21st International Conference on Circuits, Systems, Communications and Computers (CSCC 2017)

MATEC Web of Conferences Volume 125 (2017)

Heraklion, Greece
14 - 17 July 2017

Editors:

Nikos Mastorakis
Valeri Mladenov
Aida Bulucea

ISBN: 978-1-5108-4968-6

Printed from e-media with permission by:

Curran Associates, Inc.
57 Morehouse Lane
Red Hook, NY 12571

Some format issues inherent in the e-media version may also appear in this print version.

Printed by Curran Associates, Inc. (2017)

For additional information, please contact EDP Sciences – Web of Conferences at the address below.

EDP Sciences – Web of Conferences
17, Avenue du Hoggar
Parc d'Activité de Courtabœuf
BP 112
F-91944 Les Ulis Cedex A
France

Phone: +33 (0) 1 69 18 75 75
Fax: +33 (0) 1 69 28 84 91

contact-edps@webofconferences.org

Additional copies of this publication are available from:

Curran Associates, Inc.
57 Morehouse Lane
Red Hook, NY 12571 USA
Phone: 845-758-0400
Fax: 845-758-2633
Email: curran@proceedings.com
Web: www.proceedings.com

TABLE OF CONTENTS

edp sciences

MATEC Web of Conferences

Statement of Peer review

In submitting conference proceedings to MATEC Web of Conferences, I certify to the Publisher that I adhere to the **Policy on Publishing Integrity** of the journal in order to safeguard good scientific practice in publishing.

1. All articles have been subjected to peer review administered by the proceedings editors.
2. Reviews have been conducted by expert referees, who have been requested to provide unbiased and constructive comments aimed, whenever possible, at improving the work.
3. Proceedings editors have taken all reasonable steps to ensure the quality of the materials they publish and their decision to accept or reject a paper for publication has been based only on the merits of the work and the relevance to the journal.

Title, date and place of the conference

21st International Conference on Circuits, Systems, Communications and Computers (CSCC 2017)

Agia Pelagia Beach, Heraklion, Crete, Greece

July 14-17, 2017

Proceedings editor(s):

- Nikos Mastorakis, Technical University of Sofia, Bulgaria
- Valeri Mladenov, Technical University of Sofia, Bulgaria
- Aida Bulucea, University of Craiova, Romania

07-09-2017

Date and editor's signature

Transient Response of Low-Power ECG Recoding Amplifiers for Use with Un-gelled Electrodes

Martin J. Burke[1,a] Oscar Tuohy[1]

[1]*Dept. of Electronic and Electrical Engineering, Trinity College, University of Dublin, College Green, Dublin 2, Ireland.*

Abstract. This paper addresses the design of the low-frequency response of a multi-stage bioelectric amplifier intended for use in the measurement of the human electrocardiogram (ECG) using high-impedance un-gelled electrodes. The response is optimised to meet the International Electrotechnical Commission 60601 standards [1,2] for electrocardiograph recorders in both the time and frequency domains. The optimum design for a three stage amplifier, having two differential stages and a differential-to-single-ended conversion stage was established in the context of low-power ambulatory ECG monitoring. The optimum configuration was found to be two differential stages with a gain of 20dB each and a differential-to single-ended output stage with unity gain. The -3dB pole is placed at 0.013Hz and a zero at 0.0013Hz in the first and second stages to give an overall -3dB low cut-off frequency of 0.02Hz. In addition, the pole of the input ac coupling network was placed at 0.0013Hz in order to cancel the zero in the non-inverting front-end stage. This ensured that undershoot and recovery slope performance requirements in response to a narrow pulse of 3mV amplitude and 100ms duration were met.

1 Introduction

The nature of the low-frequency response of bioelectric amplifiers intended for use in recording the human electrocardiogram (ECG) is of the utmost importance because of the clinical significance of these recordings. Adequate magnitude and phase responses are required to prevent distortion of the ECG signal profile which can introduce changes into the waveform morphology that have serious diagnostic implications [3,4]. The nature of the distortion which results from poor low frequency response has a detrimental effect primarily on the T-wave, the S-T segment and the Q-T interval.

In recent years, miniaturisation and portability has meant that the use of ECG recorders has extended beyond the hospital clinics and wards to non-clinical scenarios such as general practice, sports medicine, physiology and even the factory floor. This increase in low-power, battery-operated equipment has meant corresponding changes in electronic instrumentation and circuit design. Trends have therefore changed in the design of the bioelectric amplifiers for ECG recording. Lower power supply voltages have tended to make amplifier front-end stages ac coupled rather than dc coupled as in the past. This is because of large electrode polarisation voltages that must be eliminated at the amplifier input so that they do not saturate the front-end stage of the amplifier. Recent trends towards un-gelled electrodes have increased the magnitude of these polarisation voltages.

AC coupling at the amplifier input also allows high gain to be maintained in the early stages of the amplifier for the preservation of the signal-to-noise ratio. Low-power technology has significantly reduced the gain-bandwidth product of operational amplifiers among other parameters. This means that the high gain required in ECG amplifiers must usually be distributed across several stages. This in turn has led to an increase in multi-stage amplifier configurations and an associated increase in the complexity of the low frequency response. This paper investigates the issues in the design of the low-frequency response of bioelectric amplifiers intended for ECG recording using un-gelled or dry electrodes. The aim is to optimise the response to meet both time and frequency domain performance requirements for ECG recording equipment issued by international standards authorities.

2 Background

Standards for the performance requirements of ECG recorders have been developed in the US by the American National Standards Institute (ANSI) with recommendations made by the American Heart Association (AHA). In Europe the corresponding standards are issued by the International Electrotechnical Commission (IEC). These have been developed and improved over several decades and have kept pace with technological developments and clinical requirements. Most recent standards have made an effort to merge the US and EU requirements to make them almost identical. This has, in fact, added strength to both sets of standards and increased the usage of the IEC 60601 standard, which is now accepted worldwide [1,2].

[a] Corresponding author: mburke@tcd.ie

2.1 Frequency domain requirements

Early standards for ECG recorder performance were based on recommendations issued by the AHA and the IEEE in 1967 [5,6]. These standards required that the magnitude of the frequency response be within ± 0.5 dB of the mid-band gain within the frequency range 0.67Hz–150Hz. The low-frequency limit was based on a practical lowest heart rate value of 40 beats-per-minute (bpm). The phase response was required to be no greater than that corresponding to a single-pole high-pass filter having a -3dB cut-off frequency of 0.05Hz [5,6]. These magnitude and phase response requirements are illustrated in Figure 1.

More recent standards issued by both the EU and the US [1,2] require that the amplitude response of an ambulatory ECG recorder shall be within ±3 dB of the response at 5Hz, within a frequency band of 0.05Hz to at least 55Hz. A phase response requirement is not specified but the merits of a single-pole high-pass filter having a cut-off frequency of 0.05Hz are still cited as a benchmark. Instead of the phase response requirement a time-domain specification has been introduced.

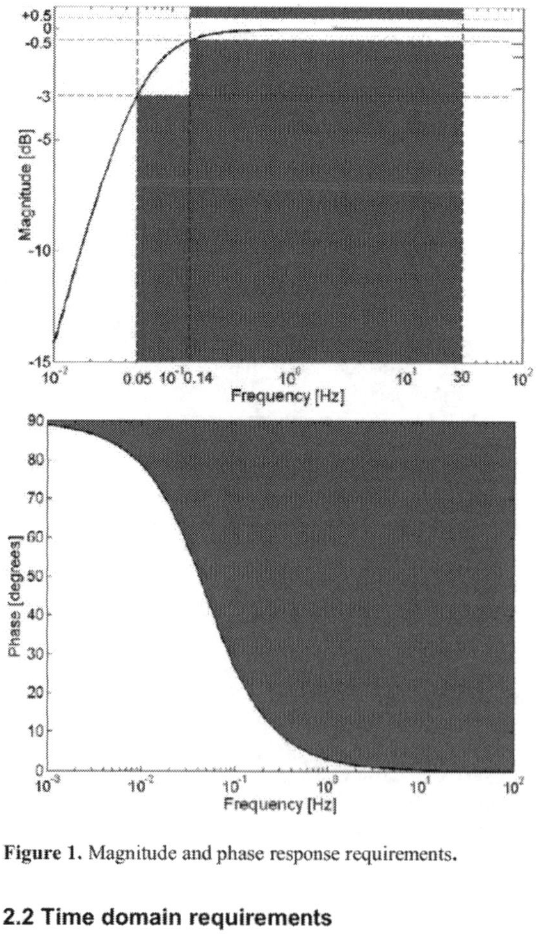

Figure 1. Magnitude and phase response requirements.

2.2 Time domain requirements

The IEC 60601 most recent standards, which are now closely aligned and merged with those of ANSI, have introduced two time-domain methods of testing ECG recorder performance. These are both shown in Figure 2. Method A was introduced in a previous IEC standard and allows a maximum baseline undershoot of 100μV in the transient response to a narrow rectangular pulse of 3mV amplitude and 100ms duration. A maximum recovery slope of 300μV/s following undershoot at the end of the pulse is allowed, as can be seen in Figure 2. The output waveform is input-referred to make it independent of amplifier gain. Method B, on the other hand, uses a triangular wave to model the QRS complex of the ECG. An isosceles triangular wave of peak amplitude of 1.5mV and a duration varying between 20ms and 200ms with a repetition rate of less than 1Hz is applied as input to the recorder. The amplitude of the peak of the triangle must maintain a variation within +0dB and -1dB (-12%) as the pulse duration is varied between 20ms and 200ms. This can be seen in Figure 2. In the studies carried out by the author, the rectangular pulse of Method A was preferred.

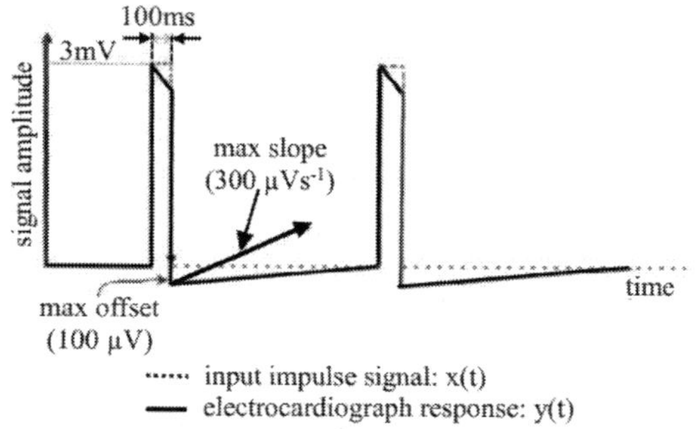

Method A: Rectangular Pulse

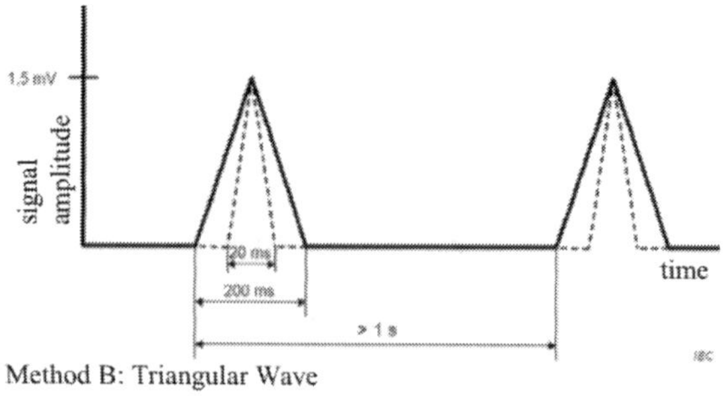

Method B: Triangular Wave

Figure 2. Transient response requirements [from 1,2]

3 Single-Ended Amplifier Stage

The first stage of interest is the single-ended non-inverting amplifier stage shown in Figure 3. This stage is ac coupled and therefore has a high-pass frequency response. It provides gain in the pass band and has a steady-state transfer function of the form:

$$\frac{V_o}{V_i} = \frac{[1 + j\omega C_1(R_1 + R_2)]j\omega C_3 R_3}{(1 + j\omega C_1 R_1)(1 + j\omega C_3 R_3)} \qquad (1)$$

Bode plots of the magnitude and phase of the frequency response of this stage are shown in Figure 3. The stage has an in-band high-frequency gain $A_{V0} = (R_1 + R_2)/R_1$. The -3dB pole in the high-pass response is located at a radian frequency of $\omega_{P1} = 1/(C_1R_1)$. An ac coupling network in the form of resistor R_3 and capacitor C_3 has been included at the input to ensure that dc electrode polarisation potentials do not appear at the amplifier input and cause it to saturate. If this network were omitted, the gain of this stage would level out at unity, at the location of the zero at a radian frequency $\omega_{Z1} = 1/[C_1(R_1 + R_2)] = \omega_{P1}/A_{V0}$, as indicated by the dashed line in the magnitude characteristic of Figure 3. The zero would also have the effect of restoring the phase to 0° as $\omega \rightarrow 0$, as shown by the dashed line in the phase characteristic of Figure 3.

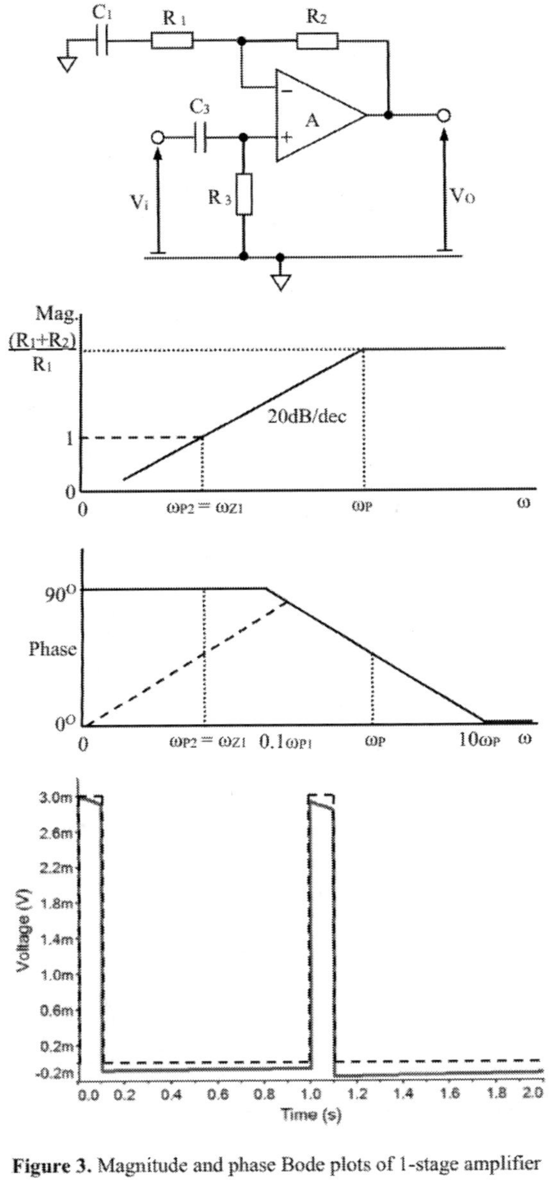

Figure 3. Magnitude and phase Bode plots of 1-stage amplifier

In order to get an overall response of the form of a high-pass filter, the lower frequency pole, ω_{P2}, of the input network is arranged to cancel the zero in the response of the feedback network by a choice of time constants such that $C_3R_3 = C_1(R_1 + R_2)$. In this case the transfer function of the stage simplifies to:

$$\frac{V_o}{V_i} = \frac{j\omega C_3 R_3}{(1 + j\omega C_1 R_1)} = \frac{j\omega C_1(R_1 + R_2)}{(1 + j\omega C_1 R_1)} \tag{2}$$

This is depicted by the solid-line magnitude and phase responses in Figure 3.

The magnitude response can be expressed as:

$$\left|\frac{V_o}{V_i}\right| = \sqrt{\frac{\left(\frac{\omega}{\omega_{Z1}}\right)^2}{1 + \left(\frac{\omega}{\omega_{P1}}\right)^2}} \tag{3}$$

The -0.5dB point in this response in absolute terms is defined as 6% below unity gain as:

$$\sqrt{\frac{\left(\frac{\omega_{-0.5dB}}{\omega_{Z1}}\right)^2}{1 + \left(\frac{\omega_{-0.5dB}}{\omega_{P1}}\right)^2}} = 0.94 \tag{4}$$

This gives the relationship between the -0.5dB and -3dB points in the magnitude response as:

$$\omega_{-0.5dB} = 2.75\omega_{P1} \tag{5}$$

This implies that if the magnitude response is to stay within ±0.5dB of the in-band value down to a frequency of 0.67Hz, then the -3dB cut-off frequency must be below 0.25Hz. This is well above the 0.05Hz limit recommended in the performance standard, which is chosen more on the basis of minimising the low-frequency phase distortion than of obtaining a flat magnitude response.

The response of this filter in the time domain to the narrow input pulse which is defined in Figure 2 can also be seen in Figure 3. The undershoot in the response is 93μV and the recovery slope is 29μV/s which meets the requirements illustrated in Figure 2. This first-order ac-coupled stage satisfies all of the performance criteria for ECG amplifiers when it is assumed that the input signal is obtained from a voltage source having zero internal impedance. The input stage of a more practical differential recording amplifier should give at least equivalent performance in order to prevent distortion of the signal. The nature of the impedance of the source must also be taken into account since this will have a profound effect on both the steady-state and the transient responses.

4 Multi-stage amplifiers

4.1 Two-stage differential amplifier

The schematic diagram of a simple differential amplifier is shown in Figure 4. This is essentially the differential version of the single-ended amplifier stage of Figure 3. This has a single cross-coupled input stage with differential input voltages V_1 and V_2. This is followed by a differential-to-single-ended conversion stage providing the output voltage, V_O. The A and B designated components will nominally have the same values.

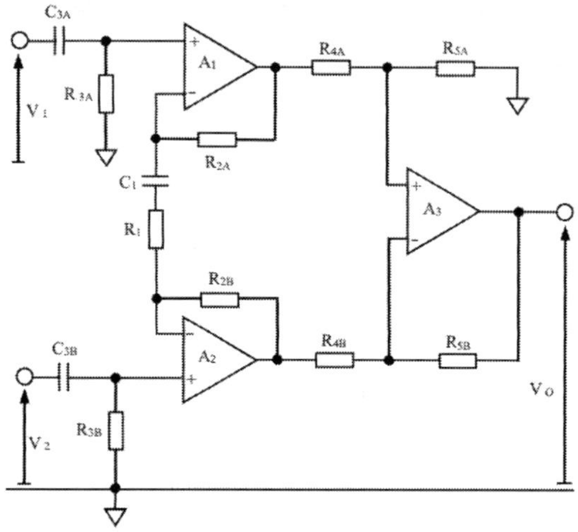

Figure 4. Schematic Diagram of 2-Stage Differential Amplifier

The steady-state transfer function of this amplifier structure is given for a differential input $V_1 - V_2$ as:

$$\frac{V_o}{V_1 - V_2} = \frac{R_5}{R_4}\frac{[1 + j\omega C_1(R_1 + 2R_2)]j\omega C_3 R_3}{(1 + j\omega C_1 R_1)(1 + j\omega C_3 R_3)} \qquad (6)$$

Very often $R_5 = R_4$ so that the output stage has unity gain, to maximize the CMRR. In this case the in-band differential gain of this stage is $A_V = (R_1 + 2R_2)/R_1$. The -3dB cut-off frequency is again located at $\omega_{P1} = 1/(C_1R_1)$ while the zero is located at $\omega_{Z1} = 1/[C_1(R_1 + 2R_2)] = \omega_{P1}/A_V$. The pole due to the input network, which is identical at each input terminal, is again located at a frequency $\omega_{P2} = 1/(C_3R_3)$. The same pole-zero cancellation that was implemented in the single stage amplifier can be replicated in the differential amplifier by choosing $C_3R_3 = C_1(R_1 + 2R_2)$. The steady-state magnitude and phase responses and the time-domain pulse response are identical to those of the single-ended amplifier stage illustrated in Figure 3 if no source impedance is taken into account.

4.2 Three-stage differential amplifier

In the low-power semiconductor technology associated with ambulatory monitoring of the ECG and the use of dry electrodes, op-amps generally have very limited gain-bandwidth product. It is consequently rarely possible to implement the overall gain needed to amplify a recorded ECG signal to the desired level in a single differential stage. The gain must therefore be distributed between two differential stages with a final output differential-to-single-ended conversion stage. This leads to the 3-stage differential amplifier shown in Figure 5. This has a high-pass input stage and a differential-to-single-ended output stage identical to the two stage amplifier. There is a second differential stage which is dc coupled to the first so that the output dc bias potentials of the first stage will carry through to the second stage. The ac coupling of the first stage is sufficient to block any electrode polarisation potentials from the amplifier input.
The steady state transfer function of this three stage amplifier is given as:

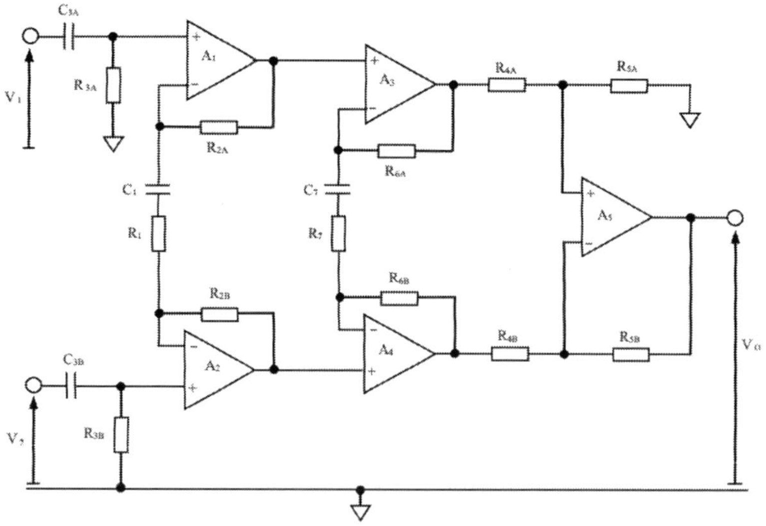

Figure 5. Schematic Diagram of a 3-stage Differential Amplifier for ECG Recording.

$$\frac{V_o}{V_1 - V_2} = \frac{R_5}{R_4} \times \frac{[1 + j\omega C_1(R_1 + 2R_2)][1 + j\omega C_7(R_7 + 2R_6)]j\omega C_3 R_3}{(1 + j\omega C_1 R_1)(1 + j\omega C_7 R_7)(1 + j\omega C_3 R_3)} \quad (5)$$

where, R_6, R_7 and C_7 are the components in the second differential stage. It can be seen that the dc coupling in the second differential stage adds an additional pole and zero to the transfer function. If the output stage has unity gain and the overall gain is distributed equally between the two differential stages then the poles and zeros of both of these stages are identical so that $\omega_{P1} = 1/(C_1R_1) = \omega_{P3} = 1/(C_7R_7)$ and $\omega_{Z1} = 1/[C_1(R_1 + 2R_2)] = \omega_{P1}/A_{V1} = \omega_{Z2} = 1/[C_7(R_7 + 2R_6)] = \omega_{P3}/A_{V2}$. In an ECG recording amplifier the gains of the individual differential stages would be in the region of 20dB so as to give an overall gain for the three-stage amplifier of 40dB. If the intention, in the first instance, is to maintain the -3dB frequency of the three-stage amplifier at the same location as for the two-stage amplifier it can be shown that:

$$\omega_{-3dB2} = \sqrt{\sqrt{2} - 1}\ \omega_{-3dB1} = 0.65\,\omega_{-3dB1} \quad (6)$$

where ω_{-3dB2} is the -3dB frequency of a single differential stage in the three-stage amplifier having two identical differential stages and ω_{-3dB1} is the -3dB frequency of a single-pole differential amplifier, and is taken as the overall -3dB frequency of the three-stage amplifier. If $f_{-3dB1} = 0.05$Hz then $f_{-3dB2} = 0.03$Hz to obtain the desired overall response. If the values of components are chosen accordingly the magnitude, phase and pulse responses of the three stage amplifier will be almost identical to those of Figure 3 and will meet all of the performance requirements when no source impedance is taken into account.

5 Effect of Electrode Impedance

5.1 Electrode Electrical Model

The purpose of the ECG recording amplifier is to provide a signal which accurately represents the electrical potential existing on the surface of the patient's body. Therefore the amplifier cannot be considered in isolation. The impedance of the electrodes used to provide the necessary interface between the patient's skin and the amplifier must be treated as an intrinsic part of the recording system. The IEC 60601 standard specifies a simple electrode model of a single parallel C-R network with C = 47nF and R = 51kΩ. This is inserted in series with each amplifier input when injecting signals from a test signal generator. This simplified model does provide an accurate reflection of all of the effects that are present when using a surface electrode. In particular, it does not accurately model the un-gelled electrodes that are becoming more popular in portable recording equipment. The IEC 60601 standard also recommends a minimum amplifier input impedance of 10MΩ.

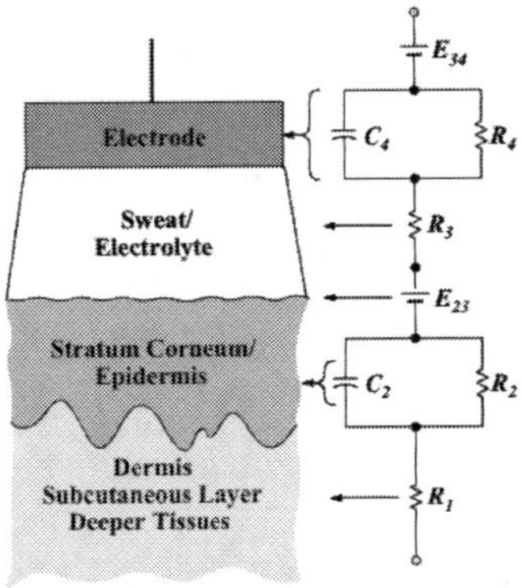

Figure 6 An Electrical Model of an Un-gelled ECG Electrode

Previous work has shown that surface bio-electrodes are modelled more accurately by the network shown in Figure 6. This model consists of two parallel C-R networks as well as a series resistance. The dc voltages represent polarisation potentials that will be blocked from the input of the amplifier by the use of ac coupling. Studies have yielded the values of the model components for a number of un-gelled or dry ECG recording electrodes [7]. For this study component values were selected that represent the extremes of the associated time constants involved. Electrode models used include: a single C-R network as specified in the IEC 60601 standard, a double C-R model with component values obtained from stainless-steel contact electrodes, and two double C-R models representative of conducting rubber electrodes. These are listed in Table 1.

Table 1: Properties of Electrode Models

Electrode Model	Single C-R (IEC)	Stainless Steel 2-CR	Conductive Rubber #1	Conductive Rubber #2
R_1+R_3 (kΩ)	NA	5	12	5
C_2 (µF)	0.047	878	220	432
R_2 (kΩ)	51	256	267	72
τ_2 (s)	0.002	225	59	31
C_4 (µF)	NA	56	23	6.9
R_4 (kΩ)	NA	380	380	158
τ_4 (s)	NA	21	8.6	1.1

5.2 Transient Response of Electrode & Amplifier

Tests were carried out to investigate the effects of varying both the impedance of the recording electrodes and the input impedance of the amplifier on the transient response to the narrow pulse of Figure 2. Each of the electrode models listed in Table 1 was used in combination with four values of common-mode input impedance of the amplifier, R_C, namely: 1MΩ, 10MΩ, 100MΩ and 1GΩ. This was done firstly for the 2-stage amplifier of Figure 4 with the -3dB frequency at 0.05Hz. The frequency response of the front-end stage of the amplifier was maintained as outlined in Section 4.1. Therefore the time-constant C_1R_1 was kept fixed as required to provide a low cut-off -3dB frequency at 0.05Hz for the 2-stage amplifier. The low-frequency pole-zero cancellation was maintained by changing the

Table 2: Pulse Response, 2-Stage Amplifier f_{-3dB}=0.05Hz

Electrode Model ↓	Amplifier R_3 (MΩ) →	1	10	100	1000
Single C-R	Undershoot (μV)	**157**	**164**	**165**	**165**
	Recov. Slope (μVs^{-1})	174	188	200	200
Stainless Steel	Undershoot (μV)	**187**	**166**	**164**	**170**
	Recov. Slope (μVs^{-1})	233	205	203	203
Conductive Rubber #1	Undershoot (μV)	**554**	**206**	**168**	**164**
	Recov. Slope (μVs^{-1})	**3400**	**498**	213	185
Conductive Rubber #2	Undershoot (μV)	**486**	**199**	**173**	**165**
	Recov. Slope (μVs^{-1})	**2000**	**449**	235	185

value of the input blocking capacitor C_3 when the value of the input resistance R_3 was altered in order to keep the time constant C_3R_3 fixed to match the time constant $C_1(R_1 + 2R_2)$. The values of the undershoot and recovery slope in response to the pulse of Figure 2 are given in Table 2. All values are referred back to the amplifier input for direct comparison with the input pulse. Values in bold indicate a violation of the requirements of the IEC 60601 performance specification. It can be seen from the table that the undershoot requirement of less than 100μV is violated by all electrode models for all values of amplifier input impedance. The recovery slope requirement of 300μVs^{-1} is satisfied by all electrode models for an input impedance of 100MΩ or greater but is violated by the conductive rubber electrodes for values of impedance below this.

The same set of tests was carried out on the 3-stage amplifier of Figure 5, with the overall -3dB low cut-off frequency f_{-3dB1} = 0.05Hz by choosing f_{-3dB2} = 0.03Hz for each of the differential stages considered individually. The results of these tests are shown in Table 3.

Table 3: Pulse Response, 3-Stage Amplifier f_{-3dB}=0.05Hz

Electrode Model ↓	Amplifier R_3 (MΩ) →	1	10	100	1000
Single C-R	Undershoot (μV)	**220**	**211**	**210**	**210**
	Recov. Slope (μVs^{-1})	**24000**	**2900**	**481**	252
Stainless Steel	Undershoot (μV)	**237**	**215**	**213**	**213**
	Recov. Slope (μVs^{-1})	281	251	248	248
Conductive Rubber #1	Undershoot (μV)	**647**	**258**	**216**	**212**
	Recov. Slope (μVs^{-1})	**3800**	**580**	281	251
Conductive Rubber #2	Undershoot (μV)	**553**	**249**	**217**	**213**
	Recov. Slope (μVs^{-1})	**3100**	**553**	276	252

A similar pattern of violations of the performance specification exist as for the 2-stage amplifier. All electrode models lead to a violation of the undershoot requirement for all values of amplifier input impedance. The recovery slope requirement is violated by the conductive rubber electrodes for an amplifier input impedance below 100MΩ, and by the single C-R model for less than 1GΩ. Several further series of tests were subsequently carried out on the 3-stage amplifier while progressively lowering the -3dB low cut-off frequency. Table 4 shows the results of the tests for f_{-3dB1} = 0.02Hz with f_{-3dB2} = 0.013Hz. It can be seen in this case that all of the electrode models meet both performance limits for an amplifier input impedance of 100MΩ or greater. This

Table 4: Pulse Response 3-Stage Amplifier f_{-3dB}=0.02Hz

Electrode Model ↓	Amplifier R_3 (MΩ) →	1	10	100	1000
Single C-R	Undershoot (μV)	**256**	**106**	90	88
	Recov. Slope (μVs^{-1})	**652**	147	100	94
Stainless Steel	Undershoot (μV)	**106**	84	81	80
	Recov. Slope (μVs^{-1})	122	94	90	90
Conductive Rubber #1	Undershoot (μV)	**537**	**129**	85	81
	Recov. Slope (μVs^{-1})	**3400**	**390**	118	91
Conductive Rubber #2	Undershoot (μV)	**399**	**122**	82	79
	Recov. Slope (μVs^{-1})	**2500**	**321**	109	88

was identified as the highest value of the low cut-off frequency for which all electrode models would meet both performance requirements and was only possible with an input impedance of 100MΩ.

5 Conclusion

The existing IEC 60601 performance specification for ECG amplifiers suggests that a -3dB frequency of 0.05Hz and an input impedance of 10MΩ will meet the performance requirements of a maximum of 100μV undershoot and a recovery slope of 300μVs^{-1} in the transient response to a narrow 3mV-100ms pulse. The authors have shown experimentally for a number of un-gelled electrode models that an amplifier needs to have a -3dB low cut-off frequency of ≤0.02Hz and an input impedance of ≥100MΩ in order to meet these specifications. Future work will be carried out to establish the amplifier requirements analytically for un-gelled electrode models as the latter are becoming increasingly more common in both clinical and ambulatory ECG measurement scenarios.

References

1. International Electrotechnical Commission, Medical Electrical Equipment Std. 2-25. IEC 60601, 2011.
2. International Electrotechnical Commission, Medical Electrical Equipment Std. 2-47. IEC 60601, 2012.
3. A. S. Berson and H. V. Pipberger, 'The Low-Frequency Response of Electrocardiographs, A Frequent Source of Recording Errors'; Amer. Heart J.; **71**, 779-789, 1966.
4. D. Tayler and R. Vincent, 'Signal distortion in the electrocardiogram due to inadequate phase response', IEEE Trans. Biomed. Eng.; **30**, 352-356, 1983.
5. C. E. Kossmann et al., 'Recommendations for standardization of leads and of specifications for instruments in electrocardiograpy and vectorcardiography.; Circulation, **35**, 583–602, 1967.
6. H. V. Pipberger et al., 'Recommendations for standardization of instruments in electrocardiography and vectorcardiograhy, IEEE Trans Biomed. Eng.; **14**, 60-68, 1967.
7. A Baba, Burke, M. J. "Measurement of the Electrical Properties of Ungelled ECG Electrodes" NAUN Int. J. Biol. & Biomed. Eng.; **2**, 89-97, 2008.

X-band Core Chip SiGe design for Phased Array T/R Modules

Valeri Timoshenkov[1,*], *Andrey Efimov*[2]

[1] University of Electronic Technology, 124498 Moscow, Russia
[2] Izhevsky radiozavod, Production Department, 426034 Izhevsk, Russia

Abstract. The structure of the Core Chip for Phased Array T R Modules is presented. Methods for the formation of a phase delay for X phase shifters are considered. An original differential design of SiGe core chip for X-band is presented. The schematic of 5 bits phase shifter and attenuator are designed. It consist of a series number LPF and HPF filters. Gain of phase shifter is 1.5 dB. Attenuator has the adjustment range from 0 to 24dB. Linear output power of the core chip is 5dBm. The total consumed current of the device is 158mA, at 5V power supply.

1 Introduction

Improving the efficiency of microwave radio and radar equipment is associated with integration increasing , mass-dimensional characteristics improving, reliability increasing due to the reduction of wire bonding between the chips, repeatability of parameters improving; unification of the transceiver equipment increasing, radiation resistance increasing due to the use of wide-bandgap semiconductors of the A_3B_5 group, increasing resistance to electromagnetic radiation by reducing the length of the connections. Regarding of that, the transceiver module parameters improving, of which core-chip is an integral part, is an important task.

The block diagram of the core-chip is shown in Fig. 1. It contains three ports switch (sw_{rt}), an attenuator, a phase shifter (Φ), signal amplifiers (A), a low-noise amplifier (LNA), a power preamplifier (PPA) and a switching device (PSSw), based on parallel or series to parallel interface.

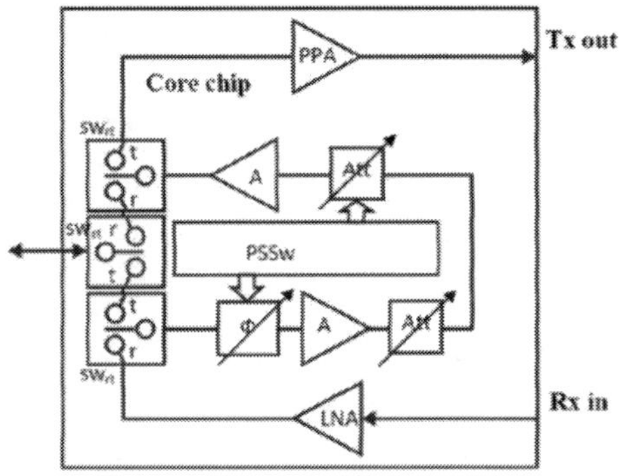

Fig. 1. Core chip block diagram

Three-port switches (SPDT) for receiving/transmitting can be realized as solid-state electronic or micromechanical switches, made by using of integrated technology.

Phase shifters are a set of, usually, sequentially connected elementary cells. Elementary phase-shift cells can be performed on the in the next configurations: delay lines (for example microstrip lines, figure2a), combinations of HPF and LPF filters (figure2b), differently loaded transmission lines (figure2c), use of vector summing of mutually orthogonal I and Q signals (Figure 2d), which can vary in amplitude.

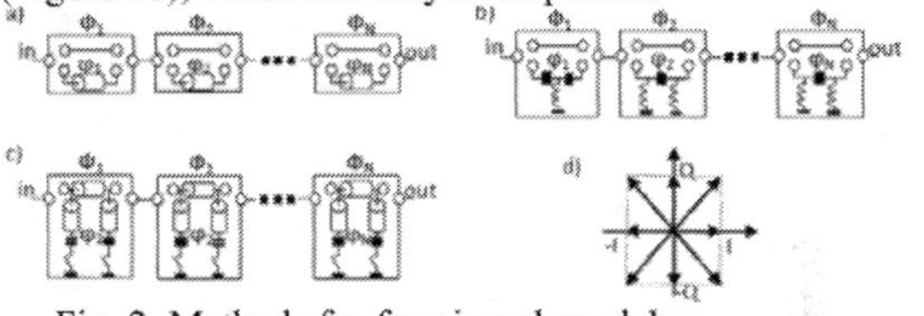

Fig. 2. Methods for forming phase delay

As a disadvantage of sequential connected elementary phase shifters is the influence of the impedance of the previous stage on the subsequent stage, which leads to a weakening of the transmitted signal, as well as to an additional phase shift.

Schematics of attenuators are also a series connection of elementary attenuators. It is most appropriate to use resistive dividers as signal attenuators.

At present, there are a large number of industrially mastered solid-state core-chips containing phase shifters and attenuators manufactured by such companies as OMMIC [1], MACCOM [10] (USA), UMS (France) [2], SELEX Sistemi Integrati SpA (Italy) [4], METDA (China) [8] based on A_3B_5 semiconductor (Table 1). There are a number of works in which silicon technology based on nanoscale CMOS [6,10] or HBT [4, 5] are used (Table 2). It should be noted the merits of using silicon technology based on SiGe bipolar transistors, which have a high upper limiting frequency [11] up to 300 GHz. This allows you to receive devices operating in the X and Ku bands

* Corresponding author: valeri04@hotmail.com

Table 1. Core chip parameters based on GaAs

Parameters	Ommic[1] GaAs	UMS[2] GaAs	Metda[8] GaAs	Micran[9] GaAs
Frequency (GHz)	8…12	8…12	8…12	8-11.5
Tx/Rx gain (dB)	8/8	23.5/12.5	11/10	15.5/16.5
Phase shift range, °	0…360	0…360	0…360	0…360
Phase step, °	5,625	5,625	5,625	5,625
Attenuation range, dB	24	34,65	48	27.9
Attenuation step, dB	-	0,55дб	0.75	0.5
TX OP1dB, dBm	11.1	13	12	20
RX OP1dB, dBm	8.5	16,5	10	16
RX noise figure, dB	7	5,8	8	5.2
Power Supply,V	-6, +6		-5, +5	-5, +5
Chip Size (mm^2)			5.06x3.8	4.0x5.1

Table 2. Core chip parameters based on Si

Parameters	[3], [6] RFcore	[4]	[5]	[7] Peregreen
Technology	CMOS	SiGe	SiGe	CMOS
Operation frequency (GHz)	9-10	8-11	8-11	8-12
Phase shift range/step (°)	360/5.6	360/11.2	360/11.2	360/5.6
Attenuation range/step (dB)	31/1	31/1	31/1	31.5/0.5
Tx/Rx gain (dB)	12/9""	17/17	30/20	-
RMS phase error (°)	2.3	6	6	8
RMS attenuation error (dB)	0.4	2	1.5	0.25
Output P1dB in TX mode	11	12	18	-
Power Supply,V	2.4.	0.8	1.5	3.3;-3.3
Chip Size (mm^2)	6.9 x 1.6	3.8 x 4.1	3.5 x 2.4	4.6x2.6

2 SIGE CORE CHIP DESIGN

The aim is to investigate the possibilities for designing a control chip (core chip) for X-frequency band using SiGe BiCMOS technology.

The chip should include the following blocks: attenuator, phase shifter, receive/transmit switches, compensating amplifiers, control circuit with parallel interface with TTL levels. Given the high high cutoff frequency of heterojunction bipolar transistors (HBT), it is advisable to design the crystal by using of SiGe BiCMOS technology [11]. Differential current switches with a stabilized reference voltage were selected for base schematic high-frequency data signal processing units.

With this approach, the implementation of switches and amplifiers with the required parameters at frequencies up to 11 GHz has not technical difficulties, with the exception of output drivers, which have fundamental limitations in signal amplitude. The most critical are two blocks: a phase shifter and an attenuator. To demonstrate the capabilities of the technology, a four-phase phase shifter with HBT as active components was analyzed. The proposed schematic of the device is shown in Figure 3.

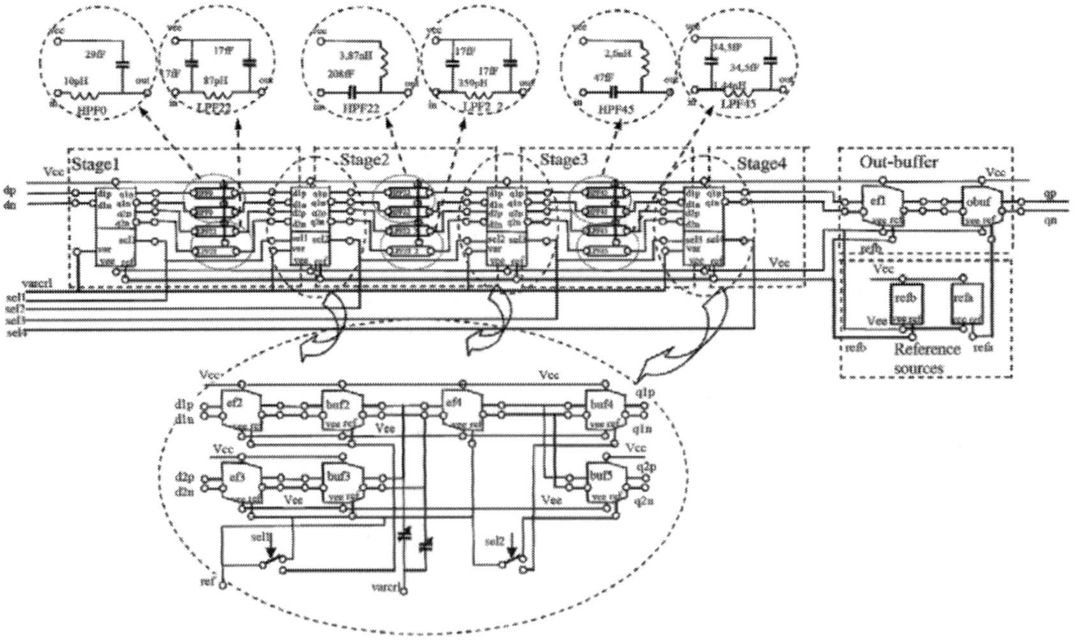

Fig. 3 Phase shifter schematic

The phase shifter contains three stages SPDT (SPDT - Single Pole, Double Throw) amplifying switches (Stage 1, 2, 3) with LC filters, providing a relative phase shift from 0 ° to 180 ° in 22.25 ° increments. The fourth stage (Stage4) is a switchable inverter. The subsequent output amplifier consists of a preamplifier and an output driver (Out buffer), both of which contain linear differential cascades.

The reference system uses stabilized reference voltage sources and special CMOS switches.

SPDT switch is a two-stage linear amplifier with a current consumption of 15.4 mA, the second stage of which performs the function of an analog demultiplexer 1:2. One of the outputs of the multiplexer is activated by the digital signal sel2, which ON/OFF the reference voltages by CMOS switch (sw2rfb25m_2v5). The principal feature of this circuit is the possibility of smooth phase adjustment within 2 ° by changing the analog voltage (varcrl) on varactors.

Two pairs of phase-shift filters are connected to the outputs of the first amplifying switch. In this schematic, the HPF0 cells are equivalent transmission line, and the LPF22a cells are LC low-pass filters.

The second and third amplifying switches (selector2to2_14m3) are identical to each other, consume 14.3 mA of current and perform the function of 2:2. Like the first switch, these have a smooth phase adjustment by changing the voltage (pin varcrl).

The inputs of the second switch are connected to the outputs of the two channels of the first switch, and its outputs are loaded on pairs of filters HPF22 and LPF22b. Similarly, the inputs of the third key are connected to the outputs of the two channels of the second switch, and its outputs are loaded onto the HPF45 and LPF45 filter pairs.

The fourth amplification switch (selector2to1_14m3), consumes 14.3 mA of current and performs the function of an analog multiplexer 2:1 with an activated or disabled inversion of the output signal.

The developed phase shifter was simulated using the Cadence system under various operating conditions in the frequency range from 9.1 GHz to 10.3 GHz. Absolute and relative phase shifts in the first three stages of the phase shifter at a frequency of 10 GHz and at two limiting temperatures of 0 ° C and + 125 °C are given in Table 5.

Table 3. Phase shift in amplification switches

Phase shift, degree	Stage 1		Stage 2		Stage 3	
	0°C	125°C	0°C	125°C	0°C	125°C
(HPF)	40.8	48.9	15.5	24.2	5.4	4.0
(LPF)	63.2	71.3	59.3	67.8	85.5	94.2
Difference	22.4	22.4	43.8	43.6	90.9	90.2

The presented data demonstrate the acceptable stability of all stages. Additional phase adjustments can be made using a varcrl test voltage, which provides an additional adjustment range of about 8 °. The relative phase shift in steps at 125 ° C (worst case) in the frequency range from 10.0 GHz to 10.3 GHz is shown in Figure 4a. The accuracy of the phase setting is not worse than ± 0.7 °. The relative phase shift in steps at 125 ° C (worst case) in the frequency range from 8.0 GHz to 12 GHz is shown in Figure 4b.

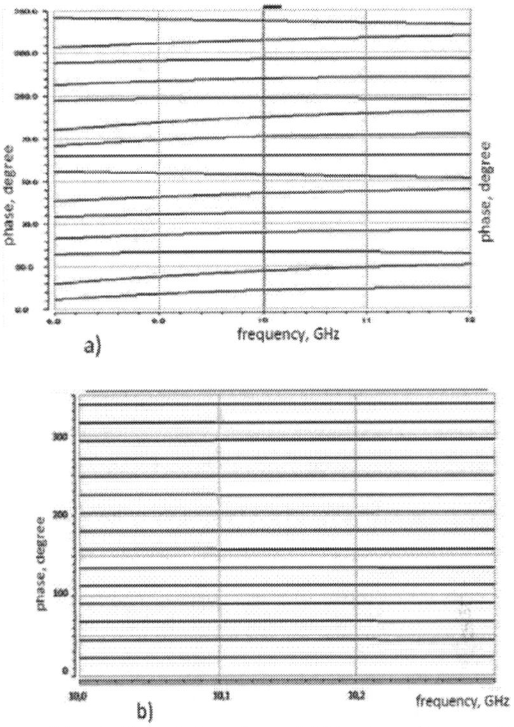

Fig. 4. The relative phase shift in steps a)- range 8-12GHz, b)- range 10-10.3 GHz

The output stage in this circuit provides a linear power of 1 dBm. In this case, four stages of the phase shifter consume a current of about 58 mA, and full circuit is about 123 mA. It is possible to increase the output power by a factor of 2 (to +4 dBm) by increasing the current consumption.

The phase shifter is the most significant block in the area of the core chip. The main area in the layout of the phase shifter is occupied by inductors, capacitors and varactors. The area of the block is 1,0x1,0 mm^2.

The main task of designing a controlled attenuator is to maintain the linearity of the input buffer at substantially different amplitudes of the input signal. For this, it is necessary to attenuate the signal before feeding it to the first amplification stage. This problem is solved by using a resistive ladder R-2R. The diagram of such ladder is shown in Figure 5. It is easy to calculate that the equivalent resistance of the ladder at node d1 is 50 Ohm. At the same time, the signal at the node d2 is divided by 2 times, at the node d3 - 4 times and at the node d4 - 8 times. Combining signals from all four nodes, you can get a total signal with a transmission factor from + 5.5dB to -18dB, which corresponds to the adjustment range from 0 to 24dB.

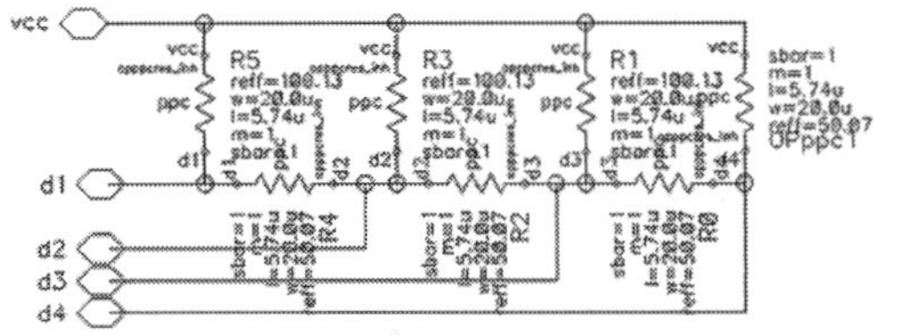

Fig. 5 The schematic of the resistive ladder R-2R

It should be noted that such system provides a binary adjustment of the attenuation, which allows simplify circuit implementation with a lower power consumption. The logarithmic adjustment system requires a much more complex circuit that contains a decoder and one or two switches per attenuator state, which contains up to 30 switches for a 4-bits. In this regard, was implemented a scheme 4-bit binary controlled attenuator. The shematic is shown in Figure 6.

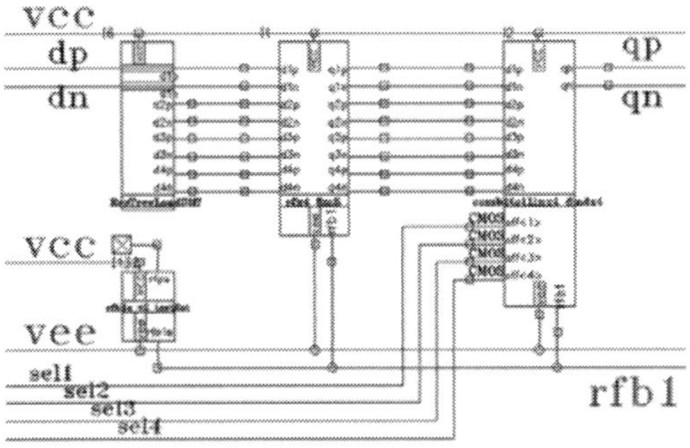

Fig. 6. Block diagram of attenuator with amplitude contro

It contains a double input resistive ladder (ResTreeLoadDiff), four double emitter followers (efx4_8m8) and a 4-bit linear differential mixer-selector (comb4to1Linx4_6m6x4). Schemes of the emitter follower and mixer-selector are shown in Figures 7 - 8 respectively.

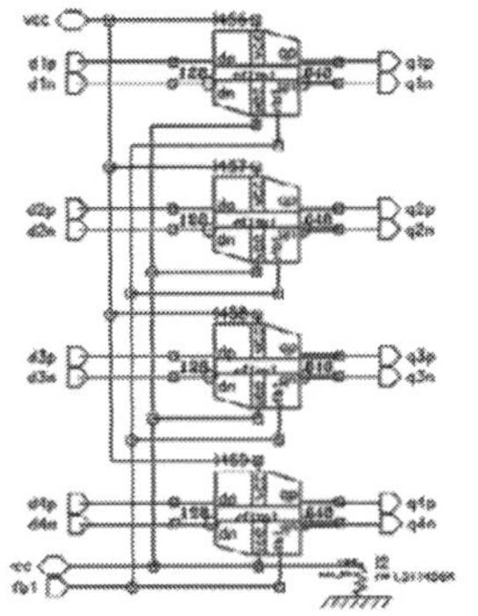

Fig. 7. Block diagram of emitter followers

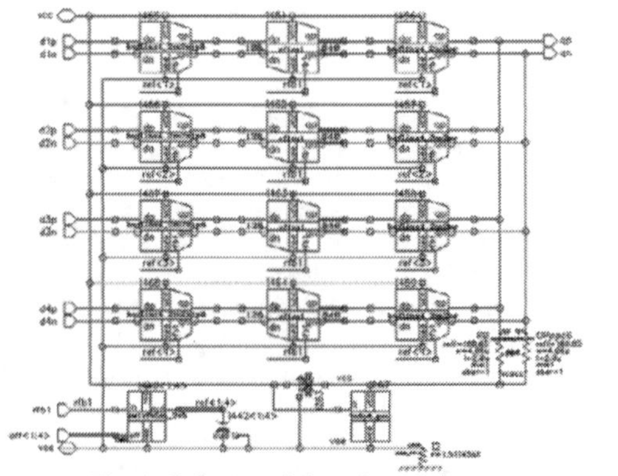

Fig. 8. Scheme of the mixer-selector

The developed attenuator was simulated by using the Cadence system under various operating conditions in the frequency range from 0 to 12 GHz. The attenuation drop by 3 dB occurs at a frequency of 11.8 GHz with a current consumption of about 35 mA.

The adjustment modes were checked by sequentially switching the binary signals sel1, sel2, sel3 and sel4 as shown in Figure 9.

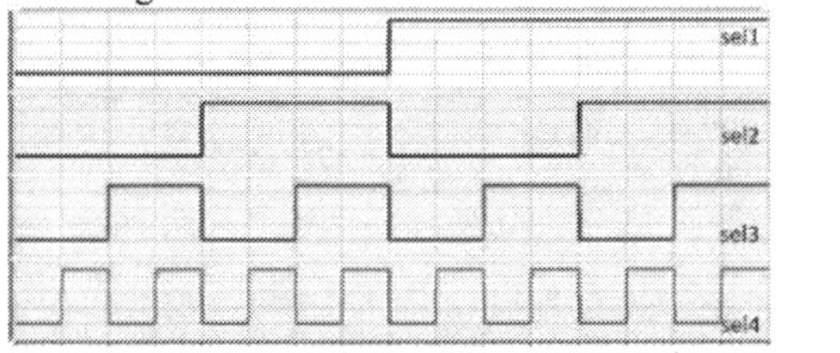

Fig. 9. Control bits at the attenuator input

The resulting differential output signal for the case of a constant amplitude of the input signal at a frequency of 10 GHz is shown in Figure 10.

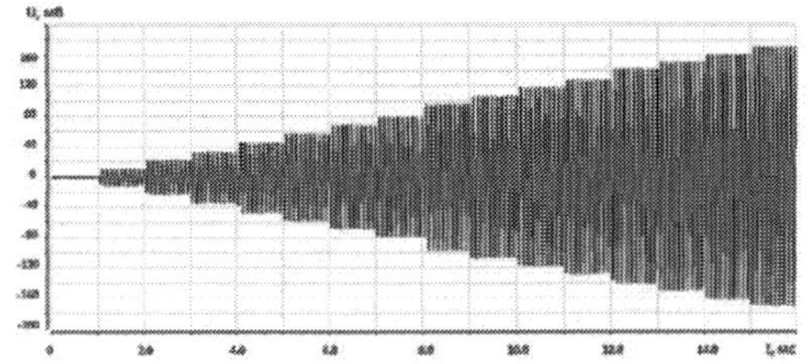

Fig.10. Attenuator output signal

The linearity of the attenuator was determined from the attenuation of the second and third harmonics with respect to the magnitude of the signal at the fundamental frequency with three values of the amplitude of the input signal. The attenuation of second harmonic is -50 dBc and third harmonic is -45 dBc.

3 Conclusions

The estimated design of the core chip, by using of SiGe technological process, satisfying the different requirements for transmitting and radar equipments.

Phase shifter provides a phase shift from 0-360 degrees, phase discrete is not worse than 11 degrees, which corresponds to 5 bits of control(at the 9.1 to 10.3 GHz). A phase shifter without a fourth stage and an output amplifier provides a gain of 1.5dB (at 125 °C). In this case, four stages of the phase shifter consume a current of about 58mA, and the complete circuit is about 123mA.

The output stage of the phase shifter provides a differential linear power of about -1dBm. It is possible to increase the output power by about 2 times (up to + 5 dBm) due to the increase in the current consumption;

The bandwidth of the attenuator (-3 dB) is 11.8 GHz in the worst case (at 125 °C) with a current consumption of about 35 mA.

The attenuator gain is from + 5.5dB to -18dB, which corresponds to the adjustment range from 0 to 24dB.

The total consumed current of the device is 158mA, (at 5V power supply) does not exceed 1W.

The using of different technologies bases (GaAs, GaN, SiGe), allow the implement of a transceiver module with optimal characteristics for any radar system.

Acknowledgment

The results of the work are obtained within the framework of the task No. 8.3459.2017/ПЧ for a research project carried out by the research center and the higher education scientific laboratory educational organization subordinated to the Ministry of Education and Science of the Russian Federation

References

1. OMMIC Preliminary Datasheet CGY2170UH 7-bit X-Band Core Chip https://www.google.ru/url?sa=t&rct=j&q=&esrc=s&source=web&cd=1&ved=0ahUKEwjq47mKpt3SAhWH2CwKHYioC3IQFggdMAA&url=http%3A%2F%2Fwww.ommic.fr%2Fdownload%2FCGY2170UH_C1.pdf&usg=AFQjCNHe1jp6qo5CwCJ_HHrz32NOIO7EVQ&bvm=bv.149760088,d.bGg&cad=rjt

2. United monolithic semiconductors X-band Core Chip GaAs Monolithic Microwave IC CHC3014-99F http://module-csums.cognix-systems.com/telechargement/2-5-1.pdf

3. A Four-Channel Bi-directional CMOS Core Chip for X-band Phased Array T/R Modules

7_4 N. Carosi, A.Bettidi, A. Nanni, L. Marescialli, and A.Centronio, "A mixed-signal X-band SiGe multi-function control MMIC for phased array radar applications," in Proc. 39th Eur.Microw. Conf., Oct. (2009), pp. 240-243.

5 J.C. Jeong, I. Yom, "X-band high power SiGe BiCMOS multifunction chip for active phased array radars," Electron. Lett., vol. **47**, no. **10**, pp. 618-619, Dec. (2011)

6 CMOS Core Chips http://www.rfcore.com/productsservices/cmos-core-chips/

7 Perigrine Semiconductor Datasheet PE1901 Monolitic Phase & Amplitude Controller. 8-12 GHz http://www.psemi.com/pdf/datasheets/pe19601ds.pdf

8 METDA Semiconductor NC1517C-812 GaAs MMIC X band T/R Multi-functional chip, 8-12GHz

9 MICRAN X-band GaAs MMICCore Chip http://www.micran.ru/sites/micran_ru/data/UserFile/File/Sertificat/2013/130615_MP001D%20Datasheet%20(v.1.0).pdf

10 MACOM Announces Industry's First Highly Integrated Plastic Packaged Control MMIC for Commercial Radar Applications https://www.macom.com/about/news-and-events/press-release-archive/row-col1/news--event-archive/macom-announces-industrys-first

11 V.Timoshenkov Ultrawide_Band Gigahertz_Range Transceiver Based on SiGe Transistors Semiconductors, (2011), Vol. **45**, No. **13**, pp. 1661–1669

Design of a full 1Mb STT-MRAM based on advanced FDSOI technology

Kotb Jabeur and *Guillaume* Prenat

Univ. Grenoble Alpes, INAC-SPINTEC; CNRS;
CEA, 17 rue des Martyrs, Grenoble, France
kotb.jabeur@cea.fr, guillaume.prenat@cea.fr

Abstract. In one hand, the shrinking of CMOS technology nodes is dramatically increasing the leakage current in integrated circuits. In the other hand, modern portable devices first concern is power-efficiency to insure a better autonomy. Thus, new device technologies and computing strategies are required in integrated systems to save power without limiting processing performances. The use of Non-Volatile Memories (NVM) seems to be a choice of a great interest in complex computing systems. But, their integration within heterogeneous technologies remains a real challenge.Among emerging NV memories, Spin Transfer Torque Magnetic Random Access Memories (STT-MRAM) is considered as one of the most attractive candidates to overcome shortcomings of conventional memories. In this paper, we describe the design of a fully embedded STT-MRAM. We developed and validated a complete MRAM platform to simulate and evaluate a 1Mb STT-MRAM based on 28nm FDSOI technology. Furthermore, we exploited body back biasing techniques offered by the FDSOI technology to achieve 60% of decrease in term of leakage power and give the possibility to increase performance up to 2x.

1 INTRODUCTION

The microelectronics industry will face major challenges related to power dissipation and energy consumption in the next years. Both static and dynamic consumption (already dominated by the leakage power) will soon start to limit microprocessor performance growth. A promising way to stop this trend is the integration of non-volatility as a new feature of memory caches, which would immediately minimize static power as well as paving the way towards normally-off/instant-on computing. The use of emerging spin-based non-volatile memory devices, such as Magnetic Random Access Memory (MRAM), in both memory hierarchy and logic (the so called "memory-in-logic") of computing systems provides a huge opportunity for low-power systems. MRAMs can be used at various levels of the memory hierarchy (memory-in-logic, register files, different levels of cache, main memory) along with traditional CMOS devices and memories to achieve ultra-low-power and provide high performance and low cost.

In this paper, we explore the potential of MRAM at advanced CMOS technology nodes by designing a full 1Mb memory based on 28nm FDSOI technology. In addition to the expected gain of MRAMs in term of power consumption, we use body bias techniques offered by the FDSOI technology to reduce further the power consumption and/or increase the performance of MRAMs.

As the Magnetic Tunnel Junction (MTJ) is the cornerstone of the MRAM, we developed a set of accurate modelling of the STT-MTJ device which has been integrated in design and simulation tools that cover the flow from the device to the circuit level to design and evaluate hybrid memory hierarchies and processor architecture.

Section 2 introduces the STT-MRAM platform design based on an accurate compact model used to integrate the device in the CMOS design flow with a bird's view of the MRAM architecture. In section 3, we validate through simulations the design of the STT-MRAM and we explore the potential of body biasing technique to decrease the power consumption and improve the performance. Section 4 is the conclusion.

2 MRAM design platform

2.1. Compact modelling of the STT-MTJ device

* Corresponding author: *kotb.jabeur@cea.fr*

The integration of the STT device into standard microelectronics design suites is a fundamental step toward the design of hybrid CMOS/MTJ circuits.

Therefore an accurate and fast SPICE compact model of the MTJ, i.e. the bit cell element, must be used for analog electrical simulations within the Process Design Kit (PDK) for the hybrid CMOS/magnetic technology, as presented in [1]. In addition to technology files for layout and physical verification, and standard cells for the design of complex logic circuits, our magnetic PDK contains a compact model of the MTJ.

The model was recently presented in [2] with emphasis on the physics behind as well as the model development and calibration flow. It is a physics-based, accurate, scalable, robust and predictive model which takes into account the temperature, the bias voltage and the impedance load of the MTJ. A special care was given to establish a PDK which is compatible with standard design suites. Thus, Verilog-AMS language has been used to develop the physical compact model. The model has been qualified on different commercials Spice and fast Spice simulators engines showing compatibility and good accuracy and speed. Concerning accuracy and speed, we described in [3] the two possible strategies to efficiently model spintronics while highlighting pros and cons of the different modeling strategies.

Fig. 1 shows the symbol and the layout views used by the analog design flow for the evaluation of the static and the transient behavior of the device at circuit level.

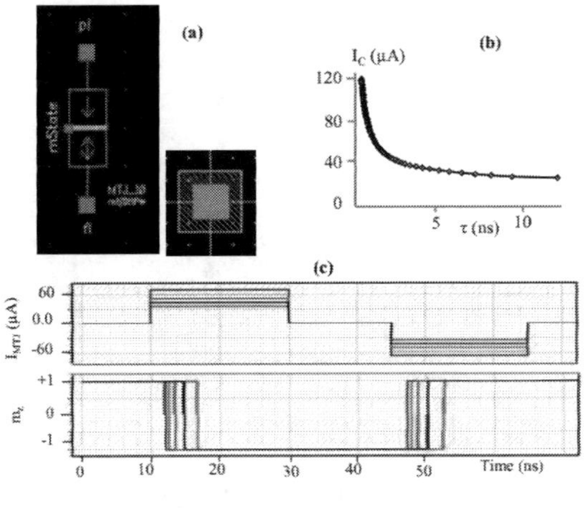

Fig. 1. Validation of the MTJ model (a) Symbol and layout of the MTJ (b) Switching current Vs pulse duration (c) Transient analysis: switching of the magnetization state m_z according to the current pulse and amplitude

Figures 1(a) illustrates the symbol and the layout as it was integrated in the commercial design tool. The switching current dynamics are presented in Fig. 1(b) describing the evolution of switching current versus the current pulse duration. Fig. 1(c) shows the magnetization switching from parallel $m_z = 1$ to anti-parallel $m_z = -1$ and back, for various amplitudes of the applied current I_{MTJ}. The model is able to predict the delay of the switching that depends on the current intensity and direction.

2.2 Magnetic Random Access Memory (MRAM)

Independently of the technology used, a standalone or an embedded memory is designed according to a combination of different blocks as shown in Figure 2. Each block fulfills a specific function and has a direct impact on the final memory performances and characteristics. The core block is the Array of BitCells where data is stored. In our case, we opt for a 1T-1MTJ BitCell architecture where each MTJ is connected in series with a n-type FET.

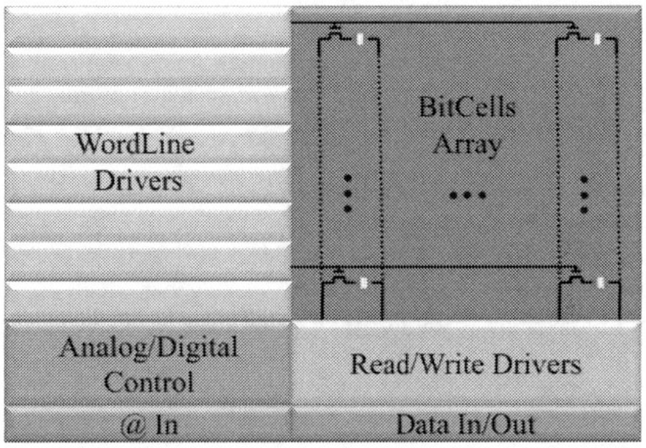

Fig. 2. Architecture of the STT-MRAM memory array based on 1T1MTJ bit cell

The function of the Inputs/Outputs drivers (Address and Controls Inputs, Data's Inputs/Outputs) is to restyle the input signals coming from the system level control and to drive the heavy loaded data bus.

The Analog/Digital Control Block represents the memory's brain; it generates all the internal control signals, decodes the address and drives the different sub-blocks. It ensures the synchronization between the different blocks by means of an accurate delays monitoring. Depending on the technology and the architecture of the MRAM, the control block may contain analog blocks such as a Biasing Block to guarantee stable voltages and currents commonly required for readout circuits.

The Read/Write Drivers are used to write (write driver) or read (sense amplifier (SA)) the bitcells.

Finally, the WordLine Driver is used to select one row of the array; the word is obtained by combining this selection with the column multiplexer or "y-mux", part of the Read/Write Driver Block. We designed, validated and characterized a full library of MRAMs ranging from 128kb to 1Mb.

All instances have been simulated and validated through different Process, Voltage, Temperature (PVT) corners while analyzing their performances (in time, power and estimated area, yield...). To guarantee an industrially-high yield of the designed circuits, 6 sigma Monte-Carlo simulations had to be carried out.

 DOI: 10.1051/matecconf/201712501003

3 MRAM specifications and evaluations

3.1 MRAM specifications

Based on the latest test chip results published in literature by industrials such as Samsung [4], Toshiba [5] and Qualcomm [6], we draw the specifications of the MRAM designed in this work. Table 1 summarizes the main specifications targeted in this work.

The model of the MTJ has been calibrated and its parameters were tuned to match the magnetic technology specifications presented in table 1. Since we target an embedded memory which may be used at one level of cache memories, the same SRAM interface has been considered to respect the compatibility with conventional CPU interfacing ports. Figure 3 describes different pins of the SRAM-like single port interface. While it is possible to add other pins for enhanced functionalities such as power gating test purposes, the interface is kept simple. However, two additional pins are used for body biasing purposes. The pin CBBIAS (Core Body Biasing) enables the biasing of the MRAM core, i.e. bitcell arrays. The pin PBBIAS (Periphery Body Biasing) enables the biasing of the MRAM periphery, i.e. world line drivers, read/write blocks, multiplexers and so on. Table 1, illustrates the system specification target and the circuit-level design considerations.

Table 1. STT-MRAM specifications

MTJ	40nm	Magnetic
TMR, Rp, Sigma	>150%, 1 KΩ, 5%	Magnetic
Retention Endurance Critical current (Ic)	10 years >10e12 Ic=40-100μA	Magnetic
Density	1Mb	System
Timing	20-100ns [10-50 Mhz]	System
IO width	32	System
Bitcell size	min MOS size, 0,0364μm²	CMOS Circuit
Bitcell architecture	1T-1MTJ	CMOS Circuit
Optimization techniques	Body Bias Quasi differential sensing SL sharing	CMOS Circuit
CMOS	28nm-FDSOI	CMOS Circuit
P.Supply	1V	CMOS Circuit

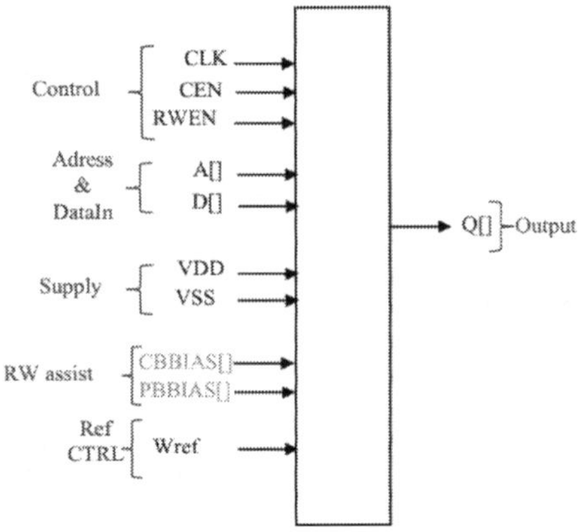

Fig. 3. SRAM-like single port interface

3.2 MRAM simulation and evaluation

We run simulations in the developed hybrid CMOS/magnetic environment of different size instances of memories from 128Kb to 1Mb. Accurate results with fast simulation time and no convergence issues have been obtained. Figure 4 depicts different access operations of the MRAM where data is written or read for each clock signal. Thanks to the body-biasing technique offered by the FDSSOI technology, we may decrease the static power consumption during sleep mode. It is also possible to improve the performance of the memory by boosting the back gate of the memory core to pass higher current through the bitcell and so write the MTJ more rapidly. In figure 5, we compare the power consumption and the performance of the MRAM with and without activating the body biasing. A 60% of static power decrease has been observed thanks to the body biasing technique of the periphery CMOS part of the memory. Also, the performance of the memory can attain 2x of improvement by body biasing the core of the MRAM (here the performance mainly related to MTJ writing time). Only 10% of dynamic power consumption has been observed when boosting the performance of the memory.

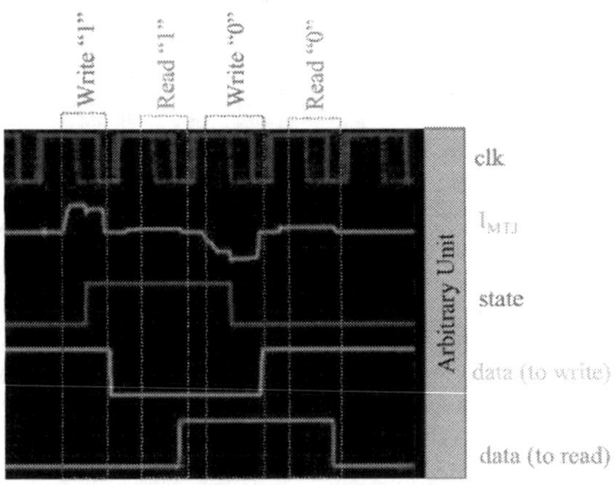

Fig. 4. Simulations of the MRAM instance and validation of its functionality

DOI: 10.1051/matecconf/201712501003

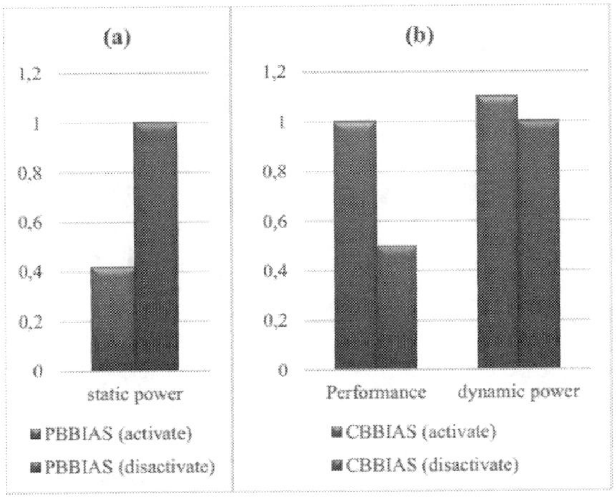

Fig. 5. Effect of body biasing on the memory power consumption and performance (a) Static power reduction by activating periphery body biasing (b) Performance improvement by activating core body biasing

4 Conclusion

As a NV emerging memory, MRAM integration in complex modern systems is a hot topic in both academic and industrial R&D. A solid design flow compatible with industrial constraints and standards is required to associate such a technology to the existing CMOS based integrated circuits systems. In this work, we depicted the complete design of a 1Mb MRAM from the single bitcell to the final memory architecture. While the static power consumption of the MRAM *core* is zero in standby mode thanks to the non-volatility of MTJs, the periphery part of the memory architecture will present a certain amount of leakage power. We proved that using FDSOI technology, the body bias possibility offered by such a technology can reduce further the static power of MRAM up to 60%. Moreover, we demonstrated that the writing time of the bitcell can be decreased by a factor of 2, leading to an improvement of 2x in terms of memory performance. Results are very supportive for future complex hybrid magnetic/CMOS system.

Acknowledgment

This work was partly supported by the French National Research Agency (ANR) under grants ANR-15-CE24-0033-01 and by the German Research Foundation (DFG) in the framework of the MASTA project.

References

1. G. Di Pendina et al., "A Hybrid Magnetic/CMOS PDK for the Design of Low-Power Logic Circuits", J. Appl. Phys., Vol. 111, 2012
2. http://www.mosak.org/grenoble_2015/presentations/T5_Bernard-Granger_MOSAK_Grenoble_2015.pdf
3. K. Jabeur et al., "Comparison of Verilog-A compact Modeling Strategies for Spintronics Devices", IEEE Electronics Letters, 2014
4. Y. J. Song et al, "Highly Functional and Reliable 8Mb STT-MRAM Embedded in 28nm Logic", IEDM 2016
5. Daisuke Saida et al, " 1×- to 2×-nm perpendicular MTJ Switching at Sub-3-ns Pulses Below 100 μA for High Performance Embedded STT-MRAM for Sub-20-nm CMOS", IEEE Transactions on Electron Devices, vol. 64, no. 2, february 2017
6. Yu Lu et al, "Fully Functional Perpendicular STT-MRAM Macro Embedded in 40 nm Logic for Energy-efficient IOT Applications", IEDM 2015

DOI: 10.1051/matecconf/201712501004

Comparative Analysis of Resonant Converters for Energy Storage Systems

Stoyan Vuchev[1*], *Dimitar Arnaudov*[1], *and Nikolay Hinov*[1]

[1] Technical university of Sofia, Faculty of Electronic Engineering and Technologies, Department of Power electronics, 1000 Sofia, Bulgaria

Abstract. The following paperwork presents a comparative analysis of multiphase resonant converters for applications in energy storage systems. Models of the examined converters are developed in the software environments of MATLAB and LTspice. Results from the simulation examination of the converters during charging of supercapacitors and rechargeable batteries are presented. These results are compared to results obtained from experimental examination of the converters via a laboratory stand. For the purposes of the experimental examination, a control system is developed on the base of a virtual instrument in LabVIEW. The advantages and disadvantages of the different converters are discussed.

1. Introduction

Resonant DC/DC converters are widely implemented in energy storage systems (ESS) for their soft switching operation and high overall efficiency. Various circuit topologies are used for charging of energy storage elements (ESE), such as supercapacitors and rechargeable batteries, providing either DC current or DC voltage [1, 2].

Due to the specificities of the charging process, the initial charging current may have to be limited via different possible means and methods. Another important issue may be the necessity of galvanic isolation. When higher output power is needed, modular system topology is often used with several converters operating in parallel to a common load [3-6].

The following paperwork considers a resonant DC/DC converter with three input inverter stages. Due to the circuit features, its operation principle remains unchanged for larger number of modules. Comparative analysis of the converter operation is carried out for different topologies of the input inverter stages. Model based design is proposed for simplified examination of the complicated processes observed in the separate stages. Models of the examined modules are developed for optimization of the analysis and the design procedure.

2. Resonant converter circuits with switching capacitor voltage limitation

The following considered circuits are all derived from the classical resonant inverter half-bridge topology with reverse diodes. As the name suggests, an operation specificity of these converters is the voltage limitation across part of the switching capacitor, which results in a limitation of the supply source current during operation at low resistance loads near the short circuit mode. This feature has a significant contribution to the overall circuit performance in applications for charging of energy storage elements (ESE). Detailed description of the voltage limitation realization and main dependencies is presented in [7].

Another privilege of these converters is their behavior as ideal current sources with respect to the load, which is very useful for obtaining the constant-current ESE charging mode.

2.1 Resonant inverter with separated input filter capacitor

Circuit of the resonant inverter with separated input filter capacitor is presented in fig. 1. It consists of a half-bridge (transistors *T1* and *T2*), input filter capacitors C_{F1} and C_{F2}, resonant tank inductance L_K, resonant tank capacitor separated into two parts (C_K and C_E), limitation diodes D_{D1} and D_{D2} and a coupling output transformer *Tr*. The inverter operation is described in detail in [7].

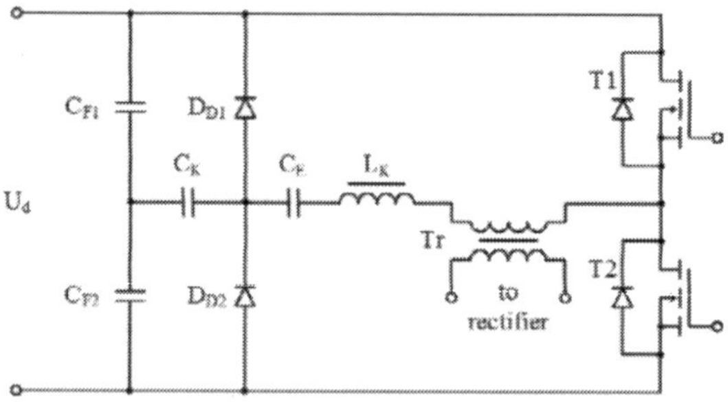

Fig. 1. Circuit of a resonant inverter with switching capacitor voltage limitation and separated input filter capacitor.

* Corresponding author: stoyan.vuchev@tu-sofia.bg

2.2 Resonant inverter with separated switching capacitor

Another version of the presented in fig. 1 inverter is the circuit with separated switching capacitor (fig. 2). Here, instead of the two large filter capacitors, two equal parts of C_K are connected directly between the limitation diodes midpoint and the input voltage power poles.

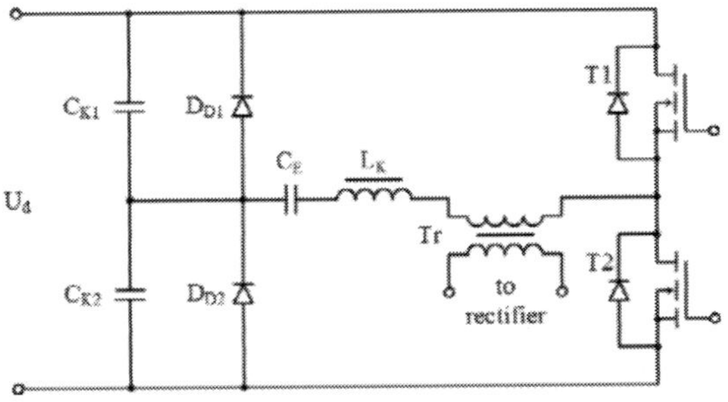

Fig. 2. Circuit of a resonant inverter with voltage limitation across separated switching capacitor.

If the input source is considered as an ideal voltage source with zero resistance, the two capacitor parts are connected in parallel with respect to the AC component. Therefore, each of the two capacitances must be half of the original C_K value.

$$C_{K1} = C_{K2} = \frac{C_K}{2} \tag{1}$$

Nevertheless, the total installed reactive power of the capacitors remains unchanged, although they share the resonant tank current.

2.3 Single-stroke resonant inverter circuit

An equivalent to the presented in fig. 2 circuit with respect to the AC component is the single-stroke resonant inverter (fig. 3). In this case, instead of two equal halves, there is a single C_K part of the switching capacitor connected to the input supply negative pole.

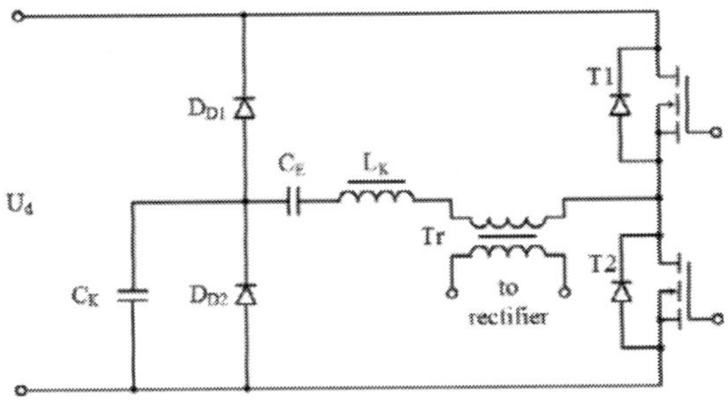

Fig. 3. Circuit of a single-stroke resonant inverter with switching capacitor voltage limitation.

An advantage of the last two inverter topologies is the absence of large input filter capacitors. Moreover, the single-stroke circuit has no capacitor pairs, which eliminates the necessity of two capacitors with well equalized values in order to balance the resonant processes.

3. Multiphase converter topology

In order to obtain high output power, a multiphase converter topology is proposed. A generalized block-diagram of the particular examined three-phase topology is presented in fig. 4. It consists of three inverter stages with coupling transformers, as well as, a three-phase bridge rectifier. The proposed topology allows the number of the input stages to be increased without violating the converter operation – only a proper phase shift of each inverter control signals should be considered.

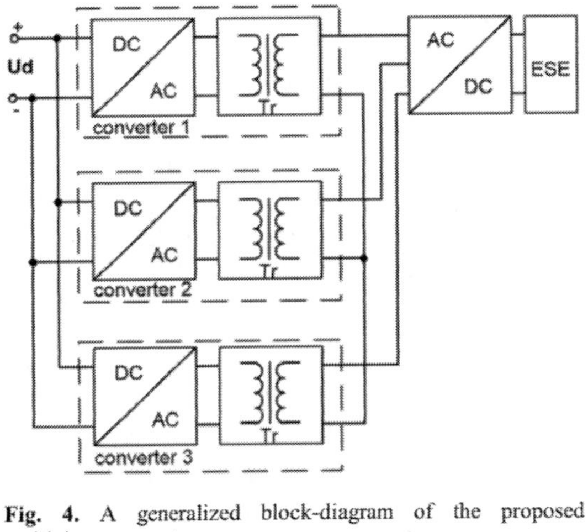

Fig. 4. A generalized block-diagram of the proposed multiphase converter.

Any of the above presented resonant inverter circuits can be implemented for realization of the converter input stages.

4. Models of the proposed converter

Models of the proposed multiphase converter are developed on a modular principle in the software environments of MATLAB Simulink and LTspice for the purposes of the circuit examination and the design procedures. This modular principle allows comparative analysis of different circuit topologies for realization of one or more converter modules to be carried out without changing the rest of the model. Thus, one and the same generalized converter model can be used for examination of specific topology parts preserving the operating conditions of the overall model.

The full MATLAB Simulink model of the examined multiphase converter is presented in fig. 5. A detailed description of this model and the separate modules in its composition is presented in [8].

Models of the three above presented resonant inverters with switching capacitor voltage limitation are also developed in MATLAB Simulink in order the circuits to be analyzed and compared during operation as input inverter stages of the proposed multiphase converter. The three models are presented in fig. 6.

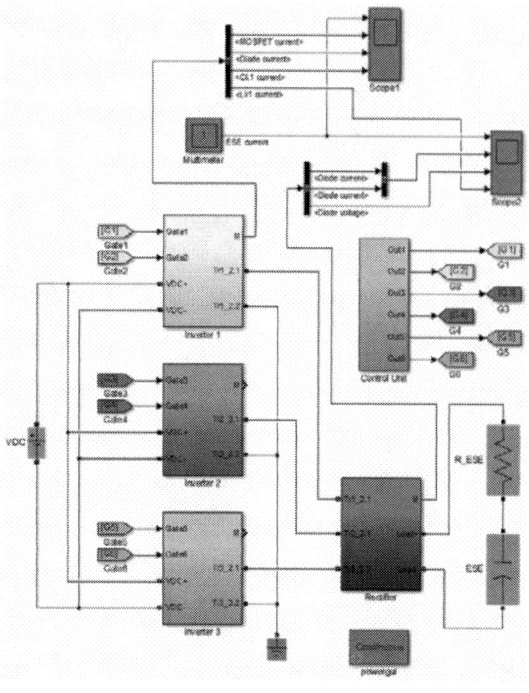

Fig. 5. Full MATLAB Simulink model of the converter.

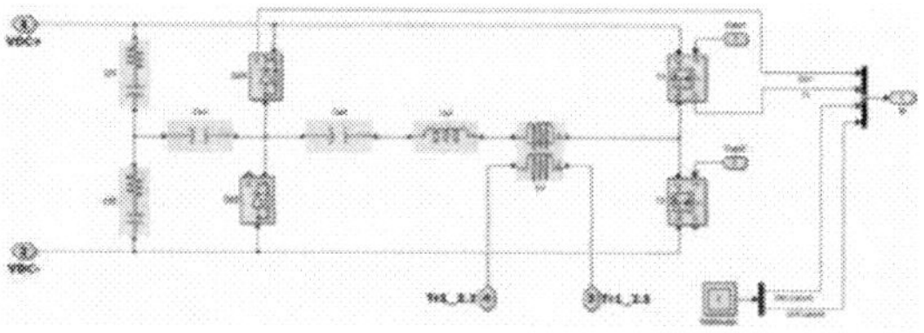

a)

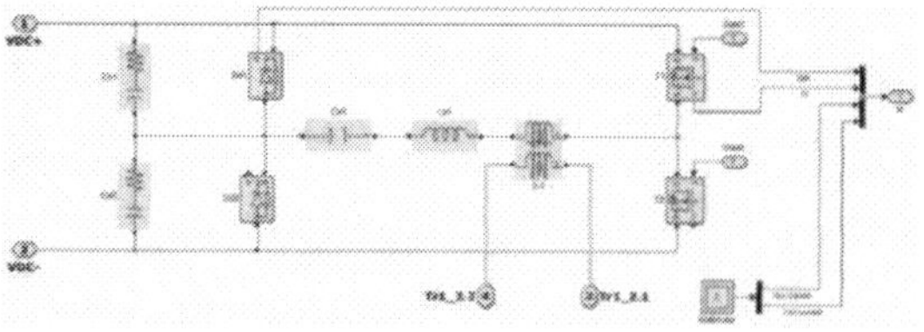

b)

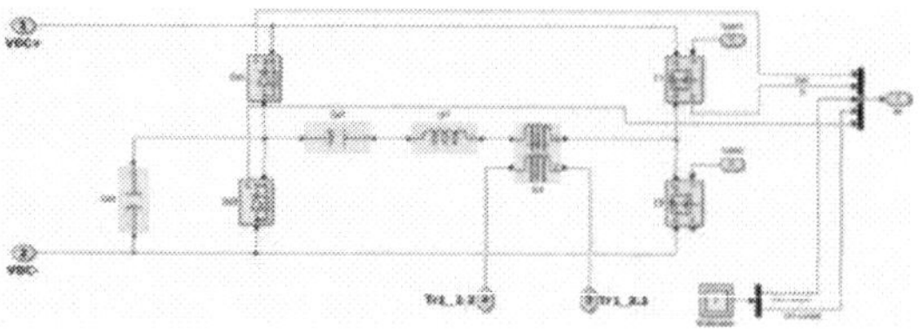

c)

Fig. 6. MATLAB Simulink models of the resonant inverters: a) circuit with separated input filter capacitor; b) circuit with separated switching capacitor; c) single-stroke circuit.

5. Simulation results

Results from computer simulations of the proposed multiphase converter are obtained for supply voltage of 30V, and the ESE is represented by a capacitance of 10mF and a resistance of 1Ω (including parasitic resistance of connections). The transformer ratio is 1. The other circuit values are as follows:

$$C_K = 2.8\mu F,\ C_E = 0.4\mu F,\ L_K = 135\mu H$$

5.1 MATLAB simulation results

The results obtained from computer simulations with the developed in MATLAB Simulink model of the proposed converter with single-stroke resonant inverter stages are presented in fig. 7, fig. 8 and fig. 9. The obtained waveforms are identical for the three examined input inverter topologies. The only difference is the maximum value of the C_K current which is twice smaller for the circuit with separated switching capacitors.

For the purposes of the present investigation, the capacitance representing the ESE is significantly reduced in order to obtain proper illustration of the whole charging process for reasonably small simulation times.

As it can be observed, the limitation diode interval of conduction strongly depends on the ESE state of charge. For lower values of the load voltage, the voltage limitation across C_K is significant, which results in limitation of the initial charging current. With increase of the ESE voltage, smaller limitation is applied.

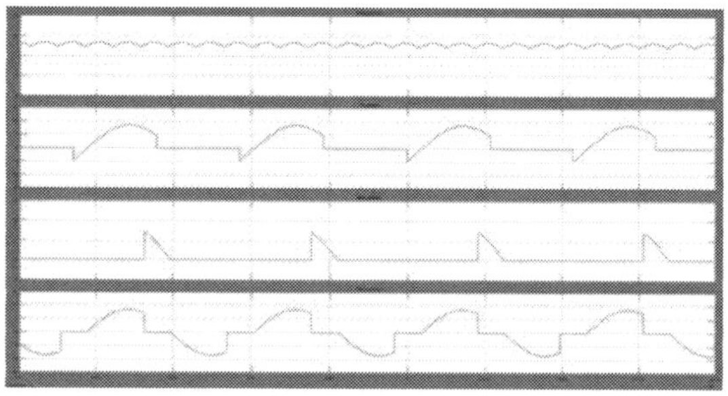

Fig. 7. Waveforms of the ESE, the transistor T1, the limitation diode D_{D1} and the switching capacitor C_{K1} currents at 10ms simulation time (MATLAB Simulink model).

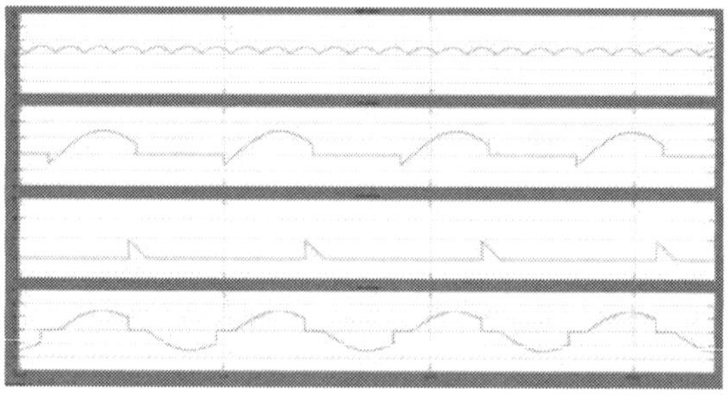

Fig. 8. Waveforms of the ESE, the transistor T1, the limitation diode D_{D1} and the switching capacitor C_{K1} currents at 20ms simulation time (MATLAB Simulink model).

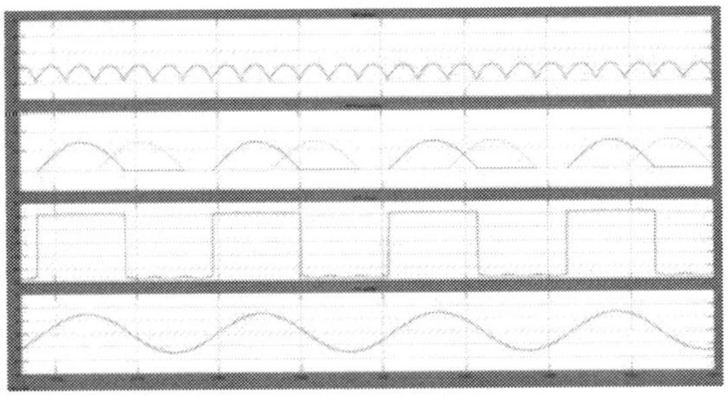

Fig. 9. Waveforms of the ESE current, the rectifier diodes D_{R1} and D_{R3} currents, the diode D_{R1} voltage and the resonant inductance L_{K1} current at 20ms simulation time (MATLAB Simulink model).

5.2 LTspice simulation results

For verification of the obtained simulation results from the model of the proposed multiphase converter in MATLAB Simulink, an identical model is developed in the software environment of LTspice. During the simulation examination, the same circuit element values are used.

Again, the capacitance representing the ESE is significantly reduced in order to obtain proper illustration of the whole charging process for reasonably small simulation times.

The results obtained from the LTspice model of the proposed multiphase converter are presented in fig. 10, fig. 11 and fig. 12. As it can be observed, they are identical to those from the MATLAB Simulink model, which verifies both their authenticity.

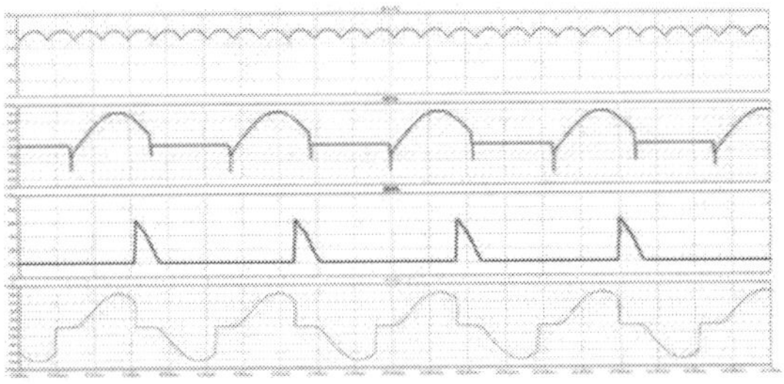

Fig. 10. Waveforms of the ESE, the transistor T1, the limitation diode D_{D1} and the switching capacitor C_{K1} currents at 10ms simulation time (LTspice model).

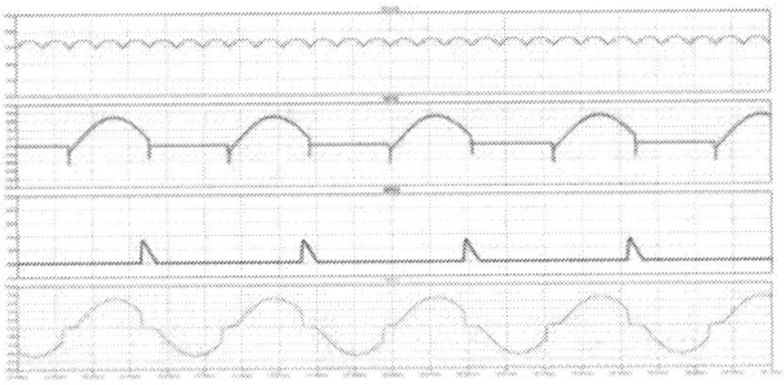

Fig. 11. Waveforms of the ESE, the transistor T1, the limitation diode D_{D1} and the switching capacitor C_{K1} currents at 20ms simulation time (LTspice model).

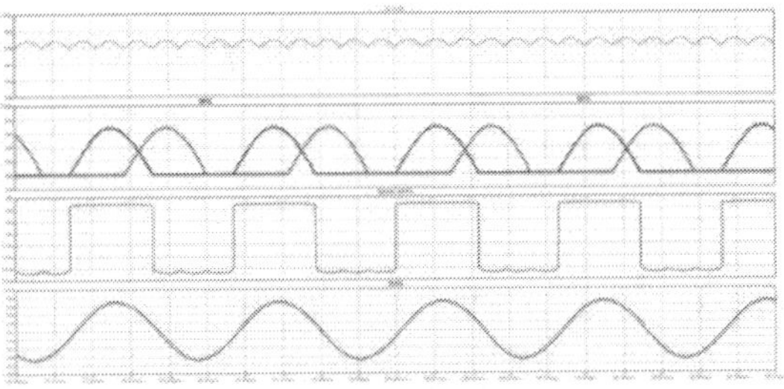

Fig. 12. Waveforms of the ESE current, the rectifier diodes D_{R1} and D_{R3} currents, the diode D_{R1} voltage and the resonant inductance L_{K1} current at 20ms simulation time (LTspice model).

5.3 Tolerances of the circuit elements

The tolerances of the elements in the examined circuits play an important role in the whole converter performance. Deviation in one or more of the resonant tank values results in a different resonant frequency, i.e. different detuning for a fixed operating frequency. As a result, lack of balance between the separate stage currents occurs.

The above can be observed in fig. 13 where simulation results from the MATLAB Simulink converter model are presented for a changed value of one of the resonant tank inductors ($L_{K1} = 155\mu H$). The other circuit component values are unchanged.

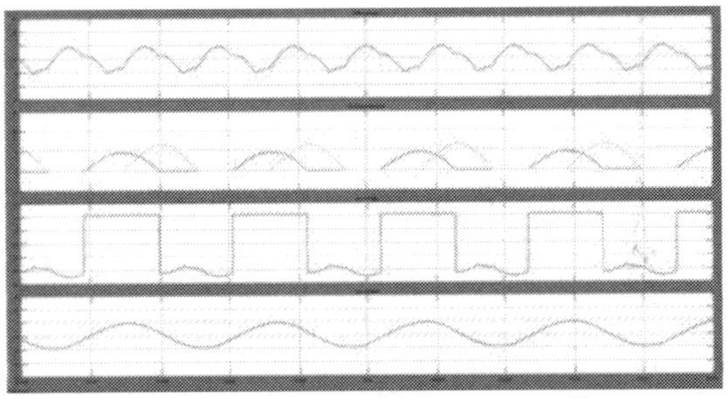

Fig. 13. Waveforms of the ESE, the transistor T1, the limitation diode D_{D1} and the switching capacitor C_{K1} currents at 20ms simulation time (MATLAB Simulink model with circuit imbalance).

An identical simulation examination is carried out in LTspice for verification of the obtained results (fig. 14).

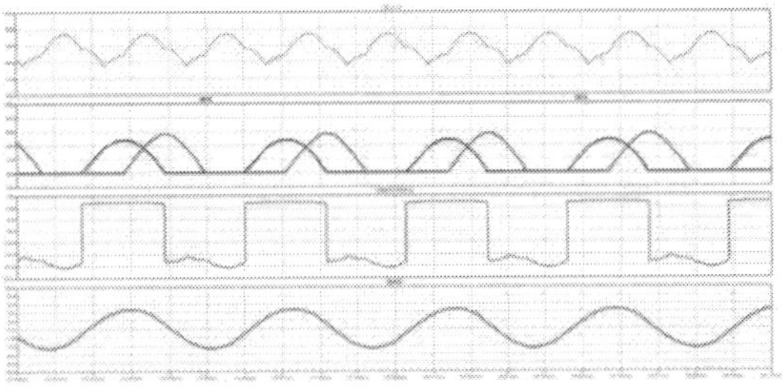

Fig. 14. Waveforms of the ESE, the transistor T1, the limitation diode D_{D1} and the switching capacitor C_{K1} currents at 20ms simulation time (LTspice model with circuit imbalance).

 DOI: 10.1051/matecconf/201712501004

6. Experimental examinations

For further verification of the obtained simulation results, experimental examinations of the proposed multiphase converter based on single-stroke resonant inverter input modules are carried out on a laboratory stand. The presented waveforms (fig. 15 to fig. 18) correspond to the charging process of a 58F/16V supercapacitor. The other circuit parameter values are identical to the ones from the two simulation models.

The experimentally obtained current waveforms present the operation of an imbalanced converter due to the tolerances of the circuit elements. As a result of these tolerances, an imbalance between the separate inverter stage currents occurs. This can easily be observed from the non-symmetric ESE current waveform, as well as, from the rectifier diode current waveforms having different maximum values.

The presented waveforms of the currents through the diodes, the transistors and the L_K inductors are obtained via a current probe with ratio of 10mA/mV. The waveform of the ESE current is obtained via a measurement shunt.

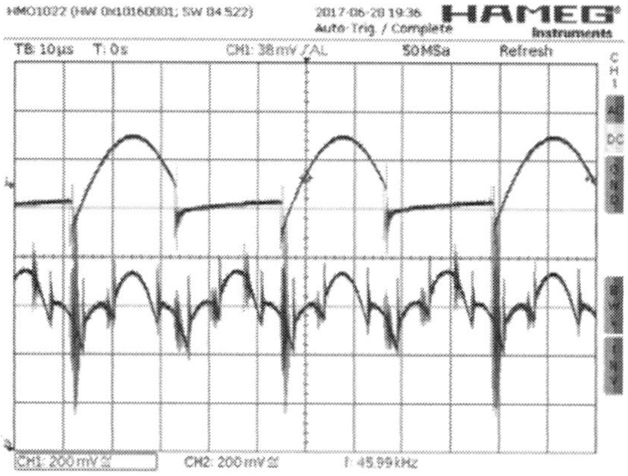

Fig. 15. Waveforms of the transistor T1 and the ESE currents.

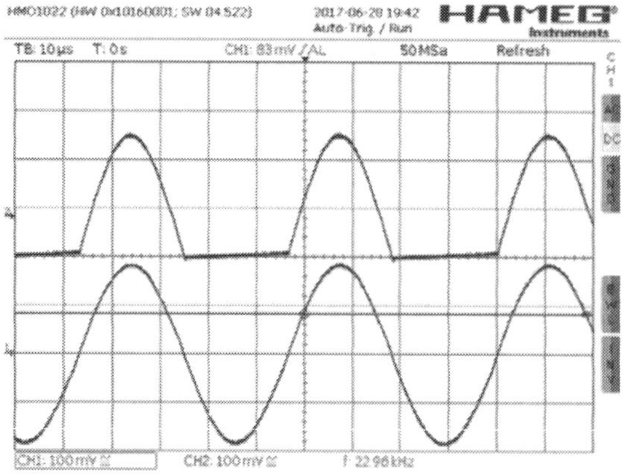

Fig. 16. Waveforms of the diode D_{R1} and the L_{K1} currents.

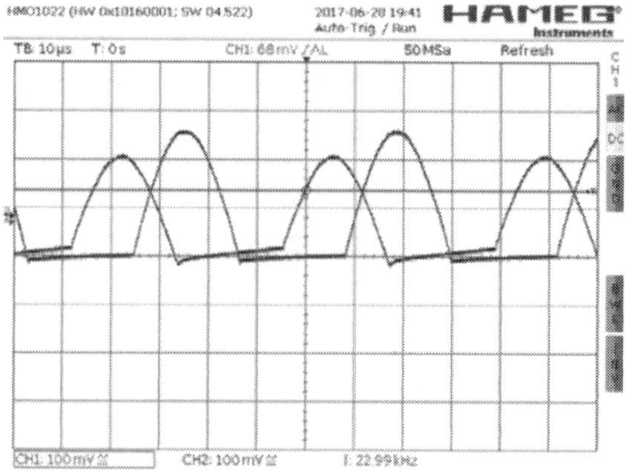

Fig. 17. Waveforms of the diodes D_{R1} and D_{R3} currents.

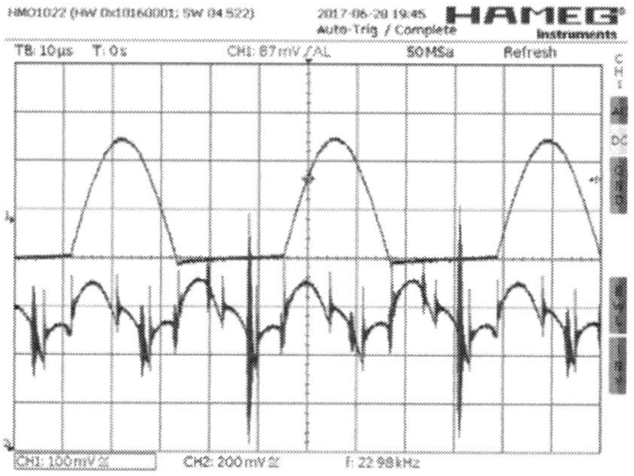

Fig. 18. Waveforms of the diodes D_{R1} and the ESE currents.

7. Conclusion

An investigation of a multiphase converter for charging of ESE is carried out. Different topologies of resonant inverters with switching capacitor voltage limitation are considered for the converter realization. These stages operate at specific load.

Another specialty is the rectifier operation with two diodes from the same group (anode or cathode) operating simultaneously during part of the time as the stage operates in current rectification mode. This can be observed from the waveforms presented in fig. 9, 12, 13, 14 and 17.

With variation of the resonant tank element values, a stage operating mode is changed with respect to those of the other modules. Moreover, this change causes different changes in the operating modes of the other two stages although they have identical component values.

By the means of the developed multiphase converters simulation models, the influence of the component values variations on the separate stages operating modes can be examined. The mutual influences can change the operating modes, and, in some cases, deviation from the limitation mode may occur. Therefore, in order to minimize these influences, topologies with least possible number of coupled reactive elements (capacitors) are necessary to be used.

The developed models allow parametric analysis to be carried out. Because of the complexity of the circuit processes and the lack of steady state operation during ESE charging, analytical expressions for the circuit currents and voltages are difficult to be obtained. For design of such converters model based design is used. In the developed model, the converter is based on a modular structure consisting of separate sub-circuits, which favors the comparative analysis for a constant configuration with different basic converter circuits. Obtaining different operating modes of the multiphase converter allows to evaluate in which cases a synchronous rectifier realization is possible in order to increase the converter efficiency.

The carried out research is realized in the frames of project *BG05M2OP001-2.009-0033*, Operational Program *Science and Education for Smart Growth* 2014-2020.

References

1. Cabrane, Z., M. Ouassaid, M. Maaroufi, *WCCS Proceedings*, pp. 380-385 (2014).
2. Madzharov, N., *Journal of Engineering Science and Technology Review*, **9**, 6 (2016).
3. Cornea, O., N. Muntean, M. Gavris, *OPTIM 2010*, pp. 589-594 (2010).
4. Zarkov, Z., I. Bachev, L. Stoyanov, V. Lazarov, *IEEE-PEMC 2016 Proceedings*, pp. 32-37 (2016).
5. Kanchev, H., F. Colas, V. Lazarov, B. Francois, *IEEE Transactions on Sustainable Energy*, **5**, 4 (2014).
6. Antoszczuk, P., R. Retegui, M. Funes, *IEEE Transactions on Industrial Informatics*, **10**, 4, pp. 2224-2232 (2014).
7. Arnaudov, D., N. Hinov, I. Nedyalkov, *ELEKTROTECHNICA & ELEKTRONICA E+E*, **50**, pp. 11-18 (2015).
8. Arnaudov, D., N. Hinov, S. Vuchev, I. Nedyalkov, *PCIM Europe 2017 Proceedings*, pp. 1130-1136 (2017).

MATEC Web of Conferences **125**, 02001 (2017) DOI: 10.1051/matecconf/201712502001
CSCC 2017

Zhou Method for the Solutions of System of Proportional Delay Differential Equations

S.O. Edeki [1*], and *G.O. Akinlabi* [1]

[1]Department of Mathematics, Covenant University, Ota, Zip Code: 112212, Nigeria

Abstract. In this paper, we consider a viable semi-analytical approach for the approximate-analytical solutions of certain system of functional differential equations (SFDEs) engendered by proportional delays. The proposed semi-analytical technique is built on the basis of the classical Differential Transform Method (DTM). The effectiveness and robustness of the proposed technique is illustratively demonstrated and the results are compared with their exact forms. We note also that using this method, the SFDEs with proportional delays need not be converted to SFDEs with constant delays before obtaining their solutions, and no symbolic calculation or initial guesstimates are required.

1 Introduction

Delay Differential Equation (DDE) is a functional differential equation (FDE) which arises when the rate of change of a time-dependent process is not only determined by its present state but also by a certain previous state in its mathematical modeling. That is, the rate of change of an unknown function depends not just on the values of the unknown function and its independent variable but also on the time values less than the independent variable [1].

This class of differential problems is encountered in many models of real life occurrences and has a wide range of applications in science and engineering. For instance, many of the processes in biology, engineering, physics, medicine, chemistry, and so on involve time delays. Different studies have been conducted by different authors on DDEs. We mention some of these as follows: Houwen and Sommeijer [2] dealt with the stability properties of Linear Multistep Methods (LMMs) for the solution of pure delay equations by making use of the three popular LMMs: Adams-Bashforth, Adams-Moulton and Backward Differentiation Formula.

Al-Mutib [3] also discussed the stability properties of numerical methods for DDEs by considering the one-step method, Runge-Kutta. In 1991, Hout and Spijker [4] analysed the stability of numerical methods for the solution of DDEs by studying the behaviour of these methods when they are applied to the linear test problem. Wille and Baker [5] considered the solution of DDEs by numerical methods and particularly, the numerical solution of state-dependent problems. Those worthy of mention in the discussion of the stability properties of numerical methods for DDEs include (but not limited to) Cryer [6], Barwell [7], Widerholt [8], Watanabe and Roth [9], Bellen and Zennaro [10], Brugnano and Trigiante [11]. Shakeri and Dehgan [12] employed the Homotopy Perturbation Method (HPM) for the solution of DDEs. Some numerical illustrations were given in which they concluded that the proposed method is very efficient and easy to use.

FDEs are basically with constant delays, proportional delays, or time-dependent (time-varying) delays. Meanwhile, we will concentrate in this work on those types with proportional delays.

2 Systems of delay differentail equations (SDDEs)

Here, we give a brief introduction with respect to SDDEs as follows:

Let $f_1(\cdot), f_2(\cdot), f_3(\cdot), \cdots, f_n(\cdot)$ be differentiable functions on a certain domain D, such that $q_i \in (0,1)$, $i = 1(1)k$, and for some dimensional functions, $\underline{w}(t) = \left(w(t), w'(t), w''(t), \dots, w^{(n)}(t)\right)$, then:

$$\begin{cases} f_1\left(t, \underline{w}(t), \underline{w}(q_0 t), \underline{w}(q_1 t), \dots, \underline{w}(q_k t)\right) = 0 \\ f_2\left(t, \underline{w}(t), \underline{w}(q_0 t), \underline{w}(q_1 t), \dots, \underline{w}(q_k t)\right) = 0 \\ f_3\left(t, \underline{w}(t), \underline{w}(q_0 t), \underline{w}(q_1 t), \dots, \underline{w}(q_k t)\right) = 0 \\ \vdots \\ f_n\left(t, \underline{w}(t), \underline{w}(q_0 t), \underline{w}(q_1 t), \dots, \underline{w}(q_k t)\right) = 0 \end{cases} \quad (1)$$

is referred to as the general form of a SDDE with proportional delays, $q_i \in (0,1)$.

Equation (1) has vital applications in real life settings. Many researchers have applied series of methods such as HAM, ADM, and so on for solving various forms of differential equations including DDEs [13-15].

* Corresponding author: soedeki@yahoo.com

3 Analysis of the DTM

The semi-analytical method (DTM) as remarked by many scholars, has been proven to be user-friendly in terms of application for differential models (linear or nonlinear), because the DTM converts the concerned problems to their equivalent forms in algebraic recursive relations, but this is not so when other semi-analytical techniques, such as VIM, HAM, ADM and so on are used [16-17]. The DTM has been modified to handle models of nonlinear types and the likes [18-21].

3.1 *The Overview of the DTM*

Let $m(t)$ be a differentiable function whose transformed form is $M(k)$. Thus, the k-th derivative of $m(t)$ is denoted as:

$$M(k)=\frac{1}{k!}\left(\frac{d^k m(t)}{dt^k}\right)_{t=t_0} . \tag{2}$$

So, the inverse form of $M(k)$ is:

$$m(t)=\sum_{k=0}^{\infty} M(k)(t-t_0)^k . \tag{3}$$

Using (2) in (3) therefore gives:

$$m(t)=\begin{cases}\displaystyle\sum_{k=0}^{\infty}\frac{(t-t_0)^k}{k!}\left(\frac{d^k m(t)}{dt^k}\right)_{t=t_0} , & t_0\neq 0\\ \displaystyle\sum_{k=0}^{\infty}\frac{t^k}{k!}\left(\frac{d^k m(t)}{dt^k}\right)_{t=0} , & t_0=0\end{cases} \tag{4}$$

Equation (4) signifies that the notion of the transformation method originated from Taylor series expansion.

3.2 *The fundamentals of DTM: theorems and properties*

Theorem 1: If $v(t)=\alpha v_a(t)\pm\beta v_b(t)$, then $V(k)=\alpha V_a(k)\pm\beta V_b(k)$

Theorem 2: If $v(t)=\frac{\alpha d^{\eta} v_+(t)}{dt^{\eta}}$, $\eta\in\mathbb{N}$, then

$$V(k)=\frac{\alpha(k+\eta)!}{k!}V_+(k+\eta)$$

Theorem 3: If $v(t)=e^{\lambda t}$, then $V(k)=\frac{\lambda^k}{k!}$

Theorem 4: If $v(t)=v_+^2(t)$, then

$$V(k)=\sum_{\eta=0}^{k} V_+(\eta)V_+(k-\eta)$$

Theorem 5a: Suppose $h(t)$ and $v(t)$ are differentiable functions whose differential functions are $H(k)$ and $V(k)$ respectively and $p\in(0,1)$, then:

$H(k)=p^k V(k)$ if $h(t)=v(pt)$

where p is the proportional delayed parameter.

Theorem 5b: If $v(t)=v_1(p_1 t)v_2(p_2 t)$, then

$$V(k)=\sum_{\eta=0}^{k} p_1^{\eta} p_2^{k-\eta} V_1(\eta)V_2(k-\eta) .$$

Note: the proof of theorems (1)-(4) can easily be found in standard texts [18], so we will briefly sketch that of theorem 5a as follows.

Proof: (Theorem 5a): Consider the derivative of $h(t)=v(pt)$ as follows for $\tau=(pt)$ and $h=h(t)$

That implies that:

$$h=v(\tau),\ \frac{dh}{d\tau}=v'(\tau) \text{ and } d\tau=pdt\ \left(\text{i.e. } \frac{d\tau}{dt}=p\right) \tag{5}$$

$$\therefore\quad \frac{dh}{dt}=\frac{dh}{d\tau}\cdot\frac{d\tau}{dt}=p\frac{dh}{d\tau}=p\frac{dv}{d\tau} . \tag{6}$$

Similarly,

$$\frac{d^2h}{dt^2}=\frac{d}{dt}\left(\frac{dh}{dt}\right)=\frac{d}{dt}\left(p\frac{dh}{d\tau}\right)$$

$$=\frac{d}{d\tau}\left(p\frac{dh}{d\tau}\right)\frac{d\tau}{dt}=p^2\frac{d^2h}{d\tau^2}=p^2\frac{d^2v}{d\tau^2} . \tag{7}$$

In general, the k-th derivative of $h(t)=v(pt)$ is:

$$\frac{d^k h}{dt^k}=p^k\frac{d^k v}{d\tau^k} . \tag{8}$$

Hence, from (2)

$$\left(\frac{d^k h}{dt^k}\right)_{t=t_0}=\left(p^k\frac{d^k v}{d\tau^k}\right)_{t=t_0}=p^k\left(\frac{d^k v}{d\tau^k}\right)_{t=t_0}$$

$$\therefore\quad \left(\frac{d^k h}{dt^k}\right)_{t=t_0}=k!\,p^k V(k) . \tag{9}$$

So, dividing both sides of (9) by $k!$, and using (2) gives:

$H(k)=p^k V(k)$ Q.E.D

4 Illustrative examples and applications

In this section, the proposed method is applied with some illustrative examples for the solutions of system of delay differential equations (SDDEs).

Case 1: Consider the following SDDE:

$$\begin{cases} h_1'(t)=e^{-t}-e^{\frac{t}{2}}+h_1\left(\frac{t}{2}\right)+h_1(t)-h_2(t)\\ h_2'(t)=e^{t}+e^{\frac{t}{2}}-h_1\left(\frac{t}{2}\right)-h_1(t)-h_2(t)\end{cases} \tag{10}$$

subject to:

$$\begin{cases} h_1(0)=1\\ h_2(0)=1\end{cases} \tag{11}$$

with the exact solutions:

$$\begin{cases} h_1(t)=e^{t}\\ h_2(t)=e^{-t}\end{cases} \tag{12}$$

Solution procedure-Case 1:
Taking the DT of (10) gives:

$$DT\left(\begin{cases} h_1'(t)=e^{-t}-e^{\frac{t}{2}}+h_1\left(\frac{t}{2}\right)+h_1(t)-h_2(t) \\ h_2'(t)=e^{t}+e^{\frac{t}{2}}-h_1\left(\frac{t}{2}\right)-h_1(t)-h_2(t) \end{cases}\right). \quad (13)$$

Therefore, for $k \geq 0$, we have the following in recurrence form:

$$H_1(k+1)=\frac{1}{k+1}\left(\frac{(-1)^k}{k!}-\frac{\left(\frac{1}{2}\right)^k}{k!}+\left(\frac{1}{2}\right)^k H_1(k)+H_1(k)-H_2(k)\right) \quad (14)$$

$$H_2(k+1)=\frac{1}{k+1}\left(\frac{(1)^k}{k!}+\frac{\left(\frac{1}{2}\right)^k}{k!}-\left(\frac{1}{2}\right)^k H_1(k)-H_1(k)-H_2(k)\right) \quad (15)$$

with

$$\begin{cases} H_1(0)=1 \\ H_2(0)=1 \end{cases}. \quad (16)$$

Thus, for $k=0$,

$$H_1(1)=\frac{1}{1}\left(\frac{(-1)^0}{0!}-\frac{(0.5)^0}{0!}+\left(\frac{1}{2}\right)^0 H_1(0)+H_1(0)-H_2(0)\right)=1. \quad (17)$$

$$H_2(1)=\frac{1}{1}\left(\frac{(1)^0}{0!}+\frac{(0.5)^0}{0!}-\left(\frac{1}{2}\right)^0 H_1(0)-H_1(0)-H_2(0)\right)=-1. \quad (18)$$

Thus, for $k=1$,

$$H_1(2)=\frac{1}{2}\left(\frac{(-1)}{1!}-\frac{(0.5)}{1!}+\left(\frac{1}{2}\right)H_1(1)+H_1(1)-H_2(1)\right)=\frac{1}{2}. \quad (19)$$

$$H_2(2)=\frac{1}{2}\left(\frac{(1)}{1!}+\frac{(0.5)}{1!}-\left(\frac{1}{2}\right)H_1(1)-H_1(1)-H_2(1)\right)=\frac{1}{2}. \quad (20)$$

Thus, for $k=2$,

$$H_1(3)=\frac{1}{3}\left(\frac{(-1)^2}{2!}-\frac{(0.5)^2}{2!}+\left(\frac{1}{2}\right)^2 H_1(2)+H_1(2)-H_2(2)\right)=\frac{1}{3!}. \quad (21)$$

$$H_2(3)=\frac{1}{3}\left(\frac{(1)^2}{2!}+\frac{(0.5)^2}{2!}-\left(\frac{1}{2}\right)^2 H_1(2)-H_1(2)-H_2(2)\right)=-\frac{1}{3!}. \quad (22)$$

Thus, for $k=3$,

$$H_1(4)=\frac{1}{4}\left(\frac{(-1)^3}{3!}-\frac{(0.5)^3}{3!}+\left(\frac{1}{2}\right)^3 H_1(3)+H_1(3)-H_2(3)\right)=\frac{1}{4!}. \quad (23)$$

$$H_2(4)=\frac{1}{4}\left(\frac{(1)^3}{3!}+\frac{(0.5)^3}{3!}-\left(\frac{1}{2}\right)^3 H_1(3)-H_1(3)-H_2(3)\right)=\frac{1}{4!}. \quad (24)$$

Thus, for $k=4$,

$$H_1(5)=\frac{1}{5}\left(\frac{(-1)^4}{4!}-\frac{(0.5)^4}{4!}+\left(\frac{1}{2}\right)^4 H_1(4)+H_1(4)-H_2(4)\right)=\frac{1}{5!}. \quad (25)$$

$$H_2(5)=\frac{1}{5}\left(\frac{(1)^4}{4!}+\frac{(0.5)^4}{4!}-\left(\frac{1}{2}\right)^4 H_1(4)-H_1(4)-H_2(4)\right)=-\frac{1}{5!}. \quad (26)$$

Hence, considering (16)-(26), we write coefficients as follows:

$$\begin{cases} H_1(0)=1,\ H_1(1)=1,\ H_1(2)=\frac{1}{2!}, \\ H_1(3)=\frac{1}{3!}, H_1(4)=\frac{1}{4!},\ H_1(5)=\frac{1}{5!},\cdots \end{cases} \quad (27)$$
$$\begin{cases} H_2(0)=1,\ H_2(1)=-1,\ H_2(2)=\frac{1}{2!}, \\ H_2(3)=-\frac{1}{3!},\ H_2(4)=\frac{1}{4!},\ H_2(5)=-\frac{1}{5!},\cdots \end{cases}$$

$$\therefore h_1(t)=\sum_{k=0}^{\infty}H_1(k)t^k=H_1(0)+H_1(1)t+H_1(2)t^2+H_1(3)t^3+H_1(4)t^4+\cdots$$
$$=1+t+\frac{1}{2!}t^2+\frac{1}{3!}t^3+\frac{1}{4!}t^4+\frac{1}{5!}t^5+\cdots. \quad (28)$$

Similarly,

$$h_2(t)=\sum_{k=0}^{\infty}H_2(k)t^k=H_2(0)+H_2(1)t+H_2(2)t^2+H_2(3)t^3+H_2(4)t^4+\cdots=1-t+\frac{1}{2!}t^2-\frac{1}{3!}t^3+\frac{1}{4!}t^4-\frac{1}{5!}t^5+\cdots. \quad (29)$$

Case 2: Consider the SDDE [17]:

$$\begin{cases}2h_1'(t)=h_1(t)+e^{\frac{t}{2}}h_2\left(\frac{t}{2}\right)\\ 2h_2'(t)=h_2(t)+e^{\frac{t}{2}}h_1\left(\frac{t}{2}\right)\end{cases} \quad (30)$$

subject to:

$$h_1(0)=1=h_2(0) \quad (31)$$

with the exact solutions:

$$\begin{cases}h_1(t)=e^t\\ h_2(t)=e^t\end{cases}. \quad (32)$$

Solution procedure- case 2:
Taking the DT of (30) gives:

$$DT\left(\begin{cases}2h_1'(t)=h_1(t)+e^{\frac{t}{2}}h_2\left(\frac{t}{2}\right)\\ 2h_2'(t)=h_2(t)+e^{\frac{t}{2}}h_1\left(\frac{t}{2}\right)\end{cases}\right). \quad (33)$$

Therefore, for $k\geq 0$, we have the following in recurrence form:

$$H_1(k+1)=\frac{1}{2(k+1)}\left(H_1(k)+\sum_{i=0}^{k}\frac{(0.5)^i}{i!}\left(\frac{1}{2}\right)^{k-i}H_2(k-i)\right), \quad (34)$$

$$H_2(k+1)=\frac{1}{2(k+1)}\left(H_2(k)+\sum_{i=0}^{k}\frac{(0.5)^i}{i!}\left(\frac{1}{2}\right)^{k-i}H_1(k-i)\right), \quad (35)$$

with

$$\begin{cases}H_1(0)=1\\ H_2(0)=1\end{cases}. \quad (36)$$

Hence, using (36) in (34)-(35) for $k\in\mathbb{N}\cup\{0\}$, we have:

$$\begin{cases}H_1(1)=1, H_1(2)=\frac{1}{2}, H_1(3)=\frac{1}{6}, H_1(4)=\frac{1}{24},\\ H_1(5)=\frac{1}{120},\cdots\end{cases}$$
$$\begin{cases}H_2(1)=1, H_2(2)=\frac{1}{2}, H_2(3)=\frac{1}{6}, H_2(4)=\frac{1}{24},\\ H_2(5)=\frac{1}{120},\cdots\end{cases} \quad (37)$$

$$\therefore h_1(t)=\sum_{k=0}^{\infty}H_1(k)t^k=H_1(0)+H_1(1)t+H_1(2)t^2+H_1(3)t^3+H_1(4)t^4+\cdots=1+t+\frac{1}{2}t^2+\frac{1}{6}t^3+\frac{1}{24}t^4+\frac{1}{120}t^5+\cdots\approx e^t. \quad (38)$$

Similarly,

$$h_2(t)=\sum_{k=0}^{\infty}H_2(k)t^k=H_2(0)+H_2(1)t+H_2(2)t^2+H_2(3)t^3+H_2(4)t^4+\cdots=1+t+\frac{1}{2}t^2+\frac{1}{6}t^3+\frac{1}{24}t^4+\frac{1}{120}t^5+\cdots\approx e^t. \quad (39)$$

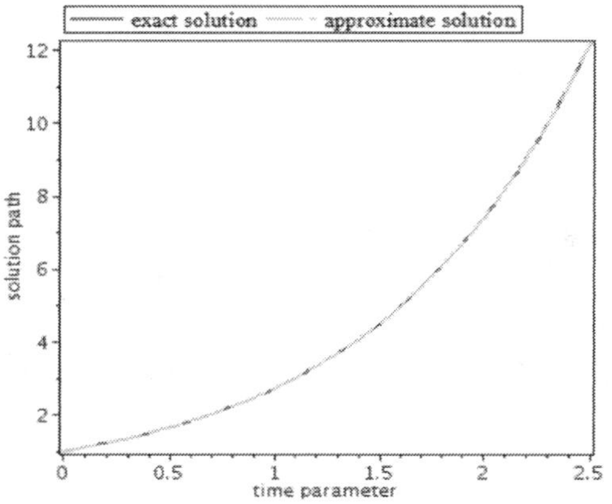

Fig. 1: Exact and Approx. Solutions of $h_1(t)$ in case 1

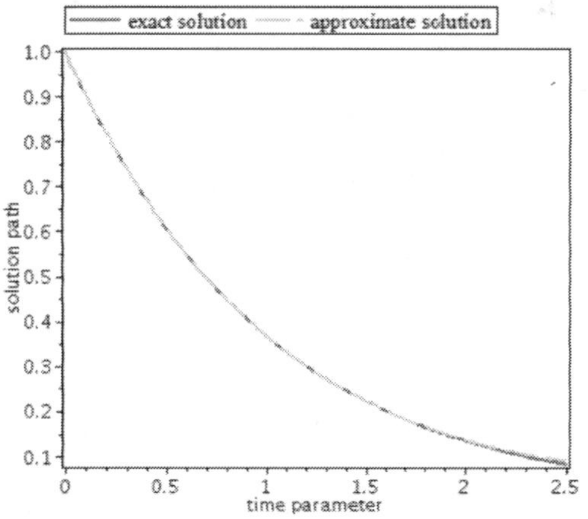

Fig. 2: Exact and Approx. Solution of $h_2(t)$ in case 1

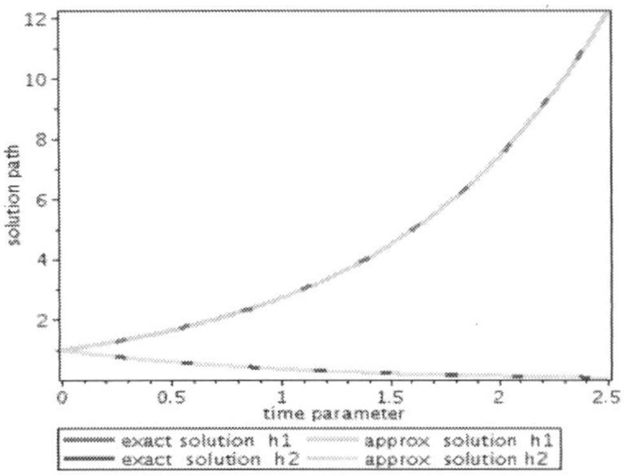

Fig. 3: Exact and Approx. Solutions of $h_1(t)$ & $h_2(t)$ in case 1

5 CONCLUSION

We considered in this work, by means of Zhou method, the approximate-analytical solutions of a certain system of functional differential equations (SFDEs) engendered by proportional delay. The effectiveness and robustness of the proposed technique was illustratively demonstrated and the results coincide approximately with their exact forms when compared. In addition, we noted that using this method, the SFDEs with proportional delays need not be converted to SFDEs with constant delays before obtaining their solutions, and no symbolic calculation or initial guesstimates, linearization or perturbation is required.

Acknowledgement

The authors are grateful to Covenant University for financial support. In addition, they also wish to thank the anonymous reviewer(s) for their constructive comments.

References

[1] J. C. Butcher, "Numerical Methods for Ordinary Differential Equations". New York: John Wiley & Sons (2008).

[2] P. J. Van der Houwen, and B. P. Sommeijer, "Stability in Linear Multistep Methods for Pure Delay Equations", J. Comput. Appl. Math., **10**, (1984): 55–63.

[3] A. N. Al-Mutib, "Stability Properties of Numerical Methods for Solving Delay Differential Equations", J. Comput. Appl. Math., **10**, (1984): 71–79.

[4] K. J. in't Hout and M. N. Spijker, "Stability Analysis of Numerical Methods for Delay Differential Equations", Numer. Math., **59**, (1991): 807–814.

[5] D. R. Wille, and C. T. H. Baker, "Stepsize Control and Continuity Consistency for State-Dependent Delay-Differential Equations", J. Comput. Appl. Math., **53**, (1994): 163-170.

[6] C.W. Cryer, "Highly-Stable Multistep Methods for Retarded Differential Equations", SIAM J. Numer. Anal. **11,** (1974): 788-797.

[7] V. K. Barwell, "Special Stability Problems for Functional Differential Equations", BIT, 15, (1975): 130–135.

[8] L. F. Widerholt, "Stability of Multistep Methods for Delay Differential Equations", Math. Comput., **30** (134), (1976): 283-290.

[9] D. S. Watanabe, and M. Roth, "The Stability of Difference Formulas for Delay Differential Equations", SIAM J. Numer. Anal., **22**, (1985): 132–145.

[10] A. Bellen, and M. Zennaro, "Strong Contractivity Properties of Numerical Methods for Ordinary and Delay Differential Equations", Appl. Numer. Math., **9**, (1992): 321–346.

[11] L. Brugnano and D. Trigiante, "Solving Differential Problems by Multistep Initial and Boundary Value Methods". Amsterdam: Gordon and Breach Science Publishers (1998).

[12] F. Shakeri, and M. Dehghan, "Solution of delay differential equations via a homotopy perturbation method", Mathematical and Computer Modelling, **48,** (2008): 486–498.

[13] M. Zennaro, "Delay Differential Equations: Theory and Numerics, in Theory and Numerics of Ordinary and Partial Differential Equations", Adv. Numer. Anal., **5,** Clarendon Press, Oxford, (1995).

[14] G.O. Akinlabi and S. O. Edeki, "On Approximate and Closed-form Solution Method for Initial-value Wave-like Models", International Journal of Pure and Applied Mathematics, **107** (2), (2016): 449-456.

[15] L. Qiu, T. Mitsui, and J.-X. Kuang, "The numerical stability of the θ-method for delay differential equations with many variable delays", Journal of Computational Mathematics, **17** (5) (1999): 523-532.

[16] S.O. Edeki, G.O. Akinlabi and S.A. Adeosun, "Analytic and Numerical Solutions of Time-Fractional Linear Schrödinger Equation", Communications in Mathematics and Applications, **7** (1), (2016): 1–10.

[17] R. K. Saeed and B. M. Rahman, "Adomian Decomposition Method for Solving System of Delay Differential Equation", Australian Journal of Basic and Applied Sciences, **4** (8) (2010): 3613-3621.

[18] J. K. Zhou, "Differential Transformation and its Application in Electrical Circuits", Huazhong University Press,Wuhan, China, (1986).

[19] S. O. Edeki, G. O. Akinlabi, S. A. Adeosun, "On a modified transformation method for exact and approximate solutions of linear Schrödinger equations", AIP Conference proceedings **1705**, 020048 (2016); doi: 10. 1063/1.4940296.

[20] Gh. J. Mohammed, F. S. Fadhel, "Extend differential transform methods for solving differential equations with multiple delay", Ibn Al-Haitham J. for Pure and Appl. Sci., **24** (3), (2011): 1-5.

[21] S. O. Edeki, O. O. Ugbebor, E. A. Owoloko, "Analytical Solutions of the Black–Scholes Pricing Model for European Option Valuation via a Projected Differential Transformation Method", Entropy, **17** (11), (2015): 7510-7521.

[22] J. Rebenda, Z. Smarda, Y. Khan, "A Taylor Method Approach for Solving of Nonlinear Systems of Functional Differential Equations with Delay", arXiv:1506.05646v1, [math.CA], 18 June, (2015).

Evaluation of Sustainable Practices within Project Management Methods

Satya Shah[1, a], *Elmira* Naghi Ganji[1] and *Alec* Coutroubis[1]

[1]*Applied Engineering and Management, Faculty of Engineering and Science, University of Greenwich, UK*

Abstract. The purpose of this research study is to investigate some of the sustainable practices within projects with a focus on social projects. The different research methodologies applied through this research consisted both primary and secondary research, including literature review and through case study. The stakeholder's behavioural needs towards acting and implementing sustainable practices led to the adoption of sustainable practices within projects which are managed across profit and non-profit organisations. Nevertheless, lack of sustainable behaviour was outlined, and henceforth the integration of sustainable development within social projects is crucially important as such projects were identified as the drivers toward educating the society in order to help to produce generations of people who would be more sustainably aware. Currently, sustainable development is very often taken into account when it comes to managing projects. Nevertheless, if the adoption of sustainable practices is well established in some sectors such as construction, literature tends to demonstrate a lack of information regarding other sectors, especially within social projects. This research aims to investigate the adoption of sustainable practices within social projects and therefore to satisfy a literature gap.

1 Introduction

The earth is facing major environmental issues mostly due to the current practices used within a world of consumption and globalization. In the last two decades, the concept of sustainability and accountability has become an emerging characteristic of the enterprises worldwide. Improving significant aspects of a company success such as economic, social and environmental performance; sustainability defines a strategy to transform businesses towards long-term prosperity. The awareness of the population is constantly increasing and a real need of change now appears as vital in order to preserve the environment but also to stimulate ethical behaviours [1]. The triple bottom line of sustainable development aims to respond to the present needs in focusing on three major aspects: the environmental, economic and social aspects [2]. Presently, most of the governments promote the positive effects of an on-going transition to a potential green economy. Nevertheless, even if the environmental sector is growing very fast, this is a long process that requires major changes at different levels. This means that several gaps have not been explored yet and there is still a considerable need of more research and improvements.

Project Management is a discipline that can be applied in every business, organisations and governments or even in everyone's private life. Adopting a new way of tackling projects integrating the concept of sustainability will impact on most of people's personal or professional habits. The benefit of the implementation of sustainability within building approaches has already been undeniably well established [3]. Literature tends to demonstrate a lack of information regarding other sectors, especially within social projects. Therefore, this research aims to examine the possible gaps within the integration of sustainable development within social projects and expects to provide recommendations in order to contribute to the success of sustainability.

Furthermore, the world literature would provide suitable secondary resources related to the application of sustainable practices within the for-profits and non-profits organisations and also makes a bridge between the two mentioned organisations, as a more reliable term called "hybrid organisation" [4]. Finally, based on a clear roadmap and its five different pillars, this study seeks to examine the concept of environmental sustainability and social awareness through the conduction of a survey questionnaire of Company AB. Hence, the research primary resources will be provided. According to the analysis and final results; a set of ultimate statements and recommendations for future research will be presented based on the limitations of this research.

2 Literature Review

The review of literature seeks to outline the conceptual framework of the research by presenting a review of advantages, disadvantages, motivations, drivers and hurdles towards the use of sustainable practices within project management methods, especially with the key focus towards social projects in particular. The key

[a] Corresponding author: s.shah@gre.ac.uk

research areas of this study aims to focus towards the following areas as highlighted in Figure 1.

Fig. 1. Research Focus of Sustainability and Social Projects

2.1 Sustainable Development

The meaning of sustainable development was defined by The World Commission on Environment and Development [5] as "development that meets the needs of the present without compromising the ability of future generations to meet their own needs". This study aims to investigate some of the sustainable practices adopted within projects with a focus on social projects. Therefore, sustainable development is considered as the major component of this research. This is why an understanding of the concept and the relevance of sustainable development is necessary in order to successfully fulfil the focus of this research.

Recent literature has identified that the issue of sustainability has increasingly influenced the business world for the past 30 years. The concept of sustainable development has been widely associated with three components called the triple bottom line: economic activity, social progress and environmental responsibility. In addition, the research asserts that a balanced approach to these three aspects and a sensible use of the planet's resources is the only way to lead to a sustainable future [2]. In order to achieve this balanced approach, numerous different practices exist. The notion of "practices" was defined by [6] as "the elements like shared routines or behaviour, models, guidelines and policies"; they may exist at different levels. Sustainable practices can be associated with the main aspects of sustainable development such as pollution, waste and recycling, climate change, corporate social responsibility, cultural dimensions, global awareness or globalisation, as examples. This study aims to identify current sustainable practices adopted within projects. However, at the start of this research study, the author's only aims to address the two important key areas of corporate social responsibility (CSR) and community awareness.

2.2 Corporate Social Responsibility (CSR)

Recent literature tends to outline that the concept of CSR is debated and argued to be unclear and hard to define. [7]. However, as it is also a growing notion, different authors have tried to define it. Other research studies explains Corporate Social Responsibility as a concept integrating a wide range of issues involved in the relationship between an organisation's actions and those affected by them [8]. Therefore, achieving corporate social responsibility is about meeting the needs of the stakeholders [9]. This author also clarifies the concept by expressing the following range of issues which should be covered through dealing with CSR: the employee relations, human rights, corporate ethics, community relations and the environment. Recent literature has also identified the concept of Corporate Social Responsibility as a main contribution to sustainable development as it encourages organisations to act socially responsibly and therefore integrate at least one of the three dimensions of the triple bottom line of sustainable development [10].

However, most of the organisations are starting to see the economic potential of the integration of sustainable development. This is why it is also important to highlight that adding economic value to corporate social actions can be considered as reducing the moral validity. In fact, [11] argues that trying to achieve superior profit through social initiatives perverts the essence of CSR. These findings provides the researchers to have a better understanding of the concept of corporate social responsibility which is one of the key areas of sustainable development this research focusses upon. Research studies define environmental awareness as the individuals' vigilance in noticing environmental problems and beliefs about their potential adverse consequences [12]. Research explains that among its principles, sustainable development encourages the mobilization of individuals, including women, youth and various communities to take an active role in achieving sustainable development [13]. Recent literature has mainly demonstrated a significant and increasing awareness of global environmental problems as well as a need of improvements to ensure the protection of the environment [1].

2.3 Project Management

Literature explains that traditionally, the management of projects is now considered as a science due to the growing number of Project Management institutions and associations. It is the discipline of managing projects successfully [14]. The research does not aim to define project management but to link it to the concept of sustainable development, mainly focusing on the two key areas mentioned previously as CSR and community awareness. Hence, the authors intend to provide the main focus on evaluating the integration of sustainable practices within projects. As discussed earlier, research studies have shown an increasing environmental awareness from the community. This is why stakeholders demand is probably one of the factors that drove the project management industry to integrate sustainability. Literature showed that government and multinational corporations are the two main customer groups currently requesting sustainability within projects [15]. In addition, it asserts that this demand will increase, which again states the importance of the integration of sustainable principles within project management. This led to the birth of a new concept termed as "*green project management*".

According to research studies by [16], Green Project Management is still considered in its infancy. In fact, the idea of applying green standards within projects is quite new. Green Project Management aims to incorporate environmental aspects into project management processes. It is about thinking green throughout the whole project and making decisions in order to reduce the possible impact on the environment with the intention of preserving it. The literature insists that the point is not to make every decision about the environment and to evaluate if it is eco-friendly enough or not; the purpose is to take into account potential environmental impacts instead of ignoring them [16].

One of the research objectives is to analyse the impact of the use of sustainable methods on the project stakeholders. Throughout research it suggests that project stakeholders are closely linked to both the concept of sustainable development and of project management. In fact, this study has identified that stakeholder management is increasing considerably in the context of sustainable development. It has also stated that in order for projects to meet stakeholders' needs and expectations, project management will have to be done in the context of sustainable development. So far, it appears that project stakeholders could be engaged with sustainable development in two slightly different ways. The first one is of course, the increasing demand of stakeholders for achieving sustainability. The second is the promotion of sustainability through the stakeholders' engagement.

2.4 For-Profit and Non-Profit Organisations

According to a study, non-profit organisation refers to "an entity that legally prohibited from disturbing profits to its shareholders or managers" [17]. These organisations operate within various fields such as charity, clothing and shelter, labour, sports, health and safety, food delivery, politics, religion, defence, altruism, liberty, business support and civil rights [18]. As it is evident from the statistics, 1,478,194 non-profit organisations existed in the US in 2006 which was 36% more than its last decade [19]. Besides, there is a tight competitiveness among these organisations, as some of the researchers have utilised the porter's five forces in order to monitor the competitor's intensity in those environments [20]. The mentioned factors act as major motivations for these organisations to move towards sustainability, especially considering their most important missions for social and moral missions.

The study aims to focus towards social sustainability and its adoption within the projects of an organisation. In addition, it intends to compare the use of the sustainable practice within profit and non-profit organisations. Hence, the research investigates the profit and non-profit organisations and the adoption of sustainability practices within these environments. A recent study investigates 10 different cases of social non-profit organisations in Australia and explores their need to develop sustainable practices both in strategic and operational levels of management in order to obtain strategies to measure social entrepreneurship theory [21]. They interviewed the CEOs and senior managers of the companies and achieved 3 propositions according to the results of their questionnaire based approach. Firstly, the environmental changes such as climate change push the businesses to adopt sustainable approaches. Secondly, achieving financial benefits leads them to adopt operational decisions and proper strategies which are compatible with sustainability. Thirdly, the need to balance the three pillars of sustainability and to adopt multiple innovation strategies persuade them towards organisational sustainability [21].

Regarding the for-profit organisations, a research paper examines the influence of stakeholder's pressures towards environmental sustainability of an adhesive manufacturing industry through a qualitative survey [22]. As reported, again competitive advantage plays a vital role in this case as a critical motivator. Profitability, business image, availability of quality management standard, minimizing environmental impacts, government regulations, customer demand and staff awareness enhancement are the parameters that are very important towards the adoption of environmental sustainability. Furthermore, high industry competition and shareholders' inspiration exert the most important influential factors for environmental management system (EMS) adoption. The shareholder's desire is due to the fact that the factors such as financial performance, energy and water consumption and recycling are their major business challenges, and hence, move them towards adoption of sustainable practices [22].

A research paper utilises the term "hybrid organisation" to make a linkage between the non-profit and for-profit organisations in order to create an effective way moving towards social and environmental changes [23], whereas, hybrid organisation also known as fourth sector, L3C, Blended value, benefit corporation and mission driven, refers to "the start-up that combines different institutional logics in unprecedented ways" [24]. In other words, the hybrid organisation mixes the parameters, value systems and action logics such as social responsibility and financial profits from different society sectors such as public sector and non-profit sector. Explaining the way that hybrid organisations contribute to the environmental protection and social impacts, a theoretical model called Sustainability-driven Business Model is defined [23]. The main factors of this model includes social change as organisational objective, effective relationship between the stakeholders and consistent interaction with markets, competitors and industry institutions. This model identifies the key distinctive factors between the traditional and hybrid organisations. In terms of corporate social responsibility (CSR) and environmental issues, the traditional ones only address these issues if they access to sufficient resources, strong business plans and gain enough profits; whereas hybrids integrate their business cases with explicit environmental objectives. In terms of stakeholder's relationship, the traditional ones rely on financial profit as a critical factor, however, hybrids firstly consider mutual benefits and sustainability results.

3 Research Methodology

This research is based on both qualitative and quantitative data which is facilitated through detailed company survey using site visits, themed interviews and questionnaire administration. Furthermore, reviewing the history and background of the company, all the publicity available materials such as company website and brochures were used within the research.

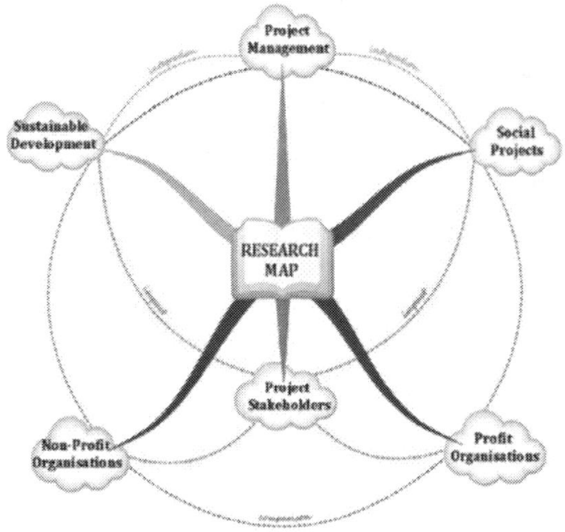

Fig. 2. Research Roadmap.

The objectives of the research which aims to satisfy by conducting primary research are as follows:

a) To understand project stakeholders' behavioural needs towards acting and implementing sustainable practices.
b) To compare the use of the identified sustainable practices and its adoption within profit and non-profit organisations.
c) To identify the importance and relevance of sustainable development within social projects.

The proposed research seeks to describe the characteristics on adoption of sustainable practices and especially within profit and non-profit based organisations. The research aims to evaluate the findings based on the collected data from document research, industry association data from the interviews and also any government environmental or sustainability regulations, therefore it would be a descriptive research. The population of the study is the personnel of Company AB consisting of the shareholders and senior managers due to their primary knowledge; current, accurate and factual data they can present for the research purpose. As a result, the researcher will be able to draw assumptions and derive findings based on the existing information and perform the analysis in the higher steps. In Company AB, seven main parties were involved in meetings and helped the authors to write up the observations and findings. The key questions identified for the qualitative data collection is as shown below in table 1 out of the given eighteen questions within the survey. The research also aims to focus on using expert interviews to develop further understanding of how the organisations behaves towards the concept of sustainable development (SD); and integrating SD while undertaking projects.

Table 1. Key Research Survey Questions.

No.	Question	Description
5	Are you familiar with the concept of sustainable development	To investigate if the respondents (as potential project stakeholders) are aware with the concept of sustainable develop.
7	How aware are you of environmental issues?	To investigate if the respondents are aware of environmental issues.
8	I consider environmental issues as a priority in today's world.	To investigate what extend the respondents agree with statements in order to understand if they consider environmental issues as a priority in today's world and if they feel like their actions as an individual impact on the environment.
13	I refuse to deal with an organisation that does not consider sustainable development.	To investigate what extend the respondent agree with statement in order to understand if they would refuse –or not- to deal with an organisation doesn't consider sustainable development.
11	Rank the following five characteristics in order of imp. For you when buying a product.	To investigate what are the priorities of the respondents when buying a product.
14	Some Orgs. Are promoting their involvement in Sust. Develop. How does this impact on your behaviour?	To understand the impact of promotion of Orgs. Involvement in sust. development on the respondents (potential stakeholders)
15	As a stakeholder, do projects integrating Sust. Develop. Increase your Env. Awareness?	To investigate if projects integrating Sust. Develop. Increase the respondent's Env. Awareness.
9	Have you heard about "CSR"?	To investigate the understanding of CSR
16	Rank the following four sustainable practices in order of importance for you when taking part of a project.	To investigate what are the most important sustainable practices for the project stakeholders.
17	How do you consider the integration of SD within social projects compared to other projects?	This question aims to gain the respondents' opinions on the relevance of SD within social projects.

4 Results and Discussions

As mentioned earlier within the paper the research focuses on the use of survey analysis methods to get a better understanding towards stakeholders' behavioural needs. In order for the results to be as representative as possible and therefore exploitable, the survey panel had been diverse.

4.1 Awareness and Knowledge of Sustainable Development

The question has been identified as key question in order to identify the awareness and knowledge of the participants towards sustainable development. The graph below in Figure 3 represents the percentages obtained for this question. As it can be identified in the graph, 90% of the respondents are familiar with the concept of sustainable development against only a small 10% who suggest they are not aware of it. This percentage is significant and demonstrates the increasing awareness of people towards the concept of sustainable development. Sustainable development is associated with three components: the economic, social and environmental aspects [2].

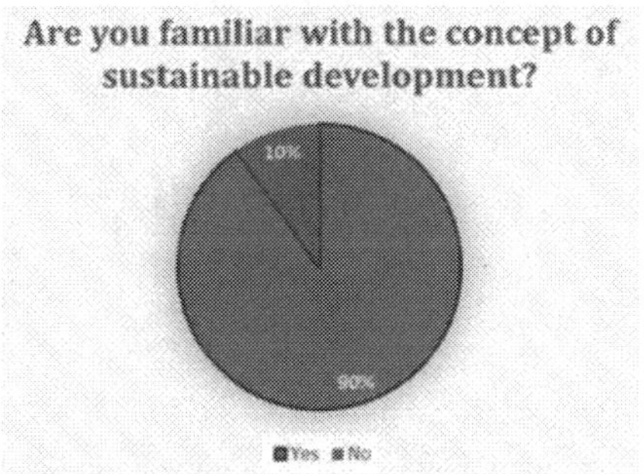

Fig. 3. Analysis towards Familiarity of Sustainable Development Concept.

4.2 Stakeholder's Behaviour towards Sustainable Development

Following the findings of the analysis of questions 5, 6 and 7, it was decided to investigate if the increasing awareness and knowledge of sustainable development had any kind of impact on the stakeholders' behaviour. In order to do so, the results of question 8 are going to be compared with questions 11 and 13.

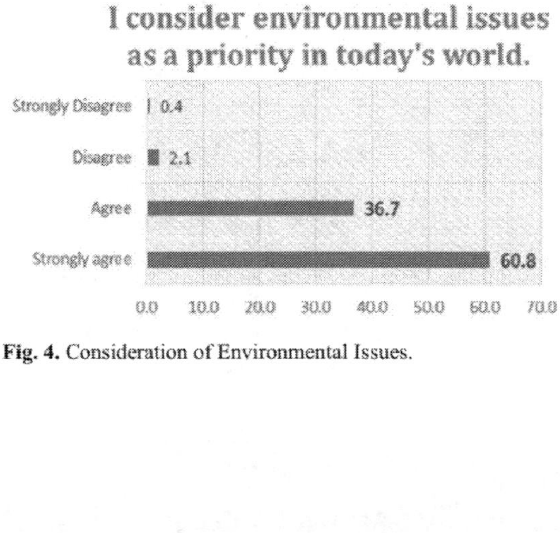

Fig. 4. Consideration of Environmental Issues.

The analysis of question 8 demonstrates that a significant number of the respondents consider environmental issues as a high priority. Indeed, as outlined in Figure 10, 60.8% of them strongly agree with the statement together with another 36.7% also agreeing to it. This, once again, confirms the result of question 7 and validates the increasing environmental awareness within the society with 97.5% of the stakeholders considering environmental issues as a priority in today's world. However, further analysis shows that this is not always very well reflected within their behaviour. Indeed, the consideration of questions 11 and 13 shows those stakeholders do not always act towards sustainability.

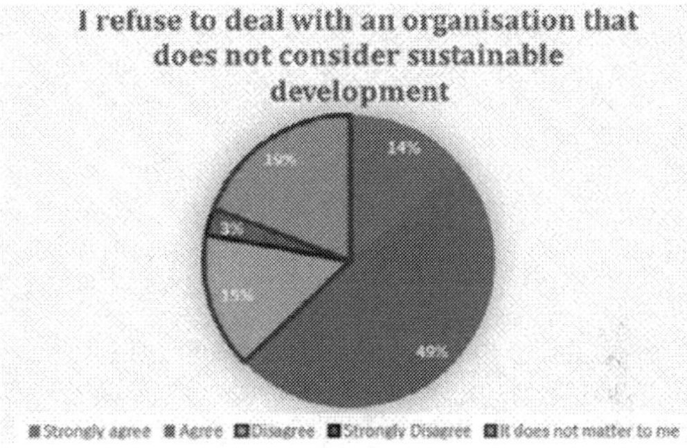

Fig. 5. Adoption of Behaviour towards Environmental Concerns.

Question 13 sought to investigate to what extent the respondents were likely to adopt a behaviour responding to their environmental concern. Reflecting on the results of question 8, it was expected that only 2.5% of the respondents would not feel the need to deal with an organisation that does not consider sustainable development. Nevertheless, it was demonstrated that 18% of the respondents would easily deal with an organisation that does not consider sustainable development. In addition to this, 19% of them suggest that this does not matter to them.

4.3 Interactions with Organisations Promoting Sustainable Development

The comparison of question 7 with questions 13 and 11 demonstrated that the awareness of the stakeholders towards sustainable development is not always reflected through their adopted behaviour. Nevertheless, further analyses seem to demonstrate a way of mobilising their sustainable behaviour. In order to do so, it was chosen to compare questions 12 and 14. Question 14 asked the respondents how likely they were to make themselves aware of an organisation's responsibility towards sustainability. As a result, 18% of the respondents would be very likely to do so. 26% of the panel would be unlikely to or would not make them aware of an organisation's responsibility towards sustainable development. Keeping these results in mind, the author then compared them with the results of question 14.

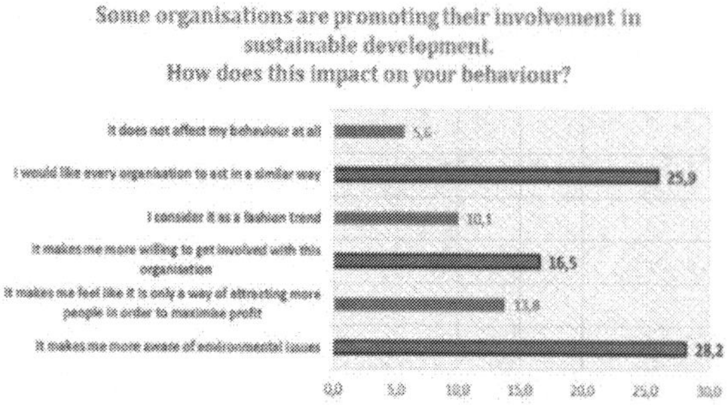

Fig. 6. Aware of Organisation's Responsibility towards Sustainability.

Indeed, question 14 sought to understand the impact of an organisation's promotion of sustainable development on the stakeholders' behaviour. As shown in Figure (6) these are the three main responses chosen by the panel:

- 28.2% of the respondents feel more aware of environmental issues;
- 25.9% of the respondents would like every organisation to act in a similar way;
- 16.5% of them would be more willing to get involved within this particular organisation.

Project stakeholders might not be willing to make them aware of an organisation's responsibility towards sustainable development; yet it is demonstrated that its promotion from the organisation itself will impact positively on the stakeholders' behaviour. Therefore, the comparison of the two questions resulted in the following conclusion: the organisations' promotion of their involvement in sustainable development can be a way of mobilising sustainable behaviour.

4.4 Sustainable Development and Project Management

The second part of the survey intended to gain further knowledge towards the integration of sustainable development within project management. The participants were asked their opinions on the integration of sustainable development within projects together with their understandings of Corporate Social Responsibility.

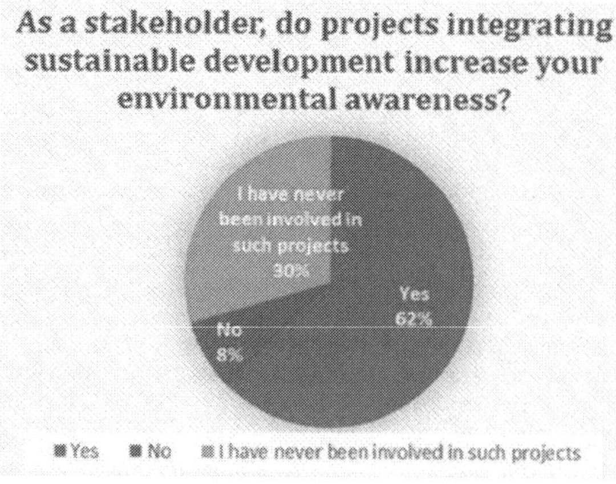

Fig. 7. Projects Integrating SD on Environmental Awareness.

Question 15 sought to investigate if projects integrating sustainable development increased the respondent's environmental awareness. As outlined in Figure 7, the majority of the respondents believe that sustainable projects increase their environmental awareness. Indeed, 89% of the respondents who were involved in such a project believe so. Therefore, this highlights the relevance of the adoption of sustainable practices within projects. Nevertheless, this question also demonstrates that 30% of the respondents have never been involved in such projects. This percentage shows that this adoption is not always well-established within projects; there is still a considerable room for improvement. First, the respondents who had already participated in a social project were questioned about the integration of sustainable development within their own. The analysis of question 20 outlines that only 39% of the social projects in which the respondents participated in integrate sustainable development (Figure 8).

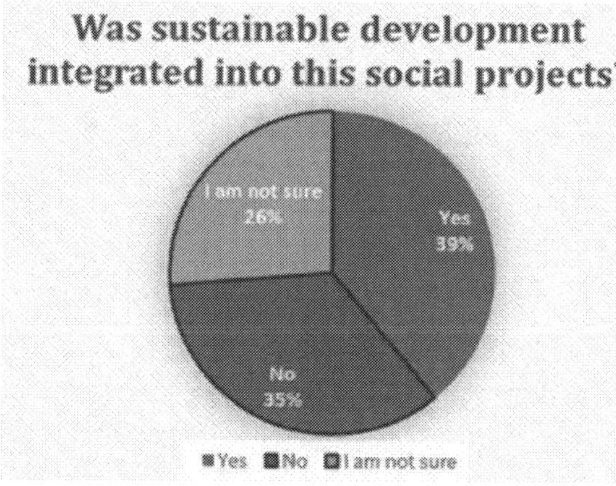

Fig. 8. Sustainable Development in Social Projects.

In addition to this, 26% of the panel are not sure whether sustainable development was integrated or not within the projects they participated in. This might demonstrate a lack of communication towards sustainability with the project stakeholders; this could also again highlight the fact that people can be aware of sustainable development but not always knowledgeable enough to recognise sustainable practices. Overall, the analysis shows that the integration of sustainable development is not well-established within social projects.

Question 17 consisted in getting the respondents' opinion regarding the importance of the integration of sustainable development within social projects. The majority of the panel (66.3%) suggested that such integration was equally important compared to other types of projects. And yet, 18.3% of the respondents believe that such integration is more important within social projects than others. The analysis of question 17 demonstrates that the panel essentially believes that sustainable development should equally been integrated within any types of projects. Nevertheless, the analysis also enabled to gather the opinion of respondents thinking that the integration of sustainable development is even more important within social projects due to their nature.

5 Conclusions

The research addresses the importance and use of sustainable practices adopted within projects, with a focus towards social projects. To achieve the aim of the study, the research derived some key research objectives. Firstly, the research focusses on identifying current sustainable practices within projects, focusing on Corporate Social Responsibility (CSR) and Community Awareness. The research also aimed to understand project stakeholders' behavioural needs towards acting and implementing sustainable practices; and to compare the use of the identified sustainable practices and its adoption within profit and non-profit organisations. Preliminary research was first outlined through literature studies, highlighting the increase environmental awareness of project stakeholders. However, lack of understanding of how their behaviour influence sustainable practices were still remaining. Further studies carried out identified the gap through analysing and discussing the results of the survey. Results highlighted that there was significant increase of environmental awareness and demand towards sustainability from the project stakeholders, including lack of sustainable behaviour; and possibility of mobilising sustainable behaviour through the organisations' promotion of their involvement in sustainable development. The study provided a brief understanding through the literature, identifying the necessity for organisations to deal with sustainability in order to maintain their project stakeholders. Nevertheless, the comparison of the adoption of sustainable practices within projects was not clearly identified through secondary research. It was understood within the literature review that no recent research had been established towards the integration of sustainable development within social projects. Therefore, further analysis of the data presented that there was a lack of integration of sustainable practices within social projects. The integration of sustainable development within social projects was identified as crucially important and relevant: social projects are the drivers towards educating the society regarding sustainable development.

It is discovered that the non-profits' core objectives and activities are more correspondent to the sustainable practices. Therefore in order to develop the social responsibility within the world businesses, the for-profit business managers require adopting managerial strategies and organisational cultures to change the neutrality of staff mind-sets regarding the sustainable practices to lead the businesses towards prosperity going greener. Further research studies towards better understanding of the economic dimension of sustainable development, rather than just the environmental and social aspects of sustainable development within projects is planned. And finally, other type of sustainable practices than CSR and community awareness such as climate change, pollution and waste management practices and effects of globalisation could be investigated in future research studies.

References

[1] M. Chavan, An appraisal of environment management systems, I.J. of MEQ, **16** (5), 444-463 (2005)
[2] M. Koukiasa, Sustainable facilities management within event venues. Worldwide Hospitality and Tourism Themes, **3** (3), 217-228 (2011)
[3] C.A. Hodges, Facility manager's approach to sustainability. Journal of Facilities Management, **3** (4), 312-324 (2005)
[4] N. Haigh, A. J. Hoffman, Hybrid organisations: The next chapter of sustainable business. Organizational Dynamics. **41**, 126-134 (2012)
[5] World Commission on Environment and Development (WCED). Our Common Future, Oxford University Press, Oxford (1987)
[6] R. Whittington, Completing the practice turn in strategy research, Organization Studies, **27** (5), 613-34 (2006)
[7] T. Mysen, Sustainability as corporate mission and strategy. European Business Review, **24** (6), 496-509 (2012)
[8] A. Murra, K. Haynes, LJ. Hudson, Collaborating to achieve corporate social responsibility and sustainability - Possibilities and problems. Sustainability Accounting, Management and Policy Journal, **1**(2), 161-177 (2010)
[9] L. Moir, What do we mean by corporate social responsibility, Corporate governance, **1** (2), 16-22 (2001)
[10] J. Moon, The Contribution of Corporate Social Responsibility to Sustainable Development. Sustainable Development, **15**, 296-306.
[11] T. Ketola, A holistic corporate responsibility model: integrating values, discourses and actions, Journal of Business Ethics, **80**, 419-35 (2007)
[12] B.M. Wiernik, D.S. Ones, S. Dilchert, Age and environmental sustainability: a meta-analysis. Journal of Managerial Psychology, **28** (7/8), 826-856 (2013)
[13] L. Swanson., D. Zhang, Perspectives on corporate responsibility and sustainable development. Management of Environmental Quality: An International Journal, **23** (6), 630-639 (2012)
[14] A.A.E. Othman, N. Sirbadhoo, An innovative partnership framework for sustainable development of rural areas in South Africa: Journal of Engineering, Design and Technology, **7** (3), pp. 243-263 (2009)
[15] F. Pelham, Will sustainability change the business model of the event industry? WHATT, **3** (3), pp. 187-192 (2011)
[16] M. Labrosse, Incorporating Green in Project Management. Employment Relations Today, **37** (3), 85-90 (2010)
[17] H. B. Hansmann, The role of non-profit enterprise. Yale Law Journal, **89** (5), 835–901 (1980)
[18] National Centre for Charitable Statistics at the Urban Institute. (2009a). Number of non-profit organizations in the United States, 1996–2006.
[19] National Centre for Charitable Statistics at the Urban Institute. (2009b). Number of non-profit organizations in the United States, 1996–2006.
[20] J. B. Ritchie, C.B Weinberg, A typology of non-profit competition: Insights for social marketers. Social Marketing Quarterly, **6** (3), 64–71 (2000)
[21] J. Weerawardena, R.E. McDonald, GS. Mort, Sustainability of non profit organisations: An empirical investigation. Journal of World Business. **45**, 346-356 (2010)
[22] S. Shah, E. Ganji, S. Hasan, Environmental management Systems and sustainability in SMEs, MATEC, **76**, (2016)
[23] N. Haigh, A. J. Hoffman, Hybrid organisations: The next chapter of sustainable business. Organizational Dynamics. **41**, 126-134 (2012)
[24] J. Battilana, S. Dorado, Building sustainable hybrid organisations: The case of commercial Microfinance organisations. AMJ. **53** (6), 1419–40 (2010)

MATEC Web of Conferences **125**, 02003 (2017) DOI: 10.1051/matecconf/201712502003
CSCC 2017

Lean Production Practices to Enhance Organisational Performance

Satya Shah[1,a], *Elmira* Naghi Ganji[1] and *Alec* Coutroubis[1]

[1]*Faculty of Engineering and Science, University of Greenwich, UK*

Abstract. Service sector organisations are constantly overcoming the challenges facing the over-production and waste reduction within their environments. Industries are also becoming very competitive thus forcing them to seek suitable production organisation strategies with the aim towards enhancing their competitiveness and efficiency. The aim of this research study is to investigate the impact of lean production practices on the performance of service based businesses through the case study of a local baked goods supplier. The research framework adopted consists of questionnaire survey method implemented with different end users, thus covering the overall production – retail – customer cycle. The research results and analysis justify the objective of the research that lean production practices enhance the performance of the supplier company and the common tool identified were JIT (Just in Time), Value Steam Mapping (VSP) and the 5S methods. The results also suggest that JIT method has a higher impact towards improvement on performance relating to quality, speed, dependability, flexibility and cost of the supplier. However, the research study also identifies that one of the major challenges faced by the organisation while adopting lean practices was the lack of commitment from top management, continuous training and employee engagement measures.

1 Introduction

The current manufacturing and production based environments are facing the key challenges towards managing and reducing over production and towards the reduction and elimination of waste within their environments. Industries are also becoming very competitive thus forcing them to seek suitable production organisation strategies with the intention of enhancing their competitiveness and efficiency. The adoption of lean production is an edge for industry to manage their operational and strategic gains thus reducing waste. Early research within this aspect suggests in order to achieve continuing competitive advantage, industries need to create appropriate production systems and technologies mainly relating to high product quality, reducing product design time, demand based production and reduction of waste and inventory management [1].

Lean production is a concept which may be viewed and implemented at a number of levels and also a commitment process of persistent improvement that can significantly impact upon an organisation's well-being, wealth and competitiveness [2]. Global competition has increased pressures on manufacturing plants towards improving different factors of operational performance. According to [3], it was deduced that organisations make use of broad production practice, and this is challenging because they are unable to improve and increase their production or even satisfy their customers. Nevertheless, for some organisation using current technologies such as Lean production practice is now becoming a critical and regular practice to achieve better performance attainments [4]. Lean organisations have the ability of producing great quality products cautiously, in lesser volumes, as well as conveying them to market quicker than mass producers. Lean management is simply all about operating the most proficient as well as effective organisation possible, with a minimal cost and zero waste and still meeting customers demand. Effective and fruitful lean producers have come to know that lean production practice is a corporate vision that helps everyone from design to product management as well as marketing and outside the four walls to involve outside suppliers and trading partners. With the correct procedure, policy and backup tools, lean organisations can access the live and up to date data that their decision makers need to attain corporate goals, together with minimizing inventory and waste, shortening lead times also producing to demand.

Currently, many service industries are faced with the problem of increasing the product quality. Considering the challenges of present competition, both locally and globally, many organisations are now improving the quality of their products, decreasing cost and meeting the unexpected need of their customers. With this focus, this study is focussed to identify the extent of Lean production practices adoption in organisations. It seeks to provide a more comprehensive knowledge about the impact of lean production practices on organisations' performance and finally, the challenges they face in the implementation of lean production practices on organisations.

[a] Corresponding author: s.shah@gre.ac.uk

2 Literature Review

This literature review aims to develop a better understanding of the concepts that seem to play a vital role in organisation's performance. Current literatures will provide relevant materials related to the specific research objectives. The review will be split into several sections and will be structured as follows; an overview of lean production, its goal and strategy, its principles and tools, seven deadly waste, benefits of adopting lean production and the barriers of implementing lean production. The study will provide a framework towards the relationship between lean production practice and organisations performance.

2.1 Lean Production

Lean production is a mixture of both mass production and craft production. According to earlier research "the machine that changed the world", the word Lean production was used contrary to the mass production system [5]. Toyota concentrated on applying the Lean production principles by using simple technologies and lower prices automation at the expense of computer technology. Lean production was founded by TPS [5, 6]. TPS focused on eliminating waste or non-value added activities, bearing in mind the entire production process and using different tools and technique to reduce the waste for example; JIT, VSM, 5S, Kanban (pull) systems, Kaizen, synchronous manufacturing, Pokayoke [3, 5], which led to the reduction of stocks and finishing time, thus increasing their delivery performance, balancing the use of space, bettering the use of resources and improving their productivity and quality [7].

Studies define Lean production as a philosophy or strategy which depends on a set of practices used to reduce waste with the intention of improving the performance of enterprises [5]. Today, Lean production has been adopted across the world by lots of major companies to stay competitive in the global market [8]. Ever since Lean production was first used, many authors have tried to describe Lean theoretically [9, 10, 11]; however, their descriptions were unclear and this led to a communication problem [12], implementation problem (in enterprises) and the problem of creating objectives that are specific [13]. The study carried out by [14] shows that since there is different theoretical approach about Lean production, identifying the use of its actual benefits becomes difficult. This implies that since there is lack of clear description, if there is need to establish it within a company will be difficult or even not in accord with Lean Production principles, thus leading to a hard evaluation of the effectiveness of the concept. Hence, it is essential for Lean production success to be estimated before it is implemented so as to avoid money and time wastage [15]. Existing research has investigated Lean production definition, goals, and approaches that are associated with the concept. In his research he categorized Lean into four different ways, namely:

1. Lean as a process of continuous effort or change or "becoming lean",
2. Lean as a process of "becoming lean",
3. Lean as a philosophy of "lean thinking" or "the Toyota way" and
4. Lean as a fixed state or "being lean [15].

The key principles behind Lean production includes specify value; identify value stream, flow, pull and perfection [1]. Hence, for continuous improvement within the organisation, organisations need to use these principles because it will help them in improving their operation.

2.2 Lean and Service Industries

Presently, the service industry is trying to improve its performance by embracing the continuous improvement process so as to stay competitive and satisfy their customers. Hence for them to achieve this there is a need for this service industry to adopt the Lean production practice as a full business strategy. Below are the deadly wastes that affect service industry. The main aim of Lean production is to eliminate all type of waste within the production process. Waste includes all activities that do not add value to organisations or customer. It is any activity that customers will not pay for; thus it is important for organisations to identify the concept of this waste and reduce it. Earlier research by *Taiicho Ohno* design of seven wastes or "Muda" which form the core of "lean philosophy" that is faced by companies on how to identify and reduce them.

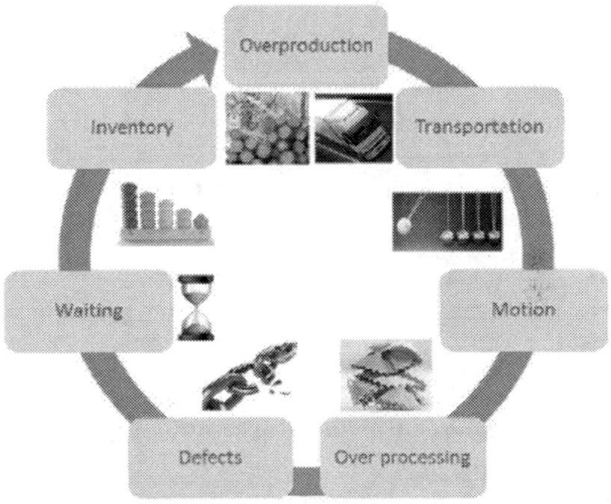

Fig. 1. The Seven Deadly Wastes of Lean Philosophy.

- **Overproduction -** Overproduction is believed to be the most dangerous among the seven wastes that were identified by Ohno;
- **Transportation** – The waste for transportation of goods between the supply chain;
- **Unnecessary Motion -** This involves the movement of workers in form of bending, reaching, stretching, walking in a distance that is very long in order to get a material, too or information or even moving to see better.
- **Unnecessary Inventory -** This is referred to as having excess raw materials or components, semi or finished goods that are not processed; hence making businesses to need additional storage area.
- **Waiting -** Waiting take place whenever time is not managed or used well. It is when the equipment,

DOI: 10.1051/matecconf/201712502003

material, customers or workers are not moving, working or not adding value to production process.

- **Over or inappropriate processing** - Over processing is referred to as taking unnecessary steps that are not required (beyond customers specification) in a production process.
- **Defect** - Defects is referred to as producing products that are faulty or imperfect thus leading to inspection, rework and fixing.

2.3 Lean Practices on Organisational Performance

Lean production has been developed and adopted by companies that wish to improve their performance globally and locally. However, in evaluating its impact on organisations performance, several authors tried this into "leanness". Hence, in this context, [16], used the model to measuring the degree of leanness in UK agricultural machining sector while another study established a model that help in determining the level of leanness by using different attributes of lean such as Kaizen, JIT and quality [17]. Another research helped in examining the impact of exact influences leanness have on manufacturing system [18]. From their study, it was seen that the component which are mostly vital to leanness consist of imperfections, cost, lead time and value. Lastly, research established a model which also helped measuring the level of leanness. The study was based on 30 criteria and fuzzy logic approach was used during the study. This implies that leanness is connected to organisations performance [19].

Due to the fact that the benefits of lean approaches are difficult to measure, an IT based system called balanced scorecard system supports the change strategies and would help managers to focus on the linkages and operational efficiencies within their organisations [20]. Probably the total life cycle time would be the most effective gauge to measure the lean progress, hence, the scorecard approach could be a good practice in this case, whereas it is evident that more than 60% of all the firms are using scorecard [21]. It could be mentioned that the scorecard would not be the best approach to define the best strategies towards going lean and hence, it is the manager's duty to handle the measurement considerations especially with the aid of the advanced software programmes.

2.4 Lean Production in Food and Beverage Industries

Presently, the food and beverage industry are faced with the challenge of not identifying waste and meeting up their market price (profit). Although, they wish to improve their productivity and take competitive advantage of the market globally. Hence, with Lean production, the food and beverage industry will be able to identify and eliminate waste through continuous improvement. Lean Production practice for food and beverage industries are altered copied from manufacturing industries. According to studies, many of these tools and technique have been used to improve the performance of organisation [22]. As shown below some of the widely used Lean production tools and how they can be used by the Company X (baked goods suppliers) to improve their quality, speed, dependability, flexibility and cost.

Table 1. Summary of Lean Production Tools.

Tool	Description	Reference
Value Stream Mapping	VSM is a tool used in designing, analysing or mapping out all actions (both value and non-value) in the production process by examining the flow of raw material from its supplier to end customers. Research studies suggest by using VSM, organisation can decrease their lead-time and production time, smoothing their production, decrease waste and improve the quality of a product. It reduce operational cost, increase flexibility and helps organisations to meet the demand of their customers.	[23]
JIT	A process which states that an organisation should produce the right product at the right time. Research studies also state that by using JIT, organisation will reduce production cost, inventory, changeover time, set up time and likely waste.	[24]
Pokayoke	This is referred to a tool which helps staff to avoid errors. The purpose of Pokayoke is to eliminate product defects by preventing, correcting or drawing attention to human errors. The Lean concept is criticized in the literature from the perspective of the personnel, because this side is less known, focusing primarily on techniques for improving the performance of the system.	[25]
Kanban	Kanban is stock controlling system which is achieved with FIFO method. An effective tool that contributes the functioning of the whole production process. According to Kanban system has many advantages over computer technologies, such as; reduced cost of information processing, it is easy to obtain and transmit information in a dynamic environment; the demand for materials is judiciously sized.	[26]

3 Research Methodology

A combination of research methods and approaches has been employed within this research. This included the use of critical literature review analysis, case study based method investigating in a local baked goods supplier and through personal interviews on the service company delivering the baked goods products to customers. The literature review conducted extensively at the initial stages of the research identified the research gaps in knowledge within this area.

3.1 Research Approach and Strategy

Methodology deals with the basic principal question of how to collect analyse and interpret data in a structured manner. The research started from theory and then moved into data, collecting qualitative information from case studies by using questionnaires and interview. The variable for this study was generated from the literature and the relationship to each other is seen within the framework. The deductive approach also includes a qualitative research method that is used to gain more insight. There is numerous research strategies used for attaining answers in any research objectives. However, due to the nature and objective of this study, the questionnaire was designed to clarify the assumption gained from the literature. The target population was chosen based on the scope of this research study. Because of this, only local baked goods supplier (Company X) were considered as possible respondents. Also interview questions were structured for the managers of a local university cafe while another questionnaire aimed at university students. According to methods, the correct sample choice and methods are important factors for collecting valid and measurable data for any research [27].

3.2 Data Collection Technique

Research states that an appropriate data collection method contributes to the success of research studies. In business research, the primary and secondary data are used to collect the necessary data. Both sources of data are used to achieve efficiency and effective research objectives. The secondary data provides an ability to save time and money, therefore it has to be analysed first before the collection of the new material [28]. The primary data have to be collected as well, as the secondary data may not always provide the needed answers to all research questions. In order to reach the research objective, the primary and secondary data were used in this study.

However, after careful consideration of the various options for data collection, author decided that two type of data collection modes been quantitative and qualitative (interview and questionnaire respectively) would be used as earlier stated. Hence, 3 steps were used to get the data for the study. Firstly, questionnaire was given to local university students (customers). This helped the researchers to find out content such as *"how satisfied customers are on the product sold on campus etc."* Secondly, an interview with the cafe managers was carried out to help understand the pattern of business such as which their suppliers are, and how often they order from their suppliers etc. Finally, questionnaire was given to local baked goods suppliers which are the main process of data collection.

3.3 Questionnaire Design

After the decision had been made to use the questionnaire and interview to collect data, the next step was to plan and design a suitable questionnaire. With the aim of producing a reliable questionnaire and minimising biases in this research, the author considered issues such as wording, appearance and appropriate categorisation of the variable in the questionnaire. The design of the questionnaire requires a good understanding of the subject matter. With an insight to the literature review conducted, the survey questions were based on the research framework. Another factor considered was the sequence of the questionnaire. The questions in the questionnaire were ordered in a logical order from the respondents' perceptions. The best way to sequence the question was to start off with more general questions to engage the respondent and then more mixed questions so that the research objectives would not be detected.

The design of the physical questionnaire/ survey plays a vital role in the overall design and affects the rate of response. It is important for the questionnaire to be of good quality to attract the response from the respondent [29]. Due to this, serious consideration was taken when producing the questionnaire, such as its layout, printing and paper quality and clarity of letters. The questionnaire questions were also designed in simple language, allowing respondents to choose from five possible answers. The questions were measured using a five-point Likert scale ranging from 'Excellent' to 'poor', ' highly satisfied' to highly dissatisfied', 'Always' to 'Never', 'strongly agree' to 'strongly disagree' and 'very large extent' to 'very small extent' adopted from [30].

3.4 Questionnaire Analysis

Quantitative research usually generates large amount of data, especially the semi-structured interviews. The authors further stated that it is very essential to acknowledge that irrespective of the kind of research (either qualitative or quantitative) a degree of subjectivity does exist. Descriptive information just like some of the data obtained during the collection of results in the research study first goes through a process called content analysis.

For the purpose of this research a process of content analysis was used to evaluate the data collected during the interview session. Content analysis is the process whereby the key themes are identified, those ones that emerge from the descriptions given by respondents or answer to the question. Content analysis is advantageous when presenting the outcomes of open-ended review questions as well as multiple interviews. Content analysis entails code groups of words that are found in transcripts of interviews which are further characterized into sections [31]. It can be added that these groups are commonly reliant on the type of research topic.

DOI: 10.1051/matecconf/201712502003

4 Results and Discussions

The following presents the results and discussions from the survey and case study within the research.

4.1 Lean Production Practices Utilised by Company X

Analysis and findings from Figure (2) demonstrates that 73.3% of respondents indicated they use VSM and JIT always while 73.3% of respondent frequently use 5S which matched to what [33] stated in their research that JIT, VSM and 5S are used by organisation to improve their operational performance. Other Lean production tools which are being used by organisation even though they are not being used frequently include TPM, Kaizen, Pokayoke, Jidoka and Kanban.

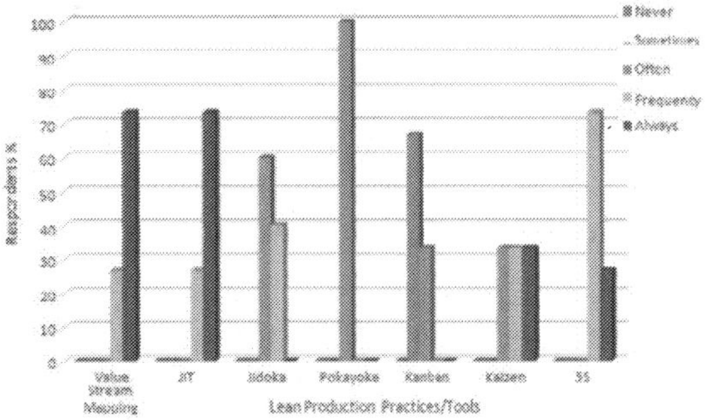

Fig. 2. Lean Production Practices/Tools.

4.2 Impact of Lean Production Practices on Performance

Respondents were asked the attributes of Lean production practice tools such as VSM, JIT, 5S, Kaizen, Pokayoke, Jidoka and Kanban in their organisations. These questions corresponded to the indicators within the framework. Below are the findings for one of the tools.

VSM

Table 2 below shows the results of the frequency analysis for VSM. It is also used to design, map out or analyse all action and has positive impact on the performance of organisation. Based on this, the question was asked "what waste do Lean production practice eradicate in your organisation".

Table 2. Frequency Analysis for Criterion VSM.

Factor	VSM	Strongly agree	Agree	Undecided	Disagree	Strongly disagree	Mean
Quality, speed, dependability, flexibility and cost	Waste reduction	40%	60%	0%	0%	0%	4.40
	Reduced production time	40%	60%	0%	0%	0%	4.40
	Reduced lead time	26.7%	73.3%	0%	0%	0%	4.27
	Enhanced quality of output	26.7%	73.3%	0%	0%	0%	4.27
	Production smoothing	66.7%	0%	33.3%	0%	0%	4.33
Average		40%	53.32%	33.3%	0%	0%	4.33
Mean (max 5.0)							86.66%

The mean from respondent answers was approximately 86.6% indicating that the contribution of the criterion is high. 40% of the respondents answered with "strongly agree", while 53.32% answered with "agree" and 33.3% with "undecided". None of respondents answered with "strongly disagree" or "disagree" in the question. This indicates that respondents believe VSM has positive impact on their performance similar to earlier research studies identified within the literature [23, 32].

4.3 Adoption of Lean Production Practices in Company X

Respondents were asked the extent in which the implementation of Lean production practice has impacted on their organisations performance.

Table 3. Frequency Analysis of Adoption of Lean Production Practices in company X.

To what extent has the Implementation of Lean production practice impacted on your organisations performance	Very large extent	Large extent	Moderate extent	Small extent	Very small extent	Mean
Work in process reduction	6.7%	46.7%	46.7%	0%	0%	3.60
Inventory reduction	0%	40%	53.3%	6.7%	0%	3.33
Lead time reduction	20%	40%	26.7%	13.3%	0%	3.67
Product and service quality improvement	20%	60.7%	13.3%	0%	0%	4.07
Improve material flow and through put	20%	53.3%	26.7%	0%	0%	3.93
Waste reduction	0%	40%	60%	0%	0%	3.40
Manufacturing cost reduction	0%	40%	53.3%	6.7%	0%	3.33
Set up time reduction	0%	33.3%	60%	6.7%	0%	3.27
Profitability improvement	26.7%	60%	13.3%	0%	0%	4.13
Sales volume improvement	0%	26.7%	60%	13.3%	0%	3.13
Labour requirement reduction	6.7%	40%	46.7%	6.7%	0%	3.47
Productivity improvement	20%	66%	20%	0%	0%	4
Average	10.01%	45.56%	40%	4.45	0 %	3.61
Mean (max 5.0)						72.2%

Table 3 above summarises the extent in which Lean production practices have been adopted by Company x. From the results, it is clear that the mean is 72.2% (high). Majority of respondents (mean =4.13) indicated that profitability improvement has significant impact on implementing Lean production practice. Again, high number of respondent (mean =4.07) believes that product and service quality improvement has significant impact on implementing Lean production practice. Again, the responses for Lead time reduction, Work in process reduction, Improve material flow and through put are all high indicating they have significant impact on implementing Lean production practice. However, Inventory reduction, Manufacturing cost reduction, Set up time reduction, Sales volume improvement, Labour requirement reduction are average indicating they have significant impact on implementing Lean production practice in moderate extent.

4.4 Challenges of Implementing Lean Practices

Respondents were asked the challenges they faced while implementing Lean practices. Table 4 shows the results of the finding. Table 4 summarises the challenges faced by company X while implementing Lean practices. From the results, it is clear that the mean (max 5.0) is high. This is because organisation experience lack of top management commitment, lack of continuous education and training, poor information/ data accuracy, employee's resistance to change, and governmental policy. The outcome for financial constraints, inexperienced technical staff, Lack of interface with existing system and solely depending on traditional system of work (between 2.5 to 3.49) is average.

Table 4. Frequency Analysis of Adoption of Difficulties for Implementing Lean Practices.

What challenges do Your organisation face while implementing Lean practices	Strongly Agree	Agree	Undecided	Disagree	Strongly Disagree	Mean
Lack of top management commitment	33.3%	66.7%	0%	0%	0%	4.33%
Lack of continuous education/ training	33.3%	66.7%	0%	0%	0%	4.33%
Poor information/ data accuracy	33.3%	40%	26.7%	0%	0%	4.07%
Solely depending on traditional system of work	40%	26.7%	33.3%	0%	0%	3.47%
Financial constraints	40%	0%	60%	0%	0%	3.20%
Inexperienced technical staff	0%	60%	0%	40%	0%	3.20%
Lack of interface with existing system	13%	13%	40%	33.3%	0%	3.07%
Government policy	46.7%	20%	6.7%	26.7%	0%	3.87%
Employees resistance to change	46.7%	13.3%	26.7%	13.3%	0%	3.93%
Average	31.81%	34.04%	21.49%	12.59%		3.72
Mean (max 5.0)						74.4%

5 Conclusions and Future Research

This research sought to explore Lean production practice on Organisation (Company X) performance. It looked at the impact of Lean production practice on organisation performance, the extent in which lean production practices have been adopted by organisation and the challenges faced by them within their pursuit to implement lean production practices. The study followed a descriptive research design using a questionnaire as the main research tool. The main data was gathered from Company X although; questionnaire and interview were given to local university students (customers) and university cafe manager respectively. The collected data was analysed using SPSS and Excel tools. An analysis of the results seems to suggest that the most popular Lean production tools used frequently by Company X are JIT, VSM, 5S and Pokayoke (automation). Furthermore, it can be concluded that JIT has a high impact on improving the overall performance (Quality, Speed, Dependability, Flexibility and Cost) of Company X. Pokayoke also plays a vital role on performance as it helps them to prevent and eliminate quality defect especially on speed, quality, dependability and cost, while Kaizen and 5S have a moderate impact on their overall performance (Quality and Speed).

Lean production practice also helped company X to deliver their products and service faster and cheaper thus reducing inventory. However, when implementing lean, most of company X are still missing out value creating activities toward their final customers. Company X still faces challenges such as lack of top management commitment, lack of continuous education/ training, governmental reforms and policies, financial constraints and employee participations when implementing lean practices. Hence, the important elements of cost-delivery-flexibility-value can be achieved through constant training, education, teamwork and desire to change. Based on the survey given to students who purchased baked goods on campus, it was seen that students were not 100% satisfied with baked goods that were available on campus. Again, from the interview conducted from cafe outlet, it was seen that before they choose their suppliers, they consider quality-product varieties, delivery time, price and consistency. These are the most decisive factors in considering a supplier, and the café outlet tends to remain with the same supplier for better customer satisfaction. This implies that the cafe always needs their supplies to be delivered with efficiency and effectively. This can be achieved with further adoption of lean production practices.

Lean production is a considered as continuous process; however, for Company X to boost their production and remain competitive in present market, they must understand their customers need and design ways on fulfilling their requirements and expectations. All waste including activities which consume resources, time, space and non-value added product or service should be eliminated. Total cost waste such as over-production which increases the inventory costs due to the storage needs should also be eliminated. Again, time waste such as time taken to start and finish the required product should be reduced. Company C should always avoid overproduction since it is a major factor towards waste. Again, since lean production is based mainly on JIT production, therefore, in all the production process, only required amount of produce depending upon the demand and the order should be produced. There should be a good relationship between the customers and suppliers. Organisations should ensure that before lean production is implemented, the entire workforce are properly informed and trained appropriately. This will enable the proper utilisation of knowledge delivery and the skills required to adopt the practices more effectively within the environment. All respective departments and business units within the business need to properly understand their roles and application of lean transformation process. Hence, more resources should be allocated towards future growth and implementation of the change management and adoption of lean production practices within the company.

References

[1] J. Womack., D. Jones, Lean Thinking: Banish Waste and Create Wealth in Your Corporation. Simon & Schuster, New York, USA (1996)

[2] A. Henderson, L. Larco, Lean Transformation: How to Change Your Business into a Lean Enterprise, Richmond, VA: The Oaklea Press (1999)

[3] J. Bicheno, The New Lean Toolbox, 5th Ed, Piscie, Publishers, ISBN: 0956830757, (2016)

[4] L. Emiliani, Linking leader's beliefs to their behaviours and competencies, Management Decision, **41** (9), 2-6 (2006)
[5] P. Womack, D. Jones, D. Roos, The machine that changed the World: The triumph of lean production, Simon & Schuster UK, ISBN: 1847370551, (2007)
[6] S. Spear. The Toyota Production System: An example of managing complex social/technical systems, Ph.D. dissertation, Harvard Business School, Boston, MA, (1999)
[7] S. Pavnaskar, J. Gershenson, A. Jambekar, Classification Scheme for Lean Manufacturing Tools, Int. J. Prod Res, **41** (13), 3075–3090 (2003)
[8] H. HosseiniNasab, T. Aliheidari, H. KhademiZare, Finding a probabilistic approach to analyse lean manufacturing, J Clean Prod, **29,** 73-81 (2012)
[9] M.A. Lewis, Lean production and sustainable competitive advantage, Int J Oper Prod Man, **20** (8), 959-978, (2000)
[10] P. Hine, M. Holweg, N. Rich, Learning to evolve: A review of contemporary lean thinking, Int J Oper Prod Man, **24** (10), 994-1011 (2004)
[11] R. Shah, P. Ward, Defining and developing measures of Lean production, J. Oper. Manag, **25** (4), 785-805 (2007)
[12] RJ. Boaden. What is total quality management...And does it matter?, Total Quality Management, **8** (4), 153-71 (1997)
[13] R. Anderson, H. Eriksson, H. Torstenson, Similarities and differences between TQM, six sigma and Lean, The TQM Magazine, **18** (3), 282-296 (2006)
[14] S. Parker, Longitudinal effects of Lean production on employee outcomes and the mediating role of work characteristics, J. Appl. Psychol. **88** (4), 620-34 (2003)
[15] J. Pettersen, Defining lean production: some conceptual and practical issues, The TQM Journal, **21** (2), 127-142 (2009)
[16] P. Forrester, U. Shimizu, H. Soriano-Meier, J. Garza-Reyes, and L. Basso, Lean Production, Market Share and Value Creation in the Agricultural Machinery Sector in Brazil, JMTM, **21** (7), 853–871 (2010)
[17] E. Bayou, A. Korvin, Measuring the Leanness of Manufacturing Systems – A Case Study of Ford Motor Company and General Motors, J Eng Technol Manage, **25** (4), 287–304, (2008)
[18] A. Anvari, N. Zulkifli, R. Yusuff, A Dynamic Modeling to Measure Lean Performance within Lean Attributes, Int J Adv Manuf Techno, **66** (5), 663–677 (2013)
[19] S. Vinodh, K. Vimal, Thirty Criteria Based Leanness Assessment Using Fuzzy Logic Approach, Int J Adv Manuf Techno, **60** (9), 1185–1195 (2012)
[20] S. Bhasin, Lean and performance measurement, Journal of Manufacturing Technology Management. **19** (5), 670–684 (2008)
[21] R. Kaplan, D.P. Norton, The office of strategic management, Strategic Finance, **87,** 56-60 (2005)
[22] S. Bhasin. Performance of Lean in Large Organisations, Journal of Manufacturing Systems, **31** (3), 349–357 (2012)
[23] W. Goriwondo, S. Mhlanga, A. Marecha, Use of the Value Stream Mapping Tool for Waste Reduction in Manufacturing. Case Study for Bread Manufacturing In Zimbabwe, In Procedia 2011 I. C. Industrial Engineering and Operations Management, **1** (1), 236–241 (2011)
[24] J. Womack, D. Jones, Lean Thinking: Banish Waste and Create Wealth in Your Corporation, Free Press, ISBN: 0743231643, (2003)
[25] M. Dudek-Burlikowska, D. Szewieczek, The Poka-Yoke method as an improving quality tool of operations in the process, J. Achiev. Mater. Manuf. **36** (1), 95-102 (2009)
[26] Y. Sugimori, K. Kusunoki, F. Cho, S. Uchikawa, Toyota production system and Kanban system Materialization of just-in-time and respect-for-human system, Int. J Prod Res, **15** (6), 553 -564 (1977)
[27] H. Maylor, K. Blackmon. Research Business and Management, Palgrave Publishers, ISBN: 0333964071 (2005)
[28] N. Malhotra., D. Birks, Marketing Research: Applied Approach, Pearson Publishers, ISBN: 0273725855, (2012)
[29] E. Fanning, Formatting a paper-based survey questionnaire: Best practices, Practical Assessment Research & Evaluation, **10** (12) (2005)
[30] R. Sanchez, V. Cortijo, U. Javed, Students' perceptions on Facebook for academic purposes, Computers & Education, **70**, 138-149 (2014)
[31] D. Carson, A. Dilmore., C. Perry., K. Gronhaug. Qualitative Marketing Research, Sage Publishers, ISBN: 0761963669, (2009)
[32] L. Rocha-Lona, J. Garza-Reyes, V. Kumar, Building Quality Management Systems: Selecting the Right Methods and Tools, CRC Press, Taylor & Francis, ISSN: 9781466564992, (2013)
[33] I. Belekoukias, A. Jose, K. Vikas, The Impact of Lean Methods and Tools on the Operational Performance of Manufacturing Organisations, Int. J Prod Res, **52** (18) 5346-5366 (2014)

Assessment of the stability of morphological ECG features and their potential for person verification/identification

Mikhail Matveev[1,*], *Ivaylo* Christov[1], *Vessela* Krasteva[1], *Giovanni* Bortolan[2], *Dimitar* Simov[1], *Nikolay* Mudrov[1], and *Irena* Jekova[1]

[1]Institute of Biophysics and Biomedical Engineering, Bulgarian Academy of Sciences, Sofia, Bulgaria
[2]Institute of Neuroscience, IN-CNR, Padova, Italy

Abstract. This study investigates the potential of a set of ECG morphological features for person verification\identification. The measurements are done over 145 pairs of ECG recordings from healthy subjects, acquired 5 years apart (T1, T2 = T1+5 years). Time, amplitude, area and slope descriptors of the QRS-T pattern are analysed in 4 ECG leads, forming quasi-orthogonal lead system (II&III, V1, V5). The correspondence between feature values in T1 and T2 is verified via factor analysis by principal components extraction method; correlation analysis applied over the measurements in T1 and T2; synthesis of regression equations for prediction of features' values in T2 based on T1 measurements; and cluster analysis for assessment of the correspondence between measured and predicted feature values. Thus, 11 amplitude descriptors of the QRS complex are highlighted as stable, i.e. keeping their strong correlation (≥0.7) within a certain factor, weak correlation (<0.3) with the features from the remaining factors and presenting high correlation in the two measurement periods that is a sign for their person verification\identification potential. The observed coincidence between feature values measured in T2 and predicted via the designed regression models (r=0.93) suggests about the confidence of person identification via the proposed morphological features.

1 Introduction

Nowadays, research on automatic person identification is a rapidly developing area, considering not only the security requirements for the cases of financial transactions, access control, travelling, but also the remote health monitoring scenarios in the clinical and emergency medicine, as well as the organization and processing of hospital databases. The efforts of many researchers are focused on the application of internal body physiological biometric characteristics, which provide robustness to hacker attacks and falsification and are available in most of the health monitoring scenarios. The analysis of the electrocardiogram (ECG) in this respect started about a decade ago, applying either methods that use measurements after detection of fiducial points or analysis of the ECG morphology.

The fiducial-based approaches are the primary considered in the field as they employ morphological features, typically measured for diagnostic purposes by ECG devices. Thus, the crucial task for precise localization of specific anchor points on the P-QRS-T segment can be managed by certified commercial ECG analysis modules with minimal intervention. The application of such a person identity approach can be easily extended to automated management of in-hospital databases. According to the data cited in literature, the identification accuracy could reach values between 97% and 100%, based on the following analysis approaches: 12 uncorrelated diagnostic features of P-QRS-T amplitudes and durations, processed by Principle Component analysis score plots applied over a database with 20 subjects [1]; 15 P-QRS-T temporal features, fed to discriminant functions over 29 subjects under various stress conditions [2]; fiducial based temporal and amplitude measurements combined with features that capture the heartbeat patterns, tested over 31 healthy subjects: 18 with a single ECG record and 13 with more than one ECG record [3].

The fiducial independent approaches for person identification are based on assessment of the P, QRS, T waveforms similarity in the analysed ECG recordings by calculation of correlation coefficients, which are subsequently processed with different techniques. The achieved identification accuracy is: 100% via discrete cosine transform over a database with 14 subjects [4]; 96.2% provided by discriminant analysis over 61 subjects [5]; 91.4% [6] and 85.7% [7] via assessment of the maximal correlation coefficient of a single-lead ECG for 11 and 14 subjects, respectively, improved to 100% while 12-lead ECG is analysed for the database with 11 subjects [6].

Majority of the cited methods are tested with small-sized ECG databases [1,2,4,7] or track intra-subject changes of ECG characteristics measured in very short distanced time intervals or even in the same session

* Corresponding author: mgm@biomed.bas.bg

[2,3,5]. This might bias the reported high identification accuracy from the real case scenario, where the influence of different factors, such as long-term ECG changes, electrode rearrangement, etc., should be considered. Our experience with large ECG databases, containing distanced in time couples of standard 12-lead ECG recordings shows lower authentication accuracies, i.e. about 86% correct verifications for a fiducial-based morphological measurements over 574 ECG couples [8]; 92.5% correct verifications for non-fiducial QRS pattern matching over 316 ECG couples [9]; 87%/78% correct verifications/identifications for non-fiducial correlation analysis of limb leads over 147 ECG couples [10].

Recently, we evaluated the inter-subject variability of morphological ECG features over large amount of time (>5 years) in a population of healthy cardiac subjects [11]. The aim of this study is to investigate the intra-individual stability of the ECG morphology using the same feature set in order to assess the potential for person identification via orthogonal ECG leads.

2 ECG database

The ECG signals used in this study are taken from a computerized ECG-ILSA database [12,13], collected for the Italian Longitudinal Study on Aging project [14]. The ECGs have been collected from individuals aged from 65 to 84 years. Each recording is with duration of 10s and includes the standard 12 leads, sampled at 500 Hz. The database contains 901 patients recorded both in the first phase (T1) and in the second phase (T2=T1+5 years). A set of 145 individuals without cardiac diseases has been selected for analysis in this study.

3 Method

Four ECG leads, forming quasi-orthogonal lead system (II&III,V1,V5) [15] are processed as follows:

1) Detection of QRS complexes in a combined ECG lead [16], heartbeat classification [17], calculation of mean RR interval between predominant beats;
2) Extraction (by best-fit correlation) of an averaged QRS-T pattern of the predominant beats for each of the 4 leads. Interval of 0.35*RR before and 0.55*RR after the detected fiducial points is considered;
3) QRS-T delineation in each of the four leads [18];
4) Calculation of 15 morphological pattern features per lead (see figure 1), as follows:
   - 12 features describing the QRS morphology that have previously been approved to provide adequate heartbeat comparison and classification [14]: QRS-width (Width); amplitudes (Ma, Mi) and offsets (Ima, Imi) of maximal positive and negative peaks; slope from QRS-onset to first peak (S1); slope from first to second peak (S2); QRS positive (ArP), negative (ArN) and total area (Ar=ArP+ArN); sum of the absolute QRS velocities values (Av); number of samples crossing 70% of the maximal peak amplitude (No);
   - 3 features describing the T-wave – width (TWidth), amplitude (Tamp), peak-to-end interval (Tp_Tend).

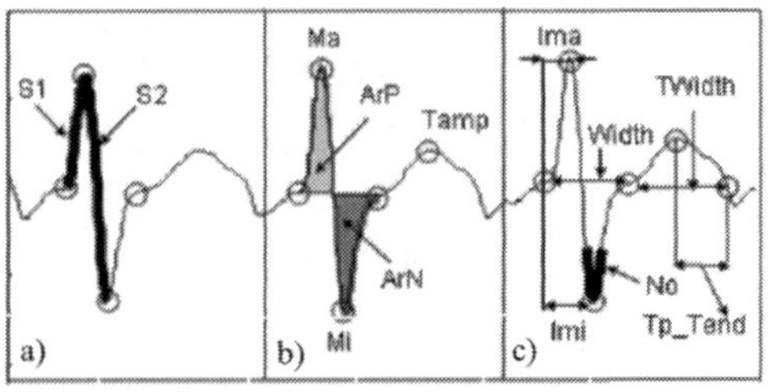

Fig. 1. Graphical representation of the morphological features calculated for the averaged delineated QRS-T pattern: a) slopes; b) amplitudes, areas; c) time intervals.

Aiming to select feature constellation, which is stable over time, thus being appropriate for the identification task, we apply the following procedures included in the multivariate analyses of the software package Statistica 12.7 (Dell Inc.):

1) Factor Analysis by Principal Components extraction method with 'varimax' rotation for providing orthogonal factors. The idea is to highlight the outstanding correlated (dependent) and uncorrelated (independent) features separated in the first 3 factors. The stability of the factors is independently verified over the data collected in the periods: T1, T2 and joint T1+T2. Presence of factor stability between the 3 datasets would indicate the factors' potential to represent the subjects' correspondence.
2) Correlation analysis for assessment of the coincidence between feature values in T1 and T2;
3) Multiple stepwise regression for synthesis of regression equations that could be applied for predicting the value of a certain feature in T2, based on data measured in T1.
4) Cluster analysis for assessment of the prediction model, e.g. the coincidence between measured and predicted feature values.

4 Results and discussion

The analysis of the designed feature space (15x4=60 features) via Factor analysis highlights 11 features that are relevant to the aim of the study and for which the following observations are valid:

- High ($\geq$0.7) and significant ($p<0.05$) factor loadings in one of the first 3 factors, combined with low and insignificant loadings in the remaining factors, when the factor analysis is performed over the joint data for 2x145 patients in T1+T2 records (see Table 1);
- The same feature distribution among the first 3 factors and comparable factor loadings, when the factor analysis is performed separately over the data collected during T1 (145 patients) and T2 (145 patients). The results are presented in Table 2 and Table 3.

Table 1. Factor loadings in the first 3 factors obtained via analysis of the data for T1 and T2.
Loadings with absolute values ≥ 0.7 are highlighted.

	Factor 1	Factor 2	Factor 3
ArN_II	*-0.889176*	0.004531	0.093518
S2_III	*-0.763494*	0.048325	-0.165169
Ar_III	*0.928569*	0.076507	0.083850
ArN_III	*-0.874855*	-0.078762	0.141749
Av_III	*0.870994*	0.011419	0.132374
Ar_V1	0.097656	*0.834255*	0.101620
ArN_V1	-0.042548	*-0.822745*	-0.167931
Av_V1	-0.009787	*0.880939*	0.125139
Ar_V5	0.044894	0.145240	*0.727179*
ArP_V5	-0.198526	0.232198	*0.723374*
Av_V5	-0.027200	-0.086195	*0.744158*

Table 2. Factor loadings in the first 3 factors obtained via analysis of the data for T1.
Loadings with absolute values ≥ 0.7 are highlighted.

	Factor 1	Factor 2	Factor 3
ArN_II	*-0.900022*	0.106638	0.069295
S2_III	*-0.716803*	-0.059771	0.006593
Ar_III	*0.929317*	0.043028	0.025345
ArN_III	*-0.884789*	0.071698	0.121484
Av_III	*0.849656*	0.059122	0.019912
S2_V1	0.155151	*-0.893559*	0.064475
Ar_V1	0.016207	*0.851458*	0.045255
ArN_V1	0.015608	*-0.821156*	-0.054854
Av_V1	-0.088712	*0.900437*	-0.005498
Ar_V5	0.044044	0.027269	*0.877656*
ArP_V5	-0.142407	0.134194	*0.834679*

Table 3. Factor loadings in the first 3 factors obtained via analysis of the data for T2.
Loadings with absolute values ≥ 0.7 are highlighted.

	Factor	Factor	Factor
ArN_II	*-0.883309*	-0.040706	0.140409
S2_III	*-0.748261*	0.013423	-0.169060
Ar_III	*0.921478*	0.108880	0.075771
ArN_III	*-0.859490*	-0.121004	0.125263
Av_III	*0.867208*	0.038183	0.118138
S2_V1	0.053774	*-0.745554*	-0.042857
Ar_V1	0.185672	*0.758675*	0.098808
ArN_V1	-0.089083	*-0.790738*	-0.226551
Av_V1	0.061571	*0.865982*	0.114185
Ar_V5	0.089063	0.206883	*0.743416*
ArP_V5	-0.181731	0.285029	*0.764283*

The Factor analysis results support the following conclusions:

1) Confirm our hypothesis that the ECG leads (II&III), V1 and V5 form quasi-orthogonal lead system, considering the fact that the features, which are strongly correlated with a certain factor are from a single axis (lead) and the features measured in different axes (leads) are distributed among the 3 factors;
2) Confirm the stability of the formed feature subsets, considering the measurements in T1 and T2, i.e. their strong correlation within a certain factor and weak correlation with the features from the remaining factors. The formed feature subsets are as follows:
   - ArN_II; S2_III; Ar_III; ArN_III; Av_III in lead (II&III);
   - Ar_V1; ArN_V1; Av_V1 in lead V1;
   - Ar_V5; ArP_V5; Av_V5 in lead V5.

Based on the above findings, it is reasonable to consider that the best features within the formed subsets are representative for person identification.

The results from the correlation analysis applied over the feature values measured in T1 and T2 (see Table 4) give a hint about the possibility for synthesis of regression equations that could be applied for predicting the value of a certain feature in T2 based on data measured in T1. The comparison between the predicted features' values and the measured ones could be considered as an adequate preliminary sign about the confidence level for person identification via morphological ECG features measured in different time moments. This is demonstrated via one of the models designed by means of stepwise multiple regression analysis, i.e. prediction of the values for ArN_III(T2) based on the values measured for ArN_II(T1) and ArN_III(T1) – see Table 5. Based even on this single model for calculation of ArN_III values in T2 we have achieved 80.7% group indistinction, when applying K-means clustering over the measured and predicted values. Only 19.3% of the predicted values have been assigned to different cluster.

Table 4. Correlations coefficients between the features included in the stable groups for both measurement periods T1 and T2.
Significant correlations are highlighted ($p < 0.05$).

T1\T2	ArN_II (T2)	S2_III (T2)	Ar_III (T2)	ArN_III (T2)	Av_III (T2)	Ar_V1 (T2)	ArN_V1 (T2)	Av_V1 (T2)	Ar_V5 (T2)	ArP_V5 (T2)	Av_V5 (T2)
ArN_II (T1)	*0.91*	*0.50*	*-0.78*	*0.82*	*-0.63*	-0.11	0.08	0.01	-0.13	0.17	-0.04
S2_III (T1)	*0.42*	*0.86*	*-0.74*	*0.66*	*-0.82*	-0.15	0.13	-0.11	-0.21	-0.10	-0.17
Ar_III (T1)	*-0.72*	*-0.74*	*0.90*	*-0.87*	*0.82*	0.25	-0.20	0.13	0.22	0.03	0.12
ArN_III (T1)	*0.74*	*0.66*	*-0.86*	*0.93*	*-0.77*	-0.24	0.14	-0.10	-0.12	0.08	-0.05
Av_III (T1)	*-0.58*	*-0.83*	*0.84*	*-0.79*	*0.86*	0.22	-0.17	0.13	0.23	0.07	0.16
Ar_V1 (T1)	0.12	-0.02	0.04	0.01	0.04	*0.70*	*-0.55*	*0.65*	0.12	0.21	0.08
ArN_V1 (T1)	-0.16	0.01	-0.02	-0.03	-0.02	*-0.70*	*0.57*	*-0.64*	-0.12	-0.23	-0.08
Av_V1 (T1)	0.18	0.01	-0.04	0.10	-0.01	*0.59*	*-0.46*	*0.65*	0.04	0.16	0.01
Ar_V5 (T1)	0.10	-0.01	0.04	-0.01	0.03	0.21	-0.27	0.18	*0.73*	*0.74*	*0.67*
ArP_V5 (T1)	0.25	0.07	-0.08	0.12	-0.06	0.23	-0.24	0.20	*0.65*	*0.76*	*0.61*
Av_V5 (T1)	0.15	0.01	-0.03	0.04	-0.02	0.12	-0.22	0.13	*0.65*	*0.66*	*0.66*

Table 5. Statistics for the regression model ArN_III (T2) = f(ArN_II(T1), ArN_III(T1)). R= .929 R^2= .862 Adjusted R^2= .860 F(2,143)=443.95 p<0.001, Std. Error of estimate: 2.158

	Beta	Std.Err. of Beta	B	Std.Err. of B	t(143)	p-level
Intercept			-0.562	0.264	-2.129	0.035
ArN_II(T1)	0.142	0.057	0.331	0.133	2.483	0.014
ArN_III(T1)	0.806	0.057	0.922	0.066	14.063	0.000

5 Conclusions

The results achieved in this preliminary study show that in general the morphological features measured from the electrocardiogram could be applied for identification of subjects in different periods of examination. This could be used in the clinical and emergency medicine, as well as for the design and management of personalized ECG databases.

Acknowledgements

This study is supported by the Bulgarian Scientific Research Fund, grant T02/11.

References

1. L. Biel, O. Pettersson, L. Philipson, P. Wide, "ECG analysis: a new approach in human identification", IEEE Trans. Instr. Meas., **50(3)**: 808-12, (2001)
2. S. Israel, J. Irvine, A. Cheng, M. Wiederhold, B. Wiederhold, "ECG to identify individuals" Pattern Recognition, **38**, 133-42 (2005)
3. Y. Wang, F. Agrafioti, D. Hatzinakos, K. Plataniotis, "Analysis of human electrocardiogram for biometric recognition", EURASIP Journal on Advances in Signal Processing, Article ID 148658 (2008)
4. K. Plataniotis, D. Hatzinakos, J. Lee, "ECG biometric recognition without fiducial detection", Proc. on Biometrics Symposium BSYM'06, 19-21, (2006)
5. F. Agrafioti, D. Hatzinakos, "ECG biometric analysis in cardiac irregularity conditions", Signal Image & Video Processing, **3**, 329-43 (2009)
6. F. Poree, A. Gallix, G. Carrault, "Biometric identification of individuals based on the ECG. Which conditions?", Comp. in Cardiol., **38**, 761-4, (2011)
7. I. Jekova. "Potential of the peripheral electrocardiogram for personal verification/ identification" Compt. Rend. de l'Acad. Bulg. des Sci., **68(4)**: 497-504, (2015)
8. I. Jekova, V. Krasteva, R. Leber, R. Schmid, R. Twerenbold, C. Müller, T. Reichlin, R. Abächerli, "Intersubject variability and intrasubject reproducibility of 12-lead ECG metrics: Implications for human verification", J. Electrocardiol., **49**: 784-9, (2016)
9. V. Krasteva, I. Jekova, R. Abächerli, "Analysis of QRS Patterns in 15-Lead ECG for Person Verification", Annual J. Electronics, **9**: 10-13, (2015)
10. I. Jekova, G. Bortolan, "Personal verification/ identification via analysis of the peripheral ECG leads. Influence of the personal health status on the accuracy", Biomed. Research Int., **2015**, Article ID 135676, (2015)
11. I. Jekova, I. Christov, V. Krasteva, G. Bortolan, M. Matveev, "Assessment of the Potential of Morphological ECG Features for Person Identification", Comput. in Cardiol., 42: 921-4, (2015).
12. S. Maggi, M. Zuchetto, F. Grigoletto, M. Baldereschi, L. Candelise, E. Scarpini, et al., "The Italian Longitudinal Study on Aging (ILSA): design and methods", Aging Clin. Exp. Res., **6**: 464-73 (1994)
13. G. Bortolan, M. Bressan, F. Golferini, ILSA Study Group, "QT dispersion in the elderly. The ILSA study", Aging Clin. Exp. Res., **16(5)**: 342–8, (2004)
14. G. Bortolan, M. Bressan, F. Golferini, "Serial analysis in the ECG-ILSA database: study of longitudinal modifications", Comput. In Cardiol., **26**: 667-70, (1999)
15. M. Matveev, L. Tomov, I. Tomov, I..Daskalov, "Lead Selection for ECG Screening", Adv. Cardiol., **19**:148-9, (1977)
16. I. Christov, "Real time electrocardiogram QRS detection using combined adaptive threshold", Biomed. Eng. Online, **3(28)**, (2004)
17. I. Christov, I. Jekova, G. Bortolan, "Premature ventricular contraction classification by the K-th nearest neighbours rule", Physiol Meas., **26**: 123-30, (2005)
18. I. Christov, I. Simova, "Q-onset and T-end delineation: Assessment of the performance of an automated method with the use of a reference database", Physiol Meas, **28**: 213-21, (2007)

State-space Coil Modelling in Plasma Magnetic Confinement Devices

Aitor J. Garrido[1,*], *Izaskun* Garrido[1], *Diego* González[1], *Odei* Molinuevo[1], *Jon* Lekube[1] and *Edorta* Carrascal[2]

[1]Automatic Control Group - ACG, Inst. of Research and Development of Processes - IIDP. Dept. Aut. Control and Systems Eng., Faculty of Engineering of Bilbao, University of the Basque Country (UPV/EHU), Pº Rafael Moreno Moreno 3, Bilbao, 48013. Spain
[2]Automatic Control Group, Department of Thermal Engineering, Faculty of Engineering of Bilbao, University of the Basque Country (UPV/EHU), 48013 Bilbao, Spain

Abstract. The need of robust and optimal control schemes is a key factor for the development of future fusion reactors. This paper has dealt with the state-space modelling of the Ultra-Low Iota Super Elongated Stellarator of the UPV/EHU, using a physical lumped parameter equivalent circuit approach. The model obtained has been validated by means of experimental output data showing an excellent matching with the real system. Besides, it has been designed a MPC scheme that has been successfully implemented both in simulation and experimentally using a real-time control platform.

1 Introduction

In the last years, it has been a considerable international effort to develop a clean technology based on magnetic confinement fusion energy, as it is the case of the ITER (International Thermonuclear Experimental Reactor) [1,2]. The process involves a nuclear reaction in which two cores of light atoms, usually hydrogen and its isotopes come together to form a heavier core. This reaction releases a great amount of energy in form of gamma rays and kinetic energy of the emitted particles that allows matter entering in state of plasma.

The final objective is to reproduce the process taking place in the stars, including the Sun, that constantly undergo nuclear fusion reactions. This represents a number of scientific and technical challenges. In particular, the automatic control composes one of the areas of interest regarding the development of a clean fusion technology, since one of the main limiting phenomena is the premature reaction decay due to instabilities of the plasma [3,4].

Nowadays there exist two main magnetic fusion devices topologies: tokamaks and stellarators. On one hand tokamak reactors confine the plasma particles in a toroidal region using magnetic fields. These particles are held in small gyrating orbits by the magnetic field. The principal magnetic field is usually toroidal and the confinement of the plasma is mainly achieved through the poloidal magnetic field. The field lines around the plasma current are combined with the toroidal field to produce helical field lines, which wrap around the torus in both directions. On the other hand, stellarators consist basically of a helically symmetric system bent into a torus with a large axisymmetric toroidal field, a moderately sized helical field and a small axisymmetric vertical field, all of them created by electromagnetic coils. In this way, the magnetic confinement in stellarators is fully achieved by the coils, so that no plasma current is needed to confine -although ohmic, non-inductive and bootstrap currents may also be present-. This fact makes stellarators a great alternative to tokamaks, with relevant progresses in the study of the physics of magnetically confined plasmas on these devices in the last years. Besides, its ability to operate in continuous mode -tokamaks are inherently pulsed devices- would allow a higher commercial profitability [5].

The studies presented in this paper have been performed for the UPV/EHU Stellarator ULISES (Ultra-Low Iota Super Elongated Stellarator), fully designed and constructed by the Automatic and Control Group of the UPV/EHU in collaboration with the EURATOM-CIEMAT (see Figure 1).

* Corresponding author: aitor.garridor@ehu.es

DOI: 10.1051/matecconf/201712502005

Fig. 1. UPV/EHU Stellarator ULISES

The rest of the paper is organized as follows: The model development is stated in Section 2. Section 2.1 describes the physical state-space model of the system considered, obtaining some relevant unknown parameter values by means of parameter identification over the real system. Then, the numerical solution achieved is benchmarking with experimental output data in Section 2.2, so as to validate the model. Section 3 is devoted to present the Model Predictive Controller (MPC) scheme used, both parameter description - Section 3.1- and design and implementation of the real time control system -Section 3.2- employed to test the controller in the next section. Section 4 presents the corresponding result, showing the correspondence between the responses of the real system and the numerical model obtained. Finally, some concluding remarks are stated in the last section.

2 Model statement

In this section, the analytical development of the plant model is provided. For this purpose, the circuit formed by the coils and resistors composing the system plant is analysed so as to derive an adequate state-space representation. Afterwards, the model is validated by comparing the numerical plant output with the real system for different shots. It is shown that the output of the numerical model presents and excellent matching with that of the real plant for all them.

2.1 System modelling

Several studies on the behaviour of the device have been carried out in order to achieve an adequate equivalent system mode [6]. It has been determined that the internal circuit of the stellarator can be represented by the following lumped parameter electrical system (Figure 2). This lumped parameter approach is widely employed when in fusion devices [7-9]:

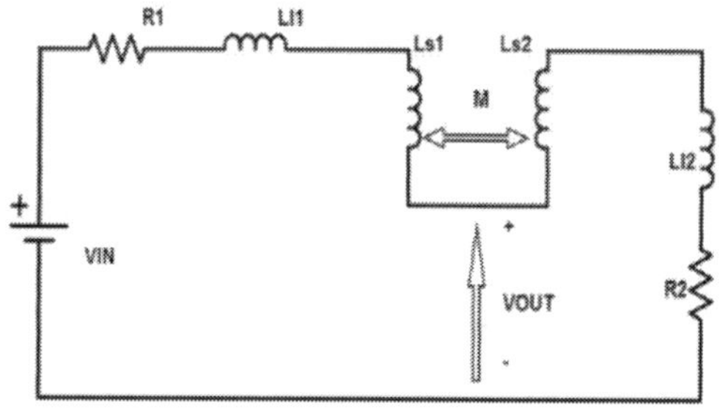

Fig. 2. Lumped parameter equivalent circuit

In this figure, R_1 represents the total resistance of the first large coil and the first small inner coil. Analogously, R_2 is the total resistance for the other two coils, so R represents the total resistance of the circuit. Note also that the inner small coils are coupled, so that total inductance of the circuit may be expressed as:

$$K = L_{l1} + L_{s1} + L_{l2} + L_{s1} \pm M, \tag{1}$$

with M being the mutual inductance of the two coupled coils and K the total inductance. The voltage input (V_{IN}) represents the DC voltage supply and the voltage output is due to the drop in the second part of coils, so that:

$$V_{OUT} = V_{R2} + V_{Ls2} + V_{l2}. \tag{2}$$

Thus, the two basic equations which govern the circuit can be written as:

$$V_{IN} = I(R_1 + R_2) + K\frac{dI}{dt} \tag{3}$$

$$V_{OUT} = I \cdot R_2 + (L_{s2} + L_{l2})\frac{dI}{dt} \tag{4}$$

where I represents the current in the circuit. In order to obtain a state-space representation, the following state variables are chosen:

$$x_1 = I \tag{5}$$

$$x_2 = \dot{x_1} = \frac{dI}{dt} \tag{6}$$

Then, from equations (3) and (5), the following expression is achieved:

$$\dot{x_1} = \frac{dI}{dt} = -\frac{(R_1 + R_2)}{K}I + \frac{1}{K}V_{IN} \tag{7}$$

Besides, deriving the equation (7) the result is:

$$\dot{x_2} = \frac{d^2I}{dt^2} = -\frac{(R_1 + R_2)}{K}\frac{dI}{dt} = -\frac{(R_1 + R_2)}{K}x_2 \tag{8}$$

Therefore, substituting equations (5) in equations (7) and then (8), the state-space model of the system can be stablished in a convenient form with non-coupled state variables as follows:

$$\begin{bmatrix}\dot{x_1}\\ \dot{x_2}\end{bmatrix}=\begin{bmatrix}-\frac{(R_1+R_2)}{K} & 0\\ 0 & -\frac{(R_1+R_2)}{K}\end{bmatrix}\begin{bmatrix}x_1\\ x_2\end{bmatrix}+\begin{bmatrix}\frac{1}{K}\\ 0\end{bmatrix}V_{IN} \quad (9)$$

$$\begin{bmatrix}I_{OUT}\\ V_{OUT}\end{bmatrix}=\begin{bmatrix}1 & 0\\ R_2 & L_{s2}+L_{l2}\end{bmatrix}\begin{bmatrix}x_1\\ x_2\end{bmatrix} \quad (10)$$

Now, is necessary to determine the real values of the parameters of the real system. For this purpose, some experimental tests are performed, collecting the results through the data acquisition system. In order to identify the elements of the matrices it is necessary to manage the differential equations of the system, so that using equations (7) and (8) it is possible to obtain an analytical expression for $x_1(t)$:

$$x_1(t)=I(t)=\frac{V_{IN}}{R}\left(1-e^{-\frac{R}{K}t}\right) \quad (11)$$

Analogously, from (6) one has:

$$x_2(t)=\frac{dI}{dt}=\frac{V_{IN}}{K}e^{-\frac{R}{K}t} \quad (12)$$

Taking into account these results, it is possible to use a set of real data from appropriate experiments to calculate the parameters of the analytical solutions of $x_1(t)$ and $x_2(t)$ obtained. In this case, a typical step voltage signal with a 6V magnitude has been used as input to the system. Considering a fixed instant during the transient response -0.05s from the enforcement of the step voltage- it is obtained a voltage output value of 2.47V and a current value of 10.94A. Besides, the steady-state current value is 25.73A, so that the total resistance of the system can be directly stablished from Ohm's law providing value of 0.2332Ω.

On the one hand, it is now possible from these data to obtain the total inductance of the circuit from equation (11), resulting in a value K=0.021. In the same way, from the solution (12) and the value of K obtained, it is possible to calculate value of the current derivative of current at this specific point of the transient regime, resulting in 163.98A/s. On the other hand, due to the symmetry of the stellarator, both large and small inner coil pairs present the same resistance, so that the value of is also known -R_1=R_2=0.1166 Ω-. Finally, from these results and equation (4) it can also be calculated the value of L_{s2}+L_{l2} -7.28mH-.

According to these results, the state-space model at this point may be expressed as:

$$\begin{bmatrix}\dot{x_1}\\ \dot{x_2}\end{bmatrix}=\begin{bmatrix}-11.1 & 0\\ 0 & -11.1\end{bmatrix}\begin{bmatrix}x_1\\ x_2\end{bmatrix}+\begin{bmatrix}47.62\\ 0\end{bmatrix}V_{IN} \quad (13)$$

$$\begin{bmatrix}I_{OUT}\\ V_{OUT}\end{bmatrix}=\begin{bmatrix}1 & 0\\ 0.1166 & 0.00728\end{bmatrix}\begin{bmatrix}x_1\\ x_2\end{bmatrix} \quad (14)$$

It has to be taken into account that the previous process has been performed for a particular state of the system during its transient response. In order to obtain a more accurate space-state model it has been used a grey-box modelling procedure, where the information acquired from the theoretical model determines the form of the identified system and the estimation of the elements of the state-space matrices is based on real input-output experimental data using the values previously obtained as initial values for the system identification algorithms [10]. In this way, it is possible to stablish a model-based grey-box state-space representing the system:

$$\begin{bmatrix}\dot{x_1}\\ \dot{x_2}\end{bmatrix}=\begin{bmatrix}-15.5 & 0\\ 0 & -15.5\end{bmatrix}\begin{bmatrix}x_1\\ x_2\end{bmatrix}+\begin{bmatrix}69.3\\ 0\end{bmatrix}V_{IN} \quad (15)$$

$$\begin{bmatrix}I_{OUT}\\ V_{OUT}\end{bmatrix}=\begin{bmatrix}1 & 0\\ 0.111 & 0.00632\end{bmatrix}\begin{bmatrix}x_1\\ x_2\end{bmatrix} \quad (16)$$

As a result, the values of the Lumped parameter equivalent circuit physical circuit are: K=0.0144H, R=0.2236Ω, R_2=0.111Ω and L_{s2}+ L_{l2} = 6.32mH.

2.2 Model validation

In this section the obtained model is compared with the real system output. For this purpose it has been used a set of validation data obtained for the same open-loop high demanding step-wise voltage input response. Results are shown in the following figures 3 and 4 both for voltage and current output, respectively. As it may be observed, the response of the grey-box model matches that of the real system, with a fit percentage of 74.2% for voltage output and 84.3% for current output case, being in part the error due to the noisy unfiltered experimental output.

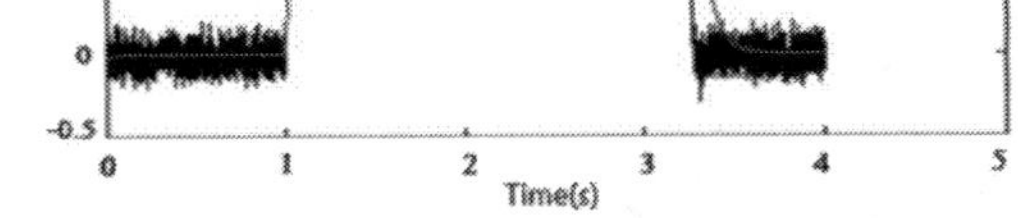

Fig. 3. Model vs real system open-loop responses (V_{OUT})

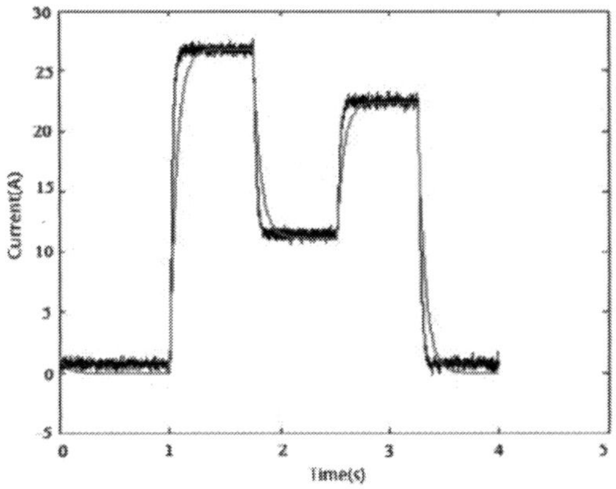

Fig. 4. Model vs real system open-loop responses (I_{OUT})

3 Model predictive control law

3.1 Controller description

The control objective is to regulate the voltage input supply to the stellarator to successfully solve the trajectory tracking problem for the voltage reference to be achieved in the chamber coils. In turn, current is controlled indirectly through voltage, as these signals are dependent each other. There exist different control approaches for this purpose, being the most used traditional PID-based schemes, robust (sliding-mode) schemes and MPC schemes [11-23]. In particular, when dealing with fusion devices where the available energy is limited, MPC is especially interesting due to its ability to ensure that both the control action and the solution error are minimal [9].

The working principle of MPC (Model Predictive Control) is to predict the future evolution of the outputs or manipulated variables [24-26]. For this purpose it is necessary to define a prediction horizon N representing the time interval in which the output predictions evolve, so that the following sequence of output predictions are calculated according with system model considered and the information of evolution of the process until time t:

$$\hat{y}\left(t+\frac{1}{t}\right), \hat{y}\left(t+\frac{2}{t}\right), \dots, \hat{y}(t+\frac{N}{t}) \quad (17)$$

Besides, a control horizon N_u representing the sequence of future control signals within N is employed:

$$u\left(\frac{t}{t}\right), u\left(t+\frac{1}{t}\right), \dots, u(t+N-\frac{1}{t}) \quad (18)$$

Usually, it is considered that the control signal remains constant for future time exceeding the control horizon ($N > N_u$).

A further feature is the sliding horizon representing the number of components of the sequence of control signals vector $\boldsymbol{u}$ to be considered, neglecting the rest of the sequence at each iteration. The MPC scheme used is shown in Figure 5.

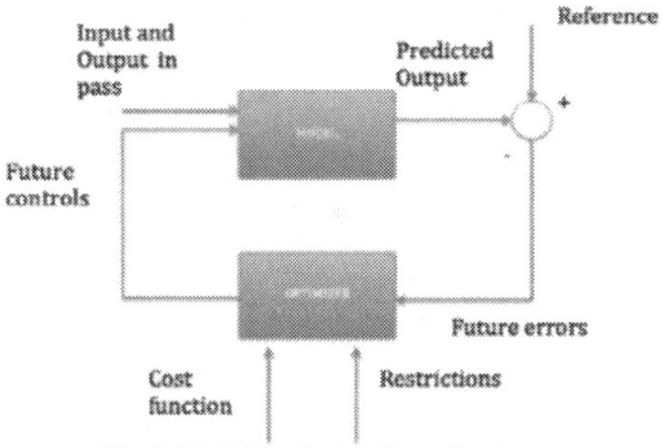

Fig. 5. Model Predictive Control scheme

The model used for the design of the MPC implementation is based on the previously obtained state-space (15-16) [27,28]. In order to develop an optimal controller, and given that the state variables are not coupled, the state-space model may be expressed as follows:

$$\dot{x_1} = -15.5x_1 + 69.3V_{IN} \quad (19)$$

$$V_{OUT} = 0.111x_1 \quad (20)$$

The control interval of the controller is stablished in accordance with the experimental sample time of the real system (0.00025s). The prediction horizon considered is set to 25 and the control horizon used is set to 13 (See Table 1). With these MPC parameters, the weight rate was 0.0225 and the weight of the output variable was stablished at 4 [29,30].

Table 1. MPC parameters.

Control Interval	0,00025s
Prediction Horizon (Intervals)	25
Control Horizon (Intervals)	13

3.2 Real-time control system

In order to demonstrate the feasibility and performance of the control scheme previously proposed, it has been implemented a real-time control design for the UPV/EHU Stellarator. The system has been designed using the real-time environment shown in Figure 6. The real-time applications are programmed and modified on an engineering PC and then launched to run on a dedicated real-time target computer connected to the physical system [31-32]. In particular, the control strategy is aimed to control a 15 kW EA-PSI 8080-510 3U power supply. A NI PCIe-6323 data acquisition device with two terminal blocks NI SCB-68A has been used for the communication between the real-time control computer and the power source, the external sensors and the stellarator. The external sensors include a Hall effect inductive current sensor able to measure up to 600A with an 1% error for measuring the current in the four-coil system of the stellarator and a scalable voltage sensor for measuring the output voltage.

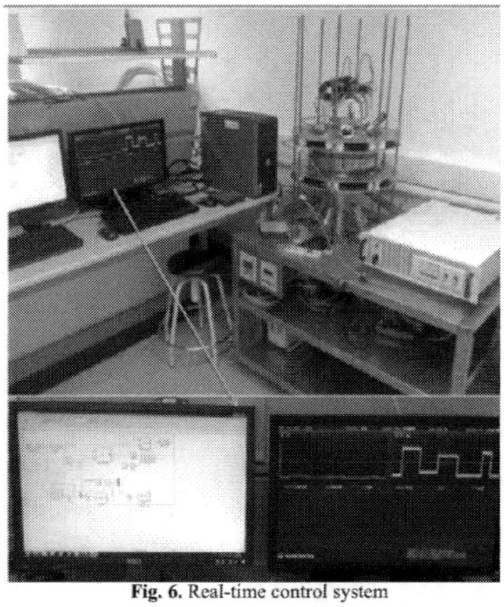

Fig. 6. Real-time control system

This structure allows to use the kernel of the real-time target computer only to run the real-time process, with an effective sample time below 250μs, updating the data in the engineering PC at a lower rate via a RJ-45 Ethernet connection.

4 Results: real system vs proposed model

As it has been stated in the introduction the final aim is to develop different controllers for the UPV/EHU Stellarator. As a first step towards achieving this goal a grey-box model has been developed. This model has been initially validated against the real system. In a second step, a model predictive control (MPC) has been designed and implemented, both in simulation with the proposed model and experimentally. In order to validate the real-time MPC over the system, experimental voltage and current output results for a demanding shot may be seen, respectively, in Figure 7 and Figure 8.

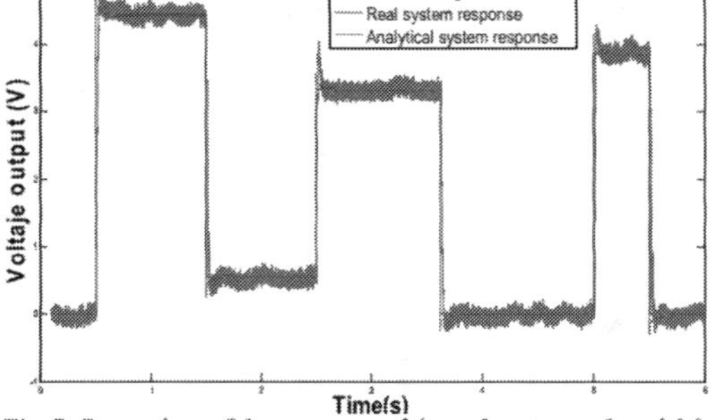

Fig. 7. Comparison of the responses of the real system and model for voltage output

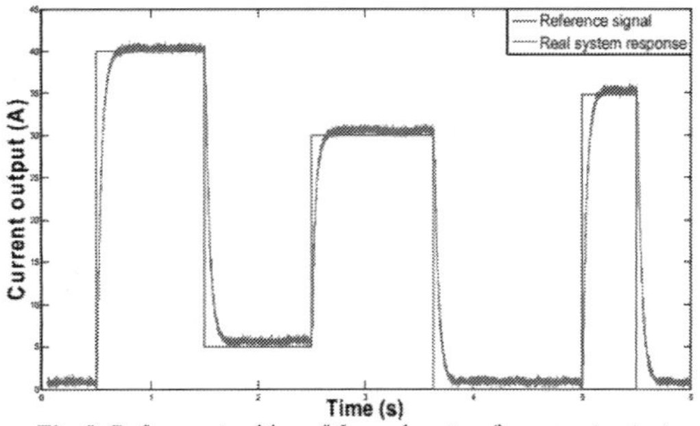

Fig. 8. Reference tracking of the real system for current output

As it may be observed, the controlled response of the real system is very similar to the desired one for both voltage and current, which shows that the real time MPC of the system provides an adequate performance over time, since the only deviation is a non-significant peak.

Besides, taking into account that the voltage is sufficiently controlled with the MPC and that the current depends basically on the voltage and on the resistance of the system, it can be assumed that this error is a result of a variation of the resistance of the system as the experiment evolves. This variation of the resistance may be due to the change of the temperature in the coils of the stellarator. Likewise, other factor that affects to the error is the environmental noise inherent to the experimental output, and in particular to the inductive current sensor of the coils.

Therefore, the real-time MPC has been proven to be an excellent candidate as a control scheme since it is able to optimize the future behaviour of the states while intrinsically minimizing the control action. In particular, Figure 7 and Figure 8 show how this scheme evidences the optimal prediction effect at each step in the reference value, where the overshoot is minimized, due to the control ability to predict the future flat-top regime.

5 Conclusions

This paper deals with the grey-box modelling of the magnetic confinement coil system of the UPV/EHU Stellarator. The state-space model obtained has been successfully validated by comparing the results of the model with those of the real system. Besides, a Model Predictive Control law has been experimentally implemented over the real-time control system using the proposed state-space model showing an excellent reference trajectory tracking behaviour. A benchmarking of the proposed MPC with a traditionally used PID controller has been also performed. It has been shown that the MPC presents a superior performance due to its ability to predict the state of the plant during the dynamic operation, while PID controller needs a fine tuning when dealing with time-delay or changing dynamics during operation. In particular, the proposed MPC scheme allows ensuring both minimal control action and solution error, which is especially relevant in the case of fusion devices where the available energy is limited.

This work was supported in part by the University of the Basque Country (UPV/EHU) through Project PPG17/33 and by the MINECO through the Research Project DPI2015-70075-R (MINECO/FEDER, UE).
The authors would also like to thank the collaboration of the Basque Energy Board (EVE) through Agreement UPV/EHUEVE23/6/2011, the Spanish National Fusion Laboratory (EURATOM-CIEMAT) through Agreement UPV/EHUCIEMAT08/190 and Stefano Coda and the TCV team for its collaboration and help.

References

1. ITER Web site. *http://www.iter.org/* (2017)
2. Teller, E. (Ed.). *Fusion Part A: Magnetic Confinement*. Elsevier (2012)
3. Sevillano, M. G., Garrido, I., & Garrido, A. J. "Control-oriented automatic system for transport analysis (ASTRA)-matlab integration for tokamaks". Energy 36 (5), 2812-2819. DOI: 10.1016/j.energy.2011.02.022 (2011)
4. Sevillano, M.G., Garrido, I., Garrido, A. J., Romero, J.A., Paley, J., Coda, S. and the TCV team "Observer-based real-time control for the poloidal beta of the plasma using diamagnetic measurements in tokamak fusion reactors", Proceedings of the IEEE Conference on Decision and Control, art. no. 6160260, pp. 7536-7542. DOI: 10.1109/CDC.2011.6160260 (2011)
5. Menard, J. E., Bromberg, L., Brown, T., Burgess, T., Dix, D., El-Guebaly et al. Prospects for pilot plants based on the tokamak, spherical tokamak and stellarator. *Nuclear Fusion*, *51*(10), 103014 (2011)
6. Neubauer, O., Panin, A., Czymek, G., & Giesen, B. Approaches to numerical modeling in development process of complex structures for fusion devices. In *Fusion Engineering (SOFE), 2013 IEEE 25th Symposium on*, pp. 1-8 (2013)
7. Romero, J.A., Moret, J. M., Coda, S., Felici, F., & Garrido, I. "Development and validation of a tokamak skin effect transformer model", Nuclear Fusion, 52 (2), art. no. 023019 (2012)
8. Garrido, A.J., Garrido, I., Goretti Sevillano, M., Alberdi, M., Amundarain, M., Barambones, O., De La Sen, M. "Nuclear fusion control-oriented plasma current linear models" Proc. Of the International Conference on Systems 2014. Corfu. Greece, pp. 145-150 (2010)
9. Garrido I, Garrido A.J., Romero J.A., Carrascal E. Sevillano-Berasategui M. and Barambones O., "Low Effort LI Nuclear Fusion Plasma Control Using Model Predictive Control Laws," Mathematical Problems in Engineering, Article ID 527420. DOI: 10.1155/2015/527420 (2015)
10. Ljung l.. "Some Classical and Some New Ideas for Identification of Linear Systems" *Journal of Control, Automation and Electrical Systems.* Volume 24, Issue 1-2 (2013)
11. Garrido, I., Garrido, A.J., Sevillano, M.G., & Romero, J.A., "Robust sliding mode control for tokamaks", Mathematical Problems in Engineering, 2012, art. no. 341405. DOI: 10.1155/2012/341405 (2012)
12. Garrido, A. J., Garrido, I., Amundarain, M., Alberdi, M., & De La Sen, M. "Sliding-mode control of wave power generation plants". IEEE Transactions on Industry Applications, 48 (6), 2372-2381. DOI: 10.1109/TIA.2012.2227096 (2012)
13. Garrido, I., Garrido, A.J., Sevillano, M.G., Romero, J.A., Amundarain, M., & Alberdi, M. "Tokamak state-space control modeling" Canadian Conference on Electrical and Computer Engineering, CCECE Vols. 1-4 0840-7789 (2008)
14. Alkorta, P., Barambones, O., Garrido, A.J., Garrido, I. "SVPWM variable structure control of induction motor drives" IEEE International Symposium on Industrial Electronics, art. no. 4374768, pp. 1195-1200 (2007)
15. Garrido, A.J., Garrido, I., Alberdi, M., Amundarain, M., Barambones, O., Romero, J.A. "Robust control of oscillating water column (OWC) devices: Power generation improvement" OCEANS 2013 MTS/IEEE - San Diego: An Ocean in Common, art. no. 6740982 (2013)
16. Garrido, I., Garrido, A.J., Alberdi, M., Amundarain, M., Barambones, O. "Performance of an ocean energy conversion system with DFIG sensorless control" Mathematical Problems in Engineering, 2013, art. no. 260514. DOI: 10.1155/2013/260514 (2013)
17. Garrido, A.J., De La Sen, M., Soto, J.C., Barambones, O., Garrido, I. "Suboptimal regulation of a class of bilinear interconnected systems with finite-time sliding planning horizons". *Mathematical Problems in Engineering*, 2008, art. no. 817063. DOI: 10.1155/2008/817063 (2008)
18. Sevillano, G., Garrido, I., & Garrido, A. J. "ASTRA-matlab integration for the control of tokamaks" (2011). Informatica, 22 (2), 241-257. ISSN: 08684952
19. Garrido, A.J., Otaola, E., Garrido, I., Lekube, J., Liria, P., Mader, J., "OWC wave power plants capture chamber modelling" OCEANS 2015 - MTS/IEEE Washington, art. no. 7401863. ISBN: 978-0-9339-5743-5 (2016)
20. Garrido, I., Garrido, A.J., Coda, S., Le, H.B., Moret, J.M., Real time hybrid model predictive control for the current profile of the tokamak à configuration variable (TCV). *Energies*, 2008, 9 (8), art. no. 609. DOI: 10.3390/en9080609 (2008)
21. Garrido, I., Garrido, A.J., Lekube, J., Otaola, E., Carrascal, E. "Oscillating water column control and monitoring". OCEANS 2016 MTS/IEEE

Monterey CA, art. no. 7761420, DOI: 10.1109/OCEANS.2016.7761420 (2016)

22. Garrido, A.J., Garrido, I., Lekube, J., De La Sen, M., Carrascal, E. "Modeling of Oscillating Water Column wave energy systems". World Automation Congress, 2016-October, art. no. 7583008, DOI: 10.1109/WAC.2016.7583008 (2016)
23. Lekube, J., Garrido, A.J., Garrido, I., Rotational Speed Optimization in Oscillating Water Column Wave Power Plants Based on Maximum Power Point Tracking (2016) *IEEE Transactions on Automation Science and Engineering,* Article in Press. DOI: 10.1109/TASE.2016.2596579 (2016)
24. Cheng, Q., Cannon, M., & Kouvaritakis, B. The design of dynamics in the prediction structure of robust MPC. International Journal of Control, 86(11), 2096-2103 (2013)
25. Morari, M., Garcia, C. E., & Prett, D. M. Model predictive control: theory and practice. In Proc./FAC Workshop on Model Based Process Control (pp. 1-12). (2014)
26. Carrascal, E., Garrido, I., Garrido, A.J., Sala, J.M. "Model Predictive Control for the heating system of a public building". World Automation Congress Proceedings, art. no. 6935986, pp. 433-438. (2014)
27. Garrido, I., Romero, J.A., Garrido, A.J., Lucchin, D., Carrascal, E., Sevillano-Berasategui, G. "Internal inductance predictive control for Tokamaks". World Automation Congress Proceedings, art. no. 6936072, pp. 628-633. DOI: 10.1109/WAC.2014.6936072 (2014)
28. Garrido, A.J., Garrido, I., Barambones, O., Alkorta, P., Maseda, F.J. "Simple linear models for plasma control in Tokamak Reactors" 2008 International Conference on Control, Automation and Systems, ICCAS 2008, art. no. 4694261, pp. 2429-2432. DOI: 10.1109/ICCAS.2008.4694261 (2008)
29. Wang, L. *Model predictive control system design and implementation using MATLAB®*. Springer Science & Business (2009)
30. Veselý, V., Rosinová, D., & Foltin, M. Robust model predictive control design with input constraints. *ISA transactions*, *49*(1), 114-120. (2010)
31. Yin, S., Luo, H., & Ding, S. X. Real-time implementation of fault-tolerant control systems with performance optimization. *Industrial Electronics, IEEE Transactions on*, *61*(5), 2402-2411 (2014)
32. Buttazzo, G. C. Hard real-time computing systems: predictable scheduling algorithms and applications (Vol. 24). Springer Science & Business Media (2011)

MATEC Web of Conferences **125**, 02006 (2017) DOI: 10.1051/matecconf/201712502006
CSCC 2017

Novel Asymmetrical Pulse Width Modulation Method

Dmitry Baimel[1,*], *Saad Tapuchi*[1], *and Nina Baimel*[2]

[1]Shamoon College of Engineering, Electrical Engineering Department, Beer-Sheva, Israel
[2]Sapir academic College, Industrial Management Department, Hof Ashkelon, Israel

Abstract. The paper proposes new asymmetrical PWM that can be used for operation of multilevel inverters. The working and construction principle of this PWM is demonstrated on 13-level PWM signal that is applied to nine-level inverter and operates it as 13-level inverter. The proposed PWM signal consists of 5-level hybrid PWM which is constructed from two PWM signals- combined parts of the standard 5-level Phase Disposition (PD) PWM and pulsed PWM. The sum of these two PWM signals produces the desired 13-level PWM signal that is applied to the 9-level cascaded inverter. The proposed PWM method allows reduction of 13-level inverter components compared to the standard topologies such as neutral point clamped or flying capacitor inverters. This results in smaller size, weight and cists of the inverter.. Extensive simulation results validate the practicability of the proposed PWM method. The proposed method can be extended to any desired number of levels.

1 Introduction

The multi-level inverters have several important advantages upon 2- and 3-level inverters: they are suitable for high voltages and high power. The output voltage wave is built of several staircases that mitigate the voltage gradient dv/dt stresses on electric machine or transformer windings connected to the multi-level inverters. Furthermore, the output voltage wave has a much lower THD factor than that of the two-level inverters.

There are several basic configurations for multi-level inverters, and each of them has its advantages and disadvantages versus the others [1-4]. One of the configurations is the Neutral Point Clamped (NPC) multi-level inverter [5-8]. The distinct DC voltages are obtained by charging several capacitors from only one DC voltage source. The principal advantage is the need for only one DC voltage source. The principal disadvantage is the need to control and regulate the capacitor charging/discharging processes to ensure that their voltage levels remain quasi constant. Another distinct type of multi-level inverters is the Cascaded H-Bridge configuration [9-11]. In this topology, each inverter phase is built of several series connected H-bridges, while each H-bridge is supplied by its own DC voltage source. The principal advantage is stable voltage levels on the H-bridge active switches, which are fixed by the DC voltage sources, while their main disadvantage is the need for several DC voltage sources.

The paper presents the proposed multilevel asymmetrical PWM that is applied to 9-level cascaded NPC inverter and operates it as 13-level inverter. The proposed method is verified by extensive simulation results.

Section II presents the 9-level NPC cascaded inverter. Section III presents the proposed Asymmetrical PWM method. Section IV shows simulation results and their discussion. Section V presents conclusions of the paper.

2 The proposed inverter

The proposed 9-level inverter consists of two series cascaded 5-level and 3-level H-bridges on each inverter phase (see Fig. 1).

The first 5-level standard NPC H-bridge is fed by Vdc voltage source. The H-bridges uses a neutral point clamping approach to get 5-level phase voltages in place of the 3-level phase voltages commonly obtained with standard H-bridges. The 5-level NPC H-bridge inverter would be an optimal solution that compromises between the number of levels (5-levels), the number of separate DC sources and the cumbersome voltage control of the clamped neutral point [11–16]. The NPC control of the 5-level NPC H-bridges is performed by sensing the voltages on the clamping capacitors and the current direction. The suitable inverter state from its possible redundant states is chosen according to these measurements. By exchanging the capacitors, the switching algorithm balances the neutral point voltage. Without voltage balancing, one of the capacitors would charge to the full Vdc voltage and the other one would discharge to the zero voltage. The voltage levels of this H-bridge are 0, Vdc/2, -Vdc/2, Vdc and –Vdc. The second bridge is standard 3-level H-bridge fed by Vdc

* Corresponding author: dmitrba@sce.ac.il

voltage source. The voltage levels of this H-bridge are 0, Vdc and –Vdc. If this inverter is operated by standard PD PWM, it provides nine voltage levels. The switching of the inverter in this case is shown Table I.

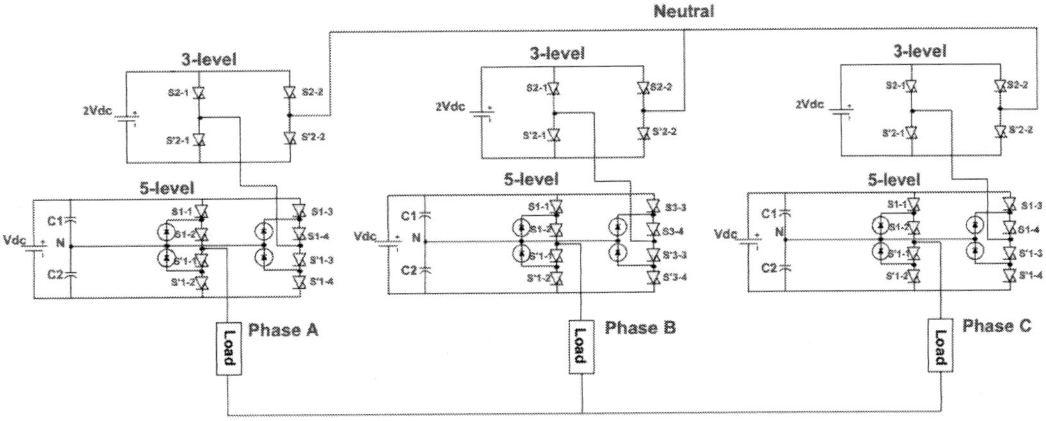

Fig. 1. The cascaded 9-level inverter.

Table 1. The switching states of the cacscaded NPC 9-level inverter when operated by PD PWM.

State	Switch/ voltage	S1-1	S1-2	S1-3	S1-4	S'1-1	S'1-2	S'1-3	S'1-4	S2-1	S2-2	S'2-1	S'2-2
1	0	0	1	0	1	1	0	1	0	1	1	0	0
2	Vdc/2	1	1	0	1	0	0	1	0	1	1	0	0
3	Vdc/2	0	1	0	0	1	0	1	1	1	1	0	0
4	-Vdc/2	0	1	1	1	1	0	0	0	1	1	0	0
5	-Vdc/2	0	0	0	1	1	1	1	0	1	1	0	0
6	Vdc	1	1	0	0	0	0	1	1	1	1	0	0
7	-Vdc	0	0	1	1	1	1	0	0	1	1	0	0
8	2.5Vdc	1	1	0	1	0	0	1	0	1	0	1	0
9	2.5Vdc	0	1	0	0	1	0	1	1	1	0	1	0
10	-2.5Vdc	0	1	1	1	1	0	0	0	0	1	0	1
11	-2.5Vdc	0	0	0	1	1	1	1	0	0	1	0	1
12	3Vdc	1	1	0	0	0	0	1	1	1	0	1	0
13	-3Vdc	0	0	1	1	1	1	0	0	0	1	0	1

3 The proposed Asymmetrical PWM method

This inverter can be operated also at 13-level voltage by application of the proposed asymmetrical PWM.

The proposed asymmetrical PWM method partially uses standard PD PWM method. In the standard PD PWM the comparison is performed separately for each phase of the inverter. The intersection points between the modulation wave and the carrier waves define the duty cycle or the switching instants of the inverter. This approach works excellently when the carrier frequency is much higher than the modulation frequency, e.g., about fifty to one hundred times higher. However, such higher switching frequencies would also yield rather high switching losses. Therefore, continuous efforts are made to lower the carrier frequencies together with raising the number of levels in multi-level inverters. The multi-level inverter of n levels uses n−1 carriers. For example, twelve carrier waves would be used with the present 13-level inverter and they are placed one upon the other. Generally, the carrier frequency is calculated according to:

$$f_{carrier} = 3(2k + 1) \times f_{modulation} \quad (1)$$

where k is a positive integer.

It is recommended that the frequency index be an odd number. Furthermore, the beginning phase between the carrier and the modulation waves should be the same for all the three phases of the inverter. Therefore, the frequency index should be a multiple of three. The proposed asymmetrical 13-level PWM signal is obtained by summing two PWM signals: the 5-level hybrid PWM signal and 3-level pulsed PWM signal. The first 5-level hybrid PWM signal is constructed from combined parts of the standard 5-level PD PWM (see Fig. 2) according to the desired pattern as shown in Fig. 3 (PWM signal for 5-level bridge). The second 3-level pulsed PWM signal is constructed in coordination with the first 5-level hybrid PWM signal is such a manner that the sum of these two PWM signals will be the desired 13-level

PWM (see Fig. 3, PWM signal for 3-level bridge). The desired 13-level PWM signal that is applied to the 9-level inverter is shown in Fig. 4.

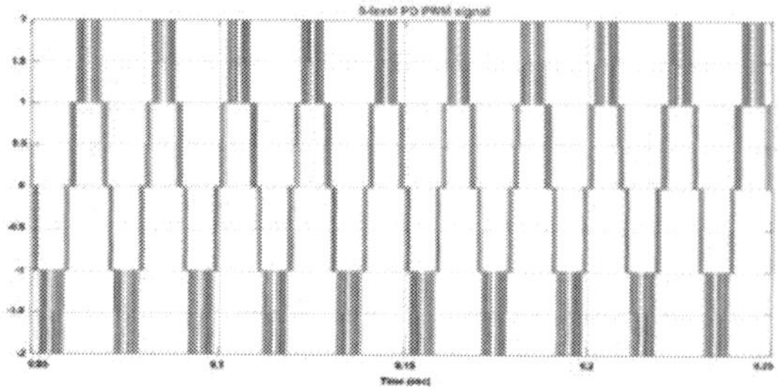

Fig. 2. The standard 5-level PD PWM signal.

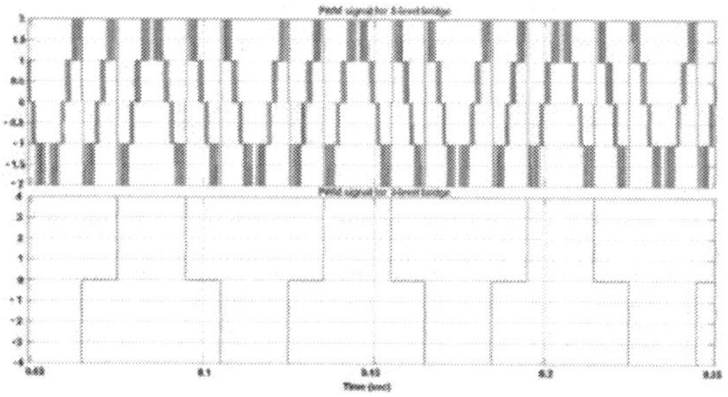

Fig. 3. The standard 5-level PD PWM signal.

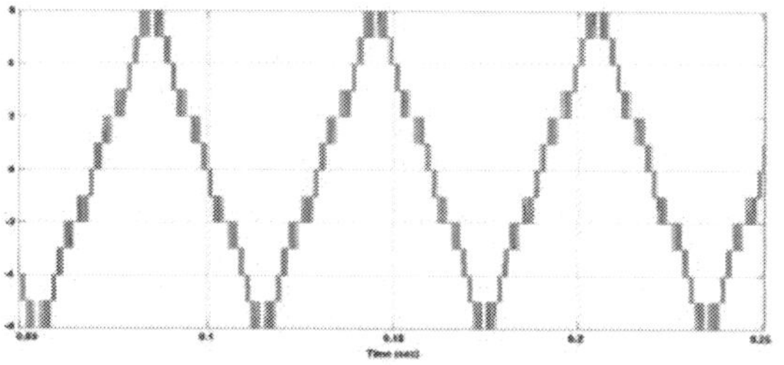

Fig. 4. The obtained 13-level PWM signal.

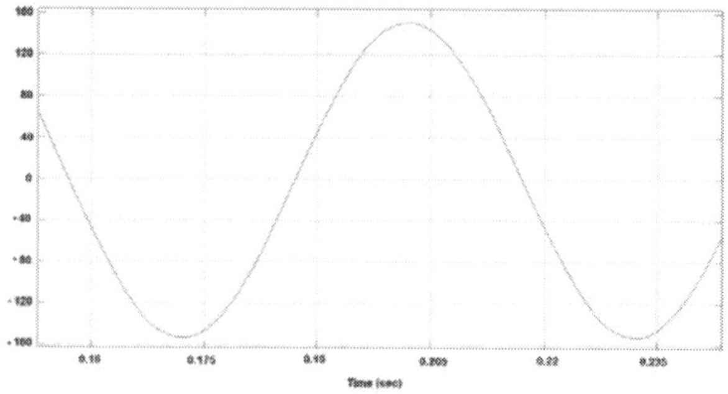

(a) Phase current, THD=0.9%

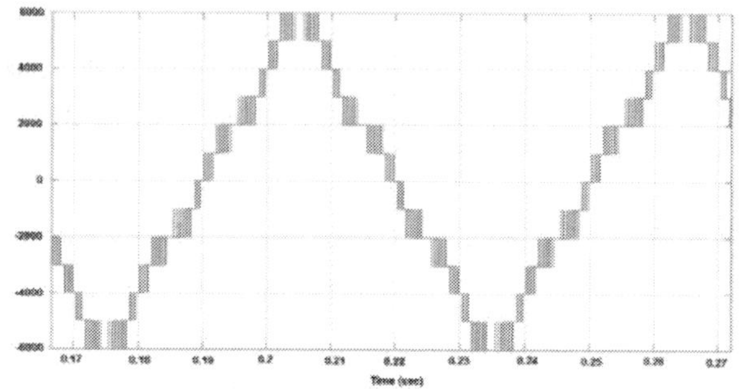

(b) Phase voltage, THD=16%

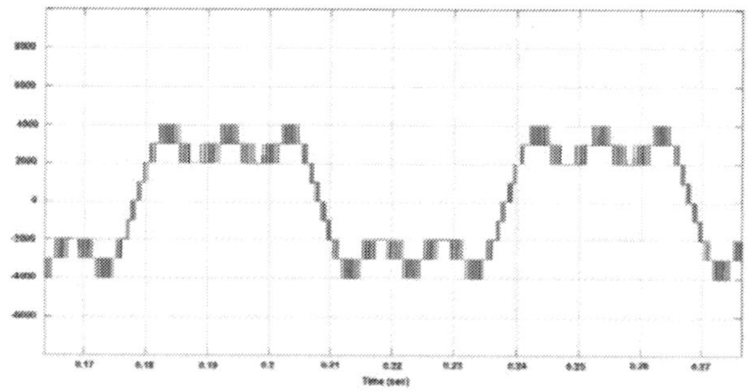

(c) Line voltage, THD=35%.

4 The Simulation results

In order to verify the proposed PWM method, extensive simulations are performed. The simulation parameters are: DC=2000V, DC link capacitors C1=C2=10mF; the load of the inverter per phase are $R = 0.19\ \Omega$, L=0.24H.

During the simulation of this 13-level PWM signal, the modulation frequency was set to 50Hz and the carrier frequency to 2100Hz. The obtained 13-level PWM signal is applied to the presented 9-level inverter. If standard 13-level PD PWM was used, it would require additional cascaded bridge. This would result in additional costs and larger size and weight.

The proposed PWM was also simulated for different modulation indexes. The simulation results are shown in Tables II and III.

Table II. Output voltage and current THD versus the level number. Modulation frequency 50Hz, carrier frequency 1050 Hz, PD PWM

Modulation index	Inverter levels (modulation index)	Phase current THD (%)	Phase volta-ge THD (%)	Line volta-ge THD (%)
1	13-level (1)	0.9	16	35
0.83	11-level (1)	0.8	21	38
0.67	9-level (1)	1	27	44
0.5	7-level (1)	0.95	33	52
0.333	5-level (1)	0.8	47	61
0.167	3-level (1)	0.85	65	78

Table II shows that the decrease in the modulation index influences the number of the voltage levels in the output voltages, e.g., there are thirteen voltage levels in the phase voltage with modulation index 1, but only three voltage levels with modulation index 0.1. As a result, the appearance of the output current and voltage waves changes as well as their spectra and harmonic content and distribution. Regarding the output voltage waves, it is seen that their waves better resemble a sinusoidal wave as the number of levels increases. As a result, their THDs decrease as well.

It can be seen that the proposed PWM method provides good THD results of the currents and voltages. The phase current THDs are below 1% which is in full accordance with IEEE 519 standard. Therefore, the proposed method is practicable and it can be implemented also to other multilevel inverter topologies. This PWM method can be extended to higher number of levels.

5 Conclusions

The paper proposes new asymmetrical PWM that can be applied to different types of multilevel inverters. The proposed 13-level PWM is constructed form the sum of two PWM signals. This PWM method operates 9-level inverter as 13-level inverter. As a result it allows reduction of the operated inverter's components compared to the standard topologies such as neutral point clamped or flying capacitor inverters. This results in smaller size, weight and cists of the inverter. However, the PWM control becomes more complicated compared to the standard PWM methods such as Phase Disposition (PD), Phase Opposition Disposition (POD) and Alternative Phase Opposition Disposition (APOD).

It can be seen that the proposed PWM method provides good THD results of the currents and voltages. The phase current THDs are below 1% which is in full accordance with IEEE 519 standard.

Extensive simulation results validate the practicability of the proposed PWM method. The proposed method can be applied to any desired number of levels.

References

1. H. Abu-Rub, J. Holtz, J. Rodriguez, and G. Baoming, "Medium-Voltage Multi-level Converters - State of the Art, Challenges, and Requirements in Industrial Applications", IEEE Trans. Ind. Electron., vol. 57, no. 8, pp. 2581-2596, 2010.
2. J. Rodríguez, S. Bernet, B. Wu, J. Pontt, and S. Kouro, "Multi-Level Voltage-Source-Converter Topologies for Industrial Medium-Voltage Drives", IEEE Trans. Ind. Electron., vol. 54, no. 6, pp. 2930-2945, 2007.
3. Krug D., Bernet S., Fazel SS, Jalili K, Malinowski M., "Comparison of 2.3-kV medium-voltage multilevel converters for industrial medium-voltage drives", IEEE Trans. Ind. Electron., pp. 2979–2992, 2007.
4. Baimel D., Rabinovici R. and S. Tapuchi, "Hybrid thirteen level cascaded H-bridge inverter", Springer Electrical Engineering, DOI 10.1007/s00202-015-0356-z, 2015.
5. J. Rodriguez, S. Bernet, P. K. Steimer, I. E. Lizama, "A Survey on Neutral Point Clamped Inverters", IEEE Trans. Ind. Electron., vol. 57, no. 7, pp. 2219-2230, 2010.
6. J. Ewanchuk, J. Salmon, B. Vafakhah, "A Five/Nine Level Twelve Switch Neutral Point Clamped Inverter for High Speed Electric Drives", IEEE Trans. Ind. Appl., vol. 4, no. 4, pp. 384-392, 2011.
7. B. Vafakhah, J. Ewanchuk, J. Salmon, "Multicarrier Interleaved PWM Strategies for a Five Level NPC Inverter Using a Three Phase Coupled Inductor", IEEE Trans. Ind. Appl., vol. 47, no. 6, pp. 2549-2558, 2011.
8. Z. Rech, C. Pinheiro, "Comparison of Neutral-Point-Clamped, Symmetrical, and Hybrid Asymmetrical Multilevel Inverters', IEEE Trans. on Ind. Electron., vol. 57, pp. 2297-2306, 2010.
9. M. Malinowski, K. Gopakumar, J. Rodriguez, M. Pérez., "A Survey on Cascaded Multilevel Inverters", IEEE Trans Ind. Electron., vol. 57, no.7, pp. 2197-2206, 2010.
10. G. Waltrich, I. Barbi, "Three Phase Cascaded Multilevel Inverter Using Power Cells With Two Inverter Legs in Series', IEEE Trans. Ind. Electron., vol. 57, no. 8, pp. 2605-2612, 2010.
11. P. Cortés, A. Wilson, S. Kouro, J. Rodriguez, H. Abu-Rub, "Model Predictive Control of Multilevel Cascaded H-bridge Inverters", IEEE Trans. on Ind. Electron., vol. 57, no, 8, pp. 2691-2699, 2010.
12. D. Holmes, T. Lipo, "Carrier Based PWM of Multilevel Inverters", Pulse Width Modulation of Power Converter Principles and Practice EBook, ch. 11, pp. 453-530, 2003.
13. A. Radan, A. H. Shahirinia, M. Falahi, "Evaluation of Carrier Based PWM Methods for Multilevel Inverters", IEEE International Symposium on Industrial Electronics, pp. 389-394, 2007.
14. F. B. Grigoletto, H. Pinheiro, "Generalized Pulse Width Modulation Approach for DC Capacitor Voltage Balancing in Diode-Clamped Multilevel Converters', IET Power Electron., vol. 4, no. 1, pp. 89-100, 2011.
15. B. Cougo, G. Gateau, T. Meynard, M. Bobrowska-Rafal, M. Cousineau, "PD Modulation Scheme for Three Phase Parallel Multilevel Inverters", IEEE Trans. Ind. Electron., vol. 59, no. 2, pp. 941-949, 2012.
16. Rabinovici, R. , Baimel, D. , Tomasik, J. , Zuckerberger, A., "Series space vector modulation for multi-level cascaded H-bridge inverters", IET Power Electronics, Vol. 3, Issue 6, pp. 843-857, 2010.

Home automation and simulation of presence in empty environments

Israel Marques[1*], *Paulo* Garcia[1]

[1]Mackenzie Presbyterian University, Electrical Engineering Department, 01302-907 Rua da Consolação 940, São Paulo-SP, Brazil

Abstract. Since their humble beginnings at the dawn of the 20th Century until contemporary age, automation and control systems have grown exponentially in both complexity and importance. Its relevance on human activities, be they mundane tasks or crucial processes, is self-evident. Among its many utilities, automated systems acquire a noble mission when put in service to protect life and property from aggressors of any kind. This paper discusses how home automation components can be utilized to implement an alternative domestic security strategy that consists in simulating the presence of an individual in an empty environment in the absence of its owner in order dissuade potential trespassing criminals, once they would feel highly discouraged to carry the criminal act should they believe the property is occupied.

1 Introduction

1.1 Origins of automation

Oxford Dictionaries defines automation as "The use or introduction of automatic equipment in a manufacturing or other process or facility" [1]. Hence, the main advantage brought by the employment of automated systems lies in the fact that the machines which compose them possess the capability of verifying their own performance and correct processes' missteps without human intervention, in the large majority of cases. Given such scenario, pre-programmed and self-correcting machines can complete their tasks at a much faster rate when compared with manual or non-automated labor.

Earlier occurrences of automated devices include the invention of float-valves to regulate liquid flow in oil-lamps, wine dispensers and water tanks in primal Greek and Arabic communities, as well as the fabrication of the Ktesibios water-clock in ancient Alexandria [2]. Greek temples from the Hellenistic period employed self-animated mechanical devices denominated as "automata" shaped like humans and animals as part of their liturgical activities [2]. By the 17th Century, Cornelis Drebbel conceived a closed loop control system to operate a furnace, thus creating an archaic thermostat [2].

The first instance of an automatized process in an industrial environment retraces to the late 1920s when Toyota Industries founder, Sakichi Toyoda developed a weaving machine capable of identifying mechanical malfunctions and cease its operation until the problem was solved, thus giving birth to toyotism and inaugurating the era of the "third Industrial Revolution" [3]. Since then, the world witnessed an expansion in the use of automated systems that are no longer restrict to factories' production lines but span through multiple commercial, governmental, academic, agricultural, medical and domestic applications [4-9].

1.2 Automation as security tool

It is an unfortunate fact that densely-populated human societies will invariably be confronted with acts of delinquency perpetrated by criminals, in higher or lowers degrees. However, the use of automated systems as allies of security can help attenuate the lethality and losses brought by criminal acts. Recent security innovations present in the domestic security automation industry include, among many others, smart locks that can be opened via smartphone, wireless video monitoring cameras that can be remotely accessed by the user, sensors kits that are able to notify the owner of invasions or domestic accidents, communication systems that notify constabulary authorities of invasions and criminal acts and even special sensors and devices that cater to specific pet necessities, all these allied with digital displays that give the proprietor complete control over home appliances and security devices in operation. [10,11].

It is noteworthy to mention that advanced home security systems are often expensive and complex. This paper presents an alternative strategy for implementing a system that uses simple home appliances devices whose operation is coordinated by a Programmable Logic Controller (PLC) that will activate appliances at arbitrary times in order to simulate the presence of the owner in an empty residential environment.

* Corresponding author: israel.avansi@gmail.com

DOI: 10.1051/matecconf/201712502007

1.3 Simulation of presence

Professionals from insurance and home protection markets warn and agree that the probability of home invasion occurrences grow a significant lot in vacation periods when families travel and temporarily leave their residences unoccupied, stimulating intruders to carry criminal acts such as invasion and theft. In a Brazilian context, Diuri explains that the number of home theft incidents increases about 30% at the beginning of the year, mostly from December to January, when school vacation time arrives and families start their touristic voyages [12]. In the same context, Davini addresses the fact that lawbreakers are often looking for situations where they can minimize their risks to conduct illegal acts with minimum effort, thus vacant residences present an easy and temptating target [13].

With the knowledge that the invasion of an occupied property is generally declined by delinquents, it is patent that simulating the presence of individuals in an empty residential environment holds the potential to decrease the probabilities of the same occurs. Silva, Campos and Lima Filho argue there is a new trend among automation developers that involves mastering the control of electro-electronic appliances in pre-programmed dates during temporal lengths can be used as a tool to increase the security of a precinct, and such systems would have the function of simulating the presence of people in the said precinct to strengthen the security of an environment [14]. The following section will describe the authors' proposed presence simulation system as well as its implementation and the details on how the components interact with each other.

2 Proposed System

2.1 System components

The automated system was envisioned as a set of electro-electronic appliances wirelessly connected through Xbee modules to a Raspberry Pi 2 single-board computer. The said appliances include one incandescent light bulb, one audio speaker connected to an Arduino Uno R3 board to play .mp3 audio files and a motion sensor to alert the user of possible trespasses. A schematic diagram of the components is shown in Figure 1. A comprehensive list of all components employed in the construction of the system follows:

- 1 Raspberry Pi 2 board;
- 4 Xbee modules;
- 1 Arduino Uno R3 board;
- 1 Arduino Mini board;
- 1 Adafruit Music Maker Arduino MP3 shield;
- 1 2GB microSD card;
- 4 Xbee modules;
- 1 Protoboard;
- 1 audio speaker;
- 1 audio amplifier;
- 1 relay switch;
- 1 incandescent light bulb;
- 1 motion sensor;
- 2 9V batteries;
- 1 Android smartphone;
- 2 medium-sized hard plastic cases;

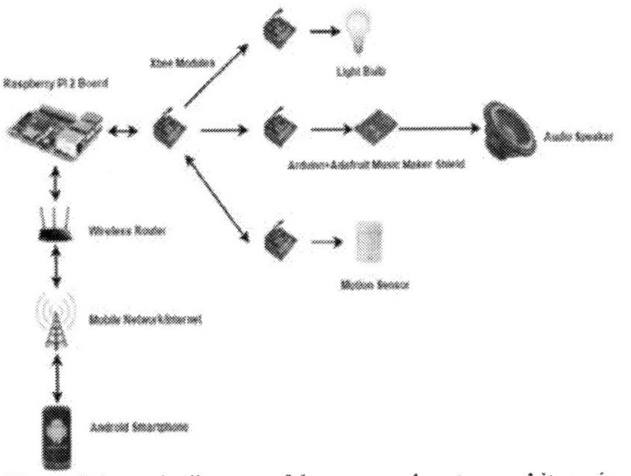

Fig. 1. Schematic diagram of the proposed system and its main components. Black arrows indicate the direction of the information traffic.

2.2 Implementation & Details

2.2.1 User Interface

The Android smartphone functions as the interface between the user and the Raspberry Pi 2 board. Through an app developed in MIT AppInventor website, all operations of the system can be controlled by pressing the buttons with the icons that represent the functions they will activate. When the buttons are pressed, the smartphone communicates with the Raspberry Pi 2 board, which in turn will then activate the components via Xbee wireless communication. The functions present in the app are: turning the light bulb on/off, activating the music player (with play/stop/pause and forward/backward buttons), activating the motion sensor (it will notify the user when it detects an intruder) and starting "simulation mode", where the user inputs an initial and final time during which the presence simulation will take place (the light bulb will be on and the Arduino R3 board will start a playlist of songs that will be heard through the speaker). A capture of the interface's initial screen can be seen in Figure 2.

2.2.2 Light Bulb

The light bulb is connected to an electric relay switch which in turn is connected to the Xbee module. As soon as the user press the light bulb icon on the app, the Raspberry Pi 2 board will send a wireless signal to the receiving Xbee module connecting to the lamp, opening the relay switch thus letting the current from the energy grid flow into the lamp, turning it on. When the button is pressed again, the same communication occurs but the relay switch will interrupt the current and the lamp turn off instead.

Fig. 2. Capture of the app's initial screen. From top to bottom, left to right: the title: "Security System", the light bulb activation button, the music player icon, the alarm activation button, which reads: "Alarm System Deactivated", an IP camera button for future system expansions, the icon for programming the initial and final moments of the simulation of presence and a last tile with information that reads: "Beginning", "End", "Time", "Activate Vibration".

2.2.3 Music Player

The music player of the proposed system was envisioned as an Arduino UNO R3 board that is connected to a speaker and plays .mp3 files through an Adafruit Music Maker Arduino shield. The music files are stored in a 2GB microSD card. The Arduino board is connected to a Xbee module that will receive signals coming from the Raspberry Pi 2 board. When the user press the buttons of the music player icon as well as its functions (play, pause, forward, et cetera) on the app, the Raspberry Pi 2 board will send signals to the receiving Xbee module connected to the Arduino board which is programmed to execute the music player functions according to the signals received.

The signals arrive in the receiving Xbee module as 3-bit packets that will be interpreted by the Arduino board, each combination of bits corresponding to one different operation mode. These include: the previously mentioned "simulation mode", where the Arduino board will command the Adafruit Music Maker shield to execute all of the .mp3 files in a row, the "music player mode", where the Arduino board will be set to read the bit packets as codes for the buttons being pressed (play, stop, pause, forward and backward buttons) and the "intimidation mode", where the music player starts executing a fearsome audio file in order to demoralize the trespasser in case an invasion actually takes place. "Intimidation mode" shall be further explained in the next subsection.

Due to the low values of current coming out from the TRS audio jack present in the Adafruit Music Maker Arduino shield, it is unwise to connect it directly to the speaker, once the signal amplitude would be too low to produce audible sounds. Therefore, an audio amplifier was included between the Adafruit shield and the speaker to boost the audio signals.

2.2.4 Motion Sensor

Likewise connected to the Raspberry Pi 2 board via Xbee module, one motion sensor was added to the system so it can detect the presence of incoming invaders. If the motion sensor icon is pressed by the operator on the app start screen, it will activate the sensor and its function: should the simulation fail to reach its purpose and the criminal individual decide to persist with the intrusion, the motion will send a signal to the Raspberry board once it detects movement. Raspberry will, in turn, send a message to the user's smartphone through an internet connection notifying him/her that an invasion is taking place. It will also force the system to go into "Intimidation mode", in which all activities of presence simulation or music reproduction are interrupted so a loud and frightful audio file can be executed. This is a last resort to alert nearby neighbours that the property is being invaded as well as to make the lawbreaker realize that his presence has been noticed.

2.2.5 Further System Technicalities

The programming software utilized in the coding of the Raspberry Pi 2 board was Python IDLE 2.0, with Python as the programming language. The software used for compilating the Arduino codes was Arduino IDE, which uses a variant of C/C++ for its functions. The Android smartphone application was developed through an open-source code from MIT AppInventor website [15].

An Arduino Mini board was added between the motion sensor and its respective Xbee module to avoid complications regarding frame multiprocessing given that "Intimidation mode" requires constant communication between the sensor and the Raspberry board.

A hard-plastic case and 9 V batteries were used to encapsulate the motion sensor and provide it with electricity. The Arduino UNO R3 board, which acted as the music player, was also encased and was powered by the common electric grid.

The Xbee modules follow a mesh network topology and have a sensitivity of -102 dBm, therefore the components attached to the Xbee can be spaced apart up to 90 meters (considering no obstacles) from the Raspberry Pi 2 board, which acts as the system's PLC. There is, naturally, a delay time between the pressing of the icons on the smartphone app and the execution of the said function, which amounts to approximately 1 or 2 seconds, depending on the selected icon.

3 Conclusion

The contribution that advances in automation, fuelled by the pursuit of new ways to increase productivity, brought to all spheres of mankind's lifestyle is undeniable. This paper, focus on one of automation's many fields that experience ongoing expansion: residential security.

As unfortunate as the reality of property breaching might be, there are many devices and systems that are capable to mitigate the number of criminal invasions. This is a niche that has acquired significant relevance and manufacturers' attention, particularly in developing countries that often face challenges like burglary and property vandalism [16]. Thus, creative ways of dealing with the aforementioned issues emerge as an answer to attend necessities of home protection and monitoring.

The system presented on this paper was designed, tested and assembled in Mackenzie Presbyterian University's facilities by the authors as a Course Conclusion Work and functioned exactly as described. The modular nature of the proposed system allows it to be expanded by adding more components (those include but are not limited to temperature sensors, gas sensors, glass break detectors, IP cameras, et cetera) to be controlled by the Raspberry Pi 2 board via Xbee connection in order to improve monitoring, if the consumer so desires. For future developments, functionality such as contacting the city's police department once criminal activity is detected is greatly recommended.

In sum, this paper has presented the construction an automated system that explores psychological warfare against criminal intruders and holds the potential to reduce home trespassing in empty environments by making use of presence simulation, deceiving lawbreakers in a non-confrontational, nonviolent fashion.

References

1. automation - definition of automation in English, *Ox.* Dict. https://en.oxforddictionaries.com/definition/automation (2017)
2. E. Hayden, M. Assante, T. Conway, An Abbreviated History of Automation & Industrial Controls Systems and Cybersecurity, A S. Anal. White. 8-9. https://ics.sans.org/media/An-Abbreviated-History-of-Automation-and-ICS-Cybersecurity.pdf (2014)
3. G. B. da Luz, D. L. Kuiawinski, Mecanização, Autonomação e Automação – Uma Revisão Conceitual e Crítica, Simp. de Eng. de Prod., 1-2. http://www.simpep.feb.unesp.br/anais/anais_13/artigos/1210.pdf (2006)
4. C. S. Filho, A Automação nos anos 2000 : Uma Análise das Novas Fronteiras da Automação, Congr. e Expo. Int. de Auto., 1-7. (2000)
5. A. Accorsi, Automação bancária e seus impactos: o caso brasileiro, Rev. de Admin. **27**, 39-46. (1992)
6. C. Magalhães, J. L. C. Dos Santos, J. I. Salém, Modelos e cenários para a Amazônia: o papel da ciência: Automação de coleções biológicas e informações sobre a biodiversidade da Amazônia, Par. Estr. **12**, 294-312. (2001)
7. J. V. L. Botega, R. A. Braga Jr., M. A. Lopes, G. F. Rabelo, Diagnóstico da Automação na Produção Leiteira, Ciên. e Agrotec., **32**, 635-639. URL: http://www.scielo.br/pdf/cagro/v32n2/45.pdf (2008)
8. R. M. Braz, V. L. Andreozzi, P. L. Kale, Detecção precoce de epidemias de malária no Brasil: uma proposta de automação, Epidemiol. Serv. Saúde **15**, (2006)
9. C. L. A. Dias, N. D. Pizzolato, Domótica: Aplicabilidade e Sistemas de Automação Residencial, Vért. **6**, 10-32. http://essentiaeditora.iff.edu.br/index.php/vertices/article/viewFile/1809-2667.20040015/86 (2004)
10. C. McCormack, The 50 Best Smart Home Security Systems, https://www.safety.com/blog/50-best-smart-home-security-products/ (2016)
11. Honeywell: Security for Your Home and Family, Home Security, http://homesecurity.honeywell.com/home_security.html#pets (2017)
12. L. Diuri, Férias sem preocupações, Allianz, https://www.allianz.com.br/-/azb-na-ferias-sem-preocupacoes (2016)
13. L. R. Davini, A importância de sistemas de segurança residencial e ação policial, Interview granted to the authors of this paper (2015)
14. T. D. Da Silva, A. L. P. S. Campos, F. S. De Lima Filho, Sistemas de Simulação de Presença Residencial, Hol., 130-140. http://www2.ifrn.edu.br/ojs/index.php/HOLOS/article/download/308/313 (2010)
15. MIT App Inventor, *Explore MIT App Inventor*. http://appinventor.mit.edu/explore/ (2016)
16. A. Farias, Os quinze bairros campeões de roubos e furtos a residências, *V. S. Paulo*. http://vejasp.abril.com.br/cidades/confira-os-15-bairros-com-mais-roubos-e-furtos-a-residencias/ (2016)

The continuous-time H_∞ model matching problem with integral control in lmi optimization

Murat Akın[1] and *Tankut* Acarman[1,*]

[1]Galatasaray University, Department of Computer Engineering, 34349, Ortaköy, İstanbul, Turkey

Abstract. In this paper, the continuous-time H_∞ model matching problem with integral control by using 2 DOF static output feedback is presented. The controller synthesis theorem and the controller design algorithm is elaborated. Simulation study illustrates the effectiveness and usability of the presented controller design.

1 Introduction

The model matching problem has attracted a lot of attention in the control theory [13-14]. If $G_m(s)$ and $G(s)$ are the model and the system matrices, respectively, the continuous-time H_∞ model matching problem (MMP) is introduced to derive a controller transfer matrix R(s) that minimizes the H_∞ norm of $G_m(s)$-$G(s)R(s)$. The model transfer matrix $G_m(s)$ has the desired performance specifications defined by its poles and zeros. Moreover, $G_m(s)$ and $G(s)R(s)$ are stable and proper transfer matrices, that is $G_m(s)$ and $G(s)R(s) \in RH_\infty$. The closed-loop performance G(s)R(s) is considered to be approximated by the desired performance $G_m(s)$ such that,

$$\gamma_{opt} = \inf_{R(s)\in RH_\infty} \left\| G_m(s) - G(s)R(s) \right\|_\infty . \qquad (1)$$

H_∞ MMP is elaborated in [5, 8, 9]. In these studies, the dynamic precompansator R(s) is obtained and then it is implemented by dynamic state feedback, [13]. Formerly, continuous-time H_∞ MMP with one degree of freedom (1 DOF) static state feedback is derived in [1], the discrete-time H_∞ MMP with 1 DOF static output feedback and the continuous-time H_∞ MMP with 2 DOF static output feedback is presented in [2-3], respectively. On the other hand, the integral control structure subject to the existence of state feedback is firstly used in [4].

In this paper, the continuous-time H_∞ MMP with integral control is proposed by using a 2 DOF static output feedback. Both the solution of the continuous-time static H_∞ optimal control problem (OCP) and continuous-time H_∞ MMP is revisited toward the solution of our presented problem, whereas continuous-time H_∞ MMP can be completely solved by the LMI-based numerical optimization.

This paper is organized as follows: In Section 2, a special formulation for the continuous-time H_∞ MMP by a 2 DOF static output feedback with integral control in linear matrix inequalities (LMIs) is elaborated. In Section 3, the main result is given by a theorem that provides two existence conditions of the solution. In Section 4, we construct the 2 DOF static output feedback with integral control by using this theorem. A numerical system example and some conclusions are finally given in Section 5 and 6, respectively.

Notations

R	The set of real numbers.
C	The set of complex numbers.
R^{nxm}	The set of nxm real matrices.
Re(α)	The real part of $\alpha \in C$.
L_∞	The functions bounded on Re(s)=0 including at ∞.
H_∞	The set of L_∞ functions analytic in Re(s)>0.
I_n	An identy matrix of nxn dimension.
0_n	A zero matrix of nxn dimension.
0_{nxm}	A zero matrix of nxm dimension.
KerM	The kernel space the linear operator M.
ImM	The image space of the linear operator M.
N^T	The tranpose of the matrix N.
P>0	P positive definite matrix.
dim(U)	The dimension of the linear space U.
$\lambda_{max}(A)$	The largest eigenvalue of the matrix A.
$\sigma_{max}(A)$	The largest singular value of the matrix A defined as $$\sigma_{\max}(A) = \sqrt{\lambda_{\max}(A^T A)}.$$
$\|G(s)\|_\infty$	The norm of the transfer matrix G(s) defined as $$\| G(s) \|_\infty = \sup_{\omega \in R} \sigma_{\max}\left[G(j\omega)\right].$$

In order to present a synthesis theorem on the LMI-based characterization of the continuous-time H_∞ model

* Corresponding author: tacarman@gsu.edu.tr

matching problem with integral control, the following lemmas are given. The first lemma is **The Bounded Real Lemma** and it is used to turn the continuous-time H_∞ optimal control problem into an linear matrix inequality (LMI):

Lemma 1.1 Consider a continuous-time transfer matrix T(s) of (not necessarily minimal) realization $T(s)=D+C(sI-A)^{-1}B$. The following statements are equivalent:

i) $\|T(s)=D+C(sI-A)^{-1}B\|_\infty<\gamma$ and the matrix A is Schur ($Re(\lambda_i(A))<0$, i=1,…,n).

ii) There is a solution X>0 to the LMI:

$$\begin{bmatrix} A^TX+XA & XB & C^T \\ B^TX & -\gamma I & D^T \\ C & D & -\gamma I \end{bmatrix}<0. \quad (2)$$

Proof: See [7]. ■

Lemma 1.2 Suppose P, Q and H are matrices and that H is symmetric. The matrices N_P and N_Q are full rank matrices satifying $ImN_P=KerP$ and $ImNQ=KerQ$. Then there is a matrix J such that,

$$H+P^TJ^TQ+Q^TJP<0 \quad (3)$$

if and only is the inequalities

$$N_P{}^THN_P<0 \quad \text{and} \quad N_Q{}^THN_Q<0 \quad (4)$$

are both satisfied.

Proof: See [10]. ■

Lemma 1.3 The block matrix

$$\begin{bmatrix} P & M \\ M^T & N \end{bmatrix}<0 \quad (5)$$

if and only if

$$N<0 \quad \text{and} \quad P-MN^{-1}M^T<0 \quad (6)$$

In the sequel, $P-MN^{-1}M^T$ is referred to as the **Schur complement** of N.

Proof: See [6]. ■

2 The continuous-time H∞ mmp by 2 dof static output feedback with integral control in lmi optimization

Toward the solution of the continous-time H_∞ MMP via LMI approach, the problem should be reformulated as standard continuous-time H_∞ OCP. The state-space representation of the system G(s) and the model system $G_m(s)$ is given:

$$G(s): \begin{cases} \dfrac{dx(t)}{dt}=Ax(t)+Bv(t) & (7) \\ y_S(t)=Cx(t) & (8) \end{cases}$$

$$G_m(s): \begin{cases} \dfrac{dq(t)}{dt}=Fq(t)+Gw(t) & (9) \\ y_m(t)=Hq(t)+Jw(t) & (10) \end{cases}$$

where $x(t)\in R^n$ is the system state, $q(t)\in R^{n_m}$ is the model state, v(t), w(t), $y_s(t)$ and $y_m(t)\in R^m$. We take that the given system is strictly proper in order to simplify the solution of the problem. The integral control is modelled by a serie integrator:

$$\frac{d\hat{x}(t)}{dt}=w(t)-y_S(t) \quad (11)$$

$$v(t)=\hat{x}(t)+u(t) \quad (12)$$

where $\hat{x}(t)$ and $u(t)\in R^m$. The control input u(t) is generated by a two degrees of freedom static output feedback controller:

$$u(t)=Ly_s(t)+Mw(t)=\begin{bmatrix} L & M \end{bmatrix}\begin{bmatrix} y_S(t) \\ w(t) \end{bmatrix}. \quad (13)$$

The block diagram of a continuous-time H_∞ MMP by a static output feedback with integral control is illustrated in Figure 1. In this formulation, the steady-output value $y_s(t)$ will follow a step function input with zero error. We will use a 2 DOF feedback control structure which is defined in the control theory, [12]:

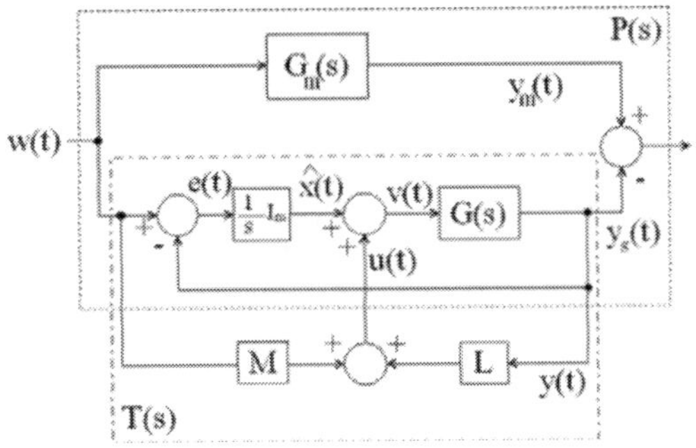

Fig. 1. The block diagram of model matching system with 2 DOF static output feedback in the integral control.

The generalized plant P(s) shown in Figure 1 can be modelled as,

$$\frac{d}{dt}\begin{bmatrix} x(t) \\ \hat{x}(t) \\ q(t) \end{bmatrix} = \begin{bmatrix} A & B & 0 \\ -C & 0 & 0 \\ 0 & 0 & F \end{bmatrix}\begin{bmatrix} x(t) \\ \hat{x}(t) \\ q(t) \end{bmatrix} + \begin{bmatrix} 0 \\ I \\ G \end{bmatrix} w(t) + \begin{bmatrix} B \\ 0 \\ 0 \end{bmatrix} u(t) \tag{14}$$

$$z(t) = \begin{bmatrix} -C & 0 & H \end{bmatrix}\begin{bmatrix} x(t) \\ \hat{x}(t) \\ q(t) \end{bmatrix} + Jw(t) \tag{15}$$

$$y(t) = \begin{bmatrix} y_S(t) \\ w(t) \end{bmatrix} = \begin{bmatrix} C & 0 & 0 \\ 0 & 0 & 0 \end{bmatrix}\begin{bmatrix} x(t) \\ \hat{x}(t) \\ q(t) \end{bmatrix} + \begin{bmatrix} 0 \\ I \end{bmatrix} w(t). \tag{16}$$

Matrices are defined as follows :

$$\underline{A} = \begin{bmatrix} A & B & 0 \\ -C & 0 & 0 \\ 0 & 0 & F \end{bmatrix} \qquad B_1 = \begin{bmatrix} 0 \\ I \\ G \end{bmatrix} \qquad B_2 = \begin{bmatrix} B \\ 0 \\ 0 \end{bmatrix} \tag{17}$$

$$C_1 = \begin{bmatrix} -C & 0 & H \end{bmatrix} \qquad C_2 = \begin{bmatrix} C & 0 & 0 \\ 0 & 0 & 0 \end{bmatrix} \tag{18}$$

$$D_1 = J \qquad D_2 = \begin{bmatrix} 0 \\ I \end{bmatrix}. \tag{19}$$

The above formulation concludes that the continuous-time H_∞ model matching problem plus integral control with the two degrees of freedom static output feedback is equivalent to the continuous-time H_∞ optimal control problem. This equivalency is drawn in Figure 2:

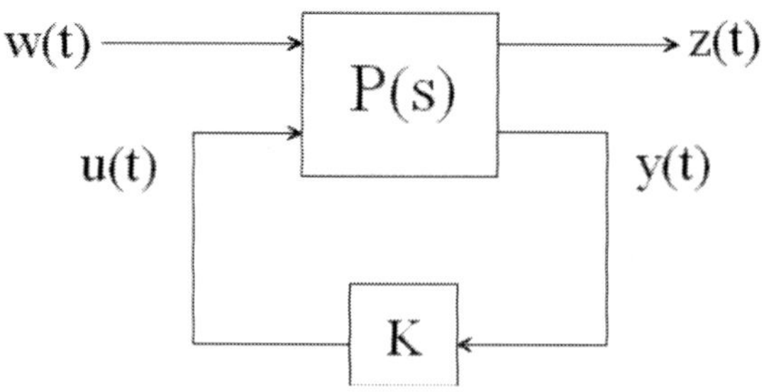

Fig. 2. The block diagram of the general form of H_∞ OCP with a static controller.

The closed-loop transfer matrix from w(t) to z(t) is derived by

$$T_{zw}(z) = D_{cl} + C_{cl}(zI - A_{cl})^{-1}B_{cl} \tag{20}$$

where

$$A_{cl} = \underline{A} + B_2KC_2 \tag{21}$$

$$B_{cl} = B_1 + B_2KD_2 \tag{22}$$

$$C_{cl} = C_1 \tag{23}$$

$$D_{cl} = D_1. \tag{24}$$

A synthesis theorem on the LMI-based solution of the problem is presented in the following section.

3 Main result

We can now present a synthesis theorem on the LMI-based solution of the continuous-time H_∞ model matching problem with integral control by two degrees of freedom static output feedback:

Theorem 3.1 A 2 DOF static output feedback plus integral controller $[L \;\; M] \in R^{mx2m}$ exists for the continuous-time H_∞ MMP if and only if there is a matrix X>0 such that,

$$\begin{bmatrix} N_o & 0 & 0 \\ 0 & I_m & 0 \\ 0 & 0 & I_{n_m} \end{bmatrix}^T \left\{ \begin{bmatrix} A & B & 0 \\ -C & 0 & 0 \\ 0 & 0 & F \end{bmatrix}^T X + X\begin{bmatrix} A & B & 0 \\ -C & 0 & 0 \\ 0 & 0 & F \end{bmatrix} + \frac{1}{\gamma}\begin{bmatrix} C^TC & 0 & -C^TH \\ 0 & 0 & 0 \\ -H^TC & 0 & H^TH \end{bmatrix} \right\} \begin{bmatrix} N_o & 0 & 0 \\ 0 & I_m & 0 \\ 0 & 0 & I_{n_m} \end{bmatrix} < 0 \tag{25}$$

$$\begin{bmatrix} \begin{pmatrix} N_c & 0 & 0 \\ 0 & I_m & 0 \\ 0 & 0 & I_{n_m} \end{pmatrix} & 0 & 0 \\ 0 & I_m & 0 \\ 0 & 0 & I_m \end{bmatrix}^T \begin{bmatrix} \begin{pmatrix} A & B & 0 \\ -C & 0 & 0 \\ 0 & 0 & F \end{pmatrix} X^{-1} + X^{-1}\begin{pmatrix} A & B & 0 \\ -C & 0 & 0 \\ 0 & 0 & F \end{pmatrix}^T & X^{-1}\begin{pmatrix} -C^T \\ 0_m \\ H^T \end{pmatrix} & \begin{pmatrix} 0_{n,xm} \\ I_m \\ G \end{pmatrix} \\ \begin{pmatrix} -C & 0_m & H \end{pmatrix} X^{-1} & -\gamma I_m & J \\ \begin{pmatrix} 0_{mxn_s} & I_m & G^T \end{pmatrix} & J^T & -\gamma I_m \end{bmatrix} \begin{bmatrix} \begin{pmatrix} N_c & 0 & 0 \\ 0 & I_m & 0 \\ 0 & 0 & I_{n_m} \end{pmatrix} & 0 & 0 \\ 0 & I_m & 0 \\ 0 & 0 & I_m \end{bmatrix} < 0 \tag{26}$$

where N_c and N_o are full rank matrices with

$$ImN_c = KerB^T \tag{27}$$

$$ImN_o = KerC. \tag{28}$$

Proof: From the Bounded Real Lemma, $K = [L \;\; M] \in R^{mx2m}$ is the two degrees of freedom static output feedback controller in Figure 2 if and only if the LMI

$$\begin{bmatrix} A_{cl}^TX + XA_{cl} & XB_{cl} & C_{cl}^T \\ B_{cl}^TX & -\gamma I & D_{cl}^T \\ C_{cl} & D_{cl} & -\gamma I \end{bmatrix} < 0 \tag{29}$$

holds for some X>0 in $R^{(ns+nm+m)x(ns+nm+m)}$. Using the expressions A_{cl}, B_{cl}, C_{cl} and D_{cl} in (21), (22), (23) and (24), this LMI can also be written as,

$$H_X+Q^TK^TP_X+P_X^TKQ<0 \qquad (30)$$

where

$$P_X=\begin{bmatrix}B_2^TX & 0 & 0\end{bmatrix} \qquad (31)$$

$$Q=\begin{bmatrix}C_2 & D_2 & 0\end{bmatrix} \qquad (32)$$

$$H_X=\begin{bmatrix}\underline{A}^TX+X\underline{A} & XB_1 & C_1^T\\ B_1^TX & -\gamma I & D_1^T\\ C_1 & D_1 & -\gamma I\end{bmatrix}. \qquad (33)$$

Lemma 1.2 eliminates the matrix K in (30). Hence, the linear matrix inequality (30) holds for some K if and only if

$$N_{Px}^TH_XN_{Px}<0 \quad \text{and} \quad N_Q^TH_XN_Q<0 \qquad (34)$$

where

$$ImN_{Px}=KerP_X \qquad (35)$$

$$ImN_Q=KerQ \qquad (36)$$

$$X>0. \qquad (37)$$

Since

$$P_X=\begin{bmatrix}B_2^TX & 0 & 0\end{bmatrix}=\begin{bmatrix}(B & 0 & 0)X & 0 & 0\end{bmatrix} \qquad (38)$$

we can write

$$P_X=P\begin{bmatrix}X & 0 & 0\\ 0 & I & 0\\ 0 & 0 & I\end{bmatrix} \qquad (39)$$

and

$$P=\begin{bmatrix}B^T & 0 & 0\end{bmatrix}. \qquad (40)$$

We can take

$$N_{P_X}=\begin{bmatrix}X^{-1} & 0 & 0\\ 0 & I & 0\\ 0 & 0 & I\end{bmatrix}N_P. \qquad (41)$$

Consequently,

$$N_{Px}^TH_XN_{Px}<0 \qquad (42)$$

is equivalent to

$$N_P^T\left\{\begin{bmatrix}X^{-1} & 0 & 0\\ 0 & I & 0\\ 0 & 0 & I\end{bmatrix}\begin{bmatrix}\underline{A}^TX+X\underline{A} & XB_1 & C_1^T\\ B_1^TX & -\gamma I & D_1^T\\ C_1 & D_1 & -\gamma I\end{bmatrix}\begin{bmatrix}X^{-1} & 0 & 0\\ 0 & I & 0\\ 0 & 0 & I\end{bmatrix}\right\}N_P<0 \qquad (43)$$

or

$$N_P^TT_XN_P<0 \qquad (44)$$

where

$$T_X=\begin{bmatrix}\underline{A}^TX^{-1}+X^{-1}\underline{A} & B_1 & X^{-1}C_1^T\\ B_1^T & -\gamma I & D_1^T\\ C_1X^{-1} & D_1 & -\gamma I\end{bmatrix}. \qquad (45)$$

Meanwhile, from (41) the bases of KerP are

$$N_P=\begin{bmatrix}N_c & 0 & 0\\ 0 & I & 0\\ 0 & 0 & I\end{bmatrix} \qquad (46)$$

where $ImN_c=KerB^T$. Therefore the condition (43) can be reduced to the inequality (26).

On the other hand, let us obtain the first inequality (25): From $ImN_Q=KerQ$ we can write,

$$Q=\begin{bmatrix}C_2 & D_2 & 0\end{bmatrix}=\begin{bmatrix}C & 0_m & 0_{mxn_m} & 0_m & 0_m\\ 0_{mxn_s} & 0_m & 0_{mxn_m} & I_m & 0_m\end{bmatrix} \qquad (47)$$

and so

$$N_Q=\begin{bmatrix}\begin{pmatrix}N_o & 0 & 0\\ 0 & I_m & 0\\ 0 & 0 & I_{n_m}\end{pmatrix} & 0\\ 0_{mx(m+n_m+r)} & 0\\ 0 & I_m\end{bmatrix} \qquad (48)$$

where the matrix N_o is defined by,

$$ImN_o=KerC \qquad (49)$$

and

$$r=dim(KerC). \qquad (50)$$

When the state space equations (17), (18), (19) and the matrix N_o are used in $N_Q^TH_XN_Q<0$, the following LMI is obtained:

$$\begin{bmatrix} \begin{pmatrix} N_o & 0 & 0 \\ 0 & I_m & 0 \\ 0 & 0 & I_{n_m} \end{pmatrix} & 0 \\ 0 & 0 \\ 0 & I_m \end{bmatrix}^T \begin{bmatrix} \begin{pmatrix} A & B & 0 \\ -C & 0 & 0 \\ 0 & 0 & F \end{pmatrix}^T X + X \begin{pmatrix} A & B & 0 \\ -C & 0 & 0 \\ 0 & 0 & F \end{pmatrix} & X \begin{pmatrix} 0_{n_s x m} \\ I_m \\ G \end{pmatrix} & \begin{pmatrix} -C^T \\ 0_m \\ H^T \end{pmatrix} \\ \begin{pmatrix} 0_{mxn_s} & I_m & G^T \end{pmatrix} X & -\gamma I_m & J^T \\ \begin{pmatrix} -C & 0_m & H \end{pmatrix} & J & -\gamma I_m \end{bmatrix} \begin{bmatrix} \begin{pmatrix} N_o & 0 & 0 \\ 0 & I_m & 0 \\ 0 & 0 & I_{n_m} \end{pmatrix} & 0 \\ 0 & 0 \\ 0 & I_m \end{bmatrix} < 0. \qquad (51)$$

Therefore we have,

$$\begin{bmatrix} \begin{pmatrix} N_o & 0 & 0 \\ 0 & I_m & 0 \\ 0 & 0 & I_{n_m} \end{pmatrix} & 0 \\ 0 & I_m \end{bmatrix}^T \begin{bmatrix} \begin{pmatrix} A & B & 0 \\ -C & 0 & 0 \\ 0 & 0 & F \end{pmatrix}^T X + X \begin{pmatrix} A & B & 0 \\ -C & 0 & 0 \\ 0 & 0 & F \end{pmatrix} & \begin{pmatrix} -C^T \\ 0_m \\ H^T \end{pmatrix} \\ \begin{pmatrix} -C & 0_m & H \end{pmatrix} & -\gamma I_m \end{bmatrix} \begin{bmatrix} \begin{pmatrix} N_o & 0 & 0 \\ 0 & I_m & 0 \\ 0 & 0 & I_{n_m} \end{pmatrix} & 0 \\ 0 & I_m \end{bmatrix} < 0 \qquad (52)$$

and if we use Schur complement argument in Lemma 1.3, the linear matrix inequality (52) can be converted to form of as follows:

$$\begin{bmatrix} N_o & 0 & 0 \\ 0 & I_m & 0 \\ 0 & 0 & I_{n_m} \end{bmatrix}^T \left\{ \begin{bmatrix} A & B & 0 \\ -C & 0 & 0 \\ 0 & 0 & F \end{bmatrix}^T X + X \begin{bmatrix} A & B & 0 \\ -C & 0 & 0 \\ 0 & 0 & F \end{bmatrix} + \frac{1}{\gamma} \begin{bmatrix} C^T C & 0 & -C^T H \\ 0 & 0 & 0 \\ -H^T C & 0 & H^T H \end{bmatrix} \right\} \begin{bmatrix} N_o & 0 & 0 \\ 0 & I_m & 0 \\ 0 & 0 & I_{n_m} \end{bmatrix} < 0. \qquad (53)$$

The proof is completed. ■

4 Controller construction

Although Theorem 3.1 is about the solvability conditions of the continuous-time H_∞ MMP by the 2 DOF static output feedback with integral control, it also provides a controller construction procedure. And The MATLAB LMI Control Toolbox [11] can be also used to solve LMIs. The controller construction procedure can be summarized as follows:

Step 1: Find a solution X>0 to the LMIs (25) and (26) for γ_{opt} which is the minimal of γ.

Step 2: Solve a 2 DOF static output feedback control law $K=[L \;\; M] \in R^{mx2m}$ from LMI

$$H_X + Q^T K^T P_X + P_X^T K Q < 0 \qquad (54)$$

where

$$P_X = \begin{bmatrix} (B^T & 0_m & 0_{mxn_m})X & 0_m & 0_m \end{bmatrix} \qquad (55)$$

$$Q = \begin{bmatrix} C & 0_m & 0_{mxn_m} & 0_m & 0_m \\ 0_{mxn_s} & 0_m & 0_{mxn_m} & I_m & 0_m \end{bmatrix} \qquad (56)$$

$$H_X = \begin{bmatrix} \begin{pmatrix} A & B & 0 \\ -C & 0 & 0 \\ 0 & 0 & F \end{pmatrix}^T X + X \begin{pmatrix} A & B & 0 \\ -C & 0 & 0 \\ 0 & 0 & F \end{pmatrix} & X \begin{pmatrix} 0_{n_s xm} \\ I_m \\ G \end{pmatrix} & \begin{pmatrix} -C^T \\ 0_m \\ H^T \end{pmatrix} \\ \begin{pmatrix} 0_{mxn_s} & I_m & G^T \end{pmatrix} X & -\gamma I_m & J^T \\ \begin{pmatrix} -C & 0_m & H \end{pmatrix} & J & -\gamma I_m \end{bmatrix} \qquad (57)$$

5 Numerical example

Theorem 3.1 and the controller construction algorithm will be used to design a controller to achieve model matching for the given system. Consider the second-order unstable system

$$G(s) = \frac{s+0.6}{(s-0.7)(s+0.5)}. \qquad (58)$$

The model system is taken as

$$G_m(s) = \frac{1}{s+1}. \qquad (59)$$

The state-space equations of G(s) are expressed in the minimum phase as

$$\frac{d}{dt}\begin{bmatrix} x_1(t) \\ x_2(t) \end{bmatrix} = \begin{bmatrix} 0 & 1 \\ 0.35 & 0.2 \end{bmatrix}\begin{bmatrix} x_1(t) \\ x_2(t) \end{bmatrix} + \begin{bmatrix} 0 \\ 1 \end{bmatrix} v(t) \qquad (60)$$

$$y_S(t) = \begin{bmatrix} 0.6 & 1 \end{bmatrix}\begin{bmatrix} x_1(t) \\ x_2(t) \end{bmatrix}. \qquad (61)$$

The state-space equations of $G_m(s)$ are again expressed as

$$\frac{dq(t)}{dt} = -q(t) + w(t) \qquad (62)$$

$$y_m(t) = q(t). \qquad (63)$$

The state-space equations of P(s) in Figure 1 can be written as

$$\frac{d}{dt}\begin{bmatrix} x_1(t) \\ x_2(t) \\ \hat{x}(t) \\ q(t) \end{bmatrix} = \begin{bmatrix} 0 & 1 & 0 & 0 \\ 0.35 & 0.2 & 1 & 0 \\ -0.6 & -1 & 0 & 0 \\ 0 & 0 & 0 & -1 \end{bmatrix}\begin{bmatrix} x_1(t) \\ x_2(t) \\ \hat{x}(t) \\ q(t) \end{bmatrix} + \begin{bmatrix} 0 \\ 0 \\ 1 \\ 1 \end{bmatrix} w(t) + \begin{bmatrix} 0 \\ 1 \\ 0 \\ 0 \end{bmatrix} u(t) \qquad (64)$$

$$z(t) = \begin{bmatrix} -0.6 & -1 & 0 & 1 \end{bmatrix}\begin{bmatrix} x_1(t) \\ x_2(t) \\ \hat{x}(t) \\ q(t) \end{bmatrix} \qquad (65)$$

$$y(t) = \begin{bmatrix} 0.6 & 1 & 0 & 0 \\ 0 & 0 & 0 & 0 \end{bmatrix} \begin{bmatrix} x_1(t) \\ x_2(t) \\ \hat{x}(t) \\ q(t) \end{bmatrix} + \begin{bmatrix} 0 \\ 1 \end{bmatrix} w(t). \qquad (66)$$

When we search for γ_{opt}, the matrix X>0 and the 2 DOF static output feedback controller, the results are obtained as follows:

$$\gamma_{opt}=0.775,\ L= -5.9578 \text{ and } M=2.6904.$$

$$X = \begin{bmatrix} 0.7179 & 0.3004 & -0.1531 & -0.2494 \\ 0.3004 & 0.6626 & -0.1936 & -0.2317 \\ -0.1531 & -0.1936 & 0.6540 & -0.1464 \\ -0.2494 & -0.2317 & -0.1464 & 1.0785 \end{bmatrix} > 0$$

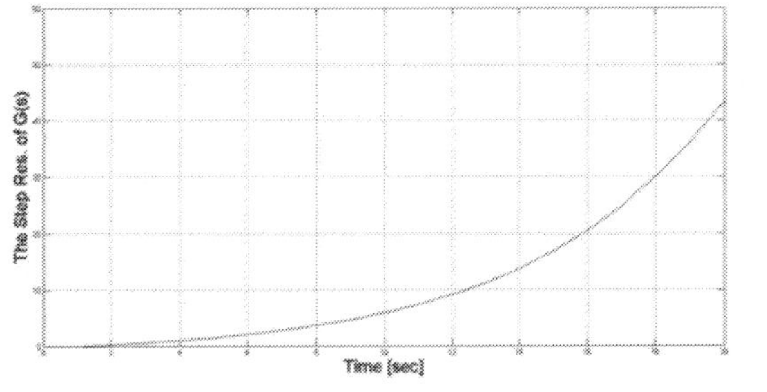

Fig. 3. The step response of the open loop system G(s).

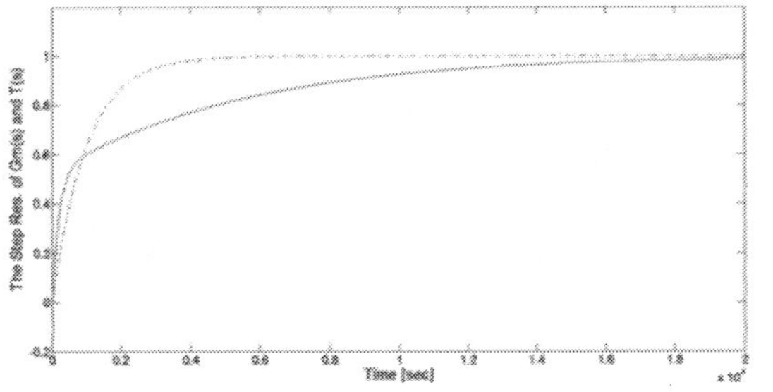

Fig. 4. The step responses of the model system $G_m(s)$:-.- and the closed system T(s):---

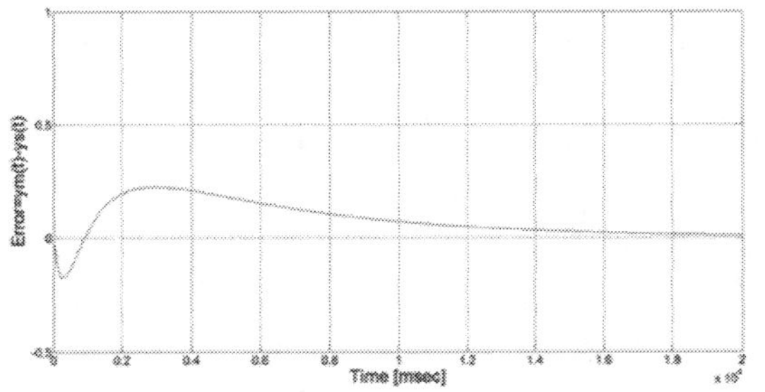

Fig. 5. The error function between the model and closed loop system outputs.

6 Conclusions

In this paper, we have studied the continuous-time H_∞ model matching problem with two degrees of freedom static output feedback. We have induced integral controller to this classical problem. The introduction of integral type of controller to this configuration naturally forces the steady-output error to zero. Moreover, the nearly proposed block diagram reduces the problem to an H_∞ optimal control problem and a theorem is proposed which provides a procedure to design the controller. Numerical simulation results have shown the expected results; that is; the steady-state error has approached to zero. However, we suppose that the two LMI conditions provided in the Theorem 3.1 can be simplified in future works.

The authors gratefully acknowledge the support of Galatasaray University, scientific research support program under grant #16.401.001

References

1. M. Akın, A. Bir, Turkish J. of Electrical Eng. and Computer Sciences, **11**, (1), 35-44, (2003)
2. M. Akın, A. Bir, *Proceedings on the 1st International Conference on Mathematics and Informatics for Industry*, Thessaloniki, Greece, 151-161, (2003)
3. M. Akın, A. Bir, *Proceedings on the 3rd IFAC Workshop DECOM-TT 2003, Automatic Systems for Building the Infrastructure in Developing Countries*, Istanbul, Turkey, 323-328, (2003)
4. M. Akın, T. Acarman, Int. J. of Control Systems and Robotics, **1**, 113-122, (2016)
5. J. C. Doyle, B. A. Francis, A. R. Tannenbaum, *Feedback Control Theory*, Macmillan Publishing Company, (1992)
6. G. R. Duan, H. H. Yu, *LMIs in Control Systems*, CRC Press, (2013)
7. G. E. Dullerud, F. Paganini, *A Course in Robust Control Theory, A Convex Approach*, Springer-Verlag, (2000)
8. B. A. Francis, *A Course in H_∞ Control Theory, No.88, Lecture Notes in Control and Information Sciences*, Springer-Verlag, (1987)
9. B. A. Francis, J. C. Doyle, SIAM J. on Control and Optimization, **4**, 815-844, (1987)
10. P. Gahinet, P. Apkarian, Int. J. of Robust and Nonlinear Control, **4**, 421-448, (1994)
11. P. Gahinet, A. Nemirovski, A. J. Laub, M. Chilali, *The LMI Control Toolbox For Use with MATLAB*, The MathWorks Inc., (1995)
12. M. J. Grimble, *Robust Industrial Control, Optimal Design Approach for Polynomial Systems*, Prentice-Hall International, (1994)
13. V. Kucera, *Analysis and Design of Discrete Linear Control Systems*, Prentice-Hall International, (1991)
14. W. A. Wolovich, *Linear Multivariable Systems*, Springer-Verlag, (1974)

MATEC Web of Conferences **125**, 02009 (2017) DOI: 10.1051/matecconf/201712502009
CSCC 2017

Simulator for testing hardware and software of the office system with RFID tags

Tadeusz Nowicki[1,*], *Krzysztof* Chlebicki[1], *Dariusz* Pierzchała[1], *Kazimierz* Worwa[1], and *Robert* Waszkowski[1]

[1]Military University of Technology, Cybernetics Faculty, 00-908 Warsaw, gen. S. Kaliskiego str., Poland

Abstract. This paper presents the method for examining the properties of the RFID-tagged document management system. The system is composed of computers, where the software for supporting processes of the RFID-tagged documents was installed. Furthermore, the system cooperates with many other elements of the office (cabinets, sluices, copiers, try rider, end so one). The examination of the properties of the RFID-tagged document management system is, in this case, complex due to the number of a possible examination scenarios. The simulator method for examining the system properties was design and implemented. It allows to conduct the examination of the properties in a short period of time for numerous testing scenarios.

1 Introduction

The paper presents a software simulator based on the method of testing the reliability and performance of a document management system with tags (tags) RFID. The system under study is composed of computers that have software for supporting document management processes with RFID tags installed. The system also cooperates with many elements of the office (closets, locks, copiers, trays, tunnels). Document ownership management system

RFID tags are complex in this case due to the large number of possible test scenarios. The built-in simulator allows you to use a simulated method to test system reliability and performance. It also allows you to carry out these property studies in a short time for a number of test scenarios.

The use of RFID tags (radio-frequency identification) for various types of applications is presented in [10], [30]-[34]. The application of this technology is found in numerous branches of the economy, including in the state administration [17] as well as in other organizations [6], including logistics [27] and [26], manufacturing [2], medical [11] .

This technology allows permanently tagged RFID tags, tags, so that the radiated waves generated from the respective antennas send signals from those tags that record their existence at a certain distance from the antennas. So documents with RFID tags are passive objects. If there is no radiation from the antennas, they do not send any signals into the ether. In the case of antennas, the reading system enables the identification of multiple tags simultaneously in the reading field. RFID tags go through the last great transformation in the sense of their size. The size of the RFID tag is constantly decreasing.

Given the fact that RFID antennas send signals at a certain frequency, you can organize a modern document management system with RFID tags, for example, in the law firm [12] and [13]. This type of system allows you to record a series of events in the room where your RFID document management system is located. The main events include:

- the emergence of new documents with RFID tags,
- the sale of a single RFID tag or package thereof outside the antenna location area,
- moving of the document with the RFID tag within the antenna
- registration of new RFID tags.

Implementing a document management system with RFID tags requires a specialized, multi-element environment to create a computer-aided process for identifying document flow. One of the most important studies of the RFID tagging system is the development of numerous experiments to test the reliability and performance of the system. Scenarios such as this can be many. This causes the number of variants of the system test scenarios to be enormous. It is worth taking into consideration that certain characteristics of using RFID tags are not uniform in time. They change quite often, which is because some RFID-tagged documents are out of system and new ones are emerging.

The concept of creating an event simulator [1], [8], [20] and [23]) generated signals of various types of activities of RFID document management system users. The simulator will operate in a network environment [24]. This allows for the preparation of a number of remotely operated user scenarios. Programmatic action scenarios can be generated automatically. Their number is not limited as they will be tested by the RFID tags management system, which will take place in virtually negligible time. The work is devoted to presenting a simulation of RFID tagging software, which will allow you to quickly perform complex tests of its essential system features related to its reliability and performance.

* Corresponding author: author@e-mail.org

2 Office with RFID tagged documents

The components of the office, apart from its typical components, using RFID technology include:

- input sluice with RFID antennas as access point to the office,
- cabinets with RFID antennas,
- document read tunnel with RFID tags,
- RFID tray reader,
- specialized copier with RFID module,
- printer server,
- RFID tagging software server,
- document flow management software system with RFID tags.

The RFID RFID input lock is intended for registration filed or removed from a law office. The person entering or leaving the office also has an RFID tag in the form of a special personal chip. RFID RFID cabinets are a natural document storage facility at the office. The document read tunnel serves the user of the law firm to submit the documents brought and left at the office with the simultaneous removal of them from the catalog already held. Similarly, a tray reader is designed to record individual documents with RFID tags. A specialized RFID printer records the fact that a document is being copied, but has a built-in verification that the document can be copied, by whom, and in how many copies. All these devices connect to the RFID document management system via a computer network controlled by a network router.

The RFID tag management system consists of the following components: Aurea BPM server business processes that describe the possible behavior of system users, a Cosmos server primarily serving the printer (copier) in the system, a Nofilis server for system configuration (setting up co-operating devices in the office) Receive signals from devices with RFID tags. Servers are a computing environment that processes document flow with RFID tags in the system.

3 Simulation method for office with RFID tagged documents investigation

For this purpose, a replacement of the original work environment of the office was shown, as shown in Figure 1. In this case, a series of event scenarios would be required for messages sent between RFID software agents from external devices to the RFID server of the system. In addition, you will have to track the response of the document flow management server to the occurrences.

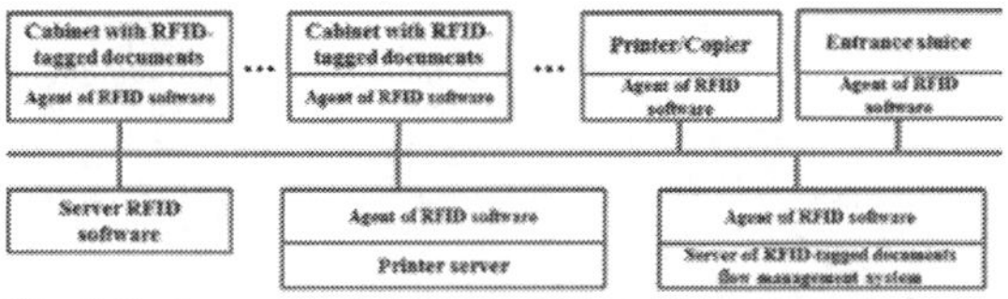

Fig. 1. System supporting the RFID-tagged document flow

It was decided to use an innovative method to test the reliability and efficiency of the system. A simulator imitating document flow events was created, in this case generating signals that change the location of documents with RFID tags in the office system. Event simulators simulating the functioning of technical systems have been described, inter alia, in the model sense in monographs [8] and [23], and in the sense of implementation in monographs [1] and [24]. In normal mode, the RFID software server is only used to configure a scanner, which defines the devices that are part of the company's office.

In turn, the existence of documents with RFID tags is recorded because RFID antennas send messages to RFID software agents and these are then transmitted by the RFID software agent to the Document Management Server. Messages are XML strings. Thus, the idea of building a simulator of XML messages imitating the existence or non-existence and movement of documents in the system. The environment of the RFID tag assisted document flow system in Figure 1 was transformed into the artificial environment illustrated in Figure 2.

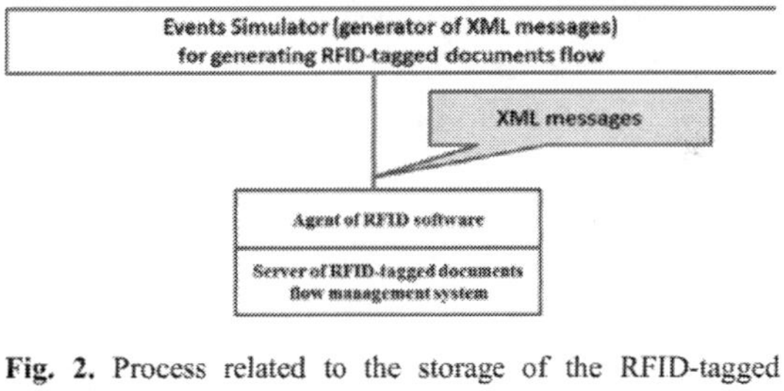

Fig. 2. Process related to the storage of the RFID-tagged documents

This makes it possible to prioritize RFID status papers in the office with their locations. This way, in the finite, soon to be able to study the reliability characteristics And the efficiency of the office system both in terms of the application software of the Document Management Server as well as the correct operation of records In the database. Without this modification, the study of characteristics would be extremely long.

4 Events in the system

The simulator should enable testing and testing of the performance and reliability of the RFID tag flow management system in a dedicated, complex system. The simulator is supposed to generate events by imitating activities carried out in a secret office equipped with specialized software. Currently, the following events are supported:

- Opening the front door - when opening the lock door, the device sends information about this event along with information about who did it and list of all RFID tags currently on the device,
- Closing the entrance door - When closing the lock outlet door, the device sends information about this event along with who it was and the list of all RFID tags currently on the device,
- Document Location - At the document location, the device sends information about this event along with a list of all RFID tags currently on the device,

- Document detection - When a document is detected, the device sends information about this event along with a list of all RFID tags currently on the device.

The simulator allows you to build the listed events into a form acceptable to the server module. The server module (monitor) in the real system communicates with devices in a secret office via http protocol. Transmitted events are XML files with a defined and structured structure. The monitoring module accepts XML files as call arguments on the services it issues.

4 Simulator architecture

An event-based scenario simulator constructs XML messages accepted by the server module and then sends them via http. The simulator has a graphical interface made using the JavaFX library and requires Java 8 virtual machine software (1.8). The simulator window is shown in Figure 3.

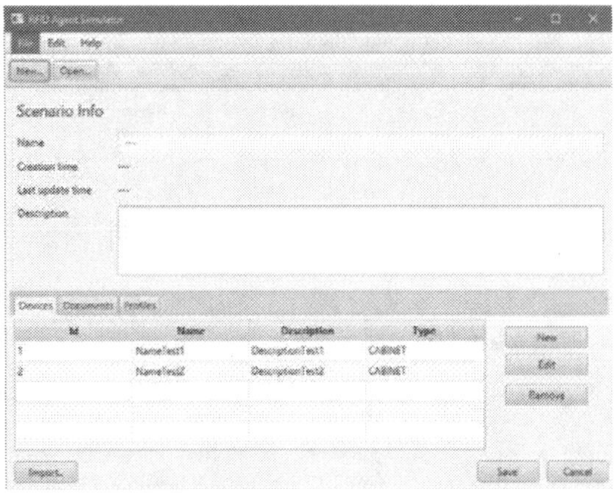

Fig. 3. Main simulator window

5.1. Description of the XML messages used in the simulator

In the real system, XML documents are used to describe events occurring in it. There are two types of these events:

- com: nofilis: crosstalk: event: tag-observation (tag-obser.vation),
- com: nofilis: crosstalk: event: read-report (read-report)

The first is generated in response to a request to read a single RFID tag, while the second one is generated in response to a request for a report. About all RFID tags read in a single session. The descriptions of the XML documents used for exchanging data between the server and agents in cabinets, mash, trays, and tunnels have been established. Communication between the server and agents is strictly defined, and involves sending messages as XML strings between them: Person ID, Document ID, a moment of identification and a number of other important measured quantities. The sample XML document specifying the way to handle the tag-observation event is as follows:

```
<?xml version="1.0" encoding="UTF-8"?>
<events>
<event type="com:nofilis:crosstalk:event:tag-
observation" timestamp="1417780363293"
uuid="CCDEDBCA-6D07-2076-5CAE-
C1DBC42DEE5D" locationId="CABINET_3.R"
objectId="C01B2916">
<id="first-read" value="1417780363291" />
<id="last-read" value="1417780363291" />
<id="observationUUID" value="73B00D24-C3B6-
25FB-CFD1-F59157FC3856" />
<id="reads" value="1" />
</event>
</events>
```

5.2 Description of simulator application packages

On Figure 4 shows the main packages of the simulator.

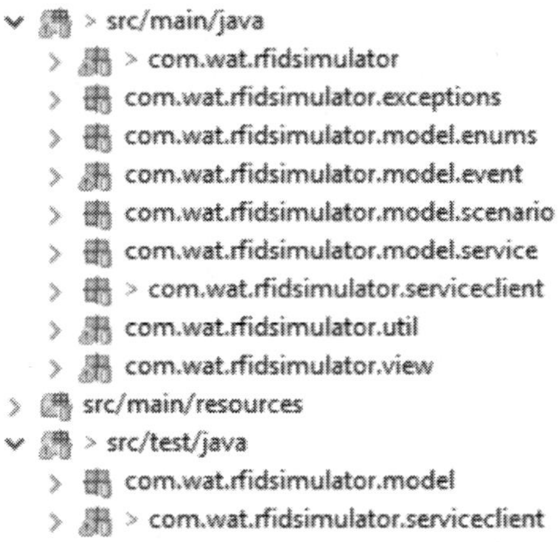

Fig. 4. Simulator application packages

Packages collect classes that perform specific and close actions. Here is an explanation of the purpose of the packages:

- com.wat.rfidsimulator - application runtime package, Com.wat.rfidsimulator.exceptions - package of classes responsible for operation and wrapping exceptions,
- com.wat.rfidsimulator.model.enums - enumerator class package,
- com.wat.rfidsimulator.model.event - a package of event classes generated by the simulation engine imitating real system events,
- Com.wat.rfidsimulator.model.scenario - JAXB class package representing the scenario being built. The script stored on the hard drive is an XML file,
- com.wat.rfidsimulator.model.service - the data model classes used by the monitoring module service client,
- com.wat.rfidsimulator.serviceclient - the client module package of the monitoring module service,
- com.wat.rfidsimulator.util - utility class package,
- com.wat.rfidsimulator.view - JavaFX GUI Class and Controller Package,

- Com.wat.rfidsimulator.model (src / test / java section) - a test suite for testing the data model used in the application,
- Com.wat.rfidsimulator.serviceclient (src / test / java section) - a package of classes that test the functionality of the monitoring client service.

5.3 The form of the simulation experiment scenario

The simulation scenario is built into a specialized application window (Figure 5). Its main features include: device definitions (Devices), user profile definitions (Profiles), event definitions, definitions of generators (nodes) and name and description.

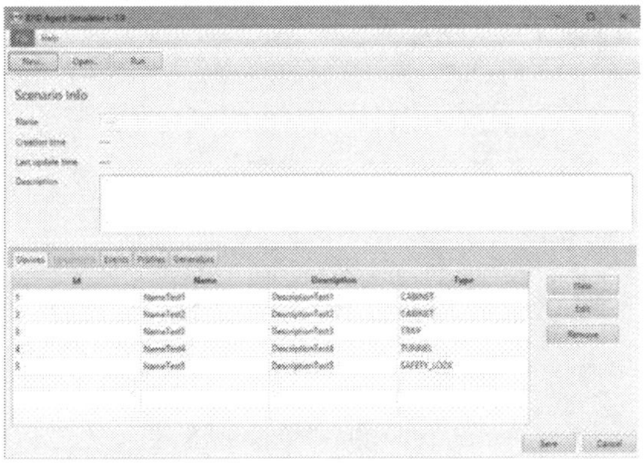

Fig. 5. Defining a new scenario

Correctly defining scenarios including used documents, devices and user profiles allow the application engine to function properly in the event design.

5.4 Running the simulator

Based on the scenario you created earlier, select the "RUN" button in the main application window. Then specify which script file to load. After this, the window will appear as shown in Figure 6. In it we can start the simulation, stop it or stop it.

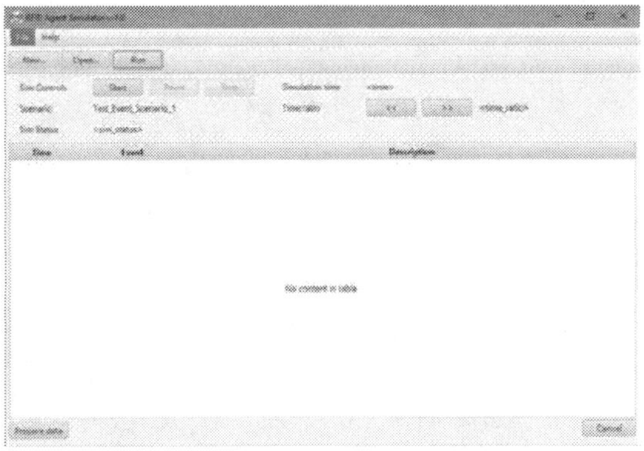

Fig. 6 Running a new scenario

In addition, you can control the rate of elapse of simulation time with special controls. Before you run the simulation, you may need to update your RFID agent data. This is done by a special button that initiates the required data based on a defined scenario. During the normal operation of the simulator, the events generated by the nodes (generators) are stored in the event log (Figure 7). In addition, they are obviously sent to the RFID agent service.

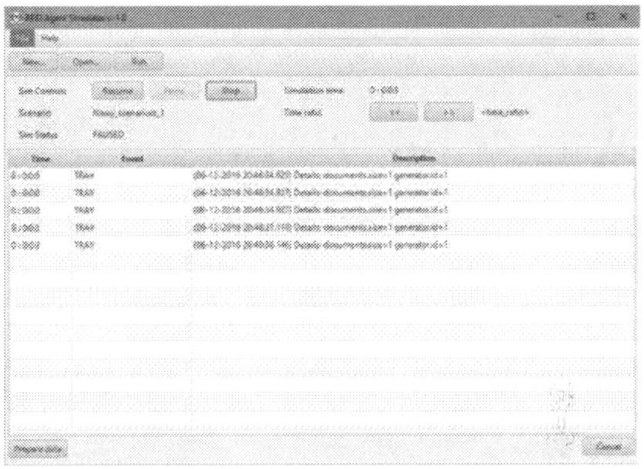

Fig. 7 Simulator activity - event log

After the simulation is complete, you can preview the report of the experiment (Figure 8).

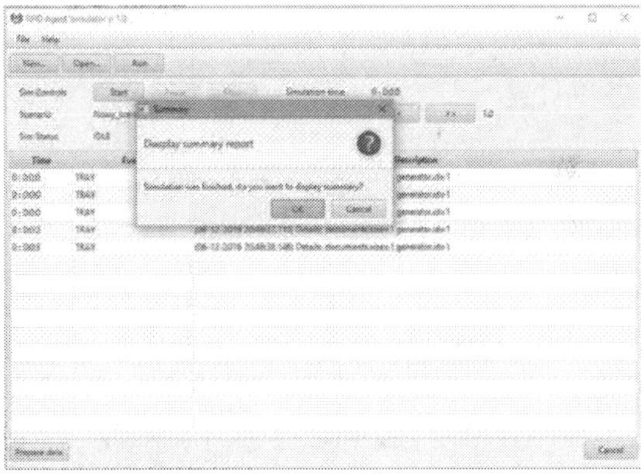

Fig. 8 End of experiment

6 Design of simulation mechanisms

Practical .implementation of Java in the first of the two presented approaches in discrete simulation, the package is implemented using recognized libraries responsible for sending messages. The main classes of the package are presented in a simplified class diagram (Figure 9). Each simulation object must inherit from the abstract BasicSimEntity class. In its set of attributes, the values of state variables are stored. Events e = <t, feS> associated with state changes are created in objects inherited from the generic BasicSimStateChange class. The main methods of this class are: corresponding to feS

DOI: 10.1051/matecconf/201712502009

state change function, which removes the non-execution event, giving the current simulation time. Attributes are control parameters: the scheduled time and priority of the status change (runSimTime, priority), and the optional time step (repetitionPeriod) - for a deterministic model with a fixed step.

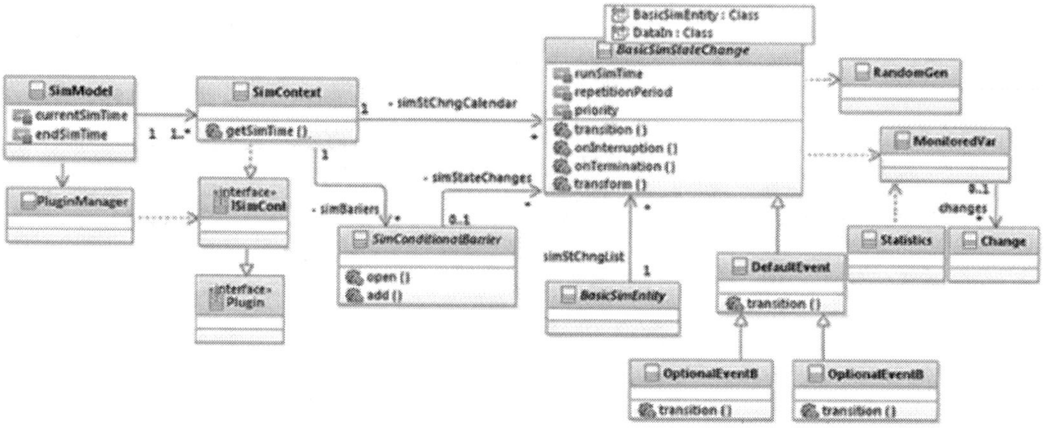

Fig. 9. Simulation classes

Depending on the constructor used, an object of one event is invoked from types: for changing the state that is scheduled only for the calendar (for runSimTime for a moment), for changing the planned state in the calendar. The accepted event broadcasting model enables you to inform all objects that are interested in a specific change in the state of the event (eg to create dependent events). The structure of the event calendar ordered by value runSimTime and priority is composed in the context object (SimContext). The package allows you to integrate many independently developed contexts modeling your various parts of the actual system into one simulation program. Each context must implement plugin interfaces (Plugin, ISimCont). Communication between objects derived from different contexts is based on a common message broker located there in the management object (SimModel). The management object, called overhead in context of the singleton pattern, is fully responsible for: start control, stop and pause in the experiment, time elapsing mode (as fast as possible, astronomical, astronomical scaling), network communication and persistent storage and recovery of states for given moments Simulation. Also, it keeps information about all contexts (so indirectly about objects and event calendars), indicates the specific event to be performed at each simulation time, and determines on this basis the current value of the simulation time that applies to all contexts and objects. Supplementing the basic functions of the package are the classes responsible for: Generating random numbers and pseudo-random processes according to given schedules (RandomGen), monitoring changes and gathering the values accepted by the indicated state variables in different simulations (MonitoredVar) and calculating different statistics on the time series monitors (Statistics). The main simulator software packages are shown in Figure 10.

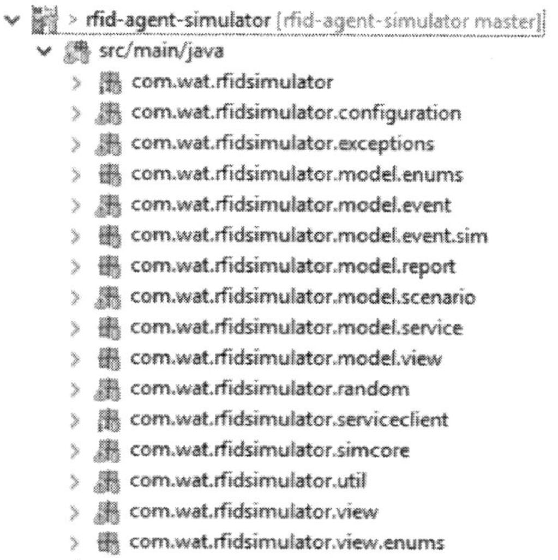

Fig. 10. Simulator application packages

Packages collect classes that perform specific and close actions. Programmable random number generators are based on computational formulas. The subsequent values generated by the generator are derived from the previous ones. The first value is called the generator seed. It can be initialized by the user (grain number) or by the system (according to the current date and astronomical time). Initialization by a grain number ensures the repeatability of the designated numbers in the unchanged initial data. It is said then about generators of pseudorandom numbers. On the other hand, initialization by date and time ensures the uniqueness of generated strings of numbers. Particularly important are generators of uniform distribution numbers, since the numbers they define are the basis for methods of generating pseudorandom numbers with any distribution. The most commonly used are linear generators based on linear algorithms. Values of random variables with other distributions are generated by the methods of inversion of the distribution, elimination and superposition of distributions.

7 Conclusions

The basic property of the proposed solution is a simulated methodology of RFID document management, document access control and copy control [28, 29, 30, 31], as well as the management of authorized people access.
An additional advantage of the designed solution, besides ensuring the process of verifying the correctness of the office system software with documents with RFID tags, will ensure the possibility of rapid testing. Implemented and undoubtedly innovative methodology for simulating the reliability and performance of computer systems with complex software can also be used in other cases of this type.

References

1. E.M.Abu-Taieh, A.A.R. El Sheikh, *Handbook of research on discrete event simulation environments: Technologies and applications*, IGI Global, Hershey, New York (2010)
2. F.W.C. Araújo Filho, X.L. Travassos, P.S. Figueiredo, *Use of the RFID technology to overcome inefficiencies in the production process: an analysis of a microcomputer company in Ilhéus – Bahia*, Journal of Information Systems and Technology Management, Vol. 11, No. 1, pp. 65–84 (2014)
3. R.E. Barlow, F.Proschan, *Mathematical Theory of Reliability*, John Wiley & Sons, New York, London, Sydney (1965)
4. R.E. Barlow, F.Proschan, *Statistical Theory of Reliability and Life Testing Probability Models*, Holt, Rinehart and Winston Inc. (1975)
5. D. Bobrowski, *Modele i metody matematyczne teorii niezawodności*, WNT, Warszawa (1985)
6. I. Bose, E.W.T. Ngai, T.S.H. Teo, S. Spiekermann, *Managing RFID projects in organizations*, European Journal of Information Systems, 18, pp. 534–540 (2009)
7. B. Dodson, B. Nolan, *Reliability Engineering Handbook*, Marcel Dekker Inc. (1999)
8. G.S. Fishman, *Discrete event simulation. Modeling, programming and analysis*, Springer, New York (2001)
9. F. Grabowski, J.J aźwiński, *Metody bayesowskie w niezawodności i diagnostyce*, WKŁ, Warszawa (2001)
10. C. Heinrich, *RFID and Beyond: Growing Your Business Through Real World Awareness* Wiley Publishing, Indianapolis (2005)
11. J. Kannry, S. Emro, M. Blount, M. Ebling, *Small-scale Testing of RFID in a Hospital Setting: RFID as Bed Trigger*, AMIA 2007 Symposium Proceedings Archive, pp. 384–388 (2007)
12. M. Kiedrowicz (ed.), *Zarządzanie informacjami wrażliwymi. Bezpieczeństwo dokumentów, wykorzystanie technologii RFID*, WAT, Warszawa (2016)
13. M. Kiedrowicz (ed.), *Zarządzanie informacjami wrażliwymi. Wybrane aspekty organizacyjne, prawne i techniczne ochrony informacji niejawnych RFID*, WAT, Warszawa (2015)
14. B. Kopociński, *Zarys teorii odnowy i niezawodności*, PWN, Warszawa (1973)
15. M.R. Lyu (ed.), *Handbook of Software Reliability Engineering*, McGraw-Hill (1996)
16. Y.K. Malaiya, M.N. Li, J.M. Bieman, R. Karcich, *Software reliability growth with test coverage, IEEE Transactions on Reliability*, Vol.51, No.4, 420–426 (2002)
17. T. Maniva, H. Sugano, M. Kato, *Mass Data Read/Write Technology for UHF-Band RFID Tags*, Fujitsu Sci. Tech. J., 43(4), 464–468 (2007)
18. J. Musa, *Software Reliability Engineering: More Reliable Software, Faster and Cheaper*, AuthorHouse, Bloomington (2004)
19. Pfefferman J.D., Cernuschi-Frias B., *A no-parametric non-stationary procedure for failure prediction*, IEEE Transactions on Reliability, Vol.51, No.4, 434–442 (2002)
20. H. Perros, *Computer simulation techniques – the definitive introduction*, North Carolina State University, Raleigh (2009)
21. H. Pham, *System Software Reliability*, Springer (2006)
22. M. Rausand, A. Hoyland, *System Reliability Theory: Models, Statistical Methods, and Applications*, Wiley Series in Probability and Statistics, Wiley-Interscience (2003)
23. S. M. Ross, *Simulation*, Elsevier Inc. (2006)
24. B. Sinclair, *Simulation of Computer Systems and Computer Networks: A Process-Oriented Approach*, University Press, Cambridge UK (2004)
25. Sołowjew A.D., *Analityczne metody w teorii niezawodności*, WNT, Warszawa 1983
26. C.T. Stambaugh, F.W. Carpenter, *Wireless innovation in inventory monitoring and accounting*, Strategic Finance, Vol. 91(6), 35–40 (2009)
27. S. Whang, *Timing of RFID Adoption in a Supply Chain*, Management Science, Vol. 56, No. 2, 343–355 (2010)
28. M. Kiedrowicz, T. Nowicki, R. Waszkowski, Z. Wesołowski, K. Worwa, *Optimization of the Document Placement in the RFID Cabinet*, EDP Science, MATEC Web of Conferences 76 02001, (2016), DOI:10.1051/matecconf/20167602001

29. M. Kiedrowicz, T. Nowicki, R. Waszkowski, Z. Wesołowski, K. Worwa, *Method for assessing software reliability of the document management system using the RFID technology*, MATEC Web Conf., 76 (2016) 04009, DOI:https://doi.org/ 10.1051/matecconf/ 20167604009
30. M. Kiedrowicz, T. Nowicki, R. Waszkowski, Z. Wesołowski, K. Worwa, *Software simulator for property investigation of document management system with RFID tags*, MATEC Web Conf., 76 (2016) 04012, DOI: https://doi.org/10.1051 /matecconf/20167604012
31. R. Waszkowski, A. Chodowska, M. Kiedrowicz, T. Nowicki, Z. Wesołowski, K. Worwa, *Data flow between RFID devices in a modern restricted access administrative office*, MATEC Web Conf., 76 (2016) 04004, DOI: https://doi.org/10.1051/matecconf/ 20167604004
32. M. Kiedrowicz, T. Nowicki, R. Waszkowski, Z. Wesolowski, and K. Worwa, *Business processes in the RFID-equipped restricted access administrative office*, MATEC Web Conf., 76 (2016) 04003, DOI: https://doi.org/10.1051/matecconf/ 20167604003.
33. M. Kiedrowicz, *Location with the use of the RFID and GPS technologies - opportunities and threats*, GIS ODYSSEY 2016, pp. 122-128, (2016).
34. M. Kiedrowicz, T. Nowicki, R. Waszkowski, *Business process data flow between automated and human tasks*, 3rd International Conference on Social Science (ICSS 2016) December 9–11 2016, pp. 471-477, (2016).

MATEC Web of Conferences **125**, 02010 (2017) DOI: 10.1051/matecconf/201712502010
CSCC 2017

Multi-faceted methodology of the risk analysis and management referring to the IT system supporting the processing of documents at different levels of sensitivity

Maciej KIEDROWICZ[1,*]

[1] Military University of Technology, Faculty of Cybernetics, Institute of Computer and Information Systems, Warsaw, Poland

Abstract. This article outlines the methodology of the IT system risk analysis and management, including various categories of risk factors significant from the point of view of the sensitive data processing and completeness of the procedure for determining the IT system risk level. The presented methodology is divided into the IT system risk analysis and the risk management method. The IT system risk level assessed by the risk analysis method described in this article constitutes an input value for the risk management method outlined in the further part hereof, referring to the IT systems used for the processing of documents at different levels of sensitivity.

Introduction

When analyzing various approaches to assessment of the risk level and proper risk treatment, a question arises whether a possibility of creating a complete and consistent methodology for analyzing the processing of documents at different sensitivity levels, including various categories of risk factors allowing their combination so that it is possible to determine the risk level of sensitive documents, while maintaining practical usability of the proposed solution, does actually exist.

This article is an attempt to answer the above question by outlining the methodology of the risk assessment and management, referring to the IT system responsible for the processing of the documents at different levels of sensitivity, which is - according to the authors - complete and consistent.

In addition, the provided methodology:

- forms grounds for the qualitative risk assessment and more detailed analysis,
- forms grounds for more detailed methodology of the risk management in the information security process,
- allows risk evaluation[1] at different levels of certainty,
- allows focus on the risk related to the processing of the documents at different levels of sensitivity; it is helpful from the perspective of both the risk resulting "from" (specific risk) and the risk "for" (a given protected value), e.g. fire risk for a certain infrastructure, regardless of the source of such risk,
- allows to apply the scenario approach,
- allows to classify the risks[2] in terms of reliability of the consequence level,
- allows to identify present risks under control and other risks that would require implementation of additional control procedures or enhancement of the present ones,
- delivers results similar to those based on the risk mitigation requirements.

Methodology concept is outlined in Chapter *2. Methodology concept*. Chapter 2.3.4. *Method for calculating the IT system risk* constitutes further elaboration of this concept. Additionally, mathematical formalism allowing to unambiguously determine the risk level of the processing of the documents at different levels of sensitivity also forms a part of the proposed methodology. Such formalism is introduced by subpoints 2.3.4.2.1. - 2.3.4.2.3.

The risk management process should be adapted to the operating organizational structure, clear to everyone and implemented in line with the adopted methodology and law.

In this article, the risk management process is an organized method of risk identification, analysis and evaluation within the framework of the entire risk assessment process, which allows to omit repeatable, rational and efficient risk management activities, as resulting from the risk management strategy.

* Corresponding author: maciej.kiedrowicz@wat.edu.pl

[1] Risk evaluation - process of comparing the results of risk analysis with risk criteria to determine whether the risk and/or its magnitude is acceptable or tolerable [1] definition 3.7.1.

[2] Risk classification - division of risks according to the previously set criteria.

1. Risk elements related to the processing of the documents at different levels of sensitivity

This chapter contains the definition and selected information about the risk and its classification (Chapter 1.1 Definition and classification of risk), with special emphasis on the IT system risks (Chapter 1.2 IT system risks). It also presents certain aspects of ensuring security of the IT systems (Chapter 1.3. Selected aspects of the IT system security), which shall be used in the following part of this document, methodology of the risk analysis and management of the IT system.

1.1. Basic definitions

For the purpose of further consideration, the following definitions have been adopted.
Def. 1. Methodology
Methodology is a set of rules, instructions and good practices intended to outline procedures (methods) in a given situation to attain a goal. It is also presented as a problem-solving approach standardized for a selected area. It is a collection of methods for performing certain activities, achieving certain goals or a set of rules and methods concerning a given action and intention to attain a certain goal. Methodology describes where and how to look for solutions to the problem.
Def. 2. Organization/Office unit - O.
The O-Organization is a deliberately created group of human, capital and ideological resources as well as business activities and information processes interrelated for the purpose of achieving certain goals/objectives of the Office.
Def. 4. set of processes related to the sensitive data processing - P(O).
The organization is also defined as "a set of variable processes with different relationships of interdependence. The organization becomes a space where people integrate around different tasks and problems to be solved. This gives rise to the need to combine various work contents, arrange tasks into processes and create organizational structures according to such processes not according to the authority centers or functional specialization" [2].
The set of the processes related to the sensitive documents processing P is a finite and countable set of processes $P(O) = \{P_1, P_2, \dots, P_i, \dots, P_N\}$, where: N – the number of the processes related to the sensitive documents processing in the O-Organization.
Def. 5. Security of sensitive document.
Security of sensitive document - the entirety of actions undertaken to protect data and information processed in the IT or ICT system against unauthorized access, starting from their preparation, through the period of their use and distribution, and ending with their destruction. A sensitive document is considered safe if it has the following properties (security attributes):

- Confidentiality (ISO 27001) - a characteristic that applies to information to ensure that it is not made available or disclosed to unauthorized persons, entities or processes, but only to authorized parties;
- Integrity (ISO 27001) - a characteristic that applies to assets (resources) to ensure their accuracy and completeness; to ensure the accuracy and completeness of information in compliance with its business importance as well as assumptions and methods adopted to process information;
- Availability (ISO 27001) - a characteristic that applies to assets, which are made available and usable upon request of an authorized entity; all these assets and information related thereto must be accessible by authorized entities whenever they need them.
- Authenticity - a characteristic that applies to data to ensure that their origin or content describing an object is in compliance with the declared information;
- Accountability - a characteristic allowing to assign specific actions in the system to a natural person or process and place them in time.
- Non-repudiation - the lack of a possibility to repudiate total or partial participation in the data exchange by one of the participants;
- Reliability (ISO 27001) - a characteristic meaning consistent, intended behavior an effects.

Def. 7. Risk management process. In compliance with the international standards, the risk management process is a process that includes the following activities: risk assessment - inclusive of its identification, analysis and evaluation, decision-making, treatment, monitoring and review. The process refers to all risks and must constitute an integral part of the practical activities of the organization. Additionally, an appropriate party - able to provide correct methods and tools - shall be vested with the execution of such process. The risk management does not only mean preparation of the risk list and actions undertaken with respect thereto. It also requires a serious approach to the risk assessment process, which involves a number of activities, such as risk identification, analysis and evaluation. This is a systematic presentation of the whole undertaking, which requires an appropriately planned strategy.

For the purpose of the methodology described herein, the risk of the sensitive documents processing is defined as a threat, susceptibility or gap (e.g. information, security), since such technologies, i.e. information, design, production, used in a given organization (regardless of its type and scope of business) do not meet the requirements adopted in the organization's strategy or policies, do not provide an appropriate level of quality, security, integrity, availability or continuity of sensitive documents processing, were not properly implemented and do not operate in compliance with the assumptions or requirements of the adopted policies.

With the above in mind, the risk of the sensitive data processing is analyzed in division into various categories [3], sources and areas:

1) possible sources of risk: natural and technical risks, deficient (lack of) legislation, inappropriate habits, human mentality, weakness of the organization, lack of training, low awareness of

risks, lack of readiness, unprepared personnel, lack of system, unrealistic security standards, quality standards, continuity of operations standards, technical and technological delays, non-compliance with technological norms, operational errors, negligence and omissions, ignorance, incompetence, (system) corruption,

2) possible risk areas: organization, organizational unit, department, natural environment, communities, business processes, security environment, information processes, etc.

1.2. Documents at different levels of sensitivity

The documents at different levels of sensitivity include such documents that require special approach to their management. They may contain confidential information as well as data that need to be specially protected due to other reasons (e.g. banking documents). The aforesaid documents are usually handled in dedicated rooms specially adapted for that purpose - therefore, such terms as "secret office or "RFID office"[3] shall be also used further on in this article. The main objective of this article is to outline major aspects of the organization and functioning of the offices responsible for the processing of confidential documents and materials, in compliance with the effective legislation in Poland, as well as the methodology of risk management with respect to the office processes, where the basic functionality is supported by implementation of the dedicated IT systems and technologies, e.g. RFID [4-6. 32- 34, 38].

The processing of documents at different levels of sensitivity by the office is based on current legislation, which defines basic activities, resources and participations of such activities. The office is the key subject of the above-mentioned process. Every office performs many activities related to the processing of various documents. As far as the secret office (SO) is concerned, the processed documents are at different levels of security classification. The acts and resolutions, which constitute basic analytical and research resources, are among the most important publications.

While developing the methodology of risk management with respect to the office responsible for the processing of classified documents and processes, and outlying the rules and methods of operations of such unit, the national legislation needs to be taken into account.

The term "sensitive document" was not legally defined on the basis of the binding provisions of law. The common language only knows the term "sensitive data", which mainly refers to personal data. Therefore, the article tackles the idea of the documents which contain some confidential information, intended not for an unlimited, but a narrow group of recipients, due to the nature and potential damages that may occur if such information is disclosed.

[3] RFID (radio-frequency identification) – a technique that uses radio frequency to send data and supply the electrical system (RFID tag), which constitutes track tags attached to objects for the purpose of their identification. It allows reading and sometimes also recording the RFID system. Depending on its structure, the technology allows to read tags from the distance of several dozen centimeters or several meters from the reader antenna.

1.3. Risk related to sensitive documents

A special type of risk discussed herein is the risk related to sensitive documents, which also has not been defined in an explicit manner. For the purpose of IT advisory and methodology presented in the article, the risk of sensitive documents defined as a threat that the IT technology or other technologies applied in a given office unit (regardless of its type and scope of business):

- have not been properly implemented and do not work in line with their assumptions,
- prevent implementation and upgrade of technical and technological infrastructure supporting the risk management process, in accordance with the present risk profile,
- do not ensure sufficient security of the Office and its resources at an acceptable level,
- do not meet the requirements included in the following policies: security policy, quality policy, business continuity management policy, etc.,
- do not provide appropriate organization structure in terms of security services,
- do not ensure appropriate maintenance of the relevant documentation concerning security, quality or continuity of operations,
- do not ensure proper integrity, confidentiality, non-repudiation and access to sensitive data.

In light of the above, the risk of sensitive documents is analyzed in division into the following categories and attributes:

1) the following attributes in the field of information security: access to sensitive documents, confidentiality of the processed data, integrity of documents, fulfillment of security requirements included in the security policy, losses understood as a costs incurred due to the loss of security attributes [7,8,35-37];
2) the following elements in the field as resulting from the legal norms regulating such security issues: appointment of a representative to protect classified information, creation of a security division in the organization to perform tasks related to the processing of sensitive documents in the organization, adaptation of the office facilities to the requirements on creation, processing, acceptance, assignment, delivery and protection of sensitive documents according to the provisions of law; organization of a secret office, organization of a special location (place, facility) for the processing of sensitive data, including ICT systems for executing and processing sensitive documents;
3) the following documents in the field of basic quality and security documents: risk analysis reports, security policy, ICT security plan, special security requirements for the ICT system, safe use procedures and business continuity plan;

4) the following attributes/measures in the field of the sensitive information security processing process: importance of the Office and its Clients, fulfillment of the requirements included in the quality policy;
5) the following attributes in the field of security of business continuity: fulfillment of the requirements included in the business continuity management policy, financial effects of suspension/interruption of the process, non-financial effects of suspension/interruption of the process, costs and time of the process unavailability;
6) In other fields: flexibility of the process of sensitive data processing, costs and time of the process of sensitive data processing, efficiency of the change management process, efficiency of the management process architecture related to the processing of sensitive data, reliability.

Last but not least, it should be stressed that the risk of sensitive documents may result from such an allegedly prosaic reason as wrongly designed user interface in the ICT system.

Therefore, it is evident that risks may not be completely eliminated from the organization. However, there are methods of risk assessment, in particular with respect to the risk related to the processing of documents at different levels of security, and methods of risk mitigation, which are described in the following part hereof.

2. Concept of the risk analysis and risk management methodology referring to the IT system supporting the processing of sensitive data

2.1. Assumptions

The methodology proposed herein constitutes a comprehensive approach to the risk analysis and management related to the processing of documents at different levels of sensitivity, including different categories of factors, whose impact on the risk is described in *Chapter 1. Risk elements related to the processing of the documents at different levels of sensitivity*. The risk of sensitive documents and security elements are often neglected in the current risk analysis approaches, which - according to the author - are characterized by significant impact on the total risk of sensitive documents.

The methodology presented in the article takes into consideration all of the sensitive documents in the organization, therefore, there is no phase of selecting the processes of sensitive documents to be included in the risk analysis and later risk management procedures. The above approach allows comprehensive and relatively objective analysis of the processing of the documents at different levels of sensitivity within the organization. Apparently, there is no reason not apply the proposed methodology in case of the selected processes related to the processing of the document at different levels of sensitivity. Additionally, the methodology described herein assumes that each change in the process of sensitive data processing that changes the risk levels has impact only on such process and does not affect any other processes related to the processing of the documents at different sensitivity levels. On the basis of such assumption, it is evident that one vector of change of the process risk may affect only one process of the processing of sensitive data.

2.2. Methodology concept

The general scheme of the proposed methodology is outlined in Fig. 1. The described methodology is composed of the following elements [7, 8]:

- The principles of risk management [3], whose comprehensive implementation within the entire office (e.g. Secret Office) and particular areas of its operations, may be translated into the risk management efficiency.
- Risk management framework [4] – a set of components that ensure foundations and organizational arrangements in terms of design, implementation, monitoring, review and improvement of the risk management process within an organization.
- Risk management process[5] - the process that falls within the scope of responsibilities of the management and personnel of an organizational unit, designated to identify risks and compare action strategies of the organization, which may have positive or negative impact on the functioning of the organization and - while considering achievement of the specific objectives - protection of the organization against the risk above its acceptable level[6]. The risk management process also refers to

[4] [1] definition 2.1.1.

[5] In compliance with the international standards, the risk management process is a process that includes the following activities: risk assessment - inclusive of its identification, analysis and evaluation, decision-making, treatment, monitoring and review. The process refers to all risks and must constitute an integral part of the practical activities of the organization. Additionally, an appropriate party - able to provide correct methods and tools - shall be vested with the execution of such process.

[6] Acceptable risk - the risk magnitude that may be accepted by the organization, without any additional remedial actions or changes in the operations. Acceptable risk level - a conventional value. It is the result of the risk assessment process, which includes a comparison of the risk level defined during an analysis with the adopted criteria. It is determined whether the expected risk falls within the limits of acceptance and tolerance or not. Each risk, whose value goes beyond the acceptable level, but falls within the tolerance limits, should increase vigilance and initiate actions aimed at monitoring, controlling and mitigating such risk. However, before undertaking any actions, it is essential to evaluate efficiency of the monitoring process, reliability of the information, correctness of the analysis, possible losses or advantages of risks, expected expenses related to the risk mitigation and cost effectiveness of the whole undertaking [9].

the reduction of uncertainties and possibilities of dealing therewith.
- Method of the IT system risk analysis and the risk management method.

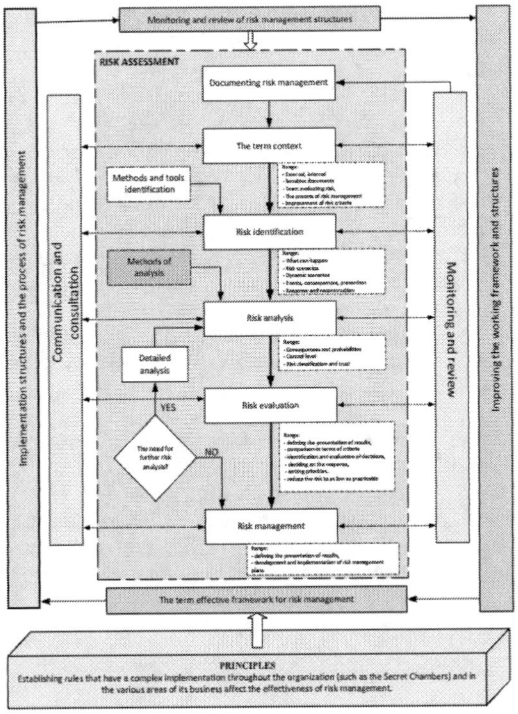

Fig. 1. Concept of the methodology of risk analysis related to the processing of the documents at different levels of sensitivity.

Taking into account the assumptions and limited number of pages of particular articles in this study, only general characteristics of individual stages of the risk management process and the method of risk assessment was presented further on herein, with respect to every process of the processing of documents at different levels of sensitivity. Special emphasis was placed, in this methodology, on the definition of the manner of presenting the risk assessment results in the form of the risk vector of the processing of the documents at different levels of sensitivity – *Chapter 2.3.4.*

2.3. Risk management process

The process includes five main tasks: communication and consultation[7], context determination, risk assessment[8], risk treatment, monitoring and review.

[7] Communication and consultation - continuous and iterative processes, which are carried out by the organization to ensure, provide or obtain information as well as to communicate with the interested parties as regards risk management, [1] definition 3.3.1.2.

[8] Risk assessment - the entire process of risk assessment, Risk analyses and risk evaluation, [1] definition 3.4.1., cf.: [10]

2.3.1. Communication and consultation

The principles of communication and consultation shall be determined before implementing subsequent elements of the process. Such activities should consider not only the issue of the risk as such (including its causes and consequences), but also the stage of the risk treatment. It is important, since this element constitutes grounds for proper communication with all involved parties and entities in the organization and its interested parties. Communication and consultation are not the goals as such - what is really important is their proper use allowing to understand the decisions being made and their expected consequences.

2.3.2. Establishing context

None of the organizations functions in empty space, therefore it is crucial to analyze external and internal correlations as well as their impact on the risk and the risk management process. While the external correlations not always depend on the organization, the internal correlations may, should and must be subject to rational approach to risk management. Therefore, it is essential to determine the context[9]. When determining the context of the risk management process, special attention should be paid to the fact that this process must refer to the defined objectives, responsibilities as well as the scope and scale of the undertaken actions. It is also essential to include the adopted method of risk assessment, ways of evaluating its results and criteria. What is more, agreement on the risk criteria constitutes an important element of such process. Above all, it allows to determine its materiality by referring to the values of the organization as well as its targets and missions. The standard shows that by determining the aforesaid criteria, the following should be taken into account[10]:

1) nature and types of causes and consequences, which may occur, and the manner of their measurement,
2) manner of defining the probability of their occurrence,
3) timeframe of the occurrence probability and/or their consequences,
4) manner of establishing the risk level,
5) acceptable or tolerable risk level.

It is necessary to answer the question whether the organization shall analyze every risk separately or in groups (after determining which correlations of such groups need to be examined). It is equally important to secure the whole process in terms of: information, personal, financial, logistic and technical data. The risk management process should be adapted to the operating organizational structure, clear to everyone and implemented in line with the adopted methodology and law. Competence and responsibility of the personnel should be precisely divided, whereas the risk criteria clearly defined and in compliance with the organization's targets.

[9] cf.: [3] pp. 43-47.

[10] [3], p. 47.

 DOI: 10.1051/matecconf/201712502010

2.3.3. Risk assessment

Another important action is the risk assessment process. It requires the preparation of an exhaustive list of risks[11]. Risk assessment may be performed in three stages:

- Definition of sensitive resources.
- Identification of susceptibility and risks of such resources.
- Risk measurement.

When defining sensitive resources, it is important to make a list of information objects or information processing processes, which require protection on the basis of an appropriate catalog of resources and common sense. The process requires knowledge of law and full understanding of the operational mechanism in the organization [7, 11, 29-31].

The aim of risk assessment is to create the broadest possible list of risk factors, which may have impact on the defined sensitive resources - regardless of whether their sources are under the control of the office unit or not. When identifying the risk, the cascading effect (Domino)[12], which stimulates the occurrence of further risks[13], needs to be taken into account.

The point of risk identification is to prepare the full list of risk factors, resulting from potential events that - depending on the circumstances - may create, prevent, limit, accelerate, delay or make it impossible to achieve a goal.

Risk identification is a continuous process, as the risks or risk factors not detected on time may not only make it impossible to achieve the goal, but also pose threat to the organization. The basis for such risk identification shall be the information that needs to satisfy certain criteria. It should be reliable, prompt, complete and - if possible - verified. Therefore, there are several requirements for the information sources and people responsible for such tasks. The sources must be reliable and safe, whereas the people well prepared. The risk components are the following:

1) sources of risks or threats,
2) events or incidents being the risk sources,
3) consequences for the organization and environment,
4) causes of current threats or occurring events,
5) efficiency of the monitoring and detection systems,
6) place and time of risk occurrence.

The aforesaid components shall be analyzed separately with respect to every event that may pose threat (hurricanes, floods, legislative risks, etc.).

1. *Possible identification methods: measurements*, discussions, experiences, expert opinions, laboratory tests, detection systems, modeling, scenarios, questionnaires, forecasts, risk analyses, structures, solutions (weaknesses and strengths, possibilities and needs).
2. *Possible sources of risk:* natural and technical risks, deficient (lack of) legislation, inappropriate habits, human mentality, weakness of the organization, lack of training, low awareness of risks, lack of readiness, unprepared personnel, lack of system, technical and technological delays, non-compliance with technological standards, operational errors, negligence and omissions, ignorance, incompetence, (system) corruption.
3. *Possible risk areas:*[14]: organizational unit, department, natural environment, development processes, security environment, information processes, etc.

Subsequently, the aggregated risk[15] needs to be analyzed. The point of risk analysis is to allow detailed understanding thereof. The knowledge gained at this stage allows to make a decision on the method of risk treatment (choice of the strategy[16] and selection of methods)[17]. The analysis should be aimed at determining potential consequences of risks and probability of their occurrence (the following data may be found as results: qualitative, semi-quantitative, quantitative or a combination thereof, depending on the needs of the organization and selected method).

2.3.4. Method of the IT system risk measurement.

2.3.4.1. Assumptions

The widely applied methods of efficient risk assessment are risk maps or matrices. They are composed of two combined (usually five step) scales: probability and consequences, allowing to define the acceptance level of a given risk.

[11] In compliance with [1], the risks are considered sources of potential damages, whereas the risk is expressed with reference to potential consequences and probability of their occurrence.
[12] Domino effect - a theory assuming that one event sets off a chain of events.
[13] This element is important, since some risks (threats) may occur only as consequences of other risks.

[14] Risk area - the area of risk factors, which are significant from the point of view of a given entity.
[15] Risk aggregation - description of a set of risks.
[16] Strategy of risk treatment - theory and practice aimed at implementing the assumed long-term targets under the risk modification process.
[17] Method of risk treatment - a way of modifying the risk, including, among other things, avoiding the risk, taking or increasing the risk, removing the risk source, changing the consequences, division of risk, risk retention. Source: own elaboration based on [1] definition 3.8.1

DOI: 10.1051/matecconf/201712502010

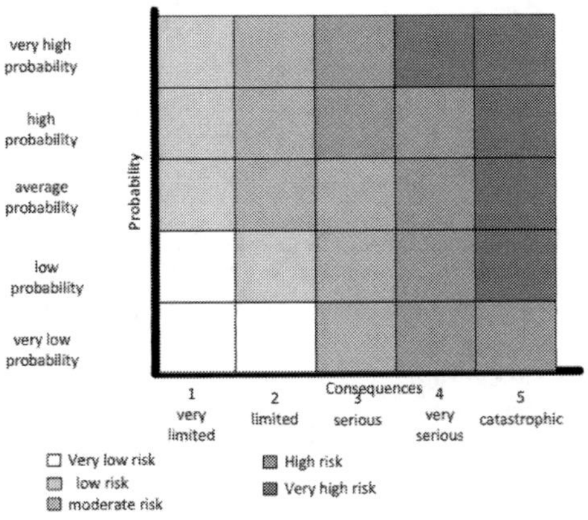

Fig.2. Risk matrix example.

The risk matrix shows that the risk is assessed on the basis of only two basic components, i.e. probability and consequences. In this approach other components/risk factors, described in Chapter 1 hereof, which include security, quality and business continuity parameters, are insignificant. With the above in mind, it seems justified to assess the IT risks by using the vector which $\overrightarrow{R_{S_i}}$ reflects the IT system risk levels in its all possible aspects. On the other hand, each considered aspect/area should specify all basic risk factors (threats, susceptibility and security mechanisms). For example, when considering the area of information security, the security of areas referring to sensitive data processing and business continuity of the IT system risk vector may be defined in the following way:

$$\overrightarrow{R_{S_i}} = \left(\overrightarrow{R^B_{S_i}}, \quad \overrightarrow{R^C_{S_i}}, \quad \overrightarrow{R^T_{S_i}}\right)$$

where:

- $\overrightarrow{R^B_{S_i}}$ - the vector coordinate $\overrightarrow{R_{S_i}}$ that characterizes an aspect of the IT system information security S_i,
- $\overrightarrow{R^C_{S_i}}$ - the vector coordinate $\overrightarrow{R_{S_i}}$ that characterizes an aspect of the IT system continuity of operations S_i, which constitutes a linear combination of the IT system risk elements S_i within the linear space $(M_{2\times 2}, R, +, \cdot)$.
- $\overrightarrow{R^T_{S_i}}$ - the vector coordinate $\overrightarrow{R_{S_i}}$ that characterizes an aspect of the security of the process of sensitive data processing in the IT system S_i,.

The selected coordinates of the risk vector represent individual risk areas (Fig. 3), each of them including several risk factors, hereinafter referred to as the composition of partial vectors of IT system risk.

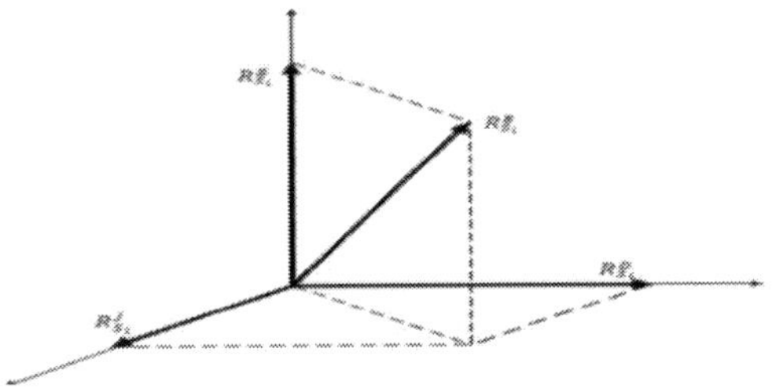

Fig. 3. Vector $R^B_{S_i}$ of IT system risk in the coordinates configuration $R^B_{S_i}$; $R^D_{S_i}$; $R^T_{S_i}$

Its visualization in the form of a "risk cube" is shown in (Fig. 4.)

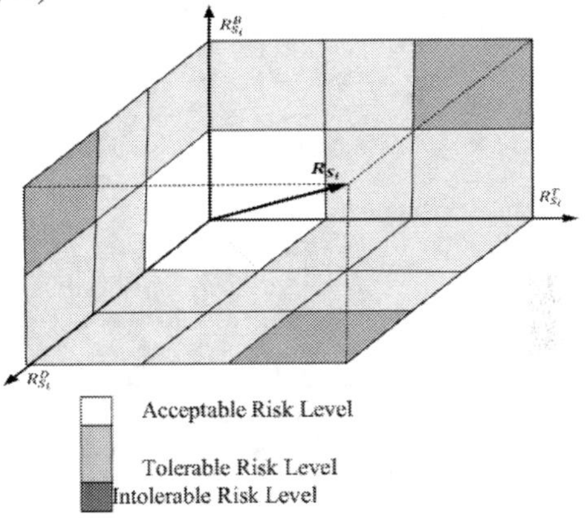

Fig.4. Risk cube of the IT system.

The method of IT system risk measurement should be also applied in such a manner so that it provides sufficient input data for risk evaluation.

2.3.4.2. Review of the procedure

The IT system risk assessment is performed in the following steps. General scheme is shown in Fig. 5.

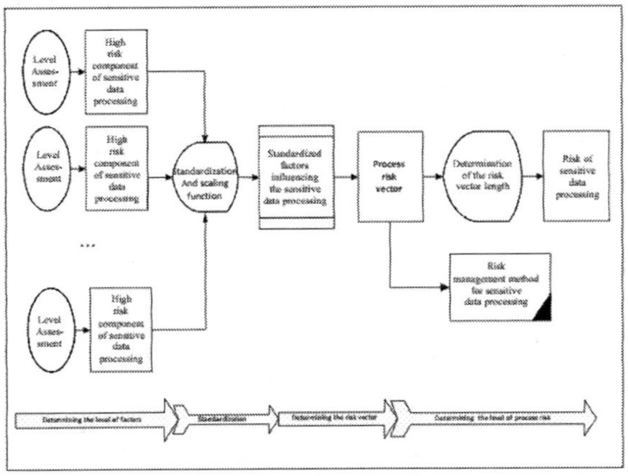

Fig. 5. General scheme of the risk assessment processes referring to the processing of the documents at different levels of sensitivity.

DOI: 10.1051/matecconf/201712502010

1) Definition of risk factors affecting the risk. The method includes several factors that, according to the author, allow a relatively objective and accurate assessment of the risk level related to the processing of the documents at different levels of sensitivity. Different elements of the risk analysis used in the methodology described herein are presented in Chapter *1*. The level of detail referring to the selected components is determined by the correlations between the risk analysis and architecture of the processes related to the processing of the documents at different levels of sensitivity.
2) Standardization of the defined factors having impact on the risk.
3) Determination of risk vector based on the standardized values of the risk components.
4) Determination of impact weights of particular factors on the total risk level for a given IT system. Such impact weights are determined depending on the confidentiality clause - the level of sensitivity, at which a given organizational unit operates.
5) Determination of the weighted risk vector. The vector includes impact of the level of the document sensitivity, at which a given organizational unit operates, on the processing process risk.
6) Determination of the final risk level referring to the processing of the documents at different levels of sensitivity. Method of risk assessment is described in Chapter*2.6*.

2.3.4.2.1. Standardization

Due to the fact that the components of the IT system risk and processes of the sensitive data processing, as a matter of principle, belong to different sets of values, it is necessary to introduce a function or a set of functions clearly transferring such components to a uniform range of values [1,..., *N*]. The adoption of such range of values [1,..., *N*] is aimed at creating the simplest possible shape of the functions that would transpose the components of the described model into a uniform range of values, additionally ensuring legibility of the risk analysis results. The exclusion of this range of values lower than 1, in particular 0 values, from such range is associated with the concept of a residual risk, [12], according to which it is impossible to completely eliminate the risk, thus, none of its components presented in the method of analysis of the process risk may have zero value. To transpose the values of the individual components of the risk of the processes of sensitive data processing into the uniform range of values, we have introduced the concept of the standardization function. The standardization function is a family of functions $\xi: X \longrightarrow [1, 2, \ldots, N]$ determined for the selected components of the business process risk.

For example, in case of the component related to the confidentiality of data processed in this process - $\boldsymbol{\alpha_{P_i}}$ function ξ_α can be defined as follows:

$$\xi_\alpha(\alpha_{P_i}) = \begin{cases} 1, if\ \alpha_{P_i} = F \\ 2, if\ \alpha_{P_i} = E \\ 3, if\ \alpha_{P_i} = D \\ 4, if\ \alpha_{P_i} = C \\ 6, if\ \alpha_{P_i} = B \\ 8, if\ \alpha_{P_i} = A \end{cases}; \quad (1)$$

$where$:
$P_i \epsilon P(O)$, $\xi_\alpha \epsilon \Xi]$, $\alpha \epsilon \mathrm{A}$ – set of confidentiality classes.

The forms of the standardization function from the family Ξ should be defined in such a manner so as to transpose their values to the range [1,..., N] and keep the right proportions of their impact on the risk of the process of sensitive data processing. Another limitation is to express the M number of the selected standardization function from the family Ξ as a product of two natural numbers larger than 1, i.e.: $\|\Xi\| = M = m \times n,\ m > 1, n > 1$. Furthermore, the point is to obtain a product $M \times N \cong 100$ - then a calculated length of the risk vector of the process of sensitive data processing could be measured in percentage and easily interpreted.

2.3.4.2.2. Risk vector of particular components of the IT system

Once the vector space is defined $(M_{m\times n}, \boldsymbol{R}, +, \cdot)$ in algebra, $(M_{m\times n}, \boldsymbol{R}, +, \cdot, \otimes)$ it is possible to introduce the concept of the risk vector for each coordinate of the IT system risk vector.

The risk of the IT system $\left(\overrightarrow{R^B_{S_i}}, \overrightarrow{R^C_{S_i}}, \overrightarrow{R^T_{S_i}}\right)$ vector $\overrightarrow{R_{S_i}}$ coordinate S_i in algebra $(M_{m\times n}, \boldsymbol{R}, +,, \otimes)$) is the number $R^B_{S_i}$; $R^D_{S_i}$; $R^T_{S_i} \in \mathcal{R}$ equal to the vector length, i.e.:

$$R^B_{S_i} = \left\|\overrightarrow{R^B_{S_i}}\right\|;\ R^D_{S_i} = \left\|\overrightarrow{R^D_{S_i}}\right\|;\ R^T_{S_i} = \left\|\overrightarrow{R^T_{S_i}}\right\| \quad (2)$$

whereas: The risk vector of any coordinate $\left(\overrightarrow{R^B_{S_i}}, \overrightarrow{R^C_{S_i}}, \overrightarrow{R^T_{S_i}}\right)$ in algebra $(M_{m\times n}, \boldsymbol{R}, +, \cdot, \otimes)$ is the vector $\overrightarrow{R^X_{S_i}} \in M^{mxn}$; gdzie $X \in \{B, C, T\}$ being a linear combination of the system risk elements S_i in the linear space$(M_{m\times n}, \boldsymbol{R}, +, \cdot)$:

$$\overrightarrow{R^X_{S_i}} = \xi_{\alpha^1}\left(\alpha^1_{P_i}\right) \cdot \overrightarrow{\alpha^1} + \xi_{\alpha^2}\left(\alpha^2_{P_i}\right) \cdot \overrightarrow{\alpha^2} + \cdots + \xi_{\alpha^M}\left(\alpha^M_{P_i}\right) \cdot \overrightarrow{\alpha^M}$$

Algebra dimension $(M_{m\times n}, \boldsymbol{R}, +, \cdot, \otimes)$ [13] is: dim $(M_{m\times n}, \boldsymbol{R}, +, \cdot, \otimes) = M$.

Due to the fact that the algebra dimension $(M_{m\times n}, \boldsymbol{R}, +,, \otimes)$ is *N*, it is evident that *N* of base vectors in the vector space does exist $(M_{m\times n}, \boldsymbol{R}, +, \cdot)$ from algebra $(M_{m\times n}, \boldsymbol{R}, +,, \otimes)$, defined in the following manner:

$$\overrightarrow{\alpha^1} = \begin{pmatrix} 1 & \cdots & 0^n \\ \vdots & \ddots & \vdots \\ 0^m & \cdots & 0^M \end{pmatrix}; \ldots; \overrightarrow{\alpha^M} = \begin{pmatrix} 0 & \cdots & 0^n \\ \vdots & \ddots & \vdots \\ 0^m & \cdots & 1 \end{pmatrix} \quad (3)$$

On the basis of the above linear combination of such formula, it is evident that the impact of all M of the selected risk analysis factors on the obtained coordinate

$\overrightarrow{R_{S_i}^X}$ of risk vector $\overrightarrow{R_{P_i}} \in M^{mxn}$ is the same. Therefore, to clarify the estimated IT system risk level, it may be necessary to determine the impact of the particular vector coordinates and risk components on the final IT system risk level as well as to modify such coordinates $\overrightarrow{R_{S_i}^X} \in M^{mxn}$ by referring to such impact weights. This article does not tackle this issue.

2.3.4.2.3. Determination of the final IT system risk level

Once the values have been set $R_{S_i}^B$; $R_{S_i}^D$; $R_{S_i}^T \in \mathcal{R}$, which define in a quantitative manner the volume of the IT system risk impact S_i. it is possible to determine the final IT system risk level. The magnitude of the IT system risks may be defined as the vector module $|\overrightarrow{R_{S_i}}|$:

$$\overrightarrow{R_{S_i}} = |\overrightarrow{R_{S_i}}| = \sqrt[2]{{R_{S_i}^B}^2 + {R_{S_i}^D}^2 + {R_{S_i}^T}^2},$$

The presented value R_{S_i} defines in a qualitative manner the magnitude of the IT system risk impact P_i, which constitutes the final value of the method of the IT system risk analysis described herein. To present the risk level in a qualitative manner, determined by the above-mentioned qualitative method, the following risk ranges may be adopted: $R_{P_i} > 70$ – catastrophic risk, $R_{P_i} \in (60, \dots, 70]$ – very high risk, $R_{P_i} \in (50, \dots, 60]$ – high risk, $R_{P_i} \in (40, \dots, 50]$ – medium risk, $R_{P_i} \in (30, \dots, 40]$ – low risk, $R_{P_i} \in (20, \dots, 30]$ – very low risk, $R_{P_i} < 20$ – residual risk.

2.3.5. Risk evaluation

Evaluation of the IT system risk consists in the comparison of the results of risk analysis, including the adopted criteria to qualify the risk into the right category (acceptable, tolerable, intolerable risk levels, Fig. 4).

The main objective is to provide data that constitute grounds for making a decision on further risk management (whether to process the risk or abandon it, and if the decision is to process the risk - determine to what extent). The risk evaluation process is a summary of the present activities (identification and analysis) and indication which risk or group of risks should be processed further and which may be handled using current control measures [14-15].

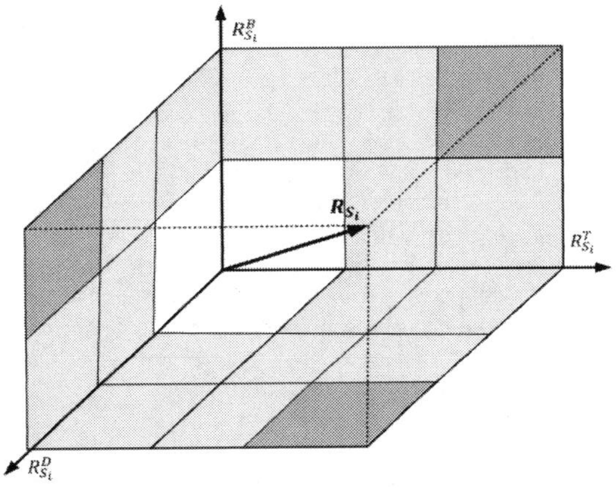

Fig. 6. Map of the IT system risk.

Risk evaluation, as the last step in the risk assessment

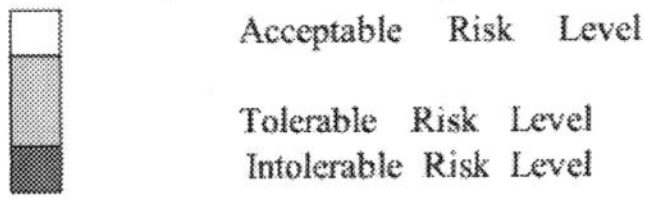

process, includes a comparison of the risk level identified during an analysis with the adopted criteria. Such comparison requires great accuracy and reliability. It is determined whether the expected risk falls within the limits of acceptance and tolerance or not. The accepted risk does not require any special attention (daily activities), whereas the risk within the tolerable limits should increase vigilance and initiate actions aimed at its monitoring, control and mitigation mechanisms. Risk tolerance does not mean acceptance of the status quo, it requires a response. However, before undertaking any actions, it is essential to evaluate efficiency of the monitoring process, reliability of the information, competency of staff, correctness of the analysis, possible losses or advantages of risks, expected expenses related to the risk mitigation and cost effectiveness of the whole undertaking. The higher the risk level, the more attention needs to be paid - preparation of special programs that may be implemented to eliminate or mitigate such risks, execution of a relevant process and scope of activities brining the risk to the tolerance or acceptance level, depending on the necessity of counteracting the costs of the effects and expenses regarding the adopted criteria. Such criteria should result from the organization's readiness, however the organization's ability to handle the risks depends on its personnel and parameters: size, structure, equipment, financial possibilities, professional approach as well as sensitivity and resistance to the expected risk. The main condition is to focus on bringing the risk to acceptable level. It is not always possible - in certain circumstances, some factors justifying the risk tolerance above its acceptable level may occur. The said circumstances may be the following:

1) the organization's possibilities go beyond its needs in terms of managing some acceptable risks, thus, it may be allowed, from time to time, to increase the risks for the purpose of benefiting from the

circumstances that may constitute an opportunity for the organization,
2) the risk level beyond the acceptable limits is so low that it does not require any special treatment or programs within the framework of the available resources,
3) the risk is not specified and does not fall within the organization's monitoring process,
4) the costs of risk management and mitigation, including the insurance and security costs, are disproportionate to potential profits; the only option would be to tolerate the risk that only slightly exceeds the acceptance limits.

During the risk assessment process, each risk has to be classified and compared with its tolerable and acceptable level. However, prior to that, it is necessary to adopt certain criteria that would help to explicitly identify significant risks, requiring resolute actions. This is a step in defining the risk that needs special attention.

2.3.6. Risk treatment

The starting point in risk management is composed of two levels: the first one - not requiring any other procedure than the monitoring process, always acceptable, and the second one - not tolerable, requiring immediate remedies aimed at brining the risks to the tolerance zone. The risk falling between those two levels shall be assessed in economic terms (costs and profits), e.g. in the management process related to residual risk. Nonetheless, the risk is not constant and may escalate towards non-tolerable level. Such risk requires more attention and needs to be monitored. Therefore, it is justified to qualify the risk as "non-tolerable". The actions need to be taken immediately, when the estimated cost/effect comparison is < 1. The risk within such range is considered reasonably practical, but needs to be monitored and the organization needs to prepare itself for appropriate reaction when the said circumstances appear. Such preparation shall include:

1) determination of the absolute scale of the expected risk,
2) broadening of knowledge, improvement of methods and arrangements related to the risk reduction or modification and its consequences,
3) ensuring appropriate readiness level to face the situations, when undesired events may occur due to the risk escalation,
4) readiness to incur any costs of potential losses, if the actions aimed at eliminating or mitigating the risks and preventing undesired events caused thereby or threats resulting therefrom proved inefficient.

Risk assessment determined the method of risk treatment. Such methods are defined in the following standard[18]:

1) avoidance of risk by making decisions on non-commencement or discontinuance 2. decrease or increase of risk to benefit from an opportunity,
2) elimination of the risk source,
3) change of probability (of risk occurrence),
4) change of consequence,
5) sharing of risk with another party or parties (including contracts and risk financing),
6) keeping the risk based on a conscious decision. To choose the right method of risk treatment, it is essential to consider all costs in terms of potential profits. However, it is not a prerequisite. According to the standard, it is recommended to include also such risks that are hard to justify, while considering only the cost effectiveness of the choice. The so-called severe risks (with high negative consequences, but low probability) should also be analyzed.

The method of risk treatment should also be articulated and properly described. The risk treatment plans are used for that purpose. They should include the majority of the previously indicated elements, i.e.[19]:

1) justified choice of a given treatment option,
2) persons responsible for its implementation,
3) proposed actions,
4) requirements concerning the resources, including those for crisis preparedness,
5) reporting and monitoring requirements,
6) time framework and schedule.

2.3.7. Monitoring and review

The last two actions are monitoring and review. The monitoring process should be included already at the plan preparation stage (periodic), even though - according to the standard - the process should be also verified ad hoc. While developing the plans, it is essential to explicitly assign responsibility for this action and include all aspects of risk management therein. The monitoring process is aimed at tracking all changes occurring in the environment, not eliminating or mitigating the risk, but providing information thereon. It also constitutes grounds for performing actions and controlling the risk. Only permanent monitoring may contribute to confidence in information. Everything is subject to change: environment, atmosphere, sensitivity, organizations, law, programs and processes. Such changes affect targets, rules, policies and risk management practices. The monitoring and review processes should be also properly documented. The point is to not only document the processes, but also, or even above all, to create appropriate conditions for improvement and refinement of the selected methods and tools. Apart from the International Standard Organization (ISO), there are also several other recommendations concerning risk management, such as the British standard published by the Federation of European Risk Management Associations (FERMA) or American Enterprise Risk Management – Integrated Framework, known as COSO_II, which was developed by the Committee of Sponsoring Organizations of the Treadway Commission (COSO).

[18] [3], p. 51.

[19] [3], p. 53.

All these norms and standards, similarly to those mentioned at the beginning hereof, are based on similar assumptions. The goal is to define links between the organization's targets, including all risk management elements, i.e. context determination, risk assessment, risk response and treatment, control actions, information and communication principles, as well as monitoring through constant evaluation of the obtained results [16-21].

2.4. Documentation of risk management

The documented[20] actions related to risk management constitute one of the last elements of the pillar related to the above-described processes. According to the standard, it is also recommended to use the available tools for consolidating the knowledge of identified risks as well as actions and decisions made during the risk management process. This element fulfills several important functions, thanks to which the organization is able to accomplish its goals. Therefore, it is even more important to be able to learn and improve internal methods and processes implemented under the risk management procedure. The documentation of data also brings some benefits in terms of management of the organization, by supporting its decision-making process thanks to a possibility of multiple use of the archived historic sensitive documents [22, 23, 5, 6, 24, 39]. The guidelines on risk documentation, applied in office units, point to at least two types of the used documents. The first type refers to identification worksheets or risk identification and assessment worksheets. They are used as basic material for risk analysis. The second type of the documents are the so-called risk registers[21]. They include extended information on the identified and assessed risks, including defined actions to be taken with respect thereto. The risk registers most often constitute integrated lists enclosed with risk reports, which are subject to verification and analysis at the stage of monitoring and review [11, 25-27].

Summary

The methodology of the risk analysis and management referring to the IT system supporting the processing of documents at different levels of sensitivity, is characterized by high complexity due to the mathematical apparatus applied. Therefore, due to the fact that a number of factors affecting processes risk level were taken into consideration, it is almost impossible to determine the risk of the process of sensitive data processing in terms of time and costs or to manage such risk in a traditional manner, without applying any IT solutions or computer techniques. Due to a variety of different factors and broad spectrum of their impact on the processes of sensitive data processing, the application of the risk analysis should constitute an integral part of the decision-making process as well as the planning of different variants of the operations of each organization. The knowledge of the risks associated in the sensitive data processing allows to shape such processes so that their security levels are acceptable [4, 28]. When analyzing the risk sources and categories in the processes of sensitive data processing, their characteristics, process architecture and its life cycle should be mainly taken into account. Such knowledge, in combination with the quality statistics concerning the security and architecture of the process for sensitive data processing, seems to be the key to risk mitigation in all its aspects – human, environmental, security-related, qualitative and economic. The considerations outlined herein are of mainly cognitive importance, thus, formal descriptions of certain issues were omitted. The objective of the article was to show the concept which differs from the traditional view on the issues related to risk quantification.

[20] ISO 31000:2009 does not recommend any model or sample documentation forms concerning risk management, but provides only general recommendations on risk identification. Given the importance of this issue, it was outlined in more detail in the article.

[21] Example of risk registers can be found in *Risk Management Guidelines Companion to AS/NZS 4360:2004*, replaced by current ISO 31000 [3].

References

1. PN-ISO Guide 73:2009, Risk Management – Vocabulary, (2009).
2. C. Sikorski, *Ludzie nowej organizacji. Wzory kultury organizacyjnej wysokiej tolerancji niepewności*, p. 23 (1998).
3. PN-ISO 31000:2012, *Zarządzanie ryzykiem -- Zasady i wytyczne*, (2012).
4. M. Kiedrowicz, *Location with the use of the RFID and GPS technologies - opportunities and threats*, GIS ODYSSEY 2016, pp. 122-128, (2016).
5. M. Kiedrowicz, J. Koszela, *Business processes modelling for the processing of classified documents using RFID technology*, Collegium of Economic Analysis Annals, vol. **42,** pp. 53-66, (2016).
6. M. Kiedrowicz, J. Koszela, *Secret office model for the processing of classified documents using RFID technology*, Collegium of Economic Analysis Annals, vol. **42,** pp. 67-81, (2016).
7. R. Hoffmann, M. Kiedrowicz, J. Stanik, *Risk management system as the basic paradigm of the information security management system in an organization*, MATEC Web of Conferences, vol. **76**, DOI: 10.1051/matecconf/20167604010 (2016).
8. J. Stanik, J. Napiórkowski, R. Hoffmann, *Zarządzanie ryzykiem w systemie zarządzania bezpieczeństwem organizacji*, Zeszyty Naukowe Uniwersytetu Szczecińskiego – Ekonomiczne Problemy Usług, (2016).
9. J. Gołębiewski, *Zarządzanie kryzysowe w świetle wymogów bezpieczeństwa*, pp. 120-121, (2011).
10. D. Wróblewski (ed.), *Przegląd wybranych dokumentów normatywnych z zakresu zarządzania kryzysowego i zarządzania ryzykiem wraz z leksykonem*, p. 161, (2014).
11. M. Kiedrowicz, J. Stanik, *Selected aspects of risk management in respect of security of the document lifecycle management system with multiple levels of sensitivity*, (in:) Information Management in Practice,

(eds) B.F. Kubiak and J. Maślankowski, pp. 231-249, (2015).

12. J. Hash, *Risk Management Guidance For Information Technology Systems*, ITL Bulletin, (2002).
13. T. Trajdos, *Matemetyka*, (1993).
14. S. Nowosielski, *Modelowanie procesów gospodarczych w literaturze i praktyce*, (in:) Podejście procesowe w organizacjach, (ed.) S. Nowosielski, (2009).
15. J. Stanik, T. Protasowicki, KKIO - Od procesów do oprogramowania: badania i praktyka, *Metodyka kształtowania ryzyka w cyklu rozwojowym systemu informatycznego*, (2015).
16. M. Kiedrowicz, J. Stanik, *Adequacy evaluation of the simulation models of system dynamics on the example of the Earned Value model*, (in:) Information Management (eds) B.F. Kubiak and A. Sieradz, pp. 9-17, (2014).
17. J. Zawiła-Nadźwiecki, *Metoda TISM-BCP – Total Security Management. Business Continuity Planning*, (2003).
18. B. Bruegge, A. Dutoit, *Inżynieria oprogramowania w ujęciu obiektowym. UML, wzorce projektowe i Java*, (2011).
19. M. Piotrowski, *Notacja modelowania procesów biznesowych*, (2007).
20. T. Nowicki, M. Marczak, *The modeling analysis and simulation of transport company functioning*. (in:) Modeling of modern enterprises logistics, (eds.) M. Fertsch, K. Grzybowska, A. Stachowiak, (2009).
21. M. Kiedrowicz, T. Protasowicki, J. Stanik, *Wybrane aspekty standaryzacji w ochronie publicznych zasobów informacyjnych i świadczonych usług w kontekście społeczeństwa informacyjnego*, Zeszyty Naukowe Uniwersytet Szczeciński.. – Ekonomiczne Problemy Usług, vol. **113**, pp. 113-130, (2014).
22. M. Kiedrowicz, *Publiczne zasoby informacyjne jako podstawa tworzenia platform integracyjnych*, (in:) INTERNET. Prawno-informatyczne problemy sieci, portali i e-usług, (ed.) G. Szpor, pp. 231-246, (2012).
23. M. Kiedrowicz, *Uogólniony model danych w rozproszonych rejestrach ewidencyjnych*, Roczniki Kolegium Analiz Ekonomicznych, vol. **33**, pp. 209-234, (2014).
24. M. Kiedrowicz, R. Waszkowski, *Business rules automation standards in business process management systems*, (in:) Information Management in Practice, (eds) B.F. Kubiak and J. Maślankowski, pp. 187-200, (2015).
25. M. Kiedrowicz, *Rejestry publiczne wykorzystywane przez organy odpowiedzialne za wykrywanie i przeciwdziałanie przestępczości*, (in:) Rejestry publiczne: Jawność i interoperacyjność, (ed.) A. Gryszczyńska, pp. 603-649, (2016).
26. R. Kasprzyk, A. Stachurski, *A concept of standard-based vulnerability management automation for IT systems*, Computer Science and Mathematical Modelling, pp. 33-38, vol. **3**, (2016).
27. R. Kasprzyk, M. Maj, Z. Tarapata, *Przestępstwa w cyberprzestrzeni. Aspekty techniczne i prawne*. (in:) Przestępczość w XXI wieku. Problemy technologiczno-informatyczne., pp. 527-539, Warszawa, (2015).
28. M. Kiedrowicz, *Objects identification in the information models used by information systems*, GIS ODYSSEY 2016, pp. 129-136, (2016).
29. Z. Tarapata, *Models and algorithms for knowledge-based decision support and simulation in defence and transport applications*, Wojskowa Akademia Techniczna, Warszawa, (2011)
30. Z. Tarapata, M. Zabielski, R. Kasprzyk, K. Szkółka, Profile Cloning Detection in Online Social Networks, Computer Science and Mathematical Modelling, vol. **3**, pp.39-46, (2016)
31. Z. Tarapata, R. Kasprzyk, Graph-based optimization method for information diffusion and attack durability in networks, *RSCTC 2010*, Lecture Notes in Artificial Intelligence, vol. **6086**, pp. 698-709 (2010)
32. M. Kiedrowicz, T. Nowicki, R. Waszkowski, Z. Wesolowski, and K. Worwa, *Method for assessing software reliability of the document management system using the RFID technology*, 20th International Conference on Circuits, Systems, Communications and Computers, MATEC Web of Conferences, vol. **76**, DOI: 10.1051/matecconf/20167604009 (2016).
33. M. Kiedrowicz, T. Nowicki, R. Waszkowski, Z. Wesolowski, and K. Worwa, *Business processes in the RFID-equipped restricted access administrative office*, 20th International Conference on Circuits, Systems, Communications and Computers, MATEC Web of Conferences, vol. **76**, DOI: 10.1051/matecconf/20167604003, (2016).
34. M. Kiedrowicz, T. Nowicki, R. Waszkowski, Z. Wesolowski, and K. Worwa, *Software simulator for property investigation of document management system with RFID tags*, 20th International Conference on Circuits, Systems, Communications and Computers, MATEC Web of Conferences, vol. **76**, DOI: 10.1051/matecconf/20167604012 (2016).
35. R. Hoffmann, M. Kiedrowicz, J. Stanik, *Evaluation of information safety as an element of improving the organization's safety management*, 20th International Conference on Circuits, Systems, Communications and Computers, MATEC Web of Conferences, vol. **76**, DOI: 10.1051/matecconf/20167604011, (2016).
36. M. Kiedrowicz, *Rejestry i zasoby informacyjne wykorzystywane przez organy odpowiedzialne za wykrywanie i przeciwdziałanie przestępczości*, (in:) Jawność i jej ograniczenia, (ed.) G.Szpor, Monografie Prawnicze, (vol. IX), pp. 170-264, (2015).
37. M. Kiedrowicz, *Dostęp do publicznych zasobów danych - Big data czy Big brother*, (in:) INTERNET. Publiczne bazy danych i Big data, (ed.) G. Szpor, pp. 15-39, (2015).
38. M. Kiedrowicz, *The importance of an integration platform within the organisation*, Zeszyty Naukowe, vol. **46**, pp.83-94, (2014).
39. M. Kiedrowicz, T. Nowicki, R. Waszkowski, *Business process data flow between automated and human tasks*, 3rd International Conference on Social Science (ICSS 2016) December 9–11 2016, pp. 471-477, (2016).

 DOI: 10.1051/matecconf/201712502011

System risk model of the IT system supporting the processing of documents at different levels of sensitivity

Jerzy STANIK[1,*]

[1] Military University of Technology, Faculty of Cybernetics, Institute of Computer and Information Systems, Warsaw, Poland

Abstract. This study outlines the system risk model of IT system oriented at the safety of the processes of sensitive data processing. The model constitutes a multi-dimensional approach to the analysis of IT system risk and IT processes implemented therein. The presented approach includes various categories of risk factors, resulting from both the architecture of the very IT system, IT security elements and security of the continued operations. The model described in this article may constitute a starting point for the development of the method for IT system risk analysis and appropriate IT security policy, which may in turn constitute input values for the methodology of IT system risk management.

Introduction

When analyzing various models, methods and approaches to assessment of the risk level and proper handling of risks, a question arises whether a possibility of creating a complex and adequate IT system risk assessment model[1], where the documents at different sensitivity levels are processed, and which includes various categories of risk factors allowing their combination so that it is possible to determine the risk level of sensitive documents, while maintaining practical usability of the proposed solution, does actually exist. This article is an attempt to answer the above question by outlining the system risk model of IT system supporting the processing of the documents different levels of sensitivity, which is - according to the authors - complete and consistent. The proposed risk model may be used at the stage of managing the IT system security and also developing the appropriate IT system security policy.

The risk related to IT systems may be considered in two different ways. Firstly, it is perceived as the design risk associated with other risks occurring at different stages of the IT system life cycle. Secondly, the approach consists in the analysis of the implemented processes of sensitive data processing to assess the risks related thereto and then in the management of the properly identified risks by accepting, transferring, avoiding or mitigating such risks. This study presents the IT system model of the office in such context. If the IT system risk level of the office is known, it is possible to efficiently manage such risk [2-6] by applying methods, methodologies and tools intended for that purpose.

1. Basic IT system risk elements

The starting point for constructing the IT system risk assessment model, as proposed in this article, reflecting systemness of the described solution, shall be the IT system security model for the office presented in Fig. 1.

The model presented in Fig. 1 covers the three following areas: security of data, security of the processes of sensitive data processing and security of the continued process operations, and is based on the following components:

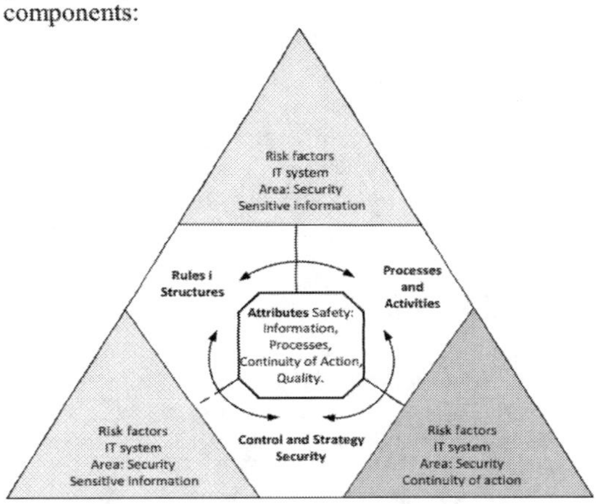

Fig. 1. The IT system security model for the office, allowing the processing of documents at different sensitivity levels.

- Rules - strategy, policies and procedures defining the rules of procedure concerning the

* corresponding author: jerzy.stanik@wat.edu.pl

[1] Risk assessment - the entire process of risk assessment, Risk analyses and risk evaluation. [1] definition 3.4.1.

DOI: 10.1051/matecconf/201712502011

security of sensitive data, processes of their processing and continuity of operations, whose comprehensive implementation within the entire office means efficient office management.
- Structures - a set of positions and organizational units within the organization and their correlations. For the purpose of this study, the following structures are of importance: risk management framework, security services, continued operations framework, quality and control management services.
- Office processes and operations - the solutions ensuring proper operations of the office, security and quality of the information processed therein, (Stanik i Protasowicki, 2015), compliance with the requirements on the business continuity, responses to infringement of the policies and procedures as well as incidents related to a breach of security of sensitive data.
- Security control and strategy - ongoing monitoring of the IT system operations, processes of sensitive data processing, verification of the level of compliance with safety rules as well as their consistency and adequacy, and solutions for residual risk reduction with respect to the assigned attributes of the security of the process of sensitive data processing and their business continuity.

The following correlations occur between the particular pillars of the above-described model:
- the rules included in the policies and procedures define the operations of the security solutions together with the ways of monitoring their work,
- the operations of the security systems - security-ensuring solutions - determine the occurrence of new security principles and affect the scope of the monitoring of the continued operations, whereas the quality of the processing processes determine the occurrence of new security principles and affect the scope of the monitoring and control,
- the events detected thanks to the security monitoring stimulate changes in the security solutions - security system as well as information security management system, and provide recommendations for the modifications of the existing solutions in terms of their security and creation of new security policies and procedures.

The model defined in such a manner shows the areas that determine the level of IT system risks and ensure completeness of the approach, which was confirmed by wide application of the model [7, 8]. The key element of the above-mentioned IT system security model is a set of basic IT security attributes, divided into the following subsets/areas:

I. Information security area. Within the framework of this component, the following elements with special impact on the IT system risk level may be distinguished:
   1. **Confidentiality**: Access to the information is limited to a group of authorized entities only. The data are protected against reading and copying by a person not authorized by the data owner. This type of security solution not only includes the protection of all data, but also of the individual elements thereof, which look "innocent", but may be used to breach the confidentiality of other information.
   2. **Data consistency**: The point is to ensure that the information is not modified in an unauthorized manner and that all potential modifications are detected. The information is protected against its removal or any modifications made without the consent of its owner. The protected information also includes such elements as settlement system records, tapes with back-up copies, times of creating files and documents.
   3. **Data availability**: The information may be accessed in any circumstances permitted by the information security policy. The offered services are protected against distortion and damage. If an authorized user needs to use the IT system, which is unavailable, the effect may be the same as in case of removing data from the system.
   4. **Data certainty:** The party undertaking some actions using the software may not deny the fact the (s)he performed some operations with the use of the software.

II. The area of the process of sensitive data processing. Within the framework of this component, the following elements with special impact on the IT system risk level may be distinguished:
   1. **Availability of the process of sensitive data processing** - a possibility of making a certain action in office available for use at a certain time and upon request of an authorized entity.
   2. **Operating safety**: The point is to ensure that the work of the IT system is in line with the users' expectations. If the IT system resources, e.g. hardware and software start operating significantly different than usually, especially after the software upgrade or removing hardware failure, a real disaster could happen (e.g. ls command, which starts removing files from time to time instead of displaying them). This type of protection may be considered a way of ensuring operating safety.
   3. **Process control**: The objective is to control access to the core IT system process. Unknown or unauthorized persons (or programs) in the system may constitute a serious problem. It is essential to learn how they got into the system. To remove the effects of such incidents may require substantial contribution in terms of time and workload, for example, related to the necessity of redesigning and reinstalling the

system as well as verifying whether any important component was changed or disclosed - even if nothing has actually happened.

4. **Audit:** The system is not only under threat from the unauthorized users. Sometimes authorized users make mistakes, commit offenses and even deliberately destroy things. In such case, it is important to check what was done, by whom and with what effects. One way to obtain such information is to use the damage-proof event records in the system, which allows identifying the offenders and their actions. In some critical applications, it is possible to undo certain operations, which may be helpful in the process of restoring proper condition of the system.

III. The area of the process of safety of sensitive data processing. Within the framework of this component, the following elements with special impact on the IT system risk level may be distinguished:

1. Fulfillment of the requirements included in the policy referring to the process continuity of operations,
2. Business Continuity Plan - BCP
3. Disaster Recovery Plan - DRP.
4. Financial effects of suspension/interruption of the process implementation,
5. Non-financial effects of suspension/interruption of the process implementation,
6. Costs and time of the process unavailability.

Among from the information security attributes, all of them were directly incorporated into the system risk model of IT system proposed in this article. The impact of confidentiality and availability on the IT system risk depends on the expected level of such attributes for a given system. If the expectations concerning availability or confidentiality of the IT system are high, a given attribute shall significantly affect the risk assessment process for such system. However, if the availability or confidentiality for a certain IT system is not a critical factor, then the impact of a given attribute on the risk of such IT system shall be marginal [12-13].

According to the authors, in case of attributes of the security of the processes of sensitive data processing, it is important to prevent the situations when the lack of integrity and continuity of business processes or information processed thereunder is knowingly accepted. Therefore, it may be assumed that the expectations for every process in terms of its integrity are comparable.

The *Rules*, presented in the model in Fig. 1, are characterized by the following elements having impact on the risk level of IT systems: · security policy, · security procedures, · – BCP (*Business Continuity Plan*) – DRP (*Disaster Recovery Plan*). Of these, the security policy and safe use procedures implemented in the office have key impact on the IT system risk. However, the manner of considering such factors in the presented model differs [9-11]. The security policy constitutes a direct component of the IT system risk in the proposed model, whereas the safe use procedures have only indirect impact on such risk. Since verification of the security procedures constitutes an integral part of the process of classifying IT systems and assigning them to appropriate safety classes, the impact of the security procedures on the IT system risk in the proposed model is expressed by assigning the IT system to a specific security class. The methodology proposed in this article does not include any evaluation of the BCP or DRP Plans. It is due to the fact that the BCP-related issues are more connected with business risk than IT system risk, whereas DRP is directly linked to the attribute of the IT system availability. Furthermore, practical experience has shown that IT systems not requiring high level of availability usually do not have any dedicated DRP Plans, which usually results from the economic account of profitability. Therefore, to include the IT system risk analysis in the method proposed herein, the DRP-related component, would raise the risk level of such systems. Another argument in favor of exclusion of the DRP-related component from this methodology is close connection of the DRP Plans with the business needs of a given organization. According to the author, evaluation of such plans in isolation from the business needs of the organization would be an abuse and would undermine the objectivity of the methodology proposed herein.

The category *Processes and Actions* in the model presented in Fig. 1 includes the following elements, which may have impact on the risk level of IT systems: protection processes, change management process, control and security mechanisms. The impact of the protection processes on the IT system risk, in particular its process of sensitive data processing is shown in Fig. 2. The impact of the change management process on the IT system risk is visible in commonly applied international standards, such ITIL and COBIT (Control Objectives for Information and Related Technology), which is reflected in the fact that the change management process is included in the proposed model as a risk component.

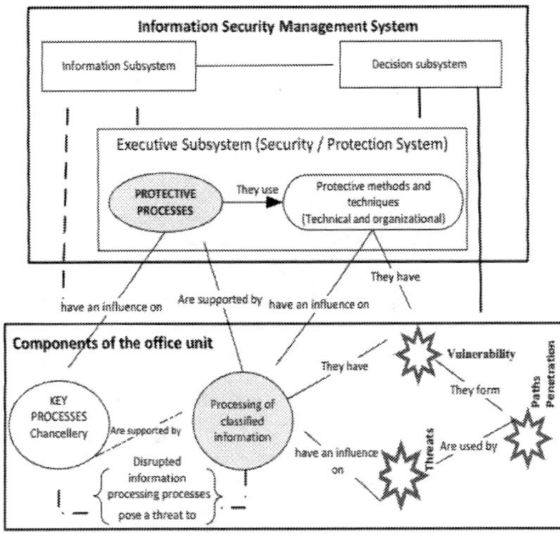

Fig. 2. The place of the protection processes in the information security management system in the office.

The control is the last of the main components of the IT system security model presented in Fig. 1. As part of this component, the following elements with special impact on the level of IT system risk may be distinguished: complexity of ICT environment, security monitoring system, physical and logical access control, impact of human factor. All of the above-mentioned elements are included in the method of IT system risk analysis proposed herein, however, the manner of their incorporation into the said method is different [14-19].

2. Components of the vector of IT system risk in the office

The system risk model of IT system for the office, presented herein, has been defined as the following vector $\overrightarrow{R_{S_i}}$:

$$\overrightarrow{R_{S_i}} = \langle \overrightarrow{R^B_{S_i}}, \overrightarrow{R^C_{S_i}}, \overrightarrow{R^T_{S_i}} \rangle \qquad (1)$$

defining the IT system risk level, which includes three composition (coordinates) partial vectors $\overrightarrow{R^B_{S_i}}$, $\overrightarrow{R^C_{S_i}}$, $\overrightarrow{R^T_{S_i}}$, reflecting the levels of IT system risks in terms of particular areas of risk factors. The selected coordinates of the risk vector represent individual risk areas (Fig. 1), each of them including several risk factors, hereinafter referred to as the composition of partial vectors of IT system risk. The components of particular partial vectors used in this IT system risk model of the office are the following:

I. Information security area - $R^B_{S_i}$:

1. Data availability in the system - $\boldsymbol{\lambda_{S_i}}$. The data availability in the IT system S_i is a possibility of making a certain action in office available for use at a certain time and upon request of an authorized entity. The data availability in the IT system S_i is expressed by assigning the system to a particular availability class $\lambda \in \Lambda$, marked as λ_{P_i}. Set L = {I, II, III, IV, V}[2] containing the following elements is called the group of availability classes of the IT system:

   I – defines the IT system S_i, in case of which the expected availability is 99.99% per year and its maximum one-time unavailability does not exceed 30 minutes,

   V – defines the IT system S_i, in case of which the expected availability is 70% per year and its maximum one-time unavailability exceeds 3 weeks.

   Every IT system $S_i \epsilon P(O)$ $i \epsilon \{1, 2, \dots N\}$belongs to one and only one availability class $\lambda \in \Lambda$. The described principle of assigning the IT system S_i to a given availability class ensures explicitness of defining the availability of the IT system S_i, which is significant for the model outlined in this article.

2. Data confidentiality - α_{P_i}

The property of data non-disclosure to any unauthorized parties S_i is the IT system data confidentiality. The confidentiality of data processed by the IT system S_i is expressed by assigning the system to a particular data confidentiality class, $\alpha \epsilon \mathrm{A}$ and marked as α_{P_i}. Every IT system $S_i \epsilon P(O)$ $i \epsilon \{1, 2, \dots N\}$ belongs to one and only one availability class of confidentiality of the business process data $\alpha \in A$. The set of confidentiality classes of data processed by the IT system S_i is called A = {A, B, C, D, E}, composed of the following elements:

A – defines the IT system and processes secret data, whose disclosure may pose threat to human life or health,

E – defines the IT system, used for processing of public data.

3. Fulfillment of the requirements defined in the information security policy -$\eta^B_{S_i}$. The set of requirements in the O's office security policy is a finite set, $W^B_{P(O)} = \{w_1, w_2, \dots w_m, \dots w_{M^B}\}$, where: M^B is the number of requirements in the security policy in terms of P(O). In case of each requirement, $w_m \epsilon W^B_{P(O)}$ we define the priority of the requirement in terms of a given IT system S_i. The requirement priority $w_m \epsilon W^B_{P(O)}$ in terms of the IT system S_i is the number $p^m_{S_i} \in \{0,1, \dots 5\}$, where:

0 – means that the requirement is inaccurate for the IT system S_i,

5 – means that the requirement is maximally significant for the system S_i.

The values from 1 to 5 are numerical expressions of the following: minimum, low, medium, high and maximum level of significance of the requirement in terms of a given IT system. To allow 0 value in the set of values $p^m_{S_i}$ means to respond to the situations, when the requirement has nothing to do with the analyzed IT system. Therefore, in case of each IT system $S_i \epsilon P(O)$, there is the following set: $W^B_{S_i}$such as that: $W^B_{S_i} \neq \emptyset$, $W^B_{S_i} \subseteq W_{P(O)}$, $w_m \epsilon W^B_{P(O)}$ belongs to $W^B_{S_i}$ when and only when $p^m_{P_i} \neq 0$.

The fulfillment of the requirement $w_m \epsilon W^B_{P(O)}$of the IT system S_i is the number, $s^m_{P_i} \in [0\%, \dots, 100\%]$, where 0% – means that the requirement has not been met in terms of the process P_i, 100% – means that the requirement has been fully met in terms of the process P_i. The fulfillment of the requirements

[2] While considering the subjectivity of interpretations of particular elements in the group of availability classes and limited number of pages in this articles, I have decided to include construction of only two extreme elements of the particular sets.

of the IT system policy S_i is the following percentage value:

$$\eta^B_{S_i} = \frac{\sum_{m=1}^{\overline{W^B_{P(O)}}} \left(p^m_{S_i} * s^m_{S_i}\right)}{\sum_{m=1}^{W^B_{P(O)}} p^m_{S_i}} \qquad (2)$$

where:

- $W^B_{S_i}$ – the set of system requirements S_i,
- $p^m_{S_i}$ – the priority of *m* system requirement S_i,
- $s^m_{S_i}$ – the fulfillment of *m* system requirement S_i,

4. *Efficiency of the system monitoring of the information security*– $\beta^B_{S_i}$,

The efficiency of the system monitoring of the data for the IT system S_i is in the form of the following product:

$$\beta^B_{S_i} = d^B_{SM}(S_i) * \sum_j \left(\delta^m_{S_i} * \upsilon^{k^j}_{S_i}\right); \qquad (3)$$

where:

j – the number of the next criterion for assessing efficiency of the security monitoring system,

$\delta^m_{S_i}$ – priority of the *j–th* criterion for assessing efficiency of the system security monitoring system S_i,

$\upsilon^{k^j}_{S_i}$ – value of the *j–th* criterion for assessing efficiency of the system security monitoring system S_i,

k^j – materiality of the *j–th* criterion for assessing efficiency of the system security monitoring system,

$d^B_{SM}(S_i)$ – multiplier of the inclusion of the IT system S_i in the security monitoring system,

whereas:

$$d^B_{SM}(S_i) = \begin{cases} 1, \text{if the IT system is covered by a monitoring system to monitor the information system} \\ 0, \text{if the IT system is not covered by a monitoring systemto monitor the information system} \end{cases}$$

If the IT system S_i is under various monitoring systems, it is essential to define the number of criteria for assessing efficiency of such monitoring systems, e.g. in the form of tables [Table 1].

Table 1. Sample criteria for assessing efficiency of the security monitoring systems

Criterion	Priority $\delta^m_{P_i}$	Materiality k^j	Value $\upsilon^{k^j}_{P_i}$
Journal of process operations (collection of logs and data archivization)	4	3	{0,1,2,3,4,5}, where: 0 – no journal of the process operations (collection of logs) and no data archivization are made; 5 – efficient, modern and reliable backup mechanisms as well as log and data archivization are implemented for the process;
Analysis of susceptibility to frauds	3	2	{0,1,2,3,4,5}, where: 0 – no mechanisms of susceptibility analysis; 5 – developed system of susceptibility analysis, detecting possible susceptibility of business processes as well as offering certain ways of removing detected gaps and supporting the process of their removal;
Reactions related to detection of frauds	3	3	{1,2}, where: 2 - allows to automatically react to an attack; 1 - sends notifications about the detected events and undertaken actions; 1 - allows interruption of suspicious sessions and processes; 2 - allows separation of the attack source from the remaining part of the ICT infrastructure;
Average time of the system's reactions to an event (from the time of occurrence of such event to the time of its reporting and starting potential automatic reactions)	4	3	{0,1,2,3,4,5}, where: 0 – over 1 hour; 1 – from 5 minutes up to 1 hour; 2 – from 30 seconds up to 5 minutes; 3 – from 5 seconds up to 30 seconds; 4 – from 1 second up to 5 seconds; 5 – up to 1 second;
Reporting and data analysis	3	1	{0,1,2,3,4,5}, where: 1 – the system offers basic functionalities related to reporting; 5 – the system has a developed data warehouse module, allowing to perform multidimensional analyses according to the predefined criteria;

Source: own elaboration.

Otherwise, in compliance with the above definitions, the efficiency of the monitoring system selected for the IT system S_i would be zero and further determination of its parameters - unjustified. The criteria presented in Table 1 with respect to assessment of the monitoring system efficiency, materiality values and priorities of particular criteria as well as sets of their available values are not obligatory and may be customized. They should be considered sample data. The point of the above-described method for assessing efficiency of the security monitoring systems is to describe, in a quantitative manner, the quality rate of a given system that would allow direct comparison of the security monitoring systems from different supplier and characterized by different qualitative, functional and operational parameters.

II. Business continuity operations area - $\mathbf{R}^{C}_{S_i}$:

1. Fulfillment of the requirements defined in the business continuity management policy - $\eta^{C}_{S_i}$

The set of requirements in the O' office BC policy is a set, $W^{C}_{P(O)} = \{w_1, w_2, \dots w_m, \dots w_{M^C}\}$, where: M^C is the number of requirements in the security policy in terms of P(O). In case of each requirement, $w_m \epsilon W^{C}_{P(O)}$ we define the priority of the requirement in terms of a given IT system S_i. The requirement priority $w_m \epsilon W^{C}_{P(O)}$ in terms of the IT system S_i is the number $p^{m}_{S_i} \in \{0,1, \dots 5\}$, where:

0 – means that the requirement is inaccurate for the IT system S_i,

5 – means that the requirement is maximally significant for the system S_i.

The values from 1 to 5 are numerical expressions of the following: minimum, low, medium, high and maximum level of significance of the requirement in terms of a given IT system. To allow 0 value in the set of values $p^{m}_{S_i}$ means to respond to the situations, when the requirement has nothing to do with the analyzed IT system. Therefore, in case of each IT system $S_i \epsilon P(O)$, there is the following set: $W^{C}_{S_i}$ such as that: $W^{C}_{S_i} \neq \emptyset$, $W^{C}_{S_i} \subseteq W_{P(O)}$, $w_m \epsilon W^{C}_{P(O)}$ belongs to $W^{C}_{S_i}$ when and only when $p^{m}_{P_i} \neq 0$.

The fulfillment of the requirement $w_m \epsilon W^{C}_{P(O)}$ of the IT system S_i is the number, $s^{m}_{P_i} \in [0\%, \dots, 100\%]$, where 0% – means that the requirement has not been met in terms of the process P_i, 100% – means that the requirement has been fully met in terms of the process P_i. The fulfillment of the requirements in the business continuity management policy of the IT system S_i is the following percentage value:

$$\eta^{B}_{S_i} = \frac{\sum_{m=1}^{\overline{W^{C}_{P(O)}}} \left(p^{m}_{S_i} * s^{m}_{S_i}\right)}{\sum_{m=1}^{\overline{W^{C}_{P(O)}}} p^{m}_{S_i}} \tag{4}$$

where:

- $W^{C}_{S_i}$ –the set of business continuity requirements of the system S_i,
- $p^{m}_{S_i}$ – the priority of *m* system requirement S_i,
- $s^{m}_{S_i}$ – the fulfillment of *m* system requirement S_i,

2. Efficiency of the system monitoring the business continuity – $\beta^{C}_{S_i}$

The efficiency of the system monitoring the business continuity of the IT system S_i is in the form of the following product:

$$\beta^{C}_{S_i} = d^{C}_{SM}(S_i) * \sum_j \left(\delta^{m}_{S_i} * \upsilon^{kj}_{S_i}\right); \tag{5}$$

where:

j – the number of the next criterion for assessing efficiency of the system monitoring the business continuity,

$\delta^{m}_{S_i}$ – priority of the *j–th* criterion for assessing efficiency of the system security monitoring the system's business continuity S_i,

$\upsilon^{kj}_{S_i}$ – value of the *j–th* criterion for assessing efficiency of the system security monitoring the system's business continuity S_i,

k^j – materiality of the *j–th* criterion for assessing efficiency of the system monitoring the business continuity,

$d^{C}_{SM}(S_i)$ – multiplier of the inclusion of the IT system S_i in the system monitoring the business continuity,

whereas:

$$d^{C}_{SM}(S_i) = \begin{cases} 1, \text{if the IT system is covered by a monitoring} \\ \quad \text{system to monitor the information system} \\ 0, \text{if the IT system is not covered by a monitoring} \\ \quad \text{systemto monitor the information system} \end{cases}$$

BCP (Business Continuity Plan) and DRP (Disaster Recovery Plan).

The model proposed in this article does not include any evaluation of the BCP or DRP Plans. It is due to the fact that the BCP-related issues are more connected with business risk than IT system risk, whereas DRP is directly linked to the attribute of the IT system availability. Furthermore, practical experience has shown that the IT systems implemented in the office, i.e. RFID, which do not require high level of availability, usually do not have any dedicated DRP Plans, which usually results from the economic account of profitability. Therefore, to include the IT system risk in the model proposed herein, the DRP-related component, would raise the risk level of such systems. Another argument in favor of exclusion of the DRP-related component from this model is close connection of the DRP Plans with the business needs of a given organization. According to the author, evaluation of such plans in isolation from the business needs of the organization would be an abuse and would undermine the objectivity of the methodology proposed herein.

3. Cost of the IT system unavailability -κ_{S_i}

The costs related to unavailability of the IT system include all expenses connected with the performance of a given portion of actions, i.e. the operations that constitute a specific information process. To estimate the costs of the IT system unavailability, it was assumed that the event causing interruption of the information processing may occur at the worst possible moment. The cost of the IT system unavailability S_i is the measure consisting of financial effects of the interrupted process and non-financial effects of suspended information processing. The financial effects of the interrupted process of sensitive data processing shall be deemed to mean maximum potential financial losses that the Office would incur due to the suspension of such process for a definite time. The financial effects may be as follows: loss of profits, contractual damages, penalty interest, fines, potentially additional costs of running the office. The non-financial costs of suspending the processes are the consequences of the suspended processed, which may not be expressed by the volume of losses. The materiality of the non-financial effects of the suspended process for a definite time is estimated by choosing one of the following levels:

- insignificant effects - unnoticeable effects or no effects,
- noticeable effects - visible effects, in case of which no actions are required,
- serious effects - effects requiring certain actions to be undertaken for the purpose of their removal,
- very serious effects - effects requiring certain actions to be undertaken for the purpose of preventing discontinuance of business operations of the whole company,
- catastrophic effects - effects that may directly lead to the company's fall.

The non-financial effects are as follows:

- potential loss of trust on the market, e.g. loss of partners' trust, loss of the office's goodwill, dissatisfaction of clients, loss of clients,
- potential legal consequences (other than financial), e.g. restraint of liberty,
- potential dissatisfaction of the company's owners,
- potential dissatisfaction of individual clients,
- potential impediment to the activities of business, e.g. inability or problematic implementation of another process in the office.

The cost of unavailability of the process of information processing is expressed by assigning the process to a particular unavailability cost class $\kappa \in \mathrm{K}$, marked as κ_{S_i}. Set K = {I, II, III, IV, V, VI} containing the following elements is called the group of unavailability classes of the business processes:

I – defines the process of sensitive data processing, in case of which the level of financial costs does not exceed 5% of the office's financial fluidity ratio, e.g. 1 000, whereas the level of the non-financial costs is insignificant; VI – defines the process of sensitive data processing, in case of which the level of financial costs exceeds 50% of the office's financial fluidity ratio, e.g. 1 000 000, whereas the level of non-financial costs is catastrophic.

Every process of sensitive data processing $P_i \epsilon P(O)$ $i \epsilon \{1, 2, \dots N\}$belongs to one and only one unavailability cost class. $\kappa \in \mathrm{K}$. The proposed scale is not obligatory, may be customized.

4. The maximum time of unavailability of the processes of sensitive data processing - π_{S_i}

Maximum time of the process unavailability is the time during which the process execution must be restored to prevent any significant financial or non-financial effects. The maximum time of unavailability of the processes of information processing is expressed by assigning the process to a particular unavailability time class $\pi \in \Psi$ and is marked as π_{S_i}. The group of unavailability time classes of the *process of sensitive data processing* is set N = {0,1,2,3,4,5}, where: 0 – less than 1 hour; 1 – 4 hours; 2 – 1 day; 3 - 1 week, 4 – more than 1 week, 5 - 1 month and more.

Every process of sensitive data processing $P_i \epsilon P(O)$, $i \epsilon \{1, 2, \dots \mathrm{T}\}$, belongs to one and only one cost class of the process of sensitive data processing. $\pi \in \Psi$. The proposed scale is not obligatory, may be customized.

III. Processing security area - $\mathrm{R}^{\mathrm{T}}_{\mathrm{S}_i}$:

1. Fulfillment of the requirements defined in the processing security policy - $\eta^T_{S_i}$

The set of requirements in the O's office processing security policy is a finite and countable set, $W^T_{P(O)} = \{w_1, w_2, \dots w_m, \dots w_{M^T}\}$, where: M^T it is the number of requirements of the security policy with respect to the processing processes $P_j \epsilon S_i \in P(O)$. In case of each requirement, $w_m \epsilon W^T_{P(O)}$ we define the priority of the requirement in terms of a given IT system S_i. The requirement priority $w_m \epsilon W^T_{P(O)}$ in terms of the IT system S_i is the number $p^m_{S_i} \in \{0,1, \dots 5\}$, where:

0 – means that the requirement is inaccurate for the IT system ; S_i,

5 – means that the requirement is maximally significant for the system S_i.

The values from 1 to 5 are numerical expressions of the following: minimum, low, medium, high and maximum level of significance of the requirement in terms of a given IT system. To allow 0 value in the set of values $p^m_{S_i}$ means to respond to the situations, when the requirement has nothing to do with the analyzed IT system. Therefore, in case of each IT system S_i $\epsilon P(O)$, there is the following set: $W^T_{S_i}$ such as that:$W^T_{S_i} \neq \emptyset$, $W^J_{S_i} \subseteq W_{P(O)}$, $w_m \epsilon W^T_{P(O)}$ belongs to $W^T_{S_i}$ when and only when $p^m_{P_i} \neq 0$. The fulfillment of the requirement $w_m \epsilon W^T_{P(O)}$of the IT system S_i is the number, $s^m_{P_i} \in [0\%, \dots, 100\%]$, where 0% – means that the requirement has not been met in terms of the process P_i, 100% – means that the requirement has been fully met in terms of the process P_i. The fulfillment of the requirements in the business continuity management policy of the IT system S_i is the following percentage value:

$$\eta_{S_i}^T = \frac{\sum_{m=1}^{\overline{W_{P(O)}^T}} \left(p_{S_i}^m * s_{S_i}^m\right)}{\sum_{m=1}^{\overline{W_{P(O)}^T}} p_{S_i}^m} \quad (6)$$

where:

- $W_{S_i}^T$ –the set of business continuity requirements of the system S_i,
- $p_{S_i}^m$– the priority of m system requirement S_i,
- $s_{S_i}^m$ – the fulfillment of m system requirement S_i,

2. Efficiency of the quality monitoring system – $\beta_{S_i}^T$
The efficiency of the quality monitoring system for the IT system S_i is in the form of the following product:

$$\beta_{S_i}^T = d_{SM}^T(S_i) * \sum_j \left(\delta_{S_i}^m * v_{S_i}^{k^j}\right); \quad (7)$$

where:

j – the number of the next criterion for assessing efficiency of the quality monitoring system,

$\delta_{S_i}^m$ – priority of the j–th criterion for assessing efficiency of the quality monitoring systemS_i,

$v_{S_i}^{k^j}$– value of the j–th criterion for assessing efficiency of the quality monitoring systemS_i,

k^j – materiality of the j–th criterion for assessing efficiency of the quality monitoring system,

$d_{SM}^T(S_i)$– multiplier of the inclusion of the IT system S_i in the quality monitoring system,

whereas:

$$d_{SM}^T(S_i) = \begin{cases} 1, \text{if the IT system is covered by a monitoring system to monitor the information system} \\ 0, \text{if the IT system is not covered by a monitoring systemto monitor the information system} \end{cases}$$

3. Duration of information processing - δ_{S_i}
It is the average time of all operations related to the information processing. The duration mainly depends on the organizational level of the implemented procedures and value added level. The time of the sensitive information processing is expressed by assigning the process to a particular execution time class $\delta \in \Delta$, marked as δ_{S_i}. The group of execution time classes of the *process of data processing* is set $\Delta = \{0,1,2,3\}$, where: 0 – insignificant; 1 – medium organizational level of the implemented procedures and low value added; 2 – medium organizational level of the implemented procedures and average value added; 3 – high organizational level of the implemented procedures and high value added.
Every process of sensitive data processing $P_i \in P(O)$, $i\epsilon\{1,2,\ldots L\}$, belongs to one and only one cost class of the process of sensitive data processing. $\delta \in \Delta$. The proposed scale is not obligatory, may be customized.

4. Processing flexibility in the IT system - ϑ_{S_i}
The processing flexibility in the IT system S_i means the process ability to change, update, change order of the performed actions, merge operations, etc. It S_i is also determined on the basis of the process susceptibility to the transformation of the used resources as well as the speed rate of responding to the clients' requests. To introduce the definition of the processing flexibility scales in the IT system, S_i the following definitions have been adopted. The group of the processing flexibility scale classes S_i constitutes set $E = \{0,1,..,9\}$, whose elements discretize the processing flexibility scale in the IT system S_i, where: 0 – no processing flexibility in the IT system S_i, 9 – processing flexibility in the IT system S_i, with maximum reach, but at variance with the scope of requirements adopted in the security and business continuity policies. The proposed scale is not obligatory, may be customized. The level of the distribution and multiplicity of the IT system architecture components is called the scale of the processing process in the IT systemS_i. The scale of the processing flexibility in the IT system S_i is expressed by assigning the system to a particular flexibility scale class $\vartheta \in \Theta$, marked as ϑ_{P_i}.

5. Importance of the IT system - ζ_{S_i}
The importance of the IT systemS_i is the measure consisting of the consumer and recipient satisfaction levels, amounts of revenue generated by the system, strength of relationships between the system and clients. The importance of the IT system S_i is expressed by assigning the system to the importance class $\zeta \in Z$ and marked ζ_{S_i}. Set ZN = {I, II, III, IV, V,VI}S_i containing the following elements is called the group of the IT system importance classes: I – defines the IT system S_i, in case of which the consumer satisfaction level is below 50% and the amount of revenue generated by the system is low, VI - defines the IT system S_i, in case of which the consumer satisfaction level is over 90% and the amount of revenue generated by the system is very high. Every IT system $S_i \in P(O)$ $i \in \{1,2,\ldots Z\}$ belongs to one and only one IT system importance class. $\zeta \in Z$.

6. Efficiency of the change management process - φ_{P_i}
The efficiency of the change management process is the level of compliance of such process in the IT system S_i with the best practices in that respect. The efficiency of the change management process in the IT system S_i is expressed by way of the percentage compliance of such process S_i with the ITIL or other standards in that respect. The efficiency of the change management process in the IT system S_i is marked as φ_{P_i}.

3. Normalized components of the IT system risk vector

Due to the fact that the particular coordinates of the IT system risk vector as well as individual risk factors belong to different sets of values, it is necessary to introduce the function ξ or group of functions$\xi\epsilon\Xi$, which would clearly transpose the components to the uniform range of values. The standardization function is the family of functions $\xi : X \longrightarrow [1, 2, \ldots, N]$. Various forms of the standardization function from the family Ξ should be defined in such a manner so that they reflect their values per range [1,..., *N*] and maintain appropriate proportions of their impact on total IT system risk, including the set X of all specialized risk factors divided into subsets X^B, X^T, X^C representing the elected areas/aspects: information security, processing security and business continuity regarding the processing of sensitive information. Another limitation is to express the numbers L^B, L^T, L^C of the selected standardization function from the family Ξ as a product of two natural numbers larger than 1 is another limitation, i.e.:

$$\|\Xi^B\| = L^B = m \times n, m > 1, n > 1, \Xi^B \subset \Xi$$
$$\|\Xi^T\| = L^T = m \times n, m > 1, n > 1, \Xi^T \subset \Xi$$
$$\|\Xi^C\| = L^C = m \times n, m > 1, n > 1, \Xi^C \subset \Xi$$

Furthermore, the point is to make the products: $L^B \times N^B, L^T \times N^T, L^C \times N^C \cong 100$, then the calculated length of the IT system risk vector $\overrightarrow{R_{S_i}}$ and its coordinates $\left(\overrightarrow{R^B_{S_i}}, \overrightarrow{R^C_{S_i}}, \overrightarrow{R^T_{S_i}}\right)$ may be measured as scaled percentages and hence may be easily interpreted.
In the model proposed herein, the following values have been adopted:

- Information security area: $L^B = 4$, N^B=24, $\xi : X^B \longrightarrow [1, 2, \ldots, 24]$ *and* $L^B \times N^B \cong 100$
- Process security area: $L^T = 6$, N^T=16, $\xi : X^T \longrightarrow [1, 2, \ldots, 8]$ *and* $L^T \times N^T \cong 100$
- Business continuity area: L^C =4, N^C=24 $\xi : X^C \longrightarrow [1, 2, \ldots, 24]$ *and* $L^C \times N^C \cong 100$.

The proposed ranges are not obligatory, may be customized. Such value ranges are aimed at creating the simplest possible shape of the functions that would transpose particular coordinates of the vector $\overrightarrow{R_{S_i}}$ and components of the described model into uniform value ranges, additionally ensuring legibility of the risk analysis results. The exclusion of the values lower than 1, in particular 0 values, from such range is associated with the concept of a residual risk, (Hash, 2002), according to which it is impossible to completely eliminate the risk, thus, none of its components presented in the IT system risk model may have zero value. To transpose the values of the individual IT system risk components into the uniform value ranges, we have introduced the concept of the standardization function.

When considering the above assumption and limitations, the standardization functions $\xi\epsilon\Xi$ shall be as follows:

A. in case of a subset of the functions $\xi\epsilon\Xi^B$ characterized by the information security:

1. for the data *availability* component, it is defined in the following manner:

$$\xi_\lambda(\lambda_{S_i}) = \begin{cases} 1,\ if\ \lambda_{S_i} = V \\ 7, if\ \lambda_{S_i} = IV \\ 13, if\ \lambda_{S_i} = III \\ 19, if\ \lambda_{S_i} = II \\ 24, if\ \lambda_{S_i} = I \end{cases}; \tag{8}$$

2. for the data confidentiality component, it is defined in the following manner:

$$\xi_\alpha(\alpha_{S_i}) = \begin{cases} 1,\ if\ \alpha_{S_i} = E \\ 7, if\ \alpha_{S_i} = D \\ 13, if\ \alpha_{S_i} = C \\ 19, if\ \alpha_{S_i} = B \\ 24, if\ \alpha_{S_i} = A \end{cases}; \tag{9}$$

3. for the component concerning the fulfillment of the requirements of the information security policy, it is defined in the following manner: $\eta^B_{S_i}$,

$$\xi^B_\eta(\eta^B_{S_i}) = 1 + 23 * \left(1 - \frac{\eta^B_{S_i}}{100\%}\right); \tag{10}$$

4. for the information security monitoring component, it is defined in the following manner: $\beta^B_{S_i}$,

$$\xi^B_\eta(\beta^B_{S_i}) = 24 - \sqrt[3]{\frac{\beta^B_{S_i}}{2}}; \tag{11}$$

B. in case of a subset of the functions $\xi\epsilon\Xi^C$ characterized by the business continuity security of the process of sensitive data processing:

1. for the component concerning the fulfillment of the requirements of the business continuity security of the process of sensitive data processing, it is defined in the following manner: $\eta^C_{S_i}$,

$$\xi^C_\eta(\eta^C_{S_i}) = 1 + 23 * \left(1 - \frac{\eta^C_{S_i}}{100\%}\right), \tag{12}$$

2. for the component concerning the business continuity security of the process of sensitive data processing in the IT system, it is defined in the following manner: $\beta^C_{S_i}$

$$\xi^C_\beta(\beta^C_{S_i}) = 24 - \sqrt[3]{\frac{\beta^C_{P_i}}{2}}, \tag{13}$$

3. for the component concerning the costs due to unavailability of the processing processes in the IT system, it is defined in the following manner: κ_{S_i}

$$\xi_\kappa(\kappa_{S_i}) = \begin{cases} 1, if\ \kappa_{S_i} = V \\ 7, if\ \kappa_{S_i} = IV \\ 13, if\ \kappa_{S_i} = III; \\ 19, if\ \kappa_{S_i} = II \\ 24, if\ \kappa_{S_i} = I \end{cases} \qquad 14)$$

4. for the maximum unavailability time component, it is defined in the following manner: π_{S_i}

$$\xi_\pi(\pi_{S_i}) = \begin{cases} 1, if\ \pi_{S_i} = 4 \\ 7, if\ \pi_{S_i} = 3 \\ 13, if\ \pi_{S_i} = 2; \\ 19, if\ \pi_{S_i} = 1 \\ 24, if\ \pi_{S_i} = 0 \end{cases} \qquad (15)$$

C. in case of a subset of the functions $\xi \epsilon \Xi^T$ characterized by the security of the processes of sensitive data processing:

1. for the component concerning the fulfillment of the requirements of the information processing security policy, it is defined in the following manner: $\eta^T_{S_i}$,

$$\xi^T_\eta(\eta^T_S) = 1 + 15 * \left(1 - \frac{\eta^T_{S_i}}{100\%}\right); \qquad (16)$$

2. for the component concerning the monitoring of the security of the processing processes in the IT system, it is defined in the following manner: $\beta^T_{S_i}$,

$$\xi^T_\eta(\beta^T_{S_i}) = 16 - \sqrt[3]{\frac{\beta^T_{S_i}}{2}}; \ , \qquad (17)$$

3. for the component concerning the duration of the information processing, it is defined in the following manner: δ_{S_i}

$$\xi_\delta(\delta_{S_i}) = \begin{cases} 1, when\ there\ is\ lack\ of\ system\ flexibility \\ 5, when\ the\ flexibilityof\ the\ system\ is\ low \\ 10, when\ the\ flexibility\ of\ the\ system\ is\ good \\ 15, when\ the\ flexibility\ of\ the\ system\ is\ maximum \end{cases}$$

4. for the system *flexibility* component, it is defined in the following manner: ϑ_{S_i}

$$\xi_\vartheta(\vartheta_{S_i}) = \begin{cases} 1, if\ \vartheta_{S_i} = 4 \\ 7, if\ \vartheta_{S_i} = 3 \\ 13, if\ \vartheta_{S_i} = 2; \\ 19, if\ \vartheta_{S_i} = 1 \\ 24, if\ \vartheta_{S_i} = 0 \end{cases} \qquad (18)$$

5. for the system importance component, it is defined in the following manner: - ζ_{S_i}

$$\xi_\zeta(\zeta_{S_i}) = \begin{cases} 1, if\ \zeta_{S_i} = VI \\ 4, if\ \zeta_{S_i} = V \\ 7, if\ \zeta_{S_i} = IV \\ 10, if\ \zeta_{S_i} = III \\ 13, if\ \zeta_{S_i} = II \\ 15, if\ \zeta_{S_i} = I \end{cases} . \qquad (19)$$

6. for the component concerning the efficiency of the change management process in the IT system, it is defined in the following manner: φ_{S_i}

$$\xi_\varphi(\varphi_{S_i}) = 1 + 15 * \left(1 - \frac{\varphi_{S_i}}{100\%}\right). \qquad (20)$$

The form of the above-mentioned standardization functions from the family Ξ was defined, for the purpose of the model presented herein, in such a manner so that they transpose their values into appropriate ranges and maintain correct proportions of their impact on the IT system risk.

4. The IT system risk vector

The following vector $\overrightarrow{R_{S_i}}$ is considered the IT system risk model:

$$\overrightarrow{R_{S_i}} = \langle \overrightarrow{R^B_{S_i}}, \overrightarrow{R^C_{S_i}}, \overrightarrow{R^T_{S_i}} \rangle \in M_{m\times n} \times M_{m\times n} \times M_{m\times n} \ (21)$$

where:

- $M_{m\times n}$ - matrix size: m x n,
- $\overrightarrow{R^B_{S_i}}$ - the vector coordinate $\overrightarrow{R_{S_i}}$ that characterizes an aspect of the IT system security S_i, which constitutes a linear combination of the IT system risk elements S_i within the linear space $(M_{2\times2}, \boldsymbol{R}, +, \cdot)$.
- $\overrightarrow{R^C_{S_i}}$ - the vector coordinate $\overrightarrow{R_{S_i}}$ that characterizes an aspect of the IT operation business continuity S_i, which constitutes a linear combination of the IT system risk elements S_i within the linear space $(M_{2\times2}, R, +, \cdot)$.
- $\overrightarrow{R^T_{S_i}}$ - the vector coordinate $\overrightarrow{R_{S_i}}$ that characterizes an aspect of the security of the processes of sensitive data processing in the IT system S_i, , which constitutes a linear combination of the IT system risk elements S_i within the linear space $(M_{2\times3}, R, +, \cdot)$.

$(M_{m\times n}, R, +, \cdot)$ - Vector space defined as a set of matrices $M^{m\times n}$ with an option of adding matrices + external operator· constitutes vector space over the body of real numbers R .

whereas:

$$\overrightarrow{R^B_{S_i}} = \xi_\lambda(\lambda_{S_i})\cdot\vec{\lambda} + \xi_\alpha(\alpha_{S_i})\cdot\vec{\alpha} + \xi^B_\eta(\eta^B_{S_i})\cdot\overrightarrow{\eta^B} + \xi^B_\beta(\beta^B_{S_i})\cdot\overrightarrow{\beta^B}$$

$$\overrightarrow{R^C_{S_i}} = \xi^C_\eta(\eta^C_{P_i})\cdot\overrightarrow{\eta^C} + \xi^C_\beta(\beta^C_{P_i})\cdot\overrightarrow{\beta^C} + \xi_\kappa(\kappa_{P_i})\cdot\vec{\kappa} + \xi_\pi(\pi_{P_i})\,\vec{\pi},$$

$$\overrightarrow{R^T_{S_i}} = \xi^J_\eta(\eta^J_{P_i})\cdot\overrightarrow{\eta^J} + \xi^J_\beta(\beta^J_{P_i})\cdot\overrightarrow{\beta^J} + \xi_\delta(\delta_{S_i})\cdot\vec{\delta} + \xi_\vartheta(\vartheta_{S_i})\cdot \vec{\vartheta} + \xi_\zeta(\zeta_{S_i})\cdot\vec{\zeta} + \xi_\varphi(\varphi_{S_i})\cdot\vec{\varphi}, \qquad (22)$$

where: $\vec{\lambda}, \vec{\alpha}, \overrightarrow{\eta^B}, \overrightarrow{\eta^C}, \overrightarrow{\eta^T}, \overrightarrow{\beta^B}, \overrightarrow{\beta^C}, \overrightarrow{\beta^T}, \vec{\kappa}, \vec{\pi}, \vec{\vartheta}, \vec{\zeta}$ - base vectors in the vector space $(M_{m\times n}, \boldsymbol{R}, +, \cdot)$ from algebra $(M_{m\times n}, \boldsymbol{R}, +, \cdot, \otimes)$,

Since the algebra dimension $(M_{2\times2}, \boldsymbol{R}, +, \cdot, \otimes)$ is (Trajdos, 1993): dim $(M_{2\times2}, \boldsymbol{R}, +, \cdot, \otimes)$ = 4 and $(M_{2\times3}, \boldsymbol{R}, +, \cdot, \otimes)$: dim $(M_{2\times3}, \boldsymbol{R}, +, \cdot, \otimes)$ = 6, therefore $\left(\overrightarrow{R^B_{S_i}}, \overrightarrow{R^C_{S_i}}, \overrightarrow{R^T_{S_i}}\right)$ 14 base vectors defined in the following way exist to define the components:

$$\vec{\lambda} = \begin{pmatrix} 1 & 0 \\ 0 & 0 \end{pmatrix};\ \vec{\alpha} = \begin{pmatrix} 0 & 1 \\ 0 & 0 \end{pmatrix};\ \overrightarrow{\eta^B} = \begin{pmatrix} 0 & 0 \\ 1 & 0 \end{pmatrix};\ \overrightarrow{\beta^B} = \begin{pmatrix} 0 & 0 \\ 0 & 1 \end{pmatrix}$$

$$\overrightarrow{\eta^C} = \begin{pmatrix} 1 & 0 \\ 0 & 0 \end{pmatrix};\ \overrightarrow{\beta^C} = \begin{pmatrix} 0 & 1 \\ 0 & 0 \end{pmatrix};\ \vec{\kappa} = \begin{pmatrix} 1 & 0 \\ 0 & 0 \end{pmatrix};\ \vec{\pi} = \begin{pmatrix} 0 & 1 \\ 0 & 0 \end{pmatrix};$$

$$\overrightarrow{\eta^C}=\begin{pmatrix}1 & 0\\ 0 & 0\\ 0 & 0\end{pmatrix};\ \overrightarrow{\beta^C}=\begin{pmatrix}0 & 1\\ 0 & 0\\ 0 & 0\end{pmatrix};\ \vec{\delta}=\begin{pmatrix}0 & 0\\ 1 & 0\\ 0 & 0\end{pmatrix};$$

$$\vec{\vartheta}=\begin{pmatrix}0 & 0\\ 0 & 1\\ 0 & 0\end{pmatrix};\ \vec{\zeta}=\begin{pmatrix}0 & 0\\ 0 & 0\\ 1 & 0\end{pmatrix};\ \vec{\varphi}=\begin{pmatrix}0 & 0\\ 0 & 0\\ 0 & 1\end{pmatrix}.$$

On the basis of the above linear combination of such formulas, it is evident that the impact of all of the selected dimensions/factors $\left(\overrightarrow{R^B_{S_i}},\ \overrightarrow{R^C_{S_i}},\ \overrightarrow{R^T_{S_i}}\right)$ of the IT system risk analysis particular risk vector coordinates $\overrightarrow{R_{S_i}}$ is the same. To clarify the estimated IT system risk level, it may be necessary to determine the impact of the particular vector coordinates and risk components on the final IT system risk level as well as to modify such coordinates $\overrightarrow{R_{S_i}} \in M_{m\times n} \times M_{m\times n} \times M_{m\times n}$ by referring to the said impact. This article does not tackle this issue.

5. Magnitude of the IT system risk

Once the IT system risk vector is defined and its coordinates determined according to algebra [20], $(M_{m\times n}, \boldsymbol{R}, +, , \otimes)$ when we want to determine total risks for the IT system, S_i it is necessary to first set the magnitude $R^B_{S_i}$; $R^C_{S_i}$; $R^T_{S_i}$ and then the value R_{S_i}.

The risk of the IT system $\left(\overrightarrow{R^B_{S_i}},\ \overrightarrow{R^C_{S_i}},\ \overrightarrow{R^T_{S_i}}\right)$ vector $\overrightarrow{R_{S_i}}$ coordinate S_i in algebra $(M_{m\times n}, \boldsymbol{R}, +, , \otimes)$) is the number $R^B_{S_i}$; $R^C_{S_i}$; $R^T_{S_i} \in \mathcal{R}$ equal to the vector length, i.e.:

$$R^B_{S_i} = \left\|\overrightarrow{R^B_{S_i}}\right\|;\ R^C_{S_i} = \left\|\overrightarrow{R^C_{S_i}}\right\|;\ R^T_{S_i} = \left\|\overrightarrow{R^T_{S_i}}\right\| \quad (26)$$

The presented values $R^B_{S_i}$; $R^C_{S_i}$; $R^T_{S_i} \in \mathcal{R}$ define the magnitude of the IT system risk S_i components in a quantitative manner. To present the risk level, in a qualitative manner, of particular vector coordinates $\overrightarrow{R_{S_i}}$, the following risk ranges may be adopted:

Component $R^B_{S_i}$	Component $R^C_{S_i}$	Component $R^T_{S_i}$
$R^B_{S_i} > 70$ - *catastrophic risk,*	$R^C_{S_i} > 70$ - *catastrophic risk,*	$R^T_{S_i} > 70$ - *catastrophic risk,*
$R^B_{S_i} \in (60,\dots,70]$- *very high risk,*	$R^C_{S_i} \in (60,\dots,70]$- *very high risk,*	$R^T_{S_i} \in (60,\dots,70]$- *very high risk,*
$R^B_{S_i} \in (50,\dots,60]$- *high risk,*	$R^C_{S_i} \in (50,\dots,60]$- *high risk,*	$R^T_{S_i} \in (50,\dots,60]$- *high risk,*
$R^B_{S_i} \in (40,\dots,50]$ - *medium risk,*	$R^C_{S_i} \in (40,\dots,50]$ - *medium risk,*	$R^T_{S_i} \in (40,\dots,50]$ - *medium risk,*
$R^B_{S_i} \in (30,\dots,40]$ - *low risk,*	$R^C_{S_i} \in (30,\dots,40]$ - *low risk,*	$R^T_{S_i} \in (30,\dots,40]$ - *low risk,*
$R^B_{S_i} \in (20,\dots,30]$- *very low risk,*	$R^C_{S_i} \in (20,\dots,30]$- *very low risk,*	$R^T_{S_i} \in (20,\dots,30]$- *very low risk,*
$R^B_{S_i} < 20$ - *residual risk.*	$R^C_{S_i} < 20$ - *residual risk.*	$R^T_{S_i} < 20$ - *residual risk.*

The above-mentioned value ranges were determined on the basis of the practical use of the model presented herein.

The volume of the IT system risks may be defined as the vector module $\left|\overrightarrow{R_{S_i}}\right|$ (Fig. 3):

$$\overrightarrow{R_{S_i}} = \left|\overrightarrow{R_{S_i}}\right| = \sqrt[2]{{R^B_{S_i}}^2 + {R^C_{S_i}}^2 + {R^T_{S_i}}^2}\,, \quad (23)$$

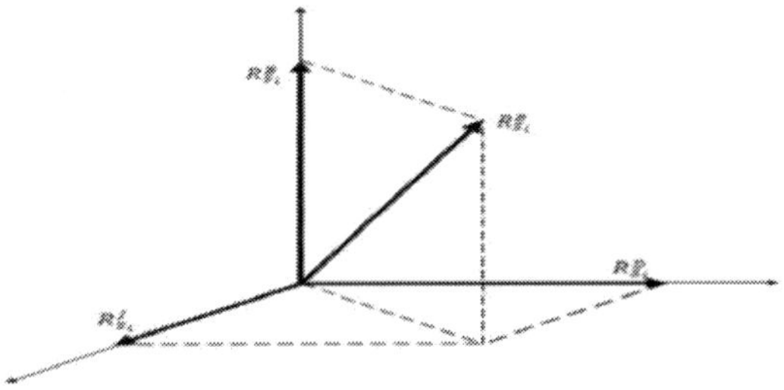

Fig. 3. Vector $\overrightarrow{\boldsymbol{R_{S_i}}}$ of IT system risk in the coordinates configuration $\boldsymbol{R^B_{S_i}}$; $\boldsymbol{R^C_{S_i}}$; $\boldsymbol{R^T_{S_i}}$

6. Evaluation of the IT system risk

Evaluation of the IT system risk consists in the comparison of the results of risk analysis, including the adopted criteria to qualify the risk into the right category (acceptable, tolerable, intolerable risk levels, Fig. 4).

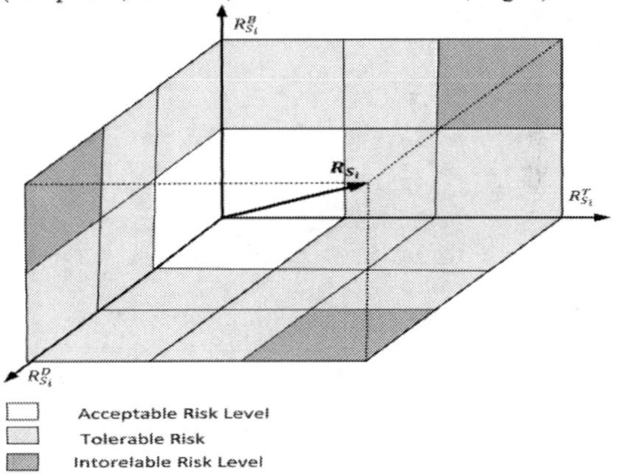

Fig. 4. Map of the IT system risk

The main objective is to provide data that constitute grounds for making a decision on further risk management (whether to process the risk or abandon it, and if the decision is to process the risk - determine to what extent). The risk evaluation process is a summary of the present activities (identification and analysis) and indication which risk or group of risks should be processed further and which may be handled using current control measures.

The risk evaluation has also significant impact on the decision making process. The results of the risk analysis help to decide which risks and to what extent make it necessary for the office to implement a special algorithm for processing such risks and to determine priorities of their processing. The determined risk levels should be then compared with their criteria, including the context agreed at the beginning. In this case, the evaluation shall allow to define the manner of processing a certain risk [21-22].

During the risk assessment process, each risk has to be classified and compared with its tolerable and acceptable level. However, prior to that, it is necessary to adopt certain criteria that would help to explicitly identify significant risks, requiring resolute actions. This is a step in defining the risk that needs special attention. The risk records to be made as a result of the risk assessment shall be helpful in streamlining the risk management process, and hence - crisis management.

Summary

The IT system risk model of the office, described in this article, which includes the process of sensitive data processing, is characterized by high complexity due to the mathematical apparatus applied. Therefore, due to the fact that a number of factors affecting the IT system risk level and its processes were taken into consideration, it is almost impossible to determine the risk of the process of sensitive data processing in terms of time and costs or to manage such risk in a traditional manner, without applying any IT solutions or computer techniques.

Due to a variety of different factors and broad spectrum of their impact on the processes of sensitive data processing, the application of the risk analysis should constitute an integral part of the decision-making process as well as the planning of different variants of the operations of every office unit. The knowledge of the risks associated in the sensitive data processing allows to shape such processes so that their security levels are acceptable (Fig. 4). When analyzing the risk sources and categories in the processes of sensitive data processing, their characteristics, IT system architecture and life cycles should be mainly taken into account. Such knowledge, in combination with the statistics concerning the security and architecture of the system for sensitive data processing, seems to be the key to risk mitigation in all its aspects - human, environmental, security-related, qualitative and economic. The considerations outlined herein are of mainly cognitive importance, thus, formal descriptions of certain issues were omitted. The objective of the article was to show the concept which differs from the traditional view on the issues related to risk quantification.

Bibliography

1. PN-ISO Guide 73:2009, Risk Management – Vocabulary, (2009).
2. R. Hoffmann, M. Kiedrowicz, J. Stanik, MATEC Web of Conferences, *Evaluation of information safety as an element of improving the organization's safety management*, vol. **76**, (2016).
3. R. Hoffmann, M. Kiedrowicz, J. Stanik, MATEC Web of Conferences, *Risk management system as the basic paradigm of the information security management system in an organization*, vol. **76**, (2016).
4. J. Stanik, J. Napiórkowski, R. Hoffmann, *Zarządzanie ryzykiem w systemie zarządzania bezpieczeństwem organizacji*, Zeszyty Naukowe Uniwersytetu Szczecińskiego – Ekonomiczne Problemy Usług, (2016).
5. M. Kiedrowicz, T. Protasowicki, J. Stanik, *Wybrane aspekty standaryzacji w ochronie publicznych zasobów informacyjnych i świadczonych usług w kontekście społeczeństwa informacyjnego*, Zeszyty Naukowe Uniwersytetu Szczecińskiego – Ekonomiczne Problemy Usług, vol. **113**, pp. 113-130, (2014).
6. M. Kiedrowicz, J. Stanik, *Selected aspects of risk management in respect of security of the document lifecycle management system with multiple levels of sensitivity*, (in:) Information Management in Practice, (eds) B.F. Kubiak and J. Maślankowski, pp. 231-249, (2015).
7. M. Kiedrowicz, *Location with the use of the RFID and GPS technologies - opportunities and threats*, GIS ODYSSEY 2016, pp. 122-128, (2016).
8. M. Kiedrowicz, *Objects identification in the information models used by information systems*, GIS ODYSSEY 2016, pp. 129-136, (2016).
9. M. Kiedrowicz, J. Stanik, *Adequacy evaluation of the simulation models of system dynamics on the example of the Earned Value model*, (in:) Information Management (eds) B.F. Kubiak and A. Sieradz, pp. 9-17, (2014).
10. T. Nowicki, M. Marczak, *The modeling analysis and simulation of transport company functioning.* (in:) Modeling of modern enterprises logistics, (eds.) M. Fertsch, K. Grzybowska, A. Stachowiak, (2009).
11. M. Kiedrowicz, Publiczne zasoby informacyjne jako podstawa tworzenia platform integracyjnych, (in:) INTERNET. Prawno-informatyczne problemy sieci, portali i e-usług, (ed.) G. Szpor, pp. 231-246, (2012).
12. M. Kiedrowicz, *Uogólniony model danych w rozproszonych rejestrach ewidencyjnych*, Roczniki Kolegium Analiz Ekonomicznych, vol. 33, pp. 209-234, (2014).
13. M. Kiedrowicz, *Rejestry publiczne wykorzystywane przez organy odpowiedzialne za wykrywanie i przeciwdziałanie przestępczości*, (in:) Rejestry publiczne: Jawność i interoperacyjność, (ed.) A. Gryszczyńska, pp. 603-649, (2016).
14. J. Hash, Risk Management Guidance For Information Technology Systems, ITL Bulletin, National Institute of Standards and Technology, Gaithersburg MD, (2002).
15. J. Stanik, T. Protasowicki, *Metodyka kształtowania ryzyka w cyklu rozwojowym systemu informatycznego*, KKIO „Od procesów do oprogramowania: badania i praktyka", (2015).
16. M. Kiedrowicz, J. Koszela, *Business processes modelling for the processing of classified documents*

using RFID technology, Collegium of Economic Analysis Annals, vol. **42,** pp. 53-66, (2016).
17. M. Kiedrowicz, J. Koszela, *Secret office model for the processing of classified documents using RFID technology*, Collegium of Economic Analysis Annals, vol. **42**, pp. 67-81, (2016).
18. J. Gołębiewski, *Zarządzanie kryzysowe w świetle wymogów bezpieczeństwa*, pp. 120-121, (2011).
19. M. Kiedrowicz, R. Waszkowski, *Business rules automation standards in business process management systems*, (in:) Information Management in Practice, (eds) B.F. Kubiak and J. Maślankowski, pp. 187-200, (2015).
20. T. Trajdos, Matemetyka, Wydawnictwa Naukowo–Techniczne, (1993).
21. PN-ISO/IEC 27005, Technika informatyczna, Techniki bezpieczeństwa. Zarządzanie ryzykiem w bezpieczeństwie informacji, (2013).
22. PN-ISO 31000:2012, Zarządzanie ryzykiem -- Zasady i wytyczne, (2012).

DOI: 10.1051/matecconf/201712502012

A Computer System for CBRN Contamination Threats Analysis Support, Prediction Their Effects and Alarming the Population: Polish Case Study

Zbigniew Tarapata[1,a], Ryszard Antkiewicz[1], Mariusz Chmielewski[1], Michał Dyk[1], Rafał Kasprzyk[1], Wojciech Kulas[1], Andrzej Najgebauer[1], Dariusz Pierzchała[1], Jarosław Rulka[1]

[1] *Institute of Computer and Information Systems, Faculty of Cybernetics, Military University of Technology, Warsaw, Poland*

Abstract. The article outlines a concept for the system supporting analyses of threats related to contamination and alarming (WAZkA), for the purpose of the National System for Detection of Contamination and Alarming (Krajowy System Wykrywania Skażeń i Alarmowania, KSWSiA) in Poland. Additionally, the article presents the point of designing such system, its concept and components. The main objective of WAZkA is to support the following processes of the KSWSiA: information exchange between the system elements and coordination of the system operations, as well as to prepare assessment and expert analyses, needed by the decision-making bodies, with respect to risk emergency situations during natural disasters, technical failures or other events resulting in biological, chemical or radioactive contamination. The selected modules included in the WAZkA system: Event Tree Analyzer, visualization module (COP) and emulators of the threats monitoring systems, were described as well as the idea of using the system for the purpose of training, including the designed emulators of the risk monitoring systems together with the scenario editor. The Event Tree Anlyzer is a graphical representation of a chronological sequence of events, significant from the point of view of the functioning of the object, which occur after a given event that initiates such sequence. COP is the GIS tool, which allows to present an operating situation on the basis of background maps. The application offers a possibility of enriching the presented operating situation with the risk data provided in the form of NATO ADat-P3 (CBRN) reports. Emulators of the threats monitoring systems allow to generate, in an artificial and user-controlled manner, data on risks, which "pretend" to be real data obtained from the monitoring systems. The above approach significantly facilitates the organization of training and learning about rare situations or situations that have never occurred, but that are potentially dangerous.

1 Introduction and Motivation

Pursuant to appropriate provisions of law [11], the National System for Detection of Contamination and Alarming (Krajowy System Wykrywania Skażeń i Alarmowania, KSWSiA) was established in Poland. The main elements of KSWSiA are functional subsystems intended for detecting the CBRN (Chemical, Biological, Radiological, Nuclear) contamination and alarming about it organizational bodies and units, which analyze the contamination and evaluate the situation to later develop, announce and introduce intervention measures. The functional systems, which constitute the system core, are the following: The System of Contamination Detection of the Armed Forces of the Republic of Poland - supervised by the Minister of National Defense, networks and systems for the epidemiological surveillance and control of communicable diseases in the country as well as national contact points for the international surveillance system to identify threats to human health and life of large populations - supervised by the Minister of Health, systems of early detection of radioactive contamination and radioactive contamination centers, whose activities are coordinated by the President of the National Atomic Energy Agency, voivodeship early detection systems supervised by Voivodes [13], systems for epizootic and phytosanitary surveillance, supervision of safety of animal products and animal feeding stuffs, supervision of safety of agro-food products controlled by the competent Ministers of Agriculture and Agricultural Markets. The Central Contamination Analysis Center (COAS) in Warsaw acts as the KSWSiA coordinator.

The above-mentioned entities included in the composition of KSWSiA use various sources of contamination data and data processing systems. However, there is no system that would integrate all data from different sources (i.e. threat monitoring systems, TMS), allow information exchange between KSWSiA system elements and support the decision-making bodies in performing the following actions: (a) assessment and expert analyses concerning the contamination risks and (b) warning and alarming the population about such risks.

[a] Corresponding author: zbigniew.tarapata@wat.edu.pl

Therefore, the article presents a concept of the system supporting analyses of threats related to contamination and alarming (WAZkA). The presented concept falls within the scope of topics of the R&D project entitled: "Integration and support of the information management processes as well as optimization of decisions of the detection and alarming system" realized under the contest of the National R&D Center BiO 7/2015 by the scientific and industrial consortium composed of: Military University of Technology in Warsaw – leader, HTRC sp. z o.o., Central State Fire Service School in Częstochowa, Cardinal Stefan Wyszyński University in Warsaw.

The main objective of WAZkA [14] is to develop and construct a highly developed ICT tool, needed by the entities of KSWSiA, which shall support the following processes: information exchange between the system elements and coordination of the system operations, as well as to prepare assessment and expert analyses, needed by the decision-making bodies, with respect to risk emergency situations during natural disasters, technical failures or other events resulting in biological, chemical or radioactive contamination.

The individual objectives are the following:

1. Development of the risk identification methodology, also with respect to international risks, including the risk assessment process in terms of risk occurrence and prioritization.
2. Development of rules for assessment of susceptibility of a given area to certain risks, including risk maps and threat maps.
3. Development of rules for collecting data from the risk monitoring systems.
4. Development of the module for collecting data by the ICT system and warnings saved by the monitoring systems.
5. Development of the module allowing to use the Regional Warning System and other systems for alarming regional population.
6. Design and implementation of a modern ICT system responsible for exchanging information on threats, preparing assessment and performing analyses of undesired events, coordinating actions, modeling scenarios, including identification of their risks, sending information to the people via available warning systems and carrying out preparatory exercises.
7. Development of the training schedule for public administration units, which use products that were created under the project, and development of the system of exercises.
8. Preparation of recommended legislative amendments to improve the functioning of the system for contamination detection and alarming.
9. Current dissemination of the project results.

The paper is organized as follows. In section 2 we present short review of threats monitoring systems, warning and alarm systems in Poland. Section 3 contains the concept of system WAZkA. In section 4 we describe a set of tools for threats analysis, visualization and training in WAZkA.

2 Threats monitoring, warning and alarm systems in Poland

The systems for the monitoring of radiological risks are supervised by the National Atomic Energy Agency. The above-mentioned systems include: PMS (Permanent Monitoring System) stations [8], ASS-500 stations [4], [8], stations of the Institute of Meteorology and Water Management, stations of the Automated Network of Radioactive Contamination Measurements (SAPOS), which belong to the military, and the System of Contamination Detection of the Armed Forces of the Republic of Poland. Furthermore, the following entities are responsible for the contamination monitoring: Provincial Sanitary-Epidemiological Stations, HACCP system, National Health Inspectorate, etc.

Regional Warning System (RSO) [16] is a service used to inform the citizens on upcoming dangers; it has been operational since 1 January 2015. The messages transmitted by the system mainly focused on meteorological warnings (e.g. strong winds, thunderstorms, icing), hydrological warnings (e.g. water levels), traffic information (e.g. traffic jams, construction works, detours), and other information relevant from a safety standpoint. Regional Warning System Messages can be seen in Polish Television programs in digital terrestrial multiplex MUX-3. The most important of them appear on a special news bar on the TV screen. All messages are also available on teletext pages in programs TVP1, TVP 2, TVP Kultura, TVP Historia and TVP Polonia from p. 190, while in the Regional TVP from p. 430. The same warnings will also appear on the websites of voivodeship (provincial) offices. Smartphone users can use a free application for mobile phones, available at shops with applications for the individual platforms (Google Play, Apple App Store, Windows Phone Store). The application may be searched for using key words "RSO" and "Regional Warning System".

The digitexCZK/IP® system [17] has been created on the basis of on up-to-date technologies, according to a PLATAN construction team's original design. This is the only one in Poland warning system which for data transmission uses not only analogue but also digital radio communication in the DMR (TDMA) and NXDN (FDMA) standards, as well as local area and wide area networks (LAN, WAN) and encoded IP. In the digitexCZK/IP® system, use of IP for data and voice transmission makes it possible to create and expand the system easily and it allows for integration with the existing analogue warning systems, i.e.: digitexCZK/FSK, DSP-50, RSSS-2000/3000, MDSA-24.

These systems use different data formats: ATP-45(d) [2], NATO ADatP-3 (eg. CBRN report), CAP (Common Alerting Protocol), IRIX 1.0, EURDEP 2.1 (UE standard), others, including non-structural (simple e-mail, fax).

3 The concept of WAZkA system

The most important expected final result of the project implementation shall be the WAZkA system demonstrator (the system supporting analyses of threats related to contamination and alarming). Figure 1 presents the WAZkA system concept. WAZkA means in polish language - the dragonfly. The dragonfly is considered a silent killer among insects - like a CBRN contamination.

The WAZkA system consists of the following modules [14]:

• Integration Module IM1 - responsible for the communication, transfer and initial processing of data from the current TMS. The data shall be obtained in an automated manner from the systems and entities having IT systems to process the risk-related information. For the purpose of other entities, an interface for semi-automatic and manual data supplementation shall be launched (e.g. serial mail dispatch);

• Integration Module IM2 - responsible for the integration with the existing detection and warning systems. The risk alerts from the WAZkA system are set through the above-mentioned module;

• Data Acquisition & Analysis Module DAAM - central module of the system responsible for the analysis of data obtained from the monitoring systems (via IM1). On the basis thereof, an assessment, arrangement in hierarchy and forecast of the risk development are made. In case of occurrence of such risks, an alert is sent to the detection and alarming systems (via IM2);

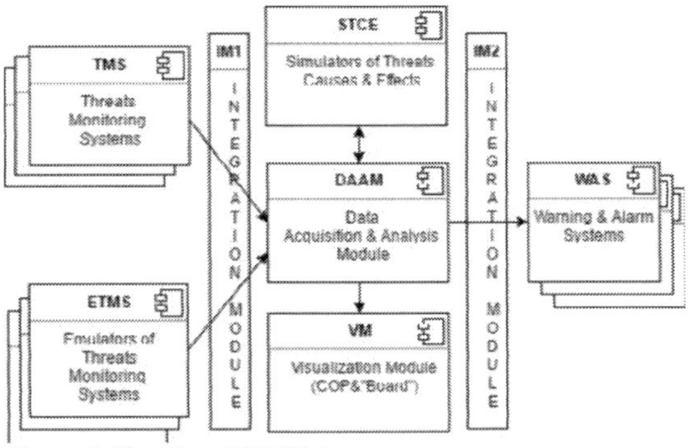

Figure 1. The idea of WAZkA system.

• Visualization Modules (VM) - responsible for the presentation of data and results of analyses (in particular - warnings about the risks), as needed by the KSWSiA entities. Two VMs are proposed:

o Board - a web portal, which facilitates quick access to the most recent information and the most serious risks. It shall be the central communication point between the KSWSiA entities. Access to the presented information shall be filtered depending on the privileges of the logged user.

o Common Operational Picture (COP) - similarly to the Board module, the COP shall be accessed via Internet. It shall present the information about the risks on a digital map.

• Simulators of Threats Causes and Effects STCE - the simulators shall support the DAAM module. They allow to simulate the processes of occurrence and development of risks, thanks to which it shall be possible to generate warning and prepare appropriate measures in advance. The simulators also allow to play different variants of the risk development scenarios, which shall contribute to faster and less risky decision-making process with respect to risk elimination. We also use existing simulators: Aloha [18] (the hazard modeling program, which is used widely to plan for and respond to chemical emergencies) and SI Promien [9].

• Emulators of the Threats Monitoring Systems (ETMS) allow to generate, in an artificial and user-controlled manner, data on risks, which "pretend" to be real data obtained from the monitoring systems. The above approach significantly facilitates the organization of training and learning about rare situations or situations that have never occurred, but that are potentially dangerous.

Practical use of the project results as regards national defense and security shall be in the form of the implementation of the WAZkA results at appropriate institutions responsible for contamination monitoring as well as warning and alarming of the population. Social benefits resulting therefrom may be compared to the implementation of, for example, the Regional Warning System, with which the WAZkA system shall naturally cooperate. The system built under this project shall allow collaboration with the military systems with similar functionalities, but shall be dedicated to civil services, in particular entities included in the National Firefighting and Rescue System under the responsibility of the State Fire Service. Therefore, the following entities may be included in the group of potential system recipients:

- Head of the National Civil Defense/Chief Commander Brigadier of the State Fire Service;
- entities subordinate to and supervised by the Minister of Interior (Emergency Management Department of the Ministry of Interior, National Police Headquarters, State Fire Service HQ, Border Guard HQ);
- voivodes (voivodeship emergency management center - especially, in terms of increasing the ability to inform civilians);
- other non-military components of KSWSiA (Radiological Incident Center "CEZAR" PAA, Central Meteorological Forecast Bureau - Institute of Meteorology and Water Management, Research Institute of the Ministry of Transport, Ministry of Agriculture and Rural Development, Ministry of Health, Ministry of Administration and Digitization, Chief Inspectorate for Veterinary and Heads of Maritime Offices).

4 A set of selected tools for threats analysis, visualization and training in WAZkA

4.1 Event Tree Analyser (ETA)

The Event Tree is a graphical representation of a chronological sequence of events, significant from the point of view of the functioning of the object, which occur after a given event that initiates such sequence (Figure 2, Figure 3, Figure 4). This is one of the forms of

the decision trees (e.g. stochastic PERT [1]). It can be used during e.g. planning of hazardous materials transport [12, sect. 3, sect. 6] for risk analysis.
Event tree [10] allows:

- Determination of probability of the occurrence of a given scenario of events;
- Assessment of the final event consequences;
- Calculation of frequency of the occurrence of particular event scenarios;
- Modification of the Event Tree characteristics in case of the occurrence of specific events.

Figure 2 presents an example of the event tree created in the Event Tree Analyser application. The tree consists of the initial element (black circle), events (rectangles with the names recorded inside), final elements, i.e. the effects (white circles) and curves joining the tree elements. Two curves described by the probability are always derived from every event. One of them determines consequences of the fact that the event occurred, whereas the other one - that the event did not occur.
The presented example describes development and consequences of the loss of integrity of a ammonia container. At the beginning, it is considered whether the bottom of the container lost integrity. If so (probability 0.99), the ammonia pool will be created, otherwise (probability 0.01) - the pool will not be created. Then, a possibility of immediate explosion or delayed ignition is considered. The above may happen on two paths of the risk development, but with high probability thereof. On the basis of the probability of occurrence and non-occurrence of certain events, the probability of occurrence of particular effects of the lost integrity is determined. In the analyzed case, three types of effects are possible, i.e. immediate explosion, explosion and chemical contamination. Together with the risk development, certain events may become more probable and some - completely improbable. In such case, the probability of occurrence of specific risk effects is also changing.
The Event Tree Analyser application allows to determine which of the events has actually occurred and to automatically calculate the probabilities. Figure 3 presents an example of such situation. The event "no pool formed" was checked, which means that the bottom of the container did not lose its integrity, thus, the events on an alternative paths become improbable, whereas the probability of occurrence of the events on the checked path significantly increases. For example, the probability of delayed ignition increased from 0.09 to 0.90. The increase was substantial - i.e. by two orders of magnitude. The probability of occurrence of every risk effect also increased, since the bottom part of the container was not damaged and no pool was formed. Figure 4 shows recalculated Event Tree from Figure 2 with situation after "Delayed ignition" event done.
The presented application constitutes an alternative to the solutions similar to the tree event analysis, e.g. Logan [15]. However, a significant difference is that the Event Tree Analyser application does not require the necessity to build complementary event in every case, even though it provides for such a possibility.

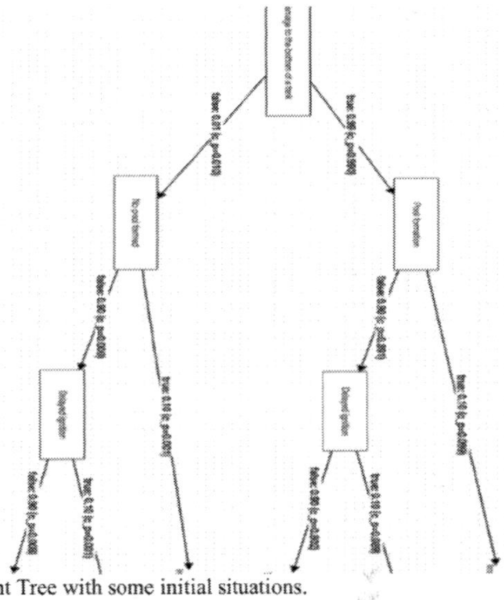

Figure 2. Event Tree with some initial situations.

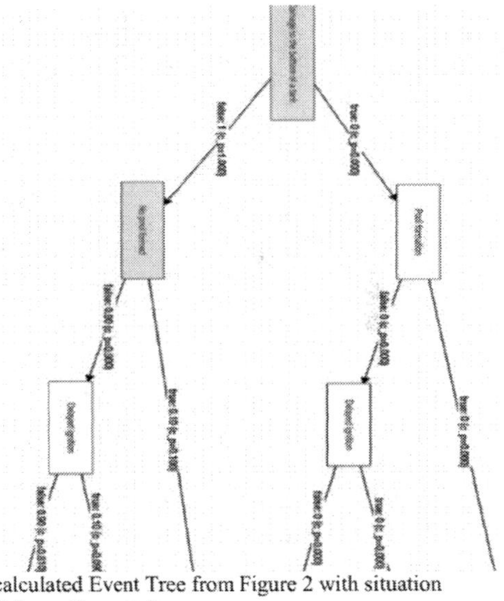

Figure 3. Recalculated Event Tree from Figure 2 with situation after "No pool formed" event done.

It allows to avoid certain artificial aspects in the constructed trees. Additionally, apart from determining the probability of occurrence of the effects, the probability of occurrence of each of the indirect events is also measured provided that predecessor of such events occurred. The following examples show the value in brackets, recorded on curves between the events.
Event Tree Analyser is the application built in the client-server architecture, which does not need any additional software to be installed by the user outside a web browser.

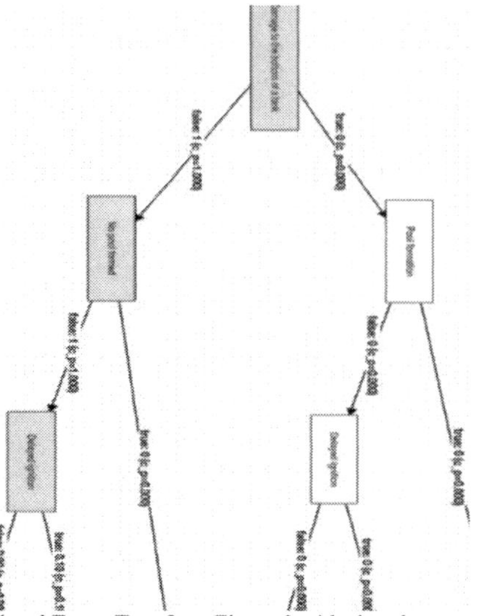

Figure 4. Recalculated Event Tree from Figure 2 with situation after "Delayed ignition" event done.

4.2 Common Operational Picture (COP)

It is the GIS tool, which allows to present an operating situation on the basis of background maps. The application offers a possibility of enriching the presented operating situation with the risk data provided in the form of NATO ADat-P3 (CBRN) reports. The map module allows to perform map measurements of the indicated routes and areas as well as provides special functions supporting the decision-making process by defining flood zones and terrain profiles (Figure 6). The map module allows to present the objects within geographical space, in accordance with the symbols of NATO APP-6A and Ministry of the Interior and Administration. When applying this property, it is possible to reflect the operating situations of military units and supporting forces (fire service, police, border guards, etc.) with respect to the emergency infrastructure elements.

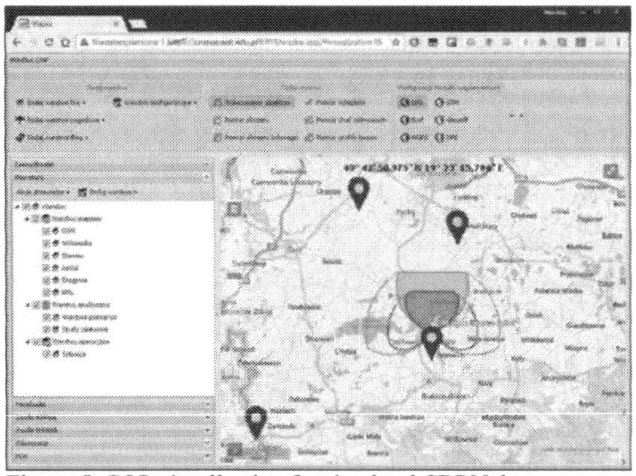

Figure 5. COP visualization for simulated CBRN threat (Chemical).

An important function for building an image of the executed operation (reaction to risk) is to manage the information about such risk. The risk data may be entered with the use of the dedicated data format system - WAZkA - or CBRN standard ADatP3 reports (Figure 5). The use of the map mechanisms of the OpenLayers component allowed to integrate many sources of the provided mapping data.

The COP visualization is provided in the form of a state application (communicating asynchronously with the data feeding services), created in Sencha GXT technology, supported by the Spring framework from services perspective. COP is delivered as 2 services: the first one is responsible for creating and feeding with data of the analyzed risk scenario, while the second one is responsible for generating visualization of a given scenario on the map, with the set geographic projection parameters.

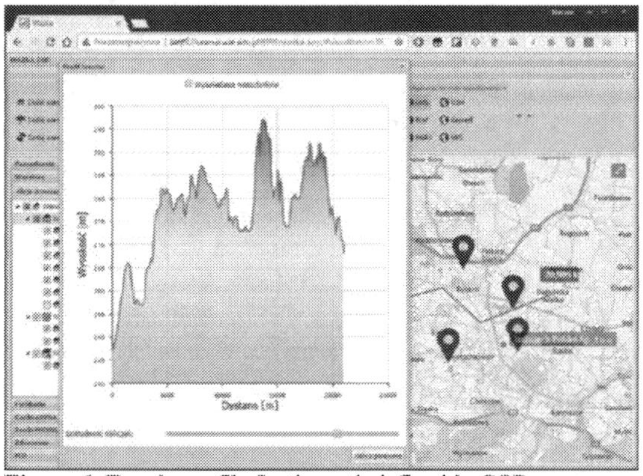

Figure 6. Terrain profile for the path defined in COP.

COP uses a possibility of visualizing any WMS (Web Map Service), allowing to enrich the operation area with satellite data, analytical maps, terrain elevation models and other analytical data related to, for example, weather information. Additional application mechanisms provide map calculation tools, which determine the lengths of the user-defined routes, fields of marked areas, terrain elevation profiles and flood zones (Figure 7). The functions supporting the decision-making process in the form of additional configurable GIS layers may be applied to the analyzed risk data, which significantly facilitates the analysis of an examined emergency situation.

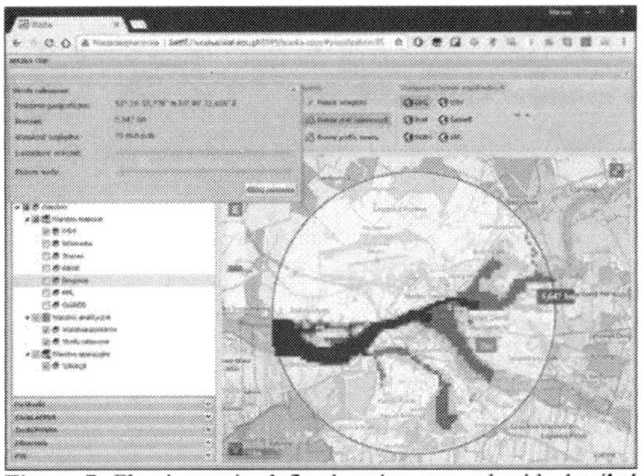

Figure 7. Flood area in defined region merged with detailed OpenStreetMap data layer fused in COP.

The COP tool provides services in the form of RESTful API and handles data serialization, in both XML and JSON formats. The tool has been equipped with additional applications supporting the manual configuration of requests to establish the scenario data and map application configuration, which additionally allows to use COP as a component of other web pages as well as automatic functional application.

4.3 Emulators of Threats Monitoring Systems (ETMS)

One of the goals of the designed WAZkA system is to use it for the purpose of training. To accomplish this goal, it is necessary to develop an artificial working environment of the system. It is aimed at providing the most exact recreation of the environment, preferably at such level of fidelity so that the trainees get the impression that they work in an actual environment. To reflect the data provider systems (in this case, the Threats Monitoring Systems), it was suggested to use the emulators (ETMS in Figure 1), i.e. the tools launched in environment other than the actual systems, aimed at providing data in the same way as real environments do.

The emulators were proposed as purely IT tool, launched in the same or identical hardware environment as the designed WAZkA system. The constructive simulation method, reduced to a simple determine data provider, in accordance with the predefined scenario, was selected as the emulation method.

Originally, the emulators should have been integrated with the whole system in the same manner as the actual systems. Thanks to that, they were supposed to be "transparent" for other system modules. Therefore, the emulators constitute an independent subsystem using the typical interfaced of the designed WAZkA system.

The above assumptions and general concept of the solution is presented in Figure 8. The requirements for the subsystem of emulators result from the requirements for the whole system. They were developed in the form of use cases.

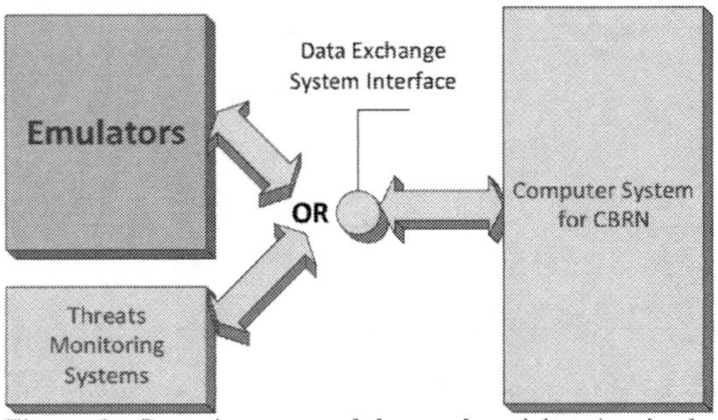

Figure 8. General concept of the emulators' location in the system *WAZkA*, *Source: own elaboration*

Emulation of the monitoring systems should be a function available to all users in the capacity of the *Emulator Operators*. Such users may influence the emulation process by controlling the simulation process for the purpose of emulation and by developing specific emulation scenarios (in this case - simulation scenarios). The process of emulation uses a typical function of the system known as the *Information Exchange*, which is aimed at integrating the whole system with the actual environment. On the other hand, the *Emulation of the Monitoring Systems* is an element of the use case - *Training*, which constitutes the function of the entire system.

During the analysis of the emulation requirements, six functional areas have been distinguished:

- Authorization;
- Emulation startup;
- Read of emulation parameters;
- Change of emulation parameters;
- Stopping emulation;
- Building of the scenario.

Each of the above areas has been specified by describing a dialog of the environment with the subsystem of emulators. Sample requirements for the manner of initiating the emulation process are presented in Table 1.

Table 1. Description of the project requirement with respect to the manner of initiating the emulation process, *Source: own elaboration*.

Emulator Operator	Emulation of the Monitoring Systems	Information Exchange
indication of the system for emulation	change of emulation parameters	
indication of the emulation scenario (sequence of events)	verification of emulation parameters (positive)	
instructions on initiating emulation at a given moment from the time of an indicated event	provision of data for emulation (correct data)	access to the system monitoring channel
	initiation of emulation at a given moment from the time of an	receipt and processing of data from

Emulator Operator	Emulation of the Monitoring Systems	Information Exchange
	indicated event; calling the interpretation service of the set type event and set parameters; sending messages to the system monitoring channel,	emulator;
	access to data of the emulation status	

The specification of functionalities, whose fragment was presented above, was developed on the basis of desired characteristics of the designed system, within the scope of the training requirements. The description in the form of interaction between the environment and emulation subsystem allowed to build a dynamic software model and hence generate the prototype template. The outline of the dynamic software mode, performed on the basis of the above table, is presented in Figure 9.

The software model developed in such a manner, executed for all functional areas and interaction variants, allowed to created the software static model, which in turn constituted grounds for generating the prototype template. After supplementing the implementation, the emulation subsystem prototype was created. The prototype form to use the above-mentioned functionality is presented in Figure 10.

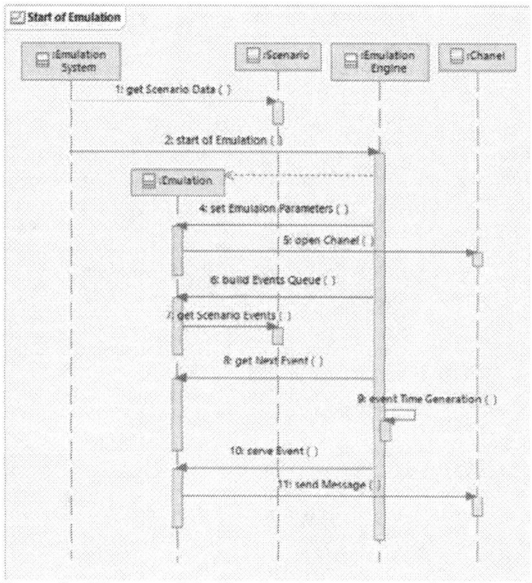

Figure 9. Diagram of the functional area sequence *Initiation of the emulation process, Source: own elaboration*

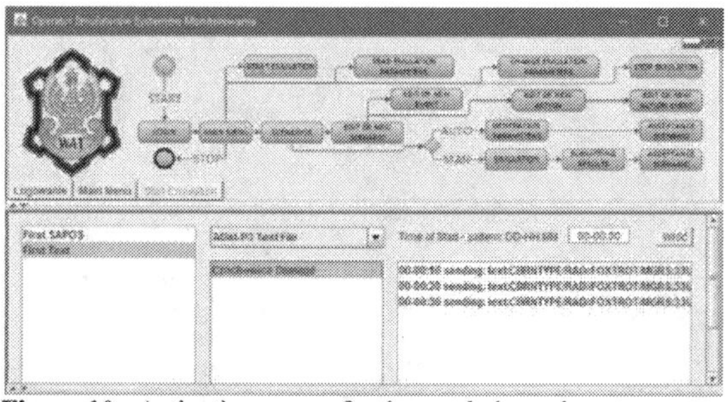

Figure 10. Activation screen for the emulation subsystem prototype, *Source: own elaboration*

5 Conclusions

The article outlined the concept of the system supporting analyses of threats related to contamination and alarming (WAZkA) for the purpose of the National System for Detection of Contamination and Alarming in Poland. Some of the selected software tools created for the WAZkA system were described.

One of the key elements for the project success is identification of the processes implemented under the National System for Detection of Contamination and Alarming, which require support by the IT services (program applications). One of the way to do it is using some approaches e.g. described in [5], [6], [7]. The main assumption is integration of KSWSiA with the existing systems (risk monitoring, warning and alarming). Furthermore, some of the KSWSiA entities are convinced that the designed system shall support the operations of KSWSiA and not replace the well-functioning areas. Therefore, numerous consultations are underway with the KSWSiA entities, in particular with the Central Contamination Analysis Center, which is at the same time the Administrative Center of KSWSiA, and State Fire Service Headquarters - the project owner.

A serious and difficult problem is to obtain access to the sources of data from the existing risk monitoring systems, managed by various institutions (IMGW, GIS, GIOŚ, RCB, PAA, etc). Additionally, the quality of the collected data shall determine the usability of the IT system and adequacy of the developed analyses and decisions. It is also worth noticing that due to the implementation of the project, new legislative and organizational solutions shall be indicated, which allow to reduce the time - from the moment of obtaining the information on an event to the time of undertaking appropriate actions by the KSWSiA entities (including, above all, the actions related to alarming and warning population), which may be an innovative solution within the European Union.

Acknowledgments

This work was partially supported by grant N°° DOB-BIO7/12/01/2015 of Polish National Center for Research and Development (NCBiR) titled „Integration and support of information management processes and decision optimization in warning and alarm system".

References

1. R. Antkiewicz, A. Gąsecki, A. Najgebauer, D. Pierzchała, Z. Tarapata, Stochastic PERT and CAST Logic Approach for Computer Support of Complex Operation Planning, *ASMTA'2010*, Lecture Notes in Computer Science, **6148**, Springer-Verlag Berlin Heidelberg, 159-173 (2010)
2. *ATP-45(d): Warning and reporting and hazard prediction of chemical, biological, radiological and nuclear incidents (operators manual)*, NATO unclassified (2010)
3. T. Binek, J. Czepiel, The National System of Contamination Detection and Alarm, Currently Operating in Poland, BiTP Vol. **36** Issue **4**, pp. 15-24 (2014)
4. D. Grabowski, W. Kurowski, W. Muszynski, B. Rubel, G. Smagala, J. Swietochowska, Radiation monitoring network in Poland, Nukleonika, **46(4)**: pp.147–149, (2001)
5. M. Kiedrowicz, J. Stanik, Selected aspects of risk management in respect of security of the document lifecycle management system with multiple levels of sensitivity, (in:) *Information Management in Practice*, (eds) B.F. Kubiak and J. Maślankowski, pp. 231-249, (2015)
6. M. Kiedrowicz, Location with the use of the RFID and GPS technologies - opportunities and threats, *Proceedings of the Geographic Information Systems Conference and Exhibition, GIS ODYSSEY 2016*, pp.122-128 (2016)
7. M. Kiedrowicz, Objects identification in the informations models used by information systems, *Proceedings of the Geographic Information Systems Conference and Exhibition, GIS ODYSSEY 2016*, pp. 129-136, (2016)
8. P. Lipiński, P. , K. Isajenko, M. Biernacka, A. Żak, Integration of Polish Monitoring Networks (ASS-500 and PMS systems), Nukleonica, vol. **46(4)**: pp. 143–146 (2001)
9. M. Mlynarczyk, P. Maciejewski, M. Szerszen, CBRN Analysis and SI Promień – Comparison of the Functionality of the Software for the Assessment of Contamination, BiTP Vol. **40** Issue **4**, pp. 133-138 (2015)
10. M.E. Pate-Cornell, Fault Trees vs. Event Trees in Reliability Analysis, Risk Analysis, Vol. **4**, Issue **3**, pp. 177–186 (1984)
11. *Regulation of the Council of Minister of October 16, 2006 on the contamination detection systems and level of competence of appropriate bodies* (Journal of Laws [DzU] of 2006 No. 191, item 1415), (2006)
12. Z. Tarapata, *Models and algorithms for knowledge-based decision support and simulation in defense and transport applications*, ISBN 978-83-62954-15-5, Military University of Technology in Warsaw (2011)
13. *Act of April 26, 2007 Journal of Laws [DzU], No. 89, item 590, as amended, and Regulation of the Council of Ministers of June 25 on the detailed scope of activities of the Head of the National Civil Defense, heads of civil defense of voivodeships, poviats and communes*, Journal of Laws [DzU] No. 96, item 850, (2007)
14. http://wazka.wat.edu.pl (2017)
15. http://loganfta.com (2017)
16. https://www.premier.gov.pl/en/news/news/a-promise-from-expose-kept-regional-warning-system-rso-is-fully-operational.html
17. https://www.publicalerting.com/products/public-warning-system/advantages-of-digitexczkip/
18. https://www.epa.gov/cameo/aloha-software

Analytical processing system of business processes, methods of exploration of business process definitions and instances

Jarosław Koszela[1,*]

[1]*Military University of Technology, Faculty of Cybernetics, Institute of Computer and Information Systems, Warsaw, Poland*

Abstract. The article tackles the topics related to systems, methods and mechanisms for storing process definitions and instances for the purpose of their analytical processing - process warehouses and general architecture of such process warehouses, including tools allowing their extract, transform, load (ETL) as well as analytical processing and exploration of stored process definitions and instances - i.e. the process mining. Furthermore, the article describes a mechanism for storing processes, with the use of a network database, and one of the methods for researching into similarities of the processes through the tagging of generic processes.

1 Introduction

The presently applied methods of modeling, designing and creating IT systems are based on three basic approaches: structural, object and process. In the structural and object approach, the system structure and resources come to the fore, whereas the issue describing the processing dynamics stays in the background, even though this aspect is equally important in terms of a complete and consistent description of the modeled system. The situation is different in case of the process approach, where the priority is the description of the processing dynamics in the form of business process models, whereas the system models as well as the descriptions of the system structures and resources recede into the background.

The most popular currently applied notations of the business process is the BPMN v2.0 (Business Process Model and Notation) [1-3] standard, developed by the BPMI (Business Process Management Initiative) and OMG (Object Management Group) in January 2011. The standard defines a set of symbols and their semantics, allowing to model a diagram of the business process definition in a graphical form (Fig. 1). The graphical notation of the process, presented in the BPMN standard, is in human-readable form. On the other hand, the following formats are used for the purpose of a notation allowing clear interpretation: XPDL (XML Process Definition Language) [4] developed by WfMC (Workflow Management Coalition) and adapted for the purpose of exchanging process definitions noted in this format between various systems, and the BPDM format (Business Process Definition Metamodel) developed by OMG, which described meta-models defining concepts, correlations and their semantics to exchange the business process models between different modeling processes. Both these formats are based on data notation in XML (Extensible Markup Language), developed by XSD (XML Schema Definition) and XMI (XML Metadata Interchange).

The modeling of business processes is a defining stage of the model that describes operations of a given organization or merged or collaborating elements of the modeled reality fragments. To perform the modeling activities in a manner allowing on one hand, their actual and physical embodiments, and on the other - necessary or desired efficiency, it is crucial to apply the automation tools. The group shall include process automation systems - the workflow systems, in particular the workflow management systems - WFMS (Workflow Management System) [5]. The main purpose of such IT systems is to process the process instances, according to the modeled business process definition. It should be mentioned that the main task realized by the WFMS systems is the processing of processes in accordance with their definitions, not activities described thereby. The implementing systems, independent of WFMS, or specialized services are responsible for performing activities and works described in the processes.

The basic scope and tasks related to the business processing IT systems have been presented by the WFMC organization, which defines workflow in the following way:

"The automation of a business process, in whole or part, during which documents, information or tasks are passed from one participant to another for action, according to a set of procedural rules" [6].

On the other hand, the workflow management system - WFMS - is defined by WFMC as:

"A system that defines, creates and manages the execution of workflows through the use of software, running on one or more workflow engines, which is able to interpret the process definition, interact with workflow

* Corresponding author: jkoszela@wat.edu.pl

participants and, where required, invoke the use of IT tools and applications" [6].

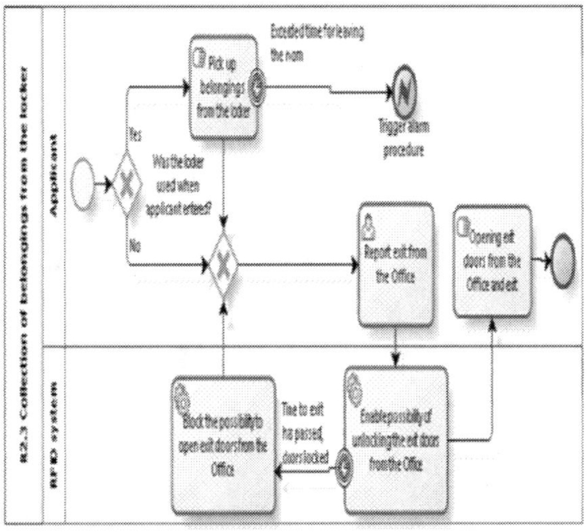

Fig. 1. Example of BPMN process.

2 Systems analysis of business processes

The system for the business process analysis (OLAP-BP) is categorized as Business Intelligence (BI), in case of solutions based or significantly supported by business processes [7-10]. The process modeling is an activity that requires constant modification, improvement and optimization of such processes. The variability of the environment, legislation, organization, economic situation makes it necessary to continuously introduce changes and upgrades of the process to increase its efficiency in broad context. The PDCA model [11] is used for the business process management. The model describes the process life cycle and consists of four main steps: Plan, Do, Check, Act. The model present a closed cycle of the process management, where the processes should be all the time modified and upgraded. The developed processes may be automated, analyzed and explored through the process automation systems (workflow systems) (Fig.2) [1,3],[5-10],[17-26],[28,33]. The use of the process warehouse, including process exploration, makes it possible to perform an in-depth analysis of the processes gathered in the warehouse [7,8], by applying special tools for process exploration, which may use various methods, e.g. analytical, forecast, simulation [12], structural, semantic, etc. The process warehouse as well as process exploration tools should be included in the group of the Business Intelligence systems.

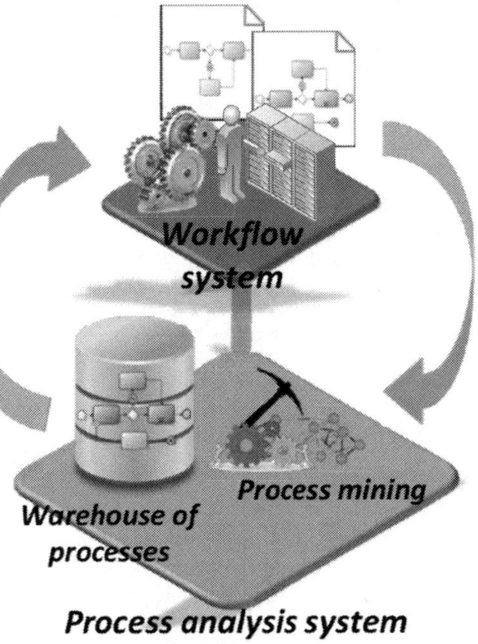

Fig. 2. Execution (workflow system) and analysis (process system architecture [18]

The functioning of the process warehouse in the organization is aimed at streamlining the management and decision-making processes by providing current data and information regarding the implementation of business processes. The main tasks of the process warehouse are, among other things, the following [18]:

- integration with the process runtime environment, allowing to transfer data in time cycles and via an online model;
- possible extraction and upload of the processes and process instances;
- processing of data with the process definitions and instances derived from the process runtime environments, in cycle and event modes (online);
- storage of data on business process, which include, among other things, the following:
- collection of unified business process definitions and instances in terms of their structure and semantics,
- collection of metadata and semantic data concerning business processes,
- collection of indirect data and results of analytical processing and process exploration,
- in forms allowing to analytically process the data, while ensuring expected capacity, in particular
- analysis of deviations of the process instances from sample paths,
- identification of deadlocks and bottlenecks in the process instances,
- analysis of execution times of the process instances and particular components,
- analysis of the decisions made during the process implementation,

- identification of the so-called dead process or process fragments and resources, which are not implemented or are implemented vary rarely,
- definition and analysis of the process similarity measures as well as event sequences,
- identification of new processes on the basis of the process execution logs,
- identification of patterns as well as rare and frequent event sequences,
- provision of apparatus and tools allowing the process analytical processing and exploration.

The process warehouse is a system which, through its software, analysis methods and process exploration, allows efficient analytical processing and exploration of the collected business processes and process instances. Fig. 3 shows the general architecture model of the process warehouse, in which the following basic subsystems may be distinguished:

- extract, transformation and load from different sources of various formats of the definition notation regarding processes and executed instances of business process, together with their structural and semantic unification,
- process warehouses as thematic composition of the unified process and process instances,
- analyses and exploration of processes and process instances,
- access to the process warehouse allowing interactive questioning and answering in the form of reports, tables, charts, etc.

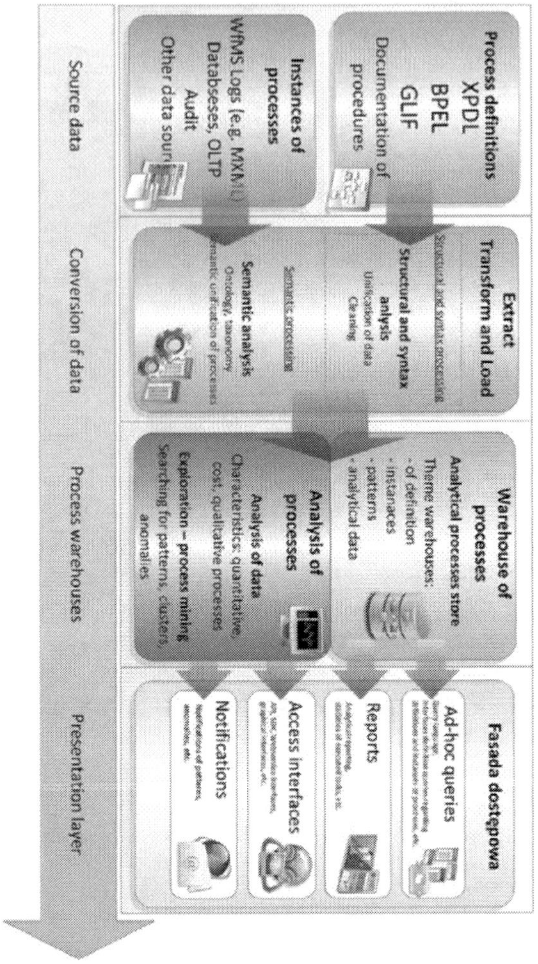

Fig. 3. Architecture of process warehouse

3 Process warehouse - analytical composition of the process definitions and instances

The process warehouse is an IT tool used for collecting, accessing and efficient processing of the business processes and process instances for the purpose of their analysis and exploration. The physical composition of the process warehouse includes the components of the process definitions and instances in the form of unified data, metadata, semantic data and analytical data (Fig. 4).

Warehouse of the unified processes and instances - a component responsible for the storage of data on the process definitions and instances, pursuant to the effective standards, e.g. XPDL [4,14], MXML [16], XES [15], which constitutes grounds for generating data on the processes stored in the analytical data warehouse. As part of the preliminary data, two variants of the warehouse structures were developed and tested - the original variant based on the physical warehouse of the

DOI: 10.1051/matecconf/201712502013

matrix process structures and the warehouse using Neo4j graph database [31].

Warehouse of metadata and semantic data - a component responsible for the storage of semantic models expressed in ontological languages, which ensures, among other things, a possibility of expressing complex links between the model elements and a possibility of expressing logical equivalence of the terms and instances as well as open world assumptions, by introducing a specific manner of interpreting the lack of knowledge in the model. Correlations between various elements of the process warehouse - a component that implements metamodel of the processes warehouse and that is responsible for storing data on the links binding individual elements of the process warehouse, ensuring its coherence.

Analytical data and process warehouses - a component responsible for storing data on the processes in the form of graphs and networks in the form of matrices, using the network databases - this method for representing data on the process definitions and instances allows to apply a mathematical apparatus for the purpose of the process analyses and streamlines analytical processing in terms of its capacity.

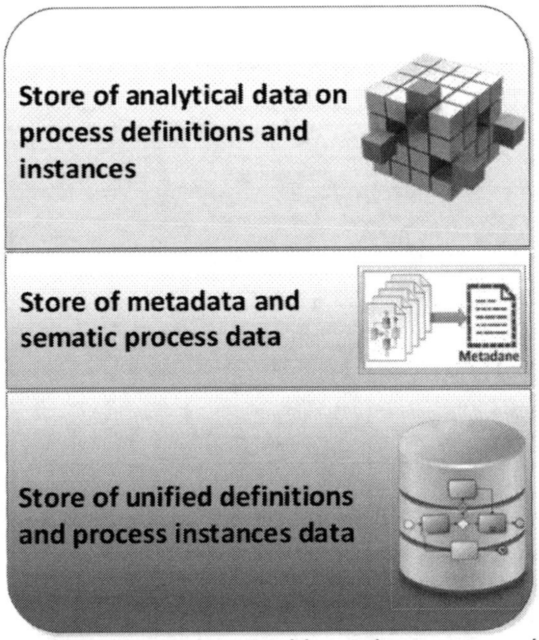

Fig. 4. Process warehouse model - storing processes and instances

Fig.5 shows a sample business process noted in graphical notation of the BPMN v2.0 standard, implemented with the use of the process modeling tools – Bizagi Modeler v3.1 [13] and the same process noted in the formal data structure, i.e. XPDL (Fig.6). The developed transformation tool is used for the business process noted in the XPDL format to be translated into Neo4j's Cypher Query Language [31,32], applied in the network environment (Fig.7). When comparing a visual embodiment of the process noted in BPMN v2.0 (Fig.5) and another visualization of the result after the transformation of such process saved in Neo4j database (Fig. 8), it may be observed that the basic information included in the definition of such process was included in the network database warehouse.

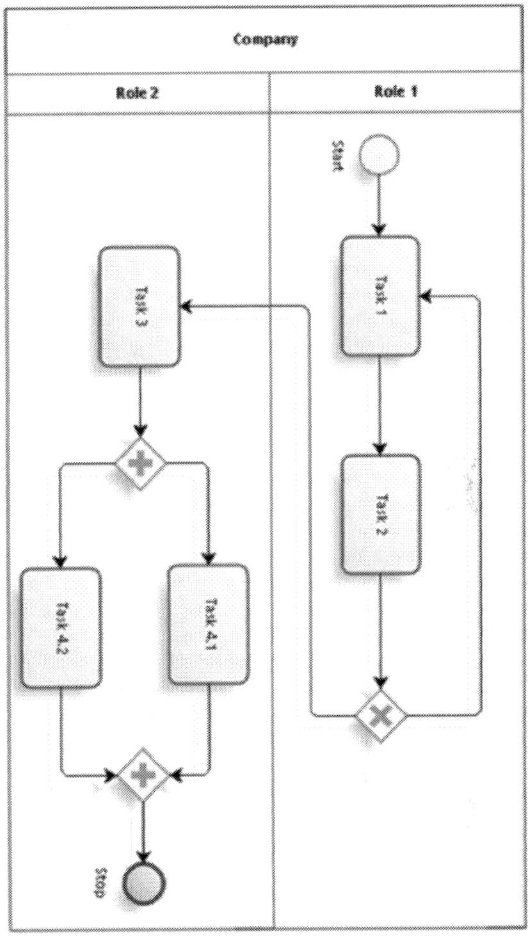

Fig. 5. Sample process in BPMN v2.0

```
<Activities>
    <Activity        Id="5df66d16-191b-4735-a618-fb5c47eeee9f"
Name="Start">
      <Description />
      <Event>
        <StartEvent Trigger="None" />
      </Event>
      <Documentation />
      <NodeGraphicsInfos>
        <NodeGraphicsInfo        ToolId="BizAgi_Process_Modeler"
Height="30"  Width="30"  BorderColor="-10311914"  FillColor="-
1638505">
          <Coordinates XCoordinate="134" YCoordinate="101" />
        </NodeGraphicsInfo>
      </NodeGraphicsInfos>
      <ExtendedAttributes>
        <ExtendedAttribute Name="RuntimeProperties" Value="{}"
/>
      </ExtendedAttributes>
    </Activity>
    <Activity        Id="732a4357-14e6-4780-981c-85b3b962714b"
Name="Task 1">
      <Description />
```

```
<Implementation>
  <Task />
</Implementation>
<Performers />
<Documentation />
<Loop LoopType="None" />
<NodeGraphicsInfos>
  <NodeGraphicsInfo ToolId="BizAgi_Process_Modeler" Height="60" Width="90" BorderColor="-16553830" FillColor="-1249281">
    <Coordinates XCoordinate="211" YCoordinate="86" />
  </NodeGraphicsInfo>
</NodeGraphicsInfos>
<ExtendedAttributes />
</Activity>
```

Fig. 6. Fragment of Fig. 5 process definition in XPDL

```
CREATE (start1:Event {Id: 1, Type: 'Start', Trigger: 'None', Pool_Name:'Organization', Lane_Name:'Role 1'})
CREATE (stop1:Event {Id: 7, Type: 'Stop', Trigger: 'None', Pool_Name:'Organization', Lane_Name:'Role 2'})
CREATE (z1:Task {Id: 2, Type: 'Activity', SubType: 'None', LoopType:'None', Name:'Task 1', Pool_Name:'Organization', Lane_Name:'Role 1'})
CREATE (z2:Task {Id: 3, Type: 'Activity', SubType: 'None', LoopType:'None', Name:'Task 2', Pool_Name:'Organization', Lane_Name:'Role 1'})
CREATE (z3:Task {Id: 4, Type: 'Activity', SubType: 'None', LoopType:'None', Name:'Task 3', Pool_Name:'Organization', Lane_Name:'Role 2'})
CREATE (z4_1:Task {Id: 5, Type: 'Activity', SubType: 'None', LoopType:'None', Name:'Taskv4.1', Pool_Name:'Organization', Lane_Name:'Role 2'})
CREATE (z4_2:Task {Id: 6, Type: 'Activity', SubType: 'None', LoopType:'None', Name:'Task 4.2', Pool_Name:'Organization', Lane_Name:'Role 2'})

CREATE (g1:Gateway {Id: 8, Type: 'XOR', Condition: '', Pool_Name:'Organization', Lane_Name:'Role 1'})
CREATE (g2:Gateway {Id: 9, Type: 'AND', Condition: '', Pool_Name:'Organization', Lane_Name:'Role 2'})
CREATE (g3:Gateway {Id: 10, Type: 'AND', Condition: '', Pool_Name:'Organization', Lane_Name:'Role 2'})

MATCH (start1 {Id:1}), (z1 {Id:2}), (z2 {Id:3}), (z3 {Id:4}), (z4_1 {Id:5}), (z4_2 {Id:6}), (g1 {Id:8}), (g2 {Id:9}), (g3 {Id:10}), (stop1 {Id:7})
CREATE (start1)-[:Transition {Id:20, Condition:''}]->(z1)
CREATE (z1)-[:Transition {Id:21, Condition:''}]->(z2)
CREATE (z2)-[:Transition {Id:22, Condition:''}]->(g1)
CREATE (g1)-[:Transition {Id:23, Condition:''}]->(z1)
CREATE (g1)-[:Transition {Id:24, Condition:''}]->(z3)
CREATE (z3)-[:Transition {Id:25, Condition:''}]->(g2)
CREATE (g2)-[:Transition {Id:26, Condition:''}]->(z4_1)
CREATE (g2)-[:Transition {Id:27, Condition:''}]->(z4_2)
CREATE (z4_1)-[:Transition {Id:28, Condition:''}]->(g3)
CREATE (z4_2)-[:Transition {Id:29, Condition:''}]->(g3)
CREATE (g3)-[:Transition {Id:30, Condition:''}]->(stop1)
```

Fig. 7. Transformation of Fig. 5 process to the Neo4j's Graph Query Language

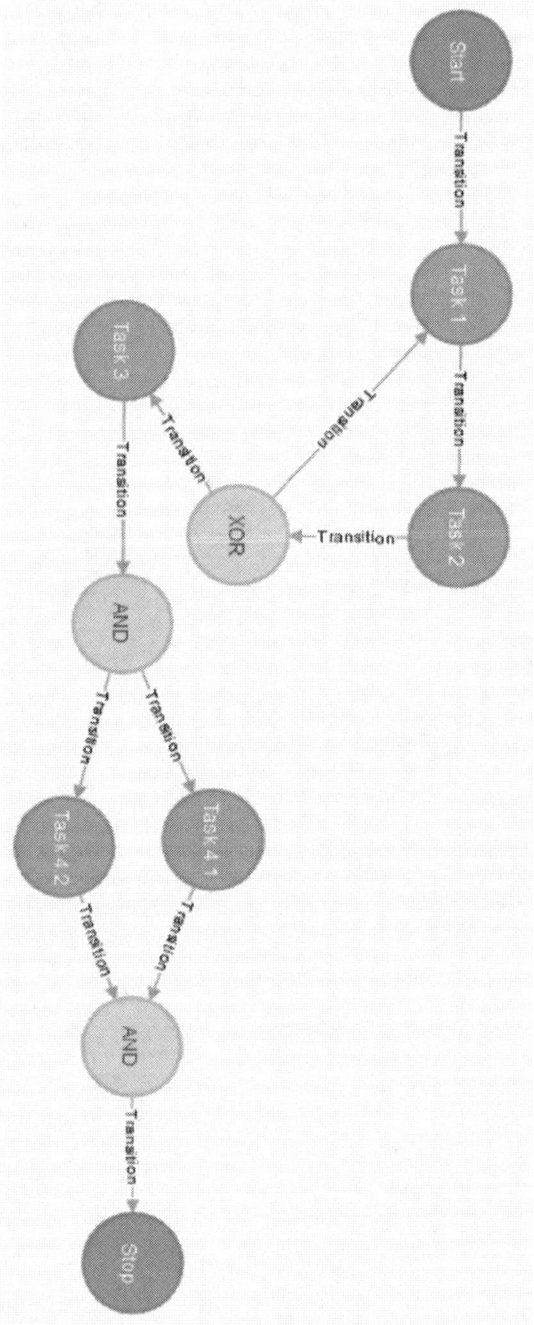

Fig. 8. Visualization of the process shown in Fig. 5 stored in the process network database

4 Method of similarity processes by genetic tagging

One of the main groups of the process analysis methods are methods used for examining similarities between the business process definitions and instances. The methods directly based on the graph and network theories [9, 27, 29, 30] as well as mixed methods may be included in the above-mentioned group. The methods are usually quite complex in terms of calculations, which means that their application for the analysis of a large number of the process definitions and instances may be rather costly as far as calculations are concerned. Therefore, the process similarity method by genetic tagging is aimed at increasing the efficiency of the processes similarity analysis in case of a significant number of the processes. The method is based on the process transformation from the form based on graphs to the form of element sequences (genes), which correspond to the model form. Generally, the similarity analysis is aimed at analyzing two "genetic" sequences of the processes.

The first step is to transform the notation of the process definition from the graph form to the linear tag sequence. Such transformation should include the relationship of a certain order, which shall transform two different notations of the same process definition into a uniform and identical process tag sequence.

$$G=(V,E) \quad (1)$$

$$E \subseteq \{(v_s,v_e,f) : v_s,v_e \in V, f \in F\} \quad (2)$$

$$v = \{(s,g) : v \in V,\ s \in S,\ g \in G\} \quad (3)$$

The process defined as graph G, in which a set of the vertices V means a set of the process active elements (i.a. process, activities, gates, events), and set E means the flowing of controls and messages between the process active elements, including the definition of such flow f. An element of the set of vertices V is defined as a well-ordered tandem of elements, where s means semantically unified feature of the process, and g means a type of the process active element.

The elements of the process genetic tag sequence are in the following form:

$$t = (v_s,f,v_e) \quad (4)$$

whereas the process genetic tag sequence is in the form of the well-ordered sequence:

$$T = (t_1,t_2, \ldots, t_i) \quad (5)$$

Transformation of Fig. 5 process noted in XPDL to the structure of the process genetic tag sequence is as follows:
<St1.Start; Tr1; Ta1.Task 1>, <Ta1.Task 1; Tr1; Ta1.Task 2>, <Ta1.Task 2; Tr1; Ga2.>, <Ta1.Task 3; Tr1; Ga3.>, <Ta1.Task 4.2; Tr1; Ga3.>, <Ta1.Task 4.1; Tr1; Ga3.>, <Ga2.; Tr1; Ta1.Task 1>, <Ga2.; Tr1; Ta1.Task 3>, <Ga3.; Tr1; Ta1.Task 4.1>, <Ga3.; Tr1; Ta1.Task 4.2>, <Ga3.; Tr1; En1.Stop>

For example, a slight modification of the process presented in Fig. 5 may be introduced by adding one activity, and we obtain the process shown in Fig. 9.

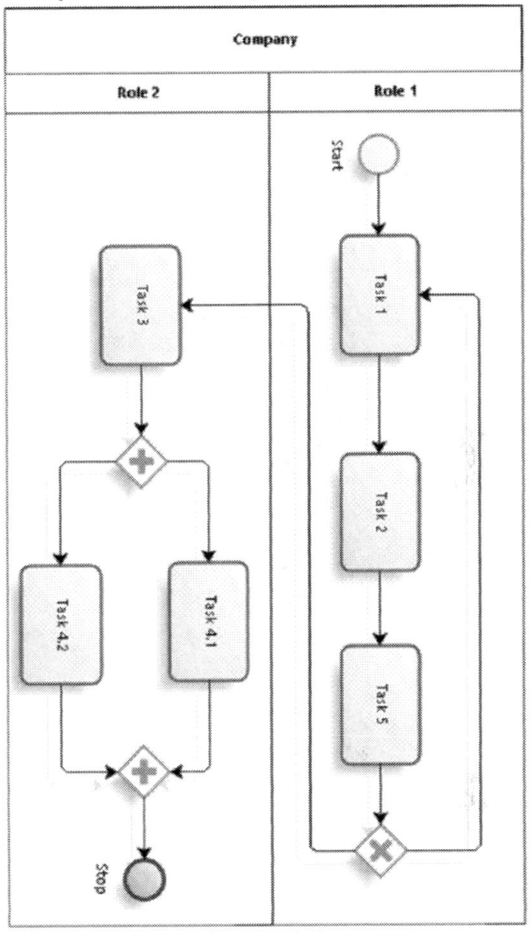

Fig. 9 Modified process Fig.5 (Task 5)

Process genetic tag sequence Fig. 9 is as follows:
<St1.Start; Tr1; Ta1.Task 1>, <Ta1.Task 1; Tr1; Ta1.Task 2>, <Ta1.Task 2; Tr1; Ta1.Task 5>, <Ta1.Task 5; Tr1; Ga2.>, <Ta1.Task 3; Tr1; Ga3.>, <Ta1.Task 4.1; Tr1; Ga3.>, <Ta1.Task 4.2; Tr1; Ga3.>, <Ga2.; Tr1; Ta1.Task 1>, <Ga2.; Tr1; Ta1.Task 3>, <Ga3.; Tr1; Ta1.Task 4.1>, <Ga3.; Tr1; Ta1.Task 4.2>, <Ga3.; Tr1; En1.Stop>

The so prepared process genetic tag sequence is in the linear form of the input data to establish the similarity measures. Basic process similarity measures have been developed on the basis of the similarities established for the corresponding process genetic tag sequence:

- General numerical similarity measure - the measure which defines the process similarity in terms of a quotient of occurrences of the types of tags in the particular process genetic tag sequences.

- Detailed numerical similarity measure - the measure which is similar to the general numerical similarity measure, except that the tags of the same type are those which have the same type of the initial active elements, including their properties, the same type of transition between the active elements and the same type of the final active element, including their properties.
- General chain similarity measure - the measure which is aimed at defining the level of similarity between two business processes noted as the genetic tag sequence, based on the number of similar subchains. The ratio of the number of positive comparisons of the subchains with the general number of the compared subchains is the results of the above-mentioned comparison. The subchains are properly compared if all of their corresponding threes are of the same type.
- Detailed chain similarity measure - the measure is similar to the general chain similarity measurement, except that - when comparing particular tags in subchains- the tags of the same type are those which have the same type of the initial active elements, including their properties, the same type of transition between the active elements and the same type of the final active element, including their properties.

Values of such similarity measurements are scalar values - number from the range [0,1], where 1 means that the compared processes are identical in terms of a given similarity measure. When applying the aforementioned process similarity measures, based on the similarities of genetic tags for the processes shown in Fig. 5 and Fig. 6, we obtain the following values of the similarity measures:

- general numerical similarity measure: 0.9091,
- detailed numerical similarity measure: 0.9091.
- general chain similarity measure: 0.7532,
- detailed chain similarity measure: 0.7532.

3 Conclusions

The above material shows the results of the studies carried out in the field of modeling, implementation and analysis of the systems based on the process approach as well as systems of analysis and automation of business processes. The presented subject related to the business processes, in particular their modeling, analysis and automation is a relatively new area of research in both IT and management. However, the implementation of the described processes in both these fields stimulates their development dynamics, as the increased demand for more efficient activities may be a powerful engine for economic growth.

The presented aspects of the systems, tools and methods of analytical business processing should be considered as an introduction to further development of this subject matter in various directions. The directions include issues related to the tools and methods for collecting data on the process definitions and instances as well as tools and methods for analytical processing in different dimensions and at different levels.

References

1. M. Weske, *Business Process Management. Concepts, Languages, Architectures*, Berlin, Springer-Verlag (2007)
2. OMG, BPMN - standard documents, [Online] http://www.omg.org/spec/BPMN/2.0/ (2011)
3. A. Arsanjani, N. Bharade, M. Borgenstrand, P. Schume, J. K. Wood i V. Zheltonogov, *Business Process Management Design Guide. Using IBM Business Process Manager*, USA, IBM Corporation (2015)
4. WFMC, XML Process Definition Language – standard XPDL documents, [Online] http://www.xpdl.org/ (2012)
5. W. van der Aalst, K. van Hee, *Workflow Management. Models, Methods, and Systems* (The MIT Press Cambridge, Massachusetts London, 2002)
6. WFMC, *Terminology & Glossary - WFMC-TC-1011*, [Online], http://wfmc.org/docs/TC-1011_term_glossary_v3.pdf (1999)
7. G. Bliźniuk, M. Chmielewski, T. Gzik, J. Koszela, Warehouse of processes, *Studia Informatica*, **33-2A**, 111-127 (2012)
8. P. Zadora, *Hurtownie danych w organizacji inteligentnej* (Akademia Ekonomiczna, Katowice, 2004)
9. W. van der Aalst, *Process Mining*, (Springer-Verlag, Berlin, 2016)
10. B. Gawin, *Systemy informatyczne w zarządzaniu procesami Workflow*, (PWN, Warszawa, 2015)
11. R. Moen, C. Norman, *Evolution of the PDCA Cycle* (2009)
12. A. Sidnev, J. Tuominen i B. Krassi, *Business Process Modeling and Simulation* (Otamedia Oy, Espoo, 2005)
13. Bizagi, [Online] http://www.bizagi.com (2017)
14. WFMC, [Online] http://www.wfmc.org (2017)
15. XES, [Online] http://www.xes-standard.org (2017)
16. MXML-Mining eXtensible Markup Language, [Online] http://www.processmining.org/logs/mxml (2003)
17. M. Kiedrowicz, *Zarządzanie informacjami wrażliwymi - wybrane aspekty organizacyjne, prawne i techniczne ochrony informacji niejawnych* (WAT, Warszawa, 2015)
18. J. Koszela, Business process modeling for processing classified documents using RFID technology in *20th International Conference on Circuits, Systems, Communications and Computers*, **76**, N. Mastorakis, V. Mladenov, and A. Bulucea, Eds. (MATEC Web of Conferences, Cedex A: E D P Sciences (2016)
19. R. Waszkowski, M. Kiedrowicz, T. Nowicki, Z. Wesolowski, and K. Worwa, Business processes in the RFID-equipped restricted access administrative office, in *20th International Conference on Circuits, Systems, Communications and Computers*, vol. 76, N. Mastorakis, V. Mladenov, and A. Bulucea, Eds. (MATEC Web of Conferences, Cedex A: E D P Sciences, 2016

20. M. Kiedrowicz, Uogólniony model danych w rozproszonych rejestrach ewidencyjnych, *Roczniki Kolegium Analiz Ekonomicznych*, vol. **33**, pp. 209-234, (2014)
21. M. Kiedrowicz, The importance of an integration platform within the organisation, *Zeszyty Naukowe*, vol. **46**, pp.83-94, (2014)
22. M. Kiedrowicz, Dostęp do publicznych zasobów danych - Big data czy Big brother, (in:) INTERNET. Publiczne bazy danych i Big data, (ed.) G. Szpor, pp. 15-39, (2015)
23. M. Kiedrowicz, R. Waszkowski, Business rules automation standards in business process management systems, (in:) Information Management in Practice, (eds) B.F. Kubiak and J. Maślankowski, pp. 187-200, (2015)
24. M. Kiedrowicz, T. Nowicki, R. Waszkowski, Z. Wesolowski, and K. Worwa, Software simulator for property investigation of document management system with RFID tags, *20th International Conference on Circuits, Systems, Communications and Computers, MATEC Web of Conferences*, Cedex A: E D P Sciences, vol. **76**, (2016)
25. M. Kiedrowicz, J. Koszela, Business processes modelling for the processing of classified documents using RFID technology, *Collegium of Economic Analysis Annals*, vol. **42**, pp: 53-66, (2016)
26. M. Kiedrowicz, T. Nowicki, R. Waszkowski, Business process data flow between automated and human tasks, *3rd International Conference on Social Science (ICSS 2016) December 9–11 2016*, pp. 471-477, (2016)
27. R. Dijkmana, *Similarity of business process models: Metrics and evaluation*, Information Systems, Elsevier, **36** (2011)
28. M. Kiedrowicz, J. Koszela, *Secret office model for the processing of classified documents using RFID technology*, Collegium of Economic Analysis Annals, **42**, 67-81 (2016)
29. M. Ehrig, A. Koschmider, A. Oberweis, *Measuring Similarity between Semantic Business Process Models*, Conferences in Research and Practice in Information, **67**, Australian Computer Society (2007)
30. R. Dijkman, M. Dumas, L. García-Bañuelos, *Business Process Graphs: Similarity Search and Matching*, Graph data management: techniques and applications, IGI Global (2012)
31. Neo4j, [Online] https://neo4j.com (2017)
32. I. Robinson, J. Webber, E. Eifrem, Graph Databases (O'Reilly Media, Sebastopol, 2015)
33. W. van der Aalst & others, *Process Mining Manifesto*, IEEE Task Force on Process Mining, [Online] http://www.win.tue.nl/ieeetfpm/downloads/Process%20Mining%20Manifesto.pdf

Dynamic business process in workflow systems

Maciej Kiedrowicz[1*]

[1] Military University of Technology, Faculty of Cybernetics, Institute of Computer and Information Systems, Warsaw, Poland

Abstract. The article presents the concept of business process modeling by using dynamic processes. An extended definition of the business process allows to construct a mechanism for dynamic selection of actions performed in order, which makes it possible to achieve the process goal assumed in the definition. The mechanism for selecting actions subsequently taken in the dynamic process constitutes extension of the functionalities in the workflow process, including the process progress status, WfMS and service environments.

1 Introduction

The process approach applied during the modeling, design, implementation and use of IT systems makes it necessary for the authors to model and design such business processes that shall constitute fundamental and necessary structure elements of the system based on the process approach [1, 2, 4, 6]. It is possible to model basically all of the processes used in the company's operations, however, such a comprehensive approach would cause a significant increase of complexity and hence the costs related to the implementation of such system. If the system based on the process approach is implemented in the incremental form, it means that the processes or groups of processes, which should be modeled or implemented in the first row, need to be distinguished. If the organization already uses the process automation systems, the analysis of definitions and instances of such processes may contribute to the decisions made with respect to their efficiency and quality, using methods and tools for process analyses - process warehouses [7-14]. The main selection criteria include the processes: that are most often implemented within the organization (quantitative factor), that have significant impact on efficiency and operating costs of the company (economic factor) and that have significant impact on the implementation of the company's main targets (strategic factor). On the other hand, the processes rarely implemented or characterized by high variability of their structure require a lot of effort on the part of creators of the business processes, which consequently results in the fact that such processes often have very complex structures. In such processes, the correlation between the cost of their implementation and potential profit during their automated processing may be largely unsatisfactory. It is possible to model and design such processes that would not require from their creators any high structural precision at the beginning [15-18]. The aforesaid processes include adaptation, generic and dynamic processes.

2 Process modeling

One of the most important stages of creating a process is its modeling. It is usually the analyst working with different business employees, responsible for a given business process implemented within the organization and specialized in a given field, who is entrusted with the task of building the aforementioned model. During the modeling process, persons responsible therefor, must identify actions in a given business process, which are both mandatory and optional. Apart from that, additional aspects of each of the aforesaid actions are determined: business owner, input and output data and their necessity, errors that may occur while performing a certain action and methods for dealing with such errors.

As a result of the business process modeling, formalized records are obtained. The format, in which the process model is presented, may differ depending on the adopted method and standard. The form is usually graphical (but may be also different), relatively easy to understand and maintain, with the support of appropriate tools. Currently, the most often applied form of graphic notation is BPMN v 2.0 [3].

The processes may be modeled in different ways, but the best results are produced by one of the verified modeling strategies [25-28]. There are many modeling strategies, but none of them is universal - for one company one strategy may be more efficient than the other, and for another company - rather contrary. We may distinguish four basic strategies [2]:

• top-down - according to this strategy, the modeling of a business process should start from the definition of general elements and then, at later stages, additional details may be added to reach the definition at the lowest level. The main advantage of this strategy is that it focuses around major business needs and then assigns particular detailed actions to be taken with respect thereto. The disadvantage is that the strategy requires

* Corresponding author: maciej.kiedrowicz@wat.edu.pl

extensive knowledge and experience - in case of complex processes, any mistakes made at a higher level may cause problems during the modeling of more detailed business processes.

• bottom-up - the strategy opposite to the one described above. The process modeling starts from the detailed elements of processes and subprocesses, which - when combined into increasingly larger groups - shall eventually create the whole business process. The advantage of such approach is the fact that it results in an accurately designed process, where all detailed actions, products and subprocesses are of great importance. However, one of the drawbacks is that the created business process model may turn out to be too detailed and complex and hence not fully compatible with the general business needs of the organization.

• inside-out (dissemination) - the strategy may constitute a compromise between the two above-mentioned approaches. First of all, the main and most important processes, including their details, are defined, and then some elements, subprocesses and supporting tasks added. The difficulty in determining which tasks (or processes) are the most important may be considered a disadvantage, since any mistakes made in this case can lead to the necessity of re-starting the modeling process.

• mixed - this approach is a hybrid of all of the above-mentioned strategies. Intelligent use of the advantages related to other strategies helps to achieve better results and more efficient modeling, while minimizing the impact of drawbacks resulting from the application of the particular strategies separately.

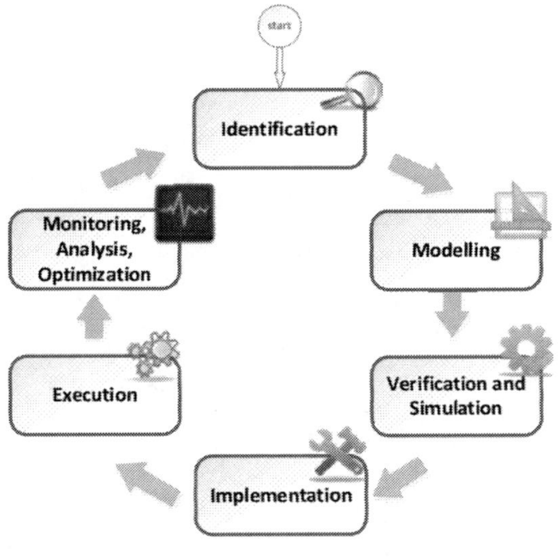

Fig. 1. Life cycle of business process.

The process approach is characterized by constant and cyclical sequence of steps, which are aimed at modeling, implementing and improving processes. The sequence of such steps executed cyclically is defined as the process life cycle (Fig. 1).

3 Ad-hoc, adaptive and generic processes

The process models applied in the mainstream process modeling must be complete in terms of achievement of the assumed goals. It means that the authors must develop business processes which include many situations and cases [19-22]. Based on such approach, the processes are usually very complex and susceptible to unexpected changes, which may occur in their environment, e.g. amended rules and regulations. Therefore, an alternative to the said approach in the process modeling might be ad-hoc, adaptive or generic processes.

The ad-hoc processes were intended to introduce an element of ambiguity and dynamics obtained during the process implementation, with initially non-defined form of such process, in whole or in part. They may be applied at a given place (as part of a certain activity) under the undefined subprocess, whose actual implementation means the choice of a particular set of processes possible to use at a given time. Currently, the most often applied method of defining subsequent processes under the ad-hoc process is manual selection of the processes by system users. Fig. 2 shows basic definition of the process using the ad-hoc process.

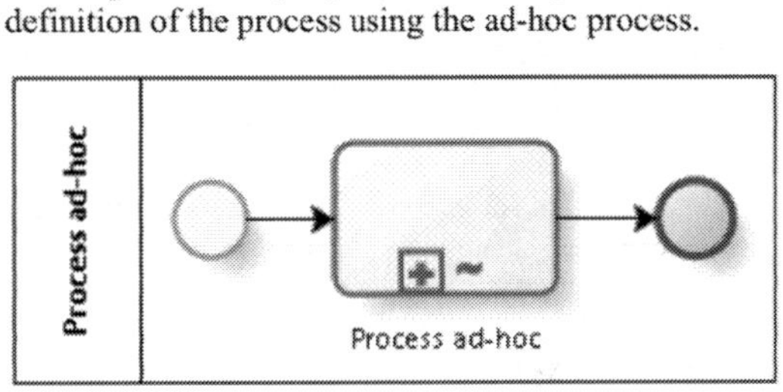

Fig. 2. Example of simple business process with ad-hoc process

Adaptive processes are the processes which may be adapted to new conditions encountered while implementing the process, in a simple manner, without any significant labor input, time consumption or financial contributions. The adaptation may be controlled by a person or automatically supported (in whole or in part). The current workflow systems support the said processes in a very limited manner, by using ad-hoc actions, which - however - need to be forecasted by the process designer prior to the process creation. Full adaptation to new, unpredicted conditions may be achieved with the help of the mechanism of dynamic processes.

Generic processes are universal and may be used to implement any general process, in case of which further clarification takes place at the time of implementing a given instance of the process. Current standards on the process modeling do not provide for a possibility of creating the aforementioned generic processes.

2.1 Dynamic business processes

The aforementioned types of processes: ad-hoc, adaptive or generic are aimed at developing a general and undetermined definition of the process, thanks to which such process would be adaptable to variable conditions [23, 24]. One of the possibilities is to dynamically adapt the process to the assumed target in the variable conditions. Such business processes may include dynamic processes. The processes may constitute extension of the idea of ad-hoc processes, where after determining the goal and indirect goals of the process, the sequence of the actions would be automatically or semi-automatically defined (Fig.4). Selection of appropriate processes and actions to be taken to achieve the process goal or goals requires definition of additional properties for each process or action, which may be used as part of dynamic selection of next steps of the process to accomplish a given objective. When selecting the processes or actions in the subsequent steps, it is necessary to consider the changing process environment, due to which the implementation of the processes with the same goal does not have to have the same form. Such selection requires fulfillment of initial conditions for the performance of a given action. The factors determining such initial conditions of the process use may include, for example, the general process status (which may be permanent or affected by individual actions), previously performed actions or data obtained from the previously performed actions. The conditions may be obligatory or needed to support the selection of a given action. In combination with the definition of weights, we shall obtain the mechanism allowing to determine the limiting conditions or conditions permitting to benefit from the possibilities of a given process, based on current status of the process instance, process definition, condition of the workflow environment and its surrounding (*pre*section – Fig.4). When checking the initial conditions (both obligatory and supporting), we may obtain a hint whether it is possible to use the said actions and processes in the process instance, at a given time of implementing such process instance. By using the aforementioned mechanisms and obtained results, we are provided with a special tool supporting the decision-making process regarding the choice of appropriate actions and processes in the next steps of a given process instance.

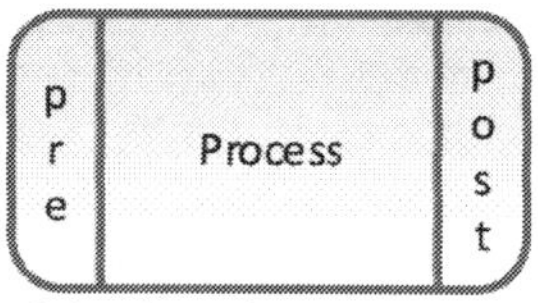

Fig. 4. Schema of the dynamic process with pre and post sections [7]

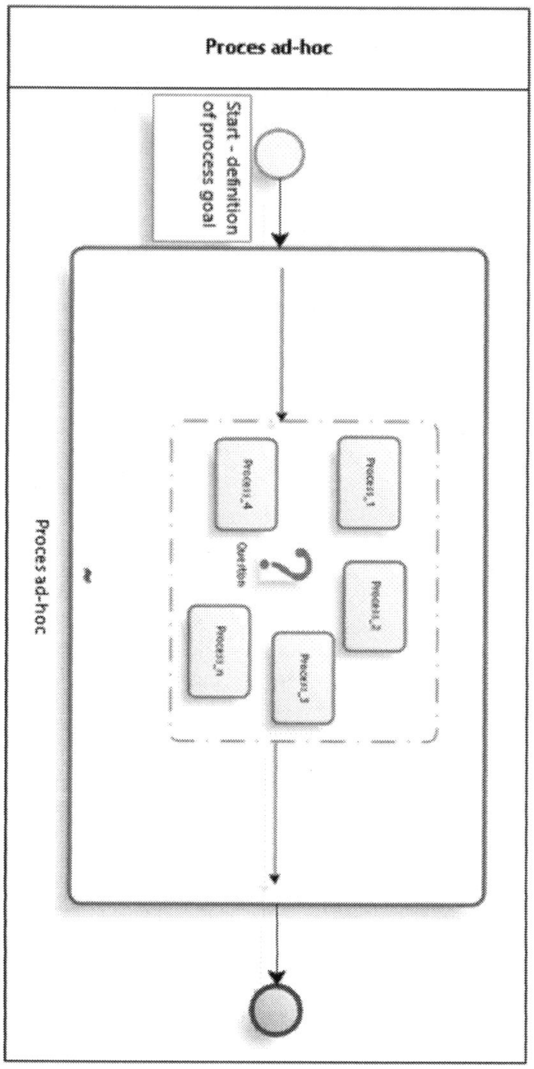

Fig. 5. Ad-hoc process as the process of dynamic selection of actions

Apart from the conditions for using a given process and their weights, the *pre* section may allow to define a set of guidelines and instructions influencing the status of a given process instance, workflow environment and its surrounding. Such a set of guidelines and instructions may be included in the *post*-section, which is activated and implemented after the workflow management system performs a given action. Such instructions may have impact on the process status and particular attributes describing the process, which shall result in greater possibilities of managing dynamic process development.

2.2 Structure of *pre* and *post* sections of dynamic process definition

The definition of the standard for recording input conditions of actions (the concept described in the previous chapter) and operations performed after completing a given action, which may be used to modify the process status, constitutes an important element of the designed extension of XPDL language [5].

The *pre* conditions may have different forms, refer to a simple process parameter, several interdependent parameters, rules, functions, general process status or its current progress. To stimulate the process progress, it is required to store the history of the previous process progress in terms of the order and number of actions performed as well as the process status at a given point in time. The definition of simple conditions regarding single parameters is rather easy and the functionality of their verification in the process runtime environment may be implemented without any problems, regardless of the form of recording. The problem occurs in case of more complex conditions of the structure of rules that may be defined in the *pre*-section. One of the solutions analyzed from the point of view of the project process itself would be to use a language, in which it is possible to record the assumed conditions and rules, e.g. by applying the first order account properties predicate. The application of such mechanism would eventually allow to implement a universal solution, similar to, for example, Prolog language. However, such solution implies the occurrence of a complex program for interpreting conditions recorded in the aforesaid language - this is the task much more complex that the scope of this study. Therefore, even though the creation of such a new language seems a bit exaggerated now, in the future it might turn out that it is quite reasonable and even necessary as part of development and popularization of the dynamic process concept. A compromise solution is to define a set of operators and functions allowing to handle the *pre* conditions and *post* operations, which need to be made available by the runtime environment of dynamic processes. The main disadvantage of the said solution is the lack of such developed universality that would be allowed by the above-mentioned solution. However, a set of the aforesaid functions may be so developed (e.g. thanks to additional libraries) that it offers sufficient universality level and, in some aspects, provides much greater possibilities, as the implementation of such functions may be definitely more extended that the implementation offered by the language of predicates (apparently, we may use another language, e.g. any programming language, which would be interpreted or complied during the implementation, but it would create rather severe problem regarding the issue of security, thus, it is not a good solution). Besides, this solution is much safer, as the implementation of the functions constitutes a part of the runtime environment, not the process itself. Apart from the security issue, another advantage of this solution is better resistance to general errors and basically complete elimination of syntactic errors. Furthermore, the processes using such solution shall be more transparent and easier to interpret.

The basis for the draft definition of the dynamic process is the XPDL standard [5], thus, in case of the basic definition of a part of the process description, the XPDL standard structure is used. Some elements of the process definition, describing the the aspects of dynamics, constitute extension of the definition of the XPDL process standard by adding supplementary structures required to save the dynamic process definition. Modification of the XPDL language refers to a number of aspects:

- recording of actions that might be used in the process,
- recording of security level of actions,
- extension of the *Activity* and *WorkflowProcess* structure by elements required due to the dynamic nature of the process.

The first element shall be implemented by adding the*Type* attribute to the *Activity* node. The attribute may have one of the two following values: *ProcessElement* and *SpareElement*. The activities of the *ProcessElement* type belong to the process flow. The process may be composed of a number of such activities. The activities of the *SpareElement* type belong to a set of activities that might be used in a given process. In case of applying such activity, it shall be copied to the process definition, whereas the *Type* attribute of the copied activity set to the *ProcessElement* value. The runtime environment of dynamic processes may provide access to a set of additional and public actions, which could be implemented in any process, by using e.g. a XPDL document containing the definition of only the *SpareElement* action type. However, every environment may implement such option in any way or not make it available at all.

The action security level shall be recorded through the *SecurityLevel* action attribute. The attribute may adopt one of the two following values:

- *Secure* - secure level
- *Unlimited* - level allowing unlimited modifications

The third aspect requires considerably greater extension of the definition structure determined in the XPDL standard. The first components to be added is the information on the process progress, i.e. actions performed. Inside of the activity node, the node called *Executions* was added, including the information on further executions of a given action in the *Execution* nodes (there might be more than one execution of a given action, e.g. due to the process loop). Every single node of the action execution shall include execution identifier, date and time of commencement of a given action as well as its end time. It may also contain some information on the input and output data of the activities in the form of copied nodes - *InputSet* and *OutputSet*, including defined values of the parameters or artifacts.

Another addition to the standard XPDL shall be the *pre* section including a description of the conditions verified during the dynamic modification of the process definition. Inside the *Activity* tag, the *PreSection* tag shall be added, which contains the *Conditions* tag, which shall include individual conditions within the framework of the *Condition* tags. Each *Condition* tag has the *Type* attribute that adopts one of the three following values:

- *Required* - the condition must be fulfilled in a security mode
- *Supporting* - the condition is a supporting condition, so its fulfillment is not required in any of the security modes

- *Sufficient* - the fulfillment of such condition is sufficient to benefit from a given activity in a security mode, regardless of the results of other *Required* type conditions.

The *Condition* tag may include a single simple condition - *SimpleCondition* or complex condition - *And* or *Or*. The *And* and *Or* tags may contain other *And* or *Or* tags as well as *SimpleCondition*. To meet the main condition, all other conditions contained in the *And* tag or any condition in the *Or* tag must be met in accordance with the principles of the Boolean algebra. The *And* and *Or* tags group other conditions, and their name defines behavior, this, they have no additional attributes. The *SimpleCondition* tag is defined by the operator in the *Type* attribute. The operator types of such operators are the following: *Eq* (equal to), *Ne* (not equal to), *Lt* (less than), *Le* (less than or equal to), *Gt* (greater than), *Ge* (greater than or equal to), *Contains*. The *SimpleCondition* tag includes two tags defining *LValue* and *RValue* of the operation. Each of them has two attributes: *DataType* - a type of the parameter data and *Type* - a type of the parameter. The *Type* attribute may adopt one of the three values:

- *Value* - a value of the feature,
- *Parameter* - a parameter used in the process as an internal *Parameter* element, with the *Type* (defining the parameter type) and *Name* (defining the name of the parameter in the process) attributes.
- *Function* - the function is used if the value is defined by the function stipulated in the *Name* attribute of the internal *Function* tag. If the function adopts certain input parameters, the *Function* tag must include a set of such parameters. The parameters are grouped through the *FParameters* tag. The single parameter is defined by the*FParameter* tag, which is a copy of the following *tags: LValue*/*RValue*, including the additional *Name* attribute, which defines name of the parameter. It should be emphasized that even though, in this case, the structure allows for practically unlimited incorporation of the results of the function operation, as an input parameter of another function, the runtime environment of the dynamic processes shall always somehow limit this possibility.

The *WorkflowProcess* tag was supplemented with the *Goal* attribute, whereas the *PreSection* tag - with a set of the *GoalWeights*/*GoalWeight* tags, including *Name* and *Weight* attributes, defining weights for particular targets.

The last element, which should be added, is the definition of the post-section, where the operations performed after the completion of a given action are defined. The post-section is defined via the *PostSection* tag, which may cover any number of operations. Every operation is represented by the *Operation* tag, with one *Type* attribute, defining the type of such operation (operator). The *Is* operator functions similarly to other operators known from the *pre* section; the sole difference is the that only the process parameter may constitute L-value. The *Procedure* operator allows to perform any function, which does not return any result - the structure of the *Function* tag is identical to the one described above. All post-section operations should be performed in order according to the record in the XPDL structure.

Below are the selected fragments of the process definition, in the form of the modified XSD structure for XPDL format, extended by the previously described tags, used to construct dynamic business processes.

```
<xsd:attribute name="Type">
 <xsd:simpleType>
  <xsd:restriction base="xsd:NMTOKEN">
   <xsd:enumeration value="ProcessElement"/>
   <xsd:enumeration value="SpareElement"/>
  </xsd:restriction>
 </xsd:simpleType>
</xsd:attribute>

<xsd:attribute name="SecurityLevel">
 <xsd:simpleType>
  <xsd:restriction base="xsd:NMTOKEN">
   <xsd:enumeration value="Secure"/>
   <xsd:enumeration value="Unlimited"/>
  </xsd:restriction>
 </xsd:simpleType>
</xsd:attribute>

<!--WorkflowProcess-->
<xsd:attribute name="Goal" type="xsd:string"/>


<xsd:element name="PreSection" maxOccurs="1">
 <xsd:complexType>
  <xsd:element name="Conditions" maxOccurs="1">
   <xsd:complexType>
    <xsd:element name="Condition" minOccurs="0">
     <xsd:complexType>
      <xsd:choice minOccurs="0">
       <xsd:element ref="xpdl:And"/>
       <xsd:element ref="xpdl:Or"/>
       <xsd:element ref="xpdl:SimpleCondition"/>
      </xsd:choice>
      <xsd:attribute name="Type">
       <xsd:simpleType>
        <xsd:restriction base="xsd:NMTOKEN">
         <xsd:enumeration value="Required"/>
         <xsd:enumeration value="Supporting"/>
         <xsd:enumeration value="Sufficient"/>
        </xsd:restriction>
       </xsd:simpleType>
      </xsd:attribute>
     </xsd:complexType>
    </xsd:element>
   </xsd:complexType>
  </xsd:element>
  <xsd:element name="GoalWeights" maxOccurs="1">
   <xsd:complexType>
    <xsd:element                    name="GoalWeight"
minOccurs="0">
     <xsd:complexType>
      <xsd:attribute name="Name" type="xsd:string"/>
      <xsd:attribute                    name="Weight"
type="xsd:integer"/>
     </xsd:complexType>
    </xsd:element>
   </xsd:complexType>
```

```
   </xsd:element>
  </xsd:complexType>
</xsd:element>

<xsd:element name="PostSection" maxOccurs="1">
 <xsd:complexType>
  <xsd:element name="Operation" minOccurs="0">
   <xsd:choice minOccurs="0">
    <xsd:complexType>
     <xsd:element ref="xpdl:Function"/>
     <xsd:attribute name="Type">
      <xsd:simpleType>
       <xsd:restriction base="xsd:NMTOKEN">
        <xsd:enumeration value="Function"/>
       </xsd:restriction>
      </xsd:simpleType>
     </xsd:attribute>
    </xsd:complexType>
    <xsd:complexType>
     <xsd:all>
      <xsd:element name="LValue">
       <xsd:element ref="xpdl:Parameter"/>
      </xsd:element>
      <xsd:element name="RValue" type="ValueType" />
     </xsd:all>
     <xsd:attribute name="Type">
      <xsd:simpleType>
       <xsd:restriction base="xsd:NMTOKEN">
        <xsd:enumeration value="Is"/>
       </xsd:restriction>
      </xsd:simpleType>
     </xsd:attribute>
    </xsd:complexType>
   </xsd:choice>
  </xsd:element>
 </xsd:complexType>
</xsd:element>

<xsd:element name="And">
 <xsd:complexType>
  <xsd:element ref="xpdl:And" minOccurs="0"/>
  <xsd:element ref="xpdl:Or" minOccurs="0"/>
  <xsd:element ref="xpdl:SimpleCondition" minOccurs="0"/>
 </xsd:complexType>
</xsd:element>

<xsd:element name="Or">
 <xsd:complexType>
  <xsd:element ref="xpdl:And" minOccurs="0"/>
  <xsd:element ref="xpdl:Or" minOccurs="0"/>
  <xsd:element ref="xpdl:SimpleCondition" minOccurs="0"/>
 </xsd:complexType>
</xsd:element>

<xsd:element name="SimpleCondition">
 <xsd:complexType>
  <xsd:all>
   <xsd:element name="LValue" type="ValueType" />
   <xsd:element name="RValue" type="ValueType" />
  </xsd:all>
  <xsd:attribute name="Type">
   <xsd:simpleType>
    <xsd:restriction base="xsd:NMTOKEN">
     <xsd:enumeration value="Eq"/>
     <xsd:enumeration value="Ne"/>
     <xsd:enumeration value="Lt"/>
     <xsd:enumeration value="Le"/>
     <xsd:enumeration value="Gt"/>
     <xsd:enumeration value="Ge"/>
     <xsd:enumeration value="Contains"/>
    </xsd:restriction>
   </xsd:simpleType>
  </xsd:attribute>
 </xsd:complexType>
</xsd:element>

<xsd:complexType name="ValueType">
 <xsd:choice minOccurs="0">
  <xsd:complexType>
   <xsd:choice minOccurs="0">
    <xsd:element ref="xpdl:Parameter"/>
    <xsd:element ref="xpdl:Function"/>
   </xsd:choice>
   <xsd:attribute name="Type">
    <xsd:simpleType>
     <xsd:restriction base="xsd:NMTOKEN">
      <xsd:enumeration value="Parameter"/>
      <xsd:enumeration value="Function"/>
     </xsd:restriction>
    </xsd:simpleType>
   </xsd:attribute>
   <xsd:attribute name="DataType">
    <xsd:simpleType>
     <xsd:restriction base="xsd:NMTOKEN">
      <xsd:enumeration value="String"/>
      <xsd:enumeration value="Number"/>
      <xsd:enumeration value="Boolean"/>
      <xsd:enumeration value="DateTime"/>
     </xsd:restriction>
    </xsd:simpleType>
   </xsd:attribute>
  </xsd:complexType>
  <xsd:complexType>
   <xsd:simpleContent>
    <xsd:extension base="xs:string">
     <xsd:attribute name="Type">
      <xsd:simpleType>
       <xsd:restriction base="xsd:NMTOKEN">
        <xsd:enumeration value="Value"/>
       </xsd:restriction>
      </xsd:simpleType>
     </xsd:attribute>
     <xsd:attribute name="DataType">
      <xsd:simpleType>
       <xsd:restriction base="xsd:NMTOKEN">
        <xsd:enumeration value="String"/>
        <xsd:enumeration value="Number"/>
        <xsd:enumeration value="Boolean"/>
        <xsd:enumeration value="DateTime"/>
       </xsd:restriction>
      </xsd:simpleType>
```

```
      </xsd:attribute>
     </xsd:extension>
    </xsd:simpleContent>
   </xsd:complexType>
  </xsd:choice>
</xsd:complexType>

<xsd:element name="Parameter">
 <xsd:complexType>
  <xsd:attribute name="Type">
   <xsd:simpleType>
    <xsd:restriction base="xsd:NMTOKEN">
     <xsd:enumeration value="String"/>
     <xsd:enumeration value="Number"/>
     <xsd:enumeration value="Boolean"/>
     <xsd:enumeration value="DateTime"/>
    </xsd:restriction>
   </xsd:simpleType>
  </xsd:attribute>
  <xsd:attribute name="Name" type="xsd:string"/>
 </xsd:complexType>
</xsd:element>

<xsd:complexType name="FunctionParameter">
 <xsd:complexContent>
  <xsd:extension base="ValueType">
   <xsd:attribute name="Name" type="xsd:string"/>
  </xsd:extension>
 </xsd:complexContent>
</xsd:complexType>

<xsd:element name="Function">
 <xsd:complexType>
  <xsd:element name="FParameters" maxOccurs="1">
   <xsd:complexType>
    <xsd:element name="FParameter" minOccurs="0"
base="FunctionParameter" />
   </xsd:complexType>
  </xsd:element>
  <xsd:attribute name="Name" type="xsd:string"/>
 </xsd:complexType>
</xsd:element>
```

3 Conclusion

The above material contains the results of studies related to the automated modeling and construction of the dynamic business processes. The presented process definitions supplemented with the *pre* and *post* sections allow to increase the automation level of the process of selecting subsequently executed actions, based on the set process goal. The application of the mechanisms for defining rules of availability of a given action in terms of the specific process progress and runtime environment and its surrounding allow to automate or support self-defining and self-organizing business processes. The presented mechanism has also adaptive properties, since - in case of the target set for the process, its implementation may be each time different. The above depends on the progress of the process, variable set of available activities, changing status of the workflow environment as well as changing status of the runtime environment. The described mechanism for defining and implementing dynamic business processes refers to the area of process modeling and supporting decisions made with respect to the automatic selection of subsequent actions aimed at realizing the target defined in the process. In the following steps, the research should be directed at verification and potential modification of the method for defining dynamic processes, development of formal method for determining selection of further steps, including, among other things, reduction of costs and time needed to implement the process. Another additional and significant aspect is the dynamic and automated selection of some executive services, available at a given time for the performed activities, including their cost, resources and time. Such a solution would allow to automate the area of the business process modeling and definition as well as the selection of executive services of such processes.

References

1. 1-M. Weske, *Business Process Management. Concepts, Languages, Architectures*, Berlin, Springer-Verlag. (2007).
2. 2-M. Sałaciński, *Modelowanie procesów biznesowych. Praktyczne wykorzystanie BPMN*, Software Developer's Journal, vol. **04** (2010).
3. 3-OMG, BPMN - standard documents, [Online] http://www.omg.org/spec/BPMN/2.0/ (2011)
4. 4-A. Arsanjani, N. Bharade, M. Borgenstrand, P. Schume, J. K. Wood i V. Zheltonogov, *Business Process Management Design Guide. Using IBM Business Process Manager*, USA, IBM Corporation. (2015).
5. 5-WFMC, XML Process Definition Language – standard XPDL documents, [Online] http://www.xpdl.org/ (2012).
6. 6-W. van der Aalst, K. van Hee, *Workflow Management. Models, Methods, and Systems,* The MIT Press Cambridge, Massachusetts London, (2002).
7. 7-G. Bliźniuk, M. Chmielewski, T. Gzik, J. Koszela, Warehouse of processes, *Studia Informatica*, vol. **33-2A**, 111-127. (2012).
8. 8-W. van der Aalst, *Process Mining*, Springer-Verlag, Berlin. (2016).
9. 9-M. Kiedrowicz, *Zarządzanie informacjami wrażliwymi - wybrane aspekty organizacyjne, prawne i techniczne ochrony informacji niejawnych* WAT Warszawa, (2015).
10. 10-J. Koszela, Business process modeling for processing classified documents using RFID technology in *20th International Conference on Circuits, Systems, Communications and Computers*, MATEC Web of Conferences, vol. **76**, (2016)
11. 11-M. Kiedrowicz, J. Koszela, *Secret office model for the processing of classified documents using RFID technology*, Collegium of Economic Analysis Annals, pp. 67-81, vol. **42**. (2016).
12. 12-R. Waszkowski, M. Kiedrowicz, T. Nowicki, Z.

Wesolowski, and K. Worwa, Business processes in the RFID-equipped restricted access administrative office, in *20th International Conference on Circuits, Systems, Communications and Computers*, MATEC Web of Conferences, vol. **76**, DOI: 10.1051/matecconf/20167604003 (2016).

13. 13-R. Dijkmana., *Similarity of business process models: Metrics and evaluation*, Information Systems, Elsevier, vol. **36** (2011).
14. 14-W. van der Aalst & others, *Process Mining Manifesto*, IEEE Task Force on Process Mining, [Online] http://www.win.tue.nl/ieeetfpm/downloads/Process%20Mining%20Manifesto.pdf
15. R. Antkiewicz, M. Dyk, R. Kasprzyk, A. Najgebauer, D. Pierzchała, Z. Tarapata, *Criminal Procedure Management Based on BPM Simulation*, Information Systems in Management, pp. 87 – 99, vol. **2**, (2013).
16. D. Pierzchała, R. Antkiewicz, M. Dyk, R. Kasprzyk, A. Najgebauer, Z. Tarapata, *Modelling, simulation and computer support of the Polish criminal procedure*, (in:) Information Systems Architecture and Technology. The Use of IT Technologies to Support Organizational Management in Risky Environment, (Eds.) Z. Wilimowska, L. Borzemski, A. Grzech, J. Świątek, pp. 51-60, (2014).
17. M. Kiedrowicz, T. Nowicki, R. Waszkowski, Z. Wesolowski, and K. Worwa, *Software simulator for property investigation of document management system with RFID tags*, 20th International Conference on Circuits, Systems, Communications and Computers, MATEC Web of Conferences, vol. **76**, DOI: 10.1051/matecconf/20167604012 (2016).
18. R. Kasprzyk, M. Zabielski, P. Kowalski, G. Oksiuta, K. Rzempołuch, *GUARDIAN – Emergency Response System with Incremental Information Delivery Model*, Biuletyn Systemów Informatycznych, pp. 1-6, vol. **11**, (2013).
19. M. Kiedrowicz, *Objects identification in the information models used by information systems*, GIS ODYSSEY 2016, pp. 129-136, (2016).
20. M. Kiedrowicz, *Uogólniony model danych w rozproszonych rejestrach ewidencyjnych*, Roczniki Kolegium Analiz Ekonomicznych, pp. 209-234, vol. **33**, (2014).
21. M. Kiedrowicz, *Location with the use of the RFID and GPS technologies - opportunities and threats*, GIS ODYSSEY 2016, pp. 122-128, (2016).
22. M. Kiedrowicz, *The importance of an integration platform within the organisation*, Zeszyty Naukowe, pp.83-94, vol. **46**, (2014).
23. M. Kiedrowicz, J. Stanik, *Selected aspects of risk management in respect of security of the document lifecycle management system with multiple levels of sensitivity*, (in:) Information Management in Practice, (eds) B.F. Kubiak and J. Maślankowski, pp. 231-249, (2015).
24. M. Kiedrowicz, T. Nowicki, R. Waszkowski, Z. Wesolowski, and K. Worwa, *Method for assessing software reliability of the document management system using the RFID technology*, 20th International Conference on Circuits, Systems, Communications and Computers, MATEC Web of Conferences, vol. **76**, DOI: 10.1051/matecconf/20167604009 (2016).
25. M. Kiedrowicz, T. Nowicki, R. Waszkowski, *Business process data flow between automated and human tasks*, 3rd International Conference on Social Science (ICSS 2016) December 9–11 2016, pp. 471-477, (2016).
26. M. Kiedrowicz, *Rejestry i zasoby informacyjne wykorzystywane przez organy odpowiedzialne za wykrywanie i przeciwdziałanie przestępczości*, (in:) Jawność i jej ograniczenia, (ed.) G. Szpor, Monografie Prawnicze, pp. 170-264, vol. **IX**, (2015).
27. M. Kiedrowicz, *Dostęp do publicznych zasobów danych - Big data czy Big brother*, (in:) INTERNET. Publiczne bazy danych i Big data, (ed.) G. Szpor, pp. 15-39, (2015). M. Kiedrowicz, R. Waszkowski, *Business rules automation standards in business process management systems*, (in:) Information Management in Practice, (eds) B.F. Kubiak and J. Maślankowski, pp. 187-200, (2015).
28. M. Kiedrowicz, J. Koszela, *Business processes modelling for the processing of classified documents using RFID technology*, Collegium of Economic Analysis Annals, vol. **42**, pp. 53-66, (2016).

MATEC Web of Conferences **125**, 02015 (2017)
DOI: 10.1051/matecconf/201712502015
CSCC 2017

On a Generalized Squared Gaussian Diffusion Model for Option Valuation

S.O. Edeki[1*] and *O. O. Ugbebor*[1,2]

[1]Department of Mathematics, Covenant University, Ota, Zip Code: 112212, Nigeria

[2,1]Department of Mathematics, University of Ibadan, Ibadan, Zip Code: 200221, Nigeria

Abstract. In financial mathematics, option pricing models are vital tools whose usefulness cannot be overemphasized. Modern approaches and modelling of financial derivatives are therefore required in option pricing and valuation settings. In this paper, we derive via the application of Ito lemma, a pricing model referred to as Generalized Squared Gaussian Diffusion Model (GSGDM) for option pricing and valuation. Same approach can be considered via Stratonovich stochastic dynamics. We also show that the classical Black-Scholes, and the square root constant elasticity of variance models are special cases of the GSGDM. In addition, general solution of the GSGDM is obtained using modified variational iterative method (MVIM).

1 Introduction

In modern finance, the importance of options in pricing theory cannot be overemphasized as they can be used for control risk and hedging. This therefore requires the attention of financial analysts when dealing with finance, actuarial sciences, and other related areas of applied sciences [1-3]. Hence, the involvement of stock options in the study of option pricing and valuation theory [4]. Black and Scholes [5, 6] assumed the underlying stock price process, S_t, to be lognormally distributed, and as such solves the following stochastic dynamics (SDE):

$$dS_t = S_t\left(\mu dt + \sigma dW_t\right) \tag{1.1}$$

where μ and σ are mean rate of return, and stock price volatility parameter respectively, while W_t represents a one-dimensional Standard Brownian Motion (SBM).
According to the Black-Scholes model, the value of a European-style option on S stock at time t, is $V = V\left(S,t\right)$ that solves the partial differential equation (PDE):

$$\frac{\partial V}{\partial t} + \frac{1}{2}S^2\sigma^2\frac{\partial^2 V}{\partial S^2} + rS\frac{\partial V}{\partial S} - rV = 0. \tag{1.2}$$

Equation (1.2) is the classical Black-Scholes model, where r is the risk-free rate, $V \in C^{2,1}\left(\mathbb{R}\times\left[0,T\right]\right)$, with a payoff function $p_f\left(S,t\right)$, and expiration price, E such that:

$$p_f\left(S,t\right) = \begin{cases} (S-E)^+, & \text{for European call option} \\ (E-S)^+, & \text{for European put option} \end{cases} \tag{1.3}$$

Black and Scholes based their model on some assumptions such as arbitrage-free opportunities, no allowance of dividend-yield paying stock, lack of transaction costs, constant mean rate and constant volatility parameter among others [7]. To be addressed here among the assumptions is that of constant volatility, that is the stock price standard deviation. The constant nature of the volatility as assumed by Black and Scholes was to make the model a linear type in order to obtain analytical solution easily. Contrary to this, constant volatility appears unrealistic in practical settings. We therefore intend to resort to a more accommodating model driven by constant elasticity of variance (CEV).

2 Basic Definitions, Theorem(s) and Existing Model

The assumption of constant volatility as in (1.1) has drawn the attention of many researchers; see [8-10] and the references therein for more details. Delbean and Shirakawa [11] proved that the CEV model permits arbitrage opportunities when the stock price is based on strict positive conditions.
Cox and Ross [12] considered the CEV diffusion process governed by the SDE:

$$dS_t = S_t\mu dt + \sigma S_t^{\frac{\xi}{2}} d\left(W_t\right) \tag{2.1}$$

* Corresponding author: soedeki@yahoo.com

whose solution is S_t, ξ represents an elasticity rate, while μ, σ, and W_t remain as earlier defined.

Beckners [13] considered the CEV and its implications for option pricing on the basis of empirical studies and concluded that the CEV class could be a better descriptor of the actual stock price in terms of behaviour than the traditionally used lognormal model. MacBeth and Merville [14] proposed a three-stage-procedure on how to estimate σ and ξ.

In what follows, the Black-Scholes model will be modified using the SDE associated with the CEV model in (2.1) to get the the GSGDM as a proposed model.

Definition 2a: Let $X:\Omega \to \mathbb{R}$ be a random variable with $\underline{E}(X)$ and $Var(X)$ denoting the mathematical expectation and the variance of X respectively. Then we denote by $SG_{\Xi}(\Omega)$, the space of all square-Gaussian random variables.

Definition 2b: [15] A random process $X=(X(t),\ t\in T)$ is said to be square-Gaussian, if for all $t\in T$ $X(t)\in SG_{\Xi}(\Omega)$ and

$$\sup_{t\in T}\left(\underline{E}(X(t))^2\right)^{\frac{1}{2}}<\infty .$$

Note: In this work, we take all stochastic processes to be square Gaussian (SG).

Theorem 2.1 : [16]
Suppose $X(t)$ an adapted stochastic process on a filtered probability space $F_{PS}=(\Omega,B,\mu,F(B))$, possesses a quadratic variation $\langle X\rangle$, is a solution of the SDE:

$$dX(t)=H_1dt+H_2dW(t) \tag{2.2}$$

where $H_1=H_1(t,X(t))$ represents the drift coefficient, $H_2=H_2(t,X(t))$ is the diffusion coefficient, $W(t)$ is a standard Brownian motion representing the intrinsic noise (white noise) in the dynamical system; and $u\in C^{1,2}(T\times\mathbb{R})$, such that $u(t,x):(0,\infty)\times\mathbb{R}\to\mathbb{R}$ is a twice continuously differentiable function with T as time at maturity, then, $u=u(t,X(t))$ is a stochastic process for which:

$$du(t,X(t))=\frac{\partial u}{\partial t}dt+\frac{\partial u}{\partial x}dX(t)+\frac{1}{2}\frac{\partial u}{\partial x}(dX(t))^2 \tag{2.3}$$

whence,

$$\begin{cases} du(t,X(t))=\left(\dfrac{\partial u}{\partial t}+H_1\dfrac{\partial u}{\partial x}+\dfrac{1}{2}H_2^2\dfrac{\partial^2 u}{\partial x^2}\right)dt \\ \qquad +H_2\dfrac{\partial u}{\partial x}dW(t)\end{cases} \tag{2.4}$$

Equation (2.4) is called an Ito formula.
Note: If $X=W$, that is $H_1\equiv 0$ and $H_2\equiv 1$, then

$$du(t,X(t))=\left(\frac{\partial u}{\partial t}+\frac{1}{2}\frac{\partial^2 u}{\partial x^2}\right)dt+\frac{\partial u}{\partial x}dW(t). \tag{2.5}$$

Equation (2.5) is called an Ito lemma.

3 VIM and the Modified VIM [17, 18]

Considering the general nonlinear PDE of the form:

$$\begin{cases} Lu(x,t)+Ru(x,t)+Nu(x,t)=f(x,t) \\ u(x,t)=h(x)\end{cases} \tag{3.1}$$

where $L=\frac{\partial}{\partial t}$, R is a linear operator whose partial derivatives are w.r.t. x, $Nu(x,t)$ is a nonlinear term associated to (3.1) and $f(x,t)$ is a source term (which may be homogeneous or inhomogeneous), thus by the classical VIM, the solution of (3.1) is expressed as:

$$\begin{cases} u_{n+1}(x,t)=u_n(x,t) \\ \qquad +\int_0^t \lambda\left(Lu_n+\overline{Ru_n}+\overline{Nu_n}-f(x,t)\right)ds\end{cases} \tag{3.2}$$

where λ is a Lagrange multiplier [19, 20] to be identified optimally via variational theory, and the terms: $\overline{Ru_n}$ and $\overline{Nu_n}$ are being considered as restricted variations such that $\delta\overline{Ru_n}=0$ and $\delta\overline{Nu_n}=0$. Hence, by calculating the variations w.r.t. u_n using the stationary conditions:

$$\begin{cases} \lambda'(x)=0 \\ 1+\lambda(x)=0,\end{cases} \tag{3.3}$$

the Lagrange multiplier is identified as $\lambda=-1$. Therefore, (3.2) becomes:

$$\begin{cases} u_{n+1}(x,t)=u_n(x,t) \\ \qquad -\int_0^t\left(Lu_n+R(u_n)+N(u_n)-f(x,t)\right)ds.\end{cases} \tag{3.4}$$

Remark: Using (3.4) for the solution of special kind of nonlinear differential equations involves the calculation of unrequired terms, repeated calculations, and time-consumption, hence, the need for meaningful modification of the VIM. The modified VIM as proposed by [17] gives the iterative formula as follows:

$$u_{n+1}(x,t)=u_n(x,t)-\int_0^t\left(R(u_n-u_{n-1})+(G_n-G_{n-1})\right)ds, \tag{3.5}$$

where

$$\begin{cases} u_{-1}=0, \\ u_0=h(x), \\ u_1=u_0-\int_0^t\left(R(u_n-u_{n-1})+(G_n-G_{n-1})-f\right)ds, \\ G_n=Nu_n+O(t^{n+1}). \end{cases} \tag{3.6}$$

3.1 *Derivation of the Generalized Model (GSGDM)*

Suppose the stock price, S_t at time t, satisfies the SDE in (2.1), with all parameters as earlier defined, and that the value of the contingent claim $V=V(S,t)$ is such that $V\in C^{2,1}(\mathbb{R}\times[0,T])$, therefore by Ito lemma, we have:

$$\begin{cases} dV=\frac{\partial V}{\partial t}dt+\frac{\partial V}{\partial S}dS+\frac{1}{2}\frac{\partial^2 V}{\partial S^2}\langle dS\rangle \\ \quad =\frac{\partial V}{\partial t}dt+\frac{\partial V}{\partial S}\left(S_t\mu dt+\sigma S_t^{\frac{\xi}{2}}dW_t\right) \\ \quad +\frac{1}{2}\frac{\partial^2 V}{\partial S^2}\left\langle S_t\mu dt+\sigma S_t^{\frac{\xi}{2}}dW_t\right\rangle \end{cases}. \tag{3.7}$$

Thus, for:

$$\left\langle S_t\mu dt+\sigma S_t^{\frac{\xi}{2}}d(W_t)\right\rangle=\sigma^2S_t^{\xi}dt, \tag{3.8}$$

we therefore write (3.7) as:

$$dV=\left(\frac{\partial V}{\partial t}+\mu\frac{\partial V}{\partial S}+\frac{1}{2}\sigma^2S^{\xi}\frac{\partial^2 V}{\partial S^2}\right)dt+\sigma S^{\frac{\xi}{2}}\frac{\partial V}{\partial S}dW. \tag{3.9}$$

Let $\Phi(t)$ be a delta-hedged-portfolio by longing a contingent, and shorting a delta unit of the underlying asset such that:

$\Phi(t)=V(S,t)-\Delta S$, $d\Phi(t)=dV(s,t)-\Delta dS$,

$$\Delta=\frac{\partial V}{\partial S}\text{ , and } d\Phi(t)=r\Phi(t)dt \tag{3.10}$$

in order to make the value of the portfolio riskless, where r is a riskless rate, say bank account.

$$\therefore\quad \begin{aligned} d\Phi(t)=&\left(\frac{\partial V}{\partial t}+\mu\frac{\partial V}{\partial S}+\frac{1}{2}\sigma^2S^{\xi}\frac{\partial^2 V}{\partial S^2}\right)dt \\ &+\sigma S^{\frac{\xi}{2}}\frac{\partial V}{\partial S}dW-\Delta\left(\alpha Sdt+\sigma S^{\frac{\xi}{2}}dW\right) \end{aligned} \tag{3.11}$$

$$\Rightarrow \begin{cases} \frac{d\Phi}{dt}=\left(\frac{\partial V}{\partial t}+\mu\frac{\partial V}{\partial S}+\frac{1}{2}\sigma^2S^{\xi}\frac{\partial^2 V}{\partial S^2}\right) \\ \quad +\sigma S^{\frac{\xi}{2}}\frac{\partial V}{\partial S}\frac{dW}{dt}-\frac{\partial V}{\partial S}\left(\alpha S+\sigma S^{\frac{\xi}{2}}\frac{dW}{dt}\right) \end{cases}$$

showing that:

$$\frac{d\Phi}{dt}=\frac{\partial V}{\partial t}+\frac{1}{2}\sigma^2S^{\xi}\frac{\partial^2 V}{\partial S^2}\equiv r\Phi. \tag{3.12}$$

Thus, using (3.10) in (3.12), we have:

$$\frac{\partial V}{\partial t}+rS\frac{\partial V}{\partial S}+\frac{1}{2}\sigma^2S^{\xi}\frac{\partial^2 V}{\partial S^2}-rV=0. \tag{3.13}$$

Hence, we refer to (3.13) as the GSGDM.

3.2 *Comparison of the models*

In this subsection, we shall compare the basic features of the two models presented above.

Suppose V^{o}_{BSM} denotes the volatility of the B-S model, V^{o}_{GSGDM} the volatility of the GSGDM associated SDE, V^{r}_{BSM} the variance of the B-S model, and V^{r}_{GSGDM} the variance of the GSGDM associated SDE. Then the following can easily be deduced:

$$V^{o}_{BSM}=\sigma\text{ , }V^{o}_{GSGDM}=\sigma S^{\frac{\xi}{2}-1}\text{ , }V^{r}_{BSM}=\sigma^2\text{ , and } V^{r}_{GSGDM}=\sigma^2S^{\xi-2}. \tag{3.14}$$

Remark 3.2:

It is obvious that $V^{o}_{GSGDM}=h(\sigma,S_t)$ is not a constant function but a function of the underlying asset price S_t.

3.3: Special Cases of the GSGDM

In this subsection, we present the B-S and the square root models as special cases of the GSGDM.

3.3a: B-S Model and GSGDM

In (3.13), if $\xi=2$ then the PDE representing the classical B-S model associated with the stochastic dynamics in (1.1) is obtained (see (1.2)).

3.3b: Square-root CEV Model and GSGDM

In (3.13), if $\xi=1$ then the PDE model and the associated with the stochastic dynamics are:

$$\frac{\partial V}{\partial t}+rS\left(\frac{\partial V}{\partial S}+\frac{1}{2}\sigma^2\frac{\partial^2 V}{\partial S^2}\right)-rV=0 \tag{3.15}$$

and

$$dS_t=S_t\mu dt+\sigma\sqrt{S_t}d(W_t) \tag{3.16}$$

respectively.

Equation (3.16) is referred to as the square-root CEV process dynamics [7, 15].

3.4 Modified VIM for the Generalized Square-root CEV Model

Comparing (3.15) with (3.1) makes it obvious that:

$$LV = V_t,\ Ru = \left\{ rS\left(V_S + \frac{1}{2}\sigma^2 V_{SS} \right) - rV \right\},$$

$Nu = 0$ and $f(x,t) = 0$. Hence, for $I_{0,t} = \int_0^t (\cdot) ds$, we have:

$$V_{n+1} = V_n - I_{0,t}\left(\begin{array}{c} \left(rS\left(V_{Sn} + \frac{1}{2}\sigma^2 V_{SSn} \right) - rV_n \right) \\ -\left(rS\left(V_{Sn-1} + \frac{1}{2}\sigma^2 V_{SSn-1} \right) - rV_{n-1} \right) \end{array} \right) \quad (3.17)$$

$$\begin{cases} V_{-1} = 0, \\ V_0 = V(S,0), \\ V_1 = V_0. \end{cases} \quad (3.18)$$

Since, $Nu = 0.$
Thus, for $n \geq 1$, we have:

$$V_2 = V_1 - I_{0,t}\left(\begin{array}{c} \left(rS\left(V_{S1} + \frac{1}{2}\sigma^2 V_{SS1} \right) - rV_1 \right) \\ -\left(rS\left(V_{S0} + \frac{1}{2}\sigma^2 V_{SS0} \right) - rV_0 \right) \end{array} \right),$$

$$V_3 = V_2 - I_{0,t}\left(\begin{array}{c} \left(rS\left(V_{S2} + \frac{1}{2}\sigma^2 V_{SS2} \right) - rV_2 \right) \\ -\left(rS\left(V_{S1} + \frac{1}{2}\sigma^2 V_{SS1} \right) - rV_1 \right) \end{array} \right),$$

$$V_4 = V_3 - I_{0,t}\left(\begin{array}{c} \left(rS\left(V_{S3} + \frac{1}{2}\sigma^2 V_{SS3} \right) - rV_3 \right) \\ -\left(rS\left(V_{S2} + \frac{1}{2}\sigma^2 V_{SS2} \right) - rV_2 \right) \end{array} \right),$$

$$\vdots \quad \vdots \qquad \vdots \qquad \vdots .$$

So, $V_{n+1}(S,t) \to V(S,t)$ as $n \to \infty$, implies that:

$$V(S,t) = \lim_{k\to\infty} \left\{ V_{k-1} - I_{0,t}\left(H(S,t) \right) \right\},\ k \geq 2. \quad (3.19)$$

where

$$H(S,t) = \left\{ \begin{array}{c} \left(rS\left(V_{Sk-1} + \frac{1}{2}\sigma^2 V_{SSk-1} \right) - rV_{k-1} \right) \\ -\left(rS\left(V_{Sk-2} + \frac{1}{2}\sigma^2 V_{SSk-2} \right) - rV_{k-2} \right) \end{array} \right.$$

Equation (3.19) represents the general solution of the GSGDM.

5 CONCLUSION

In this paper, we derived via the application of Ito lemma and the CEV stochastic dynamics, a pricing model referred to as Generalized Squared Gaussian Diffusion Model (GSGDM) for option pricing. The key merit of this model is that the stock price volatility is a function of the underlying asset price; not a constant as noted in the assumptions of the classical Black-Scholes model. We further showed that the classical Black-Scholes, and the square root constant elasticity of variance models are special cases of the GSGDM. In addition, we obtained a general solution of the GSGDM using modified variational iterative method.

Acknowledgement

The authors are grateful to Covenant University for financial support. In addition, we thank the anonymous reviewer(s) for their constructive comments.

References

[1] S.O. Edeki, I. Adinya, O.O. Ugbebor, "The Effect of Stochastic Capital Reserve on Actuarial Risk Analysis via an Integro-differential equation", *IAENG International Journal of Applied Mathematics,* **44**(2), (2014): 83-90.
[2] A. Habib, "The calculus of finance", Universities Press (India) Private Ltd., 2011.
[3] O.O. Ugbebor and S.O. Edeki, "On Duality Principle in Exponentially Le'vy Market", *Journal of Applied Mathematics & Bioinformatics*, **3**(2), (2013), 159-170.
[4] K.L. Chu, H. Yang, and K.C. Yuen, "Estimation in the Constant Elasticity of Variance Model", *British Actuar. J.* **7** (2001): 275–292.
[5] F. Black, M. Scholes, "The pricing of options and corporate liabilities", *J. Pol. Econ.* **81** (1973): 637–659.
[6] M.E. Adeosun, S.O. Edeki, O.O. Ugbebor, Stochastic Analysis of Stock Market Price Models: A Case Study of the Nigerian Stock Exchange (NSE), *WSEAS Transactions on Mathematics,* **14,** (2015): 353-363.
[7] S.O. Edeki and O. O. Ugbebor, Remarks on the Generalized Squared Gaussian Diffusion Model for Option Pricing, *Stochastic and Applications, Research and Training* (START) Workshop, Feb. 13-16, (2017).
[8] R.C. Blattberg, R.C. and N.J. Gonedes, "A comparison of the stable and student distributions as stochastic models for stock prices", *Journal of Business*, **47** (1974): 244-280.
[9] J.D. Macbeth and L.J. Merville. "An empirical examination of the Black-Scholes call option pricing model", *Journal of Finance*, **34**, (1979): 1173-1186.
[10] B. Lauterbach and P. Schultz, "Pricing warrants: an empirical study of the Black-Scholes model and its alternatives", *Journal of Finance*, **45** (1990.), p. 1181.
[11] F. Delbaen and H. Shirakawa, "A note of option pricing for constant elasticity of variance model", *Asia-Pacific Financial Markets*, **9** (2), (2002): 85-99.
[12] J. Cox and S. Ross, "The valuation of options for alternative stochastic processes", *Journal of Financial Economics*, **3**, (1976): 145-166.

[13] S. Beckers, "The Constant Elasticity of Variance Model and Its Implications for Option Pricing", *The Journal of Finance*, **35**, (3) (1980): 661-673.
[14] J.D. Macbeth and L.J. Merville, "Tests of the Black-Scholes and Cox Call Option Valuation Models", *Journal of Finance*, **35**, (1980): 285-301.
[15] Yu. V.Kozachenko and O. V. Stus, "Square–Gaussian random processes and estimators of covariance functions", *Mathematical Communications* **3** (1998): 83-94.
[16] Ito, K. (1946). On a stochastic integral equation, Proceedings of the Japan Academy, 22, 32-35.
[17] T. A. Abassy, M. A. El-Tawil, H. El Zoheiry, Toward a modified variational iteration method, Computational and Applied Mathematics, *Journal of Computational and Applied Mathematics* **207** (2007) 137–147.
[18] S. O. Edeki, G. O. Akinlabi., and A. S. Osheku, On a Modified Iterative Method for the Solutions of Advection Model, *World Congress on Engineering 2017*, WCE 2017, London, U.K. *(In-press)*.
[19] M.A. Abdou, A.A. Soliman, Variational iteration method for solving Burger's and coupled Burger's equations, *J. Comput. Appl. Math.* **181** (2) (2005) 245–251.
[20] J.H. He, Variational iteration method for autonomous ordinary differential systems, *Appl. Math. Comput.* **114** (2–3) (2000): 115–123.

Optimization of equipment deployment on fire trucks

Tadeusz Nowicki[1,*]

[1]Military University of Technology, Cybernetics Faculty, 00-908 Warsaw, gen. S. Kaliskiego str., Poland

Abstract. In this work, the problem of deploying firemen' equipment is discussed in order to achieve the best value of ergonomic indicators for fireman during anti-fire action. The equipment can be deployed on the fore truck in a different ways. We are looking for the best way to do it from the point of view of ergonomics. The multi-criterial optimization problem of equipment location on the vehicle has been formulated. It is linear integer programming problem with three criteria functions. It is able to solve that problem using formal method after some modifications. It is possible to receive several solutions from multi-criterial optimization problem and then evaluate them in a virtual simulation environment. It can then be taken into account a number of additional factors that are important for fireman and ergonomics.

1 Introduction

The issues of ergonomics in the design of technical objects are often connected with numerous problems in different applications [1, 2, 3]. If they are related to staff serving technical equipment, there are problems in the sphere of discussion:

- empirical study of human work in concrete conditions of material work environment,
- creating guidelines for new (modernized) designers, technologies, products,
- setting criteria for assessing working conditions,
- to support a systematic study of the health of employees,
- development of standards, measures and undertakings ensuring optimal working conditions,
- supporting activities aimed not only at adapting to the conditions of so called "material working environment" to man but also man to work under these conditions,
- provision of the basis for the prevention of occupational disease, including industrial poisoning, in the prevention of occupational disease prevention.

In the event of a problem with the deployment of equipment in a rescue and fire fighting vehicle taken into account, some of the above points shall be taken into account.

The development of standards, equipment and activities to optimize the working conditions is to determine the equipment to be deployed in the rescue and fire fighting vehicle and to deploy it in the useable recesses of rescue and firefighting vehicles designed for this purpose. The result of this study will be the guidelines for designers equipping new or upgraded fire trucks.

In the issue of deployment of equipment rescue and firefighting vehicles are guided by the working conditions of persons - the personnel of the vehicle. A number of factors are taken into account, but the problem is primarily dedicated to take into account ergonomic factors. It should be emphasized that these factors are particularly important in multiple actions in a relatively short time and refer to the same group of people. Possible effects of misplaced equipment in a rescue and fire fighting vehicle will be cumulatively accumulated to the health of the crew members of the vehicle. The definition of criteria for evaluating working conditions will be mainly related to the ergonomics of firefighters taking part in rescue operations.

The problem of empirical study of human work in concrete conditions of material work environment [9]-[14] is not easy to solve in a short time. It would be necessary to carry out a number of specialized personnel surveys for various equipment installations in rescue and firefighting vehicles in a large sample of various types of rescue and firefighting operations. This would not only be a long-term undertaking but would also add to the health of the staff. So decided to solve quite innovative. Computer simulations of rescue personnel actions for various types of actions will be used to simulate the various deployment variants on the vehicle in terms of ergonomics.

From the labor ergonomics point of view, the following factors are taken into account in the analysis of the human factor load:

- physical load,
- psychological load,
- environmental load,
- organizational load.

The order of the loads is not accidental here. The most important thing is physical stress, which is independent of others and is a constant problem in different types of actions. Its positive change is essential if it is possible. Other loads can be adjusted by training, treatment, organizational regulations, etc.

* Corresponding author: tadeusz.nowicki@wat.edu.pl

Therefore, workload will be considered physical and to some extent organizational. Criteria for taking into account the physical strain in the process of unloading equipment from a rescue and fire fighting vehicle for various types of rescue rescue operations, however, must be remembered that physical effort and the effects of rescue personnel work differ significantly in the vertical movement of equipment (taking off equipment from fire truck) and horizontal relocation of equipment to the place of its distribution in the rescue and firefighting operation.
Next, this time about the organizational nature of the criterion will be the time of unloading equipment at the beginning of the rescue and firefighting operation. On the one hand, the short time of unloading of equipment is a factor which additionally loads a crew member of a rescue and firefighting vehicle and, on the other hand, is an important element of a smooth operation of this type. A decision has been made to include this criterion in assessing the ergonomics of deploying equipment in a rescue and fire fighting vehicle.
You can specify a number of assumptions and requirements for the deployment problem (in the literature also referred to as localization or packing problem) equipment on a fire brigade vehicle:

- one of the problems is determining whether the equipment is to be positioned high or low in modular vehicle construction,
- another problem is whether certain sets of equipment are to be close to each other or whether they can be placed at a relative distance,
- another problem is whether certain sets of equipment are to be placed on one side of the vehicle or can be placed on two other sides of the vehicle,
- in principle, the rear of the vehicle is defined as it is an accessory for the control of water and foam feeders, etc.,
- another problem is whether certain sets of equipment are to be placed deep or shallow in the modular construction of the vehicle,
- it is important that the weight distribution of the fire truck is taken into account, as poor weight distribution can cause accidents during rapid maneuvering of vehicles on the road or in the field during various difficult maneuvers when the crew tries to position the vehicle at a suitable location,
- sprinklers used in vehicles during firefighting operations should also be considered in the problem of location of equipment on fire brigade vehicles,
- crew safety elements are dependent on: environmental conditions of the operation (icing, snow, rain, mud, etc.), order of firefighting equipment (sequence of actions to be determined), personnel load during firefighting equipment (load musculoskeletal system),
- cars should stand outside the danger zone, so at a distance from the target object, so the placement of certain equipment should take into account that fact,
- it is necessary to use roller shutters with safety belts, so packing should take into account the profile and limitations of the vehicle's construction using rescue and fire-fighting equipment.

2 Location of equipment in fire trucks

From the point of view of the manufacturer of rescue and firefighting vehicles, equipment used for rescue and firefighting operations can be deployed in the recesses of fire trucks as shown in the figure below.

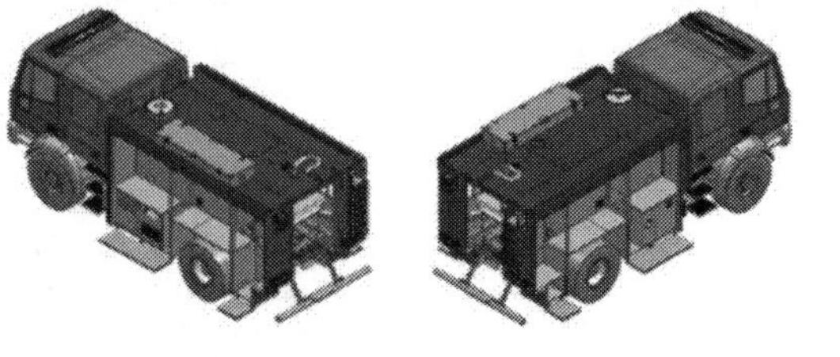

Fig. 1. Possible location of equipment on fire trucks.

As a result of these considerations we have the situation that rescue and firefighting equipment can be placed in recesses on both sides of the vehicle. But these are not many. The following two drawings (Figure 3 and Figure 4) show the recesses that may be considered in the deployment of rescue and firefighting equipment on the sides of the rescue and fire fighting vehicle.

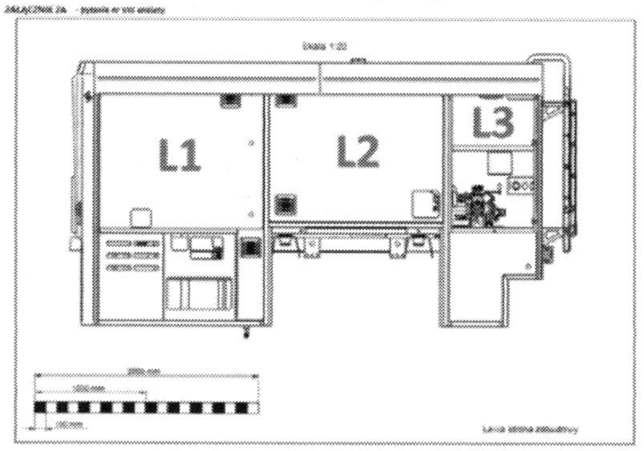

Fig. 2. Possible location of equipment on left side of fire trucks.

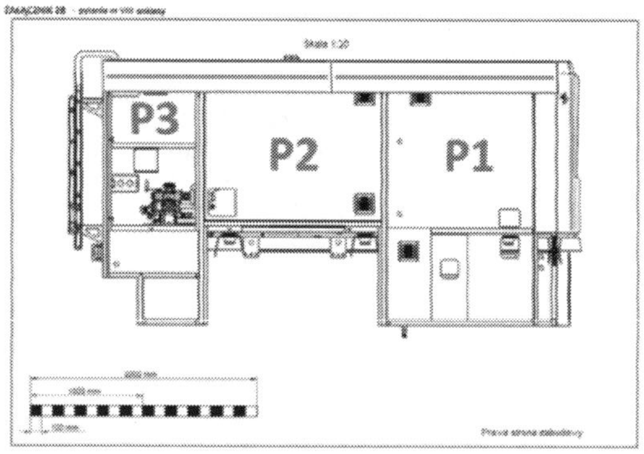

Fig. 3. Possible location of equipment on right side of fire trucks.

3 The problem of equipment location in fire trucks

It can be assumed that in the course of subsequent arrangements of the project team the set of equipment for deployment in the recesses of the rescue and firefighting vehicle (specified in special duty regulations) may change.
Assume, therefore, that we are dealing with a set of N elements of rescue and firefighting equipment whose set of numbers is defined below:

$$S = \{1,2,3,\ldots,n,\ldots,,N\} \quad (1)$$

Number N is currently specified. For each of these elements of rescue and firefighting equipment, its characteristics are:

- r_n - spatial size of n-th element of rescue and firefighting equipment,
- c_n - weight of n-th element of rescue and fire-fighting equipment,
- d_n - mean distance from the rescue and fire-fighting vehicle in which the n-th element of rescue and firefighting equipment should be placed,
- t_n - time needed for displacement of n-th element of rescue and firefighting equipment at distance d_n.

Rescue and fire-extinguishing equipment can not be deployed in full freedom from the point of view of its use in rescue and firefighting operations. Certain pieces of equipment are grouped into kits in which the equipment must be placed in the recesses of the rescue and fire fighting vehicle side by side.
Assume that there are known kits (alternatively - sets) of rescue and firefighting equipment related to each other from a functional point of view. Let's assume that number of these sets is K. The sets of sets numbers are defined as follows:

$$Z = \{1,2,3,\ldots,k,\ldots,,K\} \quad (2)$$

Each kit is defined by the elements of the primary components of rescue and firefighting equipment. The formal description of the sets is as follows:

$$Z_k = \{n \in S : \textit{selected} \text{ items from the set S}\} \quad (3)$$

These kits meet the following conditions:

$$Z_k \cap Z_i = \varnothing, i, j = 1,\ldots,N, i \neq j \quad (4)$$

and

$$\bigcup_{k \in Z} Z_k = S \quad (5)$$

Then the characteristics of the individual sets have the figures given below in the correct order with regard to the definition of the components of rescue and firefighting equipment. Total set size is:

$$r^k = \sum_{n \in Z_k} r_n, \quad (6)$$

Total weight of the set is:

$$c^k = \sum_{n \in Z_k} c_n, \quad (7)$$

Whereas the average distance from the rescue and fire-fighting vehicle in which the elements of the rescue and fire fighting equipment included in the k-th set of the formal average are to be placed:

$$d^k = \frac{1}{\overline{\overline{Z_k}}} \sum_{n \in Z_k} d_n, \quad (8)$$

Also, recount the niches in the rescue and extinguishing vehicle. There are six, so the first three to the left are numbered from 1 to 3, while the right numbered from 4 to 6. If there are additional spaces from the beech or the roof of the vehicle, let's suppose that these places will be J. Hence, the set of numbers of considered recesses in a rescue vehicle for use is defined below:

$$M = \{1,2,3,\ldots,j,\ldots,,J\} \quad (9)$$

For each of these recesses, the following characteristics are defined:

- p^j - spatial volume of the jth cavity of the rescue and fire-fighting vehicle,
- w^j - average height from the ground or from the shelf on which the vehicle personnel can stand against the j-th recess of the rescue and fire-fighting vehicle.

The following problem arises: we are looking for the deployment of rescue and firefighting equipment in the recesses of the rescue and firefighting vehicle, which is the decision matrix X:

$$X = \lfloor x_{kj} \rfloor_{KxJ} \quad (10)$$

such that x_{kj} - is equal to 1 if the k-th set of rescue and firefighting equipment is placed in the j-box (recess) or equals 0 otherwise.
Circumstances for elements of matrix X are given below:

$$x_{kj} \in \{0,1\},\ k = 1,\ldots,K, j = 1,\ldots,J \quad (11)$$

this means that the decision variables are binary variables

$$\sum_{j=1}^{J} x_{kj} = 1, k = 1,\ldots,K \quad (12)$$

that means that each kit must be in one of the recesses of the rescue and fire-fighting vehicle, and in addition only one,

$$\sum_{k=1}^{K} x_{kj} \cdot r^k \leq p_j, j = 1,\ldots,J \quad (13)$$

that means that the capacity of the kits placed in each of the recesses cannot exceed its total capacity and

$$\left| \sum_{k=1,2,3} c^k - \sum_{k=4,5,6} c^k \right| \leq \varepsilon \quad (14)$$

This means that the weight load on both sides of the vehicle axle is smaller than the assumed magnitude ε of a practically determined magnitude, so that the vehicle will not have a tendency to tilt while crossing corridors on access roads to the rescue and firefighting site. The last restriction is nonlinear. However, it can be shown that after inserting auxiliary variables this inequality can be reduced to a linear form.

The function of the criterion of distribution of rescue and firefighting kits in fire truck is vector:

$$F(X) = (F_1(x), F_2(X), F_3(X)) \tag{15}$$

where

$$F_1(X) = \sum_{j=1}^{J}\sum_{k=1}^{K} x_{jk} \cdot c^k \cdot w^j \tag{16}$$

means the total weight of vertical displacement of rescue and fire-fighting equipment during the action,

$$F_2(X) = \sum_{j=1}^{J}\sum_{k=1}^{K} x_{jk} \cdot c^k \cdot d^k \tag{17}$$

means the total weight of horizontal displacement of rescue and firefighting equipment during the action,

$$F_3(X) = \sum_{j=1}^{J}\sum_{k=1}^{K} x_{jk} \cdot \sum_{n \in Z_k} t_n \tag{18}$$

means the total time of moving rescue and firefighting equipment during the action.

Thus, the problem of multi-criterion minimization is in following form: to choose such X * to minimize

$$F_1(X^*) = \min_{X \in D} \sum_{j=1}^{J}\sum_{k=1}^{K} x_{jk} \cdot c^k \cdot w^j \tag{19}$$

$$F_2(X^*) = \min_{X \in D} \sum_{j=1}^{J}\sum_{k=1}^{K} x_{jk} \cdot c^k \cdot d^k \tag{20}$$

$$F_3(X^*) = \min_{X \in D} \sum_{j=1}^{J}\sum_{k=1}^{K} x_{jk} \cdot \sum_{n \in Z_k} t_n \tag{21}$$

where the set D of acceptable solutions takes the form:

$$x_{kj} \in \{0,1\},\ k = 1,\dots,K, j = 1,\dots,J \tag{22}$$

$$\sum_{j=1}^{J} x_{kj} = 1, k = 1,\dots,K \tag{23}$$

$$\sum_{k=1}^{K} x_{kj} \cdot r^k \le p_j, j = 1,\dots,J \tag{24}$$

$$\left| \sum_{k=1,2,3} c^k - \sum_{k=4,5,6} c^k \right| \le \varepsilon \tag{25}$$

As a result, there is the problem of multi-criterion linear binary mathematical programming [4, 5, 6, 7], which can be solved by various methods of multicriterial linear programming [7].

It is worth noticing, that this problem can be decomposed into a sequence of detailed tasks with single criteria:

- what size and where to deploy the modules in the fire brigade vehicle (unless you have already specified where and what to be),
- how to arrange certain sets of firefighting equipment on the vehicle in the fire engine vehicle modules,
- at the same time: how to arrange certain kit (s) of rescue equipment on the vehicle in the fire engine vehicle modules.

taking into account also:

- the frequency of various types of firefighting actions,
- sequences and sequences of actions performed in different types of firefighting actions,
- sets of equipment and elements used in different types of firefighting actions.

The frequency of various types of firefighting activities can be derived from the studies that determine the type of equipment and how often it is used in certain types of fire operations. These studies have been conducted for about a year and their results will be achievable in the near future.

Then let vector A denote the number of fire action types:

$$A = \{1,2,3,\dots,i,\dots,I\} \tag{26}$$

where I is the number of different types of rescue and firefighting operations.

We also assume that the numbers of rescue firefighting kits used in each type of firefighting action are known. Let the set of rescue and firefighting kit numbers used in the i-th rescue and firefighting operations take the form:

$$N^i = \{k \in S : \mathit{selected}\ \text{elements from the set S}\} \tag{27}$$

where i=1,...,I.

In turn, the frequency of occurrence of particular types of actions, learned from the research defined by the vector:

$$f = (f_1, f_2, f_3, \dots, f_i, \dots, f_I) \tag{28}$$

Then the circumstances of the decision problem will not change if it assumes in a natural way that we carry all sets of equipment in a rescue vehicle, but the vector function of the criterion function will change its form to:

$$F_1(X) = \sum_{i=1}^{I} f_i \sum_{j=1}^{J} \sum_{k \in N^i}^{K} x_{jk} \cdot c^k \cdot w^j \tag{29}$$

means the total weight of vertical displacement of rescue and firefighting equipment during various types of action,

$$F_2(X) = \sum_{i=1}^{I} f_i \sum_{j=1}^{J} \sum_{k \in N^i}^{K} x_{jk} \cdot c^k \cdot d^k \tag{30}$$

means the total weight of the horizontal displacement of rescue and firefighting equipment in the course of actions of different types,

$$F_3(X)=\sum_{i=1}^{I} f_i \sum_{j=1}^{J} \sum_{k\in N^i}^{K} x_{jk}\cdot \sum_{n\in Z_k} t_n \tag{31}$$

means the total weighted time of movement of rescue and firefighting equipment during various types of action.

Then the task of multi-criteria optimization of the choice of distribution of rescue and firefighting equipment in a rescue and extinguishing vehicle will take the form of:

To choose such X * to minimize

$$F'_1(X^*)=\min_{X\in D}\sum_{i=1}^{I} f_i \sum_{j=1}^{J} \sum_{k\in N^i}^{K} x_{jk}\cdot c^k \cdot w^j \tag{32}$$

$$F'_2(X^*)=\min_{X\in D}\sum_{i=1}^{I} f_i \sum_{j=1}^{J} \sum_{k\in N^i}^{K} x_{jk}\cdot c^k \cdot d^k \tag{33}$$

$$F'_3(X^*)=\min_{X\in D}\sum_{i=1}^{I} f_i \sum_{j=1}^{J} \sum_{k\in N^i}^{K} x_{jk}\cdot \sum_{n\in Z_k} t_n \tag{34}$$

where the set D of acceptable solutions have the form:

$$x_{kj}\in\{0,1\},\ k=1,\ldots,K,\ j=1,\ldots,J \tag{35}$$

$$\sum_{j=1}^{J} x_{kj}=1, k=1,\ldots,K \tag{36}$$

$$\sum_{k=1}^{K} x_{kj}\cdot r^k \le p_j, j=1,\ldots,J \tag{37}$$

$$\left|\sum_{k=1,2,3} c^k - \sum_{k=4,5,6} c^k\right| \le \varepsilon \tag{38}$$

3 The method for solving the problem

Taking into account that:

- the number of solutions is not large,
- it can be effectively determined by different methods of solving multi-criterion linear optimization tasks,
- assuming that the vehicle manufacturer or equipment designer does not allow for different types of placement,

this is another approach: a series of simulation experiments can be performed (using the resulting vehicle simulator and capabilities in for example VBS3 environment [8] to simulate crew operations during fire or rescue operations using vehicle equipment) to investigate whether certain sequences of crew operations with fixed deployment kits on fire brigade vehicles and sequences of activities in the various types of rescue and firefighting operations are designed to provide the greatest ergonomics and crew safety during their operations.

In simulation experiments a sequence of actions will be performed:

- we choose another type of rescue and firefighting action,
- for a selected type of rescue and firefighting operation, we perform a series of experiments to evaluate
  - the total weight of vertical displacement of life-fire extinguisher during such type of action,
  - the total weight of horizontal displacement of life-fire extinguisher during such type of action,
  - total time of moving firefighting equipment during firefighting such actions,
- we calculate
  - the total weight of vertical displacement of life-fire extinguisher during such type of action according to the formula (32),
  - the total weight of the horizontal displacement of rescue during such type of action according to the formula (33),
  - total time of moving firefighting equipment during firefighting total time of moving firefighting equipment according to the formula (34),
- we choose (the selection method) the solution giving the best estimation of the criterion functions,
- decision-makers choose the solution that will suit them to the highest degree.

4 Conclusions

The problem of fireman equipment deployment on fire truck was formulated. It is linear integer programming problem with many criterion functions. It is able to solve that problem, after its modification, using formal method, for example by Gomory cutting plane method. However, the task is large enough to propose suggestion that it is possible to obtain the solution by virtual simulation.

The new method would be based on the method of determining the approximate solutions of optimization problem, and in the virtual simulation environment these solutions would be verified.

References

1. M. Jasiulewicz-Kaczmarek, A. Saniuk, T. Nowicki, *The maintenance management in the macro-ergonomics context,* Advances in Social & Occupational Ergonomics, in series: Advances in Intelligent Systems and Computing, vol. 487, 35-46, Springer International Publishing AG (2017)
2. T. Nowicki, R. Waszkowski, A. Saniuk, *Human-Computer interaction in sanitary inspection simulation exercises,* Advances in Ergonomics Modeling, Usability & Special Populations, in series: Advances in Intelligent Systems and Computing, vol. 486, *245-254,* Springer International Publishing AG (2017)
3. M. Kiedrowicz, T. Nowicki, R. Waszkowski, Z. Wesołowski, K. Worwa, *Optimization of the Document Placement in the RFID Cabinet,* EDP Science, MATEC Web of Conferences 76, 02001 DOI:10.1051/matecconf/20167602001 (2016)

4. P. Brucker *Scheduling algorithms*. Springer, Berlin, Heidelberg (2007)
5. M.L. Pinedo, *Scheduling. Theory, algorithms and Systems*. Springer, New York, London, Heidelberg (2008)
6. M.L. Pinedo, *Scheduling. Planning and scheduling in manufacturing and services*. Springer, New York (2005)
7. T. Nowicki, *Linear Mixed Equivalent of a Stochastic Scheduling Problem with Different Processors* Journal of Military University of Technology, **4** (1994)
8. J. Koszela, R. Wantoch-Rekowski, *Designing advanced vehicle trainers using virtual simulation technology*, Journal of KONES, **22**, 265-272 (2015)
9. M. Kiedrowicz, R. Waszkowski, *Business rules automation standards in business process management systems*, (in:) Information Management in Practice, (eds) B.F. Kubiak and J. Maślankowski, pp. 187-200, (2015).
10. R. Hoffmann, M. Kiedrowicz, J. Stanik, *Risk management system as the basic paradigm of the information security management system in an organization*, MATEC Web of Conferences 76, 04010, DOI: 10.1051/matecconf/20167604010 (2016).
11. R. Hoffmann, M. Kiedrowicz, J. Stanik, *Evaluation of information safety as an element of improving the organization's safety management*, MATEC Web of Conferences 76, 04011, DOI:10.1051/ matecconf/20167604011 (2016).
12. M. Kiedrowicz, *Location with the use of the RFID and GPS technologies - opportunities and threats*, GIS ODYSSEY 2016, pp. 122-128, (2016).
13. M. Kiedrowicz, *Objects identification in the informations models used by information systems*, GIS ODYSSEY 2016, pp. 129-136, (2016).
14. M. Kiedrowicz, T. Nowicki, R. Waszkowski, *Business process data flow between automated and human tasks*, 3rd International Conference on Social Science (ICSS 2016) December 9–11 2016, pp. 471-477, (2016).

High–Level Control System for Biomimetic Autonomous Underwater Vehicle

Tomasz Praczyk[1,⋆] and *Piotr* Szymak[2,⋆⋆]

[1] *Institute of Naval Weapon and Computer Science, Polish Naval Academy, Gdynia, Poland*
[2] *Institute of Electrical Engineering and Automatics, Polish Naval Academy, Gdynia, Poland*

Abstract. Usually, a rough software architecture designed for a robot can be can be shortly presented in the form of layers. The lowest layer is responsible for direct control of the hardware, i.e. engines, energy system, sensors, navigation devices, etc. A next layer is a low–level control which knows how to use the hardware in order to achieve a desired state of the robot, e.g. to stay on a desired course. And the last layer, the layer which is the nearest to the human–operator, is a high–level control which decides how to use the low–level control and sometimes also individual pieces of the hardware to achieve predefined objectives. The paper describes architecture, tasks and operation of the high–level control system (HLCS) designed for Biomimetic Autonomous Underwater Vehicle (BAUV).

1 Introduction

Robots are usually a combination of many different devices, sensors, engines, in other words, each robot consists of different sorts of the hardware. To control the hardware, the software is necessary, and it occurs at different levels. The lowest level is responsible for direct control of the hardware, each device, sensor, battery, engine has a dedicated software which provides the interface required to control it via a definite communication protocol. For example, Vector Nav VN200 inertial navigational system (INS), used by many robots to orientate in the environment, has the software integrated with the device which communicates via RS232 and allows all external users to configure it and to read all navigational data provided by it.

At the higher level, the low–level control typically occurs, and it is responsible for achievement of low–level goals like maintaining a desired speed, direction of motion, in the case of underwater vehicle also depth. In addition to the parameters above, also other ones can be subjected to regulation by means of low–level software components, e.g. speed of engine rotation, position of manipulator, motion of artificial fin. For the purpose of regulation, different techniques can be used, e.g. traditional PID controller or fuzzy controllers.

The highest level of the software is responsible for achievement of high–level goals defined by a human–operator. When we deal with remotely operated robot, the task of the high–level control system (HLCS) is only to integrate the hardware and the software, also low–level control software,

⋆e-mail: t.praczyk@amw.gdynia.pl
⋆⋆e-mail: p.szymak@amw.gdynia.pl

into one organism. In this case, usually, the HLCS is responsible for passing commands of the operator to appropriate robot components. The operator knows, in this case, how to use the robot and all its devices and mechanisms to achieve the goals. Other situation is when an autonomous robot is in use, in such a case, the HLCS has to play the role of the operator and has to know how to use the hardware and the software of the robot to perform the task defined by the operator. Moreover, it also has to suitably respond to emergency situations which have to be detected somehow, sometimes also by the HLCS which is the only robot system which is in possession of all available information, and in consequence, it is the only system that is able to properly analyze the situation and to make a suitable decision.

(a)

(b)

Figure 1. BAUV used in experiments

Biomimetic Autonomous Underwater Vehicle (BAUV) [1, 6, 7] is a type of robot which is able to operate under the water, which is autonomous meaning that it is capable of performing some missions independently of a human–operator, and which is biomimetic, that is, it mimics appearance and behavior of living organisms, of course, to certain extend. An instance of the BAUV was constructed within the project entitled "Autonomous underwater vehicles with silent undulating propulsion for underwater ISR[1]", financed by Polish National Center of Research and Development – see Fig. 1. The autonomy of the BAUV entails the necessity of equipping the vehicle with the HLCS which is responsible for: executing orders of the operator in remotely operated mode, providing selected information to the operator, performing a mission defined by the operator, mapping, detecting emergency situations and responding to them. In addition to that, the HLCS is required to be easily scalable through adding new high–level behaviors.

[1]ISR – Intelligence, surveillance and reconnaissance

The paper describes process and implementation architecture of the HLCS mentioned above. Moreover, it also gives some algorithms of system operation. The remaining part of the paper is organized as follows: section 2 is an outline of the BAUV, section 3 is a description of the HLCS architecture and its operation in the form of algorithms, and the final section is a summary.

2 Biomimetic Autonomous Underwater Vehicle

The BAUV whose HLCS is the main subject to the paper consists of a number of hardware and software components [2]. When They all can be divided into seven functional parts, i.e. drive, energy system, sensors, collision avoidance, navigation, communication, and control.

As for the drive, the BAUV is equipped with two separate undulating propellers, i.e. two pectoral fins and one tail fin, with their engines. The pectoral fins are mainly used to control depth whereas the tail fin is applied to control course (heading). When the BAUV is on the surface the pectoral fins can be also used to change course, in that case, they work in the opposite direction, i.e. one fin pushes the vehicle forward whereas the second one backward. In addition to the fins and their engines, the drive part also includes the low–level control system (LLCS) which is the software component whose task is to implement decisions of the HLCS or the operator. In the remotely operated mode, the LLCS can force the vehicle to turn, to go ahead, and to change speed. Change of depth is not allowed in this mode. In turn, in the autonomous mode, the LLCS continuously works as a depth and course controller, desired values of course and depth it gets from the HLCS. The BAUV is not equipped with speedometer and that is why the LLCS cannot play the function of a speed controller.

The energy system consists of batteries and the software called Battery Control System whose task, as the name implies, is to ensure optimal use of the batteries, and to inform about critical and emergency situations requiring a response, e.g. low voltage on batteries, battery failure.

With regard to sensors, the BAUV has two cameras and one sonar. One camera is mounted in an external container above the hull and it is mainly used on the surface. The second camera is located in the "head" of the BAUV which is always below the surface and for that reason it is only used to observe underwater environment. The sonar is an acoustic "radar" which like the second camera is applied under the water. Currently, all the three sensors are only used to record vision data which can be then analyzed by the operator, information provided by them is not used by the BAUV in the process of making decisions. To handle the sensors two software systems are necessary, i.e. Sonar Control System (SOS) and Camera Control System (CCS), which are run on a separate auxiliary on–board PC104 computer.

The collision avoidance system consists of three echo–sounders and the software responsible for: (i) reading signals from the devices, (ii) interpretation of signals, and (iii) calculating coordinates of obstacles and sending them to the HLCS. The system is able to detect obstacles 40 meters away from the vehicle and located at the top, bottom and front of it.

Navigation system is responsible for locating the BAUV in a global Earth coordinate system. It is equipped with VN200 Inertial Navigational System (INS), Digital Compass OS5000, pressure sensor, GPS receiver, and USBL[2] transponder. As mentioned above, the BAUV does not have speedometer. All the devices mentioned above enable the BAUV to fix position in a different way. First, when the vehicle is on the surface, accurate GPS position can be recorded, second, when the vehicle works close to a mother ship or in a region where USBL system can be installed, USBL position can be used, otherwise, a dead reckoning method is applied to calculate the BAUV position based on INS, Compass and pressure sensor indications. In the latter case, speed is determined by means of odometry, that is, there are a number of propeller settings, each setting corresponds to a vehicle speed.

[2]Ultra–Short BaseLine – underwater acoustic navigational system

Navigation system is not only the hardware, it also needs software components. First, a number of device drivers is necessary with the responsibility for reading navigational data from the devices and for providing them to other software components via shared memory of the main on–board computer. Second, the system is also necessary which, depending on the situation, selects sources of navigational information (GPS, USBL, or INS, Compas, pressure sensor along with dead reckoning) and relying on them fixes or calculates position of the BAUV.

In order to communicate with the operator and with the external system which provides USBL positions to the BAUV, the vehicle is equipped with the communication system. It works in three communication channels, i.e. acoustic, radio and WiFi channel. To this end, it uses three communication devices, i.e. hydro–modem, radio–modem, and WiFi station. Effective communication requires also the software which encodes/decodes messages that the BAUV sends/receives.

Finally, the BAUV needs also the system which, on the one hand, integrates all other systems, devices, and sensors mentioned above in one super–system, but on the other hand, it also makes decisions being the consequence of mission performed by the vehicle in autonomous control mode. The role outlined above is played by the HLCS which is the main subject of this paper and which is detailed in the following section. The HLCS along with other software but except those operating on sensors, is run on the main on–board PC104 computer.

3 High Level Control System

As already mentioned the HLCS is responsible for the following tasks:

1. executing orders of the operator in remotely operated mode,
2. providing selected information to the operator,
3. performing a mission defined by the operator,
4. mapping,
5. detecting emergency situations and responding to them

In order to perform the above tasks, two–threaded implementation of the HLCS is applied [3]. One thread handles all messages and signals coming from the operator or other software components of the BAUV. There are a number of messages, i.e. configuration messages, a message with an operation to run in remotely operated mode, a message with USBL position, a message with mission definition (main or emergency mission), and messages running/stopping the mission. Signals inform the HLCS about important events, there are also a number of signals, i.e.: state signal from other BAUV systems, timer signal, obstacle detection signal. At the highest level, implementation of that HLCS thread can be presented in the form of pseudo–code shown in Fig. 2, 3, and 4.

As for the initialization, it establishes communication between the HLCS and the remaining components of the entire system, sets timers (timers are outlined further), and default emergency mission which, if not modified by the operator, is run when emergency situation is detected. Moreover, the initialization also configures all the HLCS sub–components through reading default parameters of the components from the configuration file.

When a message is received, first, it is tested whether handling messages is allowed. They cannot be handled when an emergency situation is detected which makes it impossible to use the BAUV. In

[3]A solution with only two threads is mainly due to application of four–core PC104 computers on the BAUV board. A small number of cores forced an architecture of the HLCS which is not intensely concurrent. The same applies to other BAUV software components

```
HLCS::main(parameters)
begin
initialization(parameters);
loop forever
    messageOrSignal = receiveMessage();
    if messageOrSignal is message
        handleMessage(messageOrSignal);
    else
        handleSignal(messageOrSignal);
    end if
end loop
end
```

Figure 2. Main thread of HLCS

```
HLCS::handleMessage(message)
begin
if messages are allowed
    switch(message type)
        case configuration:
                configureHLCS(message);
        case remote operation:
                runOperation(message);
        case USBL position:
                setBAUVPosition(message);
        case mission definition:
                setMission(message);
        case mission run/stop:
                runStopMission(message);
    end switch
end if
end
```

Figure 3. Handling messages

that situation, the only thing the vehicle is allowed to do is to periodically send a message with its position.

Configuration message sets different parameters of the HLCS which by default are determined in the configuration file. The message can include a single parameter to update or it can also force the system to return to default values.

In the HLCS, the assumption is made that a desired behavior of the BAUV can be achieved in two ways, i.e. either by running a single operation or running a mission which consists of the operations. An operation is a simple behavior of the vehicle, e.g. turning right, submerging, turning on the camera, moving to a way–point, whereas the mission is an organized execution of many operations, some operations are run sequentially, i.e. one after another, and the other ones are run quasi–concurrently (the mission is detailed further). In the remotely operated mode, the operator is allowed to run only a single operation by sending an appropriate message to the BAUV and the HLCS. If the operation in the message is "not blocking", that is, it does not require a longer activity from the HLCS, then, it is run in the main HLCS thread, otherwise, another thread is started with a "blocking" operation. An example of "not blocking" operation is turning right or left, which is immediately sent to the LLCS, the HLCS is not involved in its execution, whereas, moving to a way–point is an example of "blocking" operation, the HLCS has, in this case, to supervise its execution.

A next message that can be received by the HLCS is the message with USBL position. The position is given to the navigational system which decides what to do next with it.

In order to define, start or stop mission, appropriate messages have to be sent to the HLCS. There are two types of mission, i.e. main and emergency missions, the former has to be defined by the operator, whereas the latter is present in the system in a default form, however, with the possibility to change it. The message that defines the mission prepares the HLCS to run it, that is, internal representation of the mission is created in the form of appropriately organized operations ready to run. After defining the mission, it can be run by sending a proper message. It takes place by creating and running a separate mission thread which can be stopped in two situations solely, i.e. after completion of the mission or when a message is received which means intention of the operator to interrupt it.

```
HLCS::handleSignal(signal)
begin
switch(signal type)
    case timer message to operator:
                sendMessage();
    case timer emergency:
                testIfEmergency();
    case timer clear obstacles:
                clearObstacles();
    case obstacle:
                addObstacle(signal);
    case depth:
                setDistanceToBottom(signal);
    case state:
        updateStateAndTesIftEmergency(signal);
end switch
end
```

Figure 4. Handling signals

Whereas the ordinary messages are mainly used in communication between operator and the HLCS and their role is to send informations or commands requiring a greater amount of data, the signals are short, quick messages and they are used in internal communication between software components of the BAUV.

A separate class of signals are signals from a timer which is a mechanism that makes it possible to control the system by means of time. In the HLCS, the timers generate periodically, according to their setting, three types of signals. One signal activates procedure of sending message to the operator. The message includes informations about state of the BAUV, which informations are sent depends on HLCS setting. A next signal runs procedure which tests whether emergency mission should be run, and if yes, it is started. An example reason of emergency situation is missing course information for a time, or detection of water in the hull. The last signal from the timer is signal which results in browsing the set of obstacles memorized in the system and removing outdated obstacles.

The obstacles are added to a environment map managed by the HLCS by other signal generated by the collision avoidance system. During navigation, all the obstacles contained in the map are considered when maneuvers for the BAUV are calculated. The more obstacles is on the map, the slower the process of maneuver fixing is. Since positions of the obstacles in the global coordinate system can be inaccurate – it is only important for the obstacles to be accurately positioned with reference to the vehicle, outdated obstacles which are far away from the vehicle can be removed.

Apart from the signal with the obstacle, the collision avoidance system generates also a signal with current distance to the sea–bottom. As in the previous case, the information carried by the signals is necessary for save navigation, the vehicle simply should always move above the bottom, each hitting the bottom can be dangerous for the vehicle.

In order to monitor state of the BAUV, the HLCS is periodically informed by all vehicle components about their state. To this end, each component sends to the HLCS a signal with encoded state.

Lack of signal for a time or a signal with the information about an error are often the basis for starting the emergency mission.

In contrast to the main thread of the HLCS which deals with the majority of tasks assigned to the system, the second thread is used is used to run the "blocking" operations and missions. The mission consists of three lists of operations. One list includes operations which are run one after another, and they are called "A" operations. An example of an "A" operation is "go to way–point". A sequence of such operations means a path of the BAUV passing through some way–points.

```
operation::run()
begin
if condition to activate operation
    not satisfied
    reset();
    return true;
end if
switch(state)
    case state1:
        take action in state1;
        if condition in state1 satisfied
            state := state2;
        end if
        return false;
    case state2:
        take action state2;
        return false;
end switch
end
```

Figure 5. Example operation

The second list contains the so–called "B" operations which are executed quasi–concurrently. It is assumed that, one "A" operation and all "B" operations can work simultaneously. In fact, only one operation is active in a given moment, however, the effect and impression on the outside is that all mentioned operations work together. To avoid the situation in which both an "A" operation and some "B" operations at the same time try to control the BAUV propellers, with unpredictable effect, "B" operations cannot affect vehicle drive, it is only allowed to "A" and "C" operations (see further). The task of a "B" operation can be for example to turn on the camera in specified way–points and for a definite period. To this end, the operation has to continuously, for all the mission, monitor vehicle position and start the camera when the vehicle is close to any way–point.

The above–mentioned "C" operations are system operations, i.e. operations which are added to the mission not by the operator but by the system. Their responsibility is to perform tasks common to all missions, e.g. to emerge the vehicle every n meters to get GPS position, and to solve problems which can appear during the mission and which cannot be solved by "A" and "B" operations, e.g. to control the vehicle when collision or when the vehicle cannot move even though its drive is working. Since "C" operations can influence on vehicle propellers, they cannot work together with "A" operations. In consequence, once any "C" operation is started, current "A" operation is immediately interrupted.

The "C" operations are arranged according to the importance criterion. In one moment, only one "C" operation can be active. All them test, one after another, conditions necessary to activate them. Once the conditions are satisfied, the operation is started and current "A" operation is stopped. While one of "C" operations is active, the remaining "C" operations continue to test their conditions. If conditions of a "C" operation with a greater priority are also met, it takes control over the vehicle, whereas, "C" operation active so far has to be stopped. After completion of all "C" operations, an interrupted "A" operation is reseted and restarted.

```
HLCS::runMission(mission)
begin
currentAOperation := 0;
currentCOperationActive := -1;
reset := false;
loop until (currentAOperation < mission.listOfAOperations.size()
        and mission not interrupted)
    currentCOperation := -1;
    cOperationNotActive := true;
    loop until (currentCOperation < mission.listOfCOperations.size()
            and cOperationNotActive = true)
        currentCOperation++;
        cOperationNotActive := mission.listOfCOperations[currentCOperation].run();
    end loop
    if cOperationNotActive = true
        mission.listOfBOperations.runAll();
        currentCOperationActive := -1;
        reset := false;
        if mission.listOfAOperations[currentAOperation].run() is end
            currentAOperation++;
    else
        if (currentCOperationActive >=0
            and currentCOperationActive != currentCOperation)
            mission.listOfCOperations[currentCOperationActive].reset();
        end if
        currentCOperationActive := currentCOperation;
        if reset = false
            mission.listOfAOperations[currentAOperation].reset();
            reset := true;
        end if
    end if
end loop
end
```

Figure 6. Algorithm of mission

Ultimately, algorithm of mission can be presented in the form of pseudo–cod depicted in Fig. 6.

As already mentioned, operations contained in the mission can work quasi–concurrently. To achieve such an effect, the main mission loop runs all operations, which are supposed to be run concurrently, one after another. However, execution of an operation in the loop does not mean that the operation runs from the beginning to the end. If so, each operation would block other operations. Each operation is a state machine which in a single run takes only actions that correspond to a state in which the operation currently is. Example operation can be presented in the algorithm shown in Fig. 5.

To effectively control the BAUV, the operations often need information about state of different vehicle components, including the HLCS itself. For example, "go to way–point" operation has to know whether it can lead the vehicle directly to the way–point or it has to perform a collision avoidance maneuver. Providing the information to the operations is the task of the HLCS. Each component of the BAUV stores its state in the shared memory from where it can be downloaded by the HLCS which, in turn, can provide it to any operation.

The HLCS with the architecture described above confirmed its effectiveness during many tests in simulation [3–5] and with real vehicle. In fact, the tests in simulation were even more valuable because they could be carried out in any conditions. During simulation, all elements that could have the influence on the operation of HLCS were tested. The system was verified for the vehicle with different dynamics, for various underwater environments, for different vehicle and HLCS parameters, for different operations and so forth. Example paths of BAUV during tests in simulation are depicted in Fig. 7.

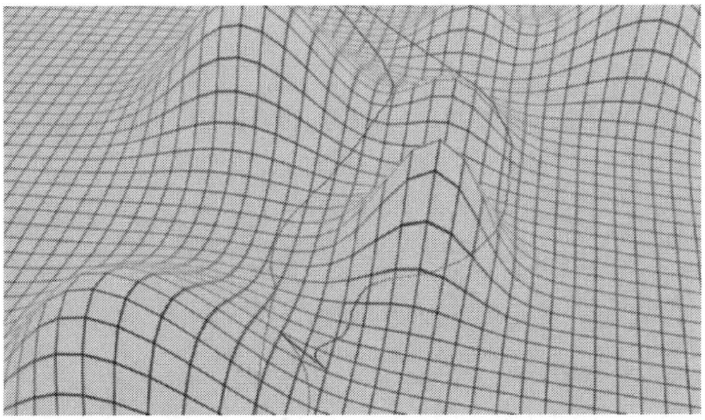

(a)

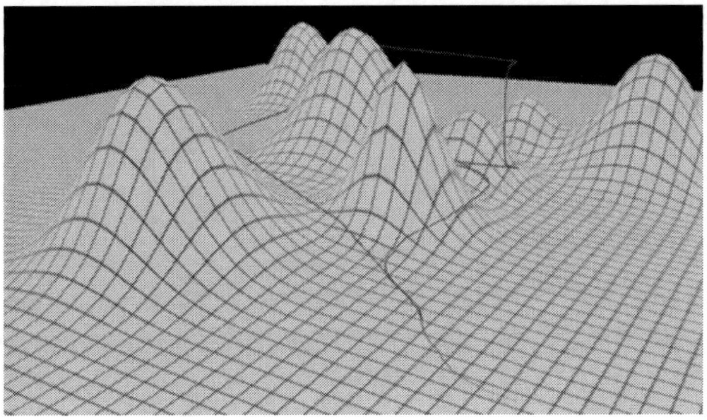

(b)

Figure 7. Example paths of BAUV during tests in simulation

Moreover, the tests in simulation made it also possible to eliminate implementation errors which appeared in the software. Appearance of the errors during tests with the real vehicle could result in damaging or losing it.

The tests on the real vehicle were also useful, first they were carried out on a pool and next in a real conditions, that is, at sea. As it appeared, the HLCS as well as the remaining components of the system passed also this exam. In the tests, the vehicle, generally behaved as we expected.

4 Summary

The paper presents the High–Level Control System for Biomimetic Autonomous Underwater Vehicle designed within the project "Autonomous underwater vehicles with silent undulating propulsion for underwater ISR", financed by Polish National Center of Research and Development. The tasks of the system are itemized and its the most crucial elements are outlined, including: handling messages and signals, cooperation with other systems, construction and modus operandi of mission, and operations. In order to allow for better understanding of the presented material, the paper includes some algorithms.

Acknowledgment

The research described in this paper were achieved in the project No. DOBR-BIO4/033/13015/2013, financed by Polish National Center of Research and Development in the years 2013-2016.

References

[1] M. Malec, M. Morawski, and J. Zajc, "Fish-like swimming prototype of mobile underwater robot", Journal of Automation, Mobile Robotics and Intelligent Systems, Vol. 4, No 3, pp. 25-30, (2010)

[2] T. Praczyk, P. Szymak, Software architecture of biomimetic underwater vehicle, Proc. SPIE 9831, Ground/Air Multisensor Interoperability, Integration, and Networking for Persistent ISR VII, doi:10.1117/12.2225871, (2016)

[3] T. Praczyk, A quick algorithm for planning a path for biomimetic autonomous underwater vehicle, Scientific Journals of Maritime University of Szczecin, no. 45 (117), pp. 23-28, (2016)

[4] T. Praczyk, Using Genetic Algorithms for Optimizing Algorithmic Control System of Biomimetic Underwater Vehicle, Computational Methods in Science and Technology (CMST), vol. 21 (4), pp. 251-260, (2015)

[5] T. Praczyk, The influence of parameters of biomimetic underwater vehicle control system on the ability of the vehicle to avoid obstacles, Scientific Journal of Polish Naval Academy, 2(205), pp. 75-91, (2016)

[6] P. Szymak, T. Praczyk, K. Naus, M. Malec, M. Morawski, Research on biomimetic underwater vehicles for underwater ISR, Ground/Air Multisensor Interoperability, Integration, and Networking for Persistent ISR VII, edited by Michael A. Kolodny, Tien Pham, Proc. of SPIE Vol. 9831, 98310K, (2016)

[7] P. Szymak, M. Malec, M. Morawski, "Directions of development of underwater vehicle with undulating propulsion", Polish Journal of Environmental Studies, Hard Publishing Company, Vol.19, No 3, pp. 107-110, (2010)

Research of the method of pseudo-random number generation based on asynchronous cellular automata with several active cells

Stepan Bilan[1,*], *Mykola* Bilan[2], and *Sergii* Bilan[3]

[1] State Economy and Technology University of Transport, Kyiv, Lukeshevicha, str., 19, 03049, Ukraine
[2] The municipal educational institution Mayakskaya Secondary School, Mayak, Moldova
[3] Win-Interactive LLC, Vinnytsia, Ukraine

Abstract. To date, there are many tasks that are aimed at studying the dynamic changes in physical processes. These tasks do not give advance known result. The solution of such problems is based on the construction of a dynamic model of the object. Successful structural and functional implementation of the object model can give a positive result in time. This approach uses the task of constructing artificial biological objects. To solve such problems, pseudo-random number generators are used, which also find wide application for information protection tasks. Such generators should have good statistical properties and give a long repetition period of the generated pseudo-random bit sequence. This work is aimed at improving these characteristics. The paper considers the method of forming pseudo-random sequences of numbers on the basis of aperiodic cellular automata with two active cells. A pseudo-random number generator is proposed that generates three bit sequences. The first two bit sequences are formed by the corresponding two active cells in the cellular automaton. The third bit sequence is the result of executing the XOR function over the bits of the first two sequences and it has better characteristics compared to them. The use of cellular automata with two active cells allowed to improve the statistical properties of the formed bit sequence, as well as its repetition period. This is proved by using graphical tests for generators built based on cellular automata using the neighborhoods of von Neumann and Moore. The tests showed high efficiency of the generator based on an asynchronous cellular automaton with the neighborhood of Moore. The proposed pseudo-random number generators have good statistical properties, which makes it possible to use them in information security systems, as well as for simulation tasks of various dynamic processes.

1 Introduction

To date, the problem of creating sources of pseudo-random numbers great attention is given [1 - 7]. A large number of different pseudo-random number generators (PRNG) have already been created, which form high-quality pseudo-random bit sequences [1 - 7]. However, modern means of information processing and protection, as well as data transmission systems require improvement of such parameters as speed, length of the repetition period of the pseudo-random sequence of numbers, and unpredictability of each element of the bit sequence. A lot of attention is paid to PRNG, which are implemented on cellular automata (CA) [8-13]. For the implementation of PRNG, CA with various forms of organization are used (one-dimensional CA, two-dimensional CA, synchronous CA, asynchronous CA, hybrid CA, etc.). The PRNG based on asynchronous CA (ACA) high quality was shown in papers [9, 14]. They were investigated using statistical tests of ENT, NIST [4, 15, 16], as well as graphical tests [4]. Such studies allowed the analysis of ACA with one active cell. However, in fact, ACA with several active cells has not been investigated. Also hybrid CA (HCA) with different forms of neighborhood organization for heterogeneous cells have not been fully investigated.

2 PRNG based on the ACA with one active cell

In their previous papers, the authors considered the PRNG based on the ACA, in which only one cell changes its state at each time point [9, 14]. The various types of neighborhoods of cells (von Neumann neighborhood and Moore neighborhood are investigated). At the initial moment of time all the cells of the ACA are set to logical "0" and "1" states, and an active cell is chosen. Each cell of the ACA is in the main informative state and can be in an additional active state (active cell).

In each time step, only the active cell can change its state in accordance with the local transition function, which it implements. After changing its state in the next time step, each active cell transmits the active signal of

* Corresponding author: bstepan@ukr.net

one of the cells in the neighborhood of the active cell. That cell of the neighborhood of the active cell to which the active signal was transmitted becomes active in the next time step of the PRNG functioning. To select the active cell in the next time step, the active cell realizes a local function, the arguments of which are the signal values at the outputs of the neighborhood cells at the current time. The result of this function is the signal on one of the active outputs of the active cell at the present time. This output is connected to the active input of one of the cells in the neighborhood of the active cell. The additional active cell performs a constant change in the general condition of the ACA in comparison with the use of one active cell. This situation reduces the number of states that lead to the formation of signal generation cycles.

In the previous papers [9, 14], the following local functions were used, which were performed by each active cell. To change the basic information state of the active cell, the XOR function is used. In this case, the arguments of such a function are the values of the own state signal. To transmit the active signal to one of the neighborhood cells, a function is used which, at an odd time step from the neighborhood cells in the logical "1" state, determines the cell with the largest number of enumeration. In addition, the local activation function determines the neighborhood cell with the largest number among the neighborhood cells that are in the logical "0" state in the odd time step.

At each time step, the active cell state signal is read. In addition, in the local function of the active cell, an additional bit is used. This bit is a signal of the state of one of the cells of the ACA at each time step of the PRNG. A cell that forms an additional bit at any time can be selected according to any previously described law. An example of the functioning of a PRNG with one active cell of the ACA on Fig. 1 is shown.

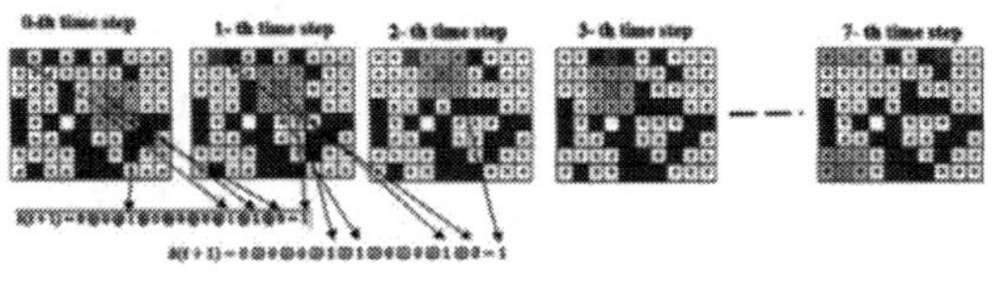

Fig. 1. An example of the functioning of a PRNG with one active cell.

In this example, the red cell is an active cell; the blue cell forms an additional bit. Condition of the active cell changes based on cells by neighborhood Moore. A red (active) cell forms a bit of a pseudo-random sequence at each time step. The sequence of bits formed after seven time steps corresponds to 0101010. The numbering of the neighborhood cells begins from the middle upper cell and increases clockwise.

The use of an additional bit as an additional argument of the function makes it possible to increase the length of the repetition period of the PRNG based on the ACA. The main characteristics that affect the quality of the PRNG on the basis of ACA with one active cell are: the dimension of the ACA, the shape of the neighborhood, the number of cells of the ACA in the initial state of the logical "1", the location of the cells in the logical "1" state on the ACA field and of the initial active cell, the local function of states of active cells and the local function of active cell transitions.

The hardware implementation of PRNG with one active cell is based on the implementation of one cell of the ACA. The cell of the ACA consists of two parts that realize the local function of states and the local function of the active signal transmission of one of the cells in the neighborhood of the active cell. In addition, the PRNG uses a switching circuit in its structure that implements the connection of the output of the active cell to the output of the generator at each instant of time.

In the papers [9, 14], the results of a test analysis of a PRNG based on ACA was described. As tests, ENT, NIST, and graphical tests were used. The obtained results confirmed the high quality of the operation of the PRNG based on the ACA with one active cell. It was determined how the performance of the PRNG affects such characteristics as the size of the ACA and the number of cells that have an initial state of logical "1". In addition, the influence of the shape of the neighborhood of ACA is been determined. In these papers, recommendations were given for the selection of high quality PRNG. It was shown that the small dimension of ACA with one active cell does not give high quality of the formed bit sequence and does not allow to form a pseudo-random bit sequence with a long repetition period.

In this regard, studies are underway to increase the length of the repetition period of the pseudo-random bit sequence based on the use of various variants of the organization ACA. Other forms of neighborhoods and other local functions of transitions to the active state are considered, and the possibility of increasing additional active cells.

3 PRNG on the basis of ACA with two active cells

PRNG based on ACA with one active cell at small dimensions have a number of shortcomings. With a small number of cells with initial states of logical "1", short cycles of bit sequences appear, and also the of single trajectories of motion of active cells are been appeared.

To eliminate such deficiencies, the ACA with two active cells are used.

The structure of PRNG based on ACA with two active cells is similar to a generator with one active cell. Only ACA is organized somewhat differently. The cell of such an ACA has a different structure since it can work in three modes.

• Standby mode,
• The mode of the first active cell,
• Mode of the second active cell.

The standby mode is characterized by the fact that the cell is set to the information state of the logical "1" or "0". In this state, the cell is located until it becomes active. In the active state, the cell can change its information state, or it may not change its own state.

This depends on the local function and on the values of the arguments for the local function of the active cell.

In the second mode, the cell is active, and it functions as well as the active cell, as described in the previous section.

If the cell is in the active state of the second active cell, then it performs the same functions as the first active cell. The only difference is that at an odd time step it performs a local function similar to that performed by the first active cell at the paired time step and vice versa. This separation of active cells in even and odd time steps is carried out in order that in the case of coincidences of the two active cells, one cell does not "disappear".

The following model describes the information state of the active cell of the ACA.

$$b_i(t+1)=\begin{cases} f\left[b^i_{N_j}(t)\right], & if\ \ \exists b^{i,act1}_{N_j}(t)=1\ \ or\ \ \exists b^{i,act2}_{N_j}(t)=1 \\ b_i(t), & in\ other\ case \end{cases} \quad (1)$$

where $b^i_{N_j}(t)$ - signals on the information outputs of the cells that constitute the cell neighborhood of i-th cell at time t;

$b^{i,actl}_{N_j}(t)$ - signal at the j-th activation input of i-th cell in i-th activity mode and this signal comes from activation output of the cell that belongs to the cell neighborhood of i-th cell at time t $\left(j=\overline{1,N}\right)$;

N – the amount of neighbor cells, that makes the neighborhood of the i-th cell.

In accordance with this model, active cells change their state regardless of the mode of functioning of the active cell. However, the transmission of the active signal of one of the neighborhood cells for the second and third modes is different. In Fig. 2 the numbering of Moore neighborhoods for an active cell is shows.

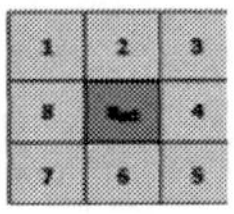

Fig. 2. The numbering of cells of the Moore neighborhood for an active cell.

The numbering of neighborhood cells and the local transition function can be chosen arbitrarily. To select an effective numbering and local transition function, it is necessary to carry out additional studies of the generator.

In Fig. 3 an example of active signal transmission by active cells in odd time step is shown.

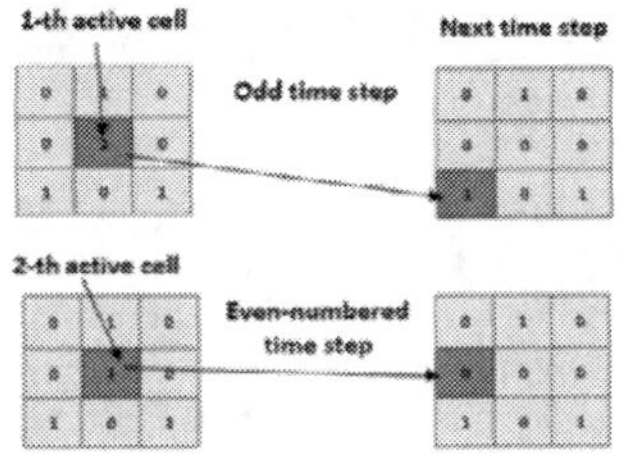

Fig. 3. An example of the transmission of an active signal by the first and second active cells in the neighborhood of Moore.

The use of two active cells avoids possible short cycles that can occur when only one active cell is used. In addition, the cell can change the direction of transmission of the active signal.

The second active cell disrupts the cycle in which the first active cell has stopped. An example of the operation of a PRNG based on ACA with two active cells on Fig. 4 is presented.

In this mode of operation of the PRNG, the active cells can coincide on one cell of the ACA. Therefore, the functions are chosen so that this coincidence does not affect the further operation.

On the example (Fig.4), it is evident that at 68 time step, two active cells converge into one active cell and at the next time step they form two active cells from one active cell. Such a work of PRNG is achieved by separating the function on even and odd time steps for each active cell.

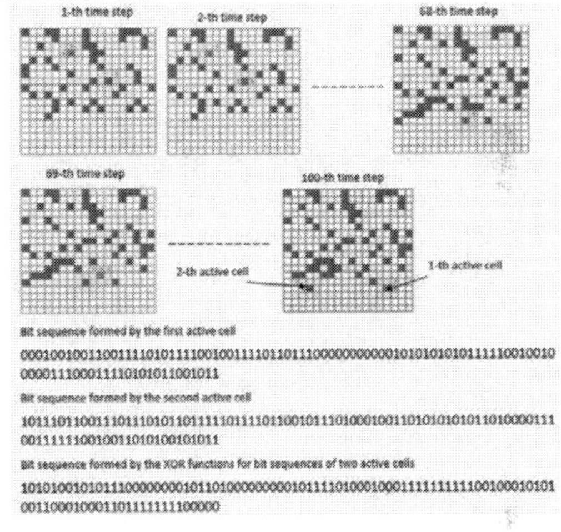

Fig. 4. An example of the functioning of PRNG based on ACA with two active cells using the Moore neighborhood.

The value of the next bit of the generated sequence at the output of the PRNG can be the state of one of the active cells of the ACA. The PRNG can also generate two pseudo-random bit sequences. In addition, such a generator can generate a pseudo-random bit sequence in which each formed bit is the result of applying the XOR function to bits of two bit of sequences that are generated by the active cells.

Thus, using the PRNG on the basis of ACA with two active cells, it is possible to form three bit sequences. The third resulting bit sequence may have a longer repetition period than the first two cells.

The hardware implementation of such a PRNG has a more complex structure, since each cell of the ACA operates in three modes. The cell of such an ACA has a different circuit realization of the active state and a scheme for transferring the active signal to the cells of the neighborhood. There are in the asynchronous cellular automata two active cells that realize different functions of the active signal transmission at each time step. In addition, the presence of two active cells complicates the switching system, which connects both active cells to the two outputs of the PRNG at the same time. In addition, there is a need to use an additional XOR gate to form a third bit sequence. However, the use of two active cells does not reduce the performance of PRNG since active cells function simultaneously.

4 Analysis of the quality of the PRNG based on ACA with two active cells

The evaluation of the quality of such generators was performed using the statistical tests ENT and NIST, as well as using graphic tests [4, 15, 16].

The analysis was carried out in the following order. First, the initial settings of the generator were set, which were described earlier. Then, two bit sequences Q_1 and Q_2 were formed by the first and second active cells. Also a third bit sequence is been generated $Q_3 = Q_1 \oplus Q_2$, Which is the result of the bitwise addition modulo 2 of the first two bit sequences. Bit sequences were formed under different initial conditions and different lengths. ACA with dimension 10×10 and 15×15 are used. An additional bit for each active cell was formed by the ACA matrix itself. After scanning all the cells of the ACA, a matrix was used whose cell states were obtained through a number of time steps that are equal to the number of cells of the ACA. As neighborhoods, the von Neumann and Moore neighborhoods were chosen for all dimensions of the ACA.

The number of initial cells equal to 53 cells for ACA with the dimension 10×10 was used and 10, 50 and 100 of cells for ACA with 15×15 dimension. The location of cells with initial states of logical "1", as well as the initial locations of active cells that were used in testing on Fig. 5 are presented.

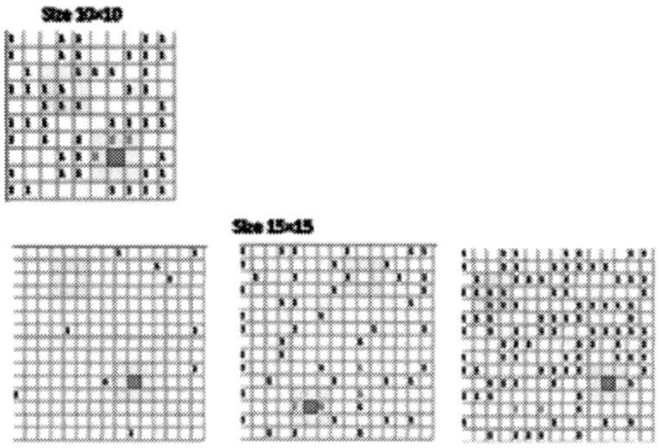

Fig. 5. The initial installation of the ACA for performance testing of the PRNG.

For each initial setup, bit sequences of length 100, 1000, 100000, 1,000,000 and 2,000,000 bits were generated, which were represented by bit files. With the help of the developed software, graphic tests were carried out, which implemented two tests:

• The histogram of distribution of the elements of sequence,

• The point's distribution on the plane.

The results of testing the bit sequences generated using the von Neumann neighborhood on Fig. 6 are presented. The sequence length corresponds to 2000000 bits.

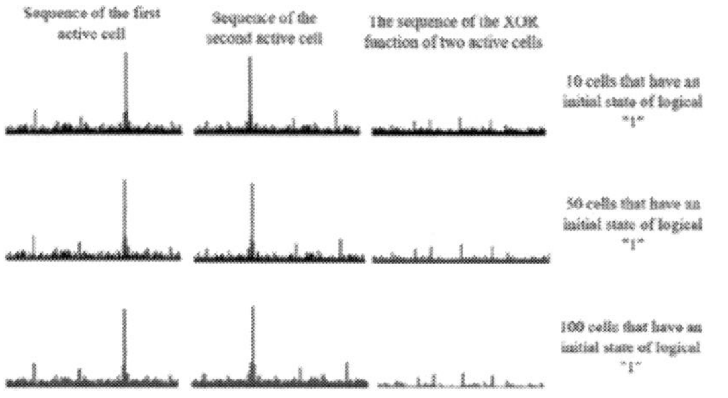

Fig. 6. The histogram of distribution of the elements of sequence for bit sequences formed using a von Neumann neighborhood.

The use of the von Neumann neighborhood does not give the desired results for small dimensions of the ACA, regardless of the number of cells in the logical "1" state. The ACA dimensions 15 × 15 also do not give good results.

The results of testing the bit sequences generated using the Moore neighborhood and have length the 2,000,000 bit on Fig. 7 are presented.

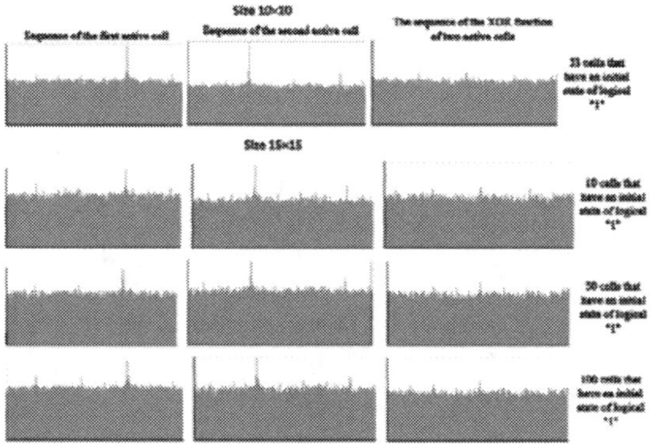

Fig. 7. The histogram of distribution of the elements of sequence for bit sequences formed using the Moore neighborhood.

The obtained histograms showed good results of the first test for the accepted sizes of ACA. It is shown that the size of the ACA 15 × 15 does not reduce the quality of the generator. It is important to note that the introduction of an additional XOR function removes defects in the bit sequences of each individual active cell. The forms of the obtained diagrams clearly shows good distribution of numbers.

The second test was carried out for sequences of 100,000, 1,000,000, 2,000,000 bits in length for the neighborhoods of von Neumann and Moore. The results of the second test for the PRNG based on the ACA with the von Neumann neighborhood on Fig. 8 are presented for a sequence with length of 1,000,000 bits.

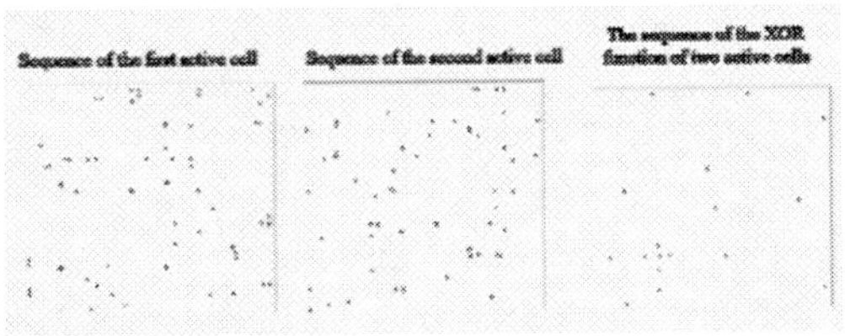

Fig. 8. Diagrams of the distribution of numbers on the plane for bit sequences formed using the von Neumann neighborhood and the length of the sequence of 1000000 bits.

Diagrams show unsatisfactory results for a sequence of 1,000,000 bits. The points are grouped in certain places on the plane, which indicates significant defects in the operation of the generator based on the von Neumann neighborhood. The results of the second test for the 2,000,000 bit sequences using the Moore neighborhood on Fig. 9 are shown. Tests were also carried out for bit sequences of shorter length (100,000 and 1,000,000 bits), which yielded positive results.

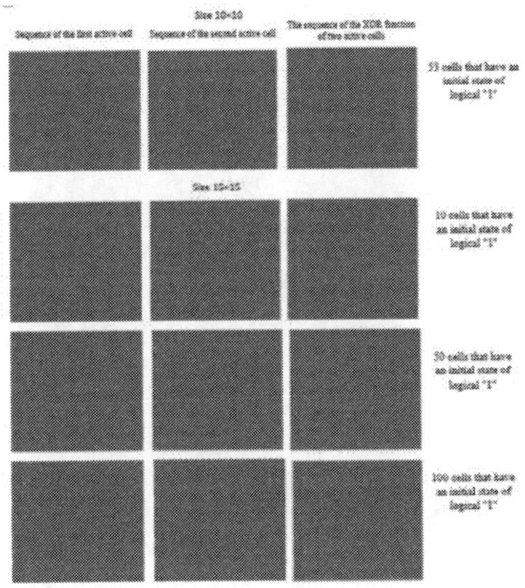

Fig. 9. Diagrams of the distribution of points in the plane for bit sequences formed using the Moore neighborhood for a sequence of length of 2,000,000 bits.

The test results showed a good distribution for the bit sequences formed by the active cells and using the XOR function.

4 Conclusion

The use of two active cells in the organization of ACA makes it possible to improve the properties of the generated pseudorandom bit sequences. Graphic tests have shown that the most effective is the neighborhood Moore. It gives a positive result for small size ACA when using graphical tests. The use of XOR functions for bit sequences formed by two active cells gives better results, which in graphical tests is proved. In addition, the length of the repetition period of the pseudo-random bit sequence is increased.

References

1. B. Schneier, Applied Cryptography, Second Edition: Protocols, Algorthms, and Source Code in C, Wiley Computer Publishing, John Wiley & Sons, Inc,. 784 (1996)
2. G. Marsaglia, Random number generators. Journal of Modern Applied Statistical Methods. **2**, 2-13 (2003)
3. W. Hörmann, J. Leydold, G. Derflinger, Automatic Nonuniform Random Veriate Generation. *Spr.-Verl., New York,* (2004)
4. E.V. Chugunkov, Methods and tools to evaluate the quality of pseudo-random sequence generators, focused on solving problems of information security: Textbook/M.: NEYAU MIFI, 236 (2012)
5. M. Matsumoto, T. Nishimura, M. Hadita, M. Saito. Cryptographic Mersenne Twister and Fubuki Stream/Block Cipher. (2005)
6. A. Tanvir, R. Md. Mahbubur. The Hybrid Pseudo Random Nimber Generator. Inter. Jour. of Hybr. Inform. Tech. **3**(1), 299-312 (2016)
7. A. Fog. Pseudo-Random Number Generators for vector Processor and Multicore Processors. Journ. of Mod. Appl. Stat. Methods. **14**(1), 308-334 (2015)
8. S. Wolfram, Cryptography with cellular automata. Lect. Not. in Comp. Scien.. **218**, p. 429-432 (1986)
9. S. Bilan, M. Bilan, S. Bilan, Novel pseudo-random sequence of numbers generator based cellular automata. Inf. Techn. and Sec. **3**, № 1, 38-50 (2015)
10. C. Fraile Ruboi, L. Hernandez Encinas, S. Hoya White, A. Martin del Rey, Rodrigues Sancher, The use of Linear Hybrid Cellular Automata as Pseudorandom bit Generators in Cryptography. Neu. Par. & Scien. Comp. **12**(2), p. 175-192 (2004)
11. K. Bhattachrjee, D. Paul, S. Das. Pseudorandom Pattern Generation Using 3-State Cellular Automata. In: El Yacoubi S., Was J., Bandini S. (eds). Cellular Automatar. ACRI 2016. Lect. Not. in Comp. Scien. **9863**, 3-13 (2016)
12. G. Sh. Sirakoulis. Parallel Application of Hybrid DNA Cellular Automata for Pseudorandom Number Generation. JCA. **11**(1), 63-89 (2016)
13. B. Martin, P. Sole, Pseudo-random Sequences Generated by Cellular Automata". International Conference on Ralations, Orders and Graphs: Interaction with Computer Scince, May 2008, Mandia, Tunisia, Nouha editions, p. 401-410 (2008)
14. S. Bilan, M. Bilan, R. Motornyuk, A. Bilan, S. Bilan, Research and Analysis of the Pseudorandom Number Generators Implemented on Cellular Automata, WSEAS TRANS. on SYS., **15**, p. 275 - 281. (2016)

DOI: 10.1051/matecconf/201712502018

15. J. Walker, ENT. A Pseudorandom Number Sequence Test Program.- [electronic resource]. January 28th, 2008. http://www.fourmilab.ch/random
16. NIST.- National institute of standarts and technology. Computer security division. Computer security resource center.- Download Documentation and Software.: http://csrc.nist.gov/groups/ST/toolkit/rng/documentation_software.html

MATEC Web of Conferences **125**, 02019 (2017) DOI: 10.1051/matecconf/201712502019
CSCC 2017

Measurement of four-pane building window filled with a PCM

Martin Kolacek[1*]

[1]*Tomas Bata University in Zlin, Faculty of Applied Informatics, Department of Automation and control Engineering, Nad Stranemi 4511, Zlin, Czech Republic.*

Abstract. The transparent building element filled with Phase change materials (PCMs) represent an innovative solution that can achieve thermal comfort in buildings lowering the cooling and heating demand. There are many different PCMs which are used in the building element. Salt hydrates can absorb a large amount of energy and have properties similar to water. Nevertheless, these materials have a tendency to supercool (supercooling effect) and to incongruent melt. This paper reports the results of the measurement specific four-pane window filled with a PMCs. Thermal properties of the window were tested in the climate simulator where the climatic conditions were dynamically controlled. The measurement confirmed high thermal inertia of the window and also reducing heat transfer through the window.

1 Introduction

There has been an increasing interest in research carried out the thermal energy storage technologies like Phase Change Materials (PCMs). PCMs enhance the energy efficiency of buildings because they can store, release or absorb a large amount of heat or cold in the small temperature range. These materials can stabilize temperature fluctuations and reduce overheating in the room.

PCMs are divided into the different groups depending on the material structure, paraffin, salt hydrates, fatty acids, polyethylene glycols etc. Each material has own advantages and limitations. Paraffin and fatty acids present no supercooling effect, low hysteresis and they are more stable than salt hydrate which can present formation of sediment [1, 9].

In recent years PCMs are applied into transparent envelope components. These building components can reduce temperature fluctuation and they are also able to release solar radiation. Additionally [2] investigated experimentally the temperature fluctuation of the interior surface and the heat entered the building, where they used PCM based on paraffin in windows. Salt hydrates are also used in transparent components as describes [3]. The transparent element can absorb visibly and also invisible radiation of the solar radiation spectrum and can convert into heat. The light transmittance of water agrees with the sensitivity curve of the human eye. Due to the fact, PCMs which contain water are selected for transparent building element [4].

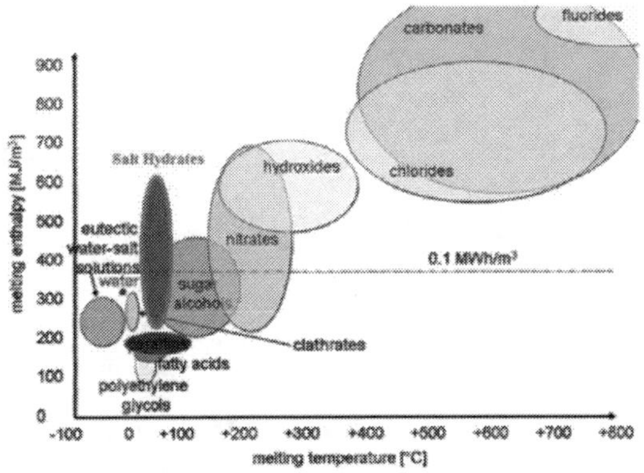

Figure 1 Types of PCM and their melting temperature [9]

Each of PCM has different physical properties. The PCMs used for transparent building elements are described in [5]. The authors [3] used a salt hydrate PCM inside the transparent window element. Calcium chloride hexahydrate was used as a PCM which was used in the window cavity in the polycarbonate container. Salt hydrates contain salts with a large and defined amount of crystal water. These materials are crystalline structures in which molecules of one type are enclosed in the crystal lattice of another [1, 9]. Salt hydrates consist of two components water and salt, there can be a problem with phase separation. That problem is known as an incongruent melting. The incongruent melting is caused released water of crystallization process, salts are not able to dissolve all the phase present and due to density difference, the lower salts settles down at the bottom of a cavity [8].

Supercooling effect is a state when PCM do not solidify upon cooling below the melting temperature, but a PCM starts crystallization when the temperature of the

* Corresponding author: kolacek@fai.utb.cz

PCM which is well below the melting temperature is reached [9]. In the study [7], experimental results confirmed supercooling tendencies of calcium chloride hexahydrate ($CaCl_2.6H_2O$). Nevertheless, salt hydrates contain nucleating agents which improve nucleating properties and also increase the rate of crystal growth [4]. Nucleating agents can decrease supercooling effect from 20°C to 5°C as is described in [4]. Carbon nanofibers, cooper, titanium oxide, potassium sulfate and borax are appropriate nucleating agents as is shown in [12].

PCM as the transparent building envelope has been studied [3]. They used the PCM window panel which contained polycarbonate containers where the PCM was placed. Due to this technology, the PCM showed high thermal inertia and the temperature difference caused by the non-linear behavior of the PCM. New technology applies the PCM inside the whole space of the window cavity and improves thermal mass and ability of the PCM to store energy as declared by the producer. Nevertheless, the technology which placed the PCM inside the whole space of the window cavity can cause incongruent melting and formation of sediment.

In this article, we will be analyzed thermal inertia of the PCM window, crystallization process and also we will try to verify the possibilities of formation the sediment.

2 Methods

The measurement was performed on four-pane glazing system incorporating the PCM. Figure 2 shows the structure of four-pane window with a specific PCM. The prismatic glass is placed in the first window cavity. This element reflects high-angle solar radiation in summer and transmits low-angle in winter. The prismatic glass can control solar radiation over the whole year. The second cavity of the window contains Krypton gas and the third cavity contains the PCM. The PCM is Calcium chloride hexahydrate which is placed inside the whole space of the window cavity. This PCM has many properties similar to water, high latent heat and thermal conductivity equal to that of water 0,5 $W/m^{-1}K^{-1}$ in the liquid phase [4]. The melting point of the PCM is around 28°C.

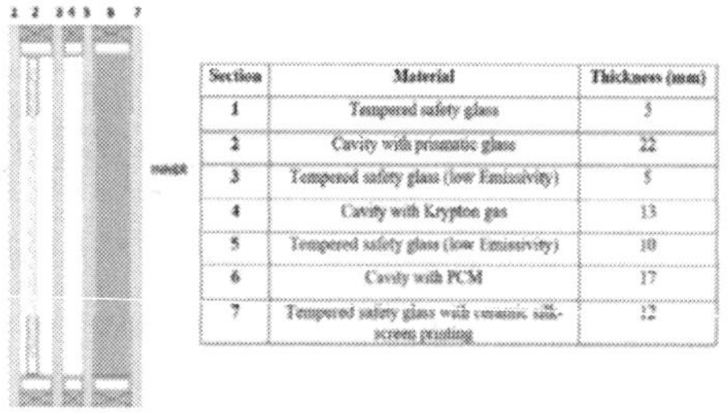

Section	Material	Thickness (mm)
1	Tempered safety glass	5
2	Cavity with prismatic glass	22
3	Tempered safety glass (low Emissivity)	5
4	Cavity with Krypton gas	13
5	Tempered safety glass (low Emissivity)	10
6	Cavity with PCM	17
7	Tempered safety glass with ceramic silk-screen printing	12

Figure 2 Structure of Four-pane building window with the PCM - Calcium chloride hexahydrate

2.1. Instrumentation

Temperatures were measured by thermocouples in four positions on each side of the window panel. Heat flows were measured on the both sides of the window. The thermal imager was used for the temperature stratification. It was important to cover the thermocouple from direct radiation. The aluminum shield covers all thermocouples.

In this work, measurements have been performed on the glazing system including the PCM using a climatic chamber. The climatic chamber is a device in which the climatic conditions on both sides of a glazing component can be dynamically controlled in the temperature range -20°C to +50°C. The climatic chamber is made up of two chambers (indoor and outdoor) separated by the partition wall. Due to the fact that the chamber is compensated, we can control heat transfer only through the partition wall. The partition wall is 20 cm wide and the value of the thermal transmittance is 0,13 $W.m^{-2}.K^{-1}$.

Figure 3 The PCM window panel placed in the partition wall of the calorimetric chamber

Figure 3 shows the window inside the calorimetric chamber where the window is installed in the partition wall.

3 Results

3.1 Surface temperature measurement

The measurement performed in three test series were carried out with the high air temperature in the outdoor chamber. Table 1 shows the climatic conditions of the calorimetric chamber, the duration of each cycle, the outdoor and indoor air temperature in the calorimetric chamber.

Table 1 Test cycle descriptions

Test	Outdoor air temperature [°C]	Indoor air temperature [°C]	Duration [hours]
1	34	21	3
2	34	21	8
3	34	21	9

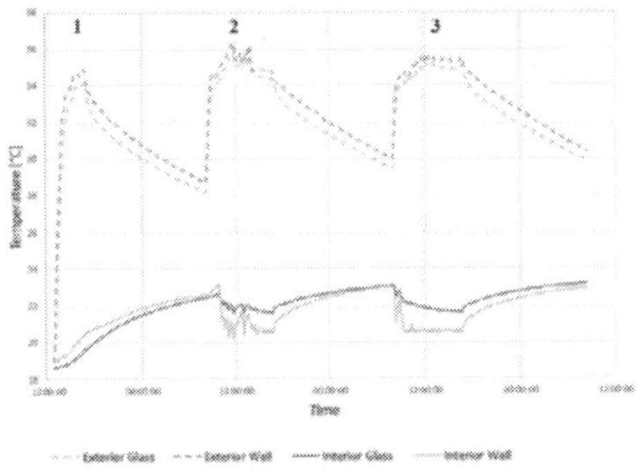

Figure 4 Surface temperature plots for test series. Exterior temperature was 34°C and interior temperature was 21°C

As can be seen in Figure 4, the thermal inertia of the window is very high. Nevertheless, it was confirmed on the third cycle which took 9 hours. Thermal storage of the latent heat was activated when the PCM start melting. It is possible to verify that the Interior Glass temperature (blue curve) decreases lower than the temperature of Interior Wall (yellow curve). The latent heat of fusion of the PCM was activated. Nevertheless, the duration of the test cycle could be higher because the PCM did not melt all over.

3.2 Heat radiation on the exterior surface

The solar radiation cannot be applied in the climate simulator. However, it was applied the infrared heater which produces a maximum radiation level of 300 W/m². The heater was placed with the distance of the window sample of 20 cm. The air gap reduced overheating of the exterior surface. The aim of this experiment was to simulate a high surface temperature on the exterior of the window.

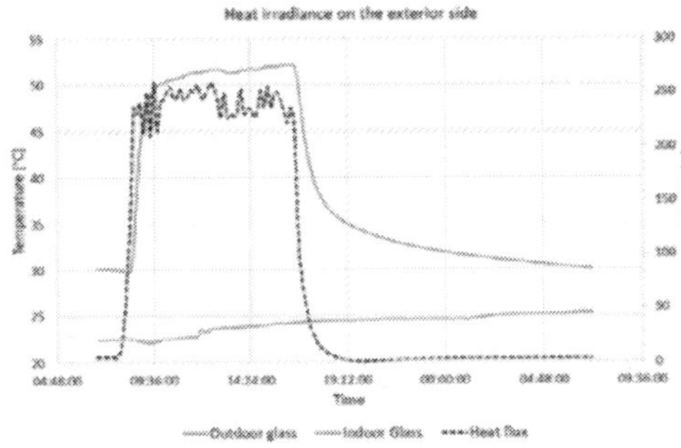

Figure 5 Measurement of heat radiation on the exterior side of the PCM window panel

Figure 5 shows the results of measurement the heat irradiance on the exterior side of the PCM window. The exterior surface temperature achieved 52°C and heat flow was 250 W/m² on the exterior side for 7 hours. When the infrared heater was turn off the surface temperature of exterior side decreased very slowly. The surface temperature on interior achieved only 25°C. The experiment confirmed very high thermal inertia and also high storage capacity.

During testing infrared heater the PCM completely melted. After that, we evaluated thermal behavior of the PCM when the outside temperature decreased up to -15°C in outdoor part of the climatic chamber. The melting process confirmed the formation of sediment that created at the bottom of the window cavity. The sediment and also the non-linear behavior of the PCM layer caused temperature differences on the surface of the window. It was important to measure the whole surface temperature of the window using a thermal imager. As can be seen in Figure 6, the 3D thermogram shows releasing of storage heat from the window. The air temperature was -15°C in outdoor and the air temperature was 21°C in indoor, meanwhile, the surface temperature on the interior of the window was almost 25°C.

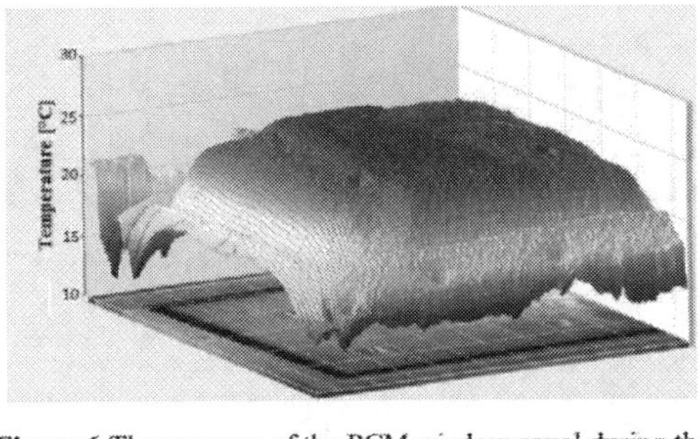

Figure 6 Thermogram of the PCM window panel during the crystallization process.

The crystallization process also confirmed supercooling tendencies of calcium chloride hexahydrate. The PCM started to crystalize when the temperature achieved 24°C. However, the melting point of the PCM is 29°C.

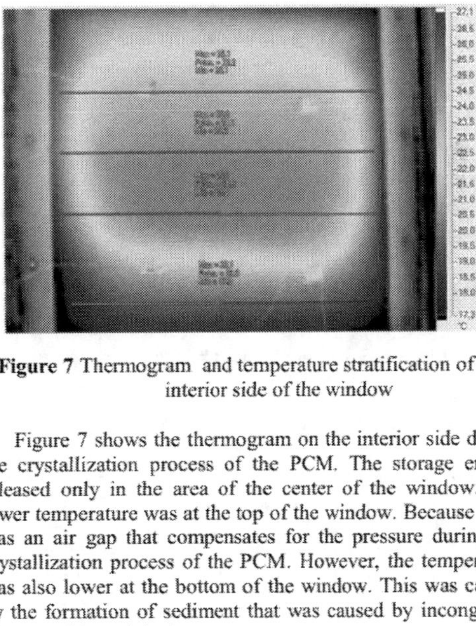

Figure 7 Thermogram and temperature stratification of the interior side of the window

Figure 7 shows the thermogram on the interior side during the crystallization process of the PCM. The storage energy released only in the area of the center of the window. The lower temperature was at the top of the window. Because there was an air gap that compensates for the pressure during the crystallization process of the PCM. However, the temperature was also lower at the bottom of the window. This was caused by the formation of sediment that was caused by incongruent melting of the salt hydrate.

DOI: 10.1051/matecconf/201712502019

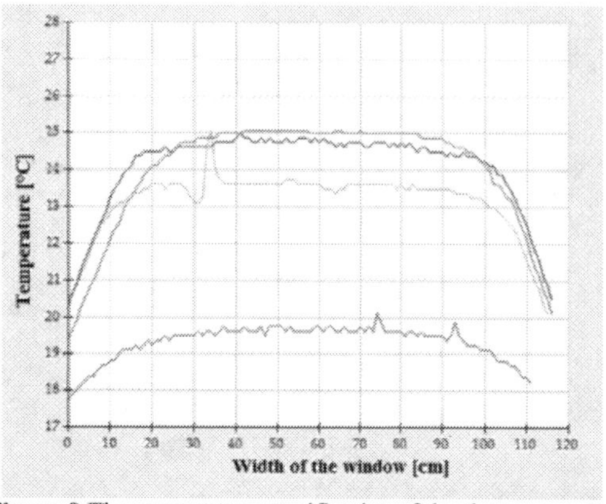

Figure 8 The temperature stratification of the thermogram in Figure 7

As can be seen in Figure 8, the temperature difference was 5°C between the sediment and the surrounding window area. The red curve represents the temperature on the sediment at the bottom of the window panel. These salts can not melt again enough and the sediment grows during repeated melting cycles. Calcium Chloride hexahydrate should be placed in a smaller volume where the incongruent melting would not occur.

The previous technology used the polycarbonate containers in which the PCM was placed. These containers improved the melting cycle of calcium chloride hexahydrate and the formation of sediment was minimized.

Conclusion

The aim of this paper has been to measure the thermal properties of the specific window panel which contained salt hydrates as a PCM. The window panel was tested with the high temperature of the exterior side. These tests were made at the different duration of each test. The infrared heater simulated high heat flow on the exterior side where it was evaluated melting process and subsequently crystallization process.

The limitation of this study is given by the infrared heater which was not used as a simulator of solar radiation but only to heat the exterior side. The results confirmed very high thermal inertia and also the high non-linear behavior of the PCM layer.

The continuation of this work will be to determine the thermal transmittance of the window panel and also it will be evaluated the window panel in the simulation module.

Acknowledgments

This work was supported by the Ministry of Education, Youth and Sports of the Czech Republic within the National Sustainability Programme project No.LO1303(MSMT-7778/2014), by the European Regional Development Fund under the project CEBIA-Tech No.CZ.1.02/2.1.00/03.0089 and also by the Internal Grant Agency of Tomas Bata University in Zlín under the project No. IGA/CebiaTech/2017/002.

References

1. de Gracia, Alvaro and Luisa F. Cabeza. (2015). "Phase Change Materials and Thermal Energy Storage for Buildings." Energy and Buildings 103: 414-419.
2. Li, Shuhong, Gaofeng Sun, Kaikai Zou, and Xiaosong Zhang. (2016). "Experimental Research on the Dynamic Thermal Performance of a Novel Triple-Pane Building Window Filled with PCM." Sustainable Cities and Society **27**: 15-22.
3. Grynning, Steinar, Francesco Goia, Egil Rognvik, and Berit Time. (2013). "Possibilities for Characterization of a PCM Window System using Large Scale Measurements." International Journal of Sustainable Built Environment **2** (1): 56-64.
4. Fokaides, Paris A., Angeliki Kylili, and Soteris A. Kalogirou. (2015). "Phase Change Materials (PCMs) Integrated into Transparent Building Elements: A Review." Materials for Renewable and Sustainable Energy **4** (2).
5. Giovannini, Luigi, Francesco Goia, Verso, Valerio R M Lo, and Valentina Serra. (2017). "Phase Change Materials in Glazing: Implications on Light Distribution and Visual Comfort. Preliminary Results." Energy Procedia **111:** 357-366.
6. Tyagi, V. V. and D. Buddhi. (2008). "Thermal Cycle Testing of Calcium Chloride Hexahydrate as a Possible PCM for Latent Heat Storage." Solar Energy Materials and Solar Cells **92** (8): 891-899
7. Taylor, Robert A., Naomi Tsafnat, and Alex Washer. (2016). "Experimental Characterisation of Sub-Cooling in Hydrated Salt Phase Change Materials." Applied Thermal Engineering **93**: 935-938.
8. Simon Furbo. *Heat Storage with an Incongruently Melting Salt Hydrate as Storage Medium Based on the Extra Water Principle*. (1980). Meddelelse Nr. 108. Technical university of Denmark.
9. Mehling, Harald and Luisa F. Cabeza. (2008). *Heat and Cold Storage with PCM: An Up to Date Introduction into Basics and Applications*. Berlin ; Heidelberg: Springer. ISBN :978-3-540-68556-2.
10. Gao, D., Deng T. (2013). "Energy storage: Preparations and physicochemical properties of solid-liquid Phase change materials for thermal energy storage". Materials and processes for energy: communicating current research and technological developments. Energy Book Series **1**. ISBN: 978-84-939843-7-3.
11. Garg H.P., Mullick S.C., Bhargava A.K. *Solar thermal energy storage*. D,Reidel Publishing Company. Dordrecht. Holland. (1985). ISBN-13 :978-94-040-8841-1. DOI :10.1007 :978-94-009-5301-7.
12. Chiu, Justin NingWei, Viktoria Martin, and Fredrik Setterwall. "A Review of Thermal Energy Storage Systems with Salt Hydrate Phase Change Materials for Comfort Cooling.". 11th International Conference on Thermal Energy Storage, Effstock, June 14-17, (2009), Stockholm, Sweden.

DOI: 10.1051/matecconf/201712502020

Active damping of multidimensional mechanic systems

Zdeněk Úředníček [1,*], and *Jaroslav* Maloch[2]
[1]Department of Automation and Control, Tomas Bata University in Zlin, Jižní Svahy, Nad Stráněmi 4511, 760 05, Zlin, Czech Republic
[2]Department of Production Engineering, Tomas Bata University in Zlin, Vavrečkova 275,760 01 Zlin, Czech Republic

Abstract. At many motion control tasks, the problem of oscillations existence in multidimensional system with limited motion control and imperfect or complicated state quantities measurement possibility exists. Paper describes active damping simple possibility of these type systems and by two-dimensional system physical model shows active damping possibility also with indirect state quantities measurement option.

1 Introduction

This paper goal is to introduce some pieces of knowledge relevant to active damping of mechanical systems with more degree of freedom with limited action interventions' possibilities and limited or complicated quantities measurement possibility. This problem often occurs at different mechanical systems motion control types serving as optical (surveillance) or other systems porter, which depend on effector systems positional state accuracy, and when actuators functions in some generalized coordinates only.

As such system example can be cameras porter, laser scanning system porter created from no ideally stiff bodies, weapons porter system with uncontrolled projectiles, but also manipulator with no ideally stiff arms for exact assembly application, not to mention, for invasive medicine application.

2 Description of system with one degree of freedom and its active damping principle

For linear system from Fig.1, where force f(t) is created by actuator according to Fig.2 reads:

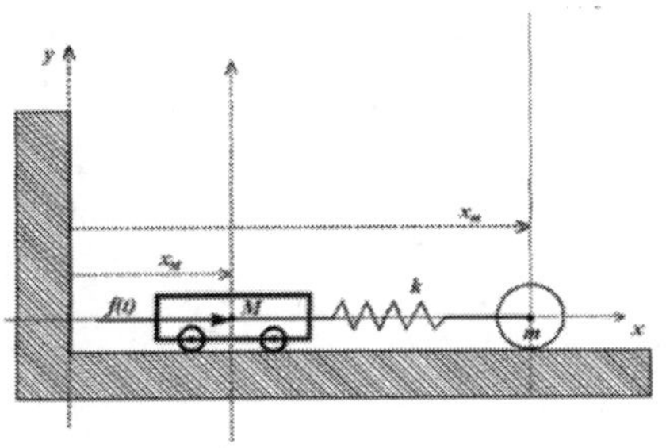

Fig. 1. Active damping principle of system with one degree of freedom.

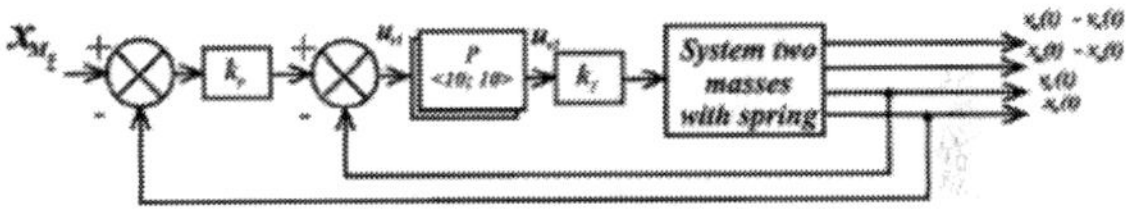

Fig. 2. Masse M cascade position control.

$$f(t)=k_f\cdot\left\{k_{pv}\cdot\left[\overbrace{k_p\cdot(x_{Mž}-x_M)}^{u_{r1}}-1/200\cdot v_M\right]\right\}= \quad (1)$$

$$=k_f\cdot k_{pv}\cdot k_p\cdot x_{Mž}-k_f\cdot k_{pv}\cdot k_p\cdot x_M-\frac{k_f\cdot k_{pv}}{200}\cdot v_M$$

and for state model reads:

$$\frac{d}{dt}\begin{bmatrix}v_m-v_M\\x_m-x_M\\v_M\\x_M\end{bmatrix}=\begin{bmatrix}0 & -\frac{k(M+m)}{M\cdot m} & +\frac{1}{200M}\cdot k_f\cdot k_{pv} & \frac{1}{M}\cdot k_f\cdot k_{pv}\cdot k_p\\1 & 0 & 0 & 0\\0 & \frac{k}{M} & -\frac{1}{200M}\cdot k_f\cdot k_{pv} & -\frac{1}{M}\cdot k_f\cdot k_{pv}\cdot k_p\\0 & 0 & 1 & 0\end{bmatrix}\cdot\begin{bmatrix}v_m-v_M\\x_m-x_M\\v_M\\x_M\end{bmatrix}+ \quad (2)$$

$$+\begin{bmatrix}-\frac{1}{M}\cdot k_f\cdot k_{pv}\cdot k_p\\0\\\frac{1}{M}\cdot k_f\cdot k_{pv}\cdot k_p\\0\end{bmatrix}\cdot x_{Mž}$$

$$c^T=[0\ \ 0\ \ 0\ \ 1]$$

If mass **m** is „extended" to **1m** in the positive direction and reference value $x_{M_ž}=0$, then after mass **m** releasing, the regulators in cascade will ensure almost mass **M** perfect still stand. Mass **m** after releasing practically oscillates undamped. Mentioned is on Fig.3.

For $M=400$ kg ; $m=1000$ kg ; $k=2.10^5 N/m$; and $k_f=2.10^6 N/1V$; $k_p=3$; $k_{pv}=3$ we obtain system poles

$$s_1=-37.498+i\cdot 209.99$$
$$s_2=-37.498-i\cdot 209.99$$
$$s_3=-0.00183+i\cdot 14.064$$
$$s_4=-0.00183-i\cdot 14.064$$

* Corresponding author: urednicek@fai.utb..cz

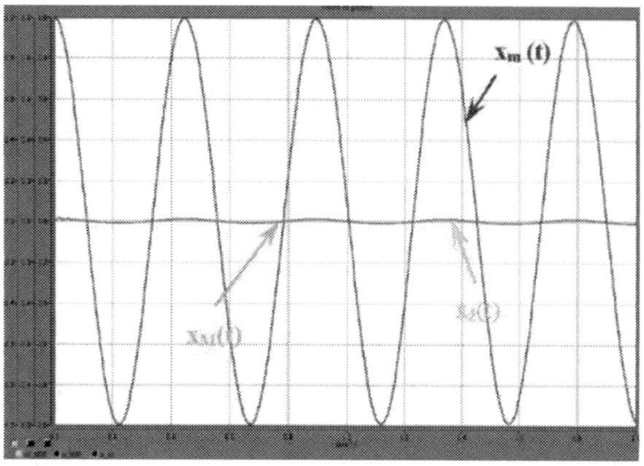

Fig. 3. The mass **m** undamped oscillation and masses **M** stabilization.

If we'll require obtaining from designed complete state regulator new required poles

$$s_1 = -50\ ; s_2 = -50$$
$$s_3 = -15 + i \cdot 15 \quad ,$$
$$s_4 = -15 - i \cdot 15$$

then is possible to create this complete state regulator as

$$\underline{r}^T = [0.010444 \quad 0.008333 \quad 0.011667 \quad -0.875] \quad (3)$$

(see Fig.4.)

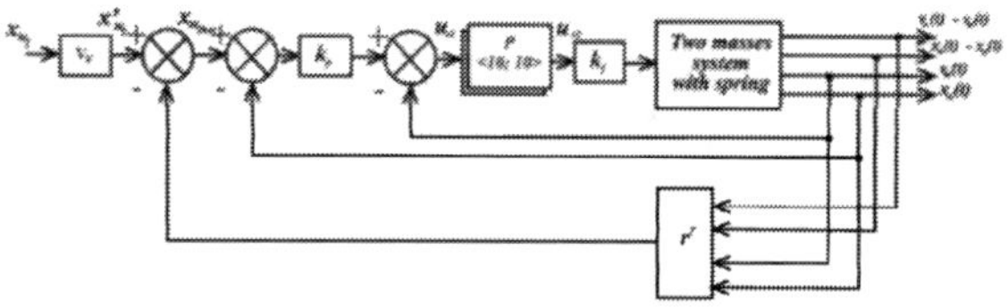

Fig. 4. Complete state regulator.

Control structure from Fig.4. will ensure the system behaviour for the same mass **m** „extending ", according to Fig.5.

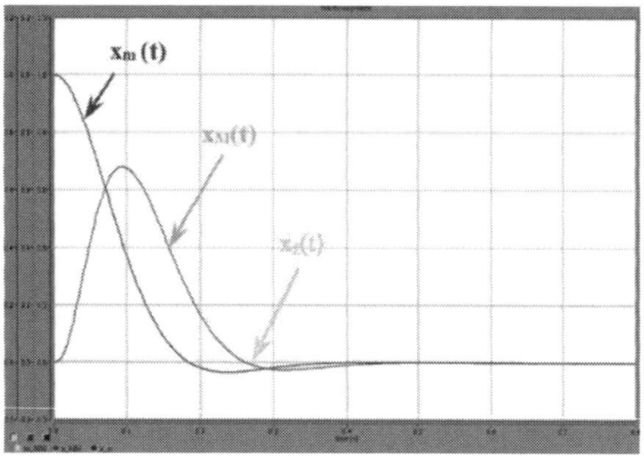

Fig. 5. Complete state regulator.

It is evident that controlled mass **M**, suppresses mass **m** oscillations now.

Fig.6 shows such system response on mass **M** desired position jump $\mathbf{x_{Mž}} = \mathbf{5\ m}$.

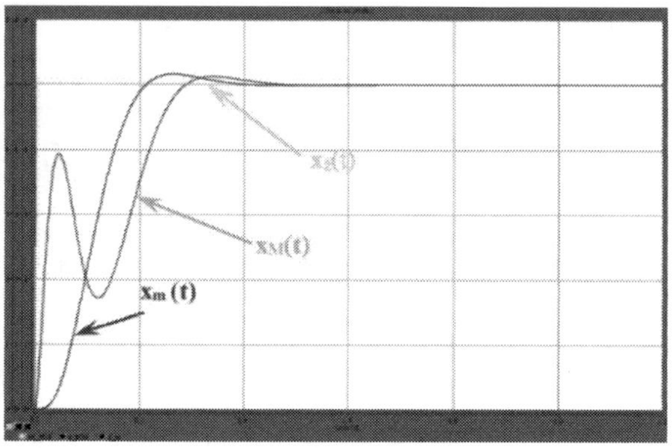

Fig. 6. Response on required **M** position jump with **m** and **M** masses oscillation active damping.

Measurement mass **m** position and speed (eventually $x_m - x_M$ and $v_m - v_M$) presents indeed problem in general.

If we design complete linear observer system with select observer matrix eigenvalues

$$s_1 = -50 + 300 \cdot i$$
$$s_2 = -50 - 300 \cdot i\ ,$$
$$s_3 = -1 + i \cdot 15$$
$$s_4 = -1 - i \cdot 15$$

and we will use only part of reconstructed state quantities from it, then structure from Fig.7 will ensure identical system behaviour as we can see on Fig. 6.

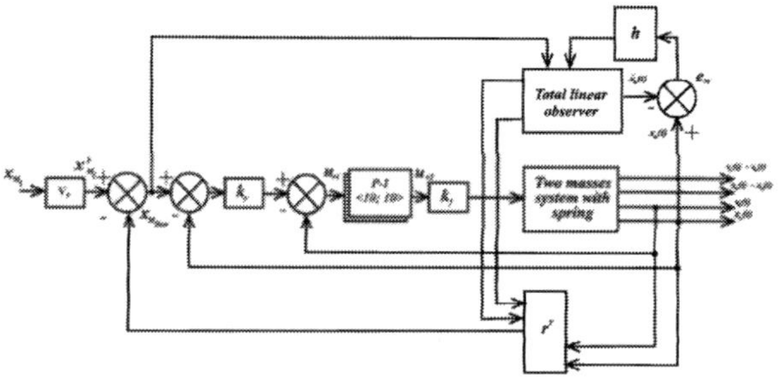

Fig. 7. Active damping with linear observer of **m** and **M** masses.

3 Active damping of mass system with two degree of freedom

Study ordering from Fig. 8. and Fig 9., so system with two degree of freedom (planar motion without friction, normal to gravitation direction), whereas external mass **M** is controlled by e.g. electrohydraulic translational positional servo system producing force **f(t)**. This mass can move only in **x** axis direction.

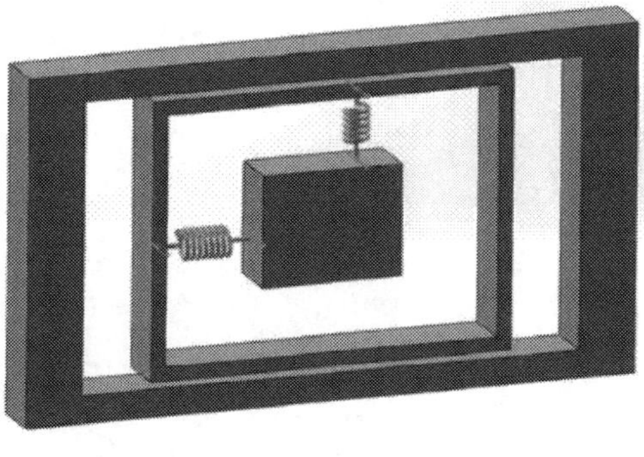

Fig. 8. Ordering of two masses system with two degree of freedom.

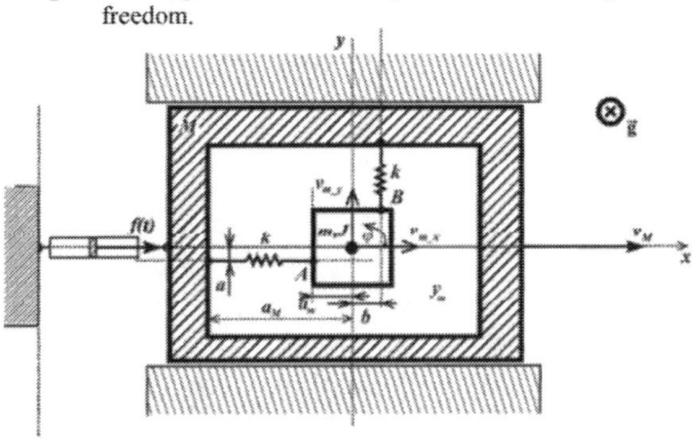

Fig. 9 Two masses system with two degree of freedom scheme.

Inside of this material „frame" is mass **m**, „hung" on two **linear springs** without dissipative damping, whose axes are, in quiescent state (mass **M** and **m** centres of gravity are in identical point, point [0, 0], angle $\varphi = 0$) displaced in a parallel way from coordinates axes. Mass **m** positive rotation direction is counter-clockwise.

Create physical simulation model of given ordering by means of simulation system for multiport simulation physical models DYNAST**

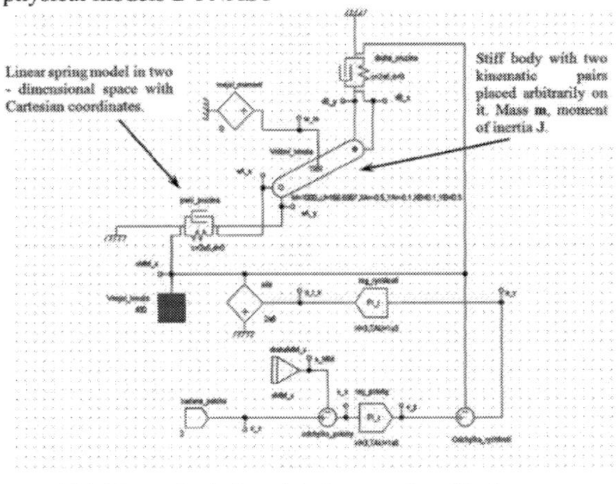

Fig. 10 Multiport physical model of system from Fig.9..

** http://virtual.cvut.cz/dyn/examples/

Graphic model setting is on Fig. 10.

Fig.11. shows system undamped response on mass **M** rerquired position jump in time **t = 0s; x_{Mz}=3m.**

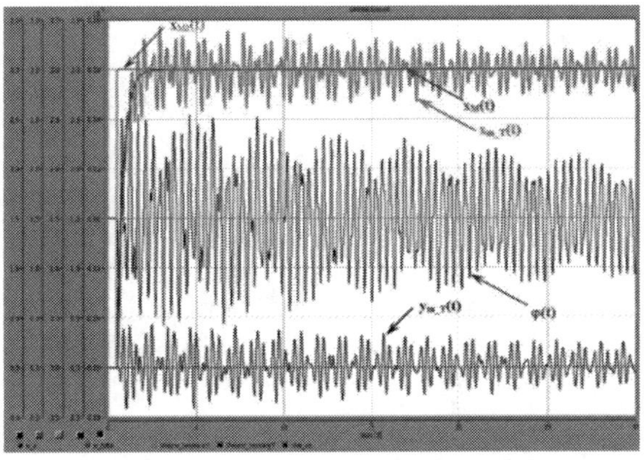

Fig. 11. Undamped system from Fig .9. and Fig.10. behaviour for desired **M** mass jump of position

It's seen that the outer **M** mass fast movement to required position produces not only mass **m** oscillations in **x** axis, but also in **y** axis. In addition, thanks to asymmetric springs bearing, at this mass **m** yawing oscillation happens and successively mechanical energy "flows" between both axes.

With regard of select ordering of both material bodies and their possible motion control way, use only **x** axis for active damping. Employ piece of knowledge from previous one-dimensional case. Design complete state regulator for control and active damping in **x** axis and subsequently propose linear observer for $x_m - x_M$ and $v_{xm} - v_{xM}$ reconstruction. It means we suppose that we are able to measure mass **M** position and speed in **x** axis and differences $x_m - x_M$ and $v_{xm} - v_{xM}$ we will obtain from observer.

Require the same mass **M** jump as in Fig. 11, but with above mentioned active dumping with state regulator and observer in **x** axis. On Fig. 12 is seen that system mechanical behaviour is damped. Not perfectly, because we dumped only part of energy.

3 Conclusions

Paper shows mechanical systems with two degree of freedom active damping simple possibility, applicable in case that the action interventions are available only in one axis. Designed one-dimensional complete state regulator is able, thanks „energy overflow" of unsymmetrical embedded springs, to damp significantly also oscillations of mass, which it is impossible to influence directly by action quantities.

 DOI: 10.1051/matecconf/201712502020

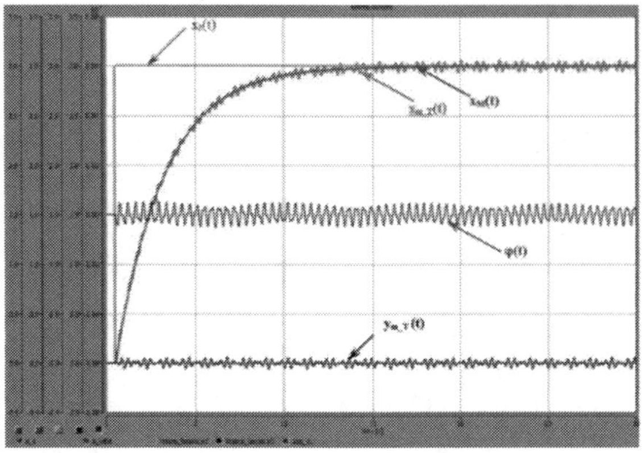

Fig.12. Behaviour of system from Fig .9. and Fig 10. damped in one axis at **M** position desired jump

Regarding to inner mass position and speed complicated measurability (respectively $x_m - x_M$ and $v_{xm} - v_{xM}$) for information about these quantities the linear observer was used.

In the event of two-dimensional model using, eventually with two-dimensional observer it is possible to achieve system complete active damping.

References

1. B. Friedland, B., *McGraw-Hill*, New York (1986)
2. L. Zboray, *Edičné stredisko VŠT v Košiciach* (1985) (In Slovak language)
3. Z. Úředníček, *T. Bata university in Zlin* (in Czech language), (2012)
4. H. A. Darweesh, M. Roushdy , H. M. Ebied, B.M. Elbagoury, *Proceedings of the WSEAS International Conference Mathematical Applications in Science and Mechanics*. (2013)
5. S. Hubalovsky, P. Kadlec, L. Mitrovic, P. Hanzalova, Proceedings of the 3rd International Conference on *Mathematical Models for Engineering Science (MMES '12)*. Paris, France, (2012)
6. http://virtual.cvut.cz/dynast/ (23.2.2017)
7. Z. Úředníček, *International journal of mechanics*, **10**, (2016)
8. Z. Úředníček, R. Drga, *MATEC Web Conf.* **76**, (2016)

MATEC Web of Conferences **125**, 02021 (2017) DOI: 10.1051/matecconf/201712502021
CSCC 2017

Utilization of 3D sensors in robotics

Miroslav Marcaník[1,*], *Michal* Šustek[1], *Pavel* Tomášek[1], and *Roman* Jašek[1]
[1]Tomas Bata University in Zlín, Faculty of Applied Informatics, Nad Stráněmi 4511, 760 05, Zlín, Czech Republic

Abstract. Recently, the interest in development of service robots highly increases. The annual turnover in this area is estimated to a number close to 17 milliard Euro in the past years. The annual turnover could rise to 0.1 billion Euro by 2020 by IFR considering 30 % growth every year. Investments are expected to flow into all areas related to service robotics, mainly into the development of assistant robots for seniors and the handicapped people, health monitoring and surgical robots, robots in agriculture, pilotless drones and helicopters and ground vehicles without a driver. Very promising years seems to be coming for all the new and already existing companies focused on this area with their software and sensor engineers together with producers of important accessories.

1. Introduction

Monitoring is used in various non-engineering applications. Tasks not only of this type are operated by service robots all over the world. Robots are equipped with a camera system for these purposes. The data from cameras are recorded and transmitted to the standpoint of an operator. Service robots can be favourably utilized wherever the environment is dangerous for a man or difficult to reach. It could be for example searching for a dangerous material, security purposes, monitoring complicated areas, undersea research.

Basic terms related to robotics, taxonomy, classification of robots and examples of complex robots are presented in the following section. The next section is focused on utilization of sensors, sensorial systems and how they work. In the last section the principle of 3D scanning of objects in free space is described together with an application in a real project.

2. Robotics

Robotics is a modern multidisciplinary field including mechanics, electronics, control theory, measurement techniques, artificial intelligence and other disciplines. Currently, robotics is mainly connected with the area of automatization. The first appliance called as a robot was produced at the beginning of the twentieth century. The word of robot is known already since 1920. Čapek brothers (Czech writers) created this word in their book with the name of R.U.R. A robot represents a non-biological artificial imitation a man [1].

2.1. Classification of robots

The robots can be divided by several different aspects.

Dividing by mobility:

- Stationary – they cannot move from one place to another (manipulators in the industry, for instance),
- Mobile – they are able to move (satellites or vehicles in the aerospace).

Mobile robots can be divided by several other criteria [2]:

- Remotely controlled – they are controlled by an operator, who has a visual information about the space around such a robot,
- Autonomous – they are supposed to solve tasks independently, for instance line tracking, ability to react on obstructions in their way, ability to move in an unknown area.

Moreover, robots can be divided by the environment in which will the robot operate:

- On the land – wheel and full-track vehicles.
- In the water – explorational submarines, robotic fish,
- In the air – quadcopters, drones, RC models, robotic birds,
- In the aerospace (outer space) – service robots, satellites.

Dividing by the purpose:

- Manipulatory – for manipulations with objects,
- Assembly – as a part of complex assembling lines,
- Service – for repairs and maintenance at places out of simple reach,
- Inspectional – for controlling of a state of an observed phenomenon,
- Explorational – for exploring of an unknown area,
- Military – pyrotechnical robots, drones,
- Medical – manipulators, laser scalpels,
- For fun – quadcopters, drones, RC models,

Dividing by the type of a running gear:

* Corresponding author: marcanik@fai.utb.cz

- Wheel,
- Full-track,
- Walking,
- Crawling,
- Climbing,
- Hybrid,
- Intelligent.

2.2. Examples of robots

ASIMO – Honda (mobile – autonomous – for walking on the land – medical aims): It is probably the best publicly known robot. It was introduced in 2000. ASIMO was constructed to imitate a human being and thus to replace him in a common human interaction. Therefore this is a humanoid. ASIMO could server as companion for elderly or ill people. It can react to a human behaviour and speech. It is not applicable in exacting environment or a terrain (compared to robots from Boston Dynamics). ASIMO is 130 cm high. It weighs 50 kg. Its maximal speed is 5.7 km/h, 2.7 km/h normally. ASIMO has 57 degrees of freedom (DOF) totally. What is very interesting about ASIMO is the fact that ASIMO can be controlled by a special head cap. Thoughts (electrical charges) are captured by sensors on the cap and then the cap transmits the signals. These signals can control the movement of the robot. Overall, operation of such a robot is very energetically exhaustive because there is a need of an actuator for every DOF. Therefore it can operate only one hour on its internal battery [2].

Fig. 1. ASIMO [2].

Mini AERCam – NASA (mobile – autonomous – for outer space – flying – inspectional/service): This robotic camera was developed by NASA in 2005 for inspections in the outer space. It is a freely flying robot equipped with 12 nozzles for compressed gas allowing movements and rotations in all directions. It is able to orientate in complex three dimensional space autonomously. It has a spherical shape. The diameter is 190 mm and it weighs 4.5kg [2].

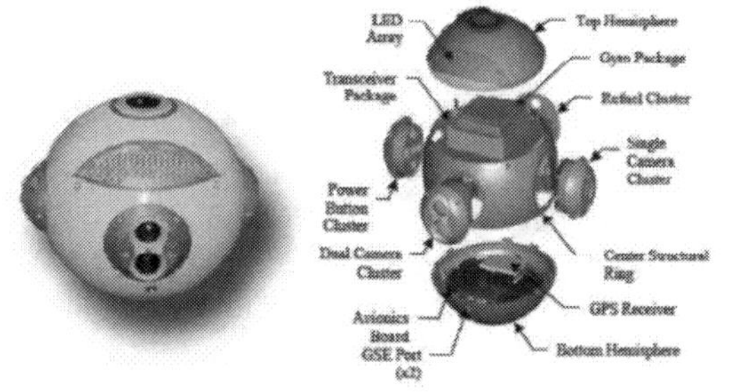

Fig. 2. Mini AERCam [2].

ATLAS – Boston Dynamics (mobile – autonomous – on the land – walking – multifunctional): Atlas is highly mobile humanoid specially constructed for exacting terrain. It was developed by Boston Dynamics with the support of Defence Advanced Research Projects Agency (DARPA). It can climg, run, manipulate and interact with a surrounding environment. It is 180 cm high. It was introduced in 2013. Its arms contain joints which allows ATLAS to use common human tools in its hands. Atlas is prepared to work in dangerous areas in which a man cannot survive. Therefore ATLAS is able to use instruments, manipulate, work with electrical appliances and perform many other similar tasks. It is equipped with a high number of sensors, stereo camera, and laser range-finder. It has implemented 28 DOF. ATLAS operates on a cable connected to an external power source [2].

Fig. 3. ATLAS [2].

An Unmanned Aerial Vehicle (UAV) or also a drone is a plane without crew which can be controlled remotely or fly autonomously using programmed flying plans or using more complex dynamic autonomous systems. These aeroplanes have a common military utilization. They can explore and also attack. They can also serve in some specific civil tasks (for example in fire fighting, monitoring used by police or for exploration of some terrain) [3].

DOI: 10.1051/matecconf/201712502021

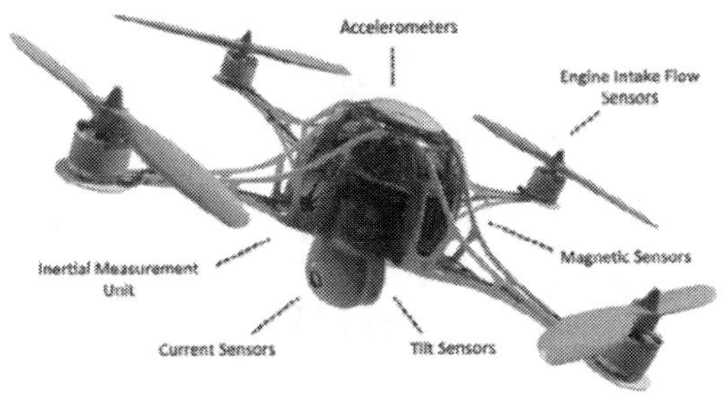

Fig. 4. Model UAV [3].

3. Sensors

Sensors are elements, which produce input block measuring chain, then this chain is in direct contact with the measured medium. Other labels of sensors are for example sensor, detector, converter, and scanner [4].

Sensors could be ordered by usability into the following categories:

- For measuring quantities,
- For physical principles,
- For the measurement environment,
- For signals according to their transformation,
- For Manufacturing Technology.

Changes of measuring quantities are scan over sensitive element mostly known as receptor, then subsequent evaluation in the sensor circuit (analog/digital converter), where the measured value is converted mostly into electric impulse, which could be processed or could be used directly as the output quantity. Principle of sensor is shown at Figure 5.

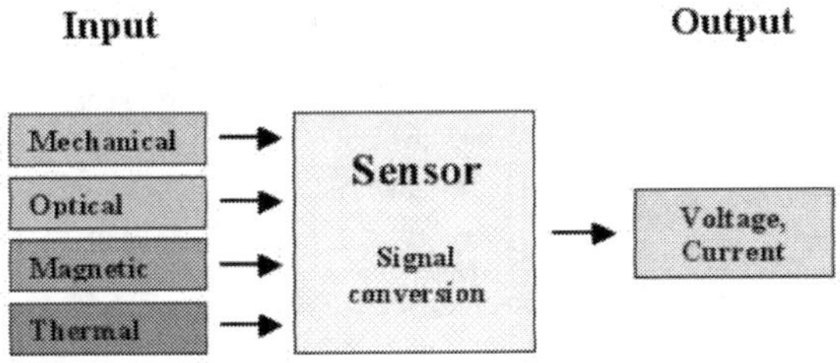

Fig. 5. Principle of a sensor [6].

First smart sensor (1978) Beckenbridge and Husson, was defined as: Smart sensor contains functions for processing measured data, automatic correction measured data, and it could automatically detect and eliminate abnormal and wrong values. It also contains a set of algorithms, which allows to respond on changes of external conditions.

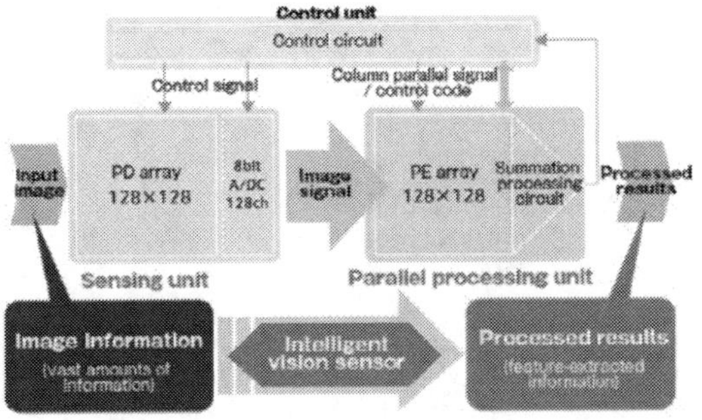

Fig. 6. The principle of an intelligent sensors [6].

3D sensor can be defined as a measuring unit which senses an object in 3D space or occupies angles X, Y and Z. 3D sensors operate on the principle of two or more video cameras, or for engaging the third dimension may be used most of the laser scanner. This makes possible a whole or only a certain part transform into 3D and 3D scene then analyses and selects the best way to handle [5].

From the above description 3D sensors can be divided into two basic categories by using various sensors. They are active and passive sensing:

- Active scanning uses laser/camera, additional information or other auxiliary devices. The concept of active sensing is very closely linked to the concept of "creating depth map".
- Passive versus active scan uses only one sensor – the camera/laser.

Since it is an improved sensor it can be categorized in a similar 3D sensors. A general allocation can be seen in Fig. 6 [5].

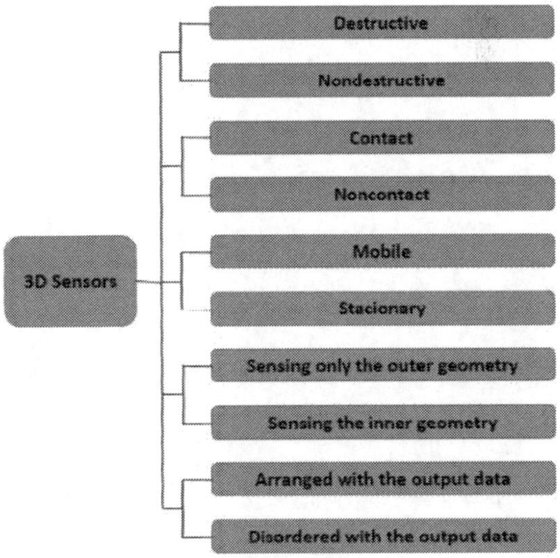

Fig. 7. Distribution of 3D sensors [5].

4. Principles of sensorial systems

Acquisition data about a space from a sensor and its processing using some tools is the main purpose of a sensorial system. Sensors providing the important data about a space:

- Photo sensors – measuring the intensity of a light, or the sensitivity of an optical device.
- Acoustic sensors – measuring of the sensitivity and frequency range of a sound.
- Mechanosensor – mechanical interactions.
- Chemosensors – detecting chemicals.
- Thermo sensors – they use thermistors and other thermoelectric sensors for measuring of the temperature.

Generally, sensorial systems can be divided into two basic groups. There are inner and outer systems. The outer systems provide data about the outer environment and the inner systems provide data only about inner status and parts of a robot. The following actions take place during scanning:

- Localization of objects,
- Studying properties of objects,
- Studying properties of the image of an environment,
- Measuring status of accumulators,
- Orientation in an environment.

5. Principles of 3D scanning

3D sensors are coming to the forefront and are more and more commonly used in all possible sectors because of the development of technology and the increasing demand and popularity of virtual reality. Some examples include construction, architecture, industrial machinery, navigation, etc. Perhaps in all applications, it is necessary to have coordinates in a 3D space. The scanning is dependent on the position of the object, its speed, colour, shape, and angle of rotation. The advent of modern technology and optics, which is still used for 2D scanning, expanded to methods for measuring the third dimension. Today, there are mainly two methods of measuring. The first one is a triangulation and the second is a light interference. The gradual development of technologies brings about the third method. This method is called Time of Light (TOF) and uses the knowledge of the speed of light.

5.1. Triangulation

Triangulation is very often used as a method which requires a very complicated structure of the measuring sensor. It is divided into two categories: active triangulation and passive triangulation.

The principle of the active triangulation involves photogrammetric reconstruction of the scanned object. The surface of scanned object is illuminated by the light source and simultaneously scanned by the CCD sensor [7].

The principle of passive triangulation involves photogrammetric reconstruction of the scanned object on the basis of its projection on the sensor surface device. One dimension is lost during projection and it is needed to renew on the basis of a common information from multiple sources [7].

The light signal is transmitted from the laser source to the object. The object reflects the light ray to the camera. The angle of the transmitted ray from the source is constant, but the CCD sensor depending on the spend ray of the dimmed sensor. The connector between the light source and the CCD sensor is called triangulation base (baseline). Thanks to the knowledge of two angles and the length of the triangular base, we can calculate the distance of a point, and then save the coordinates for later calculations and rendering [5].

To mark the surface, the following are used:

- The light beam (1D triangulation),
- Light (2D triangulation),
- Structured light beam (3D triangulation).

Disadvantages:

- Higher purchase price and better facilities,
- Time demands when evaluating the Record,
- The limiting factor may be the memory size and especially the quality of the recording,
- More necessary knowledge of issues,
- Treatment of subjects.

5.2. Interferometry

Interferometry is a method suitable for very precise measurements over a short distance. The principle is based on light interference. The principle can be seen in Figure 6. The light source – the laser – is transmitted through the polarization splitter – a part on the measured object. The reflected signal is combined with polarization ray splitter reference called carrier wave and they may interfere together. The resulting wave interference is given by equation (1) [5]:

$$I(x,y)=|I_1(x,y)|^2+|I_2(x,y)|^2+2|I_1(x,y)||I_2(x,y)|\cos(j_1(x,y)-j_2(x,y)) \quad (1)$$

Disadvantages:

- Technologically intensive production,
- Demanding quantitative interpretation of results,
- Susceptibility to interference.

5.3. Time of light

This is a method that uses the knowledge of the speed of modulated light signal that is emitted from the transmitter and subsequently reflected towards the receiver. The use of this method requires very precise time value. The principle can be seen in Fig. 7. The distance of sensing object can be computed from formula 2, where "t" is the total time from sending a signal to the one more acceptation and "c" is the speed of light (c = 2.998 * 108 m/s) [5].

$$s=\frac{c*t}{2} \quad (2)$$

Disadvantages:

- High-accuracy time measurement required,
- Measurement of a light pulse return is inexact, due to light scattering.
- Difficulty to generate short light pulses with fast rise and fall times.

6. Utilization of triangulation in a real project

The trajectory of a laser ray (using a laser module M-18B532-X-GL, for instance) impacts on objects in a space what is caught by a camera subsystem what is one of the main functional groups of a robot. A robot can contain a colour digital camera (like Go Pro Hero4) with a CMOS sensor positioned in a water and vapour resistant box or coating. The robot could be controlled remotely using a radio frequency 2.4 GHz using approved transmitter and receiver for common outdoor/indoor utilization. The communication will be done using a software programmed (in C#, for instance) providing computations and communication between the robot and an operator.

7. Conclusion

The qualities of 3D sensors became higher thanks to the progress in the modern trends in robotics. Grow in this area increases due to better digitalization, cartography, security and other aspects.

The main goal of this work lies in outlining definitions of basic terms and principles of individual categories of sensors. The authors were focused on global aspects and coping whole systems as complex units. Therefore principles of 3D sensors were described without detailed aspects of low-level technologies. Alternatives of sensors and their further utilization in real life were discussed in this work.

However, the progress in application of 3D sensors and 3D technologies generally is expected to grow more than people usually consider. This statement is based on the research data presented in this paper. The utilization of all the three dimensions (which used to be in seclusion to date) is the main advantage of 3D sensors. The authors guess that traditional 2D sensors will almost entirely vanish and will be replaced with 3D sensors in several years. New sensors will be more expensive but they will worth the money due to their possibilities in the area of visualisation and robotics.

Acknowledgment

This work was supported by the Ministry of Education, Youth and Sports of the Czech Republic within the National Sustainability Programme project No. LO1303 (MSMT-7778/2014) and also by the European Regional Development Fund under the project CEBIA-Tech No. CZ.1.05/2.1.00/03.0089. This work was also supported by Internal Grant Agency of Tomas Bata University under the project No. IGA/FAI/2017/004.

References

[1] L. Kárník, *Practical applications of service robots* (2011)
[2] J. Bartušek, *Mobile device for movement in dangerous environment* (2015)
[3] Ch. Winkler, *Design Technology* [online] (2016)
[4] Sensors & Transducers, **206** (2016)
[5] M. Marcaník, J. Dvorak, *Use of 3D sensors for the protection of critical infrastructure elements and soft targets* (2015)
[6] H. Foell, *MEMS Sensors and Actuators* [online]. (2011)
[7] S.C. Islam, M. Herrmann, R. Beigang, *IRMMW-THz2007* (2007)
[8] P. Skoupý, *3D optical measurement and scanning systems for engineering* (2007)
[9] F. Brunet, *Contributions to Parametric Image Registration and 3D Surface Reconstruction* (2010)
[10] W. Schroeder, K. Martin, B. Lorensen, *Visualization Toolkit: An Object-Oriented Approach to 3D Graphics* (2006)
[11] M. Janková, J. Dvořák, *Mathematics, Information Technologies and Applied Sciences*, (2014)

MATEC Web of Conferences **125**, 02022 (2017) DOI: 10.1051/matecconf/201712502022
CSCC 2017

Multivariate study of spectral data of oils

Hana Vaskova[1,*], and *Martina* Buckova[2]

[1]Tomas Bata University in Zlin, Faculty of Applied informatics, Department of Electronic and Measurements, Zlin, Czech Republic
[2]Tomas Bata University in Zlin, Faculty of Technology, Department of Food Technology, 760 01 Zlin, Czech Republic

Abstract. In this paper the study of structural differences and thermal degradation of edible oils during heating is presented. The study is performed on five types of vegetable oil: extra virgin olive oil, pomace olive oil, sunflower, canola and palm oil. The oils were measured by Raman spectroscopy. This method brings advantages as rapidity, independence on chemicals, provides specific information on chemical composition and structure of material and is able to detect structural changes. For the processing of large data sets multivariate analytical method as Principal component analysis and Cluster analysis are applied to find the patterns within the data. The evaluation of process of thermal degradation is also based on the major decomposition product of oxidized linoleate appearing in spectra via band 1640 cm^{-1}. Mathematically processed data indicate the least effect of heating for olive oils, the greatest degradation and loss of unsaturation for sunflower oil.

1 Introduction

Edible oils are commonly used for preparing many kinds of food and high temperatures are often applied. It is already known that extra virgin oils are more suitable for preparing "cold" meals. Others, mainly refined, are suitable for frying or baking at higher temperature. However, even the edible oils that are relatively thermal resistant should be controlled because of formation of oxidation products. Therefore, the thermal stability of edible oils is a topic of research studies using various methods.

The conventional analytical methods for edible oils quality determination require pre-treatment of samples, reagents and solvents using as well as lab equipment and skills of the lab technicians. That is why new rapid and simple methods are still demanded. Raman spectroscopy seems to be very promising technique combining rapid and relatively simple approach with sensitivity for detection of changes in molecular structure. Moreover, Raman spectra can be obtained via transparent glass or plastic vials and this measurement can be done as on-line analysis and/or by portable Raman instruments.

The objective of this study is to compare different types of edible oils and to explore their thermal stability using Raman spectroscopy. Methods that enable multivariate analysis such as Principal component analysis and Cluster analysis are used for data mining from the large spectral data sets.

2 Vegetable oils

Vegetable oils consist of triglycerides in amount of 95 – 98 %. The rest is formed by minor compounds as carotenes, tocopherols, sterols, squalene and free acids [1, 2]. The triglycerides are composed of fatty acids (FA) with characteristic number of carbon atoms in chain and amount of saturated or unsaturated bonds that are responsible for behaviour of edible oils. The main saturated fatty acids in vegetable oils are considered palmitic acid (C16:0) and stearic acid (C18:0). Oleic acid is the major monounsaturated fatty acid (C18:1). Linoleic acid (C18:2) and linolenic acid (C18:3) are the major polyunsaturated fatty acids. Each type of vegetable oil is characterized by its own specific fatty acids ratio content [2, 3].

Lipids are important and irreplaceable part of the human diet as well as proteins and carbohydrates. The role of lipids in organism is essential. Hence the intake of vegetable oils is very important. Except saturated fatty acids they also contain a substantial proportion of monounsaturated and polyunsaturated fatty acids. The unsaturated fatty acids represent health benefit of edible oils in their consumption, however, also a source of instability. Vegetable oils undergo oxidative degradation that can be caused during storage, technological operation in food production or during frying.

2.1. Thermal degradation

Thermal stress speeds up oxidative processes concerning predominantly polyunsaturated fatty acids as linoleic and linolenic acids according to high double bonds content. The major oxidation products are esters, alcohols, aldehydes, ketones, lactones and hydroxy compounds. Presence of these products strongly affects quality of edible oils (taste and aroma) and their nutritional value.

* Corresponding author: author@e-mail.org

Moreover, many of oxidation products are considered as potentially toxic in relatively low concentration [4]. According to this health risk is necessary to detect formation of oxidative products during oil heating. Some of qualitative changes of vegetable oils can be reflected in Raman spectra.

3 Materials and methods

Raman spectroscopy was used for the study of characteristics of oils and changes occurring during thermal degradation of oils. Obtained spectra were evaluated using multivariate analytical methods – Principal component analysis and Cluster analysis.

3.1. Materials

Five different types of edible oils, four refined and one extra-virgin were used for spectroscopic analysis: extra-virgin olive oil, olive pomace oil, canola, sunflower and palm. All of these oils were purchased from common markets.

At the beginning these oils were measured at lab temperature, later heated for up to 160 ± 5 °C and the temperature was maintained for 5 hours to monitor the thermal degradation process. The amount of 2 litres of each of oils was heated up The first sample of 100 ml was taken right after reaching the temperature of 160 °C other samples after every 30 minutes in the same amount. Raman microscopy measurement followed.

3.2. Raman spectroscopy and instrumentation

Raman spectroscopy provides very specific chemical „fingerprint“ of every single chemical substance in the form of the Raman spectrum. In other words Raman spectroscopy reflects chemical composition and structure of materials what makes the method proper for material identification and study of structural changes. Moreover, considering the advantages of the method, Raman spectroscopy becomes popular and valuable part of laboratories around the world in recent years.

The method is based on Raman scattering - an inelastic scattering resulting from an interaction of a photon and a molecule. Photons of inelastic scattering have slightly changed wavelengths (compared to incident laser photons), that are characteristic for specific bonds in surveyed material. Since most photons are on molecules scattered elastically (Rayleigh scattering without changing the wavelength), it is necessary to filter out of the spectrum of the strongly present wavelength of laser.

Raman spectroscopy brings many advantages as the method is relatively rapid, non-destructive, contactless, usable for measuring through transparent glass or polymeric covering layers or containers, applicable to all states of matter and different forms, without special requirements for sample preparation, usable as in situ analysis. The most often appearing drawback of the method is the fact that Raman scattering is a weak effect. Luminescence as much stronger quantum effect with bigger intensity can overlap Raman spectra and mask spectral information [5, 6].

For the measurement, inVia Basis Raman microscope form Renishaw was used. Raman instrument uses two lasers as light sources: argon ion laser with the excitation wavelength 514 nm and maximum output power of 20 mW and 785 nm NIR diode laser with maximum output power 300mW. Both were tested but more precise results were obtained using NIR laser.

A Leica DM 2500 confocal microscope with the resolution 2μm was coupled to the Raman spectrometer. All measurements were collected with 20 s exposure time and 5 accumulations. The samples were firstly scanned in range 100 to 3200 cm^{-1} with 1 cm^{-1} spectral resolution. After determining the principle peaks the spectral range was reduced approximately to the area 800 - 1800 cm^{-1}.

3.3. Principal component analysis

Raman spectral data are multivariate, since they reflect the composition of material and its structure. Raman peaks are assigned to the vibrations of chemical bonds in surveyed materials. For the evaluation it is advantageous to use multivariate mathematics.

Principal Component Analysis (PCA) is useful and powerful statistical method for analysing data. PCA finds application in various fields from chemistry via neuroscience to computer face recognition, image compression or social studies. Basically it finds and identifies patterns in datasets of high dimension and highlights hidden similarities and differences. It extracts relevant information from confusing data sets finding new variables for creation better imaginable mathematical space.

3.4. Cluster analysis

Cluster analysis (CA) is an explorative analysis offering patterns or structures recognition within the data. The method divides data into groups (clusters) in such a way, that objects in the same group are more similar to each other than to objects from other clusters.

4 Results and discussion

Raman spectral data of 5 different oils exhibit similar distribution of characteristic peaks due to their composition. However, each of oils has various ratios of saturated (SFA), monounsaturated (MUFA), polyunsaturated fatty acids (PUFA) and other components, what affects intensity and Raman shift of bands in spectra. Raman spectra of 5 oils are displayed in Fig. 1. The linear baseline correction and normalization according 1747 cm^{-1} band was applied. Raman band 1747 cm^{-1} (C=O ester carbonyl) was taken as an internal standard for normalization because it does not exhibit any changes in the structure. Essential molecular assignments for the measured spectral range

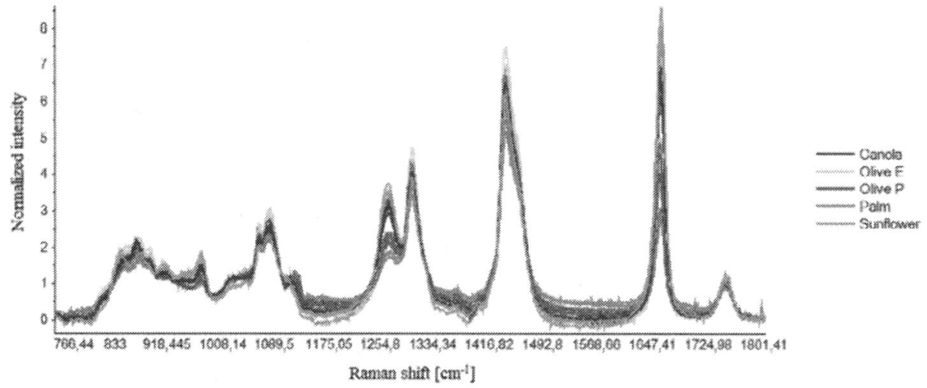

Fig. 1. Raman spectra of five types of vegetable oil, normalized.

are listed in Table 1 and are in accordance with literature [7, 8].

The cluster analysis was performed for the Raman spectra of 5 cold (room temperature before heating) oils. The hierarchical complete linkage based on correlation distance measure was used. There is the dendrogram in Fig. 2 of spectral area 1200 - 1390 cm^{-1}, which refers to bands 1267 cm^{-1} and 1303 cm^{-1}. Intensities of these bands reflect the amounts of saturated and unsaturated fatty acids with straight aliphatic chains and predominantly with 16 or 18 number of carbon atoms in chains. Various types of oils differ in the proportion of these components, what can be used for their differentiation.

The relative intensity ratio of the bands at 1265 cm^{-1} and 1303 cm^{-1} is usually used to determine the degree of unsaturation in the oil [9]. Two olive oils are the most similar. This group is enlarged by palm oil what can be affected by the similar slight higher content of palmitic and stearic acids. Second group consist of sunflower and canola oil. In comparison to the first group, sunflower and canola oils have rather higher amounts polyunsaturated fatty acids, mainly linoleic acid.

The context of saturated and unsaturated FA in oils is clearly visible also in the spectra in Fig. 1. for bands 1267 cm^{-1} and 1658 cm^{-1} (saturated) and 1303 cm^{-1} and 1442 cm^{-1} (unsaturated FA). Fig. 3 represents the dendrogram of spectral area1200 - 1800 cm^{-1}. Here, the layout within clusters is alike, but the difference is in worse correlation, especially for the connection of palm oil to the olive oils. In this area spectral characteristic are more complex what affects the pattern creation.

Table 1 Assignments for Raman bands.

Raman shift [cm^{-1}]	Molecular vibration
1267	=C-H symmetric rocking
1303	CH_2 in-plane twist
1442	CH_2 scissoring
1526	C=C stretching of carotenoids (extra virgin oils)
1640	C=C *trans, trans* 2,4 decadienal
1658	C=C cis double bond stretching
1747	C=O ester-carbonyl stretching

Thermal degradation was studied on all heated samples. In Raman spectra can be seen formation of the degradation product at 1640 cm^{-1} assigned to *trans, trans*-2,4-decadienal. It is one of the oxidative products. to the C=C stretching vibration in conjugated system [10]. The dependence of normalized intensities of band 1640 cm^{-1} on time is shown in Fig. 4. Intensities were acquired from fitting using normalization via 1747 cm^{-1} band and subtraction of the intensity at the room

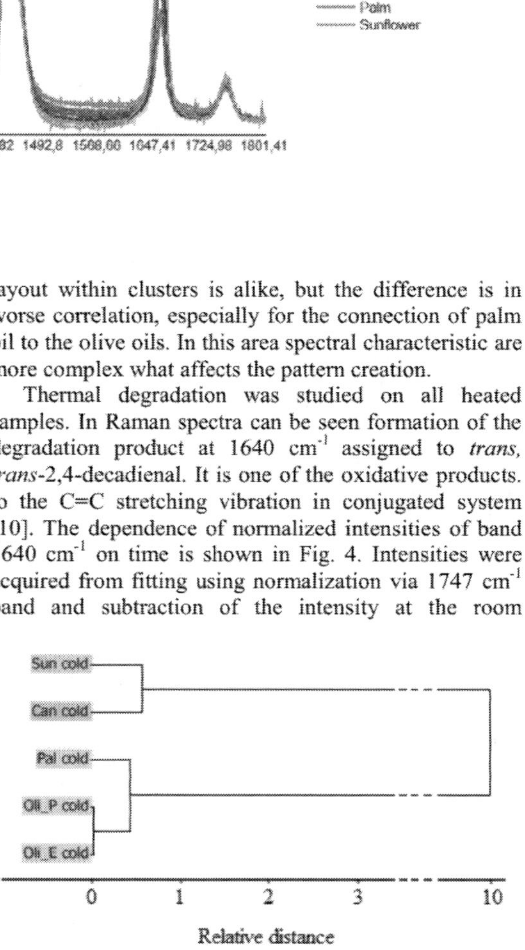

Fig. 2. Cluster analysis of cold oils in area 1200 - 1390 cm^{-1}.

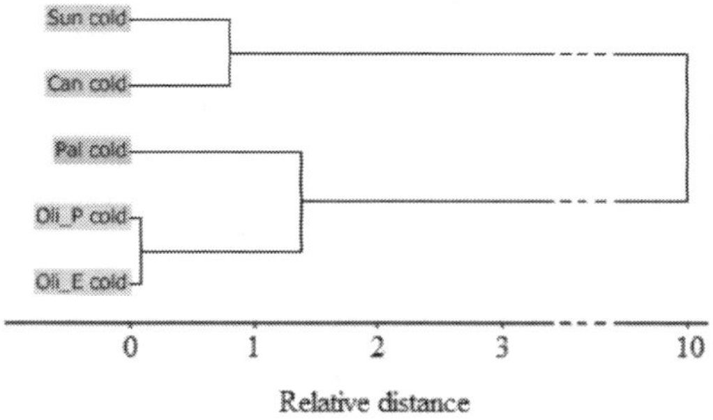

Fig. 3. Cluster analysis of cold oils in area 1200 - 1800 cm^{-1}.

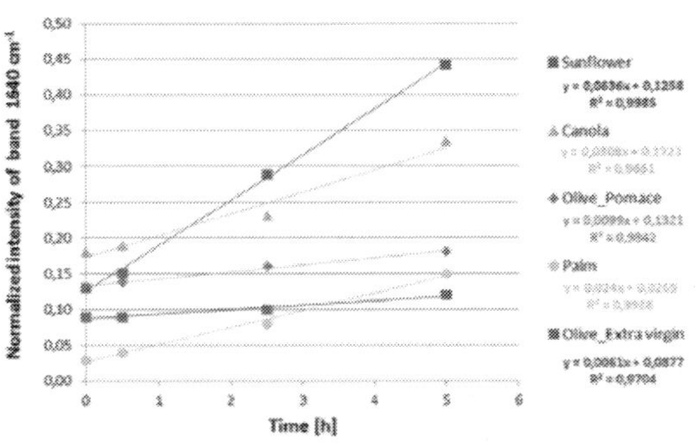

Fig. 4. Thermal degradation of edible oils according to normalized intensities of Raman band at 1640 cm^{-1}.

temperature. Results show the smallest structural changes for extra virgin olive oil followed by pomace olive oil. The biggest impact of oxidative change is observed for sunflower oil.

For the clarity of the outputs of multivariate analysis cold and heated oils for 2.5 hours and 5 hours were used. The dendrogram for named samples and the whole measured spectral area is displayed in Fig. 5. The first cluster consists of sunflower and canola oils which create clear sub-clusters with diversity of cold and heated samples. Second cluster consists of two sub-clusters of palm oil samples and olive oils.

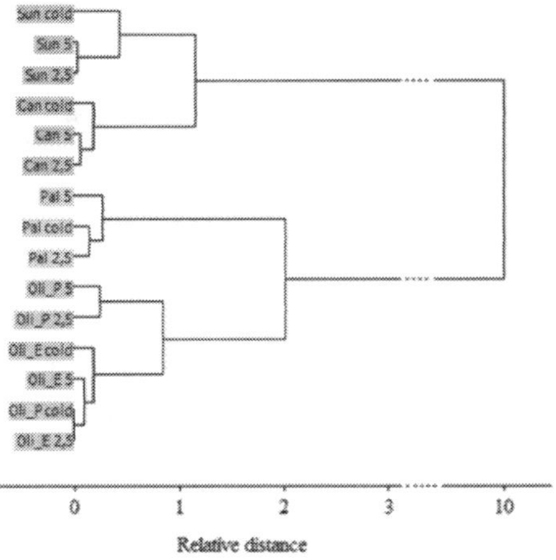

Fig. 5. Cluster analysis of cold and heated oils.

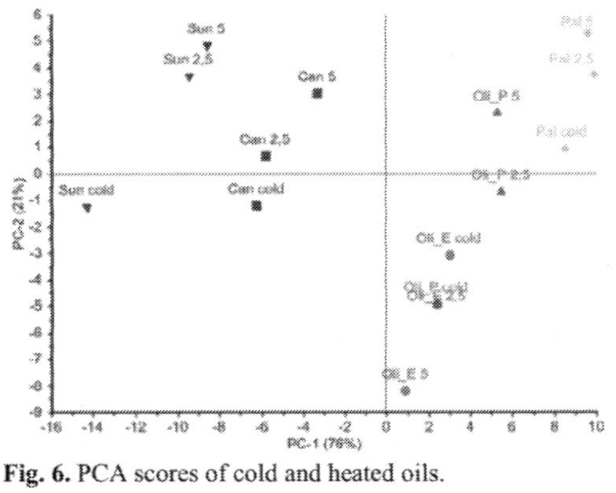

Fig. 6. PCA scores of cold and heated oils.

Spectral data of 5 cold and thermally degraded samples were used also for the PCA. The result is shown in Fig. 6. The diversity is sharply distinguished from the other species of oils. The only one overlap appears for extra virgin and pomace olive oils, what supports the closeness to their composition over other oils.

All 4 oils except of extra virgin olive oil show the same trends according to growing PC-1 and PC-2. This only one – extra virgin oil has the opposite trend.

5 Conclusions

Data reflecting structural variations of 5 types of edible oils were acquired by modern spectroscopic method Raman spectroscopy. Multivariate statistical methods Cluster analysis and Principal component analysis were used for the evaluation of the datasets. The results show good agreement with the known ratio of saturated and unsaturated fatty acids in the oils. The assessment of thermal degradation can be done via amount of arising degradation products as *trans, trans*-2,4-decadienal. The most evident degradation was observed for sunflower oil, then for canola and palm oil. The best thermal stability show extra virgin olive oil followed by pomace olive oil. However, the thermal stress speeds up undesired decomposition of vegetable oils and promotes creation of unsafe and unhealthy oxidative products in all types of tested oils. This oxidative process is more intensive with the longer period of heating.

This work was supported by the Ministry of Education, Youth and Sports of the Czech Republic within the National Sustainability Programme project No. LO1303 (MSMT-7778/2014) and also by the European Regional Development Fund under the project CEBIA-Tech No. CZ.1.05/2.1.00/03.0089.

References

1. Y. G. M. Konbonga, H. Ghalila, et al, F. N. S., 02, (2011)
2. Frank D. Gunstone, Vegetable Oils in Food Technology: Composition, Properties and Uses (Wiley-Blackwell, 2011)
3. R. C. Zambiazi, R. Przybylski, M. W. Zambiazi, C. B. Mendonca, CEPPA, Curitiba 25, 1 (2007)
4. S. A. Smith, Food Chem. 102 (2007)
5. N. B. Colthup, H. D. Lawrence, S. E. Wiberley, Introduction to infrared and Raman spectroscopy, (1990)
6. R. S. Das, Y. K. Agraval, Vibr. Spec. 57, 2 (2011)
7. S. Galier, K.C. Gordon, R. Jimenez-Flores, D.W. Everett, Int. Dairy J. 21, 6 (2011)
8. B. Muik, B. Lendl, A. Molina-Diaz, M.J. Ayora-Canada, Appl. Spectrosc. 57, 2 (2003)
9. E.C.Y. Li-Chan, Trends Food Sci. Tech. 7 (1996)
10. B. Muik, B. Lendl, A. Molina-Diaz, M.J. Ayora-Canada, Chem. Phys. Lipids 134 (2005)

Predictive control of multivariable time-delay systems

Kubalcik Marek[1,*], *Bobal* Vladimir[1]

[1] Tomas Bata University in Zlin, Faculty of Applied Informatics, Nam. T. G. Masaryka 5555, 760 05 Zlin, Czech Republic

Abstract. In technical practice often occur multivariable processes with time delay. Time-delays are mainly caused by the time required to transport mass, energy or information, but they can also be caused by processing time or accumulation. In a multivariable system each input may influence all system outputs. The design of a controller for such a system must be quite sophisticated if the system is to be controlled adequately. One of the possible approaches to control of multivariable time-delay processes is application of predictive control methods. The paper deals with design of an algorithm for predictive control of multivariable processes with time-delay. The predictive controller is based on the recursive computation of predictions which was extended for the time-delay system. The control of a multivariable system with two steps of time-delay was verified by simulation.

1 Introduction

Typical technological processes require the simultaneous control of several variables related to one system. Each input may influence all system outputs. The design of a controller for such a system must be quite sophisticated if the system is to be controlled adequately. Simple decentralized PI or PID controllers largely do not yield satisfactory results. There are many different advanced methods of controlling multi-input–multi-output (MIMO) systems. The problem of selecting an appropriate control technique often arises. Perhaps the most popular way of controlling MIMO processes is by designing decoupling compensators to suppress the interactions [1] and the designing multiple SISO controllers [2] . This requires determining how to pair the controlled and manipulated variables. One of the most effective approaches to control of multivariable systems is model predictive control (MPC) [3], [4], [5]. An advantage of model predictive control is that multivariable systems can be handled in a straightforward manner.

In technical practice often occur multivariable processes with time delay.Time-delays are mainly caused by the time required to transport mass, energy or information, but they can also be caused by processing time or accumulation. Typical examples of such processes are e.g. liquid storing tanks, distillation columns or some types of chemical reactors. Time-delay may be defined as the time interval between the start of an event at one point in a system and is resulting action at another point in a system and its resulting action at another point in the system. One older classification of techniques for the compensation of time-delayed processes is introduced in [6], [7] and newer overview of recent advances and open problems it is possible to find in [8]. Processes with time-delay in general are difficult to control using standard feedback controllers. One of the possible approaches to control processes with time delay is predictive control. The predictive control strategy includes a model of the process in the structure of the controller. The first time-delay compensation algorithm was proposed in [9]. This control algorithm known as the Smith Predictor (SP) contained a dynamic model of the time-delay process and it can be considered as the first model predictive algorithm.

When using most of other approaches, the control actions are taken based on past errors. MPC uses also future values of the reference signals. It is essentially based on discrete or sampled models of processes. Computation of appropriate control algorithms is then realized especially in the discrete domain. The basic idea of the generalized predictive control [10], [11] is to use a model of a controlled process to predict a number of future outputs of the process. A trajectory of future manipulated variables is given by solving an optimization problem incorporating a suitable cost function and constraints. Only the first element of the obtained control sequence is applied. The whole procedure is repeated in following sampling period. This principle is known as the receding horizon strategy.

An implementation of a multivariable predictive controller for control of time-delay systems based on a matrix fraction model is described in this paper. A computation of predictions for the case with the time-delay is introduced. The computation is based on a particular model of the controlled system in the form of matrix fraction which is commonly used for description of a range of processes. For the purpose of simplification it was considered equal time-delay in all particular transfer functions of the transfer matrix. The proposed algorithm is then verified by simulation.

* Corresponding author: kubalcik@fai.utb.cz

2 Model of the controlled system

Let us consider a two input – two output system. The two – input/two – output (TITO) processes are the most often encountered multivariable processes in practice and many processes with inputs/outputs beyond two can be treated as several TITO subsystems [12].

A general transfer matrix of a two-input–two-output system with significant cross-coupling between the control loops is expressed as:

$$\boldsymbol{G}(z)=\begin{bmatrix} G_{11}(z) & G_{12}(z) \\ G_{21}(z) & G_{22}(z) \end{bmatrix} \tag{1}$$

$$\boldsymbol{Y}(z)=\boldsymbol{G}(z)\boldsymbol{U}(z) \tag{2}$$

where $\boldsymbol{U}(z)$ and $\boldsymbol{Y}(z)$ are vectors of the manipulated variables and the controlled variables, respectively.

$$\boldsymbol{U}(z)=[u_1(z),u_2(z)]^T \quad \boldsymbol{Y}(z)=[y_1(z),y_2(z)]^T \tag{3}$$

It may be assumed that the transfer matrix can be transcribed to the following form of the matrix fraction:

$$\boldsymbol{G}(z)=\boldsymbol{A}^{-1}(z^{-1})\boldsymbol{B}(z^{-1})=\boldsymbol{B}_1(z^{-1})\boldsymbol{A}_1^{-1}(z^{-1}) \tag{4}$$

where the polynomial matrices $\boldsymbol{A}\in R_{22}[z^{-1}]$, $\boldsymbol{B}\in R_{22}[z^{-1}]$ are the left coprime factorizations of matrix $\boldsymbol{G}(z)$ and the matrices $\boldsymbol{A}_1\in R_{22}[z^{-1}]$, $\boldsymbol{B}_1\in R_{22}[z^{-1}]$ are the right coprime factorizations of $\boldsymbol{G}(z)$. The model can be also written in the form

$$\boldsymbol{A}(z^{-1})\boldsymbol{Y}(z)=\boldsymbol{B}(z^{-1})\boldsymbol{U}(z) \tag{5}$$

As an example a model with polynomials of second degree was chosen. This model proved to be effective for control of several TITO laboratory processes [13], where controllers based on a model with polynomials of the first degree failed. The model has sixteen parameters. The matrices $\boldsymbol{A}$ and $\boldsymbol{B}$ are defined as follows

$$\boldsymbol{A}(z^{-1})=\begin{bmatrix} 1+a_1z^{-1}+a_2z^{-2} & a_3z^{-1}+a_4z^{-2} \\ a_5z^{-1}+a_6z^{-2} & 1+a_7z^{-1}+a_8z^{-2} \end{bmatrix} \tag{6}$$

$$\boldsymbol{B}(z^{-1})=\begin{bmatrix} b_1z^{-1}+b_2z^{-2} & b_3z^{-1}+b_4z^{-2} \\ b_5z^{-1}+b_6z^{-2} & b_7z^{-1}+b_8z^{-2} \end{bmatrix} \tag{7}$$

A widely used model in general model predictive control is the CARIMA (controller autoregressive integrated moving average) model which we can obtain by adding a disturbance model as

$$\boldsymbol{A}(z^{-1})\boldsymbol{y}(k)=\boldsymbol{B}(z^{-1})\boldsymbol{u}(k)+\boldsymbol{C}(z^{-1})\boldsymbol{\Delta}^{-1}(z^{-1})\boldsymbol{n}(k) \tag{8}$$

where $\boldsymbol{n}$ is a non-measurable random disturbance that is assumed to have zero mean value and constant covariance and

$$\boldsymbol{\Delta}(z^{-1})=\begin{bmatrix} 1-z^{-1} & 0 \\ 0 & 1-z^{-1} \end{bmatrix} \tag{9}$$

in case of TITO system.

The nominal model with d steps of time-delay is considered as

$$\boldsymbol{G}(z)=\boldsymbol{A}^{-1}(z^{-1})\boldsymbol{B}(z^{-1})z^{-d}=\boldsymbol{B}_1(z^{-1})\boldsymbol{A}_1^{-1}(z^{-1})z^{-d} \tag{10}$$

For the purpose of simplification it was considered equal time-delay in all particular transfer functions of the transfer matrix. The CARIMA model for time-delay system then takes the form

$$\boldsymbol{A}(z^{-1})\boldsymbol{y}(k)=z^{-d}\boldsymbol{B}(z^{-1})\boldsymbol{u}(k)+\boldsymbol{C}(z^{-1})\boldsymbol{\Delta}^{-1}(z^{-1})\boldsymbol{n}(k) \tag{11}$$

3 Implementation of predictive controller

The basic idea of MPC is to use a model of a controlled process to predict N future outputs of the process. A trajectory of future manipulated variables is given by solving an optimization problem incorporating a suitable cost function and constraints. Only the first element of the obtained control sequence is applied. The whole procedure is repeated in following sampling period. This principle is known as the receding horizon strategy. The computation of a control law of MPC is based on minimization of the following criterion

$$J(k)=\sum_{j=1}^{N}\boldsymbol{e}(k+j)^2+\lambda\sum_{j=1}^{N_u}\Delta\boldsymbol{u}(k+j)^2 \tag{12}$$

where $\boldsymbol{e}(k+j)$ is a vector of predicted control errors, $\Delta\boldsymbol{u}(k+j)$ is a vector of future increments of the manipulated variable (for the system with two inputs and two outputs each vector has two elements), N is a length of the prediction horizon, N_u is a length of the control horizon and λ is a weighting factor of control increments.

A predictor in a vector form is given by

$$\hat{\boldsymbol{y}}=\boldsymbol{G}\Delta\boldsymbol{u}+\boldsymbol{y}_0 \tag{13}$$

where $\hat{\boldsymbol{y}}$ is a vector of system predictions along the horizon of the length N, $\Delta\boldsymbol{u}$ is a vector of control increments, $\boldsymbol{y}_0$ is the free response vector. $\boldsymbol{G}$ is a matrix of the dynamics. It is given as

$$\boldsymbol{G}=\begin{bmatrix} \boldsymbol{G}_0 & 0 & \cdots & \cdots & 0 \\ \boldsymbol{G}_1 & \boldsymbol{G}_0 & 0 & \cdots & 0 \\ \vdots & & \ddots & \ddots & \vdots \\ \vdots & & & \boldsymbol{G}_0 & 0 \\ \boldsymbol{G}_{N-1} & \cdots & \cdots & \cdots & \boldsymbol{G}_0 \end{bmatrix} \tag{14}$$

where sub-matrices $\boldsymbol{G}_i$ have dimension 2x2 and contain values of the step sequence.

The criterion (12) can be written in a general vector form

DOI: 10.1051/matecconf/201712502023

$$J = (\hat{y} - w)^T (\hat{y} - w) + \lambda \Delta u^T \Delta u \tag{15}$$

where w is a vector of the reference trajectory. The criterion can be modified using the expression (15) to

$$J = 2g^T \Delta u + \Delta u^T H \Delta u \tag{16}$$

where the gradient g and the Hess matrix H are defined by following expressions

$$g^T = G^T (y_0 - w) \tag{17}$$

$$H = G^T G \tag{18}$$

Handling of constraints is one of main advantages of predictive control. General formulation of predictive control with constraints is then as follows

$$\min_{\Delta u} 2g^T \Delta u + \Delta u^T H \Delta u \tag{19}$$

owing to

$$A \Delta u \leq b \tag{20}$$

The inequality (20) expresses the constraints in a compact form.

4 Computation of predictor

An important task is computation of predictions for arbitrary prediction and control horizons. Dynamics of most of processes requires horizons of length where it is not possible to compute predictions in a simple straightforward way. Recursive expressions for computation of the free response and the matrix G in each sampling period had to be derived. There are several different ways of deriving the prediction equations for transfer function models. Some papers make use of Diophantine equations to form the prediction equations [14]. In [15] matrix methods are used to compute predictions. We derived a method for recursive computation of both the free response and the matrix of the dynamics.

Computation of the predictor for the time-delay system can be obtained by modification of the predictor for the corresponding system without a time-delay. At first we will consider the TITO system without time-delay and then we will modify the computation of predictions for the time-delay system.

4.1. TITO system without time-delay

The difference equation of the CARIMA model without the unknown term can be expressed as:

$$\begin{aligned} y_1(k+1) &= (1-a_1)y_1(k) + (a_1 - a_2)y_1(k-1) + a_2 y_1(k-2) - \\ &- a_3 y_2(k) + (a_3 - a_4)y_2(k-1) + a_4 y_2(k-2) + \\ &+ b_1 \Delta u_1(k) + b_2 \Delta u_1(k-1) + b_3 \Delta u_2(k) + b_4 \Delta u_2(k-1) \end{aligned} \tag{21}$$

$$\begin{aligned} y_2(k+1) &= (1-a_7)y_2(k) + (a_7 - a_8)y_2(k-1) + a_8 y_2(k-2) - \\ &- a_5 y_1(k) + (a_5 - a_6)y_1(k-1) + a_6 y_1(k-2) + \\ &+ b_5 \Delta u_1(k) + b_6 \Delta u_1(k-1) + b_7 \Delta u_2(k) + b_8 \Delta u_2(k-1) \end{aligned}$$

These equations can be written into a matrix form

$$\begin{aligned} y(k+1) &= A_1 y(k) + A_2 y(k-1) + A_3 y(k-2) + \\ &+ B_1 \Delta u(k) + B_2 \Delta u(k-1) \end{aligned} \tag{22}$$

where

$$A_1 = \begin{bmatrix} 1-a_1 & -a_3 \\ -a_5 & 1-a_7 \end{bmatrix} \; A_2 = \begin{bmatrix} a_1 - a_2 & a_3 - a_4 \\ a_5 - a_6 & a_7 - a_8 \end{bmatrix}$$

$$A_3 = \begin{bmatrix} a_2 & a_4 \\ a_6 & a_8 \end{bmatrix} \tag{23}$$

$$B_1 = \begin{bmatrix} b_1 & b_3 \\ b_5 & b_7 \end{bmatrix} \; B_2 = \begin{bmatrix} b_2 & b_4 \\ b_6 & b_8 \end{bmatrix} \tag{24}$$

It was necessary to directly compute three steps-ahead predictions in a straightforward way by establishing of previous predictions to later predictions. The model order defines that computation of one step-ahead prediction is based on the three past values of the system output.

$$\begin{aligned} \hat{y}(k+1) &= A_1 y(k) + A_2 y(k-1) + A_3 y(k-2) + \\ &+ B_1 \Delta u(k) + B_2 \Delta u(k-1) \\ \hat{y}(k+2) &= A_1 y(k+1) + A_2 y(k) + A_3 y(k-1) + \\ &+ B_1 \Delta u(k+1) + B_2 \Delta u(k) \\ \hat{y}(k+3) &= A_1 y(k+2) + A_2 y(k+1) + A_3 y(k) + \\ &+ B_1 \Delta u(k+2) + B_2 \Delta u(k+1) \end{aligned} \tag{25}$$

The three steps ahead predictions can be expressed using (13) as follows

$$\begin{bmatrix} \hat{y}(k+1) \\ \hat{y}(k+2) \\ \hat{y}(k+3) \end{bmatrix} = G \Delta u + y_0 \tag{26}$$

It is possible to divide computation of the predictions to recursion of the free response and recursion of the matrix of the dynamics. The free response vector predictions can be expressed as:

$$\begin{aligned} y_0 &= \begin{bmatrix} p_{11} & p_{12} \\ p_{21} & q_{22} \\ p_{31} & p_{32} \\ p_{41} & p_{42} \\ p_{51} & p_{52} \\ p_{61} & p_{62} \end{bmatrix} \begin{bmatrix} \Delta u_1(k-1) \\ \Delta u_2(k-1) \end{bmatrix} + \begin{bmatrix} q_{11} & q_{12} & q_{13} & q_{14} & q_{15} & q_{16} \\ q_{21} & q_{22} & q_{23} & q_{24} & q_{25} & q_{26} \\ q_{31} & q_{32} & q_{33} & q_{34} & q_{35} & q_{36} \\ q_{41} & q_{42} & q_{43} & q_{44} & q_{45} & q_{46} \\ q_{51} & q_{52} & q_{53} & q_{54} & q_{55} & q_{56} \\ q_{61} & q_{62} & q_{63} & q_{64} & q_{65} & q_{66} \end{bmatrix} \begin{bmatrix} y_1(k) \\ y_2(k) \\ y_1(k-1) \\ y_2(k-1) \\ y_1(k-2) \\ y_2(k-2) \end{bmatrix} = \\ &= \begin{bmatrix} P_1 \\ P_2 \\ P_3 \end{bmatrix} \Delta u(k-1) + \begin{bmatrix} Q_{11} & Q_{12} & Q_{13} \\ Q_{21} & Q_{22} & Q_{23} \\ Q_{31} & Q_{32} & Q_{33} \end{bmatrix} \begin{bmatrix} y(k) \\ y(k-1) \\ y(k-2) \end{bmatrix} = P \Delta u(k-1) + Q \begin{bmatrix} y(k) \\ y(k-1) \\ y(k-2) \end{bmatrix} \end{aligned} \tag{27}$$

The coefficients of the matrices P and Q for further predictions are computed recursively. Based on the three previous predictions it is repeatedly computed the next row of the matrices $\boldsymbol{P}$ and $\boldsymbol{Q}$ in the following way:

$$\boldsymbol{P}_4 = \begin{bmatrix} p_{71} & p_{72} \\ p_{81} & p_{82} \end{bmatrix} = \boldsymbol{A}_1\boldsymbol{P}_{31} + \boldsymbol{A}_2\boldsymbol{P}_{21} + \boldsymbol{A}_3\boldsymbol{P}_{11} \quad (28)$$

$$\boldsymbol{Q}_{41} = \begin{bmatrix} q_{71} & q_{72} \\ q_{81} & q_{82} \end{bmatrix} = \boldsymbol{A}_1\boldsymbol{Q}_{31} + \boldsymbol{A}_2\boldsymbol{Q}_{21} + \boldsymbol{A}_3\boldsymbol{Q}_{11} \quad (29)$$

$$\boldsymbol{Q}_{42} = \begin{bmatrix} q_{73} & q_{74} \\ q_{83} & q_{84} \end{bmatrix} = \boldsymbol{A}_1\boldsymbol{Q}_{32} + \boldsymbol{A}_2\boldsymbol{Q}_{22} + \boldsymbol{A}_3\boldsymbol{Q}_{12} \quad (30)$$

$$\boldsymbol{Q}_{43} = \begin{bmatrix} q_{75} & q_{76} \\ q_{85} & q_{86} \end{bmatrix} = \boldsymbol{A}_1\boldsymbol{Q}_{33} + \boldsymbol{A}_2\boldsymbol{Q}_{23} + \boldsymbol{A}_3\boldsymbol{Q}_{13} \quad (31)$$

The recursion of the matrix $\boldsymbol{G}$ is similar. The next element of the first column is repeatedly computed and the remaining columns are shifted. This procedure is performed repeatedly until the prediction horizon is achieved. If the control horizon is lower than the prediction horizon a number of columns in the matrix is reduced. The technique is apparent from the equations (32) and (33).

$$\boldsymbol{G}\Delta\boldsymbol{u} = \left[\begin{array}{cc|cc} g_{11} & g_{12} & 0 & 0 \\ g_{21} & g_{22} & 0 & 0 \\ \hline g_{31} & g_{32} & g_{11} & g_{12} \\ g_{41} & g_{42} & g_{21} & g_{22} \\ \hline g_{51} & g_{52} & g_{31} & g_{32} \\ g_{61} & g_{62} & g_{41} & g_{42} \end{array}\right] \begin{bmatrix} \Delta u_1(k) \\ \Delta u_2(k) \\ \hline \Delta u_1(k+1) \\ \Delta u_2(k+1) \end{bmatrix} = \quad (32)$$

$$= \begin{bmatrix} \boldsymbol{G}_1 & 0 \\ \boldsymbol{G}_2 & \boldsymbol{G}_1 \\ \boldsymbol{G}_3 & \boldsymbol{G}_2 \end{bmatrix} \begin{bmatrix} \Delta\boldsymbol{u}(k) \\ \Delta\boldsymbol{u}(k+1) \end{bmatrix}$$

$$\boldsymbol{G}_4 = \begin{bmatrix} g_{71} & g_{72} \\ g_{81} & g_{82} \end{bmatrix} = \boldsymbol{A}_1\boldsymbol{G}_3 + \boldsymbol{A}_2\boldsymbol{G}_2 + \boldsymbol{A}_3\boldsymbol{G}_1 \quad (33)$$

The predictions can be written in a compact matrix form

$$\hat{\boldsymbol{y}}(k+j) = \boldsymbol{G}\Delta\boldsymbol{u}(k+j-1) + \boldsymbol{P}\Delta\boldsymbol{u}(k-1) + \boldsymbol{Q}\boldsymbol{y}(k-j+1) \quad (34)$$
$$j \le N$$

4.2. TITO system with time-delay

The nominal model with two steps time-delay is considered as

$$\boldsymbol{G}(z) = \boldsymbol{A}^{-1}(z^{-1})\boldsymbol{B}(z^{-1})z^{-2} = \boldsymbol{B}_1(z^{-1})\boldsymbol{A}_1^{-1}(z^{-1})z^{-2} \quad (35)$$

The CARIMA model for time-delay system takes the form (11) In our case d is equal to 2. In order to compute the control action it is necessary to determine the predictions from d+1 (2+1 in our case) to $d+N_2$ ($2+N_2$).

$$\begin{bmatrix} \hat{\boldsymbol{y}}(k+3) \\ \hat{\boldsymbol{y}}(k+4) \\ \hat{\boldsymbol{y}}(k+5) \end{bmatrix} = \boldsymbol{G}\Delta\boldsymbol{u} + \boldsymbol{y}_0 \quad (36)$$

The computation of free response is then modified to

$$\boldsymbol{y}_0 = \left[\begin{array}{cc|cc|cc} g_{31} & g_{32} & g_{51} & g_{52} & p_{51} & p_{52} \\ g_{41} & g_{42} & g_{61} & g_{62} & p_{61} & p_{62} \\ \hline g_{51} & g_{52} & g_{71} & g_{72} & p_{71} & p_{72} \\ g_{61} & g_{62} & g_{81} & g_{82} & p_{81} & p_{82} \\ \hline g_{71} & g_{72} & g_{91} & g_{92} & p_{91} & p_{92} \\ g_{81} & g_{82} & g_{101} & g_{102} & p_{101} & p_{102} \end{array}\right] \begin{bmatrix} \Delta u_1(k-1) \\ \Delta u_2(k-1) \\ \hline \Delta u_1(k-2) \\ \Delta u_2(k-2) \\ \hline \Delta u_1(k-3) \\ \Delta u_2(k-3) \end{bmatrix} +$$

$$+ \left[\begin{array}{cc|cc|cc} q_{51} & q_{52} & q_{53} & q_{54} & q_{55} & q_{56} \\ q_{61} & q_{62} & q_{63} & q_{64} & q_{65} & q_{66} \\ \hline q_{71} & q_{72} & q_{73} & q_{34} & q_{75} & q_{76} \\ q_{81} & q_{82} & q_{83} & q_{44} & q_{85} & q_{86} \\ \hline q_{91} & q_{92} & q_{93} & q_{54} & q_{95} & q_{96} \\ q_{101} & q_{102} & q_{103} & q_{64} & q_{105} & q_{106} \end{array}\right] \begin{bmatrix} y_1(k) \\ y_2(k) \\ \hline y_1(k-1) \\ y_2(k-1) \\ \hline y_1(k-2) \\ y_2(k-2) \end{bmatrix} =$$

$$= \begin{bmatrix} \boldsymbol{G}_2 & \boldsymbol{G}_3 & \boldsymbol{P}_3 \\ \boldsymbol{G}_3 & \boldsymbol{G}_4 & \boldsymbol{P}_4 \\ \boldsymbol{G}_4 & \boldsymbol{G}_5 & \boldsymbol{P}_5 \end{bmatrix} \begin{bmatrix} \Delta\boldsymbol{u}(k-1) \\ \Delta\boldsymbol{u}(k-2) \\ \Delta\boldsymbol{u}(k-3) \end{bmatrix} + \begin{bmatrix} \boldsymbol{Q}_{31} & \boldsymbol{Q}_{32} & \boldsymbol{Q}_{33} \\ \boldsymbol{Q}_{41} & \boldsymbol{Q}_{42} & \boldsymbol{Q}_{43} \\ \boldsymbol{Q}_{51} & \boldsymbol{Q}_{52} & \boldsymbol{Q}_{53} \end{bmatrix} \begin{bmatrix} \boldsymbol{y}(k) \\ \boldsymbol{y}(k-1) \\ \boldsymbol{y}(k-2) \end{bmatrix} =$$

$$= \boldsymbol{P}_1 \begin{bmatrix} \Delta\boldsymbol{u}(k-1) \\ \Delta\boldsymbol{u}(k-2) \\ \Delta\boldsymbol{u}(k-3) \end{bmatrix} + \boldsymbol{Q}_1 \begin{bmatrix} \boldsymbol{y}(k) \\ \boldsymbol{y}(k-1) \\ \boldsymbol{y}(k-2) \end{bmatrix} \quad (37)$$

The computation of forced response (32) remains the same. Recursive computation of the matrices is analogical to the recursive computation described in section 4.1.

4.2. Modified predictor for arbitrary time-delay

The predictor modified for an arbitrary time –delay is then given as follows.

$$\begin{bmatrix} \hat{\boldsymbol{y}}(k+1+d) \\ \hat{\boldsymbol{y}}(k+2+d) \\ \hat{\boldsymbol{y}}(k+3+d) \end{bmatrix} = \boldsymbol{G}\Delta\boldsymbol{u} + \boldsymbol{y}_0 \quad (38)$$

$$
\boldsymbol{y}_0 = \begin{bmatrix}
g_{(d+1)1} & g_{(d+1)2} & g_{(d+3)1} & g_{(d+3)2} & \cdots & g_{(d+d+1)1} & g_{(d+d+1)2} & p_{(d+3)1} & p_{(d+3)2} \\
g_{(d+2)1} & g_{(d+2)2} & g_{(d+4)1} & g_{(d+4)2} & \cdots & g_{(d+d+2)1} & g_{(d+d+2)1} & p_{(d+4)1} & p_{(d+4)2} \\
g_{(d+3)1} & g_{(d+3)2} & g_{(d+5)1} & g_{(d+5)2} & \cdots & g_{(d+d+3)1} & g_{(d+d+3)1} & p_{(d+5)1} & p_{(d+5)2} \\
g_{(d+4)1} & g_{(d+4)2} & g_{(d+6)1} & g_{(d+6)2} & \cdots & g_{(d+d+4)1} & g_{(d+d+4)1} & p_{(d+6)1} & p_{(d+6)2} \\
g_{(d+5)1} & g_{(d+5)2} & g_{(d+7)1} & g_{(d+7)2} & \cdots & g_{(d+d+5)1} & g_{(d+d+5)1} & p_{(d+7)1} & p_{(d+7)2} \\
g_{(d+6)1} & g_{(d+6)2} & g_{(d+8)1} & g_{(d+8)2} & \cdots & g_{(d+d+6)1} & g_{(d+d+6)1} & p_{(d+8)1} & p_{(d+8)2}
\end{bmatrix} \cdot
$$

$$
\cdot \begin{bmatrix}
\Delta u_1(k-1) \\ \Delta u_2(k-1) \\ \Delta u_1(k-2) \\ \Delta u_2(k-2) \\ \vdots \\ \Delta u_1(k-d-2) \\ \Delta u_2(k-d-2) \\ \Delta u_1(k-d-1) \\ \Delta u_2(k-d-1)
\end{bmatrix}
+ \begin{bmatrix}
q_{(d+3)1} & q_{(d+3)2} & q_{(d+3)3} & q_{(d+3)4} & q_{(d+3)5} & q_{(d+3)6} \\
q_{(d+4)1} & q_{(d+4)2} & q_{(d+4)3} & q_{(d+4)4} & q_{(d+4)5} & q_{(d+4)6} \\
q_{(d+5)1} & q_{(d+5)2} & q_{(d+5)3} & q_{(d+5)4} & q_{(d+5)5} & q_{(d+5)6} \\
q_{(d+6)1} & q_{(d+6)2} & q_{(d+6)3} & q_{(d+6)4} & q_{(d+6)5} & q_{(d+6)6} \\
q_{(d+7)1} & q_{(d+7)2} & q_{(d+7)3} & q_{(d+7)4} & q_{(d+7)5} & q_{(d+7)6} \\
q_{(d+8)1} & q_{(d+8)2} & q_{(d+8)3} & q_{(d+8)4} & q_{(d+8)5} & q_{(d+8)6}
\end{bmatrix}
\begin{bmatrix}
y_1(k) \\ y_2(k) \\ y_1(k-1) \\ y_2(k-1) \\ y_1(k-2) \\ y_2(k-2)
\end{bmatrix} =
$$

$$
= \begin{bmatrix}
\boldsymbol{G}_d & \boldsymbol{G}_{d+1} & \cdots & \boldsymbol{G}_{d+d-1} & \boldsymbol{P}_{d+1} \\
\boldsymbol{G}_{d+1} & \boldsymbol{G}_{d+2} & \cdots & \boldsymbol{G}_{d+d} & \boldsymbol{P}_{d+2} \\
\boldsymbol{G}_{d+2} & \boldsymbol{G}_{d+3} & \cdots & \boldsymbol{G}_{d+d+1} & \boldsymbol{P}_{d+3}
\end{bmatrix}
\begin{bmatrix}
\Delta \boldsymbol{u}(k-1) \\ \Delta \boldsymbol{u}(k-2) \\ \vdots \\ \Delta \boldsymbol{u}(k-d-2) \\ \Delta \boldsymbol{u}(k-d-1)
\end{bmatrix} +
$$

$$
+ \begin{bmatrix}
\boldsymbol{Q}_{(d+1)1} & \boldsymbol{Q}_{(d+1)2} & \boldsymbol{Q}_{(d+1)3} \\
\boldsymbol{Q}_{(d+2)1} & \boldsymbol{Q}_{(d+2)2} & \boldsymbol{Q}_{(d+1)3} \\
\boldsymbol{Q}_{(d+3)1} & \boldsymbol{Q}_{(d+3)2} & \boldsymbol{Q}_{(d+1)3}
\end{bmatrix}
\begin{bmatrix}
\boldsymbol{y}(k) \\ \boldsymbol{y}(k-1) \\ \boldsymbol{y}(k-2)
\end{bmatrix} =
$$

$$
= \boldsymbol{P}_2 \begin{bmatrix}
\Delta \boldsymbol{u}(k-1) \\ \Delta \boldsymbol{u}(k-2) \\ \vdots \\ \Delta \boldsymbol{u}(k-d-2) \\ \Delta \boldsymbol{u}(k-d-1)
\end{bmatrix} + \boldsymbol{Q}_2 \begin{bmatrix}
\boldsymbol{y}(k) \\ \boldsymbol{y}(k-1) \\ \boldsymbol{y}(k-2)
\end{bmatrix} \tag{39}
$$

The computation of the forced response is again given by equation (32)

5 Simulation example

As simulation example was chosen a system with two steps of time-delay

$$
\boldsymbol{G}(z) = \boldsymbol{A}^{-1}\left(z^{-1}\right)\boldsymbol{B}\left(z^{-1}\right)z^{-2} \tag{40}
$$

described by polynomial matrices (41) –(42)

$$
\boldsymbol{A}\left(z^{-1}\right) = \begin{bmatrix}
1 - 0.5827z^{-1} + 0.1745z^{-2} & -0.0220z^{-1} + 0.1797z^{-2} \\
0.0167z^{-1} - 0.0886z^{-2} & 1 - 0.4564z^{-1} - 0.0830z^{-2}
\end{bmatrix} \tag{41}
$$

$$
\boldsymbol{B}\left(z^{-1}\right) = \begin{bmatrix}
-0.0035z^{-1} + 0.0955z^{-2} & 0.1484z^{-1} + 0.2197z^{-2} \\
0.2783z^{-1} + 0.3107z^{-2} & -0.0371z^{-1} - 0.3489z^{-2}
\end{bmatrix} \tag{42}
$$

Control responses are in figures 1and 2.

The tuning parameters that are lengths of the prediction and control horizons and the weighting coefficient λ were tuned experimentally. There is a lack of clear theory relating to the closed loop behaviour to design parameters. The length of the prediction horizon was set to $N = 10$. The length of the control horizon was also set to $N_u = 10$. The coefficient λ was taken as equal to 0,5.

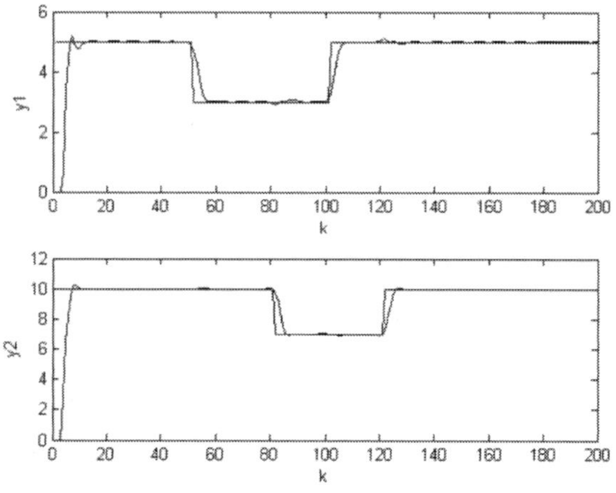

Fig. 1. Simulation results – controlled variable.

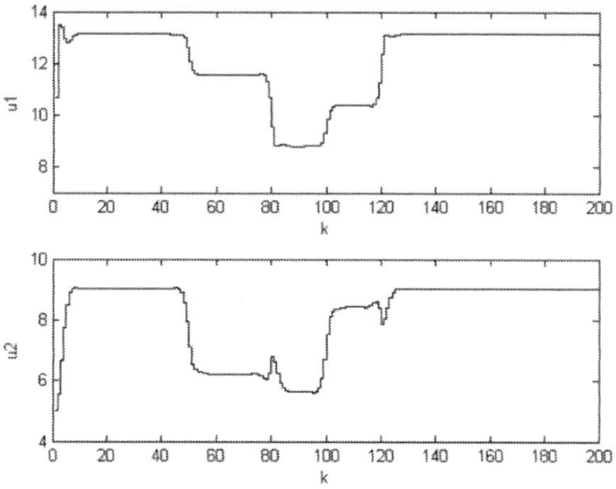

Fig. 2. Simulation results – manipulated variable.

6 Conclusions

The algorithm for control of the multivariable time-delay systems based on model predictive control was designed. The predictive controller is based on the recursive computation of predictions by direct use of the CARIMA model. The computation of predictions was extended for the time-delay system. The control of a multivariable system with two steps of time-delay was verified by simulation. The simulation verification provided good control results. Asymptotic tracking of the reference signal was achieved. The control was rather sensitive to tuning parameters. Experimental tuning of the controller was quite complicated.

References

1. P.R. Krishnawamy, et al., Ind. Eng. Chem. Res., **30**, 662 (1991)
2. W. L. Luyben, Ing. Eng. Chem. Process Des. Dev., **25**, 654 (1986)

3. E.F. Camacho, C. Bordons, *Model Predictive Control* (Springer-Verlag, London, 2004)
4. M. Morari, J.H. Lee, Computers and Chemical Engineering, **23**, 667 (1999)
5. J. Mikleš, M. Fikar, *Process Modelling, Optimisation and Control* (Berlin: Springer-Verlag, 2008)
6. A. O'Dwyer, Proc. of the 3rd IMACS/IEE International Multiconference on Circuits, Systems, Communications and Computers, 176, Athens, Greece (1999)
7. A. O'Dwyer, Proc. of the 3rd IMACS/IEE International Multiconference on Circuits, Systems, Communications and Computers, 187, Athens, Greece (1999)
8. J. P. Richard, Automatica, **39**, 1667 (2003)
9. O. J. Smith, Chem. Eng. Progress, **53**, 217, (1957)
10. D. W. Clarke, C. Mohtadi, P. S. Tuffs, Automatica, **23**,137 (1987)
11. D. W. Clarke, C. Mohtadi, P. S. Tuffs, Automatica, **23**,149 (1987)
12. F. G. Shinskey, *Process Control System* (McGraw-Hill. New York, 1996)
13. M. Kubalčík, V. Bobál, IMechE Part I: J. Systems and Control Engineering, **220(17)**, 641 (2006)
14. W.H. Kwon, H. Choj, D.G. Byun, S. Noh, Automatica, **28**, 1235, (1992)
15. J.A. Rossiter, *Model Based Predictive Control: a Practical Approach* (CRC Press, 2003)

The effect of blinds on workplace illuminance

Jiri Vincenec[1,*], and *Martin Mitas*[1]

[1] *Tomas Bata University in Zlin, Faculty of Applied Informatics, Department of Automation and Control Engineering, Nad Stranemi 4511, Zlin, Czech Republic*

Abstract. The paper explores the effect of blinds on the workplace illuminance. The blinds are used to reduce solar load from the sunshine and decrease energy consumption for cooling in the overheated room. With blinds reducing inside illuminance the standards may not be fit and it is necessary add artificial lighting in this cases. It is important to correctly regulate daylight and eventually supplement it with artificial lighting to set the system for minimum energy consumption to meet all standard requirements. This paper presents the basic effect of the blinds on the internal illuminance of the workplace in the laboratory of lighting systems. This paper indicates that with increasing angles of blinds inside illuminance is decreasing.

1 Introduction

Nowadays, when electric energy is used almost in all areas, increased energy efficiency is required not only from electrical equipment but also from entire systems; for example, house automation.

For instance, to reduce solar load, it is necessary to regulate the glazing area. Hoffmann describes twelve different coplanar shade with different geometry. She presents a simulation of energy consumption in building with those different shades [1]. Daylight control can also be done with internal blinds. For example, Sanati divided the window into two parts, the upper part is equipped with fixed blind and the bottom part is equipped with blind, which can be controlled by the occupant [2]. Shen describes lighting and daylight control as one system; in other words, daylight control communicates with the lighting system and can communicate with HVAC system. His conclusion proves that less energy for lighting and cooling is needed when using integration [3]. The influence of shading control strategic describes Yun. He looked at the issue as a whole and include quantitative and qualitative criteria [4].

For optimal energy savings, it is also necessary to take into account the regulation of the light sources for the regulation of blinds. Roisin deals with lighting energy saving in office [5]. Similar approach presents Soori [6] with lighting strategy for a typical office building in Dubai, where he describes the impact of artificial lighting and natural lighting on the HVAC system. Caicedo demonstrates daylight-adaptive lighting control [7].

The purpose of this study is to describe blinds effect in the laboratory of lighting systems. In this case, we consider only quantitative parameters of inside illuminance at measuring points. Quantitative requirements are described in Czech stands [8, 9]. Next phase of this research will contain artificial lighting and its automation with blinds to achieve optimal lighting conditions and energy consumption saving.

2 Methods

This article examines the effect of blinds on workplace illuminance in the laboratory that was built for the purpose of research on workplace lighting and home automation.

The laboratory is located at Tomas Bata University in Zlin, Faculty of Applied Informatics. GPS coordinates of the laboratory are 49°13'50" North latitude and 17°39'27" East longitude. The solar azimuth angle was set at 174°40'.

In the laboratory are six student workstations and one tutor workstation. The South wall is fitted with windows divided into smaller windows separated with inside pillars. These pillars are equipped with inside blinders.

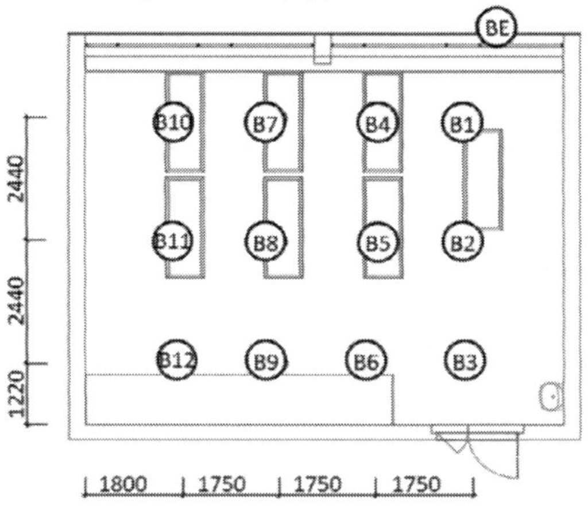

Fig. 1. The position of the measuring points in the room

* Corresponding author: vincenec@fai.utb.cz

Outside the windows are equipped with outside blinders. These blinders are equipped with electric motors for automatic functions.

In the laboratory were set twelve checking point, the positions are shown in fig. 1. Six checking points are at student's workstation, two at tutor workstation and the rest of the inside checking point near the inner wall. Outside illuminance is measured in front of the window position BE.

The measurement was supplemented by the calculation of the daily illumination level

$$D = \frac{E}{E_h} \qquad (1)$$

when D is daylight factor [%],
E inside illuminance [lx],
E_h outside illuminance [lx].

Two outdoor blinds can regulate daylight. Each blind can be controlled separately. Dimension and shape are shown in fig. 2. The blinder lamella angle can be set at an angle of 0 ° to 75 °.

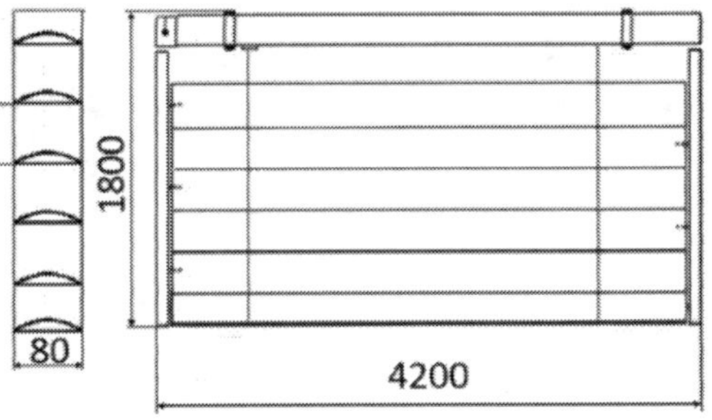

Fig. 2. Parameters of the blinds

For measurement were used data loggers Almemo and two measuring heads FLA 623VL with range 0 to 170k lx and FLA603VL2 with range 0,05 to 12k5 lx. Both measuring heads with an absolute error less than 5 %.

3 Results

This article provides measurements of inside illuminance measured according to the checking points in the fig.1. Outside illuminance was measured at the same time as the measurement of inside illuminance.

The measurement was performed for cloudy sky without blinds and for clear sky without blinds and with blinds set on angles 90°, 120° and 165°. The angle is calculated from the horizontal plane.

1.1 Daylight with cloudy sky

The measurement was carried out 12. 4. 2017 between 11:15 and 11:30 with cloudy sky. With internal and external illumination were calculated daylight factor. Measured values and calculated daylight factor are in table 1. As can be seen outdoor illuminance during measurement is approximately nineteen thousands lux. When comparing daylight factor with standard values we can see that middle row meet minimal values for daylight factor and window row met average values for daylight factor. On the other hand, daylight factor at door row does not fit.

Table 1. Measured values with cloudy sky

Window row	Inside illuminance [lx]	Outdoor illuminance [lx]	Daylight factor [%]
Bod 1	2218	19489	11,38
Bod 4	2006	19262	10,41
Bod 7	1885	18545	10,16
Bod 10	1999	18581	10,76
Middle row	Inside illuminance [lx]	Outdoor illuminance [lx]	Daylight factor [%]
Bod 2	621	19381	3,20
Bod 5	574	19187	2,99
Bod 8	510	18565	2,75
Bod 11	503	18386	2,73
Door row	Inside illuminance [lx]	Outdoor illuminance [lx]	Daylight factor [%]
Bod 3	259	19346	1,34
Bod 6	245	18525	1,32
Bod 9	186	18861	0,99
Bod 12	195	18485	1,06

1.2 Daylight with clear sky

The measurement was carried out 11. 4. 2017 between 11:00 and 13:00 with a clear sky. To determine the effect of daylight regulation several angles of the blind lamella.

The first measurement was performed for clear sky and no blinds. Measured values and calculated daylight factor are in table 2. As can be seen outdoor illuminance during measurement is approximately eighty-nine thousand lux. When comparing daylight factor with standard values we can see that in this case window row is under average values for daylight factor. For middle row, the values meet minimal values for daylight factor. On the other hand, daylight factor at door row is not fit satisfied.

Table 2. Measured values with clear sky and no blinds

Window row	Inside illuminance [lx]	Outdoor illuminance [lx]	Daylight factor [%]
Bod 1	4268	88556	4,82
Bod 4	3795,7	88590	4,28
Bod 7	3910,9	88785	4,40
Bod 10	4501,7	88918	5,06
Middle row	Inside illuminance [lx]	Outdoor illuminance [lx]	Daylight factor [%]

Bod 2	1642,3	88619	1,85
Bod 5	1638,6	88604	1,85
Bod 8	1660,9	88534	1,88
Bod 11	1543,6	88312	1,75
Door row	Inside illuminance [lx]	Outdoor illuminance [lx]	Daylight factor [%]
Bod 3	766,24	88748	0,86
Bod 6	772,41	88974	0,87
Bod 9	835,55	88543	0,94
Bod 12	713,72	87849	0,81

The second measurement was performed for clear sky and blinds set at 90°. Measured values and calculated daylight factor are in table 3. As can be seen outdoor illuminance during measurement is approximately eighty-nine thousand lux. When comparing daylight factor with standard values we can see that in this case window row is under minimal values for daylight factor. For middle and door row, the values do not meet minimal values for daylight factor.

Table 3. Measured values with clear sky and tilt of blinds 90°

Window row	Inside illuminance [lx]	Outdoor illuminance [lx]	Daylight factor [%]
Bod 1	1158	89114	1,30
Bod 4	1035	90020	1,15
Bod 7	1000	89362	1,12
Bod 10	1138	89302	1,27
Middle row	Inside illuminance [lx]	Outdoor illuminance [lx]	Daylight factor [%]
Bod 2	643	89629	0,72
Bod 5	617	89681	0,69
Bod 8	617	89203	0,69
Bod 11	568	89927	0,63
Door row	Inside illuminance [lx]	Outdoor illuminance [lx]	Daylight factor [%]
Bod 3	323	89528	0,36
Bod 6	320	89864	0,36
Bod 9	355	89189	0,40
Bod 12	238	89639	0,27

The third measurement was performed for clear sky and blinds set at 120°. Measured values and calculated daylight factor are in table 4. As can be seen outdoor illuminance during measurement is approximately eighty-seven thousand lux. When comparing daylight factor with standard values we can see that no values of daylight are fulfilled.

Table 4. Measured values with clear sky and tilt of blinds 120°

Window row	Inside illuminance [lx]	Outdoor illuminance [lx]	Daylight factor [%]
Bod 1	678	86458	0,78
Bod 4	639	87248	0,73
Bod 7	552	87348	0,63
Bod 10	586	87387	0,67
Middle row	Inside illuminance [lx]	Outdoor illuminance [lx]	Daylight factor [%]
Bod 2	346	86807	0,40
Bod 5	329	87288	0,38
Bod 8	311	87106	0,36
Bod 11	298	87095	0,34
Door row	Inside illuminance [lx]	Outdoor illuminance [lx]	Daylight factor [%]
Bod 3	192	87300	0,22
Bod 6	187	87567	0,21
Bod 9	204	87217	0,23
Bod 12	139	87266	0,16

The last measurement was performed for clear sky and blinds set at 165°, which is the maximum angle and represents the maximum shade blinds. Measured values and calculated daylight factor are in table 5. As can be seen outdoor illuminance during measurement is approximately ninety thousand lux. When comparing daylight factor with standard values we can see that in this case none of the measured points fulfils standard values.

Table 5. Measured values with clear sky and tilt of blinds 165°

Window row	Inside illuminance [lx]	Outdoor illuminance [lx]	Daylight factor [%]
Bod 1	58	90424	0,06
Bod 4	58	89958	0,06
Bod 7	55	90062	0,06
Bod 10	55	90098	0,06
Middle row	Inside illuminance [lx]	Outdoor illuminance [lx]	Daylight factor [%]
Bod 2	26	89797	0,03
Bod 5	25	90155	0,03
Bod 8	24	90236	0,03
Bod 11	23	89809	0,03
Door row	Inside illuminance [lx]	Outdoor illuminance [lx]	Daylight factor [%]
Bod 3	13	90437	0,01
Bod 6	12	90487	0,01
Bod 9	12	90292	0,01
Bod 12	9	90368	0,01

Fig. 4 show inside illuminance for blinds angle 90°, 120° and 165°. In this figure can be seen, that requirement for the illuminance of working place are fulfilled for angle 90° window row and middle row and for angle 120° is this requirement fulfilled for window row. The rest of values does not fit the standard requirements and they should be completed with artificial lighting.

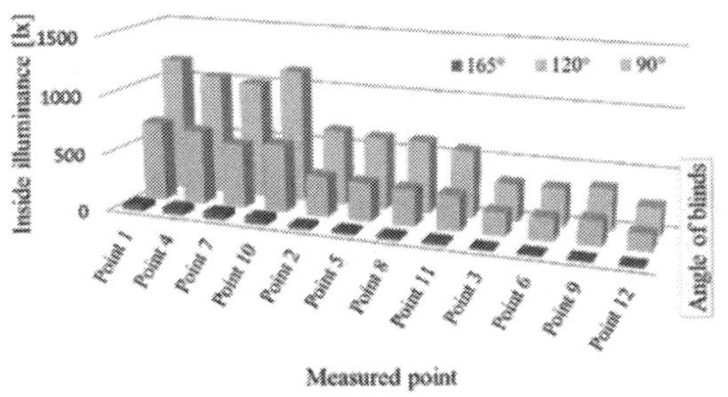

Fig. 3. Inside illuminance for blinds angle 90°, 120° and 165°

3 Conclusion

This paper describing the effect of blinds on workplace illuminance. Table 1 presents illuminance levels at 12 checking point in the laboratory without the blinders with cloudy sky. Both requirements, illuminance of workspace and daylight factor are fulfilled.

Table 2 shows illuminance levels for clear sky and no blinders. As can be seen, the illuminance of the workspace is meet for all measured points, but daylight requirement is fulfilled only for window and middle row. The disadvantage of this solution is that solar load will enormously burden inside temperature and direct sunlight will cause glare.

To eliminate solar load and glare the blinders could be used. This article provides basic measurement of blinds angle on internal illuminance. The angle was set at 90°, 120° and 165°, which present maximal shading.

Measured values of those angles are in tables 3, 4 and 5. As can be seen, daylight factor is not fulfilled except for angle 90° window row, when values meet with minimal daylight factor. On the other hand, workplace illuminance is fulfilled for angle 90° window and middle row and for angle 120°window row. This fact is also evident from the figure 4.

This study deals only with internal illuminance and it does not adequately reflect solar load savings. The main goal was to map the effect on the internal illuminance. The next step in this research is measured artificial lighting and program optimal control for combination of daylight and artificial lighting because when optimal daylight and artificial lighting is set the solar load is reduced at the minimum and inner illuminance is completed with artificial lighting.

This work was supported by the European Regional Development Fund under the project CEBIA-Tech No. CZ.1.05/2.1.00/03.0089 and also by the Internal Grant Agency of Tomas Bata University under the project No. IGA/CebiaTech/2017/002 .

References

1. S. Hoffmann, E. S. Lee, A. McNeil, L. Fernandes, D. Vidanovic, A. Thanachareonkit, Energy and Buildings **112,** 19 (2019)
2. L. Sanati, M. Utzinger, Building and Environment **64**, 10 (2013)
3. E. Shen, J. Hu, M- Patel, Building and Environment **78**, 15 (2104)
4. G. Yun, K. Ch. Yoon, K. S. Kim, Energy and Buildings **84**, 15 (2014)
5. B. Roisin, M. Bodart, A. Deneyer, P. D'Herdt, Energy and Buildings **40**, 10 (2008)
6. P. K. Soori, M. Vishwas, Energy and Buildings **66**, 9 (2013)
7. D. Caicedo, A. Pandharipande, F. M. J. Willwms, Energy and Buildings **73**, 10 (2014)
8. CSN 73 0580-1, Standard, Czech office for standards, metrology and testing, Prague, CZ (2012)
9. CSN EN 12464-1, Standard, Czech office for standards, metrology and testing, Prague, CZ (2012)

DOI: 10.1051/matecconf/201712502025

DC motors and servo-motors controlled by Raspberry Pi 2B

Michal Šustek[1,*], *Miroslav* Marcaník[2], *Pavel* Tomášek[2] and *Zdeněk* Úředníček[1]

[1]Tomas Bata University, Faculty of Applied Informatics, Department of Automation and Control Engineering, 76005 Zlín, Czech Republic
[2]Tomas Bata University, Faculty of Applied Informatics, Department of Informatics and Artificial Intelligence, 76005 Zlín, Czech Republic

Abstract. The expanding capabilities of today's microcontrollers and other devices lead to an increased utilization of these technologies in diverse fields. The automation and issue of remote control of moving objects belong to these fields. In this project, a microcontroller Raspberry Pi 2B was chosen for controlling DC motors and servo-motors. This paper provides basic insight into issue of controlling DC motors and servo-motors, connection between Raspberry and other components on breadboard and programming syntaxes for controlling motors in Python programming language.

Introduction

Nowadays, there is a high demand for wireless devices controlled by Wi-Fi, GSM or Bluetooth [1]. These technologies offer a simplification of our lives in home automation or entertainment in the form of Radio Controlled (RC) models. At the same time, the possibilities of microcontrollers have risen in many applications [2].

Current control systems are based on special purpose devices. However, little attention is given to universal microcontrollers that are able to perform a wide variety of tasks [1, 2]. The remote control via microcontrollers is more popular among researchers and "RC fans" than among the public [3].

The performance growth of microcontrollers has led to their ability to manage complex applications. At the same time, there is a variety of manufacturers of microcontrollers with many diverse types of processors and performance. Raspberry and Arduino belong to the most widely used microcontrollers [4]. Both of them provide high performance, and they can be used in many challenging automation applications.

The second generation of the Raspberry microcontroller provides enough performance to replace a standard PC in some audiovisual and automation applications [5]. With the use of the wireless extension, which can be achieved by a simple antenna, the device becomes in a complex control station.

Section 1 describes a microcontroller Raspberry Pi and its performance. Section 2 shows a basic functionality of DC motors and servo-motors. In section 3 is insight into issue of connection between components. In addition, section 4 describes basic programming in language Python for one component of each type (1 motor and 1 servo-motor).

1 Microcontroller Raspberry

A Raspberry Pi 2B is a small single-board device, which supports Linux-based operating systems, USB connections for mouse, keyboard, Ethernet adapter, and other devices. On Raspberry board are HDMI connector for attaching a monitor and general-purpose inputs and outputs [6]. A MicroSD card is used a storage device and Python is used for programming.

In history Raspberry Pi was created in UK as a low cost platform for teaching computer basics, in particular Python [8]. The first generation of Raspberry was introduced in February 2012. Since this time, a wide variety of Raspberry microcontrollers has been created. In addition, each of these variants have different performance and parameters.

Raspberry Pi 2B was chosen for the purpose of this research. It contains 4-core 900 MHz processor, 1 GB of RAM, 4 USB 2.0 ports, HDMI video output, 40-pin GPIO (General Purpose Input/Output) header.

Fig. 1. Microcontroller Raspberry PI 2B [8].

Raspberry can be used as an unpretentious and cheap replacement of a PC; however, it has wide use in home automation and remote control systems. This is

* Corresponding author: sustek@fai.utb.cz

caused by an opportunity to use GPIO pins, which function is programmable.

1.1 GPIO pins

General-Purpose Input/Output are generic pins on integrated circuit of Raspberry. Behavior of these pins is not defined and they can be programmed according to users' needs. Each pin can be configured as input or output; it can be enabled and disabled; input value can be readable and output value can be readable or writable [8]. In some applications are GPIO pins used as maskable interrupt (IRQ).

Ability of using the GPIO pins is provided by external Python module RPi.GPIO. This module must be imported into the main control program.

2 DC motors and servo-motors

DC motors and servo-motors are main actuators part in each robotic system. These components provide movement and rotation around desired axis. In deeper context, this component provide ability of movement. DC motors and servo-motors are crucial in all robotic projects. [12]

2.1 DC motors

Direct current motors are composed of three main parts (rotor, stator, and commutator). The stator circumferentially is provided with regularly spaced and mutually oppositely oriented main magnetic poles and commutation poles. The poles of the same polarity follow the poles of the given polarity in the direction of rotation of the anchor (rotor). The rotor has coils in the grooves and these coils are connected to a mechanical commutator. The commutator provides the supply of a correctly oriented current to the coils of the rotating anchor so that all currents of the flowing coil side form a torque of the same direction in the magnetic field of the main poles [12].

On magnetic neutral place between main poles of commutator, are placed carbon brushes. The number of the brushes is the same as the number of the main poles.

Current, which flows through anchor windings, creates reactionary magnetic field that deforms and weakens magnetic field around main poles and has effect on commutator magnetic field. A compensating winding is used to suppress the reactionary magnetic field. Today a stator and a rotor are created from isolated dynamo-sheet of metal in modern motors.

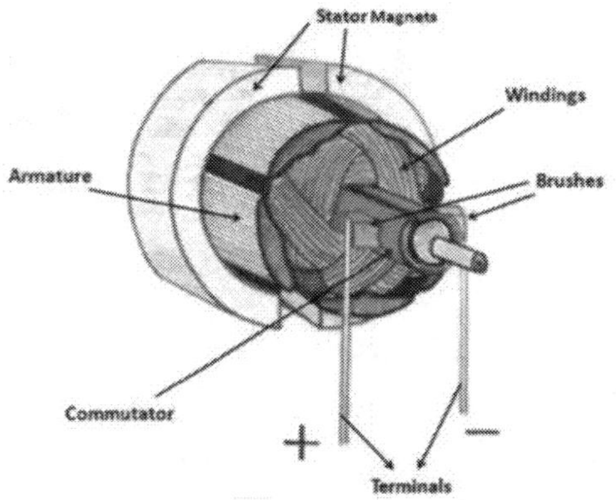

Fig. 2. Brushed DC motor [14].

Brushless DC motors are the second variant of DC motors. Brushless motors provide electrical commutation with permanent magnet rotor and stator with a sequence of coils. A permanent magnet rotates and current carrying conductors are fixed in this type of motor. Transistors or rectifiers at the correct rotor position switch the armature coils in such a way that the armature field is in space quadrature with the rotor fields [12].

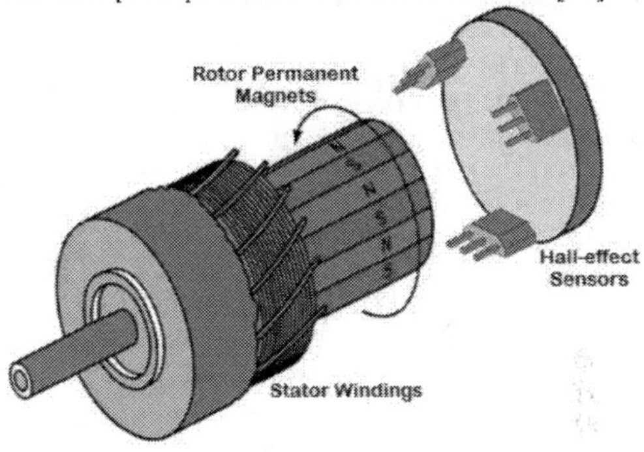

Fig. 3. Brushless DC motor [15].

2.2 Servo-motors

A servo-motor (servo) is a motor which uses a feedback to correct the output of the motor. The feedback is based on information from a sensor or from a sensors and external circuitry. The servo itself is consisted from a DC motor, a potentiometer and a control circuit. They are small but very energy-efficient devices, which are controlled by electrical impulses. Gears for controlling a shaft attach the motor. The power supply of the motor is stopped, when the motor shaft is at the desired position. If it is not in desired position, then it is turned in the appropriate direction. The motor speed is proportional to the difference between desired and actual position [12].

DOI: 10.1051/matecconf/201712502025

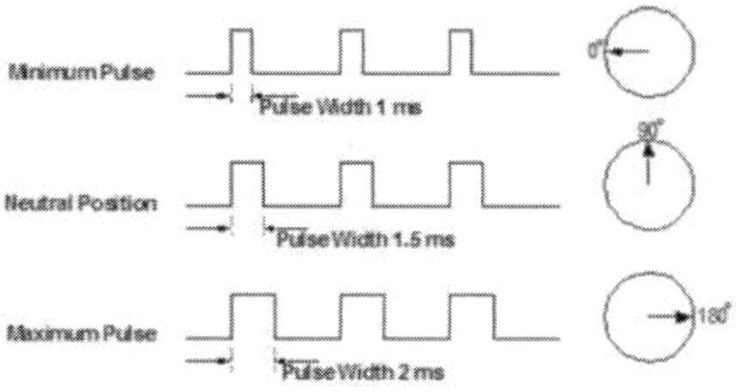

Fig. 4. Servo-motors controlling pulses [8].

Signals are send as electrical pulses with variable width, or a Pulse Width Modulation (PWM) is used. A minimal and a maximal value of pulse and repetition rate is usually distinguished. Usually servos can turn 90° in each direction for total 180°.

The neutral position is defined as the position, where the motor have amount of potential rotation equal to direction in both side (clockwise and counter-clockwise). The servo expects a signal every 20 milliseconds and the length of the electrical pulse determines how far the motor turns. When the servo moves on position, it will hold that position. If any external force try to push against the servo, while it holding a position, the servo will resist from moving out of the position. The maximum amount of force which a servo can resist is called the torque rating. The position will not be held forever, the position pulse must be repeated to instruct servo to stay in desired position.

There are two types of servos [13], AC and DC. AC servos can work with higher current surges and are used in industrial applications. On the other hand, DC servos are not designed for high current surges and are better usable for smaller applications. There are also servos for continuous rotation.

In real application servos are used in RC models (airplanes, walking robots), service robots and operating grippers.

3 Motor connection

A small 6V DC motor PERMAX 280, a microcontroller Raspberry Pi 2B, and an H-bridge L293D were used in this project. The H-bridge is a simple circuit, which contains switching elements. These elements are usually Field-Effect Transistors (FET) transistors. All switches can be turned off or on independently. The H-bridge can be used to switch a direction of a motor depending on a current flow. Table 1. presents how switch state can effect the behavior of a motor.

Tab. 1. H-bridge switch combination [8].

S-1	S-2	S-3	S-4	Motor behavior
1	0	0	1	Clockwise turns
0	1	1	0	Counter-clockwise turns
0	0	0	0	Stop
1	1	-	-	Short circuit
-	-	1	1	Short circuit
1	0	1	0	Braking
0	1	0	1	Braking

Where **1** means the switch is closed, **0** means the switch is opened, and – means it does not matter on the state of a switch.

The H-bridge L293D contains 2 H-bridges, so it is useful for 2 DC motors. The main advantages of this chip are:

- Thermal protection
- Capable with Raspberry logic (3V)
- Voltage range of 4.5 to 36V for motors
- Motor's peak current of 1.2A
- Continuous motor current of 600 mA

In this work, all the components are connected on a breadboard as depicted in Figure 5. The main advantage of using L293D with Raspberry (it has 3V logic) is that the control of pins need only a little current to control motors.

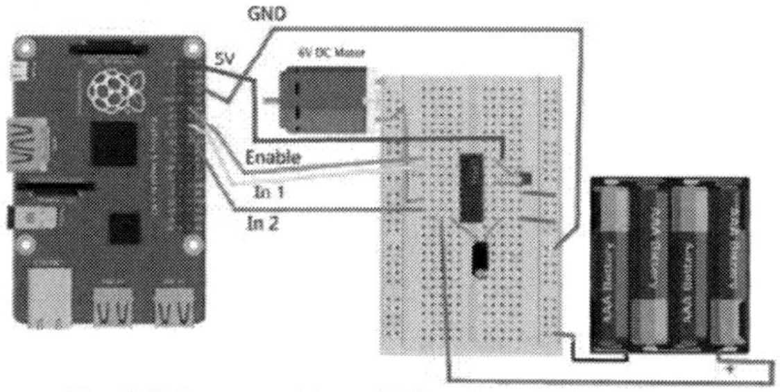

Fig. 5. DC motor wiring with Raspberry Pi 2B [8].

4 Software solution

Python has been chosen as the programming language in this work. Python is a higher programming language, which does not need to have strictly defined variables, unlike C++. In the deeper context, it is a hybrid dynamically interpreted language from a group of scripting languages. Graphic User Interface (GUI) IDLE, which is well organized, was used to develop the software itself. A module called Rpi.GPIO has been used together with basic libraries.

4.1 Solution for DC motor

At the beginning, there is a need to import a module for controlling GPIO pins, in particular RPi.GPIO, which can be downloaded from www.python.org.

```
import RPi.GPIO as GPIO
import time
```

Then the mode for GPIO pins must be set up. BOARD and BCM setup can be chosen. BOARD option specifies referring of the pins to the plug. BCM option means referring of the pins by the Broadcom SOC channel.

```
GPIO.setmode(GPIO.BCM)
```

There is also a need to select GPIO pins, which will be used. The H-bridge L293D is used as a motor driver.

Therefore, pin number 18 must be enabled to control the speed of the motor.

```
enable_pin = 18
pin_1 = 23
pin_2 = 2
```

All used pins will be configured as outputs. These pins help to control direction of the motor. We also define PWM analog output, where 500 is PWM frequency. The initial value of duty cycle is set to 0% of the frequency.

```
GPIO.setup(enable_pin, GPIO.OUT)
GPIO.setup(pin_1, GPIO.OUT)
GPIO.setup(pin_2, GPIO.OUT)
pwm_motor=GPIO.PWM(enable_pin,500)
pwm_motor.start(0)
```

In the following block of code, the movement function for each direction (forward, backward) and stop function are defined. Pin 1 is responsible for forward movement, on the other hand pin 2 is used for reverse movement.

```
def forward(duty_cycle):
  GPIO.output(pin_1, True)
  GPIO.output(pin_2, False)
  motor_pwm.ChangeDutyCycle(duty_cycle)

def reverse(duty_cycle):
  GPIO.output(pin_1, False)
  GPIO.output(pin_2, True)
  motor_pwm.ChangeDutyCycle(duty_cycle)

def stop():
  GPIO.output(in_1_pin, False)
  GPIO.output(in_2_pin, False)
  motor_pwm.ChangeDutyCycle(0)
```

The following part of the program represents the main loop which prompts the user for a command and calls direction functions and the stop function.

```
try:
  while True:
    direction = raw_input('w – forward, x – reverse, t - stop')
    if direction[0]=='t':
      stop()
      else:
        duty_cycle= input('Duty cycle (0-100%)')
        if direction [0]=='w':
          forward(duty_cycle)
        elif direction [0]=='s':
          reverse(duty_cycle)

finally:
  print("Cleaning up")
  GPIO.cleanup()
```

This is elementary program for control DC motor with the microcontroller Raspberry Pi 2B. This program is written for one motor, which is wired to the microcontroller by L293D motor driver.

4.2 Solution for servo-motor

The module RPi.GPIO must be used for GPIO control as in the previous case.

```
import RPi.GPIO as GPIO
import time
```

The number of GPIO pin on Raspberry Pi 2B has to be chosen. In addition, every servo needs a slightly different length of pulse to maximize its range of angles, two constant are used to set the pulse duration between angles 0° and 180°. Values of these variables represent duration of pulse in milliseconds. Frequency is set up to 50 Hz, therefore it is giving a pulse every 20 milliseconds.

```
servo_pin=18
0_deg = 0.5
180_deg = 2.5
frequency= 50.0
```

Some calculations, which are related to the length of pulse, were made for easier future modifications. Period is 1000 milliseconds and is divided by frequency (50 Hz in our case) so the result is 20 millisecond. In addition, if there is a need to change a duty cycle, an interval between 0 and 100 must be used and the constant k can be used to scale an angle to duty value. To convert the pulse for 0° to a corresponding value of duty between 0 and 100, is length of pulse multiplied by constant k. The value of range of duty is calculated by multiplying the span of pulse length by the constant k.

```
period = 1000/frequency
k = 100 / period
0_deg_duty = 0_deg*k
pulse_range = 180_deg-0_deg
duty_range=pulse_range*k
```

The part, which initialize the GPIO pin, is similar to the variant for DC control by Raspberry Pi 2B.

```
GPIO.setmode(GPIO.BCM)
GPIO.setup(servo_pin,GPIO.OUT)
pwm=GPIO.PWM(servo_pin,frequency)
pwm.start(0)
```

In angle definition, we convert angle into duty cycle value, and then we call *ChangeDutyCycle* to set the new pulse length.

```
def set_angle(angle):
  duty_cycle=0_deg+(angle/180.0)*duty_range
  pwm.ChangeDutyCycle(duty_cycle)
```

The main loop of control program is written below. In the following part, a value of angle between 0° and 180° is set. It could be used for steering, when 90° is forward direction, 0° is turning left and 180° is turning right.

```
try:
  while True:
    angle = input("Angle 0° to 180°")
```

```
    set_angle(angle)

finally:
  print("Cleaning up")
  GPIO.cleanup()
```

Conclusion

The high demand for wireless devices, which can simultaneously perform a wide variety of tasks has led to significant use of microcontrollers. This paper provides elementary insight into the issue of microcontrollers and the controlling of DC motors and servo-motors.

The microcontroller Raspberry Pi 2B has been chosen as the brain of this project. This microcontroller provides enough performance to run control system for DC motors and servo-motors. 6V DC motor PERMAX 280, motor driver L293D and breadboard have been chosen for creation of this system. This connection is only experimental and it is not used in real robotic platform yet. The controlling software is written in programming language Python; however, we also need to use GPIO pins. The module RPi.GPIO must be imported into the program. The submitted syntaxes in programs are the elementary way to control DC motors and servo-motors. It can be modified for controlling more motors and servo-motors.

The next work is planned to be focused on extending the control system on a cell phone as a control device, in particular, by using LTE (Long Term Evolution) technology. The main difference in LTE system will be in control software (Android, iOS application). An LTE modem must be added to the entire system. Another further work can be aimed at implementation of this control system into a 4-wheeled robotic chassis.

Acknowledgment

This work was supported by the Ministry of Education, Youth and Sports of the Czech Republic within the National Sustainability Programme project No. LO1303 (MSMT-7778/2014) and also by the European Regional Development Fund under the project CEBIA-Tech No. This work was also supported by Internal Grant Agency of Tomas Bata University under the project No. IGA/FAI/2017/004.

References

1. A. A. Asadi, S. Bagheri, A. Imam, E. Jalayeri, W. Kinsner, and N. Sepehri. *Institute of Electrical and Electronics Engineers Inc.* (2016)
2. K. Chaitanya, G. Karudaiyar, C. Deepak, S. B. Reddy, *1st International Conference on Data Engineering and Communication Technology*, **469** Springer Verlag. (2017)
3. I. Lobachev, E. Cretu *Institute of Electrical and Electronics Engineers Inc.* (2016)
4. A.C. Martinez, *International Conference on Human Factors and System Interactions,* **497** Springer Verlag. (2016)
5. P. Membrey, D. Veitch, R. K. C. Chang. *Association for Computing Machinery*, (2016)
6. M. Šustek, M. Opluštil, Z. Úředníček, 6th *International Masaryk Conference for Ph.D students and young researchers*, (2015)
7. M. Vanitha., M. Selvalakshmi, R. Selvarasu. *Institute of Electrical and Electronics Engineers Inc.* (2016).
8. S. Monk. *Make: action: Movement, light, and sound with Arduino and Raspberry Pi.* San Francisco, CA: Maker Media. (2016)
9. H.L. Dai, L. Wang. *Communications in Nonlinear Science and Numerical Simulation* **46**: 116-125 (2016)
10. K. Premkumar, K. G. J. Nigel. "Smart Phone Based Robotic Arm Control using Raspberry Pi, Android and Wi-Fi."*Institute of Electrical and Electronics Engineers Inc.* (2015)
11. D. Sanchez-Benitez, J. M. de la Cruz, G. Pajares, D. Gu. "Visual Control of a Remote Vehicle." *Intelligent Robotics and Applications*, Pt Ii 7102: 579-588 (2011)
12. M. Ghosh, S. Ghosh, P.K. Saha, G.K. Panda, *IEEE Transactions on Industrial Electronics*, **64** (2017)
13. R.S. Ashok, Y.B. Shtessel, *American Control Conference (ACC)* (2016)
14. Todd H. Hubing, Clemson University [online], Available from: http://www.cvel.clemson.edu/auto/actuators/images/chaudhary-DCmotor.png (2017.5.18)
15. Electrical Technology, UK, Birmingham, Available from: http://www.electricaltechnology.org/2016/05/bldc-brushless-dc-motor-construction-working-principle.html (2017.5.18)

Steps towards modern trends in district heating

Lubomir Vasek[1] *and Viliam Dolinay*[1,a]

[1]Tomas Bata University in Zlín, Faculty of Applied Informatics, Nad Stranemi 4511, 760 05 Zlin, Czech Republic

Abstract. This paper focuses on new trends in district heating a cooling (DHC) area and algorithms allowing incorporating new technologies and performing optimal control. Classical district heating usually means huge source (as heating plant) and set of pipes which transfer heat energy through a medium, mostly water, across whole town and chilled water is returning back to the plant. Let's imagine a modern city where buildings are consuming only a fraction of the energy contrary to what buildings required in the past. And especially during sunny or windy days, they have energy to spare. Around of such modern city is not only the one big heating plant, but perhaps solar and wind farms, waste incinerators, industrial companies with energy surpluses. Simply in this modern city are dozens, perhaps hundreds of small energy producers that share pipe network or at least part of it. In such a district energy system, production planning is more difficult. And not only production, modern houses with minimal heat loss and data connections also allow to plan consumption more effectively. The aim is to achieve the best solution evaluated by the objective function, usually determined by minimizing the production and distribution costs and providing meets the needs of energy consumers. The method presented in this paper is based on a simulation using the proposed holonic distributed model. This model also introduces the idea of general prosumers strategy, where all active elements within the modern DHC system are represented by prosumer objects. The prosumers are perceived as objects able to actively participate in the planning and realization of the production and consumption of energy. It is assumed that the general behaviour of the object in DHC is the same, no matter how they differ in size and design. Thus, all the objects are defined by two characteristics - the ability to produce and consume. The model based on this basic principle, of course, with the most accurate information about the particular values at a time, object properties and other, should provide tools for simulation and control of modern DHC. In a broader perspective model can be applied to superior units such Smart Energy Grids - understood as a system integrating electricity (Smart Grids) and heat and cool (Smart Thermal Grids) features.

1 Introduction

Modern civilization is aware that energy resources are limited and at the same time this civilization requires greater comfort and convenience, which are often more energy-demanding. Intensely are therefore addressed issues of sustainability and efficiency. In the field of energetics, it means to lower consumption of primary energy. The main obstacles to these goals are mainly technical capabilities and the economic performances of individual countries [1]. However, if the countries want to behave ecologically and foresight into the future, they must seek these goals.

An effort to energy saving also means the introduction of new principles and technologies. In the area of district heating and cooling variety of producers grows, smaller and usually more ecological sources are involved, for example geothermal, solar, wind sources, industrial waste heat recovery, etc. [2-4]. The role of consumers is also more important. The expected benefits can be achieved only by mutual cooperation of all DHC elements [5,6]. Upgraded and improved technologies require support from new and intelligent approaches in control. Nevertheless, the modern concept of control cannot be understood only as an algorithm implemented in a specific object, but the entire hierarchy in which objects collaborate to achieve common goals. Even though the elements of the system are directed towards a common goal such a large and often disparate systems as DHC is not appropriate to centralize. It seems better to distribute the competence and ensure cooperation. Distributed control approaches in the proposed model are represented by holonic structure (multi-agent), which is looking for the optimal solution of the objective function.

2 Generations of District Heating

District heating is likely the most efficient, fuel-flexible and environmentally friendly method to produce and distribute energy on the market. It is sustainable, affordable and community-based. On a larger scale district heating system began to develop as early as the 19th century. Since then, the technology and materials gradually improved also DH somehow changed its face. We can talk about generations of DH.

[a]Corresponding author: vdolinay@fai.utb.cz

2.1 Previous generation of DH

The first generation of district heating systems used steam as the heat carrier. These systems were first introduced in USA in the 1880s. Almost all district heating systems established until 1930 used this technology, both in USA and Europe. Typical components were steam pipes in concrete ducts, steam traps, and compensators.

The second generation of systems used pressurized hot water as the heat carrier, with supply temperatures mostly over 100 °C. These systems emerged in the 1930s and dominated all new systems until the 1970s. Typical components were water pipes in concrete ducts, large tube-and-shell heat exchangers, and material-intensive, large, and heavy valves.

The third generation of systems was introduced in the 1970s and took a major share of all extensions in the 1980s and beyond. Pressurized water is still the heat carrier, but the supply temperatures are often below 100 °C. This third generation is sometimes referred to as "Scandinavian district heating technology", since many district heating component manufacturers are Scandinavian. Typical components are prefabricated, pre-insulated pipes directly buried into the ground, compact substations using plate stainless steel heat exchangers, and material lean components [5].

2.2 The 4th Generation District Heating

The future 4th Generation District Heating (4GDH) system is defined as a coherent technological and institutional concept, which by means of smart thermal grids assists the appropriate development of sustainable energy systems [5]. 4GDH systems provide the heat supply of low-energy buildings with low grid losses in a way in which the use of low-temperature heat sources is integrated with the operation of smart energy systems. See Figure 1. The concept involves the development of an institutional and organizational framework to facilitate suitable cost and motivation structures [7].

In the context of the 4th generations, we can also talk about Smart Thermal Grids or in combination with electric power is also used term Smart Energy Grid.

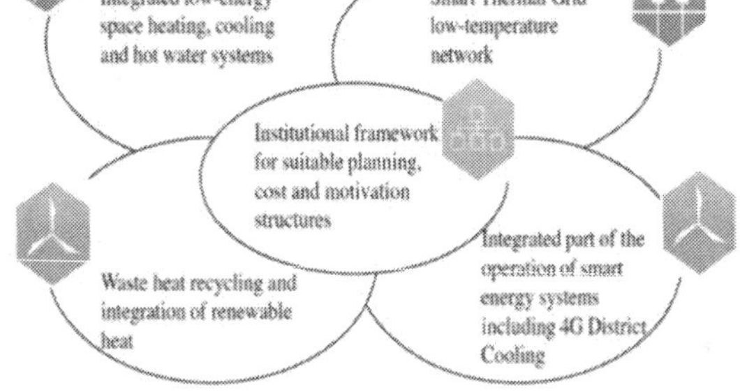

Fig. 1. Illustration of the concept of 4GDH including smart thermal grids [4].

2.3 The coming of the fifth generation

Even though the 4th generation is still called future generation and implementation only began in some large cities and many sources estimate that the main era for fourth generation will start in 2020 [13], especially the rapid development of digitization and mobile technology suggests the following directions - the features of the fifth generation [14].

3 Deployment of the 4th and 5th generation ideas into practice

The application of ideas of the 4th generation (especially rebuilding networks and building new sources) will be quite slow in the conditions of the Czech Republic (author's home country). District heating is not too prepared for this, and the investments needed to build, for example a diverse structure of smaller sources and their interconnection, will be huge and build it will take many years. Instead, the implementation of digital technologies (the character of the 5th generation) is closer, so it seems that rise of these generations will not be consecutive but concurrent.

However, a number of developmental steps can be started already. The areas of development and use of the developed means can be divided into the following three areas – heat energy production, distribution and consumption. In each of these areas, it is possible to specify the objectives and research and development activities from two areas – technical-technological and economic. Of course, both of these areas are very closely related, but it will be appropriate to use separate but closely interrelated models – technical-technological and economic.

The objectives can be formulated as follows (including the design of individual steps and stages of the solution):

3.1 Heat energy production area

3.1.1 Technical-technological objectives

a) Changes in the technological elements in DHCS.
b) Including a whole range of other possible and usable heat sources in DHC. These are different types of renewable sources (solar, wind, geothermal), waste heat from incineration plants, technological and manufacturing processes, surplus electricity in the grid and, last but not least, the thermal energy accumulators that can be used in certain phases of their activity. A special case is incorporating the thermal energy accumulators as possible sources (from the modelling point of view).
c) Adjustments to the control system of individual technological elements
d) Predictor of disposable production capacity of individual sources depending on production factors and time. The production capacities of each source are classified by priority into several categories. The use of individual sources should

be managed by their immediate effectiveness and will therefore depend on a number of influencing factors and will be time-varying. So we can talk about a system where the significant characteristics of their individual elements change over time. To model these dependencies, individual sources can be characterized in priorities that express their efficiency in obtaining thermal energy. Under this priority, resources can be categorized into the following categories:

Prio 1 ("necessary") - "residual heat" from cogeneration power generation
Prio 2 ("appropriate") - RES in case of appropriate (eg climatic) conditions
Prio 3 ("normal") - production under normal conditions
Prio 4 ("emergency") - production under critical conditions

For each category, the economic model will generally consider the different cost (production costs) of the heat produced:

3.1.2 Economic objectives

Optimizing the load of individual production sources in connection with the optimization of energy flows within the distribution of thermal energy

3.2 Area of heat energy distribution

3.2.1 Technical-technological objectives

Changes in the technological elements - distribution part of DHCS.

3.2.2 Economic objectives

Optimization of energy flows using proposed predictor of the disposable production capacities of the individual sources and heat consumption for individual types of consumers.

3.3 Heat consumption area

3.3.1 Technical-technological objectives

a) Creating an intelligent heat consumption predictor for individual types of consumers (or individual consumers) that will be based on an analysis of historical data to determine heat consumption dependencies on relevant factors:
- Time characteristics of consumption - actual values, historical trends in the previous period, trends in the analogous historical period (similar days or longer time periods), average values for analogous periods
-Type of heating operation - daily, weekly, seasonal
- Significant climate conditions (external temperature, sunshine, wind, etc.), their time characteristics, their predicted values from meteorological forecasts
b) Incorporating the heat accumulator as an consumer into the DHCS
c) The output is a time-space list of heat consumption requirements for individual consumers that will be used as input to the distribution subsystem

3.3.2 Economic objectives

Analysis of the possibilities and benefits of economic motivation of consumers for the time-varying consumption of heat energy.

This contribution, which follows up on the long-term research focused on the technical-technological area, specifically on prediction of heat consumption in DHC, focuses on a more comprehensive view of the whole DHC system, i.e. its individual parts and their interaction. So we can talk about an integrative view of DHC.

4 DHC model

Having the ability to effectively control such a complex system as the modern DHC requires having its model available to test (simulate) a number of situations in virtual conditions.

Such a model was introduced in [10] and thus only a reminder of basic terms will follow.

The proposed model is multi-agent (holonic) working with the idea of prosumer concept.

4.1 Holonic system

The holonic system can be understood as a specific implementation of multi-agent concept. Holons (agent type), could be defined as autonomous and co-operative building blocks of the system for transforming, transporting, storing and/or validating information and physical objects. The holon consists of an information processing part and often a physical processing part. A holon can be part of another holon. It is also possible to see it as a model of a particular element, i.e. part of the model of the entire system. In this sense is holon used in this article.

The internal structure of holons can be made up of a group of other holons, which can be described as "subholons". Any such subholon is, of course, full holon. This allows a very flexible way to define entire holonic system.

The most important features of holon are autonomy and co-operation. Autonomy is characterized by its ability of self-regulation, i.e. the capability to apply the flexible strategy which allows holon to respond differently to changes in its relevant environment [5]. Set of holons including their mutual relations is referred as holarchy. Holarchy is a system of holons that can cooperate to achieve a goal or objective. The holarchy defines the basic rules for co-operation of the holons and thereby limits their autonomy.

4.2 Prosumers concept

For the purpose of modelling processes in DHC in the production, distribution and consumption of heat presented in this article can be as prosumer identified as an element which acts as an energy source or(and) as a consumer. The prosumer can act on both roles, for example a heat accumulator that consumes energy when it is charging, and can be understood as a source when discharged. So the prosumer has a component of production and a component of consumption. However, any of them may be zero. Therefore prosumer, at least in the context of this article, will be used to denote all active elements in DHC.

5 DHC model structure

The proposed model of DHC consist of two fundamental components – set of **prosumer** and **distribution network**. The characteristic attributes which specify properties relevant for the modelling and analysis of DHC behaviour are defined for each element.

Description of such modelled system is shown in Figure 2.

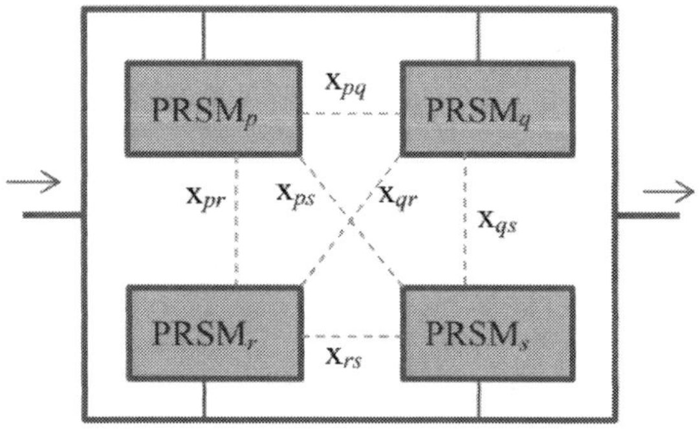

Fig. 2. A schematic description of part of DHC network topology

——	The distribution system - provides the physical energy transfer. In case of DHC may be understood as part of the piping system.
$PRSM_i$	Individual prosumers - object acting (at particular time) as supplier or consumer.
x_{ij}	Amount of energy transmitted from the supplier *i* to the consumer *j*. The interconnection formulate the resulting solution - matrix $X(t) = \{x_{ij}(t)\}$
- - - -	Logical links - possible direction and amount of supplied energy

5.1 Prosumer

Each prosumer $PRSM_i$ is characterized in relation to the analysed processes of production, distribution and consumption of heat with a number of attributes that can be divided into two groups - producer attributes and consumer attributes. Most of these attributes are function of time.

1. Producer attributes - for $PRSM_i$ it is necessary to know the following:

a. Performance data for each source as a function of time *t* and any other parameters, referred to as a vector *PP* (production parameters). They are specific for the process of heat production in a given source and affect produced

b. Price data of the supplied energy for each source, again as a function of time *t* and any other parameters referred to as a vector *PP*

The following figure illustrates the potential cost dependence on the produced amount. The costs are the lowest (optimal) if production is also within the optimum interval < P_{opt1}, P_{opt2}>. A production below (in interval <P_{min}, P_{opt1}>) or above (in interval < P_{opt2}, P_{max}>) the optimum means increased costs to produce a "unit of energy". In case that the curve will not be known throughout the interval, it can be approximated - for example the mean value for each interval is applied. It is of course also possible to apply various approximations, e.g., linear see orange dashed line in the figure.

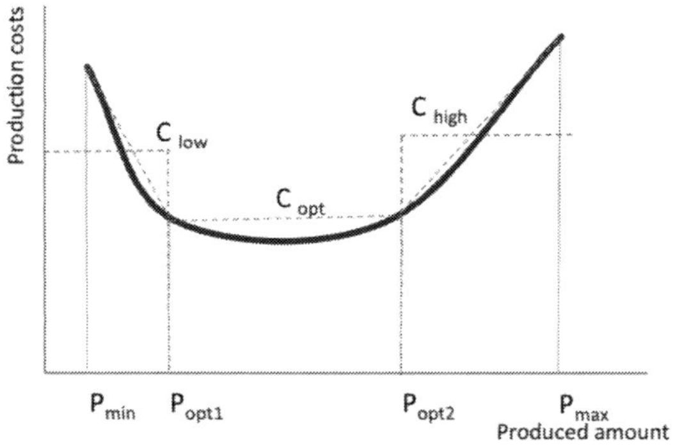

Fig. 3. The dependence of cost on the produced quantity

2. Consumer attributes

Data on the required consumption of each consumer as a function of time *t* and any other parameters *CP*

5.2 Distribution network

Another important part of DHC and therefore its model is distribution network. It connects individual prosumers and allows the transfer of thermal energy between them in a desired direction and time varying quantities. The distribution network is characterized by a topology which is generally very stable and varies, if at all, only in very specific points in time - the physical reconstruction of the network, connecting or disconnecting certain prosumer etc.

6 Optimization of energy flow in DHC

Model specified previously is used to find the optimal distribution of energy flows between the individual prosumers to satisfy their consumption demands and apply the most efficient use of production capacity of each prosumer (as produced). There should be highlighted that the solutions are being sought for dynamic system, i.e. these energy flows are changing over time. Result (solution) is captured in the matrix X(t) = $\{x_{ij}(t)\}$, which has a similar structure as the matrix R. The value of $x_{ij}(t)$ is the amount of energy transmitted from the supplier to the consumer *j* (at time t) ($x_{ij}(t) >= 0$).

The solution will satisfy the condition of minimum objective function. That is, in this case the value of the total cost CF which is calculated as sum of cost CP to produce and the cost CT to transfer whole needed amount of heat energy between prosumers for the entire time period of heating, thus

$$CF = min(CP + CT) \quad (1)$$

If the time interval TI is divided into M particular time intervals identified as $\Delta t_k = t_{k+1} - t_k$, $k = 1, 2, \ldots, M$, the equation for the production costs is

$$CP = \sum_{k=1}^{M} \left(\sum_{i=1}^{N} \sum_{j=1}^{N} x_{ij}(t) * c_i(t) \right) \Delta t_k \quad (2)$$

here $c_i(t)$ are costs (the cost of one unit of heat energy producing in source (prosumer) *i* in the corresponding time interval Δt_k.

Similarly, for transportation (distribution) is obtained equation

$$CT = \sum_{k=1}^{M} \left(\sum_{i=1}^{m} \sum_{j=1}^{n} x_{ij}(t) * ct_l(t) \right) \Delta t_k \quad (3)$$

where $cd_l(t)$ are the cost of the transport of energy unit through route *l* - their tag (index) is stored in matrix R.

Obtained solutions X must fulfil a number of conditions, see [10]

To solve such tasks usually means to define a function (target or purpose function). Very often this function is defined in economic terms as a cost function that calculates the necessary cost for given solution. A solution is determined by set of, mostly integer, parameters which characterize the process. If the values of parameters are such, that the restrictive conditions come true, the solution is defined as feasible solution. It is usually possible to find it by a heuristic method. However, very difficult is to find the optimal solution. Such solution is characterized in that the selected target function for it acquires its most extreme, usually minimum value.

Theoretically, it is easy to find the optimal solution by calculating all the possible variants and determine if it is a feasible solution. For feasible solution calculate the value of the target function and choose the one in which reaches the target function extreme value – it is so called the Brute Force algorithm. It is clear, however for the larger scheduling task the amount of possible variants is huge and this method is not due time requirements practically applicable.

In our case, when the parameters (transferred thermal power or amount of heat energy) are not integer values, the situation is more complicated becausethe number of possible variants can grow beyond all bounds. Thereafter the only possible way is to find a suitable procedure based on the heuristic methods and tries to find in reasonable time the solution, which is good enough, because there is in general unfortunately not guarantee finding the optimal one.

6.1 Methods

Searching the best variant of scheduling energy flows will be designed as a suitable procedure based on the set of heuristic methods. Methods will be developed to explore feasible solution. Such methods may vary either by using different algorithms, or, in case that the used algorithms are parametrized, only vary the values of those parameters. The search process then proceed in a way that successively, by a suitable mechanism, will individual heuristics methods propose their solutions and the best result will be sought - evaluation will be performed using the chosen target function. The mechanism to prepare sequence of used methods can be established on the basis of the results obtained previously and of course, it can interfere with human - the dispatcher. The search progress will be stopped after a predetermined time and selected the best of the calculated variants.

7 Conclusions

New trends in the field of heating and cooling systems were analyzed, built the mathematical description of the problem and prepared the first proposal of the model. The fundamental ideas of this model and algorithms to seek optimal flow of energy in modern DHC systems were presented. Since finding the optimal result is a rather complicated problem, for the solution were selected heuristic methods. They were introduced, but currently need to be more tested and verified. However, the ideas presented in this paper mostly focus the future arrangement of district heating, and also for this reason it is more or less solved in the laboratory (simulated) conditions. It is however assumed that at least the component parts will be soon confronted with real data from selected parts of the real district heating.

Acknowledgment

This work was supported by the Ministry of Education, Youth and Sports of the Czech Republic within the National Sustainability Programme project No. LO1303 (MSMT-7778/2014).

References

1. 4DH, 4GDH Definition, Available from: *<http://www.4dh.dk/about-4dh/4gdh-definition>*
2. European Commission, Energy Strategy, Available from: *<http://ec.europa.eu/energy/en/topics/energy-strategy>*
3. A. Giret, V. Botti, In *Journal of Intelligent Manufacturing*, p. 645-659 (2004)
4. H. Lund, S. Werner, R. Wiltshire, S. Svendsen, J. E. Thorsen, F. Hvelplund, B. V. Mathiesen, 4th Generation District Heating (4GDH): Integrating smart thermal grids into future sustainable energy systems, *Energy*, **68**, (2014),
5. L. Vasek, V. Dolinay, In *Recent Advances in Systems*. New Jersey, Piscataway, p. 559-563, (2015)
6. P. Navratil, J. Klapka, J. Balate, P. Konecny, In: *Proceedings of the 18th International Conference on Soft Computing MENDEL,* p. 356-362, (2012)
7. M. T. Tsaya, W. M. Linb, *Elect. Power Energy Syst.*, **22**, p. 367–373, (2000)
8. C. Johansson, F. Wernstedt, P. Davidsson, Deployment of Agent Based Load Control in District Heating Systems. *First International Workshop on Agent Technologies for Energy Systems*, (2010)
9. S. Fawkes, The Rise of the Energy Prosumer, Available from: *<http://www.heatconference.co.uk/ index.php/blog/entry/the-rise-of-the-energy-prosumer>* (2015)
10. L. Vasek, V. Dolinay, Holonic Model of DHC for Energy Flow Optimization. In *IFAC-PapersOnline. Laxenburg*, 2016, p. 413–418, (2016)
11. D. Janacova, H. Charvatova, K. Kolomazník, V Vasek, P. Mokrejs, R. Drga, In *International Journal of Mathematical Models and Methods in Applied Sciences*, **5**, p. 1094-1101, (2011)
12. J. Novak, P. Chalupa, V. Bobal, In *IEEE Transactions on Power Systems*, p. 2450-2459, **4** (2011)
13. C40 & UNEP, Good Practice Guide, In *District Energy*, (2016)
14. M. Kalli, Fifth Generation of District Heating – Energy Solutiion for Future Smart Cities, In Euro Heat & Power, p 24 – 26, **2** (2017)

DOI: 10.1051/matecconf/201712502027

Validation of new CFD release by Ground-Coupled Heat Transfer Test Cases

Stanislav Sehnalek[1,*]

[1] *Tomas Bata University in Zlin, Faculty of Applied Informatics, Department of Automation and Control Engineering, Nad Stranemi 4511, Zlin, Czech Republic*

Abstract. In this article is presented validation of ANSYS Fluent with IEA BESTEST Task 34. Article stars with outlook to the topic, afterward are described steady-state cases used for validation. Thereafter is mentioned implementation of these cases on CFD. Article is concluded with presentation of the simulated results with a comparison of those from already validated simulation software by IEA. These validation shows high correlation with an older version of tested ANSYS as well as with other main software. The paper ends by discussion with an outline of future research.

1 Introduction

Important parameter for building climate is temperature gains caused by internal and external heat sources. These gains affect comfort of people inside these buildings. A long-term research of peoples' comfort in 26 office buildings in five European Union countries was executed by [1]. Interior comfort can be provided by ventilation systems, by shading systems or by their combination. In recent years, there is a particular interest in sustainability of buildings [2] and [3]. Currently, there has been growing interest in lowering energy performance of buildings. This effort is also reflected in a new European directive, which instructs to construct near to zero energy sufficient buildings. Regardless of our experience and knowledge, there are always a risks of constructing an inconvenient building. To prevent this, appropriate design of building should be achieved. Thermal properties of a building could be calculated in a development phase, but it is limited to one-dimensional and rarely as two-dimensional problem solutions thanks to the complexity of buildings and the mathematical apparatus available. As a result of computational power increase in last decades, it is possible to design a model and implement mathematical simulation of thermal behaviour of a building also in three-dimensional space [4]. For such mathematical simulation it is used computational fluid dynamic (CFD) [5]. Thanks to the expanding performance of computers, CFD is used for solutions as a convenient way to validate building's behaviour [6]. However, first of all it is important to validate thermal simulation programs [7]. Judkoff and Neymark developed a methodology for such intention in the middle of 90s [8]. Their approach is based on the analytical solution for steady-state heat flow through the floor slab. Although it was developed by Delsante, Stokes and Walsh [9], this problem has been in focus of researchers for some time [10]. Delsante's methodology focuses only on heat flow through solids and omits above grade constructions. Standard established by ASHRAE improved Judkoff's and Neymark's methodology by adding cases which focus mainly on above grade constructions and solar radiation [10], [11].

This paper returns to previous research of this phenomenon by authors. This time the focus is on validation of new release of ANSYS Fluent 18, nevertheless that FLUENT 6 was already validated. In methods section is included outline of cases from IAE BESTEST Task 34. In results chapter are summarized outcomes of simulations. Whole paper is concluded with discussion on results and outcomes.

2 Methods

International Energy Agency Building Energy Simulation Test methodology was developed by Judkof et. al. [8] in the middle of 90's. Combination of empirical validation, analytical verification and comparative analysis techniques are main proceedings of this methodology. It operates only with slab-on-grade heat transfer and became a stepping-stone for the other approaches, such as ANSI/ASHRAE Standard 140 improved adaptation developed by ASHRAE accordingly with American National Standards Institute (ANSI).

Methodology describes 17 cases of ground-coupled heat transfers designed to be compared with verified whole-building energy simulation software. Several of those already tested by IEA are EnergyPlus, FLUENT, Matlab, TRNSys and GHT. The first case, GC10a has its base in analytical solution and it is the simplest one of all cases. Furthermore, these cases are subdivided into three series, each with its own specification. For this paper were

*Corresponding author: sehnalek@fai.utb.cz

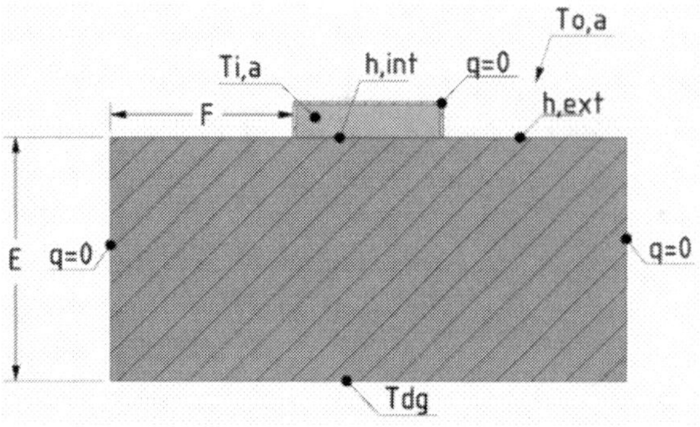

Fig. 1. Elevation section

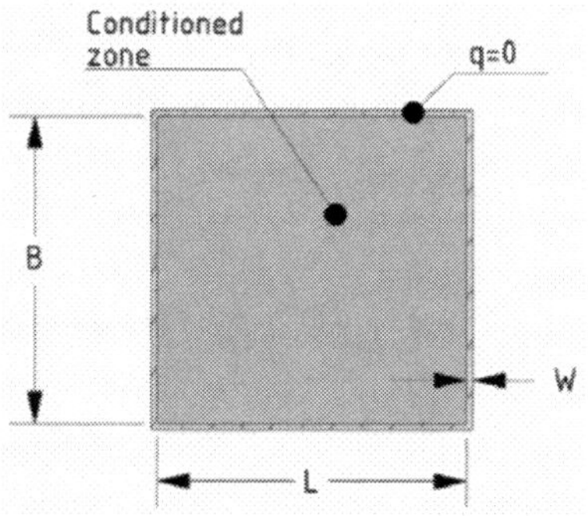

Fig. 2. Plan view

chosen six cases where all are steady-state. As mentioned before, FLUENT has been tested in past, but for version 6.0.20, in this article is tested ANSYS FLUENT 18.0 [12].

- Series a
  - The main purpose of this series is to validate whole-building simulation programs.
  - Namely: TRNSYS 16.1, SUNREL-GC 1.14.01, FLUENT 6.0.20 and MATLAB 7.0.4.365.
  - It is recommended to apply this series as the first one, if a tested software can run it.
- Series b
  - In this series, parameters are adjusted for more limited whole-building simulation programs or standard.
  - Namely: EnergyPlus 2.0.0.025 and ISO 13 370.
  - Provides basis for series "a" and "c".
- Series c
  - This series is most narrowed in use of boundary conditions, because it serves only for comparison of BASESIMP with other software.

2.1 Geometry

Geometry is similar in most cases, except for several models, which will be described later. Figure 1 depicts the elevation section of the examined test model, where F represents far field boundary distance, E stands for deep ground boundary depth, T_{dg} is deep ground temperature, $T_{o,a}$ is the outside air temperature, $T_{i,a}$ is the inside temperature and h_{int} and h_{ext} represents surface coefficients of convection [8].

Figure. 2 shows plan view of the proposed building with slab dimensions. These parameters are similar for all cases. Table 1 enlists geometrical properties for proposed cases, with inequality in GC10a, GC30a and GC30c, which vary in ground depth and far-field boundary distance [8].

Table 1: Geometry properties.

Parameter	Value [m]
B	12
E	15
F	15
L	12
W	0,24
Building height	2,7

Table 2: Thermal properties for soil, slab and above grade construction.

	Soil and Slab
Thermal conductivity $[Wm^{-1}K^{-1}]$	1,9
Density $[kg\,m^{-3}]$	1490
Specific heat $[Jkg^{-1}K^{-1}]$	1800

2.1.1 Thermal properties

Some of thermal properties are identical for all test cases aside from surface coefficients of convection, and these are enlisted in table 2 and 3.

Several parameters which are not present in table 2 also have to be taken into account:

- use slab thickness as low as software allows for a stable calculation;
- for software demanding below-grade foundation walls, use the same thermal properties as soil;
- surface radiation exchange is not included (if necessary set radiation to 0 or as low as possible);
- the ground surface and floor slab are on the same height level and both are considered to be flat and homogenous;
- for all cases water transmission via material should be turned off or reduced to its lowest level;
- adiabatic walls of the above construction are in contact with soil but do not penetrate it;
- no windows;

- no infiltration or ventilation;
- no internal gains.

2.2 Case specification

In the following section are list of used cases. Parameters for each case are enlisted as well as changes against default configuration.

2.2.1 Case GC10a – Steady-State Analytical Verification Base Case

This case if the basic one and all the other are divided from it. It was derived by Delsante et al. [9] as 3 dimensional steady-state heat flow through the floor slab. This analytical solution method with comparison of simulation software could be taken as secondary mathematical truth standard.

$$q = k(T_i - T_o)\frac{1}{\pi}F(L,B,W) \qquad (1)$$

Where is	$T_i[°C]$	is surface temperature of the floor
	$T_o[°C]$	surface temperature of the outside ground
	$k[Wm^{-1}K^{-1}]$	conductivity of floor slab and soil
	$F(L,B,W)[m]$	dimension function of L,B and W

2.2.2 Rest cases

The rest of used cases are summarized in table 3. For cases with "const T" was set boundary condition to constant temperature of surface insted of specification of heat transfer coefficient.

Table 3: Test specification

Case	$h_{,int}$ $[\frac{W}{m^2K}]$	$h_{,ext}$ $[\frac{W}{m^2K}]$	Ground Depth(E) $[m]$	Far-Field Boundary (F) $[m]$
GC10a	const T	const T	infinite	infinite
GC30a	const T	const T	30	20
GC30b	100	100	15	15
GC60b	7,95	100	15	15
GC65b	7,95	11,95	15	15
GC30c	7,95	const T	15	8

2.3 ANSYS Fluent 18.0

ANSYS Fluent is mainly used for determination of fluid flow by Navier-Stokes equations. It also contains energy calculations for heat transfer in fluids and solids as well as other parameters in scope of engineers [12].

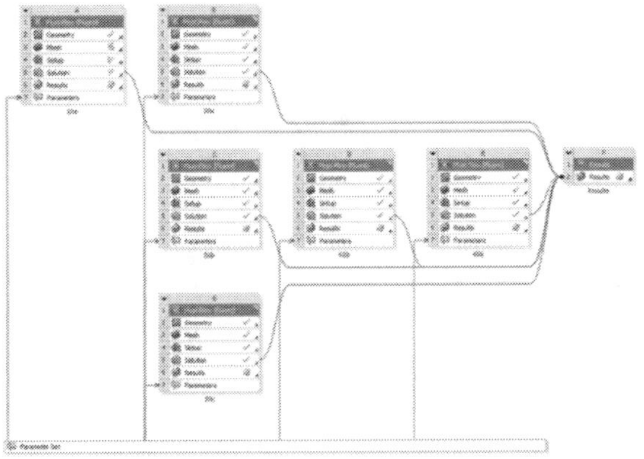

Fig. 3. Scheme of workbench configuration of cases.

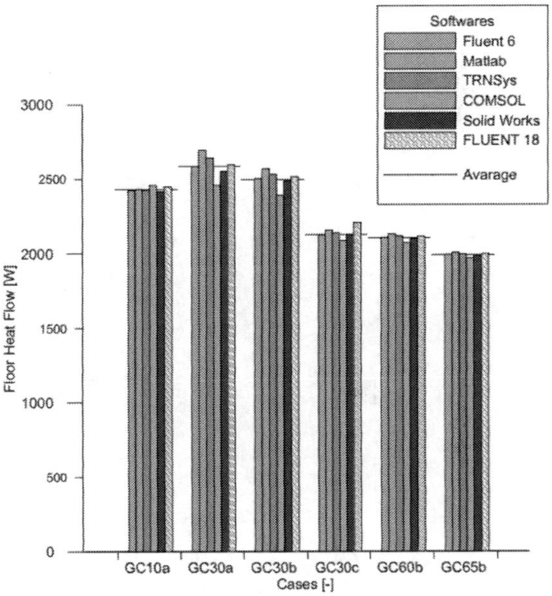

Fig. 4. IEA BESTEST Ground Coupling: In-Depth Floor Slab Steady-State Floor Conduction.

3 Results

Outcome of application of IEA BESTEST cases on FLUENT 18 will follow in this section. All mentioned cases were implemented by Workbench workspace with usage of parametrization and is depicted in Figure 3 [12].

3.1 Application of cases on ANSYS Fluent

This chapter deals with implementation of IEA BESTEST on ANSYS Fluent. Cases' main parameters initiation will be provided in subsections. First case is considered as parental for all the other cases and only changes in those will be mentioned.

Table 4: Stationary test cases calculated by SW-FS.

Case	FLUENT 18 [W]	Average [W]	Absolute difference [W]	Relative difference [%]
GC10a	2449	2435	6	<1
GC30a	2597	2588	9	<1
GC30b	2497	2501	4	<1
GC30c	2125	2138	13	3
GC60b	2112	2104	8	<1
GC65b	1988	1989	1	<1

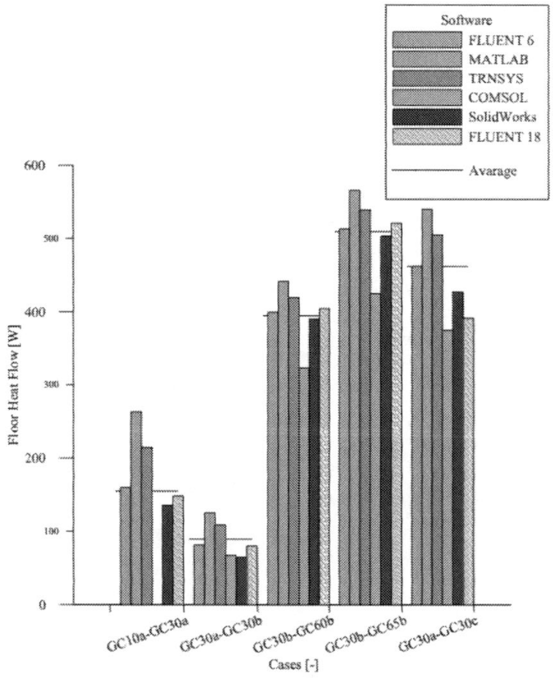

Fig. 5. IEA BESTEST Ground Coupling: In-Depth Floor Slab Steady-State Floor Conduction Sensitivity

Table 5: Stationary test case comparison calculated by ANSYS Fluent.

Case	Fluent 18 [W]	Average [W]	Absolute diff. [W]	Relative diff. [%]
GC10a - GC30a	135	159	24	15
GC30a - GC30b	65	95	31	32
GC30b - GC60b	390	396	6	1
GC30b - GC65b	504	511	7	1
GC30a - GC30c	427	471	43	9

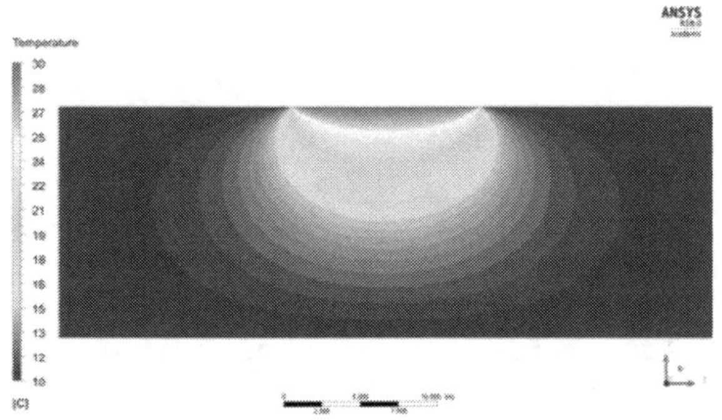

Fig. 6. Side view of temperature distribution.

After appropriate setup of the cases on Fluent, each case was executed. Results from simulation are shown in Figure. 4. Axis Y represents heat flows in Wats, on axis X are displayed used cases. The line at the top of each case is average without Fluent 18 taken in account. Results for EnergyPlus, FLUENT 6, Matlab and TRNSYS was taken from [8], results for COMSOL Multiphysics was taken from [13] and results for SolidWorks Flow Simulation (SW-FS) was taken from previous investigation of authors [14]. Results of case GC10a and GC30a was not provided for EnergyPlus.

Comparison of cases is displayed in Figure. 5. Axis Y is similar to Figure. 4, axis x represents odds between cases. Values were taken from same source as for Figure. 4. For this comparison EnergyPlus was excluded because of missing results in cases GC10a and GC30a. The evaluation for this comparison is presented in table 5. As can be seen differences vary from approximately 1% to 32%.

Side view of temperature distribution is disclosed in Figure. 6. This state is for case GC30b with basic conditions. Other cases are similar only with little differences in distribution and geometry sizes. Temperatures are displayed in °C and vary from 10 °C for exterior to 30 °C for investigated slab.

4 Conclusion

The results indicate, overall, that new release has no changes to calculation. Main reason for difference between versions is generated mesh which influence solutions. Variation of 1% is very positive for such type of benchmark. As is documented in [11], there was variety from 9% to 55% disagreement between firstly tested software with the analytical solution. However, appropriate setup of mesh should be considered along with proper analysis after generation. As next step should follow testing on remaining 10 cases from IAE BESTEST. These are similar to already tested once, but they have sinusoidal variation of outside temperature. Further research should aim comprehensive ANSI/ASHRAE Standard 140, and properly validate ANSYS Fluent with it.

This work was supported by the Ministry of Education, Youth and Sports of the Czech Republic within the National Sustain-

DOI: 10.1051/matecconf/201712502027

ability Programme project No. LO1303 (MSMT-7778/2014) and also by the Internal Grant Agency of Tomas Bata University in Zlin under the project No. IGA/CebiaTech/2017/002.

References

1. Nicol, F. and Humphreys, M. (2007). Maximum temperatures in European office buildings to avoid heat discomfort, Solar Energy 81(3): 295–304.
2. Butera, F. M. (2004). Glass architecture : is it sustainable ?, Passive and Low Energy Cooling for the Built Environment, number May 2005, Santorini, pp. 161–168.
3. Poirazis, H. (2004). Double Skin Fac¸ades for Office Buildings Literature Review, Technical report, Lund.
4. Tsai, B.-j., Lin, S.-C. and Yang, W.-C. (2012). HVAC analysis of a building installed shape-stabilized phase change material plates coupling an active building envelope system, WSEAS TRANSACTIONS on HEAT and MASS TRANSFER 7(3): 79–90.
5. Tu, J., Yeoh, G. H. and Liu, C.. *Computational Fluid Dynamics: A Practical Approach*, (Elsevier Inc., 2008), ISBN 978-0-7506-8563-4,
6. Jarungthammachote, S. (2014). Entropy Generation Analysis of Transient Heat Conduction in a Solid Slab with Fixed Temperature Boundary Conditions, WSEAS TRANSACTIONS on HEAT and MASS TRANSFER 9: 9–18.
7. Lomas, K., Eppel, H., Martin, C. and Bloomfield, D. (1997). Empirical validation of building energy simulation programs, Energy and Buildings 26(3): 253–275.
8. Neymark, J. and Judkoff, R. (2008). In-Depth Diagnostic Cases for Ground Coupled Heat Transfer International Energy Agency Building Energy Simulation Test and Diagnostic Method (IEA BESTEST) In-Depth Diagnostic Cases for Ground Coupled Heat Transfer Related to Slab-on-Grade Construction, Technical Report September 2008, NREL, Golden.
9. Delsante, A. (1987). The Development of an Hourly Thermal Simulation Program for Use in the Australian Nationwide House Energy Rating Scheme.
10. Trethowen, H. and Delsante, A. (1998). Four-Year On-Site Measurement of Heat Flow in Slab-on-Ground Floors with Wet Soils, Thermal performance of the exterior envelopes of buildings VII(December): 487–499.
11. Judkoff, R. and Neymark, J. (2006). Model Validation and Testing : The Methodological Foundation of ASHRAE Standard 140, Technical report.
12. *Ansys fluent user's guide* (2017)
13. Gerlich, V., Sulovska, K. and Zalesak, M. (2013). COMSOL Multiphysics validation as simulation software for heat transfer calculation in buildings: Building simulation software validation, Measurement 46(6): 2003–2012.
14. Sehnálek, S., Zálešák, M., Vincenec, J., Opluštil, M., Chrobák, P. Evaluation of SolidWorks Flow Simulation by Ground-Coupled Heat Transfer Test Cases. In Latest Trends on Systems. Volume II. Rhodes, 2014, s. 492-498. ISSN 1790-5117. ISBN 978-1-61804-244-6

DOI: 10.1051/matecconf/201712502028

CFD validation by measurement of specialized ventilation equipments on duct tract

Stanislav Sehnalek[1,★]

[1] *Tomas Bata University in Zlin, Faculty of Applied Informatics, Department of Automation and Control Engineering, Nad Stranemi 4511, Zlin, Czech Republic*

Abstract. This article describes measurement of HVAC distribution box on air duct track in Laboratory of Environmental Engineering (LEE). Firstly, the paper describes the LEE and then measurement apparatus with description of calculation methods. Then follows specification of sample with introduction to newly developed equipment for positioning of the anemometer. The evaluation of results of measurements with CFD comparison follows. The article is concluded with discussion over measured data with an outline for further research.

1 Introduction

Research of air mechanics is in concern of researchers for more than a century. Particulary the air flow parameters were investigated by Hagen, Reyleigh, Reynolds [1], followed up by Prandtl, Moody [2], Colebrook [3], Von Karman [4] and many others[5]. The prerequsite for a successful design technique is the knowledge of properties concerning HVAC components. Determination of parameters for specific HVAC devices are in scope of specialized laboratories. Laboratory of such capabilities is maintained by authors of this article at Tomas Bata University in Zlin, Faculty of Applied Informatics and is involved in this paper. Special interest in actual development is put on air divider for mounting in the ducts which is an important element within HVAC systems. In the authors' facility, the Laboratory of Environmental Engineering, it is possible to test the divider for all main parameters. In the presented paper, the focus is on measurement methods and comparison of results obtained by this standard with computational fluid dynamics (CFD). Mainly, the validation of CFD with measurement could lead to design better air dividers for HVAC purposes.

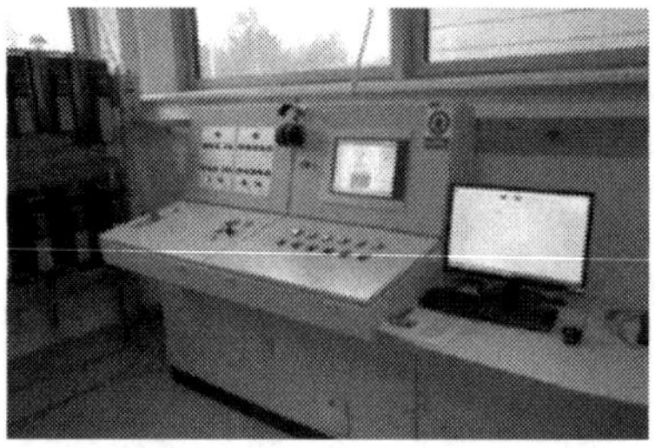

Fig. 1. Controlling board for duct tract

★Corresponding author: sehnalek@fai.utb.cz

Firstly, the article describes the methods of measurement with the test track. Above mentioned is linked with the description of the measurement method with characterization of used sample. A special device which helped with measurement process is also mentioned. Methods section is concluded with description of used CFD. Then the measured results are described, followed by discussion. The article is completed by used methods.

2 Methods

There is a possibility to measure volumetric flow of any equipment determined for installation inside a duct. For these measurements is used multiple-nozzle chamber (MNC) to resolve flow rate through the duct configuration. There is a wall taping mounted on MNC for measurement of pressure to resolve flow in accordance with ISO 5801 [6]. Calculations for air flow follows, in equations are made customization to match MNC which dispose authors at research facility.

$$Re_t = \frac{0,95\, d_n\, \sqrt{2\rho\,\Delta p}}{17,1 + 0,048\theta} 10^6 \tag{1}$$

Where	Re_t	throat Reynolds number	$[-]$
	d_n	diameter of nozzle	$[m]$
	ρp	air density	$[kg\, m^{-3}]$
	Δp	pressure difference at nozzles	$[Pa]$
	θ	temperature of air	$[°C]$

$$\alpha = 0,9986 - \frac{7,00}{\sqrt{Re_t}} + \frac{134,6}{Re_t} \tag{2}$$

Where α nozzle flow rate coefficient $[-]$

$$q_m = \pi \sum_{i=1}^{m} (\alpha \frac{d_n}{4}) \sqrt{2\rho\,\Delta p} \tag{3}$$

Where q_m mass flow $[kg\, s^{-1}]$

DOI: 10.1051/matecconf/201712502028

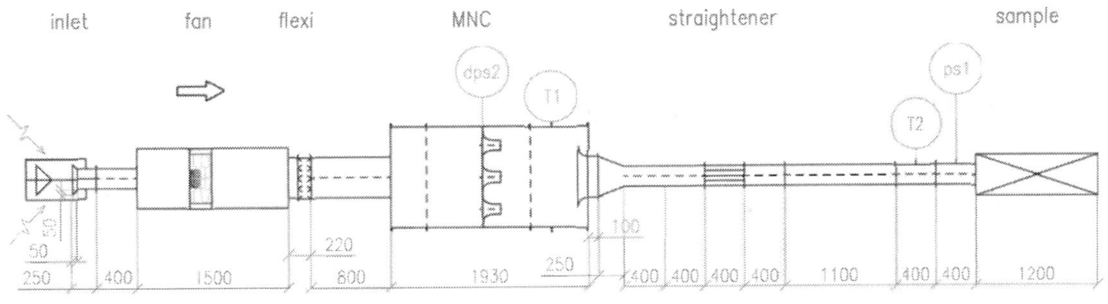

Fig. 2. Measurement track

2.1 Fan track

There are two available dimensions for the track. The diameters are 200*mm* and 400*mm*. For each dimension there are available several types of duct which can be connected with each other. This function leads to many measurement variations. The track allows measurements of fan performance curve, loss coefficient, acoustic parameters, leakage and others. All components of the track are made in accordance with International standard ISO 5801. Controlling system of the track is handled by PLC with touch panel including visualization. All measured data are periodically saved to local FTP server in form of CSV file. The whole controlling board is depicted on Figure 1. On the left can be seen frequency converters for fans, next to these are buttons for switching circuit breaker, a touch panel with visualization for setting experiment and on the right is a computer unit.

Scheme of the measurement track is depicted in Figure 2. The whole length without the sample is almost 8*m* long. The measurement track consists of inlet, ducts, fan, flexible joint, MNC, ducts, straightener, ducts and sample. Used ducts are of diameter 200*mm*.

2.2 Measured sample

As a measuring sample was used air divider for ventilation purposes. It consist of inlet with diameter of 160*mm*, inner rectangular part and ten outlets of diameter 62*mm*. To provide fully developed air, there have been added plastic pipes to each outlet. Big disadvantage of those is that it is delivered in twisted pack. That caused that it has tendency to twist. In order to prevent this from, happening a paper tube which is ordinary used for posters carrying was added. Length of outlet pipes was chosen to be 1000*mm*, which is around 16*D*, this ensured appropriate length to fully develop air profile. Final setup can be seen on Figure. 3.

2.3 Measuring equipment

Measurement of air velocity at outlets was performed with vane apparatus. This anemometer can measure velocity up to $40ms^{-1}$, with precision $\pm3\%$ from measured value. On the Figure 4 is positioning instrument with anemometer and measuring at one point.

Fig. 3. Measured sample with measurement track

2.4 Positioning instrument

To ensure appropriate position of measurement in each point, there have been made positioning arrangement. Firstly were calculated positions of measuring points for considered diameter. This calculation was done based on log-linear assumption of velocity distribution in accordance with Winternitz and Fischl [7]. They hypothesized that the velocity distribution along a diameter can be represented by the equation 4. In this assumption is duct divided to one central circular zone and number of annular zones, which all have equal area. Measuring points are at exact velocity mean zone. The reason to chose this method is based on research of Kinghorn and McHugh [8], who compared 14 traverse methods and log-linear had small-

DOI: 10.1051/matecconf/201712502028

Fig. 4. Positioning of anemometer

est mean percentage deviation with orifice plate. Final traverse positions for measurement was $15mm$ from the centre in 4 directions. Number of points and length was chose mandatory because of size of anemometer and because more points wouldn't had significant meaning.

$$v_y = A + B\,log\frac{y}{d} + C\frac{y}{d} \qquad (4)$$

Where	v_y	velocity at a distance y	$[ms^{-1}]$
	y	distance from the wall	$[m]$
	d	pipe diameter	$[m]$
	A, B, C	dimensions of velocity	

3D model was created after calculation of traverse position points in ANSYS SpaceClaim [9]. Due to complicated positions of sample outlets were modelled several configurations and then manufactured by 3D printer. Final instrument is shown on Figure. 5, above is computer model and beneath is a real model. To appropriately fix anemometer in position, a holder with magnetic base was used. This mounting have several degrees of freedom. This attribute is useful because during the measurement was mandatory to measure 4 positions at each outlet and simultaneously allow air to flow effortlessly. Fixation with anemometer was established also by 3D printed part.

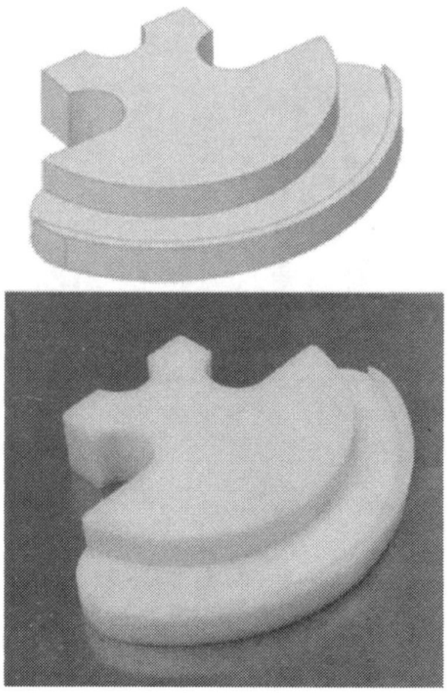

Fig. 5. Positioning instrument

2.5 CFD set-up

As computational fluid dynamic (CFD) software was used ANSYS Fluent in version 18 [10]. It was simulated only sample with boundary conditions of inlet pre-set to velocity measured by MNC to reduce computational costs. Outlet boundary conditions was set to gauge pressure of $0Pa$. Gravitational force was at Z direction and was set up to $-9,81ms^{-2}$. For calculation were used two approaches of generating mesh. In the first one was maximal face size set to $0,002m$ and edited inflation condition. Inflation boundary conditions is in high importance for fluid flow, because it generates boundary layers. First layer high (Y+) was calculated 5 based on [11] and was applied for all boundary regions same Y+. Maximum number of layers was set to 10 with default growth rate of 1, 2. In the second approach were used same conditions and was calculated first layer high for each outlet based on measured velocity.

$$\delta_v = 122\,d\frac{ln(Re)}{Re\,G(lnRe)} \qquad (5)$$

Where	δ_v	sub-layer thickness	$[mm]$
	d	pipe diameter	$[m]$
	$G(lnRe)$	function which has a limit of 1 for $Re \rightarrow \infty$	
	Re	Reynolds number	$[-]$

3 Results

3.1 Measurement on sample

The data collection was started after fixation of anemometer in appropriate point and outlet. For each point was measured velocity every second for half a minute. This

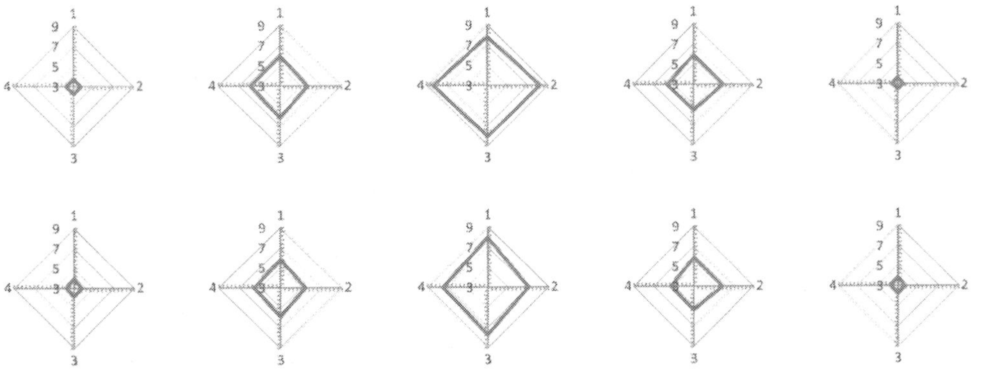

Fig. 6. Distribution of velocity at each outlet $[ms^{-1}]$

gives more then 120 values for calculating mean velocity at each outlet which is summarized in table 1. Also is calculated expanded uncertainty σ with coverage factor $k = 2$ in accordance to international standard JCGM 100:2008 [12]. The volume flow $\dot{V}$ was calculated from velocity. Total volume flow by anemometer was $(0,162 \pm 0,019)[m^3 s^{-1}]$. Measurement on MNC was performed by pressure transmitter with standard uncertainty of type A $\pm 0,577 Pa$ and type B from calibration of $\pm 0,3\%$ and of reading $\pm 0,03 Pa$. Expanded uncertainty is then $\pm 1,249 Pa$ with coverage factor of 2. When is calculated with equations 1, 2 and 3 the volumetric flow is $(0,151 \pm 0,036)[m^3 s^{-1}]$. This difference is around $6,8\%$ and is mainly due to the principle of measurement by anemometer but it is in range of uncertainty. The reason is that during the measurement process anemometer makes obstacle to the flow which then makes quicker streamlines. Next reason is due to swirling stress caused by aerodynamic forces on the rotor blading [13]. This fact and uncertainty of both methods make above mentioned difference non essential for purposes of this article. Distribution of velocities is depicted in Figure. 6, where upper left is outlet position one, next to it is second and so on. From above mentioned is apparent that air velocity distribution is not symmetrical at each outlet which leads to different air distribution in HVAC system. So is difficult to assemble such distributing box and appropriately balance each outline.

Table 1: Measured air velocity distribution at outlets

position	$v\,[ms^{-1}]$	$\sigma\,[ms^{-1}]$	$\dot{V}\,[m^3 s^{-1}]$	$Y+\,[mm]$
1	3,759	0,080	0,011	3,514
2	5,936	0,315	0,018	2,329
3	8,118	0,419	0,025	1,755
4	5,729	0,330	0,017	2,405
5	3,574	0,129	0,011	3,677
6	3,858	0,099	0,012	3,432
7	5,675	0,391	0,017	2,426
8	7,538	0,726	0,023	1,877
9	5,570	0,555	0,017	2,467
10	3,763	0,144	0,011	3,510

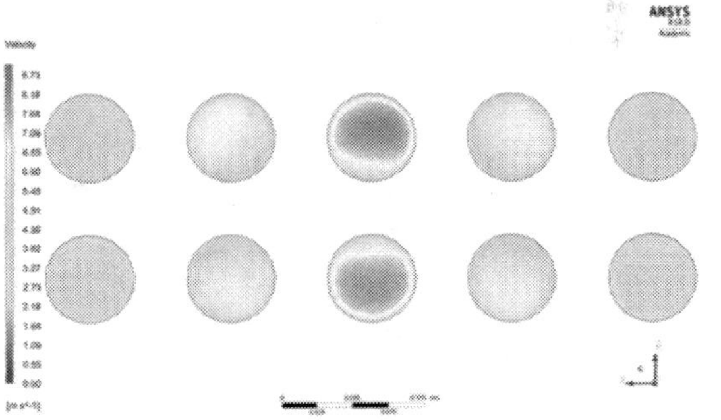

Fig. 7. Countours of velocity at outlets

3.2 CFD on sample

In previous part was measured air volume flow between $0,151$ to $0,162[m^3 s^{-1}]$ from which was taken in account measurement of MNC and so inlet air velocity for $DN200$ is around $4,8 ms^{-1}$ thus Reynolds number was calculated 64 000. Placed on before determined parameters was computed sub-layer high $(Y+)$ at inlet as $3,125\,10^{-3} m$. For outlets values was calculated at each outlet based on measured velocities and is summarized in table 1. Difference in generated mesh is summarized in table 2.

From Figure. 8 and 9 is apparent non symmetrical air distribution. This fact is in correlation with measured data as shows Figure. 7.

4 Conclusion

From above mentioned is apparent that air velocity distribution is not symmetrical at each outlet which leads to different air distribution in HVAC system. It is difficult to assemble such distributing box and appropriately balance

Table 2: Comparison of generated meshes

	one Y+ mesh	each Y+ mesh
nodes	493 384	559 048
elements	1 654 298	1 263 217

Table 3: Volumetric flow comparison $[m^3 s^{-1}]$

Position	measurement	simulation	difference
1	0,0113	0,0106	0,0008
2	0,0179	0,0160	0,0020
3	0,0245	0,0207	0,0038
4	0,0173	0,0163	0,0010
5	0,0108	0,0108	0,0000
6	0,0116	0,0110	0,0007
7	0,0171	0,0165	0,0006
8	0,0228	0,0211	0,0017
9	0,0168	0,0168	0,0000
10	0,0114	0,0111	0,0003

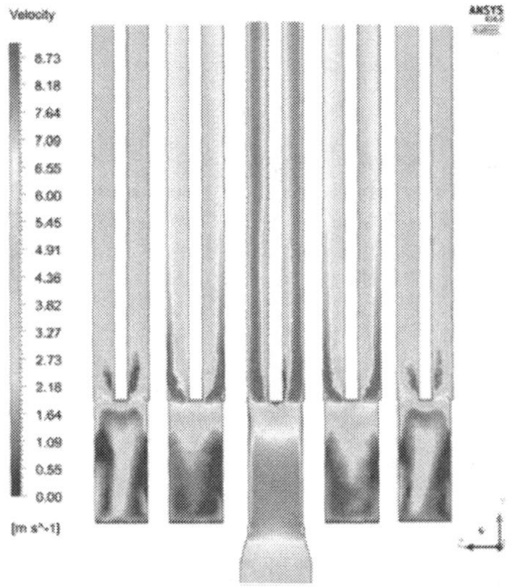

Fig. 8. Countours of velocity from simulation (side views)

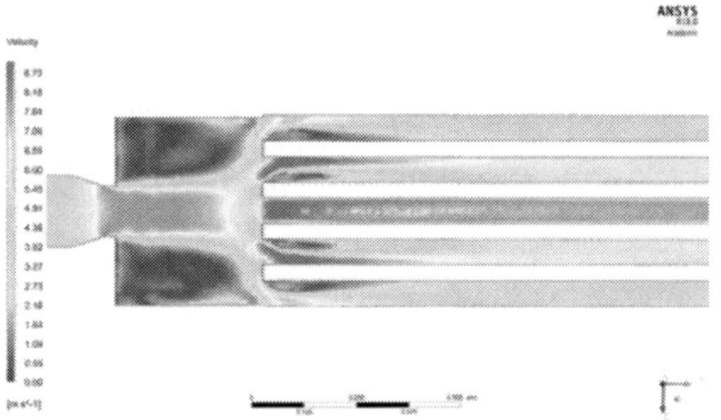

Fig. 9. Countours of velocity from simulation (top view)

each branch. The purpose of the paper was to evaluate and outline CFD simulation for HVAC equipment. Further research will focus on align air velocity equally at all outlets by CFD with later validation by measurement of final solution.

This work was supported by the Ministry of Education, Youth and Sports of the Czech Republic within the National Sustainability Programme project No. LO1303 (MSMT-7778/2014) and also by the Internal Grant Agency of Tomas Bata University in Zlin under the project No. IGA/CebiaTech/2017/002.

References

1. O. Reynolds, Proceedings of the Royal Society of London **35**, 24 (1883)
2. L.F. Moody, Transaction of the A.S.M.E. **66**, 14 (1944)
3. C.F. Colebrook, Journal of the Insitution of Civil Engineers **11**, 29 (1939)
4. T. Von Kármán, L. Edson, *The Wind and Beyond: Theodore Von Kármán, Pioneer in Aviation and Pathfinder in Space* (Little, Brown, 1967)
5. P.A. Davidson, Y. Kaneda, K. Moffatt, K.R. Sreenivasan, *A voyage through turbulence* (Cambridge University Press, 2011)
6. CSN EN ISO 5801:2009, Standard, Czech office for standards metrology and testing, Prague, CZ (2009)
7. F.A.L. WINTERNITZ, C.F. FISCHL, Water Power **9**, 225 (1957)
8. Kinghorn, F. C., McHugh, A., La Houille Blanche pp. 49–58 (1977)
9. *Ansys fluent user's guide* (2017)
10. *Spaceclaim 2015 user's guide* (2015)
11. H. Schlichting, K. Gersten, *Boundary-Layer Theory* (Springer Berlin Heidelberg, 2017), ISBN 978-3-662-52917-1
12. J.C. for Guides in Metrology, Tech. rep., JCGM (2008)
13. W. Merzkirch, *Fluid Mechanics of Flow Metering* (Springer, 2005), ISBN 9783540222422

MATEC Web of Conferences **125**, 02029 (2017) DOI: 10.1051/matecconf/201712502029
CSCC 2017

Effect of implementation quadruple glazing panel into the walls on the airborne sound insulation of building facades

Pavel Drabek[1,*]

[1] Tomas Bata University in Zlin, Faculty of Applied Informatics, Department of Automation and Control Engineering, Nad Stranemi 4511, Czech Republic

Abstract. Noise is one of the major national problems for decades. In the case of buildings, this concernment has become an issue when building structures are becoming lighter and lighter in weight. This approach does not only caused difficulties with poor sound insulation but also meant heat accumulation problems. This is due to the fact that commonly used lightweight construction materials are not able to absorb too much heat energy like massive constructions did. Production and implementation companies are trying to avoid these ailments by implementing accumulation materials into the buildings most frequently in the form of panels. A subject of this paper is to study the effect of implementation one type of facade system into the perimeter walls on the airborne sound insulation of building facades. The research is dedicated to the quadruple glazing panel which is a translucent wall element without any mechanical components or electronic devices.

1 Introduction

The general building rule is that all parts of the building must work altogether. Without the correlation between construction elements and technological equipment, the buildings are bound to have some serious defects. Therefore the individual elements which are implemented into the building must have specific properties even in terms of acoustics. In recent years the construction of lightweight buildings has grown and the sound insulation of these structures has become a serious trouble.

The sound is transmitted through most walls and floors by setting the entire structure into vibration. This vibration generates new sound waves of reduced intensity on the other side [1]. For single leaf structures, such as a homogenous concrete wall, the transmission follows the mass law, that is, the more massive the structure, the smaller the quantity of transmitted sound [2]. In case of lightweight structures consisting of multiple layers, such as a gypsum wall, the spring-mass law is applicable. If a highly absorbent material such as stone wool is used as the spring in a double leaf wall, the sound insulation improves. This fact was one of the reasons why manufacturers have started using a multilayer sandwich structures in lightweight buildings. Thus, the sound insulation structures have begun to improve over the years. However, the acoustics were not the only issue that required attention. In previous research [3], we studied the effect of the thermal accumulation on the energy efficiency of the building. One of the research intentions was to solve the light constructions and their thermal accumulation abilities which are lower compared to the more massive structures. Consequently, the energy consumption of lightweight buildings may be higher than an identical building with higher thermal accumulation. For this reason, production and implementation companies increase thermal accumulation by installing mostly PCM materials into perimeter walls.

This paper deals with the passive facade system in the form of transparent wall elements which increases both the thermal capacity of the rooms and the thermal comfort. These elements are installed instead of non-load-bearing perimeter walls. The aim of this work is to determine the impact of installation of these elements on the overall airborne sound insulation of the facade.

2 Internal environment parameters

Sound transmission paths through the structure are of diverse character. The requirements for noise level in rooms which further affect the properties of the façade are derived from the Ministry of Health decree which requires fulfilment of the two parameters, the equivalent noise level L_{Aeq} and the maximum noise level L_{Amax}. For the transmission of sound, only the structural features of the facade are not decisive but also the sound behaviour inside the space has a certain effect because multiple reflections from the walls, ceiling, floor, and object surfaces influence the sound pressure level [1]. Valid values of L_{Aeq} in front of the facade and in the internal area are listed in Table 1. In the context of this article, living rooms were preferred to be studied, since the inner environment requirements for this type of interior space

* Corresponding author: pdrabek@fai.utb.cz

places more emphasis on L_{Amax} value than to other types of indoor areas, with the exception of hospital rooms.

Table 1. The parameters considered for the noise analysis [4].

$L_{Aeq,T}$ [dB] two meters in front of the facade		
Highways, roads I. and II. class, local roads I. and II. cl.	Day time:	65 dB
	Night time:	55 dB
L_{Amax} [dB] of indoor areas		
Living rooms	Day time:	40 dB
	Night time:	30 dB
Required sound insulation value of facade R_W [dB]		
Living rooms	Day time:	33 dB
	Night time:	33 dB

3 Quadruple glazing panel

The relevant task described in the article was to evaluate theoretical and experimental aspects of acoustic properties such as airborne sound insulation and reflection of sound waves of the panel. From the point of view of acoustics, this panel can be described as glazing group of multiple safety glasses without a frame. This group contains hermetically sealed cavities filled with inert gas, prism plate and PCM material (see Fig. 1). The entirety of these elements is ensured by a structural sealant, which stands for the frame of the whole set. It can be obvious that even the type of connection method affects the acoustic properties of the whole element.

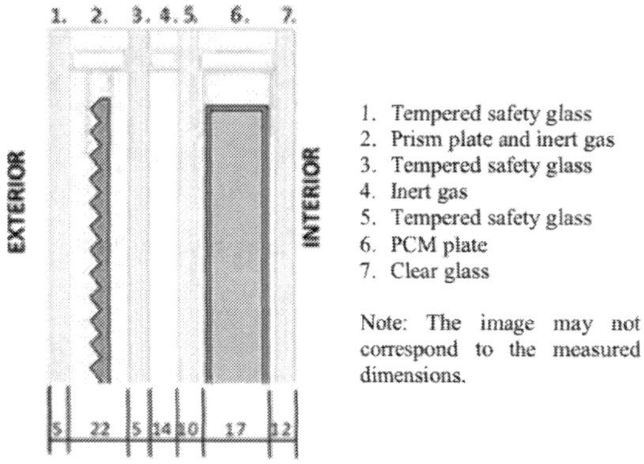

Fig. 1. Description of layers of quadruple glazing panel.

The transmission of sound energy through the weakest elements of the façade, especially the windows, is mainly due to the vibration of the glazed parts [2]. With the area density and the observed frequency, the degree of sound insulation is also changing or, more specifically, with increasing area density, airborne sound insulation also increases because the window surface is no longer so easy to vibrate, and at the same time, the amount of scattering of the incident sound energy from the surface of the window increases [1][2]. The airborne sound rate also affects the angle of the incident sound waves, discontinuities, stiffness, the number of windows and so on. However, these general assumptions are not fully applicable to a building element of this type.

Generally, the degree of airborne sound insulation is mainly dependent on the area density of the glass. Based on experimental measurements, it was found that the airborne sound insulation of a single glass only slightly increases from 6.5 kg/m^{-2} due to coincidence effect in the soundproofing area [2][5]. For double glazing with significantly different glass thicknesses, the coincidence of the thicker glass is already suppressed. And in the case of triple glazing the positive effect is reflected mainly at higher frequencies, and in the case of frequencies smaller than 500Hz, the improvement is minimal [5][6]. However, the design of this panel is different from the common windows described above. The absence of the frame, the connection method and the window surface greatly change the acoustic properties [2]. The area density of individual glasses ranges from 12.5 to 30 kg/m^{-2} and the dimensions of the panel are 1.2 x 1.2 m. From a general perspective, the panel acts as a very heavy and rigid building component. The calculated critical frequency is around 150Hz. This relatively low value, combined with different glass and gauge thicknesses, means that the coincidence effect is almost completely suppressed here.

4 Methods

The level of airborne sound insulation of the facade can be solved in several ways. The basic ones are computational models, simulation models and real measurements in the laboratory. The solution in this article is based on computational models which reflect experiences of predicting sound transmission through the facade of residential buildings and other building of a similar character [7]. The accuracy of such models depends on the accuracy of the input data, the model situation, the type of façade elements contained, the geometry of the situation and the type of the predicted variable. Likewise, the different types of external sound field used in different situations lead to different values [7]. For this reason, only the incident of the diffuse sound field was considered, because it is rationally assumed that the results are sufficiently representative for other types of external sound fields. Another important aspect for predicting the noise load in an indoor area is also the spectral character of the attenuation of sound propagation in the outdoor environment [8]. This attenuation occurs as a result of the absorption of sound in the atmosphere and its magnitude depends on specific meteorological conditions. All these parameters require the attention of acoustical engineers. The input values entering the analysis were obtained by measuring the standardized sound pressure level difference in the laboratory. These concernments will be discussed in the following.

4.1 Laboratory measurement of acoustic parameters

Airborne sound insulation measurements were performed according to the requirements of the concerned standards [8][9]. For the measurement itself, a special chamber was used, the interior space of which was divided into two parts (outdoor and indoor) by a dividing partition and a wall opening for a panel was created in it. Subsequently, wall diffusion elements were placed in the outdoor room to form a partial diffusion field at a frequency range of 50 - 10000 Hz and there was also a sound source in the room. The already built-in panel has been further modified from the indoor side so that the individual microphones can be firmly attached close to the window surface. At the same time, it was desirable to minimize the influence of lateral transmission, in particular reflections from the back wall of the indoor room. For this reason, the microphones were placed in the air gap between the panel and the board with absorbent material (see Fig. 2). Afterwards, on both sides, the average sound pressure levels in the third-octave bands at the aforementioned frequency range were measured.

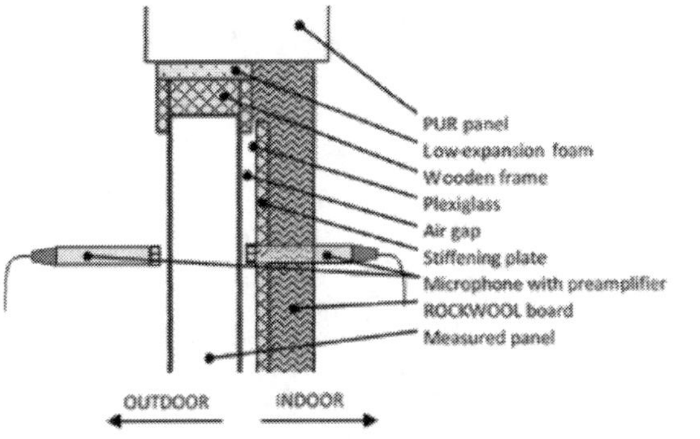

Fig. 2. Schematic representation of microphone mounts with rear-side absorption.

In the experimental measurement, only the normalized difference in sound pressure levels for the entire frequency range was found. These values need to be attributed to the influence of lateral transmission, which is also frequency dependent; however, this influence has not yet been accurately determined. Due to the risk of considerable transmission of acoustic energy by the dividing partition, an "orientation" test was conducted to determine if the acoustic power transmitted by the surrounding structure is small compared to the acoustic power transmitted over the test element. The result of this test was that the acoustic energy transmitted by the partition is even higher than the acoustic energy transmitted by the test element; consequently, it is necessary to modify the existing partition between indoor and outdoor space by installing additional material which would bring a high weight to a small thickness.

Fig. 3. Measurement of the standardized level difference in the Laboratory (a. LpA measurement in reception room, b. Microphone field, c. Norsonic MF-850).

4.2 Model situation description

To process this point, the internal area of the administration building was taken into account. The dimensional parameters of the considered area are shown in Table 2.

Table 2. Dimensional specifications of the considered area.

Room Parameters	
Dimensions in [m], (w x l x h)	7,32 x 8,70 x 3,01
Surface in [m^2]	223,81
Volume in [m^3]	191,69
Parameters of the wall in contact with the outdoor environment	
Inner surface in [m^2]	26,19
Windows surface in [m^2]	13,51
Windows frame surface in [m^2]	3,12
Other structures surface in [m^2]	12,68
Usable surface for PCM panels	8,00

Since the full mathematical description of the acoustic insulation conferred by glazed panels is extremely complicated, simplified theoretical models are frequently used [1][7]. As the predominant source of sound in the outdoor environment, the most frequent source of outdoor noise, road traffic was considered. For this situation, were served the standard values of the sound pressure levels for transport density (1000 cars/hour), which were subsequently recalculated to a reference distance of 30 m (the distance of the linear source and the facade of the model situation). Subsequently, it was necessary to determine the considered frequency range, which is prominent for the given situation. This range depends primarily on the magnitude of attenuation due to its absorption in the atmosphere for different weather conditions [10].

The very spectral nature of the attenuation of sound propagation in the outdoor environment is very important in the prediction of the noise pollution in indoor space. The output is the value of the attenuation coefficient m. Thus, attenuations in the frequency bands for the given atmospheric conditions were determined at first. From these attenuations, the sound pressure levels at the reference distance were determined, to which additional losses were added to the reference distance, and subsequently, the sound pressure level L_{pA} in front of the facade was determined. Consequently, the upper limit of the frequency range has been reduced to 4 kHz. Higher frequencies do not need to be taken into account due to atmospheric attenuation and the fact that almost all building materials are characterized by high absorption or reflection capabilities at this frequency range [10].

In order to calculate the effect of quadruple glazing panel implementation on airborne sound insulation, experimentally determined values of domestic certified laboratories were used, these values are shown in Table 3.

Table 3. The acoustic data of the implemented elements in the model situation

Element used	Frequency [Hz]					
	125	250	500	1000	2000	4000
	Airborne sound insulation R_W [dB]					
Sandwich wall of thickness 30 cm	35	40	46	52	58	64
Double glazing Window (6/16/6)	23	22	30	36	37	39
Quadruple glazing panel	25	27	28	31	41	51

5 Results

In the following the results of the measurement of the standard difference of the sound pressure levels as well as the results of the model situation are summarized.

In general, the main parameter describing the listening parameters of the room is the reverberation time [1]. It is dependent on several input parameters, of which the dimensions of the room and the sound absorption of the internal surfaces are of utmost importance. The maximum value of the sound absorption factor depends mainly on the sound absorption coefficient [2]. As this factor is higher, the higher the absorption can be achieved. Whilst on how material absorbs in the range of lower frequencies is determined primarily by its thickness and that is why the sound absorption value of the panel at low frequencies is considerably lower than the sandwich wall type. In the range of higher frequencies, the sound absorption of the panel is very similar to lower frequencies.

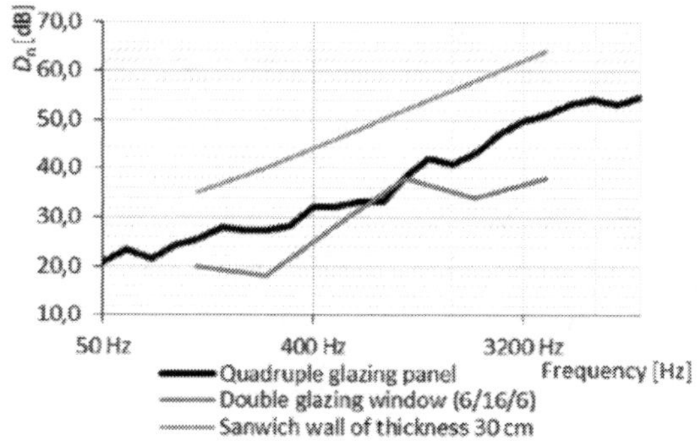

Fig. 3. Description of layers of quadruple glazing panel.

Based on this fact, it can be stated that the implementation of PCM windows into the perimeter walls will not have a significant negative impact on the overall listening parameters of the room (see Fig. 4); however, from the point of view of the soundproofing properties, it is necessary to ensure the proper fit and seal because the individual joints and gaps are the weakest facade elements.

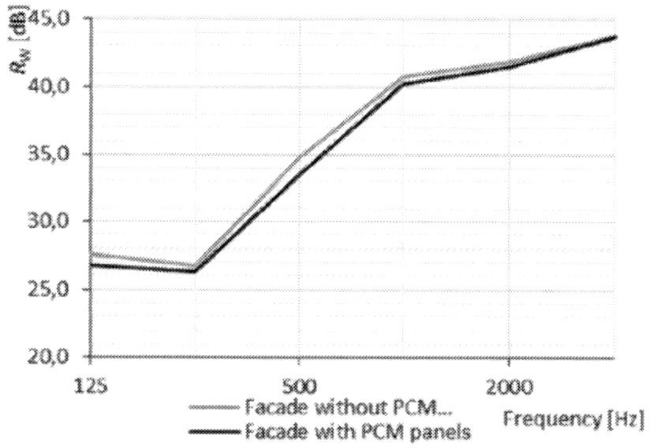

Fig. 4. Influence of quadruple glazing panel implementation on airborne soundness in the model situation.

6 Conclusion

Sound insulation between the different rooms inside a building or to the outside environment is a very complex problem [11][12]. This matter has become very topical in the recent years mainly in connection with the development of buildings constructed from lightweight materials. The aim of the study was to determine the impact of the implementation of the quadruple glazing panel with the PCM plate into the perimeter walls, instead of non-load-bearing structures, on the sound insulation properties of the facade. This goal was met with the authors' comments and that the results of the experimental measurement do not include the effect of the sound transmission by the sideways which must be added to the value of the standard difference D_n. To determine the rate of sound transmission by sideways it would be necessary to install an element of known acoustic parameters in the reduced aperture, and a substitution method could be used to determine it. The conclusion is that the correct incorporation of these types of storage elements into the perimeter walls of buildings will not significantly reduce the sound-insulating properties.

Acknowledgement

This work was supported by the Ministry of Education, Youth and Sports of the Czech Republic within the National Sustainability Programme project No. LO1303 (MSMT-7778/2014) and also by the Internal Grant Agency of Tomas Bata University in Zlin under the project No. IGA/CebiaTech/2017/002.

References

1. H. Kuttruff, Room Acoustics, **5**, (2009)
2. M. Möser, G. Müller, Handbook of Engineering Acoustics, (2013)
3. P. Drabek, M. Zalesak, WSEAS Transactions on Systems and Control, **11**, 32-38 (2016)
4. 272/2011 Sb., Regulation, Ministri, Praha (2011)
5. A. Tadeu, D. Mateus, Applied Acoustics, **62**, 307-325 (2001)
6. D. Vila, Master Thesis, (2012)
7. EN 12354, Standard, European Committee for Standardization, Brusel, (2001)
8. EN ISO 717-1, Standard, European Committee for Standardization, Brusel, (2013)
9. EN ISO 140-5, Standard, European Committee for Standardization, Brusel, (2000)
10. EN ISO 9613-1, Standard, European Committee for Standardization, Brusel, (1995)
11. N. Ashmore, D. Cabrera, C. Kocer, Australian Acoustical Society, N/A, 1-9 (2015)
12. R. Wareing, J. Davy, J. Pearse, Australian Acoustical Society, N/A, 1-10 (2014)

Comparison of two internationally recognized methods for determining the sound absorption coefficient

Pavel Drabek[1,*]

[1] Tomas Bata University in Zlin, Faculty of Applied Informatics, Department of Automation and Control Engineering, Nad Stranemi 4511, Czech Republic

Abstract. With today's growing focus on noise control issues and the emergence of sound quality as an important aspect of product design, acoustic material testing is becoming increasingly relevant to engineers, designers and manufacturers from a broad range of industries. Acoustic material testing is the process by which acoustic characteristics of materials are determined in terms of absorption, reflection, impedance, admittance and transmission loss. Many different methods can be used to determine the acoustic properties of materials. There are standing wave method, two-microphone free field and multimicrophone techniques, reverberation chamber method, in-situ methods and many other alternative methods based on measurement of internal properties of porous materials. The point is that some methods are preferred over others because the environment in which they are measured is closer to real practice. The article deals with the comparison of the results of the measurement in the reverberation chamber and in the interferometer.

1 Introduction

In recent years, great emphasis has been put on improving the quality of the environment and the well-being of a person [1]. Hence, the proposals for new production technologies and materials must take into account all factors that may have a negative impact on the environment. For this reason, it is necessary to implement a set of measures to eliminate the harmful effects. These measures are realized on the basis of experimental measurements of characteristic physical quantities and their evaluation. One of these environmental factors is noise and the protection against its excessive exposure is an object of engineering interest.

In the case of performing an acoustic assessment of the space in order to improve the sound transmission, it is necessary to work with the values of the sound absorption coefficient α of the absorbent materials in relation to the frequency.

Determination of the absorption coefficient of materials for sound absorption and absorbent structures is commonly performed according to two basic methods [1][2]. The first one is a standing waves method, which allows the determination of the coefficient only for the sound waves impinging perpendicularly. The advantage of using this method is that the material impedance can be detected simultaneously [1]. However, the values found in this way have little relevance in technical practice because when the material is placed in enclosures its sound absorption coefficient is considerably different due to the omnidirectional sound waves incidents [3]. Hence its values can not be used to design acoustic adjustments, and preference is given to the results from the reverberation chamber measurement because its internal environment is closer to the final practical application. From the same assumption, other alternative methods have been developed that have a different accuracy of results, time and financial demands on the necessary equipment, for example [4][5].

The problem is that the laboratories that carry out the measurements are following a certain piece of legislation (ASTM or ISO). The point is that these documents differ in several requirements for measuring space, used equipment and the sample itself. For example, a comparison of these two approaches is mentioned in [6]. The intention of this paper is to provide information on the different measurement techniques and its differences in results.

2 Description of the tested materials

This point specifies the properties of two materials that were selected to compare the results of the α measurement coefficient in the interferometer and the reverberation chamber. The intent was to choose the elements which are characterized by different texture, porosity, thickness and the technological process of its production.

The first sample was the mineral wool bonded with organic resin ROCKWOOL - Multirock Rockmin (see Fig. 1) insulating wadding in the form of boards with dimensions 1000x600x40 mm. These boards are mainly used for thermal, noise and fire insulation of roofs, ceilings and walls.

* Corresponding author: pdrabek@fai.utb.cz

Fig. 1. Pattern of Rockwoll - Multirock Rockmin (sample 1).

The second specimen was the NOISEFLEX Classic (see Fig. 2) acoustic panel with dimensions of 1000x500x50 mm. This panel is made of the Basotect material, which is a flexible foam with an open cell structure made of melamine resin. It is used in a wide range of applications, such as sound and heat insulation of buildings and vehicles, as well as cleaning sponges.

Fig. 2. Pattern of Noiseflex Classic (sample 2).

3 Methodology

Measurement of the above-mentioned samples was done by both methods, specific activities are described in followings.

3.1 Impedance or standing wave tube measurement

The principle of measuring the sound absorption factor of materials using this method is well known and is described in detail in [1]. The measurements were performed using the two-microphone tube Brüel & Kjaer 4206 and the three-channel PULSE multi-analyzer Brüel & Kjaer type 3560-B-030. These kits meet the standards ISO 10534-2, ASTM E1050 – 12. The measuring system consists of two cylindrical form tubes of diameter 30 and 100 mm, which allow measuring in the frequency range 0 Hz to 1.6 kHz and 500 Hz to 6.4 kHz, and a broadband loudspeaker that generates noise. With a broadband signal propagating from the loudspeaker, a frequency response function is measured between the two phase-matched condenser microphones which are placed at set distances along the length of the tube. Each measured response must be phase calibrated according to the procedure presented in the governing standard. Afterwards, the resulting absorption curve is then determined by the combined calculation over the entire frequency range. Equations (1) and (2) define the algorithm for the computation of the sound absorption coefficient, α, from H.

$$R(j\omega)=\frac{H_{12}-e^{-jkz}}{e^{jkz}-H_{12}}e^{j2k(l+z)} \quad (1)$$

where $H_{12}=p(z_2)/p(z_1)$ is the transfer function which is simply the ratio of pressures p, $k=2\pi f/c$ is the wave number, s is the center-to-center distance between the microphones, z_1 is the distance from the face of the test sample to the center of the nearest of the microphone, z_2 is the distance for the farther microphone, and $R(jw)$ is the complex reflection coefficient. The resulting α value is then given by the following equation.

$$\alpha=1-|R(j\omega)|^2. \quad (2)$$

Both materials were cut to the inner dimension of each tube. However, the carving itself needs to be done very accurately. It was hypothesized that any small difference between the diameter of the material sample and that of the inside of the tube would cause measurement errors [1]. This effect should be more visible in the narrower tube since small differences in diameter result in large differences in boundary pressure loading. In part, the question of the effect of these inaccuracies on the resulting values of the sound absorption coefficient is solved here [7].

3.1 Reverberation chamber method

As in the previous case, the reverberation chamber method is well known and does not need to be described here [2]. It is described in detail in standards [8] and [9]. The measurements were performed in a reverberation chamber at Tomas Bata University in Zlín, and the values were further compared with those obtained from a certified laboratory in Prague. At this point, it is worth to mention that the reverberation chamber in Zlín does not meet the parameters of the standards for sound absorption measurements and the measurements made in it are only indicative and serve the purpose of its further verification, which has already been carried out and published here [10]. The reverberation chamber in Zlin has a rectangular shape and volume of 93.66 m^3. To eliminate the standing waves generation and to create a partial diffusion environment, the walls and the ceiling are fitted with diffusion elements. The reverberation chamber in Prague was built according to the requirements of the standards concerned. It has a volume of 200 m^3 and also contains diffusion elements.

The test element was asymmetrically mounted directly on the floor of the chamber so that no part of it was closer than 1m from any boundary wall (see Fig. 3). The sample was rectangular with a width/length ratio of

DOI: 10.1051/matecconf/201712502030

between 0.7 and 1. The area of the sample was about 9 m^2. The outer flanks of the test specimen were enclosed by an acoustically reflective frame. Subsequently, the reverberation time with the sample and the empty room was measured.

Fig. 3. Measurement of sound absorption of sample 2 in reverberation chamber at TBU in Zlin.

In the same way, both samples were measured in a reverberation chamber in Prague. The area of the samples was about 12 m^2. The reverberation times were measured over a range of 100 Hz to 5 kHz and was determined on the basis of the impulse response, so the chamber was excitation by a pistol shot. The source was normally placed in the corner of a room, pointing into the corner, because it maximally excites the modes of the room and reduces the amount of direct radiation from the source to the test sample. Despite these measures, a diffuse field is not completely achieved, and consequently, the reverberation time is position dependent [1]. For this reason, it is normal to use multiple sources and receiver positions and to average the results to reduce the effect of nondiffuseness [2]. Even with all these measures, the measured absorption coefficients are often more inaccurate at low than high frequencies due to modal effects.

During the measurement, microclimatic conditions were also recorded to correctly determine the amount of absorbed sound in the interior of the chamber. The procedure for calculating the attenuation factor is given in the standard [11].

4 Results

This point summarizes the results of the two different comparisons. The first one shows the differences between the results of the sound absorption coefficient obtained by different methods, and the second one compares the results from measurements performed in two different environments, where the first space meets the standard requirements for the volume and shape of the room and the other does not meet these requirements. These anticoincidences will be discussed in the following.

As can be seen from the Fig. 4 and 5, the α values determined in the reverberation chamber are higher in the entire frequency range. It is mainly because the impedance tube measures the absorption only for the perpendicular incidence of sound waves and furthermore, the absorption coefficients determined in reverberation chambers are commonly exaggerated by diffraction effects and care must be taken, where it is critical, to correctly take such effects into account. The appropriate proof can be that absorption coefficient tables published in the literature often contain values greater than 1 [1]. These results only confirm this fact.

Sample 2 displays better absorption capabilities, especially at lower frequencies, where, in particular, the higher material thickness is applied. Towards higher frequencies, the increase in absorption in both samples is very similar. In the case of impedance tube results, it can be observed that absorption increases in sample 2 much earlier. This can be caused by several factors such as, for example, a better cellular structure of the material and the method of joining the individual layers. However, it is also possible that the sample was not completely cut off and the resulting leakage affected the results.

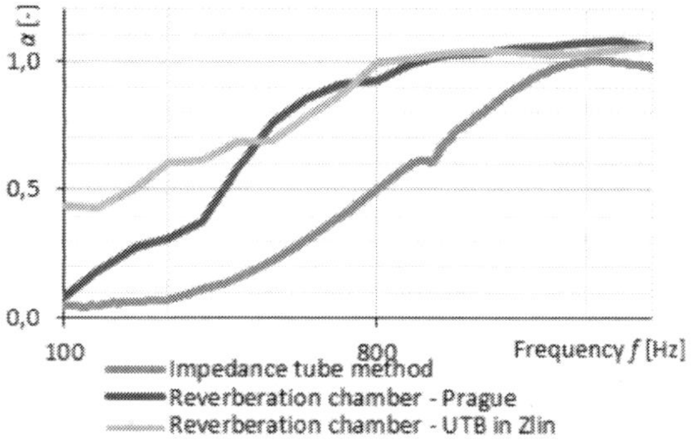

Fig. 4. Comparison of absorption curves of sample 1 for different measurement methods.

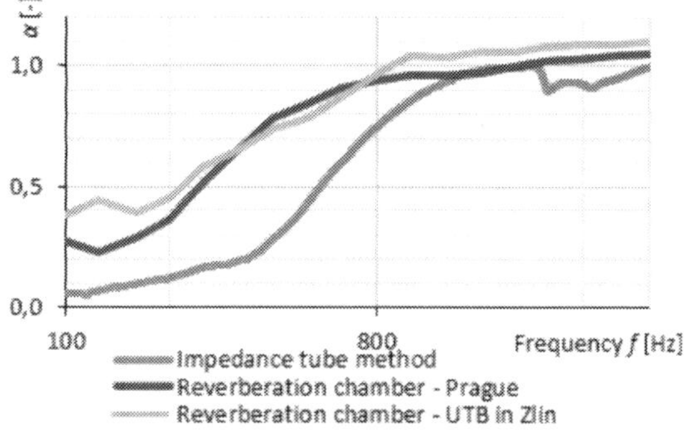

Fig. 5. Comparison of absorption curves of sample 2 for different measurement methods.

When comparing the results from both chambers, some deviations are noticeable, especially at lower frequencies. In the case of the TBU Chamber, significant fluctuations can be observed. This is due to the fact that the volume is not sufficient and the sound field is not sufficiently distributed at lower frequencies. This causes that the dispersion of reverberation times is relatively high and the uncertainty of the measurement increases considerably. And this is precisely why the internal chamber volume is required to be at least 150 m3. At higher frequencies, the values are met and the difference here is mainly due to the diffraction effect.

5 Conclusion

In most applications, the sound will be incident on an absorptive material from a multitude of incident angles at once. The random incidence absorption coefficient is the parameter used most in the design of spaces to specify the absorption performance of materials. The reverberation chamber test requires large sample sizes and a specialist test room and so it is expensive to undertake. For this reason, developers of absorptive materials will often use the impedance tube to build up an understanding of the material properties of small samples, before undertaking reverberation tests.

From the above, it is clear that it is very necessary to know what method can be used to obtain the desired results. For the development of new materials, the impedance tube method is suitable; however, for design acoustic adjustments of the space, the alpha coefficient obtained from the rectangular chamber measurements is much more relevant.

Acknowledgement

This work was supported by the Ministry of Education, Youth and Sports of the Czech Republic within the National Sustainability Programme project No. LO1303 (MSMT-7778/2014) and also by the Internal Grant Agency of Tomas Bata University in Zlin under the project No. IGA/CebiaTech/2017/002.

References

1. T. Cox, P. D'Antonio, Acoustic Absorbers and Diffusers, 2, (2009)
2. M. Möser, G. Müller, Handbook of Engineering Acoustics, (2013)
3. R. Novy, Hluk a chveni, (2009)
4. K. Kleinschmidt, Building Acoustics, **6**, 63-70 (1999)
5. O. Robin, A. Berry, O. Doutres, N. Atalla, Acoustical Society of America, **136**, 13-19 (2014)
6. M. Bischel, K. Roy, J. Greenslade, Acoustics08 Paris, **AA03**, 1669-1674 (2008)
7. A. Barnard, M. Rao, NOISE-CON, **N/A**, 1-8 (2004)
8. ASTM C423-90a, Standard, ASTM International, West Conshohocken, 2002
9. EN ISO 354, Standard, European Committee for Standardization, Brusel, (2003)
10. P. Drabek, M. Zalesak, WSEAS Transactions on Environment and Development, **12**, 377-385 (2016)
11. EN ISO 9613-1, Standard, European Committee for Standardization, Brusel, (1995)

Modeling the yield of hydrolysis process of leather shavings

Hana Vaskova[1,*], and *Pavel* Kocurek[1]

[1]Tomas Bata University in Zlin, Faculty of Applied informatics, Department of Electronic and Measurements, 760 05 Zlin, Czech Republic

Abstract. In this paper the mathematical modeling of collagen hydrolyzate yield from shavings, a leather waste material, is dealt. Besides its function, leather industry is perceived as a consumer of resources and producer of pollutants. The process of alkaline enzymatic hydrolysis offers a reasonable method of processing part of solid waste arising from leather industry with the aim of further utilization of collagenous share. The model is based on the total mass and dry matter balances of technology and its individual components to optimize the hydrolysate yields. The results are visualised in 3D. The experimental laboratory data of alkaline enzymatic hydrolysis are used for comparison with the model and are discussed.

1 Introduction

The environmental protection is a topic attracting lot of attention. Attitudes are different. Different also in terms of what each individual can or wants to do and really does, and what is the matter of larger units, such as at the level of manufacturing industries. In each production, waste is generated.

A significant amount of waste arises annually from manufacturing sector. In this paper it is dealt with waste generated in leather industry. Leather products like footwear, clothing, handbags, wallets, fashion accessories, upholstery, etc. are among the objects of our everyday needs. However a way of conversion of rawhide to leather requires many treatment processes. The diversity and amounts of produced waste represent a serious problem. The production of 200 kg of leather requires 1000 kg of raw hides, i.e. the use of feedstock is only 20%. From the input of 1000 kg about 250 kg of non-tanned waste, 200 kg of tanned wastes containing chromium is also produced [1]. A remaining share comprises modified solid waste and sludge. In the production of 200 kg of leather about 50,000 kg of waste water containing about 5 kg of chromium is generated [2].

Chrome-tanning is still the most common type of tanning worldwide. Complex salts of trivalent chromium effectively influence the desired functional properties of leather. The fibril-forming collagens are the major structural proteins of hides and skins. Salts of trivalent chromium stabilize a hide by crosslinking collagen fibres and supply required qualities. However, trivalent chromium contained in leather can be under various conditions in small amounts oxidized to another form – hexavalent chromium [3]. Hexavalent chromium belongs among toxic elements and its salts are classified as carcinogen in the contrast to the trivalent form, which is benign, safe and largely beneficial [4]. Chromium is contained in solid waste and waste water. The degradation to toxic form can occur in the environment, e.g. during landfilling [5].

There are many aspects such as losses of collagen material or energy and chemical consumption requiring changes of attitude and optimization of both, production processes and waste processing. Despite growing demand for alternative methods of tanning, and there some existing e.g. [6], none has been a competitive replacement to such a large extend [7].

The existing methods of processing waste containing chromium are often based on separation of collagenous material and chromium share. This is done by hydrolytic reaction in alkaline or acidic medium. The protein is liquified and after further treatment can be applied in forms of gelatine or protein hydrolyzates. The further use of chromium sludge is not so successful. However, for example a by thermal decomposition a reduction of chrome cake amount can be reached [8]. Anyway it is still better solution to process at least a part of waste material.

Mathematical modeling gains a great importance for the analysis and prediction of the behaviour of processes and phenomena. It seems to be useful in the optimization of waste processing as well. Although the quality of the waste material varies according to sources and type, modeling may indicate the appropriate direction for efficient processing.

2 Objective of the study

The objective of this study is mathematical modeling of yield of collagenous hydrolyzate produced by alkaline enzymatic hydrolysis, based on the physico-chemical characteristics of the inputs and intermediates within the processing and comparing with real experimental laboratory data.

* Corresponding author: vaskova@fai.utb.cz

3 Dechromation process

Hydrolysis of leather shavings in alkaline medium is used to obtain enzymatic hydrolyzate of collagen. The production system consists of three fundamental elements: reactor, filter and evaporator. When the desired degree of hydrolysis is reached, hot heterogeneous mixture is filtered and the resulting filtrate is transferred to an evaporator for increasing the concentration of hydrolysed substance.

4 Mathematical model

The physico-chemical processes occurring in the reactor can be described along with other mathematical relationships on the basis of the mass and mass fraction of dry matter. The assignments of physical quantities occurring in the model are listed in Table 1.

The yield of hydrolysates is closely related to the input materials parameters as well as the parameters of intermediates in the production process. The simulation calculations for the yield of final hydrolysates is based on mass and mass fraction of dry matter balances for the entire production system, its units and combination of these units. The balances are listed in the equations (1) – (4).

Table 1. Assignments for the model.

Designation	Quantity	Unit
m_s	Mass of shavings (feedstock)	t
m_w	Mass of water (feedstock)	t
m_{ob}	Mass of organic base	t
m_m	Mass of MgO	t
m_{fk}	Mass of filter cake	t
m_f	Mass of filtrate	t
m_{ww}	Mass of waste water	t
m_p	Mass of product	t
a_s	Dry matter of shavings	1
a_{fk}	Dry matter of filter cake	1
a_f	Dry matter of filtrate	1
a_p	Dry matter of product	1

Total mass balance of the whole system:

$$m_s + m_w + m_{ob} + m_m = m_{fk} + m_p + m_{ww} \tag{1}$$

Balance of the total dry matter of technology

$$m_s a_s + m_m = m_{fk} a_{fk} + m_p a_p \tag{2}$$

Mass balance of reactor and filter

$$m_s + m_w + m_{ob} + m_m = m_{fk} + m_f \tag{3}$$

Balance of dry matter of evaporator

$$m_{fl} a_{fl} = m_p a_p \tag{4}$$

The calculations are solved for the specific values given in Table 2. These values of mass fractions of dry matter in individual raw materials are considered to cover the range with higher probability of their achievement in the hydrolysis process. The amounts of feedstock were chosen for a real reactor in semi-industrial scale - 3 tons of leather waste material and 15 tons of water. Values of dry matters and mass rate of shavings and water are known from previous experiments. Varying value of dry matter of feedstock material due to various sources of leather waste, that also affects the filtrate, should be considered.

Masses m_{fk}, m_f, m_w and m_p represent unknown – modeled quantities.

The objective is to gain as much product as it is economically profitable with the consideration of the main operating costs.

Table 2. Dry matter values.

Quantity	Value
a_s	0.20 – 0.80
a_{fk}	0.10 – 0.50
a_f	0.02
a_p	0.30

4.1. Outputs of the model

Based on the equations (1) – (4), a 3D visualization of solution of the balance mathematical model was performed in software Wolfram Mathematica 9.

The product mass dependence on dry matter of shavings and filter cake is displayed in Fig. 1. Dependence of the product mass on the dry matter of filter cake and the water consumption for three specific dry matter values of the leather shavings in the range of 0.20 – 0.80 is shown in Fig. 2. Also product mass

DOI: 10.1051/matecconf/201712502031

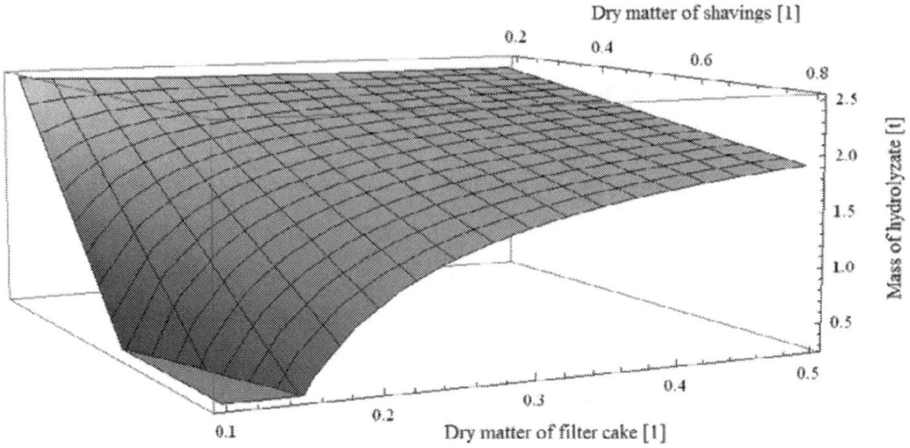

Fig. 1. 3D visualisation of product mass dependence on dry matter of shavings and filter cake.

dependence on dry matter of shavings and water consumption was dealt.

The amount of dry matter in the filter cake depends on the time of filtration and the consumption of pressure energy. As illustrated in Fig. 1., after reaching the value of the dry matter in filter cake approximately 0.3, it is not effective to continue in hydrolysis reaction. Prolongation of the process has no significant effect on the yield of the product. Contrariwise, the energy consumption is higher and hence, the operational costs [9], is increased.

In Fig. 2., 3D dependences of hydrolyzate yields on the dry matter of filter cake and the consumption of water for a specific mass of dry matter of leather shavings are displayed. Results indicate how the product yields develop in a range of dry masses of shavings. The most remarkable change occurs for lower values of dry matter of filter cake. Also the consumption of water for reaching the same product yield increase with the higher amount of dry matter in leather shavings.

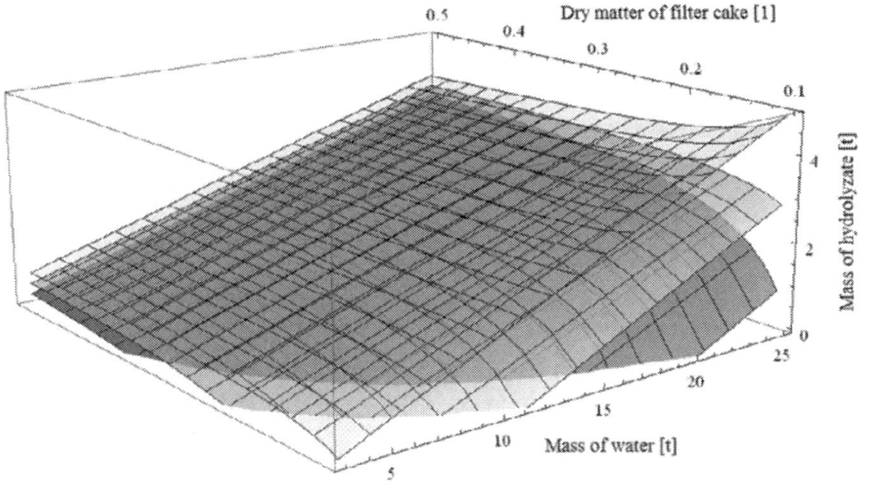

Fig. 2. 3D visualisation of dependence of product mass on the dry matter of filter cake and the consumption of water for constant mass of dry matter of chromium shavings 0.2 (upper), 0.5 (middle) and 0,8 (lower).

5 Experimental data

5.1. The experiment

The experiment included the hydrolysis phase in the batch reactor and the subsequent filtration phase, all done under laboratory conditions. For the experiment leather shavings from chrome-tanned cattle hides from a local tannery were used. Hydrolysis was done in automatically controlled batch reactor in approximately quarter size of a pilot scale.

Firstly, a reaction mixture from chromium shavings and distilled water in the ratio of 1:5 was prepared. Magnesium oxide was added to reach optimal alkaline conditions. Process of alkalinization was completed after 2 days and was followed by gradual heating of the mixture for one hour up to 70 °C. The pH was controlled and modified when necessary by cyklohexylamine to be in range 9-9.5 and Alcalase enzyme was added. The reaction mixture was hydrolysed for 4 hours, while stirred. Finally, after completion of the hydrolysis, the mixture was filtered through a fabric filter to separate the collagen hydrolysate from chromium cake.

The data obtained from experimental alkaline hydrolysis of shavings and filtration under laboratory conditions are shown in Table 3.

Table 3. Experimental data.

	Mass [kg]	**Dry matter [1]**	**Total chromium [g/kg of dry matter]**
I			
Shavings	2.00	0.639	33.700
Water	10.00	0	-
Filter cake	6.12	0.178	44.450
Filtrate	4.98	0.020	0.002
II			
Shavings	3.00	0.367	33.742
Water	15.00	0	-
Filter cake	6.04	0.176	33.137
Filtrate	10.10	0.013	0.666

5.2. Comparison of the model and experimental laboratory data

Because a real reactor was used, which is not apparently ideally isolated, the filtrate yield due to energy losses is lower than predicted. In the balance equations, losses during water evaporation are not included. However, the water content affects the dry matter and also the quantity of individual substances.

In the experiments performed, the energy losses are manifested by a difference in the weight of input and output substances of 7.5 and 10.3 %. Weight loss is mainly caused by water evaporation. The weights of the filtrate, regardless of loss, calculated from the mass balance, are m_f = 5.88 kg for experiment I and m_f = 11.96 kg for experiment II. These heat losses in terms of the amount of filtrate obtained in both cases make up about 15 % difference. The experimental results indicate the further step of the study - that some coefficient of evaporation should be considered in the mathematical model, as nothing in the world is ideal.

6 Conclusions

Development of methods for safe, environmentally friendly and economically effective reduction of waste is demanded all over the world. Model dealing with the requirement of minimizing cost in the process of hydrolysis of leather shavings in terms of yield was presented. Optimization the processing approach of leather wastes is based on thorough analysis of technological operations and on design of mathematical model describing the mechanism of physico-chemical behaviour. Comparison of the model with experimental data shows the need to include, in particular, water loss due to the design of the reactor.

This work was supported by the Ministry of Education, Youth and Sports of the Czech Republic within the National Sustainability Programme project No. LO1303 (MSMT-7778/2014).

References

1. S. Huffer, T. Taeger, JALCA, **99** 424–428 (2004)
2. D. Janacova, V. Vasek, K. Kolomaznik et. al. Automatizace, regulace a procesy, 55-66 (2010)
3. K. Kolomazník, M. Adámek, I. Anděl, M. Uhlířová, J. Hazard. Mater. **160** 514-520 (2008)
4. X. Hang, X. Zhang, X. Wang, L. Jin, Z. Yang, C. Jiang, Q. Chen, BMC Public Health. **11** 224-232 (2011)
5. J. Lopez-Luna, M. C. Gonzalez-Chavez, F. J. Esparza-Garcia, R. Rodriguez-Vazquez, . Hazard. Mater. **163** 829-834 (2009)
6. M. Crudu, V. Deselnicu, DC Deselnicu, L. Albu, Waste Manage **34** 1806–1814 (2014)
7. Proposal for a restriction. Danish Environmental Protection Agency [online] (2012)
8. P. Kocurek, K. Kolomazník, M. Bařinová, J. Hendrych, Waste Manage. Res **35** 444-449 (2017)
9. H. Vašková, K. Kolomazník, *ICCC*. (to be published)

Thermoelectric cooling in combination with photovoltaics and thermal energy storage

Jan Skovajsa[1,*] and *Martin* Zálešák[1]

[1]Tomas Bata University in Zlin, Faculty of Applied Informatics, Department of Automation and Control Engineering, Nad Stranemi 4511, Zlin, Czech Republic

Abstract. The article deals with the use of modern technologies that can improve the thermal comfort in buildings. The article describes the usage of thermal energy storage device based on the phase change material (PCM). The technology improves the thermal capacity of the building and it is possible to use it for active heating and cooling. It is designed as a "green technology" so it is able to use renewable energy sources, e.g., photovoltaic panels, solar thermal collectors, and heat pump. Moreover, an interesting possibility is the ability to use thermal energy storage in combination with a photovoltaic system and thermoelectric coolers. In the research, there were made measurements of the different operating modes and the results are presented in the text.

1 Introduction

The energy consumption of heating, ventilating and air conditioning systems (HVAC) is still increasing with the increasing demand for thermal comfort in the buildings. [1] Nowadays, the energy consumption of the building is decreasing by using the renewable energy sources. Suitable renewable sources for buildings are solar energy, wind energy, geothermal energy and heat pumps. However, these technologies are not able to deal with an insufficient thermal storage capability of the buildings.

Presently, a parameter of sufficient thermal insulation is preferred, which often does not address the thermal storage capability. Mainly buildings constructed from lightweight materials are problematic, where outside heat load variations may cause inappropriate air temperature fluctuations of the inner space. The problem is that the lightweight structures are not able to store a sufficient amount of thermal energy and thus balance the inner environment conditions. Consequently, the user's comfort can be compromised. This problem can be solved by using thermal energy storage. The best way for decreasing the energy consumption and increasing thermal comfort is using of the thermal energy storages means in combination with renewable energy sources e.g. thermal energy storage in combination with a photovoltaic system and thermoelectric coolers.

1.1 Thermal energy storage

Thermal energy storage (TES) is temporary holding of thermal energy in the form of hot or cold substances for later utilization. [2] The principle of TES is based on an increase in temperature (sensible TES) or change of phase (latent TES). Starting with an initial solid state, heat addition to the substance first causes sensible heating of the solid, followed by a solid-to-liquid phase change, a sensible heating of the liquid, a liquid-to-vapor phase change and a sensible heating of the vapor. [3]

There are two forms of heat: sensible heat and latent heat. Sensible heat can be defined as a changing of the temperature of the storage substance. The amount of stored heat that caused the temperature growth is commonly called the heat capacity of the storage medium. The main parameter of the accumulation of sensible heat is the specific heat capacity. It determines the amount of energy needed to change the temperature of 1 kg of the substance by 1 K. The amount of sensible heat energy can be calculated by equation (1).

$$Q = m \cdot \int_{T_f}^{T_i} c_p \, dT \qquad (1)$$

Where m is mass [kg]
T_i initial temperature [K]
T_f final temperature [K]
c_p specific heat capacity [$J \cdot kg^{-1} K^{-1}$]

During the phase change process, the material keeps the temperature constant so called the melting or evaporating temperature as per the case. On the other hand, the heat supplied or released in the process is called latent heat. The quantity of latent heat is derived from the difference in enthalpy of the two relevant cases. Thermal energy storage realized by phase change materials

* Corresponding author: jskovajsa@fai.utb.cz

(PCMs) exploits not only sensible, but especially latent heat. [4] That is the reason that PCMs are capable of storing and releasing large amounts of energy. PCMs are either packaged in specialized containers, such as tubes, plane panels and plastic bags, or contained in conventional building elements, such as wall boards and ceilings, or encapsulated as self-contained elements. [5]

Accumulation of latent heat exploits the specific heat capacity and the change of the accumulated medium, during the phase change process where the latent heat is released or absorbed. During the phase change, the temperature of the substance remains constant, and it is possible to store and release large amounts of energy. This is the reason why latent heat storage is one of the most efficient ways of storing thermal energy. [6] The amount of energy is determined by the enthalpy value during the phase change, in the solid state and in the liquid state, according to the following equation (2).

$$\Delta Q = m \cdot \Delta h \tag{2}$$

Where m is mass [kg]
Δh enthalpy change [$J \cdot kg^{-1}$]

Figure 1 below shows the principle of TES in the form of latent and sensible heat in the PCMs.

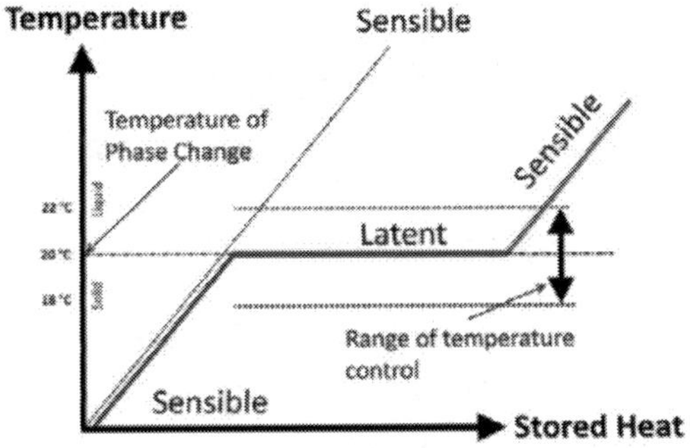

Fig. 1. Sensible heat vs. latent heat and temperature control during the phase change. [7]

1.2 Phase change material (PCM)

There are three types of PCM: organic, inorganic and eutectic PCM. The most important property is high thermal energy storage capacity.

Organic PCMs are composed of paraffin, fatty acids or sugar alcohol. The principal advantages are their chemical and thermal stability. They are usually non-corrosive, recyclable and have little or no subcooling. [8] Unfortunately, the disadvantages of using organic PCM are their flammability, low thermal conductivity and lower phase change enthalpy. [9]

Inorganic PCMs include salt hydrates, salts and metals. They cover a wide range of phase change temperatures. The main advantage is higher enthalpy per volume due to their high density. However, they have the disadvantages of corrosion, phase segregation, lack of thermal stability, subcooling and phase separation. [8]

The eutectic PCMs are a combination of chemical compounds or elements that have a single chemical composition and that solidify at a lower temperature than any other composition obtained from the same components. [10]

In fact, all materials can be considered as PCMs. However, effective and predictable energy storage allows only some of them. Figure 2 shows materials suitable for thermal energy storage. For application in buildings, it is necessary to know the specific heat of fusion and the temperature at the time when the phase change occurs. The most commonly used PCMs in buildings are paraffin and salt hydrates. [11, 12] The main advantages of the PCMs are reducing of use of cooling systems and using the stored energy during the night.

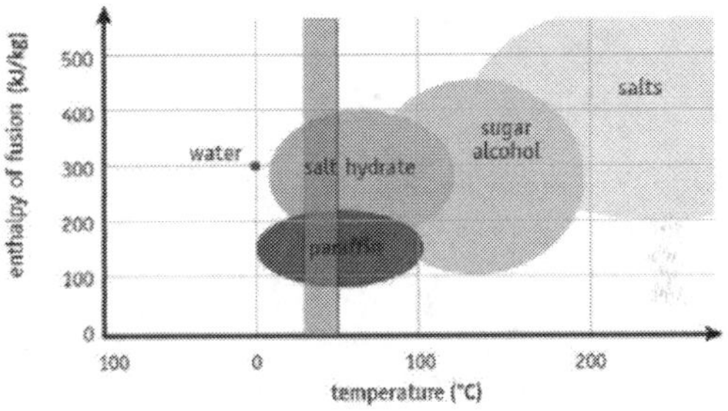

Fig. 2. Classes of materials that can be used as phase change materials and their typical ranges of melting temperatures and melting enthalpies. [13]

PCM can be incorporated in construction materials using different methods. Traditionally, the application in the envelope of the room has been studied as one of the best options because such a solution offers a large area for passive heat transfer. [14]

Efficiency increasing is possible when the PCMs is directly integrated into the energy system in the building. These active systems affect the temperature of the air flow around the element from the PCM. The use of the air flow as forced convection to obtain energy from storage materials is very important. [15] For other applications, PCMs can serve as a reservoir of excess energy for future utilization. One of the possible ways of integrating PCMs into the energy systems is presented in this paper.

1.3 Thermoelectric cooling system

Thermoelectric coolers (or Peltier coolers) are solid-state heat pumps. Thermoelectric coolers (TEC) are based on the Peltier effect (Jean Peltier, 1834) to convert electrical energy into a temperature gradient. TECs are composed of a number of n-type and p-type semiconductor junctions. When a DC power source is applied the electrical current flows from the n-type element to the p-type element. The temperature of the cold junction decreases - the electrons pass from a low energy level element (p-type) to a high energy level element (n-type) through the cold junction. At the same time, the electrons carry the absorbed heat to the hot junction. This heat is transferred to the heat sink, whilst the electrons return to a lower energy level in the p-type semiconductor (the Peltier effect). [16]

There is a possibility to use thermocouples to generate electrical energy. If there is a temperature difference between the cold and hot junction of n-type and p-type thermoelements, a voltage (Seebeck voltage) directly proportional to the temperature difference is generated. The Peltier effect and the Seebeck effect are shown on the left in Figure 3.

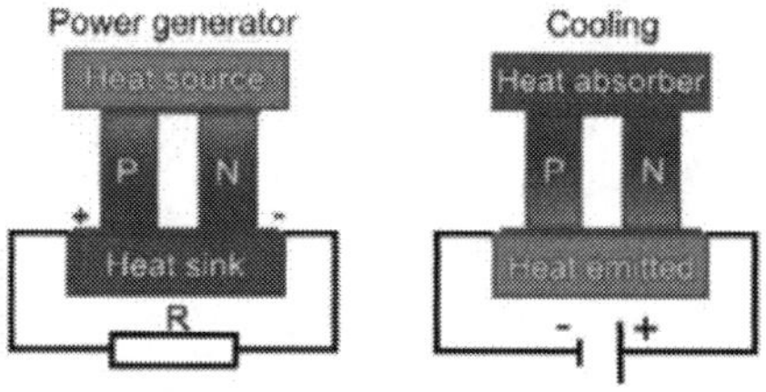

Fig.3. Thermoelectric power generator and cooling device.

Some of the recent studies are focused on TECs and thermoelectric generators (TEGs) define in combination with solar energy and PCMs. TEG is an alternative choice to convert solar energy into electricity from photovoltaic (PV) technology. New areas of research of thermoelectric technology are automotive, cooling of electric devices and buildings, etc. The technology described in this article is able to use electrical energy from PV for cooling the room by TEC in combination with PCM.

2 Methods

The proposed technology is based on the paraffin-based PCM grouped into active element. [17] The PCM DuPont Energain uses molecular encapsulation that forms a highly durable PCM with a wide operating temperature range from 0 °C to 40 °C. The mass of the thermal panels is composed of a mixture of polyethylene and paraffin wax. When the temperature of the panels rises above 18 °C, the wax begins to melt and absorbs up to 515 $kJ \cdot m^{-2}$ of heat between 18 °C and 24 °C. It corresponds to standard indoor temperature conditions.

In the following paragraphs are described the basics of the accumulation device and its operation modes, thermocouples and also photovoltaics. More specific information is described in our previous articles, for example dimensions, measurements and improving the heat transfer coefficient, and determined of the time constant. [18-20]

2.1 Accumulation device

Measurement of the parameters was done on the technology (see Figure 4 below) which is located in a laboratory at the Faculty of Applied Informatics of Tomas Bata University in Zlin in the Czech Republic. This system is composed of two thermal accumulation panels and each of them is composed of 6 layers of PCM. There are a water tube heat exchanger and three electric heating foils imposed inside the accumulation panels. As previously mentioned, the proposed technology is able to use any common energy sources, including renewable energy sources for heating or cooling, for example heat pumps, solar thermal collectors or It can use photovoltaic systems in combination with electric thermocouples, which is not common in the PCM devices. It is the biggest difference of the technology.

Fig. 4. Thermal panels and thermoelectric assembly on the right.

The whole technology and its connection with the photovoltaic system, monitoring, and controlling system are shown in Figure 5.

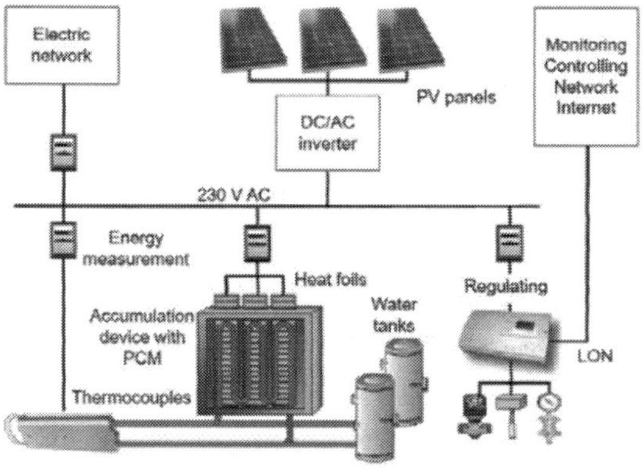

Fig. 5. Components of the technology.

The technology can work in many different modes, which depend on the requirements. The technology can be used as a standard passive system. In this mode, the technology accumulates the heat or cold. This mode can reduce the temperature peaks and keep a stable temperature in the monitored room during the day and night. The technology can also work in active mode. In this mode, the technology is able to influence the room temperature by accumulating the heat or cold obtained from the external sources. Individual operating modes are:

- removing of heat or cold from the thermal panels,
- heating of thermal panels by electric heating foils,
- heating of thermal panels from the hot water tank,
- cooling of thermal panels from the cold water tank,
- cooling of thermal panels by thermoelectric coolers.

2.2 Thermoelectric coolers

The technology includes a thermoelectric coolers powered by the photovoltaic panels or from the power grid. There is used six thermoelectric assembly type L.L.-210-24-00-00 in the technology, see Figure 6. The Liquid-to-Liquid Series thermoelectric assembly offers dependable, compact performance by cooling objects via liquid to transfer heat. Heat is absorbed through one liquid heat exchanger and dissipated thru a second liquid heat exchanger. The thermoelectric modules are custom designed to achieve a high coefficient of performance (COP) to minimize power consumption. [21]

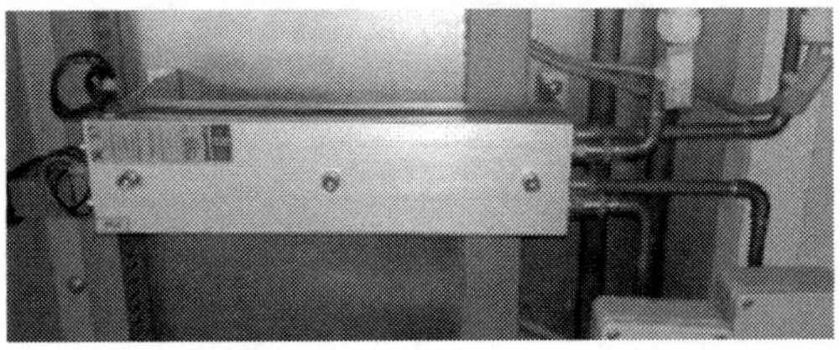

Fig. 6. Thermoelectric assembly type L.L.-210-24-00-00.

Basic specifications of the thermoelectric assembly:

- Power – Input 194 W
- Max. Cooling Power 208 W
- Current 8.1 A
- Voltage (DC) 24 V
- Max. Amb. Temp. 62 °C

To determine the number of thermocouples it was necessary to calculate the cooling capacity of the thermal panel. The average specific heat capacity of the thermal panel is about 11 kJ·kg^{-1}K^{-1} (16 to 27 °C) and its weight is about 129 kg.

$$Q = m \cdot \int_{T_f}^{T_i} c_p \, dT = 15.61 \text{ kJ} = 4.34 \text{ kWh} \quad (3)$$

When the charging of the thermal panels takes 8 h, the overall performance of the thermocouples must be about 0.55 kW. For the thermocouples with an efficiency of 50 % there is the input power for the thermocouples required about 1100 W. So, it is necessary to use six thermoelectric assembly type L.L.-210-24-00-00.

2.3 Photovoltaic system

For ensuring power supply there is installed the photovoltaic system consists of 9 polycrystalline photovoltaic panels with a total area of 11.25 m^2.

In the summer, solar radiation falling on photovoltaic panels has an average intensity of 750 Wm^{-2}. Real energy efficiency of the installed photovoltaic system was set at 10.5%. The value was measured in our another research focused on verification of the effectiveness of photovoltaic panels and their economic return. [22, 23] The real power output is a little bit lower than expected consumption of the technology. However, the real power output during the sunny day is higher than maximum power input of the thermoelectric coolers.

3 Results and discussion

Measurement of heating of PCMs has already been examined many times. The measurements of heating of the technology are shown in previous articles. [18-20] Thus, the main objective of measured was to find out how's the PCM behave in the temperature range which is specific for cooling. For this purpose, is the specific heat capacity very important parameter. The used PCM has this value around 6800 Jkg^{-1}K^{-1} in the temperature range from 10 °C to 21 °C. The main limiting factor of cooling devices is the risk of condensation of water vapor. Therefore it must be ensured that the surface temperature is at least 1 K above the dew point.

There are shown in the following text measurements and results of the both passive and active cooling modes. Cooling was made by using the heat pump and thermoelectric cooling.

The first measurement is focused on standard passive mode. In this mode, the accumulation panel is used especially to reduce the temperature fluctuation and also stabilize the indoor air temperature during a few warm days. An example of this behaviour can be seen in Figure 7. This mode ensured to stabilize the indoor air temperature between 23.2 °C and 24.0 °C when the outdoor temperature oscillated from 5.3 °C to 22.7 °C.

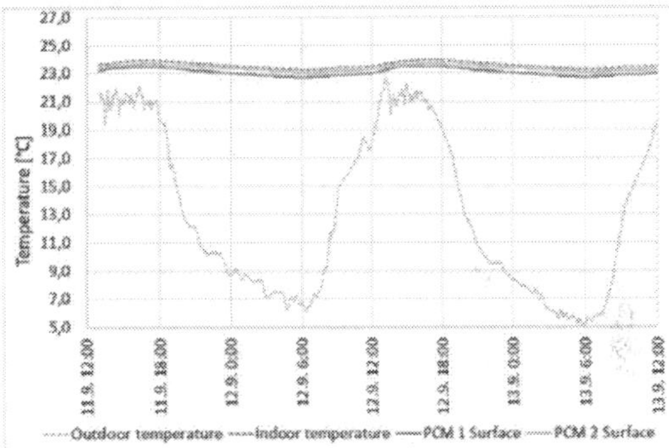

Fig. 7. Passive mode.

The next measurement is focused on the active cooling mode with using of the cooling cycle of the heat pump. Results are shown in Figure 8.

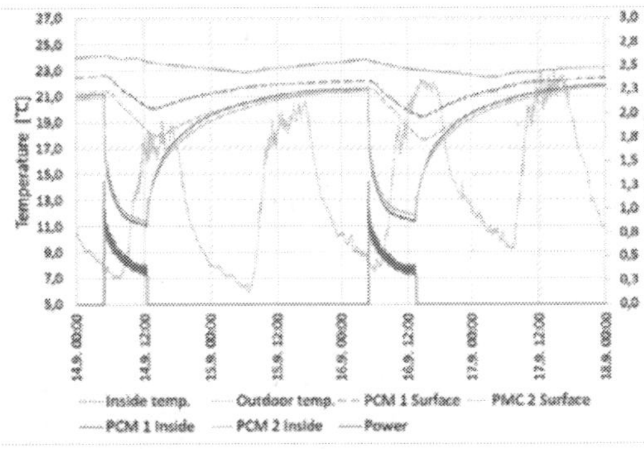

Fig. 8. Active cooling with using of the heat pump.

In the first cooling cycle, a time of change of the surface temperatures from 21.4 °C to 17.9 °C (unmodified surface) and from 22.6 °C to 20.0 °C (modified surface) was around 7.5 h. The indoor temperature was decreasing from 24.3 °C to 23.1 °C during the day with turned on the active cooling. Then the indoor temperature was still decreasing up to the following morning. The next day the technology was still turned off and the indoor temperature was increasing in accordance with the outdoor temperature.

In the following cooling cycle, the situation and results were very similar to the previous one. The outdoor temperature was higher in this case and the technology was turned on for a longer time. The time of change of the surface temperatures from 21.8 °C to 17.6 °C and from 22.4 °C to 19.3 °C was around 8.5 h. The indoor temperature was decreasing from 23.8 °C to 22.6 °C. The process of the re-heating was almost same as in the first cycle. During this cooling cycles, the total amount of energy drained from thermal panels was around 7.9 kWh.

The last measured mode is active cooling by thermoelectric coolers powered by the photovoltaic system. As in the previous case, the measurement was done in two cycles during hot days when the outdoor temperature reached up to 25 °C. In this mode, the thermal panels were able to reduce the indoor temperature from 24.0 °C to 22.9 °C and from 24.1 °C to 23.2 °C. Measured parameters are shown in Figure 9.

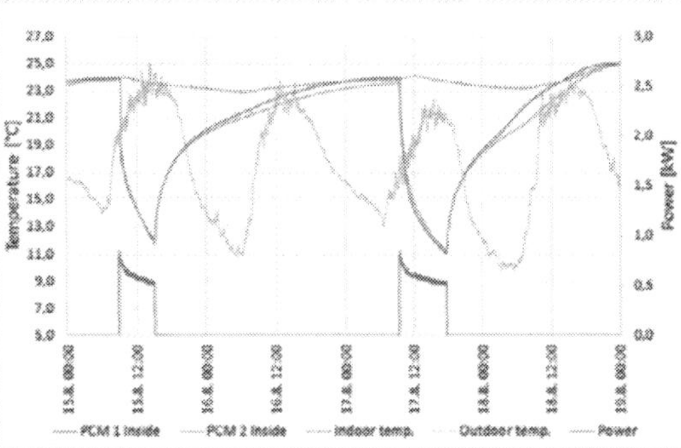

Fig. 9. Active cooling with using with the thermocouples.

In Figure 9, it is possible to see that the first cooling cycle was turned on before at 9 o'clock and it was turned off at 15 o'clock. In the beginning, the indoor temperature was increasing accordance to the outdoor temperature. After turning on the technology, the indoor temperature began to decrease. After turning off, the indoor temperature was steadily decreasing up to the next morning. After that, indoor temperature was increasing again accordance to outdoor temperature.

The following cooling cycle had the similar process. The technology was turned on after 9 o'clock and turned off before 18 o'clock. The indoor temperature decreasing as in the first cycle but then it was increasing fast during the last measured day because the high outdoor temperature and also the temperature of the thermal panel was above the phase change temperature range.

It is possible to judge that area of the thermal panels is low in comparison with the total area of the room. However, it can be resolved by higher heat flux, for example, by forced convection. The thermoelectric coolers were powered by the energy produced by the photovoltaic system. The photovoltaic system produced over 35.5 kWh during the both measured cycles (four days). The heat energy removed from thermal panels was over 8.7 kWh. The thermoelectric coolers consumed over 18.5 kWh. The energy consumption of the thermoelectric coolers and energy production from renewable energy sources are shown in Figure 10.

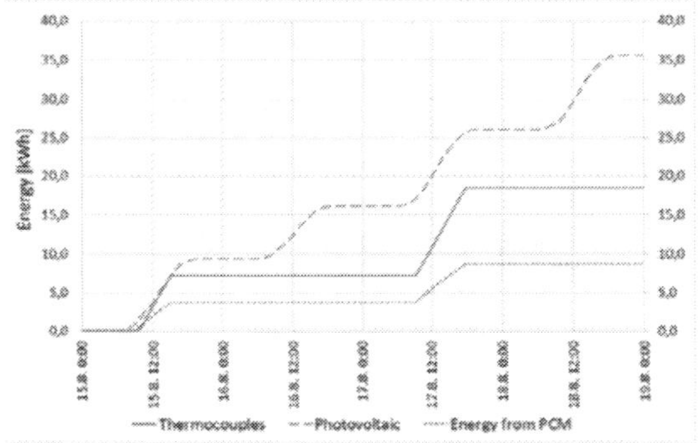

Fig. 10. Energy balance of the thermoelectric cooling.

The disadvantage of the thermoelectric cooling is producing a lot of waste heat on the opposite side of the thermocouples. The hot side of TEC is cooling by a liquid cooler connected to the cold water tank. There is an opportunity to save some energy - use the waste heat for preheating hot water to save energy.

4 Conclusion

The proposed PCM-based technology shows possibility of using the PCMs in the active system for heating and cooling. One of the advantages is the possibility to use renewable energy sources and thermoelectric coolers in combination with the photovoltaic system, which is not a common case widely used. The measurement of the proposed technology indicates farther application of the combination of the thermoelectric cooling with the photovoltaic system and other renewable energy sources. Moreover, what might be considered interesting: the utilisation of solar radiation for cooling of the building in the summer. Farther the described system efficiency could be improved by the utilisation of the waste heat from the thermoelectric assembly for preheating of the DHW, water for pool etc.

This work was supported by the Ministry of Education, Youth and Sports of the Czech Republic within the National Sustainability Programme project No. LO1303 (MSMT-7778/2014) and also by the European Regional Development Fund under the project CEBIA-Tech No. CZ.1.05/2.1.00/03.0089 and also by the Internal Grant Agency of Tomas Bata University under the project No. IGA/CebiaTech/2017/002

References

1. D. Zhou, C.Y. Zhao, Y. Tian, Appl. Energ. **92**, 593–605 (2012)
2. A.H. Abedin, A.M. Rosen, Open. Renew. Energ. J. **4**, 42-46 (2011)
3. K.O. Lee, M.A. Medina, X. Sun, Energ. Buildings, **86**, 86-92 (2015)
4. L.G. Socaciu, LEJPT, 75–98 (2012)
5. S.A. Memon, S.A, Renew. Sust. Energ. Rev. **31**, 870–906 (2014)
6. M.F. Demirbas, Energ. Source. Part B, **1**, 85–95 (2006)
7. H. Mehling, L.F. Cabeza, Heat Mass Transfer, 11-55 (2008)
8. RGEES, *An Innovation for Storing Thermal Energy and Temperature Control*, (2016)
9. S. Mondal, Appl. Therm. Eng. 1536-1545 (2008)
10. J. Giro-Paloma, M. Martinez, L.F. Cabeza, A.I. Fernandez, Renew. Sust. Energ. Rev. (2016)
11. J. Kosny, *Engineering Materials and Processes*, 64-81 (2015)
12. A. Castell, I. Martorell, M. Medrano, G. Pérez, L.F. Cabeza, Energ. Buildings, **42**, 34-40 (2010)
13. S. Grynning, F. Goia, E. Rognik, B. Time, IJSBE, **2**, 56-64 (2013)
14. L. Sánchez, P. Sánchez, A.D. Lucas, M. Carmona, J.F. Rodriguez, Colloid Polym. Sci. **12**, 1377-1385 (2007)
15. Energain, *DuPontTM Energain RPCM Guidebook*, (2010)
16. T.M. Tritt, EMSAT, (2002)
17. T. Habrovansky, *Control and monitoring of heating and cooling units in laboratory of building control systems*, (2008)
18. M. Kolacek, S. Sehnalek, Heat Mass Transfer, **11**, 56-61 (2016)
19. J. Skovajsa, M. Kolacek, M. Zalesak, Energies, **10**, 152 (2017)
20. J. Skovajsa, M. Kolacek, M. Zalesak, MATEC Web Conf. 7 (2016)
21. LairdTech, LairdTech website (2017)
22. P. Chrobak, S. Sehnalek, M. Zalesak, Electrorevue, (2014)
23. P. Chrobák, M. Zálešák, M. Opluštil, S. Sehnálek, J. Vincenec, EAD, **10**, 320-238 (2014)

Using formal methods in distributed system design

Awwama Emad, *Kadi* Mohammad, *Krayem* Said, *Lazar* Ivo, *Rihawi* Ahmad

University UTB, FAI department, Nad Stráněmi 4511, 760 05 Zlín, Czech Republic

Abstract. Distributed systems are groups of networked computers, which have the same goal for their work. The terms "concurrent computing", "parallel computing", and "distributed computing" have a lot of overlap, and no clear distinction exists between them. The same system may be characterized both as "parallel" and "distributed"; the processors in a typical distributed system run concurrently in parallel. Parallel computing may be seen as a particular tightly coupled form of distributed computing, and distributed computing may be seen as a loosely coupled form of parallel computing. Nevertheless, it is possible to roughly classify concurrent systems as "parallel" or "distributed" using the following criteria. Philosophy is centrally concerned with arguments. The first question to be asked of any argument (or inference) is whether or not it is valid: that is, does its conclusion really follow from the cited premises? Validity of inference is the central problem of deductive logic.

1 Introduction

Recently, with the increasing demand benefit of using formal methods for modeling, we started seeing large number of applications using formal methods Examples of these methods include ASM (Borger & Stark, 2003), B (Abrial, 1996), and VDM (Jones, 1990). We have choosed Event-B as a formal method to show effectiveness of this method, which has possibility for developing system free of errors by verifying using Rodin model.

Formal verification of a program is the mathematical proof that it does what is expected of it. The 21st century has seen a vast worldwide interest in formal methods [1-5].

While Rigorous descriptions promise to improve system reliability, design time and comprehensibility, they do so at the cost of an increased learning curve; the mathematical disciplines used to formally describe computational systems are outside the domain of a traditional engineering education. In addition, the meta-models used by most formal methods are often limited in order to enhance provability. There is a notable tradeoff between the need for rigor and the ability to model all behaviors.

1.1 Event-B method

1.1.1 The Event-B formalism

We present our formal development framework — Event-B (see Figure 1).

The Event-B formalism is a state-based formal approach that promotes the correct-by-construction development paradigm and formal verification by theorem proving. Event-B has been specifically designed to model and reason about parallel, distributed and reactive systems.

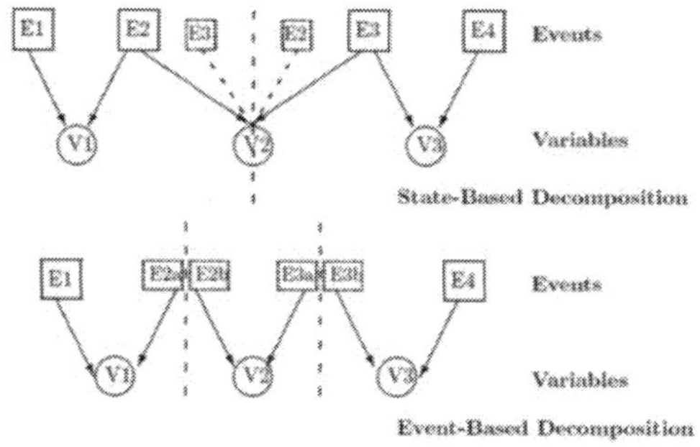

Fig. 1. Comparing event-based and state-based decomposition.

Formal verification involves the application of mathematical proofs to every possible behavior allowed by a specification (Abrial, 1996). In a state-based specification the behavior is a transformation of the system moving from one state to another. Proof obligations are generated using the specification and the language rules

These proof obligations then need to be discharged using properties of the specification.

Event-B is a mathematical approach for developing formal models of systems (Abrial & Hallerstede, 2006) [11, 7]. An Event-B model is constructed from a collection of modelling elements. These elements include invariants, events, guards and actions. The modelling elements have attributes that can be based on set theory and predicate logic. Set theory is used to

* Corresponding author: lazar@fmk.utb.cz

represent data types and the manipulation of data. Logic is used to apply conditions on the data.

1.1.2 The development of an Event-B model

The development of an Event-B model goes through two stages; abstraction and refinement. The abstract machine specifies the initial requirements of the system0 Refinement is carried out in several steps with each step adding more detail to the system, generally, but not exclusively, in a top-down manner Reactive systems (Harel & Pnueli, 1985) are systems that continually respond to changes in their environment. The focus on atomic events in Event-B creates a representation of a reactive system (Jones, 2005). The model transitions are triggered by changes in the state of the model, which can represent the system's environment. The guard on an event will allow or prevent an event from occurring depending on the state of the model. When none of the guards are true the system is deadlocked. Event-B is designed for modelling distributed systems (Abrial & Hallerstede, 2006). It implements the theory of discrete transition systems. Discrete transition systems, or action systems, model atomic actions that can be performed in parallel providing the actions do not affect the same state variables One method for specifying concurrency in Event-B is to model each update as a group of potentially interleaving atomic events (Edmunds & Butler, 2008) [1-5].

This allows the model to specify how concurrent execution can be dealt with by the system being modelled specifying a distributed system in Event-B takes a global approach. Rather than creating a specification for each component of the system it is modelled as a whole along with its environment. The model is closed in that it reacts only to changes in its internal state. Initially states are modelled abstractly with the events that describes the main goal of the system.

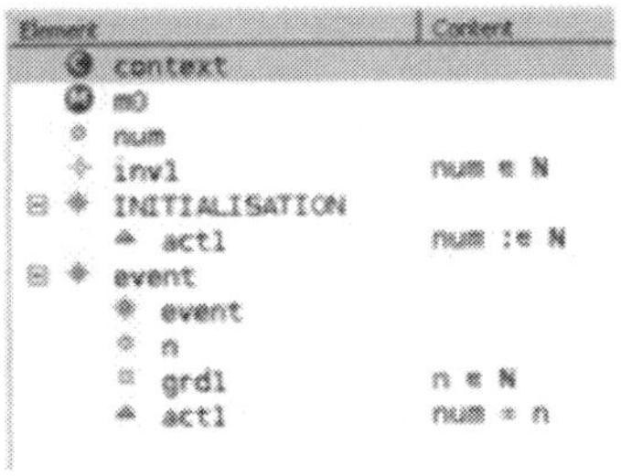

Fig. 2. Context Event-B.

Detail is added through refinement to describe the final distributed system. The ability to add new events and refine single events into multiple concrete events allows the functionality of the system to expand beyond that modelled in the abstract machine. Refinement ensures that the refined models are consistent with the abstract machine.

1.2 Event-B model

In Event-B, a system model is specified using the notion of an abstract state machine (Abrial, 2010) [6,8]. An abstract state machine encapsulates the model state represented as a collection of model variables, and defines operations on the state, i.e. it describes the dynamic behavior of the modelled system. A machine may also have the accompanying component, called context (see Figure 2). A context might include user-defined carrier sets, constants and their properties, which are given as a list of model axioms. In Event-B, the model variables are strongly typed by the constraining predicates called invariants. Moreover, the invariants specify important properties that should be preserved during the system execution. A general form of Event-B models is given in (see Figure 3).

The machine is uniquely identified by its name M. The state variables, ***v*** are declared in the Variables clause and initialised in the Init event. The variables are strongly typed by the constraining predicates. I given in the Invariants clause. The invariant clause might also contain other predicates defining properties that should be preserved during system execution.

The dynamic behavior of the system is defined by the set of atomic events specified in the Events clause. Generally, an event can be defined as follows introduction to the event-B method and the Rodin [12, 13].

We outline the general structure of an Event-B specification. A specification consists of a static part, specified in a context, and a dynamic part, specified in a machine.

An Event-B machine M1 may be declared to be a refinement of some other Event-B machine M0. In this case we refer to M0 as the abstract machine and M1 as the refined machine. Machine M1 is said to be a correct refinement of M0 if any behavior that may be exhibited by M1 is also a possible behavior of M0. Refinement represents our expectation that the behavior of M1 should conform to the behavior of M0. Of course declaring that M1 refines M0 does not on its own guarantee the correctness of a refinement. Rather the declaration gives rise to proof obligations that need to be discharged in order to guarantee the correctness of a refinement.

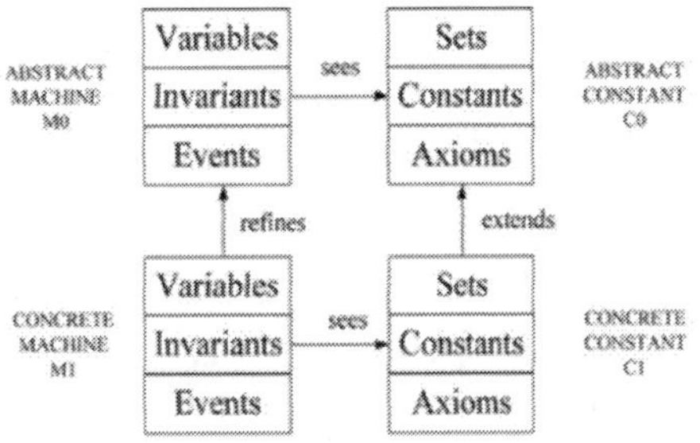

Fig. 3. Machine and context relationship.

When refining a machine, it is common to specify new types and constants to be used in the refinement.

This is achieved by specifying a new context for the refined machine. If the specification of any new types and constants depend on the types and constants used by the abstract machine, the new context is declared to be an extension of the context of the abstract model. The relationships between a machine and its refinement, as well as their respective contexts, is illustrated by Figure 2. This figure shows the refinement declaration from M1 to M0, together with the relationships with their contexts. A refined context C1 is declared as an extension of the abstract context C0 meaning context C1 may refer to types and constants specified in context C0. The dashed line from machine M1 to context C0 indicates that M1 implicitly see definitions in C0 (via C1).

An Event-B context contains the following elements:

- Sets: Abstract types used in specification to distinguish various entities
- Constants: Logical variables whose value remain constant
- Axioms: Predicates that specify assumptions about the constants.

An Event-B machine contains the following elements:

- Variables: State variables whose values can change
- Invariants: Predicates that specify properties about the variable that should always, remain true.
- Initialization: Initial values for the abstract variables
- Events: Guarded actions specifying ways in which the variables can change. Events may have parameters.

A machine may see the static elements defined in a context meaning that these elements are visible within the machine. The structure of a specification is outlined (see Figure 3).

2 Our proposed model

Our model represent a client management model verified using Rodin too.

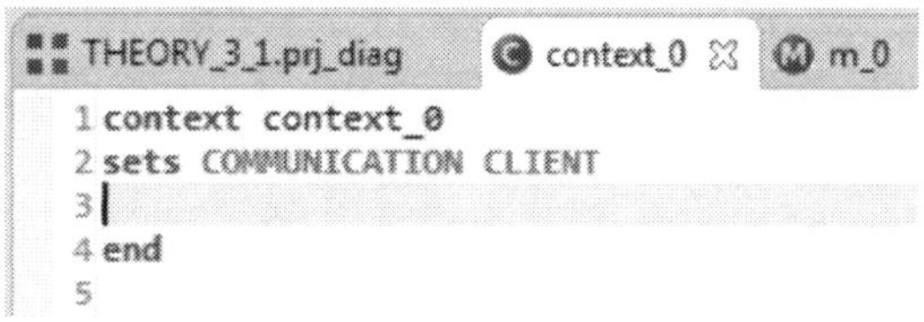

Fig. 4. Context in the machine m_0. Case study I — platform Rodin.

3 Conclusions

Communication and negotiation are very important characteristics of distributed systems; and in this paper we have presented some of the basic concepts in formal method using Event-B also we have presented verification of protocols in distributed systems., so we can say, event-B allows us to define a kind of modeling methodology by write the correct mathematical notions; wherefore we can apply event-B in modeling many different complex projects, but we should choose carefully invariants and variables to ease effort of proof.

As well as the Rodin tool offers reactive environment for constructing and analyzing models as do most modern integrated development environments, and provides integration between modeling and proving whereas this is important feature for the developers to focus on the modeling task without switch between different tools to check proving in same time.

The intent of this paper to give some insights on modelling and formal reasoning using Event-B method in distributing systems.

References

1. E. Borger, R. Stark *Abstract State Machines: A Method for High-Level System Design and Analysis*. Springer, ISBN 978-3-642-18216-7. (2003)
2. C.B Jones. *Systematic software development using VDM*. New York: Prentice Hall ISBN:0-13-880733-7, **2** (1990)
3. B. Meyer, B. In *Advances in Object-Oriented Software Engineering*, D. Mandrioli and B. Meyers, Eds. Prentice Hall, 1-50. (1991).
4. P. Behm, P. Benoit, A. Faivre, & Meynadier, J.-M. météor: A successful application of B in a large project. In *World Congress on Formal Methods*, J. M. Wings, J. Woodcock, & J. Davies, Eds. Lecture Notes in Computer Science, vol. 1708. Springer, Berlin, Heidelberg, 369–387. ISBN:3-540-66587-0, **1** (1999)
5. I. Houston, S. King, Experiences and results from the use of Z in IBM. In VDM '91: *Formal Software Development Methods*. Lecture Notes in Computer Science, vol **551**. Springer, Berlin, Heidelberg, 558–595. (1991).
6. J.-R. Abrial. *Modeling in Event-B*, Swiss Federal University (ETH), Zürich, 2010. ISBN: 978-0-521-89556-9
7. J.-R. Abrial, M. Butler, S. Hallerstede, & L. Voisin An open extensible tool environment for Event-B, *Springer*, of*LNCS*, 2006, pp 588–605, ISSN 0302-9743. Vol. **4260** (2006)
8. J.-R. Abrial. *Modeling in Event-B*, Cambridge, ISBN-13 978-0-511-72976-8, CAMBRIDGE UNIVERSITY PRESS (2010)
9. M. Jastram, M. Butler. *Rodin User's Handbook*: Covers Rodin v.2.8, CreateSpace Independent Publishing Platform, ISBN 10: 1495438147 ISBN 13: 9781495438141, USA. https://www3.hhu.de/stups/handbook/rodin/current/pdf/rodin-doc.pdf. (2014)
10. Rodin User's Handbook v. 2.8, Accessed on: 2014-02-04 https://www3.hhu.de/stups/handbook/rodin/current/html/introduction.html.

11. Hallerstede, S. *Justifications for the Event-B Modelling Notation*. B2007: Formal Specification and Developmentin B, Springer, Vol. **4355**., pp 49-63., ISSN 0302-9743. (2007)
12. http://wiki.event-b.org/index.php/Rodin_Platform_3.2_Release_NotesRodin *Platform 3.2 Release Notes*, Accessed on: 2015-11-05
13. http://www.event-b.org

```
machine m_0 sees context_0

variables replyed choosed fulfilled declined cs

invariants
  @inv1 cs∈COMMUNICATION ↔ CLIENT ∧ replyed ⊆ cs ∧ choosed ⊆ replyed ∧ fulfilled ⊆cs  ∧ declined ⊆ cs

events
  event INITIALISATION
    then
      @act1 replyed =∅
      @act2 choosed = ∅
      @act3 fulfilled = ∅
      @act4 declined = ∅
      @act5 cs =∅
  end
```

Fig. 5. Invariants and initialization in the machine m_0. Case study I — platform Rodin.

```
  event Plan_in
    any c as
    where
      @grd1 c ∈ COMMUNICATION  ∧ c ∉ dom(cs) ∧ as ∈ COMMUNICATION↔CLIENT ∧ dom(as)={c} ∧ ran(as)⊆CLIENT
    then
      @act1 cs=cs  ∪ as
  end

  event choose
    any c as
    where
      @grd1 c∈ dom(replyed) ∧ as ⊆ replyed ∧ as ∩ choosed =∅
    then
      @act1 choosed = choosed ∪ as
  end

  event decline
    any c as
    where
      @grd1 c ∈ dom(cs) ∧ c ∉ dom(declined) ∧ as ⊆ {c} ◁cs
    then
      @act1 declined = declined ∪ as
  end

  event reply
    any c a
    where
      @grd1 c ↦a ∈ cs ∧ c ↦a ∉ replyed
    then
      @act1 replyed = replyed ∪ {c↦a}
  end

  event fulfill
    any c as
    where
      @grd1 c∈dom(choosed) ∧ c ∉ dom(fulfilled) ∧ as ⊆ {c} ◁choosed
    then
      @act1 fulfilled = fulfilled ∪ as
  end
end
```

Fig. 6. Events in the machine m_0. Case study I — platform Rodin.

MATEC Web of Conferences **125**, 02034 (2017) DOI: 10.1051/matecconf/201712502034
CSCC 2017

The family house control system based on Raspberry Pi

Tomas Sysala[1,*], *David* Fogl[1], and *Petr* Neumann[2]

[1]TBU in Zlin, Dept. of Automation and Control Engineering, Faculty of Appl. Informatics, Nad Stranemi 4511, Zlin, Czech Republic
[2]TBU in Zlin, Dept. of Electronics and Measurements, Faculty of Applied Informatics, Nad Stranemi 4511, Zlin, Czech Republic

Abstract. The article deals with the design and implementation of a smart household based on simple wireless modules, which are monitoring (collecting data) and controlling smart household supporting devices. The central unit processes measured parameters, and in relation to resulting values, a pre-set action is performed. Those actions variety can be configured by user via the user interface so that a set of smart rules for reaction on by household devices generated stimuli or problems can be created. That all together composes a control system based on Raspberry Pi, which manages indoor and outdoor temperature measurement, the lighting control, RF transmitter, jalousie, motion sensor control etc. There is a GUI for a PC and for a mobile phone as a part of that system.

1 Introduction

The term "Smart house" or "Smart household" is popular already since 1980s. The term "smart building" emerged in USA at the turn of the 80s and 90s decade. That term expressed an above-standard comfort building [1]. Since then, the technology development influences the meaning and the content of that interrelatinon "smart" and "bulding". It is common that housholds are equipped with various electronic gadgets nowadays. Among many others, we can name desktop and mobile computers, smart TV sets being able to record TV broadcasts automatically, wireless garage gate control, and provide household both indoor and outdoor security. Those all are technologies taken for granted by majority of us contemporary that are forwarding the significance of smart building on.

Currently, we perceive that term as fully automated household where individual devices control is doable via an uncomplicated user interface.

Although the particular technologies are not very new, it is not easy to network them in a coherent system controllable from one location. The individual household technologies have different communication channels and interfaces according to the manufacturer. Some of the do not have any communication channel and interface. Therefore there is very complicated to install a smart system in an established household. The particular devices are not prepared and smart system compatible. For the purpose of such household automation, and to include in the smart system its existing devices, we have to create an active control of particular devices. We need also to realize modules able to communicate via various interfaces, or we need to procure brand new more advanced devices.

2 Effective household controlling

If we manage to interconnect as much as possible existing and newly installed devices, we obtain affortless access and controllability over the whole household. Thanks to unified access to all devices, we are able to create situation oriented modes and indoor environment according to user´s mood. One button touch sets the whole household particular complex setting. For instance, the morning awakening arrangement could start with jalousie slats opening, sun shine and music. All particular jalousie get open in between. On entering bathroom, lights are lit on and the favourite radio station is switched on.

As another example, the household locking could illustrate the system possibilities. When leaving, all unnecessary appliances are automatically switched off, the jalousies get partially closed, air condition stops operation, all lights go out, and all security elements get active.

We occupy ourselves with devices and relevant control algorithms for smart building control development at our department.

The building lighting control via DALI bus is one of our implemented oproject [2]. To control the whole building with a programmable logic controller (PLC) is another variant of solution [3]. Although such solution is comprehensive, its high costs represent noticeable disadvantage. Those costs comprise also mostly a complete wiring replacement and completion what means sensors and actors interlinking.

As a cheaper alternative, there is a possibility to make use of a microcontroller or of a small cheap computer together with a higher number of wireless modules [4].

* Corresponding author: sysala@fai.utb.cz

2.1 Systems on the market

There are many systems for smart household on the market nowadays. We aim at wireless communication possibility what means that PLC control does not fit in our project goals. PLC application is much more convenient for new buildings where the special wiring is indispensable.

2.1.1 Loxone

Loxone company offers both their flag ship PLC automation based on PLC Miniserver [5] and Miniserver GO [5] without the PLC link what is more advantageous for wireless communication with peripherals.

2.1.2 Fibaro

Fibaro company's products are based on miniature modules designed for easy installation without special demands on wiring.

Z-Wave protocol oriented control unit is one of Fibaro basic components for smart household. That control unit incorporates Fibaro System Home Center 2 for remote control over all connected devices. The control is executed via web interface as well as mode setting and composing rules for automation [6].

2.1.3 Control4

The core of Control4 system is a control unit offered in a few variants. Those variants differ in power, in number of ports and integrated devices like audio, and in range of controllable smart devices. Up to 50 devices can be connected to each control unit.

Control4 system does not provide any own wireless sensors and modules. That shortage is substituted for Nyce company's products represented with wireless modules communicating via ZigBee interface and protocol [7].

3 Main ideas of our design

The designed system proceeds from three basic ideas [4].

3.1 Wireless modules application

Wireless approach can be regarded as noninvasive form of household automation.

A lot of smart systems is based on PLC application what requires special wiring where a majority of devices and elements is interconnected with cable and relays or with other integrating technologies.

Those systems are advantageous in case of new building and flat construction or when we are refurbishing them including the new wiring installation.

However, if we plan to implement the smart building technology in an existing household, that system represents a costly alternative.

3.2 Open source products utilization

In pursuance of our project goals, there are employed products and applications developed as community projects so that they are freely accessible for use.

The big advantage of those projets is a numerous user base which the open discussion of problems or presentation of successful solution accompanied with detailed instructions is a standard way of improvement in.

3.3 Price

By employing open source projects and by modular solution of automation by our own, we are able not only modify the system exactly according to our needs, but we can also save money compared to commercial products employing.

3.3 Remote access and hosehold system securing

There is possible to control a smart household not merely from the household itself or its vicinity, but also from any placein the world where the link to our system is possible to establish. The remote access to our system is practicable via mobile phone technologies like GSM or via internet.

4 Project main goals

The following demands are placed on the solution of our smart household control project.

4.1 System remote management

- There is possible to address the system from any computer or mobile device in household concerned.
- To address the system outside that household is permitted exclusively with knowledge of security access data.
- It is possible to configure and monitor all connected devices.

4.2 Temperature measurement

- The temperature measurement inside any room and also outside the household.

4.3 Surroundings humidity measurement

- The humidity measurement inside any room and also outside the household
- The indoor plant soil humidity measurement.

4.4 Movement detection

- People's and animals´ movement is detected in selected rooms.

4.5 Illumination control

- The light go on/go out in any room is possible without user presence in that very room.
- The light intensity control in any room.

4. 6 Jalousie control

- The indoor jalousie complete control comprising the ful or partial opening/closing.

4. 7 Security camera system

- Any household place monitoring with streaming and recording opossibility.

4. 8 Main entrance control unit

- The whole system controllability from a fixed place at main entrance.
- The "leaving" button to switch the whole system in the mode of "deserted" household.

5 The system structure

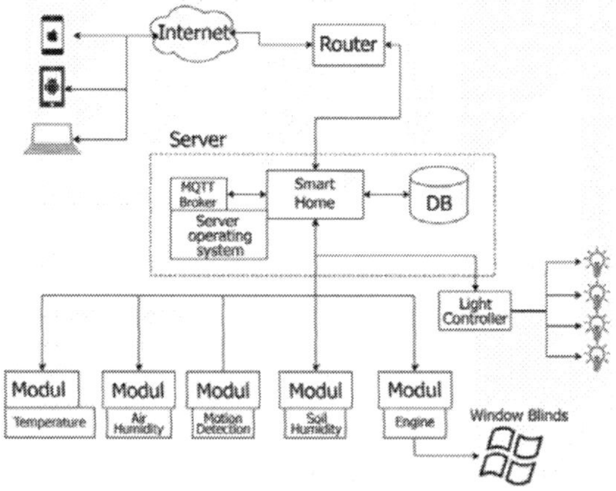

Fig. 1. Smart household architecture block diagram [4].

According to aforesaid requirements, the smart building system has been designed. The smart household, MQTT Broker, and database are carried on a server. Individual modules with connected sensors for temperature, air humidity, movement detection, indoor plant soil humidity measurement and the module for windows jalousie control are linked to the system. The light control module is also linked to the system.

5.1 Employed components

5.1.1 Raspberry Pi

Raspberry Pi is a fully-fledged miniature single-board microcomputer designed and developed by the British Raspberry Pi Foundation aimed at informatics education in highschools [8]. There is not possible to change the configuration of Raspberry Pi because all modules are soldered on one PCB. The GNU/LINUX operational system is iemployed, and it is possible to choose among a few distributions, like Debian, Ubuntu and others.

There is supplied a new model Raspberry Pi 2 in February 2015. That model is fitted out with a new SoC Broadcom BCM2836, and it includes a quadruple processor cores with clock rate of 900 MHz and a SIMD 1 GB memory to increase performance. The inbuilt graphic processor VideoCore IV supports OpenGL ES 2.0, 1080p30, MPEG-4[33]. This model is used by the system as a central control unit for our smart household system concept.

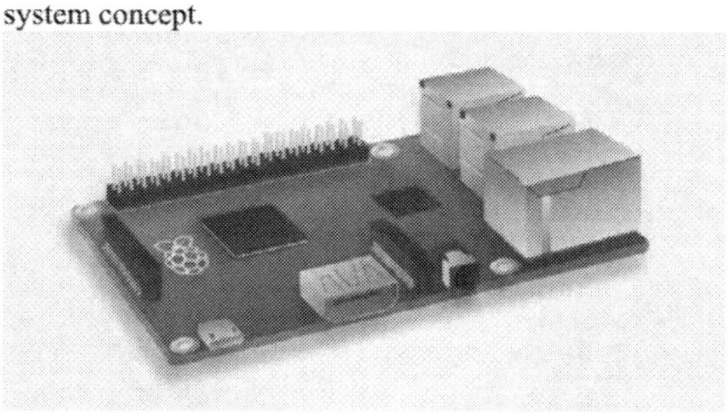

Fig. 2. Raspberry Pi 2[8].

5.1.2 GPIO

General Purpose Input Output – GPIO terminals serve to interconnection with any device with binary communicating interface.

Raspberry Pi 2 board provides following I/O pins:
- 17 I/O pins
- SPI bus pin (Serial Peripheral Interface)
- I2C bus (Inter-Integrated Circuit)

Beside I/O pins, there are also pins for peripherals power supply:
- Two 5 Volts power supply pins
- Two 3.3 Volts power supply pins
- Eight common ground pins

5.1.3 Arduino

Arduino is an open platform with a graphic user interface development environment related to the Wiring environment (similar project like Arduino, i.e. a board with microcontroller and IDE) [9, 10].

The development hardware support is represented with Atmel 8 bit microcontroller boards in many varieties, as for instance ATMega8, ATMega168, ATMega328, ATMega1280 and ATMega2560.

Unlike Raspberry Pi, Arduino is not devised as a desktop so that it does not content any operational system.

As for that, the servicing programs need to be prepared on a different device, and to load it to Arduino afterwards.

The advantage of such solution is a lower energy consumption, and in contrast to Raspberry Pi, it is possible to power those modules from batteries.

5. 1. 4 NodeMCU

NodeMCU is an open IoT platform that was developed from ESP8266 project by processing unit together with micro USB port (for power supply and communication) and with 10 I/O pins (6 digital pins, 3 analog pins and one ADC pin) insertion in a common module. The first generation employs the ESP-12 processing unit with 20 KB SRAM and 4 MB flash memory. The incorporated wifi module supports 802.11b/g/n, devkit nodemcu v0.9 standard [11].

The second generation employs the new processor ESP-12E together with devkit nodemcu v1.0 [12].

5.1.5 GPIO

Like at Raspberry Pi or at Arduino, the NodeMCU includes I/O pins for peripherals communication. The pins sorting follows [13]:
- 6 digital
- 3 analog
- 1 ADC
- Four 3.3 Volts power supply pins
- One 5 Volts power supply pin
- 4 common ground pins

5. 2. Wireless modules

The majority of wireless modules uses the NodeMCU unit.

5.2.1 The NodeMCU supporting scripts implementation

There are a repeating set of steps in creating and programming individual modules. These steps are as follows:
1. Module activation from sleep mode.
2. Module connection to WiFi.
3. The particular module task execution.
4. Communication with the central node.
5. Putting a module in the sleep mode for a set time period.

It is necessary to implement servicing LUA script for a particular function execution.

5.2.2 Module initialization

The module initialization begins with loaded firmware starting (we use basic firmware with LUA language), and with seeking out the initialization script „init.lua". Provided that script is accessible, it starts automatically.

5.2.3 Module link to the local WiFi network

Module tries repeatedly to connect to WiFi network specified in „wifi.config"file which SSID and password are also in. If connection to WiFi fails, or if DHCP server does not assigned IP address, module repets that attempt in 10 seconds interval. In case that connection fails even after that set of attempts, module is put to sleep mode for 10 minutes. After module activation, the „init.lua"script is launched again.

5.2.4 Communication with the central node

A simple HTTPrest api serves for communication between a notification module and central node. We specify module ID and data to be transferred, and data are sent to central server with the POST utility. Central server processes data, and it sends response HTTP 200 to that module, and server stores data in database or it launches other predefined action according to the implemented procedure. Providing the central application is not able to accept that message, it sends the error code HTTP 400 and saves the information about unsuccessful transaction in logs [4].

5.2.5 Putting module to sleep for a set time period

In order to serve their purpose, there is necessary to consider the power supply concept of individual modules, and how to minimize energy consumption. There are two groups of modules. First group is characterized by uninterrupted operation. This group includes sensors and modules waiting all the time for launching event, like movemen sensor, jalousie control, camera system etc. The second group includes so called notification sensors that are measuring physical quantities in regular intervals. In between, those sensors can enter the slee mode which they are consuming minimum energy in until they are activated to perform their task.

5.2.6 Temperature measurement module

There exist both simple sensors measuring only temperature and advanced sensors measuring also air humidity. The air humidity could be interesting for case of keeping constant household humidity by automatic humidifiers. Nevertheless, same rooms are not interesting for humidity control so that only temperature measurement is sufficient. In that case, we can use a cheaper sensor. DS18B20 sensor has been selected for our project. When also humidity level is of our interest, we can choose DHT11 sensor or a more expensive but more accurate sensor DHT22.

For a created module fulfils its function of temperature measurement and data passing to server, it is necessary to implement ULA language script. The function of that script is as follows:
1. Module activation from sleep mode („init.lua").
2. Module connection to WiFi („wifi.lua").
3. Temperature value reading from sensor („temp ds18b20.lua").
4. Temperature forwarding to server („data send.lua").
5. Putting module in sleep mode for a specified time period („sleep.lua").

The sleep mode after task execution saves the connected battery energy.

5.2.7 Humidity measurement module

There exist many sensors for the soil humidity measurement. The budget-wise sensor Produino LM393 has been selected for our project.

That sensor is one of the cheapest on the market (1.7 EUR). That sensor enables humidity evaluation both in digital and in analog form (relative humidity percentage in the range of 0 – 100. Nevertheless, the digital form is very inaccurate, and it indicates only exceeding of pre-set humidity limit.

The house plants soil humidity is unlike the temperature changing not so frequently so that there is not necessary to awake module every 10 minutes. It is sufficient to set sleep mode for an interval of about 60 minutes (the maximum value is about 71 minutes). The module with batteries operational time can be remarkably extended.

5.2.8 Movement detection module

One of the most frequently used sensors are the movement sensors installed in buildings and in households. Those sensors are most often used for entrance automatic lights, toilet lights and in other windowsless rooms.

The movement detection module has been realised with commercial models NodeMCU and HC-SR501. HC-SR501 module can identify movement in angle of 120° and distance of 7 meters (price 1 EUR) [14, 15].

The sensor data is read via digital pin D4 which is set to mode „gpio.INT“, and with the help of „gpio.trig()“ function, we put pin D4 in automatic detection mode. In that mode, pin D4 waits for event (callback), and in case of logic 1 reception, module calls the preset function. There takes place a notification of central node about movement detection with „data send.lua“script and „Motion“data type in our case.

5.2.9 Household lighting control module

The household lighting control requires not only module creation with wireless communication addressing ability to a mobile device, but also a wireless control of lighting itself. All foregoing modules are exclusively collecting physical quantities data, but they do not communicate with their environment. Providing that we need to control remotedly, we need to deal with a problem what to communicate at lights with. Common house light is connected to the mains voltage of 230 volts, and it is controlled with a touch switch is located at the wall or it may be located at the power supply cable.

The further requirement concerns light intensity control, so called dimming possibility [16].

There is emerging also a WiFi application for house lights remote control besides the radio controlled sockets in couple of recent years. Unlike a simple controlling element insertion between bulb and socket, there are modified light bulbs containing embodied radio receiver. Nevertheless, that system comprises another component called WiFi Hub that receives simple UDP packets initiating the radio signal for individual bulbs control. Such arrangement is easy to implement and to control via any device communicating via a WiFi link. The higher costs of such solution are compensated for much easier incorporation in our smart household system [17].

5.2.10 Window jalousie adjustment module

The last module for smart household system design is an automatic jalousie controller. There exist many jalousie system concepts. In our project, we are concentrated on the current broadly used system of indoor horizontal jalousies supplied for common plastic window design. That system is handled by means of bead pull-chain driving the shaft of window blind.

The simpliest way how to handle window blinds is a direct shaft rotation handling. That way of handling has a drawback in module mounting on pull-chain end what means a higher pull force for pulling the blind up. Thet is why we need 12 volts motor and adaptor power supply.

One of few stepping motors with operational voltage of 12 volts is 28BYJ-48 motor. Stepping motors are well applicable for jalousie handling because of stepwise controlled rotation in accurate number of steps. There is 64 steps needed for one turn of the motor shaft.

6 Camera supervising system

One of the main security elemnts for household security is without doubt camera supervising system. It guards the household both against intrusion from outside and also monitors various parts of household, like child's rooms and animals without personal presence necessity. The majority of camera systems is also detecting movement, and in case of such event, camera system can notify user, send the event documenting picture, or it can start event recording.

There exists a huge amoun of various camery systems for household security provision. The most important attributes of a quality camera is its functionality, placement variety, and also its ability to communicate with other systems. The outdoor camera required attributes set will naturaly differ from the indoor camera one.

Fig. 3. Raspberry Pi Camera module [18].

DOI: 10.1051/matecconf/201712502034

We have employed the Raspberry Pi camera for our project. Its integration in system is easy, and its performance in household projects is excellent.

6.1 Camera installation in Raspberry Pi

The Raspberry Pi camera module is capable of taking full HD 1080p photo and video and can be controlled programmatically.

If we want to use camera also during the night, it is recommended to accomplish it with two infrared light generating LEDs. Those LEDs are to be fixed with screws on the camery PCB, one LED on each side.

That camera enables also streaming services. The access to video stream is possible via a PC or via mobile application „IP Cam Viewer Lite". That application is available for both mobile platforms Android and iOS as well.

7 OpenHAB server implementation

OpenHAB (Open Home Automation Bus) is a server Java application designated for home automation. It offers both a server backend running ounder all common operational system versions (Windows, Linux, OS X) and also frontend in the form of web environment plus mobile applications for Android and iOS. It is an open code project what means that application is free of charge under the EPL licence. That is why OpenHab is becoming an excellent candidate for household automation and smart household creation starting projects.

The system is modular, and it is possible to extend it with addons serving as interface for peripherals. Among those extensions, we can find also binding to Milight system for light bulb control, binding to MQTT broker in both modes publish/subscribe, email client, bluetoth and others.

The other part represents a data repository, which stores states of all connected elements. It takes care for synchronization among all connected packages. All obtained data can be stored in a database, in a harddisk or in cloud systems to ensure durability even after system restart.

OpenHab Log serves for data storage in log files or in databases. The RRD4J (Round Robin Database for Java) is a default database serving mostly for diagram generation in user environment [21].

The other possibility is a link to SQL database or to another one. Providing we store data in files, we find them in openhab home/logs directory [22].

7.1 Graphic User Interface - GUI

OpenHab makes possible to answer individual queries directed to the databases, and to present response in predefined graphic windows. Those windows are to be displayed on a computer s, mobile phone or tablet screen with any operational system.

The windowas creation description is beyond the scope of this article. Nevertheless, the following figures illustrate resulting windows example.

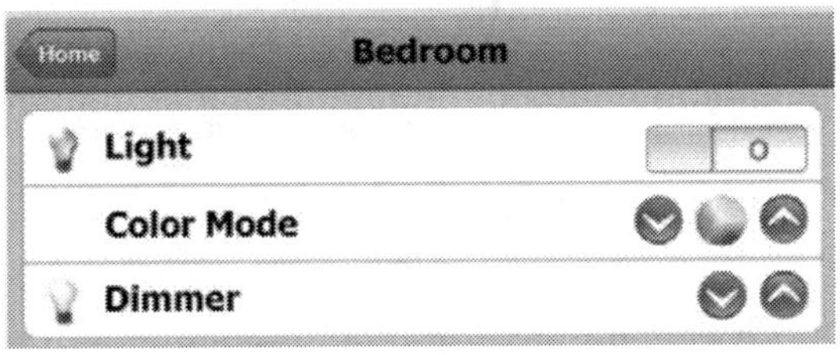

Fig. 4. OpenHab adding items – bedroom [4].

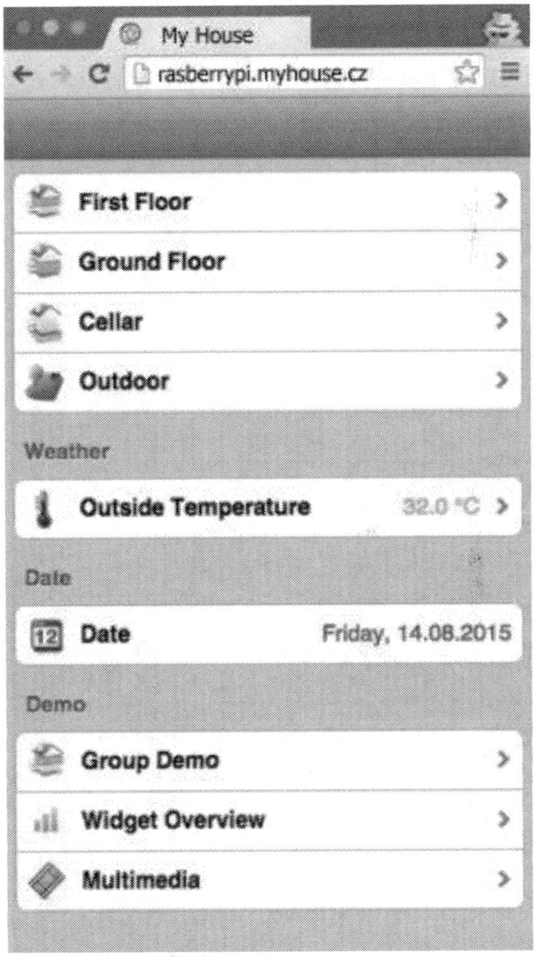

Fig. 5. OpenHab map creation – rooms [4].

This work was supported by the Ministry of Education, Youth and Sports of the Czech Republic within the National Sustainability Programme project No. LO1303 (MSMT-7778/2014) and also by the European Regional Development Fund under the project CEBIA-Tech No. CZ.1.05/2.1.00/03.0089.

Conclusion

As a result of our project, the complex household control system based on Raspberry Pi and other wireless modules has been created. The whole system is functional, and to its remarkable advantages belong prise, noninvasive implementation with further extension possibility.

The designed system increase the inhabitation comfort, it optimizes lighting energy consumption, thermal energy and other energies consumption.

It also improves the household security level either in case of a flat or a family house. The modular solution does not hamper modification and extension for sake of household control optimization.

References

1. M. Hrbacek, Martin. An Intelligent family house IV. [Online]. Available: http://bit.ly/24ndolw.
2. T. Sysala, J. Pribyslavsky, P. Neumann, *MATEC Web of Conferences*. (EDP Sciences, Les Ulis, 2016)
3. T. Sysala, M. Pospichal, P. Neumann. *17th International Carpathian Control Conference (ICCC)*. (Piscataway: IEEE Operations Center, 2016)
4. D. Fogl, *diploma work at Tomas Bata University in Zlin*, (2016).
5. Loxone smart house [Online]. Available: http://www.loxone.com/cscz/chytry-dum/prehled.html, (2017)
6. Fibaro system [Online]. Available: http://www.fibaro.com/cz, (2017)
7. Control4 system [Online]. Available: http://www.control4.cz/, (2017)
8. Raspberry Pi Products [Online]. Available: https://www.raspberrypi.org/products/, (2017)
9. Arduino Uno [Online]. Available: http://richarduino.com/specification-arduino-uno/, (2017)
10. Arduino Due [Online]. Available: https://www.arduino.cc/en/Main/ArduinoBoardDue, (2017)
11. NodeMCU v1 [Online]. Available: http://cktplus.com/NodeMCU-Lua-WiFi-Internet-of-Things-IoT-Development-Board, (2017)
12. NodeMCU v2 [Online]. Available: http://www.seeedstudio.com/depot/NodeMCU-v2-Lua-based-ESP8266-development-kit-p-2415.html, (2017)
13. NodeMCU GPIO [Online]. Available: https://github.com/nodemcu/nodemcu-devkit, (2017).
14. Motion detection (in Czech) [Online]. Available: http://vyvoj.hw.cz/automatizace/pir-cidlo-skvely-sluha-ale-zly-pan.html, (2013)
15. Sensor HC-SR501 specification [Online]. Available: https://www.mpja.com/download/31227sc.pdf, (2017)
16. Milight Light Bulb [Online]. Available: http://www.milight.com/milight-5w-rgbw-e14-screw-iphone-ios-android-controlled-light/, (2017)
17. Phillips Hue Bridge [Online]. Available: http://www2.meethue.com/en-gb/productdetail/philips-hue-bridge, (2017)
18. Raspberry Pi 2 camera [Online]. Available: https://ae01.alicdn.com/kf/HTB1_MnuKpXXXXbdXXXXq6xXFXXXC/Original-DOIT-Raspberry-Pi-2-Fisheye-Len-NoIR-Camera-1080p-Rpi-Wide-Angle-Remote-Control-Monitor.jpg, (2017)
19. P. Navratil, L. Pekar, *16th WSEAS International Conference on Circuits*, **1**, (2012)
20. R. Vala, D. Malanik, R. Jasek: *International Joint Conference CISIS'12 - ICEUTE'12 - SOCO'12 Special Sessions.* (Springer-Verlag Berlin, Germany, 2013)
21. OpenHab security [Online]. Available: https://github.com/openhab/openhab/wiki/Security, (2017)
22. OpenHab configuration [Online]. Available: https://github.com/openhab/openhab/wiki/Configuring-the-openHAB-runtime, (2017)

Testing of Method for Assessing of Room Thermal Stability

Hana Charvátová[1,*] and *Martin* Zálešák[2]

[1] *Tomas Bata University in Zlín, Faculty of Applied Informatics, Regional Research Centre CEBIA-Tech, nám. T. G. Masaryka 5555, 760 01 Zlín, Czech Republic*
[2] *Tomas Bata University in Zlín, Faculty of Applied Informatics, Department of Automation and Control Engineering, nám. T. G. Masaryka 5555, 760 01 Zlín, Czech Republic*

Abstract. The paper presents the interim results of our research on the developing methodological procedure which could be used for assessment of a thermal stability of buildings with regards to its thermal accumulative parameters. The principle of testing is based on a combination of computer simulation of cooled room model developed in COMSOL Multiphysics software and on theoretical calculations with respect to compliance with valid European and Czech technical standards used in building industry and architecture under conditions obtained by real measurement for the room to be tested. The presented example shows the effect of the heat-accumulation properties of the outside wall insulation materials on the course of the cooling room for winter conditions.

1 Introduction

Each residential building is characterized by energy consumption and energy gains. The energy demands depend on many factors such as the climatic conditions, the purpose of the object, and hence the requirements of the indoor environment, and so on. In terms of optimization, the design of the buildings is emphasis on minimizing energy consumption while minimizing investment and operating costs while keeping the required internal environment parameters. These costs strongly depend on the building's thermal storage parameters and can therefore be influenced by their construction.

However, due to the complexity of physical processes, a theoretical testing of the thermal stability in the design of new building structures or in their reconstruction is very difficult. In terms of the assessment of the heat accumulation parameters, consideration should be given to the time delay of the response of the indoor environment to changing outdoor conditions. These problems are solved in the technical standard CSN EN 13790 [1] and related CSN EN 13792 [2], CSN EN 13786 [3], CSN EN 15251 [4] and CSN 06 0220 [5] and, to a certain extent, CSN 73 0540 [6].

However, a complex solution to this problem according to CSN EN 13790 [1] and related standards is difficult and the most accurate methods are sought using modern computer tools using simulation methods based on numerical solution of non-stationary multiphysical processes on models describing studied objects under simplified conditions.

From this perspective, we deal with testing of the factors that influence thermal stability of building by combination of computer simulation in the COMSOL Multiphysics user interface and theoretical calculations with respect to above-mentioned technical standards used in the building industry. Possibilities of use Comsol Multiphysics for testing of thermal stability of buildings were verified in the papers [7], [8].

In the following text, we follow the paper [8], in which the heat flow through the uninsulated outside wall were compared by the theoretical calculation. Now, we describe the procedure by which it is possible to combine both computer simulation and theoretical calculations to determine the heat losses of the room to be taken under simplified assumptions for the assessment of thermal insulating materials of the external wall or the heat-accumulation properties of the room to be tested.

2 Theoretical description of the studied problem solving

For computer simulation by COMSOL Multiphysics software we use Laminar Flow Interface of the Conjugate Heat Transfer Module, which is used primarily to model slow-moving flow in environments where temperature and energy transport are also an important part of the system and application, and must coupled or connected to the fluid-flow in some way. The interface solves the Navier-Stokes equations together with an energy balance assuming heat flux through convection and conduction. The density term is assumed to be affected by temperature and flow is always assumed to be compressible [9].

* e-mail: charvatova@fai.utb.cz

Finite Element Equations for Heat Transfer

A basic equation of non-stationary heat transfer in an isotropic body can be described by equation (1) [10]:

$$-\left(\frac{\partial q_x}{\partial x}+\frac{\partial q_y}{\partial y}+\frac{\partial q_z}{\partial z}\right)+\Phi=\varrho c_p\frac{\partial T}{\partial t} \qquad (1)$$

where:
q_x, q_y, q_z - components of heat flow density, $\left[\mathtt{W}\cdot\mathtt{m}^{-2}\right]$;
$\Phi = \Phi(x,y,z,t)$ - inner heat-generation rate per unit volume, $\left[\mathtt{W}\cdot\mathtt{m}^{-3}\right]$;
ϱ - material density, $\left[\mathtt{kg}\cdot\mathtt{m}^{-3}\right]$;
c_p - heat capacity, $\left[\mathtt{J}\cdot\mathtt{K}^{-1}\right]$;
T - temperature, [K];
t - time, [s].

According to Fourier's law the components of heat flow can be expressed as follows [10]:

$$q_x=-\lambda\frac{\partial T}{\partial x},\ q_y=-\lambda\frac{\partial T}{\partial y},\ q_z=-\lambda\frac{\partial T}{\partial z} \qquad (2)$$

where:
λ - thermal conductivity of the media, $\left[\mathtt{W}\cdot\mathtt{m}^{-1}\mathtt{K}^{-1}\right]$.

Substitution of Fourier's relations (2) into equation (1) gives the basic heat transfer equation [10]:

$$\frac{\partial}{\partial x}\left(\lambda\frac{\partial T}{\partial x}\right)+\frac{\partial}{\partial y}\left(\lambda\frac{\partial T}{\partial y}\right)+\frac{\partial}{\partial z}\left(\lambda\frac{\partial T}{\partial z}\right)+\Phi=\varrho c_p\frac{\partial T}{\partial t} \qquad (3)$$

It is assumed that the boundary conditions can be of the following types [10]:

1. Specified temperature: $T_s = T_1(x,y,z,t)$ on S_1.
2. Heat flow density: $q_s = q(x,y,z,t)$ on S_2.
3. Convection boundary conditions: $q_xn_x + q_yn_y + q_zn_z = h(T_s - T_e) + q_r$ on S_3.

where:
h - heat transfer coefficient, $\left[\mathtt{W}\cdot\mathtt{m}^{-2}\mathtt{K}^{-1}\right]$;
T_s - unknown surface temperature, [K];
T_e - convective exchange temperature, [K];
q_s - heat flow density on the surface, $\left[\mathtt{W}\cdot\mathtt{m}^{-2}\right]$;
q_r - incident radiant heat flow per unit surface area, $\left[\mathtt{W}\cdot\mathtt{m}^{-2}\right]$;
q_x, q_y, q_z - components of heat flow density, $\left[\mathtt{W}\cdot\mathtt{m}^{-2}\right]$.

For initial temperature field for a body at the time $\tau = 0$ it holds [10]:

$$T(x,y,z,t) = T_0(x,y,z) \qquad (4)$$

By determination of the heat losses from the room we assumed that the heat transfer between the room air and the surroundings is the heat transfer through its walls.

In this case, the heat flow can be described by equation (7) [5]:

$$\Phi = A\cdot U\left(\theta_{in}(t)-\theta_{out}(t)\right), \qquad (5)$$

where:
A - heat transfer surface, $\left[\mathtt{m}^2\right]$;
U - overall heat transfer coefficient, $\left[\mathtt{W}\cdot\mathtt{m}^{-2}\mathtt{K}^{-1}\right]$;
θ_{in} - temperature of air inside the room, [°C];
θ_{out} - temperature of air outside the room, [°C];
Φ - heat flux through the external wall, [W];
t - time, [s].

The overall heat transfer coefficient (U) through the multilayer wall of the room can be computed according to equation (6) [5]:

$$U=\frac{1}{\frac{1}{h_{in}}+\frac{1}{h_{out}}+\sum_{j=1}^{n}\frac{\delta_j}{\lambda_j}} \qquad (6)$$

where:
h_{in} - heat transfer coefficient of the inner wall surface, $\left[\mathtt{W}\cdot\mathtt{m}^{-2}\mathtt{K}^{-1}\right]$;
h_{out} - heat transfer coefficient of the outside wall surface, $\left[\mathtt{W}\cdot\mathtt{m}^{-2}\mathtt{K}^{-1}\right]$;
U - heat passage coefficient, $\left[\mathtt{W}\cdot\mathtt{m}^{-2}\mathtt{K}^{-1}\right]$;
δ_j - thickness of the layer, [m];
λ_j - thermal conductivity of the layer, $\left[\mathtt{W}\cdot\mathtt{m}^{-1}\mathtt{K}^{-1}\right]$;
n - number of the layers, [−].

The degree of utilization of heat gains or thermal heat losses are directly related to the thermal inertia of the building. Based on the inner heat capacity of the building, a time response to changing environmental conditions can be determined as a time constant, which generally indicates the time at which the transient process of a monitored variable decreases from maximum to zero value, if the process proceeds at constant velocity or linearly.

According to the Czech technical standard CSN EN ISO 13790 [1], the time constant for cooling mode is given by the equation (7):

$$\tau_c=\frac{C_m/3.6}{H_{tr,adj}+H_{ve,adj}}, \qquad (7)$$

τ_c - time constant of the building or building zone in the cooling mode, [h];
C_m - inner heat capacity of the building, [kJ.K^{-1}];
$H_{tr,adj}$ - representative value of the total specific heat flux by heat transfer converted for a thermal difference between the interior and the external environment, [W.K^{-1}].
$H_{ve,adj}$ - representative value of the total specific heat flux by ventilation converted for a temperature difference between the interior and the external environment, [W.K^{-1}].

DOI: 10.1051/matecconf/201712502035

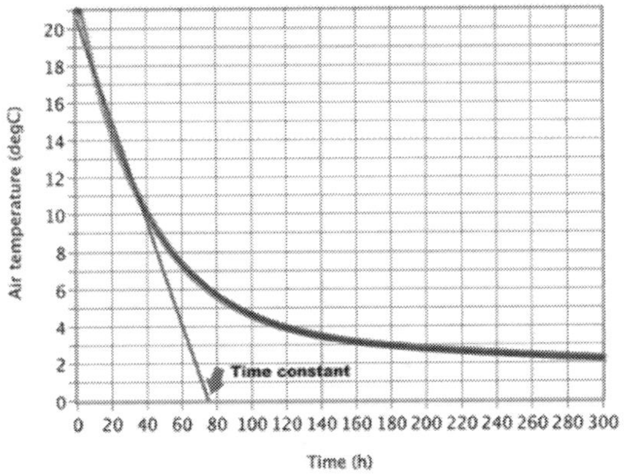

Figure 1. Principle of determining the time constant in the case of cooling down of the room.

It is obvious that the time course of heating or cooling of the room strongly depends on the outside air temperature. In this regard, it is necessary to consider the thermal accumulation properties of the room, as a result of which the response of the indoor environment is caused by some time delay in the changing environment conditions. Therefore, an effort is made to simplify the solution, for example by expressing the storage properties of a building by room time constant according to CSN 06 0220 [5] or by so-called sliding temperature running mean external temperature according to CSN EN 15251 (8) [4]:

$$\theta_{rm} = (1-\alpha)\left\{\theta_{ed-1} + \alpha \cdot \theta_{ed-2} + \alpha^2 \cdot \theta_{ed-3} \ldots\right\}, \quad (8)$$

or by equation (9):

$$\theta_{rm} = (1-\alpha)\,\theta_{ed-1} + \alpha \cdot \theta_{rm-1}. \quad (9)$$

θ_{rm} - running mean external temperature for the evaluated day, [°C],
θ_{rm-1} - running mean external temperature for the previous day, [°C],
θ_{ed-1} - daily mean external temperature for the previous day, [°C],
θ_{ed-2} - daily mean external temperature two days before the evaluated day, [°C],
θ_{ed-3} - daily mean external temperature three days before the evaluated day, [°C],
α - coefficient from 0 to 1. Its recommended value is 0.8, [1].

The aim of our research is to find a relationship between the time constant and the constant α.

3 Method used for the studied problem solving

Our currently tested principle for assessing of the room thermal stability using the theoretical calculations and computer simulations supported by experimental measurements in laboratory or real conditions is based on these steps:

- Build a simplified model of the tested room in user interface of COMSOL Multiphysics.
- Computer simulation of temperature distribution in the tested model of the room for 9 days with the initial and boundary conditions obtained by measuring on a real object of the room (the course of the outdoor air temperature, or the ambient air temperatures, if any, of the adjoining rooms).
- Exporting data describing the air temperature at the center of the room calculated in COMSOL Multiphysics to the user interface of software Maple, where the time constant is determined by Least square method from the linear part of the curve of temperature decrease (see Fig. 1).
- Numerical determination of the optimal value of the coefficient α for calculating the running mean external temperature according to equation (8) or (9) and then the heat loss through the outside wall of the room after 8 days of testing so that the heat losses calculated according to [5] equal to the heat losses determined by the computer simulation.

3.1 Example of the suggested method using

We demonstrate the above described method for assessment of thermal stability of the room which simplified geometric model is shown in Fig. 2. It contains only elements that significantly affect the heat flow between the rooms and the surroundings.

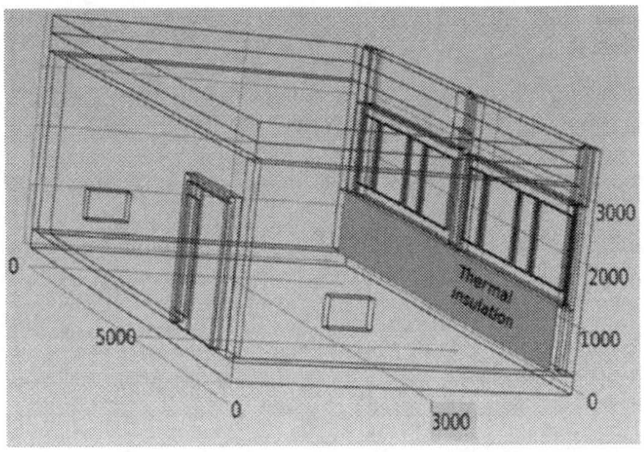

Figure 2. Geometry sketch of the tested room model.

Table 1. Physical properties of the main geometrical elements of the tested room.

Geometrical element	Thermal conductivity $\left[\mathrm{W.m^{-1}.K^{-1}}\right]$	Density $\left[\mathrm{kg.m^{-3}}\right]$	Specific heat capacity $\left[\mathrm{J.kg^{-1}.K^{-1}}\right]$
Inner and external walls	0.1765	817	953
Floor	1.43	2300	1020
Ceiling	0.8185	1251	1021
Window frame	0.20	420	2510
Ceiling insulation	0.039	30	1270
Thermal insulation of external wall	0.18	400	5000

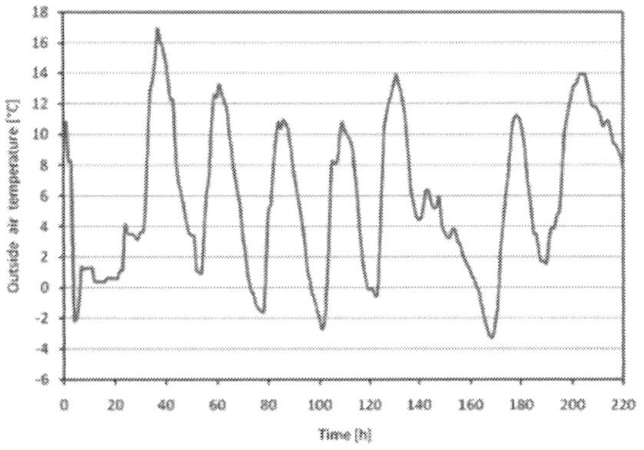

Figure 3. Course of outside air temperature used for computer simulation - measured data.

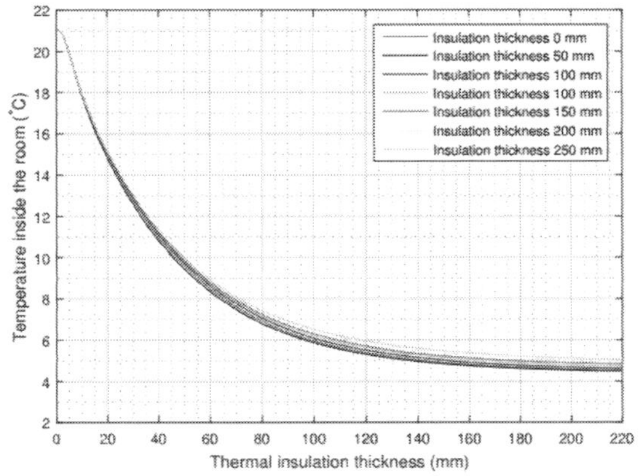

Figure 4. Dependence of the air temperature decrease on thickness of the external wall insulation.

Aim of the testing was to evaluate the influence of the thickness of the external wall and its thermal insulation on the time course of the cooling down of the room. The conditions used for computer simulation and theoretical calculations are:

- initial air temperature inside the room 21 °C,
- air temperature of all neighboring rooms 0 °C,
- heat transfer coefficient between the walls of the room and the air inside the building 8 $\mathrm{W.m^{-2}.K^{-1}}$,
- heat transfer coefficient between the walls of the room and outside air 23 $\mathrm{W.m^{-2}.K^{-1}}$,
- thickness of the inner walls, ceiling and floor was 30 cm,
- physical properties of all elements of the models shows Table 1,
- course of outside air temperature is shown in Fig. 3.

The results of our experiment are presented in Figs 4 - 6. Fig. 4 shows a decrease of the air temperature inside the room during its cooling down in dependence on the thermal insulation thickness. Simulations were compared for wall of 200 mm thickness. It is evident, that maximum temperature decrease occurred for the wall without thermal insulation and that the temperature drop has decreased with the increasing thickness of the thermal insulation.

The dependence of the time constants on the thermal insulation determined by the linear regression of the data obtained by computer simulation is shown in Fig. 5. The time constant is increased approximately by 4.6 hours for the wall with thermal insulation thickness of 300 mm compared to the time constant for the room without the thermal insulated external wall.

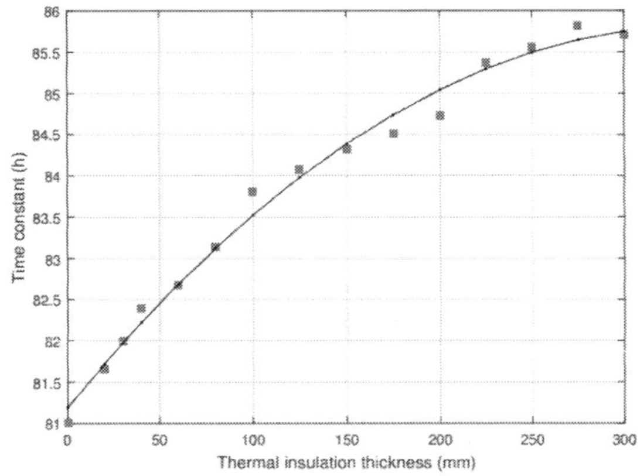

Figure 5. Dependence of the time constant τ_c on thickness of the external wall insulation.

In Fig. 6 is presented dependence of the thermal insulation on value of coefficient α which is required to calculate the daily mean temperature of the external air (8) or (9) in accordance with CSN EN 15251 [4]. It is evident that if the wall be insulated by material with higher specific heat capacity, the air temperature and the time of cooling down the room increase. The experimental results show that under the conditions considered, the coefficient α strongly depends on the thickness of the external wall thermal insulation. Under the tested conditions, its recommended value of 0.8 [4] is achieved up to a thickness of thermal insulation of about 50 mm.

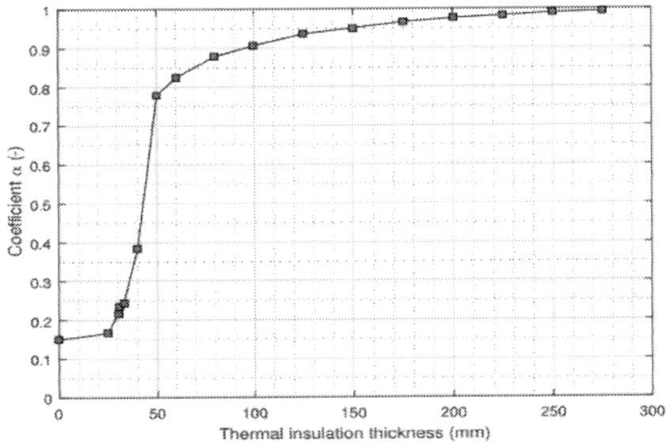

Figure 6. Dependence of the coefficient α on thickness of the external wall insulation.

4 Conclusion

In the paper was described the procedure by which it is possible to combine both computer simulation and theoretical calculations to determine the heat losses of the room under simplified assumptions with respect to Czech and European technical standards used in construction and architecture. The methodology was tested by the assessment of the heat-accumulation properties and thermal insulating materials of the external wall. The tested model of the room showed dependence of the time constant τ_c and the coefficient α on the thermal insulation thickness.

Further work will be focused on verifying the validity of our procedure for other boundary conditions as well as for other types of construction structures.

Acknowledgement
This work was supported by the Ministry of Education, Youth and Sports of the Czech Republic within the National Sustainability Programme project No. LO1303 (MSMT-7778/2014).

References

[1] *CSN EN 13790: Energy performance of buildings - Calculation of energy use for space heating and cooling* (Office for Standards, Metrology and Testing, 2009)

[2] *CSN EN 13792: Thermal performance of buildings - Calculation of internal temperatures of a room in summer without mechanical cooling - Simplified methods.* (Czech Standards Institute, Prague, 2005)

[3] *CSN EN 13786: Thermal performance of building components - Dynamic thermal characteristics - Calculation methods* (Office for Standards, Metrology and Testing, 2008)

[4] *CSN EN 15251: Indoor environmental input parameters for design and assesment of energy performance of buildings – addressing indoor air quality, thermal environment, lighting and acoustics.* (Office for Standards, Metrology and Testing, Prague, 2011)

[5] *CSN 06 0220: Heating systems in buildings – Dynamic behaviour.* (Czech Standards Institute, Prague, 2006)

[6] *CSN 73 0540: Thermal protection of buildings* (Office for Standards, Metrology and Testing, Prague, 2011)

[7] V. Gerlich, *Verification of Possibility of Using COMSOL Multiphysics as Simulation Tool for Heat Transfer Calculation in Systems with Accumulation.* (Thesis. Tomas Bata University in Zlin, Zlin, 2012) pp. 157

[8] H. Charvátová, M. Zálešák *Proceedings of the 19th International Conference on Systems. Recent Advances in Systems*, (Zakynthos Island, Greece: WSEAS Press, 2015) pp. 627-631

[9] *Heat Transfer Module User's Guide.* (COMSOL, 2012) pp. 296

[10] G. Nikishkov, *Introduction to the Finite Element Method.* (University of Aizu, 2003)

[11] H. S. Carslaw, J. C. Jaeger, *Conduction of Heat in Solids.* (Clarendon Press, Oxford, 1986) pp. 510

Calculation of Shielding Effectiveness of Materials for Security Devices

Stanislav Kovar*, *Jan* Valouch and *Hana* Urbancokova

Faculty of Applied Informatics, Nad Stráněmi 4511, 760 05 Zlín, Czech Republic
*skovar@fai.utb.cz

Abstract. Currently, electromagnetic interference constitutes one of the major complications for a function of electronic or electrical devices. Because these devices are constantly exposed to effects of electromagnetic radiation, it is desirable to increase the electromagnetic immunity of device. One of the possibilities is to applicate the suitable shielding materials which can protect the device against the radiated electromagnetic emissions. This paper devotes to finding suitable materials for shielding security devices.

1 Introduction

Electromagnetic interference has become the serious problem for all electronic and electrical devices; that is why the demand for security of devices against this danger has increased. This paper describes one of the ways how to ensure the electromagnetic immunity of device against radiated electromagnetic emissions. This way is the use of shielding material. The authors of this publication used CST Studio Suite simulation software to calculate shielding effectiveness of materials. The research is focused especially on security devices, where the great emphasis is placed on reliability.

Electromagnetic interference can be limited in three main areas, namely at the source of the disturbance, at the receiver and in the transmission route. For the purpose of this work, it is necessary to restrict noise coming into the receiver because there are many interference sources and it is not possible to eliminate all of them. Depending on the method of interference propagation, the means to reduce unwanted noise fall into two categories, namely disturbance by conduction and radiation. In the case of conducted interference, the device is equipped with EMI filters, chokes, capacitors; it is also possible to change the transmission medium or arrangement of circuits. Radiated interference is reduced by selecting a suitable shielding. [1]

Shielding can be defined as a structural means to reduce interfering electromagnetic fields within a defined area. In other words, it protects the devices against unwanted external electromagnetic interference and simultaneously it prevents leakage of electromagnetic disturbance from the device. [1]

2 Shielding Effectiveness

The significant parameter in this area is shielding effectiveness that describes how the material eliminates the effects of electromagnetic radiation from the interference source. [1] According to [2] and [3], this parameter can be described by the following equation.

$$SE = 10 \cdot \log \frac{P_1}{P_2} [dB] \tag{1}$$

Individual characters indicate:
P_1 – power generated by interference source;
P_2 - power passing through the shielding material.

This equation can be adjusted into a form which better corresponds to the physical mechanisms of the shielding effect. [1] This adjustment is described in publications [2] and [3].

$$SE = R + A + M[dB] \tag{2}$$

Individual characters indicate:
R - attenuation by reflection;
A - absorbent attenuation;
M - attenuation caused by multiplied reflection.

2.1 Attenuation by Reflection

This type of attenuation indicates how much energy is reflected at the interface between the dielectric with the impedance of Z_0 and the metal barrier with the impedance of Z_M. The same situation occurs on the output between the metal barrier and the dielectric. [1] According to [2] and [3], the attenuation can be written as follows.

$$R = 20 \cdot \log \left| \frac{Z_0 + Z_M}{2Z_M} \cdot \frac{Z_0 + Z_M}{2Z_0} \right| [dB] \tag{3}$$

$$R = R_1 + R_2 [dB] \tag{4}$$

Individual characters indicate:

Z_0 – impedance of environment (dielectric);
Z_M – impedance of material.

2.2 Absorbent Attenuation

This type of attenuation occurs by absorption of energy by the shielding material due to heat losses. [1] According to [2] and [3], the equations can be written as follows.

$$A = 20 \cdot \log e^{\frac{t}{\delta}} [dB] \quad (5)$$

$$\delta = \sqrt{\frac{2}{\omega \mu \sigma}} \quad (6)$$

Individual characters indicate:
t – material thickness;
δ – intrusion depth;
σ - conductivity;
μ - permeability;
ω – wave frequency.

2.3 Attenuation Caused by Multiplied Reflection

In the case, when the electromagnetic wave passes through the shielding material, then there are multiple reflections on the interfaces between environments. If (t >> δ), the impact of multiple reflections is negligible; conversely, if (t << δ) then the attenuation is negative and shielding effectiveness decreases. According to the information given in publications [2] and [3], the attenuation may be described by the following equation. [1]

$$M = 20 \cdot \log \left| 1 - \left(\frac{Z_0 - Z_M}{Z_0 + Z_M} \right)^2 \cdot e^{-\frac{2t}{\delta}} \cdot e^{-j\frac{2t}{\delta}} \right| [dB] \quad (6)$$

Individual characters indicate:
Z_0 – impedance of environment (dielectric);
Z_M – impedance of material.
δ – intrusion depth.

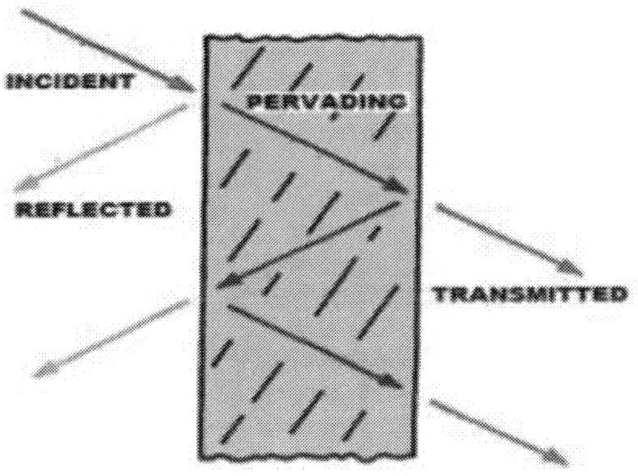

Fig. 1. Principle of Attenuation by Multiplied Reflection. [3]

3 Process of Simulation

The whole process of calculation of shielding effectiveness was performed using CST Studio Suite simulation software. The software is suitable for this experiment because it includes a wide database of materials. As representatives of shielding materials, steel and aluminium were selected. These materials are readily available and suitable for use with security devices. In addition, both materials are relatively cheap.

The process of simulation began by modelling the shielding material whose dimensions are 1x1m and thickness is 1mm. The receiver and transmitter are located facing each other on both sides of the material. The distance of transmitter and receiver from the material under test is 0.5m. The plane wave serves the source of the electromagnetic field and the probe receives the intensity of field penetrated through the shielding material. For an idea, Fig. 2 illustrates the process of testing where TX antenna replaces the source of the field and the RX antenna substitutes the probe.

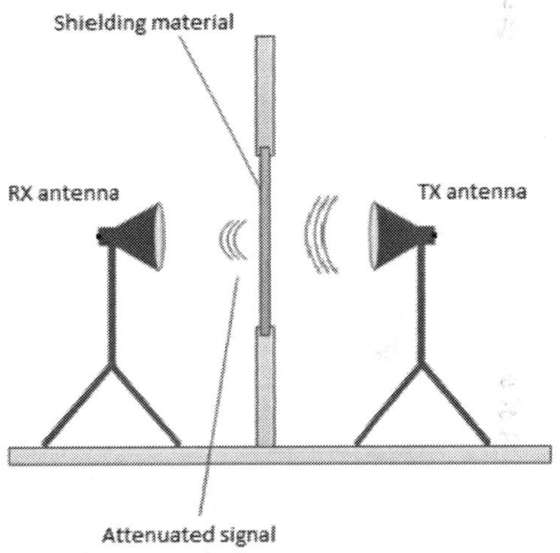

Fig. 2. Principle of Testing of Shielding Effectiveness. [4]

3.1 Shielding materials

The shielding material is one of the most famous ways of the device to protect the device against radiated electromagnetic interference. Shielding material can eliminate the level of disturbance and at the same time, it does not require intervention into the electronics of the device. As mentioned above, this paper describes only several representatives of potential materials for shielding purpose. Because CST Studio software includes a large number of materials, the paper describes the properties of selected materials in Tab. 1 and 2. It is necessary to remark that the data is taken from the software database.

Tab. 1. Parameters of Aluminum

Name	Value	Unit
Type	Lossy metal	-
Mue	1	-

 DOI: 10.1051/matecconf/201712502036

Electrical conductivity	3.56e+007	S/m
Rho	2700	Kg/m^3
Thermal conductivity	237	W/(mK)
Heat capacity	0.9	kJ/(kgK)
Diffusivity	9.75309e-005	m^2/s
Young's modulus	69	kN/mm^2
Poisson's ratio	0.33	-
Thermal expansion	23	1e-6/K

Tab. 2. Parameters of Steel

Name	Value	Unit
Type	Lossy metal	-
Mue	1	-
Electrical conductivity	6.993e+006	S/m
Rho	7870	Kg/m^3
Thermal conductivity	65.2	W/(mK)
Heat capacity	0.45	kJ/(kgK)
Diffusivity	1.84103e-005	m^2/s
Young's modulus	205	kN/mm^2
Poisson's ratio	0.29	-
Thermal expansion	13.5	1e-6/K

4 Results

This section describes the results of the electromagnetic simulation which was created by CST Studio software. A number of shielding materials for the purposes of this research is huge; despite this fact, this paper includes only several representatives. Results in this section depict attenuation of the electromagnetic field through the shielding material and it helps to create an idea which material is the suitable choice for increasing of electromagnetic immunity.

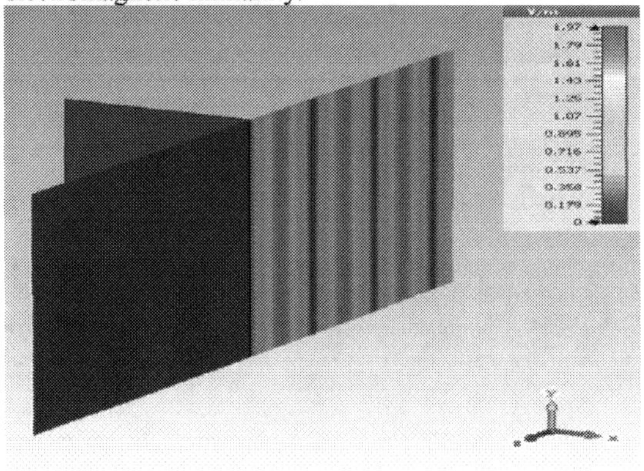

Fig. 3. Shielding Effectiveness.

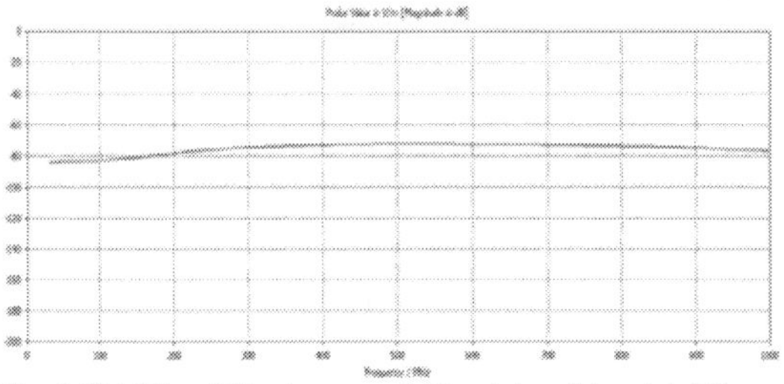

Fig. 4. Shielding Effectiveness of Aluminium Material. [1]

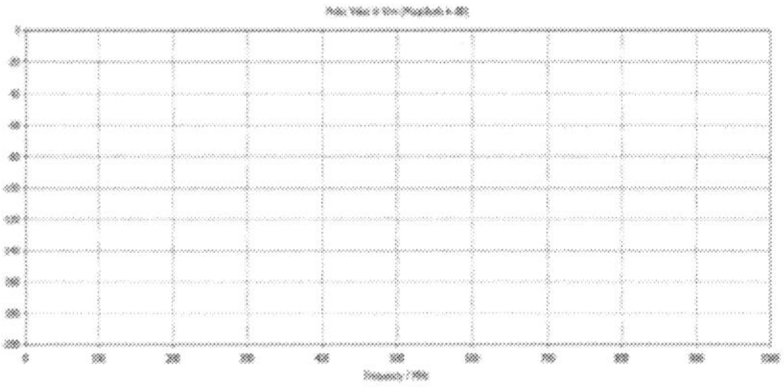

Fig. 5. Shielding Effectiveness of Steel Material. [1]

To ensure all functions of safety devices, cabling must be lead throughout the shielding material for transferring data or to supply power to the device. Therefore, copper wire with a diameter about 1mm is lead throughout the material. The results of shielding effectiveness can be affected by selected wire. It includes the shape, diameter or load of wire.

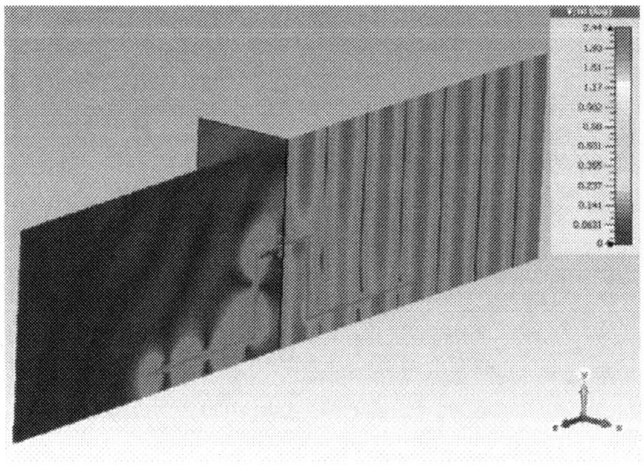

Fig. 6. Shielding Effectiveness of Aluminium when Copper Wire Passing through Material.

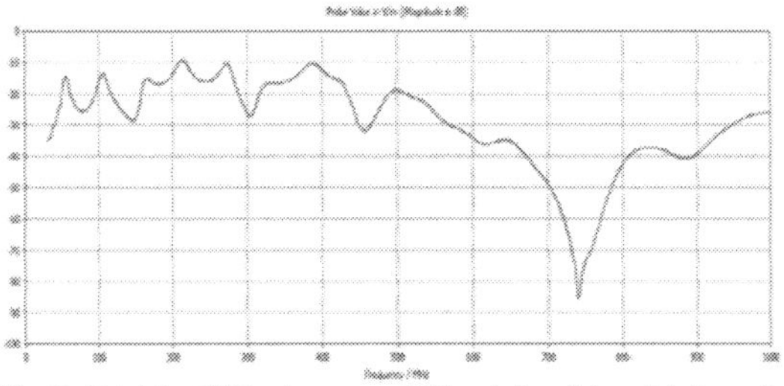

Fig. 7. Shielding Effectiveness of Aluminium Material through Which Passing Copper Wire. [1]

DOI: 10.1051/matecconf/201712502036

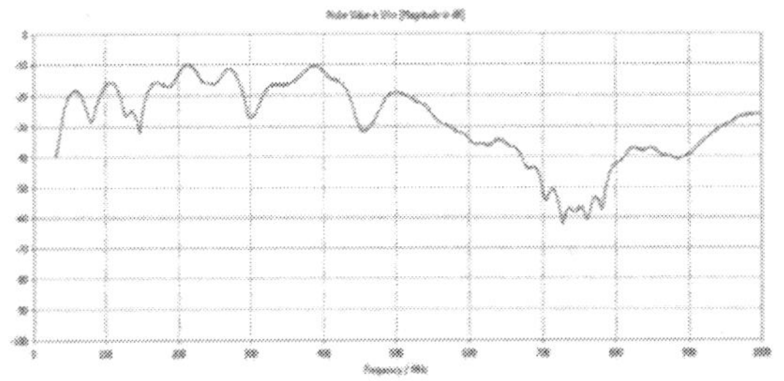

Fig. 8. Shielding Effectiveness of Steel Material through Which Passing Copper Wire. [1]

5 Conclusion

The paper describes the calculation of shielding effectiveness of material for the security device. Because the important factor of security devices is the reliability, the great emphasis should be placed on the electromagnetic immunity. This article summarises one of the ways how to protect the electronic and electric device.

Results of simulations indicate that the use of steel is the suitable way to protect device because it is able to resist the effect of the electromagnetic field. Conversely, the resistance of aluminium to the electromagnetic field is not as high as for steel. The field penetrates with certain attenuation.

In the case, that a wire is led throughout the shielding material, the field can couple to the wire and pass through a sealed material. Therefore, it is necessary to use the shielding wire to protect security devices.

The purpose of this paper is to expand the existing knowledge of shielding materials for security devices. This article will serve as a basis for future research in this research field.

The work was funded with the support of the Internal Grant Agency of Tomas Bata University under the project No. IGA/CebiaTech/2016/005, and support of research project No. LO1303 (MSMT-7778/2014) by the Ministry of Education, Youth and Sports of the Czech Republic within the National Sustainability Programme and also by the European Regional Development Fund under the project CEBIA-Tech No. CZ.1.05/2.1.00/03.0089.

References

1. S. Kovar. Immunity of camera systems against electromagnetic interference. Zlin (2017). *Treatise on doctoral thesis*. Faculty of applied informatics in Zlin. Supervisor doc. Mgr. Milan Adamek, Ph.D.
2. M. Pospislik, T. Riha, M. Adamek, Rui M. S. Silva. *W.S.E.A.S.T.C.S*, **14** (2015)
3. J. Svacina. *Electromagnetic compatibility : principles and notes*. Issue **No. 1**. (2001), 156 p. ISBN 8021418737. (in Czech)
4. Shielding Effectiveness Testing. *Rhein Tech Laboratories, Inc.* [online]. Available at : www.rheintech.com/what-we-do/our-emc-testing-services/shielding-effectiveness
5. D. Kovac, I. Kovacova, J. Kanuch. *EMC in terms of theory and applications*. ISBN 80-7300-202-7. **1** (2006)
6. H. Ott. *Electromagnetic Compatibility*. ISBN 978-0-470-18930-6. (2009)

Hybrid Extension for Advanced Technology Zone

Václav MACH[1,*]

[1] Tomas Bata University in Zlín, Faculty of Applied Informatics, Nad Stráněmi 4511, 760 05 Zlín, Czech Republic

*v2mach@fai.utb.cz

Abstract. This article deals with the software extension for metallic loops. This extension consists of using the binary signal which can be generated by the Control and Indicating Equipment (CIE) to unite analog and digital detectors. Designed improvement can be applied to all existing modes of analog CIE such as Normal Closed (NC), End of Line (EOL) or Advanced Technology Zone (ATZ). It can be also applied to all common digital bus.

1 Introduction

The main component of the Intruder Alarm System (IAS) is the CIE, which evaluates the information obtained from connected detectors. Due to the type of detector connected to the CIE, it can be divided in analog and digital. Nowadays, the most common way how to connect detectors to the CIE is using a digital bus. Using this manner brings many advantages like connecting several detectors to the one bus. That means efficient cable length. All connected detector can be also independently addressed by the CIE.

Despite these advantages, there are still some situations where analog metallic loops can be used. The analog connection is much easier than mentioned digital. Detectors connected to the analog loop must have Normal Closed (NC) contact. When the detector is activated, it automatically switches the contact to the closed state. Even this small change can be enough to evaluate a change in the circuit by the CIE. Using just one detector in one loop is not very efficient. Therefore, more detectors can be added to the single loop, but there is still a problem in addressing of each detector. This problem can be avoided by using the ATZ mode. Described circuit can be found in the following figure.

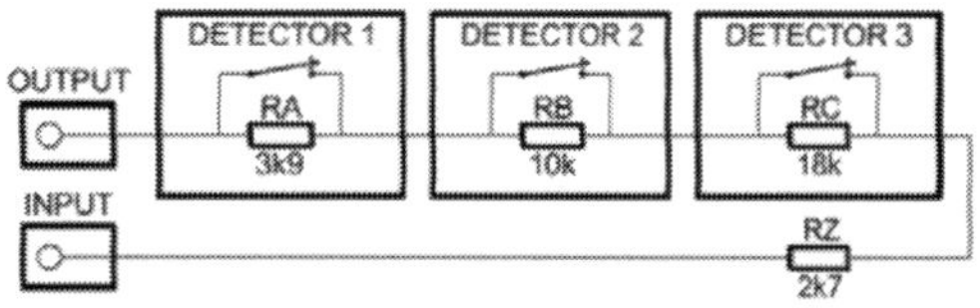

Fig. 1. Advanced Technology Zone wiring.

The ATZ is the most used mode in the metallic loop because it has the biggest number of possible states and the biggest number of connected detectors. This mode is based on the different values of used resistors. Different values of resistors allow distinguishing which detector in the loop has been activated. [4] In common situations, the loop can be divided into three or more independent zones.

The actual state of the loop is evaluated by the CIE. Commercial CIE has usually up to 16 independent analog loops. [5] The signal from the loop is in the form of the voltage which can be affected by connected resistors. Before evaluation signal must be first converted from analog to digital signal using the Analog to Digital Converter (ADC). After this conversion measured value can be evaluated by the CIE.

Another possible way how to connect detectors to the CIE is using a single digital bus, which consists of several cables. These cables are commonly used for the power voltage and data transmission. In practice, connected detector has a unique address which is saved in the CIE. Detector periodically sends its actual state with its address. [3] According to this information CIE can react to received information.

2 Hybrid Extension

The goal of this article is to connect mentioned manners together. It means that to one designed loop can be connected up to six analog detectors which using the NC contact and up to sixteen digital detectors. This is possible when created loop using Two Wire Interface (TWI). TWI consist of two wires Serial Clock Line (SCL) and Serial Data Line (SDA). [6] CIE by the SCL generates the clock signal and data to each device can be transmitted by the SDA. In this extension, SCL is used not only for the clock signal but it is also used for the analog detectors. The amplitude of generated clock signal can be affected by the resistor value which can be added to the circuit by activating NC contact.

The main improvement of this extension is that the SCL can be sent through the analog loop. This signal is periodically generated by the CIE and then it is received back to it. The CIE can compare the received signal with the transmitted. When these two signals are equal it means that the loop is not affected by the analog

 DOI: 10.1051/matecconf/201712502037

detectors. Despite of this, digital detectors are controlled by a different part of the program. None of the commercial made CIE provide official schematics of created devices. The CIE cannot be programmed. According to this limitations, a new concept is created to achieve set goals.

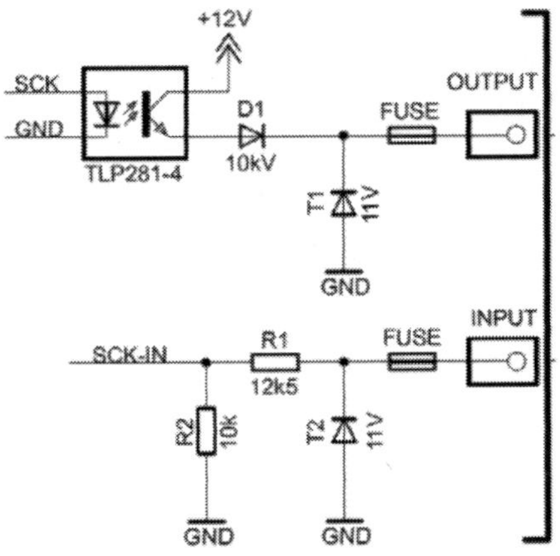

Fig. 2. Designed circuit of CIE.

In practice, the SCK signal is shifted from 3.3 V up to 12 V using the optocoupler. Magnifying the SCK signal helps to increase the range where can be added analog detectors. The amplitude of received SCK signal by the CIE can be converted to the binary number using ADC. Created number can be then evaluated by the CIE. Digital detectors can communicate with the CIE even if analog detector affects the loop. Up to six analog detectors can be connected to the loop based on resistor values. Calculated values can be found in the following table.

Table 1. Calculated threshold values [1].

Current State	Value of SCK-IN	Active resistor
-	[-]	[kΩ]
Short-circuit	1023	0
Serenity	915	2k7
Active - RA	792	3k9 + RZ
Active - RB	655	10k + RZ
Active - RC	534	18k + RZ
Active - RD	418	30k + RZ
Active - RE	284	56k + RZ
Active - RF	159	120k + RZ
Sabotage	0	Infinity

According to the high frequency of the SCK, the conversion must be done very quickly by the microcontroller. Used ATmega2560 the microcontroller can use 8-bit or 10-bit conversion. For purpose of this research, 10-bit converter was used.

Every detector connected by the TWI should have a specialized device which is able to convert states into the TWI signal. The device should consist of TWI interface, power distribution, and the microcontroller. TWI interface follows the standard and it provides interface itself. Power distribution supplies connected detector. The main component is the microcontroller, which by the TWI interface communicates with the CIE. It also response to periodical impulse and it provides the unique name of each connected detector.

Created board consists of ATtiny26 the microcontroller which has built-in TWI interface and it has enough input pins to collect all needed information from the detector. The power supply for the board is 12 V but the microcontroller operates at 5 V. On the board is voltage regulator due to mentioned problem. Voltage regulator converts 12 V to the 5 V which is suitable for the microcontroller.

The used microcontroller is fast enough to accomplish the TWI requirements. Every microcontroller has a simple program which consists of the periodical response to broadcast signal generated by the CIE. It also has conditions for every state that can occur. The final circuit can be found in the following figure.

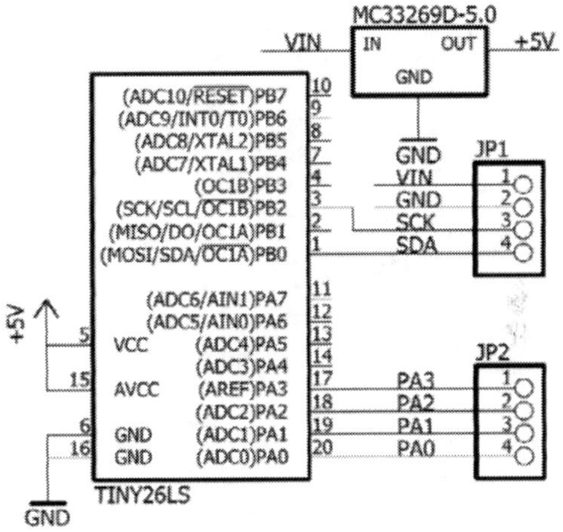

Fig. 3. TWI converting device for the detector.

The device has two terminal blocks. First is used for the power supply and the TWI interface. The second is used for the alarm states from the detector. Every possible state can be distinguished by the extension board. These states are the alarm, anti-masking, failure, battery. More states can be added in the future if needed.

Program of this board can be very simple. The microcontroller periodically checking the alarm pins (PA0 - PA3) and responding to broadcasted signal. When the alarm signal is received, the microcontroller sends the message to the CIE. The program in the CIE than process the incoming message. ATtiny26 the microcontroller was used due to its small package, low price, and small power consumptions.

3 Experiment and Measurement

The experiment was done in the laboratory of Tomas Bata University in Zlín at Faculty of Applied Informatics. Used components are listed below:

- ATmega2560 the microcontroller
- Oscilloscope Hameg Instruments HMO-722
- Digital multi-meter M-3900

The testing circuit from figure 2 with ATmega2560 the microcontroller was assembled. The circuit consists of optocoupler which shifts the voltage from 5 V to 12 V. There are also components which help to protect the circuit against the overvoltage. Receiving part consist of the voltage divider which creates the suitable voltage level for the microcontroller.

Using ATmega2560 the microcontroller was created rectangular signal by the TWI. This signal must be generated continuously. The TWI has given several speeds by the standard. In this case, the microcontroller uses frequency 100 kHz which means that 10-bit string can be transmitted within 0.1 ms. According to the legislation CSN EN 50131-1 ed. 2 CIE must be able to detect alarm signal lasting longer than 400 ms. [2] Used SCL clock is fast enough to detect the alarm signal.

The main measurement was done by using schematics from figure 2 with resistors from table 1. A single resistor and NC switch were used instead of the real detector. Each switch was activated to display the change using Hameg Instruments HMO-722 the oscilloscope. Every possible state was measured and displayed. Measurement results can be found in the following figure.

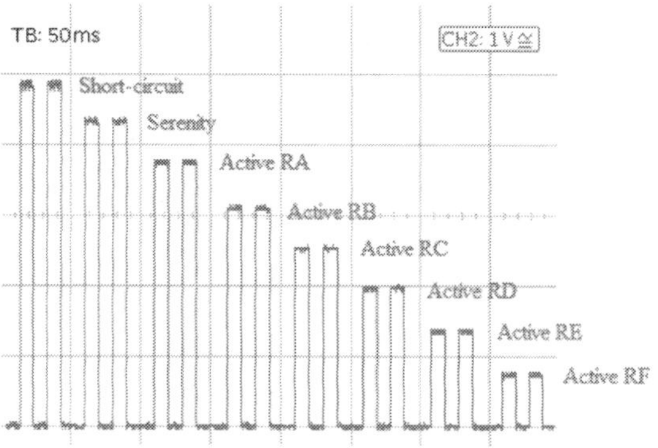

Fig. 4. Waveform of SCK on the oscilloscope.

From figure 4 can be seen the gap between each state. Each state has its own mark. The measurement proved that SCL signal is not distorted when it passes through several resistors. Another ATmega2560 the microcontroller was connected to the loop to prove flawless communication. The time base was set to 50 ms. This test was applied to all possible states which can occur. Measured voltage levels match with calculated values from table 1.

3 Conclusion

This article presents a connection between the analog and digital wiring. Designed schematic uses advantages of analog and digital connection using the TWI. The experiment proved that this method works and it can be implemented in the modern CIE. SCK signal is not affected by connecting detectors to it. More research can be done using an extension of this design to another interface.

This work was supported by the Ministry of Education, Youth and Sports of the Czech Republic within the National Sustainability Programme project No. LO1303 (MSMT-7778/2014) and also by the European Regional Development Fund under the project CEBIA-Tech No. CZ.1.05/2.1.00/03.0089 and by the Internal Grant Agency of Tomas Bata University under the project No. IGA/CebiaTech/2017/006

References

1 V. Mach. T. **5 (2)**, (2016)
2 CSN EN 50131-1 ed. 2. Alarm systems - Intrusion and hold-up alarm systems - Part 1 System requirements. Prague (2007).
3 D. Brooks. S.J., **24 (2)**, 101-117, (2011)
4 A. Hanáček, M. Sysel. S.V., 119-128, (2015)
5 T. Lovecek; A. Velas; K. Kampova, L. Maris; V. Mozer. ICCST, 2013
6 L. Jung, N. Shany, A. Emperle, T. Lehmann, P. Byrnes-Preston, N. Lovell, G. Suaning. IEEE JoSSC. 48, 2013.

MATEC Web of Conferences **125**, 02038 (2017) DOI: 10.1051/matecconf/201712502038
CSCC 2017

Advanced Hardware Protection of Metallic Loops

Václav MACH[1,*] and *Milan* ADÁMEK[1]

[1] Tomas Bata University in Zlín, Faculty of Applied Informatics, Nad Stráněmi 4511, 760 05 Zlín, Czech Republic

*v2mach@fai.utb.cz

Abstract. This article deals with the advanced protection of metallic loops using addition electronic components. The main goal of this article is to improve especially Advanced Technology Zone (ATZ), which is the most applied method. The improvement consists of protection against overvoltage which can destroy the Control and Indicating Equipment (CIE) and it consist of adding more states which have the impact of numbers of connected detectors. All ideas are introduced with technical details, schematic and every idea also comes with an explanation.

1 Introduction

The Intruder Alarm System (IAS) is a part of technical security which can indicate the intrusion to the protected building or area. The concept is driven by the standard CSN CLC/TS 50131. The standard is divided into several parts that describe single areas. The most important standard for this article is the CSN CLC/TS 50131-1 Control and indicating equipment (CIE), which consist of information and parameters which every product must accomplish.

The CIE is the main component of the IAS. It consists of several components which are responsible for each function. These functions are:

- It receives and evaluates the signals from the detectors.
- It provides the power to the connected detectors and other equipment
- It allows system diagnostics
- It controls signalling, transmission, recording, and other functions that indicate the current conditions.

According to the evaluation of incoming signal, the commercial CIE can be divided into two groups. First group using digital interface and second using analog interface. Digital CIE using only one bus which typically consists of four cables. This manner allows to connecting several detectors to one bus. Detector evaluates actual state which is then sent to the CIE in binary form. [1]

CIE using analog loops evaluates actual state of each zone. Each loop has the maximum amount of connected devices according to used mode. These modes are Normal Closed (NC), End of Line (EOL) and ATZ. The most used mode is ATZ because it provides the biggest amount of possible connected detectors from all mentioned modes. Even nowadays ATZ mode is still commonly used in many applications.

ATZ mode still has many disadvantages and possible threats. One of the biggest disadvantages is the number of connected devices which is limited usually up to four devices. [2] This is given by a huge tolerance of terminating resistor which is usually 30%. It means that states between each other must have a gap. This situation helps with the selection of terminating resistor but it inefficiently uses the working range.

The biggest threat is that every commercial CIE has only basic protection against overvoltage which can destroy CIE by the potential intruder. This protection is done using one-use fuse which is installed in each loop. [3] When higher voltage passes the fuse it becomes interrupted. The interrupted loop is not working anymore. In this case destroyed fuse must be replaced.

This article deals with mentioned disadvantages and it tries to bring a new solution. For purposes of this research, a prototype of new CIE was created. Created design is listed in following chapters.

2 Advanced technology Zone

ATZ mode uses different values of resistors. Different values can very precisely distinguish between individual detectors. Each detector has a resistor with a unique value. In real operation, multiple detectors are connected into several groups. Each group uses the same value of resistors.

In general, the ATZ variant has four states, but each individual group can be distinguishable. It can be done by using different values of resistors. This variant is limited by the final numbers of used groups. Usual ranges of values are R1 = 10 kΩ, R2 = 30 kΩ and R3 = 100 kΩ. Adding more resistors can result in difficulties in distinguishing between groups. Each group can contain up to three detectors.

Every loop should be able to distinguish between basic states. These states for every variant are as follows:

DOI: 10.1051/matecconf/201712502038

- Serenity
- Alarm
- Failure
- Sabotage

Serenity and Alarm state are very easy to identify. The tricky part comes with the detection and subsequent distinction between Failure and Sabotage. In the NC variant it is almost impossible to distinguish them. In such case, Failure must be detected as Alarm.

The connected detectors can have some additional outputs like tamper or anti-masking. These connections must be wired in the correct way according to the device manual and also an appropriate version must be used.

2 Designed Hardware Protection

Every analog CIE consists of Analog to Digital Converter (ADC) which converts the analog signal to the binary form. Usually, this converter is already embedded into the microcontroller. Every possible protection must be done outside of the microcontroller.

Designed protection consists of output part and input part. Input part should process not only the continuous signal but it also should process binary pattern. This pattern provides better protection against sabotage because is almost impossible to imitate random binary signal which is generated by the CIE. Due to this situation, every output of the CIE can be controlled. The control part is galvanically separated using an optocoupler to protect CIE from any other threats.

The diode in the forward direction is placed in the circuit to protect also the power supply against overvoltage. The diode is dimensioned up to 1 kV. Another active protection is the Transient Voltage Suppression (TVS) diode in combination with the resettable fuse. [4] TVS diode acts as a normal diode with the threshold voltage. In this case threshold voltage is set to 11 V. When this voltage is exceeded diode becomes to the short circuit mode and voltage is passed to the Ground (GND). [5] In the same time resettable fuse disconnects the circuit due to the big current from the external power supply. TSV diode can turn back from the short circuit state after the voltage drops back under 11 V. Also the resettable fuse can turn back to the connected state. It means that this protection is nondestructive. Schematic can be found in the following figure.

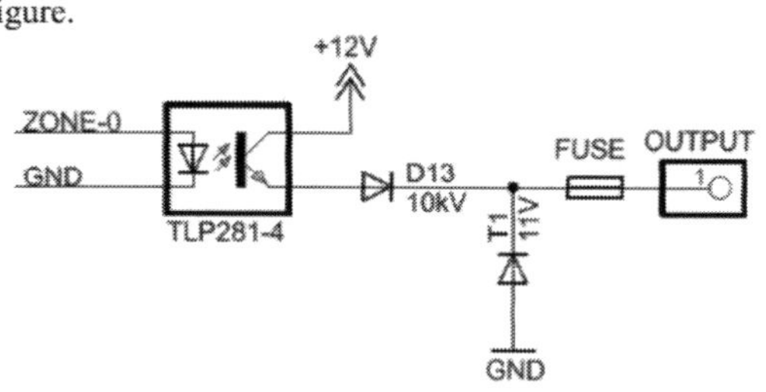

Fig. 1. Output part of created protection of analog loop.

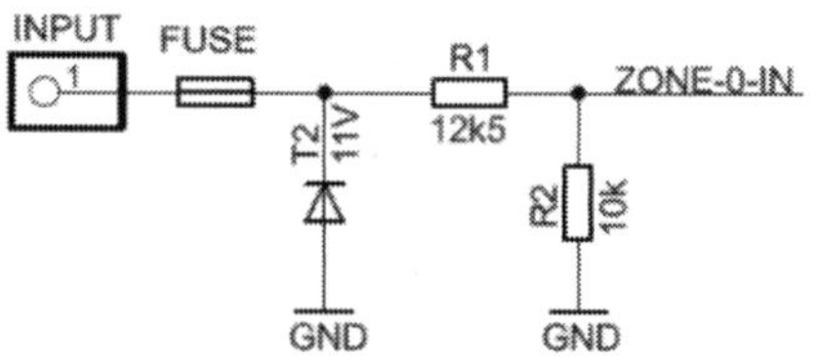

Fig. 2. Input part of created protection of analog loop.

The input part consists of a twin set of TVS diode and resettable fuse as well as the output part. Before voltage gets to the ADC it passes through the voltage divider. Operating voltage of the circuit is 10,9 V. But the maximal voltage level which can be applied to the ADC is only 5 V. The entering voltage must be lowered using the voltage divider.

Voltage divider uses resistors with values 10 kΩ and 12,5 kΩ. It means that output voltage of the voltage divider is 4,84 which is safe for the ADC built in the microcontroller. This precise value is used to evaluate short circuit state of the loop. All possible states are listed in Table 2.

All modes use NC contact and resistor in the loop. When the detector is activated, it opens the NC contact. It causes that connected resistor is no long bypassed and the resistor is connected to the loop. ATZ mode uses several resistors with different values to identify, which of these resistors were connected to the loop. The total value of the resistor in the loop is changing by adding more resistor to it. This change is detected and evaluated in the CIE.

Own values of resistors were uses to achieve the satisfying number of the possible detectors connected to the loop. Used values are listed in Table 1. These values are not very common but all these values can be found in the market. As mentioned before, commercial tolerance for the resistor value is about 30%. [6] Listed values of the resistor must have only 5% tolerance to achieve maximal states without interference or overlapping. Created schematic with detectors and resistor can be found in the following figure.

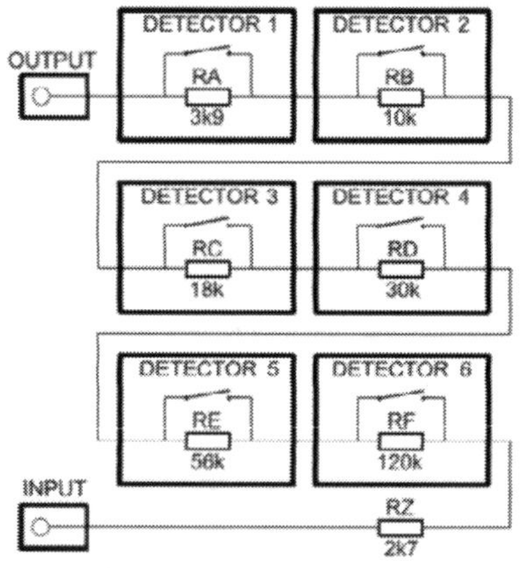

Fig. 3. Resistor values using ATZ mode.

Before final evaluation, entering voltage must be converted using ADC. Used ATmega2560 the microcontroller has a built-in 1024-bit converter. It means that range of entering voltage is converted into numbers from 0 to 1023. Conversion values are shown in the following table.

Table 1. Calculated values of resistors.

Current State	Value of ADC	Input voltage	Active resistor
-	[-]	[V]	[kΩ]
Short-circuit	1023	4,84	0
Serenity	915	4,33	2k7
Active - RA	792	3,75	3k9 + RZ
Active - RB	655	3,10	10k + RZ
Active - RC	534	2,52	18k + RZ
Active - RD	418	1,97	30k + RZ
Active - RE	284	1,34	56k + RZ
Active - RF	159	0,75	120k + RZ
Sabotage	0	0	Infinity

Selected values of used resistors have an exponential rising tendency. This tendency helps to achieve a linear order of resulting voltage. Created voltage levels are shifted from each other by 0,5 V. Created gap and 5% tolerance helps against any overlapping or distortion.

Created design needs also software extension. Used ATmega2560 the microcontroller allows using several programming platforms such as Atmel Studio or Arduino. Values of the ADC from Table 1 can be used as threshold values for the software extension. The program should consist of all possible states which are mentioned in Table 1.

2 Measurement

The experiment was done in the laboratory of Tomas Bata University in Zlín at Faculty of Applied Informatics. Used components are listed below.

- ATmega2560 the microcontrollers
- Digital multi-meter M-3900
- Power supply LBN-303 0-30V/0-3A

The Printed Circuit Board (PCB) was created, to confirm that designed system is working. Tested PCB was connected to the power supply. The pin named ZONE-0 was set to logic 1 using the test program. This change causes that optocoupler activated the loop. Each resistor was added to the loop and by the ADC in the microcontroller entering voltage was measured and displayed.

The measurement was primarily focused on the independent states, which can occur. Measured values are presented in the following Figure 4. The measurement shows designed levels of each state. Presented states are given by the resistor values in Table 1.

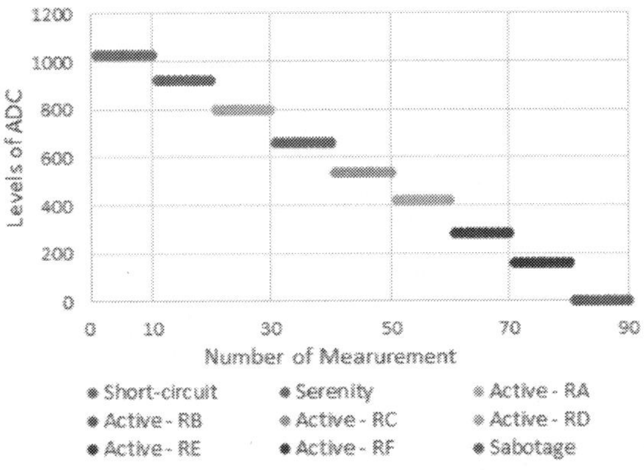

Fig. 4. Measurement results of each state.

Ten measurements of each state were taken to obtain a satisfactory amount of data. Even with this amount of values, states are very stabilized according to calculated values. From Figure 4 can be seen the gap between each state to ensure minimal possible distortion or overlapping. Another measurement was done according to the protection against overvoltage using TVS diode and resettable fuse.

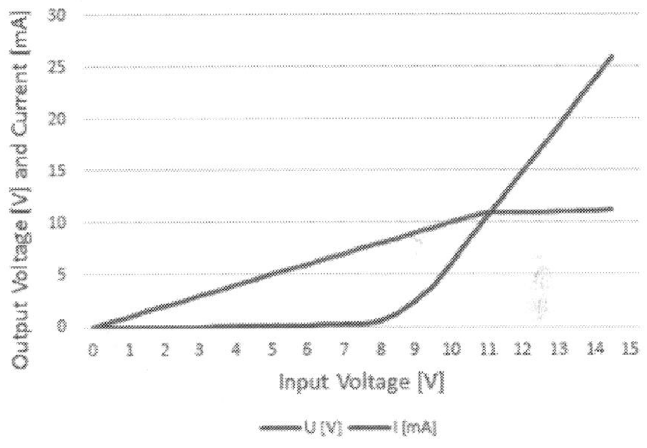

Fig. 5. Measurement results of TVS diode.

Previous Figure 5 shows the situation when the overvoltage occurs. In this case, the input voltage is limited by the TVS diode. This diode is dimensioned to the 11 V. When this voltage is exceeded TVS diode slowly becomes to the short circuit state. It means that voltage does not rise, but the current does. When current reach value approximately to 20 mA resettable fuse opens the circuit. Resettable fuse activates approximately at 13.5 V. This level protects CIE against overvoltage very well.

2 Conclusion

Created design adds to the CIE more electrical protection against sabotage by the overvoltage and it also allows to use more possible levels. All presented schematics were assembled and then tested. These measurements are listed and commented in several figures. To personal safety, the sabotage by overvoltage was tested only to 15 V. But even 15 V proved that designed schematic works. All measurements were done using the 8-bit ADC embedded in ATmega2560 the microcontroller. The TVS diode was tested using Mastech-M3900 digital multi-meter.

This work was supported by the Ministry of Education, Youth and Sports of the Czech Republic within the National Sustainability Programme Project No. LO1303 (MSMT-7778/2014) and also by the European Regional Development Fund under the project CEBIA-Tech No. CZ.1.05/2.1.00/03.0089 and by the Internal Grant Agency of Tomas Bata University under the project No. IGA/CebiaTech/2017/006.

References

1 D. Brooks. S.J., **24 (2)**, 101-117, (2011)

2 A. Hanáček, M. Sysel. S.V., 119-128, (2015)

3 I. Strašil. B.U.T. (2008)

4 D. Bouangeune, D. Cho, H. Yun, K. Shim, CH.O.I. **11**, 88-92, (2015)

5 V. Mach. T. **5 (2)**, (2016)

MATEC Web of Conferences **125**, 02039 (2017) DOI: 10.1051/matecconf/201712502039
CSCC 2017

Immunity of electronic devices against radio-frequency electromagnetic fields

Hana Urbancokova[1*], *Stanislav* Kovar[1], *Ondrej* Halaska[1], and *Jan* Valouch[1]

[1]Faculty of Applied Informatics, Tomas Bata University in Zlin, nam. T.G.Masaryka 5555, 760 01 Zlin, Czech Republic

Abstract. One of the major types of electromagnetic interference, which affect electronic devices in their normal operation, is the interference with radio-frequency electromagnetic fields. This interference is generated by the mainly radio and television transmitters, industrial equipment and other transmitters and receivers in general use for communication. Testing of electromagnetic susceptibility of electronic devices on radiated radio-frequency electromagnetic field is governed by the basic standard IEC 61000-4-3 and the equipment under test are exposed to test electromagnetic fields with an intensity from 1 V/m to 30 V/m, the most often in the frequency range from 80 MHz to 2 GHz. The aim of this paper is to explain the issue of electromagnetic susceptibility and to present sample the electromagnetic immunity tests of the basic set of the intrusion and hold-up alarm system against the radio-frequency electromagnetic field according to the relevant electromagnetic compatibility standards.

1 Introduction

Measurement and testing of electromagnetic compatibility (EMC) of electronic devices are carried out according to standardized methodologies in a precisely defined environment. An ideal environment for testing the electromagnetic susceptibility of electronic devices would be the real environment in which the devices will work. However, such the environment is variable. So because of the reproducibility of the test, a simulated environment is selected according to the instructions that are given in the standards of the individual immunity tests.

Measurement of interference which is transmitted by the radiation is performed in anechoic or semi-anechoic chambers; respectively at the test site in open space OATS - Open Area Test Site. Testing for electromagnetic immunity in the test radiated radio-frequency electromagnetic field should be always carried out in shielded chambers due to the high intensity of the generated field. But in the case of large systems or devices, the measurements must be carried out at the installation site. [1, 2]

Electromagnetic susceptibility (EMS) is the ability of a device, equipment or system to function without degradation in the presence of an electromagnetic disturbance. They must work without failures or with a precisely defined allowable influence. EMS deals with the technical measures which increase electromagnetic immunity of receivers. EMS is focused on removing the consequences of interference, without removing their causes.

The electromagnetic susceptibility of the technical system is divided into:

- Internal EMS - it is system immunity against interfering sources contained inside its own system.
- External EMS - it is the resilience of the system against external sources of electromagnetic interference (EMI). [2, 3]

This paper describes the electromagnetic immunity test of the basic set of the intrusion and hold-up alarm system (I&HAS). This basic set consisted of a control panel with an accumulator stored in a plastic box, the keypad, PIR detector and siren. This set has been tested to the effects of EMI (radiated, radio-frequency, electromagnetic field), and system failures or unintentional behaviour of components of I&HAS were monitored during the immunity tests. A semi-anechoic chamber was used for EMS tests and the test set was in two basic states (ON state and state of alarm).

2 Radio-frequency electromagnetic field

Testing of electromagnetic susceptibility of electronic devices on radiated radio-frequency electromagnetic field is governed by the basic standard IEC 61000-4-3 Electromagnetic compatibility (EMC) Part 4-3: Testing and measurement techniques - Radiated, radio-frequency, electromagnetic field immunity test.

Radio-frequency field is mostly generated by a tiny system transmitter/receiver used by staffs that ensure operation, maintenance and safety in manufacturing. Other systems that generate radio-frequency electromagnetic fields can be, for example, stable radio or television transmitters, vehicles transmitters, and other industry electromagnetic sources. In the last years, a large growth of radio-frequency interference was

* Corresponding author: urbancokova@fai.utb.cz

detected, especially in the frequency bands from 0.8 GHz up to 6 GHz. [2, 4]

2.1 Testing levels

The following table (Table 1.) shows an intensity of the testing field based on testing level according to IEC 61000-4-3. Testing levels are used for general purposes, digital radiotelephones and other devices which emit radio-frequency radiation.

Table 1. Intensity of radio-frequency radiation

Level	Intensity of testing field V/m
1	1
2	3
3	10
4	30
X	Special

"X" represents the unlimited testing level and its associated field intensity can acquire whatever value. This testing level can be given in the product standard.

The intensity of the testing field is represents as a value of an unmodulated signal. This signal is modulated by sinus wave 1 kHz with 80% modulation depth when testing of electromagnetic susceptibility. The real threat when radio-frequency fields radiating is simulated for the equipment under test (EUT) by this modulation. [4]

2.2 Environmental classes

The selection of the appropriate level for EUT is made according to environmental class selection based on the followings:

- Class 1: The environment with the low levels of the electromagnetic radiation – typical environment for the local radio stations or television stations that are further than 1 km each other and low power transmitters/receivers.
- Class 2: The environment with the moderate levels of the electromagnetic radiation – typical for business environment in which the low power transmitters are used (less than 1 W) but with close-to-device-usage limitation.
- Class 3: Then environment with the demanding levels of the electromagnetic radiation – typical for the industry environment where are transfer receivers with the higher power than 2 W, which are used in the close field of the device (up to 1 m). There is also the environment, where the radio transmitters, industry, scientific or medical devices are used.
- Class 4: Transfer systems transmitter/receiver and significant sources of interference are situated at the distance of less than 1 m from the EUT.
- Class X: The unlimited level which is defined in a standard for particular product or in a device specification. [4, 5]

2.3 Frequency range

Testing of electromagnetic susceptibility on the general purposes is mostly done in frequency range from 80 MHz up to 2 GHz. In case, when testing levels involve safety against radio-frequency radiation from digital radiotelephones and other devices which emit radio-frequency fields, the immunity tests are done in frequency range from 800 MHz up to 960 MHz and 1.4 GHz up to 6.0 GHz.

3 Workplace for EMS testing

The basic principle of testing of susceptibility against the radio-frequency electromagnetic field is the use of appropriate antennas for irradiation EUT by specific levels of the electromagnetic field. This testing should be done inside absorption places (in an anechoic chamber or semi-anechoic chamber with additional absorbers).

Workplace for EMS testing consists of technical and other equipment such as the high-frequency signal generator with amplitude modulation sinus wave 1 kHz with 80% modulation depth. The output of the generator can have a filter at the bottom sluice band for harmonic features suppression of the generated signal.

Other equipment which is needed for susceptibility testing of electronic devices is broadband powerful amplifier (for signal amplification), the transmission directional antenna which emits testing electromagnetic wave (generates electromagnetic fields), for example, biconical (double-cone) antenna, logarithmic-periodic antenna, funnel antenna or antenna with double waveguide or another linear polarized antenna system which is appropriated for frequency requirements. In all inputs and outputs of cables and conducting to the testing chamber must be plugged the electric filters EMI (the filter must not to produce additional resonance on the plugged conducting). The isotropic sensor of the field with appropriate susceptibility and auxiliary device for recording power levels, for checking and for continuous functional evaluating EUT and other equipment for ensuring specific function when testing, are needed.

In the tests of susceptibility to radio-frequency fields, most of the EUTs are placed in an absorption chamber on an 80 cm high table, or on a floor on a non-conductive pad 5-15 cm high. According to standards preferred distance of the antenna from the EUT is 3 m. If this distance is can not be met, it may be shorter, but not less than 1 m. Also, the distance of the EUT from the walls of the chamber should be greater than 1 m. The EUT should be irradiated by a homogeneous field of known and constant intensity. The area of this field is usually 1.5 x 1.5 m in height of 0.8 m above the floor. In case of testing smaller devices, the area of the field may be smaller, but it must not fall below 0.5 x 0.5 m.

The test procedure includes four points:

a) Verification of laboratory reference conditions.
b) Verification of the proper operation of the EUT.
c) Performing the test.
d) Evaluation of test results. [4, 5, 6]

3.1 Equipment under test

Fig. 1 shows the basic set of intrusion and hold-up alarm systems, which was tested for resistance against radio-frequency interference. For this type of equipment it is necessary to comply not only the basic standard IEC 61000-4-3, but also the next specialized standard EN 50130-4 Alarm systems – Part 4: Electromagnetic compatibility – Product family standard: Immunity requirements for components of fire, intruder, hold up, CCTV, access control and social alarm systems. [7]

Fig. 1. The basic set of I&HAS.

The set was powered from the mains 240V/50Hz. The control panel, accumulator and mains power module were closed in the plastic box which is usually supplied with the control panel. All components belong to the product lines Oasis. Fig. 1 shows the location of the components of I&HAS on the table which was placed on the turntable in the semi-anechoic chamber.

The set included the following components:

- Control panel JA 82-K.
- Accumulator 12V, 2.4Ah.
- Mains power module.
- Keypad JA-81E.
- PIR detector JS-20.
- Siren SA-913TM.

3.2 Measuring equipment

The measurements of electromagnetic sesceptibility were performed in the semi-anechoic chamber in the EMC laboratory at the Tomas Bata University in Zlin. The semi-anechoic chamber creates a shielded space in which all inappropriate electro-magnetic interferences from the environment that could distort the measurement results are eliminated. [8]

Used semi-anechoic chamber from manufacturer FRANCONIA was equipped with the logarithmic-periodic antenna HL046 (Rohde&Schwarz) (Fig. 2) which operates in the frequency range from 80MHz to 1.3 GHz. The distance of the antenna from the equipment under test is adjustable according to the requirements of standards.

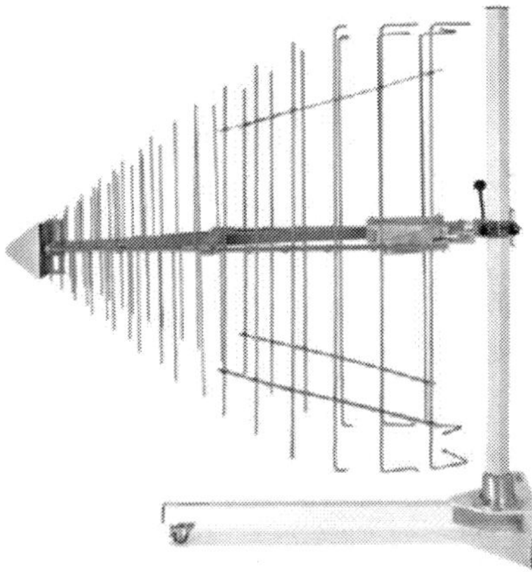

Fig. 2. Logarithmic-periodic antenna HL046.

Another device in a semi-anechoic chamber was electric field probe HI-6015 (ETS-Lindgren) which operates in the frequency range from 100 kHz to 6 GHz.

Other measuring equipment were placed outside the semi-anechoic chamber:

- Signal generator - SMB 100A (Rohde&Schwarz) - frequency range from 9 kHz to 6 GHz.
- EMI test receiver - ESU (Rohde&Schwarz) - frequency range from 20 Hz to 8 GHz.
- Amplifier No.1 - 150A250 (Amplifier Research) - frequency range from 100 kHz to 250 MHz.
- Amplifier No.2 - 150W1000 (Amplifier Research) - frequency range from 80 MHz to 1 GHz.
- Amplifier No.3 - 80S1G4 (Amplifier Research) - frequency range from 0.7 GHz to 4.2 GHz.
- Switch and control unit - OSP 130 (Rohde&Schwarz).
- Switch and control unit - OSP 150 (Rohde&Schwarz).
- EMC measurement software - EMC32 (Rohde&Schwarz). [9]

4 The results of selected measurements

The EUT, on which was measured the electromagnetic susceptibility to radiated electromagnetic fields, was tested in the semi-anechoic chamber in the EMC laboratory at the Tomas Bata University in Zlin. The set of I&HAS was measured in the mode where the whole set was in the ON state (state of guarding) or when the alarm was induced. The distance of the antenna from the EUT was 2.5 m, in order to ensure the required strength of an electromagnetic field. The testing was performed using a Peak detector which indicates the maximum value of the electromagnetic field for each measured frequency.

The selected measurements from the semi-anechoic chamber are shown in Figures 3, 4, 5 and 6. A harmonic unmodulated signal (which corresponds to the values of field strength) is amplitude modulated to a depth of 80% by the low-frequency harmonic voltage of 1 kHz. The strength of the electric field should be set to a value of 10 V/m.

DOI: 10.1051/matecconf/201712502039

Each test run is shown using two images that are outputs from the EMC32 control and display software. The x-axis shows the frequency in Hz from 80 MHz to 3 GHz. The y-axis shows either the degree of the radiated electromagnetic field (Imm Level) in V/m (volt per meter) or the level of the currently used amplifier (Amp Out Fwd) in W (watt).

According to standard IEC 61000-4-3 the frequency range from 80 MHz to 2 GHz is the most often to used, but we have set the frequency value up to 3 GHz, since standard EN 50130-4 recommends testing EMS frequencies up to 2.7 GHz.

In the first EMS test, I&HAS test set was in the ON state (state of guarding). During the test in the prescribed frequency range (80 MHz to 2 GHz - according to IEC 61000-4-3), the assembly resisted the action of a radio-frequency field of level 3, which corresponding to the intensity of the field of radiation of 10 V/m. After exceeding the 1.988 GHz frequency, the status of the EUT has changed, the system detected an error and proclaimed an alarm (the siren was activated).

In Fig. 3 the intensity of the test field at individual frequencies is shown where deviations from the required 10 V/m are usually minimal. At 175 MHz and 810 MHz the deviation was greater (-1.25 V/m). Fig. 4 shows the power of the amplifiers during the test.

In the next test, I&HAS test set was in the alarm state (when the alarm was induced and the siren has been activated). During the entire test (from 80 MHz to 3 GHz), the status of the EUT has not changed and the system did not report no errors after the test was completed. The intensity of the test field at individual frequencies and the power of the amplifiers during the second test are shown in Fig. 5 and Fig. 6.

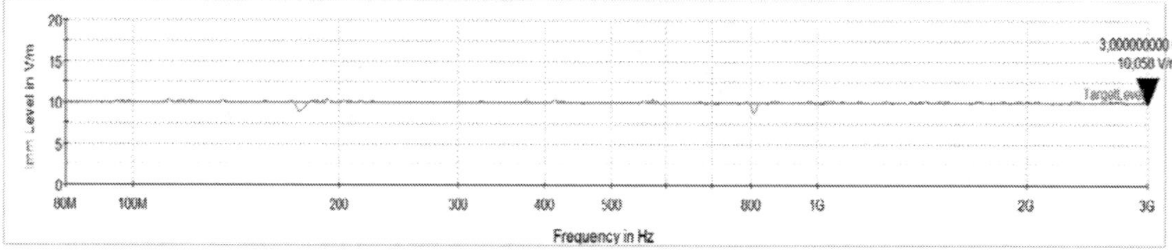

Fig. 3. Test 1 - Immunity level.

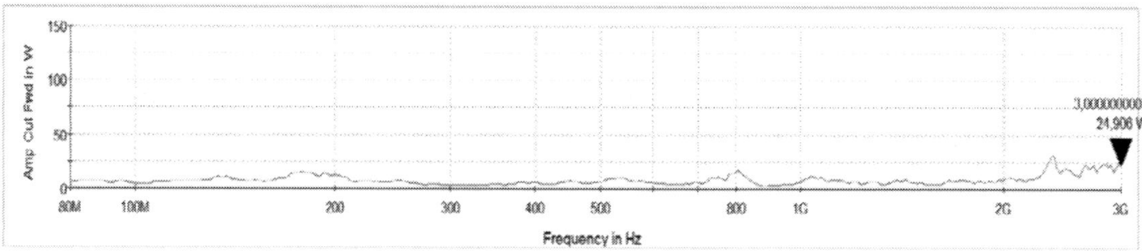

Fig. 4. Test 1 - Amp Out Fwd.

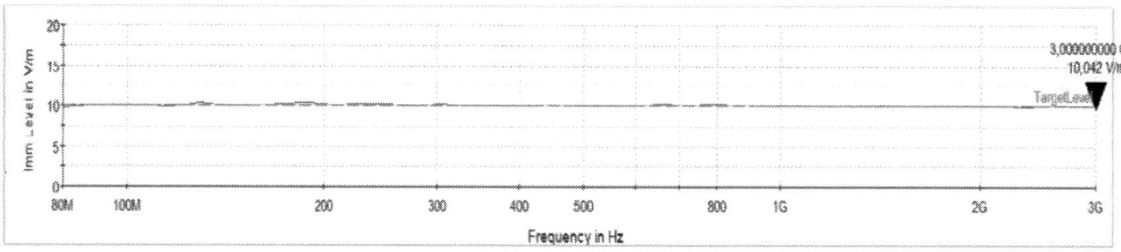

Fig. 5. Test 2 - Immunity level.

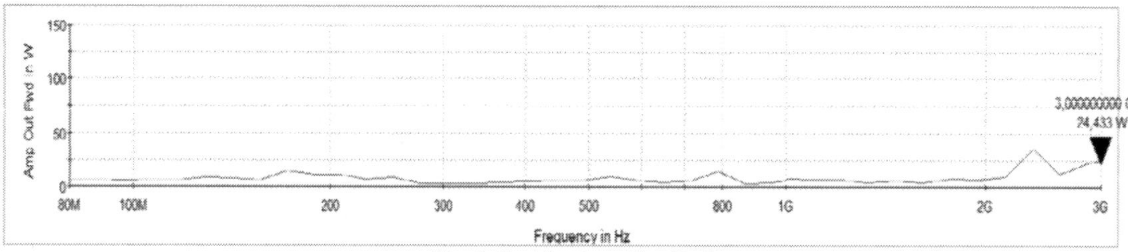

Fig. 6. Test 2 - Amp Out Fwd.

5 Conclusion

The article describes the requirements and the course of the test of electromagnetic susceptibility of electronic devices on radiated radio-frequency electromagnetic field. In our case the EUT was the basic set of the intrusion and hold-up alarm system in two basic states - ON state and state of alarm. For this type of equipment it is necessary to comply not only the basic standard IEC 61000-4-3, but also the next specialized standard EN 50130-4.

According to standard IEC 61000-4-3 the equipment under test are exposed to test electromagnetic fields with an intensity from 1 V/m to 30 V/m, the most often in the frequency range from 80 MHz to 2 GHz. Standard EN 50130-4 recommends testing EMS frequencies up to 2.7 GHz.

During our selected measurements I&HAS test set was exposed to radio-frequency fields at an intensity of 10 V/m and in the frequency range from 80 MHz to 3 GHz. During the immunity test when EUT was in the ON state, the status of the EUT has changed after exceeding the 1.988 GHz frequency - the system detected an error and proclaimed an alarm (the siren was activated). At the end of the test, it was necessary to turn off the alarm manually, but the system remained fully functional. During the immunity test when EUT was in the alarm state, no change was observed.

Acknowledgment

This work was supported by the Ministry of Education, Youth and Sports of the Czech Republic within the framework of the National Sustainable Development Program no. LO1303 (MSMT-7778/2014) as well as the European Regional Development Fund under the CEBIA-Tech project no. CZ .1.05 / 2.1.00 / 03.0089 was supported by research project VI20172019054 "Analysis of software module for real-time immunity assessment in terms of convergent security" supported by the Ministry of Interior of the Czech Republic in 2017-2019 and the Internal Grant Agency of Tomas Bata University within the project no. IGA / CebiaTech / 2017/006

References

1. J. Valouch: Technical requirements for Electromagnetic Compatibility of Alarm Systems. *In: International Journal of Circuits, Systems and Signal Processing.* **Volume 9.** USA, Oregon: North Atlantic University Union (2015). p. 186 – 191. ISSN: 1998-4464. p. 6.
2. J. Svacina: *Electromagnetic compatibility: principles and notes.* Issue No. 1. Brno: University of Technology (2001), 156 p. ISBN 8021418737. (in Czech).
3. H. Urbancokova, J. Valouch and M. Adamek: Testing of an Intrusion and Hold-up Systems for Electromagnetic Susceptibility - EFT/B. *In: International Journal of Circuits, Systems and Signal Processing.* **Volume 9.** USA, Oregon: North Atlantic University Union (2015). p. 40-46. ISSN: 1998-4464. 7 p.
4. IEC 61000-4-3: *Electromagnetic compatibility (EMC) - Part 4-3: Testing and measurement techniques - Radiated, radio-frequency, electromagnetic field immunity test.* International Electrotechnical Commission (2006).
5. T. Rybak and M. Steffka: *Automotive electromagnetic compatibility (EMC),* Boston: Kluwer Academic Publishers (2004), ISBN: 1-4020-7713-0.
6. H. Ott: *Electromagnetic Compatibility.* USA, Hoboken: WILEY (2009). ISBN 978-0-470-18930-6. 844 p.
7. EN 50130-4: *Alarm systems. Electromagnetic compatibility. Product family standard: Immunity requirements for components of fire, intruder, hold up, CCTV, access control and social alarm systems.* European Committee for Electrotechnical Standardization (2011).
8. H. Urbancokova, S. Kovar, J. Valouch and M. Adamek: Electromagnetic Interference of Components of Intrusion and Hold-up Alarm Systems. *In: Automation Control Theory Perspectives in Intelligent Systems, Advances in Intelligent Systems and Computing 466 - Proceedings of the 5th Computer Science On-line Conference 2016 (CSOC2016)* (2016). pp. 443-452 . DOI: 10.1007/978-3-319-33389-2_42. ISBN: 978-3-319-33387-8 (Print) 978-3-319-33389-2 (Online). ISSN: 2194-5357. 10 p.
9. S. Kovar and J. Valouch: Electromagnetic susceptibility of IP camera. *In: Przegląd Elektrotechniczny.* **Vol 2016, No 5.** Poland, Warszawa (2016). pp. 204-208. DOI:10.15199/48.2016.05.40. ISSN 0033-2097. 5 p.

* Corresponding author: urbancokova@fai.utb.cz

Dividing of metal and plastic components of printed circuit boards

Jiri Krenek[1], *Dagmar* Janacova[1*], *Ondrej* Liska[2], *Vladimir* Vasek[1] and *Oldrich* Suba[3]

[1] Tomas Bata Univerzity in Zlín, Faculty of Applied Informatics, nám. T.G.Masaryka 5555, 760 01 Zlín, Czech Republic
[2] Technical University of Kosice, Faculty of Mechanical Engineering, Department of Automation, Control and Human Machine Interaction, Letná 9, 04200 Košice, Slovakia
[3] Tomas Bata Univerzity in Zlín, Faculty of Technology, nám. T.G.Masaryka 5555, 760 01 Zlín, Czech Republic

Abstract. This paper contents one possibility of PCB separation due to the temperature due to the different thermal expansion of the metal path and the plastic from which the boards are made. Using the knowledge from the literary study and the simulation environments used, we have reached the maximum analysis of the problem. The separation of metal and plastic may occur due to temperature changes if the temperature difference is sufficient. We have carried out a study of printed circuit board production so we can choose the appropriate path of separation. Furthermore, we calculated the shear stress size required to tear the conductive copper paths from the epoxy resin. The temperature field in a two-layer board was modeled in the FEMLAB and Pro/ENGINEER programming environments. From the simulated temperature field simulations, conclusions can be drawn that accurately describe the condition and characteristics of materials subjected to heat shock. They derived the resulting relationship for calculating the resulting shear stress needed to separate the conductive paths and plastic materials of the PCB. In our own experiments, we used several ways to heat PCBs. The temperature is also sufficient for the separation of tin. After using the mechanical separation of the components, they were dropped from the PCB. Mechanical separation was also used when removing conductive paths. This separation is effective, but in the newer types of PCBs, the cyclical effects of thermal shock have to be applied to the separation of copper paths. Laboratory tests have demonstrated the viability of the proposed solution. The proposed method of recycling could lead to industrial use, which requires consistent sorting of waste electrical and electronic equipment.

1 Introduction

In recent years with the development of consumer electrics the recycling of electric waste has become a necessity the due to the lowering prices of electrics we experience its massive consumption as well as decrease of its lifetime. Retired electrics normally used to end in the solid and hazardous waste landfills. Because these products contain many valuable components, but also materials that are harmful to the environment, we have focused our work on the possibilities of reuse of the retired electric waste, originating mainly from computing technologies, as a source of valuable raw materials.

Electric waste is currently the fastest growing type of the waste. Globally it now constitute up to 5% of weight of the solid domestic waste which is almost as much as plastic packaging. In the European Union countries, where households annually produce about 8 million tons of electric waste, the electric waste is growing at a rate of 3-5% per year, almost three times faster than the total waste volume. Developing countries even assume that their electric waste production will triple by 2010. Experts estimate that in line with the growth in sales of electrics the European Union will have to cope with almost 11 million tons of the electric waste just in 2020. Ten years later the annual production will rise to almost 14 million tons. And we must add to this another approximately three million tons of the electric waste originating from organizations and companies [1].

According to the latest information there is currently used about one billion of personal computers in the world. Independent analytic company Gartner expects that this number will double over the next six years [2]. According to this study the sales of computers will increase by 12% worldwide per year. However in the calculation of this growth it is necessary to calculate the depreciation of old models. As the study says about 180 million of personal computers (PCs) will be replaced this year, which will be 16% of all the systems used. A fifth of them will be completely destroyed and the rest could still be used for other purposes, or travel to less developed countries.

It is assumed that in the Czech Republic is used about 5.10^6 personal computers. This means that considering the average lifetime of 11 years are

* Corresponding author: janacova@fai.utb.cz

discarded annually about 1,8.10[4] personal computers, which involves, at an average weight 24 kg of the personal computer, the 432 tons of recyclable material. This will worsen over the time because population in the world is increasing and so does the consumption of products, while the lifetime of their use dramatically reduced. Probably the most valuable raw materials that can be obtained from the electric waste and specifically from the computers are the precious metals.

2 Material of the printed circuit board (PCB)

For surface mounting the PCB material should have coefficient of linear expansion approximately the same as the material of the components used. Otherwise, due to the different thermal expansion of circuit boards and components the excessive mechanical stress on the solder joint could develop. The size of the mechanical stress is yet derived from the difference of coefficients of the linear expansion. Secure mounting of the components doesn't depend only on their size, but for example also on temperatures in the operation of the final device, in particular on the limit temperatures during operation and on changes of ambient temperature. The resistance of the soldered joints to breakage depends also on their shape. The resistance to breakage of the soldered joints depends on its shape. In some cases it is necessary to use specially adapted PCBs. Based on experience during normal application of surface mounting on glass-epoxy PCB (FR4) without the risk of subsequent cracking of soldered joints there can be fitted miniature passive components (resistors, ceramic capacitors) up to 10 mm, Integrated circuits design SO, plastic chip carrier, flat pack circuits, quad pack, TAB (Micropack) etc. It is not recommended to mount ceramic chip carrier which's coefficient of linear expansion doesn't correspond to the coefficient of linear expansion of the boards [3, 4, 9].

Thicknesses of PCBs are not different from conventional embodiments. Currently the European producers offer plates with thicknesses from 0.8 to 3.2 mm, a preferred size is 1.6 mm. Copper foil is produced in thicknesses of 35 microns, 70 microns and 105 microns or more. FR4 material is supplied with a copper foil with a thickness of 18 micron, 9 micron and 5 micron. These thinnest films are used for the finest joints which is the case of some special applications of surface mount [3, 4, 6].

3 Theory

The following figure shows the status of materials during the temperature change. It is evident that the expansion of the material 1 is much smaller than in the material 2. This is due to the different coefficients of thermal expansion of both materials. We used this property to derive a formula for the calculation of the resulting shear stress which is needed for separation of the conductive paths and plastic materials from the PCB.

Fig. 1. Linear expansion of materials.

To calculate the amount of shear stress needed to split the two boards we used the Hook's law.

$$\sigma = E \cdot \varepsilon , \tag{1}$$

where σ is the resulting shear stress [Pa],
E is modulus of elasticity [Pa],
ε is the relative elongation [-].

In the final equation it is necessary to take into account the thermal expansion of solid objects.

$$l = l_0 \cdot (\alpha \cdot \Delta T + 1) , \tag{2}$$

where α is the coefficient of linear expansion [K^{-1}],
ΔT is the temperature difference [K],
l_0 is the original length of the material [m].

By modifying and merging the two equations we get the following equation for calculation of the shear stress of one plate.

$$\sigma = E \cdot \alpha \cdot \Delta T \quad . \tag{3}$$

Resultant force F_T can be specified

$$F_T = (\sigma_1 - \sigma_2) \cdot S_j \tag{4}$$

Where F_T is a resultant force [N],
σ_1 is tensile stress of the first material [Pa],
σ_2 is tensile stress of the second material [Pa],
S_j is the contact surface of both materials [m^2].

This force must be greater than the allowable shear stress for the materials, which gives the following relationship:

$$\frac{F_T}{S_j} > \tau_s , \tag{5}$$

where τ_s is the maximum allowable shear stress of the material [MPa].

For the calculation we selected the combination of epoxy resin and copper [5].

Calculation shows the size of the force in dependence on change of the temperature which is required to peel the copper surface paths from the epoxy resin.

The required shear stress for separation of Cu path from PCB is 109°C.

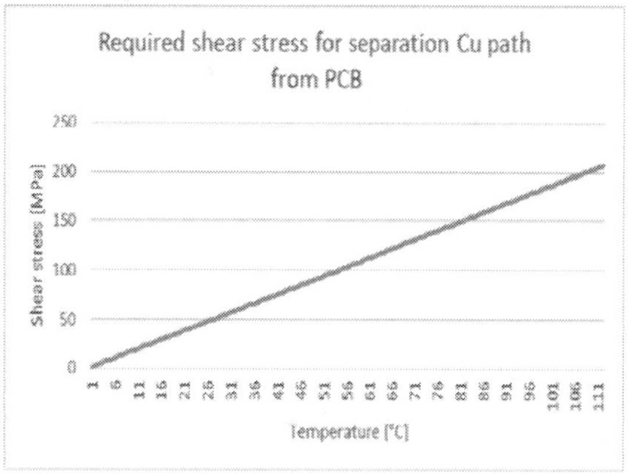

Fig. 2. Required shear stress for separation Cu path from PCB.

Table 1. Mechanical properties of materials [5]

	FR4	Copper
E (Pa)	$22\cdot10^{9}$	$11\cdot10^{10}$
α (K^{-1})	$18\cdot10^{-6}$	$17\cdot10^{-6}$

4 Modelling of transient thermal stress of layered plastic plates copper (Cu-EP) due to thermal shock

4.1 Thermal stress of multilayer walls composed of isotropic layers

The influence of temperature changes on the inhomogeneous, layered plates/shells are generally manifested in two ways. If there is any (even homogeneous) body statically stored indefinitely, preventing the imposition of free thermal expansion of the body, creating a corresponding strain. For multilayer walls thermal stress occurs as a result of the inhomogeneity, when the thermal expansion in equidistant surfaces of walls into the generally different thermal expansion coefficients in the layers.

Consider the generally layer wall, for example the wall with generally variable properties after thick, exposed thermal effects of any temperature profile $\Delta T(x)$, corresponding to a certain point transient of heat transmission of the wall.

Not only the elastic constants, but the coefficient of linear thermal expansion is generally varies discontinuously at the interface of both layers as well as continuously within each of the layers, due to any dependence of these parameters on the temperature.

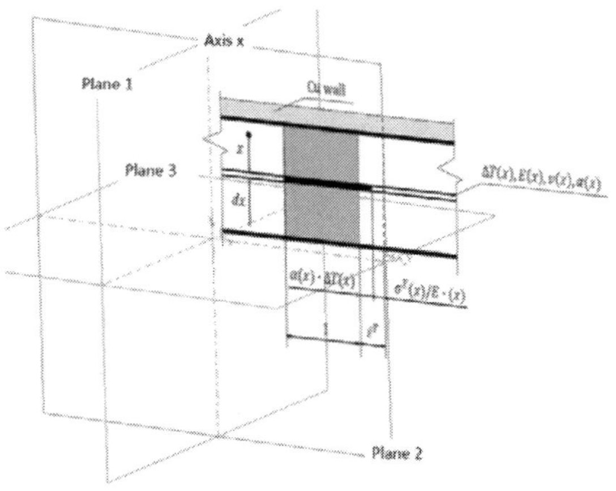

Fig. 3. Thermal stress of multilayer walls

On the case under consideration as can be seen on the wall as "thinking" composed from an infinite of the number of elementary layers of thickness *dy*. Each layer has its own values of the elastic constants and the thermal expansion coefficient. Value $\Delta T(x)$, express the difference of the actual temperature at the point "x" and reference temperature of the wall, i.e. the temperature at which assume zero stress of the wall.

Let wall is mounted so that it is prevented only warping, while membrane deformation - i.e. a deformation in the direction of the reference plane are enabled. Externally so the wall will show some overall - effective dilatation ε^T, assuming of isotropy is the same in both directions of the coordinate system (y, z) of reference plane. The resulting membrane forces in the cross-sections of the wall is equal to zero, then the equation is:

$$\int_{(s)} \sigma^T(x)dx = 0. \tag{6}$$

If no warping of the wall is the sum of thermal expansion and elastic deformation of each imaginary elemental layer dx constant, It is equal to the effective value ε^T. Considering that it is a equibiaxial stress is:

$$\varepsilon^T = \frac{\sigma^T(x)}{E^*(x)} + \alpha(x)\ \Delta T(x) \tag{7}$$

where: $E^* = E/(1-\nu)$.

Using (1) can be expressed in the resulting of unibiaxial deformation of the wall. Equation

$$\varepsilon^T = \frac{\int_{(s)} E^*(x)\,\alpha(x)\,\Delta T(x)\,dx}{\int_{(s)} E^*(x)\,dx}. \tag{8}$$

DOI: 10.1051/matecconf/201712502040

Thermal stress $\sigma_x^T = \sigma_z^T$ in the area of the ordinate y will be:

$$\sigma^T(x) = E^*(x)\left[\varepsilon^T - \alpha(x)\,\Delta T(x)\right] \quad (9)$$

Equation (9) defines stress in the equidistant planes with the plate of plane, except the edges where it is necessary to solve the corresponding boundary value problem. Are not expressed as normal and interlaminar shear stresses which representing the local stress concentrations at the edges of the layers.

4.2 FEM modeling of transient thermal stress

Diagrams of shear stresses are plotted in figure 4. Unlike normal interlaminar component the sign peak shear stress does not play any role for subsequent separation of the layers. How to heating and a subsequent rapid cooling the layered structure to cause formation of significant stress peaks, which can cause separation of the layers, applying in the recycling process.

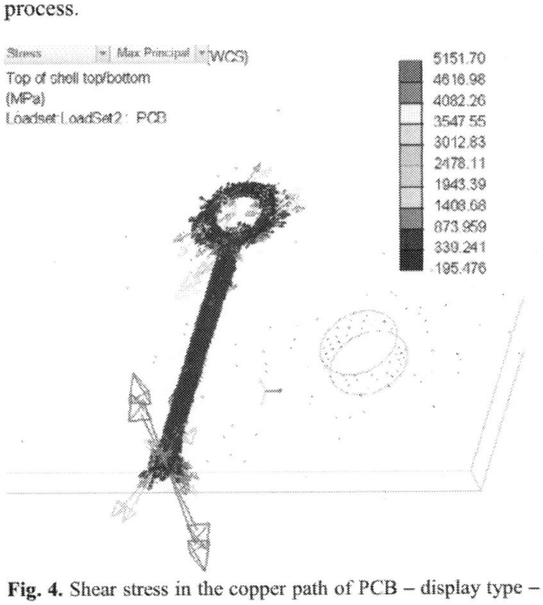

Fig. 4. Shear stress in the copper path of PCB – display type – vectors.

Based on the results of the modeling of transient thermal stress of PCBs is possible to comment on potential uses of these stress for the separation of the Cu layers in the process of recycling computer waste. The chosen procedure tempering and rapid cooling you can rate depending on the parameters (temperature, residence time) in terms of the level interlinear stress and thus its effectiveness.

5 Laboratory tests

Hot air gun has been use for the most effective heating to 370°C. The temperature was measured contactlessly using radiometer Thermopoint 64/64 plus, having a range from -30 to 900°C. The temperature is sufficient even for the separation of a tin. After using mechanical separation components dropped away from the PCB. We used mechanical separation and when you delete the conductive paths. This separation is effective, but in newer types of PCB was necessary for the separation of the copper paths applied more thermal shocks [5, 10].

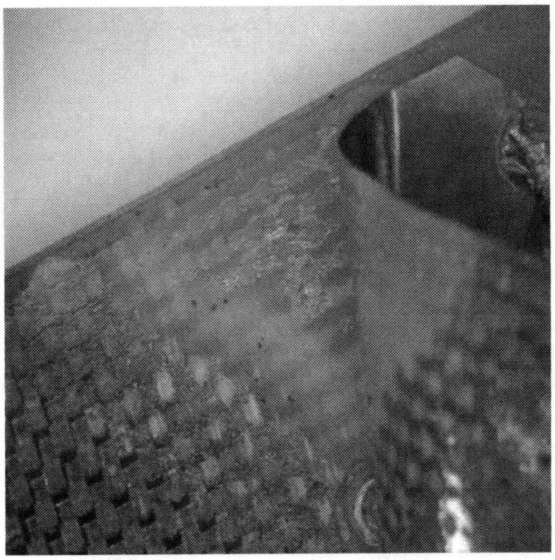

Fig. 5. PCB after heating to temperature 370°C.

5.1 Results of separation shown under microscope

Photos of separating copper paths from the PCB in the separation in the laboratory.

Fig. 6. Detailed view of the separated copper path under the microscope.

6 Conclusion

We conducted a study of the production of printed circuit board, to be able to choose a suitable way of separation electric waste. Furthermore we calculated the size of the shear stress that is necessary to separate the conductive copper paths from epoxy resin. In our own experiments we have used several methods of heating of the PCB. Heating PCB at a press tempered at 200 °C, further microwave heating. Was the most effective heating with a heat gun to 350 °C. This temperature is sufficient even for the separation of tin, because the melting point of tin is 250 °C. After using mechanical separation, parts dropped away from the PCB. We used a mechanical separation when you delete the conductive paths.

Laboratory tests showed that the temperature difference must be much greater than the calculation gives. It is due to the fact, that copper is very plastic and the calculated expansion caused by the temperature difference is smaller than expected. For newer types of PCB it was necessary inject more thermal shocks for the separation of the copper paths.

The proposed method of recycling could lead to industrial use, which requires prior diligent sorting of the electric waste.

Acknowledgement

The research work is supported by the Project of the Structural Funds of the EU, Operational Programme Research and Development, Measure 2.2 Transfer of knowledge and technology from research and development into practice and by the Ministry of Education, Youth and Sports of the Czech Republic within the National Sustainability Programme project No. LO1303 (MSMT-7778/2014) and also by the European Regional Development Fund under the project CEBIA-Tech No. CZ.1.05/2.1.00/03.0089

References

1. Ekoabeceda (in Czech) [Online]. [cit. 2017-02-10]. Available from: http://www.recyklohrani.cz
2. Recycling (in Czech) [Online]. [cit. 2017-02-10]. Available from: http://ekologie.xf.cz
3. F. Božek, R. Urban, Z. Zemánek, Recycling, 202 p. (in Czech), ISBN 80-238-9919-8 (2002)
4. Volek, J., Pospíchal, Z.: *Technický týdeník*, **48**, č. 25. p. 8 – 9, ISSN 0040-1064 (2000)
5. J. Křenek, *Diploma work*, (in Czech) FAI UTB, Zlín (2007)
6. D. Beneš, Waste, http://www.waste.cz/pdf/ (2007)
7. M. Noska, Gartner: http://computerworld.cz/, (2008)
8. P. Božek, In., ICSS 2013; Wroclaw; Poland; p. 229-240. ISSN 2194-5357. (2013)
9. P. Michal, M. Gombár, A. Vagaská, J. Piteľ, J. Kmec. In *Advanced Materials Research*, **712**, p. 382-386. Trans Tech Publications. (2013)
10. M. Maňas, D. Maňas, M. Staněk, M., Š. Šanda, V. Pata, Chemicke listy. (2011)

DOI: 10.1051/matecconf/201712502041

The influence of regression curve parameters of creep behaviour on measured data prediction

Martin Reznicek[1, a], Janostik Vaclav[1] and Ondrej Bilek[1]

[1] *Tomas Bata University in Zlin, Nam. T.G. Masaryka 5555, Zlín, 760 01 Czech Republic*

Abstract. This study deals with the study of the influence of regression curve parameters on prediction of possibilities of measured data. In this study, the necessary introduction to polymer materials issues and their material structure which influences their physical and mechanical properties, is described. Thereafter, the method of testing materials using device DMA which enables this measurement is presented. In the next part, this measured data are processed using creep modulus in which regression curves are applied. In the final part of this study, the influence of individual parameters of the regression curve on their process during the prediction is described. The study will prove the inconsiderable influence especially the last parameter of the regression curve equation and its significant influence on measured data prediction.

1 Introduction

Nowadays, polymeric materials belong to commonly used materials in a number of applications and use. In the practice it is possible to meet a number of methods which enable to study the properties of these materials and to recognize better their behaviour during different conditions of use. These measurements are often unnecessary without the need to choose a certain range of variables which can then be analyzed. It is not possible to always fully influence the choice of the density of this scale, namely the density of the points which are then passed through different lines, curves and splines. However, the density of these points significantly affects the accuracy of the interleaved geometric elements. In interleaving, each used software allows to influence the extent of this interference, and thus the extent to which the interleaved geometry matches the obtained points from the individual measurements. [1-5]

For this purpose, HDPE and LDPE materials from DOW were selected. Polymers are chemicals composed mostly of carbon, hydrogen, oxygen, nitrogen, chlorine and other elements. They are substances which are processed in the liquid state, mostly under elevated temperature and pressure. In this state, it is possible to produce a variety of shapes in the production process. Polymers can be of natural or synthetic origin, from a chemical point of view, they are mainly organic substances composed of large macromolecules. These macromolecules are composed of many repetitive cells in the string called "mer", which is a basic monomeric unit that has the ability to connect under appropriate conditions. From the suffix mer (mer = part) and poly prefix (meaning more from Greek) the word polymer was created.

The length of the macromolecules can be expressed using the molar mass, resp. relative molecular weight. By definition, the macromolecular substance is a compound whose molecular weight exceeds 10^3 g/mol, and the polymer bears a substance having a molecular weight greater than 10^4 g/mol.

The manufacture of polymers is linked to them. Nowadays, there is an increasing demand for the resulting plastic product. It should have the lowest weight, high temperature resistance, abrasion resistance, frost resistance, it should be firm and tough. These requirements give a permanent impetus to the emergence of new types of polymers, especially high-tech polymers which are now used for example in the aerospace or aerospace industry.[6-9]

Because of different mechanical properties that depend on the internal structure, it is possible to divide the polymers into:

Linear - single monomer molecules join together in a row to form a string. Such polymers have a higher density (e.g. HDPE) due to a spatial arrangement that allows molecules to come closer together.

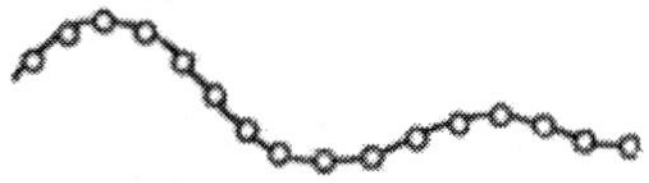

Figure 1. Linear structure

Branched - will occur if side branches are added to the basic string. These branched macromolecules cannot be as close to each other as they are in the linear branches, and thus have a lower density (e.g. LDPE). Due to branching, the mobility of the macromolecules is

[a] Corresponding author: mreznicek@utb.cz

impaired (the molten polymer has lower fluidity) and there is also a decrease in the intermolecular forces (the side chains are further apart) which lead to the worse mechanical properties of the polymer. [10-15]

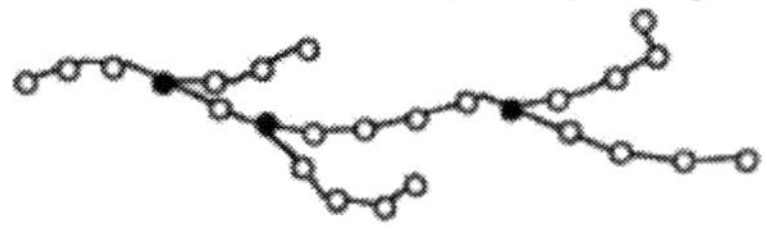

Figure 2. Branched structure

Crosslinked (block, grafted) - are formed by linking straight or branched chains by means of transverse chemical bonds. Such a cross-linked macromolecule has a limited mobility as a whole. This newly formed network results in a change in polymer properties, increases its hardness, stiffness, increased temperature resistance, but resistance to impact stresses is reduced by crosslinking. The resulting polymer is non-melting and insoluble again.

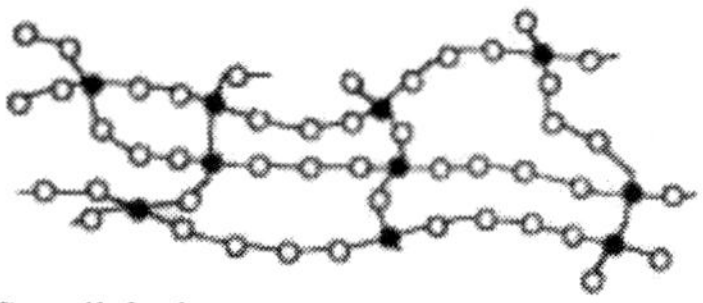

Figure 3. Crosslinked structure

Based on usable properties and possibilities of use, depending on the mechanical properties, the polymeric materials can be assembled into the following pyramid.

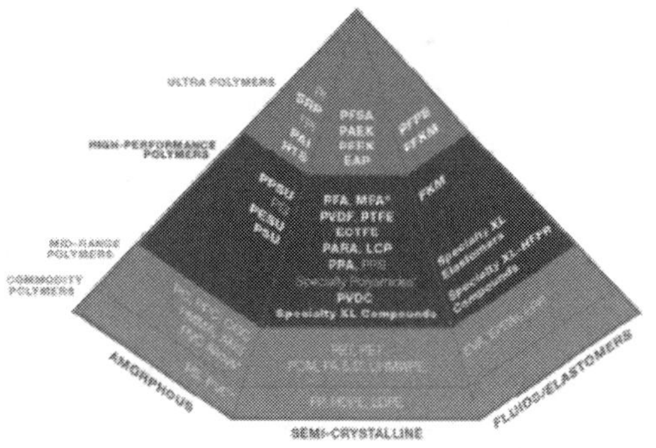

Figure 4. Separation of polymer

2 Methods

For creep tests it is necessary to prepare test specimens. These are designed to provide repeatability in predefined shapes and dimensions. For measuring mechanical tests, standard double-sided blades specimens as standard are used, for the measurement of creep properties on the DMA device samples in the shape of a block are used, which can be seen in Fig. 5. This shape and size of samples is adapted for measurement on DMA devices.

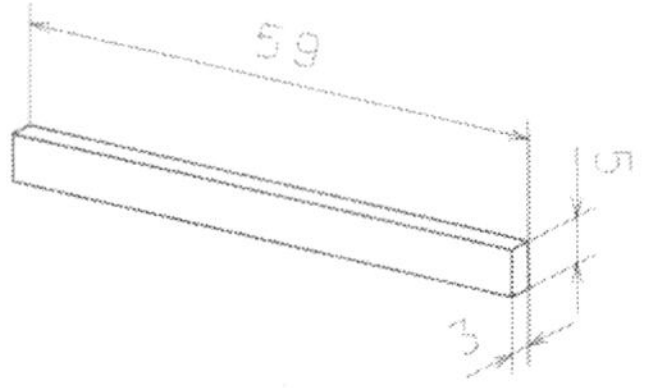

Figure 5. Sample dimensions

The crosslinked material was chosen for the measurement of creep properties for comparison of various options. High-density polyethylene from the company DOW was chosen as a material. Testing samples were made from this material according to a standard ISO 527-2 1BA for the tensile test. The processes of injection moulding and radiation cross-linking were performed with the minimum time gap to avoid the influence on the measurement surroundings.

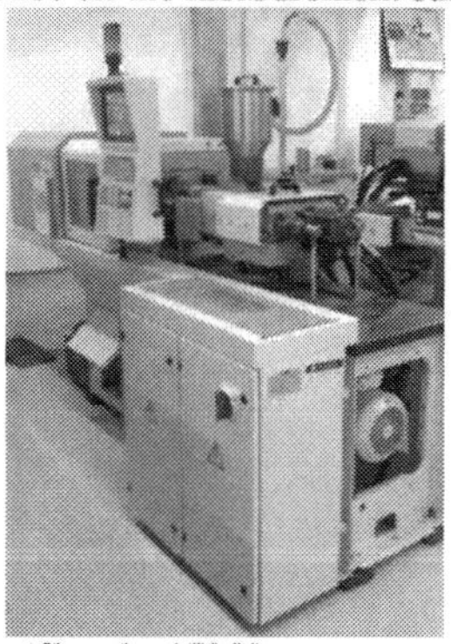

Figure 6. Arburg Allrouder 170 U

These samples were moulded by the injection moulding machine ARBURG Allrouder 170U according to the same process conditions.

Table 1. Process conditions

Parameter	Value
Injection temperature	200 °C
Barrel temperatures	195 °C, 190 °C, 180 °C
Mold temperature	40 °C
Injection velocity	40 mm/s
Injection pressure	60 MPa
Cooling time	45 s

The samples were irradiated by doses 33 kGy, 66 kGy, 99 kGy, 132 kGy, 165 kGy, 198 kGy. The concurrent measurement followed after irradiation on the device DMA1 from the Company Mettler Toledo and on the device for measurement of creep properties of own produce.

Dynamic mechanical analysis (DMA) is one of the possible methods for measurement of dynamic properties.

The samples for this kind of test can be exposed to tension, compression, bending and shear.

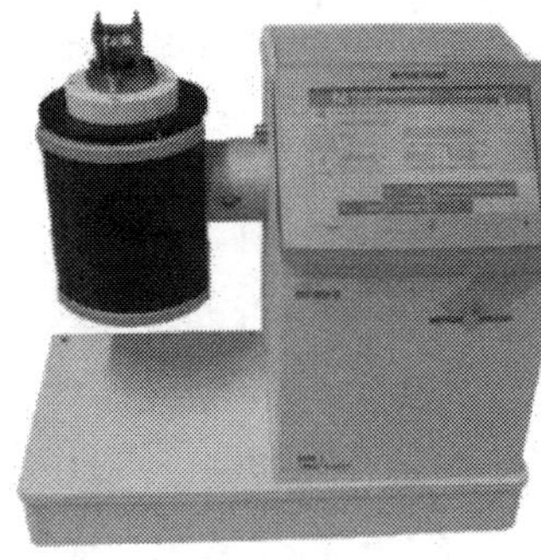

Figure 7. Mettler Toledo DMA1

The device disposes with the mode TMA, which enables to measure the expansion, creep and relaxation time. The device DMA1 in Fig. 7 was used for measurement.

The device DMA1 enables the measurement of brittle and though materials, which are suitable for these type of loading, and it enables evaluation in the program STAR. The load module enables loading from 0.001 to 10 N. The frequency generator enables the variable adjustment of oscillation from 0.001 to 300 Hz.

3 Data of results

During evaluating the results, it was necessary to proceed with a slight cut of the measured ones. As can be seen in formula 1, the resulting module is directly proportional to the loading force and initial length L_0 that are constant during measurement and calculation.

$$E_t = \frac{FL_0}{A(\Delta L)_t} \qquad (1)$$

However, this creep modulus is inversely proportional to the initial cross section of the test piece and, above all, to the elongation value.

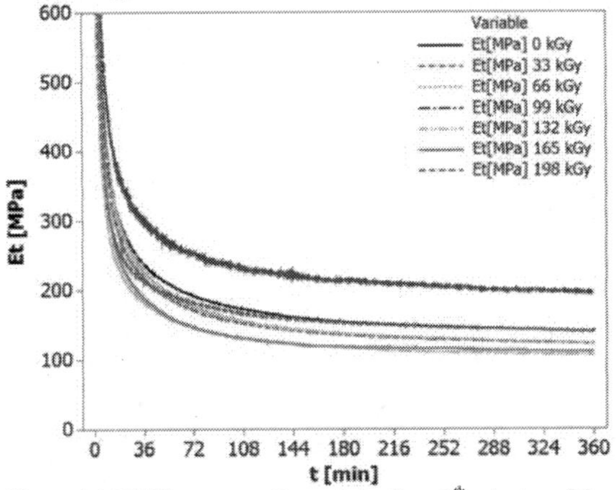

Figure 8.1 HDPE creep tensile modulus from 5th.minutes of the measurement

The value of the ΔL extension is very small at the beginning of the measurement and the subsequent recalculation of the creep modulus value is thus considerably large up to theoretically infinite. Such high values have a negative effect on the size of the scale, which then does not have sufficient telling value.

The highest initial modulus of elasticity was therefore set to 500 MPa, which corresponds approximately to the fifth minute of measurement. This reduction of only 1.3% value has contributed significantly to better interpretation of the measured data. In Fig. 8, it is possible to see the results of each creep tests. These results have already been confirmed in a number of others and are only a partial confirmation of our correct measurements. As in previous measurements, it is possible to see the dose of 99 kGy as the most appropriate dose of radiation to improve creep properties. Other doses used in these measurements have either minimal or even negative effects on these properties.

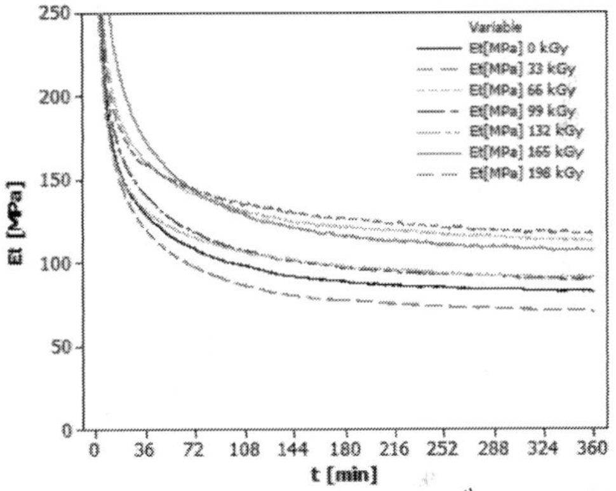

Figure 9. LDPE creep tensile modulus from 5th.minutes of the measurement

In Fig. 9, data evaluation for LDPE material irradiated by different doses can be seen. Also in this graph, the initial values were cut at 5 minutes, which significantly contributed to a better interpretation of the measured values. Compared to the results in Fig. 8 a far more compact effect of doses and far less influence on their creep properties can be seen.

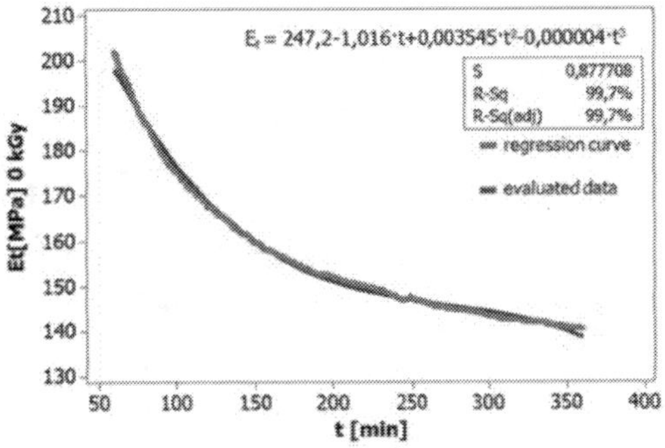

Figure 10. Placing a regression curve with measured HDPE data 0 kGy

From the above displayed graph it is possible to see the size of regression curve equations parameters which affect the size of the creep tensile modulus. It may seem that parameters (c) and (d) are almost negligible, but with increasing prediction time, these parameters become the determining value of the time.

Table 2. The regression curve reliability

Radiation dose [kGy]	Reliability value (R-Sq) [%] HDPE	Reliability value (R-Sq) [%] LDPE
0	99,7	99,6
33	99,6	99,4
66	99,5	99,6
99	99,4	99,6
132	99,5	99,5
165	99,2	99,5
198	99,7	99,5

Table 2 shows the reliability of interleaved regression curves by measured data for individual materials and doses. This reliability was in all cases above the 99% confidence limit, indicating a high degree of credibility. Fourth degree polynomial was used to find a suitable regression curve.

5 Conclusion

The effect of individual regression curve parameters over a short period of time does not greatly influence its behaviour and it is very often adjusted to match the regression curve and the measured data. This method is useful if it is only needed to break the curve with measured data.

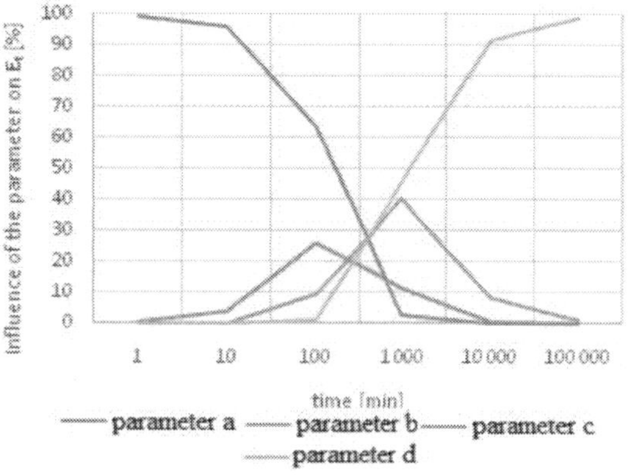

Figure 11. The influence of curve parameters on the prediction

Very often there is an attempt to predict measured data most often in terms of time. Therefore, the measured data is best passed through the regression curve with the parameters completed so that the reliability is as large as possible, and then by simply arriving at the change (e.g. time), it is judged by its behaviour over a longer period of time. However, as seen in Fig. 11, the effect of parameters is variable from the point of view of increasing time, and the initial negligible influence of parameter d has, with increasing time, a negligible effect on the duration of the regression curve. On the other hand, the initial significant effect of the parameters is reduced to a minimum over time. Parameters b and c have a significant share, especially over the medium-term. Therefore, when making regression curves, it is necessary to neglect the last parameters of the curve equations describing the data. As proved in this article, its influence is notable in the field of prediction of the measured data behaviour and can significantly affect the conclusions of the individual measurements.

Acknowledgments

This paper is supported by the internal grant of TBU in Zlin No. IGA/FT/2017/010 funded from the resources of specific university research and by the Ministry of Education, Youth and Sports of the Czech Republic within the National Sustainability Programme project No. LO1303 (MSMT-7778/2014) and also by the European Regional Development Fund under the project CEBIA-Tech No. CZ.1.05/2.1.00/03.0089.

References

1. Sefidmazgi NR, Bahia HU. Mechanisms of failure in uniaxial repeated creep test and the relationship to aggregate packing. RILEM Bookseries ,**11**:757-71, (2016).
2. Ren, W., Zhang, D., Wang, G. and CHeng, H. Mechanical and thermal properties of bamboo pulp fiber reinforced polyethylene composites. *BioResources*, **11**, pp. 4117-4127, (2014).
3. Ge H, Le J-, Mantell SC. Numerical modeling of stress corrosion cracking of polymers. *Eng Fract Mech* , **160**:199-212, (2016).
4. E. Morales, J.R. White, J. Mater. Sci., **44** (17) (2009), pp. 4734–4742
5. Ge, H., Li, H., Mantell, S.C.,Annual technical conference - ANTEC, conference proceedings, **2**, 1281 - 1286p., (2014).
6. Apollonio C, Covas DIC, de Marinis G, Leopardi A, Ramos HM. *Creep functions for transients in HDPE pipes.* Urban Water J, **11**,:160-6,(2014).
7. M. Ovsik, D. Manas, M. Manas, M. Stanek, M. Hribova, K. Kocman, D. Samek, Chem. listy, **106** (2012)
8. A. Lalande, D. Gardette Nucl. Instrum. Methods Phys. Res. B, **222** (2004)
9. D. Manas, M. Manas, M. Stanek, M. Danek, Arch. Mater. Sci. Eng., **32** (2) (2008)
10. J.G. Drobny, CRC Press, (2003).
11. O. N. Tretinikov, S. Ogata, Y. Ikada, Polymer **39**,24 (1998).
12. G. Zamfirova, V. Gaydarov, T. Zaharescu, L. G. Silva, Chemicke Listy **104** (2010).
13. W.C. Oliver, G.M. Pharr, J. Mater. Res., **19**. (2004).
14. D. Manas, M. Hribova, M. Manas, M. Ovsik, Stanek, Thin Solid Films **530** (2013).
15. G. M. Pharr, Materials Science and Engineering (1998).

Evaluation of nano-mechanical properties and morphology of filled polypropylene modified by irradiation

Martin Ovsik[1]*, *Michal* Stanek[1], and *Martin* Reznicek[1]

[1] *Tomas Bata University in Zlin, TGM 5555, 760 01 Zlin, Czech Republic*

Abstract. This paper describes the effect of electron beam irradiation on the surface properties (nano-indentation test) of glass fiber filled polypropylene (30%). These nano-mechanical properties were measured by the DSI (Depth Sensing Indentation) method on samples which were non-irradiated and irradiated by different doses of the β – radiation (33, 66 and 99 kGy). The purpose of the article is to consider to what extent the irradiation process influences the resulting nano-mechanical properties measured by the DSI method. The polypropylene tested showed significant changes of indentation hardness and modulus. The best results were achieved by irradiation at doses of 99 kGy (increase about 35%) by which the highest nano-mechanical properties of filled polypropylene were achieved. These changes were examined and confirmed by X-ray diffraction and Gel content.

1 Introduction

Polypropylene (PP) is a stereospecific polymer prepolyamydered by polymerization using an organometallic catalyst system. Commercial polypropylenes have up to 95% isotactic content, which means that pendant methyl groups are almost all on the same side of the chain.

When polypropylene is exposed to ionizing radiation, free radicals are formed and these cause chemical changes. Since PP is highly crystalline, these radicals are relatively immobile, and consequently may not be available for reaction for long periods of time.

As with other polyolefins, upon irradiation the free radicals are formed along with evolution of hydrogen gas. If the radical is formed on the pendant methyl, the resulting reaction is cross-linking. However, if the radical is formed in the main chain, the chain end may react with hydrogen, thus causing an irreversible scission. Although the processes of chain scission and cross-linking occur simultaneously, and even though the net effect is crosslinking, the overall effect is the loss of mechanical strength. [1-3].

Electron beams (β-rays) generated by accelerators are monoenergetic and the absorbed dose is greatest just below the surface of the irradiated material and falls rapidly at greater depths in the material (Figure 1). The energy range of electron beams used in radiation processing is from 0.15 to 10 MeV. Compared with gamma irradiation, electron accelerators have advantages of higher power and directional beams. The time of irradiation by β-rays is in seconds. The limited penetrating power of electron beams means that they are mainly used for irradiating relatively thin objects like wires and cable insulation [1-4].

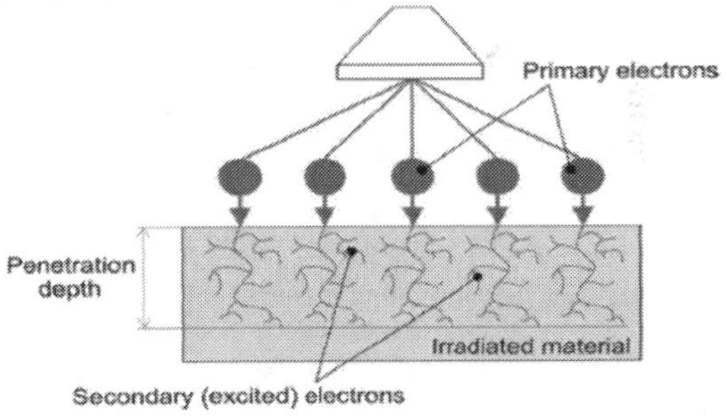

Fig. 1. Radiation crosslinking by electrons rays [2].

Common polypropylene, when exposed to the effect of the radiation cross-linking, degrades and its mechanical properties deteriorate. Using cross-linking agent TAIC (triallyl isocyanurate) produces a cross-linking reaction inside the polypropylene structure. The utility properties of polypropylene improve when the non-crystalline part of polypropylene is cross-linked. [3-5].

The aim of this paper is to study the effect of ionizing radiation with different doses, on nano-mechanical properties of polypropylene filled by 30% glass fiber (PP 30GF) and compare these results with those of non-irradiated samples. The study is carried out due to the ever-growing employment of this type of polymer (PP 30GF).

* Corresponding author: ovsik@ft.utb.cz

2 Experimental

2.1 Material

For this experiment polypropylene PP PTS - Crealen EP-865HS-M0083 filled by 30% glass fibers (PP 30GF), that were supplied by PTS Plastics Technology Service, Germany was used. The material already contained the special cross-linking agent TAIC - triallyl isocyanurate (6 volume %), which should enable subsequent cross-linking by ionizing β – radiation.

2.2 Sample preparation

The samples were made using the injection molding technology on the injection molding machine Arburg Allrounder 470H. Processing temperature 210–230 °C, mold temperature 55 °C, injection pressure 90 MPa, injection rate 50 mm/s.

2.3 Irradiation

The prepared specimens were irradiated with doses of 0, 33, 66 and 99 kGy at BGS Beta-Gamma Service GmbH & Co. KG, Germany.

2.4 X-ray diffraction.

X-ray diffraction patterns were obtained using a PAN alytical X-pert Prof X-ray diffraction system (Netherlands). The CuKα radiation was Ni-filtered. The scans (4.5 ° 2 Q/min) in the reflection mode were taken in the range 5-30 ° 2Θ. The sample crystallinity X was calculated from the ratio of the crystal diffraction peaks and the total scattering areas.

2.5 Nano-indentation

Nano-indentation test were performed using a Nano-indentation tester (Figure 2), CSM Instruments (Switzerland) according to the CSN EN ISO 14577. The tip is made of diamond having the shape of a cube corner (Vickers). In the present study, the maximum load used was 100 mN and loading rate (and unloading rate) was 200 mN/min. A holding time was 90 s at the indentation and 21600 s at the creep.

The indentation hardness (H_{IT}) was calculated as maximum load (F_{max}) to the projected area of the hardness impression (A_p) and the indentation modulus (E_{IT}) is calculated from the Plane Strain modulus (E^*) using an estimated sample Poisson's ratio (ν) according to [4-7]:

$$H_{IT} = \frac{F_{max}}{A_p} \quad (1)$$

$$E_{IT} = E^* \cdot (1 - v_s^2) \quad (2)$$

Measurement of all above mentioned properties was performed 10 times to ensure statistical correctness.

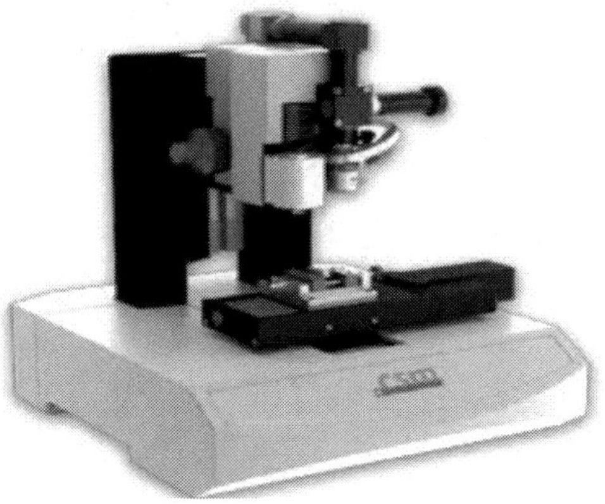

Fig. 2. Nano-indentation tester.

3 Results and discussion

3.1 X-ray diffraction

Figure 3 shows typical X-ray diffraction of the non-irradiated and irradiated polypropylene. The results of the crystallinity for non-radiated and irradiated PP 30GF are shown in the Fig. 4. The values measured show some heterogeneity of the crystallinity at individual radiation doses. When applying β-radiation the structure of PP 30GF undergoes decrease of the crystalline phase.

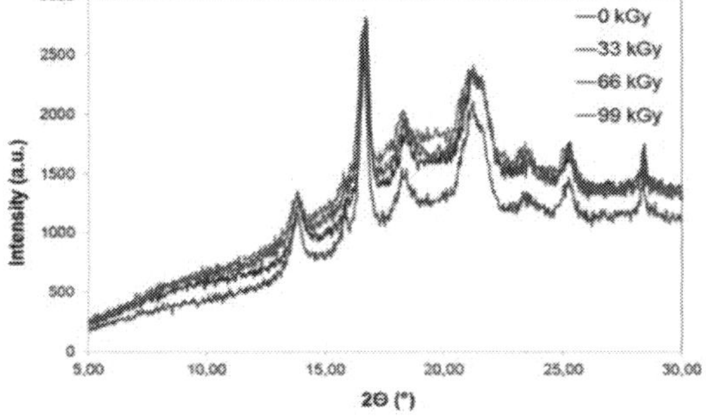

Fig. 3. X – ray diffractograms of PP 30GF.

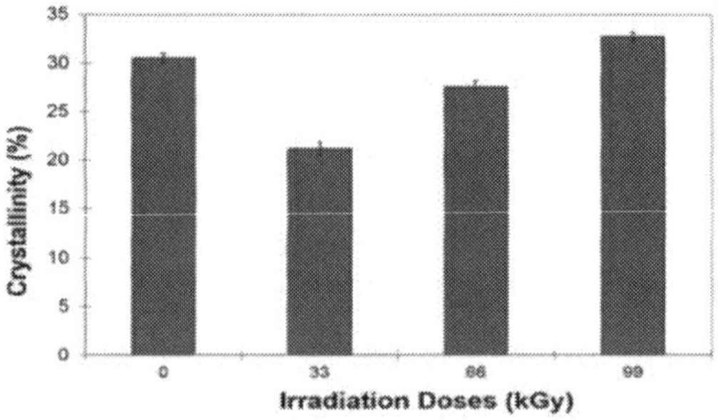

Fig. 4. Crystallinity of PP 30GF.

The smallest value of crystallinity was found in the case of the PP 30GF irradiated at the dose of 33 kGy. On the contrary the highest value of crystallinity (Fig. 4) was measured at non-irradiated and the irradiated at dose of 99 kGy.

The process of irradiation causes physical and chemical changes in the structure of PP 30GF. They are mainly changes of crystalline and amorphous phase. The measurement results show clearly that as the irradiation dose increases, the crystallinity decreases. During the amorphous phase cross-linking occurs which results in creation of very solid areas as well as considerable growth of nano-hardness values. Higher irradiation doses do not cause greater cross-linking but rather disruption of links resulting in degradation of the irradiated material.

3.2 Gel Content

Gel content showed the highest values at radiation dose of 66 kGy at which it reached 66.8% degree of cross-linking. Specimens irradiated by 99 kGy radiation dose showed very similar value 67% degree of cross-linking (Fig. 5).

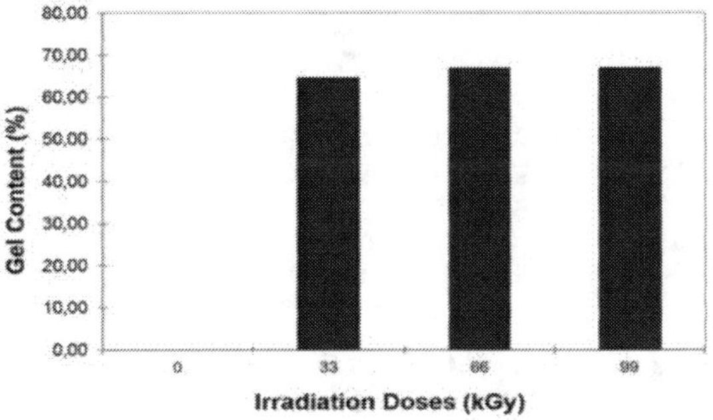

Fig. 5. Gel content of PP 30GF.

3.3 Nano-indentation test

Radiation cross-linking creates changes in the PP 30GF structure by creating 3D net. Beta radiation gradually penetrates more deeply into the PP 30GF structure through the surface layer. The surface layer undergoes changes which have a considerable influence on the nano-mechanical properties of PP 30GF.

The Figure 6 show a very important correlation between the force and the depth of the indentation. The correlations provide very valuable information on the behavior of tested material and the modified surface layer. The correlation between the force and the depth of the indentation in PP 30GF also proved very interesting. It demonstrated the influence of radiation on the change of nano-mechanical properties in the surface layer of specimens. The non-irradiated material showed low hardness as well as increasing impression of the indenter in the surface layer. On the contrary, the irradiated PP 30GF showed considerably smaller depth of the impression of the indenter which can signify greater resistance of this layer to wear.

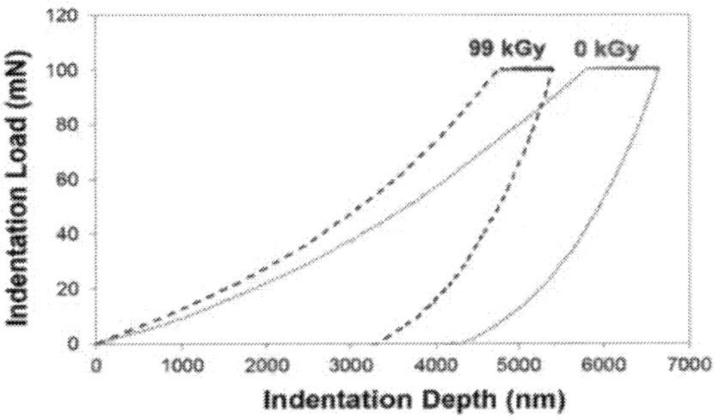

Fig. 6. Indentation characteristic of irradiated PP 30GF.

The greatest values of nano-hardness test were obtained for PP 30GF irradiated with dose of 99 kGy as is apparent in Table 1.

Table 1. Summary of measured values.

Irradiation doses	0kGy	33kGy	66kGy	99kGy
HIT (Mpa)	130.43	146.59	171.87	175.87
EIT (Gpa)	2.43	2.95	3.34	3.21
Wel (uJ)	0.09	0.08	0.07	0.08
Wpl (uJ)	0.22	0.22	0.19	0.19
CIT (%)	16.27	15.10	14.95	15.52
Gel Content (%)	0.00	64.40	66.80	67.00

Nano-indentation test of PP 30GF modified by beta radiation showed that the highest values of indentation hardness was found for PP 30GF modified by the radiation dose of 99 kGy (H_{IT} = 175.9 MPa). The smallest value of indentation hardness was found for non-irradiated PP 30GF (H_{IT} = 130.4 MPa). The increase of indentation hardness value for PP 30GF irradiated by the dose of 99 kGy was by 35% (Figure 7) in comparison with the non-irradiated PP 30GF.

Similar behaviour was found for indentation modulus E_{IT} according to Oliver and Pharr method (see Figure 8), which also increases with increasing irradiated doses. Values of stiffness showed the highest value 3.2 GPa at 99 kGy radiation dose, while the lowest stiffness value 2.4 GPa was found in non-irradiated PP 30GF. This represents increase in indentation modulus by 33%.

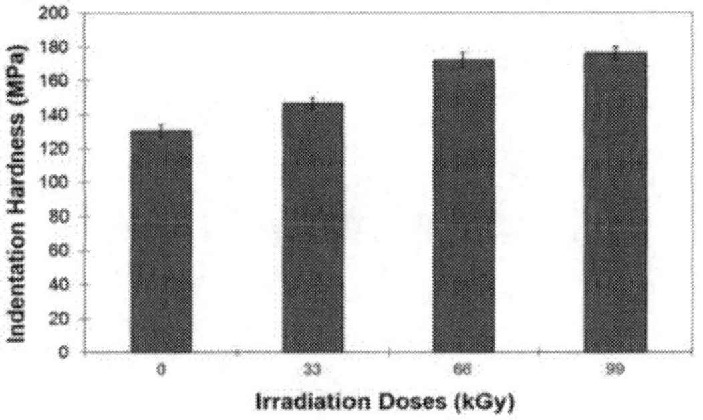

Fig. 7. Indentation hardness (H_{IT}).

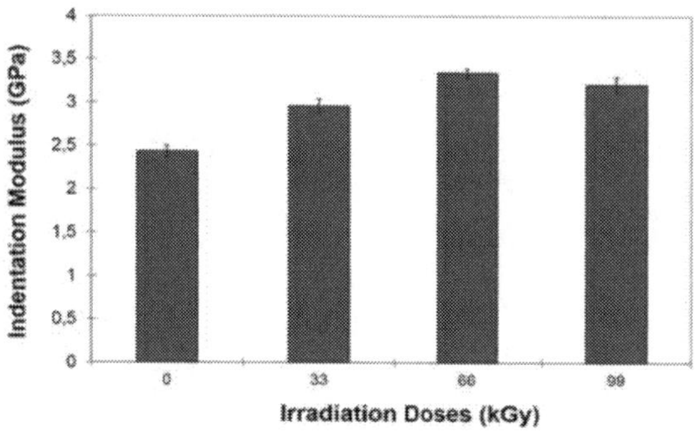

Fig. 8. Indentation modulus (E_{IT}).

Very important values were found for indentation creep (C_{IT}). The lowest value of indentation creep was measured at radiation dose of 99 kGy (C_{IT} = 15.5%). The highest indentation creep value measured at non-irradiated PP 30GF (C_{IT} = 16.2%). Decrease in creep values was 5% for irradiated PP 30GF compared to the non-irradiated one as is seen at Figure 9.

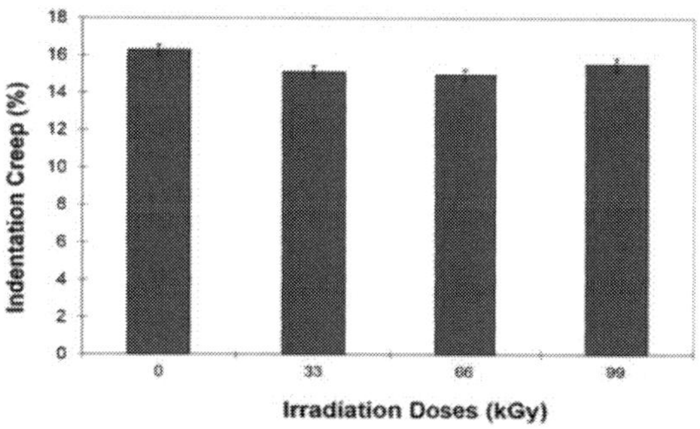

Fig. 9. Indentation creep (C_{IT}).

Interesting results were found for elastic and plastic part of deformation work. The highest value of elastic and plastic deformation work was measured for non-irradiated PP 30GF. The lowest value at both deformation work was found when the highest value of radiation dose of 99 kGy was applied (Figure 10).

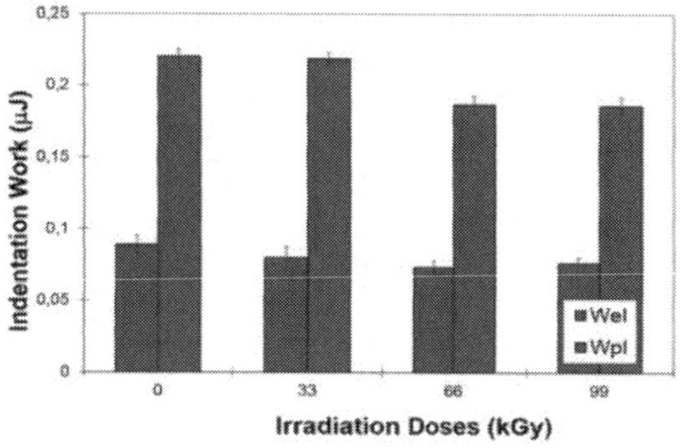

Fig. 10. Elastic and plastic part of deformation work.

Higher radiation dose does not influence significantly the nano-mechanical properties. An indentation hardness increase of the surface layer is caused by irradiation cross-linking of the tested specimen. A closer look at the nano-hardness results reveals that when the highest radiation doses are used, nano-mechanical properties decreases which can be caused by radiation induced degradation of the material.

4 Conclusion

Radiation, which penetrated through specimens and reacted with the cross-linking agent, gradually formed cross-linking (3D net), first in the surface layer and then in the total volume, which resulted in considerable changes in specimen behaviour.

The experimental study showed that glass fibber filled polypropylene modified by beta radiation doses of 0, 33, 66 and 99 kGy showed considerable increase of some nano-properties. In terms of nano-mechanical properties, the values of nano-hardness of surface layer increased by 35% at radiation dose of 99 kGy, stiffness of surface nano layer by 33% (99 kGy). Nano-creep values dropped in irradiated PP 30GF from 16.2% to 15.5% (99 kGy). Improvement of nano-mechanical properties of radiated PP 30GF has a great significance also for industry. The modified polypropylene shifts to the group of materials which have considerably better properties. Its creep and other nano-mechanical properties make PP 30GF ideal for a wide application in the areas where higher resistance to wear, creep are required. Commonly manufactured PP 30GF can hardly fulfil these criteria.

Acknowledgment

This paper is supported by the internal grant of TBU in Zlin No. IGA/FT/2017/010 funded from the resources of specific university research and by the Ministry of Education, Youth and Sports of the Czech Republic within the National Sustainability Programme project No. LO1303 (MSMT-7778/2014) and also by the European Regional Development Fund under the project CEBIA-Tech No. CZ.1.05/2.1.00/03.0089.

References

1. J.G. Drobny, CRC Press, (2003)
2. M. Ovsik, L. Hylova, D. Manas, M. Manas, M. Stanek, M, MATEC Web of Conferences, **76**, (2016)
3. O. N. Tretinikov, S. Ogata, Y. Ikada, Polymer **39**, 24 (1998)
4. G. Zamfirova, V. Gaydarov, T. Zaharescu, L. G. Silva, Chemicke Listy **104** (2010)
5. W.C. Oliver, G.M. Pharr, J. Mater. Res., **19**, (2004)
6. J. Dobransky, et al. Metalurgija. **54**, 3 (2015)
7. G. M. Pharr, Materials Science and Engineering (1998)

Influence of electron beam irradiated on the surface properties of polyamide measured by micro-indentation test

Martin Ovsik[1]*, *Michal* Stanek[1], and *Vojtech* Senkerik[1]

[1] *Tomas Bata University in Zlin, TGM 5555, 760 01 Zlin, Czech Republic*

Abstract. Cross-linking is a process in which polymer chains are associated through chemical bonds. Radiation, which penetrated through specimens and reacted with the cross-linking agent, gradually formed cross-linking (3D net), first in the surface layer and then in the total volume, which resulted in considerable changes in specimen behaviour. This paper studies the effect of different doses of ionizing beta radiation on the micro-mechanical properties of commercially available polyamide. The measured results indicate, that electron beam irradiation is very effective tool for improvement of surface properties of PA6. The micro-mechanical properties after irradiated surface treatment was increased up to 24 % compared to non-irradiated surface.

1 Introduction

Polyamides are one of the most commonly used polymers. Due to their very high strength and durability polyamides are commonly used in textiles, carpets and floor coverings or automotive. Probably more familiar name designation is nylon. Polyamide is a semi-crystalline thermoplastic material with very high toughness, good chemical stability and impact resistance. Polyamide is also a good electrical insulator and as other polyamide insulating properties will not be affected due to moisture. It is also resistant to corrosion. Polyamide has many features and enhancements in terms of plasticization of improved varieties. Polyamide is thanks to its very good mechanical properties, which can be even improved as shown in the results, suitable for applications with great demand on the stiffness and resistance of surface layers for instance friction parts used in automotive industry [1-3].

Polyamides are polymers whose repeating units are characterized by the amide group. Through radiation cross-linking, thermoplastic polyamides are turned into plastics which behave like elastomers over a wide temperature range. Cross-linking makes the originally thermoplastic product able to withstand considerably higher temperatures of up to 350 °C. The dimensional stability under thermal stress is also improved. Radiation cross-linked polyamide can often replace thermosetting plastics or high-performance plastics such as PPS, PEI, LCP, etc. One application that has proved most useful over the years is radiation cross-linked components for the electrical industry, e.g. switch components, and the automotive industry, for instance components for the engine compartment [1-3].Cross-linking is a process in which polymer chains are associated through chemical bonds. Cross-linking is carried out by chemical reactions or radiation and in most cases the process is irreversible. Ionizing radiation includes high-energy electrons (electron beam - β-rays) (Figure 1) and gamma rays (γ-rays) (Figure 2). These not only are capable of converting monomeric and oligomeric liquids into solids, but also can produce major changes in properties of solid polymers. [3]

In general, copolymers cross-link more readily than polyamide. Common polyamide 6, when exposed to the effect of the radiation cross-linking, degrades and its mechanical properties deteriorate. Mechanical properties of polyamides are modified by irradiation, as seen by reduced tensile strength (50% loss when irradiated in air, 16% under vacuum). Aromatic polyamides retain strength better than aliphatic polyamides. Using cross-linking agent TAIC (triallyl isocyanurate) produces a cross-linking reaction inside the PA6 structure. The utility properties of PA6 improve when the non-crystalline part of PA6 is cross-linked [1-4].

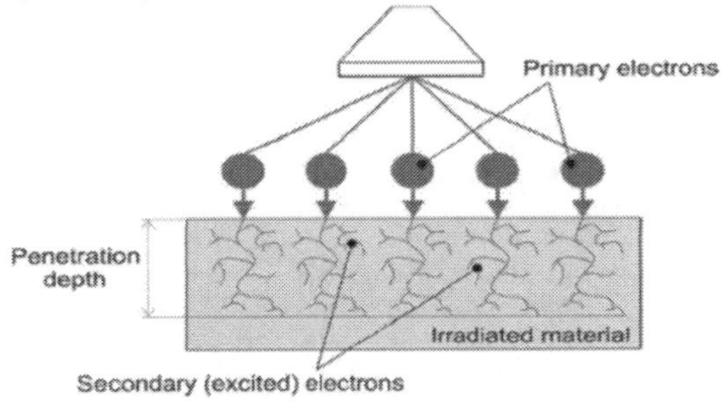

Fig. 1. Radiation crosslinking by electrons rays.

* Corresponding author: ovsik@ft.utb.cz

DOI: 10.1051/matecconf/201712502043

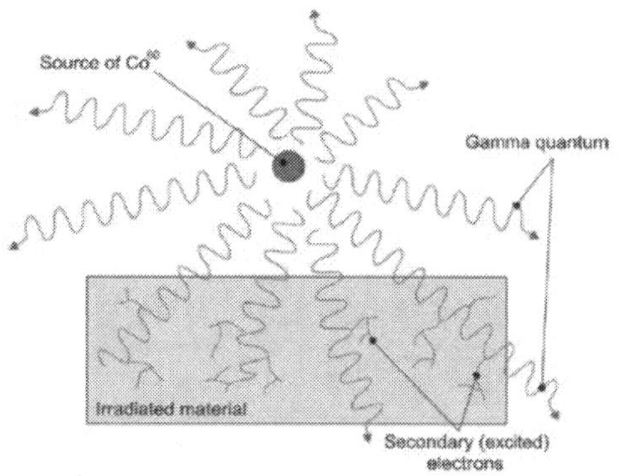

Fig. 2. Radiation crosslinking by Gamma rays.

The thermoplastics which are used for production of various types of products have very different properties. Standard polymers which are easy obtainable with favorable price conditions belong to the main class. The disadvantage of standard polymers is limited both by mechanical and thermal properties (Figure 3). The group of standard polymers is the most considerable one and its share in the production of all polymers is as high as 90% [1] [4].

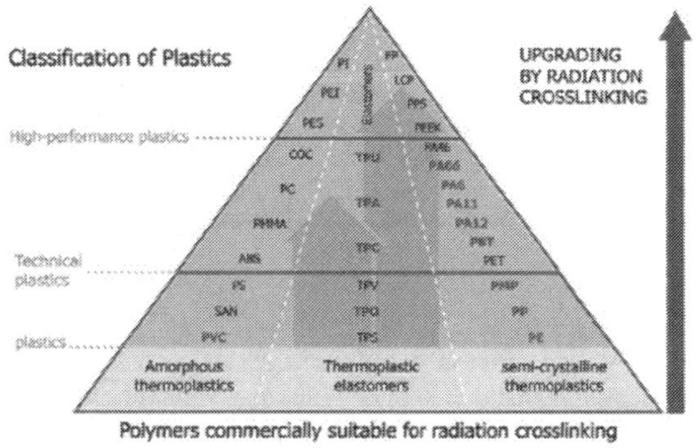

Fig. 3. Upgrading properties by radiation cross-linking.

The aim of this paper is to study the effect of ionizing radiation with different doses, on micro-mechanical properties of PA6 and compare these results with those of non-irradiated samples. These tested polymers find a broad application in many branches of industry and in daily life as well.

2 Experimental

2.1 Material

For this experiment Polyamide Duramid 9TH269 M800/13, PTS Plastics Technology Service, Germany, was used. The material already contained a special cross-linking agent TAIC (5 volume %), which should enable subsequent cross-linking by ionizing β – radiation.

2.2 Sample preparation

The samples were made using the injection molding technology on the injection molding machine Arburg Allrounder 470H. Processing temperature 245–265 °C, mold temperature 80 °C, injection pressure 90 MPa, injection rate 50 mm/s. It was used normalized specimen measuring 80x10x4 mm.

2.3 Irradiation

The prepared specimens were irradiated with doses of 0, 33, 66 and 99 kGy at BGS Beta-Gamma Service GmbH & Co. KG, Germany.

2.4 Micro-indentation

Micro-indentation test were performed using a Micro-indentation tester (Micro Combi Tester) (Figure 4), CSM Instruments (Switzerland) according to the CSN EN ISO 14577. The tip is made of diamond having the shape of a cube corner (Vickers). In the present study, the maximum load used was 0.5 N and loading rate (and unloading rate) was 1 N/min. A holding time was 90 s at the indentation and 21600 s at the creep.

Fig. 4. Micro-indentation tester.

The indentation hardness (H_{IT}) was calculated as maximum load (F_{max}) to the projected area of the hardness impression (A_p) and the indentation modulus (E_{IT}) is calculated from the Plane Strain modulus (E^*) using an estimated sample Poisson's ratio (ν) according to (Figure 5) [2-4]:

$$H_{IT} = \frac{F_{max}}{A_p} \quad (1)$$

$$E_{IT} = E^* \cdot (1 - \nu_s^2) \quad (2)$$

DOI: 10.1051/matecconf/201712502043

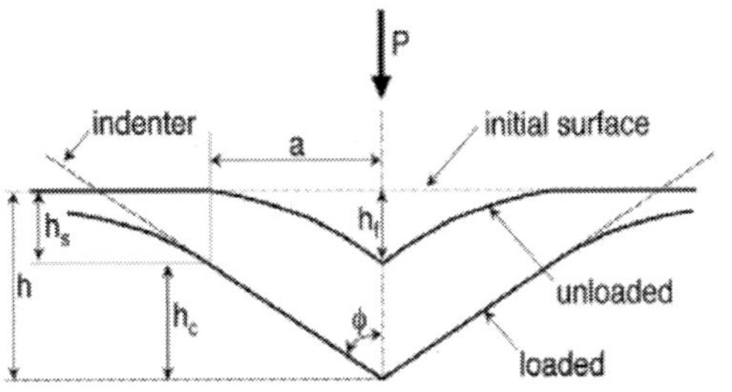

Fig. 5. Schematic illustration of unloading process.

Measurement of all above mentioned properties was performed 10 times to ensure statistical correctness.

3 Results and discussion

Gel content showed the highest values at radiation dose of 99 kGy at which it reached 60.0% degree of cross-linking (Figure 6).

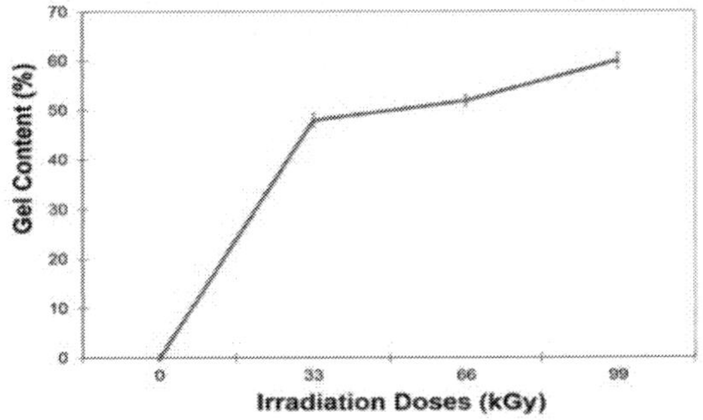

Fig. 6. Gel content of PA6.

Radiation, which penetrated through specimens and reacted with the cross-linking agent, gradually formed cross-linking (3D net), first in the surface layer and then in the total volume, which resulted in considerable changes in specimen behaviour.

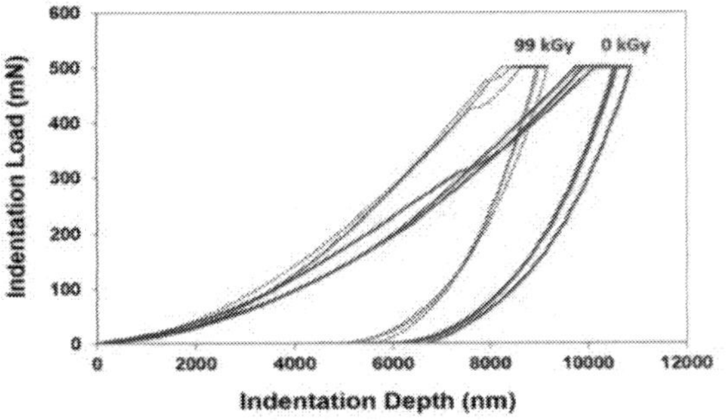

Fig. 7. Indentation characteristic of irradiated PA6.

Micro-indentation characteristics determined by DSI method are depicted in Figure 7 and Figure 8. They characterize course of loading force in dependence on indentor penetration depth, which gives an idea about course of instantaneous values of observed micro-mechanical properties.

It demonstrated the influence of radiation on the change of micro-mechanical properties in the surface layer of specimens. The non-irradiated material showed low hardness as well as increasing impression of the indenter in the surface layer. On the contrary, the irradiated PA6 showed considerably smaller depth of the impression of the indenter which can signify greater resistance of this layer to wear (Figure 7 and Figure 8).

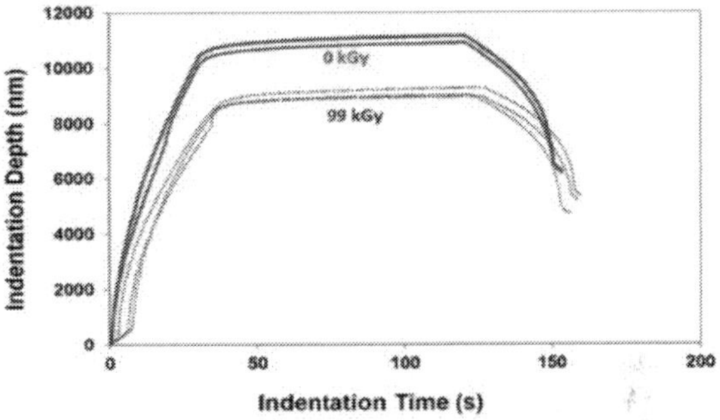

Fig. 8. Indentation characteristic of irradiated PA6.

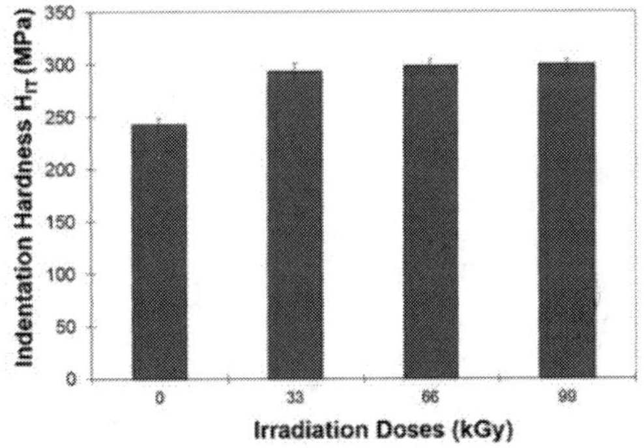

Fig. 9. Indentation hardness (H_{IT}).

The development of micro-mechanical properties of irradiated polyamide was characterized by the instrumented test of micro-indentation hardness (H_{IT}), as can be seen in Fig. 9. The highest values (300 MPa) of micro-indentation hardness were found at 99 kGy radiation dose, while the lowest value of micro-indentation hardness (242 MPa) was measured on non-irradiated polyamide 6. The increase of micro-indentation hardness at 99 kGy radiation dose was by 24% compared to the non-irradiated PA6. Similar development was recorded for micro-stiffness of specimens represented by the elastic modulus of indentation (E_{IT}) illustrated in Fig. 10. The results of measurements show clearly that the lowest values of micro-indentation modulus were measured on the non-irradiated PA6 (5.0 GPa), while the highest values were reached in PA 6 irradiated by 99 kGy dose (6.2 GPa). A significant increase of micro-indentation modulus (24%) was recorded at the radiation dose of 99 kGy compared to the non-irradiated PA6.

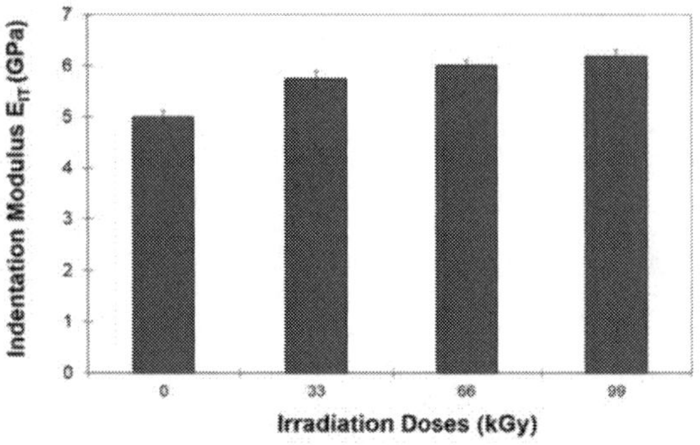

Fig. 10. Indentation Modulus (E_{IT}).

Very important values were found for indentation creep (C_{IT}). The lowest value of indentation creep was measured at radiation dose of 99 kGy (C_{IT} = 12.2%). The highest indentation creep value measured at non-irradiated PA6 (C_{IT} = 14.3%). Decrease in creep values was 17% for irradiated PA6 compared to the non-irradiated one as is seen at Figure 13.

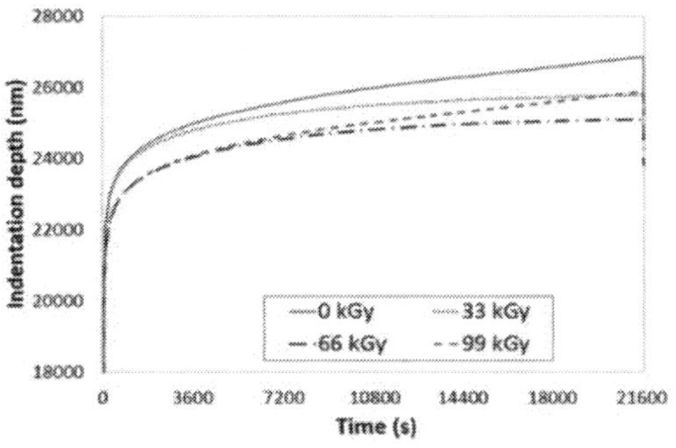

Fig. 12. Indentation creep (C_{IT}).

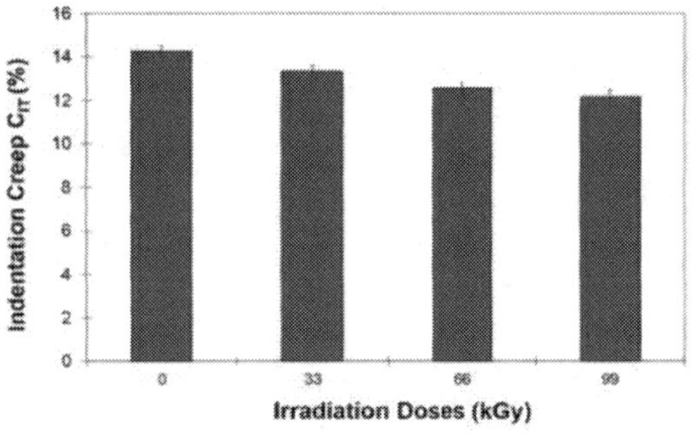

Fig. 13. Indentation creep (C_{IT}).

Radiation cross-linking creates changes in the PA6 structure by creating 3D net. Beta radiation gradually penetrates more deeply into the PA6 structure through the surface layer. The surface layer undergoes changes which have a considerable influence on the micro-mechanical properties of PA6.

Higher radiation dose does not influence significantly the micro-mechanical properties. An indentation hardness increase of the surface layer is caused by irradiation cross-linking of the tested specimen. A closer look at the micro-hardness results that when the highest radiation doses are used, micro-mechanical properties decreases which can be caused by radiation induced degradation of the material.

4 Conclusion

This research paper investigates influence of modified polymer material (beta radiation) on the micro-indentation test. The surface layer of PA6 is modified by β – radiation with doses of 33, 66 and 99 kGy.

Radiation, which penetrated through specimens and reacted with the cross-linking agent, gradually formed cross-linking (3D net), first in the surface layer and then in the total volume, which resulted in considerable changes in specimen behaviour.

The micro-mechanical properties of surface layer of PA6 modified by beta radiation improved significantly. The indentation hardness an indentation modulus values increased by about 24% (99 kGy) as a result of radiation. Also different depths of indentation in the surface layer of tested specimen were significantly different. The highest values of micro-mechanical properties were reached at radiation dose of 99 kGy. It also proved the fact that higher doses of radiation do not have very positive effects on the micro-mechanical properties, on the contrary due to degradation processes the properties deteriorate.

Improvement of micro-mechanical properties of radiated PA6 has a great significance also for industry. The modified PA6 shifts to the group of materials which have considerably better properties. Its micro-mechanical properties make PA6 ideal for a wide application in the areas where higher resistance to wear, creep are required. Commonly manufactured PA6 can hardly fulfil these criteria.

Acknowledgment

This paper is supported by the internal grant of TBU in Zlin No. IGA/FT/2017/010 funded from the resources of specific university research and by the Ministry of Education, Youth and Sports of the Czech Republic within the National Sustainability Programme project No. LO1303 (MSMT-7778/2014) and also by the European Regional Development Fund under the project CEBIA-Tech No. CZ.1.05/2.1.00/03.0089.

References

1. J.G. Drobny, CRC Press, (2003)
2. M. Ovsik, L. Hylova, D. Manas, M. Manas, M. Stanek, MATEC Web of Conferences, **76**, (2016)
3. O. N. Tretinikov, S. Ogata, Y. Ikada, Polymer **39**, 24 (1998)
4. W.C. Oliver, G.M. Pharr, J. Mater. Res., **19**, (2004)

Ultra nano-hardness of surface layer of irradiated high–density polyethylene (HDPE)

David Manas[1,a], *Jozef* Dobransky[2] and *Lenka* Chvatalova[1]

[1]*Tomas Bata University in Zlin, Nam. T.G.Masaryka 5555, Zlin, 760 01, Czech Republic*
[2]*Technical University of Košice, Faculty of Manufacturing Technologies with a seat in Prešov, Department of Automobile and Manufacturing Technologies, Štúrova 31, 080 01 Prešov, Slovakia*

Abstract. Using high doses of beta radiation for high-density polyethylene (HDPE) and its influence on the changes of micromechanical properties of surface layer has not been studied in detail so far. The specimens of high-density polyethylene (HDPE) were made by injection moulding technology and irradiated by high doses of beta radiation (0, 33, 66 and 99 kGy). The changes in the microstructure and micromechanical properties of surface layer were evaluated using WAXS and instrumented ultra nano-hardness test. The results of the measurements showed considerable decrease in micromechanical properties (indentation hardness, indentation elastic modulus) when low doses of beta radiation are used.

1 Introduction

Polyethylene is a thermoplastic consisting of crystalline domains and amorphous domains. A thermoplastic can be melted and reshaped as desired by heating it to a temperature above the melting point of the plastic crystalline domains. Crosslinking by aid of radiation or chemically results in the formation of crosslinks or bridges between the macromolecular chains. When this material is heated to a temperature above the crystalline melting point, it does not melt and flow; but exhibits a viscoelastic behaviour. The stretching or deformation of the polyethylene in this condition results in the orientation of the macromolecular chains, and elastic stress is developed in the material. If the polymer is cooled in this stretched condition, reformation of the plastic crystalline domains freezes the elastic stress in the material. The material retains the expanded shape, even on removal of the deforming force. This material is now heat shrinkable, and the stored stress can be recovered at any time by heating it to a temperature above the crystalline melting point. During the application, the heating results in the melting of the plastic crystalline domains, and the stored elastic stress is recovered [1,2]. On the other hand, the process of fabricating heat shrinkable products is based on the shape memory phenomenon.

This phenomenon occurs to some extent in non-processed thermoplastics, but its full advantage comes true in the crosslinked thermoplastics, such as the crosslinked polyethylene and its copolymers. Semicrystalline polymers such as low-density polyethylene (LDPE), high-density polyethylene (HDPE) and like other polyolefins, are common heat shrinkable polymers widely used in industry. Heat shrinkable polymers have a wide application in the packaging industry, electrical power and electronic equipment, cable industry and in the preparation of heat shrinkable tubes and connections [3–6]. Typical uses include primary electrical insulation, cable jacketing and repair, strain relief, component encapsulation and water proofing and corrosion protection [6]. In heat shrinkable products usually a hot melt adhesive as a binder is applied underneath to melt over and seal the part (e.g. cable)shortly before shrinking of polymeric cover takes place. For this reason the processing parameters should beoptimised at temperatures higher than the melting temperature of the hot melt adhesive (about 70–90 °C) [3]. Therefore it is desirable to increase the shrink temperature to as high as possible. The shrinkage is usually measured by placing the specimens in an oil/water bath or a hot air oven at a constant temperature. On the other hand, thermal mechanical analysis (TMA) is the most popular technique to obtain the thermal shrinkage under a constant heating rate. TMA is often used to study the shrinkage mechanisms and shrinkage modelling as well [7,8].

The principle of the radiation process is the ability of the high energy radiation to produce reactive cationts, anoints and free radicals in the material. The industrial application of the radiation process (Figure 1) on polymer and composites includes polymerization, crosslink-linking and degradation. The radiation process involves mainly the use of either electron beam from electron accelerators or gamma radiation from Cobalt – 60 sources.

[a] Corresponding author: dmanas@ft.utb.cz

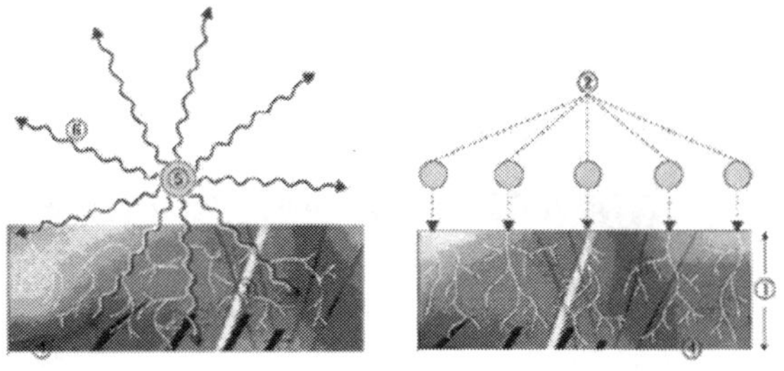

a) b)

Fig. 1. Design of Gamma rays (a) and Electron rays (b).
a) 3 – secondary electrons, 4 – irradiated material, 5 – encapsulated Co – 60 radiation source, 6 – Gamma rays
b) 1 – penetration depth of electron, 2 – primary electron, 3 – secondary electron, 4 – irradiated materiál

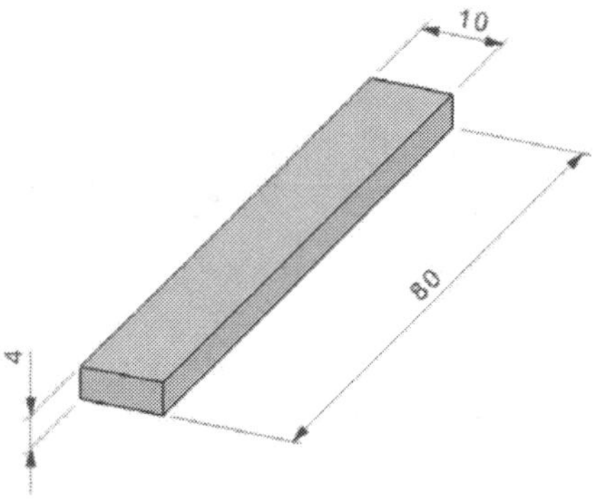

Fig. 2. Dimension of sample.

The aim of this paper is to study the effect of ionizing radiation with different doses, on ultra nano-hardness of surface layer of high-density polyethylene (HDPE) and compare these results with those of non-irradiated samples. The study is carried out due to the ever-growing employment of this type of polymer high-density polyethylene (HDPE) [3-20].

2 Experimental

2.1 Material and methods

For this experiment High Density Polyethylene (HDPE) DOW – HDPE 25055E, DOW - Chemical company, USA (unfilled, HDPE) was used. Irradiation was carried out in the company BGS Beta Gamma Service GmbH & Co, KG, Germany with the electron rays, electron energy 10 MeV, doses minimum of 0, 33, 66 and 99 kGy on air the ambient temperature.

The samples (Figure 2) were made using the injection molding technology on the injection moulding machine Arburg Allrounder 420C. Processing temperature 245–295 °C, mold temperature 85 °C, injection pressure 80 MPa, injection rate 45 mm/s. [7-29]

2.2 Ultra nano-hardness test

Nano-indentation test was done using a Ultra Nanoindenation Tester (UNHT) (Fig. 5), CSM Instruments (Switzerland) according to the CSN EN ISO 14577. Load and unload speed was 1000 N/min. After a holding time of 90 s at maximum load 500 N the specimens were unloaded. The specimens were glued on metallic sample holders (Fig. 2). [7-29]

$$H_{IT} = F_{max}/A_p \quad (1)$$

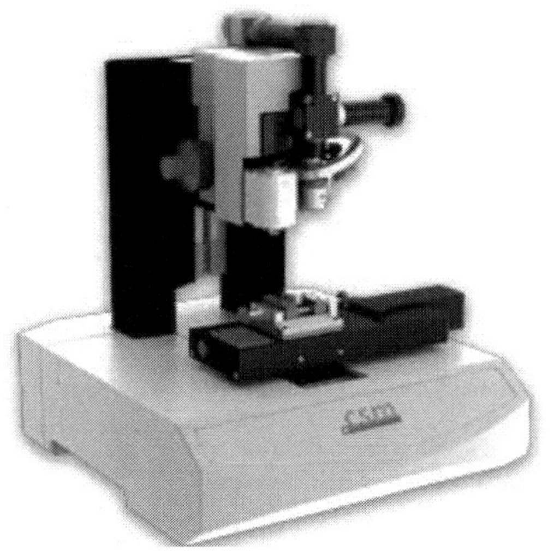

Fig. 3. Ultra Nano-indentation tester.

2.3 Wide-angle X-ray scattering

Wide-angle X-ray diffraction patterns were obtained using a PANalytical X'Pert PRO X-ray diffraction system (Netherlands). The CuKα radiation was Ni-filtered. The scans (4.5 ° 2 Θ/min) in the reflection mode were taken in the range 5–30 ° 2 Θ. The sample crystallinity (X) was calculated from the ratio of the crystal diffraction peaks and the total scattering areas. Crystall size L100 of α most intensive peak at 100 was calculated using Scherrer equation. As a standard "perfect" crystal terephthalic acid with the peak at 2 Θ = 17.4 ° and the half maximum breadth 0.3 ° 2 Θ was chosen [7-29].

2.4 Gel Content

Gel test is done to find the content of non-filtered phase – gel of the given material according to standard ČSN EN 579. The portion of 1g (of material radiated by low radiation doses) weighed with a precision of three decimal places was mixed with 100-250 ml of solvent. Xylol was used for polypropylene because it dissolves the amorphous part of HDPE, the crosslinking part does not dissolve. The mixture was extracted for 6 hours. Then solutes were separated by distillation. After removing the residual Xylol the crosslinked extract was rinsed by distilled water. The rinsed extract was dried for 6 - 8 hours in vacuum at 100°C. The dried and cooled residue was weighed again with precision to three decimal places and compared to the original weight of the portion. The result is stated in percentage as the degree of crosslinking.

$$G_I = [(m3-m1)/(m2-m1)]*100 \qquad (3)$$

Where,
G_i is the degree of crosslinking of each specimen expressed in percentage
m_1 is the weight of the cage and lid in milligrams
m_2 is the total of weights of the original specimen, cage and lid in milligrams
m_3 is the total of the weights of the residue of specimen, cage and lid in milligrams
The result of G_i is rounded to the nearest whole number [9, 14].

3 Results and discussion

The development of micromechanical properties of irradiated high density polyethylene (HDPE) was characterized by the instrumented test of ultra nanohardness (H_{IT}), as can be seen in Figure 4. The lowest values (39 MPa) of indentation hardness were found on high density polyethylene (HDPE) irradiated with radiation dose of 66 kGy radiation dose, while the highest value of indentation hardness were found on non-irradiated high density polyethylene (54 MPa). The decrease of indentation hardness at 165 kGy radiation dose was by 17 % compared to the non-irradiated high density polyethylene (HDPE).

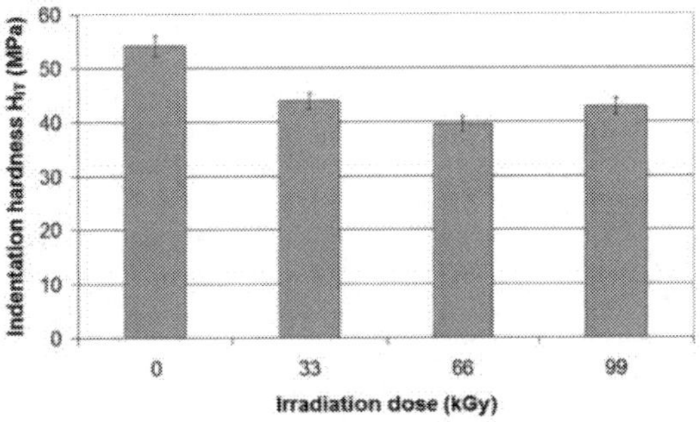

Fig. 4. Indentation hardness H_{IT} vs. irradiation doses.

Similar development was recorded for microstiffness of specimens represented by the indentation elastic modulus (E_{IT}) illustrated in Figure 5. The results of measurements show clearly that the lowest values of indentation elastic modulus were measured on the high density polyethylene (HDPE) (1.04 GPa) irradiated with radiation dose of 66 kGy, while the highest values were found on non- high density polyethylene (HDPE) (1.30 GPa). A significant decrease of indentation elastic modulus (11 %) was recorded at the radiation dose of 66 kGy compared to the high density polyethylene (HDPE).

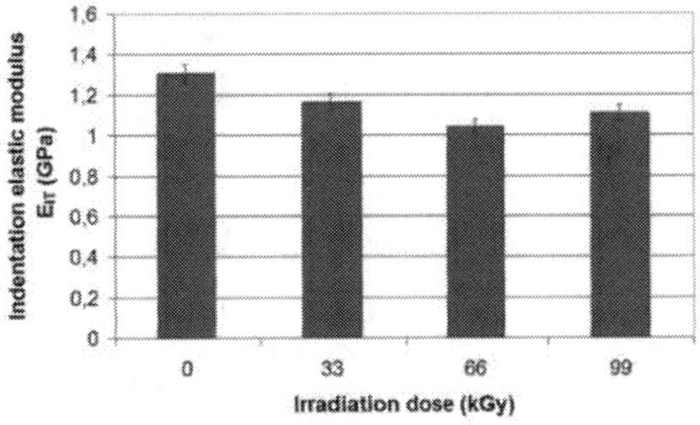

Fig. 5. Indentation elastic modulus E_{IT} vs. irradiation doses.

Other important material parameters obtained during the micro-hardness test were elastic and plastic deformation work. The mechanical work W_{total} induced by the indentation is only partly consumed as plastic deformation work W_{plast}. During the removal of the test force the remaining part is set free as work of the elastic reverse deformation W_{elast}.

Very important values were found for indentation creep. For materials which creeps as polymers, a basic calculation of that creep can be measure during a pause at the maximum force. The creep is the relative change of the indentation depth when the test force is kept constant measured by instrumented test of ultra nanohardness showed (Figure 6) that the highest creep values were measured irradiated by 33 kGy dose (27 %), while the lowest creep value was found in high density polyethylene (HDPE) irradiated by 99 kGy dose (16 %). The creep increase by 27 % as a result of radiation, which represents a considerable decrease of surface layer resistance.

When applying β-radiation the structure of polypropylene undergoes loss and then a grow of the crystalline phase. It can be assumed that the size of individual crystals will correspond with the loss of crystalline phase (crystalline value X calculated lay in the range 38-47 %). Cross-linking occurs in the remaining noncrystalline part which has a significant influence on the mechanical properties of the surface layer. The greatest size (Table 1) of crystalline phase (47 %) was found at non-irradiated high density polyethylene (HDPE). The lowest size of crystalline phase was found in the case at the radiation dose of 66 kGy (38 %). On the contrary the smaller size of crystalline phase of high density polyethylene (HDPE) was measured at radiation dose of 99 kGy (38 %). Its influence on the mechanical behavior is insignificant.

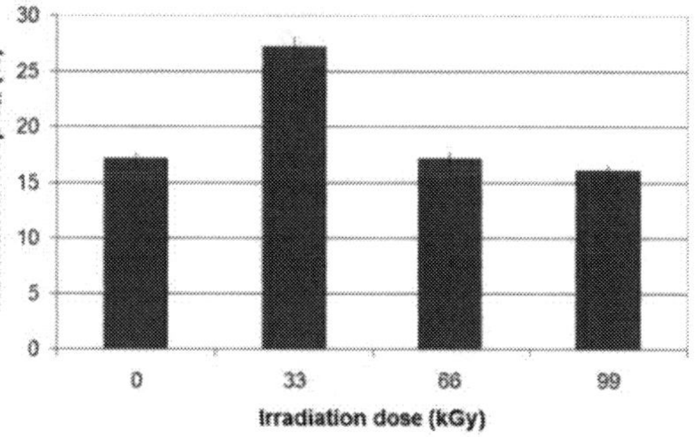

Fig. 6. Indentation creep C_{IT} vs. irradiation doses.

The highest values of plastic deformation work were obtained for non-irradiated high density polyethylene (HDPE). The highest values of elastic deformation work were obtained for high density polyethylene (HDPE) irradiated with radiation dose of 33 kGy. The lowest values of W_{el}, W_{pl} were obtained for high density polyethylene (HDPE) irradiated with dose of 0 kGy. Radiation of specimens caused lower values of plastic deformation work which is in Figure 7.

Table 1. X-ray diffraction of non-irradiated and irradiated HDPE

Sample	X X-ray, %,±1%
0 kGy	47
33 kGy	42
66 kGy	38
99 KGy	40

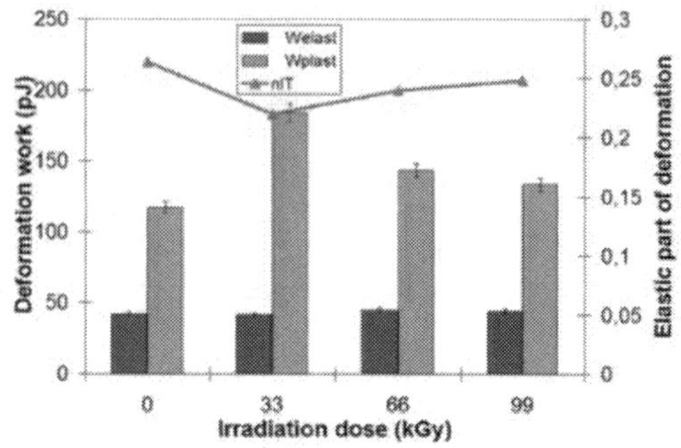

Fig. 7. Deformation work vs. irradiation dose.

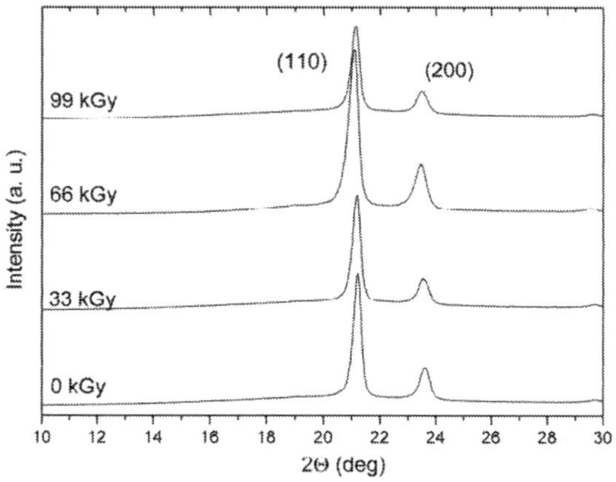

Fig. 8. X- ray diffraction non-irradiated and irradiated PBT.

The figure 8 shows typical X-ray diffraction spectrum of the non-irradiated and irradiated high density polyethylene (HDPE). There is an apparent presence of α-phase in the non-irradiated specimen. The greatest grow of α-phase is seen at the radiation dose of 66 kGy (Figure 5).

Table 2. Gel content of HDPE vs. irradiation doses.

Sample	Gi (%)	Std. Dev.
0 kGy	0	0
33 kGy	0	0
66 kGy	0	0
99 KGy	55	2.1

Gel content showed the highest values at radiation dose of 99 kGy at which it reached 55 % degree of cross-linking. Specimens irradiated by 0, 33, 66 kGy radiation dose showed very similar value 60 % degree of cross-linking (Table 1).

4 Conclusion

The experimental study deals with the effect of modification of the surface layer by irradiation cross-linking on the properties of the surface layer of high density polyethylene (HDPE). High density polyethylene (HDPE) was modified by beta irradiation at doses of 0, 33, 66, 99 kGy. The changes of micromechanical properties were found at the radiation dose of 66 kGy for indentation hardness, indentation elastic modulus (which decreased by 17 % and 11 %) compared to the non-irradiated high density polyethylene (HDPE).

Acknowledgment

This paper is supported by the internal grant of TBU in Zlin No. IGA/FT/2017/010 funded from the resources of specific university research and by the Ministry of Education, Youth and Sports of the Czech Republic within the National Sustainability Programme project No. LO1303 (MSMT-7778/2014) and also by the European Regional Development Fund under the project CEBIA-Tech No. CZ.1.05/2.1.00/03.0089. Special thanks also to Dr. Michal Danek (BGS Beta Gamma Service GmbH & Co, KG, Germany) for his kind assistance during sample preparation.

References

1. Dj. Gheysari, Eur. Polym. J. **37** (2001) 295-302, (2001)
2. K. Makuuchi, S. Cheng. Wiley, Hoboken, 2011.
3. J.G. Drobny, Elsevier, Oxford, 2013.
4. D. Dobrotə, Energy Procedia, **100**, 1160-1166, (2015)
5. G. Zamfirova, V. Gaydarov, T. Zaharescu, L. G. Silva. Chemicke Listy, **104**, 283-286, (2010)
6. D. Manas, M. Hribova, M. Manas, M. Ovsik,M. Stanek, Thin Solid Films, **530**, 49-52,(2013)
7. O. Uzuna, U. Kölemena, S. Çelebi, N. Güçlü, Journal of the European Ceramic Society. **25**, 969–977, (2005).
8. W. C. Oliver, G. M. Pharr. J Mater Res, **7**. (6) 1564–1583, (1992)
9. E. Ragan, P. Baron, J. Dobránsky. Advanced Materials Research 383-390, 2813-2818, (2012).
10. H. Wang, L. Xu, R. Li, J. Hu, M. Wang, G. Wu, Radiation Physics and Chemistry, **125**, 41-49, (2016)
11. J. Dobránsky, L. Běhálek, P. Baron, Key Engineering Materials, **669**, 36-43, (2016)
12. Dobransky, J., Běhalek, L., Baron, P., Kočiško, M., Simkulet, V., Vojnova, E., Briančin, J. Metalurgija, **55** (3), pp. 449-452, (2016)
13. Dobránsky, J., Kočiško, M., Baron, P., Simkulet, V., Běhálek, L., Vojnová, E., Nováková Marcinčinová, Ľ. Metalurgija, **55** (3), pp. 477-480, (2016)
14. J. Čop, L. Fojtl, O. Bílek, V. Pata, Manufacturing Technology, **16** (2), pp. 334-338, (2016)
15. Singh, P. Kishore, M. Singh, A. Srivastava, Radiation Effects and Defects in Solids, **170** (10), 845-853, (2015)
16. S. Kashyap, D. Datta, International Journal of Plastics Technology, **19** (1), 1-18, (2015)
17. S. Zhang, R. Dubay, M. Charest, Expert Systems with Applications, **42** (6), 2919-2927, (2015)
18. S. Ota, Radiat Phys Chem 1981;18(1–2):81–7.
19. S. Kumar, MV. Pandya, JAppl Polym Sci 1997;**64**:823–9.
20. JW. Hoffman, IEEE Electr Insulat Mag 1991;**7(3):**16–23.
21. R. Rado, P. Zelenak, Int Polym Sci Technol 1992;**19(4):**72–7.
22. KS. Wayne, Polym Eng Sci 1994;34(14):1121–8.
23. JW. Hoffman, IEEE Electr Insulat Mag 1991;**7(2):**33–8.
24. H. Kambe, T. Kato, JAppl Polym Sym 1973;**20**:365–75.
25. H. Kambe, T. Kato, M. Kochi, JMacromo l Sci-Chem 1974;**A8(1):**157–64.
26. PK. Patra, CK. Das, JPolym Eng 1997;**17(3):**231–44.
27. JK. Mishra, S. Raychowdhury, CK. Das, Polym Int 2000;**49**:1615–23.
28. JK. Mishra, CK. Das, J Elastom Plast 2001;**33**:137–53.
29. SR. Chowdhury, JK. Mishra, CK. Das, Macromol Mater. Eng 2001;**286(4):**243–7.

DOI: 10.1051/matecconf/201712502045

Mechanical properties of surface layer of unfilled polypropylene

David Manas[1,a], *Jozef* Dobransky[2] and *Lenka* Chvatalova[1]

[1]*Tomas Bata University in Zlin, Nam. T.G.Masaryka 5555, Zlin, 760 01, Czech Republic*
[2]*Technical University of Košice, Faculty of Manufacturing Technologies with a seat in Prešov, Department of Automobile and Manufacturing Technologies, Štúrova 31, 080 01 Prešov, Slovakia*

Abstract. Using high doses of beta radiation for unfilled polypropylene (PP) and its influence on the changes of micromechanical properties of surface layer has not been studied in detail so far. The testing sapmles polypropylene (PP) were made by injection moulding technology and irradiated by high doses of beta radiation (0, 15 and 33 kGy). The changes in the microstructure and micromechanical properties of surface layer were evaluated using WAXS and instrumented ultra nano-hardness test. The results of the measurements showed considerable increase in micromechanical properties (indentation hardness, indentation elastic modulus) when low doses of beta radiation are used.

1 Introduction

Polypropylene is a versatile, low cost, chemically stable and lightweight polymer, which offers attractive mechanical, electrical and thermal properties due to its relative higher degree of crystallinity. This is used in many applications such as radiation-sterilized medical and pharmaceutical components, food packaging materials and cosmetics [5]. A literature survey [6–11] indicates that effects of 14.89 MeV electron irradiation on polyethylene and polystyrene in the dose range of 57.6–576 KGy showed a greater red shift in absorption edge of polyethylene as compared to polystyrene [6]. Whereas, the enhancement in the thermal properties, dielectric constant, dielectric loss and crystallinity of 2 MeV and 1.5 MeV electron irradiated polypropylene has also shown considerable modifications [7,8]. However, more investigations are needed as far as the radiation energy, mode of energy deposition and energy densities are concerned. In particular, the effects of highenergy pulsed electron irradiation on mechanical Properties such as surface hardness and surface roughness of polypropylene needs more attention. Out of several types of radiations that can be used for radiation processing, high-energy electrons are of particular interest, especially for polymers, due to their high dose rates and consequently high-energy deposition in lesser time intervals. This not only achieves high process rates, but also allows crosslinking, as oxidation effects are relatively weak at the high dose rates. Moreover, electron beam irradiation also offers facility of easy control, maintenance of steady dose rate without any depletion and homogeneous energy deposition [2,6,12].

The principle of the radiation process is the ability of the high energy radiation to produce reactive cationts, anoints and free radicals in the material. The industrial application of the radiation process (Figure 1) on polymer and composites includes polymerization, crosslink-linking and degradation. The radiation process involves mainly the use of either electron beam from electron accelerators or gamma radiation from Cobalt – 60 sources.

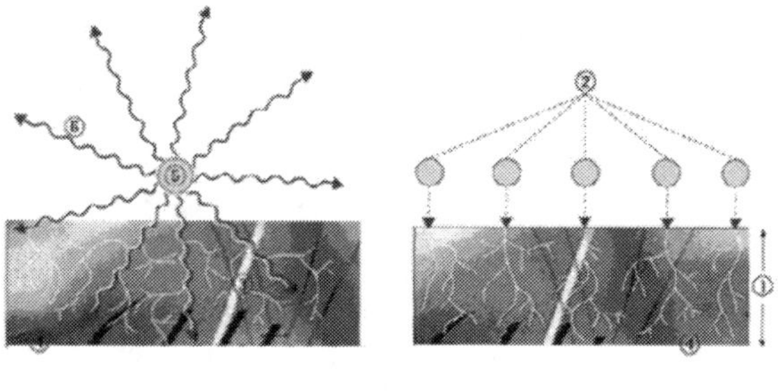

a) b)

Fig. 1. Design of Gamma rays (a) and Electron rays (b).
a) 3 – secondary electrons, 4 – irradiated material, 5 – encapsulated Co – 60 radiation source, 6 – Gamma rays
b) 1 – penetration depth of electron, 2 – primary electron, 3 – secondary electron, 4 – irradiated materiál

The aim of this paper is to study the effect of ionizing radiation with different doses, on ultra nano-hardness of surface layer of polypropylene (PP) and compare these results with those of non-irradiated samples. The study is carried out due to the ever-growing employment of this type of polymer polypropylene (PP) [3-10].

2 Experimental

2.1 Material and methods

[a] Corresponding author: dmanas@ft.utb.cz

DOI: 10.1051/matecconf/201712502045

For this experiment PTS-Crealen EP-2300L1-M800; PTS Plastics Technologie Service, Germany (unfilled, iPP+TAIC, MFR—230 °C /2,16 kg—6 g/10 min) was used. The material already contained a special cross-linking agent TAIC—triallylisocyanurate (6 volume %), which should enable subsequent cross-linking by ionizing β-radiation. Irradiation was carried out in the company BGS Beta Gamma Service GmbH & Co, KG, Germany with the electron rays, electron energy 10 MeV, doses minimum of 0, 15 and 33 kGy on air the ambient temperature.

The samples (Figure 2) were made using the injection molding technology on the injection moulding machine Arburg Allrounder 420C. Processing temperature 245–295 °C, mold temperature 85 °C, injection pressure 80 MPa, injection rate 45 mm/s. [7-17]

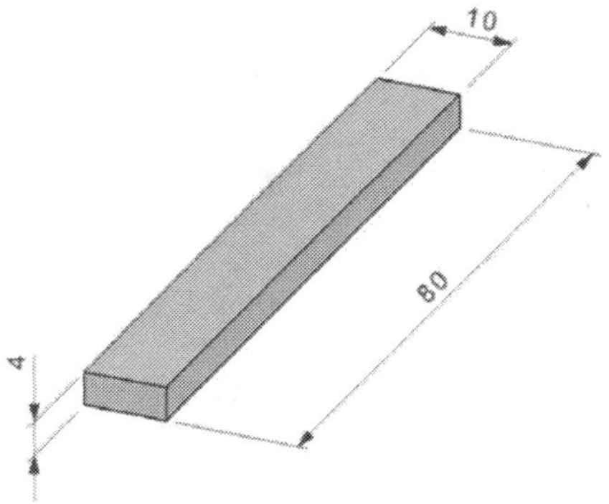

Fig. 2. Dimension of sample.

2.2 Ultra nano-hardness test

Nano-indentation test was done using a Ultra Nanoindenation Tester (UNHT) (Fig. 5), CSM Instruments (Switzerland) according to the CSN EN ISO 14577. Load and unload speed was 1000 μN/min. After a holding time of 90 s at maximum load 500 μN the specimens were unloaded. The specimens were glued on metallic sample holders (Fig. 2). [7-17]

$$H_{IT} = F_{max}/A_p \quad (1)$$

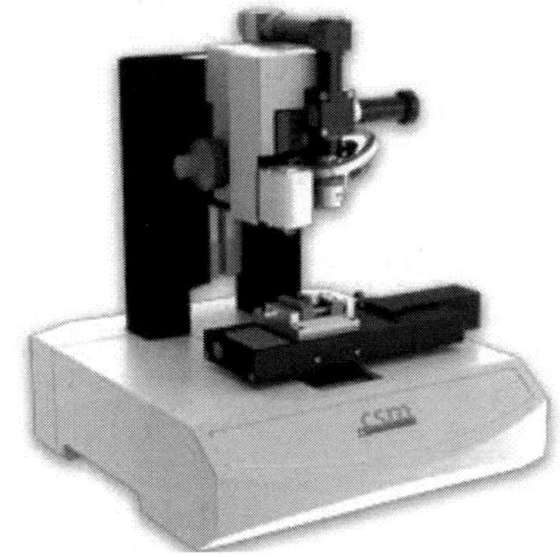

Fig. 3. Ultra nano-indentation tester.

2.3 Wide-angle X-ray scattering

Wide-angle X-ray diffraction patterns were obtained using a PANalytical X´Pert PRO X-ray diffraction system (Netherlands). The CuKα radiation was Ni-filtered. The scans (4.5 ° 2 Θ/min) in the reflection mode were taken in the range 5–30 ° 2 Θ. The sample crystallinity (X) was calculated from the ratio of the crystal diffraction peaks and the total scattering areas. Crystall size L100 of α most intensive peak at 100 was calculated using Scherrer equation. As a standard "perfect" crystal terephthalic acid with the peak at 2 Θ = 17.4 ° and the half maximum breadth 0.3 ° 2 Θ was chosen [7-17].

3 Results and discussion

The development of micromechanical properties of irradiated polypropylene (PP) was characterized by the instrumented test of ultra nanohardness (indentation hardness H_{IT}), as can be seen in Figure 4. The highest values of indentation hardness (68 MPa) were found on polypropylene (PP) irradiated with radiation dose of 15 kGy radiation dose, while the lower value of indentation hardness (56 MPa) was measured at 33 kGy radiation dose. The lowest values (49 MPa) of indentation hardness were found on non-irradiated polypropylene (PP). The increase of microhardness at 15 kGy radiation dose was by 38 % compared to the non-irradiated polypropylene (PP).

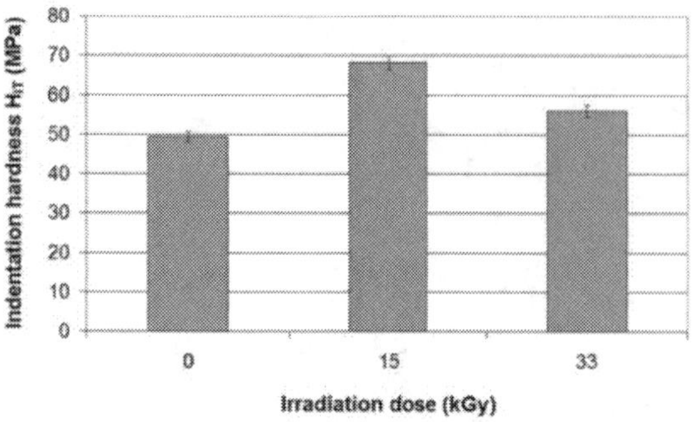

Fig. 4. Indentation hardness H_{IT} vs. irradiation doses.

Similar development was recorded for microstiffness of specimens represented by the elastic modulus of indentation (E_{IT}) illustrated in Figure 5. The results of measurements show clearly that the highest values of microstiffness were measured on the polypropylene (PP) (1.02 GPa) irradiated with radiation dose of 15 kGy, while the lower values were reached in polypropylene (PP) irradiated by 33 kGy dose (0.82 GPa). The lowest values (0.77 MPa) of microstiffness were found on non-irradiated polypropylene (PP). A significant increase of microstiffness (32 %) was recorded at the radiation dose of 15 kGy compared to the non-irradiated polypropylene (PP).

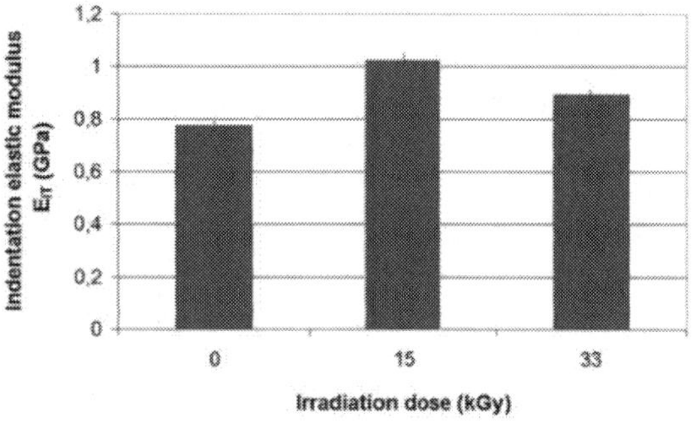

Fig. 5. Indentation elastic modulus E_{IT} vs. irradiation doses.

Other important material parameters obtained during the micro-hardness test were elastic and plastic deformation work. The mechanical work W_{total} induced by the indentation is only partly consumed as plastic deformation work W_{plast}. During the removal of the test force the remaining part is set free as work of the elastic reverse deformation W_{elast}.

Very important values were found for indentation creep. For materials which creeps as polymers, a basic calculation of that creep can be measure during a pause at the maximum force. The creep is the relative change of the indentation depth when the test force is kept constant measured by instrumented test of microhardness showed (Figure 6) that the lowest creep values were measured on non-irradiated polypropylene (PP) (10 %), while the highest creep value was found in polypropylene (PP) irradiated by 15 kGy dose (13 %). The creep increased by 35 % as a result of radiation, which represents a considerable decrease of surface layer resistance.

When applying β-radiation the structure of polypropylene undergoes loss and then a grow of the crystalline phase. It can be assumed that the size of individual crystals will correspond with the loss of crystalline phase (crystalline value X calculated lay in the range 45-67 %). Cross-linking occurs in the remaining noncrystalline part which has a significant influence on the mechanical properties of the surface layer. The greatest size (Table 1) of crystalline phase was found in the case at the radiation dose of 15 kGy (67 %). The smaller size of crystalline phase was found in the case at the radiation dose of 33 kGy (54 %). On the contrary the smallest size of crystalline phase was measured at non-irradiated (45 %). Its influence on the mechanical behavior is insignificant.

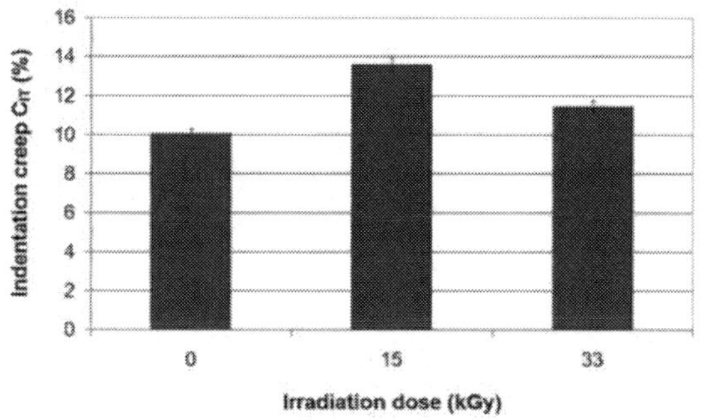

Fig. 6. Indentation creep C_{IT} vs. irradiation doses.

The highest values of elastic deformation work were obtained for non-irradiated polypropylene (PP). The highest values of plastic deformation work were obtained for polypropylene (PP) irradiated with radiation dose of 15 kGy. The lowest values of Wel, were obtained for polypropylene (PP) irradiated with dose of 15 kGy. Radiation of specimens caused lower values of plastic deformation work which is in Figure 7.

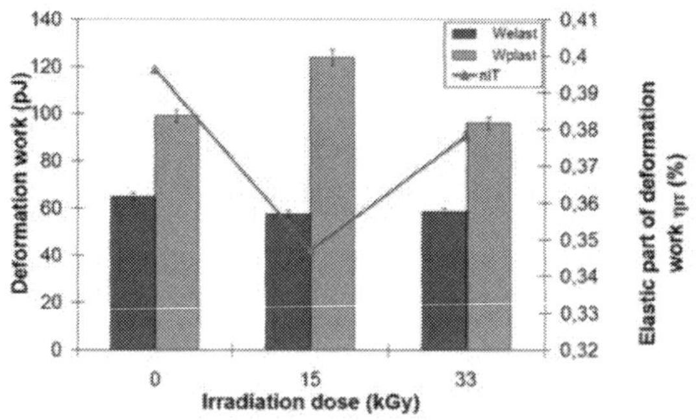

Fig. 7. Deformation work vs. irradiation dose.

Higher radiation dose does not influence significantly the micro-hardness value. An indentation hardness increase of the surface layer is caused by irradiation cross-linking of the tested specimen. A closer look at the micro-hardness results reveals that when the highest radiation doses are used, micro-hardness decreases which can be caused by radiation induced degradation of the material.

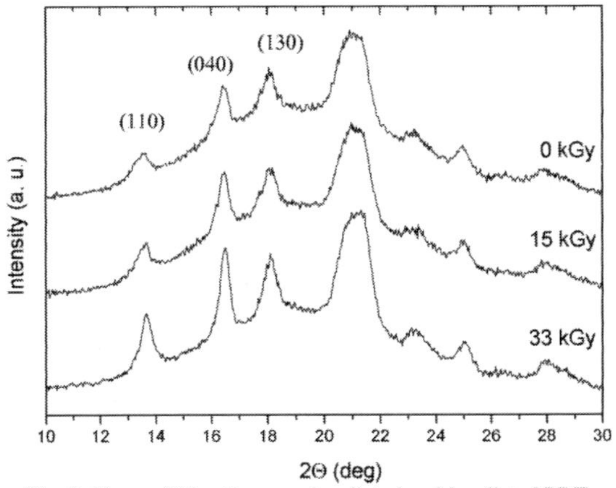

Fig. 8. X- ray diffraction non-irradiated and irradiated PBT.

The figure 8 shows typical X-ray diffraction spectrum of the non-irradiated and irradiated polypropylene (PP). There is an apparent presence of α-phase in the non-irradiated specimen. The greatest grow of α-phase is seen at the radiation dose of 15 kGy (Figure 8).

Table 1. X-ray diffraction of non-irradiated and irradiated PP.

Sample	X X-ray, %,±1%
0 kGy	45
15 kGy	67
33 kGy	54

4 Conclusion

The experimental study deals with the effect of modification of the surface layer by irradiation cross-linking on the properties of the surface layer of polypropylene (PP). Polypropylene (PP) was modified by beta irradiation at doses of 0, 15 and 33 kGy. The changes of micromechanical properties were found at the radiation dose of 15 kGy for indentation hardness which decreased by 38% compared to the non-irradiated polypropylene (PP). Improvement of mechanical properties in micro and macro scale of radiated polypropylene (PP) has a great significance also for industry. The modified polypropylene (PP) shifts to the group of materials which have considerably better properties. Its micromechanical properties make polypropylene (PP) ideal for a wide application in the areas where higher resistance to wear, scratch are required.

Acknowledgment

This paper is supported by the internal grant of TBU in Zlin No. IGA/FT/2017/010 funded from the resources of specific university research and by the Ministry of Education, Youth and Sports of the Czech Republic within the National Sustainability Programme project No. LO1303 (MSMT-7778/2014) and also by the European Regional Development Fund under the project CEBIA-Tech No. CZ.1.05/2.1.00/03.0089. Special thanks also to Dr. Michal Danek (BGS Beta Gamma Service GmbH & Co, KG, Germany) for his kind assistance during sample preparation.

References

1. Dj. Gheysari, Eur. Polym. J. **37** (2001) 295-302, (2001)
2. K. Makuuchi, S. Cheng. Wiley, Hoboken, 2011.
3. J.G. Drobny, Elsevier, Oxford, 2013.
4. D. Dobrotə, Energy Procedia, **100**, 1160-1166, (2015)
5. G. Zamfirova, V. Gaydarov, T. Zaharescu, L. G. Silva. Chemicke Listy, **104**, 283-286, (2010)
6. D. Manas, M. Hribova, M. Manas, M. Ovsik,M. Stanek, Thin Solid Films, **530**, 49-52,(2013)
7. O. Uzuna, U. Kölemena, S. Çelebi, N. Güçlü, Journal of the European Ceramic Society. **25**, 969–977, (2005).
8. W. C. Oliver, G. M. Pharr. J Mater Res, **7**. (6) 1564–1583, (1992)
9. E. Ragan, P. Baron, J. Dobránsky. Advanced Materials Research 383-390, 2813-2818, (2012).
10. H. Wang, L. Xu, R. Li, J. Hu, M. Wang, G. Wu, Radiation Physics and Chemistry, **125**, 41-49, (2016)
11. J. Dobránsky, L. Běhálek, P. Baron, Key Engineering Materials, **669**, 36-43, (2016)
12. Dobransky, J., Běhalek, L., Baron, P., Kočiško, M., Simkulet, V., Vojnova, E., Briančin, J. Metalurgija, **55** (3), pp. 449-452, (2016)
13. Dobránsky, J., Kočiško, M., Baron, P., Simkulet, V., Běhálek, L., Vojnová, E., Nováková Marcinčinová, Ľ. Metalurgija, **55** (3), pp. 477-480, (2016)
14. J. Čop, L. Fojtl, O. Bílek, V. Pata, Manufacturing Technology, **16** (2), pp. 334-338, (2016)
15. Singh, P. Kishore, M. Singh, A. Srivastava, Radiation Effects and Defects in Solids, **170** (10), 845-853, (2015)
16. S. Kashyap, D. Datta, International Journal of Plastics Technology, **19** (1), 1-18, (2015)
17. S. Zhang, R. Dubay, M. Charest, Expert Systems with Applications, **42** (6), 2919-2927, (2015)

Comparison of integrated and composed step-down converter in terms of EMC

Peter Janků[1,*], *Luboš* Lorenc[1] and *Tomáš* Dulík[1]

[1]Tomas Bata University in Zlin, Faculty of applied informatics, Nad Stranemi 4511, 760 05 Zlin

Abstract. Stabilized voltage sources, even linear or working on a switching principle, are an integral part of almost all electronic devices. Hand in hand with the pressure of environmental protection, there comes an emphasis on reducing energy consumption, resulting in preference of switching solutions. On the other hand, considering the issues on electromagnetic compatibility, each switching-mode operated power source produces considerable amount of interferences. In the framework of the hereby described experiment, the authors of the paper tested several voltage sources operating on the switching principle. This paper provides a description of the experiment and the obtained results.

1 Introduction

In a modern world, different electronic devices are unnecessary parts of a daily live. Moreover, the rising popularity of IoT devices together with a pressure on the target device size and power efficiency, it creates new challenges for a HW developers. At the opposite side of these situation the modern designs have to pass really strict EMC limitations and standards.

Mostly every electronic device has to have inbuilt power source in form of a linear stabilizer or a voltage converter. These parts of designs are usually one of the most important tasks in a HW design work. They are usually supplying highest currents in the device circuit and they could have a really significant impact on a final EMC characteristic. Therefore, the selection and construction of a suitable power source is really tricky. [4, 5]

In this paper we will deal with step-down voltage converters which are in terms of EMC usually more problematic then linear stabilizers. For the HW developers there are two possibilities how to construct a power source based on step-down voltage converter. The first one is to compose it from different discrete and integrated parts (composed step-down converter), the second one is to use it as an embeddable integrated device (integrated step-down converter) These research free follows previous presented studies [1, 2, 3] in which different step down converters were discussed with special attention on their EMC compatibility. The measurements of real characteristics of integrated step-down converter are discussed in this paper together with comparison with previous published composed step-down converters. All measurements and measures were performed to meet the requirements placed by working conditions and the standard EN 61000-6-3. [2, 3, 4, 5]

2 Description of used converters

In this paper the comparison between integrated and composed step down converters is discussed. The Traco TSR-1-2450 [7] was selected as an "integrated step-down converter" and the circuit based on AOZ1284 [6], which was published in previous research was selected as a "composed step-down converter". Both of them has nearly the same characteristic.

2.1. Converter parameters

Table 1. Electrical parameters of step-down converters

Parameter	AOZ1284	TSR-1-2450
Maximal input voltage	30 V	36 V
Output voltage	5 V	5 V
Maximal output current	800 mA	1 A
Min. power effeciency	80 %	84 %

As could be seen in Table 1, both converters has nearly the same electrical characteristics. Therefore we can simply compare their real electrical and EMC characteristics. For all measurements, the reference input voltage level was set at 12 V and 24V.

* Corresponding author: janku@fai.utb.cz

DOI: 10.1051/matecconf/201712502046

2.2. Integrated voltage converter TSR-1-2450

The selected integrated converter is an electronic device, which has integrated all necessary parts for work as nonisolated DC/DC converter. It has wide range of input voltage level (6,5 V to 36 V) and high efficiency (max. 96 %). Moreover, the output current can achieved 1 A level (5W output). It is inbuilt in package, which can directly replace standard linear stabilizers with package TO-220. The picture of this device could be seen at Fig. 1.

As stated before, the input/output filtering capacitors are inbuilt as well as other necessary parts; therefore, the usage of this part is really easy. For normal operation connection of one simple input capacitor is recommended by manufacturer. In order to accomplish international EMC standard EN 55022, it is recommended to connect simple LC filter at the input of this device. [7]

Fig. 1. Integrated step-down converter TSR-1-2450.

2.3. Composed step-down converter based on AOZ1284

As a second device for this comparison the step-down converter composed from passive parts and based on AOZ1284 was chosen. Its construction and detailed characteristics were published in the previous paper [2].

The whole circuit is based on a previous mentioned integrated device complemented by set of passive electronic parts. The main current loop consisting of inductor, switching N-MOSFET transistor and Schottky diode are placed outside of IO. Moreover, other capacitors are used for setting the converter's working frequency, for stabilizing input and output voltage level and for feedback compensation. The feedback resistors are also place outside of the IO. These facts means, that the electronic circuit of this step-down converter is significantly more complex than in previous case. At the other hand, the developer is able to tune more parameters of power source in order to fit specific characteristics of supplied device. [12, 13]

3 Measurements and results

The described converters were constructed and/or prepared as a functional sample and tested for achieving of the request parameters. Consequently, the sets of measurements were performed in order to gain data set needed for implementation of these converters into final products.

Since the target use of circuits was not specified, the standard EN 61000-6-3 had been chosen as a base requirement for EMC tests.

The predefined tests were as follows:

- output voltage stability vs. output load,
- power efficiency at different output loads and input voltages ,
- interference currents on the input cables measured by LISN ENV216,
- electromagnetic interference without a cover according to EN 61000-6-3.

3.1 Measurement configurations

The predefined sets of measurements from previous chapter were performed at three different measurement networks:

- Network configuration for measurement DC characteristics,
- Network configuration for measurement of interferences on input wires,
- Network configuration for measurement of radiated electromagnetic field.

3.1.1 Network for measurement of DC characteristic

The first measurements of DC characteristics were performed at a network composed from the laboratory power source Velleman PS3010, the measured converter and the programmable load Array 3721A. As is depicted in Fig. 2 the input voltages and currents were measured by using two true RMS multimeters connected directly at controlled converter's input. The precise output values were measure directly by programmable load.

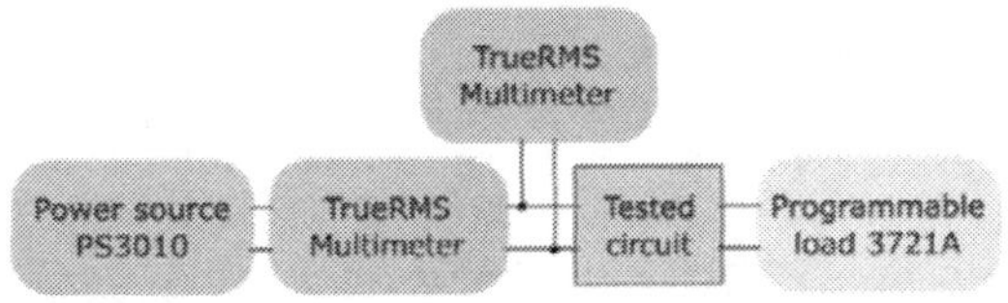

Fig. 2. Measurement network for comparison of DC characteristics

3.1.2 Radiated electromagnetic field

The measurement network used for measurement of radiated electromagnetic field is visualized in Fig. 3. As can be seen, measured sample was placed in a semi anechoic chamber which limits the signals naturally presented in environment.

The measurement network was composed of a bilogarithmical antenna Teseq Bilog CBL 6112 connected through interconnection network to the Rohde&Schvartz ESU 8 test receiver and spectral analyser. Data obtained by ESU 8 were processed by using EMC32 software.

Because of measurement need to be performed in different working conditions, the measured sample were connected to the laboratory power source and loaded by programmable load. [9, 10, 11]

In order to eliminate of electromagnetic field emitted by power source and programmable load, the last measurement was performed with bypassed measured sample.

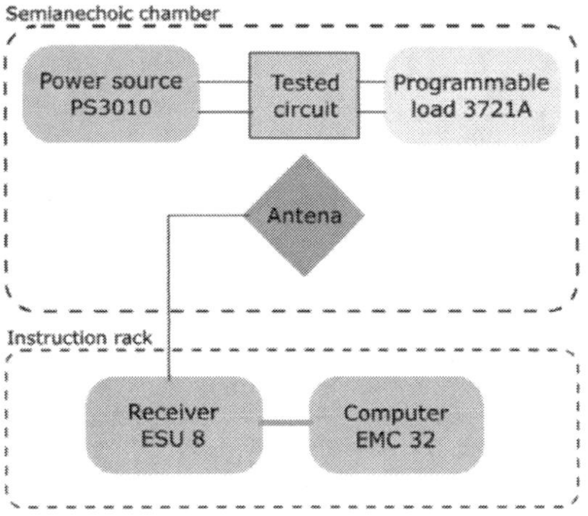

Fig. 4. Measurement network used for measure of radiate electromagnetic field.

3.1.3 Interferences on input wires

The measurement of interferences on input wires was performed in the standard combination used in previous cases. The measured sample is powered by using laboratory power source and it is connected to the programmable loads set in continuous current mode. Moreover, the LISN Rohde & Schwarz ENV216 was connected between power source and measured sample. This device can meet the requirements of CISPR 16-1-2, EN 55016-1-2. Because of performed measurements were not final (measured converters are usually only one part of final device) the current probe could be used as in previous researches [2].

The obtained data were collected in EMC 32 software and post procced by using MS Excel and Wolfram Mathematica.

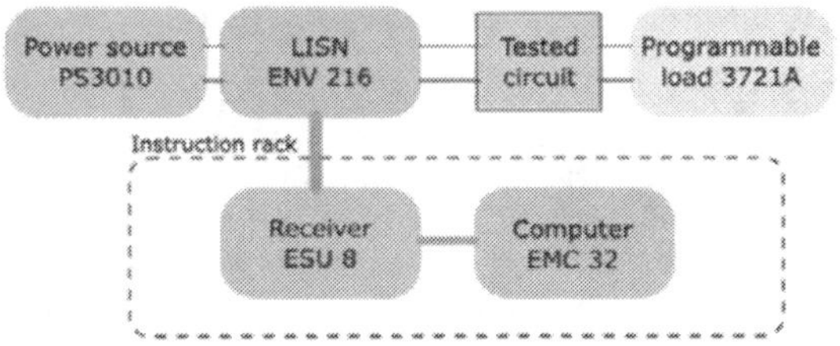

Fig. 3. Configuration of measurement network for measure of interferences on input wires.

3.2 Results

The measurement networks descripted in previous chapters were used in order to obtain real data. Both observed step-down converters were placed into same working conditions and same values were checked.

3.2.1 DC parameters

As was told before, compared step-down converters were constructed with nearly same output parameters. By using the DC measure network, described in the section 3.1.1, these parameters and its characteristics were measured. These measurements were done in two steps. At first time the converters efficiency was checked and at second the stability of output voltage was compared.

The graphs of converters efficiency in different working conditions are depicted in fig. 5. As could be seen, both of converters are able to achieve nearly the same efficiency. The composed step-down converter based on AOZ 1284 has the lower level of efficiency (78%) with 12V input and 800mA output load. This point is probably caused by limitation of some selected parts. At the other hand, integrated converter Traco achieved even lower level of efficiency – 76%. It has to be notice that this result is lower than typical values provided by manufacturer's datasheet.

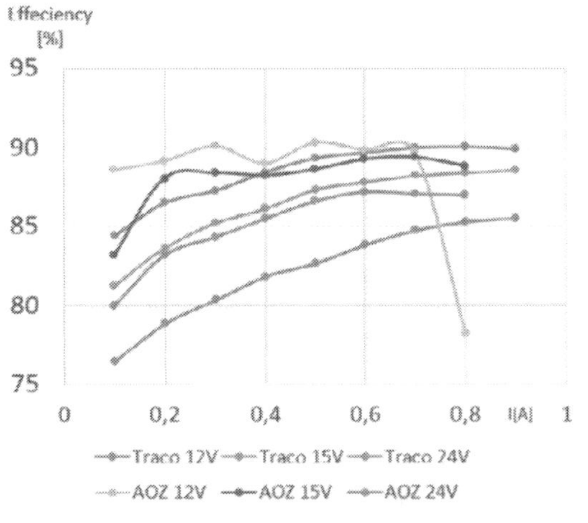

Fig. 5. Comparison of converters efficiency in different working conditions.

DOI: 10.1051/matecconf/201712502046

The dependencies of output voltage level on output load are shown in Fig. 6. As can be seen the maximum difference in output voltage for step-down converter Traco is 35 mV and for composed converter AOZ is 44 mV. Moreover, the average value of output voltage level is lower in AOZ converter then Traco. This could be problem for some installation; at the other hand, in case of composed converter this parameter could be fine-tuned by of resistors in feedback divider.

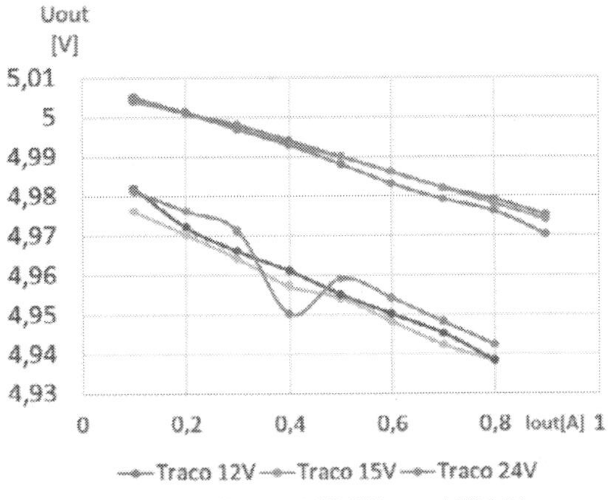

Fig. 6. Output voltage dependence on output current measured with different level of input voltage.

3.2.2 Radiated electromagnetic field

As it was mentioned in previous sections, the measurement of radiated electromagnetic field was one part of this comparison. The measurement method and base bade was used according to standard EN 61000-6-3. The base bend was used in rang of 30MHz to 1GHz.

One of the worst measured outputs can be seen in Fig. 7. This graph describes the level of radiated electromagnetic field for integrated converter Traco. Even if there is a problematic point around the 180 MHz, these don't have to be strictly problem – the radiated field is strictly depend on cases in which is measured. This means, that for our purposes we measured just only converter without any cover or case. In real usage this converts will be probably inbuilt in device placed in cover, box or case.

The results of a corresponding measurement performed at composed step-down converter AOZ could be seen in previous the paper [2]. There was the same case – one problematic point but measurement without case.

3.2.3 Interferences on input wires

According to a principle of operation of the step down converters, the current ripples and/or voltage peaks at input wires are expected. The set of measurements required by standard EN 61000-6-3 is really large. Therefore, due to size limit of this paper, only two measurements at positive input wire are presented. As was told before, these measurements were performed by using measure network defined in standard EN 61000-6-3. The base of this network was ENV 2016 LSN.

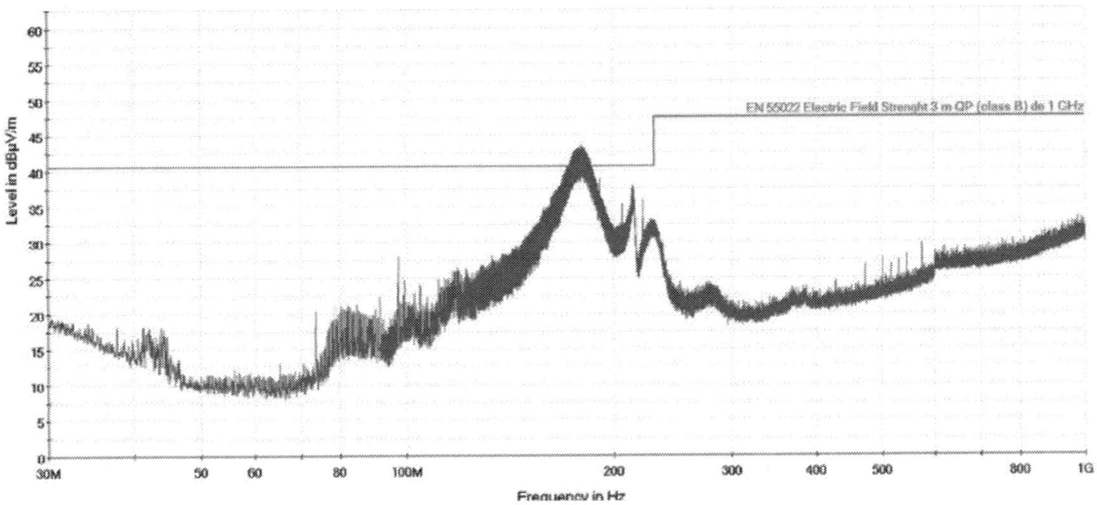

Fig. 6. Output voltage dependence on output current measured with different level of input voltage.

DOI: 10.1051/matecconf/201712502046

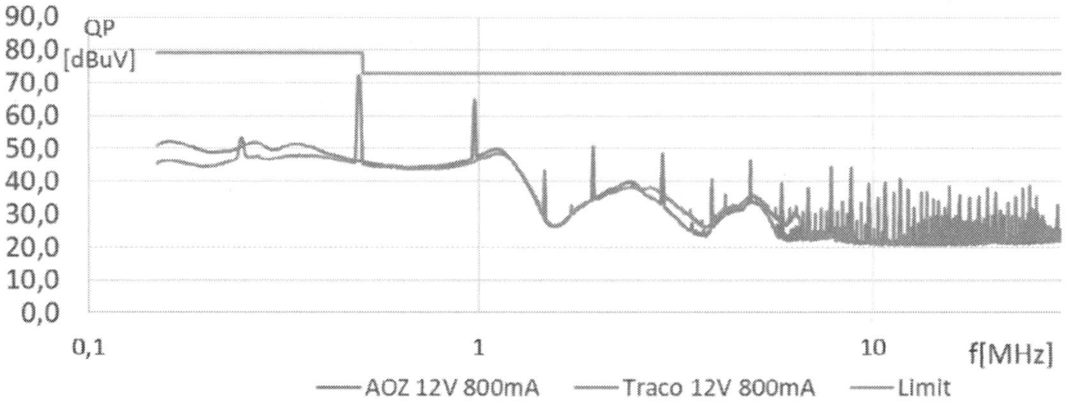

Fig. 7. Output voltage dependence on output current measured with different level of input voltage.

The comparison of spectrums of interferences on input wires can be seen in Fig. 7 and Fig. 8. Both this measurements were performed with maximum output load set at level of 800 mA. The fig. 7 depicted the state, when the 12 volts are used as an input into converters. The measurement was performed in frequency range from 150 kHz to 30 MHz.

For both converters, the first peak is measured at the converters working frequency – for AOZ it is 961 kHz, while for Traco it is 580 kHz. The next peaks mostly correspond with harmonic multiplies of working frequency. Even though the peaks, both of converters are able to full-fill the limit define by standard. It has to notice, that these measurements were performed with power filters included into input wires. The characteristic of filter used for AOZ step down converter was described in previous research. The filter used together with Traco converter corresponds to recommendations defined in manufacture datasheet.

The results of second measurement is shown in Fig. 8. This measurement was performed in the same configuration as the previous one, but the input voltage was changed to 24 V. The position of frequency peaks and it's level is nearly the same as in the previous case. Even if there is a lot of peaks, no one exceeds the limit defined by the standard.

All performed measurements were done by using Quasi-peak detector. In fact, the standard defines the same set measurements performed by using average detector with different limits. Both of them has to pass. Due to limit size of this paper, only QP measurements are discussed. Moreover, the interferences on input wires could slightly depend on characteristic of load. This mean that in real case – in real device, the level of interferences could be different.

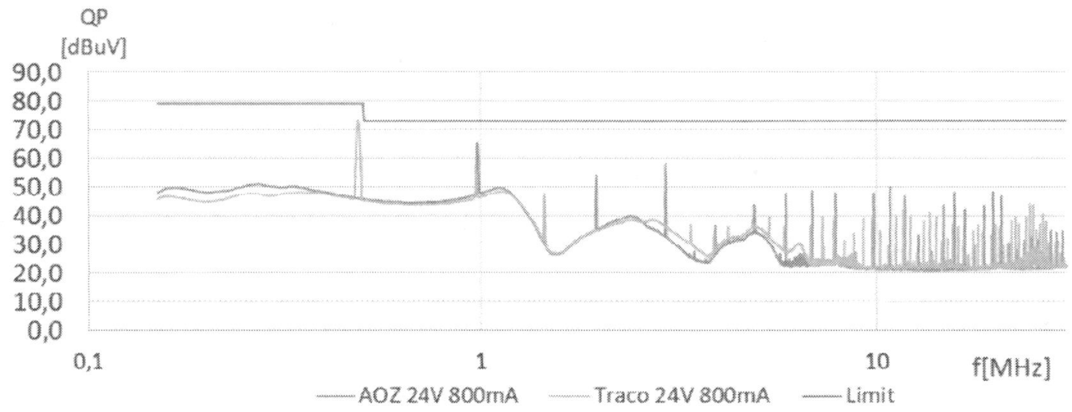

Fig. 8. Output voltage dependence on output current measured with different level of input voltage.

4 Conclusions

This paper provides comparison of two small cheap step-down converters. The converter composed from discreet parts and based on AOZ 1284 was chosen as the first one compared device. Its construction and basic characteristics were discussed in previous published paper. The integrated step-down converter Traco TSR-1-2450 was chosen as the second device. It is nonisolated fully integrated step down converter, which can be used as a replacement to a well-known linear stabilisers 78xx.

Both converters were construct/prepared as a functional sample and the same set of measurement were performed on them. The DC measurements agree that both converters has nearly the same characteristics and that they are able to full-fill requirements of different electronical devices. The radiated electromagnetic field measurement shown, that both of them are likely to meet the requirements defined by standard. The interferences on input wires were in both cases performed on devices with connected input filters. Thanks to this, no significant problems were founded when the quasi-peak detector was used.

According the data we obtained it can be suspected that both converters will be able to pass all requirements defined by standard EN61000-6-3 after small tuning of input filters.

Because of the voltage converter is usually only one part of electronic device and all its EMC characteristics depends on the connected load, performed measurements are only tentative. At the other hand, they can provide basic overview of device characteristics for electronic device designers.

As was described in previous text, the used standard defines significantly larger set of needed tests. These measurements was not performed due to limit size of this paper and they could be interesting subject of future research. Moreover, there is a set of isolating converters at the market with the nearly the same parameters which can be the subjects for future research.

Acknowledgement

This work was supported by the Ministry of Education, Youth and Sports of the Czech Republic within the National Sustainability Programme project No. LO1303 (MSMT-7778/2014).

References

1. M. Pospisilik, M. Adamek, R. M. S. Silva, *Different constructions of step down voltage converters in terms of EMC*, International Journal of Circuits, Systems and Signal Processing, Volume 10, (2016), p. 190-199, ISSN: 1998-4464

2. P. Janku, M. Pospisilik, T. Dulik, *Construction of compact step down voltage converter in terms of EMC*, MATEC Web Conf. 76 01010 (2016),DOI: 10.1051/matecconf/20167601010

3. J. Svacina, *Electromagnetic Compatibility [Elektromagneticka kompatibilita]*, Brno: VUT Brno, (2002).

4. C. R. Paul, *Introduction to Electromagnetic Compatibility*, New York: John Wiley, (1992).

5. P. A. Chatterton, M. A. Houlden, *EMC – Electromagnetic Theory to Practical Design*, New York: John Wiley, (1991).

6. ALPHA & OMEGA Semicondutor (2012, March), AOZ1284 Datasheet[online]. Available: http://aosmd.com/res/data_sheets/AOZ1284PI.pdf

7. Traco Power DC/DC Converters, TSR-12450. (2015, October) Datasheet [online] Available: http://www.tracopower.com/products/tsrn1.pdf

8. M. Pospisilik., T. Dulik, International Journal of Circuits, Systems and Signal Processing, **8**, (2014), pp 518 – 528

9. M. Mann, B. Gutheil, J. Zastrau, P. Weiss, "*Electromagnetic field measurements – Means of verification*", In Proc. of the 5th WSEAS/IASME Int. Conf. on Electric Power Systems, High Voltages, Electric Machines, Tenerife, Spain, December **16-18**, (2005), pp 591-595

10. M. Pospisilik, J. Soldan, M. Adamek, *Influence of the Properties of a Real Semi Anechoic Chamber on an Internal Electromagnetic Field Distribution*, WSEAS Transactions on Systems, **14**, (2015), pp 174 – 186, E-ISSN: 2224-2678

11. J. A. Cartrysse, "*Measuring method for the characterization of shielding gaskets*", in 8th International Conference on Electromagnetic Compatibility, pp 251 – 253, Heriot-Watt University, Edinburgh, UK, September (1992).

12. Z. Trnka, *Theory of Electrical Engineering [Teoretická elektrotechnika]*. Bratislava: SNTL Alfa, (1972)

13. V. Kus, *Effects of Converters with Semiconductors to the Power System [Vliv polovodičových měničů na napájecí soustavu]*, Prague: BEN-Technicka literature, (2002), ISBN: 80-730-0062-8

* Corresponding author: janku@fai.utb.cz

DOI: 10.1051/matecconf/201712502047

An analytical dynamic model of heat transfer from the heating body to the heated room

Jana Mižáková[1] and *Ján* Piteľ[1,*]

[1]Technical University of Košice, Faculty of Manufacturing Technologies with a seat in Prešov, Bayerova 1, 080 01 Prešov, Slovakia

Abstract. On the base of mathematical description of thermal balance the dynamic model of the hot-water heating body (radiator) was designed. The radiator is mathematically described as a heat transfer system between heating water and warmed-up air layer. Similarly, the dynamic model of heat transfer through the wall from the heated space to the outdoor environment was design. Both models were interconnected into dynamic model of heat transfer from the heating body to the heated room and they will be implemented into simulation model of the heating system in Matlab/Simulink environment.

1 Hot-water heating body

An analytic identification method based on mathematical description of a heat exchanger was chosen for design of the hot-water heating body dynamic model [1].

A hot-water heating body can be described as a heat transfer system between heating water and warmed-up air layer [2]. Heating water circulates inside radiator and delivers a heat through surface layer. External side of radiator is surrounded by air layer, which is warmed-up and heated air naturally flows up due to difference of specific weight [3]. It was considered ideal mixing of the heating water in internal space of the radiator and ideal air mixing in boundary layer of the radiator.

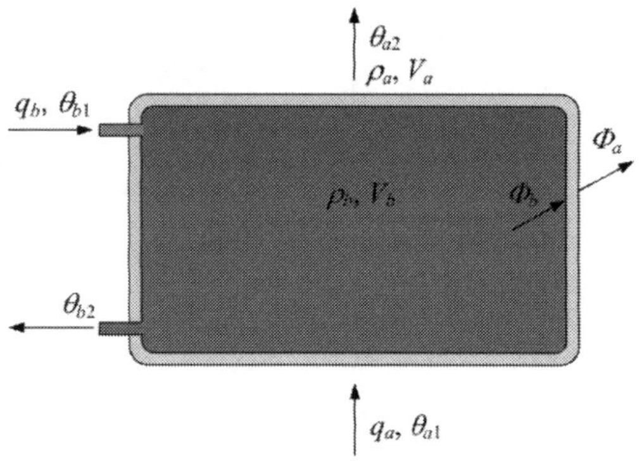

Fig. 1. Heat transfer in the heating body.

The heating water with mass flow q_b and temperature θ_{b1} inputs into radiator (Fig. 1). At every time point there is the volume of heating water V_b with density ρ_b in internal space of radiator. This water delivers a heat through surface layer of the radiator with plane A_r which is surrounded by air layer. Temperature of the return heating water from radiator is θ_{b2}. The air flow rate is q_a, volume of air in boundary layer of the radiator is V_a, its input temperature to the radiator surface is θ_{a1} and its output temperature after heating is θ_{a2}. Exchanged heat flow from heating water to the radiator wall is Φ_b and from the radiator wall to room space is Φ_a [4,5].

1.1 Mathematical description of heat transfer in the heating body

Generally, for dynamic balance describing of heat energy increasing or decreasing in system it is valid, that difference of input and output heat flows is equal to the time variation of the accumulated energy in a system [6]. Then the heat accumulation equation is valid for air heating in the boundary layer of the radiator:

$$\Phi_a - q_a \cdot c_a \cdot (\theta_{a2} - \theta_{a1}) = \rho_a \cdot V_a \cdot c_a \cdot \frac{d\theta_{a2}}{dt} \quad (1)$$

where Φ_a is heat flow from the radiator wall to the surrounding [W], q_a is air flow in the boundary layer of the radiator [kg·s^{-1}], c_a is specific heat capacity (specific heat) of air [J·kg^{-1}·K^{-1}], θ_{a1} is input air temperature [K], θ_{a2} is output air temperature [K], ρ_a is air density [kg·m^{-3}] and V_a is air volume in the boundary layer of the radiator [m^3].

For heat exchanging from the heating water to the radiator wall this heat accumulation equation is valid:

$$q_b \cdot c_b \cdot (\theta_{b1} - \theta_{b2}) - \Phi_b = \rho_b \cdot V_b \cdot c_b \cdot \frac{d\theta_{b2}}{dt} \quad (2)$$

where Φ_b is heat flow from the heating water to the radiator wall [W], q_b is mass flow rate of the heating water [kg·s^{-1}], c_b is specific heat capacity (specific heat) of water [J·kg^{-1}·K^{-1}], θ_{b1} is input water temperature into the radiator [K], θ_{b2} is temperature of the return heating

* Corresponding author: jan.pitel@tuke.sk

water from the radiator [K], ρ_b is water density [kg·m^{-3}] and V_b is volume of water in the radiator [m^3].

It is necessary for design of automatic control to know the dynamic dependence of the control deviation according to changes of variables which have effect on the deviation [7-10]. For that reason, we express dependent variables in equations (1) and (2) by their values in initial steady-state and their increments. Next, to simplify computation, we express each of dependences in non-dimensional form as relative changes of variables and we get system of differential equations describing the radiator:

$$x_{\Phi a} - x_{\theta a2} + x_{\theta a1} - x_{qa} = \tau_{ma} \cdot \frac{\mathrm{d}x_{\theta a2}}{\mathrm{d}t} \tag{3}$$

$$-x_{\theta b2} + x_{\theta b1} + x_{qb} - x_{\Phi b} = \tau_{ma} \cdot \frac{\mathrm{d}x_{\theta b2}}{\mathrm{d}t} \tag{4}$$

where $\tau_{ma} = \frac{\rho_a \cdot V_a}{q_{a0}}$ and $\tau_{mb} = \frac{\rho_b \cdot V_b}{q_{b0}}$ are time constants.

1.2 Dynamic model of the hot-water heating body

After Laplace transform of differential equations (3) and (4) and other mathematical operations it is valid for relative change of air output temperature:

$$\begin{aligned} X_{\theta a2}(s) &= \frac{1}{\tau_{ma} \cdot s + 1}\left[X_{\Phi a}(s) + X_{\theta a1}(s) - X_{qa}(s)\right] = \\ &= G_a(s) \cdot \left[X_{\Phi a}(s) + X_{\theta a1}(s) - X_{qa}(s)\right] \end{aligned} \tag{5}$$

$$\begin{aligned} X_{\theta b2}(s) &= \frac{1}{\tau_{mb} \cdot s + 1}\left[-X_{\Phi b}(s) + X_{\theta b1}(s) + X_{qb}(s)\right] = \\ &= G_b(s) \cdot \left[-X_{\Phi b}(s) + X_{\theta b1}(s) + X_{qb}(s)\right] \end{aligned} \tag{6}$$

where $\tau_{ma} = \frac{\rho_a \cdot V_a}{q_{a0}}$ and $\tau_{mb} = \frac{\rho_b \cdot V_b}{q_{b0}}$ are time constants.

To make mathematical description of dynamic characteristics of the radiator complete, it is necessary to supplement equation (5) and (6) with relations for relative changes of heat flows $x_{\Phi a}$ and $x_{\Phi b}$. If heat transfer coefficients h_a and h_b are constant in unsteady-states, relative variations of heat flows are dependent only on temperature changes of the heating water and air. Generally, we can express it as:

$$X_{\Phi a}(s) = W_{ab}(s) \cdot X_{\theta b2}(s) - W_{aa}(s) \cdot X_{\theta a2}(s) \tag{7}$$

$$X_{\Phi b}(s) = -W_{ba}(s) \cdot X_{\theta a2}(s) + W_{bb}(s) \cdot X_{\theta b2}(s) \tag{8}$$

Transfer functions in relations (7) and (8) are [2]:

$$W_{ab}(s) = \frac{k_b}{1 + \tau_r \cdot s} \qquad W_{aa}(s) = k_a \cdot \frac{1 + \tau_b \cdot s}{1 + \tau_r \cdot s} \tag{9}$$

gains k_b, k_a:

$$k_b = \frac{A_r}{q_{b0} \cdot c_b} \cdot \frac{1}{\frac{1}{h_a} + \frac{1}{h_b} + \frac{d_r}{\lambda_r}} \tag{10}$$

$$k_a = \frac{A_r}{q_{a0} \cdot c_a} \cdot \frac{1}{\frac{1}{h_a} + \frac{1}{h_b} + \frac{d_r}{\lambda_r}} \tag{11}$$

and time constants τ_b, τ_r:

$$\tau_b = \rho_r \cdot c_r \cdot d_r \cdot \left(\frac{1}{h_b} + \frac{d_r}{2\lambda_r}\right) \tag{12}$$

$$\tau_r = \rho_r \cdot c_r \cdot d_r \cdot \frac{1 + \frac{(h_a + h_b) \cdot d_r}{2\lambda_r} + \frac{h_a \cdot h_b \cdot d_r}{6\lambda_r^2}}{h_a + h_b + \frac{h_a \cdot h_b \cdot d_r}{\lambda_r}} \tag{13}$$

where other variables not mentioned above are: A_r is plane of the radiator surface [m^2], h_a is heat transfer coefficient between radiator surface and air [W·m^{-2}·K^{-1}], h_b is heat transfer coefficient between heating water and radiator body [W·m^{-2}·K^{-1}], d_r is thickness of the radiator wall [m], λ_r is heat conductivity coefficient of the radiator body material [W·m^{-1}·K^{-1}], ρ_r is specific weight of the radiator body material [kg·m^{-3}] and c_r is specific heat capacity (specific capacity) of the radiator body material [J·kg^{-1}·K^{-1}] [11,12].

Transfer functions $W_{ba}(s)$ and $W_{bb}(s)$ we get by reciprocity of indexes „a" and „b" in terms (9).

Based on the terms (5) till (9) for non-dimensional variables the block diagram of dynamic model of the hot-water heating body was designed (Fig. 2).

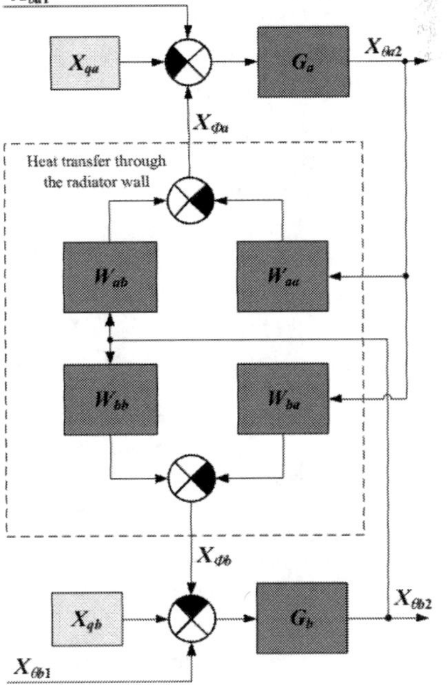

Fig. 2. Block diagram of dynamic model of the hot-water heating body.

Input variables into model are non-dimensional variables or constants: input temperature of air $X_{\theta a1}$, air flow rate X_{qa}, temperature of the input heating water into radiator $X_{\theta b1}$ and mass flow rate of the heating water X_{qb}. Output variables from model are non-dimensional variables: output temperature of air after heating by the radiator surface $X_{\theta a2}$ and temperature of the return heating water from the radiator $X_{\theta b2}$.

2 Heat transfer through the wall

For design of the dynamic model of heat transfer through the wall we have considered a plane wall, where the wall has been considered as continuum with continuously distributed thermal resistance and capacity [13,14]. We have chosen elementary layer with following parameters (Fig. 3): thickness of the plane wall dw [m], layer thickness in the plane wall dy [m], distance of layer from the heated surface y [m]. The heat flow Φ_1 [W] is supplied into heated wall surface which temperature is θ_{w1} [K], the heat flow Φ_2 [W] is taken away from the refrigerated wall surface which temperature is Φ_2 [W]. The heat flow Φ inputs into the unit surface of layer dy, and the heat flow Φ + dΦ outputs from it. Temperature of the elementary layer is θ_w [K].

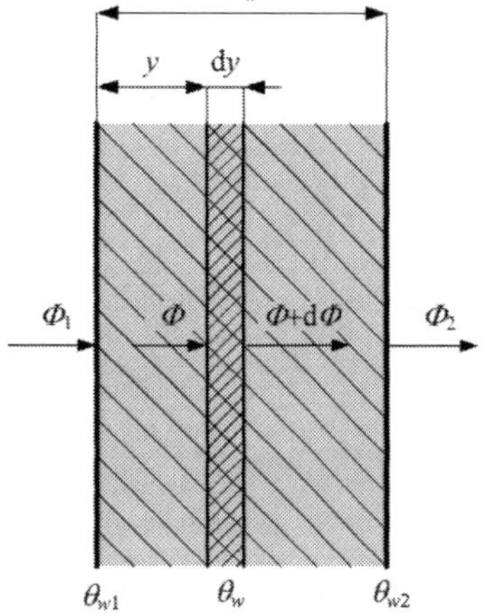

Fig. 3. Heat transfer through the plane wall.

2.1 Mathematical description of heat transfer through the wall

The heat energy does not originate either does not lose in considered elementary layer of the wall. Then difference of the input heat and output heat in the layer has to be equal to the time variation of the energy in the layer [15].

Let's c is specific heat capacity (specific heat) and ρ is volume weight of the wall material, then:

$$\Phi-(\Phi+\mathrm{d}\Phi)=\frac{\partial}{\partial t}(c\cdot\rho\cdot\theta_w\cdot\mathrm{d}y) \tag{14}$$

Considering that heat flow dΦ is:

$$\mathrm{d}\Phi=\frac{\partial\Phi}{\partial y}\mathrm{d}y \tag{15}$$

If specific heat capacity c and volume weight ρ of the used wall material are constant, then [16]:

$$-\frac{\partial\Phi}{\partial y}=c\cdot\rho\cdot\frac{\partial\theta_w}{\partial t} \tag{16}$$

According to Fourier's law the heat flow is directly proportional to the temperature gradient:

$$\Phi=-\lambda\frac{\partial\theta_w}{\partial y} \tag{17}$$

where λ is heat conductivity coefficient of the used wall material.

Partial differential equations (16) and (17) with relevant initial and border conditions completely describe non-stationary one-dimensional heat flow [17].

As we mentioned above we have expressed dependent variables by their values and increments and by substitutions and subtractions we have got partial differential equations system of heat transfer dynamics through the wall:

$$-\frac{\partial\Delta\Phi}{\partial y}=c\cdot\rho\cdot\frac{\partial\Delta\theta_w}{\partial t} \tag{18}$$

$$\Delta\Phi=-\lambda\frac{\partial\Delta\theta_w}{\partial y} \tag{19}$$

To simplify computation, we have expressed each of dependences in non-dimensional form and then we can express partial differential equations (18) and (19) in a form:

$$\frac{\partial x_{\Phi}}{\partial y}+c\cdot\rho\cdot\frac{d_w}{\lambda}\frac{\partial x_{\theta w}}{\partial t}=0 \tag{20}$$

$$x_{\Phi}+d_w\frac{\partial x_{\theta w}}{\partial y}=0 \tag{21}$$

Equations (16), (17) or (20), (21) still need to be supplemented by equations of heat transfer on both sides of the wall surfaces. In dimensionless form for indoor surface area it is valid:

$$x_{\Phi 1}=x^{*}_{\Phi 1}-\kappa_1\cdot x_{\theta w1}=(x_{\theta a2}-x_{\theta w1})\cdot h_1-\kappa_1\cdot x_{\theta w1} \tag{22}$$

where $x^{*}_{\Phi 1}$ includes also external effects on the heat flow transfer into the wall (temperature changes or heat transfer coefficient changes, etc.), $\kappa_1=\frac{h_1\cdot d_w}{\lambda}$ and h_1 is heat transfer coefficient between air and wall surface [W·m^{-2}·K^{-1}].

Similarly, for outdoor surface area it is valid:

$$x_{\Phi 2} = x_{\Phi 2}^{*} + \kappa_2 \cdot x_{\theta w2} = \left(x_{\theta w2} - x_{\theta o}\right) \cdot h_2 + \kappa_2 \cdot x_{\theta w2} \quad (23)$$

where $x_{\Phi 2}^{*}$ includes external conditions of the heat flow transfer from the wall, $\kappa_2 = \frac{h_2 . d_w}{\lambda}$ and h_2 is heat transfer coefficient between wall surface and air [W·m^{-2}·K^{-1}].

2.2 Dynamic model of heat transfer through the wall

By the Laplace transform of partial differential equations (20) and (21) and by the other mathematical operations it has been possible to get a system of equations, which describes dependence of non-dimensional variables for heat flows Φ_1, Φ_2 and temperatures θ_{w1}, θ_{w2}.

Laplace transform image of partial differential equations system is:

$$\overline{\overline{X}}_{\Phi} = \frac{q}{q^2 - p} \overline{X}_{\Phi 1} - \frac{p}{q^2 - p} \overline{X}_{\theta w1} \quad (24)$$

$$\overline{\overline{X}}_{\theta w} = -\frac{1}{q^2 - p} \overline{X}_{\Phi 1} + \frac{q}{q^2 - p} \overline{X}_{\theta w1} \quad (25)$$

Using inverse Laplace transform we have got following equations:

$$\overline{X}_{\Phi} = \cosh\sqrt{p} \cdot \overline{X}_{\Phi 1} - \sqrt{p} \cdot \sinh\sqrt{p} \cdot \overline{X}_{\theta w1} \quad (26)$$

$$\overline{X}_{\theta w} = -\frac{\sinh\sqrt{p}}{\sqrt{p}} \cdot \overline{X}_{\Phi 1} + \cosh\sqrt{p} \cdot \overline{X}_{\theta w1} \quad (27)$$

Let denote $\overline{X}_{\Phi} = \overline{X}_{\Phi 2}$ and $\overline{X}_{\theta w} = \overline{X}_{\theta w2}$. And simultaneously because that the unknowns variables are the heat flow Φ_2 taken away from the refrigerated wall surface and temperature θ_{w1} of the heated wall surface, we express $\overline{X}_{\Phi 2}$ and $\overline{X}_{\theta w1}$ [2]:

$$\overline{X}_{\Phi 2} = \frac{1}{\cosh\sqrt{p}} \overline{X}_{\Phi 1} - \sqrt{p} \cdot \mathrm{tgh}\sqrt{p} \cdot \overline{X}_{\theta w2} \quad (28)$$

$$\overline{X}_{\theta w1} = -\frac{\mathrm{tgh}\sqrt{p}}{\sqrt{p}} \overline{X}_{\Phi 1} + \frac{1}{\cosh\sqrt{p}} \overline{X}_{\theta w2} \quad (29)$$

with transfer functions:

$$G_1(p) = \frac{1}{\cosh\sqrt{(p)}} \quad (30)$$

$$G_2(p) = \sqrt{(p)} \cdot \mathrm{tgh}\sqrt{(p)} \quad (31)$$

$$G_3(p) = \frac{\mathrm{tgh}\sqrt{p}}{\sqrt{(p)}} \quad (32)$$

Next problem is to find function which corresponds to (26) and (27) using inverse Laplace transform. Due to the fact, that transfer functions (28)-(30) are not defined as images, we have to use Taylor series and substitution $p = T_s \cdot s$. Thus we get transfer functions:

$$G_1(p) = \frac{24}{24 + 12T_s s + T_s s^2} \quad (33)$$

$$G_2(p) = \frac{4\left(6T_s s + T_s s^2\right)}{24 + 12T_s s + T_s s^2} \quad (34)$$

$$G_3(p) = \frac{120 + 20T_s s + T_s s^2}{5\left(24 + 12T_s s + T_s s^2\right)} \quad (35)$$

where $T_s = \frac{d_w^2 \cdot \rho \cdot c}{\lambda}$ is constant which is depended on the wall properties.

Based on the terms (28) till (35) for non-dimensional variables the block diagram of dynamic model of heat transfer through the wall was designed (Fig. 4).

Input variables into model are non-dimensional variables: temperature of the heated air in the room $X_{\theta a2}$ and outdoor temperature $X_{\theta o}$. Output variables from model are non-dimensional variables of the wall temperatures $X_{\theta w1}$ and $X_{\theta w2}$ [18-20].

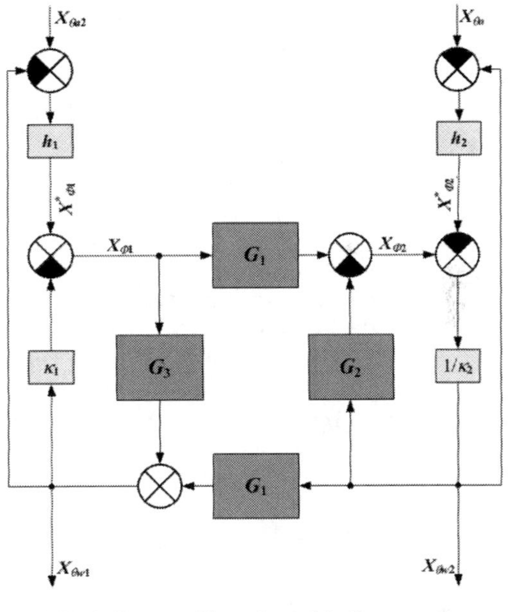

Fig. 4. Block diagram of dynamic model of heat transfer through the wall.

3 Conclusion

Dynamic model of heat transfer from the heating body to the heated room consists of two relative separated models: model of the heating body and model of heat transfer through the wall to the outdoor environment. Interconnection of these two models is presented in Fig. 5.

The designed dynamic model will be the basis for creating the simulation model of the heating system in Matlab/Simulink environment [21-25].

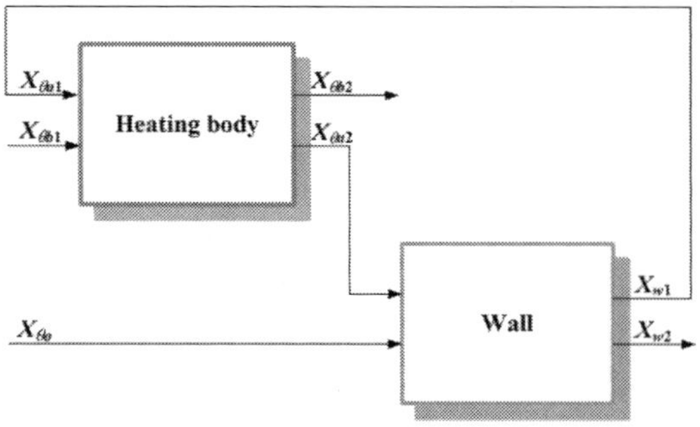

Fig. 5. Block diagram of dynamic model of heat transfer from the heating body to the heated room.

Acknowledgment

This work was supported by the Slovak Research and Development Agency under the contract No. APVV-15-0602 and also by the Project of the Structural Funds of the EU, ITMS code: 26220220030.

References

1. H. Charvatova, D. Janacova, R. Drga, O. Liska, V. Vasek, M. Zalesak, Computer modeling of heat balance in counterflow tube heat exchanger. International Journal of Mechanics, **7** (4), pp. 385-392 (2013)
2. J. Čermák, V. Peterka, J. Závorka, *Dynamika regulovaných soustav v tepelné energetice a chemii*, 584 p. (1968)
3. I. Čorný, Ľ. Straka, J. Mihalčová, Konvekčné modely a ich aplikácia v simulačných programoch v technike prostredia. Strojárstvo extra, **12** (5), pp. 6/1-4 (2009)
4. F. Hruška, Model konvekčního topného tělesa, *in MATLAB 2002*, Praha, pp. 202-206 (2002)
5. F. Hruška, J. Piteľ, Analytický model prostředí interiéru jako regulované soustavy, *in Workshop "Human Factor and Environmentalist"*, Vienna-Košice, pp. 41-42 (2002)
6. D. Janacova, H. Charvatova, K. Kolomaznik, M. Fialka, P. Mokrejs, V. Vasek, Interactive software application for calculation of nonstationary heat conduction in a cylindrical body. Computer Applications in Engineering Education, **21** (1), pp. 89-94 (2013)
7. V. Vasek, K. Kolomaznik, D. Janacova, Tannery wastes processing distributed control system, *in International Conf. on CAD/CAM, Robotics and Factories of the Future*, Durban, pp. 894-900 (2001)
8. M. Rimár, I. Čorný, M. Fedák, Analýza a syntéza riadenia tepelných sústav, 190 p. (2013)
9. V. Vasek, P. Dostalek, J. Dolinay, D. Janacova, K. Kolomaznik, Microcontrollers and modern control methods, *in WSEAS International Conference on Computer Engineering and Applications*, Mexico, pp. 195-198 (2008)
10. A. Hošovský, J. Piteľ, Základy automatického riadenia, 97 p. (2013)
11. J. Pitel, J. Borzikova, Model of the heating body for heating process control using, *in MMTT 20*, Jaroslavl, pp. 78-80 (2007)
12. J. Piteľ, T. Saloky, Simulačný model teplovodného vykurovacieho telesa. Acta Metallurgica Slovaca, **13**, pp. 301-306 (2007).
13. H. Charvatova, D. Janacova, K. Kolomaznik, Study of non-stationary heat conduction in a plane plate for symmetric and asymmetric problem. WSEAS Transactions on Heat and Mass Transfer, **6** (1), pp. 51-60 (2011)
14. J. Pitel, Model of the heated space for heating process control using, *in MMTT 19*, Voronez, pp. 141-143 (2006)
15. I. Corny, M. Fedak, Equation model of thermal comfort parameters, *in Energy transformation in industry*, High Tatras, pp. 25-27 (2013)
16. I. Corny, Mathematical model of thermal parameters, *in Operation and diagnostics of machines and production systems operational states*, Brno, pp. 15-18 (2008)
17. J. Piteľ, Matematický model prestupu tepla stenou pre simuláciu riadenia procesu vykurovania, Acta Metallurgica Slovaca, **13**, pp. 296-300 (2007).
18. H. Charvatova, M. Zalesak, S. Sehnalek, D. Janacova, V. Vasek, R. Drga, Computer simulation of parameterized module for testing of thermal stability in the room. International Journal of Mathematics and Computers in Simulation, **9**, pp. 53-59 (2015)
19. J. Mizakova, S. Hrehova, A. Hosovsky, Simulation model of heat transfer through the wall, *in International conference on Applied Mathematics and Computational Methods*, Venice, pp. 195-200 (2013)
20. J. Mizakova, J. Pitel, S. Hrehova, Some simulation results of heat transfer through the wall. International Journal of Mathematical Models and Methods in Applied Sciences. **8**, pp.1-8, (2014)
21. M. Balara, M. Tóthová, Símulačný model riadenia vykurovacieho systému s kaskádnou regulačnou štruktúrou, in *ARTEP 2015*, Stará Lesná, pp. 32-1 – 7 (2015).
22. I. Corny, Application of simulation control in building energy system. Acta Technica Corviniensis, **2** (3), pp. 25-31 (2009)
23. M. Tóthová, M. Balara, Simulácia riadenia vykurovacieho systému s kaskádnou regulačnou štruktúrou (1). iDB Journal, **5** (2), pp. 44-45 (2015)
24. M. Fedak, I. Corny, Building energy performance simulation and its evolution, *in MMS 2014*, Stary Smokovec, pp. 42-46 (2014)
25. M. Tothova, M. Balara, J. Dubjak, Simulation model of cascade control of the heating system. International Journal of Engineering Research in Africa, **18**, pp. 20-27 (2015)

 DOI: 10.1051/matecconf/201712502048

Impact behaviour of acrylonitrile-butadiene-styrene after temperature and humidity load

Lenka Hylova [1,*], *Miroslav* Manas[1]

[1]Tomas Bata University in Zlin, nam. T. G. Masaryka 5555, 76001 Zlin, Czech Republic

Abstract. This study deals with acrylonitrile-butadiene-styrene (ABS) which was subjected the drop-weight test before and after temperature and humidity load. ABS is an engineering plastic and also an important engineering terpolymer, which has butadiene part uniformly distributed through the acrylonitrile-styrene matrix and is commonly used in production of automotive interior components. The injection moulded ABS samples were subjected the penetration test at fall height 100 J before and after temperature and humidity load and the results were subsequently evaluated and discussed. It was found out that ABS after temperature and humidity load has lower impact resistance.

1 Introduction

Acrylonitrile-butadiene-styrene (ABS) is an engineering plastic and also an important engineering terpolymer, which has butadiene part uniformly distributed through the acrylonitrile-styrene matrix. ABS was commercialized at the latter of 1940s by U.S. Rubber and originally was made by blending of polystyrene-co-acrylonitrile (SAN) and NBR acrylonitrile-butadiene rubber (NBR), while nowadays ABS of the graft-type is made by copolymerization of styrene and acrylonitrile monomers in the rubber presence. Some of SAN is grafted to the rubber during the polymerization process and the grafted SAN behaves as a dispersing agent. The rubber phase, which is the part of ABS (generally polybutadiene grafted with SAN) is dispersed in the form of spherical particles in grafted SAN. Physical properties of ABS are influenced by the rubber particle size and content, molecular weight of SAN matrix and also by the grafting degree. The origin of ABS can be set to mid-1940s. Acrylonitrile-styrene copolymer was used since 1940s and the disadvantages of this copolymer led to the incorporation of third monomer namely butadiene rubber, which imparted higher impact resistance and higher strength to this terpolymer. ABS has great mechanical properties, chemical resistance, excellent toughness, easy processing ability, good dimensional stability, durability, cheapness and low coefficient of thermal expansion. The low mechanical strength, vulnerability to environmental conditions and non-conductivity are the disadvantages of ABS. It is also possible to enhance mechanical properties such as tensile strength, hardness and flexural modulus of ABS using fibre-reinforcement. This polymeric material has various application as in the architecture, construction, computer and business equipment, personal care products, toys, medical devices and in automotive interior components [1-3].

Brazilian scientists investigated three types of commercial ABS, namely GP (ABS for general-purpose use), HI (an ABS high impact) and HH (ABS high heat resistance). They studied activation energy of all three ABS and they realized that it is much higher than reported in the literature. One reason can be the fact that ABS terpolymer is produced worldwide by a large number of producers and for different application of use. They also found out that ABS HH is a little more thermally resistant than ABS HI and much more than ABS GP because of its highest acrylonitrile content. ABS HI and ABS HH also exibit high activation energy because of high butadiene content, this is probably because the SAN matrix is directly bonded to butadiene and the liberation of butadiene is very difficult during the degradation reaction [1].

The scientists from China dealt with the influence of polybutadiene-grafted styrene-acrylonitrile (PB-g-SAN) impact modifiers content on mechanical behaviour and morphology of ABS blends. They found out a big influence of PB-g-SAN content on impact strength, the higher PB-g-SAN content, the higher impact strength is, unlike the flexural strength, flexural modulus, melt flow index, tensile strength, and Rockwell hardness decrease with the increase of PB-g-SAN content [4].

M.A. Peydro, F. Pares, R. Navarro and S. Sanches-Caballero dealt with ABS contaminated with LDPE which obtained using a twin-screw extruder. Four ABS/LDPE blends of 1, 3, 4 and 8 % of LDPE were obtained and then other ABS/LDPE blends with adding of styrene-ethylene/butadiene-styrene (SEBS) was made

* Corresponding author: hylova@utb.cz

in 1, 2, 4 and 8 wt% of SEBS. The flat specimens were injection moulded and subsequently tested. It was found that the higher content of LDPE, the lower tensile strength, tensile modulus, elongation at break, Charpy notched impact strength are, unlike the shrinkage increases with the content of LDPE. After adding of SEBS, elongation at break and Charpy notched impact strength increase with the content of SEBS and also the shrinkage slightly decreases [5].

A team of Chinese scientists investigated impact behaviour of two ABS samples. ABS-1 sample was toughened with 10 wt% compounded rubber (low-cis PB rubber/styrene-butadiene block copolymer) and ABS-2 sample was made with 12 wt% linear random styrene-isoprene-butadiene rubber (SIBR) as a toughening modifier. ABS-2 has much higher impact strength and elongation at break than ABS-1 sample, unlike ABS-1 has higher tensile strength and break strength in comparison with ABS-2 sample [6].

Cooperation of Chinese and Canadian scientists has brought interesting results. These scientists dealt with ABS blends with a constant rubber concentration of 15 wt% compounded with polybutadiene-grafted styrene-acrylonitrile (PBD-g-SAN) impact modifiers with SAN resin in a twin-screw extruder. The blend with small rubber particles is called ABS-S and with large rubber particles ABS-L. The ABS-L has slightly lower yield strength in comparison with ABS-S, while ABS-S has more than four times lower impact strength than ABS-L which shows that small rubber particles with the diameter of 92 nm cannot toughen SAN resin [7].

This study can bring a big benefit for the deeper knowledge about ABS after temperature and humidity load, which is useful to apply for both the indoor and outdoor applications of this material.

2 Experimental

ABS was used as the basic polymer material (STAREX ABS, HF-0660IW). An ARBURG Allrounder 470H Advance Injection moulding machine was used for sample preparation, with the processing conditional to comply with acrylonitrile-butadiene styrene (ABS) producer's recommendations, as can be seen in Tab. 1. The samples were in the shape of plates with dimensions 100×100×3 mm according to ISO 6603-2.

Table 1. Setting of injection moulding machine parameters

Injection Parameters	Values
Injection Pressure [MPa]	70
Injection velocity [mm.s^{-1}]	40
Holding Pressure [MPa]	65
Cooling Time [s]	17
Mould Temperature [°C]	40
Melt Temperature [°C]	225

A part of injection moulded samples was put into the climatic chamber, type DISCOVERY from company Angelantoni. These samples were 168 hours in environment at temperature 75 °C and humidity 98 %. After this time the samples were cooled on 23 °C and 50 % of humidity with rate of cooling 10 °C per hour and rate of humidity decreasing 10 % per hour.

Drop weight test carried out on temperature and humidity loaded samples after 24 hours acclimatization at ambient temperature (23 °C) and humidity (50 %). Gain results were compared with non-loaded samples, which was tested at the same conditions. For these tests drop weight test machine HIT230F from company Zwick was used. The test carried out at 100 J impact energy of penetrator, falling surface of penetrator has shape of hemisphere with diameter 20 mm. Test was performed according to ISO 6603-2. TestExpert II was used for evaluation of results, which were maximum impact force and all consumed work for whole deformation. At the end crack surface after the test was evaluated.

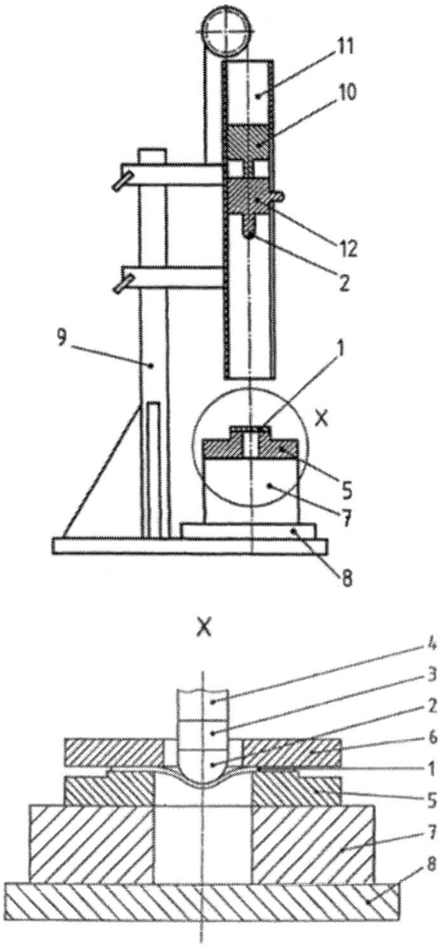

Fig. 1. Falling-dart system.

1 – Test specimen; 2 – Hemispherical striker tip 10 mm; 3 – Force sensor; 4 – Shaft; 5 – Test specimen support; 6 – Clamping ring (optional); 7 – Base; 8 – Acoustic isolation

(optional); 9 – Stand for falling-dart system; 10 – Holding and release system for weighted striker; 11 – Guide shaft for weighted striker; 12 – Weighted striker 23,77 kg.

3 Results and discussion

This study is concentrated on comparison ABS before and after temperature and humidity load. Injection moulded ABS samples were penetrated by penetrator with potential energy 100 J before and after load.

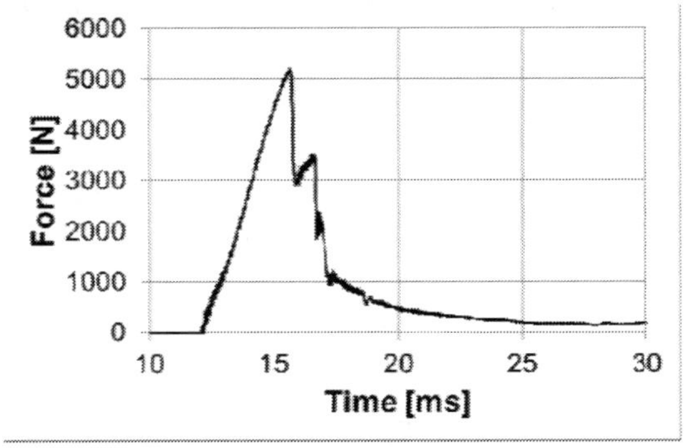

Fig. 2. ABS force record in time before temperature and humidity loading.

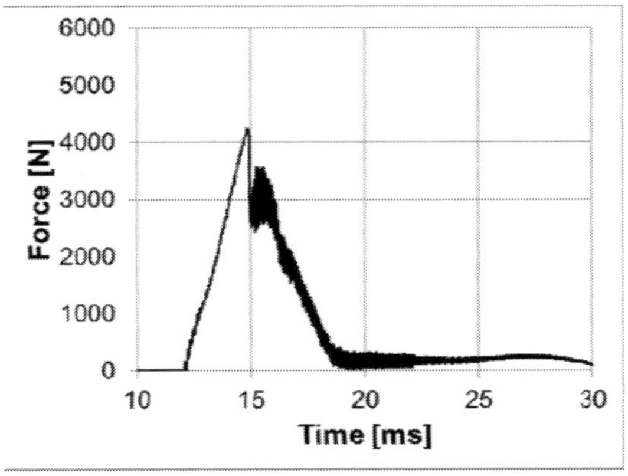

Fig. 3. ABS force record in time after temperature and humidity loading.

From the Figure 2 and 3 it is clearly visible that ABS after temperature and humidity load has lower impact resistance because the small force for penetration is needed.

In Figure 4 it is visible that the smaller impact force is needed for ABS penetration after humidity and temperature load. The difference is 959 N. The similar material behaviour is also in Figure 5 where the all consumed work in J is displayed, there is the difference 3,5 J.

In Figure 6 and 7 the up and side view before climate test is displayed. From the pictures it is clear that the growth of the main crack continuing around the edge occurs.

In Figure 8 and 9 the up and side view after climate test is displayed. In comparison with the crack growth before climate test it is visible, that after lowering of the impact resistance caused by temperature and humidity load the crack growth differs.

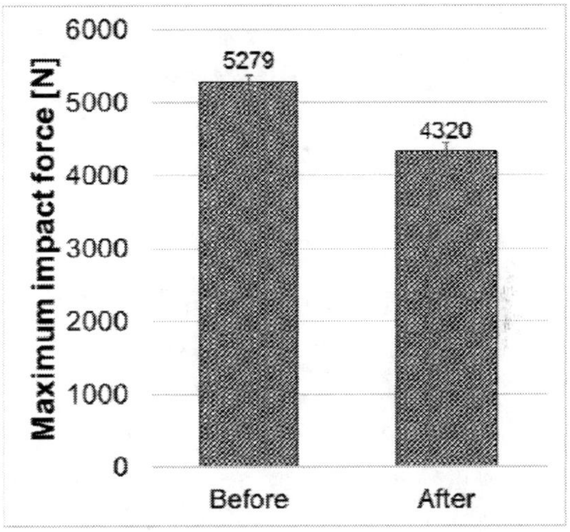

Fig. 4. ABS maximum impact force before and after temperature and humidity loading.

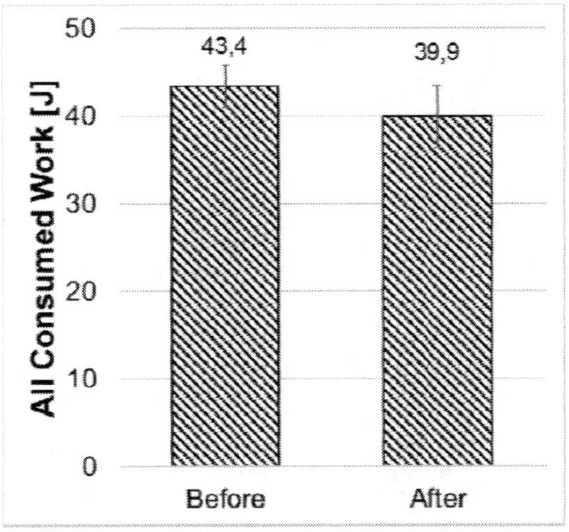

Fig. 5. ABS all consumed work before and after temperature and humidity loading.

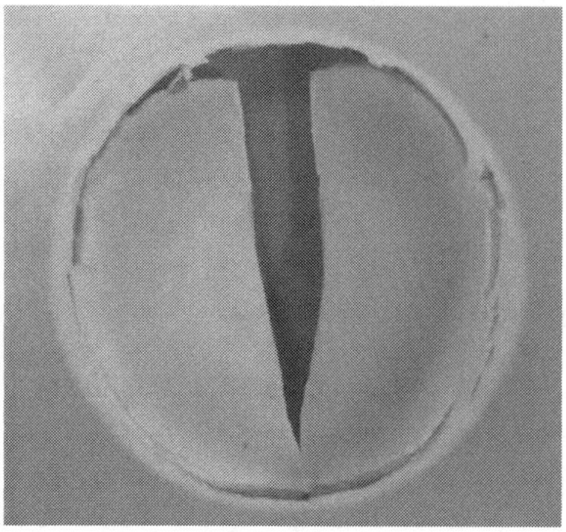

Fig. 6. ABS deformation after drop weight test at 100 J before climate test (up view).

Fig. 7. ABS deformation after drop weight test at 100 J before climate test (side view).

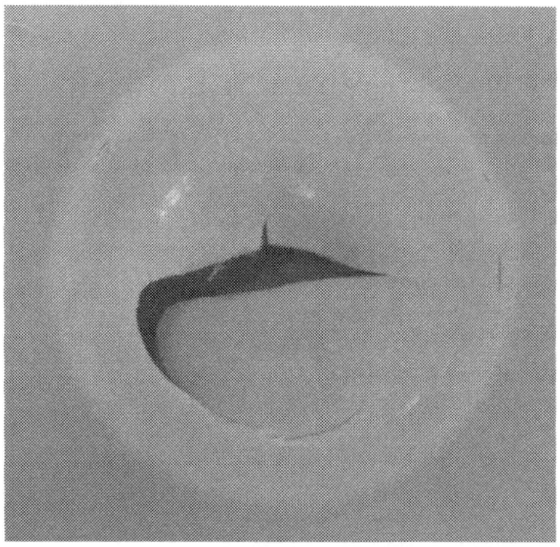

Fig. 8. ABS deformation after drop weight test at 100 J after climate test (up view).

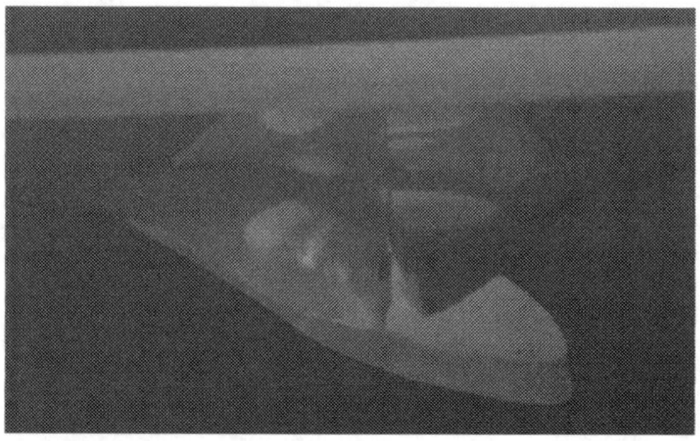

Fig. 9 ABS deformation after drop weight test at 100 J after climate test (side view).

4 Summary

In this study the injection moulded ABS samples were subjected the test of falling penetrator at fall height 100 J after and before temperature and humidity load. The results show that after 168 hours in environment at temperature 75 °C and humidity 98 % the material does not have the same properties as before load. The impact resistance decreased significantly.

Acknowledgment

This paper is supported by the internal grant of TBU in Zlin No. IGA/FT/2017/010 funded from the resources of specific university research and by the Ministry of Education, Youth and Sports of the Czech Republic within the National Sustainability Programme project No. LO1303 (MSMT-7778/2014) and also by the European Regional Development Fund under the project CEBIA-Tech No. CZ.1.05/2.1.00/03.0089.

References

1. H. Polli, L.A.M. Pontes, A.S. Araujo, J.M.F. Barros, V.J. Fernandes Jr., J. Therm. Anal. Calorim. **95** (2009), 131-134
2. S. Olivera, H.B. Muralidhara, K.Venkatesh, K. Gopalakrishna, C.S. Vivek, J. Mater. Sci. **51** (2016), 3657-3674
3. Y. Aoki, Chem. Phys. **7** (2017), 1935-2492
4. F.L. Jin, S.L. Lu, Z.B. Song, J.X. Pang, L. Zhang, J.D. Sun, X.P. Cai, Mater. Sci. Eng., A **527** (2010), 3438-3441
5. M.A. Peydro, F. Parres, R. Navarro, S. Sanches-Caballero, Polym. Eng. Sci. (2014), DOI 10.1002/pen.23680, 1313-1324
6. J. Yang, Ch.X. Wang, Z.S Yu, Y. Li, K.K. Yang, Y.Z. Wang, J. Appl. Polym. Sci. **121** (2011), 2458-2466
7. X.Y. Xu, X.F. Xu, Polym. Eng. Sci. (2011), DOI 10.1002/pen.21908, 902-907

Optimization of fall height setting for drop weight tested polypropylene

Lenka Hylova[1,*], *Miroslav* Manas[1]

[1]Tomas Bata University in Zlin, nam. T. G. Masaryka 5555, 76001 Zlin, Czech Republic

Abstract. This study deals with polypropylene (PP) which was subjected the drop-weight test. PP is a semicrystalline thermoplastic polymer which is commonly used in many indoor applications and also in the automotive industry in the car interiors. The injection moulded PP samples were subjected the penetration test at different fall heights and the results were subsequently evaluated and discussed. It was found out that the fall heights from 100 to 230 J are suitable for PP penetration, but the optimal one is 100 J. Higher heights are not needed because of increasing power consumption of the test device.

1 Introduction

Polypropylene (PP) is a nonpolar thermoplastic semi-crystalline polymer, it is the most consumed polymer globally and has light weight and low density. PP is widely used because of its low cost and being non-toxic and non-hazardous. PP has a great resistance to acids and alkalis, good processing features, electrical insulation, good chemical stability and its bending fatigue resistance is also great. However, PP has low mechanical properties, which is possible to improve by reinforcing with fillers [1, 2].

Siti Rohana Ahmad, Chengzhe Xue and Robert J. Young from United Kingdom dealt with the reinforcement of PP by graphene nanoplatelets (GNP). An average particle diameter of GNP was 15 µm and the average thickness was 6-8 nm. They found out that the blending of GNP to PP led to a huge modification of both mechanical properties and also the microstructure. The thermal stability, the melting temperature and degree of crystallinity were increased. It was found that the Young´s modulus of PP/GNP nanocomposites increased with the loading of GNP [1].

Jia-Horng Lin, Chien-Lin Huang, Chi-Fan Liu, Chih-Kuang Chen, Zheng-Ian Lin and Ching-Wen Lou used as a filler for PP short glass fibres (SGF) and because PP is nonpolar polymer, it was necessary to use a coupling agent for better adhesion between PP and filler. SGF´s average length was 3.2 nm and diameter was 13 µm. This filler was treated with a silane coupling agent. Maleic anhydride grafted polypropylene (PP-g-MA) and maleic anhydride grafted styrene-ethylene-butylene-styrene block copolymer (SEBS-gMA) were used as coupling agents. They blended various amounts of PP, a specified amount of 25 wt% of SGF and 2, 4, 6 or 8 wt% of a coupling agent (PP-g-MA or SEBS-gMA) together to the form different PP/SGF/PP-g-MA blends and PP/SGF/SEBS-g-MA blends and they successfully improved the compatibility between PP and SGF by using previously mentioned coupling agent. The flexural strength, tensile strength, impact strength, compatibility and thermal behaviour were increased. They found out that SGF is a good reinforcing fibre and the connection of 25 wt% of SGF improves the flexural, tensile and impact strengths of PP [2].

Because PP presents low mechanical performance and low impact resistance at temperatures below its glass transition, it is beneficial to create PP blends with elastomeric compounds. The scientists from Mexico dealt with one of these types of blend, namely with PP/EVA (poly[ehtylene-co-(vinyl acetate)]) blend and they studied the effect of compatibilizers on the impact behaviour of this blend. They found out the relationship between the impact resistance and both EVA concentration in the blend and particle size of the dispersed EVA phase. In content of 40 % of EVA in the blend, the impact resistance increased of more than 270 % with the addition of 6.2 phr of compatibilizers at ambient temperature. Moreover, with increasing the compatibilizer content to 10 phr, an additional rise in the impact resistance was obtained [3].

The scientists Lu Wang and Douglas J. Gardner from USA studied the difference between injection moulded PP samples and PP samples created by fused layer modelling (FLM) device. They used two printing process parameters a layer height and extrusion temperature and explored to examine their influence on the Izod impact strength of printed PP samples. The higher proper printing process control, the more similar Izod impact strength to injection moulded PP is. The higher extrusion

* Corresponding author: hylova@utb.cz

temperature and the smaller layer height, the smaller cell sizes and higher degree of diffusion is [4].

Ying-Guo Zhou, Bei Su, Lih-Sheng Turng investigated PP/LDPE blended parts with a chemical blowing agent (CBA). They fabricated super-ductile PP/LDPE blended parts by conventional injection moulding machine with CBA. They found out that PP/LDPE blend tends to create super-ductile parts using the chemical foaming method. They also found out a close relationship between morphological structures which were influenced by the packing pressure and time, dosage of the blowing agent and ratio of the composition and mechanical properties [5].

The Brazilian scientists studied a lignin as a green primary antioxidant for PP and they found out that lignin showed an appropriate dispersion in PP matrix without heterogeneities of the cryogenic fracture surface of test samples. To obtain this dispersion, it is needed to use a twin-screw extruder. They also realized that it is possible to use lignin as a stabilizer for PP exposed to humid and warm conditions [6].

This study deals with pure PP and its impact behaviour. There is a small number about research concentrated on pure PP mechanical behaviour. It is important to know well the mechanical behaviour of pure PP and then it is possible to improve the properties using some filler or some kind of polymer modification.

2 Experimental

Polypropylene was used as the basic polymer material (TATREN, IM 25-75). An ARBURG Allrounder 470H Advance Injection moulding machine was used for sample preparation, with the processing conditional to comply with polypropylene (PP) producer's recommendations, as can be seen in Tab. 1. The samples were in the shape of plates with dimensions 100×100×3 mm according to ISO 6603-2.

Injection moulded polypropylene samples were tested on drop weight test machine Zwick HIT230F according to ISO 6603-2 at ambient temperature 23 °C. As a main parameter was used fall height, which was optimized. However, for easier explanation in this article is used impact energy, which is calculated from fall height, weight and gravity acceleration constant. 15 samples at each height (30, 50, 100, 150, 200 and 230 J) were tested and then maximum impact force was statisticaly evaluated in program TestExpert II and MiniTab. At the end crack surface after the test of each height was evaluated.

Table 1: Setting of injection moulding machine parameters.

Injection Parameters	Values
Injection Pressure [MPa]	70
Injection velocity [mm.s^{-1}]	50
Holding Pressure [MPa]	60
Cooling Time [s]	20
Mould Temperature [°C]	30
Melt Temperature [°C]	225

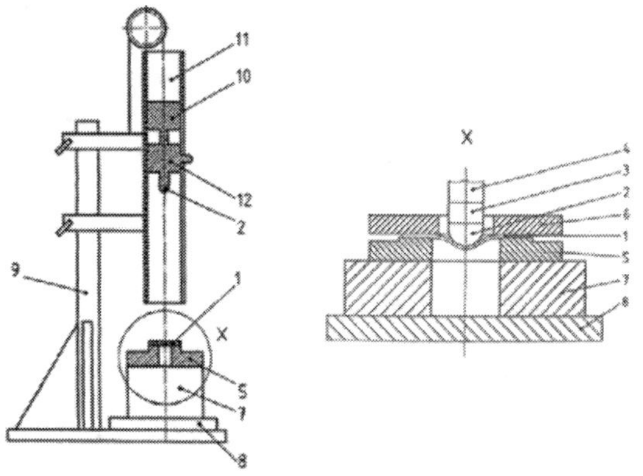

Fig. 1. Falling-dart system.

1 – Test specimen; 2 – Hemispherical striker tip 10 mm; 3 – Force sensor; 4 – Shaft; 5 – Test specimen support; 6 – Clamping ring (optional); 7 – Base; 8 – Acoustic isolation (optional); 9 – Stand for falling-dart system; 10 – Holding and release system for weighted striker; 11 – Guide shaft for weighted striker; 12 – Weighted striker 23,77 kg.

3 Results and discussion

This study is concentrated on optimization of fall high

Table 2. PP statistical evaluation of the maximum force at the height of the fall.

Set energy of fall [J] / Statistical characteristics [N]	30	50	100	150	200	230
Number of measurements	15	15	15	15	15	15
Arithmetic mean	3296	3556	3716	3768	3820	3850
Type error A	1	4	4	8	5	5
Standard deviation	5	13	12	24	16	16
Minimum value	3289	3540	3701	3728	3804	3822
Median	3296	3553	3712	3773	3813	3851
Maximum value	3304	3578	3739	3801	3844	3868
Variation range	14	38	38	73	40	47

DOI: 10.1051/matecconf/201712502049

during drop weight test of PP. Injection moulded PP samples were penetrated by penetrator with fall heights in the range from 30 to 230 J and the results were subsequently evaluated. The conditions of injection moulding are displayed in Table 1 and PP statistical evaluation of the measurements is shown in Table 2.

3.1. Maximum impact force

The height of fall was set at all measurements differently and the results are then discussed.

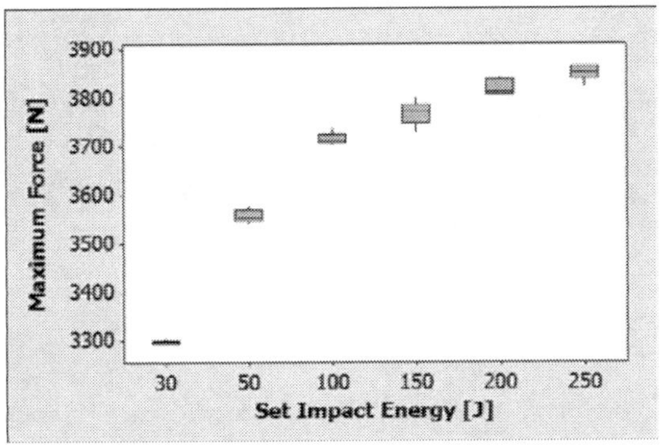

Fig. 2. PP Boxplot graph of maximum force at fall height.

In Figure 2 the maximum force at fall height is displayed. At the height of 30, the sample was not penetrated, there occurs just plastic deformation. It is probably caused by too small fall height for penetration of this material. Penetration occurred at 50 J, but the force is smaller than at the material with the higher fall height what can be caused by the friction of the penetration along the material. Because of that the value 100 J looks like the optimal fall height, because there the penetration occurs and the variation range is small. At the heights from 150 to 230 J the penetrations are also, but it is not needed to use these heights because of increasing power consumption of the test device.

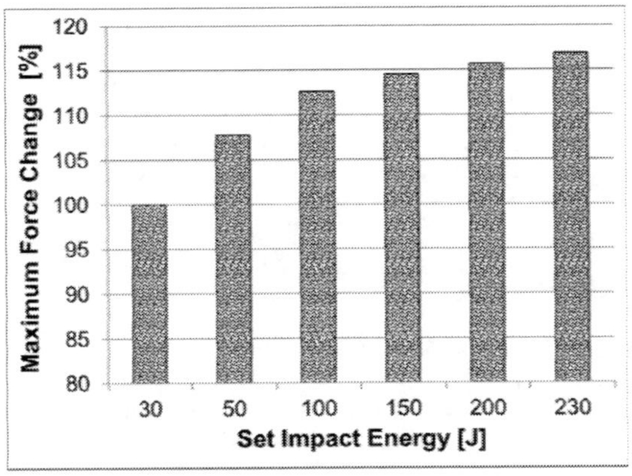

Fig. 3. PP percentage change in maximum force to the prescribed base energy of fall 30 J.

The force change in % during the test can be seen in Figure 3. The changes move in 17 % from the sample with no penetration to last penetrated sample. The sample with the optimal fall height 100 J in comparison with the first penetrated sample at 50 J shows the change around 6 %. The last penetrated sample´s height 230 J increases by 4 % in comparison with the sample with the optimal fall height 100 J. Also in this case it is enough to use the fall height 100 J for the sample penetration.

3.2. Deformation after the test

After the drop weight test the samples were photographed for better idea about the crack growth.

Fig. 4. PP deformation after drop weight test at 30 J.

In Figure 4 it is clearly shown that the material was not penetrated because of too small fall height needed for penetration.

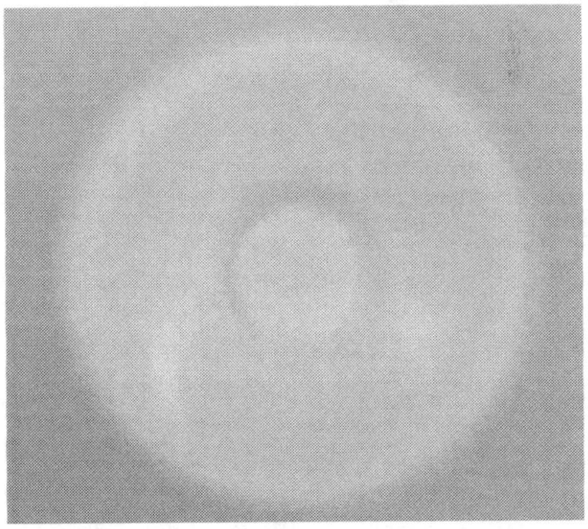

Fig. 5. PP deformation after drop weight test at 50 J.

From Figure 5 to Figure 9 the crack growth at different fall heights can be seen. The crack growth is similar at all samples, because all these fall heights were high enough for this material penetration. However, the fall height 100 J looks like optimal as was already mentioned and explained above.

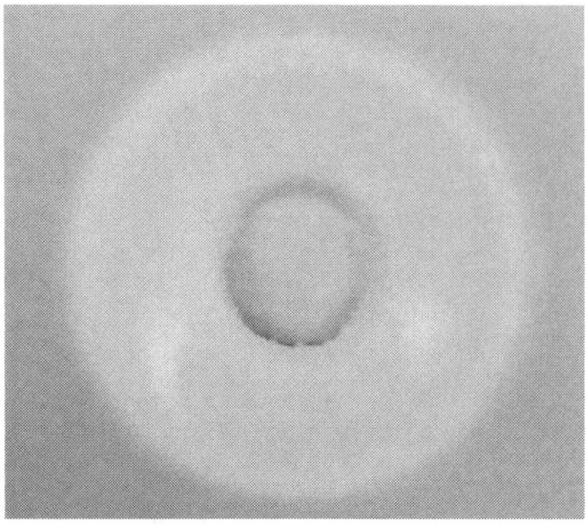

Fig. 6. PP deformation after drop weight test at 100 J.

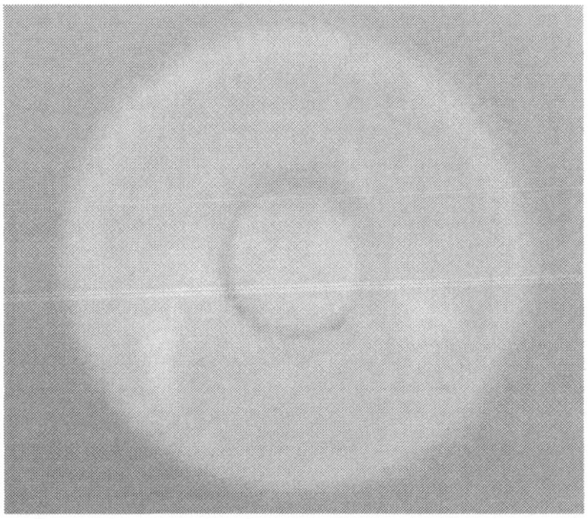

Fig. 7. PP deformation after drop weight test at 150 J.

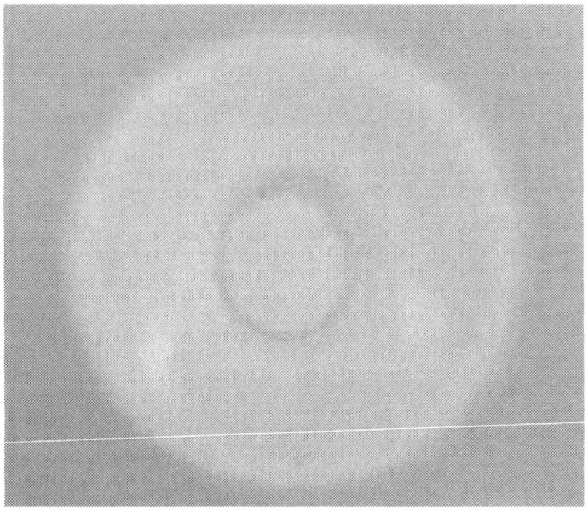

Fig. 8. PP deformation after drop weight test at 200 J.

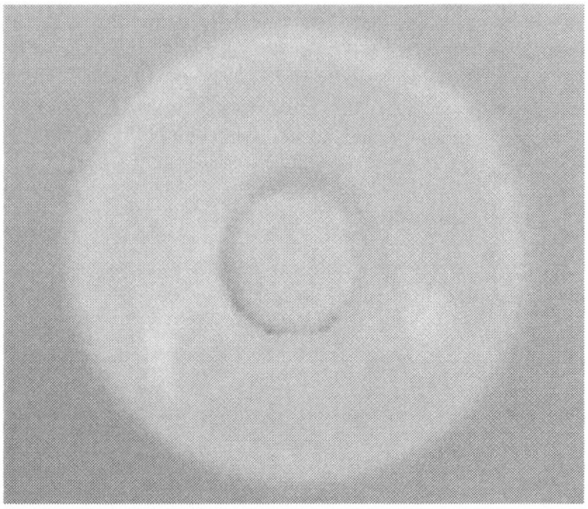

Fig. 9. PP deformation after drop weight test at 230 J.

4 Summary

In this study the injection moulded PP samples were subjected the test of falling penetrator at different fall heights. The range of fall heights was from 30 to 230 J. At the value of fall height 30 J the sample was not penetrated because of too small fall height. The value 50 J was enough for the sample penetration but was smaller than it was expected which could be caused by the friction of the penetrator along the material during the test. From 50 to 230 J the material was always penetrated, but the values from 150 to 230 J are not needed to use because of increasing power consumption of the test device. The conclusion of this study is that the fall height 100 J is the optimal for the penetration of PP material.

Acknowledgment

This paper is supported by the internal grant of TBU in Zlin No. IGA/FT/2017/010 funded from the resources of specific university research and by the Ministry of Education, Youth and Sports of the Czech Republic within the National Sustainability Programme project No. LO1303 (MSMT-7778/2014) and also by the European Regional Development Fund under the project CEBIA-Tech No. CZ.1.05/2.1.00/03.0089.

References

1. S.R. Ahmad, C. Xue, R.J. Young, Mater. Sci. Eng. B **216** (2017), 2-9
2. J.H. Lin, C.L. Huang, C.F. Liu, C.K. Chen, Z.I. Lin, C.W. Lou, Materials **8** (2015), 8279-8291
3. A. Maciel, v. Salas, O. Manero, Adv. Polym. Tech. **24** (2005), 241-252
4. L. Wang, D.J. Gardner, Polymer **13** (2017), 74-80
5. Y.G. Zhou, B. Su, L.S. Turng, J. Appl. Polym. Sci. (2016), DOI 10.1002/app.44101
6. R. Gadioli, W.R. Waldman, M.A. de Paoli, J. Appl. Polym. Sci. (2016), DOI 10.1002/app.43558

DOI: 10.1051/matecconf/201712502050

Impact resistance of high-density polyethylene against falling penetrator with different potential energy

Ales Mizera[1,*], *Petr* Chalupa[1], and *Ivan* Hudec[2]

[1]Tomas Bata University in Zlin, nam. T. G. Masaryka 5555, 76001 Zlin, Czech Republic

[2]Faculty of Chemical and Food Technology STU in Bratislava, Radlinskeho 9, 812 37 Bratislava 1, Slovakia

Abstract. This study deals with high-density polyethylene (HDPE) which was subjected the drop-weight test. HDPE is a semicrystalline thermoplastic polymer which is commonly used in many applications and mainly in the automotive industry because of its properties. The injection moulded HDPE samples were subjected the penetration test at different potential energies and the results were subsequently evaluated and discussed. The samples were tested in the range of potential energies from 30 to 230 J. The first sample penetration occurred at the energy 50 J. It was found out that the potential energy 30 J is too small for penetration of this material, which shows the impact resistance of HDPE.

1 Introduction

Polymers in comparison with small molecules have rare properties that are very often difficult to predict. For dealing with polymeric materials it is desirable to have some knowledge background of the physical chemistry of polymers. For the industrial practice it is important to know the properties such as heat capacity or melt viscosity for establishing polymerization and processing conditions. Polymers are omnipresent and they are used in a huge number of the applications, from consumer products to high-temperature industrial use to medical devices under a wide-range of conditions. Multilayer films, nanomaterials, electronic devices and electro-optical are being developed in modern polymer science for end-use performance evaluation. These applications require much more complex and specialized testing [1].
Polyethylenes are commodity polymers which account for more than 70 % of total plastics consumption and are low cost, easily processable and available. Typical applications of these polymers are packaging, household items, net ropes, medical applications, fishing rods, water pipes, etc. There are many types of polyethylenes, such as linear low density polyethlyene, low density polyethylene, ethyl vinyl acetate copolymer, polyolefinic elastomer, high density polyethylene and more other polyethylenes [2].

In our study is as a material used high density polyethylene (HDPE) because of its material properties such as impermeability to water, chemical resistance, low cost and easy processing, etc. HDPE is a semicrystalline linear thermoplastic polymer which is commonly used for tubing, shrinkable products, electrical insulation, cable jacketing, waterproofing, corrosion protection against corrosion and for many other applications [3].
HDPE is often used in variety of impact strength demanding applications such as pipe protection for oil and gas transportation, load-bearing biomedical implants, liquid food containers, industrial vessels and automotive fuel tanks. HDPE during these applications may be subjected to drop or crash loading. The scientists from Argentina and Austria J.P. Torres, P.M. Frontini, M. Machado and Z. Major proposed and validated a thermomechanical constitutive model that aims to achieve a compromise between formulation simplicity and prediction accuracy. They found out that initial linear elastic response coupled with a temperature-dependent power-law viscoplastic flow element and a non-linear strain-hardening element are appropriate to model biaxial stress scenarios. They provided experimental infrared thermography data connected with digital image correlation to realize temperature development during HDPE deformation at high velocity. A first try was made at modelling HDPE failure using an element effacement technique. A force-time curve and fracture patterns were well predicted. However, they found out that their experimental information obtained in their study is not sufficient and they are going to continue in their study in the future [4].

A.A. Baulin, A.A. Baulin, A.V. Kalandin, N.A. Kudryavtseva from St. Petersburg improved a good stabilization method of HDPE blends during its preparation to obtain significantly increased stress cracking resistance with retention of physicomechanical

* Corresponding author: mizera@utb.cz

properties of the composites which are of a practical importance. They used 0.15 % each of complex antioxidants and light stabiliser together with a copolymer of ethylene with vinyl acetate and linear low-density polyethylene to achieve the stabilization of HDPE blend [5].

The scientists from Iraq dealt with filling of HDPE with lignocellulose (LC), calcium carbonate (CC) and fibre glass (FG) and they studied their mechanical properties. They used 0, 5, 10, 15, 20 and 25 wt% of filling with all three fillers. It was found that LC filler increases mechanical properties as the tensile strength, impact strength, Shore D hardness, Young modulus and elongation in % of HDPE. The composite consisted of HDPE and this filler is eco-friendly, low density and has high mechanical properties [6].

This study may become a big benefit for the deeper knowledge of HDPE behaviour, which can be consequently applied in practice applications.

2 Experimental

High-density polyethylene (HDPE) was used as the basic polymer material (DOW HDPE 25055E). An ARBURG Allrounder 470H Advance Injection molding machine was used for sample preparation, with the processing conditional to comply with high density polyethylene (HDPE) producer's recommendations, as can be seen in Tab. 1. The samples were in the shape of plates with dimensions 100×100×3 mm according to ISO 6603-2.

Table 1: Setting of injection moulding machine parameters.

Injection Parameters	Values
Injection Pressure [MPa]	80
Injection velocity [mm.s^{-1}]	60
Holding Pressure [MPa]	65
Cooling Time [s]	30
Mould Temperature [°C]	30
Melt Temperature [°C]	185

Injection moulded high density polyethylene samples were tested on drop weight test machine Zwick HIT230F according to ISO 6603-2 at ambient temperature 23 °C. As a main parameter was used 30, 50, 100, 150, 200 and 230 J potential energy of penetrator with weight. For each potential energy 15 samples were tested and then maximum impact force was statisticaly evaluated in program TestExpert II and MiniTab. At the end crack surface after the test of each height was evaluated.

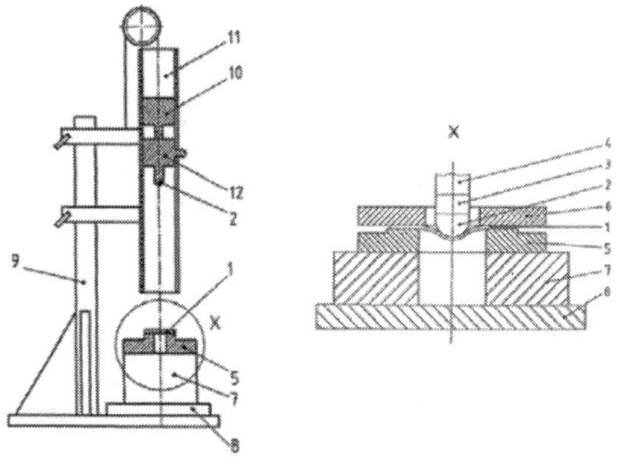

Fig. 1. Falling-dart system.

1 – Test specimen; 2 – Hemispherical striker tip 10 mm; 3 – Force sensor; 4 – Shaft; 5 – Test specimen support; 6 – Clamping ring (optional); 7 – Base; 8 – Acoustic isolation (optional); 9 – Stand for falling-dart system; 10 – Holding and release system for weighted striker; 11 – Guide shaft for weighted striker; 12 – Weighted striker 23,77 kg.

3 Results and discussion

This study is concentrated on impact resistance of HDPE against penetrator with different potential energies. Injection moulded HDPE samples were penetrated by penetrator with potential energies in the range from 30 to 230 J and the results were subsequently evaluated. The conditions of injection moulding are displayed in Table 1 and HDPE statistical evaluation of the measurements is shown in Table 2.

3.1. Maximum impact force

The energy of fall was set at all measurements differently and the results are then discussed.

Table 2. HDPE statistical evaluation of the maximum force at the energy of the fall.

Set energy of fall [J] / Statistical characteristics [N]	30	50	100	150	200	230
Number of measurements	15	15	15	15	15	15
Arithmetic mean	3554	3675	3780	3840	3754	3890
Type error A	2	3	3	9	18	18
Standard deviation	7	9	10	27	56	55
Minimum value	3543	3655	3761	3768	3657	3786
Median	3553	3675	3783	3853	3767	3918
Maximum value	3564	3688	3792	3899	3851	3929
Variation range	21	33	32	80	194	143

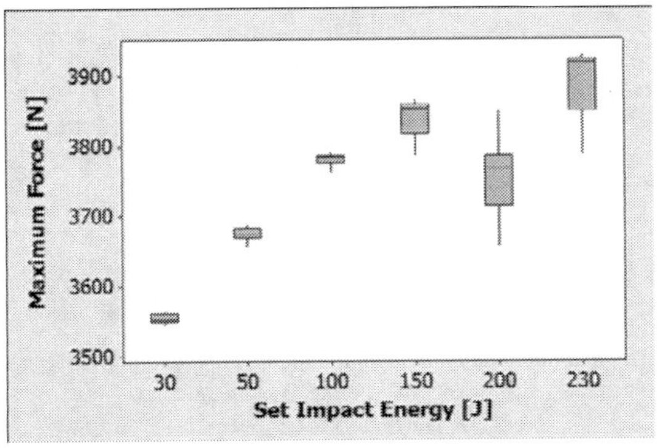

Fig. 2. HDPE Boxplot graph of maximum force at potential energy.

In Figure 2 the maximum force at potential energy is displayed. At the energy of 30, the sample was not penetrated, there occurs just plastic deformation. It is probably caused by too small potential energy for penetration of this material. Penetration occurred at 50 J, but the force is smaller than at the material with the higher impact energy what can be caused by the friction of the penetration along the material. Because of that the value 100 J looks like the optimal potential energy, because there the penetration occurs and the variation range is small. At the energies from 150 to 230 the penetrations are also, but the variation ranges at these measurements are too high.

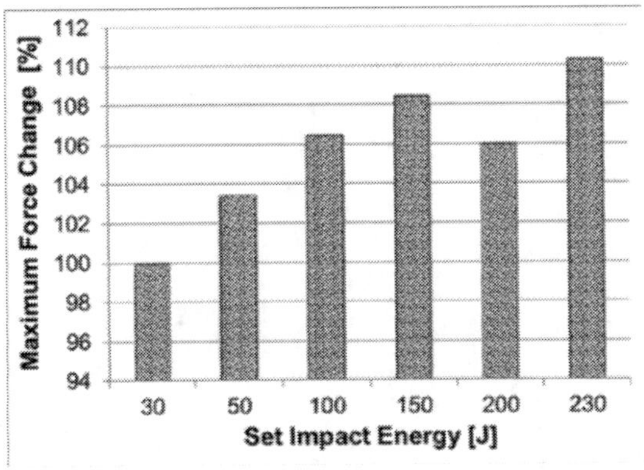

Fig. 3. HDPE percentage change in maximum force to the prescribed base energy of fall 30 J.

The force change in % during the test can be seen in Figure 3. The changes move in 10 % from the sample with no penetration to last penetrated sample. The sample with the optimal impact energy 100 J in comparison with the first penetrated sample at 50 J shows the change around 3 %. The last penetrated sample´s energy 230 J increases by 3 % in comparison with the sample with the optimal potential energy 100 J.

3.2. Deformation after the test

After the drop weight test the samples were photographed for better idea about the crack growth.

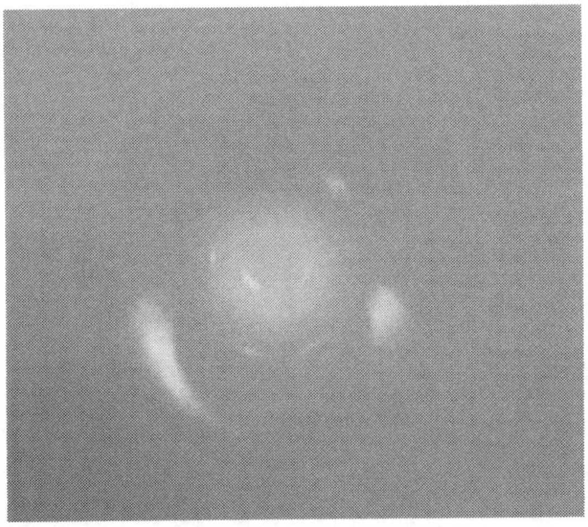

Fig. 4. HDPE deformation after drop weight test at 30 J.

In Figure 4 it is clearly shown that the material was not penetrated because of too small potential energy needed for penetration.

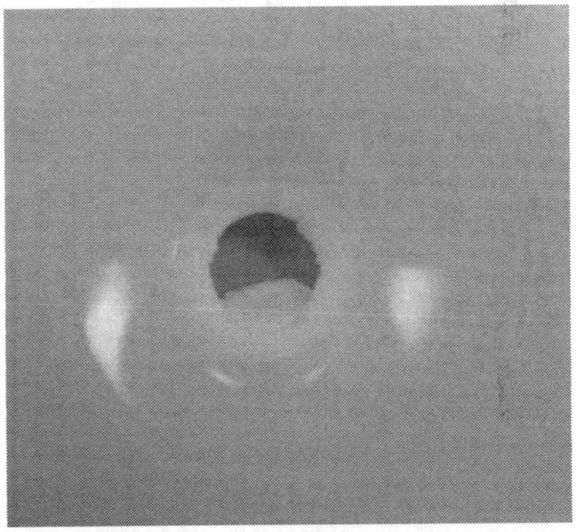

Fig. 5. HDPE deformation after drop weight test at 50 J.

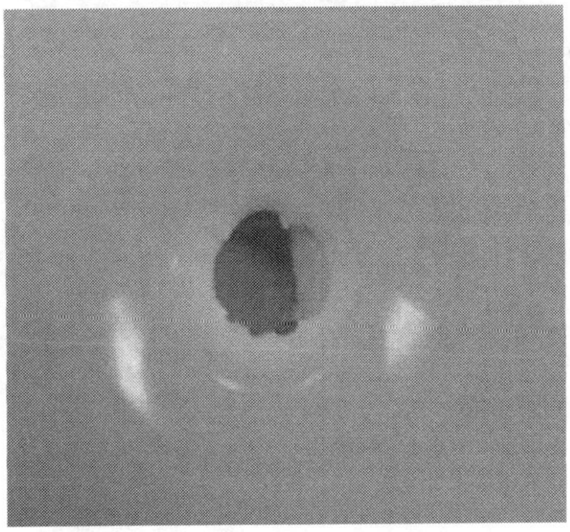

Fig. 6. HDPE deformation after drop weight test at 100 J.

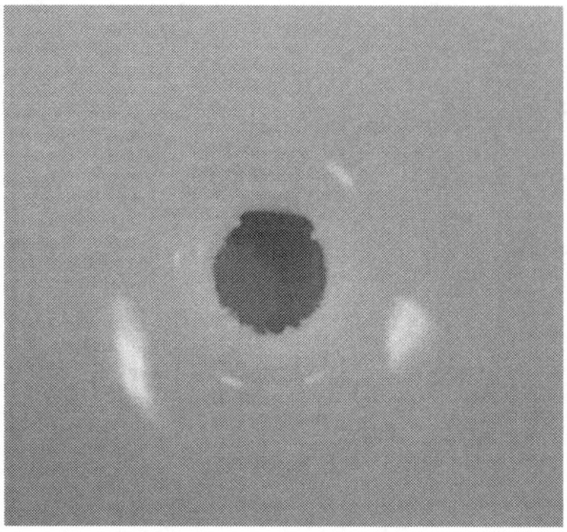

Fig. 7. HDPE deformation after drop weight test at 150 J.

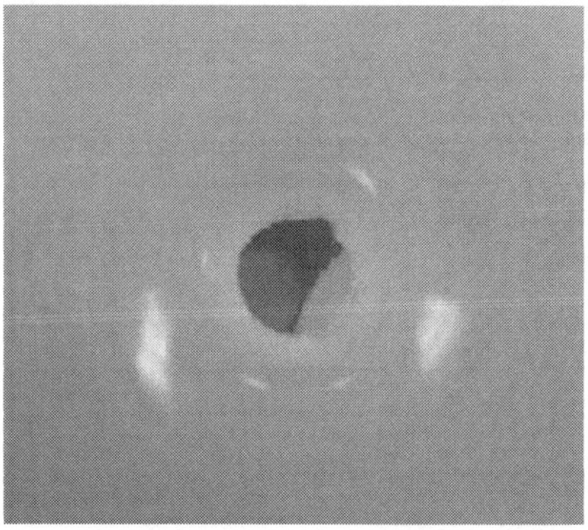

Fig. 8. HDPE deformation after drop weight test at 200 J.

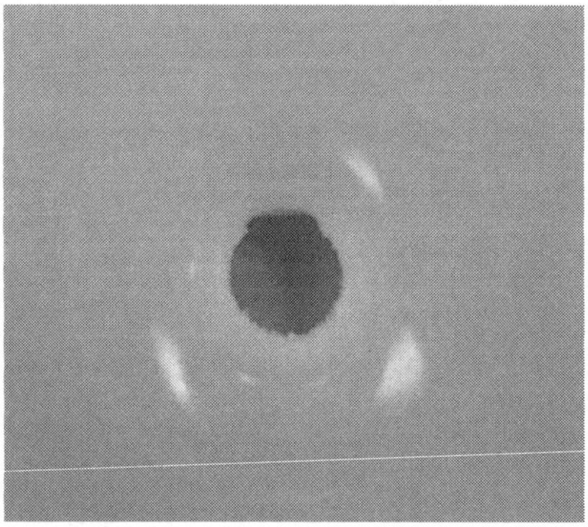

Fig. 9. HDPE deformation after drop weight test at 230 J.

From Figure 5 to Figure 9 the crack growth at different potential energies can be seen. The crack growth is similar at all samples, because all these potential energies were high enough for this material penetration. However, the potential energy 100 J looks like optimal as was already mentioned and explained above.

4 Summary

In this study the injection moulded HDPE samples were subjected the test of falling penetrator at different potential energies. The range of potential energies was from 30 to 230 J. At the value of potential energy 30 J the sample was not penetrated because of too small energy. The value 50 J was enough for the sample penetration but was smaller than it was expected which could be caused by the friction of the penetrator along the material during the test. From 50 to 230 J the material was always penetrated, but the values from 150 to 230 J had too high variation ranges. The conclusion of this study is that the potential energy 100 J is the optimal for the penetration of HDPE material and the lowest potential energy for penetration is 50 J.

Acknowledgment

This paper is supported by the internal grant of TBU in Zlin No. IGA/FT/2017/010 and funded from the resources of specific university research and by the Ministry of Education, Youth and Sports of the Czech Republic within the National Sustainability Programme project No. LO1303 (MSMT-7778/2014) and also by the European Regional Development Fund under the project CEBIA-Tech No. CZ.1.05/2.1.00/03.0089.

References

1. B. Ellis, R. Smith, Polymers: a property database. 2nd ed. Boca Raton, Fla.: CRC Press/Taylor & Francis Group, **12** (2009), ISBN 9781420005707.
2. S.M. Tamboli, S.T. Mhaske, D.D. Kale, Indian J. Chem. Technol. **11** (2004) 853-864.
3. H.A. Khonakdar, J. Morshedian, M. Mehrabzadeh, U. Wagenknecht, S.H. Jafari, Eur. Polym. J. **39** (2003) 1729-1734.
4. J.P. Torres, P.M. Frontini, M. Machado, Z. Major, Int. J. Impact. Eng. **98** (2016), 52-61
5. A.A. Baulin, A.A. Baulin, A.V. Kalandin, N.A. Kudryavtseva, Int. Pol. Sc. Tech. **43** (2015), 21-25
6. M.N. Khalaf, J. Saudi. Chem. Soc. **19** (2019), 88-91

Influence of fall height on high impact polystyrene deformation and characteristics of drop weight test

Ales Mizera[1,*], *Petr* Chalupa[1], and *Ivan* Hudec[2]

[1]Tomas Bata University in Zlin, nam. T. G. Masaryka 5555, 76001 Zlin, Czech Republic

[2]Faculty of Chemical and Food Technology STU in Bratislava, Radlinskeho 9, 812 37 Bratislava 1, Slovakia

Abstract. This study deals with high impact polystyrene (HIPS) which was subjected the drop-weight test. HIPS is a polymer produced by the reaction between butadiene synthetic elastomer and styrene (5-14 %) which contains the crystal polymer in certain amounts and is commonly used in mechanical engineering applications where machine parts are exposed to impact loading. The injection moulded HIPS samples were subjected the penetration test at different fall heights and the results were subsequently evaluated and discussed. It was found out that all fall heights are suitable for HIPS penetration, but the optimal one is 50 J because of the smallest variation range. Higher heights are not needed because of increasing power consumption of the test device. From the results, it is clear, that HIPS is not so highly impact resistant material as for example HDPE, because of that is this material suitable for applications where is not often exposed to too big impacts at high velocities.

1 Introduction

After adding of an elastomer, brittle polystyrene (PS) becomes more ductile. This is how high impact polystyrene (HIPS) arises. HIPS is one of the first toughened systems. In 1948 a process of adding elastomers to rigid plastics in order to increase their fracture resistance was firstly used. The big success of HIPS led to the development of similar blends. HIPS is a polymer produced by the reaction between butadiene synthetic elastomer and styrene (5-14 %) which contains the crystal polymer in certain amounts. This polymer has higher impact resistant in comparison with unfilled PS and it is also durable against organic liquids, solid oils and liquid oils. End-use properties of HIPS are dependent on many factors such as the concentration and composition, particle size and distribution of the rubber. It has been found out that one of the main factors which affect the impact strength and toughness of this material is the rubber-phase size distribution and particle size. HIPS is mostly used in mechanical engineering applications where machine parts are exposed to impact loading [1-3].

The scientists from Turkey studied the effect of previous impacts on the impact behaviour of HIPS. They measured instrumented Charpy impact tests and set the falling angles of Charpy hammer as 5, 10, 13, 15, 16, 17, 18, 19 and 20 °. It was realized that there was noticeable crack propagation at 20 °. Subsequently, all samples were put into the impact tester and fractured by the Charpy hammer again, but this time at angle of 35 °. The scientists called this impact as "final impact". The sample which was firstly impacted at 20 ° was fractured during the final impact with a very small energy. This small energy the tester could not measure. It was also found out that crack initiation energies were almost the same for each sample, unlike crack propagation energies increased for the samples previously impacted at 5 and 10 ° [2].

Jin Hwan Choi, Kyung Hyun Ahn and Sang Yong Kim studied how the graft degree affects the tensile and dynamic behaviour of HIPS, they found out that the tensile modulus and the yield stress decrease with the graft degree up to 120 % and then increase. The earlier part of this behaviour occurs because of the increase in the stress transferred to the rubber particles and the latter part arrives from huge occlusions which are not enclosed by rubber layers. It was also revealed that the degree of graft depresses the moves of the rubber chain and because of that the glass transition temperature increases [4].

V. Serpoosha, S. Zokae and R. Bagheri dealt with the rubber particle cavitation in HIPS and its influence on mechanical properties and deformation behaviour of this polymer at various temperatures. The samples were subjected of thermal cycles and the creep behaviour was studied. The creep curve of specimen at – 23 °C and of the ambient temperature had also zero difference, but after lowering the temperature from the ambient temperature to – 44 °C, the creep deformation increased. Three-point-bending test was also measured up to a

* Corresponding author: mizera@utb.cz

constant load of 200 N. During cooling from the ambient temperature to − 20 °C, the load-displacement curve shifts to the left, it shows that the cooled material is more rigid than the control specimen. The Charpy impact test showed that the Charpy impact strength decreases with an increasing cavitation degree in cooled HIPS specimens and the zones of notch-tip damage in three-point-bending specimens become larger [5].

It is also possible to fill the HIPS with fibres. A team of scientists from Argentina and Spain dealt with HIPS reinforcement with short sisal fibres and with mechanical behaviour of HIPS after this type of filling. They found out that the sisal fibres in HIPS caused an increasing trend in stiffness, while deformation at break and tensile strength decreased. It was probably caused by the poor adhesion between fibres and polymeric matrix. All composites of polymeric matrix and sisal fibres displayed ductile behaviour under both impact loading and quasi-static conditions and in composites, impact fracture toughness decreased in comparison with the polymeric matrix [6].

This study becomes a big benefit for the practice, because it is concentrated on the observation of crack growth an on HIPS behaviour during this process.

2 Experimental

Polystyrene was used as the basic polymer material (EDISTIR SR 550 07). An ARBURG Allrounder 470H Advance Injection moulding machine was used for sample preparation, with the processing conditional to comply with polystyrene (PS) producer's recommendations, as can be seen in Tab. 1. The samples were in the shape of plates with dimensions 100×100×3 mm according to ISO 6603-2.

Table 1. Setting of injection moulding machine parameters.

Injection Parameters	Values
Injection Pressure [MPa]	70
Injection velocity [mm.s^{-1}]	50
Holding Pressure [MPa]	60
Cooling Time [s]	20
Mould Temperature [°C]	30
Melt Temperature [°C]	225

Injection moulded polystyrene samples were tested on drop weight test machine Zwick HIT230F according to ISO 6603-2 at ambient temperature 23 °C. As a main parameter was used fall height, however this parameter was re-calculated on impact energy, which was set on the machine. 15 samples at each height (30, 50, 100, 150, 200 and 230 J) were tested and then maximum impact force was statisticaly evaluated in program TestExpert II and MiniTab. At the end crack surface after the test of each height was evaluated.

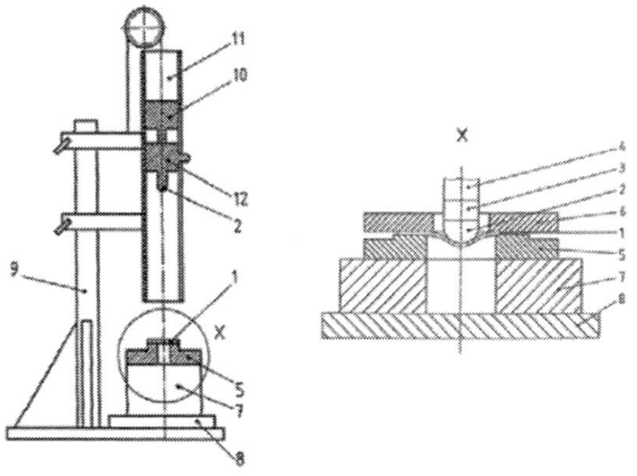

Fig. 1. Falling-dart system.

1 – Test specimen; 2 – Hemispherical striker tip 10 mm; 3 – Force sensor; 4 – Shaft; 5 – Test specimen support; 6 – Clamping ring (optional); 7 – Base; 8 – Acoustic isolation (optional); 9 – Stand for falling-dart system; 10 – Holding and release system for weighted striker; 11 – Guide shaft for weighted striker; 12 – Weighted striker 23,77 kg.

3 Results and discussion

This study is concentrated on the influence of fall height on high impact polystyrene deformation. Injection moulded HIPS samples were penetrated by penetrator with fall heights in the range from 30 to 230 J and the results were subsequently evaluated. The conditions of injection moulding are displayed in Table 1 and HIPS statistical evaluation of the measurements is shown in Table 2.

3.1. Maximum impact force

The height of fall was set at all measurements differently and the results are then discussed.

Table 2. HIPS statistical evaluation of the maximum force at the height of the fall.

Set energy of fall [J] / Statistical characteristics [N]	30	50	100	150	200	230
Number of measurements	15	15	15	15	15	15
Arithmetic mean	2171	2246	2228	2245	2209	2186
Type error A	16	8	9	10	9	9
Standard deviation	50	25	29	33	27	27
Minimum value	2073	2207	2180	2187	2177	2160
Median	2188	2251	2232	2245	2200	2179
Maximum value	2227	2273	2267	2307	2251	2243
Variation range	154	67	86	119	74	83

DOI: 10.1051/matecconf/201712502051

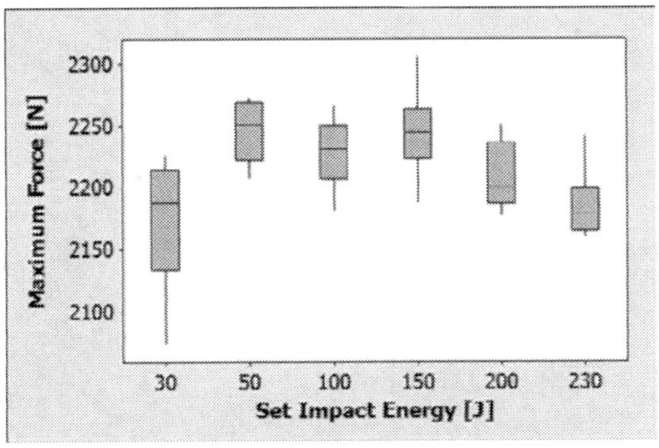

Fig. 2. HIPS Boxplot graph of maximum force at fall height.

In Figure 2 the maximum force at fall height is displayed. Penetration occurred at all fall heights of this material. The value 50 J looks like the optimal fall height, because the variation range is there the smallest. It is not needed to use higher heights because of increasing power consumption of the test device.

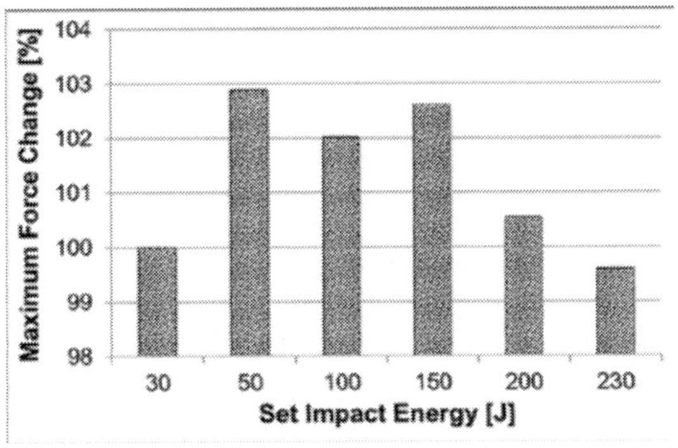

Fig. 3. HIPS percentage change in maximum force to the prescribed base energy of fall 30 J.

The force change in % during the test can be seen in Figure 3. The changes move in 3 % from the sample with fall height 230 J and 50 J. The sample with the optimal fall height 50 J in comparison with 230 J shows the change around 3 %. Also in this case it is enough to use the fall height 50 J for the sample penetration.

3.1. Deformation after the test

After the drop weight test the samples were photographed for better idea about the crack growth.

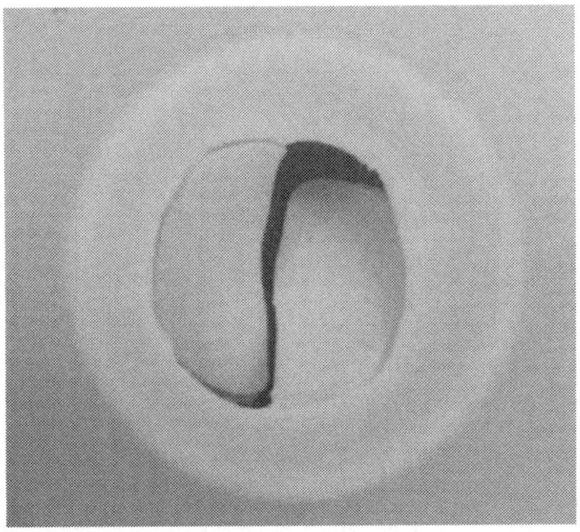

Fig. 4. HIPS deformation after drop weight test at 30 J.

In Figure 4 the growth of the main crack continuing around the edge is displayed.

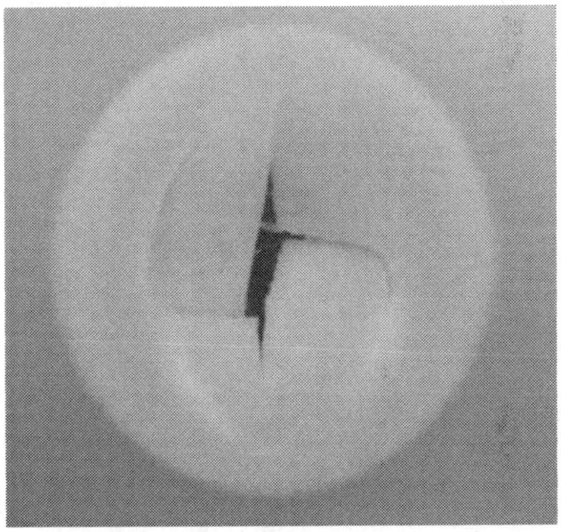

Fig. 5. HIPS deformation after drop weight test at 50 J.

In Figure 5 the growth of the main crack and perpendicular crack with continuing around the edge is shown.

In Figure 6 and 7 the growth of the main crack and perpendicular crack with brake around the edge on one side is shown.

In Figure 8 and 9 there is clearly visible that these fall heights cause complete hole in the sample which copies the penetrator shape.

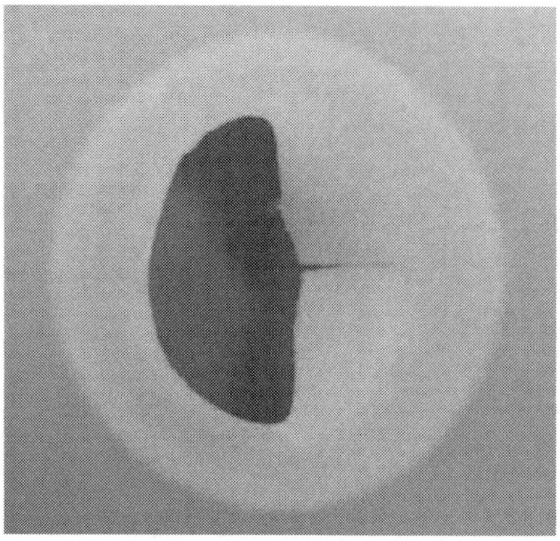

Fig. 6. HIPS deformation after drop weight test at 100 J.

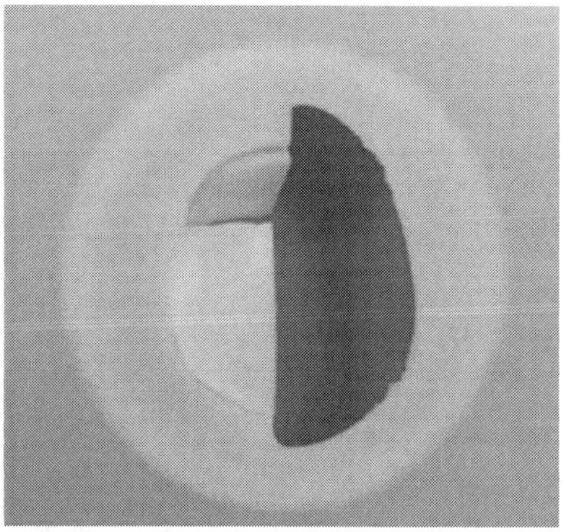

Fig. 7. HIPS deformation after drop weight test at 150 J.

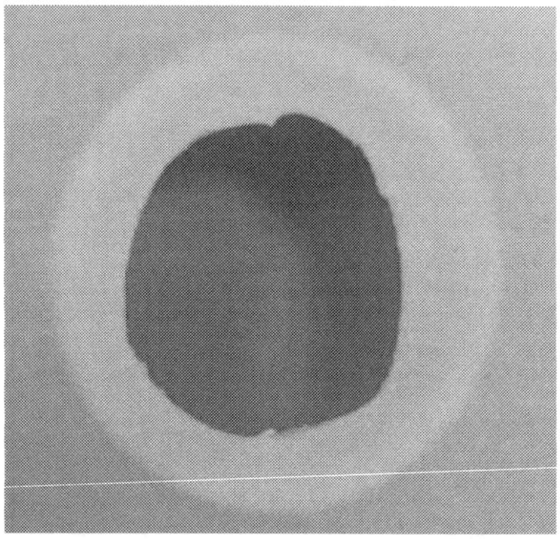

Fig. 8. HIPS deformation after drop weight test at 200 J.

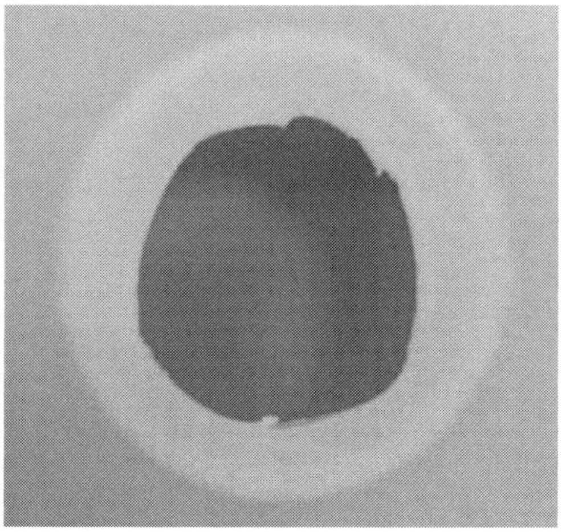

Fig. 9. HIPS deformation after drop weight test at 230 J.

4 Summary

In this study the injection moulded HIPS samples were subjected the test of falling penetrator at different fall heights. The range of fall heights was from 30 to 230 J. All these fall height cause the sample penetration. The value 50 J looks like the optimal because of the smallest variation range. The values from 100 to 230 J are not needed to use because of increasing power consumption of the test device. The conclusion of this study is that the fall height 50 J is the optimal for the penetration of HIPS.

Acknowledgment

This paper is supported by the internal grant of TBU in Zlin No. IGA/FT/2017/010 funded from the resources of specific university research and by the Ministry of Education, Youth and Sports of the Czech Republic within the National Sustainability Programme project No. LO1303 (MSMT-7778/2014) and also by the European Regional Development Fund under the project CEBIA-Tech No. CZ.1.05/2.1.00/03.0089.

References

1. T.V. Khanh, Theor. Appl. Fract. Mec. **29** (1998), 75-83
2. T. Sahin, T. Sinmazcelik, A. Arici. J. Mater. Sci. **39** (2004), 2543-2546
3. T. Yilmaz, T. Sahin, T. Sinmazcelik, J. Mater. Sci **44** (2009), DOI 10.1007/s10853-009-3640-3, 4308-4314
4. J.H. Choi, K.H. Ahn, S.Y. Kim, Polymer **41** (2000), 5229-5235
5. V. Serpooshan, S. Zokaei, R. Bagheri, J. Appl. Polym. Sci. **104** (2007), 1110-1117
6. P. Antich, A. Vázquez, I. Mondragon, C. Bernal, Composites: Part A **37** (2006), 139-150

Effect of Pigment Concentration on Mechanical Properties of Polycarbonate

Vaclav Janostik[1,*] and *Vojtech* Senkerik[1]

[1] *Tomas Bata University in Zlin, TGM 5555, 760 01 Zlin, Czech Republic*

Abstract. This experimental study deals with the influence of pigments on the mechanical properties of polymeric polycarbonate material Lexan 923c, which is commonly used in industry and is being processed with injection technology. This material was stained with three different pigments from Lifokolor. It was also stained with 6 different concentrations of selected pigments. Emphasis was placed on measuring the tensile strength, impact strength and hardness of polyurethane mixtures.

1 Introduction

Nowadays polymeric materials are irreplaceable in many industries. They are exclusive material for their mechanical properties and shaping capabilities. To obtain higher effectivity of production, a number of complicated parts is made by injection technology. Often, customer requirements are too high. Above all, the biggest problem is adhering to the desired color range and the mechanical properties of the part. Therefore, compromise between materials and pigments should be found.

There are several basic color methods. However, these methods are associated with the final process. We are focusing on the injection process, which has a high ability to reproduce complicated parts.

The granulate for injection can be colored in a dry manner. This is a direct mixing of the natural granulate with the pigments in the mixing device. Thereafter, this prepared mixture is transferred in the hopper of the injection moulding machine. The distribution of the colored concentrate of this mixture is not perfect. Even further strained and sedimentation of the colored concentrate is observed due to the shock of the injection unit. Therefore, this method is suitable for products with lower demands on color accuracy. To obtain more precise distribution of color concentrate, bulk or mass dispensers are used.

The colored concentrate consists of a polymeric carrier which is miscible with the polymer. In the polymeric carrier, the pigment is incorporated up to 90%. The final colour effect must be consist with the customer's requirements. The way of dosing and mixing of the coloured concentrate is important for desired values of the colour shade. The way of dosing is also very important for the final mechanical properties of the part.

2 Methods

2.1 Type of polymeric material and pigment

Lexan 923 polycarbonate (PC) from SABIC was selected for studying of mechanical properties. This material is characterized by high impact resistance, it is strong and flexible. Excludes the possibility of cracks. In contact with fire, products become soft and melt, fire is not support and it is not expand. Low weight with good mechanical properties guarantee a long service life. The test specimens were made by injecting this polymeric material with a different concentration of three kinds of pigment colors.

For the coloring of the natural polymeric material, three color pigment types have been used, which are commonly used in industry. These pigments were purchased from LIFOCOLOR s.r.o. in basic color shades. This pigment is stable up to 290 °C

2.2 Formation of the mixture

Dry blending was used for preparing of the mixture. Stirring was always carried out in the exact ratio of Lexan 923 polymer granulate with a certain type of pigment. Mixing systems commonly used in industry were used. The mixtures were mixed in concentrations (1-6)% ; total weight of the final mix was 1500g. The precision laboratory height of the HELAGO HL - 2000i was used for weighing.

Table 1. Formation of the mixture.

$C_{pigment}$	$C_{polymer}$	$m_{pigment}$	$m_{polymer}$	M_{mix}
1%	99%	15g	1485g	1500g
2%	98%	30g	1470g	1500g
3%	97%	45g	1455g	1500g
4%	96%	60g	1440g	1500g
5%	95%	75g	1425g	1500g
6%	94%	90g	1410g	1500g

* Corresponding author: vjanostik@utb.cz

DOI: 10.1051/matecconf/201712502052

2.3 Production of test specimens

The test samples were created by injection molding technology on the ARBURG Allrounder 470H 1000-400 Injector. This machine can be optimally dimensioned for applications of all known injection technologies.

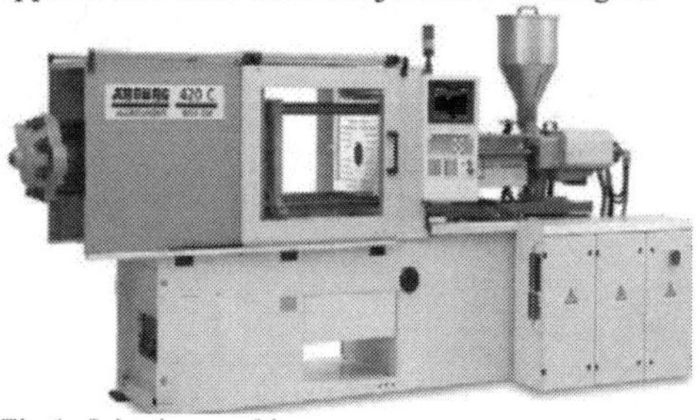

Fig 1. Injection machine

Two types of standardized test bodies were selected. The first body is designed for tensile testing according to ČSN EN ISO 527-1 type 2 and the second body for impact strength is degined according to ČSN EN ISO 179-1

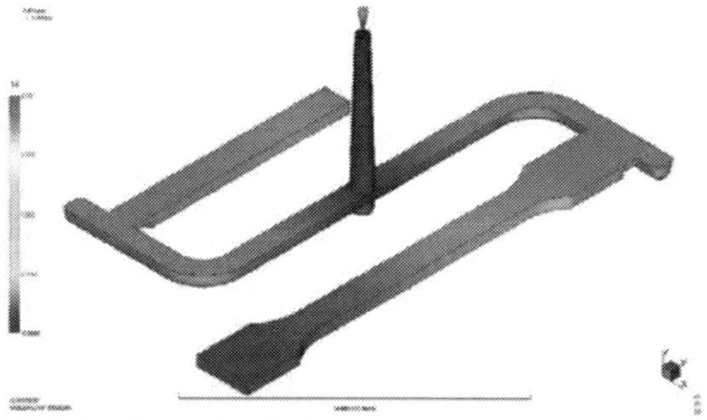

Fig 2. Injection molded bodies

Injection of test bodies was always carried out under the same technological conditions.

Table 2. Injection Parameters.

mold temperature	60	°C
plastication pach	24	Mm
injection pressure	800	Bar
touch pressure	300	Bar
time touch pressure	15,5	S
injection speed	40	mm/s
patch	8	mm
cool time	30	S
1.zone temperature	40	°C
2. zone temperature	270	°C
3. zone temperature	275	°C
4. zone temperature	280	°C
5. zone temperature	285	°C
nozzle temperature	290	°C

3 Experiment

Materials were tested by tensile test, flexural impact test, hardness test, and dimensional measurements to evaluate shrinkage. To compare the physical (mechanical) properties of polymer materials (PC) which was influenced by different pigment concentrations, a tensile test machine, charpy hammer, portal gauge and hardness hardness tester (Shore D) was used.

3.1 Impact bending test

The HIT impact hammer automatically detects the used pendulum. Therefore, HIT provides accurate measurement data within the specified range and corresponding to the standard. A double carbon rod was used to make the pendulums. High impact strength and high mass concentration at the point of impact are achieved. The impact hammer has an optional pendulum brake. The electronics include a high-resolution digital sensor for accurate angular swing measurement. Each set of measurements was performed on 20 test bodies

Fig 3. Impact bending test

3.1 Tensile stress machine

After producing of the testing samples a test was carried out to determine the tensile stress-strain properties and also the test to determine the tear strength. In both cases the testing samples were clamped into jaws at both ends in the tensile stress machine Tensometer 2000 by Alpha Technologies. (Fig. 5). Test sample dumbbell was stretched by the prescribed constant speed 50 mm/min until they were torn. In case of test sample crescent, graves and trouser, stretching speed was 100 mm/min.

Fig 4. Tensile stress experiment

4 Results

4.1 Bending impact test

The bending impact test was measured according to EN ISO 179-1. The test bodies were set up horizontally on the supports and hammered by impact hammer strikes. The test bodies were 80x4x10 and were fitted with a notch type V at a depth of 2 mm. Twenty test bodies were used for each set of measurements.

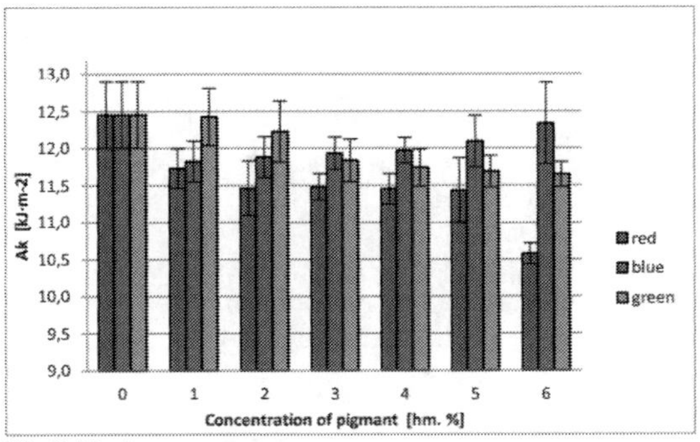

Fig 5. Noch tougness

The bending impact test determines the stiffness of the test body. When adding a red (Lifocolor-CR-Red 3620 F/PC) (red) or green (Greocolor-CR-Green 4842 F/PC) natural green polymer pigment (lexan 923) a decrease in notched toughness can be observed with increasing pigment concentration. On the other hand, the addition of blue (Lifocolor -CR-Blue 50009 F / PC) (blue) pigment increased the notch toughness. It has also been shown that by adding the pigments, the toughness was reduced in comparison with the natural material.

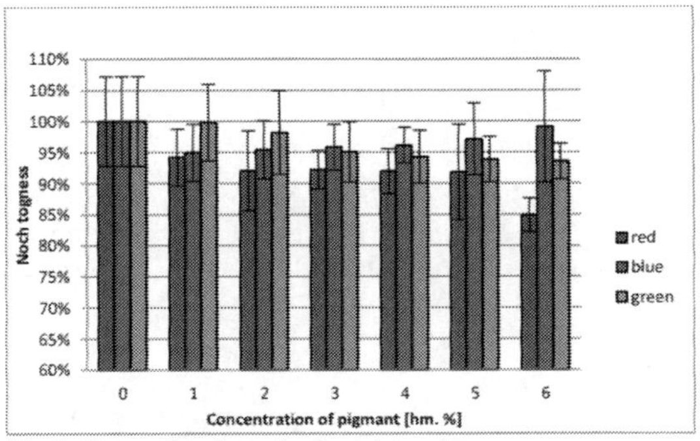

Fig 6. Proportional graph of notch toughness

At 1% concentration of the red pigment there was a 6% decrease in notch toughness. Also a negative trend can be seen. As the concentration of red pigment increases, the impact strength decreases. At 6% concentration of the red pigment, the toughness decreases by up to 15%

At 1% concentration of the green pigment, the impact strength value is the same as the value of the transparent material. At 6% concentration there was a 7% decrease in impact strength. The green pigment creates a more stable mixture with a decrease in the impact strength of the transparent material, and the stiffness of the test body has decreased.

At 1% concentration of the blue pigment, the toughness dropped by 5%. Further, the increasing trend is observed, at 6% concentration, the notched toughness value approaches the value of the transparent material. There was a 1% drop on the reference sample.

4.2 Tension test

The tensile test was performed according to the standard CSN EN ISO527-1 on the ZWICK Roell 1456 Testing Machine. The test bodies were shaped in the form of blades - type II. Twenty test specimens were used for each set of measurements. The temperature in the test room was 22 ° C.

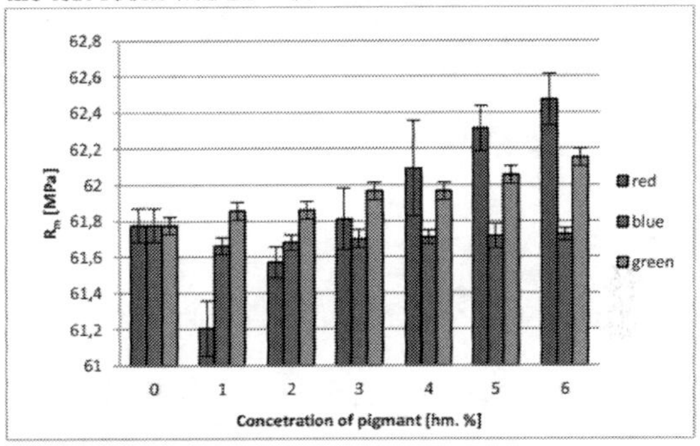

Fig 7. Limit of strength

249/5000

The tensile test indicates the strength of the material. When the red or green pigment was added to the natural polymer (lexan 923), the tensile strength was increased. On the other hand, when the blue pigment was added, a slight decrease in the tensile strength is observed.

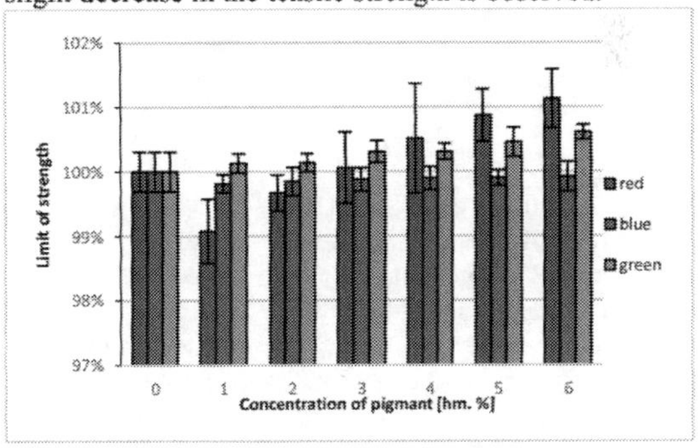

Fig 8. Proportional graph Limit of strength

At 1% concentration of the red pigment, the strength limit was decreased by 1%, where a growing tren is evident. At 6% pigment concentration, the 1% strength limit was increased.

At 1% concentration of the green pigment, the strength limit was slightly increased. The 6% concentration increased by 0.6%.

In the blue pigment, the tensile strength of the tensile strength dropped. This value fluctuated within a range of 0.5%.

4.3 Shore D

The hardness test (Shore D) was performed according to ISO 7619-1 standard on the Omag Affri ART 13 hardness tester. The test bodies had a thickness at the test site of 8 mm and their surface was smooth and clean. Ten test bodies were used for each set of measurements and 10 measurements were performed. The temperature in the test room was 22 °C.

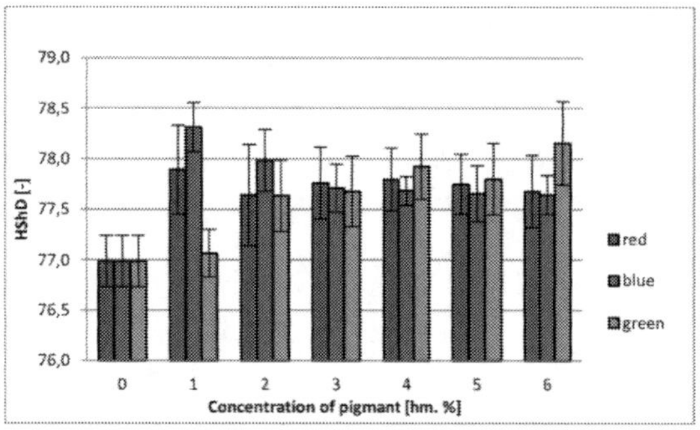

Fig 9. Shore D

Hardness results (Shore D) show that when a red pigment was added to the PC material (Lexan 923), the hardness increased and the trend was decreasing with increasing concentrations. A similar phenomenon occurred with the use of a blue pigment. On the other hand, the green pigment showed a growing trend.

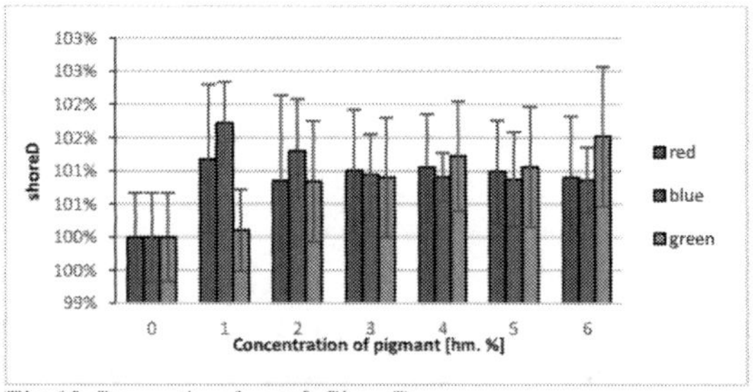

Fig 10. Proportional graph ShoreD

The change of the hardness is the most notably with 1% blue pigment concentration. When concentration grew by 2%, the trend slightly declining. A similar phenomenon occurs when the red pigment is used. At 1% concentration the hardness increased by 1%. However, with the increasing concentration of the pigment, there was a slight decrease in hardness. The intense phenomenon occurred with the green pigment. At 1% concentration there was a slight increase in hardness. He was also watching the growing trend. At a concentration of 6%, the hardness increased by 2% with a transparent material

5 Conclusion

Impact strength evaluation shows that the type of pigment selected significantly influences the stiffness of the body. When red pigments were used at higher concentrations, the stiffness decreased up to 15%. The blue pigment influenced the stiffness of the material to a minimum.

The tensile test evaluation shows that pigments do not significantly affect the tensile strength. Selection of the right concentration will result in minimal deviations from the strength limit.

Hardness is also influenced but only on a small scale. We are in the area of minimum deviations when a 3% pigment concentration is used. At this concentration, the materials have very similar mechanical properties.

Acknowledgement

This paper is supported by the internal grant of TBU in Zlin No. IGA/FT/2017/010 funded from the resources of specific university research and by the Ministry of Education, Youth and Sports of the Czech Republic within the National Sustainability Programme project No. LO1303 (MSMT-7778/2014) and also by the European Regional Development Fund under the project CEBIA-Tech No. CZ.1.05/2.1.00/03.0089

References

1. M. Ovsik, D. Manas, M. Manas, M. Stanek, M. Hribova, K. Kocman, D. Samek, Irradiated Polypropylene Studied by Microhardness and WAXS, Chemicke listy 106, (2012)
2. M. Stanek, M. Manas, D. Manas, V. Pata, S. Sanda, V. Senkerik, A. Skrobak, How the Filler Influence the Fluidity of Polymer, Chemicke listy, (2011)
3. M. Stanek, D. Manas, M. Manas, O. Suba, Optimization of injection molding process, Intl. J. of Math. and Computers in Simul., Vol.5, No.5, (2011)
4. J. Javorik, M. Stanek, The shape optimization of the pneumatic valve diaphragms, Intl. J. of Math. and Computers in Simul., Vol.5, No.4, (2011)
5. M. Stanek, D. Manas, M. Manas, J. Javorik, Simulation of injection molding process by cadmould rubber, Intl. J. of Math. and Computers in Simul., Vol.5, No.5, (2011)
6. M. Ovsik, D. Manas, M. Manas, M. Stanek, M. Bednarik, P. Kratky, Effect of beta irradiation on microhardness of polyamide 6, Key Engineering Materials, vol. 586, (2014)
7. M. Manas, D. Manas, M. Stanek, A. Mizera, M. Ovsik, Modification of polymer properties by irradiation properties of thermoplastic elastomer after radiation cross-linking, Asian Journal of Chemistry, vol. 25, Issue 9, (2013)
8. Tim A. Osswald, International Plastics Handbook: the Resource for Plastics Engineers (fourth ed.) Hanser Publishers, Munich (2006)
9. Dobransky, J., et al. Comparison of Cooling Variants by Simulation Software. Advanced Materials Research. Vol. 801 (2013). pp. 75-80. ISSN 1022-6680.
10. Behalek, L. and Dobránsky, J. Conformal cooling of the injection moulds. Applied Mechanics and Materials. Vol. 308 (2013). pp. 127-132. ISSN 1660-9336.

Catalytic oxidation using nitrous oxide

Beltran-Prieto Juan Carlos[1,*], *Kolomaznik* Karel[1]

[1] Faculty of Applied Informatics, Tomas Bata University in Zlín, nám. T. G. Masaryka 5555, 760 01 Zlín, Czech Republic

Abstract. Nitrous oxide is a very inert gas used generally as oxidant as it offers some advantage compared with other oxidants such as O_2 but a considerably higher temperature (> 526 °C) is often required. For particular cases such as the oxidation of sugar alcohols, especially for the oxidation of primary alcohols to aldehydes, N_2O has the advantage over O_2 of a higher reaction selectivity. In the present paper we present the modelling of oxidation reaction of sugar alcohols using an oxidizing agent in low concentrations, which is important to suppress subsequent oxidation reactions due to the very low residual concentrations of the oxidizing agent. For orientation experiments we chose nitrous oxide generated by thermal decomposition of ammonium nitrate. Kinetic modeling of the reaction was performed after determination of the differential equations that describe the system under study.

1 Introduction

In heterogenous catalysis, several metal oxides have been extensively used in chemical reactions. Among the most effective catalysts are iron-containing acidic zeolites which yield surface-activated iron-oxo species (α-Oxygen). Ohtani reported that the oxidation of organic compounds at room temperature can be performed by the reductive decomposition of N_2O to produce hydroxyl radical (·OH) selectively, however it is observed only under limited reaction conditions, such as γ-radiolysis, photolisis or electrolisis [1]. N_2O is used as a trap for hydrated electron as well as hydroxyl radical (·OH) generated by γ-radiolysis of water via reactions (1) and (2)

$$H_2O \xrightarrow{\gamma\ ray} \dot{}OH + e^-_{aq} + H^+ \quad (1)$$

$$N_2O + e^-_{aq} + H_2O \rightarrow N_2 + \dot{}OH + OH^- \quad (2)$$

The oxidation kinetics is based on the idea of the reaction mechanism, quantitative description of the dependences of the reaction rates on the concentration of the reacting components. The description is realized by vector differential equation, the solutions of which are time dependent of the concentrations of the oxidation intermediate products. [2]–[6] Generally, chemical reactions are accompanied by various relatively complex simultaneous reactions resulting in a complicated blend of intermediate products. As a general model, the oxidation reaction of sugar alcohols (S) using nitrous oxide (N) for the production of derivatives (A) and (B) in isothermal conditions is discussed next. The diagram of the system is presented in Fig. 1 having three inputs (F, C_{N0}, and C_{S0}), four state variables (A, N, S and B) and four output variables (A, N, S, and B).

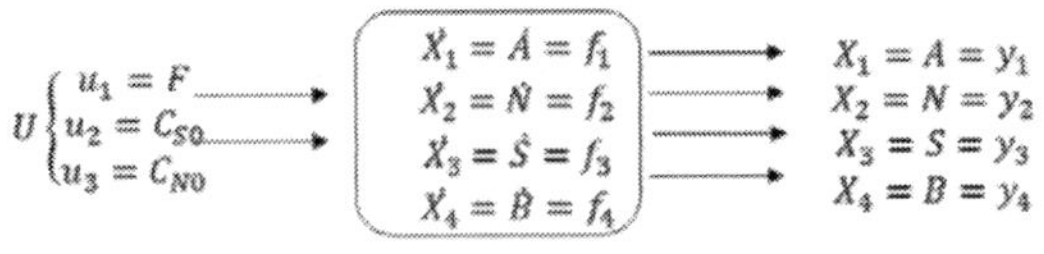

Fig. 1. Scheme of the oxidation of glycerol with NO_2 describing the input, state variable and output

2. Mathematical model of oxidation with NO_2

The set of equations that describe the mass balance, including of chemical reactions in which are supposed to be of the first order mechanism, of the components is presented in (3) to (6)

$$\frac{dA}{dt} = k_1 \cdot S \cdot N - k_2 \cdot A \cdot N - \frac{F}{V}A \quad (3)$$

$$\frac{dN}{dt} = -k_1 \cdot S \cdot N - k_2 \cdot A \cdot N + \frac{F}{V}C_{N0} - \frac{F}{V}N \quad (4)$$

$$\frac{dS}{dt} = -k_1 \cdot S \cdot N + \frac{F}{V}C_{S0} - \frac{F}{V}S \quad (5)$$

$$\frac{dB}{dt} = k_2 \cdot A \cdot N - \frac{F}{V}B \quad (6)$$

The described system is non-linear. The elements of matrix A, B, are the following [7]–[9]:

$$a_{11} = \frac{\partial {f_1}^0}{\partial A} = -k_2 N^0 - \frac{F^0}{V}; a_{12} = \frac{\partial {f_1}^0}{\partial N} = k_1 S^0 - k_2 A^0; a_{13} = \frac{\partial {f_1}^0}{\partial S} = k_1 N^0; a_{14} = \frac{\partial {f_1}^0}{\partial B} = 0 \quad (7)$$

$$a_{21} = \frac{\partial {f_2}^0}{\partial A} = -k_2 N^0; a_{22} = \frac{\partial {f_2}^0}{\partial N} = -k_1 S^0 - k_2 A^0 - \frac{F^0}{V}; a_{23} \frac{\partial {f_2}^0}{\partial S} = -k_1 N^0; a_{24} = \frac{\partial {f_2}^0}{\partial B} = 0 \quad (8)$$

$$a_{31} = \frac{\partial {f_3}^0}{\partial A} = 0; a_{32} = \frac{\partial {f_3}^0}{\partial N} = -k_1 S^0; a_{33} = \frac{\partial {f_3}^0}{\partial S} = -k_1 N^0 - \frac{F^0}{V}; a_{34} = \frac{\partial {f_3}^0}{\partial B} = 0 \quad (9)$$

* Corresponding author: prieto@fai.utb.cz

$$a_{41}=\frac{\partial f_4{}^0}{\partial A}=k_2N^0;a_{42}=\frac{\partial f_4{}^0}{\partial N}=k_2A^0;a_{43}=\frac{\partial f_4{}^0}{\partial S}=0;a_{44}=\frac{\partial f_4{}^0}{\partial B}=-\frac{F^0}{V} \quad (10)$$

Considering the control variables, equations (11) to (14) are obtained:

$$b_{11}=\frac{\partial f_1{}^0}{\partial F}=-\frac{A^0}{V};\ b_{12}=\frac{\partial f_1{}^0}{\partial C_{S0}}=0;\ b_{13}=\frac{\partial f_1{}^0}{\partial C_{N0}}=0 \quad (11)$$

$$b_{21}=\frac{\partial f_2{}^0}{\partial F}=\frac{(C_{N0}-N^0)}{V};\ b_{22}=\frac{\partial f_2{}^0}{\partial C_{S0}}=0;\ b_{23}=\frac{\partial f_2{}^0}{\partial C_{N0}}=\frac{F^{\circ}}{V} \quad (12)$$

$$b_{31}=\frac{\partial f_3{}^0}{\partial F}=\frac{(C_{S0}-S^0)}{V};\ b_{32}=\frac{\partial f_3{}^0}{\partial C_{S0}}=\frac{F^{\circ}}{V};\ b_{33}=\frac{\partial f_3{}^0}{\partial C_{N0}}=0 \quad (13)$$

$$b_{41}=\frac{\partial f_4{}^0}{\partial F}=-\frac{B^0}{V};\ b_{42}=\frac{\partial f_4{}^0}{\partial C_{S0}}=0;\ b_{43}=\frac{\partial f_1{}^0}{\partial C_{N0}}=0 \quad (14)$$

Therefore, the representation of the state vector is given by:

$$\begin{pmatrix}\frac{dA}{dt}\\ \frac{dN}{dt}\\ \frac{dS}{dt}\\ \frac{dB}{dt}\end{pmatrix}=\begin{pmatrix}-\left(k_2N^0+\frac{F^{\circ}}{V}\right) & k_1S^0-k_2A^0 & k_1N^0 & 0\\ -k_2N^0 & -\left(k_1S^0+k_2A^0+\frac{F^{\circ}}{V}\right) & k_1N^0 & 0\\ 0 & -k_1S^0 & -\left(k_1N^0+\frac{F^{\circ}}{V}\right) & 0\\ k_2N^0 & k_2A^0 & 0 & -\frac{F^{\circ}}{V}\end{pmatrix}\begin{pmatrix}\Delta A\\ \Delta N\\ \Delta S\\ \Delta B\end{pmatrix}+\begin{pmatrix}-\frac{A^0}{V} & 0 & 0\\ \frac{(C_{N0}-N^0)}{V} & 0 & \frac{F^{\circ}}{V}\\ \frac{(C_{S0}-S^0)}{V} & \frac{F^{\circ}}{V} & 0\\ -\frac{B^0}{V} & 0 & 0\end{pmatrix}\begin{pmatrix}\Delta F\\ \Delta C_{S0}\\ \Delta C_{N0}\end{pmatrix} \quad (15)$$

The multiplication procedure leads to the next group of equations:

$$\frac{d\Delta A}{dt}=-\left(k_2N^0+\frac{F^{\circ}}{V}\right)\Delta A+(k_1S^0-k_2A^0)\Delta N+(k_1N^0)\Delta S-\frac{A^0}{V}\Delta F \quad (16)$$

$$\frac{d\Delta N}{dt}=-(k_2N^0)\Delta A-\left(k_1S^0+k_2A^0+\frac{F^{\circ}}{V}\right)\Delta N+(k_1N^0)\Delta S+\frac{(C_{N0}-N^0)}{V}\Delta F+\frac{F^{\circ}}{V}\Delta C_{N0} \quad (17)$$

$$\frac{d\Delta S}{dt}=-(k_1S^0)\Delta A-\left(k_1N^0+\frac{F^{\circ}}{V}\right)\Delta S+\frac{1}{V}(C_{S0}-S^0)\Delta F+\frac{F^{\circ}}{V}\Delta C_{S0} \quad (18)$$

$$\frac{d\Delta B}{dt}=(k_2N^0)\Delta A+(k_2A^0)\Delta N-\left(\frac{F^{\circ}}{V}\right)\Delta B-\left(\frac{B^0}{V}\right)\Delta F \quad (19)$$

For the purpose of control, it is necessary to introduce the following dimensionless parameters

$$A^*=\frac{A}{S^0}\therefore A=A^*\cdot S^0 \quad (20)$$

$$N^*=\frac{N}{N^0}\therefore N=N^*\cdot N^0 \quad (21)$$

$$S^*=\frac{S}{S^0}\therefore S=S^*\cdot S^0 \quad (22)$$

$$B^*=\frac{B}{S^0}\therefore B=B^*\cdot S^0 \quad (23)$$

$$F^*=\frac{F}{F^0}\therefore F=F^*\cdot F^0$$

$$C_{S0}{}^*=\frac{C_{S0}}{S^0}\therefore C_{S0}=C_{S0}{}^*\cdot S^0 \quad (24)$$

$$C_{N0}{}^*=\frac{C_{N0}}{N^0}\therefore C_{N0}=C_{N0}{}^*\cdot N^0$$

After substitution of dimensionless dependencies, equations (25) to (28) are obtained:

$$\frac{d\Delta A^*\cdot S^0}{dt}=-\left(k_2N^0+\frac{F^{\circ}}{V}\right)\Delta A^*\cdot S^0+(k_1S^0-k_2A^0)\Delta N^*\cdot N^0+(k_1N^0)\Delta S^*\cdot S^0-\frac{A^0}{V}\Delta F^*\cdot F^0 \quad (25)$$

$$\frac{d\Delta N^*\cdot N^0}{dt}=-(k_2N^0)\Delta A^*\cdot S^0-\left(k_1S^0+k_2A^0+\frac{F^{\circ}}{V}\right)\Delta N^*\cdot N^0+(k_1N^0)\Delta S^*\cdot S^0+\frac{(C_{N0}-N^0)}{V}\Delta F^*\cdot F^0+\frac{F^{\circ}}{V}\Delta C_{N0}{}^*\cdot N^0 \quad (26)$$

$$\frac{d\Delta S^*\cdot S^0}{dt}=-(k_1S^0)\Delta A^*\cdot S^0-\left(k_1N^0+\frac{F^{\circ}}{V}\right)\Delta S^*\cdot S^0+\frac{1}{V}(C_{S0}-S^0)\Delta F^*\cdot F^0+\frac{F^{\circ}}{V}\Delta C_{S0}{}^*\cdot S^0 \quad (27)$$

$$\frac{d\Delta B^*\cdot S^0}{dt}=(k_2N^0)\Delta A^*\cdot S^0+(k_2A^0)\Delta N^*\cdot N^0-\left(\frac{F^{\circ}}{V}\right)\Delta B^*\cdot S^0-\left(\frac{B^0}{V}\right)\Delta F^*\cdot F^0 \quad (28)$$

Accordingly, multiplying either by V/F^0G^0 or by V/F^0N^0, the next sets of equations are obtained:

$$\frac{d\Delta A^*}{dt^*}=-\left(\frac{k_2N^0V}{F^0}+1\right)\Delta A^*+\left(\frac{Vk_1N^0}{F^0}-\frac{Vk_2A^0N^0}{F^0S^0}\right)\Delta N^*+\frac{Vk_1N^0}{F^0}\Delta S^*-\frac{A^0}{S^0}\Delta F^* \quad (29)$$

$$\frac{d\Delta N^*}{dt^*}=-\frac{Vk_2S^0}{F^0}\Delta A^*-\left(\frac{Vk_1S^0}{F^0}+\frac{Vk_2A^0}{F^0}+1\right)\Delta N^*+\frac{Vk_1S^0}{F^0}\Delta S^*+\frac{(C_{N0}-N^0)}{N^0}\Delta F^*+\Delta C_{N0}{}^* \quad (30)$$

$$\frac{d\Delta G^*}{dt^*}=-\frac{Vk_1G^0}{F^0}\Delta A^*-\left(\frac{Vk_1N^0}{F^0}+1\right)\Delta S^*+\frac{(C_{S0}-S^0)}{S^0}\Delta F^*+\Delta C_{S0}{}^* \quad (31)$$

$$\frac{d\Delta B^*}{dt^*}=\frac{Vk_2N^0}{F^0}\Delta A^*+\frac{Vk_2A^0N^0}{F^0S^0}\Delta N^*-\Delta B^*-\frac{B^0}{S^0}\Delta F^* \quad (32)$$

where the term $t^*=(F^{\circ}\cdot t/V)$ implies a dimensionless parameter (dimensionless time). As a result, the system transforms into (33)

$$\begin{pmatrix}\frac{d\Delta A^*}{dt^*}\\ \frac{d\Delta N^*}{dt^*}\\ \frac{d\Delta S^*}{dt^*}\\ \frac{d\Delta B^*}{dt^*}\end{pmatrix}=\begin{pmatrix}-\left(\frac{Vk_2N^0}{F^{\circ}}+1\right) & \frac{Vk_1N^0}{F^0}-\frac{Vk_2A^0N^0}{F^0S^0} & \frac{Vk_1N^0}{F^{\circ}} & 0\\ -\left(\frac{Vk_2S^0}{F^{\circ}}\right) & -\left(\frac{Vk_1S^0+Vk_2A^0+F^{\circ}}{F^{\circ}}\right) & \left(\frac{Vk_1S^0}{F^{\circ}}\right) & 0\\ -\left(\frac{Vk_1S^0}{F^{\circ}}\right) & -\left(\frac{Vk_1N^0}{F^{\circ}}+1\right) & 0 & 0\\ \left(\frac{Vk_2N^0}{F^{\circ}}\right) & \left(\frac{Vk_2A^0N^0}{F^{\circ}S^0}\right) & 0 & -1\end{pmatrix}\begin{pmatrix}\Delta A^*\\ \Delta N^*\\ \Delta S^*\\ \Delta B^*\end{pmatrix}+\begin{pmatrix}-\frac{A^0}{S^0} & 0 & 0\\ \frac{(C_{N0}-N^0)}{N^0} & 0 & 1\\ \frac{(C_{S0}-G^0)}{G^0} & 1 & 0\\ -\left(\frac{B^0}{S^0}\right) & 0 & 0\end{pmatrix}\begin{pmatrix}\Delta F^*\\ \Delta C_{S0}\\ \Delta C_{N0}\end{pmatrix} \quad (33)$$

Furthermore, as the transfer function G(s) is given by $G(s)=(sI-A)^{-1}B$, firstly it is necessary to calculate (sI − A). Therefore, we need to define the next elements of matrix *A*:

$$a_{11}=\left(\frac{Vk_2N^0}{F^{\circ}}+1\right);\ a_{12}=\frac{Vk_1N^0}{F^0}-\frac{Vk_2A^0N^0}{F^0S^0};\ a_{13}=\frac{Vk_1N^0}{F^{\circ}} \quad (34)$$

DOI: 10.1051/matecconf/201712502053

$$a_{21} = \left(\frac{Vk_2N^0}{F^\circ}\right); a_{22} = \left(\frac{Vk_1S^0+Vk_2A^0+F^\circ}{F^\circ}\right); a_{23} = \left(\frac{Vk_1S^0}{F^\circ}\right) \quad (35)$$

$$a_{31} = \left(\frac{Vk_1S^0}{F^\circ}\right); a_{32} = \left(\frac{Vk_1N^0}{F^\circ}+1\right) \quad (36)$$

$$a_{41} = \left(\frac{Vk_2N^0}{F^\circ}\right); a_{42} = \left(\frac{Vk_2A^0N^0}{F^\circ S^0}\right) \quad (37)$$

$$(sI - A) = \begin{pmatrix} s+a_{11} & -a_{12} & -a_{13} & 0 \\ a_{21} & s+a_{22} & -a_{23} & 0 \\ a_{31} & a_{32} & s & 0 \\ -a_{41} & -a_{42} & 0 & s+1 \end{pmatrix} \quad (38)$$

In order to simulate the process, the next input parameter values are taken into account: F=0.1 $m^3 \cdot s^{-1}$, C_{S0}=1 $mol \cdot m^{-3}$, C_{N0}=1 $mol \cdot m^{-3}$ k_1=0.32 h^{-1}, k_2=0.49 h^{-1}, k_3=0.27 h^{-1}, V=1 m^3, N=0.2 $mol \cdot m^{-3}$, S=0.3 $mol \cdot m^{-3}$, A=0.5 $mol \cdot m^{-3}$, B=0.2 $mol \cdot m^{-3}$. As a result, the respective transfer functions are given by the following set of equations:

From input u_1=F to output

$$y1=A: G(s) = \frac{-1.6667s^3-11.49s^2-12.2919s-2.4619}{s^4+7.39s^3+15.8504s^2+12.8288s+3.3684} \quad (39)$$

$$y2=N: G(s) = \frac{4s^3+16.61s^2+18.8436s+6.2336}{s^4+7.39s^3+15.8504s^2+12.8288s+3.3684} \quad (40)$$

$$y3=S: G(s) = \frac{2.3333s^3+12.2833s^2+20.7807s+10.8307}{s^4+7.39s^3+15.8504s^2+12.8288s+3.3684} \quad (41)$$

$$y4=B: G(s) = \frac{-0.6667s^3+0.64s^2+4.656s+5.2533}{s^4+7.39s^3+15.8504s^2+12.8288s+3.3684} \quad (42)$$

from input u_2=C_{S0} to output

$$y1=A: G(s) = \frac{0.6400s^2+2.5088s+1.8688}{s^4+7.39s^3+15.8504s^2+12.8288s+3.3684} \quad (43)$$

$$y2=N: G(s) = \frac{0.9600s^2+1.9200s+0.96}{s^4+7.39s^3+15.8504s^2+12.8288s+3.3684} \quad (44)$$

$$y3=S: G(s) = \frac{1s^3+7.39s^2+13.6616s+7.2716}{s^4+7.39s^3+15.8504s^2+12.8288s+3.3684} \quad (45)$$

$$y4=B: G(s) = \frac{2.1952s+3.3994}{s^4+7.39s^3+15.8504s^2+12.8288s+3.3684} \quad (46)$$

from input u_3=C_{N0} to output

$$y1=A: G(s) = \frac{-0.9933s^2-2.0429s-1.0496}{s^4+7.39s^3+15.8504s^2+12.8288s+3.3684} \quad (47)$$

$$y2=N: G(s) = \frac{s^3+2.98s^2+2.5944s+0.6144}{s^4+7.39s^3+15.8504s^2+12.8288s+3.3684} \quad (48)$$

$$y3=S: G(s) = \frac{-1.64s^2-3.9336s-2.2936}{s^4+7.39s^3+15.8504s^2+12.8288s+3.3684} \quad (49)$$

$$y4=B: G(s) = \frac{1.6333s^2+2.2605s-0.0251}{s^4+7.39s^3+15.8504s^2+12.8288s+3.3684} \quad (50)$$

Finally, the inverse Laplace transformation leads to equations (165) to (176)

input u_1=F

$$y_1(t) = 0.723e^{-4.4235t} - 3.0361e^{-1.4364t} + 0.6464e^{-0.5301t} \quad (51)$$

$$y_2(t) = 2.4697e^{-4.4235t} + 1.3396e^{-1.4364t} + 0.1907e^{-0.5301t} \quad (52)$$

$$y_3(t) = 1.0725e^{-4.4235t} - 0.4997e^{-1.4364t} + 1.7604e^{-0.5301t} \quad (53)$$

$$y_4(t) = -1.3854e^{-4.423t} + 1.8044e^{-1.436t} - 3.0969e^{-t} + 2.0111e^{-0.53t} \quad (54)$$

input u_2=C_{S0}:

$$y_1(t) = 0.0827e^{-4.4235t} - 0.3507e^{-1.4364t} + 0.4335e^{-0.5301t} \quad (55)$$

$$y_2(t) = -0.2826e^{-4.4235t} + 0.1548e^{-1.4364t} + 0.1278e^{-0.5301t} \quad (56)$$

$$y_3(t) = -0.1227e^{-4.4235t} - 0.0577e^{-1.4364t} + 1.1804e^{-0.5301t} \quad (57)$$

$$y_4(t) = 0.1585e^{-4.423t} + 0.2084e^{-1.436t} - 1.7154e^{-t} + 1.3485e^{-0.5301t} \quad (58)$$

input u_3=C_{N0}:

$$y_1(t) = 0.2876^{-4.4235t} - 0.1393e^{-1.4364t} - 0.1482e^{-0.5301t} \quad (59)$$

$$y_2(t) = 0.98226e^{-4.4235t} + 0.0615e^{-1.4364t} - 0.0437e^{-0.5301t} \quad (60)$$

$$y_3(t) = 0.4266e^{-4.4235t} - 0.0229e^{-1.4364t} - 0.4036e^{-0.5301t} \quad (61)$$

$$y_4(t) = -0.550e^{-4.4235t} + 0.082e^{-1.4364t} + 0.929e^{-t} - 0.461e^{-0.5301t} \quad (62)$$

The response to a step function for the input u_1 is presented as an example in Fig. 2,

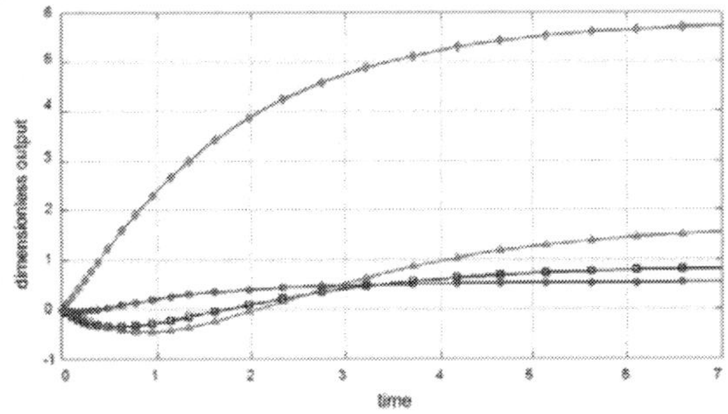

Fig. 2: Step response for the system of glycerol oxidation with NO_2. Input u_1=F to respective outputs y_1=A □; y_2=N o; y_3=S ◊; y_4=B △

3 Conclusions

Today, special attention is paid to partial oxidation of several sugar alcohols because it gives oxidation intermediate products with high utility value. However, a major problem of partial oxidation of these compounds lies in its low reactivity and high oxidation reactivity of intermediates, which is expressed by different values of the rate constants of oxidation in the first step of the reaction and in subsequent steps of the oxidation reaction. The yield depends on the ratio of rate constants. For simulation purposes, specified constants and initial concentrations of nitrous oxide and reactant can be specified.

This work was supported by the Ministry of Education, Youth and Sports of the Czech Republic within the National Sustainability Programme project No. LO1303 (MSMT-7778/2014).

References

1. B. Ohtani, S.-I. Takamiya, Y. Hirai, M. Sudoh, S.-I. Nishimoto, and T. Kagiya, J. Chem. Soc. Perkin Trans, **2**, 175-179, [1992].
2. H. S. Fogler, *Elements of Chemical Reaction Engineering*, (Prentice Hall, New Jersey, 1999).
3. B. A. Finlayson, *Introduction to Chemical Engineering Computing*. (John Wiley and Sons, Inc, 2006).

4. I. Tosun, *Modeling in Transport Phenomena*, (Elsevier, 2007).
5. R. L. Burden and J. D. Faires, *Numerical Methods*, (Brooks Cole, 2002).
6. A. S. Foust, L. A. Wenzel, C. W. Clump, L. Maus, and L. B. Andersen, *Principles of unit operations*, (John Wiley & Sons, Inc, New Delhi, 1980).
7. G. Stephanopoulos, *Chemical Process Control: An Introduction to Theory and Practice*. (Prentice-Hall, 1984).
8. E. D. Seborg, T. F. Edgar, and D. Mellichamp, *Process Dynamics and Control*. (John Wiley and Sons, Inc., 1989).
9. R. Aris, *Elementary Chemical Reactor Analysis*. (Dover Publications, Boston 2000).

Study of dissolution process and its modelling

Beltran-Prieto Juan Carlos[1,*], *Beltran-Prieto* Luis Antonio[1]

[1] Faculty of Applied Informatics, Tomas Bata University in Zlín, nám. T. G. Masaryka 5555, 760 01 Zlín, Czech Republic

Abstract. The use of mathematical concepts and language aiming to describe and represent the interactions and dynamics of a system is known as a mathematical model. Mathematical modelling finds a huge number of successful applications in a vast amount of science, social and engineering fields, including biology, chemistry, physics, computer sciences, artificial intelligence, bioengineering, finance, economy and others. In this research, we aim to propose a mathematical model that predicts the dissolution of a solid material immersed in a fluid. The developed model can be used to evaluate the rate of mass transfer and the mass transfer coefficient. Further research is expected to be carried out to use the model as a base to develop useful models for the pharmaceutical industry to gain information about the dissolution of medicaments in the body stream and this could play a key role in formulation of medicaments.

1 Introduction

Dissolution is a process in which a solute forms a solution in a solvent. In the study of dissolution we normally come across with several factors that affects this process, namely surface area, agitation, temperature, enthalpy and entropy which affects dissolvability of salts as well as the nature of solvent and solute.[1], [2]

Understanding the dissolution processes of any compound considers the study of kinetic rates, controlling factors, products of dissolution, kinetics of precipitation, chemical equilibrium, mechanism of crystallization among other factors [3], [4]. During the formation of dissolutions, homogenous materials are formed with the combination of more than one chemical species that achieve equilibrium. The components of dissolution (solute and dissolvent) form a homogenous mixture and have a regular distribution of their physicochemical properties. As a result, every portion has the same chemical and psychical characteristics but the quantity of solute and dissolvent are in proportions that varied within some limits. This can be exemplified by the capacity of solubilization that every compound has in a specific solvent. The physical properties are given by the concentration of the components, which can be separated by changes of phases such as evaporation, condensation, or fusion, however, they are not able to be separated by sedimentation or centrifugation. This is normally caused due to the size of the particles, which is normally lower than 10 Angstroms. The stability of materials can be influenced by several factors such as transport process. Additionally, the presence of elements like oxygen or other oxidants (i.e. Fe_2O_3, MnO_2, nitrogen compounds) and proper characteristics of the materials such as structure, surface, reactive area, presence of ligands, temperature affect their dissolution rate. [5]–[7]

The formation of dissolution is strongly related to the attraction between the solute and the solvent. A solution is formed when attractive forces between different particles are bigger than the attractive forces between particles that are similar. Therefore, the amount of solute solubilised depends on the strength of attraction. The attractive intermolecular forces between particles keep the particles together; as a result, these intermolecular forces have to be broken in order to form a solution. [8], [9]

Dissolution process is important in several fields. In the pharmaceutical industry gives information about the disposition of a pharmaceutical compound within an organism or drug release (adsorption, distribution, metabolism and excretion). This is extremely important in cases where drug release should be controlled in time or gradual after specific time of administration. Several systems aimed to control drug delivery try to minimize degradation of compounds prevention of side effects and increment of drug bioavailability. Research in this field has been carried out by the application of micelles as drug carriers, soluble polymers and liposomes. Bioavailability is the fraction of a drug dose in its active form or some of the metabolites absorbed from the site of administration that reaches the systemic circulation or a particular place where it performs the main function. This property can be increased using micellar systems which have the potential to solubilise drugs with low solubility. It also depends on the properties of the pharmaceutical form and its formulation. Drugs can be administrated by various routes, such as oral, rectal, parenteral, topical, inhalational, etc.). They require being in solution to be adsorbed after crossing several semipermeable cell membranes before reaching the systemic circulation. There exists several alternatives to cross cell membranes, among the most important are passive diffusion, facilitated passive diffusion, active

* Corresponding author: prieto@fai.utb.cz

transport and pinocytosis. Low bioavailability can be present in cases where metabolism of the drug occurs before reaching the required plasmid concentration. This is frequent in oral administration of low hydrosoluble drugs with low adsorption. [10]

2. General model of dissolution process

The general model of dissolution is a first order model, described by the differential equation given in (1)

$$\frac{dC(t)}{dt} = a(C_S - C(t)), \quad C(0) = 0 \qquad (1)$$

where a > 0 is constant and C_S is the limit concentration achieved after the solvent is dissolved or the solute is saturated.

When a liquid is flowing through the inner tube formed with crystals of a solute, a gradient of concentrations exist in the solid surface. The solute starts to dissolve slowly and gradually according to the solubility of the material in the respective solution (Fig. 1). For the analysis of the system, we consider a plug flow model with perfect radial mixing, isothermal conditions and constant fluid physical properties. The concentration of the solid varies along the tube (axial coordinate) with absence of radial diffusion and resistance to mass transfer due to liquid phase contribution. The diameter of the cylindrical tube remains constant.

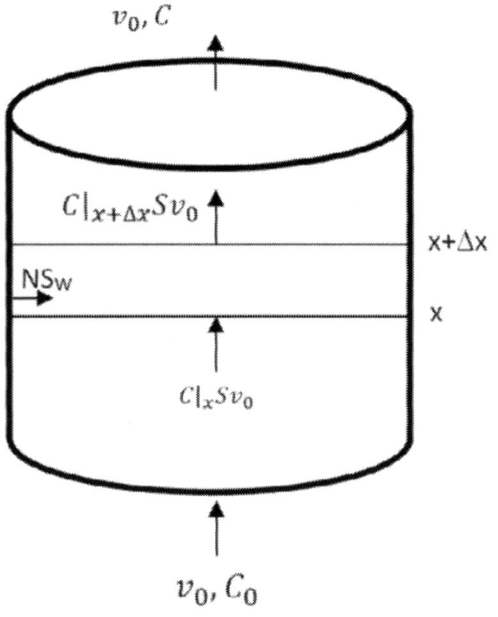

Fig. 1. General representation of the system under study

To describe the process, we consider a differential element (shell) of thickness Δx, with constant cross section area and derive the macroscopic mass balance around the elemental volume. If the process is in steady state, there is no accumulation of mass. There is no chemical reaction but there is transfer of mass between the surface of the solid and the fluid. Additionally, we assume that the system remains infinitesimally close to an equilibrium state at all times. This implies that the process is slow enough to allow the system to adjust itself internally and the properties in one part of the system do not change any faster than those at other parts[11]. As a result, the general conservation law is as expressed in (2):

$$C_x S\vartheta_0 - C_L S\vartheta_0 + \Delta R = 0 \qquad (2)$$

where C is the concentration of the solid, with a distance (x) and a thickness (L), ϑ represents the superficial fluid velocity, S the surface area of the solid, ΔR express the incremental rate expression given by the mass flux [product of the mass transfer coefficient (k), the composition linear driving force (C^*-C)] and the surface area of the tube (A_W).

Equation (2) takes the form of (3)

$$C|_x\left(\frac{\pi D^2}{4}\right)\vartheta_0 - C|_L\left(\frac{\pi D^2}{4}\right)\vartheta_0 + k[C_S - C(x)]A_W = 0 \qquad (3)$$

Where D is the diameter of the tube, k the mass transfer coefficient, C and C_S are the concentration of the substance and solubility respectively.

Dividing equation (3) by $\pi D\Delta x$ gives

$$C|_x\left(\frac{D}{4\Delta x}\right)\vartheta_0 - C|_L\left(\frac{D}{4\Delta x}\right)\vartheta_0 + k[C_S - C(x)] = 0 \qquad (4)$$

$$\left(\frac{-D\vartheta_0}{4}\right)\frac{[C|_L - C|_x]}{\Delta x} + k[C_S - C(x)] = 0 \qquad (5)$$

Taking the limit when Δx→0 gives the concentration profile with distance, as expressed in equation (6)

$$\left(\frac{-D\vartheta_0}{4}\right)\frac{dC}{dx} + k[C_S - C(x)] = 0 \qquad (6)$$

The system is described by the previous ordinary differential equation, which can be integrated with the following initial condition: $x = 0, C = 0$

The solution can be performed by separation of variables

$$\frac{dC}{C_S - C(x)} = \frac{4k}{D\vartheta_0}dx \qquad (7)$$

$$\int\frac{dC}{C_S - C(x)} = \frac{4k}{D\vartheta_0}\int dx \qquad (8)$$

$$-\ln|C_S - C(x)| = \frac{4k}{D\vartheta_0}x + B \qquad (9)$$

$$e^{\ln|C_S - C(x)|} = e^{-\frac{4k}{D\vartheta_0}x + B} \qquad (10)$$

$$C_S - C(x) = B' e^{-\frac{4k}{D\vartheta_0}x} \qquad (11)$$

$$C(x) = C_S - B' e^{-\frac{4k}{D\vartheta_0}x} \qquad (12)$$

At the boundary, when $x=0$, the concentration corresponds to zero (C=0), therefore the value of the constant B' is equal to C_S. Substituting the value of the constant gives

$$C(x) = C_S\left(1 - e^{-\frac{4k}{D\vartheta_0}x}\right) \quad (13)$$

Equation (13) can be used to evaluate the concentration at the boundary, when X=L

$$C(L) = C_S\left(1 - e^{-\frac{4k}{D\vartheta_0}L}\right) \quad (14)$$

The variation of weight (ΔW) according to time (Δτ) can be calculated by determining the rate at which the compound is being dissolved (υ), as expressed in (15)

$$\Delta W = \upsilon \Delta\tau \quad (15)$$

Accordingly, the rate of dissolution [g/s] is determined by multiplying the volumetric flow rate through the cylinder [m^3/s], the concentration at the boundary *C(L)*[mol/m^3] and the molecular weight of the substance [g/mol] as expressed in (16)

$$\upsilon = \frac{\pi D^2}{4}\vartheta_0 C(L) M_W \quad (16)$$

Substituting (16) in (15) and using equation (14) leads to equation (17)

$$\Delta W = \frac{\pi D^2}{4}\vartheta_0\, C_S\left(1 - e^{-\frac{4k}{D\vartheta_0}L}\right) M_W \Delta\tau \quad (17)$$

Equation (17) can be rearranged to have

$$\frac{4\Delta W}{\pi D^2 \vartheta_0\, C_S M_W \Delta\tau} = 1 - e^{-\frac{4k}{D\vartheta_0}L} \quad (18)$$

For any value of *x*, the exponential function can be represented as a power series as indicated in (19)

$$e^x = \sum_{n=0}^{\infty}\frac{x^n}{n!} = 1 + x + \frac{x^2}{2} + \cdots \quad (19)$$

Using the approximation of equation (19) gives (20)

$$e^{-\frac{4k}{D\vartheta_0}L} \approx 1 - \frac{4k}{D\vartheta_0}L \quad (20)$$

From (20) we can obtain (21)

$$1 - e^{-\frac{4k}{D\vartheta_0}L} \approx \frac{4k}{D\vartheta_0}L \quad (21)$$

Substituting equation (21) into (18)

$$\frac{4\Delta W}{\pi D^2 \vartheta_0\, C_S M_W \Delta\tau} \approx \frac{4k}{D\vartheta_0}L \quad (22)$$

Finally, obtaining for *k* gives (23)

$$k \approx \frac{\Delta W}{\pi D\, C_S M_W \Delta\tau L} \quad (23)$$

Since equation 23 is an approximation, the maximum error can be estimated according to equation (24)

$$\varepsilon_k = \left|\frac{\partial k}{\partial \Delta W}\right|\varepsilon_{\Delta W} + \left|\frac{\partial k}{\partial \Delta\tau}\right|\varepsilon_{\Delta\tau} + \left|\frac{\partial k}{\partial D}\right|\varepsilon_D \quad (24)$$

where

$$\left|\frac{\partial k}{\partial \Delta W}\right| = \frac{1}{\pi D\, C_S M_W \Delta\tau L} \quad (25)$$

$$\left|\frac{\partial k}{\partial \Delta\tau}\right| = -\frac{\Delta W}{\pi D\, C_S M_W \Delta\tau^2 L} \quad (26)$$

$$\left|\frac{\partial k}{\partial D}\right| = -\frac{\Delta W}{\pi D^2\, C_S M_W \Delta\tau L} \quad (27)$$

The substitution of the values of the partial derivatives using equations (25-26), the experimental errors $\varepsilon_{\Delta W}$, $\varepsilon_{\Delta t}$,ε_D and simplifying we obtain equation (28)

$$\varepsilon_k = \frac{\Delta W}{\pi D\, C_S M_W \Delta\tau L}\left(\frac{\varepsilon_{\Delta W}}{\Delta W} + \frac{\varepsilon_{\Delta\tau}}{\Delta\tau} + \frac{\varepsilon_D}{D}\right) + \left|\frac{\partial k}{\partial \Delta\tau}\right|\varepsilon_{\Delta\tau} + \left|\frac{\partial k}{\partial D}\right|\varepsilon_D \quad (28)$$

2 Discussion

Initially, pure water is passed through a tube constructed of a solid. Considering that the solid is slightly soluble in water (*C** moles solid/cm^3 solution), the inner walls of the tube will dissolve very slowly. By weighing the dried tube before and after exposure, it is possible to calculate the rate of mass transfer. As an example to this process, if a crystal of barium hydroxide is dipped into a rapidly stirred solution of dilute acid containing phenolphthalein, a thin layer of solution at the surface of the crystal becomes pink. The thickness of the alkaline layer varies with the stirring speed, and, if the latter is very low, irregular streamers of alkaline solution may extend one or two centimeters out into the solution. With a very soluble base, as sodium hydroxide, even a high stirring speed cannot confine the alkaline solution to a thin, even layer.

Considering that a monomolecular film of liquid next its surface is saturated by the base rapidly, as expressed in the Nernst diffusion layer theory of dissolution rates, a layer is formed in which concentration gradients of both acid and base exist. This type of system has been discussed by other researchers but no systematic study of such cases has been made.

If solid benzoic acid is immersed in an alkaline solution a similar gradient of acid and base concentrations should exist near the surface.

3 Conclusions

We analyzed the dissolution process of solids in a fluid by determining the quasi steady state material balance for velocity profile, the profile of compound concentration through the space dimension and time. We discussed the assumptions implied in the analysis and deduced a method of estimating the maximum possible experimental error in calculating kc

Using mathematical modeling allows evaluating equations based on this assumption that account satisfactorily for the dissolution rate of solid benzoic acid in dilute sodium and potassium hydroxide solutions. Many investigators believe that the outer surface of the diffusion layer is diffuse and ragged and that the average concentration gradient is not linear over a considerable fraction of the total layer thickness. The experiment described with barium and sodium hydroxides indicates that the lower the concentration differences and the better the stirring, the sharper the boundary of the diffusion layer. It is possible to consider two cases: the zone in which solutes are transported both by convection and diffusion may be negligibly thin compared to the entire layer in which concentration gradients exist; or that the distance from the surface at which neutralization occurs may be considered as "effective thicknesses" without destroying the validity of the relation to be derived

This work was supported by the Ministry of Education, Youth and Sports of the Czech Republic within the National Sustainability Programme project No. LO1303 (MSMT-7778/2014)..

References

1. P. Acero, K. A. Hudson-Edwards, and J. D. Gale, Chem. Geol., 419, 1–9, [2015].
2. A. E. Post, B. Arnold, J. Weiss, and J. Hinrichs, J. Dairy Sci., 95, 4, 1603–1616, [2012].
3. H. H. Teng, P. M. Dove, and J. J. De Yoreo, Geochim. Cosmochim. Acta, 64, 13, 2255–2266, [2000].
4. A. Lttge, U. Winkler, and A. . Lasaga, Geochim. Cosmochim. Acta, 67, 6, 1099–1116, [2003].
5. D. E. Giammar, J. M. Cerrato, V. Mehta, Z. Wang, Y. Wang, T. J. Pepping, K.-U. Ulrich, J. S. Lezama-Pacheco, and J. R. Bargar, Water Res., 46, 18, 6023–6032, [2012].
6. J. M. Senko, S. D. Kelly, A. C. Dohnalkova, J. T. McDonough, K. M. Kemner, and W. D. Burgos, Geochim. Cosmochim. Acta, 71, 19, 4644–4654, [2007].
7. M. Ginder-Vogel, B. Stewart, and S. Fendorf, Environ. Sci. Technol., 44, 1, 163–169, [2010].
8. H. K. Shaikh, R. V. Kshirsagar, and Patil S. G., World J. Pharm. Pharm. Sci., 4, 4, 324–338, [2015].
9. P. Costa and J. M. Sousa Lobo, Eur. J. Pharm. Sci., 13, 2, 123–133, [2001].
10. S. S. Jambhekar and P. J. Breen, Drug Discov. Today, 18, 23, 1173–1184, [2013].
11. Y. Cengel and M. Boles, Thermodynamics: an Engineering Approach, (McGraw-Hill, New York 1994).

MATEC Web of Conferences **125**, 02055 (2017) DOI: 10.1051/matecconf/201712502055
CSCC 2017

Detecting fire in video stream using statistical analysis

Karel Koplík[1], *Peter* Janků[2,*], *Olga* Voznyuk[2], *Tomáš* Dulík[2], *Petr* Snopek[3]

[1]Brno University of Technology, Faculty of Information Technology, Czech Republic
[2]Tomas Bata University in Zlin, Faculty of applied informatics, Nad Stranemi 4511, 760 05 Zlin, Czech Republic
[3] UNIS, a.s., Jundrovská 33, 624 00 Brno, Czech Republic, Czech Republic

Abstract. The real time fire detection in video stream is one of the most interesting problems in computer vision. In fact, in most cases it would be nice to have fire detection algorithm implemented in usual industrial cameras and/or to have possibility to replace standard industrial cameras with one implementing the fire detection algorithm. In this paper, we present new algorithm for detecting fire in video. The algorithm is based on tracking suspicious regions in time with statistical analysis of their trajectory. False alarms are minimized by combining multiple detection criteria: pixel brightness, trajectories of suspicious regions for evaluating characteristic fire flickering and persistence of alarm state in sequence of frames. The resulting implementation is fast and therefore can run on wide range of affordable hardware.

1 Introduction

In this paper, we present new algorithm for detecting fire in video based on tracking suspicious regions in time with statistical analysis of their trajectory. Our goal was to develop a fast algorithm which can run on an affordable hardware with minimum rate of false alarms.

The purpose of detecting fire in video is to improve current systems based on traditional fire and smoke detection sensors, which are limited in several ways: e.g., they cannot be used in industrial plants, where burning is an inherent part of the manufacturing process and/or where the occasional occurrence of smoke cannot be avoided. The current sensors have also relatively short range: they need to be close to the potential fire, so there must be many of them in order to cover all dangerous places.

Cameras can monitor much larger areas and their operation can be more reliable then chemical or optical smoke sensors, which need to be regularly checked, cleaned or exchanged. Therefore, it is desirable to develop a camera-based fire detection system which can become a welcomed alternative to traditional fire and smoke detection sensors.

Of course, there are already other systems for fire detection in video streams. What makes our system different is that it is very fast and doesn't require too much computation power.

2 Detailed description

The entire algorithm is very simple. It consists of the following steps:

1. Detect suspicious regions
2. Find bounding rectangles
3. Track rectangles in time
4. Analyse trajectories
5. Check for persistence

In the following sections we will look at each step. To demonstrate, let's use a video of a burning tree as an example.

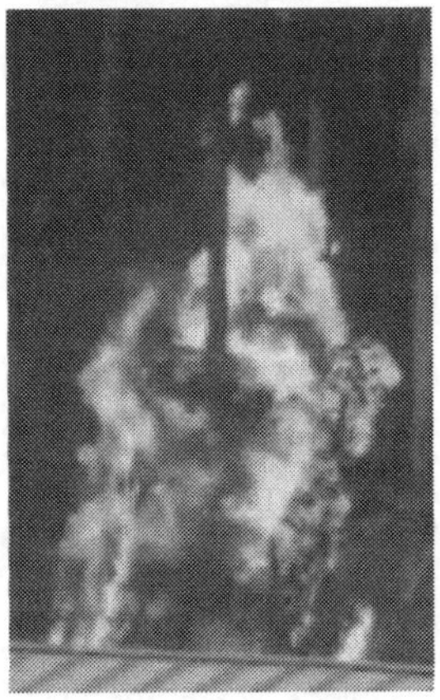

Fig. 1. Burning fire.

2.1 Detecting suspicious regions

The regions of interest in this case would be those pixels which have fire-like colour and also pixels which change

* Corresponding author: janku@fai.utb.cz

visibly in time (i.e. contain movement). Suspicious pixels are then a union of these two sets.

2.1.1 Detecting pixels with fire-like colour

Finding pixels based on colour is very simple and it can be done using different colour models like RGB, YUV, YCbCr HSI or HSV. [1][6][7] First two focus on colour spectrum and latter two on colour intensity. Fire is usually the brightest part in the video so using brightness as an additional criterion is very useful.

In our algorithm we work with RGB colour model and the procedure looks like this: We take red (R), green (G), and blue (B) channels and calculate colour saturation (S).

Then the following rules are applied:

$$R > G > B$$
$$S > ST$$

where:

S_T is saturation threshold.

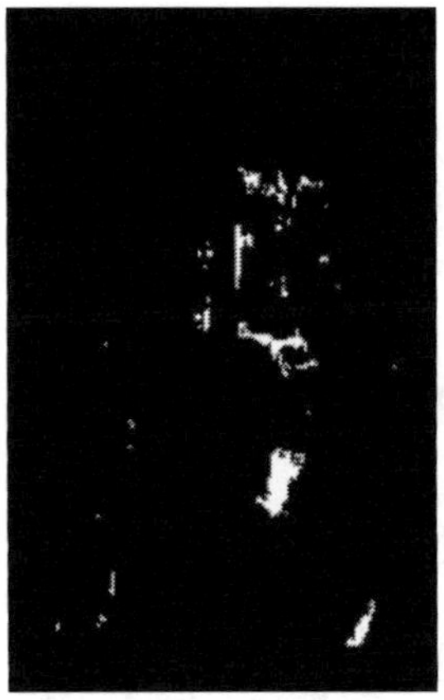

Fig. 2. Fire colour map-

2.1.2 Detecting movement

To detect movement we actually need three frames. Because we need the previous, current and the next frame, the algorithm is always one frame behind a real-time video stream from a camera.

Taking only greyscale frames, we basically subtract the background to detect motion in foreground. First we calculate an absolute difference between previous (fi-1) and next (fi+1) frame. This will subtract the background. Then we calculate an absolute difference between current (fi) and the next frame. This will update that information. Then we apply binary AND operator on the two calculated differences to obtain information about the movement in the foreground.

$$|f_{i-1} - f_{i+1}| \wedge |f_i - f_{i+1}| \quad (1)$$

It is also necessary to filter out lone pixels (i.e. noise) in the result movement map. The amount of noise depends on camera and lighting conditions.

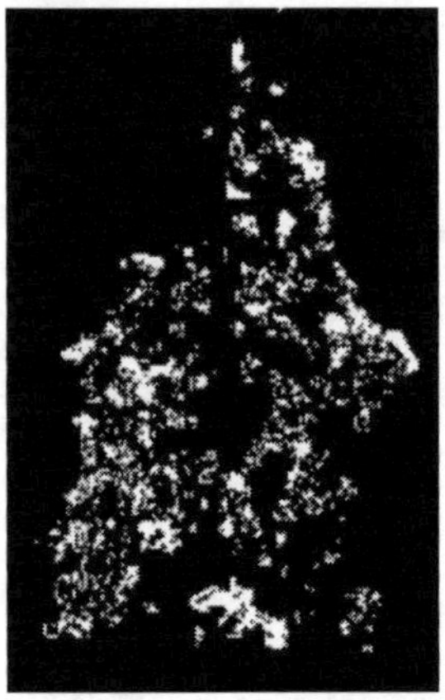

Fig. 3. Movement map.

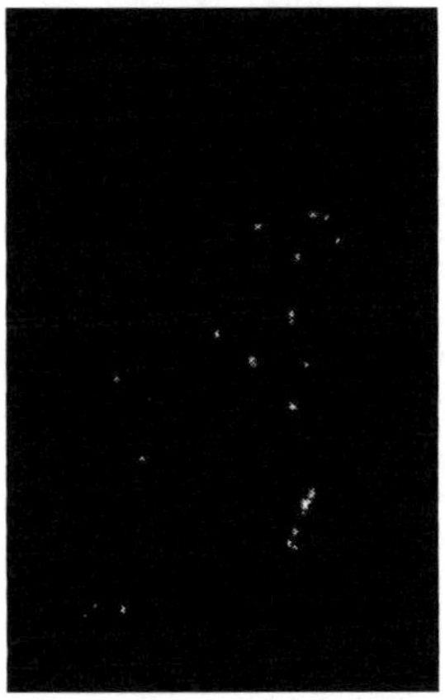

Fig. 4. Suspicious areas.

2.2 Founding bounding rectangles

The binary map of suspicious pixels will most likely consist of lots of small disconnected areas concentrating in separated larger regions. In one of our first attempt, we tried to find bounding rectangles for each of them and then to connect them into larger bounding rectangle if they were close enough to each other. This worked but also turned out to be very costly in terms of processing time. The solution was to dilate the small areas using a morphology operator.

Dilatation (as a morphological operation) consists of convoluting an image with a small kernel shaped like a simple shape (circle, square, etc.).

This results into much fewer bounding rectangles to be found and aggregated in the next step and significantly increases the algorithm speed.

2.3 Tracking suspicious regions in time

DOI: 10.1051/matecconf/201712502055

Similarly to [8] we test suspicious regions fire-like characteristic in time. Our method consists of tracking. Before we start we need to aggregate found areas in space and then link them in time.

2.3.1 Aggregating regions in space

After we are done marking up areas of interest in each frame we need to look into previous frames to find out if we can link them to previously marked areas.

For that we use a tree data structure consisting of two layers of bounding rectangles.

In first frame, we add rectangles to the root of the tree. If a rectangle to be added overlaps (with added tolerance) any rectangles stored in the tree, they are all replaced with a rectangle which is based on the largest one and is large enough to contain all of them. The parent rectangle is not reduced in size in this step and they are added as its children.

If they already have children, the children are moved to the new parent and the original parent is discarded.

Once all the rectangles have been added to the tree, the bottom layer is removed. Before that we check if each top-layer rectangle has any children.

If it has, we find the smallest bounding rectangle for all children and resize the parent to the average between the original and the smallest size.

2.3.2 Linking regions in time

If the parent ends up with no children, we reduce its RTL (right to live) parameter. If it has at least one child, we will set RTL to predefined maximum value.

The RTL parameter basically tells us how long we will keep a rectangle which has not been updated (e.g. for 3 frames).

In all of the following frames, we repeat the same steps as with the first frame, but now we have preexisting first-layer.

2.3.3 Tracking regions in time

The tracking is based on keeping the history of middle points. These are not the centre points of bounding rectangles. Instead, we take the original map of suspicious regions (without applied dilatation) and average the coordinates of suspicious pixels. The new average point is then added to stack.

The reason we use the stack is that we remove points if their count surpasses defined limit.

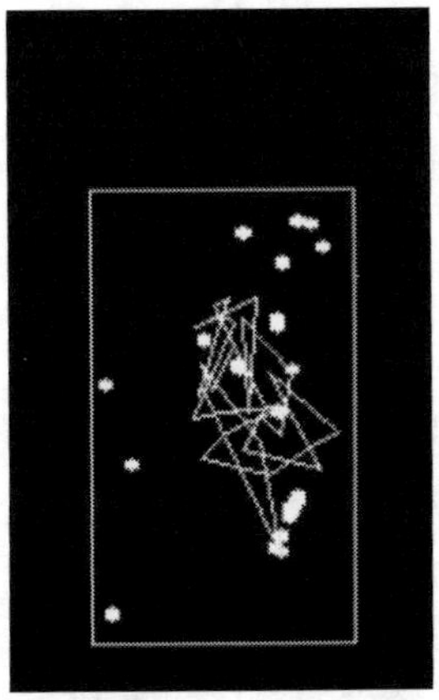

Fig. 4. Suspicious region's trajectory.

2.4 Analysing trajectories

This and the following step are very important. Without them, we would be detecting a large spectrum of objects and features which are similar to fire in colour and in "not being static". The fire, however, has a very specific way of moving. First of all, it stays in one place and is characteristic by constant flickering. This is very useful because it's hard to find anything else what is (yellow and bright and) constantly changing shape while staying in one location. The trajectory of the middle points should basically fit the normal distribution.

To test this with our suspicious regions, we use horizontal and vertical coordinates of the middle points. First we calculate the mean value μ and the standard deviation σ for each axis. If the distribution is normal, according to the gaussian curve, 68.2% of values should belong to the interval:

$$(\mu-\sigma,\mu+\sigma) \quad (2)$$

Since we work with object that doesn't only change shape but also size over time, it is not wise to rely on too many values to increase precision. Instead, we work with fewer values (according to our tests, the optimal number seems to be around 100) and expect some reasonable error. That is why we had settled to expecting 60% of data to fall into the above specified interval.

2.5 Checking for persistence

To further eliminate false alarms, we apply the last criterion, which is persistence. If the previous step gives us positive result, we don't trigger the alarm yet but save it. This we do for each frame.

Depending on the video source quality and captured scene properties, we usually set the persistence limit to at least 15 seconds (which would be 375 frames for 25 fps video source) or even more. With such setting, we found our algorithm gives satisfactory low false alarm rates.

Longer persistence limit could result in longer delay or missing short positive detections.

To evaluate persistence, we don't require the positive test on normal distribution in each frame. It can be just some higher percentage. Empirically, we had set it to the top quarter.

Fig. 6. Output screen.

3 Algorithm parameters

There are several parameters which need to be set after a camera providing video stream for our algorithm is installed into a new environment.

3.1 Brightness threshold

Defines the minimum brightness needed for classifying pixels as fire-coloured. Normally the best value would be around 225 (out of 255) but in some test videos it had to be adjusted because the fire was too dark due to the type of video source.

3.2 Movement threshold

During the movement detection processing the camera noise is reduced by filtering out some lone pixels. This parameter sets the threshold. Usually in badly illuminated areas the threshold needs to be set higher. This is important because noise has normal distribution so it could cause a false alarm.

3.3 Small regions gap size

Maximum distance between two bounding rectangles of small regions that can be aggregated. This parameter should have a small value (e.g. 10 px) and depends on video resolution.

3.4 Regions minimal size

If there are too many very small regions found because of camera noise, we eliminated them by setting a minimal bounding rectangle size. If the size is set too high, small flames will not be detected. If it's too low, the noise can trigger false alarm.

3.5 Region "right to live"

As was explained in the previous chapter, this parameter sets how long we keep a region appearing to be empty in a few frames.

This mostly happens when there is no movement detected. Since the fire has multiple independently moving flames it can be expected that with high probability, it will not stop moving for more than few (e.g. 3) frames.

3.6 Number of middle points

The parameter defines how many middle points we want to remember for each region before we test them for normal distribution. It should be enough for this criterion to be calculated relatively accurately but also not too many so we adapt to changes in the scene quickly. We use empiric value of 100.

3.7 Persistency interval

This parameter determines the number of frames, for which a positive detection has to persist before triggering the alarm. This parameter needs to be changed according to number of frames per second in each video stream.

The higher this number is the harder it is to fool the algorithm but also the longer delay we get. Fire keeps its characteristic movement all the time, but most other objects and phenomena move chaotically and in short intervals. In our tests, 15 seconds turned out to be sufficient minimal length.

4 Performance

To test our algorithm, we had acquired several videos containing flames, moving bright objects and phenomena similar to fire.

4.1 Algorithm speed

Our algorithm is very simple so when optimized, it runs in real time on average hardware. It does not rely on frequency of fire flickering unlike some algorithms so the frame rate doesn't have to be that high either.

How fast the algorithm detects flame really depends on the camera setting and scene characteristics, but in ideal conditions it depends solely on the defined length of the minimal persistence interval.

Not ideal conditions would be e.g. the flame is too small or too far from the camera, if the flame is not fully visible in camera's field of view or the flame movement is being distorted by another moving object (in one test video it was a burning piece of wire rolling out of flames).

4.2 Strengths and weaknesses

Similarly to other fire-detecting algorithms, the most concerning weakness is false alarm ratio. Avoiding false alarms is implemented by combining multiple criteria

[2][3][4][5]. If all criteria are fooled, the false alarm occurs.

During our testing we had encountered some problematic scenes. To test the constant movement with normally distributed middle points of suspicious regions we had used some videos of dancing people. Interestingly, some types of dance don't have the normal distribution of movement and some do.

In the end, none of these videos triggered the alarm but some were really close. When dancing, the movement often briefly stops and that makes the persistence criterion come out negative.

What was most problematic was white background in some videos. Anything what moves in front of such background can pass the movement-and-brightness criterion because even when the object is not bright the algorithm sees only bright areas changing shape as the object covers and uncovers the background.

Other concern we have is with natural phenomena similar to fire. When testing the algorithm on videos of sunset being reflected on moderately moving ocean surface, the false alarm was triggered every time. This means that our algorithm cannot be used at locations where something like this occurs. However, it can be useful in locations such as a factory hall or a tunnel where these phenomena don't appear.

Other than that, our algorithm proved to work without problems and was almost impossible to fool intentionally when processing real time camera input.

5 Conclusion

We had developed and successfully tested a new algorithm. In this stage in can be used with any camera system and will work mostly without error. However, there are certain situations in which the algorithm triggers false alarm. This will be the subject of our future research.

Acknowledgement

This paper is supported by Technology Agency of the Czech Republic (TA ČR) within the Visual Computing Competence Center - V3C project No. TE01020415, by Ministry of Education, Youth and Sports of the Czech Republic within the National Sustainability Programme project No. LO1303 (MSMT-7778/2014) and also by the European Regional Development Fund under the project CEBIA-Tech No. CZ.1.05/2.1.00/03.0089.

References

1. T. Chen, P. Wu, and Y. Chiou, "An Early Fire-Detection Method Based on Image Processing," *Proc. IEEE Int. Image Process.*, (2004), pp. 1707-1710.
2. B.U. Toreyin, Y. Dedeoglu, and A.E. Cetin, "Flame Detection in Video Using Hidden Markov Models," *Proc. IEEE Int. Conf. Image Process.*, (2005), pp. 1230-1233, 2005.
3. W. Krüll et al., "Design and Test Methods for a Video-Based Cargo Fire Verification System for Commercial Aircraft," *Fire Safety* J., **41**, no. 4, (2006), pp. 290-300.
4. T. Celik, "Fast and Efficient Method for Fire Detection Using Image Processing," ETRI Journal, **32**, no. 6, (Dec. 2010), pp. 881-890.
5. L., Zhigang, G.Hadjisophocleous, G. Ding and Ch.S. Lim. Study of a Video Image Fire Detection System for Protection of Large Industrial Applications and Atria [online]. (cit. 2013-12-01).
6. Poobalan, Kumarguru and Liew, Siau-Chuin. Fire Detection Algorithm using Image Processing Techniques. In: E-Proceeding of the 3rd International Conference on Artificial Intelligence and Computer Science (AICS2015), 12-13 (October 2015) , BayView Hotel, Penang, Malaysia. pp. 160-168.. ISBN 978-967-0792-06-4.
7. Jiang, B., Lu, Y., Li, X. et al. Multimed Tools Appl (2015) **74**: 689. doi:10.1007/s11042-014-2106-z.
8. A. E. Gunawaardena, R. M. M. Ruwanthika, A. G. B. P. Jayasekara, "Computer Vision Based Fire Alarming System", in Proceedings of the 2nd International Moratuwa Engineering Research Conference (MERCon), pp. 325-330, Moratuwa, Sri Lanka, (April 2016).

DOI: 10.1051/matecconf/201712502056

Change of notch impact strength depending on radiation dose and test temperature

Bednarik Martin[1,*] and *Stoklasek* Pavel[1]

[1] Tomas Bata University in Zlin, TGM 5555, 760 01, Zlin, Czech Republic

Abstract. The main purpose of this paper has been determine the effect of radiation crosslinking on the notch impact strength of polyamides filled with fiberglass. These properties were examined in dependence on the dosage of the ionizing beta radiation (non-irradiated samples and those irradiated by dosage 66 and 132 kGy were compared) and on the test temperature (23 – 150 °C).

1 Introduction

The modification of polymer properties by irradiation is constantly evolving area. Ionic and ionizing radiation are the main types of radiation which are used for the polymer modification. Gamma radiation created from radioactive isotope Co-60 (60Co) belongs to ionizing radiation as well as beta radiation (electron beam) and X-ray radiation. All of these types significantly differ, however during these all process the energy transfer to atoms of irradiated material occurs [1-6].

As stated in previous investigations [6-16], it is possible to effectively change physical, mechanical and biological properties of irradiated material by ionizing radiation. These changes are probably caused by primary and secondary processes which are created due to interaction of ionizing radiation with polymer [1,2].

The crosslinking level can be adjusted by irradiation dosage and often by means of a crosslinking booster. The main difference between electron beta and photon gamma is in their different abilities of penetrating the irradiated material. Gamma rays have a high penetration capacity. The penetration capacity of electron rays depends on the energy of the accelerated electrons. Due to accelerated electron the required dose may be applied for seconds, whereas several hours are required on the gamma radiation plant. The electron accelerators operate on the principle of the Braun tube, whereby a hot cathode is heated in vacuum to such a degree that electrons are released [17-21].

This study deals with the influence of different doses of ionizing beta radiation (66 and 132 kGy) on notch impact strength of polyamides under thermal loading and follows previous studies [3, 5, 7, 9, 10], which described the change of mechanical properties of selected types thermoplastics.

The previous study [3, 5, 7, 9, 10] proved the positive irradiation effect on mechanical of selected types polymers. Nevertheless, some findings are not explained yet, namely the change of dynamic properties during the application of beta radiation on material under thermal loading. Each new finding on the effect of radiation crosslinking on the properties of polymer materials may thus contribute to a better understanding of the issue and can extend the field of new applications.

2 Experimental

2.1 Materials

For this experiment two types polyamides were used. Both materials are filled with glass fibers and their commercial names are:

- Polyamide 66 GF 30 – V – PTS – CREAMID A3H7.2G 6*M0129A Schwarz
- Polyamide 7T GF 56 – V – DURAMID TH7 G12.0SZB*9207

The basic properties of used materials are shown in Table 1 and 2.

Table 1. Properties of PA 66 GF 30.

PA 66 GF 30	
Density [g/cm^3]	1.37
Impact toughness [kJ/m^2]	8
Tensile modulus [MPa]	10000
Bending strength [MPa]	260
Softening temperature [°C]	255

The samples were made using the injection molding technology on the injection molding machine Arburg Allrounder 470H 1000-400. The samples had the shape and dimensions according to the CSN EN ISO 179. Processing conditions during the injection moulding

* Corresponding author: mbednarik@utb.cz

DOI: 10.1051/matecconf/201712502056

were according to the recommendation of the procedures.
Test specimens were equipped with a notch type V (size 2 mm).

Table 2. Properties of PA 7T GF 56.

PA 7T GF 56	
Density [g/cm^3]	1.63
Impact toughness [kJ/m^2]	25
Tensile modulus [MPa]	19000
Bending strength [MPa]	290
Softening temperature [°C]	229

All samples were irradiated with electron (beta) rays (electron energy 10 MeV, radiation doses: 66 and 132 kGy) in the firm BGS Beta Gamma Service GmbH & Co, Saal am Danau – Germany [7, 14, 15].

2.2 Determination of mechanical characteristic

For testing the mechanical properties there was used a dynamic test on the test machine Zwick HIT50P. Test conditions were according to the CSN EN ISO 179. The energy of the hammer was 50 J and test data was processed by Test Xpert II software.

3 Results and discussion

3.1 Notch impact strength – PA 66 GF 30

Comparison of notch impact strength and maximum force (at 23, 50, 75, 100, 125, and 150 °C) of PA 66 GF 30 before and after irradiation is given in the Figures 1 to 6.

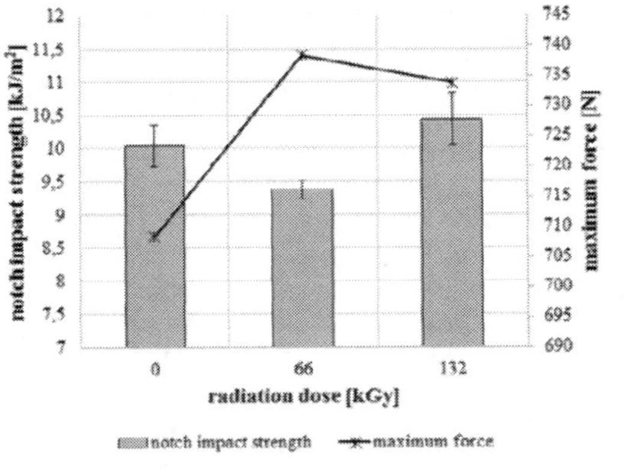

Fig. 1. Notch impact strength and maximum force (PA 66 GF 30, test temperature – 23 °C).

In the case of test temperature 23 °C the highest value of notch impact strength was achieved by the irradiation with dose of 132 kGy and the highest value of maximum force was achieved by the irradiation with dose 66 kGy (referring to: Fig. 1).

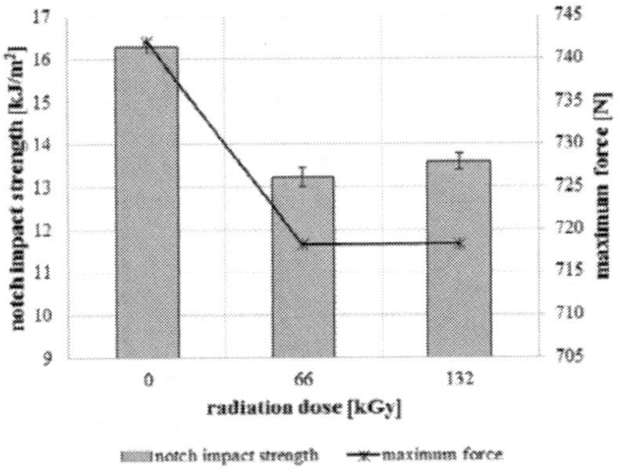

Fig. 2. Notch impact strength and maximum force (PA 66 GF 30, test temperature – 50 °C).

In the case of test temperature 50 °C the highest value of notch impact strength and maximum force was achieved at non-irradiated samples (referring to: Fig. 2).

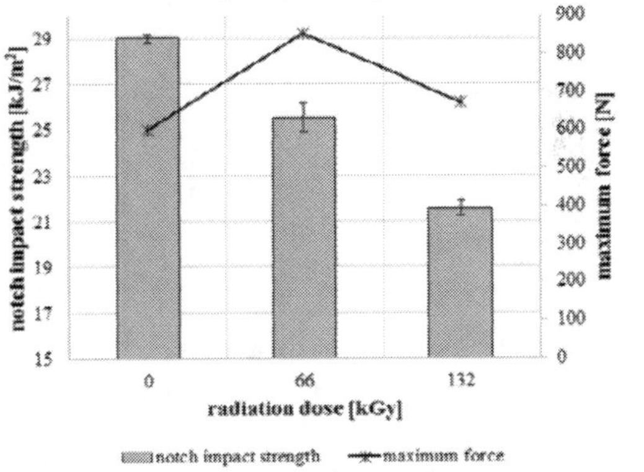

Fig. 3. Notch impact strength and maximum force (PA 66 GF 30, test temperature – 75 °C).

In the case of test temperature 75 °C the highest value of notch impact strength was achieved at non-irradiated samples and the highest value of maximum force was achieved by the irradiation with dose 66 kGy (referring to: Fig. 3).

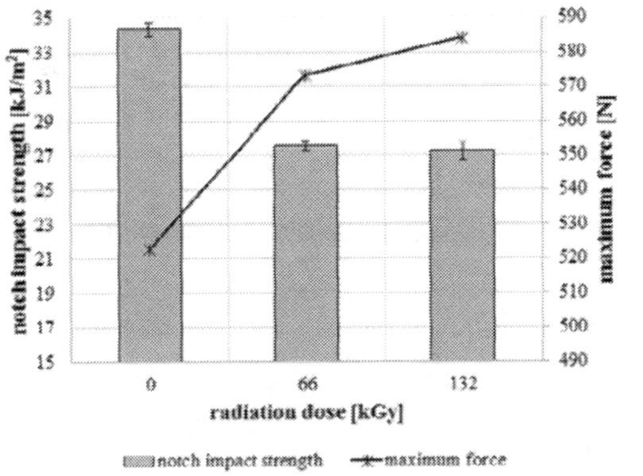

Fig. 4. Notch impact strength and maximum force (PA 66 GF 30, test temperature – 100 °C).

In the case of test temperature 100 °C the highest value of notch impact strength was achieved at non-irradiated samples and the highest value of maximum force was achieved by the irradiation with dose 132 kGy (referring to: Fig. 4).

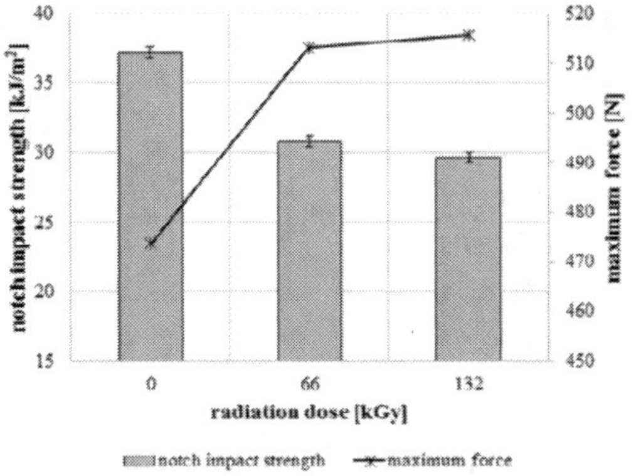

Fig. 5. Notch impact strength and maximum force (PA 66 GF 30, test temperature – 125 °C).

In the case of test temperature 125 °C the highest value of notch impact strength was achieved at non-irradiated samples and the highest value of maximum force was achieved by the irradiation with dose 132 kGy (referring to: Fig. 5).

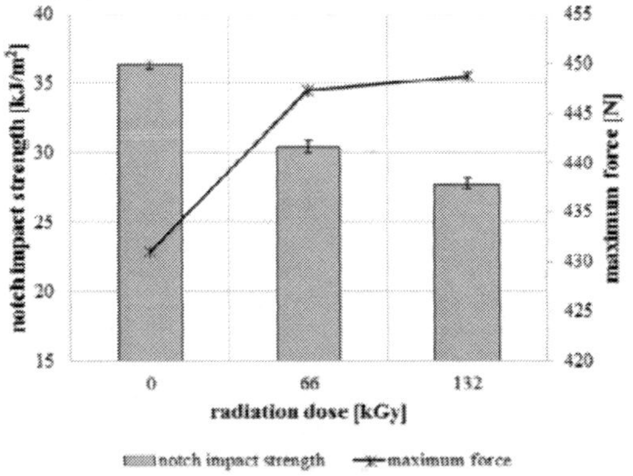

Fig. 6. Notch impact strength and maximum force (PA 66 GF 30, test temperature – 150 °C).

In the case of test temperature 150 °C the highest value of notch impact strength was achieved at non-irradiated samples and the highest value of maximum force was achieved by the irradiation with dose 132 kGy (referring to: Fig. 6).

3.2 Notch impact strength – PA 7T GF 56

Comparison of notch impact strength and maximum force (at 23, 50, 75, 100, 125, and 150 °C) of PA 7T GF 56 before and after irradiation is given in the Figures 7 to 12.

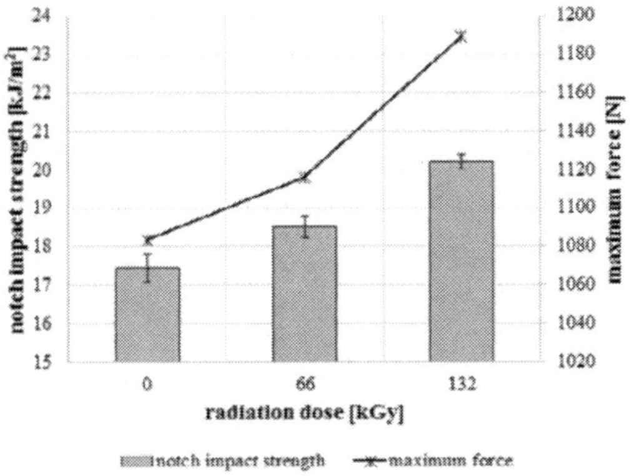

Fig. 7. Notch impact strength and maximum force (PA 7T GF 56, test temperature – 23 °C).

In the case of test temperature 23 °C the highest value of notch impact strength and maximum force was achieved by the irradiation with dose of 132 kGy. The value of notch impact strength increased from 17.5 kJ/m^2 (non-irradiated samples) to 20.2 kJ/m^2 (dose of 132 kGy), which is a hike of approximately 15 % (referring to: Fig. 7).

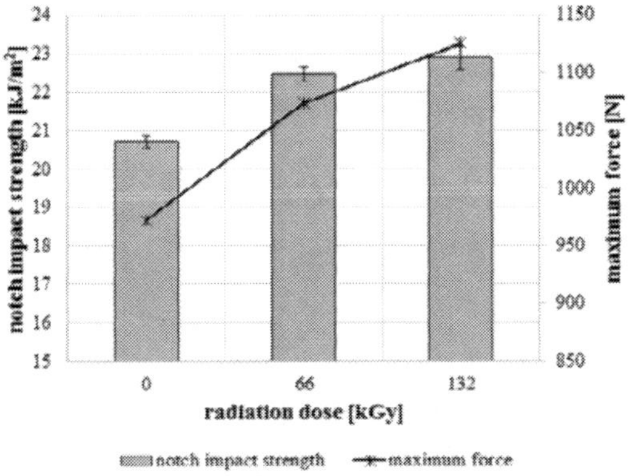

Fig. 8. Notch impact strength and maximum force (PA 7T GF 56, test temperature – 50 °C).

In the case of test temperature 50 °C the highest value of notch impact strength and maximum force was achieved by the irradiation with dose of 132 kGy. The value of notch impact strength increased from 20.7 kJ/m^2 (non-irradiated samples) to 22.9 kJ/m^2 (dose of 132 kGy), which is a hike of approximately 10 % (referring to: Fig. 8).

In the case of test temperature 75 °C the highest value of notch impact strength and maximum force was achieved by the irradiation with dose of 132 kGy. The value of notch impact strength increased from 27.2 kJ/m^2 (non-irradiated samples) to 32.2 kJ/m^2 (dose of 132 kGy), which is a hike of approximately 18 % (referring to: Fig. 9).

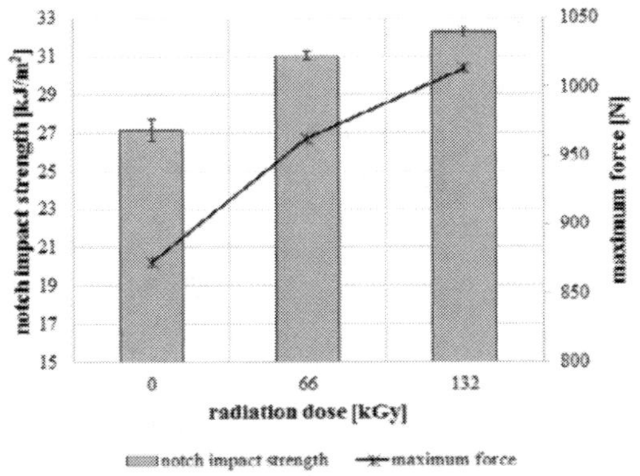

Fig. 9. Notch impact strength and maximum force (PA 7T GF 56, test temperature – 75 °C).

In the case of test temperature 100 °C the highest value of notch impact strength and maximum force was achieved by the irradiation with dose of 66 kGy. The value of notch impact strength increased from 34.9 kJ/m^2 (non-irradiated samples) to 36.7 kJ/m^2 (dose of 66 kGy), which is a hike of approximately 5 % (referring to: Fig. 10).

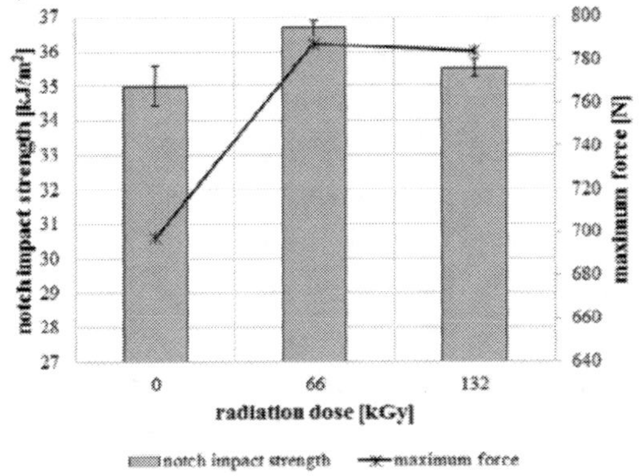

Fig. 10. Notch impact strength and maximum force (PA 7T GF 56, test temperature – 100 °C).

In the case of test temperature 125 °C the highest value of notch impact strength and maximum force was achieved by the irradiation with dose of 66 kGy. (referring to: Fig. 11).

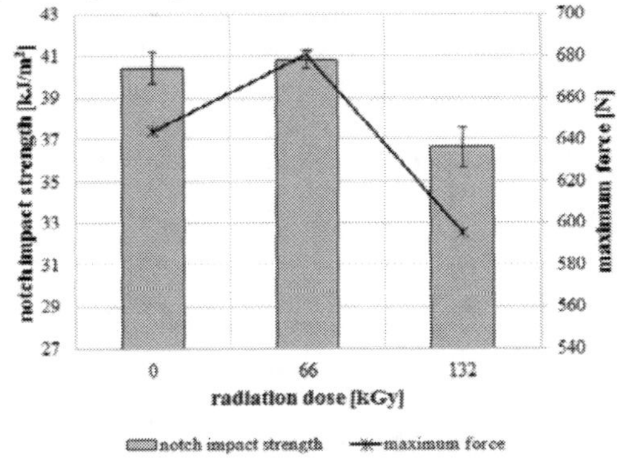

Fig. 11. Notch impact strength and maximum force (PA 7T GF 56, test temperature – 125 °C).

In the case of test temperature 150 °C the highest value of notch impact strength and maximum force was achieved by the irradiation with dose of 66 kGy. (referring to: Fig. 11).

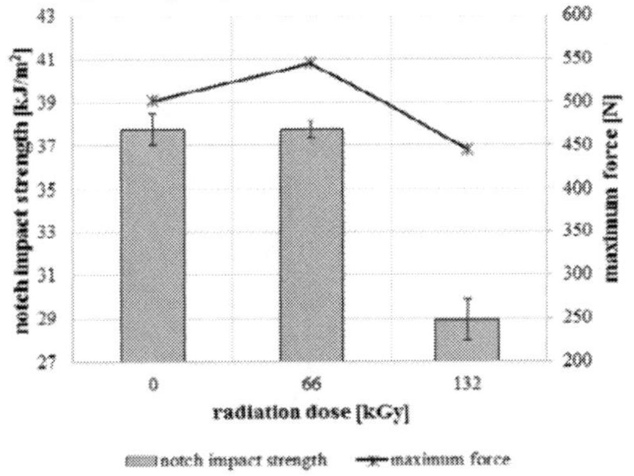

Fig. 12. Notch impact strength and maximum force (PA 7T GF 56, test temperature – 150 °C).

4 Conclusion

This article describes the effect of radiation crosslinking on the notch impact strength of polyamides (with glass fiber filler) under thermal stress. Changes due to irradiation were seen primarily in material with higher content of filler (PA 7T GF 56).

Acknowledgments

This paper is supported by the internal grant of TBU in Zlin No.IGA/FT/2017/010 funded from the resources of specific university research and by the Ministry of Education, Youth and Sports of the Czech Republic within the National Sustainability Programme project No. LO1303 (MSMT-7778/2014) and also by the European Regional Development Fund under the project CEBIA-Tech No. CZ.1.05/2.1.00/03.0089.

References

1. K. Makuuchi, S. Cheng, Radiation processing of polymer materials and its industrial applications, Wiley, Hoboken, N.J. (2012)
2. J.G. Drobny, Ionizing Radiation and Polymers: Principles, Technology and Applications, Elsevier, Oxford (2013)
3. M. Bednarik, A. Skrobak, V. Janostik, Key Eng. Materials (to be published)
4. Dj. Gheysari, A. Behjat, M. Haji-Saeid, European Polymer Journal **37**, 8 (2001)
5. A. Mizera, M. Manas, D. Manas et al., Key Eng. Materials **662**, 4 (2015)
6. S. Satapathy, S. Chattopadhyay, K.K. Chakrabarty et al., Journal of Applied Polymer Science **101**, 12 (2006)

7. Z. Holik, M. Manas, M. Danek, J. Macourek, Chem. Listy **103**, 4 (2009)
8. J. Navratil, M. Manas, M. Stanek, et al., Key Eng. Materials **662**, 4 (2015)
9. M. Ovsik, D. Manas, M. Manas, et al., Key Eng. Materials **699**, 6 (2016)
10. P. Stoklasek, A. Mizera, M. Manas, M. Bednarik, MM Science Journal **2016**, 5 (2016)
11. M. Bednarik, D. Manas, M. Manas, et al., Defect and Diffusion Forum **368**, 4 (2016)
12. J. Gehring, A. Zyball, Radiation Physics and Chemistry **46**, 6 (1995)
13. J. Navratil, M. Manas, A. Mizera, et al., Radiation Physics and Chemistry **106**, 5 (2015)
14. Z. Holik, M. Danek, M. Manas, et al., International Journal of Mechanics **5**, 8 (2011)
15. M. Bednarik, D. Manas, M. Manas, et al., MATEC Web of Conferences **76** (2016)
16. D. Manas, M. Manas, A. Mizera, et al., Key Eng. Materials **662**, 4 (2015)
17. J.G. Drobny, Radiation Technology for Polymers, CRC Press, Boca Raton (2003)
18. D. Manas, M. Manas, M. Stanek, T. Drga, Chem. Listy **101**, 2 (2007)
19. D. Manas, M. Ovsik, M. Manas, M. Stanek, J. Javorik, P. Kratky, Key Eng. Materials **586**, 4 (2014)
20. M. Manas, M. Stanek, D. Manas, M. Danek, Z. Holik, Chem. Listy **103**, 5 (2009)
21. M. Ovsik, P. Kratky, D. Manas, M. Manas, M. Stanek, M. Bednarik, Key Eng. Materials 606, 4 (2014)

 DOI: 10.1051/matecconf/201712502057

Influence of temperature and moisture on the mechanical properties of irradiated thermoplastics materials

Stoklasek Pavel[1] and *Bednarik* Martin[1,*]

[1] Tomas Bata University in Zlin, TGM 5555, 760 01, Zlin, Czech Republic

Abstract. This study deals with the effect of ionizing beta radiation on notch impact strength of polyamides filled with glass fiber under the influence of temperature and moisture. These properties were examined in dependence on the dosage of this ionizing beta radiation (non-irradiated samples and those irradiated by dosage 66, and 132 kGy were compared).

1 Introduction

The modification of polymer properties by irradiation is constantly evolving area. Ionic and ionizing radiation are the main types of radiation which are used for the polymer modification. Gamma radiation created from radioactive isotope Co-60 (60Co) belongs to ionizing radiation as well as beta radiation (electron beam) and X-ray radiation. All of these types significantly differ, however during these all process the energy transfer to atoms of irradiated material occurs [1-6].
As stated in previous investigations [6-16], it is possible to effectively change physical, mechanical and biological properties of irradiated material by ionizing radiation. These changes are probably caused by primary and secondary processes which are created due to interaction of ionizing radiation with polymer [1,2,3].

Ionization	$P \rightarrow P^{+} + e^{-}$
Excitation	$P \rightarrow P^{*}$
Thermal stabilization of electron	$e \rightarrow e_{th}^{-}$
Neutralization	$P^{+} + e_{th}^{-} \rightarrow P^{*}$
Free-radical generation	$P^{*} \rightarrow R_1^{\bullet} + R_2^{\bullet}$
	$\rightarrow R^{\bullet} + H^{\bullet}$

Fig. 1. Primary processes (P-polymer, R-radical) [1].

Hydrogene abstraction	$R^{\bullet} + P \rightarrow RH + P^{\bullet}$
Double-bond addition	$^{\bullet}RCH = CH_2 + H^{\bullet} \rightarrow RCH_2CH_2^{\bullet}$
Crosslinking or branching	$R_m^{\bullet} + R_n^{\bullet} \rightarrow R_m - R_n$
Chain scission	$R^{\bullet} \rightarrow R_k^{\bullet} + R_l$
Oxidation	$R^{\bullet} + O_2 \rightarrow ROO^{\bullet}$
	$ROO^{\bullet} \rightarrow -C = O, -OH, -COOH$
Grafting	$R^{\bullet} + M \rightarrow RM^{\bullet}$
	$RM^{\bullet} + nM \rightarrow RM_{n+r}$

Fig. 2. Secondary processes (M-monomer) [1].

Ionization, excitation and free radicals generation belong to primary interactions. Secondary reactions include crosslinking or branching, chain scission, oxidation and grafting, which follow after the free radical generation [1,2,3]. The primary and secondary processes are shown in the Figure 1 and 2 [1].
Various polymeric materials have various reactions on radiation, especially in case of crosslinking and chain scission (refer with: Table 1). Crosslinking and chain scission are two competitive processes, which always coexist during irradiation and the overall irradiation effect depends on which process predominate in given time (crosslinking or chain scission) [1-6].

Table 1. Classification of polymers according to their response to ionizing radiation [2].

Polymers predominantly crosslinking	Polymers predominantly degrading
Polyethylene	Poly(tetrafluoroethylene)
Polystyrene	Poly(vinyl fluoride)
Polypropylene	Poly(methyl methacrylate)
Polyamides	Polyoxymethylene
Poly(vinyl chloride)	Poly(ethylene sulfide)
Polyesters	Polyisobutylene
Poly(vinyl methyl ether)	Polyacrylonitrile
Poly(vinyl acetate)	Poly(propylene sulfide)

The crosslinking level can be adjusted by irradiation dosage and often by means of a crosslinking booster. The main difference between electron beta and photon gamma is in their different abilities of penetrating the irradiated material. Gamma rays have a high penetration capacity. The penetration capacity of electron rays depends on the energy of the accelerated electrons. Due to accelerated electron the required dose may be applied for seconds, whereas several hours are required on the gamma radiation plant. The electron accelerators operate

* Corresponding author: mbednarik@utb.cz

on the principle of the Braun tube, whereby a hot cathode is heated in vacuum to such a degree that electrons are released [17-21].
This study deals with the influence of different doses of ionizing beta radiation on notch impact strength of polyamides filled with glass fiber under the influence of temperature and moisture and follows previous studies [3, 5, 7, 9, 10], which described the change of mechanical properties of selected types thermoplastics.
The previous study [3, 5, 7, 9, 10] proved the positive irradiation effect on mechanical of selected types polymers. Nevertheless, some findings are not explained yet, namely the change of dynamic properties during the application of beta radiation on material under thermal loading. Each new finding on the effect of radiation crosslinking on the properties of polymer materials may thus contribute to a better understanding of the issue and can extend the field of new applications.

2 Experimental

2.1 Materials

For this experiment two types polyamides were used. Both materials are filled with glass fibers and their commercial names are:
- Polyamide 66 GF 30 – V – PTS – CREAMID A3H7.2G 6*M0129A Schwarz
- Polyamide 7T GF 56 – V – DURAMID TH7 G12.0SZB*9207

The basic properties of used materials are shown in Table 2 and 3.

Table 2. Properties of PA 66 GF 30.

PA 66 GF 30	
Density [g/cm^3]	1.37
Impact toughness [kJ/m^2]	8
Tensile modulus [MPa]	10000
Bending strength [MPa]	260
Softening temperature [°C]	255

The samples were made using the injection molding technology on the injection molding machine Arburg Allrounder 470H 1000-400. The samples had the shape and dimensions according to the CSN EN ISO 179. Processing conditions during the injection moulding were according to the recommendation of the procedures.
Test specimens were equipped with a notch type V (size 2 mm).

Table 3. Properties of PA 7T GF 56.

PA 7T GF 56	
Density [g/cm^3]	1.63
Impact toughness [kJ/m^2]	25
Tensile modulus [MPa]	19000
Bending strength [MPa]	290
Softening temperature [°C]	229

All samples were irradiated with electron (beta) rays (electron energy 10 MeV, radiation doses: 66 and 132 kGy) in the firm BGS Beta Gamma Service GmbH & Co, Saal am Danau – Germany [7, 14, 15].

2.2 Determination of crosslinked phase (gel) and mechanical characteristic

For determination the crosslinked phase (gel) there was used a gel test. Test conditions were according to the CSN EN 579 [3].
For testing the mechanical properties there was used a dynamic test on the test machine Zwick HIT50P. Test conditions were according to the CSN EN ISO 179. The energy of the hammer was 50 J and test data was processed by Test Xpert II software.
After irradiation, the test specimens were exposed to the effects of temperature and moisture (168 hours at 75 °C and 98% moisture).

3 Results and discussion

3.1 The content of crosslinked phase

As it is apparent from measurement results, the ionizing beta radiation significantly increases the content of crosslinked phase (refer with: Fig. 3).

DOI: 10.1051/matecconf/201712502057

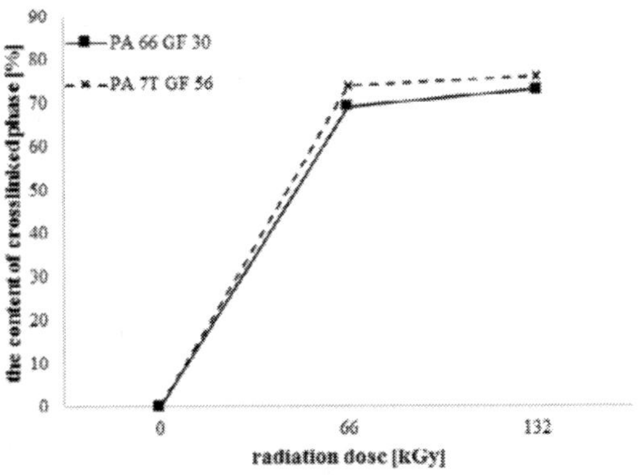

Fig. 3. Variation of content of crosslinked phase.

From this can be deduced that the higher amount of crosslinked phase (gel) the higher amount of structural net created mainly in the amorphous phase of PA 66 GF 30 and PA 7T GF 56 as a result of irradiation [1-3].
These changes have resulted in improvement of mechanical properties of tested materials.

3.2 Notch impact strength – PA 66 GF 30

Comparison of notch impact strength and maximum force (at 75 °C and 98% moisture) of PA 66 GF 30 before and after irradiation is given in the Figures 4 and 5.

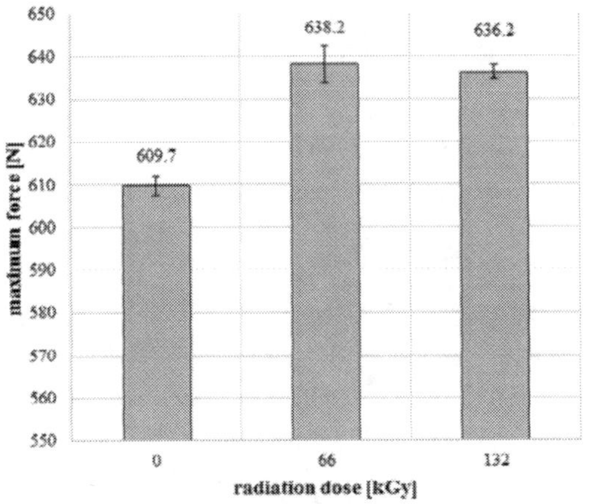

Fig. 4. Maximum force – PA 66 GF 30.

In the case of maximum force the highest increase was achieved at a dose of 66 kGy and the lowest change of maximum force was measured at a dose of 132 kGy. In the case of irradiated with a dose of 66 kGy the maximum force increased from 609.7 N (non-irradiated samples) to 638.2 N (dose of 66 kGy), which is a hike of approximately 5 % (referring to: Fig. 4).

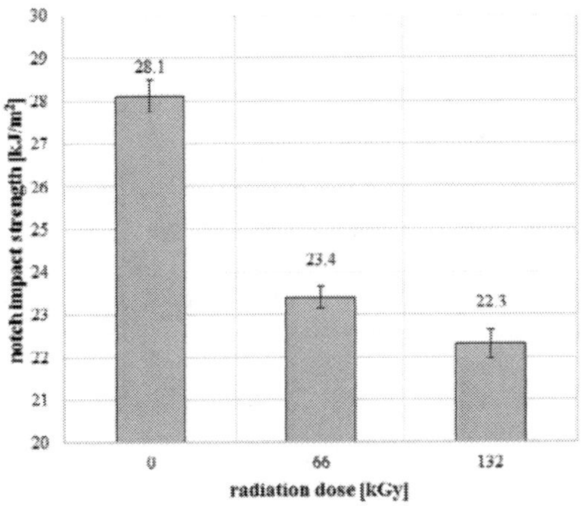

Fig. 5. Notch impact strength – PA 66 GF 30.

In the case of notch impact strength, the observed values decreased (due to irradiation). The highest decrease was achieved at a dose of 132 kGy. In the case of irradiated with a dose of 132 kGy the notch impact strength decreased from 28.1 kJ/m^2 (non-irradiated samples) to 22.3 kJ/m^2 (dose of 132 kGy), which is a drop of approximately 20 % (referring to: Fig. 5).

3.3 Notch impact strength – PA 7T GF 56

Comparison of notch impact strength and maximum force (at 75 °C and 98% moisture) of PA 7T GF 56 before and after irradiation is given in the Figures 6 and 7.

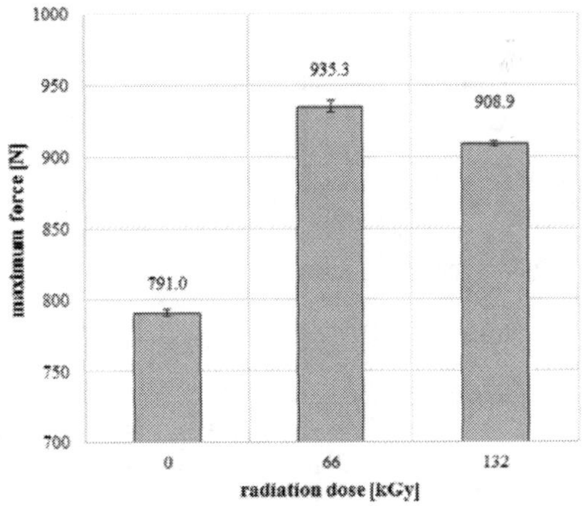

Fig. 6. Maximum force – PA 7T GF 56.

In the case of maximum force the highest increase was achieved at a dose of 66 kGy and the lowest change of maximum force was measured at a dose of 132 kGy. In the case of irradiated with a dose of 66 kGy the maximum force increased from 791.0 N (non-irradiated samples) to 935.3 N (dose of 66 kGy), which is a hike of approximately 20 % (referring to: Fig. 6).

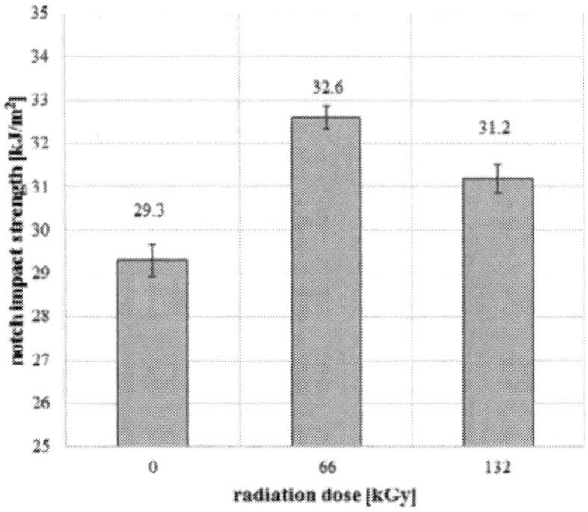

Fig. 7. Notch impact strength – PA 7T GF 56.

In the case of notch impact strength the highest increase was achieved at a dose of 66 kGy and the lowest change of notch impact strength was measured at a dose of 132 kGy. In the case of irradiated with a dose of 66 kGy the notch impact strength increased from 29.3 kJ/m^2 (non-irradiated samples) to 32.6 kJ/m^2 (dose of 66 kGy), which is a hike of approximately 10 % (referring to: Fig. 7).

4 Conclusion

This study deals with the influence of different doses of ionizing beta radiation on notch impact strength of polyamides filled with glass fiber under the influence of temperature and moisture. From the measurement results follows, that the ionizing beta radiation appears to be a very effective way to increase the mechanical properties. The consequence of irradiation is the creation of the covalent bonds among the macromolecular strings which are more flexible during thermal load than intermolecular forces [2,3,7,14,15]. These changes (together with the rise of content of crosslinked phase) have resulted in an significant improvement in mechanical properties of tested polyamides.

Changes due to irradiation were seen primarily in material with higher content of filler (PA 7T GF 56).

Acknowledgments

This paper is supported by the internal grant of TBU in Zlin No.IGA/FT/2017/010 funded from the resources of specific university research and by the Ministry of Education, Youth and Sports of the Czech Republic within the National Sustainability Programme project No. LO1303 (MSMT-7778/2014) and also by the European Regional Development Fund under the project CEBIA-Tech No. CZ.1.05/2.1.00/03.0089.

References

1. K. Makuuchi, S. Cheng, Radiation processing of polymer materials and its industrial applications, Wiley, Hoboken, N.J. (2012)
2. J.G. Drobny, Ionizing Radiation and Polymers: Principles, Technology and Applications, Elsevier, Oxford (2013)
3. M. Bednarik, A. Skrobak, V. Janostik, Key Eng. Materials (to be published)
4. Dj. Gheysari, A. Behjat, M. Haji-Saeid, European Polymer Journal **37**, 8 (2001)
5. A. Mizera, M. Manas, D. Manas et al., Key Eng. Materials **662**, 4 (2015)
6. S. Satapathy, S. Chattopadhyay, K.K. Chakrabarty et al., Journal of Applied Polymer Science **101**, 12 (2006)
7. Z. Holik, M. Manas, M. Danek, J. Macourek, Chem. Listy **103**, 4 (2009)
8. J. Navratil, M. Manas, M. Stanek, et al., Key Eng. Materials **662**, 4 (2015)
9. M. Ovsik, D. Manas, M. Manas, et al., Key Eng. Materials **699**, 6 (2016)
10. P. Stoklasek, A. Mizera, M. Manas, M. Bednarik, MM Science Journal **2016**, 5 (2016)
11. M. Bednarik, D. Manas, M. Manas, et al., Defect and Diffusion Forum **368**, 4 (2016)
12. J. Gehring, A. Zyball, Radiation Physics and Chemistry **46**, 6 (1995)
13. J. Navratil, M. Manas, A. Mizera, et al., Radiation Physics and Chemistry **106**, 5 (2015)
14. Z. Holik, M. Danek, M. Manas, et al., International Journal of Mechanics **5**, 8 (2011)
15. M. Bednarik, D. Manas, M. Manas, et al., MATEC Web of Conferences **76** (2016)
16. D. Manas, M. Manas, A. Mizera, et al., Key Eng. Materials **662**, 4 (2015)
17. J.G. Drobny, Radiation Technology for Polymers, CRC Press, Boca Raton (2003)
18. D. Manas, M. Manas, M. Stanek, T. Drga, Chem. Listy **101**, 2 (2007)
19. D. Manas, M. Ovsik, M. Manas, M. Stanek, J. Javorik, P. Kratky, Key Eng. Materials **586**, 4 (2014)
20. M. Manas, M. Stanek, D. Manas, M. Danek, Z. Holik, Chem. Listy **103**, 5 (2009)
21. M. Ovsik, P. Kratky, D. Manas, M. Manas, M. Stanek, M. Bednarik, Key Eng. Materials 606, 4 (2014)

DOI: 10.1051/matecconf/201712502058

Computer networks in education

Milan Adamek [1,a] *Miroslav* Matysek[1] and *Michaela* Barinova[1]

[1] *Tomas Bata University in Zlin, Faculty of Applied Informatics, Nam. T. G. Masaryka 5555, 760 05 Zlin, Czech Republic*

Abstract. In order to deepen practical knowledge of students within the subject "Computer Networks", a monitoring network system has been developed which is able to read, collect and distribute data describing real technological process. The monitoring system design is based on a client/server architecture. The system was verified on a model chemical reactor used for hydrolysis of chrome-tanned wastes from tanneries.

1 Introduction

University students educated in the field of Informatics attend either during their bachelor or master study in various forms the subject "Computer Networks". The basic content of the courses is to acquaint the students with the problems and administration of computer networks from a user's viewpoint. Usually, the courses more or less copy the following structure: explanation of the types of computer networks, topology and architecture of computer networks, communication protocols, and inseparable problems of computer networks security. However, computer networks represent broad and dynamically developing area which is difficult to compass in the limited time dedicated to this subject so that students could acquire practical skills through practical tasks and applications.

A client – server architecture was chosen for the system design, which meets the requirements for the separation of the parts executing data reading, collecting, distribution and presentation [1]. The said system architecture works on the assumption that reading of technological data is executed by the first client, data collection and distribution is realized by the server, and data presentation is performed by the second client. This system structure enables us to achieve the necessary freedom in the selection of the environment, in which any part of the system can be realized.

Selection of the operating system was a very important step in the monitoring system development. This especially applies to the server, since realization of any of the client is not as strongly dependent on the type of operating system. Generally it can be stated that the client application can be realized on any platform for which is available the BSD Sockets network library. The selection process of the operating system for the server application was determined by the following parameters:

1. Support of inter-process communication (IPC),
2. simultaneous processing of multiple programs,
3. means of network communication based on the TCP/IP protocol,
4. reasonable hardware demands.

As a result, for the realization of both the server and individual clients we gave preference to Linux operating system. This operating system showed best match with the above listed criteria [2, 3].

2 ARCHITECTURE OF THE MONITORING SYSTEM

In network applications, the model client - server is a standard [4]. The term server in this case denotes a process that expects a contact from the client in the sense that the server can perform an operation for the client. The client in the said model also represents a certain process. In the developed monitoring system, the behavior of the server and client can be described as follows:

- Process server is running on a PC. It initializes itself, then goes into a sleep mode and waits for a contact from the client.
- Process client is running on the same or another PC. In the event that the client and server are running on the same PC (under one OS), the communication between them is performed by means of the OS. In the case that the client and server run on different PCs, the communication between them is mediated through a computer network. The process client sends its request toward the server and waits for the result of the processing sent back by the server.
- After completing the request of the client, the server goes into a sleep mode and waits for further requests from the client.

2.1 Client

The role of the client in the proposed monitoring system is reading technological data and their visualization. A standard client works with a known port,

[a] Corresponding author: adamek@fai.utb.cz

which in this case is referred to as the reserved port. The reserved ports are installed in order to establish a connection with the server. To establish a connection, the client must know the number of the port on which the service is offered by the server (for example ftp). Other programs of a client type operate as non-standard clients. Therefore, after establishing a connection between the client and server it is not necessary to use the reserved port (it is even not desirable due to liberation of the port for further communication) and the communication is performed on randomly selected and mutually conflict-free ports from the range of dynamic and private ports. The reserved port is after establishing the connection released immediately for possible communication with another client.

Reading of technological data is ensured by the recording client that is realized as a controller of the device reading the relevant technological process quantity, which it subsequently sends to the server. It is possible to run multiple recording clients under one operating system (PC). In this case, each client ensures reading and transfer of different technological quantity. There are no specific requirements of the environment, in which this part is realized, except for the ability to use the TCP/IP protocol for the connection with the server program.

The presenting client then receives the current copies of the data of the technological process quantities from the server and ensures their presentation. It is possible to have more presenting clients running within the network – one presenting client under one operating system (PC).

2.2 Server

Collection and distribution of data is performed by the server program. Its functions can be divided into three main points:

1. Receiving data from the recording clients
2. Maintaining the current copies of the read data
3. Sending the current data to the presenting clients.

The proposed system uses two kinds of servers depending on the time needed to perform the required processes. Their function can be characterized as follows:

1. In the event the server is able to handle the clients' requests in a short period of time, the server processes these requests itself. This type of processes in the model is called iterative server. A typical example of an iterative server is a service providing date and time.
2. If the time for the processing of a client's request is unlimited, the server processes the request in a competitive way. This type of server is called competitive. The competitive server - parental process (master server) creates its copy – the descendant. The descendant then further processes the client's request, so the original (parental) process of the server may again go into a sleep mode and wait for the next client's request. This type of server of course requires an operating system, which allows simultaneous running of multiple processes. The competitive servers are widely used for example in ftp and Telnet services. The established connection between the client and the server usually contains multiple requests – in other words, multiple exchanges of queries and answers take place between the client and the server.

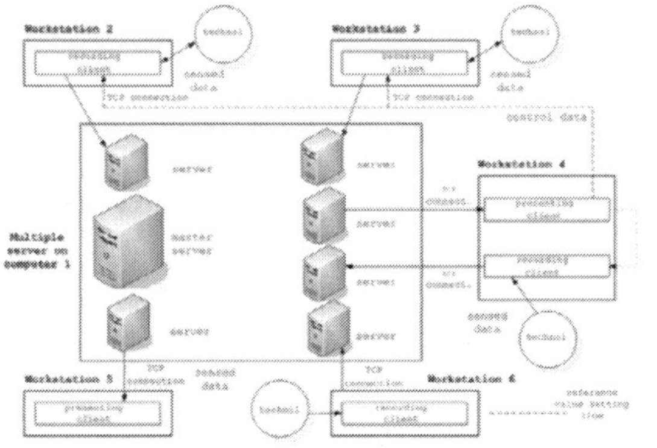

Fig. 1. The designed model of the monitoring and controlling system.

3 SOFTWARE

3.1. Program Client

Communication between the client and server through the TCP protocol is carried out according to the following algorithm:

1. Finding the IP address of the server from the specified name or address input in dot notation.
2. Creation of a mailbox for communication - function socket()
3. Connection to the server - function connect()
4. Data exchange with the server - functions read() or write()
5. Termination of communication with the server.

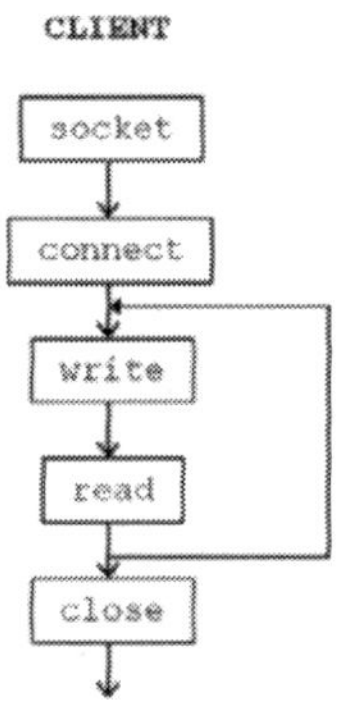

Fig. 2. The basic algorithm for the communication between a client and the server

3.2. Program Server

Processing of the clients' requirements is performed by the server in a competitive way. In most cases it is an apparent competition, which is achieved by sharing the process in time.

The basic algorithm of the Server program is as follows:

1) Immediately after starting, the Master server program creates mailboxes for communication and these are associated with the reserved ports - functions socket()

DOI: 10.1051/matecconf/201712502058

and bind(). The ports for the connection with the clients are defined in the server configuration file.

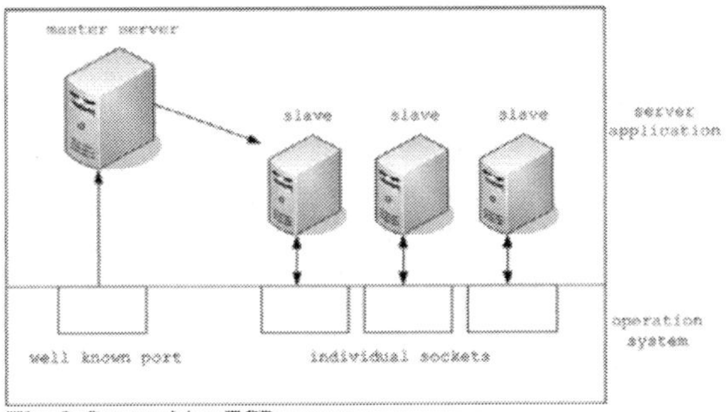

Fig. 3 Competitive TCP server.

2) After they have been created, the mailboxes are set into a passive state in which they are waiting for connections from the clients - functions listen() and select(). Using the select() function, the kernel can put the master server process into a standby mode. In this mode it waits until an event occurs, then it is activated. In the proposed model, the kernel notifies the master server process only in the case when data for connection initialization (i.e. data for reading) appear on any of the mailboxes.

3) At the occurrence of the event "connection request", the master server receives the request on the related port - function connect(). If the case of a recording client, the master server makes a checkout of the number of the connected recording clients. If a new client exceeds the maximum number of the recording clients, the connection is closed and the master server again puts itself into a sleep mode. It the event there is enough room for the connection of a new recording client, a call to the kernel function fork() is executed, resulting in the creation of a descendant to see to the operator's requirements. If a presentation client is connected, the way of the processing of the connection request is the same except for the checkout of the maximum number of connected recording clients. After that, the master server closes the no more necessary mailbox that was created by the prior calling of the connect() function.

4) Message exchange between a client and the server through the established connection

• The server (descendant) serving the recording client waits for the data sent by the client. After receiving the data, the server writes them in the shared memory. The synchronization of the access to the shared memory with other processes is ensured by semaphores. After entering the data in the shared memory, the server sends a signal that indicates to all other servers (descendants) that new data has been written in the shared memory.

• Server serving the recording client sends immediately after establishing the connection the contents of all slots to the client. Then it goes to sleep until it is awakened by a signal that initializes entering new data in the shared memory. Consequently, the server gains access to the control structure (header) of the shared memory, checks which slots contain new data and sends this data immediately to the client.

The described activities are carried out by both types of descendants cyclically until the connection is closed by the client or the Server program operation is terminated (by termination of master server).

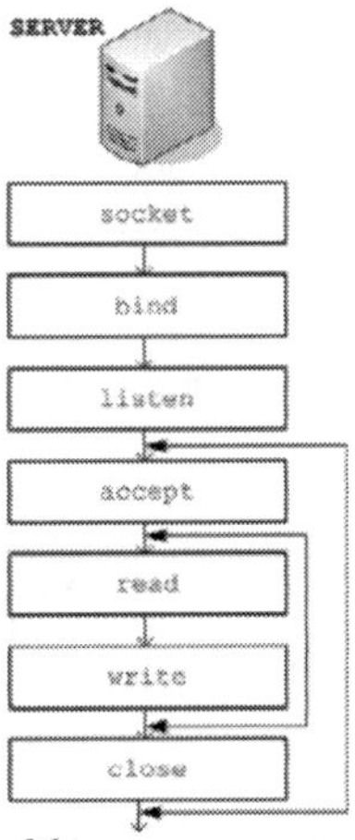

Fig. 4 Basic structure of the server program

3.3. Structure of the shared memory

The shared memory was used in the model in order to preserve the data obtained from the recording clients. The main reason for using this tool for inter-process communication was the possibility of a simultaneous access of multiple processes (descendants of the master server) to the data stored in the shared memory. A synchronization of the access, for example by semaphores, is necessary to enable access of multiple processes to the shared memory. The shared memory is divided into two parts as is shown in Figure 5.

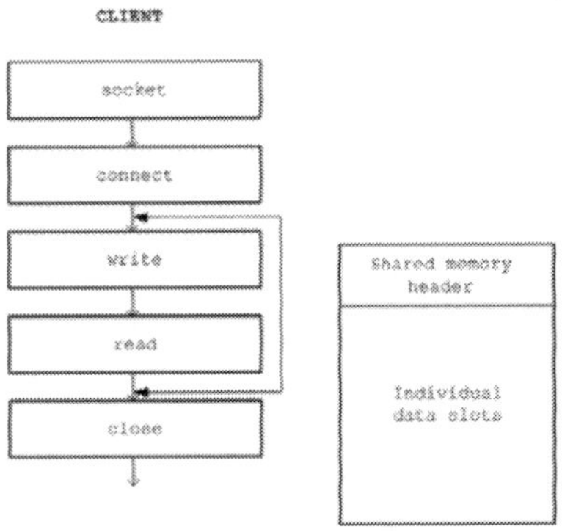

Fig. 5 Shared memory structure

The area of each data slot represents a data area into which data is written by individual recording clients, with just one slot reserved for each recording client. The server serving this client records only in the one related slot and in the header. The server serving the presenting client performs only reading from the shared memory from both the slot and the header areas.

The data describing individual slots are stored in the header. These particularly include entries indicating the time of the slot last modification. This data is used by the server operating the presentation client to decide whether the data from this slot has already been sent to the client or whether it is newly received data to be sent.

3.4. Process synchronization methods

Within the Server program it is necessary to ensure synchronization of the processes by which the data in the shared memory are accessed. The following rules must be observed in order to maintain data consistency:

1. In one moment a slot cannot be modified by more than one process.
2. If the slot is being modified, no process is allowed to read this slot.
3. The slot from which the data are just being read cannot be accessed by a process that wants to modify the data. On the other hand, a situation may occur in which two or more processes read data from the same slot.

Synchronization of all processes is based on methods using semaphores and signals.

The basic critical conditions include: termination of the connection between the client and the server, termination of work or system failure. To any of the named conditions the program Server responds by a proper termination, including the release of all tools used. For the determination of a failure or disconnection of the client program uses the primary method of sending data out of range, which evaluates the client and closes the connection. For cases where the process server does not manage to inform the client about the failure data outside the range is used symptom clipboard SO KEEPALIVE that this situation highlights the client process. Another condition which should be treated in the process of the master server, the termination of a child. In this case it is necessary to call the kernel function wait() system to avoid zombie processes.

4 NETWORK LOAD

When implementing network applications, the network load must be evaluated from two perspectives. It is necessary to consider to which extent the deployed applications will load the overall operation of the network and vice versa, to evaluate the effect of the network load on the application performance. These are the basic viewpoints on the performance issues of both the application and network.

With respect to the minimum network load, a method for the data transfer between the server and clients was selected that uses small packets which are sent in longer time intervals. This prevents the network from a stress load, since the network could be busy with other user applications.

To assess the effect of a long-term network load it is necessary to consider the time interval in which the data in the monitoring system must be presented. In the monitoring of a technological process it mainly concerns obtaining data for further calculations or verification of the course of the process control. The proposed monitoring system will not be significantly affected by crash network loads, which may be caused for instance by a short-term failure of the file - server.

5 IMPLEMENTATION OF THE MONITORING SYSTEM

For educational purposes and more detailed study on the monitoring system properties and behavior, the developed monitoring system was implemented on a real model of a technological process. This gives students the opportunity to verify the functioning of the monitoring system on a real technological device and get closer insight into the data transfer process, the functioning of the server and both the recording and presenting client. The study on real processes is still an important part of engineering education in various fields and in many cases it cannot be fully substituted by mere simulations of individual physical/chemical phenomena [7]. The need for and importance of practical experience with real systems, e.g. in the form of remote laboratories, is repeatedly reflected in technical literature in the field of the role of computer technology in university education [e.g. 8].

5.1. Monitoring of a technological process

The realistic model was represented by a chemical reactor, which was constructed for model studies on enzymatic hydrolysis of potentially hazardous chrome-tanned wastes generated during leather manufacturing. Disposal of chrome-tanned waste at open landfills where it is subjected to climatic and other external conditions is not suitable since there is a risk of oxidation of trivalent chromium present in this waste into carcinogenic hexavalent chromium salts [9]. Processing of chrome-tanned waste, the most typical representative of which is chromium shavings, and its conversion into valuable products is therefore advantageous not only from environmental, but mainly from health protection point of view.

One of the most advanced and industrially implemented procedures so far is the technique of two-step hydrolysis under alkali conditions in the presence of a proteolytic enzyme [10]. The process is done in two stages, namely alkali treatment and consecutive enzymatic hydrolysis. The results of the reaction after the first step is gelatable protein and intermediate filter cake. The cake is then subjected to enzymatic hydrolysis, giving insoluble filter cake with concentrated chromium and soluble protein hydrolyzate, which is in the terminal phase dried in vacuum evaporator. Dependent on the way in which the reaction is controlled, the reaction gives protein solution of various qualities, given specifically by gel strength (Bloom value). The model reactor allows studying the hydrolysis conditions at which it is possible to obtain desired properties of final products.

The monitoring system is implemented in the first stage of the technological process, i.e. alkaline treatment (denaturation) of chrome shavings in the chemical reactor. Simplified models of the used chemical reactor

DOI: 10.1051/matecconf/201712502058

and its control are depicted in the following Figs. 6 and 7, respectively.

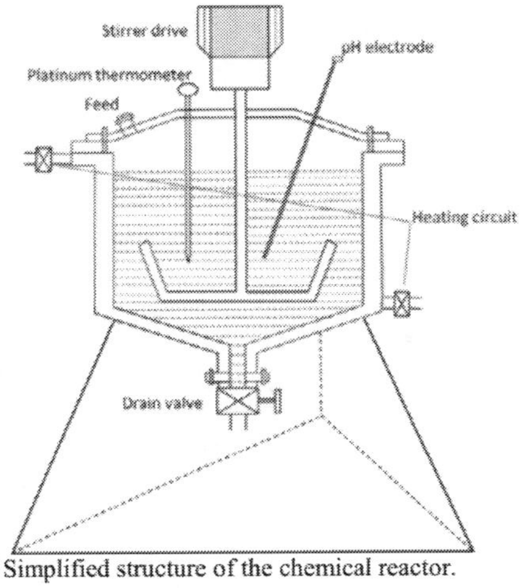

Fig. 6 Simplified structure of the chemical reactor.

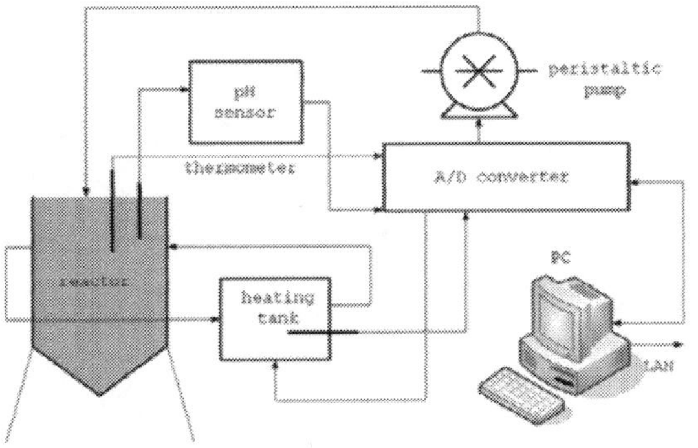

Fig. 7 Block diagram of the chemical reactor control.

The reactor, a cylindrical tank of a type of fermentation reactor, represents a non-flow isothermal heterogeneous reactor with hollow shell, through which flows the heating liquid which is heated in a separated tank outside the reactor. The alkaline treatment takes place at a pH of 12 and a temperature of 70°C. If the pH decreases below the required level (due to the buffering effect of protein), it is adjusted by addition of an alkali. At the said pH and temperature, the hydrolysis is most efficient; an increase of either value above or below this optimal level reduces the reaction rate or affects the resulting products.

The peristaltic pump (type PS 10) is used for dosing of the reaction components. Sensor PHR01 for the measurement of pH consists of a measuring glass electrode and a reference silver-chloride electrode, which are conjugated in a common stem. The potential of the measuring electrode after it is immersed in the solution is dependent mainly on hydrogen ion concentration. The platinum thermometers Pt 100 are used for the measuring of the reaction mixture temperature and the temperature of heating liquid in the heating tank. The measured data are converted from the analogue to digital form via the ADVANTECH PCI 1716 technological card and subsequently used as input data for the control circuit.

6 CONCLUSIONS

The communication based on the TCP protocol guarantees a sufficient integrity of the transferred data. The system architecture makes possible the dynamic connecting and disconnecting of both the monitoring places and the programs for monitored processes data presentation. The modularity of the system has prepared good precondition for implementing the client application in the environment of any operating system equipped with the support of communication based on the TCP/IP protocol. The local network monitoring and control system has been debugged in the C-language in the OS Linux Slackware 1.2.13 and RedHat 7.1 environment and verified on the laboratory hydrolysis/fermentation reactor installed within the premises of the Faculty of Applied Informatics.

The system has been successfully implemented at the Faculty of Applied Informatics of Tomas Bata University in Zlín, Czech Republic within the framework of the subject "Computer Networks". Extended practical knowledge contributes to higher employment opportunities of the graduates on the labor market, especially in technical branches. Students can also use the system for their bachelor and master theses; in addition to the educational benefits, the theses contribute to gradual upgrading and development of the monitoring network system including its extension for example to mobile applications.

5 Conclusion

Online software tools for designing CCTV systems are tools that are easier to use and in most cases solved by means of calculators. The tools can usually calculate the basic parameters of a CCTV system, which are often not sufficient for modeling of objects in which the CCTV system is to be located. Second type is represented by software tools which, once installed on a PC, are much more sophisticated environment with support of a wide range of libraries. They allow creating of 3D models of buildings and their interior equipment. Cameras with defined parameters are subsequently placed into the models. The tools can then simulate the images captured by the cameras and show previews of real footage. The last type of software are mobile applications. They predominantly operate on the same principle as the online tools.

Acknowledgement

This work was supported by the Ministry of Education, Youth and Sports of the Czech Republic within the National Sustainability Programme project No. LO1303 (MSMT-7778/2014) and also by the European Regional

Development Fund under the project CEBIA-Tech No. CZ.1.05/2.1.00/03.0089

References

1. Tanenbaum, *Modern operating systems*, 2nd edition, Prentice Hall, Englewood Cliffs, NJ, 2001.
2. W. R. Stevens, *Advanced Programming in the UNIX Environment*, 2nd Ed. Addison-Wesley, Reading, MA, 2005.
3. W. R. Stevens, *TI - UNIX network programming*, Prentice-Hall, Englewood Cliffs, NJ, 1998.
4. S. Tanenbaum & A. S. Woodhull, *Operating Systems*: Design and Implementation, Prentice-Hall, Englewood Cliffs, NJ, 2006.
5. Silberschatz, P. B. Galvin, G. Gagne, *Operating systems concepts*, 7th Ed. John Wiley & sons, Inc., NY, 2002.
6. S. J. Bigelow, Troubleshooting, *Maintaining & Repairing Networks*, 1st Ed. Osborne/McGraw-Hill, NY, 2002.
7. Z. Nedic, J. Machotka, A. Nafalski, *Remote laboratories versus virtual and real laboratories*, Frontiers in Education, 2003. FIE 2003. 33rd Annual 1 (2003), T3E-1-T3E-6.
8. M. Domínguez, J. J. Fuertes, M. A. Prada, S. Alonso, A. Morán, *Remote laboratory of a quadruple tank process for learning in control engineering using different industrial controllers*, Comput. Appl. Eng. Educ., Vol. 22, No. 3, 2011, pp. 375-386.
9. K. Kolomazník, M. Adámek, I. Anděl, M. Uhlířová, *Leather waste - Potential threat to human health, and a new technology of its treatment*. J. Haz. Mat., Vol. 160, No. 2-3, 2008, pp. 514-520.
10. K. Kolomaznik, M. Mladek, F. Langmaier, D. Janacova, M. M. Taylor, *Experience in industrial practice of enzymatic dechromation of chrome shavings*, J. Am. Leather Chem. As., Vol. 94, No. 2, 1999, pp. 55-63.

DOI: 10.1051/matecconf/201712502059

Intensity of EMF generated by electronic safety system devices

Martin Pospisilik[1,*], *Eva* Vnencakova[2], and *Milan* Kutaj[2]

[1]Tomas Bata University in Zlin, Faculty of Applied Informatics, Nad Stranemi 4511, 760 05 Zlin, Czech Republic
[2]University of Zilina, Faculty of Security Engineering, 1st May Street 32, 010 26 Zilina, Slovakia

Abstract. As the importance of wireless networks based on radio frequencies increases in time, a space for discussion on harmfulness of the electromagnetic radiation has occurred. On the one hand there are studies showing that a direct influence of non-ionizing electromagnetic waves on the human organism was not confirmed until a certain intensity has been reached. On the other hand, critical voices appear, warning that even low intensities of non-ionizing electromagnetic fields are harmful to the human body, if it is exposed to the radiation for a prolonged time. The authors of this paper have no ambition to resolve this dispute. However, they provide data on the intensity of the electromagnetic fields generated by several components of electronic security system that are operating on the basis of the wireless network. The data have been gained in a specialized workplace and will allow the reader to imagine how intensive the radio signals generated by the battery-operated devices are compared to the current hygienic and technical limits.

1 Introduction

Electromagnetic field (EMF) is a physical field produced by electrically charged objects. Its principle and the relevant mechanisms have been studied since 17th century and the first complete theory to describe this phenomenon was published in 1873 by James Clerk Maxwell. The EMF also include radio waves that have become an object of interest at the turn of the 19th and 20th centuries and currently their importance continues to grow. Physically, the radio waves can be understood as an energy-carrying matter. Its oscillating particles are of a very low weight but they embody great momentum. The energy of the radio waves in quantized. The smallest amount of energy is represented by a photon. The photon's energy is directly proportional to a frequency it oscillates on:

$$W_f = hf \; [J] \qquad (1)$$

Where $h = 6.625 \cdot 10^{-34}$ [Js] is a Planck's constant. The relationship between the weight of a photon and its propagation velocity can be expressed by the well-known Einstein's equation (2). The propagation velocity of EMF is given by the permittivity and the permeability of the ambience (3).

$$W = mc^2 \; [J] \qquad (2)$$

$$c = \frac{1}{\sqrt{\varepsilon_0 \varepsilon_r \mu_0 \mu_r}} \; [m/s] \qquad (3)$$

Where:
$\varepsilon_0 = 8.85 \cdot 10^{-12}$ [F/m] is the vacuum permittivity,
ε_r is the permittivity of the ambient material,
$\mu_0 = 4\pi \cdot 10^{-7}$ $[N/A^2]$ is the vacuum permeability,
μ_r is the permeability of the ambient material.

As the EMF (radio waves respectively) is the carrier of energy, it has effects on the mass which it interacts. This is useful for information transmissions as the energy of the modulated EMF drives the input of the receiver with no need of wired connection. The direct consequence of this phenomenon is a thermal action on the irradiated matter (microwave ovens) when the EMF intensity is high enough. In a free environment, the EMF intensity is usually expressed in [V/m] although the EMF consists of two components, the electrical field and the magnetic field. The intensity of electrical field is expressed in Volts per meter [V/m] while the intensity of the magnetic field is expressed in Amperes per meter [A/m]. However, in the free environment the ratio between the electric and the magnetic fields is fixed. Therefore only one unit [V/m] can be used to describe the EMF intensity correctly. The EMF intensity decreases with the distance from its radiator approximately according to the following equation:

$$E = \frac{\sqrt{30P}}{r} \; [V/m] \qquad (4)$$

Where:
P is the transmitting power of the radiator in Watts,
r is the distance from the radiator in metres.

1.1 Standardization

Concerning the issues on EMF, thorough technical standardization has been implemented in the past, mostly because of the problems arising from the electromagnetic compatibility of the relevant systems.

* Corresponding author: pospisilik@fai.utb.cz

Generally, the standardization covers two large groups of issues:

- Electromagnetic compatibility of technical systems,
- Electromagnetic compatibility of biological systems.

Although the scientists usually find consensus concerning the technical systems, there are many ambiguous issues on the electromagnetic compatibility of biological systems. Although the effects of EMF on the human organism have been observed for a long time, the results of existing biophysical and biophysical research in this area are not unambiguous. The biological effects of the electromagnetic field depend on its nature, the duration of action, and the properties of the organism. Since field receptors (ie, inputs of the electromagnetic field into the organism) are not known, these effects are only assessed by non-specific reactions of the organism. [1]

In the Czech Republic, the Government Regulation 1/2008 Sb. defines requirements for work and occurrence of persons in the electromagnetic field in the frequency range 0 Hz to 300 GHz. It also specifies the limits on permissible values of induced currents, absorbed power and irradiance density as enlisted in Table 1.

Table 1. Limits defined by the GR 1/2008 Sb. [7]

Quantity	Employed persons	Other persons
Induced current density $[A/m^2]^{1)}$	$\sqrt{2}\cdot 0.01$	$\sqrt{2}\cdot 002$
Areal power density $[W/m^2]^{2)}$	50	10
Specific absorbed power $[W/kg]^{3)}$	$0{,}4^{4)}$	$0{,}08^{5)}$

1) Valid for frequencies from 300 to 10^7 Hz.
2) Valid for frequencies from 1 to 3 GHz.
3) Valid for frequencies from 10^5 to 10^{10} Hz.
4) If only a part of a human body is exposed, the limit is increased to 10 W/kg or 20 W/kg for hands, feet and ankles).
5) If only a part of a human body is exposed, the limit is increased to 10 W/kg or 20 W/kg for hands, feet and ankles).

1.2 Radio Interfaces of Safety Systems

Usually, the wireless sensors of electronic safety systems employ standardized radio bands 434 and 868 MHz. According to the standard EN 300 220 [6], the frequency bands of 868.6 to 866.7 MHz is recommended for these purposes. The relevant radio bands and limits suitable for operation of the wireless sensors of electronic safety systems according to [6] are enlisted in the Table 2.

For the purposes of the paper, let us assume that the wireless sensors use antennas that are close to the isotropic ones, i.e. they radiate almost equal amount of power at all directions. Then the appropriate areal power density can be calculated as follows [5]:

$$S = g\frac{P_t}{4\pi r^2}\ [W/m^2] \qquad (5)$$

Where:
g is the antenna gain (1 for isotropic antennas),
P_t is the transmitted power,
r is the distance from the transmitter.

Table 2. Suitable radio bands for wireless safety sensors [6]

Frequency [MHz]	Effective radiated power limit [W]
433.05 – 434.04	0.01
868.0 – 868.6	0.025
868.7 – 869.2	0.025

When compared to the limits enlisted in Table 1, it can be stated that the transmitting power of these devices is quite negligible.

2 Tested devices

For the purposes of the experiment, the below enlisted devices were selected. All of them were provided by the manufacturer as subjects for testing and educational purposes. Primarily, these devices were indented to be tested on their operating ranges and possible vulnerability of their wireless communication. Once they were delivered to the laboratory, the intensity of EMF they transmitted was measured as well.

2.1 Jablotron JA-160PC

Jablotron JA-160PC (see Figure 1) is a wireless motion detector with embedded camera. When the alarm is launched, the detector creates a picture of the observed scene. This picture can be transmitted to the control station. The wireless connection is performed in the band of 868 MHz. The device is battery operated.

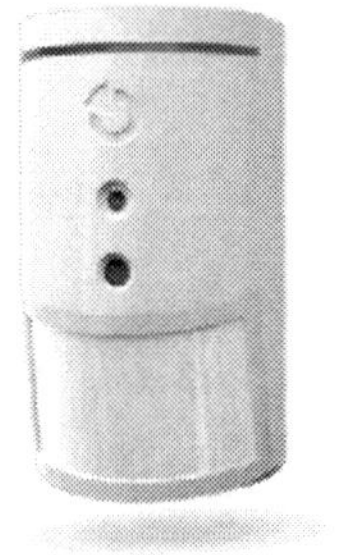

Fig. 1. Jablotron JA-160PC.

2.2 Jablotron JA-151M

This is a wireless opening magnetic detector with minimized dimensions. It is a component of JA-100 Alarm system and it is intended to detection of opening of window, doors etc. of protected area. The power supply is ensured by a single lithium battery of CR2032 type. It operates in the radio band of 868 MHz.

Fig. 2. Jablotron JA-151M.

2.3 Jablotron JA-180B

The JA-180B is a component of JA-100 Alarm system and it is intended to detection of glass breaking of glass surfaces of protected area by intruder. Its power supply is provided by an internal battery. It operates at the frequency of 868.1 MHz.

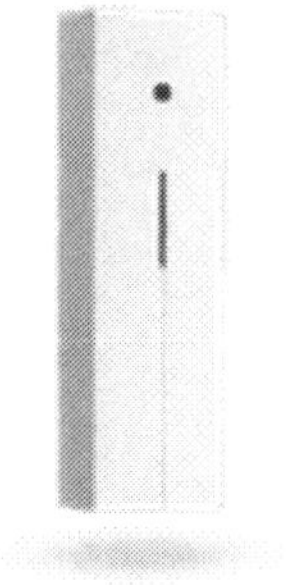

Fig. 3. Jablotron JA-180B.

3 Experiment description

The experiment took place in the Laboratory of electromagnetic compatibility at the Faculty of Applied Informatics of Tomas Bata University in Zlin. The measurement was processed inside a semi anechoic chamber Frankonia SAC-3 plus by means of the following equipment:

- EMI test receiver Rohde & Schwarz ESU 8,
- EMI antenna Teseq CBL 6112.
- Controlling software Rohde & Schwarz EMC 32.

The construction of the chamber is specific for its cylindrically shaped ceiling. The manufacturer claims that the dome shaped roof as well as its optimized absorber layout, with ferrite and partial hybrid absorber lining, minimizes the reflections in between 26 MHz and 18 GHz [8].

Fig. 4. Frankonia SAC 3 plus.

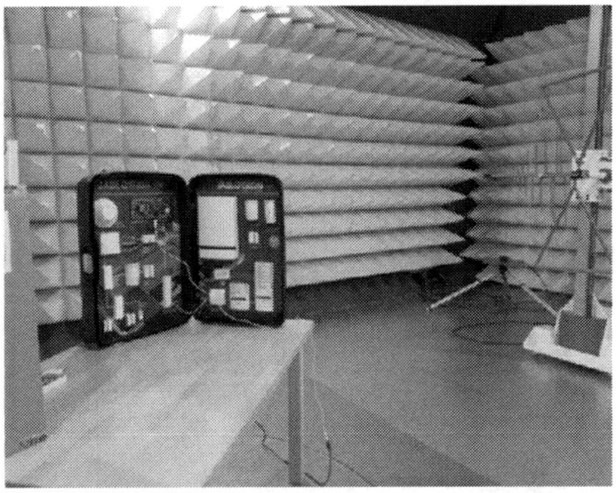

Fig. 5. Safety system Jablotron JA 100 inside the semi anechoic chamber.

3.1 Configuration

The configuration of the experiment was as depicted in Figure 5. The tested device was placed at the test table inside the semianechoic chamber and the receiving antenna was placed at an appropriate distance. The test receiver was set to continuously scan the narrow frequency band around the frequency of 868 MHz and to record the maximum measured value (MaxHold). MaxPeak detector was selected for this kind of measurement. During the measurement, the measured device was forced to launch alarm in order to obtain its attempt to establish radio connection between the device and its controlling exchange. Both, the vertical and the horizontal antenna polarization were used. The measurement was processed until no increase of the recorded values was observed. For each of the components, one measurement for vertical and one measurement for horizontal antenna polarization were processed separately.

3.2 Interpretation of the results

Inside the chamber, the intensity of the EMF radiated by the device was measured. Assuming that the manufacturer of the device constructed its transmitting antennas in order to radiate omnidirectionally, the device was treated as the isotropic EMF radiator. The EMF intensity was measured in the distance of 4 metres and transmitting power was calculated according to the equation (5).

4 Results

The results obtained by the experiment are enlisted in the Table 3. All the final measurements were processed in the distance of 4 metres.

Table 3. Results obtained by the experiment

Device	Radio Frequency [MHz]	Distance [m]	Measured Intensity [dBμV/m]	Transmitting power [W]
JA-160PC	868.090	4	101.2	0.00707
JA-151M	868.129	4	99.7	0.00495
JA-180B	868.089	4	100.5	0.00594

According to [2] and the relevant standards, the irregularity of EVF measurement inside the semi anechoic chamber can be as high as ± 4 dB (relative to the voltage units). Due to the complexity of the problem, this uncertainty is allowed even for officially certified test laboratories. For example, if the measured intensity is 100 ± 4 dBμV/m, it means that the real value of EVF may lie somewhere between 63.096 and 158.489 mV/m, resulting in the calculated transmitting power from 2.123 to 13.4 mW. Of course, there are methods to increase the accuracy of the measurement, but they needs a lot of time and expenses in orders of thousands of Euro. Therefore the authors consider the obtained results as satisfying.

Table 4. Power densities calculated from the measured intensities

Device	Radio Frequency [MHz]	Power density [μW/m^2]		Transmitting power [W]
		Distance of 1 m	Distance of 4 m	
JA-160PC	868.090	562.6	35.16	0.00707
JA-151M	868.129	393.9	24.62	0.00495
JA-180B	868.089	472.7	25.54	0.00594

Finally, let us concern the issues on the areal power density as it is expressed in the Table 1. This can be calculated by the equation (5). The calculated power densities in the distance of 1 and 4 metres from the devices are enlisted in the Table 4. It can surely be stated, that in the distance of 1 m from the device, even the short-term peak value of the transmitting power is lower than 1 mW. This is 10 000x lower value than required by the Regulation 1/2008 Sb [7].

5 Conclusions

This paper provides description of the experiment that consisted of measurement of the intensity of the electromagnetic field radiated by various wireless sensors of an electronic safety system. During the experiment it was observed that the intensities of radiated EMF of the observed devices were below the limits prescribed by relevant standards [6] and very low when hygienic limits is taken into consideration [7].

In fact, this is not a surprising result. The wireless sensors are battery-operated and therefore they cannot waste the energy pointlessly. To lower the power consumption, the communication between the sensor and the base station is performed periodically with the interval as long as tens of minutes. And, of course, the transmitting power is limited. On the other hand, it turned out that the operating ranges of the devices were shorter than the manufacturer declared.

This work was supported by the Ministry of Education, Youth and Sports of the Czech Republic within the National Sustainability Programme project No. LO1303 (MSMT-7778/2014) and also by the European Regional Development Fund under the project CEBIA-Tech No. CZ.1.05/2.1.00/03.0089.

References

1. J. Svacina, *Electromagnetic Compatibility [Elektromagneticka kompatibilita],* Brno: VUT Brno, (2002).
2. C. R. Paul, *Introduction to Electromagnetic Compatibility*, New York: John Wiley, (1992).
3. P. A. Chatterton, M. A. Houlden, *EMC – Electromagnetic Theory to Practical Design*, New York: John Wiley, (1991).
4. M. Mann, B. Gutheil, J. Zastrau, P. Weiss, *"Electromagnetic field measurements – Means of verification"*, In Proc. of the 5th WSEAS/IASME Int. Conf. on Electric Power Systems, High Voltages, Electric Machines, Tenerife, Spain, December 16-18, (2005), pp 591-595.
5. Z. Trnka, *Theory of Electrical Engineering [Teoretická elektrotechnika].* Bratislava: SNTL Alfa, (1972).
6. European standard EN 300 220.
7. Czech Government Regulation No. 1/2008 Sb.
8. Frankonia: *Anechoic Chambers / RF-Shielded Rooms*, 2012.

The balance model for heat transport from hydrolytic reaction mixture

Dagmar Janacova[1*], *Karel* Kolomaznik[1], *Pavel* Mokrejs[2], *Vladimir* Vasek[1], *Jiri* Krenek[1] and *Ondrej* Liska[3]

[1] Tomas Bata Univerzity in Zlín, Faculty of Applied Informatics, nám. T.G.Masaryka 5555, 760 01 Zlín, Czech Republic
[2] Tomas Bata Univerzity in Zlín, Faculty of Technology, nám. T.G.Masaryka 5555, 760 01 Zlín, Czech Republic
[3] Technical University of Kosice, Faculty of Mechanical Engineering, Department of Automation, Control and Human Machine Interaction, Letná 9, 04200 Košice, Slovakia

Abstract. The content of the paper is the industrial application of enzyme hydrolysis of tanning solids waste with a view to minimizing the price of enzyme hydrolysate product, which has widely used. On the base of the energy balance of the enzymatic hydrolysis we estimated the critical minimal charge of a tanning drum. We performed of the critical minimal on the basis of a balance model for heat transport from reaction mixture into the environment through reactor wall. Employing a tanning drum for hydrolytic reaction allows to process tanning wastes in the place of their origin. It means thus considerably to enhancing economics of the whole process.

1 Introduction

Although the leather industry is environmentally important as a user of the byproduct of the meat industry, it is perceived as a consumer of resources and a producer of pollutants. In order to reach the status of future sustainability the industry must aim to the treatment of inorganic and organic waste. Czech Republic as potential member of EU is also required to operate within strict legislative boundaries [1]. A sustainable industry for the future most radically change the philosophy of the leather making process through optimal resource management within the tannery. The result of this will be closed loop, clean systems operating towards zero waste for the production of high quality niche leather and other valuable collagenic materials. The function of the beam-house is to clean, purify and retain structural integrity of the collagen protein in preparation for subsequent tanning process, which technically coverts protein to leather.

2 Heat balance of enzymatic hydrolysis

Enzymatic hydrolysis: At present this method offers the best prospects for the future. The main advantage of using proteolytic enzymes as the catalyst for the process of hydrolysis is that moderate reaction conditions can be employed. The reaction takes place at a temperature 70°C, a pH value between 8 and 9, and under atmospheric pressure. Furthermore, the molecular weight of the resulting proteineous product can be influenced by altering the composition of the reaction mixture and adjusting the addition of enzymes. This provides the flexibility to the process allowing it to produce products of different specifications in response to customer requirements.

The industrial application can came to the reality in case of connection with the preparation of regenerated tanning liqueur from chromium filtrate sludge, because the price of natrium dichromate is relative expensive. Another possibility to degrease the operating costs is in using of solar pans for the concentration or drying dilute protein hydrolyzates. A further possibility in reducing prices of protein hydrolyzates consists in reducing investment costs. The chief problem consisted in holding the temperatures of reaction mixture within such limits as to arrive at a comparable yield of soluble protein after the practically same time as when an isothermal reactor was used. A further effort of ours aimed at the tanning drum not having to be constructionally adapted. In theory, our tanning drum represents a non isothermal and non adiabatic reactor.

In order to try out various possibilities of setting up parameters, preliminary calculations were performed simulating the course of reaction mixture temperature in time dependently on its initial value, and on content of drum.

The temperature of reaction mixture in dependence on time may be calculated by resolving a mathematical model representing the hydrolytic reaction. In an effort at reaching a fast solution we set up a determinist model in accordance with simplified conditions as follow:

- the reaction mixture is intimately stirred by motion of drum
- heat transfer is perfect on both sides of drum wall
- reaction heat of hydrolysis is negligible

* Corresponding author: janacova@fai.utb.cz

- drum has the shape of a cylinder, its radius being at least 10 times greater than thickness of wall so that the temperature field in wall may be described by an "infinite plate" model
- dependence of all physical parameters of the model on temperature is negligible
- assuming these, we applied the following mathematical model.

$$\frac{\partial t(x,\tau)}{\partial \tau} = a\frac{\partial^2 t}{\partial x^2}(x,\tau);\ 0<x<b;\ \tau>0 \quad (1)$$

$$m_0 c_0 \frac{\partial t_0(\tau)}{\partial \tau} = S\lambda \frac{\partial t}{\partial x}(0,\tau) \quad (2)$$

$$t(x,\,0) = t_p \quad (3)$$

$$t(b,\tau) = t_p \quad (4)$$

$$t(0,\tau) = t_0 \quad (5)$$

$$t_0(0) = t_{op} \quad (6)$$

Equation (1) describes a non-stationary temperature field in the wall of drum. Heat balance expressing equilibrium between rate of decrease in reaction mixture temperature and transfer of heat through reactor wall is described by equation (2). Equations (3) and (4) are initial conditions, and equations (4) and (5) describe conditions of perfect heat transfer. For analytical solution of the given model, Laplace transformation was applied yielding:

$$\frac{t_0 - t_p}{t_{op} - t_p} = 2\sum_{n=1}^{\infty} \frac{\cos(q_n)\sin\left[(1-X)q_n\right]}{q_n + \sin(q_n)\cos(q_n)} e^{-Fo q_n^2} \quad (7)$$

where q_n are roots of the following equation,

$$cot\,(q) = q.\ Ra \quad (8)$$

F_o is the Fourier criterion (dimensionless time)

$$F_0 = \frac{a\tau}{b^2} \quad (9)$$

$$X = \frac{x}{b} \quad (10)$$

and Ra is a dimensionless number expressing the ratio of reaction mixture enthalpy and enthalpy of drum wall.

$$Ra = \frac{m_o c_o \Delta t_o}{m\ c\Delta t} \quad (11)$$

Equation (7) is the calculated temperature dependence of reaction mixture on time in a dimensionless expression of both variables. The course of reaction mixture temperature in time depends on thickness of wall b, its coefficient of thermal conductivity a, mass m, specific heat c and also on the mass of reaction mixture m_o and on its specific heat c_o. The dimensionless value of reaction mixture $t_0(\tau)$ then depends on its initial temperature top and ambient temperature t_p, which is identical with the temperature of tanning drum wall. The only value among all those mentioned that we can practically change is the mass of charge into reactor (reaction mixture) m_o by means of which the value of dimensionless parameter Ra can be affected. Hence, such a charge of reaction mixture m_o and its initial temperature top have to be selected that temperature during the necessary reaction time does not drop under a limit where reaction rate would be very small. The minimal charge is given by value Ra, i.e. point K, and all other charges by value of parameter Ra of curves to the right of point K. When practically performing hydrolysis in a tanning drum, its walls can be preheated with hot water or thermally insulated. The minimal drum charge can thus be reduced and even smaller plant put to use. In case the drum walls are heated, critical charge quantity may be estimated by employing a quasi-stationary model.

$$-c_0 m_0 \frac{dt_0}{d\tau} = \frac{\lambda}{b} S(t_0 - t_p) \quad (12)$$

Its solution gives

$$ln\left(\frac{t_{op} - t_p}{t_0 - t_s}\right) = \frac{\lambda S\tau}{b m_0 c_0} \quad (13)$$

The non-stationary temperature field in drum wall is shown in Fig. 1 (for Ra = 4), and the time course of temperature of the reaction mixture in drum in Figure 2 (equation 7 for x = 0).

3 Practical part

3.1 Description of test

Plant at our disposal comprised a tanning drum of 2 m diameter, 1-m width, wall thickness 5 cm. We filled the drum with hot water of known mass and starting temperature of 70°C.

An aperture was drilled in the drum wall and an alcohol thermometer fixed/tightly inserted/therein so that its tip reached sufficiently far into hot liquid.

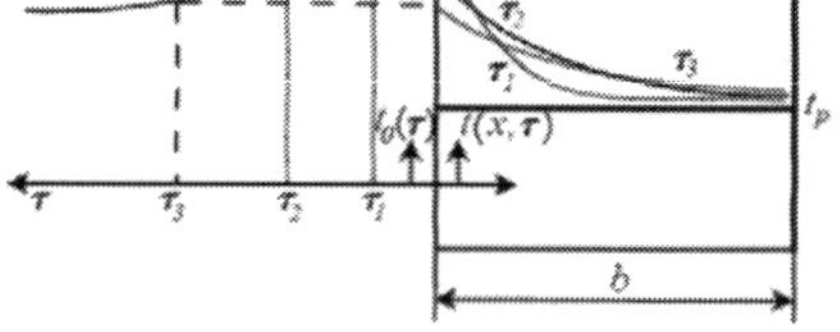

Fig. 1. The non-stationary temperature field in drum wall.

DOI: 10.1051/matecconf/201712502060

Temperature of water inside the rotating drum was measured at regular intervals. As soon as rate of temperature decrease sank/got under 0.05 °C/min, cooled water was let out and drum refilled with hot water of known starting temperature and mass.

3.2 Determining the coefficient of heat conductivity through drum wall

When determining the coefficient of drum heat conductivity, we start from relation (7) and from experimental data of the dependency of water temperature inside the rotating drum on time. In case the time is long enough, members of the infinite series on the right side of equation (7) except for the first, may be neglected, and from the condition thus simplified the value of temperature parameter may be calculated.

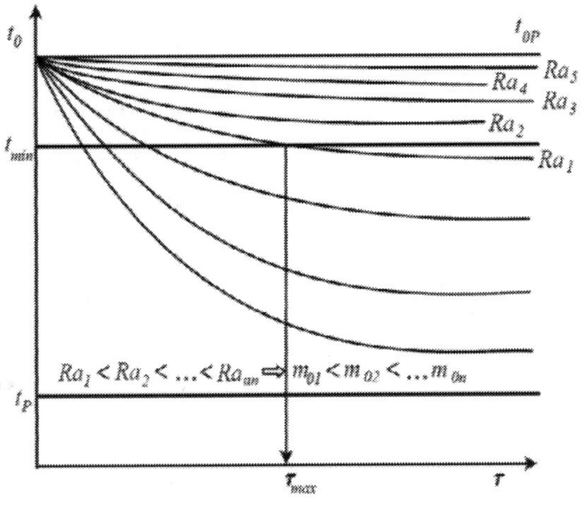

Fig. 2. The non-stationary temperature field in drum wall for variable *Ra*.

Considering that the pre-exponential member is independent of time, plotting the logarithm of dimensionless temperature against time produces a straight line from which we may determine the sought-after heat conductivity of drum wall.

$$\frac{t_0 - t_p}{t_0 - t_p} = t^* = K\, e^{-\frac{a\tau}{b^2}q_1^2} \qquad (13)$$

$$\ln t^* = \ln K - \frac{aq_1^2}{b^2}\tau \qquad (14)$$

Following table 1 presents experimentally measured temperatures of water in the drum dependently on time.

Table 1. Test measurements of water temperature inside drum.

τ	t_0	t^*	$\ln t^*$
40	52.8	0.589	-0.530
50	51.5	0.565	-0.571
60	50.4	0.544	-0.608
70	49.5	0.528	-0.639
80	48.7	0.513	-0.668
90	48.1	0.506	-0.689
100	47.5	0.491	-0.712
110	46.9	0.480	-0.735
120	46.5	0.472	-0.750
130	45.8	0.459	-0.778
140	45.2	0.448	-0.803

The same is graphically displayed in following Figure 3.

The figure 4 serves to determine gradient of linear time dependence of the natural logarithm of dimensionless water temperature in the drum.

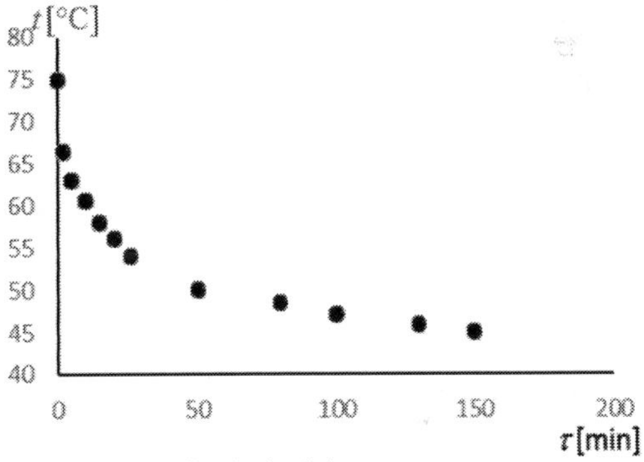

Fig. 3. Experimentally obtained data.

Applying regression analysis to experimentally obtained data presented in Fig.3 and Table.1, we determined the line gradient -0.0026 min^{-1}.

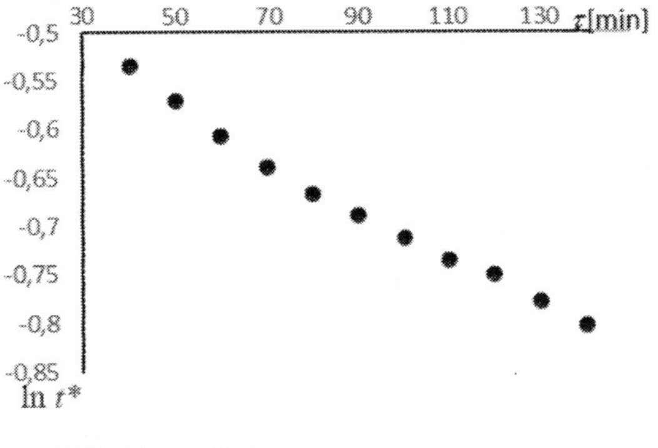

Fig. 4. The line gradient

According to (13), the mentioned value equals $-\frac{aq_1^2}{b^2}$. If we estimate criterion *Ra* equals 0.6 with a water content of 165 kg in drum and the corresponding first root of equation (8) q_1 equals 1.02.

We may calculate effective heat conductivity $a = 9.5.10^{-8}\ m^2\ s^{-1}$. Comparing this value to that of oak wood, $1.3.10^{-7}\ m^2\ s^{-1}$, we may claim our calculated value is realistic.

Modified enzymatic hydrolysis of chrome shavings under conditions of an isothermal stirred reactor was described in detail in the work [3]

4 Conclusion

Tests in a preheated drum demonstrated the process of hydrolysis could be realised on this plant, thereby making possible the direct processing of tanned wastes where these immediately originate. Investment costs will also be considerably reduced in this way and thus also the price of hydrolysis products. An approximate estimate of minimal charge for a heated drum can utilise a quasi-stationary model. The critical minimal charge of a tanning drum was estimated. An estimate was performed of the critical minimal on the basis of a balance model for heat transport from reaction mixture into the environment through reactor wall. Employing a tanning drum for hydrolytic reaction allows to process tanning wastes in the place of their origin, thus considerably enhancing economics of the whole process.

List of used symbols

t - temperature of drum wall [^{0}C],
t^* - dimensionless temperature [1],
t_0 - temperature of reaction mixture [^{0}C],
t_p - initial temperature of drum wall [^{0}C],
t_{op} - initial temperature of drum charge [^{0}C],
t_s - drum ambient temperature [^{0}C],
τ - time [s],
a - temperature conductivity coefficient [$m^2\ s^{-1}$],
x - coordinate of drum wall [m],
b - thickness of drum wall [m],
m_o - mass of reaction mixture in drum [kg],
c_o - specific heat of reaction mixture [J $kg^{-1}K^{-1}$],
c - specific heat of drum walls [[J $kg^{-1}K^{-1}$].
S - total area of drum inner walls (exchange area) [m^2],
λ - heat conduct. coefficient of drum wall [W $m^{-1}K^{-1}$],
m - mass of drum walls [kg]

Acknowledgement

The research work is supported by the Project of the Structural Funds of the EU, Operational Programme Research and Development, Measure 2.2 Transfer of knowledge and technology from research and development into practice and by the Ministry of Education, Youth and Sports of the Czech Republic within the National Sustainability Programme project No. LO1303 (MSMT-7778/2014) and also by the European Regional Development Fund under the project CEBIA-Tech No. CZ.1.05/2.1.00/03.0089

References

1. K. Kolomazník et al., ERB 3512 PL 940974 (COP 974) Northampton, (1996)
2. L. Vasek, V. Dolinay, *IFAC-PapersOnLine*, **49** (27), pp. 413-418, (2016)
3. D. Janáčová, K. Kolomazník, V. Vašek, *In 14th International Congress of Chemical and Process Engineer. Praha* : CSChE. ISBN 80-86059-30-8, (2000)
4. L. Vasek, V. Dolinay, *27th European Conferenc*, ECMS 2013, pp. 453-458. (2013)
5. W. H. Hartford *Proccedings Chromium Symposium 1986*: Inc. Pittsburg, Pa. p. 112, (1986)
6. O. Kirk *Encyclopedia of Chemical Technology*, 4th. Ed., Vol. 6, p. 269, N.Y. Willey, (1992)
7. A. J. Dean *Lange's Handbook of Chemistry* 14th. Ed., Mc. Graw-Hill, INC, N.Y, (1992)
8. C. S. Cantera, M. Giuste, A. Sofia *CITEL*, Gonnet-Argentina, (1997)
9. M. Maňas, D. Maňas, M. Staněk, M., Š. Šanda, V. Pata, *Chemicke listy*, **105** (17), p. 713-716 . (2011)
10. P. Božek, ICSS 2013; Wroclaw; Poland; p. 229-240. ISSN 2194-5357, (2013)
11. P. Božek, P. Pokorny, *In Applied Mechanics and Materials*. **611** p. 339-345. ISSN 1660-9336, (2014)

Adaptive Control of Neural Network Synthesis

Pavel Vařacha[1]

[1]Tomas Bata University in Zlín, Faculty of Applied Informatics, Zlín, Czech Republic

Abstract. Neural Network Synthesis is a method based on based on Analytic Programming and asynchronous implementation of Self-Organising Migration Algorithm. This synthesis woks as an algorithm capable of creating and learning and artificial neural networks as well as optimizing their structures and connections. This paper introduce an idea of adaptive control of Self-Organising Migration Algorithm based on complexity of processed neural network structure. Such approach already recorded several successful application in modelling and simulation.

1. Introduction

Neural Network Synthesis (ANN synthesis) is an algorithm capable of creating and learning and artificial neural networks as well as optimizing their structures and connections. To describe this method in all details would significantly exceed a possible extend of this paper. Nevertheless ANN synthesis mechanisms are very well elaborated in papers [1] and [2]. An interested reader is respectfully asked to study this previous publications as are referred at the end of the paper.

ANN synthesis is based on Analytic Programming (AP) and asynchronous implementation of Self-Organizing Migration Algorithm (SOMA). Important facts about AP which are necessary for basic understanding of an idea proposed in the paper as an adaptive individual handling are described in chapters 2. And 3. For better understanding of SOMA, please, refer paper [3] or [4].

This paper explores a possibility to make it more effective by adaptive control of SOMA parameters. The main idea is an intelligent control of the ANN synthesis based on complexity of processed neural network structure.

2. Analytic Programming

The main principle (core) of AP is based on a discrete set handling (DSH) (Fig. 1). DSH shows itself as a universal interface between the EA and the symbolically solved problem. This is why AP can be used almost by any evolutionary algorithm. In the case of ANN synthesis the algorithm is SOMA.

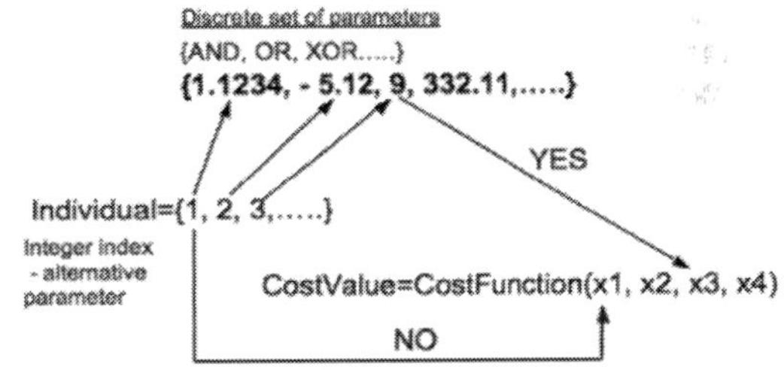

Figure 1. DSH principle

Briefly stated, in AP, individuals consist of non-numerical expressions (operators, functions,...) which are represented within the evolutionary process by their integer indexes. Each index then serves as a pointer into the set of expressions and AP uses it to synthesize the resulting function-program for the Cost Function evaluation.

=All simple functions and operators are in the so called General Function Set (GFS) divided into groups according to the number of arguments which can be inserted during the evolutionary process to create subsets GFS3, GFS2...GFS0.

Table 1. Example of GFS and its subsets

GFS Degree	Contains
GFSall	f(x1, x2, x3), +, -, *, /, Power, Abs, Round, Sin, Cos, t, K, τ, 1, 2
GFS3	f(x1, x2, x3)
GFS2	+, -, *, /, Power
GFS1	Abs, Round, Sin, Cos
GFS0	t, K, τ, 1, 2

* Corresponding author: varacha@fai.utb.cz

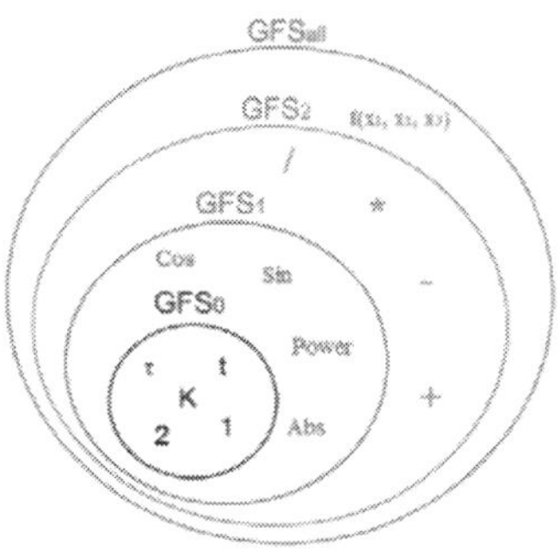

Figure 2. GFS subsets hierarchy

The functionality of AP can be seen in the specific example in Fig. 3:

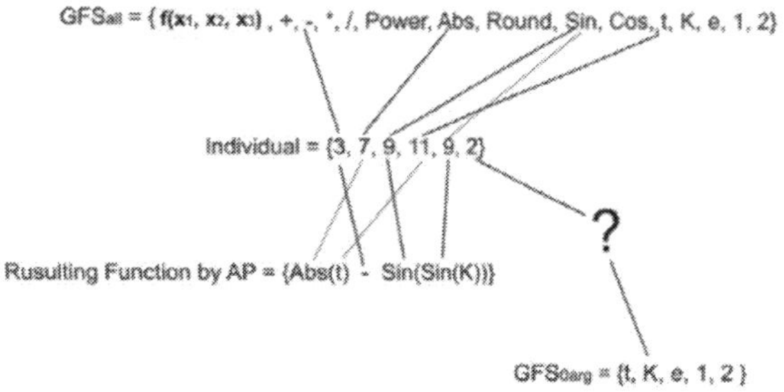

Figure.3. Main principles of AP

The individual consists of 6 arguments (indices, pointers to GFS). The first index is 3, meaning that it is taken from the set of functions GFS_{all}. The function *minus* has two arguments; therefore indexes 7 and 9 are arguments of *minus*.

$$6 + 7 \tag{1}$$

Index 7 is then replaced by *Abs* and index 9 by *Sin*.

$$Abs + Sin \tag{2}$$

Abs and *Sin* are one-argument functions. Then, index 9 follows index 11, which is replaced by *t*.

$$Abs(t) + Sin \tag{3}$$

Sin is also a one-argument function. Then, after index 11, the individual takes index 9, which is replaced by *Sin* and this *Sin* becomes an argument of the previous *Sin*.

$$Sin(Tan) + Sin(Sin(\tag{4}$$

The last index is 2, but in this case there is the function *Plus*. *Plus* needs two arguments to work properly. AP will not allow this, as there is not any other free pointer to be used as the argument. Instead of *Plus*, AP will jump into the subspace, in this case directly to the GFS_{0arg}. In the GFS_{0arg} it finds the second element, which is *K*. And by doing so, we get (5).

$$Abs(t) + Sin(Sin(K)) \tag{5}$$

The number of pointers actually used from an individual before the synthesized expression is closed is called *depth*. This example is based on the relevant and previously published work in.

3. Neural Network Synthesis

The previous chapter described basic concepts of AP. Such concepts can be easily employed to synthetize different ANN structures as can be seen from Fig. 4. This process of structural synthesis as well as ANN learning is well described for example in [3] and [4].

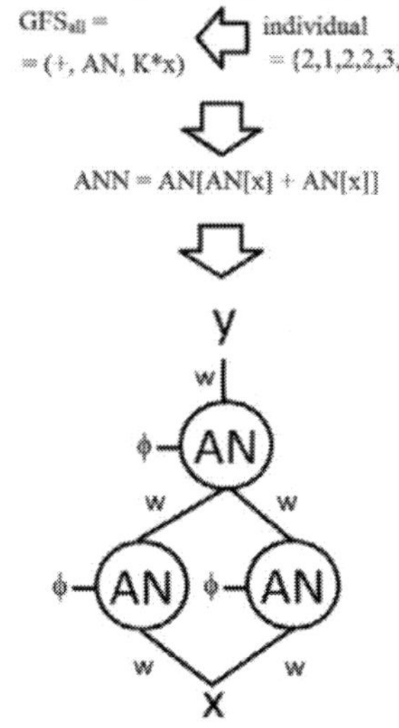

Figure 4. An Example of ANN synthesis

4. Experiment Designed for Adaptive Control

Processes described in chapters 2. and 3. have to be optimized by a specific evolutionary algorithms. In case of ANN synthesis it basically means to try variously complex ANN structures (individuals in AP) to improve them in evolutionary way. In place of such evolutionary algorithm ANN synthesis commonly employ SOMA. An algorithm which is well described in [3] and [4]. However SOMA is not anyhow adaptive to coop with various lengths of individuals in AP. SOMA simply treat all such individuals as an individual of constant length (typically 100). For this paper one control parameter of SOMA was chosen to improve this behavior.

An adaptive control proposed in this paper aim to influence control parameter of SOMA named PRT to improve its ability to deal with different lengths of individuals. For each individual SOMA will used different setting of PRT bases on length of a solved individual itself.

Commonly, SOMA is set on PRT = 0.1. In contradiction this paper proposes adaptive strategy so PRT will differ from individual to individual PRT = 1 / depth.

In order to statistically evaluate this new adaptive handling approach the function approximation problem was chosen as an aim of the experiment. The function (6) proposed by [5] as an appropriate approximation benchmark was chosen to be approximated by the ANN.

$$y = x_i^5 - 2\,x_i^3 + x_i \tag{6}$$

where x_i *is in* <-1,*by the step* 0.04 ,1>

Fig. 5 (automatically generated by ANN synthesis software) shows an example of synthetized ANN approximating (6). The difference between the ANN and

DOI: 10.1051/matecconf/201712502061

(7) is depicted as a red area which could be minimized by the process of synthesis. An goal of ANN synthesis in this case can be simply described as founding smallest possible ANN able to approximate given function. Simplicity of such function is purely purposeful here as the main goal is not test ability of ANN synthesis to solve complicated tasks but to test how the method improve while applying proposed adaptive strategy.

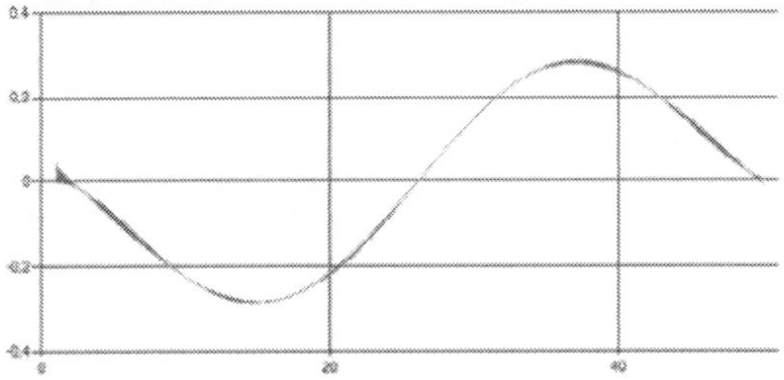

Figure 5. Approximation of (7) by synthetized ANN

AP was executed 100 times (physically on 8 cores of the Super Micro Server) to produce an ANN with the RMSD < 0.005. The main intention was to find such an ANN which met this condition and which simultaneously used as few AN as possible. All SOMA's control parameters required for repetition of this experiment are described in following tables. The setting of Asynchronous SOMA used as the EA for AP can be seen in Table 1. and SOMA setting used for ANN learning in Table 2.

Table 1. Setting of SOMA used as EA for AP

Number of Individuals	48
Individual Parameters	100
Low	0
High	3
PathLength	3
Step	0,11
PRT	Based on **experiment**
Divergence	0.01
Period	1

Table 2. Setting of SOMA used to optimize Kn

Number of Individuals	number ofKn* 0.5 (at least 10)
Individual Parameters	100
Low	-10
High	10
PathLength	3
Step	0,11
PRT	$1/K_n$
Divergence	0.01
Period	6

Based on experiment setting PRT which SOMA used to optimize Kn is set either conservatively to PRT = 0.1 or adaptively PRT = 1 / depth.

5. Results

The control of SOMA parameters consists in replacement of the static PRT value by the value which inversely depends on depth of a currently operated individual.

Table 3. Static PRT vs. adaptive control

	PRT = 1/ depth	PRT = 0.1
Average time needed for synthesis	194 s	373s
Average number of used AN	9	13

A total of 1,189,870 evaluations of AP individual fitness were completed during 100 AP executions while the PRT was set to 0.1 and the separate SOMA run was performed for all of them to set their Kn value. Without the adaptive PRT, AP was able to find an optimal ANN in only 1 case in comparison with 4 successful cases in the original experiment.

Conclusion

ANN synthesis already recorded several successful application considering practical casers of modelling and simulation [6] – [9]. It was also applied on large set of widely recognized benchmark functions [10], [11] with respect to the function approximation, prediction and problems. This results vindicate efforts for its further development.

Obtained results of experiment considered in this paper proves an ability of proposed adaptive control to further improve ANN synthesis. It can significantly improve ANN synthesis ability to overshadow concurrent method of ANN optimization as are [12] – [17].

The method of adaptive individual handling proved in this paper are going to be applied on a practical industrial example and comparison of the improved ANN synthesis is to be subjected by a future study.

Acknowledgements

This work was supported by the Ministry of Education, Youth and Sports of the Czech Republic within the National Sustainability Programme project No. LO1303 (MSMT-7778/2014).

References

1. Zelinka I., Vařacha P., Oplatková Z., Volná, E. *Structural Synthesis of Neural Network by Means of Analytic Programmig*. In 12th International Conference on Soft Computing. Czech Republic, VUT Brno, p. 25-30 (2006)
2. Vařacha P. *Neural Network Synthesis Dealing with Classification Problem*. In Recent Researches in Automatic Control. Montreux : WSEAS Press, p. 377-382 (2011)
3. Šenkerik R., Zelinka I., Davendra D., Oplatkova Z. *Utilization of SOMA and differential evolution for robust stabilization of chaotic Logistic equation*, Computers & Mathematics with Applications, Volume 60, Issue 4, Pages 1026-1037, ISSN 0898-1221, doi 10.1016/j.camwa.2010.03.059. (2010)
4. Šenkeřík R. Oplatkova Z., Zelinka I, Davendra D., *Synthesis of feedback controller for three selected chaotic systems by means of evolutionary techniques: Analytic programming*, Mathematical and Computer Modelling, ISSN 0895-7177, 10.1016/j.mcm.2011.05.030 (Available online 27 May 2011)
5. Vařacha P., Zelinka I. *Analytic Programming Powered by Distributed Self-Organizing Migrating Algorithm Application*. In IEEE Proceedings 7th International Conference Computer Information Systems and Industrial Management Applications. Ostrava : IEEE Computer Society, p. 99-100 (2008)
6. Prechelt L., *Proben1—A Set of Neural Network Benchmark Problems and Benchmarking Rules*, Universität Karlsruhe, Germany (1994)
7. Mangarianm O.L., Wolberg W.H., *Cancer diagnosis via linear programming*, SIAM News, **Volume 23**, Number 5, , p. 1-18 (1990)
8. Král E., Dolinay V., Vašek L., Vařacha P. *Usage of PSO Algorithm for Parameters Identification of District Heating Network Simulation Model*. In 14th WSEAS International Conference on Systems. Latest Trands on Systems.Volume II, Rhodes, WSEAS Press (GR) . p. 657-659 (2010)
9. CHRAMCOV, Bronislav. *Identification of time series model of heat demand using Mathematica environment*. In Recent Researches in Automatic Control. Montreux : WSEAS Press, s. 346-351 (2011)
10. Zelinka I., *Studies in Fuzziness and Soft Computing*, New York : Springer-Verlag, (2004)
11. Koza J. R., *Genetic Programming*, MIT Press, ISBN 0-262-11189-6 (1998)
12. Jui-Yu W., *MIMO CMAC neural network classifier for solving classification problems*, Applied Soft Computing, **Volume 11**, Issue 2, The Impact of Soft Computing for the Progress of Artificial Intelligence, p. 2326-2333 (2011)
13. Falco D.I., Cioppa E., Tarantino, *Discovering interesting classification rules with genetic programming*, Applied Soft Computing 1, p. 257–269 (2002)
14. Brameier M., Banzhaf W., *A comparison of linear genetic programming and neural networks in medical data mining*, IEEE Transactions on Evolutionary
15. Turner et al., *Grammatical Evolution of Neural Networks for Discovering Epistasis among Quantitative Trait Loci Evolutionary Computation, Machine Learning and Data Mining in Bioinformatics Book Series Title*: Lecture Notes in Computer Science Publisher: Springer Berlin / Heidelberg, p: 86 – 97 (2010)
16. Vonk E., Jain L.C., Johnson R.P., *Automatic Generation of Neural Network Architecture Using Evolutionary Computation*, Advances in Fuzzy Systems – Applications and Theory, **Volume 14**, World Science, ISBN: 981-02-3106-7 (1997)
17. Koza J. R. et al. *Genetic Programming III*; *Darwinian Invention and problem Solving,* Morgan Kaufmann Publisher, (1999)

MATEC Web of Conferences 125, 02062 (2017) DOI: 10.1051/matecconf/201712502062
CSCC 2017

Non-stationary behavior of roof drainage systems

Martin Koláček[1,*]

[1]Tomas Bata University in Zlin, Faculty of Applied Informatics, Department of Automation and control Engineering, Nad Stranemi 4511, Zlin, Czech Republic.

Abstract. This paper reports the non-stationary behavior of a roof drainage during experimental measurement in the climate simulator. Many buildings use a fully or partially flat roof where it is necessary to use the roof drainage. Thermal behavior of roof drainage is very important from the point of view of heat transfer and potential condensation. The placement of a roof drain slightly deteriorates thermal transmittance of the roof. This experiment evaluates roof drains in the specific climate simulator where thermal conditions were dynamically controlled in the specific temperature range. The measurement was performed for two types of roof drains. The first drainage is a simple single-shell and the second is double-shell drainage. The results show the effect on the thermal transmittance of the roof section and also the minimal effect of condensation on the non-insulation part of the drainage. Both roof drains showed minimal deterioration of thermal transmittance of the roof construction.

1 Introduction

Drainage systems of roof areas are an important task in modern residential, industrial or commercial construction. The use of internal rainwater drains is very common not only for flat roofs. The roof drainage is important in term of the thermal insulation properties of the roof.

Some studies verify modification of the length of the downpipe and its impact on increasing the flowrate [5]. Roof drainage systems are designed to the size of the roof, the number of drains and also the estimated amount of water as is described in [4].

There are not so many studies that investigate the influence of roof drainage on the thermal parameters of the roof. However, there are standards to indicate requirements for surface indoor temperatures due to the possibility of condensation of water inside buildings as describes [1].

Many roof designs have exposed to heavy seasonal rain and designers need to take increased rainfall intensity. The roofs may be drained by two basic methods, towards the outer edges and into external gutters or towards internal gutters or drainage outlets within the main roof area [3]. Gutters can be blocked by hail or due to rainfall intensity. Therefore it is important to evaluate and to compare the width of the drainage. The requirements for the location of roof drains are described in [7,6]. Thermal transmittance describes the insulation capacity of a building structure. The roof drain slightly deteriorates the insulation properties of a building structure. Due to this fact, we try to evaluate the influence of roof drain in the roof.

Roof drain causes a thermal bridge through the roof structure. Such a construction may cause the surface temperature of the structure to fall below the dew point. Therefore it is important to measure surface temperature on the surface that is directly in contact with the outside environment.

In this paper, the thermal properties of the roof drainage will be investigated and the surface temperature will be measured on the critical parts of the roof drainage under the different climatic conditions.

2 Methods

The measurement was performed on the two types of roof drains. The inlet of the first drain is 212 mm wide and is formed by a one-sided layer. The second drainage has inlet 130 mm wide and the wall is double-shell. Both drains are used for a 100 mm drainage line. These roof drains were measured in specific measuring box which was installed in the calorimetric chamber. The thermal parameters of the measuring box are similar to the actual roof structure. The both drains were equipped with a 100 mm strong polystyrene for testing the thermal behavior. This allows for a view of the heat transfer towards the connected duct pipe and only the part of the inlet body, which usually adjoins with the ceiling concrete slab. The dimension of tested sample and roof of the box are described in Table 1.

Table 1 Dimensions of constructions

Construction	Surface [m^2]
Roof of the box	2,25
Single-shell roof drainage	0,035
Double-shell roof drainage	0,013

* Corresponding author: kolacek@fai.utb.cz

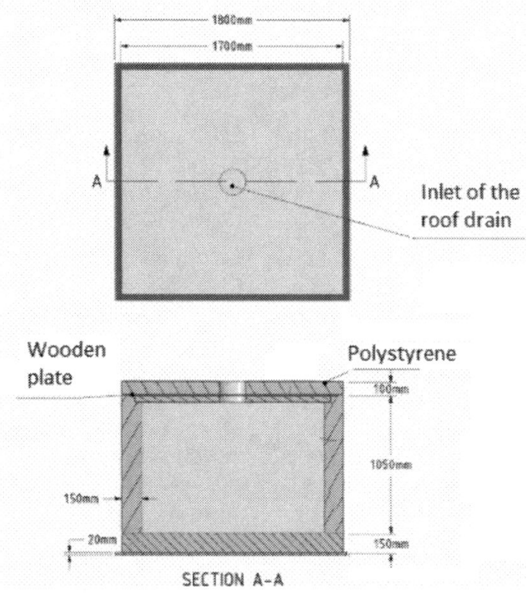

Figure 1 Measuring box where the roof drains were installed

Figure 1 shows dimensions of measuring box and position of the roof drainage.

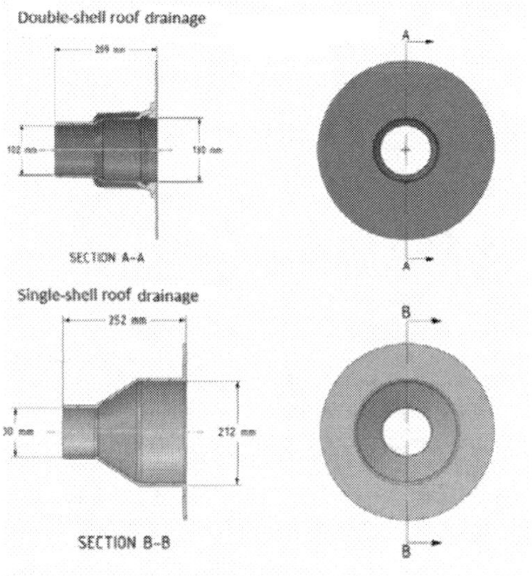

Figure 2 pictures of the roof drains

As can be seen in Figure 2 the roof drains have a different dimension of the inlet and different depth.

The calorimetric chamber is a device in which the climatic condition can be controlled in the specific temperature range from –20 °C to +50 °C. Each of the roof drains was placed in the measuring box and was exposed to three climatic tests as described Table 2

Table 2 The conditions of thermal tests

Test	The air temperature outside the box [°C]	The initial air temperature inside the box [°C]
1	10	20
2	0	20
3	-15	20

The heating element regulated the air temperature inside the measuring box for all tests. The thermal performance of this device represented heat loss of the box. The cooling curve was measured by the insulating effect of the inlet at the time-varying non-stationary air temperature inside the box. The air temperature of the exterior was stable during each experiment because temperature fluctuations are minimal during the day in winter. The decrease of the air temperature inside the box on the warm side of the inlet is similar to that of the space heating operation in the space below the flat roof, it can be simulated by switching off the heater.

The thermal transmittance was calculated by equation (1):

$$U = 1/(1/h_i + d/\lambda + 1/h_e) \quad (1)$$

Where U is the thermal transmittance [W.m^{-2}.K^{-1}]
h_i the heat transfer coefficient on the inside of the structure [W.m^{-2}.K^{-1}]
h_e the heat transfer coefficient on the exterior of the structure [W.m^{-2}.K^{-1}]
d thickness of the structure [m]
λ thermal conductivity coefficient [W.m^{-1}.K^{-1}]

Het loss was calulated by equation (2)

$$\phi = \Sigma(A \cdot U) \cdot (\Theta_i - \Theta_e) \quad (2)$$

where ϕ is heat loss of heated space [W]
A surface of construction [m^2]
Θ_i internal temperature [°C]
Θ_e external temperature [°C]

Table 3 Heat transfer coefficient

Surface	Construction	Heat transfer coefficient [W.m^{-2}.K^{-1}]
Exterior	Single-skinned	25
Interior	wall	7,7
	roof	10
	floor	5,9

DOI: 10.1051/matecconf/201712502062

The thermal transmittance was calculated for the Czech Technical Standard – Thermal protection of buildings [1]. It was necessary to calculate the average thermal transmittance of the entire roof area with the roof drainage. The thermal transmittance of the roof drainage was established by heat loss of the object and the conversion to the given area.

3 Results

The non-stationary behavior of roof drains was measured for three climatic test for each roof drain. The heat loss were firstly measured for the measuring box without roof drainage in graphs is described as Insulation plate. The thermal transmittance of insulation plate was calculated to evaluate deterioration of heat transmission due to the implementation of roof drainage.

The thermal performance of heating source was tested under the different thermal condition of the measuring box. It was done three tests where the temperature conditions were stably maintained inside and outside the box and this corresponds to the heat performance. The chart directive indicates heat loss of the box without the drainage. Heat loss is 28,5 W for 10°C temperature difference. Application of single-shell drainage increased heat loss up to 32 W and for double-shell up to 30 W.

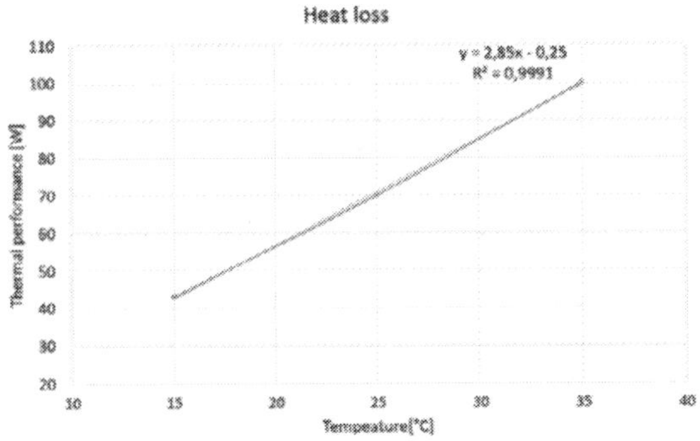

Figure 3 Heat loss of measuring box without roof drainage

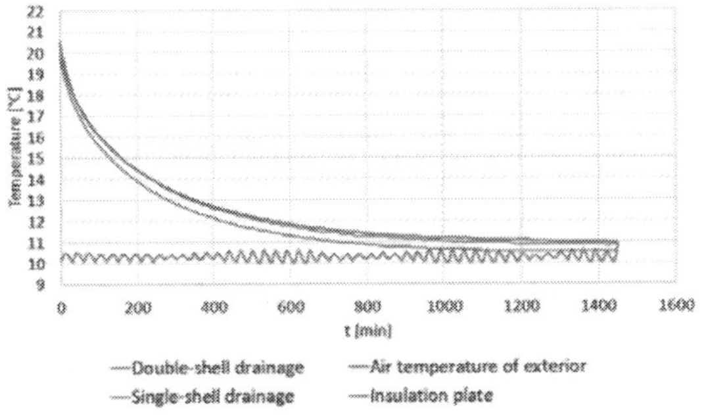

Figure 4 The cooling curve for the air temperature after the heater turned inside the box, Thermal test 1, Exterior air temperature 10°C

As can be seen in Figure 4, the air temperature decrease faster by using Single-shell drainage than the double-shell drainage. The higher thermal transmittance of single-shell drainage caused faster cooling process inside the box.

Table 4 The results of the thermal transmittance

Thermal transmittance without drainage	0,257 W/m²K
Thermal transmittance with Single-shell drainage	0,318 W/m²K
Thermal transmittance with Double-shell drainage	0,296 W/m²K

The thermal transmittance is shown in Table 4. These values are related to the roof area of the box. The thermal transmittance is only reduced by 7%. However, it is the value of the thermal transmittance of the entire roof structure. The results can be recalculated to the example of a flat roof of 100 m². This roof should be drained using roof drains with corresponding thermal insulation compared to the insulation which was used in the measuring box. The total thermal transmittance of such a roof can be calculated. The single-shell drainage causes a deterioration of the thermal transmittance by 0,2% than the double-shell drainage. Comparison of the roof without roof drainage with single-shell drainage, a deterioration of the thermal transmittance is by 0,05% and for double-shell is only by 0,03%.

A heat transfer area that does not have additional insulation is for single-shell drain 0,055 m² and for double-shell drainage 0,045 m². The surface temperature of this area was measured on the both roof drains. During the thermal test 3, the surface temperature was 17 °C for single-shell drain and 17,6 °C for double-shell drainage, the exterior air temperature was -15 °C and inside the box was 20 °C. This experiment confirmed high insulation properties of the both roof drainage and the possibility of condensation is minimal at the surface of the drainage.

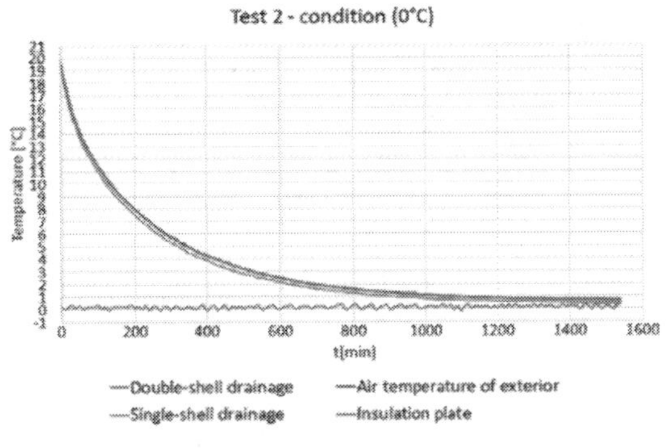

Figure 5 The cooling curve for the air temperature after the heater turned inside the box, Thermal test 2, Exterior air temperature 0°C

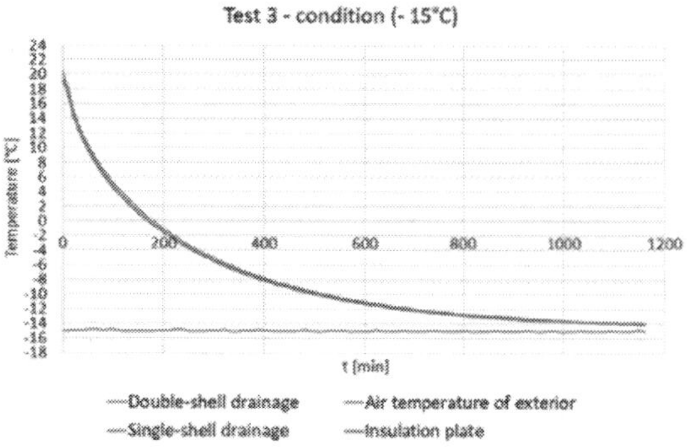

Figure 6 The cooling curve for the air temperature after the heater turned inside the box, Thermal test 3, Exterior air temperature -15°C

Figure 5 and Figure 6 show minimal temperature differences between single and double-shell roof drainage. It is difficult to verify the cooling process of the box when the exterior air temperature is so low. Due to the minimal difference in the thermal transmittance of the roof drains.

Conclusion

The experiment was conducted to investigate the non-stationary behavior of the roof drainage system. These systems are used in flat roofs where can deteriorate thermal properties of the roofs and can cause condensation on the surface of the roof drain. The thermal transmittance was calculated for two types roof drains. These roof drains were tested under three different climatic conditions and were compared. The measurement confirmed minimal deterioration of thermal properties of the roof. The placement of the roof drain has a minimal effect on the deterioration of the thermal transmittance.

The difference between the roof drains is evident in cooling at an exterior air temperature 10 °C. The surface temperatures were much higher than the dew point on the non-insulated part of the roof drain during the experimental test when the surrounding temperature was -15°C.

The temperature stratification through the roof drainage will be the subject of the future studies. These studies will be evaluated in simulation software.

Acknowledgments

This work was supported by the Ministry of Education. Youth and Sports of the Czech Republic within the National Sustainability Programme project No.LO1303(MSMT-7778/2014), by the European Regional Development Fund under the project CEBIA-Tech No.CZ.1.02/2.1.00/03.0089 and also by the Internal Grant Agency of Tomas Bata University in Zlín under the project No. IGA/CebiaTech/2017/002.

References

1. Czech technical standard CSN 730540. Thermal protection of buildings – Part 2: Requirements (2011). Czech normalisation institute Prague.
2. Czech technical standard CSN EN 12831. Heating systems in buildings – Method for calculation of the design heat load (2005). Czech normalisation institute Prague.
3. HR Wallingford. Roof Drainage Systems. Tech Talk. Volume **9.** (2012). Alianze Global Corporate and Specialty AG.
4. Manual for the Design of Roof Drainage Systems. A guide to the use of European Standard BS EN 12056-3:2000. Report SR 620. (2003)
5. Arthur, S. and J. A. Swaffield. (2001). "Siphonic Roof Drainage System Analysis Utilising Unsteady Flow Theory." Building and Environment **36** (8): 939-948
6. Czech technical standard CSN EN 1253-2. Gullies for buildings – part 2: Roof drains and floor gullies without trap. (2016). Czech normalization institute Prague
7. Howard, C. Massey. *Plumber's handbook.* Revised Edition. Craftsman Book Company. (1998). Carlsbad. ISBN: 1-57218-056-0.

Comparative Study of Intelligent Systems for Management of GIT Cancers

Nevine Labib [1,*] , *Edward Wadid* [2,*]

[1] Associate professor at Computer and IS Department, Sadat Academy for Management Sciences.

[2]Lecturer at Computer and IS Department, Sadat Academy for Management Sciences.

Abstract. Intelligent Systems contribute in the management of different GIT cancer types. The paper discusses different types of intelligent systems, classified according to the medical task achieved, such as early detection, diagnosis and prognosis. It is found out that these types include rule-based and case-based expert systems, artificial neural networks, genetic algorithms, machine learning, in addition to data mining techniques and statistical methods. The study focuses on comparing between different techniques and tools used. The comparison results in identifying the benefits of using data mining techniques for the diagnosis task, since it is based on huge amounts of data in order to discover new patterns hence new predisposing factors. It also points out the use of expert systems in the prognosis task, since this task is mainly based on the specialist experience that should be transferred to less- experienced medical professionals. Based on the previous results, it is recommended to develop an Intelligent Tutoring System (ITS) that focuses on the early diagnosis of GIT cancers, since managing the disease depends mainly on proper diagnosis, and also to build an expert system that helps transferring GIT cancers management knowledge to medical doctors in different hospitals.

Keywords: Intelligent Systems, Data Mining, GIT Cancer, Cancer Management, Expert System, Machine Learning, Artificial Neural Networks, Artificial Intelligence

1 Introduction

1.1 Background

Nowadays, Healthcare systems are focusing on the management of Cancer since it is spreading enormously. However, based on the World Health Organization (WHO), nearly one third of the cases may be prevented and another third may be treated successfully [1]. This needs the contribution of Information technology specialists so as to provide the decision makers with data, information, and knowledge, in order to have insights that help them with discovering risk factors, early detection of the disease, proper diagnosis, treatment, prognosis, and survival rate prediction.

Managing cancer requires huge amounts of accurate and updated clinical data. This is only made possible by using IT tools and techniques [2].

The study focuses on Gastro-Intestinal (GI) cancers, since they are the most common cancers. GIT cancer indicates different types of cancer that affect the digestive system; they include "cancers of the esophagus, gallbladder, liver, pancreas, stomach, small intestine, bowel (large intestine or colon and rectum), and anus" [3].

1.2 Problem Definition

The Health care forum of 2016 declared "War on Cancer" [1]. It requires more efforts to design strategies that work on decreasing cancer burden. These strategies require assembling government and industry key persons, in addition to academic professionals to work on finding measures to fight this wide spreading disease.

To deal with different types of GIT cancer management, healthcare professionals need to have sufficient data related to patient and disease details and knowledge management techniques related to new algorithms. Moreover, there is a need for intelligent systems to support different medical tasks.

Although there are several types and techniques related to management of GIT cancer, there is no clear-cut definition of the most suitable type and

* Corresponding author: nevmakram@gmail.com & edwardwadid@gmail.com

technique based on the required task, whether it is diagnosis, treatment or prognosis

1.3 Importance

Cancer management consumes huge amounts of funds in any country. The main cost is for treating the disease [4] Economic **Impact of Cancer**, American Cancer Society). Therefore, governments are working on strategies that deal with this disease in order to reduce the costs and improve the quality of life of cancer patients.

1.4 Objectives

Based on the problem definition, the study aims at achieving the following objectives:

a-Discussing the current intelligent systems of the GIT cancer domain.

b- Comparing between various techniques used to decide on the suitable technique related to the medical task.

1.5 Structure of the paper

The paper will discuss the various types of intelligent systems, such as Expert Systems, Case-based learning, Intelligent Decision Support Systems, and others. Then it will discuss recent studies related to the domain, classified based on the medical task they are achieving, then make a comparison among them based on technique and tool used. Finally, results are presented and conclusions and recommendations are drawn.

2 State of the Art

2.1 Intelligent Systems

"Intelligent System (IS) can be defined as the system that incorporates intelligence into applications being handled by machines. Intelligent systems perform search and optimization along with learning capabilities. Different types of machine learning such as supervised, unsupervised and reinforcement learning can be modeled in designing intelligent systems. Intelligent systems also perform complex automated tasks which are not possible by traditional computing paradigm. Various diagnostic, robotics and engineering systems are results of intelligent procedures implemented in Intelligent System Design"

"An intelligent system is a system that can imitate, automate some intelligent behaviors of human being. Expert systems, intelligent agents and knowledge-based systems are examples of intelligent systems. Currently, intelligent systems is a discipline that studies intelligent behaviors and their implementations as well as their impacts on human society". [5]

2.2 Gastrointestinal (GIT) Cancer

GIT cancer is found out to be one of the most commonly diagnosed malignancies and a major cause of mortality [6]. Some of the problems related to this major health problem worldwide are poor prognosis and limited treatment options. Hence, the main focus is on preventing this serious disease in order to reduce its incidence and mortality.

Some of the predisposing factors are diet such as eating dried fish and meat and refined carbohydrates, genetic factors, infectious diseases such as H. pylori infection, in addition to alcohol consumption and smoking [3].

3 Comparison from IS perspective

The following table show the different types in IS used in the field of GI cancer, classified by the three different tasks (Algorithm, Diagnosis, Prognosis)

Table 1. Comparative of different types of IS systems according to tasks.

Task	Type of IS	Technique used	Tools	Results
Algorithm	Data Mining	Association rules	MATLAB	data mining algorithm based on ontology makes rules more intuitive, appealing and understandable [8]

 DOI: 10.1051/matecconf/201712502063

	Decision Support System	Machine learning	N/A	The outcome of the specific implementation is a set of clinico-genomic profiles, which are employed for decision support, automated diagnosis, prognosis, treatment and follow-up in colon cancer. [9]
	Expert systems	Genetic Algorithms	C-MANTEC algorithm	Better cancer outcome prediction results were obtained using the GA framework noting that this approach, in comparison to the SFS [10]
Diagnosis	Decision Support System	knowledge base	C ++ &MySQL	creation of the computer knowledge base containing the data of histological, cytologic, and clinical researches. The system is focused on improvement of diagnostics quality of stomach cancer [11]
	Expert systems	Case-Based Reasoning (CBR) Rule-Based Reasoning (RBR).	Java object-oriented	this approach would be useful for general practitioners. [12]
	Artificial Intelligence	Artificial Neural Network (ANNs),	N/A	The ANN model built with the six serum tumor markers could distinguish lung cancer, not only from lung benign disease and normal control, but also from other common gastrointestinal cancers, [13]
	Artificial Intelligence	Image processing	Vector Machine Algorithm	The suggested system by using a combination of mentioned methods was succeeded to achieve 91.8% accurate diagnosis. Although available methods are accurate but they are expensive and time consuming, by comparing this method with those mentioned above are will have a better understanding of its accuracy and usefulness. [14]
	Data Mining	Artificial Neural Network (ANNs), decision trees, and logistic regression	N/A	present a new validated discriminative GERD questionnaire using data mining techniques. The questionnaire is useful, friendly, and short, and therefore can be easily applied in clinical practice for choosing the appropriate diagnostic workup for patients with upper gastrointestinal complaints. [15]
	Machine Learning	Decision Tree, Majority, Nearest Neighbors, and Best Z-Score	Python	the Decision Tree would perform best simply because it is a very widespread machine learning algorithm. [16]
	Decision Support System	Image analysis & decision fusion	N/A	The objective of this research is to improve the overall abnormality detection ability and provide the decision support by using artifcial intelligent techniques [17]
	Expert systems	genetic algorithm	N/A	the algorithm provides a list of biomarkers that play the most important role in this lethal disease as a by-product. [18]
	Artificial Intelligence	Artificial Neural Network (ANNs)	Maruyama computer program	Using an ANN, LNM in each LNG can be accurately predicted. Additional knowledge about one lymph node

			(MCP)	improves the results [18]
	Data Mining	Cluster analysis	SAS Enterprise Miner 6.1	Enterprise Miner predictive modeling nodes were great at easily and quickly implementing classification models for colorectal cancer [19]
Prognosis	Artificial Intelligence	Artificial Neural Network (ANNs) Cox regression models	Utilizing R 2.12.0	This study showed that ANN model is a more powerful tool in survival prediction and influential factors of the CRC patients compared to the Cox regression model [20]
	Knowledge-based system	Bayesian model, Artificial Neural Network (ANNs)	MATLAB	This study focused on the classification problem of high-dimensional patterns and especially of socio-demographic cancer questionnaires [21]
	Artificial intelligence	Machine Learning	N/A	the use of machine learning classifier will become much more commonplace in many clinical and hospital settings. [22]
	Decision Support System	decision-theoretic model	N/A	The model has been incorporated into a computer-based system, that can be used as a decision-support system. Preliminary evaluation results indicate that the performance of the model in its present form matches the performance of experienced clinicians. [23]
	Expert systems	artificial neural network (ANN) and Cox regression hazard (CPH) models	N/A	study demonstrated that the ANN model is a more powerful tool in determining the significant prognostic variables for GC patients, compared to the CPH model. Therefore, this model is recommended for determining the risk factors of such patients [24]
	Artificial intelligence	Machine-learning	MATLAB	Machine learning applied to information from a disease-specific (cancer) database and the EAR can be used to predict clinical outcomes. [25]
	Expert systems	Artificial Neural Network (ANNs)	N/A	The performance of ANN model in predicting the probabilities of death is consistently high for all time points according to the accuracy and the area under the receiver operating characteristic curve. [26]
	Expert systems	Artificial Neural Network (ANNs)	N/A	by using trained ANN, we can prognosis cancer with least clinical and laboratory features and without requirement of much time. [27]

4 Discussion and Future Work

4.1 Discussion

Based on the results extracted from the table, it was found out that Expert Systems, Machine Learning and statistical methods are used for both diagnosis and prognosis. However, data mining techniques are mainly used for diagnosis since they are good in the classification and clustering tasks.

Regarding algorithms, data mining, machine learning and expert systems are used.

Therefore, although there is no single technique or tool that is used to perform a specific medical task, expert systems are mainly used for prognosis because GIT cancers follow many protocols to be treated and the prognosis relies mainly on the expertise of oncologists whereas data mining techniques contribute to the diagnosis since they mainly rely on big amounts of data in order to discover new patterns.

5. Conclusion and Future Work

Regarding the recommendations for future work, the following projects are suggested:

a) Developing an Intelligent Tutoring System that teach and train junior medical doctors on the early diagnosis of GIT cancer since all of the other medical tasks depend on the right diagnosis.

b) Designing an Expert System that incorporates different protocols used to treat GIT cancers in order to transfer such important knowledge from senior Oncologists to others less experienced in various governmental and private hospitals.

References

1. *Health Care Forum: War on Cancer*, The Economist Group,(2016).
2. Elham Maserat, Reza Safdari, Marjan Ghazisaeidi, Elahe Maserat, Sima Ghezelbash, *Simulation models of gastrointestinal cancers: strategic approach to predicting and decision making*, AME Publishing Company, Transl Gastrointest Cancer (4):174-177 ,(2014).
3. https://gicancer.org.au/gi-cancer/what-is-gastro-intestinal-cancer
4. https://www.cancer.org/cancer/cancer-basics/economic-impact-of-cancer.html
5. http://www.igi-lobal.com/dictionary/intelligent-system/15045
6. Deepika ponnal, sujatha madireddi, *evaluation of risk factors for gastric cancer*, International Journal of Applied Biology and Pharmaceutical Technology, Volume: I: Issue-1 May-July – (2010)
7. D. Compare, a. Rocco, g. Nardone, *risk factors in gastric cancer*, european review for medical and pharmacological sciences,(2010)
8. Seyed Abbas Mahmoodi, Kamal Mirzaie and Seyed Mostafa Mahmoudi , *A new algorithm to extract hidden rules of gastric cancer data based on ontology*, SpringerPlus (2016)
9. T.p. exarchos, n. Giannakeas and y. Goletsis , *a framework for cancer decision support based on profiling by integrating clinical and genomic data: application to colon cancer*,
10. Rafael Marcos,Luque-Baena, Daniel Urda2, Jose Luis Subirats, Leonardo Franco, Jose M Jerez, *Application of genetic algorithms and constructive neural networks for the analysis ofmicroarray cancer data*, Luque-Baena et al. Theoretical Biology and Medical Modelling(2014)
11. E V Polyakov,O G Sukhova , P Y Korenevskaya , V S Ovcharova,I O Kudryavtseva , S V Vlasova, O P Grebennikova , D A Burov, G S Yemelyanova and V Y Selchuk , *Computer decision support system for the stomach cancer diagnosis*, International Conference on Particle Physics and Astrophysics(2017)
12. Renata Saraiva , Mirko Perkusich , Lenardo Silva , Hyggo Almeida , Clauirton Siebra, Angelo Perkusich, *Early diagnosis of gastrointestinal camncer by using case-based and rule-based reasoning*, Elsevier Ltd.(2016).
13.]Feifei Feng & Yiming Wu & Yongjun Wu & Guangjin Nie & Ran Ni, *The Effect of Artificial Neural Network Model Combinedwith Six Tumor Markers in Auxiliary Diagnosis of Lung Cancer* , Springer Science+Business Media(2012).
14. Danial Ahmadzadeh , Mohammad Fiuzy, Javad Haddadnia, *Stomach Cancer Diagnosis by Using a Combination of Image Processing Algorithms, Local Binary Pattern Algorithm and Support Vector Machine*, Journal of Basic and Applied Scientific Research www.textroad.com(2013).
15. Noya Horowitz , Menachem Moshkowitz , Zamir Halpern , Moshe Leshno, *Applying Data Mining Techniques in the Development of a Diagnostics Questionnaire for GERD*, Springer Science + Business Media, Inc.(2006).
16. Abraham Karplus , Machine Learning Algorithms for Cancer Diagnosis,(2012)
17. M.M. Zheng,S.M. Krishnan, M.P. Tjoa, *A fusion-based clinical decision support for disease diagnosis from endoscopic images*, Computers in Biology and Medicine 35 (2005)
18. Charalampos Moschopoulos, Dusan Popovic, Alejandro Sifrim, Grigorios Beligiannis, Bart De Moor and Yves Moreau, *A genetic algorithm for pancreatic cancer diagnosis*,
19. Elfriede H. Bollschweiler,, Stefan P. Mönig, Karin Hensler, *Artificial Neural Network for Prediction of Lymph Node Metastases in Gastric Cancer:* A Phase II Diagnostic Study, Annals of Surgical Oncology(2004)
20. Pedro G. Ramos, University of Louisville, Louisville KY , Pedro G. Ramos, *Gastrointestinal Diseases: Diagnoses, Misdiagnoses, and Comorbidities* ,(2010).
21. Mahmood Reza Gohari, Akbar Biglarian, Enayatollah Bakhshi, Mohammad Amin Pourhoseingholi, *Use of an Artificial Neural Network to Determine Prognostic Factors in Colorectal Cancer Patients*, Asian Pacific Journal of Cancer Prevention, Vol 12, (2011)

22. Marios Poulos, *Knowledge-based system for prognosis of specific types of cancer using Elman neural network,* Artificial Intelligence Research, , **Vol. 2**, No. 2,(2013)
23. Joseph A. Cruz, David S. Wishart, *Applications of Machine Learning in Cancer Prediction and Prognosis,* Cancer Informatics:2 59–77,(2006).
24. Peter Lucas,Henk Boot & Babs Taal, *Computer-based Decision Support inthe Management of Primary Gastric non-Hodgkin Lymphoma,* Methods of Information in Medicine **37**, (1998)
25. Lucheng zhu, wenhua luo, meng su, wei, juan wei, xuebang zhang and changlin zou, *Comparison between artificial neural network and cox regression model in predicting the survival rate of gastric cancer patients, biomedical reports* 1: 757-760,(2013)
26. A Biglarian,E Hajizadeh, A Kazemnejad, *Application of Artificial Neural Network in Predicting the Survival Rate of Gastric Cancer Patients,* Iranian J Publ Health, Vol. 40, No.2, pp.80-86,(2011).
27. Hamid Nilsaz-Dezfouli1, Mohd Rizam Abu-Bakar, Jayanthi Arasan,Mohd Bakri Adam and Mohamad Amin Pourhoseingholi, *Improving Gastric Cancer Outcome Prediction Using Single Time-Point Artificial Neural Network Models,*(2017)
28. Saeid Afshar, Fahime Abdolrahmani, Fereshte vakili tanha, Mahin Zohdi seaf, Kobra Taheri, *Quick and reliable diagnosis of stomach cancer by artificial neural network,* Proceedings of the 10th WSEAS International Conference on MATHEMATICS and COMPUTERS in BIOLOGY and CHEMISTRY,(2009).

DOI: 10.1051/matecconf/201712502064

Cascode-based voltage-amplifier stage

Martin Pospisilik[1*]

[1]Tomas Bata University in Zlin, Faculty of Applied Informatics, Nad Stranemi 4511, 760 05 Zlin, Czech Republic

Abstract. Voltage-amplifier stages are the basic components of commonly used high gain amplifiers the bias and other parameters of whose are set by the external negative feedback. The typical device that uses the voltage-amplifier stage is the operational amplifier. Similar constructions can also be created on the basis of discrete transistors. From the circuit designer's point of view, the voltage-amplifier stage defines the crucial parameters of the whole unit - the amplification factor, dominant pole of its transfer function and the slew rate. In this paper the proposal on construction of the voltage-amplifier stage based on discrete transistors is described. When connected between the input differential amplifier and the output stage, it allows creating of cheap amplifier for HiFi applications with considerable performance.

1 Introduction

The typical structure of an operational amplifier is depicted in Fig. 1. It consists of three basic parts – the differential input front-end, voltage-amplifier stage and the output circuit that increases the output current delivery capability.

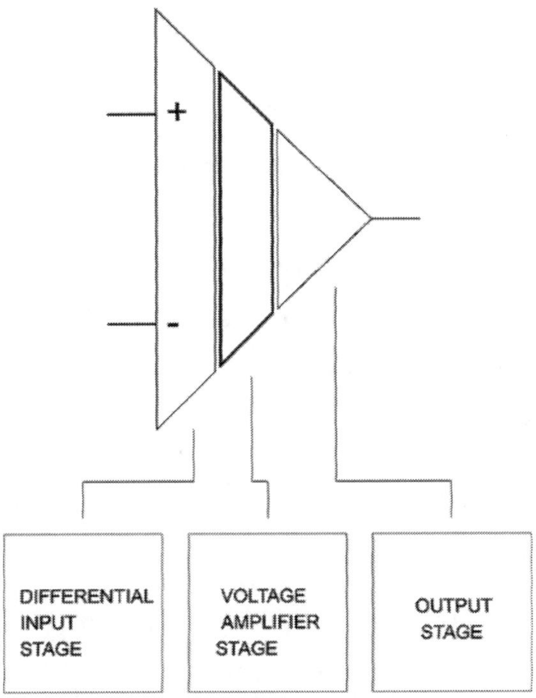

Fig. 1. Stages of a conventional operational amplifier.

Not only in power amplifiers, the voltage-amplifier stages are considered as one of the most critical parts, since they not only provide considerable gain but also must give the full output voltage swing [1]. Typical constructions of the voltage-amplifier stage are depicted in Fig. 2.

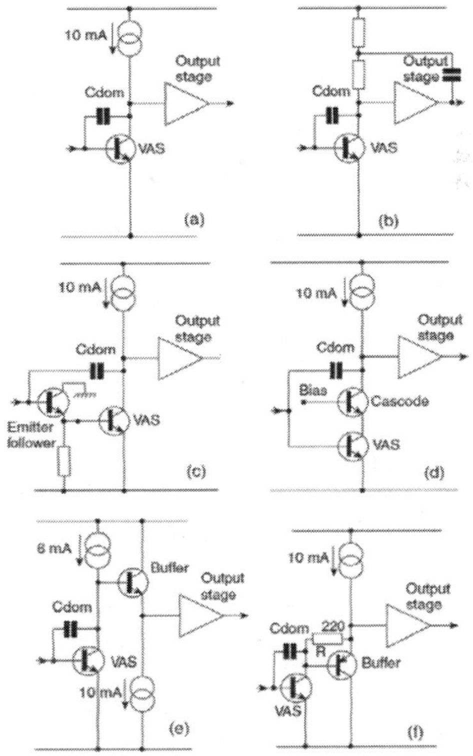

Fig. 2. Typical approaches to the construction of the conventional voltage-amplifier stages (see text).

* Corresponding author: pospisilik@fai.utb.cz

DOI: 10.1051/matecconf/201712502064

According to [1], the approaches depicted in figure 2 can briefly be described as follows. The approach (a) represents a typical solution with a current source load to the transistor's collector. Similar results can also be obtained by the approach (b) that is based on collector load bootstrapping. The emitter follower applied in the approach (c) allows increasing of the transistor's beta, resulting in higher local negative feedback. The feedback increase can also be performed by means of a cascode, as depicted in Fig. 2d. This solution also allows increasing of the power supply voltage as the voltage spreads across the transistors. The approach (e) consists in buffering the transistor's collector from the output stage. Another form of buffering is introduced by the approach (f).

The following goals are pursued by all of the above mentioned approaches: There is a need for high voltage amplification factors together with local negative feedback that allows linearization of the stage. Additional linearization is provided by means of the global negative feedback that defines operating parameters of the circuit. Due to the high amplification factor, the Miller's effect at the capacity between the transistor's collector and base acts as the dominant capacity (C_{dom}) to define the dominant pole of the transfer function of the whole amplifier.

In the past, several enhancements of the voltage-amplifier stage construction have been introduced. An example of such improvement is presented in the figure 3.

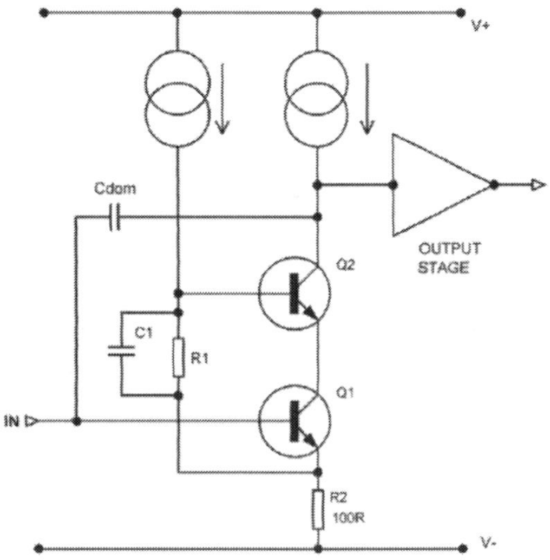

Fig. 3. Hawksford's variation of the cascoded voltage amplifier stage.

The Hawksford's solution [2] depicted in figure 3 consists in bootstrapping of the cascode transistor Q2 from the emitter of the transistor Q1 which leads to reduction of variations of the V_{CE} voltage across the transistor Q1.
Many more approaches to the construction of the voltage-amplifier stage can be found in the appropriate literature [3], [4], [5].

2 Alternative approach

The authors of this paper decided to apply an alternative approach. The circuit diagram of their cascode is depicted in the figure 4. The basis of the circuit is derived from the relevant circuit diagram disclosed in [6]. It is a common-emitter common-base cascode.

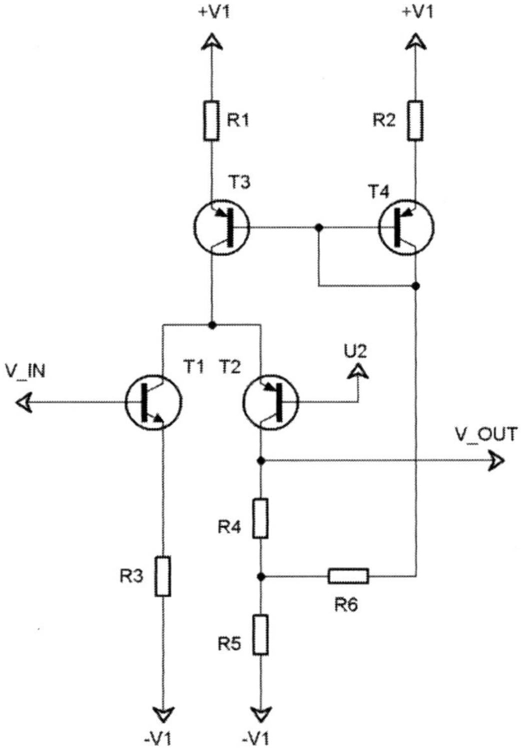

Fig. 4. The voltage-amplifier stage proposed by the authors of this paper.

The cascode depicted in the figure 4 consists of the transistors T1 and T2. While the base of the transistor T2 is connected to a fixed voltage V2, the base of the transistor T1 is biased by the voltage V_IN. The circuit's driving signal is also superimposed to this voltage. Both transistors are fed from the collector of the transistor T3 which represents a current source in this structure. The quiescent current of the cascode is defined by means of the current mirror composed of the transistors T3 and T4 and it is influenced by the negative feedback bounded between the resistors R4 and R5. Since symmetrical power supply ±V1 is expected, the target output voltage bias V_OUT is expected to lie near 0 V. In order to achieve large signal amplitudes, the front end's output voltage is expected to lie close to the value of –V while the fixed bias V2 of the transistor T2 is expected to lie close to the value of +V.

When compared to the stages described above, the hereby presented design employs large local negative feedback which eliminates its harmonic distortion and helps to stabilize the circuit's bias, even when the global negative feedback must also be applied. While the voltage amplification factor is quite low, the circuit shows excellent performance at high frequencies.

3 Simulation

The hereby described voltage-amplifier stage has been implemented in an audio frequency preamplifier. The design of the circuit was processed with the aid of simulation software Multisim, which is based on SPICE algorithms and libraries. Several simulation outputs are provided within this chapter.

3.1 Creating the basis

The basis of the circuit depicted in the figure 4 has been inserted into the simulation software. The following points have been assumed:

- The circuit is based on BC550/BC560 low-cost low-noise transistors.
- The quiescent currents of the transistor T1 and T2 are both approximately 1 mA.
- The power supply voltage is ± 24 V.
- The front-end stage's bias is – 20 V.
- The T2 bias is + 20 V.

The values of the appropriate resistors can be defined by means of the following procedure:
The emitter current of the transistor T1 should be approximately 1 mA. Therefore:

$$R_3 = \frac{V_{IN} - V_{BE\_T1} - V^-}{I_{E\_T1}} \approx 3.3\ k\Omega \quad (1)$$

Where:
V_{IN} = -20 V (input bias voltage),
V_{BE_T1} = 0.65 V (BE voltage of T1),
V^- = -24 V (negative power supply voltage),
I_{E_T1} = 1 mA (emitter current of T1).

Because the required output voltage is 0 V, the voltage across the resistors R4 and R5 should be one half of the total power supply voltage, i.e. 24 V. When the feedback current through the resistor R6 is neglected, the following assumption can be made:

$$(R_4 + R_5) = \frac{0 - V^-}{I_{E\_T2}} \approx 24\ k\Omega \quad (2)$$

Where:
I_{E_T2} = 1 mA (emitter current of T2).

The following points must be taken into consideration:

- Also the collector current of the transistor T4 flows through the resistor R5.
- The ratio between R5 and R4 defines the strength of the local negative feedback.

According to the above mentioned, the feedback current through the resistor R6 must be chosen before the values of R4 and R5 are assigned. Supposing the transistors R3 and R4 have the same current gain β, the ratio between their collector currents is as follows:

$$\frac{I_{C\_T3}}{I_{C\_T4}} = \frac{R_2}{R_1} \quad (3)$$

Moreover the following assumption should be fulfilled:

$$I_{C\_T3} = I_{C\_T1} + I_{C\_T2} \approx 2\ mA \quad (4)$$

Considering the voltage drop at the resistor R1 should not be higher than 1 V, so the peak-to-peak signal voltage was not limited, it seems reasonable to choose R1 = 470 Ω. As the feedback current should be lower in order to decrease the circuit's power consumption, the following value of R2 has been chosen: R2 = 2.2 kΩ. Now, according to (3), the estimated collector current of the transistor T4 should be approximately 430 μA. Compared to I_{C_T2}, this current cannot be neglected. Therefore the equation (2) must be transformed into the following form:

$$(0 - V^-) = R_4 I_{C\_T2} + R_5 (I_{C\_T2} + I_{C\_T4}) \quad (5)$$

Considering the conventional resistor values, the following combination fits well: R4 = 15 kΩ, R5 = 5.6 kΩ, R6 = 82 kΩ.

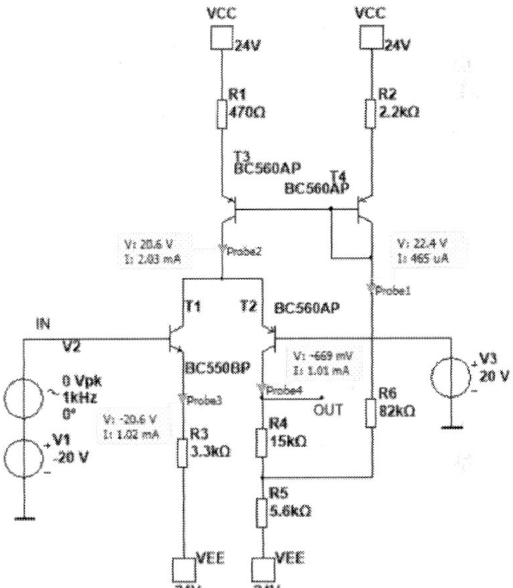

Fig. 5. Simulation diagram of the basis of the proposed voltage-amplifier stage.

The diagram of the simulated circuit is depicted in the figure 5 together with the probes showing voltages and currents in the relevant nodes. The input bias is given by the voltage source V1 while the bias of the transistor T2 is given by the voltage source V3. The voltage source V2 represents the driving signal of the circuit.

The performance of the basic circuit depicted in the figure 5 is as follows: the AC gain is 13.5 dB, the –3dB bandwidth is 5 MHz and the total harmonic distortion is lower than 0.015 % for the output magnitude of 1 V at the frequency of 1 kHz. It is worth mentioning that the overall performance of the whole amplifier will be improved by the global negative feedback.

3.2 Gain increasing

Usually, the gain of 13.5 dB would not be satisfying in real application. There are two ways to increase the AC gain of the simulated circuit:

1. Decreasing of the local negative feedback established by the current mirror T3/T4.
2. Decreasing of the local negative feedback established by the resistor R3.

There are several technical reasons to choose the second option:

- The simple way to decrease the local negative feedback established by the resistor R3 is to bridge it by a serial combination of another resistor and a capacitor.
- The adjustments of the negative feedback introduced by the current mirror can further be made in order to improve the overall transfer function of the whole amplifier and/or to modify its slew rate.

In the figure 6 the simulation diagram of the circuit with the increased gain is depicted. The resistor R7 = 1 kΩ and the capacitor C1 = 47 μF have been added in order to increase the AC gain of the circuit to 26 dB in the range from 4.5 Hz to 4.5 MHz (- 3 dB). For the output magnitude of 1 V the total harmonic distortion is approximately 0.05 %.

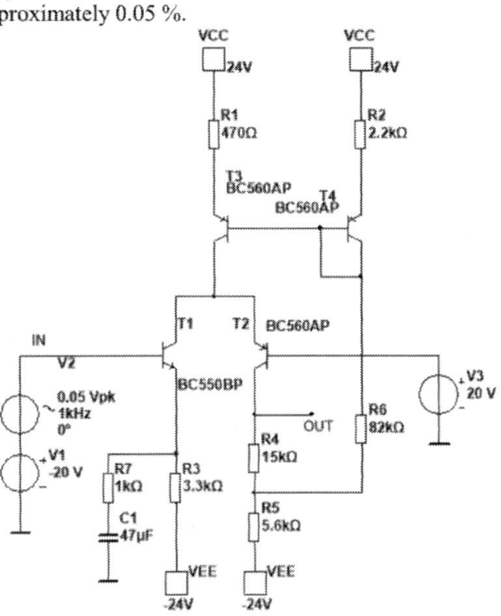

Fig. 6. Simulation diagram of the basis of the proposed voltage-amplifier stage with increased gain.

3.3 Temperature stability

The temperature drift of the output DC voltage for the circuit depicted in the figure 6 is approximately - 11 mV/°C. The temperature dependence of collector currents of the transistors T1 and T2 is depicted in the figure 7, provided the input bias is not temperature-dependent. However, this condition is rarely fulfilled in practice. The front end and back end circuits of the voltage-amplifier stage are temperature-dependent as well. Therefore this issue must be solved in the framework of the whole amplifier. For illustration, in the figure 7 there is a simulation result of temperature dependencies of collector currents of the transistors T1 and T2 if the stage's front end employs a current mirror at its output, which is quite usual for the input differential amplifiers (see below).

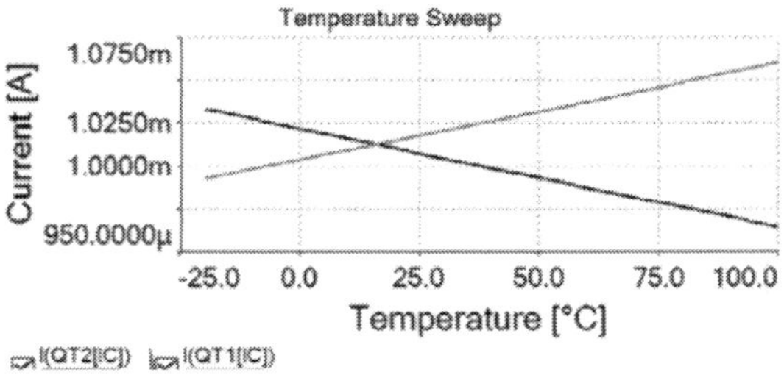

Fig. 7. Temperature dependence of T1 and T2 collector currents provided the input voltage bias is not temperature-dependent.

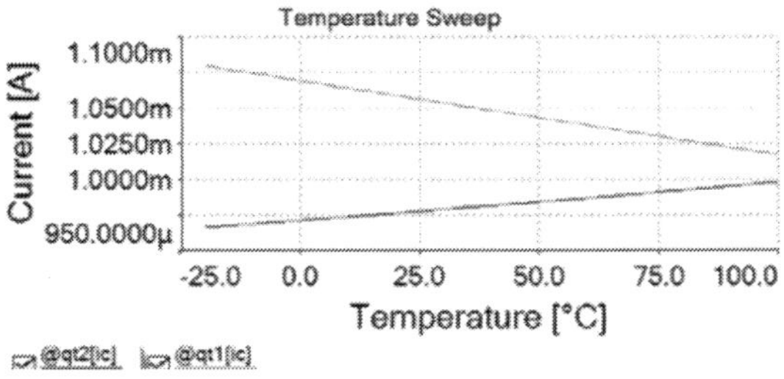

Fig. 8. Temperature dependence of T1 and T2 collector currents provided the input voltage bias is obtained from a simple current mirror.

3.4 Creating a whole

The designs of the differential input stage as well as of the output voltage follower are not the subjects of this paper. However, in practice, the voltage-amplifier stage cannot operate alone. In order to check how this stage affects the behaviour of the whole amplifier, the structure of which is depicted in the figure 1, the circuit depicted in the figure 9 has been simulated. It consists of ideal input differential stage the gain of which is 20 dB and the output bias voltage of which is -20V, the hereby described voltage-amplifier stage and the output stage the voltage gain of which is as high as 0 dB. The internal gain of this circuit is expected to be as high as 46 dB but the set of resistors R7, R8 sets the total value to the level of 20 dB.

First of all, the open-loop transfer function of the whole circuit must be known in order to determine the stability of the circuit when the feedback loop is closed. Because the DC feedback is still necessary to process this simulation, the inverting input of the differential unit is blocked by the capacity as high as 1F. This ensures the feedback loop will not affect the transfer function at the operating frequencies. According to the simulation, the circuit would not be stable with the closed feedback loop.

 DOI: 10.1051/matecconf/201712502064

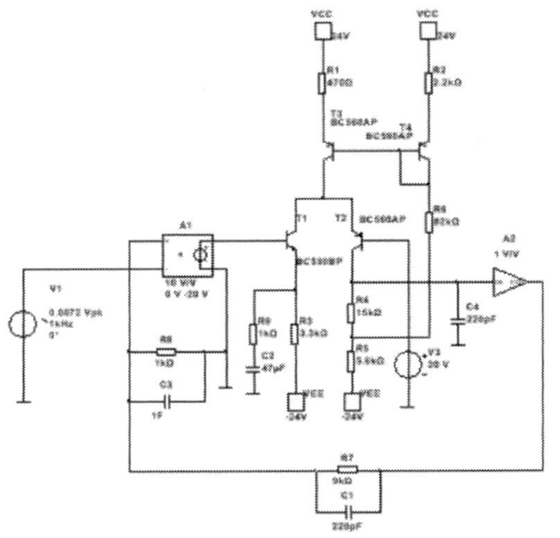

Fig. 10. A test bench for the hereby described voltage-amplifier stage.

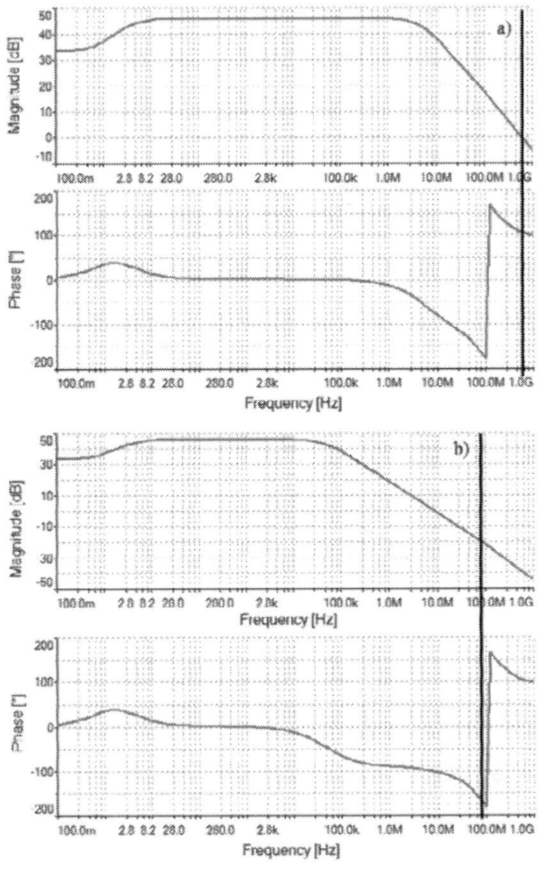

Fig. 10. Transfer function of the circuit depicted in Fig. 9 with opened feedback loop: a) without dominant pole, b) with dominant pole.

In order to fulfil the Nyquist's stability criterion, the capacitor C4 was added into the circuit depicted in the Figure 9. It implements the dominant pole of the circuit's transfer function. In the Figure 8b it can be seen how the transfer function is affected.

Now the circuit is expected to be stable with the closed feedback loop and the capacitor C3 (1 F) can be disconnected in order to let the feedback loop operate. Within this configuration, the simulated parameters of the circuit are as follows:

- The gain is 19.5 ± 0.5 dB for frequencies from 1 Hz to 40 kHz.
- The phase shift within the frequency range from 20 Hz to 20 kHz is lower than ± 15°.
- The total harmonic distortion at the frequency of 1 kHz and the output magnitude of 1 V is as low as 0.0025 %.

4 Implementation

The hereby described voltage-amplifier stage was implemented in several designs of audio-frequency amplifiers, such as universal amplifier for an equaliser or a preamplifier for MM phono cartridge. It was observed that it operated according to expectations. The application examples is depicted below.

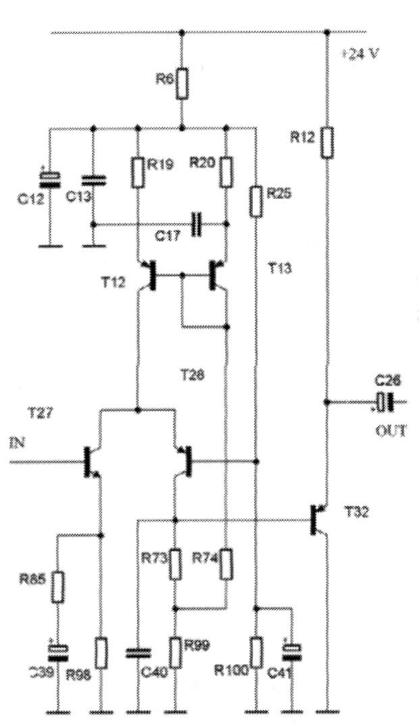

Fig. 11. Application example of the cascade-based voltage-amplifier stage. This connection has been used in an MM phono preamp with non-symmetrical power supply voltage of 24 V.

5 Conclusions

This paper provides an example of design of a voltage-amplifier stage assembled of discrete transistors. The authors provide comparison of their solution together with the usually applied solutions as well as simulations on their stage's behaviour. Obviously, this topic is too large to be fully described within a framework of a single paper. The hereby described voltage-amplifier stage has been implemented in several amplifier circuits and it can be stated that it operated as expected. However, once the stage is a part of a complex circuit obtained with one global feedback loop, it is not easy to specify how much does it causes that the whole circuit is not strictly ideal. Therefore we provided simulations showing what behaviour of the whole circuit can be expected once the hereby proposed voltage-amplifier stage is employed together with other components that show strictly ideal behaviour.

The most likely objection against this approach is probably the following one: why would anyone assembly the audio frequency amplifier using lots of discrete devices when there are suitable operational amplifiers obtainable at the market. Of course, this is true. There are, however, also arguments against this objection: The typical operational amplifiers target to as high internal amplification factor as possible. This has lots of positive effects, but there are also the negative ones – the dominant pole of the transfer function lies at low frequencies, the complex structure of the operational amplifier embodies considerable phase shifts etc. On the other hand, sensitive designer can, using discrete devices, produce any operational amplifier he likes, even that one with quite low amplification factor, but having the dominant pole of the transfer function at considerably high frequency. Moreover, when the price of a single transistor can be as low as 0.025 €, who would resist the temptation?

This work was supported by the Ministry of Education, Youth and Sports of the Czech Republic within the National Sustainability Programme project No. LO1303 (MSMT-7778/2014).

References

1. Douglas Self, *Audio Power Amplifier Design Handbook (Focal Press, 2009).* ISBN: 978-0-240-52162-6
2. M. Hawksford, *Reduction of transistor slope impedance dependent distortion in large-signal amplifiers*, JAES 36 (**4**) (April 1988)
3. P.P. Gray , R.G. Meyer, *Analysis and Design of Analog Integrated Circuits* (Wiley, 1984),
4. J. Hefley, *High fidelity, low feedback, 200W* (Electronics & Wireless World, June 1992)
5. G. Stochino, *Ultra-fast amplifier* (Electronics & Wireless World, October 1996)
6. P. Neumann, J. Uhlir, *Electrical circuits and functional units [Elektricke obvody a funkcni bloky]* (Prague, CVUT, 2005), ISBN 80-01-03281-7

Single Stator Dual PM Rotor Synchronous Machine with two-frequency single-inverter control, for the propulsion of hybrid electric vehicles

Marcel Topor[1], *Fabrizio* Marignetti[2], *Sorin Ioan* Deaconu[1], and *Lucian Nicolae* Tutelea[1]

[1]Politechnica University of Timisoara, Electrical Engineering Department
[2]University of Cassino, Electrical Engineering Department

Abstract. This paper introduces a novel brushless, single winding and single stator, dual PM rotor axial-air-gap machine capable to deliver independently torque at the two rotors by adequate dual vector control. The proposed topologies, the circuit model, controlled dynamics simulation and preliminary 3D FEM torque production on a case study constitute the core of the paper. The proposed dual mechanical port system should be instrumental in parallel (with planetary gears) or series hybrid electric vehicles (HEV) aiming at a more compact and efficient electric propulsion system solution.

1 Introduction

Vehicles equipped with internal combustion engine (ICE) have been in existence for over a hundred years. Although ICE vehicles (ICEVs) are being improved by modern automotive electronics technology, they need a major change to significantly improve the fuel economy and reduce the emissions [1].

Electric vehicles (EVs) and hybrid EVs (HEVs) have been identified to be the most viable solutions to fundamentally solve the problems associated with ICEVs [2]–[4]. Electric drives are the core technology for EVs and HEVs [5]–[10].

A key problem with HEV is the electric propulsion corroboration with the thermal engine traction (ICE) such that the latter is allowed to operate close to the sweet point (torque and speed for maximum efficiency or minimum emission) indifferent to the vehicle speed [11]–[12].

A so called continuously variable transmission (CVT) is required for the scope.

The Toyota Prius e-CVT solution for the parallel HEV requires two electric machines, two inverters, and a planetary gear [1].

A distinct electric generator and a propulsion electric motor, both with full power converters, are typical for a series HEV.

The present paper proposes a new, dual PM rotor, SM drive with basically single a stator and dual rotor with different pole counts and high winding factors, to reduce volume, weight and cost in either planetary-gear parallel HEV or in series HEV. The paper is organized as follows: Section 2: proposed dual PM rotor machine topology, Section3: the dual PM rotor single stator phase coordinate model, Section 4: 3D FEM torque production analysis, Section 5: proposed dual two-frequency vector control and dynamic simulations, Section 6: conclusions.

2 The proposed dual PM rotor machine topology

In an effort to simplify the planetary-geared e-CVT for the parallel HEV or the series HEV we hereby propose to replace the basically two electric machines and their two power converters by a single, axial-air-gap, electric machine central stator, fed from a single PWM converter with dual frequency voltage output ($V_1(f_1)$, $V_1(f_2)$) and two independent PM rotors with $2p_1$ and $2p_2$ poles, placed on the sides of the central stator provided with N_s slots and a tooth-wound (or Gramme) winding (Fig. 1).

The mixture of two frequencies in the inverter output voltage (with corresponding phase angles) leads to two different speeds ω_{r1} and ω_{r2} in the two rotors and different positive (or negative) torques, as required.

The two frequency voltages and their currents travel the whole single stator winding coils sides, though only the left side (in fig. 1) produces torque at ω_{r1} speed and only the right side interacts to produce torque at ω_{r2} speed.

This implies some additional copper losses in the stator but if the end connections are kept small, part of this inconveniency is removed.

On the other hand, the single inverter has to handle the entire apparent power related to the interaction of stator magnetic fields with both rotors at different speeds.

Only when the two frequencies are equal to each other and electric rotor speeds related by $\omega_{r1} = \omega_{r2}$ ($n_1p_1 = n_2p_2$), a direct transfer of power through the winding,

* Corresponding author: sorin.deaconu@fih.upt.ro

 DOI: 10.1051/matecconf/201712502065

for say, one motoring and one generating operation modes, seems to be possible.

Apart from the evident simplification and compactness of the proposed solution, attempts to reduce somewhat the inverter power rating based on motor/generator simultaneity are worth trying (for medium speeds one rotor is less active).

Though there will be $\omega_2 - \omega_1$ torque pulsations from one rotor to the other, the torque stress on the stator will be reduced when one rotor is motoring and one is generating.

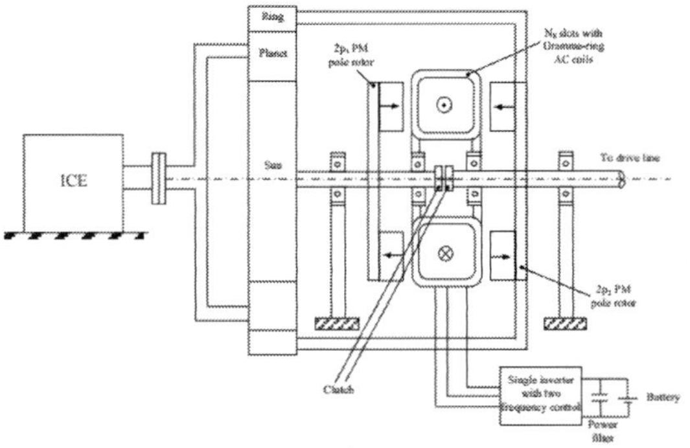

a)

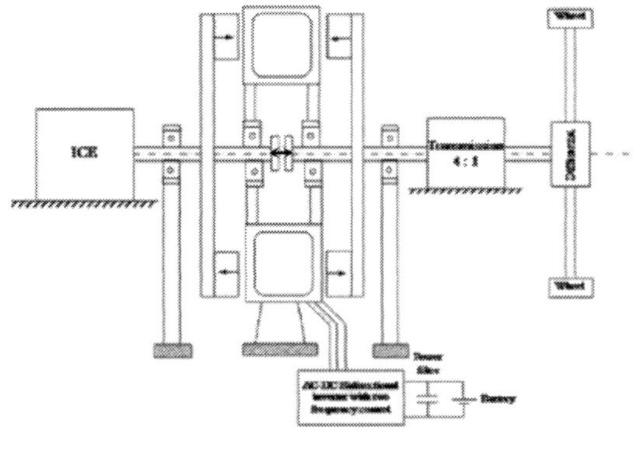

b)

Fig. 1. Proposed e-CVT with single electric machine stator and single inverter a) for planetary gear parallel HEV; b) for series, HEV.

The proposed e-CVT topology in detail is presented in figure 2.

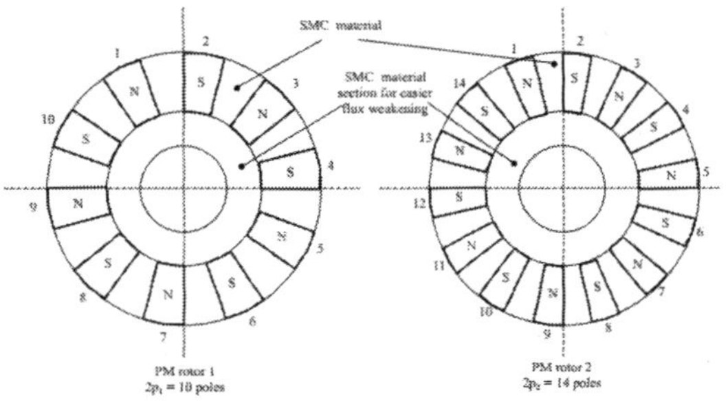

a) b)

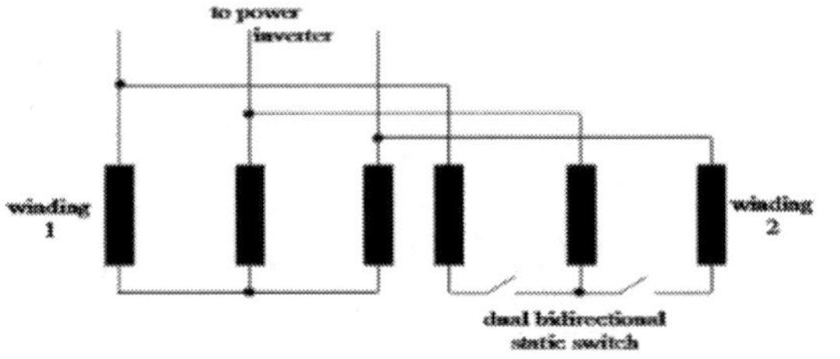

c)

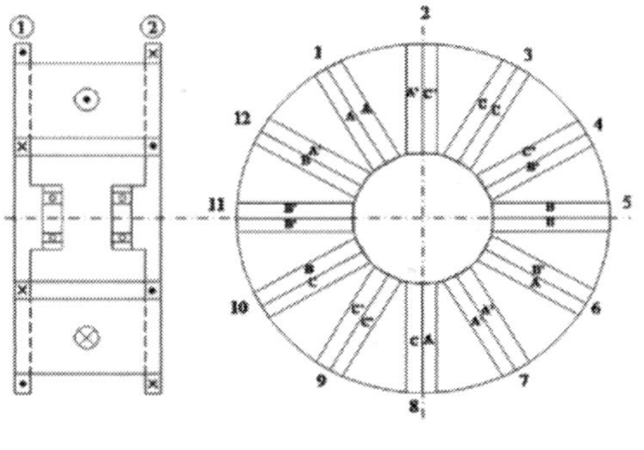

d)

Fig. 2. Dual PM rotor (10 poles/14 poles) axial air-gap single stator (12 slots) PMSM proposed typical topology:
a) 10 PM poles rotor with SMC back iron and small-air-gap SMC zone for flux weakening; b) 14 PM poles rotor with SMC back iron; c) SMC stator with machined slots and Gramme ring ("through") AC coils; d) opening half of the winding in fig. 4e; e) two layers "non-through" coil winding.

Though fig. 2 is rather self-explanatory, here are few remarks:

- the stator core magnetic circuit SMC material is suggested, but a rolled-lamination magnetic core is also feasible, especially for the case of "non through" coils (fig.2e); the same rationale is valid for the rotor magnetic core.

- either "through" or "non through" coil shapes may be adopted; it seems that if the number of turns/coil is small, "non through" coils may be mounted easily.

- it may be, however, possible to adopt double layer coils along tangential direction with opposite polarity on the two stator axial sides (fig. 2d). In this case a dual TRIAC switch might be used to disconnect one half winding when only motoring or only generating is needed, with only one rotor being active (typical to average vehicle speeds).

The stator m.m.f. flux lines in the stator close circumpherentially in the back iron and thus avoid severe flux fluctuations in the two rotors; besides, the PM flux fluctuation effects from one rotor to the other ($2p_1 \neq 2p_2$), should be small for surface PMs, for the same reason.

The axial flux permanent machines with double rotor and single stator have smaller axial length than the corresponding solution with radial flux, for given, larger than 6, number of poles and diameter, as it is mentioned in both references [13-14].

Figure 3 shows the two rotors with different number of permanent magnet poles. The different number of

DOI: 10.1051/matecconf/201712502065

poles may impose a rather different amount of permanent material but if we select the arc pole ratio adequately, it is possible to use the same amount of permanent magnet material in both rotors.

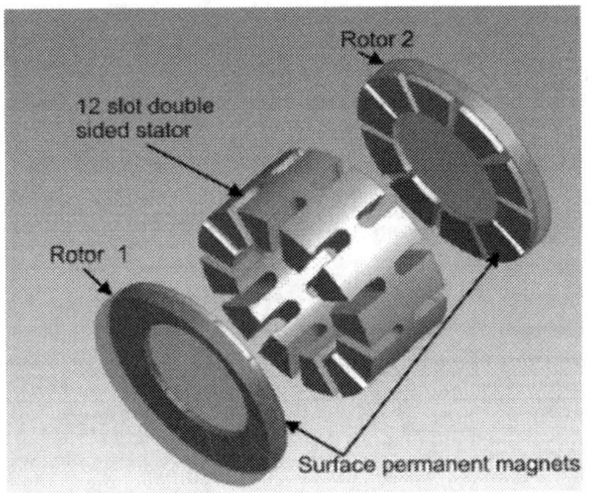

Fig. 3. Proposed configuration exploded view

3 The proposed phase-coordinate model

The stator phase supply voltages $V_{s\,a\,b\,c}$ contain two frequencies

$$V_{s\,a\,b\,c} = V_{s_1}^{*}\cos(\theta_{er_1} + \gamma_1) + V_{s_2}^{*}\cos(\theta_{er_2} + \gamma_2), \quad (1)$$

$$\frac{d\theta_{er_1}}{dt} = \omega_{r_1}, \quad \frac{d\theta_{er_2}}{dt} = \omega_{r_2}, \quad (2)$$

$$\gamma_1 = \frac{\pi}{2} + \delta_{v_1}, \quad \gamma_2 = \frac{\pi}{2} + \delta_{v_2}, \quad (3)$$

where δ_{v1}, δ_{v2} are the voltage power angles (positive for motoring, negative for generating); θ_{er1}, θ_{er2} rotors 1 and 2 electrical position angles (PM rotor axes).

The small SMC rotor pole parts (with some anisotropy) (Fig. 2a) are used to facilitate PM flux weakening and also (by proper pole span segmentation), to facilitate rotor position estimation in case of sensorless control.

Let us neglect here the small rotor saliency (left in the rotors SMC pole section, for easier flux weakening) and discuss here the Gramme ring winding case. The total phase inductance L_S and resistance R_S (considering both rotors with all phase coils in series), though different, are rather straightforward (as for constant air-gap AC machines):

$$L_S \cong 6 \cdot \frac{(N_S \cdot n_c \cdot k_{w1}/3)}{\pi^2 \cdot g_m(1+k_S)\cdot k_c} \cdot \left[\frac{(1+k_{diff1})}{p_1} + \frac{(1+k_{diff2})}{p_2}\right] + L_{ls} + L_{lEC},$$
$$R_S = \rho_{co} \cdot \frac{(N_S \cdot n_c/3)\cdot l_{coil}}{I_{rated}} \cdot j_{co\ rated}, \quad g_m = g + h_{PM}, \quad (4)$$

with

L_{ls} – slot leakage inductance;
L_{lEC} – end connection inductance;
ρ_{co} – copper resistivity;
N_S – number of stator slots;
n_c – number of turns/coil;
l_{coil} – turn length;
g – mechanical gap;
h_{PM} – PM axial thickness;
$j_{co\ rated}$ – rated copper current density;
I_{rated} – rated current;
k_{w1}–fundamental winding factor: 0.933 for the 12 slots/10 pole and for 12 slots /14 poles configurations;
$k_{diff\ 1,2}$ – differential leakage inductance coefficients for the rotor with $2p_1$ and, respectively, $2p_2$ poles (which we know are large in tooth-wound windings because the stator m.m.f. is rich in space harmonics).

The e.m.f. per phase, produced by PMs is:

$$E_{1,2abc} = \omega_{r1,2} \cdot \varphi_{PM\ 2p_1(2p_2)} \cdot k_{w1} \cdot \frac{N_S}{6} \cdot n_c \cdot \cos\left[\theta_{er\ 1,2} - (i-1)\frac{2\pi}{3} + \frac{\pi}{2}\right]. \quad (5)$$

With $|L_S|$ a diagonal matrix with constant terms, the matrix stator voltage equations are straight forward:

$$|i_{abc} \cdot R_S| - |V_{abc}| = -L_S\frac{d}{dt}|i_{abc}| - |E_{1\ abc} + E_{2\ abc}|,$$

$$\frac{J}{p_1}\cdot\frac{d\omega_{r1}}{dt} = \frac{p_1}{2}\cdot\frac{(E_{1a}\cdot i_a + E_{1b}\cdot i_b + E_{1c}\cdot i_c)}{\omega_{r1}} - T_{1\ load}, \quad (6)$$

$$\frac{J}{p_2}\cdot\frac{d\omega_{r2}}{dt} = \frac{p_2}{2}\cdot\frac{(E_{2a}\cdot i_a + E_{2b}\cdot i_b + E_{2c}\cdot i_c)}{\omega_{r2}} - T_{2\ load}.$$

This circuit model has been developed for controlled dynamics investigation as only a full 3D Finite Element Analysis (FEA) can accurately analyze the complex geometry of the proposed electric machine.

4 3D FEM Analysis For Torque Production

The main purpose of this analysis is to find out torque in the proposed axial flux machine using 3D field analysis method. The main parameters of the model are given in table 1.

A full scale model using commercial software was built for the 3D nonlinear magneto-static solution. Using the full scale model with an average mesh of 500 000 nodes, the flux density solution was obtained.

Figure 4 shows the PM air-gap flux density of the machine. It can be seen from the plot that maximum air-gap flux density is nearly 0.8T and the average air-gap flux density is 0.55 T, at mean diameter.

It can also be noted from the air-gap flux density plot that the flux density becomes greater at the edges of the magnets because of the fact that the leakage flux between the magnets gains importance and causes some concentration of flux (shorter than pole-pitch wide PMs might overcome this difficulty).

Table 1. Parameters and machine dimensions.

Frequency (f)	50 Hz
Number of poles rotor 1 ($2p_1$)	10 poles
Number of poles rotor 2 ($2p_2$)	14 poles
Current density (Js)	4.33 A/mm2
Air-gap length (g)	1 mm
Pole-arc-ratio rotor 1 (α_{i1})	0.6944
Pole-arc-ratio rotor 2 (α_{i2})	1
Outer diameter (D_o)	300 mm
Inner diameter (D_i)	180 mm
Slot depth (h_{ss})	30 mm
Axial length of stator core (h_{cs})	90 mm
Axial length of rotor core (h_{cr})	10 mm
Magnet axial length (h_{PM})	5 mm
Permanent magnet material	NeFeBr40

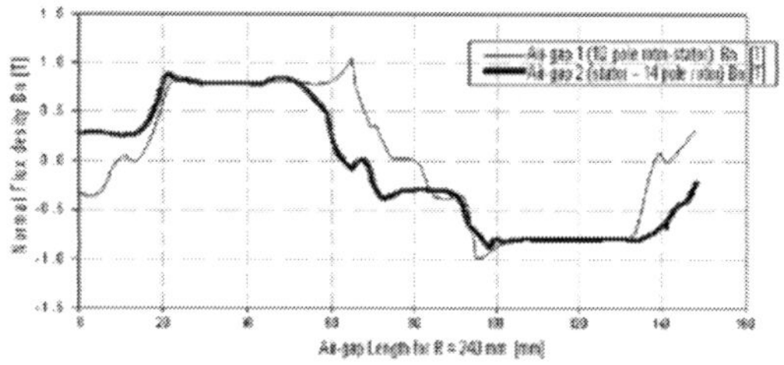

Fig. 4. No load air-gap flux density variation from finite element analysis.

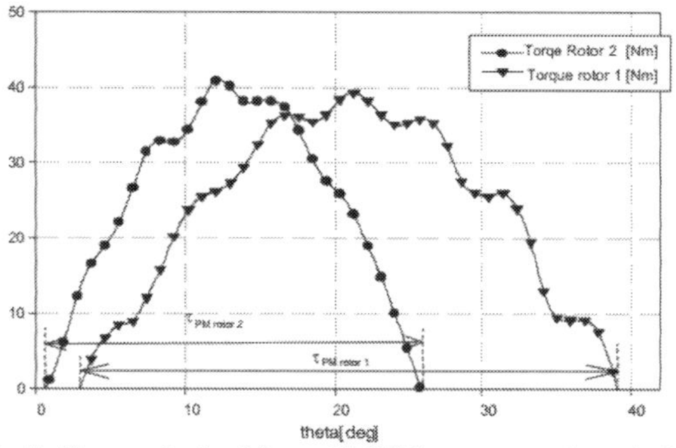

Fig. 5. Torque obtained from 3D FEM magnetostatic analysis for the two rotors.

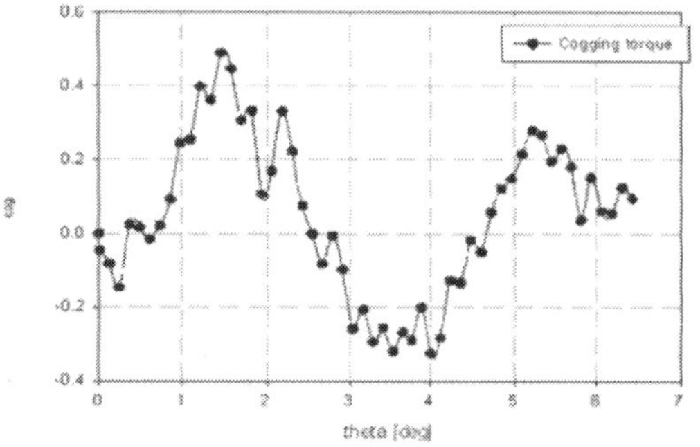

Fig. 6. Cogging torque from 3D analysis.

In general, the total torque of a PM machine is characterized by cogging torque, average torque and on-load (total) ripple torque. Since the considered prototype has a slotted topology, the pulsating torque comprises both cogging and on-load ripple torque components.

The two output torques at zero speed for constant amperturns (3744 dc Aturns per slot) is presented in fig 5. The torque for each rotor was computed separately by means of Maxwell stress tensor.

As the calculations in fig. 5 have been done at standstill, with DC currents, the torque pulsations created by one frequency voltage in both rotors do not occur.

The cogging torque may affect the torque quality of the permanent magnet machines. In our case the two rotors are decoupled from each other. We have analyzed the cogging torque by rotating the two rotors simultaneously and we have evaluated the torque in the central stator. The resulting cogging torque presented in figure 6 is the summation of the two cogging torques produced by the two rotors, which, obviously do not overlap. It is however fairly small.

5 Proposed Dual Vector Control Strategy and Dynamic Simulation

The proposed dual (two-frequency) vector control strategy is illustrated in fig. 7, for the speed control mode.

The objective of the dynamic simulation is to evaluate the dynamic and steady state operation of the dual vector control algorithm using two frequency modulation operation.

Fig. 7 illustrates in fact an indirect DC current control vector control strategy with open loop (voltage) PWM strategy after rotor coordinate transformations back and forth to ω_{r1} and ω_{r2}.

The PI + SM (sliding mode) speed and current controllers (with chattering elimination by the addition of a PI signal, applied to the sliding mode functional, which is active only close to the target) provide for robust control, without e.m.f. compensation, so usual with DC current regulators.

Based on the machine circuit model in paragraph 3, the dual vector control strategy dynamic behavior is simulated here via a dedicated Matlab Code. The complete set of parameters (obtained by trial and error) used in simulations are given in table 2.

The case evaluated is the drive startup behavior for rotor 2 with the speed ramping from 0 to 1000rpm at no load and a step load of 15Nm at t = 1s. Rotor 1 is driven by the IC engine in controlled generator mode (-30N·m) - (Fig. 8a, b, c).

Fig. 8a is presenting the stator current for the startup of rotor 2 and the machine 15 Nm step load which occurs at 1s from startup. The torque for rotor 2 at startup and step load is shown in figure 8b and negative (generating) torque of rotor 1 in fig.8c. The torque pulsations (of the two frequency m.m.f.s. in the two rotors) are mild in this particular case but not so in for all situations.

Table 2. Dual vector control drive system parameters.

Motor Parameters		Phase Resistance	2.87Ω
		Phase inductance	8.50E-003H
		Rotor PM flux 1	0.18 Wb
		Rotor PM flux 2	0.13 Wb
		Pole pairs rotor 1	5
		Pole pairs rotor 2	7
		Inertia (including reduction of translating mass)	0.018kgm^2
		Power (rotor 1)	2.5kW
		Power (rotor 2)	1.7kW
IGBT Inverter		Snubber resistance	1.00E+005Ω
		Ron	2.00E-004Ω
		Tf	1.00E-006s
		Tt	2.00E-006s
Control parameters of PI controllers	controller 1	Kp speed	1
		Ki speed	1
		Kp current	0.06
		Ki current	0.3
	controller 2	Kp speed	1
		Ki speed	5
		Kp current	0.06
		Ki current	0.3

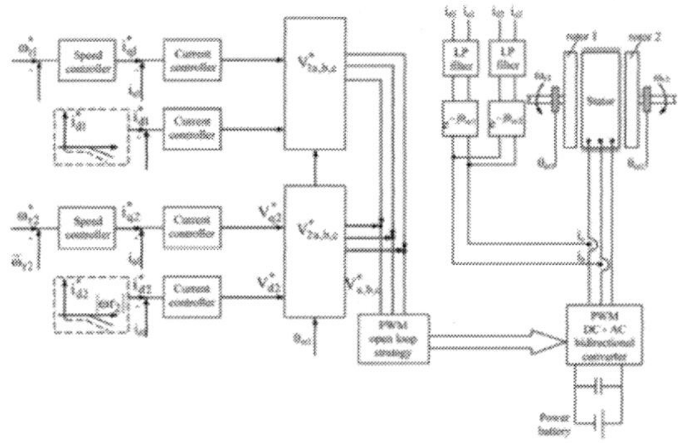

Fig. 7. Generic dual vector control strategy.

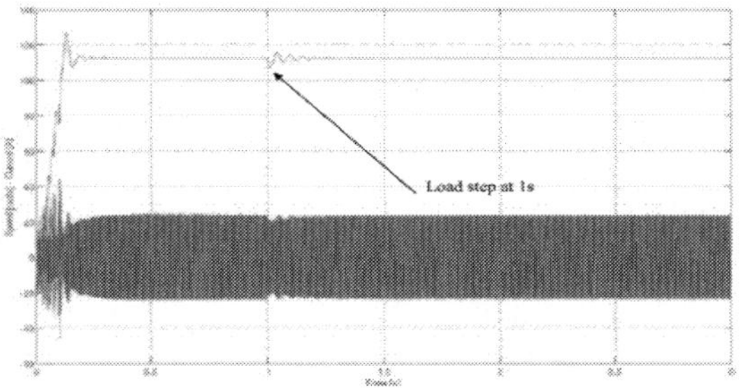

a) Rotor 2 speed for startup (0 -110rad/s) with load variation (from no load to 15 Nm) at 1s and three phase currents.

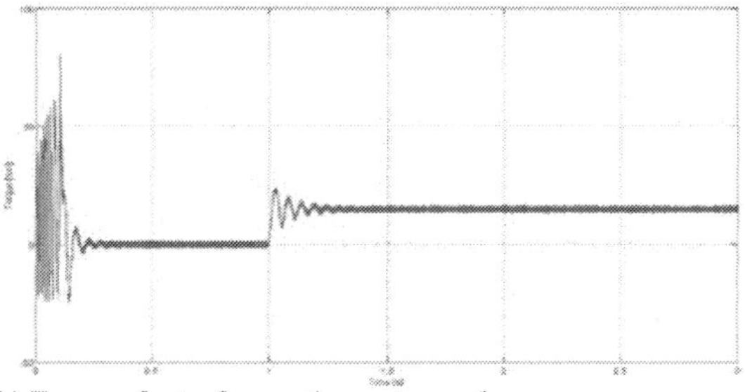

b) Torque of rotor 2 operating motor mode

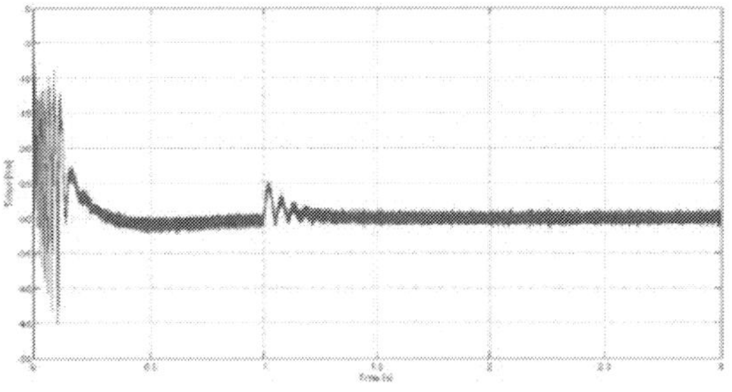

c) Torque of rotor 1 operating in generator mode at 1500 rpm.
Fig. 8.

6 Conclusions

In this paper, a drive system to produce dual, independent, electromechanical torque output using an axial-air-gap machine with a single stator and winding and two different PM rotors has been introduced in terms of topologies, circuit model, control method (from a single inverter), and preliminary 3D-FEM torque production analysis.

Rather extended steady state and dynamics simulations have been proposed. The dual vector control for the independent rotors with one common stator is presented and proven to be effective.

These preliminary results prove the concept quantitatively but further studies, which are already under way, in relation to prototyping, dynamic model, and control and optimization design are needed to fully prove the eventual practicality of the proposed system.

References

1. K.T. Chau, C.C. Chan, C. Liu, *Overview of PM brushless drives for electric and hybrid electric vehicles*, IEEE Transactions on IE, vol. 55, no. 6, June 2008, pp. 2246-2257 (2008).
2. C. C. Chan and K. T. Chau, *Modern Electric Vehicle Technology*, Oxford, U.K.: Oxford Univ. Press, (2001).
3. M. Ehsani, K. M. Rahman, and H. A. Toliyat, *Propulsion system design of electric and hybrid vehicles*, IEEE Trans. Ind. Electron., vol. 44, no. 1, pp. 19–27, Feb. (1997).
4. K. T. Chau and C. C. Chan, *Emerging energy-efficient technologies for hybrid electric vehicles*, *Proc. IEEE*, vol. 95, no. 4, pp. 821–835, Apr. (2007).
5. C. C. Chan and K. T. Chau, *An overview of power electronics in electric vehicles*, IEEE Trans. Ind. Electron., vol. 44, no. 1, pp. 3–13, Feb. (1997).
6. Z. Q. Zhu and D. Howe, *Electrical machines and drives for electric, hybrid and fuel cell vehicles*, Proc. IEEE, vol. 95, no. 4, pp. 746–765, Apr. (2007).
7. M. Terashima, T. Ashikaga, T. Mizuno, K. Natori, N. Fujiwara, and M. Yada, *Novel motors and controllers for high-performance electric vehicle*

with four in-wheel motors, IEEE Trans. Ind. Electron., vol. 44, no. 1, pp. 28–38, Feb. (1997).

8. K. T. Chau and Y. S. Wong, *Hybridization of energy sources in electric vehicles*, Energy Convers. Manag., vol. 42, no. 9, pp. 1059–1069, Jun. (2001).
9. K. T. Chau and Y. S. Wong, *Overview of power management in hybrid electric vehicles*, Energy Convers. Manag., vol. 43, no. 15, pp. 1953–1968, Jun. (2002).
10. M. Ehsani, Y. Gao, S. E. Gay, and A. Emadi, *Modern Electric, Hybrid Electric, and Fuel Cell Vehicles: Fundamentals, Theory, and Design*, Boca Raton, FL: CRC Press, (2005).
11. C. C. Chan, K. T. Chau, J. Z. Jiang,W. Xia, M. Zhu, and R. Zhang, *Novel permanent magnet motor drives for electric vehicles*, IEEE Trans. Ind. Electron., vol. 43, no. 2, pp. 331–339, Apr. (1996).
12. J. M. Miller, *Hybrid electric vehicle propulsion system architectures of the e-CVT type*, IEEE Trans. Power Electron., vol. 21, no. 3, pp. 756–767, May (2006).
13. P. Zheng, R. Liu, P. Thelin, E. Nordlund, C. Sadarangani, *Research on the Parameters and Performances of a 4QT Prototype Machine Used for HEV*, IEEE Transactions on Magnetics, Jan. 2007 Volume: 43 Issue: 1, pp: 443–446, (2007).
14. A. Cavagnino, M. Lazzari, F. Profumo, A. Tenconi, *A Comparison Between the Axial flux and the Radial-flux Structures for PM Synchronous Motors*, In Proceedings of IEEE Industry Applications Conference, 36th IAS Annual Meeting, pp. 1611-1618 (2001).

MATEC Web of Conferences **125**, 02066 (2017) DOI: 10.1051/matecconf/201712502066
CSCC 2017

Energy efficiency tools for residential users

Emmanouil Zacharioudakis [1,*], *Helen C.* Leligou[1], *Aikaterini* Papadopoulou[1]

[1]Synelixis Solutions Ltd., Perissou 157, Nea Chalkidona, 14343, Athens, Greece, {zacharioudakis, nleligou, kpapadopoulou}@synelixis.com

Abstract. Residential energy consumption reserves a significant portion of the total energy consumption in modern cities. The rates of construction of new buildings as well as the rates of renovation on existing ones are generally very low. At the same time, unlike centrally operated large commercial buildings, the installation of energy management systems is a rather expensive solution leaving residential users with limited means to improve their energy efficiency as results are not evident. Considering that to drive energy efficient behaviour, we have to first raise awareness, then provide evidence through measurements and then support further, more elaborate, energy efficiency actions, we capitalise on ICT as soft measures towards reaching hard goals. We propose a novel incremental solution starting from a rather simple mobile application exploiting the sensors available in our smartphones and tablets to proceed to more intelligent advice provisioning towards energy efficiency. We present its implementation architecture and discuss certain market-wise challenges to prove its potential.

1 Introduction

Energy consumed in the buildings' sector consists of residential and commercial end users and accounts for 20.1% of the total delivered energy consumed worldwide[1]. Buildings in the EU are responsible for 40% of primary energy consumption [2]. In households in particular it is 26.2% of total final energy consumption for EU28 [3]. By improving the energy efficiency of residential and public buildings, the EU's total energy consumption can be reduced by about 6% and lower CO_2 emissions by about 5%, [4], [5]. However, reducing energy use in buildings by introducing new technologies is very challenging; across Europe, the rates of construction of new buildings as well as the rates of renovation of existing ones are generally very low [6].

In order to achieve the energy reduction targets set for a sustainable future, affecting the behavioral characteristics of the citizens' interaction within the buildings where they live and work, will have a more tangible impact [6]. Human beings need knowledge and motivation to change and Information and Communication Technologies (ICT) can assist in both providing knowledge and communicating the motivation. Raising awareness of the importance of efficient use of energy is a major target in many countries as this is the most long-lasting measure towards energy consumption reduction. ICT is a low-cost solution in shaping behaviours and achieving energy efficiency. This approach is currently pursued by different initiatives among which the EU-GAIA project focuses on a particular target group as essential for designing a successful behavioral-change strategy [7]. Observing that educational buildings constitute 17% of the non-residential building stock in the EU [8], GAIA focuses on the educational community, aiming to instill behavioral change towards energy efficiency and sustainability through an educational approach, combined with a set of applications.

Targeting energy efficiency in residential setting can yield significant results because a) motivating people to embrace energy-efficient habits has sustainable results on energy consumption, as these people are highly unlikely to abolish their habits in the future as well as in other environments and b) people tend to imitate behaviours which leads to a multiplicative effect. Research interviews conducted [9] made clear that once learned, energy conservation insights can be applied everywhere.

To shape the behaviour of EU residents, a set of ICT tools can be exploited. First, knowledge needs to be acquainted about the importance of behaving in an energy efficient manner and actions that can lead in significant energy reductions. This can be achieved through relevant games and/or quizzes prompting the reader to visit sites with appropriate information, towards achieving the goal of spreading knowledge in an enjoyable manner. Second, practical advice on how to reduce energy consumption in specific real-life circumstances needs to be provided. Again, ICT can accomplish this e.g. through mobile phone applications, for specific real-life situations, either manually entered by the user or sensed by the device itself. Third, advice

* Corresponding author: zacharioudakis@synelixis.com

taking into account real energy consumption information is highly valuable and can result in significant energy savings. Psychologists agree that you have to measure before you act, since measurements provide quantifiable information about the benefits of acting green. This can be achieved either through participatory sensing or through the installation of measurement infrastructure (e.g. power meters, temperature, luminosity sensors) whose cost can range from few hundreds of euros (2017) to few thousands, depending on the measurement points, accuracy and intelligence of the accompanying software.

The rest of the paper is organized as follows: in section 2, we provide a short introduction to participatory sensing and on currently available solutions for residential use. In section 3, we present a set of applications towards shaping behaviours and assisting residential users in being energy efficient. In section 4, we present the implementation architecture of the application set, in section 5 we present the challenges, and finally in section 6 we conclude discussing the potential of such an application set.

2 Currently available solutions –State-of-the-art

2.1 Participatory sensing

Participatory sensing is the concept of communities (or other groups of people) contributing sensory information to form a body of knowledge. The ideas behind participatory sensing is rather than design and build fancy (and expensive) occupancy sensors, we instead rely on the building's occupants to participate in the sensing process. Apart from collecting valuable information, having the occupants insert information about temperature, luminosity and power consumption helps them realise how their behaviour impacts energy consumption and its interplay with the experienced comfort. Additionally, participatory sensing has been shown to create wisdom in many different sectors from weather, urban mobility, congestion as well as any other sensory information that collectively forms knowledge.

The idea is to collect measurements through a mobile device or a laptop/desktop computer in a central repository and process/visualise the readings so as to support intelligent decision making. In a building context, a simple smartphone (android/iOS/SMS-based) application where building occupants can provide real-time feedback on room-level building comfort could be considered as participatory sensing information for collecting comfort level information. The app would prompt the user to enter the building and room number and then allow them to rate the comfort of the room using a (rather limited) thermal sensation scale, e.g. from (-3) very cold to (+3) very hot (0 means comfortable; this scale is the "industry standard" for measuring thermal comfort). These reports would then be collected in a central database for analysis. A web-based interface would then be created to visualize the data. One visualization could be a dynamic overlay of recent thermal comfort reports on the building floorplan; other visualizations could show the historical comfort of different rooms at different times of the day while more advanced analyses are also possible by collecting additional data and performing more sophisticated processing.

2.2 ICT applications for energy efficiency

Energy efficiency relevant applications span diverse disciplines and may have different objectives all aiming at contributing towards the major goal of energy consumption reduction. Among them are energy consumption simulators for building/districts/countries, energy management systems for buildings (suitable mainly for big buildings where dedicated personnel for building management exists), smart home applications enabling remote control of devices towards enhancing comfort and reducing energy consumption, e.t.c. Up to now, solutions for energy management and thus efficiency in buildings rely on sensing and actuating infrastructures which are rather expensive for residential users who however, could create a significant impact on energy consumption if they had the means to collect data, receive recommendations and act upon the provided input.

Example applications for participatory or user-based sensing are Meter Readings and MobilizingCS. Meter Readings is a tool that makes it easy to regularly monitor the energy usage of the household. The user is allowed to add the types of meters to monitor, and to select an interval. Then the app will notify the user when it is time to read the meters. Based on the readings entered, it is possible to get a graphical overview of the monthly usage as well as total average and usage per day. MobilizingCS is a data collection tool; it provides mobile-based data capture through inquiry-based surveys and temporarily triggered reminders. All captured data are automatically timestamped, geocoded and uploaded to a centralized MobilizingCS server for analysis and visualization. The current application is the first step towards realizing the vision of a planetary nervous system. In this version, users are able to collect real-time data from their mobile phone with a user-controlled frequency. The data are stored in the phone and can also be pushed to a remote location that users self-determine. The sensor data can be visualized in real-time. Moreover, the application provides two levels of privacy control to users in the data collection process: (i) privacy by determining which sensor data are locally stored in the phone and (ii) privacy by determining which sensor data are anonymized and remotely shared.

ICT-based solutions relevant to energy management systems for buildings include systems that come with sensing and actuating infrastructures along with software capable of visualising the readings, of providing recommendations and of supporting building manager decision making and execution in a user friendly manner. Such systems have been developed by numerous industrial stakeholders like ABB and Honeywell and include BuildingIQ [10], Decathlon, EnergyCAP [11], eSightenergy [12] Rockwell

Automation [13], Energy Lens [14], and many others. For example, BuildingIQ reduces Heating, ventilation and air conditioning (HVAC) energy costs in commercial buildings, works with a Building Management System (BMS) for actuating purposes, continuously monitors inputs including weather, occupancy, energy prices and demand response events, makes small changes at the air handler unit (AHU) level that result in large HVAC energy savings, without impacting occupant comfort, improves a building's energy performance and usage without incurring CapEx expenses, reduces a building's carbon footprint and improving its sustainability score by up to 20 LEED points or a full NABERS point, enables a building to be Smart Grid-ready without requiring an upgrade or custom engineering.

3. A scalable solution for residential users

Our aim is to exploit state-of-the-art technologies to build a scalable solution that can guide residential users behave in a more energy efficient manner. To do so, they would be supported to track and control their home's energy consumption and to make efficiency aware decisions.

3.1 Raising awareness

As the *first step* in behavioural change is to raise awareness, the elementary component of the proposed solution consists of a smartphone application which focuses on luminosity and temperature conditions and user guidance to adjust them: saving energy while preserving their comfort. With respect to luminosity, it exploits the currently available in all smartphone devices luminosity sensors, captures the luminosity value, displays it to the user and prompts them to choose among a set of activities. Depending on the selected activity and combining it with the current time, the application notifies the user if the luminosity is adequate for their activity, if more than the suitable value for the activity it provides a message informing them about potential savings. It would tell them that regulating the luminosity could save them a certain amount of energy (and possibly, relevant cost, if inserted at the application initialisation time) and could also reduce the CO_2 footprint by a certain amount. With respect to temperature, unfortunately the temperature sensor existing in mobile devices cannot be exploited because it is placed close to the device's processor aiming at sensing its temperature and avoid overheating. Thus, the user is prompted to enter the temperature values on their own. Once entered, they are, similarly with the previous case, provided with recommendations about taking action to reduce the energy consumed to reach the desired indoor temperature. For example, they are notified about the target values ensuring comfort by widely accepted standards, they are informed about the energy expenses associated with every degree in the temperature and how this correlates with the external temperature as well as about easy to take actions.

The proposed solution provides recommendations based on the wide literature and statistics available today, while additional recommendation or exchange of ideas could take place through social networking among all users of the specific application.

3.2 Systematic monitoring and measurement

On top of the previous application, a web-based mobile application that allows for manual uploads of home energy sources values-electricity, oil, natural gas- can assist residential users in closer monitoring of the energy consumption in their houses. Through this application, the user is prompted to insert power consumption values entering readings from the power meter either through a dedicated user interface or by uploading power consumption information through a structured file e.g. an excel file. The readings are uploaded to a cloud infrastructure where they are processed and visualised. Apart from the visualisation of the reading, the application provides additional information such as statistics about average consumption of other residential users and comparison to historical reading from the same house, if available. This way the residential user can a) observe peaks of energy consumption and take action if not justified by their activities, b) observe the base energy consumption and identify which devices consume energy even if no other load is active and c) study whether specific loads can be shifted in time to match demand-response programs put in place by the power provider. Analysis of historical data is provided via attractive diagrams and important metrics such as mean values, peak and base loads depicted in a daily, weekly or monthly basis according to the user preference.

3.3 Semi-automated Energy Management

The next step is a) more elaborate monitoring and b) user guidance based on specific rules, assuming the absence of actuators. For more elaborate monitoring, the installation of sensing devices (power meters and possibly temperature sensors) should be placed in the building tracking energy consumption, temperature and humidity levels in order to automate the procedure. Two options arise here: either the infrastructure provider delivers software capable of extracting the reading in some structured file, in which case, this can be imported in the above mentioned participatory sensing part of the solution; or enable the integration of the sensors with the provided cloud infrastructure, assuming this will have an open Application Programming Interface implemented for this reason. This way, more elaborate monitoring can be achieved guiding more elaborate decisions. It is worth stressing that sensing equipment can be nowadays installed by the users themselves, i.e. it does not require the intervention of specialised personnel. This is an important element as one can buy a one-phase power meter and use it to monitor different power lines each day/week/month. Additionally, in certain markets, it is possible to rent equipment which allows for elaborate monitoring for a specific time span. According to the observation during this time span, specific rules can be defined, upon which the user is notified and instructed to act appropriately.

With respect to actions, assuming that no actuators are in place, the application allows the user to define rules upon which they are notified. Alerts notify the user when rules are triggered via text or email allowing them to take appropriate action. A social networking feature for users to compare similar buildings is possible while the application can also be available through desktop computers. For example, "If the temperature exceeds 22 degrees Celsius, send an SMS". While this seems to be over simplistic, there are still buildings where no thermostat in the rooms exists and the thermostat is only installed where the HVAC central system is installed. Additionally, there are many cases where the building thermal profile has radically changed from the time the initial study had been performed, leading to an apartment being over-heated while other remain at low temperatures. A flexible notification generation engine enabling the user to specify rules at will, can become a powerful tool since all major energy management systems are in essence executing specific rules.

While the main motivation can be considered the combination of environment sustainability with the reduction of energy bills, additional motivation can be provided by gamification/rewarding schemes which can be implemented on top of the previous application components and potentially combined with social networking flavours. This can be considered as a separate component which compares current with past user behaviour and energy bills and creates a hall of fame among users so that more energy efficient users become known and they can gain popularity.

4. The implementation architecture

The proposed application set exploits the sensing elements of the mobile device, sensing devices installed at home, visualisation and web technologies and the abundant processing and storage facilities offered at cloud infrastructures. As shown in Fig. 1, so as to raise awareness a mobile application is proposed which can be executed on the mobile phone while, by communicating with the cloud, the repertoire of the recommendations provided can be continuously enriched and updated. To be able to read the sensors existing in the mobile devices, native apps have to be developed for Android and iOS devices, as these are the ones exhibiting high penetration to the populations.

To support participatory sensing in the targeted environment, a web-based application can be used (which can be executed both at desktop/laptop computers and at mobile devices, e.g. smartphones and

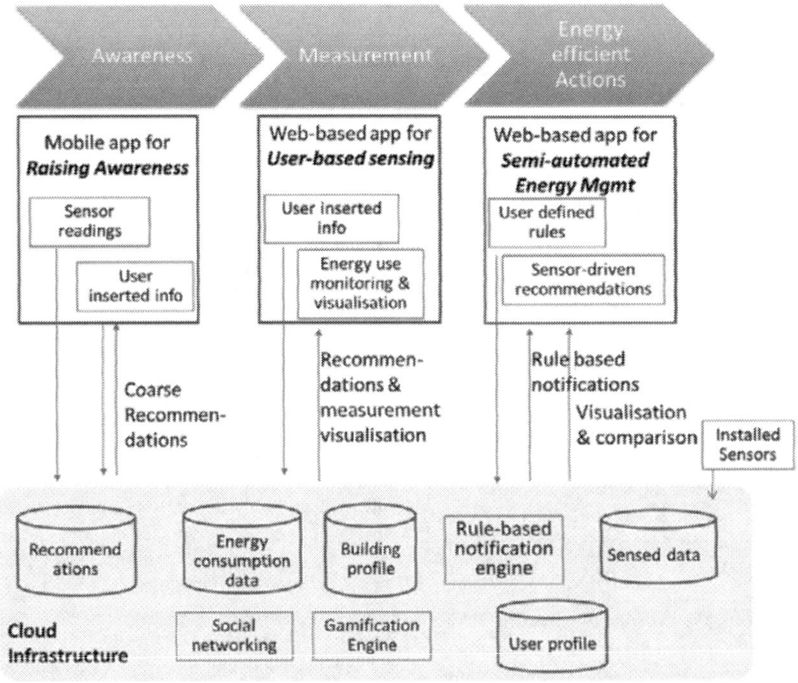

Fig.1. The implementation architecture of the application set realising the concept of raising awareness, measure and act in a efficient manner

tablets). Through a user friendly interface this application allows for a) inserting user-read data from power meters and/or temperature/humidity sensors b) inserting reading from power utilities or exported from sensing devices and c) inserting building specific information. Specifically, to create enhanced user experience, the user interface can be based on HTML5, CSS3 and on the materialize CSS (material design) framework. Also AngularJS framework version 1.5 can be used for the further necessities.

The user is furthermore able to insert building specific information including building/apartment ID, number of floors/areas in the building, number of individual rooms (e.g. classrooms) in the floor/area, geographic location, surface (m^2) per area, number of inhabitants per house/area, age of the building, whether there was intervention /Date of intervention per building, orientation, energy types available (electricity, gas, etc.).

With respect to the energy consumption, the user is allowed to insert yearly consumption per energy type, yearly energy cost and footprint.

The user will receive valuable information including:

- Visualised building performance information allowing for comparing the performance among days/months/years as well as for comparing the performance of the currently monitored house/apartment with others of the same typology. By typology we refer to houses/apartments of the same/similar geographical location (as it is not objective to compare an apartment in Athens with an apartment in Sweden), of the same age/thermal characteristics which strongly depend on the material used for its construction and of similar use (residential buildings should be compared to residential buildings). As the number of inhabitants, strongly affects the consumed energy, in the analytics the capability to present energy consumption per inhabitant will be offered.
- Receive suggestions for energy savings. These can range from suggestions for long-term actions and interventions (such as "you consume too much for heating, consider changing the central heating to another method") to suggestions like "electricity consumption is higher than other days; is it justifiable? Consider making out the most of natural light".

The visualisation itself is expected to provide adequate insight to the users to seek ways to reduce the peaks as well as average energy consumption values. For example, as shown in Fig. 2, it is evident that in the period visualised at the top graph, the peak energy is higher even through the average of the two graphs may be quite close one another.

Such comparisons may lead to valuable observation suggesting devices that have highly fluctuating energy demand patterns which may drive the user to activate these devices in time periods that the power utility offers more attractive tariffs. As regards the intelligence of the suggestions, this depends on the collected readings as well as on the implementation of a relevant recommendation engine.

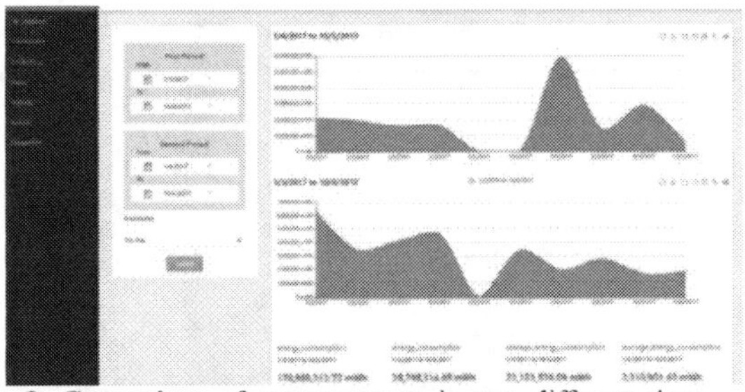

Fig. 2. Comparison of measurements in two different time periods

Finally, the 3rd step incorporates reading from sensing devices. As Internet of Things (IoT) technologies invade our everyday lives, interconnected sensing devices become a commodity and interfaces are getting standardised. Each installation may consist of a multitude of IoT nodes, which communicate with a cloud infrastructure via a gateway device. The IoT nodes include multiple sensing devices, while the gateway nodes coordinate communication and enable interaction with cloud-based services and other Internet-connected devices. All devices use a wireless interface to communicate locally, while gateways use wired connectivity to report measurements and receive commands or configuration updates.

The overall design pattern for the installation of IoT infrastructure in the considered buildings is as follows:

- IoT nodes installed to monitor the power consumption of the building/house as a whole, or specific areas/sectors (e.g. individual power lines).
- IoT nodes installed in rooms to monitor a set of environmental parameters such as temperature, humidity, activity and noise levels (see Fig. 1).
- One or a set of IoT gateway nodes installed in central points of the house/building to bridge the IoT nodes that communicate using IEEE 802.15.4 with the Internet.

Assuming that a) the IoT gateways communicate directly with some cloud infrastructure which can be accessed by our applications or b) at least the relevant readings can be exported and re-inserted in our cloud infrastructure, continuous monitoring of energy consumption and environmental parameters is possible. If these data are available in near real time, then the user can define rules upon which they receive a notification triggering their actions. Default rules will be offered by the application itself although greater savings can be achieved if the user takes the advice of an expert and sets accordingly their own rules. The same notification engine residing in the cloud can be exploited to generate alerts, e.g. when inhabitants are away and temperature values exceed a predefine threshold or water consumption is not zero. It needs not pointing out that comparison with other similar residences is still possible and all previously defined suggestions are still enacted. An example of the information accompanying an alert is shown in Fig. 3.

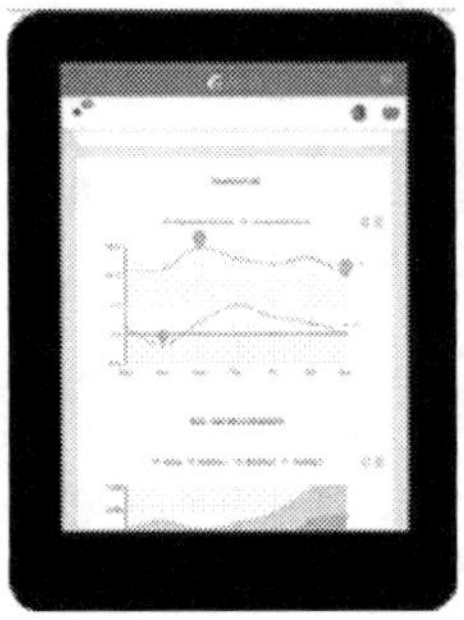

Fig. 3. Information provided together with an alert about detected consumption anomalies

5 Challenges

As the aforementioned applications capitalise on state-of-the-art technologies, the main challenges in their implementation and mass deployment stems from business relevant matters. The first application outlined above is a mobile app which can either be offered for free to trigger the audience's interest or advertisement of Energy Services COmpanys (ESCOs) can pay off its deployment. ESCOs are entities that primarily invest in building interventions and are paid off by the energy savings achieved. In the second step, for users to be willing to pay for using it or downloading it, it is necessary to enrich the recommendation engine with sophisticated and high-value recommendations which mandates cooperation with building energy management experts. Finally, in the third step, it is important to ensure integration of a wide set of available in the market sensing devices in the infrastructure used by the presented applications. This mandates the implementation of so-called wrappers for popular sensing device interfaces.

6 Conclusions

Residential buildings consume an important percentage of total energy consumption in modern cities. Towards reducing the consumed energy and increasing the efficiency of energy use, first, awareness about energy efficiency should be raised, then, this should be supported by measurements to provide adequate evidence to users and finally, suggestions at all timescales, (from intervention to real-time actions) should be provided to the users.

In this paper, we have proposed an incremental solution that can be used by residential users to achieve high energy efficiency and reduce energy bills obviating the need for installing expensive energy management systems. The proposed solution capitalises on state-of— the-art technology to ensure low cost, while initial business aspects have been explored to check business viability.

Acknowledgment

The work presented in this paper is partially funded by the Green Awareness in Action (GAIA) project funded by the European Commission under the H2020-EE-2015-2-RIA call and contract number 696029.

References

1. EIA, *International Energy Outlook 2016, Chapter 6 Building Energy Consumption* (2016) https://www.eia.gov/forecasts/ieo/buildings.cfm
2. European Commission, Energy, Buildings, https://ec.europa.eu/energy/en/topics/energy-efficiency/buildings
3. F. Christian, *Statistics on Energy Consumption in Households* (2014)
4. https://ec.europa.eu/energy/en/topics/energy-fficiency/buildings
5. SIEMENS, *Building Automation Impact on Energy Efficiency, Application per EN 15232 eu.bac product certification*
6. Buildings Performance Institute Europe, *Europe's buildings under the microscope: A country-by-country review of the energy performance of buildings,* Technical report, (2011)
7. J. Stromback, C. Dromacque, M. H. Yassin, *The potential of smart meter enabled programs to increase energy and systems efficiency: a mass pilot comparison*, Technical report, VaasaETT Global Energy Think Tank, Funded by European Smart Metering Industry Group (2013)
8. http://gaia-project.eu/index.php/en/homepage-3/
9. K. Crosby, A. B. Metzger, *Powering down: A toolkit for behavior-based energy conservation in k-12 schools*, Technical report, U.S. Green Building Council (2012)
10. https://www.buildingiq.com/solutions
11. http://www.energycap.com
12. http://www.esightenergy.com/uk/software
13. http://www.rockwellautomation.com
14. http://www.energylens.com/

A performance comparison of two emotion-recognition implementations using OpenCV and Cognitive Services API

Luis Antonio Beltrán Prieto[1,a] and Zuzana Komínkova-Oplatková[1]

[1]*Faculty of Applied Informatics, Department of Informatics and Artificial Intelligence, Tomas Bata University in Zlín, Nad Stráněmi 4511,76005 Zlín, Czech Republic*

Abstract. Emotions represent feelings about people in several situations. Various machine learning algorithms have been developed for emotion detection in a multimedia element, such as an image or a video. These techniques can be measured by comparing their accuracy with a given dataset in order to determine which algorithm can be selected among others. This paper deals with the comparison of two implementations of emotion recognition in faces, each implemented with specific technology. OpenCV is an open-source library of functions and packages mostly used for computer-vision analysis and applications. Cognitive services is a set of APIs containing artificial intelligence algorithms for computer-vision, speech, knowledge, and language processing. Two Android mobile applications were developed in order to test the performance between an OpenCV algorithm for emotion recognition and an implementation of Emotion cognitive service. For this research, one thousand tests were carried out per experiment. Our findings show that the OpenCV implementation got a better performance than the Cognitive services application. In both cases, performance can be improved by increasing the sample size per emotion during the training step.

1 Introduction

The aim of this paper is to compare the performance of two emotion-recognition implementations. The first application consists of Python code which uses OpenCV face-recognizer classes combined with Fisher Face technique. The second one is a C# application which makes requests to a Cognitive Services API. 500 facial expressions from the Cohn-Kanade (CK+) dataset were examined by each program for evaluation purposes.

Facial emotion recognition seeks to predict the real feeling that a person expresses based on facial images, with a wide range of possible applications, such as improving student engagement [1], building smart health environments [2], analyzing customers' feedback [3] and evaluating the quality of children's games [4], just to name a few.

Deep learning is a recent, revolutionary technique in machine learning which pursues the objective of bringing artificial intelligence to solve practical applications across different, diverse fields, such as recommender systems [5], plasma tomography reconstruction [6], facial age estimation [7], and neuroimaging [8], among others. Recognizing faces within images and videos has been one of the challenges that deep learning has tested thoroughly, with significant performance and improvement. This progress has been achieved thanks to development of Convolutional Neural Networks and the availability of huge training datasets [9].

As a consequence, detecting the emotion expressed by a person is the next step into facial analysis. Recent research [10] has proven that emotion detection can be achieved by the usage of machine learning and artificial intelligence algorithms. While it is not an easy task, several open-source libraries and packages, such as OpenCV, TensorFlow, Theano, Caffe and CNTK (Microsoft Cognitive Toolkit) simplify the process of building deep-learning-based algorithms and applications. Emotions such as anger, disgust, happiness, surprise, and neutrality can be detected.

This paper is organized as follows. In the first section, a theoretical background on emotion recognition, OpenCV, Fisherfaces algorithm, Cognitive Services, and the extended Cohn-Kanade (CK+) database is presented. Afterwards, the methods and methodology that was used for this comparison are described. Then, evaluation results, comparison and discussion are presented together. Finally, conclusions are shown at the end of the paper.

2 Background Information

Emotions are strong feelings about people's situations and relationships with others. Most of the time, humans show how they feel by using facial expressions. Speech, gestures, and actions are also used to describe a person's current state.

Emotion recognition can be defined as the process of detecting the feeling expressed by humans from their

[a] Corresponding author: beltran_prieto@fai.utb.cz

facial expressions, such as anger, happiness, sadness, deceitfulness, and others. Even though a person can automatically identify facial emotions, machine learning algorithms have been developed for this purpose. Emotions play a key role in decision-making and human-behaviour, as many actions are determined by how a person feels at some point.

Typically, these algorithms use either a picture or a video (which can be considered as a set of images) as input, then they proceed to detect and focus their attention on a face and finally, specific points and regions of the face are analysed in order to detect the affective state.

Machine Learning (ML) algorithms, methods and techniques can be applied to detect emotions from a picture or video. For instance, a deep learning neural network can perform effective human activity recognition with the aid of smartphone sensors [11]. Moreover, a classification of facial expressions based on Support Vector Machines was developed for spontaneous behavior analysis.

2.1 OpenCV and Fisherfaces

OpenCV [12] is a free, yet powerful, open-source library developed by Intel Corporation which has been widely used in computer vision and machine learning tasks, such as image processing, real-time image recognition, and face detection. With more than 2500 optimized algorithms included, this library has been extensively used for research and commercial applications from both global and small entrepreneurs. OpenCV contains an optimized set of libraries written in C language, with bindings to other languages and technologies, including Python, Android, iOS, and CUDA (for GPU fast processing), and wrappers in other languages, such as C#, Perl, Haskell, and others. Moreover, it works under Windows and Linux.

Among its capabilities, OpenCV contains a FaceRecognizer class which, as the name suggests, is helpful for face recognition tasks. There are three algorithms available for this purpose: Eigenfaces, Fisherfaces, and Local Binary Patterns Histograms. While the first technique considers a linear combination of facial features in order to maximize total variance in data, thus representing data in a powerful, but classless, way, Fisherfaces takes a Linear Discriminant Analysis approach in which class-specific dimensionality reduction is performed so the combination of features that separate the best classes is taken into account. If there exists any external source, such as light, which affects the representation of the image, the Eigenfaces technique is not able to accurately classify the faces. Fisherfaces, on its side, is not affected by this factor.

The algorithm goes as follows: First, let $V = \{V_1, V_2, \ldots, V_c\}$, $V_i = \{v_1, v_2, \ldots, v_N\}$ be a random vector with samples obtained from c classes. Then, the total mean, μ, and the mean of class i, μ_i, where $i \in \{1, 2, \ldots, c\}$ are computed as described in equations (1) and (2). These values are used in equations (3) and (4) in order to calculate the Scatter matrices, S_B and S_W.

$$\mu = \frac{1}{N}\sum_{i=1}^{N} v_i \qquad (1)$$

$$\mu_i = \frac{1}{|V_i|}\sum_{v_j \epsilon V_i} v_j \qquad (2)$$

$$S_B = \sum_{i=1}^{c} N_i(\mu_i - \mu)(\mu_i - \mu)^T \qquad (3)$$

$$S_W = \sum_{i=1}^{c}\sum_{x_j \epsilon x_i}(x_j - \mu_i)(x_j - \mu_i)^T \qquad (4)$$

A projection W maximizes the class separability criterion by following equation (5):

$$W_{opt} = \arg max_W \frac{|W^T S_B W|}{|W^T S_W W|} \qquad (5)$$

The General Eigenvalue Problem solves this optimization task (6):

$$S_B v_i = \lambda_i S_W v_i$$
$$S_W^{-1} S_B v_i = \lambda_i v_i \qquad (6)$$

The rank of the scatter matrix, S_w, is at most (N samples – c classes). In problems such as pattern recognition tasks, the number of samples is smaller than the dimension of the data input. Thus, S_W becomes singular and can be solved using a linear discriminant analysis. At the end, the optimization problem is rewritten to equations (7) and (8)

$$W_{pca} = arg\ max_W |W^T S_T W| \qquad (7)$$

$$W_{fld} = \arg max_W \frac{|W^T W_{pca}^T S_B W_{pca} W|}{|W^T W_{pca}^T S_W W_{pca} W|} \qquad (8)$$

And the transformation matrix W, projecting a sample into the $(c - 1)$ dimensional space is given by equation (9):

$$W = W_{fld}^T W_{pca}^T \qquad (9)$$

2.2 Cognitive Services

Cognitive Services [13] are a set of machine learning algorithms developed by Microsoft which are able to solve artificial intelligence problems in several fields, such as computer vision, speech recognition, natural language processing, machine learning search, and recommendation systems, among others. These algorithms can be consumed through Representational State Transfer (REST) calls over an Internet connection, allowing developers to use artificial intelligence research to solve problems. These services are open-source and can be consumed by many languages, including C#, PHP, Java, Python, and implemented in desktop, mobile, console, and web applications.

The Computer Vision API of Cognitive Services provides access to machine learning algorithms capable of image processing tasks. Either an image stream is uploaded or an image URL is specified to the service so the content can be analyzed for label tagging, image categorization, face detection, color extraction, text detection, and emotion recognition. Video is also supported as input. The Emotion API analyses the sentiment of a person in an image or video and returns the confidence level for eight emotions mostly understood by a facial expression, including anger, contempt, disgust, fear, happiness, neutrality, sadness and surprise.

2.3 The Extended Cohn-Kanade database

The Cohn-Kanade AU-Coded Facial Expression Database [14, 15] is a well-known repository of face images used for research purposes into the facial recognition field, with an increased interest in emotion detection research. An Extended version 2 of the database, also known as CK+, was developed in order to address some limitations of version 1, such as non-validation of emotion labels, the absence of a common performance metric against which to evaluate the latest algorithms and standard protocols for typical databases and quantitative meta-analysis. It contains the facial expressions of 210 adults between 18 and 50 years of age, from which 31% were male, 81% Euro-Americans, 13% Afro-Americans, and 6% from other groups. For each participant, 23 facial displays were performed. 593 sequences were labelled with a basic emotion from a pool of seven categories: anger, contempt, disgust, fear, happiness, sadness, and surprise.

3 Methods and Methodology

The objective of this experiment is to compare the performance of 2 emotion-recognition implementations. The first one (Experiment A) is a Python-based application which makes use of the OpenCV machine learning algorithms for facial and emotion detection. The second one (Experiment B) is a C# software application which makes requests to a Cognitive Services API for emotion detection. In both cases, the Extended Cohn-Kanade dataset of images was used as input for the analysis. Both applications were developed by the authors for this experiment.

For Experiment A, we considered 327 sequences which actually show a relevant sequence of emotion, from a neutral feeling to the emotion itself. First step is then to obtain both the neutral and emotional images. From this subset, OpenCV library is used to detect the face on each picture by using a custom Haar-filter. Effective object detection is possible thanks to the Haar feature-based cascade classifiers proposed in [16], a machine learning based approach which takes advantage of cascade functions training from both positive and negative images. OpenCV already provides several Haar-filter functions; however, a cascade function of boosted classifiers was used for this experiment in order to detect the faces in the pictures. Thereafter, all images were standardized by converting them to grayscale and resized to the same dimensions. Table 1 presents how half of the subset, i.e., 327 images, were distributed among the different labelled emotions. The other half corresponds to 327 emotionless faces, i.e., showing neutrality. Then, we proceeded to randomly split the subset in two new sets: training set and prediction set. For training, we considered 523 images, which corresponds to 80% of the pictures. The remaining 20% was considered for the prediction set. For better evaluation purposes, 10 random training and classification sets were generated. The training process consists of getting the characteristics of each face along with the labelled emotion, i.e. the expression shown by the person. This data is used to create and train a Fisherface classifier. Then, evaluation of the classifier proceeds by comparing the outcome of its predict function of each face with the actual labelled emotion.

Table 1. Sample size of each labelled emotion

Labelled Emotion	Number of faces
Anger	45
Contempt	18
Disgust	58
Fear	25
Happiness	69
Sadness	28
Surprise	84

Experiment B starts with the 654 images extracted with the Python code from Experiment A. 10 random groups consisting each of 20% of the collection were generated in order to evaluate samples of the same size as in Experiment A. For each experiment, every face was submitted to the Cognitive Services API for its evaluation, as its training has already been developed by Microsoft. A C# application was developed for running this experiment. The service returns a JSON content which contains the score for each emotion. Only the highest score, considered as the predicted facial expression detected by the service, was compared with the actual labelled emotion for evaluation purposes. Fig. 1 shows the application developed in C# for this experiment. It takes a previously provided picture, then finds a face on it and finally submits a request in order to detect the emotions expressed by the person in the photo. The analysis is performed by the Emotion Cognitive Service.

5 Results and Discussion

After running each of the 10 tests from Experiment A, the results which are presented in Table 2 were obtained. An average of 75.87% correct predictions was calculated as an outcome. On the other side, Table 3 illustrates the results of each test in Experiment B. As a result, a 68.93% average of efficiency was obtained after running 10 tests of this implementation.

The findings of the experiments show that the Python-based implementation with OpenCV using Fisherfaces proved to be more accurate than the Cognitive Services implementation in C# by approximately a 7% difference. For experiment A, several of the mistakes occurred when trying to predict emotions with low occurrences in the dataset, such as fear and contempt mistakenly classified as neutral expressions. Moreover, there were a few errors when trying to predict a neutral face, most of the time identified as a sad face. Regarding experiment B, neutral images were wrongly identified as either contempt or sadness emotions; however, by looking closely to the scores obtained by the Cognitive Services, a minimum difference between the wrong prediction and the actual emotion was detected. Thus, in most cases, the second best prediction was correct. However, for evaluation purposes, this was considered as an error.

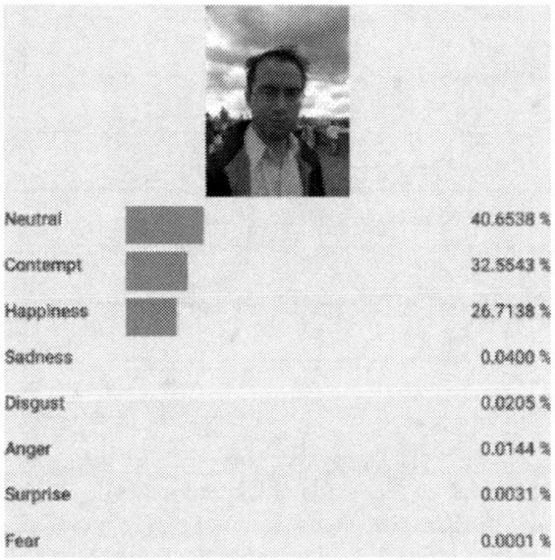

Fig. 1. Analysis of emotions detected on a picture by the Emotion Cognitive Service.

Table 2. Evaluation results of experiment A

Test Number	Correct (%)	Incorrect (%)
1	103 (78.62%)	28 (21.37%)
2	100 (76.33%)	31 (23.66%)
3	98 (74.80%)	33 (25.19%)
4	104 (79.38%)	27 (20.61%)
5	96 (73.28%)	35 (26.71%)
6	95 (75.25%)	36 (27.48%)
7	99 (75.57%)	32 (24.42%)
8	100 (76.33%)	31 (23.66%)
9	97 (74.04%)	34 (25.95%)
10	102 (77.86%)	29 (22.13%)

Table 3. Evaluation results of experiment B

Test Number	Correct (%)	Incorrect (%)
1	89 (67.93%)	42 (32.06%)
2	95 (72.51%)	36 (27.48%)
3	86 (65.64%)	45 (34.35%)
4	91 (69.46%)	40 (30.53%)
5	88 (67.17%)	43 (32.82%)
6	90 (68.70%)	41 (31.29%)
7	95 (72.51%)	36 (27.48%)
8	93 (70.99%)	38 (29.00%)
9	84 (64.12%)	47 (35.87%)
10	92 (70.22%)	39 (29.77%)

5 Conclusion

The objective of this experiment was to compare the performance of two different implementations of emotion-recognition applications by using OpenCV and Python with a Fisherface technique in the first case, while considering a C#-based solution which makes requests to a Cognitive Services API for Emotion detection for the second solution. While the first implementation got the best results, the performance could be improved either by increasing the sample size of those emotions with few faces, so the training phase gets benefited, or by removing them from the subset, as not enough cases were collected.

Acknowledgement

This work was supported by the Ministry of Education, Youth and Sports of the Czech Republic within the National Sustainability Programme project No. LO1303 (MSMT-7778/2014) and also by the European Regional Development Fund under the project CEBIA-Tech No. CZ.1.05/2.1.00/03.0089, further it was supported by Grant Agency of the Czech Republic—GACR 588 P103/15/06700S and by Internal Grant Agency of Tomas Bata University in Zlin under the project No. IGA/CebiaTech/2017/004. L.A.B.P author also thanks the doctoral scholarship provided by the National Council for Science and Technology (CONACYT) and the Council for Science and Technology of the State of Guanajuato (CONCYTEG) in Mexico.

References

1. A. C. Garn, K. Simonton., T. Dasingert, A. Simonton, Psychol. Sport Exerc. **29** pp. 93-102 (2017)

2. A. Fernandez-Caballero, A. Martinez-Rodrigo, J. M. Pastor, J. C. Castillo, E. Lozano-Monasor, M. T. Lopez, R. Zangroniz, J. M. Latorre, A. Fernandez-Sotos, J. Biomed. Inform. **64** pp. 55-73 (2016)
3. A. Felbermayr, A. Nanopoulos, J. Interact. Mark. **36** pp. 60-76 (2016).
4. R. Gennari, A. Melonio, D. Raccanello, M. Brondino, G. Dodero, M. Pasini, S. Torello, Int. J. Hum-Comput. St. **101** pp. 45-61 (2017)
5. J. Wei, J. He, K. Chen, Y. Zhou, Z. Tang, Expert Syst. Appl. **69** pp. 29-39 (2017)
6. F. A. Matos, D. R. Ferreira, P. J. Carvalho, Fusion Eng. Des. **114** pp. 18-25 (2017)
7. H. Liu, J. Lu, J. Feng, J. Zhou, Pattern Recogn. **66** pp. 82-94 (2017)
8. S. Vieira, W. H. L. Pinaya, A. Mechelli, Neurosci. Biobehav. R. **74** pp. 58-75 (2017)
9. O. M. Parkhi, A. Vedaldi, A. Zisserman: *Proceedings of British Machine Vision Conf.* (BMVA Press, Durham 2015)
10. C. K. Yogesh, M. Hariharan, R. Ngadiran, A.H. Adom, S. Yaacob, K. Polat, Appl. Soft. Comput. **3** (2017)
11. C. A. Ronao, S. Cho, Expert Syst. Appl. **59** (2016)
12. OpenCV library. http://opencv.org [Online: accessed 01-Jun-2017]
13. Cognitive Services. http://microsoft.com/cognitive [Online: accessed 03-Jun-2017]
14. T. Kanade, J. F. Cohn, Y. Tian. *Proceedings of the Fourth IEEE Int. Conf. on Automatic Face and Gesture Recognition* (Grenoble, 2000).
15. P. Lucey, J. F. Cohn, T. Kanade, J. Saragih, Z. Ambadar, I. Matthews. *Proceedings of the Third Int. Workshop on CVPR for Human Communicative Behavior Analysis* (San Francisco, 2010).
16. M. Turk, A. Pentland. J. Cognitive Neurosci **3** pp. 71–86 (1991)

An approach for estimation of optimal energy flows in battery storage devices for electric vehicles in the smart grid

Gergana Vacheva[1,*], *Hristiyan* Kanchev[1], *Nikolay* Hinov[1] and *Rad* Stanev[2]

[1]Technical University of Sofia, Department of Power Electronic, Sofia, 1000, bul. Kl. Ohridsky 8, Bulgaria
[2] Technical University of Sofia, Electrical Power Engineering Department, Sofia, 1000, bul. Kl. Ohridsky 8, Bulgaria

Abstract. While the number of the vehicle actuated with liquid fuels are settled, the count of electric vehicles is increasing. For the present moment most of them are scheduled for daily urban usage. This paper presents an analytical approach for estimation of the impact of electrical vehicle (EV) battery charging on the distribution grid. Based on the EV charge profile, load curve and local distributed generation the grid nodes, the time variation of grid parameters is obtained. A set of typical load profiles of EV charging modes is studied and presented. A software implementation and a 24h case study of low voltage distribution network with EV charging devices is presented in order to illustrate the approach and the impacts of EV charging on the grid. In the current paper an approach using variable nonlinear algebraic equations for dynamic time domain analysis of the charge of the electric vehicles is presented. Based on the results, the challenges due to EV charging in distribution networks including renewable energy sources are discussed. This approach is widely applicable for various EV charging and distributed energy resources studies considering control algorithms, grid stability analysis, smart grid power management and other power system analysis problems.

1 Introduction

In order to preserve the environment through a reduction of harmful emissions, in our days the usage of the electric vehicles is growing. And thus it is established that their charge stations are a major challenge for low voltage distribution networks stability [1, 2]. The simultaneous operation of multiple EV charge stations represents a significant load for which most of the distribution grids are not designed for. For this reason, the influence of various EV charge profiles on microgrids is a topic of interest [3]. In the case of unidirectional charging devices (the ones that only consume power and do not provide grid support) the charging process can be represented as a distributed load to reduce grid congestion. The growing number of EV leads to a considerable increase of the load in distribution networks and difficulties in managing overloads and dispatching of the grid.

A novel approach for charging stations control in order to decrease peak loads and optimize energy flows in distribution networks is presented in this paper. Objective of the proposed solution is the implementation of a schedule which supports the grid at peak load periods using the energy storage elements of electric vehicles. This can be done by using bidirectional charging devices for EV – in this way they can consume energy in periods of excess production and supply it to the local grid afterwards. As a result, balancing of the daily energy flows can be achieved.

2 Description of the studied microgrid

Recently a variety of techniques and methodologies for power system analysis exist. Even in a system with multiple branches, the classical analysis of energy flows can provide a precise solution to the given problem, at the cost of increased computational time. Nevertheless limitations based on the availability of the electric vehicles are imposed – their usage is based on different repetitive patterns in weekdays and the weekend.

In the current paper an approach using variable nonlinear algebraic equations for dynamic time domain analysis of the charge of the electric vehicles is presented. On Fig.1 is shown the studied system: a three-phase 0,4 kV distribution network with 21 nodes located in a small village near the city of Sofia [4]. The grid is equally distributed, the loads are considered symmetrical in all phases and with power factor correction (predominantly active load) therefore the compensation of reactive power is not taken into consideration in this study. The minimal and the maximal load of the system without EV charging are respectively P_{min} = 33,2 kW and P_{max} = 110,8 kW.

* Corresponding author: gergana_vacheva@tu-sofia.bg

At node 10 and 18 of the grid are connected two photovoltaic (PV) arrays: one with a peak power $PG1$ = 30 kW connected at node 10 and the second is connected at node 18 and has a peak power $PG2$ = 50 kW.

2.1 Types of electric vehicles present in the system

For this study are considered four common models of electric vehicles: Mitsubishi i-MiEV family, Nissan Leaf, Tesla Model S and BMW i3. Those models were also chosen because of the fact that their characteristics and charging profiles (in normal charge and fast charge modes) are accessible from numerous sources including documentation provided by the producers. In future, the number EV in urban areas is expected to increase, each model having different charge profile, therefore the impact of an increased number of different models and charging profiles can be examined.

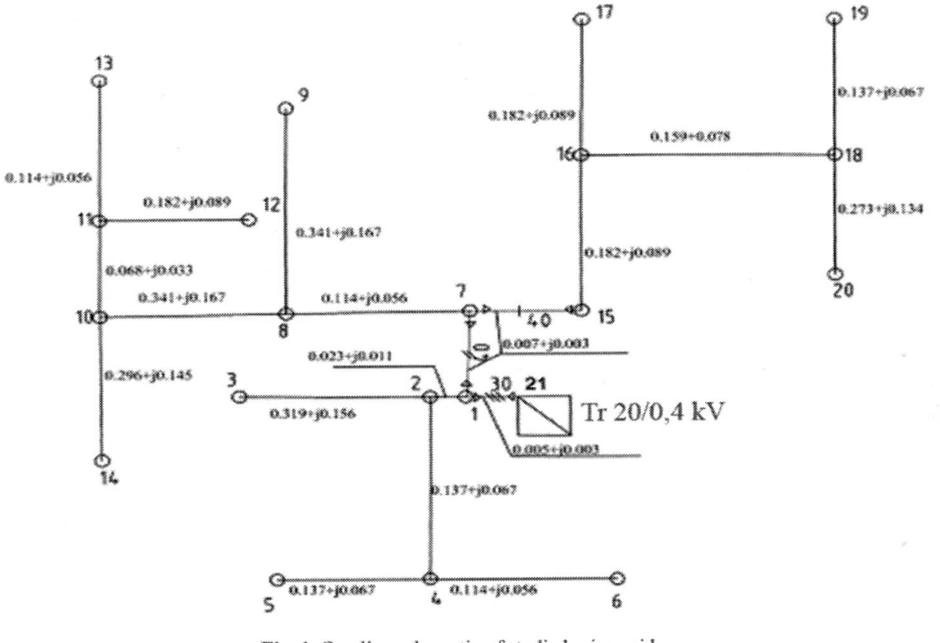

Fig. 1. One line schematic of studied microgrid

The values used for analysis of the electrical system are the magnitudes and phase angles of the voltages, the active and reactive powers. The following equations describe the state of each node in the studied microgrid [3].

$$P_k = \sum_{m \in k} V_k V_m (G_{km} \cos\theta_{km} + B_{km} \sin\theta_{km}) \qquad (1)$$

$$Q_k = \sum_{m \in k} V_k V_m (G_{km} \sin\theta_{km} - B_{km} \cos\theta_{km}) \qquad (2)$$

Where

- Pk is the active power in node k;
- Qk is the reactive power in node k;
- Vk is the magnitude of the voltage in node k;
- Vm is the magnitude of the voltage in node m;

$$\dot{Y}_{km} = G_{km} + jB_{km} \qquad (3)$$

is element k, m from the bus admittance matrix;

- θk voltage angle at node k;
- θm voltage angle at node m;

and $\theta_{km}=\theta_k - \theta_m$

2.2 Profiles of EV charging

At the following figures (fig. 2 to fig. 10) are presented the characteristic charging profiles of the considered vehicles in different charge modes and by different values of the initial State Of Charge (SoC) - the maximum charging power is given as a function of the batteries SoC. From those characteristics and the daily grid congestion and PV production profiles, the optimal time for full charge of the vehicles is determined.

The charging stations have a significant impact on the time and mode of charging the EV batteries. The charging devices should provide relatively high instantaneous power, low cost and high efficiency of the power conversion. A classification of charging devices storage station can be made by the following parameters:

- location of the storage devices: on-board and off-board charger;
- direction of the energy flows: unidirectional and bidirectional charging devices;

- mode of charge: normal and fast (high-power) charge.

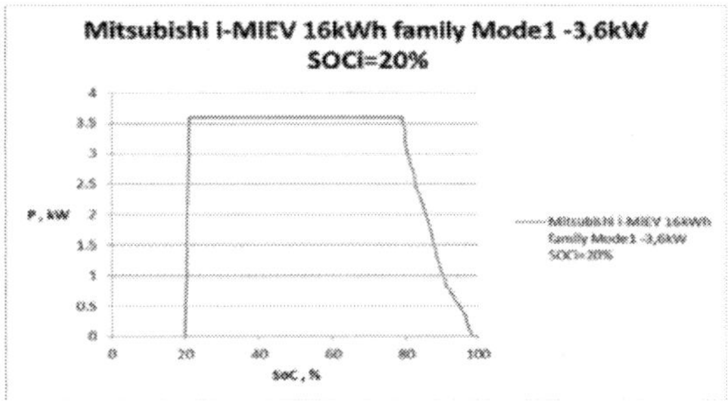

Fig. 2. State of charge profile of Mitsubishi i-Miev -3,6 kW

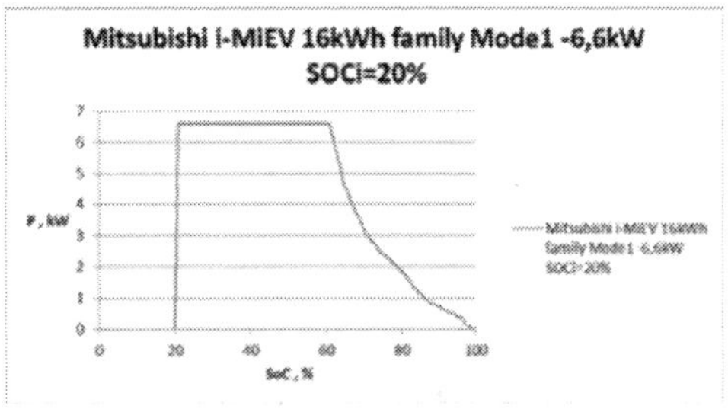

Fig. 3. State of charge profile of Mitsubishi i-Miev - 6,6 kW (fast charge)

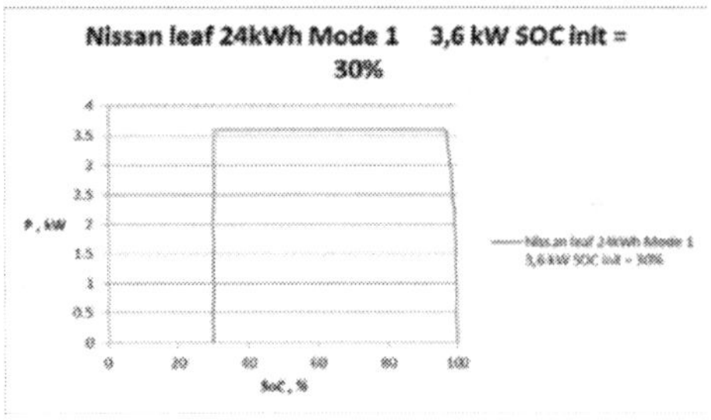

Fig. 4. State of charge of Nissan leaf - 3,6 kW

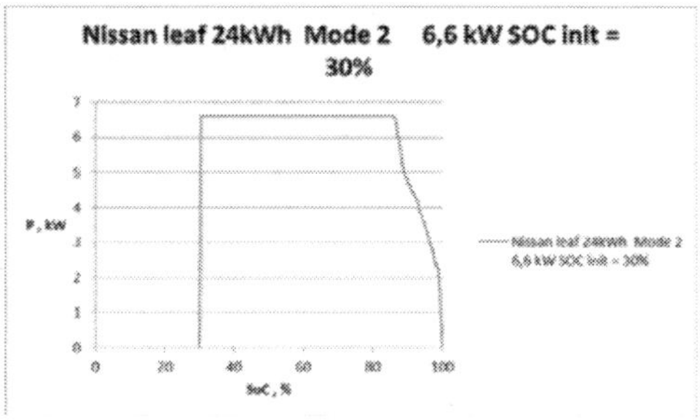

Fig. 5. State of charge of Nissan leaf - 6,6 kW (fast charge)

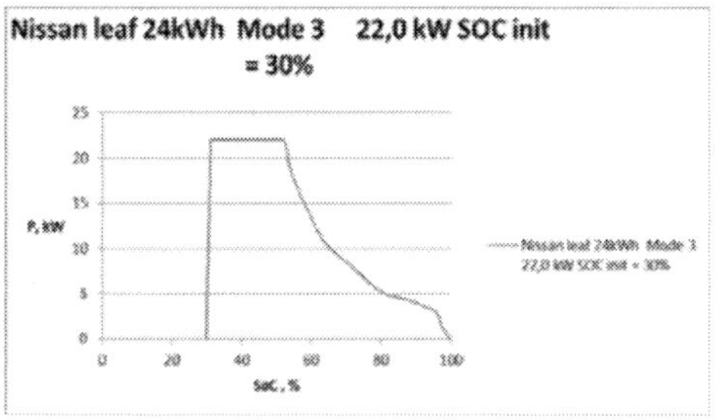

Fig. 6. State of charge of Nissan leaf - 22 kW (fast charge)

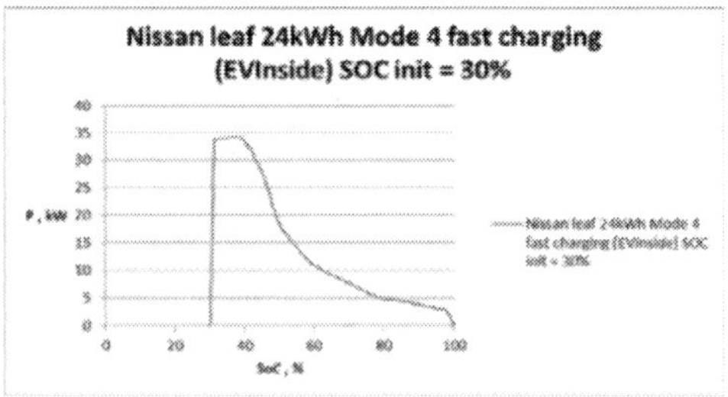

Fig. 7. State of charge of Nissan leaf - 24 kW (fast charge)

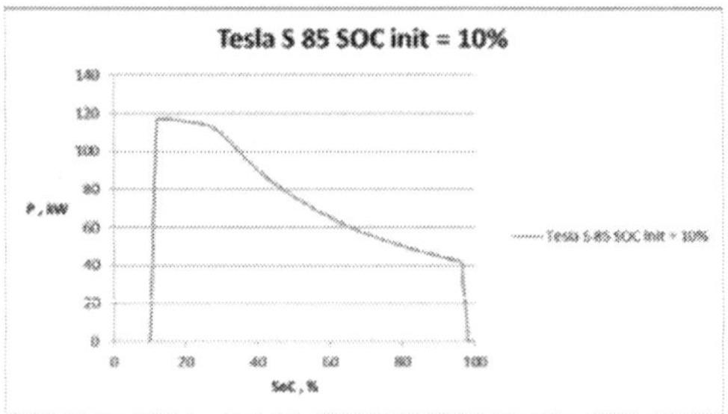

Fig. 8. State of charge of Tesla S 85

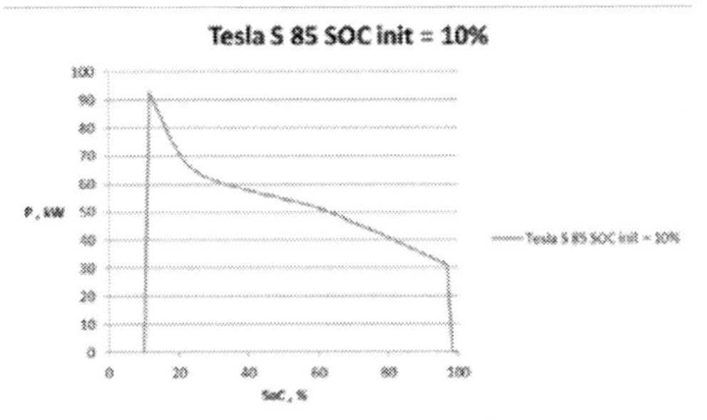

Fig. 9. State of charge of Tesla S 85.

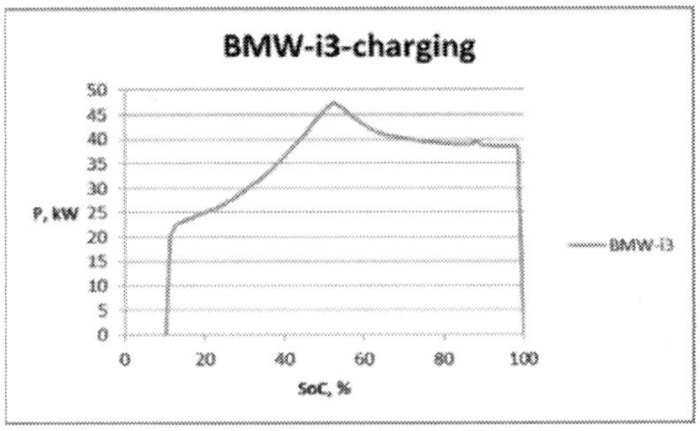

Fig. 10. State of charge of BMW i3 (fast charge)

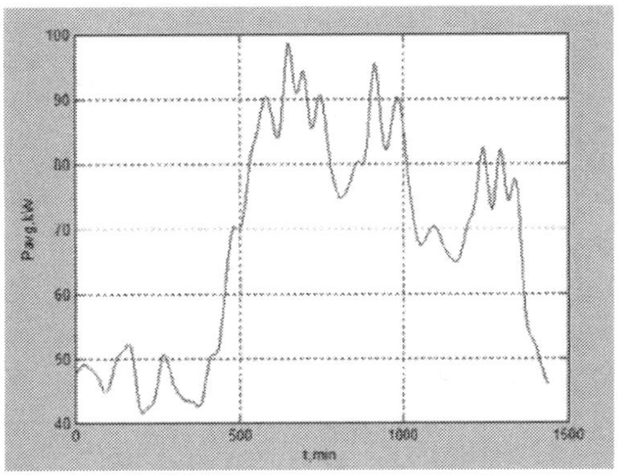

Fig. 11. Load profile forecast for a sample 24 hour period

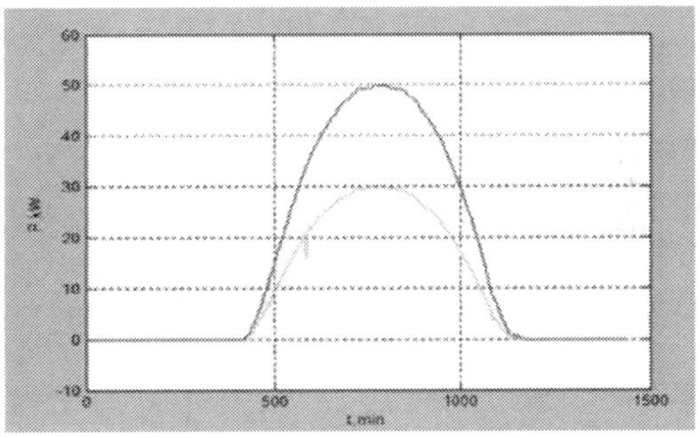

Fig. 12. PV production forecast for a sample 24 hour period

3 Load profile and PV generation profiles

At the figure 11 is presented the average predictive load schedule in the studied microgrid without presence of electric vehicles for a sample 24 hour period. The forecasted power generated by the PV arrays during a sample summer day is presented on fig. 12. The data from those figures is used for assessment of the grid stability without EVs and then the impacts of EV charging in the system is assessed.

4 Resulting load profile in the microgrid

A presence of 10 electrical vehicles totaling 7% of the vehicles in the village is assumed. The average daily run

Bus №	t_i, min	Charging device load pattern
12	187	Mitsubishi i-Mi, Mode1, SOCi=20% 3,6kW
14	300	Mitsubishi i-MiEV, Mode2, SOCi=20% 6,6kW
13	245	Mitsubishi i-Mi, Mode1, SOCi=20% 3,6kW
17	821	Mitsubishi i-Mi, Mode2, SOCi=20% 6,6kW
4	400	BMW i3, SOCi=10%, Mode fast charge
20	420	Nissan Leaf Mode2, SOCi=40%, 6,6 kW
18	130	Nissan Leaf Mode3, SOCi=40%, 22 kW
10	972	Nissan Leaf Mode4, SOCi=40%, fast charge
16	1115	Tesla S 60, SOCi=10%, Mode fast charge
8	800	Tesla S 85, SOCi=10%, Mode fast charge

per vehicle is 64 km. A distribution of the nodes of EV

charger placement, starting moment of the charging and the initial SOC are presented in table 1. It is supposed that the most of the EV users will start charging their vehicles after returning home which is considered to occur most probably at 18:30h. The resulting load profile of the grid (fig. 13) contains several peaks of the load due to EV charging, although the grid parameters remain in the operational limits, imposed by the operator.

Table 1. The scenario of the operation mode

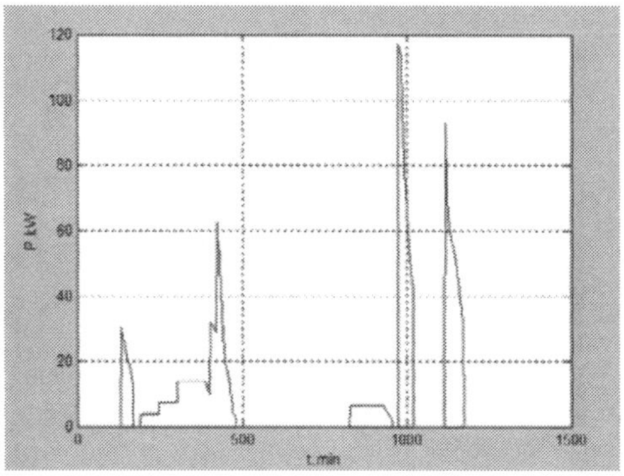

Fig. 13. Resulting load profile for the sample 24 hour period, including EV charging

5 Conclusion

An analytical approach for assessment of the impact of electrical vehicle battery charging on the distribution grid. Based on various EV charge profiles, a sample load curve and PV generators in various nodes of the grid, the time variation of grid parameters is obtained. A set of typical load profiles of EV charging modes is studied and presented. A software implementation and a 24h case study of low voltage distribution network with EV charging devices demonstrate the impacts of EV charging on the low-voltage grid. Based on these results, the interest for future researches on bidirectional EV charging stations providing grid support in the daily periods of peak consumption is proven.

This research is funded in the framework of project BG05M2OP001-2.009-0033 of the EU Structural Funds and „Gestion intelligente des flux énergétiques dans des micro- et nano-réseaux" funded by Agence Universitaire de la Francophonie and the Bulgarian National Fund for Scientific Research.

References

1. P. Papadopoulos, "Integration of electric vehicles intro distribution Networks," Ph.D. thesis, Cardiff University, 2012.
2. Yijia Cao, Shengwei Tang, Canbing Li, Peng Zhang, et al., "An optimized EV charging model considering TOU price and SOC curve", IEEE Transactions on smart grid, Vol. 3, NO. 1, p. 388-393, March 2012
3. R. Stanev, M. Georgiev, A. Krusteva, "An approach for estimation of the impact of electric vehicle charging devices on distribution networks", VI-th Scientific Conference „EF 2014", Sozopol, Bulgaria, pp. 251-260, 22 – 25 September, 2014
4. R. Stanev, "Voltage control strategies for distribution networks with distributed energy resources", Proceedings of the Technical University of Sofia, Vol. 63, Issue 6, pp. 263-271, 2013
5. A. G. Neagoe-Stefana, A. C. Neagoe, and Al. C. Mandis, "Impact of Charging Electric Vehicles in Residential Grid on the Power Losses and Voltage Plan", International Symposium on Fundamentals of Electrical Engineering, Polytechnical University of Bucharest, Romania, November 28-28, 2014
6. S. Schey, D. Scoffield, J. Smart, "A First Look at the Impact of Electric Vehicle Charging on the Electric Grid in The EV Project", EVS26 International Battery, Hybrid and Fuel Cell Electric Vehicle Symposium, Los Angeles, California, May 6–9, 2012
7. S. Habib, M. Kamran, U. Rashid, "Impact analysis of vehicle-to-grid technology and charging strategies of electric vehicles on distribution networks - A review", Journal of Power Sources, vol. 277 pp. 205-214, March 2015
8. J. Balcells, J. Garcia, "Impact of plug-in Electric Vehicles on the supply grid", IEEE Vehicle Power and Propulsion Conference (VPPC), Lille, France, 1-3 September, 2010

MATEC Web of Conferences **125**, 02069 (2017) DOI: 10.1051/matecconf/201712502069
CSCC 2017

Triangulation positioning system network

Marios Sfendourakis[1], *Rajagopal* Nilavalan[1], and *Emmanuel* Antonidakis[2]

[1] University of Brunel - Dept of Electronic and Computer Engineering ,UB8 3PX Kingston Lane, Uxbridge Middlesex United Kingdom

[2] Technological Educational Institute of Crete (TEI of Crete) - Dept of Electronic Engineering, Romanou 3 Chalepa Greece

Abstract—This paper presents ongoing work on localization and positioning through triangulation procedure for a Fixed Sensors Network - FSN.The FSN has to work as a system.As the triangulation problem becomes high complicated in a case with large numbers of sensors and transmitters, an adequate grid topology is needed in order to tackle the detection complexity.For that reason a Network grid topology is presented and areas that are problematic and need further analysis are analyzed.The Network System in order to deal with problems of saturation and False Triangulations - FTRNs will have to find adequate methods in every sub-area of the Area Of Interest - AOI.Also, concepts like Sensor blindness and overall Network blindness, are presented. All these concepts affect the Network detection rate and its performance and ought to be considered in a way that the network overall performance won't be degraded.Network performance should be monitored contentiously, with right algorithms and methods.It is also shown that as the number of TRNs and FTRNs is increased Detection Complexity - DC is increased.It is hoped that with further research all the characteristics of a triangulation system network for positioning will be gained and the system will be able to perform autonomously with a high detection rate.

Keywords— Fixed Stations Network, Triangulation, Localization, Network Blindness, Triangulation Area.

1. Introduction

The problem of localization is under research last years, whereas the applications of Sensors Networks are spread year by year in many fields, ways to find the position of a Sensor or a Transmitter with high accuracy are still tested and remain of high importance. One of the localization techniques is the process of Triangulation which was analyzed in [1]. It was also shown that in a large network with a great number of Sensors (SRs) there are cases of pseudo transmitters (PTRNs) which need to be examined on a case by case basis. The goal of this paper is to shed light on various issues that should be put into consideration when a Sensors Network (SN) has to work as an automated system. Various cases will be analyzed and it will be shown that for an automated network with many SRs and a great number of TRs that operate in an area of interest, there are attributes that need great attention and need to be examined and integrated in the system.A fixed stations network isn't able to move it's SRs but with logical programming it can analyze and combine the SRs data and provide valuable results. When results with high accuracy are collected the positions of new transmitters that entered the A OI will be acquired.So far,bearing only estimation is one of the fundamental and challenging problems in target tracking and Multisensor–multitarget bearing–only tracking is a challenging problem with many applications [5],[6],[7].

2. Contributions

Prior research has yielded mixed findings mainly related with SR to SR position in Wireless Sensor Networks - WSNs and WSNs with mobile SRs.The main problem of that research is not to find the SRs positions after their random deployment in an area.In our research we focus in finding new TRs positions who enter a Fixed Sensors Network - FSN area, with known positions of SRs, and with an initial state of TRs positions in that area. We show that a FSN, in order to localize TRs in an initial state and being able to tracking the new TRs in a new state the network should focus in processing of SR to SR data and each SR's state. Not only a SR might become blinded by degrading the detection performance in an area but also the overall state of the network might become blinded or saturated.It is also showed that the network ought to combine various ways in order to remain in a high detection performance.In addition, network detection rate and network detection performance are presented for this type of network and its function for transmitters - TRs detection.

DOI: 10.1051/matecconf/201712502069

3. Sensors Blindness

Every Sensor- SR in the network will collect some data of Bearings-BRNGs which are related with the Transmitters-TRs that will be detected in one area. Each SR has a circular region with radious r for detection. The problem is that as the number of existing TRs increase then the SRs become blind and many new TRs in it's area of responsibility might not be detected. As it is depicted in Fig.1 the SR1 and SR2 have a number of bearings which are black colored. The fact is that if a new TR enter a SR's radius, in a bearing similar with the previous, then it might only be detected by another SR. In Fig.2a SR1 and SR2 have certain sets of BRNGs. Then two new TRs appear in the area, TR3 and TR4 which are detected by SR2 Fig.2b.SR1 has already BRNGs at those radials.

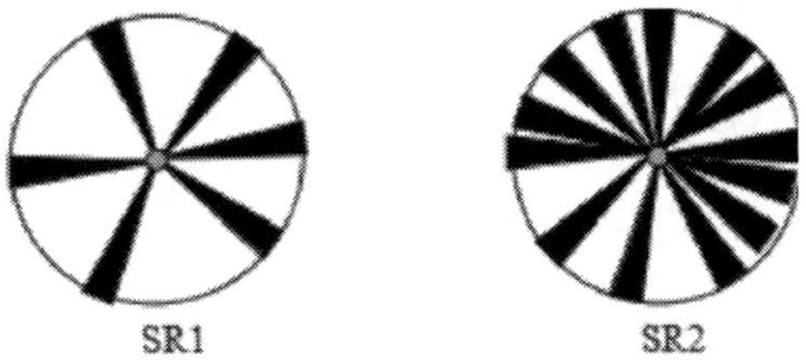

Figure 1

For that reason we have to define a SR parameter that affects the detection through TRN and which is the Sensor Blindness - SR_{BL} . SR_{BL} is related with the number of BRNGs already acquired and the SR detection accuracy error.We take for granted an average network error for detection for each SR ,S_{ER} which might be 2^0 to 5^0 degrees.

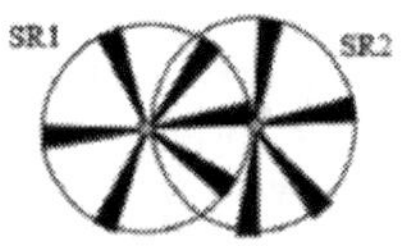

Figure 2a

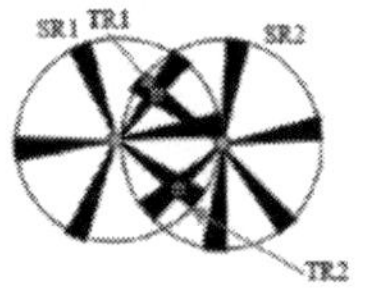

Figure 2b

So,Sensor Blindness SR_{BL} is defined as:

$$SR_{BL} = R_{SRs} \times 2S_{ER} /360 \quad * \quad 100\%$$

For example ,if a SR has 6 BRNGs (30,60,120,224,330,10) and the network has an average detection error for each SR, 4^0 then the SR blindness will be:

SR1 Blindness : 6 x (2x 4) / 360 * 100 = 13.33%

That means that at a percentage of 13.33% , SR1 will not detect a new TR but only another SR,within its region will find that new TR.In Fig.1, SR2 has a high level of blindness of 28.8%.

4. Network Parameters

An FSN in order to be operational a lot of parameters should be examined and checked not only before it's operation but also when it operates. SRs characteristics should be checked and also it's topology need to be carefully designed as problematic areas might degrade it's performance.Areas of TRN whilst will detect TRs ,synchronously will saturate it's state. For that reason parameters like Network Blindness, Network Saturation, Network Detection rate etc. should be approached.

4.1 Network Blindness

As it was previously mentioned, every SR of the network has a level of blindness. Summing the blindness of all the SRs then we have a picture of the network Blindness,which is a factor that characterizes the detection performance of the network.In Fig.3 we see a grid network with SRs that have a low level of blindness.We see that there exist enough free area for detection. Comparing Fig.3 with Fig.4 we see that in Fig.4 the free area for detection is far more less, and by that way the process of detection is more complicated.
Network Blindness Definition -N_{BL} where n is the number of SR_s

$$N_{BL} = B_1 + B_2 + \ldots + Bn/n$$

(Example 1 Sensor Network Blindness)

We have a Network of 4 SRs with various BRNGs,[SR1 4 (170,200,320,46),SR2 6(30,60,120,224,330,10),SR3 3 (210,
240,300), SR4 2(18,70). SRs Average Error =4.

The total of SRs BRNGs is:

BRNGs Total : 4 + 6 + 3 + 2 = 15 BRNGs

N_{BL} is the sum of all the SRs blindness of the network divided with the number of SRs-N_{SRs}.

$$N_{BL} = B_1 + B_2 + B_3 + B_4 / N_{SRs}$$

N_{BL} = 13,33 + 16,4 + 10 + 6 / 4 = 11,43

So,in this case the overall Network Blindness is:

N_{BL} = 11,43%

DOI: 10.1051/matecconf/201712502069

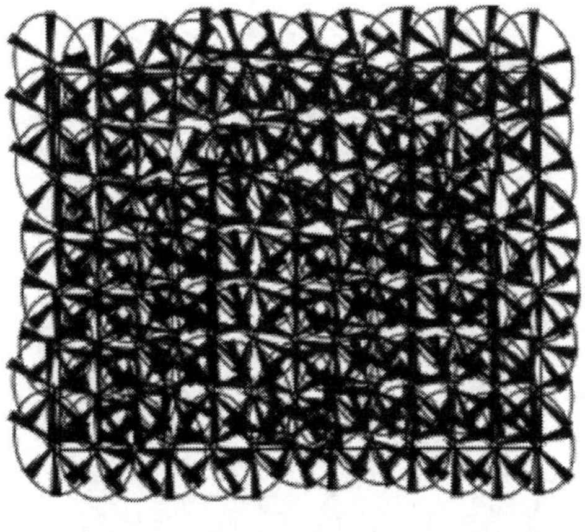

Figure 3

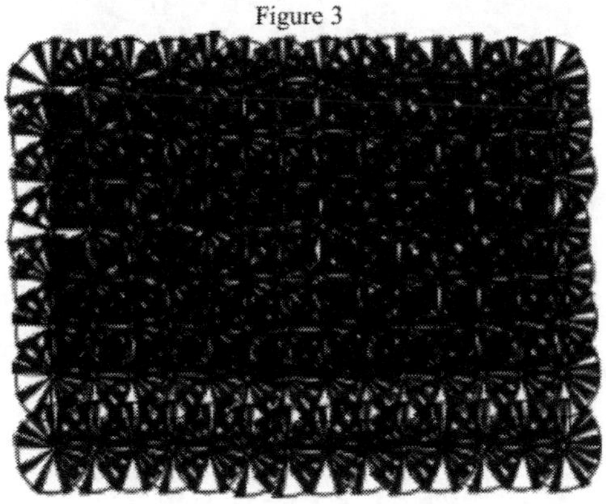

Figure 4

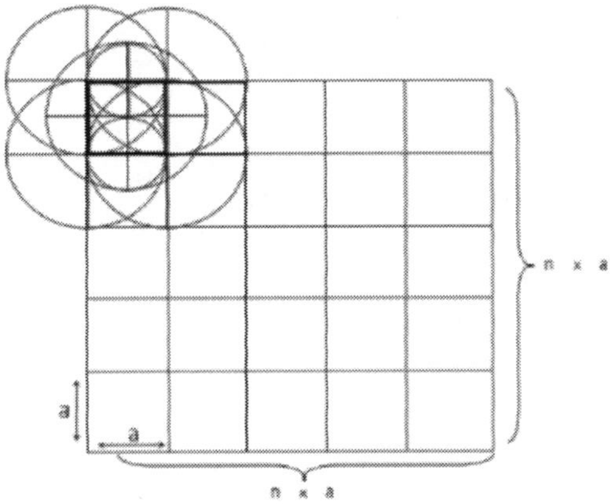

Figure 5

Although the distance between SR4 and TR1 is high, the TR1 is detected due to its high power. A TR which isn't detected due to its low power, will be detected by other SRs which are at close distance.

4.2 Network Saturation

Another attribute of the network which need further analysis is the number of TRN_s .As the number of TRNs in the network AOI increases, then the network approaches a saturation state that degrades it's performance.We define the network saturation state with the following parameters:

Network Area Saturation State: N_{AST}

Area Size:A_S

$$N_{AST} = \text{Total Area of TRNs} / \text{Area Size}$$

So, N_{TAST} is given by the equation (1),

$$N_{AST} = \sum_{i=1}^{n} TRNi / A_S \qquad (1)$$

Where n is the number of TRNs of the network in a current state.In order to deal with the various cases of TRNs the system has to find the number of TRNs in each sub-area in the grid and then process the Network Area Saturation State - N_{AST} ,for that sub-area. Assuming that an AOI of the Network has n sub-areas, then the Total Network Saturation State , N_{TAST} is given by the equation (2),

$$N_{TAST} = \sum_{i=1}^{n} N_{ASTi} / A_{TS} \qquad (2)$$

where A_{TS} is the total area size.

4.3 Network Detection rate

Another parameter that need to be defined for a FSN for localization via triangulation is the Network Detection Rate - ND_{rate} . We define ND_{rate} with the equation (3):

$$ND_{rate} = 100 - [(SRD_F + NB_{BL}(2-k)) + ETRN_s] / 3 \qquad (3)$$

where $ETRN_s$ is the number of Existing Triangulations.We define k as a quotient", $k = 1/ETRN_s$, where: $0 < k < 1$, assuming that as the number of $ETRN_s$ increase, then N_{BL} is affected. SRD_F is the Sensors Detection Failure and it is the number of SRs of the Network which will fail to detect TRs.

4.4 Network Grid topology

In Fig.5 ,it is depicted the Area of Interest - AOI for detection.In this area we see a grid perspective of squares where clusters of SRs cover the whole area and form regions of coverage .In each individual square there are seven circles which cover each sub-region, Fig.6.

DOI: 10.1051/matecconf/201712502069

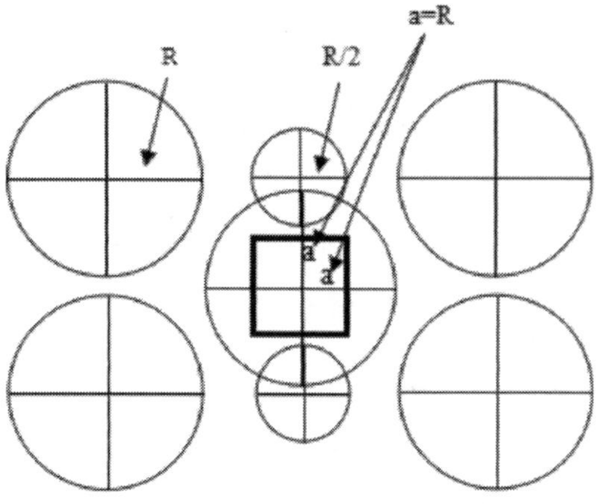

Figure 6

Their coverage intersect with each other and by that way the whole area is monitored, Fig.8.Each circle is the peripheral area of coverage of a SR. We have two types of SRs. One type that has a circular coverage of radius r, where r =a, and a second type with a circular coverage of radius r/2 = a/2. By that way, SRs with a small radius coverage are minimizing the area of TRN in each square. Additionally, SRs with radius coverage can monitor four square regions by each of their four quadrant, except circles that are located in the peripheral area of the grid which monitor two squares.Circles located at the AOI grid corners monitor only one quadrant.In the following Fig.7 we have a depiction of a Grid with twenty five sub-areas.

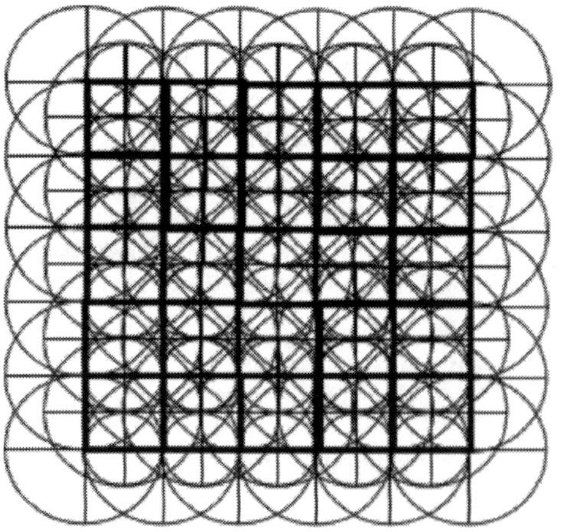

Figure 7

Each sub-area is monitored by the seven SRs and an additional SR that overlaps the area. A similar splitting procedure is applied in a GSM network, where an area is monitored by TRs that operate in hexagonal cells as it is depicted in Fig.9.The actual radio coverage of a cell is called footprint.The radio network operates in a bundle of frequencies, in this case (A,B,C,D,E,F,G) [2],[3],[4].

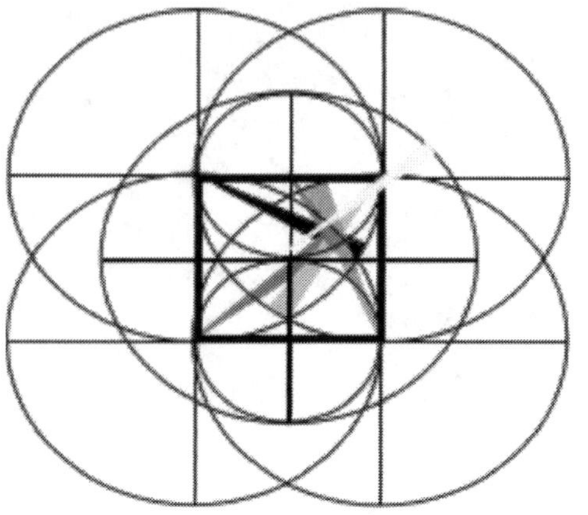

Figure 8

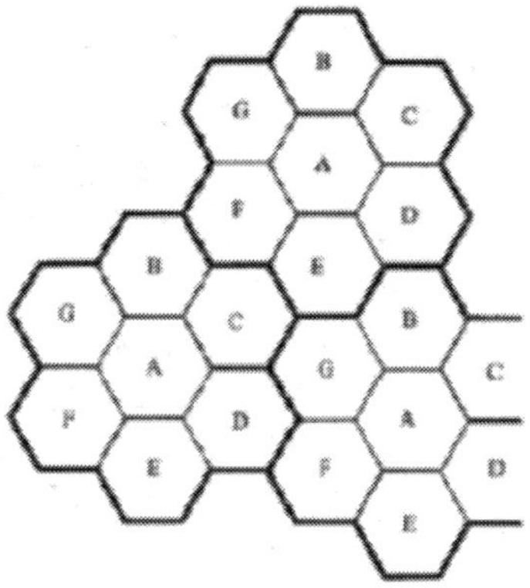

Figure 9

The size of cells might vary and often the size of cells might be splitted. By Cell splitting Fig.10, it is achieved capacity improvement by rescaling the system and the number of times that channels are reused is increased. Due to smaller cells, capacity increases and that is due to additional number of channels per unit area [3].

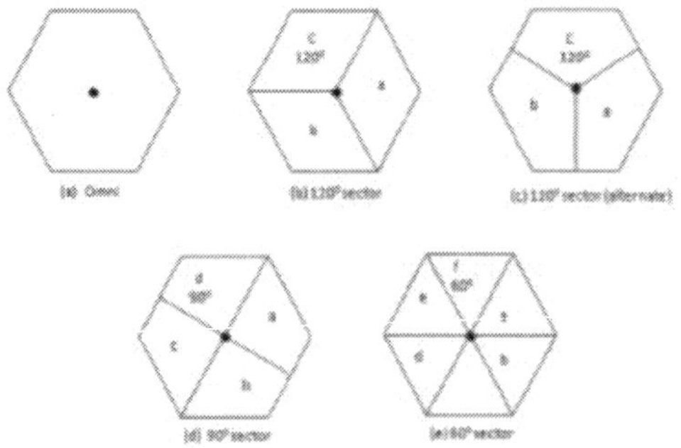

Figure 10

In the Fixed Station Network - FSN the area is monitored by SRs that operate in the same frequency whilst vary in sensitivity. During processing of data acquired, every area is processed independently from the other.All the parameters of the network are also acquired and at the same time the SRs parameters are checked. If inside an area a SR has problem of high blindness then its operation might be degraded. Thresholds of blindness have to be applied for each SR.

4.5 Network Detection Performance

In the following figures, Fig.11 initial State, and Fig.12, actual State 1,TRNs are depicted with red color FTRNs with black and new TRNs with green color.As the number of TRNs and FTRNs is increased Detection Complexity - DC is increased. We define DC as the level of easiness to detect a new TR in the area.The system has to deal with the detection of new TRs while the areas of TRNs and false TRNs that probably exist, have to be tackled on a case by case basis.There is a high probability that the number of TRNs and FTRNs will be increased, (in Fig.12 we see that TRNs and FTRNs are increased) and that presupposes that every area should be monitored by a minimum number of SRs. These SRs should be able to find a new TR and synchronously reject a FTRN.In Fig.12 it is depicted the actual state 1 which is a problematic area with FTRNs and new TRs that entered the area. The system will detect the new TRs with a detection algorithm which we name Sensors Cluster Detection - SCD. Its name implies that Clusters of SRs are working as groups to process one area and seek for new TRs.This algorithm will be presented and analyzed in a future paper.A problematic situation appears when SRs have a high rate of saturation which also means that the area is saturated. For these reasons, like in the case of Centralized Intrusion Detection Systems - CIDS where a centralized computer monitors all the activities in the network and detects intrusions by analyzing the monitored network activity data. [8] SRs Clusters should monitor each area and send their data to a central computer. Data fusion and adequate data analysis should provide results with high accuracy.The problem of target tracking with the process of triangulation deteriorates more in the case that exist many TRNs which block detection beyond the area of TRN.

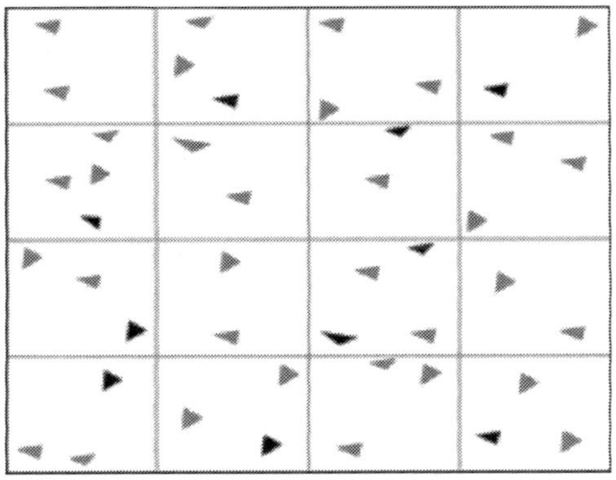

Figure 11

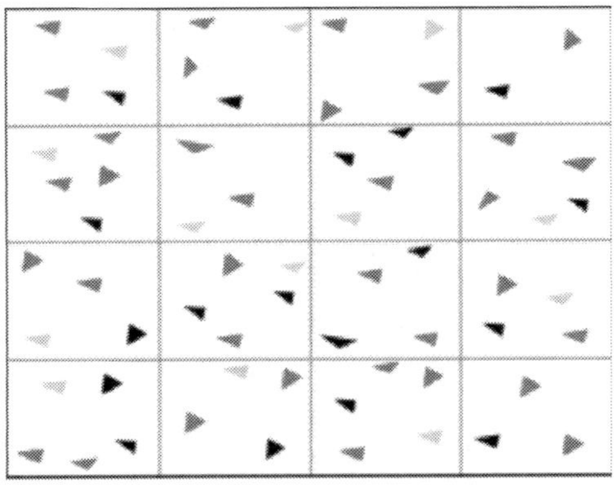

Figure 12

References

[1] M.Sfendourakis, N.Rajagopal, E.Antonidakis "Automatic Triangulation Positioning System for wide area coverage from a Network of Stations in Fixed Positions". *In Proceedings of the 19th International Conference on Systems (part of CSCC '15),* Recent advances in Systems (2015): (pp.650-660).

[2] R.P. Yadav et.al, 'Wireless Communication', 2008.

[3] Nura Muhammad Shehu 'Coverage and Capacity Improvement in GSM Network' [IJNREME -2015] 2, pp: (57-62).

[4] Patel, Sheshhan R., and A. K. Sisodia. "Techniques for Improving Channel Capacity of Downlink in GSM Systems." (2014).

[5] E. Taghavi, R. Tharmarasa, T. Kirubarajan, and M. McDonald. Multisensor multitarget bearing only sensor registration". *IEEE Transaction on Aerospace and Electronic Systems*, vol. 52, no. 4, August 2016.

[6] Y. Bar-Shalom, X. R. Li, and T. Kirubarajan, Estimation with Applications to Tracking and Navigation: Theory, Algorithms and Software, Wiley, NY,2001.

[7] Y. Bar-Shalom, P. K. Willett, and X. Tian, Tracking and Data Fusion: A Handbook of Algorithms, YBS Publishing, Storrs, CT, 2011.

[8] Butun, I., Morgera, S.D. and Sankar, R., 2014. A survey of intrusion detection systems in wireless sensor networks. *IEEE Communications Surveys & Tutorials, 16*(1), pp.266-282.

Self-propelled autonomous 2D parallel robots for sliding cupping-glass massage for back and chest

Sergey Sayapin[1,*], Elena Sayapina[2]

[1] Institute for Machine Science named after A.A. Blagonravov of the Russian Academy of Science, 101990 Moscow, Russia
[2] A. Tsyb Medical Radiological Research Centre, 249036, Obninsk, Russia

Abstract. There are numerous examples of effective using of sliding cupping-glass massage for disease prevention, treatment, rehabilitation, and removal of weariness. This is kind of massage including combination influences to patient's back and chest by cupping-glasses and massage. However, work of masseur is connected with a big physical stress. Moreover, masseur can make the massage only with one patient by two hands. As a result daily productivity of the masseur is limited. Therefore advanced intelligence carried massage robots are needed for sliding cupping-glass massage, being able to work autonomously without the presence of the masseur. In this paper, a novel approach to a creation of intelligence self-propelled autonomous portable massage robot based on original 2D parallel mechanism is presented. This robot based on triangular parallel structure with 3 d.o.f., called the Triangle, is designed for sliding cupping-glass massage for back and chest. Main massage manipulations of robot are presented along with a description of proposed locomotion algorithms. Locomotion and manipulation experiments are performed by pneumatic prototypes. We examine design principles of the Triangle as future intelligent base block for various rehabilitation and other robotic systems that can self-propelled and self-reconfigure.

1 Introduction

It is known that a massage is now considered one of the most effective non-drug methods of effective means of disease prevention, treatment, rehabilitation, removal of weariness. Therefore now massage is used in clinics, hospitals, and medical centers of many countries. All kinds of the massage are made by a masseur or a patient (self-massage) manually or by massage apparatuses [1]. In order to augment an effect of traditional manual techniques, the masseur may use other massage techniques, for example, such as a sliding cupping-glass massage (SCGM) for back and chest. However, usually SCGM is independent kind of manual massage including combination influences to patient's back and chest by the cupping-glasses and massage. There are numerous examples of effective using of SCGM in practice medicine [1]. In Fig. 1 (a) basic massage movements for SCGM by vacuum massage cupping glass (VMCG) are shown. These movements include following: I - straight, II - zigzag, III - spiral, and IV - figure-of-eight. The masseur makes the massage personally. Therefore the presence of the masseur is required, but he can make the massage only with one patient by two hands. As a result a daily productivity of the masseur is limited. Moreover, the masseur usually performs laborious and monotonous manipulations all day long that lead to his fatigue. A work of the masseur is connected with a big physical stress that can be cause of pathological changes in spine and lumbar one. The self-massage also demands from patient of the big physical stress that is inadmissible for separate categories of patients. Therefore labor-intensive procedures of the massage should be robotized.

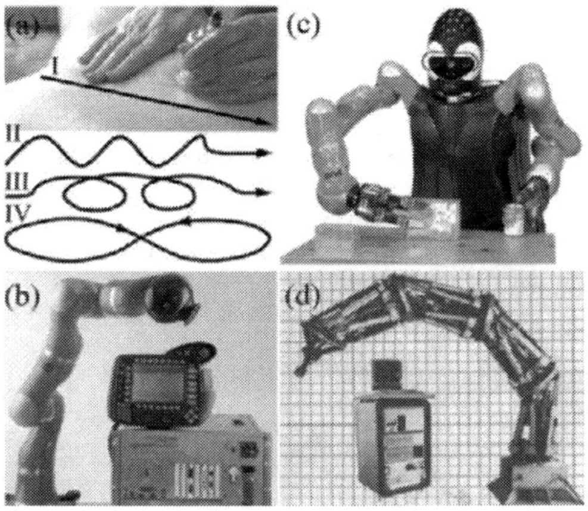

Fig. 1. Basic massage movements by VMCG (a); the KUKA lightweight robot with controller (b); mobile dual arm robot with 3-finger hands (c); the multi-module parallel robot Logabex LX4 (d).

Currently, there are variable robots, which can be used as base of half-autonomous or autonomous massage robots, for example, such as anthropomorphic one/two-armed robots (similar to the KUKA lightweight robot) [2] or multi-module parallel robots (similar to the

* Corresponding author: S.Sayapin@rambler.ru

Logabex robot LX4) [3], which are shown in Fig. 1 (b, c, and d). Unfortunately, now there are only few examples of practical use of anthropomorphic one-armed massage robots which was created similar to the industrial robots [4]-[6]. However, these one-armed robots have large sizes and weight, and therefore, they cannot be used in carried massage robotic systems. Furthermore, in case of the patient's body movements, the programmed motion of massage robot is not suitable. Thus, a creation of the carried massage robots for SCGM for back and chest being able to work autonomously without the presence of the masseur is an urgent task. Therefore modern rehabilitation medicine is needed of advanced intelligence carried massage robots, being able to work autonomously without the presence of the masseur. I propose new concept of a self-propelled multifunctional intelligence autonomous carried planar massage robot for SCGM for back and chest based on a triangular parallel structure with 3 d.o.f., called the Triangle [7]. The description of design principles of the Triangle as future intelligence base block for various rehabilitation and other robotic systems that can self-propelled and self-reconfigure is presented below.

2 Description of Triangle

The Triangle is based on the 2D triangular parallel mechanism and therefore it has higher a specific stiffness and a bearing capacity, and lower specific weight. In Fig. 2 a structural scheme of the Triangle is shown. The proposed concept will allow be robotize the process of SCGM. As a result there are the following advantages:

- The Triangle is able to organize autonomous conduction of SCGM to several patients simultaneously, and holding cupping massage by several vacuum massage cupping-glasses (VMCG) in the sitting or standing, for example by three VMCG on chest and three VMCG on back of patient at the same time and, as a result the daily productivity of the masseur increases.
- There is massage by sliding and stretching of muscle tissues at the same time the three VMCG that improves the performance of the process of massage.
- There is the autonomous SCGM to hard reached areas of the body such as back, and ensure the controlled movement of VMCG and VMCG bypass the moving parts of body that are not valid for massage effects, such as moles, sensitive and damaged skin, post-operative wounds, etc.
- The autonomous SCGM does not require special facilities and can be performed at the bedside and at the home.
- The Triangle released extra time, which can be used to conduct other types of massage and, as a consequence, there is a possibility of increasing the number of patients served per shift.
- There is the reduction of the physical fatigue of the masseur, thereby increasing his productivity and improving health at the end of the work shift.

The Triangle (Fig. 2) has a massage device based on the active triangular module ABC with the parallel structure. The sides AB, BC and CA are made in the form of similar rods. The ends of rods are pivotally connected at the vertices of the active triangular module ABC with the VMCG 1. Thus, each of the rods is provided a linear drive 2, a force sensor 3, a relative-displacement sensor 4, and a relative-velocity sensor 5. All vertices of triangle module ABC are executed with possibility of connection the like rods through them 2 for the formation of the additional active triangular parallel structures. Each of VMCG 1 is pivotally connected at the vertices of the active triangular module ABC and forms its device discrete fixation to the patient's body. In addition, each of the VMCG 1 is hermetically connected by a flexible hose 6 to a mated canal of an air distributor 7 of a degassing system provided with a pressure sensor 8, the air distributor 7 and a vacuum pump 9 electrically connected to a control system 10 in the form of a neural computer 11 with digital-to-analogue converters (DAC), and relevant software (the main advantages of neural computer are associated with massively parallel processing, and as the result is high speed, low requirements for stability and accuracy of the parameters of the elementary nodes, resistance to interference and destruction). The inputs of the control system 10 are connected through the data buses of analog–digital converters (ADC) to the outputs: of ADC 12, 13, 14 and 15 of the force sensors 3 for ADC 12; the relative-displacement sensors 4 for ADC 13; the relative-velocity sensors 5 for ADC 14; and the pressure sensors 8 for ADC 15. The outputs of the control system 10 are connected through the output data buses to the corresponding inputs of software and the following units, connected in series: DAC 16, power amplifiers 17, linear drives 2, air distributor 7, and vacuum pump 9. The control system 10 made with the possibility of operational control and management in real-time.

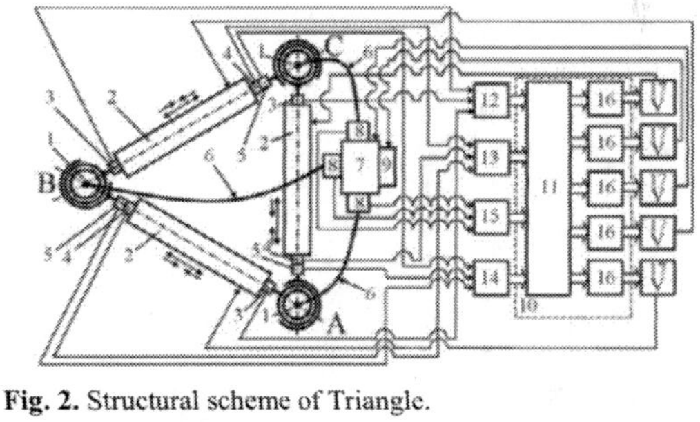

Fig. 2. Structural scheme of Triangle.

The Triangle works as follows. On surface of the patient's body [1] an active triangle module ABC applied with VMCG 1 in its vertices (Fig. 3, a, b). The initial position of the active triangle module ABC is mounted on the massaged area of the patient's body arbitrary. Then the VMCG 1 degas by the vacuum pump 9 (Fig. 2) and after their individual suction and retraction of the skin on the value for reliable fixation of VMCG 1 and excluding injury of the patient's skin, which is determined visually, close the corresponding valve (in the figures not shown) of the air distributor 7 and record the value of the minimum allowable pressure with pressure sensors 8. Then, using the appropriate valves (on the pictures conventionally are not shown) of the air distributor 7 is produced depressurization of VMCG 1 to the maximum pressure inside them, which ensures the possibility of their sliding mobility according to the patient's body without detachment from him. At this point, these valves of the air distributor 7 and with the help of pressure sensors 8 are fixed values, the maximum allowable pressures inside the VMCG 1. Further, control system 10 enters data, which include the contours of body areas massaged, associated with the base coordinate system and the coordinates of the areas of the body that are not valid for massage effects, such as moles, sensitive and damaged skin, surgical wound, etc. Then the control system 10 gives the command to the vacuum pump 9 and the air distributor 7 to degas through the flexible hoses 6 and the respective valves of the air distributor 7 two fixed VMCG 1 on surface of the patient's body and one sliding VMCG. After reaching in these fixed and sliding VMCG the minimum allowable and maximum allowable pressures from the respective pressure sensors 8 through the ADC 15 receives analog signals into the control system 10 in which the control commands are formed, which through the corresponding DAC 16 and power amplifier 17 are fed to the closure of the valves of the air distributor 7 and the shutdown of the vacuum pump 9. After that, relative to the base coordinate system entering coordinates of the centers of the two fixed VMCG and one sliding VMCG and the distance between them. Then, the masseur gives a command to perform the programmed massage movements for the sliding VMCG.

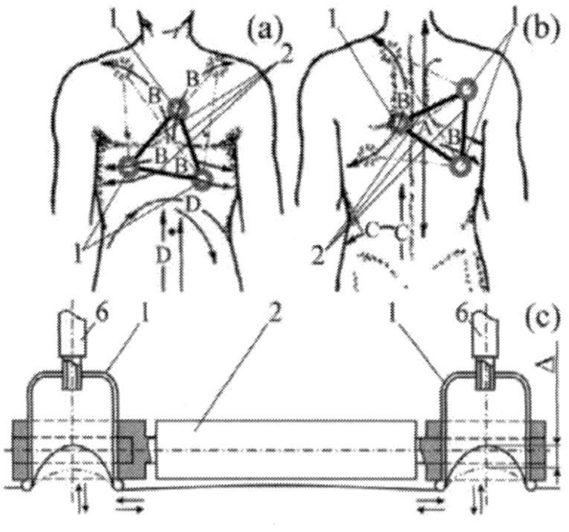

Fig. 3. Structural scheme of Triangle.

In Fig. 3 (a, b) schemes of the SCGM in various diseases are shown: spinal osteochondrosis and lumbago (A); pneumonia and bronchitis (B); myositis and sciatica (C); colitis and hypertension (D) [1]. As we can see in the above diseases impose the straight movements of the one sliding VMCG 1 and its movements along the circular arcs. After receipt of the command to the control system 10 in the computer 11 (taking into account the previously entered data) the initial coordinates of the VMCG 1 for carrying out massage movements of the VMCG 1 are calculating, for example arcuate movements (B) (Fig. 3, a, b), from the condition of ensuring a minimum number of VMCG rearrangements required to convert the selected path of movement, which depend on the maximum strokes of the linear drives 2. The active triangle module ABC can be installed in the initial position in such way that each of his VMCG 1 will be able to alternately perform the rolling massage movement on different trajectories of the movements of b without its permutations (Fig. 3, b). The movement of the VMCG 1 on the surface of the patient's body is carried out by appropriately changing the lengths of the linear drives 2, controlled relative-displacement sensor 4. Thus the required speed of the massage movements of the VMCG 1 on the patient's body is provided by the speed control of axial movements of the linear drives 2 according to signals from the respective relative-velocity sensors 5. The geometric resistance of the active triangular module ABC (Fig. 3) allows you to define the coordinates of its vertices A, B and C by measuring by the relative-displacement sensor 4 of the lengths of all rods and control their movements similarly to the organization of spatial movements of the *I*-coordinate manipulator [8]. The relative-velocity sensor 5 allow to control the speed of movement of the sliding VMCG 1 at this stage of massage in accordance with the valid values, defined for this type of massage movements and introduced to the control system 10. It should be noted that all of the VMCG 1 in the course of their rearrangements through sliding motions on the massaged surface of the patient body, alternately become floating and unmoveable. Here in, the process of their permutation. In the active triangular module ABC one of the VMCG 1 closest to his move) and the other two are roaming and unmoveable, respectively. While the maximum allowable air pressure sets in one roaming sliding VMCG, and in two fixed VMCG – minimum allowable air pressure. After that, the control system is commanded to switch on the linear drives 2, is connected to the sliding VMCG 1 and produced a consistent change in their lengths at a given speed controlled by the relative-speed sensor 5. After moving the sliding VMCG 1 to a specified destination (or intermediate) point, determined by the relative-displacement sensor 4 associated with linear drive 2, the command is made to switch them off. Then displacement of the sliding VMCG becoming the fixed VMCG, and one of the two fixed VMCG is becoming roaming. The pressure in the displaced VMCG is the minimum, and another is allowable maximum. Further, similar to the previous cycle from the control system is commanded to switch on the linear drive 2, is connected to the moving VMCG and produced a consistent change in their lengths at a given speed controlled by the relative-speed sensor 5. Then similarly do the movement of third VMCG in final or intermediate point. After displacement of all VMCG in the calculation the initial coordinates two of the VMCG are made unmoveable, and the third lying on the trajectory massage movements, for example the arc B (Fig. 2, b), make sliding cupping-glass and make her massage movements. Thus, depending on the desired massage

DOI: 10.1051/matecconf/201712502070

motions, the estimated initial coordinates of VMCG can be computed in such way that all VMCG will be on the trajectories required of massage movements, for example on the arcs **B** (Fig. 3, b). In this case, the massage can be performed sequentially and alternately. Permutations of triangular ABC module can be arranged in such way that the trajectory of all movements VMCG will coincide with the specified trajectory of massage movements in the process of permutations, i.e. there will not be "spurious" passages of VMCG.

Using the Triangle it's also able to produce a local vacuum massage and the massage by sliding and stretching of the muscle tissue [1]. In Fig. 3 (c) the scheme of their conduct is shown. Local vacuum massage is performed at a fixed on the patient's body VMCG 1 by the vacuum in the air up to a pressure whose value is in the range from the maximum pressure to the minimum pressure. For its implementation by commands from the control system in the VMCG with established frequency and amplitude of the pressure change from the minimum permissible to the maximum and Vice versa. Management of alternate higher and lower pressure is carried out using the diffuser 7 and vacuum pump 9 according to the commands from the control system 10, formed as a result of processing the signals from the pressure sensors 8. The distance between the involved skin surface at the maximum pressure inside the jar and the involved skin surface with minimal pressure is Δ (Fig. 3). The distance Δ corresponds to the maximum value of the amplitude in the conduct to local vibration by varying the pressure in the VMCG.

Massage by sliding and stretching the muscle tissues is produced, while still fixed on the patient's body VMCG 1 by discharging air to the minimum allowable pressure. It is possible to carry out this type of massage as alternate movement of the linear actuators, as the simultaneous movement of two or more linear actuators. After fixing the VMCG 1 on the massaged area of the body of the patient (Fig. 3) at the position at which the length of the linear actuator 2 correspond to their average values, the control system 10 is commanded to the linear drive 2 on decrease (increase) its length at a predetermined value, after reaching which the linear actuator 2 is stopped and is switched on for reverse, increasing (decreasing) its length to a set value. The process is repeated at a given rate, the required number of cycles. The maximum change in length of the linear actuator 2 corresponds to a given vibration amplitude of the massage movements of compression-tension. Changing the length of the linear actuator 2 and the amplitude are controlled by the relative movement of the sensor 4 and the speed – with the help of relative velocity sensor 5. The efforts of the mechanical effects of VMCG 1 on the muscle tissue of the patient performing all types of massage are controlled by the force sensor 3. In case of exceeding the set value of the effort in conducting a moving cupping massage, on command from the control system 10 produces an increase in pressure in the VMCG 1 by the amount of the established step and take him for the maximum allowed pressure value and continue massage. In case of exceeding a predetermined force value during the massage by sliding and stretching of muscle tissue, control system 10 reduces the magnitude of the amplitude which is set by the permissible forces in the extreme positions of the linear actuator 2 and continue the massage.

In case of spontaneous detachment of one of vacuum massage cupping-glasses from the patient's body during the massage unplanned increase in her pressure happens, as in the control system 10 receives the corresponding signal from the pressure sensor 8. In response to the situation the control system 10 will give the appropriate command to the distributor valve 7 and vacuum pump 9. It should be noted that the active triangular bearing module ABC on the massaged area of the body of the patient occurs at three points in the form of VMCG 1. Therefore, in the case of the horizontal position of the patient gravity from 1/3 the weight of the active triangle module ABC will be enough for a snug fit to the surface of the seal body VMCG 1 and subsequent suction to the body after lowering the pressure to the minimum allowable value. This will mean that the VMCG 1 is recorded on the patient's body and the massage will continue in accordance with the established program. In case of the pressure decrease in the cupping-glass is not going to happen, from the control system 10 will receive the signal about the movement of the VMCG to a new location and repeat the procedure vacuum. And, in case of repeated unsuccessful attempts, from the control system 10 the massage therapist will receive the signal about emergency situation, for correction of which requires his involvement. After the liquidation of the emergency situation massage therapist, the massage procedure will be continued offline.

We implemented the Triangle concept with a real pneumatic prototype that uses nine syringes (60.0 ml) and three barrels (60.0 ml) as three linear pneumatic actuators with three pneumatic pumps and as three VMCG with three vacuum pumps (Fig. 4, a). The pneumatic prototype is operated manually.

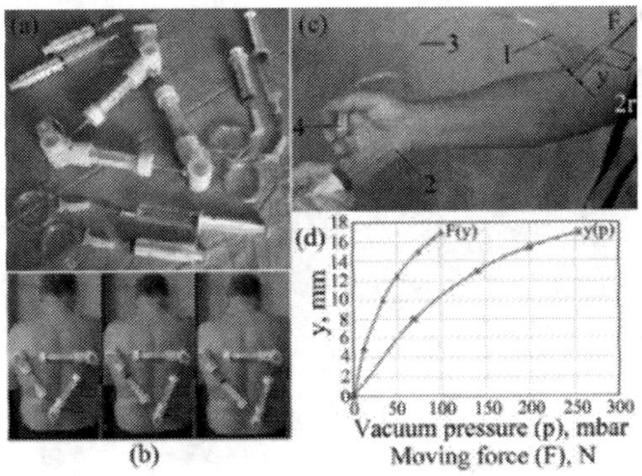

Fig. 4. The pneumatic prototype of Triangle (a); SCGM of the back by the pneumatic prototype of Triangle (b); the prototype of VMCG (c); the experimental relationships between (y) and (p), and (F) and (y) for the prototype of VMCG (d).

We also performed locomotion experiments and SCGM of the patient's back by the pneumatic prototype

DOI: 10.1051/matecconf/201712502070

(Fig. 4, b). In Fig. 4 (c) a prototype of VMCG is shown, which consists of one barrel 1, one syringe 2, and tubing 3 with a roller clamp 4 of an infusion system. This prototype is the same as VMCG with vacuum pump of the real pneumatic prototype (Fig. 4, a, b). Fig. 4 (d) illustrates the experimental relationships between skin uplift (y) and a vacuum pressure (p), and also between skin uplift (y) and moving force (F). Fig. 4 (d) also illustrates the relationship between moving force (F) and vacuum pressure (p). In the experiments, vacuum pressure loadings applied using the prototype of VMCG was subjected to the male's shoulder skin in the 60 year age range. The experiments were conducted by gently pressing barrel 1 of diameter 29.0 mm against the skin to ensure a good initial contact and then activating syringe 2 (vacuum pump) to create the vacuum inside the barrel of syringe 2 so that the skin is drawn into the barrel 1 (Fig. 4, c). The bulging of the skin as a result of cupping is shown in Fig. 4; all images were captured using a Canon digital camera IXUS 990 15. Moving forces (F) were measured using the Dynamometer 5029 DPU-0.1-2 (GOST 13837-79). The vacuum pressures (p) developed inside the prototype of VMCG were calculated using Boyle's Law:

$$p_iV_i=p_fV_f,$$

where the subscripts i and f refer to initial (before pumping, p_i=1000 mbar) and final (after pumping) states and measured volumes of barrel 1 (prototype of VMCG, 60.0 ml) with tubing 3 (3.18 ml) and barrel (60.0 ml) of syringe 2 (vacuum pumping chamber) which is decreased by volume of skin uplift (V_{su}). The volumes of skin uplift (Fig. 4, c) were calculated as volumes of ball segment ($V_{su}=\pi y^2(3r\text{-}y)/3$).

3 Other kinds of locomotion of Triangle

The Triangle can locomote also without vacuum pressure using other types of locomotion, for example, such as a leopard crawl (Fig. 5, a), a vertical rolling (similar to the tetrahedral walker movement) [9], and a shuffle (Fig. 6). The leopard crawl (Fig. 5, a) can be used when locomotion of the Triangle on a horizontal or inclined surface.

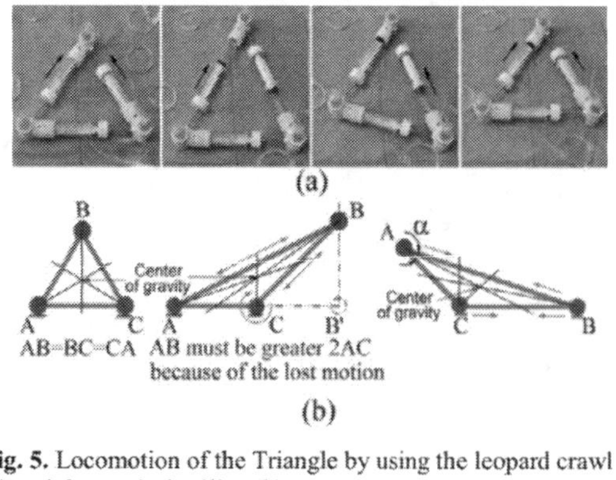

Fig. 5. Locomotion of the Triangle by using the leopard crawl (a) and the vertical rolling (b).

The Triangle can shuffle one's feet when moving in a vertical plane as shown in Fig. 6. The movement cycle of the Triangle includes following stages: initial position (a), a displacement of the center of gravity left (b), forward translation of right joint by using the shuffle (c), the displacement of the center of gravity right (d), forward translation of left joint by using the shuffle (e), final/initial position (a). Also the pneumatic prototype of the Triangle can be rotated by the plunger installed in right or left prototype of the VMCG (f).

Fig. 6. The movement cycle of the Triangle by using the shuffle (a-e) and the ability of rotation (f).

The locomotion of the Triangle in the vertical plane (Fig. 5, b and Fig. 6) can be used when movement in narrow aisles, for example between the walls. The angle α is chosen based on design parameters of the Triangle.

4 Conclusions

Any suitable robots for autonomous SCGM haven't found.

We presented the novel approach to a creation of intelligence self-propelled autonomous portable massage robot for SCGM for back and chest based on original planar parallel mechanism. The proposed novel concept of SCGM robot, called the Triangle, can be used in physiotherapy offices, hospitals, rehabilitation, sports and Wellness centers, as well as at home to conduct autonomous self-massage hard to reach areas of the body.

The use of the Triangle will allow you to automate the process of SCGM and to improve its efficiency by increasing the number of simultaneously roaming the VMCG up to three more (with the capacity of moving massager additional linear actuators and the VMCG), as well as significantly increase the number of concurrent patients with a single therapist and reduce his physical weariness and fatigue. Thus it's possible additional installation of sensors at the vertices of a triangular active module ABC, e.g. ultrasound, which will allow you to extend the functionality of the massager moving.

The Triangles could be used as future intelligent base block for various rehabilitation and other robotic systems that can self-propelled and self-reconfigure.

Current objective is to design software and equip the Triangle with reliable and miniature electronics, linear drives and communication hardware.

Another future task is in applying of the Triangle

towards on-line diagnostics of patient's health during the rehabilitation procedure.

References

1. V.I. Dubrovsky, A.V. Dubrovskaya, *Therapeutic massage*. GEOTAR-Media, Moscow (2004)
2. R. Bischoff, J. Kurth, G. Schreiber, R. Koeppe, A. Albu-Schäffer, A. Beyer, O. Eiberger, S. Haddadin, A. Stemmer, G. Grunwald, and G. Hirzinger, The KUKA-DLR Lightweight Robot arm-a new reference platform for robotics research and manufacturing, in: *Proceedings of the Robotics (ISR), 2010 41st international symposium on and 2010 6th German conference on robotics (ROBOTIK)*, pp. 741-748. VDE Verlag GmbH, Berlin (2011)
3. J.-P. Merlet, *Parallel Robots. 2nd ed.* Springer, Dordrecht (2006)
4. V. Golovin, M. Arkhipov, V. Zhuravlev, Force training for position/force control of massage robots. *In: New Trends in Medical and Service Robots*, pp. 95-107. Springer Int. Publ., Switzerland (2014)
5. Y. Huang, J. Li, Q. Huang, and C. Liu, Design and control of anthropomorphic BIT soft arms for TCM remedial massage, in: *Proceedings of the 2013 IEEE/RSJ International Conference on Intelligent Robots and Systems, Tokyo, Japan, November 3-7, 2013*, pp. 1960-1965. IEEE (2013)
6. EMMA, The Robot Therapist. *Innovation - The Singapore Magazine of Research and Technology and Education*, **15**, 1 (2016)
7. S.N. Sajapin, M.S. Sajapina, Russian Patent 2551939, *Byull. Izobret.*, **16** (2015)
8. A.Sh. Koliskor, *Stanki i Instrument*, **12** (1982)
9. R. Belisle, C.H. Yu, R. Nagpal, Mechanical Design and Locomotion of Modular-Expanding Robots, in: *Proceedings of the 2010 IEEE International Conference on Robotics and Automation,Anchorage, USA, May 3-8, 2010*, pp. 17-23. IEEE (2010)

Online Adaptive Coronary Heart Disease Risk Prediction Model

Jostinah Lam[1], *Eko* Supriyanto[1,*], *Faris* Yahya[1], *Muhammad Haikal* Satria[1], *Suhaini* Kadiman[2], *Aizai* Azan[2], and *Amiliana* Soesanto[3]

[1] Advanced Diagnostics and Progressive Human Care Research Group, IJN-UTM Cardiovascular Engineering Centre, Faculty of Biosciences and Medical Engineering, Universiti Teknologi Malaysia, 81310 Skudai, Malaysia.
[2] National Heart Institute, Kuala Lumpur, Malaysia
[3] National Cardiovascular Centre, Jakarta, Indonesia

Abstract. Coronary Heart Disease (CHD) is the leading causes of death worldwide. Life style changing is one of the important methods to delay the incidence of CHD. The awareness of life style changing is however still low. In order to improve awareness of life style changing, some CHD risk prediction models have been introduced. The existing models however either not well structured, not completed, static or offline. This paper introduces a new online CHD risk prediction model. The model is structured according to three risk factor groups including molecular structure, body system vital sign and bioenergy symphony. The model had also been compared with 5 existing models. Comparison results show that the model has better structure, adaptability and accessibility. Validation test using 120 subjects shows that the model prediction accuracy is 96.2%. This shows that the model is suitable to be used widely for CHD risk prediction both healthy and risk subjects as a preventive method in getting CHD in the earlier age.

1 Introduction

Coronary heart disease according to WHO are diseases that related to blood vessels supplying the heart muscle [1]. Coronary heart disease (CHD) is usually caused by blockage that stops the process of supplying blood to the heart. The main reason for the blockage formation is due to the buildup of plague in the walls of coronary arteries over the years. CHD events can be specified including stable and unstable angina, acute myocardial infarction and coronary death [2].

In 2012, out of the 17.5 million (31% of all global deaths) cardiovascular deaths, 7.4 million people died from CHD [1]. In Malaysia, CHD is the leading cause of death where it contributes 23.10% of total deaths [3]. The high percentage has put Malaysia in the 33 rank in the world [3]. The worrying numbers of deaths from CHD in Malaysia has alarmed the country to put more efforts on the preventive measures. A number of preventive measures had been carried out through modifiable risk factors such as smoking, hypertension, cholesterol level, diabetes, obesity, diet and physical activity [4]. One of the preventive measures taken is to predict the chances of an individual of getting CHD with the help of risk predictor. By knowing the probability of one having CHD, further actions can be carried out to prevent the occurrence of the disease. Hence, early detection and prevention of CHD is vital in reducing the number of CHD deaths.

There are a variety of risk prediction models throughout the advancement of cardiovascular risk assessment research. One of the most well-known and long-standing risk prediction models would be the Framingham risk score [5]. Nearly all of the risk prediction models were developed based on multiple variables since the happening of CHD event does not depend on solely one but many risk factors. The prediction variables used in the original Framingham CHD risk score include age, gender, total cholesterol, HDL cholesterol, blood pressure, smoking status and diabetes mellitus. The other risk prediction models like SCORE [6], QRISK [7], Reynolds [8], ACC/AHA risk calculator [9] have more or less similar prediction variables with each other [10]. Nevertheless, the existing risk predictors are not well-structured. All of the risk factors are not properly classified into specific category which makes it difficult to track and understand the root of the CHD event. Without a thorough understanding of CHD event and systematic approach to educate public about CHD event, it is challenging to increase public's awareness and hence the difficulty to reduce CHD mortality rate.

Another weakness found in the existing risk prediction model is the elasticity of the model. Most of the risk prediction models use data collected in the past which can be as short as 1 to 3 years ago or as long as 10 to 20 years ago. By the time the prediction model is ready to use, the predicted risk may not be suitable for individuals at that time anymore since the weight of risk

* Corresponding author: eko@utm.my

factor changes over time. Consequently, there is a need to develop a more dynamic risk prediction model to ensure the flexibility and adaptive of the model in future. Therefore, this study takes the initiative to develop a novel online adaptive CHD risk prediction model. In order to improve trust and increase awareness of people to live on healthier lifestyle, a new risk factor structure based on energy level classification was incorporated in this prediction model. The prediction model was also constructed based on the concept of being adaptive. This adaptive prediction model includes dynamic database, adaptive weighted risk factor and dynamic interpolation.

2 CHD risk factor

2.1. Physiology of CHD

There are many factors that influence the occurrence of CHD event. All of the risk factors are interrelated with each other and cannot be ruled out. A physiological diagram of CHD was illustrated in Fig. 1. The fundamental of CHD event is that coronary arteries was blocked by plague buildup for years and disable the oxygen supply process to the heart muscle. Therefore, the diagram starts with cardiovascular system in the middle and DNA cell in the centre symbolizes the molecule structure that forms the blood, vessel and heart. The molecular structure carries the DNA of an individual and it is not able to be changed for the whole life. Age, gender and genetic are risk factors that are non-modifiable.

The primary component that causes the buildup plague is cholesterol; hence measurement of total cholesterol, HDL and LDL is very important in determining CHD risk. Other cardiovascular related risk factors like blood pressure, heart rate, and blood sugar is definitely significant in predicting CHD incidence. Besides cardiovascular system, the whole body system is actually involving in the CHD events indirectly. It is the bioenergy symphony that manipulates the operation of body system. As we can see from Fig. 1, food, fluid, air, mental activity, environment and physical activity influence the operation of specific body system. These bioenergy symphonies can influence the body system either positively or negatively. Therefore, people can gain benefits from knowing the physiological of CHD incidence and make a change towards healthy lifestyle.

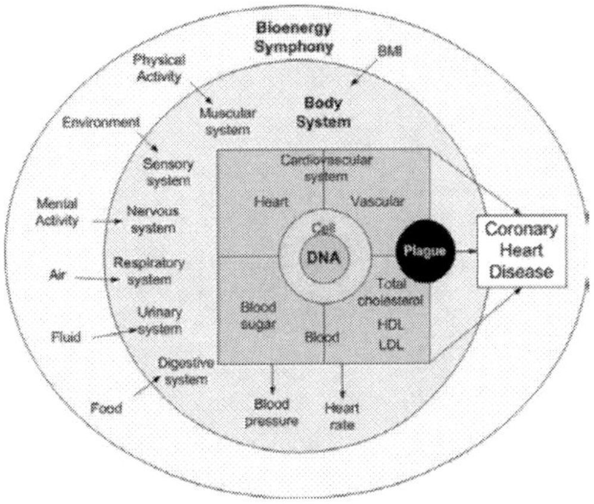

Fig. 1. Physiological diagram of CHD.

2.2 Energy Level Classification of Risk Factor

Based on the physiology of CHD event, the risk factors involved can be classified into 3 categories which are molecular structure, body system, and bioenergy symphony. These 3 classes can also be sorted out according to their energy level: low, middle, and high energy level. The energy level indicates the amount of energy required to function in the universe.

The first class of risk factors is molecular structure class which consists of non-modifiable risk factors like age, gender, and heredity. Non-modifiable risk factors can be linked directly to DNA and genetic of an individual where the risk factors in this category cannot be altered anymore. This fundamental molecular structure uses very low energy level to operate.

Next, the second class of risk factor would be body system class where it consists of every related body systems like cardiovascular system, respiratory system, digestive system to CHD. The risk factors in this category indirectly associated to the body system of an individual.

The third class is the high energy level category: bioenergy symphony. Bioenergy symphony class associate with the entire universe. Risk factors that fall on this category are food, fluid, air, environment, physical activity, and mental activity. This category is a significant class in determining the risk factor as all of these risk factors can either increase or decrease the possibility of one in getting CHD depending on their lifestyles. Table 1 shows classification of CHD risk factors.

Table 1. Classification of Risk Factor.

Risk Factors		
Low Energy Level (LEL): ***Molecular Structure***	*Middle Energy Level (MEL):* ***Body System***	*High Energy Level (HEL):* ***Bioenergy Symphony***
• DNA Telomere (Age/A) • Chromosome (Gender/G) • Genetic (N) (Abnormalities, Race, Parent history)	• Cardiovascular system (Heart rate/HR, systolic (SB) & diastolic (DB) blood pressure) • Body Mass Index (BM) • Blood lipid (Total cholesterol/TC, LDL, HDL) • Blood sugar (BS)	• Food (FD) • Fluid (FL) • Air (AR) • Environment (EN) • Physical activity (PA) • Mental activity (MA)

3 CHD prediction model

CHD risk is currently calculated using static risk equation as follow:

$$CHDRisk_{static} = f(LEL) + f(MEL) + f(HEL) \quad (1)$$

In order to improve the accuracy of the prediction, a new dynamic risk equation ($CHDRisk_{dynamic}$) is proposed with considering region (R) and time (T).

$$CHDRisk_{dynamic} =$$

$$f(LEL,R,T) + f(MEL,R,T) + f(HEL,R,T) \quad (2)$$

Where:

$$f(LEL,R,T) = (a_0 + a_1 A_{G,R,T} + a_2 A^2_{G,R,T}) a_3 N \quad (3)$$

$$f(MEL,R,T) = f(SB) + f(DB) + f(TC) +$$

$$f(HDL) + f(LDL) + f(BM) + f(BS) \quad (4)$$

Where:

$$f(DB) = a_4 DB^3 + a_5 DB^2 + a_6 DB + a_7 \ ;$$

$$f(SB) = a_8 SB^3 + a_9 SB^2 + a_{10} SB + a_{11} \ ;$$

$$f(TC) = a_{12} TC + a_{13} \ ; f(HDL) = a_{14} HDL + a_{15} \ ;$$

$$f(LDL) = a_{16} LDL + a_{17} \ ;$$

$$f(BM) = a_{18} BM^3 + a_{19} BM^2 + a_{20} BM + a_{21} \ ;$$

$$f(BS) = a_{22} BM^4 + a_{23} BM^3 + a_{24} BM^2 + a_{25} BM + a_{26};$$

$$f(HEL,R,T) = f(FD) + f(FL) + f(AR) + f(EN) + f(PA) + f(MA) \quad (5)$$

The coefficient a_n can be obtained from dynamic interpolation of epidemiological and individual data. Fig. 2, Fig. 3, and Fig. 4 show the examples of CHD risk for each energy level and its interpolation equation respectively.

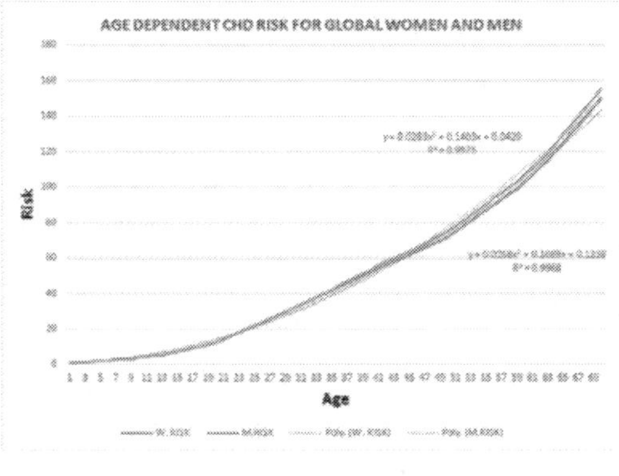

Fig. 2. Age dependent CHD risk for global men and women.

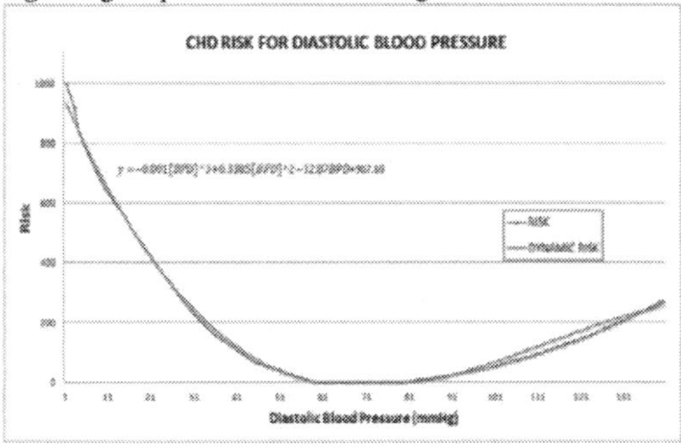

Fig. 3. CHD risk for diastolic blood pressure.

These graphs were generated from 10900 people with 3 different race groups (Caucasian, Mongolian and Negroid) [2]. This epidemiological data and interpolation equation were inputted in the webserver. This model is used as first condition or static model. In order to calculate the risk, a subject can input the risk factors data via mobile user interface. After risk calculation by the equation in the webserver, the subject can get the information about the current risk, the risk at certain age, the age at 100% risk and list of bioenergy symphony activities to increase age at 100% risk. In addition, the admin can always update the database using new epidemiological data to ensure that the risk is up to date. The model implementation algorithm can be seen in the Fig. 5.

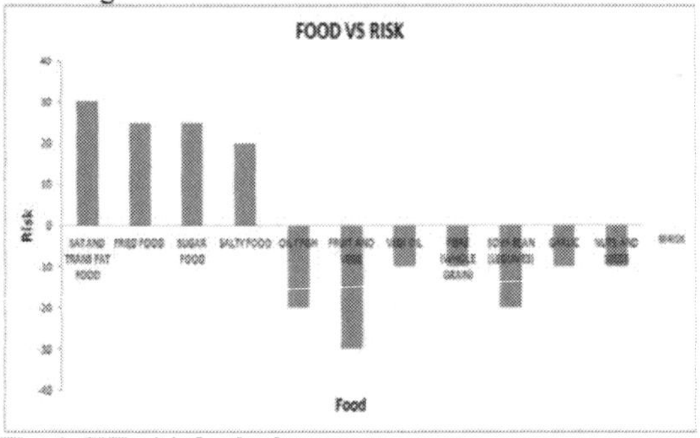

Fig. 4. CHD risk for food.

The backend system was done by using MySQL as main database. The web server for front end was done with Apache 2.0 and coded with PHP version 5.5.1. In order to improve the accuracy of the model to be used in Malaysia, 2410 CHD patients' data from Malaysia was inputted in the model. This input has changed the equation coefficients in the model and the model become dynamic model.

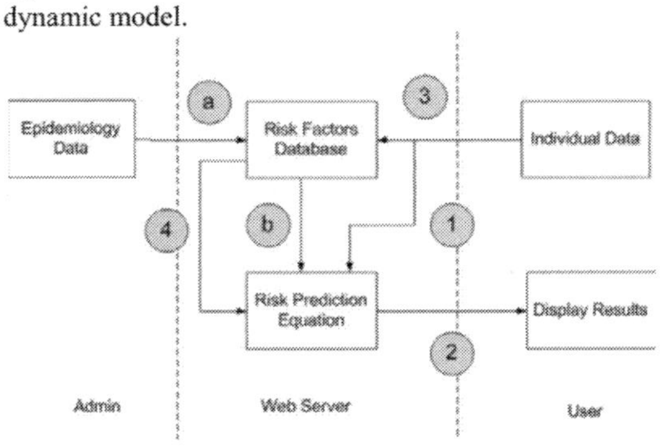

Fig. 5. Model Implementation Algorithm.

4 Result and analysis

In order to verify the newly developed adaptive risk prediction model, we did comparison study with 5 existing models including Framingham Risk Score [5], QRISK [7], SCORE [6], Reynolds [8], and WHO/ISH [11]. The comparison includes structure, adaptability and accessibility. The structure analysis is based on criteria of physiological pathway including: completeness, redundancy, connectivity, time analysis and spatial analysis. As for the adaptability analysis, it is conducted based on adaptive weighted risk factor and epidemiology dependent risk calculation. The accessibility analysis includes data enter human error, personalized risk, accountability and real time access.

Table 2 shows the results of structure test carried out with 5 different risk prediction models and one static model. As we can see from Table 2, our dynamic model obtained the highest score among the other existing models. The main criterion that influences the results is the adaptability of the model. The other models scores lower than dynamic model since they have inadequate adaptive weighted risk factor and epidemiology dependent risk calculation. The completeness of the dynamic model also increased the total score in the structure test. However, there are redundancies of structure in the dynamic model because there are some factors that might exist more than one time to be used for different risk factors category. Overall, the adaptive model is up to 41% better than 5 existing models in terms of structure, adaptability and accessibility.

Table 2. Physiological diagram of CHD.

	FRS	QRISK	SCORE	Rey	WHO	Static	Dynamic
Structure	3.6	4.1	3.5	3.9	3.6	3.6	4.7
Adaptability	0.6	0.6	0.6	0.6	0.6	0.6	2
Accessibility	2.3	2.3	2.3	2	2	2	3
Total Point	6.5	7	6.1	6.8	5.7	6.6	9.7
Percentage Different (%)	33	28	37	30	41	32	0

The risk prediction results have also been validated with Electrocardiography and Echocardiography stress test results. There are 120 subjects with age from 15 to 95 years old participated in the validation study. The results from five existing models, static model and dynamic model are shown in Table 3.

Table 3. a) Results of 120 Subjects with existing models.

	FRS	QRISK	SCORE	Rey	WHO	Static	Dynamic
VLR[a]	22	34	18	14	15	23	32
LR[b]	29	26	41	32	46	27	22
MR[c]	43	51	55	42	25	44	46
HR[d]	20	9	4	32	18	19	16
VHR[e]	6	0	2	0	16	7	4

a. VLR = very low risk b. LR = low risk c. MR= middle risk
d.HR = high risk e. VHR = very high risk

Table 3. b) Results of 120 Subjects with ECG and ECHO tests

	Dynamic	ECG	ECHO	AVG(ECHO+ECG)
VLR	32	28	31	29.5
LR	22	23	20	21.5
MR	46	50	47	48.5
HR	16	15	18	16.5
VHR	4	4	4	4

Table 3. c) Accuracy Results

	FRS	QRISK	SCORE	Rey	WHO	Static	Dynamic
VLR	74.57	84.75	61.02	50.85	47.48	77.96	92.19
LR	74.14	79.07	9.30	13.95	51.16	79.63	97.73
MR	88.66	94.85	86.60	51.55	86.60	90.72	94.57
HR	78.79	54.55	24.24	90.91	6.06	86.84	96.88
VHR	66.67	0	50	25	0	57.14	100
AVG	76.57	62.64	46.23	46.45	38.26	78.46	96.27

The risk level was divided into five categories: very low risk, low risk, middle risk, high risk, and very high risk. All of the subjects were also tested with ECG stress test and Echo stress test. Table 3. a) and b) shows the risk prediction results of 120 subjects with existing models and ECG and Echo stress tests. The average of ECG and Echo stress test were then calculated and compared with the other risk prediction models. The accuracy results were shown in Table 3. c). The result of accuracy test show that the prediction accuracy for dynamic model is 96.2%.

Although the model had shown promising results from verification and validation test, this model still has some weaknesses that need to be confronted. First, this model requires bigger resources for its database and processing to produce dynamic equation. Another disadvantage is that there is a possibility for dynamic interpolation error to happen because the new data group has different trend or far distance from existing equation. For example, the new data group comes from huge nuclear radiated area; this will change the trend drastically and introduce error in the interpolation. Generalization of data will also produce inaccuracy if the previous epidemiology data is originated from a specific region. Therefore, in order to improve the model, artificial intelligence can be applied for the interpolation or risk calculation.

5 Conclusion

In this study, a new online adaptive CHD risk prediction model had been developed. The model had been developed based on 10900 patient data from available global data and 2410 patients' data from Malaysia. This model had been tested by 120 subjects and validated with ECG and ECHO stress tests. Test result shows that the model just show error less than 4% compared with result from ECG and ECHO stress tests. When compared to other existing models, the model had shown up to 41% better results in term of structure, adaptability and accessibility.

Acknowledgement

The authors would like to thank Ministry of Education Malaysia for the providing financial support of this project. The authors would also like to express gratitude to National Heart Institute, Malaysia and National Cardiovascular Centre, Indonesia, for the data support.

References

1. http://www.who.int/mediacentre/factsheets/fs317/en
2. N. D. Wong, Nat. Rev. Cardiol., **11.5**, pp. 276-289 (2014)
3. http://www.worldlifeexpectancy.com/country-health-profile/malaysia/
4. S. M. Grundy, R. Pasternak, P. Greenland, S. Smith and V. Fuster., J. Am. Coll. Cardiol., **34.4**, pp. 1348-1359 (1999)
5. P. W. Wilson, et al., Circulation, **97.18**, pp. 1837-1847. (1998)
6. I. Graham, et al., Eur. Heart J., **28.19**, pp.2375-2414 (2007)
7. J. Hippisley-Cox, et al., BMJ **335.7611**, pp. 136 (2007)
8. P.M. Ridker, et al., Circulation, **118.22**, pp. 2243-2251 (2008)
9. D.C. Goff, et al., J. Am. Coll. Cardiol. (2014)
10. P.W.F. Wilson, and B. F. Culleton., UpToDate Inc. *Textbook of Medicine* (2010)
11. S. Mendis, et al., J. Hypertens., **25.8** , pp. 1578-1582 (2007)

MATEC Web of Conferences 125, 03001 (2017) DOI: 10.1051/matecconf/201712503001
CSCC 2017

Convergecast with Unbounded Number of Channels

Roman Plotnikov[1,*], *Adil* Erzin[1,2], and *Vyacheslav* Zalyubovskiy[1]

[1]Sobolev Institute of Mathematics, 4 Acad. Koptyug Avenue, Novosibirsk, Russia
[2]Novosibirsk State University, 2 Pirogova Str., Novosibirsk, Russia

Abstract. We consider a problem of minimum length scheduling for the conflict-free aggregation convergecast in wireless networks in a case when each element of a network uses its own frequency channel. This problem is equivalent to the well-known NP-hard problem of telephone broadcasting since only the conflicts between the children of the same parent are taken into account. We propose a new integer programming formulation and compare it with the known one by running the CPLEX software package. Based on the results of a numerical experiment, we concluded that our formulation is more preferable in practice to solve the considered problem by CPLEX than the known one. We also propose a novel heuristic algorithm, which is based on a genetic algorithm and a local search metaheuristic. The simulation results demonstrate the high quality of the proposed algorithm compared to the best known approaches.

1 Introduction

In wireless sensor networks (WSNs), collecting data from all sensor nodes to a distinguished node, called the sink, is one of the most fundamental problems. Due to the limited transmission range of sensor nodes, which follows, in particular, from the need to minimize a communication energy consumption [1], multi-hop communication over a tree-based routing topology is usually used to gather data. Such a pattern is known as convergecast [2].

Since radio communication is the main source of energy consumption, it is important to minimize the amount of transmitted data. One of the ways to optimize communication overhead for sensor nodes is to merge their own data with the received packets by means of some aggregation function. Aggregation convergecast is possible when data are spatially correlated or the goal is to collect some summarized information (e.g. maximum, mean, etc.) In such a scenario, each sensor node needs to send only one packet during the aggregation session.

Because of its ability to provide time bounds, TDMA-based scheduling algorithms are widely used. In a TDMA scheduling, time is divided in equal-length slots under assumptions that each slot is long enough to send or receive one packet [3]. Minimizing time for the aggregated convergecast in this case is equivalent to minimizing the number of time slots required for all packets to reach the sink.

Another important factor of the convergecast protocol is aggregation latency, which is defined as the required number of time slots of the whole data collection process. The problem of minimization of latency is known in literature as minimum-latency aggregation scheduling (MLAS) [4]. The solution of MLAS typically includes two components: a spanning tree rooted at and directed towards the sink node, and schedule, which assigns a transmitting time slot for each tree link so that (1) every node transmits only after all its children in the tree have, and (2) potentially interfered links are scheduled to transmit in different time slots. The last condition means that the TDMA schedule should be interference free, i.e. no receiving node is within the interference range of the other transmitting node. There are two types of interferences or collisions in wireless networks: primary and secondary. A primary collision occurs when more than one node transmits to the same destination. In tree-based aggregation, it corresponds to the case when two or more children of the same parent send their packets in the same time slot. A secondary collision occurs when a node overhears transmissions intended for other node. Such kind of collision is caused by links in the underlying communication graph, but not in the aggregation tree.

The MLAS problem was proven to be NP-hard [5]. Finding an optimal time slot assignment for a given tree is still NP-hard [6]. Therefore, all existing results in literature are heuristic algorithms for finding approximate solutions. Most of them contain two relatively independent phases: aggregation tree construction followed by link scheduling [4, 5, 7].

In this paper, we mainly focus on the first phase – finding the minimum delay aggregation tree assuming that the proper chosen tree would lead to a good solution. Additionally, in this stage we take into account only conflicts between the children of the same parent, i.e. primary collisions. First, such a model is suitable for multichannel transmissions, where secondary interference can be avoided by assigning different frequencies under the assumption that the number of channels is big enough. Moreover, the solution of such a "relaxed" problem can be used as a lower bound of the

* Corresponding author: prv@math.nsc.ru

aggregation latency for the original MLAS, so a tree with a smaller delay can be considered as a better candidate to produce a shorter schedule.

It is worthwhile to mention that the considered problem is equivalent to the problem of finding the optimal broadcasting tree in a graph, also known as a telephone broadcasting problem, which has been proved to be NP-hard [8]. Most existing algorithms construct an aggregation tree based on the shortest path tree (SPT) or connected dominated set (CDS), but as was shown in [9] an optimal solution could be neither SPT nor CDS based. To overcome this issue, we propose a novel heuristic algorithm, which combines a genetic algorithm performing broad search among various aggregation trees with a local search procedure aimed at the pruning of the currently found tree.

In summary, we provide the following contributions towards a better understanding of the aggregated convergecast problem:

- We present an alternative IP formulation for the MLAS problem in case of the absence of secondary collisions and compare it with previously known model.
- We propose a novel heuristic Genetic Local Search (GLS). In contrast to traditional genetic algorithms, GLS uses an embedded local search procedure to further improve the current feasible solution.
- Through extensive simulation experiments, we demonstrate the quality of the solutions achievable by the GLS algorithm vs. the current state-of-the-art methods.

The rest of the paper is organized as follows: The recent research results are overviewed in Section 2. The mathematical formulation of the problem and the comparative analysis of two IP-formulations are given in Section 3. In Section 4, the new heuristic algorithm is described. Simulation results are presented in Section 5, and the paper is concluded in Section 6.

2 Related work

Data aggregation for WSNs has been proposed to improve energy efficiency of sensor nodes and consequently prolong network lifetime [10]. Some surveys considering different aspects of the problem have been published [11, 12].

The MLAS problem was first introduced in [5]. The authors proved that the problem is NP-hard even for unit disk graphs, and proposed a $(\Delta - 1)$-approximation algorithm, where Δ is the maximum node degree in the network graph. In this algorithm, the Shortest Path Tree is created first, which later is used as an input for the scheduling algorithm. In the nearly constant approximation proposed by Huang et al. [7], the data latency bounded by $23R + \Delta - 18$, where R is the network's radius. The algorithm in [13] aims to minimize the data aggregation time by using a Connected Dominated Set (CDS). Moreover, the authors choose the network topology center as the aggregation tree root instead of sink. This allows them to reduce the upper bound to $16R + \Delta - 14$. Wang et al. designed a Peony-tree-based data aggregation algorithm with latency bound $15R + \Delta - 15$ [14]. Based on the properties of neighboring dominators in CDS, Nguyen et al. have improved the algorithm from [13] and have given a proof of upper bound $12R + \Delta - 12$ for their algorithm [15].

In [16], the authors proved that minimizing the schedule length for an arbitrary network in the presence of multiple frequencies is NP-hard and proposed approximation algorithms with worst-case performance bound for geometric networks. They also showed that finding the minimum number of frequencies required to remove all interfering links in an arbitrary network is NP-hard problem. Pan et al. considered convergecast for low-duty-cycled multi-channels WSNs aimed to find a time slot and frequency channel assignment that can minimize the data aggregation delay [17]. The authors proved NP-completeness of the problem and proposed a heuristic scheme, which contains three consecutives phases: tree formation, slot assignment, and channel assignment.

As mentioned earlier, a relaxed version of the MLAS problem, which takes into account only primary collisions, is equivalent to the broadcast time problem. The NP-hardness of this problem is proved in [8]. In [18] it is shown that the problem remains NP-hard even for 3-regular planar graphs. Polynomial-time algorithms for the exact solution are known only for few special graphs: trees [8], complete graphs [19], and unicyclic graphs [20]. An algorithm based on a combinatorial approach with $O(\log n)$ approximated ratio were presented in [21]. As for heuristics, simulation results suggest that the best results are achieved by the algorithms presented in [22] and [23].

3 Problem formulation

We consider a WSN consisting of stationary sensor nodes with one sink. All sensors are homogeneous. We use a protocol interference model [24], which is a graph theoretic approach that assumes correct reception of a message if and only if there is no simultaneous transmission within proximity of the receiver. For simplicity, we assume that the interference range is equal to the transmission range. Then the WSN with sink node s can be represented as a graph $G = (V, E)$, where V denotes all the sensor nodes and $s \in V$. An edge $(u, v) \in E$ if and only if the distance between the nodes u and v is within the transmission range.

The problem considered in this paper is defined as follows. Given a connected undirected graph $G = (V, E)$, $|V| = n$, $|E| = m$ and a sink node $s \in V$, find the minimum length schedule of data aggregation from all the vertices of $V \setminus \{s\}$ to s under the following conditions:

- at the same time slot any vertex can either receive or send a message;
- each vertex can receive at most one message during one time slot;
- each vertex can send a message only once.

Since it is convenient to consider the directed edges (*arcs*) when constructing an aggregation tree, we also introduce a directed graph $G_{or} = (V, A)$ constructed from G by replacing each edge with two oppositely directed arcs and excluding the arcs starting from s.

3.1 Integer Programming formulations

3.1.2 IP formulation 1

Tian et al. [9] proposed an IP formulation for the general problem when the elements use the same channel (frequency) and collisions between the vertices (not only between the children of the same parent) are taken into account. The IP-formulation of the problem with an unbounded number of channels may be obtained from this formulation by excluding the corresponding set of constraints as follows.

Let us consider a directed graph $G_{or}' = (V \cup \{s'\}, A \cup (s,s'))$ which is constructed from G_{or} by adding a fictive node s' and an arc (s,s'). Let us introduce the variables $x_{a,t}$ for any $a \in A \cup (s,s')$ and $t \in \{1, \ldots, n\}$: $x_{a,t} = 1$ if an arc a is scheduled to transmit a packet during the time slot t, and $x_{a,t} = 0$ otherwise. Let us also denote the set of all arcs starting from $v \in V$ as $S(v)$ and all arcs ending at $v \in V \cup \{s'\}$ as $D(v)$. Then the problem is the following:

$$\sum_{t=0}^{n} t * x_{(s,s'),t} \rightarrow_{x} \min \qquad (1)$$

$$\sum_{a \in S(v)} \sum_{t=0}^{n} x_{a,t} = 1, \ \forall v \in V \qquad (2)$$

$$\sum_{t'=t+1}^{n} x_{a't'} \leq 1 - \sum_{a \in S(v)} x_{a,t}, \quad \forall v \in V \cup \{s'\} \ \forall a' \in D(v) \ \forall t \qquad (3)$$

$$\sum_{a \in S(v)} x_{a,t} + \sum_{a' \in D(v)} x_{a',t} \leq 1 \ \forall v \in V \cup \{s'\} \ \forall t \qquad (4)$$

In this formulation the time slot when s sends a message to s' is taken as an objective function (1). Constraints (2) guarantee that each vertex can transmit data only once. Constraints (3) ensure that, once a vertex transmits, it can no longer receive messages. Constraints (4) hold the requirement that each vertex can only transmit or receive a message during each time slot. Note that the formulation (1)-(4) contains $O(nm)$ variables and $O(n^2 + nm)$ constraints.

3.1.1 IP formulation 2

The solution space of the formulation (1)-(4) is rather large: in the case of dense graph G the number of variables may be close to $O(n^3)$ as well as the number of variables of the dual problem. For the efficiency of branch and bound-based exact methods IP formulations of less size are more preferable. Therefore below we propose another IP formulation with $O(n^2)$ variables and $O(n^3)$ constraints.

Let us number all vertices $V = \{v_0 = s, v_1, \ldots, v_{n-1}\}$ and introduce the following variables. Let $t_i \in \{1, \ldots, n - 1\}$ be the time slot of data sending by the vertex $v_i \in V$; u_i be the number of edges in the path from v_i to s in the convergecasting tree ($u_0 = 0$); L be the length of a schedule; x_{ij} be equal to 1 if v_i sends a message to v_j and 0 otherwise; y_{ij} is equal to 1 if $t_i \geq t_j$ and 0 otherwise. Then the IP-formulation can be written in the following form:

$$L \rightarrow_{x,u,t,y,L} \min \qquad (5)$$

$$L \geq t_i, \ i = 1, \ldots, n \qquad (6)$$

$$\sum_{j=0}^{n} x_{ij} = 1, \ i = 1, \ldots, n \qquad (7)$$

$$1 - (n+1)(1 - x_{ij}) \leq u_i - u_j \leq \leq 1 + (n+1)(1 - x_{ij}), \ (i,j) \in E \qquad (8)$$

$$t_j - t_i \leq -1 + (n+1)(2 - x_{ik} - x_{jk}) + (n+1)(1 - y_{ij}) \quad i, j, k = 1, \ldots, n, \ i < j \qquad (9)$$

$$1 - (n+1)\, y_{ij} \leq t_j - t_i \leq (n+1)(1 - y_{ij}), \quad i, j = 1, \ldots, n, \ i < j \qquad (10)$$

$$t_i + 1 - (n+1)(1 - x_{ij}) \leq t_j, \ (i,j) \in E \qquad (11)$$

Constraints (7) guarantee that each vertex sends a message only once during the aggregation session. Constraints (8) ensure that the subgraph which is defined by the variables **x** is a tree. With the constraints (9) and (10) the conflicts between children of a same parent are eliminated. The constraints (11) hold the requirement that each vertex can transmit data only after receiving messages from all of its children in the aggregation tree.

3.2 Comparison of the IP formulations

We have tested the both IP formulations using the IBM ILOG CPLEX package. We launched CPLEX on commonly used interconnection topologies: butterfly graph (BF_d), cube connected cycle (CCC_d) and shuffle-exchange graph (SE_d) (Table 1). More detailed information about these graph classes can be found in [25]. We also launched CPLEX for instances generated randomly using GT-ITM Pure Random model [26]. Results of the experiments are presented in Table 1 and Table 2, respectively. $\text{CPLEX}_{\text{IP1}}$ stands for the CPLEX using formulation (1)-(4) and $\text{CPLEX}_{\text{IP2}}$ stands for the CPLEX using formulation (5)-(11). The calculation time was limited by 1000 seconds. If CPLEX failed to find an optimal solution during 1000 seconds, then the best found feasible solution was returned. In this case the objective value is marked in italics.

The results of the experiment show that the both IP formulations are suitable to solve the considered problem in acceptable time in cases of small dimension (10-25 vertices and 20-50 edges). When $n \geq 40$ and $m \geq 60$ $\text{CPLEX}_{\text{IP2}}$ is unable to complete the process during 1000 seconds (except one case when $n = 40$, $m = 64$), but it always finds an optimal or near-optimal solution. This means that $\text{CPLEX}_{\text{IP2}}$ finds a near-optimal solution rather fast, and spends the majority of running time for the proof of its optimality. Although $CPLEX_{IP1}$ appeared to outperform $CPLEX_{IP2}$ in some cases, the results of $CPLEX_{IP1}$ were significantly worse when the calculation process was aborted due the time limit. Additionally, $CPLEX_{IP1}$ was often unable to find any feasible solution (see, e.g. cases when $n \geq 50$ in Table 2). In summary, we conclude that the IP formulation (5)-(11) is more preferable in practice to solve the considered problem by CPLEX than the formulation (1)-(4). Even if CPLEX fails to find an optimal solution for the formulation (5)-(11) in a specified time, it always provides a decent near-optimal feasible solution.

Table 1. CPLEX performances on the popular network topologies.

	n	m	$CPLEX_{IP1}$		$CPLEX_{IP2}$	
			Time (sec.)	Obj	Time (sec.)	Obj
CCC_3	24	36	8.92	6	4.99	6
CCC_4	64	96	1000	*60*	1000	*10*
SE_3	8	10	0.02	5	0.01	5
SE_4	16	21	0.67	7	0.19	7
SE_5	32	46	44.73	9	159.1	9
BF_3	24	48	96.44	5	87.49	5
BF_4	64	128	1000	*58*	1000	*8*

Table 2. CPLEX performances on the pure random graphs.

n	m	$CPLEX_{IP1}$		$CPLEX_{IP2}$	
		Time (sec.)	Obj	Time (sec.)	Obj
10	29	2.329	4	2.16	4
10	26	0.703	4	0.856	4
25	35	3.96	5	0.85	5
25	40	8.29	6	10.82	6
25	47	10.99	5	119.1	5
40	64	1000	*30*	965	7
40	68	67,6	7	1000	7
40	70	46,4	6	1000	6
50	158	1000	*42*	1000	*7*
50	127	1000	-	1000	*6*
50	126	1000	-	1000	*7*
100	232	1000	-	1000	*9*
100	233	1000	-	1000	*10*
100	367	1000	-	1000	*9*

4 Heuristic algorithm GLS

In this section, we propose the new heuristic algorithm, Genetic Local Search (GLS), which combines a genetic algorithm approach [27] with a local search meta-heuristic. Similar to a conventional genetic algorithm, GLS maintains a set of feasible solutions (*population*) and imitates an evolutionary process as follows: at each iteration the pairs of solutions are chosen from the population and reproduce an *offspring*. As soon as a new solution is generated, it can be modified by the Mutation procedure. After this, the Local Search procedure tries to improve the current solution. Each time the best solutions are kept in the population of the next generation. This process continues until some predefined stopping condition is met.

The pseudocode of the GLS algorithm is presented in Fig. 1. The starting population is generated at the *Initialization* step in line 1. After that in lines 3-9 the following steps are sequentially repeated until a stopping condition is met: *Selection*, *Crossover*, *Mutation*, *LocalSearch*, *FitnessCalculation* and *Join*.

As an input the algorithm takes a communication graph G_{or} and the following set of parameters:

- *PopSize* – the size of population;
- *OffspSize* – the size of offspring;
- *FPItCount* – the number of iterations in the first population construction procedure;
- *SPProportion* – the ratio of shortest-path trees in the starting population;
- *PM* – the probability of mutation;
- *PLS* – the probability of local search.
- k_{max} – the maximum possible number of iterations in mutation procedure

The next subsections contain detailed descriptions of the algorithm steps.

4.1 Initialization

At the *Initialization* step the first population is generated. The first tree, which is added into the first population, is the shortest-path tree constructed by the Dijkstra algorithm. After this tree is constructed, the length of the shortest path from each vertex to the sink is known. Let $l(v)$ be the length (number of edges) of a shortest path from vertex $v \in V$. Let us consider a directed graph $G_1 = (V, A_1)$, where $A_1 = \{(u,v) \mid (u,v) \in A,\ l(u) = l(v) - 1\}$. Note that any spanning tree which is rooted in s and contains only arcs from A_1 is a shortest-path tree. The next trees added to the population are generated by two procedures: *RandomShortestPath* and *RandomMinDegree*. The procedure *RandomShortestPath* starts with a tree $T = (\emptyset, \{s\})$; an arc from A_1 which connects a vertex from the current tree with a vertex from V which is not in the current tree is sequentially chosen at random and added to the current tree. In the procedure *RandomMinDegree*, the tree is constructed in a similar manner, but with the following difference: at each step an arc is chosen randomly from A, and the probability of an arc choice is inversely proportional to the degree of a corresponding vertex in the current tree. A new tree is added to the population only if it is not a copy of an existing one. The *Initialization* step requires three parameters: *PopSize* – the maximum size of the population, *SPProportion* – an approximate part of the trees generated by the procedure *RandomShortestPath*, and *FPItCount* – the maximum number of successive attempts to generate a tree. The pseudocode of the *Initialization* step can be found in Fig. 2.

```
INPUT: Gor = (V, A) - communication graph, PopSize, OffspSize, FPItCoun, SPProportion, PM, PLS, kmax - additional parameters;
OUTPUT: T - spanning tree on G rooted in s;
Initialization;
FitnessCalculation(population);
while (stop condition is not met)
  Selection;
  Crossover;
  Mutation;
  LocalSearch;
  FitnessCalculation(offspring);
  Join;
  T = the best tree among the current population
end while
```

Fig. 1. Genetic local search (GLS).

```
INPUT: Gor = (V, A) - communication graph, SPProportion, FPItCount, PopSize - additional parameters;
OUTPUT: p - population (a set of spanning trees on G rooted in s);
i = 0;
T0 = Dijkstra(); // Dijkstra algorithm
p = {T0}; // population
while (i < FPItCount and p.Size < PopSize)
  p = random real value between 0 and 1
  if (p < SPProportion)
    T = RandomShortestPath();
  else
    T = RandomMinDegree();
  if (p contains T)
    i++; // clones are forbidden
  else
    p.add(T);
end while
```

Fig. 2. GLS: Initialization.

4.2 Fitness calculation

In order to estimate the quality of every solution in the population its *fitness* should be calculated. Fitness is a positive value which is higher when the solution is closer to the optimal solution. Let $L(T)$ be the minimum convergecasting schedule length for a spanning tree T. Then the fitness is $1 / L(T)$.

Note that the convergecasting schedule of minimum length on a spanning tree T can be found in time $O(n)$ for example using the procedure described in [8] with a small modification, because the position of the broadcast center is known in our case.

4.3 Selection

In the Selection step a set of parents is filled by the solutions from the current population in the following way. Sequentially a tree is taken from the current population with proportion to fitness probability. Note that the same solution can be added to the parent set several times. The number of elements in the parent set exceeds twice the maximum number of elements in offspring *OffspSize*, which is the parameter of GLS.

4.4 Crossover

At first a set of parents is divided randomly into *OffspSize* pairs. After that each pair of parents $T_p^1 = (V, A_p^1)$ and $T_p^2 = (V, A_p^2)$ generates a child tree T_c in the following way. Let us consider a vertex $v \in V \setminus \{s\}$ and two vertices $v_1, v_2 \in V$: $a_1 = (v, v_1) \in A_p^1$, $a_2 = (v, v_2) \in A_p^2$. The goal is to choose an arc from $\{a_1, a_2\}$ and to add it to T_c. If $v_1 = v_2$ then the arc a_1 is chosen. If adding of one arc from $\{a_1, a_2\}$ to T_c leads to the appearance of cycles, then another arc is chosen. In the remaining case let us introduce the weight $w_i = 1 / \delta(v_i) + 1 / |l(v) - l(v_i) - 2|$, where $\delta(v_i)$ is a degree of the vertex v_i in the tree T_p^i, $i \in \{1, 2\}$. Then the arc is chosen randomly from $\{a_1, a_2\}$ with probability $P(a_i) = w_i / (w_1 + w_2)$, $i \in \{1, 2\}$.

4.5 Mutation

Mutation is a randomized procedure which is applied to the solutions in the current offspring. The Mutation procedure is applied with probability P_M (a parameter of GLS) to each offspring. The Mutation procedure takes as an argument (an integer parameter) k – the maximum difference (number of different arcs) between the initial tree and the modified one. This parameter is taken randomly from the interval $[0, \ldots, k_{max}]$, where k_{max} is another algorithm parameter, inverse to its value probability (i.e., smaller modifications are more possible). The pseudocode of the mutation procedure is given in Fig. 3.

DOI: 10.1051/matecconf/201712503001

```
   INPUT: G = (V, A) - communication graph, T = (V,
A(T)) - spanning tree on G rooted in s, k - an integer
parameter;
   OUTPUT: T - spanning tree on G rooted in s;
   do k times:
      (i,j) = random arc from A \ A(T);
      if (j is not descendant of i)
         T.SetParent(i, j);
```

Fig. 3. GLS: Mutation.

4.5 Local search

As well as mutation, the local search procedure is applied to a subset of offspring defined by the probability P_{LS} – another algorithm parameter. The pseudocode of the local search procedure is presented in Fig. 4. At each iteration the procedure performs a search of such arc $a = (v_1, v_2) \in A \setminus A(T)$ whose addition of T (together with detaching of v_1 from its parent in T) leads to the maximum decrease of the objective function. The method *CalculateEffect*(T, u, v) calculates the change of the schedule length after detaching of v from its parent in T and adding an arc (v, u). Method *T.SetParent* performs the mentioned reattaching. The whole procedure continues while the solution is improved.

```
   INPUT: G = (V, A) - communication graph, T = (V,
A(T)) - spanning tree on G rooted in s, k - an integer
parameter;
   OUTPUT: T - spanning tree on G rooted in s;
improved = true;
   while (improved)
      improved = false;
      best_u = NULL; best_v = NULL; bestImpr = 0;
      for each arc (u, v) in A \ A(T)
        effect = CalculateEffect(T, u, v);
        if (effect < bestImpr)
          best_u = u;
          best_v = v;
          bestImpr = effect;
          improved = true;
        end if
      end for
      if (improved)
        T.SetParent(best_u, best_v);
        CalculateSchedule(T);
        break;
      end if
   end while
```

Fig. 4. GLS: Local search.

4.6 Join

At the join step *PopSize* solutions from the current population and the current offspring, which have the highest fitness, are chosen to fill the population of the next generation.

5 Simulation

The proposed algorithm has been implemented in C++. Also, we implemented two of the most efficient previous heuristics: the Round Heuristic (RH) [22] and the Tree Based Algorithm (TBA) [23] in order to compare them with our GLS algorithm. As test instances, the following commonly used interconnection topologies have been considered: BF_d – butterfly graph, CCC_d – cube connected cycle, SE_d – shuffle-exchange graph. The results can be found in Tables 3-5. In addition, we ran all algorithms on random graphs generated using three well-known network models: GT-ITM Pure Random, GT-ITM Transit-Stub [26] and BRITE Top-Down Waxman [28], see Tables 6-8. OPT stands for the optimal value of the objective either known previously [25] or obtained by us using CPLEX launched on one of the IP formulations proposed in Section 3 (as for GT-ITM Pure Random model when $n \le 25$). If the optimal value of the objective is not known, then the lower bound (LB) is mentioned. For graphs CCC_d and BF_d the best known lower bounds are taken from [25]. For other models the maximum of the following two values are taken: (a) $\lceil \log_2 n \rceil$ [25]; (b) a value obtained by calculating for each vertex its minimum receiving time plus the length of the shortest path to the root. The minimal values of convergecasting time are marked bold in the tables below.

The following algorithm's parameters allow us to get the best results: *PopSize* = 50, *OffspSize* = 25, *FPItCount* = 3, *SPProportion* = 0.6, *PM* = 0.6, *PLS* = 0.8, $k_{max} = \lfloor n/3 \rfloor$. As a stopping criterion we used the following rule: the minimum and the maximum values of fitness among all solutions in the current population are not changed during last 10 iterations.

For some reason in several cases we failed to reproduce the results of TBA presented in [23]. For example, in CCC_6, CCC_8, BF_6, BF_7, BF_8, SE_8, the length of the schedule yielded by TBA in our implementation appeared to be greater by 1 than the length of the schedule constructed by RH, although the authors of TBA state that they are the same in those cases.

Table 3. Results in CCC_d.

d	*n*	*m*	LB	RH	TBA	GLS
3	8	12	6	**6**	**6**	**6**
4	24	36	9	**9**	**9**	**9**
5	160	240	11	**11**	**11**	**11**
6	384	576	13	**13**	14	**13**
7	896	1344	16	**16**	**16**	**16**
8	2048	3072	18	**18**	19	**18**

Table 4. Results in BF_d.

d	*n*	*m*	LB	RH	TBA	GLS
3	24	48	5	**5**	**5**	**5**
4	64	128	7	**7**	**7**	**7**
5	160	320	8	**9**	**9**	**9**

 DOI: 10.1051/matecconf/201712503001

6	384	768	10	**10**	11	**10**
7	896	1792	11	**12**	13	**12**
8	2048	4096	13	**14**	15	**14**

Table 5. Results in SE_d.

d	*n*	*m*	OPT	RH	TBA	GLS
3	8	10	5	**5**	**5**	**5**
4	16	21	7	**7**	**7**	**7**
5	32	46	9	**9**	**9**	**9**
6	64	93	11	**11**	**11**	**11**
7	128	190	13	**13**	**13**	**13**
8	256	381	15	**15**	16	**15**

Table 6. Results in GT-ITM Pure Random model.

n	*m*	LB	OPT	RH	TBA	GLS
10	29	4	4	**4**	**4**	**4**
10	23	4	4	**4**	**4**	**4**
25	35	5	5	6	6	**5**
25	40	6	6	**6**	7	**6**
25	47	5	5	**5**	**5**	**5**
25	42	5	6	**6**	**6**	**6**
100	277	7	-	**7**	**7**	**7**
100	232	7	-	8	8	**7**
100	233	7	-	**8**	9	**8**
500	1497	9	-	**10**	**10**	**10**
500	1259	9	-	**10**	**10**	**10**

Table 7. Results in BRITE Top-Down Waxman model.

n	*m*	LB	RH	TBA	GLS
100	208	8	**10**	11	**10**
100	307	9	11	**10**	**10**
100	407	9	**10**	**10**	**10**
500	1529	9	**11**	12	**11**
500	1529	9	**12**	**12**	**12**
500	1530	10	**12**	13	**12**
1000	1028	22	**22**	**22**	**22**
1000	2020	17	**19**	**19**	**19**
1000	3027	10	**13**	14	**13**

Table 8. Results in GT-ITM Transit-Stub model.

n	*m*	LB	RH	TBA	GLS
100	287	7	**8**	9	**8**
100	261	7	**9**	**9**	**9**
100	267	7	**9**	11	**9**
100	273	7	9	9	**8**
100	275	7	9	**8**	9
600	1004	11	**14**	**14**	**14**
600	1208	10	14	**13**	**13**
600	1250	10	15	14	**13**
600	1234	10	15	**14**	**14**
600	1235	10	13	13	**12**
1020	2533	10	**16**	**16**	**16**
1020	3366	10	17	17	**16**
1020	3515	10	17	**16**	**16**
1020	2563	10	18	**17**	**17**
1020	2550	10	17	17	**16**

The results of the experiment show that our algorithm GLS performs better or the same as other known heuristics. The most noticeable advantage of GLS can be observed on the GT-ITM Transit-Stub model: in 10 cases out of 15 it outperforms at least one of the other algorithms, in 4 cases it outperforms both of them, and in 2 cases its convergecasting time is less by 2 than the convergecasting time obtained by one of other algorithms. We found only one case when another algorithm outperforms GLS: in the fifth instance of the BRITE Transit-Stub model the aggregation latency obtained by TBA is less by 1 than the one obtained by

GLS. In total, GLS appeared to be extremely efficient for all tested topologies and network models.

Obviously, GLS is more time-consuming than RH and TBA, but its running time remained acceptable in all tested cases. Thus, it solves a problem with 100 vertices and 300 edges in about 1.5 seconds, and it solves a problem with 1000 vertices and 3000 edges in about 30 seconds. It should be noticed that we launched it on one thread although it is well-parallelizable and therefore it may be significantly speeded-up according to the machine hardware and operation system properties. Moreover, the variety of parameters of GLS provides flexibility, and more thorough tuning of these parameters may also improve the algorithm.

6 Conclusion

In this paper, we addressed an aggregated convergecast problem in WSNs for a case when the number of channels is unbounded. The objective is to minimize the data aggregation time. We proposed a new heuristic algorithm, which is based on the genetic algorithm and the local search metaheuristic. Our scheduling algorithm has lower latencies than the previous best approaches, Round Heuristic [22] and Tree Based Algorithm [23] especially for such widespread network model as GT-ITM Transit–Stub. We also proposed a new IP-formulation to this problem and compared it with a variant from [9] using IBM CPLEX package. Our formulation appeared to be more suitable for moderate-size instances (up to 100 vertices and 300 edges), where it always finds a near-optimal feasible solution in a reasonable time.

The research of R. Plotnikov is partly supported by the Russian Foundation for Basic Research (grant no. 16-37-60006). The research of A. Erzin and V. Zalyubovskiy is partly supported by the Russian Foundation for Basic Research (grant no. 16-07-00552).

References

1. A.I. Erzin, N. Mladenovich, R.V. Plotnikov, Computers & Operations Research **78**, 557-563 (2017)
2. B. Malhotra, I. Nicolaidis, M.A. Nascimento, Wireless Netw. **17**, 319-335 (2011)
3. I. Demirkol, C. Ersoy, F. Alagoz, IEEE Comm. Mag. **44**, 115-121 (2006)
4. P.-J. Wan, S.C.-H. Huang, L. Wang, et al., *Proc. ACM MOBIHOC*, 185-194 (2009)
5. X. Chen, X. Hu, J. Zhu, *Lecture Notes Comput. Sci.* **3794**, 133-142 (2005)
6. A. Erzin, A. Pyatkin, *IEEE Int. Symp. On Comm. Systems, Networks and DSP (CSNDSP)*, 7574007 (2011)
7. S.C.-H. Huang, P.J. Wan, C.T. Vu, et al., *Proc. IEEE INFOCOM*, 366-372 (2007)
8. P.J. Slater, E.J. Cockayne, S.T. Heditniemi, Information dissemination in trees, SIAM J. Comput. **10**, 692-701 (1981)
9. C. Tian, H. Jiang, C. Wang, et al., IEEE Trans. Veh. Technol. **60**, 3462-3472 (2011)
10. B. Krishnamachari, D. Estrin, S. Wicker, *IEEE ICDCS*, 575-578 (2002)
11. R. Rajagopalan, P.K. Varshney, IEEE Commun. Surveys & Tutorials **8**, 48-63 (2006)
12. M. Bagaa, Y. Challa, A. Ksentini, et al., IEEE Commun. Surveys & Tutorials **16**, 1339-1368 (2014)
13. X. Xu, X. Mao, IEEE Trans. Parallel Distr. Syst. **22**, 163-175 (2011)
14. P. Wang, Y. He, L. Huang, Ad Hoc Networks, **11**, 1287-1296 (2013)
15. T.D. Nguyen, V. Zalyubovskiy, H. Choo, *IEEE Globecom*, 6133827 (2011)
16. A. Ghosh, O.D. Incel, V.S.A. Kumar, et al., *IEEE MASS*, 363-372 (2009)
17. M.-S. Pan, Y.-H. Lee, Ad Hoc Netw. **40C**, 1-14 (2016)
18. M. Middendorf, Information Processing Letters **46**, 281-287 (1993)
19. C. Cheng, C.K. Tse, M. Lau, IEEE Sensors J. **11**, 699-710 (2011)
20. H.A. Harutyunyan, E. Maraachlian, J. of Combinatorial Optimization, **16**, 307-322 (2008)
21. M. Elkin, G. Kortsarz, *STOC 2002*, 438-447 (2002)
22. R. Beier, J.F. Sibeyn, *SIROCCO*, 17-36 (2000)
23. H.A. Harutyunyan, B. Shao, J. Parallel Distrib. Comput. **66**, 68-76 (2006)
24. P. Gupta, P. Kumar, IEEE Trans. On Information Theory **IT-46**, 388-404 (2000)
25. J. Hromkovic, R. Klasing, B. Monien, R. Peine, *Combinatorial Network Theory*, 125-212 (Springer, 1996)
26. E.W. Zegura, K. Calvert, S. Bhattacharjee, *IEEE INFOCOM*, (1996)
27. S.N. Sivanandam, S.N. Deepa, *Introduction to genetic algorithms* (Springer, 2008)
28. A. Medina, A. Lakhina, I. Matta, J. Byers, *Proc. Ninth Int. Symp. on Modeling, Analysis and Simulation of Computer and Telecommunication Systems (MASCOTS)*, 346 (2001).

Zero-knowledge universal lossless data compression

Rodolfo A. Fiorini*

Politecnico di Milano University, 20133 Milano, Italy

Abstract. Advanced instrumentation, dealing with nanoscale technology at the current edge of human scientific enquiry, like X-Ray CT, generates an enormous quantity of data from single experiment. The very best modern lossless data compression algorithms use standard approaches and are unable to match high end requirements for mission critical application with full information conservation (a few pixels may vary by com/decom processing). In previous papers published elsewhere, we have already shown that traditional *Q* Arithmetic can be regarded as a highly sophisticated open logic, powerful and flexible bidirectional formal language of languages, according to "Computational Information Conservation Theory" (*CICT*). This new awareness can offer competitive approach to guide more convenient algorithm development and application for combinatorial lossless compression. To achieve true lossless com/decom and to overcome traditional constraints, the universal modular arithmetic approach, based on *CICT* Solid Number (SN) concept, is presented. To check practical implementation performance and effectiveness, an example on computational imaging is benchmarked by key performance index and compared to standard well-known lossless compression techniques. Results are critically discussed.

1 Introduction

Advanced instrumentation, dealing with nanoscale technology at the current edge of human scientific enquiry, like X-Ray CT, generates an enormous quantity of data from single experiment [1]. Even in MicroCT or Discrete Tomography (DT) by electron microscopy, 2-D projection images are acquired from various angles, by tilting the sample, generating new challenges associated with the problem of formation, acquisition, compression, transmission, and analysis of an enormous quantity of data [2], [3]. During this time of exploding data growth, disk manufacturers have begun running into the physical limitations of current storage technology (e.g., disk platter bit density, data transfer, etc.) and to seek new technologies to rely on [4].

Contemporary approaches to data compression vary in time delay or impact on application performance as well as in the amount of compression and loss of data. Two approaches that focus on data loss are lossless (no data loss) and lossy (some data loss for higher compression ratio). Different from natural images, advanced technology imaging and medical images generally have two special issues that should be noted in compression. First, they are sensitive to compression errors. Large distortion arising from lossy compression may invalidate their interpretation and diagnostic values. Second, especially the monochromatic images usually have extended dynamic range. Each pixel typically contains 16 or 12 bits per channel, compared to the 8-bit-depth pixels of common natural images. Nevertheless, both lossless and lossy compression schemes have been proposed to compression image application. Lossy compression (irreversible, i.e. information dissipation) schemes can achieve much higher Compression Ratio (CR) than lossless ones, by allowing some distortion in reconstruction. However, for mission critical application, the lossy distortion level must have to be supervised by qualified experts to avoid possible legal and diagnostic problems, especially for medical application [5],[6].

Lossless compression (reversible, i.e. information conservation) schemes provide reconstructed images identical to the original ones, but suffer from relative lower compression ratio, typically between 2:1 and 4:1. Furthermore, a single compression ratio (CR) cannot serve as a guideline for the compression of medical images, as compression artifacts vary considerably with image content, scanning technique, and compression algorithm [7]. Some image compression schemes have been adopted by the DICOM standard [8], among which JPEG 2000 [9]. It is based on a reversible integer wavelet transform and it is considered to have the best performance and a few good properties. JPEG 2000 provides both lossy and lossless compressions for images with bit depth no more than 16 bit per channel, and allows progressive transmission with SNR (Signal to Noise Ratio) and spatial scalability. In particular, it supports ROI (Region Of Interest) coding, so that image regions with diagnostic importance can have much higher quality than the other parts.

The codestream obtained after compression of an image with JPEG 2000 is downscalable in nature, meaning that it can be decoded in a number of ways; for instance, by truncating the codestream at any point, one may obtain a representation of the image at a lower resolution, or signal-to-noise ratio. However, as a

* Corresponding author: rodolfo.fiorini@polimi.it

consequence of this flexibility, JPEG 2000 requires encoders/decoders that are complex and computationally demanding. JPEG 2000 has been published as an ISO standard, ISO/IEC 15444. According to Wikipedia, as of 2013, JPEG 2000 is not widely supported in web browsers, and hence is not generally used on the Internet [10]. Traditional lossless compression techniques can be mapped to three main reference areas according to their compression underlining principle: a) Entropy encoding; b) Dictionary; c) Others. The very best modern lossless compressors use probabilistic models, such as prediction by partial matching.

2 Contemporary techniques limitations

As a matter of fact, we can say that almost all contemporary data compression techniques are still based on binary code uncertainty probabilistic evaluation, by treating messages to be encoded as a sequence of independent and identically distributed random variables, according to the probabilistic approach of the father of probabilistic communication theory [11]. Their major points of weakness for contemporary data compression techniques to be used for high demanding lossless applications are:

1) context and data type compression effectiveness and efficiency strong dependence for algorithm optimization;
2) centralized data size compression/decompression speed and space limitations;
3) fixed bit depth for image com/decom processing or just downgrading.

Third point is especially inadequate for discrete tomography and advanced biomedical imaging applications where high data reliability is required, at different bit depth output representation scenarios (for instance, a network with many different output devices with different output bit depth each).

Our main interest is most focused on convenient zero-knowledge universal lossless comp/decomp algorithm for advanced applications as discrete tomography, computed tomography and medical images with true "Arbitrary Bit Depth" (ABD) resolution [5],[6]. No contemporary lossless comp/decomp algorithm is able to satisfy this kind of specification yet. Furthermore it would be a plus to use traditional BD (Bit Depth) settings of images, more efficiently, so that only a small part of the coded bit-stream is needed at the decoder to lossless regenerate and display the original image, with recommended BD parameters for specific need.

3 Combinatorial lossless compression

Human biological transducers, by which we acquire information on the outer world interacting with it, are intrinsically discrete. This means that our perception of continuous shapes is just an illusion created by our mind. From this ground we can infer that an illusion of continuity can be achieved by discrete optimized support, without even noticing any difference, maintaining thus a maximum representation coverage property.

In general, optimization problems can be divided into two large categories depending on whether the variables are continuous or discrete. In solving a classical linear optimization problem (continuous), one can exploit the fact that, due to the convexity of the feasible region, any locally optimal solution is a global optimum.

An optimization problem with discrete variables is known as a combinatorial optimization problem. In a combinatorial optimization problem, we are looking for an object such as an integer, permutation or graph from a finite (or possibly countable infinite) set [12]. In many such problems, exhaustive search is not feasible. It operates on the domain of those optimization problems, in which the set of feasible solutions is discrete or can be reduced to discrete, and in which the goal is to find the best solution. In finding global optima for integer optimization problems, one is required to prove that a particular solution dominates all others by arguments, other than the calculus-based approaches of convex optimization.

While in linear optimization problems, the feasible region is convex, the feasible regions of classical integer optimization problems consists of either a discrete set of points or, in the case of general MILP (Mixed Integer Optimization Problem), a set of disjoint convex polyhedra [13]. Some common problems involving combinatorial optimization are the Traveling Salesman Problem (TSP) and the minimum spanning tree problem. TSP is NP-hard problem in combinatorial optimization, notoriously, and P versus NP problem is a major unsolved problem in computer science [14]. Nevertheless, when a discrete optimized solution is obtained, the discrete approach reveals to be, in this sense, highly convenient because it strongly decreases the computational cost and the complexity of the system for representation modelling. According to computational information conservation theory (*CICT*) [15],[16], in Arithmetic the structure of closure spaces (across an Outer-Inner Universe boundary) is self-defined by Natural Numbers Reciprocal Space (RS) representation [17],[18]. By this way, Natural Number can be thought as both structured object and symbol at the same time.

3.1. Linear arithmetic closure

As a simple example, let us consider a generic fraction N/D, where N and D $\in \boldsymbol{Z}$, and D = $\bar{0}7.\bar{0}$, L an integer counter, N the dividend, Q the quotients and R the remainders of the long hand division. In traditional arithmetic long division algorithm (the one you learn to divide at elementary school), usual dominant result (quotient, Q) is important, and minority components (remainders, R) are always discarded. We can write the L, N, Q and R sequences as from Table 1.

Table 1. L, N, Q, R SEQUENCES.

L	1	2	3	4	5	6	7	8	9	10	11	12	13	14	15...
N	10	20	30	40	50	60	70	80	90	100	110	120	130	140	150...
Q	1	2	4	5	7	8	10	11	12	14	15	17	18	20	21...
R	3	6	2	5	1	4	0	3	6	2	5	1	4	0	3...

for L = 1, 2, 3, ...

In this specific case, we see that the remainder **R** sequence repeats itself after 7 remainders with R(L) given by:

R(1+7n) = R1 = 3, R(2+7n) = R2 = 6, R(3+7n) = R3 = 2, R(4+7n) = R4 = 5, R(5+7n) = R5 = 1, R(6+7n) = R6 = 4, R(7+7n) = R7 = 0 for n = 0,1,2,3,...

Accordingly, we can rearrange the quotients with respect to their cyclic remainder value respectively, obtaining the **R1**, **R2**, **R3**, **R4**, **R5**, **R6**, **R7** sequences as from Table 2.

Table 2. R1, R2, R3, R4, R5. R6, R7 SEQUENCES.

R1	Q1,	Q8,	Q15,	Q22,	Q29,	Q36,	Q43,	Q50,...
R2	Q2,	Q9,	Q16,	Q23,	Q30,	Q37,	Q44,	Q51,...
R3	Q3,	Q10,	Q17,	Q24,	Q31,	Q38,	Q45,	Q52,...
R4	Q4,	Q11,	Q18,	Q25,	Q32,	Q39,	Q46,	Q53,...
R5	Q5,	Q12,	Q19,	Q26,	Q33,	Q40,	Q47,	Q54,...
R6	Q6,	Q13,	Q20,	Q27,	Q34,	Q41,	Q48,	Q55,...
R7	Q7,	Q14,	Q21,	Q28,	Q35,	Q42,	Q49,	Q56,...

In a more compact modular format, we can write:
R(L) = 3 L mod(07) and
D Q(L) = N – R(L), where N = 10 L.
We can interpret the remainders R(L) as the linear (unfolded) arithmetic closure to N with respect to D Q(L).

3.2. Exponential rational closure

For sake of simplicity, at elementary level, let us consider fraction 1/D, where D in ***Z***, or Egyptian fraction, with no loss of generality for common fraction (common fraction is given by Egyptian fraction multiplied by N $\in$ ***Z***, where N is the Numerator) is considered a simple integer division. In traditional rational representation, rational proper quotient is represented by infinite repetition of a basic digit cycle, called "reptend" (the repeating decimal part) [19]. The first repetition of basic digit cycle corresponds to the first full scale interval where number information can be conserved; *CICT* calls it "Representation Fundamental Domain" (RFD) [20]. In general, D, the denominator of the considered OSR (Outer Symbolic Representation) is given by a finite decimal word of length W_D digits. From IOR (Inner OpeRational Representation) X, the related RFD_L can be obtained, by a word length of L_X digits. Elementary number theory considerations give us the usual worst case word length L_X for RFD_L, with no loss of information, by:

$$L_X = D - 1 \qquad (1)$$

digits, if and only if 10 is a primitive root modulo D. Otherwise Lx is a factor of (D-1). If the period of the repeating decimal of 1/D for prime D is equal (D−1) then the repeating decimal part is called "cyclic number" and D can be referred as "primitive number" or "solid number" (SN) in *CICT*, or "full reptend prime" elsewhere [21]. Thus a SN is necessarily prime. It is a sufficient qualification, only. Conversely a prime number may not be a SN. So, the usual worst case word length L_X for X, given by eq.(1), can get RFD_L with no loss of information, related to D, just in case D is SN. With no loss of generality, let us consider, the first Integer to show SN property manifestly, that is number "$\overline{0}7.\overline{0}$". In this case D = 7, so that worst case length analysis gives L_X = D–1 = 6 digits.

By realizing that the remainder R_1 is the fixed multiplicative ratio of a formal power series [06], the computation from generator 3^n (mod7) for n = 1, 2, 3,...., till its exponential closure, gives the sequence the "Fundamental Cyclic Remainder Sequence" (FCRS):

$$R_1 = 3, R_2 = 2, R_3 = 6, R_4 = 4, R_5 = 5, R_6 = 1, \qquad (2)$$

from which the "Fundamental Cyclic Quotient Sequence" (FCQS) can be readily regenerated by 7 * R_n (mod10):

$$Q_1 = 1, Q_2 = 4, Q_3 = 2, Q_4 = 8, Q_5 = 5, Q_6 = 7. \qquad (3)$$

So, quotient and remainder information can always be regenerated anew by remainder information only, but not vice-versa [20].

Therefore, 7 is just a SN and its full information content is usually captured by a six-digit word length RFD_6, for Q_6 and the same for R_6, and the full-information content of long division 1/7 would be stored into two decimal coupled words <Q, R> having length M_{QR} = (6 + 6) digits in total, for exact arbitrary precision computation. As a matter of fact, for all rational sequences, the Remainder R_L, at any computation evolutive stage L_X (accuracy), is the fixed multiplicative ratio of a formal power series associated to the optimized decimal representations of their elementary generators [20]. Thus 1/7 associated information content can be lossless compressed down to minimal M_{QR} = (1 + 1) digits in total, in this specific case. As a matter of fact, any word couple $<Q_L, R_L>$ can be thought to be equivalent to and can represent a different real measurement instrument class, defined by RFD word length L_X. It is easy to see that, in general for SN of order 1 (SN_1 for short), the greater D, the lengthier L_X, and higher the achievable compression ratio E_w.

In this simple case E_w = (2*6)/2 = 6:1, for number 7. By this way, finite length coupled words can provide both finite arbitrary computational precision and relative precision exact error computability in a finite amount of time. By remainder knowledge, it is always possible to regenerate exact quotient and new remainder information at any arbitrary accuracy, with full information conservation. Thanks to the above arithmetic properties, the division algorithm can become free from trial and error like in finite segment *p*-adic representation system, but with no usually associated coding burden [21]. According to our humble knowledge, this is the first time that these arithmetic properties allow this kind of numeric awareness for arithmetic computational system.

All the other members of the 1/7 RFD "Word Family Group" can be derived immediately, by cyclic permutation only, obtaining our result of Fig. 1. So, the final SN_1 Family Group overall information compression ratio is given by $E_f = (2 * 6 * 6)/2 = 36:1$. It does not take a large leap in imagination to suspect that the next larger prime number p to show SN property might be a good candidate for exhibiting cyclic-number property on an even larger scale. Unfortunately there does not seem to be any simple rule dictating which prime number p will have SN_1 property and which will not, so that one just has to check each prime out by long division to see. It turns out that the next higher prime number with the desired SN_1 property is $p = D = 17$ where $T_p = 16$ digits. A search for still larger prime numbers with the same cyclic properties reveals that they are not at all rare. In fact no less than seven more prime numbers smaller than 100 generate cyclic numbers of order one or SN_1. They are: 19, 23, 29, 47, 59, 61 and 97.

1/7	0.	$Q_1=1$	$Q_2=4$	$Q_3=2$	$Q_4=8$	$Q_5=5$	$Q_6=7$
		$R_1=3$	$R_2=2$	$R_3=6$	$R_4=4$	$R_5=5$	$R_6=1$
2/7	0.	$Q_1=2$	$Q_2=8$	$Q_3=5$	$Q_4=7$	$Q_5=1$	$Q_6=4$
		$R_1=6$	$R_2=4$	$R_3=5$	$R_4=1$	$R_5=3$	$R_6=2$
3/7	0.	$Q_1=4$	$Q_2=2$	$Q_3=8$	$Q_4=5$	$Q_5=7$	$Q_6=1$
		$R_1=2$	$R_2=6$	$R_3=4$	$R_4=5$	$R_5=1$	$R_6=3$
4/7	0.	$Q_1=5$	$Q_2=7$	$Q_3=1$	$Q_4=4$	$Q_5=2$	$Q_6=8$
		$R_1=5$	$R_2=1$	$R_3=3$	$R_4=2$	$R_5=6$	$R_6=4$
5/7	0.	$Q_1=7$	$Q_2=1$	$Q_3=4$	$Q_4=2$	$Q_5=8$	$Q_6=5$
		$R_1=1$	$R_2=3$	$R_3=2$	$R_4=6$	$R_5=4$	$R_6=5$
6/7	0.	$Q_1=8$	$Q_2=5$	$Q_3=7$	$Q_4=1$	$Q_5=4$	$Q_6=2$
		$R_1=4$	$R_2=5$	$R_3=1$	$R_4=3$	$R_5=2$	$R_6=6$
7/7	0.	$Q_1=9$	$Q_2=9$	$Q_3=9$	$Q_4=9$	$Q_5=9$	$Q_6=9$
		$R_1=7$	$R_2=7$	$R_3=7$	$R_4=7$	$R_5=7$	$R_6=7$

Fig. 1. Q_n and R_n values for each component of SN_1 Word Family Group 1/7 [06].

Till now we discussed a peculiar number property focusing our attention, for simplicity of presentation, on SN_1 only, but it does not imply that a number has to be a SN_1 in order to generate intriguing cycles. For instance, Family Group 1/13 contains the smallest cyclic-numbers of order two or SN_2. What about more second order cyclics? The basic ones are also generated by a subset of prime fractions $1/p$. The other prime numbers smaller than 100 which generate second order cyclics are 31, 43, 67, 71, 83 and 89. In the same manner one can now go on to define, and find, cyclic numbers of order three, four, five, and higher and higher, according to his own computational needs. The smallest prime number producing the Family Group of third order or SN_3 cyclic-number is 103. In this case, $T_p = 34$ digit string (so we have $3 * 34 = 102$, instead of the unique 102 digit string a first order cyclic would have). The seven smallest primes generating cycles of order four through ten are respectively 53, 11, 79, 211, 41, 73, and 281, but you must reach prime number 353 to get the first prime generating cycle of order 11 or SN_{11}. All the prime numbers less than 100 have now been covered with the exception of $p = 37$, with $T_p = 3$ digits. Therefore 37 is a cyclic number of order 12 or SN_{12}. Multiplication composition of prime numbers can generate an entire universe of new number-cycles. So any modular group can be better represented by generators and relations. One of the earliest presentations of a group by generators and relations was given by the Irish mathematician William Rowan Hamilton in 1856, in his Icosian Calculus, a presentation of the icosahedral group [22], [23]. The first systematic study was given by German mathematician Walther Franz Anton von Dyck (1856–1934) [24], student of German mathematician Christian Felix Klein (1849–1925), in the early 1880s, laying the foundations for combinatorial group theory [25]. Every group has a presentation, and in fact many different presentations; a presentation is often the most compact way of describing the structure of the group. In abstract algebra, the "fundamental theorem of cyclic groups" states that every subgroup of a cyclic group G is cyclic. Moreover, the order "k" of any subgroup of a cyclic group G of order n is a divisor of n, and for each positive divisor "k" of n, the group G has exactly one subgroup of order "k". This is just the first step to start an intriguing voyage from the concept of "presentation of a group" to the concept of "representation theory" for combinatorial modular group theory [26]. Traditional rational number system $\boldsymbol{Q}$ can be regarded as a highly sophisticated open logic, powerful and flexible formal language, with self-defining consistent words and rules, starting from elementary generators and relations [20].

4 Application example

The rich operative scenario offered by combinatorial modular group theory is full of articulated solutions to information processing problems.

Table 3. PICTURE BENCHMARK DATABASE LIST [27].

N.	NAME	PIXELS	SIZE (MB)	BPP
01	artificial	3072x2048	36.80	24
02	big_building	7216x5412	223.36	24
03	big_tree	6088x4550	158.50	24
04	cathedral	2000x3008	34.42	24
05	fireworks	3136x2352	42.21	24
06	flower_foveon	2268x1512	19.62	24
07	hdr	3072x2048	36.80	24
08	leaves_iso_1600	3008x2000	34.42	24
09	leaves_iso_200	3008x2000	34.42	24
10	nightshot_iso_100	3136x2352	42.29	24
11	nightshot_iso_1600	3136x2352	42.29	24
12	spider_web	4256x2848	69.36	24

For instance, Word Family Group SN_1, discussed in the previous section, shows peculiar, cyclical properties that can be conveniently used to get interesting image lossless comp/decomp algorithm. Please, note from Fig.1 that remainder $R_n = a = 1,2, \ldots, p - 1$, can be thought as pointer to Q_n+1 to get the beginning of *a*/D quotient cyclical string immediately, with no computation at all, but the initial one for SN_1 Word Family *p*. Combinatorial optimization is achieved by finding the best $SN_1 = p$ which allow to minimize a desired constraint within a specified interval for each image. Then, *a*/*p* will be best in that no other rational in that specified interval will have a smaller numerator or a smaller denominator. To check our idea, we used an Internet public picture database for 24 bpp color images [27] as reported by Table 3 and Fig.2. Twelve original colour pictures with different dynamic range and different overall content were considered. They are lossless compressed from 24 to 16 bpp by JPEG-LS (Lossless JPEG), JPEG 2000, HD Photo (JPEG XR) algorithms and by ours that is called UC (Universal Compression).

4.1. Lossless compression technical details

Lossless JPEG was developed as a late addition to JPEG in 1993, using a completely different technique from the lossy JPEG standard developed previously. It uses a predictive scheme based on the three nearest (causal) neighbors (upper, left, and upper-left), and entropy coding is used on the prediction error.

Fig. 2. Pictures in Benchmark Database as from Table 1, for our application example [27].

The standard Independent JPEG Group libraries cannot encode or decode it, but Ken Murchison of Oceana Matrix Ltd. wrote a patch that extends the IJG library to handle Lossless JPEG. It has some popularity in medical imaging, and is used in DNG (Adobe) and some digital cameras to compress raw images, but otherwise was never widely adopted. It might be used as an umbrella term to refer to all lossless compression schemes developed by the Joint Photographic Expert group. They include JPEG 2000 and JPEG-LS.

JPEG-LS is a lossless/near-lossless compression standard for continuous-tone images. Its official designation is ISO-14495-1/ITU-T.87. It is a simple and efficient baseline algorithm which consists of two independent and distinct stages called modeling and encoding. It was developed with the aim of providing a low-complexity lossless and near-lossless image compression standard that could offer better compression efficiency than JPEG. At the time, the Huffman coding-based JPEG lossless standard and other standards were limited in their compression performance. Total decorrelation cannot be achieved by first order entropy of the prediction residuals employed by these inferior standards. JPEG-LS, on the other hand, can obtain good decorrelation. Part 1 of this standard was finalized in 1999. Part 2, released in 2003, introduced extensions such as arithmetic coding. The core of JPEG-LS is based on the LOCO-I algorithm [28] that relies on prediction, residual modeling and context-based coding of the residuals. Most of the low complexity of this technique comes from the assumption that prediction residuals follow a two-sided geometric distribution (also called a discrete Laplace distribution) and from the use of Golomb-like codes, which are known to be approximately optimal for geometric distributions. Besides lossless compression, it also provides a lossy mode ("near-lossless") where the maximum absolute error can be controlled by the encoder. Compression for JPEG-LS is generally faster than JPEG 2000 and much better than the original lossless JPEG standard. Here JPEG-LS is used for historical reason comparison, JPEG 2000 provides lossless compressions for images with bit depth no more than 16 bit per channel, and allows progressive transmission with signal-to-noise ratio (SNR) and spatial scalability. In particular, it supports ROI (Region Of Interest) coding, so that image regions with diagnostic importance can have much higher quality than the other parts. The codestream obtained after compression of an image with JPEG 2000 is downscalable in nature, meaning that it can be decoded in a number of ways; for instance, by truncating the codestream at any point, one may obtain a representation of the image at a lower resolution, or SNR. However, as a consequence of this flexibility, JPEG 2000 requires encoders/decoders that are complex and computationally demanding.

HD Photo slgorithm is based on technology originally developed and patented by Microsoft. It supports deep color images with 48-bit RGB, both lossy and lossless compression, and is the preferred image format for Ecma-388 Open XML Paper Specification documents. HD Photo offers several major key improvements over JPEG, including better compression, lossless compression, tile structured support, more color accuracy, transparency map and metadata support. HD Photo is conceptually very similar to JPEG: the source image is optionally converted to a luma-chroma colorspace, the chroma planes are optionally subsampled, each plane is divided into fixed-size blocks, the blocks are transformed into the frequency domain, and the frequency coefficients are quantized and entropy coded. In July 2007, the Joint Photographic Experts

Group and Microsoft announced HD Photo to be under consideration to become a JPEG standard known as JPEG XR. On 16 March 2009, JPEG XR was given final approval as ITU-T Recommendation T.832 and starting in April 2009, it became available from the ITU-T in "pre-published" form. On 19 June 2009, it passed an ISO/IEC Final Draft International Standard (FDIS) ballot, resulting in final approval as International Standard ISO/IEC 29199-2. The ITU-T updated its publication with a corrigendum approved in December 2009, and ISO/IEC issued a new edition with similar corrections on 30 September 2010. In 2010, after completion of the image coding specification, the ITU-T and ISO/IEC also published a motion format specification (ITU-T T.833|ISO/IEC 29199-3), a conformance test set (ITU-T T.834|ISO/IEC 29199-4), and reference software (ITU-T T.835|ISO/IEC 29199-5) for JPEG XR. In 2011, they published a technical report describing the workflow architecture for the use of JPEG XR images in applications (ITU-T T.Sup2|ISO/IEC TR 29199-1). In April 2013, Microsoft released an open source JPEG XR library under the BSD licence. As of August 2014, there were still no cameras that shoot photos in the Jpeg XR (.JXR) format.

UC provides lossless compressions for images with arbitrary bit depth (ABD) per channel, and allows progressive transmission with SNR and spatial scalability, at no extra cost. Specifically, it supports ROI (Region Of Interest) coding, so that image regions with diagnostic importance can have much higher quality than the other parts. The codestream obtained after compression of an image with UC is downscalable and upscalable in nature, meaning that it can be decoded in a number of ways; for instance, by truncating the codestream at any point, one may obtain a representation of the image at a lower resolution, or signal-to-noise ratio. Different from all other algorithms, this time, if you have local computational resources, you can regenerate the original information arbitrarily to higher BD. As a consequence of this flexibility, you do have to pay no extra cost!

4.2. Results and discussion

Compression results for 24 to 16 bpp lossless compression of the twelve database pictures reported in Table 3, with different content and different extended dynamic each, show that, on average, UC takes about 17% more space than JPEG 2000. Nevertheless UC shows compression speed about 17% faster than JPEG 2000 on average. In order to achieve an overall evaluation and a fair comparison between so different algorithms, we define the key performance index (KPI) given by compressed bit-per-pixel (bpp) times compression time (s, in second) for each picture, where:

$$KPI = bpp \times s \quad . \qquad (4)$$

Our first raw results, with no further algorithm refinement out of cyclic family computation only, as described in Section 3.2, show that overall UC KPI compare quite well to HD Photo and it is better than traditional JPEG 2000, with no further algorithmic development effort or computational load.

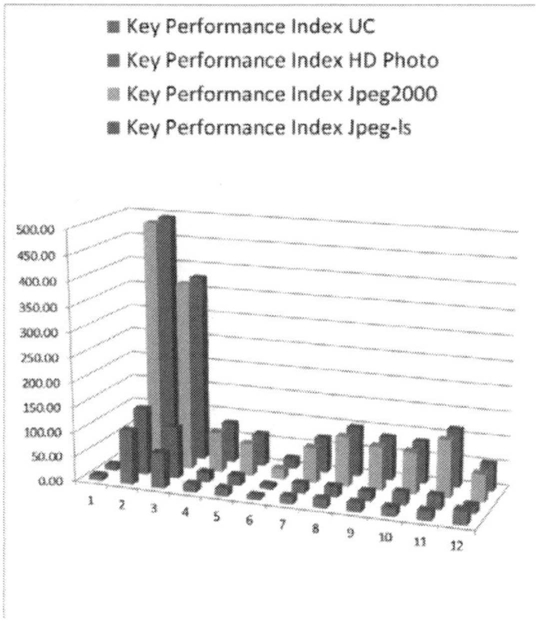

Fig. 3. KPI 24 to 16 bpp lossless compression result for JPEG-LS, JPEG 2000, HD Photo and UC algorithms (from back to front respectively): ordinate in KPI units, abscissa number ordering refers to picture list as from Table 1.

The only image where UC KPI is greater than HD Photo KPI is picture number 12, the "spider_web" picture shown in Fig.4. As you can see from that picture, different from all other picture in our Benchmark Database, there are a lot of linear, finer details with delicate superpositions embedded in it and HD Photo algorithm can take advantage from them quite easily.

Fig. 4. Spider_web picture as n.12 test picture in our Picture Benchmark Database.

UC is a zero-knowledge universal lossless compression algorithm that does not use linear a priori knowledge to achieve better result. Therefore, for general purpose application raw UC on average can perform better than HD Photo, but for pictures full of superposed linear, finer details it cannot compete with HD Photo. Nevertheless, raw UC algorithm parameters have not yet been quite tuned for overall optimum performance, so there is still room for further improvement. UC exploits arbitrary bit depth (ABD) per channel and full information conservation and regeneration by design. UC method differs from the existing ones in three main features. First, it is not a traditional extended bit depth encoding/decoding and does not use Gray-Golomb coding to support progressive transmission as in VOI (Value Of Interest) approaches [29].

Second, UC scheme can utilize dynamic BD settings for original images to support dynamic BD scalability, which allows pixels to be progressively reconstructed in the order according to their display importance. Pixel reconstruction can be centralized or decentralized, local or global. Third, we can consider end-user display computational resource availability, for end-point information regeneration and network bandwidth minimization. Different from all other algorithms, not only a downscaling, but even an upscaling is possible by UC information conservation and regeneration. For images with extended bit-depth, the pixel values can be displayed after BD mapping to fit the display bit depth. Thus only pixels with interested values can be visually important, under certain predefined BD parameters.

5 Conclusion

We have presented results on an universal zero-knowledge combinatorial lossless compression scheme called UC, for extended dynamic range images, with arbitrary bit depth, based on information conservation and regeneration according to *CICT* by design. Its raw overall zero-knowledge lossless compression performance compare quite well to standard ones, but offering true ABD and achieving full image information conservation and regeneration, at no extra cost, without complex and computationally demanding encoders/decoders.

References

1. N. Reims, T. Schoen, M. Boehnel, F. Sukowski, M. Firsching, Proc. of SPIE "Optics + Photonics", Soc. Photo-Opt. Instr. Eng., 921209 (2014).
2. K.J. Batenburg, J. Sijbers, IEEE Trans. Image Process. **20**(9), 2542 (2011).
3. K.J. Batenburg, S. Bals, J. Sijbers, C. Kübel, P.A. Midgley, J.C. Hernandez, U. Kaiser, E.R. Encina, E.A. Coronado, G. Van Tendeloo, Ultramicr. **109**, 730 (2009).
4. M.H. Kryder, S.K. Chang, IEEE Trans. Mag. **45**(10) (October 2009). Available at:<URL= http://isites.harvard.edu/fs/docs/icb.topic1195323.files/After_Hard_Drives.pdf>.
5. D.A. Koff, H. Shulman, Can. assoc. of radiologists jour. **57**, 211 (2006).
6. M.J. Zukoski, T. Boult, T. Iyriboz, Int. J. of Bioinf. Research and Applications **2**(1), 89 (2006).
7. T.J. Kim, K.H. Lee, B. Kim, E.J. Chun, V. Baipal, Y.H. Kim, S. Hahn, K.W. Lee, Eur. J. Radiol. **69**(3), 483 (2009).
8. The DICOM standard, (2009). Available at:<URL= http://dicom.nema.org/dicom>.
9. ISO/IEC 15444 (2007). Available at:<URL= https://www.iso.org/standard/41570.html>.
10. Wikipedia, Jpeg2000 (2017). Available at:<URL= https://en.wikipedia.org/wiki/JPEG_2000>.
11. C.E. Shannon, Bell Syst. Tech. J. **27**(3) 379 (July/October 1948).
12. A. Schrijver, (2017). Available at:<URL= http://homepages.cwi.nl/~lex/files/dict.pdf>.
13. K.L. Hoffman, T.K. Ralphs, (2012). Available at:<URL=http://coral.ie.lehigh.edu/~ted/files/papers/ICO-EORMS11.pdf>.
14. L. Fortnow, Comm. ACM **52**(9), 78 (2009).
15. R.A. Fiorini, in N.E. Mastorakis, M. Demiralp, N. Mukhopadhyay, F. Mainardi, Eds., *Advances in Applied mathematics, Modelling and Simulation, Mathematical and Computers in Science and Engineering Series n.34* (Florence, Italy, WSEAS Press, 385-394, 2014).
16. R.A. Fiorini, Intern. J. Syst. Applications, Eng. and Dev. **9**, 93 (2015). Available at:<URL= http://www.naun.org/main/UPress/saed/2015/a305994003.pdf>.
17. R.A. Fiorini, Fundam. Inform. **135**(1-2),135 (2014).
18. R.A. Fiorini, G. Laguteta, in V. Mladenov, Ed., *Proceedings of the 19th International Conference on Systems* (Zakynthos Island, Greece, 648-655, 2015).
19. E.W. Weisstein, (1999-2012). Available at:<URL= http://mathworld.wolfram.com/FullReptendPrime.html>.
20. R.A. Fiorini, G. Laguteta, Fundam. Inform. **125**(3-4), 261 (2013).
21. D.M. Young, R.T. Gregory, *A Survey of Numerical Mathematics, vol.I and II* (Reading, Mass.: Addison Wesley, 1973).
22. W.R. Hamilton, Phil. Mag. **12**, 446 (1856).
23. B. Chandler, W. Magnus, *The History of Combinatorial Group Theory: A Case Study in the History of Ideas, Studies in the History of Mathematics and Physical Sciences* (1st ed., Springer, 234, December 1, 1982).
24. W. von Dyck, Math. Ann. **20**(1), 1 (1882).
25. J. Stillwell, *Mathematics and its history* (Springer 2002).
26. C.W. Curtis, *Pioneers of Representation Theory: Frobenius, Burnside, Schur, and Brauer, History of Mathematics* (Providence, R.I.: American Mathematical Society, 2003).
27 The New Test Images for Image Compression Benchmark (Jan 2008). Available at:<URL= http://www.imagecompression.info/test_images>.
28. M. Weinberger, G. Seroussi, G. Sapiro, IEEE Trans. Im. Proc. **9**(8), 1309 (Aug. 2000). Available at:<URL= http://www.labs.hp.com/research/info_theory/loco/>. <URL= http://www.labs.hp.com/research/info_theory/loco/HPL-98-193R1.pdf>.
29. W. Sun, Y. Lu, W. Feng, L. Shipeng, IEEE, ICIP, 1749, (2009). Available at:<URL: http://toc.proceedings.com/07230webtoc.pdf>.

Design and study of a microstrip slot antenna operating at 2.8/3.1/3.6/4.7/5.4 GHz

Angel Lozada[1*], *Andrés* Piedrahita[2], *Gloria* Russi

[1]Electronic Engineering, Faculty of Engineering, Central Unit of the Valley of Cauca, Tuluá, Colombia.
[2]Informatic Engineering, Faculty of Engineering, Central Unit of the Valley of Cauca, Tuluá, Colombia.

Abstract. A novel design of a multi band microstrip antenna is presented in this work. The double modified U slots planar patch antenna is designed, simulated and fabricated to operate at 2.8 GHz (between 2.794 to 2.846 GHz), at 3.1 GHz (between 3.145 to 3.196 GHz), at 3.6 GHz (between 3.56 to 3.3.644 GHz), at 4.7 GHz (between 4.684 to 4.772 GHz) and at 5.4 GHz (between 5.423 to 5.526 GHz) for WiMAX/WLAN applications. One of the main challenges was keeping a low profile and low cost substrate (1.2mm and FR4 respectively) with penta-band frequency response without scarifying these characteristics. Each resonant frequency is accomplished by modifying each U slot and patch radiator itself. Simulations had been conducted using HFSS software and measured parameters such as reflection coefficient (S11 parameter) was performed with a vector network analyzer. Measured results confirm simulated results that the antenna could work within mentioned frequencies. Parametric study was conducted in order to study the effect of slots variation over the design.

1 Introduction

As a result of development of wireless and satellite communication systems, came out the miniaturization of electronic components and therefore the appearance of microstrip technology and its antennas [1]–[4]. These miniaturization in telecommunications has become more evident during the last 35 years impulsed by low profile devices such as smartphones [5], radio frequency identification systems (RIFD) [6], wearable devices [7], and so on; reason why studying, designing and fabricating microstrip antennas (MSA) still receive attention by researchers around the world. Part of this attention recalls to overcome MSA disadvantages such as low gain, narrow bandwidth and so on; and improve its advantages such as low profile, low cost, capable to work at multi-frequency bands, among other characteristics; enabling these structures to be applied on current wireless communication system.

Multiband microstrip antennas are required because current and future devices must be able to communicate each other through different standards, which mean different frequencies band [8], also the antennas used at base stations use array microstrip antenna to deploy telecommunications networks, satellite communication antennas, along with other applications. In order to achieve multi-frequency response several techniques have been applied such as electromagnetic band gap structure (EBG) [9], ring resonator, defected ground structure antenna (DGS) [10], multilayer antenna, reconfigurable antennas [11], slots antennas [12], etc. Among these variety of designs, slot antennas offer several advantages such as keeping a low profile structure, single designs (which makes available for mass fabrication), bandwidth improvements, multi-frequency response along other antenna improvements. But within slots antenna technique there are options designs to achieve researcher's goal. Some of these options are design the patch radiator with alphabet letter shape such as, L shape [13], S shape [6], F shape [14] and U shape [15]–[17] among others. In this paper, a modified double U slot planar microstrip antenna is designed, simulated and fabricated to operate at 2.8/3.1/3.6/4.7/5.4 GHz for wireless communication such as WiMAX/WLAN applications.

2 Antenna design

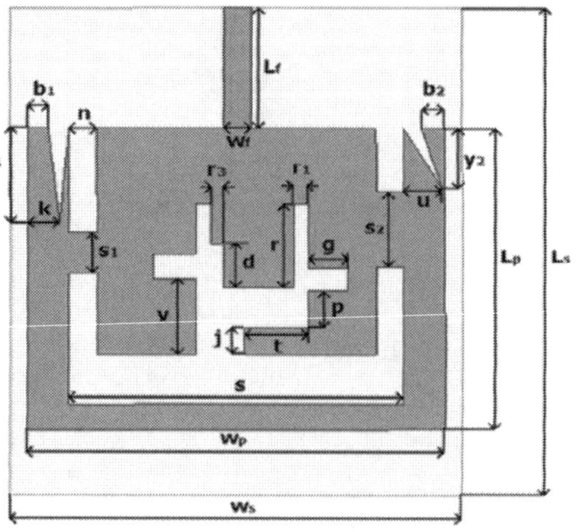

Fig. 1 Antenna Design Parameters

* Corresponding author: alozada@uceva.edu.co

DOI: 10.1051/matecconf/201712503003

The geometry of the proposed antenna is shown in Fig. 1. The antenna is designed and simulated on a FR4 substrate with relative permittivity $\varepsilon_r = 4.4$; the substrate is easy to get in domestic market and also less expensive than other used antenna substrates for high-frequency applications, with a thickness h = 1.2mm, and a loss tangent δ = 0.02 using HFSSv17.2 which is based on Finite Element Method (FEM), the rest of parameters are summarized in Table 1and Table 2.

Table 1 Parameters Design

Parameter	Value (mm)	Parameter	Value (mm)
Ls	38.8	n	2
Ws	32.5	k	2.3
h	1.2	s1	3.2
Lp	24	s	24
Wp	30	s2	6
Wf	2	b2	1.7
Lf	9.6	y2	4.8
b1	1.5	u	2.8
y1	5.5	r2	0.9

Table 2 Parameters Design

Parameter	Value (mm)
d	3.5
v	6
j	2.1
t	4.6
p	3
g	2.9
r3	6.7
r2	1.1

Based on [15]–[20], the U slot technique offers the opportunity to get multi-frequency operation in the same way as the slots allow to add one or more resonance frequency or shift them to desired ones keeping a low profile antenna, however most of those designs are fed by coaxial connector and either patch radiator or slots are no modified in deed. Moreover, other designs [21]–[23] shows U slots patch antenna feeding by stripline getting compact design and multi-frequency response. For this reason the mentioned technique is used to get multiband operation in current research.

3 Simulation results

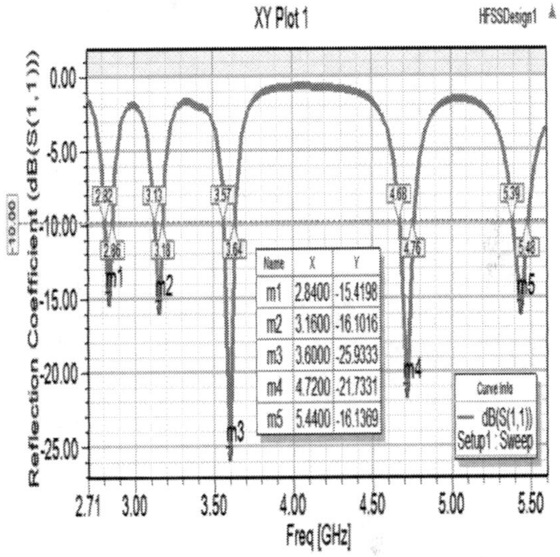

Fig. 2 Reflection Coefficient (S11 Parameter)

Based on reflection coefficient results (S11 parameter curve) of Fig. 2, it is emphasized that at the 1st frequency band of 2.8 GHz the resulting impedance bandwidth is going from 2.817 to 2.863 GHz, getting the lower reflection coefficient of -15.4198dB at 2.84 GHz, at 2nd frequency band of 3.1 GHz the impedance bandwidth is going from 3.131 to 3.184 GHz with the lower reflection coefficient of -16.1016dB at 3.16 GHz, at the 3rd frequency band of 3.6 GHz the impedance bandwidth is going from 3.565 to 3.636 GHz with the lower reflection coefficient of -25.9333dB at 3.6 GHz, at the 4th frequency band of 4.7 GHz the impedance bandwidth is going from 4.677 to 4.76 GHz with the lower reflection coefficient of -21.7331dB at 4.72 GHz, and at the 5th frequency band of 5.4 GHz the impedance bandwidth is going from 5.389 to 5.483 GHz with the lower reflection coefficient of -16.1369dB at 5.44 GHz to operate for WiMAX and WLAN applications.

In order to further study the penta-band operation properties of the proposed antenna, surface current distributions (A/m) of the whole antenna at frequencies of 6 (solution frequency), 2.8, 3.1, 3.6, 4.7 and 5.4 GHz are given in Fig. 4–9.

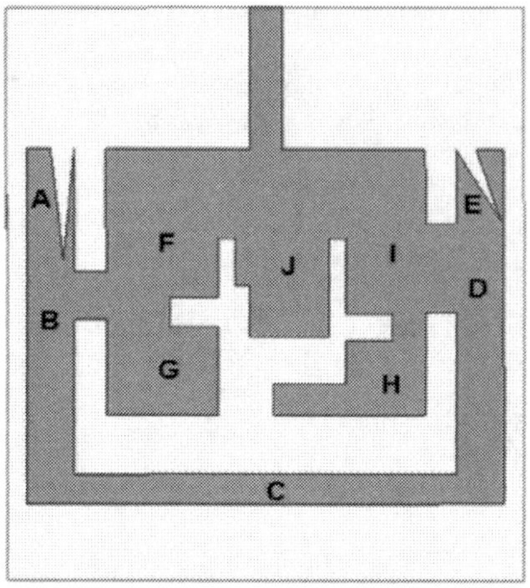

Fig. 3 Antenna Regions

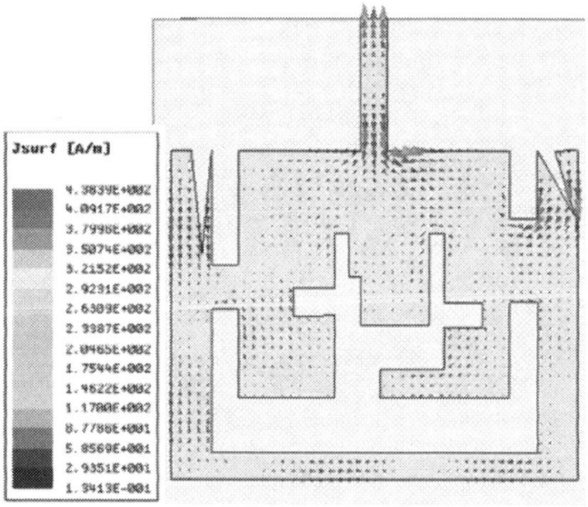

Fig. 4 Vector of Surface Current Density at 6 GHz

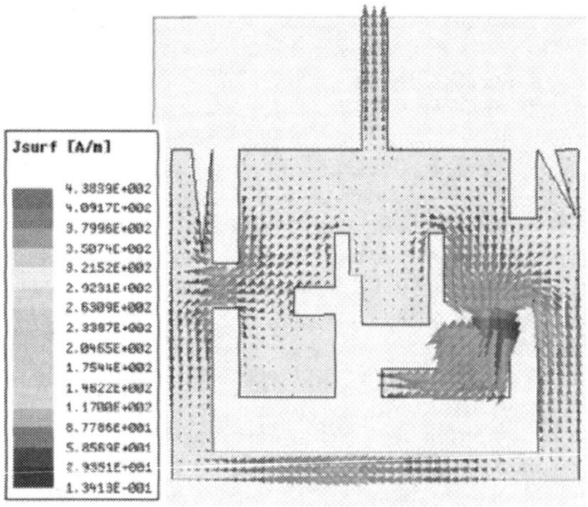

Fig. 5 Vector of Surface Current Density at 2.84 GHz

It can be clearly seen from these figures that the current distributions are different in all frequencies. The antenna has been divided in several regions (A~J) as is shown in Fig. 3 for better understanding on current density paths.

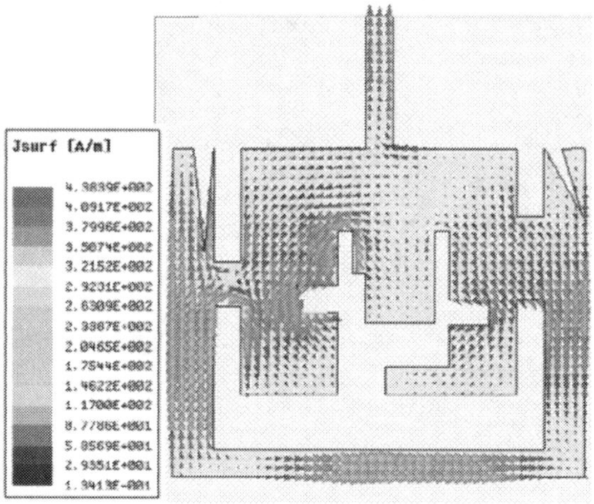

Fig. 6 Vector of Surface Current Density at 3.16 GHz

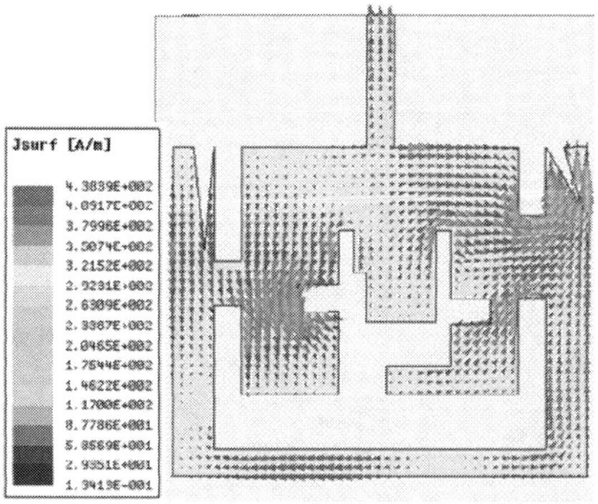

Fig. 7 Vector of Surface Current Density at 3.6 GHz

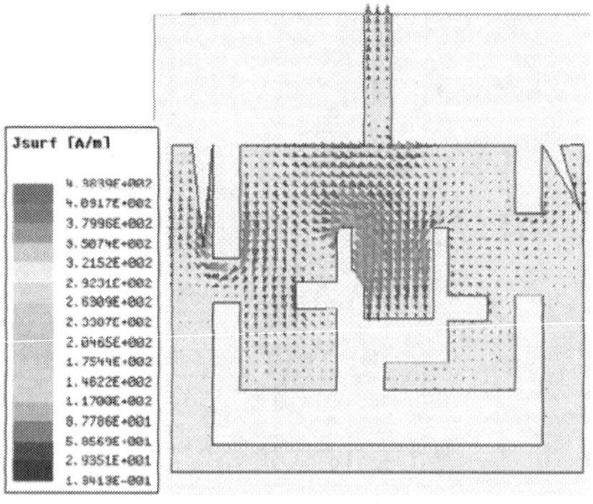

Fig. 8 Vector of Surface Current Density at 4.72 GHz

In Fig. 4 for instance, the current has a very low flow and magnitude, which means that the patch radiator is not excited at this frequency as is it was expected. But, when the antenna operates at 2.8 GHz it was noticed that the current flows from I and D to H region where is mainly concentrated having the strongest magnitude, also is possible to observe a moderate current density flowing from F to B region and from right to left of C region as is shown in Fig. 5. This clearly indicates the importance of the slots defined by g, p, s_2 and t parameters on the proposed antenna resonance response.

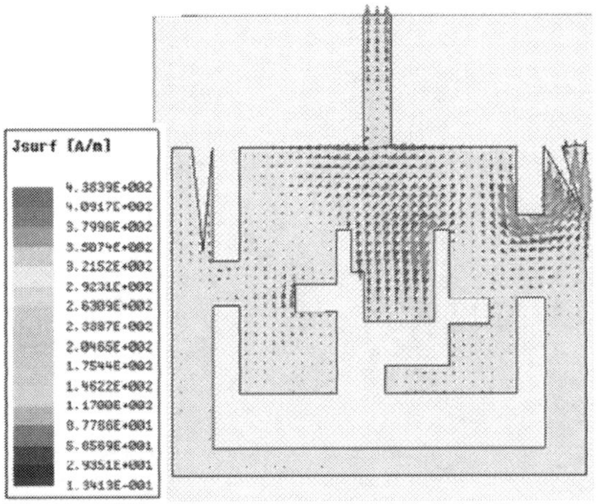

Fig. 9 Vector of Surface Current Density at 5.44 GHz

Fig. 6 shows that the current has uniform distribution at B, C, D, F and G regions. The current paths flows from upper to lower side of B region, from left to right side of C region, from lower to upper side of D region and from F to G region, acting these areas as the resonator for the antenna at 3.6 GHz. At 3.6 GHz the current is flowing from I, H and D regions to E region, also from F to G region, making possible to observed the highest current magnitude at E and G regions and weak magnitude at A, B and C regions, making E and G regions antenna resonate at mentioned band as is shown Fig. 7 which makes the antenna resonate at this frequency.

Fig. 8 shows that the surface current is going from F to J region with highest magnitude and concentration at J region which mean this area is excited and resonate at 4.7 GHz. The J and E regions acts as resonator at 5.4 GHz as the flow path of surface current is going from I to E region and from upper side to lower side of J region, concentrating the highest density and magnitude at mentioned frequency as is shown in Fig. 9.

Controlling the reactance inductive and reactance capacitive contributions of each slot it is possible to do by modifying width, length and position of these structures, which mean that currents path is also modified. Therefore, resonance frequencies can be controlled towards higher and or lower ones.

Introducing slots on the antenna patch modified the current path and so can be used to generate and multiple resonance frequencies band, for WiMAX and WLAN applications.

The gain radiation pattern at solution frequency is shows in Fig. 10. Maximum gain occur at $\varphi = 190$ and $\varphi = 360$ degrees.

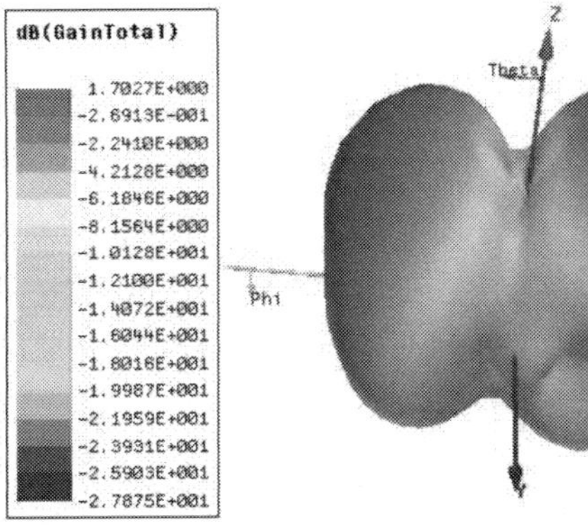

Fig. 10 Gain-Radiation Pattern

4 Parametric Study

Parametric study of planar patch microstrip antenna is conducted by varying the width, length and position of slots antenna to understand how it does affects these variations over the resonance frequencies, impedance bandwidth and reflection coefficient values

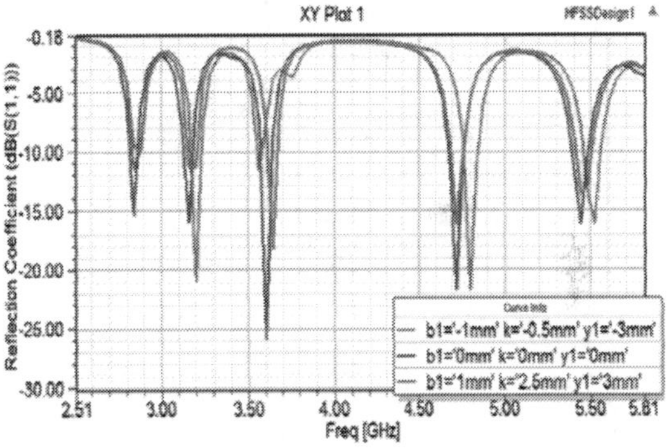

Fig. 11 Parameters b1, k and y1.

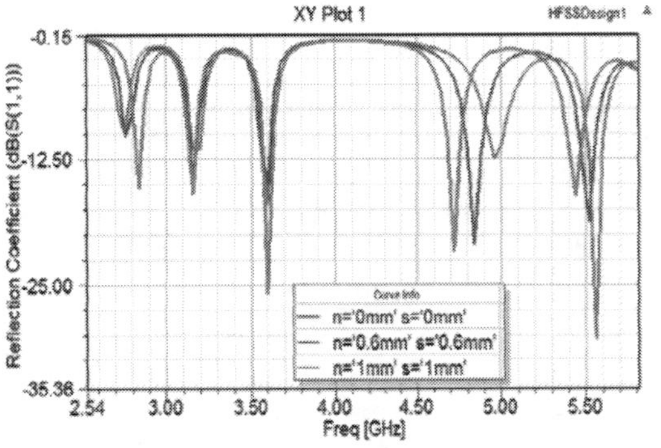

Fig. 12 Parameters n and s.

As it can be seen from Fig. 11 it is possible to study the effects of the slot variations defined by parameters *b1*, *k* and *y1*.

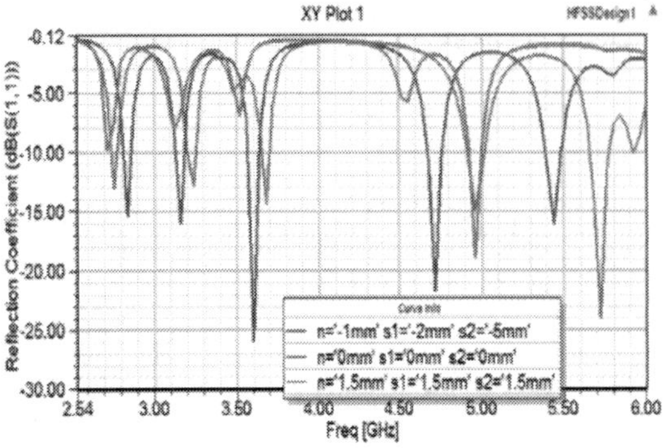

Fig. 13 Parameters n, s1 and s2

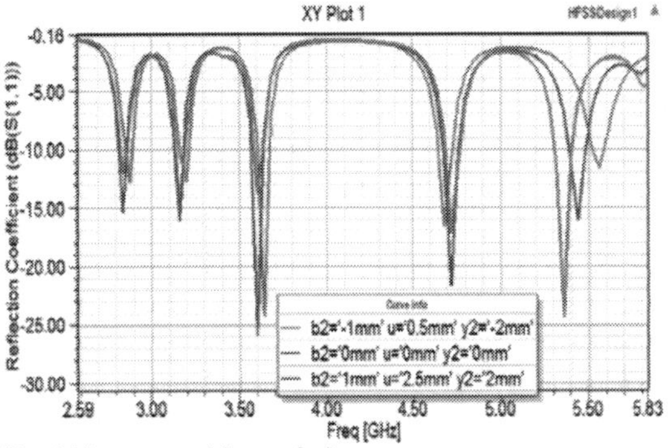

Fig. 14 Parameters b2, u and y2

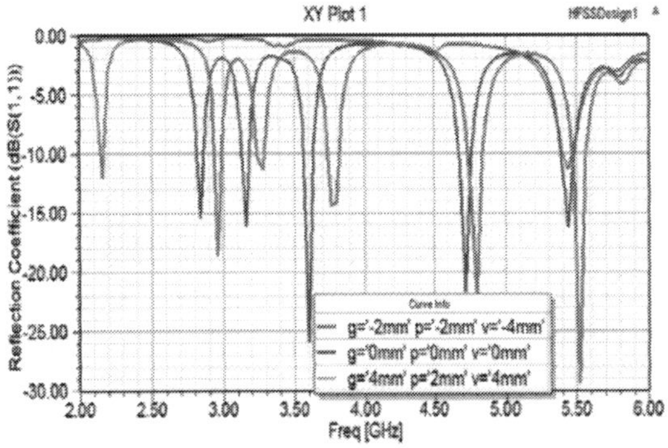

Fig. 15 Parameters g, p and v

When mentioned parameters decrease, the reflection coefficient values for all frequencies increase compare with same parameters without modifications, and the 1st frequency is suppressed; but when the parameters increase their dimensions is possible to observe that the 4th and 5th resonant frequencies are moved toward higher ones and 1st and 3rd frequencies have higher reflection coefficient values. It is also possible to observe that at 2nd, 4th and 5th frequency the reflection coefficient values are lower or equal than without modifications.

As either parameters increase or decrease, the impedance bandwidth shown in most cases a decrement. When parameters *n* and *s* increase their dimensions from 0 to 0.6 and then to 1 mm, the 4th and 5th frequency changes toward higher ones, also is possible to evidence that the 1st, 2nd, 3rd and 4th frequencies increase their reflection coefficient values suppressing the 1st frequency band as is shown in Fig. 12.

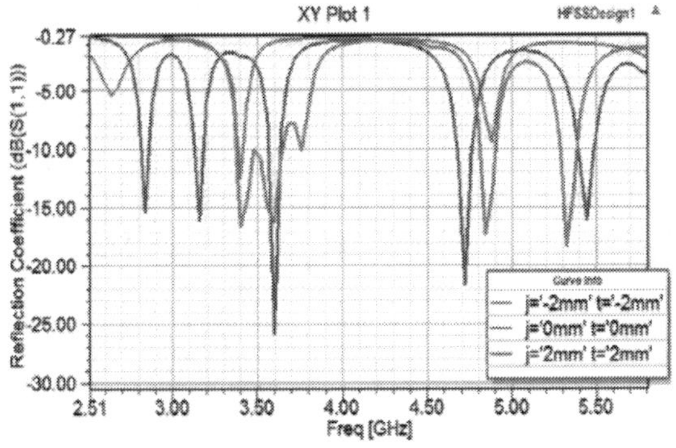

Fig. 16 Parameters j and t

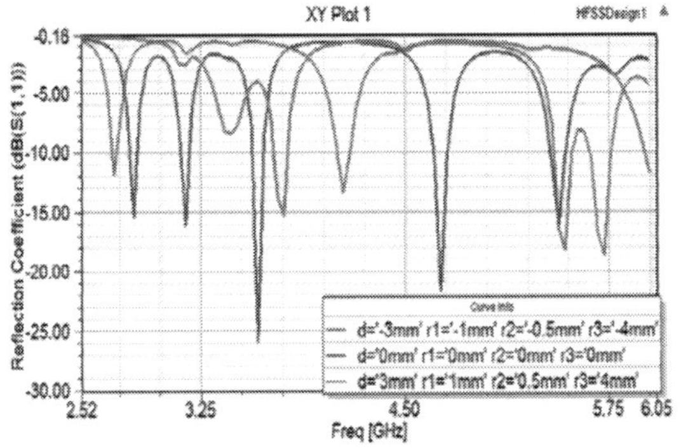

Fig. 17 Parameters d, r1, r2 and r3.

Fig. 13 shows the results of variation parameters of *n*, *s1* and *s2*. When the slot parameters decrease, it shows the suppression of frequencies 1st to 4th (return loss greater than -10B) and the 5th frequency is shifted to 4.9 GHz, but when slots dimension increase the resonating frequency is shift to higher frequency band (from 2nd to 5th frequency band) but the 1st frequency changes to lower resonance frequency).

The effects of slot parameters defined by *b2*, *u* and *y2* are simulated as is shown in Fig. 14. Decreasing slots dimension defined by the mentioned parameters are reflected by the increment of reflection coefficient values for 1st to 4th frequency band and decrement and shifting to lower resonating of 5th frequency band, but the increment of slot dimension mean an increment of reflection coefficient for all frequencies.

When slot dimension defined by *g*, *p* and *v* decreases the antenna exhibit a shift to higher frequencies for the five bands, however when variations include the increment of slot dimensions the antenna resonate at two bands at 2.2 GHz and 5.4 GHz band as the other three frequencies are suppressed at all as is shown in the Fig. 15.

As Fig. 16 shows, there is a shift toward to higher resonance frequencies when parameters g, p and v decrease their values and the antenna become a dual band antenna when mentioned parameters decrease their values suppressing the other three frequencies band.

DOI: 10.1051/matecconf/201712503003

A suppression of four frequencies is shown in Fig. 17 when the parameters d, r_1, r_2 and r_3 present a decrement of their dimensions making the antenna resonate at only one frequency band (3.7 GHz) suppressing the other four; but when parameters increase their values, the antenna resonate at four frequencies. It can be also observed a remarkable difference between parameters variations results, indicating a highly sensitivity of mentioned parameters to these variations.

5 Fabrication and Measurement

The antenna was made using the LPKF ProtoMat S103 circuit board plotter for producing PCB/antenna prototypes. Once the antenna was fabricated (top and bottom view of fabricated antenna are shown in Fig. 18, the reflection coefficient parameter was measured (S11).

As shown in Fig. 19 there is a good agreement between simulated and measured results. Some discrepancies can be seen between the simulated and measured results, which may occur because the effect of the SMA connector, the fabrication imperfections and the measurement calibration while using the VNA.

Fig. 18 Top View Fabricated Microstrip Antenna

The antenna resonate at 2.8 GHz (between 2.794 to 2.846 GHz), at 3.1 GHz (between 3.145 to 3.196 GHz), at 3.6 GHz (between 3.56 to 3.3.644 GHz), at 4.7 GHz (between 4.684 to 4.772 GHz) and at 5.4 GHz (between 5.423 to 5.526 GHz) for WiMAX/WLAN applications.

In this design, if the slots are absent, the antenna will only have one major current path on each of the patch elements. However, in the presence of the current slots, the current path on each of the patch elements is disturbed and perturbed, hence creating the penta-band operation.

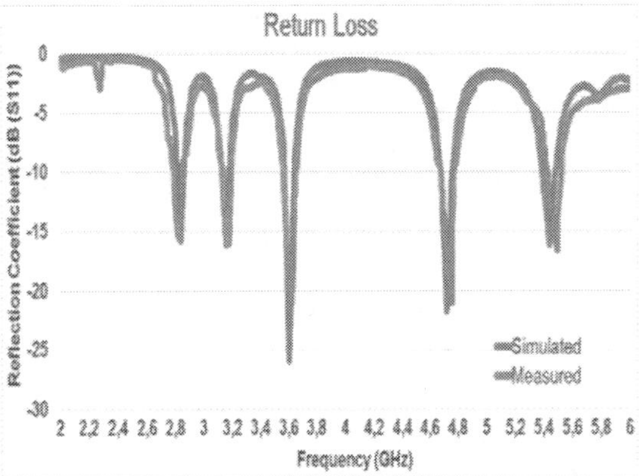

Fig. 19 Simulated vs Measured Results

3 Conclusions

In the current work, a penta-band antenna with two modified U slots is designed, simulated and fabricated without modifying the ground plane, keeping a low profile (1.2mm) and using a low cost substrate (FR4). The antenna parameters were simulated using HFSS software and measurements were developed with a Vector Network Analyzer for impedance matching. Simulated and measured results shows that the antenna resonate at 2.8 GHz (between 2.794 to 2.846 GHz), at 3.1 GHz (between 3.145 to 3.196 GHz), at 3.6 GHz (between 3.56 to 3.3.644 GHz), at 4.7 GHz (between 4.684 to 4.772 GHz) and at 5.4 GHz (between 5.423 to 5.526 GHz) for WiMAX/WLAN applications.

Slots played a key role as they control the resonance frequencies. Adjusting accordingly width length and position modified current distribution concentrated at slots and then modifying the resonance frequencies, facilitating the antenna resonate at other three frequencies.

Therefore, the designed antenna can work within WiMAX and WLAN compliance applications. Current antenna may work as a reference for future works related to optimization and improvement of slotted planar patch antennae looking to miniaturize current dimensions, improve gain or modifying other desired characteristic aiming to improve it

References

[1] G. Kumar and K. P. Ray, Broadband Microstrip Antenna. Artech House, (2003).

[2] T. Milligan, Modern Antenna Design, 2nd Ed. Jhon Wiley & Sons, Innc., (2005).

[3] C. Balanis, Antenna Theory. Analysis and Design. John Wwiley & Ssons, INC., (2005).

[4] A. Lozada and S. Donglin, “Microstrip Antenna for Satellite Communications,” in International Symposium on Antennas, Propagation and EM Theory, (2008), pp. 1–3.

[5] S. Sultan, S. Imran, C. Xiaodong, and P. Clive, “Compact and Printed Multiband Antennas for 2G/3G/4G Smartphones,” in International Symposium

on Antennas and Propagation & USNC/URSI National Radio Science Meeting, (2015), pp. 1138–1139.
[6] M. A. Ennasar, I. Aznabet, M. Essaaidi, and M. Group, "A Compact Modified S-Shaped RFID Tag Antenna for Metallic Applications," in IEEE 15th Mediterranean Microwave Symposium (MMS), (2015), pp. 8–10.
[7] S. Ha and C. W. Jung, "Single patch beam steering antenna with U-slot for wearable fabric applications," in IEEE International Symposium on Antennas and Propagation (APSURSI), (2011), pp. 1560–1562.
[8] U. Shameem, M. Ur-rehman, Q. H. Abbasi, and K. Qaraqe, "A Low Profile Penta-band Antenna For Portable Devices," in International Workshop on Antenna Technology (iWAT), (2016), pp. 174–177.
[9] L. Peng, C. L. Ruan, and J. Xiong, "Compact EBG for multi-band applications," IEEE Trans. Antennas Propag., vol. 60, no. 9, pp. 4440–4444, (2012).
[10] L. X. Truong and Tran Minh Tuan, "Design A Microstrip Antenna With Defected Ground Structure," in 2015 International Conference on Advanced Technologies for Communications (ATC) Design, (2015), pp. 160–163.
[11] M. Borhani, P. Rezaei, and A. Valizade, "Design of A Reconfigurable Miniaturized Microstrip Antenna for Switchable Multiband Systems," IEEE Antennas Wirel. Propag. Lett., vol. 1225, no. c, pp. 1–1, (2015).
[12] M. Chang and W. Weng, "A Printed Multi-band Slot Antenna for LTE / WLAN Applications," in IEEE International Symposium on Antennas and Propagation & USNC/URSI National Radio Science Meeting, (2015), pp. 1144–1145.
[13] M. Nirmen and I. H. Ehab K., "Tri-Band Microstrip Antenna with L-Shaped Slots for Bluetooth / WLAN / WiMAX Applications," 33 rd Natl. Radio Sci. Conf. (NRSC (2016)), no. Nrsc, pp. 73–80, (2016).
[14] A. K. Gautam, L. Kumar, and B. K. Kanaujia, "Design of Compact F-Shaped Slot Triple-Band Antenna for WLAN / WiMAX Applications," Trans. Antennas Propag., vol. 64, no. 3, pp. 1101–1105, (2016).
[15] Y. Zimu, Z. Hou, Z. Leiming, and W. An, "A U-shaped Slot Antenna for WLAN and WiMAX Applications," in 7th Asia Pacific International Symposium on Electromagnetic Compatibility, (2016), pp. 152–154.
[16] C. Bhan, A. K. Dwivedi, B. Mishra, and A. Kumar, "Quad Bands U-Shaped Slot Loaded Probe Fed Microstrip Patch Antenna," (2015) Second Int. Conf. Adv. Comput. Commun. Eng., pp. 409–412, (2015).
[17] Q. Wu, L. Shi, and G. Zhao, "Design of a Ku-band broadband U-slot microstrip antenna," in IEEE International Conference on Microwave Technology and Computational Electromagnetics, (2013), pp. 212–215.
[18] H. F. Abutarboush and A. Shamim, "Paper-based inkjet-printed tri-band U-slot monopole antenna for wireless applications," IEEE Antennas Wirel. Propag. Lett., vol. 11, pp. 1234–1237, (2012).
[19] S. Bansal and J. B. Sharma, "Hexa Band Asymmetrical U-Slot Microstrip Patch Antenna for Wireless Applications," in Annual IEEE India Conference (INDICON), (2015), pp. 25–28.
[20] R. Tej and C. Brajlata, "Single Layer Dual band Microstrip Patch Antenna using Probe Feed," Int. J. Comput. Appl., vol. 92, no. 12, pp. 1–5, 2014.
[21] H. F. AbuTarboush, H. S. Al-Raweshidy, and R. Nilavalan, "Triple Band Double U-Slots Patch Antenna for WiMAX Mobile Applications," (2008) 14Th Asia-Pacific Conf. Commun. (Apcc), Vols 1 2, pp. 140–142, (2008).
[22] T. Alam, M. R. I. Faruque, and M. T. Islam, "Probe-fed rectangular patch antenna for wireless communication," (2015) Int. Conf. Netw. Syst. Secur., pp. 1–4, (2015).
[23] R. Jothi Chitra, A. Suganya, and V. Nagarajan, "Enhanced gain of double U-slot micro strip patch antenna array for WiMAX application," (2012) Int. Conf. Commun. Signal Process. ICCSP-(2012), pp. 141–144, (2012).

5G technologies boosting efficient mobile learning

Helen C. Leligou[1,*], *Emmnouil* Zacharioudakis[2], *Louisa Bouta*[2], *Evangelos Niokos*[2]

[1]Technological Education Institute of Sterea Ellada, Electrical Eng. Dept. Psahna Evias, 34400, Greece, leligou@gmail.com
[2] OTE Academy, Pelika & Spartis 1, Maroussi, 151 22, Athens, {manos.otea@gmail.com, lbouta, vniokos}@oteacademy.gr

Abstract. The needs for education, learning and training proliferate primarily due to the facts that economy becomes more and more knowledge based (mandating continuous lifelong learning) and people migrate among countries, which introduces the need for learning other languages, for training on different skills and learning about the new cultural and societal framework. Given that in parallel, time schedules continuously become tighter, learning through mobile devices continuously gains in popularity as it allows for learning anytime, anywhere. To increase the learning efficiency, personalisation (in terms of selecting the learning content, type and presentation) and adaptation of the learning experience in real time based on the experienced affect state are key instruments. All these user requirements challenge the current network architectures and technologies. In this paper, we investigate the requirements implied by efficient mobile learning scenarios and we explore how 5G technologies currently under design/testing/validation and standardisation meet these requirements.

1 Introduction

Lifelong learning becomes more and more important for the EU economy in its way towards an innovation-based economy where disruptive out-of-the-box thinking and fast adoption of new (including digital) technologies plays an ever increasing role. In parallel, EU society is becoming more and more multi-national as large flows of immigrants arrive in diverse countries making it hard to design training programs and even harder (and very expensive) to realise them. At the same time, in the so-called new EU member states (like Hungary, Bulgaria, Romania, Slovakia) high unemployment coexists with skills shortages; business and industry criticise quality and relevance of current training programs; low image and attractiveness of Vocational Educational Training (VET) has impeded its penetration even though higher-level qualifications bring higher returns. Hence, there is a clear market need for reinforcing vocational education and training, providing incentives to better match skills and jobs, offering attractive VET programmes to engage both young and older people, even with poor prior education, low aspirations and motivation and/or from deprived backgrounds.

The exploitation of state-of-the-art information technologies, and more specifically those relevant to mobile devices, can significantly assist in increasing the effectiveness of all types of education while lowering its cost, meeting the needs of both learners and tutors. The learners want to be able to easily access learning material at anytime, anywhere so that they productively use all their available time. At the same time, attractive learning material employing gamification concepts strengthen user engagement and improve the learning experience. Finally, social interactions have become an indispensable flavor of all our daily activities and in education contexts they could be exploited to cultivate competition.

From the tutor perspective, being able to reach the learner at any time contributes to the faster achievement of educational goals. Additionally, being able to easily develop customized (or even personalized) learning curriculum and material, reusing already available ones, significantly accelerates their work. With the assessment of learner performance being another time consuming task, its easy (automated) assessment exploiting Information Technologies becomes important; even more so, the automated assessment of the learner's behaviour (exploiting sensing devices and data fusion) can drive further personalization of the learning experience.

Towards meeting these needs, the ever increasing penetration of mobile devices (smart phones and tablets) throughout the world can be leveraged. Learners of all ages are familiar with mobile apps including games and cloud-based applications. Mobile apps enable the seamless communication among the learners, and between learner and tutor. Furthermore, the large cloud infrastructures can be used for big (learning) data storage and complex processing. State-of-the-art smartphones are equipped with sensors enabling a) the creation of more attractive learning materials (e.g. games using gyroscopes and other sensors of the smart devices) and b) the assessment of user engagement. Emotion recognition based on facial expressions analysis is possible [1]. Distinguishing boredom in real time allows

* Corresponding author: leligou@gmail.com

DOI: 10.1051/matecconf/201712503004

for triggering experience adaptation to personal needs in real-time.

The development of smart mobile applications that use the sensors available on these devices to detect and personalise the learning experience and communicate with a cloud infrastructure to perform heavier storage and processing tasks is nowadays feasible. Such smart educational solutions are expected to increase the effectiveness of education [2] at all levels and reduce the relevant cost through the sharing of learning resources.

These trends are not at all EU specific and this is proven by the global statistics and forecasts for the e-learning market: PRNewswire stated (in March 2017) that "the Global E-Learning Market is poised to grow at a CAGR of around 7.2% over the next decade to reach approximately $325 billion by 2025" with mobile learning market growing fast (to reach $12.2 billion in 2017 [3]). Education is the third most popular industry in the app development market which is 9.44% of all active apps in the Apple App Store. Organizations use more and more mobile devices in their training programs to save time from their employees' lives, to have more and more answers in their fingerprints through their smartphones, to enable Bring Your Own Device (BYOD) paradigm in training allowing them to benefit of any timeslot in their busy schedule. Gartner predicts that 45% of businesses will have a BYOD policy by 2020 (Gartner forecasts). This is also becoming true for children education (k-12 training) that can enjoy playful experiences at home strengthening their education. MarketsandMarkets forecasts the Global mobile learning market to grow from $7.98 billion in 2015 to $37.60 billion by 2020, at a Compound Annual Growth Rate (CAGR) of 36.3%. Additionally, 70% of learners felt more motivated when training on a mobile device [4]. Mobile e-learners typically study for 40 minutes longer than students using a desktop or tablet [5]. Smartphone learners complete course material 45% faster than those using a computer. Especially, younger people seem to prefer robot-based learning or combination of laptop/mobile/robot learning sessions, with interactive whiteboards also being widely used to offer an enhanced learning experience.

Mobile learning owes its attractiveness to three key features, all tightly coupled with the mobile network performance and features. Firstly, it enables self-directed anytime, anywhere learning; secondly, convenience during the busy day supporting personalisation of training schedules and thirdly but most importantly, it leads to better outcomes: increased retention, reduced training times, and boosts productivity than more traditional training models. Serious games and real-time adaptation of learning experiences are the cornerstones of this last feature.

In this paper, we identify the key features of 5G technologies that open the way for improved mobile learning solutions to the benefit of both the society and the market. The rest of the paper is organised as follows: section 2 presents typical architectures of mobile learning solutions specifying requirements for improved learning solutions and technical points where improvements are possible; section 3 presents key advantages of 5G technology while section 4 attempts to guide engineers in exploiting 5G innovation for delivering mobile learning solutions with advanced efficiency.

2 Mobile Learning architectures

The fast growing mobile learning sector includes many different solutions and applications ranging from mobile apps downloaded and executed in mobile devices (smartphones and tablets) running any operating system, to fully connected experiences where multiple learners interact in real time (play training games) through different and diverse devices-obviously mediated by a cloud infrastructure. In between the two boundaries, solutions where learning materials and/or schedules and/or other learning relevant information is kept in some cloud infrastructure accessed by the learner to initiate a new learning session can be found. While the first type of mobile learning does not really challenge the network operation, internet-enabled or internet-based solutions can impose really demanding requirements on the network performance.

Different architectures are surveyed in [6] where they are finally evaluated and compared with respect to a set of factors that include: 1) device mobile support, 2) heterogeneity support, 3) wireless communication technology, 4) adaptability, 5) traceability and control, 6) learning as a collaborative process and 7) learning integrated with formal or realising informal learning. The reason for selecting these factors is that they are tightly coupled with the user requirements for contemporary mobile learning scenarios and foremost learning process personalisation.

2.1 Learning process personalisation

The personalisation of the learning process is crucial for high learning performance. The performance depends on what the user experiences which in turn is reflected in his affect state. Personalization can involve allowing learners to customize the learning experience by selecting a visual theme or accommodating individual comfort and accessibility or by enabling learners to control volume and screen text font sizes. Personalization can be taken further by capturing a learner's name during registration and using it throughout the course or by streaming specific content to an individual. To increase learning efficiency, the learning infrastructure has to provide the appropriate content for every person at each time, in the appropriate for every person presentation form and level of difficulty. To decide the "appropriateness" of content and presentation, pedagogical models are used, which take into account the person's skills and more interestingly the person's emotional state. To decide the affect state, the sensors of the device in use have to be exploited to collect readings to feed affect-state detection modules so as to decide on keeping or changing certain parameters of the learning experience, such as difficulty, or even changing the learning material itself to boost the learner's engagement. With regards to skill acquaintance towards personalising the learning experience, the performance of the learner has to be continuously traced. The intelligence of adapting the learning experience to the learner's skills and emotional state needs also to take into account past behaviours and process evolutions and thus cannot be implemented (locally) in the mobile devices. In this case placing the personalisation decision module to some cloud infrastructure, introduces the requirement for exchanging important volumes of data between the mobile devices and the cloud.

The volume of the data communicated between the mobile device and the intelligent components residing in the cloud as well as the relevant latency requirements, depend on the type of sensors used to extract emotion information as well as on the type of learning material and learner performance metrics of interest. If camera readings are used for emotion detection, the volume of data is quite big while emotion detection is still possible (at coarser levels) using gyroscope and accelerometer readings. [7] Up to now, streaming the mobile device's camera reading to the cloud is considered an impractical solution which however, would result in higher accuracy in emotion detection. With respect to the learner's performance, pedagogists and trainers are responsible for identifying key moments, where the interactions between the learner and the learning material has to be captured so as to drive learning performance personalisation. For example, if the learning material is a video demonstrating the assembly of a certain device, the "performance" is expressed just as "video watched" while the case is significantly different if the learning material is an interactive game where the two trainees are immerged in the same critical situation and the aim is to assess their reactions towards crisis management. To respond to individual needs, pre-testing is an effective method based on existing competencies. The pre-test assessment can consist of a series of questions linked to course topics and allow learners to skip topics linked to correctly answered questions.

2.2 Collaboration and gaming

Collaboration during learning was initially considered as one of the disadvantages of distant learning. However, collaboration either for assisting one-another or even for solving the same problem can be considered today a mainstream app. On the other side, gamification is introducing competition and has been shown to increase engagement as it usually offers a playful experience. Both real-time collaboration and gamified learning content impose strict requirements on the network supporting the communication between the different learners in terms of latency. The difference of this situation from any other multi-player gaming app from the network perspective is that apart from information regarding the players' interactions, information about the learners' performance needs to be traced and communicated to/through the cloud as well as the data from the devices sensors to enable affect detection and learning process adaptation in real-life.

The situation becomes even more challenging when the collaborating or playing tenants use diverse devices which can either be any mix among mobile (smartphones and tablets), fixed (like whiteboards) and robots. In this case, the information needs to be communicated in a standardised manner (e.g. xAPI statements) to enable appropriate processing in the cloud towards tailoring the presentation of the interaction to the learner and device combination in place each time.

3 Critical Requirements

- Personalised learning involving mobile devices imposes the following requirement on the network: Enhanced mobility support to enable learners exercise everywhere and anytime, even when in the bus or train, so as to exploit all available timeslots in their busy schedules.
- High capacity/low latency to enable data from the sensing elements of the mobile devices to reach cloud infrastructures where "intelligence" allowing personalisation and real-time adaptation based on affect detection resides.
- High capacity/low latency to enable performance relevant data reach the cloud where the learning experience is decided andcontrolled. The modern learner wants to know how information relates to and benefits them directly. Learner-centered eLearning provides opportunities for learners to relate content to their role or personal situation through thought-provoking self-reflective learning checks. These are particularly powerful when interspersed within a scenario at pivotal moments to provoke learners to think how they would handle the situation.
- High security and privacy support: Privacy and security become more and more important in our lives, challenging the networks as they become more and more heterogeneous and as they rely on decoupling physical from logical topologies.
- Quality of Service: The data exchanged between the mobile device and the cloud infrastructure can be distinguished in data relevant to the execution of the learning material (game or other), data relevant to affect detection (generated by the mobile device's sensors) and data relevant to the performance of the learning allowing for self-reflection as well as for experience personalisation. These three types of data need differentiated treatment if resources are to be efficiently used over any network that connects the mobile device with its peers.
- Long battery lifetime: Having the mobile devices executing learning materials (e.g. games) with almost all sensors operating in parallel to enable affect detection and learning experience personalisation, prolonging the lifetime of the battery becomes mandatory to accomplish e.g.

an one-hour experience while on move (e.g. at train).

These requirements should be considered on top of the continuous connectivity and network reliability and availability which are also imposed by traditional learning scenarios.

4 5G-features relevant to the mobile learning use case

5G will provide an order of magnitude improvement in performance in the areas of more capacity, lower latency, more mobility, more accuracy of terminal location, increased reliability and availability. 5G will allow the connection of many more devices simultaneously and to improve the terminal battery capacity life. Lastly, 5G will help European citizens to manage their personal data, tune their exposure over the Internet and protect their privacy.

5G offers more capacity: 5G architectures envision capacity in the range of 1-10Gbps to the wireless edge network part with multiple 10Gbps for the access part and even higher for the metro part. What is even more interesting and important is not the capacity itself but the capability to manage the capacity enjoyed by each service and the capability to isolate traffic in each so-called network slice. ***Network slicing,*** in 5G vision, is also an important part of the overall 5G architecture that addresses the deployment of multiple logical networks as independent business operations on a common physical infrastructure. One of the goals would be to provide network slices flexibly meeting the wide range of use cases that the 2020 timeframe will demand [8]. To this end, a "5G slice" could be composed of a collection of 5G network functions (NF) and specific radio access technology (RAT) settings that are combined together for a specific use case and/or business model. In that context, network slices must fulfil a set of requirements such as the need for sharing and efficiently reusing resources (including radio spectrum, infrastructure, and transport network); differentiation of traffic per slice; visibility of slices; protection mechanisms among slices (a.k.a. slice isolation); and support for slice-specific management. Isolating traffic of different logical networks allows for achieving lower latency for service that require it as is the case for the interactive mobile learning scenario in combination with the bulk of data that need to be exchanged not only for the execution of the learning material but equally importantly for the communication of sensed and performance-relevant data.

Transport slices should also support seamless VNF mobility within the slice. 5G Converged Data Plane functions are distributed to the edges of a common core network, resulting in creating a distributed flat network. The control plane functions, which are responsible for mobility management, QoS control, etc., direct the user traffic to be served agnostically to the access networks to which it is attached.

Network functions in 5G will be more strongly decoupled from physical architecture than in legacy systems Traditionally, mobile network functions are implicitly grouped into network entities via specification of their interconnections, where each entity is responsible for a pre-defined set of functions. A balance between flexibility and complexity needs to be taken into account. In 5G systems, network functions are to be designed to allow a maximally flexible instantiation or even dynamic (re)allocation of functions (i.e. logical entities) to physical entities, enabled by the principle such as a) avoidance of strict timing relations between network functions and protocol stack layers, and design of network functions and b) design of network functions such that these are either able to adapt to the physical architecture in which they are used or are replaceable by alternate network functions specifically optimized for these non-ideal environments. Furthermore, the support of the design, implementation, deployment, management and maintenance of network functions by software programming, exploiting characteristics of software such as flexibility and rapidity of design, development and deployment throughout the lifecycle of network functions etc. can be seen as replacing a "network of entities", as in legacy systems, by a "network of (virtual) functions."

These network functions certainly include mobility, traffic control, authentication, authorisation, accounting and security as well as Intrusion Prevention and Intrusion Detection. Mobility management function design and selection may be service-specific, to allow for a higher degree of customization, e.g., network-slice-specific or radio-access-specific mobility management. This perfectly suits learning sector requirements for enhanced mobility, as a significant part of users exploit the time they spend traveling/commuting between office and home to learn, imposing stringent requirements on the network with respect to mobility management.

With respect to security aspects, the decoupling of logical functionality from its physical realization has always required dedicated security mechanisms. The fact that 5G networks and functions will, to an even higher degree, be provided as logical/virtualized concepts, emphasizes both the required scope and the criticality of security. Most of the necessary security functions in current networks are flexible in the sense that they can "move along" with the motion of the functionality that they protect. But this does not mean that security is agnostic of the physical realization of the logical architecture. 5G vision is to offer enhanced security and flexible AAA over heterogeneous networks. Service-specific access control and accounting/charging policy functionality and placement will be supported as well as service specific security (e.g. a slice with no encryption and/or with added data integrity). 5G aims at designing a security architecture that is flexible and extensible, allowing e.g. functional end-points to be re-allocated due to mobility or traffic optimization. Nevertheless, a complete independence of the physical architecture cannot be obtained. It plans for service-specific access control to allow or block access to deployed services and service-specific monitoring to detect suspicious traffic. Configuration of the Intrusion Prevention and Intrusion Detection VNFs will depend on the type of services that require protection and on the security policies set.

Decentralised security and privacy are of utmost importance to the 5G vision.

Other key characteristics of 5G architectures to be exploited in mobile learning scenarios are the increased reliability and availability as well as the improved terminal battery capacity. Reliability and availability rely on the multi-connectivity technology implemented in 5G in combination with the network function virtualisation which will promptly decide on the physical network reconfiguration. On the other hand, terminal battery capacity improvements primarily depend on the sleep time and patterns that can be enforced on a service specific manner.

5 How 5G meets learning requirements

The growing demand for learning through mobile devices in diverse environments moving (as in train) or not (at home) presents challenges to cellular networks. The imposed requirements are already addressed by use cases from other vertical industrial sectors on which currently ongoing projects focus on. In this framework, they have narrowed down the generic goals of the 5G PPP group vision to concrete target values for Key Performance Indicators. These are listed in the following table.

Starting from the increased user data rates, the means to achieve this goal are to use more frequency spectrum and more dynamic spectrum access. Towards reducing significantly the end-to-end latency, the primary methods are to use more efficient network architectures, more efficient air interface designs, signaling and procedures, better QoS differentiation, and direct device to device communication, where possible. With respect to network architectures, low-latency network architectures are concerned with shortening the distances and number of hops between the user and the content; for example, by distributing some network functions that are centralized today. On the other hand, the air interface may adapt the frame structures in order to reduce the Transmission Time Interval (TTI) and/or Hybrid Automatic Repeat reQuest (HARQ) round trip times. While this can efficiently be implemented at the higher frequencies where more bandwidth is available, this can become very inefficient for wide area coverage. Signaling and procedures can be thinned out, by simplifying their components. Turning our attention to better QoS differentiation, as the low-latency transmission usually comes with inefficient resource utilisation, it should only be applied with the services that require such low latencies.

Starting from the requirement to support fast service deployment, activation and further management, this is in essence the efficient mapping of service functions onto a virtualized substrate, possibly belonging to multiple infrastructure operators. For the service deployment time, in other words, the duration required for setting up end-to-end logical network slices characterized by respective network level guarantees (such as bandwidth guarantees, End-to-End (E2E) latency, reliability), stringent target values are imposed by media and automotive use cases.

With respect to the battery longer lifetime, the primary methods to address its prolongation are to improve air interface, procedures and signaling, and to reduce the distance between the Massive Machine Communications devices and the access node. Techniques to improve the air interface include the use of sleep modes, energy-efficient modulation, coding and multiple access schemes, for example, use of constrained modulation techniques, very robust coding and/or spreading allowing very low transmission powers, and simplified procedures such as those introduced for the previous goal [9]. As far as security is concerned, tailored security at the service and device level is envisioned in 5G vision. 5G might consider dynamic control and data plane support for different security system instantiations to be able to provide differentiated security services on request.

Table 1 5G technology responses to Use Case requirements

Mobile Learning Use Case Requirements	5G Architecture Response
Enhanced mobility support to enable learners exercise everywhere and anytime	Fast Service deployment Support Velocity >50km/h (currently targeted in automotive use cases projects)
High capacity/low latency to support data handling differentiation for sensed data and performance related data; these requirements are tightly bound to Quality of Service differentiation capabilities	5G target : 1000 times higher mobile data volume per area The user data rates considered in the 5G use case go beyond $\geq$ 1 Gbps while for latency, three different levels are distinguished with the low one ranging from 1-10ms Furthermore, multiple traffic types are supported between them bursty, periodic and event driven.
High security and privacy support	Increasing importance in the highly heterogeneous, rapidly changing, network architecture
Long battery lifetime	10 times longer battery life based on sleep time and patterns that can be enforced on a service specific manner.
Network reliability and availability	Target reliability ranges from low (<95%) to high (>99%) Target availability also ranging from low (<95%) to high (>99%)

The dynamic composition of the 5G infrastructure needs security guarantees within the system: beyond the mutual authentication and secure communication channel establishment, and despite the decoupling between logical and physical network topologies, it is necessary to delve into topics of infrastructure/system integrity and operational security assurance. As the system dynamics are key to achieve the agility of stakeholders (as recent Network Function Virtualisation and Software Defined Networking initiatives suggest), then the survivability must be increasingly understood as the major operational security model.

6 Conclusions

As the realm of mobile learning augments, it is important to identify technologies that best meet the user requirements. Supporting personalisation and real-time adaptation to the temporal user needs leads to enhanced user satisfaction, reduces significantly the achievement of the learning goals to the benefit of the individual, the society and the economy. Our investigation shows that 5G technologies are anticipated to significantly boost mobile learning as it efficiently satisfies high priority user requirements providing the tutors/trainers with richer means to define efficient learning scenarios. Among the most important 5G features, high data rates enable communication of performance and affect-state relevant data which fuel learning experience personalisation and adaptation; high battery lifetime offers the user the opportunity to learn throughout long journeys; quality of service differentiation and high network availability and reliability contribute in enhancing the learning experience through a variety of learning content types from simple videos and files to interactive possibly collaborative learning games. 5G provides the engineers with abundant tools to implement an unprecedented number of novel learning solutions meeting learners' and trainers' requirements making learning more enjoyable and efficient than ever.

Acknowledgment

This work has been co-financed by the EU H2020 MaTHiSiS project.

References

1. ICT-317669 METIS project, *Scenarios, requirements and KPIs for 5G mobile and wireless system* (Deliverable D1.1, May 2013), available at: https://www.metis2020.com/documents/deliverables
2. L. Duan, D. Xu, I. W. Tsang, *Learning with Augmented Features for Heterogeneous Domain Adaptation, Proceedings of the 29th International Conference on Machine Learning* (Edinburgh, Scotland, UK, 2012)
3. https://elearningindustry.com/surprising-mobile-learning-statistics-elearning-professionals-know
4. Lynda.com, *The benefits of mobile learning*, white paper, (2014), available at: http://cdn.lynda.com/cms/asset/text/lyndacom-whitepaper-mobile-learning-benefits-20151245042329.pdf.
5. http://mnalearning.com/resource_view.php?id=70
6. S. Baccari, F. Mendes, C. Nicolle, F. Soualah-Alila, N. Mahmoud, *Comparative Study of the Mobile Learning Architectures, e-LEOT 2nd EAI International Conference on e-Learning e-Education and Online Training*, (Novedrate, Italy,2015)
7. A. Færøvig Olsen, *Detecting Human Emotions Using Smartphone Accelerometer Data*, (Master Thesis, 2016)
8. 5G PPP Architecture Working Group, *View on 5G Architecture* (2016), available at: https://5g-ppp.eu/wp-content/uploads/2014/02/5G-PPP-5G-Architecture-WP-July-2016.pdf
9. J. F. Monserrat, G. Mange, V. Braun, H. Tullberg, G. Zimmermann, Ö. Bulakci, *METIS research advances towards the5G and wireless system definition* (EURASIP, 2015)
10. M. Maternia, S. E. El Ayoubi, *5G PPP use cases and performance evaluation models* (2016), available at: https://5g-ppp.eu/wp-content/uploads/2014/02/5G-PPP-use-cases-and-performance-evaluation-modeling_v1.0.pdf
11. M. Suk, B. Prabhakaran, *Real-time Mobile Facial Expression Recognition System – A Case Study, IEEE Conference on Computer Vision and Pattern Recognition Workshops* (2014)
12. Conference on e-Learning e-Education and Online Training (Novedrate, Italy, 2015)
13. A. Mecke, I. Lee, J.R. Baker jr., M.M. Banaszak Holl, B.G. Orr, Eur. Phys. J. E **14**, 7 (2004)
14. CEDEFOP, *Spotlight on VET in Hungary*(2014)
15. CEDEFOP, *Spotlight of VET Romania* (2013)

* Corresponding author: leligou@gmail.com

DOI: 10.1051/matecconf/201712503005

General Data Acquisition Platform for Wireless Sensor Network Based on CC2538

Zhi-Jun Yang[1,2], Yang-Yang Ding[1] , Hong-Wei Ding[1] and Yang Su[1]

[1]School of Information Science and Engineering, Yunnan University, Kunming, 650091, China
[2]The Academy for Educational Science Research, Educational Department of Yunnan Province, Kunming , 650223,China

Abstract. Wireless sensor networks are the hotspots of current research and have very wide application prospects. Its front end is a sensor that can sense and check the external world. This paper takes temperature and humidity as the research object, and builds a wireless sensor network data acquisition platform by combining the Internet of things and the WeChat public platform. The platform uses DHT11 temperature and humidity sensors and CC2538 sensor nodes to obtain the relevant data, through the server and database for data access. The combination with WeChat public platform not only allows us to view the temperature and humidity in the WeChat public, but also allows us to understand the environmental changes of the relevant detection area more conveniently and quickly. The effectiveness of the platform is also demonstrated by the collection of temperature and humidity data.

1 Introduction

With the continuous improvement of living standards, people pay more attention to their own living environment. Temperature and humidity are two of the more sensitive parameters of human environment. We can use the wireless sensor network to get environmental parameters to serve people. The front end of a wireless sensor network is a network communication system consisting of sensors and their nodes that can perceive and acquire external world data. It can not only a variety of real-time monitoring, sensing and collecting in the regional distribution of monitoring data, but also to the Internet through wired or wireless mode to connect and transmit the data to the observer.So as to further analysis and use of the collected information.

This paper develops a data acquisition platform based on cc2538 wireless sensor network. The platform using the Internet of things technology to monitor the temperature and humidity. At the same time it can be free from time and geographical constraints, users can quickly understand the monitoring site temperature and humidity changes and respond in a timely manner.

2 System Overall Design

The whole system consists of the sensing layer, the network layer and the user application layer. The sensing layer is mainly CC2538cb sensor nodes and DHT11 temperature and humidity sensors and other sensing devices, used to obtain the monitoring area of the relevant monitoring information, and through the access device and other devices in the Internet solid resource sharing. The network layer mainly sends the information obtained by the sensing layer to the Internet. Through the establishment of the networking platform in the network information resources integration can become a interoperability of intelligent network, the establishment of an efficient, reliable and credible infrastructure platform for large-scale monitoring and management. Through the central computer platform, the sensor network to obtain a variety of monitoring information for real-time management and control, and for the upper application to provide a good user interface. The main function of the user application layer is to build a practical application for monitoring, where the use of WeChat public platform to achieve real-time monitoring, early warning and other functions. The system structure is shown in Fig. 1.

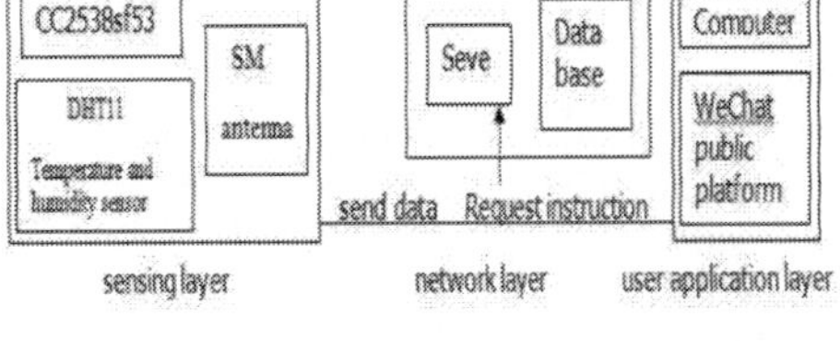

Fig. 1

The working process of the system is as follows: firstly, the data of temperature and humidity in the environment are collected by DHT11 temperature and humidity sensor, and the temperature and humidity data obtained from the node's SM antenna module is sent to the nearest sink node. And then the aggregation node after the reunification of the data will be sent and stored in the database for the WeChat public platform for data calls. Finally, when the user in the WeChat public

* Corresponding author: 18213977051@163.com

 DOI: 10.1051/matecconf/201712503005

platform to send a request, the server will send the current data in the database to the WeChat public number, so that users can get the latest temperature and humidity data.

3 Hardware component

There are a lot of wireless sensor network related to the hardware, the hardware part of the system adopts CC2538 as ordinary sensor nodes and sink node to form a wireless sensor network, through the node's SMA antenna data sent to the server side. The main difference between common sensor nodes and sink nodes is whether serial communication can be carried out. CC2538 node RAM reached 32k, so the use of the process do not have to worry about the problem of insufficient RAM. Besides CC2538 node prices to be relatively cheap, more suitable for beginners to use. CC2538 node physical map shown in Fig. 2.

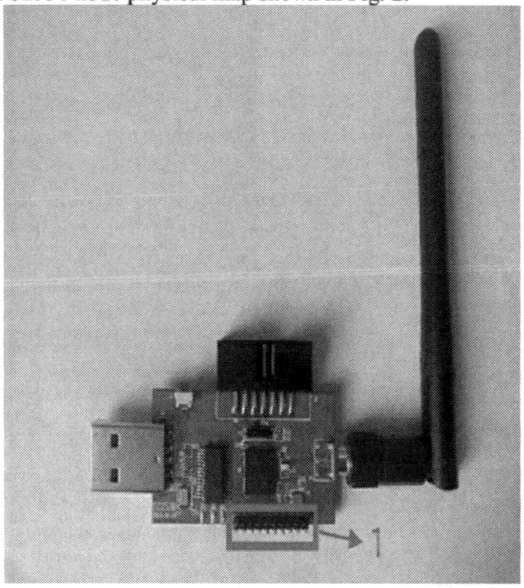

Fig. 2

The IO port is reserved in the design of the node, as shown in Figure 3, which is indicated as 1, from left to right: VDD • PA2 • PA3 • PA4 • PA5 • PA6 • PA7 • PD0 • PD1 • GND. Reserved IO port can be programmed according to the need to develop functions, such as UART, SPI, I2C, SSI, ADC, input, output, etc., high flexibility. Therefore, we can use the reserved IO port to complete the required sensor access. Cc2538 main chip circuit shown in Fig. 3.

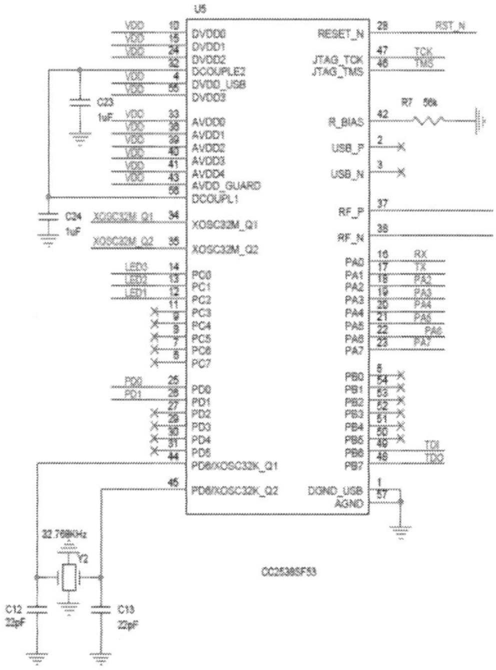

Fig. 3

The node design does not directly use 2538 USB function instead of using the PL2030 USB conversion chip, mainly because of 2030 for the Linux/Ubuntu virtual machine, Android is a free drive, we can use it more simple and fast. The circuit shown in Fig. 4.

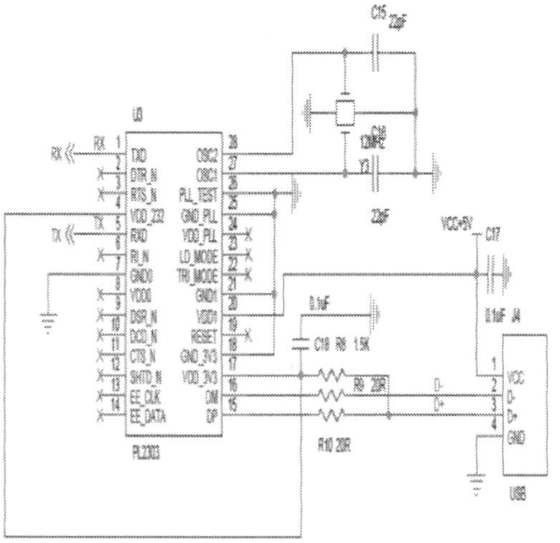

Fig. 4

The system through the DHT11 temperature and humidity sensor to collect environmental data. DHT11 digital temperature and humidity sensor is a composite sensor, including the calibration of digital signal output temperature and humidity. Using the digital module acquisition technology and temperature and humidity sensing technology to ensure product reliability and long-term stability. Its core is a resistive moisture

DOI: 10.1051/matecconf/201712503005

element and an NTC temperature measuring element. DHT11 sensors are calibrated in extremely accurate humidity calibrators and the calibration coefficients are stored in OTP memory in the form of a program. These calibration coefficients are called internally during the processing of the detection signal. Using single-wire serial interface, easy to system integration. In addition, DHT11 has been widely used because of its small size, low power consumption and convenient connection between 4 pins.

4 Software Part

4.1TinyOS Operating System

TinyOS is the mainstream operating system in wireless sensor networks. It is an open source operating system developed by University of California at Berkeley, designed for embedded wireless sensor networks. TinyOS is based on the event-driven mechanism, with less code, low energy consumption, high concurrency, fast response and so on, can better meet the specific application. And NesC programming language is used to support component programming.Taking into account the general characteristics of wireless sensor nodes: simplified hardware architecture, low storage capacity, CPU performance and battery power. Making the TinyOS operating system very suitable for wireless sensor networks.

TinyOS is a component-based programming architecture which is widely used in embedded operating system, and its components are an abstraction of hardware and software functionality. The whole system consists of components, through the components to improve software compatibility. The system itself provides a set of components for user invocation, which can be divided into underlying hardware abstraction components, intermediate composite hardware components and upper software components (including main components and application components) from bottom to top, as shown in Fig. 5.

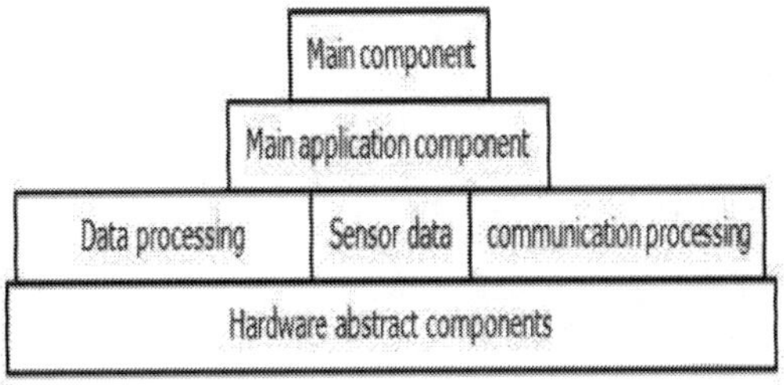

Fig. 5

The underlying hardware abstraction component maps the physical hardware to the TinyOS component module and is responsible for reporting events to the upper layer. The intermediate hardware components simulate the advanced hardware behavior, which is responsible for parsing the data and passing the data parameters. The upper software components mainly implement component control, routing and data transmission, protocol analysis, etc., the upper component to the underlying components issued a command.

4.2 Send and receive data between nodes

4.2.1 Send the data

The data transmitting and receiving between the common node and the sink node are mainly through SM antenna. In the node programming process used six components, respectively, MainC components, timing components TimerMillliC, control the sending of AMSendC components, control the receiving AMReceiverC components and LedsC components.

Sensor through the cc2538 reserved IO port access, select the temperature and humidity sensor DHT11 to measure the temperature and humidity in the environment, connect the DHT11's 3 (1 floating) pins to the IO port according to the corresponding relationship.

Because TinyOS can directly use the C file, so the driver here by the C language.In the compilation process, we need to add DHT11 driver to the TinyOS compiler environment. First copy the driver to the tinyos-main-release_tinyos_2_1_2 \ tos \ chips \ cc2538 directory, the driver contains DHT11.c and DHT11.h files. And then modify the tinyt-main-release tinyos 2 1 2 \ tos \ platforms \ cc2538cb .platform (Ctrl + h can show hidden files) file, increase the path% T / chips / cc2538 / DHT11. Finally, modify the cc2538cb.rules file under tinyos-main-release_tinyos_2_1_2 \ support \ make \ cc2538cb and add EXTRA_MODULES + = $ (CHIP DIR) / DHT11 / DHT11.c after EXTRA_MODULES + = ... After compiling, programming, we can read DHT11 data.

4.2.2 Receive the data

Through the receive interface to achieve data reception, receive interface to provide basic information to receive and forward information function, the entire process achieved by the ActiveMessageC components. In this way, we can complete the transmission of information to the sink node, the sink node is directly connected with a computer, using the serial port to read the information of the software you can see to the sensor node data acquisition.

4.3 Server and Database

The temperature and humidity data collected by the sensor are stored in the database through the server, so the stability, practicability and convenience of the server and the database are very important. The system uses the MySQL database and the Baidu cloud server, the server and the database through the GET request way to transmit the sensor to send the data. In the Baidu cloud server to build a server environment, install the MySQL database, through the preparation of the code can communicate with the mobile client. The data collected from the sensor nodes are observed on the computer as shown in Fig. 6.

```
UDP - IP.recv: len: 21 (21, 21) srcport: 10210 dstport: 10210
 rx_cksum: 0xc11a my_cksum: 0xc11a
 TestLinkLocalC: recv from: fe80::212:6d4c:4f00:2
 humidity: 14%RH  temperature: 21℃
 TestLinkLocalC: reply seqno: 15
 IPProtocolsP: Sending IPv6 Packet
  source: fe80::212:6d4c:4f00:1
  dest:  ff02::1
 IPNeighborDiscovery: Converting to 15.4 addresses
  source: IEEE154_ADDR_EXT:  0:12:6d:4c:4f: 0: 0: 1
  dest:  IEEE154_ADDR_SHORT: 0xffff
 fragment length: 78 offset: 61
 fragment length: 0 offset: 61
 sendDone: was not delivered! (0 tries)
 UDP - IP.recv: len: 21 (21, 21) srcport: 10210 dstport: 10210
 rx_cksum: 0xc01a my_cksum: 0xc01a
 TestLinkLocalC: recv from: fe80::212:6d4c:4f00:2
 humidity: 14%RH  temperature: 21℃
 TestLinkLocalC: reply seqno: 16
```

Fig. 6

4.4 WeChat Public Platform

The use of WeChat's public platform to the sensor data collected real-time monitoring.Because compared with the computer, WeChat public account is more suitable for simple and easy to observe the various data collected by the sensor, in addition to the cost of the development of the WeChat public number, easy to use.

Users in the network environment landing personal WeChat, concerned about the corresponding WeChat public number can enter the system.WeChat public numbers need to be bound to the server, the request can be sent to respond. After binding, WeChat public number to send a request to the server, the server according to the instructions to read the corresponding data in the database provided to the WeChat public number, you can view the corresponding environmental data at the WeChat side. Send and receive schematic diagram shown in Fig. 7.

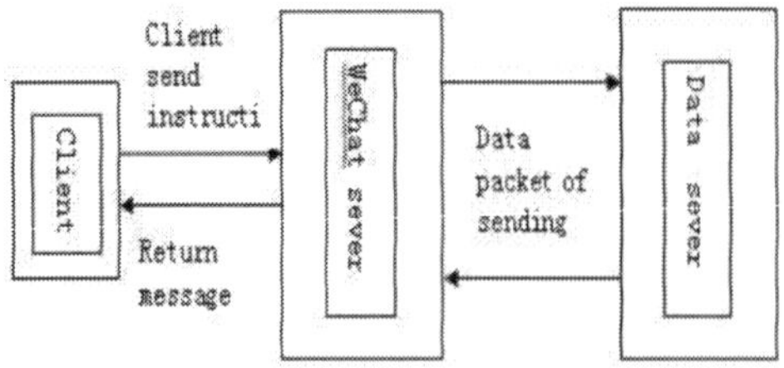

Fig. 7

5 Concluding

The environmental data acquisition platform in this paper makes full use of the flexibility and scalability of wireless sensor to designs the platform. The effectiveness of the platform is also demonstrated by the collection of temperature and humidity data. The introduction of TinyOS operating system greatly simplifies the hardware platform construction and development difficulties. The combination of the Internet of things and the WeChat public platform allows us to get rid of computers without time and geographical constraints, and easier to understand the changes in the environment. At the same time, it has simple operation, high efficiency and can share monitoring data externally. However, there are still some deficiencies in the design. There is also a need to extend the different types of sensors for full monitoring. For the problem of delay in data acquisition and transmission, the next step will be to improve the issue by adding a new transceiver mechanism.

Acknowledgements

This work was supported by the National Natural Science Foundation of China under Grant Nos.61461054 and 61461053.

References

[1]. Zhi Jun Yang, Hong Wei Ding, Zheng Guan ,L.Z.Zh u, A New Transportation Control System Based On Prior ity Differentiated Polling Strategy, Proceedings of 2015 World Conference on Control, Electronics and Electrical Engineering,vol.116,38-44,(2015).

[2]Zhi Jun Yang, Hong Wei Ding, Characteristics of a T wo-Class Polling System Model, Tsinghua Scienc and Technology, vol.**19**,no.5,516-520,(2014).

[3]Zhi Jun Yang, Hong Wei Ding, C L Chen, Research o n E(x) Characteristics of Two-Class Polling System of E xhaustive-Gated Service, *Acta Electronica Sinica,* no.4,7 75-778,(2014)

[4]TIAN Aijun, WANG. Deming Design of universal sig nal acquisition system in wireless sensor network[J]. Mo dern Electronics Technique,2017,40(2)

[5] LI Song-tao, YIN Qing-shuang. Design and Implem entation of Mobile Environmental Monitoring System B ased on Android and ZigBee [J]. Computer Technology and Development,2017,(3).

[6]XU Jiang-chun, YUE Qiu-yan, REN Xiang-yang. Gre enhouse Environment Detection System Based on the Vi rtual Instrument and WeChat Public Platform[J].Journal of Anhui Agri,2016,44(4)

[7] XU Zi-jing. Design of Zigbee Low Power Greenhouse Monitoring System Based on Solar-Power[J]. Automation technology and Application,2017,36(2).

[8]GAO Renzhi, SHANG Lihui, TU Xuan. Environment Monitoring System Software Development Based on An droid[J]Electronic Science and Technology,2017,30(1).
[9] Liu Chengtao, Wang Zhen. Intelligence environment monitoring system based on WeChat public platform For eign Electronic Measurement Technologh,2017,36(2).
[10]Liu Lian, Zhou Fengxing. Design and Implementatio n of Environment Monitoring System at Smart Home Ba sed on APP,2014,22(7).
[11]WANG Hua-bin, LUO Zhong-liang. Design of Data Acquisition and Monitoring System Based on Zigbee,20 11,(8).
[12]GAO Junfeng, WANG Fangyi, YIN Xiangyu. Desig n and Implementation of Environmental Information Ac quisition Systemfor Campus,2014,4(11).

Efficient Secret Key Delivery Using Heartbeats

Kwantae Cho[1,*], and *Byungho* Chung[2]

[1, 2] Information Security Research Division, Electronics and Telecommunications Research Institute, Republic of Korea

Abstract. Recently many researchers have employed physiological signals like heartbeats as a source of the key seed used in key establishment protocols. The physiological signals make it easy to establish a secret key between implantable (or attachable) medical devices which can sense physiological signals. A key establishment protocol is a fundamental requirement to support the security of the healthcare and medical services such as diagnosis, treatment, prevention, and follow-up services. However, existing key establishment protocols demand high computational and communication costs or need long key establishment time. In this paper, we propose an efficient IPI-based key establishment protocol that requires relatively short time while keeping the strength of security close.

1 Introduction

Recent advances of sensor technologies have enabled the emergence of small types of sensor devices, especially, called biometric sensors. Generally, biometric sensors are small enough and they can be attached on or implanted in the human body in order to monitor physiological signals. Once integrated with wireless network modules, biometric sensors can construct a special kind of wireless sensor networks in a human body, called as body sensor networks (BSNs). The biometric sensors check the health status of the human body and, as needed, they may carry out intelligent treatment via their mutual communication automatically. The information covered by BSNs not only involves individual privacy, but it may even be life threatening in the worst case. For example, if an attacker with malicious intent can control the insulin injector implanted in a particular patient at will and it excesses insulin into the patient's body, the patient will be in a very dangerous situation. Thus, privacy and security protection of the BSNs is an essential requirement to popularize medical and healthcare services.

In BSNs, the use of biometrics, specifically, physiological signal, makes it possible to provide stronger security more easily. We can imagine that a long-term secret key is embedded in implantable medical devices before deployment. If a malicious attacker gets the long-term key by unpredicted accidents or a compromise attack, the patient with the implantable medical device will have to undergo surgery to update the long-term secret key. If asymmetric cryptosystem is applied to the implantable medical device, it may not be necessary to store the secret key in advance, but it will bring a huge energy problem to the medical device. For these reasons, many security researchers have proposed symmetric key-based cryptographic protocols that does not required storing secret information in advance.

Most of physiological-signal-based key establishment schemes [1-6] have been designed based on fuzzy-vault scheme [7]. However the fuzzy-vault scheme fundamentally requires significant computation and communication costs by a number of polynomial calculations and the transmission of numerous chaff points. For these reasons, most researchers have tried to deal with the issues. The work [3] reduced computational costs by not calculating lagrangian interpolation coefficients only by transmitting matched points to the other party. The work [4] employs simple arithmetic operators instead of Euclidean distance formula which requires squaring and square root, for vault unlocking. Above these, the works [5-6] have been enhanced the security of fuzzy-vault. In the works, chaff points are chosen from not 1-dimensional space but 2-dimensional space in order to increase the number of available points and make it difficult for a brute force attack to be successful.

In this paper, we propose a lightweight key establishment scheme using inter-pulse interval (IPI) of photoplethysmogram (PPG), in order to avoid the above disadvantages of the fuzzy-vault scheme. Here, an IPI means the interval between two peaks of the PPG signals. If the IPIs are used for key establishment scheme, it is not necessary to derive the polynomial, unlike the fuzzy-vault, and there is no need to transmit chaff points, so the amount of computation and the amount of traffic can be greatly reduced. Although various IPI-based key establishment schemes [8-12] have been proposed so far, the work [13] recently proposed a simple and efficient IPI-based key delivery protocol. The work [13] encodes the secret key generated by biometric sensor A using an error correction code (ECC), then A hides it in a witness, which is generated from the biometric information measured by itself, and transmits it securely to another biometric sensor B. Then B recovers the secret key using its own witness. However, since the work has to collect

* Corresponding author: kwantaecho@etri.re.kr

biometric information for witness generation as long as the bit length of the encoded output, the secret key exchange takes a relatively long time.

In this paper, we have reduced the key generation time by lessening the length of witness, while maintaining the advantages of the IPI-based key establishment schemes. Biometric sensor A encodes the generated witness using the ECC and it transmits only the parity code of the encoded outputs to another biometric sensor B. Also, in order to hide a secret key in the witness, A needs a witness equivalent to the key length, not the encoded output length. The main contributions of the paper are outlined as follows.

1) *Relatively short key establishment time:* we shortened the key establishment time by reducing the number of IPIs needed to generate a secret key. It will be possible to access the medical device (biometric sensor) faster in an emergency.
2) Low *computational and communication cost:* The proposed protocol adopts a symmetric cryptosystem, not an asymmetric cryptosystem. Furthermore, the proposed protocol does not transmit a large amount of data like chaff points of the fuzzy-vault.

The remainder of this paper is organized as follows. Section 2 introduces backgrounds of the proposed key delivery protocol. After explaining our IPI-based key delivery protocol in Section 3, we discuss the performance of the proposed protocol in Section 4. Finally, we conclude this paper in Section 5.

2 Backgrounds

In this section, we explain our system and adversary models, and we briefly introduce related works.

2.1. Overview of System model

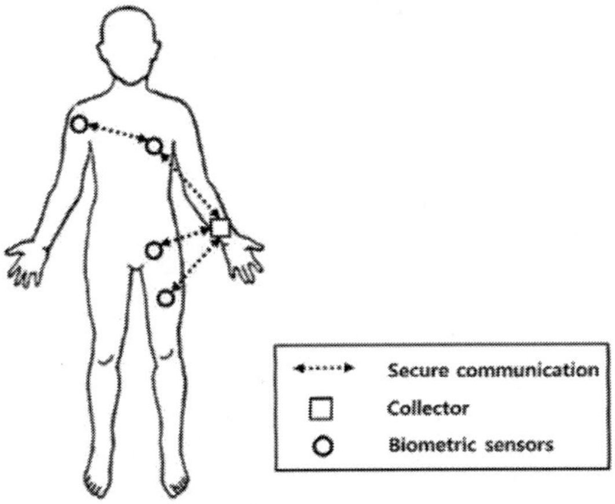

Fig. 1. Our System Model

Fig. 1 depicts our system model, which can be applied to biometric-based systems such as u-Healthcare service system, a BSN (a Body Sensor Networks), and a WBAN (a Wireless Body Area Network). Such systems are mainly made up of two types of devices: a Collector and several biometric sensors. Each biometric sensor can be attached to a body or implanted in the body as necessary. The collector can be wirelessly connected to an external management server. Each biometric sensor measures biometric information of the body for various tasks such as health status monitoring and medical decision support, while offering the biometric information to the collector. The collector periodically aggregates the biometric information from each biometric sensor installed in the same body, and then it sends the aggregated data to the external management server.

In our system model, the collector as well as the biometric sensors can measure the inter-pulse interval (IPI) of the photoplethysmogram (PPG). Here, IPIs can be measured in / above the human body [14]. In biometric-based systems, since biometric sensors handle private medical information of patients, it is necessary to construct secure communication between them. The secret key delivery protocol, which proposed in this paper, allows two biometric sensors (or between a biometric sensor and a collector) to share a secret key for secure communication between themselves.

2.2. Adversary model

The type of an adversary A can be divided into two types as follows. The first is to find who possess a certain biometrics even though A does not have any secret which is shared between a collector and each biometric sensor and used in process of authentication. The second is to make a valid response even though A is not a legitimate participant. More specifically, A wants to be not only authenticated by a collector or biometric sensors of the attack target, but also participate in a secret delivery protocol by pretending to be a legitimate participant. Accordingly, we can define two adversary types: a *passive adversary* and an *active adversary*.

A passive adversary is an adversary that can just eavesdrop and collect the exchanged messages between legitimate participants but cannot inject and modify their messages because A has no ability to make a valid challenge and response of the secret key delivery protocol. For instance, tracing through continuous eavesdropping is one of passive attacks. Meanwhile, an active adversary is defined as A who can fabricate messages and insert them into the normal authentication process to achieve his/her malicious purpose. Here, we assume that an active adversary cannot physically access a biometric sensor because physical access to a biometric sensor implanted in a body or attached on a body is quite difficult. The attack target will probably be able to easily recognize the physical access. For example, impersonation and spoofing attacks belong to this attack.

2.3. Related works

The feasibility of IPIs for key establishment between biometric sensors have been studied steadily. It relies heavily on the randomness of IPIs and their disparity between IPIs obtained by different subjects. In this subsection, we discuss these IPI characteristics and then we introduce some of the representative IPI-based key delivery protocols.

In many previous works [8-12], it is already evaluated that each IPI, which is obtained from healthy subjects as well as patients with cardiovascular diseases, has a high degree of entropy and it therefore can be used as a security key. However, all bits of an IPI does not have a high degree of entropy. Although the length of IPIs is from eight to ten bits in accordance with the sampling rate of a biometric sensor and each IPI is time-variant, it is known that only the three or four least-significant bits (LSBs) of all its bits are independent random variables [12-13].

One of the most important consideration when IPIs are used for key establishment is the disparity between IPIs which are simultaneously obtained from the same body. Most related works [13, 15-17] have focused on how to efficiently synchronize IPIs having such a property. The work [15] firstly proposed the key establishment scheme using IPIs while the works [16] and [17] did not share any secret information between two parties in advance for key exchange. Compared with these works, the work [13] does not use pre-deployed secret information while reducing the number of communication rounds considerably.

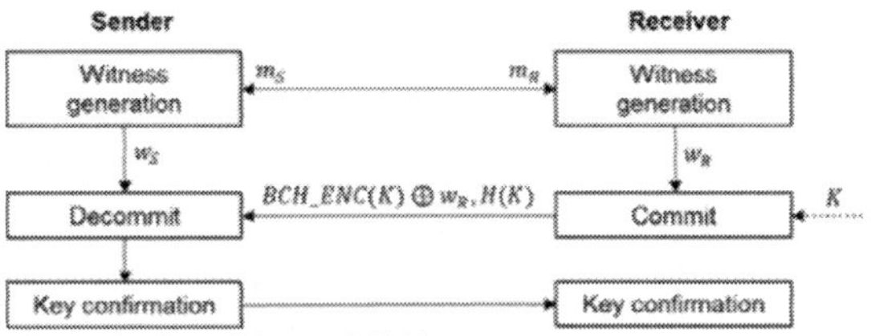

Fig. 2. Outline of the work [13]

Fig. 3 shows the outline of the work [13]. It is assumed that two biometric sensors (Sender and Receiver) are attached to the same subject. Both biometric sensors measure IPIs in real time and they periodically exchange misdetection flag (m_S, m_R) for the block consisting of several trimmed IPIs. The sender and the receiver generate witness values (w_S and w_R, respectively) generated from the blocks. The receiver creates nonce K used as a symmetric key between itself and the sender. After encoding the nonce using the BCH (Bose–Chaudhuri–Hocquenghem) code, the receiver computes XOR operation with the encoded codes and its witness w_R, and then it transmits the computed results to the sender. The sender runs XOR operation with the received value and its witness w_S, decodes the encoded codes. Finally, the sender checks whether a derived key is correct through the key confirmation step. However, the work [13] requires a relatively long time to exchange a secret key. For example, it takes between 60 and 77.6 seconds to generate a 80-bit key with using three LSBs and (204, 80, 37) BCH codes; that is, a 204-bit witness is required to make a 80 bit key and it is derived from about 68 IPIs. The key-exchange time should be reduced for practical use. In this paper, we significantly reduced the expected key-exchange time by modifying the commit step effectively.

3 Proposed secret key delivery protocol

In this section, we explain the proposed secret key deliver protocol between two biometric sensors (a Sender and a Receiver) using IPIs. The proposed protocol is composed of several steps: witness generation, ECC encoding & decoding, key generation, key transmission, key derivation, key verification, and key confirmation. The three steps (ECC encoding, key generation, and key transmission) accord with the Commit step of Fig. 2 while other three steps (ECC decoding, key derivation, and key transmission) accord with the Decommit step of that. Fig. 3 depicts our proposed secret key deliver protocol. The notation is shown in Table 1.

Table 1. Notation

Notation	Description
n	The number of IPIs (or witnesses) needed to generate a key
IPI_i	The i-th of n IPIs
$w_{x,i}$	The i-th witness piece of biometric sensor x
w_x	Witness of biometric sensor x
BCH_ENC / BCH_DEC	Normal In brackets
P	Parity code of the encoded output using BCH code
K	A symmetric session key between Sender and Receiver
TS	Timestamp
$MAC_K(M)$	A message authentication code to authenticate message M with key K
$\oplus$	A XOR operator
X ‖ Y	The concatenation of X and Y
SUCCESS	A flag to mean that a pairwise key between Sender and Receiver is established successfully

3.1. Witness generation

Each biometric sensor makes its own witness from its own measured IPIs in this step. Sender S consecutively measures n IPIs (IPI_1, IPI_2, …, IPI_n), each of which is the time difference between two sequential heartbeats. Like the work [13], we assume that only three LSBs of each IPI is used to produce a witness piece. The selected IPI bits are reprocessed through the Gray coding, which can lower the disparity between two IPIs. We then call the Gray-coded bits as a *witness piece*, i.e., an IPI is a source of a witness piece and n witness pieces ($w_{S,1}, w_{S,2}, \dots\dots, w_{S,n}$) become a witness (w_S). In the same way as S, Receiver R also generates its own witness w_R (where $w_S \approx w_R$), providing a basis for trust establishment.

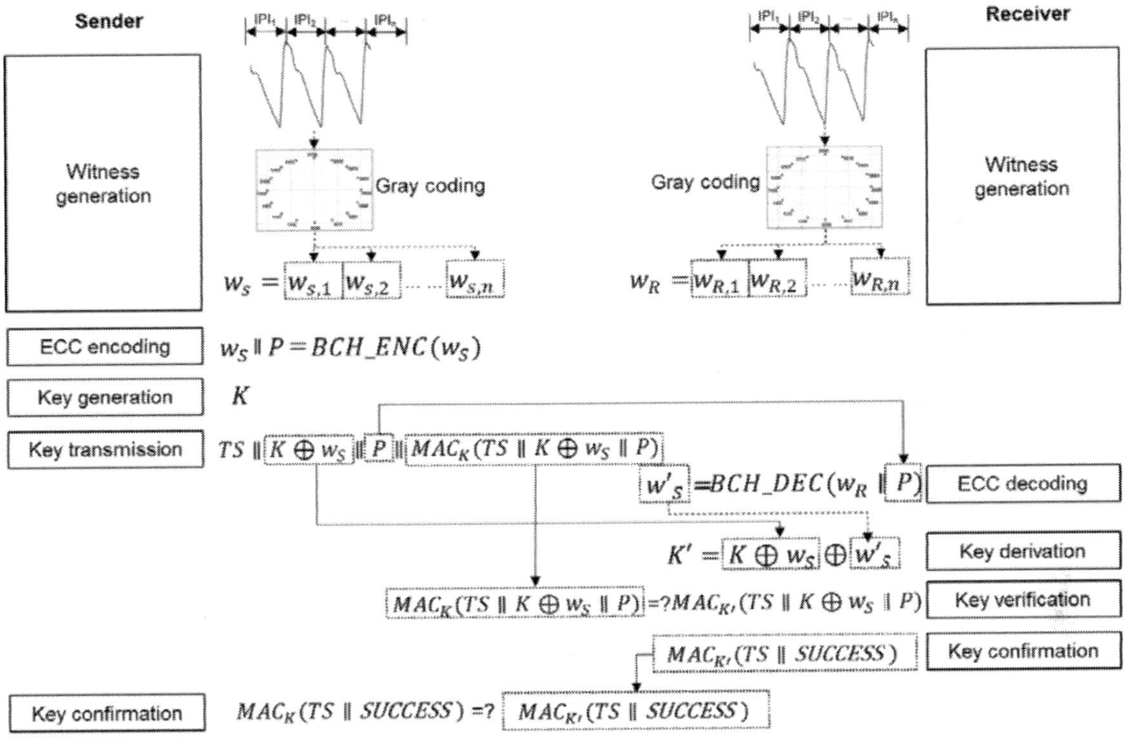

Fig. 3. Proposed key delivery protocol

3.2. ECC encoding & decoding

In this step, S generates parity code P for its w_S using an error correcting code. We employ an error correcting code as the BCH code. The encoded output of the BCH code is separated into its original data w_S and its parity code P. In the key transmission step, only P is sent to R for BCH decoding.

3.3. Key generation & transmission

S generates a secret key and then it provides R with supplementary information required for key derivation and key verification. S selects a nonce used as a symmetric session key K between itself and R. After computing supplementary information $TS \parallel K \oplus w_S \parallel P \parallel MAC_K(TS \parallel K \oplus w_S \parallel P)$, S sends R the computed result, which helps R to the end that R recovers the K.

3.4. Key derivation & verification

R derives the same key K using its own witness w_R. On receiving the supplementary information, R decodes it using w_R together with P. Consequently, R can obtain $w'_S\ (= w_S)$. If the bit difference between w_S and w_R is within the correctable range of the BCH code, w'_S and w_S will be exactly the same. Using w'_S, R computes $K \oplus w_S \oplus w'_S$ and it finally get secret key $K'(= K)$.

For the validation check of K', after calculating $MAC_{K'}(TS \parallel K \oplus w_S \parallel P)$, R checks whether the calcaulted result is equal to the received value $MAC_K(TS \parallel K \oplus w_S \parallel P)$. If same, R determines K' as a session key during the session associated with S.

3.5. Key confirmation

S confirms that S and R has the identical session key. In this step, R computes $MAC_{K'}(TS \parallel SUCCESS)$ using its own session key K' and then transmitting it to S. On receiving it, S computes $MAC_K(TS \parallel SUCCESS)$ and it then checks whether the computed value and the received value are the same. If same, S and R begin secure communication using the session key. Otherwise, they start the entire steps again.

4 Discussion

In this section, we discuss the performance of the proposed key delivery protocol through the comparison with the representative existing work [13]. Fig. 4 compares the security strength between the proposed protocol and the protocol in the existing work. The security strength of the existing work is always the same as the generated key length, that is $2^{-80} (\approx 8.2718 \times 10^{-25})$. However, the security strength of the proposed

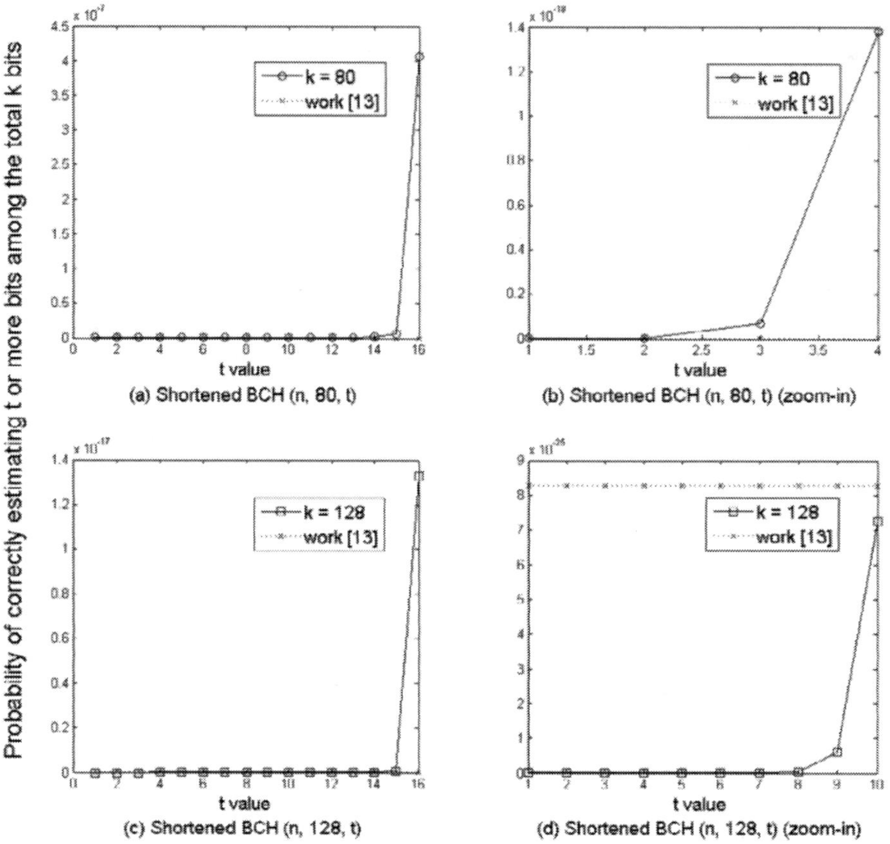

Fig. 4. Key extimation probability according to *t* and a key length

protocol depends on the parameter value, specifically, *k* and *t*, of the BCH code (*n, k, t*); here, *n* is the total bit length of the BCH-encoded data, *k* is the bit length of the BCH input data, and *t* is the number of correctable bits.

In order to get some profitable information, a passive or active adversary should find out a valid session key or guess it accurately. Since it is very difficult for the adversary to directly obtain the biometric information from the body of the attack target, the adversary has to predict the key without a given biometric information. If the adversary can precisely estimate (*k-t*) bits or more, then he/she get a valid session key. Accordingly, we can compute the probability (*P*) of correctly estimating (*k - t*) bits ore more among the total *k* bits as below,

$$P = \sum_{i=k-t}^{k} {}_kC_i \left(\frac{1}{2}\right)^k . \qquad (1)$$

Fig. 4 stands for the key prediction probability according *k* and *t* in the proposed protocol and the existing protocol. Figs. 4(b) and 4(d) are enlarged versions of Figs. 4(a) and 4(c), respectively. As shown in Figs. 4(a) and 4(b), when $k = 80$, the key prediction probability is higher in the proposed protocol than in the work [7] at all *t* values. However, in case that $k = 128$ and $t \leq 10$, the key prediction probability of the proposed protocol is lower than that of the existing work. Besides, as the error correction rates of the proposed protocol and the existing protocol are about 0.078 and 0.088, respectively, they are almost similar.

Next, let's look at the key generation time. We assume that 3-bit IPIs are used for a key generation and 70 IPIs are measured per a minute. A 128-bit key for the proposed protocol requires 36.57 secs ($= \frac{128}{3} \times \frac{60}{70}$), while a 80-bit key for the existing protocol needs 58.28 secs ($= \frac{204}{3} \times \frac{60}{70}$). As already expected, the proposed protocol can significantly reduce the key establishment time, compared with the existing protocol, by approximately 35%.

5 Conclusion

In this paper, we proposed an efficient key delivery protocol. Compared to the existing work, we have significantly reduced key generation time by decreasing the size of the witness required to generate a secret key. This advantage will enable faster response by reducing the time to access a secure medical device in an emergency.

In the near future, we will perform real-time testing using actually measured photoplethysmogram in order to investigate the availability of the proposed protocol. Furthermore, we will demonstrate how high probability that a session key between two biometric sensors is established on a simulator to be built in the near future.

Acknowledgements

This work was supported by the ICT R&D program of MSIP/IITP[2016-0-00575-002, Feasibility Study of Blue IT based on Human Body Research]

References

1. K. K. Venkatasubramanian, A. Banerjee, S. K. S. Gupta, *PSKA: Usable and Secure Key Agreement Scheme for Body Area Networks*, IEEE Trans. Information Technology in Biomedicine (2010)
2. N. Jammali, L. C. Fourati, *PFKA: A Physiological Feature based Key Agreement for Wireless Body Area Network*, International Conf. Wireless Networks and Mobile Communications (2015)
3. C. Hu, X. Cheng, F. Zhang, D. Wu, X. Liao, D. Chen, *OPFKA: Secure and Efficient Ordered-Physiological-Feature-based Key Agreement for Wireless Body Area Networks*, IEEE INFOCOM, pp. 2274-2282 (2013)
4. M. Khalil-Hani, R. Bakhteri, *Securing Cryptographic Key with Fuzzy Vault based on a new Chaff Generation Method*, International Conf. High Performance Computing and Simulation (2010)
5. Y. Lu, S. Bao, *Efficient Fuzzy Vault Application in Node Recognition for Securing BSNs*, IEEE International Conf. Communications (2014)
6. Y. Lu, S. Bao, M. Chen, R. Jin, *Fuzzy Vault Based Automatic Secret Sharing in BSNs*, International Conf. Biomedical Engineering and Informatics (2013)
7. A. Juels, M. Sudan, *A Fuzzy Vault Scheme*, Designs, Codes and Cryptography (2006)
8. C. C. Poon, Y. T. Zhang, S. D. Bao, *A novel biometrics method to secure wireless body area sensor networks for telemedicine and m-health*. IEEE Commun. Mag., pp. 73–81 (2006)
9. S. D. Bao, C. C. Y. Poon, Y. T. Zhang, *Using the timing information of heartbeats as an entity identifier to secure body sensor network*, IEEE Trans. Information Technology in Biomedicine, **12**, pp. 772-779 (2008)
10. G. H. Zhang, C. C. Y. Poon, Y. T. Zhang, *Analysis of using interpulse intervals to generate 128-bit biometric random binary sequences for securing wireless body sensor networks*, IEEE Trans. Information Technology in Biomedicine, **16**, pp.176-182 (2012)
11. G. H. Zhang, Y. X. Zhang, Y. T. Zhang, A Comparison of Binary Number Generators for Wireless Body Sensor Networks Security, IEEE-EMBS International Conf. Biomedical and Health Informatics (BHI), pp.782-784 (2012)
12. M. Rostami, A. Juels, F. Koushanfar, *Heart-to-heart (H2H): authentication for implanted medical devices*, ACM CCS, pp. 1099–1112 (2013)
13. R. M. Seepers, J. H. Weber, Z. Erkin, I. Sourdis, C. Strydis, *Secure Key-Exchange Protocol for Implants Using Heartbeats*, ACM International Conf. Computing Frontiers, pp. 119-126 (2016)
14. C. Y. P. Carmen, Z. Yuan-Ting, B. Shu-di, *A Novel Biometrics Method to Secure Wireless Body Area Sensor Networks for Telemedicine and M-Health, IEEE Communications Magazine*, pp. 73-81 (2006)
15. S. Cherukuri, K. K. Venkatasubramanian, S. K. S. Gupta, *BioSec: A Biometric Based Approach for Securing Communication in Wireless Networks of Biosensors Implanted in the Human Body*, International Conf. Parallel Processing Workshops (2003)
16. K. Cho, D. H. Lee, *Biometric Based Secure Communications without Pre-deployed Key for Biosensor Implanted in Body Sensor Networks*, International Workshop on Information Security Applications, pp.203-218 (2011)
17. K. Cho, B. Chung, *Lightweight Biometric Key Agreement Scheme for Secure Body Sensor Networks*, International Journal of Communications, **1**, pp.218-222 (2016)

MATEC Web of Conferences **125**, 03007 (2017) DOI: 10.1051/matecconf/201712503007
CSCC 2017

An improved technique for the detection of pilot contamination attacks in TDD wireless communication systems

Dimitriya Mihaylova[1,*], *Zlatka* Valkova-Jarvis[1], and *Georgi* Iliev[1]

[1]Faculty of Telecommunications at Technical University of Sofia, 8 Kl. Ohridski Blvd, Sofia 1000, Bulgaria

Abstract. One of the problems phasing the physical layer security of a wireless system is its vulnerability to pilot contamination attacks and hence schemes for its detection need to be applied. A method proposed in the literature consists of training with two N-PSK pilots. Although the method is effective in most of the cases, it is not able to discover an attack initiated during the transmission of the second pilot from the pair if both the legitimate and non-legitimate pilots coincide. In this current paper, an improvement to this method is proposed which detects an intruder who misses the first pilot transmission. The suggested improvement eliminates the usage of threshold values in the detection – a main drawback of previously existing solution.

1 Introduction

One of the major problems in wireless networks relates to ensuring their security. In an endeavour to achieve this a new strategy, called physical layer security (PLS), has been developed. Instead of using crypto-algorithms, PLS relies on the changes in the physical properties of the channel when an intruder attempts to participate in the communication.

In spite of the fact that PLS improves secrecy without using the complex computational systems that are typical of cryptographic schemes, some of its weaknesses, as observed in [1], require extensive additional research. One of these weaknesses is the capability of the malicious user to interfere with the process of channel estimation. This vulnerability can be exploited in what is known as a *pilot contamination attack*, a comprehensive description of which can be found in [2].

A time division duplex (TDD) system such as massive MIMO (MaMIMO), where the uplink and downlink channels are reciprocal and the channel state information (CSI) is obtained during a training phase, is particularly vulnerable to such a pilot contamination attack. Different levels of CSI at the transmitter and the eavesdropper (ED) and their influence on the confidentiality of a system are discussed in [3]. The process of channel estimation on MaMIMO consists of the receiver sending pilot signals to the transmitter, which then computes the CSI and, based on this result, designs its precoder. The objective of a prospective eavesdropper is to send pilots together with the legitimate receiver and thus to produce incorrect channel estimation at the transmitter end, resulting in an erroneous precoder, which also sends the data signal in the direction of the attacker. By this active attack the intruder could overcome the passive eavesdropping resistance of a MaMIMO system, as is observed in [4].

A pilot contamination attack undermines security at the physical layer and consequently has a detrimental effect on the security capability of the whole system. Hence the significance of introducing schemes for the detection of a pilot contamination attack and the need to terminate the communication in the event that one is detected.

2 System model

The current paper is focused on a technique for the detection of pilot contamination attacks. The system is TDD, composed of a single cell in which a base station (BS) with multiple antennas - M in number – communicates with a legitimate user (LU) and where an ED tries to circumvent the security. The model, used for the sake of simplicity, is composed of a single LU and one ED in the cell, both of them equipped with a single antenna transceiver. In addition, the channels are assumed to be static and subject to Additive White Gaussian Noise (AWGN), and user mobility is not included.

The system model is depicted in Fig.1.

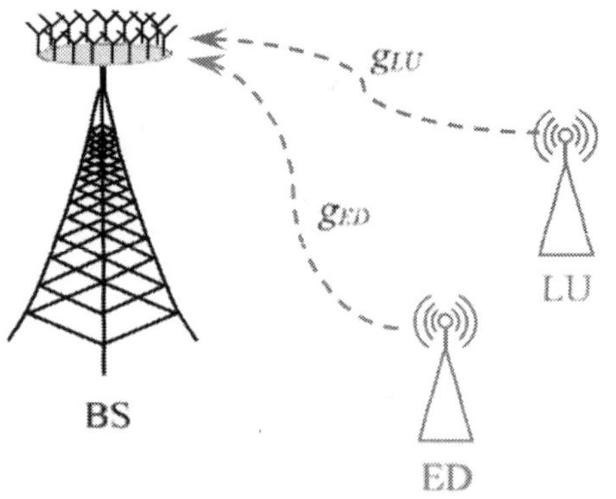

Fig. 1. The system model.

* Corresponding author: dam@tu-sofia.bg

DOI: 10.1051/matecconf/201712503007

During the uplink TDD phase, the LU and ED synchronically send their pilot sequences to the BS, where the CSI is computed. The uplink channels of the LU and ED, denoted as g_{LU} and g_{ED} respectively, follow Eq. 1:

$$\begin{aligned} g_{LU} &= \sqrt{P_{LU} d_{LU}}\, h_{LU} \\ g_{ED} &= \sqrt{P_{ED} d_{ED}}\, h_{ED}, \end{aligned} \tag{1}$$

where P_{LU} and P_{ED} are the transmit powers of the LU and ED, d_{LU} and d_{ED} are scalars for the large-scale fading, and h_{LU} and h_{ED} are $M \times 1$ vectors for the small-scale fading.

3 Two random N-PSK pilots detection method (2-N-PSK)

A simple and effective technique for the detection of a pilot contamination attack is suggested in [5]. This method consists in sending random PSK pilot signals during the uplink channel estimation phase of a TDD system. An 8-PSK constellation is shown in Fig. 2, where the relationship between the coordinates of a complex number, its trigonometric form, and its module and argument representation is given by Euler's equation:

$$q = x + iy = r(\cos\varphi + i\sin\varphi) = re^{i\varphi}. \tag{2}$$

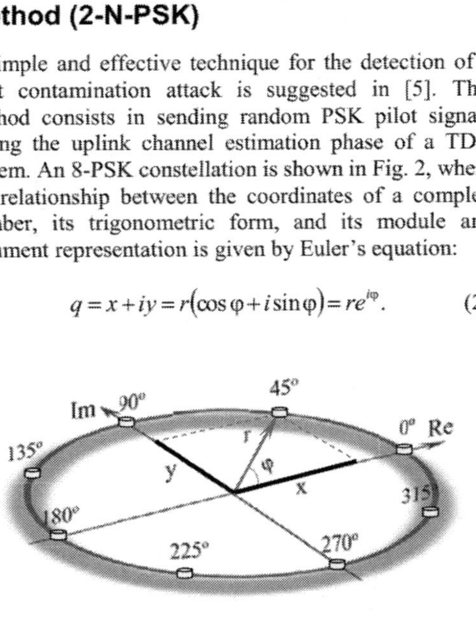

Fig. 2. Eight Phase Shift Keying (8-PSK) constellation diagram. Geometric representation of a complex number.

This method makes a decision about the presence of an ED via the following procedure. The LU sends two N-PSK pilot symbols to the BS, the first of which could be publicly known, with the second being chosen at random. The signals received at the BS for the first and second pilots, denoted as y_1 and y_2 respectively, are given in Eq. (3):

$$\begin{aligned} y_1 &= g_{LU} p_1^{LU} + g_{ED} p_1^{ED} + n_1 = \\ &= \sqrt{P_{LU} d_{LU}}\, h_{LU} p_1^{LU} + \sqrt{P_{ED} d_{ED}}\, h_{ED} p_1^{ED} + n_1 \\ y_2 &= g_{LU} p_2^{LU} + g_{ED} p_2^{ED} + n_2 = \\ &= \sqrt{P_{LU} d_{LU}}\, h_{LU} p_2^{LU} + \sqrt{P_{ED} d_{ED}}\, h_{ED} p_2^{ED} + n_2, \end{aligned} \tag{3}$$

where the pilots sent from the LU during the first and the second training periods are p_1^{LU} and p_2^{LU}, the pilots from the ED are p_1^{ED} and p_2^{ED}, and the AWGN in the first and second time slots are n_1 and n_2 respectively.

In the BS the CSI is obtained by processing the received signals. Their correlation is computed by Eq. (4), where $(\cdot)^H$ means Hermitian matrix and n_{12} is the noise result:

$$\begin{aligned} z_{12} &= \frac{y_1^H y_2}{M} = \\ &= \frac{1}{M}\left(\sqrt{P_{LU} d_{LU}}\, h_{LU} p_1^{LU} + \sqrt{P_{ED} d_{ED}}\, h_{ED} p_1^{ED}\right)^H \times \\ &\left(\sqrt{P_{LU} d_{LU}}\, h_{LU} p_2^{LU} + \sqrt{P_{ED} d_{ED}}\, h_{ED} p_2^{ED}\right) + n_{12} \end{aligned} \tag{4}$$

The scalar product of the correlation result is then analysed.

If its phase converges to a phase of a valid N-PSK symbol, two possible scenarios exist: either the ED is absent during both of the training periods or the ED is present in only one of the time slots.

If the scalar product of the correlation result has an angle that does not converge to a valid N-PSK phase, a definite decision is taken that the pilot contamination attack appears in both the training periods.

Summarising the simulation results of the 2-N-PSK, the method reveals the intervention of a non-legitimate user in the channel estimation procedure when either one or both of the ED's pilots differ from the pilots of the LU. When the ED sends a pilot which equals the one sent from the LU in only one of the training intervals, the 2-N-PSK technique undertakes additional verification to determine if this intervention is non-legitimate in nature. The worst case scenario, which the method is not able to detect, is when both of the attacker's pilots coincide with the legitimate pilots or when the first is the same and the second is shifted by 180 degrees, i.e. the complex number of the second ED's pilot is reciprocal to that of the LU.

The main advantages and drawbacks of the method are discussed in [6], where other solutions which have been proposed in the literature are also analysed and compared.

4 An improved technique for the 2-N-PSK detection method

As described in the previous sections, the objective of the pilot contamination attack is to compromise the CSI and thus to reveal the legitimate channel to the malicious user. So, once the ED starts sending pilots to the BS synchronically with the LU this process would continue until all of the information about the channel is revealed. However, the ED could participate in the communication at a later stage and thus miss one or more of the training periods. This is exactly the case when, despite the presence of the ED in the second slot, the angle of the correlation result converges to a valid N-PSK phase if the ED guesses either the pilot of the LU or the reciprocal number.

When this situation occurs, the authors in [7] suggest a revision of the amplitude of the received signals, since the received power of the contaminated pilot will be larger than that of the non-contaminated pilot. To decide if the difference in the received power is a result of a pilot contamination attack in one of the slots or is simply a consequence of the natural imperfections of the channel, the ratio of the received signals is compared with some thresholds. A decision that a malicious user has sent a pilot during one of the slots is made if the result of the ratio is outside the range defined by the thresholds. Otherwise, the conclusion is that there is no ED present during the channel estimation procedure.

Since the assignment of thresholds requires previous channel knowledge, the reference values are difficult to obtain and their definition is subject to possible error. Therefore, in the case of pilot contamination during only one of the slots the use of the 2-N-PSK detection method is not effective.

In the current paper we propose another solution for the detection of a pilot contamination attack initiated during the second training period, which avoids the use of threshold values. We will consider the scenario in which the ED duplicates the pilot of the LU or sends its reciprocal value. Hence, if the phase of the correlation result z_{12} is a valid N-PSK angle, the technique described below is applied. It is illustrated in Fig. 3.

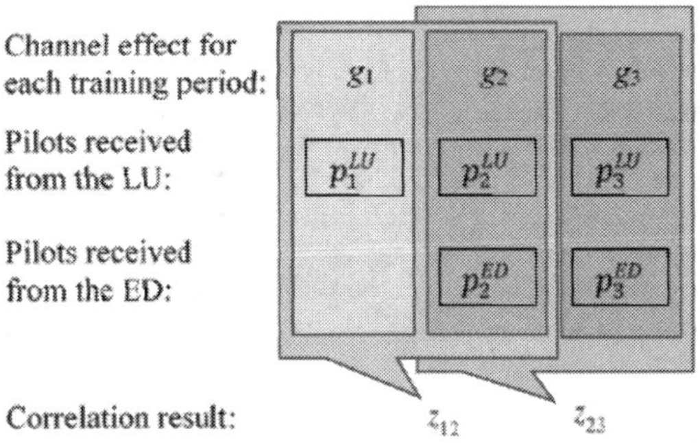

Fig. 3. Channel gain comparison for the received pilots.

Considering the first pilot transmission, according to Eq. (3) apart from the noise, the signal received at the BS in the absence of an ED is:

$$y_1 = p_1^{LU} g_{LU}, \tag{5}$$

which defines the value of the channel gain as:

$$g_1 = g_{LU} = \frac{y_1}{p_1^{LU}}. \tag{6}$$

In the second training slot the ED's contamination with $p_2^{ED}=p_2^{LU}$ forms:

$$y_2 = p_2^{LU} g_{LU} + p_2^{ED} g_{ED} = p_2^{LU}\left(g_{LU} + g_{ED}\right), \tag{7}$$

leading to channel gain:

$$g_2 = g_{LU} + g_{ED} = \frac{y_2}{p_2^{LU}}. \tag{8}$$

Since the BS is familiar with both the sent pilots and the received signals, the values of the channel gains can be calculated and the channel knowledge from the two training periods can be compared. Different values correspond to an attack in one of the slots. However, as

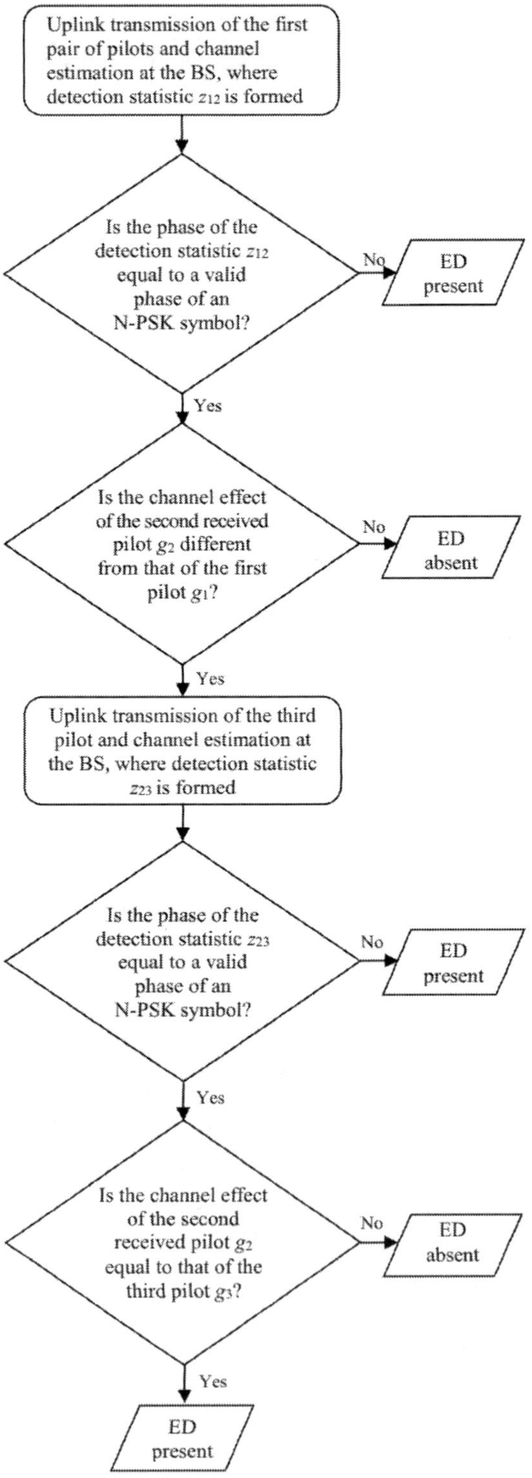

Fig. 4. Flow chart of the improved 2-N-PSK method.

the impact of noise could give rise to some limited variations, in order to avoid setting thresholds of an acceptable range of alteration, the values of the channel gain could be compared to those calculated during the next training interval.

First, the correlation of the next two pilots is computed. In the worst case, where the ED manages to guess the third pilot, the received signal is:

$$y_3 = p_3^{LU} g_{LU} + p_3^{ED} g_{ED} = p_3^{LU}\left(g_{LU} + g_{ED}\right). \quad (9)$$

The argument of the correlation z_{23} between the second and the third pilot is also a valid N-PSK phase. Then the effect of the channel gain for the third received pilot is calculated:

$$g_3 = g_{LU} + g_{ED} = \frac{y_3}{p_3^{LU}} \quad (10)$$

and the intrusion is confirmed in the case of equal channel gain values in the second and the third received pilots, i.e. when $g_2 = g_3$.

The block diagram depicted in Fig. 4 illustrates the proposed approach.

Another interpretation of the proposed technique can be observed in Fig. 5, where a geometric representation of the 8-PSK pilots is shown together with the correlation results. For simplicity, the simulation is carried out with a single antenna BS, a static channel is assumed and noise influence is not taken into account. The amplitudes of the pilots from the LU and ED are regarded as being equal and their value is set to 1. For the purposes of the simulation, the channel between the BS and LU is assumed to be g_{LU}= 1 and that between the BS and ED to be g_{ED}= 0.7.

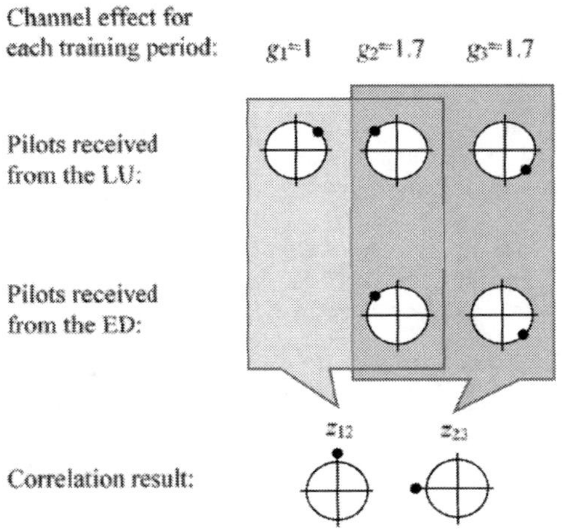

Fig. 5. Example interpretation of the proposed technique.

As can be seen from the example in Fig. 5, when no ED is present the channel gain at the BS equals the gain of the legitimate channel. When an attack is under way, the resulting channel gain equals a larger value, which continues to show up during the next pilot sessions. Even in the worst case, when the ED's pilots coincide with those of the LU and the phase of the correlation result is a valid 8-PSK angle, the second appearance of the channel gain g_2 indicates the presence of an intruder.

In addition, the proposed complement to the 2-N-PSK method could be used to indicate the presence of an attacker whose first pilot repeats the LU's pilot and whose second pilot is reciprocal to the LU's second pilot. This situation could not be detected by the 2-N-PSK itself, since the phase of the detection statistic coincides with the angle of a symbol from the N-PSK constellation. However, the value of the channel gain computed from the first received pilot differs significantly from the channel gain of the second pilot, which demonstrates the presence of malicious intervention.

5 Conclusion

Effective schemes for the detection of pilot contamination attacks are recommended for use in wireless systems and the communication needs to be interrupted if such an attack is discovered.

In this paper a complement of the 2-N-PSK method for the detection of pilot contamination attacks is proposed. The improvement does not cover the case when the attacker repeats both the pilots of the legitimate user and further investigation is needed in this direction. Although the solution improves the accuracy of the detection when the channel is static, its efficiency needs to be tested in the presence of noise.

In the case of low power noise, it is possible to outline an area around the N-PSK symbols in which there is no ED present. In this situation the proposed technique will provide a good detection performance. When the signal-to-noise ratio is very low, comprehensive information about the noise power at the BS is necessary in order to improve the success rate of the method. These elements are important considerations for future studies.

Acknowledgment: This work is supported by the Project № BG05M2OP001-2.009-0033-C01

References

1. W. Trappe, IEEE Commun. Mag., **53**, 16-20, (2015)
2. X. Zhou, B. Maham, A. Hjorungnes, IEEE TWC, **11**, 903–907, (2012)
3. Ta-Yuan Liu, Pin-Hsun Lin, Shih-Chun Lin, Y.-W. Peter Hong, Eduard Axel Jorswieck, IEEE Commun. Mag., **53**,19–25, (2015)
4. D. Kapetanovic, A. Al-Nahari, A. Stojanovic, F. Rusek, *Proc. IEEE Int. Symp. PIMRC*, 2014
5. D. Kapetanovic, G. Zheng, K.-K. Wong, B. Ottersten, *Proc. IEEE Int. Symp. PIMRC*, 2013
6. D. Mihaylova, G. Iliev, Z. Valkova-Jarvis, *Proc. BalkanCom* (Tirana, Albania 2017)
7. D. Kapetanovic, G. Zheng, F. Rusek, IEEE Commun. Mag., **53**, 21–27, (2015)

Communication Framework for Tele-rehabilitation Systems with QoS Guarantee

Nikolay Dandanov[1], *Plamen* Semov[1], *Antoni* Ivanov[1], *Nicole* Christoff[1,2], *Vladimir* Poulkov[1]

[1]Technical University of Sofia, Faculty of Telecommunications, Sofia 1756, Bulgaria

[2]Aix-Marseille Université, CNRS, LSIS UMR 7296, France

Abstract. Nowadays, there is great interest in developing telemedicine technologies. These technologies will provide health care from distance swiftly and lightly, as well as reduce the expenses for activities, such as rehabilitation. Telemedicine applications are possible due to the advances in information technologies and the ever-expanding communication network infrastructure. The network characteristics bandwidth, packet loss, latency, jitter and policies are crucial for the performance of tele-rehabilitation systems. Because in tele-rehabilitation human lives are at stake, guaranteeing the Quality of Service (QoS) is important. In this paper, an approach for assuring the QoS for information transmission in tele-rehabilitation systems is proposed.

1 Introduction

In the recent years, a great advancement in the development of technological and rehabilitation methods was observed. By combining rehabilitation and the advancements in Information and Communications Technologies (ICT), tele-rehabilitation arises. This is a subpart of telemedicine, consisting of a system for controlled rehabilitation "via the Internet" – an actual application possibility with a promising development in the future. A tele-rehabilitation system is a bilateral system, consisting of master and slave devices, which interact through a bidirectional communication channel, as shown in Figure 1.

Various communication media can be used in tele-rehabilitation: transmission lines, wireless transmission or the Internet. Depending on the different environments, based on their performance, a decision for using TCP (Transmission Control Protocol) or UDP (User Datagram Protocol) for transporting the information has to be made.

TCP provides reliable two-way communication and guarantees data delivery at the cost of retransmissions and long timeouts that are detrimental to the performance of real-time applications, such as teleoperation. UDP does not require reception acknowledgments, eliminating unnecessary waiting time, which makes it appealing for teleoperation.

In tele-rehabilitation, improved quality video-assisted telecommunication services and devices, such as videoconferencing, webcams and telepresence, assist in treatments. Sensors and body monitoring data, voice, sounds, medical images and information related to tele-haptics (the sense of touch), as well as virtual reality, can also be transmitted for rehabilitation purpose. Moreover, with the massive utilization of portable smart terminals, such as smartphones, laptops and tablets, web-based approach and mobile applications are becoming ever more common and can potentially be used for tele-rehabilitation.

In tele-rehabilitation, human lives are at stake. Hence, the consequences of an error or delays in information transmission could be serious. This is the reason why reliable techniques of networking must be developed and applied [1]. Particular stress should be laid on the importance of availability and reliability of the communication networks. Interruptions in network operation, e.g. introduced by a power cut, could cause errors or delays in the transmitted data. These specifics pose strong requirements for the bandwidth, delay, jitter, reliability and availability of the network connection for tele-rehabilitation.

Five fundamental network characteristics are crucial for the performance of tele-rehabilitation systems.

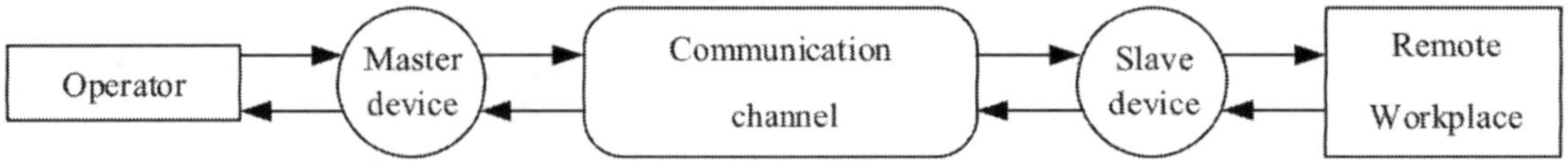

Fig. 1. Tele-rehabilitation concept

* Corresponding author: n_dandanov@tu-sofia.bg

Bandwidth is a fundamental requirement that there is enough capacity in a network path for all of the packets to get through unimpeded. Packet loss is the amount of packets, which do not arrive correctly at their destination, and it should be less than 1-2%. Latency is the time delay between an event occurring on one site and the remote end seeing it. For a voice transmission with good quality, a latency of less than 150 ms is needed. Jitter is the time variation of latency among the packets, which can result in packets arriving in different order than transmitted. Jitter should be under 50 ms. Policies are introduced by network elements like firewalls and Network Address Translation (NAT) devices. If the traffic is encrypted for security, some additional aspects should also be considered.

The rest of the paper is organized as follows. In the next section, some telecommunication approaches for tele-rehabilitation purposes ensuring the required QoS are considered. We present the problem definition and motivations in section 3. In section 4, various categories of telemedicine data and their Quality of Service (QoS) requirements are described. The proposed approach for assuring the QoS for information transmission in tele-rehabilitation systems is described in section 5. Finally, we conclude the paper in section 6.

2 State of the art

In this section, some telecommunication approaches for tele-rehabilitation purposes guaranteeing the required QoS are considered.

In [2] to overcome instability, caused by unknown and varying time delay, an event-based teleoperation system is employed for synchronization of the robot and the operator. The developed teleoperation system could be easily adjusted to be useful for a tele-rehabilitation robot. UDP is used for sending operator commands and forcing feedback. Additionally, the size of packets for UDP compared to TCP puts less load on the communication channel. To avoid breakings in the control cycle, a server application monitors the control cycle's duration.

The effect of time delay can be reduced with latency tolerant control methods as presented in [3]. The proposed architecture is evaluated with three models of the system components: a master device, a slave device and a communication system. The master includes a controller and the human operator, which are connected via a high-delay medium to the slave model. The master side is where the "human operator" or the replacing automatic control device is located. The surgical staff can be found here, providing the control signals for the actuators of the slave. The communication system includes a transmitter, a receiver and a communication medium. In the deriving cascade setup, the time delay can be partially alleviated using appropriate predictive controllers, tuned to the master and slave systems [3].

In [4], the authors discuss the importance of provisioning QoS and information security in the field of medical care, focusing on the use of data communications, Internet, cloud and Smart Ubiquitous Computational Devices (SUCDs). They present possible scenarios, related to remote control of Medical Surgical Robots via the Internet. The main idea is to lay stress on the importance of QoS provisioning and cyber security in the field of telemedicine, which also applies to tele-rehabilitation.

To assess the convenience of the remote tele-laboratory technique, different configuration architectures have been tested in [5]. For each of these configurations, experiments have been performed, consisting of 400 remote movements of a robot. These experiments use TCP and UDP protocols. Performance details, obtained from these experiments, show that the configuration with UDP is fastest and the most convenient one for traditional tele-robotic applications. A new software protocol, called Interoperable Telesurgical Protocol (ITP), has been developed, which is open and meant for sharing. The first data interface in ITP is a packet of 84 bytes, using the UDP network protocol for fast transmission. The small size of the ITP packet makes it suitable for high packet rates.

In [6], the Secure ITP enciphers communications between the master and slave. The communications use TLS (Transport Layer Security), DTLS (Datagram TLS) protocols and the AES (Advanced Encryption Standard) cipher.

Analysis of the possibilities for providing real-time services for bilateral teleoperation systems on existing wireless infrastructures, using only application layer measurements without any information from the network layer, is presented in [7]. Since teleoperation systems should have a video feedback channel, the influence of video transmission on the transmission quality in the other two periodical channels is analysed. Based on the delay variation measurements of the two opposite directions, data channels identify WLAN (Wireless Local Area Network) problems.

The packet latency is observed and analysed in [8]. Teleoperation latency becomes noticeable to human users for delays above about 200ms, starts to be annoying at around 500ms, and significantly impacts the performance of tasks at 1s and longer. In order to provide true tele-surgical care, software systems need to be in place to protect the integrity of the signal and minimize the latency of data transmission between the surgeon and the patient. One way to protect remote surgery's connectivity is to send information over multiple communication pathways or routes.

An investigation into the use of SIP (Session Initiation Protocol) protocol for a telemedicine transition system was proposed in [9]. According to standard computing platforms and operating systems, it is easier to integrate SIP protocol into the application program. Second, SIP is an extensible protocol. Therefore, it is able to run a wide range of applications with a variety of media formats and loads. In the SIP protocol, a number of criteria have been developed for instant messaging, resource management, media streaming (video) and online friend management applications.

In [10], a robotic tele-rehabilitation system has been developed to perform both interactive and cooperative bilateral rehabilitation. The system has been evaluated using four computer games, each with different specification of the data transmission and event management. In addition, robotic teleoperation techniques have been implemented to evaluate the performance and stability of the force reflecting strategy in the cooperative bilateral configuration. The internet communication between the robots has been performed through sockets, using the TCP/IP protocol stack.

A classification of the security threats against mobile surgical tele-robotic systems is presented in [11]. Communication networks security is an active research area and many existing strategies may be also applicable to tele-rehabilitation systems. Identifying those, as well as developing novel, specialized mitigation strategies, and analysing their impact on system's performance, security and safety, is an emerging research question.

3 Problem Definition

Based on the specifics of tele-rehabilitation and the resulting requirements on the network performance and QoS, a method for conforming to these demands for information transmission in tele-rehabilitation systems should be provided. The approach has to satisfy the requisites for bandwidth, latency, packet loss, jitter, policies, reliability and availability of network connection.

4 QoS Requirements

The data for telemedicine, which is transferred through a communication channel, can be divided into five main categories with different QoS demands:

- Voice;
- Video;
- Data from sensors;
- Teleoperation;
- Virtual reality.

4.1 Voice over IP (Internet Protocol)

In order to digitize human voice effectively, a sampling rate of 8 kHz with 8 bits per sample is needed, which results in a minimum data transfer rate of 64 kbps (kilobits per second). The delay must be less than 100 – 150 ms. Some notable low bit rate compression algorithms used are ITU G.723.1 and G.729A. It is common to use silence compression to reduce the payload dramatically.

4.2 Video

The type of video, which is most important in telemedicine, is the video, which is transmitted in real-time. The throughput in raw format, without compression, varies depending on three main features – resolution, frame rate and bits per pixel. For video with resolution 1920×1080 pixels, 30 frames per second, RGB (Red, Green and Blue) color components and 8 bits per pixel per color, a total video stream with data rate of 1.5 Gbps in raw format is produced. Techniques, which compress individual frames, have been developed. In addition, motion prediction is used to compress the data even further. Most of the time, the throughput for video transmission is dependent mainly on the motion within the images. Factors, such as resolution and scanning rates, are not so relevant. A full-resolution HDTV (High-Definition TeleVision) stream, compressed with the MPEG2 method, requires 19.3 Mbps of data bandwidth. For online video streaming with 720p resolution, a 2.4 Mbps channel is required.

Every computation for compressing and decompressing the video adds delay to the total transmission delay. The greater the compression ratio used, the greater the latency introduced. The total delay requirement for video transmission is less than 150 ms.

4.3 Data from sensors

For this type of information, the requirements for throughput and delays are not so stringent. However, high requirements for data integrity are set. Efficient transport protocols are needed to provide correctly received sensors' data.

4.4 Teleoperation and Virtual reality

This category includes a mix of video, voice, text, sensors data and remote device commands, which are to be multiplexed and transferred through the communication channel simultaneously in real-time. A list of provisional network requirements for teleoperation and virtual reality can be identified. These QoS requirements include [1], [4]:

- reliability and integrity;
- an acceptable end-to-end delay;
- multiplexing of various data rates resulting in high network bandwidth;
- low data error rate (BER – Bit Error Rate);
- low latency;
- constant jitter.

Studies show that the acceptable limit of time delay in terms of a surgeon's perception of safety is roughly 330 ms [1]. A study in [1] shows how the interactive Internet gaming is affected by the end-to-end delay. The results are presented in Table 1.

Table 1. Perception of interactive Internet gaming as a function of end-to-end delay [1]

End-to-end delay	***< 50 ms***	***50-100 ms***	***100-150 ms***	***100-150 ms***	***> 200 ms***
Per-cep-tion	Excel-lent game-play	Good game-play	Noticea-bly decreased gameplay	Signifi-cantly effected gamep-lay	Intole-rable game-play

5 Approach for assuring QoS for information transmission in tele-rehabilitation systems

Because of the various transport protocols and telemedicine technologies existing, we propose adaptable and scalable framework for tele-rehabilitation. Its main functions are:

1) providing abstraction and generalization of the transmitted data among telemedicine devices from different vendors. This way, the network infrastructure is transparent;

2) Data Tunneling for meeting various QoS requirements;

3) M2M communication capabilities for tele-rehabilitation devices from different vendors;

4) General and scalable application software for all telemedicine technologies;

5) Adaptation of the transport layer for reaching target QoS requirements.

The proposed framework is illustrated on Figure 2.

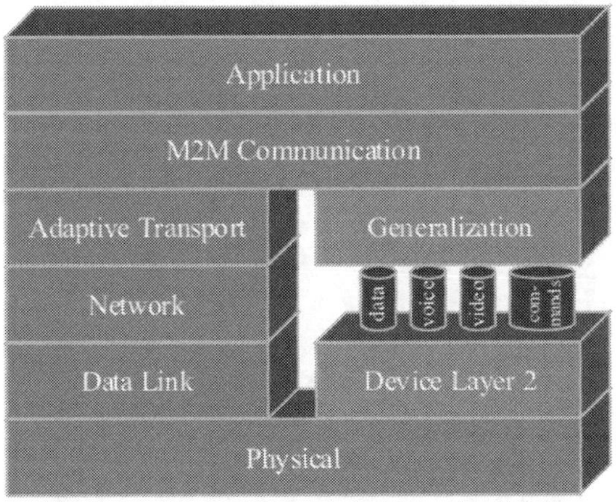

Fig. 2. Proposed framework for assuring QoS for information transmission in tele-rehabilitation systems

The layer "Generalization" has the main responsibility to set the parameters for each data stream generated by a tele-rehabilitation device. It controls tele-rehabilitation devices, or more specifically – their output data streams. Another main responsibility is to adapt or translate different teleoperation and sensors data streams, which are sometimes unique for the device itself. The layer gives a compatibility function for all tele-rehabilitation devices to work together.

The main responsibility for the "M2M Communication" layer is to give tele-rehabilitation devices abilities to share and request data from each other, which is needed for taking an overall decision by a given tele-rehabilitation device. This functionality can be realized as a sublayer of the Application layer.

"Application" layer is the man-machine interface, which sets QoS requirements for the data streams. It works also like a SIP server to negotiate data stream parameters between different vendor-specific or technology-specific devices. Another function is to track communication KPIs (Key Performance Indicators), such as delays, throughput, error rate, latency, etc. This acts as a feedback for the "Generalization" and "Adaptive Transport" layers, so they can further modify data and communication parameters and thus meet QoS requirements.

The "Adaptive Transport" layer has the task to fulfill the QoS requirements for every data stream on the transport layer by using various transport protocols – existing or novel. For transporting information, which is insensitive to delays but should be received with no errors, TCP can be used, for example for controlling a remote workplace or receiving measurements from sensors.

Because of the broad development of the Internet and associated IP networks and protocols, this is one of the candidates for providing such transport. In this case, one appropriate protocol for transporting media in real-time is SIP in addition with Session Description Protocol (SDP) and Real-time Transport Protocol (RTP) or Secure RTP (SRTP). For a transport protocol, either TCP, UDP, Stream Control Transmission Protocol (SCTP) or any other suitable implementation can be leveraged.

By implementing this multilayer framework, we separate the communication channel functions from the tele-rehabilitation devices functions. Hence, tele-rehabilitation technologies can be developed independently from the network infrastructure. This method will be a common interface for all tele-rehabilitation technologies, providing network communication capabilities.

With the use of data tunneling, QoS requirements for the transmission of different information types are met. For meeting stringent QoS requirements, a tailored protocol on the transport layer can be developed. The M2M communication capabilities assure compatibility between tele-rehabilitation devices from different vendors. This unity enables general and scalable application software for all telemedicine technologies.

The information with particular requirements for network performance can be separated into different traffic flows. Each of these flows should use a distinct stack of protocols, tailored to fulfilling the requirements posed by this type of information.

As the technologies and services in the networks evolve, backward compatibility should be maintained, so that devices from both newer and older generations can interoperate together.

6 Conclusions and Future Work

The proposed communication framework for tele-rehabilitation systems with QoS guarantee provides abstraction and generalization of the transmitted data among various tele-rehabilitation devices. Hence, the network infrastructure is transparent to the communicating devices. Data tunneling is leveraged for meeting various QoS requirements. M2M communication capabilities are added for interoperability. Adaptation in the transport layer protocols is a means to reach target QoS requirements.

As a result, the framework can serve to develop generalized and scalable application software for all tele-rehabilitation technologies.

The communication between tele-rehabilitation systems has to be designed in such way, so that it allows compatibility between devices from different vendors and of various generations, and provides openness of the underlying protocols and methods.

The next steps in the development of the common communication framework for tele-rehabilitation systems would include a more elaborate selection and design of the protocols in each layer should be performed. After a protocol stack has been chosen, the integrity of the whole stack shall be tested and evaluated. This can be done by simulating the interoperation of separate protocols and devices or by implementing the stack in tele-rehabilitation systems and devices.

Acknowledgment

This work is supported by Project № BG05M2OP001-2.009-0033-C01.

References

1. J. Marescaux, J. Leroy, M. Gagner, F. Rubin, D. Mutter, M. Vix, S. Butner, M. K. Smith. Transatlantic Robot-Assisted Telesurgery. Nature, **413**, 379–380 (2001)
2. I. Petrović, F. Kolonić, P. Korondi. Internet Based Teleoperation for Cooperative Navigation and Manipulation. Mec. Eng., **6**, 356-368 (2009)
3. S. Jordán, A. Takács, I. Rudas, T. Haidegger. Modelling and Control Framework for Robotic Telesurgery (2013)
4. M. Smithwick, Network Options for Wide-Area Telesurgery. Telemed. and Tel, **1** (3), 131-38 (1995)
5. R. Marín, P. J. Sanz, P. Nebot, R. A. Wirz. Multimodal Interface to Control a Robot Arm via Web: A Case Study on Remote Programming. IEEE Transactions on Industrial Engineering, **52** (6), 1506-1520 (2005)
6. G. Lee, B. Thuraisingham. Cyberphysical systems security applied to telesurgical robotics. Comp. St. & Int. **34**, 225–229 (2012)
7. P. Haller, T. Vajda, Z. Szanto, L. Marton. Communication Performance Evaluation of Bilateral Teleoperation systems Implemented over WLAN. http://www.ms.sapientia.ro/~martonl/Research_TE_Documents/WLAN_Meas.pdf (2013)
8. T. Lendvay, J. Rosen, B. Hannaford. Telerobotics: Its Future in Clinical Application. Pediatric Robotic and Reconstructive Urology: A Comprehensive Guide, *Blackwell Publishing Ltd.*, 314-327 (2012)
9. T. Long. Telemedicine Transmission System Design Research Based on Session Initiation Protocol. Soft. Eng., 9, 298-307 (2015)
10. A. A. Siqueira, K. P. Michmizos, H. I. Krebs. Development of a robotic system for bilateral telerehabilitation. In Proceedings of 22nd International Congress of Mechanical Engineering (COBEM 2013), Ribeirão Preto, SP, Brazil. ABCM, Rio de Janeiro, Brazil, 8427-8436 (2013)
11. T. Bonaci, H. J. Chizeck. Surgical Telerobotics Meets Information Security. RSS 2012 Workshop on Algorithmic Frontiers in Medical Robotics: Manipulation in Uncertain, Deformable, Heterogeneous Environments. Sydney, Australia (2012)

DOI: 10.1051/matecconf/201712503009

State-of-the-art on Virtualization and Software Defined Networking for Efficient Resource Allocation on Multi-tenant 5G Networks

Christos Tsirakis[1*], *Panagiotis* Matzoros[1], and *George* Agapiou[2]

[1]OTE Academy S.A., Maroussi-Athens, Greece
[2]OTE S.A., Maroussi-Athens, Greece

Abstract. Global data traffic explosion is expected to set stringent requirements for next generation networks in the next decades. Besides, very low latencies will have to be guaranteed for enabling new delay critical services. However, current Software Defined Networking (SDN) solutions have limitations in terms of separating both data and control planes among tenants/operators, and the capability to adapt to new or changing requirements. Moreover, some virtualization schemes do not ensure isolation of resources and do not guarantee bandwidth across the entities. While some others fail to provide flexibility to the slices to customize the resource allocation across the users. Therefore, novel SDN and virtualization techniques should be implemented to realize the upcoming 5G network that will facilitate at least efficient resource allocation and multi-tenancy among the plethora of different requirements.

1 Introduction

Currently, mobile networks are a key element of society, enabling communication, access and information sharing. In future, the number of smart devices connected to the Internet is projected to expand to somewhere between 20 and 46 billion by 2020, and in turn the mobile data traffic, that these smart devices generate, will determine a 1000-fold capacity increase by 2020 [1]. In addition, except from the constantly increasing traffic demand from the end users, one of the major concerns of wireless networks comes from the spectrum scarcity. Studies show that spectrum resources owned by a single operator are often underutilized; as in [2], where macro-cell utilization seems to be typically around 20-40%. Thus, current wireless and mobile networks should evolve to become more intelligent, efficient, secure, and extremely scalable to deal with a torrent of data communications without deteriorating the quality and reliability of the provided services and effectively reducing capital and operational costs if possible.

On the one hand, this challenge has led to the consideration of new access technologies or the need to improve the efficiency of the existing ones. Paradigms such as Heterogeneous Networks (HetNets) (e.g., femtocells and small cells), the combination of different Radio Access Technologies (RATs) and the use of the cognitive radio concept have appeared as candidate alternatives to increase the efficiency of wireless networks. On the other hand, these paradigms will potentially increase the costs of network operators (CapEx and OpEx) by requiring the deployment of more infrastructure, and consequently making network management more complex [3].

Not long ago, the fifth generation (5G) cellular network was defined and discussed globally. The 5G-PPP group released its plan and perspectives for future mobile networks until 2020. It considers virtualization and SDN to be two major trends in the evolution of the mobile network and serve as key enablers for future 5G cellular networks [4, 5]. There is a close relationship between virtualization and SDN. They are mutually beneficial, highly complementary to each other, and share the same feature of promoting innovation, creativity, openness and competitiveness [6].

However, it is emphasized that the virtualization and deployment of network functions do not necessarily rely on SDN technologies, and vice versa [7]. While both network virtualization and SDN manage networks, they rely on different methods. While SDN separates the control and data/forwarding planes to offer a centralized view of the network, virtualization is a complementary approach to SDN for network management primarily and focuses on optimizing the network services themselves.

Indeed, due to the strong coupling between control and data planes (and its physical embedding in the network elements) in conventional networks, the development and deployment of new networking features would imply a modification of the control plane of all network devices through the installation of new firmware and, in some cases, hardware upgrades. This approach would imply very long periods of deployment and unaffordable costs, therefore the new networking features are commonly introduced via expensive, specialized, and hard-to-configure equipment (also

* ctsirakis@oteacademy.gr

known as middleboxes). Also, the centralization of the control logic in a controller with global knowledge of the network state simplifies the development of more sophisticated networking functions (e.g., routing algorithms), services, and applications.

In that sense, the network virtualization is a promising solution that will allow for realizing the vision of 5G and includes many advantages [9]. First of all, it has the advantage of separating the physical infrastructure from its services. More specifically, physical mobile network infrastructure resources, such as radio access networks (RANs), core networks (CNs), and physical radio resources (licensed spectrum), can be abstracted and sliced into virtual cellular network resources, and shared by multiple tenants/operators through isolating each other. As a result, network infrastructure can be decoupled from the services it provides, and differentiated/customized services can be provided to customers, enhancing the Quality of Service (QoS) management. Also, virtualization enables the hostage of multiple virtual base stations on a physical one, so there is no need to deploy new infrastructure and avoid payments for constructing new base stations and their maintenance. Furthermore, efficient resource utilization is achieved by keeping the scarce wireless channels occupied as much as possible when allowing usage of unused resources by one entity to other entities and assigning wireless resources intelligently based on the actual need [10].

However, wireless network virtualization (WNV), in comparison with wired network virtualization, introduces a number of challenges that do not exist in the wired domain: signal propagation, interference, user mobility, radio access technology. Wireless links are less reliable, suffer from interference and have a fluctuating capacity depending on the channel quality. All these challenges make the problem more complicated and will have to be taken into account when developing a proper solution to meet the expected requirements [11].

In this context, a key business model for reducing future deployment and operational costs is network sharing. There are different approaches to network sharing:

1) *Spectrum sharing*: It refers to the licensed spectrum owned by operators that can be utilized by multiple contracted operators based on agreements. The total available radio spectrum is considered as a whole resource and is virtualized as the abstracted access medium.

2) *Infrastructure sharing*: Only infrastructures are shared in this case. Infrastructure sharing can be classified into two categories: (a) passive sharing and (b) active sharing. Passive sharing refers to the reuse of components such as physical sites, tower masts, cabling, cabinets, power supply, and so on. Active RAN sharing involves sharing base stations among multiple mobile virtual network operators (MVNOs) with either separate spectrum resources for each entity or shared spectrum resources through spectrum pooling.

3) *Full network sharing*: It is the combination of spectrum sharing and infrastructure sharing, which means both radio resource and network infrastructure can be shared among multiple mobile network operators (MNOs) based on agreements.

Thus, a survey of resource sharing deployments is a key building block for virtualizing future mobile networks in order to address the explosive capacity demand of mobile traffic, reduce infrastructure investments, and enhancing the overall resource utilization by utilizing the wireless resources more efficiently. In this work, state-of-the-art virtualization and SDN solutions, that attempt to address the aforementioned challenges and meet the requirements of the upcoming 5G technology, are presented.

2 Virtualization and Resource Allocation

This work focuses more on RAN virtualization and ways to efficiently share the available spectrum among multiple tenants. In fact, when implementing slicing on a wireless network, the main issue is how to assign resources to the different slices [11]. This is known as the resource allocation problem. In this section, we present current proposals for resource allocation and multi-tenancy support in wireless networks, and explain the characteristics of these solutions.

As already mentioned, the WNV concept can be applied at different layers and degrees, from only virtualizing the core network to virtualizing the radio spectrum and physical layer of base stations (BSs).

One option for the implementation of spectrum virtualization could be to share the RF front end and antenna of the BS, like in [12], where the flexible slicing of a radio into multiple slices, each operating on different spectrum fragments, is enabled. Modifying the scheduling software in use is another option. In fact, the vast majority of approaches modify the frame scheduler to assign Physical Resource Blocks (PRBs) to the slices [13, 14, 15, and 16]. The PRB structure is described in [13]. As a result, BS virtualization can allow each tenant to have its own customized schedulers over its slice.

The BS is the entity responsible for accessing the radio channel and scheduling the air interface resources between the users. In order to effectively allocate resources, these should be virtualized first. Therefore, the BS has to be virtualized to virtualize in turn the air interface. Virtualizing the BS is similar to node virtualization. The physical resources of the node (e.g., CPU, memory, I/O devices) are shared between multiple virtual instances. A hypervisor, which is a well-known virtualization solution, is added on the top of the physical layer of the BS and is responsible for virtualizing the BS and the spectrum as well. In summary, the hypervisor accomplishes two tasks:

1) Hosts several virtual BSs onto a physical BS.

2) Schedules the wireless resources (PRBs) among the different virtual BSs.

Following this way, two different versions of the hypervisor exist [17]:

1) *Static version:* the hypervisor allocates the PRBs among the different tenants just once at the beginning. The number of the allocated PRBs for each tenant is equal, where each virtual BS will get the exact same

amount of PRBs and keeps it regardless if it is being actually used or not.

2) *Dynamic version:* the PRBs are allocated to the different tenants in a dynamic manner at equal time intervals. The amount of the allocated PRBs will depend on the load that each tenant is experiencing during the last time instance. In this way, each operator will only get his required share of the PRBs and less waste of resources will occur.

Decades of experience with Internet has reinforced a general rule of thumb: it is nearly always more preferable to dynamically allocate resources over static resource allocations. Dynamic resource allocation can allow for more efficiency and flexibility in situations where the demand on scarce resources is not predictable. The multi-tenant model defines that each tenant is dynamically assigned and reassigned all the physical and virtual resources according to its consumers' demand [18].

This solution uses the PRB as the minimum resource granularity that can be allocated, and assigns PRBs among the different virtual nodes, and not among the users (as typically done by a scheduler). The PRBs are scheduled to the different virtual BSs based on previously arranged contracts (SLAs), which specify different guarantees for the operator owning a virtual BS. After the hypervisor allocates PRBs to the virtual BSs, each virtual BS allocates the PRBs to its users. In other words, the hypervisor is responsible for scheduling the air interface (between BSs and user equipment) resources (e.g., OFDMA sub-carriers).

Some other works, trying to avoid such a low-level strategy as in [13], propose mechanisms that schedule the resources between slices in a higher layer. This approach is generally done at the MAC layer or at the Network-layer. Such kind of work is the solution proposed in [15], where the authors define the Network Virtualization Substrate (NVS) that is a substrate on BSs enabling effective virtualization of the wireless resources. The NVS integrates virtualization into the WiMAX base station uplink/downlink scheduler software.

For efficient resource allocation, the BS includes a collection of schedulers. More specifically, the NVS is designed as a hierarchical scheduler divided in two steps, slice scheduling and flow scheduling:

- *Slice scheduling* is the process of selecting which slice has to transmit at every moment. Every slice can request a certain amount of resources or bandwidth. Given that by maximizing the total utility of the slices directly maximizes the revenue of the MNO, the slice that maximizes the total utility will be selected.

- *Flow scheduling* can be customized by the selected slice (controlled by each tenant), selecting this way which flow should transmit in the first position. Basically, a traffic classifier splits packets in flows, according to their different QoS. More specifically, a downlink flow scheduler determines the sequence of packets to be transmitted in the downlink direction based on flow priorities, like VoIP traffic, video traffic, file sharing, and Web traffic with decreasing priority. Similarly, an uplink flow scheduler determines uplink slot allocation based on the bandwidth requests from clients, channel quality, and QoS.

Finally, when both decisions have been taken, the frame scheduler will be invoked to perform the allocation of the resources to the resulting packet (mapping PRBs to specific slots in the MAC frame).

A similar framework is demonstrated in [19]. However, those researchers claim that instead of performing prioritization between different applications for each SP separately after allocation of RBs (post-allocation priority), prioritization between different traffic types should be performed for the multiple Service Providers (SPs) jointly prior to the allocation of resources (pre-allocation priority). The reason is that a SP would possibly have insufficient resources to serve all real-time (RT) requests if the scheduler assigns resources on a fair-throughput basis without considering the traffic heterogeneity.

In another work [16], the authors take one step further and propose a spectrum-sharing framework to exploit virtualization in real LTE networks. They introduce the Virtual Resource Manager (VRM), which is responsible for collaborative spectrum allocation for different tenants, as a replacer of the LTE Radio Resource Manager (RRM) in a virtual network, in order to improve the system performance in a multi-tenant collaborative network. The VRM includes the fundamental radio resource scheduling feature, which distributes radio resources among Mobile Units (MUs), taking into account channel conditions and QoS requirements. The researchers develop an innovative approach called Time Domain Muting (TDM) Radio Resource Virtualization (RRV). This approach combines Radio Resource Virtualization (RRV) and enhanced Inter-Cell Interference Coordination (eICIC) to improve spectrum usage while protecting SPs from excessive interference. RRV, eICIC, and HetNet as well, are shortly explained below.

A HetNet consists of a mixture of different base station types such as high power base stations (macro cell) and low power base stations (small cell). Small cell BSs are typically deployed in hotspots to offload traffic from the macro cell. So, HetNet is regarded as an efficient solution to increase the network capacity in order to be able to carry the forecasted increase of data traffic [20].

For explaining the different spectrum allocation schemes, the following example is used [21]:

A simple two-cell model is used in a virtualized HetNet. It consists of the BS-A of a large cell, belonging to SP-A, and a small cell of SP-B that is located within BS-A coverage. A traditional network would distribute distinct spectrum bands for each SP in these two cells. In contrast, a virtualized network does not separate the bandwidth.

In the case of Separate Spectrum Virtualization (SSV), SP-A and SP-B can get varying amounts of spectrum every time interval based on their requirements, agreements, and policies. In SSV, the spectrum slices allocated to the two SPs in the same time interval do not overlap. This is an easy way to ensure isolation, but it does not make full use of the complex characteristic of spectrum since it creates an interference-free set of spectrum slices.

In the case of Radio Resource Virtualization (RRV), considering the radio resources as a function of geography and signal strength, it seems that the spectrum can be reused with varying levels of interference. This means that the same slice of spectrum can be reused by multiple SPs in the same time interval in overlapping geographical areas (that is, there is some interference).

One of the technical challenges, that needs to be addressed in order to fully benefit from HetNet deployments, is the interference management. Thus, the technique proposed is called eICIC with TDM muting for downlink co-channel deployment of macro and small cells [20].

The basic principle of TDM eICIC is to prevent the macro cell BSs from transmitting on certain subframes, meaning that they are periodically muted. During these subframes, no data signal will be sent from the macro cell BSs. As a result, the small cell BSs can schedule MUs, which would otherwise experience too high interference from the macro cell BS. However, the macro-BS should still transmit critical system information and Common Reference Signals (CRS).

3 SDN and Multi-tenancy

In the previous section, the state-of-the-art in mobile networks virtualization was provided. Below, the same concepts are extended to IP networks for enabling multi-tenancy.

SDN can be deployed on any traditional network environment, from home and enterprise networks to data centers. As the recent research on SDN shows that it is a promising technology, different commercial virtualization platforms based on SDN concepts have started to appear.

VMWare has proposed a network virtualization platform (NVP) [22] that provides the necessary abstractions to allow the creation of independent virtual networks for large-scale multi-tenant environments. NVP is a complete network virtualization solution that allows the creation of virtual networks, each with independent service model, topologies, and addressing architectures over the same physical network. With NVP, tenants do not need to know anything about the underlying network topology, configuration, or other specific aspects of the forwarding devices. NVP's network hypervisor translates the tenants' configurations and requirements into low-level instruction sets to be installed on the forwarding devices.

IBM has also recently proposed SDN VE [23], another commercial and enterprise-class network virtualization platform. SDN VE uses OpenDaylight as one of the building blocks of the so-called software-defined environments (SDEs). This solution also offers a complete implementation framework for network virtualization. Like NVP, it uses a host-based overlay approach, achieving advanced network abstraction that enables application-level network services in large-scale multitenant environments.

FlowVisor [24] is one of the early technologies to virtualize an SDN. Its basic idea is to allow multiple logical networks share the same OpenFlow networking infrastructure. For this purpose, it provides an abstraction layer that makes it easier to slice a data plane based on off-the-shelf OpenFlow-enabled switches, allowing multiple and diverse networks to coexist. Five slicing dimensions are considered in FlowVisor: bandwidth, topology, traffic, device CPU, and forwarding tables. Moreover, each network slice supports a controller, i.e., multiple controllers can coexist on top of the same physical network infrastructure. Each controller is allowed to act only on its own network slice. In general, a slice is defined as a particular set of flows on the data plane. From a system design perspective, FlowVisor is a transparent proxy that intercepts OpenFlow messages between switches and controllers. It partitions the link bandwidth and flow tables of each switch. Each slice receives a minimum data rate, and each guest controller gets its own virtual flow table in the switches.

Similar to FlowVisor, OpenVirteX [25] acts as a proxy between the NOS and the forwarding devices. However, its main goal is to provide virtual SDNs through topology, address, and control function virtualization. All these properties are necessary in multitenant environments where virtual networks need to be managed and migrated according to the computing and storage virtual resources. Virtual network topologies have to be mapped onto the underlying forwarding devices, with virtual addresses allowing tenants to completely manage their address space without depending on the underlying network elements addressing schemes.

AutoSlice [26] is another SDN-based virtualization proposal. Differently from FlowVisor, it focuses on the automation of the deployment and operation of virtual SDN (vSDN) topologies with minimal mediation or arbitration by the substrate network operator. Additionally, AutoSlice targets also scalability aspects of network hypervisors by optimizing resource utilization and by mitigating the flow-table limitations through a precise monitoring of the flow traffic statistics. Similarly to AutoSlice, AutoVFlow [27] also enables multi-domain network virtualization. However, instead of having a single third party to control the mapping of vSDN topologies, as is the case of AutoSlice, AutoVFlow uses a multiproxy architecture that allows network owners to implement flow space virtualization in an autonomous way by exchanging information among the different domains.

FlowN [28] is based on a slightly different concept. Whereas FlowVisor can be compared to a full virtualization technology, FlowN is analogous to a container-based virtualization, i.e., a lightweight virtualization approach. FlowN was also primarily conceived to address multitenancy in the context of cloud platforms. It is designed to be scalable and allows a unique shared controller platform to be used for managing multiple domains in a cloud environment.

Each tenant has full control over its virtual networks and is free to deploy any network abstraction and application on top of the controller platform.

4 Conclusion

Cellular technology is expected to be a critical tool for future connectivity. In 5G cellular networks of the future, virtualization and SDN are expected to be on the frontline, and it is a challenge to find ways to exploit them to handle the vast increase in data traveling across both the access and the core network. The IoT era will require extended automation of network functions, via virtualization, QoS-aware differentiation of different classes of IoT traffic, and the collection and analysis of data to enable virtualization and SDN to optimize the network. It is thus imperative for the future 5G architectural models to be designed having in mind the IoT data explosion.

After reviewing the proposed approaches above, some conclusions can be done for the design of next wireless virtualization solutions. As it has been shown throughout the state-of-the-art review, virtualization can be done at different parts of the network and also different levels: flow level, sub-carrier or time slot level, or even at the lowest level of hardware components. Virtualization at higher levels leads to a better multiplexing of resources across slices (and hence increased utilization with fluctuating traffic), and simplicity of implementation, but at the same time can reduce the efficiency of isolation and the flexibility of resource customization. Whereas, virtualization at lower level leads to a reverse effect.

As described throughout this work, there have been recent efforts to introduce wireless network virtualization, explain its performance requirements, architecture, uses cases and potential approaches to challenges. While both industry and academia embrace virtualization at unprecedented speeds, the development is still at an early stage, with many open questions. Although the combination of SDN with virtualization in future wireless access networks is expected to support the anticipated vast increase in the number of mobile devices, the heterogeneity in devices, requirements, and usage scenarios, leaves many hurdles yet to be taken. There are important unexplored research challenges such as resource management, inter-operability, instantiation, heterogeneity support, which should be addressed in order to realize an a virtualized 5G network that facilitates efficient resource allocation and multi-tenancy.

This work has received funding from the European Union Horizon 2020-MCSA-ITN-2015 Innovative Training Networks (ITN) under grant agreement No 675806 (5G-AURA) and No 641985 (5G-Wireless).

References

1. CISCO White Paper, *Cisco visual networking index: Global mobile data traffic forecast update, 2016-2021*, (2017)
2. A.J. Staring, *Applying the Cloud Computing Model in LTE based Cellular Systems*, (2012)
3. M. Richart, et al., *Resource Slicing in Virtual Wireless Networks: A Survey*, IEEE Trans. on Network and Service Management, **13**, 15 (2016)
4. N. Bizanis, F.A. Kuipers, *SDN and Virtualization Solutions for the Internet of Things: A Survey*, IEEE Access, **4**, 16 (2016)
5. E. Hossain, M. Hasan, *5G Cellular: Key enabling technologies and research challenges*, IEEE Instrumentation & Measurement Mag, **18**, 11 (2015)
6. S. Sun, et al., *Integrating network function virtualization with SDR and SDN for 4G/5G networks*, IEEE Network, **29**, 6 (2015)
7. Y. Li, M. Chen, *Software-Defined Network Function Virtualization: A Survey*, IEEE Access, **3**, 12 (2015)
8. P. Rost, et al., *Benefits and Challenges of Virtualization in 5G Radio Access Networks*, IEEE Communications Mag., **53**, 8 (2015)
9. J. Cadir, et al., "Resource Pooling for Wireless Networks: Solutions for the Developing World", ACM SIGCOMM Computer Communication Review, **46**, 6 (2016)
10. P. Rost, et al., "Benefits and Challenges of Virtualization in 5G Radio Access Networks," IEEE Comms Magazine, **53**, 8 (2015)
11. M. Richart, et al., *Resource Slicing in Virtual Wireless Networks: A Survey*, IEEE Trans. on Network and Service Management, **13**, 15 (2016)
12. S.S. Hong, et al., *Picasso: Flexible RF and Spectrum Slicing*, Proc. of the ACM SIGCOMM, 12 (2012)
13. Y. Zaki, et al., *LTE Wireless Virtualization and Spectrum Management*, WMNC, (2011)
14. C. Liang, F.R. Yu, *Wireless Virtualization for next generation mobile cellular networks*, IEEE Wireless Comms, **22**, 9 (2015)
15. R. Kokku, et al., *NVS: A Substrate for Virtualizing Wireless Resources in Cellular Networks*, IEEE/ACM Trans. on Networking, **20**, 14 (2012)
16. X. Wang, et al., *A Collaborative Spectrum-Sharing Framework for LTE Virtualization*, IEEE Conf. on CIC, (2015)
17. Y. Zaki, et al., *LTE mobile network virtualization: Exploiting multiplexing and multi-user diversity gain*, Jour. Mobile Networks and Applications, **16**, 9 (2011)
18. J. Cadir, et al., *Resource Pooling for Wireless Networks: Solutions for the Developing World*, ACM SIGCOMM Comp. Comm. Rev., **46**, 6 (2016)

19. A. Abdelhamid, et al., *Resource Allocation for Heterogeneous Traffic in LTE Virtual Networks*, IEEE Int. Conf. on MDM, (2015)
20. Y. Wang, K.I. Pedersen, *Performance Analysis of Enhanced Inter-cell Interference Coordination in LTE-Advanced Heterogeneous Networks*, IEEE 75th VTC Spring, (2012)
21. X. Wang, et al., *On Radio Resource Sharing in Multi-Antenna Virtualized Wireless Networks*, Proc. of ACM Int. Workshop on MSWiM 2013, 10 (2013)
22. T. Koponen, et al., *Network virtualization in multi-tenant datacenters*, in Proc. 11th USENIX Symp. Netw. Syst. Design Implement., 14 (2014)
23. S. Racherla, et al., *Implementing IBM Software Defined Network for Virtual Environments*, Durham, NC, USA: IBM RedBooks, (2014)
24. R. Sherwood, et al., *Can the production network be the testbed?* , in Proc. 9th USENIX Conf. Oper. Syst. Design Implement., 6 (2010)
25. A. Al-Shabibi, et al., *OpenVirteX: A Network Hypervisor*, (2014)
26. Bozakov, P. Papadimitriou, *AutoSlice: Automated and scalable slicing for software-defined networks*, in Proc. ACM Conf. CoNEXT Student Workshop, 2 (2012)
27. H. Yamanaka, et al., *AutoVFlow: Autonomous virtualization for wide-area OpenFlow networks*, in Proc. 3rd Eur. Workshop Softw. Defined Netw., (2014)
28. D.A. Drutskoy, *Software-defined network virtualization with FlowN*, Ph.D. dissertation, Dept. Comput. Sci., Princeton Univ., Princeton, NJ, USA, (2012)

Load balancing in 5G Networks

Christos Tsirakis[1*], *Panagiotis* Matzoros[1], *Petros* Sioutis[2] and *George* Agapiou[3]

[1]OTE Academy S.A., Maroussi-Athens, Greece
[2]Voice Research Lab, OTE S.A., Maroussi-Athens, Greece
[3]Wireless Research Lab, OTE S.A., Maroussi-Athens, Greece

Abstract. The expected huge increase of mobile devices and user data demand by 2020 will stress the current mobile network in an unprecedented way. The future mobile networks must meet several strong requirements regarding the data rate, latency, quality of service and experience, mobility, spectrum and energy efficiency. Therefore, efforts for more efficient mobile network solutions have been recently initiated. To this direction, load balancing has attracted much attention as a promising solution for higher resource utilization, improved system performance and decreased operational cost. It is an effective method for balancing the traffic and alleviating the congestion among heterogeneous networks in the upcoming 5G networks. In this paper, we focus on an offloading scenario for load balancing among LTE and Wi-Fi networks. Additionally, network graphs methodology and its abstracted parameters are investigated in order to better manage wireless resource allocation among multiple connections. The COHERENT architectural framework, which consists of two main control components, makes use of such abstracted network graphs for controlling or managing various tasks such as traffic steering, load balancing, spectrum sharing and RAN sharing. As a result, the COHERENT project eventually develops a unified programmable control framework used to efficiently coordinate the underlying heterogeneous mobile networks as a whole.

1 Introduction

The COHERENT project [1] focuses on developing a next generation unified control and coordination framework for various heterogeneous radio access networks, but with focus on LTE and Wi-Fi. It adopts the concept of resource and service virtualization across technology domains, while the key innovation of the project is the development of a unified programmable control framework used to coordinate the underlying heterogeneous mobile networks as a whole.

The flexibility, programmability and efficient control and coordination have been promised by the COHERENT architecture for RAT, by using abstracted network graphs, central control and coordinator (C3) and real time controller (RTC). The COHERENT architectural work targets to exploit these advantages in addressing different goals of PHY and MAC layers, by proposing varied abstraction and control methodologies.

In the COHERENT framework, the communication between entities is primarily envisioned using abstracted network graphs. More specifically, it describes the network graphs and the potential applications of them. It also describes a wide variety of metrics for abstractions that can be utilized in building different network graphs. These include measurements based, probabilistic or statistics based, simulations based, and existing standards based abstractions.

The COHERENT coupling of network virtualization with software defined networking (SDN) control facilitates efficient operation using abstract network views (which are referred to as network graphs) that can be used for network monitoring and optimization, as well as for sharing of physical resources among various virtual operators, introducing new business models and enabling new exploitation opportunities. The potentials of network virtualization and SDN could be applied in several domains, such as offloading and load balancing.

Offloading has been proposed as a candidate solution for improving the cellular utilization by delivering data originally targeted for cellular networks via complementary network technologies [3]. This promising solution can significantly lower the operational cost of a network operator, especially when existing deployed infrastructure is exploited.

Femtocell technique was initially proposed to improve indoor voice and data services of cellular networks [5], [6] and [9]. First, the usage occurs primarily indoors (homes or offices). Thus, the operators get the opportunity to offload heavy users through femtocells. Femtocells operate on the same licensed spectrum as the macrocells of cellular networks and thus do not require special hardware support on mobile phones. Additionally, femtocells can be deployed quickly, unlike traditional macrocellular deployments. The disadvantages include the need to install short-range base stations in residential or small-business environments, and the solution is usually for indoor environments and cannot handle macroscopic mobility.

* ctsirakis@oteacademy.gr

Also, opportunistic peer-to-peer offloading technique was proposed in [7]. It is used to offload traffic from the cellular network to opportunistic peer-to-peer mobile network by selecting some users as the initial set to push the contents. Afterward, the initial set of users aids the propagation of the contents to further users through short-range wireless connectivities (e.g., Bluetooth and ad hoc Wi-Fi). Simulation results have shown that a large fraction of data can be offloaded from the cellular network.

In this work, we propose Wi-Fi for outdoor offloading. In general, Wi-Fi networks operate on the unlicensed frequency bands and cause no interference with 3G cellular networks. Wi-Fi is usually ubiquitously available in urban areas, either deployed by operators as commercial hotspots or deployed by users for residential usage. In [2], [8] and [10], research work is focused on the performance of Wi-Fi offloading on environments with high mobility, like large metropolitan areas.

The paper is organized as follows: Section II briefly presents two main architectural components, which are used as control mechanisms, and the network graphs are introduced as well. Section III presents a set of use case groups that the COHERENT could be applied and their implementation to a real example is described. Section IV focuses on an offloading use case for load balancing purposes. Finally, Section V consists of the conclusion and the future work that could be done for next generation mobile networks.

2 Control Components and Network Graphs

2.1 Architectural control components

According to the defined COHERENT layered architecture, a heterogeneous physical infrastructure layer includes a hybrid wireless domain composed by LTE/Wi-Fi access networks. Some examples of physical radio transceivers include LTE eNBs in cellular networks or Wi-Fi APs in the WLANs. LTE and Wi-Fi technologies were selected as they are expected to play an important role in the next generation wireless access networks.

COHERENT proposes two main architectural components used as control mechanisms:

The *Central Controller and Coordinator (C3)* is a logically centralized entity in charge of logical centralized network-wide control and coordination among entities in RAN based on centralized network view. C3 could be implemented with distributed physical control instances sharing network information with each other. Sharing network information among C3 instance creates the logically centralized network view and therefore achieves logical centralized control and coordination. In other words, C3 is one of the most critical architectural entity that allows flexible management of all network infrastructures (physical or virtual) at runtime and provides all the functionalities for the management and dynamic provisioning of multi-layer network connections.

The *Real-Time Controller (RTC)* is logical entity in charge of local or region-wide control, targeting at real-time control operations, e.g., MAC scheduling, queuing methods, etc. It has local network view. It could run directly on one Radio Transceiver (RT) or on a virtualized platform and receives monitoring information gathered from one RT or multiple RTs. It can delegate control functionality to the RTC agent which resides in the RTs. RTC communicates with an RTC agent/RTC agents on one RT or multiple RTs. A more detailed analysis for COHERENT architecture is presented in [4].

2.2 Network graphs and integration to C3

One of the main innovations in COHERENT is the way to aggregate abstracted information from radio network entities and to represent it as different types of network graphs. Information stored in the network graphs is exposed to the C3 control layers for high-level resource allocation and spectrum management. From an implementation point of view, the network graphs will be supported by a database infrastructure. A specific interface will be provided for the interaction of the Network Graphs Database with the C3 control plane, as shown in figure 1.

Note that there are different types of databases which are categorized according to their functions. For our analysis we consider:

- Structured Query Language (SQL)
- Non-SQL or, relational databases and non-relational databases.
- Graph databases

Their difference is about the way they are built, the type of information they store, and how they store it. Relational databases are structured, while non-relational databases are document-oriented and distributed. Open-source options for SQL databases include MySQL, PostgreSQL and SQLite, while for Non-SQL candidate solutions are MongoDB and Redis. While many documents describe the characteristics of each type in COHERENT we are particularly interested in the Non-SQL type and the Graph Database type. While great documentation and great software solutions describe the SQL and Non-SQL types, the Network Graphs databases are relatively new and in the following we provide a note for this type of database.

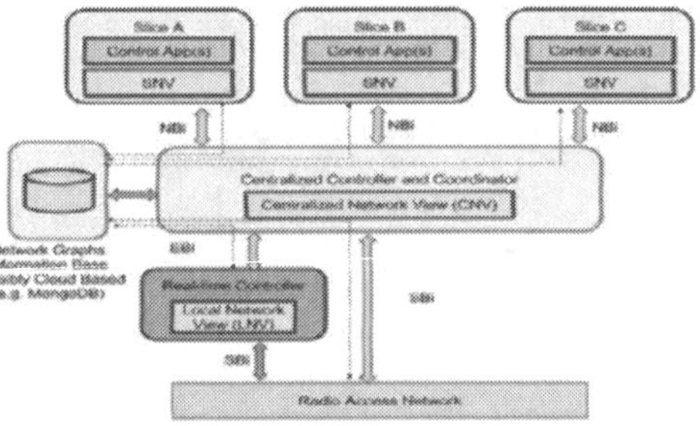

Fig. 1. C3 and supporting information database

While traditional databases compute relationships expensively at query time, a graph database stores connections, readily available for any "join-like" navigation operation. Accessing those already persistent connections is an efficient, constant-time operation and allows to quickly traversing millions of connections per second per core [Neo4j]. A graph database uses graph structures for semantic queries with nodes, edges and properties to represent and store data. Examples of Network Graph Database include: Neo4J, AllegroGraph, ArangoDB, OrientDB, Titan, Apache Giraph.

In our approach, the RTs will talk with the C3 and in turn the C3 will talk with the Network Graph Database. A direct access to the network elements will be also possible (without the interleaving of the C3), for actions that require fast responsiveness.

In COHERENT project, we are targeting extremely complex environments with hundreds of network elements and thousands of end users that are connected through multi-RAT infrastructures. In addition the runtime statistics that we are interested in for both the LTE and the Wi-Fi network can be used to define complex relationships while being exploited in various use cases.

3 Use Cases and Scenarios

3.1 COHERENT use cases

The use cases reflect the different perspectives of the COHERENT actors and highlight the benefits and new opportunities that could derive from the overall COHERENT framework. These use cases have been carefully selected due to their importance towards integrated 5G communications. It should be also noted that preliminary results for each use case are provided. Below, we present a set of use cases where the COHERENT approach could be applied:

Offloading for Load balancing: In this use case we consider an open design platform for LTE and Wi-Fi load balancing or/and offloading scenarios based on network information interworking.

Spectrum management: Due to the potentially large area to be considered, we identify a set of sub use cases:

- Spectrum sharing within the Coherent architecture,
- Spectrum sharing between microwave links and WiMAX networks, and
- Spectrum sharing between two TD-LTE networks.

RAN sharing: In this use case we exploit the unique programmability features of OpenAirInterface (OAI) by considering scenarios where the eNodeB is virtualized and supports concurrent operation of multiple Mobile Virtual Network Operators (MVNOs) with specific scheduling principles per operator.

Throughput improvement: In this use case we consider for per-user-throughput improvement using distributed antennas designs (DAS). This paradigm includes deployment of RRH, UE pairing based on a selection transmission technique for improving/maintaining per user throughput and coverage extension.

3.2 Multi-connectivity use case: SINR network graphs

In general, the Network Graphs are supported by a database infrastructure. Thus, the information related to the way user and base station transmissions affect neighbouring transmissions are stored in an Interference graph, while the base stations deployment and user locations are stored in a Topology Graph. Because of extreme LTE system complexity, these graphs are then used to facilitate efficient resource allocation, to make handover decisions and promote agility in decision making by the C3.

Maximizing the performance through effective resource optimization and load balancing under the conditions of heterogeneity, multi-connectivity and strict QoS requirements is key for enabling 5G. Here, heterogeneity can refer to: mixed use of cells (base stations or access points) of different sizes for the purpose of optimizing the network capacity; interworking of cellular systems with non-cellular short-range communications (inter-RAT); and, different node capabilities such as resource availability and signal processing capabilities. In general, user equipment (UEs) are typically capable of connecting to several access technologies, and hence the type of access should be selected based on which network can provide the best connection to a specific application. In multi-connectivity settings where each user can have multiple connections at the same time, the load of each base station can also be dynamically adjusted via allocation of the data rate to the same user but through different base stations. In this sense, the overall load can be balanced while the quality of service (QoS) is maintained.

Specifically, the multi-connectivity technique is proposed to utilize radio resources scheduled by multiple distinct base stations for a single user to enhance the throughput. In this way, the user equipment (UE) can exploit different eNodeBs (eNBs) resources for the uplink (UL) and the downlink (DL) transmissions. Another important characteristic of multi-connectivity is that it supports seamless mobility by eliminating handover interruption delays and errors, and optimizes capacity for devices connected in a heterogeneous network. Moreover, these multiple connections between each user and base stations (BS) can support multiple

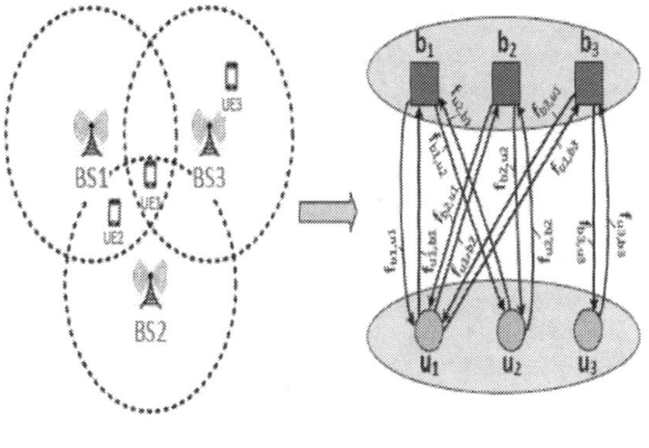

Fig. 2. From original network to network graph

traffic flows between users (video dissemination, gaming, social networking, etc.). Based on intended multi-connectivity application, the underlying L1/L2/L3 information is required to be abstracted and further computed. We establish network graphs of the underlying LTE RAN and we formulate an optimization problem for throughput maximization running as a control application that utilizes the network graph as an input under multi-connectivity use-case.

In figure 2, we observe the transformation of the original network to network graph, which represents the physical connectivity formed at the abstraction layer by extracting the radio access layer parameters.

In the multi-connectivity use case, the following parameters of interest are the abstracted parameters in both uplink and downlink directions that are extracted from the underlying network based on the LTE system:

- Reference signal received power of BS/UE
- Total number of PRBs of BS
- Maximum number of PRBs of UE
- Bandwidth per PRB
- Thermal noise power
- UE Aggregated maximum bit rate

The main focus is on a new problem of modelling of interference between adjacent BSs in frequency systems. An example of interference graph and required PHY-level measurements are shown, which can be used to increase spectral efficiency.

A visualization of the corresponding network graph is presented in figure 3 with 3 BSs and 18 UEs. For simplicity, only the SINR element is depicted in dB form on the edge (directed links between nodes). If there is no connectivity, i.e., SINR is smaller than the SINR threshold, then the property set is empty and no edge exists (e.g., 7 UEs in this case do not have any connection to all BSs). Then, the network graph that contains all properties of edges is provided as input to the algorithm of the applications for optimization.

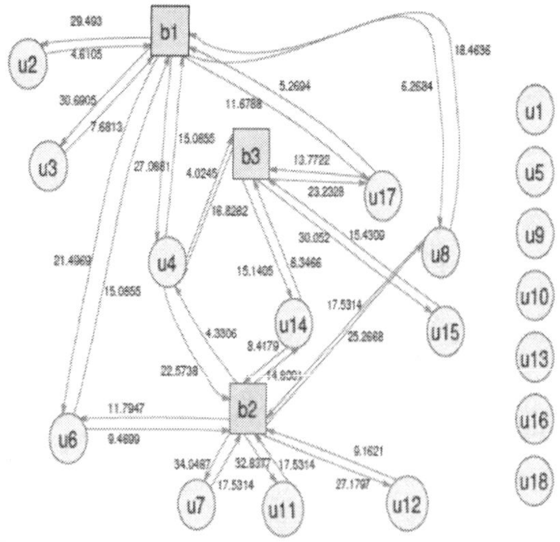

Fig. 3. SINR (in dB) of network graphs from underlying network

4 Load Balancing and Offloading Scenario

The unprecedented increase in the mobile data traffic volume, as well as the need for network coverage expansion are major concerns for mobile operators. Hence, it is becoming important to be able to offload data from the mobile network to the Wi-Fi network. Today 20% of data is landing on Wi-Fi in outdoor environment while 60% of data is landing in Wi-Fi in indoor environments. In highly populated areas even an 80% of data is landing in Wi-Fi networks. Therefore, the offloading from an eNodeB to Wi-Fi AP can lead to be able to load balance the overloaded commercial eNodeBs.

To show in COHERENT that services like video and voice can be offloaded from a mobile to a Wi-Fi network which can lead to load balance the mobile and cellular networks. Today in commercial networks it has been proven that these services like voice over LTE (VoLTE) and video over LTE (ViLTE), which are IMS-based services that can offer mobility and value added services, can be offloaded from a commercial mobile network to Wi-Fi network and have VoWiFi and ViWiFi respectively. The offloading process for application services is shown in figure 4.

Besides, an important key aspect of 5G is also the ability to effectively manage heterogeneous infrastructures in a unified programmable manner via proper RAT-agnostic abstractions capable of supporting crucial mobility management operations, such as load balancing and resource optimization.

The requirements at the process of load balancing between eNodeB and Wi-Fi AP can be as:

- A common user interface for any available service through the mobile or Wi-Fi network.
- Seamless service connectivity between the two networks.
- The latency at the offloading-load balancing process should be minimum.

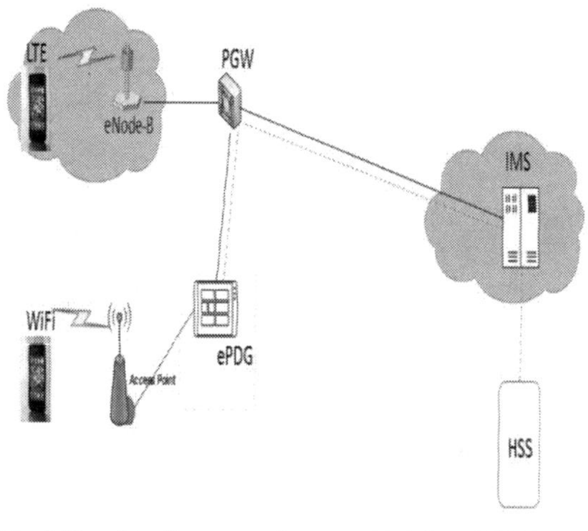

Fig. 4. The offloading process between eNodeB and Wi-Fi

Load balancing using commercial eNodeB and Wi-Fi AP is targeted to investigate the opportunities of finding technology agnostic abstractions. In this regard, a brief description of potential parameters for abstraction is provided. The abstraction parameters that can be utilized from the physical interface are the basic ones:

• For Wi-Fi the abstraction parameters can be ***RSSI, access point transmit power, frequency bandwidth***, etc., while for the mobile interface the abstraction parameters can be ***CQI, QCI, BW, Pt***, etc.

• ***Available Node Capacity*** = Available bandwidth x Spectral efficiency

• ***Available bandwidth*** (in Hz) indicates the amount of frequency resources that are available at RAN node. Available bandwidth is also impacted by backhaul load, control channel capacity, HW load, and current QoS satisfaction requirements.

• ***Spectral efficiency*** (in bps/Hz) is the average bit rate that can be transmitted over a given bandwidth. It is a measure how efficiently frequency resources are utilized at RAN node. Both available bandwidth and spectral efficiency are measured and averaged before reporting. Reporting and averaging is executed in time-scale of seconds.

• ***SINR***: The channel measurements are technology-specific. LTE UE measurements are RSRP and RSRQ, while Wi-Fi measurements are RSSI, respectively. Technology-specific measurements should be abstracted to SINR be comparable.

The connection of the abstractions and the mapping of the network graph to the application layer is shown in Figure 5.

5 Conclusion

This work presented the process where low level abstractions defined in heterogeneous RAN systems are transferred to higher layers in which the RTC and the central controller C3 are using them for controlling or managing various tasks such as traffic steering, load balancing, spectrum sharing, RAN sharing etc. Low level abstractions are provided in a form of network graphs which are stored in a database and invoked by the controller for the benefits of producing a manageable and self-organized network. Abstraction mechanisms and control methodologies are proposed in alignment to the COHERENT architecture to achieve the targeted goals.

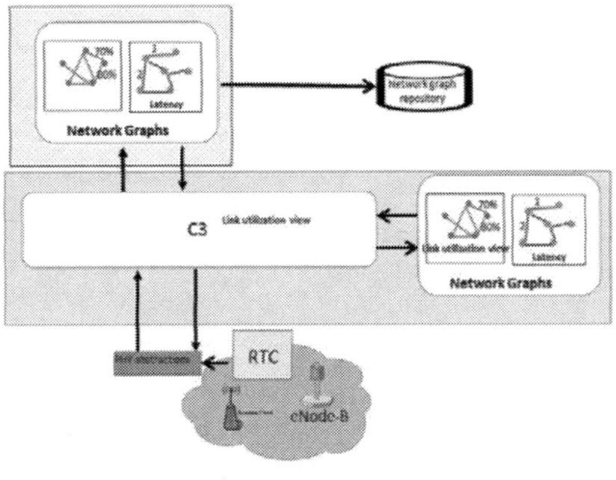

Fig. 5. Network graph mapping to the upper layer

To show their applicability, we formulated a throughput maximization problem for the multi-connectivity problem of local-routed inter-user traffic under user mobility in LTE systems, where the necessary abstracted information is exposed to network graphs as the input for the optimization problem. The proposed algorithm can utilize the RTC/C3 architecture to allocate the technology agnostic user rate and technology dependent air-interface resources such as the MCS, PRB number in LTE system. The multi-connectivity technique not only has advantage in user perspective (i.e., more UEs can be reached through multiple BSs) but also in the network perspective (i.e., larger aggregated rate). However, the multi-connectivity will take more resources out of all BSs in order to achieve the improved aggregated user rate and more connected pairs than in the single-connection case. To sum up, the control and coordination plane of RTC/C3 architecture enables the data rate and resource allocation among multiple connections for inter-user traffic.

Furthermore, the next generation wireless access network, 5G, will be composed by evolved LTE for below 6 GHz, Wi-Fi and also New Radio for above 6 GHz that are expected to converge. Due to the increased complexity, the project focus was on the evolved LTE network and Wi-Fi, nevertheless effort should be given to provide generic solutions for the heterogeneous wireless domain whenever possible.

This work was conducted within the framework of the 5G-PPP COHERENT project, which is partially funded by the Commission of the European Union (Grant Agreement No. 671639). Also, this work has received funding from the European Union Horizon 2020-MCSA-ITN-2015 Innovative Training Networks (ITN) under grant agreement No 675806 (5G-AURA) and No 641985 (5G-Wireless).

References

1. *Coordinated control and spectrum management for 5G heterogeneous radio access networks (COHERENT)*, EU H2020 5G-PPP project, website http://www.ict-coherent.eu/.
2. K. Lee, J. Lee, Y. Yi, I. Rhee, and S. Chong, *Mobile data offloading: How much can wifi deliver?*, IEEE/ACM Trans. on Netw., **21**, 15 (2013)
3. A. Aijaz, A. Aghvami, M. Amani, *A survey on mobile data offloading: Technical and business perspectives*, IEEE Wirel. Commun., (2013)
4. *COHERENT: Coordinated Control and Spectrum Management for 5G Heterogeneous Radio Access Network*, Deliverable 2.2 "System Architecture and Abstractions for Mobile Networks", (2016)
5. V. Chandrasekhar, J. G. Andrews, and A. Gatherer, *Femtocell networks: A survey*, IEEE Commun. Mag., **46**, 9 (2008)

6. J. G. Andrews, H. Claussen, M. Dohler, *Femtocells: Past, Present, and Future*, IEEE Jour. on Selected Areas in Comms, **30**, 12 (2012)
7. B. Han, P. Hui, V. Kumar, M. V. Marathe, G. Pei, A. Srinivasan, *Cellular Traffic Offloading through Opportunistic Communications: A Case Study*, ACM CHANTS, (2010)
8. S. Dimatteo, P. Hui, B. Han, *Cellular Traffic Offloading through WiFi Networks*, IEEE 8th Int. Conf. on MASS, (2011)
9. *Femtocells—Natural Solution for Offload,* whitepaper by Femto Forum, (2011)
10. E. Bulut, B. K. Szymanski, *WiFi Access Point Deployment for Efficient Mobile Data Offloading,* Proc. of the 1st Int. Workshop on PINGEN, 6 (2012)

Considerations for IP Interconnection of Power Grid Components

Velissarios Gezerlis[1], *Maria* Belesioti[1,*], *Tilemachos* Doukoglou[1], *Ioannis* Chochliouros[1]

[1]Hellenic Telecommunications Organization S.A. (OTE), 1, Pelika & Spartis Street, 15122 Maroussi-Athens, Greece

Abstract. The foreseen capabilities of 5G, such as reliable and robust handling of data management can be commonly utilized by different sectors. The Electricity sector has remained for many years a stable industry using the same operational and maintenance regimes and dependable infrastructure. The need to integrate communication network domains in the Smart Grids context with 5G is considered as the next generation regarding power grids, and it is bidirectional as far as electricity and information is concerned, aiming to create a widely distributed automated energy delivery network (as in [1]). In this paper, a Communication-as-a-Service scenario is presented as a proposal of a telecom operator in order to "address" scalability, security and interoperability that a Smart grid network requires, by using communication solutions provided by 5G.

1 Introduction

Back in 2007, National Institute of Standards and Technology (NIST) has been assigned to coordinate the development of a framework that includes protocols and model standards for information management, based on research that has been previously made so as to create frameworks flexible, uniform and technology-neutral, able to achieve interoperability of smart grid devices and systems 2. The electrical power supply started more than a century ago with decentralized isolated networks, and has been evolved to a European centralized mixed network. Since the beginning of the 21st century, more and more decentralized energy systems are being introduced into the network again, so future architectures will have to support both centralized and decentralized concepts 3. Nowadays electricity constitutes the most versatile used form of energy and its demand is growing continuously, in a global level. Traditional electrical power systems delivering energy to commercial and residential consumers are about to exceed their limits.

Smart grids can "meet" the need of the ever-growing demand by combining communications and information technology with production, delivery and consumption of electrical energy and, *at the same time*, by improving system's reliability and stability without increasing maintenance costs.

This paper is organized as follows: Section II introduces the general idea of distributed energy systems and the proposed overlay network architecture. Also the model of the proposed scenario is presented, by using the SGAM (Smart Grid Architecture Model) tool. Section B briefly describes VPN (Virtual Private Network) technology and the deployment of a VPN network in this scenario, as well as the IPsec protocol suite. Section III is referred to the usability of 5G networks in the Smart Grid Sector. Finally, Section IV contains the relevant conclusions.

2 Development of a complete simulation environment

Distributed energy systems have a great role to play and will have a huge impact on future electrical supply systems as well as lead to many financial benefits. Up to now, energy systems are integrated into electric grids. Special designed topologies and/or control for almost each particular case is required, which means waste of money and time for debugging **Error! Reference source not found.**. *The SmarterEMC2* H2020 EU-funded research effort under Grant Agreement No.646470 proposes the implementation of ICT tools that support Customer Side Participation and Renewable Energy Sources (RES) integration and facilitate open access in the electricity market. The consumers would be part of the scheme through an advanced Demand Response system that will be able to manage consumption and effectively communicate in a multi-level hierarchically organized Smart Grid, involving other entities as well as, *for example*, ESCOs (Energy Services Companies).

From the ICT point of view, smart grids involve the integration of an information infrastructure with the existing power systems (generation, transmission and/or distribution physical systems). This integration arises from the need of a more advanced level of automation in the Smart Grids, when compared to existing grids of today and will require the deployment of a vast telecommunication infrastructure leading to the

* Corresponding author: mbelesioti@oteresearch.gr

increased introduction of ICT in the power grids. The main goal in the area of Smart Grids is to create a complete-simulation environment (encompassing Power & Communication infrastructures) to evaluate the implementation of different distributed algorithms, advanced grid control policies and their performance in near-real life conditions. Initially, the time restrictions and/or limitations imposed by the communications' infrastructure will be identified, by creating heavy data applications related to the power grid operation, such as power quality indices and billing.

Additionally, applications based on reliable two-way communications to gain access to the data of smart meters and other measurable components of the power grid will be performed. More specifically, control commands will be sent to various appliances, after ensuring that they are ready to accept commands, in order to implement the smart control operations of the power grid and gain access to detailed measurements, regarding the impact of these operations on the power quality.

For the power grid so far classic simulated operations -such as the state estimation or the reconfiguration of the power grid structure according to the real condition of the system- are getting different importance and meaning, due to the deployment of telemetry projects and the installation of smart meters and other devices capable of storing data and communicating as often as it is required.

Furthermore, the need for more hosting capacity of renewable resources dictates the need for supervising "more closely" the power grid, in order to avoid the power quality loss, as well as the need to be able to issue control orders and implement distributed algorithms on the power grid actors to "maintain" the balance.

The effectiveness of such control schemes has to be proven within the framework of the telecommunication technologies to be used in two different time scales. Specifically, we should examine the minimum telecommunication requirements (round-trip delay, bit rate, reliability, QoS – as well as impact of failures and failover to backup routes) to obtain an acceptable level of management over the power grid in near real-time applications, by measuring the upper limit of the information required to be exchanged. On the other hand, we should also define the threshold of time resolution for facilitating appropriate applications, which are requiring the exchange (mainly one-way communications) of huge amount of data in an "offline" mode (i.e.: store and forward operation).

The integration of these technologies facilitates convergence of standards and implementation of necessary analytical capabilities. SmarterEMC2 proposes a system which will stand as an overlay communication network for the interconnection of the Power Grid elements (off-net management). During the past years, this type of network has evolved as the most commonly used way to share data and services, among a network of loosely connected components 4.

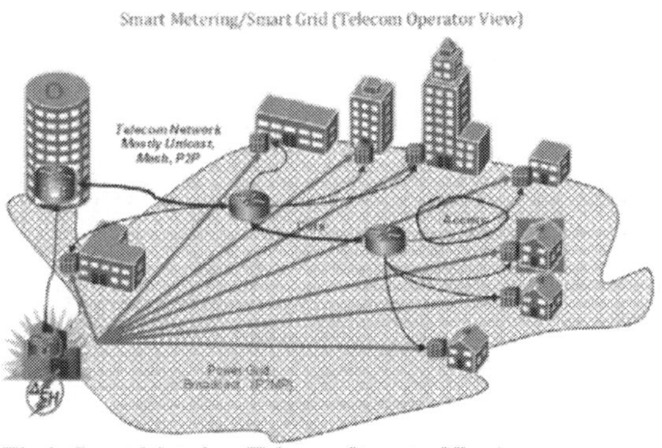

Fig.1: Smart Metering (Telecom Operator View)

This overlay communication system, as far as transmission is concerned, can be either wireless using LTE, 3G and GPRS or wired (copper cable and/or fiber optics). At this point, it should be clarified that the above mentioned communication system is divided into two major networks, that is: home network and Wide Area Network (WAN). As far as the latter is concerned, SmarterEMC2 will use the already broadband (wired/wireless) network of the telecommunication operator participating in the project, in order to establish communication between home networks, ESCOs and power generators (see Fig.1). Home network will be the one having direct impact to the consumer, since it is located inside his house. ZigBee protocol is the one that will most probably be used for the deployment of this kind of network. ZigBee is a specification for small, low power radios based on *IEEE 802.15.4 – 2003 Wireless Personal Area Networks standard* **Error! Reference source not found.** and is considered ideal for energy monitoring and home automation 6. In the following scheme (as in Fig.2), the modelling of communication layer is presented.

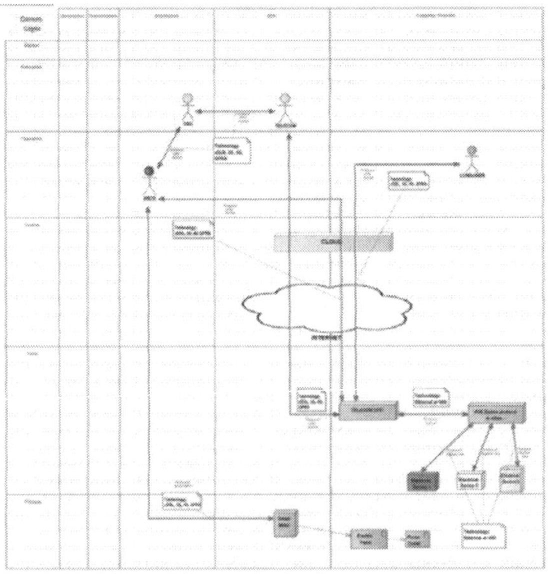

Fig. 2: Modelling of Communication Layer

Smart grid is a complex system, consisting of many processes and levels both in the area of energy and in the communication field. The connections among the electrical and telecom equipment are imprinted along with the relation among consumers, telecom operators and DSOs (Distribution System Operators). All, protocols that will be used as well as the home network and the WAN are described thoroughly in this SGAM model.

The above depicted communication layer is divided into zones and domains. In the vertical axis, the TelCo's communication system uses all zones, except for the market. Every actor of the horizontal domain should correspond to the vertical zone. Thus, in the distribution and DER (Distributed Energy Resources) domains and enterprise zone, DSOs and telecom operators are listed. Energy service companies have operational role and are responsible for distributing energy so are corresponded to the specified point.

As far as the customer premises domain is concerned, all telecom and electrical equipment is located. More specifically, all electrical physical equipment (outlets, electric panels, etc.) are in the process zone and all physical communication equipment are in the field zone. Home electrical devices, through *ZigBee Protocol* will send signals/messages to ZigBee Hub, which also will be located inside the house. By using Ethernet or/and WiFi the information will be transferred to operator's CPE (Customer-premises equipment) and then through separated VPNs each of the actors will be able to have access to the information. The technology used for this final transmission can be either wired (e.g. xDSL) or wireless (3G/4G). Internet Protocol (IP) will be used and different means of access depending on availability and traffic demand -such as Copper and Optical Fiber- will be utilized. One or more VPNs will be created for communication between the "energy/utilities" grid elements, with respect to the privacy and security of the data and "grid elements" using cryptography and Tunnel connections (i.e., Internet Protocol Security (IPsec)).

2.1 VPN deployment

IP-*based* user applications are becoming increasingly popular and the Internet technology has emerged as the major "driving force" behind new developments in the area of telecommunication networks. In an environment where clients are connecting to ever-growing networks, security requirements are of high importance. VPNs have become the logical solution for remote-access connectivity, since they provide secure communications with access rights tailored to individual users, such as employees, contractors or partners, and with reduced communications costs and increased flexibility. In remote-access VPNs, deployment can use two primary methods: IP Security (IPsec) and Secure Sockets Layer (SSL), each one with its advantages mainly based on access requirements needed. In the specific case of the *Communication-as-a-Service* deployment, the related VPN deployment is based upon the IPsec protocol suite, a developing standard for security at the network or packet processing layer. It provides encryption and integrity protection of packets on both IPv4 and IPv6, as well as authentication of the communicating entities.

VPNs allow for private data to be transmitted securely over public networks. They can also offer enormous versatility and customizability through modification of the VPN client software. Besides security, VPNs encompass an entire spectrum of technologies such as quality of service (QoS) and network management (NM). IPsec allows secure communication, by using authentication and encryption in each IP packet of a session. It provides encryption on IPv4 and IPv6, as well as authentication of the communicating entities.

IPsec grants two choices of security service: Authentication Header (AH) 8 where it provides data origin authentication, but does not provide secrecy, and; Encapsulating Security Payload (ESP) 9, where confidentiality is supported and data origin authentication is optional. Finally, IPsec supports two modes of operation, that is: Transport Mode, which is used to protect communication between two hosts, and; Tunnel Mode which is used to build virtual tunnels, commonly known as VPNs 10. In the latter mode, both the header and the payload are encrypted and for decryption there is an IPSec-compliant device on the receiving side.

2.2 Simulation environment

The simulation scenario of Demand Response Service will be tested and the communication procedure will be analysed. At first, a simplified demand response mechanism will be simulated. The Demand Response platform requests measurements from multiple devices, such as smart meters. The data acquired is used to perform calculations and, according to the results, control signals are sent. Next smarter algorithms will be tested that solve the same technical problem, but are adapted to the constraints posed by the telecommunication infrastructure. The main objective of the simulation is to analyse the effect of the telecommunication infrastructure on the various control algorithms and so to design new algorithms that are able to utilize effectively the underlying telecommunication infrastructure. Thus, networks where: up to hundreds of nodes are organized in a specific topology; point-to-point, unicast and also multicast (or even broadcast) communication, between nodes is being considered, and; traditional layer 3 Internet protocols (TCP/IP) with IPv4 (and probably IPv6) address space are used 11 .

A tree-star network topology can be considered as a combination of two or more star networks connected together. In each of star network comprising the tree, there is a central server to which all the nodes are directly linked. The central computers of the star networks are connected to a main cable called as the "bus". Thus, a tree network is a bus network of star networks. This topology is ideal when the nodes are located in groups, with each group occupying a relatively small physical region. The tree topology structure relies on the main bus cable. In case it fails, the whole network is crippled.

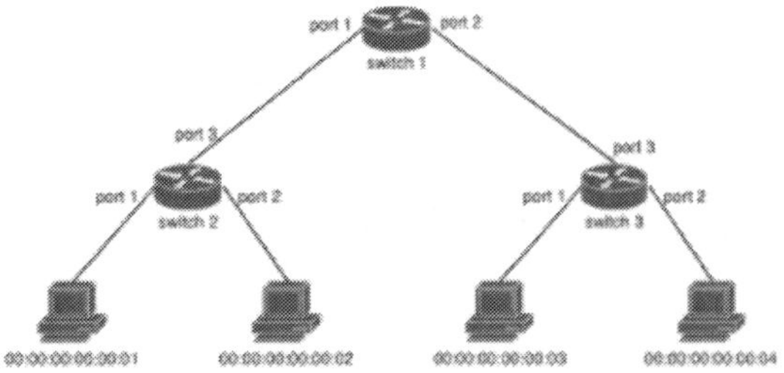

Fig. 3: Tree Network Structure

3 How 5G can act as "catalyst" in the future smart grid networks

Communication networks for Smart Grids and Smart Meters need to be able to control distributed energy, while simultaneously fulfilling specific performance requirements, as the demand for efficient and reliable communication solutions is expected to grow due to the emergence of smart grids especially in the medium-voltage and low-voltage substations, since these assets currently have no communication or measurement equipment.

The fifth generation of mobile communications -or 5G- actually envisioned as an evolution in mobile communications, can provide economically viable mobile and effective solutions. Verticals like energy are expected to be the new "end-user" thus enabling new applications and/or businesses. In the context of SmarterEMC2, the potential of introducing 5G could be very high, especially in the applications of energy grid control and smart metering; thus, the anticipated performance of 5G will enable communication infrastructure to actively participate in the emerging smart grid and energy scenarios. In order to resolve the new challenges, such as increase of energy demand and storage, smart energy grids will have to focus in data transmission and distributed networks, in the most cost-efficient way.

Due to the development of power plants, new challenges are appearing both for DSO's and telecom operators. Energy production based on solar power plants is more disturbed than traditional power plants, based for example on fossil, while in addition is not stable and varies from day-to-day due to weather conditions (e.g., sun, wind). The need for increased resilience can be met through 5G networks together with increased control, monitoring and protection.

In order to optimize the use of these distributed power plants, a real time dynamic routing of electricity flows is necessary. This routing will require a monitoring and control network, able to transmit distributed data such as measures from smart meters in real time. 5G technology could support efficiently all these services required by the energy sector, providing sufficient flexibility in order to deploy specific virtual network functions and ensure dedicated technical performances with related Service Level Agreements (SLAs) such as latency and Bit-Error Rate (BER).

Smart Grid communication networks consist of multiple domains, each one serving a specific area, for example a distribution network or location such as a secondary substation (where transformation between medium and low voltage takes place). The domain where 5G is expected to play a significant role, is the one of access and backhaul networks, as described in the proposed tree-like topology in the previous Section 2.

Three European Standards Organizations (ESOs), that is CEN (European Committee for Standardization), CENELEC (European Committee for Electrotechnical Standardization) and ETSI (European Telecommunications Standards Institute) have been developing a proper framework to enable energy operators to provide standard enhancement and development in the Smart Grid and Smart Metering fields of the energy market 12, 13.

4 Conclusions

The SmarterEMC2 project proposes diverse use cases, some of them requiring ultra-reliability while others requiring low latency communication to smart meters and support of massive number of connected devices. Smart Metering and tree topology as proposed in this paper, demand support of a wireless network that can provide wide area connectivity, optimized for low data rates with high penetration and lower cost at the same time. In this respect, the flexible network architecture proposed by 5G can guarantee reliability, security and performance requirements opening the door to new business roles and responsibilities both on energy and telecom sector.

Acknowledgments

The research leading to the actual results has received funding from the European Community's Horizon 2020 Framework Program "SmarterEMC2", under Grant Agreement (GA) No.646470.

The project consortium members are: Intracom S.A. Telecom Solutions (ICOM), University of Durham, Institute of Communication and Computer Systems (ICCS), INESC Porto, Thales Italia S.p.A., Aydem Guneybati Anadolu Enerji Sanayi ve Ticaret Anonim Sirketi (AYDEM), Elektrik Dagitim Hizmetleri Dernegi Baskanligina (ELDER), University of Aalborg (AAU), Hellenic Telecommunications Organization S.A. (OTE) and Fujitsu Laboratories of Europe Ltd. (FLE).

References

1. X. Fang, S. Misra, G. Xue, D. Yang, IEEE Com. Surv. & Tut. **14**(4), 944-980 (2012)
2. National Institute of Standards and Technology (NIST), *NIST Framework and Roadmap for Smart Grid Interoperability Standards, Release 1.0* (U.S.

Department of Commerce, 2010, November). Available at: https://www.nist.gov/sites/default/files/documents/public_affairs/releases/smartgrid_interoperability_final.pdf

3. CEN-CENELEC-ETSI Smart Grid Coordination Group, *Smart Grid Reference Architecture* (2012, November) Available at: https://ec.europa.eu/energy/sites/ener/files/documents/xpert_group1_reference_architecture.pdf
4. A. Mohd, E. Ortjohann, A. Schmelter, N. Hamsic, and D. Morton, *Proceedings of IEEE ISIE, Cambridge, U.K., June 30 - July 02, 2008, 1627–1632)* (2008)
5. J. Ren, Y. Li, T. Jiang and T. Li, Sec. Com. Netw. **9**(3), 229-240 (2016, February). DOI: 10.1002/sec.539
6. https://www.engineersgarage.com/articles/what-is-zigbee-technology
7. ZigBee Alliance website. Available at: http://www.zigbee.org/
8. S. Kent and R. Atkinson, *RFC 2402: IP Authentication Header* (The Internet Society, 1998, November)
9. S. Kent and R. Atkinson, *RFC 2406: IP Encapsulating Security Payload (ESP)* (The Internet Society, 1998, November)
10. S. Kent and R. Atkinson, *RFC 2401: Security Architecture for the Internet Protocol* (The Internet Society, 1998, November)
11. M. Salehi, J. Proakis, *Digital Communications* (McGraw-Hill Education, 2007, November)
12. CEN-CENELEC Sector, Smart grids found at: https://www.cencenelec.eu/standards/Sectors/SustainableEnergy/SmartGrids/Pages/default.aspx
13. CEN-CENELEC Sector, Smart meters found at: https://www.cencenelec.eu/standards/Sectors/SustainableEnergy/SmartMeters/Pages/default.aspx

A Novel Architectural Concept for Enhanced 5G Network Facilities

Ioannis P. Chochliouros[1,*], *Ioannis* Giannoulakis[2], *Anastasia S.* Spiliopoulou[1], *Maria* Belesioti[1], *Alexandros* Kostopoulos[1], *Evangelos* Sfakianakis[1], *Anastasios* Kourtis[2], *Emmanouil* Kafetzakis[3] and *Stelios* Agapiou[4]

[1]Hellenic Telecommunications Organization (OTE) S.A., 15124 Maroussi Athens, Greece
[2]National Center for Scientific Research "Demokritos", Greece
[3]ORION Innovations Private Company, Greece
[4] E.P.F.L., Switzerland

Abstract. The 5G ESSENCE project's context is based on the concept of Edge Cloud Computing and Small Cell-as-a-Service (SCaaS) -as both have been previously identified in the SESAME 5G-PPP project of phase 1- and further "promotes" their role and/or influences within the related 5G vertical markets. 5G ESSENCE's core innovation is focused upon the development/provision of a highly flexible and scalable platform, offering benefits to the involved market actors. The present work identifies a variety of challenges to be fulfilled by the 5G ESSENCE, in the scope of an enhanced architectural framework. The proposed technical approach exploits the profits of the centralization of Small Cell functions as scale grows through an edge cloud environment, based on a two-tier architecture with the first distributed tier being for offering low latency services and the second centralized tier being for the provision of high processing power for computing-intensive network applications. This permits decoupling the control and user planes of the Radio Access Network (RAN) and achieving the advantages of Cloud-RAN without the enormous fronthaul latency restrictions. The use of end-to-end network slicing mechanisms allows for sharing the related infrastructure among multiple operators/vertical industries and customizing its capabilities on a per-tenant basis, creating a neutral host market and reducing operational costs.

1 Introduction

Up to now several visions of 5G have been proposed and their basic features, *apparently*, converge to the idea that "*any person or item can connect at arbitrarily high data rates, from any place, and with extremely low latency*" [1, 2]. How these traits can be realised depends on several factors, including combinations of existing types of communication networks, as well as new and ground-breaking implementations. 5G solutions envisage consolidation of cellular, Internet of Things (IoT), and Wi-Fi networks; this list may be enriched with broadcast networks and automotive systems. Furthermore, in order to achieve higher transmission rates, new wireless solutions, such as exploitation of millimeter-Wave (mmWave) bands, are expected to be utilized [3]. The reasons behind these developments are well grounded in practical requirements. Separate radio interfaces are required for the different solutions, such as cellular over IoT and, *additionally*, the exigency for extremely low latency drives inexorably to ultra-dense deployments and usage of higher frequencies [4].

The main problem of the proposed 5G solutions is that they neither have been adequately tied to a solid business case, nor well integrated to the legacy infrastructure of network operators and the rest of actors within the communications ecosystem. This is not surprising, considering the lack of new monetisable revenue streams [5]. For years, operators have been making efforts to launch new services, such as image messaging, video calls, location-based services and so on (and even some examples of Over-The-Top (OTT) players like *Skype* have achieved to deliver added value solutions); however, the average revenue per user remains low. Therefore, 5G needs not only to target to new technological solutions, it should also take into account current economic position of telecom operators and also to "pave the way" for producing new benefits that will create new markets and services, so that additional 5G actors -such as multimedia content providers and vendors- are also able to increase their profits.

If there are no new revenues, there arises the ultimate necessity that 5G reduces operators' costs. To "address" this requirement, 5G ESSENCE introduces innovations in the fields of network softwarization, virtualization, and cognitive network management. It also provides a highly flexible and scalable platform, capable of supporting new business models and revenue streams by creating a "neutral host market" and ultimately reducing

* Corresponding author: ichochliouros@oteresearch.gr

operational costs by providing new opportunities for ownership, deployment, operation and amortisation.

Entering the second phase of 5G-PPP program activities suggests that communication networks become sufficiently flexible to handle a range of applications and services, originating from different domains/verticals. At the same time, a transformation towards a significant reduction in cost and the optimal allocation of available resources takes the place of initial Key Performance Indicators (KPIs) for "driving" capacity growth and coping with the numerous barr6iers on the infrastructure and management domains. On the users' side, a high level of personalized services, along with edge mobile capabilities and innovative services are anticipated, since customers require added value to their choices, in order to accommodate specialized requirements with greater quality of both perception and experience The 5G ESSENCE approach allows new stakeholders to dynamically "enter" the network value chain by building upon and leveraging the outcomes of 5G-Public Private Partnership (PPP) Phase-1 SESAME project [6], as well as several other Phase-1 research activities. Small Cell operators, network operators, and OTT players, are offered access on-demand to "evolved" Small Cell platforms, enhanced with mobile edge computing capabilities. Moreover, 5G ESSENCE will provide advanced network virtualization, distributed service management, and the full potential of a network embedded cloud, by building upon network slicing and isolation and then providing this capability to multiple operators (tenants).

2 The 5G ESSENCE conceptual approach

2.1 Market positioning and vision

During 5G-PPP Phase-1, the ongoing SESAME project evolves the small cell concept by integrating processing power (i.e., a low-cost micro server) and by enabling the execution of applications and network services, in accordance to the Mobile Edge Computing (MEC) paradigm [7]. It also provides network intelligence and applications by leveraging the Network Function Virtualization (NFV) concept [8]. The SESAME platform consists of one or more clusters of "Cloud – Enabled" Small Cells (CESCs) [9], which are devices that include both the processing power platform and the small cell unit. CESCs can be deployed at low- and medium-scale venues and support multiple network operators (i.e.: multitenancy) and further, network services and applications at the edge of the network.

In this context, SESAME has developed several small cell related functions as Virtualized Network Functions (VNFs) [10], such as the GPRS Tunnelling Protocol (GTP) en-/de-capsulation of data packets. Also, SESAME has demonstrated so far that some network related functions (such as content caching, firewalls and monitoring) perform adequately well when running as VNFs in the developed micro-server infrastructure (coined as "Light Data Centre" - Light DC) [11].

The 5G ESSENCE proposal leverages results from the SESAME project, as well as from other 5G-PPP Phase-1 projects (i.e.: COHERENT, SPEED 5G, and SONATA mainly), in order to provide an evolution of the SESAME platform and to "meet" the 5G-PPP Phase-2 requirements (i.e., to cover the specific network needs of the vertical sectors and their interdependencies). It enhances the processing capabilities for data that have immediate value beyond locality, it "addresses" the processing-intensive small cell management functions such as Radio Resource Management (RRM) / Self Organising Network (SON) and, *finally*, it culminates with real-life demonstrations. For all the above, 5G ESSENCE suggests clear breakthroughs in the research fields of wireless access, network virtualisation and end-to-end (E2E) service delivery. The existing virtualized resources of small cells will be exploited to their full potential and in a dynamic way, thus supporting extremely low-latency and the delivery of high-performance services, greater network resiliency and substantial capacity gains at the access network for the next 5G stage. To achieve these important goals, 5G ESSENCE will build on the SESAME project by developing a distributed edge cloud environment (coined as "Edge Data Centre" -Edge DC-), based on a two-tier architecture: the first tier (i.e., Light DC), will remain distributed inside the CESCs for providing latency-sensitive services to users, directly from the network's edge. The second tier will be a more centralized, "high-scale" cloud, namely the Main Data Centre (Main DC), which will provide high processing power for computing intensive network applications. It will also have a more centralized view so as to host efficient Quality of Service (QoS) enabled scheduling algorithms. Both these cloud tiers will form the Edge DC in the 5G ESSENCE terminology, which will be "viewed" as an integrated cloud infrastructure from the upper management and orchestration layers.

With respect to the radio resources of the wireless access network it is well known -and from the results of SESAME project it became even clearer- that the capacity offered from small cells does not scale beyond a specific threshold due to interference. Existing radio resource allocations remain "inadequate" due to the lack of a centralized coordination, especially in urban areas and environments with high density of users. As a remedy, the Cloud-Radio Access Network (C-RAN) approach [12-14] has introduced centralized BaseBand Units (BBUs) for processing both the control and user planes, in order to support flexible scaling and sophisticated interference coordination techniques. However, the significant capacity gains proposed by C-RAN come with a high cost for the fronthaul network since the fronthaul requirements for C-RAN are in the order of 6 Gbps bandwidth for small cell sites and of latency less than 0.5ms Round Trip Time (RTT) [15]. In other words, direct fibre lines (i.e., without switching or buffering) or mmWave links are necessary for the small cell fronthaul connections.

In the case of macro-base stations the fronthauling cost can be affordable; but in the small cell case, it is too expensive and not realistic. Small cells can be connected to fronthaul through a variety of technologies (cable, public fibre, and microwave) and there are scenarios in which they are deployed without a central planning. Even if public leased fibre or multi-gigabit Ethernet were available everywhere, that would not be sufficient (mainly because of the latency requirements).

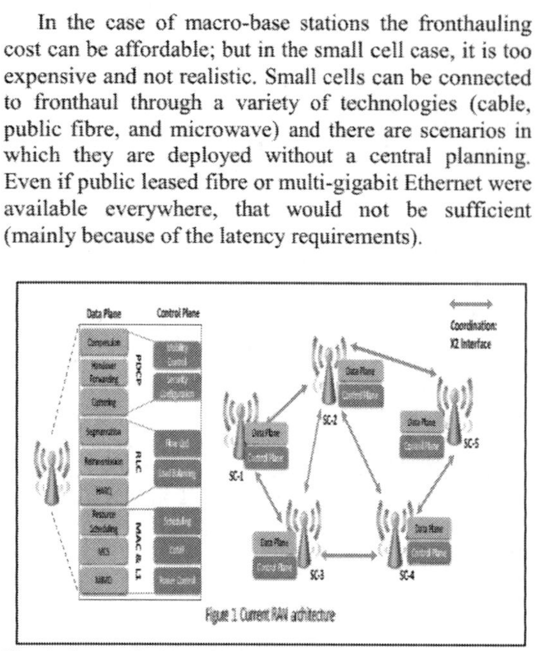

Fig. 1. Current RAN Architecture

Correspondingly, the SESAME project applies some advantageous distributed RRM/SON techniques for managing interference and increasing capacity. The coarse coordination achieved through X2 interface targets to reduce interference but it is less efficient for allocating resources in a unified fashion among multiple cells in comparison with the C-RAN approach (see, e.g., Fig. 1).

2.2 Challenges for growth

5G ESSENCE proposes a pioneering approach to alleviate the consequences of extreme network densification and of the insufficient management

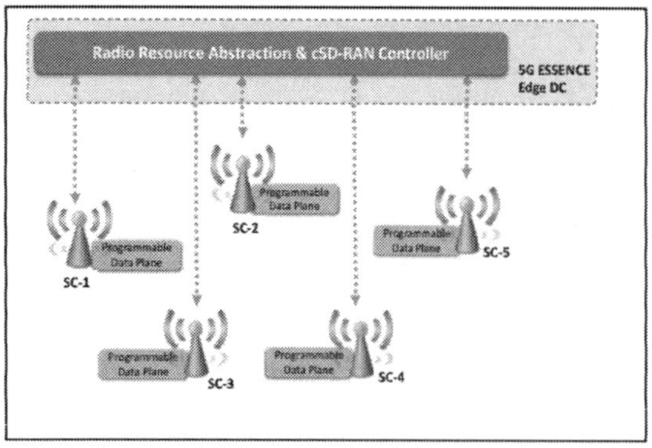

Fig. 2. 5G ESSENCE Approach to Radio Resource Abstraction

It suggests decoupling the control and user planes for the Radio Access Network (RAN), similarly to Software Defined Networking (SDN) in data networks [16] and claiming the benefits of C-RAN without the enormous latency restrictions in the fronthaul [17]. Thus, the project envisages that the small cell network functions related to the user/data plane will remain distributed [18], while the control plane functions will be disaggregated from the RAN and hosted at the Main DC by using Commercial-of-the-Self (COTS) hardware. Although the design of such a centralized Software Defined-RAN (cSD-RAN) controller is a challenging task, since also real-time feedback of radio conditions should be taken into account, the distributed and network-integrated cloud inherited by SESAME so far is adequate for hosting controllers based on spatial segmentation, so this aspect can accelerate research results achieved to date. In particular, centralization "brings" immediate benefits for operators seeking to improve network efficiency and quality as well as coming to grips with digital convergence transformation [19]. Further, 5G ESSENCE aspires to include multiple Radio Access Technologies (RAT) in its network architecture [20], representing an important step towards fulfilling the vision of 5G wireless networks, where intelligent deployments aim to achieve higher performance and flexibility and to offer more efficient spectrum utilization.

Clear breakthroughs are also foreseen in the fields of high-performance virtualization, service delivery and resource orchestration, targeting the critical issues of resource efficiency and latency reduction. These would be achieved through the support of a converged cloud-radio environment, the orchestration of diverse types of lightweight virtual resources and the support of live VNF migration. The approach of network control centralization [21] will not remain only in the radio resource abstraction part, since given the needs for fast resource provisioning and mapping -and for increased abstraction in the management of services- 5G ESSENCE will provide even tighter mapping and closer interactions between the resource orchestration (i.e., deployment, placement and scaling of VNFs) and service orchestration (i.e., building, coordinating and exposing services to upper layers).

On the domain of hardware technologies, the processing power attached to small cells brings new capabilities to the network as well as new challenges; in the perspective of 5G ESSENCE, the placement of low power/low cost processors to small cells, even with hardware acceleration, will be revised. Although the Cloud-Enabled Small Cell (CESC) platform in SESAME is based on non-x86 architectures (ARMv8), the potential use of x86-based, low-cost and low-power processors will also be leveraged due to their efficiency (small form factor, low powered, passively cooled, low price) and their important share in the market.

The mentioned research domains cover only the technical aspects of the proposed novel 5G ESSENCE activities. However, a significant part of the project is also devoted to the actual demonstration of the outcomes in vertical industries, as they have been identified by 5G-PPP [22].

In order to showcase that "5G will be able to create a whole new ecosystem for technical and business innovation", 5G ESSENCE "unifies" computing and storage resources into a programmable and unified small cell infrastructure that can be provided *as-a-Service* to all related stakeholders [23]. To that end, it provides a clear plan for real life demonstrations in the fields of: (a) multimedia entertainment; (b) mission critical communications at emergency events, *and;* (c) in-flight connectivity and entertainment.

In addition to actual demonstrations, 5G ESSENCE is expected to accommodate a much wider range of use cases, especially in terms of ameliorated latency, resilience, coverage and bandwidth. One of its major innovations is that it provides E2E network and cloud infrastructure slices over the same physical infrastructure, in order to fulfil vertical-specific requirements as well as mobile broadband services, *in parallel*. 5G ESSENCE "opens the door" to venue owners (e.g., municipalities, stadiums, site owners, and virtually anyone who manages a property) and can install and run a local small cell network, to deploy a low cost infrastructure and to act as neutral host network and service provider.

Although probably none of such entities would offer static network coverage, many of them could foresee adequate chances for profits generated by exploiting the 5G ESSENCE concepts of multitenant small cells, able to provide wireless network coverage coupled with added-value services in close proximity to customers and visitors that belong to multiple network operators and vertical industries.

3 Proposed architectural framework

3.1 Architectural framework

The architecture provided so far by the SESAME project (see Fig.3) acts as a solid reference point for 5G ESSENCE ([24-29]). It combines the current 3GPP framework for network management in RAN sharing scenarios and the ETSI NFV framework for managing virtualized network functions [8]. The CESC offers virtualized computing, storage and radio resources and the CESC cluster is considered as a cloud from the upper layers ([27-28]).

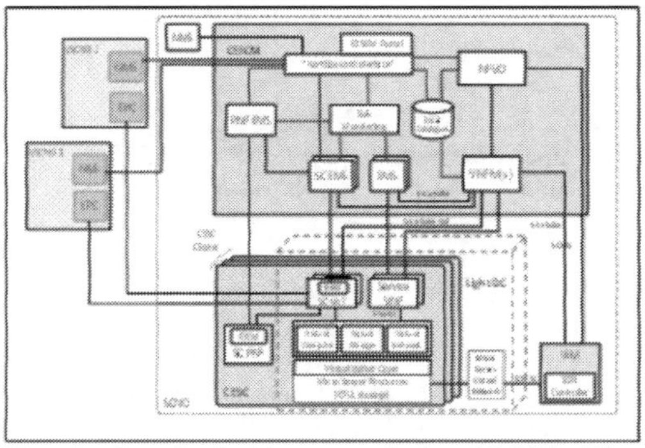

Fig. 3. Overall Architecture of the 5G-PPP (Phase-1) SESAME Project

This cloud can also be "sliced" to enable multi-tenancy. The execution platform is used to support VNFs [10] that implement the different features of the Small Cells as well as to support for the mobile edge applications of the end-users. Evolving the high-level architecture of Fig.3, the technical approach of 5G ESSENCE is shown in Fig.4, where the working architecture is illustrated, with emphasis on the functional elements and interfaces. The examination that follows, describes the work split in the proof-of-concept design and implementation. The 5G ESSENCE architecture will allow multiple network operators (tenants) to provide services to their users through a set of CESCs deployed, owned and managed by a third party (i.e., the CESC provider). In this way, operators can extend the capacity of their own 5G RAN in areas where the deployment of their own infrastructure could be expensive and/or inefficient, as it would be the case of, *for example*, highly dense areas where massive numbers of Small Cells would be needed to provide the expected services. In addition to capacity extension, the 5G ESSENCE platform is equipped with a two-tier virtualized execution environment, materialized in the form of the Edge DC, that allows also the provision of MEC capabilities to the mobile operators for enhancing the user experience and the agility in the service delivery. The first tier (i.e., the Light DC hosted inside the CESCs), is used to support the execution of VNFs for carrying out the virtualization of the Small Cell access.

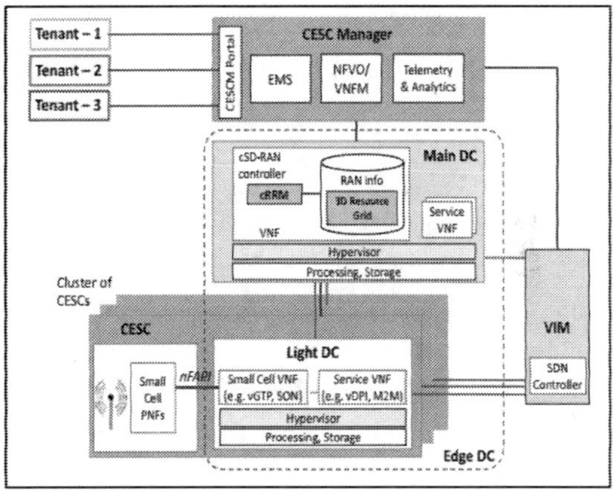

Fig. 4. The 5G ESSENCE Architectural Composition

In this regard, network functions supporting traffic interception, GTP encapsulation/decapsulation and some distributed RRM/SON functionalities are expected to be executed therein. VNFs that require low processing power (e.g., a Deep Packet Inspection (DPI), a Machine-to-Machine (M2M) Gateway and so on), could also be hosted here. The connection between the Small Cell Physical Network Functions (PNFs) and the Small Cell VNFs can be realised through, e.g., the network Functional Application Platform Interface (nFAPI). Finally, backhaul and fronthaul transmission resources will be part of the CESC, allowing for the required connectivity. The second cloud tier, i.e., the Main DC, will be hosting more computation intensive tasks and processes that need to be centralized in order to have a global view of the underlying infrastructure. This encompasses the cSD-RAN controller which will be delivered as a VNF running in the Main DC and makes control plane decisions for all the radio elements in the geographical area of the CESC cluster, including the centralized Radio Resource Management (cRRM) over the entire CESC cluster. Other potential VNFs that could be hosted by the Main DC include security applications, traffic engineering, mobility management and, *in general*, any additional network E2E services that can be deployed and managed on the 5G ESSENCE virtual networks, effectively and on-demand.

3.1 High level architecture aligned to proposed scenarios of use

At the network's edge, each CESC is able to host one -or more- service VNFs, directly applying to the users of a specific operator. Similarly, VNFs can be instantiated inside the Main DC and be parts of a Service Function Chaining (SFC) procedure. The Light DC can be used to "implement" different functional splits of the Small Cells, as well as to support the mobile edge applications of the end-users. Simultaneously, 5G ESSENCE proposes the development of small cell management functions as VNFs, which run in the Main DC and coordinate a fixed "pool" of shared radio resources, instead of considering that each small cell station has its own set of resources.

The CESC Manager (CESCM) is responsible for coordinating and supervising the use, the performance and the delivery of both radio resources and services. It controls the interactions between the infrastructure (CESCs, Edge DC) and the network operators. Also, it handles Service Level Agreements (SLAs) while on an architectural basis CESCM encompasses telemetry and analytics as "fundamental tools for efficiently managing the overall network". The Virtualised Infrastructure Manager (VIM) (see Fig.5) is responsible for controlling the NFV Infrastructure (NFVI), which includes the computing, storage and network resources of the Edge DC.

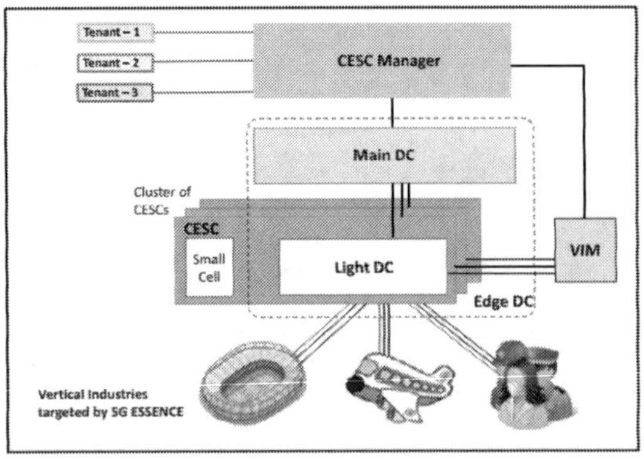

Fig. 5. The 5G ESSENCE High-Level Architecture

It should be mentioned that 5G ESSENCE does not only propose the development and adaptation of the multitenant CESC platform, the virtualization infrastructure and the centralization of the software-defined radio resource management described above; it also "addresses" several aspects that affect performance in 5G virtualized environments such as virtual switching [30], VNF migration [31] and Machine Learning algorithms [32], which allow for orchestrating diverse types of lightweight virtual resources.

Last but not least, it is worth noting that the abovementioned two-tier architecture of 5G ESSENCE is well aligned with the current views on 5G architecture described by 5G-PPP in [33], where the infrastructure programmability and the split of control and user planes are identified as two "key logical architecture design paradigms for 5G" (as in [34]). First, 5G ESSENCE achieves infrastructure programmability by leveraging the virtualized computation resources available at the Edge DC. These resources will be used for hosting VNFs, tailored according to the needs of each tenant and on a per-slice basis [35]. Network slicing enables network operators and service providers to realize, operate and manage different logical networks (slices) on top of the same physical infrastructure, while providing a diverse set of network/service level differentiation [36]. Second, the Main DC allows centralizing and softwarizing control plane small cell functions to enable more efficient utilisation of radio resources coordinated among multiple CESCs [37]. In addition to the abovementioned aspects, 5G ESSENCE contributes to other 5G architectural concepts identified in [33], such as for example the realization of the network slicing concept [38], which is a fundamental requirement of 5G ESSENCE for enabling that multiple tenants and vertical industries "share" the same CESC infrastructure.

Actors in the European telecom scene are at a major turning point, that is: mobile network traffic is rising and subscribers' revenue is declining [39]. In this context, 5G ESSENCE will explore the means to deliver its achievements to the market, with emphasis in the quantification of benefits, especially in terms of total cost of ownership, revenues and profits. It will allow the sharing of existing and new infrastructure by many operators in a multitenant environment, thus enabling new business models that will help new entrant market players to develop and analyse the perspectives of potential "win-win" strategies based on the developed solutions ([40-41]).

Key actors, revenue streams, and cost/performance drivers of the various RAN partitioning options will also be identified. The main benefits of 5G ESSENCE include the maximization of resource usage, the reduction of equipment and management costs and QoS improvement, thus encouraging network innovation and the deployment of distinct network services ([42-43]). These features can be applied directly into the 5G ESSENCE architecture and result in many general "key benefits", such as CAPEX and OPEX reduction, easy management and operation, speedy innovation deployment without interfering in-service networks and efficient resource utilization.

4 Conclusions and overview

In the planned 5G ESSENCE approach, the Small Cell concept has been further evolved as not only to offer multi-operator radio access but, also, to realize an increase in the capacity and the performance of existing RAN infrastructures and to "spread" the range of the delivered services while simultaneously maintaining its agility. To attain these ambitious aims, the 5G ESSENCE approach leverages the paradigms of RAN scheduling and, furthermore, provides an enhanced, edge-*based*, virtualized execution environment attached to the small cell, taking advantage and reinforcing the concepts of MEC and network slicing. Based upon the innovative framework of the previous 5G-PPP (phase 1) SESAME project, we identify the respective challenges and we propose a more enhanced architectural framework so that to fulfil the new challenges with the aim of satisfying real life demonstrations in the fields of multimedia and entertainment, mission-critical communications at emergency events, and in-flight connectivity and entertainment. We focus upon the essential components of the new architecture and identify perspectives for growth and development.

The paper has been based on the context of the 5G-PPP phase 2 "5G ESSENCE" ("*Embedded Network Services for 5G Experiences*") Project (GA No.761592), funded by the European Commission.

References

1. European Parliament Think Tank, *5G network technology: Putting Europe at the leading edge*, (2016, January)
2. European Commission and 5G-PPP, *5G Vision: The 5G-PPP Infrastructure Private Public Partnership: The Next Generation of Communication Network and Services* (2015)
3. T.S. Rappaport, S. Run, R. Mayzus, H. Zhao, Y. Azar, K. Wang, G.N. Wong, et *al.*, IEEE Acc. **1**, 335-349, (2013)
4. Ericsson AB, *White Paper on 5G Radio Access, (Uen 284 23-3204 Rev C)* (2016, April)
5. W. Bock, P. Soos, M. Wilms, M. Mohan, *Five Priorities for Achieving Europe's Digital Single Market* (The Boston Consulting Group Inc., 2015)
6. SESAME H2020 5G-PPP Project (Grant Agreement No.671596). [http://www.sesame-h2020-5g-ppp.eu/Home.aspx]
7. European Telecommunications Standards Institute (ETSI), *Mobile-Edge Computing Introductory Technical White Paper* (2014)
8. European Telecommunications Standards Institute (ETSI), *Network Functions Virtualisation - Introductory White Paper* (2012)
9. SESAME 5G-PPP Project, *Deliverable 2.5 ("SESAME Final Architecture and PoC Assessment KPIs")* (2016)
10. SESAME 5G-PPP Project, *Deliverable 2.4 ("Specification of the Infrastructure Virtualisation, Orchestration and Management")* (2016)
11. SESAME 5G-PPP Project, *Deliverable 4.1 ("Light DC Architecture Design")* (2016)
12. A. Maeder, M. Lalam, et *al.*, *Proceedings of EuCNC-2014, Bologna, Italy, June 26-29, 2014. IEEE, 1-5*, 2014)
13. P. Rost, C.J. Bernardos, A. De Domenico, et. *al.*, IEEE Com. Mag, **52**(5), 68-76 (2014)
14. A. Checko, H.L. Christiansen, Y. Yan, L. Scolari, G. Kardaras, M.S. Berger and L. Dittmann, IEEE Com. Surv. & Tut. **17**(1), 405-426 (2015)
15. Fujitsu Network Communications Inc., *The Benefits of Cloud-RAN Architecture in Mobile Network Expansion* (2014). Available at: http://www.fujitsu.com/downloads/TEL/fnc/whitepapers/CloudRANwp.pdf
16. M.Y. Arslan, K. Sundaresan, and S. Rangarajan, IEEE Com. Mag. **53**(1), 50-156 (2015)
17. B.N. Astuto, M. Mendon, et *al.*, IEEE Com. Surv. and Tut. **16**(3), 1617-1634 (2014)
18. S. Chia, M. Gasparroni, and P. Brick, IEEE Micrw. Mag. **10**(5), 54-66 (2009)
19. Huawei Technologies Co. Ltd., *Centralized Operations: Strategies for Today and Tomorrow* (Managed Services White Paper, 2014)
20. R. Wang, H. Hu, and X. Yang, IEEE Acc., **2**, 1187-1195 (2015)
21. H. Yan, *A Practical System for Centralized Network Control, CMU-CS-10-149, Thesis*. (Carnegie Mellon University, Pittsburgh, PA, 2010, November)
22. *White Papers* from the 5G Infrastructure Association. Available at: https://5g-ppp.eu/white-papers
23. Small Cell Forum (SFC), *Small cells – what's the big idea? (White Paper)* (SFC, 2012, February)
24. I.P. Chochliouros, I. Giannoulakis, et *al.*, *Proceedings of AIAI-2016 Int. Conf., IFIP AICT **475**, L. Iliadis and I. Maglogiannis (Eds.), Springer International Publishing Switzerland, 666-675* (2016)
25. L. Goratti, et *al.*, *Proceedings of AIAI-2016 Int. Conf., IFIP AICT **475**, L. Iliadis and I. Maglogiannis (Eds.), Springer International Publishing Switzerland, 676-685* (2016)
26. SESAME 5G-PPP Project, *Deliverable 2.2 ("Overall System and Arcchitecture"* (2016). Available at: http://www.sesame-h2020-5g-ppp.eu/Deliverables.aspx
27. SESAME 5G-PPP Project, *Deliverable 2.3 ("Specification of the CESC Components – First Iteration")* (2016)
28. SESAME 5G-PPP Project, *Deliverable 3.1 ("CESC Prototype design specifications and initial studies on Self-X and virtualization aspects")* (2016). Available at: http://www.sesame-h2020-5g-ppp.eu/Deliverables.aspx
29. I.Giannoulakis, et *al.*, *Proceedings of the EuCNC-2016 Conference, Athens, Greece, June 27-30, 2016*
30. J. Pettit, J. Gross, et *al.*, *Proceedings of the 23rd International Teletraffic Congress (ITC23) / The*

2nd Workshop on Data Centre Converged and Virtual Ethernet Switching (DC-CAVES). San Franciosco, September 08, 2011 (2011)

31. Huawei Technologies Co. Ltd., *White Paper – Huawei Observation to NFV* (2014)
32. M. Mohri, A. Rostamizadeh, and A. Talwakar, *Foundations of Machine Learning* (The MIT Press, 2011)
33. S. Redana, A. Kaloxylos et al., *Views on 5G Architecture", White paper of the 5G-PPP architecture WG* (2016, July)
34. F.Z. Yousaf, and T. Taleb, IEEE Netw. **30**(2), 110-115 (2016)
35. P. Rost, A. Banchs, I. Berberana, M. Doll, et *al.*, IEEE Com. Mag. **54**(5), 84-91 (2016)
36. M. Richart, J. Balosian, J. Serrat, and J.-L.Gorricho, IEEE Trans. on Netw. and Serv. Mgmt. **13**(3), 462-476 (2016, September)
37. C.-L. I, J. Huang, R. Duan, C. Cui, J.(X.) Jiang, and L. Li, IEEE Acc. **2**, 1030-1039 (2014)
38. P. Hedman, *Decription of Network Slicing Concept (NGMN 5G P1)* (NGMN (Next Generation Mobile Networks) Alliance, 2016)
39. X. Costa-Perez, J. Swetina, T. Guo, R. Mahindra, and S. Rangarajan, IEEE Com. Mag. **51**(7), 27-35 (2013)
40. I.P. Chochliouros, et *al.*, *Proceedings of the EuCNC-2016, Athens, Greece, June 27-30, 2016* (2016)
41. G.A. Khan, et *al.*, IEEE Com. Mag. **49**(10), 134-142 (2011)
42. K. Samdanis, X. Costa-Perez, and V. Sciancalepore, IEEE Com. Mag. **54**(7), 32-39 (2016)
43. A. Khan, W. Kellerer, K. Kozu, and M. Yabusaki, IEEE Com. Mag. **49**(10), 134-142 (2011)

DOI: 10.1051/matecconf/201712503013

Modeling and simulation of botnet based cyber-threats

Rafał Kasprzyk[1,a], Marcin Paź[1], Zbigniew Tarapata[1]

[1] *Institute of Computer and Information Systems, Military University of Technology, Warsaw, Poland*

Abstract. The paper presents an analysis of cyber-threats, with particular emphasis on the threats resulting from botnet activity. Botnets are the most common types of threats and often perceived as crucial in terms of national security. Their classification and methods of spreading are the basis for creating cyberspace model including the presence of different types of cyber-threats. A well-designed cyberspace model enables to construct an experimental environment that allows for the analysis of botnet characteristics, testing its resistance to various events and simulation of the spread and evolution. For this purpose, dedicated platforms with capabilities and functional characteristics to meet these requirements have been proposed.

1 Introduction

The challenges posed by cyber-threats are now the main issues delineated in both preparatory and operational concepts of security strategies implemented in the majority of countries and international organizations [11]. The developed strategies highlight the need of paying special attention to the new area, where today's societies mainly function, i.e. cyberspace. Many academic and military centers in the majority of countries worldwide conduct research aimed at developing new methods and specialized tools to increase the efficiency of detection, prevention and neutralization of effects of cyber-threats [1]. The need to develop more of such methods and tools is due to the continuously increasing dependence of state administration, private institutions and the whole society on the correct functioning of communication networks and IT systems [14][15][16][17][18].

The Internet, which is the foundation of cyberspace, is now more and more often perceived as an incredibly sensitive infrastructure, whose functioning determines the state security within social, economic and military fields [1]. In accordance with the report entitled *We are social media*, the Internet has around 3.01 billion users, which is 42% of the world's population. Furthermore, we may observe an upward trend in the number of Internet users. To efficiently attack the online infrastructure, it is no longer necessary to mobilize any armed forces. Any person with standard computer technologies and appropriate knowledge may prepare cyber attack having catastrophic results for the contemporary political and economic system. Therefore, it is absolutely essential to identify in time, prevent and neutralize the effects of such cyber-threats, which are generally certain events in cyberspace that may result in undesired consequences, causing damages to the systems of both individual users and organizations.

[a] Corresponding author: rafal.kasprzyk@wat.edu.pl

2 Botnet based cyber-threats

When analyzing historical data on cyber attacks [5], we may see that in the majority of cases, the sources of such attacks were botnets, which are basically computers (*zombies, bots*) infected with malicious software (*malware*), which provide their creators with a certain level of control over the infected devices [23]. A number of the infected computers within the framework of one botnet usually differs from several to even several hundred thousands bots. The largest observed networks contained even a couple of millions of the infected computers. Such an army of bots allows to make a lot attacks, without the knowledge of the users. Low maintenance cost of botnets and more accessible knowledge required for their management increases the popularity and hence number of such botnets.

No.	Botnet name	No. of IP addresses	Percentage
1	*Conficker*	62 221	21.19%
2	*ZeroAccess*	32 460	11.57%
3	*Zeus (incl Citadel)*	25 311	9.03%
4	*Sality*	14 003	4.99%
5	*Zeus GameOver*	12 513	4.46%
6	*Ircbot*	10 768	3.84%
7	*Bankpatch*	6 086	2.17%
8	*Banatrix*	5 385	1.92%
9	*Virut*	4 014	1.43%
10	*Kelihos*	3 922	1.40%
	Other	103 750	37.00%

Table 1. A listing of botnet activities in Poland in 2014. Source: CERT Polska, Report 2014

Botnets are usually used for [21][23]:

- Sending massive amounts of unsolicited e-mail (SPAM), the most popular way of using botnet, allowing to send millions of messages in a very short period of time. It is estimated that 80% of spam is sent by zombie computers. The e-mail addresses used for sending spam are put on blacklists, whereas any incoming mail is blocked by mail servers. The use of botnets allows to circumvent this problem by sending spam from e-mail addresses belonging to the owners of infected *zombie* devices.
- *Distributed Denial of Service* (DDoS), which means blocking access to Internet services by generating false traffic. Consequently, the attacked server is overloaded and becomes unavailable. Cybercriminals usually demand money to stop the attack. Unfortunately, at a time when a lot of companies operate online, the company owners often pay such ransom, without any involvement of the law enforcement authorities.
- Stealing confidential and private data, e.g. credit cards numbers, information allowing to get access to bank accounts, wide spectrum of logins and passwords. The collected data are then used for other illegal activities, for example, may be sold.
- Generating false clicks on pop-up ads, i.e. *Pay-Per-Click* (PPC) by advertising agencies at various websites. The owners of such websites charge a commission per every click. By using zombie networks, it is also possible to generate thousands of such clicks within one day only, and each click comes from a different computer so as not to raise any suspicion. Therefore, the money spent on advertising campaigns go straight into the pockets of website owners.

Botnets have become the source of income for large cybercriminal groups, allowing them to generate large profits from such illegal actions. For example, *DNSChanger* [19], with over 4 mln bots, used to inject ads, generated income of USD 14 mln within 5 years of operations, whereas *Storm* [19], with approx. 5 mln bots, used to send SPAM, had a total income of USD 3,5 mln every year. What is more, the botnet risk shall significantly increase, when we consider a possibility of hiring the already existing botnet network to make such cyber attacks. Estimated costs [19]: DDoS full-day attack - between USD 30 and USD 70; email SPAM - USD 10 per 1 mln messages; purchase of 2000 bots: USD 200; purchase of a botnet capable of efficient DDoS attack - USD 700; purchase of 1000 website visits - USD 7-15.

3 Botnet network classification

Botnets are usually classified according to their architecture and protocols used for communication between infected computers. When classifying the botnets in terms of their architecture, we may distinguish centralized and decentralized botnets [23].

In the **centralized models**, all infected computers communicate with the *Command and Control* servers (C&C). Every infected computer, upon establishing communication with C&Cs, is registered in the special database, where, among other things, all data on IP address and locations of botnet computers, are stored. By using the C&C panel, the *botmaster* may send commands to all or some of the selected *zombie* computers, which meet certain criteria (e.g. based on their location). Centralized botnets may be easily implemented and later managed. However, due to the highlighted role of C&Cs, it is relatively easy to neutralize them, as the only action that needs to be undertaken is to render C&Cs harmless and seize the server responsible for the management of the whole botnet.

In the **decentralized model** called also ***peer-to-peer* (P2P) model**, the botnet network has a distributed structure, within the framework of which every *zombie* computer may play the role of the managing server. In the P2P architecture, it is enough when the *botmaster* has access to any *zombie* computer. The idea of such approach is to provide a single bot with a list of "neighboring" devices and once it receives a message, it shall resend it to such "neighbors". Therefore, it is possible to spread a command within the entire botnet network, without highlighting the C&C role. In practice, it is rather difficult to create decentralized botnets. Every recently infected computer must be provided with the list of bots - "neighbors", with which it shall connect in the botnet network. However, to eliminate decentralized botnets is much more difficult than eliminating centralized networks. Active P2P botnet has no specific zombie computer, whose seizure would allow to neutralize the botnet network as a whole. Every *zombie* computer may play the role of the management center.

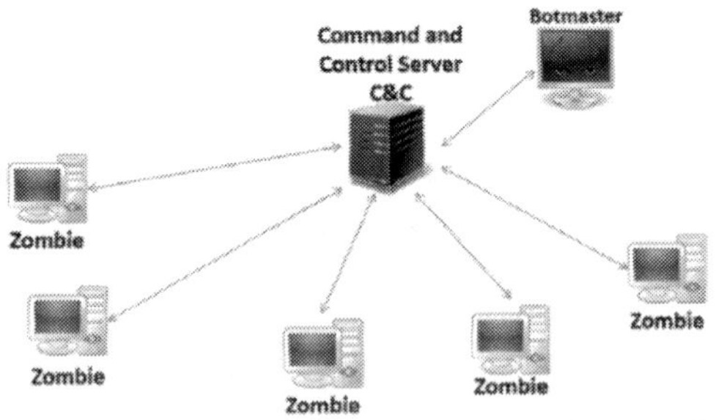

Figure 1. Centralized botnet network model. Source: Own elaboration.

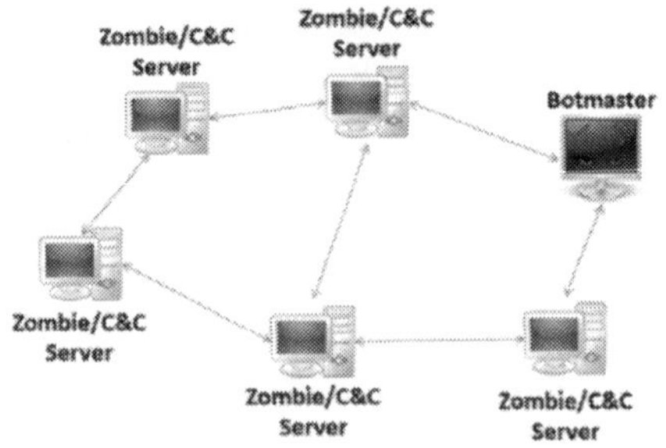

Figure 2. Decentralized botnet network model. Source: Own elaboration.

Botnet networks with mixed architecture are also sometimes created. This approach facilitates the sending of the "neighbors" list to recently infected computers, which first communicate with C&C to obtain such list and then switch into the P2P communication. The mixed architecture is also categorized as the decentralized model, even though C&Cs are used at a certain stage of the botnet's "lifetime".

All network connections are based on protocols that define the rules of interaction between particular network devices. While considering this property, we may distinguish the following classes of botnets [23]:

- *Internet Relay Chat* (IRC) oriented, the chat most often used by botnet designers, every infected computer connects with the indicated IRC server. The botnet control is exercised by giving commands in the form of conversation on the dedicated IRC channel - connected bots listen to the text on the channel and if they recognize it as a command, start executing it.
- WWW-oriented botnets, a relatively new, but quite popular type of botnets. It is based on the HTTP protocol by sending requests and responses. It is also characterized by low traceability by security systems. A bot connects with the predefined server, obtains certain commands from such server and while responding - sends its own data.
- *Instant Messenger* (IM) oriented, a rarely used type, communicating via online communicators, such as AOL, MSN, ICQ, etc. Relatively low popularity of such botnets is due to the fact that creating an individual IM account, for every infected device, is quite difficult.
- other types, which communicate via own TCP/IP-based protocols, i.e. only use the protocols of transport layer, such as: TCP, ICMP and UDP.

4 Spreading methods of Botnet networks

One of the most important stages of the botnet life cycle is its spreading. The spreading methods are planned already at the development stage of the software, which constitutes the bot code. The most frequently seen methods for spreading botnets, and hence device viruses, are the following:

- Computer worms - special programs automatically spreading and most often using errors of operating systems.
- Electronic mail and communicators - by sending an e-mail containing malicious code, e.g. in the form a holiday card, the HTML content with a link to programs with malware, information on changed login data to an account on one of the most popular services, etc.
- Warez - files downloaded from the websites with illegal software, which hide malware under crack files to popular applications and games.
- Social networks - portals, where fake accounts are created to send messages to other users, containing links to scripts with codes connecting to botnets.
- *Blackhat Search Engine Optimization* (*Blackhat* SEO), the technology that allows to adapt WWW content and location of key words to subpages of a web service for the purpose of obtaining higher index position in search engines. The user visiting such website gets a software installed on his/her computer, which connects the device to a botnet network.

5 Modeling of botnet networks

Along with the development of cybercrimes, whose sources are botnets, the need to develop models, methods and tools for detection, prevention and neutralization of their effects is also growing. There are several levels of a potential analysis of cyberspace phenomena [10]:

- Host (device) analysis - the analysis which is mainly based on raising awareness among users with respect to various cyber-threats, installation of anti-virus software and *firewall* software, and keeping used software up to date (latest updates always installed).
- Analysis of incoming/outcoming traffic - the analysis which is mainly based on the network traffic monitoring via *Intrusion Detection System* (IDS) and *Intrusion Prevention System* (IPS).
- Analysis of botnet network and communication between the infected computers and C&C server - the analysis is aimed at monitoring the functioning of the Internet as a whole and may be performed by specialist institutions, such CERT, in particular with the assumption of their collaboration to ensure cyber security at a state level.

The subsequent part of this article contains an outline of the **cyberspace model**, intuitively understood as space for creating, collecting, processing and exchange of information, which is "generated" by collaborating ICT system and external entities (e.g. people) that interact with such systems [1]. The cyberspace is modeled to allow description and analysis, including simulation, of the botnet cyber-threats. The cyberspace model must constitute grounds for developing methods for detection, prevention and neutralization of negative effects related to the botnet cyber-threats.

Currently, the model, developed methods and constructed tool (simulation environment) allow to:

- analyze structural characteristics of an identified/hypothetical botnet network to estimate the scope of a potential attack made via a given botnet network (e.g. the volume of the traffic that may be generated in case of the DDoS attack);
- evaluate resistance of the botnet network to accidental events (e.g. updated antivirus software by the *zombie* computer user) and take deliberate actions to combat/capture the botnet network (e.g. turning off a computer identified as C&C, turning off *zombie* computers located in key spots of the

botnet network from the point of view of its structure);

- describe and analyze, including simulation, spreading of malware and evolution of the botnet network in cyberspace;
- describe and analyze, including simulation, effects of selected attacks on real/hypothetical Internet targets (e.g. DDoS attack with specific parameters on the ICT network of the analyzed organization).

As the *CyberSpace* model, the following vector is proposed:

$$CyberSpace(t) = \left\langle \begin{matrix} CNet(t), CAs(t), CTs(t), \\ AMs(t), SMs(t) \end{matrix} \right\rangle$$

where:

$CNet(t)$ – the model describing topology and quantitative characteristics of the Internet (or its part that could be of interest for the purpose of modeling);

$CAs(t)$ – cyberspace actors, e.g. users, administrators, hackers;

$CTs(t)$ – cyber-threats that occur or might potentially occur (e.g. botnet network, malware);

$AMs(t)$ – methods/mechanisms of attacks that are possible realizations of cyber-threats (i.e. DDoS attack realized through botnets);

$SMs(t)$ – security methods/mechanisms for the Internet components (e.g. installation of antivirus software or firewall, IDS/IPS).

Parameter $t \in T = \{1, 2, 3, \ldots\}$ means discretized time, where: T – a set of discrete moments.

The Internet modeling network [20] is ordered as a three:

$$CNet(t) = \left\langle \begin{matrix} G(t) = \langle V(t), B(t), I(t) \rangle, \\ \{f_i(v,t)\}_{\substack{i\in\{1,\ldots,NF\}, \\ v\in V(t)}} \\ \{h_j(b,t)\}_{\substack{j\in\{1,\ldots,NH\} \\ b\in B(t)}} \end{matrix} \right\rangle$$

where:

$G(t)$ – graph [20] describing topology of the Internet (or its part that could be of interest for the purpose of modeling) at the time *t*; where: $V(t)$ – vertices of the graph $G(t)$; $B(t)$ – branches of the graph $G(t)$; $I(t) \subset V(t) \times B(t) \times V(t)$ and $I(t)$ is called incidence relationship. Vertices (active elements of the Internet) and branches (wired and wireless connections between active elements of the Internet) constitute a set of functions defining values of their attributes:

$f_i(v,t): V(t) \times T \to X_i$ – *i*-th function described at vertices of the graph $G(t)$;

$h_j(b,t): B(t) \times T \to Y_j$ – *j*-th function described at branches of the graph $G(t)$;

NF – a number of functions described at vertices $G(t)$;

NH – a number of the functions described at branches $G(t)$;

The X_i i Y_j sets, i.e. values of the $\{f_i(v,t)\}$ and $\{h_j(b,t)\}$ function may be from different spaces, which shall in particular depend on the adopted manner of the description of the Internet functioning or its analyzed part.

Formal description of cyber-threats must include features characterizing each of the possible types of cyber-threats. Therefore, the cyber-threats vector may be defined in the following manner:

$$CTs(t) = \left[CT(t,k)_{k \in K(t) = \{botnet, malware, \ldots\}} \right]$$

$CT(t,k)$ – model of the *k*-th type of cyber threat;

$\overline{\overline{K(t)}}$ – number of threat types, which occurred or might potentially occur.

As a model of the botnet cyber-threats, the following pair is proposed:

$$CT(t, k = botnet) = \langle BN(t), Diff(t) \rangle$$

$BN(t)$ – evolving network describing the typology and quantitative characteristics of the botnet network;

$Diff(t)$ – model of the botnet network evolution on the Internet.

The botnet network is modeled as an ordered three:

$$BN(t) = \left\langle \begin{matrix} BG(t) = \langle BV(t), BE(t) \rangle, \{bf_i(bv,t)\}_{\substack{i\in\{1,\ldots,NBF\}, \\ bv\in BV(t)}} \\ \{bh_j(be,t)\}_{\substack{j\in\{1,\ldots,NBH\} \\ be\in BE(t)}} \end{matrix} \right\rangle$$

where:

$BG(t)$ – graph describing the topology of the botnet network at time *t*. Note! The graph $BG(t)$ constitutes a framework of the graph's subgraph $G(t)$, whose vertices are those vertices $V(t)$ that constitute infected computers – i.e. *zombie*, whereas the edges reflect communication channels between *zombies*, which occurred based on the branches $B(t)$. The described vertices and edges of the graph $BG(t)$ constitute a set of functions defining values of their attributes.

$bf_i(bv,t): BV(t) \times T \to Z_i$ – *i*-th function described at vertices of the graph $BG(t)$;

$bh_j(be,t): BE(t) \times T \to Q_j$ – *j*-th function described at edges of the graph $BG(t)$;

NBF – a number of the functions described at vertices $BG(t)$;

NGH – a number of the functions described at branches $BG(t)$;

The Z_i i Q_j sets, i.e. the values of the $\{bf_i(bv,t)\}$ and $\{bh_j(be,t)\}$ function may be from different spaces. In particular, it is contemplated whether such attributes of the botnet network vertices as: role, status and location, and attributes of the botnet network edges as: communication protocol, communication frequency within the stipulated timeframe, size of the message, should be taken into account or not.

The model of the botnet network evolution on the Internet was defined in the following manner [4][12][13]:

$$Diff(t) = \left\langle \begin{matrix} CNet(t), \{MDM\}_{l\in\{1,\dots,NMDM\}}, \\ Gen(v,t) \end{matrix} \right\rangle$$

where:

$CNet(t)$ – the model describing topology and quantitative characteristics of the Internet (or its part that could be of interest for the purpose of modeling), which constitutes a component of the *CyberSpace(t)* model;

MDM_l – a probabilistic state machine describing the *Malware Diffusion Model* responsible for the evolution of the *l*-th botnet type, $l \in \{1,\dots,NMDM\}$;

$Gen(v,t)$ – the function of interaction modeling (sending messages) between vertices in the network $CNet(t)$.

The above-mentioned framework of the cyberspace model allows for the quantitative analysis of the botnet network by using the characteristics and algorithms from the field of graph and network theory; as a result, it is possible to develop methods of efficient detection, prevention and neutralization of the effects of the botnet cyber-threats.

6 Complex networks theory vs botnet network topology

It is worth noting that the present research into the botnet networks shows that they have typology of the *Complex Networks* [7]. Therefore, the algorithms developed to generate complex networks may be used to analyze the properties of the botnets. The above observation is extremely valuable, as it allows to conduct experiments, which would be otherwise impossible or too difficult to perform due to limited possibilities of collecting data on the botnet networks active at a given time.

The algorithms commonly used to generate complex networks are *Random Graphs* [8][9] and *Scale Free* networks [2][3][6]. In the already classic model - *RG(n,p)*, the random graph is generated by way of a procedure, which includes two stages. At the first stage, the n number of the graph vertices is established, and at the second stage, each of the C_n^2 pairs of vertices is combined with the p probability through the edge. The network created in such a manner has a homogeneous nature of vertices, i.e. without any highlighted vertices (with high degree in comparison with the average value of the vertices degree), which significantly affect the functioning of the network as a whole. Therefore, networks having this type of structure are hard to destroy, i.e. to unbind into multiple compound bondings. The classic model of random graphs only allows to generate static networks, which makes it difficult to analyze evolving networks, such as botnets.

The *Scale Free* network model takes account of the fact that actual networks are not static, but evolving structures. The actual networks "grow" by adding the following nodes, whereas new nodes are attached, with higher probability, to the nodes with higher degree. This type of behavior is known as *preferential attachment*, which means that the nodes are attached to the existing network according to the predefined hierarchy. There are numerous modifications of the basic algorithm for generating the *Scale Free* network and new modifications are all the time made, which reflect the growing interest in the complex networks. The modifications mainly refer to the change of the linear rules of preferential attachments into other (sometimes very complex) non-linear rules. Another idea is to include in the linear rule of preferential attachments the so-called initial "attractiveness" of the nodes or the "aging" effect of the nodes as well as a possibility of their deactivation (lack of possibility to attach new nodes thereto). Additionally, the same network evolution algorithm is modified in different ways. Thus, for example, at the following stages of evolution, we may have to deal not only with adding new nodes with new edges, but also with adding only new edges to the existing nodes or re-attaching some of the selected edges. In case of adaptation of the algorithm for generating the *Scale Free* network to the process of the botnet network modeling, a number of parameters is included (e.g. geographical location, average "lifetime" of *zombie* before it is detected, temporary deactivation caused by e.g. turning off an infected device for the night).

The research into the *Scale Free* networks prove that such networks are resistant to random attacks [22]. It is different in case of targeted attacks on the so-called hubs, i.e. the vertices with high degree. Such attacks may significantly affect integrity of the network and its functioning as a whole [22].

7 Experimental environment to research the botnet network

The program platform for the development experimental environment is *Framework Gephi* – an interactive platform for visualization and exploration of graphs and networks, with modular structure, implemented in the *Model-View-Controller* architecture, by using the

Inversion of Control pattern. *Gephi* evolves by adding new *plugins* to the existing environment. It is worth noticing that the plugins to the *Gephi* implementation, somehow forced by its designers, are in compliance with the best practices of the object programming, which often comes down to the principle of SOLID (*Single responsibility, Open-closed, Liskov substitution, Interface segregation, Dependency inversion*). Another interesting aspect is also the differentiation between *Application Programming Interface* (API) of the same *Gephi's Framework* and API offered by way of adding of the *Service Provider Interface* (SPI) thereto. *Gephi's API* is created by the platform designers (or under their supervision) and, as a matter of principle, rarely changed. On the other hand, SPI is a set of interfaces or services implemented in the form of special plugins, thus, the designers of the *Gephi's Framework* are not responsible for their proper functioning. Such approach is a tribute to the contemporary needs in terms of the necessity to quickly create software based on the existing components. However, on the other hand, the adopted solution ensures high quality of the software, at the same time guaranteed that its plugins may be used by already numerous *Gephi* users.

The experimental environment was created as a set of original *Gephi* plugins, and its functionality was presented by the *Use Cases* [13].

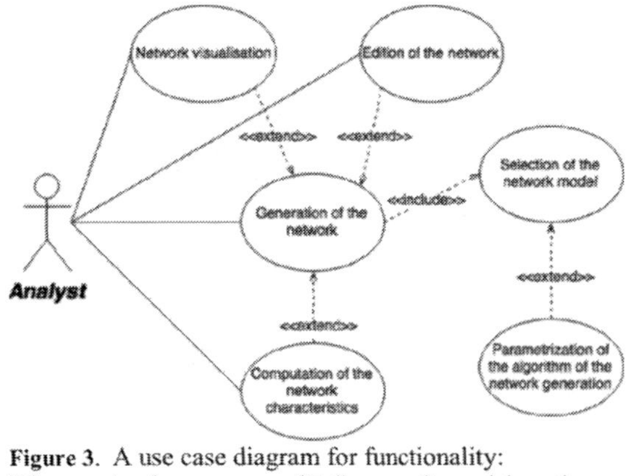

Figure 3. A use case diagram for functionality: "*Generating botnet network*". Source: Own elaboration.

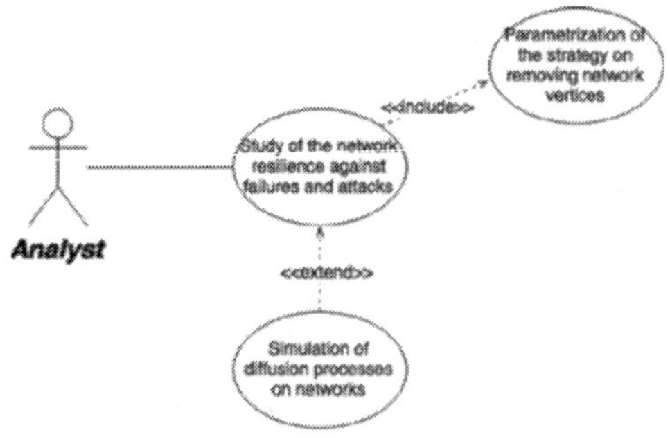

Figure 4. A use case diagram for functionality: "*Testing botnet network resilience to failures and attacks*". Source: Own elaboration.

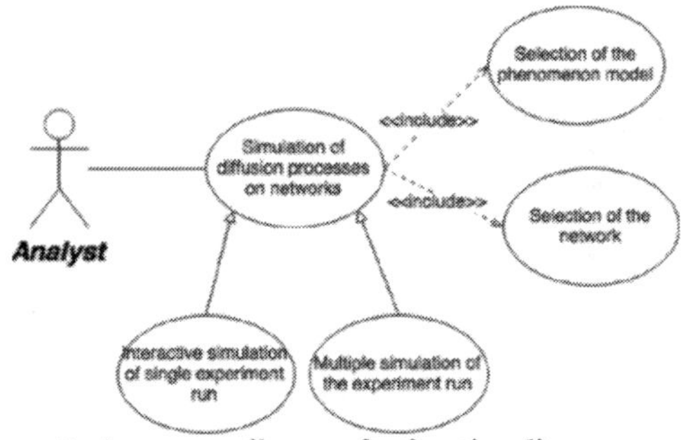

Figure 5. A use case diagram for functionality: "*Simulation of botnet network evolution*" - a special case of diffusion process simulation in the network. Source: Own elaboration.

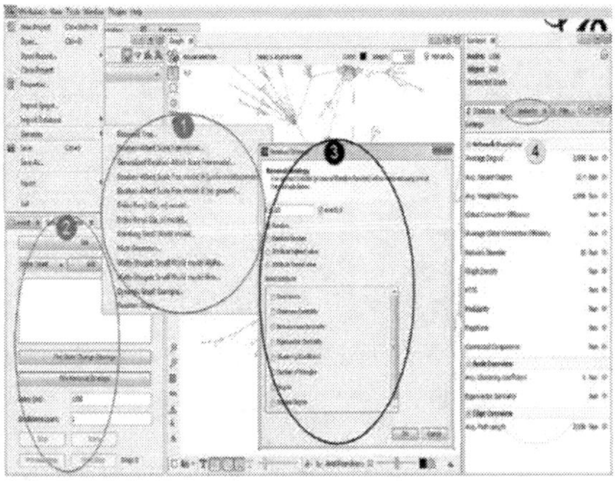

Figure 6. A main window of experimental environment software. Source: Own elaboration.

Figure 6 shows the main window of the experimental environment, with the highlighted interface elements, which correspond in terms of their functionalities to the presented use cases. The submenu with a list of implemented network generators was marked in red (area no. 1). The tab for parametrization of the network diffusion process was marked in blue (area no. 2). Finally, the window allowing to analyze the networks resistance to failures and attacks was marked in black (area no. 3). Attention should be also paid to the tab presenting graph statistics (yellow - area no. 4) available on the *Gephi* platform. Such algorithms constitute an integral part of the platform and are successively added and upgraded by the community of *Gephi* programmers, including authors of this study. In conclusion, the environment build on the basis of *Gephi* allows to:

- analyze the characteristics of the identified/ hypothetical botnet networks;
- assess resistance of the botnet network to accidental events and deliberate actions aimed at combating/ capturing the botnet network;

- describe and analyze, including simulation, spreading of malware and evolution of the botnet network.

The ICT network simulation environment, which was used for the purposes of modeling and analysis, including simulation, effects of the selected attacks on the actual/ hypothetical target on the Internet, complements the presented experimental environment. When choosing the simulation environment, the key criterion was its scalability and expansion. Furthermore, the simulator should allow efficiency analysis of the security methods/ mechanisms with respect to methods/ mechanisms of attacks based on the modeled infrastructure. There are many environments allowing to model the actual ICT networks (e.g. OMNeT++, CNet, NS-2, PRIME SSF, Möbius, etc.). In academic circles, as far as the analysis of the effects of attacks on the ICT infrastructure is concerned, OMNeT++ is often used. Since the aforementioned tool includes all ISO OSI protocols and layers, it is possible to accurately reflect the target of an attack as well as the attack itself. OMNeT++ is generally available under the APL license, and has modular structure, simulation engine with discrete event model as well as open architecture (implementation in C++). The extended programmer's tools and good documentation, from the design, through implementation, start-up and collection of results, are of great help. The programmer may choose from a variety of ready libraries.

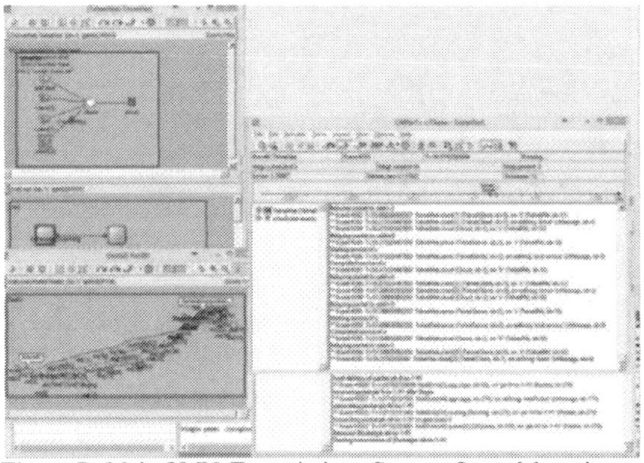

Figure 7. Main OMNeT++ window. Source: Own elaboration.

8 Summary

The threats resulting from the botnet network are really important in terms of cyberspace security. Additionally, great dynamics of changes in the manner of the botnet operations and methods of attacks resulting therefrom increase the need of their in-depth analysis. Observations and analysis of the web traffic as well as reactions to the emerging anomalies are not enough. It is more and more necessary to have special skills for predicting attacks and launching protection methods right for the great dynamics of changes in the types of cyber attacks.

The established framework of the mathematical model of cyberspace, which includes the cyber-threats present therein, constituted grounds for creating the experimental environment and concept of using the OMNeT++ simulation environment.

Another step shall be to extend the model and programming tools, forming a kind of a research laboratory to analyze the botnet networks and develop methods for their efficient elimination.

References

1. Antkiewicz R., Dyk M., Kasprzyk R., Najgebauer A., Pierzchała D., Tarapata Z., Maj M.: *„Koncepcja rozwoju zdolności w obszarze cyberbezpieczeństwa infrastruktur krytycznych państwa"*, in report of Kościuszko Institute *„Bezpieczeństwo infrastruktury krytycznej wymiar teleinformatyczny"*, ISBN 978-83-63712-15-0, pp. 93-102, Warsaw, (2014)
2. Barabási A.L., Albert R.: "*Emergency of Scaling in Random Networks*", Science, 286, pp. 509-512 (1999)
3. Barabási A.L., Albert R., "*Topology of Evolving Networks: Local Events and Universality*", Physical Review Letters, Vol. 85, No 24, 5234-5237 (2000)
4. Bartosiak C., Kasprzyk R., Najgebauer A.: "*The graph and network theory as a tool to model and simulate the dynamics of infectious diseases*", BAMS, Vol. 9, Issue 1, 17-28, (2013)
5. CERT.GOV.PL, (2015), *The report on the state of cyber security in Poland for the year 2014*
6. Chen Q., Chang H., Govindan R., Jamin S., Shenker S.J., Willinger W.: "*The origin of power laws in Internet topologies revisited*", Proceedings of the 21st Annual Join Conference of IEEE Computer and Communication Societies (2002)
7. Dagon D., Gu G., Zou C., Grizzard J., Dwivedi S., Lee W., Lipton R.:, *A Taxonomy of botnet structures – lecture: Computer Security Applications Conference*, 2007. ACSAC 2007
8. Erdös P., Rényi A.: "*On random graphs*", Publicationes Mathematicae 6, 290-297 (1959a)
9. Erdös P., Rényi A.: "*On the evolution of random graphs*", Publications of the Mathematical Institute of the Hungarian Academy of Sciences 5, 17-61, (1959)
10. Godkin T., (2013), *Statistical Assessment of Peer-to-Peer Botnet Features*, University of Victoria
11. Grzelak M., Liedel K., (2012), *Bezpieczeństwo w cyberprzestrzeni. Zagrożenia i wyzwania dla Polski - zarys problemu, Bezpieczeństwo Narodowe no 22, II*
12. Kasprzyk R.: "*Diffusion in Networks*", Journal of Telecommunications and Information Technology, 2/2012, 99-106, (2012)
13. Kasprzyk R.: "*Modele ewolucji systemów złożonych i metody badania ich charakterystyk dla potrzeb komputerowej identyfikacji potencjalnych sytuacji kryzysowych*", PhD thesis, supervisor A. Najgebauer, Faculty of Cybernetics, Military University of Technology in Warsaw, (2012)
14. Kiedrowicz M.: *Publiczne zasoby informacyjne jako podstawa tworzenia platform integracyjnych*, (in:) INTERNET. Prawno-informatyczne problemy sieci, portali i e-usług, (ed.) G. Szpor, pp. 231-246, (2012).
15. Kiedrowicz M., Stanik J.: *Selected aspects of risk management in respect of security of the document lifecycle management system with multiple levels of sensitivity*, (in:) Information Management in Practice,

(eds) B.F. Kubiak and J. Maślankowski, pp. 231-249, (2015)

16. Kiedrowicz M., *Dostęp do publicznych zasobów danych - Big data czy Big brother*, (in:) INTERNET. Publiczne bazy danych i Big data, (ed.) G. Szpor, pp. 15-39, (2015)
17. Kiedrowicz M.: *Location with the use of the RFID and GPS technologies - opportunities and threats*, GIS ODYSSEY 2016, pp. 122-128, (2016)
18. Kiedrowicz M.: *Objects identification in the informations models used by information systems*, GIS ODYSSEY 2016, pp. 129-136, (2016)
19. Kijewski A.: Secure 2013 *CERT Polska vs botnets*
20. Korzan G., *Elementy Teorii grafów i sieci – metody i zastosowania*, WNT, Warsaw, (1978)
21. Namiestnikow J., *Ekonomia botnetu,* Kaspersky Lab, (2009)
22. Tarapata Z., Kasprzyk R.: *Graph-based optimization method for information diffusion and attack durability in networks*, Lecture Notes in Computer Science, Volume 6086/2010, p. 698-709, Springer, (2010)
23. Vitaly Kamluk *„Biznes botnetowy"* Kaspersky Lab

Free and Open Source Chemistry Software in Research of Quantitative Structure-Toxicity Relationship of Pesticides

Vesna Rastija[1,*], *Dejan* Agić[1], *Kristian* Brlas[1], *Vijay* Masand[2]

[1] Faculty of Agriculture, J. J. Strossmayer University of Osijek, Vladimira Preloga, Osijek, Croatia
[2] Department of Chemistry, Vidya Bharati Mahavidyalaya, Camp, CK Naidu Road, Amravati, 444 602, Maharashtra, India

Abstract. Pesticides are toxic chemicals aimed for the destroying pest on crops. Numerous data evidence about toxicity of pesticides on aquatic organisms. Since pesticides with similar properties tend to have similar biological activities, toxicity may be predicted from structure. Their structure feature and properties are encoded my means of molecular descriptors. Molecular descriptors can capture quite simple two-dimensional (2D) chemical structures to highly complex three-dimensional (3D) chemical structures. Quantitative structure-toxicity relationship (QSTR) method uses linear regression analyses for correlation toxicity of chemical with their structural feature using molecular descriptors. Molecular descriptors were calculated using open source software PaDEL and in-house built PyMOL plugin (PyDescriptor). *PyDescriptor* is a new script implemented with the commonly used visualization software PyMOL for calculation of a large and diverse set of easily interpretable molecular descriptors encoding pharmacophoric patterns and atomic fragments. *PyDescriptor* has several advantages like free and open source, can work on all major platforms (Windows, Linux, MacOS). QSTR method allows prediction of toxicity of pesticides without experimental assay. In the present work, QSTR analysis for toxicity of a dataset of mixtures of 5 classes of pesticides comprising has been performed.

1 Introduction

Pesticides are used extensively to control agricultural pest and to improve crop yields. However, small fraction of the pesticides is moving up from surface into stream, rivers and lakes and cause of considerable environmental concern as a result from application drift, rainfall runoff, or residue leaching through the soil into groundwater [1]. The contamination of water by pesticides increasing around the world, so the knowledge of eco-toxicological effects for aquatic organisms for the environmental risk assessment is essential.

Before pesticides are registered they must undergo laboratory testing on animals for short-term (acute) and long-term (chronic) health effects. Laboratory animals are purposely fed doses high enough to cause toxic effects. Small planktonic crustaceans *Daphnia,* fish, and algae are the most common organisms tested for the evaluation of toxic effects of pesticides. In order to reduce expensive and time-consuming experiments and reduce animal testing quantitative structure-toxicity relationship (QSTR) method is valuable [2]. Two-dimensional (2D) and three-dimensional (3D) molecular structure considerable influence on properties of pesticides, such as, absorption, distribution, metabolism, and excretion (ADME). QSTR method allows prediction of environmental toxicity derived from the molecular structure and fills an important gap in risk assessment studies (REACH) [3].

QSTR method involves representations of molecules or molecular patterns in the form of numerical descriptors that capture the structural features and properties of molecules, generally known as molecular descriptors. Molecular descriptors describe: chemical properties (electrophilicity, hydrogen bonding), physical-chemical properties (lipophilicity, polar surface area), 2D structure (topological, information, connectivity, information indices, 2D frequency fingerprints), 3D structure (RDF, WHIM, GETAWEY, geometrical descriptors). Correlation of toxicity of molecule and molecular descriptors is most often expressed by linear equation calculated by multiple linear regression (MLR), or partial least squares (PLS) [4]. Computational neural networks (CNN) is usually performed if there is an assumption about a nonlinear and a highly complex relationship between the structure and the observed toxicity [5].

There are many commercial and free academic packages developed for calculation of molecular descriptors. Most of the molecular descriptors can be calculated by using commercial software packages such as CODESSA [6] and DRAGON [7]. Limitations of most of those packages are high price and hardly interpretable calculated molecular descriptors in terms of structural features. To overcome this, we have developed, *PyDescriptor*, a new script implemented with the commonly used visualization software PyMOL for calculation of a large and diverse set of easily interpretable 1D- to 3D- descriptors. They are also easy interpreting in terms of structural moieties, applicable for representing local environment or structure, simple to understand, independent of experimental properties, sensitive to changes in conformation molecule. PyMOL is free open source molecular graphics tool for 3D visualization of proteins, small molecules, density, surfaces, and trajectories [8]. *PyDescriptor* is a useful addition to the currently existing molecular descriptor calculation software. It has several advantages like free

* Corresponding author: vrastija@pfos.hr

and open source and it is able to works on all major platforms (Windows, Linux, MacOS). The script is freely available for academic use [9].

In the present paper we have generated QSTR models using molecular descriptors calculated by *PyDescriptors* for estimation of toxicity of 43 pesticides obtained on aquatic vertebrates bluegill sunfish (*Lepomis macrochirus*) [1].

	Chemical	Exp. endpoint	Prediction fitting
		$logLC_{50}$ mol/L	$logLC_{50}$ mol/L
1	bensulfuron	2.43	-0.26
2	chlorimuron	0.59	1.39
3	chlorsulfuron*	0.92	0.86
4	flumetsulam	2.97	-0.36
5	halosulfuron	2.22	0.01
6	imazapyr*	3.19	-0.03
7	imazaquin	3.13	0.11
8	imazethapyr	3.17	-0.14
9	metsulfuron*	2.61	-0.35
10	nicosulfuron	3.39	0.36
11	primisulfuron*	2.34	-0.99
12	prosulfuron	2.57	-0.96
13	sulfometuron	2.22	-0.48
14	triasulfuron	2.40	-0.49
15	atrazine*	2.22	-0.19
16	cyanazine	1.97	-0.28
17	metribuzin	2.65	-0.33
18	prometon	2.12	0.29
19	prometryn	1.62	0.36
20	simazine	2.53	-0.68
21	acetochlor	0.74	0.25
22	alachlor*	1.31	0.03
23	metolachlor	1.64	-0.51
24	propachlor	0.86	0.55
25	azinphos-methyl	-1.19	0.40
26	chlorpyrifos	-1.25	0.26
27	diazinon	-0.13	-0.53
28	disulfoton	-0.34	-0.24
29	ethoprophos	1.19	-0.16
30	fonofos	-1.35	-0.22
31	malathion	-0.45	0.49
32	parathion	-0.24	-0.47
33	parathion methyl	0.86	0.51
34	phorate*	-1.82	1.25
35	terbufos	-1.89	0.92
36	butylate*	1.39	-0.62
37	carbaryl	1.69	0.25
38	carbofuran	0.45	0.85
39	EPTC	2.13	-0.40
40	molinate	1.87	0.25
41	pebulate*	1.54	0.35
42	thiobencarb	0.84	-0.52
* member of the test set			

Table 1. Experimentally obtained toxicity endpoint and estimated values by eq. (1) of pesticides for *Lepomis acrochirus*.

2 Methods

2.1 Toxicity data

Toxicity data for aquatic vertebrates bluegill sunfish (*Lepomis macrochirus*) were retrieved from literature. Toxicity of 43 pesticides is expressed as LC_{50} (lethal concentration that kills 50 % of the animals in a test population / $molL^{-1}$). LC_{50} were converted in the form of a logarithm (log LC_{50}) (Table 1).

2.2 Calculation of molecular descriptors

Molecular descriptors were calculated using open source software PaDEL [9] and a new in-house built PyMOL plugin (PyDescriptor) [8] followed by extensive objective and subjective feature selection to avoid redundant descriptors.

2.3 Regression analysis and validation of models

For model building, the dataset was divided into training (80%) and test (20%) sets. The best QSAR models were obtained using a Genetic Algorithm using QSARINS v 2.2 [11].

The models have been assessed by: fitting criteria; internal cross-validation using leave-one out (LOO) method and Y-scrambling; and external validation. Fitting criteria included: the coefficient of determination (R^2), adjusted (R^2_{adj}), cross-validate R^2 using leave-one-out method (Q^2_{LOO}), global correlation among descriptors (Kxx), difference between global correlation between molecular descriptors and y the response variable, and global correlation among descriptors (ΔK), standard deviation of regression (s), and Fisher ratio (F). Internal and external validations also included the following parameters: root-mean-square error of the training set ($RMSE_{tr}$); root-mean-square error of the training set determined through cross validated LOO method ($RMSE_{cv}$), root-mean-square error of the external validation set ($RMSE_{ex}$), concordance correlation coefficient of the training set (CCC_{tr}), test set using LOO cross validation (CCC_{cv}), and of the external validation set (CCC_{ex}), mean absolute error of the training set (MAE_{tr}), mean absolute error of the internal validation set (MAE_{cv}) and mean absolute error of the external validation set (MAE_{ex}) [12], predictive residual sum of squares determined through cross-validated LOO method ($PRESS_{cv}$) in the training set and in the external prediction set ($PRESS_{ex}$). The analysed external validation parameters also include the coefficient of determination (R^2_{ex}). Robustness of QSAR models was tested by Y-randomisation test. New parallel models were developed based on fit to randomly reordered Y-data (Y scrambling), and the process was repeated several times (2000 iterations) [12]. Investigation of the applicability domain of a prediction model was performed by leverage plot or Williams plot (plotting residuals vs. leverage of training compounds). Detection of outliers was carried out for compounds that have values of standardized residuals greater than two standard deviation units using QSARINS. The leverage h

of a compound is the measure of its influence on the model.

3 Result and discussion

The best three-descriptor based QSTR model for prediction of toxicity for the *Lepomis acrochirus* is:

$$\log LC_{50} = 1.948 - 0.588\ \mathrm{ALog}P + 1.223\ FP747 - 0.375\ fPH3A \quad (1)$$

$N_{\text{training set}} = 34 \quad N_{\text{prediction set}} = 9$

The statistical results of the obtained QSTR model are presented in Table 2. Satisfaction of fitting criteria implies the following: the closer R^2 values are to unity, the more similar calculated values are to the experimental ones, that is, $R^2 \geq 0.60$. Also, larger F statistic and lower standard deviation means that the model is more significant. In order to avoid overfitting, inter-correlation between the descriptors included in the equation is detected based on Kxx and ΔK. Low Kxx and $\Delta K \geq 0.05$ implies no chance correlation between descriptors. The minimum acceptable statistical parameters for internal and external predictivity include the following conditions: $R^2_{\text{ext}} \geq 0.60$; $CCC_{\text{ext}} \geq 0.85$; $RMSE_{\text{cv}}$ and MAE_{cv} close to zero; and $RMSE_{\text{tr}} < RMSE_{\text{cv}}$. Robust QSAR models should have low $R^2_y\text{scr}$ and low $Q^2_y\text{scr}$ values and $R^2_y\text{scr} > Q^2_y\text{scr}$. In order to investigate the applicability of a prediction model and detect possible outliers, the applicability domain of the selected model was evaluated by a leverage analysis expressed as Williams plot, in which residuals and the leverage values were plotted. Williams plot is given in Figure 1. A scatter plot of experimentally obtained toxicity calculated by QSTR model versus values calculated by Eq. (1) is presented in Figure 2.

Table 2. Statistical parameters of the obtained QSAR models.

	Statistical parameters	Value
Fitting criteria	R^2	0.87
	R^2_{adj}	0.86
	F	68.24
	Kxx	0.35
	ΔK	0.19
	$RMSE_{\text{tr}}$	0.51
	MAE_{tr}	0.43
	CCC_{tr}	0.93
Internal cross-validation	Q^2_{loo}	0.84
	$RMSE_{\text{cv}}$	0.56
	MAE_{cv}	0.48
	$PRESS_{\text{cv}}$	0.92
	CCC_{cv}	0.92
Y-scrambling	$R^2_y\text{scr}$	8.67
	$Q^2_y\text{scr}$	-19.05
External validation	R^2_{ext}	0.79
	$RMSE_{\text{ext}}$	0.66
	MAE_{ext}	0.52
	$PRESS_{\text{ext}}$	3.95
	CCC_{ext}	0.85

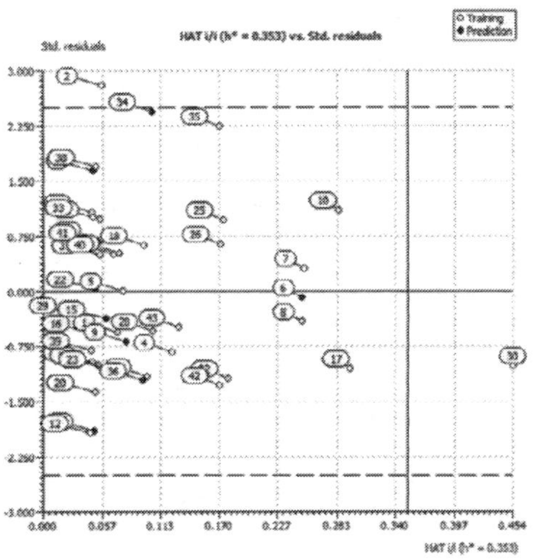

Fig. 1. Applicability domain of the QSAR model for loglC$_5$0 expresses by eq. (1).

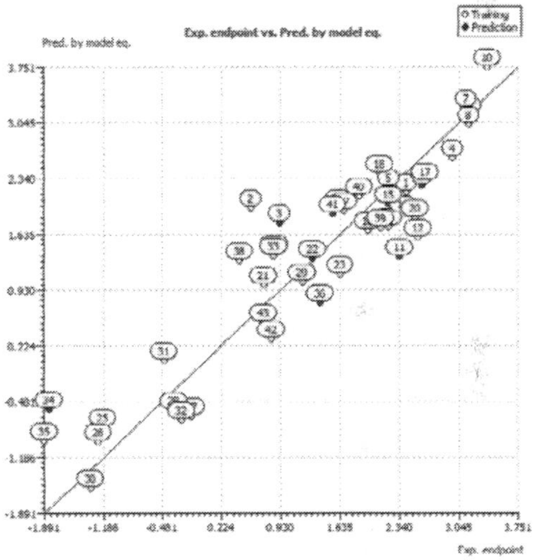

Fig. 2. A scatter plot of experimentally obtained toxicity calculated by QSTR model versus values calculated by eq. (1).

Obtained model has satisfactory results of fitting parameters and internal validation and low collinearity between the three descriptors. The results of Y-scrambling demonstrated that model wasnot obtained by chance correlation. Model 1 may be considered as predictive due to the high values of R^2_{ext} and CCC_{ext}, as well as small difference between $RMSE_{tr}$ and $RMSE_{ex}$, and between MAE_{tr} and MAE_{ex}. As can be seen from the Williams plot (Figure 1), toxicity of pesticides **30** (fonofos) predicted my model (1) must be used with reserve, because its leverage value is greater than the warning leverage ($h^* = 0.353$). Also, the same model has generated one outliers, pesticides **2** (chlorimuron) because its standardized residual is greater than ± 2.5.

The best QSTR model obtained include the following descriptors: lipophilicity (ALog*P*), PaDEL fingerprint descriptor *FP747* and PyMOL descriptor *fPH3A*. Considering the negative coefficient of ALog*P* in Eq. (1) highly toxic compounds have a high lipophilicity. High lipophilic compounds my easily pass lipidous membranes and accumulate in fat tissue, therefore cause enhanced toxic effect [13]. Negative coefficient of PyDescriptor *fPH3A* implies that frequency of occurrence of hydrogen within 3 Å from phosphorus positively influence on increased toxicity of pesticides. QSAR study of toxicity of phoshorhydrazide (PHA) derivates revealed that the NH–P(X) moiety has a much higher inhibitory activity than the NH–C(X) moiety. The presence of the electron acceptor substituent around the P=X group increases the inhibitory potential of the PHA derivatives [14]. Obtained results are in accordance with previous findings of QSTR modeling of toxicity of organic molecules to *Daphnia magna* [4]. Obtained PLS models suggests that higher lipophilicity and electrophilicity, and hydrogen bond donor groups are responsible for greater toxicity.

Figure 3a presents a chemical structure of the most toxic compound (**35**), an aliphatic organothiophosphate insecticide, terbufos. Thiophosphates are a very toxic class of organophosphorus compounds, especially if possess reactive functional groups such as: methyl, phosphate ester (P=O type) and unsubstituted phenyl group [15]. QSTR study of some organophosphorus compounds performed by using the quantum chemical and topological descriptors relieved that the sulphur atoms instead of oxygen atoms improved toxicity [16].

Figure 3b shows a structure of minimum toxic compound (**6**) imazapyr, an imidazolinone herbicide. Imazapyr does not contain phosphorus atom. According a positive coefficient of fingerprint descriptor *FP747* in eq. (1) imply that higher values of this descriptors mean lower toxicity.

4 Conclusion

In the present work, we have used an open source molecular descriptor calculation PyMOL plugin *PyDescriptor* for calculation easily interpretable and informative molecular descriptors. Robust QSTR models with good external predictive ability have been developed for the toxicity of pesticides for the fish, bluegill sunfish. The developed models, since, satisfy the threshold values for many statistical parameters could be useful for the prediction of experimentally undermined toxicity of known pesticides, as well as new pesticides. The model can also be employed to better understand the mechanism of toxicity of the various families of pesticides on the aquatic organisms, as well as the identification of potential aquatic pollutant.

Our results indicates that future QSTR analysis of pesticides should apply a specific group of descriptors relates with lipohilicity and structure fragment involved in electron transfer.

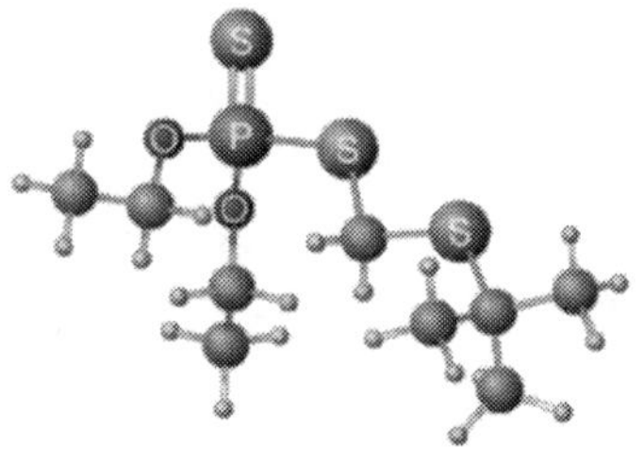

a)

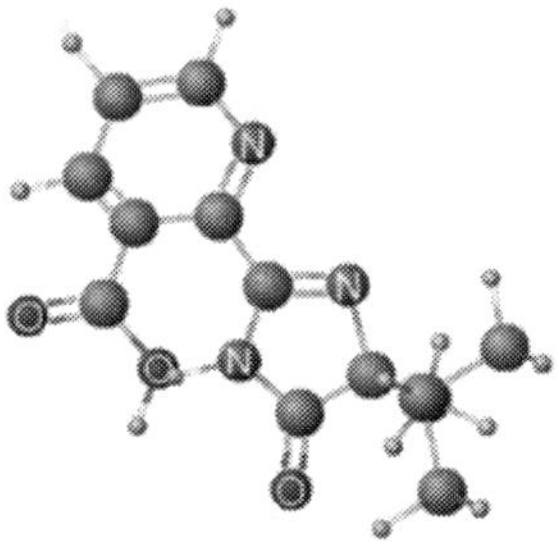

b)

Fig. 3. Structure of: a) the most toxic pesticide, terbufos (**35**); b) the least toxic pesticide imazapyr (**6**).

Acknowledgements

Authors are thankful to Josip Juraj Strossmayer University of Osijek, Osijek, Croatia for financial support to the project INGI-2015-20 to complete the present work.

References

1. W. Battaglin, J. Fairchild, Water Sci. Technol. **45**, 95 (2002)
2. S. Cassani, S. Kovarich, E. Papa, P. P. Roy, L. van der Wal, P. Gramatica, J. Hazard. Mater. **258**, 50 (2013)
3. EC Proposal for a Regulation of the European Parliament and of the Council concerning the Registration, Evaluation, Authorisation and Restriction of Chemicals (REACH), establishing a European Chemicals Agency and amending Directive 1999/45/EC and Regulation (EC) on Persistent Organic Pollutants (Brussels, Belgium) (2003)
4. S. Kar, K. Roy, J. Hazard. Mater. **177**, 344 (2010)
5. D. V. Eldered, P. C. Jurs, SAR QSAR Environ. Res. **10**, 75 (1999)
6. A. R. Katritzky, V. Lobanov, M. Karelson, CODESSA Reference Manual. University of Florida, Gainesville, (1996)
7. Dragon Professional Version 5.5, Talete srl, (2007) (http://www.talete.mi.it/dragon.htm).
8. PyMOL, Schrödinger, LLC. (2007) (http://www.pymol.org/).

9. PyDescriptor, http://www.unios.hr/wp-content/uploads/2016/06/PyDescriptors-Tutorial.pdf
10. C. W. Yap, J. Comput. Chem. **35**, 1466 (2010)
11. P. Gramatica, N. Chirico, E. Papa, S. Cassani, S. Kovarich, J. Comput. Chem. **34,** 2121 (2013)
12. P. Gramatica, QSAR Comb. Sci. **26**, 694 (2007)
13. O. G. Kolumbin, L. N. Ognichenko, A. G. Artemenko, P. G. Polischuk, M.A. Kulinskyb, E. N. Muratov, V. E. Kuz'min, V. A. Bobeica, Chem. J. Mold. **8**, 95 (2013)
14. K. Gholivand, L. Asadi, A. A. E. Valmoozi, M. Hodaii, M. Sharifi, H. M. Kashani, H. R. Mahzouni, M. Ghadamyari, A. A. Kalate, E. Davari, S. Salehi, M. Bonsaii, RSC Adv. **6**, 24175 (2016)
15. A.-M. Petrescu, G. Ilia, Ecoterra **14**, 90 (2015)
16. S. A. Senior, M. D. Madbouly, A.M. El Massry, Chemosphere **85**, 7 (2011)

MATEC Web of Conferences **125**, 04002 (2017)
CSCC 2017
DOI: 10.1051/matecconf/201712504002

Diagnostic System of Drill Condition in Laminated Chipboard Drilling Process

Bartosz Swiderski[1], *Jaroslaw* Kurek[1,*], *Stanislaw* Osowski[2,3], *Michal* Kruk[1], *Albina* Jegorowa[1]

[1]University of Life Sciences, Warsaw, Poland
[2] Warsaw University of Technology, Warsaw, Poland
[3] Military University of Technology, Warsaw, Poland

Abstract. The paper presents an on-line automatic system for recognition of the drill condition in a laminated chipboard drilling process. Two states of the drill are considered: the sharp enough (still able to drill holes acceptable for processing quality) and worn out (excessive drill wear, not satisfactory from the quality point of view of the process). The automatic system requires defining the diagnostic features, which are used as the input attributes to the classifier. The features have been generated from 5 registered signals: feed force, cutting torque, noise, vibration and acoustic emission. The statistical parameters defined on the basis of the auto regression model of these signals have been used as the diagnostic features. The sequential step-wise feature selection is applied for choosing the most discriminative set of features. The final step of recognition is done by support vector machine classifier working in leave one out mode. The results of numerical experiments have confirmed good quality of the proposed diagnostic system.

1 Introduction

Use Tool Condition Monitoring (TCM) is an important automatic system to improve the quality and productivity of machine tools without interrupting normal operations [1,2,3]. TCM is aiming in detecting or predicting the tool failure. It is composed of sensors, which monitor the signals coming from force, torque, vibration, temperature, acoustic emission, electric current, etc. Many sensors are used for monitoring machining processes and yield an extended set of sensitive features. The registered sensor signals are analysed, transformed and selected by the system to yield the most sensitive features to the monitoring purposes [4,5]. On this basis the decision system is built up to generate automatically the control parameters for the production process. The information from the learning procedure is stored in the system and is used to classify the newly obtained exploitation data. The newly acquired data may be used in retraining the system. With this increasing experience, the system will become more and more reliable in monitoring/control the production.

The paper proposes new solution of TCM in wood industry, directed to monitoring the condition of the drill. Drill wear results in decreasing the cutting edge properties and worsening the product quality [6,7]. The blunting of drill is caused by the mechanical, thermal and chemical influence of the work piece. This is especially important, when the wood based materials with large amount of glue are drilled [6].

Different types of sensors are used in monitoring the sharpness of the drills. The most often applied are the sensors reacting on force, electrical power, acoustic emission, vibration and acoustic pressure [4,8,9]. The signals of the mentioned above sensors are more or less correlated with the condition of the tool. However, they are also susceptible to the random interferences and background noise. Many types of sensors are used in a parallel to reduce the influence of the noise. However, the force or torque sensors are relatively complex and difficult in mounting to the cutting tool. On the other side the vibration sensors and current or power sensors are easy to install, but less accurate. The sound signal is similar to the vibration. The acquisition of the sound, usually in the range of frequencies from 20kHz to 80kHz, can be easily done applying the microphone. However, the acoustic pressure sensors (microphones), are even more sensitive to the background noise.

On the basis of the registered sensor signals the diagnostic features are created and assessed. They will serve as the input attributes to the final classification system. In some publications the diagnostic features are defined directly on the basis of sensor signals in time domain or after their transformation using either Fourier or wavelet transformation [6,10]. Different statistical measures, such as mean value, root mean squared value, power, energy, skewness, kurtosis, etc., are applied. The better correlation of these parameters with the degree of sharpness of the cutting edge of drill the better quality of the features, applied as the input signals to the neural

* Corresponding author: jaroslaw_kurek@sggw.pl

classifiers responsible for the recognition of the tool condition [11,12,13].

In this work we apply the diagnostic features defined on the basis of the autocorrelation principle. Five sensor signals, registered in a laminated chipboard drilling process, are exploited. They include feed force (F), cutting torque (M), noise (C), vibration (V) and acoustic emission (A).

The features generated on the basis of these signals should differentiate two classes of drill state: the sharp drill (class 1) and blunt drill (class 2). The first class refers to the tool which is able to drill holes of proper parameters, acceptable from the processing quality point of view. The second class means the drill condition resulting in a not satisfactory quality of the final product.

The paper will present the process of building an automatic diagnostic system for assessing the sharpness of the drill on the basis of the above registered signals. The procedure begins from the acquisition of the sensor signals, then describes the generation of diagnostic features, selection of the best set of these features and final recognition of the condition of drill (sharp or blunt). The support vector machine (SVM) is used as the pattern recognition and classification tool. We used SVM, since it belongs to the most efficient classifiers of good generalization ability.

2 Data base in experiments

The data used in experiments have been acquired using Buselatto JET 100 CNC vertical machining centre with a maximum spindle speed of 4500 rpm. The data acquisition were done on the laminated chipboard of the dimension 150x35x18mm using Faba HW drills of the 12 mm diameter. The movement of the working unit was caused by a pneumatic actuator with the feed speed equals 1.35m/min. The following sensor devices have been applied in experiments: A - acoustic emission measuring system (contact sensor Kistler 8152B, amplifier Kistler 5125B), V - mechanical vibration measuring system (accelerometer Kistler 8141A, amplifier Kistler 5127B), C - noise (sound pressure) measuring system (microphone and preamplifier B&K 4189, amplifier B&K NEXUS 2690), F and M – dynamometer with Kistler 9345A sensor and ICAM5073A amplifier. The samples have been registered by using two data acquisition cards (NI PCI-6111 and NI 6034E) through connection boxes (NI BNC-2110), as shown in Fig. 1. Two acquisition cards of different sampling frequencies: 2MHz for acoustic emission signal and 50 kHz for vibration and noise signal, respectively, have been applied using the LabVIEW 7 National Instruments application. The measurement system was fully automatic and all measurements have been done on-line in the production process of laminated chipboard drilling.

The acquired data were associated with two conditions of drills. The sharp state (class 1) refers to the tool which is able to drill holes, acceptable from the processing quality point of view. The second state of drill, called blunt, reflect the drill resulting in a processing quality regarded as not satisfactory.

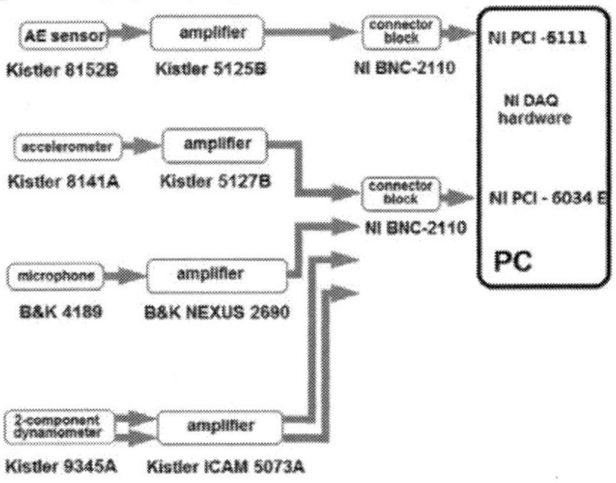

Fig. 1. The general scheme of devices used in the proposed on-line diagnostic system of the drill in laminated chipboard drilling process.

The quality of drilling results was controlled manually by human expert, who took into account the smoothness of the circumference and tolerance parameters specified in furniture manufacturing. The examples of acceptable and unacceptable holes drilled in a laminated chipboard are shown in Fig. 2.

The database for numerical experiments was prepared using 6 drills. All of them were used repeatedly to generate the proper size of learning data. In the first phase the new drills were used in laminated chipboard drilling process.

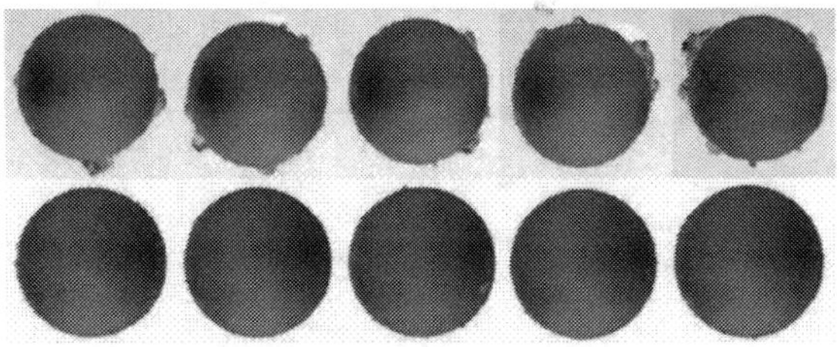

Fig. 2. The typical examples of unacceptable (upper row) and acceptable (lower row) holes drilled in a laminated chipboard.

The results were assessed by the human expert, responsible for the product quality. These samples represented observations belonging to class one. In the next phases the drills were successively blunted few times in a controlled way under the microscope Mitutoyo TM-505. The drills have been blunted, every time exacerbating the degree of drill blunting. After each blunting the drilling process was repeated 5 times and the signals of five sensors were registered, delivering the samples representing class 2. In this way the class 2 was represented by the data corresponding to different degree of blunting. The registered time samples were arranged in a vector forms and the size of all vectors was the same and equal 60000.

The performed experimental trials have created the database, which was used in further numerical experiments. Totally 102 measurements of five sensor signals referring to class one have been registered. The database of blunted drill states contained 145 observations belonging to second class. This way the total number of observations, each representing five time series, was equal 247.

3 Generation of diagnostic features

The diagnostic features used in classification have been created on the basis of 5 measured signals: feed force (F), cutting torque (M), noise (C), vibration (V) and acoustic emission (A). Because of different sampling frequencies: 50kHz for F, M, C, V and 2MHz for A. The A signal was re-interpolated into common 50kHz.
An examples of typical force signals representing the sharp and blunt states of the drill are presented in Fig. 3.

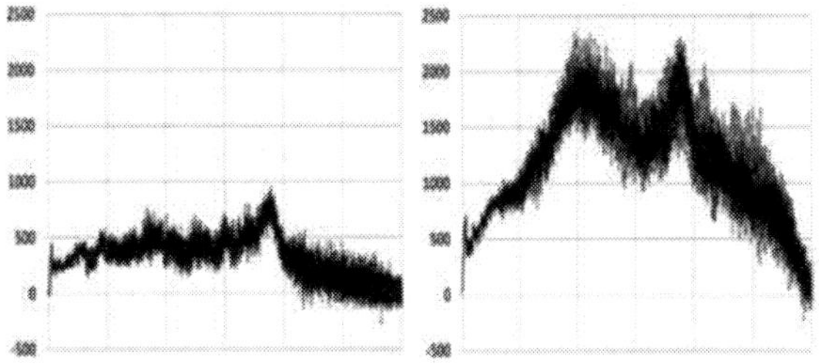

Fig. 3. The signals of the force registered for sharp (left) and blunt (right) states of the drill.

All five types of signals have been organized in the form of
multidimensional time series **Y**

$$\mathbf{Y} = [\mathbf{F} \quad \mathbf{M} \quad \mathbf{C} \quad \mathbf{V} \quad \mathbf{A}] = \begin{bmatrix} F_1 & M_1 & C_1 & V_1 & A_1 \\ F_2 & M_2 & C_2 & V_2 & A_2 \\ \vdots & \vdots & \vdots & \vdots & \vdots \\ F_N & M_N & C_N & V_N & A_N \end{bmatrix} \quad (1)$$

where N represents the size of the time series (60000 in experiments). The vector auto regression model (VAR) was applied in the generation of the diagnostic features [14]. VAR is a natural extension of the univariate autoregressive model to dynamic multivariate time series and forms one of the most successful, flexible, and easy to use model for the analysis of multivariate time series. Let

$$\mathbf{y}_t = [F \quad M \quad C \quad V \quad A]^T \quad (2)$$

denotes an (5×1) vector of time series variables. The basic p-lag vector autoregressive VAR(p) model has the form

$$\mathbf{y}_t = \mathbf{A}_1\mathbf{y}_{t-1} + \mathbf{A}_2\mathbf{y}_{t-2} + \ldots + \mathbf{A}_p\mathbf{y}_{t-p} + \boldsymbol{\varepsilon} \quad (3)$$

where $\mathbf{A}_i$ are (5×5) coefficient matrices and $\boldsymbol{\varepsilon}$ represents an (5×1) unobservable zero mean white noise vector process. The first order VAR(1) model of auto regression was used in our solution. This rank was chosen arbitrarily to reduce the risk of overfitting the model. In this case the auto regression process is defined as follows

$$\begin{bmatrix} F_t \\ M_t \\ C_t \\ V_t \\ A_t \end{bmatrix} = \begin{bmatrix} a_{11} & a_{12} & a_{13} & a_{14} & a_{15} \\ a_{21} & a_{22} & a_{23} & a_{24} & a_{25} \\ \vdots & \vdots & \vdots & \vdots & \vdots \\ a_{51} & a_{52} & a_{53} & a_{54} & a_{55} \end{bmatrix} \begin{bmatrix} F_{t-1} \\ M_{t-1} \\ C_{t-1} \\ V_{t-1} \\ A_{t-1} \end{bmatrix} + \begin{bmatrix} \varepsilon_{Ft} \\ \varepsilon_{Mt} \\ \varepsilon_{Ct} \\ \varepsilon_{Vt} \\ \varepsilon_{At} \end{bmatrix} \quad (4)$$

or in a compact matrix form

$$\mathbf{y}_t = \mathbf{A}_1\mathbf{y}_{t-1} + \boldsymbol{\varepsilon}_t \quad (5)$$

The auto regression coefficients forming matrix $\mathbf{A}_1$ have been estimated using maximum likelihood method [14,15]. In the case of data used in this work the matrices **A** obtained for the sharp and worn out drills are as following

- Sharp drills

$$\mathbf{A} = \begin{matrix} 0.9873 & 0.0015 & -0.0946 & -0.0041 & -0.0015 \\ 0.0016 & 0.9938 & -0.0253 & -0.0003 & -0.0046 \\ -0.0006 & 0.0018 & -0.0041 & 0.0052 & -0.0058 \\ 0.0006 & 0.0011 & -0.0029 & 0.8805 & 0.0042 \\ -0.0001 & -0.0010 & 0.0041 & 0.0005 & 0.2000 \end{matrix}$$

- Blunt drill

$$\mathbf{A} = \begin{matrix} 0.9894 & 0.0012 & -0.1284 & -0.0089 & -0.0041 \\ 0.0030 & 0.9983 & 0.0410 & 0.0027 & 0.0042 \\ -0.0027 & 0.0012 & 0.4894 & 0.0050 & -0.0002 \\ 0.0079 & -0.0001 & 0.0030 & 0.8943 & -0.0066 \\ 0.0000 & 0.0000 & -0.0010 & -0.0011 & 0.4947 \end{matrix}$$

The highest differences between the elements of **A** matrix for both types of drills are observed in the third (noise) and fifth (acoustic emission) columns. It means that these two signals will represent the highest ability of class discrimination.

The elements of auto regression matrix will form the basis for computation of the diagnostic features of the process. Three groups of features have been considered.

- Features equal to the autoregressive coefficients a_{ij} of the matrix $\mathbf{A}_1$.
- Features based on the statistical description of each signal.
- Features based on the statistical description of the residual signals from VAR(1) auto regression.

The following statistical parameters have been applied in definition of the last two groups of features:

1. Mean
2. Median
3. Standard deviation (std)
4. Interquartile ranges (IQR)
5. Interquartile coefficient of variation defined as the ratio of IQR/median
6. Coefficient of variation defined as the ratio std/mean
7. Skewness
8. Cumulant of the third order
9. Cumulant of the fourth order
10. Cumulant of the fifth order.

On the basis of these descriptors 125 potential diagnostic features have been defined. Not all of them represented good class discrimination ability. After introductory experiments we have found that the most class distinctive are the features defined on the basis of residual signals from VAR(1) auto regression. They are defined for all 5 signals. Hence their total number is 50. Only this set of features was investigated in the next stages of selection.

4 Selection of diagnostic features

The feature selection is the process of selecting a subset of relevant features, called also variables or predictors, for use in construction of the classification model. The most important reason of this step is to enhance the generalization ability of the classifier system by reducing the possible overfitting.

The central premise when using a feature selection technique is that the data contain features which are either redundant or irrelevant. Therefore, such features can be removed without significant loss of information [16,17].

In our solution we have applied the sequentially repeated step wise approach. Let us assume n potential features x_i (i=1, 2, …., n) subject to selection. The algorithm starts from some randomly chosen set of m features ($m \leq n$). Let us assume some measure of the quality Q of the model. It might be the accuracy, sensitivity, area under ROC curve or their weighted combinations, reflecting the performance of the classifier at application of this subset as the input attributes. The higher is the value of this measure the better set of diagnostic features. By sequential adding and removing the features to the tested subsets of features we find the subset of the highest quality measure.

In this particular application the quality of the feature set was defined as the average of accuracy (ACC) of class recognition and the area under ROC curve (AUC) [16,17], so Q=0.5(ACC+AUC). The values of ACC and AUC are estimated as the average of the results of 10-fold cross validation of the data in the classification mode. The classification system applied in this and other phases of signal processing was built on the basis of support vector machine of the Gaussian kernel.

5 SVM classifier

The diagnostic features selected in the previous stage are applied as the set of input attributes to the SVM classifier [18]. This solution of the classification system was chosen due to its very high efficiency in pattern recognition problems.

The support vector machine, developed by Vapnik, is a classification and regression system, characterized by very good generalization properties. It works in a space formed by the non-linear mapping of the original input vectors **y** into a feature space using the kernel function $K(\mathbf{x},\mathbf{x}_i)$. The learning problem of SVM is defined as the optimization task of separating the learning vectors $\mathbf{x}_i$ into two binary classes of the destination values either d=1 (one class) or d=−1 (the opposite class), with the maximal separation margin. The SVM training algorithm creates a model that assigns new data vectors into one class or the other on the basis of their location towards the separating hyperplane.

The important advantage of SVM is the special formulation of the learning problem, which leads to the quadratic programming with linear constraints. This type of optimization is very well developed and easy to solve. The separation margin introduced in the formulation of the minimized cost function provides some immunity of this classifier to the noise. Therefore, this approach to the classification problems has a reputation of very good generalization ability [18].

The effectiveness of SVM depends on the selection of the type of kernel, the kernel's parameters and the regularization parameter C. A common choice is a linear or Gaussian kernel, treated as the most universal and robust. Both are controlled by a single parameter γ. The optimal values of C and γ have been selected by a grid search of their predefined values.

6 Results of numerical experiments

6.1 Experimental setup

The data set taking part in experiments contained 102 observations regarding the sharp state of drills and 145 observations representing different degrees of blunting (worn out state) [19]. They resulted in the total number of n=247 patterns, each representing 5 types of signals. They have been mixed and taken part in learning and testing the classification systems by applying leave-one-out mode of operation. Three variants of the investigations have been performed on the available measured data set.

- Selection of feature applying the whole data set and performing the classification in leave one out mode on the same set of patterns. One common set of selected features was used in learning all classification systems.
- Selection of the features combined with learning the SVM classifier on n-1 patterns. The remaining nth pattern is left for testing the adapted system. The experiments are repeated n times, each time with a new testing sample. The succeeding trials were performed at the newly selected sets of features.
- The data split into two separate parts. 40% of them are used in feature selection and the remaining 60% used only in learning and testing the classification property of the system in leave one out mode. One common set of features chosen in the selection phase is used in all these learning procedures of the SVM.

6.2 Results of experiments

The results of experiments will correspond to these three selection methods. In the first variant of investigation the selection process was done on the whole set of observations. On the basis of these results the selected features were fixed and applied as the input attributes in leave one out mode of classification. The samples used in classification were the same as in the feature selection. Two features have occurred to be the best: the interquartile ranges IQR of the noise C (notation C4) and the ratio IQR/median of the acoustic emission (notation A5). The other features have been assessed by the selection algorithm as not important in this variant of investigations. The application of the linear SVM of the regularization constant equal 100 has allowed to obtain the average accuracy equal ACC=0.976.

The second variant of investigations is more demanding, since the selection of features and the process of learning was repeated *n* times (*n* – the number of observations). Each time the learning procedure was performed on *n*-1 cases, leaving the *n*th one for testing. In all runs of experiments the set of selected features was under change. Fig. 4 presents the relative histogram of how often the particular features have been chosen by the selection algorithm. The notations of the features correspond to the name of signal (V, C, F, M, A) and the succeeding number of the statistics (from 1 to 10) used in generation of the particular feature. As it is seen the statistics of the features C4 and A5 have been the most often chosen by the selection algorithm in all runs of the leave one out experiments. The average accuracy rate obtained in the experiments in this variant was similar to the previous case and equal ACC=0.967.

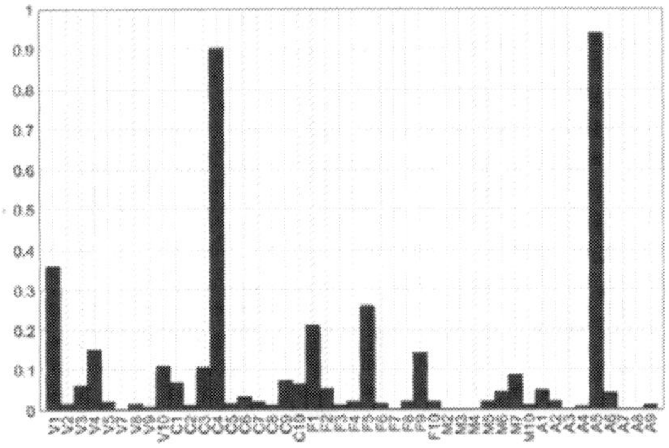

Fig. 4. The percentage of times the features have been selected in the second variant of the experiments

The last variant of experiments was the most demanding. The selection stage was separated from the classification and testing. The data set was split into 40% used only in selection of the features and the remaining 60% of the data used only in the classification and testing. The classification of the data has been also done in leave one out mode of operation. This variant of investigation is the most similar to the future application of the system in industry.

Fig. 5 shows the percentage of times the particular features have been chosen by the selection algorithm in 2000 repetitions of the experiments. It is seen that larger population of features has been selected as the input attributes in this variant of experiments.

The accuracy of class recognition varied from run to run. Fig. 6 shows the histogram of this accuracy values in 2000 repetitive runs of algorithm. The average accuracy of class recognition obtained in these experiments was equal ACC=0.950.

Another quality measure of the classification system is the Receiver Operating Characteristics (ROC). Especially important is the area under curve (AUC). Good classifier should have this value close to one. On the other side the random classifier is characterized by this value equal 0.5. In our solution the AUC was equal 0.947, which is very close to be ideal.

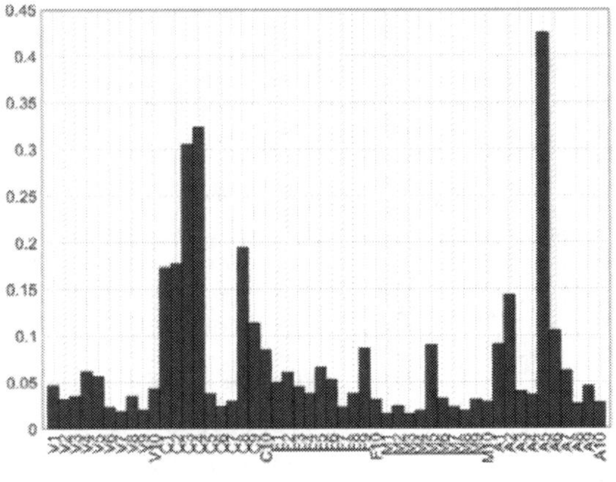

Fig. 5. The percentage of times the features have been selected in the third variant of the experiments

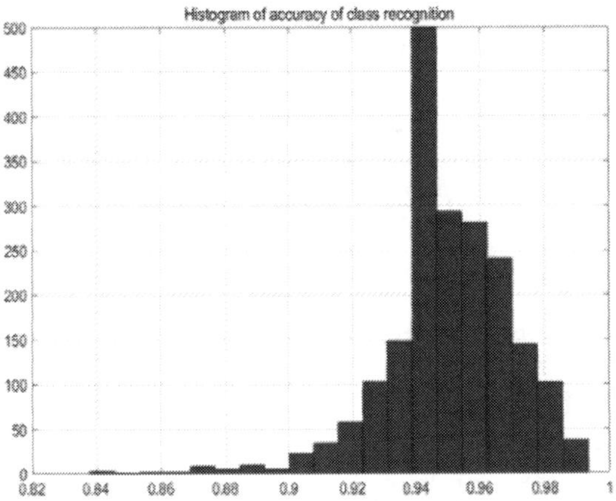

Fig. 6. The histogram of accuracy of class recognition in 2000 runs of the third variant of experiments

7 Conclusions

The paper has presented an automatic system for recognition of the condition of drill in a standard laminated chipboard drilling process. Two states of drill have been recognized: the sharp one, allowing the process of drilling to continue and blunt one, which should lead to stop the production. The recognition process is done on-line without interrupting the drilling process.

The presented solution shows that the satisfactory results of recognition of drill condition are possible on-line by proper processing the sensor signals registering the feed force, cutting torque, noise, vibration and acoustic emission. On the basis of these signals the diagnostic features have been defined using the multivariable auto regression model VAR(1). The selection process following the generation of these features was responsible for selecting the most significant ones, which were used as the input attributes to the classification system.

The support vector machine classifier was used for the class recognition. Its choice was dictated by very good generalization ability of this solution. The results of its application are acceptable in practice. The relative testing error of recognition in leave-one-out mode of operation was changing from 3% to 5%, depending on the organizational variant of the investigations.

References

[1] C. Scheffer, H. Kratz, P.S. Heyns, F. Klocke, Development of a tool wear-monitoring system for hard turning, International Journal of Machine Tools & Manufacture, **43**, 973–985 (2003).

[2] D. E. Dimla, P. M. Lister, On-line metal cutting tool condition monitoring. I: force , vibration analyses, International Journal of Machine Tools & Manufacture, **40**, 739–768 (2000).

[3] K. Jemielniak, T. Urbański, J. Kossakowska J., S. Bombiński, Tool condition monitoring based on numerous signal features, Int J. Adv. Manuf. Technol., **59**, 73–81 (2012).

[4] N. H. Abu-Zahra, G. Yu, Gradual wear monitoring of turning inserts using wavelet analysis of ultrasound waves, International Journal of Machine Tools & Manufacture, **43**, 33–343 (2003).

[5] R. Lemaster, L. Lu, S. Jackson, The use of process monitoring techniques on a CNC wood router. Part 1. Sensor selection, Forest Products Journal, **50,** 7/8, 31–64 (2000).

[6] J. Wilkowski, J. Górski, Vibro-acoustic signals as a source of information about tool wear during laminated chipboard milling, Wood Research, **56,** 1, 57–66 (2011).

[7] R. G. Silva, K. J. Baker, S. J. Wilcox, The adaptability of a tool wear monitoring system under changing cutting conditions, Mechanical Systems, Signal Processing, **14,** 2, 287–298 (2000).

[8] R. J. Kuo, Multi-sensor integration for on-line tool wear estimation through artificial neural networks, fuzzy neural network, Engineering Applications of Artificial Intelligence, **13**, 249–261 (2000).

[9] A. Noori-Khajavi, R. Komandur, Frequency, time domain analyses of sensor signals in drilling-Part I, *International* Journal of Machine Tools, Manufacture, **35,** 6, 775–793 (1995).

[10] J. H. Zhou, C. K. Pang, Z. W. Zhong, F. L. Lewis, Tool wear monitoring using acoustic emissions by dominant-feature identification, IEEE Transactions on Instrumentation, Measurement, **60,** 2, 547–559 (2011).

[11] S. S. Panda, A. K. Singh, D. Chakraborty, S. K. Pal, Drill wear monitoring using back propagation neural network, Journal of Materials Processing Technology, **172**, 283–290 (2006).

[12] K. Patra, S. K. Pal, K. Bhattacharyya, Artificial neural network based prediction of drill flank wear from motor current signals, Applied Soft Computing, **7**, 929–935 (2007).

[13] P. Lezanski, An intelligent system for grinding wheel condition monitoring, Journal of Materials Processing Technology, **109**, 258–263 (2001).

[14] H. Lutkepohl, *Introduction to Multiple Time Series Analysis*, Berlin Springer-Verlag (1991).

[15] *Matlab user manual*, Natick: MathWorks, (2014).

[16] P.N. Tan, M. Steinbach, V. Kumar, *Introduction to data mining*, Boston: Pearson Education Inc. (2006).

[17] J. Kurek, S. Osowski, Support vector machine for fault diagnosis of the broken rotor bars of squirrel-cage induction motor, Neural Computing and Applications, **19**, 557-564 (2010).

[18] V. Kecman, *Learning, Soft Computing: Support Vector Machines, Neural Networks,, Fuzzy Logic Models*, Cambridge, MA: MIT Press (2001).

[19] M. Kruk, A. Jegorowa, J. Kurek, S. Osowski, J. Górski, Automatic recognition of drill condition on the basis of images of drilled holes, in Proc. Conference "Computational Problems of Electrical Engineering", Sandomierz, 2016, pp. 1-4

Evaluation of diagnostic classifiers using artificial clinical cases

Karol Antczak[1], *Andrzej* Walczak[1,*] and *Michał* Paczkowski[1]

[1]Institute of Computer and Information Systems, Military University of Technology, Warsaw, Poland

Abstract. Evaluation of classifiers in diagnosis support systems is a non-trivial task. It can be done in a form of controlled and blinded clinical trial, which is often difficult and costly. We propose a new method for generating artificial medical cases from a knowledge base, utilizing the concept of so-called medical diamonds. Cases generated using this method have features analogous to that of double-blinded trial and, thus, can be used for measuring sensitivity and specificity of diagnostic classifiers. This is easy and low-cost method of evaluation and comparison of classifiers in diagnosis support systems. We demonstrate that this method is able to produce valuable results when used for evaluation of similarity-based classifiers as well as shallow and deep neural networks.

1 Introduction

1.1 Evaluation of diagnostic tests

Diagnostic and screening tests are important tools of medical diagnosis, especially in evidence-based approach. They serve two main purposes. The first one is to establish presence of some medical condition, while the second purpose is to determine absence of it. No diagnostic test is 100% accurate. Instead, there is always a possibility that given test can yield a wrong result. It is a significant risk factor and, as such, has to be minimized or at least identified. This is why it is so important to evaluate diagnostic tests.

Evaluation of diagnostic test should be done in a form of a *controlled trial* [1]. Such trial involves a group of people, typically divided into two subgroups: test and control. People from test group are diagnosed using diagnostic test being evaluated, while control group is diagnosed using the best currently available test serving the same purpose. This test is also called *gold standard test*. It is important to remember that, as it was already mentioned, even gold standard test is not fully accurate. Because of this, test is always evaluated in comparison to current gold standard.

Controlled trial can be randomized, meaning that patients are assigned to control and test groups randomly. Randomization of trial provides several benefits [2], the most important one being prevention of bias. Another benefit is increase of statistical power of evaluation. There are many randomization techniques, developed for maximizing specific benefits at the cost of others. The simplest one is just "coin-tossing" and assigning patients to either group with equal probability. More sophisticated approaches involve restricting allocations of patients or adaptive methods.

Another important technique for minimization of observer bias is blinding the trial. *Blinded trial* means that every patient from test and control groups does not know his assignment. If tester does not know the patient's assignment, too, then the trial is double-blinded.
Evaluation of diagnostic test in the controlled trial is mostly performed by comparison of quality measures of test under evaluation and gold standard. There are various quality measures for diagnostic tests. Most of them are based on cardinalities of four subsets: True Positives (cases where test properly identified presence of disease), False Positives (where test incorrectly identified presence of disease), True Negatives (where test properly excluded disease) and False Negatives (where test incorrectly excluded disease). Two basic quality measures are sensitivity and specificity. They are defined as:

$$sensitivity = \frac{|TP|}{|TP|+|FN|} \quad (1)$$

$$specificity = \frac{|TN|}{|TN|+|FP|} \quad (2)$$

Sensitivity serves as an indicator how good the test is in identifying existing diseases. Specificity, on the other hand, measures ability of the test to identify patients without disease. In practice, these two measures are exclusive: increasing the sensitivity results in lower specificity and vice versa. Typically, diagnostic tests should have high sensitivity, while screening tests should be characterized by high specificity. Dependency between sensitivity and specificity can be visualized in a form of ROC curve.

1.2 Diagnosis Support Systems

* Corresponding author: andrzej.walczak@wat.edu.pl

Modern diagnosis relies not only on diagnostic tests and physician's knowledge, but also computer-based support systems. They can aid physician in retrieval and processing of medical data as well as support the very diagnosis process. Such systems can be viewed as a diagnostic test – given set of medical data, it can provide proposed diagnosis.

Typical *diagnosis support system* relies on two components: knowledge base and inference engine (classifier). *Knowledge base* represents information about the domain the system was created for support. In the domain of medical diagnosis, it can be information about symptoms, diseases, risk factors, etc. Knowledge can be represented in various ways. Some of the techniques used are ontologies, semantic networks, rules, frames and scripts. The input for the knowledge base can be achieved manually or semi-automatically by retrieving information from physicians, medical sources or by performing controlled trials.

Another component of diagnosis support system is inference engine, usually in a form of a *classifier*. Mathematically, classifier can be viewed as function v mapping a power set of input features X (e.g. symptoms) to a set Y of output classes (e.g. diseases):

$$f: P(X) \rightarrow Y \quad (3)$$

The parameters of function f are adjusted basing on information from knowledge base in a process of training.

The number of output classes can vary for different classifiers. For $|Y| = 2$, we deal with binomial (binary) classifier. For diagnostic classifiers, this usually means that classifier can diagnose only one disease, and provides one of two possible outputs:

- 1 - if patient have a disease
- 0 - if patient does not have a disease

Of course, there are also classifiers able to return a set of classes, i.e. $|Y| > 2$. They are known as multinomial classifiers.

Classification can be also achieved using regression models returning continuous values rather than binary ones. In such case, it is necessary to perform a quantization, for example, by choosing class with maximum value. Another way is to apply threshold function on values (decision threshold) or class ranks (rank threshold).

1.3 Evaluation of diagnostic classifiers

Diagnostic classifiers can be viewed as a specific kind of diagnostic tests, and, therefore, can be evaluated using the same methods. For binomial classifier, we can calculate its sensitivity and specificity using formulas (1) and (2). In case of multinomial classifiers, these measures are calculated per each of possible classes. There are, however, several problems with practical evaluation of diagnostic classifiers.

The first one is a need for real clinical cases for test and control groups. Organization of controlled clinical trial is a difficult task, involving many groups of stakeholders, and resources such as time, money and personnel. Moreover, clinical trials are not necessary for creation of knowledge base, and therefore, training of the classifier. As a result, many diagnosis support systems don't have properly measured quality metrics. This is a serious risk factor for the patient. What is worse, these systems are often publicly available. Safety concerns of such systems are described further in [3].

The second problem of classifier evaluation is uneven distribution of cases, leading to bias. It is important factor in case of rare diseases, but can also occur when there are specific requirements for patients. As a result, performed trial can have low statistical power.

2 Proposed approach

2.1 General assumptions

Each of problems mentioned in previous section occurs not only in a field of classifiers but is also relevant to evaluation of all kinds of medical tests. However, using knowledge base it is possible to generate clinical cases "artificially". It is relatively easy to generate artificial case by choosing random subset of symptoms. However, it is not trivial to determine whether it is a positive or negative case – this is caused by lack of "gold standard" test. To overcome this, we propose a method based on concept of "medical diamonds" introduced by Walczak and Paczkowski [4].

The general idea is very simple. Let us consider knowledge base with graph-based structure, containing two types of nodes: conditions and symptoms. Each disease is connected with one or more symptoms. Such connection means that given symptom can occur in associated disease. Symptoms are not exclusive - they can be connected with multiple diseases. Connections are also unweighted, meaning that each symptom has the same "strength". Example of such knowledge base is shown in Figure 1.

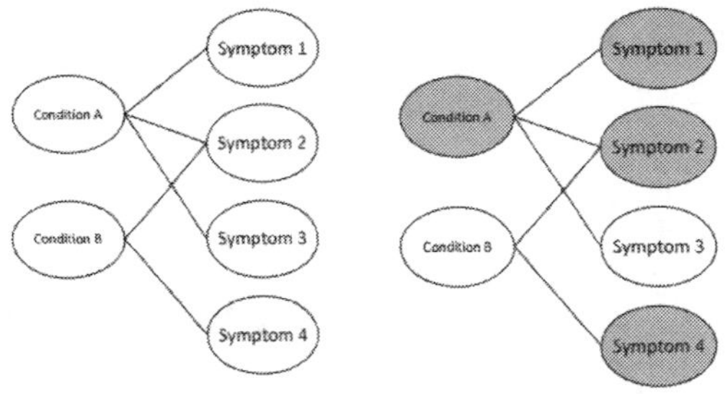

Fig. 1. Example of graph knowledge base (left) and sample case (right)

Note, that in order to ensure a proper quality of knowledge base, it should be verified by experts (diagnosticians) in order to exclude all inconsistencies and fill gaps. It should also be compatible with standards like International Classification of Diseases (ICD) 9 or 10.

2.2 Generating positive and negative cases

Now consider what a typical clinical case looks like in knowledge base of given structure. It will be a random subset of all available symptoms. In general, we are not able to certainly determine whether the patient has one disease or another. Thus, we are not able to identify Positive (P) and Negative (N) sets. However, it is possible that case will have one or more so-called medical diamonds. There are three kinds of medical diamonds, proposed by Walczak and Paczkowski [4]:

- 1st kind: symptom which identifies uniquely disease
- 2nd kind: symptom which identifies disease, but is also present in few others
- 3rd kind: group of symptoms always determining presence of disease

For knowledge base with graph-like structure, we are able to identify diamonds of the 1st kind. Presence of diamond in case determines, by definition, its disease. Hence, we are able to generate positive case for given disease *D* just be ensuring it will have at least one diamond of the 1st kind for *D* and some other symptoms not being diamonds for other diseases.

Using this method we are able to generate negative cases as well. It will be any case not having diamond (of the 1st kind) for *D* and having, among other symptoms, diamond for any other disease.

With positive and negative cases, we can now use them to test classifiers. Knowing which cases belong to each group, we can calculate sets TP, FP, TN and FN, and then sensitivity and specificity. This method has several advantages over clinical trial. We can generate set of any size, limited only by computational power. Additionally, set of such cases will have the features of double-blinded trial, thus reducing the bias. Thanks to this, it can be used to generate test and control sets.

3 Tests results

3.1 Test methodology

We have performed a series of experiments, measuring sensitivity and specificity of various classifiers for detecting psoriasis. We used artificial cases generated with proposed method. Three classifiers were tested: Jaccard index, shallow neural network and deep neural network. We analysed how sensitivity and specificity changes for different sizes of patient's symptoms.

3.2 Datasets

For case generation, we used knowledge base from SWD system. It is a system developed on Military University of Technology in Warsaw for diagnosis support for skin and respiratory diseases [5]. The knowledge base consists of 91 diseases, 766 symptoms and 112 possible values of symptoms. Data is stored in a form of triplets <disease, symptom, symptom value>, for example <psoriasis, lesions in the vicinity of the elbow, present>. There are 14086 such triplets in total. Data was entered by medical experts and reviewed multiple times in order to ensure its consistency. Moreover, all data is fully compliant with ICD-9 standard.

Positive set consisted of 500 cases identifying psoriasis. Each of them was generated with following algorithm:

- choose random diamond of the 1st kind associated with psoriasis
- choose remaining symptoms from other symptoms not being diamonds

Negative set consisted of 500 cases associated with scabies, generated with algorithm:

- choose random diamond of the 1st kind associated with scabies
- choose remaining symptoms from other symptoms not being diamonds

The number of symptoms in each case was a parameter N with values 1 to 300. For each value of N, sets were re-generated. Hence, for all tests, 350 000 random cases were generated. As one can see, this is much more than used in typical clinical trial.

3.3 Jaccard Index

First evaluated classifier was *Jaccard index*. It is a set similarity measure defined as:

$$J(A,B) = \frac{|A \cap B|}{|A \cup B|} \qquad (3)$$

In formula 3, sets A and B are compared. As a classifier, Jaccard index chooses a disease for which set of associated symptoms is the most similar to symptoms in the case.

The measured sensitivity and specificity for this classifier are presented in Figure 2.

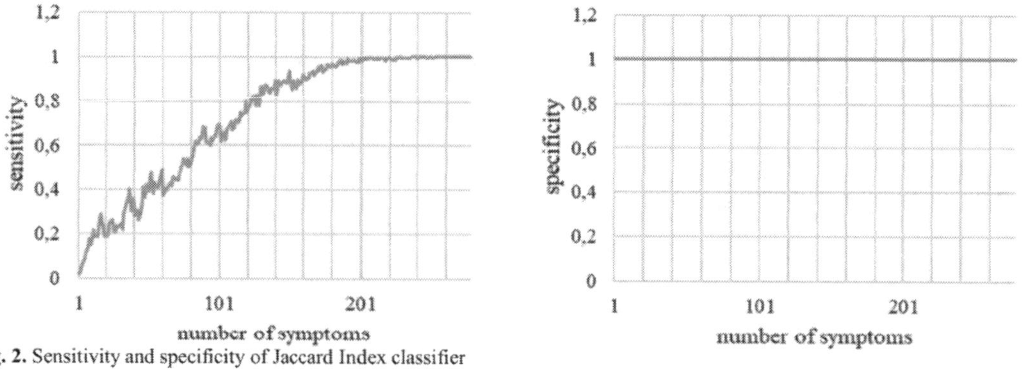

Fig. 2. Sensitivity and specificity of Jaccard Index classifier

DOI: 10.1051/matecconf/201712504003

One can observe that the sensitivity of Jaccard index increases with the number of symptoms. This is consistent with nature of this classifier. For large number of symptoms, many of them will be associated with correct disease. As a result, positive patient's symptoms will be the most similar to set of symptoms characteristic for psoriasis. This dependency is roughly monotonic, however there are several slopes. They can be identified as moments of appearance of diamonds of 2nd and 3rd kinds. They are more important than regular symptoms, but for Jaccard index, all symptoms have the same "importance". Thus, we revealed hidden feature of our dataset, which our classifier, due to its simplicity, was not able to discover.

Jaccard Index had constant specificity of 1, meaning that there were not any false positive cases. At the first sight, this can be quite surprising, given the fact that in tested model there are 275 common symptoms for psoriasis and scabies. However, there are more than 2 diseases in our knowledge base. Some of them, for example mycosis fungoides, have the same symptoms as

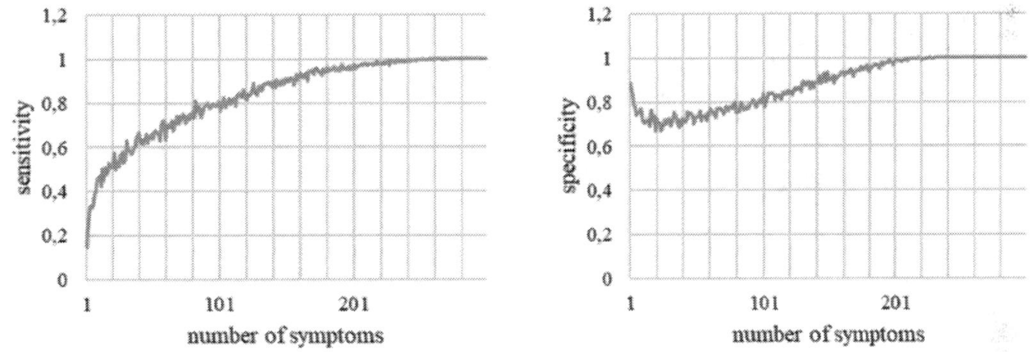

Fig. 3. Sensitivity and specificity of Neural Network classifier

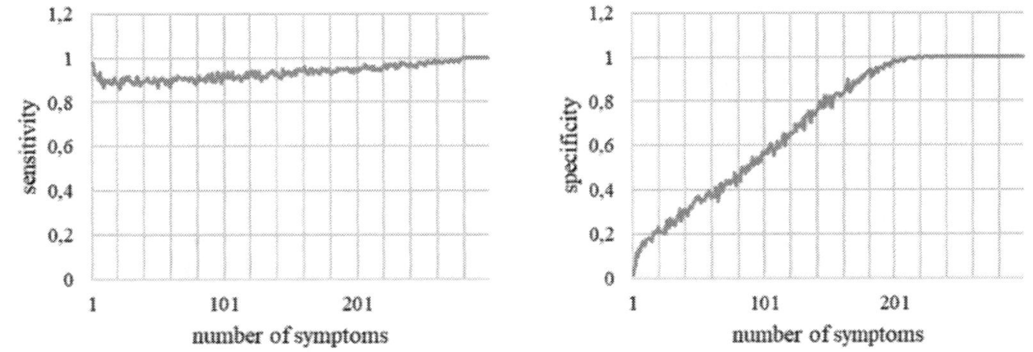

Fig. 4. Sensitivity and specificity of Deep Neural Network classifier

common set for psoriasis and scabies as well as additional common symptoms associated with scabies (see figure 5). Generated case is always at least as similar (in terms of Jaccard index) to these diseases, as it is similar to psoriasis. As a result, there were no cases from negative set that were classified as the most similar to psoriasis by Jaccard index.

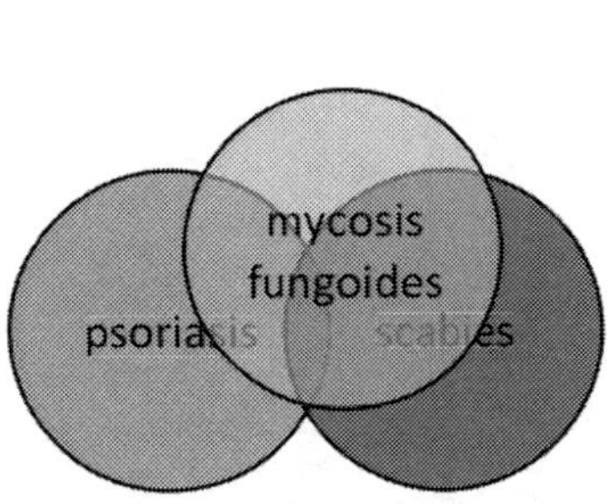

Fig. 5. Covering common symptoms of psoriasis and scabies by mycosis fungoides

3.4 Neural network

The second tested classifier was a shallow *neural network*. It consisted of 880 input neurons (all symptoms + symptoms values), 256 hidden neurons (with sigmoid activation function) and 91 output neurons (one for each disease). The network was trained with generated dataset (500 positive and 500 negative cases of various lengths) using 10000 iterations of gradient descent with learning rate 0.1. The loss function used during training was cross-entropy. We also added weight decay penalty (L2) to loss function in order to prevent overfitting.

Trained neural network performed better than Jaccard index in terms of sensitivity, especially for small case size. This indicates that network was able to identify "diamonds" and use them to correctly classify cases even for small number of other symptoms. Jaccard index could not utilize this property and required higher number of symptoms to perform as good. However Jaccard index had higher specificity than neural network for number of symptoms < 200. It is caused by the fact that Jaccard index is good representation of natural way of thinking of diagnosticians [3].

3.5 Deep neural network

The last model was a *deep neural network*. It represents an increasingly popular branch of machine learning, known as deep learning. Deep models attempt to extract and utilize high level features from data. We tested this classifier in order to determine whether it could extract diamonds, which can be viewed as multilevel features in medical data. Deep networks are typically multi-layered. Our deep network consisted of 3 hidden layers, 256 neurons each, with sigmoid activation function. It was trained using the same method as previous network.

Test results (Figure 4) showed that deep neural network had significantly better sensitivity than both of previous models. Additionally, sensitivity had stable values regardless of number of symptoms, however, at the cost of low specificity. Nonetheless, it seems that deep neural network was able to extract diamonds and use them even more efficiently than shallow network.

4 Discussion

4.1 Classifier evaluation

As we demonstrated, our method of measuring performance of classifiers can be successfully used for comparison of various models. Our results confirmed the prediction that the more "sophisticated" model, the more is it able to utilize hidden features of data. Additionally, we showed that there is no "silver bullet" in diagnostic classification. The higher sensitivity is achieved at the cost of lower specificity and vice versa. In this perspective it seems reasonable to use multi-classifier systems, for example in a form of classifiers ensembles [6].

4.2 Conclusions

We have presented a method for generating artificial patient cases from knowledge base. Such cases will be doubly blinded, since they will not be biased by patient (which is artificial) or classifier (which does not have a priori knowledge of the case). We have shown that it is possible to generate cases "medically plausible", meaning that they have one and only one, clearly determined, correct diagnosis. This is done by extracting hidden features of the knowledge base, in the form of medical diamonds. Because we can generate cases in any number, it is possible to use them for measuring sensitivity and specificity of classifier. Then, evaluation of classifier can be viewed as measuring its ability to uncover hidden features from dataset. Test results show that it is indeed possible to evaluate and compare various classifiers with our method.

We have not performed a meta-evaluation of proposed method. It seems reasonable to perform such meta-evaluation in a form of clinical trial, measuring sensitivity and specificity of given classifier on generated cases and comparing it to values obtained from performing classification on real cases. One can also think of performing "Turing Test"-like evaluation [7]. In this approach, artificial and real cases would be presented to expert, who should determine whether the case is a real one. This can be used as a quality measurement for knowledge base.

4.3 Other works

Generating artificial patient cases is a known task, existing nearly as long as knowledge-based diagnosis support systems. One of the first attempts was described in 1987 by Parker and Miller [7]. They used INTERNIST-1/QMR knowledge base to create simulated patient cases. The case was generated by choosing random disease, and then selecting random subset of all illnesses (other diseases, subdivisions and facets) linked to the selected disease. Next, a list of findings was generated, using knowledge of frequencies of finding given symptoms. The generated cases were then used for training of medical students. They also proposed using them for medical "Turing Test" described in previous section.

As for the newer attempts, in 2010 Buczak and others proposed a data-driven approach for generating artificial electronic medical records (EMRs) [8]. They were, similarly to us, motivated by difficulties in obtaining real-life medical data as well as privacy concerns regarding EMRs. The EMRs were generated for use in development of bio-surveillance algorithms. Other data-driven approaches included generating fictional clinical timeline [9] or entire population for modelling spreading of diseases [10].

The general problem of using synthetic data in supervised classification task was researched by Nonnemaker and Baird [12]. They concluded that using such data for classifiers training is for the most part safe and will not result in worsening of classifier's accuracy. A practical method for learning image classifiers from synthetic data was presented by Zhang and others [13]. They identified a problem of *distribution gap* between real and synthetic data. As a solution, they proposed using a deep learning model, namely Multichannel Autoencoder.

References

1. M. Rodger, T. Ramsay, D. Fergusson, Diagnostic

randomized controlled trials: the final frontier, *Trials,* **137**, 13 (2012)

2. G. D. Schulz KF, Generation of allocation sequences in randomised trials: chance, not choice, *Lancet,* **359**, 9305 (2002)
3. A. Walczak. K. Antczak, Patient Safety versus Computer Diagnosis, *MATEC Web of Conferences,* **76** (2016)
4. A. Walczak, M. Paczkowski, Medical data preprocessing for increased selectivity of diagnosis, *Bio-Algorithms and Med-Systems,* **12**, 1 (2016)
5. System Wspomagania Diagnostyki do informatycznego wspomagania badań naukowych w medycynie, *Wojskowa Akademia Techniczna*, [Online] http://www.isi.wat.edu.pl/sites/default/files/zalaczniki/swd.pdf.
6. K. Antczak, Rank thresholds in classifier ensembles in medical diagnosis, *Computer Science and Mathematical Modelling,* **3** (2016)
7. R. C. Parker, R. A. Miller, Using Causal Knowledge to Create Simulated Patient Cases: The CPCS Project as an Extension of INTERNIST-1, *Proceedings of the Annual Symposium on Computer Application in Medical Care* (1987)
8. A. Buczak, S. Babin, L. Moniz, Data-driven approach for creating synthetic electronic medical records, *BMC Medical Informatics and Decision Making,* **10**, 1, (2010)
9. D. M. Eddy, L. Schlessinger, Archimedes: An Analytical Tool for Improving the Quality and Efficiency of Health Care, *Building a Better Delivery System: A New Engineering/Health Care Partnership.*, Washington, National Academies Press (2005)
10. V. Ravichandran, D. Janes, Models of Infectious Disease Agent Study (MIDAS), National Institute of General Medical Sciences (2016). [Online] https://www.nigms.nih.gov/Research/SpecificAreas/MIDAS/Pages/default.aspx.
11. M. Kiedrowicz, T. Nowicki, R. Waszkowski, Business process data flow between automated and human tasks, *3rd International Conference on Social Science (ICSS 2016) December 9–11 2016*, pp. 471-477, (2016).
12. J. Nonnemaker, H. S. Baird, Using Synthetic Data Safely in Classification, *Proc. IS&T/SPIE Conf. on Document Recognition and Retrieval (DRR 2009)* (2009)
13. X. Zhang, Y. Fu, S. Jiang, L. Sigal, and G. Agam. Learning from synthetic data using a stacked multichannel Autoencoder, *2015 IEEE 14th International Conference on Machine Learning and Applications (ICMLA)* (2015)

DOI: 10.1051/matecconf/201712504004

A Comparative Study of Control Methods for a Robotic Manipulator with Six DOF in Simulation

Georgia P. Smyrnaiou, Michail Papoutsidakis and Dimitrios Tseles*

Piraeus University of Applied Sciences, Department of Automation Engineering, 12244, P. Ralli & Thivon 250, Athens, Greece

Abstract. In this paper a comparative study of the classical control methods for the testing of a mathematical model, which controls six actuators of a six degrees of freedom robotic arm with a single controller, is illustrated, aiming to the constructive simplification of the system. In more detail, a mathematical model of the system is designed which simulates all mechanical parts, including 5-way directional pneumatic valve, the pneumatic actuators/pistons and the mathematical model of the controller. The purpose of the above is the tuning of a Single Input, Multiple Output (SIMO) controller which will direct the motion of the six pneumatic pistons. The thorough analysis of the implementation of the pneumatic system in Matlab/Simulink environment is followed by experimentation and results using Proportional (P), Proportional-Integral (PI), Proportional-Derivative (PD) and Proportional-Integral-Derivative (PID) controllers. The simulation results show the advantages of the above classical control methods on the robotic human arm which imitating human motion and made by a well-known company in the field of pneumatic automation.

1 Introduction

In modern industry pneumatic systems are used with an increased rate. A pneumatic system uses compressed air as a mean to transfer the motion, and have as a final result the movement of a piston or in rare cases the rotation of a motor. Pneumatic Systems find application in cases where small forces should be applied and great velocity is needed. This is the main reason they are widely used in the industry. Pneumatic systems also store and transfer energy with ease and can produce low cost, linear movement with relatively high speed, easily adjustable [1].

Cylinders are considered the basic elements of motions in Pneumatic Systems, which convert the pneumatic force into a linear motion. With the pneumatic cylinders achieve the reciprocating motion by means of compressed air.

Pneumatic cylinders consist of a chamber and ports from where the air enters and exeunt, performing, that way, the linear movement. The piston's chamber is tight to avoid any leakage and is highly durable so that it can endure the high pressure [2].

There are three distinguished categories for the pneumatic cylinders:

- The single-acting cylinders
- The double-acting cylinders
- The Tandem cylinder.

For the correct function of the pneumatic actuators a controller is required. The valves are devices that help regulate the starting or stopping of the piston, and also assist in determining the compressed air flow direction. The valve controls the motion of the rod and the valve respectively is tuned by a classic controller [3].

Valves are distinguished in the following categories:

- Directional valves.
- Signal valves.
- Pressure control valves.
- Return / check valves [2].

2 Control appliance in Simulation environment

2.1 Non-linear mathematical model

A pneumatic system consists of a cylinder, a valve, exhaust and supply tubes, position sensors and pressure sensors. The load is the rest of the mechanical parts that are connected to the pneumatic piston. A non-linear pneumatic system is illustrated in the following Figure.

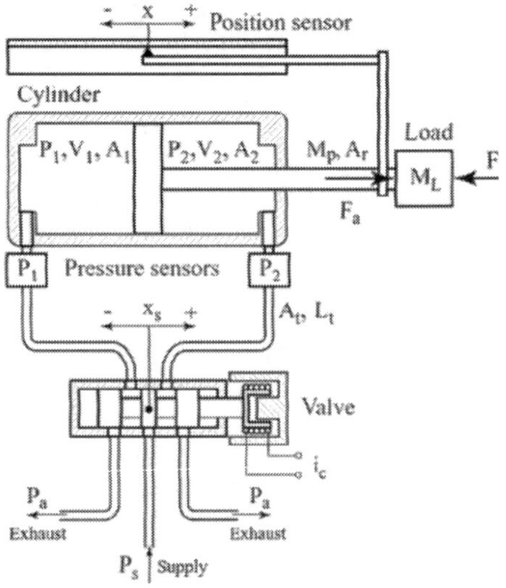

Fig. 1: Standard pneumatic cylinder-valve model

* Corresponding author: giouli.smyrnaiou@gmail.com

The equation of motion for the piston-rod-load assembly can be expressed as:

$$(M_L + Mp)\cdot\ddot{x} + B\cdot\dot{x} + F_f + F_L = P1\cdot A1 - P2\cdot A2 - P_a\cdot A_r$$

Where M_L is the external mass of the load, Mp is the piston and rod assembly mass, x is the piston position, $\dot{x}$ is the velocity of the piston, $\ddot{x}$ is the acceleration of the piston, B is the friction coefficient, F_f is the friction force (Coulomb), F_L is the external force, P1 and P2 are the absolute values of the air pressure of the actuator's chambers, P_a is the absolute value of the environment pressure, A1 and A2 are the piston effective areas, A_r is the rod cross sectional area.
The above equation represents the force of the actuator generated by different pressures acting on the opposite sides of the piston, in order to control the actuator's output.

The time derivative for the pressure in the pneumatic cylinder chambers can be expressed as:

$$\dot{P}_i = \frac{RT}{V_{0i} + A_i\left(\frac{1}{2}L \pm x\right)}\left(a_{in}\dot{m}_{in} - a_{out}\dot{m}_{out}\right) - a\frac{PA_i}{V_{0i} + A_i\left(\frac{1}{2}L \pm x\right)}\dot{x}$$

Where P is the piston's pressure, R is the ideal gas constant, T is the temperature, V_{0i} is the inactive volume at the end of stroke and admission ports, A_i is the piston effective area, L is the piston stroke, x is the piston position, m_{in} and m_{out} are the mass flows entering and leaving the chamber, and a_{in} ,a_{out} taking values between 1 and k, depending on the actual heat transfer during the process.
The first term of the above equation represents the effect of the pressure of the air flow into or out of the cylinder chamber, while the second term describes the effect of the motion of the piston.

The pressure drop across the valve orifice is usually large, and the flow has to be treated as compressible and turbulent. If the upstream to downstream pressure ratio is larger than a critical value P_{cr}, the flow will attain sonic velocity (choked flow) and will depend linearly on the upstream pressure. If the pressure ratio is smaller than P_{cr} the mass flow depends nonlinearly on both pressures. The standard equation for the mass flow through an orifice of area A_u is:

$$\dot{m}_u = \begin{cases} C_f A_u C1 \dfrac{P_u}{\sqrt{T}} & \text{if } \dfrac{P_d}{P_u} \le P_{cr} \\ C_f A_u C2 \dfrac{P_u}{\sqrt{T}}\left(\dfrac{P_d}{P_u}\right)^{\frac{1}{k}}\sqrt{1-\left(\dfrac{P_d}{P_u}\right)^{\frac{(k-1)}{k}}} & \text{if } \dfrac{P_d}{P_u} > P_{cr} \end{cases}$$

Where $\dot{m}_u$ is the mass flow through valve orifice, C_f is the supply rate, P_u is the value of the upstream pressure and P_d is the value of the downstream pressure. C1 and C2 are constants of a given fluid, in this case the air:

$$C1 = \sqrt{\frac{k}{R}\left(\frac{2}{k+1}\right)^{\frac{k+1}{k-1}}}, C2 = \sqrt{\frac{2k}{R(k-1)}} \text{ and } P_{cr} = \left(\frac{2}{k+1}\right)^{\frac{k}{k-1}}$$

Where k is the constant of air value [4].

2.2 Simulation of the Pneumatic System with six-pistons and Proportional controller (P)

The pneumatics' system simulation model with six parallel connected pistons with analog control is illustrated in the figure below.

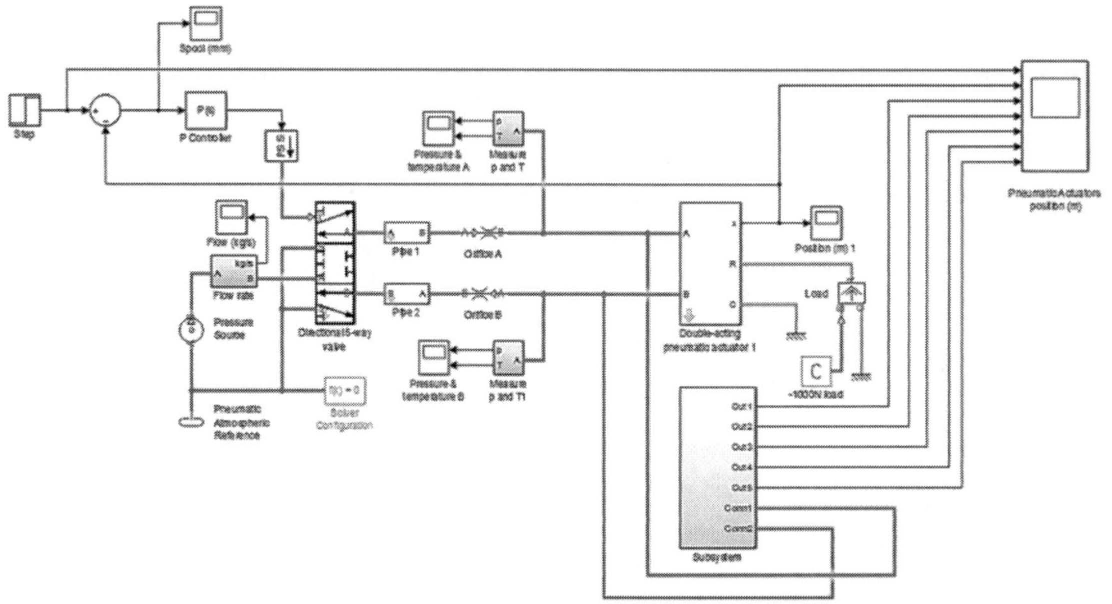

Fig. 2: Simulation model of the pneumatic system with six pistons and P controller

This model represents an integrated pneumatic system with six controllable actuators/ pistons. The components are described below:

1. A directional control valve 5/3

This is a five-way valve and three-position (5/3 valve) which is used to control the compressed air's flow into and out the pistons, having as an output the return of the rods.

As shown in Fig.2, the supplied pressure is inserted in port P and the pneumatic actuators are connected to ports A and B. R and S are return paths of the A and B ports respectively.

2. Double-acting Cylinders

The Pneumatic System uses six double-acting cylinders with a single rod that forces the compressed air to move the rod in both directions.

3. Flow Rate

As shown from Fig. 2, the block diagram of the flow rate of the pneumatic system is connected with the directional valve to drive the compressed air to the actuators ports so that they can move accordingly. The Flow rate block diagram contains a subsystem which consists:

- Mass & Heat Flow Sensor, which is a device that converts the mass flow rate and heat flow rate between the two pneumatic nodes into physical measurement signals G and Q. The positive direction of the sensor is from the port A to port B.
- PS-Simulink Converter which converts the input Physical Signal to a unit less Simulink output signal in this case Kg/s.

4. Pressure Source

This is an ideal air compressor which maintains a fixed pressure differential, irrespectively the flow rate. The compressor does not add extra heat to the system. A positive pressure difference results in the pressure in port B to be greater than the pressure in the port A. The compressor differential pressure is 6 bar.

5. Subsystem block and Time scope block

For the pneumatic system Simulation, the Simulink library was used. Time scope block is used and the six actuators are connected and also the input step. A Subsystem block is created which includes the five pneumatic pistons and it's connected with the first one (Master-slaves) as illustrated in the following figure.

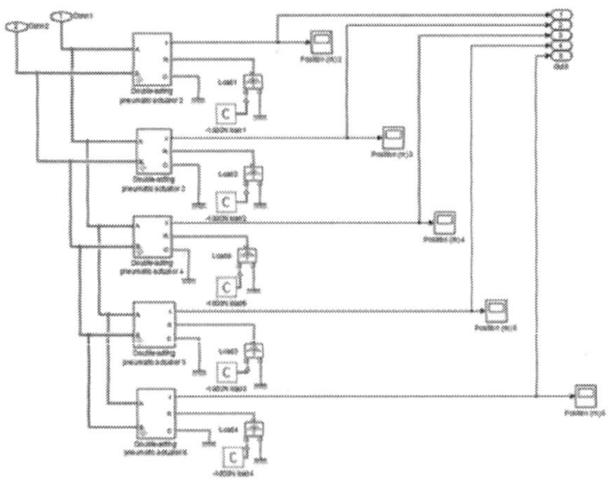

Fig. 3: Subsystem block

The Step input is set to start from 0 sec. Step's range value starts from 0 to 1.
As final value in the stoke parameter of the pistons is set 0.05 m height and the stroke length is set in 0.1 m.
From the Simulink library a PID controller is selected (Proportional–Integral–Derivative). The P value is set to $K_P = 120$ and the rest of the parameters are eliminated (0) to achieve Proportional control. Simulation time is set to T=0.5 sec, air supply pressure is set to 6 bar, $[6 \cdot 10^5$ Pascal].
The systems response and the position of the six actuators with Proportional control are shown in the following figure.

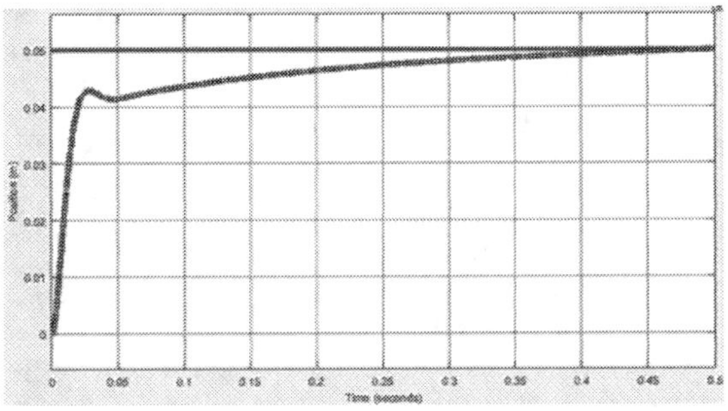

Fig. 4: P controller's Step Response

The fig. 4 results for $K_P = 120$, where the pistons have settled in the Set value. For lower K_P values a steady state error occurs in the systems response with values on the position of the pistons less than 0.05 m. For greater K_P values the steady state error is lifted. At this point it should be mentioned, that the steady state error is not erased completely, but instead it is getting smaller.

2.3 Simulation of the Pneumatic System with six-pistons and Proportional-Integral controller (PI)

The PID controller is tuned (Proportional–Integral–Derivative) to $K_P = 120$ and $K_I = 5$ to achieve Proportional-integral control. The following figure illustrated the pneumatic system response.

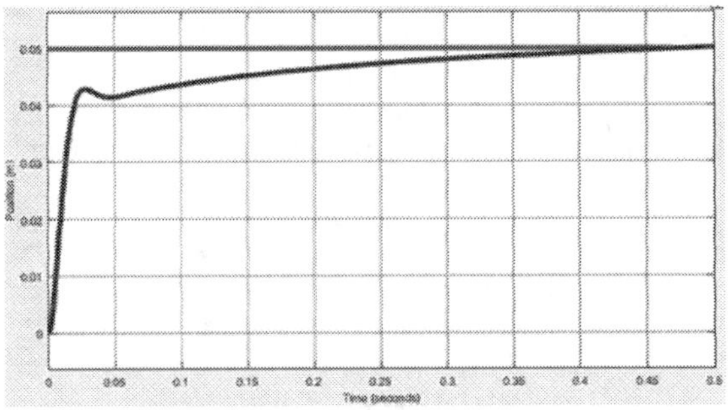

Fig. 5: PI controller's Step Response

The above figure's results for $K_P = 120$ and $K_I = 5$, where the pistons have settled in the Set value.

For increased the K_I gain, a steady state error appears in the system with values of the position of the pistons greater than 0.05 m.

2.4 Simulation of the Pneumatic System with six-pistons and Proportional-Derivative controller (PD)

The PID controller is tuned (Proportional–Integral–Derivative) to $K_P = 120$ and $K_D = 0.6$ to achieve Proportional-Derivative control in the pneumatic system. The following figure illustrated the pneumatic system response.

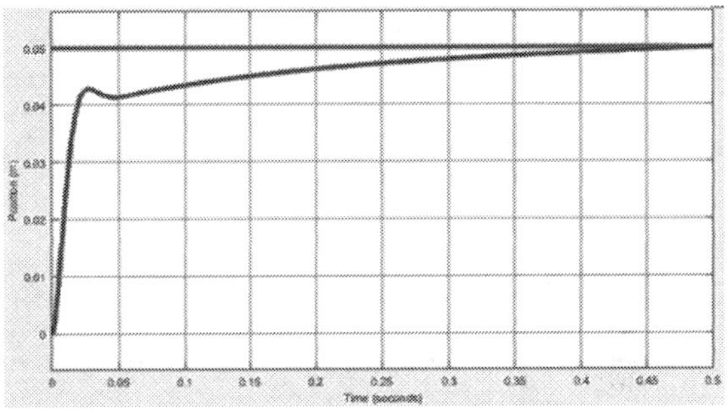

Fig. 6: PD controller's Step Response

The above figure, results for $K_D = 0.6$ and $K_P = 120$ and filter coefficient N=100, where the pistons have settled in the Set value.
Increasing the K_D coefficient a steady state error occurs with values on the position of the pistons less than 0.05 m.

2.5 Simulation of the Pneumatic System with six-pistons and Proportional-Integral-Derivative controller (PID)

The PID controller is tuned (Proportional–Integral–Derivative) to $K_P = 120$, $K_I = 5$ and $K_D = 0.6$ to achieve Proportional-Integral-Derivative control in the pneumatic system.
The system response and the position of the six actuators with Proportional-Integral-Derivative control is shown in the following figure.

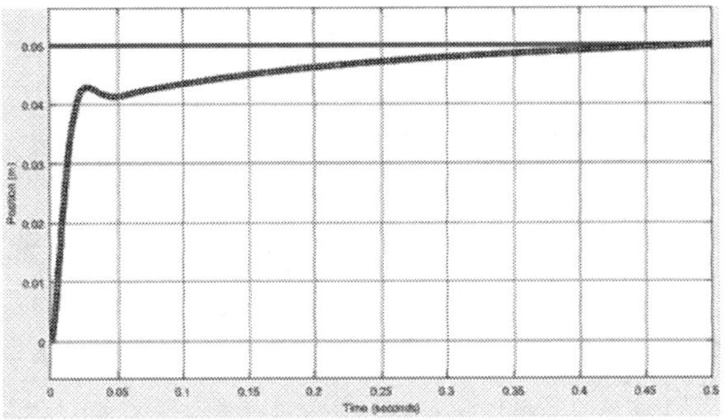

Fig. 7: PID controller's Step Response

The above figure results for $K_P = 120$, $K_I = 5$ $K_D = 0.6$ and filter coefficient N=100, the pistons have settled in the Set value.

Increasing the gains values a steady state error occurs with values on the position of the pistons less than 0.05 m.

Increasing the Proportional gain while leaving the other two gains aside it is observed, that the system's response tries to follow the input set to it but a steady state error occurs. Increasing its value the steady state error is getting smaller but it is never eliminated.

Increasing the Integral gain and leaving the other coefficients intact a steady state error appears in the system with values of the position of the pistons greater than 0.05 m.

By increasing the Derivative gain and leaving the other coefficients intact a steady state error appears in the system with values of the position of the pistons less than 0.05m.

3 Results

With the Proportional control method the Pneumatic system response gets accurate by choosing the correct value and acts fast with settling time T_S=492.4 ms (Fig.4). When the application requirements are increased then this method of control gets unsuitable and the systems response with a load gets unpredictable [5]. Therefore this method of control cannot deal with all the scenarios that can occur in the industrial environment and needs furthermore assistance from a subsystem.

The second method of control that was used in the pneumatic system was the Proportional-Integral method which according to the theory using the integration term is intended to eliminate the steady state error in the system. The steady state error theoretically should have been eliminated by the integral term while adding some minor distortion on the systems response, has settling time T_S=488.6 ms doesn't eliminate the stead state error E_{SS}=0.05 m as expected even at the maximum value (Fig 5).

In simulation environment the PI controller doesn't add oscillating behavior, nor creates overshoot in the pneumatic system. In reality studies have shown that the Integral coefficient on a Non-linear system adds constantly force in the system creating disturbances [5-8], and unbalancing the systems response. That is the main reason that the PI controller is avoided in general in both simulation experiments as well as in real once.

The next method of control that was applied in the pneumatic system was the PD controller (Proportional-Derivative). The-D coefficient should minimize the systems overshoot. With experimental testing it is confirmed that the PD controller helps stabilize the Pneumatic system response with T_S=498.7 ms and eliminates the over shoot with a E_{SS}=0.05 m (Fig.6).

The last controller tested was the three-term PID controller (Proportional-Integral-Derivative) to complete the comparison between all the controllers. The response time of the PID controller it's the same as the PD's. T_S=498.5 ms (Fig.7). In simulation environment, PID controller has distortion when the coefficients value are too high but he is eliminating the overshoot effect.

In reality the presents of the I-term is creating low frequency signals that are hard to eliminate and adds unpredictable behavior in the system's response [5-8], making it hard to justify its usage on a non-linear model as this one.

Therefore the most optimal response for the six actuator pneumatic systems is given by PD controller in Simulation as well as in real experiments.

4 Further upgrades

By taking advantage of the possibilities given by Matlab/Simulink the pneumatic system that was designed for the purpose of finding the most optimal method of control, could be benefit by adding fuzzy logic controller. The particular controller is not found in the literature, but could be used to control the position of the six pistons of the system, providing new comparison data and therefore new results.

Fuzzy control occurred from the need for a control strategy that is not based on a mathematical model system, which usually differs from the real. The main structural elements of a fuzzy logic controller are the knowledge base, the fuzzy sets, the fuzzifier, the inference engine and the defuzzifier [9].

5 Conclusion

In the current study a comparison was performed between classic methods of control in simulation environment that included a six actuator robotic arm with six degrees of freedom and a single classic controller. The design and implementation of the pneumatic system was described (Matlab/Simulink).

The mathematical models of the directional valve, the actuators and the controllers were described. The experimental result where Proportional (P), Proportional-Integral (PI), Proportional Derivative (PD), and Proportional-Integral-Derivative (PID) were used, were illustrated.

The innovative pneumatic system simulation model of an input and multiple output (Single Input, Multiple Output - SIMO), gives the user the ability to tune in a single controller that can simultaneously drives six parallel connected drive pistons.

After the experiments completion it was shown that the Proportional Derivative (PD) provided the system with the most optimal response.

Moreover, the specific pneumatic system with the given robustness and repeatability, as recorded by the experimental procedure, created a clear practical promises for the usage of the robotic hand ExoHand of Festo which can be used as an outer skeleton that can be worn as a glove by the human hand.

The fingers can be actively moved and their strength amplified the operator's hand movements are registered and transmitted to the robotic hand in real time.

The exoskeleton hand has all the principal physiological degrees of freedom of its human counterpart. It thus

supports the human hand's diverse techniques for grasping and handling objects.
The objectives are to enhance the strength and endurance of the human hand, to extend humans' scope of action and to secure them an independent lifestyle even at an advanced age.
Since all the joints and their drive units are located outside the actual hand in the form of the exoskeleton, this manual orthosis can be fitted not only over the human hand, but also over an artificial handmade of silicone. Using the same hardware, this enables a scenario that creates a link between robotics and orthotics in a completely new way.
The ExoHand combines human intelligence with the capabilities of a robot. While machines are precise, robust and powerful, their responses to complex situations are limited. They normally rely on the visual and tactile perception and decision-making capacity of a human operator.
With the ExoHand the operator has the sensation of feeling the shape of the remote object. The human sense of touch can thus be implemented over long distances and can even be applied at the interface of the real to the virtual world. The system amplifies the strength of the human hand and helps employees remain in the work process for a longer time without suffering permanent physical effects. To prevent fatigue, the ExoHand can be worn for activities carried out in the assembly process, thereby functioning as an assistance system that makes for more pleasant working conditions in the assembly environment.
The ExoHand moving by eight pneumatic actuators which ensure the precise movement of the robotic arm. The forces, the angles and distances recorded by sensors [10].

Given the fact that the construction is fully operational, but there is no literature to be found with some effort to make simulations in the MatLab Simulink, neither any experimental results of its usage. The model of this paper performs robust control and can simulate human movement using six pneumatic actuators, which in fact will ensure the accurate movement of the robotic hand in real time.

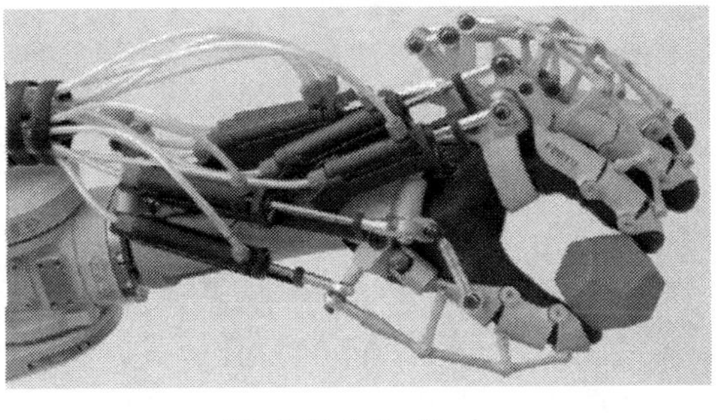

Fig. 8: Festo ExoHand

All authors would like to express their gratitude to the Piraeus University of Applied Sciences for providing the funding in order to undertake and complete this research project as part of: "Automation of Production and Services" Post graduate program of studies.

References

[1] *Hydraulic-Pneumatic systems and Applications*, Athanasios T. Routoulas, Contemporary Publications, Athens, Greece (2008)
[2] Movement control in the pneumatic systems, N. Themelis, Department of Mechanical Engineering, National Technical University of Athens, Greece (2007)
[3] *Automation and Automatic Control Systems*, Part A, I. Lignos, P. Bouslis, G. Politis, G. Chamilothoris, Electrical Sector, Athens (2001)
[4] A High Performance Pneumatic Force Actuator System Part 1 - Nonlinear Mathematical Model, Edmond Richer and Yildirim Hurmuzlu, Southern Methodist University, School of Engineering and Applied Science, Mechanical Engineering Department, Dallas (2001)
[5] "A comparative Investigation Into Proportional-Integral-Derivative Control Methods for Accurate Position Control of Linear Pneumatic Actuators", M.G. Papoutsidakis, University of the West of England, Bristol, UK (2004)
[6] An Analysis of a Pneumatic Servo System and Its Applications to a Computer-Controlled Robot, S. Liu and J. E. Bobrow, Journal of Dynamic Systems, Measurement and Control, **vol 110**, PP 228-235 (1988)
[7] Non-conventional adaptive control of a servopneumatic unit for vertical load positioning, C. Ferraresi, P. Giraudo, G. Quaglia, West Technical Conference (1994)
[8] Variable Structure Control of a Pneumatic Actuator, Tang J. and Walker G., Transactions of the ASME, **vol.117**, pp.88-92 (1995)
[9] Control wind turbine induction motor squirrel cage using fuzzy logic, C. Kokkotas, Department of Electrical and Computer Engineering, University of Patras, Greece (2013)
[10] https://www.festo.com/net/SupportPortal/Files/156734/Brosch_FC_ExoHand_EN_lo. pdf

Software for Assessing the Performance of Anti-plagiarism Programs

Marius Popescu[1], Csiki Laszlo[1] and Antoanela Naaji[1,a]

[1]*"Vasile Goldis" Western University of Arad, Engineering and Computer Science Department, 86 Rebreanu St., Arad, Romania*

Abstract. Detecting plagiarism is one of the current issues concerning the process of publishing scientific papers. There are numerous anti-plagiarism programs on the market, some of which are free, other proprietary. However, with a few exceptions, they cannot detect changes brought to original texts, but can only identify copy-pasted paragraphs of a certain length (number of words). The software that we developed and which we are presenting in this paper is based on an original algorithm using Java, and is aimed at assessing the performance of anti-plagiarism software. This program shows that such software has vulnerabilities and can be easily sidestepped, especially by programmers. The algorithm's method consists of reading a .docx document, and then replacing every fifth word in the sentence with a synonym existing in text files attached to the software. At the end, when the algorithm completes its cycle, the result is saved in a new .docx document. In order to demonstrate the effectiveness of our program as a tool for assessing the performance of anti-plagiarism software, the paper presents a comparative analysis of 4 such programs, based on the percentages of originality and similarity obtained.

1 Introduction

Since 1980, governments, universities, research institutes and other institutions have been facing an increasing amount of research misconduct. Consequently, policies and procedures have been designed to investigate, adjudicate and prevent such cases. According to the US Office of Research Integrity, misconduct in research means [1]:

"- Fabrication – making up data or results and recording or reporting them;

- Falsification – manipulating research materials, equipment or processes, or changing or omitting data or results, such that the research is not accurately represented in the research record;

- Plagiarism – the appropriation of another person's ideas, processes, results, or words without giving appropriate credit;

- Research misconduct does not include honest error or differences of opinion (45CFR 93.103)" [1].

The new approach to misconduct, which is more effective than attempting to catch and punish, is prevention by encouraging good conduct in research.

As regards plagiarism, it is the appropriation of ideas, methods, procedures, technologies, results or texts of another person, regardless of how they were obtained, and the presentation of such as one's own creation [2]. This is a severe infringement of moral rules in these professional communities in which the originality of creations is acknowledged and rewarded.

Generally speaking, plagiarism is an infringement of both the author's moral rights and intellectual property rights over their creation. Nowadays, the phenomenon is enhanced by the possibility to access Internet and the ease with which texts, ideas or images can be copied from doctoral theses, research papers, or articles existing online. Although there are numerous previous examples, in the 1980s it can be seen a slow increase in plagiarism, for about 8 years, followed by a sudden rise before 1990, which lasted for almost 10 years. In last years, the number of cases decreased, largely due to the development of new methods for detecting plagiarism, using specialized software [3].

Plagiarism based on texts derived from the Internet is currently called online plagiarism. Due to the increasing number of online publications, the methods of detecting plagiarism should be more diverse. Thus emerged new services and specialized software to detect plagiarism, free or for payment, some directly accessible on various websites, others through computer programs. In general, websites and programs can detect copying-and-pasting from texts found on the internet or in own databases, not considering punctuation (usually inverted commas), but they cannot detect rephrased sentences or translations from foreign languages [4]. Since anti-plagiarism software cannot pronounce itself on the plagiarism of ideas, but only of texts [5], it does not provide high performance.

Linguistic phenomena underlying plagiarism were analyzed only after these systems were designed, and are a key issue in improving such software. Various types of plagiarism were identified [2], such as plagiarism of ideas, references, authorship, word-by-word and paraphrases.

[a] anaaji@uvvg.ro

DOI: 10.1051/matecconf/201712504005

In the first case, ideas, knowledge or theories are reclaimed without appropriate citation. Reference and authorship plagiarism includes entire citations or documents, with no mention of authorship. Word-by-word plagiarism is known as copy-paste, or textual copy, and consists of the exact copy of a text (fragment) from a source in the plagiarized document. As regards paraphrase plagiarism, it is often used to conceal the act of plagiarism, and expresses the same content under a different form. Paraphrasing is generally defined as invariability between different formulations and is the linguistic mechanism underlying many acts of plagiarism. [6].

The paper presents a software application, based on an original algorithm, which modifies a certain text by automatically replacing words with their synonyms. Its primary role is to detect vulnerability in anti-plagiarism software, as well as to evaluate its performance. As method, the original text is checked by four anti-plagiarism programs, three of them free and one proprietary. Subsequently, they can be modified using our program (by replacing words with their synonyms), and then proceed to a new check.

The following sections present the algorithm and how it is implemented, its testing on the four anti-plagiarism programs, the discussions on results, and conclusions.

2 Description and implementation of the algorithm

The program was created in Java and has two classes, namely, *DocumentHandle* and *App*. After reading the paragraphs in a .docx file, each fifth word is replaced with a synonym in text files [7], and if no synonym is found, then it proceeds to the following word, until it reaches the end of the document. The program ends, and the result is saved in a new docx document. The most important of the two classes is the *DocumentHandle* class, which manages the entire algorithm. This is where variables are declared (`String inputFilePath`, `String outputFilePath`, `XWPFDocumentdoc`) and implemented (*DocumentHandle* class requires 2 parameters: `String inputFilePath` and `String outputFilePath`), while also establishing the necessary methods (`String smallInput()`, `String get_sin_file()`, `String getFirstLetter()`, `String changeWord()`, `void rebuildDocument()` and `StringBuilder mainEngine()`). Thus, the `smallInput` method reads a parameter which is the word *inputWord*.

```
private String smallInput(String fullWord){
 String smallInput=null;
 if(fullWord.length()<4){smallInput=fullWord;}
 else
if((fullWord.length()>3)&&(fullWord.length()<6)){
smallInput=fullWord.substring(0,fullWord.length()-
1);;} else
if((fullWord.length()>5)&&(fullWord.length()<8)){
smallInput=fullWord.substring(0,fullWord.length()-
2);;} else if(fullWord.length()>=8){
smallInput=fullWord.substring(0,fullWord.length()-
2);;} return smallInput;}
```

For a more accurate search, the methods checks the length of the word and if it is longer than three, then the last (one or two) letters are deleted.

```
private String get_sin_file(String letter){
 String letterFilePath=null; File dir=new
File("C:/Desktop/Plagiarism/synonyms/");
 FileFilter fileFilter=new
WildcardFileFilter("*_"+letter+".txt");
 File[] files=dir.listFiles(fileFilter);
 for (int i=0;i<files.length;i++){
letterFilePath=files[i].getAbsolutePath();}
 if(letterFilePath==null) {letterFilePath=
"C:/Desktop/Plagiarism/synonyms/litera_a.txt";}
 return letterFilePath;}
```

The method `get_sin_file()` reads a parameter which is the first letter of the word and then looks for the file containing words beginning with that letter and their synonyms.

```
private String getFirstLetters(String word){
 String firstLetters="";
 word=word.replaceAll("[.,-]","");
 if(word.equals("")){return null;}
 else{for(String s:word.split(" "))
 {firstLetters+=s.charAt(0);}}
 return firstLetters;}
```

The method `getFirstLetter()` reads a parameter which is the word *inputWord* and returns a *string* which contains the first letter in the word.

```
private String changeWord(String
unformattedInput){String inputWord=
 unformattedInput.replaceAll("[.,"]","");
 String outputWord=null;
 String firstLetter=getFirstLetters(inputWord);
 if(firstLetter!=null){
  String filePath=get_sin_file(firstLetter);
  File file=new File(filePath);
  if (inputWord.length()<3){return inputWord;}
  else{try{Scanner scanner=new Scanner(file);
  int lineNum=0;
  while (scanner.hasNextLine()){
  String lineFromFile=scanner.nextLine();
  String[] splitLine=lineFromFile.split(" ");
 if (splitLine[0].contains(smallInput(inputWord)))
 {Stringline=lineFromFile;outputWord="["+inputWord
  +">"+line.substring(line.indexOf(":")+2)+"]";
  return outputWord;}}
  if (outputWord==null){outputWord="[Change this
    ->"+inputWord+"]";}}
  catch (FileNotFoundException e){
      e.printStackTrace();}}}
  else{outputWord="[Change this-
>"+inputWord+"]";} return outputWord;}
```

Likewise, the `changeWord()` method reads a parameter which is a *inputWord* and then runs the method `getFirstLetter()` and the method `get_sin_file()`. Then, the word is changed if it exists in that file, and the synonym is returned. If the word does not exist in the list, then a square bracket is returned containing the following line: `[Change this->inputWord]`.

```
private void rebuildDocument(){try{
   this.doc.write(new
FileOutputStream(this.outputFilePath));
   System.out.println("File saved to:"+
```

DOI: 10.1051/matecconf/201712504005

```
this.outputFilePath);}
    catch(IOException e){e.printStackTrace();}}
```

The `rebuildDocument()` method recreates the formatted .docx document and saves it.

```
public StringBuilder mainEngine(){
  StringBuilder returnString=new StringBuilder();
  int counter=1;
  for(XWPFParagraph p:this.doc.getParagraphs()){
  List<XWPFRun> runs=p.getRuns();
  if(runs!=null){for (XWPFRun r:runs){
    String text=r.getText(0);
    if(text!=null) {//find the fifth words
    String[] split=text.split(" ");
    for (int i=4;i<split.length;i=i+5){
    System.out.print("original world:"+split[i]);
    String currentWord=split[i];
    returnString.append(counter+".Original
world:"+currentWord);returnString.append("changed
to:"+changeWord(currentWord)+"\n");
text=text.replace(currentWord,changeWord(currentWor
d));counter++;}
    r.setText(text,0);}}}}
```

The `mainEngine()` method is the engine of the entire algorithm, where all major events occur. Firstly, we take each paragraph and look for the *n*-th word, which will be replaced. In the end, when no paragraph is left, we call on the method `rebuildDocument()`, which ends the algorithm and returns the result; this can be seen on the interface of the software. The *Synonym file* contains the synonyms of all words in the Romanian language. The algorithm flow is illustrated in a logical schema (Fig.1).

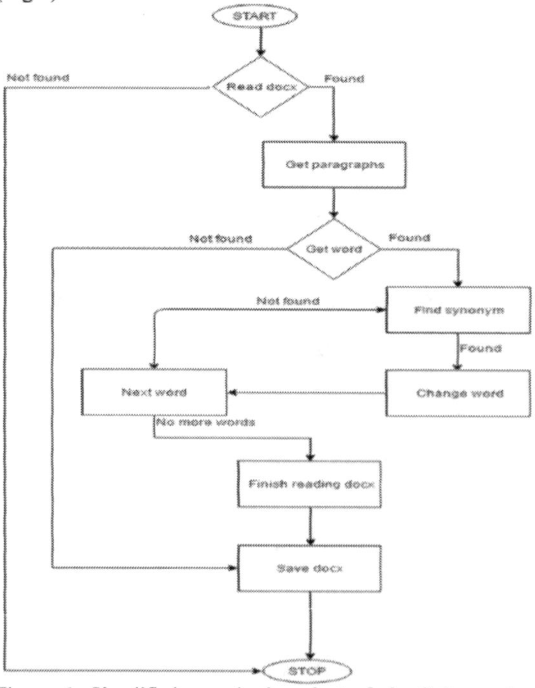

Figure 1. Simplified organization chart of *the Software for Assessing the Performance of Anti-plagiarism Programs.*

In the first step the *input* file, meaning the document which is meant to be modified, is read. In the second step the existence of the document is checked. If it does not exist then the program is stopped with no error. If it does exist, then the most complex part comes along, meaning opening and reading a paragraph, which means – for example – one line, and from there takes each *n*-th word which is *inputWord.* Then, the first letter of the word is taken and that particular file is open, containing synonyms – for each letter there is a separate file which contains the synonyms. For example, *letter_a.txt* which contains the words beginning with the letter *"a"*. After this stage the word is searched in the file and if it does not exist, then it moves to the following word in the paragraph. If it does exist, then the *inputWord* is changed with the synonym. Going further, the following word is taken from the paragraph and the loop is run again until no word remains unevaluated in the paragraph. Then, the following paragraph is taken and the loop is started again. This flow is reprised until the paragraph is finalized. If there is no paragraph left, then the program saves the file and the algorithm is stopped. The program uses the libraries *.apache.poi.xwpf* and *org.apache.commons*; among the most important was the *org.apache.poi.xwpf* library. The program works with this open-source API and can manage a *.docx* document. The software is written under a *Maven* structure, therefore the application can run without error on other *compilers*.

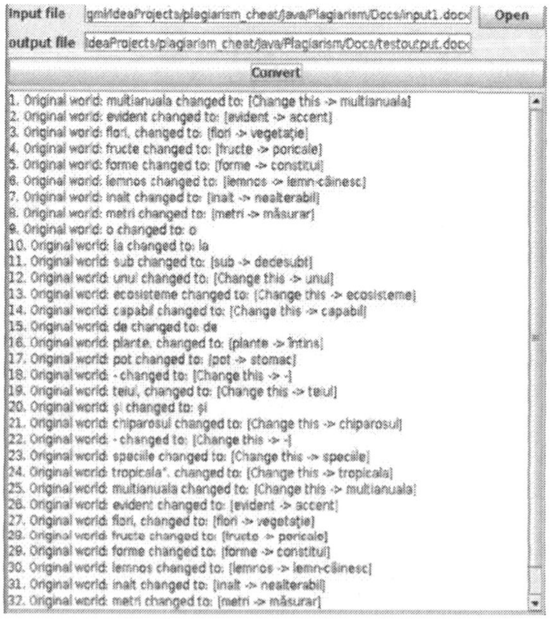

Figure 2. The primary interface of the *Software for Assessing the Performance of Anti-plagiarism programs.*

The graphic interface (GUI) of the *Software for Assessing the Performance of Anti-plagiarism programs* is user-friendly (Fig.2). The *Convert* button starts the engine in the background. The desired file is placed in the *input file*, specifying the path/location where it is found in the computer, and the *output file* specifies the location where to save the new document. The program runs and changes words that are found in the dictionary, and those which are not found are placed between braces.

3 Testing the program and discussions on results

The *Software for Assessing the Performance of Anti-plagiarism programs* is based on an original algorithm, being an open-source program, available on Github, at: https://github.com/laszlocsiki/plagiarism_cheat/tree/development/Java/Plagiarism/src/main/java/plagiarism. To test the performance of the software, a plagiarized document was checked using several online anti-plagiarism websites and a proprietary anti-plagiarism software application.

It is worth mentioning that modifying a document using the algorithm presented only occurs in the case of copy-paste plagiarism. Submitting a plagiarized document to the *Software for Assessing the Performance of Anti-plagiarism programs* does not eliminate plagiarism, but results in a paraphrase plagiarism, which conceals the act of plagiarism, while the document expresses the same content under a different form. The syntactic correctness of the text submitted to the algorithm depends on the synonyms imported from the *Synonyms* file. The new text requires a review or grammatical proofreading, even if it proceeds to check the existence of synonyms for the words found in the sentence on positions "x+1", "x+2" etc., when no synonym is found for the word at position "x", with $x \in [4 \div 9]$. Otherwise, the content of sentences can be distorted or unintelligible.

To begin with, we selected and ran the document in the free plagiarism detection software called *PlagScan* [8], which proved to be a very precise light-weight plagiarism tester. After scanning the plagiarized document, the result was 57% plagiarized, which means that more than half of the content was plagiarized (Fig.3a). After running the document through the *Software for Assessing the Performance of Anti-plagiarism programs*, the result obtained is more than satisfactory, namely, a 2% similarity with the original document (Fig.3b).

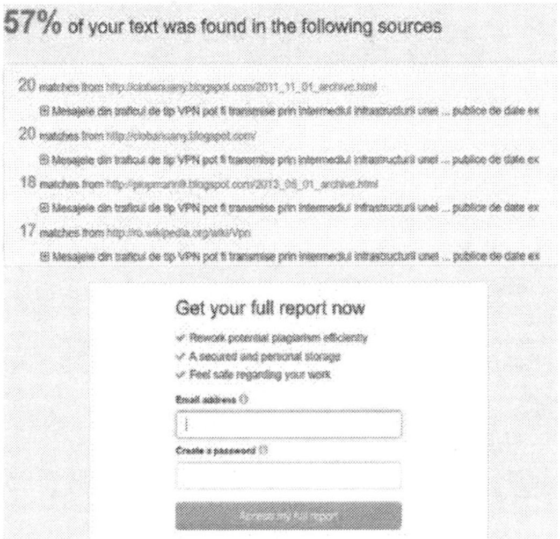

a)

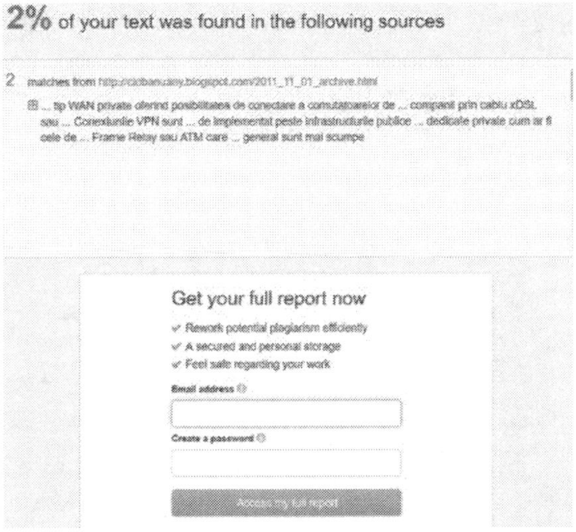

b)

Figure 3. Interface of the *PlagScan* software [8]: a) before running the document through the *Software for Assessing the Performance of Anti-plagiarism programs* b) after running the document through the *Software for Assessing the Performance of Anti-plagiarism programs.*

With the result returned for the chosen document, the program was ran and checked again for two other free applications used to check plagiarism, called *Plagiarism Checker* [9] and *Plagiarisma* [10]. The difference is illustrated in Figures 4 and 5. After the first scanning of the original document with the *Plagiarism Checker* software (Fig.4a), the result was 70% original, meaning that only 30% of the content was copied from other sources. After running the *Software for Assessing the Performance of Anti-plagiarism programs,* the similarity coefficient was null (Fig.4b), meaning that 100% of the text was unique/original, no information was copied from other sources.

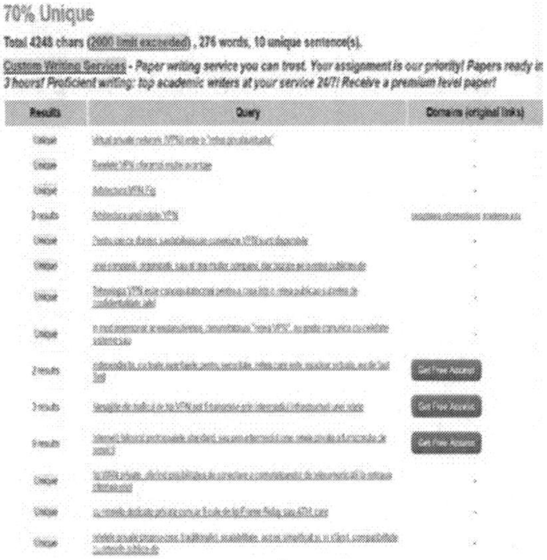

a)

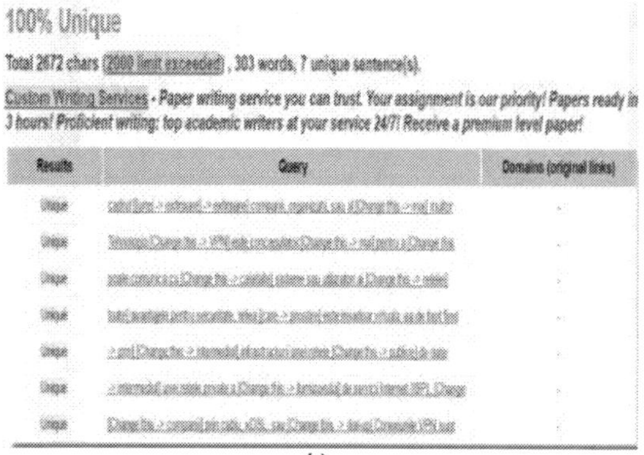

b)

Figure 4. Interface of the *Plagiarism Checker* Program [9]: a) before running the document through *Software for Assessing the Performance of Anti-plagiarism programs* b) after running the document through *Software for Assessing the Performance of Anti-plagiarism programs.*

Small SEO Tools is a tester which has many services connected to SEO, such as *Plagiarism Checker, Keyword Position Checker, Grammar Checker, Spell Checker,* etc. By checking the document with *Plagiarisma,* it initially found that 87% of the content was unique and 15% was plagiarized, meaning from other sources (Fig.5a).

The *Software for Assessing the Performance of Anti-plagiarism programs* was run, then the document was submitted again to the anti-plagiarism software and we can see that the new document is no longer plagiarized (Fig.5b). In other words, the anti-plagiarism software detects a 15% similarity, and after using our software, the anti-plagiarism software established the document to be unique/original.

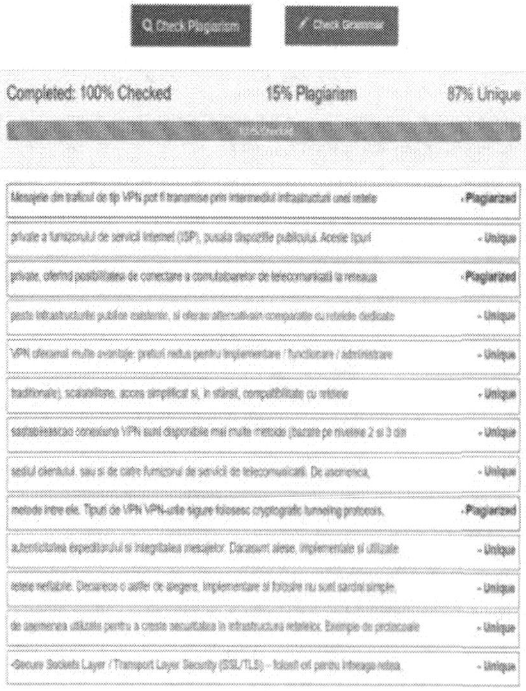

a)

b)

Figure 5. Interface of *Plagiarisma* [10]: a) before running the document through *Software for Assessing the Performance of Anti-plagiarism programs*; b) after running the document through *Software for Assessing the Performance of Anti-plagiarism programs.*

As followed we analyzed the performance of the software by testing the plagiarized document checked with the help of a high-performance anti-plagiarism software application, *Sistem antiplagiat (Anti-plagiarism System)* [11], which evaluates the degree of originality of the text for the document. Details of the Similarity Report refer to concrete aspects concerning plagiarism, such as: fragments found in documents within the database are highlighted in red, those found in Internet sources are colored in green, and those identified in databases of legal documents are marked in a blue background.

After the first scanning of the original document with the *Sistem antiplagiat* software (Fig.6a), the result was 0.1% original, meaning that almost 100% of the content was copied from other sources.

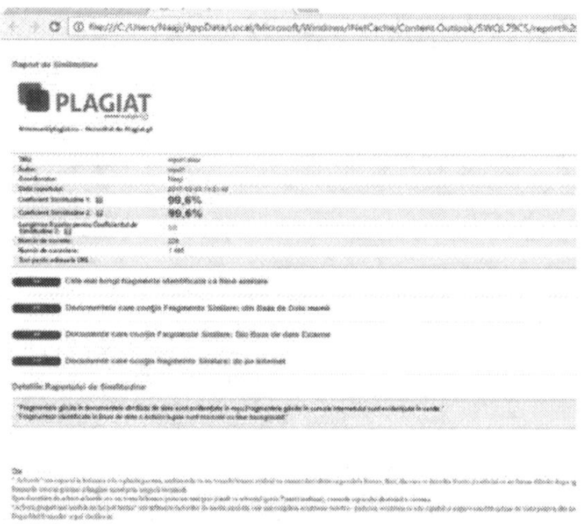

a)

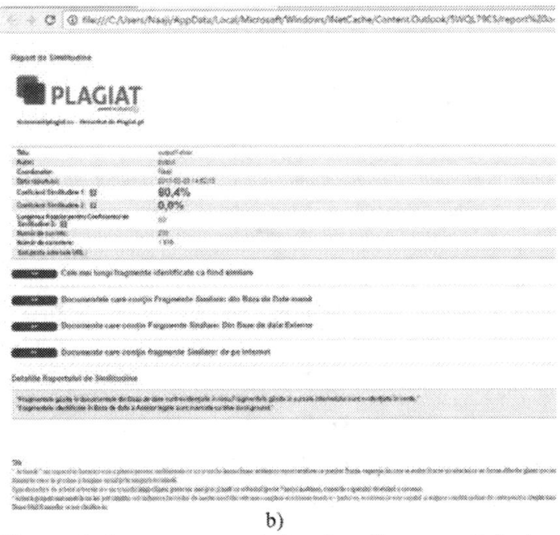

b)

Figure 6. Report generated by the *Sistem antiplagiat* software [11]: a) before running the document through *Software for Assessing the Performance of Anti-plagiarism programs*; b) after running the document through *Software for Assessing the Performance of Anti-plagiarism programs*.

After running the *Software for Assessing the Performance of Anti-plagiarism programs,* the similarity coefficient was still 80.04% (Fig.6b), meaning that only about 20% of the text was unique/original.

For this software, it can be noted that the application calculated 2 similarity coefficients, but the first coefficient is not sufficient, given the small decrease after applying the *Software for Assessing the Performance of Anti-plagiarism programs* (Fig.7). When opting for x=4, changing every fourth word, then the similarity coefficients are improved significantly. Sources marked in bold letters contain fragments which can be plagiarized and exceed the limit of the *Similarity Coefficient 2* in length [11].

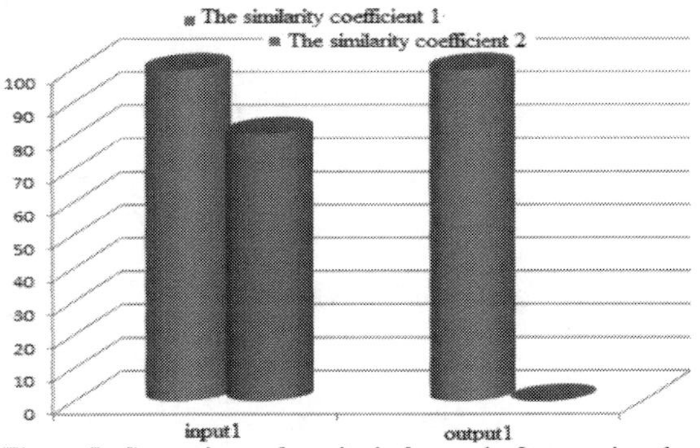

Figure 7. Comparison of results before and after running the document through the *Software for Assessing the Performance of Anti-plagiarism programs*.

A comparative analysis of results obtained by using the free anti-plagiarism programs demonstrates that most of these programs can be "fooled" especially by programmers or even by authors which are not IT specialists, through the simple replacement of words with their synonyms.

Likewise, by performing an analysis of performance on the anti-plagiarism software mentioned above, it can be noted that *Plagiarisma* is not as precise/efficient as *PlagScan*, but it is enough to test plagiarized documents (Fig.8). The explanation of the difference between the results of anti-plagiarism programs resides in the fact that each program uses another method to check the content of the document. For example, one method takes 10 words from a statement and checks that paragraph in other existing sources, and the other method takes only 5 words per statement. For this reason there is a very large difference between anti-plagiarism programs. The users raise the question of using the most precise anti-plagiarism software. Running the *Software for Assessing the Performance of Anti-plagiarism programs* shows that the program which checks 5 words in a paragraph is much more precise than a program checking 10 words in a paragraph.

Thus, results obtained indicate the fact that the *PlagScan* program is more precise, noting that after running *Software for Assessing the Performance of Anti-plagiarism programs*, only 2% of the content was plagiarized.

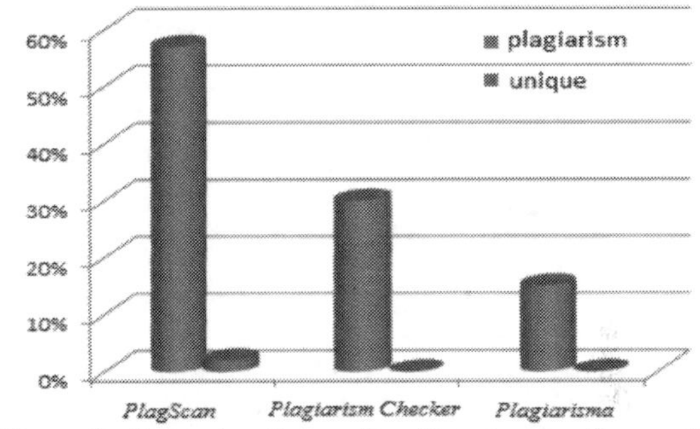

Figure 8. Comparing the results obtained using three anti-plagiarism programs.

Tests conducted previously illustrate the fact that plagiarism testers can be sidestepped, with a simple algorithm and manual review, whereas if the algorithm is more developed, a document can be created to avoid "copy-paste" plagiarism.

The main purpose of *Software for Assessing the Performance of Anti-plagiarism programs* is to compare and detect the most efficient anti-plagiarism software applications.

4 Conclusions

Software for Assessing the Performance of Anti-plagiarism programs is based on an original algorithm, being an open-source program. The software was developed only for testing anti-plagiarism programs and it proves that, with a few manual touch-ups, plagiarism tests can be avoided. Any plagiarized document which goes through the algorithm described above may elude detection by anti-plagiarism software, which illustrates that establishing the plagiarism of a document, or ideas from a certain field of expertise must be made by experts from that field and not only by anti-plagiarism programs. Since resulting similarity coefficients vary according to the anti-plagiarism software, it follows that our software can be a good indicator for the performance of software existing on the market to detect plagiarism. It also can be developed with a vocabulary that is richer in synonyms and with a more advantageous interface, as well as to avoid changes in citation. Likewise, it can be improved by creating a script section for keeping quotes in the document, since quotes are important and should not be modified. For the time being, the software can only be used for texts written in Romanian, but it can be easily adapted to any other language.

References

1. A.E. Shamoo, D.B. Resnik, *Responsible Conduct o Research*, Oxford University Press, (2009)
2. M. Potthast, B. Stein, A. Barrón-Cedeño, P. Rosso, An Evaluation Framework for Plagiarism Detection, *Proceedings of the 23rd International Conference on Computational Linguistics*, COLING 2010 Beijing, China, (2010)
3. D. Pecorari, Good and original: Plagiarism and patchwriting in academic second-language writing, *Journal of Second Language Writing* 12, p.317–345, (2003)
4. J. Mariani, G. Francopoulo, P. Paroubek, A Study of Reuse and Plagiarism in Speech and Natural Language, *Processing papers, BIRNDL 2016* Joint Workshop on Bibliometric-enhanced Information Retrieval and NLP for Digital Libraries, (2016)
5. W. Sutherland-Smith, R. Carr, Turnitin.com: Teachers' Perspectives of Anti-Plagiarism Software in Raising Issues of Educational Integrity, *Journal of University Teaching and Learning Practice,* 2(3), (2005)
6. M. Vila Rigat, *Paraphrase Scope and Typology. A Data-Driven Approach from Computational Linguistics*, Phd Thesis, Universidad de Barcelona, 2013.
7. *** Dictionar online (Online Dictionary), available at: http://dexonline.net, accessed December 2016.
8. *** *PlagScan*, available at: http://www.plagscan.com/plagiarism-check/, accessed January 2017
9. *** *Plagiarism Checker*, available at: http://smallseotools.com/plagiarism-checker/, accessed January 2017
10. *** *Plagiarisma*, available at: http://plagiarisma.net, accessed January 2017.
11. *** *Sistem antiplagiat*, available at: http://sistemantiplagiat.ro/pagina-principala, accessed February 2017.

Intellectual Capital and Predefined Headings in Swedish Health Care Sector

Annika Terner[1], and *Amra* Halilovic[2]

[1]Uppsala Region, Uppsala and Department of Public Health and Caring Sciences, Uppsala university, Uppsala, Sweden
[2]Dalarna County Council, Falun, Sweden

Abstract. The heavily decentralized Swedish health care sector is facing massive challenges, e.g. to even out differences in health care performance. Intellectual Capital can partly be used to explain these differences. In the research field it is difficult to find contributions regarding the study of intellectual capital management in the health care sector and there is also a lack of studies on semantic interoperability. It is semantic interoperability which allows the right information to be available to the right people at the right time across products and organizations. Structured and standardized headings can be a tool to enable semantic interoperability. The aim of this article is to argue for predefined headings as intellectual capital and as base for a national shared and standardized terminology in the health care sector. The study shows that there is a lack of national management of predefined headings deployed in both electronic health records and national quality registries. This lack causes multiple documentation which is time-consuming, impacts health professionals' workloads, data quality and partly the performance of health care. We argue that predefined headings can be a base for semantic interoperability and that there is a need for the management of predefined headings on a national level.

1 Introduction

Sweden, when compared with other countries, produces high quality health care and takes first place in the efficiency index where the overall quality of health care is related to the cost of achieving this quality [1].

The health care sector in Sweden is heavily decentralized with 21 county councils and regions responsible for financing and providing good health care for all inhabitants in the country. The principle of local self-government gives each county council and region the right to design health care services with reference to local conditions. [2]

However, this principle enables differences between county councils and regions in terms of both organizational infrastructure and IT infrastructure. The National Board of Health and Welfare has recently pointed out remarkably large differences between county councils and regions regarding access to health care services, medical results and financial results. [3]

In addition to these differences between county councils and regions, the Swedish health care sector, like health care sectors in other countries, is facing massive challenges: demographic changes, medical and technological advances, growing expectations of citizens, and stablizing financial resources [4-6]. However, as Elg et. al. express; 'financial resources allocated to health care are not expected to increase' [4] p. 102]

The health care sector is a complex system involving different stakeholders: health care professionals, patients, researchers, IT suppliers, government, administrators and others. Health care professionals, such as physicians and nurses, have to work together in order to deliver good quality health care for their patients. Their decisions are dependent on knowledge and it is important that knowledge created by one part is shared with other parts as there is the need *'to deliver the right information, at the right time, to the right person, and in the right format.'* [7], p. 497]

The health care sector is a knowledge-intensive sector with valuable assets. This stock of knowledge is defined as intellectual capital (IC) [8]. Chang et. al. describe IC as the knowledge-related intangible assets embedded in an organization [9]. It is widely accepted that IC is a crucial factor for organizational success [10]. Effective management of IC, together with physical capital, contributes to sustainable and competitive advantages [11]. IC is also perceived as a factor which can partly explain variations in the performance of healthcare organizations [8].

In the literature, it is difficult to find contributions regarding the study of IC management in the health care sector. The research field has focused mostly on single organizations, for example hospitals. [11-13]

Management of IC in the health care sector faces several challenges; particularly challenging is the lack of integration between the different IT systems and thereby the lack of integrated information [7].

Over the years different solutions of technical interoperabilitet have been invented and implemented. However these solutions are ineffective because they do not solve the lack of semantic interoperability. Semantic interoperability allows the right information to be available to the right people at the right time across products and organisations [14, 15].

In a recent study we argued that structured and standardized headings (defining health information similar to physical labels on boxes [16]) can be a tool to enable access to health-related information at the right time, to the right person and in the right format.

2 Aim

The aim of this article is to argue that predefined headings are intellectuell capital and therefore can be a base for a national shared and standardized terminology in the health care sector.

3 Intellectual Capital

Traditionally IC is described as the stock or sum of knowledge which organizations use for value creation and competitive advantage [8, 17, 18]. There are three different types of IC: human, structural and relational capital, see Figure 1.

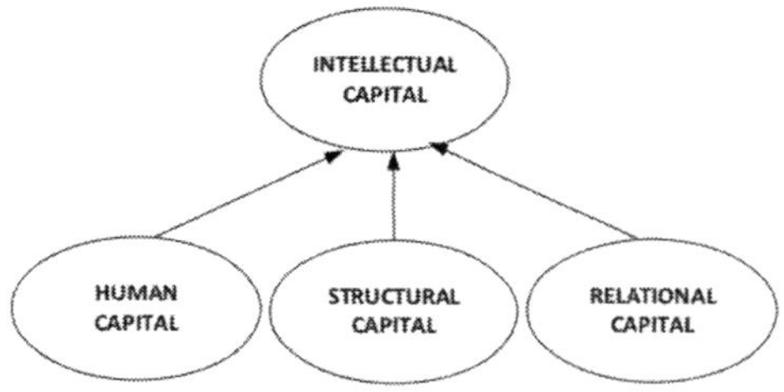

Figure 1: Conceptualisation of Intellectual Capital (after Bontis, N., 1999)

Human capital is defined as the knowledge, skills and experiences owned and utilized by individuals. In the health care context this knowledge is an important factor in achieving high performances [20].

Structural capital, also called organizational capital, is defined as institutionalized knowledge. The individual knowledge is codified, stored and shared. This knowledge together with routines, procedures, IT systems, research and organizational culture constitutes organizational capital. [11]

Relational capital, also called social, is defined as the knowledge available through, derived from, and utilized by networks of relationships. It is the knowledge at group level. [19]

These three types of IC are interdependent and they form the stock of knowledge in an organization [8]. IC is created by individuals and needs to be shared before it becomes knowledge at the group or organizational level [8, 20].

According to Nonaka it is important to highlight the distinction between information and knowledge. Information is defined as a flow of messages and knowledge; '*...created and organized by the very flow of information, anchored on the commitment and beliefs of its holder. This understanding emphasizes an essential aspect of knowledge that relates to human action.*' [20].

Nonaka's 'Spiral of organizational knowledge creation' explains how tacit and explicit knowledge held by individuals can be transformed, legitimized, enlarged and enriched [20].

4 Predefined Headings and Electronic Health Records

Predefined headings are an expression of knowledge-based healthcare. As early as in 1730 criteria for proper documentation of disease progression was the focus in a medical thesis [21]. At the first hospital in Sweden, Serafimerlasarettet in Stockholm, 50 rules governed the health care activities in 1755. Some of these rules governed the documentation in health records. The documentation should include diagnosis, therapy, cure, surgery, food and disease progression. [22] One hundred years later, at the same hospital, health records were structured by predefined headings; previous diseases, cause of disease, symptoms, diagnosis and prognosis are examples of predefined headings employed in 1851 [22]. In 1984 a structure of predefined headings for a basic health record was introduced to the Swedish health care sector. The structure of predefined headings was developed by physicians and examples of predefined headings include hereditary, previous diseases, hypersensitivity and symptoms. [23]

The health care professionals have defined the headings based on their knowledge and experience of what information is necessary to provide good health care [24].

Previous research has shown that predefined headings are employed to structure health information about patients in electronic health records (EHRs) [25, 26]. Underneath each predefined heading, the health care professional enters narrative text, one or more predefined statements, or a numeric value.

EHR is defined as an electronic record of health-related information on an individual which conforms to nationally recognized interoperability standards and which can be created, managed, and consulted by health care professionals across health care organizations. Health-related information means, among others, treatment and discharge summaries, investigation results and reports, prescriptions and health care professional notes. [27]

The primary purpose of EHRs is to support the continuity, efficiency and quality of health care. The information in an EHR is retrospective, concurrent, and prospective [28]. For health care professionals and patients, the EHR represents opportunities in terms of accessible, systematic, and comprehensive patient information. [29]

The EHR is expected to provide information when and where it is needed about the patient [30, 31]. Most EHRs in Sweden are similar to the previous handwritten health records structured by predefined headings in predefined templates [32].

The problem is that each county council and region has their own terminology of predefined headings in their EHRs. The result of a recent study showed that the number of shared and standardized predefined headings in EHRs across three county councils and regions was just 2% [33]. This means that health information about the same patient cannot be exchanged between county councils and regions. The solution is semantic interoperability, which means that the information is unambiguously understood in content, meaning, and purpose by the receiver [34, 35]

5 Predefined Headings and National Quality Registries

Predefined headings are also employed in National Quality Registries (NQRs). In Sweden, NQRs have a long history. From the beginning, they were created by the individuals who themselves would benefit from them in their professional lives. Today there are about one hundred NQRs in Sweden; examples include the Swedish Hip Arthroplasty Register, National Quality Registry of Stroke and National Diabetes Registry. The NQRs contain individualized data concerning health information about patients. The data is protected by the Patient Data Act [36] and all county councils and regions are recommended to register data in NQRs.

Reports from NQRs are available to health care professionals and managers in county councils and regions [37]. Some NQRs are also freely available to all inhabitants via the Internet. On a national level the reports from NQRs constitute an important input to monitoring and comparing performance of health care among county councils and regions; an example is 'Open Comparison and Assessment' [38].

NQRs are sources of "knowledge of improvement" because they contain aggregated data which, after analysis, can lead to documented evidence for or against e.g. methods and material used in health care. This, in turn, leads to better outcomes for patients. This improvement of knowledge is an important part of knowledge-based health care [33].

Each NQR has defined their headings based on the indicators which are important to follow up for their specialty, e.g. diabetes. The consequence of this is a lack of shared predefined headings across the NQRs, which also indicates a lack of semantic interoperability between NQRs. [33]

6 Conclusions

Predefined headings are expressions for health care professionals' knowledge, skills and experiences. When deployed in EHRs the information and knowledge can be shared within the county council or region, and by deployment in NQRs the information and knowledge can be shared among county councils or regions; as a result predefined headings should be regarded as intellectual capital.

There is an assumption that there is semantic interoperabilty between EHRs and NQRs, e.g. that the predefined headings in NQRs are shared with EHRs. However, the fact is that each county council and region has its own terminology of predefined headings in their EHRs and each NQR has its own termninolgy of predefined headings which means a lack of semanic interoperability between EHRs and NQRs.

Thus, there is a lack of national management of predefined headings deployed in both EHRs and NQRs. This lack results in multiple documentation, eg health care professionals must first document in an EHR and then register the same information in another way in a NQR. Consequently this is time-consuming and impacts the workload and data quality and partly the performance of health care.

Over the years different solutions of technical interoperability have been invented and implemented. However these solutions have been ineffective because they do not solve the problem of lack of shared and standardized predefined headings across EHRs and NQRs.

We believe that predefined headings can be a base for a shared and standardized terminology for the health care sector in Sweden and therefore we recommend management of predefined headings on a national level.

References

1 Sveriges Kommuner och Landsting, Svensk sjukvård i internationell jämförelse. (Swedish health care in international comparison.), Stockholm(2015).

2 Ministry of Health and Social Affairs, Health and medical care in Sweden, Ministry of Health and Social Affairs, Ed., ed. Stockholm: The Government Offices of Sweden (2011, updated 30 January 2012).

3 Socialstyrelsen, Öppna jämförelser 2016 - En god vård? Övergripande uppföljning utifrån sex frågor om hälso- och sjukvårdens resultat (Comparisons 2016 - A good health care? Overall follow-up based on six questions about health care results), Stockholm(2017).

4 M. Elg, J. Stenberg, P. Kammerlind, S. Tullberg, J. Olsson, Swedish healthcare management practices and quality improvement work: development trends, Int J Health Care Qual Assur, vol. **24**, pp. 101-23 (2011).

5 G. Bronzetti, M. A. Baldini, G. Sicoli, Intellectual Capital Report in the Healthcare Sector: An Analysis of a Case Study, in *Handbook of Research on Human Resources Strategies for the New Millennial Workforce*, P. O. d. Pablos and R. D. Tennyson, Eds., ed: Business Science Reference (2017).

6 A. Garlatti, M. Massaro, V. Bruni, Intellectual capital evaluation in a health care organization. A case study., presented at the XIX IRSPM Conference, Birmingham (2015).

7 C. El Morr, J. Subercaze, Knowledge management in healthcare, in *Handbook of Research on Developments in e-Health and Telemedicine: Technological and Social Perspectives*, ed: IGI Global (2010), pp. 490-510.

8 J. M. Evans, A. Brown, G. R. Baker, Intellectual capital in the healthcare sector: a systematic review and critique of the literature, BMC Health Serv Res, vol. **15**, p. 556 Dec 15 (2015).

9 S.-C. Chang, S.-S. Chen, J.-H. Lai, The effect of alliance experience and intellectual capital on the value creation of international strategic alliances, Omega, vol. **36**, pp. 298-316 (2008).

10 L. Moore, L. Craig, *Intellectual capital in enterprise success: strategy revisited*: John Wiley & Sons (2008).

11 S. Veltri, G. Bronzetti, G. Sicoli, Reporting intellectual capital in health care organizations: Specifics, lessons learned, and future research perspectives, (2011).

12 J. Van Beveren, Does health care for knowledge management?, Journal of knowledge management, vol. **7**, pp. 90-95 (2003).

13 D. Jelonek, A. Halilovic, From intangible assets to management of intellectual capital within health care industry. A comparative study between Sweden and Poland, International Journal of Economics and Statistics, vol. **4**, (2016).

14 M. P. Stroupe. (2013). What is EHR Interoperability and Why Should I Care? A reference document for Urgent Care and Occupational Health Providers. Available: http://www.nethealth.com/wp-content/uploads/2013/11/What-is-EHR-Interoperability.pdf

15 M. Schweitzer, A. Hoerbst, Dynamic User Interfaces for Service Oriented Architectures in Healthcare, Stud Health Technol Inform, vol. **228**, pp. 795-7 (2016).

16 M. Nordman, Överskrift, titel, namn eller rubrik? Några beteckningar i teori och praktik (Caption, title, name or heading? Some indications of the theory and practice), in *I terminologins tjänst Festskrift för Heribert Picht på 60-årsdagen*, A. Nuopponen, B. Toft, and J. Myking, Eds., ed Vaasa: Vasa universitet (2000), pp. 110-7.

17 N. Bontis, Managing organizational knowledge by diagnosing intellectual capital: Framing and advancing the state of the field, in *The Strategic Management of Intellectual Capital and Organizational Knowledge*, N. Bontis and C. W. Choo, Eds., ed New York: Oxford University Press (2002).

18 M. Subramaniam, M. A. Youndt, The Influence of Intellectual Capital on the Types of Innovative Capabilities, The Academy of Management Journal, vol. **48**, pp. 450-463 (2005).

19 P. Ordóñez de Pablos, Measuring and reporting structural capital: Lessons from European learning firms, Journal of Intellectual Capital, vol. **5**, pp. 629-647 (2004).

20 I. Nonaka, A Dynamic Theory of Organizational Knowledge Creation, Organization Science, vol. **5**, pp. 14-37 (1994).

21 N. Rosén von Rosenstein, De historiis morborum rite consignandis, Harderwijk, (1730).

22 I. Nilsson, *Medicinsk dokumentation genom tiderna (Medical documentation through the ages)*. Lund: Lunds universitet (2007).

23 R. Hynninen, B. Wadman, H. Åberg, *Att skriva patientjournaler (Writing patient records)*, 2nd ed. Lund: Studentlitteratur (1984).

24 A. Terner, H. Lindstedt, M. Pless, K. Sonnander, A Retrospective Analysis of Health, Health Care, and Legal Requirements as Reflected in Predefined Headings in an EHR, e-Journal of Health Informatics vol. **9**, (2015).

25 D. L. Andreen, L. J. Dobie, J. C. Jasperson, T. A. Lucas, C. L. Wubbenhorst, The conversion to electronic hospital notes at Mayo Clinic. Overcoming barriers and challenges, J Healthc Inf Manag, vol. **24**, pp. 57-64 Summer (2010).

26 J. C. Denny, A. Spickard, 3rd, K. B. Johnson, N. B. Peterson, J. F. Peterson, R. A. Miller, Evaluation of a method to identify and categorize section headers in clinical documents, J Am Med Inform Assoc, vol. **16**, pp. 806-15 Nov-Dec (2009).

27 The National Alliance for Health Information Technology, Report to the Office of the National Coordinator for Health Information Technology on

Defining key health information technology terms, (2008).

28 International Organization for Standardization, Health informatics - Electronic health record - Definition, scope and context, (2006).

29 A. Terner, Predefined Headings in a Multi-professional Electronic Health Record: Professionals' Application, Aspects of Health and Health Care and Correspondence to Legal Requirements, Uppsala universitet, (2014).

30 W. W. Stead, Rethinking electronic health records to better achieve quality and safety goals, Annu Rev Med, vol. **58**, pp. 35-47 (2007).

31 C. M. Cusack, Electronic health records and electronic prescribing: promise and pitfalls, Obstet Gynecol Clin North Am, vol. **35**, pp. 63-79, ix Mar (2008).

32 A. Terner, H. Lindstedt, K. Sonnander, Predefined headings in a multiprofessional electronic health record system, J Am Med Inform Assoc, vol. **19**, pp. 1032-8 Nov-Dec (2012).

33 A. Halilovic, A. Terner, Standardized headings as a foundation for semantic interoperability in EHR, MATEC Web Conf., vol. **76**, p. 04001 (2016).

34 Healthcare Information and Management Systems Society. (2005). Interoperability Definition and Background. Approved by HIMSS Board of Directors 06/09/05. Available: http://www.himss.org/sites/himssorg/files/HIMSSorg/Content/files/AUXILIOHIMSSInteroperabilityDefined.pdf

35 European Commission, European Interoperability Framework (EIF) for European public services, European Commission, Ed., ed. Bruxelles, Belgique: European Commission (2010).

36 *Patientdatalag (Patient Data Act),* Socialdepartementet (2008).

37 Nationella Kvalitetsregister. (2016, 24 March). *Swedish National Quality Registries.* Available: http://kvalitetsregister.se/englishpages.2040.html

38 Sveriges Kommuner och Landsting. (2016). *Öppna jämförelser (Open Comparison and Assessment).* Available: https://skl.se/tjanster/merfranskl/oppnajamforelser.275.html

Design and Implementation of Application for the Hearing Impaired People

ChoulWoo Kim[1], *Dongyun* Kim[1], *Hyundo* Lee[1], *Hanseong* Park[1], *Giung* Kwon[1], *Eunju* Park[1], *Hankyu* Lim[1,*]

[1]Dept of Multimedia Engineering, Andong National University, Andong, Republic of Korea

Abstract. With the development of various information and communication technologies, numerous applications are being developed and used in various fields in this modern society. However, these applications are mostly designed to provide convenience to general users, and applications for people with disabilities are small in number and inconvenient to use. Therefore, this study designed and implemented an application for the hearing impaired in particular. This application is intended to enable users with hearing impairment to communicate more easily with other people and to provide convenience in everyday life and emergency situations. We believe that many applications should be developed in various fields to provide the convenience of life to those who are experiencing information gap due to disability.

1 Introduction

The number of people with disabilities is increasing and the occurrence rate of hearing impairment among the disabilities is the third highest after physical disability and visual impairment [1]. According to the Ministry of Health and Welfare's '2014 Survey on the Status of People with Disabilities', the number of hearing-impaired people in South Korea was approximately 310,000 in 2014. Most of the people with hearing impairment acquired the disability and the higher the age, the higher the incidence became [2]. Among the various applications of information and communication technology, smart devices have become an essential part of everyday life such as educational and administrative services, shopping, and banking [3]. Applications in various fields are being developed for the increasing number of smartphone users and user-oriented smartphone applications for user convenience are also increasing [4]. However, smartphones are not convenient communication tools for people with hearing impairment, who have difficulty using even the most basic voice calls on a smartphone [5]. Even though there are some applications that can be used by people with disabilities who have limited physical and cognitive functions through education and training, the number and types of applications for the disabled in South Korea are very limited compared to other countries [3]. Furthermore, even the applications developed for the hearing-impaired are inconvenient to use because their services do not consider the hearing-impaired users properly [6].

Consequently, this study designed and developed an application for the hearing impaired people who need special functions that are not provided by most of the applications made for general users. In order to develop this application, we examined the lacking features of existing applications for the hearing-impaired and investigated the daily lives of hearing-impaired people to find and improve their inconveniences. The application developed in this study implemented a feature to easily communicate through the sign language to solve the daily discomfort of the hearing impaired people, SOS feature to alert an emergency situation, a feature to set alarms by vibration to alert the hearing impaired people, and a feature to search the voices of non-disabled people and communicate them by sign language. Moreover, we added other features to help the hearing impaired such as food ordering and guidance to nearby welfare facilities for the hearing impaired. This application was implemented using Android Studio to allow the hearing impaired to use it more conveniently with various smart devices.

One limitation of this study is that it may be less usable for the disabled because people who responded to the questionnaire survey to investigate the feasibility of application development were non-disabled people. The usability of this application will be improved in our follow-up study.

The application developed in this paper is expected resolve the information gap and improve the convenience of living for the disabled people.

2 Related Research

2.1 Hearing impairment

Hearing impairment refers to a disorder in the ability to hear due to a damage of the hearing organ. Hearing impairment varies widely according to the severity from mild hearing loss, which cannot hear small sounds, to

* Corresponding author: hklim@anu.ac.kr

DOI: 10.1051/matecconf/201712504007

severe hearing loss, which cannot hear loud sounds [1]. Whereas the non-disabled people communicate by speech, the hearing impaired communicates in a different language according to their degree of disability.

There are various communication methods for the hearing impaired, such as sign language, oral method, total communication, and bilingual approach [7].

2.2 Android Studio

Android is a software stack and an operating system for smartphones and other mobile devices, which includes middleware, user interfaces, and standard applications [8]. Android allows developers to write applications in Java language and provides runtime library for running complied byte codes. Furthermore, they provide various tools and APIs required to develop applications through the Android Software Development Kit (SDK). Android Studio is an Android development tool based on IntelliJ IDEX which is a famous integrated development environment (IDE). Therefore, developers can easily use various functions provided by IntelliJ.

In this study, we developed an application using Android Studio and created a virtual machine through the emulator which is a feature of Android Studio to implement it in an environment that is identical to the actual mobile phone.

3 Requirement Analysis

To develop the app for the convenience of the hearing impaired in this study, we added and improved various functions by conducting a questionnaire survey and benchmarking.

3.1 Survey Investigation

The survey was conducted between October 1 and 6, 216 using Naver Form. The number of respondents was 96 in total, consisting of 73 males and 23 females. Figure 1 to 4 show the graphs of significant results obtained from the survey.

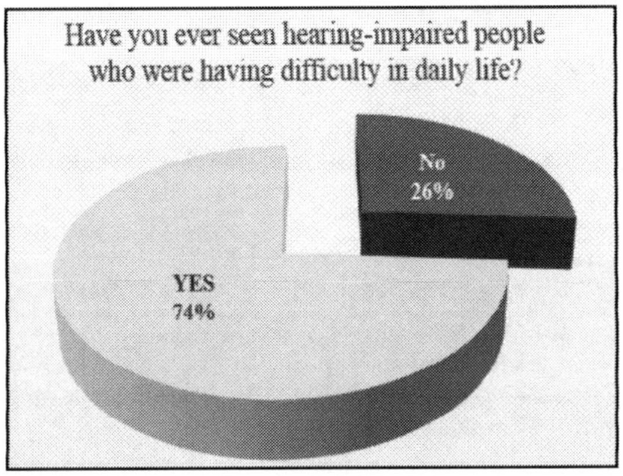

Fig. 1. Survey Result 1

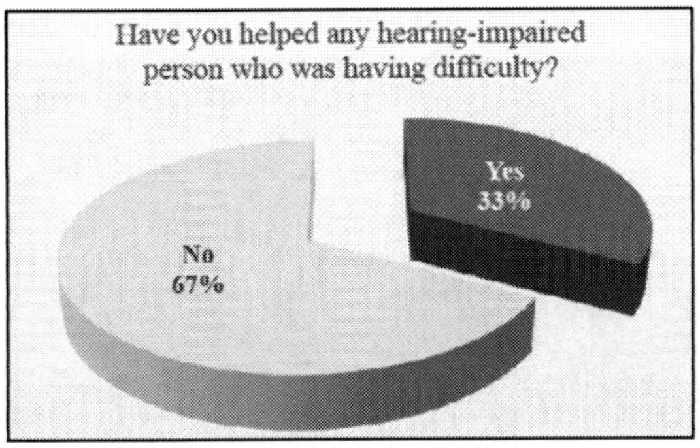

Fig. 2. Survey Result 2

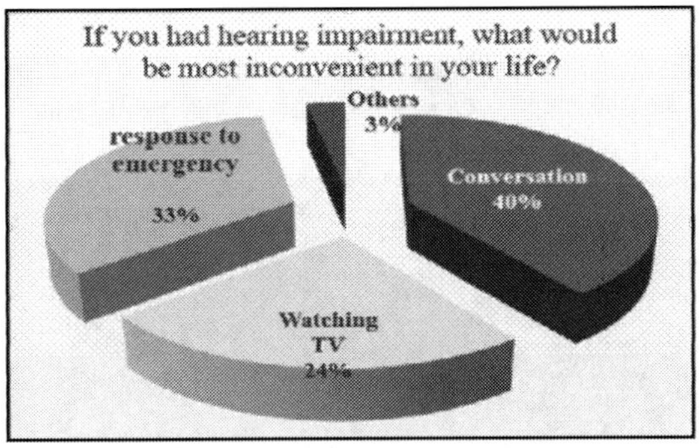

Fig. 3. Survey Result 3

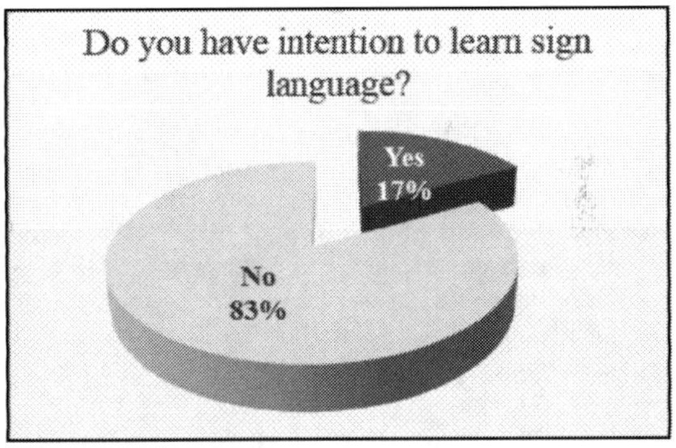

Fig. 4. Survey Result 4

As a result of the survey, 74% of the respondents answered yes to "I have seen hearing-impaired people who were having difficulty in daily life." To the question, "Have you helped any hearing-impaired person who was having difficulty?" 67% answered that they have not. To the question, "If you had hearing impairment, what would be most inconvenient in your life?" the largest number of respondents answered 'conversation,' followed by 'response to emergency,' 'watching TV,' and 'Others.' Furthermore, 83% of the respondents answered that they have no intention to learn sign language.

The survey results showed that many respondents have seen hearing impaired people but did not help them. Many respondents thought that conversation would be the most difficult if they had hearing impairment. In addition, most of the respondents had no intention to learn sign language for communication with the hearing impaired people. Therefore, the survey results suggest that information and communication technology and other helpful devices are needed for communication between the non-disabled and the hearing impaired.

3.2 Benchmarking

To improve the usefulness of the application developed in this study, the currently used applications for the hearing impaired were investigated for benchmarking and their weak points were noted for supplementation. Figure 5 shows the benchmarked applications.

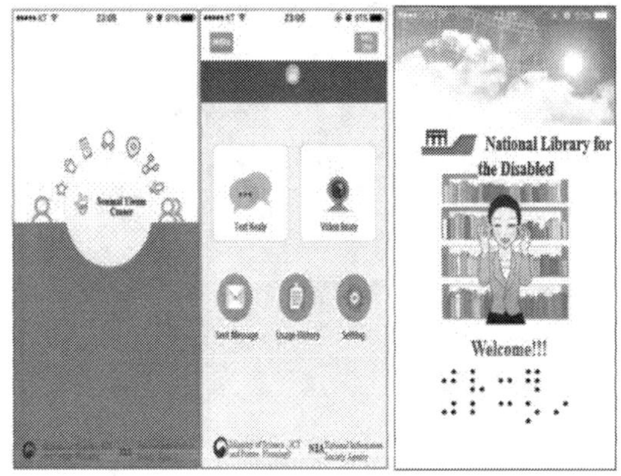

Fig. 5. 'Sonmal Yieum Center' and 'National Library Video Data Pavilion for the Disabled'

As a result of benchmarking, 'Sonmal Yieum Center' helped communication between hearing impaired people and relay person by translating or converting sign language into texts. 'Share Typing' provides real-time subtitles and stenographers delivered messages through real-time typing at schools, churches, seminars, etc. 'National Library Video Data Pavilion for the Disabled' provided sign language and subtitles to allow the hearing impaired to read library materials anywhere. The benchmarking results showed that applications to help the daily life of the disabled were insufficient and the translation feature using sign language was difficult to use because it required a relay person. Therefore, the application for the hearing impaired developed in this study added a feature to search dialogues and information for general users as well as for the hearing impaired during conversations where the hearing impaired feel most discomfort. Sign language dictionary, sign language search and browsing, and expert connection features were added to design and implement a more convenient and fast application.

4 Design

4.1 Flowchart

Figure 6 shows the flowchart of the application developed in this study. The numerical word search, voice translation, vibration alarm, SOS, substitute order, and welfare facility search features were defined.

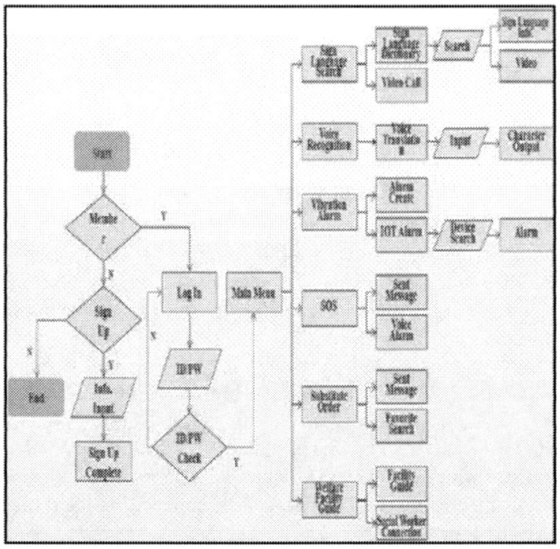

Fig. 6. Flowchart of the Application

4.2 UI Design

The following shows the user interface (UI) of the application developed in this study. The image at left in Figure 7 is the 'Log In' UI for logging in to or signing up for the application, which consists of password input field, sign up and log in buttons. The image at right in Figure 7 shows a page where you can choose any function of the application to run the function.

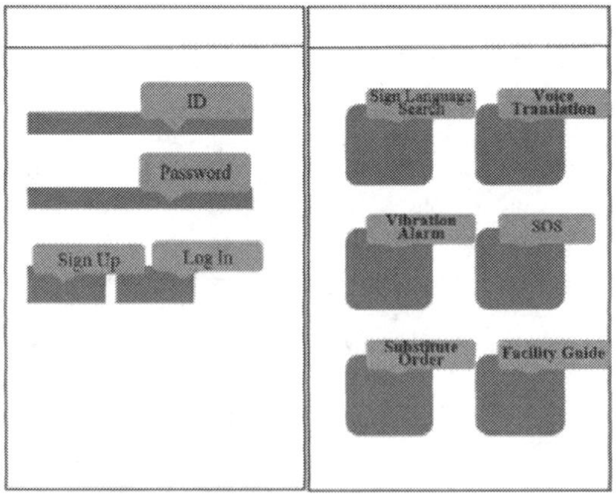

Fig. 7. 'Log In' and 'Main Screen' UI

The UI page for 'sign language search' is shown at left in Figure 8. It consists of a sign language dictionary where users can search sign language by connecting with a sign language search site and a feature for making a video call with a sign language expert.

The UI at right in Figure 8 shows a page that can be used by the hearing impaired in an emergency or to seek help from surrounding persons. It includes messaging feature for sending text messages to the stored phone number and alarm feature to notify emergency to other people in the vicinity by large siren sound.

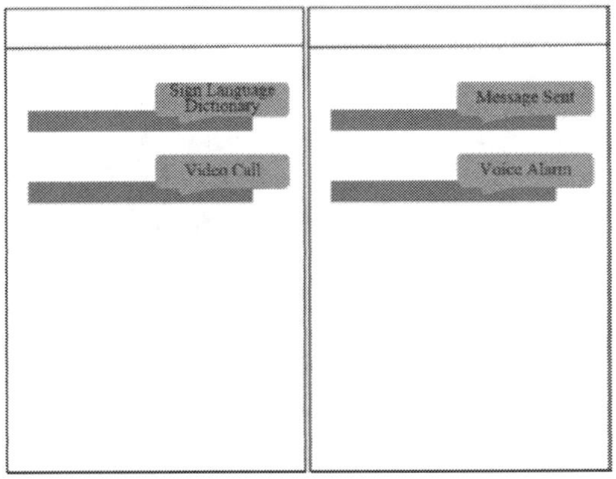

Fig. 8. 'Sign Language Search' and 'SOS Page' UI

5 Implementation

In this study, eight functions were implemented as prototype, including log in, sign up, sign language search, void translation, vibration alarm, SOS, substitute order, and welfare facility guide.

5.1 Log In and Sign Up

Figure 9 below shows the screens for Log In and Sign Up. The application developed in this study was designed to ask for the minimum personal information, considering that the users are disabled people who have difficulty using the application When the ID that a user wants is already taken by another user, a message requesting recently is displayed. When user clicks the JOIN button, the sign-up process is completed and the Log In page appears. When user clicks the 'CANCEL' button, the main page appears.

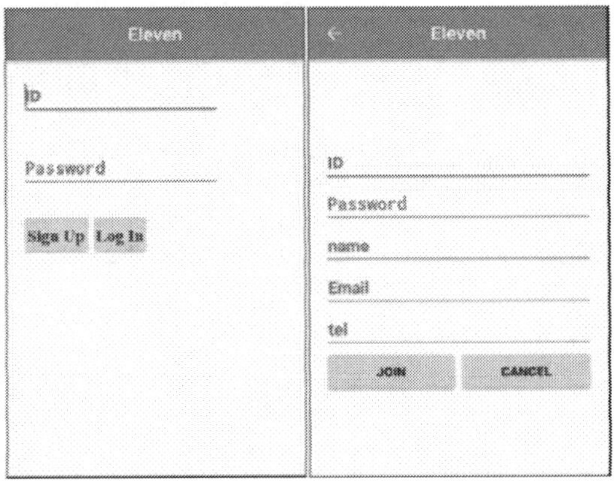

Fig. 9. 'Log In' and 'Sign Up' Implementation screen

5.2 Intro and Main Screen

Figure 10 below shows the intro and main screens of the application. The intro screen was named Eleven (11) by rotating the equal sign '=' which means equality by 90 degrees. When the main screen appears after log in, the menu icons appear, including sign language search, voice translation, vibration alarm, SOS, substitute order, and welfare facility guide. Users can click an icon to go to the desired menu.

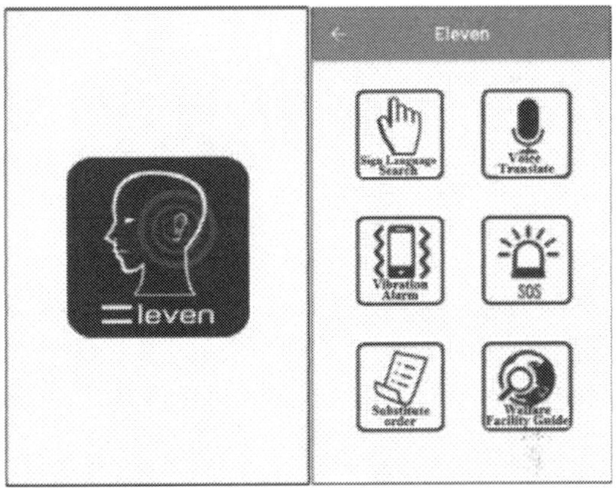

Fig. 10. 'Intro' and 'Main' Implementation Screen

5.3 Sign Language Search and Sign Language Dictionary

Figure 11 below shows the sign language search screen. This screen appears when the sign language search icon is clicked in the main screen. The sign language dictionary screen shows the Korean Sign Language Dictionary page where you can enter a sign language to search and play videos.

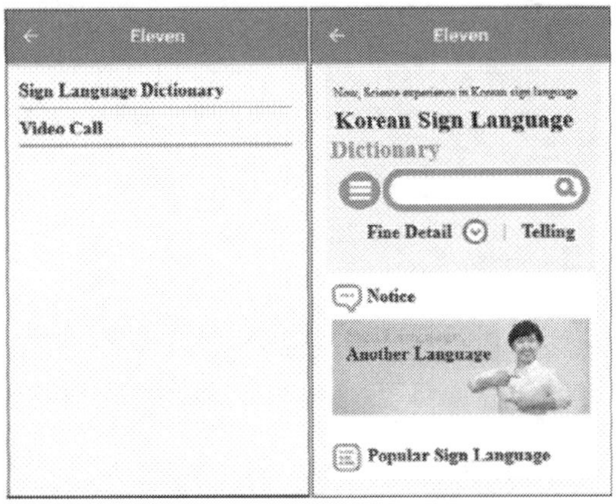

Fig. 11. 'Sign Language Search Screen' and 'Sign Language Dictionary Screen' Implementation

5.4 Voice Translation Recognition

Figure 12 below shows the voice translation recognition screen. When you click the mic button and say words, they are recognized and displayed as texts in TextView.

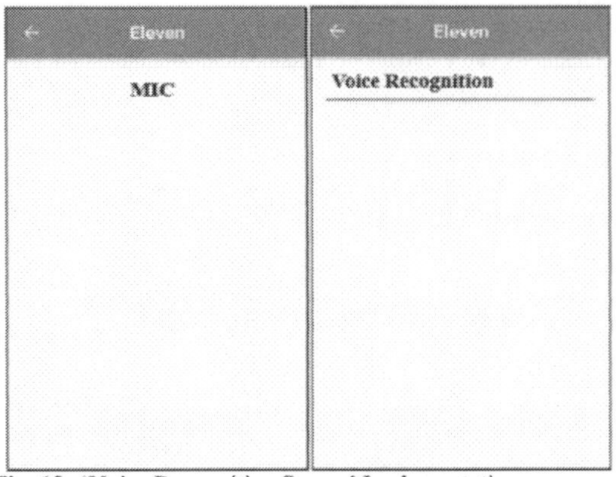

Fig. 12. 'Voice Recognition Screen' Implementation

5.5 Vibration Alarm and Alarm Generation screen

Figure 13 below shows the vibration alarm and alarm generation screens. This screen appears when you click the vibration alarm icon in the main screen. When you select a date and time and click the SET button in the alarm generation screen, the alarm goes off by vibration at the selected time.

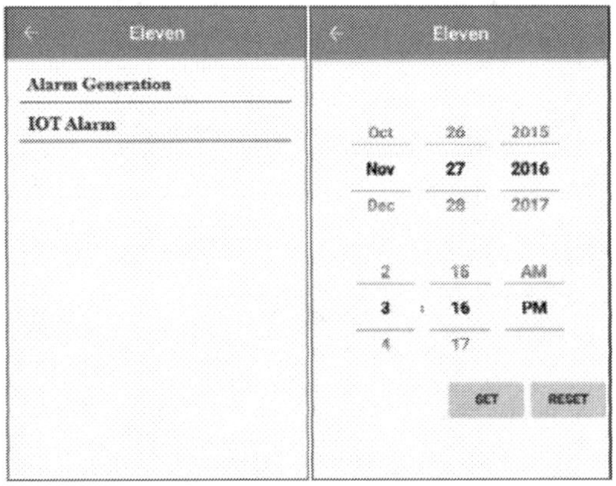

Fig. 13. 'Vibration Alarm' and 'Alarm Generation Screen' Implementation

5.6 SOS and Substitute Order

Figure 14 below shows the SOS screen. A preset text message is sent to the pre-set number in an emergency. When you select the siren icon, the emergency is notified to people in the vicinity by outputting a siren sound. When you click the siren button once again, the siren sound will stop.

Figure 15 below shows the substitute order screen. When you click the 'Substitute Order' button, select the connected restaurant phone number and order item, and click the Order button, a text message is sent to the restaurant.

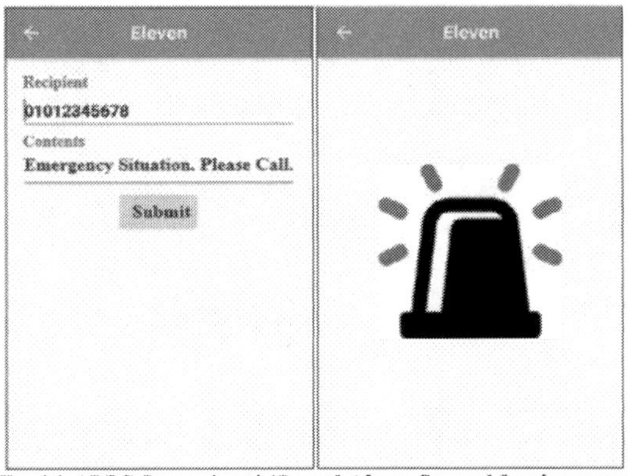

Fig. 14. 'SOS Screen' and 'Sound Alarm Screen' Implementat ion

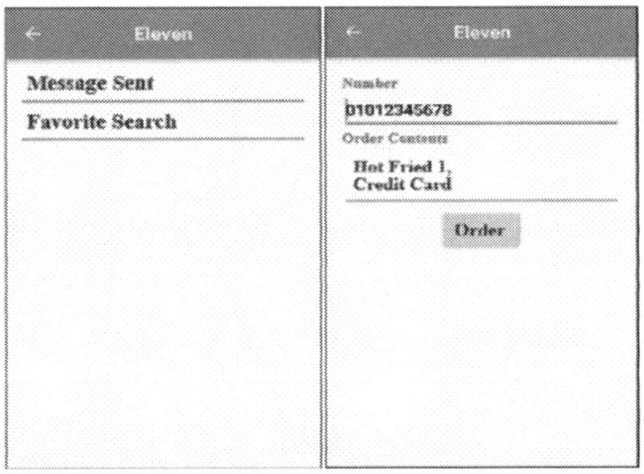

Fig. 6. 'Substitute Order Screen' and 'Message Sent Screen' I mplementation

5.7 Welfare Facility Guide

Figure 16 below shows the welfare facility guide screen. When you click the Facility Guide or Social Worker Connection button, the website of Korean Association of the Welfare Institutes for the Disabled appears.

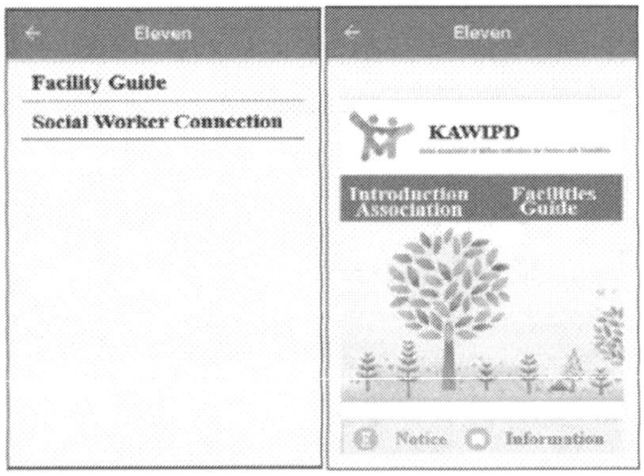

Fig. 7. 'Welfare Facility Guide Screen' Implementation

6 Conclusion

An application for the smooth communication and convenient life of the hearing impaired people was designed and implemented. For this application, searching sign language search feature and voice to text translation feature were designed to facilitate communication between the hearing impaired and non-disabled people. In addition, vibration alarm and SOS alert features were designed and implemented for the safety of the hearing impaired. In addition, welfare facility guide feature was added to help users easily find welfare facilities.

In South Korea, smartphones have become popular among the disabled, but there are not many applications that have considered the environment for the disabled. This study intended to help the hearing impaired people to lead more convenient and safe life and to communicate easily with non-disabled people. This application will help bridge the information and communication gap of the disabled.

The development and propagation of smartphone applications for the disabled are not as active as those for general users. However, more smartphone applications for the disabled should be developed because they have constant demand. Furthermore, many applications in various areas are required to resolve the information gap and improve the convenience of living for people with various disabilities.

Acknowledgment

"This research was supported by the MSIP(Ministry of Science, ICT and Future Planning), Korea, under the Seoul Accord Vitalization Program(IITP-2017-2011 0 00559) supervised by the IITP(Institute for Information & communications Technology Promotion)"

References

[1] E. Jang, B. Kim, "The study on the GUI guideline in the survey of deaf needs. - Focused on municipal seodaemun deaf community welfare center.-," Design Convergence Study 43, Vol. **12**, pp, 214-217, No. 6 (2013)

[2] Ministry of Health and Welfare's, "2014 Survey on the Status of People with Disabilities," Ministry of Health and Welfare's, pp. 149-154 (2015)

[3] Ablenews, http://www.ablenews.co.kr/News/NewsContent.aspx?CategoryCode=0002&NewsCode=003420130320093247143741(03, 2017)

[4] J. Oh, B. An, "Android Based Mobile Smart Alarm," The Journal of the Institute of Internet, Broadcasting and Communication, Vol, **12**, No. 3, pp. 141-147 (2012)

[5] J. Kim, "Research studies on user's needs on screen mobile phone for people with hearing disorder," The Graduate School of Design Ewha Womans University, pp. 14-20 (2008)

[6] K. Kim, "A design guideline to develop an application for cultural facility in consideration of the deaf," Graduate School of Industry and Engineering Seoul National University of Science and Technology, pp. 7-12 (2014)

[7] S. Woon, Kyungjin Kim, Il Heo, "The Study on Proposal to Apply Sign Language in the Field of Education for Deaf Students," The Journal of Special Education: Theory and Practice, Vol. **14**, No. 4, pp. 113-132 (2013)

[8] S. Kim, "*Android programming complete guide 1*," Hanbit Media (2016)

MATEC Web of Conferences **125**, 04008 (2017) DOI: 10.1051/matecconf/201712504008
CSCC 2017

Automatic Regulation of Wastewater Discharge

Yolanda Bolea, *and Antoni* Grau

Automatic Control Dept, Technical University of Catalonia, UPC, 08034 Barcelona, Spain

Abstract. Wastewater plants, mainly with secondary treatments, discharge polluted water to environment that cannot be used in any human activity. When those dumps are in the sea it is expected that most of the biological pollutants die or almost disappear before water reaches human range. This natural withdrawal of bacteria, viruses and other pathogens is due to some conditions such as the salt water of the sea and the sun effect, and the dumps areas are calculated taking into account these conditions. However, under certain meteorological phenomena water arrives to the coast without the full disappearance of pollutant elements. In Mediterranean Sea there are some periods of adverse climatic conditions that pollute the coast near the wastewater dumping. In this paper, authors present an automatic control that prevents such pollution episodes using two mathematical models, one for the pollutant transportation and the other for the pollutant removal in wastewater spills.

1 Introduction

Beaches and coastal waters are very sensitive areas to be polluted and problems can appear in those areas near pollution sources after a heavy rainfall or when a sewage treatment plant malfunctions. Pollution can also occur from disruption or damage of wastewater collection and treatment infrastructure due to severe natural events like hurricanes or flooding.

Untreated storm water runoffs from cities and rural areas can be another significant source of beach water pollution. In some areas, boating wastes and malfunctioning septic systems can also be important local sources of beach water pollution. Combined sewer systems are designed to carry both raw sewage and storm water runoff to sewage treatment plants. New control methods are implemented in wastewater treatment plants [1-3], and effects of environmental factors have been also studied [4]. However, even with the proposed methodologies, during heavy rainstorms these systems can become hydraulically overloaded and discharge a mixture of raw sewage and polluted runoff from streets into local waterways. The discharges pollute water around the outfalls and at downstream beaches. Heavy rainfall can also hydraulically overload separate sanitary sewer systems, which carry raw sewage to wastewater treatment plants. This is especially a problem for systems with excessive infiltration of rainfall through the ground into leaky sanitary sewers and with large inflows from sources such as roof drains connected directly to sewers. When flows exceed the capacity of the system, sewers can overflow and discharge untreated sewage from manholes and bypasses at pump stations and sewage treatment plants. The discharges flow into local waterways and therefore they pollute water. People who swim in waters near storm drains can become ill. Polluted runoff and untreated sewage released into the water can expose swimmers to bacteria, viruses, and protozoans. These pathogens (disease-causing organisms) can be present at or near the site where polluted discharges enter the water. Children, elderly, and people with weakened immune systems are most likely to develop illnesses or infections after swimming in polluted water [5].

Due to the high concentration of touristic resorts and a big city such as Barcelona, its coastal waters are very sensitive to pollution. Specifically, in the Mediterranean an estimated 85% of sewage flows into the sea without adequate treatment [6], creating risks of diseases such as viral hepatitis, dysentery, poliomyelitis and typhoid, all of which are endemic in the region. In fact, it is widely accepted that the Mediterranean Sea has several features, meteorological and oceanographic among others, that configure a system of complex phenomenology. It is worth noting also that the Mediterranean sea's physical features, as being almost closed to other water masses, make its ecosystems vulnerable to problems associated to the lack of water circulation and renewal, as excessive pollutant concentration, being derived from human activities or natural processes. The release of pollutants into coastal zones from municipal and/or industrial drainage systems is a problem with a considerable environmental impact. The use of submarine outfalls constitutes at the same time a procedure for wastewater

* Corresponding author: antoni.grau@upc.edu

treatment, usually complementing operations on sewage treatment plants, given the appropriate weather conditions. In some environmental limit cases, the high level of pollution in water that arrives to the beach causes diseases and damages to swimmers. Specifically, this fact occurs in the beaches of the city of Barcelona (capital of Catalonia) because of the Besòs wastewater plant. For this reason, when the emergence warning is generated, an automatic control system for regulating the water pollution (E.coli) in Besòs outfall output in an efficient and rapidly way is proposed. This automatic control system consists on a Smith Predictor (SP) scheme using a PI computed by Ziegler-Nichols method [7].

The outfall studied in this work dumps wastewater processed by Besòs sewage treatment plant. This plant is able to process up to 520,000 m3 of sewage water a day. Daily, in average more than 390,000 m3 are treated in the plant and about 80% of this sewage volume comes from population living in Barcelona Metropolitan Area and its industry. The urban wastewater plant ejects treated water to the see by an outfall about 3km away from the coast. This outfall is formed with hundreds of short segments assembled in a unique pipe that enters to the sea to throw the processed wastewater in the plant. This water received a secondary treatment (physical and biological treatment) meaning that the output water is not drinking water, still biologically polluted (bacteria, viruses...). This wastewater is dumped at 50m depth in the Mediterranean Sea.

The wastewater is pumped to the submarine outfall, and the secondary sludge, containing up 60% of initial organic matter, is removed to be dehydrated and moved to Montcada sludge treatment plant.

Wastewater pollutant diffusion is originated in the dumping spot area, with a given initial concentration C_0, and as the wastewater is dragged and diluted by water currents, concentration is reduced and dispersed around the area. In a general case, organic pollutant will reach coastline with very low concentrations, almost negligible. In fact, most of the days, this negligible pollution will disperse mainly towards south, in response to northern winds dominance, and the circulation currents usually present in the area. But given south eastern and especially eastern winds, there exists the risk that biological pollution disperses towards the coast. This risk increases under certain meteorological conditions, as cloudy skies blocking solar radiation incidence, or cold waters inhibiting micro-biota which normally predates upon bacteriological pollutants. These particular conditions use to take place during storms with some stationary effects due to year's season.

The paper is organized as follows. In section 2 the mathematical models used in this research are presented. The first is a control model, a simplified one for contaminants transportation to be implemented in real time, and the other model for the bacteriological concentration at the outfall exit. Both models are used in the main contribution part of this paper, pollution detection in the sampled areas, that is, in the beaches in front of the outfall, which are described in section 3. Based on real data, a set of results are presented during periods of beach pollution. These data have been used to test our model and as a validation method to prove the feasibility and reliability of the pollution approach that is presented in the paper. Section 4 collects and discusses those experiments and validation with real data.

2 Plant Control Model: Outfall Pollution and Bactericidal Model

The pollutant components concentration decreases along the trail formed by water currents, due transport and transformation processes which affect differently each pollutant component [8-9]. These coast pollutant concentrations can be studied through a mass conservation equation, introducing transport and transformation processes, and external gain/loss gives place to a general form mass conservation equation, or convection-diffusion-reaction equation, Eq. (1):

$$\frac{\partial C}{\partial t} = -U\frac{\partial C}{\partial x} - V\frac{\partial C}{\partial y} - W\frac{\partial C}{\partial z} + \frac{\partial}{\partial x}\left[K_x\frac{\partial C}{\partial x}\right] + \frac{\partial}{\partial y}\left[K_y\frac{\partial C}{\partial y}\right] + \frac{\partial}{\partial z}\left[K_z\frac{\partial C}{\partial z}\right] + \lambda C + I \quad (1)$$

where C is the pollutant component concentration (mass/volume); U, V, and W are considered water speed vector components (length/time) in x, y and z axis respectively; K_x, K_y and K_z denote turbulent diffusion coefficients (area/time) in x, y and z axis respectively; and finally I refers to external gain/loss contribution speed (mass/volume·time).

It is assumed that water currents induce a constant speed horizontal advection process, which along turbulence phenomena, yields a dilution plume. This plume grows along x axis, describing depth through z axis, and y axis perpendicular to both. Vertical diffusion is not accounted under the assumption that the formed diffusion plume will expand through the depth, considering the sea a well-mixed mass of uniform density. All these assumptions allow to simplifying Eq. (1) into Eq. (2):

$$-U_a\frac{\partial C}{\partial x} + \frac{\partial}{\partial y}\left[K_y\frac{\partial C}{\partial y}\right] + \lambda C = 0 \quad (2)$$

Solving this equation by the finite differences numerical method [10], being U_a the advective velocity and C the pollutant concentration at each point (x,y) of the outfall output, these values are calculated and E.coli measured in CFU/100ml.

2.1. Modeling bactericide system

Chlorine-based disinfectants are commonly used in wastewater treatment [11]. In order to manage coastal pollution due to the wastewater that arrives from a submarine outfall under extreme weather conditions as mentioned in previous sections, authors have developed a simplified mathematical model that represents this process of disinfection. The bactericidal model is formulated by means of the Conservation Mass Law and the Chick's Law [12] that state:

$$C_{in}(t) - C_{out}(t) = \frac{1}{k}\frac{dC_{out}(t)}{dt} \qquad (3)$$

From Eq. (3), the rapidity of the variation of the biomass is proportional to the quantity of microorganisms (in our case, basically E.coli) present in a certain moment. The variables and parameters are the following: C_{in} is the input pollutant concentration of the wastewater, C_{out} is the output concentration of the wastewater, and k is the biomass variation parameter [t^{-1}] (disinfection constant) initiating at the wastewater input and the water pollution concentration at the wastewater output has been developed, following the next equation:

$$G_b(s) = \frac{C_{out}(s)}{C_{in}(s)} = \frac{1}{(s+k)} \qquad (4)$$

Usually, this parameter is formulated in an empirical way: $k = k_d + k_s I$ where k_d [d^{-1}] is the background or 'dark' disinfection rate, k_s [$cm^2 cal^{-1}$] is the 'light only' disinfection rate coefficient and I is the radiation [$cal\ cm^{-2}\ d^{-1}$]. A good review of models can be found in [13].
In the cases where the variation of temperature is the most important parameter, authors use Marais formulation [14] because the temperature is the only environmental factor considered, $k_d = 2.6 \times 1.19^{(T-20)}$, $k_s = 0$, with temperature T [°C]. In the experiments presented in this paper water temperature is considered at 21°C and 10°C, in summer and winter respectively, and the disinfection constant is $k = 0.1289$ [h^{-1}] and $k = 0.019$ [h^{-1}], respectively.
In the cases where the irradiation is the most important parameter usually the Mayo, [15], formulation is used:

$$k_d = 0.108\,, k_s = \frac{5.74\times10^{-4}}{Z} \qquad (5)$$

where Z [cm] is the sea depth. The value that authors use in these experiments for the coefficient k is set to 0.7687 [h^{-1}].
Initially, water coming from the sewage system is treated in the wastewater plant and it is thrown away to the sea by the submarine outfall. When water goes through the outfall (like a pipe in control system), a delay is introduced that can be represented as $\tau = L/v$, with $v = Q/A$, where L is the outfall length, v is the water velocity, Q is the water flow and A is the outfall pipe area. In Besòs outfall, with the present geometry and conditions, the estimated delay is $\tau = 0.3949$h (23m,41s,64cs).
In Figure 1, the diagram for water concentration system is shown; this system contains chlorine-based disinfection applied in the wastewater plant that later on is transported to the sea by the outfall. Therefore, the transfer function that relates the outfall output pollutant concentration with the input wastewater concentration is:

$$G_s(s) = \frac{C_{outd}(s)}{C_{in}(s)} = \frac{1}{(s+k)}e^{-s\tau} \qquad (6)$$

which corresponds to a first order plus delay time (FOPDT) plant. This FOPDT transfer function in canonical form has a gain, $K = 1/k$, a time constant, $T = 1/k$ and a delay τ.

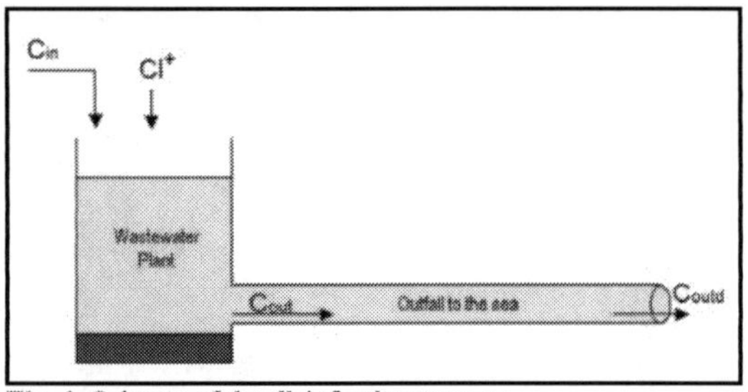

Fig. 1. Scheme of the disinfection system

3 Automatic Control System

In order to control water pollution at the output of the outfall when there are emergency warnings, a suitable option is to dose chlorine (Cl^{+}) to lower the E.coli concentration in treated water before it goes to the sea by the outfall. This water, at the end, can reach the beaches of the city of Barcelona causing an unnecessary and hazardous problem to population.
The control strategy that was decided by the plant officers was carried out using a supervisor and a low level controller [16]. The supervisor is in charge of activating the control system when any warning is detected. This control system has to generate the desired reference concentration at the output of the outfall in order that the polluted water arrives to the beach without any biological danger independently of the climate conditions present in the sea in that moment. If the biological charge at the output of the outfall is too high, the sea cannot kill enough bacteria before the water reaches the coast pushed by the storm and strong associated winds. The low level controller is in charge of supplying chlorine (Cl^{+}) to the concentration C_{in} before this water leaves the plant to the sea. The amount of chlorine to dose is controlled until the desired reference is reached. In order to guarantee the system internal stability and to compensate the system delay, an Internal Model Control (IMC) scheme is used (see Figure 2).

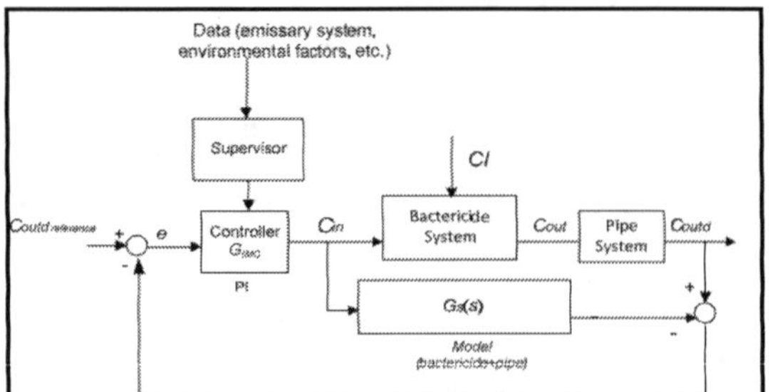

Fig. 2. IMC scheme of the disinfection system.

When an IMC scheme is used and the system is represented by an FOPDT model, the naturally achieved controller is a simple classical PI controller. Through the IMC scheme most of the delay is compensated but, as

obvious, there is a delay modelling error. In the worst case, the delay estimation error is 2.37 minutes.
It is represented by an unstructured multiplicative uncertainty [17-18]. Recently, a growing interest in the derivation of simple rules that offer a high level of robustness in IMC approach has appeared. In this sense, the rule SIMC is of special interest, proposed in [19] and it is oriented to improve the efficiency of regulation. Generally, developed tuning methods based on control techniques with internal model use pole cancellation and therefore they produce very slow responses. Taking into account this effect, in this new procedure the IMC tuning rules are modified in order to achieve swift responses in front of setpoint changes. For the PI controller tuning, a FOPDT model is used as a basis. The SIMC tuning for a PI controller (with K_p controller proportional constant and Ti controller integrator time) can be expressed as:

$$K_p K = \frac{1}{2\tau}, \quad \frac{T_i}{T} = \min\{1{,}8\tau\} \tag{7}$$

Detailed information can be found in [20].

4 Results and Discussion

In order to test the feasibility of the automated control system using a PI controller presented in this paper, authors have prepared a set of cases that simulates real situations that happen along the year in the Mediterranean Sea. The presented control methodology is applied for these cases.
Table 1 and Table 2 show the different cases divided into 2 big sections: winter and summer cases. This division is done because there are clearly separated weather conditions in the area. The Mediterranean area, due to its location, has a mild climate without extreme conditions, but nonetheless there are some differences regarding the water temperature, wind conditions and solar radiation.
The bound values for water pollution have been taken according to the Directive [20] of the European Parliament and of the Council of 15 February 2006 concerning the management of bathing water quality and repealing Directive 76/160/EEC, and it specifies a limit of 500 CFU/100ml to consider safe water to human activities.
The parameters that are used to select the setpoint to obtain a suitable water quality according the present European directive are the wind direction (WD, in degrees), wind velocity (WV, in m/s), total suspended solids (TSS, in kg/m^3), cloud coverage (CC, unity), water temperature and solar altitude (in degrees).
For these experiments, the values that authors have chosen for each season are: 1) Winter season: water temperature 10°C, this is an average value for the most cold months of year; the sun altitude has been taken as 20° respect the horizon, a representative value for those months of the year although Barcelona is at 41° 24'N latitude; 2) Summer season: water temperature 21°, average value for summer months, sun altitude of 45°, much higher than in winter time, and also very representative of Barcelona sun irradiation.

For the remainder parameters values, the following values have been taken, as representative values. Authors chose two values for most of them, quite different one from the other, to see the model behaviour in front those combination of values.

Table 1. Parameters and Output Model Concentration (winter).

Winter cases for water temp.=10°C; solar altitude=20° WD= wind direction (degrees); WV= wind velocity (m/s); TSS= total suspended solids (g/m³); CC= cloud coverage (unitary); C=concentration (CFU/100ml)					
Case	*WD*	*WV*	*TSS*	*CC*	*C*
1	45°	2	799	0.99	268.30
2	45°	2	799	0.15	268.80
3	45°	2	100	0.99	54.81
4	45°	2	100	0.15	25.97
5	45°	20	799	0.99	1868.90
6	45°	20	799	0.15	660.00
7	45°	20	100	0.99	381.70
8	45°	20	100	0.15	360.00
9	311°	2	799	0.99	256.80
10	311°	2	799	0.15	257.00
11	311°	2	100	0.99	133.75
12	311°	2	100	0.15	125.36
13	311°	20	799	0.99	559.70
14	311°	20	799	0.15	533.70
15	311°	20	100	0.99	302.90
16	311°	20	100	0.15	253.70

Each combination has a real meaning and it appears during the year at least once. For the winter season values the chosen values have been:

- Wind direction: 45° and 311°.
- Wind velocity: 2 and 20 m/s.
- Total suspended solids: 799 and 100 g/m^3, this parameter is considered as a water quality measurement.
- Cloud coverage: 0.99 and 0.15 over 1. This fraction corresponds to the amount of clouds in sky, a value of 1 corresponds to complete coverage of the sky, and a value of 0 means clear sky.

For the summer season, the chosen values have been:

- Wind direction: 0° and 311°.
- Wind velocity: 2 and 20 m/s.
- Total suspended solids: 799 and 100 g/m3.
- Cloud coverage: 0.90 and 0.1(over 1) which are more realistic values for this season.

Table 2. Parameters and Output Model Concentration (summer).

Summer cases for water temp=21°C; solar incidence=45° WD= wind direction (degrees); WV= wind velocity (m/s); TSS= total suspended solids (g/m3); CC= cloud coverage (unitary); C=concentration (CFU/100ml)					
Case	*WD*	*WV*	*TSS*	*CC*	*C*
1	0°	2	799	0.90	279.10
2	0°	2	799	0.10	279.08
3	0°	2	100	0.90	134.40
4	0°	2	100	0.10	75.68
5	0°	20	799	0.90	765.30
6	0°	20	799	0.10	654.06
7	0°	20	100	0.90	461.92
8	0°	20	100	0.10	265.60
9	311°	2	799	0.90	364.40
10	311°	2	799	0.10	364.80
11	311°	2	100	0.90	258.97
12	311°	2	100	0.10	142.47
13	311°	20	799	0.90	725.77
14	311°	20	799	0.10	625.78
15	311°	20	100	0.90	397.10
16	311°	20	100	0.10	247.80

The wind direction is restricted to those orientations that really can carry bacteriological material to the beach, because the outfall is located to the east of the shore, and only a range of directions are of interest to study the pollution at the beach; those values range from 280° to 60°. Moreover, the Catalan coast is slightly oriented from NNE to SSW, having its normal at 311° in the area of study.

The choice of wind velocity is based on realistic values, ranging from a gentle breeze (2m/s) during most of the time in this area to storms (20m/s) that appear at the end of summer (2nd-3rd week of September mainly) and in winter. Those winds can happen with rain (a high cloud coverage ratio) or in sunny days (low cloud coverage ratio). The value for suspended solids also appears from the experience in the Mediterranean shores, happening episodes of high pollution some days of the year or low pollution other periods. Authors consider that the values chosen for the experiments cover a wide range of combination that in fact cover most of the time of winter and summer periods.

The behaviour of the model using the parameters representing the winter season can be seen in Table 1. The output of the model, expressed as the microbial contamination by bacteria, which is expressed in Colony Forming Units (CFU), a measure of the bacterial population, can be seen in column with "*C*", concentration. As a reference of this output, the limits set by the European Community for the quality of coastal waters correspond to concentration values below 500 CFU/100ml representing accepted concentrations to consider the beaches as allowed bathing areas, whereas those values above this limit represent coastal pollution and therefore the bath ban in beaches. In some cases, the limit of 500CFU/100ml is reached, and thus the beach should be closed for bathing activities. Fortunately, this limit is achieved only in very special conditions and it happens in average 2-3 times a year. During the winter season, it is not very significant the coastal pollution because the null activity in the beaches but it is reached in cases 5, 6, 13 and 14. In those cases, the wind velocity was high (20m/s) as well as the suspended solids (799g/m^3) and it does not depend on the cloud coverage, the wind is so high that the sun cannot kill enough bacteria during their travel to the beach. For the rest of cases, the output concentration of the model is always below the allowed limit.

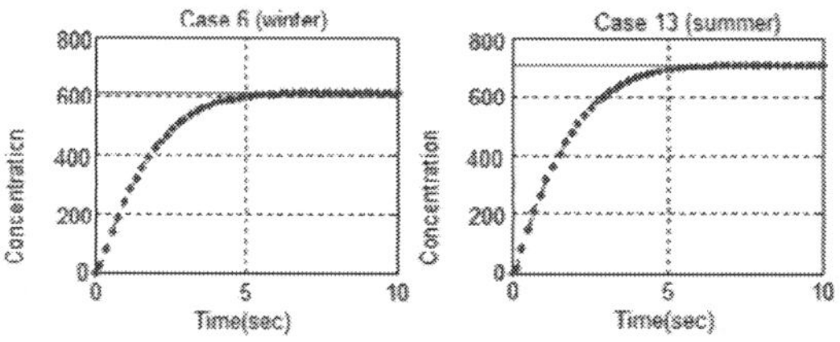

Fig. 3. Control results in case 6 (winter) and case 13 (summer). The concentration is expressed in CFU/100ml, reaching values above the recommended ones for bathing.

During the summertime, the output concentration values are higher than in winter because the water temperature and the irradiation in summer permit that bacteria can develop more rapidly. However, the pollution episodes are still rare and only in cases 5, 6, 13 and 14 the output values are above the pollution limits. In summertime, the values are in general in the range of good-sufficient quality due to the mentioned reasons. Those values have been compared with the historic values registered in the monitoring stations and there is a high coincidence with the episodes forecasted with the proposed model. Once the meteorological parameters are known, it is possible to select the setpoint to achieve a suitable water quality in the coast when there is any warning of pollution in the beach; in that moment the automatic control is activated to avoid that polluted water arrives to the coast.

The control results of the cases 6 and 13 for winter and summer, respectively, can be seen in Figure 3. The plant (wastewater and outfall) pollutant concentration has a different behaviour in case 6 (winter) and case 13 (summer), but in both cases the biological charge that arrives to the coast is above the allowed values in the European Directive for safe bathing. The automation of the disinfection system by the control scheme that cancels the delay and supplies the needed chlorine amount takes in average 5 minutes in both cases, when in regular circumstances, after a manual process, could take 2-3 hours to act and regulate the pollution in the water.

5 Conclusions

A novel automatic control system has been presented in order to cancel the water pollution in the coast. Under certain weather conditions, the biologically polluted water that the outfall of the Besòs wastewater plant throws to the sea arrives with bacteria levels higher than the recommended ones by a European Directive of safe bathing. In those cases, the beaches have to close the access to the population until the hazard disappears. With the new control system that authors present in this research, when those weather conditions are present, the wastewater is chlorinated in the plant before been thrown to the sea with a potential danger to pollute the coast. The automatic system is based in a Smith Predictor that cancels the delays in the outfall and seawater transport, reducing drastically the time to act before any emergence warning is generated.

This work has been funded by the Spanish Ministry of Science Project "ColRobTransp" MINECO DPI2016-78957-R.

References

1. S.I. Samsudin, M.F. Rahmat, N.A. Wahab, Nonlinear PI Control with Adaptive Interaction Algorithm for Multivariable Wastewater Treatment Process. Mathematical Problems in Engineering, Volume 2014 (2014), Article ID 475053, 13 pages.
2. Y. Zhang, T. Zhao, A. Zhou, Z. Zhang, W. Liu, Scenario Based Municipal Wastewater Estimation: Development and Application of a Dynamic Simulation Model. Modelling and Simulation in Engineering, Volume 2016 (2016), Article ID 1746310, 13 pages.
3. M. Meneses, H. Concepción, R. Vilanova, Joint Environmental and Economical Analysis of Wastewater Treatment Plants Control Strategies: A Benchmark Scenario Analysis. Sustainability 2016, 8(4), 360; doi:10.3390/su8040360.
4. L. Liu, G. Hall, P. Champagne, Effects of Environmental Factors on the Disinfection Performance of a Wastewater Stabilization Pond Operated in a Temperate Climate. Water 2016, 8(1), 5; doi:10.3390/w8010005.
5. United States Environmental Protection Agency EPA, Pollution in beaches. Available online: http://water.epa.gov/type/oceb/beaches/pollution.cfm (accessed on 24 March 2017).
6. M. Kellis, I.K. Kalavrouziotis, P. Gikas, Review of Wasterwater Reuse in the Mediterranean Countries, focusing on Regulations and Policies for Municipal and Industrial Applications. Global NEST Journal, Vol 15, No 3, pp 333-350, 2013.
7. J. Gámiz, J. Gámiz, PID parameters tuning in control loops for industrial processes, Revista Técnica Industrial, vol. 290, pp. 46-50, December, 2010, (in Spanish).
8. J.M. Abril, M.M. Abdel-Aal, A modelling study on hydrodynamics and pollutant dispersion in the Suez Canal, Ecological Modelling, vol. 128(1), pp.1-17, April 2000.
9. P.E. Carreras, A.N. Menéndez, Mathematical simulation of pollutant dispersion, Ecological Modelling, vol. 52, pp. 29-40, 1990.
10. R. LeVeque, Finite Difference Methods for Ordinary and Partial Differential Equations: Steady-State and Time-Dependent Problems (Classics in Applied Mathematic), Siam Ed., 2010.
11. J. Gamiz, Y. Bolea, A. Grau, J. Gamiz, F. Luque, J.M. Vargas, Automation of chlorination process for drinking water treatment plant: Control strategies. In Proceedings of the 10th IEEE International Conference on Industrial Informatics, INDIN, pp. 337-341, 2012.
12. H. Chick, An investigation of the Laws of Desinfection, The Journal of Hygiene, vol. 8(1), pp.92-158, 1908.
13. S. Liu, Fecal Coliform Decay and Regrowth Kinetics in an Anearobic Dairy Wastewater Environment, MsC. Thesis, Louisiana State University, May 2002.
14. G.R. Marais, Faecal bacteria kinetics in stabilization ponds, J. Env. Engrg Div., Am. Soc. Civ. Engrs, 100 (1) , pp. 139–199, 1974.
15. A.W. Mayo, Effect of pond depth on bacterial mortality rate, J. Envir. Engrg. ASCE, 155 (5), pp. 964–997, 1989.
16. A. Leva, A.M. Colombo, On the IMC-based synthesis of the feedback block of ISA PID regulators, Transactions of the Institute of Measurement and Control 26(5), pp.417-440, 2004.
17. S. Skogestad, I. Postlethwaite, Multivariable Control. Analysis and Design, John Wiley & Sons, New York, 1997.
18. R.S. Sanchez Peña, M. Sznaizer, Robust Systems Theory and Application, John Wiley & Sons, New York, 1998.
19. S. Skogestad, Simple analytic rules for model reduction and PID controller tuning, Journal of Process Control 13, pp.291-309, 2003.
20. Directive 2006/7/EC, Official Journal L 064, 04/03/2006, pp. 37–51. 2006.

Liquid Storage Cylindrical Tank - Earthquake Analysis

Kamila Kotrasová[1,*], and *Eva* Kormaníková[1]

[1]Department of Structural Mechanics, Institute of Structural Engineering, Faculty of Civil Engineering, The Technical University of Kosice, Vysokoskolska 4, 042 00 Kosice, Slovak Republic

Abstract. The ground-supported cylindrical tanks are used to store a variety of liquids. This paper provides the theoretical background for concrete containers fixed to rigid foundations due to earthquake events, describing of fluid hydrodynamic impulsive and convective (sloshing) effects on tank. Seismic responses: base shear, the bending moment and overturning moment are calculated by using the response spectra for Slovak republic risk region. As the examples is analysed the ground supported cylindrical concrete tanks for variable fluid filling.

1 Introduction

Industrial facilities contain a large number of constructions and structural components. Both building and non-building structures typically can be found in an industrial/chemical plant. Above ground pressurised tanks are typical examples of non-building structures of such sites.

Ground-supported storage tanks are built for storing a variety of liquids, e.g. water for drinking and fire-fighting, petroleum, oil, liquefied natural gas, chemical fluids, chemical and radioactive fluid wastes. Liquid storage containers are strategically very important structures, since they have vital uses in industries, nuclear power plants and are connected to public life. Seismic safely of liquid tanks is of considerable importance [1–7]. Water storage tanks should remain functional in the post earthquake period to ensure potable water supply to earthquake-affected regions and to cater the need for fighting demand. Industrial liquid tanks containing highly toxic and inflammable liquids and these tanks should not lose their contents during the earthquake. Satisfactory performance of tanks during strong ground shaking is crucial for there modern facilities. The seismic behaviour of liquid storage tanks is highly complex problem due to liquid-structure interaction [9, 13-19].

The liquid storage containers on basis of their structure with respect to ground can be classified into three categories: underground tanks, tank resting on grounds, overhead tanks – elevated tanks supported on standing. The Liquid storage tanks may be from the shape point of view following types: circular, rectangular, square, polygonal, spherical, conical, funnel tanks. I most cases the underground and on ground container are cylindrical or rectangular is shape but the shape of construction. Rectangular tanks are used to store small capacity of fluid. For economy these thanks should square in plan and their height should half of the side. Rectangular tanks are uneconomical for large capacities [8, 10-12].

2. Cylindrical of fluid filled tank due to earthquake events

A typical cylindrical tank is shown in Fig. 1. It essentially consists of a base plate rested on the ground and a vertically erected shell wall. Optionally, there may be a floating or fixed roof to protect the liquid content from the outside air, column(s) inside the tank to support the roof, ring girders to enhance the stiffness of the wall and to improve its stability, and anchorage along the border of the base plate to prevent uplift. For a broad tank with its diameter, and therefore the tank is generally left unanchored.

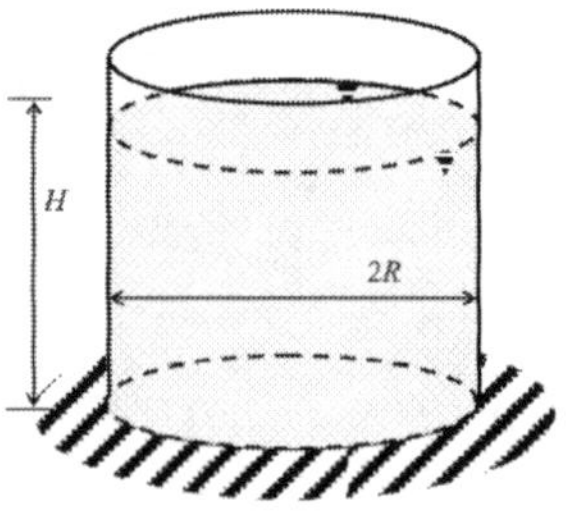

Fig. 1. Cylindrical tank.

Under the static condition, a cylindrical liquid storage tank is subjected to axisymmetric hydrostatic pressure caused by the liquid content acting radially outwards on the vertical tank shell wall. Hoop tensile force is developed in tank shell wall to withstand this pressure. In static design of a cylindrical tank, the required shell thickness of the shell wall is determined

[*] Corresponding author: author@e-mail.org

DOI: 10.1051/matecconf/201712504009

by the magnitude of this hoop tensile force. Under the static condition the base plate and the other parts of the tank structure bear no significant load and thus can be designed just to comply with the minimum structural requirements.

When a liquid storage tank is subjected to seismic load, vibrational motion of the liquid content is developed due to the ground excitation acting on it via the tank structure. The first one, defined as the "impulsive mode", consists of the liquid particles moving in unison with the motion of the tank structure. The second one, defined as the "convective mode" or usually called "sloshing", consists of the liquid particles near the free surface oscillating vertically. The resultant load effect of the liquid motion is generally represented by a total base shears and an total bending and overturning moments. In response to the hydrodynamic load, axial compressive and tensile stresses as well as additional hoop stress are developed in the tank shell wall. These stresses are asymmetric and much greater than that due to the hydrostatic pressure under the static condition. For an unanchored tank subjected to a sufficiently large resultant of total overturning moment, a portion of the base plate will separate from the support foundation. Accompanying with the base plate uplift, extensive deformations with significant out-of round distortion occur in the tank shell wall. The phenomenon is called the "uplift mechanism". The "uplift mechanism" is highly nonlinear to the applied load.

3 Seismic analysis of fluid filled tank

The problem of fluid-structure interaction is very important in case of fluid filled tanks. The motion of fluid in the tank is possible to define using the simple quasistatic model, in which the inertial forces are defined by hydrostatic and hydrodynamic pressure on the tank wall.

3.1 Hydrodynamic pressure

The seismic loads acting on wall and bottom of flexible cylindrical tanks (Figure 2) can be divided into the following components:

- the rigid impulsive component, caused by the inertia of the liquid, if the rigid tank moves together with the foundation,
- the convective load component, where the fluid vibrates in the rigid tank (sloshing),
- the impulsive flexible component tank shell of fluid (e.g. steel tanks).

The motion of the fluid contained in a rigid cylinder may by expressed as the sum of two separate contributions, which called "rigid" impulsive and convective, respectively. The "rigid" impulsive component satisfies exactly the boundary conditions at the walls and the bottom of the tank, but gives (incorrectly, due to the presence of the waves in the dynamic response) zero pressure at the original position of the free surface of the fluid in the static situation. The "convective" term does not alter those boundary conditions that are already satisfied, while fulfilling the correct equilibrium condition at the free surface. Use is made of a cylindrical coordinate system: r, z, θ, with origin at the centre of the tank bottom and the radius are denoted by H and R, respectively, ρ is the mass density of the fluid, while $\xi=r/R$ is non-dimensional radius and $\zeta=z/H$ is non-dimensional coordinate.

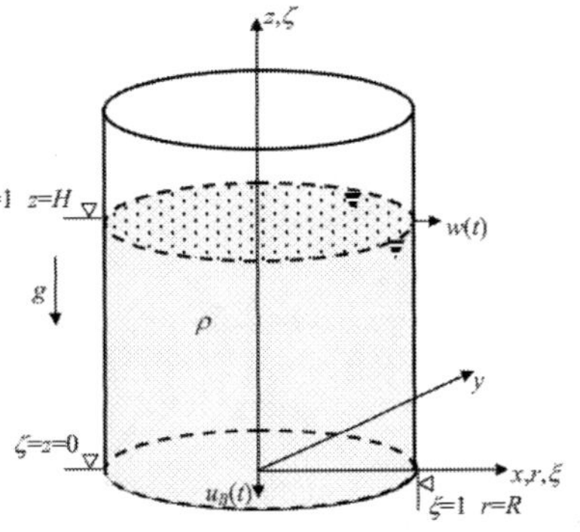

Fig. 2. Cylindrical tank.

3.1.1 Rigid impulsive component

The spatial-temporal variation of the "rigid" impulsive pressure is given by the expression

$$p_i(\xi,\zeta,\theta,t) = C_i(\xi,\zeta)\rho H \cos\theta A_g(t), \tag{1}$$

where

$$C_i(\xi,\zeta) = 2\sum_{n=0}^{\infty} \frac{(-1)^n}{I_1'(\nu_n/\gamma)\nu_n^2}\cos(\nu_n\zeta)\, I_1\left(\frac{\nu_n}{\gamma}\xi\right), \tag{2}$$

$\nu_n = \pi\dfrac{2n+1}{2}$ and $\gamma = H/R$, $I_1(\cdot)$ is the modified Bessel function of order 1 and $I_1'(\cdot)$ is derivate can be expressed in terms of modified Bessel function of order 0 and 1 $I_1'(x) = \dfrac{dI_1(x)}{dx} = I_0(x) - \dfrac{I_1(x)}{x}$. The function C_i gives the distribution along the height of p_i. θ is angle of circumference, $\gamma=H/R$ is tank slenderness parameter, $A_g(t)$ is the horizontal ground acceleration time-history in free-field with peak value denoted by a_g as a result of an equivalent single-degree-of-freedom system with a impulsive period T_i.

3.1.2 Convective pressure component

The spatial-temporal variation of the convective pressure component is given

$$p_c(\xi,\zeta,\theta,t) = \rho\sum_{n=1}^{\infty} \psi_n \cos(\nu_n\gamma\zeta)\, J_1(\nu_n\xi)\cos\theta A_{cn}(t), \tag{3}$$

where

$$\psi_n = \frac{2R}{(\lambda_n^2-1)J_1(\lambda_n)\cosh(\lambda_n\gamma)} \tag{4}$$

DOI: 10.1051/matecconf/201712504009

J_1 is Bessel function of the first order, λ_n are the roots of the first-order Bessel function of the first kind (λ_1=1.8412; λ_2=5.3314; λ_3=8.5363, λ_4=11.71, λ_5=14.66 and $\lambda_{5+i}=\lambda_5+5\,i$ for i is given 1,2,...). $A_{cn}(t)$ is acceleration time-history of the response of a single degree of freedom oscillator having a circular frequency ω_{cn} given by

$$\omega_{cn} = \sqrt{\frac{g\lambda_n \tanh(\lambda_n \gamma)}{R}}, \tag{5}$$

so

$$T_{cn} = \frac{2\pi}{\sqrt{\frac{g\lambda_n \tanh(\lambda_n \gamma)}{R}}} \tag{6}$$

and a 0.5% damping ratio appropriate for the sloshing of the fluid.

Only the first oscillating (sloshing) mode and frequency of the oscillating liquid (n=1) needs to be considered in expression for design purposes.

$$\omega_{c1} = 4.2/\sqrt{R} \tag{7}$$

which, for the usual values of R yields periods of oscillation of the order of few seconds.
Only the first convective mode of vibration needs to be considered for practical applications in the analysis.

3.1.3 Flexible component.

It is normally unconservative to consider the tank as rigid. In flexible tanks the fluid pressure is usually expressed as the sum of tree contributions, referred to as: "rigid" impulsive, sloshing and flexible. The third satisfied the condition that the radial velocity of the fluid along the wall equals the deformation velocity of the tank wall, as well as the conditions of zero vertical velocity at the tank bottom and zero pressure at the free surface of the fluid. The dynamic coupling between the sloshing and the flexible components is very weak, due to the large differences between the frequencies of the sloshing motion and of the deformation of the wall, which allows determining the third component independently of the others.

The radial distribution of the flexible impulsive pressure on the tank bottom is qualitatively the same as for the rigid impulsive pressure. Assuming the modes as known, the flexible pressure distribution on the walls has the form

$$p_f(\zeta,\theta,t) = \rho H \psi \cos\theta \sum_{n=1}^{\infty} \cos(\nu_n \zeta) A_{fn}(t) \tag{8}$$

For a horizontal earthquake ground motion, the response of various SDOF systems may be calculated independently and then combined to give the base shear and overturning moment. The most tanks have the parameter tank slendernes γ, whereby $0.3 < \gamma < 3$. The parameter tank slendernes is given by relation $\gamma = H/L$, where H is the filling height of fluid in the tank and $2L$ is inside width of tank.

Values m_i, h_i, h_i^*, m_{cn}, h_{cn}, and h_{cn}^* for rigid vertical circular tanks on ground, fixed to the foundation in Eurocode 8 - 4 [13] are shown in Fig. 7 – 10.

4 Mechanical model of fluid cylindrical filled tank due to earthquake events

The dynamic analysis of a liquid - filled tank may be carried out using the concept of generalized single - degree - of freedom (SDOF) systems representing the impulsive and convective modes of vibration of the tank - liquid system as shown in Fig. 3. For practical applications, only the first convective modes of vibration need to be considered in the analysis, mechanical model. The impulsive mass of liquid m_i is rigidly attached to tank wall at height h_i. Similarly convective mass m_{cn} is attached to the tank wall at height h_{cn} by a spring of stiffness k_{cn}. The mass, height and natural period of each SDOF system are obtained by the methods described in [17].

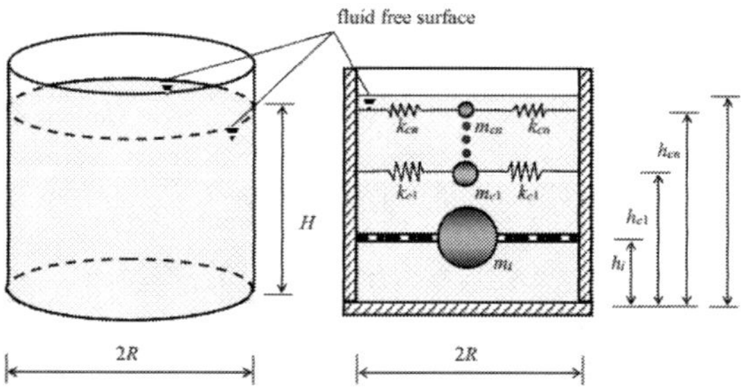

Fig. 3. Liquid-filled tank modeled by generalized single degree of freedom systems.

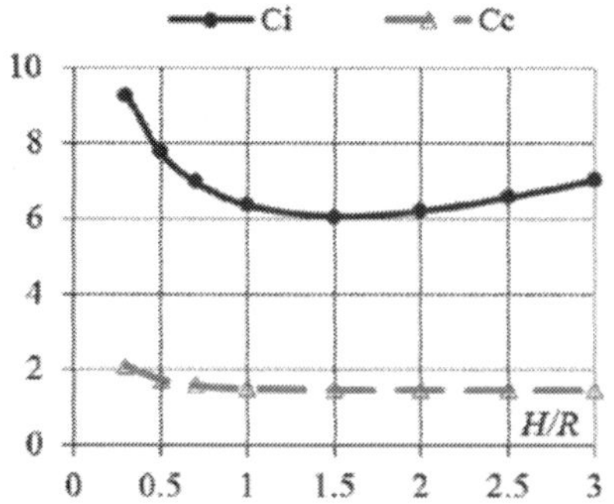

Fig. 4. Coefficients C_i and C_c as function of the tank slenderness parameter $\gamma = H/R$.

For a ground supported cylindrical tank, in which the wall is rigidly connected with the base slab, time period of impulse mode of vibration T_i in [s] is given by

$$T_i = C_i \frac{H\sqrt{\rho}}{\sqrt{t/R}\sqrt{E}} \tag{9}$$

DOI: 10.1051/matecconf/201712504009

where C_i is coefficient of time period for impulsive mode.

$$T_c = C_c\sqrt{R} \quad (10)$$

C_c is coefficient of time period for convective mode. The values of C_i, C_c are given from Fig. 4.

The values of the masses m_i and m_c are given from Fig. 5.

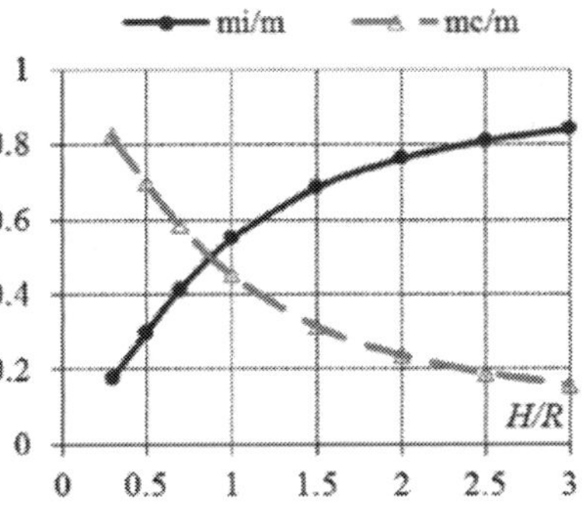

Fig. 5. Ratios m_i/m and m_c/m as function of the tank slenderness parameter $\gamma = H/R$.

The values of the corresponding heights of masses above the base h_i, h_c are given from Fig. 8 and h_i^*, h_c^* from Fig. 11.

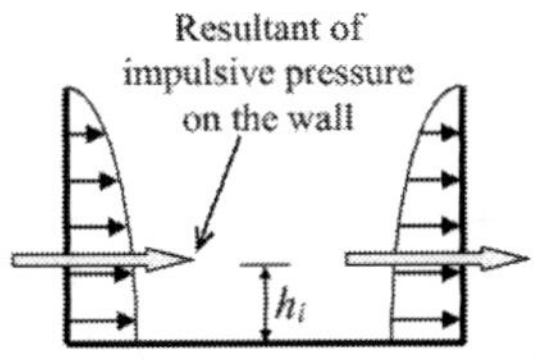

Fig. 6. Resultant of impulsive pressure on the wall.

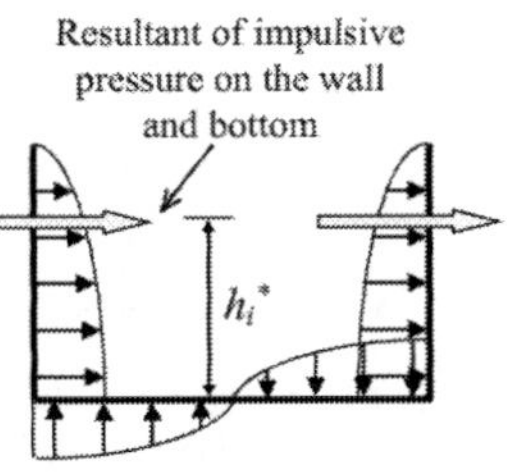

Fig. 7. Resultant of impulsive pressure on the wall and bottom.

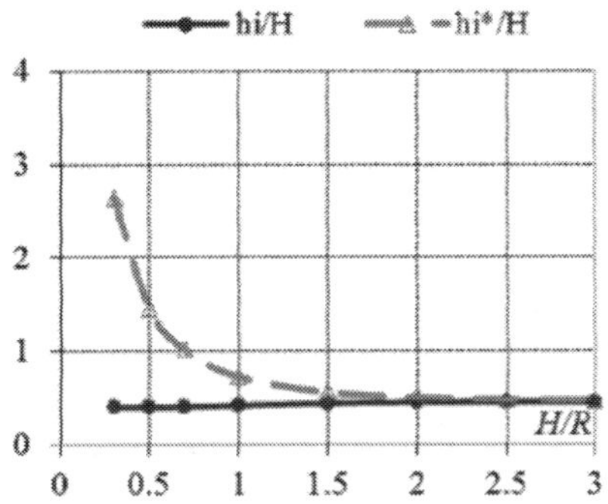

Fig. 8. Ratios h_i/H and h_i^*/H as functions of the parameter tank slenderness $\gamma = H/R$.

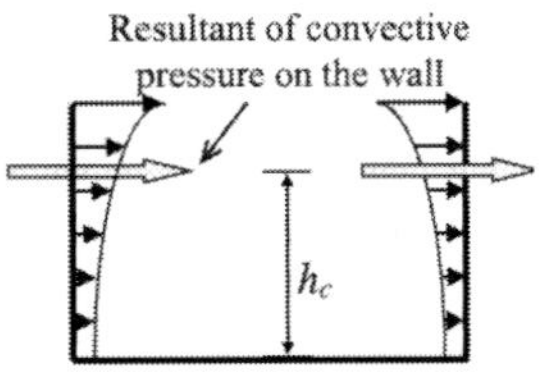

Fig. 9. Resultant of convective pressure on the wall.

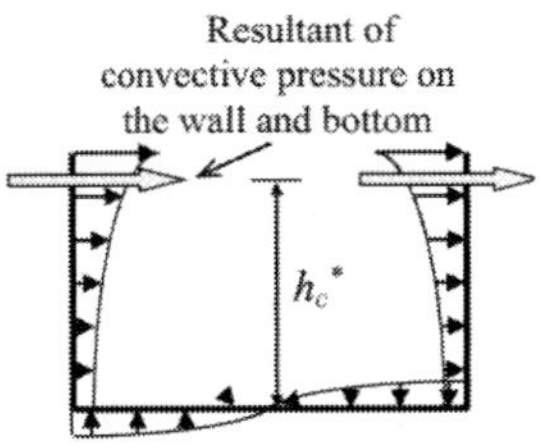

Fig. 10. Resultant of convective pressure on the wall and bottom.

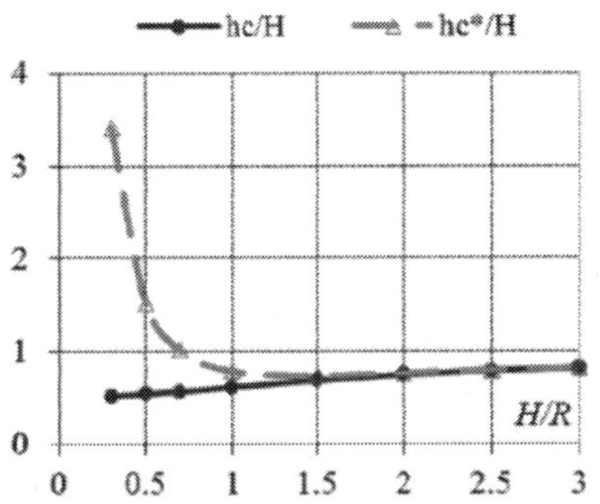

Fig. 11. Ratios h_c/H and h_c^*/H as functions of the tank slenderness parameter $\gamma = H/R$.

Seismic coefficient $S_e(T)$ will be calculated separately for impulsive $S_e(T_i)$ and convective mode $S_e(T_c)$. The impulsive horizontal seismic coefficient is obtained from 2 % damped elastic response spectrum for steel or pre-stressed concrete tanks and 5 % damped elastic response spectrum for concrete and masonry tanks. The convective seismic coefficient is obtained from 0.5 % damped elastic response spectrum [17].

The total base shear of ground supported tank at the bottom of the wall can be obtained by combining the overturning moment in impulsive and convective mode:

$$V = (m_i + m_w + m_r)S_e(T_i) + (m_c)S_e(T_c) \quad (11)$$

The total base shear given by base shear in impulsive mode and base shear in convective mode at the bottom of base slab

$$V^* = (m_i + m_w + m_b + m_r)S_e(T_i) + (m_c)S_e(T_c), \quad (12)$$

where m_i is impulsive mass of water, m_c is convective mass of water, m_w is mass of tank wall, m_b is mass of base slab and m_r is mass of roof of tank.

The base moment of ground supported tank at the bottom of the wall is given by base moment in impulsive mode and base moment in convective mode

$$M = (m_i h_i + m_w h_w + m_r h_r)S_e(T_i) + (m_c h_c)S_e(T_c) \quad (13)$$

The total overturning moment can be obtained by combining the overturning moment in impulsive and convective mode to be used for checking the tank stability at the bottom of base slab/plate, and is given by

$$M^* = \left(m_i h_i^* + m_w h_w^* + m_r h_r^* + m_b (t_b / 2)\right) S_e(T_i) + \left(m_c h_c^*\right) S_e(T_c) \tag{14}$$

5 Numerical example and results

A ground supported concrete cylindrical tank has inner dimensions: diameter $D = 20$ m and height $H = 6.5$ m. Wall has uniform thickness $s = 0.25$ m. The base slab thick d is 0.4 m. There is no roof slab on the tank. Tank is made from concrete, therefore, $E = 3.40 \cdot 10^7$ kNm^{-2}, $\rho = 2540$ kg/m^3. The reservoir is filled with water (H_2O), with density $\rho_w = 1\,000$ kg/m^3 to height 6.0 m. We consider only horizontal seismic load only in horizontal direction. The elastic response spectrum was used for Slovakia.

A ground supported concrete cylindrical tank has capacity 1885 m^3. The tank slenderness parameter given is by relation $\gamma = H/L$. In this case, where tank slenderness parameter is 0.3, substantial amount of mass - 18 % participates in impulsive and 82 % participates in convective mode. The elastic response spectrums Elastic response spectrum is determined for Slovak republic region of seismic risk 2. The impulsive spectral accelerations are obtained from a 5% damped elastic response spectrum (for concrete tanks) and the convective spectral accelerations are obtained from a 0.5% damped elastic response spectrum.

The base shear above the tank bottom plate is 2,196 kN, the base shear below the tank bottom plate 2,883 kN, the total bending moment above the tank bottom plate 5,814 kNm, the total overturning moment below the tank bottom plate 15,769 kNm.

6 Conclusions

This paper presented the results from the hydrodynamic analysis of the reinforced concrete circular tank. Using of theoretical background for definition of impulsive and convective effects of fluid in liquid storage circular container was calculated the seismic response of tank due to earthquake even: the total base shears of the wall and the total base bending and overturning moments, immediately above and below the tank bottom plate, for full water filling of tank 6 m. As ground motion was determined the elastic response spectrum for Slovak republic region of seismic risk 2.

This work was supported by the Scientific Grant Agency of the Ministry of Education of Slovak Republic and the Slovak Academy of Sciences the project VEGA 1/0477/15 "Numerical analysis and modeling of interactive problems in multilayered composite structural members".

References

[1] A. Di Carluccio, G. Fabbrocino, E. Salzano, G. Manfredi, *ICSV18* (2008), Beijing, China.

[2] N. Jendzelovsky, N., L. Balaz, *Applied Mechanics and Materials*. **617** (2014)

[3] K. Kralik, J. Kralik jr., *Advanced Materials Research*, **715** (2013)

[4] M. Krejsa, Z. Kala, S. Seitl, *Procedia Engineering*. **142** (2016)

[5] K. Kotrasová, I. Grajciar, E. Kormaníková, *Journal of Vibration Engineering and Technologies*. **3** (2015)

[6] M. Krejsa, P. Janas, V. Krejsa, *International Journal of Mathematics and Computers in Simulation*. **8** 1 (2014)

[7] G. Lajcakova, J. Melcer *Comunications : Scientific Letters of the University of Žilina*. **13** 3 (2011)

[8] R. Livaoğlu, A. Durmuş, *Structural Engineering and Mechanics*, **53** 1 (2015)

[9] S. Medvecka, O. Ivankova *Applied Mechanics and Materials* **769** (2015)

[10] J. Melcer, *Applied Mechanics and Materials*, **486** (2014)

[11] J. Michel, M. Mihalikova, *Acta Metallurgica Slovaca*. **6** 2 (2000)

[12] O. Sucharda, M. Pajak, T. Ponikiewski, P. Konecny *Construction and Building Materials*, **138** (2017)

[13] V. Valašková, J. Melcer, G. Lajčáková, *Procedia Engineering*. **111** (2015)

[14] B. Taraba, Z Michalec, V. Michalcova, T. Blejchar, M Bojko, M Kozubkova. *Fuel*. **118** (2014)

[15] K. Tvrdá, J. Dický, *Journal of Civil Engineering*. ISSN: 1336-9024

[16] M. Zmindak, I. Grajciar, *Computers and Structures*. **64** 5-6 (1997)

[17] Eurocode 8 – Design of structure for earthquake resistance – Part. 4: Silos, tanks and pipelines. Januar 2006.

Laminate circular cylindrical shell

Eva Kormaníková[1,*], and *Kamila* Kotrasová[1]

[1]TUKE Košice, Civil Engineering Faculty, Vysokoškolská 4, 042 00 Košice, Slovakia

Abstract. The paper deals with a numerical approach of optimal design modelling of laminate circular cylindrical shell. For thin-walled shells the classical shell theory is capable of accurately predicting the shell behaviour. In the frame of numerical optimization of circular cylindrical shell there is made the minimization of weight subject to displacement constraint. Thickness of layers is taken as design variable. In the example there is found the thickness of the shell laminate roof under constant pressure loading using Modified Feasible Direction method.

1 Introduction

For many years, designers have treated optimization problems involving composite materials. The design of a composite laminate stacking sequence generally involves selecting discrete layer thickness – a discrete optimization problem. The directionality of fibre composites needs the optimization in the process of design of these materials. Many works have been done on optimization of cylindrical shells, for example, Park et al. [1] used optimization of laminate stacking sequence to maximize the strength. Adali and Verijenko [2] optimized the stacking sequence design for hybrid laminates. Soremekun et al. [3] used optimization algorithm for stacking sequence blending of multiple composite laminates to minimize the weight and the cost of the panels. Weaver [4] used computational study for designing the laminate composite cylindrical shells under axial compression to minimize the mass with local and global constraints.

2 Classical shell theory

Thin-walled laminate shells can be also modelled as two-dimensional structural elements but with single or double curved reference surfaces (Fig. 1).

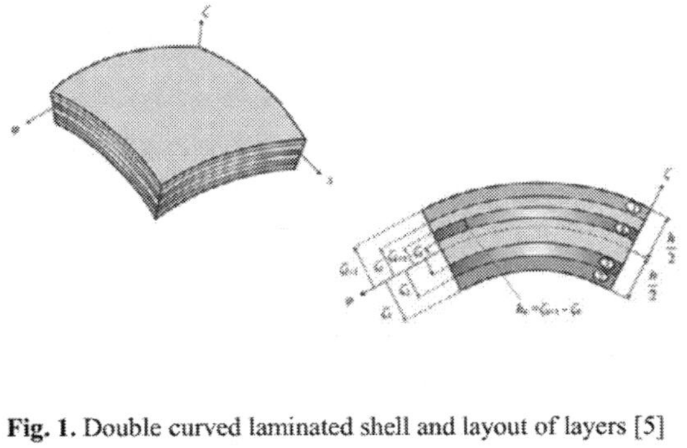

Fig. 1. Double curved laminated shell and layout of layers [5]

The modelling and analysis of laminate circular cylindrical shells fabricated from fibre composite material depends on the radius/thickness ratio (Fig. 2).

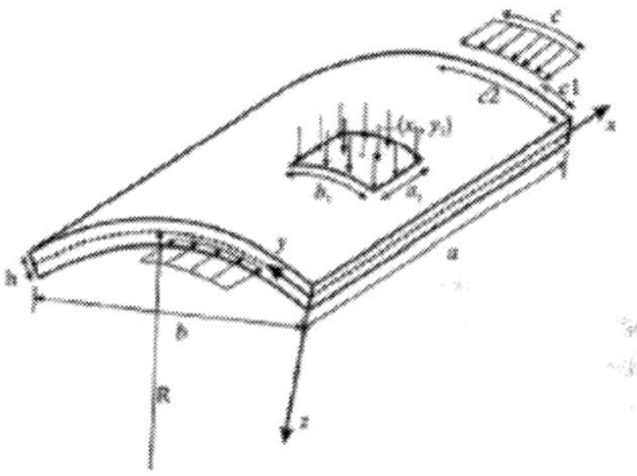

Fig. 2. Circular cylindrical shell under general loading [6]

The strain displacement relations for a circular cylindrical shell using Love´s first approximation are given by

$$\bar{\varepsilon}_x = \frac{\partial u}{\partial x},$$

$$\bar{\varepsilon}_s = \frac{\partial v}{\partial s} + \frac{w}{R}, \quad \bar{\varepsilon}_{xs} = \frac{\partial u}{\partial s} + \frac{\partial v}{\partial x},$$

$$\kappa_x = -\frac{\partial^2 w}{\partial x^2}, \quad \kappa_s = -\frac{\partial^2 w}{\partial s^2} + \frac{1}{R}\frac{\partial v}{\partial s},$$

$$\kappa_{xs} = -2\frac{\partial^2 w}{\partial x \partial s} + \frac{1}{R}\frac{\partial v}{\partial x}. \quad (1)$$

The total strains at a arbitrary distance z of the middle surface are written by

$$\varepsilon_x = \bar{\varepsilon}_x + \kappa_x z,$$

$$\varepsilon_s = \bar{\varepsilon}_s + \kappa_s z,$$

[*] Corresponding author: eva.kormanikova@tuke.sk

$$\varepsilon_{xs} = \bar{\varepsilon}_{xs} + \kappa_{xs} z \,. \tag{2}$$

Each individual layer is assumed to be in a state of generalized plane stress, the Hooke's law yields

$${}^n\sigma_i = {}^n E_{ij}\varepsilon_j, \quad i,j = (x, s, xs), \tag{3}$$

where n is number of one layer and E_{ij} is component of elasticity matrix defined in [7].
The force and moment resultants (Fig. 3) are defined by

$$N_i = \int_{-h/2}^{h/2} \sigma_i dz, \quad M_i = \int_{-h/2}^{h/2} \sigma_i z dz, \quad i,j = (x, s, xs). \tag{4}$$

The constitutive equations are written in the matrix form

$$\begin{pmatrix} \boldsymbol{N} \\ \boldsymbol{M} \end{pmatrix} = \begin{pmatrix} \boldsymbol{A} & \boldsymbol{B} \\ \boldsymbol{B} & \boldsymbol{D} \end{pmatrix} \begin{pmatrix} \bar{\boldsymbol{\varepsilon}} \\ \boldsymbol{\kappa} \end{pmatrix}, \tag{5}$$

where $\boldsymbol{A}$ is the extension matrix, $\boldsymbol{B}$ is the bending-extension coupling matrix, $\boldsymbol{D}$ is the bending matrix.
The components of ***A, B, D*** matrix are

$$A_{ij} = \sum_{n=1}^{N} {}^nE_{ij}\left({}^nz - {}^{n-1}z\right), \quad B_{ij} = \frac{1}{2}\sum_{n=1}^{N} {}^nE_{ij}\left({}^nz^2 - {}^{n-1}z^2\right),$$

$$D_{ij} = \frac{1}{3}\sum_{n=1}^{N} {}^nE_{ij}\left({}^nz^3 - {}^{n-1}z^3\right) \tag{6}$$

where N is number of layers.

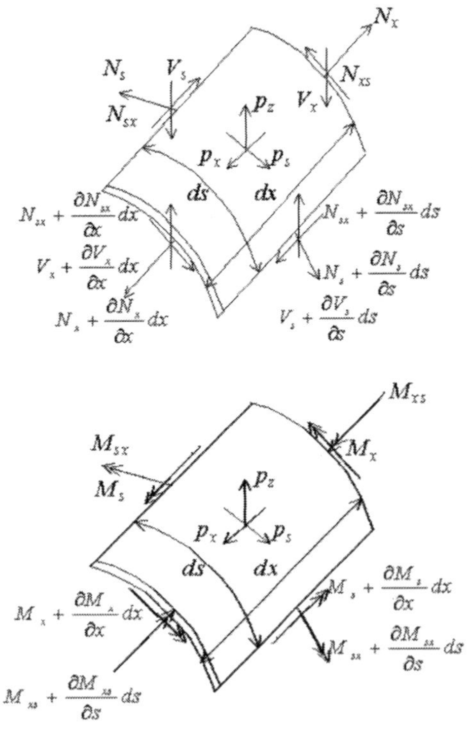

Fig. 3. Force and moment resultants of the differential shell element.

The equilibrium equations for differential shell element on Fig. 3 are given by

$$\frac{\partial N_x}{\partial x} + \frac{\partial N_{xs}}{\partial s} = -p_x,$$

$$\frac{\partial N_{xs}}{\partial x} + \frac{\partial N_s}{\partial s} + \frac{1}{R}\left(\frac{\partial M_s}{\partial s} + \frac{\partial M_{xs}}{\partial x}\right) = -p_s,$$

$$\frac{\partial^2 M_x}{\partial x^2} + 2\frac{\partial^2 M_{xs}}{\partial x \partial s} + \frac{\partial^2 M_s}{\partial s^2} - \frac{N_s}{R} = -p_z \,. \tag{7}$$

Substituting the constitutive equations into the equilibrium equations yields a set of three coupled partial differential equations for the three displacements u, v, w which can be written in matrix form

$$\begin{pmatrix} L_{11} & L_{12} & L_{13} \\ L_{21} & L_{22} & L_{23} \\ L_{31} & L_{32} & L_{33} \end{pmatrix} \begin{pmatrix} u \\ v \\ w \end{pmatrix} = -\begin{pmatrix} p_x \\ p_s \\ p_z \end{pmatrix}. \tag{8}$$

The linear differential operators L_{ij} are defined in [5]. The governing equations are solved by the help of Finite Element Method (FEM).

3 Finite element analysis

The basic idea of the FEM is a discretisation of the continuous structure. The discretisation is defined by finite element mesh make up of elements nodes. The starting point for elastostatic problems is the total potential energy. In accordance with the Ritz method the approximation is used for displacement field vector by notation

$$\tilde{\boldsymbol{u}}(x) = \boldsymbol{N}(x)\boldsymbol{v}, \tag{9}$$

where $\boldsymbol{N}(x)$ is the matrix of the shape functions, that are functions of the position vector $\boldsymbol{x} = (x, s, z)$ and $\boldsymbol{v}$ is the element displacement vector.
For the stresses and strains we obtain from Eq. (9) the Eq. (10)

$$\boldsymbol{\sigma}(\boldsymbol{x}) = \boldsymbol{E}\boldsymbol{\varepsilon}(\boldsymbol{x}) = \boldsymbol{EDN}(\boldsymbol{x})\boldsymbol{v},$$

$$\boldsymbol{\varepsilon}(\boldsymbol{x}) = \boldsymbol{Du}(\boldsymbol{x}) = \boldsymbol{DN}(\boldsymbol{x})\boldsymbol{v} = \boldsymbol{B}(\boldsymbol{x})\boldsymbol{v} \,. \tag{10}$$

With the approximation (Eq. 9) the total potential energy is a function of all the nodal displacement components arranged in the element displacement vector $\boldsymbol{v}$. The variation of the total potential energy

$$\delta\Pi = \delta\boldsymbol{v}^T\left(\int_V \boldsymbol{B}^T\boldsymbol{E}\boldsymbol{B}\boldsymbol{v}dV - \int_V \boldsymbol{N}^T\boldsymbol{p}dV - \int_{O_q} \boldsymbol{N}^T\boldsymbol{q}dO\right) \tag{11}$$

leads to

$$\delta\boldsymbol{v}^T\left(\boldsymbol{K}\boldsymbol{v} - \boldsymbol{f}_p - \boldsymbol{f}_q\right) = 0, \tag{12}$$

where p, q are volume and surface loadings, respectively and $\boldsymbol{K}$ is the symmetric stiffness matrix given by

$$K = \int_V B^T E B dV \cdot \qquad (13)$$

The vectors of the volume forces and the surface forces are written by

$$f_p = \int_V N^T p dV ,$$

$$f_q = \int_{O_q} N^T q dO \cdot \qquad (14)$$

If the components of δv are independent of each other, we obtain from Eq. (12) the system of linear equations

$$Kv = f ,$$

$$f = f_p + f_q \cdot \qquad (15)$$

All equations considered above are valid for a single finite element and they should have an additional index *E*. We have the inner element energy

$$U_E = \frac{1}{2} v_E^T \int_{V_E} B^T E B dV v_E = \frac{1}{2} v_E^T K_E v_E , \qquad (16)$$

with the element stiffness matrix

$$K_E = \int_{V_E} B^T E B dV ,$$

$$E = \sum_{n=1}^{N} {}^n E ,$$

$${}^n E = \overline{T}^T({}^n\beta)^{(n)} E_L \overline{T}({}^n\beta), \qquad (17)$$

where E is the elasticity matrix obtained with suitable transformations in two stages, firstly from the principal material directions to the element local directions and secondly to the global directions. B is the strain matrix, T is the transformation matrix with

$$\overline{T}(\beta) = (T^T(\beta))^{-1} . \qquad (18)$$

Because the energy is a scalar quantity, the potential energy of the whole structure can be obtained by summing the energies of the single elements. By a Boolean matrix L_E the correct position of each single element is determined. The element displacement vector v_E is positioned into the system displacement vector by the equation

$$v_E = L_E v , \qquad (19)$$

then we obtain the system equation by summing over all elements [8-11]

$$\left(\sum_i L_{iE}^T K_{iE} L_{iE} \right) v = \left[\sum_i L_{iE} \left(f_{iEp} + f_{iEq} \right) \right] \cdot \qquad (20)$$

The system stiffness matrix is also symmetric, but it is a singular matrix. After consideration of the boundary conditions of the whole system, K becomes a positive definite matrix and the system equations can be solved.

4 Sizing optimization problem

The basic problem is the minimization of a function subject to inequality constraints [12]:
Minimize objective function

$$Z = F(X) \rightarrow \min, \qquad (21)$$

Subject to constraints

$$\overline{X}_i^L \le X_i \le \overline{X}_i^U \qquad i = 1,2, ..., N_d, \qquad (22)$$

$$g_j(X) \le 0 \qquad j = 1,2, ..., N_c, \qquad (23)$$

where X_i is a design variable [13].

We make use of the existing response at a number of points in the design space to construct a polynomial approximation to the response at other points. The optimization process is applied to the approximate problem represented by the polynomial approximation

$$F = a_0 + \sum_{i=1}^{N_d} a_i X_i + \sum_{i=1}^{N_d} b_i X_i^2 + \sum_{i=1}^{N_d - 1} \sum_{j=i-1}^{N_d} c_{ij} X_i X_j + \sum_{i=1}^{N_d} d_i X_i^3 \qquad (24)$$

where N_d is the number of design variables, a_i, b_i, c_{ij}, d_i are coefficients to be determined by a least squares regression.

When the objective function and constraints are approximated and their gradients with respect to the design variables are calculated based on chosen approximation, it is possible to solve the approximate optimization problem. Using the Modified Feasible Direction method (MFD) the solving process is iterated until convergence is achieved. To find the search direction, active and violated constraints have to be identified.

Convergence to the optimum is checked by criteria of maximum iterations and criteria changes of objective function. Besides these criteria, the Kuhn-Tucker conditions necessary for optimality must be satisfied by using the Lagrangian multiplier method. The Kuhn-Tucker conditions are sufficient for optimality when the number of active constraints is equal to the number of design variables and if objective function and all of the constraints are convex. Otherwise, sufficient conditions require the second derivatives of the objective function and constraints [14-16]. Convergence or termination checks are performed at the end of each optimization loop. The optimization process continues until either convergence or termination occurs.

5 Example and results

There is needed to find the thickness of the shell roof fabricated from laminate $[0/45/-45/90]_S$ under constant pressure loading p_z in the example (Fig. 4). The material properties of each layer were used from homogenization techniques:

E_1 = 142 GPa, E_2 = 10.3 GPa, G_{12} = 7.2 GPa, ν = 0.27, ρ = 1.58 g.cm^{-3}.

Each layer of the laminate has the same thickness ${}^n h$.

 DOI: 10.1051/matecconf/201712504010

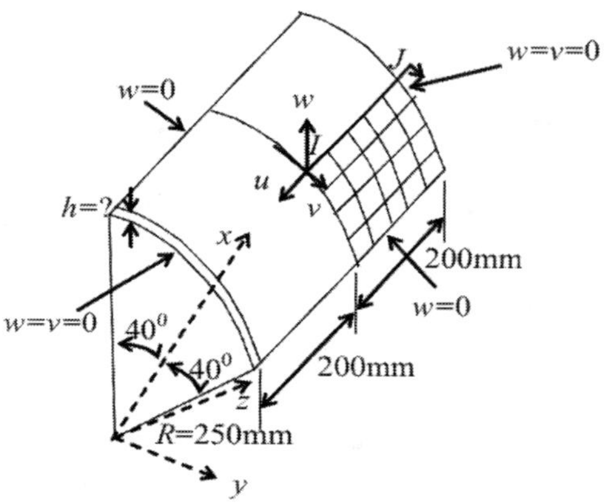

Fig. 4. Problem sketch and finite element model.

Due to symmetry, a quarter of the shell is considered for modelling (Fig. 4).
The mathematical optimization problem we can write:
Minimize objective function

$$F(X)=G(^{n}h)\rightarrow \min \quad [\mathrm{N}]$$

Subject to constraints

$$0.0125\leq {}^{n}h \leq 0.625 \quad [\mathrm{mm}]$$

$$-3.0\leq w(^{n}h)\leq 0.0 \quad [\mathrm{mm}]$$

where ^{n}h is the thickness of one layer.

The general optimization contains:

1. Initial analysis with input data (Tab. 1).
2. Mathematical optimization problem.
3. Linear approximation.
4. Algorithm of MFD method with convergence criteria.
5. Convergence or termination checks of general optimization.

Table 1. Optimization parameters.

Optimization parameters	Initial values	Final values	Tolerance
Design variables - thickness of one layer [mm]	0. 25	0. 1619	$1\cdot10^{-3}$
Objective function - weight [N]	4.4064	2.8532	0.01
Constraint - displacement w [mm]	-1.2478	-3.0296	0. 03

Results of the optimization process are listed in the Table 1.

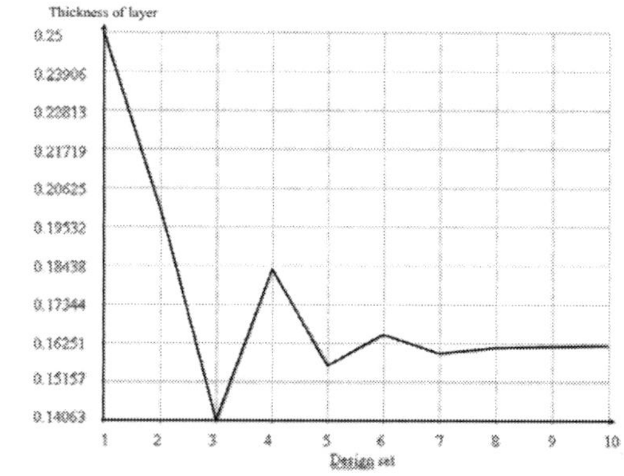

Fig. 5 Variation of the design variable values – thickness [mm] during the optimization process.

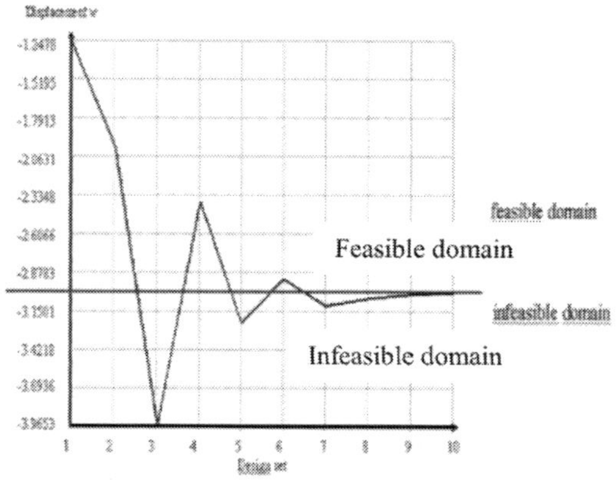

Fig. 6 Variation of the constraint values – displacement w [mm] during the optimization process.

6 Conclusion

The proceeding deals with a numerical approach of modelling of circular cylindrical shell fabricated from fibre composite material. The theory of circular cylindrical shells is described in the frame of classical shell theory. In the paper there are involved the strain displacement relations, constitutive equations and differential equilibrium equations.
There was used homogenization for calculating the material characteristics given in the example [17-19].
In the frame of numerical optimization it was made the minimization of weight subject to displacement constraint. Design variable is thickness of layers of laminate circular cylindrical shell. The initial and final values of design variables, constraints and the objective function are shown in the Table 1.
Maximum number of iterations of MFD was 100. The general optimization process was stopped after 10 design sets (Fig. 5, Fig. 6), because the difference between the current value and the one or two previous designs was less than tolerance specified in the Table 1.
The final value of design variable is $^{n}h = 0.16187\,\mathrm{mm}$ (Fig. 5). The total thickness of laminate circular

cylindrical shell is $8^{\pi}h = 1.3$ mm. Figure 6 shows the feasible and infeasible domain in the usable design space.

The optimization is very useful way for design of laminate structural elements including circular cylindrical shells.

This work was supported by the Scientific Grant Agency of the Ministry of Education of Slovak Republic and the Slovak Academy of Sciences under Projects VEGA 1/0477/15 and 1/0078/16.

References

1. JH. Park, JH. Hwang, CS. Lee, W. Hwang, Stacking sequence design of composite laminated for maximum strength using genetic algorithms, *Compos Struct* **52**, p. 217–31, (2001)
2. S. Adali, V. Verijenko, Optimum stacking sequence design of symmetric hybrid laminates undergoing free vibration. *Compos Struct* **54**, p. 131–8, (2001)
3. G. Soremekun, Z. Gurdal, C. Kassapoglou, D. Toni, Stacking sequence blending of multiple composite laminates using genetic algorithms, *Compos Struct,* **56,** p. 53–62, (2002)
4. PM. Weaver, Design of laminated composite cylindrical shells under axial compression. *Composites Part B* **31,** p. 669–79, (2000)
5. http://file.scirp.org/Html/1-4900125_27735.htm
6. https://www.researchgate.net/publication/26121884 8
7. H. Altenbach, J. Altenbach, W. Kissing, *Structural analysis of laminate and sandwich beams and plates.* Lubelskie Towarzystwo Naukowe, Lublin, (2001)
8. J. Kralik, Optimal design of npp containment protection against fuel container drop, *Adv. Mat. Res.* **688**, p. 213-221, (2013)
9. M. Krejsa, P. Janas, I. Yilmaz, M. Marschalko, T. Bouchal, The use of the direct optimized probabilistic calculation method in design of bolt reinforcement for underground and mining workings, *The Scientific World Journal*, Article number 267593, (2013)
10. M. Zmindak, Z. Pelagic, M. Bvoc, Analysis of high velocity impact on composite structures, *Appl. Mech. and Mat.* **617**, p. 104-109, (2014)
11. J. Melcer, G. Lajcakova, Comparison of finite element and classical computing models of reinforcement pavement, *Adv. Mat. Res.* **969**, p. 85-88, (2014)
12. E. Kormanikova, I. Mamuzic, Optimization of laminates subjected to failure criterion, *Metal.* **50** (1), p. 41-44, (2011)
13. Z. Gürdal, R. T. Haftka, P. Hajela, *Design and Optimization of Laminated Composite Materia,* J. Wiley & Sons, (1999)
14. A. M. Valuev, Models and methods of multiobjective optimization in problems of quarry design and planning, *WSEAS Trans. on Math.*, **13**, p. 557-566, (2014)
15. E.A. Vorontsova, A projective separating plane method with additional clipping for non-smooth optimization, *WSEAS Trans. on Math.*, **13**, p. 115-121, (2014)
16. J. Lovíšek, J. Králik, Optimal Control for Elasto-Orthotropic Plate, *Contr. and Cyber.* **2**, p. 219-278, (2006)
17. M. Sejnoha, J. Zeman, Micromechanical modeling of imperfect textile composites, *Int. Jour. of Eng. Scien.* **46** (6), p. 513-526, (2008)
18. J. Ma, S. Sahraee, P. Wriggers, , L. De Lorenzis, Stochastic multiscale homogenization analysis of heterogeneous materials under finite deformations with full uncertainty in the microstructure, *Comp. Mech.* **55**, Issue 5, p. 819-835, (2015)
19. C. Maruccio, L. De Lorenzis, L. Persano, D. Pisignano, Computational homogenization of fibrous piezoelectric materials, *Comp. Mech.* **55**, Issue 5, p. 983-998, (2015)

 DOI: 10.1051/matecconf/201712504011

Testing of Process Control Systems in Mining using simulation

V.V. Okolnishnikov, S.V. Rudometov, S.R. Shakirov, and S.S. Zhuravlev*

Institute of Computational Technologies SB RAS, 6, Ac. Lavrentieva ave., Novosibirsk, Russia, 630090

Abstract. This paper describes a visual interactive simulation system specialized in simulation of technological processes in mining. A new model of the crushing-grading mill was developed with the help of this simulation system. The model was integrated with an actual process control system of the crushing-grading mill into a software/hardware test bed. The process control system of the crushing-grading mill was debugged and test with the help of this model.

1 Introduction

Institute of Computational Technologies of Siberian Branch of the Russian Academy of Sciences in Novosibirsk (ICT) develops process control systems for mining and coal mining.

Arising problems are the following:

- The complete testing of control system using the programmer's tools is almost impossible because of inability to connect to actual equipment.

- There is no way to make the complete testing of control system on-site because of inability to reproduce alarm situations or emergency situations.

- Start-up and live testing time of control system on-site is limited.

The most suitable way to solve these problems is simulation [1]. A means for solving these problems is a model integrated with an actual process control system. The model can be run as a part of the actual process control system. On the other hand, the model can use software and hardware components of the actual process control system, for example, control programs, the operator workstation, or a programmable logic controller (PLC) in which the control programs executed, and others. The model can emulate processing equipment of the actual process control system.

Because of the importance of these problems, there are a large number of papers on the use of simulation in the development and optimization of mining systems [2-5]. There are also a large number of simulation tools both universal simulation systems and specialized systems and packages for simulation of mining systems.

A number of models for the simulation of the following subsystems of coal mines were developed [6, 7] such as: belt conveyor subsystem, power supply subsystem, ventilation subsystem, pumping subsystem and longwall mining subsystem. These models are used at ICT for developing of process control systems for underground coal mines in Kuznetsk Coal Basin (Russia, Western Siberia).

A new model of the crushing-grading mill was developed. This model is used at ICT for developing of process control system of the crushing-grading mill "Apatite" (Russia, Kola Peninsula). All models were developed with the help of our own simulation system.

2 The simulation system

A visual interactive Manufacturing and Transportation Simulation System (MTSS) is a process-oriented discrete simulation system intended to development and execution of models of technological processes [8, 9]. MTSS is a set of program interfaces for creating elemental models as well as forming complex models from them. The elemental model is verified according to its specifications, ready-to-use simulation model of an equipment unit with capability of low-level control for it.

The elemental model consists of the following parts:

- Two-dimensional and three-dimensional animated graphic images.

- Input and output parameters.

- Functionality algorithm describing dependence between parameters.

- States that the elemental model can reach during the simulation process.

- Control commands defining switching process between elemental model states.

A model in MTSS is created by graphical connection of images of elemental models with the help of visual interactive interface. MTSS is also a tool for running of complex models built from elemental models. The running model performs the movement of the model time and visualization. Statistics is collected as well. Statistics are available as a short overview when model runs, and more statistics are available after model completion.

Elemental models can be then combined in a libraries forming simulation goal-specific tool, used by field specialists.

* Corresponding author: okoln@mail.ru

Such tool can be an application for rapid creation of correct simulation model by mining engineers. Usually engineers have not enough qualification to create simulation models in details, but they know how to connect correctly elemental models to create the required topology. MTSS uses 2D as a graphical editor and 2D, 3D for visualization of model running. Such approach seems more natural for mining engineers, when all installations and machines appear first on 2D plans. 3D is more useful for visualizing complex vertical movement.

Process control systems often have two levels: the low level of equipment and simple control logic in it and the upper level of complex control of production. One of the distinguishing features of MTSS is a division of the logic of a simulation model into two parts: a low-level logic and an upper level logic.

Such division allows us not only to correlate to the usual structure of the process control systems but also to use such models for embedding them into actual process control systems in the following ways: to emulate equipment, to simulate upper level logic, and to send commands to actual process control system for debugging and testing. The division into upper and lower logics let us also organize a switch between various implementations of decomposition. It makes possible coexisting simulation of upper level logic and a proxy that allows communicating with the upper level logic of actual process control system.

The model of mining can communicate with a new process control system developed in ICT, to be a source of input signals, emulate equipment, test actual control program with simultaneous visualization of overall process of mining. This allows debugging and tuning of a new process control system in accordance with behaviour of simulated system, even simulating various accidents. This permits to minimize time and costs on site for commissioning.

3 The model of crushing-grading mill

A new library of elemental models of equipment of the crushing-grading mill was developed within MTSS. This library contains the following elemental models:

- Product source. The product source provides the possibility to specify parameters of input stream of stone ore.
- Stone ore pass. This elemental model simulates a bunker-like object that takes and stores product from product source.
- Hydrohammer. The hydraulic hammer melts product portions what contain fractions that are not acceptable for stone ore pass.
- Vibrofeeder. The vibrofeeder gets the portion of product from stone ore pass and sends it to the next elemental model.
- Screw crusher. The screw crusher melts product again.
- Shaking grizzly. The shaking grizzly is transportation equipment.
- Conveyor. The conveyor is a long belt conveyor to deliver product on the long distances. The conveyor requires power supply chain to function (wires, transformer, and power generator).
- Bunker. The bunker is used for an intermediate storage of the end product.
- Crusher chamber. The crusher chamber is a simple object that just stores the product what may be loose during transportation and melting of the product in various elemental models.

The product (stone ore) is presented in the simulation like a portion of the product defined by product amount in kg, its own fraction, amount of add-ons, and density. The product portions are generated in "Product source" according to its scenarios. Then these portions can be changed during their pass through the simulation model: its fraction can be changed (when it is melting), other product portions can be generated resulting in product split or product uniting, and add-ons can be excluded by a special elemental model. A product movement is presented in Fig. 1.

Product portions are generating in "Product source" ("input" in Fig. 1), then they are passing to "Stone ore pass", decreasing their space left (originally it is 3 m3 in this simulation. 158 kg of the product with the density 1350 kg/m3 takes 0.12 m3 which can be seen in fields "stp-approx space left m3", "in stone ore pass, kg"). Some amount of the product cannot be passed to "Stone ore pass" because it only accepts the product with fractions less than 800 mm. So it is passed to "hydrohummer". "The hydrohummer" is manually controlled, it is turned off now, and we see that 25.5 kg of the product will be melted ("Melt, kg") and nothing is melted yet (counting property "Melted, kg"). On each step, 1.9 kg of the product is passed to working "Vibrofeeder". It can function only if "Screw crusher" is started. It passes its product portions to "Screw crusher" that melts everything to fractions of 350 mm. "Shaking Grizzly" delivers melted product to "Conveyor" that is turned on. "Conveyor" takes every portion of a product and delivers it to the bunker. 1344 kg of the product is already processed as we may see, but 1631 kg is generated as a source product. A part of the product is in "Stone ore pass", the most of the rest is on "Conveyor" (that moves slowly and has a significant length). Other elements have big productivity in this configuration of the simulation model; therefore the product amount on them is small.

Since "Stone ore pass" has a limited capability, at some moment it can be not enough to handle the product portions. In this case, amount of a generated product that was not accepted by "Stone ore pass" will be shown in "input not accepted kg" variable. This product will be passed to "Stone ore pass" on the next simulation step.

During the simulation, each elemental model can be started or stopped which will immediately lead to the change in the product amount in the bunker. "Vibrofeeder", "Screw crusher" and "Shaking grizzly" have their own max input capabilities and their advance speed.

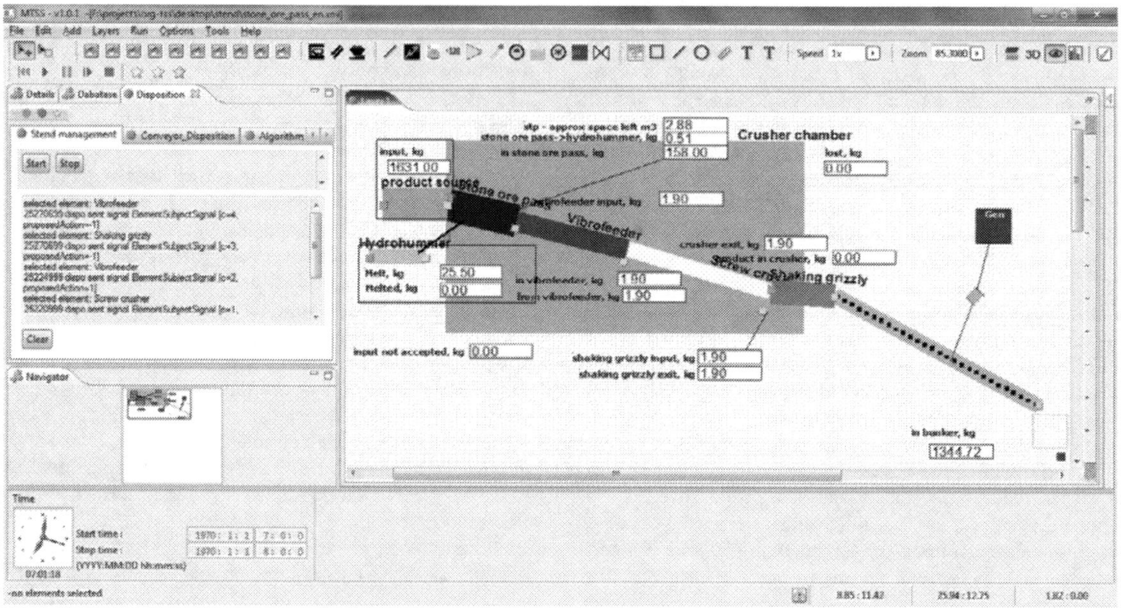

Fig. 1. The main windows of model of crushing-grading mill.

Small capabilities will lead to overflowing of "Stone ore pass", and big ones will lead to always empty "Stone ore pass". Also the "Conveyor" has the length and the speed that can lead to lots of the product to be stuck on it and not appear in the bunker.

4 Testing of process control system of crushing-grading mill

A software/hardware test bed for testing the process control systems using a simulation model is developed at ICT. The structure of software/hardware test bed is shown in Fig. 2.

The process control system of crushing-grading mill is developed at ICT employing Wonderware InTouch. The Simulation System MTSS includes the corresponding OPC client allowing the model of crushing-grading mill to interact with the process control system of the crushing-grading mill.

The model simulates the coordinated values for input signals from the processing equipment sensors of the crushing-grading mill in physical units of measurement and sends them to the process control system. An operator of the process control system sends commands to the processing equipment of the crushing-grading mill. In accordance with the logic of the control program of the process control system these control commands are sent to the actuators of the real system, but they arrive at the model. In the model this commands "is executed" generating the corresponding changes in the state of the processing equipment. The new values of the input signals are sent to the process control system, which tests the correctness of the command information execution. Thus the process control system "doesn't know" in what environment - actual or simulated - it works.

All this helps to debug and test the upper level of the process control system, control programs, executed in PLC, with incomplete set of processing equipment as well as in the case of emergencies.

The own SCADA-System is implemented in ICT, with its help a number of process control systems were developed. Each process control system was supplied with its own model for testing.

In order to test the low level of process control systems with using the model and the test bed we have an opportunity to generate the values of certain input signals in electrical units in the form they are read directly from the sensors. These simulated signals are directly sent to the input of the corresponding input/output modules and PLCs. So the functionality of the whole scheme shown in Fig. 2 is checked.

5 Conclusion

Simulation system MTSS enables engineers with little experience in simulation, investigation and optimization of mining systems to solve complex engineering problems to assess the effectiveness of automation and choice of the optimal technology, which eventually will reduce the costly risks during the design and optimization technological processes in the mining.

Simulation system MTSS can be used not only for simulation of existing mining techniques but also for perspective robotized techniques [10, 11].

This research was financially supported by the Russian Foundation for Basic Research (project 16-47-420490 r_a, and project 16-07-01179 a).

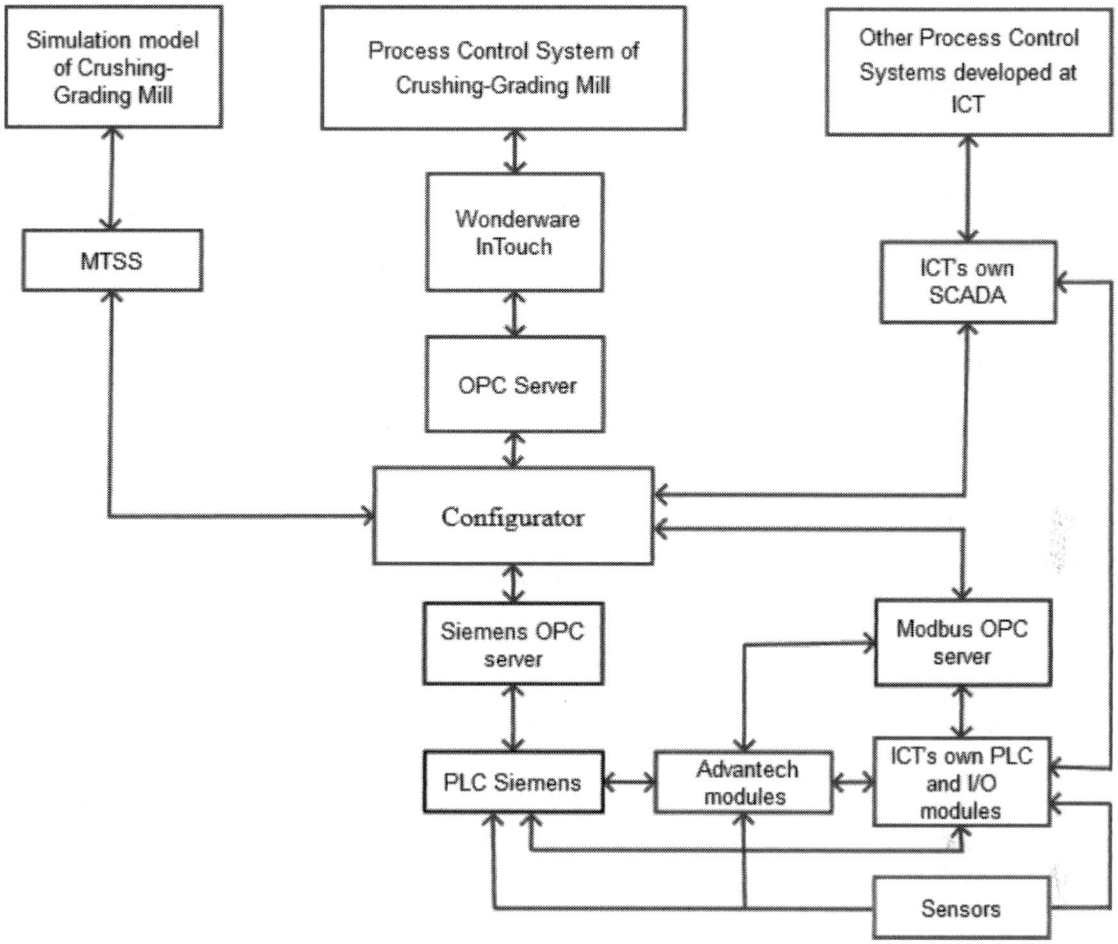

Fig. 2. The scheme of testing of process control system.

References

1. J.R. Sturgul, Simulation, **76(5)**, 286–288 (2001)
2. J. Greberg, F. Sundqvist, *Proceedings of Second International Future Mining Conference*, 273–278 (2011)
3. D. Cai, E. Baafi & I. Porter, Mine planning and equipment selection, 107–114 (2012)
4. C. Meng, S.S. Nageshwaraniyer, A. Maghsoudi, Y. Son, and S. Dessureault, Computers & Industrial Engineering, 766–779 (2013)
5. M. Fioroni, L. Santos, L. Franzese, I. Santana, G. Telles, J. Seixas, B. Penna, G. Alkmim, *Proceedings of the 2014 Winter Simulation Conference*, 1855–1865 (2014)
6. V. Okolnishnikov, S. Rudometov, S. Zhuravlev, Engineering, Technology & Applied Science Research, **6**, 993–999 (2016)
7. V. Okolnishnikov, S. Rudometov, S. Zhuravlev, V. Sinoviev, *Proceedings of the 28TH European Modeling and Simulation Symposium. Simulation in Industry*, 212–215 (2016)
8. V.V. Okolnishnikov, S.V. Rudometov, *Proceedings of 7th IFAC Conference on Manufacturing Modelling, Management, and Control*, 653–658 (2013)
9. V.V. Okolnishnikov, S.V. Rudometov, St. Petersburg State Polytechnic University Journal. Computer Science. Telecommunications and Control Systems, **1 (181)**, 62–68 (2014)
10. V.V. Sinoviev, A.N. Starodubov, M.U. Dorofeev, V.V. Okolnishnikov, *Mathematics and Computers in Science and Engineering*, **50**, 75–77 (2015)
11. V.V. Sinoviev, V.V. Okolnishnikov, A.N.Starodubov, Dorofeev, International Journal of Mathematics and Computers in Simulation, **10**, 123–128 (2016)

MATEC Web of Conferences **125**, 04012 (2017) DOI: 10.1051/matecconf/201712504012
CSCC 2017

Molecular Dynamics on FPGA Based Accelerated Processing Units

Mihaela Maliţa[1,3,*], *David* Mihăiţă[2,**], and *Gheorghe M.* Ştefan[3,***]

[1] *Computer Science Dept., Anselm College, Manchester, NH*
[2] *Faculty of Electronics, Tc. & IT, Politehnica University of Bucharest, Bucharest, Romania*
[3] *Faculty of Electronics, Tc. & IT, Politehnica University of Bucharest, Bucharest, Romania*

Abstract. One of the main problems in providing the amount of computation requested by the Molecular Dynamic domain is to offer an appropriate architectural environment for solving ***all*** the aspects of the intense parts of the involved computation. Current solutions accelerate only partially the intense computation – forces computation & position and speed updates, which represents around 75% from the total computational effort – thus limiting the help provided by the parallel computing resources involved. The aim of this paper is to introduce a parallel accelerator featured with functions able to add to the accelerated functions the neighbourhood list building, which represent around 25% from the total computation. Thus, accelerations higher than the current $\sim 4\times$ are expected. Our proposal, the ***MapReduce Accelerator***, is evaluated using the Gromacs system. The Martini water example, running on a cycle accurate simulator, is used to evaluate the speed-up and the energy.

1 Introduction

The Molecular Dynamics computational domain belongs to the 4-th dwarf – *N-Body Methods* – emphasized in the Berkeley's View [2]. A short description of the problem considers N particles, p_i for $i = 1, \dots N$, each characterized by a small set of parameters, let say, for example, position, speed, charge and mass ($p_i : (x_i, y_i, z_i, v_x^i, v_y^i, v_z^i, q_i, m_i)$). Each simulation cycle, in the brut force approach, consists of the following two steps:

1. for each p_i is computed the force vector resulting from the forces exerted by all the other $N-1$ particles (in time belonging to $O(N^2)$)
2. the particles are let free to change their state (position and speed) for a very short time interval; the shorter the interval the more accurate the simulation is (in time belonging to $O(N)$).

While, for N bodies, the brute force approach leads to $O(N^2)$ computation for each simulation cycle, applying various strategies, the computational complexity are reducible to $O(NlogN)$ or even $O(N)$. For the particular case of Molecular Dynamics, the computational complexity is given by the huge number of simulation cycles requested for an accurate simulation of the molecular folding process. Thus, any optimization applied to the first step of the simulation cycle is welcome. There are various ways to reduce the number of forces considered as acting on each particle, such as *Barnes-Hut Algorithm*, *Fast Multipole Method* or *Particle Mesh Method*. We selected, for investigating how the Molecular Dynamics can be accelerated using hybrid computation, the Gromacs[1] system whose main idea is to limit the interactions of each particle p_i to a small neighbourhood of $M << N$ particles whose actions on the particle p_i worth taking into consideration. Thus, a three-step approach is currently practiced:

1. neighborhood search (in time belonging to $O(N^2)$)
2. forces computation (in time belonging to $O(N \times M)$)
3. up-date (in time belonging to $O(N)$)

There are many solutions for accelerating the Molecular Dynamics applications. The most radical one is to build ASICs based specialised engines, like the *Anton* machine build by D. E. Shaw Research [10]. At the other end, meaningful accelerations are also obtained by using the last Intel's families of multi cores processors supported by SSE[2] units.

A good compromise performance vs. price is provided by using hybrid computation solutions embodied in Accelerated Processing Units (APU). An APU integrate in the same system a PU with an accelerating parallel engine, such as a GPU[3], a MIC[4] or, increasingly more frequently, a FPGA. The small accelerations provided by the use of the current parallel accelerators are mainly due to the fact that only the last two of the previously listed steps are submitted to the parallel accelerator, while the first step – the neighbourhood search – which is theoretically the most

*e-mail: mmalita@anselm.edu
**e-mail: David.Mihaita@infineon.com
***e-mail: gheorghe.stefan@upb.ro

[1] GROningen MAchine for Chemical Simulations, see http://www.gromacs.org/
[2] Streaming SIMD Extensions
[3] Graphic Processing Units such as Nvidia or ATI products.
[4] Many Integrated Core such as Intel's Xeon Phi family of processors

time consuming, is left to the PU. Usually, the weight of the first step is minimized by the compromising solution of applying it only once at 10-50 state up-dates.

Our proposal refers to an APU based on a parallel accelerator having a Map-Reduce architecture, implemented in FPGA, able to perform efficiently on *all* the previously emphasized three steps.

The next section discuss the state of the art. In the third section is a short description of the proposed *mapReduce* accelerator. The fourth section describe the use of the accelerator in running the Gromacs system, a widely used Molecular Dynamics environment. Final comments concludes the paper.

2 State of the Art

2.1 Multi-Core Approach

Current CPU are already parallel machines. Intel's processors, for example, are multi-core engines featured with Streaming SIMD Extensions (SSE) accelerators. We used an Intel i5 system for running Gromacs for Martini water [8]. Table 1 shows us the effects of this kind of two-level parallelism: multi cores, each accelerated by an SSE.

Table 1. The performance on i5 multi-core [8].

CPU type	Performance [μ/day]	Acceleration
1-Core, no SSE: 1 EU	5.84	1.00×
1-Core, with SSE: 1+4 EUs	9.78	1.67×
4-Core, no SSE: 4 EUs	18.94	3.24×
4-Core, with SSE: 4+16 EUs	31.48	5.39×

It looks like the SSE accelerator (with its 4 execution units, EU) is not of great use. The multi-core aspect is more useful. The overall acceleration, 5.39×, is higher than the acceleration provided by the hundred of EUs of a GPU or the 60 cores of a MIC, because all stages of the Gromacs computation are submitted to the acceleration. But, from architectural point of view, the acceleration provided by $p = 20$ EUs is too small, $0.27 \times p$.

2.2 Hybrid Solutions

In this paper we deal with systems, distributed or not, based on APU, but we consider only the task executed by one APU. We discuss and provide a hybrid solution for accelerating the Gromacs system.

The current hybrid solutions [1] [6], using GPUs or MICs to accelerate a CPU, develop an algorithm (see Figure 1) containing the following sections:

1. Build the neighbor lists; runs on CPU
2. Compute forces for the bonded interactions and update; runs on CPU
3. Compute forces for the non-bonded interactions and update; runs on GPU or MIC
4. Integrate the results; runs on CPU

The section 1 of the algorithm runs only once at 10-50 updates of the state. The Gromacs team decided experimentally that each update of the positions provides too small chances of positions to be considered in redefining the neighbourhood of each particle. Only the section 3 of the algorithm is sent to the accelerator. Because the force computation and update computation represent $\sim 75\%$ form the total computation [8], the acceleration provided by a hybrid system is theoretically limited by the Amdahl rule to $\sim 4\times$.

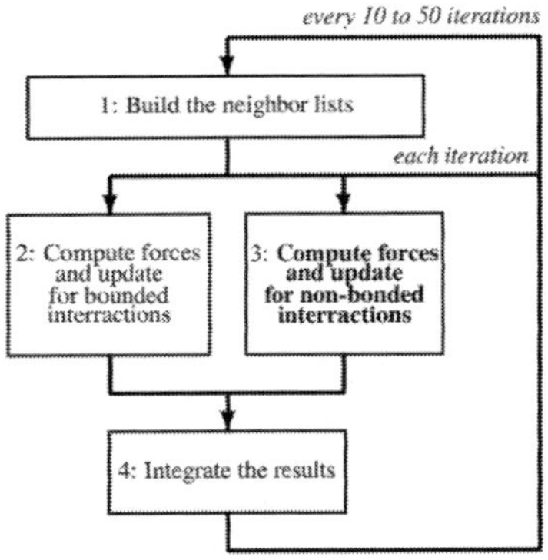

Figure 1. The hybrid algorithm. Only the section 3 is performed by the accelerator part of the hybrid system.

The current performances published for the hybrid systems are the following:

- using GPU as accelerator no more than 3× acceleration with GPUs equipped with hundred of cores [6] [4] [1]
- using the Intel Xeon Phi MIC as accelerator 1.8× acceleration is provided [9] [1]

The performances reported for the hybrid systems based on GPU and MIC are limited mainly due to the weak involvement of the accelerator part of the hybrid system in all the sections of the computation represented in Figure 1. We consider that there are more computation stages appropriated for parallel treatment. Therefore, we propose that, at least, **aspects related with the building of the neighbor list can be reconsidered in order to allow the accelerator to contribute more to the overall computation.** The architecture of the accelerator we propose is featured with mechanisms able to compute efficiently both, the neighbor list and the updates under the forces acting in the identified neighbourhood.

3 APU Based on the *mapReduce* Accelerator

3.1 The System

Figure 2 shows the block schematic of our proposal: an APU designed as a hybrid system where ACCELERATOR is based on the cellular system ***mapReduce*** [7] [11] [12] [13]. It consists (in the initial FPGA implementation) of:

 DOI: 10.1051/matecconf/201712504012

- HOST: a general purpose computing system with its CPU, MEMORY, I/O system
- INTERFACE: a DMA (direct memory access) unit for data and program transfer between MEMORY and the internally distributed memories in ACCELERATOR
- ACCELERATOR: the ***mapReduce*** system with its:
  - MAP section: an array of p cells, C_i for $i = 1, 2, \ldots, p$, each containing:
    - *eng*: a 32-bit execution unit
    - *mem*: a 1KW of 32-bit words data memory
  - REDUCE: a *log*-depth circuit performing vector-to-scalar reduction operations (addition, maximum, ...)
  - CONTROL: a special cell containing
    - *eng*: a 32-bit execution unit (identic with those from the MAP section)
    - *mem*: a 1KW of 32-bit words data memory
    - *prog mem*: a 4KW of 32-bit words memory used to store the program executed by the accelerator

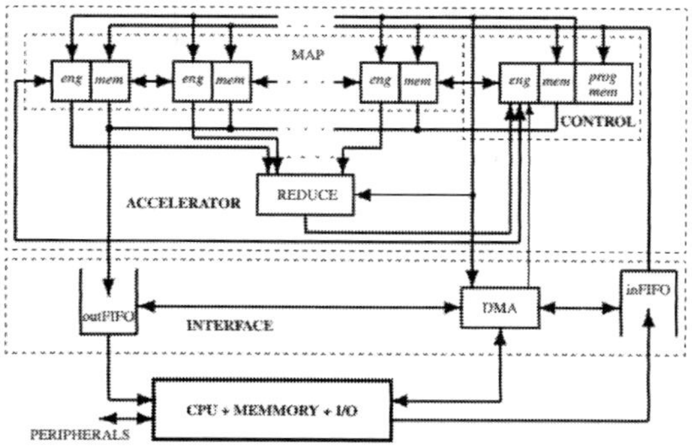

Figure 2. APU as a Hybrid Computing System based on the *mapReduce* Accelerator.

INTERFACE, connected between ACCELERATOR and the HOST is controlled by a DMA unit and the transfer is performed through the two FIFOs. DMA loads the program in CONTROL section and transfers data between ACCELERATOR's distributed memory along the cells and MEMORY. In each clock cycle the MAP section receives an instruction from CONTROL. There are two operating modes:

- slave mode: CPU loads the program(s) in *prog mem*, starts running the program(s) and controls the data transfer between ACCELERATOR and MEMORY
- autonomous mode: CPU loads the program(s) and starts running the program, but now the data transfer is completely under the control of ACCELERATOR.

3.2 Implementation

In this initial stage of the project, the ***mapReduce*** accelerator is implemented using the FPGA technology. For an advanced stage of the project, we are based on previous implementations of the mapReduce accelerator [11] and on evaluations for the 32*nm* technology. The FPGA technology evolved from a pure programmable structure to a mixed solution putting together frequently used ASIC blocks with the in field programmable blocks used mainly for interconnections. Thus, besides the usual Configurable Logic Blocks, the designers have access to memory blocks, DSP units, advanced micro-controllers (for example: Dual-ARM Cortex 9), and a lot of standard interfaces. Such FPGAs could be a wonderful support for a hybrid computing system centered on the micro-controller and based on the mapReduce accelerator developed on the programmable part.

3.3 The Architecture

Because each cell has its m-word memory, the data in the p-cell MAP section is represented as an array of m p-scalar full ***horizontal vectors*** as follows:

```
v[1] = <s[11], s[12], ..., s[1p]>
v[2] = <s[21], s[22], ..., s[2p]>
...
v[m] = <s[m1], s[m2], ..., s[mp]>
```

where: each "column":

```
w[j] = <s[1j], s[2j], ..., s[mj]>
```

is the full ***vertical vector*** of scalars associated to cell j, for $j = 1, 2, \ldots p$. We call *vector memory* this distributed memory in the MAP array. Distributed along the array of cells there are also the following vectors:

```
IX = <1,    2,    ..., p   >
B  = <b[1], b[2], ..., b[p]>
A  = <a[1], a[2], ..., a[p]>
```

Vector `IX` is the constant *index vector* (used to identify each cell), while `B` is a *Boolean vector*, used to enable or disable every cell ($b_i = 1$ the cell C_i executes the current instruction). Vector `A` is the *accumulator vector* distributed along the cells. CONTROL section has two special registers: `a`, the accumulator, and `pc`, the program counter.

Each cell, C_i, in MAP and CONTROL executes instructions from a similar ISA. The ISA is accumulator centered in this initial stage of the project. of The main difference is related with the control instructions. In the MAP section there are executed *spatial control* instructions (the cells are enabled or disabled acting on the content of the vector `B`, at the clock cycle level, according to locally tested conditions). In CONTROL the program counter `pc` ensures the *temporal control*. Thus, the ACCELERATOR's ISA is the Cartesian product of two ISAs:

$$ISA = (cISA \times aISA)$$

Besides the usual arithmetic & logic and control instructions, the controller's instruction set, *cISA*, contains specific instructions related with the REDUCE unit:

```
cCLOAD(0):
 a <= reduceSum = a[0]*b[0]+ ... +a[p]*b[p]
cCLOAD(1):
 a <= reduceMax = max(a[0]*b[0], ...,a[p]*b[p])
cCLOAD(2):
 a <= reduceBool = b[0] | ... | b[p]
cCADD(0):
 a <= a+reduceSum
```

where the output of the REDUCE section is the co-operand provided by the ARRAY.

Here are few samples from aISA, which are executed only in the cells where `b[i] = 1`:

```
ADD(val):  a[i] <= b[i] ? a[i]+mem[val] : a[i]
VADD(val): a[i] <= b[i] ? a[i]+val : a[i]
CADD:      a[i] <= b[i] ? a[i]+a : a[i]
MULT(val): a[i] <= b[i] ? a[i]*mem[val] : a[i]
WHERE(cd): b[i] <= cd ? 1 : 0
ENDWHERE:  b[i] <= 1
```

where, `a` is the co-operand, i.e., the accumulator of the CONTROL section.

The program is organized in pairs of instructions, one for CONTROL prefixed with `c`, and one for the cells in MAP. Here is an example of the assembler code which performs the scalar multiplication of the index vector with itself delivering the result in the controller's accumulator:

```
      cNOP;              ENDWHERE; // b[i] <= 1 overall
      cNOP;              IXLOAD;  // a[i] <= i
      cNOP;              IXMULT;
// a[i] <= acc[i]*i
      cVLOAD(latency);   NOP;
// a <= latency size
LB(1) cBRNZDEC(1);       NOP;
// wait for latency
      cCLOAD(0);         NOP;      // a <= reduceSum
```

The left column of instructions are executed by the CONTROL unit, while the right column instructions are executed in each active cell. The first line activates all the cells in the array, the second load the value of the index vector in accumulator, then the content of the accumulator is multiplied in the accumulator with the value of the index vector. The next two instructions delays the load of the accumulator a with the reduction sum provided by the REDUCE unit with a latency in $O(log\,p)$. The last line loads in the accumulator of the CONTROL unit the value of the reduction sum computed from the content of the accumulator vector **A**.

4 Gromacs on *mapReduce* based APU

The Gromacs simulations are defined for two cases: (1) in the simulated space, a cellular periodic structure of identic three-dimension boxes is defined, and (2) in the simulated space, the cellular approach considers a number of different boxes. In this paper the first case is considered.

The main difference from the actual algorithms consists in the fact that the parallel approach is considered for both, neighborhood selection and upgrade computation.

Each particle is represented by a *particle vector* of the form: `<x, y, z, vx, vy, vz, t, s>` where: `x, y, z` are spatial coordinates, `vx, vy, vz` are the three components of the velocity, `t` is a parameter and `s` is an integer. Initially, in MEMORY there is a string of unstructured particle vectors.

4.1 The Case of Periodic Cell Structure in the Simulation Space

In the Gromacs molecular dynamic simulation, periodic boxes of particles are considered for bulk glasses, liquids, crystals or mixtures. The computation considers only one box for which periodic boundary conditions are computed.

4.1.1 The Main Tasks

There are four tasks to be defined for describing the algorithm. For the sake of simplicity, we consider the number of particles equal with the number, p, of cells, C_i, in the MAP array.

LOAD task

It loads, from MEMORY, the vector memory of the accelerator with 8 horizontal vectors, each of $p/8$ particle vectors. Then, the $p/8$ 8×8 resulting matrices are transposed. Thus, each of the p cells, in the ***mapReduce*** accelerator, gets a particle vector as a partial 8-element vertical vector:

```
pw[j] = <x, y, z, vx, vy, vz, t, s>
```

for $j = 1, 2, \ldots, p$. This task is performed in time $O(p)$.

SEARCH task

It builds in each cell C_i the particle list of neighbourhood, `pl[i]`, for the associated particle `pw[i]`, as follows:

```
/*******************************************
task name: SEARCH

r[ij]: distance between particles i and j
rc: cutoff radius defining the neighbourhood
pl[i]: neighbourhood list of pw[i]
*******************************************/
    for (i=1; i<p+1; i=i+1) begin
        transfer pw[i] in CONTROL;
        doInParallel compute r[ij];
        where (r[ij] =< rc)
            add pw[i] to pl[i];
        endwhere
    end
```

At the end of this process, in each cell C_i, besides its particle vector `pw[i]`, there is stored a particle list `pl[i]` of various lengths, for example:

```
w[1]   = < pw[1], pl[1]> =
         < pw[1], <pw[6], pw[20], pw[131]>>
w[2]   = < pw[2], pl[2]> =
         < pw[2], <pw[3], pw[32],..., pw[50]>>
...
w[46]  = < pw[46], pl[46]> =
         < pw[46], <pw[4], pw[50], pw[100]>>
...
w[p] = < pw[p], pl[p]> =
       < pw[p], <pw[65],..., pw[315]>>
```

where, for example, the neighbourhood of particle 46 is: `pl[46] = <pw[4], pw[50], pw[100]>`.

The execution time of this task is in $O(p)$, because the search of cells where $r[ij] \leq rc$ is performed in $O(1)$ and the update of the neighbourhood list, `pl[i]`, in all the active cells is performed also in constant time. The number of particle vectors in `pl[i]` is no bigger than $q < p$.

UPDATE task

It consists, mainly, in two stages. In the first stage, the program computes the force exercised by the particles from `pl[i]` on the particle `pw[i]`. Then, in the second stage, for a very short period of time, the force is applied on the particle and its new particle vector `pw[i]` is computed. The execution time for this task is in $O(p \times q)$.

STORE task

It is performed on the result of the last update on 8 horizontal vectors containing p vertical 8-component partial vectors. First, the $p/8$ 8×8 matrices, contained in the 8 horizontal vectors, are transposed. Then the resulting 8 horizontal vectors, each of $p/8$ vectors, are stored in MEMORY.

4.1.2 The Algorithm

The algorithm which uses the previously defined tasks is:

```
LOAD
loop (how many times are needed)
    SEARCH
    loop (L times)
        UPDATE
    repeat
repeat
STORE
```

The main loop is repeated so many times how may times the application requires, while the inner loop runs a number of cycles, L, determined by the accuracy imposed to the simulation. The Gromacs team recommends $L \in [10, 50]$ updates of the positions at one neighbour search. The execution time of the algorithm is in $O(p \times q)$.

4.1.3 Evaluation

Using, in the Vivado environment, our *mapReduce* accelerator instantiated for $p = 400$, the Gromacs molecular dynamic simulation for the Martini water was done. The data, corresponding to 400 particles, are loaded and *all* the stages of simulation are computed on the parallel accelerator.

At the end of the SEARCH task, in each cell C_i, besides its particle vector `pw[i]`, there is stored a particle list `pl[i]` of various lengths, containing from 0 to 60 particle vectors, so as in each cell are stored no more than $61 \times 8 = 480$ scalars. The mean value is 41×8.

The degree of parallelism achieved for each main stage of the computation are presented in Table 2. The figures are provided from the simulation, programmed in assembly language for FPGA implementation. The architecture performs pretty good for the neighbour search, the stage we added to be submitted to the parallel accelerator. Forces are computed in parallel with a smaller degree of parallelism because the mean length of the neighbourhood list is 40 while the maximal length is 60. the architecture are presented in Table 2 and Table 3. Because the neighbour search is performed once for 10 updates, its weight in the full simulation is diminished, and consequently, the overall degree of parallelism we measured in simulation is only $\varepsilon = 0.64$, instead of $\varepsilon = 0.756$.

Table 2. Degree of parallelism for running Gromacs for Martini water on the *mapReduce* accelerator [8].

Simulation part	Cycles	Percentage	Degree of Parallelism
Box periodicity	80	0.24%	66.8%
Neighbour search	26410	79.93%	79.2%
Force computation	6409	19.40%	60.4%
Thermostat	91	0.28%	51.0%
Update	50	0.14%	100%
Mean degree of parallelism ε	33040	100%	**75.6%**

Table 3 shows the performance of the two extreme solutions, CPU and specific circuit implemented as ASIC, in order to pe compared with our architectural solution in two implementations, FPGA and ASIC. The computation performance is expressed in microseconds of dynamic simulation performed per one day of computation, $\mu s/day$, while the energy use is expressed in Watts-hours per microseconds of dynamic simulation, $Wh/\mu s$.

Table 3. Comparing *mapReduce* based APU solution with PU and ASIC solutions [8].

Machine	Technology	Freq	$\mu s/day$	$Wh/\mu s$
Intel I5: one core no SSE	22nm	2.7 GHz	5.84	267.1
Intel I5: four cores & SSE	22nm	2.7 GHz	31.48	72.4
Anton	ASIC 65nm	0.4 GHz	572.32	3.1
mapReduce	FPGA 28nm	0.5 GHz	187.01	3.5
mapReduce	ASIC 22nm	2.7 GHz	1010.34	0.3

Theoretically, the acceleration for p execution cells is:

$$\alpha = p \times \frac{f_{CK\_Intel}}{f_{CK\_FPGA}} \times \varepsilon \times \frac{1}{CPI}$$

With of CPI[5] of 1.5, because the cells execute floating point operations in few clock cycles (to keep *eng small & simple*), we compute $\alpha = 31.6$. The acceleration measured in simulation for the FPGA solution, with 400 execution cells, is $\alpha = 32$ compared with one Intel core without SSE, i.e., one execution cell.

For the ASIC implementation of the *mapReduce* accelerator (with $f_{CK\_ASIC} = 2.7MHz$), the acceleration is

$$\alpha_A = 0.426p = 170.66$$

Let's call this acceleration, α_A, the *architectural acceleration*, i.e., acceleration which compares engines working

[5]CPI stands for Cycles Per Instruction.

DOI: 10.1051/matecconf/201712504012

at the same frequency, thus emphasizing the effects of the architectural design decisions. Indeed, for our case, the acceleration is limited because of $\varepsilon < 1$ (limited by the problem and by our ability to provide an efficient algorithm) and because we decided to execute floating point operations with a sequence of specific instructions.

Compared with a 4-core Intel PU with SSE, i.e., 4+16 execution units, the FPGA acceleration is 5.94×. In the section 2.2 we provided performances published for GPU and MIC based hybrid solutions. Our FPGA hybrid system performs at least 2× better than GPU, which provides 3×, or MIC which provides 1.8× acceleration. Do not mention the power of hundred of Watts consumed by GPU or MIC accelerators, compared with tenth of Watts of our FPGA solution.

The comparison with the *Anton* ASIC looks not too bad. Our FPGA implemented programmable solution has performances in the same range with this specialized circuit which is only 3× more efficient.

5 Final Remarks

The degree of parallelism achieved by the *mapReduce* accelerator in running Gromacs is 60% for force computation and 80% for neighbour search. The overall degree of parallelism is 64%. The current hybrid solutions accelerate only the force computation. Our solution brings a substantial improvement, because it involves the accelerator in the neighbour search also, for which its degree of parallelism is higher than for force computation.

We defined the *architectural acceleration* of an APU as the acceleration provided by an APU with both, one-core PU and the accelerator implemented in the same technology and running at the same frequency. Thus, the architectural acceleration of our proposal is $0.43p\times$. The acceleration is limited only by the degree of parallelism and by the weight of floating point operations, both specific to the application.

The acceleration provided by our *mapReduce* accelerator implemented in 28nm FPGA, related to the performance of an 22nm 4-core Intel CPU with SSE, is 6×. The simulation estimates, for an ASIC implementation of the ***mapReduce*** accelerator, 30× improvement.

The energy efficiency of the *mapReduce* accelerator is improved 20× for the FPGA version, and 300×, for ASIC version.

A promising compromise between FPGA and ASIC in implementing ***mapReduce*** accelerators for Gromacs system is the eASIC technology.

Acknowledgments

The authors got meaningful support from Nicolae Goga, in understanding important details about the Gromacs system, and form Lucian Petrică an exigent reader of the intermediary forms of the text.

References

[1] S. Alam, U. Varetto, *GROMACS on Hybrid CPU-GPU and CPU-MIC Clusters: Preliminary Porting Experiences, Results and Next Steps,* At: http://www.prace-ri.eu/IMG/pdf/wp120.pdf

[2] K. Asanovic, *et al.*, The landscape of parallel computing research: A view from Berkeley (2006) http://www.eecs.berkeley.edu/Pubs/TechRpts/2006/EECS-2006-183.pdf

[3] Călin Bîra, *Programming environment for parallel accelerators*, PhD Thesis, UPB, ETTI, Department of Electronic Devices, Circuits and Architectures (2013) http://arh.pub.ro/papers/LucrareDoctorat_v9d.pdf

[4] L. Jianguo, *Running GROMACS on GPUs: a Benchmark Study* (2014) At: https://www.acrc.a-star.edu.sg/docs/ASTAR

[5] S. C. Kleene, "General Recursive Functions of Natural Numbers", in *Math. Ann.*, 112, (1936)

[6] E. Lindahl, *Molecular Simulation with GROMACS on CUDA GPUs* (2013) At: http://on-demand.gputechconf.com/gtc/2013/webinar/gromacs-kepler-gpus-gtc-express-webinar.pdf

[7] M. Malita, G. Ştefan, D. Thiébaut, "Not Multi-, but Many-Core: Designing Integral Parallel Architectures for Embedded Computation" *ACM SIGARCH Computer Architecture News*, Volume 35 , Issue 5, pp. 32-38 (2007)

[8] D. Mihăiţă, *N-Body Problem. Application, on a Map-Reduce Accelerator, to Molecular Dynamics*, Master Thesis, Politehnica University of Bucharest, (2016)

[9] M. Plotnikov, *GROMACS for Intel Xeon Phi^{T}M Coprocessor* At: https://software.intel.com/en-us/articles/gromacs-for-intel-xeon-phi-coprocessor

[10] D. E. Shaw, *et al.*, "Anton, A Special-Purpose Machine for Molecular Dynamics Simulation". *Communications of the ACM*. 51 (7): 91–97 (2008)

[11] G. Ştefan, *et al.*, "The CA1024: A Fully Programmable System-On-Chip for Cost-Effective HDTV Media Processing", in *Hot Chips: A Symposium on High Performance Chips*, Memorial Auditorium, Stanford University (2006) At: https://youtu.be/HMLT4EpKBAw 35:00

[12] G. Ştefan, "One-chip TeraArchitecture", *Proceedings of the 8th Applications and Principles of Information Science Conference*. Okinawa (2009) http://arh.pub.ro/gstefan/teraArchitecture.pdf

[13] G. Ştefan, M. Maliţa, "Can One-Chip Parallel Computing Be Liberated From Ad Hoc Solutions? A Computation Model Based Approach and Its Implementation", *18th Inter. Conf. on Ciruits, Systems, Communications and Computers*, Santorini, 582-597 (2014)

DOI: 10.1051/matecconf/201712504013

Milk duct segmentation in microscopic HE images of breast cancer tissues

Bartosz Świderski[1], *Michał* Kruk[1], *Stanisław* Osowski[2,3], *Grzegorz* Wieczorek[1], *Jarosław* Kurek[1], *Leszek J.* Chmielewski[1], and *Arkadiusz* Orłowski[1]

[1] Faculty of Applied Informatics & Mathematics, Warsaw University of Life Sciences, Warsaw, Poland
[2] Faculty of Electrical Engineering, Warsaw University of Technology, Warsaw, Poland
[3] Faculty of Electronics, Military University of Technology, Warsaw, Poland

Abstract. The aim of the paper is to recognize and extract the milk duct in haematoxylin and eosin (HE) stained breast cancer tissues. The paper presents the modified K-means approach to segmentation of the milk duct in HE stained images. Instead of using single pixels we propose to consider the defined region of pixels in the process. Thanks to such modification more accurate extraction of the milk ducts has been achieved. To compare the results in a numerical way the GT images prepared by the medical expert have been subtracted from the corresponding images created by the segmentation methods. The numerical experiments performed for many preparations have confirmed the superiority of such approach. The proposed method has allowed reducing significantly the error of duct segmentation in comparison to the classical K-means approaches. The results show, that our method is superior to the standard K-means and to the K-means preceded by averaging or Gaussian filtration at different size of filtration mask.

1. Introduction – medical background

Ductal carcinoma in situ (DCiS) belongs to the most frequently appearing type of non-invasive breast cancer [1,2]. It is "non-invasive" because is limited to the milk duct and is regarded as not life-threatening. However, DCiS increases the risk of developing an invasive breast cancer later on (around 1/3 od DCiS are ended in an invasive cancer). More than 90% of cases are without any visible symptoms in normal life.

The first signs of the illness can be recognized in the mammogram. After noting them the biopsy is usually made and the pathologist analyzes the piece of breast tissue and reports back on the type and grade of the DCIS, describing how abnormal the cells look when compared with the normal breast cells.

The image shown in Fig.1 [4] presents possible types of findings, starting from the normal cells and ending on the invasive ductal cancer. They include normal cells, ductal hyperplasia (too many cells present), atypical ductal hyperplasia (too many cells starting to take on an abnormal appearance), ductal carcinoma in situ (too many cells but still confined to the inside of the duct), DCiS with micro-invasion (few of the cancer cells breaking through the wall of the duct) and finally invasive ductal cancer (many cancer cells broken beyond the breast duct transferring DCiS into an invasive ductal carcinoma,).

Automatic recognition of the milk ducts is an important task in computerized approach to the problem. The aim is to separate individual milk ducts existing in the preparation. On the basis of many extracted ducts the medical expert can diagnose the particular case. Our task in this presentation is to develop computerized system which is able to extract the individual ducts from the whole image with the highest precision comparable to the precision of human expert.

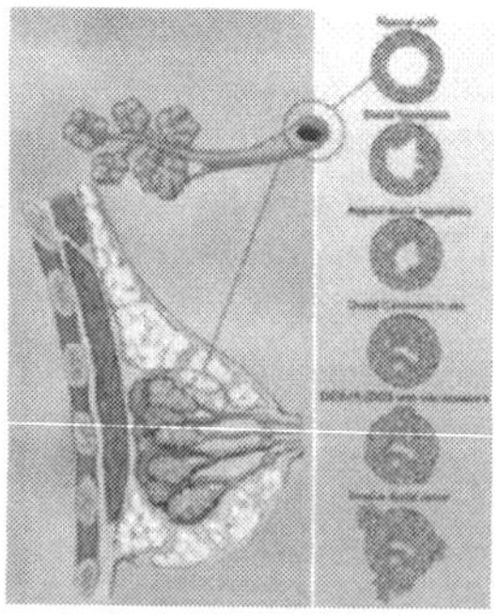

Fig. 1 Different phases of development of the DCiS. The images on the right represent the views of milk ducts in different stages of cancer advancement [4].

2. Problem statement

The aim of the paper is to recognize and extract the milk duct in haematoxylin and eosin (HE) stained breast cancer tissues. They form the region of interest in our analysis. An example of the analyzed image is presented in Fig. 2. It depicts the cross area of many milk ducts of different sizes and shapes. The arrows point to two chosen ducts. The group of ducts are located in the background of the tissue.

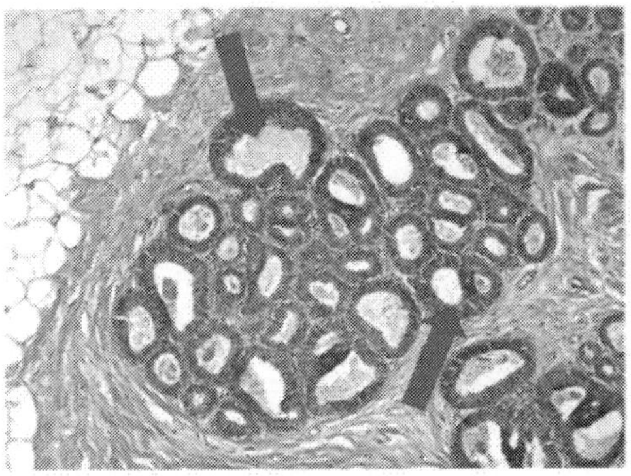

Fig. 2 An example of the image subject to the analysis in the paper. Many milk ducts of different size and shape, which should be extracted, are present in the image.

The most important factor in medical decision taking is precise determination of the shape, size, degree of filling the inside, width of the walls and channel patency. On the basis of values of these parameters the decision of the advancement of the breast cancer is taken. Therefore, the task of extraction of all milk ducts should be done as precise as possible.

The popular method of doing it is the K-means algorithm [3,5,6]. However, its direct application to this problem is not efficient, since it results in a lot of artifacts in the background. The remedy to this problem is application of the morphological operations, which allow removing the residual noise in the resulting image. This process has some negative aspects - changing the shape and size of the milk duct. Our work presents some modification of K-means which eliminates the need for additional image processing. Thanks to this we are able to achieve better accuracy in the milk duct reconstruction. This will be confirmed by comparing our results with the ground truth (GT) pattern pointed manually by the medical expert for the same images.

3. Materials

The HE images of the breast cancer tissues, which are subject to analysis, have been prepared in the Military Medical Institute in Warsaw. The biopsy material has been acquired from the patients suffering from breast cancer of different grade and then prepared using HE technology. The preparations have been scanned using high definition 3D Histech scanner and obtained images stored in the data base. The size of each image was equal 55808×82688. Fig. 3 presents some examples of images representing three grades of cancer advancement.

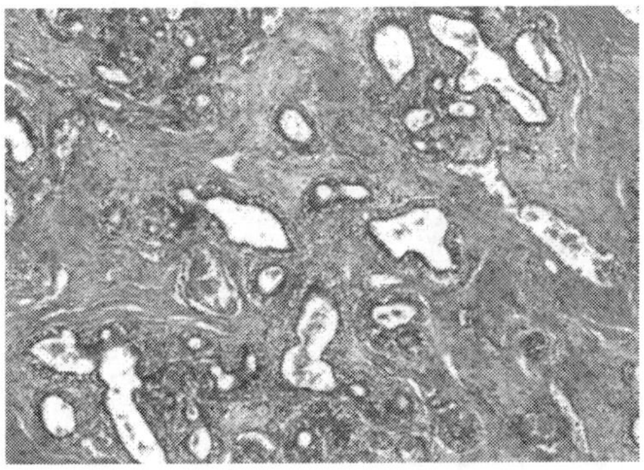

a)

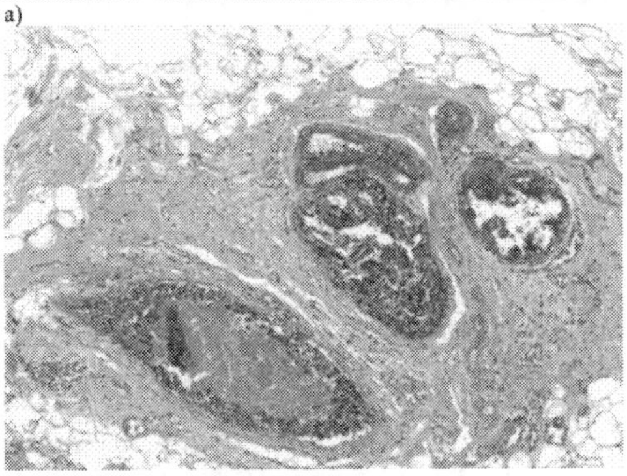

b)

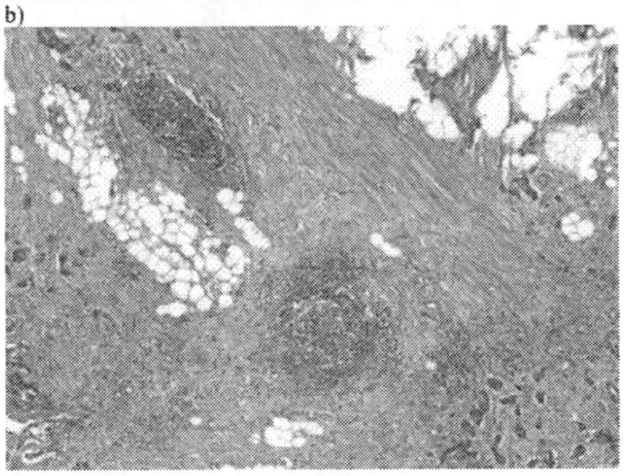

c)

Fig. 3 The examples of HE images of breast cancer tissues representing three different grades: a) ductual hyperplasia, b) ductual carcinoma in situ (DCIS), c) invasive ductual cancer.

4. Methods

The aim of clusterization is to separate the analyzed image into clusters representing the milk ducts existing in the image. Classical K-means operates on individual pixels in RGB channels, searching for the nearby pixels of similar intensity [5,6]. In our proposition we extend the representation of individual pixel to the region around it, including N neighboring pixels. In the case of RGB image each pixel will be represented by the vector of the length 3N, **x**=[R_0, R_1, …, R_N, G_0, G_1, …, G_N, B_0, B_1, …, B_N], where the elements within R, G an B family are arranged in a non-decreasing order of pixel intensity values. An example of vector creation is shown below. Let us assume the RGB representation of image in the following matrix form.

48	**108**	**53**	**117**	**215**	**222**
73	**164**	**181**	**169**	**213**	**67**
23	**165**	**60**	197	**65**	**81**
147	**173**	**30**	**89**	**157**	**30**
174	**162**	**155**	**169**	**149**	**240**
139	241	115	106	138	165

122	**133**	**103**	**238**	**134**	**189**
163	**254**	**114**	**249**	**135**	**133**
139	**55**	**93**	49	**220**	**89**
165	**27**	**195**	**35**	**124**	**38**
139	**28**	**160**	**178**	**100**	**150**
184	16	197	24	171	67

11	**188**	**84**	**227**	**96**	**112**
193	**101**	**108**	**100**	**55**	**213**
62	**174**	**69**	196	**202**	**196**
113	**180**	**50**	**101**	**243**	**42**
176	**113**	**210**	**206**	**83**	**220**
91	5	110	193	171	253

We will create vector representation for the marked RGB pixels of the intensity levels equal 197, 49 and 196, respectively. Assume N=25, which means that each pixel of the image has 2 neighbors from left and right as well as from the top and bottom. The vector representation of the marked pixels neighborhood region in RGB channels arranged in a non-decreasing order will look as following.

$\mathbf{X}_1$=
[30,30,53,60,65,67,81,89,108,117,149,155,157,162,164,165,169,169,173,181,197,213,215,222,240,
27,28,35,38,49,55,89,93,100,103,114,124,133,133,134,135,150,160,178,189,195,220,238,249,254,
42,50,55,69,83,84,96,100,101,101,108,112,113,174,180,188,196,196,202,206,210,213,220,227,243]

This vector represents pixels of the image region denoted in the matrix form by bold. To prepare vector representation for the boundary pixels (for example position (1,1)) we extend the image by replicating the neighboring n columns and n rows in vertical and horizontal fashion. An example of such replication for red channel is shown below. Now the element (1,1) of the previous red matrix of the intensity 48 has the required number of neighbors.

48	108	48	108	53	117	215	222	215	222
73	164	73	164	181	169	213	67	213	67
48	108	48	**108**	**53**	**117**	**215**	**222**	215	222
73	164	73	**164**	**181**	**169**	**213**	**67**	213	67
23	165	23	**165**	**60**	197	**65**	**81**	65	81
147	173	147	**173**	**30**	**89**	**157**	**30**	157	30
174	162	174	**162**	**155**	**169**	**149**	**240**	149	240
139	241	139	241	115	106	138	165	138	165
174	162	174	162	155	169	149	240	149	240
139	241	139	241	115	106	138	165	138	165

To avoid the outlier problem p extreme elements from both sides of each RGB vector can be rejected, making the clusterization problem more resistant to different type of noise, that might exist in the image. Assuming for example p=2 we get the previous vector in the form

$\mathbf{X}_2$=
[~~30,~~30,53,60,65,67,81,89,108,117,149,155,157,162,164,165,169,169,173,181,197,213,215,~~222,240~~,
~~27,~~28,35,38,49,55,89,93,100,103,114,124,133,133,134,135,150,160,178,189,195,220,238,~~249,254~~,
~~42,50~~,55,69,83,84,96,100,101,101,108,112,113,174,180,188,196,196,202,206,210,213,220,~~227,243~~]

Searching for the nearest neighbors of the particular pixels we use the Euclidean distance between its vector representation. For example the distance between the marked RGB pixels of intensity (197, 49, 196) and the pixels of intensity (60, 93, 69) of the first row of matrix is equal d= 101.5185.

The alternative solution that will be compared in this work is application of the standard K-means algorithm, or K-mean algorithm preceded by the low-pass filtration of the image. The filtration might apply different filtering masks, for example averaging or Gaussian filters.

5. Results

The aim of numerical experiments was to make comparative analysis of the results of our automatic extraction of milk ducts to the classical K-means methods, all related to the results of medical expert. Fig. 4 presents three examples of original images containing the milk ducts of different shape and size.

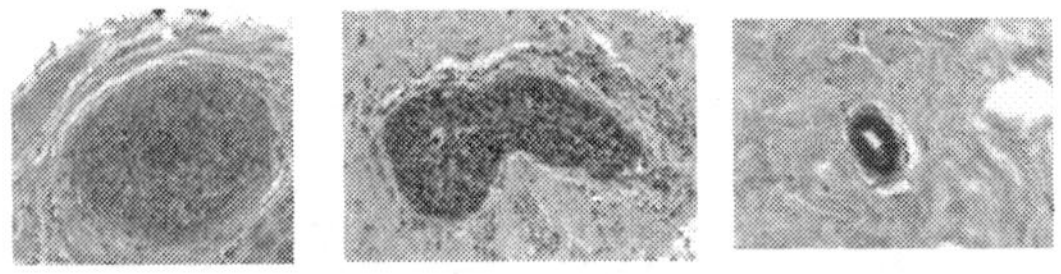

Fig. 4 The examples of original HE images of the milk duct used in numerical experiments

The results of our automatic system for these three images are presented in Fig. 5 (upper row). The boundary of the extracted images are clean and the background is without any artifacts. The bottom row presents the corresponding results obtained by using the standard K-means algorithm.

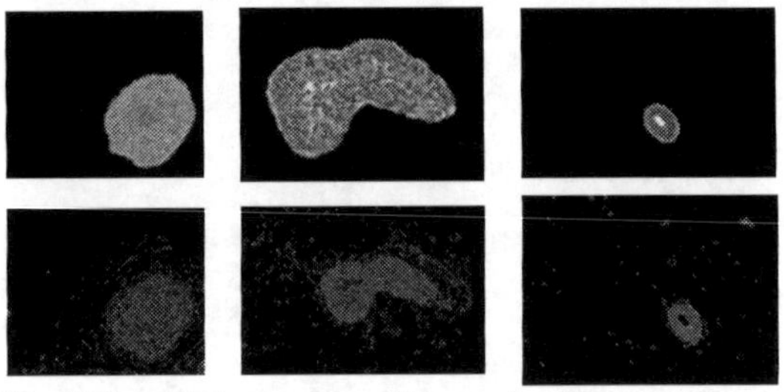

Fig. 5 The milk ducts extracted by our algorithm (upper row) and by standard K-mean (lower row)

The difference of the quality of extraction is evident. The results of our approach do not need any additional post-processing, while the application of standard K-means results in many artefacts, that should be eliminated by morphological operations.

Fig. 6 presents the details of graphical comparison of the extraction results of one chosen duct due to our algorithm and to the other existing approaches. Fig. 6a presents the original input image, Fig. 6b – the milk duct extracted using our method, Fig. 6c – the result of application of standard K-means and Fig. 6d – the standard K-means combined with application of the averaging filter with the 3x3 filtering mask.

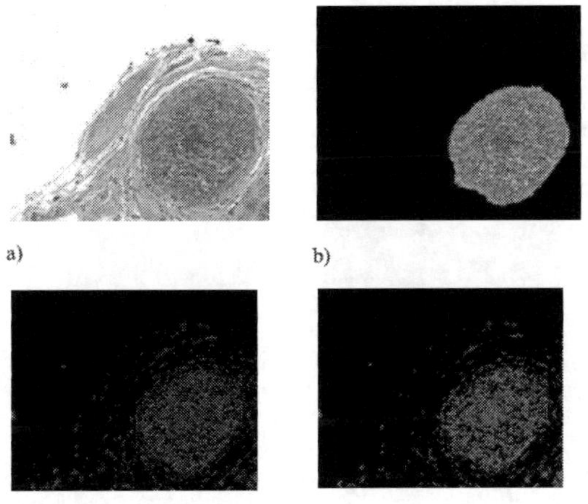

Fig. 6 The images of the milk duct: a) the original input image, b) the milk duct extracted using our method, c) the result of application of standard K-means, d) the standard K-means with application of the averaging filter with the 3x3 filtering mask.

To compare the results in a numerical way the GT images prepared by the medical expert have been subtracted from the corresponding images created by the segmentation methods. The differential images have been defined on the basis of the binary masks. The sum of the nonzero pixels in the differential image was divided by the total sum of pixels in the GT image. The statistical results of such comparison have been done for the data base of 10 preparations, from which more than 80 milk ducts have been extracted. The statistical results are presented at application of different number of clusters used in K-means algorithm. Different variants of K-means (our approach, standard K-means and K-means with application of filtering) are depicted in Table 1.

Table 1 The relative difference of segmented image and GT image prepared by medical expert at application of different clustering methods.

Method	Number of clusters			
	3	4	5	6
Proposed method n=10	62,77%	**25,37%**	28,57%	39,82%
Proposed method n=5	67,14%	36,71%	**36%**	43,32%
Proposed method n=3	90,32%	39,32%	**39,18%**	42,17%
Average filter 3x3	141,83%	**41,37%**	58,61%	78,3%
Average filter 5x5	604,87%	514,21%	358,68%	**82,27%**
Gaussian filter 3x3	133,05%	**37,17%**	49,7%	75,08%
Gaussian filter 5x5	132,8%	**37,18%**	49,7%	75,95%
Standard kmeans	141,07%	**35,39%**	50,61%	66,35%

The values higher than 100% might have happened in the case when the size of the extracted ducts were much larger than the GT result.

The results show, that our method is superior to the standard K-means and to the K-means preceded by averaging or Gaussian filtration at different size of filtration mask. The advantage of the proposed method is very well seen in the best case, when at n=10 (mask size N=21×21).

6. Conclusions

The paper has presented the modified K-mean method for extracting the milk ducts in HE images of breast cancer. The main point of the method is substitution of the single pixel in K-mean algorithm by the region around this pixel and concatenation of RGB regions into common vector.

The proposed method has allowed reducing significantly the error of duct segmentation in comparison to the classical K-means approaches. Future research will be directed to test the method on larger population of HE images and compare the results with the GT patterns prepared by different experts. At the same time the numerical measures characterizing the basic parameters of extracted ducts will be proposed.

References

[1] C.Y. Chen, L.M. Sun, B.O. Anderson, Paget disease of the breast: changing patterns of incidence, clinical presentation, and treatment in the USA, *Cancer*, 107(7),1448, (2006).

[2] D.D. Dershaw, A. Abramson, D.W. Kinne, Ductal carcinoma in situ: mammographic findings and clinical implications, *Radiology*,170(2), 411–415, (1989).

[3] K. Anil Jain, Data clustering: 50 years beyond K-means, *Pattern Recognition Letters*, 31(8), 651–666, (2010).

[4] http://www.breastcancer.org/symptoms/types/dcis/diagnosis.

[5] C. Tse-Wei, C. Yi-Ling, C. Shao-Yi, Fast image segmentation based on K-means clustering with histograms in HSV color space, *2008 IEEE 10th Workshop on Multimedia Signal Processing* (MMSP), Cairns, Queensland.

[6] P.N. Tan, M. Steinbach, V. Kumar, *Introduction to data mining*, Boston: Pearson Education Inc., 2006.

MATEC Web of Conferences **125**, 04014 (2017) DOI: 10.1051/matecconf/201712504014
CSCC 2017

Network model of risk analysis in the technical structures

Andrzej Walczak[1], Jarosław Napiórkowski[1*], Piotr Adamczyk[1], Grzegorz Kiryk[1]

[1] Faculty of Cybernetics, Military University of Technology (WAT), Gen. Sylwestra Kaliskiego 2 Str., 00-908 Warsaw, Poland

Abstract. The aim of the article is to present the possibilities offered by network models. This article discusses the network model of risk analysis in technical structures. We are discussed some network centrality measures and their use in risk analysis. We have proposed a mixed, expert-formal model for analyzing the risk of asset risk in technical structures based on own methodology of network building. We shown that mathematically model of structure of the network and its corresponding physical are linked by bijection. This creates a unequivocal model for quantitative risk analysis.

1 Introduction

Generally known and common development and describing the concept of the risk assessment process is PN-EN 31010: 2010 (Risk management - risk assessment techniques. Standard is not intended for certification, regulatory or contractual use but provides guidance on the selection and application of systematic and methodological risk assessment techniques [1]. Risk assessment carried out in accordance with this standard supports other measures of risk management. It shows the use of certain techniques, referring to other international standards, which describe in more detail the concept and application of these techniques.

As examples of such techniques the norm indicates, for example: "brainstorming", Delphi technique, preliminary analysis of threats, Failure Mode and Effects Analysis, FMEA, Fault Tree Analysis, FTA, methods based on Bayesian statistics and Bayesian networks.
The techniques are classified according to their use at different stages:

- risk identification;
- analysis of the consequences at the stage of risk analysis;
- qualitative, quantitative or semi-quantitative estimation of the probability at the stage of risk analysis;
- analysis of control effectiveness at the stage of risk analysis;
- evaluation of risk level at the stage of risk analysis;
- risk assessment;

At each stage of risk assessment, it is possible to use various tools and methods.

This standard, Table A.1 (Applicability of tools used for risk assessment) contains special classification, proposal of the techniques that can be applied at each stage of risk assessment and their usefulness.

Methods based on Bayesian statistics and Bayesian networks are classified as non-applicable to risk identification of qualitative, quantitative or semi-quantitative estimation of the probability at the stage of risk analysis or risk assessment at the stage of risk analysis. At the same time, the standard shows them as having application to the analysis of the consequences at the stage of risk analysis and risk assessment.

According to the standard, one of the strong points of this approach is the fact that only the Bayes rule and knowledge of a priori probabilities are required.

What is more, the language is easy to understand and the method provides a mechanism for using subjective beliefs.

At the same time, it has some limitations, such as:

- defining dependency on the Bayesian network may not be feasible due to the complexity and costs related thereto;
- the Bayesian approach requires knowledge of a number of conditional probabilities, which are generally determined on the basis of expert knowledge. The software based on the Bayesian network can provide answers only on the basis of such assumptions.

The advantage of network models is the simplicity of their interpretation. Network models presented in graphical form are understandable not only for those involved in their creation. In case of risk assessment, the undoubted advantage of the network model is the ability to visualize the links between the effects of threats.

Taking an inventory of resources and identifying the processes of vulnerability and risks, the scale effect

* Corresponding author: jaroslaw.napiorkowski@wat.edu.pl

should be taken into account [4]. The size of the network representing expertise knowledge can also be a problem.

However, for network models supported by the fact that if we build a network model is the ability to obtain estimates of the probability distributions which should be used on the network. Given the above, it is true to define dependencies in the Bayesian network is troublesome but developing methods for building the network security models may prove to be a truly cost-effective method of analysis of potential security despite the above-mentioned limitations.

2 What we get by building network model of technical infrastructure?

The construction of a network model of technical infrastructure should begin with the development of a methodology for the production of a network model of the examined technical structure, which will result in each expert product the same graphical image of the examined technical structure. As a result, we obtain a graphic form of the model examined structure with each node environment analysis. This will give us the opportunity:

- quantitative characterization of the effect of each node in this structure for asset security risk,
- simulate changes in the network structure of the so that through structural changes control the risk of failure. For example, in the analysis of the security of strictly law [15] regulated information we can simulate the impact of statutory changes or standards on selected elements of the information loss,
- build a simulator of real situations, which by their nature (crisis situations) are not repetitive, that in the simulation can occur under varying conditions of risk.

A particularly interesting element of the network model of technical infrastructure (including critical infrastructure) is the ability to enumerate characteristics that uniquely indicate the impact of the network structure and individual nodes on the propagation of threat in such a structure.

The impact of individual network elements has of both local features, resulting from the immediate environment of the test element and the global features (or rather non-local) resulting from the nature of the network structure in the wider environment of the examined element.

3 Network centrality measures

Centrality measure defines how important is a node in the network. Centrality measures serve to measure the intuitive feeling that in most real composite networks, some vertices or edges are more important / prestigious than others. Centrality can affect both nodes and the entire network. There are a vast number of different centrality measures that have been proposed over the years.

In the network structure, the numerical values of selected characteristics of its components (in particular network nodes) which describe the influence of these elements in its structure can be determined. Defining centrality in networks that analysis security can help identify key vulnerabilities and vulnerabilities.

In the literature, these items are illustrated on basic network models such as linear structure, star structure, linear cyclic structure.

These will be respectively: centrality degree, betweenness centrality and closeness centrality. These three centrality measures are developed and tested in many different ways creating slightly different parametric characteristics of network elements. We will refer to their definitions and applications to the sample technical infrastructure. Each of these parameters will be called a centrality of node - according to the terminology accepted in the literature.

We will introduce a measure of degree centrality node, closeness and betweenness for work Borgatti, Everett, Freeman (2002). Similar measures have been introduced centrality of the analysis of complex networks. [8].

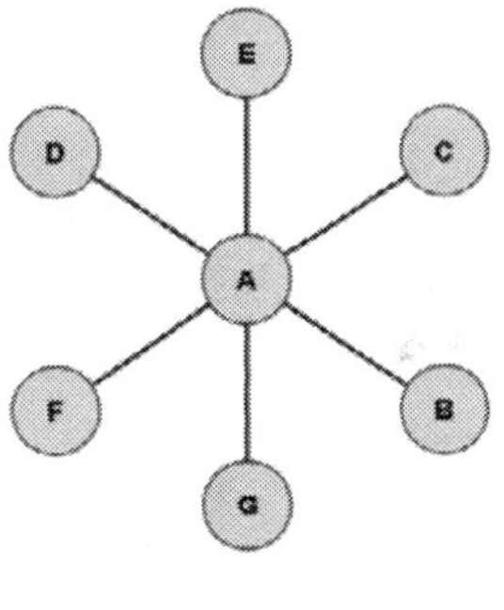

Fig. 1. Star structure. Source: own elaboration.

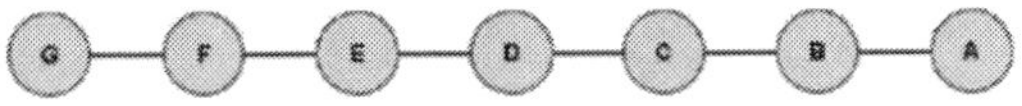

Fig. 2. Linear structure. Source: own elaboration.

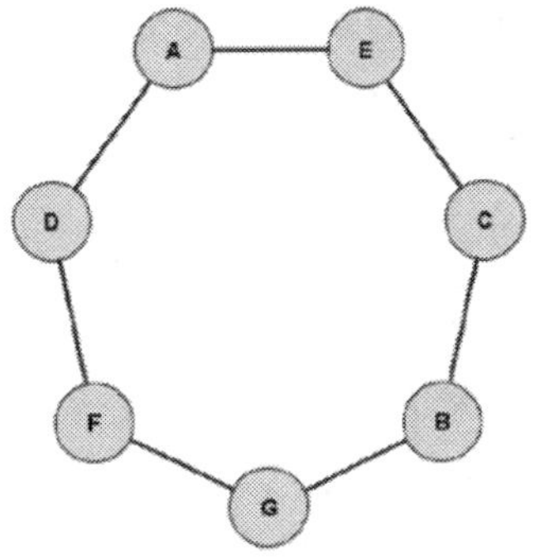

Fig. 3. Ring (linear cyclic) structure. Source: own elaboration.

Let us consider the typical characteristics computed for network nodes.

The degree (or valency) - deg(v) - of a vertex of a graph is the number of edges incident to the vertex, with loops counted twice. [10, 12].

In directed graphs we can distinguish degree called in-degree and out-degree [5]. We call the number of edges entering or leaving the node (for non-directed graphs we use the vertex degree term).

In star topology network (Fig. 1) node called A has a degree higher than any other node. This gives it more possibilities to create different relationships than any other node in this structure.

3.1 Degree Centrality

Degree is a simple centrality measure that counts how many neighbours a node has. It can be used to illustrate the popularity or influence of nodes. It is useful for determining which nodes are critical (key node) for spreading information or influencing nodes located in the immediate neighbours.

Let us note that the simple enumeration of degree of node does not yet give the essence of this characteristic. Only when we add a descriptive creation of a large (more than the other nodes) number of relations in the analysed network is "node degree centrality" becomes a descriptive characteristic. It can be used for further analysis of the properties of network elements because it points to clearly defined properties in the real case of the network. Because the node degree is easy to calculate with a known network structure, assigning it a parametric measure of degree centrality allows for the transfer of the obtained numerical characteristic to descriptive characteristics of the network used in separate analyzes of its properties.

In linear networks, the degree of node A is not significantly higher than the degrees of other nodes, and the number of relationships created by node A with other nodes does not open a special preference for node A in its power to influence other network elements.

In the real world there are many interpersonal relationships and people think that a large number of relationships with others (key figure) are the most important.

For undirected graph degree C_d is:

$$C_d(v_i) = d_i \tag{1}$$

where

d_i – number of edges at v_i.

If the network is directed, we have two versions of the measure: in-degree is the number of in-coming links, or the number of predecessor nodes; out-degree is the number of out-going links, or the number of successor nodes.

3.2 Prestige and gregariousness

Prestige (popularity) and gregariousness of node are measures that showing which node is more important because it communicates with more nodes. Nodes with more outgoing edges are preferred., in this way we determine the publicity of the node. When we using in-degrees d_i^{in}, degree centrality measures how popular a node is and its value shows prominence or prestige.

$$C_d(v_i) = d_i^{in} \tag{2}$$

Similar calculations should be performed to calculate gregariousness node d_i^{out}.

$$C_d(v_i) = d_i^{out} \tag{3}$$

When we join the in-degree (d_i^{in}) and out-degree d_i^{out} as a result, we ignore the direction of the edges. In fact, when we remove the direction of the edge we get $C_d(v_i)=d_i$.

$$C_d(v_i) = d_i^{in} + d_i^{out} \tag{4}$$

Simple standardization methods include normalization by the maximum possible degree:

$$C_d^{norm}(v_i) = \frac{d_i}{n-1} \tag{5}$$

where n is the number of nodes.

We can also normalize by maximizing the degree of node:

$$C_d^{max}(v_i) = \frac{d_i}{\max_j d_i} \tag{6}$$

Finally, we can normalize by the sum of degrees:

$$C_d^{sum}(v_i) = \frac{d_i}{\sum_j d_i} \tag{7}$$

We can also normalize by the maximum degree. For the purpose of this work, we will adopt the following designation.

$$C_D = \frac{\deg(v)}{n-1} \tag{8}$$

where

v - node index,

n - the number of nodes,

deg(v) is number of adjacent edges

3.3 Closeness, reach

Closeness centrality is a measure of centrality in a network, calculated as the sum of the length of the shortest paths between the node and all other nodes in the graph. This is therefore the expected distance between the node and any other node. Thus the more central a node is, the closer it is to all other nodes.

In star type network (Fig. 1) node A is closer to each network node than any other node. Such a structural advantage of node A translates into the strength of its

DOI: 10.1051/matecconf/201712504014

impact on other nodes in the network. Parameter called „closeness" is , Just like the node degree calculated from the definition given in a later section of this article. Obtaining numerical characteristics describing the closeness of nodes gives us another ability to use this parameter in the structure of the network to analyze its properties.

Just like earlier, in a star-type network, the closeness of node A to other nodes in the network is much higher than in acyclic and cyclic (ring) linear structures. In ring structure of network each node other than A is actually closer to this node than in the acyclic network. A small change in the structure has a significant impact on this parameter because it is higher than in the acyclic linear structure but it is significantly lower than in the star structure.

$$C_C(v) = \frac{n-1}{\sum_{i=1, v\neq k}^{n-1} d(v,k_i)} \qquad (9)$$

So we have to count all distances $d(v, k_i)$ from node v to all other nodes and calculate $C_C(v)$,

3.4 Betweenness

Especially important for us is the betweenness centrality.

Betweenness is the ability of a node in the network to create connections with other nodes. A node with a higher value of this parameter than other nodes in the network is often called a hub. In a star-type and a ring topology network, node A can connect much more nodes than a linear network - although the latter is also located between the other nodes. But the connection structure is in a cyclic network other than the star network.

In the descriptive definition, we mean that this measure shows the strength of the network node to the extent that it belongs to the roads in the network graph such that they join two other nodes. If we assign all the roads connecting each pair of nodes and calculate how often the node "x" lies on these roads, we define its betweenness centrality. To summarize, if a node is on all or nearly all the roads connecting two arbitrarily selected nodes in the network its betweenness is high. It is easy to see that this node property strongly depends on the network structure.

$$C_B(v) = \sum_{i\neq j\neq k} \frac{\sigma_{jk}(v)}{\sigma_{jk}} \qquad (10)$$

In formula (10) j and k these are indexes of two arbitrary nodes in the network between which there is a path in the network graph. The numerator of an equation is the number of shortest paths from j to k that pass through v.

An example network built for the analyzed example of any technical infrastructure (in our example, the technical equipment of the office with automatic document flow control [17]) is based on constructing a triangle (Fig. 4) asset – vulnerability – threat.

Fig. 4. Network reference model. Source: [7]

The threat is passed on to the resource through its single susceptibility or a subset of individual, independent vulnerabilities. Individual nodes of susceptibility need not be interrelated, i.e. there is no obligatory relationship in the network graph between nodes of vulnerability.

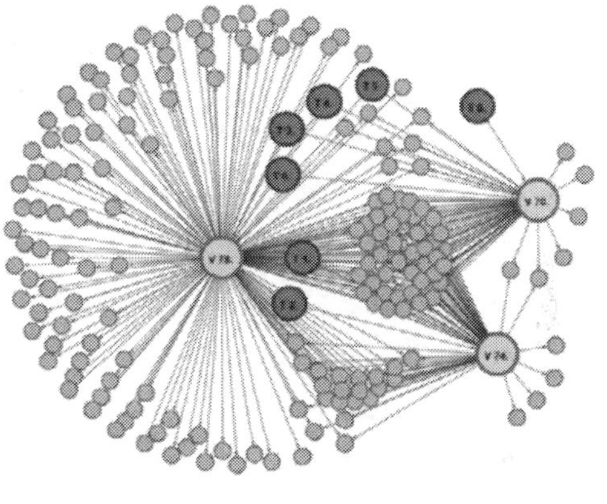

Fig. 5. Network graph [6, 7, 16] for security model described in the office - selected portion of the assets. (black - asset node, green - vulnerability node, red - threat node). Source: own elaboration, Gephi ver. 0.9.1

Table 1. Betweenness Centrality of sample nodes.

Node	Node degree	Betweenness Centrality	Normalized Betweenness Centrality [0,1]
V 70.	65	239.333333	0.007108
V 74	75	70.333333	0.002089
V 78	170	667.333333	0.019819

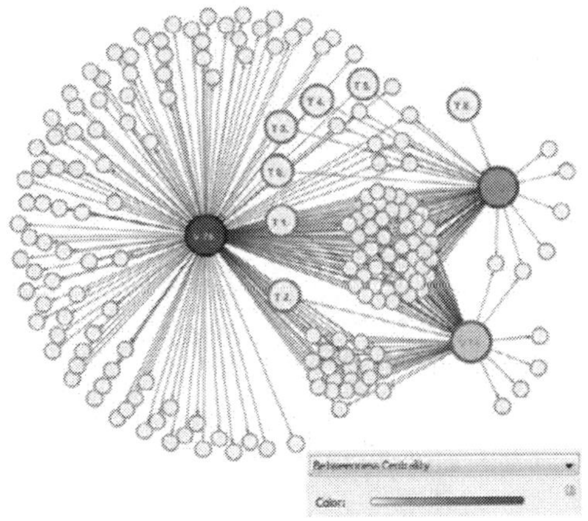

DOI: 10.1051/matecconf/201712504014

Fig. 6. Coloured illustration of Betweenness Centrality Distribution for example network. Source: own elaboration, Gephi ver. 0.9.1

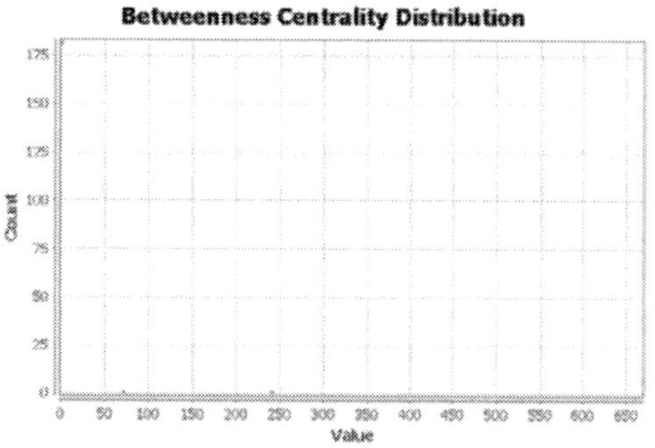

Fig. 7. Betweenness Centrality Distribution. Source: own elaboration, Gephi ver. 0.9.1

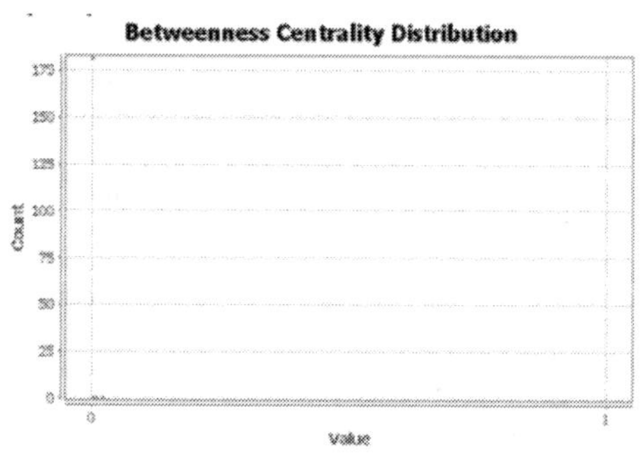

Fig. 8. Normalized Betweenness Centrality Distribution. Source: own elaboration, Gephi ver. 0.9.1

For our model are possible situations when for an asset to have one and only one susceptibility, or one common vulnerability has a group (subset) of assets (Fig. 5). If such single vulnerability is activated by a subset of threats, betweenness for the node illustrating this structure vulnerability will be equal to 1 because this node belongs to all designated routes linking assets and threats nodes. We do not take into account the routes theoretically possible but not created in the network graph.

Fig. 9.. Assets that may be affected by the occurrence of one of the six above-mentioned threats in the context of vulnerability V 70. - "uncontrolled remote access of third party users." Source: own elaboration, Gephi ver. 0.9.1

Table 2. Closeness and Betweenness Centrality of nodes from Fig. 9. Source: own elaboration, Gephi ver. 0.9.1

Node	Node Degree	Closness Centrality	Betweeness Centrality
T 1.	3	0.504249	0.000000
T 2.	2	0.502906	0.000000
T 3.	2	0.502906	0.000000
T 4.	2	0.502906	0.000000
T 5.	2	0.502906	0.000000
T 6.	1	0.504201	0.000000
T 8.	1	0.504201	0.000000
V 70.	65	1.000000	239.333333

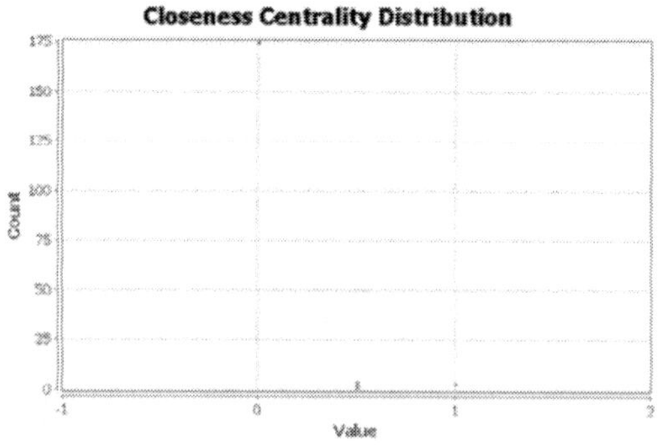

Fig. 10. Closeness Centrality Distribution. Source: own elaboration, Gephi ver. 0.9.1

The second situation is when an asset is characterized by several vulnerabilities shared with other assets (Fig. 6). Betweenness at the time will be less than 1 for each of the nodes describing vulnerability, because the number of all routes in the graph between pairs of nodes

 DOI: 10.1051/matecconf/201712504014

will always be greater than the number of routes that pass through the selected single node of vulnerability.

So the model adopted for determining the risk enforce structure for created network in the convention "asset - vulnerability - threat" and by that on the range of values of the individual centrality measures for the vulnerability nodes in this network. We can easily see that the betweenness for vulnerability nodes is less or equal than 1 in constructed network models.

In our network, if the degree of vulnerability node is high (its connects many assets nodes with a large number of threat nodes), at the same time it will have closeness too high because a large number of nodes can achieve it in one step. Betweenness for each node of vulnerability will be depend only on the network structure. The closer to 1 will be value of betweenness for node that have high degree, it such vulnerability in the risk analysis structure will be a very important node with high impact.

But if the vulnerability node has a low degree, i.e. it connects a small number of assets nodes with threat nodes, then the closeness factor in this case will be not high, but betweenness factor may be closer to 1. This means that even with a small group of threats they are transferred to the asset nodes. So, the value of the betweenness parameter indicates the significance of the vulnerability node in the forwarding of threats to the asset. This means that the vulnerability node can be a hub even with a relatively small value of degree centrality or closeness centrality of that node.

4 Risk of exposure assets to the threat

This risk is defined in a classic form:

$$R = p(T) * con(A) \tag{11}$$

Probability of threat occurrence p(*T*) is usually estimated based on experts' knowledge of threats. However, whether and to what extent the occurrence of a threat will mean the occurrence of a risk on a particular resource depends on the structure of the network and, in particular, on the location of the vulnerability nodes of the asset at risk. The first approximation will be the dependency of the asset threat function F(*A*) on the vulnerability structure of the examined asset. With a certain probability of threat p(*T*) its influence on asset may be described by following equation:

$$F(A) = B * p(T) \tag{12}$$

where *B* is the calculated value of the betweenness of vulnerability in the examined network for the vulnerability node that transport the threat to the resource. This equation does not raise doubts when there is a single vulnerability node between a group of assets and a threat node. We see here that the network structure model has a decisive influence on obtained values of B. But, if vulnerability nodes have relations in the network graph, then the proposed probability calculation is inadequate since each of the vulnerabilities will have in that case their influence in relation together with the others.

Likewise, it will also be when there are no relationships between vulnerability nodes , but we arrive at a given asset node via several possible vulnerabilities activated by threat with its probability *p*(*T*) (Fig.5). In this case each of the vulnerabilities has own influence, and the threat function *F*(*T*) can be summed up after all vulnerabilities. The risk of an asset threat will then be the result of the aggregation of the impact of the threats.

The dependencies (relations) between the vulnerabilities theoretically could be of various types. However, let's note that in the adopted network build-up method, the asset always has the vulnerabilities as a set of own properties. We are also always starting to build a network model with assets and their vulnerabilities in the semantic model: noun-adjective (or in Polish - adjective participle or adjective phrase).

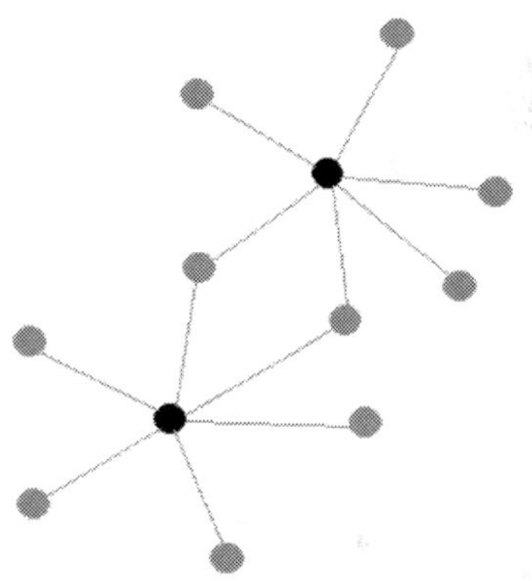

Fig. 11. Asset node (black) is always the center of the structure of the star formed from the nodes of his vulnerability (green). Source: own elaboration, Gephi ver. 0.9.1

This means that any possible relationship between vulnerabilities can result from their coexistence as in Fig. 8 created during the description of the asset. We can imagine a vulnerability such as „brake fluid leak" or „damaged seal in brake pump", which can be related by the relationship in the network graph.

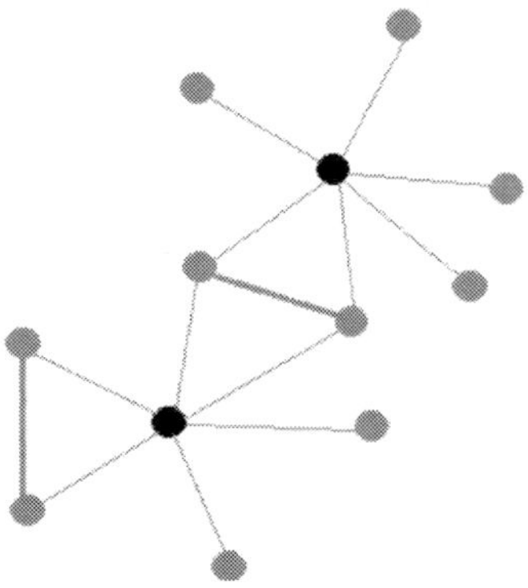

Fig. 12. In the star network some vulnerabilities may coexist in the examined technical structure. We will create at the time an edge illustrating this relation in the network graph (blue). Source: own elaboration, Gephi ver. 0.9.1

However, it should be clarified whether the application of the proposed model asset – vulnerability - threat in a version of single and independent nodes of vulnerability must be really extended to relationship-related vulnerabilities. We can't rule out this situation. However, one should strive for such a definition of vulnerability with adjective or adjective phrase [6, 7, 11, 16], so to eliminate build-up interdependent vulnerabilities. This is the role of an domain expert and therefore the presented model will always be in fact a mixed (formal-expert) model.

This is a leading feature of the presented network model of technical infrastructure. The vulnerabilities of assets in this model is independent of each other. However, it is possible that we can reach the selected asset from the activated threat through several vulnerabilities at the same time. This situation requires a separate probability model in the risk description. In such model of network we can (for a single vulnerability) we can describe it with a formula:

$$R_j = con(A) * F(z) = con(A) * \sum_i B_i * p(z_j) \tag{13}$$

The risk is assumed in this model of vector properties because we assign it to the threat node indexed by *j* cooperating by index *i* with sum of vulnerability nodes activated by the threat node indexed by *j*. The full risk in the infrastructure should be sum respectively by the indexes i and j, but we are practically interested in the risk from the selected threat indexed by *j*. Separating the risk associated with the occurrence of the selected threat *j* allows us to describe the effects attributed to the asset. In the model shown we can see that the structure of the relationship in the network graph selects the group of assets affected by the selected threat. This shows how complex is the process to define the effect. It also shows that the risk should be defined by the two-indicators function:

$$R_{jk} = con(A_k) * F(z) = con(A_k) * \sum_i B_i * p(z_j) \tag{14}$$

One indicator refers to the selected resource item and the other to the selected threat. The effects in this formula are a vector, but the components of this vector may be different for each resource k.

Impact models are always a feature of a particular system in which we investigate the risk and there is no universal impact model. In addition, more than one value or feature is required in many cases to determine the consequences and their probability for different periods, locations, groups, or situations.

The consequences can be expressed in material and non-material effects. In each system the effects measure may be different. A universal measure can usually be financial for an organization that is the owner of a system under test. At that point, however, we need to set the risk for all the resources and collect the total financial impact because, as shown above, even a single threat can affect many collections of resources [13, 14].

The effect is also treated as an immediate (operational) or postponed (business) effect, including financial and market consequences. Immediate (operational) effect can be direct or indirect [2]. The first of these is, for example, the financial value of replacing any asset or the cost of acquiring, configuring, and installing new assets [11]. It may also be the cost of suspended operations caused by an incident before the service provided by the asset is restored. Indirect effects include, for example, the cost of lost profits, interrupted operations, potentially misuse of information obtained through a security breach, or breach of regulatory obligations.

5 Summary

We have proposed a mixed, expert-formal model for analyzing the risk of asset risk in technical structures. The expert component of the model, is always present at the stage of creating a triad of "asset - vulnerability - threat". It results from the methodology of building a network model of the examined technical infrastructure [7] and principles of risk analysis. We get a mathematical network model that is typical for complex networks, where we introduce a new concept of asset-threat function. It depends on network structure. We also see that the accepted methodology in the task of risk analysis determines the structure of the network. The numerical value of risk is calculated with the specified probability of occurrence of hazards and effects on the resource determined by the expert description, but we show (what cannot be done without a network model) how it depends on the mathematical model of the network structure. We also showed that even when the threat is certain ($p(T)$=1). The importance of this threat depends strongly on the structure of the network of links between the assets, its vulnerabilities and threats exploiting its vulnerabilities. We can calculate this importance accurately.

Mathematically the structure of the network and its corresponding physical are linked by bijection. This means that the build model of the technical structure corresponds to one and only one graph assuming that the model will be made using the given methodology [7]. This creates an unequivocal model for quantitative risk analysis.

References

1. *PN-EN 31010:2010 Risk management - Risk assessment techniques*
2. *PN ISO/IEC 27005 Information technology. Security techniques. Information security risk management*
3. M. Kiedrowicz, Uogólniony model danych w rozproszonych rejestrach ewidencyjnych, *Roczniki Kolegium Analiz Ekonomicznych*, vol. **33**, pp. 209-234, (2014).
4. K. Liderman, *Risk Analysis and protection of information in computer systems* (2008)
5. A. Fronczak, P. Fronczak, *Świat sieci złożonych. Od fizyki do Internetu*, (Wydawnictwo Naukowe PWN, 2009)
6. P. Adamczyk, G. Kiryk, J. Napiórkowski,. A. Walczak, Sieciowy model systemu bezpieczeństwa., *Zarządzanie informacjami wrażliwymi. Bezpieczeństwo dokumentów, wykorzystanie technologii RFID, 9-24*, (Wojskowa Akademia Techniczna, 2016).
7. P. Adamczyk, G. Kiryk, J. Napiórkowski,. A. Walczak, Network model of security system. *MATEC Web of Conferences, vol.* 76, 02002,. DOI: 10.1051/matecconf/20167602002, (2016)
8. C. Bartosiak, R. Kasprzyk, Z. Tarapata., Application of Graphs and Networks Similarity Measures for Analyzing Complex Networks, *Biuletyn Instytutu Systemów Informatycznych*, **7**, 1–7 (2011).
9. S.P. Borgatti, M.G. Everett, L.C. Freeman, Ucinet 6.0 for Windows: Software for Social Network *Analysis. Harvard: Analytic Technologies.*
10. R. Diestel, *Graph Theory* (3rd ed.), (Berlin, New York: Springer-Verlag, 2005).
11. M. Kiedrowicz M. (Editor). *Zarządzanie informacjami wrażliwymi. Wybrane aspekty organizacyjne, prawne i techniczne ochrony informacji niejawnych.* (Warszawa, Wojskowa Akademia Techniczna, 2015).
12. R.J. Wilson, *Wprowadzenie do teorii grafów.* (Warszawa, PWN, 2007)
13. R. Hoffmann, M. Kiedrowicz, J. Stanik, Risk management system as the basic paradigm of the information security management system in an organization, *20th International Conference on Circuits, Systems, Communications and Computers, MATEC Web of Conferences*, Sciences, vol. **76**, 04010, DOI: 10.1051/matecconf/20167604010, (2016).
14. R. Hoffmann, M. Kiedrowicz, J. Stanik, Evaluation of information safety as an element of improving the organization's safety management, *20th International Conference on Circuits, Systems, Communications and Computers, MATEC Web of Conferences*, vol. **76**, 04011 DOI: 10.1051/matecconf/20167604011, (2016).
15. M. Kiedrowicz, Objects identification in the informations models used by information systems, *GIS ODYSSEY 2016*, pp. 129-136, (2016).
16. M. Kiedrowicz (Editor). *Zarządzanie informacjami wrażliwymi: Bezpieczeństwo dokumentów, wykorzystanie technologii RFID*, (Warszawa, Wojskowa Akademia Techniczna, 2016).
17. M. Kiedrowicz, T. Nowicki, R. Waszkowski, Z. Wesolowski, and K. Worwa, Method for assessing software reliability of the document management system using the RFID technology, *20th International Conference on Circuits, Systems, Communications and Computers, MATEC Web of Conferences*, vol. **76**, 04009 DOI: 10.1051/matecconf/20167604009, (2016).

MATEC Web of Conferences **125**, 04015 (2017) DOI: 10.1051/matecconf/201712504015
CSCC 2017

Optimization of wave pattern of corrugation on plates of heat exchanger

Václav Dvořák[1,*]

[1]Technical University of Liberec, Faculty of Mechanical Engineering, Department of Power Engineering Equipment. Address: Studentska 2, 46117, Liberec, Czech Republic

Abstract. The article deals with optimization of undulated heat transfer surface of plate heat exchanger. The goal of optimization is not only to increase effectiveness of heat transfer but also to reduce the pressure drop. Using four optimization parameters, the function describing the shape of corrugations is defined and these parameters are optimized. A simple steepest descent gradient method and stochastic Monte Carlo method are used, the optimum shape of the heat exchange surface is searched for four values of the pressure drop. It was found that a simple steepest descent method quickly gets stuck in a local extreme and the resulting configurations were found only by changing the slope of the waves. The stochastic method enables full optimization through the optimization space and find completely different waveforms with similar values of target function. The question, which shape of the waves on the heat transfer surface is the best, is still open.

1 Introduction

Energy recovery during air ventilation is one of the ways to reduce the energy consumption of buildings. Heat recovery can substantially reduce energy consumption needful for heating during cold seasons or air conditioning during hot seasons. The main component of any energy recovery devices are heat exchangers. Development of recuperative heat exchangers in recent years has focused on increasing their effectiveness. Another challenge is the development of so-called enthalpy exchangers for simultaneous heat and moisture transport, i.e. transport of both sensible and latent heat, as presented by Vít et al. in work [1]. To develop heat exchangers, methods of computational fluid dynamics are increasingly used, but there are still some problems to transfer the calculation results to the design and manufacturing processes.

To simulate a heat exchanger, it is necessary to create a model and a computational mesh and then use a Computational Fluid Dynamics (CFD) software. When assembling the heat exchanger, complicated and irregular narrow channels are created. These channels are split into small volumes (elements). The final meshes are structured or unstructured with different element sizes. Most of researchers use unstructured meshes for their calculations. Gherasim et al., in work [2], presented a comparison of various grids for a plate heat exchanger modeled by a tetrahedral mesh.

Subsequent researchers have used numerical simulations to investigate plate heat exchangers with chevron (undulated) profiles. Tsai [3] and Liu [4], for example, dealt with these heat exchangers and their different geometries. Similarly Giurgiu et al. in work [5] used CFD to study the influence of geometric characteristics of the two plates on the intensification process of heat transfer. They used SST k-ω turbulence model and non-structural high-density mesh and modeled only small part of the heat exchanger. They carried out also a session of experimental measurements which confirms the results obtained through numerical simulation. Kumar et al. [6] experimentally investigated the effect of symmetric and mixed chevron angles in a plate heat exchanger on heat transfer rate ratio, friction losses and many others quantities.

Rios Iribe et al. [7] investigated, using CFD and hexahedral meshes, momentum and heat transfer of a non-Newtonian fluid in steady laminar regime through a plate heat exchanger at constant wall temperature. Although the flow pattern was highly complex, under an adequate definition of the characteristics parameters, it was possible to establish simple correlations between the dimensionless numbers that characterize the thermal-hydraulic behavior of plate heat exchangers. Al-Waked et al. [8] investigated numerically conjugate heat and mass transfer processes across membrane heat exchangers of variable mass transfer resistance. A hybrid mesh was used.

Novosád and Dvořák [9], investigated the influence of oblique waves in herringbone pattern on the heat transfer surface. The main difficulty faced in this work was the creation of custom geometry. Each version had to be modelled, meshed, loaded into the solver, set the boundary conditions and subsequently perform the numerical simulation separately.

Waves in herringbone pattern are widely used for steal plate heat exchanger. The reason is that forming the plates

* Corresponding author: vaclav.dvorak@tul.cz

DOI: 10.1051/matecconf/201712504015

provides efficient and reliable way to increase the heat transfer area of the heat exchanger. Another pattern is the wavy pattern, visible down in Figure 1, which provides the same advantages. Although it is often used in plastic and aluminium plate heat exchangers in air ventilation systems, it is overlooked by researchers and it is not clear, which of both patterns is better, i.e. has higher heat transfer and lower pressure drop.

It is not even clear whether there is a completely different shape of waves that would be even better. Therefore the aim of this work is to optimize the shape of wavy pattern and answer which of these patter is the ideal one for the most intensive heat transfer and lowest pressure drop.

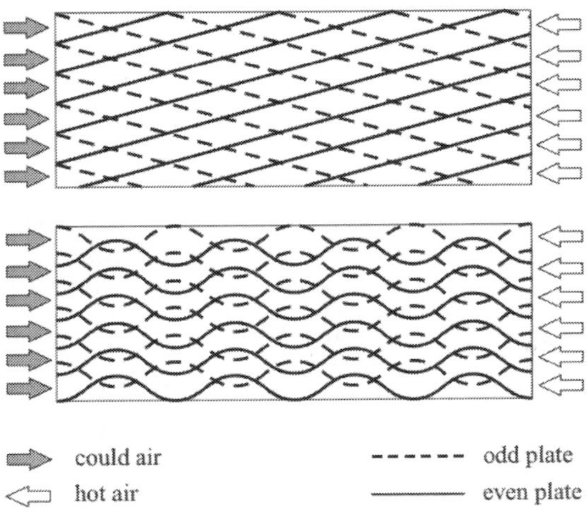

Fig. 1 Two basic types of undulation; up – herringbone pattern, down – wavy pattern with sinusoidal waves.

1 Methods

2.1 Methods of grid generation

To optimize a plate heat exchanger, we needed to model, mesh and compute a lot of computational variants. However, there are several disadvantages of repeated generation of computational meshes: Demanding and time consuming work and parameterization of the model is problematic. Further, even a small change of geometry requires to do again the whole process of model creation and mesh generation. Furthermore, meshes are not similar, i.e. the size, shape, and height of cells adjacent to walls are not the same for different topologies and numerical error which is added to the solution and influence evaluation of objective function.

Therefore, we used method, developed by Dvořák [10], for generating computational variants. This method is based on a dynamic mesh, which is provided by Ansys Fluent software. The meshes were created by pull procedure, which is similar to the own production process, i.e. the pulling direction is perpendicular to the plates. The main advantage is that this type of mesh generation is automatic and controlled by in-house software. All computational variants thus have the same mesh.

In this paper, we discuss the case of a counter flow heat exchanger, which does not have a symmetrical heat transfer area. It is because undulation cross each other, as it is obvious form Figure 1. To simulate flow and heat transfer in such heat exchanger, we need to create model containing two plates, as it is shown in Figure 2.

The heat transfer surface was divided into two parts. Input and output portions with length of $L_0 = 0.05$ m were fixed, remained flat and served for developing velocity profiles before and after central part.

The central part which was provided by undulation had length $L = 0.15$ m. Input boundary conditions were specified by velocities of 3 m/s, the output boundary conditions were specified as pressure outlets with static pressure 0 Pa. Bottom and upper boundary conditions were periodic, thus a heat exchanger with infinite number of plates was simulated. The width of the model was $B = 0.05$ m. We used mesh density, element size and count of cell layers according to recommendations from Dvořák and Novosád [11].

In this study, we used turbulence model SST k-ω, medium was air considered as incompressible gas. As a results, we obtained pressure, velocity, turbulence fields and temperature fields inside the computational domain for given inlet velocity.

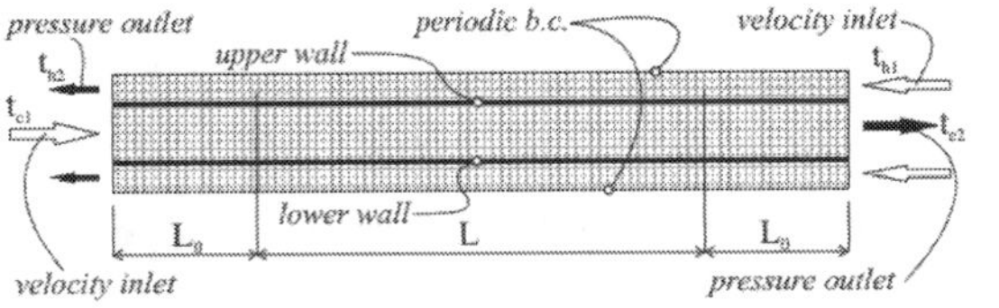

Fig. 2 Model of heat exchange surface of counter flow recuperative heat exchanger.

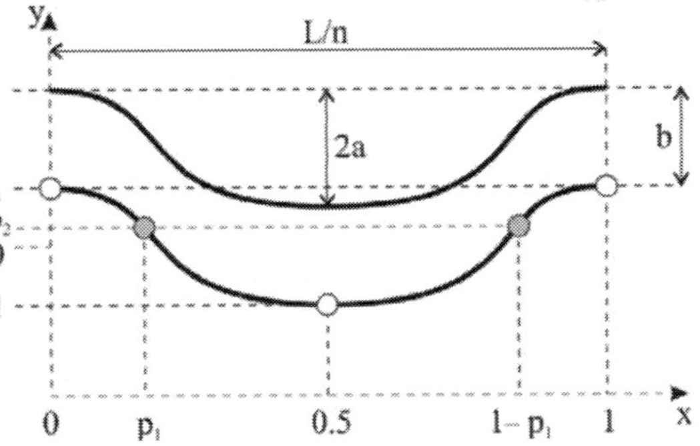

Fig. 3 Definition of parameters defining the wave curve.

In this work, the longitudinal corrugations was formed by the curve in Figure 3. The curve consisted of five points and associated by natural cubic spline. The curve is axially symmetrical. To create a curve, it is necessary to know the length L (m) of the heat exchanger, number of longitudinal waves n (1), the wave pitch b (m), their amplitude a (m) and parameters π_1 and π_2. Parameter π_1 expresses the longitudinal coordinate of the control points, while the parameter π_2 represents vertical position of the two control points. As will be seen later, these two parameters allow creation of a wave curve similar to a sine curve and broken wave pattern similar to herringbone pattern.

The shape of the middle part of plates was defined as vertical displacement z (m) of points on the wall according to equation

$$z = \frac{p}{2}\left[\cos\left(2\pi\, m\right) + s\right], \tag{1}$$

where $p = 0.003$ m is plate pitch, $s = 1$ for upper wall of the model and $s = -1$ for lower wall, m (1) represents wave number which is calculated from horizontal coordinates (x, y) of points on the wall and set of parameters according to relation

$$m = \frac{1}{b}\left[s\,y + \frac{a}{2} f\left(2\pi \frac{n\,x}{L}\right) + y' \right], \tag{2}$$

where f (1) is function describing wave shape according Figure 3.

Amplitude of wavy corrugation a (m) was not determined directly, but as multiple of the length of longitudinal waves

$$a = \pi_3 \frac{L}{n}, \tag{3}$$

It is, because properties of waves depends on count of waves only slightly, while the dependency on the wave steepness is more significant. Therefore, the steepness of waves, i.e. parameter π_3(1) become the third optimization parameter. The forth optimization parameter was count of longitudinal waves, i.e. $\pi_4 = n$.

The method of grid transformation according to relations (1) to (5) are described in work [10].

2.2 Method for optimization of plate heat exchanger

To optimize the shape of heat transfer surface of a heat exchanger, we need an objective or target function F. Producers of heat exchangers often require as high heat transfer as it is possible for given pressure drop. Therefore and according to previous works [12], we used linear combination of two main characteristic properties of a heat exchanger in the form of

$$F = \eta - C_F \left(\frac{|\Delta p - \Delta p_R|}{\Delta p_R} \right)^R, \tag{4}$$

where Δp (Pa) is calculated or measured pressure drop, Δp_R (Pa) is reference or required pressure loss, η (1) is calculated or measured coefficient of effectiveness, C_F (1) penalty coefficient and R (1) is parameter by which we can control peak of objective function. Values $C_F = 5$ and $R = 2$ were found in previous work [13]. Thus, obtained effectiveness is penalized by the difference between obtained and required pressure drop. Suggested function has quite flat peak which simplifies searching for an optimum.

The pressure drop was defined as pressure difference

$$\Delta p = \overline{p}_{01} - \overline{p}_2, \tag{5}$$

where $\overline{p}_{01}$ (Pa) is mass-averaged total pressure at the inlet and $\overline{p}_2$ (Pa) is area-averaged static pressure at the pressure outlet.

The coefficient of effectiveness (or effectiveness) is the efficiency of sensible heat transfer. Most recuperative heat exchangers in air conditioning systems work in isobaric mode, where mass flow rates of hot and cold air are equal, i.e. $\dot{m}_h = \dot{m}_c$. Assuming parity between specific heat capacities $c_{p\,h} = c_{p\,c}$, we can write the effectiveness as

$$\eta = \frac{t_{h1} - t_{h2}}{t_{h1} - t_{c1}}, \tag{6}$$

where t_{h1} (°C) and t_{h2} (°C) are inlet and outlet temperatures of hot air, t_{c1} (°C) is outlet temperature of cold air.

The task of optimization dealt with finding of optimal values of four parameters according to Figure 3; x-coordinates π_1 and y-coordinates π_2 of control points on the wave, steepness of waves π_3 and number of longitudinal waves $\pi_4 = n$, while plate pitch p, often defined by requirement on material consumption, and pitch of undulation b, which is usually defined by deformability of plate material and technology of pressing, remained constant during optimization.

As optimization method, we first used common steepest descent gradient optimization method [14] which belongs to so-called local method, because these method are capable to find only a local optimum. Since it was found during research that the problem has a lot of optimums, a global optimization method was applied.

As global optimization method, we used a simple stochastic Monte Carlo algorithm described in work [15]. To emphasize searching for local optimum, we used modification described in previous work [14] that favoured variants closer to the last best variant found according to relations

$$\pi_i^n = \pi_i^{best} - ran^2(\pi_i^{best} - \pi_i^{low}), \tag{7}$$

$$\pi_i^n = \pi_i^{best} + ran^2(\pi_i^{up} - \pi_i^{best}), \tag{8}$$

where π_i^n is a new value of optimization parameter π_i, π_i^{best} is the value of the parameter for the last best variant, π_i^{low} and π_i^{up} are lower and upper limit of the same parameter respectively, and $ran = \langle 0;1 \rangle$ is random number. The use of equations (7) and (8) were alternated also randomly.

The model of plate heat exchanger was optimized for four values of reference pressure, $\Delta p_R = 100, 150, 200$ and 250 Pa.

3 Results

3.1 Steepest descent method

First the optimization was performed using a simple gradient method, which is able to find only a local optimum of the objective function. The optimization was initialized by values of parameters:, $\pi_1 = 0.3$, $\pi_2 = 0.5$ and $\pi_3 = 0.08$, while $\pi_4 = 5$. In this optimization, the parameter π_4 remained constant.

The results in the figures show that the steepest descent gradient optimization method is very fast and relatively quickly leads to the goal. The method relatively quickly finds a local minimum.

Table 1. Results of optimization no. 1, steepest descent method, $\pi_4 = 5$, and four values of reference pressure Δp_R.

Δp_R (Pa)	100	150	200	250
No. of steps	19	72	76	78
η(1)	0.7816	0.8079	0.822	0.8335
Δp (Pa)	102.3	150.95	200.72	250.62
F (1)	0.7789	0.8047	0.822	0.8335
π_1(1)	0.3	0.3329	0.3414	0.3464
π_2(1)	0.504	0.4942	0.4944	0.4931
$\pi_3 = a \cdot n / L$ (1)	0.0798	0.1972	0.227	0.2454
$\pi_4 = n$ (1)	5	5	5	5

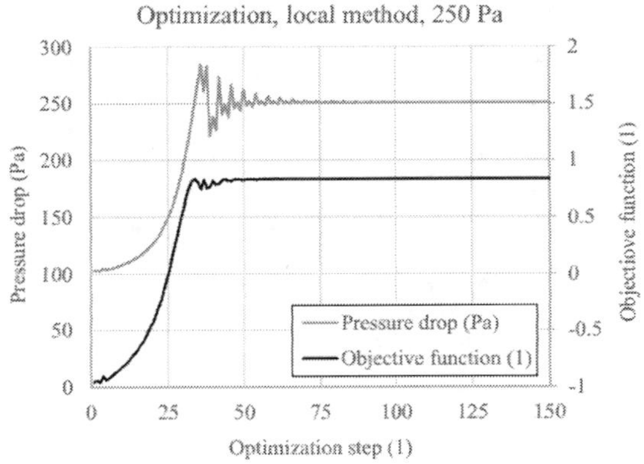

Fig. 4 Course of optimization for reference pressure $\Delta p_R = 250$ Pa, while steepest descent method is used.

Optimization results are summarized in Table 1, examples of the course of the objective function and the diagrams are in Figures 4 and 5. As can be seen in the course of the objective function F, and the pressure drop Δp in Figure 4, the search for wave configuration was very fast, the desired pressure is achieved in practice after 34 steps.

However, this method consists in finding the gradient direction in which the target function is changing most rapidly. It turned out that the objective function is most sensitive on parameter π_3, i.e. on the slope of the waves. Therefore, during the optimization, the optimum value of parameter π_3 was found soonest, while other parameters remained practically unchanged, see diagram in Figure 5.

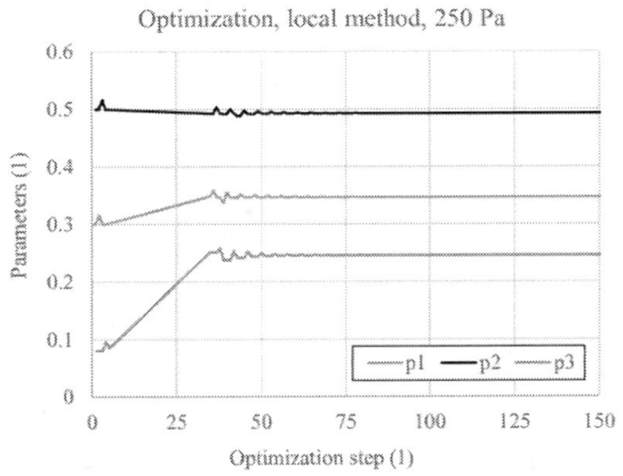

Fig. 5 Development of parameters during optimization for reference pressure $\Delta p_R = 250$ Pa by steepest descent method.

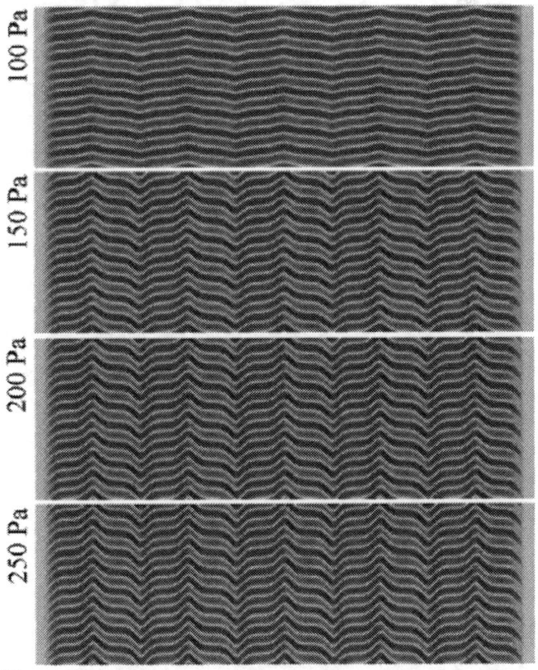

Fig. 6 Optimized shapes of heat transfer surfaces for various values of reference pressure, steepest descent method is used.

As it is apparent from the results of optimization and especially Figure 6, the result of optimization was largely influenced by the initial values of parameters. Because the value of the objective function is strongly dependent on the amplitude of the waves, the third parameter π_3 was the most developed. In contrast, the parameter π_2 changes only slightly and parameter π_1 only negligibly. This situation did not change in the further optimization, which should take place already in the other direction.

Also found shapes of waves indicates that only a local optimum was found. We can observe in Figure 6 that found shapes differ only in the third parameter, i.e. steepness of the waves. It is therefore obvious that optimization method got stuck in local extreme and we need to use a method capable to identify a global maximum.

3.2 Stochastic Monte Carlo global method

The results of applying stochastic Monte Carlo method are summarized in Table 2. From this it follows that the optimization takes incomparably longer, but the value of the objective function do not different too much from the values that can be found in Table 1 for much simpler and quicker gradient method.

Table 2. Results of optimization no. 2 for stochastic method, four values of reference pressure Δp_R.

Δp_R (Pa)	100	150	200	250
No. of steps	312	217	411	712
η (1)	0.7814	0.8088	0.8295	0.8414
Δp (Pa)	101.07	150.55	199.41	252.29
F (1)	0.7809	0.8087	0.8295	0.8410
π_1 (1)	0.4408	0.2034	0.1895	0.4484
π_2 (1)	0.5487	0.2439	0.6622	0.9397
$\pi_3 = a \cdot n / L$ (1)	0.0293	0.2046	0.2022	0.294
$\pi_4 = n$ (1)	2	8	4	6

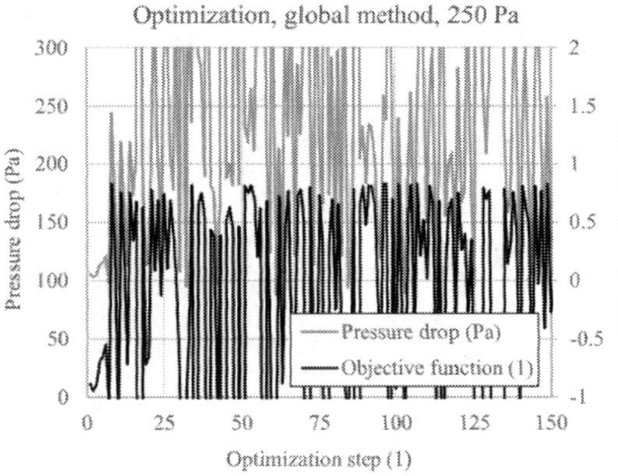

Fig. 7 Course of optimization for reference pressure $\Delta p_R = 250$ Pa, while stochastic method is used.

The advantage of used stochastic method is that it does not get stuck in a local extreme, but it can leave it. As can be seen from Figure 7, the method is able to find relatively quickly a configuration of heat transfer area with the required pressure drop, moreover, it is able to explore other options too.

Yet, according to Figure 8, it appears that even this method has a tendency to remain in the first found optimum, i.e. with the height of the target function found it is less likely that other configurations of heat exchange surface is explored. As we can see on the development of the optimization parameters in Figure 8, optimization parameters cease to evolve in time.

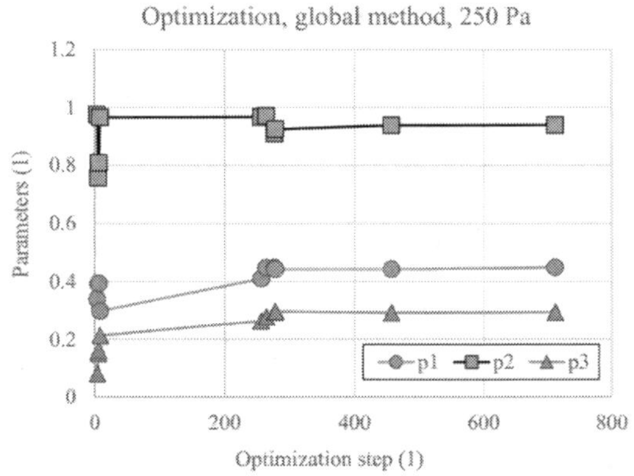

Fig. 8 Development of parameters during optimization for stochastic method and reference pressure $\Delta p_R = 250$ Pa.

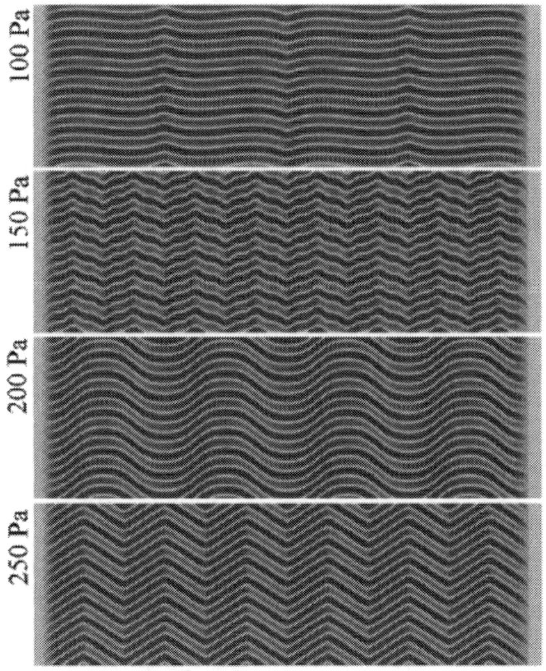

Fig. 9 Optimized shapes of heat transfer surfaces for various values of reference pressure, stochastic method is used.

As seen from the results of the individual and particularly from Figure 9, in which the resulting shapes are shown, stochastic method can find advantageous shapes in virtually any point of the optimization space. The result can thus be for example very long waves ($\pi_4 = 2$ for $\Delta p_R = 100$ Pa) or very short and corrugated ($\Delta p_R = 150$ Pa) or rounded smooth waves ($\Delta p_R = 200$ Pa) or even variation of the herringbone pattern ($\Delta p_R = 250$ Pa). It follows that the optimization method works and allows to find the variation of the heat exchange surface. However, the question whether the global optimum was found in not answered. Also, we still do not know whether the waves are better rounded, or shaped in herringbone patter or in other design.

DOI: 10.1051/matecconf/201712504015

Interesting is certainly the recognition that totally different configurations can reach very similar results. Since this run of optimization did not reply asked questions, one more optimization was conducted, in which the values of only three parameters were sought, while the number of waves remained the same, i.e. $\pi_4 = 5$.

Table 3. Results of optimization no. 3, stochastic method is used, $\pi_4 = 5$, four values of reference pressure Δp_R.

Δp_R (Pa)	100	150	200	250
No. of steps	179	217	176	190
η (1)	0.7798	0.8073	0.8333	0.8378
Δp (Pa)	100.85	151.96	203.74	250.57
F (1)	0.7794	0.8065	0.8316	0.8378
π_1 (1)	0.2433	0.2561	0.1972	0.4439
π_2 (1)	0.3807	0.3834	0.4089	0.9264
$\pi_3 = a \cdot n / L$ (1)	0.0668	0.2024	0.2446	0.308
$\pi_4 = n$ (1)	5	5	5	5

As can be seen in Table 3, the resulting value of the objective function is not very different from the values found for the four parameters. Found shapes this time are much more similar and have the shape of a fish bone, see Figure 10.

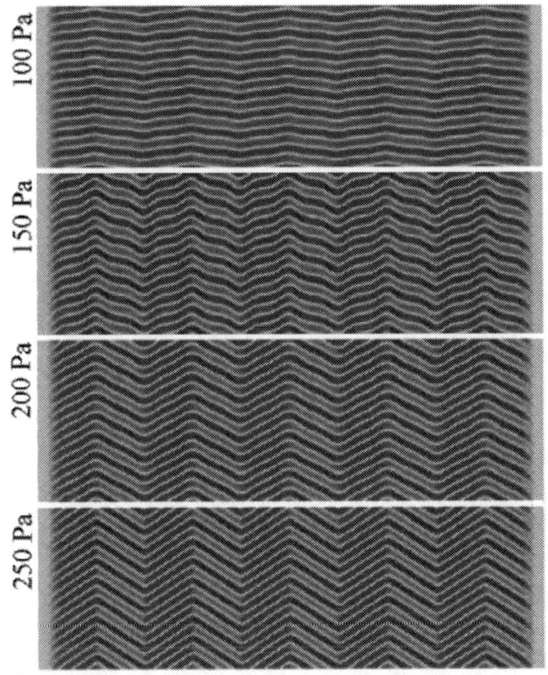

Fig. 10 Optimized shapes of heat transfer surfaces for various values of reference pressure, stochastic method is used, three parameters are optimized.

From the course of the development of optimization parameters in Figure 11, it seems that when it finds a high value of the objective function, there is only a slight shift values of optimization parameters.

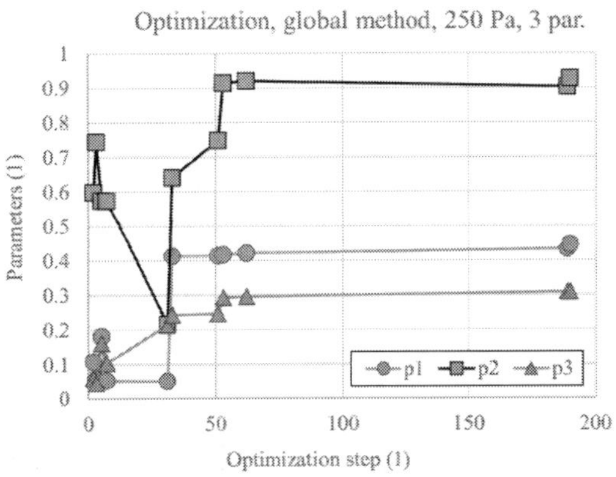

Fig. 11 Development of parameters during optimization for stochastic method and reference pressure $\Delta p_R = 250$ Pa.

4 Conclusions

An undulated heat transfer surface of recuperative heat exchanger was optimized to obtain as high coefficient of effectiveness of heat transfer as possible. The shape of waves of corrugation for surface of heat exchanger was optimized.

The task of optimization was to find optimal values of four parameters of wavy pattern: x-coordinate and y-coordinate of control points on wave curve, steepness of waves and count of longitudinal waves.

The optimization procedure looked for maximum of objective function which was a linear combination of effectiveness and pressure drop. First we used simple steepest descent method and then stochastic Monte Carlo method and the optimum was searched for four values of reference pressure drop. Three different optimization were run and we investigated the resulting shapes of undulation.

It was found that simple steepest descent method is fast, but only a local minimum is found and it is reached simply by altering steepness of waves.

The stochastic Monte Carlo method is more capable to search through the optimization space. Very different shapes were found as optimal – sharp waves, rounded, or even waves in herringbone pattern. It was verified that a global optimization method is necessary to use, preferably in conjunction with local method.

In further work, it would be also beneficial to carried out an analysis of flow around optimal shapes.

Acknowledgment

This publication was written at the Technical University of Liberec, Faculty of Mechanical Engineering with the support of the Institutional Endowment for the Long Term Conceptual Development of Research Institutes, as provided by the Ministry of Education, Youth and Sports of the Czech Republic in the year 2017.

References

1. T. Vít, P. Novotný, V.V. Nguyen, V. Dvořák, WSEAS, Recent Advances in Energy, Environment, Economics and Technological Innovation, 34-38 (2013)
2. I. Gherasim, N. Galanis, C.T. Nguyen, Int. Jour. of Thermal Science. **50**, 1499-1511 (2011)
3. Y.Ch. Tsai, F.B. Liu, P.T. Shen, Int. Commun. in Heat and Mass Transfer **36**, 574–578 (2009)
4. F.B. Liu, Y.Ch. Tsai, Heat Mass Transf. **46**, 585–593 (2010)
5. O. Giurgiu, A. Pleşa, L. Socaciu. Energy Procedia **85**, 244-251 (2016)
6. V. Kumar, A.K. Tiwari, S.K. Ghosh. Energy Conversion and Manag. **118**, 142–154 (2016)
7. E.Y. Rios-Iribe, M.E. Cervantes-Gaxiola, E. Rubio-Castro, O.M. Hernández-Calderón, Applied Thermal Eng.
8. R. AL-Waked, M.S. Nasif, G. Morrison, M. Behnia, Applied Thermal Eng. **84**, 301–309 (2015)
9. J. Novosád, V. Dvořák, EPJ Web of Conferences **67**, 020 85 (2014)
10. V. Dvořák, Recent Advances in Computer Science **1**, 193-198 (2014)
11. V. Dvořák, J. Novosád, Recent Advances in Computer Science, pp 115-120 (2015)
12. V. Dvořák, Applied Mechanics & Materials **752-753**, 820-827 (2015)
13. V. Dvořák, MATEC Web of Conferences **76**, 04027 (2016)
14. R. Fletcher M. J. D. Powell, A Rapidly Convergent Descent Method for Minimization. Computer J. **6** (2): 163-168 (1963).
15. Metropolis P., Ulam S.: The Monte-Carlo method. J. of the American Statistical Assoc. **44**, 335, (1949)

DOI: 10.1051/matecconf/201712504016

Homogeneity of the Test Variants in Entrance Exams

Jindřich Klůfa[1]

[1] University of Economics, Department of Mathematics, 13067 Prague, Czech Republic

Abstract. The problem of homogeneity of test variants in mathematics, which are used in admission process, is solved in present paper. The analysed data are the results of entrance examination in mathematics at University of Economics in Prague. Different statistical methods (test of hypothesis, correlation, regression) were used for this analyse. These results will be used to further improve of the preparation of test variants in the coming years.

Keywords. Entrance exams in mathematics, homogeneity of test variants, regression and correlation.

1. Introduction

For entrance examinations are frequently used the multiple choice question tests. Advantages of these tests: the multiple choice question tests are objective (there is clearly no impact of any subjective factor in evaluation) and results can be evaluated quite easily for large number of students. On the other hand, a student can obtain certain number of points in the test purely by guessing the right answers. This problem was analysed in [7], [16] and [18]. In [7] it was shown that risk of success of students with lower performance levels at University of Economics in Prague is negligible.

The difficulty of test variants for students is poorly measured. If we use the multiple choice question tests, the difficulty of test variants depends also on variants of answers from which the correct answer is chosen, e.g. the example

"combinatorial number $\binom{7}{3}$ is (a) 21, (b) 35, (c) 49"

is more difficult than the example

"combinatorial number $\binom{7}{3}$ is (a) negative number, (b) zero, (c) positive number".

This problem shall be analysed for the test variants in mathematics which are used for the entrance examinations at University of Economics in Prague.

Test variants in mathematics are generated from a database created by the Department of Mathematics. The tests in mathematics at University of Economics have 10 questions for 5 points and 5 questions for 10 points (100 points total) – see [8]. Questions are independent. Each question has 5 answers (one answer is correct), wrong answer is not penalized. The number of points in the test in mathematics can be

$$0, 5, 10, 15, 20, 25, 30, 35, 40, 45, \ldots, 90, 95, 100.$$

These tests are used to the three faculties of the Prague University of Economics (Faculty of Informatics and Statistics, Faculty of Finance and Accounting, Faculty of Business Administration). Analysis of the entrance examinations in mathematics in 2013 is provided in this paper (similar problems are solved in [2-6], [9-10], [12-13] and [15]. These results will be used to further improve of the preparation of test variants in the coming years.

2. Entrance examinations at University of Economics

The analysed data are the results of 4614 students in mathematics in 2013. Seventeen test variants were used for the entrance examinations in mathematics in 2013 (these test variants we can find in [8]). Part of one of them is on Figure 1.

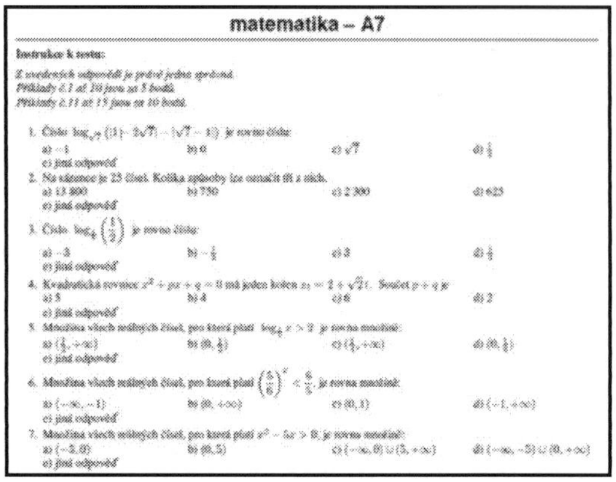
matematika – A7

Fig. 1. Part of the variant A7 in mathematics in 2013

The test variants have 15 questions, each question has 5 answers – see Figure 1. Between these answers is the answer "e) another answer". If e) is correct answer, to mark the letter e may be for the students more complicated than to mark the letters a, b, c, d. For example solution of the question 1 in the test variant A7 (see Figure 1) is

$$\log_{\sqrt{7}}((-1+2\sqrt{7})-(\sqrt{7}-1))=\log_{\sqrt{7}}(\sqrt{7})=1,$$

i.e. the correct answer is e). The question 1 in the test variant A7 with variants of answers e.g.

a) 1 b) 0 c) $\sqrt{7}$ d) $\frac{1}{2}$ e) another answer

may be easier for students. Therefore we shall study the dependence of the number of points in the test in mathematics (denoted Y) on the number of answers e) in tests variants (denoted X).

3. Results

The number of answers e) in tests variants which were used for the entrance examinations at University of Economics in Prague in 2013 is 1, 2, 3, 4 and 5. Now we shall compare distributions of number of points in the test in mathematics in test variants with 1, 2, 3, 4 and 5 answers e) - see Figure 2 and Table 1.

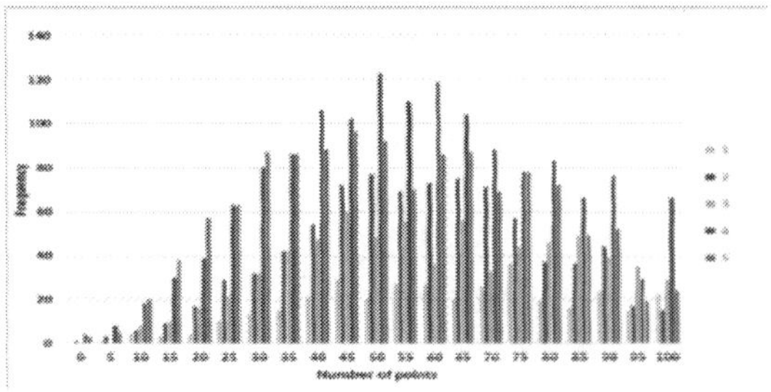

Fig. 2. Distribution of number of points in test in mathematics in 2013 in test variants with 1, 2, 3, 4 and 5 answers e) (histogram)

Tab 1. Distribution of number of points in test in mathematics in 2013 in test variants with 1, 2, 3, 4 and 5 answers e) (source: own calculation)

Number of answers e)	Frequency n_i	Average number of points	Variance
1	352	62.699	506.655
2	836	57.829	419.742
3	707	60.184	528.578
4	1478	56.712	532.850

Now we shall test null hypothesis

$$H_0: \mu_1 = \mu_2 = \mu_3 = \mu_4 = \mu_5, \quad (1)$$

where $\mu_1, \mu_2, \mu_3, \mu_4, \mu_5$ is mean number of points in mathematics in test variants with 1, 2, 3, 4 and 5 answers e), i.e. mean number of points in test variants with 1, 2, 3, 4 and 5 answers e) is the same.

To verify the validity of the hypothesis we use ANOVA. In the first step we verify assumption of this method by Bartlett's test (see e.g. [1]). The hypothesis "variance of number of points in mathematics in test variants with 1, 2, 3, 4 and 5 answers e) is the same" is not rejected at 1% significance level, assumption of ANOVA can be considered to have been met.

Results of ANOVA we got with MS Excel (e.g. [14]) – see Table 2. Since

$$F = 19.422 > 2.374,$$

the null hypothesis (1) is rejected at 5% significance level. There are some differences between the test variants with 1, 2, 3, 4 and 5 answers e), the differences between average number of points in test variants with 1, 2, 3, 4 and 5 answers e) in Table 1 are statistically significant.

Tab 2. Results of ANOVA (source: own calculation)

Source of variability	Test variants	Rezidual	Sum
Sum of Squares	39486	2342608	2382094
Degrees of freedom	4	4609	4613
Fraction	9871.58	508.27	
F	19.422		
p value	7.31E-16		
F crit	2.374		

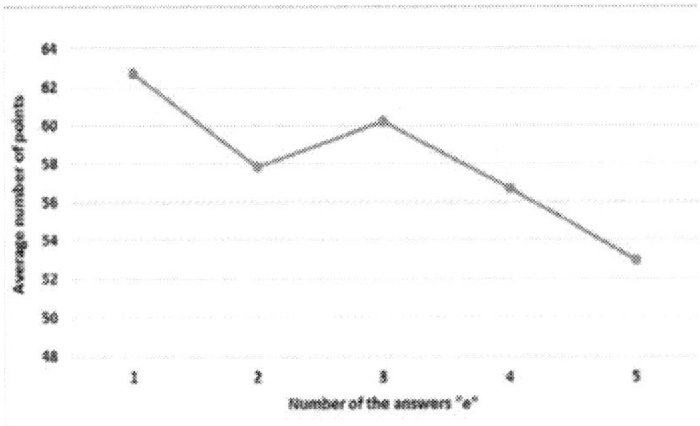

Fig. 3. Dependence of the average number of points in the test in mathematics on the number of answers e) in tests variants

From results of ANOVA it seems that Y=the number of points in the test in mathematics depends on X=the number of answers e) in tests variants. From Figure 3 it seems that dependence is linear, therefore we shall compute the correlation coefficient r and regression line $y = a + bx$. Using MS Excel we have

$$r = -0.112$$

From this result follows that the dependence of the number of points in the test in mathematics on the number of answers e) in tests variants is weak or the dependence does not exist. Therefore we shall test null hypothesis

$$\text{Ho: } \rho=0, \qquad (2)$$

i.e. the number of points in the test in mathematics does not depend on the number of answers e) in tests variants. We shall compute - see e.g. [17]

$$t = \frac{r}{\sqrt{1-r^2}}\sqrt{n-2} = -7.66$$

Critical value of t distribution for $n-2=4612$ degrees of freedom and significance level $\alpha = 0.01$ is $t_{0.01}(4612) = 2.58$. Since

$$|t| > 2.58,$$

the null hypothesis (2) is rejected at 1% significance level, i.e. the dependence of the number of points in the test in mathematics on the number of answers e) in tests variants exists. Using MS Excel we obtain furthermore regression line

$$y = 63.974 - 2.009x$$

From this regression line follows that expected the number of points in mathematics in the test variant with 0 answers e) is 63.974 and if the number of answers e) in tests variants increases by 1, then the expected the number of points in mathematics decreases by 2.009.

4. Conclusion

The differences between number of points in mathematics in test variants, which were used for the entrance examinations in mathematics at University of Economics in Prague in 2013, were analysed in present paper. The differences may arise due to the varying difficulty of the test variants, but also because of the different level of knowledge of students who write these variants. From [11] it follows that differences between results of tests variants may arise due to different level of knowledge of the students who wrote these variants. On the other hand, the difficulty of test variants for students is poorly measured. This problem was solved in the present paper. From results of the paper it follows that the number of points in the test in mathematics depends on the number of answers "e) another answer" in tests variants, but the dependence is very weak.

Acknowledgements. This paper was processed with contribution of long term institutional support of research activities by Faculty of Informatics and Statistics, University of Economics, Prague.

References

1. Anděl, J. (1978) *Matematická statistika*. Praha: SNTL/ALFA.
2. Brožová, H., Rydval, J. (2013) 'Analysis of the exam test quality', *Efficiency and Responsibility in Education*, Proceedings of the 10th International Conference, Prague, pp. **47–54**.
3. Hrubý, M. (2013) 'Extended elements of the question objects', *Efficiency and Responsibility in Education*, Proceedings of the 10th International Conference, Prague, pp. **204–209**.
4. Hrubý, M. (2016) 'Feedback improvement of question objects ', International Journal of Continuing Engineering Education and Lifelong Learning, vol. 26, no 2, pp. **183–195**.
5. Kaspříková, N. (2012) 'Data analysis of students' performance', *Efficiency and Responsibility in Education,* Proceedings of the 9th International Conference, Prague, pp. **213–218**.
6. Kaspříková, N., Klůfa, J. (2015) 'AOQL Sampling Plans for Inspection by Variables and Attributes Versus the Plans for Inspection by Attributes', Quality Technology and Quantitative Management, vol. 12, no. 2, pp. **133-142**.
7. Klůfa, J. (2012) 'Tests from probability point of view', *Efficiency and Responsibility in Education*, Proceedings of the 9th International Conference, Prague, pp. **229–233**.
8. Klůfa, J., Eliášová, L. (2013) *Matematika – příprava k přijímacím zkouškám na VŠE*, Prague: Ekopress.

9. Klůfa, J. (2013) 'Comparison of entrance examinations in mathematics', *Efficiency and Responsibility in Education*, Proceedings of the 10th International Conference, Prague, pp. **270–275**.
10. Klůfa, J. (2015) 'Dependence of the Results of Entrance Examinations on Test Variants', Procedia - Social and Behavioral Sciences, vol. 174, pp. **3565–3571**.
11. Klůfa, J. (2016) 'Analysis of the differences between results of test variants', *Efficiency and Responsibility in Education, Proceedings of the 13th International Conference,* Prague, pp. **279–285**
12. Kohanová, I. (2012) 'Analysis of university entrance test from mathematics', Acta Didactica Universitatis Comenianae Mathematics, vol. 12, pp. **31-46**.
13. Kučera, P., Svatošová, L., Pelikán, M. (2015) 'University study results as related to the admission exam results' *Efficiency and Responsibility in Education*, Proceedings of the 12th International Conference, Prague, pp. **318–324**.
14. Marek, L. (2013) *Statistika v příkladech*, Prague: Professional Publishing.
15. Mošna, F. (2013) 'E-learning and interactive dynamical figures for teaching of mathematics', *Efficiency and Responsibility in Education*, Proceedings of the 10th International Conference, Prague, pp. **449–454**.
16. Premadasa, I. (1993) 'A reappraisal of the use of multiple-choice questions', Medical Teacher, vol. 15, no. 2-3, pp. **237-242**.
17. Rao, C.R. (1973) *Linear Statistical Inference and Its Applications*, New York: John Wiley
18. Zhao, Y. (2006) 'How to design and interpret a multiple-choice-question test: A probabilistic approach', International Journal of Engineering Education, vol. 22, no. 6, pp. **1281-1286**.

Using Machine Learning Methods Jointly to Find Better Set of Rules in Data Mining

Hyontai SUG[1*]

[1]Division of Computer Engineering, Dongseo University, 47 Jurye-ro, Sasang-gu, Busan 47011, Korea

Abstract. Rough set-based data mining algorithms are one of widely accepted machine learning technologies because of their strong mathematical background and capability of finding optimal rules based on given data sets only without room for prejudiced views to be inserted on the data. But, because the algorithms find rules very precisely, we may confront with the overfitting problem. On the other hand, association rule algorithms find rules of association, where the association resides between sets of items in database. The algorithms find itemsets that occur more than given minimum support, so that they can find the itemsets practically in reasonable time even for very large databases by supplying the minimum support appropriately. In order to overcome the problem of the overfitting problem in rough set-based algorithms, first we find large itemsets, after that we select attributes that cover the large itemsets. By using the selected attributes only, we may find better set of rules based on rough set theory. Results from experiments support our suggested method.

1 Introduction

Rough sets are one of widely accepted machine learning technologies. Good property of rough set theory is that it can describe uncertain facts solely based on data. As a result, there is no room for prejudiced views to be inserted in the discovered knowledge [1, 2, 3]. For example, assume that we have a decision table T like table 1. A decision table T is a table having conditional attributes and decision attributes in a fixed setting. Each attribute has corresponding values. In our example T contains the universe U of objects, x_1, x_2, x_3, x_4, and x_5. The set of attributes A has 2 attributes, a_1 and a_2. The set of decision class d has two values, 1 and 2. V_i is the set of values that each attribute has where i = 1, 2, and $V_1 = \{1, 2, 3\}$, $V_2 = \{1, 2\}$.

Table 1. A decision table T.

U	a1	a2	d
x_1	1	1	1
x_2	1	2	1
x_3	2	1	2
x_4	2	2	2
x_5	3	2	1

Possible set of minimal rules for T are as follows :

Rule 1. If (a_1 = 1) Then (d = 1)

Rule 2. If (a_1 = 2) Then (d = 2)

Rule 3. If (a_1 = 3) Then (d = 1)

As we can see from the example, rules based on rough set theory reflect the available data quite honestly.

There are also some other data mining or machine learning techniques solely based on data. Association rules [4, 5, 6] are one of representative techniques of such kind. Association rules find rules of association, where the association resides between sets of items in database. For example, assume that we have a simple database of transaction records like table 2 that shows the records of items purchased together in a supermarket.

Table 2. A simple transaction database.

Tr #	items
t_1	1, 3
t_2	2, 3
t_3	1, 2, 3
t_4	2, 5

* Corresponding author: sht@gdsu.dongseo.ac.kr

If minimum support that represents how many times an itemset occurs in a transaction record is two, the large itemset of length one can be found as in table 3. Itemset means the set of items that occur in the same records, and large itemset means that the itemset that occurs at least over given minimum support.

Table 3. Large itemset of length one.

itemset	support
{1}	2
{2}	3
{3}	3

Table 4 shows large itemset of length two.

Table 4. Large itemset of length two.

itemset	support
{2, 3}	2

There are no large itemset of length three, so we can stop the iteration. From the found large itemsets, we may generate association rules like; if item 2 has been purchased, then item 3 will be purchased also with the confidence of 67%, and if item 3 has been purchased, then item 2 will be purchased also with the confidence of 67%. As we see from the example, association rule algorithms find itemsets that occur more than given minimum support. This fact allows the algorithms to find the itemsets practically even for very large databases by supplying the minimum support appropriately.

2 Method and experiment

Because rough set theory-based algorithms find rules very thoroughly, it may confront with the overfitting problem. Overfitting training data set is a very well-known problem [7]. Overfitting in machine learning algorithms occurs, because a training data set usually does not cover data space fully. For example, assume that we have a data set that has 10 attributes and each attribute can have 10 discrete values. So the possible data space is 10^{10} = 10,000,000,000. If we have one instance for each data point in the 10 dimensional data space, we have 10 billion objects. Assuming each object occupies four bytes, the size becomes 40GB. As we see from this even simple example, the training data from real world usually occupy very small portion of their data space.

Therefore, if we apply the rough set-based rule discovery method directly to real world data sets, we may not get such good results as we expected, especially the size of data set is small compared to the domain of the data set, and the data set values are very specific for some attributes values. In other words, the data values are subdivided very much. In order to prove our assertion we'll perform an experiment with a real world data set. For our experiment, a data set called 'zoo' from UCI machine learning depository [8] is used. Zoo data has 17 conditional attributes and one decision attribute. The decision attribute has 7 different class values which classify animals in a zoo. The total number of instances is 101. Table 5 shows the meaning of each attribute.

Table 5. The attributes of data set 'zoo'.

No.	attribute	domain
1	Animal name	Unique for each instance
2	Hair	Boolean
3	Feathers	Boolean
4	Eggs	Boolean
5	Milk	Boolean
6	Airbone	Boolean
7	Aquatic	Boolean
8	Predator	Boolean
9	Toothed	Boolean
10	Backbone	Boolean
11	Breathes	Boolean
12	Venemous	Boolean
13	Fins	Boolean
14	Legs	Numeric (0, 2, 4, 5, 6, 8)
15	Tail	Boolean
16	Domestic	Boolean
17	Catsize	Boolean

In order to generate rough set-based rules for the data set MODLEM [9] algorithm was used, and test was based on 10-fold cross validation. MODLEM is a standard method that can find rules based on rough set theory.

MODLEM generated 7 rules with the accuracy of 42.6% as follows:

Rule 1. If milk in {1} Then class = 1 (41/41, 100%)

Rule 2. If name in {chicken, crow, dove, duck, flamingo, gull, hawk, kiwi, lark, ostrich, parakeet, penguin, pheasant, rhea, skimmer, skua, sparrow, swan, vulture, wren} Then class = 2 (20/20, 100%)

Rule 3. If name in {pitviper, seasnake, slowworm, tortoise, tuatara} Then class = 3 (5/5, 100%)

Rule 4. If name in {bass, carp, catfish, chub, dogfish, haddock, herring, pike, piranha, seahorse, sole, stingray, tuna} Then class = 4 (13/13, 100%)

Rule 5. If name in {frog, newt, toad} Then class = 5 (4/4, 100%)

Rule 6. If name in {flea, gnat, honeybee, housefly, ladybird, moth, termite, wasp} Then class = 6 (8/8, 100%)

Rule 7. If name in {clam, crab, crayfish, lobster, octopus, scorpion, seawasp, slug, starfish, worm} Then class = 7 (10/10, 100%)

The percentage in parentheses shows the confidence of the rule, and the fraction represents the number of classified instances over the number instances having the same condition part. As we see in the rules, rough set-based method found rules precisely and rules are very accurate. But, the test result is not good.

Even though MODLEN can handle continuous values, because association rule algorithms cannot deal with continuous values, discretization method by Fayyad et al. [11] was applied for later application of the association rule algorithms. MODLEM generated the same 7 rules and with the same accuracy for the discretized data also like the original data set.

In order to find association rules class association rule algorithm [11] was used, because the data set has several conditional attributes and a decision attribute. Table 6 shows the large itemsets when minimum support is 10.

Table 6. Large itemsets.

itemset	support
hair=1 feather=0 eggs=0 milk=1 airborne=0 aquatic=0 predator=1 toothed=1 backbone=1 breathes=1 venomous=0 fins=0 legs='(3-4.5]' tail=1 domestic=0	12
hair=1 feather=0 eggs=0 milk=1 airborne=0 aquatic=0 predator=1 toothed=1 backbone=1 breathes=1 venomous=0 fins=0 legs='(3-4.5]' tail=1 catsize=1	11
hair=1 feather=0 eggs=0 milk=1 airborne=0 aquatic=0 predator=1 toothed=1 backbone=1 breathes=1 venomous=0 fins=0 legs='(3-4.5]' domestic=0 catsize=1	12
hair=1 feather=0 eggs=0 milk=1 airborne=0 aquatic=0 toothed=1 backbone=1 breathes=1 venomous=0 fins=0 legs='(3-4.5]' tail=1 domestic=0 catsize=1	16
hair=1 feather=0 eggs=0 milk=1 airborne=0 predator=1 toothed=1 backbone=1 breathes=1 venomous=0 fins=0 legs='(3-4.5]' tail=1 domestic=0 catsize=1	11

According to the large itemsets in table 6, the collection of items in the found large itemsets is { hair, Feather, eggs, milk, airborne, aquatic, toothed, backbone. breathes, venomous, fins, legs, tail, catsize}. MODLEM algorithm was applied using these attributes only to see the effect of attribute selection. Eight rules with the accuracy of 96.0% were generated as follows:

Rule 1. If milk in {1} Then class = 1 (41/41, 100%)

Rule 2. If feather in {1} Then class = 2 (20/20, 100%)

Rule 3. If toothed in {1} AND fins in {0} AND legs in {'(-inf-1]'} Then class = 3 (3/3, 60%)

Rule 4. If legs in {'(3-4.5]'} AND hair in {0} AND aquatic in {0} Then class = 3 (2/2, 40%)

Rule 5. If fins in {1} AND eggs in {1} Then class = 4 (13/13, 100%)

Rule 6. If aquatic in {1} AND legs in {'(3-4.5]'} AND hair in {0} AND toothed in {1} Then class = 5 (4/4, 100%)

Rule 7. If legs in {'(4.5-inf)'} AND aquatic in {0} AND eggs in {1} Then class = 6 (8/8, 100%)

Rule 8. If backbone in {0} AND airborne in {0} Then class = 7 (10/12, 100%)

Comparing the previous two results from the original data set and the modified data set by selecting the 15 attributes only, we doubt that the attribute 'name' might have negative effect for accuracy, because the attribute occurs very often in the rule set from the original data set. After omitting 'name' attribute, and we ran MODLEM again, resulting in 10 rules with accuracy of 94.1% as follows:

Rule 1.If milk in {1} Then class = 1 (41/41, 100%)

Rule 2. If feather in {1} Then class = 2 (20/20, 100%)

Rule 3. If toothed in {1} AND fins in {0} AND legs in {'(-inf-1]'} Then class = 3 (3/3, 60%)

Rule 4. If legs in {'(3-4.5]'} AND hair in {0} AND aquatic in {0} Then class = 3 (2/2, 40%)

Rule 5. If fins in {1} AND eggs in {1} Then class = 4 (13/13, 100%)

Rule 6. If aquatic in {1} AND legs in {'(3-4.5]'} AND hair in {0} AND toothed in {1} Then class = 5 (4/4, 100%)

Rule 7. If legs in {'(4.5-inf)'} AND predator in {0} Then class = 6 (7/7, 87.5%)

Rule 8. If legs in {'(4.5-inf)'} AND airborne in {1} Then class = 6 (6/6, 75%)

Rule 9. If backbone in {0} AND airborne in {0} AND predator in {1} Then class = 7 (8/8, 80%)

Rule 10. If backbone in {0} AND legs in {'(-inf-1]'} Then class = 7 (4/4, 40%)

When we removed attribute 'predator' only that is the other attribute not having been selected, MODLEM generated the same result with the original data discretized and un-discretized as well. The above experiments prove that our assertion is true and show the property of overfitting in rough set theory-based rule generation method.

One more experiment after eliminating the two attributes, 'name' and 'predator' in the original data set without discretization was performed, and we found similar result with accuracy of 96.0% by MODLEM, and the found 8 rules have slight different shape with the one after discretization as follows:

Rule 1. If milk in {1} Then class = 1 (41/41, 100%)
Rule 2. If feather in {1} Then class = 2 (20/20, 100%)
Rule 3. If toothed in {1} AND fins in {0} AND legs < 1Then class = 3 (3/3, 60%)
Rule 4. If legs >= 3 AND tail in {1} AND eggs in {1} AND aquatic in {0} Then class = 3 (2/2, 40%)
Rule 5. If fins in {1} AND eggs in {1} Then class = 4 (13/13, 100%)
Rule 6. If aquatic in {1} AND legs >= 3 AND toothed in {1} AND hair in {0} Then class = 5 (4/4, 100%)
Rule 7. If legs >= 5.5 AND aquatic in {0} AND eggs in {1} Then class = 6 (8/8, 100%)
Rule 8. If backbone in {0} AND airborne in {0} Then class = 7 (10/12, 100%)

Our method is also effective for a representative rule learner like RIPPER [12] as we can see in table 17. The experiment was also based on 10-fold cross validation

Table 7. The result of RIPPER.

Data set	Accuracy (%)	Number of rules
The original	88.1	6
Data set whose 'name' and 'predator' attribute have been removed	91.1	7

Table 8 summarizes all the previous experiments using MODLEM for the data set.

Table 8. The summary of the experiments with rough set algorithm.

	Data set	Accuracy (%)	Number of rules
No discretization	The original	42.6	7
	Data set whose 'name' and 'predator' attribute have been removed	96.0	8
With discretization	The original	42.6	7
	Data set whose 'predator' attribute have been removed	42.6	7
	Data set whose 'name' attribute have been removed	94.1	10
	Data set whose 'name' and 'predator' attribute have been removed	96.0	8

3 Conclusions

Rough sets are one of widely accepted machine learning technologies because of their strong mathematical background and capability of finding optimal rules based on given data sets. Good property of rough set theory is that it can describe uncertain facts solely based on data. As a result, there is no room for prejudiced views to be inserted in the found knowledge from the data. But, because rough set theory-based algorithms find rules very thoroughly, it may confront with the overfitting problem. Overfitting may occur because the theory find rules very precisely, but, on the other hand, it is not easy to find a training data set that covers its data space fully, even for big data.

On the other hand, association rules find rules of association, where the association resides between sets of items in database. Association rule algorithms find itemsets that occur more than given minimum support. The algorithms can find the itemsets practically in reasonable time even for very large databases by supplying the minimum support appropriately.

In order to overcome the problem of overfitting problem in rough set theory-based algorithms, we find large itemsets using class association rule algorithm, then we select attributes that cover the large itemsets. By using the selected attributes only, we may find better set of rules in accuracy. Various experiments have been done using a public data set called 'zoo' in UCI machine learning repository to support our suggested method.

This work was supported by Dongseo University, "Dongseo Frontier Project" Research Fund of 2016.

References

1. Z. Pawlak, Int. J. of Parallel Programming, **11**, 5, 341-356 (1982)
2. M. Bal, Inf. Sci. Lett., **2**, 1, 35-47 (2013)
3. J. Stefanowski, *Rough Sets in Knowledge Discovery 1: Methodology and Application,* 500-529. (Heidelberg: Physica-Verlag, 1998)
4. R. Agrawal, T. Imieliński, A. Swami, *Proceedings of the 1993 ACM SIGMOD international conference on Management of data - SIGMOD '93,* 207-216 (1993)
5. J. Hipp, U. Güntzer, G. Nakhaeizadeh, ACM SIGKDD Explorations Newsletter, **2**, 58, 58-64 (2000)
6. M. Hasher, http://michael.hahsler.net/research/association_rules/measures.html (2015)
7. D.J. Leiwever, The J. of Investing, **16**, 15-22 (2007)
8. A. Frank, A. Suncion, UCI Machine Learning Repository [http://archive.ics.uci.edu/ml]. Irvine, CA: University of California, School of Information and Computer Sciences (2010)
9. J. Stefanowski, *6th European Congress on Intelligent Techniques and Soft Computing*, 109-113 (1998)
10. U. M. Fayyad, K.B. Irani, *Thirteenth International Joint Conference on Articial Intelligence*, 1022-1027 (1993)
11. L.T.T. Nguyen, B. Vo, T. Hong, H. Thanh, Expert Systems with Applications, **40**, 6, 2305-2311 (2013)
12. T. Lehr, J. Yuan, D. Zeumer, S. Jayadev, M.D. Ritchie, BioData Mining, **4**, 4, doi : 10.1186/1756-0381-4-4 (2011)

Crowdsourcing as an IT help tool to determine impact in the health sector

Juan Diego López[1,*], *Roberto Osorio*[2], *Luis Moreno*[3], *Jorge Gomez*[4], *Francisco López*[5], *Aldo Vilardy*[6], *Jairo Gutierrez* [7], *Liliana Gomez*[8] *and Francisco Veléz*[9]

[1]UCEVA Asesor, Vicerrectoria de Investigaciones, Tuluá - Valle, Colombia
[2]ECCI Asesor Vicerrectoria de Investigaciones, Bogotá, Colombia
[3]LUMON Ceo, Dirección, Bogotá, Colombia,
[4]UCEVA Vicerrector, Vicerrectoria de Investigaciones, Tuluá - Valle, Colombia
[5]LV Consultores, Departamento de Informática, Tuluá - Valle, Colombia
[6]LV Consultores, Departamento de Informática, Bogotá, Colombia
[7] UCEVA Rector, Rector Institucional, Tuluá - Valle, Colombia
[8] UNIMUNUTO Departamento de Informática y Electrónica, Director, Bogotá, Colombia
[9] UCEVA Docente, Vicerrectoria de Investigaciones, Tuluá - Valle, Colombia

Abstract. The aim of this research was to propose a solution which applies the Crowdsourcing concept as the use of Information Technology to determine the perception of a social environment, which can perform a raised topic by an entity. In this case, the perception of Ruben Cruz Velez hospital with respect to: What opinion would you give about the Hospital Prevention and Promotion program?, in order to evaluate throughout Crowdsourcing, the Monitoring and Control Inspection (IVC) mechanisms for the provision of health services and component effectiveness, processes and standards of the Mandatory Quality Assurance System and their impact on provision of health services to users in an accessible and equitable manner.It is important to highlight that the development of a web platform that allows citizen participation to evaluate the mechanisms of Inspection of Monitoring and Control (IVC) of the provision of health services, analyzing the effectiveness of corrective actions and their impact on The provision of services to users in an accessible and equitable manner. Undoubtedly, in order to understand the current development and situation of traditional medicine in diverse geographical and cultural contexts, the way it adapts to its environment, and the type of health care available, it is necessary to locate it in the context of the models Health care in which it is inserted. The analysis of the current situation of traditional health systems, seen as subsystems of the total system, serves as a starting point for a more detailed reflection of their dynamics in Colombia, so thanks to the development of the CROWDSOURCING methodology as a tool To understand the current situation will help us to make valuable decisions for the future of the health sector particularly the beneficiary entities.

1 Introduction

The present research is based on work carried out in the Ruben Cruz Velez Hospital of Tuluá, Valle del Cauca-Colombia. Work funded by Unidad Central del Valle-UCEVA.

One of this work motivation is to evaluate, throughout crowdsourcing, the provision of health service and component effectiveness, processes and standards of the mandatory system of quality assurance and its impact on the provision of these services to users in an accessible and equitable manner. And in turn, evaluate and value citizen participation, in order to identify possible gaps and shortcomings of the general health system.

Studies with the use of new technologies, in particular, all those advances related to the internet, have allowed the birth of a new multitude processes and applications, which were based on the network of networks: Web 2.0, evolution of the traditional web (1.0), after the .com bubble sites, and the applications which represent its principles and currently some of their fruits.

It is important to note that "Web 2.0" concept, was coined by O'Really[1] in the year of 2005 and although it is a difficult term to define[2], the truth is that it has meant a radical change in the way to use the Internet. Specifically, Web 2.0 refers both to a way of using web and technological paradigm, comprises both a set of new web technologies, a set of business strategies as well as a series of social trends [3].

* Corresponding author: jdlopez@uceva.edu.co

Undoubtedly, within the history and evolution of Crowdsourcing[4], this was defined for the first time, by an American journalist, Jeff Howe, where in 2006 he defined it as the open call initiated by a company or institution normally performed by an employee directed to an indefinite group of individuals ("crowd"), often large in order to outsource a function,[5]. Therefore, Several authors have tried so far to elaborate a definition, some focusing on the use of crowdsourcing as a process of problem solving 6,[7], others as a way to outsource tasks[8]. However, Crowdsourcing refers to a collective intelligence 9, and does not have a theoretical basis which is based in this research[4], although this problem is being remedied.

Nevertheless, within the context of health care, various forms of crowdsourcing have been used for disaster response10 and a disease outbreak[11]. These forms of crowdsourcing relied on unpaid volunteers to provide services such as language translation or geolocation. One example is the 23andMe company, which is the largest community of personal genotype, with more than 100,000 subscribers serving the genome, and more than 75% of the community has expressed its willingness to participate in research studies organized by the company[12]. In addition, a large case led by the National Human Genome Research Institute, referring to associated tests like type 2 diabetes, prostate cancer, cholesterol levels, and multiple sclerosis[12]. It can be highlighted that according to what PatientsLikeMe and 23andMe companies perform, these are types of research studies based on crowdsourcing [13].
Therefore, PatientsLikeMe & 23andMe, are crowdsourcing operators in health and research studies, studies carried out in improvement areas of disease characterization and measurement, research aspects of drugs use, exploration of social health experience in terms of network user, disease establishment and the basis of traits with genetic associations.

One of the cases of crowdsourcing in health was developed by World Community Grid[14], a non-profit project which aimed to support scientific research projects for the benefit of humanity. The project started in 2004 to accelerate the discovery of a cure for smallpox. The crowdsourcing approach, have allowed researchers to examine the effect of 35 million pharmacological compounds, and finally select 44 of particular therapeutic interest. Since then, WCG has extended its objectives to other areas, such as the human immunodeficiency virus, and two promising inhibitors, which have promoted the AIDS treatment advance. Similarly, WCG Have an active project since November 2011, the GO project Fight Against Malaria, whose objective is to discover pharmacological compounds, which are effective against the more resistant forms of malaria[15].

Nevertheless, scientists of The Scripps Research Institute, La Jolla-California, USA, used IBM network in the World Community to computationally evaluate millions of candidate compounds against different molecular pharmacological systems of the malaria parasite. Another project is the GO16, where Malaria is just one example of the potential that crowdsourcing offers us, as a proven methodology in other fields, addressed to find solutions to this and other diseases.

2 Material and methods

The present case is addressed to propose a solution, which applies the Crowdsourcing concept for weighting of surveys and determination of the perception, which have allowed a social environment in front of a subject that an entity raises.

In this case, several alternatives are evaluated and the feeling evaluation is selected throughout an application of regular expressions to the opinion expressed by a community, as well as a weighting of the responses selected to one or more questions that an entity raise.

To obtain the above, the themes are defined as follows:

a) Implement a security system and database profiles.

b) Implement an option for handling regular expressions.

c) Implement an administration for creation of survey topics, creation of questions, opinion topics and association of regular expressions.

d) Implement a survey processing and opinion processing system with bar graph presentation with the obtained result.

e) Implement options to allow the people registration in a community who want to participate in the process throughout surveys and opinion.

f) Implement options to allow surveys to be answered and provide input from the registered community.

Starting from what is stated in the description, the following architecture for the solution is presented as shown in Figure 1.

Fig. 1. Architecture

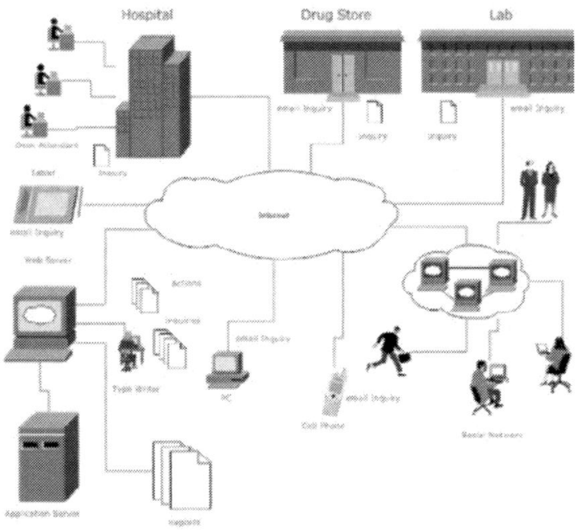

The architecture is based on a JEE Enterprise Java Web Design, using the following components: Front-End: Framework JSF adding to framework PrimeFaces 5.0. Back-End: Framework JSF with EJB 3.0 (JEE). Respectively, allows access to Relational Database: Framework JPA, specifically the EclipseLink component.

The project structure, as shown in Figure 2, is a general structure for developing the solution, creating and locating sources in its packages.

Fig. 2. Project structure

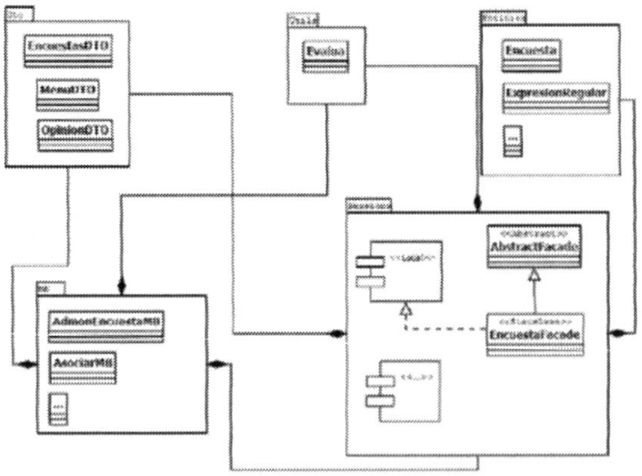

For development a project is created Web JSP using IDE Netbeans 8.0.2 full version. To open the project, simply select the option to open projects from the IDE.

Within the requirements for installation is needed as Software:

-Java development kit version 7 update 80. http://www.oracle.com/technetwork/es/java/javase/downloads/jdk7-downloads-1880260.html
-Mysql5.5
https://dev.mysql.com/downloads/windows/installer/5.5.html
-Glassfish4.1
https://glassfish.java.net/download-archive.html

3 Results

The project considered for the case study, a question to be developed using the crowdsourcing methodology, at the Ruben Cruz Velez Hospital in Tuluá - Valle del Cauca – Colombia, which were performed to get the following results.

Fig. 3. Option "Theme"

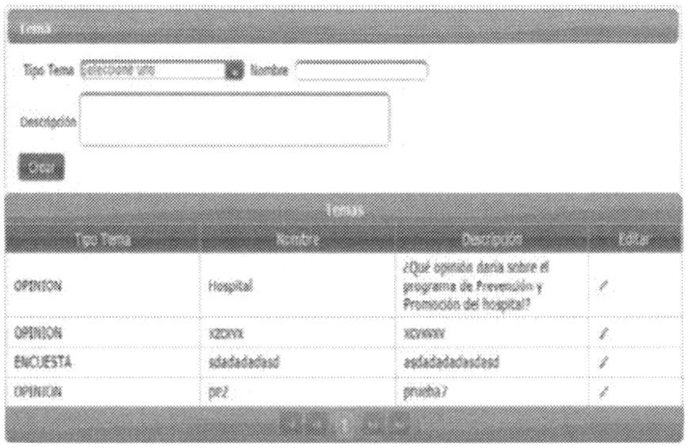

To create a theme, you must select one of the options of type, which are Survey or Opinion type. In addition, gives a name to the subject, which is typed in the text box called name. To facilitate a more precise objective, it describes what is wanted with the subject and finally it is pressed the button create with which, a subject is stored in database. The description should be as telling as possible so that those who are going to conduct the survey or say understand what you want with your answers or comments.

Once created the theme, is displayed in the grid which allows a future modification.

If you want to change, press the pencil icon in the grid next to the profile name, after which you can modify the profile. To be stored after modifying, the ✓ icon is

DOI: 10.1051/matecconf/201712504018

pressed. Otherwise, if you want to cancel, press the X icon. Note that every time you create a theme of a specific type, the previous theme will be closed and the new theme, will be active.

Given these concerns, Crowdsourcing is used as a methodology for health, where an opinion question is performed throughout web and social networks in such a way the Ruben Cruz Hospital users in Tuluá, Valle – Colombia. A particular theme of the hospital, for this case was asked:

What opinion would you give about the Hospital Prevention and Promotion Program?, in order to evaluate, throughout Crowdsourcing, the Surveillance and Control Inspection (SCI) mechanisms for provision of health services and the component effectiveness, processes and standards of the Mandatory Quality Assurance System and its impact on the provision of health services to users in an accessible and equitable manner.

Fig.4. Crowdsourcing for health

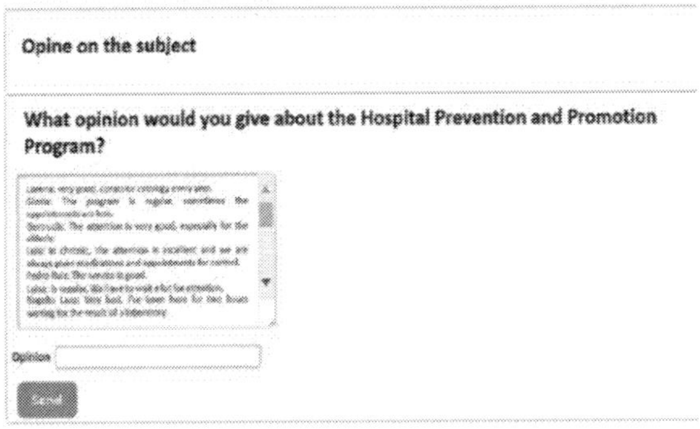

In this process, each user gave his opinion as shown in Figure 4. From there, each of them made their opinion reaching about 400 users who opined and it was given as a general result, users are not at ease with the Service, as shown in Figure 5. Given this concerns, a report was presented to the hospital management to take the corresponding corrective, and will continue to use the tool for decision-making senior management.

Fig.4. Result

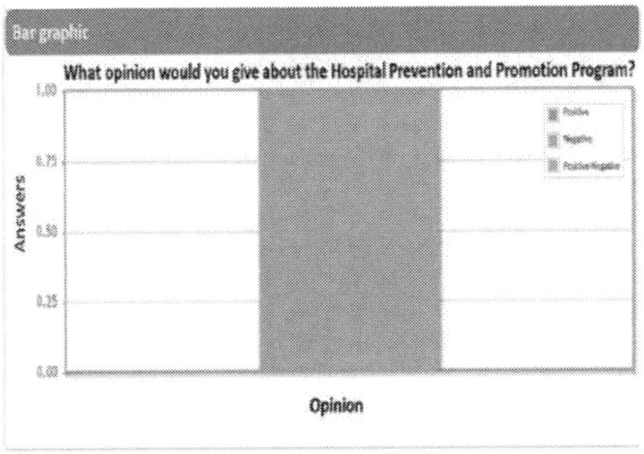

Considerations

Crowdsourcing facilitates the implementation of innovation models and development of actions, which support improvements and the achievement of benefits in innovation processes, this provides more accurate and reliable estimates for a company or organization to base some of their decisions or actions on knowledge and work group of external groups.

Undoubtedly, to understand the current development and situation of traditional medicine in diverse geographic and cultural contexts, the way in which it adapts to its environment, and the type of health care available, it is necessary to locate it in the models context of health care in which is inserted.

It is important to note that the current situation analysis of traditional health systems, seen as subsystems of the total system, serves as a starting point for a more detailed reflection of its dynamics in Colombia. In this way, throughout the development of Crowdsourcing methodology, have allowed to understand the current situation and provides more accurate and reliable estimates of valuable decisions for the future of the health sector, particularly the two beneficiary entities.

It is noteworthy that the implementation and validation of a technological strategy to address and solve problems for the general social security system in health programs in health promotion and disease prevention in high rural and territorial environments Dispersed territories. Case study center of the cauca valle.

Final considerations

We describe the results of Crowdsourcing implementation in the health case study at Ruben Cruz Velez Hospital in the city of Tuluá, Valle – Colombia. Given these concerns, this paper is derived from the project "Control system, inspection, health services surveillance in Colombia for the general system of social security in health throughout ICT services and processes management", a project funded by ICT (Information and Communication Technologies) Ministry and Colciencias in Colombia.

Acknowledgements

Mainly to UCEVA- Unidad Central del Valle Del Cauca and their valuable contribution for research realization as a pioneering project in Latin American, and also an acknowledgement to Dr. Julio Cesar Toro, for opening the doors of the Ruben Cruz Velez Hospital as beneficiary.

References

1. O'Reilly, T. (2007) what is Web 2.0: Design Patterns and Business Models for the Next Generation of Software. Communications & Strategies, 1, 17
2. Cormode, G. and Krishnamurthy, B. (2008) Key differences between Web 1.0 and Web 2.0. First Monday, 13 (6).
3. Murugesan, S. (2007) Understanding Web 2.0. IT Professional, 9(4), 34-41
4. Lopez Juan D. González F. Estelles E. Prieto F. Crowdsourcing: Para la Prevención y Promoción de la Salud en Colombia. www.laccei.org/LACCEI2013Cancun/Referee Papers/RP056.pdf Eleventh LACCEI Latin American and Caribbean Conference for Engineering and Technology (LACCEI'2013)
5. Howe, J. (2006) Crowdsourcing: A definition. http://crowdsourcing.typepad.com/cs/2006/06/crowd sourcing_a.html (Last access, april, 2016).
6. Brabham, D. C. (2008). Crowdsourcing as a model for problem solving. Convergence: The International Journal of Research into New Media Technologies, 14(1), 75
7. Vukovic, M. and Bartolini, C. (2010) Towards a Research Agenda for Enterprise crowdsourcing. In: M. Tiziana and S. Bernhard (eds) Leveraging Applications of Formal Methods, Verification, and Validation (Springer, Berlin/Heidelberg, 2010) 425-434 [Lecture Notes in Computer Science 6415].
8. Oliveira, F., Ramos, I., Santos, L. (2010) Definition of a crowdsourcing Innovation Service for the European SMEs. In: Daniel F. et al. (eds.) Current Trends in Web Engineering (Springer, Berlin/Heidelberg, 2010), pp. 412-416.
9. Schenk, E. and Guittard, C. (2011) towards a characterization of crowdsourcing practices. Journal of innovation economics, 1(7), 93-107.
10. Denyer, D., Tranfield, D. and Van Aken, J.E. (2008) Developing design propositions through research synthesis. Organization Studies, 29(3), 393-413.
11. Gao & Barbier, 2011) Harnessing the Crowdsourcing Power of Social Media for Disaster Relief. Ieee InTeLLIGenT SySTemS Published by the IEEE Computer Society Cyber-physical-social systems ISSN 1541-1672, 2011 IEEE.
12. Freifeld, C. C., Chunara, R., Mekaru, S. R., Chan, E. H., Kass-Hout, T., Ayala Iacucci, A., & Brownstein, J. S. (2010). Participatory Epidemiology: Use of Mobile Phones for Community-Based Health Reporting. PLoS Medicine, 7(12).
13. J.Y. Tung, N. Eriksson, A.K. Kiefer, J.M. Macpherson, B.T. Naughton, A.B. Chowdry, C.B. Do, D.A. Hinds, A. Wojcicki, J.L. Mountain Characteristics of an Online Consumer Genetic Research Cohort. 23andMe, Inc, Mountain View, CA http://blog.23andme.com/wpcontent/uploads/2011/10/ASHG2011poster-JYT.pdf (Last access, March, 2016).
14. Swan, M. (2012). Crowdsourced Health Research Studies: An Important Emerging Complement to Clinical Trials in the Public Health Research Ecosystem. Journal of Medical Internet Research, 14(2). ISSN:1439-4456
15. WCG 2004." Proyecto GO Viruela", worldcommunitygrid. http://www.worldcommunitygrid.org/research/gfam/overview.do (Last access, March, 2016).
16. WCG 2011." Proyecto GO Fight against Malaria", worldcommunitygrid. http://www.worldcommunitygrid.org/research/gfam/overview.do. (Last access, March, 2016).

Strategies for Improving the Quality of Polling Service in Wireless Metropolitan Area Network

Zhi-Jun Yang[1,2], *Yang* Su[1,*], *Hong-Wei* Ding[1] and *Yang-Yang* Ding[1]

[1]School of Information Science and Engineering, Yunnan University, Kunming, 650091, China.

[2]The Academy for Educational Science Research, Educational Department of Yunnan Province, Kunming , 650223,China.

Abstract. Four kinds of service types are defined in IEEE 802.16. In order to provide the Quality of Service (Qos) for different services, the system must use a reasonable resource allocation method and scheduling algorithm to efficiently and fairly allocate bandwidth resources. Although in the IEEE 802.16 MAC, for the uplink real-time polling service (rtPS) and non-real-time polling service (nrtPS) business type of data transmission are used to polling, but do not provide business-based services. In this paper, the distinction between priority service of rtPS and nrtPS is carried out, and the simulation experiment is used to analyze the performance characteristics of the protocol under the distinction of high and low priority. Wherein the theoretical values of the average delay and the information packets are compared with the experimental values. The average query cycle and throughput are also evaluated. Which proves the validity of the improved service strategy and improves the service characteristics of the system.

1 Introduction

In the fields of industrial control, computer time division multiplexing, communication system protocol and computer network protocol, the control mode of polling system has been widely used because of its fairness and usability. The analysis and research of the polling system are also developing continuously. With the deepening of the research, the application of the polling system has been further expanded. The strategy of the polling service can be divided into three categories: exhaustive service, gated service and limited-k service. In practice, priority-based services have a wide range of needs, so the distinction priority service is very necessary. In the broadband network, it is necessary to provide end-to-end service quality assurance for different types of service flows to satisfy the requirements of the traffic flow for broadband, delay jitter and packet loss rate. IEEE802.16[1,2], also known as the IEEE Wireless MAN air interface standard, it regulates the underlying standards (including the physical layer and the media access control layer) of the wireless access system in the 2-66 GHz frequency range, and analyzes the system coexistence background, gives the system design, configuration and frequency use scheme.

With the rapid growth of wireless data services and multimedia applications, providing QoS support in the systembusiness has become a basic requirement that must be met. The MAC protocol in IEEE 802.16 defines four types of services, specifying different QoS parameters and basic bandwidth allocation mechanisms for them. However, the standard does not specify the principles of resource allocation and scheduling between services and similar services. Therefore, how to make effective use of system resources and ensure that different QoS requirements of various services become important and challenging research work. In this paper, we focus on the scheduling problem of real-time polling service (rtPS) non-real-time polling service (nrtPS) in 802.16, and study

* Corresponding author: sy064615@163.com

DOI: 10.1051/matecconf/201712504019

the resource scheduling strategy between two kinds of services. At the same time,we propose a service strategy that prioritizes the two businesses. Among them, the high-priority service will use the exhaustive service operation mechanism, and low priority will use the gated service way. What's more, this kind of mixed service strategy can ensure the QoS demand and the system bandwidth allocation fairness.

2 The development of IEEE802.16 series standards

IEEE802.16 standard committee in July 1999 began to discuss the global unified wireless broadband metropolitan area network access standards, so far has been established including 802.16, 802.16a, 802.16c, 802.16d, 802.16e, 802.16f, etc. and a series of standards. According to the different frequency band, 802.16 system can divide into two kinds of line of sight and non line of sight, in which the 2-11 GHz band system applies to the non line of sight range, and the 10-66GHz band system is used in line of sight range. According to whether to support mobile features, IEEE 802. 16 standard series can also divide into fixed broadband wireless access air interface standard and mobile broadband wireless access air interface standard. So, the 802.16, 802.16a, 802.16d are fixed wireless access air interface standard, the 802.16e belongs to the mobile broadband wireless access air interface standard. As the current standard 802.16j, there is a backward compatibility for the earlier established IEEE802.16 standards. It uses multi-hop relay technology as the core, using a relay-based network architecture, can achieve high coverage at low cost. The technical fields corresponding to the IEEE 802. 16 part of the series of standards are shown in Table 1 below.

Table 1. The technical fields corresponding to the 802. 16 part of the series of standards

Standard number	Corresponding technical areas
802.16	10-66GHz fixed broadband wireless access system air interface
802.16a	2-11GHz fixed broadband access system air interface
802.16c	10-66GHz Compatibility of fixed broadband access system
802.16d	2-66GHz fixed broadband access system air interface
802.16e	2-11GHz fixed and mobile broadband wireless access system air interface management information base
802.16f	2-11GHz fixed broadband wireless access system air interface management information base (MIB) requirements

3 IEEE 802.16 MAC protocol analysis

IEEE 802.16 broadband wireless metropolitan area network consists of base station (BS) and Subscriber Station (SS). The BS is the central station, which is responsible for all communication between the network and the network. SS connects all types of users and the BS through the air interface. IEEE 802.16 MAC layer specification uses a hierarchical structure, divides into three sub-layers:

(1) Convergence Sub layer (CS), responsible for high-level interface, convergence of the upper different business. IEEE 802.16 MAC is connection-oriented, and the protocol defines two CS sub layers to map the upper layer business as a connection. The ATM CS sub layer provides service support for ATM; Packet CS provides mapping of packet-based services such as IEEE 802.3, 802.1Q, and IP. The Packet CS sub layer defines the concept of a classifier. The classifier is a set of mapping standards. Each packet enters the network is mapped to a connection according to the rules defined by the classifier. Each connection consists of a unique connection identifier (CID) of 16 bits, according to the service quality requirements, they associate with the appropriate connection to ensure that different business QoS.

(2) Common Part Sub layer (CPS), which implements the main MAC function, is responsible for SS initialization and entry network, physical layer support and channel information management, connection and service flow management, radio resource management, data processing and retransmission, etc.. It supports Point to Multi-Point (PMP) network topology, downlink only BS to send, uplink broadband with multiple SS sharing, BS is responsible for uplink and downlink broadband resource allocation. The uplink adopts way that is composed of time-division multiple access (TDMA) and

DOI: 10.1051/matecconf/201712504019

Demand Assigned Multiple Access (DAMA), and the downlink mainly adopts Time-Division Multiplex (TDM) mode. As shown in Figure 1 below: shows the uplink and downlink transmission of data.

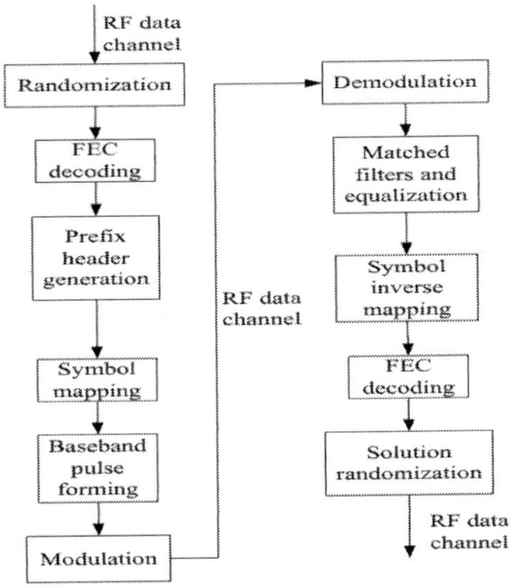

Fig.1. The uplink and downlink transmission of data.

(3) Safety Sub layer (SS), responsible for authentication and encryption.

IEEE 802.16 MAC layer implementation of the principle of QoS[3] is to map the MAC packet transmission to the business flow, and map to the connection that has the CID logo. It can be based on the QoS parameters of the business scheduling to guarantee the MAC QoS characteristic. According to the different features and requirements of the business, IEEE 802.16 MAC in the uplink direction defines four different levels of business scheduling service type:

1) Unsolicited Grant Service (UGS) are used to support real-time business needs for fixed bandwidth, such as E1, T1, VoIP, and so on.

2) Real-Time Polling Service (rtPS), rtPS is mainly used to meet the variable bandwidth real-time business needs, such as MPEG video stream.

3) Non-Real-Time Polling Service (nrtPS), nrtPS applies to the data size variable non-real-time business flow, with a certain cycle of polling connection.

4) Best Effort Service (BE), BE according to the network status for the general business to provide the greatest possible business, but it cannot guarantee QoS.

4 Traffic service strategy based on service priority for wireless metropolitan area networks

4.1 Protocol model analysis

As shown in Figure 2, the wireless computer network consists of N sites, each site's business is divided into two types of priority, λ_{i1} for the high priority service arrival rate, under the condition that the arrival process is Poisson process, the arrival process probability generation function is $A_h(z)$, where the mean value and the variance are $\lambda_{i1}(i=1,2, ...,N)=\lambda_h=A'_h(1)$ and $\sigma^2_{\lambda h}=A''_h(1)+\lambda_h-\lambda^2_h$. $\lambda_{i2}(i=1,2,...,N)$is the arrival rate of the low priority service for each site. The generation function, mean value and variance of each station for low priority service arrival process are $A(z)$, $\lambda_{i2}(i=1,2,...,N)=\lambda=A'(1)$ and $\sigma^2_\lambda=A''(1)+\lambda-\lambda^2$. The low priority queues of the site i ($i = 1, 2, ..., N$) obtain the transmission right at time t_n and send the information packets arriving before time t_n by the gated service rule, the transmission service time of an information packet in the queue follows the identical independent probability distribution with the generation function, mean value and variance are $B(z)$,$\beta=B'(1)$ and $\sigma^2_\beta=B'(1)+\beta-\beta^2$. When the site i completes the low-priority service information packet transmission before the station time t_n arrives, after a switch time γ [its generation function, the mean value and variance are $R(z)$, $\gamma=R'(1)$ and $\sigma^2_{\beta h}=B''_h(1)+\beta_h-\beta^2_h$], AP(BS or Master) through the multi-point scheduling method to check whether the high priority queue is empty, and query $i+1$ site. If the high priority service queue is not empty, the high priority service of each station is unified according to the exhaustive service rule at time t^*_n to send information packets, and the generation function, the mean value and variance are $B_h(z)$, $\beta_h=B'_h(1)$ and $\sigma^2_{\beta h}=B''_h(1)+\beta_h-\beta^2_h$. After the high priority business of each station is empty, the $i+1$ site starts the low priority service transmission at time t_{n+1}. The transmission of the high priority service and the low priority service of each site are alternately accepted service by the AP (BS or Master) and are accessed according to the rules of the exhaustive service and the gated service respectively.

At the time of t_n, t^*_n and t_{n+1} ($t_n<t^*_n<t_{n+1}$), the

whole system state can be expressed by the variables $\{\xi_1(n), \xi_2(n), \ldots, \xi_N(n), \xi_h(n)\}$, $\{\xi_1(n^*), \xi_2(n^*), \ldots, \xi_N(n^*), \xi_h(n^*)\}$ and $\{\xi_1(n+1), \xi_2(n+1), \ldots, \xi_N(n+1), \xi_h(n+1)\}$. The state of the system can be described by the Markov chain, which is aperiodic and experienced.

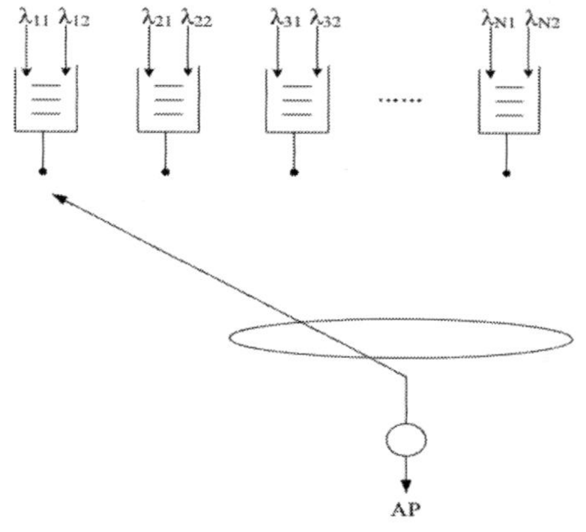

Fig.2. Distinguish the priority MAC protocol system diagram.

4.2 Protocol model characteristics

According to the Markov chain theory, under the condition of $\sum_{i=1}^{N}\lambda_i\beta_i + \lambda_h\beta_h < 1$, the system generation function is:

$$G_{i+1}(z_1,z_2,\cdots,z_N,z_h)=$$

$$R\left[\prod_{j=1}^{N}A_j(z_j)A_h\left(B_h\left(\prod_{j=1}^{N}A_j(z_j)F\left(\prod_{j=1}^{N}A_j(z_j)\right)\right)\right)\right]\bullet$$

$$G_i\left[z_1,z_2,\cdots,B_i\left(\prod_{j=1}^{N}A_j(z_j)A_h\left(B_h\left(\prod_{j=1}^{N}A_j(z_j)F\left(\prod_{j=1}^{N}A_j(z_j)\right)\right)\right)\right),\right.$$

$$\left.z_{i+1},\cdots,z_N,B_h\left(\prod_{j=1}^{N}A_j(z_j)F\left(\prod_{j=1}^{N}A_j(z_j)\right)\right)\right]$$

$$i=1,\ 2,\ \ldots,\ N \tag{1}$$

Where $F(z)$ is the probability generation function of the transmission time distribution for the information packets arriving in any time slot according to the exhaustive service rule. And it is assumed that the memory capacity of each site is large enough and don't cause loss of information packets.

The average information packets stored is $g_i(j)$ in the j station memory, when the service starts at t_n.

$$g_i(j)=\lim_{z_1,\cdots,z_N,z_h\to 1}\frac{\partial G_i(z_1,z_2,\cdots,z_N,z_h)}{\partial z_j}$$

$$i=1,\ 2,\ldots,\ N,\ h;\ j=1,2,\ldots,N,\ h \tag{2}$$

4.2.1 Mean queue length

The derivatives of Eqs (1) and (2) give the mean queue length as:

The mean queue length of the low priority service is:

$$g_i(i)=\frac{N\lambda\gamma}{1-\rho_h-N\rho} \tag{3}$$

The mean queue length of the high priority service is:

$$g_{ih}(h)=\frac{\lambda_h\gamma(1-\rho_h)}{1-\rho_h-N\rho} \tag{4}$$

4.2.2 The average delay

The average delay of the information packet is the time from the arrival of the information packet into the site memory until it was sent.

The average delay for each site's low priority business information packet is:

$$E(w)=\frac{(1+\rho)g_i(i,i)}{2\lambda g_i(i)} \tag{5}$$

The average delay for each site's high priority business information packet is:

$$E(w_h)=\frac{g_{ih}(h,h)}{2\lambda_h g_{ih}(h)}-\frac{(1-2\rho_h)A_h''(1)}{2\lambda_h^2(1-\rho_h)}+\frac{\lambda_h B_h''(1)}{2(1-\rho_h)} \tag{6}$$

4.2.3 The average query cycle and throughput

The average query cycle for N sites is:

$$E(\theta)=\frac{N_\gamma}{1-\rho_h-N\rho} \tag{7}$$

The throughput of the system is the number of

DOI: 10.1051/matecconf/201712504019

packets transmitted by the system per unit of time.

The throughput of the system is:

$$T = N\rho + \rho_h \tag{8}$$

4.3 Method of improving QoS guarantee

Based on the traffic priority of the polling mechanism: in the original IEEE 802.16 MAC, the IP head of the Taxonomy of Service (ToS) field that has 3bit priority sub field mapping into the above four different Qos level, see Table 2. The same level of business uses the same type of scheduling, no longer distinguish priority, here we will further subdivide the rtPS business and nrtPS business to distinguish priority services. "011" of rtPS and "001" of nrtPS in the ToS field are the high priority service identifier in the same service, and "100" of rtPS and "010" of nrtPS are used as low priority service identifier in the same business. In the IEEE 802.16 MAC polling mode, the BS periodically queries the different business queues of the SS site. First, the higher priority[8,9] business queue is authorized to send the information in the exhaustive service mode, that is, it sends the full information packets of the queue and the packets of information to be reached during the transmission, until the class of business queues on the query SS site is empty. When the SS high priority service queue is empty, the BS starts to query the service queue with the lower priority and sends the information according to the policy of the gated service. That is, it sends the information packets that arrive before the transmission start. The information packets arriving during transmission will wait for the next chance to send. In this way, the service of the polling mode in the IEEE 802.16 MAC is distinguished by the different service policies of the exhaustive service and the gated service, which makes it have better flexibility and QoS guarantee.

Table 2. Correspondence table for ToS field and IEEE 802.16 service type

Business type	ToS field	Scheduling strategy	Business
UGS	111-101	reserve resources	VoIP
rtPS	100-011	real-time polling	MEPG video stream
nrtPS	010-001	non-real-time polling	interactive game
BE	000	FIFO	WWW、E-mail

5 Analysis and evaluation

Based on the Markov chain and the probability generation function of the wireless computer network MAC protocol model, combined with the characteristics of IEEE 802.16, the length of a slot is defined as 200 microseconds, the uplink TDMA frame length is 0.01 seconds, that is, Contains 50 time slots. SS station number is set to 50, through the theoretical calculation and simulation experiments, the average information packets stored and the average delay are as follows.

Table 3. Average information packets stored

$\lambda=\lambda_h$ (Information packets / Time slot)	High priority business theoretical value	High priority business experimental value	Low priority business theoretical value	Low priority business experimental value
0.00050	0.00057	0.00057	0.02865	0.02863
0.00100	0.00134	0.00132	0.06711	0.06715
0.00150	0.00241	0.00242	0.12146	0.12172
0.00200	0.00404	0.00411	0.20408	0.20461
0.00250	0.00405	0.00404	0.34014	0.34065
0.00300	0.01257	0.01269	0.63829	0.63714

Table 4. Information packets average delay

$\lambda=\lambda_h$ (Information packets / Time slot)	High priority business theoretical value	High priority business experimental value	Low priority business theoretical value	Low priority business experimental value
0.00050	0.39131	0.39624	28.59122	28.61720
0.00100	0.80956	0.79581	34.08481	34.06318
0.00150	1.27151	1.27191	41.84967	41.90759
0.00200	1.81122	1.80871	53.65867	53.65264
0.00250	2.47724	2.50196	72.71238	72.65779
0.00300	3.63032	3.64774	115.73909	115.60939

Table 5. Average query cycle and throughput

$\lambda=\lambda_h$ (Information packets / Time slot)	Query cycle theoretical value	Query cycle experimental value	Throughput theoretical value	Throughput experimental value
0.00050	57.30660	57.29980	0.12750	0.12490
0.00100	67.11409	67.11825	0.25500	0.25014
0.00150	80.97166	80.91685	0.38250	0.37551
0.00200	102.04082	102.17950	0.51000	0.50062
0.00250	136.05442	136.17320	0.63250	0.62541
0.00300	212.76596	212.45540	0.76500	0.74973

Table 3 to table 5 shows that the improved protocol theoretical analysis is consistent with the experimental results, through the IEEE 802.16 MAC protocol IP head ToS sub field settings, providing services to the SS site in business priority. Table 3 shows that the average information packets increases with the increase of the arrival rate, the information packet arrival rate is from 0.0005 to 0.003, and the information packets stored in the high priority service and the low priority service is increased by more than 20 times, but the distinction between high-priority and low-priority services remains clear. Table 4 shows the same rule on the average delay of the information packet. High-priority and low-priority services are clearly differentiated as the arrival rate and system load increase. Table 5 verifies the consistency between theoretical and experimental analysis of query cycles and throughput.

6 Conclusions

This paper based on the four original types of service scheduling makes some improvements in wireless metropolitan area network IEEE 802.16 MAC protocol, and further provides polling scheduling strategies based on service priority. Then, the theoretical value of the average number of information packets and the average delay of the information packet is compared with the experimental value, in the case of high priority business and low priority business. And the theoretical value and the experimental value of the query cycle and throughput are basically consistent. So, they are proved that the improved scheduling strategy improves the flexibility of protocol scheduling and better guarantees the QoS of different service flows. Compared with the traditional wired network, although the existing wireless network service quality and performance there are still some gaps. However, with the popularity of wireless networks and the development of a variety of business applications, the research and improvement of MAC layer QoS mechanism in wireless metropolitan area network has clear practical significance and application value. In the future work, we will continue to study the priority of the polling service strategies, the use of new hybrid services, such as gated-exhaustive service, gated-gated service, exhaustive-exhaustive service to guarantee the service quality of data service, and improve the utilization rate of system resources.

Acknowledgements

This work was supported by the National Natural Science Foundation of China under Grant Nos.61461054 and 61461053.

References

1. YaNan Sun, ZhongQiang Pan, Effective Bandwidth Allocation Mechanism of Supporting QoS in IEEE 802.16 Standard, *Computer and Modernization*, vol.**9**,25-29,(2016).
2. Jun Yu, GuangWei Bai, Hang Shen, DiffServ-based congestion control mechanism in IEEE 802.16 Mesh networks, *Application Research of Computers*, vol 31,no.9,(2014).
3. ZhiJun Yang, HongWei Ding, Zheng Guan, LongZheng Zhu, A New Transportation Control System Based On Priority Differentiated Polling Strategy, *Proceedings of 2015 World Conference on Control, Electronics and Electrical Engineering*,vol.**116**,38-44,(2015).
4. ZhiJun Yang, HongWei Ding, Characteristics of a Two-Class Polling System Model, *TSINGHUA SCIENCE AND TECHNOLOGY*, vol.**19**,no.5,516-520,(2014).
5. ZhiJun Yang, HongWei Ding, ChanLong Chen, Research on E(x) Characteristics of Two-Class Polling System of Exhaustive-Gated Service, *Acta Electronica*

Sinica, no.4,775-778,(2014).

6. Jia Guo, JiaLong Xiong, ZhiJun Yang, HongWei Ding, The analysis of performance for a priority distinction double-queue and single-server communication network, *International Conference on Control Engineering and Electronics Engineering*, Vol. **95**,(2014).

7. JiaLong Xiong, ZhiJun Yang, HongWei Ding, MengYao Wang, The Analysis of Performance for Priority Distinction Double-queue and Triple-server Communication Network, *2015 International Conference on Computer Science and Software Engineering*,810-826,(2015).

8. Zheng Guan, Zhijun Yang, Wenhua Qian, Min He, Research Article On Two-Level State-Dependent Routing Polling Systems with Mixed Service, *Mathematical Problems in Engineering*,1-9,(2015).

9. Min He, Zheng Guan, Liyong Bao, An Analysis of Polling Access Protocol for Wireless Sensor Networking, The *5th Annual IEEE International Conference on Cyber Technology in Automation, Control and Intelligent Systems*,720-724,(2015).

MATEC Web of Conferences **125**, 04020 (2017) DOI: 10.1051/matecconf/201712504020
CSCC 2017

Fuzzification of facial movements to generate human-machine interfaces in order to control robots by XMPP internet protocol

Jesús A. Romualdo Ramírez[1,*], *Enrique* Mendéz Franco[1,**], and *David* Tinoco Varela[2,***]

[1]UNAM Facultad de Estudios Superiores Cuautitlán, ITSE. San, Sebastián Xhala, Cuautitlán Izcalli Edo. De Mex. México
[2]UNAM Facultad de Estudios Superiores Cuautitlán, Departamento de Ingeniería. San Sebastián Xhala, Cuautitlán Izclli.

Abstract. The classic human-machine interfaces require mechanical or electronic elements which can be cumbersome or complex in their uses and implementations. As a result, interfaces of such kind can present a rigid communication with devices which we want to control, additionally they may not be a usable tool by people who have lost a body limb and who present different types of corporal disabilities.

In this work is showed the development of a human-machine interface which can control a remote device by the characterization of natural human facial movements employing artificial vision and fuzzy logic.

Due to the characteristics of the proposed interface, it permits that disabled, untrained, and even illiterate persons can use it easily.

This implementation is able to establish a remote communication with any electronic device through the internet by the XMPP protocol, which gives it a dynamism of control over practically any geographical position in the world where internet connection exist, in this way, it is possible to integrate it into the internet of things.

Keywords - Human-machine interfaces, Fuzzy control systems, Artificial vision, Internet of things.

1 Introduction

Many human-machine interfaces are developed and used every day to control various electronic and mechanical devices, such as Smart TVs, drones and terrestrial, marine and even space reconnaissance robots. However, such kind of control needs of unnatural elements to work, for example: joysticks, radio frequency control (RF), teach pendants, and others.

This causes that a disabled or an untrained person can be confused and rigid when he tries to control any type of robot or technological device.

One of the biggest disadvantages of the classical interfaces is the fact that most of them are technological element which can be manipulated by hands, this presents an adversity when people who have lost their hands, or don not have mobility on them, tries to manipulate such interfaces.

Due to the above, the generation and developing of human-machine interfaces which respond naturally and which can be controlled by different types of corporal behaviors, such as facial expressions, permits that any person can operate any device intuitively. In fact, almost any invalid person can use this kind of devices, because the interfaces don not require a body extremity to manipulate these controllers.

Human body, and in a general form any biological entity, possess unique traits and biological signals which can be used to manage a robotic system in a natural, e intuitive way. Many of these signals can be given by the facial movements of any person.

When common expressions or daily movements from a human face are used as controllers, a robot can be more easily handled, due to there is no necessity to learn commands or sequence of instructions.

Nowadays with the emergence of the *internet of things,* and the connection of any technological device to the internet, there is a great importance to be able to

* gsusitto@gmail.com, ** itse.enrique@gmail.com, *** dativa19@hotmail.com

control robotic systems in big distances through a communication global network, for this reason a human-machine interface which can control and monitor any electronic device by the network of networks could has a great scientific and commercial impact. The advantages of this schema can increase with respect to the inclusion of population sectors with body disabilities, and population who cannot read or write. All of this, just because there is a more natural communication between the human and the device to control.

In the present paper, it is demonstrated that through the use of techniques of artificial vision it is possible to generate more ergonomic e intuitive controllers which can perform command actions in any kind of environments. The presented controller uses fuzzy logic to interpret the facial movements in order to convert them to control words.

It is important to mention, it is necessary that the system be of low cost, and it needs to have the basic infrastructure to exchange information in order to have a penetration in population sectors of different social levels. Due to this situation, a project which uses the internet communication protocol XMPP (*Extensible Messaging and Presence Protocol*) is proposed. XMPP was originally destined to send and to receive instant messaging. This protocol permits us, among other things, to transmit control signals between two separated identities, and to make easier their connection because anybody can use the free servers destined to this kind of tasks.

2 Preliminaries

2.1 Fuzzy logic

Fuzzy logic arises between the 60s and 70s, proposed by *Lofti A Zadeh* [1]. This logic permits to simulate the mechanisms of human reasoning in order to control the proposed system. It provides a mathematical model which can process the uncertainty from the human cognitive process, and in this way it can be possible to solve different kind of problems using mathematical and computational methods.

Basically, fuzzy logic is a manner to mathematically represent the uncertainty, and vagueness of a problem. When we are looking for a solution of a given problem, we have input and output variables, fuzzy logic allows the transformation of the input variables into its corresponding output privileging the significance characteristics instead of the precision ones.

Fuzzy logic uses real values between 0 and 1 to indicate if a fact is completely false (0), or totally true (1), this is the membership degree corresponding to an input value in a fuzzy set. Being multivalued, an input can belong to more than one fuzzy set at the same moment, with a different membership value for each one. In this way, it provides a smooth transition between a pair of characteristics. All values which can take an input variable are called *universe of discourse*.
Once we have determined the different membership values of an entry to each of the sets in the universe of discourse we say that the variable has been *fuzzified*.

A standard control system based in fuzzy logic is showed in figure 1.

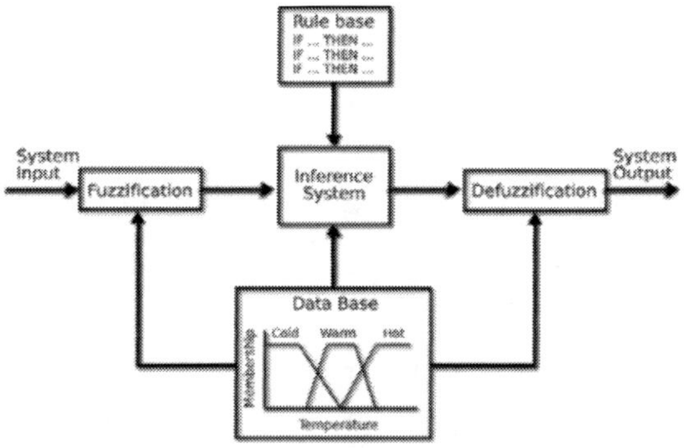

Fig. 1. Basic scheme of a fuzzy system.

2.2 Artificial vision and OpenCV

Artificial vision (AV) is a scientific discipline which consists in acquiring, processing, and mathematical modeling the processes of visual perception in living beings, capturing images from the real world in order to generate numerical or symbolic data that can be quantified and codified and then used that information in algorithms and software. Collected data can be used in the decision-making needed to carry out a given process. A system which uses artificial vision recognize figures and patterns, among other things.

Nowadays, artificial vision has great popularity over many technological, industrials, and services sectors due to the large amount of applications in which can be directed. AV can solve problems of supervision in fruits and vegetables [2], obstacles detection systems in vehicles and smart transportation [3, 4], and even it is usefulness in the design, development, and generation of systems which can be helpful as prosthesis for blind people [5] [6].

Due to the big amount of uses that this kind of systems can has, there is many computing tools developed in order to facilitate the work of new researchers and developers in this knowledge area.

The number of software instruments to work with these schemes is in fact varied, ranging from the costly to the free, and from the private to the open access, however, for the development of this project we had used the Open CV (*Open Source Computer Vision*) library due to it is no restricted just to one operative system, it is compatible with *Linux*, *Windows* and *Mac OS X*, it has big dynamism, and additionally it has interfaces to work with Python[a], Ruby[b], Matlab[c], and other languages.

Open CV is an open source library developed by *Intel* to be used in C language. It is oriented to work with real-time applications, for this reason it is a really good option to use it in facial recognition [7], tracing movements and objects detecting tasks [8], and functionality on mobile devices [9]. The last of great importance and interest for the development of the proposed project.

2.3 XMPP, communication protocol

Extensible Messaging and Presence Protocol XMPP, is an open protocol based on XML (*eXtensible Markup Language*), designed to give solutions related to real-time communications. This protocol is daily used by many companies[d].

Some of the most notable advantages of XMPP are:

1. *Decentralization*, XMPP Works with decentralized client-server networks, due to this fact anyone can install their own XMPP server, and make a connection to the rest of the network using the internet infrastructure or by a subscription to a public server.
2. *Safe*, the protocol core has SASL (*Simple Authentication and Security Layer*) and TSL (*Transport Layer Security*), which provides encryption and safe authentication algorithms.
3. *Extensible*, due to the XMPP cores is based in XML, it is possible to obtain custom applications such as instant messaging services, voice over IP, communication between machines, notifications, and alerts. In order to maintain the interoperability of the XMPP applications, *software foundation* manages the most of the extensions.
4. *Open standard*, Internet Engineering Task Force (IETF)[e] has formalized the XMPP protocol as an instant messaging standard [10].
5. XMPP protocols are free, public and easy to understand.

All the presented advantages of the XMPP protocol are useful in the development of human-machine interfaces which can control technological devices remotely.

2.3.1 Basics of XMPP

Each XMPP entity requires an identifier called a JID (*Jabber identifier*), which is composed of the user name, and the domain to which the resource is connected. The format of this identifier is like that of an email address "user @ domain / resource".

Using XML transmission technology, XML elements known as *stanzas* are exchanged between two entities in a network. A stanza can be understood as a basic unit of information. There are three types of stanzas in XMPP:

a. The *message stanza*, transmits information from one user to another, contains information from the sender and recipient, as well as the content and subject of the message.
b. The *Presence stanza* reports on the availability and status of a user on the network. Only those who have the contact of a user can see their status.
c. The *IQ* (Information / Query) *stanza*, provides a request-response structure between network users.

2.3.2 Process of delivery of the messages.

Assuming two users with subscriptions in different domain, quijote@lamancha.net and dulcinea@toboso.net, when Quijote sends a message to Dulcinea the following events are triggered (see figure 2).

1. Quijote connects to lamancha.net server.
2. The server lamancha.net negotiates and opens a connection with toboso.net, in case that the connection is not achieved, the message is discarded.
3. The server toboso.net delivers the message to Dulcinea, if it is not online, the message will be delivered later.

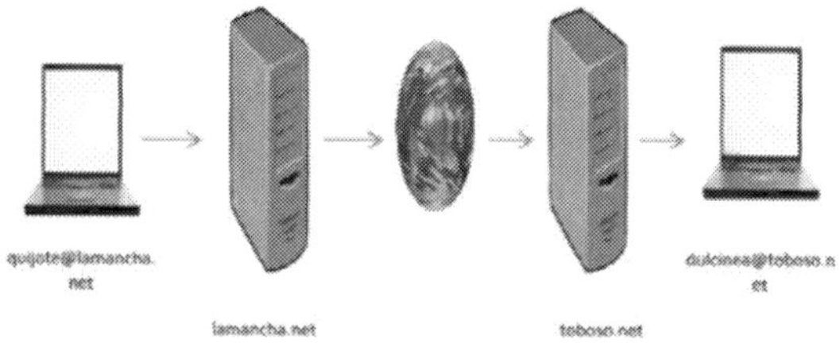

Fig. 2. Basic scheme of sending and receiving data through XMPP.

2.4 Internet of things

The *Internet of Things* (IoT) is a paradigm that quickly gains ground in the world of modern wireless telecommunications. The main idea of this paradigm is that many elements such as sensors, TV devices, appliances, telephones, among others, are able to interact between each of them through the internet [11].

In this area, XMPP can not only be used as a protocol to send instant messages between two humans, but can

---

[a] https://www.python.org/
[b] https://www.ruby-lang.org/
[c] https://www.mathworks.com/products/matlab.html
[d] https://xmpp.org/uses/social.html
[e] https://www.ietf.org/

be used to send commands between humans to objects, sensors or actuators and in this way, an automated remote control.

2.5 Raspberry Pi

Raspberry Pi[f] is a reduced-board computer, meaning that all its components, including processor, memory and ports of entry and exit, are integrated into a single board. The processor that has the board is an ARM[g] that runs at about 700 MHz, its RAM is 1 GB, and both in addition to the graphics processor are encapsulated in a single chip. Raspberry has user-configurable input and output pins that are programmable by the user, allowing you to interact with sensors and actuators. System storage is done on a micro SD card in which the operating system is also installed, this allows to change the functionalities of the card only by changing micro SD card. Raspberry can connect to the internet through an Ethernet port or in some models using WiFi, allowing you to interact with remote applications too.

The software that can be installed in Raspberry Pi as an operating system is commonly based on Linux distributions for ARM, such as Android, Firefox OS, Pidora but the most common and also officially supported is Raspbian[h], based on Debian[i], which has preinstalled features destined to the development of applications, like Python and Mathematica among others.

Raspberry Pi was developed by the *Raspberry Pi Foundation* in the UK, intended to bring young people to the development of skills in computer science, but the low cost, small size, ease of connection to the internet and interaction with sensors and actuators have expanded the uses that can be given to this computer. In this sense the applications can go from a personal computer, an entertainment center or a system dedicated to specific tasks in the scientific, academic or industrial sphere [12].

An important fact to use Raspberry Pi is that it has been analyzed as an element that can be linked quickly within the IoT network [13].

3 Development

A remote control system was developed by means of Internet protocol XMPP, the control commands are obtained by means of an artificial vision system and fuzzy logic that identifies the facial movements of a person.

The prototype is composed of two entities, one whose function is to generate the control words for the mobile robot through artificial vision and a fuzzy inference process, this will be called « console ». The second entity is responsible for receiving control words from the console and activating the actuators in the mobile robot. This entity will be called "mobile receptor".

Communication is done using the internet as a transmission channel, using the XMPP protocol for sending data. This protocol is used in order to save resources by avoiding installing an own server and making development faster by taking advantage of existing infrastructure and internet services, the basic scheme of this system can be seen in figure 3.

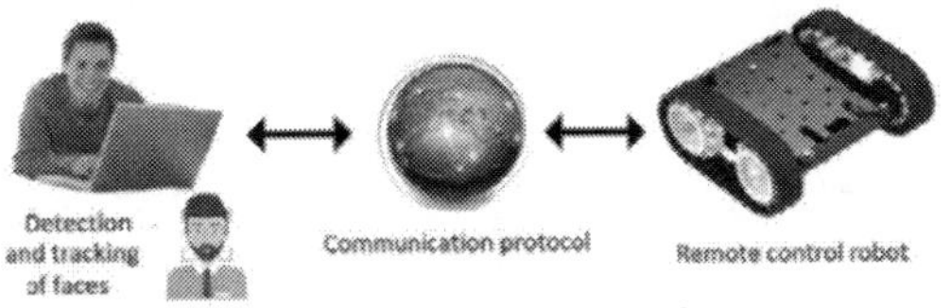

Fig. 3. Basic scheme of the developed prototype.

3.1 Console

The console is the part of the prototype from where the mobile receiver is controlled. This entity is executed on a computing system complemented with an image receiving and capturing element such as a webcam.

The first step that the console performs is the acquisition of data through the camera, when recognizing that there is a face in its field of vision, the position of the center of the face is calculated, a value that is used as a reference point to determine the commands that control the mobile receiver.

One of the main features of the application is that once it has detected the face that will give the orders, the software follows the movement of the face within its particular field of vision, and this situation allows the operation to be performed in real time.

Once the system has defined that a particular facial movement has been a command and not a sporadic movement, the facial position is calculated and the control word is obtained, it is at this time when the control word is sent as a text message through the internet to the robot or element to be controlled, as can be seen in figure 4.

Fig. 4. Detection and sending of messages through XMPP to a remote robot.

---
[f] https://www.raspberrypi.org/
[g] https://www.arm.com/
[h] https://www.raspbian.org/
[i] https://www.debian.org/index.es.html

To make the interface, the OpenCV library was used to generate facial recognition, and Gloox as an XMPP client.

The program follows the steps showed in Figure 5.

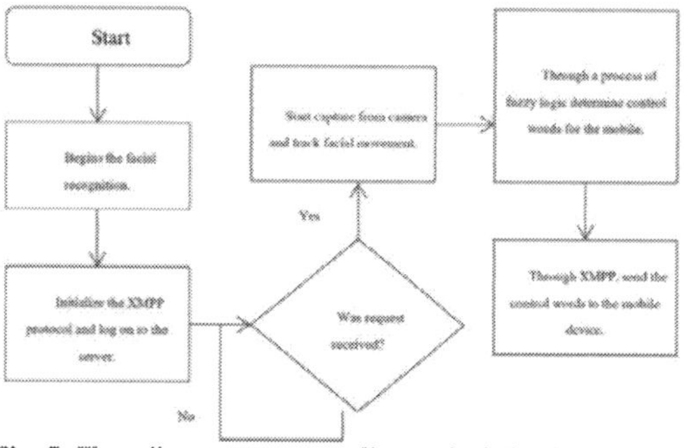

Fig. 5. Flow diagram corresponding to the behavior of the face detection system and sending control signals to a robot positioned in a different geographical area.

2.3.1 Creation of the instant messaging session.

When the console is run, it connects to the messaging server and creates a remote session in which it reports its availability online, waiting to receive a message to open a chat session with the mobile receiver. Once session is opened, it starts facial detection and the process of generating and transmitting control words to any remotely connected device.

2.3.2 Detection and facial tracking

The description of the process completed by the console to make the facial recognizing and tracing is listed below.

1) Capture the image from the camera.
2) Convert the image to grayscale.
3) Equalize the histogram of the grayscale image to standardize the brightness and contrast of the image, so that in different lighting conditions the image content is not affected.
4) Once the image is processed, the classifier to be processed is loaded.
5) When the face has been identified, a pair of XY coordinates are generated for the upper left and lower right corners, these coordinates serve to generate a recognition frame in the area where the face is located, and therefore, to calculate the center of this area, as can be seen in figure 6. The center coordinates will be used as inputs for the diffuse inference system.

3.2 Inference system

It was decided by fuzzy inputs as they allow a gradual transition between variables, also if the user is into the camera's viewing and he makes a subtle facial movement but without the intention of generating a change in the state in which the robot is, the fuzzy input allows a tolerance rage to avoid fake commands.

Fig. 6. Face identification by coordinates XY.

The camera's viewing area is divided into two axes, X, and Y, being the origin the upper left corner so that the values of the X axis grow to the right and those of the Y axis to the left both in a positive way.

Each axis as outputs universe of discourse is divided into three membership functions which can be observed in figure 7.

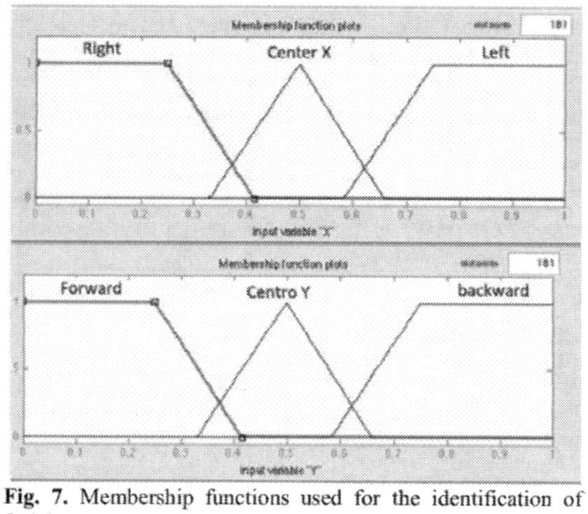

Fig. 7. Membership functions used for the identification of facial movements.

For the inference system was developed a sugeno-type fuzzy inference with just one output variable, the variable has nine sets with constant value. With the inputs, and outputs sets were generated the rules showed in the figure 8.

With the rules showed in figure 8, it has been generated 9 different control words which will be sent to the mobile receptor. These words indicate to the robot the movement it needs to do. There is a rule classifier with the velocities and directions programmed from the beginning in the mobile receptor.

	Left	Center X	Right
Fordward	Fordward Left	Fordward	Fordward Right
Center Y	Left	Stop	Right
Backward	Backward Left	Backward	Backward Right

Fig. 8. Used rules in the inference system.

The inference system can be modified in order to have two continues output sets, a set by each actuator. Each set has to transmit to the actuators, or CD motors, the gradualness in the velocities and directions of the controlled robot.

When the inference process has generated the output command, this is passed as argument to the method which send it through the messaging session that has been created previously. When it is ended the sending of the command, the program continues in a loop generating new commands until the session is finalized.

The session ends when the robot sends a message indicating to the console "terminate the connection".

3.2 Mobile receptor

The mobile receptor is formed by the unit of control, power stage, and actuators.

Unit of control is formed by the Raspberry Pi board which receive, process, and manage the commands that have been sent through the internet. Raspberry uses the processed data to activate the actuators, cameras or any device connected to the robot, and controller them according to the received instructions.

It is very important to say that the Raspberry PI GPIO pines are unbuffered and it has the level voltage of 0 volts for the logic zero, and 3.3 volt for the logic one, limited to 500mA. These levels are good enough to connect LED's (Light Emitting Diode), but they can destroy the board if a motor is directly connected, for that reason it is necessary to have a power stage between the board and the actuators. The power stage in this prototype is made with a simple electronic device: the H bride[j] which generates the necessary energy to turn on the actuators.

In the proposed model, Raspberry was loaded with Raspbian[k] as operating system because it has development tools such as a Python[l] interpreter.

The mobile receptor is ready to start a chat session and information exchange with the console when it has been successfully connected to the jabberes.org server, these steps can be seen in the figures 9, and 10.

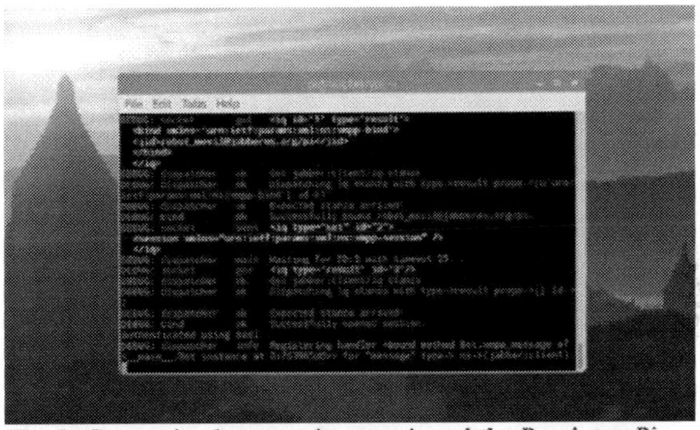

Fig. 9. Connection between the console and the Raspberry Pi installed in the remote robot to control.

Fig. 10. Reception and interpretation of control commands, execution made by the remote Raspberry Pi.

4 Results

From integrating techniques and methods described through the paper was achieved:

1. It was established a control system using artificial vision. In this, fuzzy logic allows generating command words through the interpretation of facial movements.
2. It was made a connection between two identities using a free real-time communication protocol

[j] An H bride is an electronic circuit which allows that a DC electric motor can rotate in both ways forward and backward.

[k] https://www.raspbian.org/

[l] https://www.python.org/

DOI: 10.1051/matecconf/201712504020

through the internet, sending and receiving command words.

3. It was made a remote control of a robot using a computing reduced system as interface to generate access to the internet.
4. We could control a robot in a different geographical position by just making face movements, the robot started, moved to different directions, and turned off. It could be possible to monitoring the environment in which it was moving.
5. The generated system can easily connect to the internet of things, and so, interact with any connected element.
6. It was developed a control system easy and intuitive for final users. It can be used for people with corporal disabilities, untrained, and even can be used by people who cannot read and write. This is a very important fact due to this system is easily incorporated in any population sector.
7. It was developed a low cost system, and for that, accessible to population sectors with low economic resources.

5 Conclusions

Artificial vision as means of capture of the input variables in a control system gives to users a different experience in which there is no necessity to use only fingers or hands as control elements, but they involve a different mobility for its execution.

Fuzzy logic permitted processing efficiently the information obtained by the camera, mainly because this logic is more tolerant to errors than classical logic, it allows an adequate and flexible control in reference with the image capture, and so a better recognition of command words. By means of fuzzy logic, it is possible to avoid mistakes when the control words are generated because the proposed system can distinguish between movements that indicate a command and those movements that just are generated by a reaction not related to the control of the mobile receptor.

The XMPP instant messaging protocol as means to send commands through internet allowed to facilitate the process. The fact that it is possible to use the free servers represents a considerable saving in the economic and in the temporal. It is not necessary to have an own server, and it is not necessary to waste time in develop an information exchange protocol.

The use of a reduced computer such as Raspberry Pi facilitates the development of prototypes which requires of functionalities more complex in comparison with a microcontroller which has not many resources. Its multiple forms of connection, and its integration with standard peripherals via USB or low-level hardware make it ideal to interact with the real world through sensors and actuators. The easy form to connect it to internet positions it as a suitable device to control different technological, electronic, and mechanical systems remotely.

One of the most interesting advantages of the proposed system is the fact that it allows an easy, and fast interaction with the internet of things, due to it can make hardware-hardware communications in a manual or autonomous way.

The most important advantage of the proposed model with respect to classical human-machine interfaces is that it can be easily used by people with corporal disabilities, even it can be used by illiterate people because this system does not need complex instructions or previous technical knowledge, it is not necessary to include hands, fingers, foots or any corporal extremity to control it, the system is entirely controlled just by natural facial expressions. All of this allows that almost anyone can use it. By means of the inputs data fuzzification, it is possible to particularize the gestures that can be used as control words for anyone.

It is important to say that the development of this project was made by using free use hardware and software.

Acknowledgment

The authors thank PAPIIT IN113316 and the program PIAPI1634 of the FESC-UNAM.

References

1. Zadeh, L. A. (1965). Fuzzy sets. Information and control, **8**(3), 338-353.
2. Cubero, S., Aleixos, N., Moltó, E., Gómez-Sanchis, J., & Blasco, J. (2011). Advances in machine vision applications for automatic inspection and quality evaluation of fruits and vegetables. *Food and Bioprocess Technology*, **4**(4), 487-504.
3. Bertozzi, M., Broggi, A., Cellario, M., Fascioli, A., Lombardi, P., & Porta, M. (2002). Artificial vision in road vehicles. *Proceedings of the IEEE*, **90**(7), 1258-1271.
4. Bertozzi, M., Broggi, A., & Fascioli, A. (2000). Vision-based intelligent vehicles: State of the art and perspectives. *Robotics and Autonomous systems*, **32**(1), 1-16.
5. Dobelle, W. H. (2000). Artificial vision for the blind by connecting a television camera to the visual cortex. *ASAIO journal*, **46**(1), 3-9.
6. Chader, G. J., Weiland, J., & Humayun, M. S. (2009). Artificial vision: needs, functioning, and testing of a retinal electronic prosthesis. *Progress in brain research*, 175, 317-332.
7. Youssif, A. A., & Asker, W. A. (2011). Automatic facial expression recognition system based on geometric and appearance features. *Computer and Information Science*, **4**(2), 115.

8. Uke, N., & Thool, R. (2013). Moving vehicle detection for measuring traffic count using opencv. Journal of Automation and Control Engineering, **1**(4).
9. Pulli, K., Baksheev, A., Kornyakov, K., & Eruhimov, V. (2012). Real-time computer vision with OpenCV. Communications of the ACM, **55**(6), 61-69.
10. Saint-Andre, P. (2011). Extensible messaging and presence protocol (XMPP): Core.
11. Atzori, L., Iera, A., & Morabito, G. (2010). The internet of things: A survey. Computer networks, **54**(15), 2787-2805.
12. Upton, E., & Halfacree, G. (2014). Raspberry Pi user guide. John Wiley & Sons.
13. Maksimović, M., Vujović, V., Davidović, N., Milošević, V., & Perišić, B. (2014). Raspberry Pi as Internet of things hardware: performances and constraints. Design issues, 3, 8.
14. Hjelmås, E., & Low, B. K. (2001). Face detection: A survey. Computer vision and image understanding, **83**(3), 236-274.

MATEC Web of Conferences **125**, 04021 (2017) DOI: 10.1051/matecconf/201712504021
CSCC 2017

Big Data Analytics in the Management of Business

Dorota Jelonek[1,*]

Czestochowa University of Technology, Poland

Abstract. Data, information, knowledge have always played a critical role in business. The amount of various data that can be collected and stored is increasing, therefore companies need new solutions for data processing and analysis. The paper presents considerations on the concept of Big Data. The aim of the paper is to demonstrate that Big Data analytics is an effective support in managing the company. It also indicates the areas and activities where the use of Big Data analytics can bring the greatest benefits to companies.

1 Introduction

Over the past decade, the "Big Data" era has quietly descended on many communities, from governments and e-commerce to health and sports organisations [1].

These data are generated from the Web, online transactions, emails, videos, audios, images, click streams, logs, posts, search queries, health records, social media, science data, sensors and mobile phones and their applications.

Within the next decade, the amount of information will increase by 50 times while the number of information technology specialists who keep up with all that data will increase by 1,5 times.

Information overload [2] is one of the most serious problems in the Big Data environment. For information users, searching for what they need from the vast amounts of information accurately is becoming more difficult [3]. However, if companies are able to collect, process and analyse large datasets, then gathered information can be extremely valuable. In the era of exponential growth of business information, the acceleration of data accessibility is becoming vital.

Enterprise database systems, search systems, advanced data, text and Web analytics are becoming important for turning data into actionable knowledge and intelligence. As the data volume is large, the analytics can only be possible if we have highly efficient algorithms and software.

Highly skilled executives in terms of gathering and using knowledge, who also have analytical skills, are nowadays among most competitive factors of the company.

In the turbulently changing environment, making a decision is associated with a high risk, which may hinder the access to relevant information and reliable analysis, delivered when you need them. Advanced analytical tools, supported by innovative ways of processing Big Data become necessary to expand enterprises. Research of Brynjolfsson, Hitt and Kim [4] confirmed that the efficiency is higher in organisations which base their decisions on data and analytics systems. This is facilitated by basing decision-making process on data obtained from analytical systems what is referred to as "data-driven decision-making approach (DDD)" [5].

The purpose of this paper is to demonstrate that Big Data analytics is an effective support in the management of business. The following sections present the essence of Big Data, traditional data analysis vs. Big Data analytics methods as well as the role of Big Data analytics in the management of business. The results of empirical research about priorities for the application of Big Data are also presented.

2 The essence of Big Data

The current explosion of data that is being generated is due to three main reasons [6, 7]:

1. Hundreds of applications such as mobile sensors, social media services, and other related devices are collecting information continuously.
2. Storage capacity has improved so much that collecting data is cheaper than ever, making preferable to buy more storage space rather than deciding what to delete.
3. Machine Learning and information retrieval approaches have reached a significant improvement in the last years, thus enabling the acquisition of a higher degree of knowledge from data.

Figure 1 shows the relations between increasing data variety and complexity and the memory size of databases from megabytes to petabytes. It is shown that ERP systems generate data which companies collect and process in databases or data warehouses. Nevertheless CRM and Web systems have the biggest influence on the rapid increase in the amount of data.

Figure 1 also presents the main sources of data for Big Data.

* Corresponding author: jelonek@zim.pcz.pl

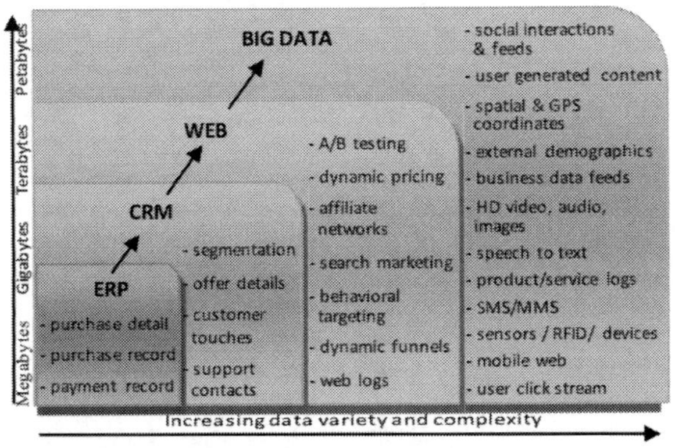

Fig. 1. Big Data – variety and complexity [8]

The concept of Big Data is, however, broader than just large data sets. The most important challenge is not to increase data sets but to search for a new approach to the analysis.

Wielki [9] indicates, that Big Data is mainly characterised by:

- type of data - data unstructured,
- size of data - 100 terabytes to petabytes,
- way of information flow - a permanent inflow of data to the organisation (in real time),
- basic analytical method - machine learning,
- primary purpose – a creation of new products.

The phenomenon called "Big Data" differs as a data source from the previously used sources such as databases or data warehouses. Davenport and others [10] emphasise that organisations which capitalise on big data stand apart from traditional data analysis environments in three key ways:

1. They pay attention to data flows as opposed to stocks.
2. They rely on data scientists and product and process developers rather than data analysts.
3. They are moving analytics away from the IT function and into core business, operational and production functions.

Big Data requires a revolutionary step forward from traditional data analysis, characterised by its four main components: volume, velocity, veracity, variety [11 – 13]. These are shown in Figure 2.

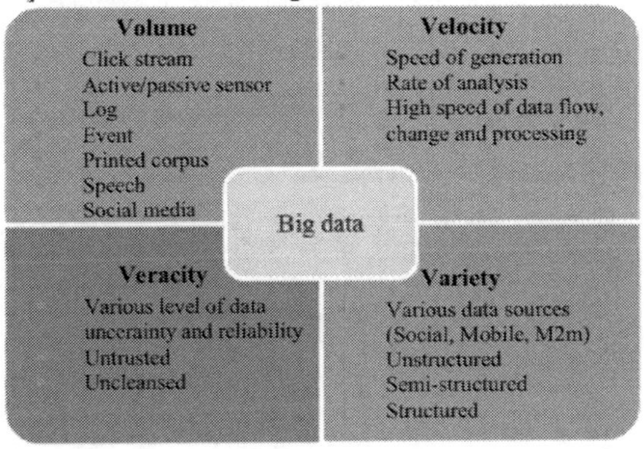

Fig. 2. Four Vs of Big Data.

Each component presented in Figure 2 is shortly expressed below.

Variety makes Big Data really big. Big Data come from a great variety of sources and generally has three types: structured, semi-structured and unstructured. Structured data insert a data warehouse already tagged and easily sorted but unstructured data are random and difficult to analyse. Semi-structured data do not conform to fixed fields but contains tags to separate data elements [14, 15].

Volume or the size of data now is larger than terabytes and petabytes. The grand scale and rise of data outstrip traditional store and analysis techniques [14, 15].

Velocity is required not only for Big Data, but also all processes. For time limited processes, big data should be used as it streams into the organisation in order to maximise its value [14, 15].

Veracity: Big Data are sourced from many different places, as a result you need to test the veracity/quality of the data.

B. Frank states that all of the above-mentioned definitions of the "V" dimensions are secondary to the importance of data value. This parameter was defined by B. Frank as "Uber-V" because it points out the business value that data are for the company. The other dimensions are merely ancillary. B. Frank believes that the complicity, volume and format of data are not important, however the knowledge of how to process them in a way relevant to the enterprise is essential [16].

All these facts are known as the 4V's of Big Data, [17] which lead to the definition given by Steve Todd at Berkeley University: Big Data is when the normal application of current technology does not enable users to obtain timely, cost-effective, and quality answers to data-driven questions.

Other examples of definitions underline the unstructured character of data, i.e. accordingly to Rouse [18] Big Data is a general term used to describe the voluminous amount of unstructured and semi-structured data a company creates - data that would take too much time and cost too much money to load into a relational database for analysis.

Pawełoszek and Wieczorkowski [19] proposed "three-aspect approach", identifying three essential aspects of big data: technological, business and social. The technological aspect in the above classification represents a focus on the methods of big data analysis and information technology used. The business aspect of the described classification focuses on applications of Big Data, especially on they role in decision support. The social aspect of Big Data is associated with social consequences of data processing results. When making decisions on implementing solutions for Big Data analytics all three mentioned aspects should be considered.

3 Traditional data analysis vs. Big Data analytics methods

Big Data are not just data, but also IT infrastructure, analytical systems and employees with high analytical skills.

Big data analytics is the process of examining large data sets to uncover hidden patterns, unknown correlations, market trends, customer preferences and other useful business information.

Big Data analytics may show new relations between data, reveal unseen earlier trends and contribute to the creation of new knowledge, which can then be used to increase the effectiveness and improve the profitability of the company. In the long term, these can compensate for the costs associated with the purchase of specialised software and hiring specialists [20, 21].

There are many differences between the conventional and Big Data analytics. Even though some of them are very fuzzy, Table 1 presents a summary of differences.

Table 1. The differences between Big Data analytics and Traditional analytics [22].

	Big Data analytics	Traditional analytics
Type of data	Unstructured formats	Formatted in rows and columns
Volume of data	100 terabytes to petabytes	Tens of terabytes or less
Flow of data	Constant flow of data	Static pool of data
Analysis methods	Machine learning	Hypothesis-based
Primary purpose	Data-based products	Internal decision support and service

Changes in the analysis of Big Data relate to three main areas [23]:

- the ability to analyse large amounts of data, while not having to use smaller data sets,
- readiness to deal with unstructured data, characterised by low accuracy,
- rising importance of correlations, which tend to look for relations between phenomena rather than their causes.

While analysing Big Data the focus should be placed on the search for correlations and patterns, which indicate that "something is happening", instead of explaining the reasons "why it is happening". This means that previously used method of hypothesis and seeking arguments to verify them is reversed. The discovery of unexpected correlations can only be a stimulus to formulate hypotheses.

Big Data process continuously incoming data from the environment and from inside the company. Thus, the Big Data analytics is based on data collected in real time, and that is why the results of the analysis are accurate and generated without delay.

Analytic applications are universal and have a wide range of functionality, useful in both large companies and small companies from the SME sector. They allow for integration of complex business processes and quick response to any changes on the operational level, as well as in the business environment. Thanks to them, companies are able to track on a regular basis the status of each process and rapidly response to events through flexible modification of the processes.

The analysis of Big Data involves analytical methods for traditional data and Big Data, analytical architecture for Big Data, and software used for analysis of Big Data. In the analysis of huge volumes of data multiple analyses are being applied such as: association rule learning aimed at discovery of relationships in databases; A/B testing allowing for comparison of control group with a test group; cluster analysis enabling classification of objects divided into smaller groups; crowdsourcing enabling gathering data generated by communities; data fusion and data integration which data analysis coming from different sources; genetic algorithms based on the process of natural evolution and having its application mainly in optimization; machine learning and natural language processing creating the field of artificial intelligence; neural networks based on the functionality of human's nervous system and finding its application in optimization and pattern recognition; analysis of nodes in networks; predictive modelling and analysis of regression based on mathematical models; spatial analysis and simulations; supervised and unsupervised learning and visualization boards including cloud tags, history and spatial information flows and managerial dashboards [24].

This long list of methods for analysing Big Data is probably not complete as new methods of extracting information and knowledge from the sets of Big Data constantly appear. Enterprises from almost every sector develop the concept of information and data as company's strategic asset [25].

4 Big Data in the management of business

Managers increasingly adopt strategies based on acquiring, processing and using high-quality data for the decision-making (data-driven decision-making approach).

Research carried out by EMC Forum 2013 indicate that:

- 39% of entrepreneurs believe that Big Data provide business success,
- 19% of entrepreneurs are of the opinion that with Big Data they have achieved a competitive advantage,
- 36% of entrepreneurs believe that the introduction of Big Data will increase the safety and security of their data.

The researchers from the Economist Intelligence Unit survey [26], sought the answer to the question "Which of the following business processes do you believe are the most important priorities for the application of big data now, and which will be most important in three years?". The results of their study are presented in Figure 3.

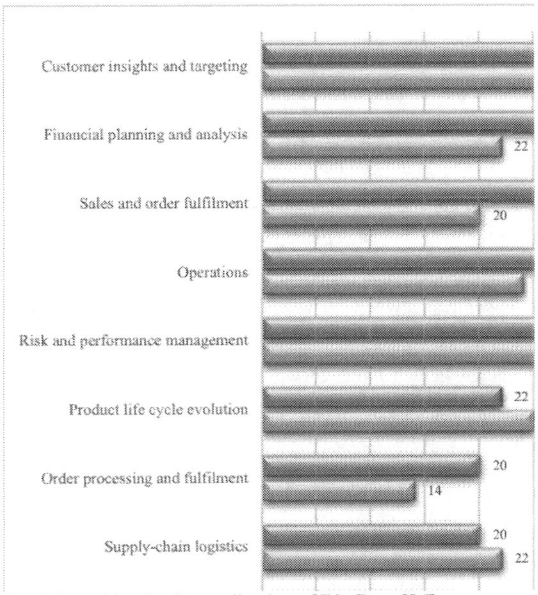

Fig. 2. Priorities for the application of Big Data [26]

Customer processes are currently a priority for the application of big data, according to 42% of the C-level executives. Financial planning with 32% and sales with 29% are the following indications for big data analytics. Other priorities include operations, risk management and performance management as well as the evolution of product life cycle and same others. A long list of priorities suggests broad opportunities for Big Data solutions enterprise-wide. In three years, these priorities will become even harder to segregate. According to respondents a customer insights and targeting will remain the top priority, however it will drop in relative terms as several others emerge.

Big Data are produced in every segment in manufacturing. For enterprise performance, Big Data help to identify the product demands, productivity and performance via diverse business objectives. For production, Big Data make it possible to detect the right facility causing the product flaw [27].

Big Data analysis is used in enterprise management in the following areas and activities [28, 29]

- transformation of key organisational business processes,
- strategic decision support,
- identification of the most cost-effective suppliers in delivering products on-time,
- product development,
- flag machinery and process variances that might be indicators of quality problems,
- analysis of receivables, an anticipation of payments, asset management,
- identification of which marketing promotions and campaigns are most effective in driving customer traffic, engagement, and sales,
- predictions of customer behaviour,
- customer relations management,
- optimization of marketing mixes given marketing goals,
- optimization of sales resource assignments, product mix,
- redefinition of product,
- collaborative filtering,
- supply-demand analysis.

The concept of Big Data is still relatively new, so its implementation in companies often faces barriers. The Big Data + Report indicated that Polish companies, primarily face the following difficulties [30]:

- shortage of qualified specialists - 29%,
- high exploitation costs - 27%,
- unclearly defined purpose and justification for the implementation of Big Data - 22%,
- complicated technology, which does not bring the expected profits - 7%.

Some institutions take steps to eliminate identified barriers. For example, universities educate "data science" and "data analysis" specialists while IT companies try to develop cheaper, more effective and "user-friendly" solutions. Nevertheless, the most difficult barriers to overcome are the mental barriers, lack of knowledge about Big Data and resistance to change.

5 Architecture for Big Data Analysis

Four main components of Big Data: volume, velocity, veracity and variety are the reason why Big Data are difficult to process, and what's more analyse and draw conclusions. For effective use of Big Data companies need new IT architectures, that is a configuration of hardware and software in a way which ensures efficient processing of Big Data. Cloud computing technologies can provide unlimited resources on demand. It could be a solution to the problem of growing volume of data and could allow effective data management [31]. The most common architecture for Big Data is Apache Hadoop.

Many organisations looking to collect, process and analyse Big Data have turned to a newer class of technologies that includes Hadoop and related tools such as YARN, MapReduce, Spark, Hive and Pig as well as NoSQL databases [32].

Hadoop is essentially a distributed data infrastructure: It distributes massive data collections across multiple nodes within a cluster of commodity servers, which means you don't need to buy and maintain expensive custom hardware. It also indexes and keeps track of that data, enabling Big Data processing and analytics far more effectively than was possible previously.

Hadoop quickly emerged as a foundation for Big Data processing tasks, such as scientific analytics, business and sales planning, and processing enormous volumes of sensor data, including from internet of things sensors.

Apache Hadoop is used by large corporations such as Yahoo, Facebook, Amazon, eBay, The New York Times, Chevron and IBM.

6 Conclusions

The practical usefulness of Big Data analytics is evident in many areas of company management, especially in strategic management and stakeholders management. Big Data analytics can lead to more effective marketing, new revenue opportunities, improved operational efficiency, competitive advantages over rival organisations and other business benefits.

As a conclusion, a list of recommendations for companies that wish to implement Big Data solutions is presented below:

1. Verify company's information strategy in terms of Big Data requirements, which include hardware platform, software, application landscape of Big Data analytics and human resources - "data science" and "data analyst" specialists.
2. Adjust the "new" information strategy to the business strategy and the business strategies to new business processes opportunities.
3. Create flexible business models.
4. Build information culture in the organisation. The first question a data- driven organisation asks itself is not "What do we think?" But "What do we known?"
5. Change the decision-making model. Data-driven decisions tend to be better decisions.
6. Collect, process and use data which already exist in the information resources of the company.
7. Identify other data that should be collected.
8. Identify new sources of data.
9. Use Big Data analyses in real time, because with time some data cease to be useful.

In the era of Big Data and new, more advanced analytical capabilities, companies can gain a competitive advantage on the market, by competing on analytics. The analysis is a part of the increasingly exposed current studies on decision-making on the basis of data.

References

1. M. Beyer, *Gartner says solving 'big data' challenge involves more than just managing volumes of data.* (2011) http://www.gartner.com/it/page.jsp?id=1731916
2. D. Jelonek, *The problem of information overload in the information society (in Polish),* Zeszyty Naukowe Ekonomiczne Problemy Usług Uniwersytet Szczeciński, T.1, **650** (2011)
3. J. Dong, Y. Qin, X.Y. Sun, L.M. Du, *Research on Improved Collaborative Filtering Recommendation Algorithm on MapReduce.* In MATEC Web of Conferences, **63**, p. 04018, EDP Sciences (2016)
4. E. Brynjolfsson, L.M. Hitt, H.H. Kim, *Strength in numbers: How does data-driven decisionmaking affect firm performance?* (2011)
5. F. Provost, T. Fawcett, *Data science and its relationship to big data and data-driven decision making*, Big Data, **1(1)** (2013)
6. T. Kraska, *Finding the needle in the big data systems haystack.* IEEE Internet Comput **17** (2013)
7. A. Fernández, S. del Río, V. López, A. Bawakid, M.J. del Jesus, J.M. Benítez, F. Herrera, *Big Data with Cloud Computing: an insight on the computing environment, MapReduce, and programming frameworks*, Wiley Interdisciplinary Reviews: Data Mining and Knowledge Discovery, **4(5)** (2014)
8. J. Bloem, M. Van Doorn, S. Duivestein & E. van Ommeren, *Creating clarity with big data.* Sogeti VINT, (2012).
9. J. Wielki, *Analysis of the possibilities of using big data in e-business* (in Polish), Prace Naukowe/ Uniwersytet Ekonomiczny w Katowicach (2014)
10. T. Davenport, P. Barth, R. Bean, *How 'Big Data' is Different,* MIT Sloan Management Review, **54(1)** (2012)
11. Big Data. What it is and why it matters, http://www.sas.com/en_us/insights/big-data/what-is-big-data.html (10.01.2017)
12. A. McAfee, E. Brynjolfsson, T.H. Davenport, D.J. Patil, D. Barton, *Big data. The management revolution.* Harvard Bus Rev, *90(10)* (2012)
13. IBM, *Big Data at the Speed of Business*, (2014) [Online]. Available: http://www.01.ibm.com/software/data/bigdata/. (12.01.2017).
14. S. Sagiroglu, D. Sinanc, *Big data: A review. In Collaboration Technologies and Systems (CTS)*, 2013 International Conference on IEEE, (2013)
15. C. Eaton, D. Deroos, T. Deutsch, G. Lapis and P.C. Zikopoulos, *Understanding Big Data: Analytics for Enterprise Class Hadoop and Streaming Data,* Mc Graw-Hill Companies, 978-0-07-179053-6, (2012)
16. http://www.forbes.com/sites/teradata/2014/11/19/defining-big-data-in-two-words-who-cares (2017.01.22).
17. R. Gupta, H. Gupta, M. Mohania, *Cloud computing and big data analytics: what is new from databases perspective?,* In: 1st International Conference on Big Data Analytics (BDA), New Delhi, India, (2012)
18. M. Rouse, "Big data", http://searchcloudcomputing.techtarget.com /definition/big-data-Big-Data, 2011. (2017.02.20)
19. I. Pawełoszek, J. Wieczorkowski, *Big data as a business opportunity: an Educational Perspective*, In: Computer Science and Information Systems (FedCSIS), 2015 Federated Conference on. IEEE, (2015)
20. S. LaValle, *Big data, analytics and the path from insights to value,* MIT Sloan Management Review, (2011) http://sloanreview.mit.edu/article/big-data-analytics-and-the-pathfrom-insights-to-value/ (20.02.2017)
21. J. Liebowitz, *Big data and business analytics*, Boca Raton FL [etc.]: CRC Press: Taylor & Francis Group. (2013)

22. T. Davenport, *Big Data @ Work: Dispelling the Myths*, Uncovering the Opportunities, Harvard Business School Press, Boston (2014)
23. V. Mayer-Schonberger, K. Cukier, *Big Data. Revolution which will change the way we think, work and live* (in Polish), MT Biznes, Warszawa (2014)
24. A. Chluski, L. Ziora, *The role of big data solutions in the management of organizations. Review of selected practical examples*, Procedia Computer Science **65** (2015)
25. F. Provost, T. Fawcett, *Data Science for Business: What you need to know about data mining and data-analytic thinking*, O'Reilly Media, Inc. (2013)
26. Economist Intelligence Unit survey, September 2014 https://www.eiuperspectives.economist.com/sites/default/files/Whosbigonbigdata.pdf (2017.01.20)
27. B. Qing, J. Wang, J. Cheng, *Research on Ontology Modeling of Steel Manufacturing Process Based on Big Data Analysis*, MATEC Web of Conferences, **45**, EDP Sciences (2016)
28. B. Schmarzo, *Big Data. Understanding how data powers big businesses*, Wiley (2013)
29. T. Davenport, J. Dyché, *Big data in big companies*, International Institute for Analytics (2013)
30. Computerworld Polska (2014). Raport Big data +, Systemy analityki wielkich zbiorów danych w polskich organizacjach. Computerworld Polska.
31. D. Jelonek, C. Stępniak, T. Turek, L. Ziora, *Identification of mental barriers in the implementation of cloud computing in the SMEs in Poland,* In Computer Science and Information Systems (FedCSIS), 2014 Federated Conference on IEEE (2014)
32. http://searchbusinessanalytics.techtarget.com/definition/big-data-analytics (2017.02.10)

Results of Implementing ERP System in a Multi-plant Enterprise

Elzbieta Wyslocka[1,*]

[1]Czestochowa University of Czestochowa, Department of Management, ul. Dabrowskiego 69, 42-201 Czestochowa, Poland

Abstract. Enterprise Resource Planning (ERP) systems enhance productivity and working quality by offering integration, standardization and simplification of multiple business transactions. The article discusses company's internal processes and their complexity resulting from expansion of the company to new plants. Using a case study of the implementation of one of the Polish ERP systems of Macrologic in several multi-plant enterprises, it demonstrates how it improved the functioning and organization of processes in these companies.

Introduction

In-depth analysis and interpretation of data is nowadays one of the most important elements of decision-making for most businesses. Due to growing amount of information and needs related to their analysis, companies are increasingly investing in IT solutions that allow not only collection of records in data warehouses but also their compilation, interpretation and graphic presentation. The ERP (Enterprise Resource Planning) system facilitates making strategic business decisions based on reliable data. It is a key element in maintaining business continuity. It provides easy access to data from all possible areas of the business. In literature, factors influencing the success of enterprise ERP implementation have been quite widely discussed, as well as the need to improve approaches and implementation methods. [1-4] Some of the works are also devoted to the specifics of multi-plant enterprise management and the functioning of their ERP systems [5-7]. In the article using a case study of the implementation of one of the Polish ERP systems of Macrologic in several multi-plant enterprises, it demonstrates how it improved the functioning and organization of processes in these companies.

1 ERP system as a tool supporting planning and decision-making in enterprise management

Decision-making process in modern businesses requires access to up-to-date and accurate information. This is one of the challenges companies face and a key factor in corporate decision-making. Often, company information is dispersed in several databases or several programs. For example, inventory data is in one database and customer information in another. In many cases, databases are isolated or autonomous systems (not integrated and independent) (Figure 1).

Warehouse	Production	Sales department
• physical location of products, • current inventory, • quantity of products booked	• quantity of scheduled products for production, • quantities currently produced , • production capacity	• quantity of finished goods for sale , • confirmed sales orders, • customer information

Fig. 1. Structure of the isolated databases systems.

As illustrated in Figure 1, in case of isolated systems, storage, production, sales, and customer information are stored in several databases / programs. Since it is not possible to share information within a single system, it is difficult to use it. Enterprise Resource Planning (ERP) is very useful for making business decisions. This system collects data, organizes and integrates all areas of company's operations and supports resource management, accounting for maximum efficiency. Integration involves use of a common database within a single system, so that the company uses only one set of data. ERP system optimizes costs and inventory, accelerates information exchange, and streamlines communication, helping to improve customer service and shortening fulfillment of orders. The process-based (modular) structure of the ERP System integrates information from various processes taking place in the enterprise, which provides full support for relevant business decisions in companies from different industries, so this system is applicable in both manufacturing, trading and service providing enterprises. Such a structure of ERP system allows to deploy all or selected items simultaneously or in the right order.
Each of the modules can support handling of individual processes in different areas of the company: in sales,

* Corresponding author: wyslocka@zim.pcz.pl

supply, stock, production or accounting. The advantage of modular structure of the system, however, is its integrity. Modules linked together represent a functional system, making it more efficient by sharing information in real time.
A complete ERP system with all modules, regardless of industry, is usually chosen by medium and large companies. They receive support for resource management and process monitoring, business operations settlement, and assessment of financial standing.
The use of ERP systems in enterprise management is steadily increasing, however, the quality of data provided by them should be taken into consideration. Conducted research [8] shows that it is very important to match technology to tasks (task-technology fit - TTF). Organizations are embedded in developing environments that poses new challenges. They require continuous adaptation of information systems or organizations to contextual understanding of data quality. Although ERP systems are considered durable, it is important to remember to modify them as their mismatch can affect data quality beyond typical functionality. Ensuring TTF will be an increasingly challenging task with growing non-routineness.
In order to fully utilize the potential of ERP system, its functionality should be extended to include the planning of resources of its customers and suppliers. The process of creating an extended ERP system must include business partners (customers and suppliers), taking into account different technological and financial statuses of their customers and suppliers. Thus, an effective and flexible, extended ERP system must contain both high-end and low-end solutions, and also understand that full inter-organizational integration may not be possible [9].
Research conducted on the ERP implementation process in enterprises indicate that the assistance provided by external consultants during ERP implementation is essential. Knowledge transfer is an extremely important factor in the success of an ERP system. It has also been proven that passing on knowledge about the technical aspects of ERP systems is more important than effective communication and conflict resolution among members of an organization. It also seems that top management assistance in ERP implementation is less important than acceptance by its users [3]. ERP systems enable businesses to run accounting and manage different areas of business. They can, for example, support distribution, service and production. The ERP system is often set up to match the business processes in the company. As a rule, companies operating in a particular industry are pursuing similar business processes. However, some of them implement their own specific processes. The ERP system can be modified and configured to meet the company's requirements in this area.

2 Management in multi-plant company

Managing an enterprise involves making many difficult decisions. Especially in multi-plant companies, managers encounter various dilemmas. Particularly those involved in human resources management are important. The question arises as to how industrial relations in subordinate plants are controlled, but at the same time leaving them with some degree of flexibility? One way to solve this problem is to negotiate at the plant level, but to address certain issues, solutions from the central human resources department can be implemented [10]. It is important to take initiatives in personnel management and to use factors that seem to provide stable industrial relations in circumstances that, as evidenced by experience, tend to favor conflicts. Problems are associated, for example, with the high proportion of the workforce rewarded for the results, the differentiation of earnings and the difference in earnings between factories [11].
Modern production management allows for higher efficiency of production processes. By using the right IT tools, companies can cut costs, increase productivity, and improve relationships with customers and suppliers. To increase the productivity of all plants in the network, multinational corporations develop and implement multi-sector management improvement programs. Numerous studies described in the literature on systems for improving the quality and effectiveness of multiple facilities are systematically carried out [6]. A decisive step towards improving the productivity of multi-plant companies is to embrace their operations with one link, which is the ERP production system.
A separate problem with the operation of large companies is the coordination of multi-site purchasing activities to minimize the total cost of purchase. In the literature, an integrated model of linear programming and multitasking approach has been proposed, which are ideally suited to coordinating purchases in multi-component organizations to achieve global profitability. Proposed model provides an effective coordination mechanism that helps multi-plant organizations and suppliers maintain availability of materials in the right amount, at the right quality and at a minimal cost [5]. On the other hand, it should be noted that supply chain management is suitable both for large multi-plant enterprises and for small organizations [12].
It also seems that problems of material flow management in the supply chain, where links belong to the same owner, are similar to those that occur in the supply chain where organizations are not linked by a single owner [13]. In addition, the level of integration between independent companies may be greater than that of formally dependent companies. With this in mind, companies can choose between vertical integration and supply chain management, that is, between the costs and benefits of control, from the owner's position, and those that are rooted in indirect control through relations [7].
In solving all of these and other problems that arise in managing a multi-plant enterprise, ERP system may be helpful. It should be well configured, adapted to the

processes taking place in the enterprise and its organizational structure.

3 Structure and functions of Macrologic ERP system

A classic, integrated ERP system allows to manage all business operations. It supports top executives - generating statistics, reports, and analyzes, providing information needed to make decisions.

With the use of information technology and modern systems, business processes conducted in operational management - production, logistics, sales and marketing as well as in auxiliary activities - accounting, wages and fixed assets are modeled. Thanks to sharing and exchanging information (information flow), it helps to forecast and plan future activities using the full knowledge within the enterprise (finance, controlling) and the maintenance of quality standards (quality management).

In response to growing competition and declining margins, companies increasingly use optimization of production processes. The whole company benefits because Macrologic ERP Manufacturing provides data relevant to other the areas of management: sales, personnel, finance, and fixed assets. The comprehensive solution makes it easy to record and plan production staff working time, optimize utilization of machines and equipment, and manage budgets in production processes. ERP Manufacturing module provides effective management support at all stages of production: planning, product manufacturing, accounting and reporting for the board. Management information generated in Macrologic ERP Production is used by other Macrologic ERP modules: Sales, Logistics and Personnel.

The amount of knowledge that companies gather in collecting data makes it often difficult to use the data effectively. Effective customer relationship management, sales processes and logistics within the company are possible through the use of tools provided within the Macrologic ERP Logistics. Two solutions are used to support sales processes: Macrologic CRM and Macrologic ERP Logistics. Used separately or together, support activities in the area of customer acquisition, sales and warehouse management.

Using software in the area of customer relationship management allows preparation of proposals that meet customer needs and requirements, building contact history, and supporting businesses in developing effective promotional campaigns. These activities complement the analysis of the cost and profitability of sales processes for which the logistics department is responsible. In contrast, the use of ERP in the management of sales processes allows companies to increase efficiency of their trading activities, which in practice translates to shorter sales cycles, improved market forecasts, and analysis of shopping carts. This enables total sales management, from procurement, through execution, to delivery to the client.

Human resources processes, starting from selection and employment, through ongoing updating of employee records, payroll, social security and tax settlements, are all needed to begin the process and deliver them effectively. In Macrologic ERP Personel staff management is not divided into individual tasks. The program works on the entire personnel management process: from the recruitment process to the end of the contract. This allows control of all events to flow smoothly, and supervisors receive all information necessary to consciously shape the future personnel policy.

Especially in multi-plant enterprises, benefits of implementing the program are significant:

- fast data flow between people involved in the recruitment and servicing process,
- ability to adapt the program to needs of organization's staff both at the headquarters and in the subsidiaries,
- faster access to essential employee data for all authorized people,
- ability to react quickly to staff changes in the organization.

Also in the area of enterprise financial management, planning and analysis is much easier thanks to the use of the Macrologic ERP Finance system. It allows to track financial situation, streamline payments and settlement processes, support company's asset management, create current financial reports and forecasts. Multidimensional analysis provides managers with decision-making knowledge and help to develop new strategies in businesses. In every company, a lot of information concerning the business "wanders" down the corridors, between plants, departments, branches, employees. If this information is organized, one can plan systematic operational activities. If the company and its managers are able to analyze this information in the most intricate levels, then forecast, plan and settle accounts, we are talking about an action strategy, and support for this project is the Macrologic Controlling Information System. Controlling system allows to create multidimensional OLAP analysis. Data are collected in many dimensions in the so-called OLAP cubes, which can be freely formed. Multidimensional analyzes enable strategic decision making from the company's point of view. They may be associated with optimizing costs in selected areas of business or choosing the best deals for business partners.

The software base contains a rich set of predefined, standardized processes that allow for quick launch. Each organization has its own habits and requirements resulting from its "know-how". Therefore, standard processes are defined in the first step. However, if they require changes - any modifications to the processes are possible. This facilitates the BPMN process modeler - a tool that allows to change defined processes, and most importantly, every change is immediately reflected in the ERP system. Managers can quickly adapt existing processes in the company to Macrologic ERP, because the modeler allows to create very different processes tailored to the individual needs of the enterprise. The process modeler, built into the ERP system, and constant process information provide a bird's eye view on the company. It is an easy way to identify barriers and blockades in the business. Recognizing what needs to be improved (with measurable indicators in the process diagrams), each manager can simultaneously make changes to the way the company operates and the ERP system. If an organization, for example, develops (creates new plants) or restructures, the manager can easily change processes by modifying diagrams. By using a process modeler, any company can easily adapt existing processes and add new ones to the system. The program will automatically reflect changes for all employees affected by the process.

4 Examples of implementation of Macrologic ERP in multi-plant enterprises

There are many companies where implementation of ERP system has brought tangible benefits. Some of them will be discussed on the example of ERP Macrologic implementations in selected multi-plant enterprises. The Industry Group, which is a world-class expert in implementing projects involving machinery and equipment for the mining industry, can be the first example. The quality of company's products has been confirmed by numerous Polish and international certifications and customer trust expressed in long-term business relationships. Implementing Macrologic ERP enabled the company to reduce IT maintenance costs. In addition, Industry Group has significantly improved the implementation of financial management processes, which is particularly important in the case of a parent company. Implementation of the Production module contributed to the improvement of production processes, especially in strategic planning, which translated into unit productivity growth of 20%, production increase of 30% and reduction of failure compensation buffer up to 24 hours. The company had also succeeded in increasing the efficiency of warehouse management and improving customer service, which helped to reduce inventory by 40%. The benefits of raising the work culture of the organization are also important.

In another example of ATLAS Group one of the dynamic growth drivers are new acquisitions that are important both in expanding the offer and in increasing the scale of operations. Following the centralization of human resources operations at the ATLAS Group, it was necessary to introduce a common IT system that would improve HR and payroll while preserving the specifics of individual companies. Diversified personnel policies, several work systems, and various wage regulations required the use of IT solutions that would enable evolutionary staffing and payroll adjustments in the companies they acquired to be in line with company rules. Also, in a distributed organization like ATLAS, it was necessary to introduce employee self-service, which facilitated access to their own HR-payroll data. The decision to introduce extended billing periods prompts us to look for tools to automate the activities of creating graphics and to facilitate the control of planning and accounting of working time in accordance with the Labor Code. The company headquarters also needed improvements in delegation service. Each year, ATLAS accounts for several thousands of domestic and overseas business trips. On the one hand, the Company sought to facilitate the control of the use of company and private car delegations and, on the other, would ensure compliance with legal regulations.

Due to the fact that the companies of the Group have different business profiles - production, mining, transportation or power industry - and their own organizational characteristics (e.g. different remuneration systems), ATLAS has sought a solution that would take these differences into account.

Implementing a system that supports group management usually means "stiffening" the rules of action to unify principles throughout the group or even centralizing HR and payroll. The Company wanted the system to allow organizing the service in subsidiaries in a way that have a common environment within the Group, but at the same time maintaining its own, effective logic. Macrologic proposed a flexible solution that met these expectations. The proposed system allowed, among others handling various remuneration systems within the Group.

In the case of the Polonia Logistyka company, dynamic development of the company and establishment of new locations in the field have led to a situation, in which previously used IT solutions became ineffective. Difficult flow of information on transport orders, their profitability, use of transport fleet, and the exchange of this information between departments have been serious barriers to operations of the company. Therefore, the management board has decided to purchase and implement a solution that would collect all relevant information regarding transport and forwarding orders on the one hand, and on the other it would allow access to them from various locations of the Company. Additional requirement expected by the management board was that the solution managing transport operation should communicate on-line with other systems used by the Company. As a result of works carried out, the basic aim of the project was to connect all branches of the company to a single information exchange system. Thus, the management of Polonia Logistyka was given the opportunity to analyze the current condition of the whole company through cross-analysis reports on, among other things, orders, costs of service or sale of services.

This is the basis for taking strategic activities for faster and more effective business development. Employees of Polonia Logistyka have been able to work remotely from virtually anywhere where is access to the Internet. The vehicle loading visualization mechanism allows for better planning of the use of means of transport, and the route planning mechanism facilitates optimization of journeys. This greatly improved the work of sales representatives who at any time can check the load on cars and properly plan further orders. It has managed to largely eliminate empty passages of cars, which significantly influenced the optimization of costs. On the other hand, the route planning mechanism allows firstly to optimize the route, and secondly, drivers receive a fully-defined route, which in turn affects their performance. This creates a possibility to handle more transport orders. In addition, any driver, regardless of the car used, has the possibility to accurately record fuel and route settlements. The cost analysis of car usage (also from the finance and accounting program) provides accurate accounting for drivers. Communication between forwarding software and accounting and finance programs have completely eliminated errors that had occurred earlier when transmitting data between the previous system was done manually, and significantly improved performance of accounting department.

5 Conclusion and Future Work

Modern management can be considered as a single sequence of decisions and creation of conditions for effective implementation of the decision. Management should be treated as a form of practical decision-making activity concerning the best use of existing assets, capital, and human resources in order to fulfill the assumed tasks to ensure sustainable business growth. Making decisions requires transforming information into a collection of variants and choosing the best one - final decision (optimal), instruction for further action. So the quality of information, its up-to-date, becomes crucial in the management decision-making process. IT is an indispensable tool of modern management. Supporting the decision-making process by an ERP system brings measurable benefits. This system collects data, organizes and integrates all areas of a company's operations and supports resource management, accounting for maximum efficiency. The case study of the implementation of ERP Macrologic discussed in this work confirms this thesis. Especially in the case of multi-plant enterprises, the effects of information integration are clearly visible. It is important that the ERP system allows unification of certain solutions, at the same time individualizing and adjusting them to the needs of individual plants.

ERP software is designed to help companies streamline their operations, but can also complicate them if the new system does not meet user expectations as a result of incorrect decisions during implementation. We need to involve employees in cooperation with the managerial staff and the system vendor so that the company gets practical software that improves the efficiency of its business processes.

In order to better analyze the impact of ERP system implementation in multi-plant enterprises on management effectiveness in the future, quantitative studies assessing the change in economic categories, such as costs and revenues, must be conducted. On the other hand, the implementation of an ERP system based on processes occurring in the enterprise requires a detailed analysis of these processes.

References

1. N. Elkhani, S. Soltani, M.N. Ahmad, Journal of Enterprise Information Management **27**, 759 (2014)
2. K. Jagoda, P. Samaranayake, International Journal of Accounting & Information Management **25**, 91 (2017)
3. D. Maditinos, D. Chatzoudes, C. Tsaridis, Journal of Enterprise Information Management **25**, 60 (2011)
4. D.A. Almajali, R. Masa'deh, A. Tarhini, Journal of Enterprise Information Management **29**, 549 (2016)
5. T. Oboulhas, X. Xu, D. Zhan, Journal of Manufacturing Technology Management **16**, 654 (2005)
6. T.H. Netland , A. Aspelund, International Journal of Operations & Production Management **34**, 390 (2014)
7. H. Hoakansson, I. Snehota, *Developing relationships in business network* (Routledge, London, 1995)
8. P. Glowalla, A. Sunyaey, Journal of Enterprise Information Management **27**, 668 (2014)
9. P. Ekman, P. Thilenius, T Windhal, Business Process Management Journal **20**, 480 (2014)
10. N. Kinnie, Employee Relations **4**, 23 (1982)
11. E.G.A. Armstrong, J.F.B. Goodman, J.E. Davis, A. Wagner, Personnel Review **7**, 19 (1978)
12. V.A. Marbet, M.A. Venkataramanan, Decision Science **29**, 539 (1998)
13. S. Kot, M. Starostka-Patyk, D. Krzywda, *Zarzadzanie lancuchami dostaw* (Wydawnictwo Politechniki Czestochowskiej, Czestochowa, 2009)

MATEC Web of Conferences **125**, 04023 (2017) DOI: 10.1051/matecconf/201712504023
CSCC 2017

3D model of flow in micro channels

Tatiana Kudryashova* and *Sergey* Polyakov

Keldysh Institute of Applied Mathematics RAS, Miusskaya sq. 4, Moscow 125047, Russia

Abstract. The micro channels are important components in many micro - electro - mechanical systems (MEMS) and technical systems. They are used to transport a gas or a liquid into devices and the systems. In our work, the gas flows into a micro channel have been studied for various shapes and sizes of the micro channels. Numerical simulations of compressible flows through a micro channel are performed by solving the Navier–Stokes equations and the quasigasdynamic equations (QGD). The numerical approaches are realized on hybrid parallel computer systems. The software includes the Domain Decomposition technique, the Message Passing Interface (MPI) for organization of interprocess data exchange and an application programming interface Open Multi-Processing (OpenMP). The calculations are performed on the Heterogeneous Computer Systems with Video Processing Units (VPU) and the classical microprocessors - Central Processing Unit (CPU).

1 Introduction

Earth's limited resources make resource saving and energy saving not only a priority for the development of civilization, but also the guarantee of its survival. One of the main directions of realization of this priority is the creation of micro and nanotechnologies with enhanced performance characteristics. The advantages of these technologies are diminutiveness, low power consumption, low material consumption, reliability, demand across all sectors of the economy.

These technologies can be applied in medicine, for creation of new materials, for computer techniques of a new generation, for purification of water and air and etc.

MEMS technologies have typical sizes from 1 micrometer (μm) up to a few millimetres. The complexity of such systems depends on the number of components. Nowadays, MEMS can include about several millions of units. Today, there are nano - electro - mechanical systems (NEMS). These systems have submicron sizes. MEMS and NEMS have the same functional part, but NEMS work with spatial (or time) scales about 2-3 orders less.

MEMS and NEMS technologies are applied to create micro sensors, engines, generators, pumps, filters and etc. These complicated systems are needed to study in details. For this analysis, we should join the experiment results and mathematical modelling. In contrast to many other computational challenges, applications in micro and nano technologies typically have specific problem size [1].

This paper deals with approaches to calculate gas flows in the micro channels of the technical systems. We study the flows for various configurations of the micro channels. The calculations were performed for laminar flow in the micro channels with the cross sections: circular, rectangular and annular channel [2].

There are many studies about circular micro channels although the rectangular micro channels have more prospects for being used in the technical systems. They are easier to produce, more technological and more simple for mathematical modelling.

The goal of this study is investigation of characteristics of flow for various configurations of the micro channels and comparison of two numerical approaches. For computing we used the QGD equations and the Navier–Stokes equations.

The numerical results will be compared with the flow regimes into the micro channels of the various sizes and shapes of the cross-section.

In technical applications the problems with the large Knudsen numbers and the high Reynolds numbers have appeared. These tasks have a complex real geometry. To solve these problems, fine unstructured (irregular) grids and hybrid grids are used. Such computational challenges require the utilization of modern hybrid parallel computer systems. In our work, two computing systems are implemented with VPU and CPU microprocessors.

2 Governing equations

The numerical interpretation is based on the system of the QGD equations [3, 4]. The QGD equations are obtained by a kinetic approach. The Boltzman equation is integrated with collision invariants, using a special variant of serial expansion for the distribution function. The system of QGD equations has been constructed as an extension of the traditional Navier-Stokes system of equations. This model generalizes the Navier-Stokes

* Corresponding author: kudryashova@imamod.ru

DOI: 10.1051/matecconf/201712504023

system and it is different from the Navier-Stokes system in additional dissipative terms with a small parameter τ. The system of the QGD equations is used for the flow field calculations [5]. Efficiency and precision of this method are provided by validity of conservation laws and entropy balance. With the usual notations, the general form of the QGD system is written as:

$$\frac{\partial \rho}{\partial t} + \mathrm{div}\,\mathbf{j} = 0, \quad \mathbf{j} = \rho(\mathbf{u} - \mathbf{w}),$$
$$\mathbf{w} = \tau\left[\frac{1}{\rho}\mathrm{div}(\rho\mathbf{u})\right]\mathbf{u} + \mathbf{w}^*, \qquad (1)$$
$$\mathbf{w}^* = \tau\left[(\mathbf{u}\nabla)\mathbf{u} \;\; \frac{1}{\rho}\!\!+ \;\; p\right],\nabla$$

$$\frac{\partial}{\partial t}(\rho u_k) + \mathrm{div}(\mathbf{j}u_k + \mathbf{e}_k p \;\; \mathbf{\Pi}_k) \;\; 0, \qquad =$$
$$\mathbf{\Pi}_k = (\Pi_{j,k}), \quad \Pi_{k,j} = \Pi^{NS}_{k,j} + \Pi^{AD}_{k,j},$$
$$\Pi^{NS}_{k,j} = \mu\left(\frac{\partial u_k}{\partial x_j} + \frac{\partial u_j}{\partial x_k} + \delta_{k,j}\left(\zeta \;\; \frac{2}{3}\right)\mathrm{div}(\mathbf{u})\right), \qquad (2)$$
$$\Pi^{AD}_{k,j} = \rho u_k w^*_j + \delta_{k,j}\tau((\mathbf{u} \;\;)p),$$
$$j,k = 1,2,3;$$

$$\frac{\partial}{\partial t}E + \mathrm{div}(\mathbf{j}H + \mathbf{q} \;\; \mathbf{\Pi}\mathbf{u}) - 0, \qquad =$$
$$\mathbf{q} = -\kappa\nabla T - \tau\left[(\mathbf{u}\nabla)\varepsilon\nabla\, p(\mathbf{u} \;\;)\left(\frac{1}{\rho}\right)\right]\rho\mathbf{u}, \qquad (3)$$

$$E = \rho\left(\frac{1}{2}|\mathbf{u}|^2 + \varepsilon\right), \quad \varepsilon = c_V T,$$
$$H = \frac{E + p}{\rho}, \quad p = Z\rho \;\; T, \quad \Re$$
$$\gamma = \frac{c_p}{c_V}, \quad \tau = \frac{\mu}{p\mathrm{Sc}}, \qquad (4)$$
$$\mathrm{Pr} = \frac{\mu c_p}{\kappa}, \quad \mathrm{Sc} = \frac{\mu}{\rho D}.$$

Here ρ is the density, **u** is the velocity vector, $p = \rho RT$ the pressure, $\Re$ is the universal gas constant, T is the temperature, ε is the internal energy, γ is the specific heat ratio, H is the enthalpy, μ, ζ, κ, τ are the kinetic coefficients of gas (μ is the coefficient of dynamic viscosity, ζ is the coefficient of relative volume viscosity, κ is the coefficient of thermal conductivity of gas, τ is the relaxation time of the flow to a quasi-equilibrium state). Dependencies of these coefficients on the governing parameters are written as follows: $\mu = \mu(T)$, $\zeta = \zeta(T)$, $\chi = \chi(T)$ and $\tau = \tau(T,\rho)$. $Z = Z(T,\rho)$ is compressibility factor, $\gamma = \gamma(T,\rho)$ is adiabatic index, $c_V = c_V(\;T)$, $c_p = c_p(\;T)$ are specific heat capacity and $\Re = k_B / m$ is the gas constant, (k_B is the Boltzmann's constant, Sc and Pr are the Schmidt and the Prandtl numbers); **j** and **Π** are modified fluxs of density and viscous stress tensor; $\rho\mathbf{w}$ and $\rho\mathbf{w}^*$ are vectors of the QGD corrections $\rho\mathbf{u}$; **q** is heat flux vector; $\mathbf{e}_k$ ($k = 1,2,3$) are the orthogonal unit vectors, div and ∇ are the operators of divergence and gradient. To analyze the results of calculations, we need the values of flow parameters such as the Mach number, the Reynolds number and the Knudsen number.

$$a^2 = \gamma\frac{p}{\rho}, \quad \lambda \approx \frac{\mu}{\rho\sqrt{Z\Re T}}A,$$
$$\mathrm{Ma} = \frac{|\mathbf{u}|}{a}, \quad \mathrm{Re} = \frac{\rho|\mathbf{u}|\lambda}{\mu}, \quad Kn = \frac{L}{\lambda}. \qquad (5)$$

Where a – the speed of sound and λ – the mean free path. The system (1) – (3) can be completed by initial and boundary conditions. The initial conditions correspond to an equilibrium state of the gas medium without interaction with external factors.

The initial conditions are :

$$\rho = \rho_0, \quad \mathbf{u} = 0, \quad P = P_0, \quad T = T_0. \qquad (6)$$

Here ρ_0 and p_0 – initial gas density and pressure, T_0 is the initial temperature. Inlet parameters are:

$$(\mathbf{u},\mathbf{n}) = u_{in}, \quad \rho = \rho_{in}, \quad T = T_{in}. \qquad (7)$$

On free surfaces of the computational domain, the so-called "soft" boundary conditions can be written as:

$$\frac{\partial \rho}{\partial n} = 0, \quad \frac{\partial(\rho\mathbf{u})}{\partial n} = 0, \quad \frac{\partial p}{\partial n} = 0. \qquad (8)$$

For solid walls sliding conditions were applied.

If τ is equal to 0, we have the Navier-Stokes system of equations.

3 Problem description

The problem is considered for calculation of the nitrogen flow across the nozzle in a micro channel. The experimental data for the issue was published in [6]. The computational domain is shown in Figure. 1.

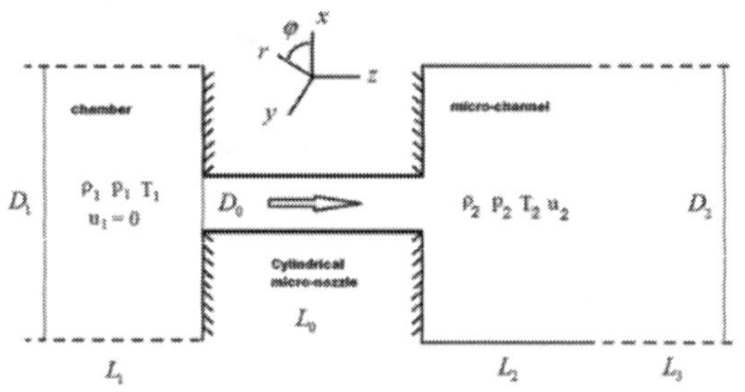

Fig. 1. Computational domain.

The cylindrical micro nozzle has the diameter D_0 and length $L_0 = 6D_0$. The computational domain has the diameter $D_1 = 6D_0$ and lengths $L_1 = 10L_0$, $L_2 = 30L_0$ and $L_3 = 20L_0$. It connects the chamber with nitrogen and micro-channel. At an initial moment t=0 the gas is at rest: $u_1 = u_2 = 0$. In the chamber nitrogen is located under standard normal conditions: $T_1 = 295.15\,K$, $p_1 = 101325\,Pa$. The gas is disposed in the nozzle and chamber with temperature $T_2 = 295.15\,K$ and the pressure, $p_2 = \delta_0 p_1$, δ_0 $10^{-3} \div 10^{-5}$. The nozzle on the left is blocked by a partition, which opens instantly at the beginning of the calculation. The inner surface of the nozzle is perfectly smooth and thermally insulated. The diameters of the computational areas of the cylinder micro nozzle and the vacuum chamber were equal: $D_1 = D_2 = 6D_0$. The calculated part length of the cylinder micro nozzle is $L_1 = 10L_0$; the calculated area length of the vacuum chamber is $L_2 = 50L_0$.

For computing, various sizes were implemented. In particular, the value of diameter D_0 was varied from 3.1 - 310 micrometers. The results of the numerical experiments are presented in the sections below.

4 Numerical method

The grid numerical method has a finite volume method as basis and is used to calculate the macro parameters on the QGD equations [7-9]. For this purpose, in the computational domain D, the spatial grid Ω_D with cells C_m ($m = 1,\dots,M$) and time grid ω_t with variable step Δt was introduced. The grid Ω_D is a hybrid mesh, that is, it includes several element types.

All parameters of the gas components (density, pressure, temperature, velocity vector components, etc.) have been carried to the centers of mass of grid elements, that is, to the centers of cells. Stream variables have been set in the centers of the cells sides. Spatial approximations of the main terms have been executed by the technique presented in work [10]. The computing scheme on time is obvious. The resulting grid equations at a predictor stage have view:

$$
\begin{aligned}
&\hat{\rho}_{l,m} = \rho_{l,m} + \frac{\Delta t}{|V_m|}\sum_{p=1}^{M_m} W^{(\rho)}_{l,n,m,p}\left|S_{m,p}\right|,\\
&W^{(\rho)}_{l,n,m,p} = \left(\mathbf{W}^{(\rho)}_{l,m,p}, \mathbf{n}_{m,p}\right),\\
&\hat{\rho}_{l,m}\hat{u}_{l,k,m} = \rho_{l,m}u_{l,k,m} + \frac{\Delta t}{|V_m|}\sum_{p=1}^{M_m} W^{(\rho u)}_{l,n,m,p,k}\left|S_{m,p}\right|,\\
&W^{(\rho u)}_{l,n,m,p,k} = \left(\mathbf{W}^{(\rho u_k)}_{l,m,p}, \mathbf{n}_{m,p}\right), \quad k = x, y, z,\\
&\hat{E}_{l,m} = E_{l,m} + \frac{\Delta t}{|V_m|}\sum_{p=1}^{M_m} W^{(E)}_{l,n,m,p}\left|S_{m,p}\right|,\\
&W^{(E)}_{l,n,m,p} = \left(\mathbf{W}^{(E)}_{l,m,p}, \mathbf{n}_{m,p}\right), \quad m = 1,\dots,M, \quad l = a, b.
\end{aligned}
\qquad (9)
$$

Here f_m, $\hat{f}_m$ – values of the corresponding functions on the lower and upper layers on time in the center of the control volume V_m (coinciding into effect of the selected approximation with grid cell C_m), $|V_m|$ – value of the control volume V_m, $|S_{m,p}|$ – faces squares $S_{m,p}$ of the control volume V_m, M_m – faces number of the control volume V_m, $W^{(\alpha)}_{n,m,p}$ – scalar multiplication of flux $\mathbf{W}^{(\alpha)}_{m,p}$ via the face $S_{m,p}$ by the external normal $\mathbf{n}_{m,p}$ to this face $(\alpha = \rho, \rho u_x, \rho u_y, \rho u_z, E)$. The fluxes approximations $\mathbf{W}^{(\alpha)}_{m,p}$ are similar to the proposals in [10], but do not use artificial viscosity.

5 Parallel implementation

Parallel realization uses supercomputers (or clusters) with hybrid architecture [11, 12]. Such computer systems have several multi-core central processors (CPUs) on each node, as well as several vector or graphics processors (VPUs or GPUs). Parallelization is performed on principles of geometric parallelism, splitting of computational area into subdomains and uses algorithms for dynamic load balancing of the calculators.

The calculation is performed on the discrete QGD equations on a grid distributed among cluster nodes using the "domain decomposition" technique. For a Cartesian grid, when parallelizing, a grid of calculators corresponding to the spatial dimension of the problem is used. For irregular hybrid grid, for parallelization, software packages are applied, such as: METIS [13], ParMETIS [14, 15]. Within each compute node, the grid cells are distributed among the CPU threads by the same algorithms as among the nodes. The QGD computations are strongly coupled and therefore they are executed on the CPU [16].

For computing two systems were implemented:

1) MVS-10P (JSCC RAS). The calculations were performed on the central processors Intel Xeon E5-2690 E5-2690 v0 @ 2.90GHz and vector processors Intel Xeon Phi 7110X. The number of CPU cores ranged from 16 to 2048. The number of VPU cores ranged from 60 to 7680. Interconnect Infiniband FDR (56 Gb/s);

2) MVS-5P (JSCC RAS): This system based on Intel Xeon E5-2697A v4 @ 2.60GHz (88 nodes, 2 processors per node, 16 cores per processor, 2 threads per core). Interconnect is OmniPath (100 Gb/s).

6 Results

An analysis of the numerical results was carried out. The problem was researched in details for (*z*,*r*) geometry and $D_0 = 310$ μm. The grids with the number of square ($23424 {*} 2^k$) x ($192 {*} 2^k$) cells were used (parameter k=1, 2, 3). The analysis included three questions: accuracy of mathematical model, accuracy of numerical method, efficiency of parallel implementation.

Firstly, we have compared the QGD and the Navier-Stokes models. For this purpose, we have calculated the norms of the density difference, pressure difference, temperature difference and velocity difference for some fixed time moments. One result of these calculations is presented in Table 1. Analysis of data showed that the solutions obtained by these models may differ significantly, especially in the areas of rapid development of the flow. However, if the flows are stationary and the Mach numbers are moderate (for example, $0.1 \le Ma \le 3$) then from a certain instant in time, these solutions practically coincide. The difference is in only time to reach the steady-state.

Table 1. Comparison of the models (t=8 μs).

№ grid	$\|\rho_{QGD}-\rho_{NS}\|_C$	$\|p_{QGD}-p_{NS}\|_C$	$\|T_{QGD}-T_{NS}\|_C$
1	1.49e-04	3.61e-05	6.70e+01
2	3.33e-04	4.86e-05	2.61e+01
3	5.43e-04	4.31e-05	2.14e+01

At second, we have considered the accuracy of the numerical method for the grid sequence. We have compared the norms of the density difference, pressure difference, temperature difference and velocity difference for the grids with the space steps h, $h/2$, $h/4$. The obtained results are presented in Table 2. These results confirm the grid convergence of the numerical procedure.

Table 2. Comparison of the accuracy.

Grids	$\|\rho_h-\rho_{h/2}\|_C$	$\|p_h-p_{h/2}\|_C$	$\|T_h-T_{h/2}\|_C$
1 and 2	3.25e-4	6.34e-5	8.21e-3
2 and 3	9.87e-5	1.96e-5	2.61e-3

At third, we have analyzed the efficiency of parallel implementation of the presented numerical method. Computing times and efficiency of the parallelization are shown in Figures 2 and 3 for (z,r) geometry and grid with k=2. These data demonstrate a possibility of calculations of gasdynamic tasks on big configurations. At the same time, sharp falling of efficiency on small configurations illustrates the known problem of data processing of large volume by one thread of CPU. The use of both the CPUs and the VPUs on the same node allows us to reduce the computing time by 1.5-1.7 times. However, the efficiency degrades rapidly because of the VPUs cores have slow network exchanges.

The plots of some numerical results are displayed in Figure 4 and 5. They show the density distribution and concentration distribution obtained at the time t=27.6 μs. Calculations were performed on the supercomputer system MVS10P. The pressure and the temperature profiles do not have strong gradients at the time, and therefore are not shown. In fact, an isothermal flow is established here.

The calculations were carried out in the three-dimensional case in the (z, x, y) coordinates The main part of the numerical experiments was carried out on a grid with the cubic cells (23424 * 2^k) x (384 * 2^k) x (384 * 2k) (parameter k = 1,2,3). For this variant, the efficiency of parallelization was tested. It increased for the maximum configurations of used supercomputers by 1.5 times [17, 18]. At the same time, we can not use VPUs in full due to their small RAM. In generally it is possible to note that results of 3D and 2D calculations coincide for average sizes of the flow parameters, but differ in dynamics of the process.

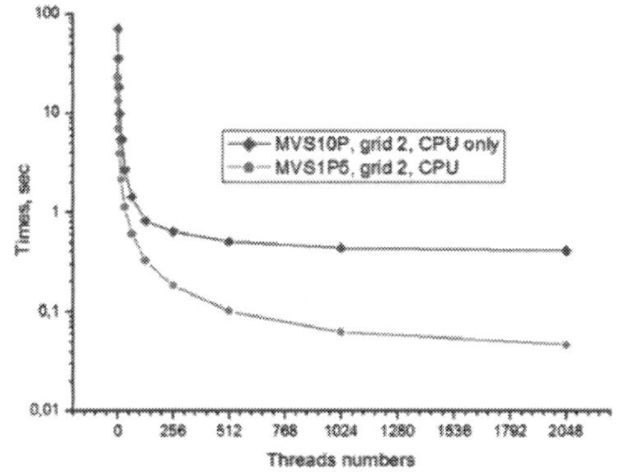

Fig. 2. Computing time.

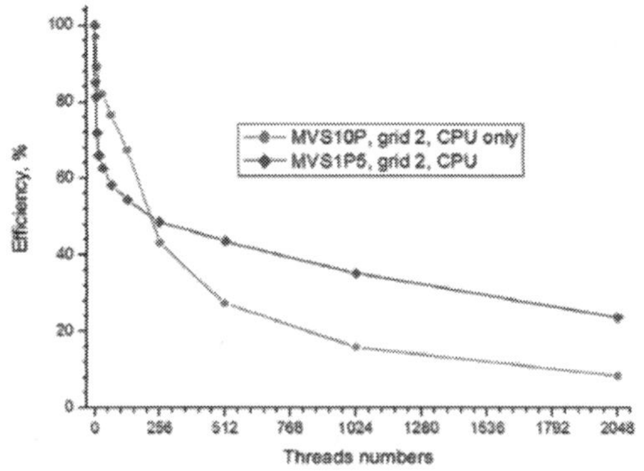

Fig. 3. Efficiency of calculations.

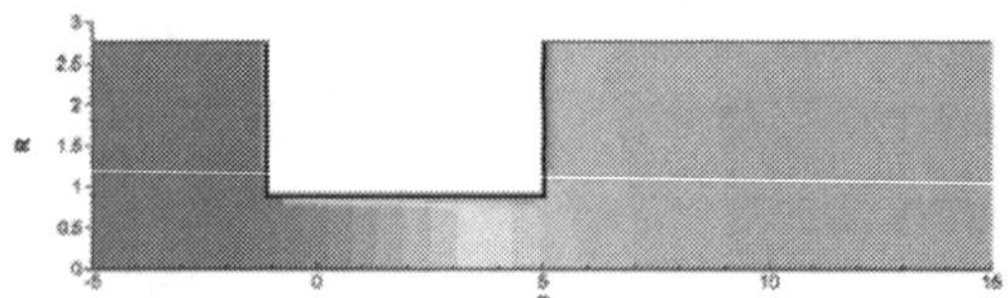

Fig. 4. Gas density distribution near the micro nozzle entry.

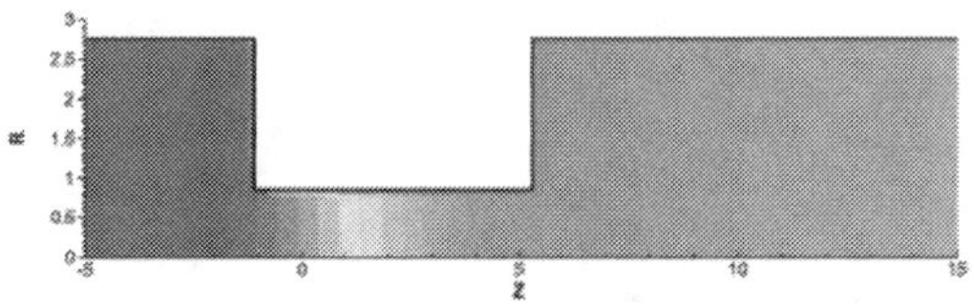

Fig. 5. Decimal logarithm of gas concentration near the micro nozzle entry.

7 Conclusion

The problem of gas flows simulation in the micro channels of the technical systems for a real geometry is considered. To solve it, the numerical parallel algorithm is supported. This one is based on the QGD equations and the finite volume method applied to cells of different shapes The algorithm was tested for the case of an axially symmetric and complete three-dimensional Cartesian geometry of the problem. The calculations confirmed the robustness and effectiveness of the developed common approach. The development of the work will be connected with the calculations of the flows for more complex variants. It can be a curvilinear geometry of the computational domain or the use of hybrid grids.

This work was supported by Russian Foundation for Basic Research (grant № 16-07-00206-a, № 17-01-00973-a).

References

1. D. Resnick. Nanoimprint lithography, in "Nanolithography. The art of fabricating nanoelectronic and nanophotonic devices and systems" / Edited by Martin Feldman. Woodhead Publishing Limited, P. 315-345, (2014).
2. A. Aota, T. Kitamori, Micro- and Nanofluidics, in "Nanofabrication handbook" / Edited by Stefano Cabrini, Satoshi Kawata. CRC Press, 2012. - P. 379-398; (2012).
3. T.G. Elizarova Quasi-Gas Dynamic Equations. Springer-Verlag, Berlin Heidelberg New York (2009).
4. B.N. Chetverushkin, Mathematical modeling of problems in the dynamics of a radiating gas, Moscow, Science, In Russian (1985).
5. I.A. Graur, T.G. Elizarova, T.A. Kudryashova, S.V. Polyakov. *Numerical investigation of jet flows, using multiprocessor computer systems* // J. Mathematical Modelling, 14(6), p. 51-62, (2002).
6. A. Ramos, G. Tejeda, J.M. Fernandez, S. Montero. *Nonequilibrium Processes in Supersonic Jets of N2, H2, and N2 + H2 Mixtures: (I) Zone of Silence*. J. Phys. Chem. A, 113, p. 8506–8512, (2009).
7. I.V. Fryazinov, Balance method and variational-difference schemes. Differentsial'nye uravneniya, 7, 1332–1343, (1980).
8. A.A. Samarskiy, A.V. Koldoba, Yu.A. Poveshchenko, V.F. Tishkin, A.P. Favorskiy, *Difference schemes on irregular grids*. Minsk, Publishing of Closed Joint Stock Company "Criterion", (1996).
9. R. Eymard, T.R. Gallouet, R. Herbin, The finite volume method. *Handbook of Numerical Analysis, Amsterdam, North Holland,* **7**, 713–1020, (2000).
10. I.V. Popov, I.V. Fryazinov, Method of adaptive artificial viscosity for the equations of gas dynamics on triangular and tetrahedral grids. *Mathematical Models and Computer Simulations*, **1**, 50–62, (2013).
11. T.A. Kudryashova, S.V. Polyakov, V. Podryga, Yu. Karamzin. *Multiscale modeling of nonlinear processes in technical microsystems.* // J. Mathematical modelling, № 7, V **27** (2015).
12. T.A. Kudryashova, S.V. Polyakov, V. Podryga. CFD *Problems Solving Parallel Approaches on Supercomputers*. 20th International Conference on Circuits, Systems, Communications and Computers (CSCC 2016), Corfu Island, Greece, July 14-17, 2016. N. Mastorakis, V. Mladenov and A. Bulucea (Eds.). MATEC Web of Conferences **76** 04025(2016).
13. METIS-Family of Multilevel Partitioning Algorithms, http://glaros.dtc.umn.edu/gkhome/views/metis, (2009).
14. Karypis G., Schloegel K., Kumar V. *ParMETIS – Parallel Graph Partitioning and Sparse Matrix Ordering Library*. URL: http://glaros.dtc.umn.edu/gkhome/metis/parmetis
15. Satish Balay, Kris Buschelman, William D. Gropp, Dinesh Kaushik, Matthew G. Knepley, Lois Curfman McInnes, Barry F. Smith, Hong Zhang, PETSc Web page, http://www.mcs.anl.gov/petsc, (2001).
16. Hang Si, TetGen: A Quality Tetrahedral Mesh Generator, http://tetgen.berlios.de/, (2009).
17. http://www.mcs.anl.gov/research/projects/mpi/
18. http://www.parallel.ru

An experimental design to study decommitment in a collaborative multi-agent system in a scheduling domain

Michele Van Dyne[1,*], *Costas* Tsatsoulis[2]

[1]Computer Science Department, Montana Tech, 1300 W. Park St. Butte, MT 59701
[2]Department of Computer Science and Engineering, University of North Texas, 1155 Union Circle #310440, Denton, TX 76203-5017

Abstract. Based on previous multi-agent research, this paper describes the experimental design of extending that research to an additional domain. The original work used collaborative agents, each controlling a radar, to negotiate with each other to perform the task of target tracking. Agents were allowed to schedule their own tasks, commit to tasks requested by other agents, and then, dependent on experimental condition, either always honor commitments, unilaterally decommit if another higher priority commitment occurs, or negotiate whether to drop a commitment or not is another apparently higher priority request is received. In the original research, the domain was highly time constrained, and agents were required to operate in a real-time environment. This research extends the concept of agent decommitment into a resource scheduling domain. The problem is no longer time constrained, however, the number of agents is increased dramatically. In this paper, we describe the theoretical background and experimental design of the new research.

1 Background

Previous multi-agent research has assumed that in collaborative multi-agent systems when an agent makes a commitment, then it would honor it. However, there may be situations where circumstances change and honoring the commitment would lead to a lowering of the social welfare of the system; in such situation it is preferable not to honor a commitment. In the multi-agent systems of interest agents are multitasking and can perform certain actions in parallel. Since the agents are collaborative they must be able to request that another agent perform a task, and thus are capable of communication. When an agent in the system attempts to achieve a goal, it decides to perform a set of tasks to reach the goal. Each decision to perform a task is a commitment to the task. Our work follows the Belief-Desire-Intention (BDI) model of agent architecture defined by Rao and Georgeff [1], where the commitment to a task is viewed as an "intention," and the goal that must be attained is viewed as a "desire" in the BDI framework. Finally, the information available to the agent is known as "beliefs" in [1][2] and indicate to the agent the feasibility of the task as well as the subsequent attainment of the goal. An agent may also commit to a task because another agent has requested it. Thus, we have task commitments either to oneself or to another agent.

Schut and Wooldridge extend the BDI model to include a decision theoretic approach to what they call "intention reconsideration" [3]. Their approach allows an agent to decide for itself whether to perform an action or to deliberate over its intentions. Two conditions are defined under which reconsideration may be appropriate: when conditions have changed such that an intention can no longer be achieved, and when better opportunities arise. While this approach moves the decommitment decisions from design-time to runtime, it only allows an agent to consider what should be done "next", a default action or a reconsideration. This approach studied only the effects on a single-agent system, and thus disregards effects on a multi-agent system.

Decommitment may happen if a task becomes impossible to complete, or if an alternate task that has is of higher importance is presented, or, finally, if conditions indicate that the performance of a task is no longer a productive or needed activity. The goal of our work was to study what would be the best way for an agent to drop a previous commitment to perform a task for another agent in the multi-agent system. We wanted to study the effects of two different types of decommitments to the overall social welfare of the multi-agent system: (1) unilateral, where the agent drops a task to which it has committed itself without informing the other agent, and (2) negotiated, where the agent will inform the other agent that it is planning to drop its commitment, but it is open to negotiate and be convinced not to do so. Finally, we compared the two decommitment approaches to the effects on the social welfare of the system if no commitments were ever dropped.

To perform our previous research, we developed an architecture of a multi-agent system that operated in an environment of hard real time, using sensors that had to

* Corresponding author: mvandyne@mtech.edu

collaborate to track multiple targets [4]. An agent controlled a sensor and had to commit to tracking a target over a period of time, and then switch to another target, and so on. If a more important target, though, appeared, it may have to decommit from tracking a previous target and move to the new one. Commitments were made to the first agent to sense a target, as multiple agents needed to track in order to establish a precise target location. Since targets would move out of a sensor's area, commitments had to be flexible and fluid, and move with the target across the sensor and agent network.

We found the architecture to be very useful in creating multiple decommitment experiments by varying the number of targets and sensors in the environment, as well as the target speed [5]. We computed the social welfare of the multi-agent system as the utility of the target tracking schedule of the whole network, which is a function of accuracy, number of measurements per target per second, and the balance of managing to track multiple targets.

Using our experimental set up we demonstrated that both unilateral and negotiated decommitment performed as hypothesized, that is, overall performance improved, and that negotiated decommitment provided additional benefit over the performance of unilateral commitment. Graceful degradation of performance was also demonstrated in all conditions as the constraints on the system. Finally, under all conditions, agents demonstrated rationality in decision making and both negotiated decommitment and unilateral decommitment provided a higher locally assessed utility than did the baseline condition.

Our previous research provided an architecture on which to test the concept in different domains. In particular, the fact that agents may hold resources that other agents need opens to possibility of using this architecture in the domain of scheduling. In work by Sen and Durfee, an agent schedules tasks to be performed at a given point in time. These tasks may originate from the agent itself, or may be committed to at the request of another agent. The distributed task scheduling problem is defined in [6] as a group of tasks to be scheduled requiring the use of a set of resources controlled by a set of agents. The design described in this paper uses the domain of classroom scheduling for a university. Thus, the requirement that a task be scheduled at a specific time can be dropped, however the framework of agents holding resources that are needed by others remains a criterion.

2 The Problem Domain

Classroom scheduling at the university being used as a test case uses a process where course offerings scheduled in a particular room at a particular time for the corresponding previous semester have priority in continuing to use that room in subsequent semesters. If no course offerings changed, this approach would yield a conflict-free schedule every semester. Unfortunately, course offering requirements do change, making it necessary to change at least a portion of the previous schedule.

The possible changes to a course offering that will affect future schedules are:

- Offering has been cancelled
- New course offering added
- Additional sections of a course added
- Expected enrollment in the course has changed (either increased or decreased)
- Time/days course is offered has changed
- Classroom requirements (equipment/facilities) have changed

The following sections discuss the effect on the scheduling process when each of the conditions has occurred.

2.1 Course Offering Cancelled

A course that was offered in a previous semester schedule that has been cancelled in the future schedule frees up a resource (classroom/days/time) that can be used for other courses. In the architecture of the system, this creates a free resource as opposed to one that is currently held by a current course offering agent. Free resources will be consumed before a course scheduling agent requests that another one give up its holdings, if at all possible.

2.2 New Course Offering Added

When a new course is added to the schedule, it holds no resources from a previous semester. Generally, a newly added course will have a request for a specific set of days and a time, along with an estimate of the enrollment, and a request for a particular room, along with particular requirements for the offering, including capabilities and facilities present in the room. If that room is a free resource at that time, the request can be fulfilled as-is. If not, however, negotiation between the agent holding that resource from the previous schedule, and the agent requesting the resource as a newly added course will be necessary.

2.3 Additional Sections of a Course Added

Adding additional sections of a course is very similar to adding a new course. These new sections hold no resources from a previous semester and generally will request a specific set of days and a time, along with an estimate of the enrolment, and a request for a particular room, the same as with a wholly new course offering. As before, if that room is a free resource at that time, the request can be fulfilled as-is. If not, however, negotiation between the agent holding that resource from the previous schedule, and the agent requesting the resource as a newly added course will be necessary.

2.4 Expected Enrollment Changed

If the expected enrollment of a course decreases, it may be possible to move that course offering to a smaller room, if one is available. The previous course offering still holds the resources it was schedule for, but now has less priority over those resources.

On the other hand, if the expected enrollment increases and the increase is too much for its previous room to handle, one of two things can happen. The course enrollment may simply be capped by the room capacity, or the course offering experiencing an expected increase can negotiate with other course offering agents for a larger room.

2.5 Time/Days of Offering Changed

On occasion, the department offering a course may need to change the days/time that a course is offered so that it fits the schedule of the students taking the course, or so that it fits the schedule of the instructor teaching the course. Individual academic departments keep track of the other courses students in a cohort are normally taking and thus has an idea of when offerings can be scheduled to work for that cohort. Additionally, individual departments are aware of the teaching schedules of their instructional faculty, and can work out when a course offering can be scheduled to meet those requirements also.

Individual academic departments look at day/time changes from a local viewpoint, however. They do not have an overview of what rooms may be available at given times, nor the requirements of courses offered by other departments.

2.6 Classroom Requirements Changed

Changes in how a course is taught can change the classroom requirements of that course. This may include requiring computing workstations for each student, or other laboratory equipment. It may also include changes to the instructor's podium equipment, including computing and projection. Some of these changes may be possible to accommodate by enhancing the equipment of the currently scheduled classroom, while others may necessitate the change to a different room already so equipped.

3 Architecture

Our previous work was concerned with individual independent agents each holding access to a resource (radar) which may be used to assist other agents. To map this architecture to the current domain, we can view each course offering in a previous schedule as an agent holding a resource, and each changed course as an agent requesting resources from those agents holding them. In our previous work, agents were constrained by timing, and had to maintain a task schedule during which time a request had to be honoured (that is, a radar sector must be enabled at a specific time in order to track an expected target). In the current domain, this timing constraint is removed, so individual agents do not need to maintain a task list. Nor do agents in the current domain need to respond to requests in a hard real time limit as they did in the previous work.

The abstracted goal of the overall agent system is, however, the same as before. Agents in the new scheduling domain collaborate to maximize the overall social welfare of the system, just as they did in the previous domain. One major difference, however, is the number of agents. In the previous work, we experimented with 4-12 independent agents controlling radars. In the current work, with each course offering and changed course acting as an agent, we have on the order of 1500 agents. Fortunately, only a small subset of these will be involved in negotiations – only those that have a conflict between a currently held resource and a requested one.

3.1 System Architecture

The data for this problem resides in three data sets. The first is the complete schedule for all course offerings held in the previous semester corresponding to the current one. The second is the list of requests for all (or at least most) of the course offerings to be held in the upcoming semester. In both of these datasets, the requirements of the course offering for the resource are contained in the data. The final dataset contains information about all rooms and their capacities and facilities.

The first pass of the overall system is to identify all course offerings that are exactly the same in the previous and current schedule and eliminate those from the "request" dataset since they pose no conflicts. These are stored in a new dataset – the "potential" schedule. The next pass is to look at requests that are different from the previous schedule. Any of these that do not cause a conflict may be added to the potential schedule. What remains to be dealt with are the requests that do cause conflicts.

An agent is spawned for each of the requests that cause conflicts along with an agent for each of the courses on the potential schedule with which they conflict. Note that a single course offering request may conflict with more than one offering on the potential schedule.

Following the formalization introduced by Soh and Tsatsoulis, the social agent environment can be expressed as follows [7]:

Ω a multi-agent system

Ψ a "neighborhood" in the system

$\lambda(\alpha,\beta)$, predicate indicating agent α knows about agent β.

A neighborhood is defined as:

$$\Psi \subseteq \Omega \ , \ \Psi \neq \varnothing \qquad (1), (2)$$

Every agent, α_i in neighborhood Ψ knows about all other agents in that neighborhood. That is:

$$\lambda(\alpha_i, \alpha_j) \forall i \forall j \alpha_i, \alpha_j \in \Psi \qquad (3)$$

There may be any number of neighborhoods, they need not have the same number of members, and neighborhoods may overlap. Thus,

$$\Omega = \{\Psi_1, \Psi_2, \ldots, \Psi_N\} \qquad (4)$$

Agents may communicate with other agents within their neighborhood, that is, an agent may only communicate with those that it is aware of. Thus negotiation is also restricted to agents within the same neighborhood.

Neighborhoods are defined not necessarily by proximity, but by areas of conflict. For example, all agents negotiating for the use of rooms with the same capabilities at the same times can define a neighborhood, as can agents negotiating for a specific space. Neighborhoods are not static, and as commitments to relinquish or exchange resources are made, neighborhood boundaries may change. The implication of this constraint is that broadcast requests are not made to all agents, reducing the communication load on the system as a whole. The overhead of recalculating neighborhoods is considered inconsequential in comparison to the cost of mass communications.

3.2 Agent Architecture

Each agent has the capacity to communicate with other agents in its neighborhood, to negotiate the relinquishment or exchange of resources with another agent, and to make final decisions on whether to grant requests or not. Each of these processes is carried on by individual threads within the agent, while each agent is implemented as an independent process.

Similar to our previous work, a priority is assigned to the resources held by a particular agent and to the agent requesting that resource. The difference in this research is that it is the importance of holding a resource to a particular resource that is prioritized, and not the priority of performing a particular task.

A resource priority, with respect to a given agent, is represented by the tuple:

$w_i = (p_i, vh_i, c_i, wh_i)$, where:

p_i is the calculated priority of a particular resource (defined below);

vh_i is the agent A_i's assessment of the validity of the requesting agent h_i's information;

c_i is the constrainedness of the task, comprised of the number of other agents also in the conflict set and the specificity of resource requirements for that offering;

wh_i is h_i's assessment of the priority of its need for the resources;

The calculated priority, p_i, of a particular resource is a combination of the capabilities and facilities of a particular classroom and the needs of the current agent. The closer the resource to the needs of the agent, the higher the priority of keeping that resource, and the further the resource to the needs of the agent, the lower the priority. For example, if an agent needs a room with a capacity to hold 50 students and requires a podium computer and projection system, and the room it currently holds has the capacity for 150 students and has PCs at each student station and has a podium computer and projection, the resource clearly meets the need of the agent, but also exceeds the minimum need, therefore, it will have a lower calculated priority to that agent.

Agent negotiation is initiated by a requesting agent to an agent holding resources it desires. The initial request contains the requesting agent's evaluation of its own priority in having the resources held by the agent currently in possession of those resources. If the possessing agent agrees that the priority of the requesting agent is higher than its own priority, the "negotiation" between these two agents can stop at this point and the possessing agent tentatively relinquishes its resources and becomes a requesting agent. If this new requesting agent is successful at finding resources to meet its needs, then it fully relinquishes its former resource and the conflict is resolved. If not, however, agents must do additional work.

Clearly, the requesting agent is the one who must do the bulk of the work. If another agent is unwilling to give up resources currently held, the requesting agent must then investigate other options. These can include finding another room that will meet its needs, changing the day/time of the course offering, or possibly splitting the offering into smaller sections (essentially spawning two or more processes with less restrictive needs). If any of these activities is successful, the conflict is resolved and no additional negotiation is needed. If not, the requesting agent can go back to the possessing agent again, now with a higher priority to its request since it has investigated other avenues and has found no possible solution. If this requesting agent is one who had formerly held resources and has only tentatively relinquished them to another requesting agent, it may choose to decommit those resources and take them back for itself, or it may choose to continue negotiations with other agents, dependent on the conditions of the experiment begin run.

4 Experimental Design

The ultimate goal of the agent system is to find a schedule of course offerings that meets the needs of all, that is, there are no conflicts, and all course offerings are holding adequate resources. This defines the optimal measurement of the overall social welfare for the system. Therefore, the actual overall measurement of social welfare is a function of the best possible scenario less factors for any unscheduled course offerings and any course offerings assigned resources that are less than optimal. Individual agents, or even groups of agents in a conflict set, are unable to calculate this overall social welfare score, but do so with local approximations in attempting to negotiate with each other to secure resources

There are three conditions to be tested to determine the potential of commitment/decommitment in producing optimized solutions. The first condition is that once an agent relinquishes resources, it does so completely rather than tentatively, and thus becomes a true requesting agent. This condition is the baseline in which a committing agent always honors its commitments. The second condition is where an agent makes a tentative commitment, investigates whether it can secure resources elsewhere, and if not, simply drops the tentative commitment. This is the unilateral decommitment condition in which the requesting agent has no recourse but to accept the unilateral decision of the possessing agent. The final condition is where the possessing agent, having made a tentative commitment to a requesting agent, but not being able to secure other resources, goes back into negotiation with the original requesting agent rather than simply dropping the commitment. This is the negotiated decommitment condition.

Datasets representing the three data sources (prior schedule – fall semester 2016, current requests – fall semester 2017, and room capabilities) have been secured for testing purposes. The experiment will be run on a High Performance Computing (HPC) platform which has 22 nodes each with 32 process elements per node, for a total of 704 process elements. Two of the nodes have Nvidia Tesla K20 GPUs installed, and with these, we can provide an additional 2496 cuda cores per K20.

5 Future Work

While this paper has described the theoretical basis for applying a multi-agent system with decommitment parameters, and has outlined the experimental design to be used to test the system, the actual experimentation is yet to be performed. Results of the experimentation will be reported in a future paper.

In addition to the work outlined in this paper, extensions to the system include factoring in additional scheduling constraints. Course instructors may have preferences and requirements that are unrelated to the course offering itself. Preferences might include classrooms that are near that instructor's office, not teaching courses back to back, and if so, back to back courses should be near each other, and familiarity with a particular room and its operation. Requirements may include handicap accessibility among other things.

Acknowledgements

The authors would like to thank Montana Tech Enrollment Services staff Leslie Dickerson, Registrar; Janet Friesz, Supervisor; and Abigail Peterson, Administrative Evaluator III, for their assistance in obtaining course offering and scheduling test data for use in this research.

References

1. A. S. Rao and M. P. Georgeff. 1995. "BDI Agents: from theory to practice", Proceedings of the 1st International Conference on Multi-Agent Systems (ICMAS '95), June 12-14, San Francisco, CA, pp. 312-319.
2. Parsons, T.S., Sierra, C. and Jennings, N.R., Agents that reason and negotiate by arguing, Journal of Logic and Computation, Vol. 8 No. 3, 1998, pp. 261-292.
3. Schut, M. and Wooldridge, M., Principles on intention reconsideration, Proceedings of the Fifth International Conference on Autonomous Agents, 2001, pp. 340-347.
4. M. Van Dyne and C. Tsatsoulis. 2010. "A Comparison of Agent Decommitment Techniques in a Real-Time Environment", Proceedings of the 9th Conference on Artificial Intelligence, Knowledge Engineering, and Databases (AIKED 2010), University of Cambridge, UK, Feb. 20-22, pp. 271-279.
5. M. Van Dyne and C. Tsatsoulis. 2011. "Effect of agent decommitment in a target tracking domain", Proceedings of the 2011 IEEE Aerospace Conference, Big Sky, MT, Mar. 5012.
6. Sen, S. and Durfee, E., A contracting model for flexible distributed scheduling, Annals of Operations Research, Vol. 65, 1996, pp. 195-222.
7. L-K. Soh and C. Tsatsoulis, A Real-Time Negotiation Model and a Multi-Agent Sensor Network Implementation, Autonomous Agents and Multi-Agent Systems, Vol. 11, No. 3, 2005, pp. 215-271.

Website Clickstream Data Visualization Using Improved Markov Chain Modelling In Apache Flume

Amjad Jumaah Frhan

PhD Candidate, Department of Telecommunication and Information Technology, University Politehnica of Bucharest, Romania.

Abstract- Clickstream data analysis is considered as the process of collecting, analysing and reporting the aggregate data about the web pages a visitor clicks. Visualizing the clickstream data has gained significant importance in many applications like web marketing, customer prediction, product management, etc. Most existing works employ different tools for visualizing along with techniques like Markov chain modelling. However the accuracy of the methods can be improved when the shortcomings are resolved. Markov chain modelling has problems of occlusion and unable to provide clear display of data visualizing. These issues can be resolved by improving the Markov chain model by introducing a heuristic method of Kolmogorov– Smirnov distance and maximum likelihood estimator for visualizing. These concepts are employed between the underlying distribution states to minimize the Markov distribution. The proposed model named as WebClickviz is performed in Hadoop Apache Flume which is a highly advanced tool. The clickstream data visualization accuracy can be improved when Apache Flume tools are used. The performance evaluation are made on a specific website clickstream data which shows the proposed model of visualization has better performance than existing models like VizClick.

Keywords- Clickstream data, VizClick, WebClickviz, Apache Flume, Markov chain, Kolmogorov–Smirnov distance.

1 Introduction

Click data analytics [1] devices to mine websites, social media and online transactions are helping companies maximize customer interactions. A clickstream is a series of page requests; every page requested generates a flag [2]. These signs can be graphically represented for clickstream reporting. The principle purpose of clickstream taking after is to give webmasters understanding into what guests on their site are doing. There are two levels of clickstream investigation, traffic analytics and e-commerce analytics. Traffic analytics [3] operates at the server level and tracks what number of pages is served to the user, to what extent it takes each page to stack [4], how often the user hits the browser's back or stop catch and how much data is transmitted before the user moves on [5]. E-commerce-based examination [6] uses clickstream data to determine the effectiveness of the site as a channel-to-market. It's concerned with what pages the shopper lingers on, what the shopper puts in or takes out of a shopping basket, what items the shopper purchases, whether or not the shopper belongs to a dependability program and uses a coupon code and the shopper's preferred method of payment [7].

Because an extremely large volume of data can be gathered through clickstream investigation, numerous e-businesses rely on enormous data analytics and related apparatuses [8], for example, Hadoop [9] to help interpret the data and generate reports for specific areas of interest. Clickstream investigation is considered to be best when used in conjunction with other, more standard, market evaluation resources. Inaugurating clickstream or snap way data must be gleaned from server log files. Because human and machine traffic were not differentiated, the investigation of human snaps required a considerable effort. Subsequently, Javascript technologies [10] were developed which use a taking after cookie to generate a series of signs from browsers.

Analysing the information of clients that visit an organization website can be imperative in order to remain competitive [11]. This analysis can be used to generate two discoveries for the organization, the first being an analysis of a user's clickstream while utilizing a website to reveal usage patterns, which thus gives a heightened understanding of customer behaviour [12]. This use of the analysis creates a user profile that guides in understanding the types of people that visit an organization's website [13]. Clickstream analysis can be used to predict whether a customer is likely to purchase from an e-commerce website. Clickstream analysis can also be used to improve customer fulfilment with the website and with the organization itself [14]. This can generate a business advantage, and be used to assess the effectiveness of advertising on a web page or site. Clickstreams can likewise be used to enable the user to see where they have been and enable them to easily return to a page they have already visited, a capacity that is already incorporated in many browsers.

Unauthorized clickstream information collection is considered to be spyware. However, authorized clickstream information collection comes from associations that use select in panels to generate market research utilizing panelists who agree to share their clickstream information with other companies by downloading and introducing specialized clickstream collection agents. VizClick [16] attempted to visualize the website clickstream data using a systematic approach which was performed on www.adobe.com to analyse the market behaviour of customers. However this model does provide only nominal clarity in clickstream data visualization. Hence this paper developed improved Markov chain based clickstream data visualization model named as WebClickviz, which is explained in the following sections. The proposed visualization model utilizes a heuristic determination method in general Markov chain to overcome the issues of display clarity and occlusion. The remainder of the article is organized as: Section 2 discusses some the most related research works. The improved markov chain modelling is discussed in Section 3. Section 4 focuses on the webclickviz visualization methodology while section 5 presents the visualization performance and evaluation results. Finally, Section 6 explains a conclusion about the proposed work.

2 Related Works

Website clickstream data visualization is a step by step procedure by which the user propagation is tracked from the server log files and clickstream files. In [17], an extensive survey has been made to clickstream data analysis. This work discussed about the scientific visualization and information visualization creates graphical models on the KDD process. More than offering resources for interactive visual exploration of databases, visual mapping techniques are presently being used to enhance user interpretation of mining errands and furthermore as an integrated some portion of expository DM calculations. Many mining techniques require user intervention at different stages and representation is beginning to be used to bolster the decision processes involved in making such interventions.

In [18], Moe has proposed an empirical two-stage choice model with the varying decision rules of the clickstream data. The author proposes and applies an empirical two-stage choice model to Internet clickstream information that captures observed choices for two choice stages: items viewed and items purchased. The model takes into account interdependences between choices inside a stage and the use of changing decision rules in each stage. The author accommodates heterogeneity in preferences and in decision rules. The proposed model uses observed choices to infer both attribute preference evaluations and criterion attributes, examinations and criterion attributes.

In [19], the authors proposed a practical methodology for the prediction of demographic web site guest profiles that can be used for web advertising targeting purposes. The methodology involves the change of web site guests' clickstream patterns to a set of features and the preparation of Random Forest classifiers that generate predictions for gender, age, educational level and occupation category. These demographic predictions can bolster online advertisement targeting (i) as an extra contribution to personalized advertising or behavioral targeting, in order to restrict promotion targeting to demographically defined target gatherings, or (ii) as a contribution for aggregated demographic web site guest profiles that bolster marketing managers in selecting web sites and achieving an ideal correspondence between target gatherings and web site audience piece.

In [20], the authors employed a big data approach to discover the user interests in e-commerce. The authors of [21] also employed similar approach to extract customer shopping types from online sites. In [22], the authors introduced VisMOOC, a visual analytic system to help analyse user learning behaviours by using video clickstream data from Massive Open Online Courses (MOOC) platforms. They work closely with the instructors of two Coursera courses to understand the data and collect task analysis requirements. In [23], the authors applied some standard algorithms to CFA prediction in this setting, and showed how one type of behavioural data collected about students – video-watching clickstream events – can be used as learning features to improve prediction quality. This can be taken as motivation for the future researches of clickstream data. Though there have been various techniques been utilized successfully for data analysis, most techniques relied on standard Markov chain. As stated earlier, the drawbacks in standard Markov chain reduces visualization quality and hence this research model focuses on eliminating them.

3 Improved Markov Chain Modelling

The shortcomings of standard Markov chain [24] for the website clickstream data visualization led to the development of the Improved Markov chain. This improved version overcomes the occlusion and display problems by heuristic determination of the grid spacing distributions. The Kolmogorov– Smirnov distance and maximum likelihood estimator are used between the underlying distribution states to minimize the Markov distribution. Considering the probability space $(\Omega, \mathbb{F}, \mathbb{P})$, equipped with a filtration $\mathbb{F} = \{\mathcal{F}(t): t \geq 0\}$. Let the continuous stochastic process $X(t) = \{X_t, t \geq 0\}$ be the solution of the univariate jump-diffusion process

$$dX_t = \mu(X_t;\vartheta)dt + \sigma(X_t;\vartheta)dW_t + \int_{\zeta(X_t)} \eta(X_t, v;\vartheta)P(X_t, dt, dv;\vartheta) \quad (1)$$

with an preliminary value $X_0 = x_0$, where ϑ denotes the unknown parameter set; $\mu(.)$ and $\sigma(.)$ define the drift and diffusion functions; W_t is the Wiener process; $P(.)$ represents a Poisson random measure with intensity $\mu(X_t;\vartheta)$. Given a mark set ζ, the jump coefficient η has a mark density $\phi\zeta(v, X_t)$.

For a continuous time Markov chain with a finite support, the grid elements are assumed to be monotonically increasing. Let h denotes the grid spacing between two adjacent grid elements on a n grid points Markov chain while I be the unit matrix.. Define a n×n rate generator matrix by $Q = (q_{i,j}: i \neq j)$, with the rate elements $q_{i,j}$ subject to the conditions: $q_{i,i} \leq 0$, $q_{i,j} \geq 0$ and $\sum_j q_{i,j} = 0$. The transition probability from state x_i^h to x_j^h in time t, for a homogeneous continuous time Markov chain, is obtained by

$$P(t) = \left(p_{i,j}(t)\right) = e^{tQ} = \sum_{k=0}^{\infty} \frac{(tQ)^k}{k!} =$$

$$I + \textstyle\sum_{k=1}^{\infty} \frac{(tQ)^k}{k!} \quad (2)$$

For the jump-diffusion in Eqn.(1), because of the freedom of the continuous parts from the hop parts, we can compose the comparing rate generator network Q as $Q = Q^c + Q^j$. Q^c and Q^j signify the generator framework that approximates the continuous part $\mu(.)dt + \sigma(.)dWt$ and jump part $\int_\zeta \eta(.)P(.)$ individually. Since in continuous time, a stochastic differential condition is completely portrayed by its mean and fluctuation, a very much characterized Q-rate network will coordinate the chain's first and second prompt minutes to those of the fundamental procedure. The approximation for Q^c matrix for univariate diffusion and the rate elements are given by

$$q_{i,i-1} = \frac{1}{2h^2}\sigma^2(x_i^h) + \frac{1}{h}\mu^-(x_i^h), q_{i,i=} - \frac{1}{h^2}\sigma^2(x_i^h) - \frac{1}{h}|\mu(x_i^h)|,$$

$$q_{i,i+1} = \tfrac{1}{2h^2}\sigma^2(x_i^h) + \tfrac{1}{h}\mu^+(x_i^h) \; q_{i,j=}0 \; \forall j \neq i, i-1, i+1 \quad (3)$$

where the ± denotes the respective absolute value. However, when the grid spacing is too coarse, the proposed rate matrix formula exhibits an approximation error of $h|\mu(x_i^h)|$ in matching the second moment. Hence the corrected formula is presented to address this error

$$q_{i,i-1} = \frac{1}{2h^2}\sigma^2(x_i^h) - \frac{1}{2h}\mu(x_i^h), q_{i,i=} - \frac{1}{h^2}\sigma^2(x_i^h),$$

$$q_{i,i+1} = \tfrac{1}{2h^2}\sigma^2(x_i^h) + \tfrac{1}{2h}\mu(x_i^h) \quad (4)$$

subject to the necessary condition of

$$h < \frac{\sigma^2(x_i^h)}{|\mu(x_i^h)|} \quad (5)$$

Considering the empirical distribution of the data, the generalized Q^c formula is needed to accommodate a non-equidistant grid setting while satisfying the local consistency condition. For a n-state non-equidistant Markov chain with n −1 associated grid spacing of h, the Q^c is given by

$$q_{i,i-1} = \frac{1}{h_i}\mu^+(x_i^h) + \frac{\sigma^2(x_i^h) - \left(h_{i-1} \times \mu^-(x_i^h) + h_i \times \mu^+(x_i^h)\right)}{h_{i-1}(h_{i-1} + h_i)},$$

$$q_{i,i} = -q_{i,i-1} - q_{i,i+1}$$

$$q_{i,i+1} = \frac{1}{h_i}\mu^+(x_i^h) + \frac{\sigma^2(x_i^h) - (h_{i-1} \times \mu^-(x_i^h) + h_i \times \mu^+(x_i^h))}{h_i(h_{i-1} + h_i)}$$

$$q_{i,j=}0\ \forall j \neq i, i-1, i+1 \qquad (6)$$

The following condition is needed to be satisfied for a well-defined probability matrix to be guaranteed.

$$sup\ (h) \leq \frac{\sigma^2(x_i^h)}{|\mu(x_i^h)|} \qquad (7)$$

Then the jump part is approximated, in which the matrix elements for the jump-diffusion generator matrix are given by

$$q_{i,j} = \lambda(x_i)\phi_\zeta(x_i; \zeta(x_i) \cap (x_j - x_i - h_{i-1}/2, x_j - x_i + h_{i+1}/2]), \quad for\ j \neq 1, i, n,$$

$$q_{i,j} = \lambda(x_i)\phi_\zeta(x_i; \zeta(x_i) \cap (-\infty, x_1 + h_1/2]),$$

$$q_{i,j} = \lambda(x_i)\phi_\zeta(x_i; \zeta(x_i) \cap (x_n - h_{n-1}/2, \infty)),$$

$$q_{i,i} = -\sum_{j \neq i} q_{j,i.} \qquad (8)$$

This setting can have a state-subordinate jump force and a jump distribution, which considers a conduct back translation, is hard to fuse with conventional numerical strategies. The execution of a model will be touchy to matrix separating and the lower and upper limits of the lattice. The benefits of the non-equidistant (non-uniform) lattice have been recorded in the exploration territory of finite difference methodology (FDM) and partial differential equations (PDE).

The improved model acquaints a heuristic approach with examining the matrix components for a n-states Markov chain, to such an extent that the Kolmogorov–Smirnov distance between the first distribution function G(X) and the Markov distribution function $\tilde{G}(X^h)$ is limited. In such a case, we show that a non-equidistant Markov model can accomplish more elevated amount of exactness than an equidistant Markov display. The subsequent network x^h as for the Kolmogorov–Smirnov distance is given by

$$x_i^h = G^{-1}(\frac{2i-1}{2n}) \qquad (9)$$

A repercussion of the Markov chain move likelihood network is the semi-explanatory log-likelihood function, which can be utilized to align the parameters of a jump-dispersion. The maximum likelihood estimator (MLE) of Improved Markov chain is characterized by

$$\hat{\vartheta}MCA := arg\ max\mathcal{L}(\vartheta), \qquad (10)$$

where $\mathcal{L}(\vartheta)$ is the log-likelihood. Given m discretely checked time arrangement data $x_{t1}, x_{t2}, \ldots x_{tm}$, the log-likelihood value produced by a period homogeneous transition probability matrix is given by

$$\mathcal{L}(\vartheta) = \sum_{i=1}^{m-1} ln\left(e'(t_i)P(t_{i+1} - t_i)e(t_{i+1})\right) \qquad (11)$$

This principle of the improved Markov chain model can significantly enhance the visualization performance.

4 WebClickviz Visualization Methology

4.1 Tool and Data

The analysis of the website clickstream data has been carried out worldwide using many tools. Google analytics is one of the famous tools which have the basic functionality of clickstream data visualization. In this paper, Apache Flume is utilized to load, analyse the clickstream data and visualize it. Apache Flume is a distributed, reliable, and available service for productively gathering, aggregating, and moving a lot of streaming data into the Hadoop Distributed File System (HDFS). It has a straightforward and adaptable engineering in light of streaming data streams; and is robust and fault tolerant with tunable dependability instruments for failover and recuperation. Apache flume ingests the streaming data from multiple sources into the Hadoop storage and analysis and then insulates the buffer storage.

Flume utilizes channel-based transactions to ensure reliable message delivery. At the point when a message moves starting with one operator then onto the next, two transactions are begun, one on the specialist that conveys the occasion and the other on the specialist that gets the occasion. This guarantees ensured delivery semantics. The data used to load Apache Flume is the data that describes the page visits of users who visited msnbc.com [25]. Visits are recorded at the level of URL

DOI: 10.1051/matecconf/201712504025

category and are recorded in time order. The data comes from Internet Information Server (IIS) logs for msnbc.com and news-related portions of msn.com for an entire day. The categories are "frontpage", "news", "tech", "local", "opinion", "on-air", "misc", "weather", "health", "living", "business", "sports", "summary", "bbs" (bulletin board service), "travel", "msn-news", and "msn-sports". A total of 989818 users have been recorded with average visits of 5.7 per user. Fig.1 shows the sample view from the input data collected from msnbc.com.

Fig.1. Input data

4.2 Loading Data

Each sequence in the dataset corresponds to page views of a user during that twenty-four hour period. Each event in the sequence corresponds to a user's request for a page. Requests are not recorded at the finest level of detail--that is, at the level of URL, but rather, they are recorded at the level of page category (as determined by a site administrator). Fig.2a & 2b shows how the data are loaded into Apache flume.

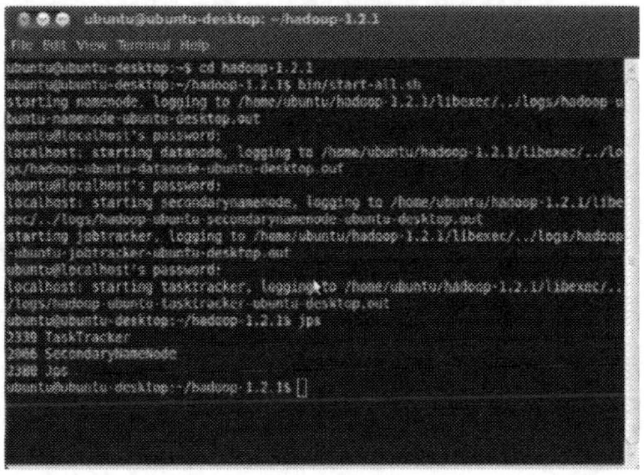

Fig.2a

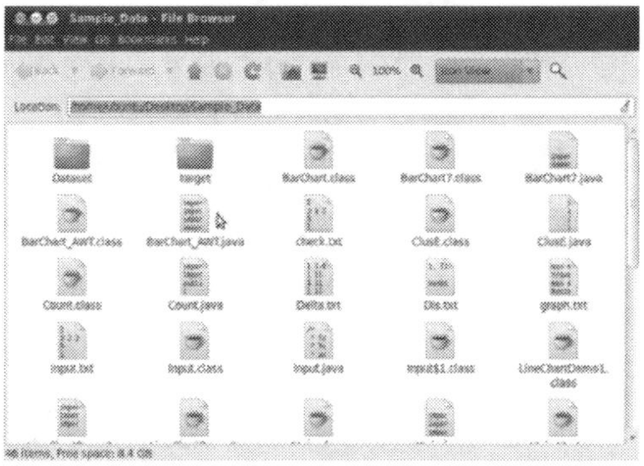

Fig.2b

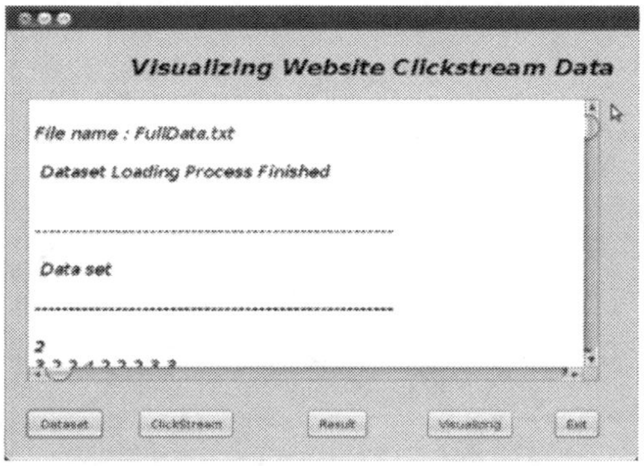

Fig.3. View Loaded data

Fig.3 shows the loaded data while the Fig.4 shows the aggregated data. The data is loaded by means of loaddata() command which asks for the folder location of the data. When given, the data is loaded into the tool and can be viewed.

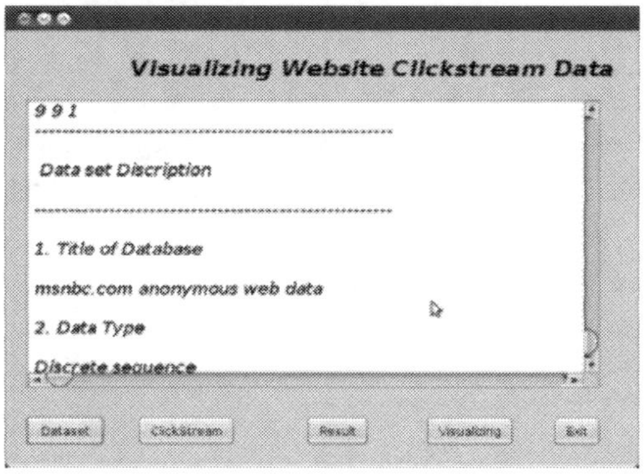

Fig.4. Aggregation of CRM data

Any page requests served via a caching mechanism were not recorded in the server logs and, hence, not present in the data. Fig.5 shows the visualized categories.

The clickstream process is executed once the data are loaded. This includes the aggregation and categorization view.

An implementation of Flume's RpcClient interface encapsulates the RPC mechanism supported by Flume. The user's application can simply call the Flume Client SDK's append(Event) or appendBatch(List<Event>) to send data and not worry about the underlying message exchange details.

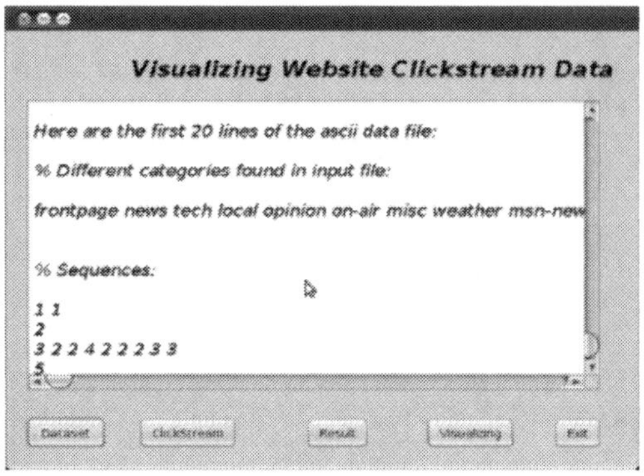

Fig.5. Categories of msmbc.com data

The user can provide the required Event arg by either directly implementing the Event interface, by using a convenience implementation such as the SimpleEvent class, or by using EventBuilder's overloaded withBody() static helper methods.

Data visualization helps to optimize the website and improve the business sales and values. Fig.6a & 6b shows the Visualized results. It can be seen that the categorization is accurately completed and the visits of the users are recorded as shown.

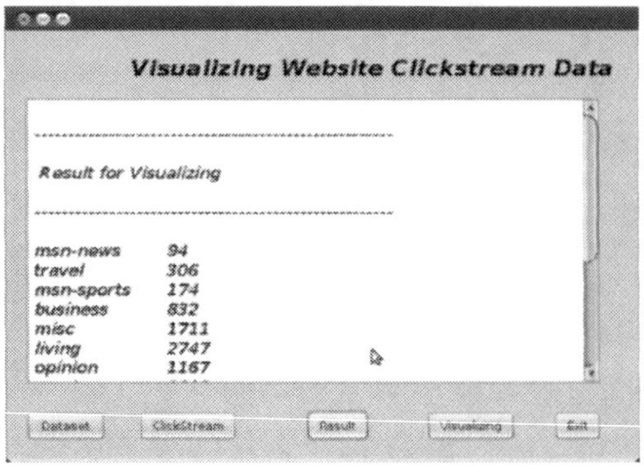

Fig.6a. Visualization Result 1

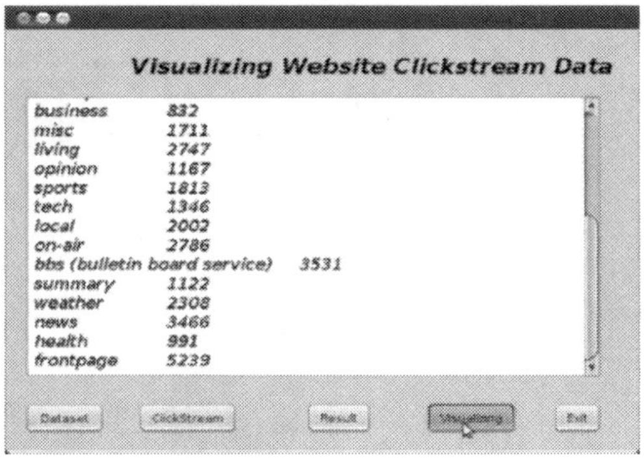

Fig.6b. Visualization Result 2

4.3 Geographic Representation

The visualization is complete only when the data are visualized either in graphical or association representation. Fig.7a shows the global representation of the clickstream data while Fig.7b shows the graphical representation in USA specifically.

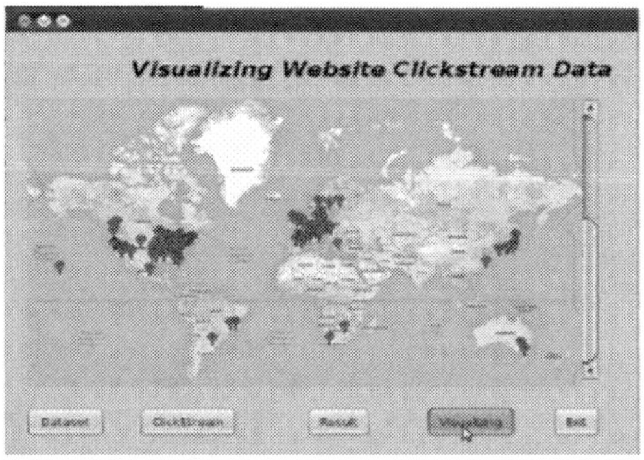

Fig.7a. Geographical Visualization 1

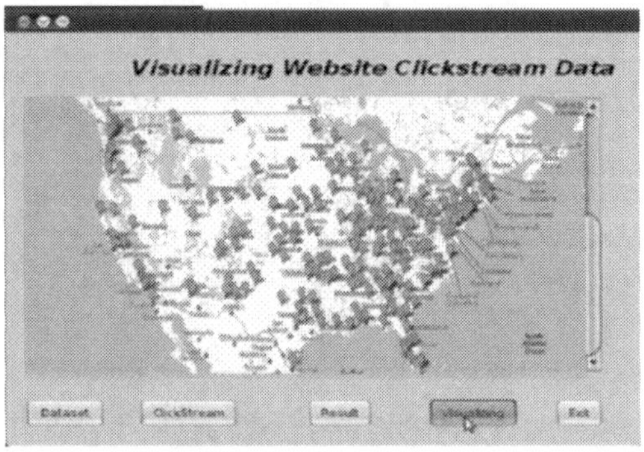

Fig.7b. Geographical Visualization 2

DOI: 10.1051/matecconf/201712504025

5 Visualization Performances

The performance of the WebClickviz is visualized in the charts given below. The charts are generated for the sample set of the msnbc.com website clickstream data.

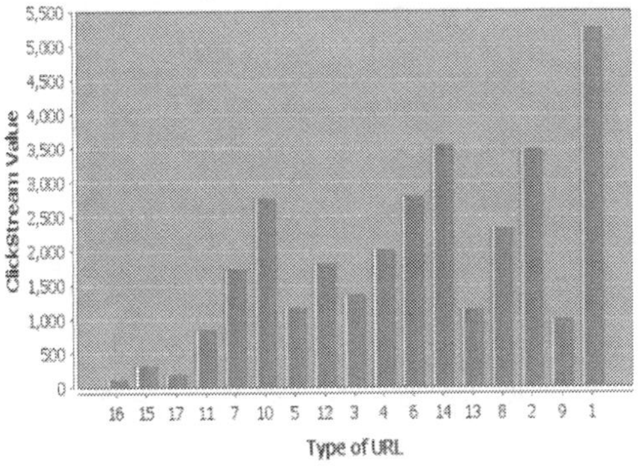

Fig.8. Clickstream value vs. type of URL

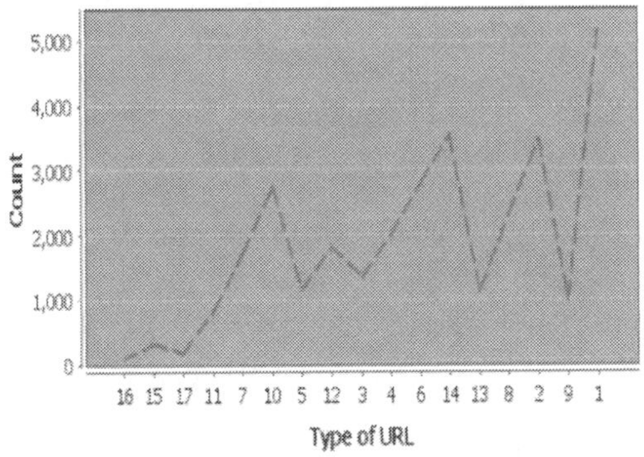

Fig.9. Count vs. type of URL

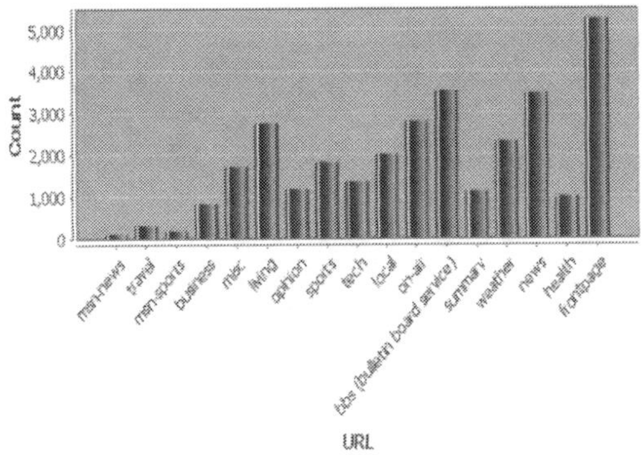

Fig.10. Count vs. URL specified

From the figures 8, 9 & 10, it can be seen that the charts clearly indicate the performance of the proposed model in visualization of clickstream data. As the visualization is highly improved in Hadoop Apache Flume, this work can serve as the initial step in making sense out of large web analytics data.

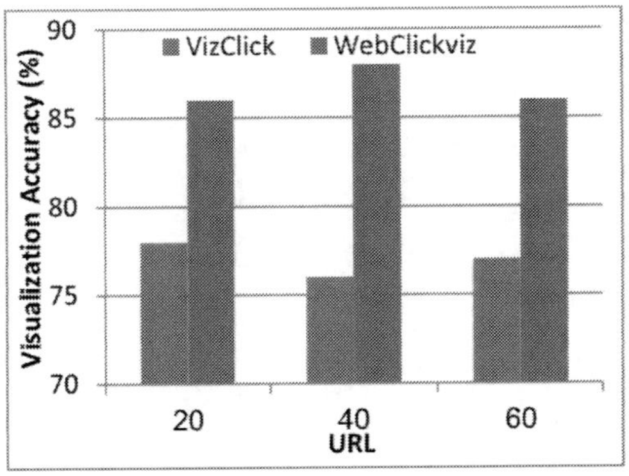

Fig.11. Visualization Accuracy

Fig.11 shows the comparison of visualization accuracy of existing VizClick versus the proposed WebClickViz. It is seen that the accuracy is higher in the proposed model at all counts of urls. The fundamental reason for existing was to examine measurable methodologies on clickstream information, as the accumulated arrangement of site visit demands executed by a specific client, and other client route components, can give understanding into their expectations, particularly as for purchase engagement and real-time purchase likelihood prediction. This can enhance the web analytics techniques by employing different strategies.

6 Conclusions

As stated in this article, these results are very encouraging as new methods of targeting customers could be derived from this solution. The proposed model consisting of the Improved Markov chain based visualization (WebClickviz) improves the web analytics by providing accurate visualization of the website clickstream data. This article suggested the method of interactive visualization in order to utilize these results in the analysis of data for different applications. In the field of clickstream data research is still in its earliest stages, much research still should be finished. With the rebellion of new and speedier innovation, the idea of big data is exceptionally hot right now, particularly on the grounds that companies can, more than ever, make an interpretation of customer data into higher revenue. In the future researches, it will be analysed how to utilize these results for different applications. Likewise the use of new learning algorithms to fit clickstream data, namely, by introducing other models such as neural networks, support vector machines [26], genetic algorithms, etc will be investigated.

REFERENCES

1. Farney, T. A. Click analytics: Visualizing website use data. Information Technology and Libraries, **30**(3), 141, (2011)
2. Kimball, R., & Merz, R. The data webhouse toolkit. Wiley (2000).
3. Phippen, A., Sheppard, L., & Furnell, S. (2004). A practical evaluation of Web analytics. Internet Research, **14**(4), 284-293.
4. Gonçalves, B., & Ramasco, J. J. (2008). Human dynamics revealed through Web analytics. Physical Review E, 78(2), 026123.
5. Plaza, B. Monitoring web traffic source effectiveness with Google Analytics: An experiment with time series. In Aslib Proceedings (Vol. **61**, No. 5, pp. 474-482), (2009). Emerald Group Publishing Limited.
6. Kohavi, R., Rothleder, N. J., & Simoudis, E. Emerging trends in business analytics. Communications of the ACM, **45**(8), 45-48, (2002).
7. Hasan, L., Morris, A., & Probets, S. Using Google Analytics to evaluate the usability of e-commerce sites. Human centered design, 697-706, (2009).
8. Kohavi, R., Mason, L., Parekh, R., & Zheng, Z. Lessons and challenges from mining retail e-commerce data. Machine Learning, **57**(1), 83-113, (2004).
9. White, T. Hadoop: The definitive guide. "O'Reilly Media, Inc.", (2012).
10. Flanagan, D. JavaScript: the definitive guide. "O'Reilly Media, Inc.", (2006).
11. Bucklin, R. E., & Sismeiro, C. Click here for Internet insight: Advances in clickstream data analysis in marketing. Journal of Interactive Marketing, **23**(1), 35-48, (2009).
12. Montgomery, A. L., Li, S., Srinivasan, K., & Liechty, J. C. Modeling online browsing and path analysis using clickstream data. Marketing science, **23**(4), 579-595, (2004).
13. Moe, W. W., & Fader, P. S. Capturing evolving visit behavior in clickstream data. Journal of Interactive Marketing, **18**(1), 5-19, (2004).
14. Van den Poel, D., & Buckinx, W. Predicting online-purchasing behaviour. European journal of operational research, **166**(2), 557-575, (2005).
15. Danaher, P. J., Mullarkey, G. W., & Essegaier, S. Factors affecting web site visit duration: a cross-domain analysis. Journal of Marketing Research, **43**(2), 182-194, (2006).
16. Kateja, R., Rohith, A., Kumar, P., & Sinha, R. VizClick visualizing clickstream data. In Information Visualization Theory and Applications (IVAPP), 2014 International Conference on (pp. 247-255). IEEE, (2014).
17. De Oliveira, M. F., & Levkowitz, H. From visual data exploration to visual data mining: a survey. IEEE Transactions on Visualization and Computer Graphics, **9**(3), 378-394, (2003).
18. Moe, W. W. An empirical two-stage choice model with varying decision rules applied to internet clickstream data. Journal of Marketing Research, **43**(4), 680-692, (2006).
19. De Bock, K., & Van den Poel, D. Predicting website audience demographics forweb advertising targeting using multi-website clickstream data. Fundamenta Informaticae, **98**(1), 49-70, (2010).
20. Chen, L., & Su, Q. Discovering user's interest at E-commerce site using clickstream data. In Service systems and service management (ICSSSM), 2013 10th international conference on (pp. 124-129). IEEE, (2013).
21. Schellong, D., Kemper, J., & Brettel, M. Clickstream data as a source to uncover con-sumer shopping types in a large-scale online setting, (2016).
22. Shi, C., Fu, S., Chen, Q., & Qu, H. VisMOOC: Visualizing video clickstream data from massive open online courses. In Visualization Symposium (PacificVis), 2015 IEEE Pacific (pp. 159-166). IEEE, (2015).
23. Brinton, C. G., & Chiang, M. Mooc performance prediction via clickstream data and social learning networks. In Computer Communications (INFOCOM), 2015 IEEE Conference on (pp. 2299-2307). IEEE, (2015).
24. Gilks, W. R., Richardson, S., & Spiegelhalter, D. (Eds.), Markov chain Monte Carlo in practice. CRC press, (1995).
25. http://www.msnbc.com
26. Steinwart, I., & Christmann, A. Support vector machines. Springer Science & Business Media, (2008).

MATEC Web of Conferences **125**, 04026 (2017)
CSCC 2017
DOI: 10.1051/matecconf/201712504026

Deployment of SIP in MANET: challenges and circumvention

Salma R. Abdelhamid[1,2], *Hossam-Eldeen* M. Shamardan[2], and *Atef* Z. Ghalwash[2]

[1]Faculty of Computers and Information Technology, Future University in Egypt, Cairo, Egypt
[2]Faculty of Computers and Information, Helwan University, Cairo, Egypt

Abstract. The immense growth in wireless network applications has encouraged the researchers to enhance and propose new approaches that facilitate the deployment of the widely used services, protocols, and applications of the wired networking area in the wireless networks. Among which, the Session Initiation Protocol (SIP) is a signaling protocol that allows the establishment of multimedia sessions and calls between different parties. SIP functionality totally depends on a centralized infrastructure, and complexity arises when deploying such a protocol in a special type of wireless networks, namely Mobile Ad-hoc Networks (MANET), due to the absence of a centralized infrastructure, and the dynamic topology of the later. This paper highlights the the challenges arising when deploying SIP in MANETs and presents an overview of different proposed approaches to overcome these challenges.

1 Introduction

The field of wireless networks has experienced an unprecedented growth during the past decades. The internet and Internet Technology (IT) devices such as laptops, Personal Digital Assistant (PDA), Internet Routers, and Smart Mobile phones play a vital role nowadays for a huge portion of persons. The presence of such a fast rate development of the used wireless networking technologies has persuaded the researchers to focus on an important type of networks, which is the MANET. The MANET is widely used over the globe due to the low cost of deployment and the flexibility of the network [1]. A MANET consists of a group of wireless mobile nodes (MNs) such as laptops, mobile devices, and PDAs connected together through wireless links. Unlike the traditional infra-structured wireless networks which mainly depend on centralized routers and fixed access points, MANETs are formed spontaneously and are mainly characterized with the absence of a centralized infrastructure [2]. In addition to that, the topology of the network faces rapid and frequent changes due to the mobility of the nodes, or sometimes their failures. These MNs of the MANET are self-organized and self-configured devices, and are able to communicate together despite this absence of an underlying structure or a centralized administrative support [3,4].

This de-centralized infrastructure-less attribute, directed the researchers towards proposing new approaches and modifications that facilitate the use of the world wide wired networks applications and protocols, one of which is the Voice over Internet Protocol (VoIP). The VoIP can be used to establish video or voice calls over the internet, taking over the role of the usual Public Switched Telephone Network (PSTN) [5]. When it comes to telephone communications, VoIP has proven to revolutionize this field, as one of its major advantages is saving end users from highly charged international calls. [6,7]. VoIP also provides additional features such as free long-distanced calls, determining caller ID, blocking certain callers or video-conferencing. However, the use of VoIP applications requires the establishment of a session between end users and for such establishment; the Session Initiation Protocol (SIP) is considered as a key element.

The Session Initiation Protocol (SIP) is a signaling protocol that is used to control multimedia communication sessions such as initiating, modifying, or terminating and interactive session. In other words, it is a signaling protocol that enables one party to call another party and to negotiate the parameters of a multimedia session. SIP is totally built upon a centralized infrastructure including

 DOI: 10.1051/matecconf/201712504026

different entities such as Proxies and Registrars, typically owned by the network operator. Due to this major contradiction between the decentralized architecture of ad-hoc networks and the SIP, the later cannot be directly deployed into MANETs. And it is an undeniable fact that SIP multimedia services over MANETs can be indisputably exploited in different business areas, the thing that highlighted the exploration of its deployment in MANETs and different approaches were proposed [8]. This paper presents an overview of different approaches used for signaling SIP over MANET.

The rest of the paper is organized as follows. Section 2 presents an overview of the SIP, along with its entities and functionalities. MANET is briefly discussed in section 3, highlighting some of the routing protocols concepts. Section 4 wraps up the problem of deploying SIP in MANET. A literature review is presented in Section 5. Finally, the overall conclusion is summarized in Section 6.

2 SIP overview

Standardized by the Internet Engineering Task Force (IETF), SIP is a text-based and HTTP-like application-layer signaling protocol that is used for controlling multimedia communication sessions between end users [9]. It is independent on the underlying transport layer and is the most widely used protocol in wired networks IP-telephony. SIP is responsible of determining user location, confirming or denying user availability, and establishing and managing the sessions between users. These functions are totally dependent on a centralized architecture including Proxies and Registrars, typically owned by the network operator.

2.1 SIP architecture

SIP relies in its operation on a centralized architecture. Each entity is in charge of a certain function and means of communications between the entities are provided. The entities of SIP are divided into two main components, user agents and SIP servers [10].

2.1.1 SIP user agents

The SIP user agents are the end points in the network. They could be phones, gateways, or various types of computers. These end points exchange SIP messages and thereby manage a SIP session. The user agent can be a client, and thereby called User Agent Client (UAC) or can be a User Agent Server (UAS). The UAC initiates the session establishment requests and generates requests, such as REGISTER, INVITE, CANCEL, ACK, or BYE, whilst the UAS receives SIP requests and send SIP responses. [10].

2.1.2 SIP servers

SIP has four main servers, Proxy Servers, Registrars, Location Servers and Redirect servers [11]. Proxy servers are SIP intermediate entities. Depending on the dataflow; it could act both as a server and a client. Upon receiving the SIP request, the proxy server is responsible of selecting the best possible route to the desired UAS and forwarding the request to it. If the proxy server did not find the location of the targeted destination in its domain, it shall forward it to the responsible proxy server. It is also responsible for assuring the authentication of the end user and whether it is allowed to make a call or not. SIP Registrars are the servers at which SIP users should first register themselves. The users should provide their addresses, transport parameters, and their capabilities. Location Servers are the serves used by the registrars to store the locations of the registered users. And as obvious from their names, Redirect Servers are responsible of redirecting SIP users to another entity allowing them to connect to different set of addresses.

2.2 SIP functionality

The main role of SIP almost ends with the session establishment between the end users, and the actual data flow is directly carried out between the end users using the underlying transport layer, whether Transmission Control Protocol (TCP), or User Datagram Protocol (UDP). To identify SIP users, each of them is given a SIP address-of-record (AOR) Uniform Resource Identifier (URI). This address can be resolved at SIP proxy that is responsible for the users' domain. Each user is supposed to register its address, using the SIP method REGISTER, at the SIP registrar in his domain, and thus allowing the identification of this user's actual location in terms of IP addresses [12].

The nodes of the networks exchange different SIP messages, either requests or responses. When a node wants to initiate a connection, it sends an initiation request INVITE to its local proxy server without knowing the exact location of the called party. The proxy will determine the route to be taken to the callee after consulting the registrar and location server. The INVITE request is then forwarded by the proxy, and possibly through other number of proxies, until it gets to its destination. The callee could either accept or reject the incoming call. If accepted, the session initiation is then finalized by having the caller acknowledging the reception of the callees answer [10, 12]. After finalizing the session establishment, and as mentioned earlier, the data exchange between the two parties takes place without the involving of SIP proxy, and using the agreed upon transport protocol. Figure (1) illustrates a simple voice connection using SIP. The two involved end users are in different domains and have different proxies.

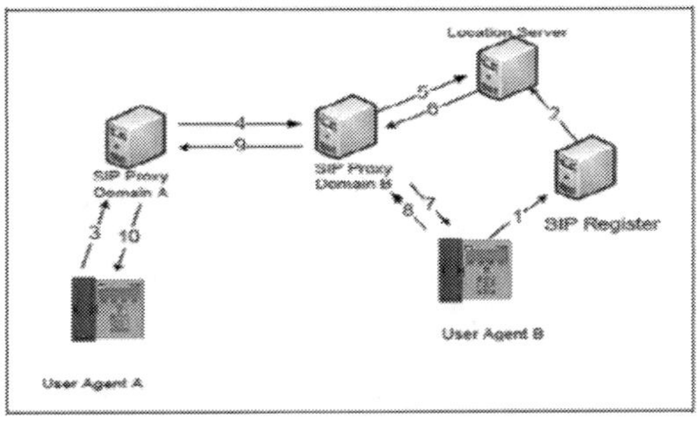

Fig. 1, Setting up a voice call using SIP [13]

The numbered steps are explained as follows [13]:

(1) User Agent "B" registers itself at its local SIP registrar.
(2) The Registrar stores the location at the location server.
(3) User Agent "A" sends an INVITE request to its local Proxy.
(4) The Proxy of user A translates the destination address domain and forwards the request to the proxy of user B domain.
(5) Proxy in Domain B looks up the address of user B in the location server.
(6) The Location server replies with the required IP-Address.
(7) Proxy in Domain B sends the request to the desired user agent.
(8-10) The response message from A to B takes the reverse route back and then after finalizing the session establishment the media content is to be exchanged directly between the end points.

3 MANET overview

The MANET is a collection of two or more devices or nodes or terminals with wireless communications and networking capability that communicate with each other without the aid of any centralized administrator [14].

3.1 MANET characteristics

Unlike traditional wireless networks, the nodes of a MANET do not have fixed locations, instead, they move from one position to another causing an unpredicted dynamic change in the topology of the network. Also besides the nodes mobility within the network, MANET nodes can anytime leave the network completely due to their movement or failure. In addition to that, one of the challenges that exist in MANET is the limitation of the available bandwidth. The MANET nodes do not have the privilege of transmitting within a large bandwidth as the devices in the wired networks. Moreover, the fading of the signal, noise effect and signal interference degrade the wireless link capacities [3, 14].

3.2 MANET routing protocols

As a result of the challenging MANET characteristics, the protocols designed for centralized wired or wireless networks cannot be directly applied to MANET. The end users of ad-hoc networks compensate the decentralized infrastructure-less architecture by relying on each other in routing. Each node contributes in routes discovery, and data sending from the source to the desired destination usually relies on multiple hops.

MANET routing protocols take into consideration the dynamic topology of the network, as well as the absence of a fixed network infrastructure [15-17]. And for the protocol to be effective, lots of operations and properties should be supported, amongst which are reactive and demand based operations, distributed operations, multiple routes providence, security measures and looping avoidance [16-18]. A lot of classifications exist for Ad-hoc networks Routing Protocols [18]. The most common classification is based upon how routing information is acquired and maintained by the nodes of the network. Accordingly, the Ad-hoc routing protocols can be divided into three types: Proactive, Reactive, and Hybrid routing protocols [4, 2, 15, 16, 19].

3.2.1 Proactive (Table-Driven) routing protocols

In this type of protocols, each node maintains the routes to all possible reachable destinations of the network in its routing table, and these tables are periodically updated by propagating update messages with the help of a sequence number created by the destination to disseminate fresh routes in case any change in the network topology occurred. The node should keep up-to-date routing information so that the packet is directly forwarded when required to the destination. The routing protocols based on this methodology differ in the way nodes update the topology change of the network and the routing information maintained in the routing tables.

However, this type of protocols does not perform effectively in highly dynamic networks as for each topology change; the MNs are obliged to update their routing tables causing an increase in the control message overheads thus leading to an overall network performance degradation [4]. Examples of this protocol are Destination sequence Distance Vector (DSDV) [14, 20, 21], Wireless Routing Protocol (WRP) [22, 14] and Clusterhead Gateway Switch Routing [14, 18, 23].

3.2.2 Reactive (On-Demand) routing protocols

In the reactive routing protocols, the routes to the destinations are not gathered a priori. The route discovery process takes place only when a node "demands" the route to a certain destination. When a node wants to send a packet to a certain destination, it applies the route discovery mechanism which mainly depends on the idea of flooding the network with route query requests to this destination [4]. The determined route remains valid until the destination is reached or any link breakage occurs in it. The drawback of the reactive protocols is the delay caused during the route discovery process which makes it inconvenient for time sensitive applications. An example of this protocol is the Ad hoc On-demand Distance Vector Routing (AODV) [16, 24, 25].

3.2.3 Hybrid routing protocols

The hybrid protocol is a merge between both proactive and reactive protocols. The routing is initially established using the proactive approach, and then the route requests from additionally added nodes are provided using the reactive approach. This approach tends to reduce the overhead of the proactive protocols as well as the time delay of the reactive protocols [4]. An example to such protocol is the Zone Routing Protocol (ZRP) [15, 26].

4 Problem definition

Ad-hoc networks have a great advantage of designing flexible networks. However, as mentioned earlier, the mobility of the nodes and the lack of a centralized infrastructure remains a challenging constraint in some research areas. Due to such constraints, the nodes are not familiar with the topology of their networks. Instead, they have to enter a discovery phase first. When joining the network, each node should be able to announce itself and discover neighboring nodes to be able to send its data to the required destination. Afterwards, Routes should be discovered and transmission takes place using cooperative multi-hops between source and destination. Another key problem with ad-hoc networks is that their dynamic un-centralized architecture makes it difficult to implement any form of communication requiring sessions instead of the best-effort dissemination of independent packets from and to multiple nodes.

SIP on the controversy to Ad-hoc networks requires centralized entities, such as the Proxy server, the Registrar or the Location Server. Each one of SIP servers has its own specific role in setting up the connection and defining the routes between sources and destinations. This centralized SIP architecture is obviously not straightforwardly applicable to ad-hoc networks. As mentioned, ad-hoc networks are wireless dynamic networks formed by peer nodes while SIP proxies and registrars are static, fixed, and centralized entities. SIP users in MANETs cannot reach other parties, as they do not have support from proxy servers. Moreover, they cannot be reached by other nodes, as there are no SIP registrars where they can register their contact information. Nevertheless, the Quality of Service (QoS) metrics of VoIP such as bandwidth consumption, delays, jitters, packets loss, and signaling are severely degraded as the traffic and number of multiple hops to the gateway increase. Consequently, several problems arise when directly deploying SIP services in ad-hoc networks, and altering the SIP main centralized architecture should first take place.

5 Deployment of SIP in MANET

This section presents an overview of some of the existing literature on researches addressing SIP signaling over MANET.

The main idea proposed by Leggio et al. in [27] is to decentralize SIP to be able to deploy it in MANETs. Decentralizing was fulfilled by embedding a limited set of SIP server functionalities into SIP user agents. Thus, the support originally provided by centralized SIP entities is merged in all end users in the ad-hoc networks, and each node carries out the required function in order to establish the session.

The authors present two methods to discover the users' AOR and thus allow session establishment. Those two methods are Fully Distributed SIP (dSIP) and SIP with Service Location Framework (sSIP). dSIP is to dispense the need of centralized SIP entities, but rely on SIP methods to acquire user contact information. When a broadcasted REGISTER message is received, it is stored in the local cache of the node, and when an INVITE message is received, the local proxy modules plays the role of binding between the specified address and SIP AOR. sSIP on the other hand depends on Service Location Protocol (SLP) [28]. In such a case, each node receiving the broadcasted SLP request replies back with SLP reply including its binding. Scalability is not an advantage of this approach due to the message broadcasting which leads to bandwidth consumption and flooding in large MANETs.

Stuedi et al. [29] handled the setup and management of the sessions in MANETs using SIPHoc, a middleware infrastructure. SIPHoc is completely decentralized, which eliminated the need of centralized components, or assigning special functionalities to some elected nodes of the network. Independent on the underlying network topology, SIPHoc supports mobile and static ad hoc networks, and it does not require any modifications in the existing applications. Moreover, this approach is based upon MANET SLP for registration and look-up operations which works by piggybacking techniques that provides an efficient messaging system.

L. Chang et al. in [30] embedded a server in the transport layer of each MN called pseudo Session Initiation Protocol (p-SIP) server. This server is meant to provide VoIP services over ad-hoc networks. The p-SIP includes the user discovery module, the session management module, the user-list cache, the SIP presence module, and moreover, the problem of the nodes mobility is resolved by means of an additional introduced mobility management module that allows each node to maintain the intended SIP information. The ad-hoc discovery mechanisms are handled via standard SIP protocol. The implementation of p-SIP is done on real devices, and the performance measurements prove the feasibility to realize the VoIP services over ad-hoc using the designed p-SIP server.

H. Chu and W. Chen proposed in [31] an integrated middleware to play the role of SIP servers and takes over their responsibilities and functions. The client registration step is to take place at this middleware instead of SIP servers. The used underlying routing protocol is AODV, which delivers the exchanged SIP messages. The authors refined the registration process by forcing the middleware to act as a registrar server, thus locally binding the IP address with the AOR. The process of forwarding the SIP messages which is supposed to be performed by the SIP proxy server is also carried out by the proposed middleware. The goal of this approach was enabling SIP applications in MANETs in addition to minimizing the signaling overhead in the network.

Mourtaji et al. proposed in [32] building a Virtual Network for Session Initiation Protocol (VNSIP). The main idea was to self-organize the Ad-hoc Network using a virtual backbone. The virtual network was constructed using specific nodes within the ad-hoc network. The SIP servers' functionalities are to be embedded into all nodes of the MANET, and according to a Virtual Network Algorithm (VNA); each node gets the function of a certain SIP server activated so that at the end, all SIP servers would be included in the network to accomplish the address distribution task. During the registration process and depending on whether the node is a member of the VN or not, the SIP are either locally sent to the node itself or broadcasted to all of the 1-hop neighboring nodes. This broadcasting is known as the Replication Mechanism. The replication mechanism allows searching in multiple SIP Proxies at the same time, and thus ensuring short response time. The simulations prove that the performance of VNSIP was remarkable at the session establishment time and failure tolerance, but when it comes to Bandwidth consumption; the performance is unsatisfactory. This behavior is a result of the high number of exchanged replicated SIP messages.

In order to overcome the unsatisfactory bandwidth consumption of the previously mentioned VNSIP [32], Mourtaji et al. proposed an enhancement later in [33]. The problem mainly arises because it is not possible to simultaneously accept all communications due to MANET bandwidth limitations. The proposed algorithm, MANET Call Admission Control (MCAC), is used to permit the establishment of calls to a number that agrees with the available bandwidth of the MANET, otherwise it rejects the calls by a certain SIP error code resulting in a busy tone. The decision of establishing or denying communications is based upon a specific threshold which is related to the network gateways responsible of providing connectivity to the MANET. When this threshold is exceeded, the establishment of new sessions is refused, and thus the already established communications remain undisrupted.

Almobaideen et al. presented an application layer called; Fuzzy and Cluster based SIP Protocol (FCSIP) [34]. FCSIP is independent on the underlying routing protocol and the MANET in which this protocol is applied is assumed to be clustered. The main idea of clustering is to divide the nodes of the network into virtual zones called cluster. Each cluster comprises a group leader called Cluster Head. The cluster head is responsible for managing its cluster and coordinate with other clusters in the network. Other members of each cluster are either cluster gateways which have access to neighboring clusters and are used to forward information between them or cluster members which are neither CH nor gateways [18, 35].

Aside from several used algorithms for electing the CH [36], the authors define a couple of criteria in their fuzzy algorithm, one of which resembles the VoIP activeness of this elected node. The main advantage of using an underlying cluster-based routing protocol is the significant reduction of transmitted SIP control messages, and this comes as a result of the hierarchical level represented by the CH and the members falling beneath it. The enhancement is proven by the simulation that compared FCSIP to a fully distributed version of SIP which they refer to as FDSIP.

6 Conclusion

Being a worldwide used protocol for supporting VoIP applications, the inherently centralized SIP encouraged the researchers to intentionally expand in proposing new approaches to facilitate the deployment of SIP in wireless networks. This paper presented a survey on the implementation of SIP functionality over a simultaneously formed and a decentralized wireless network such as the MANET. These implementations require a lot of adaptations and amendments. Some researchers proposed fully decentralizing the SIP functionalities while others proposed a middleware infrastructure to play the role of SIP servers. And incontestably, the future work in this field of interest is highly promising.

References

[1] L. Raja and S. Baboo , "An Overview of MANET: Applications, Attacks and Challenges", IJCSMC, **3**, 408 (2014)

[2] S. Dhenakaran and A. Parvathavarthini, "An Overview of Routing Protocols in Mobile Ad-Hoc Network", IJARCSSE, **3**, 251 (2013)
[3] D. Ahmed and O. Khalifa, "An Overview of MANETs: Applications, Characteristics, Challenges and Recent Issues", IJEAT, **3**, 128 (2017)
[4] A. Hinds, M. Ngulube, S. Zhu, H. Al-Aqrabi, "A Review of Routing Protocols for Mobile Ad-Hoc NETworks (MANET), IJIET, **3**, 223 (2013)
[5] A. Aburumman , K. R. Choo, and I. Lee, "Nomination-based Session Initiation Protocol Service for Mobile Ad Hoc Networks", ASOR, 149 (2013)
[6] L. Jallow, I. Hwang, A. Nikoukar, A. Liem, "A SIP - based VoIP Application in Enhanced Ethernet Passive Optical Network Architecture", *Proc. of IMECS*, **2** (2014)
[7] S. Kale and V. Khairnar, "SIP Implementation for Ad-hoc Network", IJCSET. **6**, 191 (2016)
[8] A. Hacha, S. Bah and Z. Bakkoury, "A New Cluster-Based Paradigm for SIP Routing in MANET", MedCT, **2**, 211 (2016)
[9] M. Handley, H. Schulzrinne, E. Schooler and J. Rosenberg, "SIP: Session Initiation Protocol", IETF, RFC 2543 (1999)
[10] P. Sheeba and C. Vandana, "New SIP-Based Application Layer Protocol for VoIP in MANET", IJERT, **4**, 733 (2015)
[11] L. Abdullah, I. Almomani, and A. Aburumman, "Secure Cluster-Based SIP Service over Ad hoc Networks", AEECT (2013)
[12] L. Andel, J. Kuthan and D. Sisalem, "Distributed Media Server Architecture for SIP using IP Anycast", *IPTCOMM* (2009)
[13] M. Arafat, M. Alam, and F. Ahmed, "SIP-Based QoS in IP Telephony", JNW, **9**, 3415(2014)
[14] S. Al-Omari and P. Sumari , "An overview of Mobile Ad-hoc networks for the existing Protocols and Applications", GRAPH-HOC, **2**, 87 (2010)
[15] S. Lalar and A. Yadav, "Comparative Study of Routing Protocols in MANET", OJCST, **10**, 174 (2017)
[16] R. Jha, P. Kharga, "A Comparative Performance Analysis of Routing Protocols in MANET using NS3 Simulator", IJCNIS, **4**, 62 (2015)
[17] A. Gupta, H. Sadawarti and A. Verma, "Performance analysis of AODV, DSR & TORA Routing Protocols", IJET, **2**, 226 (2010)
[18] D. Ahmed and O. Khalifa, "A Comprehensive Classification of MANETs Routing Protocols", IJCAT, 6, 141 (2017)
[19] G. Walia, "A Survey on Reactive Routing Protocols of the Mobile Ad hoc Networks", IJCA, **64**, 45 (2013)
[20] J. Bhatt and N. Hemrajani, "Effective Routing Protocol (DSDV) for Mobile Ad Hoc Network", IJSCE, **3**, 4 (2013)
[21] C. Perkins and P. Bhagwat, "Highly Dynamic Destination-Sequenced Distance-Vector Routing (DSDV) for Mobile Computers", *Proc. ACM SIGCOMM* , 234 (1994)
[22] S. Murthy and J. Garcia-Luna-Aceves, "An efficient routing protocol for wireless networks", MONET, **1**, 183 (1996)
[23] C. Chiang, H. Wu, W. Liu and M. Gerla, "Routing in Clustered Multihop, Mobile Wireless Networks With Fading Channel", *Proc. of IEEE SICON*, 197 (1997)
[24] S. Raut and H. Ambulgekar, "Proactive and Reactive Routing Protocols in Multihop Mobile Ad hoc Network", IJARCSSE, **3**, 152 (2013)
[25] C. Perkins, E. Royer and S. Das, "Ad hoc On-Demand Distance Vector (AODV) Routing", IETF, RFC 3561 (2003)
[26] S. Raju, K. Runkana and J. Mungara, "ZRP versus AODV and DSR: A Comprehensive Study on ZRP Performance on MANETs", IJCA, **1**, 194 (2010)
[27] S. Leggio, J. Manner, A. Hulkkonen and K. Raatikainen, "Session Initiation Protocol Deployment in Ad-Hoc Networks: a Decentralized Approach", IWWAN, **5** (2005)
[28] J. Veizades, E. Guttman, and C. Perkins, "Service Location Protocol," IETF, RFC 2165 (1997)
[29] P. Stuedi, M. Buhr, A. Remund, and G. Alonso, "SIPHoc: Efficient SIP Middleware for Ad Hoc Networks", IFIP (2007)
[30] L. Chang, C. Sung, S. Chiu, and Y. Lin, "Design and Realization of Ad Hoc VoIP with Embedded p-SIP Server", JSS, **83**, no. 12, 2536 (2010).
[31] Chu and W. Chen, "Enabling SIP-Based Services in Ad Hoc Networks", IJIE, **2**, 158 (2012)
[32] I. Mourtaji, M. Bouhorma, M. Benahmed, A. Bouhdir," A New Technique for Adapting SIP Protocol to Ad Hoc Networks: VNSIP (Virtual Network for SIP) Illustration and Evaluation of Performance", IJCNCS, **1**, 23 (2013)
[33] I. Mourtaji, M. Bouhorma, M. Benahmed, A. Bouhdir, "Performance Enhancement of VNSIP approach, using MCAC Algorithm", IJCNCS, **1**, 68 (2013)
[34] W. Almobaideen, N. Kubba and A. Awajan, "FCSIP: Fuzzy and Cluster based SIP Protocol for MANET", NGMAST, 169 (2014)
[35] E.M. Belding-Royer, "Hierarchical routing in ad hoc mobile networks", WCMC, **2**, 515 (2002)
[36] C. Solegaonkar, B.Prajapat, "An Overview on Cluster Head Election Techniques in Mobile Ad-Hoc Networks", IJCA, **162**, 10 (2017)

MATEC Web of Conferences **125**, 04027 (2017) DOI: 10.1051/matecconf/201712504027
CSCC 2017

Optimized UAV object tracking framework based on Integrated Particle filter with ego-motion transformation matrix

Wesam Askar[1,*], *Osama* Elmowafy[2], *Aliaa* Youssif[3], and *Gamal* Elnashar[4]

[1]Department of Electrical Engineering, Military Technical College, Egypt
[2]Computer Engineering Department, New Cairo Academy, Egypt
[3]Computer Engineering Department, Helwan University, Egypt
[4]Electrical Department, Military Technical College, Egypt

Abstract. Vision based object tracking problem still a hot and important area of research specially when the tracking algorithms are performed by the aircraft unmanned vehicle (UAV). Tracking with the UAV requires special considerations due to the flight maneuvers, environmental conditions and aircraft moving camera. The ego motion calculations can compensate the effect of the moving background resulted from the moving camera. In this paper an optimized object tracking framework is introduced to tackle this problem based on particle filter. It integrates the calculated ego motion transformation matrix with the dynamic model of the particle filter during the prediction stage. Then apply the correction stage on the particle filter observation model which based on two kinds of features includes Haar-like Rectangles and edge orientation histogram (EOH) features. The Gentle AdaBoost classifier is used to select the most informative features as a preliminary step. The experimental results achieved more than 94.6% rate of successful tracking during different scenarios of the VIVID database in real time tracking speed.

1 Introduction

Tracking objects in Unmanned Aerial Vehicle (UAV) camera image had been an important area of research many years ago. Many applications still require improvements in the performance of the video trackers due to many challenges related to this topic. The fast-abrupt motion, low resolution, noisy imagery, cluttered background, low contrast, and small target size are common issues that should be taken into considerations [1, 2]. There are also many factors govern the selection of the suitable object tracker such as the environment nature, object scale and types of the object motion [11, 12].

Thanks to a “bird’s eye view” delivered by the UAV camera, the UAV images is a vital choice for many critical application including traffic planning and surveillance, road conditions and emergency response, search and rescue operations, counter-terrorism and fighting against illegal immigration missions. The aerial images provide detailed information about the interesting target/targets that can be considered as the first and important step in the implementation of these application systems [2, 3, 5, 10].

The detection and tracking algorithms can be divided into single object or multi-object tracking [1]. Single target detection and tracking is very important in many critical applications. For instance, in military applications, the process of alignment of the enemy target in the center of the camera field of view (FOV) is necessary for shooting purpose. However, the difficulty of the tracking will increase in case of tracking using UAV camera images. This is due to the moving of this platform which produce an ego motion effect between the moving object and the background. Also, the changing of the altitude of the UAV results a change in object scale which adds extra challenges on the tracking algorithms.

In most cases the tracking systems occurs in highly environments disparity. Not all the features components extracted by certain feature extraction method may be considered as an optimum feature to contribute in an object representation model. For this reason, the proposed system performs a preliminary classification step to determine the best feature components using boosting algorithm [11].

The particle filter is a Bayesian-based framework that gives an optimal solution for tracking problem involving a recursive prediction and correction step [1, 6]. The prediction step computes the prior probability density function (PDF) of the current state based on the system dynamics of the target and the PDF of the previous state. The correction step gives the posterior distribution of the object current state through the likelihood of the measurement (in the new frame) and the Bayes' rule. The particle filter uses a set of weighted samples (particles)

* Corresponding author: wesamaaa@gmail.com

to represent the target object PDF. Each particle represents a potential state for the object candidate state. In each time step, the particles will be updated based on the dynamics of the target object, and per their measurements, they will be re-weighted. a higher particle weight represents a higher probability state of the object. The next section will survey some of related work to the proposed system which is discussed in section 3. In section 4 the experimental results and discussion will be clarified and section 5 will contain the conclusion.

2 Related works

M. Josh et.al implemented an algorithm for victim detection and tracking in search and rescue operations using Unmanned Ground Vehicle (UGV) [3]. They aimed to reduce the operator effort by developing a semi-autonomous system that can follow the victim. This system consisted of two main stages includes Ego motion compensation stage and particles filter and clustering stage. The ego motion compensation algorithm tracks good selected features from frame to frame then constructs compensation matrix and compensated image. They improve the system performance by adapting the pyramidal level per velocity feedback.

In 2015 M. Abdelwahab et. al proposed a real-time technique for detecting, tracking and counting vehicles in simultaneously manner for airborne and stationary camera video [4]. They used Kanade–Lucas–Tomasi (KLT) Feature tracker to detect good features to track in the image frame. The non-stationary background points were removed by measuring the changes in the histogram of the pixels around each feature point with time to obtain the foreground features (FGF). Then they clustered and grouped them into separate trackable vehicles per the movement angles and displacement magnitudes. Their algorithm achieved real time performance for tracking vehicles in airborne videos without any prior knowledge for their locations and independent on their number.

Cao et.al use the KLT features and Random sample consensus (RANSAC) method to separate background features from moving objects and estimate the ego motion of the moving camera fixed in UAV [6].. They incorporated ego motion transformation matrix with the system model of the particle filter prediction step. The HSV color histogram and Hu moments were weighted and combined for computing the similarity measure and used them in the observation model of the particle filter correction step. The performance of their algorithm achieved tracking rate of 95%. However, the average tracking speed of the proposed method is 13.1 frames per second which is may not satisfy some application requirements.

Saif et.al presented and updated framework to handle six Uncertainty Constraint Factors (UCF) issues and challenges for moving object detection and tracking problems from UAV aerial images [2]. Theas six UCFs including the illumination change, environment clutter, object type, Camera motion, moving object direction and motion complexity. They also dealt with the feature extraction problem as a separate unsolved issue because of the increasing of computation time related to the selections of large feature vector that suitable for optimum detection performance. They proposed a general framework for object detection problem from UAV aerial images. They employed a combination of frame difference and segmentation techniques for motion vector estimation and blob detection respectively. After that they suggested to use clustering to give physical meaning of overall detection. Finally, they recommended a proper classification step to distinguish between different types of objects that may include humans, vehicles, etc.

Moti et.al proposed a tracking method based on arbitration between Optical Flow (OF) and Kalman Filter (KF) techniques that can predict a target position in an efficient manner even it turns suddenly during its motion [7]. Their attention had been drawn to different situations where either the OF worked better or the KF did. They measured the distances to the nearest obstacle using the laser and used infrared camera images to detect the target object. Then fused these two types of data with the arbitrate OFKF filter for real-time tracking of a man in an indoor lab environment. By the same way, Shantaiya et. al proposed a simultaneously multiple objects tracking algorithm using Kalman Filter and improved Optical Flow [8]. They achieved better tracking accuracy using this improvement and combination relative to using each other separately, but the computation time still not suitable to track objects in UAV tracking requirements frame works.

3 Proposed Framework

In this paper the tracking framework can be divided into four stages includes pre-tracking, prediction, correction and post-tracking stages as illustrated in Fig. 1. The following sub-sections will give detailed descriptions for these stages.

3.1 Pre-Tracking Stage

The pre-tracking stage consists of four steps aimed to select the best features to represent the target from the first frame in the search area as illustrated in the following.

3.1.1 Target detection

The pre-tracking stage is executed to extract the best features indices vector before start tracking process. Many tracking systems proposed algorithms to detect the target object from image sequence using manual or automatic manners. The proposed framework starts with manual selection for the target object by the user as the region inside a rectangular region from the whale image frame. This region of interest (ROI) is considered as a target object template that will be exposed to the feature extraction step as illustrated in the following sub-sections.

where T is the number of all candidate features components.

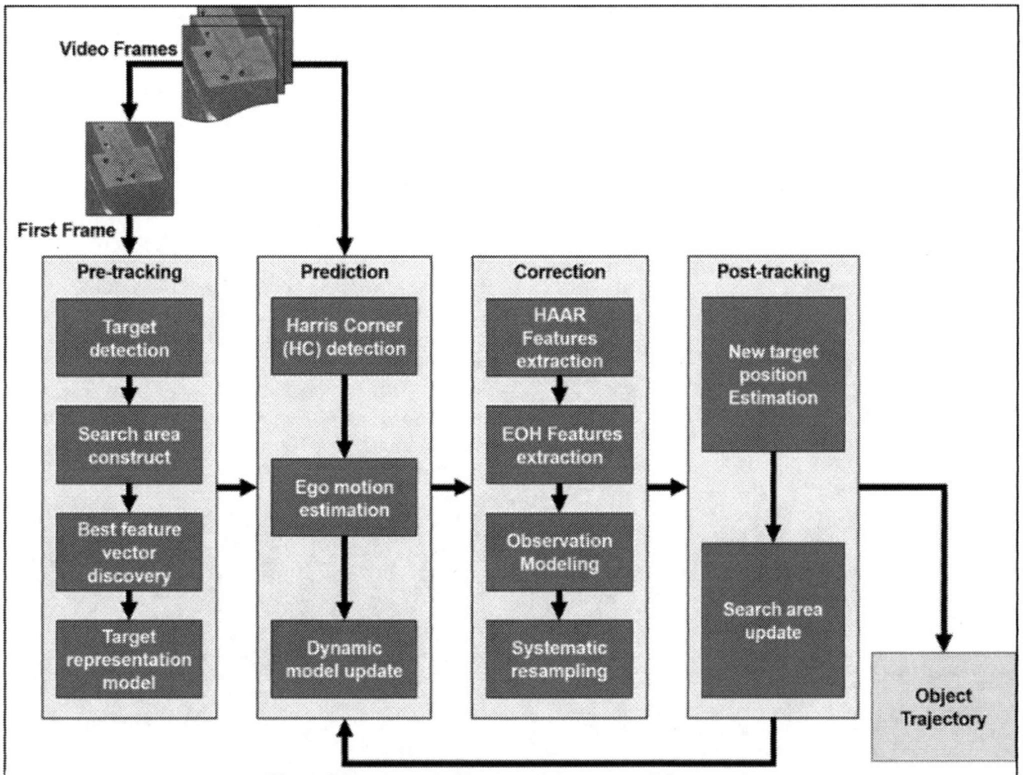

Fig. 1. The schematic diagram of the proposed framework.

3.1.2 Search area construction

The proposed framework starts with the construction of padding image IP before constructing the search area due to the possibilities of existing the target object position near the image boarders. This may restrict formation of the search area to have the same bounding box during tracking process for all frame sequence. By finding the width w and height h of the ROI, the padding value P can be determined as n multiples of w or h (which one is bigger). Then search area can be constructed based on the ROI bounding box and P.

3.1.3 Best feature vector discovery

In this step the proposed system applies the Gentle AdaBoost classifier on a pre-constructed training dataset based on the search area foregrounds and backgrounds. By knowing target ROI, the f foregrounds can be extracted by different random views or positions around the ROI center and the b backgrounds can be extracted from different location the rest of the search area. All foregrounds and backgrounds have the same size of ROI w and h The features extraction step based on Haar rectangles (HR) and edge orientation histogram (EOH) is applied on all foregrounds and backgrounds to extract all candidate features. These candidates are concatenated together to form a meas input vector of size $(f + b)\times T$,

The Gentle AdaBoost classifier trains T week classifiers (the same number of the candidate features components) and combines them into a linear fashion. Each classifier $h_i(x)$ is a simple threshold function trained on one feature only. They are weak in the sense that they can only decide whether a value is below or above a given threshold. Although one-week classifier is not accurately to describe a whole dataset alone, a combination of them would lead to a strong classifier. A simple weak classifier example used in this paper is as the following:

$$h_i(x) = \begin{cases} 1 & if\ f_i(x) < \theta_i \\ -1 & otherwise \end{cases} \quad i = 1,2, \dots T \quad (1)$$

Where f_i is the selected feature and θ_i is the learned threshold. The output of the classifier $(F_{idx.})$ is in the form of vector with size $T_{opt.}\times 1$, where $T_{opt.}$ Is a pre-selected number of the strongest week classifiers (i.e. candidate features components).

3.1.4 Target representation model

As illustrated above, the target is represented by a rectangle region that contains $w\times h$ pixels which is difficult to deal with them directly. So, a feature extraction process should be applied and specifically on the features with the index numbers inside $F_{idx.}$ vector. There are many types of features can describe the target

DOI: 10.1051/matecconf/201712504027

object. Due to the real-time requirements of the UAV tracking system, in this paper the Haar-like rectangles (HR) and the edge orientation histogram (EOH) are used because of their simplicity and fast computation cost [13, 14].

3.1.4.1 Haar-like Rectangles (HR) features

The HR features can describe the object with its color and much spatial information. They can be defined as a filter that computes the gray level difference between two defined white and black areas as the following:

$$Haar(x, y, w, h, type, C) = E_w(ROI) - E_k(ROI) \quad (2)$$

Where x, y are the coordinates of the top-left corner for any candidate ROI and w and h are its width and height respectively, the $type$ is one of the Haar-like rectangles patterns listed in Fig. 2, the channel of the color space is represented in term C and $E_w(ROI)$ and $E_k(ROI)$ are white and black parts of ROI. The pool of the features consists of various HR per patterns, sizes and color channels. Thanks to the integral image (II) technique, the HR features can be extracted in very lower executional time. Using II, the summed values of a certain ROI can be efficiently computed by only four II accesses.

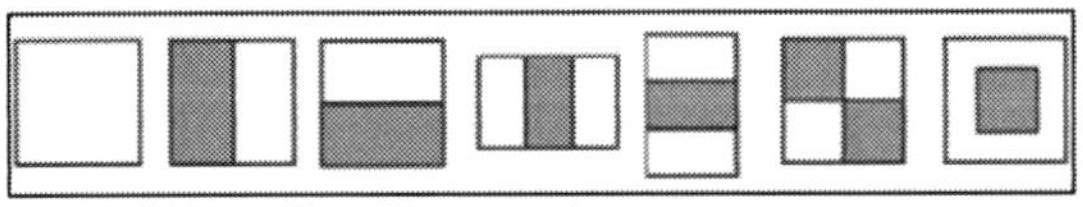

Fig. 2. different Haar-like rectangles patterns

3.1.4.2 Edge Orientation Histogram (EOH)

The EOH features are invariant with color and local spatial information. So, they are good for tracking targets in low light where the colors can be hard to distinguish [14]. To compute EOH first the search area is converted to grayscale image and is convoluted with the horizontal and vertical Sobel kernels to detect the edges on it. After that, the magnitude and direction are calculated for all pixels. Only pixels that have the magnitude greater than a pre-defined threshold (T) are considered and the rest considered as noise. Then all edge directions fall between 0 to 2π are quantized into (M) number of bins and calculate. Using the integral image technique of the Mth bin matrix, the system can compute all possible components of EOH features as the sum of the magnitude for each bin relative to ROI.

3.2 Prediction stage

The prediction stage is the first step in the Particle filter algorithm that concerns for estimating the new position of each particle using a state transition model (dynamic model). In many cases the first order auto-regressive model is used and achieves good results in tracking systems [6, 7, 8]. However, in case of tracking objects using moving platform (UAV), this model should be optimized to compensate the ego motion resulted by the moving UAV camera. The proposed system uses the optical flow technique and k-means clustering method for calculating the ego motion transformation matrix to increase the tracking rate. Then the transformation matrix is combined with the dynamic model to produces the proposed state transition model for the particle filter technique as discussed later.

3.2.1 Harris Corner (HC) detection

To calculate the ego motion, the system starts with dividing the current frame into sub-frame regions (blocks) then detecting the Harris Corner points (HC) [15] on them. This HC points may relate to fixed objects (background) or moving objects (foregrounds). However, we first assume that the most of them are related to the background. The optical flow method is used to estimate the new position of HC points in the next frame. Fig. 3(a, b) shows HC points and their correspondences in all frame blocks.

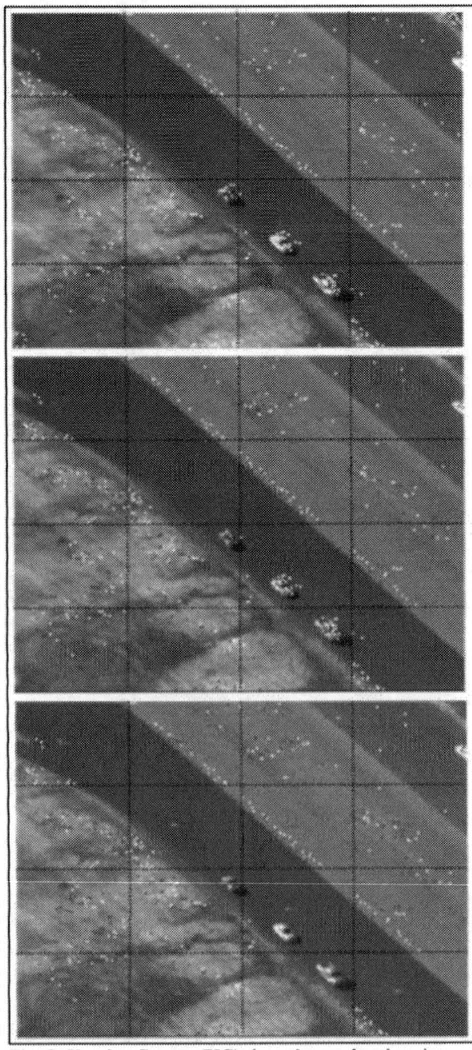

Fig. 3. Harries Corner (HC) detection and estimation.

3.2.2 Ego Motion Estimation

After having the new HC points and their correspondences, the Euclidian distance (ED) and angles (θ) are calculated for each HC pairs ((x_i, y_i) and (y_i', y_i')) per equation 3, 4. The proposed system applies the k-means method on all HC points belong to each block. It aims to cluster the HC data (θ and ED) into two groups representing the foreground (moving objects) and backgrounds. The group contains of the most HC points is considered as a background and the foreground points are removed as shown in Fig. 3(c).

$$ED = \sqrt{(x_i - x_i')^2 + (y_i - y_i')^2} \quad (3)$$

$$\theta = \frac{y_i - y_i'}{x_i - x_i'} \quad (4)$$

The Maximum Likelihood Estimation SAmple Consensus (MLESAC) method is applied on the background HC pairs to estimate the affine geometric transform for each block. The MLESAC is a generalization of RANSAC estimator with a maximization of the likelihood rather than just the number of inliers [16]. Due to the possibilities of image rotation, skewing, and warping, not all blocks have the identical affine transformation. So the median value of all affine transformations is computed and is considered as the ego motion transformation(E). The transformation E is an 3x3 affine transformation matrix with the following form:

$$E = \begin{bmatrix} a & c & e \\ b & d & f \\ 0 & 0 & 1 \end{bmatrix} \quad (5)$$

where a, b, c, d, e and f are the matrix components which determine the values of translation, scale, sheer and rotation transformation types.

3.2.3 Dynamic model update

As mentioned above the calculate ego motion transformation matrix is cooperated with auto-regression model to formulate the state transition model for the (N) particles. Each particle can represent a candidate object state (X) as the following:

$$\boldsymbol{X} = (x, y, 1, \dot{x}, \dot{y}, w, h)^T \quad (6)$$

Where x and y are the left-top coordinate of the ROI rectangle and w and h are its width and height respectively. The velocity information is represented by $\dot{x}$ and $\dot{y}$ components. The constant number 1 inserted for matrix operations convenient. The proposed first-order auto-regression model can be expressed by the following equations:

$$x_t = x_{t-1} + \dot{x}_{t-1} + Gx_{t-1}(0, \sigma_x) \quad (7)$$

$$y_t = y_{t-1} + \dot{y}_{t-1} + Gy_{t-1}(0, \sigma_y) \quad (8)$$

$$\dot{x}_t = \dot{x}_{t-1} + G\dot{x}_{t-1}(0, \sigma_{\dot{x}}) \quad (9)$$

$$\dot{y}_t = \dot{y}_{t-1} + G\dot{y}_{t-1}(0, \sigma_{\dot{y}}) \quad (10)$$

$$w_t = w_{t-1} + Gw_{t-1}(0, \sigma_w) \quad (11)$$

$$h_t = h_{t-1} + Gh_{t-1}(0, \sigma_h) \quad (12)$$

Where $G_*(*)$ is zero mean white Gaussian noise components for several unidentified dynamic factors that may happened during tracking (sudden random motion, slight acceleration, …). σ_* is the variance of $G_*(*)$. After calculating the ego motion transformation matrix $E_{3\times3}$, the system takes only the first two rows in E and updates only the two position components in the state **X** (i.e. x_t and y_t) as the following equation:

$$\begin{bmatrix} xe_t \\ ye_t \end{bmatrix}_{2\times N} = \begin{bmatrix} a & c & e \\ b & d & f \end{bmatrix}_{2\times3} \times \begin{bmatrix} x_t \\ y_t \\ 1 \end{bmatrix}_{3\times N} \quad (13)$$

Where xe_t and ye_t are the two updated position components of the target object at current frame t.
The equations (11, 12) are updated by inserting the effect of scale change represented by a and d components in the ego motion transformation matrix E as the following:

$$we_t = w_t * a \quad (14)$$

$$he_t = h_t * d \quad (15)$$

Empirically, the nominal values of a and d components were between (0.97 – 1.3) which denotes to decreasing or increasing the object scale.

3.3 Correction Stage

The main objective of the correction stage is to calculate the weights corresponding to the new samples in each time step. It consists of three steps including the first two HR and EOH features extraction steps as discussed before. In the observation modeling step, the system assigns weights to all particles according to a similarity score between the target object and the candidate particle ROI.

Based on the new weights of the particles (samples), the systematic resembling step is applied to reject samples which have very low weight and to concentrate on particles with large weights. In the beginning the system assigns equal weights to the particles. Then, by calculating the observation likelihoods in the next frames, each particle represents a good candidate to the object will be assigned to a high weight.

3.4 post-tracking

In this stage the proposed system can predict the new state of the target by taking the median of all candidate states represented by the particles. Because of the probability that the particles may have status positions relatively far from the object center, the median filter is used. It achieves good results better than average filter due to the minimal influence to the noise. Based on the estimated new position of the target object, the new

DOI: 10.1051/matecconf/201712504027

search area is determined again to use in object tracking in the next frame.

4 Experimental results

To evaluate the proposed object tracking framework in different scenarios, the VIVID database [17] is used with small modification to simulate more difficult environments. This modification performed by adding some drifting noise in each new frame. This drift can be considered as UAV vibrations or camera shacking. The VIVID includes civilian and military vehicles moving on a runway with different kinds of motions (straight and loop) and changing speed. Also, the scale of them are changing in the image due to the change of UAV altitude. In some situations, the tracked vehicle looks very similar to another when it passes.

The algorithms implemented using MATLAB and all the experiments were executed on a 2.6 GHz computer with 4 GB RAM. The performance results achieved 94.6% successful tracking rate with calculation speed more than 48 frames per second (fps) for 640×480 pixels images.

At the first frame the system selects randomly 20 different sub-images around the object as foregrounds and 200 sub-images from the background. Then a pool of 106 extracted features (90 HR and 26 EOH) are created to be the inputs for the AdaBoost classifier for selecting the best F features that represent the object. In calculating the ego motion the system divides the image frame into 4×4 sub-image and choose only the strongest 20 HC in each. Finally, the particle filter set at 500 particles to represent the candidate object locations.

To evaluate the system the recall and precision are calculated in same manner as in [6]. Fig. 4 and Fig. 5 show the average accuracy and the speed of the system using different values of F.

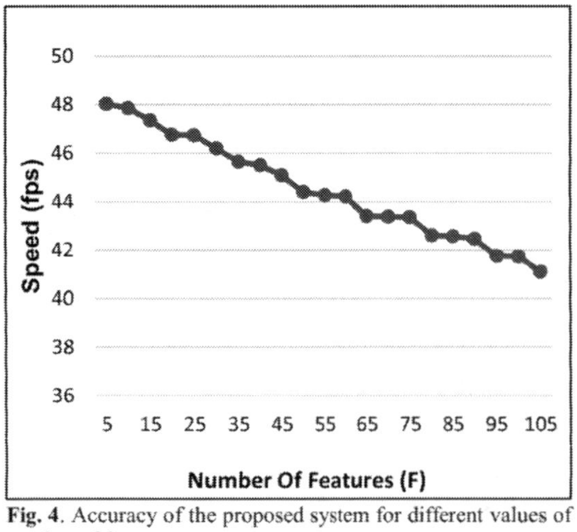

Fig. 4. Accuracy of the proposed system for different values of number of features.

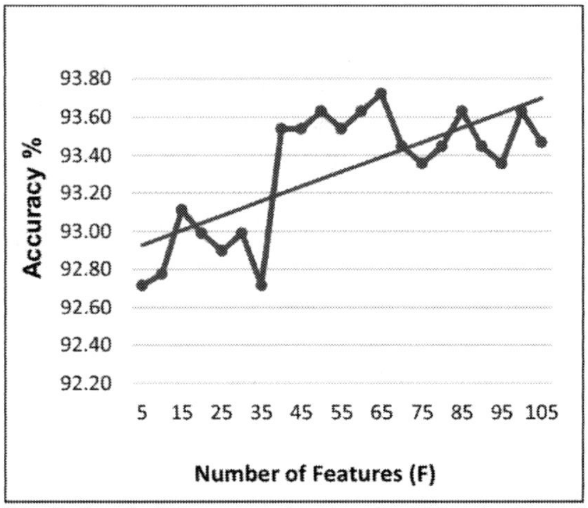

Fig. 5. Speed of the proposed system for different values of number of features.

As mentioned before the ego motion incorporation with the dynamic model improves the accuracy of the framework. Fig. 6. Illustrates the accuracy of the system for the first image sequence of VIVID database (egtest01) which contain vehicles that loop around on a runway, then drive straight. Starts from frame 900 vehicle being tracked speeds up and passes very similar to another vehicle. When the vehicle speeds up the particles lags the center of which means that the dynamic model does not guides these particles and predicts the new position as better as before. So, the accuracy values are decreasing (red curve). By incorporating the ego motion transformation matrix with the dynamic model, the particles directed to closer position to the vehicle center resulted in improving the accuracy value (green curve).

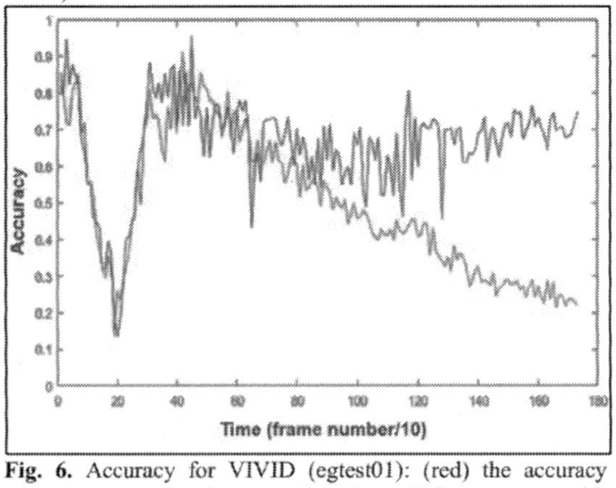

Fig. 6. Accuracy for VIVID (egtest01): (red) the accuracy without ego motion incorporation, (green) the accuracy with ego motion incorporation.

The effect of scale change appears obviously when we examine the recall and precision measures separately as shown in Fig. 7. Approximately after frame 1300 the UAV altitude was slightly decreasing results in increasing in the object scale which leads to decreasing in recall results.

DOI: 10.1051/matecconf/201712504027

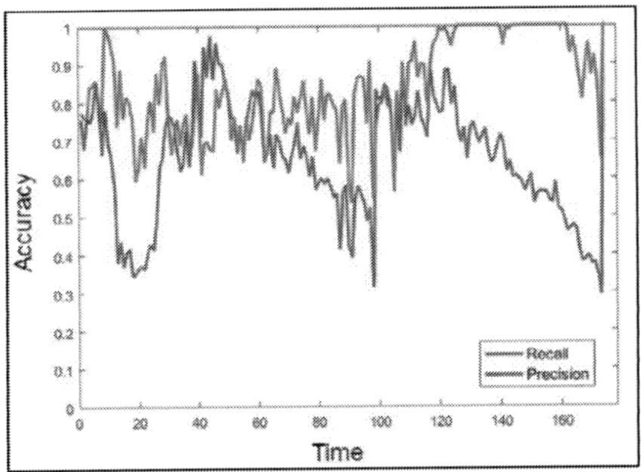

Fig. 7. Recall and Precision Accuracies without compensating the scale change effect.

As mentioned before by updating the dynamic model again using equations (13) and (14), the width and the height of each candidate particle bounding box will get closer values as the object ground truth. Then the recall and precision accuracies will increase as shown in Fig. 8.

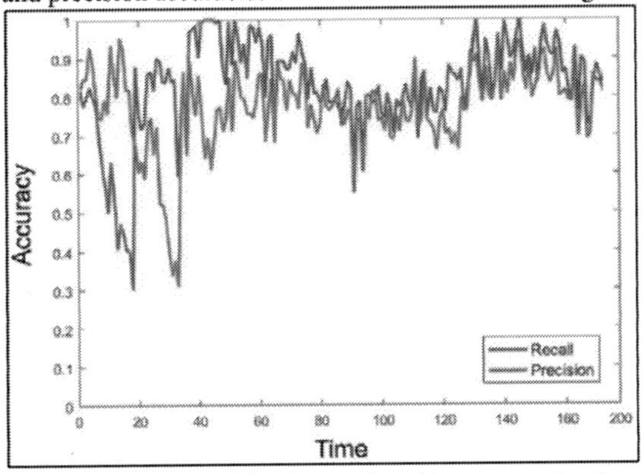

Fig. 8. Recall and Precision Accuracies with compensating the scale change effect.

Table 1 is showing a comparison between the proposed framework and the tracking method in [6] in both speed and accuracy to illustrate the improvement of the performance specially the real-time requirement with the satisfactory accuracy. The tracking speed using the proposed framework is approximately four times the speed in the other method. The accuracy didn't reduce by large value and can be consider the same in the both methods due to the probabilistic nature of the experiments.

Table 1. Comparison between the proposed tracking framework and the classical particle filter.

Tracking Method	Speed (fps)	Accuracy %
Classical Particle Filter tracking method	13.1	95.1
Proposed Particle Filter tracking framework	47.6	94.6

There are many factors for the improvements in the speed. The use of the integral images for calculating the HR and EOH features reduced the execution time significantly. However, this execution time is directly proportional to the image size. In single object tracking purposes using UAVs, the object size is small. So, it is intuitively to concentrate the calculations on a search area as minimum as possible to reduce the calculations but as maximum as possible to includes the object candidate positions. In this paper, the search area was chosen first to be three times greater than the object size while the object speed per frame not exceeds this value.

5. Conclusion

In this paper an optimized object tracking framework is introduced to achieve the UAV vision based object tracking requirements. The tracking process starts with selecting the best features form a pool of Haar-like rectangles (HR) and edge orientation histogram features (EOH). This is done by applying AdaBoost classifier to all features that extracted from a pre-created set of foregrounds and backgrounds in the first frame. The selected features are considered as the observation model of the target object. This observation model is used for the particle filter correction stage to compare with candidate position denoted by each particle. Before the correction step the new position of the object is predicted using a modified dynamic model of the object. This modification is done by calculating the ego motion of the UAV using fixed background points and comparing between them to extract the affine transformation matrix which incorporates with the object dynamic model. By using this framework, the tracking speed and accuracy achieves better results than most of recent UAV tracking methods.

References

[1] A. Yilmaz, O. Javed and M. Shah, ACM Computing Surveys, *"Object Tracking: A Survey"*, Vol. **38**, No. 4, Article 13, (2006).

[2] A.F.M. Saifuddin Saif, A. Prabuwono, Z. R. Mahayuddin and H. Himawan, International Journal of Advancements in Computing Technology (IJACT), *"A Review of Machine Vision based on Moving Objects Object Detection from UAV Aerial Images"*, Vol. **5**, (2013).

[3] M. Joshi, R. Madri and M. Joshi, TENCON 2013 - 2013 IEEE Region 10 Conference (31194), *"Real time motion tracking algorithm for search and rescue robots"*, (2013).

[4] M. A. Abdelwahab and M. M. Abdelwahab, Multimedia (ISM), IEEE International Symposium on, *"A Novel Algorithm for Vehicle Detection and Tracking in Airborne Videos"*, (2015).

[5] P. Burdziakowski, M. Przyborski and J. Szulwic, 1st Int. Con. on Innovative Research and Maritime App. of Space Technology IRMAST, *"A Vision-Based Unmanned Aerial Vehicle Navigation Method"*, (2015).

[6] X. Cao, C. Gao, J. Lan, Y. Yuan and P. Yan, Neurocomputing, "*Ego motion guided particle filter for vehicle tracking in airborne videos*", Vol. **124**, pp. 168–177, (2014).

[7] Y. Motai, S. K. Jha and D. Kruse, Image Communication, "*Human tracking from a mobile agent: Optical flow and Kalman filter arbitration*", Vol. **27**, pp. 83–95, (2012).

[8] A. Shantaiya, K. Verma and K. Mehta, Europ. J. of Adv. in Eng. and Tech., "*Multiple Object Tracking Using Kalman Filter And Optical Flow*", pp. 34-39, (2015).

[9] P. Perez, C. Hue, J. Vermaak, and M. Gangnet, ECCV 2002, LNCS 2350, "*Color-Based Probabilistic Tracking*", pp. 661–675, (2002).

[10] H. Yang, L. Shao, F. Zheng, L. Wangd and Z. Song, Neurocomputing, "Recent advances and trends in visual tracking: A review", Vol. **74**, pp. 3823–3831, (2011).

[11] S. Sivaraman and M. M. Trivedi, IEEE transactions on intelligent transportation systems, "*Looking at Vehicles on the Road: A Survey of Vision-Based Vehicle Detection, Tracking, and Behavior Analysis*", Vol. **14**, no. 4, (2013).

[12] M. Coskuna, S. Ünala, 9th Int. Conf. Inter. Eng., "*Implementation of Tracking of a Moving Object Based on Camshift Approach with a UAV*", (2015).

[13] B. L. Sefidgari, Int. J. of Artificial Intelligence & App. (IJAIA), "*Feed-Back Method Based On Image Processing for Detecting Human Body Via Flying Robot*", Vol. **4**, No. 6, (2013).

[14] D. Geronimo, A. Sappa, A. Lopez and D. Ponsa, Proc. 5th Int. Conf. Comput. Vis. Syst., "*Adaptive image sampling and windows classification for on-board pedestrian detection*", (2007).

[15] J. Shi and C. Tomasi, IEEE Conf. on Computer Vision and Pattern Recognition, "*Good Features to Track*", (1994).

[16] P. H. S. Torr and A. Zisserman, Computer Vision and Image Understanding, "*MLESAC: A New Robust Estimator with Application to estimating Image Geometry*", (2000).

[17] R. T. Collins, X. Zhou, and S. K. Teh, IEEE International Workshop on Performance Evaluation of Tracking and Surveillance (PETS 2005), January, 2005. "*An Open Source Tracking Testbed and Evaluation Web Site,*", *available online until 14th June 2017 at:* http://vision.cse.psu.edu/data/vividEval/main.html

Adaptive algorithm for solution of early exercise boundary problem of American put option implemented in Mathematica

Ladislav Lukáš[1,*]

[1]University of West Bohemia, Faculty of Economics, Univerzitni 22, 30614 Pilsen, Czech Republic

Abstract. The paper is focused on American option pricing problem. Assuming non-dividend paying American put option leads to two disjunctive regions, a continuation one and a stopping one, which are separated by an early exercise boundary. We present variational formulation of American option problem with special attention to early exercise action effect. Next, we discuss financially motivated additive decomposition of American option price into a European option price and another part due to the extra premium required by early exercising the option contract. As the optimal exercise boundary is a free boundary, its determination is coupled with the determination of the option price. Therefore, a closed-form expression of the free boundary is not attainable in general. We discuss in detail a derivation of an asymptotic expression of the early exercise boundary. Finally, we present some numerical results of determination of free boundary based upon this approach. All computations are performed by sw Mathematica, and suitable numerical procedure is discussed in detail, as well.

1 Introduction

American option pricing problems given with different levels of abstraction are presented in [3], [4], [6], and [7]. We know that in contrast to European options, American options can be exercised at any time between the writing and the expiration of the option contract. Exercising flexibility gives American option more profiteering opportunity than European option offers, and it means that payoff functions of American options take the following general form, where a subscript C, and P denotes an option type, i.e. *call*, and *put*, respectively

$$V_c(S,t) \geq \max(S-K,\ 0) \qquad (1)$$

$$V_p(S,t) \geq \max(K-S,\ 0) \qquad (2)$$

here $S \geq 0$, is an underlying risky asset price, e.g. stock price, $0 \leq t \leq T$, T is the option expiration date, and K is the option exercise price, called strike price, too.

Now, let us focus on non-dividend paying American put option. In fact, when S falls below a certain point, one should exercise the option immediately to avoid loss. For example, if at time t, the current stock price S_t is $S_t < K(1 - e^{-r(T-t)})$, then the option holder should exercise the option immediately. Here, r denotes a risk-free interest rate. In fact, the payoff at the option expiration data T will never exceed K in any case. Though, if the option is exercised at the time t, the immediate gain is $K - S_t > K - K(1 - e^{-r(T-t)}) = Ke^{-r(T-t)}$, and by depositing this gain in a saving account, assuming a regular compounding process applies, the total payoff will exceed K at $t = T$, clearly.

Hence, a thorough inspection of relation (2) provides an idea that for American put option there exist two disjunctive subregions, denoted Σ_1 and Σ_2, covering $\Sigma = [0,+\infty) \times [0,T]$, i.e. $\Sigma_1 \cup \Sigma_2, = \Sigma$.

Let $\partial\Sigma_i$, denotes boundary of Σ_i, $i = 1, 2$, being defined as $\partial\Sigma_i, = \mathrm{cl}(\Sigma_i)\backslash\Sigma_i$, where $\mathrm{cl}(\Sigma_i)$ is usual pointwise closure of set Σ_i. Hence, a common piece of their boundaries, denoted $\Gamma = \partial\Sigma_1 \cap \partial\Sigma_2$, is called optimal exercise boundary.

The optimal exercise boundary is reasonably defined by mapping $\Gamma:[0,T] \rightarrow \Gamma(t)$, thus specifying the underlying asset price at Γ, denoted $S_\eta = \Gamma(t_e)$, precisely. Here, we adopt the subscript η instead of usual t in order to point out the specific asset price at the optimal exercise time t_e, in particular.

The optimal exercise boundary is not given a priori, and has to be determined together with option pricing function $V(S,t)$ by solving the corresponding option pricing problem. Here, we already drop the subscript P for simplicity, as we are handling the American put option in the paper excusively.

Using optimal exercise boundary $\Gamma(t)$, the subregions Σ_1 and Σ_2 are defined in following way

$$V(S,t) > \max(K-S,\ 0),\ \ (S,t) \in \Sigma_1, \qquad (3)$$

$$\Sigma_1 = \{(S,t) \mid \Gamma(t) \leq S < +\infty\},\ \ t \in [0,T],$$

$$V(S,t) = \max(K-S,\ 0),\ \ (S,t) \in \Sigma_2, \qquad (4)$$

$$\Sigma_2 = \{(S,t) \mid 0 \leq S \leq \Gamma(t)\},\ \ t \in [0,T],$$

where Σ_1 is called the continuation subregion, since the payoff is zero when $S > S_\eta$, and the holder should

* Corresponding author: author@e-mail.org

continue to keep the option, whereas Σ_2 is called the stoping subregion. strike price.

Noting, the continuation subregion Σ_1 is sometimes called retained subregion alternatively, whereas the stopping subregion Σ_2 is called selling subregion, or exercise subregion, as well. In Figure 1, there are depicted both subregions Σ_1, Σ_2, the expiration date T, and the option exercise price, all schematically. The horizontal axis represents an underlying asset price S, and the vertical axis carries the time t elapsed from entering the option contract into power.

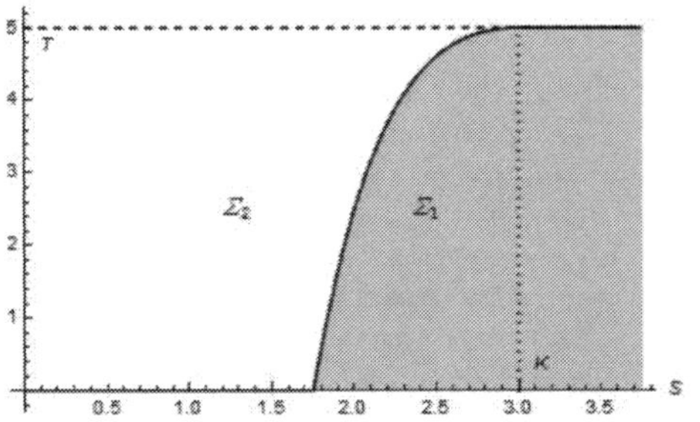

Fig. 1. Subregions Σ_1, Σ_2, and early exercise boundary.

Following classical procedure based on construction of self-financing portfolio, Δ-hedging principle, and Itô's formula, which is common and typical for derivation of almost all models within the field of financial option pricing problems, we can infer that function $V(S,t)$ satisfies the Black-Scholes PDE in the subregion Σ_1

$$\frac{\partial V}{\partial t} + rS\frac{\partial V}{\partial S} + \frac{1}{2}\sigma^2 S^2 \frac{\partial^2 V}{\partial S^2} - rV = 0, \quad (S,t) \in \Sigma_1, \quad (5)$$

provided $V(S,t)$ belongs to $C^{2,1}(\Sigma_1)$ class of functions, in classical formulation framework, see for example [3] and [6].

The boundary conditions on $\partial\Sigma_1$ are specified in following way. First, on the optimal exercise boundary Γ, it holds

$$V(S,t) = \max(K - S, 0) \;\Rightarrow\; \frac{\partial V(S,t)}{\partial S} = -1,$$

$$S = S_\eta \in \Gamma(t), \quad t \in [0,T). \quad (6)$$

Further, the terminal condition at $t = T$, and the condition when $S \to +\infty$, are following

$$V(S_T,T) = \max(K - S_T, 0),$$

$$\lim V(S,t) = 0, \; S \to +\infty, \; t \in [0,T]. \quad (7)$$

Concluding, we see that American put option pricing problem leads to finding a function pair $\{V(S,t), \Gamma(t)\}$ in subregion Σ_1 satisfying the PDE (5) and boundary-terminal conditions (6) and (7).

Following [7], we are able to get more compact form of the problem and to elucidate its setting, too. First, it is reasonable to introduce so called Black-Scholes differential operator $\mathfrak{L}_{BS}$ as follows

$$\mathfrak{L}_{BS} F(S,t) = \frac{\partial G}{\partial t} + rS\frac{\partial G}{\partial S} + \frac{1}{2}\sigma^2 S^2 \frac{\partial^2 G}{\partial S^2} - rG, \quad (8)$$

for any function $F(S,t)$ belonging to $C^{2,1}[(0,+\infty) \times (0,T)]$ class of functions

Using (3), (4) and the operator $\mathfrak{L}_{BS}$, we can rewrite properties of function $V(S,t)$ in subregions Σ_1, Σ_2, in compact form

$$\mathfrak{L}_{BS}V(S,t) = 0, \; V(S,t) > \max(K - S,0), \; (S,t) \in \Sigma_1, \quad (9)$$

$$\mathfrak{L}_{BS}V(S,t) = -rK < 0, \; V(S,t)=\max(K-S,0), \; (S,t) \in \Sigma_2. \quad (10)$$

Since (10) holds on Γ, being tackled as a part of $\partial\Sigma_2$, we can conclude by direct computation that both the pricing function $V(S,t)$ and its first derivative $\partial V/\partial S$ are continuous on the optimal exercise boundary Γ. Now, combining relations (9) and (10) together, we get the variational formulation of American put option pricing problem in strong case, see [4], Chapter 6.2, for more details

$$\min\{-\mathfrak{L}_{BS}V(S,t), V(S,t)-\max(K-S,0)\} = 0, \; (S,t) \in \Sigma, \quad (11)$$

$$V(S_T,T) = \max(K - S_T, 0), \; S_T \in [0, +\infty),$$

$$\lim V(S,t) = 0, \; S \to +\infty, \; t \in [0,T].$$

2 Decomposition formula for American put option

Early exercise premium is discussed from several viewpoints in [1], and [2]. Following [4], Chapter 6.3, we present an interesting decomposition formula for American put option price $V(S,t)$ which gives a link to European put option price $V^E(S,t)$ in following way

$$V(S,t) = V^E(S,t) + e(S,t), \quad (12)$$

here $V^E(S,t)$ is the well-known European put option price on the same underlying asset, which is computed by closed Black-Scholes formula, see for example [2], [3], and [6], as well, and $e(S,t)$ is the early exercise premium given as follows

$$e(S,t) = rK \int_t^T d\eta \int_0^{S_\eta} G(S,t;\xi,\eta) d\xi. \quad (13)$$

The function $G(S,t;\xi,\eta)$ is fundamental solution, sometimes called Green function, too, of the well-known Black-Scholes PDE, being expressed explicitly in relation (5). Inspecting (13) thoroughly, we reckon the upper bound S_η of the inner integral to cause direct dependence of early exercise premium $e(S,t)$ upon the optimal exercise boundary Γ, evidently.

Now, we refer to [4], Chapter 6.3, and Theorems 6.3 and 6.4 therein, for more technical details regarding the function $G(S,t;\xi,\eta)$. However, we ought to present here at least the function $G(S,t;\xi,T)$ in explicit form

$$G(S,t;\xi,T) = \frac{e^{-r(T-t)}}{\xi\sigma\sqrt{2\pi(T-t)}} e^{\varphi(S,t;\xi,T)}, \quad (14)$$

$$\varphi(S,t;\xi,T) = -\frac{1}{2\sigma^2(T-t)}[\ln\frac{S}{\xi} + (r - \frac{\sigma^2}{2})(T-t)]^2 .$$

which represents a solution of the Black-Scholes PDE with special terminal condition expressing concentrated effect at an arbitrary point ξ

$$V(S,T) = \delta(S-\xi),\ S = S_T,\ \xi \in [0, +\infty), \qquad (15)$$

where $\delta(.)$ is the well-known Dirac function being given by its properties $\delta(x) = +\infty$, if $x = 0$, otherwise $\delta(x) = 0$, and $\int_{-\infty}^{+\infty} \delta(x)dx = 1$.

3 Early exercise boundary equation

As the optimal early exercise boundary Γ is not known a priori but has to be determined together with pricing function $V(S,t)$, therefore, in general, the problem is called free-boundary value problem for parabolic PDE. Albeit we have already formulated the problem by expressions (5)-(7) explicitly, the main difficulty therein is that one needs to solve both for unknown function $V(S,t)$ and unknown boundary $\Gamma(t)$, simultaneously.

Since any American option has early exercise term in the contract, the determination of $\Gamma(t)$ is of special importance to the holder of American options, put ones in particular. In [4], Chapters 6.3-6.5, and [8], there are several interesting results related to both qualitative and quantitative properties of the optimal exercise boundary.

Except other ones, as for example position of $\Gamma(T)$, the monotonicity of $\Gamma(t)$, upper and lower bounds of $\Gamma(t)$ and convexity of $\Gamma(t)$, the most important are following two ones. First, asymptotic expression of $\Gamma(t)$ near $t = T$, and at second, the particular equation for determination of $\Gamma(t)$, which is given in [4], Chapter 6.3, Theorem 6.5.

Solution of that equation by successive approximations realized by an adaptive iteration algorithm implemented in sw package Mathematica, there is the core of our paper.

Following [4], Theorem 6.5, the equation for determination of optimal exercise boundary $\Gamma(t)$ for American options is following

$$\Gamma(t) = K + \Gamma(t)e^{-q(T-t)}\Phi[-g_2(t;K,T,\sigma,\beta_2)]$$

$$- Ke^{-q(T-t)}\Phi[-g_1(t;K,T,\sigma,\beta_1)]$$

$$-rK\int_t^T e^{-r(\eta-t)}\{1-\Phi[h_1(t;\Gamma(\eta),\eta,\sigma,\beta_1)]$$

$$+rK\int_t^T e^{-r(\eta-t)}\{1-\Phi[h_2(t;\Gamma(\eta),\eta,\sigma,\beta_2)]\}d\eta, \qquad (16)$$

here q is dividend rate, $\Phi(x)$ is cumulative distribution function of standard normal distribution $N(0,1)$, parameters β_1, β_2, are defined as follows

$$\beta_1 = r - q - \sigma^2/2,\quad \beta_2 = r - q + \sigma^2/2,$$

and functions $g_i(t;K,T,\sigma,\beta_i)$, $h_i(t;\Gamma(\eta),\eta,\sigma,\beta_i)$, $i = 1, 2$, are given by following expressions

$$g_i(t;K,T,\sigma,\beta_i) = \frac{-\ln\frac{\Gamma(t)}{K}+\beta_i(T-t)}{\sigma\sqrt{T-t}},\quad i = 1,2, \qquad (17)$$

$$h_i(t;\Gamma(\eta),\eta,\sigma,\beta_i) = \frac{\ln\frac{\Gamma(t)}{\Gamma(\eta)}+\beta_i(\eta-t)}{\sigma\sqrt{\eta-t}},\quad i = 1,2. \qquad (18)$$

However, it is a nonlinear Volterra integral equation of the second kind. In general, solving such type of equation is a rather challenging problem for numerical mathematics. Regarding (16), we remark that it is applicable in any case of American options when early exercise is interesting, i.e. in case of American put options, and in case of American call options paying dividends.

4 Solution algorithm

The first step is time discretization. Let t_i, $i = 0, \ldots, n$, such that $t_0 = 0$, $t_n = T$, denote regular mesh of time points with a mesh size $\Delta t = T/n$. As the $\Gamma(t)$ represents a uncountable set of points (t,S_t) laying on the optimal early exercise boundary Γ, then adopting time discretization turns the problem to solve equation (16) directly to looking for a finite set of points $\{t_i,S_i\}$, $i = 0, \ldots, n$, satisfying a discrete version of (16), where we just introduce shorter notation S_i instead of cumbersome $S_t|_{t=ti}$.

Time discretization being applied upon (16) yields the following set of fixed-point looking problems

$$S_i = \Psi(S_i;\ t_i,\ \Gamma(\eta)),\ i = 0, \ldots, n, \qquad (19)$$

here symbol Ψ expresses formally the right-hand side of (16) after discretization thus denoting its proper dependence upon variable S_i, but also upon parameters t_i and $\Gamma(\eta)$ thereby making the numerical solution of (19) rather involved.

In order to overcome numerically a complication caused by function $\Gamma(\eta)$ appearing in (19), which is itself a solution of equation (16) being seeked, we propose the following algorithm based upon successive approximation of $\Gamma(\eta)$ starting with some initial guess.

Adaptive iterative algorithm – steps:

1. Set initial approximation $\Gamma_0(\eta)$, $\eta \in [t_i,T]$, and set index $k = 0$,
2. Increment current k by 1, for loop t_i, $i = 0, \ldots, n$, solve $S_{i,k} = \Psi(S_{i,k};t_i,\Gamma_{k-1}(\eta))$, $k \geq 1$, until convergence of $S_{i,k}$ appears with given tolerance ε_1,
3. Build $\Gamma_k(\eta)$, $\eta \in [0,T]$ using available set $\{t_i,S_{i,k}\}$, $i = 0, \ldots, n$, by spline approximation,
4. Check convergence,
   if $\| \Gamma_k - \Gamma_{k-1} \|_{L_2(0,T)} \leq \varepsilon_2$ then *Stop*
   else *GoTo* step 2.

Our first attempt to solve (10) for a given t_i, which is a core of the step 2 within the proposed algorithm, was simply lured by computational power of sw Mathematica to be able to solve it just by two following commands

```
eq6318 = S[t] == eqSt := K + # Exp[-q (T - t)] CDF[
```

DOI: 10.1051/matecconf/201712504028

```
NormalDistribution[0,
1], -(-Log[#/K] + \[Beta]2 (T - t))/(\[Sigma] Sqrt[T - t])] -
K Exp[-r (T - t)] CDF[
NormalDistribution[0,
1], -(-Log[#/K] + \[Beta]1 (T - t))/(\[Sigma] Sqrt[T - t])] -
K r Integrate[
Exp[-r (\[Eta] - t)] (1 -
CDF[NormalDistribution[0,
1], (Log[#/
S\[Eta][\[Eta]]] + \[Beta]1 (\[Eta] -
t))/(\[Sigma] Sqrt[\[Eta] - t])]), {\[Eta], t, T}] +
+q # Integrate[
Exp[-q (\[Eta] - t)] (1 -
CDF[NormalDistribution[0,
1], (Log[#/
S\[Eta][\[Eta]]] + \[Beta]2 (\[Eta] -
t))/(\[Sigma] Sqrt[\[Eta] - t])]), {\[Eta], t, T}] &

FindRoot[eqSt[s] == s, {s, s1}]
```

However, it failed with a Mathematica process control message SystemException["MemoryAllocationFailure"] signalizing an extreme demand of internal Mathematica procedures upon memory allocation when executing such complex command. It was simply over the memory capacity of our Dell Latitude E6510 computer with 4GB RAM. Hence, we turned to break the given algorithm into a sequence of less complex steps and control manually their performance and convergence in adaptive way, too.

Following [4], Chapter 6.5, we also know some advanced information about optimal exercise boundary. First, the location point at $t = T$

$$\Gamma(T) = \min(rK/q, K), \tag{20}$$

and second, an asymptotic expression of $\Gamma(t)$ near $t = T$, in case of $q = 0$, i.e. for non-dividend paying American put option,

$$(K - \Gamma(t))/K \approx \sigma \sqrt{[(T-t)\,|\ln(T-t)|]}. \tag{21}$$

As already stated above, we know that $\Gamma : t \rightarrow \Gamma(t)$ is a convex and monotone increasing function on $(0,T)$.

Numerical example:
For numerical determination of the optimal early exercise boundary $\Gamma(t)$, we select the American put option with following data: strike price $K = 40$, risk-free rate $r = 0.05$, underlying asset price $S \in (0,65]$, with volatility $\sigma = 0.3$, option expiration date $T = 1$ [year], and dividend rate $q = 0$, i.e. non-dividend paying case.

In Figures 2 and 3, we show two different initial variants of $\Gamma_0(t)$, constructed either by using asymptotic expression (21) with a proper prolongation, or by ad-hoc way using a cubic polynomial with proper interpolation conditions maintaining $\Gamma(T) = K$ as required by (20), and both qualitative properties, i.e. monotonicity and convexity of $\Gamma_0(t)$, on (0,T), as well.

In Figure 2, we present an idea of construction of $\Gamma_0(t)$ using (21) with proper prolongation. A curve given

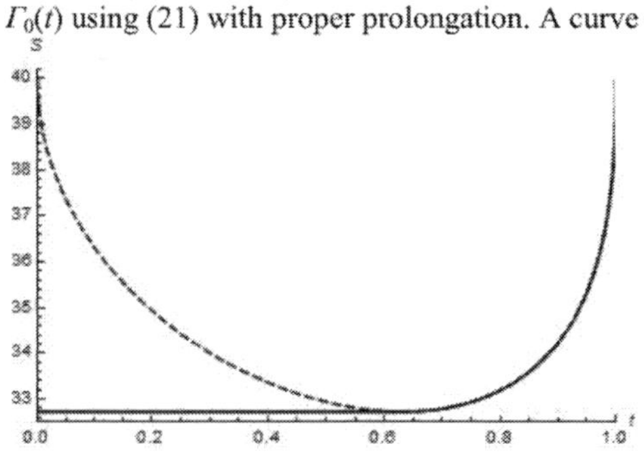

Fig. 2. $\Gamma_0(t)$ – initial early exercise boundary asymptotic-derived with proper prolongation (full line); $\Gamma(t)|_{asymp}$ – curve given by (21) on $(0,T)$ (dashed line).

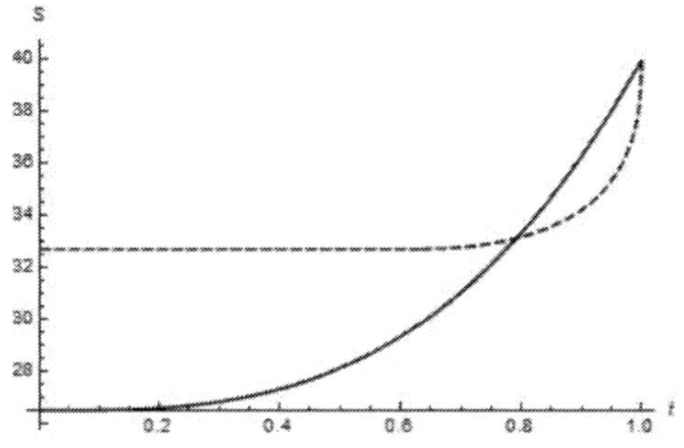

Fig. 3. $\Gamma_0(t)$ – variants: 1) ad-hoc guess cubic curve (full line); 2) asymptotic-derived with proper prolongation one (dashed line).

by (21) is convex on (0,T), but it violates the monotonicity. Hence, to fix that defect, we propose the following procedure. First, we find a global minimum point t_{min} of function (21) on (0,T) issuing the minimum value Γ_{min} of that function. Second, we make a smooth prolongation from $t = 0$ to $t = t_{min}$ by a horizontal line keeping the calculated minimal value Γ_{min}, as it is depicted in Figure 2. Finally, we bond both branches together to get a feasible guess for $\Gamma_0(t)$, $0 \leq t \leq T$.

Assumption $q = 0$, i.e. the case of non-dividend paying option, simplifies the equation (16) for determination of optimal early exercise boundary $\Gamma(t)$ so that the first term is modified and the last one is dropped completely. Hence, we obtain another set of fixed-point looking problems, written formally in the same form (19), however, with a slightly different form of Ψ. It is defined as the right-hand side of the following equation

$$\Gamma(t) = K + \Gamma(t)\Phi[-g_2(t; K, T, \sigma, \beta_2)]$$

$$- Ke^{-q(T-t)}\Phi[-g_1(t; K, T, \sigma, \beta_1)]$$

$$-rK \int_t^T e^{-r(\eta-t)}\{1 - \Phi[\, h_1(t; \Gamma(\eta), \eta, \sigma, \beta_1)]\,, \tag{22}$$

here parameters β_1, β_2, are defined as follows

$$\beta_1 = r - \sigma^2/2, \quad \beta_2 = r + \sigma^2/2,$$

DOI: 10.1051/matecconf/201712504028

and functions $g_i(t; K, T, \sigma, \beta_i)$, i = 1, 2, are given by (17), and function $h_1(t; \Gamma(\eta), \eta, \sigma, \beta_1)$ by (18), correspondingly.

Classical trapeziodal rule is used for numerical approximation of integral $\int_t^T \omega(\eta) d\eta$, which appears in equation (22), as the third term on its right-hand side. Because of the time discretization, we point out that the lower bound $t = t_i$, in particular case, whereas the upper bound T is fixed in any case.

Using function $h_1(t; \Gamma(\eta), \eta, \sigma, \beta_1)$, and $\Phi(x)$, we can define the function $\omega(\eta)$ in following way

$$\omega(\eta) = e^{-r(\eta-t)}(1 - \Phi[h_1(t; \Gamma(\eta), \eta, \sigma, \beta_1)\ ]). \quad (23)$$

For trapezoidal rule, let m is a number if intervals covering $[t_i, T]$ with a step $\Delta\eta = (T - t_i)/m$, thus providing

$$\int_t^T \omega(\eta) d\eta \approx$$
$$\frac{\Delta\eta}{2}\{\omega(t_i) + 2\left[\sum_{j=1}^{m-1} \omega(t_i + j\Delta\eta)\right] + \omega(T)\} = Q_i. \quad (24)$$

Now, we formulate the inner-most problem. For given set of points $\{t_i, S_{i,0}\}$, find $\{t_i, S_{i,k}\}$, $k \geq 1$, such that equation (25) holds, with given tolerance appearing in convergence criterion (26)

$$S_{i,k} = \Psi(S_{i,k};\ t_i, \Gamma_{k-1}(\eta))$$
$$= \mathrm{K} + S_{i,k}\Phi[-\frac{-\ln\frac{S_{i,k}}{K}+\beta_2(T-t_i)}{\sigma\sqrt{T-t_i}}]$$
$$-Ke^{-r(T-t_i)}\Phi[-\frac{-\ln\frac{S_{i,k}}{K}+\beta_1(T-t_i)}{\sigma\sqrt{T-t_i}}] - r\,KQ_{i,k-1}, \quad (25)$$

$$|\ S_{i,k} - \Psi(S_{i,k};\ t_i, \Gamma_{k-1}(\eta))\ | \leq \varepsilon_1. \quad (26)$$

Now, we present some snippets of our Mathematica code we developed for numerical solution of the problem to find optimal early exercise boundary for American put option.

First, it is a construction of the initial early exercise boundary $\Gamma_0(t)$ based upon asymptotic expression of $\Gamma(t)$ near $t = T$, as given by (21)

```
eebAsymp:=K (1-σ Sqrt[(T-#)Abs[Log[T-#]]])&
Plot[eebAsymp[t],{t,0,T}]
FindMinimum[{eebAsymp[t], t > 0, t < 1}, {t,.5}]
tm=t/.Last[%]
eebm=%%[[1]]
eeb1:=If[#<tm,eebm,eebAsymp[#]]&;
Plot[{eeb1[t],eebAsymp[t]},{t,0,T},PlotStyle-
>{Automatic,Dashed},PlotRange->{{0,1},{32.5,40.2}}]
eeb2[t_]:=Piecewise[{{eebm,t<tm},{eebAsymp[t],t>=tm}
}]
Plot[Evaluate[eeb2[t]],{t,0,T},PlotStyle-
>{Red},PlotRange->{{0,1},{32.5,40.2}}]
```

Second, we present a main part of code computing the right-hand side of (25)

```
Δt=(T-t)/(n-1);
ψ3:=With[{s=sLast,t=tLast},Exp[-r(#-t)](1-
CDF[NormalDistribution[0,1],(Log[s/Evaluate[Sη[#]]]+β1
(#-t))/(σ Sqrt[#-t])])&];
fstη=Table[ηη=t+j Δt;ψ3[ηη]//Evaluate,{j,n-1}];
fL=PadLeft[fstη,n,fstη[[1]]];
fR=PadRight[fstη,n,fstη[[n-1]]];
f3is=Δt (Total[fL]+Total[fR])/2  (* <Trapezoidal Rule *)
(* <Compute 1-st & 2-nd terms *)
ψ1:=With[{s=39.181,t=.98},K+# Exp[-q(T-
t)]CDF[NormalDistribution[0,1],-(-Log[#/K]+β2(T-t))/(σ
Sqrt[T-t])]&];
ψ2:=With[{s=sLast,t=tLast},-K Exp[-r(T-
t)]CDF[NormalDistribution[0,1],-(-Log[#/K]+β1(T-t))/(σ
Sqrt[T-t])]&];
sRhs=ψ1[s]+ψ2[s]+f3is
```

Results of our calculations are depicted in Figures 4 and 5. Setting $\varepsilon_1 = 10^{-3}$, we computed two variants of optimal early exercise boundary using from two initial functions $\Gamma_0(t)$, as discussed above and shown in Figure 3, respectively.

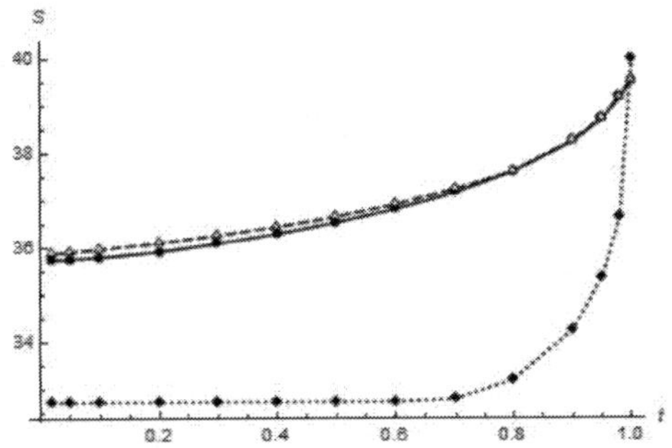

Fig. 4. Local comparison of computed optimal early exercise boundaries $\Gamma(t)$ computed from two initial curves $\Gamma_0(t)$ given in Figure 3 (full line and dashed one), and location of asymptotic-derived with proper prolongation curve $\Gamma_0(t)$ (doted line), with set of nodal points $\{t_i, S_i\}$.

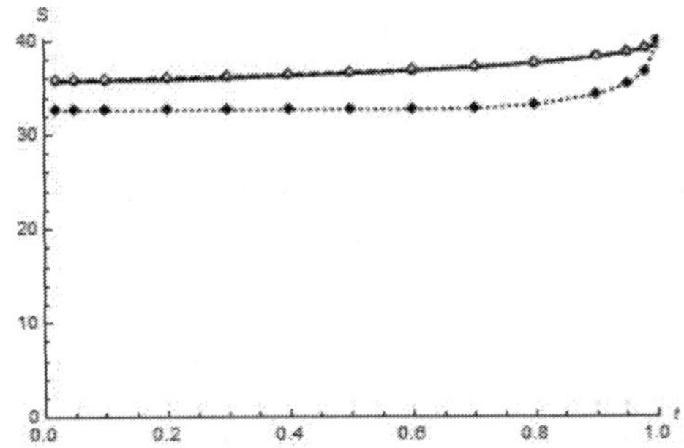

Fig. 5. Global comparison of computed optimal early exercise boundaries $\Gamma(t)$ computed from two initial curves $\Gamma_0(t)$ given in Figure 3 (full line and dashed one), and location of asymptotic-derived with proper prolongation curve $\Gamma_0(t)$ (doted line), with set of nodal points $\{t_i, S_i\}$.

In Figures 4 and 5, we show also the selected set of points for time discretization, i.e. $\{t_i\}$, $i = 0, \ldots, n$, which are used for basic time discretization of nonlinear Volterra integral equation (16), in general. Inspecting the results presented, we may conclude that different initial functions $\Gamma_0(t)$ cause almost negligible differences between our computed approximations of the optimal early exercise boundary $\Gamma(t)$. , which sounds rather

5 Conclusions

In the paper, we discuss briefly a variational formulation of American put option problem, in strong sense. Next, we are focused upon the early exercise premium, which is an integral part of pricing function of that options. However, the most attention is devoted to problem of finding optimal early exercise boundary for American put option, which is formulated by nonlinear Volterra integral equation of the second kind. We propose the adaptive iteration algorithm for solving that problem. The numerical procedure implementing that algorithm is coded in Mathematica, and it seems to work satisfactory. So, it presents a promising platform for our future research, as no doubt, the further and more complicated numerical experiments are necessary to investigate the computational behaviour and performance of the proposed algorithm in more details.

In particular, we acknowledge the financial support of our research by the grant SGS2017-004 "Finance and sustainable development from viewpoint of theory and practice", registered in and provided by the Internal Grant System of the University of West Bohemia in Pilsen, Czech Republic.

References

1. A. Doffou, Int. J. Banking and Fin. **6** (1), 31-47 (2008)
2. M. Dueker, Directly Measuring Early Exercise Premiums Using American and European S&P 500 Index Option, Working Paper Series, https://research.stlouisfed.org/wp/2002/2002-016.pdf
3. Ch. Fries, *Mathematical Finance – theory, modeling, implementation* (John Wiley & Sons, Hoboken, New Jersey, 2007)
4. L. Jiang, *Mathematical Modeling and Methods of Option Pricing* (World Scientific Publ. Co, Singapore, 2005)
5. L. Lukáš, *Conf. Proc., 34-th Int. Conf. Math. Methods in Economics 2016* (Tech. Univ. of Liberec, Liberec, Czech Republic, 2016), 512-517
6. S.N. Neftci, *An Introduction to the Mathematics of Financial Derivatives* (2-nd Ed., Academic Press, London, 2000)
7. O. Pironneau, Y. Achdou, *PDE for Option Pricing*, In *Mathematical Modeling and Numerical Methods in Finance* (Spec. Vol., Handbook of Numer. Analysis, North-Holland, Elsevier, Amsterdam, 2009)
8. R. Stamicar, D. Ševčovič, J. Chadam, Canad. Appl. Math. Quarterly, **7** (4), 427-444, (1999)

Universal language extension for conducting laboratory experiments on analogue and digital circuit design

George Popov[1*], *Filip* Krastev[2]

[1]TU FCST, Information Technology for the Industry, 8 Kliment Ohridski Blvd, 1000 Sofia, Bulgaria

[2]TU FCST, Information Technology for the Industry, 8 Kliment Ohridski Blvd, 1000 Sofia, Bulgaria

Abstract. The article examines in a specialized language different variants of software provision in a specialized environment for conducting laboratory experiments on analogue and digital circuits. A universal language for ULLE laboratory experiments was developed as a resident driver. When declaring an I / O variable (to connect to lab model), it is transmitted to the driver, which is invoked similarly to the system interrupt dispatcher. This way, each time a call is invoked, the model's output channels and input variables are refreshed. Such a conversion allows the driver to work with programs written in different programming languages.

1 Introduction

Despite the diversity and complexity of the specialized company software of automated systems for conducting laboratory experiments [1,2,3,4], it can be said that there are two basic approaches:

- monolith systems – these are hardware systems whose functionality is available through user menus, as data is entered/displayed in windows or charts are to be taken;
- soft systems – these are systems that use a specialized language for conducting laboratory experiments.

Monolithic systems are menu-oriented and perform a strictly defined function. Their main advantage lies in the rapid convening with the system and the easier conduct of laboratory experiments. On the other hand, they follow a certain model from which they cannot deviate, which deprives them of the ability to adapt to different types of tasks and applications.

Systems that are based on programming language are more "agile", enabling the researcher to set up a specific research program according to the needs of the experiment. Another advantage of the software systems is that to them it is possible to emulate through a program code part of the studied electronic circuit (or hardware research). Examples of this is to set OOB (Negative Feed Back) in source code or the signal from a research output hardware to be read by the software, to get redesigned and passed to the input entrance of another scheme.

The proposed method in the article was carried in the microcomputer system for the conduct of laboratory experiments Micro Lab [5,6]. It consists of a general-purpose PC and a non-intelligent (non-CPU control) laboratory model containing a constant analog-digital periphery, having 4 analogue inputs, 4 analogue outputs and a removable module (Fig. 1) as well, which is different for each laboratory experiment.

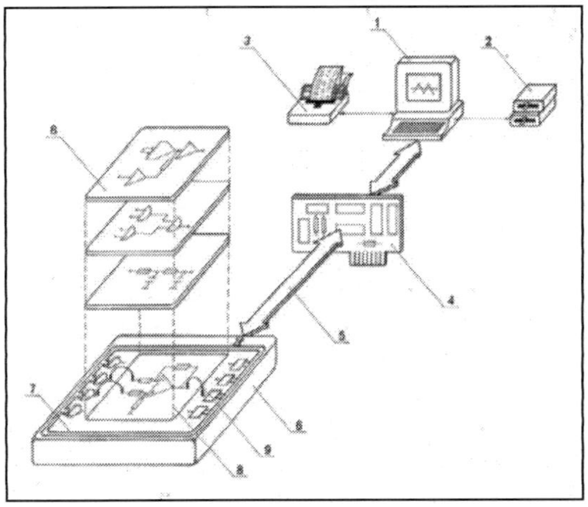

Fig.1. System for laboratory experiments Micro Lab. It can be observed constant (7) and exchangeable modules (8).

The researcher realizes the experimental layout of the laboratory model by performing the necessary connections with commutating(switching) lines (Fig. 2). The study is conducted using the stimulus-response method with the help of a special program written for the specific experiment, that sets values of voltage of output channels and read voltages of input channels.

* Corresponding author: popovg@tu-sofia.bg

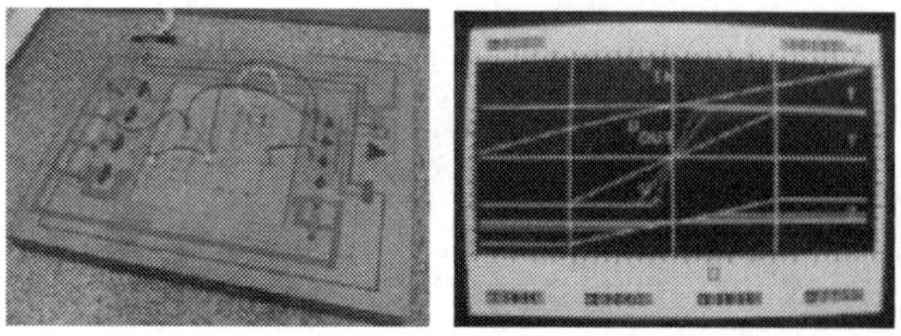

Fig. 2. Associated experimental staging and result output of the experiment. The transmission characteristics at different OA gain values are observed.

The described system provides a complete functional basis for conducting the experiments described in [7].

2 Description of languages for the conduct of laboratory experiments.

The universal language for laboratory experiments ULLE was established in 1988 at the Technical University of Sofia, developed over the years adequately to the software and hardware standards of the modern computer systems. The main idea of most versions of the language consist in the possibility to declare input/output variables of a type model. Another feature is that these variables are refreshed automatically without engaging the researcher.

2.1. ULLE for PCs Apple II, IBM PC with DOS operating system.

For an Apple II PC, ULLE is an extension of the built-in language BASIC. The idea of realization comes from the built-in language operator & that transmits governance in a specific point (address) where the processing of the additional command from the special user program can be performed. BASIC usability is that the researcher can send special commands in programming and dialog mode, i.e. to stop and continue the process of implementation (interpretation) of the program. In the IBM PC with DOS operating system, a ULLE universal resident driver has been implemented, working with most of the programming languages of its time: BASIC of C and Pascal.

The idea of the realization is the following: after declaring a variable of type model, its address is intercepted by the extension of the language. Two types of actions are being carried out:

- If the variable is of type OUTPUT, its value is constantly fed by the dedicated hardware at the output of the model;
- If the variable is of type INUPT, it is constantly refreshed by the output of the model. In this case, the manufacturer (the lab model) continuously produces data and update it in memory cells, which are really addresses of variables in the language of high level, and the user (the program written in the language for conducting laboratory experiments) read them only when needed.

In order to achieve the above features two conversions have been made. In the earlier version, the driver is called out by an interruption 1C h or 70 h, thus refreshing the corresponding input/output variables [8]. Hence the term "live variable" and "Live Variables BASIC" or "LVBASIC" as a version of ULLE.

The later version imposed use of special hardware that monitors for change in values of the "living" variables and generates the interruption that invokes driver execution. This implementation seems modern, but unfortunately it would complicate greatly the laboratory staging. Examples of code for these versions of ULLE (LVBASIC version).

2.1.1 Declaration of variable

- For the input channel on the laboratory staging
&INP (<CHANNEL>, <VAR>, < VALUE>);

- For the output channel
&OUT (<CHANNEL >, <VAR>, < VALUE>);
where:

CHANNEL – the ID number of the input or output channel in Micro Lab periphery;

VAR – the given name of the "living" variable, which will monitor (and transmit) value in the chosen channel;

VALUE – the actual value in millivolts. If the input voltage on the specified entrance changes with a bigger value than stated, an interruption with VALUE is generated to refresh the variable.

2.1.2 Variable release

Release is done with the command:

& KILL <VAR>

After release, the "live variable" stops tracking the channel by becoming a regular variable and retaining its last value. This can be used to memorize value at a time and is extremely convenient when working with arrays.

2.1.3 Notation of data structures and operations

A living variable can participate in an arithmetic expression similar to an ordinary variable. For example, if UI is the input voltage and U2 is the output and are both defined as "live variables", the transmission characteristic can be plotted with:

100 DRAW (*Ul*, *U2*): GOTO 100,

and the dependence of the output power with load R on the output voltage is plotted with:

100 DRAW (*U2*, (*U2**U2*)/*R*): GOTO 100

Filling a buffer (array) with data from an input channel is realized as follows:

10 DIM *A* [100]

20 FOR TO 100

30 *&INP* (1, *A*[I], 200)

40 NEXT *I*

Here the process of "come to life" on each new element of the array, the previous one holds its constant value. In case the following line is inserted:

25 NOT STROBE THEN GOTO 25

It can be performed software strobing to data entry through the living variable STROBE, reading at the input channel of the system.

Similarly, the output of a predefined data buffer is implemented in the following way:

10 DIM *A* [100] ; Array to output

20 &OUT (1, *X*) ; Define living variable X for output channel 1

30 FOR *I*=1 TO 100: *X*=*A*[I]: NEXT ; Send the array through the output channel 1

When it is necessary to remember the current value of a "living" variable, for example X, it can be done in several ways:

- release the variable

&KILL *X*

- assign to a different variable (e.g. TEMP):

TEMP= *X*

-define another "live" variable on the channel:

&INP (1, *Y*, 150)

It is possible that a "living" variable X is simultaneously defined as input and output. Then it will output to the output channel the magnitude that is observed on the input.

LVBasic makes it easy to describe an experimental set-up and to implement linked data structures. The following example illustrates the implementation of a large-scale amplifier (through a real operational amplifier of the removable module) and a feedback with a coefficient of transmission specified by the constant FB. The entrance of the inverting scale amplifier is connected to an output channel 1 and its exit to input channel 2.

10 *&OUT* (1, O_1) ; Voltage output 1 will be equal to the value of the variable IN_1

20 *INP* (2, IN_2) ; The variable IN_2 tracks the value of channel 2.

30 *INP* (1, *C*) ; The variable C tracks the value of channel 1.

40 *&O_1* = IN_2**FB*;

50 PRINT IN_2 ; Print the current result.

60 IF *C* < 10000 THEN 40 ; While C is less than 10000 mV, the cycle 40-60 is running.

2.2. ULLE for PC with Windows OS

In order to make full use of the increased capabilities of the computer systems, the following ULLE implementations were made.

- Realization based on multithreading environment, developed in TU-Sofia. The environment represents the core which supports time share arrangement and co-op mode as well as synchronization and communication of user level threads. New features have been added to the kernel resident module API, supporting the entrances and exits of the model. The essential advantage of this realization is the better structure of the code, which allows for the base of this ULLE version to build a newly designed hard system for the conduct of laboratory experiments.
- Implementation of Open MP. The underlying disadvantage of its own multithreading environment is that it represents itself as a process to Windows and cannot efficiently use the resources of multicore platforms. For this purpose, the last modification of ULLE was made.

3. Conclusion

System for laboratory exercises MicroLab is used to conduct laboratory experiments on analogue and digital circuitry disciplines for more than 30 years and has gained considerable experience. For the sake of brevity of the exhibition, not all the features of ULLE are given. Software provisioning was changing with different computer generations, following two main concepts: MicroLab Integrated (Monolithic) Environment and Universal Language for Laboratory Experiments ULLE. The conclusions drawn are:

- To enhance the experiment and put it in the forefront, the tools used should not be too complicated and distracting the learner;
- To add a part of the laboratory experiment in cloud [9] and make option for distance learning;
- There's been a comparative survey among students in analogue circuitry, as most of them prefer the language extension with live variables instead of a library with corresponding functions;
- Using of BASIC is convenient, because it has automatic declaration of variables, provides opportunities for direct work with the interpreter, i.e. the ability to directly set/read out values from the model, including interrupting and continuing a program as well as inserting a code during the execution.

Acknowledgment

This work is supported by the Project № BG05M2OP001-2.009-0033-C01

References

1. H. Austerlitz, AP, *Data Acquisition Techniques Using PC*, San Diego, California, (1991)

2. Nuno Sousa, Gustavo R. Alves, and Manuel G. Gericota, *An Integrated Reusable Remote Laboratory to Complement Electronics Teaching*, IEEE TRANSACTIONS ON LEARNING TECHNOLOGIES, VOL. 3, NO. 3, JULY-SEPTEMBER 2010

3. V.J. Harward et al., *"The iLab Shared Architecture: A Web Services Infrastructure to Build Communities of Internet Accessible Laboratories," Proc. IEEE,* vol. 96, no. 6, pp. 931-950, June 2008

4. D. Magin and S. Kanapathipillai, *"Engineering Students' Understanding of the Role of Experimentation"*, European Journal of Engineering Education, 2000, Vol. 25, no. 4, pp. 351-358

5. Mechkov K.,, *Computer Based Technical Laboratory for Conduction of Laboratory. Experiments, Announcements,* VMEI, 44th, Book 9 (1989)

6. Zhekov Z., K. Mechkov. Modular System for Automation of Practical Laboratory Experiment., 3rd Nat. Ass.: Syst. Auto. Eng. Labour and Sci. Res. SAITNI-89, B.G. Albena, 10 (1989)

7. https://wiki.analog.com/university/courses/electronics/labs

8. Popov G., *"Parallel Data Exchange Through Living Variables"*, SAITNI-93, Albena, 1989 (bulg. version)

9. Hakima Mostefaoui,.Abdelhalim Benachenhou and Abderrahmane Adda Benattia, *"Design of a low cost remote electronic laboratory suitable for low bandwidth connection"* , Computer Applications in Engineering Education Volume 25, Issue 3, pages 480–488, May 2017

DOI: 10.1051/matecconf/201712504030

A cluster expansion for interacting spin-flip processes

Massimo Campanino[1,*] and *Michele* Gianfelice[2,**]

[1] *Dipartimento di Matematica, Università degli Studi di Bologna, P.zza di Porta San Donato 5, 40126 Bologna, Italy*
[2] *Dipartimento di Matematica, Università della Calabria, Campus di Arcavacata, Ponte P. Bucci - cubo 30B, 87036 Arcavacata di Rende, Italy*

Abstract. We consider a system of spin flip processes, one-for each point of $\mathbb{Z}$, interacting through an Ising type interaction. We construct a cluster expansion and prove that it is convergent when the intensity h of the spin-flip processes is sufficiently high. The system is relevant in the study of the ground state of a quantum Ising process with transverse magnetic field.

1 Introduction

The ground state of the Quantum Ising model with a transverse magnetic field can be represented as a classical Ising model with one added continuous dimension ([DLP]). In its turn this classical Ising model can be represented via a suitable FK random cluster model ([F] [CKP]). This last representation has been used for example in [GOS] to study the entaglement of the ground state.

Here we consider an Ising model in 1+1 dimensions, where the second dimension is continuous. We introduce a representation of this model as a Gibbs random field in $\mathbb{Z}^2$, in which the spins take values in a space of trajectories. We construct a cluster expansion based on this representation and prove that it satisfies the conditions for convergence (see [KP] when the parameter h corresponding to the transverse magnetic field is sufficiently large.

2 Definition of the system

We consider a Gibbs random field on $\mathbb{Z}$ in which the spins take values in a space of processes with values in $\{-1, 1\}$.

Let us first define the finite volume distribution. We consider on $\mathbb{R}$ a Poisson point process with intensity h. Given an interval $\left[-\frac{\beta}{2}, \frac{\beta}{2}\right]$, the Poisson point process induces a measure on piecewise constant functions on $\left[-\frac{\beta}{2}, \frac{\beta}{2}\right]$ with values in $\{-1, 1\}$. The spin configuration $\sigma(t)$ at $t = \pm\frac{\beta}{2}$ is obtained by taking the values equal to -1 or 1 with probability $\frac{1}{2}$ and switching the value of $\sigma(t)$ at each point of the point process configuration. It is not important which extreme of $\left[-\frac{\beta}{2}, \frac{\beta}{2}\right]$ one chooses and which value one assigns to the spin at switwing times..

[*] e-mail: Massimo.Campanino@unibo.it
[**] e-mail: gianfelice@mat.unical.it
[0] *AMS Subject Classification* : 60K35, 60F15, 60K15, 82B43.
Keywords and phrases: Spin-flip processes, Gibbs random fields, cluster expansion

Let us denote by X_I the set of piecewise constant functions with values in $\{-1, 1\}$ defined on the interval I and by μ_I the measure just described on X_I.

Let Λ a finite subinterval of $\mathbb{Z}$. We define a boundary condition for $\Lambda \times \left[-\frac{\beta}{2}, \frac{\beta}{2}\right]$ as two configurations η_1, η_2 in $X_{\left[-\frac{\beta}{2}, \frac{\beta}{2}\right]}$ for the horizontal boundary and two configuration $\xi_1, \xi_2 \in \{-1, 1\}$ for the lower and the upper boundary.

The conditional Gibbs measure is a measure on the space $X^{\Lambda}_{\left[-\frac{\beta}{2}, \frac{\beta}{2}\right]}$ whose density w.r.t. $\bigotimes_{i\in\Lambda} \mu^{(i)}_{\left[-\frac{\beta}{2}, \frac{\beta}{2}\right]}$ is given by

$$
\begin{aligned}
& Z^{-1}_{\eta_1,\eta_2,\xi_1,\xi_2} \times \\
& \exp(-J \sum_{x,y\in\Lambda:|x-y|=1} \int_{-\frac{\beta}{2}}^{\frac{\beta}{2}} dt \sigma_x(t)\sigma_y(t) \\
& -J \sum_{x\in\Lambda} \sum_{y\in\partial\Lambda:|x-y|=1} \int_{-\frac{\beta}{2}}^{\frac{\beta}{2}} dt \sigma_x(t)\eta_y(t)) \\
& \times \prod_{x\in\Lambda} \delta_{\sigma_x\left(-\frac{\beta}{2}\right),\xi_1(x)} \delta_{\sigma_x\left(\frac{\beta}{2}\right),\xi_2(x)}
\end{aligned}
$$

where $Z_{\eta_1,\eta_2,\xi_1,\xi_2}$ is the normalizing constant.

We first define a conditional measure on the trajectories $\sigma(t)$ with values in $\{-1, 1\}$ for t belonging to some interval $[a, b]$ and boundary conditions $\sigma(a) = \varepsilon_1$ and $\sigma(b) = \varepsilon_2$ with $\varepsilon_1, \varepsilon_2 \in \{-1, 1\}$.

Let μ be a Poisson point process in the interval $[a, b]$ with intensity h. If $\varepsilon_1 = \varepsilon_2, \mu^{\varepsilon_1,\varepsilon_2}$ is the measure μ conditioned to the presence of an even number of jumps, while if $\varepsilon_1 \neq \varepsilon_2$ then $\mu^{\varepsilon_1,\varepsilon_2}$ is the measure μ conditioned to the presence of an odd number of jumps. Hence the trajectory corresponding to this realization is a piecewise constant function which is equal to ε_1 in a and to ε_2 in b and has jumps in each point of the point process configuration.

It doesn't matter the value at the jump points since it has no consequence.

3 The cluster expansion

We perform a cluster expansion on the model and verify that, when h is sufficiently large, we can ensure that, for a suitable choice of the parameter, the condition of Kotezky and Preiss are satisfied and the cluster expansion is therefore convergent.

Set $\delta = \frac{\beta}{N}$ for some N. We subdivide each "vertical segment" into closed subintervals of lenght δ. We associate a lattice to the subdivision and to each site of the lattice a *spin* in the space of the piecewise function on the interval $[0, \delta]$ with values in $\{-1, 1\}$. The *spins* on neighbouring sites in the vertical directions must satisfy the compatibility condition that the final value of the trajectory of one *spin* must agree with the initial value of the trajectory of the other.

Therefore, we consider a spin model on $\mathbb{Z} \times \delta\mathbb{Z}$. If $x = (x_1, x_2)$ and $y = (x_1, x_2)$ with $x_2 \in \delta\mathbb{Z}, x_1, y_1 \in \mathbb{Z}$ with $|x_1 - y_1| = 1$, then

$$W\left(\sigma_x, \sigma_y\right) := J \int_0^\delta \sigma_x(t)\,\sigma_y(t)\,dt. \tag{1}$$

If $x = (x_1, x_2)$ and $y = (x_1, y_2)$ with $y_2 = x_2 + \delta$, then

$$W\left(\sigma_x, \sigma_y\right) := \delta_{\sigma_x(t), \sigma_y(t)}\,. \tag{2}$$

The finite volume distribution on a volume Λ with boundary conditions η on $\partial\Lambda$ has density w.r.t. the reference measure $\bigotimes_{x\in\Lambda} \mu(d\sigma_x)$ given by

$$Z_\eta^{-1} \exp\left(-\sum_{x,y\in\Lambda:|x-y|=1} W\left(\sigma_x, \sigma_y\right) - \sum_{x\in\Lambda}\sum_{y\in\partial\Lambda} W\left(\sigma_x, \eta_y\right)\right) \tag{3}$$

with Z_η a normalizing constant.

We perform a first expansion: if $x = (x_1, x_2)$ and $y = (y_1, y_2)$ with $|x_2 - y_2| = 1$, we write

$$e^{-W(\sigma_x, \sigma_y)} = 1 + \left[e^{-W(\sigma_x, \sigma_y)} - 1\right] \tag{4}$$

and perform the expansion

$$Z = \sum_{\ell\subset\Lambda^n} \int \left(\prod_{e\in\ell\,:\,e=\{x_2, y_2\}} \left[e^{-W(\sigma_x, \sigma_y)} - 1\right]\right) \bigotimes_{x\in\Lambda} \mu(d\sigma_x)\,. \tag{5}$$

Given $\ell \subset \Lambda^n$ on each vertical segment we look at those sites A that belong to some $e \in \ell$. If two sites in A are not consecutive we integrate over over the intermediate sites. This integral can be explicitely performed: if the sites are $x = (x_1, x_2)$ and $y = (y_1, y_2)$ with $y_1 > x_1$, the integral is

$$\begin{cases} \frac{1+e^{-2h(y_1-x_1)}}{2} & \text{if } \sigma_x(\delta) = \sigma_y(0) \\ \frac{1-e^{-2h(y_1-x_1)}}{2} & \text{if } \sigma_x(\delta) \neq \sigma_y(0) \end{cases}\,. \tag{6}$$

We take $\delta = \frac{1}{\sqrt{h}}$. Therefore, the activity of a polymer R

can be estimated by

$$\left(e^{\frac{1}{\sqrt{h}}} - 1\right)^{\#\{horizontal\ bonds\}} \frac{e^{-2\sqrt{h}\#\{vertical\ bonds\}}}{2}\,. \tag{7}$$

If we denote by

$$V(R) := \#\{horizontal\ bonds\ of\ R\} + \#\{vertical\ bonds\ of\ R\}\,, \tag{8}$$

We have proved the following theorem.

Theorem. The activity of a polymer $\zeta(R)$ can be bounded by

$$\zeta(R) \leq c(h)^{V(R)} \tag{9}$$

where

$$c(h) := \max\left\{e^{\frac{1}{\sqrt{h}}} - 1, e^{-2\sqrt{h}}\right\}. \tag{10}$$

Remark. The bounds in (9) and (10) imply that cluster expansion (see [KP]) is convergent. In particular they imply that two point correlation functions decay exponentially with the distance when h is large with decay constant going to ∞ as $h \to \infty$.

4 Conclusions

The result of this paper can be extended without problems to $\mathbb{Z}^d$ and should be appliable to study the ground state of the quantum Ising model with a transverse magnetic flield and in particular the entanglement.

References

[KP] R. Kotecky, D. Preiss *Cluster expansion for abstract polymer models.* Comm. Math. Phys. **103**, 491-498 (1986)

[CKP] M. Campanino, A. Klein, F. Perez *Smoothness of the density of states in the Anderson model at high disorder.* Comm. Math. Phys. **114**, 439-461 (1988)

[DLP] W. Driessler, L. Landau, J.F. Perez *Estimates of critical lengths and critical temperatures for classical and quantum lattice systems* J. Statist. Phys. **20**123-162 (1979)

[F] C. M. Fortuin et al. *On the Random cluster model. I. Introduction and relation to other models* Physica **57** 536-564 (1972)

[GOS] G. R. Grimmett, T. J. Osborne, P. F. Scudo *Entanglement in the quantum Ising model.* J. Statist. Phys. **131** 305-339 (2008).

Hierarchical Motion-Compensated Frame Rate Up-Conversion Using Gaussian Pyramid and Guidance Motion Vector

Bumjun Park[1], and *Jechang* Jeong[2,*]

[1]Department of Electronics and Computer Engineering, Hanyang University, Seoul, Korea
[2]Department of Electronic Engineering, Hanyang University, Seoul, Korea

Abstract. This paper proposes fast and accurate frame rate up-conversion algorithm for both software and hardware. The proposed algorithm first construct Gaussian pyramid structure using 3×3 Gaussian mask. After constructing Gaussian pyramid, forward and backward unilateral motion estimation is implemented at the top level of the pyramid. Then, motion vector field that is obtained at the top level is projected onto the middle level and the bottom level of the pyramid with unilateral motion vector refinement. Next, on the bottom level, we implement motion vector smoothing and proposed motion vector shifting with bilateral motion vector refinement. By shifting unilateral motion vector to bilateral motion vector, we could avoid generating holes and overlapped regions. Finally, we select final MV between forward and backward MVs according to their reliability. After all the processes, we interpolate new frames by using overlapped block motion compensation. Experimental results show that proposed algorithm is up to 80 times faster than conventional algorithm with 0.1dB peak signal-to-noise gain in average.

1 Introduction

Frame rate up-conversion (FRUC) is the technique that interpolates virtual frame which exists in the middle of two original frames' time interval. As a result of FRUC process, we can get high frame rate video with low frame rate video.

There have been proposed many FRUC algorithms. In the early stage, FRUC was implemented by copying original frames. However, simply copying frames couldn't make video that has enough quality to be used. As the research progresses, motion compensated frame rate up-conversion (MC-FRUC) was proposed. MC-FRUC is composed of two parts, motion estimation (ME) and motion compensated interpolation (MCI) [1]. ME is the process that finds motion vector (MV). There are many ME algorithms but block matching algorithm (BMA) is mainly used because it is easy to implement both in software and hardware [2]. BMA finds the MV by finding the block that is most similar to the current block in the search range. Using BMA, MC-FRUC finds MV with two methods, unilateral ME and bilateral ME. Unilateral ME finds the MV from the view point of one original frame to other original frame. On the other hand, bilateral ME finds the MV from the view point of interpolated frame to two original frames. In general, unilateral ME finds more accurate MV than bilateral ME because bilateral ME can find incorrect MV when there exist periodical or uniform background. However, unilateral ME generates holes and overlapped regions in the interpolated frame which doesn't appears to bilateral ME. Therefore, unilateral ME need additional process to handle holes and overlapped regions. The MCI is the process that interpolates new frames by using MV information. When interpolating frames, blocking artifact occurs because of BMA. To solve this problem, overlapped block motion compensation (OBMC) was proposed [3]. OBMC reduces blocking artifact by using bilinear window.

Up to this point, many MC-FRUC algorithms were proposed [4] - [6]. Choi et al. proposed bi-directional MC-FRUC (BI_FRUC) using subsampled image which is a simple kind of pyramid structure [7]. However, their subsampling method was too simple to find correct MV. More than that, they used only forward unilateral MV as an initial MV. As a result, their algorithm estimated less accurate MV. Furthermore, when shifting unilateral MV to bilateral MV, they only used MV that is located in the same position of the current block in the reference frame. Consequently, miss match between unilateral MV and bilateral MV caused loss of quality despite of their refinement process. To overcome their weakness, Yoo et al. proposed direction-select ME (DSME) which use both forward and backward unilateral MV as an initial MV to estimate accurate MV [8]. However, they also used simple subsampling method for reducing computational complexity which is not proper to find accurate MV. In addition, they couldn't propose the solution to minimize error that occurs when shifting unilateral MV to bilateral MV.

In this paper, we propose hierarchical MC-FRUC using Gaussian pyramid and guidance motion vector to

* Corresponding author: jjeong@hanyang.ac.kr

solve existing defects [9]. To reduce computational complexity, conventional algorithms used simple subsampling which causes loss of accuracy of ME. To solve this problem, we adopted 3-level Gaussian pyramid to make subsampled image that contains a local average of lower level image at every pixel. In addition, we consider nine MV candidate and propose guidance MV to get rid of miss match that occurs when shifting unilateral MV to bilateral MV.

This paper is organized as follows. Section 2 describes details about proposed algorithm. Section 3 shows experimental results and compares proposed algorithm with conventional algorithms. Finally, section 4 concludes the paper.

2 Proposed algorithm

Fig. 1 shows overall flow chart of proposed algorithm. At first, proposed algorithm make 3-level Gaussian pyramid using 3×3 Gaussian mask. Fig. 2 shows the structure of 3-level Gaussian pyramid. Next, forward and backward unilateral ME is implemented at the top level. Then, MV field that is obtained at the top level is projected onto the middle level and the bottom level of the pyramid with unilateral MV refinement. Next, on the bottom level, we implement weighted MV smoothing and proposed MV shifting with bilateral MV refinement. MV shifting is the process that shifts unilateral MV to bilateral MV. Finally, in the MV selecting process, we select MV between forward and backward MVs according to their reliability. After all the process, we interpolate new frames with OBMC.

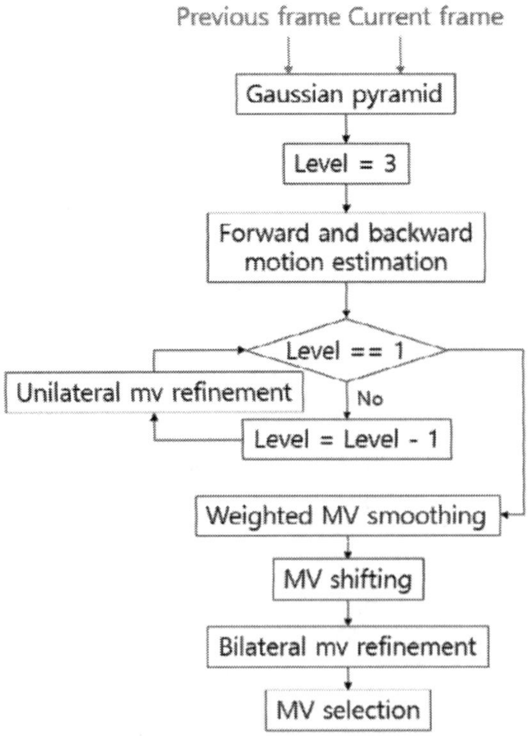

Fig. 1. Overall flow chart of proposed algorithm.

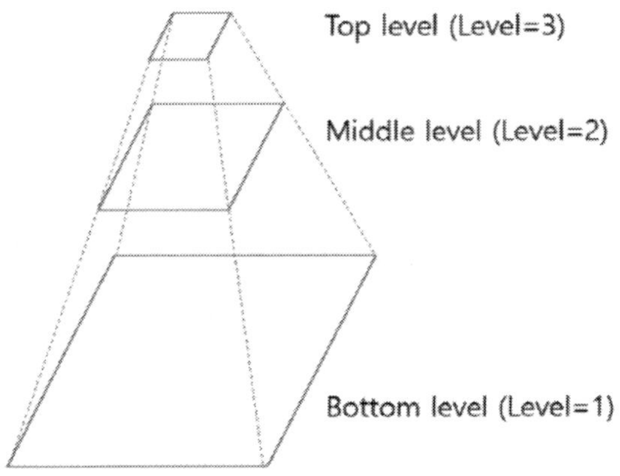

Fig. 2. Structure of 3-level Gaussian pyramid.

2.1. Gaussian pyramid

Many algorithms have been proposed to reduce computational complexity. Among them, pyramid structure is most popular because it is easy to implement both for software and hardware [9]. However, conventional algorithms used simple subsampling method which reduces accuracy of ME [7] – [8]. To overcome this weakness, our proposed algorithm uses 3-level Gaussian pyramid structure using 3×3 Gaussian mask. By using Gaussian mask, our subsampled images contain local average of lower level image which increases accuracy of ME. 3×3 Gaussian mask is defined as follows.

$$G = \begin{pmatrix} 1 & 2 & 1 \\ 2 & 4 & 2 \\ 1 & 2 & 1 \end{pmatrix} \times \frac{1}{16} \tag{1}$$

where G denotes Gaussian mask.

2.2 Forward and backward motion estimation

After Gaussian pyramid structuring, forward and backward ME is implemented at the top level of the pyramid. Forward ME finds the MV from the view point of previous frame to current frame and backward ME finds MV from the view point of current frame to previous frame. When finding MV, we calculate sum of absolute difference (SAD). MV is achieved by finding position that has minimum SAD in the search range. SAD and MV for forward and backward directions are defined as follows.

$$\begin{gathered} SAD_f(dx,dy) = \sum_{x,y\in B} |f_{n-1}(x,y) - f_n(x-dx,y-dy)| \\ SAD_b(dx,dy) = \sum_{x,y\in B} |f_{n-1}(x-dx,y-dy) - f_n(x,y)| \\ v_f = \arg\min_{dx,dy\in R}\{SAD_f(dx,dy)\} \\ v_b = \arg\min_{dx,dy\in R}\{SAD_b(dx,dy)\} \end{gathered} \tag{2}$$

where SAD_f and SAD_b denotes forward and backward SAD respectively. (dx,dy) denotes candidate MV position, B denotes current block, and f_{n-1} and f_n denote previous and current frame respectively. v_f and v_b denote forward and backward MV respectively and R denotes search range.

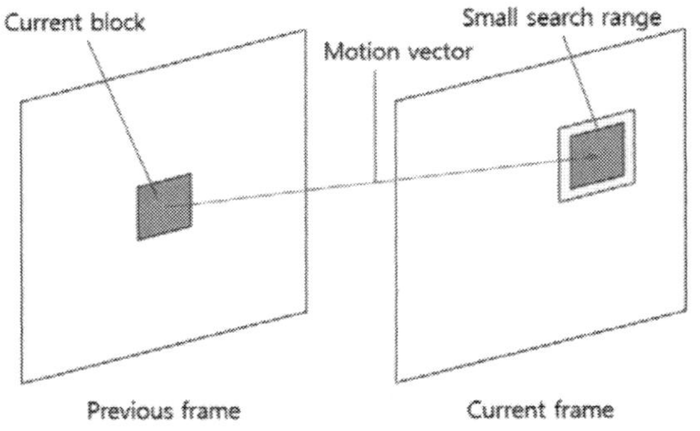

Fig. 3. Example of unilateral motion vector refinement.

2.3 Motion vector projection

After obtaining MV field at the top level, we project MV field onto the middle level and the bottom level of the pyramid. When projecting MV field, MVs should be doubled every time the level increases. However, simply doubled MV field does not fit at the next level. To solve this problem, unilateral MV refinement is implemented every time the level increases. Fig. 3 shows an example of unilateral MV refinement. Using (2), we refine MV by finding minimum SAD in the small search range.

2.4 Weighted motion vector smoothing

After projecting MV field onto the bottom level, we implement weighted MV smoothing. Weighted MV smoothing contains two parts, detecting outlier MV and MV smoothing. In the detecting outlier MV process, we detect outlier MV by calculating (3).

$$
\begin{aligned}
v_{avg} &= \frac{1}{9}\sum_{i=0}^{8} v_i \\
D_i &= abs(v_{avg} - v_i) \\
D_n &= \frac{1}{8}\sum_{i=1}^{8} D_i
\end{aligned}
\tag{3}
$$

where v_{avg} denotes average of nine MVs, D_i denotes difference between v_{avg} and v_i, D_n denotes average MV difference of neighboring MVs. If D_0 is bigger than D_n, we set current block MV v_0 as outlier MV. Fig. 4 shows notation of motion vectors.

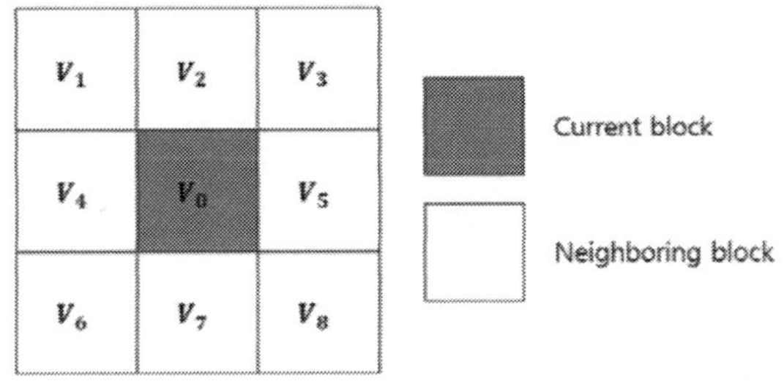

Fig. 4. Notation of motion vectors.

After detecting outlier MVs, we smoothen outlier MVs with weighted sum of neighboring inlier MVs. Weights of neighboring inlier MVs are assigned in inversely proportional to Euclidian distance. The weight window and smoothing method is defined as follows.

$$
\begin{aligned}
w_i &= \begin{cases} \frac{1}{\sqrt{2}}, & i = 1,3,6,8 \\ 1, & i = 2,4,5,7 \end{cases} \\
v_{0s} &= \frac{\sum_{i=inliers} v_i \times w_i}{\sum_{i=inliers} w_i}
\end{aligned}
\tag{4}
$$

where w_i denotes weight window of neighboring MVs and v_{0s} denotes smoothen v_0.

2.5. Motion vector shifting

In this step, we shift unilateral MV to bilateral MV. In the conventional algorithms [7] – [8], they considered only one MV that is located on the same position of current block in the reference frame. However, considering only one MV candidate caused MV shifting error despite of their additional process to refine it. In this paper, we consider additional eight MV candidates that is neighboring with current block. By considering additional MV candidates, we could use symmetrical properties to reduce miss match between unilateral MV and bilateral MV. Proposed MV shifting consists of two process, finding guidance MV and bilateral MV refinement. When finding guidance MV, first thing to do is comparing the area of nine MV candidates that overlaps with current block. Fig. 5 shows an example of finding guidance MV. In proposed MV shifting method, we choose most overlapped MV as a guidance MV. However, we can encounter three kinds of cases as we process proposed method. First, if we have no MV that overlaps with current block, we choose MV that is located on the same position of the current block as a guidance MV. Second, if we have only one MV that overlaps most, we choose that MV as a guidance MV. Finally, if we have more than two MV that overlaps most, we calculate sum of bilateral absolute difference (SBAD) of each MV. After calculating SBAD, we choose the MV that has minimum SBAD as a guidance MV. In this case, SBAD and guidance MV is defined as follows.

$$
\begin{aligned}
& SBAD(v_{hx}, v_{hy}) \\
&= \sum_{x,y\in B} \left| f_{n-1}(x - v_{hx}, y - v_{hy}) - f_n(x + v_{hx}, y + v_{hy}) \right| \\
& v_g = \arg\min_{v_i \in M}\{SBAD(v_{hx}, v_{hy})\}
\end{aligned}
\tag{5}
$$

Where v_{hx} and v_{hy} denote half of x directional coefficient and y directional coefficient of v_i. M denotes the set of MV that overlaps most.

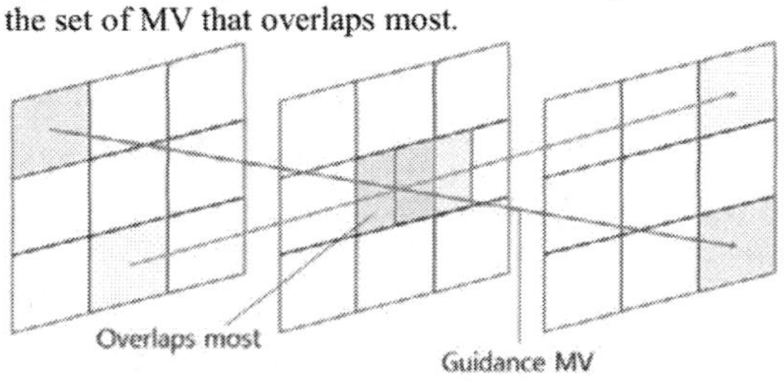

Fig. 5. Example of finding guidance motion vector.

In the proposed algorithm, we minimized motion vector shifting error by finding proper guidance MV. However, to reduce remaining errors, we implement bilateral MV refinement. This process is similar to unilateral MV refinement. The difference is that we use SBAD when implementing bilateral MV refinement instead of SAD. Using (5), we refine guidance MV by finding the position that has minimum SBAD in the small search range.

2.6 Motion vector selection

In the proposed algorithm, all processes are applied both to forward and backward MVs respectively. In this step, after applying all processes, we choose one MV that is more reliable. To select more reliable MV, we calculate SBAD of forward and backward MV and use it as a reliability. Reliability and final MV are defined as follows.

$$r_f = SBAD(v_{fx}, v_{fy})$$
$$r_b = SBAD(v_{bx}, v_{by}) \quad (6)$$
$$v_{final} = \min(r_f, r_b)$$

where r_f and r_b denote reliability of forward and backward v_g. v_{fx} and v_{fy} denote x directional coefficient and y directional coefficient of forward v_g. v_{bx} and v_{by} denote x directional coefficient and y directional coefficient of backward v_g. v_{final} denotes final MV.

3 Experimental results

In this paper, we interpolate even frames by using two odd frames of original sequence. When interpolating frames, we interpolated frames by using OBMC [3]. For the test sequences, we used HEVC test sequences. When experimenting, we set block size as 8pixel and search range as 33pixel at the top level. Small search range was set to 5pixel. When evaluating quality of algorithm, we calculated peak signal to ratio (PSNR) with original even frames and interpolated even frames.

Table 1 and Table 2 shows PSNR and time results comparing with conventional algorithms [7], [8] and proposed algorithm. As we used 3-level Gaussian pyramid, proposed algorithm is about 80 times faster than [7] with 0.1dB PSNR gain in average. Also, proposed algorithm is about 2 times faster than [8] with 0.17dB PSNR gain in average.

Fig. 6 shows result image of conventional algorithms and proposed algorithm. In this image, DSME and BI_FRUC couldn't interpolate lines of playground clearly because they found incorrect MV. Furthermore, both DSME and proposed algorithm interpolated foot of player smoothly but BI_FRUC interpolated with incorrect MV. More than that, the method BI_FRUC used to interpolate frames couldn't reduce blocking artifact when the movement is fast. This kind of weakness also can be detected on the basketball. DSME and proposed interpolated moving basketball smoothly. However, basketball of BI_FRUC was distorted by blocking artefact. Overall, proposed algorithm shows better performance than conventional algorithms in both objective and subjective comparison.

Table 1. PSNR(dB) results

Class	Sequence	DSME	BI_FRUC	Proposed
Class A	*PeopleOnStreet_2560x1600*	27.91	26.86	27.61
	Traffic_2560x1600	37.20	37.72	37.28
Class B	*BasketballDrive_1920x1080*	30.64	30.30	31.02
	BQTerrace_1920x1080	32.68	31.77	32.5
	Cactus_1920x1080	31.8	32.01	31.93
	Kimono1_1920x1080	36.2	35.61	35.97
	ParkScene_1920x1080	34.59	35.10	35.22
Class C	*BasketballDrill_832x480*	29.67	30.80	30.88
	BQMall_832x480	32.93	33.01	32.93
	PartyScene_832x480	30.68	30.02	30.49
	RaceHorses_832x480	27.05	26.98	27.05
Class E	*FourPeople_1280x720*	40.49	40.58	40.27
	Johnny_1280x720	41.52	41.39	41.75
	KristenAndSara_1280x720	41.32	41.50	41.31
Average		33.90	33.83	34.01

Table 2. Time(sec) results

Class	Sequence	DSME	BI_FRUC	Proposed
Class A	*PeopleOnStreet_2560x1600*	522	67	30
	Traffic_2560x1600	340	49	26
Class B	*BasketballDrive_1920x1080*	1322	149	98
	BQTerrace_1920x1080	10427	180	73
	Cactus_1920x1080	1029	137	57
	Kimono1_1920x1080	11040	72	36
	ParkScene_1920x1080	462	69	26
Class C	*BasketballDrill_832x480*	158	21	12
	BQMall_832x480	179	26	13
	PartyScene_832x480	160	25	10
	RaceHorses_832x480	138	17	10
Class E	*FourPeople_1280x720*	12842	48	24
	Johnny_1280x720	569	75	27
	KristenAndSara_1280x720	478	66	26
Average		2833	71.61	33.43

4 Conclusion

In this paper, we proposed fast and accurate FRUC algorithm by using 3-level Gaussian pyramid and guidance MV. Proposed algorithm can find more accurate MV when implementing ME process because we used Gaussian pyramid structure instead of simple subsampling. Moreover, we proposed new MV shifting method using guidance MV. By adopting guidance MV, we could reduce errors that occurs when shifting unilateral MV to bilateral MV. As a result, proposed algorithm showed 0.1dB PSNR gain with up to 80times faster than conventional algorithm in average.

"This research was supported by Basic Science Research Program through the National Research Foundation of Korea(NRF) funded by the Ministry of Science, ICT and future Planning(NRF-2015R1A2A2A01006004)"

(a)

(b)

(c)

Fig. 6. Result image: (a) DSME, (b) BI_FRUC and (c) proposed

References

[1] C. Cafforio, F. Rocca, and S. Turbaro, "Motion compensated image interpolation," *IEEE Trans. Communications*, vol. 38, no. 2, pp. 215 - 222, Feb. 1990.

[2] F. Dufaux and F. Moscheni, "Motion estimation techniques for digital TV : a review and a new contribution," *Proc. IEEE*, vol. 83, pp. 858 - 876, June 1995.

[3] M.T. orchard and C.J. sullivan, "Overlapped block motion compensation : an estimation-theoretic approach," *IEEE Trans. Image Processing*, vol. 3, no. 9, pp. 693 - 699, Sept. 1994.

[4] S.H. Lee, Y.C. Shin, S. Yang, H.H. Moon, and R.H. Park,"Adaptive motion-compensated interpolation rate-up-conversion," *IEEE Trans. Consumer Electronics*, vol. 48, no. 3, pp. 444 - 450, Aug. 2002.

[5] S.H. Lee, O. Kwon, and R.H. Park, "Weighted-adaptive motion compensated frame rate up-conversion," *IEEE Trans. Consumer Electronics*, vol. 49, no. 3, pp. 485 - 492, Aug. 2003.

[6] S.-J. Kang, K.-R. Cho, and Y.H. Kim, "Motion Compensated Frame Rate Up-Conversion Using Extended Bilateral Motion Estimation," *IEEE Trans. Comminications*, vol. 53, no. 4, pp. 1759 - 1767, Nov. 2007.

[7] B.-T Choi, S.-H Lee, and S.-J Ko, "New Frame Rate Up-Conversion Using Bi-Directional Motion Estimation," *IEEE Trans. Consumer Electronics*, vol. 46, no. 3, pp. 603 – 609, Aug. 2000.

[8] D.-G. Yoo, S.-J. Kang, and Y.H. Kim, "Direction-Select Motion Estimation for Motion-Compensated Frame Rate Up-Conversion," *Journal of Display Technology*, vol. 9, no. 10, pp. 840 - 850, Oct. 2013.

[9] Adelson, Edward H., et al. "Pyramid methods in image processing." *RCA engineer* 29.6 (1984): 33-41.

MATEC Web of Conferences **125**, 05002 (2017) DOI: 10.1051/matecconf/201712505002
CSCC 2017

Multidirectional motion estimation algorithm for frame rate up-conversion

Songhyun Yu[1], *Jechang* Jeong[1]

[1] Department of Electroincs and Computer Engineering, Hanyang University, Seoul, Korea

Abstract. In this paper, we propose a new motion estimation algorithm for motion-compensated frame rate up-conversion. To reduce computational complexity, it constructs a hierarchical structure using Gaussian image pyramid and unidirectionally estimates motion vectors (MVs) between two original frames at the top level. Since the accuracy of the motion vector may deteriorate at low resolution, each block has five candidates for motion vector so that disadvantages of hierarchical motion estimation are reduced. After motion estimation (ME), MVs of bottom level are corrected based on the sum of absolute difference (SAD) values of the blocks. All unidirectional MVs are assigned to bidirectional MVs, and new frames are interpolated using these MVs. As a result, proposed algorithm shows up to 1.3 dB increase in PSNR compared with conventional algorithm with low computational complexity, and it shows clearer images than conventional algorithms.

1 Introduction

Frame rate up-conversion (FRUC) is a technique which interpolates frame by inserting new frames between originally existed frames. In the early days of technology, frame interpolation was performed using frame repetition or simple averaging of two frames. However, this causes image quality deterioration. In recent years, motion-compensated FRUC (MC-FRUC) algorithm has been developed [1-3]. This algorithm generally has three steps: motion estimation (ME), motion vector smoothing (MVS), and motion compensated interpolation (MCI).

ME is a process of finding motion of each object using original frames, and motion vectors (MVs) are obtained in this step. Depending on the direction in which the motion is predicted, ME is divided into two major categories: unidirectional motion estimation (UME), bidirectional motion estimation (BME). Motions are predicted unidirectionally in the viewpoint of the original frame, and overlapped areas and hols occur in the interpolated frame. BME bidirectionally predicts motions in the viewpoint of the interpolated frame, so there are not holes and overlapped areas. However, it can find false MVs since there in no information about the current reference block.

Basically, ME has a high computational complextiy, so for real-time processing of high-resolution video, it is essential to reduce the complexity. Several studies proposed low-complexity FRUC algorithms; [13] used Gaussian pyramid structure and Laplacian pyramid structure in ME step, and [15] used subsampling of the original image for ME. These algorithms, however, have reduced the accuracy of MVs due to the resolution changes of the original images. In this paper, we propose a multidirectional motion estimation (MME) algorithm to reduce complexity and maintain the accuracy of the motion vector.

For the MVS process, [4] used mean and variance of neighboring MVs and weighted sum of these motion vectors replace the current motion vector, and in [6], current motion information is used to correct false motion vectors. However, when the current block is at the boundary of an object or when the current motion vector is not correct, these algorithms can cause an error. In this paper, an adaptive global MVS algorithm is proposed to overcome these limitations.

The remainder of this paper is organized in the following order; secsion 2 reveal the proposed algorithm in detail, section 3 shows experimental results compared with other algorithms, and section 4 concludes this paper.

2 Proposed algorithm

Fig. 1 shows overall flowchar of the proposed algorithm. Two original frames form a pyramid structure using [7]. The unidirectional motion estimation is performed at the top level, in which five candidate positions are designated. At the lower levels, the candidates are modified by small search range motion estimation around each position. Once the MVs of the all blocks are determined, these MVs are modified according to the sum of absolute difference (SAD) value. Final MVs are converted to the bidirectional MVs using [5]. As a result, a new frame is interpolated in the MCI step. The details of the proposed algorithm are described in the following subsections.

2.1. Motion estimation

Prior to the motion estimation process, each frame forms an image pyramid as shown in Fig. 2. As shown in Fig. 3,

* Corresponding author: jjeong@hanyang.ac.kr

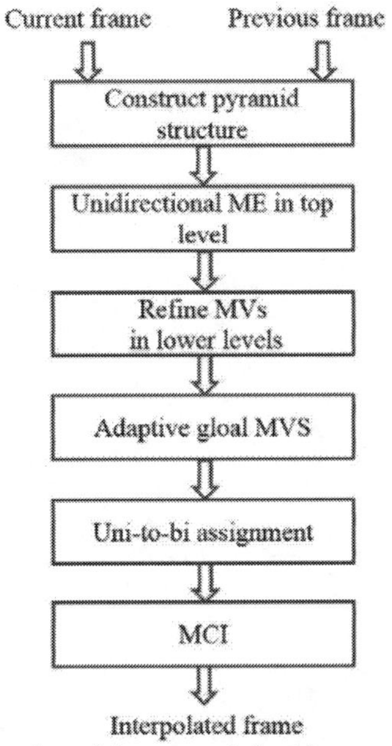

Fig. 1. Flowchart of the proposed algorithm.

the proposed MME algorithm divides the search range into four regions according to directions and finds the candidate positions with the smallest SAD for each region. SAD is given by:

$$SAD_u(B, v_m) = \sum_{p \in B} |f_p(p) - f_c(p + v_m)|$$
$$v_o = \arg \min_{v_m \in SR_o} \{SAD(B, v_m)\}, \qquad o = 1,2,3,4 \tag{1}$$

where SAD_u denotes the SAD value in unidirection, B is the current block, p is a pixel position in the block B, and v_o means candidate MVs of the current block in each search range "SR_o". Four resions of the search range are represented as n.

After top level processing , each candidates points are updated using ME with small search range. The size of this small search range is determined based on the SAD value of each candidates, and it is given by :

$$SR_{small}(S) = \alpha(S - 255)^2 + \beta \tag{2}$$

where S is a SAD value, and SR_{small} is the size of the search range. β means maximum size of the search range, and α is weighting factor. We set $\beta = 50$, $\alpha = 0.0007689$.

At the bottom level, current block decides final motion vector which has the smallest SAD among the candidates

2.2. Adaptive global motion vector smoothing

When the ME process of one frame is ompleted, the MVS is performed to reduce an erorr generated in the ME.

Fig. 2. Pyramid structure.

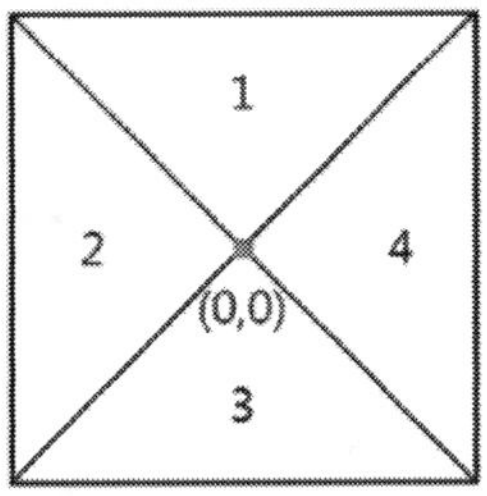

Fig. 3. Four regions of the search area.

Proposed algorithm utilizes SAD values of final MVs to determine which MV is incorrect one. This process is shown as follows:

$$\begin{aligned} R(B) &= 1 \qquad && if\ SAD(B) > Th \\ R(B) &= 0 && otherwise \end{aligned} \tag{3}$$

where $R(B)$ indicates reliability of the current block B, and Th means threshold value.

To determine threshold value, we used recursive algorithm in [8], and it is shown in Fig. 4.

3 Experimental results

Objective and subjective evaluations are performed in this section. For the objective ecaluation, peark signal to noise ratio (PSNR) is used, and complexity of each algorithms are considered. High efficiency video coding (HEVC) standard test sequences were chosen for the test so that high resolution videos are includes in the experiment. Block size is set to 16×16, and search range of the top level is set to ± 12 pixels.

Table 1 shows PSNR results compared with conventional algorithms [15, 4, 10]. In all sequences, the proposed algorithm shows the highest PSNR value; up to 1.17 dB compared to [15], up to 1.34 dB compared to [4], and up to 1.05 dB compared to [10]. Average values also shows that proposed algorithm has highest PSNR value.

DOI: 10.1051/matecconf/201712505002

1. Select initial threshold value T
2. Segment histogram of SAD using T
-> It generates two resiong ($Z_1 > T, Z_2 \leq T$)
3. Calculate the average values w_1, w_2 in Z_1, Z_2, respectively
4. Compue a new threshold $T_{new} = \frac{(w_1+w_2)}{2}$
5. Repeat step 2-4 until $\Delta T = |T_{new} - T| < \gamma$

Fig. 4. Algorithm to determine threshold.

Table 2 shows computational complexity of the algorithms. N means block size (16), R means search range (25), and R_s denotes small search range (2). The small search range of the proposed algorithm is adaptively determined, but approximated to an average value of 2. Ratio represents the relative amount of computation when the computation complexity of the proposed algorithm is 1. It can be seen that the proposed algorithm has less computational complexity than the other algorithms. [15] does not make much difference; however, when MV is modified at lower levels, there are many overlapping parts, so the actual computational complexity of the proposed algorithm is smaller than 1.

Fig. 5 shows results images in *BasketballDrive* sequence. In the square part, the result image of the proposed algorithm is clearer than the other algorithms.

Table 1. PSNR comparison

	[15]	[4]	[10]	Proposed
PeopleOnStreet (2460×1600)	26.86	26.69	27.91	28.03
BasketballDrive (1920×1080)	30.30	30.39	30.46	30.84
ParkScene (1920×1080)	35.10	34.95	34.30	35.35
Johnny (1280×720)	41.39	41.40	41.52	41.62
BQMall (832× 480)	33.01	32.53	32.94	33.01
Average	33.33	33.19	33.43	33.77

Table 2. Computational complexity

Algorithm	Complexity	Ratio
[15]	$(\frac{N}{2})^2(R+1)^2$	1.01
[4]	$2(1.5N)^2(2R+1)^2$ $-((1.5N)^2-1.5N)^2$	63.03
[10]	$2N^2(2R+1)^2$ $+2N^2(2R_s+1)^2$	31.48
Proposed	$\left(\frac{N}{4}\right)^2\left(\frac{R}{2}+1\right)^2$ $+5(\frac{N}{2})^2(2R_s+1)^2$ $+5(N)^2(2R_s+1)^2$	1

(a)
(b)
(c)
(d)

Fig. 5. Result images (a) [15], (b) [4], (c) [10], (d) proposed.

4 Conclusion

In this paper, ME algorithm and MVS algorithm for the MC-FRUC were proposed. In the ME process, multidirectional motion estimation was proposed to find accurate MVs with low computational complexity, and adaptive global motion vector smoothing algorithm was proposed in the MVS step, so the error of the MVs is corrected by adaptively determining the threshold value in frame unit. As a result, the proposed algorithm shows high PSNR in objective evaluation and clear image in subjective evaluation while keeping the computational complexity low.

This research was supported by Basic Science Research Program through the National Research Foundation of Korea(NRF) funded by the Ministry of Science, ICT and future Planning(NRF-2015R1A2A2A01006004)

References

1. C. Cafforio, F. Rocca, and S. Tubaro, "Motion compensated image interpolation," *IEEE Trans. Communication*, vol.**38**, no.2, pp.215 -222, Feb.(1990).
2. S. H. Lee, Y. C. Shin, S. Yang, H. H. Moon, and R.H. Park,"Adaptive motion-compensated interpolation rate-up-conversion," *IEEE Trans. Consumer Electronics*, vol.**48**,no.3, pp.444-450, Aug. (2002).
3. S. H. Lee, O. Kwon, and R. H. Park, "Weighted-adaptive motion compensated frame rate up-conversion," *IEEE Trans. Consumer Electronics*, vol.**49**, no.3, pp.485-492, Aug. (2003).
4. D. G. Yoo, S. J. Kang, and Y. H. Kim, "Direction-select motion estimation for motion-compensated frame rate up-conversion," *J. Display Technol.*, vol. **9**, no. 10, pp. 840–850, Oct. (2013).
5. Y. Guo, L. Chen, Z. Gao, and X. Zhang, "Frame rate up-conversion using linear quadratic motion estimation and trilateral filtering motion smoothing," J. Display Technol., vol. **12**, no. 1, pp. 89-98, Jan. (2016).
6. D. Wang, L. Zhang, and A. Vincent, "Motion-compensated frame rate up-conversion—Part I: Fast multi frame motion estimation," *IEEE Trans. Broadcast*, vol. **56**, no. 2, pp. 133–141, Jun. (2010).
7. P. J. Burt, and E. H. Adelson, "The laplacian pyramid as a compact image code," *IEEE Trans. Commun.*, vol. **31**, no. 4, pp. 532-540, Apr. (1983).
8. R. C. Gonzalez, and R. E. Woods, *Digital Image Processing*, Pearson Prentice Hall. (2010).
9. C. Wang, L. Zhang, Y. He, and Y. P. Tan, "Frame rate up-conversion using trilateral filtering," *IEEE Trans. Circuits Syst. Video Technol.*, vol. **20**, no. 6, pp. 886-893, Jun. (2010).
10. S. J. Kang, S. Yoo, and Y. H. Kim, "Dual motion estimation for frame rate up-conversion," *IEEE Trans. Circuits Syst. Video Technol.*, vol. **20**, no. 12, pp. 1909–1914, Dec. (2010).
11. D. Wang, A. Vincent, P. Blanchfield, and R. Klepko, "Motion-compensated frame rate up-conversion—Part II: New algorithms for frame interpolation," *IEEE Trans. Broadcast.*, vol. **56**, no. 2, pp. 142–149, Jun. (2010).
12. S. J. Kang, K. R. Cho, and Y. H. Kim, "Motion compensated frame rate up-conversion using extended bilateral motion estimation," *IEEE Trans. Consumer Electron.*, vol. **53**, no. 4, pp. 1759–1767, Nov. (2007).
13. B. W. Jeon, G. I. Lee, S. H. Lee, and R. H. Park, "Coarse-to-fine frame interpolation for frame rate up-conversion using pyramid structure," *IEEE Trans. Consum. Electron.*, vol. **49**, no. 3, pp. 499-508, (2003).
14. M. T. Orchard and G. J. Sullivan, "Overlapped block motion compensation: An estimation-theoretic approach," *IEEE Trans. Image Process.*, vol. **3**, no. 5, pp. 693-699, (1994).
15. B. Choi, S. Lee, and S. Ko, "New frame rate up-conversion using bi-directional motion estimation," *IEEE Trans. Consumer Electronics*, vol. **46**, no. 3, pp. 603-609, (2000).

Sensor-based supporting mobile system Parkinson disease clinical tests utilising biomedical and RFID technologies

Mariusz Chmielewski[1,a], *Michał* Nowotarski[1,b]

[1]Military University of Technology, Cybernetics Faculty, gen. S. Kaliski Street, Warsaw, Poland

Abstract. This paper discusses method and tool for assisting clinical tests of pharmaceutical drugs utilising sensors and mobile technologies. Emerging sensor and mobile technologies deliver new opportunities to gather and process medical data. Presented analytical approach implements such observations and delivers new, convenient means for remote patient monitoring. Clinical tests are highly specialised process requiring methodology and tools to support such research. Currently available methods rely mostly on analogue approach (booklets), requiring the clinical test participant to fill in health state daily. Such approach often can be biased by unpunctual, not precise reporting. The mobile device can support this process by automatic scheduling and recording an actual time of reports and most of all it can record the inertial and biometric sensor data during the survey process. Presented analytical method (tremors recognition) and mobile tool offers consistent approach to clinical test assistance transforming and Android smartphone into remote reporting and notification tool. The tool offers additionally features for sensor based diagnostics support for PD tremor recognition as well as specific clonic and tonic symptoms (dedicated for further system extensions towards epilepsy). Capabilities of the system delivers also RFID mechanisms for efficient on-site clinical test authorisation and configuration. This feature simplifies application installation and automatic set-up considering the participant, clinical test configuration, schedule, smartphone and sensor data. Such a composition delivers convenient and reliable tool which can assist patients and medical staff during the process objectifying the clinical tests results and helping to ensure good quality of the data, quickly available and easily accessible.

1 Introduction and main concept

The main idea presented in the work is to utilise handhelds and wearable biometric and inertial sensors in order to assist clinical tests and medical examinations [1][7][8]. Such an approach can deliver promising results in order to obtain objective data during massively executed clinical tests. The tool can also lower costs of conducting and analysing results of clinical tests, as the logistics of the tests can be simplified. Presented method, algorithms and its implementation delivers handheld application and a sensor armband, which are managed by the central server service. The central server service can be further integrated with any SOA infrastructure delivered by clinical test provider. Such construct is flexible easily configurable and can be deployed as a cloud services to support scalability.

The use of accelerometer and/or electromyography in neurological diseases treatment were mentioned in various publications. There were discussed ideas to monitor Parkinson's disease with the smartphone [2] or to provide automatic detection of tremors and dyskinesias with accelerometer and electromyographic signal of specified monitoring device [3]. Idea of use an accelerometer during detection of epilepsy's seizures were mentioned in [4][5][6]. What is more, since 2012 Military University of Technology has developed several sensor based solutions for neurological disease assistance and monitoring - SENSE [7], PATRON [8] utilising smartphone's inertial sensors proprietary wireless biometric sensors.

2 Tool for assisting clinical tests

PATRON [8] (smartphone-based mobile system utilising wearable sensors) offers innovative approach of Parkinson's Disease symptoms examination delivered through application of myography and inertial sensors integrated with handheld devices. The utilisation of sensor-assisted diagnostics of tremors and motor skills, delivers new opportunities for neurological research especially in the domain of effective drug usage and clinical testing of pharmaceutical therapies. The developed hardware, the PATRON multi-sensor is first fully mobile, wireless sensor fusing several channels of data gathered from surface electromyography, mechanomyography, 3-axis inertial sensor and magnetometer. The sensor can be seamlessly attached to a forearm or calf in order to remotely gather, filter and transfer the data to a handheld. The multistage DSP analysis of the data is performed in real time, delivering

[a] Mariusz Chmielewski: mchmielewski@wat.edu.pl
[b] Michał Nowotarski: michal.nowotarski@wat.edu.pl

DOI: 10.1051/matecconf/201712505003

data of tremors frequency and magnitude, the intensity of muscle tensions and the orientation of the sensor. Fused data describing the neurological examination is than stored, aggregated with the time and location and uploaded to the reporting server. The mobile application delivers two main functionalities ad-hoc tremor examination and on-demand clinical test surveying. Therefore, the application can be used for examining, the tremor intensity and limb movement fluency, evaluating the Parkinson's Disease on-off fluctuations and dyskinesia. System supports the PD patient by estimating current health state and in consequence providing recommendation for medicine usage. PATRON can also be used as a clinical test support toolkit for researchers and pharmaceutical companies guiding patients through the complete process of reporting the drug effectiveness. Sensor-based tests complement the patient's surveys, delivering objective information about the patient's health state therefore evaluating the effectiveness of a drug and applied treatment. The system offers also a server based reporting services which serve as a clinical tests warehouse. Web portal visualizes the clinical test process organizes the data and evaluates the characteristics of the medicine effectiveness [13][17]. PATRON server has been deployed on Microsoft Azure Cloud environment, which provides high-scalability and security characteristics. Web application can be accessed by the researchers, medical staff and pharmaceutical companies in order to inspect and monitor current state of clinical test process.

3 Utilisation of inertial and myography sensors

The MYO armband is a gesture and movement control device. Its purpose is to receive signals during hand's movement and gestures. The device contains eight EMG sensors (device segments) detecting muscle tension with sample rate 200 Hz and accelerometer, gyroscope and magnetometer inside built-in IMU with sample rate 50 Hz (Invensense MPU-9150 9-dof motion sensor). It is controlled by the Free-scale Kinetis Cortex M4 120MHz processor and communication is realized with Micro USB port or Bluetooth LE protocol. Armband can be expandable between 7.5 - 13 inches (19 - 34 cm) forearm circumference and weights 93 grams [9][10].

The vendor has provided SDKs dedicated for various mobile platforms and capabilities. For example, the iOS SDK contains methods providing ability to read data from EMG sensors, while the Android SDK lacks such features. According to [11], sensors of the Myo have the following characteristics:

- electromyograph – unit of measurement: mV, range: +/- 0.45 mV,
- accelerometer – unit of measurement: g, range: +/- 16 g,
- gyroscope – unit of measurement: °/s, range: +/- 2000 °/s,
- position sensor – unit of measurement: quaternion.

The manufacturer claims that sensor's battery should last a whole day of continuous use (which is one of crucial requirements for the clinical test assistance). For the band in a sleep mode, disconnected from any devices, expected operating time is about a week. There are two batteries inside, with a capacity of 260 mAh each. The communication range via Bluetooth is up to 15 meters. Armband's sensors can work on the leg what can be useful in various diagnostic purposes.

Myo was mentioned before as an device to medical use. It was proposed to help hand-amputees recover functionality using non-invasive method [12]. Its surface electromyography accuracy was compared and defined as similar to more expensive devices.

4 Clinical test support

The main purpose of the application is to continuously monitor the patient's condition. Therefore, at a time specified according to the schedule, application displays a notification asking the user to complete a short survey about his health. The schedule can be configured according to the patient's individual diagnostic needs. The survey initially contains the following questions:

- Are You able to perform survey? (Yes, No)
- Rate your state (On, On-Off, Off)
- Do you have dyskinesias? (Yes, No)
- Are these dyskinesias inconvenient?(Yes, No)

The list of survey questions can be remotely configured, modifying questions and possible answers – with respect to versioning of entities (required for analytical processing). Additionally the functionality of system delivers advanced scheduling of surveys depending on the day and night cycle and the intensity of the disease. These questions were developed on the basis of questionnaires that are presented to patients to assess the effectiveness of their drugs. The application can record also drugs intake (time and dose) reported for further correlation analysis.

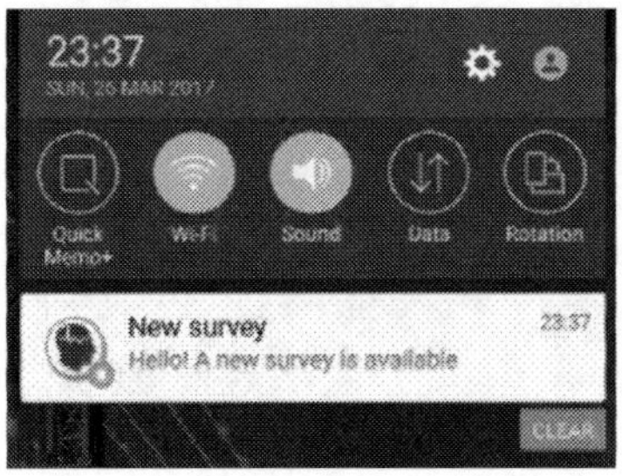

Fig. 1. New survey to fill notification displayed in the smartphone's notification toolbar

User-supplied responses are stored in the device memory and optionally sent to reporting-acquisition service. Depending on the user abilities and handheld capability the process manager can choose the preferred form of report gathering (on-site and remote method). During the survey the device and additional sensors

DOI: 10.1051/matecconf/201712505003

placed on the participant's body record answers and sensor signals (inertial and EMG). Each and every survey can take from 30-50 seconds in order to record and store statistically significant data. In addition, the application reminds the patient to take his medications and to schedule a consultation visit. The variety of reported events can be further extended as the reported data can be used as a form of detailed treatment assessment report – correlating patient's comfort and health state with environment and psychiatric state. Such data are stored automatically utilising built-in sensors or manually reported events on which the server inference system is able to recognise correspondences. The inference system has been designed as an ontology with stored rules performing patient health state data classification.

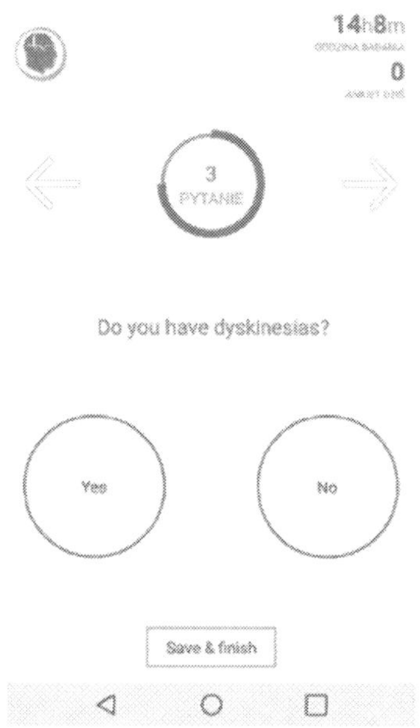

Fig. 2. Patron Droid survey screen, question number 3

The application generates all notifications (with proper vibration signalling and survey presentation) about pending survey requests. All requests store time of generation and time of recorded answers which is further used by the analytical engine. System's mechanisms try to encourage the user to constantly and regularly report good quality data rather than penalty any unwanted and faulty behaviour. To identify and overcome such data, the server side provides mechanism tagging such surveys, leaving the final decision to clinical test process manager [13][17]. The system delivers also conventional application mode, in which the user can request sensor assisted medical diagnostics, record and evaluate current health state. Patron delivers also mechanisms to identify some neurological symptoms of Parkinson's Disease using assessment of symptoms during diagnostic exercises (the flow of forearm movement, etc.). The clinical test participant is able to self-start an examination procedure which will be guided by the application using voice generated notifications. Before the test start, the user has to choose the basic configuration, such as utilised sensors and evaluated body (arm) side. The medical examination mechanisms starts to guide the user through the process of properly placing the sensors, preparing for examination, the examination itself and its assessment. The data gathered in the whole process are stored in form of CSV and binary files for further extraction and processing. This application mode, can be used to evaluated current participant state on-demand or to confirm possible tremors and dyskinesias.

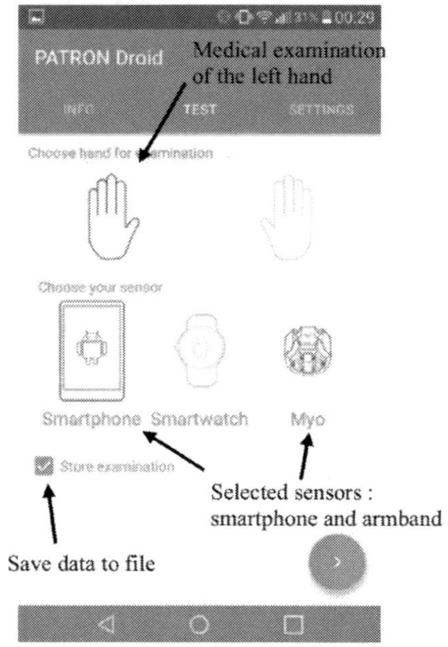

Fig. 3. Patron Droid examination's configuration main screen. Selected configuration is: medical examination of the left hand, use smartphone and armband sensor and save data to a CSV file

Before the test, the paired band is searched and connected. The user can see a screen presenting the selected hand on which he choose to test and status of sensors that he has chosen. Then the user has time to prepare for the test. If he is ready, he has to press the start button. The countdown occurs, and then the test begins.

The test has a specified time set by the user. At the top of the examination screen is a clock counts the remaining time to complete the test. Below, real-time charts for each signal type and for each sensor are drawn with their current values displayed as a number. During the test, all signals received from the sensors are passed to the algorithm receiver. At the same time, if the user has marked the option of saving to a file, the data is passed to the file writer component.

The test continues until the user-defined time has elapsed. If this is a one hand test, the test is completed. If the user set up a test for both hands, he can review the test for the selected hand and then he is asked to change his hand. After making the change, he has to press the start button again and the test is carried out for the second hand.

There is presented a screen of the application during performing an examination on the Fig. **4**.

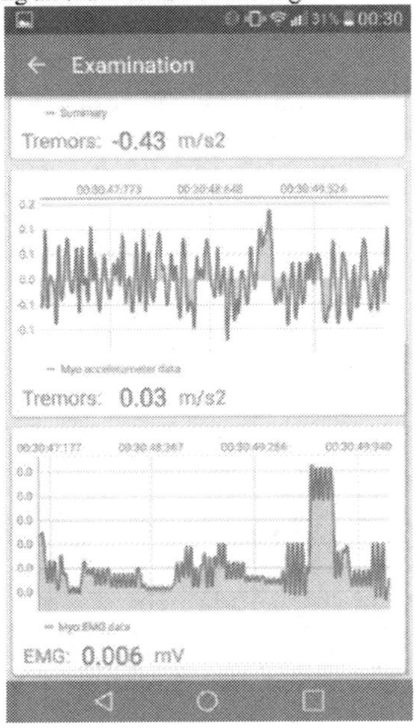

Fig. 4. Patron Droid examination screen

During the examination, the algorithm determines the individual parameters for specified time frame. At the end of the operation time, the reasoning is performed on the obtained parameters, and the result of the test is displayed to the user.

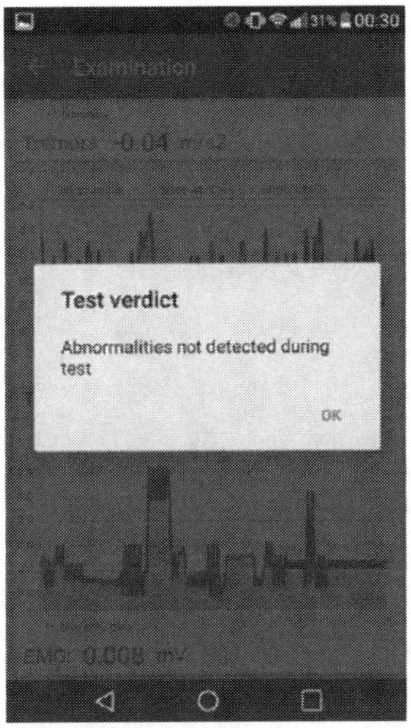

Fig. 5. Patron Droid examination result screen

If user chose to save test data, there is a file created in a device's memory. It holds the user data, test configuration and received data. Below is an example of a CSV file's fragment with data obtained during an examination.

First name	Michal					
Last name	Nowotarski					
Hand	LEFT					
Sensor	MYO					
DATE	MYO_ORIENT_X	MYO_ORIENT_Y	MYO_ACC_X	MYO_ACC_Y	MYO_GYRO_X	MYO_GYRO_Y
15-06-2016 00:28:01:731	0,1755	-0,1383	3,065	-2,199	0,375	1,202
15-06-2016 00:28:01:743	0,1755	-0,1385	2,406	-1,836	0,250	1,203
15-06-2016 00:28:01:779	0,1754	-0,1388	1,928	-1,469	0,250	1,313
15-06-2016 00:28:01:781	0,1754	-0,1389	1,516	-1,160	0,875	1,063
15-06-2016 00:28:01:783	0,1754	-0,1391	1,205	-0,874	0,000	0,750
15-06-2016 00:28:01:828	0,1755	-0,1392	0,941	-0,688	0,438	0,563

Fig. 6. Part of Patron Droid examination's data saved file

DATE	MYO_EMG_1	MYO_EMG_2	MYO_EMG_3	MYO_EMG_4	MYO_EMG_5	MYO_EMG_6
15-06-2016 00:28:01:921	0,004	-0,011	-0,007	-0,007	0,000	-0,025
15-06-2016 00:28:01:921	-0,004	0,000	-0,004	0,014	-0,011	-0,035
15-06-2016 00:28:01:927	-0,007	-0,011	-0,014	0,000	-0,014	0,025
15-06-2016 00:28:01:927	0,000	-0,014	-0,007	0,007	-0,011	-0,028
15-06-2016 00:28:01:932	-0,007	-0,011	-0,014	0,000	-0,014	0,025
15-06-2016 00:28:01:932	0,000	-0,014	-0,007	0,007	-0,011	-0,028

Fig. 7. Part of Patron Droid examination's data saved file

DOI: 10.1051/matecconf/201712505003

Before performing the first examination, user has to configure the application properly. In the "settings" tab user has to fill his personal data and configure the examination. User can choose hand configuration to test (one hand or both hands), examination time and set thresholds necessary for the proper work of the algorithm. At the tab, user can also pair his armband sensor with the application, what is required to use it during examinations.

4.1 PD Examination algorithm

The idea was to use both, an accelerometer and an electromyographic signals during diseases detection. It was targeted to detect symptoms of the Parkinson's disease and epilepsy. Both are related to dyskinesias but with slightly different intensification. The Parkinson's disease is associated with light limbs movements without increased muscle tension while the epilepsy is related to muscle tension without body movement (tonic phase) or tensioning and relaxing muscles with rapid movement (clonic phase). On the basis of the research it has been found that it is worth to measure the correlation between test results of both hands.

First step of algorithm's use is to set limit values for electromyograph and accelerometer data in the "settings" tab. These are values in mV or m/s^2 which are thresholds for exceeded limit value counters. They have to be float values, greater than zero.

Before an examination start, user has to set up a configuration:

- one or both hand test,
- which hand user want to test,
- use of smartphone and/or smartwatch and/or armband sensors.

The algorithm receives data from sensors during examination and calculate parameters separately for both hands (left, right) and every enabled sensor (ACC, EMG). Every five seconds the following parameters: minimum, maximum, deviation value and number of samples which exceeded limit values are being calculated.

```
if (!(timePartObject.getTimePartCounter() == lastTimeValue[i])) {
  devValue[i] = maxValue[i] - minValue[i];
  if (lastTimeValue[i] >= 0) { addToList(dataType); }
  lastTimeValue[i] = timePartObject.getTimePartCounter();
  timestamp[i] = timePartObject.getTimePartTimestamp();
  counter[i] = 1;
  minValue[i] = value;
  maxValue[i] = value;
  sumValue[i] = value;
} else {
  if (value < minValue[i]) { minValue[i] = value; }
  else if (value > maxValue[i]) { maxValue[i] = value; }
  sumValue[i] += value;
  switch (dataType) {
    case "acc":
      if (value >= accLimitValue) { counter[i]++; }
      break;
    case "emg":
      if (value >= emgLimitValue) { counter[i]++; }
      break;
  }}
```

Fig. 8. Code fragment for calculating parameters for a time frame

After the examination's end, these parameters are checked: if there is an exceed of values, appropriate flags are set to true.

Last step of the algorithm is flags check. They are compared to the test's configuration and based on these information, the final result of the examination is being raised.

As was mentioned before, different measurement devices have various sensors: smartphone and smartwatch have accelerometer, gyroscope and orientation sensor, while the armband has all of the above with an additional electromyographic sensor. It causes that different devices can provide results of different accuracy. What is more, both hands examination can provide more specific data than one hand examination.

As it was mentioned before, the test result is being determined on the basis of a comparison of flags set during the processing and configuring of the test. Based on the examination configuration:

- For all configurations user can receive result "no abnormalities detected".
- For one hand without electromyographic data it could be "Parkinson's disease or epilepsy suspicion", because the result is based only on the movement signal.
- Testing both hands without the armband sensor, allows the algorithm to distinguish Parkinson's disease suspicion from epilepsy suspicion, because of Parkinson's only one side (hand or leg) trembling.
- with use of the armband sensor, it could detect Parkinson's disease, epilepsy tonic phase or epilepsy clonic phase suspicion based on the ACC and EMG signals.

 DOI: 10.1051/matecconf/201712505003

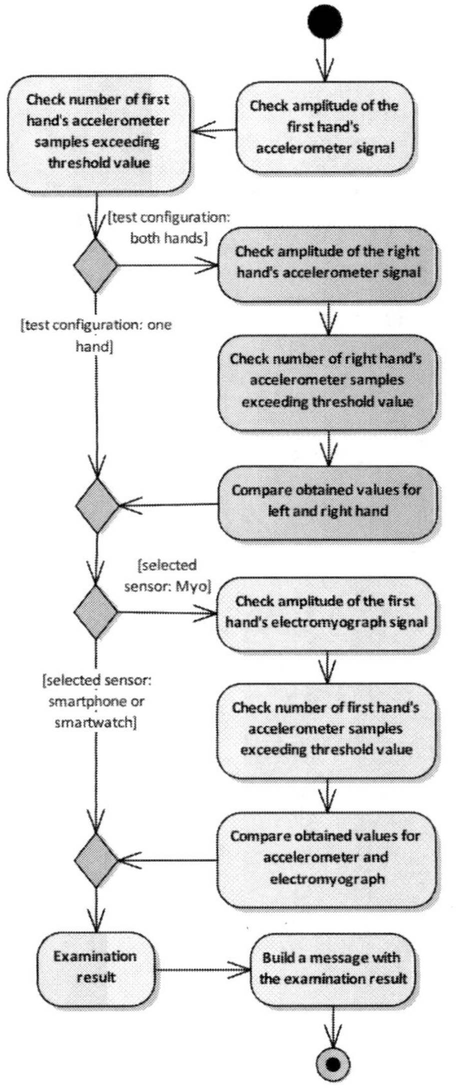

Fig. 9. Flow of the algorithm

Obtained results depend on the occurrence of the problems identified during the examination:

- No abnormalities means there was not set any of the examination flags.
- The Parkinson's disease or the epilepsy suspicion based on hand trembling during examination of one hand without the armband sensor.
- The Parkinson disease suspicion implies that there was hand trembling without muscle tension during examination of one hand with the armband sensor or only one hand trembling during any examination of both hands.
- The epilepsy tonic phase suspicion is based on increased muscle tension without hand trembling during an examination with the armband sensor.
- The epilepsy clonic phase suspicion means that there was variable muscle tension and hand trembling during an examination with armband sensor use.

```
for (int i = 0; i < accArraySize; i++) {
  if ((accLeftHandList.get(i).devValue >= accLimitValue * 2)
      && accLeftHandList.get(i).counter > 20
      && emgLeftHandList.get(i).devValue >= emgLimitValue
      && emgLeftHandList.get(i).counter > 20) {
    writeToCsv("Dyskinesia and muscle tension at: "
        + accLeftHandList.get(i).timestamp);
    emgAccFlg = true;
  } else if ((accLeftHandList.get(i).devValue >= accLimitValue * 2)
      && accLeftHandList.get(i).counter > 20
      && emgLeftHandList.get(i).devValue < emgLimitValue) {
    writeToCsv("Dyskinesia without muscle tension at: "
        + accLeftHandList.get(i).timestamp);
    accFlg = true;
  } else if ((accLeftHandList.get(i).devValue < accLimitValue * 2)
      && emgLeftHandList.get(i).devValue >= emgLimitValue
      && emgLeftHandList.get(i).counter > 20) {
    writeToCsv("Muscle tension without dyskinesia at: "
        + accLeftHandList.get(i).timestamp);
    emgFlg = true;
  }
}
```

Fig. 10. Code fragment for checking calculated parameters and making a test result

4.2 Second stage of the algorithm

The current algorithm is not sufficient for advanced diagnosis purposes, so a plan for its further development has already been prepared. In the next stage the algorithm will be significantly expanded. The diagnosis of Parkinson's disease will use an actigraphy to measure mobility of the limb. In the case of epilepsy, the purpose is to detect particular types of seizures. To achieve this, during the test will be determined muscle activation function and measured intervals between succeeding slopes on the signal record. Based on these data and accelerometer the tonic and clonic phases will be detected. The algorithm will search for similar characteristics as currently (described in 4.1). Atonic seizures will be detected by sensors located on the patient's neck, as a best place to observe their characteristics. This is a sudden momentary stroke of muscle tension along with the following drop on the EMG signal. It will be correlated with patient's behaviour (usually a fall-off) found on the inertial sensor. The algorithm will also detect myoclonic seizures that are characterized by sudden muscle spasms in the electromyographic signal. It is also intended to use the machine learning technique in patterns comparing.

At the moment, software authors do not have large sets of research data yet. At this point the research is done in several dozen attempts on two patients who reported to study.

In addition, research are still conducted to make it possible to identify if obtained sensors data allows to accurately identify conditions in patients' behaviour

DOI: 10.1051/matecconf/201712505003

which are needed to diagnose properly. One of the issues is to determine the visibility of Parkinson's tremors in the electromyography record

4.3 Data receive

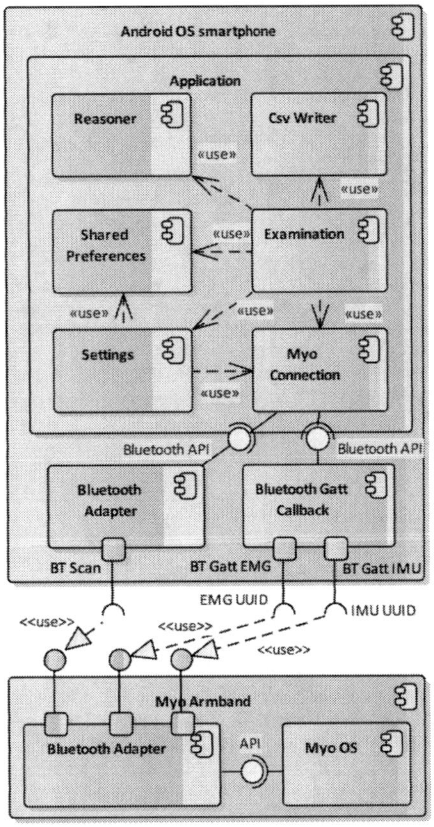

Fig. 11 Component model of the application

The main difficulty was to receive an EMG data on a mobile device straight from the armband due to lack of EMG capture methods in the official Android SDK. The solution was an own implementation of Bluetooth connection, without using the official SDK. There is released file in C++ which describes commands used in Bluetooth communication with the Myo [11]. Having used content of the file, it was possible to write a full connection with the Myo in Java using built-in Android's Bluetooth LE libraries. The connection implementation is based on a Meleap's code shared on the GitHub website[a]. The connection is being realized by a component called Myo Connection. It contains methods related to establishing and keeping a connection, receiving and parsing a data. It uses android Bluetooth components: the Bluetooth Adapter and the Bluteooth Gatt Callback. The Bluetooth Adapter searches for nearby Bluetooth devices or connect to saved one and passes connection parameters to the Gatt Callback. The Callback registers the application in armband's services (control service, IMU service, EMG service), receives data from them and sends messages to the Myo's control service.

Data received from services is provided as byte data and has to be parsed to appropriate form described in the Myo Bluetooth protocol file. Having parsed data, there is an ability to use it in the algorithm. Data consists of a accelerometer, gyroscope, magnetometer, orientation and electromyographic signal values is processed with appropriate timestamps.

The test execution is implemented as follows:

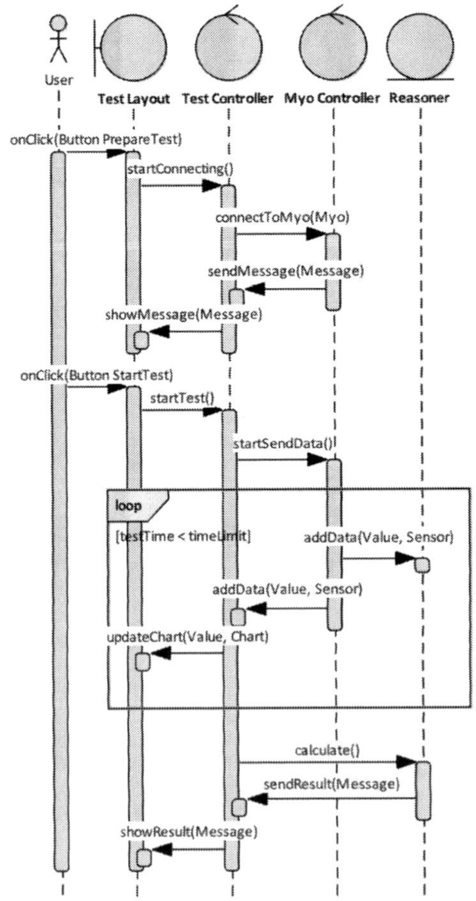

Fig. 12. Sequence diagram of the examination execution

```
public byte[] sendEmgAndImu() {
  byte command_data = (byte) 0x01;
  byte payload_data = (byte) 3;
```

[a] https://github.com/meleap/myo_AndoridEMG

```
    byte emg_mode   = (byte) 0x02;
    byte imu_mode   = (byte) 0x01;
    byte class_mode = (byte) 0x00;
    send_bytes_data  =
        new byte[]{command_data,
            payload_data,
            emg_mode, imu_mode,
            class_mode};
    return send_bytes_data;
}
```

Fig. 13. Code fragment for configuring sensor working mode to send accelerometer, orientation, gyroscope and electromyograph data

4.4 Restrictions

To work properly, the algorithm has to be used in a prepared environment. It means some constraints:
- user has to provide valid threshold data for the algorithm,
- the examination must be carried out on a person who is not moving during whole test,
- application cannot be closed or minimized,
- detection of diseases is based on selected symptoms,
- symptoms are consistent with these described before,
- the examination is done with a sensor placed on a hand with disease symptoms.

5 Experiments and tests

Tests were made by the application developer and was simulated to cover different examination cases. Every test was made with different hand movement, different muscle tension and the same test configuration. Test were conducted with the armband sensor use. Charts were made based on the data received and saved from sensors during examination. Test verdict is a result presented to user by the application. Limit values was set to 0.8 m/s^2 for an accelerometer and 0.06 mV for an electromyograph.

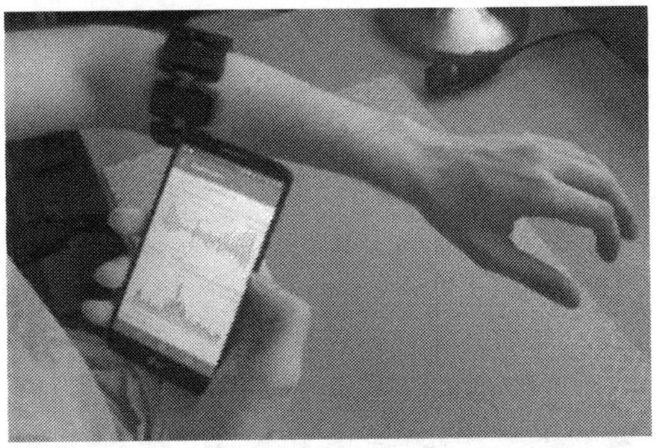

Fig. 14. A sensor test (diagnostics) processed using 2 inertial data sources and EMG – smartphones and MYO biometric sensor

5.1 Test case 1

The simulation of a healthy person's behaviour. It means that there is not any excessive handshake or muscle tension. The hand was held stably, without any movement and the accelerometer signal (blue) was maintained throughout the examination at a low level. Low values on the electromyograph chart (orange) indicates that throughout the study muscles were not significantly tightened. That shape of the graph should be achieved for a healthy person. The algorithm did not detect any irregularities in the movement of the hand or muscles tense. Both accelerometer and electromyography parameters were not exceeded enough to set flags to true. Only 3 accelerometer samples have greater value than limit value and none of electromyographic samples was greater than limit. That induced final result: Abnormalities not detected during test.

Table 1. Statistics of the Test case 1

	ACC	EMG
No. of samples	1004	1002
No. of samples exceeded limit values	3	0
Minimum value	-0.214 m/s^2	0.001 mV
Maximum value	1.378 m/s^2	0.035 mV
Deviation between min and max	1.593 m/s^2	0.034 mV

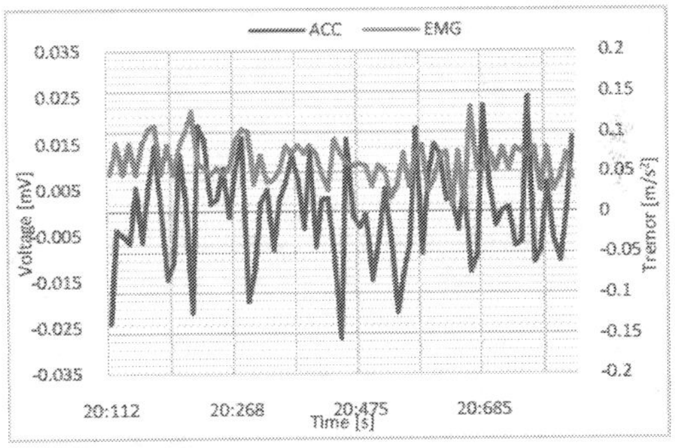

Fig. 15. Graph of extracted 150 samples started at 1000th sample of the Test case 1. Blue line is an accelerometer signal, orange line is an electromyograph signal.

5.2 Test case 2

The simulation of a person suffering from the Parkinson's disease. During the test, arm was still raised and entered in a gentle tremor. Muscles were relaxed during whole examination. Compared to the test of a healthy person, a signal from the accelerometer has higher values. It can be seen the effect of delicate hand shake on the value of the received signal. Together with the accelerometer, it is possible to see a slight increase in the value of the electromyographic signal. The algorithm detects handshake without significant change of the muscle tension. Handshake can be observed as 385

DOI: 10.1051/matecconf/201712505003

samples exceeded limit values. This amount could not have been a random hand movement, so the 20 exceeded samples in a 5 second time window condition was fulfilled and an accelerometer flag was set to true. The electromyographic signal were not significantly increased as none of samples was greater than threshold values. The algorithm detected the undesired movement of the hand without significant changes in muscle tension so the result was suspicion of the Parkinson's disease.

Table 2. Statistics of the Test case 2

	ACC	EMG
No. of samples	982	970
No. of samples exceeded limit values	385	0
Minimum value	-2.321 m/s^2	0.003 mV
Maximum value	1.962 m/s^2	0.059 mV
Deviation between min and max	4.284 m/s^2	0.056 mV

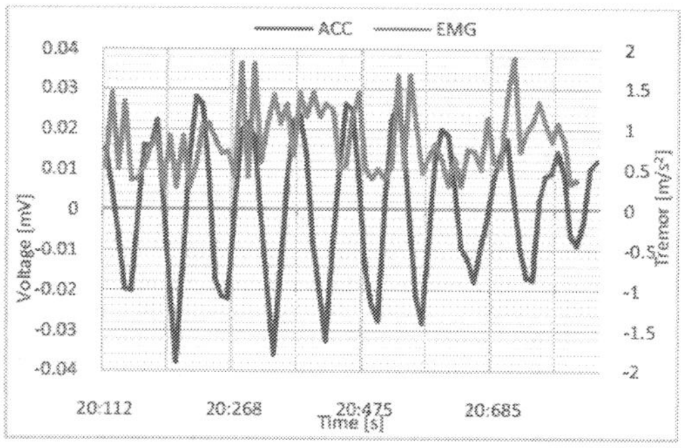

Fig. 16. Graph of extracted 150 samples started at 1000th sample of the Test case 2. Blue line is an accelerometer signal, orange line is an electromyograph signal.

5.3 Test case 3

The simulation of a person in the tonic phase of epilepsy. Hand was held in one position. To keep muscles tightened, a fist was clenched. Muscles were tensed all the time with a full strength. During the examination there was not any hand shake. The signal from the accelerometer confirms the lack of hand movement during the test. However, the flow of the electromyographic signal clearly indicates a significant and constant increase in muscle tension. After muscles having tensed, this state was maintained for about 8 seconds and then muscles were relaxed. The algorithm detected a strong muscle tension with the stillness of the hand. It is based on nearly none of accelerometer samples exceeded threshold value. It caused to keep accelerometer flag set to false. With nearly 450 electromyograph samples with values greater than limit, 20 samples in a 5 second time window condition was fulfilled and an electromyograph flag become true. That led to conclusion as the suspected was the tonic phase of epilepsy.

Table 3. Statistics of the Test case 3

	ACC	EMG
No. of samples	979	970
No. of samples exceeded limit values	3	445
Minimum value	-0.990 m/s^2	0.002 mV
Maximum value	0.977 m/s^2	0.280 mV
Deviation between min and max	1.968 m/s^2	0.283 mV

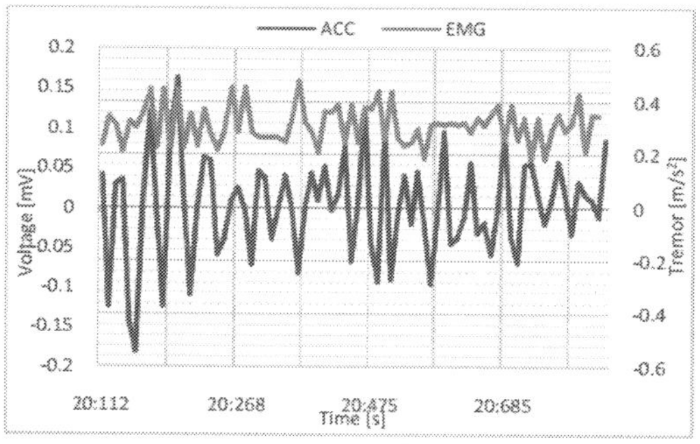

Fig. 17. Graph of extracted 150 samples started at 1000th sample of the Test case 3. Blue line is an accelerometer signal, orange line is an electromyograph signal.

5.4 Test case 4

The simulation of a person in the clonic phase of epilepsy. During the test execution, there were performed some rapid hand movements with tensioning and relaxing of muscles. The graph shows the movements of the hand on the accelerometer signal and tensioning and relaxing muscles on the record of the electromyograph signal. Algorithm detected in this case rapid hand movements with significant changes in muscle tension. Both accelerometer and electromyograph signals were significantly greater than thresholds on a large number of samples. Both flags, for accelerometer and electromyograph were set to true due to its met requirements of 20 samples exceeded limit values in a 5 second time window. Conclusion for the situation was: epilepsy clonic phase suspicion.

Table 4. Statistics of the Test case 4

	ACC	EMG
No. of samples	977	973
No. of samples exceeded limit values	573	589
Minimum value	-11.680 m/s^2	0.004 mV
Maximum value	19.484 m/s^2	0.296 mV
Deviation between	31.164 m/s^2	0.293 mV

min and max

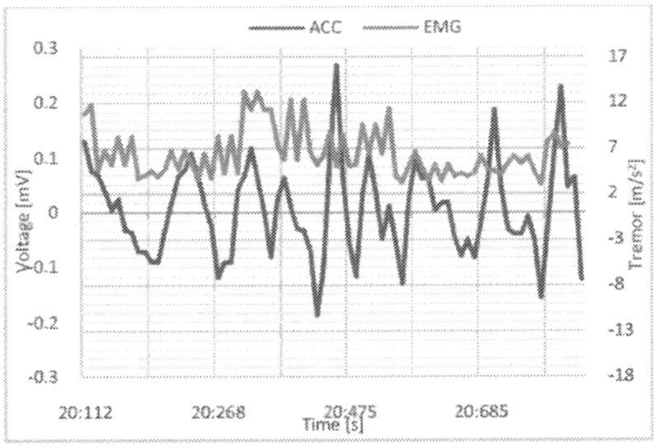

Fig. 18. Graph of extracted 150 samples started at 1000th sample of the Test case 4. Blue line is an accelerometer signal, orange line is an electromyograph signal.

6 Summary

Presented in the paper method and tool offers proprietary algorithms to support acquisition, analysis and medical diagnostics of selected neurological symptoms. The mechanisms cannot replace the professional help and detailed medical diagnostics. During system tests implemented algorithms proved their usefulness especially in the range of tremors intensity evaluation. Such information can be used for PD's drug usage forecast, as the pharmaceuticals have specific action time.

many but can assist clinical tests, but can be helpful when Application of sensors and complex algorithms requires specific configuration and environment preparation (described in 4.4.).

Results received during tests were consisted with theoretical expectations. Signals that were picked up by the application from the armband sensor reflected the behaviour of the tested person. With increased muscle tension, electromyographic signal significantly increased its value and vary depending upon the strength of the tension. A similar situation was observed in the accelerometer signal. Values were changing with the movement of the hand and band sensor obtained values corresponded to smartphone accelerometer signal. This allows to state that data received from the band were correct.

In addition, results of tests were consistent with the assumptions. On the basis of signals' characteristics, algorithm properly diagnosed diseases. This allows to evaluate that produced diagnostic tool has been implemented correctly. It is a good base for further development or research related to the diagnosis of neurological disorders with mobile devices. RFID technology [15][16] proved to be useful channel for clinical test initial configuration and on-site clinical test collection mechanisms. It has been used to authenticate and preconfigure transmission channel while maintaining patient's clinical records anonymous. Further extensions of RFID usage for automatic drug dose configuration and drug repository maintenance.

What is more, the way the application was built allows to expand it with another measurement devices or to implement more complex mechanisms for inferring and analysing user behaviour.

The system has been officially deployed after successful beta tests on population of 10 patients which have been using the application for at least 4 months. At the time of paper submission a formal acceptance of system and sensor clinical tests have been approved.

References

1. M. Nowotarski: Opracowanie algorytmów decyzyjnych wykorzystujących wybrane sygnały inercjalne oraz biomedyczne do identyfikacji zaburzeń neurologicznych oraz oprogramowania mobilnego na platformę Android, master's thesis, M. Chmielewski (supervisor), MUT (2016),
2. R. LeMoyne: Wearable and wireless accelerometer systems for monitoring Parkinson's disease patients—A perspective review, Advances in Parkinson's Disease, **2**, 113-115 (2013)
3. S.H. Roy, B.T. Cole, L.D. Gilmore, C.J. De Luca, C.A. Thomas, M.M. Saint-Hilaire, S.H. Nawab: High-Resolution Tracking of Motor Disorders in Parkinson's Disease During Unconstrained Activity, Movement Disorders, **28**, 1080-1087 (2013)
4. S. Beniczky, T. Polster, T. W. Kjaer, H. Hjalgrim: Detection of generalized tonic–clonic seizures by a wireless wrist accelerometer: A prospective, multicenter study, Epilepsia, 54, 58-61 (2013)
5. M.M. Velez, R.S. Fisher, V. Bartlett, S. Le: Tracking generalized tonic-clonic seizures with a wrist accelerometer linked to an online database, Seizure, 39, 13-18 (2016)
6. J.R. Villar, M. Menendez, J. Sedano, E. de la Cal, V.M. Gonzalez: Analyzing accelerometer data for epilepsy episode recognition, 10th International Conference on Soft Computing Models in Industrial and Environmental Applications. Advances in Intelligent Systems and Computing, 368, 39-48, Springer, Cham (2015)
7. SENSE project Wiki: http://uranus.wat.edu.pl:8808/wiki/index.php/SENSE (access: 2017.05.05)
8. PATRON project wiki: http://uranus.wat.edu.pl:8808/wiki/index.php/PATRON (access: 2017.05.05)
9. Myo tech spec: https://www.myo.com/techspecs
10. B. Stern: Inside Myo, adafruit.com (2016): https://learn.adafruit.com/myo-armband-teardown/inside-myo
11. Myo Bluetooth Low Energy specification file: https://github.com/thalmiclabs/myo-bluetooth/blob/master/myohw.h
12. M. Abduo, M. Galster: Myo Gesture Control Armband for Medical Applications, University of Canterbury (2015)

13. R. Hoffmann, M. Kiedrowicz, J. Stanik, Risk management system as the basic paradigm of the information security management system in an organization, 20th International Conference on Circuits, Systems, Communications and Computers, MATEC Web of Conferences, Cedex A: E D P Sciences, vol. 76, (2016).
14. M. Kiedrowicz, T. Nowicki, R. Waszkowski, Z. Wesolowski, and K. Worwa, Method for assessing software reliability of the document management system using the RFID technology, 20th International Conference on Circuits, Systems, Communications and Computers, MATEC Web of Conferences, Cedex A: E D P Sciences, vol. 76, (2016).
15. M. Kiedrowicz, Location with the use of the RFID and GPS technologies - opportunities and threats, GIS ODYSSEY 2016, pp. 122-128, (2016).
16. M. Kiedrowicz, Objects identification in the informations models used by information systems, GIS ODYSSEY 2016, pp. 129-136, (2016).
17. M. Kiedrowicz, T. Nowicki, R. Waszkowski, Business process data flow between automated and human tasks, 3rd International Conference on Social Science (ICSS 2016) December 9–11 2016, pp. 471-477, (2016).

Splitting Magnitude Response into Real and Imaginary Parts

Vairis Shtrauss*, *Aldis* Kalpinsh, and *Uldis* Lomanovskis

Institute for Material Mechanics, University of Latvia, Riga LV 1006, Latvia

Abstract. The determination of real and imaginary parts from magnitude responses is studied for causal linear time-invariant systems having monotonic impulse responses. It is demonstrated that the problem can be interpreted as a special filtering task in the Mellin transform domain having a diffuse magnitude response bounded by the magnitude responses of the filters corresponding to zero and maximum imaginary parts prescribed by the Kronig-Kramers relations. Discrete-time filters processing geometrically sampled magnitude responses are designed for determining the real and imaginary parts. Testing results are presented verifying the performance of the filters.

1 Introduction

Interconversion filters [1-3] operating with geometrically sampled data and executing an algorithm

$$y(\omega_0 q^m) = \sum_{n=-(N-1)/2}^{(N-1)/2} h[n] x(\omega_0 q^{m-n}) \qquad (1)$$

are used for converting monotonic and locally monotonic material functions interrelated to each other by the Mellin convolution transform (MCT)

$$y(\omega) = \int_0^\infty x(u) k\left(\frac{\omega}{u}\right) \frac{du}{u}, \qquad (2)$$

where $x(.)$ is input function, $y(.)$ is output function, $k(.)$ is kernel, $h[n]$ is impulse response of filter (1), and $q > 1$ is the common ratio for geometrically sampled data.

Interconversion filter (1) is related with the Mellin transform domain, where it has a periodic frequency response [1-3]

$$H(e^{j\mu}) = \sum_{n=-(N-1)/2}^{(N-1)/2} h[n] \exp(-j\mu \ln q), \qquad (3)$$

which approximates the ideal frequency response, expressed by the Mellin transform of kernel $k(u)$

$$H(j\mu) = M[k(u); -j\mu] = \int_0^\infty k(u) u^{-j\mu-1} du, \qquad (4)$$

where parameter μ, named the *Mellin frequency* [2,3], is an equivalent of the angular frequency for signals on the logarithmic time domain.

Theoretical basis of the interconversion filtering [1-3] comes from the fact that MCT (2) for logarithmically transformed variables alters into the Fourier convolution type transform, which may be identified with an ideal interconversion filter operating on logarithmic time or frequency domain.

In this paper, we study the use of interconversion filters (1) for the determination of the real $J'(\omega)$ and imaginary $J''(\omega)$ parts of the frequency response

$$\tilde{J}(\omega) = J'(\omega) + jJ''(\omega) \qquad (5)$$

from its magnitude response

$$|\tilde{J}(\omega)| = \sqrt{[J'(\omega)]^2 + [J''(\omega)]^2} \qquad (6)$$

for causal linear time-invariant systems (LTI) having monotonic impulse responses.

Although magnitude response (6) contains information about the real and imaginary parts, due to the operations of rising to the power and taking square root, neither the real part nor the imaginary part can be related to magnitude response (6) through MCT. Hence, converting the magnitude response into the real and imaginary parts does not represent a filtering task. On the other hand, the real and imaginary parts of frequency responses of causal physical systems are not wholly independent, but are linked by the Kramers-Kronig (KK) relations [4] ensuring the consistent magnitude responses. It points to a potent feasibility of converting the magnitude response into the real and imaginary parts. At present no methods known for the splitting the magnitude response into the real and imaginary parts. Nevertheless, development of such methods are of particular interest, because they may considerably simplify the determination of the real and imaginary parts, thanks to the fact that magnitude responses are relatively easily and accurately measurable signals, for example, by measuring the amplitudes of the steady-state responses to harmonic excitations [5-7].

Therefore, the final purpose of this study was to construct discrete-time transformers for converting magnitude response into the real part (further, *MR-Re*

* Corresponding author: strauss@pmi.lv

transformer) and into the imaginary part (further, *MR-Im transformer*).

The rest of this paper is organized as follows. Theoretical background for converting the magnitude response into the real and imaginary parts is given in Section 2. Design of discrete-time MR-Re and MR-Im transformers are considered in Section 3. Testing results of the designed transformers are also presented here. Section 4 contains conclusions.

2 Theoretical Background

Two limiting cases may be considered for magnitude response (6): (i) – when the imaginary part is small and tends to zero $J''(\omega)\to 0$, and (ii) – when the imaginary part takes the maximum value $J''(\omega)=J''_{max}(\omega)$.

2.1 Limiting Case with Imaginary Part Tending to Zero

In this case, the magnitude response approaches to the real part $|\tilde{J}(\omega)|\to J'(\omega)$ allowing to estimate the imaginary part by the KK relation [4]

$$J''(\omega)\approx -\frac{2\omega}{\pi}\int_0^\infty \frac{|\tilde{J}(u)|}{u^2-\omega^2}du\,, \qquad (7)$$

while the real part may be taken approximately equal to the magnitude response

$$J'(\omega)\approx|\tilde{J}(\omega)|\,. \qquad (8)$$

As shown in [8], by dividing the numerator and denominator on u^2, KK relation (7) takes the MCT form (2) with $x(\omega)=|\tilde{J}(\omega)|$ and $y(\omega)=J''(\omega)$, and kernel

$$k''(u)=-2u/(1-u^2)/\pi\,,$$

which according to (4) gives the frequency response [8]

$$H''_{min}(j\mu)=M[k''(u);j\mu]=\tan(j\pi\mu/2)\,. \qquad (9)$$

In its turn, Eq. (8) can be considered as the determination of $J'(\omega)$ from $|\tilde{J}(\omega)|$ by an all-pass filter with a constant (unity) frequency response

$$H'_{min}(j\mu)=1\,. \qquad (10)$$

2.2 Limiting Case with Maximum Imaginary Part

The phenomenological theories [9-11] state the following upper bound for the imaginary part of an elementary causal system with monotonic impulse response

$$J''_{max}(\omega)=\frac{\Delta J\omega\tau}{1+\omega^2\tau^2} \qquad (11)$$

with the corresponding real part $\Delta J/(1+\omega^2\tau^2)$ according to KK relation [4,8]. Since frequency responses of real systems, such as materials [9-11], contain, as a rule, constant instantaneous values, we consider the real part with added constant J_∞

$$J'_{max}(\omega)=J_\infty+\frac{\Delta J}{1+\omega^2\tau^2}\,. \qquad (12)$$

The parts (11) and (12) create magnitude response

$$|\tilde{J}_{max}(\omega)|=\sqrt{\left(J_\infty+\frac{\Delta J}{1+\omega^2\tau^2}\right)^2+\left(\frac{\Delta J\omega\tau}{1+\omega^2\tau^2}\right)^2}= \sqrt{J_\infty^2+\frac{2\Delta JJ_\infty}{1+\omega^2\tau^2}+\frac{\Delta J^2}{1+\omega^2\tau^2}}\,, \qquad (13)$$

where τ is characteristic time of the system.

Neither the real part (12) nor the imaginary part (11) can be related to the magnitude response (13) through MCT (2). We propose to approximate magnitude response (13) by a Mellin transformable function

$$A(\omega)=\sqrt{J_\infty^2+\frac{2\Delta JJ_\infty}{\sqrt{1+\omega^2\tau^2}}+\frac{\Delta J^2}{1+\omega^2\tau^2}}= J_\infty+\frac{\Delta J}{\sqrt{1+\omega^2\tau^2}}\,, \qquad (14)$$

which slightly overestimates magnitude response (13).

Contrary to the functions of pairs $\{J'_{max}(\omega),|\tilde{J}(\omega)|\}$ and $\{J''_{max}(\omega),|\tilde{J}(\omega)|\}$, the functions of pairs $\{J'_{max}(\omega),A(\omega)\}$ and $\{J''_{max}(\omega),A(\omega)\}$ may be related to each other in the terms of the Mellin transforms

$$M[J'_{max}(\omega);-j\mu]=M[A(\omega);-j\mu]\cdot H'_{max}(j\mu)\,; \qquad (15)$$

$$M[J''_{max}(\omega);-j\mu]=M[A(\omega);-j\mu]\cdot H''_{max}(j\mu)\,, \qquad (16)$$

where $H'_{max}(\mu)$ and $H''_{max}(\mu)$ are frequency responses of MR-Re and MR-Im transformers in the limiting case with maximum imaginary part. According to (15) and (16), frequency responses $H'_{max}(\mu)$ and $H''_{max}(\mu)$ may be determined as follows

$$H'_{max}(j\mu)=M[J'_{max}(\omega);-j\mu]/M[A(j\mu);-j\mu];$$

$$H''_{max}(j\mu)=M[J''_{max}(\omega);-j\mu]/M[A(j\mu);-j\mu].$$

By using the Mellin transforms

$$M[J'_{max}(\omega);-j\mu]=\frac{\pi}{2}\frac{\Delta J}{\sin(-j\pi\mu/2)};$$

$$M[J''_{max}(\omega);-j\mu]=\frac{\pi}{2}\frac{\Delta J}{\cos(j\pi\mu/2)};$$

$$M[A(j\mu);-j\mu]=\frac{2^{-j\mu}\Gamma(2+j2\mu)\Gamma(-j\mu)\Delta J}{\Gamma(2+j\mu)},$$

the following frequency responses were obtained for the MR-Re and MR-Im transformers in the limiting case with maximum imaginary part:

$$H'_{max}(\mu)=\frac{\pi\Gamma(2+j\mu)}{2^{1-j\mu}\Gamma(2+j2\mu)\Gamma(-j\mu)\sin(-j\pi\mu/2)};$$

$$H''_{max}(\mu)=\frac{\pi\Gamma(2+j\mu)}{2^{1-j\mu}\Gamma(2+j2\mu)\Gamma(-j\mu)\cos(j\pi\mu/2)},$$

where $\Gamma(.)$ is gamma function.

2.3 Diffuse Magnitude Responses

In Fig. 1, functions $|H'_{min}(\mu)|$ and $|H'_{max}(\mu)|$ are shown, which form the bounds for the magnitude response of ideal MR-Re transformer. Hence, MR-Re transformer may be interpreted as an interconversion filter with a *diffuse* magnitude response with the constant – equal to (10) – lower bound and an increasing upper bound.

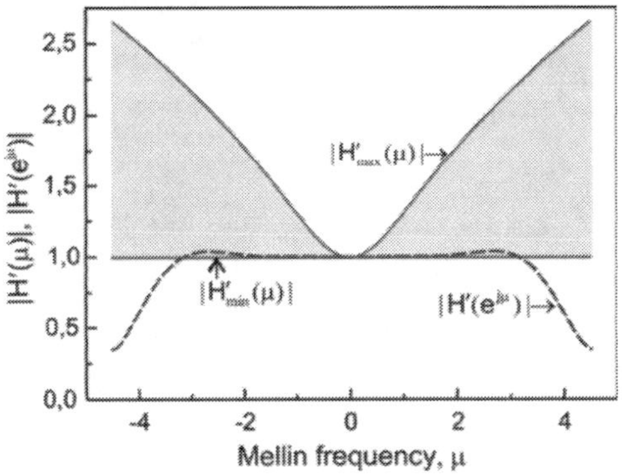

Fig. 1. The diffuse magnitude response of ideal MR-Re transformer (shaded area) and the magnitude response of 8-points discrete-time transformer (dashed).

In Fig. 2, functions $|H''_{min}(\mu)|$ and $|H''_{max}(\mu)|$ are shown, which also create the bounds of the diffuse magnitude response for ideal MR-Im transformer. In this case, the frequency response (9) establishes the lower bound, while the upper bound is again an increasing magnitude response with the shape likes to that of a differentiator of fractional order. At low Mellin frequencies $|\mu|<0.5$, MR-Im transformer has a united – not diffusing – magnitude response. This indicates actually on a practical feasibility of using KK transformers for computing the imaginary part from the magnitude response for narrow-band signals.

An important point is that MR-Im transformer has zero frequency response at zero frequency $H''(j0)=0$, which ensures cutting out zero frequency component (DC component) of an input magnitude response and, thus, minimizing the effect of constant J_∞.

3 Design and Testing of Discrete-Time Transformers

Discrete-time MR-Re and MR-Im transformers were designed by learning based on the system identification principle [1-3] to use pairs of the exact functions $\{J'(\omega),|\tilde{J}(\omega)|\}$ and $\{J''(\omega),|\tilde{J}(\omega)|\}$ corresponding to the Cole-Cole model [12] with the width parameter 0.7. Based on the experience with discrete-time Kramers-Kronig transformers [8], we chose the common ratio $q=2$ and filter length $N=8$.

In Table, coefficients are given for the obtained discrete-time transformers. As seen the transformers are non-linear phases filters [13] having non-symmetric impulse responses. The appropriate magnitude responses are shown in Fig. 1 and Fig. 2 as dashed lines.

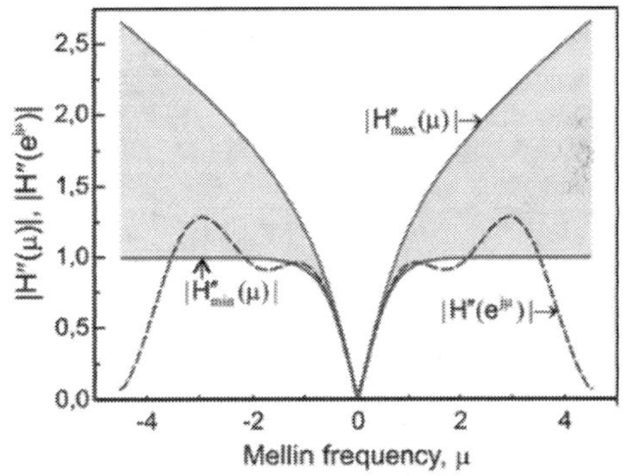

Fig. 2. The diffuse magnitude response of ideal MR-Im transformer (shaded area) and the magnitude response of 8-points discrete-time transformer (dashed).

Table. Coefficients for MR-Re and MR-Im transformers

n	Coefficients $h[n]$	
	MR-Re transformer	**MR-Im transformer**
-3.5	-0.00862702	0.109042
-2.5	0.0474832	0.0134620
-1.5	-0.143979	0.165268
-0.5	0.480793	0.601015
0.5	0.759683	-0.372957
1.5	-0.185825	-0.470905
2.5	0.0656697	0.136201
3.5	-0.0153284	-0.178838

To verify the performance, the transformers were tested by computing the real and imaginary parts of different shapes. We use the Havriliak-Negami model [14] with the following frequency response

$$\tilde{J}(\omega)=J_\infty+\Delta J[1+(j\omega\tau)^\alpha]^{-\beta},$$

which allows to change shapes of the real and imaginary parts, as well as of the magnitude responses within a wide range by varying parameters α, β, J_∞ and ΔJ.

In Figs. 3 and 4, as examples, the exact real and imaginary parts (solid) and the computed ones (dashed) by the designed 8-points transformers are shown for $\beta=1$ and $\beta=0.5$, and five values of α to keep constant parameters $J_\infty = 3, \Delta J = 1, \tau = 1$. The chosen values for the parameters α, β, J_∞ and ΔJ are close to those used for describing complex dielectric permittivity of typical polymers [9,10].

As seen, the accuracy of computing the real and imaginary parts is quite high, particularly, for the real parts at $\beta = 0.5$, where it is hard to distinguish between the exact and computed curves.

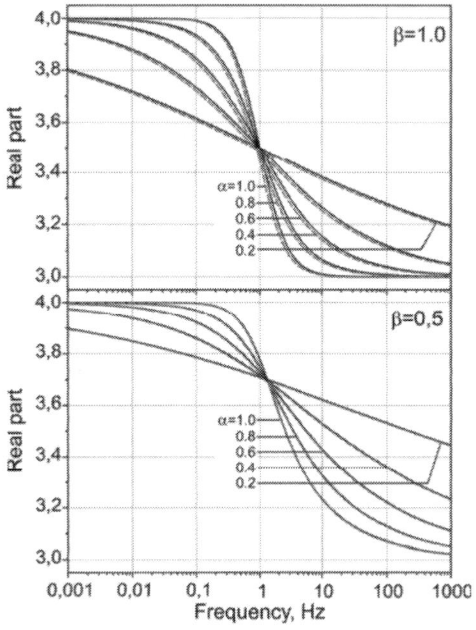

Fig. 3. Exact (solid) and computed (dashed) real parts.

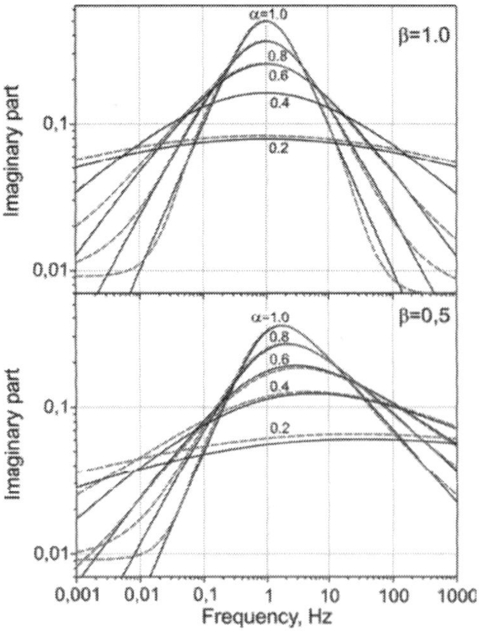

Fig. 4. Exact (solid) and computed (dashed) imaginary parts.

4 Conclusions

The use of interconversion filters [1-3], intended for transforming monotonic and locally monotonic material functions by executing the Mellin convolution transforms, is studied for the determination of the real and imaginary parts from the magnitude response for causal linear time-invariant systems having monotonic impulse responses. Since the problem cannot be described in the terms of a Mellin convolution, it does not represent an interconversion filtering task. It is demonstrated, however, that the problem in the limiting cases, when the imaginary part tends to zero and takes the maximum value, can be approximated by Mellin convolutions, which establishes the basis for interpretation the problem in the light of special interconversion filtering with diffuse frequency responses. The bounds of the diffuse frequency responses are found for determining the real and imaginary parts.

Discrete-time transformers are designed for converting the magnitude responses of causal linear time-invariant systems into the real and imaginary parts. Testing results of the transformers are presented.

This work was supported in part by the European Regional Development Fund under project No. 1.1.1.1/16/A/008.

References

1. V. Shtrauss, Signal Process. **45**, 293 (1995).
2. V. Shtrauss, J. Non-Cryst. Solids **351**, 2911 (2005).
3. V. Shtrauss, Digital Interconversion between Linear Rheologic and Viscoelastic Material Functions. In: *Advances in Engineering Research* **3**, 91 (2012)
4. N. M. Nussenzveig, *Causality and Dispersion Relations* (1972)
5. V. Strauss, A. Kalpins, U. Lomanovskis, Patent WO2015047065A1, Method and device for estimating the real and imaginary parts of the frequency response (2013)
6. V. Shtrauss, A. Kalpinsh, WSEAS Trans. Appl. Theor. Mech. **7**, 1, 29 (2012)
7. V. Shtrauss, A. Kalpinsh, *Proc. 15th WSEAS International Conference on Systems. Recent Researches in System Science (CSCC '11)* 106 (2011)
8. V. Shtrauss, Signal Process. **86** 2887 (2006)
9. N. G. McCrum, B. E. Read, G. Williams, *Anelastic and Dielectric Effects in Polymer Solids* (1967)
10. A. K. Jonscher, *Dielectric Relaxation in Solids* (1983)
11. J. D. Ferry, *Viscoelastic Properties of Polymers* (1980)
12. K. S. Cole, R. H. Cole, J. Chem. Phys. **9**, 341 (1941)
13. A. V. Oppenheim, R. V. Schafer, *Discrete-Time Signal Processing* (1999)
14. S. Havriliak, S. Negami, Polymer **8**, 4, 161 (1967)

On the representation of signals series by Faber-Schauder system

Tigran Grigoryan[1], and *Martin* Grigoryan[2]

[1] Yerevan State University, Chair of Higher Mathematics, , 1 Al. Manukyan str., Yerevan, 0025, Armenia
[2] Yerevan State University, Chair of Higher Mathematics, , 1 Al. Manukyan str., Yerevan, 0025, Armenia

Abstract. We prove that : if $f(x)$ is a measurable function, finite almost everywhere on $[0,1]$ then there is a Schauder series, which converges unconditionally to f almost everywhere on $[0,1]$ and for every $\varepsilon > 0$ there is a measurable set E contained in $[0,1]$, with $|E| > 1-\varepsilon$, such that for each $f \in C(E)$ there is a Schauder series, which unconditionally converges to f in the uniform norm.

1 Introduction

First, we recall the definition of the Faber-Schauder system (see [2]):

$$\{\varphi_n(x): n = 0,1,\ldots\}, x \in [0,1],$$

where

$$\varphi_0(x) = 1,$$

$\varphi_1(x) = x$ and for $n = 2^k + i;\ k = 0,1\ldots;\ i = 1,2,\ldots,2^k$:

$$\varphi_n(x) = \varphi_k^{(i)}(x) = \begin{cases} 0 \text{ if } x \notin \left(\frac{i-1}{2^k}, \frac{i}{2^k}\right), \\ 1 \text{ if } x = x_n = x_k^{(i)} = \frac{2i-1}{2^{k+1}}, \\ \text{linear and continuous on } \left[\frac{i-1}{2^k}, \frac{2i-1}{2^{k+1}}\right], \left[\frac{2i-1}{2^{k+1}}, \frac{i}{2^k}\right]. \end{cases}$$

For $2 \le n = 2^k + i$ we set $\Delta_n = \Delta_k^{(i)} = \left(\frac{i-1}{2^k}, \frac{i}{2^k}\right)$, the set of points, where the function $\varphi_n(x)$ is different from zero.

We also recall that the Faber-Schauder system forms a basis in the space $C[0,1]$ (see [2]) that is, any function $f \in C[0,1]$ can be uniquely represented by the series Fourier series

$$f(x) = \sum_{n=0}^{\infty} A_n(f)\varphi_n(x)$$

with respect to the Faber-Schauder system, which converges to f uniformly on $[0,1]$. The $A_n(f)$ coefficients of this series are defined by $A_0(f) = f(0)$, $A_1(f) = f(1) - f(0)$,

$$A_n(f) = A_{k,i}(f) = f\left(\frac{2i-1}{2^{k+1}}\right) - \frac{1}{2}\left[f\left(\frac{i-1}{2^k}\right) + f\left(\frac{i}{2^k}\right)\right].$$

There are number of interesting results on the properties of the Faber-Schauder system (see [2-9]).

Definition 1. A basis $\{f_k : k = 1,2\ldots\}$ of a Banach space B is said to be unconditional if for an arbitrary permutation $\{\sigma_k : k = 1,2\ldots\}$ of the natural numbers, the system $\{f_{\sigma(k)}(x) : k = 1,2\ldots\}$ is also a basis of B.

Let $E \subset [0,1]$ be a measurable set and let $C(E)$ be the class of all continuous functions defined on E, and let $b_n(x) \in C(E), n = 1,2\ldots$.

Definition 2. The series $\sum_{n=1}^{\infty} b_n(x)$ is said to be unconditionally convergent to $f(x)$ in $C(E)$ if for any permutation $\{\sigma(k) : k = 1,2...\}$ of the natural numbers, the series $\sum_{n=1}^{\infty} b_{\sigma(k)}(x)$ converges to $f(x)$ uniformly on E.

Definition 3. The system $\{f_k : k = 1,2\ldots\}$ is said to be an unconditional system of the representation of functions in the class $C(E)$ if for every function

* Corresponding author: gmarting@ysu.am

$f(x)\in C(E)$ there exists a series $\sum_{n=1}^{\infty} a_n f_n(x)$ such that it unconditionally converges to $f(x)$ in $C(E)$.

We note that in the space $C[0,1]$ there exists no unconditional basis (see [10]).

And what is more, in the article [3] M. G. Grigorian and A. A. Sargsyan, constructed a continuous function $f_0(x)\in C[0,1]$ and a permutation $\{\sigma(k): k=1,2...\}$ of natural numbers, such that the series $\sum_{k=0}^{\infty} A_{\sigma(k)}(f_0)\varphi_{\sigma(k)}(x)$ diverges in measure on $[0,1]$ and $|A_{\sigma(k)}(f_0)|<|A_{\sigma(k-1)}(f_0)|, k>1$ (where $\sum_{n=0}^{\infty} A_n(f_0)\varphi_n(x)$ -is Fourier series of function $f_0(x)\in C[0,1]$ with respect to the Faber-Schauder system).

From this follows: there exists a function $f_0(x)\in C[0,1]$, whose greedy algorithm with respect to the Faber-Shauder system diverges in measure.

But, nevertheless, for every $0<\varepsilon<1$ there exists a measurable set $E\in[0,1]$ with measure $|E|>1-\varepsilon$, such that for each $f\in C(E)$ one can find a function $g\in C[0,1], g(x)=f(x), \forall x\in E$ equal to f on E such that the greedy algorithm with respect to the Faber-Shauder system of signal g converges it in the $C[0,1]$ - norm.

Now we recall the definition of the greedy algorithm.

Let $\Psi=\{\psi_k\}_{k=1}^{\infty}$ be a normalized basis in Banach space $\sigma\in D(f,\psi)$. Then for each element $f\in X$ there exists a unique series by system $\Psi=\{\psi_k\}_{k=1}^{\infty}$ converging to f in the norm of space X:

$$f=\sum_{k=0}^{\infty} c_k(f)\psi_k$$

Let an element $f\in X$ be given. We call a permutation $\sigma=\{\sigma(k): k=1,2..\}$ of nonnegative integers decreasing and write $\sigma\in D(f,\psi)$, if

$$|c_{\sigma(k)}(f)|<|c_{\sigma(k-1)}(f)|, k>1.$$

In the case of strict inequalities here $D(f,\psi)$ consists of only one permutation.

We define the m-th greedy approximant of f with regard to the basis Ψ corresponding to a permutation by formula

$$G_m(f,\zeta)=\sum_{k=1}^{m} c_{\sigma(k)}(f)\psi_{\sigma(k)}$$

This nonlinear method of approximation was considered in the article [10] and is known as greedy algorithm.

We say that the greedy approximant of element f by system Ψ converges, if for some $\sigma\in D(f,\psi)$ we have

$$\lim_{m\to\infty} \|G_m(f,\psi)=f\|_X=0.$$

Greedy algorithms in Banach spaces with respect to normalized bases have been investigated by Temlyakov, DeVore, Konyagin, Wojtaszczyk, Korner and other authors (see [11]-[16]).

Note that $G_m(f,\psi)=\sum_{k=1}^{m} c_{\sigma(k)}(f)\psi_{\sigma(k)}$ gives the best m-term approximation in $L^2[0,1]$ - norm.

We present some results which have an immediate bearing on our investigations.

In the article [12] T. W. Korner answering a question raised by Carleson and Coifman constructed a continuous function, whose greedy algorithm with respect to the trigonometric systems diverges almost everywhere.

In the article [13] V. N. Temlyakov constructed a function f that belongs to any $L^p, p>0$ (respectively p>2), whose greedy algorithm with respect to the trigonometric system diverges in measure (respectively in $L^p[0,1], p>2$).

In the article [3] M. G. Grigorian and A. A. Sargsyan, constructed a continuous function $f\in C[0,1]$, whose greedy algorithm with respect to the Faber-Shauder system diverges in measure.

The following question arises here.

Question 1. Does there exist a set e of arbitrarily small measure such that, after modifying the values of an arbitrary function in $f\in L^p[0,1], p>2$, $p>1$, on e, the greedy algorithms for the modified function with respect to the Walsh and trigonometric systems converge to it (almost everywhere, in the norm of $L^p[0,1]$ uniformly)?

Note that the answer to Question 1 on the one hand depends on the prescribed system and the type of convergence, and on the other hand depends on whether the exceptional set on which the modification is performed depends on the function f(x) to be corrected or is universal.

We shall consider two versions of Question 1:

a) when the values of the function $f(x)$ are modified on a set of arbitrarily smallmeasure depending on the function;

b) when the exceptional set e on which the modification is performed is independent of the modified function $f(x)$ (that is, is universal and serves for a whole function class).

Note the following question, which arises when we investigate the convergence of the greedy algorithm for the new, corrected function e $f(x)$ and is also of independent interest. Can the values of any function $f(x)$ in $L^p[0,1]$], $p>1$, be modified on a set of small measure so that all the nonzero elements in the sequence of the Fourier coefficients of the function thus obtained with respect to the classical systems (in particular, the Walsh and trigonometric systems) are arranged in decreasing order?

It is important to note that, as was shown in the article [15], M. G. Grigoryan, K. S. Kazaryan and F. Soria, there exist a complete orthonormal system $\Phi=\{f_k(x)\}_{k=1}^{\infty}$ and a function $f\in L^p[0,1], p>2$, such that if g(x) is any function in $L^p[0,1], p>2$ with measue $|\{x\in[0,1], g(x)=f(x)\}|>0$ then it's greedy algorithm with respect to the system $\Phi=\{f_k(x)\}_{k=1}^{\infty}$ diverges in $L^p[0,1], p>2$.

Note also that well-known classical theorems by N. N. Luzin and D. E. Men'shov "on correction" of functions (see [17,18]). We have considered the behavior greedy algorithm after modification of functions (see [19-22]).

For Haar system we obtained:

For any ε>0 there exists a measurable set $E\subset[0,1]$, with measure $|E|>1-\varepsilon$ such that for any function $f(x)\in L^1[0,1]$ one can find a function $g(x)\in L^1[0,1]$ equal to $f(x)$ on E such that its greedy algorithm with respect to the Haar system converges to $g(x)$ in the $L^1[0,1]$-norm.

In the paper [3] M. G. Grigorian and A. A. Sargsyan was obtained

Theorem 1. For any ε>0 there exists a measurable set $E\subset[0,1]$, with measure $|E|>1-\varepsilon$ such that for any function $f(x)\in C[0,1]$ one can find a function $g(x)\in C[0,1]$ equal to $f(x)$ on E such that its greedy algorithm with respect to the Faber-Schauder system converges to $g(x)$ uniformly on [0,1].

But, nevertheless, for every $0<\varepsilon<1$ there exists a measurable set $E\subset[0,1]$ with measure $|E|>1-\varepsilon$, such that the Faber-Schauder system is an unconditional system of representation of functions of the class $C(E)$ (see [4]). This result is a consequence of the more general Theorem 1(see [9]), which is stated as follows:

Theorem 2. For every $\varepsilon>0$ there is a measurable set E contained in [0,1], with $|E|>1-\varepsilon$, such that for each $f\in C(E)$ one can find a function $g\in C[0,1], g(x)=f(x), \forall x\in E$ equal to f on E such that the Fourier series with respect to the Faber-Schauder systemof signal g unconditionally converges it in the $C[0,1]$-norm and

$$\sum_{n=0}^{m}|A_n(g)|\varphi_n(x)<2|g(x)|, \forall x\in[0,1], \forall m>0.$$

2 Proof of theorems

In this article we prove the following theorems.

2.1 Results

Theorem 3. Corresponding to each $f\in C[0,1]$ there is a Schauder series that converges to f on a set of full measure, such that for every $\varepsilon>0$ there is a measurable set E contained in [0,1], with $|E|>1-\varepsilon$, on which the series converges unconditionally to f in $C(E)$.

This theorem is a consequence of the more general Theorem 4, which is stated as follows:

Theorem 4. If $f(x)$ is a measurable function, finite almost everywhere on [0,1] then there is a Schauder series, which converges unconditionally to f almost everywhere on [0,1].

Of course, these results can not be improved by replacing the set E with [0,1], since as Karlin has shown, there is no unconditional basis for $C[0,1]$ (see [2]).

2.2 Proof of the Theorem 4

Let $f(x)$ is a measurable and finite almost everywhere function on [0,1] be given, and let f_1 be a binary step function such that

$$\left|\left\{x\in[0,1], |f-f_1|>\frac{1}{4}\right\}\right|<\frac{1}{4}.$$

By virtue of Lemma 3 of [4], there is a measurable set $E_1\subset[0,1]$ and a Schauder polynomial

$Q_1(x)=\sum_{n=2}^{m_1}A_n\varphi_n(x), |A_n|\le\frac{1}{2}$ such that

$Q_1(x)=f_1(x)$ for all $x\in E_1$, $|E_1|>1-\frac{1}{4}$, for each $B_1\subset\{2,\dots m_1\}$,

$$\left|\sum_{n\in B_1}A_n\varphi_n(x)\right|\le|f_1(x)| \text{ for all } x\in E_1.$$

Let the binary step function f_2 satisfy

$$\left|\left\{x\in[0,1], |(f-Q_1)-f_2|>\frac{1}{8}\right\}\right|<\frac{1}{8},$$

and again applying lemma 3 of [4] we find the Schauder polynomial of the form $Q_2(x)=\sum_{n=m_1+1}^{m_2} A_n\varphi_n(x), |A_n|\le\frac{1}{3}$, which coincides with f_2 on the measurable set $E_2\subset[0,1]$, where $|E_2|>1-\frac{1}{8}$ and for each $B_2\subset\{m_1+1,\dots,m_2\}$

$$\left|\sum_{n\in B_2} A_n\varphi_n\right|\le|f_2(x)| \text{ for all } x\in E_2,$$

where $|A_n|\le\frac{1}{2}$ for each $n\in(m_1,m_2]$.

Then

$$|f(x)-(Q_1+Q_2)(x)|<\frac{1}{8} \text{ for all } x\in G_2\cap E_2,$$

where

$$G_2=\left\{x\in[0,1], |(f-Q_1)-f_2|<\frac{1}{8}\right\}.$$

From this we obtain

$$\left|\sum_{n\in B_2} A_n\varphi_n(x)\right|\le|f_2(x)|\le|(f-Q_1)(x)-f_2(x)|+$$
$$+|(f-Q_1)(x)|<\frac{3}{8}; \forall x\in G_2\cap E_1\cap E_2.$$

Proceeding thus inductively, one determines a sequence $\{Q_j(x)\}_{j=1}^{\infty}$ of Schauder polynomials

$$Q_j(x)=\sum_{n=m_{j-1}+1}^{m_j} A_n\varphi_n(x), |A_n|\le\frac{1}{j+1}; \forall n\in(m_{j-1}m_{j,}],$$

and a sequences $\{E_j\}_{j=1}^{\infty}$ and $\{G_j\}_{j=1}^{\infty}$ are measurable subsets of $[0,1]$ such that

$$|G_j\cap E_j|>1-\frac{1}{2^{j+1}}; j=1,2\dots\left|f(x)-\sum_{j=1}^{n} Q_j(x)\right|<\frac{1}{2^{n+1}};$$
$\forall x\in G_n\cap E_n; n\ge1$,

and for each B_j contained in the set $\{m_{j-1}+1,\dots,m_j\}$,

$$\left|\sum_{n\in B_j} A_n\varphi_n(x)\right|<\frac{3}{2^{n+1}}\forall x\in G_j\cap E_{j-1}\cap E_j; j\ge1 .$$

Let

$$\left|\sum_{j=1}^{\infty} A_n\varphi_n\right|=\left|\sum_{j=1}^{\infty}\sum_{n=m_{j-1}+1}^{m_j} A_n\varphi_n\right|.$$

We set $B=\bigcup_{n=1}^{\infty}\bigcap_{k=n}^{\infty}(E_k\cap G_k)$.

Let $x\in B$, then for some $n_0\in N$ we have $x\in G_n\cap E_n, \forall n>n_0$. Indeed if π be a permutation of N, and if N_n be chosen so that $\{\pi(k):1\le k\le N_n\}\supset\{i:1\le i\le m_n\}\,\forall n>n_0$ then for arbitrary $M>N_n$ and $x\in G_n\cap E_n, \forall n>n_0$ it is true:

$$\left|f(x)-\sum_{k=1}^{M} A_{\pi(k)}(x)\right|\le\left|f(x)-\sum_{j=n+1}^{m_j} Q_j(x)\right|+\sum_{j=n+1}^{\infty}\frac{3}{2^{j+1}}<\frac{1}{2^{n+1}}+$$
$$+\frac{3}{2^{n+1}}=\frac{1}{2^{n-1}}.$$

I. e. the series $\sum_{i=1}^{\infty} A_n\varphi_n=\sum_{j=1}^{\infty}\sum_{n=m_{j-1}+1}^{m_j} A_n\varphi_n$ converges unconditionally to f almost everywhere on $[0,1]$ and $A_n\to0$ as $n\to\infty$.

2.3 Remark.

Repeating the argument in the proof theorem 3 we arrive at following Theorem

Theorem 5. There is a Schauder universal series of the form $\sum_{i=1}^{\infty} b_n\varphi_n(x), |b_k|\searrow 0$ with the following properties:

1. For each measurable function $f(x)$ one can find a sequence $\{\xi_k\}_{k=1}^{\infty}, \xi_k=0, or 1, k=1,2,\dots,$ such that the series, $\sum_{n=1}^{\infty}\xi_n b_n\varphi_n(x)$ converges unconditionally to f almost everywhere on $[0,1]$.

2. For every $\varepsilon>0$ there is a measurable set E contained in $[0,1]$, with $|E|>1-\varepsilon$, such that for each $f\in C(E)$ one can find a function $g\in C[0,1], g(x)=f(x), \forall x\in E$ equal to f on E such that the Fourier series with respect to the Faber-Schauder system of signal g unconditionally converges it in the $C[0,1]$ -norm, and

$$A_n(g)=b_n, \forall n\in spec(g)=\{n\in \mathrm{N}, A_n(g)\ne0\}$$
$$\sum_{n=0}^{m}|A_n(g)|\varphi_n(x)<2|g(x)|, \forall x\in[0,1], \forall m>0.$$

References

1. G. Faber, Uber die ortogonalen functionen des Hern Haar, Iahrscber Deutsch, Math. Verein, BD.**195,** 104-112 (1910).
2. J. Schauder, Zur Theorie stetiger Abbildungen in Funktionalraumen, Math. Z., **26**(1927), 47-65.
3. M. G. Grigorian, A. A. Sargsyan, Nonlinear approximation of continuous functions by the

Faber-Schauder system, Mat. Sb.vol. **199**:5, p 629-653 (2008).

4. T. M. Grigoryan, On the unconditional convergence of series with respect to the Faber-Schauder system, Analysis Mathematica, **39**, 179-188 (2013).
5. A. A. Talalyan, Representation of measurable functions by series, Usp. Mat. Nauk, **15**, no. 5 Russian Math. Surveys, 1, (Russian) (1960).
6. Casper Goffman,"Remark on a problem of Lusin", Acta Math.,vol **111**, p. 63--72S (1964).
7. V. G. Krotov "On the series by the Faber-Schauder system and by bases in C[0,1]", Mat. Zamet.,vol. **14**, p. 185--195 (1973).
8. M. G. Grigoryan, V. G. Krotov, Luzin's Correction Theorem and the Coefficients of Fourier Expansions in the Faber-Schauder System, Mat. Zametki **93**, no. 2, 172-178 (2013).
9. M. G. Grigorian and T. M. Grigoryan, On the absolute convergece Schauder series, Advances in Theoretical and Applied Mathematics,V. **9**, n. 1 (2014),
10. Karlin, Bases in Banach spaces, Duke Math. J., **15**, 971-985 (1948).
11. R. A. DeVore, V. N. Temlyakov, "Some remarks on greedy algorithms", Advances in Computational Math., **5**, 173-187 (1996).
12. T. W. Korner, Decreasing rearranged Fourier series, J. Fourier Anal. Appl. **5**, no. 1, 1-19 (1999).
13. S. V. Konyagin and V. N. Temlyakov, "A remark on Greedy approximation in Banach spaces", East Journal on Approximations, **5:1**, 1-15 (1999).
14. P. Wojtaszczyk, "Greedy Algorithm for General Biorthogonal Systems", Journal of Approximation Theory, **107,** 293-314 (2000).
15. M. G. Grigoryan, K. S. Kazaryan and F. Soria, "Mean convergence of orthogonal Fourier series of modified functions", Trans. Amer. Math. Soc. **352**:8, 3777—3798 (2000).
16. M. G. Grigoryan and R. E. Zink, "Greedy approximation with respect to certain subsystems of the Walsh orthonormal system", Proc. Amer. Math. Soc. **134,** 3495-3505 (2006).
17. N. N. Luzin, On the fundamental theorem of the integral calculus, Sb. Math. **28**, 266-294 (in Russian) (1912).
18. D. E. Menchoff [D. E. Men`shov], Sur la convergence uniforme des series de Fourier, Sb. Math. **53**, no. 11, 67-96 (1942).
19. M. G. Grigoryan, Modifications of functions, Fourier coefficients and nonlinear approximation, Sb. Math. **203,** no. 3, 49-78 (2012).
20. M. G. Grigorian (Grigoryan), On the convergence of Fourier series in the metric of L^1, Anal. Math. **17**, no. 3, 211-237 (1991).
21. M. G. Grigorian, Uniform convergence of the greedy algorithm with respect to the Walsh system, Studia Math. **198,** no. 2, 197-206 (2010).
22. M. G. Grigoryan, L. N. Galoyan, On the uniform convergence of negative order Cesaro means of Fourier series, J. Math. Anal. Appl. **434**, no. 1, 554-567 (2016).
23. M. G. Grigoryan, A. A. Sargsyan, On the universal functions for the class Lp[0,1], J. Funct. Anal. **270**, 3111-3133 (2016).

A New Stochastic Inner Product Core Design for Digital FIR Filters

Ming Ming Wong[1,⋆], *M. L. Dennis* Wong[2], *Cishen* Zhang[3], and *Ismat* Hijazin[3]

[1]*Faculty of Engineering, Computing and Science, Swinburne University of Technology, Sarawak Campus, Malaysia.*
[2]*Heriot Watt University Malaysia, Wilayah Persekutuan Putrajaya, Malaysia.*
[3]*School of Software and Electrical Engineeing, Swinburne University of Technology, Hawthorn VIC 3122, Australia.*

Abstract. Stochastic computing (SC) is a computational technique with computational operations governed by probability instead of arithmetic rules. It recently found promising applications in digital and image processing areas and attracted attentions of researchers. In this paper, a new stochastic inner product (multiply and accumulate) core with an improved scaling scheme is presented for improving the accuracy and fault tolerance performance of SC based finite impulse response (FIR) digital filters. The proposed inner product core is designed using tree structured multiplexers which is capable of reducing the critical path and fault propagation in the stochastic circuitry. The designed inner product core can lead to construction of SC based light weight and multiplierless FIR digital filters. As a result, an SC based FIR digital FIR filter is implemented on Altera Cyclone V FPGA which operates on stochastic sequences of 256-bits length (8-bits precision level). Experimental results show that the developed filter has lower hardware cost, better accuracy and higher fault tolerance level compared with other stochastic implementations.

1 Introduction

Stochastic computing (SC) [1] is a computational technique with operations based on probability instead of arithmetic rules [2–4]. This technique can simplify mathematical functions, which are computationally demanding in binary computation, with simple logic operations and reduced hardware requirement. It is robust against noise. And it has a progressive precision characteristic that the precision of stochastic numbers (bit streams) increases as computation proceeds [2]. These advantages enabled SC's recent applications in signal and image processing, in particular, in realization and implementation of digital filters [5, 6]

In this paper, a new stochastic inner product core with an improved scaling scheme is presented for improving the accuracy and fault tolerance performance of SC based finite impulse response (FIR) digital filters. The proposed inner product core is designed using tree structured multiplexers which is capable of reducing the critical path and fault propagation in the stochastic circuitry. The designed inner product core can lead to construction of SC based light weight and multiplierless FIR digital filters.

The performance of the proposed SC based FIR filter is tested via hardware implementation on an FPGA using a case study on a $6th$-order FIR digital filter. With the filter's order varying from $4th$ to $8th$ order and each having cutoff frequencies ranging from 0.2π to 0.8π, empirical analysis is performed to evaluate the proposed FIR filter's accuracy levels, fault tolerance capabilities as well as the associated hardware costs. The obtained results show that our proposed SC filter design outperforms other existing higher precision stochastic FIR filter designs.

The rest of the paper is organized as follows. Section 2 reviews stochastic computational elements of SC. The motivation and problem statement of proposed SC based FIR filter design are presented in Section 3. Next, an improved stochastic inner product is presented in Section 4. The proposed function is later employed to design a new SC digital FIR design and the case study is reported in Section 5. The experimental results (accuracy and fault tolerance analysis) as well as the hardware implementation for the application is reported and discussed in Section 6. Finally, some conclusion remarks are drawn in Section 7.

2 Basic Theory of Stochastic Computation

The basic rule of SC is that the computational data (in bit-streams) are represented as stochastic sequences and are processed in form of digitized probabilities [3]. Naturally, the representations and all the involved computations always lie within the real-number unit interval [0, 1]. Stochastic representation can be coded in two formats: *SC-unipolar* and *SC-bipolar* [1].

In SC-unipolar format, the input s is a real number within the unit interval, i.e. $0 \leq s \leq 1$. As an example, a 2's complement binary input bit-stream $\{0100\}_2$ is represented in stochastic bit-streams S, consisting of 4 of bit '1' out of $2^4 = 16$ bits (remaining bits are zeros). This stochastic bit-streams S, is also interpreted as $p = P(S = 1) = 4/16$. On the other hand, in SC-bipolar format, the range of the real number input, s, is extended to

⋆Corresponding author: wmingming7@gmail.com

$-1 \leq s \leq 1$. Consider a 2's complement binary input bit-stream $\{1100\}_2$. In SC-bipolar bit-streams S, the deterministic value is mapped to $p = P(S = 1)/2 = 12/(16 \times 2) = 6/16$.

In other words, stochastic representation observes the probability of 1s at arbitrary bit position in S. Such representation serves as the main reason for having high fault tolerance in SC. A single bit-flip in a long bit-stream causes a minor change in original logical value. On the contrary, a single bit-flip in the conventional 2's complement computation will result in huge error especially if the bit-flip occurs on the higher-order bit.

Multiplication of two inputs streams, which is computational intensive in conventional signed binary computing, can be performed using single logical gate in SC. Consider two stochastic input bit-streams, X_1 and X_2 and the output for their multiplication, Y, is derived as,

$$\begin{aligned} y &= P(Y = 1) \\ &= P(X_1 = 1)P(X_2 = 1) \\ &\quad +(1 - P(X_1 = 1))(1 - P(X_2 = 1)) \end{aligned}$$

Stochastic multiplication in bipolar format is clearly a logical XNOR operation between input bit-streams, X_1 and X_2 in digital circuit. For unipolar format, the multiplication is performed using a logical AND operation instead. Stochastic multiplier for both unipolar and bipolar formats are as depicted in Figure 1.

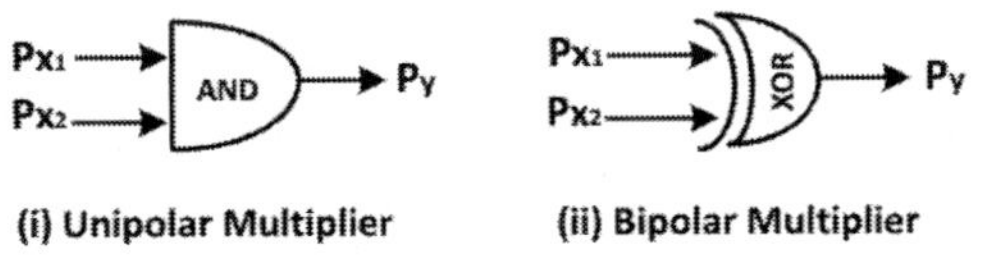

Figure 1. Stochastic Multiplier for (i) SC-unipolar and (ii) SC-bipolar formats.

Addition in SC is performed using a special operation, termed as scaled addition. The addition is scaled such that the value always lies between the probability interval [0, 1]. With S being a constant scale, the sum of two independent stochastic bit-streams X_1 and X_2, produces Y, defined as,

$$\begin{aligned} y &= P(Y = 1) \\ &= P(S = 1)P(X_1 = 1) + (1 - P(S))(P(X_2 = 1)) \\ &= SX_1 + (1 - S)X_2 \end{aligned}$$

Thus, multiplexer with conditional select line S, set as $P(S) = \frac{1}{2}$ can be used to realize the scaled addition of two stochastic bit-streams in digital circuit. **Subtraction** in SC is similar to the adder except that the stochastic scaled substractor requires an additional inverter and this only feasible in SC-bipolar format. Both the stochastic scaled adder and scaled substractor are illustrated in Figure 2.

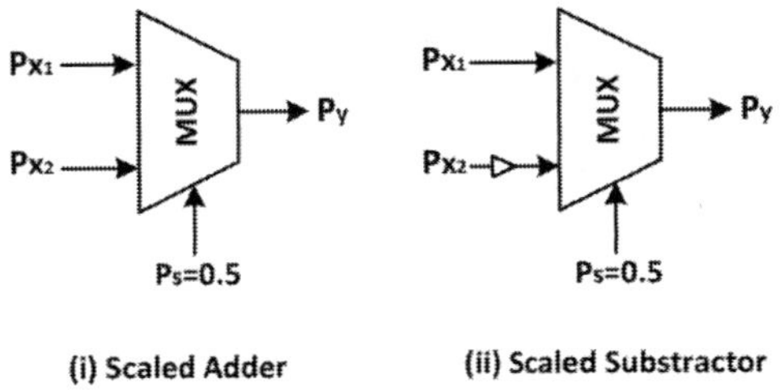

Figure 2. Stochastic scaled adder/substractor

3 Problem Statement

FIR filter is widely used in many classical DSP applications in order to achieve filtering stability and linear-phase property. FIR filters are generally characterized by their impulse response coefficients which perform multiplication with the input signals, i.e. the inner product.

Alternatively, these computationally expensive operations can be well approximated through SC. To be precise, the summation of the multiplication between input vectors $\{X_0, X_1\}$ and filter coefficients $\{a_0, a_1\}$ can be derived using a single stochastic operation, the *stochastic scaled addition*, i.e. $\frac{1}{2}(a_0X_0 + a_1X_1)$.

Through SC, the computational data are represented in stochastic bit-streams of 2^n bits (n is precision level) and are processed in the form on digitized probabilities [2]. In terms of hardware, a stochastic scaled addition can be realized using a *multiplexer* with its conditional select line, S set as the scaling factor [2].

Unfortunately, when repetitive computations are involved, the implicit scaling of $\frac{1}{2}$ in stochastic scaled addition will severly degrade the filter's output accuracy [5]. An alternative stochastic inner product architecture was reported in [5, 6] where the scaling is performed using with unevenly weightings. However, significant accuracy degradation is observed as the filter's order increases. Therefore, to address this issue, a new scaling scheme in stochastic inner product is required.

4 An Improved Stochastic Inner Product

In this work, an improved stochastic inner product is designed using a new scaling scheme which considers the weight distribution of the filter's coefficients. Under this scheme, the coefficients of equal (or near equivalent) weightings are paired together and form the scaling factor in the stochastic scaled addition. For instance, coefficients $\{a_0, a_1\}$ is paired when $a_0 \approx a_1$ and this produce scaling factor $\frac{|a_0|}{|a_0|+|a_1|}$.

A causal discrete-time FIR filter of order N (length $M = N+1$) is generally described as $y[n] = \sum_{k=0}^{N} a[k]x[n-k]$, with $y[n]$ as the output signal, $x[n]$ is the input signal and $\{a_0, a_1, a_2, a_3, \ldots, a_N\}$ are the filter coefficients. All the 4 types of linear phase FIR filters have symmetric parameters in absolute value. Therefore, the distribution of the absolute value of the filter's impulse response coefficients resembles a bell curve. The largest value is weighted at the center of the distribution and decreases gradually towards the first and the last coefficients, i.e $a_0 \approx a_N < a_1 \approx a_{N-1} < a_2 \approx a_{N-2} < \cdots < a_{\frac{N-1}{2}}$. Hence, the scaled additions are performed according to the pairs of the FIR filter coefficients arranged such as follows.

- $P_0 = \{a_0, a_N\}, P_1 = \{a_1, a_{N-1}\}, P_2 = \{a_2, a_{N-2}\}, \ldots$ and
- $P_{N'=\frac{N-1}{2}} = \left\{a_{\frac{N-1}{2}}, a_{\frac{N+1}{2}}\right\}$ for even length (such as FIR Types II and IV),
- $P_{N'=\frac{N}{2}} = \left\{a_{\frac{N}{2}}\right\}$ for odd length (such as FIR Types I and III).

Furthermore, note that $P_0 < P_1 < P_2 < \cdots < P_0 < P_{N'}$ with $N' = \frac{N-1}{2}$ for even filter length and $N' = \frac{N}{2}$ for odd filter length. With that, the next round of scaled additions are performed following the pairing shown below.

- $P'_0 = \{P_0, P_1\}, P'_1 = \{P_2, P_3\}, \ldots$ and
- $P'_{N''=\frac{N'-1}{2}} = \left\{P_{N'-1}, P_{N'}\right\}$ for N' is odd,
- $P'_{N''=\frac{N'}{2}} = \left\{P_{N'}\right\}$ for N' is even.

The similar addition process is repeated until the inner product computation is completed. An example of the resultant stochastic inner product using the proposed approach is shown in (7).

5 Case Study of New SC FIR Filter Design

Consider a $6th$-order linear phase Type I FIR filter with its taps coefficients labeled as $\{a_0, a_1, a_2, a_3, a_4, a_5, a_6\}$ and the input vectors listed as $\{X_0, X_1, X_2, X_3, X_4, X_5, X_6\}$. The inner product of the filter is derived as $y = a_0X_0 + a_1X_1 + a_2X_2 + a_3X_3 + a_4X_4 + a_5X_5 + a_6X_6$.

Using the proposed stochastic inner product, the final computation is described in (7) and is illustrated in Figure 3. Note that, both of the input vectors and filter coefficients are first converted into stochastic bit-streams using SNG modules [1], which are not shown in the figure.

$$Y_{11} = \Big(\frac{|a_0|}{|a_0| + |a_6|}\Big)X_0 + \Big(\frac{|a_6|}{|a_0| + |a_6|}\Big)X_6 \quad (1)$$

$$Y_{12} = \Big(\frac{|a_1|}{|a_1| + |a_5|}\Big)X_1 + \Big(\frac{|a_5|}{|a_1| + |a_5|}\Big)X_5 \quad (2)$$

$$Y_{13} = \Big(\frac{|a_2|}{|a_2| + |a_4|}\Big)X_2 + \Big(\frac{|a_4|}{|a_2| + |a_4|}\Big)X_4 \quad (3)$$

$$Y_{14} = \big(|a_3|X_3\big) \quad (4)$$

$$Y_{21} = \Big(\frac{|a_0| + |a_6|}{|a_0| + |a_1| + |a_5| + |a_6|}\Big)Y_{11} + \Big(\frac{|a_1| + |a_5|}{|a_0| + |a_1| + |a_5| + |a_6|}\Big)Y_{12} \quad (5)$$

$$Y_{22} = \Big(\frac{|a_2| + |a_4|}{|a_2| + |a_3| + |a_4|}\Big)Y_{13} + \Big(\frac{|a_3|}{|a_2| + |a_3| + |a_4|}\Big)Y_{14} \quad (6)$$

$$Y = \Big(\frac{|a_0| + |a_1| + |a_5| + |a_6|}{|a_0| + |a_1| + |a_2| + |a_3| + |a_4| + |a_5| + |a_6|}\Big)Y_{21} + \Big(\frac{|a_2| + |a_3| + |a_4|}{|a_0| + |a_1| + |a_2| + |a_3| + |a_4| + |a_5| + |a_6|}\Big)Y_{22} \quad (7)$$

With such filter's coefficients, $a_0 \approx a_6, a_1 \approx a_5$ and $a_2 \approx a_4$, the scaled addition in (1), (2) and (3) can be performed using fixed scaling factor $\frac{1}{2}$. Therefore, the conditional probability selection line (which is determined by the scaling factor) of the correspondence multiplexers can share the same SNG modules to promote hardware cost reduction. The savings will be more prominent in higher order filter where there is a large amount of identical coefficients. In addition, our SC FIR filter is designed with precision level of 8-bits, whereby the computations are performed using $2^8 = 256$ bits only. The filter designs in [5, 6] are computed using $2^{10} = 1024$ bits instead.

6 Experimental Results

Several simulations were performed to test the effectiveness and the efficiency of the proposed SC FIR filter. The metric of measurements included the output accuracy (error-to-signal power ratio), the fault tolerance and the hardware requirement and performance in FPGA implementation.

6.1 Accuracy Analysis

The new SC low-pass FIR filters, implemented in three different orders and each having four different cutoff frequencies, are evaluated for their accuracy levels. A total of 256 samples of input test signal is used in the test simulation. The test signal consists of a mixture of four sinusoidal waves of different frequencies padded with white noise. The accuracies of the proposed filters are measured in term of the error-to-signal power ratio and are benchmarked with the work reported in [5]. These results are as summarized in Table 1.

The results from [5] showed the error ratio increases with higher filters' order. In constrast, our SC FIR filter presents consistently lower error ratio regardless of the filters' order. Further accuracy justification can be deduced by comparing the frequency response and the power spectral density (PSD) of the output signal deduced from both our SC filter and the ideal filter (see Figure 4). It is observed that the spectrum of our SC filter is very close to that of the ideal filter.

6.2 Fault Tolerance Analysis

Apart from low hardware cost, SC is well recognized for being insusceptible towards fault as opposed to the conventional binary computing. Fault tolerance testing is conducted on our proposed SC $6th$-order FIR filter with cutoff frequency at 0.4π. The test is performed by randomly injecting various percentage of bit-flipping error in the input signals and the corresponding error-to-signal power ratio is measured and summarized in Table 2.

The results show that percentage of random bit-flipping error ranging from 0.5% to 3.0% has minimal

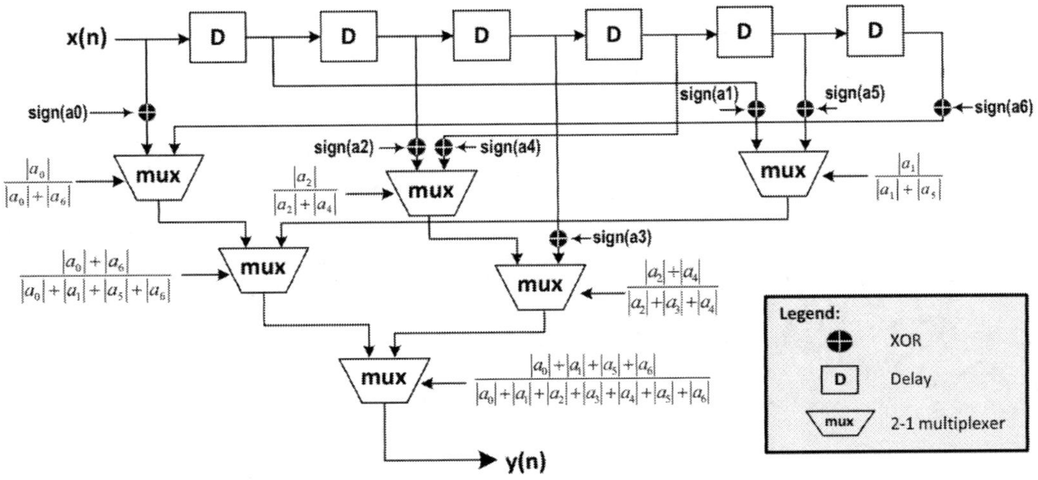

Figure 3. The new SC 6*th*-order FIR filter.

Table 1. Accuracy test results of (i) our proposed design (precision level of 8-bits) compared with (ii) [5] (precision level of 10-bits).

Filter Order	Filter Cutoff Frequency							
	0.2π		0.4π		0.6π		0.8π	
	(i)	(ii)	(i)	(ii)	(i)	(ii)	(i)	(ii)
2	0.0050	0.0037	0.0046	0.0025	0.0058	0.0013	0.0069	0.0004
4	0.0192	0.0597	0.0123	0.0314	0.0120	0.0465	0.0070	0.0145
6	0.0136	0.0648	0.0075	0.0462	0.0080	0.0637	0.0048	0.0626
8	0.0095	-	0.0107	-	0.0114	-	0.0076	-

Table 2. Error-to-signal power ratio analysis resultant from various percentage of random bit-flipping error in 6*th*-order FIR filter with cutoff frequency at 0.4π.

Filter Implementation	Percentage of Bit-Flipping					
	0.5%	1.0%	1.5%	2.0%	2.5%	3.0%
Our Work	0.0076	0.0160	0.0209	0.0292	0.0355	0.0514
Conventional Filter	0.1180	0.1874	0.3033	0.3351	0.4409	0.4843
Direct Form [6]	0.0488	0.0540	-	-	-	-
Lattice Form [6]	0.0563	0.0820	-	-	-	-

Table 3. Hardware review for the FPGA implementation of the SC 6*th*-order FIR filter with cutoff frequency at 0.4π.

Hardware Requirement/ Performance	**SC FIR Filter**	Inner Product Core	SNG Module
Combinational ALUTs (112,960)	**128**	4	26
Memory ALUTs (56,480)	**0**	0	0
Dedicated Logic Register (225,920)	**159**	1	33
Total Register (225,920)	**159**	1	33
Fmax (MHz)	**306.0**	0	429.92
Dynamic Thermal Power Dissipation (mW)	**2.11**	0.04	0.94

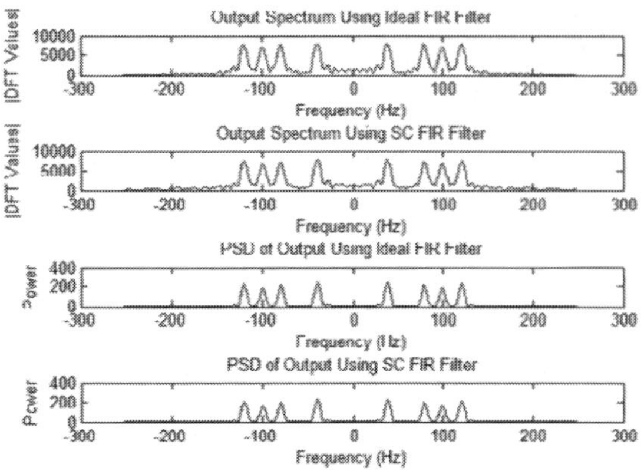

Figure 4. Output spectrum and PSD derived using the FIR ideal filter and our SC FIR filter. Both filters are low-pass with $6th$-order and the cutoff frequency at 0.4π.

impact on the output accuracy of our proposed SC FIR filter. On the contrary, the conventional ideal FIR filter shows significant accuracy degradation as the injected bit-flipping error increases at every 0.5%. These results are further benchmarked with the work reported in [6]. The authors presented two SC $7th$-order FIR filter with cutoff frequency at 0.1π using direct form and lattice form. Both of their filters also exhibited higher error percentages in comparison to our work.

The multiplexers in our proposed inner product core are positioned in tree structure to avoid error propagation that tends to occur in long critical path. Therefore, with short critical path, the presented SC FIR filter has higher fault tolerance in comparison to the conventional FIR filter as well as the existing SC FIR filters.

6.3 Hardware Complexity

The proposed SC FIR filter is implemented in Cyclone V 5CGXFC7D6F31C6 using Quartus II 11.1. The full hardware synthesis result of the filter as well as its core units; the inner product and the SNG Module are summarized in Table 3.

7 Conclusion

A case study of a new SC FIR filter design using an improved stochastic inner product core was presented in this paper. Without the use of multiplier, the inner product core unit employed stochastic scaled addition with a new scaling scheme that paired the filter's coefficients in according to their weightage. The computation was realized using multiplexers positioned in tree structure, which in turn reduces the critical path as well as the fault propagation in the stochastic circuitry. Such design enhanced the computational accuracy and offered high fault tolerance in SC filter system. For hardware evaluation, a new SC $6th$-order FIR filter with the cutoff frequency at 0.4π on FPGA platform has been implemented and tested. Experimental results have shown that the presented SC FIR filter outperforms the conventional filter and the existing works in both metrics and also has low hardware cost.

References

[1] B. R. Gaines,'Stochastic computing', *Proceedings of the Spring Joint Computer Conference, New York, NY, USA*, pp. 149-156,(1967).

[2] A. Alaghi, and J. P. Hayes,'Survey of Stochastic Computing', *ACM Trans. Embed. Comput. Syst.*, vol. **12**, no. 2, pp. 19, (2013), .

[3] W. Qian, X. Li, M. D. Riedel, K. Bazargan, and D. J. Lilja, 'An architecture for fault-tolerant computation with stochastic logic',*IEEE Transactions on Computers*, vol. **60**, no. 1, pp. 93-105, (2011).

[4] B. Moons, and M. Verhelst, 'Energy-efficiency and accuracy of stochastic computing circuits in emerging technologies', *IEEE Journal on E,merging and Selected Topics in Circuits and Systems*, vol. **4**, no. 4, pp. 475-486, (2014).

[5] Y. N. Chang, and K. K. Parhi, 'Architectures for digital filters using stochastic computing', *2013 IEEE International Conference on Acoustics, Speech and Signal Processing (ICASSP)*, pp. 2697-2701, (2013).

[6] Y. Liu, and K. K. Parhi,'Lattice fir digital filter architectures using stochastic computing', *2015 IEEE International Conference on Acoustics, Speech and Signal Processing (ICASSP)*, pp. 1027-1031, (2015).

Application of Enhanced Hadamard Error Correcting Code in Video-Watermarking and his comparison to Reed-Solomon Code.

Andrzej Dziech[1], *Jakob* Wassermann[2, *]

[1] Dept. of Telecommunication, AGH University of Science and Technology, 30-059 Krakow, Poland
[2] Dept. of Electronics and Telecommunications University of Applied Sciences Technikum Wien, 1200 Wien Austria

Abstract. Error Correcting Codes are playing a very important role in Video Watermarking technology. Because of very high compression rate (about 1:200) normally the watermarks can barely survive such massive attacks, despite very sophisticated embedding strategies. It can only work with a sufficient error correcting code method. In this paper, the authors compare the new developed Enhanced Hadamard Error Correcting Code (EHC) with well known Reed-Solomon Code regarding its ability to preserve watermarks in the embedded video. The main idea of this new developed multidimensional Enhanced Hadamard Error Correcting Code is to map the 2D basis images into a collection of one-dimensional rows and to apply a 1D Hadamard decoding procedure on them. After this, the image is reassembled, and the 2D decoding procedure can be applied more efficiently. With this approach, it is possible to overcome the theoretical limit of error correcting capability of $(d-1)/2$ bits, where d is a Hamming distance. Even better results could be achieved by expanding the 2D EHC to 3D. To prove the efficiency and practicability of this new Enhanced Hadamard Code, the method was applied to a video Watermarking Coding Scheme. The Video Watermarking Embedding procedure decomposes the initial video trough multi-Level Interframe Wavelet Transform. The low pass filtered part of the video stream is used for embedding the watermarks, which are protected respectively by Enhanced Hadamard or Reed-Solomon Correcting Code. The experimental results show that EHC performs much better than RS Code and seems to be very robust against strong MPEG compression.

1 Introduction

Many applications in telecommunication technologies are using Hadamard Error Correcting Code. Plotkin [1] was the first who discovered in 1960 error correcting capabilities of Hadamard matrices. Bose, Shrikhande[2] and Peterson [3] also have made important contributions. Levenshstein [4] was the first who introduced an algorithm for constructing a Hadamard Error Correcting Code. The most famous application of Hadamard Error Correcting Code was the NASA space mission in 1969 of Mariner and Voyager spacecrafts. Thanks to the powerful error correcting capability of this code it was possible to decode properly high-quality pictures of Mars, Jupiter, Saturn, and Uranus [5].
In this paper we introduced a new type of multidimensional Hadamard Code, we called it Enhanced Hadamard Error Correcting Code (EHC). It can overcome the limit of error correcting capability of n/2-1 bits of standard Hadamard Code, where the codeword length and the Hamming distance d have the same value n. The application of this Code in Video Watermarking gives also a strong prove of its effectiveness. The reason for selecting Video Watermarking lies in strong compression ratio, normally factors greater than 1:200, which are applied to the video sequences. For example, an uncompressed HDTV video stream has a data rate of 1.2Gbit/s and for distribution reason, it must be compressed to 6Mbit/s. For embedded watermarks, it is a big challenge to survive such strong compression ratio. Error correcting code plays a decisive role in surviving of the embedded Watermarks.
This paper has followed the structure: In Chapter 2 contains the introduction to the enhanced Hadamard Error Correcting Code and its error correcting capabilities.
In Chapter 3, the authors explain the Video Watermarking Scheme and the Chapter 4 presents the results and discussion.

2 Enhanced Hadamard Error Correcting Code

In this chapter, we will give an overview of one-dimensional and two-dimensional Hadamard Code. Then

* Corresponding author: jakob.wassermann@technikum-wien.at

DOI: 10.1051/matecconf/201712505007

the authors explain the enhanced version.

2.1 One-Dimensional Hadamard Code

The Hadamard code of n-bit is a non-linear code, which is generated by rows of a n*n Hadamard Matrix H_n. It can encode $k=log_2(n)$ messages and is denoted as (n,k). The Hamming distance is $n/2$, and it can correct $n/2$-1 errors. In the case of n=8 we obtain the following matrix:

$$H_8 = \begin{pmatrix} 1 & 1 & 1 & 1 & 1 & 1 & 1 & 1 \\ 1 & -1 & 1 & -1 & 1 & -1 & 1 & -1 \\ 1 & 1 & -1 & -1 & 1 & 1 & -1 & -1 \\ 1 & -1 & -1 & 1 & 1 & -1 & -1 & 1 \\ 1 & 1 & 1 & 1 & -1 & -1 & -1 & -1 \\ 1 & -1 & 1 & -1 & -1 & 1 & -1 & 1 \\ 1 & 1 & -1 & -1 & -1 & -1 & 1 & 1 \\ 1 & -1 & -1 & 1 & -1 & 1 & 1 & -1 \end{pmatrix} \quad (1)$$

The code words are the rows of this Matrix H_8. In Table 1 the Code Book of the linear Code (8,3) is depicted. The Hamming distance of this code is h=4.

Message	Code Words							
0 0 0	1	1	1	1	1	1	1	1
0 0 1	1	-1	1	-1	1	-1	1	-1
0 1 0	1	1	-1	-1	1	1	-1	-1
0 1 1	1	-1	-1	1	1	-1	-1	1
1 0 0	1	1	1	1	-1	-1	-1	-1
1 0 1	1	-1	1	-1	-1	1	-1	1
1 1 0	1	1	-1	-1	-1	-1	1	1
1 1 1	1	-1	-1	1	-1	1	1	-1

Table 1. Code Book of Hadamard Code (8,3)

The decoding procedure is based on Hadamard Spectrum. The spectral component with the highest value determines the decoding message. The received code word is used to build the Hadamard spectrum vector, which enables to determine the corresponding message. The spectrum vector d is calculated by multiplying the code vector c by the Hadamard Matrix H_8.

$$d = c \cdot H_8 \quad (2)$$

Supposed we received the code word:

$$c = [1 \ \ 1 \ \ -1 \ \ -1 \ \ 1 \ \ 1 \ \ -1 \ \ -1]$$

According to the Eq.(2), the decoded Hadamard Spectrum vector is:

$$d = [1 \ \ 1 \ \ -1 \ \ -1 \ \ 1 \ \ 1 \ \ -1 \ \ -1] * H_8$$

$$d = [0 \ \ 0 \ \ 8 \ \ 0 \ \ 0 \ \ 0 \ \ 0 \ \ 0]$$

The third component of the vector d has the highest value in the spectrum; all others are zeroes, $d(3)$=8, $d(i)$=0 for i=1,..8 and $i \neq 3$. It implicates that the code word at the position i=3 was received. The codebook at that position gives us the ultimate information of the message (010).

In the case of one error, the third component of the spectrum vector d still remains the highest one. In the case of a corrupted codeword c=[***-1*** 1 -1 -1 1 1 -1 -1], the Hadamard spectrum vector delivers:

$$d = [-1 \ \ 1 \ \ -1 \ \ -1 \ \ 1 \ \ 1 \ \ -1 \ \ -1] * H_8$$

$$d = [-2 \ \ -2 \ \ 6 \ \ -2 \ \ -2 \ \ -2 \ \ -2 \ \ -2]$$

The third component is still the highest one, so the message can be decoded.

In the case of two errors, it is already impossible to decode the message unambiguously.

What is interesting about Hadamard Code is that in the case of seven and eight errors it is possible again to decode the codewords. In case of eight errors, our codeword

c=[-1- 1 1 1 -1 -1 1 1]

is completely corrupted. In this case, the absolute value of the third component of the Hadamard spectrum is the highest one, and it has a negative sign. A negative sign means that the decoded code word must be inverted.

$$d = [-1 \ \ -1 \ \ 1 \ \ 1 \ \ -1 \ \ -1 \ \ 1 \ \ 1] * H_8$$

$$d = [0 \ \ 0 \ \ -8 \ \ 0 \ \ 0 \ \ 0 \ \ 0 \ \ 0]$$

In the case of seven errors, we have exactly the same situation as with one error, however, with one small difference: the third component has a negative sign, what means the decoded word must be inverted.

The following figure shows the error correcting capability of an 8 bit Hadamard code.

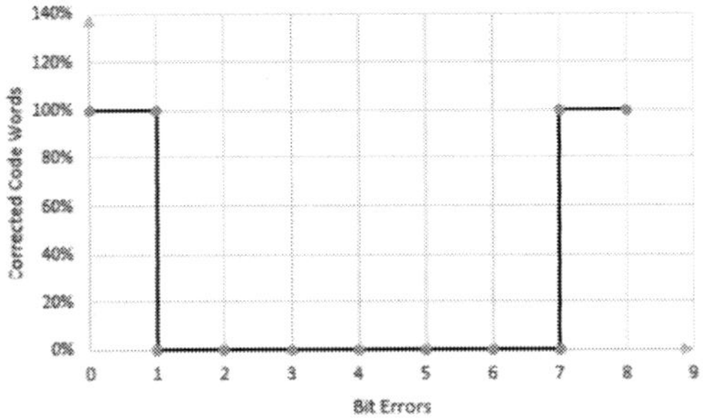

Fig. 1. Error Correcting Capability of 8 Bit Hadamard Code

The 8 bit Hadamard code can correct 1,7 and 8-bit errors regardless where they occur within the code words. Generally, we can say that n bit Hadamard code can correct totally n/2-1 types of errors. The number of error bits occurring in the range

$$\text{from } \left[1, \cdots, \frac{n}{4} - 1\right] \text{ to } \left[\frac{3}{4}n + 1, \ldots, n\right]$$

2.2 Two-Dimensional Hadamard Error Correcting Code

The 2D Hadamard Error Correcting Code uses so-called

DOI: 10.1051/matecconf/201712505007

basis images instead of Hadamard vectors. The basis images functions are orthogonal to each other, and they can be generated from the Hadamard matrix by multiplication of columns and rows. Generally, we can write

$$A_{ml} = H_n(:,l) * H_n(m,:) \qquad (3)$$

In case of 4x4 Hadamard matrix

$$H_4 = \begin{pmatrix} 1 & 1 & 1 & 1 \\ 1 & -1 & 1 & -1 \\ 1 & 1 & -1 & -1 \\ 1 & -1 & -1 & 1 \end{pmatrix}$$

We can calculate the complete set of 16 such basis images.

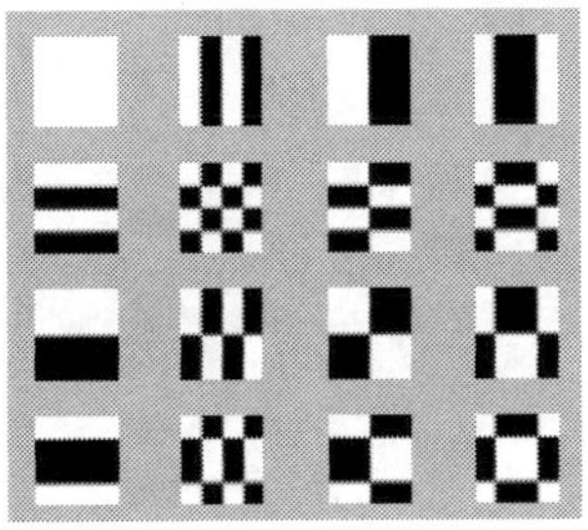

Fig. 2. Basis Images of 2D Hadamard Transform (4x4)

For instance, the pattern A_{31} is generated by Eq.(1) and has the numerical presentation

$$A_{31} = \begin{pmatrix} 1 \\ 1 \\ -1 \\ -1 \end{pmatrix} \cdot \begin{pmatrix} 1 & 1 & 1 & 1 \end{pmatrix} = \begin{pmatrix} 1 & 1 & 1 & 1 \\ 1 & 1 & 1 & 1 \\ -1 & -1 & -1 & -1 \\ -1 & -1 & -1 & -1 \end{pmatrix}$$

It can be visualized as

Fig. 3. Basis Image A_{31}. The "1" is interpreted as 255 (White) and "-1" as 0 (Black)

The 2D Hadamard Spectrum of such basis images, which is denoted by C, delivers a matrix where only one coefficient differs from zero. It represents a 2D spectrum of the corresponding basis image. For example, the Hadamard spectrum matrix of the pattern A_{31} is

$$C = H_4 * A_{31} * H_4^{-T} = \begin{pmatrix} 0 & 0 & 0 & 0 \\ 0 & 0 & 0 & 0 \\ 16 & 0 & 0 & 0 \\ 0 & 0 & 0 & 0 \end{pmatrix} \qquad (4)$$

The component C_{31}=16 and all others are zero. This fact, identification of the basis image trough its spectral coefficient, can be utilized to construct error-correcting code. The codewords are the pattern of basis images, and they can be decoded unambiguously by detecting the highest absolute coefficient value inside of 2D Hadamard Spectrum according to Eq.(4).

Message	Basis Image	Matrix Element	Pulse Stream (code word)
0000	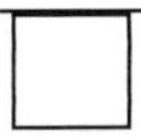	C_{11}	0000000000000000
0001		C_{12}	0101010101010101
0010	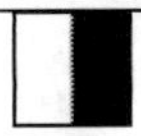	C_{13}	0000000011111111
0011	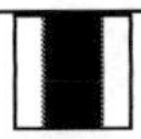	C_{14}	0000111111110000
0100	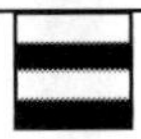	C_{21}	0000111100001111
0101		C_{22}	0101101001011010
0110		C_{23}	0011110000111100
0111	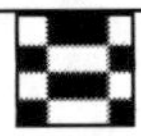	C_{24}	01101001101101001
1000	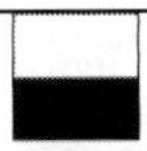	C_{31}	0011001100110011
1001		C_{32}	0101010110101010
1010	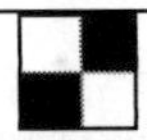	C_{33}	0011001111001100
1011		C_{34}	0011110011000011
1100	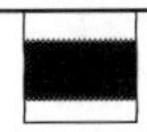	C_{41}	0110011001100110
1101		C_{42}	0101101010100101
1110	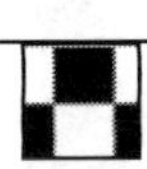	C_{43}	0110011010011001
1111		C_{44}	0110100110010110

Table 2 : 2D Code Book constructed from Basic Images

DOI: 10.1051/matecconf/201712505007

To apply the basic images as codewords, we have to map their two-dimensional structure into one-dimensional pulse stream which will be denoted by the codeword. In Table, 2 such 2D Hadamard codebook is depicted.
In case that the basis image A_{31} is corrupted by some perturbation and looks like it depicted in Figure 4

Fig. 4. Corrupted Basic Image A_{31}

It is still possible to recover the original pattern completely. To understand this, let us consider this corrupted Basic Image:

$$\widetilde{A}_{31} = \begin{pmatrix} -1 & -1 & 1 & 1 \\ 1 & 1 & 1 & 1 \\ -1 & -1 & -1 & -1 \\ 1 & -1 & -1 & -1 \end{pmatrix}$$

The Hadamard Spectrum we obtain from

$$C = H * \widetilde{A}_{31} * H^{-T} = \begin{pmatrix} -2 & 2 & -2 & 2 \\ -6 & -2 & -6 & -2 \\ 10 & -2 & -6 & -2 \\ -2 & 2 & -2 & 2 \end{pmatrix} \quad (6)$$

the absolute value of $|C_{31}| = 10$ and it still stays the highest one between the other spectral coefficients of matrix C, hence the corresponding message word could be read out from the code book depicted in Table 2. It is "1000" (see the row for coefficient C_{31}).

The total number of errors that can be corrected is n/2-1 and correspond completely to the one-dimensional case. The simple enlargement from 1D to 2D doesn't bring any improvement. To overcome this limit, a new enhance Hadamard decoding procedure for 2D and 3D Hadamard Code is introduced.

2.3 Enhanced 2D Hadamard Error Correcting Code

The enhanced 2D Hadamard Code makes it possible to correct more errors as with the standard Hadamard method. With this approach is possible to overcome the theoretical limit of error correcting capability of n/2-1 errors.

The basic idea is to map the 2D basis images into a collection of one-dimensional rows and applying them 1D decoding procedure. After this, the image is reassembled, and the 2D decoding procedure (Eq.(4)) can be applied more efficiently.

To show the functionality of this method we consider the basis images A_{71} of 8x8 2D Hadamard Transform. This basic image (Fig.5) can be derived from Eq.(3).

$$A_{71} = H_8(:,1) \cdot H_8(7,:) = \begin{pmatrix} 1 & 1 & 1 & 1 & 1 & 1 & 1 & 1 \\ 1 & 1 & 1 & 1 & 1 & 1 & 1 & 1 \\ -1 & -1 & -1 & -1 & -1 & -1 & -1 & -1 \\ -1 & -1 & -1 & -1 & -1 & -1 & -1 & -1 \\ -1 & -1 & -1 & -1 & -1 & -1 & -1 & -1 \\ -1 & -1 & -1 & -1 & -1 & -1 & -1 & -1 \\ 1 & 1 & 1 & 1 & 1 & 1 & 1 & 1 \\ 1 & 1 & 1 & 1 & 1 & 1 & 1 & 1 \end{pmatrix}$$

Fig. 5. Basic Image A_{71} of 2D Hadamard Transform (8x8) and its visualization. "1" is interpreted as white (255), "-1" as black (0)

This image is now corrupted by noise (Fig.6). The corresponding error matrix contains 17 errors. According to the consideration from chapter 2.1, it is not possible to recover this pattern because the number of errors exceeds the limit of n/2-1=15.

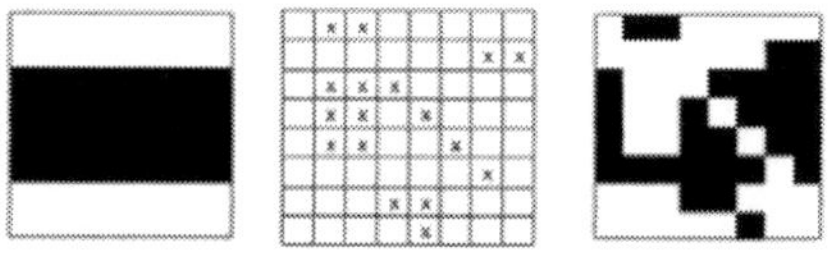

Fig. 6. Original Basis Pattern A_{71}, Error Mask, and the Corrupted Pattern

The functionality of the enhanced Hadamard decoding procedure is depicted in Figure 7.

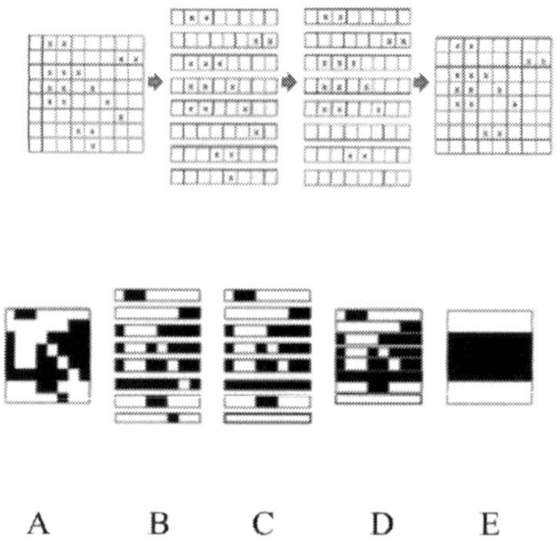

Fig. 7. Enhanced Hadamard Decoding Procedure on Error Mask and on Corrupted Basis Image

DOI: 10.1051/matecconf/201712505007

The steps of the algorithm could be described as followes:

- The corrupted basis image (A) is separated into its rows (B).
- On each row is applied 1D Hadamard decoding procedure. Rows which contain only one error are decoded error free (because of each row has the length of n=8). Rows No. 6 and No. 8 are now without any errors (C).
- Reassemble the pattern again (D). The renewed pattern contains now fewer errors as before, namely 15.
- Apply the 2D Hadamard decoding procedure according to Eq.(4). The result will be error free pattern (E).

We simulated the error correcting performances of the enhanced and standard Hadamard Error Correcting Codes with the codewords of the length n=64. The results are depicted in Fig. 8. On the x-axis, we have the number of bit errors, on the y-axis the number of corrected codewords in percentage. The enhanced Hadamard Code is depicted with a continuous line and standard Hadamard with dashed line. As described in chapter 2.1 the standard Hadamard Error Correcting Code has the following features: It can correct 100% of all corrupted codewords of the length n if the number of error bits occurring in the range [1,.., n/4-1] to [3n/4+1,…,n]. In case n=64 we can see, that standard Hadamard Code corrects all errors if their number is between 1 and 15 and between 49 and 64. In the case of Enhanced Hadamard Correcting Code, we can correct beyond these limits. For example, in the case of 16 errors, we correct 92% of all possible error pattern inside the codeword. In the case of 17 errors, it is still 83% of all error pattern that can be corrected. If we have 48 errors, in the case of Standard Hadamard Code no errors could be corrected on the contrary to the Enhanced Hadamard Code. It can correct 92% of all error pattern.

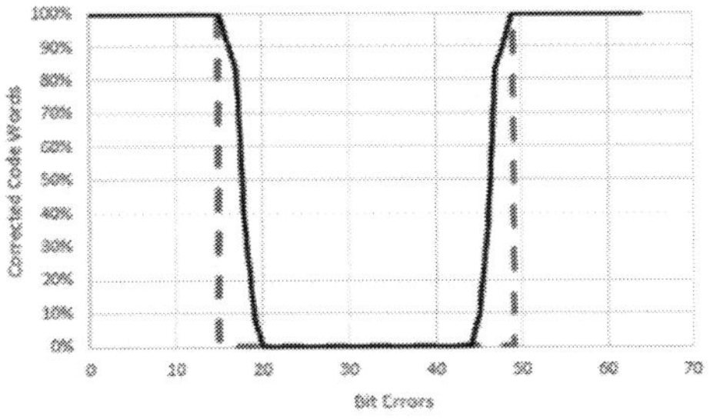

Fig. 8. Comparison of Error Correcting Capabilities of Standard Hadamard (dashed line) with 8x8 2D Enhanced Hadamard Code

2.4 Enhanced 3D Hadamard Error Correcting Code

The performance of Enhanced Hadamard Code can be improved by diluting it to three dimensions. Instead of using basic images, we can use basic cubes for generating a code book.
A Hadamard cube is a basis image expanded in the third dimension by multiplying the pattern with Hadamard vectors.

$$D_{mlk} = A_{ml} \cdot H_k(:) \quad (7)$$

where the basis image is represented by A_{ml} and $H_k(:)$ is the k Hadamard vector. For example the pattern A_{41}

$$A_{41} = \begin{pmatrix} 1 & -1 & -1 & 1 \\ 1 & -1 & -1 & 1 \\ 1 & -1 & -1 & 1 \\ 1 & -1 & -1 & 1 \end{pmatrix}$$

and the Hadamard vector $H_2 = [1 \;\; -1 \;\; 1 \;\; -1]$ generates the cube D_{412}

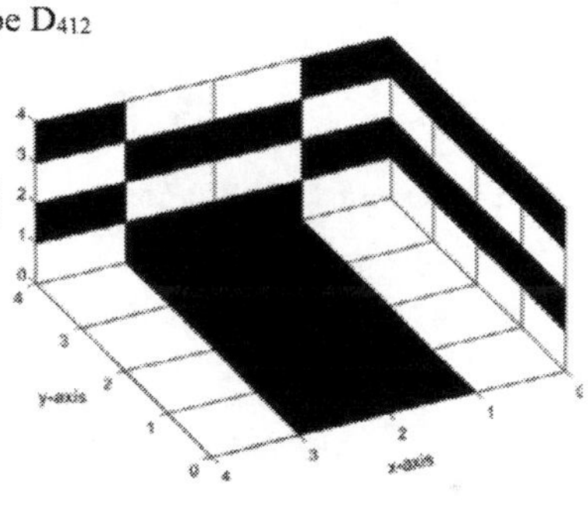

Fig. 9. Hadamard Cube D_{412}

The decoding procedure and the corresponding error correction work similar to the correcting procedure described in Chapter 2.3. Before it can be applied the cube is resolved from the front side in separate layers. On each layer, the enhanced 2D Hadamard decoding procedure is applied. The Performance of the 3D Hadamard Code was simulated and compared with the Standandard Hadamard Code of the length n=512.The Cubes have the dimension 8*8*8. The results are depicted in Figure 10.

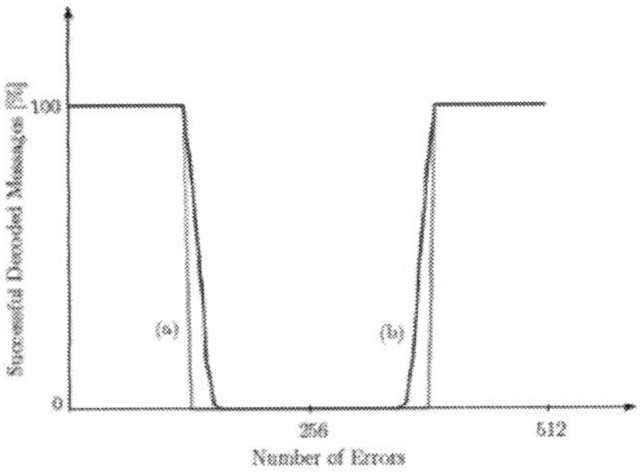

Fig. 10. Comparison of Error Correcting Capabilities of Stanard Hadamard (a) with 3D Enhanced Hadamard Code (b).

3 Application of Enhanced Hadamard Code in Watermarking Technology

Digital Watermarking is a very prospective new technology, that offers a huge number of new applications [6]. Especially the challenge to protect intellectual properties of multimedia data against illegal usage or tempering can be solved by watermarking technologies [7]. One of the important components is an error correcting code. Especially when watermarked video sequences undergo a very hard compression the error correcting code used in the watermarking scheme plays a decisive role in surviving of watermarks[8]. For this reasons, we choose these techniques to demonstrate the efficiency of Enhanced Hadamard Error Correcting Code (EHC). To underline the performance of EHC, it was compared with the well known Reed-Solomon Code [9,10] used in the same watermarking scheme.

3.1 Proposed Watermarking Scheme

The proposed watermarking scheme works in the spectral domain and uses an Interframe Discrete Wavelet Transform (DWT) [11] of video sequences and an Intraframe Discrete Cosine Transform (DCT) for embedding procedure [12,13]. In the Fig. 11, the whole encoding process is illustrated. The raw format of the luminance channel of the original video stream is decomposed by multi-level Interframe DWT with Haar Wavelet. This low pass filtered part of the video stream undergoes a block-wise DCT Transform. From DCT spectrum, special coefficients are selected and used for embedding procedure with 2D Hadamard coded watermarks. The embedding procedure itself is realized through QIM (Quadrature Index Modulation) techniques [14].

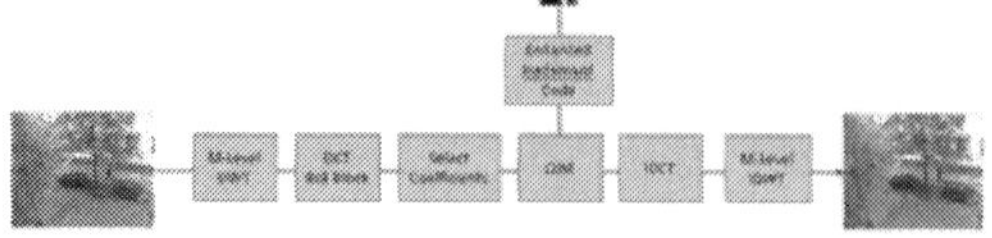

Fig. 11. Watermarking Encoding Process

The decoder procedure is depicted in Fig.12. At the beginning of the decoding procedure, the embedded video sequence undergoes the same multi-level Interframe DWT and Intraframe DCT transforms as on the encoder side.

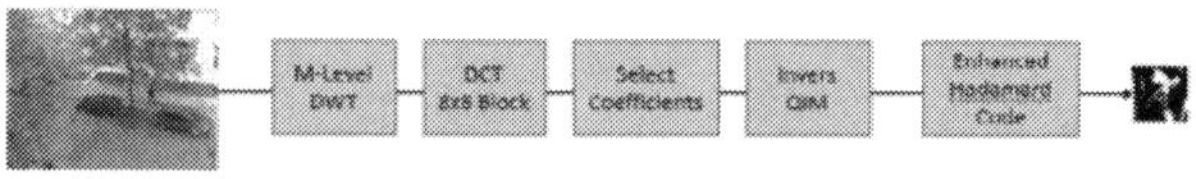

Fig. 12. Watermarking Decoding Process

After the selection of the proper DCT coefficients, the inverse QIM (IQIM) is applied. It delivers the decoded code words (pulse stream). Through the help of Enhanced Hadamard Error Correcting Code, the original watermark is extracted.

3.1.1 Multi-Level DWT

As mentioned above a multi-Level Interframe DWT with Haar Wavelet was used to deliver a low pass filtered video. The Fig.13 illustrates the operating principle of this transform. In the first level, the two consecutive frames are averaged. In the second level, the frames from level one are averaged and so forth. In this watermarking schemes, we used DWT levels from 12 till 16.

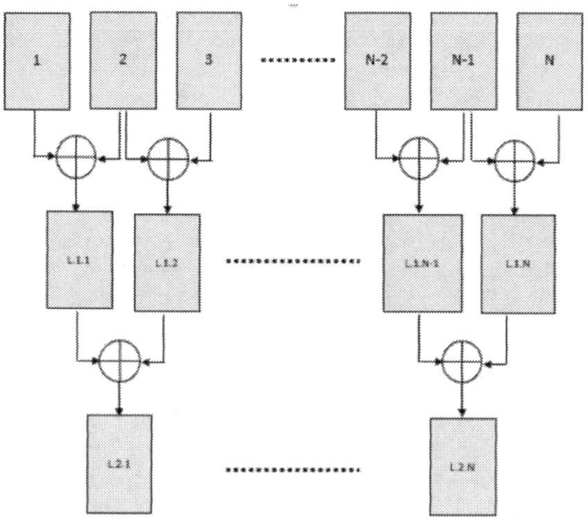

Fig. 13. Multi-Level Interframe DWT. At the first level, the two consecutive frames are averaged. At level two the consecutive frames from level one are averaged and so forth.

3.1.2 Selection of Embedded Coefficients

To realize the embedding procedure, some coefficients from the DCT spectrum of DWT filtered video sequence must be selected. The Fig.14 shows which coefficients are qualified for watermarking. These are mostly from the yellow area.

1	9	17	25	33	41	49	57
2	10	18	26	34	42	50	58
3	11	19	27	35	43	51	59
4	12	20	28	36	44	52	60
5	13	21	29	37	45	53	61
6	14	22	30	38	46	54	62
7	15	23	31	39	47	55	63
8	16	24	32	40	48	56	64

Fig. 14. Coefficients of DCT Spectrum which fits for embedding

3.2 Investigation with 3D Enhanced Hadamard Error Correcting Code

The investigation was done with HDTV video sequence with the resolution of 1080x1920 and 25fps. The video was captured with an AVCHD Camera. The watermarking processing was performed only for the luminance channel (after converting RGB into YCrCb color space) because it is more robust against distortions than any other channels. It was investigated how many embedded watermark bits survive compression attacks without causing significant impairments. The degradation of the watermarked output video was measured with SSIM (Structural Similarity) index. SSIM is based on the human eye perception and so the expressiveness about distortion is better than in the traditional methods like PSNR (Peak Signal to Noise Ratio) or MSE (Mean Square Error) [15].

It was chosen the Enhanced 3D Hadamard Code of the size of 8x8x8, which means the code word length of 512 bits. This implies the message code length of 8 bit (*$log_2(n)$* messages). The DCT block size was 8x8 and from each block were selected 16 coefficients. With these, information is easy to calculate the total number of embedded watermark bits for each frame.

$$E = \frac{H \cdot W}{B^2} \cdot \frac{M}{W} \cdot C = \frac{1920 \cdot 1080}{8^2} \cdot \frac{9}{512} \cdot 16 = 9112\,\text{Bit/Frame}$$

Where H is, the height and W is the width of the frame. The letter B denotes the block size of DCT transform; the letter M is the message code length; the letter W represents the code word length of the 3D Hadamard Code and the letter C is the number of selected spectral coefficients.

In Table 3, the results of capacity and robustness measurements are presented. The compression attacks were done by H.264 codec with different compression ratios. Because the method works in the raw video, the original data rate is 1.2 Gbit/s. As a watermark was used a chessboard pattern of the size of 30x30 Pixel.

The watermarks were inserted successively into the frames. The Delta QIM gave the width of the quantization steps and was tuned to value 11. Generally, the Delta value determines the noise distortion in the host video.

The embedded video sequence was compressed with different compression ratios. In the case of compression to 5 Mbit/s, which correspond to a compression ratio of 1:240 it is still possible to extract all watermarks error free. The quality comparison between originally compressed video and embedded and compressed shows, that there is only slightly difference. The SSIM index Video is in this case 98%.

Data Rate	Compression Ratio	DWT Levels	Delta QIM	Selected Coefficients	Embedded Bits	Extracted Watermark	SSIM Watermarking	SSIM Video
6 Mbit/s	1:200	16	11	9	9112		1	0,95
5 Mbit/s	1:240	16	11	9	9112		1	0,95
4 Mbit/s	1:300	16	11	9	9112		0,92	0,93
3 Mbit/s	1:400	16	11	9	9112		0,89	0,91
2 Mbit/s	1:600	16	11	9	9112		0,56	0,90

Table 3. Results for 3D Enhanced Hadamard Code

3.3 Comparison of 3D Enhanced Hadamard with Reed-Solomon Code

In order to show the performance of Enhanced Hadamard Code, a comparison between EHC and well known Reed-Solomon Code was carried out. Reed-Solomon Code is well known as an error correcting code and it has a plenty of practical implementations for example in consumer electronics like CD, DVD, Blu-Rays, QR-Code or in data transmission.

To make the Reed-Solomon Code comparable to Enhanced Hadamard Code we have to select two parameters: the length of the symbol and the redundancy. The symbol length (block length) is equal to the message of 9 bit. The 3D Enhanced Hadamard Code has a codebook, where to every message of 9 bit a cube is assigned with codeword length of 512 bits. The Reed-Solomon Code has a codebook, where for each message of 9 bit a string of 4599 bits (512 Symbols, each symbol is 9 bit long) is assigned. The redundancy of Reed-Solomon Code was selected in such a way, that the number of correctable symbols should approximately correspond to the number of correctable bits of Hadamard Code, which is n/2. So we get an RS Code of [511, 255] with a codeword length of n=511 symbols and the message of k=255 symbols, where a symbol is 9 bit long.

The comparison of the performance of both codes is documented in Table 4. At the data rate of 5Mbit/s, which correspond to the compression ratio of 1:240, the EHC Code can still recover the whole watermark without errors. In contrary the RS Code shows a recovered watermark with 17% errors.

 DOI: 10.1051/matecconf/201712505007

At the data rate of 3Mbit/s, the performance advantage of EHC is even more visible. EHC Watermark has an error of 1,7%. In contrary the RS Watermark is barely visible and has an error of 27,6%.

Data Rate	EHC	Err. %	Reed-Salomon	Error %
5 Mbit/s		0	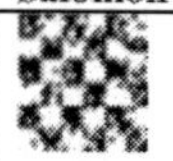	17,5
4 Mbit/s		1,7		27,6
3 Mbit/s		6,8		35,3
2 Mbit/s		41,2		40,8

Table 4. Comparison of Enhanced Hadamard with Reed-Salomon Code

In all these considerations we should take into account, that concerning the capacity EHC code is superior against RS code because the EHC codeword length is much shorter (512 bits) than an RS codeword (4599 bits).

4 Conclusion

In this paper a new type of multidimensional Hadamard Error Correcting Code, we called it Enhanced Hadamard Error Correcting Code (EHC) was introduced. It has remarkable property, it can overcome the limit of n/2-1 correctable bit errors of a standard Hadamard Code, where the codeword length and the Hamming distance d have the same value n. The application of this Code in Video Watermarking gives also a strong prove of its effectiveness.

Compared to Reed-Solomon Code the Enhanced Hadamard Code is much more effective. The watermarks of a video, protected by EHC, can survive a very strong compression attack, in opposite to RS-Code.

EHC protected watermarks can be easily recovered error-free from a video with a compression ratio of 1:240, which corresponds to a data rate of 5 Mbit/s.

If the same embedding process is using RS Code instead of EHC the error free recovery of the watermarks is not possible. It has an error of about 17,5% and the content of a watermark can barely be recognized.

All these results are very promising, and they show that the new Enhanced Hadamard Code is very powerful and can be successfully used in video watermarking.

Performed research was supported by National Science Centre, Poland, Amis project number 2015/16/Z/ST7/00559.

References

[1] PLOTKIN, M.: *Binary Code with specified minimum distance, IRE Transactions, IT-6:445-450, 1960*

[2] BOSE, R.C., SHRIKHANDE, S.S.: *A note on the result in the theory of code construction. Inf. And Control 2, 183-194 (1965)*

[3] PETERSON, W.W.: Error correcting codes. The M.I.T. Press, Massachusetts Institute of Technology & J.Wiley & Sons, New York 1961

[4] LEVENSHTEIN, V.I.: Application of Hadamard matrices to a problem in coding. *Problems of Cybernatics, 5*, 166-184, 1964

[5] Combinatoric in Space, The Mariner 9 Telemetry System, http://www.math.cuden.edu/~wcherowi/courses/m6409/mariner9talk.pdf

[6] SWANSON, M.D., K. M. T. A.: Multimedia Data-Embedding and Watermarking Technologies. In: *Proceeding of IEEE* 86 (1998), S. 1064-1087

[7] LIN, S. D., S. C.-F.: A Robust DCT-Based Watermarking for Copyright Protection. In: *IEEE Transactions on Consumer Electronics* 46 (2000), S. 415

[8] SWANSON, M.D., K. M. T. A.: Multimedia Data-Embedding and Watermarking Technologies. In: *Proceeding of IEEE* 86 (1998), S. 1064-1087

[9] SHU LIN, DANIEL J.COSTELLO, JR.: Error Control Coding, *Prentice-Hall, Inc. Englewood Cliffs, New Jersey 07632* (1983)

[10] MACWILLIAMS, F.J., Sloane, N.J.A.: The theory of error-correcting codes. *North Holland, New York, 1977*

[11] PIK-WAH CHAN, M. R. L.: A DWT-Based Digital Video Watermarking Scheme with Error Correcting Code. In: *Information and Communications SecurityLecture Notes in Computer Science* 2836 (2003), S. 202-213

[12] ZHAO, D., C. G. L. W.: A Chaos-Based Robust Wavelet-Domain Watermarking Algorithm. In: *Chaos, Solutions and Fractals* 22 (2004), S. 792

[13] I.J.COX, J. KILLIAN, F. L. & VOL.6 PP., T. S.: Secure Spread Spectrum Watermarking for Multimedia. In: *IEEE Transactions on Image Processing* 6 (1997), S. 1673-1687

[14] CHEN, B., W. G., WORNELL: Quantization Index Modulation for Digital Watermarking and Information Embedding of Multimedia. In: *Journal of VLSI Signal Processing* 27 (2001), S. 7-33

[15] HARTUNG, F. & KUTTER, M.: Multimedia Watermarking Techniques. In: *Proceeding of IEEE* 87 (1999), S. 1079-1107

[16] HO ANTONY T.S., SHEN JUN, SOON HIE TAN, KOT ALEX C..: Digital image-in-image watermarking for copyright protection of satellite images using the fast Hadamard transform. In: *Geoscience and Remote Sensing Symposium* 6 (2002), S. 3311 – 3313

Statistical and Learning Aided Classifier for ECG Based Predictive Diagnostic Tool

Sumi Bharali[1], *Manash Pratim Sarma*[1], *Kandarpa Kumar Sarma*[2] *and Nikos Mastorakis*[3]

1 Department of Electronics and Communication Engineering, Guwahati, Assam, India
2 Departments of Electronics and Communication Technology, Gauhati University, Guwahati-781014, Assam, India. email- kandarpaks@gmail.com
3 Technical University - Sofia, Sofia 1000, "Kl. Ohridski" 8, Bulgaria. email- mastor@tu-sofia.bg

Abstract. Early diagnosis and classification of long term cardiac signals are crucial issues in the treatment of heart related disorders. The available number of medical professional are not sufficient to deal with the increase patients for which design of certain machine based diagnostics tools have been accepted as a viable option. Typical Electrocardiogram (ECG) machine is helpful for monitoring the heart abnormalities only for short interval of time. Therefore, it becomes necessary to design a system which captures relevant features of the ECG signal for use with certain classifiers. In our proposed system, ECG signal elements like Q, R and S peaks are detected and heart rate estimated using Linear Discriminant Analysis (LDA), Adaptive Linear Discriminant Analysis (ALDA) and Support Vector Machine (SVM). For our work we have been used MIT BIH (Standard Arrhythmia Database).

1 Introduction

Electrocardiograph (ECG) is an instrument used in the detection and diagnosis of heart abnormalities that occur in human's body. Early diagnosis and classification of long term cardiac signals are crucial issues in the treatment of heart related disorders [1]. The available number of medical professional are not sufficient to deal with the increasing number of patients for which design of certain machine based diagnostics tools have been accepted as a viable option. ECG is used for the diagnosis of heart related disorders. Such a machine measures the electrical potentials of a patient by placing electrodes on body surface and in this way system records continuous activity of heart muscle. The study of ECG signal deals with its morphology (such as amplitude, duration, segments). Normal frequency and amplitude range of ECG signal is in between 0.05-100 Hz and 1-10 mv. Fig. 1 shows a normal ECG signal. However, the ECG signal is non-stationary; it is very difficult to analyze such a big volume of data. Therefore, it becomes necessary to design a system which captures relevant features of the ECG signal for use with certain classifiers. In our proposed system, ECG signal elements like Q, R and S peaks are detected and heart rate estimated using Linear Discriminant Analysis (LDA), Adaptive Linear Discriminant Analysis (ALDA) and Support Vector Machine (SVM). For our work we have been used MIT BIH (Standard Arrhythmia Database).

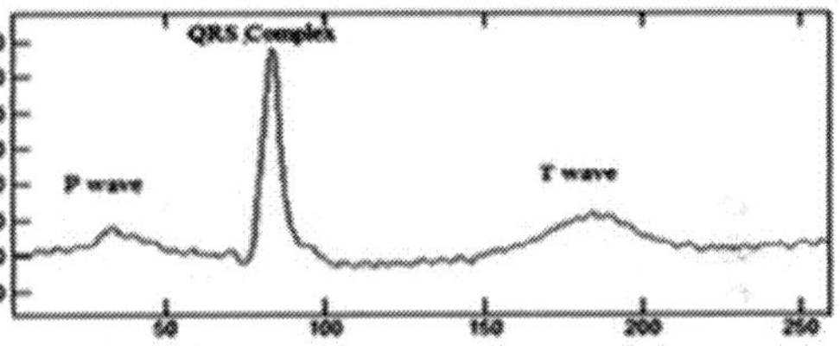

Fig.1 ECG signal.

Section II describes about the detection of QRS complex using Pam-Tompkins Algorithm and gives formulation of proposed classifiers LDA, ALDA and SVM. Section III gives description of simulation result and comparison of classifier schemes. Section IV gives the conclusion. Some of the relevant literature are [1]-[10]

2 Proposed Method

Several algorithms have already been proposed yet there are challenges which are the primary motivation behind this work for automatic detection of QRS complex. The QRS complex corresponds to the largest wave, since it represents the depolarization of the right and left ventricles, which are the chambers with the most substantial mass in the heart. Variabilty of heart rate is calculated from the parameter R-R interval which is the time difference between two succesive R

* Corresponding author: kandarpaks@gmail.com

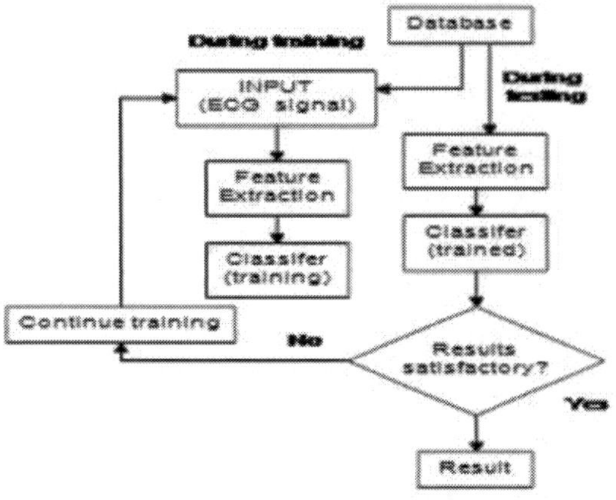

Fig.2 Overall block diagram of the system.

waves. The QRS complex is the fundamental feature of ECG signal. The peaks detected in the signal are considered as feature vector. In this work, QRS complex waveform is detected using Pam-Tompkins algorithm which also is applicable real time enviornment [2]. Heart rate is calculated from the position of consecutive R-R interval. R-R interval is calculated by subtracting consecutive location of R positions.

A. System Block Diagram

The architecture is divided into two parts feature extraction and classification of Q, R, S and HR beats using three methods LDA, ALDA analysis and SVM. It is shown in fig. 2. There are two aspects first during training, the system becomes familiar with the samples and during testing, and the ability of the system is ascertained.

Next we discuss the method of extraction of QRS complex positions and calculation of the heart rate. Here, ECG signal is taken as input and processes performed for feature extraction over each normal ECG signal. As the signals are normal and database is clean, so there is no need to do the preprocessing part of the signals. Fig. 2 show systematic stages for extracting feature from ECG signal. ECG signals have undergone differentiation operation for highlighting the QRS complex and zero crossing of ECG signal. Differentiated signal is next passed through squaring the signal for making all the negative points positive. The squaring function is given by

$$y(nT) = x(nT) \quad (1)$$

The next block of Pam-Tompkins algorithm is moving average integrator. In this block, a window is specified for detection of number of peaks within the duration of single QRS complex. The equation of moving average window is given by

$$y(nT) = \left(\frac{1}{N}\right)[x(nT-(N-1)T) + x(nT-T) + \cdots + x(nT)] \quad (2)$$

where N is the number of samples in window. Window width defines the number of samples present in the QRS complex. The processed signal at this stage thresholded for identification of QRS complex. Threshold value is based on rising edge of QRS complex. Here it is taken in between 20- 25. QRS complex is further searched after 293 sample points from the previous cycle. If the signal is greater than threshold value then the position of QRS complex is chosen as the position of original ECG signal. Now plotting both original and QRS complex in a same plot we have seen that within a window, QRS complex is obtained. The position of Q and S peaks are the first and last position of window and R peak is the middle one. Now we get the location of peaks but the peaks values are not in the expected physiological range. Since each sample of the signals are digitized into 2N levels where N is the resolution of the device for collecting signal into computers the memory segment is a factor. So one way to convert digital data into physical units is to subtract the baseline and then divide by its gain for its channel to obtain physical units. So in these way features are obtained in physical range. Baseline and gain information of the signal is obtained from the MIT-BIH database. Fig. 3 shows the detected QRS complex.

The heart rate is calculated using equations as follows

$$\text{HR}=60\times\, sampling\ frequency/(R-R\ interval) \quad (3)$$

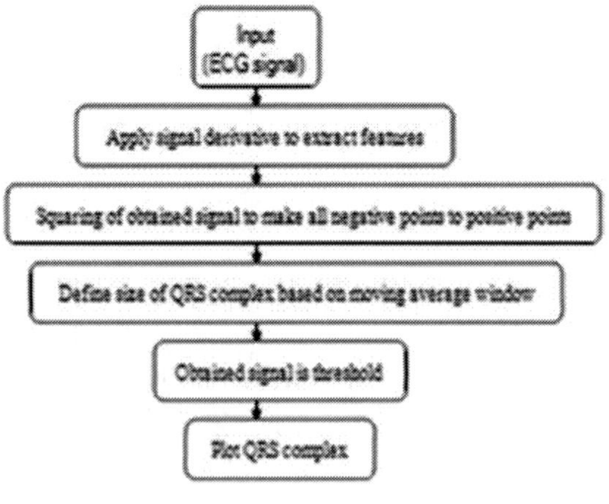

Fig.3 Evaluating QRS Complex

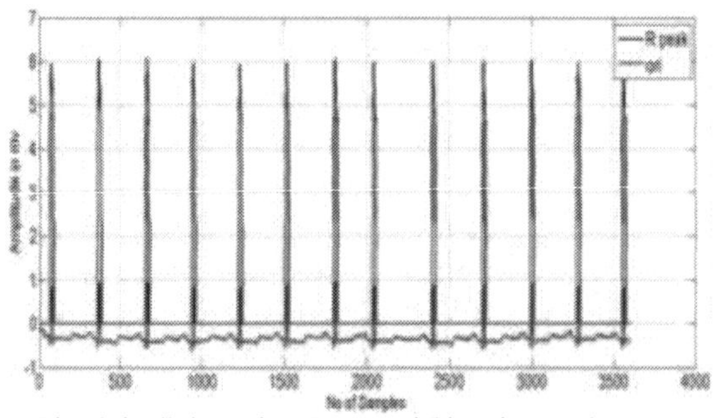

Fig. 4 QRS Complex Detected Signal no 100

DOI: 10.1051/matecconf/201712505008

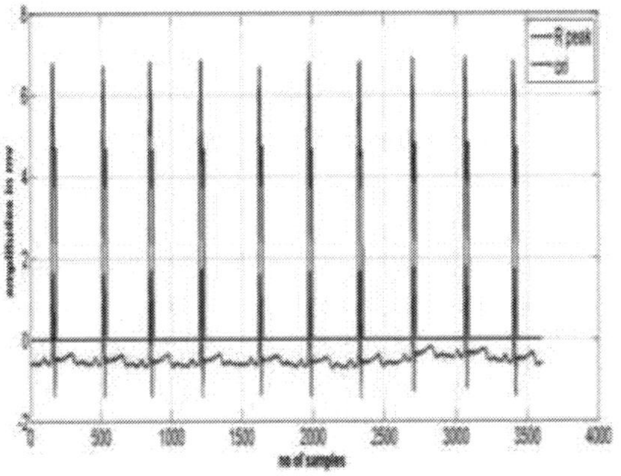

Fig.5 QRS Complex Detected Signal no 115

B. Classifier design

In this work, three classifiers are used i.e. LDA, ALDA and SVM classifier. The description is as below.

i) LDA Classifier-

LDA is a supervised method used in statistics, pattern recognition and machine learning for separating two or multiple classes into their desired classes. LDA is linear transformation technique [3]. Here classification is totally dependent on projection vector. Training data sets are projected in the direction of projection vector to maximize its separability. System model is tested by evaluating the Euclidean distance between train and test dataset. Let's say that we have m- classes and each class has n-dimensional sample points (x_1, x_2, x_3, ... , x_n). So stacking all sample values in one matrix where each row represents one feature values of different samples we get a sample matrix. Each row signifies one class. We are intend to do separation up to four classes hence we have four rows in the matrix. Fig. 6 shows the logic approaches to evaluate projection vector of LDA classifier. The system model of LDA classifier as shown in fig. 7

ii) ALDA classifier

This is a technique for prediction of how much actual and predicted data of a classifier are identical by varying its weights using weight update equation. The purpose of ALDA is to analyze [4] the closeness of the current value to the reference samples and also to minimize the error between true and obtained prediction. Fig. 8 shows logical approaches to update the weight vector. Here X's, Y_{new} are the train data and test data respectively. Initially W is taken as random weight vector.

The system model of ALDA classifier as shown in fig. 9

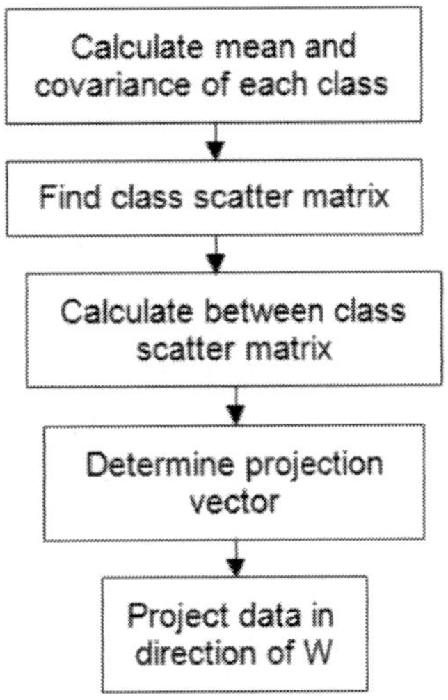

Fig.6 Logical steps to find projection vector of LDA

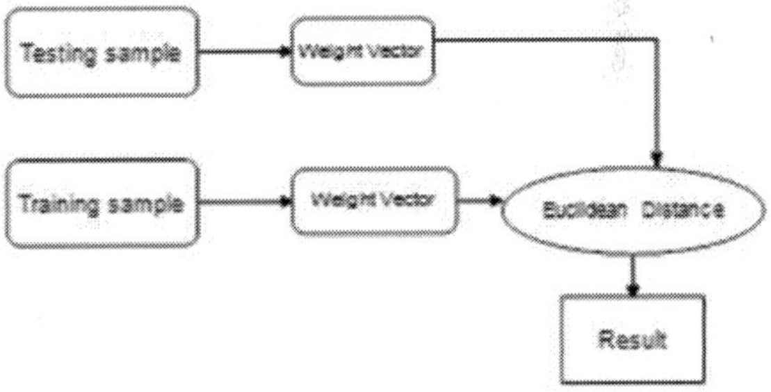

Fig.7 Block diagram of LDA classifier

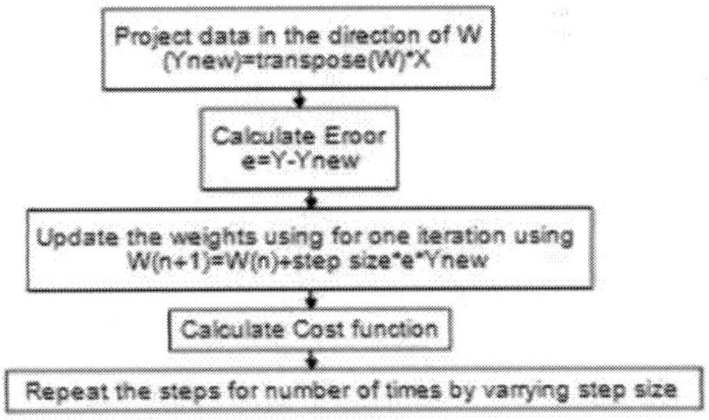

Fig.8 Block diagram for obtaining weight vector

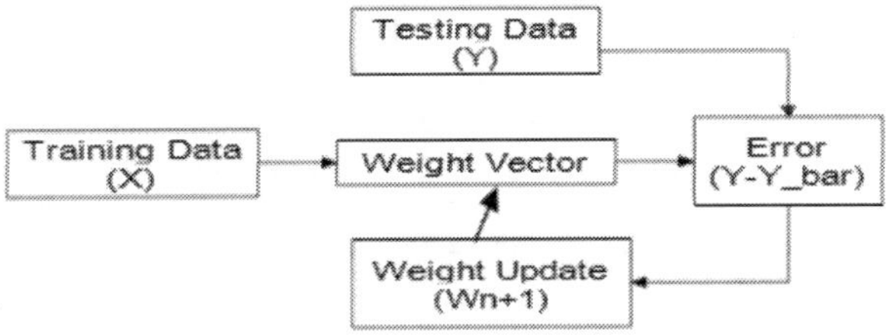

Fig.9 Block diagram of ALDA Classifier

 DOI: 10.1051/matecconf/201712505008

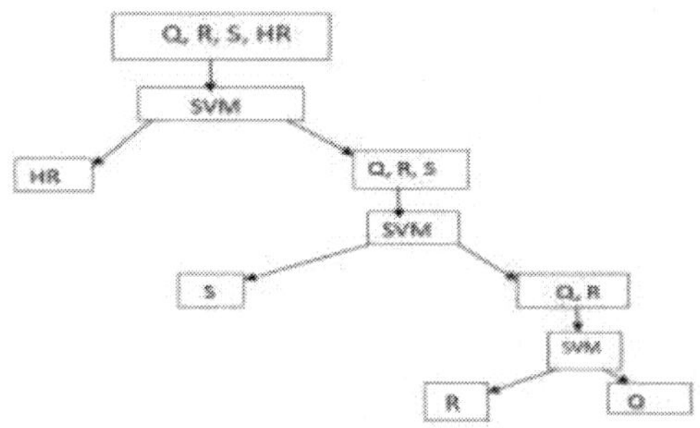

Fig.10 Block Diagram of SVM Classifier

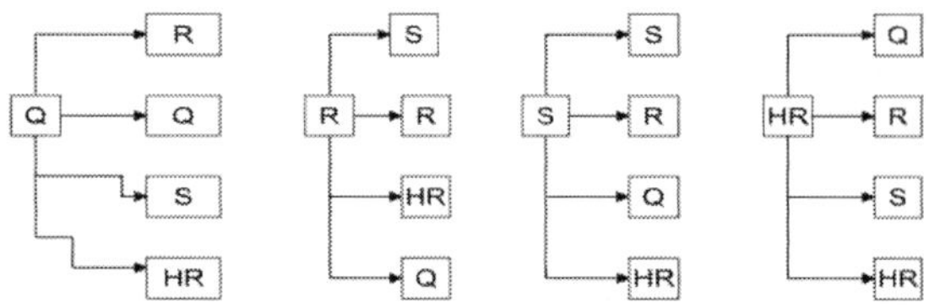

Fig.11 Euclidean distance computed using LDA classifier

iii) SVM classifier

Support Vector Machine is a supervised learning machine [6]. The main objective of SVM is to separate of two or multiple classes based on hyper-plane. With SVM kernel function, we can transform non-linear data into higher dimensional space. SVM focuses on data points which are difficult to classify. Such difficult points are close to decision boundary or hyper planes identified by support vectors. The proposed multiclass SVM uses three SVM to classify Q, R, S and HR beats of normal patient. The system model of SVM classifier as shown in fig. 10

3 Experimental Details and Results

Here we discuss the results derived. Initially database is divided into two sets testing and training data sets one for testing and other for training. Sizes of both the data sets are $(N \times M)$, where N stands for number of features and M stands for feature length. Calculated features are fed in to LDA classifier. Sizes of both data sets are made equal for calculating the Euclidean distance for each sample value of testing and training data sets. Both sets are projected in the direction of projection vector. Initially the projection vector is found to be one. So taking one as weight vector both testing and training data sets are projected in the direction of weight vector and finally computing the Euclidean distance for measuring similarity score among features. Euclidean distance is computed among this combination as shown in fig. 11. Before finding Euclidean distance data should be in normalized form, otherwise small feature values are dominated by higher values and gives fluctuating results.

Confusion matrix takes simply two values one of which is the target values of each feature of test data and the other is the predicted value of each feature generated after calculating Euclidean distance between two vectors. Here diagonal elements represent the true prediction each class given test data. In Table 2 some parameters like sensitivity, specificity, accuracy, misclassification rate and precision are calculated. Overall accuracy of the system is found to be is 88.9 %. For calculating the five parameters the following equations are used:

$$Sensitivity = TP/(TP + FN) \quad (4)$$

$$Speccificity = TN/(TN + FN) \quad (5)$$

$$Accuracy = TP + TN/(TN + FP + TP + FN) \quad (6)$$

$$Misclassification\ Rate = FP + FN/(TN + FP + TP + FN) \quad (7)$$

$$Precision = TP/(TP + FP) \quad (8)$$

where TP is true positive, TN is true negative, FP is false positive and FN is false negative. In Table 1, confusion matrix values are shown derived from LDA classifier during Q, R, S and HR estimator. The next sets of results are derived using ALDA classifier. Initially a random weight vector is taken and projected the first sample point of training data set (X) in the direction of given weight vector. After that an error is calculate between testing data set and projected data set for updating the weight vector. The obtained new weight vector is now ready projecting the next sample point of training data. Similarly, again the error difference between known and predicted sample points for updating the next weight vector. This process will continue for every sample point of training and testing data sets. Now, for repeating these steps for multiple iteration, we take the last weight vector of the respective cycles of entire data set and feed this vector in to the next cycle. In this way, we will get mean square error for every cycle of iteration. The MSE is used as the cost function. The results show variation when step size of weight update is varied. First we take a step size of 0.004. Fig. 12 shows cost function for 10 numbers of iteration by taking step size 0.004. Table 3 show confusion matrix generated for step size 0.004 using ALDA for Q, R, S and HR calculator. Results are also derived for step sizes of 0.001 and 0.0001. Results are shown in fig.s 13 and 14 and confusion matrix values are shown in Tables 4 and 5.

From fig.s 12 to 14 we see that with decreasing step size and increasing the iteration, system is responding well and error difference between known and unknown data sets are becoming less. This process is the basis of ALDA. Table 6 shows some parameters are calculated for step size .004, 0.001 and 0.0001. Table X shows different parameters calculated using SVM.

DOI: 10.1051/matecconf/201712505008

Table 1 : Confusion matrix of LDA with Q, R, S and HR estimate

Actual/ Predicted	Q	R	S	HR
Q	31	0	7	0
R	3	35	0	0
S	7	0	31	0
HR	0	0	0	38

Table 2 : Parameters obtained from the LDA classifer

Parameters	LDA
Sensitivity	0.887
Specificity	0.962
Accuracy	.887
Misclassification Rate	0.2233
Precision	0.8827

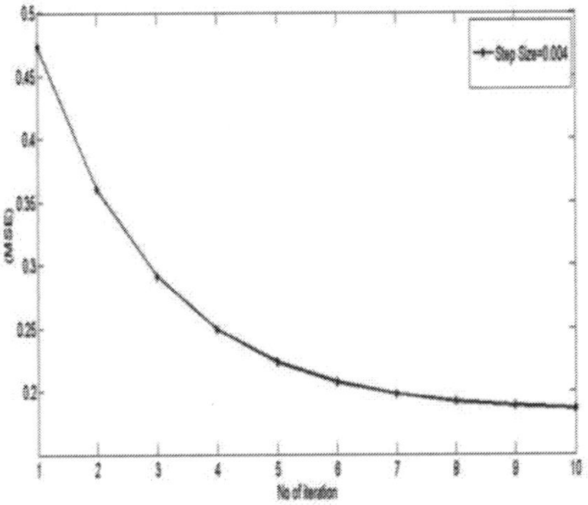

Fig.12 Cost function obtained for step size 0.004 and 10 number of iteration

Table 3. Confusion matrix

Actual/ Predicted	**Q**	**R**	**S**	**HR**
Q	29	0	9	0
R	0	35	0	3
S	7	0	31	0
HR	0	0	0	38

In this paper, feature classification has been done using LDA, ALDA and SVM technique. Overall accuracy of the LDA system is found to be 88.7%. We also define a cost function to quantify the error between actual and predicted data by varying its step size and updating the weight vector for various numbers of times. The best result come when step size is change to 0.0001 and iterates the system for 550 numbers of

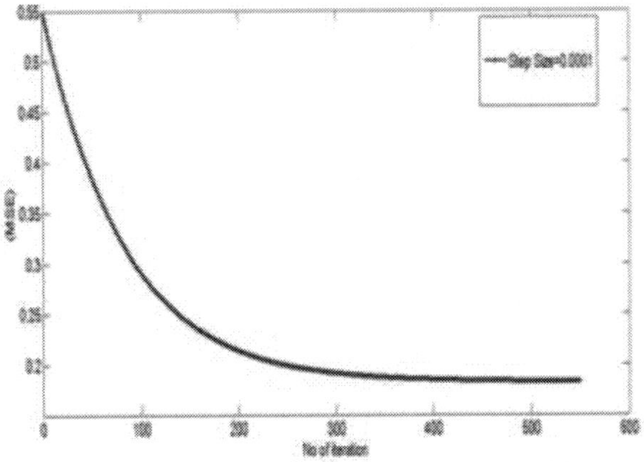

Fig.13 Cost function obtained for step size 0.001 and 20 number of iteration

Table 3- Confusion matrix

Actual/ Predicted	Q	R	S	HR
Q	28	0	10	0
R	0	35	0	3
S	6	0	32	0
HR	0	0	0	38

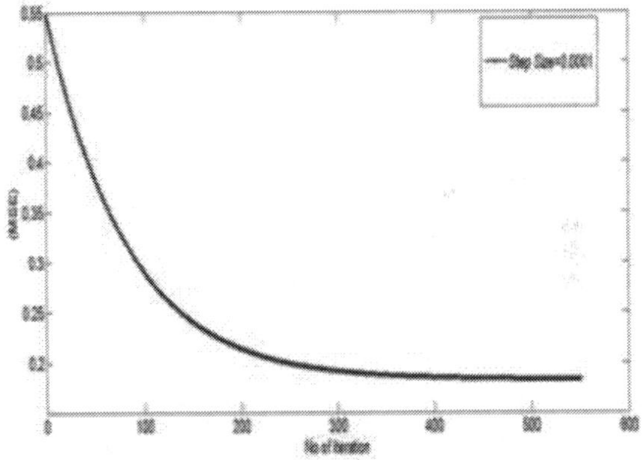

Fig.14 Cost Function obtained for step size 0.0001 and 550 number of iteration

Table 4 : Confusion matrix

Actual/ Predicted	Q	R	S	HR
Q	31	0	7	0
R	0	35	0	3
S	4	0	34	0
HR	0	0	0	38

Table 5 : Parameters calculated for a LDA classifier

Parameters	ALDA Step size=0.004	ALDA Step Size=0.001	ALDA Step size=0.0001
Sensitivity	0.8749	0.8747	0.9082
Specificity	0.958	0.9585	0.9541
Accuracy	0.8749	0.88	.9078
Misclassification Rate	0.23	0.2495	0.1835
Precision	0.876	0.8776	.9101

Table 6 : Confusion matrix from IRST node (HR beat detected)

Actual/ Predicted	No HR (Remaining)	Yes HR
No HR (Remaining)	101	0
Yes HR	0	6

Table 7 : Confusion matrix from second node (S beat detected)

Actual/ Predicted	**NoS (Remaining beat)**	**Yes S**
NoS (Remaining beat)	62	8
Yes S	14	17

Table 8 : Parameters calculated from SVM

Parameters	**SVM**
Sensitivity	0.911
Specificity	0.9535
Accuracy	0.9455
Misclassification Rate	0.059
Precision	0.9015

Finally, another set of results derived using SVM. Initially data is divided into two groups and one grpup labeled as +1 and another as -1. In fig. 10, first node contains all the features to classify the classes into their receptive groups. So after training, labeling and testing the system six sample points are detected as belong to one group i.e. (+1) and 101 sample points were detected as belong to another group (-1). Now 101 test sample points are from test set data for testing remaining classes. At second node system is trained and labeled as +1 (when train data<-0.48) and -1 (when train data>-0.48). At third node again SVM is applied to the remaining trained dataset and misclassified data obtained from the second node. Here system is trained and labeled as +1 if (train data is greater zero) and as -1(when train data is less than zero but greater than -0.48. In Tables 6 and 7, confusion matrices for first node for predicting HR and second node with S beat detected are shown respectively. Table 8 includes some of the parameters derived from the SVM. Table 9 includes a comparion of the performance.

Table 9 : Comparison of classifier performance in terms of accuracy

Classifier		
Linear Discriminant Analysis	***Adaptive Linear Discriminant Analysis***	***Support Vector Machine***
88.7 %	90.8%	94.55%

In this paper, features classification has been done using LDA, ALDA and SVM technique. Overall accuracy of the LDA system is found to be 88.7%. We also define a cost function to quantify the error between actual and predicted data by varying its step size and updating the weight vector for various numbers of times. The best result come when step size is change to 0.0001 and iterates the system for 550 numbers of times and accuracy of the system is increased to 90.8%. Finally a combination of both linear and non-linear classifier SVM is used to classify both linear and non-linear data using linear kernel, polynomial kernel and RBF kernel. SVM yield 94.55% when kernel parameters of RBF are set to 0.9 for sigma and 0.2 for penalty parameter C. Hence comparing three methods we find that the SVM provides better accuracy compared to LDA and ALDA classifier.

4 Conclusion

Here, Pam-Tompkins algorithm is used for features extraction of ECG Signal. With this algorithm Q, R and S peak is searched for every cycle of ECG signal and the heart rate of patients. The calculated features vectors are fed to the LDA, ALDA and SVM classifier. The outcome of this work is that results derived from LDA and ALDA are compared with that obtained from SVM while estimating QRS and HR of patients taking ECG signals. The proposed approach shall be helpful in designing a diagnostic support tool.

References

[1] E. J. S. Luz, W. R. Schwartz, G. C. Chavez and D. Menotti, "ECG-based Heartbeat Classification for Arrhythmia Detection: A Survey", in proceeding of Computer Methods and Programs in Biomedicine, Vol.127, pp 2-22, April 2016.

[2] A. Kaushik and P. Sabherwal, "Monitoring Electrocardiogram using Android based Smart phone", in

preceding of Annual IEEE India Conference (INDICON), pp 1-6, 2015.

[3] S. Balakrishnama, A.Ganapathiraju, "Linear discriminant analysis-a brief tutorial", in Institute for Signal and information Processing , vol. 18, pp. 1-8, 1998.

[4] M. H. Hayes, "Statistical Digital Signal Processing and Modelling", 1st edition, Wiley, 1996.

[5] U. Desai, R. J. Martis, C. G. Nayak and G. Seshikala, "Machine Intelligent Diagnosis of ECG for Arrhythmia Classification Using DWT, ICA and SVM Techniques", in proceeding of IEEE INDICON, pp 1-4, 2015.

[6] A. S. Thakare, R. Ghongade and Prof. A. S. Barhatte, "QRS Complex Detection and Arrhythmia Classification using SVM", in preceding of International Conference on Communication, Control and Intelligent Systems (CCIS), pp 239-243, 2015.

[7] E. M. Imah, F. A. Afif and M. Ivan.Fanany, "A Comparative Study on Daubechies Wavelet Transformation, Kernel PCA and PCA as Feature Extractors for Arrhythmia Detection Using SVM", in proceeding of IEEE Region 10 Conference, pp 5-9, 2011.

[8] P. Sarma, S. R. Nirmala and K. K Sarma, " ECG Classification using Wavelet Subband", in preceding of International Conference on Signal Processing and Integrated Networks (SPIN), pp 785-790, 2014.

[9] P. Sarma, S. R.Nirmala and K. K.Sarma, " Classification of ECG using Some Novel Features", in Proceeding of IEEE ICETACS, 2013.

[10] K. Lochan , P. Sah and K. K. Sarma, "Innovative feature set for retinopathic analysis of diabetes and its detection", IEEE NCETACS, 2012.

Divergence coding for convolutional codes

Zolotarev Valery[1], *Ovechkin* Gennady[2], *Satybaldina* Dina[3], *Tashatov* Nurlan[3] and *Egamberdiyev* Eldor[3]

[1]Space Research Institute RAS, Moscow, Russian Federation
[2]Faculty of Computer Engineering, Ryazan State Radio Engineering University, Ryazan, Russian Federation
[3]Department of Computer Engineering, L.N. Gumilyov Eurasian National University, Astana, Kazakhstan Republic

Abstract. In the paper we propose a new coding/decoding on the divergence principle. A new divergent multithreshold decoder (MTD) for convolutional self-orthogonal codes contains two threshold elements. The second threshold element decodes the code with the code distance one greater than for the first threshold element. Error-correcting possibility of the new MTD modification have been higher than traditional MTD. Simulation results show that the performance of the divergent schemes allow to approach area of its effective work to channel capacity approximately on 0,5 dB. Note that we include the enough effective Viterbi decoder instead of the first threshold element, the divergence principle can reach more. *Index Terms* — error-correcting coding, convolutional code, decoder, multithreshold decoder, Viterbi algorithm.

1 Introduction

Error correcting coding has become an integral part of the modern information communication and storage systems. This was made possible thanks to significant breakthroughs achieved coding theory in recent years. Presented in [1, 2] the main achievements of optimization coding theory shows that nowadays a multithreshold decoding (MTD), built on new axioms of this theory, provides a very high efficiency level at the moderate complexity. For the Gaussian channel MTD algorithms provides the error probability per bit P_b (e) $<10^{-5}$ at the bit energy level E_b/N_0 ~ 1,3 dB. To organize such an effective work of decoders for Low-Density Parity Check (LDPC) codes, which recently remained the unique competitors for MTD algorithms in the Gaussian channels with this noise level is already very difficult, and for the high-throughput channels is even impossible. It is much harder for these algorithms to decode a convolutional code. On the other hand, the possibility of implementation of MTD decoders on the basis of technical solutions [3] fully removes from them the rate problem, because it allows to keep high decoding characteristics for any channel throughput rate including 1 Gbit/s and more [4, 5]. And the resources to enhance the performance for MTD algorithms are not fully exhausted, allowing in the future expect from them further improvement of working efficiency at high noise levels. It is possible to remind that the MTD efficiency used in non-binary channels with symbol codes or in channels with erasures (in all cases at a very low complexity) was initially at the creation of these algorithms so great that for such applications there are no any competing methods for MTD decoders at the moment and probably in the future as well.

We had analyzed the performance of the currently known demonstration programs of all popular decoding methods (the Viterbi algorithm (AV), LDPC and Reed-Solomon decoders, MTD, and some others). All programs are available on our websites [6, 7]. In most cases we see that all modifications on MTD algorithms provide in a few orders higher reliability decoding fidelity than other methods, and at the same time also show in a few decimal orders greater decoding rate than their former potential competitors. The main reason of such a serious advantage of MTD decoders is always that at very high levels noise they provide the same decoding, as the optimal methods, but our decoders have a linear complexity. And the last fact allows to MTD algorithms use very long codes, which determines their advantage on AV [1, 2].

And finally, most importantly, that for many combinations of codes and channel the efficiency of different MTD modifications at a low level of E_b/N_0 is so great that there are no any other methods that could be efficient in these conditions. Thus, breaking the level of efficiency of real LDPC codes decoder, MTD algorithms actually declared their superiority in efficiency and complexity of implementation in general for all major applications in the digital data transmission, storage and recovery systems.

At increase in code distance of the used convolutional self-orthogonal codes in a limit it is possible to receive the big efficiency, but thus the area in which MTD starts optimum them to decode is shifted aside smaller noise. The given property essentially complicates reduction of decoding BER at the big noise in the channel [8, 9]. It's known that for providing the same high reliability, the calculations space will be increase with decreasing channel energy. But the use of majority logic only, obviously, will not let to closer significantly to the channel capacity.

It is possible to apply some approaches to the decision of the considered problem, based on MTD using in structure of various concatenated coding schemes. Analytical calculations and simulation results show, that application of the concatenated schemes allows reduce the probability of error decoding for 1.. 4 decimal orders without a significant complication of the decoding scheme [10, 11, 12]. Also it is possible to use MTD in schemes with the parallel coding [13] which allow to approach area of its effective work to channel capacity approximately on 0,5 dB. Unfortunately the use of cascade schemes leads to the transmission necessity of the additional check bits, thereby reducing the final code rate of the concatenated codes [1, 2].

In [14] we offers a method to improve convolutional self-orthogonal codes (CSOC) decoding efficiency due to decoding of received data by several MTDs having different settings with consequent forming of decoding result on the basis of majority votes. Such decoder was called multilevel MTD. New modifications of the decoder provided coding gain improving by a few tenths of dB due to better using of the bits soft information are offered [15].

In the paper we propose the new directions of the multithreshold algorithm development that can allow bringing the permissible levels of the code rates closely to the channel capacity.

2 Proposed methods

This section presents the traditional structure of the encoder and decoder, as well as the proposed new coding and decoding schemes based on the divergence principle. The description of the traditional decoder is given for comparison with the new schemes and corresponds to the description in [12].

MTD decoder for convolutional self-orthogonal codes (CSOC) is development of the elementary threshold decoder of Massey [16]. For implementation of operation of encoding CSOC it is possible to use the elementary diagrams constructed on the basis of shift registers. The example of the encoder scheme for CSOC, set by an ancestor polynomial $g(x) = 1+x+x^4+x^6$, is shown in a Figure 1. This code is characterized by parameters of code length, length of information sequence, code rate and the minimum code distance of n=26, k=13, R=1/2, d=5, respectively.

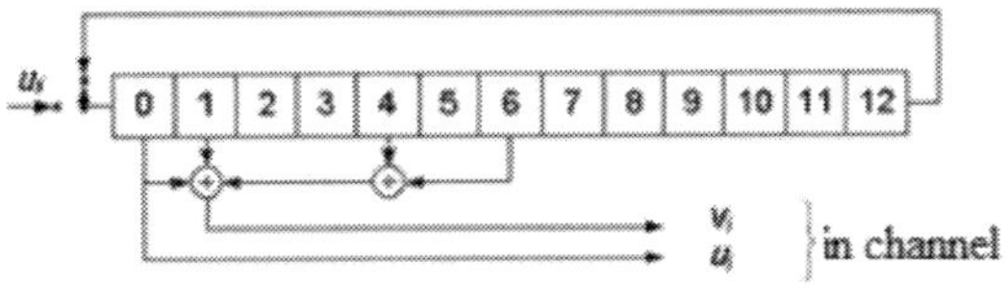

Fig. 1. Encoder for the CSOC with R = 1/2, k=13, d = 5 and n = 26 [1].

Consider the a operation principle of the convolutional coding scheme shown in Figure 1. Actually it consists of the shift register, where in the left side there are grouped cells, from the outputs of which there come the value of its contents to the inputs of the half-adder (mod 2 is an adder), from its output a check symbol v_i are sent to the channel. To simplify the description, we will assume a code to be systematic. Therefore, together with the a check symbol in the channel on each cycle of the code work the one informational symbol u_i from zero shift register cell is going away.

Check symbol generates in the encoder during operation in accordance with the following algorithm:

- Before starting to encode code block key K is in state 1.
- Information vector u = (u_0, u_1, ..., u_{k-1}) applied one character input shift register. As a result, information symbol u_0 is located in cell k-1, u_1 - the cell k-2, etc. There k - a length of information sequence, k=13 for encoder shown in Figure 1.
- Key K is transferred to state 2.
- For j from 0 to k-1 to perform cyclic shift register, and then calculates the j-th checking bit v_j:

$$v_j = \sum_{k=1}^{4} u_{(j-g_k) \bmod k} \quad (1)$$

As a result of the algorithm generated a checking vector $v = (v_0, v_1, ..., v_{k-1})$, which, together with an information vector defines the code word $c = (u, v)$, which is transmitted through the channel.

Let's describe the principle multithreshold decoding of CSOC. In a situation, where the decoder after transmission of a binary symmetric channel (BSC) rather than a distorted codeword noises message $y = (u', v')$ of length n. First calculated syndrome s = Hy (here H - check matrix code) of the received message, and for each information symbol u_j, $1 \le j \le k$, stands set $\{s_p\}$ syndrome elements with numbers $\{p\}$, called checks relative to the character u_j and containing error e_j in this symbol.

First, as in the usual threshold decoder is calculated syndrome $s = Hy$ (here H - check matrix CSOC) of the received message, and each information symbol u_j, $1 \le j \le k$, find the set of elements $\{s_p\}$ syndrome with numbers

DOI: 10.1051/matecconf/201712505009

{*p*} called checks against symbol u_j and containing, as an error term e_j in this symbol.

In addition to the threshold decoder in MTD injected binary vector *d* of length *k*, called the difference, initially filled with zeros. The basic step is to decode that for arbitrarily chosen symbol u_j computed likelihood function L_j, independent of its related inspections and *j*-th element of vector *d*:

$$L_j = \sum_{p \in \Theta_j} S_p + d_j \qquad (2)$$

where d_j - a symbol of the difference vector, related to decoded symbol u_j (0 or 1); S_p - *p*-th element of the syndrome vector, which is part of a number of checks regarding decoded symbol u_j; Θ_j - a set of of numbers of checks, controlling the *j*-th information symbol. The example of MTD decoder for encoder from Figure 1 is given in Figure 2.

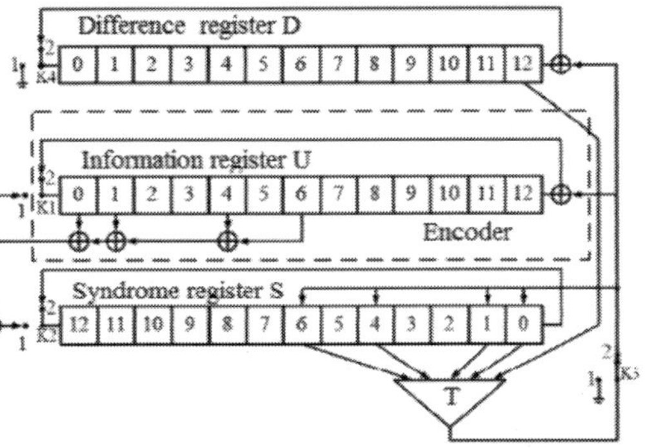

Fig. 2. MTD decoder for the CSOC [1].

Let's consider the new modification schemes for the coding and decoding procces. Figure 3 shows a new proposed divergent encoder for the CSOC with $R = 1/2$. The important point to describe the work of this encoder is the presence at far right side of the encoding register another cell, its content is also comes to the input of the half-adder, where data goes into the channel from. Of course, the code can be non-systematic, and there could be a lot of cells in the right side of the register, where the data go to multi-entranced half-adder from.

Figure 4 shows a new proposed decoder corresponding to the divergent encoder on Figure 3. It is built on the ideas of the MTD (see Figure 2) but new decoder contains two threshold elements (T) located in the left and right sides of the decoder. Left T1 and the relevant parts of the information register and syndrome, which it interacts, are square marked and called as decoder1.

Full decoder with second threshold element T2 in the right side of the registers is similar to the decoder1. Additional code checks are transferred to an input of the T2. These checks occur in the decoder much later than the symbols from the compact checks group related to the T1.

At decoding of the symbol stream received from the channel, the T1 makes decisions about information errors on the basis of their own group only checks. If the codes are chosen correctly, the density of such mistakes will be less than before the T1, and reaching the T2, these errors according to the MTD operation principles will be corrected. The number of checks are transferred to an input of the T2 is one larger than for the first threshold element. And the second threshold decodes the code with the code distance one greater than for the T1. Therefore, the correction possibility of the T2 will be higher, which will strengthen the correction process. It is important that this has been achieved without the involvement of the concatenated methods that decrease the redundancy of the first code (and the first threshold element), which significantly reduces the correcting possibilities of the first decoder.

It is obvious that the proposed divergent code can be an initial part of the code with a larger length and same structure. Then at two such the conditional "concatenated" encoding / decoding schemes the minimum distance *d* will be increased on 2, etc. Indeed, such schemes work successfully, they corresponds to the MTD operation principles and the Fundamental Theorem of the multithreshold decoding [1] and shows the satisfactory results.

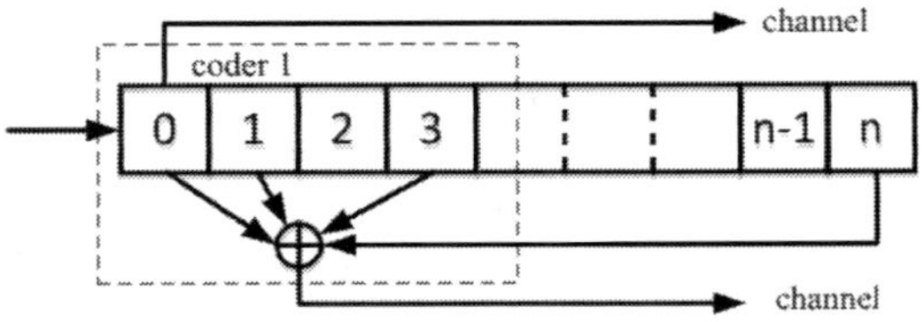

Fig. 3. Encoder for the divergent code

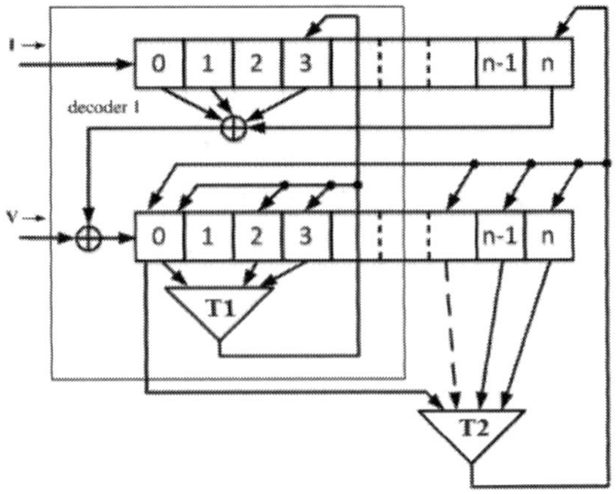

Fig. 4. Decoder for the divergent code

But actually the received decoding scheme has become much more complicated, because the effect of growth of code distance, a valuable resource, can't be easy achieved. The decoder 1 transfers no corrected errors to the right, to second threshold element T2 (see Fig. 4). Then the errors from the last cell (with number *n* in Figure 4) after the two half-adder are entered into the syndrome register.

So, the first T1 work at a bit increased noise level, which degrades its characteristics. But if T1 can to work with this increased errors and its performance degrades a little bit, and the second T2 helps to the first, then we could expect that together they can to correct the complex error flow. That fact allows continuing the analysis of divergent code scheme to determine its capabilities at high noise level.

3 Experimental studies

Consider the performance of the divergent schemes (with the growing, "divergent" values of code distance *d*). Dependences of bit error rate (BER) for Viterbi decoder (AV) and MTD for SOC with a code distance d and d + 1 shown in Figure 5. The dependence curves are typical bends in the points where the decoding error probability reaches optimum minimum values (in case when noise level decreases to the right side) for the used codes. To the left of the bend points algorithms can't work due to high channel noise.

Figure 5 shows the ability of the divergent coding scheme, when MTD for the code with the distance $d + 1$ provides decoding at level noise ~ 1.7 dB, although the traditional MTD works normally only at the noise level of the order 1.8 dB. Let's consider the MTD for the code with the minimum distance d. Its characteristics are close to the optimum up to E_b/N_0 = 1.6 dB. Let's fix the noise level of 1.7 dB for the decoder. This is the point 1 in the Figure 3.

Now we can to include in the encoder and decoder the additional faraway checks, its influence we discussed in Figure 3 and Figure 4. If additional noise from this checks is a small value and it can be expressed as an increase of channel noise in about 0.1 dB, when the D1 (for the code with the distance *d*) still copes, then the characteristics of the decoder will be displaced from the point 1 to the point 2, and its will remain optimal. But then in the second decoder with T2 really enter the error flow from the D1 with a lower density than the error probability in the channel. And this creates the conditions under which the T2 really also reduces further the error density from the first threshold element (point 3 in Figure 5).

Note that it will happen at the noise level that is approximately in 0.1 dB greater than that when T2 could work without supporting of T1. Thus, it is a really possible to advance towards higher channel noise by applying this principle for a few times.

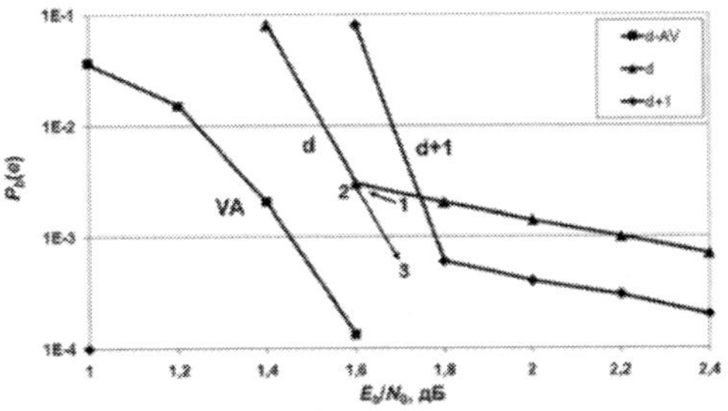

Fig. 5. Performance of the proposed coding scheme at the diferent parameters of the divergent code

Turning now to the curve for AV, shown in Figure 5, we can see that it has no such bend as the curves for MTD. In addition, for long codes which are still implemented in terms of the AV decoder's complexity, the curves usually lie to the left of the curves for MTD, as it is shown in Figure 4. It means that if we include the enough effective AV decoder instead of the D1, the divergence principle can reach more effect. Simulation results show that such schemes are functionally realizable.

4 Conclusion

In present paper some new important properties of multithreshold decoding (MTD) algorithm for convolutional code are discussed. The proposed MTD decoders allows bringing the permissible levels of the code rates closely to the channel capacity.

Various comparing the many decoding algorithms effectiveness show that only Viterbi algorithm, MTD and QMTD (a multithreshold decoding for non binary codes) are in the group of methods that change the distance of its decisions prior to the accepted information. We combine them into the class of the codes with direct check metrics and they have already been successfully applied together, in the divergence coding schemes as well. Works in this direction are expanding.

The present work has been executed under financial support of the Russian Foundation For Basic Research (grant 14-07-00859).

References

[1] V.V. Zolotarev, Y.B. Zubarev, G.V. Ovechkin, Published in Switzerland by ITU, *Optimization Coding Theory and Multithreshold Algorithms,* **158,** (March 2016).

[2] V.V. Zolotarev, Y.B. Zubarev, G.V. Ovechkin, *Multilevel decoders and optimization coding theory,* Moscow, Hot line - Telecom, 2012, 239 p.

[3] V.V. Zolotarev, *A method for decoding error-correcting code.* Patent RF №2377722, 21.06.2007, **BI №36**, (2009).

[4] V. Zolotarev, G. Ovechkin, D. Satybaldina, N.T ashatov, A. Adamova, V. Mishin, *Efficiency*

multithreshold decoders for self-orthogonal block codes for optical channels, International Journal of Circuits, Systems and Signal Processing, **V.8**, pp.487-495, (2014).

[5] V. Zolotarev, G. Ovechkin, D. Satybaldina, N. Tashatov, A. Issainova, *Effective Multithreshold Decoding Algorithms for Wireless Communication Channels*, Proc. of the 10th IEEE International Conference on Application of Information and Communication Technologies (AICT 2016), pp. 539-543, (12-14 October 2016).

[6] www.mtdbest.iki.rssi.ru

[7] www.mtdbest.ru.

[8] G.V. Ovechkin, V.V. Zolotarev, S.V. Averin, *Algorithm of multithreshold decoding for self-orthogonal codes over Gaussian channels*, 11-th ISCTA'09, July, UK, Ambleside, (2009).

[9] V. Zolotarev, G. Ovechkin, *Algorithm of multithreshold decoding for Gaussian channels*, Automation and Remote Control, No. **69**, pp. 1086-1100, (2008).

[10] V. Zolotarev, D. Satybaldina, N. Tashatov and Z. Sautbekova, *Soft Decision Decoding Techniques in Multithreshold Decoding of Self-Orthogonal Codes*, Proceedings of the 18th International Conference on Digital Signal Processing (DSP2013), Santorini, Greece, 1-3 July, (2013).

[11] G. Ovechkin, V. Zolotarev, P. Ovechkin, D. Satibaldina, N. Tashatov, *The Performance of Concatenated Schemes Based on Non-binary Multithreshold Decoders*, Advances in Systems Science. Springer International Publishing, (2014). Volume **240**, pp. 251-259.

[12] G. Ovechkin, P. Ovechkin, D. Satybaldina, A.Beisebekova, N. Tashatov, *Improving Performance of Non-Binary Multithreshold Decoder's Work Due to Concatenation*, Proc. of the 18th Int. Conf. on Communications (part of CSCC '14). Santorini Island, Greece, pp. 100–104, July. (2014).

[13] G.V. Ovechkin, *Teoriya kaskadnogo dekodirovaniya lineinykh kodov dlya tsifrovykh radiokanalov na osnove mnogoporogovykh algoritmo (Theory of concatenated decoding of linear codes based on multithreshold algorithms for digital radiochannels)*, Doct. of sciense dissertation. Russian Federation, Ryazan, p. 301, (2011).

[14] N. Tashatov, D. Satybaldina, N. Grinchenko, Van Toan Cao, G. Ovechkin, *Multilevel Multithreshold Decoding of Self-Orthogonal Codes for High-Speed Communications*, Proc. of the 2nd International Conference on Innovative Trends in Multidisciplinary Academic Research(ITMAR-2015), Volume **2**, pp.187-190.

[15] N. Grinchenko, Van Toan Cao, G. Ovechkin, *Increase efficiency of multilevel multithreshold decoder for self-orthogonal codes*, 2016 International Siberian Conference on Control and Communications (SIBCON), Moscow, (2016), pp. 1-5.doi: 10.1109/SIBCON.2016.7491819

[16] J.L. Massey, *Threshold decoding*, M.I.T. Press. Cambridge, Massachusetts, (1963).

MATEC Web of Conferences **125**, 05010 (2017) DOI: 10.1051/matecconf/201712505010
CSCC 2017

An IoT-based system that aids learning from human behavior: A potential application for the care of the elderly

Unai Saralegui[1], *Miguel Ángel* Antón[1] and *Joaquín* Ordieres-Meré[2,*]

[1]TECNALIA Research & Innovation, Sustainable Construction Division, Area Anardi 5, 20730 Azpeitia, Gipuzkoa, Spain
[2]Universidad Politécnica de Madrid, ETSII, PMQ Research Group, José Gutierrez Abascal 2, 28006 Madrid, Spain

Abstract. The goal of this paper is to describe the way of taking advantage of the non-intrusive indoor air quality monitoring system by using data oriented modeling technologies to determine specific human behaviors. The specific goal is to determine when a human presence occurs in a specific room, while the objective is to extend the use of the existing indoor air quality monitoring system to provide a higher level aspect of the house usage. Different models have been trained by means of machine learning algorithms using the available temperature, relative humidity and CO_2 levels to determine binary occupation. The paper will discuss the overall acceptable quality provided by those classifiers when operating over new data not previously seen. Therefore, a recommendation on how to proceed is provided, as well as the confidence level regarding the new created knowledge. Such knowledge could bring additional opportunities in the care of the elderly for specific diseases that are usually accompanied by changes in patterns of behavior.

1 Introduction

To maintain the health of people, it can be useful to monitor their health status in their daily lives. Ambient assisted living (AAL), a term that first appeared in the European Framework Program for research funding, are systems that are intended to improve the quality of life of special groups of people, including the elderly. Such systems make use of information and communication technologies to develop applications and services for the elderly, in order to help them in their daily activities.

When implementing an AAL system, several features should be considered [1]. First, the sensors should be non-invasive systems. They can be embedded in wearable items, like shoes, etc., or can be part of the infrastructure. In any event, it is important that these systems respect the privacy of the users.

Elderly people who live alone usually suffer more accidents than other people. For example, in the district of Kaiserslautern, Germany, 30 per cent of persons who are more than 65 years of age and living alone at home suffer at least one fall per year. Therefore, being able to identify either sudden or progressive changes in their routines by using the existing infrastructure, will help in providing specific care to such a population segment without a need for additional investment.

The intention of this paper is to analyze the opportunity to pursue additional goals and obtain further and relevant information by means of an already deployed infrastructure, in order to bring higher value to the user, in connection with the Internet of Things (IoT) paradigm.

As we seek to monitor the behavior of the elderly to detect changes in their patterns of behavior, it is important to be able to record the movements throughout the building in order to detect changes in the everyday patterns that may indicate dementia. With that objective in mind, we show in this paper how to detect human presence in a room by use of the sensors that are already there to monitor the air quality.

A network of wirelessly connected sensors is used to obtain the data from rooms in an elderly caring institution. Such sensors are designed to monitor the air quality and measure temperature, relative humidity and CO_2 concentrations. The data is analyzed and some models are trained with the data to detect the presence of a person in a room. This requires machine learning algorithms.

In order to better understand the work being done, the structure of the paper will first introduce the problem by analyzing the present state of the art in the following section. The methodology that is adopted for this on-going research will be presented in the third Section. The fourth section will provide the selected study case, the main assumptions made in this work and details of the sensor type and implementation. Section five will include the discussion and the analysis of the findings. Finally, the last section will give the main conclusions of the work and discuss future developments and research.

2 State of the Art

There are several paths for research of the use of IoT technology to acquire greater knowledge of different behaviors. In this area, studies of air quality and energy

* Corresponding author: j.ordieres@upm.es

efficiency in buildings have received much attention as in [2-3] where indoor monitoring is proposed and occupancy is related to comfort measurements.

Another interesting trend involves monitoring the indoor air quality, where contributions like [4] propose the development of a compact battery-powered system that monitors the carbon dioxide level, temperature, relative humidity, absolute pressure and intensity of light in indoor spaces, and sends the measurements by means of the existing wireless infrastructure based on the IEEE 802.11 b/g standards. The idea of promoting low cost solutions instead of those that require extensive deployment was deeply investigated in [5-6]. The latter used a monitoring system that was based on an Arduino platform with six sensors.

Not only has energy efficiency or comfort–related topics been analyzed, but also IoT technologies have been used to monitor pollutant levels in indoor areas. A correlation between the concentration of pollutants and health problems in schoolchildren has also been shown in some studies [7-8]. Researchers in this area have also been able to link sleepiness or an impact on health to CO_2 levels on campuses or in offices, thereby showing the physiological effects that a high concentration of CO_2 indoors has on workers or students [9-10].

An area that is receiving increasing attention is the demand-driven HVAC (Heat Ventilation and Air Conditioning) control, for both energy efficiency and indoor comfort. This is seen in the case of [11], where the estimation of a building's occupancy by use of a wireless CO_2 sensor network is investigated. The HVAC system can take advantage of the information, acquired about non-occupancy, in order to save energy and resources.

Another trend that is more closely related to our research interest involves using an existing air quality monitoring system to derive occupancy information in a non-intrusive scenario. The key aspect is to work under long term service principle. Various approaches have been examined to determine the occupancy information as video-image based detection [12] or detection by passive infrared (PIR), sensors [13]. However, both approaches have limitations. These involve privacy or computational cost in the case of video, and a lack of movement in the case of PIR sensors. Those limitations have caused CO_2–based presence detection methods to receive increasing attention.

In our area of research interest, mixed approaches, such as [14], have been presented. They are based on analytical models that were calibrated on empirical data, with a decision tree that defines the final inference model for occupancy. Other authors have proposed the use of a Hidden Markov Model (HMM) as a convenient and effective approach for occupancy estimation by use of Multinomial Logistic Regression (HMM-MLR) [15]. Some research to determine binary occupancy information also has been undertaken, as in [16] where a binary presence detection framework is proposed using an indoor weather station's data and Hidden Markov Models. The approach in this paper will benefit from artificial intelligence based techniques, as the sampling system cannot be reconfigured from its primary application and somehow is limited in its operating life.

3 Methodology

The adopted framework relies on the existing infrastructure for air quality monitoring.
In addition, the data is collected and uploaded to the cloud. Therefore, data can be accessed from any place and models for derivation of the behavior rules can be implemented.

The framework will use as many sensors as are available, as well as the most convenient techniques for data processing and modeling based on machine learning techniques. In this first step, we will analyze the data that is obtained and determine possible relationships that may help in building the monitoring framework. When sufficient knowledge is available and the desired information can be obtained, the decision-making processes will be applied, depending on the case of interest. (See Fig. 1.)

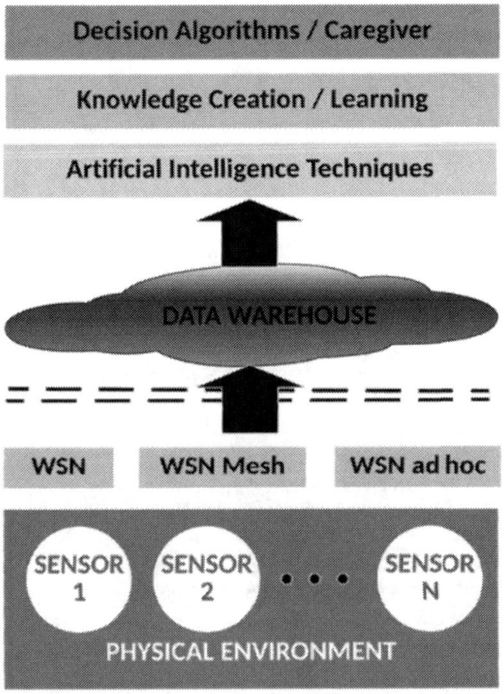

Fig. 1. The framework adopted for the research.

It is worth remembering that the main goal here is to determine human presence in specific areas as an example of a higher level of information. Our main hypothesis in this phase of the study is that it is possible to determine the binary occupancy based on the local data available at room level. As the goal is to use an already available infrastructure, the monitoring frequency is kept at the same value as in its initial application. That is a sampling frequency of 10 minutes, which means that the system is not sensitive to high frequency movements. However, it makes it possible to maintain a low energy consumption.

It will be also interesting in this research to determine the best set of algorithms to predict the occupancy values, in order to obtain the model can provide the best results for this problem. To this end, the problem is treated as a supervised learning process, in which linear and nonlinear techniques will be used with the models, in a first approach that is being built for each monitored room.

4 Study case

An agreement with a caring institution for the elderly has permitted us to collect the data that is necessary for this study. The institution has allowed us to install and monitor sensors in five different rooms in the building. The monitored rooms include the main hall, the living room, the dining room and two bedrooms.

The monitoring period lasted for one year and respected the national laws regarding non-intrusiveness and confidentiality. Five identical wireless sensors were placed in the rooms to measure and report levels of ambient temperature (ºC), relative humidity (%) and CO_2 concentration (ppm). The monitoring frequency was set at ten minutes to maintain the energy requirements.

During normal operation, the sensors are powered by ambient room light by means of an energy harvesting solar cell. In prolonged periods of low light, security backup batteries provide power to the sensors. The sensors support the open EnOcean® standard protocol (ISO/IEC 14543-3-10) for wireless communications [17]. The data is transmitted wirelessly to a central node that uploads it to the cloud.

Doors separate the rooms in the monitored building. While the data was being collected, thirteen residents were living in the building's monitored rooms. Because of the condition of the residents, their routines are well–defined and maintained throughout the year. Thus, abnormalities are easy to measure. In general, the bedrooms are used during the night and are empty during the day. The residents remain in the living room during the day, except at breakfast, lunch and dinner times when they congregate in the dining room.

5 Results and Discussion

By performing a visualization of the data for each room that each sensor generates, interesting relationships are suggested. From the brief overview in Fig. 2 it becomes clear that the dining-room is used mainly used at around 9:00 a.m., 1:00 p.m. and 8:00 p.m., which agrees with the scheduled times for breakfast, lunch and dinner in the institution.

The effect of the doors being opened or closed has also been visualized. As can be seen in the line that represents Room 2 in Fig. 2, the CO_2 concentration levels increase continually, whereas the concentration in Room 1 remains more stable and even decreases in some phases. Such behavior is expected in a room that has an open door, as the air flows through rooms whose entrances present no barrier.

The evolution of the temperature values appears in Fig. 3. The evolution is quite stable over time as the temperature values do not change much. This indicates that they will not provide sufficient information to detect changes in the occupancy of a room.

The data visualization enables us to see the impact on adjacent spaces when the doors remain open and the air flows from room to room. It becomes possible to visualize the effects as ventilation in the values of relative humidity around 9:00 a.m. in both rooms, see Fig. 4, showing a noticeable change in the relative humidity values at those moments. Consequently, the visualization of data shows that it is possible to detect when a window is open, allowing to monitor such activity.

In Fig. 5, a straight line with no change is observed during the night for Room 1. This means that there has been a problem in communication and the last measured value is provided.

By visualizing the time series that the sensor values describe, it appears that, when the doors are opened, the air flows between the rooms making the concentration of CO_2 to create different patterns. That is why it will be interesting in further research to add additional information to model the air flow between the rooms.

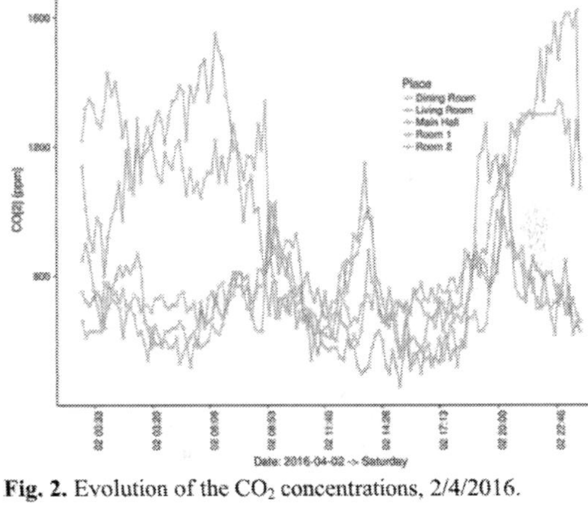

Fig. 2. Evolution of the CO_2 concentrations, 2/4/2016.

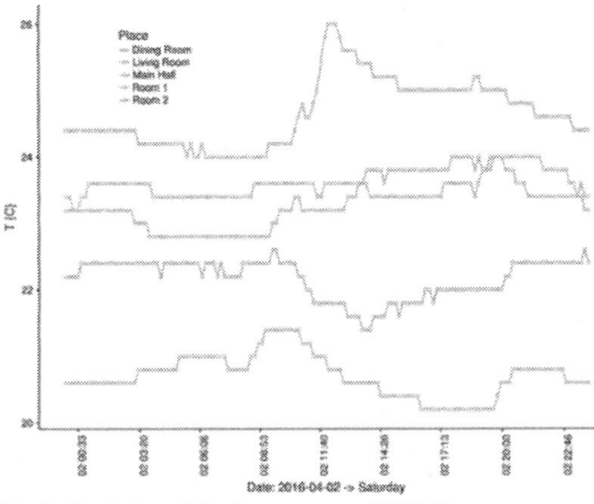

Fig. 3. Evolution of the Temperature, 2/4/2016.

DOI: 10.1051/matecconf/201712505010

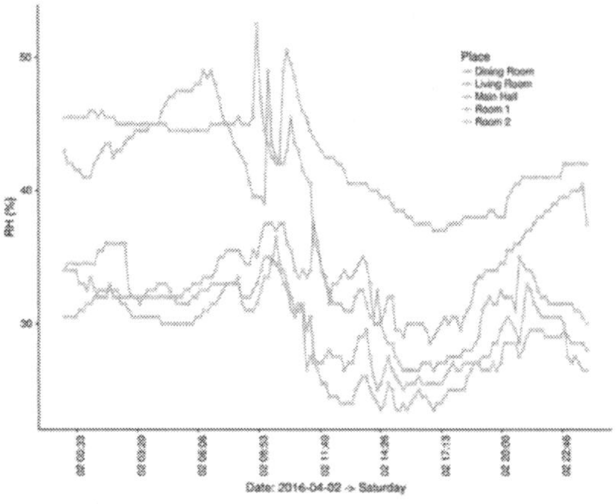

Fig. 4. Evolution of the Relative Humidity, 2/4/2016.

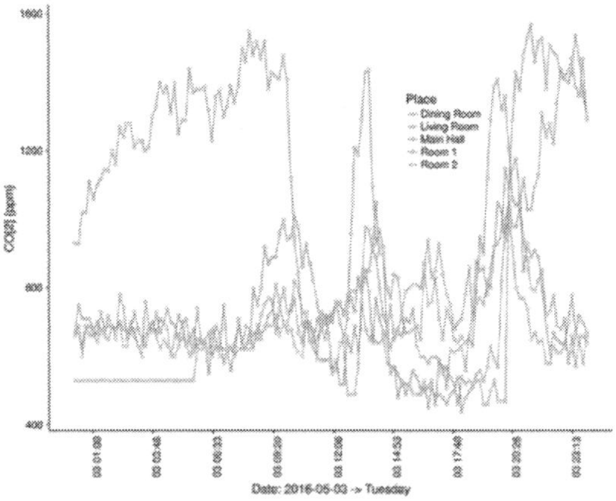

Fig. 5. Evolution of the CO_2 concentrations, 3/5/2016.

As mentioned, the main objective in this phase of the study is to determine occupancy based on the data of an already available infrastructure in a real scenario. For this purpose, several classification models have been trained after pre-processing the data. The R project's language [18] was used for this purpose. A common organization of models was established by using the Caret package in R [19]. The models that were used to build the classifiers include classical classification trees, the gradient boosting method, the multiclass Adaboost with bagging, the C5.0 classification tree, the Support Vector Machines, Quadratic Discriminant Analysis, and Neural Networks with one principal component analysis step. The machine that was used to train the models was a Linux based SMP server with twenty cores running in parallel and 48 GB of available RAM.

As an example of the capability of the models that were trained, Fig. 6 shows the performance of different models, as well as accuracy and Cohen's kappa coefficient, which relates the obtained and expected accuracy of qualitative (categorical) items, on the case of the dining-room when validated against a dataset that was not previously seen during the training phase. It can be seen that, in this case, the model that performs better is the one that was based on supported vector machines. In general, it can be said that it performs noticeably better than the classical lineal models, ctree2 in the case of trees or the C5.0 rules. Bagging methods, such as random forest (RF), the extreme gradient boosting (xgbtree) and Adaboost with bagging (Adabag) also obtain remarkably accurate values. However, the model that was based on supported vector machines with a radial kernel performs slightly better. It obtains greater accuracy and Cohen's kappa coefficient values.

The most accurate models obtained with the set of classifiers that were trained, give accuracy values of about 80%. This is quite a good value, as some effects, such as the air flow between the rooms, have not been considered. It is expected that the accuracy values will increase when taking those effects into account, which is considered for further research activities.

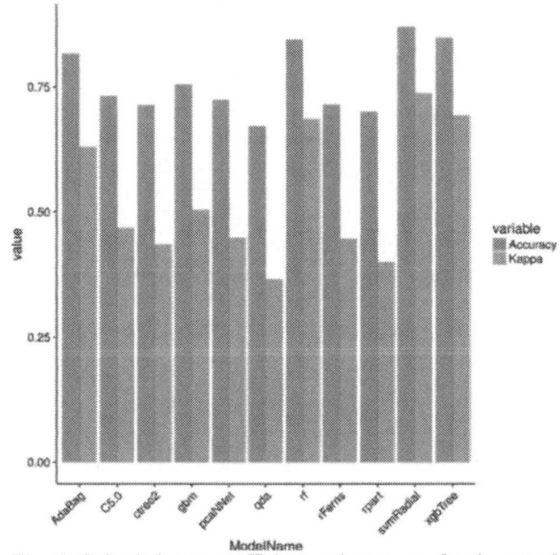

Fig. 6. Cohen's kappa coefficient and accuracy for the set of models that were trained.

6 Conclusions

The accuracy obtained by the models that were built gives confidence in the identification of binary occupancy in the rooms. However, there is room for improvement in reducing the confusion rate, although it has been reduced already in the case of non-linear classifiers. The main reasons for the confusion are that the bare variables and their intrinsic variations only enforce basic rules, but reality is more complex. For instance, indoor climate control enforces temperature within a short range. However, differences occur when the residents breathe with the room door open or closed. Actually, when the door remains open, the CO_2 levels and humidity spread to the adjoining areas and cause a rise in the concentration of such values in those areas. Of course, this effect does not occur in the same way when the doors are closed as the concentrations only rise in rooms that are occupied.

The previously identified effects of the air flow through the rooms suggest including specific information about variable trends over time. They also suggest considering the building's semantic as a key element in order to learn from the different patterns and avoid false positives due to the air flow between adjoining rooms.

All of those improvements will be considered for further development and research in the near future, in order to reduce uncertainty and provide stronger foundations for the development of a decision making system framework.

References

[1] J. Lloret, A. Canovas, S. Sendra, L. Parra, *A smart communication architecture for ambient assisted living*, IEEE Commun. Mag., **53(1)**, p. 26–33 (2015)

[2] K. Akkaya, I. Guvenc, R. Aygun, N. Pala, A. Kadri, *IoT-based occupancy monitoring techniques for energy-efficient smart buildings*, Wireless Communications and Networking Conference Workshops (WCNCW), **2015**, p. 58–63 (2015)

[3] A. Kumar, G. P. Hancke, *An energy-efficient smart comfort sensing system based on the IEEE 1451 standard for green buildings*, IEEE Sens. J., **14(12)**, p. 4245–4252 (2014)

[4] S. C. Folea, G. Mois, *A low-power wireless sensor for online ambient monitoring*, IEEE Sens. J., **15(2)**, p. 742–749 (2015)

[5] S. Abraham, X. Li, *A cost-effective wireless sensor network system for indoor air quality monitoring applications*, Procedia Comput. Sci., **34**, p. 165–171 (2014)

[6] M. Kotol, A. Heller, C. Orthmann, *Introduction of flexible monitoring equipment into the Greenlandic building sector*, ARTEK Event 2014 (2014)

[7] S. K. Wang, S. P. Chew, M. T. Jusoh, A. Khairunissa, K. Y. Leong, A. A. Azid, *WSN based indoor air quality monitoring in classrooms*, AIP Conference Proceedings, **1808(1)**, p. 20063 (2017)

[8] G. de Gennaro, P. R. Dambruoso, A. D. Loiotile, A. Di Gilio, P. Giungato, M. Tutino, A. Marzocca, A. Mazzone, J. Palmisani, F. Porcelli, *Indoor air quality in schools*, Environ. Chem. Lett., **12(4)**, p. 467–482 (2014)

[9] T. Vehviläinen, H. Lindholm, H. Rintamäki, R. Pääkkönen, A. Hirvonen, O. Niemi, J. Vinha, *High indoor CO2 concentrations in an office environment increases the transcutaneous CO2 level and sleepiness during cognitive work*, J. Occup. Environ. Hyg. **13(1)**, p. 19–29 (2016)

[10] K. Tijani, S. Ploix, B. Haas, J. Dugdale, Q. D. Ngo, *Dynamic Bayesian Networks to simulate occupant behaviours in office buildings related to indoor air quality*, arXiv Prepr. arXiv1605.05966 (2016)

[11] Q. Huang, C. Mao, *Occupancy estimation in smart building using hybrid CO2/light wireless sensor network*, J. Appl. Sci. Arts, **1(2)**, p. 5 (2017)

[12] G. Diraco, A. Leone, P. Siciliano, *People occupancy detection and profiling with 3D depth sensors for building energy management*, Energy and Buildings, **92**, p. 246–266 (2015)

[13] X. Guo, D. K. Tiller, G. P. Henze, C.E. Waters, *The performance of occupancy-based lighting control systems: A review*, Lighting Research & Technology, **42(4)**, p. 415–431 (2010)

[14] M. Jin, N. Bekiaris-Liberis, K. Weekly, C. Spanos, A. Bayen, *Sensing by proxy: Occupancy detection based on indoor CO2 concentration*, UBICOMM 2015, p. 14 (2015)

[15] Z. Chen, Q. Zhu, M. Masood, C. S. Yeng, *Environmental Sensors based Occupancy Estimation in Buildings via IHMM-MLR*, IEEE Trans. Ind. Informatics (2017)

[16] D. Wörner, T. von Bomhard, M. Röschlin, F. Wortmann, *Look twice: Uncover hidden information in room climate sensor data*, 2014 International Conference on the Internet of Things, p. 25-30 (2014)

[17] ISO/IEC Standard 14543-3-10, *International standard ISO/IEC 14543-3-10: Wireless Short-Packet (WSP) protocol optimized for energy harvesting—architecture and lower layer protocols*, edition 1.0 (2012)

[18] R Core Team, *R: A Language and Environment for Statistical Computing*, Vienna, Austria (2016)

[19] M. Kuhn C. from Jed Wing, S. Weston, A. Williams, C. Keefer, A. Engelhardt, T. Cooper, Z. Mayer, B. Kenkel, the R Core Team, M. Benesty, R. Lescarbeau, A. Ziem, L. Scrucca, Y. Tang, C. Candan, *caret: Classification and Regression Training* (2016)

Extraction of Human Stepping Pattern Using Acceleration Sensors

Takayuki Toyohira[1*], *Kiminori* Sato[1] and *Mutsumi* Watanabe[1]

[1]Graduate School of Science and Engineering, Kagoshima University, Kagoshima,890-0065, Japan

Abstract. Gait analysis plays an important role in characterizing individuals and each condition and gait analysis systems have been developed using various devices or instruments. However, most systems do not catch synchronous stepping actions between right foot and left foot. For obtaining a precise gait pattern, a synchronous walking sensing system is developed, in which a pair of acceleration and angular velocity sensors are attached to left and right shoes of a walking person and their data are transmitted to a PC through a wireless channel. Walking data from 19 persons of the age of 14 to 20 are acquired for walking analysis. Stepping time diagrams are extracted from the acquired data of right and left foot actions of stepping-off and-on the ground, and the time diagrams distinguish between an ordinary person and a person injured on left leg, and a stepping recovery process of the injured person is shown. Synchronous sensing of stepping action between right foot and left foot contributes to obtain precise stepping patterns.

1 Introduction

Gait pattern of person characterizes individual and each condition. The precise gait pattern may be one of the measures for recognizing individuals [1][2][3][4]. Gait analysis systems using acceleration sensor were developed for medical rehabilitation [5] and identification of portable device user [6], etc. However, most systems do not catch synchronous stepping actions between right foot and left foot. In this paper, a synchronous walking sensing system is developed, where a pair of acceleration and angular velocity sensors are attached to left and right shoes of a walking person and their data are transmitted to a PC through a wireless channel. Walking data from 19 students of the age of 14 to 20 are acquired for walking analysis. From acquired data, stepping time diagrams are extracted and the difference of stepping patterns between an ordinary person and a person injured on left leg and the recovery process of the injured person are shown.

2 Human walking

Human is an only creature who moves by erect bipedal walking. Always birds as ostrich and penguin and temporarily animals as dog, bear, monkey and ape move by bipedal walking, but they cannot move in an erect posture. Human walking action is classified into walk and trot [7]. Usually human walking features trot in which pivot foot alternately changes and either foot touches on the ground. Fig.1 shows an example of surface touchdown positions of left and right feet when a person stands and starts walking from the right step and moves forward.

Fig. 1. Feet touch positions of walking movement.

A trot action is regarded as a rotation movement around the touched ground or floor. In this case, the rotation energy does not exceed the gravity energy, as follows:

$$mv^2 / r \leq mg \tag{1}$$

where v , r and m are the walking velocity, the gravity centre and the mass of a person, and the acceleration of the gravity is $g = 9.80[m/s^2]$. Then the maximum value of trotting velocity is obtained as

$$v_{max} = \sqrt{rg}. \tag{2}$$

For the height $r = 1[m]$ of the gravity centre of a person, the trotting velocity is limited to $v_{max} = 3.13[m/s]$.

If the moving velocity of a person exceeds v_{max} , the moving action becomes running. In the case of trot, the horizontal momentum is delivered to the next action at a full efficiency, and the vertical momentum disappears by collision between the foot and the ground, while the gravity energy of the gravity centre is preserved by Achilles' tendon and delivered to the next action by kicking the ground. In the case of walk, the weight is supported by both feet and the velocity vector of the gravity centre is restricted toward one way and the left and right momentum by zigzag movement is vanished in

* Corresponding author: toyohira@kagoshima-ct.ac.jp

addition to the vertical momentum and so the energy efficiency of walk is inferior to trot.

In this paper, we use the term of walking for the moving action which mainly consists of trot rather than walk. Real walking accompanies with so complicated actions interlinked by feet, leg, body and moving velocity, etc, that walking patterns can be utilized to identification of individuals and each condition.

3 Walking data acquisition system

Fig.2 shows a walking data acquisition system using a couple of acceleration and angular velocity sensors. A person taking a pair of shoes attached with sensors moves by walking at a flat ground or floor, while the respective sensor transmits data to a PC through Bluetooth wireless channel. Table 1 shows specifications of the sensor TSND121 which detects 3-axes accelerations and 3-axes angular velocities and additionally earth magnetism and atmospheric pressure. The PC controls sensors by instructions of start and stop and processes the acquired data of 6-axes accelerations and angular velocities. Fig.3 shows an overview of the sensor in comparison with a 500yean coin of 2.65cm diameter, where x, y and z axes in acceleration sensing are drawn on the surface. Fig.4 shows directions of rotation angles around x, y and z axes in angular velocity sensing. Fig.5 shows a picture of shoes attached to the sensors with x axis of acceleration directed forward. The sensors are attached firmly to the shoes at the stable position [8][9].

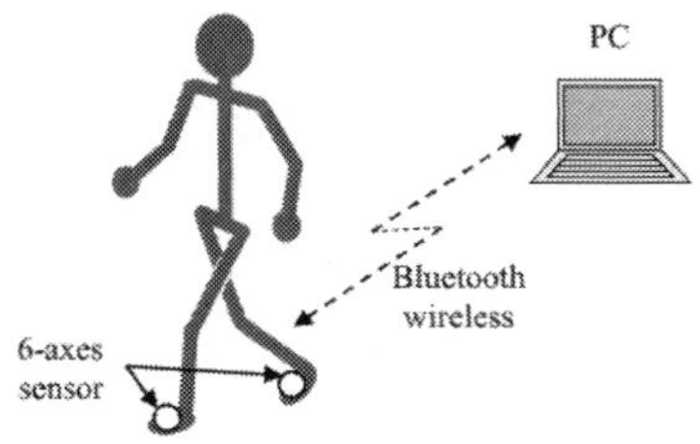

Fig.2. Walking data acquisition system.

Table 1. Specifications of sensor.

Acceleration sensor Sampling rate Accelerometer Feature Gyroscope Feature	InvenSense MPU-6050 max 1000Hz (1 to 255msec) ±2G, ±4G, ±8G and±16G ±250dps, ±500dps, ±1000dps and ±2000dps
Magnetic Field sensor	Aichi Steel AMI306
Barometer	Freescale MPL3115A2

Fig. 3. Overview of sensor.

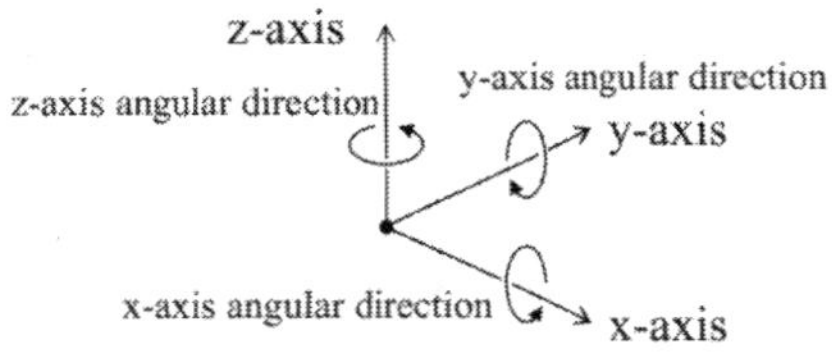

Fig.4. Angular directions in angular velocity sensing.

Fig.5. Shoes attached to sensors.

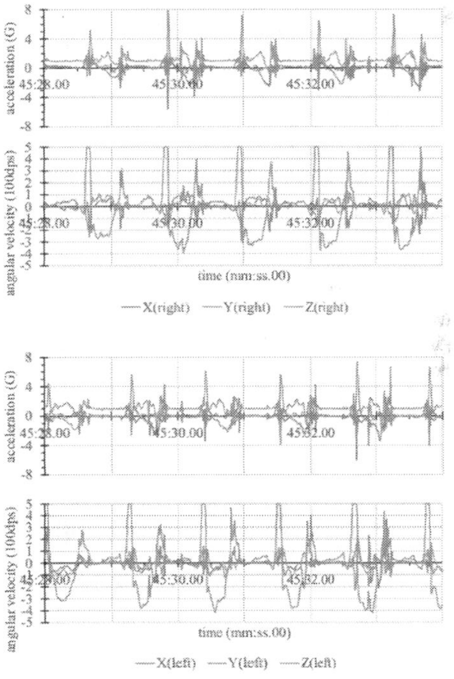

Fig.6. Acceleration and angular velocity responses for an ordinary person.

4 Data acquisition of walking

At the floor of the college building, walking data were acquired from 19 male and female students of the age of 14 to 20, one of whom had been injured on left leg but could join in the experiments. The walking manner is explained as follows: a subject person stands at the start point and raises both tiptoes in order to synchronize between left and right sensors and then begins to walk

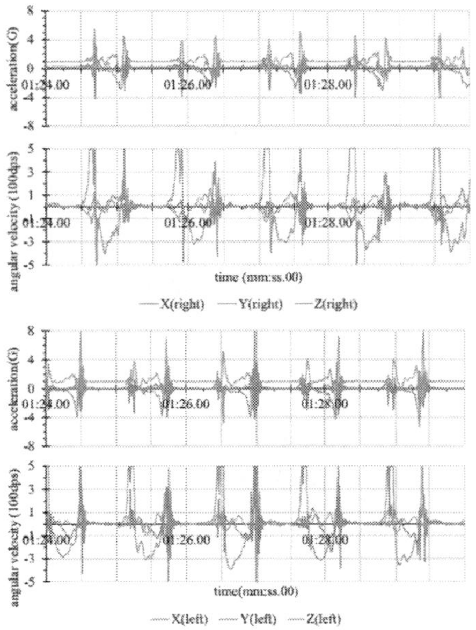

Fig.7. Acceleration and angular velocity responses for an injured person

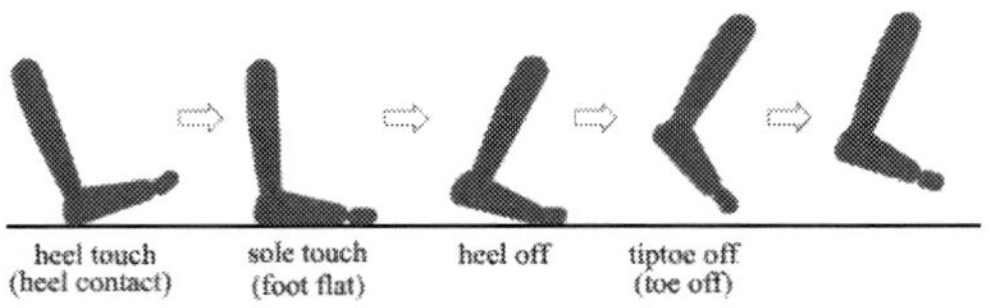

Fig.8. Stepping action of a foot.

from the right or left foot. Fig.6 shows partial waveforms of x, y and z components of acceleration and angular velocity on right foot and left foot of an ordinary person, and Fig.7 shows those of a person injured on left leg, where each waveform indicates almost steady response after initial irregular response. The responses for the injured person seem to be more irregular than those for the ordinary person. In these responses, the stepping order is indicated by numbering and the marked time positions of x and z components of accelerations and y component of angular velocity are regarded as unique changing points of stepping off and on the ground [10]. We consider that the negatives short pulse of x acceleration and the positive short pulse of z acceleration occurs simultaneously with the positive to negative rebound pulse of y angular velocity and so the time when the stepping-on changes to stepping-off is the time on the peaks of x and z acceleration pulses and the zero-crossing of y angular velocity rebound pulse. And we consider that the negative pulses of x and z accelerations occurs simultaneously and so the time when the stepping-off changes to stepping-on is the time on the peaks of x and z acceleration negative pulses. The above stepping-off and -on interpretations are supported by the foot actions of Fig.8. There, first a heel touches on the ground, a sole adheres to the ground, the heel rises with a tiptoe on the ground, and at last the tiptoe rises off the ground with the heel. The first action gives

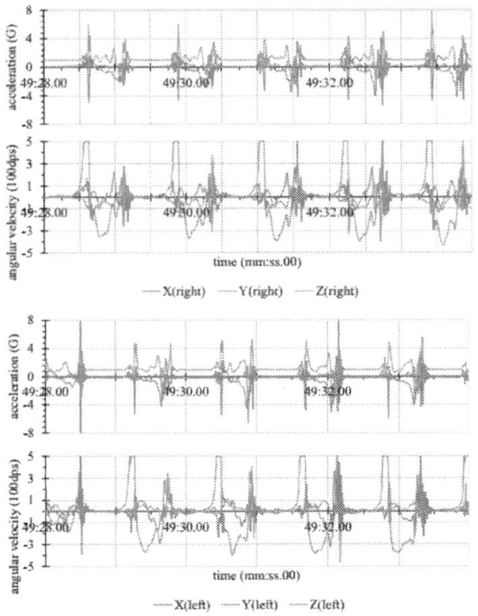

Fig.9. Acceleration angular velocity responses for the injured person at the second experiment.

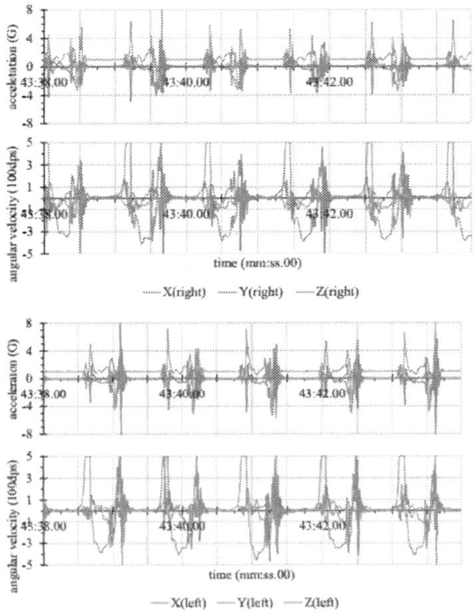

Fig.10. Acceleration and angular velocity responses for the injured person at the third experiment.

downward x and z accelerations and the last action gives the rebound rotation around y axis. Fig.9 and Fig.10 show x and z components of acceleration and y components of angular velocity for the injured person at the second experiment and the third experiment, respectively, at the interval of two weeks.

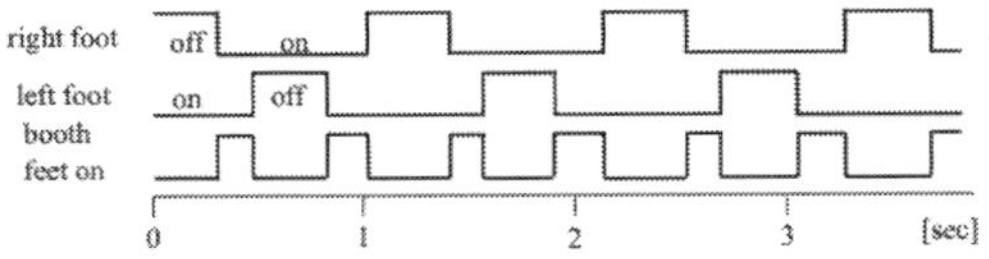

Fig.11 Stepping time diagram for the ordinary person.

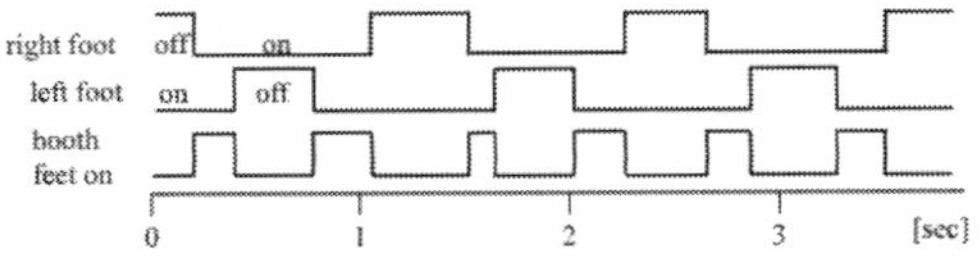

Fig.12. Stepping time diagram for the injured person.

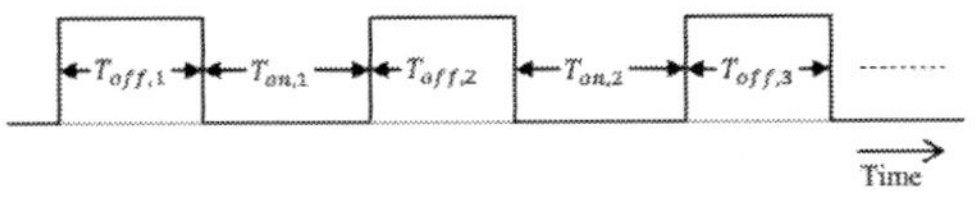

Fig.13. Stepping-off and-on time intervals.

Table 2. Statistics of time intervals of stepping-off and-on.

	Ordinary person			Injured person		
	Right foot	Left foot	Both feet	Right foot	Left foot	Both feet
$\overline{T}_{off}$	0.395	0.367		0.379	0.378	
σ_{off}	0.015	0.030		0.031	0.017	
$\overline{T}_{on}$	0.759	0.790		0.828	0.830	
σ_{on}	0.038	0.046		0.034	0.018	
$T_{on\text{-}right\text{-}left}$			0.182			0.212
$\sigma_{on\text{-}right\text{-}left}$			0.021			0.028
$T_{on\text{-}left\text{-}right}$			0.214			0.238
$\sigma_{on\text{-}left\text{-}right}$			0.036			0.013

5 Evaluation of stepping time diagrams

In order to evaluate the stepping actions, we extract the time intervals of stepping off and on the ground from the acceleration and angular velocity responses. As mentioned in the above chapter, from the unique changing points in Fig.6 and Fig.7, we obtain the stepping time diagrams of the right and left feet. Fig.11 and Fig.12 show the stepping time diagrams of the ordinary person and the injured person, respectively, where another time diagram illustrates the time intervals simultaneously stepping on the ground. The simultaneously stepping-on time diagram of the ordinary person is more balanced than that of the injured person. The simultaneous stepping-on occurs two times in a pair of the right and left steps. The stepping-off and-on time intervals are evaluated by a model of Fig.13, where $T_{off,k}$ is stepping-off time interval and $T_{on,k}$ is stepping-on time interval. The respective N intervals give the average values

$$\overline{T}_{off} = (1/N)\sum_{k=1}^{N} T_{off,k} \quad (3)$$

$$\overline{T}_{on} = (1/N)\sum_{k=1}^{N} T_{on,k} \quad (4)$$

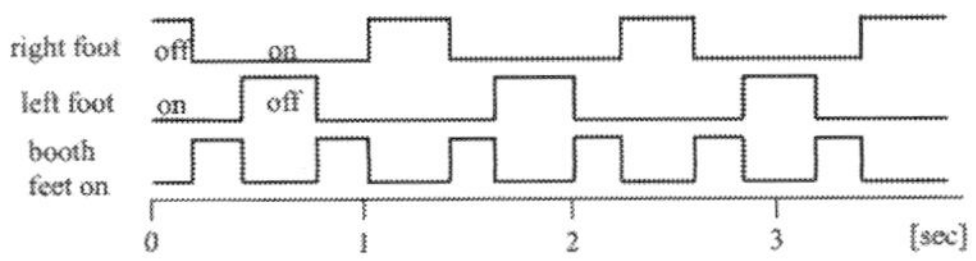

Fig.14. Stepping time diagram of 2nd experiment for the injured person.

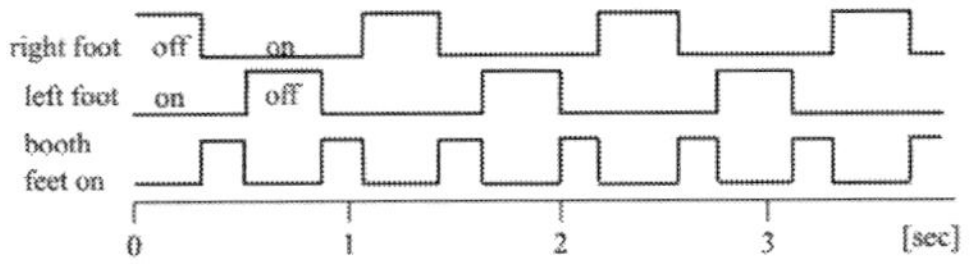

Fig.15. Stepping time diagram of 3rd experiment for the injured person.

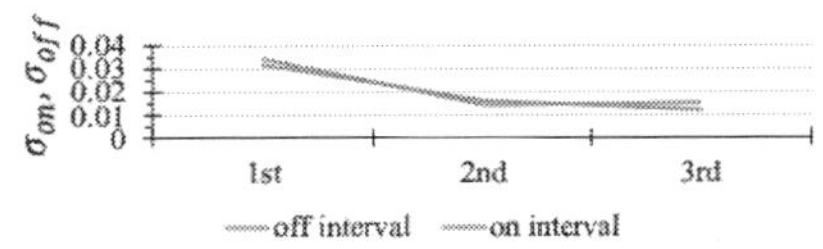

Fig.16. Standard deviations of right foot stepping time interval in second.

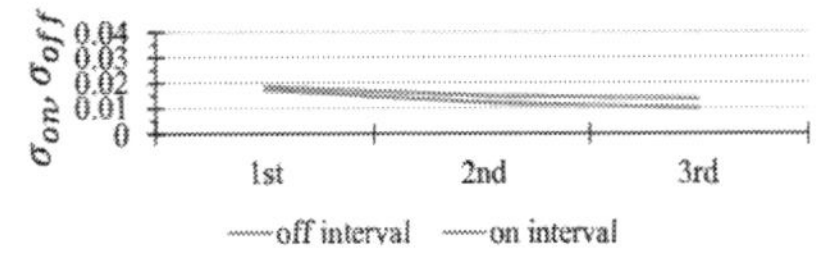

Fig.17. Standard deviations of left foot stepping time interval in second.

and the variances

$$\sigma_{off}^2 = (1/N)\sum_{k=1}^{N}(T_{off,k} - \overline{T}_{off})^2 \quad (5)$$

$$\sigma_{on}^2 = (1/N)\sum_{k=1}^{N}(T_{on,k} - \overline{T}_{on}).^2 \quad (6)$$

From the time intervals in Fig.11 and Fig.12, we obtain the average values and the standard deviations of stepping-off and -on time intervals of the right foot and the left foot for the ordinary person and for the injured person. Similarly, we define the simultaneously stepping-on time intervals and obtain the average values and standard deviation of the simultaneously stepping-on time intervals for the ordinary person and for the injured person. Table 2 shows the average values and the standard deviations of these time intervals in second. Fig.14 and Fig.15 shows the stepping-off and -on time diagrams derived from Fig.9 and Fig.10. From the time intervals in Fig.12, Fig. 14 and Fig.15 for the injured person, we obtain the average value and the standard deviations of the stepping-off and stepping-on time intervals of the 1st, 2nd and 3rd experiments of the right foot as $\overline{T}_{off,n,right}$, $\overline{T}_{on,n,right}$, $\sigma_{off,n,right}$, $\sigma_{on,n,right}$ and those of the left foot as $\overline{T}_{off,n,left}$, $\overline{T}_{on,n,left}$, $\sigma_{off,left,n}$, $\sigma_{on,n,left}$

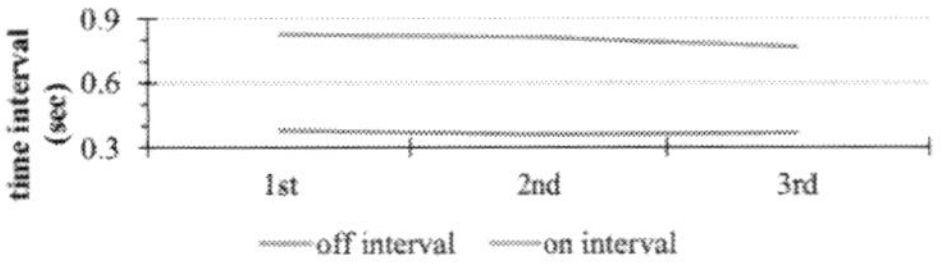

Fig.18. Average values of right foot stepping time interval.

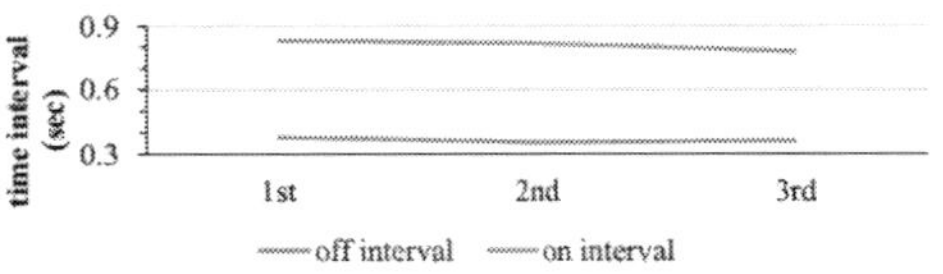

Fig.19. Average values of left foot stepping time interval.

$(n = 1,2,3,\ N = 11)$. Fig.16 and Fig.17 show convergence process of standard deviations of stepping-off and stepping-on time intervals of the right foot and the left foot, respectively. Fig.16 and Fig.17 show that the stepping action of the injured person recovers and become stable according to time progress. Fig.18 and Fig.19 show convergence process of average values of stepping-off and stepping-on time intervals. From the 3rd values of $T_{off,3,right} = 0.367[s]$, $T_{on,3,right} = 0.769[s]$ and $T_{off,3,left} = 0.360[s]$, $T_{on,3,left} = 0.779[s]$, we obtain the average step time interval $(T_{off,3,right} + T_{off,3,left} + T_{on,3,right} + T_{on,3,right})/2 = 1.14[s]$.

Moreover, we obtain the average values and the standard deviations of the simultaneously stepping-on time intervals at the 1st, 2nd and 3rd stages for the injured person, as $T_{on-right-left,1} = 0.212[s]$, $T_{on-left-right,1} = 0.238[s]$, $T_{on-right-left,2} = 0.234[s]$, $T_{on-left-right,2} = 0.234[s]$, $T_{on-right-left,3} = 0.222[s]$, $T_{on-left-right,3} = 0.190[s]$. From these results, the stepping pattern of the injured person approaches those of the ordinary person.

6 Conclusions

A walking data acquisition system using a couple of acceleration and angular velocity sensors attached to each foot is developed. The system is applied to acquisition of walking data from 19 male and female students including a male student in the recovery process of injured left leg. In the sensor data, x and z components of accelerations and y component of acceleration are used for analysis of walking. The stepping-off and -on time diagrams characterizes the walking of the ordinary student and injured student, and gives a recognition of the recovery process of the injured student. Synchronous sensing of stepping action between right foot and left foot contributes to obtain precise stepping patterns. The other data of accelerations and angular velocities may be used for the recognitions of individual and each condition in the future.

Acknowledgement

The authors appreciate greatly the helpful suggestions of Dr. Yoshihiro Tanada of Kyoto University and students' cooperation and assistance of the experiments.

References

1. J. Han, B. Bhanu, Individual Recognition Using Gait Energy Image, Trans. on Pattern Analysis and Machine Intelligence, Vol. 28, No.2, pp. 316-322 (2006).
2. Y. Makihara, R. Sagawa, Y. Mukaigawa, T. Echigo, Y. Yagi, Gait Recognition Using a View Transformation Model in the Frequency Domain, Proc. of the 9th European Conf. on Computer Vision, Graz, Austria, pp. 151-163 (2006).
3. K. Bashir, T. Xiang, S. Gong, Gait recognition without subject cooperation, Pattern Recognition Letters, Vol.31, No. 13, pp.2052-2060 (2010).
4. T. H. W. Lam, K. H. Cheung, J. N. K. Liu, Gait flow image: A silhouette-based gait representation for human identification , Pattern Recognition, Vol.44, pp. 973-987 (2011).
5. T. Kobatyashi, Y. Miyake, Y. Wada, M. Matsubara, Kinematic Analysis System of Walking by Acceleration Sensor, Trans. Inst. Auto. Contl. Japan, Vol.42, No.5(2006).
6. J. Manyjarvi, M. Lindholm, E.Vildjounaite, S. Makela, H.Alisto, Identifying Users of Portable Devices from Gait Pattern with Accelerometers, ICAPSSP'05, March (2005).
7. R. M. Alexander, Principles of Animal locomotion, Princeton University Press (2003).
8. Y. Ohtaki, K. Sagawa, H. Inooka, A Method for the Long-Term Gait Assessment Utilizing Accelerometers and Gyroscopes, Trans. of the JSME (in Japanese), Series C, Vol. 67, No. 655, pp. 192-198 (2001).
9. A. R. Jimenz, F. Seco, C Prieto, J. Guevara, A Comparison of Pedestrian Dead-Reckoning Algorithms using a Low-Cost MEMS IMU, In Proceedings of Intelligent Signal Processing, pp.37-42 (2009)
10. K. Sagawa, Y. Sato, H. Inooka, Non-Restricted Measurement of Distance during Level Walk, Trans. of the SICE , Vol. 36, No. 11, pp. 909-915 (2000).

DOI: 10.1051/matecconf/201712505012

Control of framed structures using intelligent monitoring networks

Dora Foti[1,*], *Massimo* La Scala[2], *Silvia* Lamonaca[2] and *Vitantonio* Vacca[1]

[1]Polytechnic University of Bari, Department of Civil Engineering Sciences and Architecture, Via Orabona 4, 70125 Bari, Italy
[2]Polytechnic University of Bari, Department of Electrical and Computer Science Engineering, Via Orabona 4, 70125 Bari, Italy

Abstract. The paper proposes the integration of structural monitoring with Building Management Systems for electricity and gas distributions. To assess the state of damage of existing buildings the technics of Structural Health Monitoring (SHM) is adopted. SHM as well as to record the occurrence of sudden structural damage resulting from exceptional events (earthquakes, explosions, shocks and collisions with vehicles, etc.), allows the monitoring of the progressive damage and structural performance under operating conditions through the extraction of the modal parameters of the structure. This approach requires time to process acquired data that, depending on the size of the building and the number of monitored points, varies from minutes to hours. In this paper, an intelligent system is proposed to immediately communicate during an earthquake the overrun of a certain ground shaking threshold so that gas delivery and selected power loads are interrupted, as suggested by current national regulations on structures. The use of low-cost and reduced size accelerometric sensors integrated with Energy Monitoring Systems is proposed in both high-risk earthquake centers and in all "strategic" buildings that must ensure their operation use immediately after the earthquake. The procedure for calibrating the horizontal and vertical acceleration threshold is also sketched.

1 Introduction

In the last two decades, a revolution occurred in the energy sector. Energy systems moved from "operation-centric" grids to "customer-centric" ones, where the final users aim to become independent of the main distribution grid and act as a "prosumer" i.e. a producer and consumer of electricity, heat/cool, and more recently of natural gas or biogas, too. Nowadays, the technology shows the promise to overcome the many technical issues involved in this approach. Furthermore, distributed generation, demand response programs, storage availability and advanced smart metering show the potential to create new business models built around active customers who have reached higher level of awareness and have been enabled to participate directly in the management of energy grids [1-2]. In such scenario, Demand Response (DR) programs constitute the main economical driving force that can break the inherent inelasticity that characterizes end-users energy behaviour, pushing them towards the achievement of higher efficiency goals in the energy use.

This is not the only revolution occurring in this field. Since advanced and evolutionary monitoring systems are implemented in this "customer–centric" transition, it has been realized that the developed applications can handle functions besides the energy-related ones. As an example, these systems can be used for security and safety purposes, surveillance, senior citizen monitoring, anti-intrusion, civil protection, etc.

In this paper, a monitoring system, which can be easily embedded in a Building Energy Monitoring System (BEMS), is presented. The rationale is to use it to gather data about seismic activity and to reduce the earthquakes secondary effects such as fire, explosions, floods. The aim of the paper is to identify a suitable system able to recognize an earthquake and shut down main energy carriers such as electricity and natural gas, avoiding as much as possible false alarms and improper supply interruption. The paper reports some preliminary results obtained through a research activity developed by Polytechnic of Bari and a cluster of firms within the so-called "Energy Router" project and analyses developed in a research project of relevant interest about the mitigation of the impacts of natural hazards and earthquakes.

The interest in this field arises from the fact that Italy is one of the countries in the Mediterranean that most is subject to seismic risk because of its geographic location. The Seismic Hazard Harmonization in Europe (SHARE) project determined the seismicity of the entire European territory and maps have been drawn up in which it is confirmed that Italy, Turkey and Greece are the most threatened seismic areas across Europe (Fig. 1).

* Corresponding author: dora.foti@poliba.it

In recent years, Italy has been affected by a series of seismic events that have interested the territories from North to South causing major damage to construction structures and people (i.e. Central Italy earthquakes: Emilia 2012, Aquila 2009, San Giuliano of Puglia 2002, Umbria-Marche 1997, Irpinia 1980, etc.).

On March 20th 2003, the O.P.C.M./3274 code [3] "First Elements on General Criteria for Seismic Classification of National Territories and Technical Standards for Seismic Buildings", was issued. It marked a historic breakthrough at national level for building construction directives. One of the innovations introduced concerns the obligation for designers to analyze not only the structural aspect of the building, but also all the non-structural elements, including at first the life-lines. Over the years it has been possible to see how buildings can withstand seismic action without collapsing, but unfortunately are made unusable due to the damage suffered by life-lines and other elements inserted within the volume. Specifically, in Annex 2 to O.C.M. 3274, the following is stated: "gas installations rated for more than 50 m^3/h must be equipped with valves for automatic shutdown in case of an earthquake. Gas supply pipes, when moving from the ground to the building, have to be designed to withstand the maximum relative building-ground displacements due to the seismic design action without breaking".

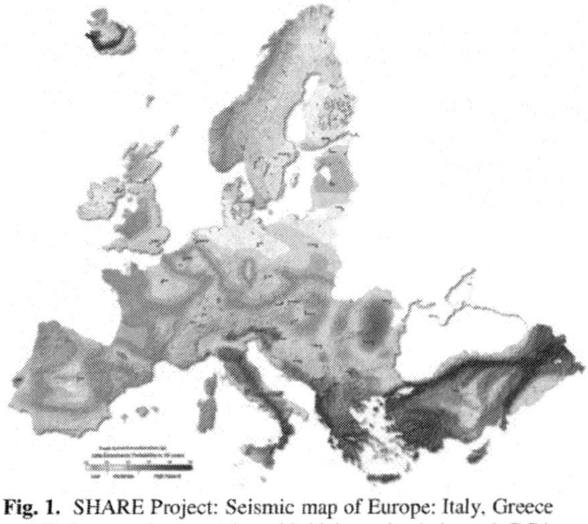

Fig. 1. SHARE Project: Seismic map of Europe: Italy, Greece and Turkey are the countries with higher seismic hazard (PGA with a probability of 10% to be overcome in 50 years, that is. earthquakes with a return period of 475 years).

It is interesting to note that in OPCM 3274/2003, this obligation was imposed only for life-lines with a gas flow of 50 Nm^3/h or more (corresponding to a power of approximately 400 to 500 kW), while during the Legislative updates, and in particular the current NTC 08 [4,5] this limit has been eliminated, leading to intrinsically increasing the safety even for all buildings that do not have large installations. This is of great importance because, while up to a few years ago large buildings required great thermal power, at present, and in light of the international commitments undertaken by Italy, in the years to come we will find buildings with elevate volumes, with high levels of crowding, but with smaller and smaller generators because they are getting less energetic. From these assumptions, it is believed that a conscientious choice has been made and the degree of safety has been increased. In addition in [4,5] it is also specified that the risk of uncontrolled gas leaks should be limited, particularly close to electrical and flammable materials by using breakers.

After about fifteen years, we are aware of a new and profound knowledge of the structural aspect, the effects that an earthquake can cause, and what are the strategies that can be adopted to reduce the risks, but there still does not seem to be full awareness of the strategies, which must be adopted for the protection of non-structural elements and, in particular, systems and technologies for the protection of gas and electricity distribution systems [6].

The aim is to ensure the stability of the life-lines, paying particular attention to the context in which they operate. There are buildings that require special attention and are defined as strategic for which, both during and after the earthquake (hospitals, civil protection co-ordination centres, firefighters, etc.) their operation must be guaranteed. It is therefore of utmost importance to avoid uncontrolled gas leakage, particularly close to electrical and flammable materials. To do this, it is necessary to adopt automatically interrupting gas distribution devices. Gas supply pipes, from land to construction, must be designed to withstand the maximum relative displacements between the building and the ground without breaking.

Starting from these considerations, we propose a possible, innovative and intelligent automated system for interrupting electricity and gas supply in a building when hit by a disruptive earthquake.

The opportunity is also given by the recent regulation in Italy about the use of smart meters. A massive electricity smart meter deployment occurred in Italy starting from year 2000 (35 million meters installed). Nowadays, the second nation-wide deployment is going on for the installation of a second generation of smart meters linked to optical fibre telecommunication grids (Open Fiber project).

Contemporaneously, a large deployment of gas smart meters has been promoted by the Energy Regulator in Italy ending up in 2018 through the so-called "Directives for the installation of gas smart meters" as modified by the Deliberation of the Autorità Energia Elettrica e Gas 575/2012/R/gas [7]. The installation of an electro-valve remotely controllable is required among minimal features of gas smart meters.

Consequently, the rationale behind the proposed architecture is to use electro-valves available on gas smart meters and electrical switches to interrupt the supply in order to avoid secondary effects due to earthquakes.

2 Energy Router architecture

The Energy Router is a hardware/software system for managing and optimizing the complex of input or output energy flows from distributed generation devices, storage systems for electricity and user equipment in buildings. Cloud-based software components are adopted for field data analysis and optimization of energy resources. By means of the Energy Router, a small intelligent distribution system, and therefore a small smart grid or a nanogrid at a building or housing level, can be created that can generate an economic benefit for the user in terms of increase in the self-consumption, energy efficiency, renewable productivity, loss reduction, and sales of auxiliary services to the network.

The architecture of the energy router is hybrid and consists of two modules communicating with each other:

• the field section, installed in the building, and designed to control generation, storage and utilization systems, and to control energy flows;

• the cloud section that uses advanced software supervision and control software solutions using forecasting and optimization models that take into account the main input parameters (renewable generation, loads, etc.) and, on the other hand, they permit to optimize the use and management of distributed energy resources (distributed energy resources or DER), while ensuring safe plant management.

The performance that the system assures is related to intelligent energy distribution within the smart grid of the building, optimizing the use of storage systems and ensuring optimum use of the systems in order not to degrade their performance.

The potential of this equipment cannot be confined to the energy sector but it shows the possibility to develop further services for citizens and smart city applications.

Hereby the system is conceived to provide a source of information about seismic activity and control functions to shut down energy services, to eliminate or at least mitigate the secondary effects of earthquakes.

In fact, an additional function of the Energy Router is the management of the gas and power network in the presence of seismic events. The idea is to equip the device with an accelerometer able to detect seismic events and to intervene on the gas network by closing a solenoid valve and switch off power.

In particular, based on numerous studies that have experienced the use of accelerometers typical of electronic devices (smartphones) for detecting seismic events [6], the idea is to install a Micro Electro-Mechanical Systems (MEMS) type accelerometer in the Energy Router. Some experiments, for example [8], have shown how the LIS331DLH accelerometer type produced by STMicroelectronics is capable of faithfully recording earthquakes of moderate to severe magnitude.

In general, MEMS accelerometers in the 90s have revolutionized the automotive industry in the airbag industry and are now largely used in laptops, gaming peripherals and mobile phones. Numerous studies have been conducted on MEMS sensors in this field, even in previous years, with appreciable results [9-12]. Thanks to their low cost (few euros) and the small size (few millimeters), they could now be used in earthquake monitoring and alert systems for high-risk earthquake centres.

The device will be sized according to predetermined acceleration ranges, which will require earthquakes with magnitude and intensity of some relevance. The energy router, therefore, detected the hazard signal, will close the user's gas network to which it is connected, by means of a remote controlled solenoid valve. Many of the latest generation gas smart meters are equipped with such solenoid valves, otherwise they may opt for existing commercial systems that can interact with the wireless energy router. The same approach can be more easily applied to switch off power loads characterized by a higher risk to yield short circuits and consequently fires. Power loads linked to the connectivity, i.e. power supply to wireless or telecommunication systems, should not be switched off during earthquakes since experience showed that they resulted very useful to send emergency messages or to localize missing people under ruins.

3 Monitoring system

As usual, classical monitoring systems permit to detect the critical structural parameters of the structure (natural oscillation periods and modal shapes) in order to ensure effective maintenance/repair and a high safety standard [13-15]. These systems require a processing time of the acquired data that, depending on the size of the building and the number of monitored points, varies from minutes to hours. It therefore appears evident that the same technology cannot be used for the system proposed here, the objective of which is to immediately communicate during an earthquake the overcoming of a certain ground shaking threshold. Therefore, the field section and the energy cloud section of the energy router must communicate very quickly the order to shut down the gas grid and the power distribution network of the user to which it is connected.

To reach this objective, no checks on the spectral shapes or the contents of the recorded seismic signal (both at the base of the building and at the different levels) can be performed, since this kind of processing requires that all the seismic signal is exhausted [16]. In light of the above, the only control parameters that can be used are the instantaneous values of horizontal and vertical accelerations measured at the foundation's level (Figure 2). This is the only point where a real-time fast comparison can be made between the acceleration values measured by the sensor and those provided by the codes that define the "project earthquake". The structural dynamics on the upper levels depend on many variables that are difficult to evaluate especially for existing buildings: structural typology, materials composing the structure and their mechanical properties, geometry in plan and elevation, local ductility and global structure, distribution and mechanical properties of the partition walls, etc. [17].

The device, integrated into the energy router, will be sized based on predetermined acceleration ranges, which will require magnitude and intensity earthquakes of

DOI: 10.1051/matecconf/201712505012

some relevance. Criteria for selection of critical earthquakes are outlined in sect. 3. The energy router, once detected the hazard signal, will then shut down gas distribution and selected power loads.

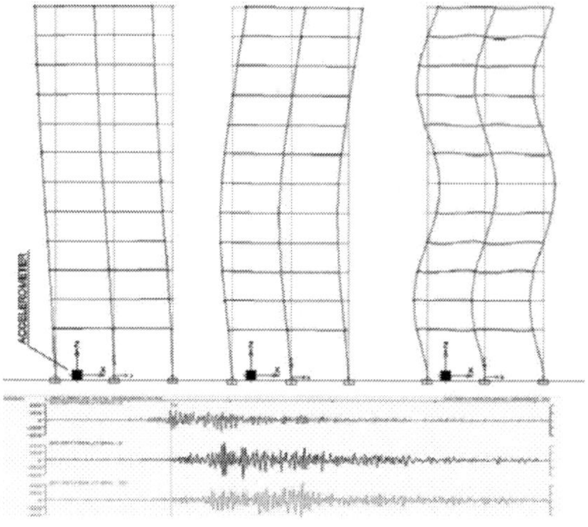

Fig. 2. A triaxial accelerometer must be positioned on the foundation ground of the building for a fast and immediate comparison of the acceleration peaks.

4 Definition of the vertical and horizontal acceleration thresholds

In the "New Technical Standards for Construction" D.M. Infrastructures 14/01/08 [4], sect. 3, the operational phases to define the design seismic actions to be considered for the design or verification of a building are introduced. These rules apply to both new and existing buildings.

The parameters that permit to deduce the "seismic load" are defined on the basis of a reference grid (Annex B, D.M. 14/01/08), which has been traced on Italian territory with a mesh of about 10 Km and that at each node it matches the values. Starting from the values in the nodes, for each point located on the territory by its geographic coordinates (longitude and latitude), it is possible to detect the seismic hazard parameters for a given return period T_R [4,5]. The return period is evaluated according to the Reference Life V_R function of the building and depending on its overcoming probability P_{VR} corresponding to the limit state that has to be analyzed [18]. It is clear from the outset that, for the purposes of this work, the limit state to which reference will be the damage one, that is to say, after an earthquake the construction as a whole, including structural and non-structural elements, equipment relevant to its function, is such that it does not endanger users and does not significantly compromise the strength and stiffness to vertical and horizontal actions, while keeping it in use, even if the equipment is partly interrupted.

Therefore, in order to determine the peak values of the expected horizontal and vertical accelerations to the ground for the Limit State of Damage, the following data are needed, but are easily obtainable:

1 - Municipality in which the building (longitude and latitude) insists;

2- Nominal life of the building (indicated in the structural design of the building);

3- Building Use Class (indicated in the structural design of the building, depending on the consequences of a breakdown of operation or a possible collapse of the building);

4- Stratigraphic and topographic nature of the layout (indicated in the structural design of the building by a coefficient S as defined in point 3.2.3.2.1 NTC-08).

From these, it is possible to obtain the return period TR of the seismic action for the State Limit of Damage, the corresponding horizontal acceleration values of the ground ag and the maximum value of the amplification factor F_0 [4, 5]. In Fig. 3, exemplifying, for example, the a_g and F_0 trends as the return period T_R varies. In the latter case, it is possible to obtain the values of the maximum horizontal $a_{max,O}$ and vertical $a_{max,V}$ accelerations through the following relationships:

$$a_{max,O} = a_g S \quad (1)$$

$$a_{max,V} = a_g S \cdot 1.35 \left(\frac{a_g}{g} \right)^{0.5} \quad (2)$$

where S is the recalled descriptive coefficient of the stratigraphic and topographic nature of the foundation soil.

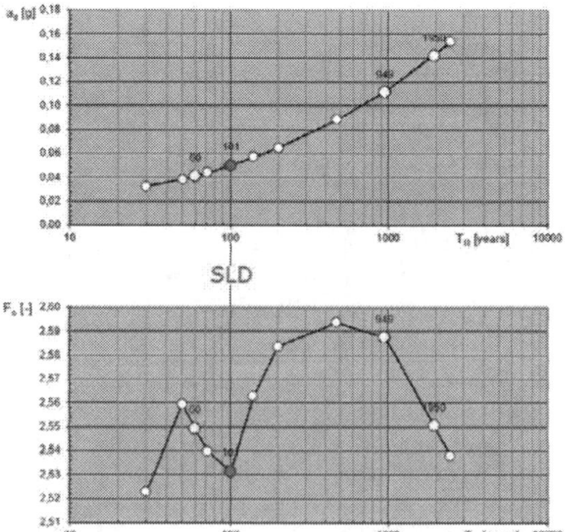

Fig. 3. a_g and F_0 vs. T_R (return period) for a building located in Verona (Italy) (long=11.2113; lat=45.193), with a Nominal Life equal to 100 years, Class of use II (constructions with normally crowded so as defined in sect. 2.4.2 NTC -08), foundation ground category of type C (point 3.2.2 NTC-08) and topographic condition T1 (table 3.2.IV NTC-08).

In order to determine the peak acceleration beyond which the system must interrupt the supply of electricity and gas, it must be considered that the horizontal motion of the ground occurs at the same time according to the two orthogonal directions x and y set by the designer being the direction of the earthquake completely generic. This is taken into account, considering that the, accelerations measured in both directions X and Y at any instant must respect the following ratio:

$$a_X^{\ 2} + a_Y^{\ 2} \leq a_{\max,O}^{\ \ 2} \tag{3}$$

For the vertical acceleration peak, instead, the following expression (4) must be applied:

$$a_Z \leq a_{\max,V} \tag{4}$$

All of the process described above can be briefly summarized with the block diagram shown in Fig. 4.

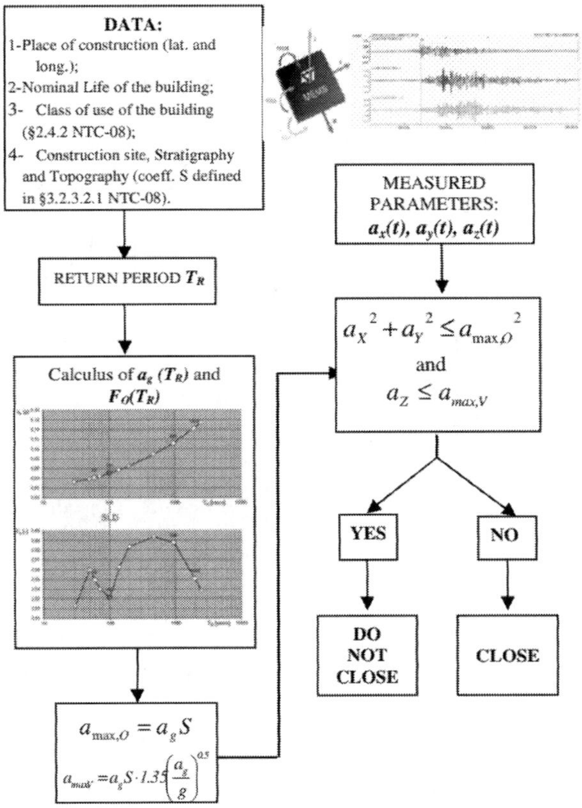

Fig. 4. Process to determine the horizontal and vertical thresholds.

5 Conclusions

In the present paper, an intelligent system has been introduced that, through the use of the Energy Router, enables to detect and communicate immediately to the gas and electricity distribution systems the occurrence of an earthquake whose accelerated peak has exceeded a certain threshold, appropriately calibrated. As mentioned in the first section, the existing structural legislation in Italy obliges designers to provide gas valve installations for automatic shutdown in case of earthquake. It is also specified that the risk of uncontrolled gas leaks should be limited, particularly close to electrical and flammable materials, by using breakers.

The system presented here envisages the use of MEMS (Micro Electro-Mechanical Systems) accelerometers typically used in laptops, gaming peripherals and mobile phones which, due to their low cost and small size, could now be used in large-scale earthquake monitoring and alert systems in high seismic areas.

For the field section and the cloud section of the energy router to communicate in real time the possibility of an earthquake and overcoming a certain acceleration threshold to close the gas grid and the power distribution network of the building, it is necessary to measure the horizontal and vertical accelerations at the foundation's level. Structural dynamics in the upper levels depend on many variables that are difficult to assess especially for existing buildings and therefore require a complex and long series of cognitive investigations that would undo the economic benefits of the system here presented.

In this paper is also presented a first algorithm that allows to determine the value of the horizontal and vertical acceleration threshold as a function of few and clear parameters, yet easily found in the structural design:

1. Municipality where the building is located;
2. Use Class of the building;
3. Nominal life of the building;
4. Stratigraphic and topographical nature of the foundation soil.

This procedure permit to personalize the acceleration peaks based on the nature, type and use destination of the building, in extremely fast times and maintaining the same level of reliability in terms of probability of overcoming the "project earthquake".

Acknowledgements

Massimo La Scala as Principal Investigator of the project "Energy Router" gratefully acknowledge Regione Puglia for funding the project under grant number HX8HXI1 and all the industrial partners participating in the project activities.

Dora Foti as Principal Investigator of the project "Mitigating the impacts of natural hazards on cultural heritage sites, structures and artefacts (MICHe)" acknowledges the Italian Ministry of Education, University and Research for support under a Project of Relevant National Interest PRIN 2015.

References

1. M. La Scala, S. Bruno, "From Smart Grids to Smart Cities: New Paradigms for Future Networks", introduction to M. La Scala, From Smart Grids to Smart Cities: New Challenges in Optimizing Energy Grids, pp. xvii-xliii, ISTE-Wiley, London-Hoboken(NJ), 2017.
2. S. Bruno, G. Giannoccaro, M. La Scala, Predictive control of demand and storage for residential

prosumers, to be presented at the 7th IEEE Technologies (IEEE PES ISGT Europe 2017), Turin, Italy, 26-29 September 2017.

3. O.P.C.M. 20/03/2003, n. 3274 (Suppl. Ord. alla G.U. 8.5.2003, N. 105), "Primi elementi in materia di criteri generali per la classificazione sismica del territorio nazionale e normative tecniche per le costruzioni in zona sismica". (*in Italian*)
4. NTC 2008 – Norme tecniche per le costruzioni – D.M. Infrastrutture 14 gennaio 2008. (in Italian)
5. Circolare 2 febbraio 2009, n. 617 (G.U. n. 47 del 26-2-2009 – Suppl Ord. n. 27) Istruzioni per l'applicazione delle "Nuove norme tecniche per le costruzioni" di cui al D.M. 14 gennaio 2008. (*in Italian*)
6. M. Cudicio, La protezione sismica degli elementi impiantistici: analisi, strategie, modelli ed esempi applicative. Legislazione tecnica, Ottobre (2014). (*in Italian*)
7. "Deliberazione 28 Dicembre 2012, 575/2012/R/GAS, Disposizioni in materia di piano di messa in servizio di gruppi di misura elettronici nell'ambito della distribuzione gas", Autorità per l'Energia Elettrica e il Gas. (*in Italian*)
8. Q. Kong, Y. Kwony, L. Schreierz, S. Allen, R. Allen, J.r Strauss, Smartphone-based networks for earthquake detection, 15th International Conference on Innovations for Community Services (I4CS), (2015).
9. A. D'Alessandro and G. D'Anna, Suitability of Low-Cost Three-Axis MEMS Accelerometers in Strong-Motion Seismology: Tests on the LIS331DLH (iPhone) Accelerometer, Bulletin of the Seismological Society of America, 103, 5, 2906–2913, October (2013).
10. A. D'Alessandro, D. Luzio, G. D'Anna, Urban MEMS based seismic network for post-earthquakes rapid disaster assessment, Adv. Geosci., 40, 1–9, (2014).
    International Conference on Innovative Smart Grid
11. A. D'Alessandro, Monitoring of earthquakes using MEMS sensors, Curr. Sci., 107, 733–734 (2014b).
12. A. Holland, Earthquake Data Recorded by the MEMS Accelerometer: Field Testing in Idaho, Seismological Research Letters, 74, 1, January/February (2003).
13. A. Mufti, Guidelines for Structural Health Monitoring, University of Manitoba, ISIS Canada (2001).
14. A.E. Aktan, S.K. Ciloglu, P.Q. Grimmelsman, F.N. Catbas, Opportunities and challenges in health monitoring of constructed systems by modal analysis, Proc. of the International Conference on Experimental Vibration Analysis for Civil Engineering Structures, Bordeaux, France (2005).
15. D. Foti, M. Diaferio, N.I. Giannoccaro, S. Ivorra, Structural identification and numerical models for slender historical structures. In: p. Asteris & V.Plevris (Eds.), Handbook of research on Seismic Assessment and Rehabilitation of Historic Structures. Hershey, PA: Eng. Science Reference, Chap 23, pp.674-703 (2015).
16. M. Diaferio, D. Foti, N.I. Giannoccaro, Non-destructive characterization and identification of the modal parameters of an old masonry tower. Proc. EESMS 2014-2014 IEEE Workshop on Environmental, Energy and Structural Monitoring Systems, Naples, Italy, 17-18 September (2014).
17. L. Zhang, R. Brincker, P. Andersen, An Overview of Operational Modal Analysis: Major Development and Issues, Proc. of the 1st IOMAC Conference, Copenhagen, Denmark (2005).
18. C. Rainieri, G. Fabbrocino, E. Cosenza, G. Manfredi, Implementation of OMA procedures using LabView, Proc. of the 2nd IOMAC Conference, Copenhagen, Denmark (2007).

MATEC Web of Conferences **125**, 05013 (2017) DOI: 10.1051/matecconf/201712505013
CSCC 2017

Development of Seasonal ARIMA Models for Traffic Noise Forecasting

Claudio Guarnaccia[1,*], *Nikos E.* Mastorakis[2], *Joseph* Quartieri[1], *Carmine* Tepedino[1] and *Stavros D.* Kaminaris[3]

[1]Department of Civil Engineering, University of Salerno, via Giovanni Paolo II 132, Fisciano, Italy
[2]Department of Electrical Engineering and Computer Science, Hellenic Naval Academy, Piraeus, Greece
[3]Department of Electrical Engineering, Piraeus University of Applied Sciences, Athens, Greece

Abstract. In this paper, a time series analysis approach is adopted to monitor and predict a traffic noise levels dataset, measured in a site of Messina, Italy. In general, acoustical noise shows a high prediction complexity, since its slope is strongly related to the variability of the sources and to intrinsic randomness. In the analysed site the predominant source is road traffic, that has a periodic and non-stationary behaviour. The study of the time evolution of this hazardous agent is very useful to assess the impact to human health and activities. The time series models adopted in this paper are of the stochastic seasonal ARIMA class; these types of model are based on the strong periodicity registered in the acoustical equivalent levels. The observed periodicity is related to the highly variability of urban traffic in the different days of the week. Three different seasonal ARIMA models are proposed and calibrated on a rich dataset of 800 sound level measurements. The predictive capabilities of these techniques are encouraging. The implemented models show a good forecasting performances in terms of low residuals, i.e. difference between observed and estimated noise values. The residuals are analysed by means of statistical indexes, plots and tests.

1 Introduction

The health of the population of urban areas is often threatened by the action of different pollutants [1]. Among them, the most common and dangerous are gases from combustion phenomena, high intensity electromagnetic fields and acoustical noise produced by transportation infrastructures and other human activities [2]. It is therefore essential to constantly monitor these pollutants but it is generally expensive and not always easy to implement. In addition, mitigation actions on pollution sources are usually adopted only when malicious agents are particularly high and hence have already influenced the health of citizens. High and dangerous acoustic levels are mainly caused by anthropic activities, in particular vehicular traffic and other transportation infrastructures. Therefore, it is clear that it is useful to implement analytical models that can provide a reliable assessment of the levels of pollution (see for instance [3-13]). If a reliable forecast is available, it is possible to limit the overcoming of certain levels of pollution by mitigation measures, also acting on the sources, before physical agents can affect the population. The authors gave a large contribution to transportation noise assessment and prediction (see for instance [14-30]).

Largely adopted forecasting models are often based on the study of correlations or causal effects that influence the sources of the noise pollution levels. However, due to the nature of the physical phenomenon, in the case of acoustic noise, it is very difficult to predict the effects in a restricted area by studying only the sources. Such a method can be strongly influenced either by the architecture of the area where the measurements are acquired or other environmental interferences which are random and variable over time. Therefore, the interest in predictive models that exploit the information contained in measurements at the receiver, is increasing: these techniques include analytical models of time series. The authors have developed and improved various deterministic and stochastic models useful for modelling and predicting univariate time series, see for example [31-37].

In this paper, three different models of time series analysis, useful for predicting the noise level in urban areas, have been developed. The predictive models considered here are of the stochastic class: in particular three different types of Seasonal Auto-Regressive Integrated Moving Average (SARIMA) functions have been developed. The SARIMA can predict the evolution of noise levels for a given time interval in a specific area of interest, i.e. the area where the data used to estimate the parameters (calibration) of the forecasting function have been acquired.

A set of noise measurements recorded during the daytime in the city of Messina, Italy, is used to calibrate the models. These data consist of daily equivalent sound pressure levels ($L_{A,eq}$), averaged over sixteen hours (from 6:00 a.m. to 10:00 p.m.).

* Corresponding author: cguarnaccia@unisa.it

To determine the best model to describe the analysed time series, a complete statistical characterization of the 800 measured data was realized. The noise level series is characterized by an high auto-correlation for a seven-day lag: this characteristic is due to the strong dependence of vehicular traffic from the day of the week. In fact, since on Saturdays and Sundays the traffic flows are lower than during working days, the measured acoustic levels were significantly influenced by this periodicity and during the weekend showed lower values with respect to other days of the week. For this periodic behaviour, seasonal stochastic models are adopted that take into account the high periodicity of the series studied. Due to the non-stationary nature of the data, some models provide for the adoption of differences operators that make the proposed models of the "integrated" type. To point at the best model, a comparison between the measured data and the forecasted level is performed. Therefore, in the final part of the paper, the analysis of the residuals is carried out both qualitatively by graphs and quantitatively using different error metrics. The three models provide a good approximation of the observed series and may indeed be useful to describe and predict the acoustic noise in the studied site.

2 Methods

In many scientific fields, it is useful to mathematically describe and predict the evolution over time of a given variable under study. This univariate time series can be modelled, for instance, by a deterministic decomposition model, able to extend the forecast to many periods in the future. Such model typology has been widely adopted by authors for the study of acoustic noise [31-35], concentration of gaseous pollutants [36] and for the evolution of electricity consumption [37].

However, when the studied phenomenon presents rapid fluctuations and a short-term forecast is useful, a stochastic model can be more suitable. In this paper, three different stochastic models of the auto-regressive moving-average type have been implemented, also using differentiation operators on an acoustical noise dataset. The proposed models are of the seasonal class, so they use the weekly periodicity present in the analysed data. Therefore, the adopted models belongs to the multiplicative Seasonal ARIMA type, generally indicated by the acronym ARIMA (p, d, q)x(P, D, Q)$_s$, where p indicates the degree of autoregressive polynomial, d indicates the number of applied differentiations, q indicates the degree of the moving average polynomial. The seasonality period is indicated by the number s, with its seasonal autoregressive (P) and moving average (Q) polynomials, and D seasonal differentiations.

In general such a model is defined as a model with AR characteristic polynomial $\phi(x)\Phi(x)$ and MA characteristic polynomial $\theta(x)\Theta(x)$, [38], where:

$$\begin{cases} \phi(x) = 1 - \phi_1 x - \phi_2 x^2 - \cdots - \phi_p x^p \\ \Phi(x) = 1 - \Phi_1 x^s - \Phi_2 x^{2s} - \cdots - \Phi_P x^{Ps} \end{cases}; \quad (1)$$

$$\begin{cases} \theta(x) = 1 - \theta_1 x - \theta_2 x^2 - \cdots - \theta_q x^q \\ \Theta(x) = 1 - \Theta_1 x^s - \Theta_2 x^{2s} - \cdots - \Theta_Q x^{Qs} \end{cases}. \quad (2)$$

The forecast is built using the latest available data in the series, so the model is able to easily track the time fluctuations of the studied series by adapting rapidly to data changes. In addition, it is necessary to estimate few coefficients to construct the model function, so the principle of parsimony is respected. In this paper, the method of likelihood function maximization is adopted to estimate model coefficients, using the 800 acoustical data measured in Messina in the calibration phase.

3 Models accuracy evaluation

Model diagnostics is concerned with testing the goodness of fit of a proposed predictive technique. An effective methodology to test model performance is based on the residual analysis: graphs and plots, statistical indexes and error metrics are good strategies to test models adequacy. Estimated residuals ($\hat{e}_t$), in the ideal situation, correspond to the stochastic component present in a time series (e_t) that is considered to take into account irregularity of the dataset and it is not deterministic predictable.

Estimated residuals may be computed in the calibration phase of the modelling process, i.e. when the measurements are available, as the subtraction between actual data and predicted values at a given period t:

$$\hat{e}_t = Y_t - \hat{Y}_t \,. \quad (3)$$

The general assumption is that the irregular term e_t is normally distributed and, if the model is correctly specified and the parameter estimates are reasonably close to the true values, estimated residuals should appear distributed like white noise. They should behave roughly like independent, normally distributed variables, characterized by a null mean [38].

In the next sections, a comparison between the residuals of the three proposed SARIMA models, calibrated in the same data range, will be presented.

In order to estimate the models accuracy, the statistical features of the estimated residuals, will be studied. Descriptive plots of the computed residuals will be shown to perform a qualitative analysis; frequencies histograms will be presented together with quantile-quantile plots and autocorrelation plots. A quantitative analysis will be performed using residual statistics, that are mean, standard deviation, median, min and max values. In addition, skewness and kurtosis indexes will be calculated to evaluate the normality of the distributions.

To evaluate residuals distortion from the mean value and dispersion around mean, quantitative metrics of error are given by the "Mean Percentage Error" (MPE) and "Coefficient of Variation of the Error" (CVE), according to the definition reported in [32].

An effective measurement of forecast accuracy is also the "Mean Absolute Scaled Error" (MASE) [39]. The MASE for seasonal time series is computed according to the following formula:

$$MASE = \frac{1}{n}\sum_{t=1}^{n}\frac{|e_t|}{\frac{1}{n-k}\sum_{i=k+1}^{n}|Y_i-Y_{i-k}|} \quad . \qquad (4)$$

MASE is computed using as "naïve" model [40] in the denominator, the value measured in the series k periods before the period t , assuming that the period t can replicate the observed value at time t-k.

Considering the fact that parameters of the models are estimated using the method of the likelihood maximization, also the Akaike's Information Criterion (AIC) is proposed to evaluate models performances. This criterion suggests to select the model that minimizes:

$$AIC = -2\log(maximum\ likelihood) + 2k \ , \quad (5)$$

where $k = p + q + 1$ if the model has an intercept or a constant terms, $k = p + q$ otherwise.

4 Data analysis and model specification

An acoustical data set related to the city of Messina, located in Sicily, in the south of Italy, has been analysed with the proposed forecasting models. The main sources of noise pollution are car traffic and typical anthropic activities of a medium-sized city. Indeed, the city of Messina has about 240000 inhabitants and, among the various problems of pollution distinctive of a medium urban agglomeration, also shows persistent acoustical noise caused by vehicular traffic. In different areas of the city the local administration has located noise monitoring stations, in which fixed and mobile sound level meters are installed. Therefore, time series of acoustical levels are available to study the noise pollution phenomenon. In this paper, the authors have taken into account the equivalent daily level, weighted with the "A" weighting curve, registered in the site of "Via La Farina".

The measurement of road traffic noise was carried out by the "Environmental Monitoring Service" of Messina.

The noise series used for this study refers to the daily time period: from 6:00 am to 10:00 pm and 800 data will be used in the calibration phase of the models. This time series is composed by 628 measured data and 172 data imputed using the technique described in [41]. The observational period starts on the 22nd of April 2008 and finishes on the 30th of June 2010. The summary statistics of the data are shown in Table 1. The observed mean level of about 71 dBA is very high considering the urban residential area under study and this level, considering the low standard deviation and spread, is persistent during the observation period.

In Fig. 1, the analysed series is plotted in the time domain: the seasonal nature of the acoustical level is evident. The weekly periodicity is confirmed also by the correlogram plot of the observed data, that shows the maximum autocorrelation for a lag of seven days (Fig. 2).

To infer the structure of a stochastic process from the time series of that process is necessary to make some simplifying and reasonable assumptions; the most important of these is stationarity [38]. Thus, to build an effective seasonal ARMA model is useful that the series is stationary: to achieve this goal, the technique of the differentiation is adopted. Figure 3 shows the autocorrelation plots of the series after three diverse differentiations choices: 3(a) refers to a difference at lag one; 3(b) refers to a difference at lag seven (seasonal difference); 3(c) refers to the series after a first difference at lag one and a second difference at lag seven.

Table 1. Summary statistics of the 800 observed acoustical levels measured during the calibration period.

Mean [dBA]	Std. Dev. [dBA]	Median [dBA]	Min [dBA]	Max [dBA]	Skew	Kurt
70.78	1.50	71.25	66.0	74.0	-1.18	0.48

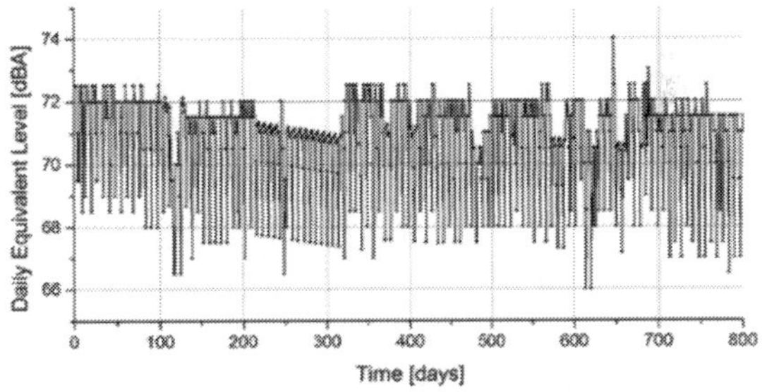

Fig. 1. Observed daily equivalent levels in the 800 calibration periods.

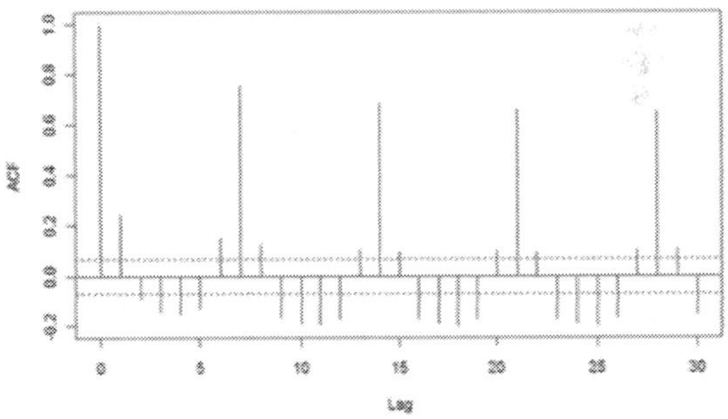

Fig. 2. Correlogram plot for the first 800 days of the series. The value of autocorrelation is plotted as a function of the lag.

5 SARIMA models details

In the previous section, the time series under study has been described from the statistical point of view. In this section three different SARIMA models are designed and applied to mathematically reproduce the observed acoustical phenomenon. Two models use the differencing technique to obtain a stationary series. All the three adopted models belong to the seasonal multiplicative class. Parameters estimation for all the proposed models is obtained using the maximum likelihood method implemented in the *R* software.

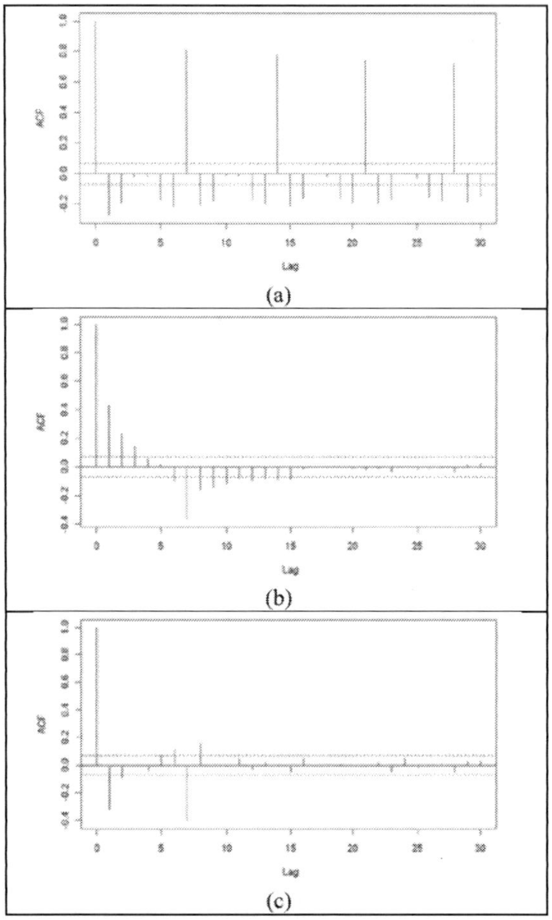

Fig. 3. Correlogram plots for the first 800 days of the series after differencing. (a) correlogram of the series after a difference at lag one; (b) correlogram of the series after a difference at lag 7; (c) correlogram of the series after a first difference at lag one and a second difference at lag 7.

5.1 Seasonal autoregressive moving average (0,1,1)x(0,1,1)$_7$ model

The first model adopted is a Seasonal ARIMA with seasonal lag equal to seven days ($s = 7$): according to the most used notation the model is a SARIMA (0,1,1)x(0,1,1)$_7$ type. Recalling what presented in Section 2, the model can be formulated as follows:

$$Y_t = Y_{t-1} + Y_{t-7} - Y_{t-8} + e_t - \theta e_{t-1} - \Theta e_{t-7} + \\ + \theta\Theta e_{t-8} \quad (6)$$

$$\hat{Y}_{t+1} = Y_t + Y_{t-6} - Y_{t-7} - \theta\hat{e}_t - \Theta\hat{e}_{t-6} + \\ + \theta\Theta\hat{e}_{t-7} \quad (7)$$

Looking at Fig. 3(c) seems reasonable that a simple model is adequate, so after taking both a first difference at lag one and a second difference at lag seven, only a negative autocorrelation remains, for lag 1 and 7. In table 2, the numerical values of the two moving average coefficients are reported. Those two estimated coefficients have a low standard error with respect to their absolute value, so the null value for the coefficients can be neglected. Figure 4 shows that this parsimonious model is able to correctly reproduce the general behaviour of the studied seasonal series. The measured acoustical level is tellingly lower than predicted one around the 550th period, but usually, in this kind of environmental application, a model that overestimates a pollutant level is preferable than an underestimating one.

Table 2. Estimated value of the coefficients adopted by the SARIMA (0,1,1)x(0,1,1)$_7$ model.

Coefficients	**Estimated Value**	**Standard Error**
MA1(θ)	0.7078	0.0387
SMA1(Θ)	0.8966	0.0306
Log likelihood = -974.39; AIC = 1954.78		

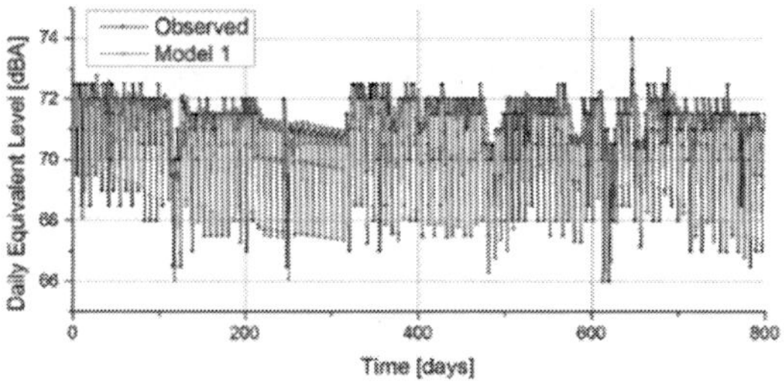

Fig. 4. Comparison between the observed 800 calibration data and the levels in the same periods predicted by the SARIMA (0,1,1)x(0,1,1)$_7$ model.

5.2 Seasonal autoregressive (7,1,0)x(0,1,0)$_7$ model

The second model adopted is again a Seasonal ARIMA with seasonal lag equal to seven days ($s = 7$); more precisely the model can be identified as a SARIMA (7,1,0)x(0,1,0)$_7$ type. In the following formulas, y_t is the differenced (i.e. "stationarized") series:

$$y_t = Y_t - Y_{t-1} - Y_{t-7} + Y_{t-8} \quad (8)$$

$$\hat{y}_{t+1} = \phi_1 y_t + \phi_2 y_{t-1} + \phi_3 y_{t-2} + \phi_4 y_{t-3} + \\ + \phi_5 y_{t-4} + + \phi_6 y_{t-5} + \phi_7 y_{t-6} \quad (9)$$

This second model is based on the assumption that all the useful information is contained in the past seven periods of the series respect to the forecasted day. The model adopt both first and seasonal differentiation and only autoregressive terms. In table 3, it is possible to notice that the coefficients of the AR5 and AR6 terms are not different from zero by a statistical point of view, thus one can conclude that noise levels measured five and six days before do not significantly affect the forecasts of acoustical levels. The good predictive performances of this model, in a one step ahead forecasting during the 800 observed days, is shown in figure 5.

Table 3. Estimated values of the coefficients adopted by the SARIMA (7,1,0)x(0,1,0)$_7$ model.

Coefficients	Estimated Value	Standard Error
AR1(ϕ)	-0.3921	0.0330
AR2(ϕ)	-0.2703	0.0359
AR3(ϕ)	-0.1987	0.0375
AR4(ϕ)	-0.1524	0.0377
AR5(ϕ)	-0.0442	0.0374
AR6(ϕ)	0.0020	0.0362
AR7(ϕ)	-0.3763	0.0337
Log likelihood = -1052.27; AIC = 2118.54		

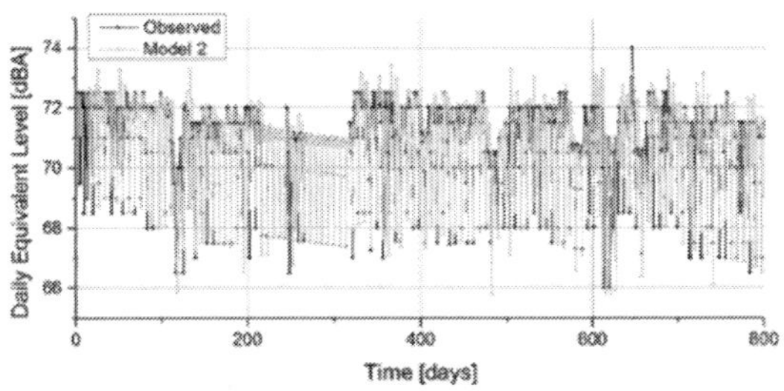

Fig. 5. Comparison between the observed 800 calibration data and the levels in the same periods predicted by the SARIMA (7,1,0)x(0,1,0)s$_7$ model.

5.3 Seasonal autoregressive moving average (0,0,1)x(1,0,0)$_7$ model

The third model adopted is a SARIMA (0,0,1)x(1,0,0)$_7$, that is slightly different from the previous, since the intercept m is not null. The basic model and the forecast equation are:

$$Y_t = m + \Phi(Y_{t-7} - m) + e_t - \theta e_{t-1} \qquad (10)$$

$$\hat{Y}_{t+1} = m + \Phi(Y_{t-6} - m) - \theta \hat{e}_t \qquad (11)$$

Table 4. Estimated values of the coefficients adopted by the SARIMA (0,0,1)x(1,0,0)$_7$ model.

Coefficients	Estimated Value	Standard Error
Intercept	70.7876	0.1924
MA1(θ)	-0.3535	0.0295
SAR1(Φ)	0.7833	0.0218
Log likelihood = -1052.88; AIC = 2111.77		

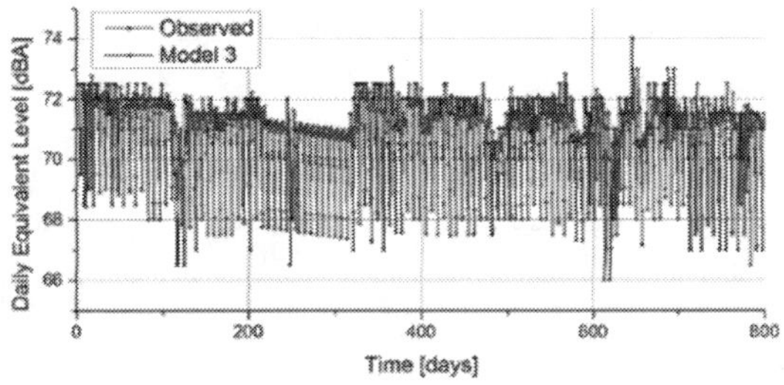

Fig. 6. Comparison between the observed 800 calibration data and the levels in the same periods predicted by the SARIMA (0,0,1)x(1,0,0)$_7$ model.

This third model differs from the others because it does not apply the differentiation operator on the time series under study. In general, the differentiation has the aim to make the data stationary and the standard assumption is that stationary series have a zero mean. In the adopted model, a nonzero constant mean is fulfilled introducing the intercept term m, in this case about 70.8 dBA as shown in Table 4.

Also the third proposed model, with the intercept term, shows good predictive performances: in Figure 6 the general behaviour of the series is well reproduced.

6 Model diagnostics and residual analysis

In this section a statistical analysis of the forecasting errors, denoted in the calibration phase whit the term "residuals" and defined in the formula (3), is performed. In table 5, measurements of central tendency and dispersion for the three models are reported, together with the minimum and maximum value of the residuals and skewness and kurtosis indexes. These results show that all the three models are capable of a good forecasting in the calibration dataset: mean and standard deviation are very low and the distributions of the error are almost symmetrical. In some specific periods, the three models are not able to follow drastic fluctuations of the acoustical noise, so the minimum and maximum values of the residuals exceed 5 dBA. An outlier detection and removal analysis could improve these parameters, reducing the value of minimum and maximum residuals.

In table 6, values of the error metrics presented in section 3 are shown. No one of the three models appears to be better than the others: MPE and CVE are always very low, MASE is lower than 1 for all the models and AIC values are similar.

Table 7 reports the values of Shapiro-Wilk [42] and Jarque-Bera [43] normality tests. Both the tests reject the null hypothesis of a normal distributed sample: rapid fluctuations of the acoustical noise are not well described by the three models, so the tails of the residuals distribution deviate from a normal shape.

Table 5. Summary statistics of the residuals distribution evaluated on the calibration dataset for the three models.

	Mean [dBA]	Std. Dev. [dBA]	Median [dBA]	Min [dBA]	Max [dBA]	Skew	Kurt
Mod1	0.02	0.84	0.03	-5.46	5.00	-0.67	8.44
Mod2	0.00	0.89	0.00	-5.12	5.09	-0.22	6.90
Mod3	-0.01	0.88	0.02	-5.10	4.35	-0.41	6.40

Table 6. MPE, CVE, MASE (error metrics) and AIC values calculated in the calibration phase, for the three different models.

	MPE	CVE	MASE	AIC
Model 1	0.013	0.012	0.905	1954.78
Model 2	-0.008	0.000	0.972	2118.54
Model 3	-0.026	0.000	0.983	2111.77

Table 7. Shapiro-Wilk and Jarque-Bera normality tests performed to residuals of the models applied to the 800 calibration data.

	Shapiro-Wilk statistic	Shapiro-Wilk p-value	Jarque-Bera statistic	Jarque-Bera df	Jarque-Bera p-value
Mod1	0.8771	2.2e-16	2403.7	2	2.2e-16
Mod2	0.8968	2.2e-16	1576.5	2	2.2e-16
Mod3	0.9028	2.2e-16	1306.6	2	2.2e-16

In figures 7, 8 and 9, three plots that describe the features of the residual distributions are reported, respectively for the three models. The almost normal distribution of residuals for all the models is a good result, since it is characteristic of casual and not systematic forecasting errors. In figure 7a, a residual autocorrelation for lags of one and seven days is still present. The second model shows a significant negative autocorrelation in the residuals, only for a lag of 14 days (see figure 8a). Finally, the third adopted model has autocorrelation in the residuals for lags of two and seven days (figure 9a).

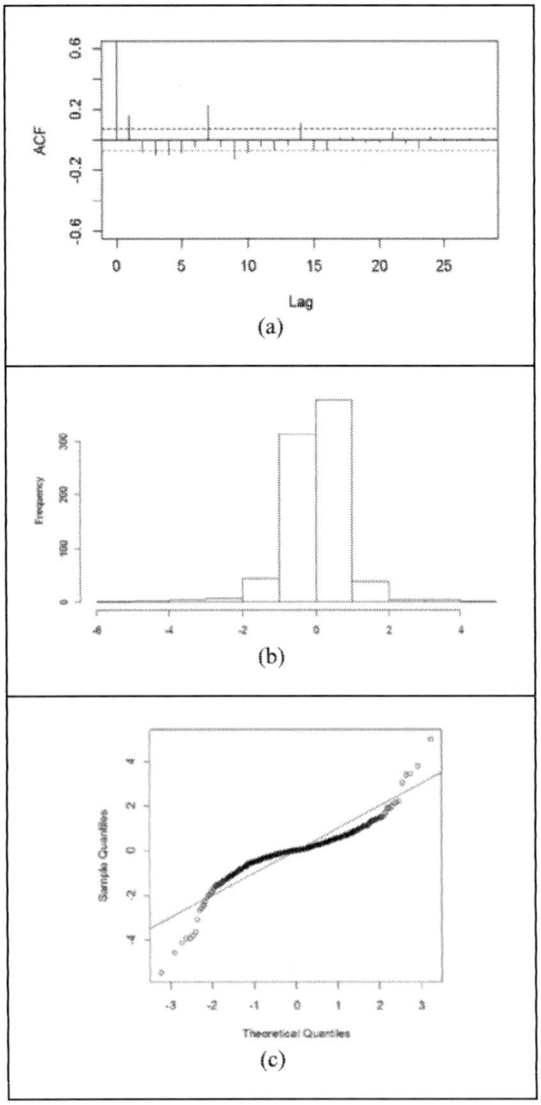

Fig. 7. Residuals of the first model applied to the 800 calibration data: (a) correlogram plot; (b) histogram; (c) normal probability plot that describes the residuals behaviour compared to a normal distribution.

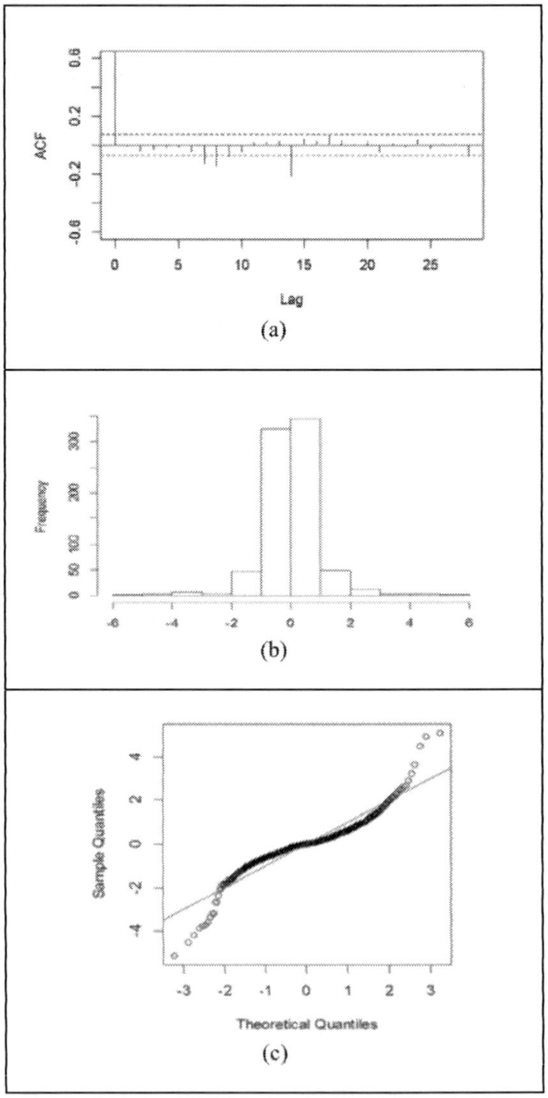

Fig. 8. Residuals of the second model applied to the 800 calibration data: (a) correlogram plot; (b) histogram; (c) normal probability plot that describes the residuals behaviour compared to a normal distribution.

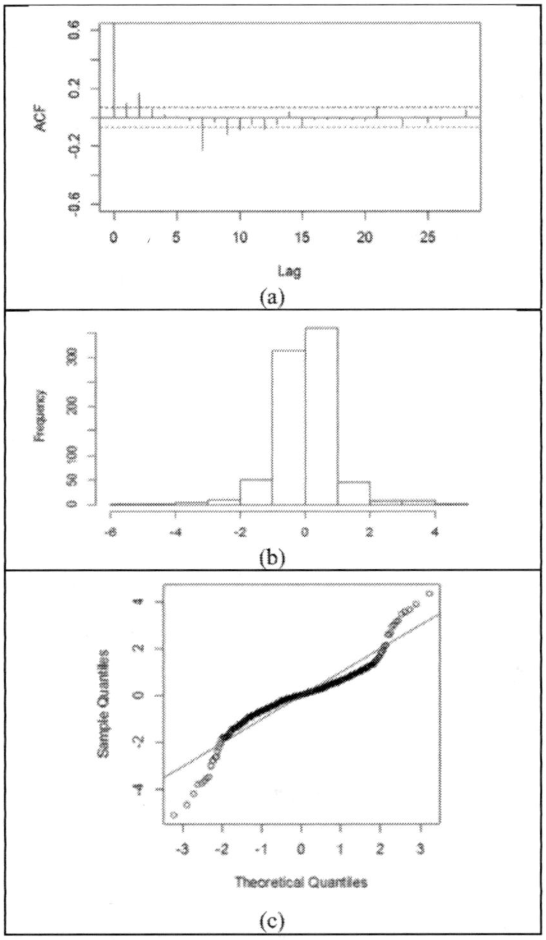

Fig. 9. Residuals of the third model applied to the 800 calibration data: (a) correlogram plot; (b) histogram; (c) normal probability plot that describes the residuals behaviour compared to a normal distribution.

7 Conclusions

In this work a time series of urban noise levels has been analysed. The aim of this analysis was the design of a forecasting model able to monitor and predict noise pollution in any urban area. The studied time series was composed by sound level measurements registered in a large and crowded road of the city of Messina, Italy.

Since the analysed series showed an evident periodic behaviour, the three proposed models were of the seasonal ARIMA typology. Higher noise levels have been measured during working days of the week, while, on the contrary, Saturday and Sunday the reduction of the anthropogenic activities (and of the traffic flows) implicated a lower level of noise pollution. The mean value of the measured acoustical levels (70.78 dBA) was quite high considering that the studied location was near many residential buildings.

Two of the three proposed models used the data differentiation technique to achieve better stationarity of the time series. The 800 daily acoustical levels of the studied time series have been used to estimate the coefficients of the adopted models in the calibration phase of the modelling procedure.

These calibration data have been also used for a quantitative comparison between the performances of the three models. The comparison was performed by means of residuals analysis. The three models showed good performances in terms of low standard deviation and close to zero mean value of the residuals distributions. Frequency histograms and Q-Q plots of the residuals showed that the residuals are quite normally distributed. However, no one of the proposed models was able to follow casual and sudden fluctuations of noise level, thus the tails of residuals distributions differed from the normal shape.

Finally, thanks to the MASE error metric, it has been observed that the three proposed models offered a prediction that on average was better than the chosen naive model. As naive model, taking into account the strong autocorrelation of seven period, it was assumed that a reference forecast can be obtained by assuming that the period *t* may replicate the observed value at period *t*-7. The MASE confirmed this remark since for the three proposed models this error metric is less than one.

References

1. E. Kahn, *Brookings Institution Press*, Washington, DC, USA, (2006)
2. J. Quartieri, A. Troisi, C. Guarnaccia, P. D'Agostino, S. D'Ambrosio, G. Iannone, Proc. of the WSEAS Int. Conf. EED'09, (Puerto de la Cruz, Tenerife (Spain), 14-16 December 2009)
3. M. Cárdenas Rodríguez, L. Dupont-Courtade, W. Oueslati, Renewable and Sustainable Energy Rev. Vol. 53, Pages 1–9, January (2016)
4. P. E. Kirrian Fiedler, P. H. Trombetta Zannin, Environmental Impact Assessment Rev. Vol. **51**, Pages 1–9, February (2015)
5. J. Prezelj, J. Murovec, Appl. Acou. Vol. **127**, pp. 160-168, December (2017)
6. V. Barone, D. W. Edvige Mongelli and A. Tassitani, J. of Adv. Transp., in press, (2017)
7. Bao-Lin Ye, W. Wu, H. Gao, Y. Lu, Q. Cao and L. Zhu, Appl. Sci. Vol. **7**(6), 588, pp. 1-17, (2017)
8. C. Guarnaccia, WSEAS Trans. on Systems Vol. **12**(2), pp. 121-130 (2013)
9. J. Quartieri, N.E. Mastorakis, G. Iannone, C. Guarnaccia, S. D'Ambrosio, A. Troisi, T.L.L. Lenza, Proc. of the 5th WSEAS *Int. Conf.* MECHANICS'09, Puerto de la Cruz, Tenerife, Spain, December 14-16 (2009)
10. C. Guarnaccia, N. E. Mastorakis, J. Quartieri, Int. J. of Mech. Vol. **7**(2), pp 37-44 (2013)
11. C. Guarnaccia, J. Quartieri, A. Ruggiero, Int. J. of Mech. Vol. **8**, pp. 298-306 (2014)
12. F. Bunn, P. H. Trombetta Zannin, Appl. Acou. Vol. **104**, Pages 16–23, (March 2016)

13. A. Ruggiero, J. Quartieri, C. Guarnaccia, S. Hloch, Int. J. of Environmental Research, Vol. **9** (4), pp.1277-1286, (2015)
14. J. Quartieri, A. Troisi, C. Guarnaccia, T.L.L. Lenza, P. D'Agostino, S. D'Ambrosio, G. Iannone, WSEAS Trans. on Systems Vol. **8**(6), pp. 673-682 (2009)
15. J. Quartieri, A. Troisi, C. Guarnaccia, T.L.L. Lenza, P. D'Agostino, S. D'Ambrosio, G. Iannone, WSEAS Trans. on Systems Vol. **8**(4), pp. 481-490 (2009)
16. J. Quartieri, A. Troisi, C. Guarnaccia, T.L.L. Lenza, P. D'Agostino, S. D'Ambrosio, G. Iannone, in Proc. of the 10th WSEAS *Int. Conf. AMTA '09*, Prague (Rep.Ceca), 23-25 March (2009)
17. J. Quartieri, A. Troisi, C. Guarnaccia, T.L.L. Lenza, P. D'Agostino, S. D'Ambrosio, G. Iannone, Proc. of the 10th WSEAS *Int. conf.* AMTA '09, Prague (Rep.Ceca), 23-25 March (2009)
18. C. Guarnaccia, T.L.L. Lenza, N.E. Mastorakis, J. Quartieri, Int. J. of Mech. Vol. **5**(4), pp. 379-386, (2011)
19. C. Guarnaccia, WSEAS Trans. on Systems Vol. **9**(8), pp.865-874, (2010)
20. G. Iannone, C. Guarnaccia, J. Quartieri, Env. Eng. And Manag. J. Vol. **12**(3), pp. 493-501 (2013)
21. J. Quartieri, G. Iannone, C. Guarnaccia, Proc. of the 11th WSEAS *Int. Conf.* AMTA '10, Iasi, Romania, June 13-15 (2010)
22. C. Guarnaccia, J. Quartieri, Int. J. of Math. Models and Methods in Applied Sciences **6**(8), pp. 926-933, (2012)
23. G. Iannone, C. Guarnaccia, J. Quartieri, *in Recent Researches in Geography, Geology, Energy, Environment and Biomedicine*, Proc. of the 4th WSEAS *Int. Conf.* EMESEG '11, Corfù Island, Greece, July 14-16 (2011)
24. J. Quartieri, N.E. Mastorakis, C. Guarnaccia, G. Iannone, Proc. of the 12th *Int. Conf.* ACMOS '10, Catania (Italy), May 29-31 (2010)
25. C. Guarnaccia, Proc. of the 11th WSEAS *Int. Conf.* AMTA '10, (Iasi, Romania, June 13-15 2010)
26. J. Quartieri, N.E. Mastorakis, C. Guarnaccia, A. Troisi, S. D'Ambrosio, G. Iannone, Proc. of the 5th WSEAS *Int. Conf.* MECHANICS '09, Puerto de la Cruz, Tenerife, Spain, December 14-16 (2009)
27. C. Guarnaccia, J. Quartieri, N.E. Mastorakis, C. Tepedino, Int. J. of Mech. Vol. **10**, pp. 14-22, (2016)
28. C. Guarnaccia, J. Quartieri, J.M. Barrios, E.R. Rodrigues, J. of the Acou. Society of America Vol. **136**, (2014)
29. C. Guarnaccia, J. Quartieri, C. Tepedino, E.R. Rodrigues, Appl. Acou. Vol. **91**, pp. 33-39, (2015)
30. J.M. Bandeira, C. Guarnaccia, P. Fernandes, M.C. Coelho, Int. J. of Intelligent Transportation Systems Research Vol. **7**, (2016)
31. C. Guarnaccia, J. Quartieri, C. Tepedino, E. R. Rodrigues, Appl. Acou. Vol. **114**, pp. 203–212 (2016)
32. C. Guarnaccia, J. Quartieri, N.E. Mastorakis, C. Tepedino, WSEAS Trans. on Systems Vol. **13**, pp. 745-756, (2014)
33. C. Guarnaccia, J. Quartieri, E.R. Rodrigues, C. Tepedino, Int. J. of Math. Models and Methods in Applied Sciences Vol. **8**, pp 384-393, (2014)
34. C. Guarnaccia, J. Quartieri and C. Tepedino, in Proc. of the Int. Conf. on Applied Mathematics and Computer Science, AIP Conference Proceedings 1836, pp. 1-7, (2017)
35. C. Guarnaccia, J. Quartieri and C. Tepedino, in Proc. of the Int. Conf. on Applied Mathematics and Computer Science, AIP Conference Proceedings 1836, pp. 1-8, (2017)
36. C. Guarnaccia, J.G. Cerón Bretón, J. Quartieri, C. Tepedino, R.M. Cerón Bretón, Int. J. of Math. Models and Methods in Applied Sciences Vol. **8**, pp 505-515, (2014)
37. C. Tepedino, C. Guarnaccia, S. Iliev, S. Popova and J. Quartieri, Int. J. of Math. Models and Methods in Applied Sciences Vol. **9**, pp 432-445, (2015)
38. P.D. Cryer, K. Chan, Second Edition, Springer, (2008)
39. P.H. Franses, Int. J. of Forecasting **32**, pp. 20–22 (2016)
40. R.J. Hyndman, G. Athanasopoulos, OTexts, (2013)
41. C. Guarnaccia, J. Quartieri, C. Tepedino, L. Petrovic, Int. J. of Mech. Vol. **9**, pp. 272-278, (2015)
42. Shapiro S.S., Wilk M.B., *Biometrika* Vol. **52**, N. 3/4, pp. 591-611 (1965)
43. Jarque C. M., Bera A. K., *International Statistical Review* 55, 163–172 (1987)

Acoustic Emissions analysis of a four-point bending test on a Reinforced Concrete beam

Corrado Chisari[1], *Claudio* Guarnaccia[1,*], *Nicola* Lamberti[2], *Vincenzo* Piluso[1], *Joseph* Quartieri[1], and *Gianvittorio* Rizzano[1]

[1]University of Salerno, Department of Civil Engineering, via Giovanni Paolo II, 132 - 84084 Fisciano (SA), Italy
[2]University of Salerno, Department of Industrial Engineering, via Giovanni Paolo II, 132 - 84084 Fisciano (SA), Italy

Abstract. Assessment of existing structures by means of non-destructive techniques is an important research topic in modern engineering, because of its potential in estimating structural health status without introducing undesired damage. Among several recognized techniques, Acoustic Emission (AE) analysis is growing interest in the scientific community, since it can be used to detect the initiation of cracking processes, to determine cracking typology and to extract other information from the specimen. In this paper, the authors present the results of a four-point bending test on a Reinforce Concrete (RC) beam, performed at the University of Salerno. The test has been conducted according to a loading protocol characterised by several loading-unloading cycles, and both mechanical and acoustic data have been recorded. The results will be presented in terms of standard AE parameters, commonly adopted in literature, such as Felicity ratio, signal strength and cumulative signal strength, historic index and b value. It will be underlined that these parameters allow to detect interesting moments of the phenomenon (cracking onset and development) and to assess the damage of the structure.

1 Introduction

The development of non-destructive tests for the damage assessment of Reinforced Concrete (RC) and other materials structures is arising interest among researchers and stakeholder. Many structures, such as bridges, buildings, tanks, etc., built in the past decades, increasingly show signs of decay and need to be monitored.

Real scale tests have been pursued by some of us, in the framework of seismic response of structures [1, 2]. On the other hand, FEM modelling has been performed by some of us, to evaluate damaging and breaking behaviour of steel and steel/concrete structures [3, 4].

Among the recognized non-destructive techniques, Acoustic Emissions (AE) is one of the most interesting to be studied and improved, since it is able to furnish several details on the status of the material and on the cracking pattern.

Several studies are present in literature, in which the AE analysis has been studied, mainly in laboratory tests. In [5], the authors investigate the possibility to use Acoustic Emission (AE) techniques to estimate the damage in single-edge notched beam tests. The Weibull damage function is assumed, based on earlier research, and it is calibrated onto the AE counts results. The comparison study indicated that the Weibull damage function calibrated from the acquired AE data can describe the damage response of both normal strength and high performance concrete. An interesting auxiliary procedure to determine the attenuation of AE signals due to the medium is also described.

[6] presents a review on the use of AE for structural health monitoring of concrete structures. Two approaches for the analysis of AE data are described: (i) parametric analysis, which makes use of parameters as counts, maximum amplitude, energy of the signals, and (ii) signal waveform analysis, which allows better noise discrimination, 3D localization and source mechanism identification. As approach (ii) requires a large amount of data to be stored and treatment of the data by specialised tools, it is less common than parametric analysis in the analysis of concrete structures. It must be pointed out that source localization may be achieved by means of parametric analysis also (by comparing arrival times of the signals), even though a number of shortcomings have been highlighted in [7], i.e. mode conversions, dispersion and attenuation of waves may result in sensors recording the arrival of different wave modes that have travelled with different velocities. Some authors [8] show that parametric analysis may also be used to reveal the type of cracking, i.e. tensile or shear cracking, based on rise time and frequency. At this stage, thus, it seems useful to focus on parametric analysis, which is simpler and requires less data to be stored. The most common use of AE data processed by means of parametric analysis, apart from the previously mentioned task of source localization and damage mechanism identification, is damage severity evaluation of existing structures. To this aim, [6] distinguishes five methods:

* Corresponding authors: cguarnaccia@unisa.it

DOI: 10.1051/matecconf/201712505014

1. Correlation of calm and felicity ratio, exploiting the phenomenon of Kaiser effect [9]. This has been codified by the Japanese standard [10];
2. The use of b-value [11-14], and, more recently, by Carpinteri et al. [15], which proposed analytical correlation with theory of fracture [16] and numerical models [17] [18]. The approach of linking AE experimental data to numerical simulations seems interesting, and quite unexplored at this stage;
3. Historic and severity indices [19, 20];
4. The use of relaxation ratio, which measure the release of AE energy during unloading [21];
5. The use of cumulative signal strength ratio [22], accounting for Kaiser and Felicity ratio and in positive relationship with the growth of the level of damage.

In this paper, the authors present the results of the analysis of AE measured during a four-point bending test on a Reinforced Concrete (RC) beam.

After presenting the main parameters of the analysis (section 2), the experimental setup, together with some details on the offline data processing, will be briefly described (section 3). In section 4, the results of the analysis will be reported, with particular care to the parameters that exhibit the most interesting performances in terms of damage assessment.

2 Parameter-based AE analysis

2.1 Single event parameters

In the AE analysis described in this paper, the signals received from the piezo-electric sensors were recorded by an oscilloscope after threshold exceeding as voltage-time data. The generic basic parameters describing the features of a signal are qualitatively illustrated in Fig. 1.

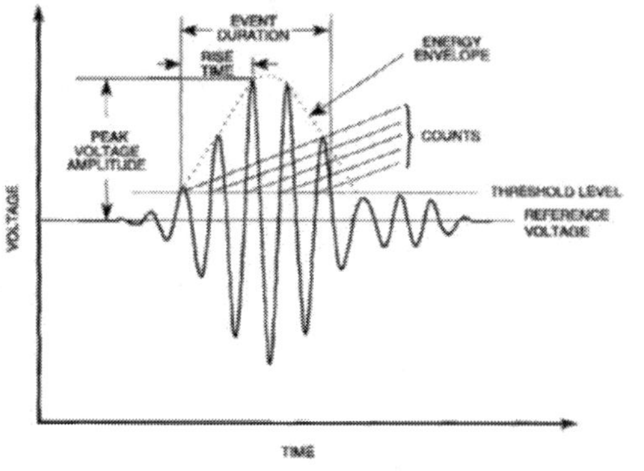

Fig. 1. Typical AE signal, with time-domain parameters [23].

From these we can define:
- Peak voltage amplitude (in V): A_{max};
- Peak voltage amplitude (in dB) [7]:

$$A_{dB} = 20\log\left(\frac{A_{max}}{A_{ref}}\right) - 20\log\left(g_f\right) \tag{1}$$

where g_f is the gain factor due to the amplifier, and $A_{ref} = 1\mu\text{V}$ is a reference value.
- Duration $d = t_f - t_i$(with t_i, t_f = time of the first and last threshold passing respectively), counts c, rise time t_r and damping time t_d (Fig. 1)
- Count rate: c/d;
- Count to peak: number of peaks from t_i and $t(A_{max})$ maximum amplitude;
- Signal strength: $S = \int_{t=t_i}^{t_f} A_{env}(t)dt$ where $A_{env}(t)$ is the positive signal envelope.

2.2 History parameters and *b*-value

After reducing the data collected by the oscilloscope for the single event to an ensemble of synthetic parameters as those outlined in the previous subsection, damage assessment may be performed by studying the following parameters which account for the evolution of signal characteristics:

- Cumulative Signal Strength $CSS(t) = \sum_{j=0}^{t} S_j$;
- Historic index [19]: $H(t) = \frac{N}{N-K}\frac{\sum_{i=K+1}^{N} S_i}{\sum_{i=1}^{N} S_i}$

where $K = \begin{cases} 0 & N > C_1 \\ C_3 N & C_1 \leq N < C_2 \\ N - C_1 & N \geq C_2 \end{cases}$

N number of events occurred up to time t
C_1, C_2, C_3 numerical constants;
- Felicity ratio (or load ratio [10]), defined as the ratio of the load at the onset of AE activity in subsequent loading to the previous load;
- b-value.

It is observed by many authors that the cumulative distribution of event magnitudes A_{dB} varies with increasing damage, and events of larger magnitude occur less frequently than events of smaller magnitude. In analogy with seismology, this statement is expressed by the Gutenberg-Richter relationship [13] [16]:

$$\log_{10} N = a - b\, M_L \tag{2}$$

where the magnitude M_L is proportional to the logarithm of the maximum amplitude A_{max}, N is the cumulative number of events with magnitude $\geq M_L$ and a, b parameters of the curve. From (1) and (2) it follows that:

$$\log_{10} N = a - b'\, A_{dB} \tag{3}$$

and thus, in line with [13], $b = 20\, b'$.

Some authors [16] suggest that, based on the fractal geometry approach in the mechanics of damage and fracture of heterogeneous materials, b-value should approach 1.0 with the evolution of damage. However, this conclusion is only partly supported by experimental observations [13, 24-27], while all authors report high fluctuation of the b-value during the test.

DOI: 10.1051/matecconf/201712505014

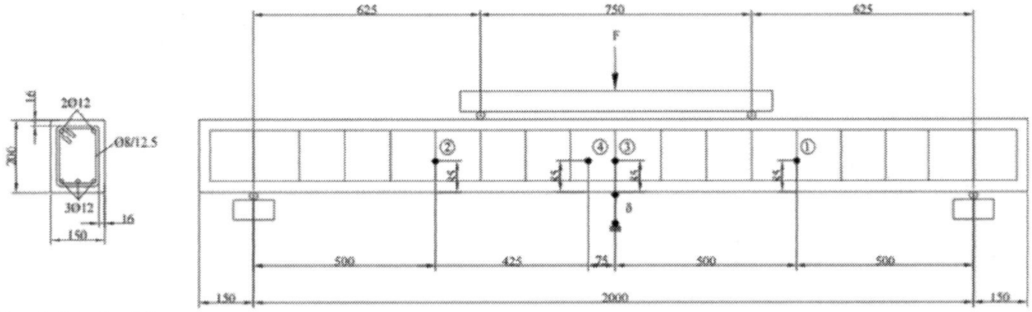

Fig. 2. Details of the test.

3 The experimental test

3.1 Description of the test and measurement setup

A four-point bending test on a reinforced concrete beam was performed at the Laboratory of Materials and Structures of the Department of Civil Engineering of the University of Salerno (Fig. 2). The simply supported, $150 \times 200 mm^2$ cross-section beam with length equal to 2000mm, was loaded in two points 625mm far from the supports by means of a stiff steel beam transferring the load from a hydraulic jack (Fig. 3). The load was applied in displacement control, according to a protocol involving preliminary increasing cycles and then a ramp until failure.

Compressive tests on 150mm-deep concrete cubes provided a mean strength equal to 40.62MPa, while tensile tests on steel bars resulted in mean yielding strength equal to 560.23MPa.

The central unit recorded the total force F transferred by the hydraulic jack and the displacement δ at mid-span. Furthermore, four piezoelectric transducers, marked in Fig. 2 by a circle around the number, were placed on the front surface of the beam, 85mm far from the bottom edge. Sensors 1 and 2 (see Fig. 2) have a 40 kHz resonance frequency; sensor 3 has a wider range of resonance (40-80 kHz); sensor 4 is centred on higher frequencies (200 kHz resonance).

Fig. 3. View of the experimental setup.

The signals detected by sensors 1, 2 and 3 were filtered and pre-amplified (factor 38) by a custom circuit. Signals from sensor 4 were not filtered and pre-amplified of a factor 10. All the signals were collected by a LeCroy oscilloscope, that stored data included in a 10 ms window from the pre-trigger. The trigger was set on sensor 3, i.e. the one supposed to be closest to the cracking region and that should have the highest signals. The instruments and the data acquisition have been provided by the personnel of the TAU lab of the University of Salerno.

The final load-displacement plot is shown in Fig. 4, together with the analytical values of first-cracking and ultimate loads, F_{cr}=10.05kN and F_u=91.97 kN respectively. The former is evaluated considering the uncracked cross-section and tensile strength equal to 2.61MPa for concrete (estimated by means of Model Code [28] formulation starting from the compressive strength); conversely, F_u was calculated according the usual hypotheses of reinforced concrete at the ultimate state, assuming a stress block approximation for the stress-strain relationship of concrete and elastic-plastic behaviour for steel.

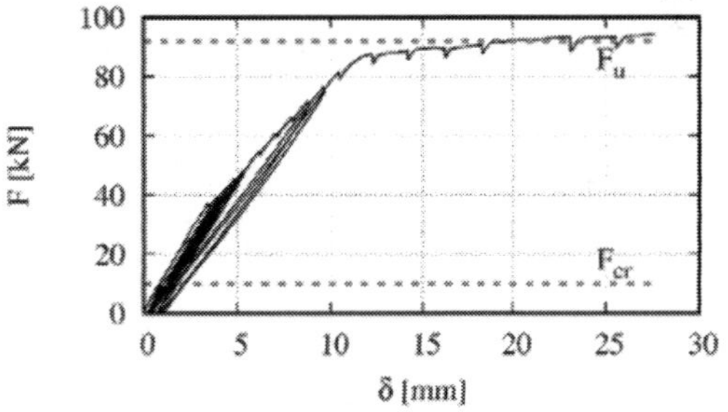

Fig. 4. Load-displacement plot in the four-point bending test.

3.2 Offline data processing

Any signal recorded was not used as-is in the parameter-based analysis, but underwent a cleaning process consisting of:

- pre-amplification removal (scaling);
- shifting of the signal to make median equal to zero (to remove low-frequency fluctuations which in the event window considered may be approximated as constant noise);
- setting any value under the threshold equal to zero.

The noise threshold is critical for the definition of many parameters but rather case-dependent. In this work, it was set as 0.01V.

 DOI: 10.1051/matecconf/201712505014

4 Results

4.1 Felicity effect and cumulative signal strength

For the sake of simplicity, only the data recorded by sensor 3, placed in the mid-span, will be discussed. The total number of events recorded was 1212, but after cleaning they were reduced to 414 only. In Fig. 5 the force and displacement histories are plotted as lines, while the events are highlighted as point markers. The grey vertical lines represent the attainment of 10, 20, ...% of total number of events.

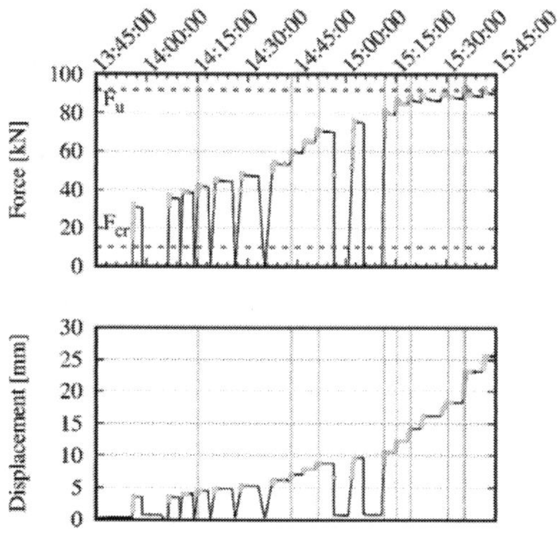

Fig. 5. Force and displacement histories.

Looking at Fig. 5, it is possible to observe that the first events, occurring when the lowest cross-section points reach concrete tensile strength, were recorded in correspondence of the evaluated F_{cr} value. Furthermore, the Kaiser effect, stating that in undamaged conditions the acoustic emissions appear only when the maximum load previously attained is exceeded, is generally confirmed (Felicity ratio equal to 1). In the latest stages of the test (basically in the last two unloading-reloadings) the Felicity effect is conversely evident, and AE events are recorded for loads below the maximum load attained so far. No events were recorded in the unloading branches, except for a single event at 14:47.

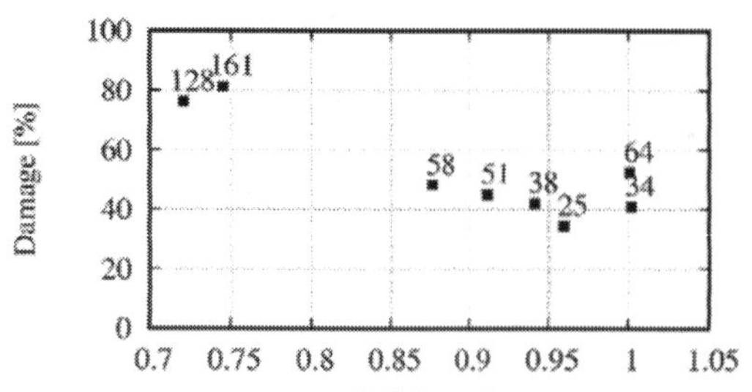

Fig. 6. Felicity effect as function of the damage (the numbers identify the events).

In Fig. 6, the Felicity ratio, evaluated for the eight unloading-reloading cycles performed in the test, is plotted against the damage D, defined in a simplified way here as:

$$D = \frac{F_{max}}{F_u} \quad (4)$$

where F_{max} is the maximum load attained so far and F_u is the ultimate load for the specimen, considering the whole test. Even though no clear trend is observable, it is evident that for damage under 60%, the Felicity ratio is greater than 0.85, while when the specimen is significantly damaged (D>70%), the Felicity ratio is under 0.75. The threshold of 0.85 for damaged/undamaged specimens is similar to that reported in [29] and recommended in [30].

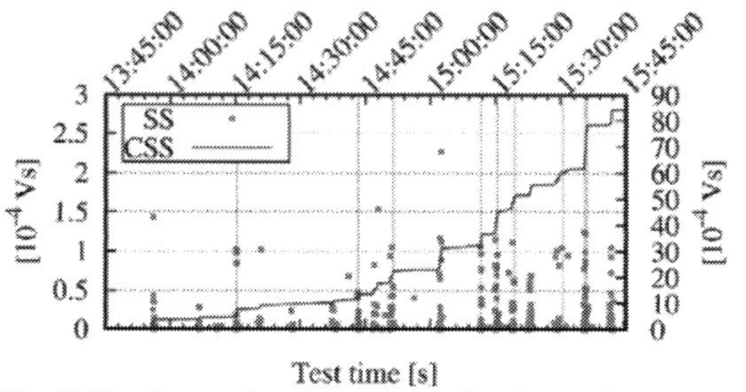

Fig. 7. Signal strength and cumulative signal strength.

In Fig. 7 signal strength and cumulative signal strength are plotted as function of time. It is possible to see that the most energetic events do not occur necessarily at the end of the test, i.e. in the damaged state, but may appear at the beginning. On the contrary, aggregated results show a clearer picture of the damage evolution, as the sudden increment in the CSS plot (wide cumulative AE activity) at around 15:35 which corresponds to the attainment of the maximum load (Fig. 5). CSS plot, thus, appears as a reliable indicator of damage onset.

4.2 Historic index

Another aggregated measure of the acoustic energy released during the damage process is represented by the historic index. Historic index is the ratio between the average SS in the last events and the average SS during the all history. As described in Section 2.2, the variable K, which represents the event number from which computing the numerator of H, depends on three constants C_1, C_2 and C_3 varying with the number of hits and material type. Generally, it is assumed that $1\text{-}C_3=C_1/C_2$. In [19, 31] the values C_3=0.8 and C_1=200 are suggested (thus implying C_2=1000), with the rationale that the numerator should be the average signal strength of the last 20% or 200 hits, whichever is smaller. Given the low number of events recorded for the test setup described in this work, it was chosen to evaluate K considering C_3=0.8 and C_1=65, hence C_2=325.

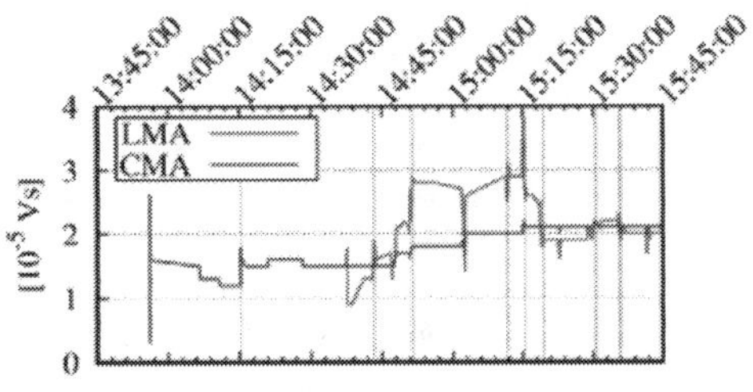

Fig. 8. Historic index: numerator and denominator evolution.

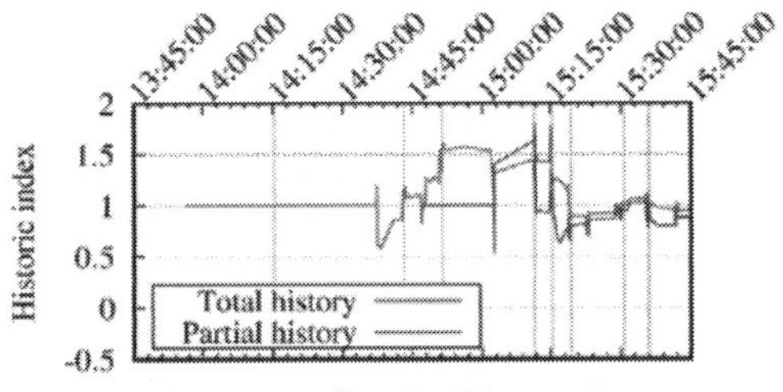

Fig. 9. Historic indices for total and partial history.

In Fig. 8, the evolution of numerator (last 65 events SS moving average, LMA) and denominator (cumulative SS moving average, CMA) is displayed. At the beginning ($N< C_1$) the two terms are equal as per the definition of historic index. After that point, the two terms show differences, with CMA being clearly smoother than LMA. CMA becomes stable at 15:15, which corresponds to damage D=87%. On the other hand, any large scattering in LMA is a symptom of occurrence of events with SS markedly different from the previous history. Since average is sensitive to outliers, the occurrence of *isolated* energetic events leads to rapid increase and decrease of LMA, as for instance at 15:03 (compare this to Fig. 7, where the isolated energetic event is represented in the SS plot). Conversely, mainly monotonic LMA increase is detected between 14:39 and 14:50: comparing this trend to the history loading, it is possible to observe that in that phase AE activity is stably increasing due to the application of load not previously experienced by the specimen. After 15:15, a decrease and then stabilization of LMA is calculated. It is interesting to notice that the large step encountered in Fig. 7 at 15:35 for CSS does not have correspondence in the LMA plot of Fig. 8. This happens because LMA considers the last events regardless of their temporal distribution: the large increase of CSS plot is due to a large number of on-average-energy events and not to low number of large-energy events, as for instance at 15:03. The simultaneous use both indices may help identify these different cases. In the final stages of the test CMA and LMA reach similar values, meaning that the historic index is approaching unity. This trend was also observed in [19] in a corrosion test.

Finally, the historic index is reported in Fig. 9, in red line. The same historic index is then evaluated assuming as starting point 14:45, which represents approximately the middle of the test (with damage D=67%). This approach aims at investigating the feasibility of the historic index as parameter describing damage evolution even when the past history is not known, as for existing structures. In this case, the number of events considered is 325; all parameters C_1, C_2, C3 were left identical as in the previous analysis.

This preliminary analysis shows that at incipient collapse (from 15:18 onwards) the historic indices evaluated in both cases are similar and close to unity, even though the partial-history plot shows higher scattering due to reduced number of events.

Even though definitive conclusions cannot be drawn at this stage, the use of partial-history historic index seems an interesting point which should be developed in future investigations.

4.3 b-value

As stated above, b-value represents the slope of the cumulative frequency plot of the magnitude distribution in logarithmic scale. Assuming the magnitude proportional to A_{dB}, the *b*-value may be obtained by multiplying the slope of amplitude cumulative frequency plot by 20. If one wants to monitor the evolution of b-value with time, this evaluation must be carried out considering all events from the beginning to the instant of interest. The cumulative frequency plot of amplitude for five stages of the test are reported in Fig. 10.

It is possible to notice that at each stage the relationship between log$N$ and A_{dB} is almost linear only in the region comprised between 80 and 95 dB. Furthermore, the slope of the quasi-linear region is not very much different in the different phases of the test, and this was also recognised in the tests reported in [24]. In the cited work, in which a shaking-table test was performed on a RC frame, large oscillation for the *b*-value was observed, with peaks and valleys that could be associated with instants of slow micro-cracking (low damage generation) and fast macro-cracking (high damage generation), respectively. For this reason, the authors suggested to revise the value 1.0 assumed as limit value for fully damaged specimen. In this work, given the behaviour reported in Fig. 10, no further analysis was then performed on b-value.

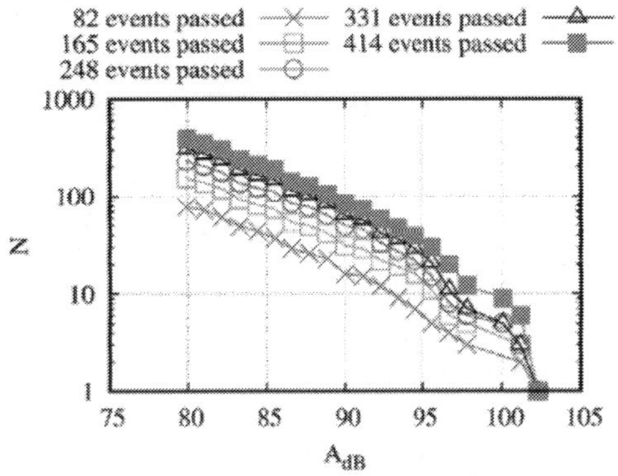

Fig. 10. Amplitude cumulative frequency at several stages.

5 Conclusions

In this paper, damage assessment of Reinforced Concrete (RC) structures is studied by means of non-destructive techniques. In particular, Acoustic Emission (AE) analysis is adopted in a four-point bending test on a RC beam.

The main parameters reported in the specific literature have been resumed and evaluated on the data collected during the test. Interesting information were obtained, concerning the cracking status and the damage occurred.

The analysis of the Felicity ratio showed that this ratio drop down to 0.7-0.75 when the damage surpasses a 60% threshold. The Signal Strength (SS) has also been analysed and compared with the Cumulative Signal Strength (CSS). It has been noticed that when the maximum load was attained, a large rise in the CSS occurred.

The historic index showed very interesting features, being a ratio of Last 65 events SS Moving Average (LMA) and Cumulative SS Moving Average (CMA). The variations of numerator and denominator have been analysed and plotted separately, in order to understand what happened approaching the crack of the specimen

Finally, the procedure to evaluate the *b*-value has been performed, but, since no evident variation were measured, the authors decided to postpone a detailed analysis on this parameter to further works.

In the end, it can be affirmed that the presented test and AE data analysis showed the possibility to help in assessing the damage of RC structures. Up to the authors opinion, the main challenge in this research domain will be the implementation and adjustment of well-established lab tests on specimen, to real and operating structures.

References

[1] M. Latour and G. Rizzano, Journal of Earthquake Engineering, 19, 1 (2015).

[2] M. Latour and G. Rizzano, Journal of Constructional Steel Research, 104 (2015).

[3] M. Latour, G. Rizzano, A. Santiago and D. Simoes, Journal of Constructional Steel Research, 101 (2014).

[4] P. Colajanni, L. La Mendola, M. Latour, A. Monaco and G. Rizzano, Journal of Constructional Steel Research, 111 (2015).

[5] Q. Dai, K. Ng, J. Zhou, E. L. Kreiger and T. M. Ahlborn, Construction and Building Materials, 31 (2012).

[6] A. Behnia, H. K. Chai and T. Shiotani, Construction and Building Materials, 65 (2014).

[7] M. Kaphle, Queensland University of Technology: PhD Thesis, 2012.

[8] S. Shahidan, R. Pulin, N. M. Bunnori and K. M. Holford, Construction and Building Materials, 45 (2013).

[9] M. Ohtsu, M. Uchida, T. Okamoto and S. Yuyama, ACI Structural Journal, 99, 4 (2002).

[10] NDIS-2421, Recommended Practice for In-Situ Monitoring of Concrete Structures by Acoustic Emission, Japanese Society for Non-Destructive Inspection, 2000.

[11] A. A. Pollock, International advances in nondestructive testing, 7 (1981).

[12] M. Ohtsu and H. Watanabe, Construction and Building Materials, 15, 5-6 (2001).

[13] S. Colombo, I. G. Main and M. C. Forde, J. Mater. Civ. Eng., 15, 3 (2003).

[14] J. H. Kurz, F. Finck, C. U. Grosse and H.-W. Reinhardt, Structural Health Monitoring, 5, 1 (2006).

[15] A. Carpinteri, G. Lacidogna and N. Pugno, Magazine of Concrete Research, 58, 9 (2006).

[16] A. Carpinteri, G. Lacidogna and S. Puzzi, Chaos, Solitons and Fractals, 41 (2009).

[17] I. Iturrioz, G. Lacidogna and A. Carpinteri, International Journal of Damage Mechanics, 23, 3 (2014).

[18] G. Birck, I. Iturrioz, G. Lacidogna and A. Carpinteri, Engineering Failure Analysis, 70 (2016).

[19] M. D. Benedetti, G. Loreto, F. Matta and A. Nanni, J. Mater. Civ. Eng., 26, 9 (2014).

[20] A. Abouhussien and A. Hassan, Structural Control and Health Monitoring, 24, 3, 2017.

[21] S. Colombo, M. Forde, I. Main and M. Shigeishi, Construction and Building Materials, 19, 10 (2005).

[22] A. R. Ridge and P. H. Ziehl, ACI Structural Journal, 103, 6 (2006).

[23] G. G. Clemeña, M. G. Lozev, J. C. J. Duke and M. F. J. Sison, Virginia Transportation Research Council, Charlottesville, Virginia (USA), 1995.

[24] F. Sagasta, A. Benavent-Climent, T. Fernández-Quirante and A. Gallego, J Nondestruct Eval, 33 (2014).

[25] G. Ma and H. Li, Construction and Building Materials, 144 (2017).

[26] D. Li, F. Du and J. Ou, Smart Materials and Structures, 26 (2017).

[27] G. Ma, H. Li and Z. Duan, J. Compos. Constr., 16, 6 (2012).

[28] International Federation for Structural Concrete, Model Code 2010 - Final draft. fib 65, FIB, 2012.

[29] M. Ohtsu, M. Uchida, T. Okamoto and S. Yuyama, ACI Structural Journal, 99, 4 (2002).

[30] 212-ACD RILEM Technical Commitee, Materials and Structures, 43 (2010).

[31] S. C. Lovejoy, Final report SPR 633, Oregon Dept. of Transportation Bridge and Engineering Section,, Salem, OR (USA), 2008.

MATEC Web of Conferences **125**, 05015 (2017) DOI: 10.1051/matecconf/201712505015
CSCC 2017

Experimental Validation Of An Innovative Procedure For The Rolling Noise Correction

Massimo Viscardi*[1], Pasquale Napolitano[1], Stefano Ferraiuolo[2]
[1] University of Naples "Federico II", Dept. of Industrial Engineering, Via Claudio, 21 – 80125 Napoli – Italy
[2] HITACHI RAIL – Via Argine, 425 - 80147, Napoli - Italy

Abstract. Among the wide contest of the train vehicles rolling noise evaluation, the aim of the paper is the development, implementation and experimental testing of a new method for roughness calculation according to FprCEN/TR 16891:2015 and the successive evaluation of the correction parameters of the measured rolling noise due to the presence of not compliant rail roughness. It is, in-fact, a very often operative condition, the execution of rolling noise tests over standard in-operation rails that are characterized by roughness profiles very different from standard one as those prescribed within the ISO 3095 procedure. Very often, this difference lead to the presence of an exceeding noise that needs to be evaluated and revised for a correct definition of the phenomena. Within the paper, the procedure implementation is presented and later on verified in operative experimental contest; forecasted and measured data are compared and successively commented.

1 GENERAL CONTEST OF THE RESEARCH

In railway sector noise is a really relevant problem. Often trains, especially low speed trains, walk trough cities or near houses. For this reason the noise produced by trains must be kept under control. The maximum admissible Sound Pressure Level (SPL) is the value frequently constrained and the norms, in last years, has shown a decreasing trend for maximum admissible value. According to this trend manufacturers have developed ever better method for noise control and reduction.

In railway sector there are three relevant noise sources; they are listed below:

- Traction Noise;
- Aerodynamic Noise;
- Rolling Noise;

and the noise, as function of speed, is shown in Figure 1.

For low speed trains, less than 100 kph, the aerodynamic noise can be neglected and the most relevant sources are the traction noise, almost constant with speed variation, and rolling noise that is linearly increasing, more or less, according to speed. The traction noise and aerodynamic noise can be easy kept under control; the first one using a more quite engine or a best insulation engine bay; the second one depends, in first approximation, by the shape of frontal area of the train.

Rolling noise generation is more complex. In that process are involved two main components:

- Wheel;
- Rail;

In most country, Italy is one of them, company in charge for wheel is not in charge for rail and vice versa.

When the noise generated by wheel/rail interaction is higher than maximum admissible level it is hard to identify clearly if it is due to wheel or rail.

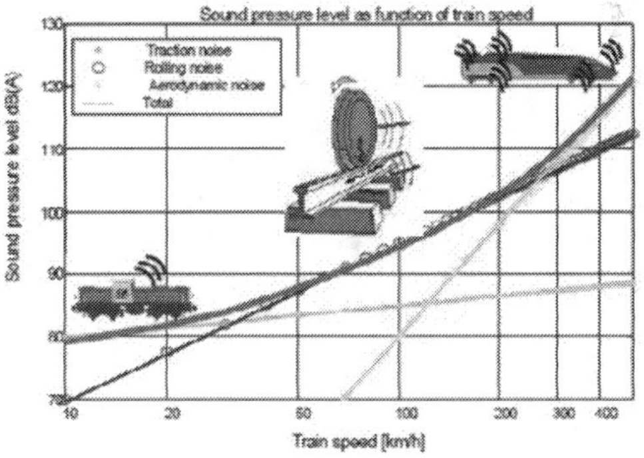

Figure 1 : Sources SPL vs. speed.

An example of rolling noise spectrum is given in Figure 2. To make general background more complex the company in charge for rail is the one who establish the maximum allowable value for rolling noise SPL. In this situation it is important for customer have a procedure and a tool to split rolling noise between rail and wheel.

In previous work [7] a computational tool that, according to UNI EN ISO FPRCEN/TR,16891 [6] can correct, eliminating it, the contribute of rail to rolling noise has been preliminary developed and implemented.

*Corresponding author: massimo.viscardi@unina.it

DOI: 10.1051/matecconf/201712505015

2 THEORETICAL BACKGROUND

There are four mechanisms that are suggested in the literature, as the main causes of rolling noise.

These are:

- Rail and wheel roughness,
- Parameter variation, or moduli heterogeneity,
- Creep,
- Aerodynamic noise.

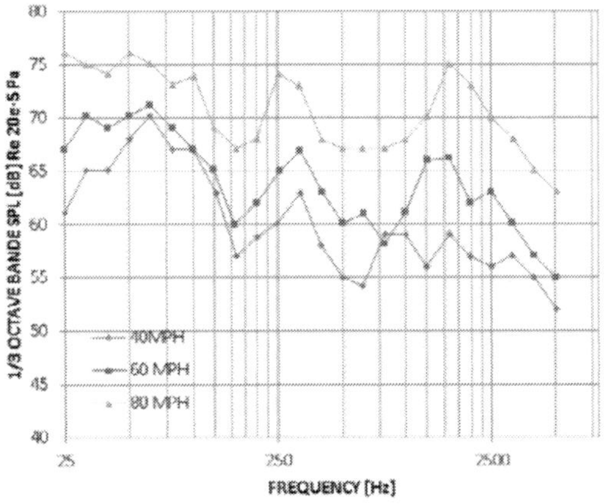

Figure 2 : Pass-by noise for single car vehicle with aluminum centered wheels on ballast and tie track.

2.1. Wheel/Rail Roughness

Is probably the most significant cause of the wheel/rail noise. The surface roughness profile may be decomposed into a continuous spectrum of wavelengths. At wavelengths short relative to the contact patch dimension, the surface roughness is attenuated by averaging of the roughness across the contact patch, an effect which is described as contact patch filtering. Thus, fine regular grinding marks of dimensions less than, perhaps, 1.5mm should not produce significant noise compared to lower frequency components.

2.2 Parameter Variation

Parameter variation refers to the variation of rail and wheel steel moduli, rail support stiffness, and contact stiffness due to variation in rail head transverse radius-of-curvature. The influence of fractional changes in elastic moduli and of radius-of-curvature of the rail head as a function of wavelength necessary to generate wheel/rail noise equivalent to that generated by surface roughness is illustrated in the figure. Experimental data for the effect of modulus variation at this frequency have not yet been found. Rail head ball radius heterogeneity also induces a dynamic response in the wheel and rail. The variation of rail head curvature would have to be -on the order of 10% to 50% to produce a noise level similar to that produced by rail roughness alone. Data on rail head radii of curvature as a function of wavelength have not been obtained nor correlated with wayside noise. Also, rail head ball radius variation will normally accompany surface roughness, so that distinguishing between ball radius variation and roughness may be difficult in practice.

2.3 Dynamic Creep

Dynamic creep may include both longitudinal and lateral dynamic creep, roll-slip in a direction parallel with the rail, and spin-creep of the wheel about a vertical axis normal to the wheel/rail contact area.

2.3.1 Longitudinal Creep

It is not considered significant by some researchers, as rolling noise levels are claimed to not increase significantly during braking or acceleration on smooth ground rail. However, qualitative changes of the sound of wheel/rail noise on newly ground rail with a grinding pattern in the rail running surface is observable to the ear as a train accelerates or decelerates, in contradiction to the notion that longitudinal creep is of no significance.

2.3.2Lateral creep

It occurs during curve negotiation, and is responsible for the well-known wheel squeal phenomena resulting from stick-slip. Lateral creep may not be significant at tangent track, but lateral dynamic creep may occur during unloading cycles at high frequencies on abnormally rough or corrugated rail. Lateral dynamic creep is postulated by some to be responsible for short-pitch corrugation at tangent track. Therefore, lateral creep, at least in the broad sense, may be a significant source of noise.

2.3.3Spin-creep

It is caused by wheel taper which produces a rolling radius differential between the field and gauge sides of the contact patch.

2.4 Aerodynamic Noise

Aerodynamic noise is caused by turbulent boundary layer noise about the wheel circumference as it moves forward and by under car components which exhibit substantial aerodynamic roughness. Noise due to air turbulence about the wheel is usually not significant at train speeds representative of transit systems, while noise due to air turbulence in the truck area may be significant.

Among these possible cause, the one that generally requires more attention is the roughness where/rail roughness and, if referred to the acceptance test to be performed at the train delivery from the manufacture to the customer, mainly the rail roughness as the wheel is generally considered as a smooth profile at this operational stage.

During these acceptance test, pass-by acoustic measurements are generally performed at different speeds and train is generally required to not exceed limit noise level at specific measurement station (generally 7,5 m @1,2 m height form the centerline). Measurement site is always a straight portion of track line, that is the reason why other phenomena are generally negligible and only rail roughness may strongly influence the measured noise level.

ISO 3095 prescribe the limit roughness to be acceptable during the test performance, but very often these strong requirements cannot be satisfied because real portion of in service tracks are used for test and rectification process are extremely expensive and time consuming as well require the stop of service operation along the train line.

Hence the reason for a correct evaluation of rail roughness and the implementation of a correction procedure [7].

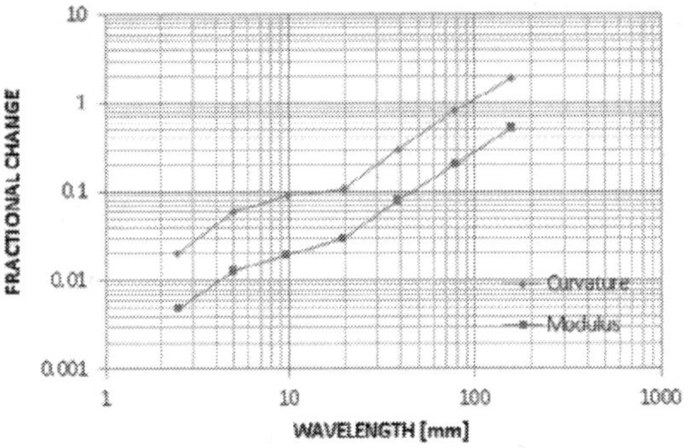

Figure 3 : Change in elastic modules and railhead curvature required to generate wheel/rail excitation.

3 Test Specimen Definition

Along this work, a medium weight metro passenger vehicle has been considered. The vehicle present the following main characteristics:

- Composition: M-R-M+M-R-M;
- Max Length: approx. 110 meters;
- Max Width: approx. 3 meters;
- Structure Material: Aluminum;
- Seats: approx. 200;
- Stand up passengers: approx. 1000;
- Maximum Speed: 90 kph;

Vehicle profile is presented in the following figure 4 and 5.

In real operative conditions a wide list of configuration are available for the train according to different equipment status. To answer at reference technical specifications, the test and relative data post processing and comparison of a single condition has been identified as standard condition. This operative condition presented:

- HVAC: on;
- Traction System: on;
- Auxiliary Inverter: on;
- Engine and Reducer: on;
- Compressor: on;
- speed: 60kph;

This condition will be used for all tests showed in this paper and will be reference condition for data post processing and comparison.

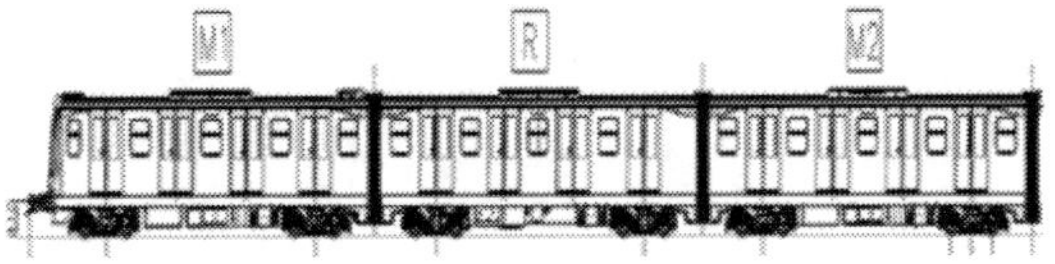

Figure 4 : Side view of half vehicle

Figure 5 : Front view

4 General Test Description

The test site was located near in Italy and it was accurately chosen to best fulfill the standard requirements. In the specific, two factors have been considered:

- Straight configuration of the track
- No reflecting surfaces near the measurement point

4.1 Rail Conditions

According to the UNI EN ISO 3381/3095 the rail must have a maximum roughness, for third band octave, less than a threshold value. This requirement is really important for noise tests acceptance. In Figure 6 the standard roughness curve according to UNI EN ISO 3095_2005.

As said before the roughness spectrum of rail was not known at test moment and its calculation was one of the scope of the tests.

4.2 Vehicle Conditions

During the test the train was considered empty, no passenger on board except people necessary for text execution. The wheel was in good condition and nor

 DOI: 10.1051/matecconf/201712505015

fatigue or excessive roughness was observed. During tests all the train equipment were settled as specified in chapter 3.

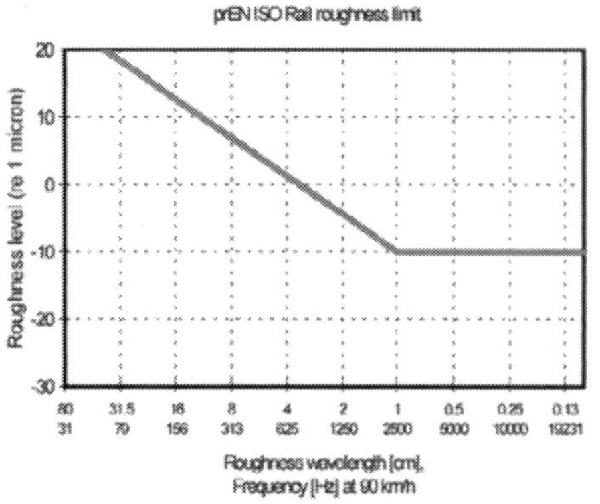

Figure 6 : Limit Roughness spectra

5 Acceleration Test Description

The acceleration was measured during multiple train pass-by to obtain a mean value of acceleration. For this test all general condition expressed in chapter 4 are applied to obtain a general standard result that can be compare with other tests. For accelerometer measurements a set of accelerometers was used. According to reference norm they were place on the railway is appropriate positions. As shown in Figure 7 the accelerometer position is defined by norm and have been repeated on experimental test as shown in Figure 8. Acceleration spectra along the z axis will be the basic input for the track decay calculation [6-7]; with acceleration along y, with a similar process, the longitudinal decay rate may be calculated. Because this parameter is less useful , it will be not presented within this paper.

In this specific test, three tri-axial accelerometers have been used also to avoid problem related to the need of compensating profiles. Also, an extra accelerometer has been positioned on the rail web for further consideration; it has not been used for the purposes of the work.

5.1 Acceleration Result

According to train configuration (see chapter 3), to test environment specification (see chapter 4) and accelerometer position (see chapter 5) shown above the acceleration has been measured for all accelerometers for more than one passage.
An acceleration example in shown in Figure 9 where a typical passage is plotted as function of time.

For decay rate calculation only vertical acceleration will be considered and only decay rate used for roughness calculation.

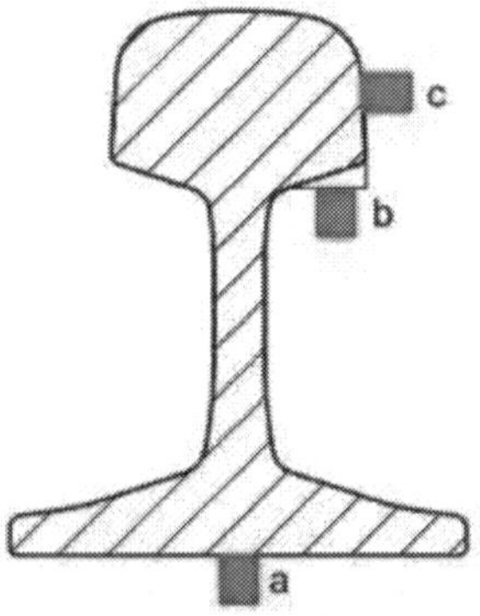

Figure 7 : Norm suggested points

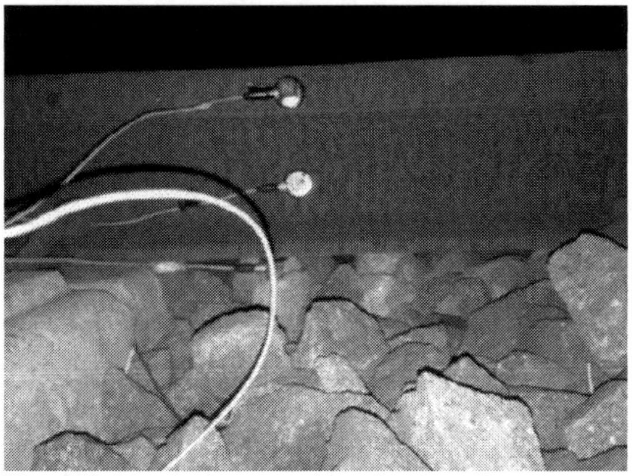

Figure 8 : Accelerometers positioned on the rail

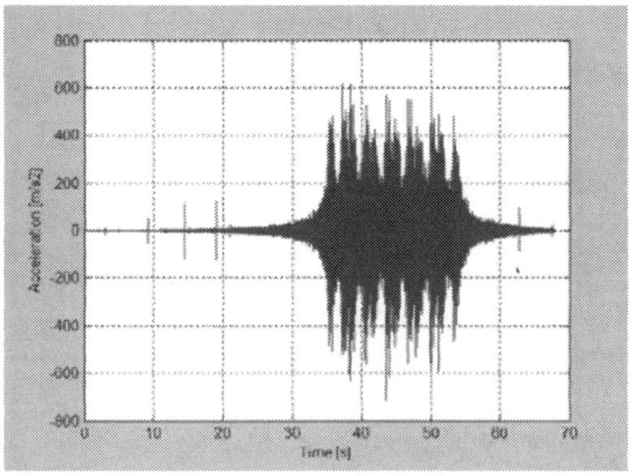

Figure 9 : Time history spectrum for single passage. Refers to accelerometer position C in reference norme

6. Roughness Calculation

Once that acceleration has been measured, according to normative the first step for roughness calculation is the decay rate calculation that depends from the FRF of the system. The FRF has been calculate on whole train passage and around a single wheel passage. The difference between two are shown in figure 10 and 11.

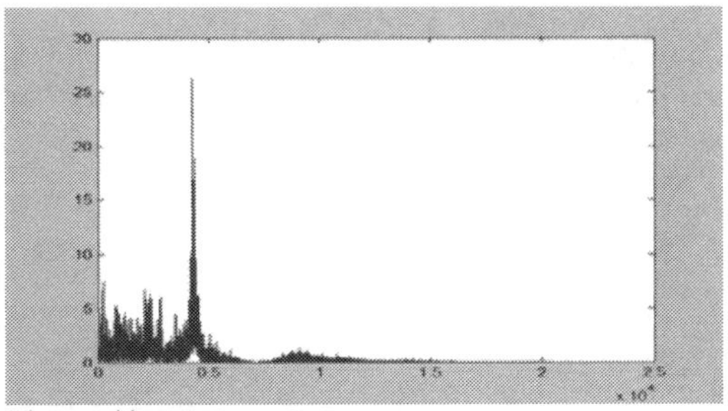

Figure 10 : FRF on whole passage

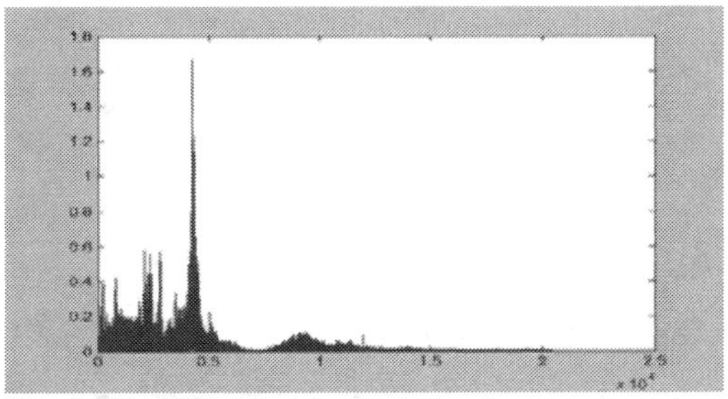

Figure 11 : FRF referred at a single wheel

Using the iterative method and a residual error of 10-5 the decay rate is than calculate for a wide number of measures as shown in Figure 12.

The mean value of decay rate is than used for roughness calculation.

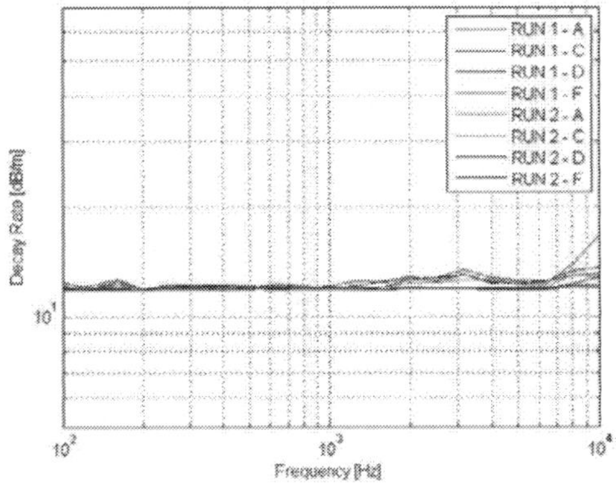

Figure 12 : Decay rate for several measures

The calculated roughness, if compared with the threshold level of Figure 6, has a really relevant value and cannot be neglect during noise tests.

As prescribed within the ISO 3095, the excess roughness need in-fact to be corrected by the use of a specific procedure that will introduced in the following chapter 8.

7. Acoustic Tests Description

Acoustic test were performed according to the pass-by noise reference EN ISO 3095. For every train passage the SPL was measured at 7.5 meters away from the center of railway seat in orthogonal direction and at 1.2 meters from ground.

The test speed was fixed at 60 Km/h according to the technical requirement even if measurement were also performed at different speed for research purposes (from 20 Km/h to 60 Km/h step 10 Km/h).

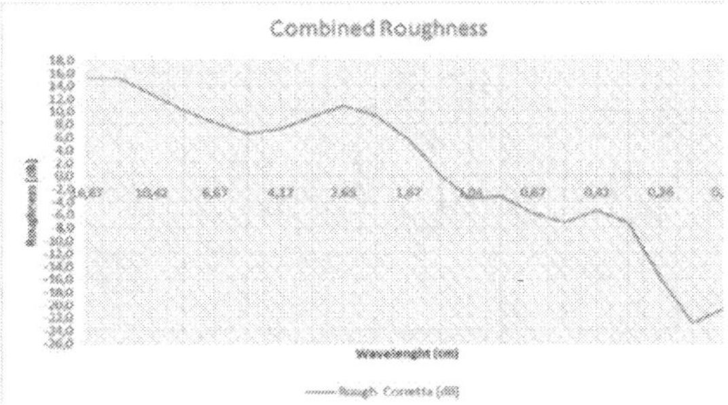

Figure 13 : Combined roughness calculated

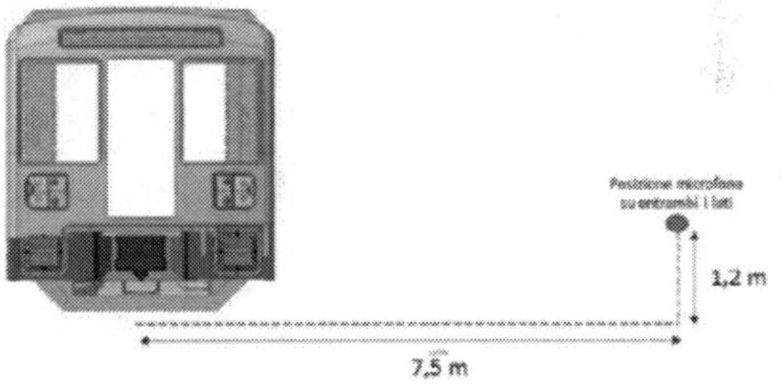

Figure 14 : Noise test scheme

7.1 Noise Measurements Results

In the following pictures, some typical results are reported. Figure 15 show the typical pass-by noise profile; also the pressure fluctuation in correspondence of the single boogie axles is evident if a zoom on the maximum levels is performed (figure16).

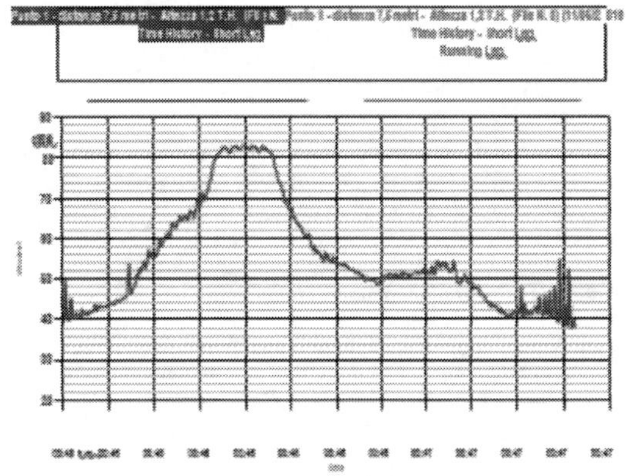

Figure 15 : Time history typical passage

Data show an equivalent level over the passage (intended as the time window when the train pass through the measurement station that is approximately 6 seconds for the specific speed) Laeq of about 82.3 dB(A).

DOI: 10.1051/matecconf/201712505015

This value has been measured over 6 passage with a difference among them of less than 0,5 dB(A). Within the next pictures, the Equivalent and maximum noise spectra are presented.

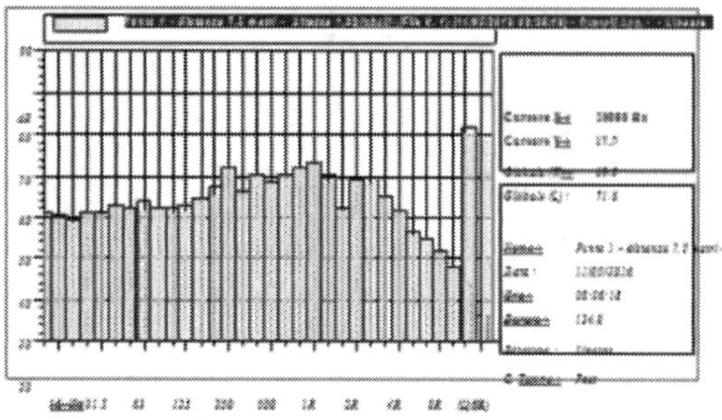

Figure 16 : Leq for typical passage

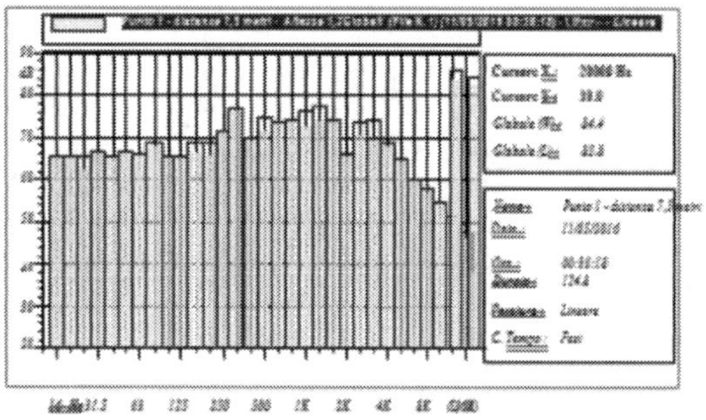

Figure 17 : Leq for typical passage

8 Noise Correction Procedure

The noise correction procedure, involves three steps. The first one is the FRF calculation to relate the noise measured to the actual roughness (to allow this passage the system will be considered linear).

The second step consist in the new roughness calculation. According to norm the noise should be measured when the roughness is less or equal at threshold roughness. The actual roughness over come the limit one and needs to be compensated.

The third step consist in noise evaluation and will involve the FRF and the roughness calculated in step one and two.

8.1 FRF Calculation

The FRF will be estimated according to following equation

$$L_{HpRtot,nl}(f_c) = L_{peq,tp}(f_c) - L_{Rtot}(f_c, v) - 10lg\left(\frac{N_{ax}}{l}\right)$$

where LHpRtot,nl(fc) is the FRF we want estimate, Lpeq,tp the measured noise, LRtot the total roughness, Nax the number of wheels and l the train length.

The total transfer function L_(HpRtot,nl) (f_c) is independent from the roughness, train length and number of axles. It characterizes the vibro-acoustic properties of the vehicle, the track and the propagation area.

The FRF result is shown in Figure 18.

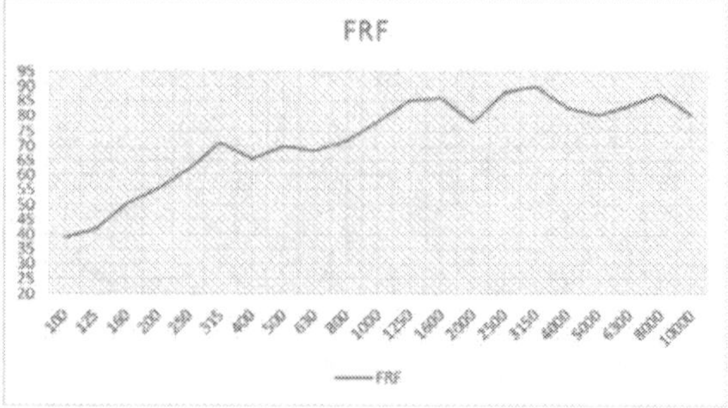

Figure 18 : Estimated FRF

8.2 Roughness Correction

The roughness is corrected according to UNI EN ISO 3095. For UNI EN ISO 3095 two revision are available. The first one from 2005 and the second one from 2013. The two curves, as shown in Figure 19, are slightly different. According to literature the most relevant zone for rolling noise generation is between 0.033 [m] and 0.010 [m] and in this range the curves are approximately the same. In any case the most recent curve will be used as reference.

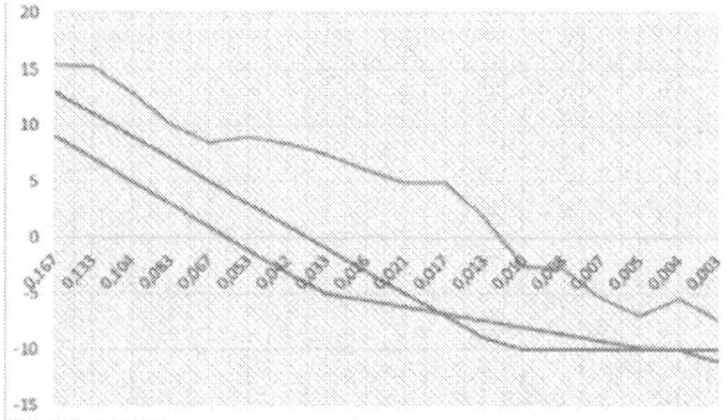

Figure 19 : Calculated roughness (grey), UNI EN ISO 3095:2005 (red) and UNI EN ISO 3095:2013 (blue) comparison versus wavelength domain

8.3 Correct Noise Evaluation

The correct noise evaluation will be done according to [7] and simply resolving Equation 1 respect to the SPL. According to results shown up to now the correct noise, compared to measured noise, is shown in Figure 20.

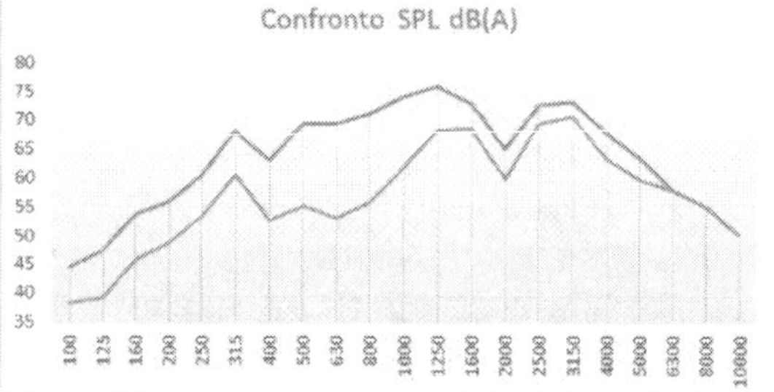

Figure 20 : Original noise (overall level 82.4 [dBA]) and corrected noise (overall 75.9 [dBA]) comparison

9 Conclusions

As shown in this paper the rolling noise is a relevant problem for train sector and must be taken under control. In the first part of the paper it has been underlined that not compliant rail conditions, with presence of severe roughness profiles may lead to exceeding noise level.

In the second part of paper an innovative procedure for exceeding rail roughness has been proposed and experimented. A dedicated test campaign has been conducted and acoustic as well as vibrational data have been acquired as these latter need to be used within the correction procedure. It has been demonstrated that in the specific rail configuration, the exceeding noise due to the rail roughness was about 6 dB(A).

From presented data is so evident the importance of keeping into account the rail rail parameters as they may strongly influence the emitted noise with severe consequence over the acceptance vehicle test.

References

1. Thompson, D.J., Wheel-Rail Noise Generation, Part I: Introduction and Interaction Model, Journal of Sound and Vibration,161, 1993a.

2. Thompson, D.J., Wheel-Rail Noise Generation, Part II: Wheel Vibration, Journal of Sound and Vibration,161, 1993b.

3. Thompson, D.J., Wheel-Rail Noise Generation, Part I: Inclusion of wheel rotation, Journal of Sound and Vibration,161, 1993c.

4. Thompson, D.J., Experimental Analysis of Wave Propagation in Railway Propagation in Railway Track, Journal of Sound and Vibration, 203(5), 1997.

5. James T. Nelson, Transit Cooperative Research Program - Wheel/Rail Noise Control Manual TCRP report 23.

6. Ente Italiano di Normazione, UNI/CT 050 , FprCEN/TR 16891 "Railway applications - Acoustics - Measurement method for combined roughness, track decay rates and transfer functions".

7. Viscardi M., Napolitano P., Ferraiuolo S. - An Innovative Procedure for the Rolling Noise Evaluation (2016) MATEC Web of Conferences, 76, art. no. 05013 Doi. 10.1051/matecconf/20167605013

8. Siano D., Viscardi M., Panza, M.A., Acoustic Optimization of a High-speed Train Composite Sandwich Panel Based on Analytical and Experimental Transmission Loss Evaluation Integrated by FE/Test Correlation Analysis Energy Procedia 81:689-703 · December 2015 DOI: 10.1016/j.egypro.2015.12.075

9. Viscardi, M., Napolitano, P., Arena, M. -Simulation and experimental validation of fatigue endurance limit of copper alloy for industrial applications (2016) International Journal of Mathematical Models and Methods in Applied Sciences, 10, pp. 340-346

10. Viscardi M., Rusciano N., Iadevaia M., Siano D. - An optimization process experience for HVAC noise emission and flows distribution inside a passenger's train wagon (2009) 16th International Congress on Sound and Vibration 2009, ICSV 2009, 6, pp. 3334-3341.

11. Massimo Viscardi, Pasquale Napolitano and Maurizio Arena – An innovative numerical approach for railway rolling noise forecast (2017)– Proceedings of the 24th International Congress on Sound And Vibrations ICSV24

MATEC Web of Conferences **125**, 05016 (2017) DOI: 10.1051/matecconf/201712505016
CSCC 2017

Specificity in the Optical Excitation Lock-in Thermography Results Processing

Anna Stoynova[1], and *Borislav* Bonev[1,*]

[1]Technical University of Sofia, Department of Microelectronics, Sofia, Bulgaria

Abstract. The aim of the paper is to study some factors influence on the contrast decreasing of the ampligram and phasegram obtained after optical lock-in thermography. It is analysed the effect of delay between excitation source modulated parameter changing and modulated signal due to thermal inertia of halogen lamp filament. Two software corrections for decreasing the effect of these factors are developed. In order to evaluate the effect of these corrections, lock-in thermography measurement is performed and multiple results processing at different correction parameters values are performed. The contrast dependence from correction parameters is presented in graphical form. Multiple results processing with random correction parameters values using the both corrections are performed for determination of maximum possible contrast An iterative method with less number of results processing for choosing appropriate values of correction parameters using the both corrections is proposed. The effect of this method is presented and compared in tabular and graphic form.

1 Introduction

In recent years, there has been a growing interest in active thermography methods, particularly lock-in thermography. Active thermographic methods use a forced temperature change (heating or cooling) of the tested object and simultaneously capture the process of temperature change with an infrared (IR) camera [1]. Excitation source is used for temperature change. In lock-in thermography is used a periodic temperature change.

The advantages of the lock-in thermography such as its non-destructivity and contactlessness in some cases, noise suppression and other, are a precondition for its wide application [2].

Any source of heating or cooling that can give or take heat for a long time can be used as excitation source:

- optical excitation sources (halogen lamp, LED, laser);
- mechanical excitation source (ultrasound source);
- electrical (for example – modulating the power supply voltage);
- hot air source.

The halogen lamp is one of the most commonly used optical excitation sources for lock-in thermography mainly because of its relatively low cost, high output power and relatively easy modulation of the light intensity.

The use of a halogen lamp as excitation source requires some peculiarities in the processing of the received data relating to the thermal inertia of the lamp [3].

A significant disadvantage in the use of a halogen lamp as excitation source is the poor energy efficiency of the measurement process. The efficiency of the halogen lamp is relatively low, which, combined with the long duration of the measurement process, leads to significant electricity consumption.

The energy efficiency of the process can be improve by increasing the sensitivity of the method, i.e., obtaining the same contrast at a lower light intensity of the lamp. Sensitivity is decreasing due to a number of factors whose origin and effect requires thorough analysis and finding ways to reduce their effect on the obtained result.

The LED optical excitation sources can be used also for energy efficiency improvement in cases, where it is not needed high output power of excitation source.

If it is needed heating of very small objects or spot of the tested object it can be used laser excitation source.

2 Principle of lock-in thermography

The principle of the lock-in thermography is based on the principle of synchronous phase detection. The first variants of lock-in thermography used analogue processing of the received signal by synchronous phase detectors. It was used a system with a sensor for infrared radiation and a modulated laser beam. This pair of emitter-receiver scans test surface [1]. Obviously, this system has been very slow. When IR thermal cameras become cheaper, they are used instead of the one receiver and the whole tested object surface is captured at once.

* Corresponding author: bonev@ecad.tu-sofia.bg

An important point in the principle of the lock-in thermography is the need to know each thermogram of the sequence at which instantaneous value of the excitation source modulated parameter is captured.

The simplest way to realize this is the synchronization between the modulating signal of the excitation source and capturing thermograms from the IR camera.

An ampligram and a phasegram, as well as some other images, are obtained as a result from the lock-in thermography measurement. These are obtained by processing all or part of the thermograms from sequence.

There are basically two methods for processing the sequence of thermograms - digital lock-in correlation and Fourier analysis.

The principle of digital lock-in correlation is shown on fig. 1.

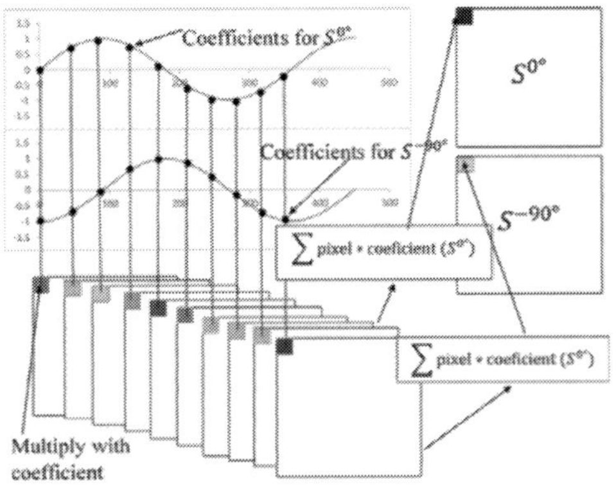

Fig. 1. The principle of digital lock-in correlation.

For one pixel of the images $S^{0°}$ and $S^{-90°}$ is obtained [2]:

$$S^{0°}(x,y)=(1/Nn)\sum_{k=1:N}\{\sum_{m=1:n}[F_{k,m}(x,y)K^{0°}]\} \quad (1)$$

$$S^{-90°}(x,y)=(1/Nn)\sum_{i=k:N}\{\sum_{m=1:n}[F_{k,m}(x,y)K^{-90°}]\} \quad (2)$$

$$K^{0°}=2\sin[2\pi(m-1)/n] \quad (3)$$

$$K^{-90°}=-2\cos[2\pi(m-1)/n] \quad (4)$$

where:
$S^{0°}(x,y)$ – value of the pixel (x,y) from image $S^{0°}$;
$S^{-90°}(x,y)$ – value of the pixel (x,y) from image $S^{-90°}$;
x – row of thermogram;
y – column of thermogram;
N – number of periods for which the calculation is performed;
n – number of captured thermograms per period;
$F_{i,j}(x,y)$ – value of the pixel (x,y) of image i from period j;
$K^{0°}$ - correlation coefficient for computation of $S^{0°}$;
$K^{-90°}$ - correlation coefficient for computation of $S^{-90°}$.

The ampligram and phasegram are obtained from images $S^{0°}$ and $S^{-90°}$:

$$S_{amplidute}=\sqrt{[S^{0°}(x,y)^2+S^{-90°}(x,y)^2]} \quad (5)$$

$$S_{phase}=\mathrm{arctg}[S^{-90°}(x,y)/S^{0°}(x,y)] \quad (6)$$

When it is used Fourier method for computation of ampligram and phasegram, first it is needed to calculate the first harmonic image:

$$S(x,y)=(1/Nn)\sum_{k=1:N}\{\sum_{m=1:n}[F_{k,m}(x,y)K]\} \quad (7)$$

$$K=\exp[-j(2\pi m/n] \quad (8)$$

The ampligram and phasegram are obtained from the first harmonic image:

$$S_{amplidute}=\sqrt{[\mathrm{Re}(S(x,y))^2+\mathrm{Im}(S(x,y))^2]} \quad (9)$$

$$S_{phase}=\mathrm{arctg}[\mathrm{Im}(S(x,y))/\mathrm{Re}(S(x,y))] \quad (10)$$

3 Specificity in the use of an optical excitation source

There are lot of specificities in thermogram sequence processing when it is used optical excitation source.

The direction of the voltage supplied to the halogen lamp is irrelevant. If it is supplied reverse voltage to the LED, it is off and can be damaged. Therefore, only one polar voltage is applied to halogen lamp and when it is used LED – only forward voltage. In the used experimental setup, halogen lamp voltage has the time diagram, shown on fig. 2.

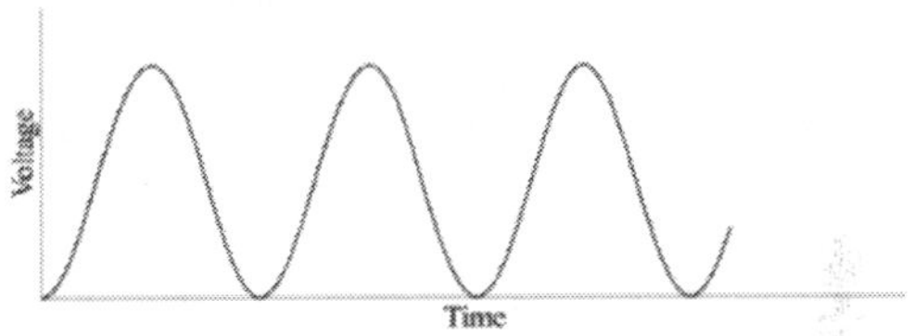

Fig. 2. The voltage waveform applied to halogen lamp.

When it is used digital lock-in correlation method, the closest correlation function to this signal is (1–cos) for computation of image $S^{0°}$ and (1-sin) for computation of image $S^{-90°}$.

As mentioned above, it is necessary to know the instantaneous value of the heat source modulated parameter for each thermogram of the sequence capturing time. The instantaneous value of the modulation signal is known for each image of the sequence capturing time. In the halogen lamp, the change in the light intensity does not fully follow the modulation signal, but with some delay due to the thermal inertia of the lamp filament. A solution in this case is the use of a light detector and the synchronization being the signal of the detector. However, software compensation may also be used. It changes initial delay of correlation function.

This delay, however, changes over time - at the start time, when the filament is cold, this delay is greatest. In subsequent periods, this delay is decreasing. This can be compensated by changing the frequency of the correlation function in combination with the initial delay.

Equations (3) and (4) are changed as follows:

$$K^{0^\circ}=1-\cos[2\pi(100+d)(m-1)/(100n)-2\pi t_{delay}f_{lock\text{-}in}] \quad (11)$$

$$K^{-90^\circ}=1-\sin[2\pi(100+d)(m-1)/(100n)-2\pi t_{delay}f_{lock\text{-}in}] \quad (12)$$

where:
t_{delay} – delay time;
$f_{lock\text{-}in}$ – excitation source modulation frequency;
d – percentage change in frequency.

This choosing of values of delay and percentage frequency change depends not only on halogen lamp parameters, but also from many other factors – environment parameters, tested object thermal parameters and other.

Automated determination of the most appropriate values for delay and percentage change of frequency can be realized. An indication that the most appropriate values for delay and percentage change of frequency are chosen is to achieve maximum contrast between two points or areas of the ampligram or phasegram. This includes multiple results processing and contrast comparison.

This can be applied in the case that in the results has a contrast, albeit low between the areas of the image. In this case, by varying the delay and frequency deviations, the contrast of the image can be increased.

When it is used Fourier method can also be used percentage frequency change correction. Equation (8) is changed as follow:

$$K=\exp\{-j[2\pi m(100+d)/(100n)]\} \quad (13)$$

In the case of using a LED excitation source there are no delay between modulation signal and the change of light intensity due to low on/off time of LEDs, but the tested object thermal parameters and environment parameters affect and applying of corrections can be increase the contrast.

4 Experiment and results

To study the effect of the factors described above, a lock-in thermography measurement of a one-layer printed circuit board (PCB) was performed.

The halogen lamp and the camera are located opposite the PCB side without paths.

Characteristics of PCB:
- material – FR4;
- thickness – 1 mm;
- material of PCB paths – copper;
- thickness of PCB paths – 35 μm.

Approximately calculation of the lock-in thermography measurement parameter is performed by using software Automation Technology IrNDT. A frequency of 0.2 Hz is chosen. At this frequency the heat wave penetration is approximately the thickness of the board [4].

The lock-in measurement is controlled by IRX-Box hardware and IR-NDT software of Automation Technology. The thermogram sequence is processed by own developed software in the environment of Matlab. It is used equations (1), (2), (11), (12), (5) and (6) for digital lock-in correlation method and (7), (13), (9) and (10) for Fourier method.

The used IR camera is FLIR SC640 with resolution of 640 × 480 pixels and frame rate of 30 frames per second.

The parameters of measurement are:
- lock-in frequency – 0.2 Hz (5s period);
- measurement duration – 50s (10 lock-in periods);
- frame rate of IR camera – 10 frames per second.

It is not used all lock-in periods for computation of ampligram and phasegram, because the thermal process during the first few periods is far from thermal equilibrium and this leads to decreasing of contrast.

To determine the influence of the described error sources, a comparison of the contrast between two areas of the phasegram at different values of the percentage frequency change and delay time is performed. The areas used for contrast computation are shown on fig. 3.

The contrast is calculated using equation (14).

$$Contrast=(S_{phase}(a_1)+S_{phase}(a_2)+\ldots+S_{phase}(a_{10}))/10-(S_{phase}(b_1)+S_{phase}(b_2)+\ldots+S_{phase}(b_{10}))/10 \quad (14)$$

where:
$a_1, a_2, \ldots, a_{10}$ – pixel of area (a);
$b_1, b_2, \ldots, b_{10}$ – pixel of area (b).

The averaging of 10 pixels is used for decreasing of noise.

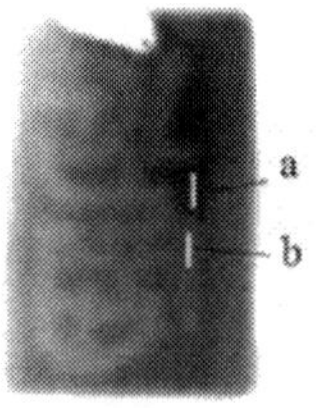

Fig. 3. Areas used for contrast computation.

The dependence between contrast and delay time is shown on fig. 4. It can be seen that the contrast depends on the phase angle of the correlation function, as the output voltage in the synchronous phase detector depends on the phase angle between the reference signal and the frequency component of the input signal, the frequency of which is equal to the frequency of the reference signal. It can be seen that the maximum is not at zero delay, due to the delay between the change of the lamp light intensity and the modulation signal.

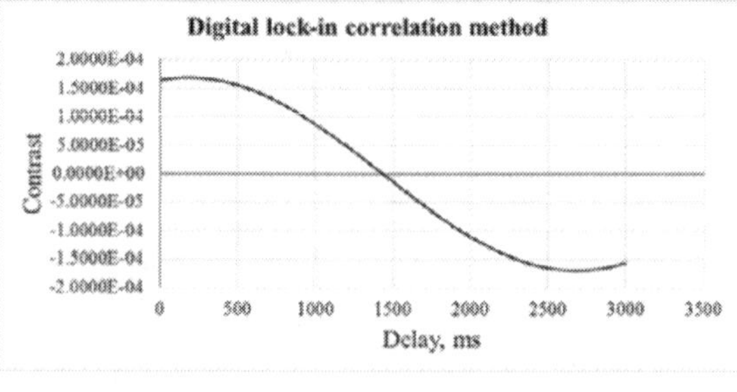

Fig. 4. Dependence between contrast and delay.

DOI: 10.1051/matecconf/201712505016

The dependences between contrast and percentage change in frequency are shown on fig. 5. It is seen that the maximum is not at the frequency of the modulation signal. This is due to the variations in the delay between changing the light intensity of the lamp and the modulation signal.

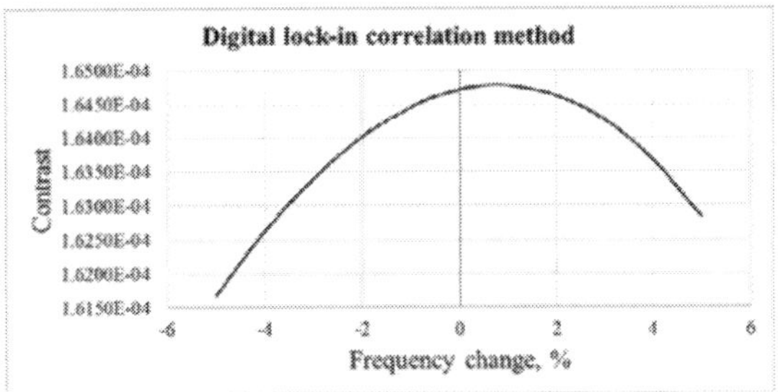

a)

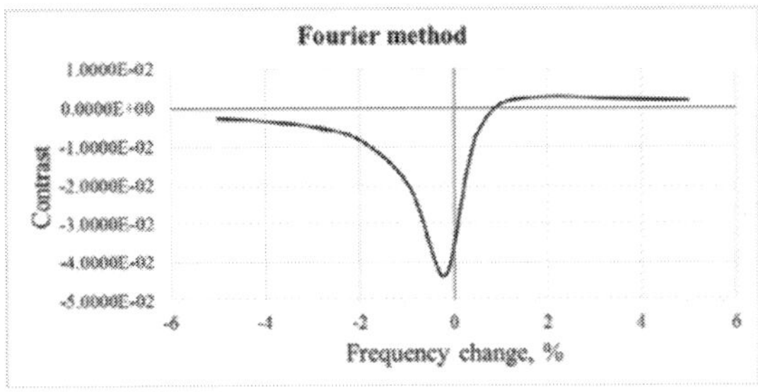

b)

Fig. 5. Dependence between contrast and percentage frequency change (a – digital lock-in correlation method, b – Fourier method).

The combination of the both corrections (delay and percentage change of frequency) can increase the contrast of phasegram more than if it is used one correction.

To determine the effect of the both corrections on the contrast, 50 phasegram calculations were performed using the digital lock-in correlation method at different random combinations of the delay and percentage frequency change values. A highest contrast is obtained at delay of 600 ms and percentage frequency change of 19 % - $1.7999.10^{-4}$. Since the contrast depends on many factors such as lamp parameters, thermal parameters of the tested object, etc., the definition of dependence on which the values of delay and percentage frequency change can be calculated is difficult and the accuracy will be low. In this case can be used iterative method, whose block algorithm is shown on fig. 6. The obtained values in this method are 200 ms for delay and 7 % for percentage frequency change (the step for delay is 50 ms and for percentage frequency change – 0.5 %) after 18 computations of the phasegram and the obtained contrast is $1.7362.10^{-4}$. The contrast without correction is $1.6472.10^{-4}$. The comparison of obtained contrast at different values of delay and percentage frequency change is presented in table 1.

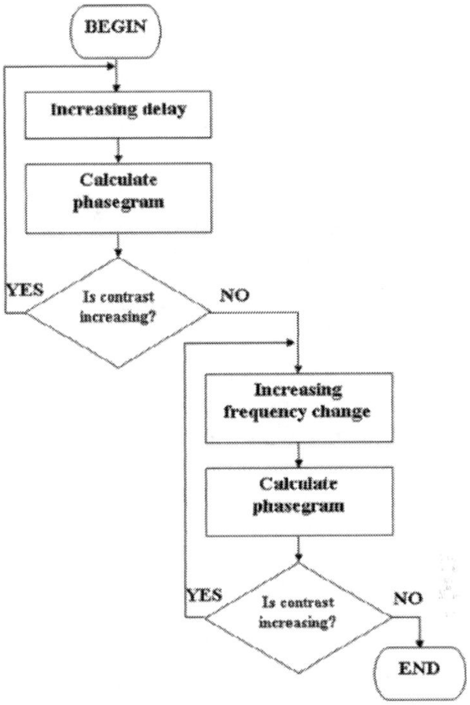

Fig. 6. Block algorithm of method for contrast increasing.

Table 1. Comparison between corrections.

Correction	Number of computations	Contrast
Without	1	$1.6472.10^{-4}$
200 ms 7 %	18	$1.7362.10^{-4}$
600 ms 19 %	50*	$1.7999.10^{-4}$

* This is a number of computations at random values of parameters. At other values it can be needed more computations for obtain the same contrast.

The phasegrams before and after using this method are shown on fig. 7.

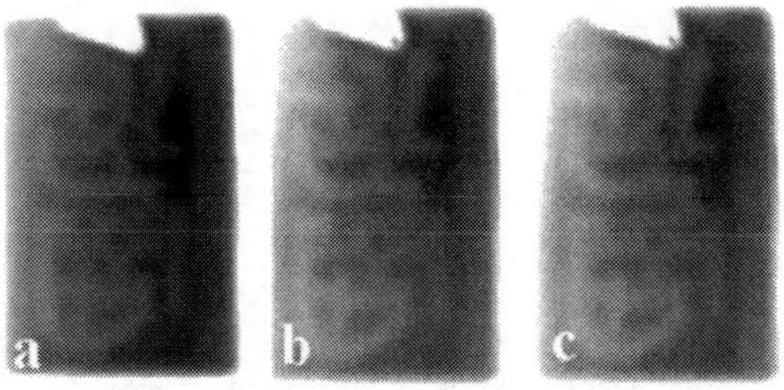

Fig. 7. Phasegrams before (a) and after using method for contrast increasing (b – 200 ms, 7 % and c – 600 ms, 19 %).

The phasegrams before and after using percentage frequency change correction at Fourier method using equation are shown on fig. 8. The contrast without percentage frequency change correction is $-3.5213.10^{-2}$ and with correction - $-4.3634.10^{-2}$ at percentage frequency change 0.2 %.

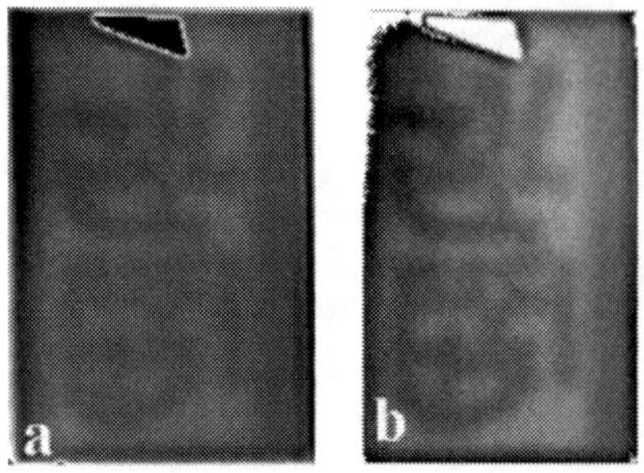

Fig. 8. Phasegrams before (a) and after (b) using percentage frequency change method at Fourier method.

5 Conclusion

The contrast of the images obtained after the lock-in measurement results processing is increased by using software compensation of the delay between the light intensity change of the lamp and the modulation signal in combination with a percentage change in frequency.

To obtain the same contrast as when no compensation is used, a lower lamp power is used which increases the energy efficiency of the method, as well as prolongs the life of the lamp.

Acknowledgment

The authors would like to thank for the support of Scientific Investigation Found under which Project No. BG05M2OP001-2.009-0033, the present work was conducted.

References

1. X. Maldague, Chapter XIV of the book: "Ultrasonic and Advanced Methods for Nondestructive Testing and Material Characterization", ed. Chen CH, (2007)
2. O. Breitenstein, W. Warta, M. Langenkamp, *Lock-in Thermography: Basics and Use for Evaluating Electronic Devices and Materials* (Springer, New York, 2010)
3. G. Busse,, QIRT (2014), http://www.ndt.net/article/qirt2014/papers/QIRT-2014-E.pdf
4. S. Delanthabettu, M. Menaka, B. Venkatraman, B. Raj, Quantitative InfraRed Thermography Journal, **12**, 1, (2015)

A Method for Strict Remote User Identification Using non - Reversible Galois Field Transformations

Nikolaos G. Bardis[1,*], *Oleksandr P. Markovskyi*[2], and *Nikolaos Doukas*[1]

[1]Department of Mathematics and Engineering Science, Hellenic Military Academy, Vari - 16673, Greece
[2]Department of Computer Engineering, Igor Sikorsky Kyiv Polytechnic Institute | National Technical University of Ukraine, Peremohy pr., Kiev 252056, KPI 2003, Ukraine

Abstract. This article proposes an approach that accelerates the realization of strict remote user identification using non reversible Galois field transformation. The proposed approach is based on using finite field arithmetic to replace the usual modular arithmetic. The application of this efficient method that was developed using Galois Fields, renders feasible an exponential reduction of the computation time required for classical zero knowledge identification methods, such as FFSIS, Schnorr and Guillou & Quisquater. The new method for user registration and identification procedure for obtaining access to the system, are illustrated. It is shown, both theoretically and experimentally that the proposed method attains a per order acceleration of the execution time required for the user identification by 2 – 3 orders of magnitude, via a hardware implementation.

1 Introduction

Given the current conditions of the widespread use of distributed systems for the collection, processing and management of information, both in the military and civil context, objectively underlines the importance of efficient and effective user rights access control methods. The rapid progress of information technology motivates the dynamic expansion of the use in the military field of multiple user distributed systems that perform operations of collection and processing of information, decision support and continuous control. The successful application of such systems depends to an important extent to the efficient identification of the users. The analysis of countermeasures in the context of information technology during military conflicts in recent years provides convincing evidence that the user identification subsystems in distributed command and control systems are increasingly becoming enemy targets.

Their practical use is limited by the fact that their implementation demands significant computational resources, given that they are founded on modular exponentiation operations, applied on numbers with lengths 1024 to 2048 bits, with a prospect for increase in the near future to 4096. In the application of modular exponentiation, an increase in the word length results to an exponential increase in the required calculation time. In this case, the rate of increase of the volume of calculations would demand an increase in the speed of computing equipment.

A particularly acute problem, is the problem of fast algorithms for identification architectures based on the concept of "zero – knowledge" in mobile devices and embedded microcontrollers, with limited energy consumption possibilities, that are commonly end user devices [1] [2]. In this context, the problem of acceleration of user identification based on zero knowledge is imminent and has a wide range of practical applications.

2 Identification Algorithms Based On The Zero – Knowledge Concept

According to current trends in technological development and its applications, there exist increased possibilities for unauthorized access to sensitive information resources of the integrated systems, possibilities that are enabled by interventions to the user identification procedures. It is a well understood fact that the increased use of wireless data transmission technologies makes it feasible for illegitimate users to mount attacks during the stage of user identification. Specifically in the case of wireless communications actions like the sniffing of passwords for access of legal subscriber, as well as his replacement after the session of identification are facilitated. A robust defense mechanism against imitation of legitimate users is the periodical repetition of the user identification procedures during the interaction of the system with a subscriber. For this reason the process of identification should be such that it enables fast implementations. Additional ways for illegitimate interventions during the identification process are the side-channel directed interactions with the system simultaneously with

* Nikolaos G. Bardis: bardis@ieee.org.org

legitimate users, the use of viruses or via the actions of irresponsible personnel. For the broad class of commercial multi-subscriber systems the elimination of the possibility of impersonation of user access by imitation of access codes is important. On the basis of the circumstances indicated, the current means for subscriber identification must satisfy the following requirements.

1. The identifying information message (password) must change with each access to the system and the passwords used must be statistically independent;
2. The length of password should be such that it completely excludes the possibility of a brute force attack;
3. The information, which is stored in the system must not be sufficient for the reproduction of subscriber passwords;
4. identification procedures must be carried out sufficiently rapidly

In literature identification methods, which satisfy the first three of the given requirements are classified as "strict", in contrast the remaining schemes that are classified as "weak". In the class of the weak schemes belong, for example, the procedure of identification which used in the UNIX operating system. This procedure involves the storage in the system of only the hash value of the passwords of users, that, with the use of the one way hash functions, excludes the possibility of the reproduction of password of the system; however, passwords themselves do not change, which makes it sufficient simple to intercept them. The class of strict procedures is principally composed by methods of identification that are based the concept "zero knowledge". The most commonly known of these methods are the FFSIS (Feige Fiat Shamir Identification Scheme) [3], Guillou- Quisquater [4] and Schnorr identification schemes [5].

FFSIS is a relatively simple and at the same time sufficiently effective scheme for the identification of the subscribers of multi-user systems, on the basis of which a number of more practical to use modified algorithms have been proposed. In the attempts of using this scheme in practice, the main disadvantage of FFSIS is the need for a large number of data exchanges during the user identification process, which noticeably loads the communication channels used. Other existing identification schemes, which implement the zero knowledge concept, require a substantially smaller volume of data transfers, but the procedures provided by them involve large computational complexity, since instead of the operation of squaring, they use the modular exponential operation.

The essence of the FFSIS consists of the following steps. The subscriber selects two prime numbers p and q and calculates the module $m=p\cdot q$. For the generation of public and private keys the subscriber selects the number v, which is been the quadratic residue on the module m. In other words, a v is selected for which $d^2 \bmod m=v$ and there exists v^{-1} such that $v\cdot v^{-1} \bmod m=1$. Then the smallest s is calculated for which: $s^2 \bmod m=v^{-1}$. The number v is the public key, while the number s is the private key. During registration, the subscriber only submits their public key - the number v to the system.

In the cycle of identification the subscriber selects a random number r and calculates the value $x=r^2 \bmod m$. The calculated value x is then sent to the system. System initiates a protocol of t cycles of accreditation. In each cycle of accreditation the following actions are carried out:

The system sends a random bit b to the subscriber. If $b=0$ then the subscriber sends to the system the number r, otherwise if $b=1$ then the subscriber uses their private key s in order to calculate $y=r\cdot s \bmod m$ and sends it to the system.

If $b=0$ then the system verifies $x=r^2 \bmod m$, otherwise if $b=1$, the system verifies $x=y^2\cdot v \bmod m$, which confirms that the subscriber possesses $s=\sqrt{v^{-1}}$ since

$$y^2\cdot v\cdot \bmod m=(r^2\cdot(\sqrt{v^{-1}})^2\cdot v) \bmod m=$$
$$=(r^2\cdot v^{-1}\cdot v) \bmod m=r^2 \bmod m=x$$

If the intruder knows the public key v of the legitimate subscriber, then they can select a random g and calculate $g^2\cdot v \bmod m=\xi$ and then send ξ, as if it were x. If the system sends as an answer the random bit $b=1$, then the intruder sends instead of y the code g. Hence the system calculates $g^2\cdot v \bmod m$, compares it with ξ and obtains a positive comparison result. However if $b=0$, then the intruder must send to the system the code $g^2 \bmod m\neq\xi$, which implies that they will have to attempt to use the fake code. If the intruder sends as x the code $g^2 \bmod m$, then the verification will proceed for $b=0$, but will fail for $b=1$.

It is obvious that the identification with the positive result is accessible only if the attacker selected the private key s. Solution of this problem is equivalent to finding the value v^{-1} of a known v. The most significant drawbacks in the described version of FFSIS identification scheme are the need for several cycles of accreditation and the low speed, caused by the fact that on each cycle of accreditation it is necessary to perform three operations of modular multiplication over multi-digit numbers. This deficiency becomes especially perceptible, if the terminal devices of subscribers are implemented as portable controllers (smart - cards), for which the completion of a modular multiplication operation presents a significant computational burden.

Another zero knowledge identification scheme has been proposed by C. Schnorr [5]. For the production of the keys, two prime numbers are considered, p and q, with q being a factor of p-1. A simple example is the case $q=11$ and $p=89$. Following that an a must be chosen, such that $a^q \bmod p=1$. E.g. for $a=45$: $45^{11} \bmod 89=1$. A random number is chosen $s<q$ e.g. $s=7$, and the calculation of $-s=q-s=11-7=4$ takes place. The number s is considered the private key. The public key v is calculated as $v=a^{-s} \bmod p$. For the example given $v=45^4 \bmod 89=39$.

The identification procedure based on the Schnorr architecture consists of the following steps:

1) The subscriber chooses a random $r<q$, e.g $r=5$ and calculates $x=a^r \bmod p$, e.g. $45^5 \bmod 89=64$, sending the number x to the system.

2) The system produces a random number $e<2^t-1$ and sends the calculated value to the subscriber. In the context of the previous example, consider $t=6$ and the corresponding $e=29$.

3) The subscriber calculates $y=(r+s\cdot e) \bmod q$ and sends the value y to the system. In the above example $y=(5+29\cdot 7) \bmod 11=10$.

4) The system verifies the equality $x = a^y \cdot v^e \bmod p$. For the above example, this equality is valid for $45^{10}\cdot 39^{29} \bmod 89= =2\cdot 32 \bmod 89=64$.

The fundamental and most computationally expensive operation in the Schnorr architecture is the modular exponentiation $a^y\cdot v^e \bmod p$.

Another classical zero-knowledge architecture, is the Guillou-Quisquater architecture [4]. The key production is carried out in the following way. The subscriber owns a public password J, which is in practice a hash signature of the symbols of a sequence containing the subscriber's name. Consider as an example the case of $J=18$. The public key of the system is the number n, which is the product of two prime numbers that are kept secret, similarly to number v. The private key is the code B such that $(J\cdot B^v) \bmod n=1$. E.g. $p=11$ and $q=19$, $p\cdot q=n =11\cdot 19=209$, $B=13$ and $v=63$ so that $J\cdot B^v \bmod n=18\cdot 151 \bmod 209=1$.

The identification sequence involves the following procedure:

1. The subscriber choses a random number r such that $1< r <n-1$, calculates the value T=rv mod n and sends the value T to the system. E.g., consider r = 22, then T=2263 mod 209=132.
2. The system produces a random number d, which must be chosen from the range $0<d<n-1$, e.g d=5 and sends it to the subscriber.
3. The subscriber calculates $D=r\cdot B^d \bmod n$ and sends it to the system. E.g. $D = 132\cdot 13^5 \bmod 209 = 176$.
4. The system calculates $T' = D^v\cdot J^d \bmod n$ and if $T = T'$, then the result of the identification is considered to be positive. For the example $T' =176^{63}\cdot 18^5 \bmod 209=132$.

Similarly to the Schnorr architecture, the fundamental operation in the case of the Guillou-Quisquater architecture is the modular exponentiation operation: $D^v\cdot J^d \bmod n$.

Hence the Schnorr and Guillou-Quisquater schemes demand a significantly smaller volume of data exchanges compared to the FFSIS, but their implementation involves a significantly large computational volume, as the squaring operation has been replaced by the modular exponentiation. The FFSIS is considered more economic in terms of the volume of the calculations involved, but its application demands several cycles of information exchange.

The purpose of this research is the development of strict remote user authentication using non reversible Galois field transformation, which involves significantly smaller computational complexity and increases the speed of identification with software and hardware implementations.

3 Mathematical Basis

In order to achieve this goal it is necessary to employ a non – reversible Galois field transformation. Using classical algebra as the basis for non – reversible transformations, the modular exponentiation operation is most commonly used: $A^E \bmod M$. Correspondingly, using Galois field algebra for constructing such transformations, the Galois field exponentiation may be utilized as: $A|^E \text{ rem } M$ [1].

This operation involves two fundamental computational procedures: polynomial multiplication or multiplication without carry – MWC hence denoted as $\otimes$ and the polynomial division operation that calculates the remainder of the polynomial reduction of a polynomial $U(x)$ with the base polynomial $M(x)$ of the field, with the reduction operation hence denoted as U rem M.

In conventional algebra, a significant part of cryptographic mechanisms, including RSA, have modulo M as a foundation the product of two prime numbers: $M=p\cdot q$. Similar approaches may be applied concerning the creation of cryptographic mechanisms based on Galois fields. More specifically, such an approach is proposed in the context of the present research for the purpose of zero-knowledge identification of remote users.

The foundation of the proposed method lies in the following mathematical proposals.

If $q(x)$ is a prime polynomial degree w, then for every element k of the field $GF(2^w)$ that is formulated from this polynomial, the operation executed is:

$$k|^{h-1} \text{ rem } g = 1, \quad (1)$$
where $h=2^w$.

Lemma: if the polynomial $M(x)$ formulated by the field is a polynomial product $M(x) = q(x)\otimes g(x)$, of two prime polynomials $q(x)$ of degree w and $g(x)$ of degree v then for every k such that $0<k<h$ and for every l such that $0< l< u$, where $h=2^w$, $u=2^v$ then it is true that:

$$(k \otimes g)|^h \text{ rem } M = k \otimes g \quad (2)$$
$$(l \otimes q)|^u \text{ rem } M = l \otimes q$$

Proof:

From (1) it is true that $k|^h = \mu\otimes q \oplus 1$, where μ is an integer.

It hence follows that (2) may be transformed as follows:

$(k\otimes g)|^h \text{ rem} M=(k|^h\otimes g|^h) \text{ rem } M=((\mu\otimes q)\oplus 1)\otimes g|^h) \text{ rem} M= =(\mu\otimes g^{h-1}\otimes q\otimes g) \text{ rem } M\oplus g|^h \text{ rem } M=(\mu\otimes g^{h-1}\otimes M) \text{ rem } M\oplus g|^h \text{ rem } M$.

Since $(\mu\otimes g^{h-1}\otimes M) \text{ rem } M = 0$, expression (2) may be simplified as: $(k\otimes g)|^h \text{ rem } M=g|^h \text{ rem } M$.

Taking into account (1), $g|^h$ is reformulated as: $g|^h=\lambda\otimes q\oplus 1$, where λ is an integer.

Consequently, $g|^{h+1}=\lambda\otimes q\otimes g\oplus g$, and $g|^{h+1}$ rem $M=(\lambda\otimes q\otimes g\oplus g)$ rem $M=g$.

It follows directly from the Lemma that exponentiation in the field defined using a polynomial $M(x)=q(x)\otimes g(x)$, the numbers that are a polynomial product of numbers smaller that k with the number g, have a repetition equal to 2^w-1. Since from the point of view of authentication, the number g and consequently the respective period are not known for a value M, then property (2) may be used for the creation of method for strict cryptographic identification.

4 Registration And Identification Procedures

The proposed method involves two procedures: the user registration procedure and the procedure of a user identification procedure for obtaining access.

The proposed user registration procedure involves the following steps:

1. The user randomly selects two prime polynomials of different degrees; $q(x)$ of degree w: $q(x)=x^w+q_{u-1}\cdot x^{w-1}+...+q_1\cdot x+q_0$ and $g(x)$ of degree v: $g(x)=x^v+g_{v-1}\cdot x^v+...+g_1\cdot x+g_0$, where $g_0,g_1,...,g_{v-1}\in\{0,1\}$, $q_0,q_1,...,q_{w-1}\in\{0,1\}$ and $w>v$.
2. The user formed the base polynomial $m(x)$ in the form of a polynomial product of the selected prime polynomials $g(x)$ and $q(x)$: $M(x)=g(x)\otimes q(x)$.
3. The user selects a random number $k\in\{1,..,2^w-1\}$ and performs the calculation of f as the exponent in the Galois field with the transformation of the polynomial $M(x)$: $f=g|^k$ rem M.
4. The user encrypts the codes M and f of the public key of the system and submits them to the system. The system receives and stores the codes M and f that are subsequently used as the public key of the authentication of the given user.

The proposed registration procedure is presented in the following example using small length numbers.

According to Step 1 of the proposed user registration procedure, two prime polynomial are selected of degrees w=6 and v=4: $q(x)=x^6+x^4+x^2+x+1$ and $g(x)=x^4+x+1$; the first polynomial $q(x)$ corresponds to the number $q=1010111_2=87$, and the second polynomial $g(x)$ – to the number $g=10011_2=19$. Subsequently, according to Step 2, the polynomial product of the selected polynomials is calculated $M(x)=g(x)\otimes q(x)=x^{10}+x^8+x^7+x^3+1$. The calculation of the polynomial corresponds to the number $M(x)=g(x)\otimes q(x)=x^{10}+x^8+x^7+x^3+1$. Following that, according to Step 3 of the procedure, the user selects the random number $k=55\in\{1,..,2^6-1\}$, and calculates $f=g|^k$ rem $M=19|^{55}$ rem 1417=465. This number, together with the number M encrypts the public key of the system and sends it to the system.

The expanded procedure of a cycle of user identification involves the following steps:

1. The system forms a random number ξ and sends it to the user.
2. The user receives the code ξ from the system and calculates η such that the expression $\xi\cdot\eta$ mod $(2^w-1)=k$ is true.
3. The user calculates the session password p for current session in the form $p=g|^\eta$ rem M and the resulting p is sent to the system.
4. The system receives from the user the session password p and calculates $r=p|^\xi$ rem M. The result obtained is compared with the fixed for the particular code f of the user. If the two codes are identical, i.e. $r=f$ then the identification cycle is considered successful.

The proposed identification cycle procedure is illustrated using the following example that continues the previously given example.

The system randomly selects the number $\xi=34$ and sends it to the user.

The user receives the code $\xi=34$ from the system and finds η such that $\xi\cdot\eta$ mod $(2^w-1)=k$, or equivalently $34\cdot\eta$ mod 63 = 55. This condition is satisfied for $\eta=22$. According to Step 3, the proposed identification procedure user calculates the session password for session p in the form:

$$p=g|^\eta \text{ rem } M=19|^{22} \text{ rem } 1417=641.$$

The obtained password p=641 is sent to the system.

The system according to Step 4 receives from the user session password p and calculates

$$r=p|^\xi \text{ rem } M=641|^{34} \text{ rem } 1417=465.$$

Since the calculated code r = 465 is identical to the stored fixed code for the particular user f= 465, the identification cycle is considered successful.

5 Estimation of the Efficiency

The principal factors used for measuring the effectiveness of the proposed method for the proposed zero – knowledge remote user identification technique are:

- the level of security against attempts to acquire unauthorized access to system resources;
- the total amount of computational resources required for the execution of a cycle of identification. In reality, critical effectiveness factor is the time required for the execution of a identification cycle by system, as such systems typically have to serve extremely large numbers of user requests.

The repeated using of already transmitted session password p is impossible, as this changes after every new identification session. In effect, for by passing the proposed identification scheme, i.e. the production of a valid session password for the user, one of the polynomials $q(x)$ or $g(x)$ is necessary to be exposed.

With external intruders that may only have available a sequence t of session passwords p_1, p_2... p_t, the information they possess is insufficient and does not enable the recovery of the $g(x)$. The system possesses only the fundamental polynomial $M(x)$ and by pass of the identification in this context involves analyzing it into simple multipliers, which for high enough powers of $M(x)$ is not realistically feasible in practice.

The fundamental advantage of the proposed method is the remote user identification based on the zero – knowledge principle, using Galois field algebra and hence obtaining increased possibilities for efficiency during user authentication. Efficiency is due to the following factors:

- Operations in the Galois fields are easily executable and require less time. More specifically, the fundamental operation of exponentiation of n bit numbers both in conventional and Galois field algebra involve in general operations of calculating squares and multiplication operations. Calculating squares in a Galois field does not require computational resources in practice and involves insertions of zeros between the bits of the number [1].
- During execution of operations in Galois fields, any processing of bits is independently executed without involving the transfer of any carry bits. The simulation in software showed that exponentiation in Galois fields is significantly faster compared to exponentiation in conventional algebra. Simulation in hardware [6] demonstrated an increase in efficiency by 2 – 3 orders of magnitude and a simultaneous simplification of the circuit necessary by 3 – 4 times.
- The research conducted demonstrated that the realistic values for the magnitude of the number ξ may be significantly smaller than the order of the polynomial $M(x)$, without effecting the level of security. In reality, the level of security is maintained even for a value of ξ equal to 2. For this reason, the magnitude of ξ is determined by the actual number of possible identification cycles. The use of relatively small values for the magnitude of ξ multiply reduces the time required for exponentiation.
- The proposed method, contrary to existing techniques uses a single session for the identification of the user by system.

6 Conclusions

In this paper, zero – knowledge user identification using non – reversible transformation in Galois fields was investigated and a scheme for such identification was proposed. For this purpose a theoretical study was conducted of the properties of specific cycles that appear during exponentiation in the context of special cases of Galois fields. The theoretical results enabled the development of procedures for the registration and identification of remote users. It was theoretically determined that the level of security attained does not differ from existing zero knowledge systems. The principal advantage of the proposed method is the possibility of achieving significantly higher rates of identification. This increased rate is of vital importance in current applications with ever growing numbers of system users and the necessity for remote information processing. Maximum effectiveness of the proposed method is attained by implementation in hardware.

References

1. Bardis, Nikolaos, Nikolaos Doukas, and Oleksandr P. Markovskyi. "Fast subscriber identification based on the zero knowledge principle for multimedia content distribution." International Journal of Multimedia Intelligence and Security 1.4 363-377, (2010)
2. Stavroulakis Peter, et al. Efficient zero—Knowledge identification based on one way Boolean transformations. In: GLOBECOM Workshops (GC Wkshps), 2011 IEEE.,. p. 275-280. (2011)
3. Feige U.,Fiat A.,Shamir A. "Zero knowledge proofs of identity" // Journal of Cryptology, Vol.1, No.2, P.77-94, (1988)
4. Guillou L.C., Quisquater J.-J. A Paradoxical Identity-Based Signature Schemes Resulting from Zero Knowledge // Advances of Cryptology - Crypto-88. Proceeding.- Springer-Verlag.- P. 216-231,(1990)
5. Schnorr C.P. Efficient Signature Generation for Smart Cards // Journal of Cryptology, Vol. 4, No.3.- pp.161-174, (1991)
6. Brey B.B. The Intel Microprocessors. Sixth Edition. Prentice Hall: New Jersey.- 1328 p., (2005)

A Translation of the Malia Altar Stone

Peter Z. Revesz[1,a]

[1] *Department of Computer Science, University of Nebraska-Lincoln, Lincoln, NE, 68588, USA*

Abstract. This paper presents a translation of the Malia Altar Stone inscription (CHIC 328), which is one of the longest known Cretan Hieroglyph inscriptions. The translation uses a synoptic transliteration to several scripts that are related to the Malia Altar Stone script. The synoptic transliteration strengthens the derived phonetic values and allows avoiding certain errors that would result from reliance on just a single transliteration. The synoptic transliteration is similar to a multiple alignment of related genomes in bioinformatics in order to derive the genetic sequence of a putative common ancestor of all the aligned genomes.

1 Introduction

Cretan Hieroglyph is a writing system that existed in eastern Crete c. 2100 – 1700 BC [13, 14, 25]. The full decipherment of Cretan Hieroglyphs requires a consistent translation of all known Cretan Hieroglyph texts not just the translation of some examples. In particular, many authors have suggested translations for the Phaistos Disk, the most famous and longest Cretan Hieroglyph inscription, but in general they were unable to show that their translation method is also applicable to the other known Cretan Hieroglyph texts. As one of a few exceptions, the author proposed both a translation of the Phaistos Disk [18] and a consistent translation of some short Cretan Hieroglyph inscriptions [19]. However, the translation of medium length Cretan Hieroglyph inscriptions remained an open problem, which is addressed in this paper.

The Malia Altar Stone, which was found by a farmer in 1937, is a blue limestone slab with a cuplike cavity on its top and a medium length Cretan Hieroglyph inscription consisting of sixteen letters on its side as described by Chapouthier [7]. The Malia Altar Stone is thought to be an offering table with some liquid placed in its cuplike cavity. The exact date of the Malia Altar Stone cannot be determined, but it is considered to be a Minoan artifact. Olivier et al. [14] list the Malia Altar Stone as item number 328 in the *Corpus Hieroglyphicarum Inscriptionum Cretae* (CHIC).

Many authors noted some visual relationships between the Cretan Hieroglyph script symbols and the Linear A, the Linear B and the Anatolian Hieroglyph script symbols. The common assumption was that the known sound values of Linear B and Anatolian Hieroglyph script symbols could be projected back to similar-looking Cretan Hieroglyph and Linear A script symbols. These attempts so far were not successful in deciphering the later two scripts.

Using ideas and methods from bioinformatics, Revesz [20] analyzed the evolutionary relationships within the *Cretan script family,* which includes the following scripts: Cretan Hieroglyph, Linear A, Linear B [6], Cypriot, Greek, Phoenician, South Arabic, Old Hungarian [9, 10], which is also called *rovásírás* in Hungarian and also written sometimes as Rovas in English language publications, and Tifinagh.

Revesz [20] found that Cypriot and Old Hungarian were closest to Cretan Hieroglyph. This study implied that Cypriot and Old Hungarian phonetic values could be more fruitful than Linear B phonetic values to project back to Cretan Hieroglyphs. That approach was used to translate the Phaistos Disk [18] and some short Cretan Hieroglyph inscriptions [19]. (In addition, Linear B was evolutionarily closest to Linear A, giving some justification for projecting Linear B phonetic values to Linear A.)

Using a specific projection of Linear B phonetic values to Cretan Hieroglyphs, Boutsikos translated both the Phaistos Disk and the Malia Altar Stone as an ancient Greek writing [3]. In particular, for the Malia Altar Stone, he obtained the following translation: *"Cares for trust and quantity goddess Mene path you correct."*

Using a combination of projections from Anatolian Hieroglyph script phonetic values and Linear B script phonetic values, Best and Woudhuizen [23] translated the Malia altar stone as a Luwian document with the following meaning: *"This inscribed altar stone for Baluzitis, delivery: Skheria."*

Lia Rietveld in [1], pages 94-95, used a similar projection from Anatolian Hieroglyphs to translate the Phaistos Disk as a Luwian letter written to King Nestor of Pylos. Further extending this approach with some

[a] Corresponding author: revesz@cse.unl.edu

phonetic projections from Egyptian Hieroglyph, Woudhuizen [23] translated several other Cretan Hieroglyph texts, including the Arkalochori Axe inscription as a Luwian text.

The approaches of Boutsikos and of Woudhuizen and his co-workers are noted here as some of the more serious translation attempts because they consider several Cretan Hieroglyph texts. A discussion of other translation attempts and their limitations can be found in Duhoux [8].

This paper is organized as follows. Section 2 describes the translation method. Section 3 presents a translation of the Malia Altar Stone inscription. Finally, Section 4 gives some conclusions and directions for future work.

2 The translation method

Our translation method is necessarily based on some assumptions about the Cretan Hieroglyph writing system. In particular, we need to classify the Cretan Hieroglyph writing system among the known categories.

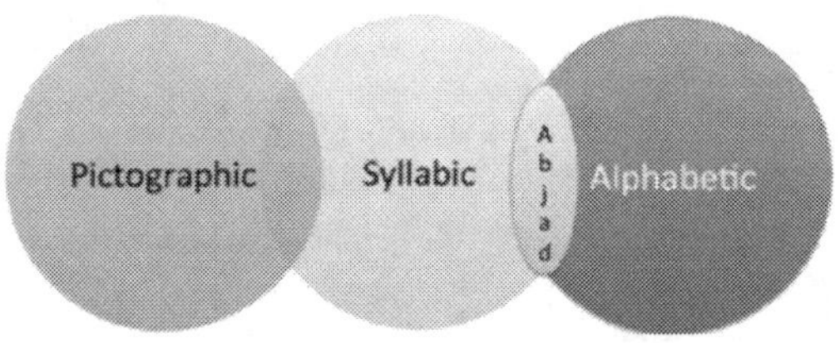

Fig. 1. A classification of writing systems.

In general, writing systems can be divided into pictographic, syllabic and alphabetic system as shown in Fig. 1. In pictographic writing systems, each symbol denotes a single word. Pictographic writing systems are limited in vocabulary and cannot express grammatical features.

In syllabic writing systems, each symbol denotes a single syllable. For example, Linear B is a syllabic writing system where in general each syllable begins with a single consonant C, which is followed by a single vowel V to form simple CV-type syllable. Such a syllabic writing is conveniently represented in a syllabic grid, where each row stands for a consonant and each column stands for a vowel.

In alphabetic writing systems, each symbol represents a single sound. In abjad writing systems each symbol represents a consonant, but when the text is read the vowels that implicitly lie between the consonants are pronounced together with those consonants. Arabic and Hebrew are examples of abjad writing systems, although they also use occasionally some symbols that represent vowels to avoid potential ambiguities. Abjad writing systems can be thought of as the intersection of syllabic and alphabetic writing systems because they share some features with both of those writing systems.

Old Hungarian [9, 10] can be characterized as a partial-abjad script because most of the time only the consonants are explicitly written down while the vowels are only implicit. However, Old Hungarian has more number of vowels than Arabic or Hebrew have. Hence in Old Hungarian the chance of ambiguity is always higher if in a word a vowel is omitted. On the other hand, Old Hungarian inscriptions take advantage of vowel harmony within words. In languages with vowel harmony, each word contains only all high or deep vowels and in fact frequently all the vowels are the same. Hence it is enough to indicate only the first vowel and omit the rest of the vowels. Table 1 illustrates the various writing systems.

Table 1. Different types of writing systems.

Type	Possible Way of Writing "Knossos"	Writing System Examples
Syllabic	Ko-no-so	Linear B
Partial Abjad	K-n-o-s-s-s	Old Hungarian
Abjad	K-n-s-s-s	Arabic, Hebrew
Alphabetic	K-n-o-s-s-o-s	English, Latin

What is the type of the Minoan writing system? Most experts say that writing developed from some initial pictogram writing, to syllabic writing, then partial-abjad writing, then abjad writing and finally an alphabetic writing. Most experts also agree that the Minoan writing seems more complex than pictograms and is not an alphabetic writing. It is therefore usually assumed that the Minoan writing is syllabic. Linear B is syllabic and it would seem impossible to that Linear A is a partial-abjad or an abjad, when Linear B is a later development of Linear A and Cretan Hieroglyphs.

However, we would like to propose that the Minoan writing system is a partial-abjad. As writing advances from pictograms, the next stage could be either syllabic—in case there is no vowel harmony and a larger set of vowels in the underlying language—or a partial-abjad—in case there is vowel harmony or only a few vowels. The rational of this hypothesis is that with either vowel harmony or with few vowels, the implicit vowels become easily guessable hence a partial-abjad or abjad writing can be efficiently applied. We believe that the Minoan language had either vowel harmony or few vowels and could naturally develop into a partial-abjad. In contrast, Mycenaean Greek had a larger number of vowels and lacked vowel harmony. Hence Mycenaean Greek naturally developed into a syllabic writing.

Our translation method uses the following steps. First, we use what we call *synoptic transliteration* to identify the phonetic values of all the symbols. Synoptic transliteration means that we compare each symbol with several different cognate symbols from other alphabets and syllabaries. Although individual symbols may change their phonetic values, when the phonetic values agree, then it is highly probable that the phonetic value of the

 DOI: 10.1051/matecconf/201712505018

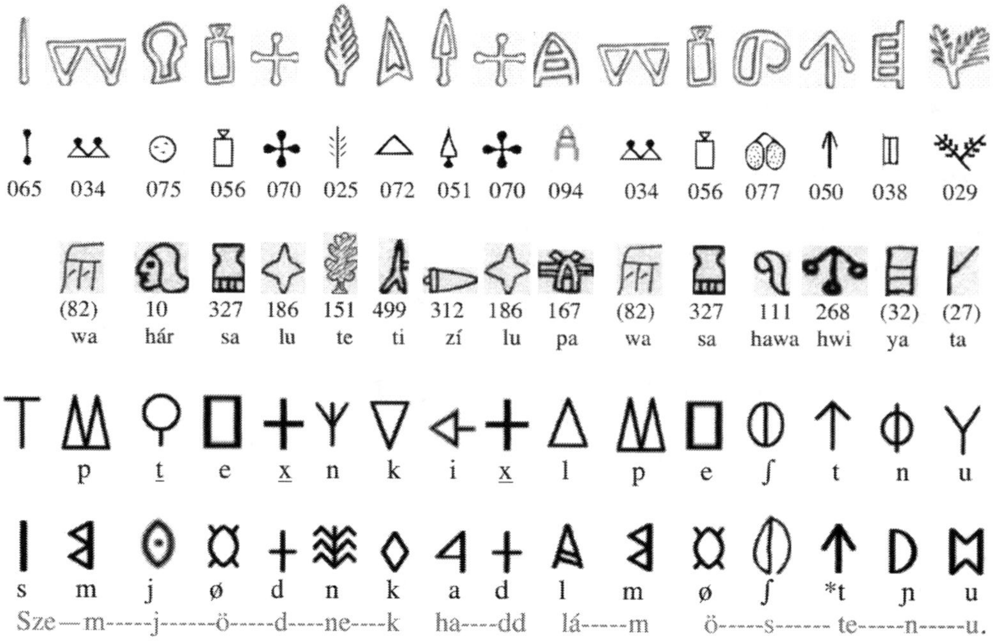

Fig. 2. The Malia Altar Stone inscription (first row), its transliteration into Cretan Hieroglyphs (second row), Anatolian/Luwian Hieroglyphs (third row), the Carian alphabet (fourth row) and the Old Hungarian alphabet (fifth row). The syllabic values are indicated below the Anatolian (Luwian) symbols, and the IPA sound values are indicated below each Carian and the Old Hungarian letter. In the bottom the translation is shown with root words in red and suffixes in blue.

Malia Altar Stone symbol was the same as the phonetic value of its cognate symbols. In case of disagreements, we consider which phonetic value may be the original.

Second, we fill in the missing vowels as is required by a partial abjad writing system, the main guide here is that with the additions, we obtain meaningful words and sentences in the Proto-Finno-Ugric, Proto-Ugric and Proto-Hungarian languages, which were also used to aid in the translation of the Phaistos Disk [17, 18], under the assumption that the Minoan language could be classified to also belong to the Finno-Ugric group of languages. The fill-in process was partially automated by the use of a database of proto-words from Zaicz [26] to aid searching for proto-words that match the phonetic values in the text.

3 The translation result

Chapouthier [7] assumed a right-to-left reading direction of the Malia altar stone inscription. The top of Fig. 2 shows a reordering of the signs of his drawing to allow a left-to-right reading direction. Several other Cretan Hieroglyph inscriptions have the same sequence of three or two signs. For example, the beginning sequence

of CHIC 118a matches the 4th, 5th, 6th and perhaps also the 7th sign of the Malia altar stone. Similarly, the sequence

occurs within CHIC 49 and 61 followed by a number, which suggests that this pair can denote some commodity. Since the first sign may depict breasts and the second sign some container, the commodity may be bottles of milk. CHIC 178, 238, 244, 248, 260, 281, 295, 296 and 310 also contain the above pair of signs, in each case following the x sign.

The third sign of the Malia altar stone inscription denotes some head. A sheep head followed by a sign occurs in CHIC 013, 015, 024 and 297, while a cow head followed by a sign occurs in CHIC 002. In some of these cases, the heads may be logograms indicating sheep milk or cow milk, respectively. However, in the Malia Altar Stone inscription the head sign may denote a human head. A human torso follows a sign in CHIC 058.

Finally, like the Malia Altar Stone, CHIC 072 may end with or it may begin with . These similarities with the other Cretan Hieroglyph inscriptions indicate a high probability that the reading direction suggested by Chapouthier [7] is correct.

The second row of Fig. 2 shows a transliteration of the Malia Altar Stone into a Cretan Hieroglyph script. The number below each Cretan Hieroglyph symbol is its numbering following Olivier et al. [14].

The third row of Fig. 2 shows a transliteration of the Malia Altar Stone into Anatolian Hieroglyph (or in parentheses Luwian) script. This transliteration as well as the number and syllabic value below each symbol follows the numbering by Woudhuizen [23].

The fourth and fifth rows of Fig. 2 show a transliteration of the Malia Altar Stone into the Carian alphabet [22] and the Old Hungarian alphabet [9, 10], respectively. For the Old Hungarian transliteration, the symbol is a version of from the Nagyszentmiklós gold treasure's cup number 23, which is variously dated between the 8th and the 10th centuries (see [10], page 157). Similarly, is a version of from the Constantinople Old Hungarian inscription from 1515 (see [10], page 193).

Table 2 lists the sound values of the Cretan Hieroglyph symbols that are known from previous translations [18, 19]. There is generally a phonetic agreement among the Cretan Hieroglyph, the Carian and the Old Hungarian symbols with only a few exceptions. The exceptions appear in the underlined Carian sound values. We believe that the Carian letters and originally had sound values closer to the corresponding Old Hungarian letters and their listed /t/ and /x/ sound values are likely later developments under the influence of the Greek letters for theta θ and chi χ.

The initial sounds of the Anatolian Hieroglyph syllabic values often differ from the rest of the sound values. Hence our translation is based on the Cretan Hieroglyph symbol and the Old Hungarian sound values because they seem to support each other and appear more reliable than either the Anatolian Hieroglyph or the Carian sound values.

Our translation is shown at the bottom of Fig. 2. The translation reads "Szem-jödnek hadd lá-m östenu," after filling in the missing vowels, the word beginning /h/ and the second /d/. Forrai [9] gives examples where word beginning /h/ and doubling of consonants are omitted. The translation means in English *"For your eyes that you may see God."*

The translation makes sense considering the possible use of the Malia Altar Stone. The cup-like cavity of the Malia Altar Stone was likely filled with some liquid that was sprinkled on the face and eyes of the people as part of some religious ceremony. The people attending the ceremony may have felt that their spiritual eyes were cleansed and afterwards could see God. The liquid could even have had hallucinogenic powers and may have been also drunk by the Minoan faithful.

In the first word of the translation, the root is the Proto-Ugric *szem (eye). It is followed by an agglutinative suffix, where *-jeid > -jöd denotes 'second person possessive case and plural number of objects' and –nek denotes the preposition 'for.' Hence szem-jödnek means 'for your eyes.'

The expression 'hadd lám' means 'let me see' or 'let you see.' The word 'hadd' contains a Proto-Uralic root with cognates Hungarian 'hagy' (to let) and Mansi 'kolj' (to let) with a second person imperative mood, meaning 'you let.' The word 'lám' derives from a Proto-Uralic root from which the Proto-Hungarian 'lát' (to see) derives.

Finally, the word 'östenu' seems cognate with Hungarian 'isten' (god) and Hattian 'istanu' (sungod).

A possible variation of the above translation assumes that the last letter in the Old Hungarian transliteration is with a phonetic value /t/. In that case the last word would be isten-t. Since –t is the Hungarian accusative suffix, the meaning of isten-t would be 'to see god-accusative-suffix.'

Table 2. Cretan Hieroglyph symbols and their IPA phonetic values.

001	m	041	ʃ	081	
002	m	042	s	082	
003	k	043	s	083	
004	a	044		084	
005	f	045		085	
006		046	n	086	
007	s	047	j	087	
008	ɛ	048	i	088	p
009	ɛ	049		089	ɲ
010	l	050	*t	090	
011	b	051	a	091	
012		052	l	092	ɲ
013		053	é	093	g
014		054	v	094	l
015		055	g	095	
016		056	ø	096	
017		057		Logogram	
018		058		153	l
019	h	059		154	ʒ
020	m	060	p	156	
021		061	k	161	
022		062	d	162	
023	ʒ	063	d	164	
024	r	064		166	
025	n	065	s	168	ɲ
026		066	ɟ͡ʝ	169	
027	t	067	nd	170	
028	p	068	u	171	
029	u	069	c͡ç	172	
030	z	070	d	173	
031	ʒ	071		179	
032	z	072	k	180	
033		073		304	
034	m	074		305	
035		075		308	
036		076		309	
037	z	077	ʃ	1	
038	ɲ	078	k	10	
039		079		100	
040	o	080		1000	

The precise origin of the Hungarian –t accusative suffix is unknown because it is not shared with Khanty and Mansi but still occurs in some of the earliest extant texts such as a funeral sermon from 1192 [2]. On the other hand, the –t accusative suffix is not applied consistently in the early texts and is often omitted.

Either translation implies a belief in the spiritual power of liquids. That belief recalls Minoan and later Greek libation offerings and several ancient Near Eastern parallels [12]. Libations may have been intended to revivify the dead by some magic power of the offered liquid, which was often blood, wine, oil or milk.

4 Conclusions and future work

In this paper, we presented a translation of the Malia Altar Stone inscription. Our translation uses a synoptic transliteration into scripts whose phonetic values are at least partially known. After a synoptic transliteration, it is easier to guess the original phonetic values of the symbols in the unknown script. That is similar to how in bioinformatics, the multiple alignment of related genomes can be used to generate a hypothetical genomic sequence of the common ancestor of the aligned genomes [20, 21].

The present translation extended our previous translations of the Phaistos Disk [17] and some shorter Cretan Hieroglyph inscriptions [18]. Like our earlier Phaistos Disk translation, the present translation also yielded a religious text. It requires more study whether our synoptic transliteration method can be applied to other Minoan inscriptions in order to develop a translation.

References

1. W. Achterberg, J. Best, K. Enzler, L. Rietveld, and F. Woudhuizen, *The Phaistos Disc: A Luwian Letter to Nestor*, Publications of the Henri Frankfort Foundation **13** (Amsterdam, Dutch Archaeological and Historical Society, 2004)
2. L. Benkő, *Az Árpád-kor magyar nyelvű szövegemlékei* (Budapest, ELTE, Régi Magyar Irodalomtudományi Intézet 1980)
3. S. Boutsikos, Malia altar stone, Available at: http://the-phaistos-disk.webnode.com/malia-altar-stone/, (2014), downloaded May 11, 2017.
4. G. Brandt et al., Science, 342, 6155, 257-261 (2013).
5. J. Campbell, *Occidental Mythology: The Masks of God* (Viking Penguin, New York 1962)
6. J. Chadwick, *The Decipherment of Linear B*, (Cambridge University Press, 1958)
7. F. Chapouthier, Inscription hiéroglyphique gravée sur un bloc de calcaire, Bulletin de Correspondance Hellénique 62, 104-109, (1938)
8. Y. Duhoux, American Journal of Archaeology, **104**, 3, 597–600 (2000)
9. S. Forrai, *The Old Hungarian Writing from Ancient Times to the Present*, (in Hungarian), (Antológia Kiadó, Budapest, Hungary 1994)
10. G. Hosszú, *Heritage of Scribes: The Relation of Rovas Scripts to Eurasian Writing Systems*, (Rovas Foundation Hungary, Budapest, Hungary 2013)
11. P.C. Kanellakis, G.M. Kuper, P.Z. Revesz, J. of Comp. and Sys. Sciences, **51**, 1, 26-52 (1995)
12. N. Marinatos, *Minoan Kingship and the Solar Goddess: A Near Eastern Koine*, (University of Illinois Press, 2010).
13. J.-P. Olivier, Cretan writing in the second millennium B.C., World Archaeology. **17**, 3, 377–389 (1986).
14. J.-P. Olivier, L. Godart and J.-C. Poursat, *Corpus Hieroglyphicarum Inscriptionum Cretae* Études Crétoises **31**, (De Boccard, Paris 1996)
15. P.Z. Revesz, *Introduction to Databases: From Biological to Spatio-Temporal*, (Springer, New York, 2010)
16. P.Z. Revesz, Proc. 4th ACM Int. Conf. on Bioinfo. and Comp. Bio., 731-734, (ACM Press, New York, USA, 2013)
17. P.Z. Revesz, A computational translation of the Phaistos Disk, In: Mathematical Models and Computational Methods (joint proceedings of AMCSE-MMMAS-EAS, Agios Nikolaos, Crete, Greece), Imre J. Rudas, editor, INASE Press, 53-57, (2015)
18. P.Z. Revesz, A computer-aided translation of the Phaistos Disk, Int. Journal of Computers, **10**, 94-100, (2016)
19. P.Z. Revesz, A computer-aided translation of the Cretan Hieroglyph script, Int. Journal of Signal Processing, **1**, 127-133 (2016)
20. P.Z. Revesz, Bioinformatics evolutionary tree algorithms reveal the history of the Cretan script family, Int. Journal of Applied Mathematics and Informatics, **10**, 67-76, (2016)
21. M. Shortridge, T. Triplet, P.Z. Revesz, M. Griep, R. Powers, Comp. Bio. and Chem., **35**, 1, 24-33, (2011)
22. Wikipedia, "Carian alphabets," downloaded April 5, 2017. Available: https://en.wikipedia.org/wiki/Carian_alphabets
23. F. Woudhuizen, *The Earliest Cretan Scripts*, (Innsbrucker Beiträge zur Kulturwissenschaft 2006)
24. J. G. Young, Minos 31-32 (1996-1997[1999]) 379-400.
25. P. Yule, *Early Cretan Seals: A Study of Chronology*, Marburger Studien zur Vor und Frühgeschichte **4** (Mainz 1981)
26. G. Zaicz, chief editor, *Etimológiai Szótár: Magyar Szavak és Toldalékok Eredete, (Etymological Dictionary: Origin of Hungarian Words and Affixes)*, (Tinta Könyvkiadó, 2006).

The Cretan Script Family Includes the Carian Alphabet

Peter Z. Revesz[1,a]

[1] *Department of Computer Science, University of Nebraska-Lincoln, Lincoln, NE, 68588, USA*

Abstract. The *Cretan Script Family* is a set of related writing systems that have a putative origin in Crete. Recently, Revesz [11] identified the Cretan Hieroglyphs, Linear A, Linear B, the Cypriot syllabary, and the Greek, Old Hungarian, Phoenician, South Arabic and Tifinagh alphabets as members of this script family and using bioinformatics algorithms gave a hypothetical evolutionary tree for their development and presented a map for their likely spread in the Mediterranean and Black Sea areas. The evolutionary tree and the map indicated *some unknown writing system in western Anatolia* to be the common origin of the Cypriot syllabary and the Old Hungarian alphabet. This paper argues that the missing link may be some ancestor of the Carian alphabet because several Carian alphabet letters show an intermediate stage between the corresponding Cypriot syllabary signs and the Old Hungarian letters.

1 Introduction

In the study of ancient scripts, Crete plays a major role as the location of origin of three different types of scripts: Cretan Hieroglyphs, Linear A and Linear B [2, 7, 8, 17, 18]. Moreover, Arthur Evans already proposed the spread of these Cretan scripts to Cyprus because of their resemblance to the later Cypro-Minoan and Cypriot syllabaries.

Recently, Revesz [12] noted further resemblances of the Cretan scripts with the Greek, Old Hungarian (native '*Rovásírás*') [4, 6, 12, 13, 15], Phoenician, South Arabic and Tifinagh alphabets. By using phylogenetic algorithms from bioinformatics [9], Revesz [12] gave, as shown in Fig. 1, a hypothetical evolutionary tree for all the above-mentioned scripts, which he collectively named the *Cretan Script Family*. He also illustrated the hypothetical spread of these scripts on a map of the Eastern Mediterranean and Black Sea areas. The evolutionary tree suggested that the Cypriot syllabary and the Old Hungarian alphabet had a common immediate ancestor, which was putatively located in western Anatolia, which seemed a likely place before a presumed split towards the northern Black Sea areas, where Hungarians are first mentioned in written history, and Cyprus in the Eastern Mediterranean.

Western Anatolia was strongly influenced by the Minoan culture. In the early and middle Bronze Age, Miletus was a Minoan colony. In the late Bronze Age, Miletus became a Carian city. By the 8th century BC, Miletus came under Greek influence and itself established many colonies in the Black Sea region (Gabrielson et al. [5], Tsetskhladze [14]). The above historical outline suggests the following hypothesis:

Minoan writing spread first to western Anatolia, where it influenced the development of the Carian alphabet [1, 16], *which spread with Milesian and other Carian settlers to various native groups of people who lived at that time on the northern shores of the Black Sea. Early Hungarian tribes were either included among those groups of people or they acquired the writing when they arrived to the northern Black Sea region.*

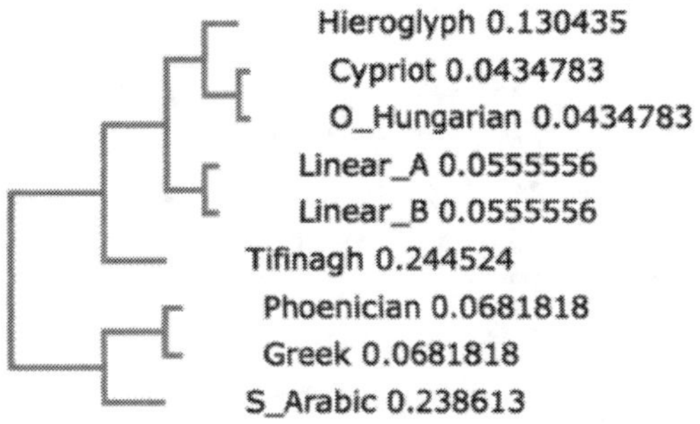

Fig. 1. The Cretan Script Family tree generated by the UPGMA phylogenetic algorithm (Revesz [12]) shows that Old Hungarian and Phoenician are in different branches of the tree. That suggests that Old Hungarian does not derive from Phoenician, and any similarity between these two alphabets is only due to their common origin.

Earlier alternative hypotheses regarding the origin of Old Hungarian include the Old Turkic (Orkhon) origin hypothesis by Sebestyén [13] and the Phoenician origin hypothesis elaborated in Hosszú [6]. More precisely, Hosszú [6] presents an encyclopedic study about Old Hungarian and its Steppean and Carpathian-Basin

[a] Corresponding author: revesz@cse.unl.edu

relatives, which collectively can be referred to as the *Rovas group*. (We do not deal with the members of this group separately because the differences among them seem relatively minor.) Chapter 4 of Hosszú [6] gives a genealogy or derivation of all Old Hungarian and related Rovas symbols from twenty Phoenician letters, four Old Turkic (Orkhon) ideograms and the Greek letter Φ.

In contrast to Hosszú [6] and Sebestyén 13], our previous study (Revesz [12]) placed Old Hungarian and Phoenician in two separate branches of the Cretan Script Family. Hence any similarity of these two alphabets is only due to their common origin. Forrai [4] and Varga [15] also questioned the assumption that Old Hungarian derives from Phoenician or Old Turkic, but they did not specify a Cretan origin of Old Hungarian.

This paper is organized as follows. Section 2 describes a similarity function between pairs of script symbols. It also uses this function to place the Carian alphabet [1, 16] into a scripts comparison table (Table 1). Finally, Section 3 gives some conclusions and directions for future work.

2 A Similarity Function for Symbol Pairs

In this section, we present a modified version of the similarity function for pairs of script symbols given in Revesz [12]. Then we apply this modified function to the Carian alphabet [16]. That is, we place each Carian letter into Table 1 according to where it has the largest similarity to its Old Hungarian neighbor. The modified function is based on the following rules that give positive scores for various similarities between pairs of symbols.

Rule 1. If both symbols contain some curved lines or both symbols contain only straight lines, then the reward is one point.

Rule 2. If both symbols enclose some region or neither symbol encloses any region, then the reward is one point.

Rule 3. If both symbols contain slanted straight lines or neither symbols contains slanted straight lines, then the reward is one point.

Rule 4. If both symbols have two or more parallel lines, then they get a half point reward for each of the shared parallel lines.

Rule 5. If both symbols contain a cross X, then the reward is one point.

Rule 6. If both symbols contain a wedge Λ independent of any cross, then the reward is half point. If they both contain a wavy line (composed of repetitions of wedges), then the reward is one point.

Rule 7. If both symbols have similar sound values, then the reward is one point.

Rule 8. If both symbols have the same meaning, then the reward is one point.

The main modification in the above rules compared with those of Revesz [12] is that the scores given are now half of the scores given previously. In Rule 8 by 'have the same meaning' we mean that the two symbols depict the same object or action. Clearly, Rule 8 can be applied only in case the original object or action depicted by the symbol is not lost. Similarly, Rule 7 can be applied only in case the sound values of the symbols are both known.

The above set of rules gives us a scoring function *s(x, y)* for any pair *x* and *y* of symbols. For example, let us find the similarity between the Carian letter 王 and the Old Hungarian letter ‡. Both letters contain only straight lines (one point by Rule 1), neither symbol encloses any region (one point by Rule 2), neither symbol contains slanted straight lines (one point by Rule 3), the Carian letter has three and the Old Hungarian letter has two horizontal parallel lines, that is, they share two parallel lines (one point by Rule 4), both symbols contain a cross (one point by Rule 5). Rule 6 does not apply because neither letter has a wedge. The sound values of /j/ and /ɟ/ are different but related. In fact, in many Proto-Ugric words that Khanty and Mansi, the closest language relatives of Hungarian, preserve with a /j/ beginning has changed into a word with a /ɟ/ beginning in Hungarian. This implies at least a partial score, let's say half point, by Rule 7. Finally, we do not apply Rule 8 because it is not clear to us what objects the two letters are intended to depict. Hence by tallying up the scores, we obtain the following:

$$s(王, ‡) = 1 + 1 + 1 + 1 + 1 + 0 + 0.5 + 0 = 5.5$$

which is a relatively high score. In fact, s(王, x) < 5.5 for any other Old Hungarian symbol *x*. Hence 王 needs to be put into the table in the same row where ‡ is. The best-fit row for each of the other Carian letters can be found similarly. In general, this placement also fits well with the other symbols in the same row.

The most striking feature of Carian is that it is often the closest to Old Hungarian among all the other script symbols in a row. For example, consider the Old Hungarian X /b/. Comparing it with its Phoenician counterpart, we get:

$$s(X, ⊴) = 1 + 0 + 1 + 0 + 0 + 0 + 1 + 0 = 3$$

Hosszú [6] and Sebestyén [13] assume the Orkhon 𐰉 /b to be the origin of the Old Hungarian X /b/. However, their similarity is only slightly higher:

$$s(X, 𐰉) = 1 + 0 + 1 + 0 + 1 + 0 + 1 + 0 = 4$$

Note that the Carian ч with phonetic value /β/ (from Adiego [1], p. 229), which is a labial sound related to /b/, provides a similarly good alternative because

$$s(X, ч) = 0 + 1 + 1 + 0 + 1 + 0 + 1 + 0 = 4$$

Table 1. A comparison of the symbols of the Cretan Hieroglyphs, Linear A, Linear B, Cypro-Minoan, Cypriot, Carian, Old Hungarina, Tifinagh, South Arabic, Phoenician, and Greek scripts. This table is modified from (Revesz [12]) mainly with the addition of the Carian alphabet. Next to each symbol in blue is its known phonetic value. Here 'unk' means the value is unknown.

C. Hieroglyphs	Linear A	Linear B	Cypro-Minoan	Cypriot	Carian	Old Hungarian	Tifinagh	South Arabic	Phoenician	Greek
		QA		KI	K	K	X	Q	Q	Ϙ
		A		I U	U	A		?	?	A
		WI		VA	W	U,V			W	Υ
		KU		RO	E Y	E E>H		H	H	E
		RA		RA	RR	N	R	R	R	P
		TI		TI	T	ts	ş	ş	ş	Μ
		I		WO	I	I J		J	J	I
		QE		JA	Ñ	J λ	ç	ç	ç	O
		PTE		MI	P	M	M	M	M	M
				SA	ʃ	ʃ	ʃ	ʃ	ʃ	Σ
		DA		TA	D	D, T	D	D	D	Δ
				MU	G	U X	Z	Z	Z	Z
		KE		GA	G	G	G	G	G	Γ
		RO		LO	unk	D	T	T	T	T
		TA		LU	T	O				Ω
		PO		PE	B	P			P	Π
					unk	S				
		NWA		PU	MB	B	F	B	B	B
		NE		NO		NT	NT	N	N	N
		PU		LI	L	L	L	L	L	Λ
	NE	TE		TO	J	ʝ	ḍ ʃ'	S	S	Ξ
		NI		NA	N	NAP	N			
		RU		RU	λ R	R				
		KI		KU	K	K	K	K	K	K
		KA		MO	Q	F	B	W F		Φ
		RE		RI	unk	ʃ>ʒ		H		Ψ
					ʃ	Uʃ	S			
		PA		PA	W	U		ḍ ʃ'	H	H
		RA		ZO	δ	ʃ, C		T'	T'	Θ

3 Conclusions and future work

This paper identified the Carian alphabet as a script evolutionary missing link that was conjectured by Revesz [12] to have existed somewhere in western Anatolia as a common ancestor of the Cypriot syllabary and the Old Hungarian alphabet. That new identification greatly strengthens the Cretan Script Family hypothesis, that is, the idea that Crete is the origin a set of related scripts that spread throughout the eastern Mediterranean and the Black Sea regions in ancient times.

The more complete and improved understanding of the evolutionary tree of the Cretan Script Family has a bearing on the still continuing efforts to 'decipher' aka translate the unknown Cretan Hieroglyph and Linear A scripts, for it seems most fruitful to substitute for the symbols of these unknown scripts the phonetic values of the evolutionarily closest known scripts. Using that simple but essential idea, it has become possible to give some preliminary translations of the Phaistos Disk (also spelled Disc) [10], and some short Cretan Hieroglyph inscriptions [11].

It remains an outstanding open problem to carry on the translation work for other prominent Minoan texts such as the Malia Altar Stone inscription [3].

References

1. I.J. Adiego, *The Carian Language*, (Koninklijke Brill NV, Leiden, The Netherlands, 2007)
2. J. Chadwick, *The Decipherment of Linear B*, (Cambridge University Press, 1958)
3. F. Chapouthier, Inscription hiéroglyphique gravée sur un bloc de calcaire, Bulletin de Correspondance Hellénique **62**, 104-109, (1938)
4. S. Forrai, *The Old Hungarian Writing from Ancient Times to the Present*, (in Hungarian), (Antológia Kiadó, Budapest, Hungary 1994)
5. V. Gabrielson, J. Lund, & T. Madsen (Eds.), The Black Sea in Antiquity: Regional and Interregional Economic Exchanges, (Sandbjerg, Denmark: Oxbow Books 2007).
6. G. Hosszú, *Heritage of Scribes: The Relation of Rovas Scripts to Eurasian Writing Systems*, (Rovas Foundation Hungary, Budapest, Hungary 2013)
7. J.-P. Olivier, Cretan writing in the second millennium B.C., World Archaeology. **17**, 3, 377–389 (1986).
8. J.-P. Olivier, L. Godart and J.-C. Poursat, *Corpus Hieroglyphicarum Inscriptionum Cretae* Études Crétoises **31**, (De Boccard, Paris 1996)
9. P.Z. Revesz, Proc. 4th ACM Int. Conf. on Bioinfo. and Comp. Bio., 731-734, (ACM Press, New York, USA, 2013)
10. P.Z. Revesz, A computer-aided translation of the Phaistos Disk, Int. Journal of Computers, **10**, 94-100, (2016)
11. P.Z. Revesz, A computer-aided translation of the Cretan Hieroglyph script, Int. Journal of Signal Processing, **1**, 127-133 (2016)
12. P.Z. Revesz, Bioinformatics evolutionary tree algorithms reveal the history of the Cretan script family, Int. Journal of Applied Mathematics and Informatics, **10**, 67-76, (2016)
13. G. Sebestyén, *Rovás és Rovásírás*, (Magyar Néprajzi Társaság, 1909)
14. G. Tsetskhladze, (Ed.), *The Greek Colonization of the Black Sea Area*, (Franz Steiner, Stuttgart 1998)
15. G. Varga, *Bronzkori Magyar Írásbeliség*, (Írástörténeti Kutató Intézet, 1993)
16. Wikipedia, "Carian alphabets," downloaded April 5, 2017. Available: https://en.wikipedia.org/wiki/Carian_alphabets
17. J. G. Young, Minos 31-32 (1996-1997[1999]) 379-400.
18. P. Yule, *Early Cretan Seals: A Study of Chronology*, Marburger Studien zur Vor und Frühgeschichte **4** (Mainz 1981)

MATEC Web of Conferences **125**, 05020 (2017) DOI: 10.1051/matecconf/201712505020
CSCC 2017

Mean Square Consistency On Numerical Solutions of Stochastic Wave Equation with Cubic Nonlinearities on 2D Rectangles

Haziem M. Hazaimeh
Department of Mathematics and statistics, Zayed University, Dubai, UAE

***Abstract*—Abstract. In this article we study the mean square consistency on numerical solutions of stochastic wave equations with cubic nonlinearities on two dimensional rectangles. In [8], we proved that the strong Fourier solution of these semi-linear wave equations exists and is unique on an appropriate Hilbert space. A linear-implicit Euler method is used to discretize the related Fourier coefficients. We prove that the linear-implicit Euler method applied to a solution of nonlinear stochastic wave equations in two dimensions is mean square consistency under the geometric condition.**

I. Introduction

In this article we study the linear-implicit Euler method for the numerical solution of semi-linear stochastic wave equations

$$u_{tt} = \sigma^2 \triangle u + A(u, u_t) + B(u, u_t)\frac{dW}{dt}$$

with cubic nonlinearities in two dimensions in terms of all systems parameters, i.e., with non-global Lipschitz continuous nonlinearities. Our study focuses on numerical solution using linear-implicit Euler method (LIEM) under the geometric condition

$$\sigma^2 \pi^2 (\frac{1}{l_x^2} + \frac{1}{l_y^2}) - a_1 = \frac{\sigma^2 \pi^2 (l_x^2 + l_y^2) - a_1 l_x^2 l_y^2}{l_x^2 l_y^2} := \gamma > 0,$$

where $0 \leq x \leq l_x$ and $0 \leq y \leq l_y$ such that $\mathbb{D} = [0, l_x] \times [0, l_x]$. (Note that l_x and l_y are the dimension parameters of a vibrating plate or a membrane). We shall impose the following boundary conditions: (note that $t > 0$)

TABLE I: Boundary Conditions

l_1	$u(x, 0, t) = 0$	or	$u_x(x, 0, t) = 0$	or	$u_y(x, 0, t) = 0$
l_2	$u(l_x, y, t) = 0$	or	$u_x(l_x, y, t) = 0$	or	$u_y(l_x, y, t) = 0$
l_3	$u(x, l_y, t) = 0$	or	$u_x(x, l_y, t) = 0$	or	$u_y(x, l_y, t) = 0$
l_4	$u(0, y, t) = 0$	or	$u_x(0, y, t) = 0$	or	$u_y(0, y, t) = 0$

where $l_1, l_2, l_3,$ and l_4 as in the following figure

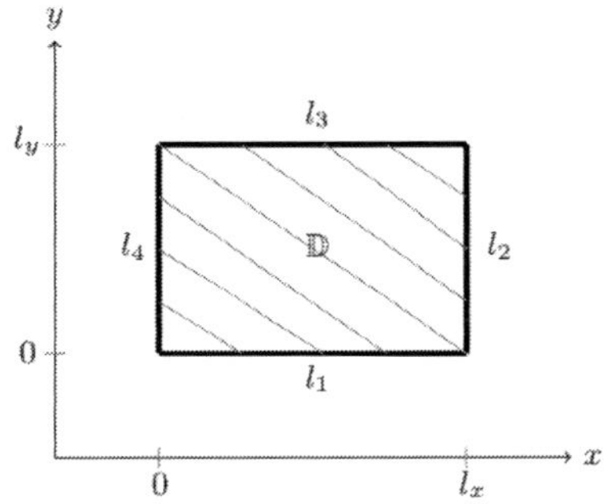

Also the initial conditions are $u(x, y, 0) = f(x, y)$ with $f \in \mathbb{L}^2$ (initial position) and $u_t(x, y, 0) = g(x, y)$ with $g \in \mathbb{L}^2$ (initial velocity). Recall that

$$\mathbb{L}^2(\mathbb{D}) = \{f : \mathbb{D} \to \mathbb{R} \mid \int_{\mathbb{D}} |f(x, y)|^2 \, d\mu(x, y) < \infty\},$$

where μ is the Lebesgue measure in two dimensions.

There is a little information about the numerical solution of nonlinear stochastic wave equations. However, Schurz [17] proved that the linear-implicit method for the nonlinear stochastic heat equation just in $\mathbb{R}$ is mean square consistent with rate $r_0 = 1.5$. Also, Higham [11] studied the mean square stability of stochastic theta method and plotted the mean square stability when the test equation has real parameters. Higham, D.J., Mao, X., Stuart, A.M. [12] proved that strong convergence results but they took less restrictive conditions. To my information and since there are a few researcher work on mean square consistent of LIEM of nonlinear stochastic wave equations in two dimensions, which make me interested in working that.

Consider the stochastic nonlinear wave equation with both additive and multiplicative noise

$$\begin{aligned} u_{tt} &= \sigma^2(u_{xx} + u_{yy}) + (a_1 - a_2\|u\|^2_{\mathbb{L}^2(\mathbb{D})})u - \kappa v \\ &\quad + \left(b_0 + b_1\|u\|_{\mathbb{L}^2(\mathbb{D})} + b_2\|v\|_{\mathbb{L}^2(\mathbb{D})}\right) \frac{dW}{dt} \end{aligned} \quad (1)$$

with $v = u_t$, where

$$W(x, y, t) = \sum_{i,j=1}^{2} \sum_{n,m=1}^{\infty} \alpha^{i,j}_{n,m} W^{i,j}_{n,m}(t) e^i_n(x) e^j_m(y)$$

and $e^{i,j}_n$ and $e^{i,j}_m$ are orthonormalized eigenfunctions of Laplace operator Δ on $\mathbb{D} = [0, l_x] \times [0, l_y]$, driven by *i.i.d.* standard Wiener processes $W^{i,j}_{n,m}$ with $\mathbb{E}[W^{i,j}_{n,m}(t)] = 0$, $\mathbb{E}[W^{i,j}_{n,m}(t)]^2 = t$. Recall

 DOI: 10.1051/matecconf/201712505020

that $e_n^i(z)$ and $e_m^j(z)$ are one of the functions $\sqrt{\frac{2}{l_z}}sin(k\pi z/l_z)$ or $\sqrt{\frac{2}{l_z}}cos(k\pi z/l_z)$, with $z = x$ or y, $k = n$ or m, and $i, j = 1, 2$. The solution of equation (1) in term of Fourier series is

$$u(x, y, t) = \sum_{i,j=1}^{2} \sum_{n,m=1}^{\infty} c_{n,m}^{i,j}(t)\, e_n^i(x)\, e_m^j(y). \qquad (2)$$

The form of Fourier solutions u and its approximate Fourier solutions u_N given by

$$u_N(x, y, t) = \sum_{i,j=1}^{2} \sum_{n,m=1}^{N} c_{n,m}^{i,j}(t) e_n^i(x) e_m^j(y) \qquad (3)$$

with its coefficients $c_{n,m}^{i,j}$ satisfying

$$\begin{aligned} \ddot{c}_{n,m}^{i,j}(t) &= \left[-\sigma^2 (\lambda_n + \beta_m) + a_1 - a_2\|u\|^2_{\mathbb{L}^2(\mathbb{D})}\right] c_{n,m}^{i,j}(t) \\ &\quad -\kappa\, v_{n,m}^{i,j}(t) + \Big(b_0 + b_1\|u\|_{\mathbb{L}^2(\mathbb{D})} \\ &\quad + b_2\|\dot{u}\|_{\mathbb{L}^2(\mathbb{D})}\Big)\alpha_{n,m}^{i,j}\dot{W}_{n,m}^{i,j}(t) \end{aligned} \qquad (4)$$

where $\lambda_n = \frac{\pi^2 n^2}{l_x^2}$, $\beta_m = \frac{\pi^2 m^2}{l_y^2}$, $\|u\|_{\mathbb{L}^2(\mathbb{D})} = \sqrt{\sum_{i,j=1}^{2}\sum_{n,m=1}^{N}[c_{n,m}^{i,j}]^2}$, and $\|\dot{u}\|_{\mathbb{L}^2(\mathbb{D})} = \sqrt{\sum_{i,j=1}^{2}\sum_{n,m=1}^{N}[\dot{c}_{n,m}^{i,j}]^2}$. Note that equation (4) is equivalent to the following system

$$\begin{aligned} \dot{c}_{n,m}^{i,j} &= v_{n,m}^{i,j} \\ \dot{v}_{n,m}^{i,j} &= \left[-\sigma^2(\lambda_n + \beta_m) + a_1 - a_2\sum_{i,j}^{2}\sum_{k,l=1}^{N}[c_{k,l}^{i,j}]^2\right] c_{n,m}^{i,j} \\ &\quad -\kappa\, v_{n,m}^{i,j}(t) \\ &\quad + (b_0 + b_1\|u\|_{\mathbb{L}^2(\mathbb{D})} + \|\dot{u}\|_{\mathbb{L}^2(\mathbb{D})})\, \alpha_{n,m}^{i,j}\dot{W}_{n,m}^{i,j}. \end{aligned} \qquad (5)$$

subject to the initial conditions

$$\left(c_{n,m}^{i,j}(0), v_{n,m}^{i,j}(0)\right) = \left(c_{n,m,0}^{i,j}, v_{n,m,0}^{i,j}\right)_{n,m\geq 1,\, i,j=1,2}.$$

The solution of system (5) is exist and unique [8]. Now, we introduce the following standard definitions.

Definition 1: For $k \in \mathbb{N}$, take the partition $0 = t_0 < t_1 < t_2 < \ldots < t_k = T$ of $[0, T]$ with current step sizes $h_k = t_{k+1} - t_k > 0$, then , as in Schurz [18], the **linear-implicit Euler-type method (LIEM)** is governed by the iterative scheme

$$\begin{aligned} c_{n,m}^{i,j}(t_{k+1}) &= c_{n,m}^{i,j}(t_k) + h_k\, v_{n,m}^{i,j}(t_{k+1}) \qquad (6) \\ v_{n,m}^{i,j}(t_{k+1}) &= v_{n,m}^{i,j}(t_k) + h_k\Big[f_{n,m}(u(t_k))\, c_{n,m}^{i,j}(t_{k+1}) \\ &\quad -\kappa\, v_{n,m}^{i,j}(t_{k+1})\Big] + g_{n,m}(u(t_k))\triangle_k W_{n,m}^{i,j} \qquad (7) \end{aligned}$$

where

$$f_{n,m}(u(t_k)) = -\sigma^2(\lambda_n + \beta_m) + a_1 - a_2\sum_{i,j=1}^{2}\sum_{n,m=1}^{N}[c_{n,m}^{i,j}(t_k)]^2$$

and

$$g_{n,m}(u(t_k)) = \Big(b_0 + b_1\sqrt{\sum_{i,j=1}^{2}\sum_{n,m=1}^{N}(c_{n,m}^{i,j}(t_k))^2} + b_2\sqrt{\sum_{i,j=1}^{2}\sum_{n,m=1}^{N}(\dot{c}_{n,m}^{i,j}(t_k))^2}\Big)\alpha_{n,m}^{i,j}$$

and

$$\triangle_k W_{n,m}^{i,j} = W_{n,m}^{i,j}(t_{k+1}) - W_{n,m}^{i,j}(t_k) \in \mathcal{N}(0, h_k),\ h_k = t_{k+1} - t_k.$$

In [10], we proved that the explicit representation of LIEM as in the following theorem

Theorem 1: Assume that $\left|c_{n,m}^{i,j}(t_k)\right| < \infty$, $\left|v_{n,m}^{i,j}(t_k)\right| < \infty$, and $a_2 \geq 0$, $\kappa \geq 0$, and

$$\forall n, m \in \mathbb{N} : \left[-\sigma^2(\lambda_n + \beta_m) + a_1\right] h_k^2 < 1 + h_k\,\kappa.$$

Then the method (LIEM) governed by equation (6) and equation (7) has the non-exploding explicit representation

$$1) c_{n,m}^{i,j}(t_{k+1}) = \frac{(1 + h_k\kappa)\, c_{n,m}^{i,j}(t_k) + h_k v_{n,m}^{i,j}(t_k)}{1 + h_k\,\kappa - h_k^2 f_{n,m}(u(t_k))} + \frac{h_k\, g_{n,m}(u(t_k))\triangle_k W_{n,m}^{i,j}}{1 + h_k\,\kappa - h_k^2 f_{n,m}(u(t_k))} \qquad (8)$$

and

$$2) v_{n,m}^{i,j}(t_{k+1}) = \frac{v_{n,m}^{i,j}(t_k) + h_k f_{n,m}(u(t_k))\, c_{n,m}^{i,j}(t_k)}{1 + h_k\,\kappa - h_k^2 f_{n,m}(u(t_k))} + \frac{g_{n,m}(u(t_k))\triangle_k W_{n,m}^{i,j}}{1 + h_k\,\kappa - h_k^2 f_{n,m}(u(t_k))} \qquad (9)$$

where $f_{n,m}(u(t_k)), g_{n,m}(u(t_k))$, $\triangle_k W_{n,m}^{i,j}$, and h_k as above.

Proof 2: (Theorem 1) See [10]

II. Mean Square Consistency of Numerical Methods

Definition 2: A numerical method with the scheme

$$\hat{u}(t + h) = \hat{u}(t) + h\, f(\hat{u}(t)) + g(\hat{u}(t))\, \triangle W(t) \qquad (10)$$

where $h = t_{k+1} - t_k = \int_{t_k}^{t_{k+1}} ds$, $\triangle W^k = W(t_{k+1}) - W(t_k) = \int_{t_k}^{t_{k+1}} dW(s) \in \mathcal{N}(0, h)$ and $f(u(t))$ and $g(u(t))$ as above applied to SDE (5) is said to be **mean square consistent** with rate $r_2 > 0$ on $\mathbb{D}$ iff $\exists K_2^c =$ consistency constant $\forall\, 0 \leq t \leq t + h \leq T$ where h is sufficiently small, i.e., $0 < h \leq \delta \leq 1$, $\forall\, u(t) \in H$, where $H := \{u \in \mathbb{L}^2(\mathbb{D}) | \dot{u} \in \mathbb{L}^2(\mathbb{D})\}$, and $\|u\|_H = \sqrt{\|u\|^2_{\mathbb{L}^2(\mathbb{D})} + \|\dot{u}\|^2_{\mathbb{L}^2(\mathbb{D})}}$: $(\mathcal{F}_t, \mathcal{B}(\mathbb{L}^2))$– measurable, then

$$\left(\mathbb{E}\left[\|u(t+h) - \hat{u}(t+h)\|^2_{N\times N}\Big|\mathcal{F}_t\right]\right)^{\frac{1}{2}} \leq K_2^c\,(V(u(t)))\, h^{r_2}$$

where

$$\hat{u}(t+h|t, u(t)) = \hat{u}(t) + \int_t^{t+h} f(u(s))ds + \int_t^{t+h} g(u(s))\, dW(s)ds$$

Lemma 3: (The Burkholder-Davis-Gundy Inequality)

$$\mathbb{E}\|\int_0^t g(s)\, dW(s)\|^p \leq C_B\, \mathbb{E}\left(\int_0^t \|g(s)\|^2\, ds\right)^{\frac{p}{2}} \qquad (11)$$

Proof 4: (Lemma 1) See Karatzas and Shreve [13].

Lemma 5: Let $X \sim \mathcal{N}(0, h_k)$, $\forall n \in \mathbb{N}$, $n \geq 1$, we have

$$\mathbb{E}(X)^{2n} = (2n - 1)!!\, h_k^n,$$

where $(2n - 1)!! = (2n-1)\times(2n-3)\times(2n-5)\times\ldots\times 5\times 3\times 1$.

Proof 6: (Lemma 2) See [9].

Theorem 7: The method (LIEM) given by

$$c_{n,m}^{i,j}(t_{k+1}) = c_{n,m}^{i,j}(t_k) + h_k\, v_{n,m}^{i,j}(t_{k+1}) \qquad (12)$$

$$v_{n,m}^{i,j}(t_{k+1}) = v_{n,m}^{i,j}(t_k) + h_k\Big[f_{n,m}(u(t_k))c_{n,m}^{i,j}(t_{k+1}) -\kappa\, v_{n,m}^{i,j}(t_{k+1})\Big] + g_{n,m}(u(t_k))\triangle_k W_{n,m}^{i,j} \qquad (13)$$

is locally mean square consistent with rate $r_2 \geq 1$, where $f(u(t_k))$ and $g(u(t_k))$ as above and $\triangle_k W_{n,m}^{i,j} = W_{n,m}^{i,j}(t_{k+1}) - W_{n,m}^{i,j}(t_k) \in \mathcal{N}(0, h_k)$, $h_k = t_{k+1} - t_k$.

Proof 8: (Theorem 2) We want to prove that

$$1)\left(\mathbb{E}\left[\|c(t+h)-\hat{c}(t+h)\|_N^2|\hat{u}(t)\right]\right)^{\frac{1}{2}} \leq K_{c_2}^c V(u(t))\, h^{r_2} \quad (14)$$

$$2)\mathbb{E}\left[\|v_{n,m}(t+h)-\hat{v}_{n,m}(t+h)\|_N^2|\hat{u}(t)\right]^{\frac{1}{2}} \leq K_{v_2}^c V(u(t))h^{r_2} \quad (15)$$

Provided that $c(t) = \hat{c}(t)$ and $v(t) = \hat{v}(t)$. To prove inequality (14), we know from [10] that

$$c(t+h)-\hat{c}(t+h) = \int_t^{t+h}\left(v(s)-\hat{f}_c(u(t))\right)ds - \int_t^{t+h}\hat{g}_c(u(t))dW(s).$$

Thus,

$$\begin{aligned}&\|c_{n,m}(t+h)-\hat{c}_{n,m}(t+h)\|_N^2\\ &= \left\|\int_t^{t+h}\left(v(s)-\hat{f}_c(u(t))\right)ds-\int_t^{t+h}\hat{g}_c(u(t))dW(s)\right\|_N^2\\ &\leq 2\left\|\int_t^{t+h}\left(v(s)-\hat{f}_c(u(t))\right)ds\right\|_N^2\\ &+2\left\|\int_t^{t+h}\hat{g}_c(u(t))dW(s)\right\|_N^2,\end{aligned}$$

by using the fact that $(a+b)^2 \leq 2a^2+2b^2$. So

$$\begin{aligned}\mathbb{E}\,\|c(t+h)-\hat{c}(t+h)\|_N^2 &\leq 2\,\mathbb{E}\left\|\int_t^{t+h}\left(v(s)-\hat{f}_c(u(t))\right)ds\right\|_N^2\\ &+2\,\mathbb{E}\left\|\int_t^{t+h}\hat{g}_c(u(t))dW(s)\right\|_N^2\end{aligned}$$

which implies that

$$\begin{aligned}\mathbb{E}\,\|c(t+h)-\hat{c}(t+h)\|_N^2 &\leq 2\int_t^{t+h}\mathbb{E}\left\|v(s)-\hat{f}_c(u(t))\right\|_N^2 ds\\ &+2\mathbb{E}\left\|\int_t^{t+h}\hat{g}_c(u(t))dW(s)\right\|_N^2 \quad (16)\end{aligned}$$

First, we will find the first part of the right hand side of inequality (16),

$$\begin{aligned}\|v(s)-\hat{f}_c(u(t))\|_N^2 &= \|v(s)-v(t)+v(t)-\hat{f}_c(u(t))\|_N^2\\ &\leq 2\,\|v(s)-v(t)\|_N^2+2\|v(t)-\hat{f}_c(u(t))\|_N^2 \quad (17)\end{aligned}$$

Step 1: We know that

$$\begin{aligned}&dv_{n,m}(r)\\ &= \left[-\sigma^2(\lambda_n+\beta_m)-a_1+a_2\|u(r)\|_{\mathbb{L}^2(\mathbb{D})}^2\right]c_{n,m}(r)dr\\ &-\kappa\, v_{n,m}(r)dr+g(u(r))\,dW_{n,m}(r)\end{aligned}$$

thus

$$\begin{aligned}&v_{n,m}(s)-v_{n,m}(t)\\ &= \int_t^s\left[-\sigma^2(\lambda_n+\beta_m)-a_1+a_2\|u(r)\|_{\mathbb{L}^2(\mathbb{D})}^2\right]c_{n,m}(r)dr\\ &-\kappa\int_t^s v_{n,m}(r)dr+\int_t^s g(u(r))dW_{n,m}(r)\end{aligned}$$

so

$$\begin{aligned}&\|v_{n,m}(s)-v_{n,m}(t)\|_N^2\\ &\leq 4\left[\sigma^2(\lambda_n+\beta_m)-a_1\right]^2\left\|\int_t^s c_{n,m}(r)dr\right\|_N^2\\ &+4\,a_2^2\left\|\int_t^s\|u(r)\|_{\mathbb{L}^2(\mathbb{D})}^2\,c_{n,m}(r)\,dr\right\|_N^2\\ &+4\,\kappa^2\left\|\int_t^s v_{n,m}(r)\,dr\right\|_N^2\\ &+4\left\|\int_t^s g(u(r))dW_{n,m}(r)\right\|_N^2\end{aligned}$$

therefore,

$$\begin{aligned}&\mathbb{E}\|v_{n,m}(s)-v_{n,m}(t)\|_N^2\\ &\leq 4\left[\sigma^2(\lambda_n+\beta_m)-a_1\right]^2\mathbb{E}\left\|\int_t^s c_{n,m}(r)\,dr\right\|_N^2\\ &+4\,a_2^2\mathbb{E}\left\|\int_t^s\|u(r)\|_{\mathbb{L}^2(\mathbb{D})}^2\,c_{n,m}(r)\,dr\right\|_N^2\\ &+4\,\kappa^2\mathbb{E}\left\|\int_t^s v_{n,m}(r)\,dr\right\|_N^2\\ &+4\,\mathbb{E}\left\|\int_t^s g(u(r))\,dW_{n,m}(r)\right\|_N^2\\ &\leq 4\left[\sigma^2(\lambda_n+\beta_m)-a_1\right]^2\int_s^t\mathbb{E}\|c(r)\|_N^2\,dr\\ &+4\,a_2^2\int_s^t\left(\mathbb{E}\|u(r)\|_{\mathbb{L}^2(\mathbb{D})}^8\right)^{\frac{1}{2}}\left(\mathbb{E}\|c(r)\|_N^2\right)^{\frac{1}{2}}\,dr\\ &+4\,\kappa^2\int_s^t\mathbb{E}\|v(r)\|_N^2\,dr\\ &+4\,C_B\,\mathbb{E}\int_s^t\|g(u(r))\|_N^2\,dW(r)\end{aligned}$$

by using Hölder and Burkerholder-Davis-Gundy inequalities, Lemma 3, then substituting

$$g(u(t)) = \left(b_0+b_1\|u(t)\|_{l^2}+\|v(t)\|_{l^2}\right)\alpha^2,$$

we get

$$\begin{aligned}&\mathbb{E}\|v_{n,m}(s)-v_{n,m}(t)\|_N^2\\ &\leq 4\left(\left[\sigma^2(\lambda_n+\beta_m)-a_1\right]^2+\kappa^2\right)\mathbb{E}V(u(s))|s-t|\\ &+12\,C_B\,\alpha^2\left[b_0^2+(b_1^2+b_2^2)\mathbb{E}V(u(t))\right]|s-t|\\ &+4\,a_2^2\,\mathbb{E}V^2(u(t))\mathbb{E}V(u(s))|s-t|\\ &\leq \max_{1\leq n,m\leq N}4\left(\left[\sigma^2(\lambda_n+\beta_m)-a_1\right]^2+\kappa^2\right)\mathbb{E}V(u(s))|s-t|\\ &+12\,C_B\,\alpha^2\left[b_0^2+(b_1^2+b_2^2)\mathbb{E}V(u(t))\right]|s-t|\\ &+8\,a_2\,\mathbb{E}V^2(u(t))\mathbb{E}V(u(t))|s-t|,\end{aligned}$$

and, if N is sufficiently large, we find

$$\begin{aligned}&\mathbb{E}\|v_{n,m}(s)-v_{n,m}(t)\|_N^2\\ &\leq 4\left(\left[\sigma^2\,\pi^2\,N^2\left(\frac{1}{l_x^2}+\frac{1}{l_y^2}\right)\right]^2+\kappa^2\right)\mathbb{E}V(u(s))|s-t|\\ &+12\,C_B\,\alpha^2\left[b_0^2+(b_1^2+b_2^2)\mathbb{E}V(u(t))\right]|s-t|\\ &+8\,a_2\,\mathbb{E}V^2(u(t))\mathbb{E}V(u(t))|s-t|\end{aligned}$$

taking the conditional expectation gives us

$$\begin{aligned}
&\mathbb{E}\left(\|v_{n,m}(s)-v_{n,m}(t)\|_N^2|u(t)\right)\\
&\leq 4\Big(\sigma^4\pi^4N^4(\frac{1}{l_x^2}+\frac{1}{l_y^2})^2+\kappa^2+3C_B\alpha^2(b_1^2+b_2^2)\Big)\,V(u(t))|s-t|\\
&+12C_B\alpha^2b_0^2V(u(t))|s-t|+8a_2V^2(u(t))V(u(t))|s-t|\\
&\leq K_5\,(1+V(u(t)))|s-t|\\
&\leq K_5\,\tilde V(u(t))|s-t|
\end{aligned}$$

where

$$\begin{aligned}
K_5 \;=\;& 4\left(\sigma^4\pi^4N^4(\frac{1}{l_x^2}+\frac{1}{l_y^2})^2+\kappa^2+3\,C_B\,\alpha^2(b_1^2+b_2^2)\right)\\
&+12\,C_B\,\alpha^2\,b_0^2+8\,a_2\,V^2(u(t))
\end{aligned}$$

therefore,

$$\begin{aligned}
\int_t^{t+h}&\mathbb{E}\big[\|v_{n,m}(s)-v_{n,m}(t)\|_N^2|u(t)\big]ds\\
&\leq k_5\,\tilde V(u(t))\frac{h_k^2}{2}\\
&\leq k_5\,\tilde V(u(t))h_k^2. \qquad (18)
\end{aligned}$$

Step 2: Also, we know that,

$$\begin{aligned}
&v_{n,m}(t)-\hat f_c(u(t))\\
&=\frac{\left(h_k\kappa+h_k\left[\sigma^2(\lambda_n+\beta_m)-a_1\right]\right)v_{n,m}(t)}{1+h_k\kappa+h_k^2\left[\sigma^2(\lambda_n+\beta_m)-a_1+a_2\sum_{i,j=1}^{2}\sum_{n,m=1}^{N}[c_{n,m}^{i,j}(t_k)]^2\right]}\\
&+\frac{h_k^2\,a_2\left(\sum_{i,j=1}^{2}\sum_{n,m=1}^{N}[c_{n,m}^{i,j}(t_k)]^2\right)v_{n,m}(t)}{1+h_k\kappa+h_k^2\left[\sigma^2(\lambda_n+\beta_m)-a_1+a_2\sum_{i,j=1}^{2}\sum_{n,m=1}^{N}[c_{n,m}^{i,j}(t_k)]^2\right]}\\
&+\frac{h_k\left[\sigma^2(\lambda_n+\beta_m)-a_1\right]c_{n,m}(t)}{1+h_k\kappa+h_k^2\left[\sigma^2(\lambda_n+\beta_m)-a_1+a_2\sum_{i,j=1}^{2}\sum_{n,m=1}^{N}[c_{n,m}^{i,j}(t_k)]^2\right]}\\
&+\frac{h_k\,a_2\left(\sum_{i,j=1}^{2}\sum_{n,m=1}^{N}[c_{n,m}^{i,j}(t_k)]^2\right)c_{n,m}(t)}{1+h_k\kappa+h_k^2\left[\sigma^2(\lambda_n+\beta_m)-a_1+a_2\sum_{i,j=1}^{2}\sum_{n,m=1}^{N}[c_{n,m}^{i,j}(t_k)]^2\right]}
\end{aligned}$$

to simplify, let

$$\begin{aligned}
F(u(t))=\quad & 1+h_k\,\kappa+h_k^2\left[\sigma^2(\lambda_n+\beta_m)-a_1\right]\\
&+a_2\sum_{i,j=1}^{2}\sum_{n,m=1}^{N}[c_{n,m}^{i,j}(t_k)]^2,
\end{aligned}$$

which gives $F(u(t))\geq 0$. Now, if we pulling the expectation over the squared norm of the latter identity, we find that

$$\begin{aligned}
&\mathbb{E}\|v_{n,m}(t)-\hat f_c(u(t))\|_N^2\\
&\leq 4\,h_k^2\,\left(\kappa+h_k\left[\sigma^2(\lambda_n+\beta_m)-a_1\right]\right)^2\mathbb{E}\left\|\frac{v(t)}{F(u(t))}\right\|_N^2\\
&+4\,h_k^4\,a_2^2\,\mathbb{E}\left\|\frac{\|u(t)\|_N^2\,v(t)}{F(u(t))}\right\|_N^2\\
&+4\,h_k^2\left[\sigma^2(\lambda_n+\beta_m)-a_1\right]^2\mathbb{E}\left\|\frac{c(t)}{F(u(t))}\right\|_N^2\\
&+4\,h_k^2\,a_2^2\,\mathbb{E}\left\|\frac{\|u(t)\|_N^2c(t)}{F(u(t))}\right\|_N^2
\end{aligned}$$

but we know that $F_c(u(t))\geq 0$, so

$$\begin{aligned}
&\mathbb{E}\|v(t)-\hat f_c(u(t))\|_N^2\\
&\leq\; 4\,h_k^2\left(\kappa+h_k\left[\sigma^2(\lambda_n+\beta_m)-a_1\right]\right)^2\mathbb{E}\|v(t)\|_N^2\\
&\quad+4\,h_k^4\,a_2^2\,\mathbb{E}\left\|\|u(t)\|_N^2v(t)\right\|_N^2\\
&\quad+4\,h_k^2\left(\sigma^2(\lambda_n+\beta_m)-a_1\right)^2\mathbb{E}\|c(t)\|_N^2\\
&\quad+4\,a_2^2\,h_k^2\mathbb{E}\left\|\|u(t)\|_N^2\,c(t)\right\|_N^2\\
&\leq\; 4\,h_k^2\left(\kappa+h_k\left[\sigma^2(\lambda_n+\beta_m)-a_1\right]\right)^2\mathbb{E}V(u(t))\\
&\quad+4\,h_k^4\,a_2^2\,\left(\mathbb{E}\|u(t)\|_N^4\right)^{\frac12}\left(\mathbb{E}\|v(t)\|_N^2\right)^{\frac12}\\
&\quad+4\,h_k^2\left[\sigma^2(\lambda_n+\beta_m)-a_1\right]^2\mathbb{E}V(u(t))\\
&\quad+4\,h_k^2a_2^2\,\left(\mathbb{E}\|u(t)\|_N^4\right)^{\frac12}\left(\mathbb{E}\|c(t)\|_N^2\right)^{\frac12}\\
&\leq\; 4\,h_k^2\left(\kappa+h_k\left[\sigma^2(\lambda_n+\beta_m)-a_1\right]\right)^2\\
&\quad+h_k^2\left[\sigma^2(\lambda_n+\beta_m)-a_1\right]^2\mathbb{E}V(u(t))\\
&\quad+4\,h_k^4\,a_2^2\,\left(\mathbb{E}V(u(t))\right)^{\frac12}\left(\mathbb{E}V(u(t))\right)^{\frac12}\\
&\quad+4\,h_k^2\,a_2^2\,\left(\mathbb{E}V(u(t))\right)^{\frac12}\left(\mathbb{E}V(u(t))\right)^{\frac12}
\end{aligned}$$

thus

$$\begin{aligned}
&\mathbb{E}\,\|v(t)\,-\,\hat f_c(u(t))\|_N^2\\
&\leq\; 4\,h_k^2\Big(\kappa+h_k\Big[\sigma^2(\lambda_n+\beta_m)-a_1\Big]\Big)^2\mathbb{E}V(u(t))\\
&\quad+h_K^2\left[\sigma^2(\lambda_n+\beta_m)-a_1\right]^2\mathbb{E}V(u(t))\\
&\quad+4\,h_k^2\,a_2^2\,(1+h_k^2)\mathbb{E}V(u(t))\\
&=\; 4\,h_k^2\Big(\kappa+h_k\Big[\sigma^2(\lambda_n+\beta_m)-a_1\Big]\Big)^2\mathbb{E}V(u(t))\\
&\quad+4\,h_k^2\Big[\sigma^2(\lambda_n+\beta_m)-a_1\Big]^2\mathbb{E}V(u(t))\\
&\quad+4\,h_k^2\,a_2^2(1+h_k^2)\mathbb{E}V(u(t))\\
&\leq\; 4\,h_k^2\Big(\kappa+\sigma^2(\lambda_n+\beta_m)-a_1\Big)^2\mathbb{E}V(u(t))\\
&\quad+4\,h_k^2\Big[\sigma^2(\lambda_n+\beta_m)-a_1\Big]^2\mathbb{E}V(u(t))\\
&\quad+8\,h_k^2\,a_2^2\,\mathbb{E}V(u(t)),
\end{aligned}$$

for large N and take the conditional expectation, then we get

$$\begin{aligned}
&\mathbb{E}\left[\|v(t)-\hat f_c(u(t))\|_N^2|u(t)\right]\\
&\leq\; 4\Big[\kappa+\sigma^2N^2\pi^2(\frac{1}{l_x^2}+\frac{1}{l_y^2})^2\Big]\,(1+V(u(t)))\,h_k^2\\
&\quad+4\Big[\sigma^4N^4\pi^4(\frac{1}{l_x^2}+\frac{1}{l_y^2})^2+2\,a_2^2\Big]\,(1+V(u(t)))\,h_k^2
\end{aligned}$$

thus

$$\mathbb{E}\left[\|v(t)-\hat f_c(u(t))\|_N^2|u(t)\right]\;\leq K_6\,\tilde V(u(t))\,h_k^2$$

where

$$K_6 = 4\Big[\kappa + \sigma^2 N^2 \pi^2 (\frac{1}{l_x^2} + \frac{1}{l_y^2})^2 + \sigma^4 N^4 \pi^4 (\frac{1}{l_x^2} + \frac{1}{l_y^2})^2 + 2a_2^2\Big].$$

Therefore,

$$\int_t^{t+h} \mathbb{E}\left[\|v(t) - \hat{f}_c(u(t))\|_N^2 | u(t)\right] ds \leq K_6\, \tilde{V}(u(t))\, h_k^2 \int_t^{t+h} ds \leq K_6\, \tilde{V}(u(t))\, h_k^3$$

and since $h_k \leq 1$, then

$$\int_t^{t+h} \mathbb{E}\left[\|v(t) - \hat{f}_c(u(t))\|_N^2 | u(t)\right] ds \leq K_6 \tilde{V}(u(t)) h_k^2. \quad (19)$$

Form inequalities (20) and (21), we have

$$\begin{aligned}\int_t^{t+h} \mathbb{E}\left[\|v(s) - \hat{f}_c(u(t))\|_N^2 | u(t)\right] ds &\leq K_5\, \tilde{V}(u(t))\, h_k^2 + K_6\, \tilde{V}(u(t))\, h_k^2 \\ &\leq K_7\, \tilde{V}(u(t))\, h_k^2 \quad (20)\end{aligned}$$

where $K_7 = K_5 + K_6$. Now, the second part of inequality (16) is

$$\begin{aligned}\mathbb{E}\| \int_t^{t+h} \hat{g}_c(u(t))\, dW(s)\|^2 &= \mathbb{E}\| \int_t^{t+h} \frac{h_k\Big(b_0 + b_1\|u(t)\|_{l^2} + b_2\|v(t)\|_{l^2}\Big)\alpha^2}{F_c(u(t))} dW(s)\|_N^2 \\ &= \mathbb{E}\| \frac{h_k\Big(b_0 + b_1\|u(t)\|_{l^2} + b_2\|v(t)\|_{l^2}\Big)\alpha^2}{F_c(u(t))} \int_t^{t+h} dW(s)\|_N^2.\end{aligned}$$

Then

$$\begin{aligned}\mathbb{E}\| \int_t^{t+h} \hat{g}_c(u(t)) dW(s)\|_N^2 &\leq \mathbb{E}\Big[\| \frac{h_k\Big(b_0 + b_1\|u(t)\| + b_2\|v(t)\|\Big)\alpha^2}{F_c(u(t))}\|_N^2 \| \int_t^{t+h} dW(s)\|_N^2\Big] \\ &\leq \left(\mathbb{E}\| \frac{h_k(b_1\|u(t)\| + b_2\|v(t)\|)\alpha^2}{F_c(u(t))}\|_N^4\right)^{\frac{1}{2}} \left(\mathbb{E}\| \int_t^{t+h} dW(s)\|_N^4\right)^{\frac{1}{2}}\end{aligned}$$

using Lemma 5.1, $F_c(u(t)) \geq 0$, and

$$(a+b+c)^4 = ((a+b+c)^2)^2 \leq (3(a^2+b^2+c^2))^2 \leq 27(a^4+b^4+c^4),$$

then we find

$$\begin{aligned}\mathbb{E}\| \int_t^{t+h} \hat{g}_c(u(t))\, dW(s)\|_N^2 &\leq h_k^2\, \alpha^4 \Big(27\Big[b_0^4 + b_1^4 \mathbb{E}\|u(t)\|^4 + b_2^4 \mathbb{E}\|v(t)\|^4\Big]\Big)^{\frac{1}{2}} (3\, h_k^2)^{\frac{1}{2}} \\ &\leq 9\,\alpha^4 \Big(b_0^4 + b_1^4\, \mathbb{E}V(u(t)) + b_2^4\, \mathbb{E}V^2(u(t))\Big)^{\frac{1}{2}} h_k^3.\end{aligned}$$

Hence, by redoing above steps for the conditional expectation, we arrive at

$$\begin{aligned}\mathbb{E}\Big[\| \int_t^{t+h} \hat{g}_c(u(t))\, dW(s)\|_N^2 \Big| \mathcal{F}_t\Big] &\leq 9\,\alpha^4 \Big(b_0^4 + b_1^4\, V(u(t)) + b_2^4\, V^2(u(t))\Big)^{\frac{1}{2}} h_k^3 \\ &\leq 9\,\alpha^4 \Big(b_0^2 + b_1^2 \sqrt{V(u(t))} + b_2^2\, V(u(t))\Big) h_k^3 \\ &\leq 9\,\alpha^4 \Big(b_0^2 + \frac{b_1^4}{2} + \frac{V(u(t))}{2} + b_2^2\, V(u(t))\Big) h_k^3,\end{aligned}$$

because we know from the Young's inequality that if $p = 2$ and $q = 2$, that $a \cdot b \leq \frac{a^2}{2} + \frac{b^2}{2}$, then

$$\mathbb{E}\Big[\| \int_t^{t+h} \hat{g}_c(u(t)) dW(s)\|_N^2 \Big| \mathcal{F}_t\Big] \leq 9\,\alpha^4 \Big(b_0^2 + \frac{b_1^4}{2} + (\frac{1}{2} + b_2^2)\, V(u(t))\Big)\, h_k^3$$

and therefore

$$\mathbb{E}\Big[\| \int_t^{t+h} \hat{g}_c(u(t))\, dW(s)\|_N^2 \Big| \mathcal{F}_t\Big] \leq 9\alpha^4 \max\left\{b_0^2 + \frac{b_1^4}{2} + \frac{1}{2} + b_2^2,\ \frac{1}{2} + b_2^2\right\} V(u(t)) h_k^2.$$

Thus

$$\begin{aligned}\mathbb{E}\| \int_t^{t+h} \hat{g}_c(u(t))\, dW(s)\|_N^2 &\leq K_8\, V(u(t))\, h_k^2 \\ &\leq k_8\ (1 + V(u(t)))\ h_k^2 \\ &\leq k_8\, \tilde{V}(u(t)))\, h_k^2. \quad (21)\end{aligned}$$

where

$$K_8 = 9\alpha^4 \max\left\{b_0^2 + \frac{b_1^4}{2} + \frac{1}{2} + b_2^2,\ \frac{1}{2} + b_2^2\right\}.$$

Thus inequality (16) equivalent to

$$\begin{aligned}\mathbb{E}\big[\|c(t+h) - \hat{c}(t+h)\|_N^2 \big| \mathcal{F}_t\big] &\leq 2\left(K_7\, \tilde{V}(u(t))\, h_k^2 + 2\, K_8\, \tilde{V}(u(t))\, h_k^2\right) \\ &\leq K_{c_2}^c\, \tilde{V}(u(t))\, h_k^2 \quad (22)\end{aligned}$$

where $K_{c_2}^c = 2\left(K_7 + K_8\right)$, which is implies that

$$\left(\mathbb{E}\left[\|c(t+h) - \hat{c}(t+h)\|_N^2 \big| \mathcal{F}_t\right]\right)^{\frac{1}{2}} \leq (K_{c_2}^c)^{\frac{1}{2}} \left(\tilde{V}(u(t))\right)^{\frac{1}{2}} h_k. \quad (23)$$

2) To prove inequality (15), from [10] we know that,

$$v(t+h) - \hat{v}(t+h) = \int_t^{t+h} \Big[f_v(u(s)) - \hat{f}_v(u(t))\Big] ds + \int_t^{t+h} \Big[g_v(u(s)) - \hat{g}_v(u(t))\Big] dW(s)$$

thus

$$\begin{aligned}v(t+h) - \hat{v}(t+h)\|_N^2 &\leq 2\| \int_t^{t+h} \Big[f_v(u(s)) - \hat{f}_v(u(t))\Big] ds\|_N^2 \\ &\quad + 2 \int_t^{t+h} \Big[g_v(u(s)) - \hat{g}_v(u(t))\Big] dW(s)\|_N^2 \quad (24)\end{aligned}$$

and we know that

$$\begin{aligned}f_v(u(s)) - \hat{f}_v(u(t)) &= f_v(u(s)) - f_v(u(t)) + f_v(u(t)) \\ &\quad - f_v(\hat{u}(t)) + f_v(\hat{u}(t)) - \hat{f}_v(\hat{u}(t))\end{aligned}$$

and, by using the local property that $u(t) = \hat{u}(t)$, hence

$$\begin{aligned}\|f_v(u(s)) - \hat{f}_v(u(t))\|_N^2 &\leq 2\|f_v(u(s)) - f_v(u(t))\|_N^2 \\ &\quad + 2\|f_v(\hat{u}(t)) - \hat{f}_v(\hat{u}(t))\|_N^2 \quad (25)\end{aligned}$$

where

$$\begin{aligned}f_v(u(s)) - f_v(u(t)) &= \Big[\sigma^2(\lambda_n + \beta_m) - a_1\Big](c(t) - c(s)) \\ &\quad + a_2\left(\|u(t)\|_N^2\, c(t) - \|u(s)\|_N^2\, c(s)\right) \\ &\quad + \kappa\,(v(t) - v(s))\end{aligned}$$

thus

$$\|f_v(u(s))-f_v(u(t))\|_N^2 \leq 3\Big(\sigma^2(\lambda_n+\beta_m)-a_1\Big)^2\|c(t)-c(s)\|_N^2 + 3a_2^2\|\|u(t)\|_N^2 c(t)-\|u(s)\|_N^2 c(s)\|_N^2 + 3\,\kappa^2\,\|v(t)\,-\,v(s)\|_N^2.$$

Also, from [10], we have

$$\|\|u(t)\|_N^2\,c(t)\,-\,\|u(s)\|_N^2\,c(s)\|_N \leq 3\,\|c(\gamma)\|_N^2\|v(\gamma)\|_N\|c(t)\,-\,c(s)\|_N$$

hence

$$\begin{aligned}\mathbb{E}\|\|u(t)\|_N^2\,c(t)-\|u(s)\|_N^2\,c(s)\|_N &\leq 9\mathbb{E}\Big(\|c(\gamma)\|_N^4\|v(\gamma)\|_N^2\|c(t)\,-\,c(s)\|_N^2\Big)\\ &\leq 9\Big[\mathbb{E}\Big(\|c(\gamma)\|_N^8\|v(\gamma)\|_N^4\Big)\Big]^{\frac{1}{2}}\Big[\mathbb{E}\|c(t)-c(s)\|_N^4\Big]^{\frac{1}{2}}\\ &\leq 9\Big[\mathbb{E}\|c(\gamma)\|_N^{16}\Big]^{\frac{1}{2}}\Big[\mathbb{E}\|v(\gamma)\|_N^8\Big]^{\frac{1}{2}}\Big[\mathbb{E}\|c(t)-c(s)\|_N^4\Big]^{\frac{1}{2}}\\ &\leq \frac{36}{a_2^2}\Big[\mathbb{E}V^4(u(t))\Big]^{\frac{1}{2}}\Big[\mathbb{E}V^4(u(t))\Big]^{\frac{1}{2}}\Big[\mathbb{E}\|c(t)-c(s)\|_N^4\Big]^{\frac{1}{2}}\end{aligned}$$

therefore

$$\mathbb{E}\|\|u(t)\|_N^2\,c(t)-\|u(s)\|_N^2\,c(s)\|_N \leq \frac{36}{a_2^2}\mathbb{E}V^4(u(t))\Big[\mathbb{E}\|c(t)-c(s)\|_N^4\Big]^{\frac{1}{2}} \tag{26}$$

but we can find that

$$\begin{aligned}\mathbb{E}\|c(t)-c(s)\|_N^4 &\leq \mathbb{E}\Big(\int_t^s\,[\mathbb{E}V(u(r))]^{\frac{1}{2}}\,dr\Big)^4\\ &\leq \int_t^s\,[\mathbb{E}V(u(r))]^2\,dr\,(s-t)^2\\ &\leq [\mathbb{E}V(u(t))]^2\,(s-t)^2\int_t^s\,dr\end{aligned}$$

and so

$$\mathbb{E}\|c(t)-c(s)\|_N^4 \leq [\mathbb{E}V(u(t))]^2\,(s-t)^3. \tag{27}$$

Substituting inequality (27) in inequality (26), we find that

$$\mathbb{E}\|\|u(t)\|_N^2\,c(t)-\|u(s)\|_N^2\,c(s)\|_N \leq \frac{36}{a_2^2}\mathbb{E}V^4(u(t))\,[\mathbb{E}V(u(t))]^2\,(s-t)^3 \tag{28}$$

and we know that

$$\mathbb{E}\|\|c(t)-c(s)\|_N^2\,c(s)\|_N \leq \mathbb{E}V(u(t))\,(s-t)^2. \tag{29}$$

Also from Theorem 2 part 1), we know that

$$\int_t^{t+h}\mathbb{E}\|v(t)-v(s)\|_N^2\,d\,s \leq K_5\,\tilde{V}(u(t))\,h_k^2. \tag{30}$$

Therefore, by using inequalities (28), (29), and (30), we find that

$$\begin{aligned}\int_t^{t+h}\mathbb{E}\|f_v(u(s))-f_v(u(t))\|_N^2\,ds &\leq 3\Big[\sigma^2(\lambda_n+\beta_m)-a_1\Big]^2\int_t^{t+h}\mathbb{E}\|c(t)-c(s)\|_N^2\,ds\\ &+3\,a_2^2\int_t^{t+h}\mathbb{E}\|\|u(t)\|_N^2\,c(t)-\|u(s)\|_N^2\,c(s)\|_N^2\,ds\\ &+3\,\kappa^2\int_t^{t+h}\mathbb{E}\|v(t)\,-\,v(s)\|_N^2\,d\,s,\end{aligned}$$

hence

$$\begin{aligned}\int_t^{t+h}\mathbb{E}\left[\|f_v(u(s))-f_v(u(t))\|_N^2|u(t)\right]\,ds &\leq 3\Big[\sigma^2(\lambda_n+\beta_m)-a_1\Big]^2\int_t^{t+h}V(u(t))(s-t)^2\,ds\\ &+108\int_t^{t+h}V^4(u(t))\mathbb{E}V(u(t))|s-t|^3\,ds\\ &+3\,K_5\,\kappa^2\,\tilde{V}(u(t))\,h_k^2\\ &\leq \Big[\sigma^2\,(\lambda_n+\beta_m)\,-\,a_1\Big]^2\,V(u(t))\,h_k^3\\ &+\frac{108}{4}\,V^4(u(t))V(u(t))\,h_k^4+3\,K_5\,\kappa\,\tilde{V}(u(t))\,h_k^2\\ &\leq \Big[\sigma^2\,(\lambda_n+\beta_m)\,-\,a_1\Big]^2\,V(u(t))\,h_k^2\\ &+27\,V^4(u(t))V(u(t))\,h_k^2+3\,K_5\,\kappa\,\tilde{V}(u(t))\,h_k^2.\end{aligned}$$

Thus, for large N, we have

$$\begin{aligned}\int_t^{t+h}\mathbb{E}\left[\|f_v(u(s))-f_v(u(t))\|_N^2|u(t)\right]\,ds &\leq \sigma^4\,N^4\,\pi^4(\frac{1}{l_x^2}+\frac{1}{l_y^2})^2\,V(u(t))\,h_k^2\\ &+27\,V^4(u(t))V(u(t))\,h_k^2+3\,K_5\,\kappa\,\tilde{V}(u(t))\,h_k^2\\ &\leq \sigma^4\,N^4\,\pi^4(\frac{1}{l_x^2}+\frac{1}{l_y^2})^2\,(1+V(u(t)))\,h_k^2\\ &+27\,V^4(u(t))\,(1+V(u(t)))\,h_k^2+3\,K_5\,\kappa\,\tilde{V}(u(t))\,h_k^2\end{aligned}$$

therefore

$$\int_t^{t+h}\mathbb{E}\left[\|f_v(u(s))-f_v(u(t))\|_N^2|u(t)\right]ds \leq K_9\tilde{V}(u(t))h_k^2 \tag{31}$$

where

$$K_9=\sigma^4N^4\pi^4(\frac{1}{l_x^2}+\frac{1}{l_y^2})^2+27V^4(u(t))+3K_5\,\kappa.$$

The second part of inequality (25) is,

$$
\begin{aligned}
&\|f_v(\hat{u}(t)) - \hat{f}_v(\hat{u}(t))\|_N^2 \\
&\le h_k^2\Big[\|\frac{\kappa\left[\sigma^2(\lambda_n+\beta_m) - a_1 + a_2\|\hat{u}(t)\|_N^2\right]\hat{c}(t)}{F(\hat{u}(t))}\|_N^2 \\
&+\|\frac{h_k\left[\sigma^2(\lambda_n+\beta_m)-a_1+a_2\|\hat{u}(t)\|_N^2\right]^2\hat{c}(t)}{F(\hat{u}(t))}\|_N^2+\|\frac{\kappa^2\,\hat{v}(t)}{F(\hat{u}(t))}\|_N^2 \\
&+\|\frac{h_k\kappa\left[\sigma^2(\lambda_n+\beta_m)-a_1+a_2\|\hat{u}(t)\|_N^2\right]\hat{v}(t)}{F(\hat{u}(t))}\|_N^2\Big] \\
&\le 4h_k^2\Big[\kappa^2\left[\sigma^2(\lambda_n+\beta_m) - a_1 + a_2\|\hat{u}(t)\|_N^2\right]^2\|\frac{\hat{c}(t)}{F(\hat{u}(t))}\|_N^2 \\
&+h_k^2\left[\sigma^2(\lambda_n+\beta_m) - a_1 + a_2\|\hat{u}(t)\|_N^2\right]^4\|\frac{\hat{c}(t)}{F(\hat{u}(t))}\|_N^2 \\
&+\kappa^4\|\frac{\hat{v}(t)}{F(\hat{u}(t))}\|_N^2 \\
&+h_k^2\kappa^2\left[\sigma^2(\lambda_n+\beta_m) - a_1 + a_2\|\hat{u}(t)\|_N^2\right]^2\|\frac{\hat{v}(t)}{F(\hat{u}(t))}\|_N^2\Big] \\
&\le 4h_k^2\Big[\kappa^2\Big(\left[\sigma^2(\lambda_n+\beta_m) - a_1 + a_2\|\hat{u}(t)\|_N^2\right]^2\|\frac{\hat{c}(t)}{F(\hat{u}(t))}\|_N^2 \\
&+\kappa^2\|\frac{\hat{v}(t)}{F(\hat{u}(t))}\|_N^2\Big) \\
&+h_k^2\left[\sigma^2(\lambda_n+\beta_m)-a_1+a_2\|\hat{u}(t)\|_N^2\right]^2\Big(\left[\sigma^2(\lambda_n+\beta_m)-a_1 \right.\\
&\left.+a_2\|\hat{u}(t)\|_N^2\right]^2\|\frac{\hat{c}(t)}{F(\hat{u}(t))}\|_N^2 + \kappa^2\|\frac{\hat{v}(t)}{F(\hat{u}(t))}\|_N^2\Big)\Big]
\end{aligned}
$$

hence

$$
\begin{aligned}
&\|f_v(\hat{u}(t)) - \hat{f}_v(\hat{u}(t))\|_N^2 \\
&\le 4h_k^2\Big[\Big(\kappa^2 + h_k^2\left[\sigma^2(\lambda_n+\beta_m) - a_1 + a_2\|\hat{u}(t)\|_N^2\right]^2\Big) \\
&\Big(\left[\sigma^2(\lambda_n+\beta_m) - a_1 + a_2\|hatu(t)\|_N^2\right]^2\|\frac{\hat{c}(t)}{F(\hat{u}(t))}\|_N^2 \\
&+\kappa^2\|\frac{\hat{v}(t)}{F(\hat{u}(t))}\|_N^2\Big)\Big]
\end{aligned}
$$

using $F(\hat{u}(t)) \ge 1$, and pulling the expectation over the last identity, then we find

$$
\begin{aligned}
&\mathbb{E}\|f_v(\hat{u}(t)) - \hat{f}_v(\hat{u}(t))\|_N^2 \\
&\le 4h_k^2\mathbb{E}\Big[\Big(\kappa^2+h_k^2\left[\sigma^2(\lambda_n+\beta_m)-a_1+a_2\|\hat{u}(t)\|_N^2\right]^2\Big)\Big(\left[\sigma^2(\lambda_n+\beta_m)\right.\\
&\left.-a_1 + a_2\|\hat{u}(t)\|_N^2\right]^2\|\frac{\hat{c}(t)}{F(\hat{u}(t))}\|_N^2 + \kappa^2\|\frac{\hat{v}(t)}{F(\hat{u}(t))}\|_N^2\Big)\Big]
\end{aligned}
$$

therefore,

$$
\begin{aligned}
&\mathbb{E}\|f_v(\hat{u}(t)) - \hat{f}_v(\hat{u}(t))\|_N^2 \\
&\le 4h_k^2\mathbb{E}\Big[\Big(\kappa^2+\left[\sigma^2(\lambda_n+\beta_m)-a_1+a_2\|\hat{u}(t)\|_N^2\right]^2\Big) \\
&\Big(\left[\sigma^2(\lambda_n+\beta_m)-a_1+a_2\|\hat{u}(t)\|_N^2\right]^2\|\frac{\hat{c}(t)}{F(\hat{u}(t))}\|_N^2 \\
&+\kappa^2\|\frac{\hat{v}(t)}{F(\hat{u}(t))}\|_N^2\Big)\Big]
\end{aligned}
$$

hence

$$
\begin{aligned}
&\mathbb{E}\|f_v(\hat{u}(t)) - \hat{f}_v(\hat{u}(t))\|_N^2 \\
&\le 4h_k^2\Big(\mathbb{E}\Big[\kappa^2+\left[\sigma^2(\lambda_n+\beta_m)-a_1+a_2\|\hat{u}(t)\|_N^2\right]^2\Big]^2\Big)^{\frac{1}{2}} \\
&\Big[\mathbb{E}\Big(\left[\sigma^2(\lambda_n+\beta_m)-a_1+a_2\|\hat{u}(t)\|_N^2\right]^2\|\frac{\hat{c}(t)}{F(\hat{u}(t))}\|_N^2 \\
&+\kappa^2\|\frac{\hat{v}(t)}{F(\hat{u}(t))}\|_N^2\Big)^2\Big]^{\frac{1}{2}}
\end{aligned}
$$

for large N, we have

$$
\begin{aligned}
&\mathbb{E}\|f_v(\hat{u}(t)) - \hat{f}_v(\hat{u}(t))\|_N^2 \\
&\le 4h_k^2\Big(\mathbb{E}\Big[\kappa^2+\left[\sigma^2N^2\pi^2(\frac{1}{l_x^2}+\frac{1}{l_y^2})^2+a_2\|\hat{u}(t)\|_N^2\right]^2\Big]^2\Big)^{\frac{1}{2}} \\
&\Big[\mathbb{E}\Big(\left[\sigma^2N^2\pi^2(\frac{1}{l_x^2}+\frac{1}{l_y^2})^2+a_2\|\hat{u}(t)\|_N^2\right]^2\|\frac{\hat{c}(t)}{F(\hat{u}(t))}\|_N^2 \\
&+\kappa^2\|\frac{\hat{v}(t)}{F(\hat{u}(t))}\|_N^2\Big)^2\Big]^{\frac{1}{2}}. \qquad (32)
\end{aligned}
$$

First, I will calculate the first part of the right side of inequality (32) which is

$$
\begin{aligned}
&\Big(\mathbb{E}\Big[\kappa^2 + h_k^2\left[\sigma^2N^2\pi^2(\frac{1}{l_x^2}+\frac{1}{l_y^2})^2 + a_2\|\hat{u}(t)\|_N^2\right]^2\Big]^2\Big)^{\frac{1}{2}} \\
&\le \Big(\mathbb{E}\Big[2\kappa^4 + 2\left[\sigma^2N^2\pi^2(\frac{1}{l_x^2}+\frac{1}{l_y^2})^2 + a_2\|\hat{u}(t)\|_N^2\right]^4\Big]\Big)^{\frac{1}{2}} \\
&\le \Big(\mathbb{E}\Big[2\kappa^4+2\Big[4\Big(\sigma^2N^2\pi^2(\frac{1}{l_x^2}+\frac{1}{l_y^2})^2\Big)^4+4a_2^4\|\hat{u}(t)\|_N^8\Big]\Big]\Big)^{\frac{1}{2}}
\end{aligned}
$$

hence

$$
\begin{aligned}
&\Big(\mathbb{E}\Big[\kappa^2+h_k^2\left[\sigma^2N^2\pi^2(\frac{1}{l_x^2}+\frac{1}{l_y^2})^2+a_2\|\hat{u}(t)\|_N^2\right]^2\Big]^2\Big)^{\frac{1}{2}} \\
&\le \Big(2\kappa^4+2\Big[4\Big(\sigma^2N^2\pi^2(\frac{1}{l_x^2}+\frac{1}{l_y^2})^2\Big)^4+4a_2^4\mathbb{E}\|\hat{u}(t)\|_N^8\Big]\Big)^{\frac{1}{2}} \\
&\le \Big(2\kappa^4 + 8\Big[\Big(\sigma^2N^2\pi^2(\frac{1}{l_x^2}+\frac{1}{l_y^2})^2\Big)^4 + a_2^4\mathbb{E}V^2(u(t))\Big]\Big)^{\frac{1}{2}} \\
&= \Big(2\kappa^4 + 8\Big(\sigma^2N^2\pi^2(\frac{1}{l_x^2}+\frac{1}{l_y^2})^2\Big)^4 + 8a_2^4\mathbb{E}V^2(u(t))\Big)^{\frac{1}{2}} \\
&\le \sqrt{2}\Big(\kappa^2+2\Big(\sigma^2N^2\pi^2(\frac{1}{l_x^2}+\frac{1}{l_y^2})^2\Big)^2+2a_2^2[\mathbb{E}V^2(u(t))]^{\frac{1}{2}}\Big) \\
&\le \sqrt{2}\Big(\kappa^2 + 2\sigma^4N^4\pi^4(\frac{1}{l_x^2}+\frac{1}{l_y^2})^4 + 2a_2^2[\mathbb{E}V^2(u(t))]^{\frac{1}{2}}\Big).
\end{aligned}
$$

Now, the second part of the right side of inequality (32) is

$$
\begin{aligned}
&\mathbb{E}\Big(\left[\sigma^2N^2\pi^2(\frac{1}{l_x^2}+\frac{1}{l_y^2})^2+a_2\|\hat{u}(t)\|_N^2\right]^2\|\frac{\hat{c}(t)}{F(\hat{u}(t))}\|_N^2+\kappa^2\|\frac{\hat{v}(t)}{F(\hat{u}(t))}\|_N^2\Big)^2 \\
&\le 2\mathbb{E}\Big(\left[\sigma^2N^2\pi^2(\frac{1}{l_x^2}+\frac{1}{l_y^2})^2+a_2\|\hat{u}(t)\|_N^2\right]^4\|\frac{\hat{c}(t)}{F(\hat{u}(t))}\|_N^4\Big) \\
&+2\kappa^2\mathbb{E}\|\frac{\hat{v}(t)}{F(\hat{u}(t))}\|_N^2 \\
&\le 2\Big(\mathbb{E}\left[\sigma^2N^2\pi^2(\frac{1}{l_x^2}+\frac{1}{l_y^2})^2+a_2\|\hat{u}(t)\|_N^2\right]^8\Big)^{\frac{1}{2}}\Big(\mathbb{E}\|\frac{\hat{c}(t)}{F(\hat{u}(t))}\|_N^8\Big)^{\frac{1}{2}} \\
&+2\kappa^2\mathbb{E}\|\frac{\hat{v}(t)}{F(\hat{u}(t))}\|_N^2 \\
&\le 2\Big(16\sigma^{16}N^{16}\pi^{16}(\frac{1}{l_x^2}+\frac{1}{l_y^2})^{16}+a_2^8\mathbb{E}\|\hat{u}(t)\|_N^{16}\Big)^{\frac{1}{2}} \\
&\Big(\mathbb{E}\|\frac{\hat{c}(t)}{F(\hat{u}(t))}\|_N^8\Big)^{\frac{1}{2}} + 2\kappa^2\mathbb{E}\|\frac{\hat{v}(t)}{F(\hat{u}(t))}\|_N^2
\end{aligned}
$$

but $F(\hat{u}(t)) \geq 1$, then

$$\begin{aligned}&\mathbb{E}\Big(\Big[\sigma^2 N^2 \pi^2 (\frac{1}{l_x^2}+\frac{1}{l_y^2})^2 + a_2\|\hat{u}(t)\|_N^2\Big]^2 \|\hat{c}(t)\|_N^2 + \kappa^2 \|\hat{v}(t)\|_N^2\Big)^2\\
&\leq 2\Big(16\sigma^{16}N^{16}\pi^{16}(\frac{1}{l_x^2}+\frac{1}{l_y^2})^{16}+a_2^8\mathbb{E}\|\hat{u}(t)\|_N^{16}\Big)^{\frac{1}{2}}(\mathbb{E}\|\hat{c}(t)\|_N^8)^{\frac{1}{2}}\\
&+2\kappa^2\,\mathbb{E}\|\hat{v}(t)\|_N^2\\
&\leq 2\Big(4\sigma^8N^8\pi^8(\frac{1}{l_x^2}+\frac{1}{l_y^2})^8+a_2^4\mathbb{E}\|\hat{u}(t)\|_N^8\Big)(\mathbb{E}\|\hat{c}(t)\|_N^8)^{\frac{1}{2}}\\
&+2\kappa^2\,\mathbb{E}\|\hat{v}(t)\|_N^2,\end{aligned}$$

hence

$$\begin{aligned}&\Big[\mathbb{E}\Big(\Big[\sigma^2 N^2 \pi^2 (\frac{1}{l_x^2}+\frac{1}{l_y^2})^2 + a_2\|\hat{u}(t)\|_N^2\Big]^2 \|\hat{c}(t)\|_N^2 + \kappa^2 \|\hat{v}(t)\|_N^2\Big)^2\Big]^{\frac{1}{2}}\\
&\leq\Big[2\Big(4\sigma^8N^8\pi^8(\frac{1}{l_x^2}+\frac{1}{l_y^2})^8+a_2^4\mathbb{E}\|\hat{u}(t)\|_N^8\Big)(\mathbb{E}\|\hat{c}(t)\|_N^8)^{\frac{1}{2}}+2\kappa^2\mathbb{E}\|\hat{v}(t)\|_N^2\Big]^{\frac{1}{2}}\\
&\leq\sqrt{2}\Big(4\sigma^8N^8\pi^8(\frac{1}{l_x^2}+\frac{1}{l_y^2})^8+a_2^4\mathbb{E}\|\hat{u}(t)\|_N^8\Big)^{\frac{1}{2}}(\mathbb{E}\|\hat{c}(t)\|_N^8)^{\frac{1}{4}}\\
&+\sqrt{2}\kappa\,(\mathbb{E}\|\hat{v}(t)\|_N^2)^{\frac{1}{2}}\\
&\leq\sqrt{2}\Big(2\sigma^4N^4\pi^4(\frac{1}{l_x^2}+\frac{1}{l_y^2})^4+a_2^2\,(\mathbb{E}\|\hat{u}(t)\|_N^8)^{\frac{1}{2}}\Big)(\mathbb{E}\|\hat{c}(t)\|_N^8)^{\frac{1}{4}}\\
&+\sqrt{2}\kappa\,(\mathbb{E}\|\hat{v}(t)\|_N^2)^{\frac{1}{2}}\\
&\leq\sqrt{2}\Big(2\sigma^4N^4\pi^4(\frac{1}{l_x^2}+\frac{1}{l_y^2})^4+2a_2\,(\mathbb{E}V^2(u(t)))^{\frac{1}{2}}\Big)\\
&\Big(\frac{2}{a_2}\mathbb{E}V^8(u(t))\Big)^{\frac{1}{4}}+\sqrt{2}\kappa\,(\mathbb{E}V(u(t)))^{\frac{1}{2}}.\end{aligned}$$

Thus inequality (32) equivalent to

$$\begin{aligned}&\mathbb{E}\|f_v(\hat{u}(t))-\hat{f}_v(\hat{u}(t))\|_N^2\\
&\leq 4h_k^2\cdot\sqrt{2}\Big(\kappa^2+2\sigma^4N^4\pi^4(\frac{1}{l_x^2}+\frac{1}{l_y^2})^4+2a_2^2[\mathbb{E}V^2(u(t))]^{\frac{1}{2}}\Big)\\
&\Big[\sqrt{2}\Big(2\sigma^4N^4\pi^4(\frac{1}{l_x^2}+\frac{1}{l_y^2})^4+2a_2\,(\mathbb{E}V^2(u(t)))^{\frac{1}{2}}\Big)\\
&\Big(\frac{2}{a_2}\mathbb{E}V^8(u(t))\Big)^{\frac{1}{4}}+\sqrt{2}\kappa\,(\mathbb{E}V(u(t)))^{\frac{1}{2}}\Big].\end{aligned}$$

Pulling the conditional expectation over the last identity, we find that

$$\begin{aligned}&\mathbb{E}\Big[\|f_v(\hat{u}(t))-\hat{f}_v(\hat{u}(t))\|_N^2|u(t)\Big]\\
&\leq 8h_k^2\Big(\kappa^2+2\sigma^4N^4\pi^4(\frac{1}{l_x^2}+\frac{1}{l_y^2})^4+2a_2^2[V^2(u(t))]^{\frac{1}{2}}\Big)\\
&\Big[\Big(2\sigma^4N^4\pi^4(\frac{1}{l_x^2}+\frac{1}{l_y^2})^4+2a_2\,(V^2(u(t)))^{\frac{1}{2}}\Big)\\
&\Big(\frac{2}{a_2}V^8(u(t))\Big)^{\frac{1}{4}}+\kappa\,(V(u(t)))^{\frac{1}{2}}\Big].\end{aligned}$$

Thus

$$\begin{aligned}&\mathbb{E}[\|f_v(\hat{u}(t))-\hat{f}_v(\hat{u}(t))\|_N^2|u(t)]\\
&\leq 8h_k^2\Big(\kappa^2+2\sigma^4N^4\pi^4(\frac{1}{l_x^2}+\frac{1}{l_y^2})^4+2a_2^2V(u(t))\Big)\\
&\Big[\Big(2\sigma^4N^4\pi^4(\frac{1}{l_x^2}+\frac{1}{l_y^2})^4+2a_2V(u(t))\Big)\\
&\Big(\frac{2}{a_2}\Big)^{\frac{1}{4}}V^2(u(t))+\kappa V^{\frac{1}{2}}(u(t))\Big]\\
&\leq 8h_k^2\cdot\Big(\kappa^2+2\sigma^4N^4\pi^4(\frac{1}{l_x^2}+\frac{1}{l_y^2})^4+2a_2^2V(u(t))\Big)\\
&\Big[\Big(2\sigma^4N^4\pi^4(\frac{1}{l_x^2}+\frac{1}{l_y^2})^4+2a_2V(u(t))\Big)\\
&\Big(\frac{2}{a_2}\Big)^{\frac{1}{4}}V^{\frac{3}{2}}(u(t))+\kappa\Big]V^{\frac{1}{2}}(u(t))\end{aligned}$$

hence

$$\begin{aligned}&\mathbb{E}[\|f_v(\hat{u}(t))-\hat{f}_v(\hat{u}(t))\|_N^2|u(t)]\\
&\leq K_{10}(1+V(u(t)))\,h_k^2\\
&\leq K_{10}\tilde{V}(u(t))\,h_k^2.\end{aligned}\tag{33}$$

where

$$\begin{aligned}K_{10}=8\cdot&\Big(\kappa^2+2\sigma^4N^4\pi^4(\frac{1}{l_x^2}+\frac{1}{l_y^2})^4+2a_2^2V(u(t))\Big)\\
&\Big[\Big(2\sigma^4N^4\pi^4(\frac{1}{l_x^2}+\frac{1}{l_y^2})^4+2a_2V(u(t))\Big)\Big(\frac{2}{a_2}\Big)^{\frac{1}{4}}V^{\frac{3}{2}}(u(t))+\kappa\Big],\end{aligned}$$

therefore

$$\begin{aligned}&\int_t^{t+h}\mathbb{E}[\|f_v(\hat{u}(t))-\hat{f}_v(\hat{u}(t))\|_N^2|u(t)]\,ds\\
&\leq K_{10}\tilde{V}(u(t))h_k^3\\
&\leq K_{10}\tilde{V}(u(t))h_k^2.\end{aligned}\tag{34}$$

To complete the proof, we have to simplify the second part of the right side of inequality (24) which is

$$\begin{aligned}&\|\int_t^{t+h}\Big[g_v(u(s))-\hat{g}_v(u(t))\Big]dW(s)\|_N^2\\
&\leq C_B\int_t^{t+h}\|g_v(u(s))-\hat{g}_v(u(t))\|_N^2ds\end{aligned}$$

but from [10] we know that

$$\begin{aligned}&\|\int_t^{t+h}\Big[g_v(u(s))-\hat{g}_v(u(t))\Big]dW(s)\|_N^2\\
&\leq C_B\int_t^{t+h}\|g_v(u(s))-g_v(u(t))\|_N^2\,ds\\
&+C_B\int_t^{t+h}\|g_v(u(t))-\hat{g}_v(u(t))\|_N^2\,ds.\end{aligned}\tag{35}$$

We start with the first part of the right side of inequality (35) which is

$$\begin{aligned}
&\int_t^{t+h} \|g_v(u(s))-g_v(u(t))\|_N^2\, d\,s \\
&\leq \int_t^{t+h} \|b_1\,(\|u(s)\|_{l^2} - \|u(t)\|_{l^2}) + b_2\,(\|v(s)\|_{l^2} - \|v(t)\|_{l^2})\,\|_N^2\, d\,s \\
&\leq \int_t^{t+h} \left[2b_1^2\,(\|u(s)\|_{l^2} - \|u(t)\|_{l^2})^2 + 2b_2^2\,(\|v(s)\|_{l^2} - \|v(t)\|_{l^2})^2\right] ds \\
&\leq \int_t^{t+h} \max\{2b_1^2, 2b_2^2\}\left[(\|u(s)\|_{l^2} - \|u(t)\|_{l^2})^2 + (\|v(s)\|_{l^2} - \|v(t)\|_{l^2})^2\right] ds \\
&\leq \int_t^{t+h} 2\max\{2\,b_1^2, 2\,b_2^2\}\,\left[\|u(\gamma)\|_{l^2}^2|s-t| + \|v(\gamma)\|_{l^2}^2|s-t|\right]\, d\,s \\
&\leq \max\{2\,b_1^2, 2\,b_2^2\}V(u(t))\,h_k^2
\end{aligned}$$

thus

$$\begin{aligned}
&\int_t^{t+h} \mathbb{E}\|g_v(u(s))-g_v(u(t))\|_N^2\, ds \\
&\qquad \leq K_{11}V(u(t))h_k^2 \leq K_{11}\tilde{V}(u(t))h_k^2 \qquad (36)
\end{aligned}$$

where $K_{11} = \max\{2\,b_1^2, 2\,b_2^2\}$. Also, the second part of the right side of inequality (35), we start with

$$\begin{aligned}
&\mathbb{E}\left[\|g_v(u(t)) - \hat{g}_v(u(t))\|_N^2\right] \\
&= h_k\mathbb{E}\left[\|\frac{[\kappa+h_kF(u(t))]\,[b_0 + b_1\|u(t)\|_{l^2} + b_2\|v(t)\|_{l^2}]}{1 + h_k\,\kappa + h_k^2\,F(u(t))}\|_N^2\right] \\
&\leq h_k\,(\mathbb{E}\|\kappa+h_kF(u(t))\|_N^4)^{\frac{1}{2}}(\mathbb{E}\|b_0 + b_1\|u(t)\|_{l^2} + b_2\|v(t)\|_{l^2}\|_N^4)^{\frac{1}{2}} \\
&\leq 81\,h_k(\mathbb{E}[\kappa^4 + h_k^4\,\sigma^4\,N^4\pi^4(\frac{1}{l_x^2} + \frac{1}{l_y^2})^4 + a_2^4\|u(t)\|_{l^2}^8])^{\frac{1}{2}} \\
&\quad \cdot (\mathbb{E}[b_0^4 + b_1^4\|u(t)\|_{l^2}^4 + b_2^4\|v(t)\|_{l^2}^4])^{\frac{1}{2}},
\end{aligned}$$

hence

$$\begin{aligned}
&\mathbb{E}\left[\|g_v(u(t)) - \hat{g}_v(u(t))\|_N^2|u(t)\right] \\
&\leq 81\,h_k\left(\kappa^4 + h_k^4\,\sigma^4N^4\pi^4(\frac{1}{l_x^2} + \frac{1}{l_y^2})^4 + a_2^4\mathbb{E}\|u(t)\|_{l^2}^8\right)^{\frac{1}{2}} \\
&\quad \cdot (b_0^4 + b_1^4\mathbb{E}\|u(t)\|_{l^2}^4 + b_2^4\mathbb{E}\|v(t)\|_{l^2}^4)^{\frac{1}{2}} \\
&\leq 81h_k\left(\kappa^4 + h_k^4\sigma^4N^4\pi^4(\frac{1}{l_x^2} + \frac{1}{l_y^2})^4 + 4a_2^2\mathbb{E}V^2(u(t))|u(t)\right)^{\frac{1}{2}} \\
&\quad \cdot \left(b_0^4 + \frac{2\,b_1^4}{a_2}\mathbb{E}V(u(t))|u(t) + b_2^4\mathbb{E}V^2(u(t))|u(t)\right)^{\frac{1}{2}} \\
&\leq 81\,h_k\left(\kappa^4 + h_k^4\,\sigma^4N^4\pi^4(\frac{1}{l_x^2} + \frac{1}{l_y^2})^4 + 4\,a_2^2\,V^2(u(t))\right)^{\frac{1}{2}} \\
&\quad \cdot \left(b_0^4 + \frac{2\,b_1^4}{a_2}\,V(u(t)) + b_2^4\,V^2(u(t))\right)^{\frac{1}{2}} \\
&\leq 81\,h_k\left(\kappa^2 + h_k^2\,\sigma^2N^2\pi^2(\frac{1}{l_x^2} + \frac{1}{l_y^2})^2 + 2\,a_2\,V(u(t))\right) \\
&\quad \cdot \left(b_0^2 + \frac{\sqrt{2}\,b_1^2}{\sqrt{a_2}}\,(V(u(t)))^{\frac{1}{2}} + b_2^2\,V(u(t))\right) \\
&\leq 81\,\left(\kappa^2 + h_k^2\,\sigma^2N^2\pi^2(\frac{1}{l_x^2} + \frac{1}{l_y^2})^2 + 2\,a_2\,(V(u(t)))^{\frac{1}{2}}\right) \\
&\quad \cdot \left(b_0^2 + \frac{\sqrt{2}\,b_1^2}{\sqrt{a_2}} + b_2^2\,(V(u(t)))^{\frac{1}{2}}\right)(V(u(t)))^{\frac{1}{2}}\,h_k \\
&\leq 81\,\left(\kappa^2 + h_k^2\,\sigma^2N^2\pi^2(\frac{1}{l_x^2} + \frac{1}{l_y^2})^2 + 2\,a_2\,(V(u(t)))^{\frac{1}{2}}\right) \\
&\quad \cdot \left(b_0^2 + \frac{\sqrt{2}\,b_1^2}{\sqrt{a_2}} + b_2^2\,(V(u(t)))^{\frac{1}{2}}\right)(1 + V(u(t)))\,h_k
\end{aligned}$$

thus

$$\mathbb{E}\left[\|g_v(u(t)) - \hat{g}_v(u(t))\|_N^2|u(t)\right] \leq K_{12}\tilde{V}(u(t))\,h_k \qquad (37)$$

where

$$\begin{aligned}
K_{12} &= 81\,\left(\kappa^2 + h_k^2\,\sigma^2N^2\pi^2(\frac{1}{l_x^2} + \frac{1}{l_y^2})^2 + 2\,a_2\,(V(u(t)))^{\frac{1}{2}}\right) \\
&\quad \cdot \left(b_0^2 + \frac{\sqrt{2}\,b_1^2}{\sqrt{a_2}} + b_2^2\,(V(u(t)))^{\frac{1}{2}}\right)
\end{aligned}$$

therefore

$$\int_t^{t+h} \mathbb{E}\left[\|g_v(u(t)) - \hat{g}_v(u(t))\|_N^2|u(t)\right] d\,s \leq K_{12}\tilde{V}(u(t))\,h_k^2. \qquad (38)$$

Thus by using inequalities (31), (34), (36), and (38) we can write inequality (15) as

$$\begin{aligned}
&\mathbb{E}\left[\|v_{n,m}(t+h) - \hat{v}_{n,m}(t+h)\|_N^2|\hat{u}(t)\right] \\
&\qquad \leq [4(K_9 + K_{10}) + 2\,C_B(K_{11} + K_{12})]\tilde{V}(u(t))\,h_k^2 \\
&\qquad \leq K_{v_2}^c\tilde{V}(u(t))\,h_k^2 \qquad (39)
\end{aligned}$$

where $K_{v_2}^c = 4(K_9 + K_{10}) + 2\,C_B(K_{11} + K_{12})$. Thus

$$\begin{aligned}
\left(\mathbb{E}\left[\|v_{n,m}(t+h) - \hat{v}_{n,m}(t+h)\|_N^2|\hat{u}(t)\right]\right)^{\frac{1}{2}} &\leq K_{v_2}^c\left(\tilde{V}(u(t))\right)^{\frac{1}{2}}h_k \\
&\leq K_{v_2}^c\tilde{V}(u(t))h_k. \qquad (40)
\end{aligned}$$

III. Conclusion

In this article we prove that the linear-implicit Euler method is mean square consistent with rate $r_0 = 2$ on nonlinear stochastic wave equations in 2 dimensions. In the future, we will continue to show that the LIEM is mean square and asymptotic stability, and convergence.

Also, we will study the stability and mean square consistency of the solution of stochastic heat equation, Burger equation.

References

[1] L. Arnold, *Stochastic Differential Equations: Theory and Applicants*, John Wiley and Sons, Inc., New York, 1974.
[2] P.L. Chow, *Stochastic Partial Differential Equations*. Chapman and Hall/CRC, Boca Raton, 2007.
[3] R. Dalang and N.E. Frangos, *The stochastic wave equation in two spatial dimensions*. Ann. Probab. *26* (1998), 187-212.
[4] G. Da Prato and J. Zabzcyk, *Stochastic Equations in Infinite dimensions*, Cambridge University Press, Cambridge, 1992.
[5] A. Friedman, *Stochastic Differential Equations and Applications*, Dover Publications, Inc. Mineola, New York, 1975.
[6] T. C. Gard, *Introduction to Stochastic Differential Equations*, Marcel Dekker, Basel, 1988.
[7] W. Grecksch and C. Tudor, *Stochastic Evolutions: A Hilbert Space Approach*, Akademie-Verlag, Berlin, 1995.
[8] Schurz, H., and Hazaimeh, H. M. (2014). Existence, uniqueness, and stability of stochastic wave equation with cubic nonlinearities in two dimensions. Journal of Mathematical Analysis and Applications, 418(2), 775-795.
[9] Hazaimeh, H. M. (2012). Stochastic Wave Equations With Cubic Nonlinearities in Two Dimensions.
[10] H. M. Hazaimeh, Local Mean Consistency on Numerical solution of stochastic wave equation with cubic nonlinearities in two dimensions. Applied Institute of Physics, 2017.
[11] Desmond Higham, Mean?square and asymptotic stability of the stochastic theta method, SIAM J. Numer. Anal. , 38 (2000), 753?769
[12] Higham, D.J., Mao, X., Stuart, A.M.: Strong convergence of Euler-like methods for nonlinear stochastic differential equations. SIAM J. Numer. Anal. 40, 1041?1063 (2002)
[13] I. Karatzas and S.E. Schreve, *Brownian Motion and Stochastic Calculus*, Second Edition. Springer-Verlag, New York, 1991.
[14] B. Oksendal, *Stochastic Differential Equations: An Introduction With applications*, Six Edition, Springer-Verlag, Berlin, 2003.
[15] A. Millet and M. Sanz-Solé, *A stochastic wave equation in two space dimension: Smootheness of the law*, Ann. Probab. *27* 1999, 803-844.
[16] X. Mao, *Stochastic Differential Equations and Applications*, Horwood Publishing, Chichester, 1997.
[17] H. Schurz, Nonlinear Stochastic heat equations with cubic nonlinearity and Additive Q-regular Noise in $\mathbb{R}^1$, *Electronic Journal of Differential Equations*, Conf. 19 (2010), 221-233.
[18] H. Schurz, Stochastic wave equations with cubic nonlinearity and Q-regular Additive Noise in $\mathbb{R}^2$, *Discrete and Continuous Dynamical Systems*, Suppl. Vol. 2011 (2011), 1299-1308.
[19] A. N. Shiryaev, *Probability* (2nd edition), Springer-Verlag, Berlin, 1996.
[20] J. B. Walsh, *An introduction to stochastic partial differential equations*, École d'été de probabilités de Saint-Flour, XIV-1984, 265-439, Lecture Notes in Math. 1180, Springer-Verlag, Berlin, 1986.

AUTHOR INDEX

AUTHOR INDEX

AUTHOR INDEX